# WISDEN
## Anthology 1900-1940

# WISDEN

## Anthology 1900-1940

EDITED BY BENNY GREEN

Macdonald
Queen Anne Press

A QUEEN ANNE PRESS BOOK

Original Wisden material © John Wisden & Co Ltd
Additional introductory material © Benny Green 1980
This Anthology © Queen Anne Press 1980

First published in Great Britain in 1980 by
Queen Anne Press, a division of
Macdonald & Co (Publishers) Ltd
Orbit House
1 New Fetter Lane
London EC4A 1AR
A member of Maxwell Macmillan Pergamon Publishing Corporation

Reprinted 1983, 1990

ISBN 0 356 19501 5

Reproduced, printed and bound in Great Britain by
Bookcraft Limited, Bath, Avon

# FOREWORD

As a friend of mine – not wont to be demonstrative – assured me the other day that he had no pleasanter evenings in the whole year than when the appearance of *Wisden* enabled him to fight the battles of the cricket season over again, I am fortified in the belief that the Almanack fulfils its mission and preserves in a readable and attractive form a record of all that is essential in connection with our glorious game. Lest there should seem to be any suspicion of vanity or egotism in my saying this, I may point to the ever-increasing favour with which *Wisden* is received, and to a constantly-growing circulation.

*Sydney H. Pardon 1893*

To Dominic

# CONTENTS

# Introduction

The contents of this anthology have been ordered differently from those of the first volume in the series. Readers will recall that that first volume covered the years between the first edition of Wisden, in 1864, and the end of the nineteenth century, by which time an insignificant yearbook padded with comically irrelevant information about the English Civil War, the length of canals, and certain facts pertaining to the Wars of the Roses, had evolved into the least imperfect sporting almanack in history, having steadily added to its virtues in the form of comprehensive match reports, coherent methods of listing averages, the introduction of "Births and Deaths of Cricketers", the incorporation of photography, the establishment of a full obituary section, and so on. In fact, so rapid was the evolution of the almanack, and so magisterial the authority of the Pardon brothers, Charles and Sydney in their style of editing, that there was very little to be found in the editions of the twentieth century that had not been there before.

All this would seem to argue for a duplication of method in this second volume of anthology. However, there is one supreme difference between the two periods which dictates a reconsideration of how best to orchestrate the contents. The years from 1864 to 1900 comprise what might loosely be defined as a regular march of time. This is not to say that nothing profound happened to the British in that period, but that a sporting enthusiast raised in the climate of 1864 would have no difficulty in recognising the contours of the world thirty-six years later. There were more balls to an over by the end of the century, more first-class counties, a formalised championship, the ascendency of overarm bowling. But, reform bills and colonial wars notwithstanding, the period from 1864 to 1900 will no doubt be seen by historians as a time of freakish stability, both in the cricketing and in the national sense. To sum up, the period covered by my first volume possessed a homogeneity which is reflected in the arrangement of the anthology.

This second volume covers a period which, so far from possessing homogeneity, was sundered by the most tragic convulsion in Europe's history. It would not be unreasonable to say that nothing in British life survived the drift from 1914 to 1919 without undergoing changes so profound as to imply new personalities, fresh beginnings, or, in too many cases, irrevocable endings.

For several seasons there was no county championship, no Test series, indeed no first-class cricket at all as we generally tend to think of that nebulous institution. Careers were breached and in some cases, destroyed. The great age of the Gentleman cricketer was buried in the mud of Flanders, and an ever-more mechanised postwar world began to throw up more and more rivals to cricket in the public affection. There were changes of a subtler kind, two of which may perhaps be suggested as symbolic of all the others. They concern the two greatest English batsmen, Jack Hobbs, who later testified that after the Great War some of the brilliance in his batting was replaced by the caution of mature responsibilities, and Dr Grace, who, according to the testimony of his friend Sir Arthur Conan Doyle, was as much a war casualty as any of the young men blown to pieces on the Western Front. The Doctor, said Doyle, simply died of bewilderment and a broken heart at the spectacle of homicidal lunacy before him.

Clearly such a confusion demanded an amended style of anthology. Readers of the first volume will know that in covering the years 1864-1900, I arranged the material to create an effect of one everlasting season, with the sections succeeding each other in the identical order to be found in the old almanacks. All the MCC matches from 1864-90, therefore, came at the front of the book in one section, followed by all the visiting tourist matches, then the counties, then the universities and so on, through to the closing items of obituary at the end of the book listed, not in chronological order but alphabetically, as though the thirty-seven seasons had been one. The general effect was, I hope, of reading one vast edition of Wisden embracing a summer stretching across an entire generation.

For the period 1900-1940 I have kept to the same method of arrangement but broken it down into its component parts, so that the years up to the outbreak of the Great War are seen as an entity, and the years from the armistice to the outbreak of the Second World War as another, with the hiatus of the war years seen as a bloody interlude during which spectral cricket proceeded against a backdrop of casualty lists and much insane oratory equating the playing of ball games in wartime with acts of the most heinous treason. Each of these three periods possessed its own distinct personality, and it is my hope, indeed by conviction, that these personalities cannot fail to emerge, of their own volition, as it were, from the small print of an almanack which at all times, on occasions accidentally, on others deliberately, reflects the flavour of life that the British people were living.

*Benny Green*

# 1900-1914

The Golden Age is always behind us. There is no question that the jeremiahs who sat
in the county pavilions of the 1930s gazing so glumly at the off-drives of Walter
Hammond and sighing for the great days of Fry and Foster would then go home to be
reproached by grandfathers who told them that if it was batting they wanted then
they should have seen Grace in his prime — a remark which a *real* connoisseur would
have taken to mean the Coroner, not the Doctor. The disease is by no means peculiar
to cricket. Readers of Wells and Bennett were constantly being referred back to
Meredith and Hardy, whose advocates were persistently maddened by allusions to
Dickens and Thackeray. It was Bernard Shaw who once said of a maiden aunt whose
soul had been rendered arthritic with snobbery that "she would have refused an earl
because he was not a duke", just as there were those who refused Larwood and
Voce because they were not Gregory and Macdonald, or Richardson and Lockwood.
    However, having conceded that the location of golden ages is a purely subjective
business, the student of cricket history knows that the period covered by this volume
is almost always regarded even by the most unsentimental witnesses as a true
golden age. Most of the historians select as the apogee of English cricket the time
between the death of Victoria and the outbreak of the Great War; a less vociferous
lobby prefers the prolific period between the wars which told of Hammond and
Sutcliffe, Bradman and Ponsford, Verity and Freeman, Hutton and Compton. At least
one critic, Sir Neville Cardus, has propagated to great effect the theory that the years
under discussion comprise *two* golden ages, the first ending with the First World
War, the second ending with the second, although of course there are several great
cricketers, among them Hobbs, Rhodes and Woolley, whose careers span both ages.
    As the new century began, the greatest career in the history of the game, perhaps
of any game, was drawing to its close. As the 1900 season opened, Dr Grace had
already scored all but eight of his 126 first-class centuries, taken all but 180 of his
2,864 wickets. He was now nearly 52 years of age, and was no longer attached to
the county of his birth, having severed his connections with Gloucestershire after the
Middlesex match at Lord's in May, 1899. The move to London, embodying the
extraordinary attempt to create single-handed a new cricketing county operating
from the Crystal Palace, may be seen as the belated cricketing image of the national
migration from the country to the town. By 1851, for the first time in the nation's
history, the urban population outnumbered the rural, and perhaps it is not too fanciful
to suggest that this irrevocable change was symbolised at last by the shift of
England's most famous athlete from Clifton to Eltham.
    That he was indeed England's most famous athlete, and something much more
than that, there can be no question. If by 1900 Grace's technique was a shade
arthritic, if he no longer bent down in the field to make contact with the passing ball
with quite the old dexterity, the shadow of his personality was more massive than
ever. By the turn of the century Grace was a kind of secular diety, one of the tiny
handful of Englishmen instantly recogniseable to a generation yet to be bludgeoned
into insensitivity by the engines of modern publicity. One of his protégés later wrote:

> The three most easily recogniseable public men in the period 1894-1904 in my
> opinion were the Old Man, the G.O.M; and General Booth. I put W.G. first because
> the man in the street would have distinguished him just as readily even if the Old

Man had changed apparel with either of the other two notabilities, and I really don't think the same could be said were the situation reversed. Like those figures of one's nursery days, he could strike terror into one's soul by the grimness of a look.

That Gilbert Jessop is not overstating the case for Grace's eminence is suggested by the fact that in 1894 Bernard Shaw, reviewing the art of England's leading singer, a man called Santley, wrote that "to the Briton with a turn for music he is just what Dr Grace is to the Briton with a turn for cricket", and that two years earlier, when a successful comedy called *Walker, London* had opened at Toole's Theatre with a character in the cast-list described simply as "W.G.", it never for a moment occurred to the dramatist, J. M. Barrie, to offer any more detailed explanation. In one of the most revealing entries ever to appear in Wisden, describing the match at Sydenham in May 1900 between London County and Surrey, we learn that at least one model of a modern major-general, on returning home from spectacular exploits out on the farflung frontiers of Empire, considered it both wise and pleasurable to arrange, as one of his very first public engagements an audience with Dr Grace.

Regarding some of the other great figures of the age Wisden is less perceptive, especially concerning the great Sidney Barnes. When first confronted by the enigma of that formidable man, the almanack did no better than the nonplussed Lancashire county committee which at the end of the 1903 season was foolish enough to try conclusions with him. With a magisterial disdain positively comic to a later age, Wisden mourns the fact that if only Barnes had "possessed the enthusiasm for the game that characterised Barlow and Johnny Briggs he might have made a great name for himself", after which Barnes went on to outsnarl, outbowl, outlive, every one of his detractors. Unwitting comedy of a different kind but stemming from the same paternalism may be found at the heart of a lavish eulogy of young Herbert Strudwick, who, for all his promise, has "a regrettable habit of chasing the ball to the boundary. I would suggest to the Surrey captain a system of modest fines, the amount being increased for each offence". Strudwick's views about this remain unknown.

We are perhaps less inclined to smile when coming across the strictures aimed at the Essex captain for committing the heresy of opening the innings with two fast bowlers, but laughter breaks through again when we hear about the Hampshire side of 1908 which found itself confronted by a Sussex team consisting of only three players. It is at moments like this that we crave more information, cursing the reticence of Pardon and his band of chroniclers whenever there were tracks to be covered, skeletons to be closeted, walls to be whitewashed. How inexpressible our feelings are at the tantalising promise of Wodehousean subterfuge when we read that in the game between MCC and Yorkshire in 1900 Mr C. O. H. Sewell suffered a spasm of schizophrenia. But what is the point of an assumed name when the assumption is such public knowledge that even Wisden feels emboldened to publicise it? Answer comes there none, although with regard to a previous instance of *nom de crease*, the famous masquerade of Mr T. C. O'Brien as J. E. Johnston in a match at the Oval in 1891, the apocrypha of the game do offer their explanation. It seems that there were moments when the magnitude of O'Brien's thirst alarmed the Surrey committee to such great effect that it barred him from the pavilion – at which O'Brien, displaying that Jeevesian ingenuity for which his class and his generation is so well remembered, gatecrashed the forbidden precincts by borrowing the persona of his own butler. But if O'Brien is a joke, then he is a magnificent joke, witness the breathtaking gallantry of his exploits in the 1914 match between Mr Robinson's side and Oxford University; posterity could not wish for a more spectacular instance of a generation taking its leave.

That it did take its leave in that last pre-war season there can be no doubt, but it is too easy to assume that the years up to 1914 constituted an idyll. On the contrary, so exacting were the social problems of the time that at least one historian, that elegant stylist George Dangerfield, has suggested that so far from smashing a peaceful world, the Great War actually saved England from the sundering effects of a great revolution. Faint echoes of that threat may be discerned in the altered venue of the Lancashire v Sussex match of 1911, and the novel method of transport resorted to in the same troubled summer by the Northamptonshire team en route to fulfil an engagement with Gloucestershire.

In fact the 1911 season appears to have been eventful in several ways: apart from the occasional intrusion of political issues, there was the instance of Jack Hobbs playing the unlikely role of demon bowler against Gloucestershire; F. R. Foster's brilliant all-round cricket against Yorkshire; the extraordinary performance of Mr C. J. B. Wood of Leicestershire in a county game at Bradford; the desperation of Hampshire a month later at Huddersfield when even the wicketkeeper went on to bowl; All India's rigorous introduction to the implications of Western pragmatism in the shape of Sidney Barnes; and, most astonishing, the sudden virtuosity of Edwin Boaler Alletson down at Hove, where in an hour or two he fashioned a monument to himself which will stand so long as the game is played — after which superhuman feat he had the dubious pleasure of reading in the Nottinghamshire county notes the sad regret of Wisden that he had proved incapable of erecting similar monuments every time he went into bat. But if editorial tact here seems wanting, it was not a very good year for etiquette anyway. In the match against Worcestershire, the Gloucestershire opening batsman, Board, must have walked back to the pavilion after his first innings dismissal wondering what, if anything, the world was coming to, while at Canterbury of all havens, Mr C. B. Fry put on a display of petulance at the expense of Colin Blythe which history has mercifully agreed to forget — except of course that Sydney Pardon did *not* forget, and very properly included the details in his match report. Further evidence of asperities in Eden are hinted at in the sad fate of Mold for Lancashire against Somerset in 1901; judicial confusions in the Somerset v Sussex match of 1910; the eccentric interpretation of the rules in the Sussex v Oxford University match of 1913; and, most uproarious of all, the resort to carpentry demanded by the sharp practices in evidence at the Surrey v London County game of 1903. And whose was the sinister hand behind the crime of the Yorkshire v Essex game of 1904?

Faced with such an array of men, problems and events, it is understandable that there should have come moments in the life of the average county secretary when he raised his hands to heaven and appealed, not for an LBW decision, but for guidance from on high. The Surrey committee, for example, was obliged to endure the ignominy of being spurned by J. N. Crawford, to expose itself to the lunacies of the English climate in the 1908 match against the Gentlemen of England, and, most trying of all, to be forced to question the fundamental assumptions of those very gentlemen in the curious case of the great fast bowler Mr N. A. Knox, who, in mid-Edwardian stride, took his leave of the cricket fields of England for the most spectacularly incongruous reason even recorded in the annals of the game. Once again Wisden gives only the barest details, so it is perhaps incumbent on an editor to record at least one fact which Wisden does not, which is that by 1910 Knox had progressed so far in his new career that he had reached the eminence of being selected to serve as an understudy in the production of *The Dollar Princess* at Daly's Theatre. Symbolically *The Dollar Princess* was the story of how a young English gentleman was won over by the blandishments of the New World. These operatic overtones in the life of a renowned cricketer are not quite as gaseous as they might seem, for the man Knox was understudying at Daly's was Basil Foster of Worcestershire. Nor should it be forgotton that Knox's earliest bowling successes came at Dulwich, where he had opened the College bowling in harness with the lyricist of the famous ballad *Bill*, from *Show Boat*.

Among the more prosaically cricketing events of the period, there are the bizarre changes of role, for instance Ranjitsinhji and Mead as demon bowlers. There are the wonderful exhibitions of all-round cricket, particularly from Tarrant, Hirst, J. R. Mason, and B. J. T. Bosanquet. George Gunn plays his brilliant tricks of temperament against Yorkshire in 1913; the Aborigine bowler Marsh is no-balled for the pristine innocence of his action; Victor Trumper blazes his trail across the damp English fields of 1902; the Triangular Tournament, prehistoric harbinger of the multi-national contests of a later age, becomes a great English triumph; the trailblazing West Indians are reduced to comic disarray by Gilbert Jessop; and, at Lord's, the immortal Fowler puts his name to a schools' match whose fortunes read as though they had been orchestrated by Frank Richards in one of his more reckless moods.

And at the end of it all, after international events had so fluttered the cricketing dovecotes that Surrey and Kent found themselves contesting a county championship match at Lord's, what was Wisden to say? What could it say? Its solemn observation that "never before has the game been in such a plight" might sound unforgiveably Panglossian to a later generation, but if Wisden was foolish enough to believe the war was no more than a brief intrusion, it was at least a foolishness to which Mr Asquith and his generals also subscribed. Of all the might-have-beens of cricket history, none is more pregnant with pathos than the proposed visit to Australia of an England team in 1915-16, unless it is the request from South Africa that "the Imperial programme should be put forward by a year," the sporting world's neat distillation of the "home by Christmas" school of armchair strategy. It is against this backdrop of a world marching unwittingly to its end that I have included an otherwise undistingished match between MCC and Western Province at Cape Town. On the final day, thanks to a last-wicket partnership between a couple of the locals called Short and Minaare, Western Province saved the game. And, as the shadows lengthened across the Newlands ground, Douglas's men walked off the field, unaware that those shadows were to be very last ever cast by any England touring side in the age of the Pax Britannica.

There is one other, utterly vital aspect of the Wisden of this period. By 1900 the annual obituary notices, which had first appeared, almost as an afterthought, as late as the 1892 edition, had already flowered into one of the glories of English sporting literature – which poses an awkward question for the anthologist. To what extent was this glory calculated and to what extent fortuitous? How much was literary artifice and how much blimpish imperception? When diverted by the news that a Mr Ford hit the ball so hard that it disturbed some partridges, or that some worthy lived in a house called "Wickets", are we smiling at Pooter or at the Grossmiths? It is not always easy to say, except that Sydney Pardon does not seem to have been the man to indulge in what might have appeared to his own age as unseemly jests at that grave juncture of a man's life, his death. But there were times when that fell event was delayed apparently indefinitely. We gaze for example, at the stupefying career in

club cricket of Charles Absolon and ask ourselves how many appointments in
Samarra that ancient worthy failed to keep. Wisden is unable to show us the famous
photograph of Absolon, overcoated and tophatted on his ninetieth birthday,
demonstrating his batting stance against the backdrop of the laurels of some
suburban back garden long since wiped off the face of the map. What the almanack
can do is to record the astonishing persistence with which this flannelled Methuselah
pursued the great love of his life. At the age of sixty-five he took four wickets in four
balls; at sixty-six he took all ten wickets in an innings; at sixty-seven he took five
wickets in six balls; at sixty-eight he took seventeen wickets in a match; at
seventy-one he again took four wickets in four balls, and in his eightieth year he took
one hundred wickets. Wisden pointedly closes the account with the reminder that
"he had been a total abstainer since 1857 and never smoked".

Whimsicality of a different kind attends the obsequies of the great footballing
Alcock, who stands for all time as the exemplar of the Englishman as world leader in
team games by captaining the French cricket side against Germany in a match at
Hamburg. Fame of yet another kind descended on the Reverend Arthur Butler, who
one day took the doctrine of Muscular Christianity to faintly excessive lengths by
becoming the only man ever to leap across the River Cherwell. The reason for leaping
across it remains unknown. Then there are the public schoolboys whose only claim to
immortality is that they served as the inspiration for some minor character in *Tom
Brown's Schooldays*.

We thrill to the dizzying effects of the Earl of Leicester's convoluted geneology,
and laugh out loud over the notoriety of the only rowing blue ever to stand in danger
of being drowned during the Boat Race. We are suitably impressed by the sporting
prowess of a Kentish veteran called Banks, whose most notable accomplishment
appears to have been his ability to ride a tricycle in his ninetieth year. A batsman
called Fison clearly qualifies for the honour of inventing the most ridiculous mode of
dismissal in the history of cricket, and one of his contemporaries called Hemingway
stakes his claim as the holder of the record for the most runs scored off a single
delivery. The famous varsity batsman Yardley wins later fame as the author of farces;
a Colonel Rhodes dies of natural causes some years after being sentenced to death
for his part in the Jameson Raid; a relation of the Graces goes into colonial politics
and creates a family record for stonewalling by delivering a speech lasting twenty
hours; the Surrey wicketkeeper Pooley dies in the workhouse; there is the curious
case of the disappearance of Henry Pickett of Essex, whose only legacy to posterity
was the bundle of clothes lying abandoned on the beach at Aberavon, while Mr
Elford becomes one of the earliest sacrificial victims of the internal combustion
engine. It is rather like reading history by flashes of intuition.

Two deaths above all others in this section commend themselves for what might
be termed extra-cricketing reasons, the first as a sketch of a familiar literary
archetype, the second as an example of the victim of the ironies of history. Of the life
of C. S. Buller, of Harrow and Middlesex, posterity remembers nothing apart from
that which Wisden has preserved, two facts which comprise a claim on behalf of his
greatest glory and the degradation to which that glory apparently led him. Buller
receives the most incongruous compliment which the almanack has ever paid, that
"he was perhaps the handsomest man the cricket field has ever known," but then
closes with "into the scandals that marred Buller's private life and caused his social
eclipse this is obviously not the place to enter," although it would seem that by
dredging up the subject, Wisden had entered already, at least far enough to put us in
mind of the kind of patrician dégringolade suffered by anti-heroes of Victorian fiction

like Trollope's George Vavasor and Copperfield's friend Steerforth. As to the flukes which attend historical events, none is more poignant that that affecting the last hours of Middlesex's Australian Albert Trott, one of these cricketers whose career seems in retrospect to have been crowded with indiscretion. After apparently losing his great bowling powers, Trott selected the most perverse day of all on which to rediscover them, his own benefit match, against Somerset at Whitsun, 1907. By taking four wickets in four balls and then ending the match with a hat-trick, Trott ruined any last chance he had of financial security, which is what Sir Neville Cardus was thinking of when he coined that wonderful remark, "Trott bowled himself into the bankruptcy court." Not being one of those cricketers who could face with equanimity the anti-climax of retirement, Trott decided to take his own life, an act of desperation which was erased from the public memory a few days later by an event of rather more significance. Albert Edwin Trott killed himself on July 30, 1914. Five days later the rest of Europe followed suit.

*Benny Green*

# JOHN WISDEN

## Born September 5, 1826; Died April 5, 1884

Wisden played his first match for Sussex, against Kent at Brighton, in July, 1845, and his last, against the MCC and Ground at Brighton, in August, 1863. After 1863 he did not take part in first-class cricket. He made his first appearance at Lord's in 1846. His first Gentlemen v Players' match was in 1848, and his last in 1859. He and James Dean founded in 1852 the United All-England Eleven, whose famous matches with the All-England Eleven began in 1857. In conjunction with George Parr, Wisden took an England Eleven to Canada and the United States in 1859 – two years before the first English team, with H. H. Stephenson as captain, went to Australia.

## PERSONAL RECOLLECTIONS

Sir Kenelm Digby writes: – I am glad to have the opportunity of noting down a few reminiscences of John Wisden, who was engaged as professional bowler at Harrow School during the four years 1852 to 1855. As those were the years in which I was a member of the Harrow eleven and captain for the last three of them, I was during the cricket season brought into close and daily connection with Wisden. I have the pleasantest recollection of his quiet, modest, and unassuming character, his unfailing good temper, his keenness in and enjoyment of his work, his genial disposition which made him a great favourite with all the present and former members of the school with whom he came in contact. He was engaged by old Harrovians not so much as a cricket coach, as for the purpose of giving the young cricketers constant practice in dealing with moderate-paced, first-class bowling. The actual teaching of cricket was mainly carried on by Frederick Ponsonby, afterwards Earl of Bessborough, whose thorough mastery of the theory and practice of the game no one who had the advantage of his instruction could ever forget. With wonderful insight and quickness he saw at a glance the weak and the strong points of each young player, and taught him how to correct the one and develop the other. As a batsman Wisden was a learner rather than a teacher, and greatly improved during the four years he was at Harrow. As a bowler he was quite in the first rank, and though other bowlers might occasionally bowl more brilliant and difficult balls, no one surpassed him in the steadiness of his attack on the wicket, in command of the ball, in straightness, and in length. He was probably the most useful member of the United All-England Eleven; and from time to time it was necessary to give him leave to be absent for some great match, in which his services could not be dispensed with. It was, it must be remembered, the day of round-arm bowling, when the raising of the arm above the level of the shoulder was prohibited. The alteration of this rule has, it seems to me, largely altered the characteristics of first-class bowling. Wisden had a perfect delivery; with a short but rapid run, a graceful and easy sweep of the arm, moderate pace, hardly a loose ball, varying his pace occasionally, but always "on the spot," he was unsurpassed as the standby of a side in first-class cricket. In round-arm bowling there was not, I imagine, the same power of manipulating the ball with the fingers, so as to make it break from the off, or come in from the leg, at pleasure, as can be done by the "windmill" bowlers of the present day. On the other hand, what was a prominent feature of the bowling of the past, seems, so far as my observation goes, to have entirely disappeared. I do not believe that any one under the age of fifty has ever seen a real shooter. I attribute this largely to the alteration in the mode of delivery, aided no doubt by the greater smoothness and diminished vivacity of the wicket. On which side lies the greater gain, or the least loss? I confess, if the gods could bring back to earth an eleven of the past to contend with an eleven of the present, I should like to see a side containing Wisden and W. Clarke as bowlers, and Fuller Pilch and George Parr as batsmen, matched against a first-class team of the present day, whether British or Colonial.

**Sir Spencer Ponsonby Fane writes:** – I knew Jack Wisden very well and played with or against him for about ten years in the important matches of those days, for which I was able to get away from the Foreign Office, such as Gentlemen and Players, North and South, Kent and England, etc. He was a very fine and accurate bowler, perfect length, but with little work, except what the ground gave it. He was a fast medium, but I think he was classed as a fast bowler – and played on that side in the match, Fast v Slow. He was a delightful bowler to play against, but required very careful watching, for he was apt to send in occasionally a very fast shooter, then so fatal on Lord's Ground. I have no recollection of his bowling a "yorker" called a "Tice" in those days – a mode of attack not in vogue at the time. I believe he was the first of the players to play in a straw hat, instead of the white topper worn by the older players. He was a good field, and an excellent bat, which was rather exceptional for a bowler at that time, when bowlers were not expected to be very able performers with the bat. He was a genial, pleasant, and respectable fellow in every way, liked and respected by every one with whom he came in contact.

**Canon McCormick says:** – Wisden was small of stature, but well made. He was too small to be a brilliant fieldsman. He made his mark as a bowler. He bowled moderately fast, and he was as fair a round arm bowler as could be seen. His delivery was quite easy. The best balls he bowled broke back slightly, and his style of delivery tended to make them shoot. He kept a good length and with a spin and a quick-rising ball he always had to be carefully watched. He was consistent rather than brilliant or original. Though a good bowler, he was not as difficult to play as Jackson or Willsher. His averages show that he always took wickets and in the best matches. As a batsman he was not in the first rank, but it was not easy to get him out. He had a very straight bat and was wonderfully patient. He often stayed in while his partner made a large score. At The Oval on one occasion he and Lillywhite got over 100 runs for the last wicket. He was a thorough cricketer and always did his very best to win. As a professional he was universally liked by Gentlemen and Players. He was modest and good tempered and never pushed himself forward.

I very well remember a celebrated match in which Wisden and I took part. It was at Lord's. The match was "MCC and Ground" against the County of Sussex, at a time when Sussex was about the best county in England. John Lillywhite was then in his prime as a batsman, and Wisden as a bowler. What made the match so remarkable was that Nixon and I, in the second innings, bowled Sussex out for 23 runs! The last big match in which I played against Wisden was Gentlemen and Players. Wisden bowled at the Pavilion end of Lord's: the second ball I cut for 4 and the third was a leg stump shooter, and it took my wicket.

On another occasion I played with Wisden for the United England XI against XVI of Southgate. This was no common match, as the XVI contained some of the best players in England. I was not put on early in the innings but, having started bowling, I bowled throughout, taking seven wickets in the first innings and nine in the second, and nearly all bowled. Though we lost it was a most interesting match, and an exhibition of first-class cricket.

Wisden was a mainstay of the United England Eleven, and did good service against George Parr's Eleven of England, a very powerful team. Wisden has left a very good record as a cricketer and a pleasant memory as a sportsman, a companion, a friend.

**The Rev. H. B. Biron writes:** – The first time I saw Wisden play was on the old ground at Canterbury just beyond the Barracks. This was before the present St. Lawrence Ground was in use. I was then a boy at school and I never imagined then that eleven years afterwards I should be playing against him for Kent, or that after another 55 years I should be asked to give a few remembrances of this famous cricketer on the 50th Anniversary of the invaluable *Cricketers' Almanack* which bears his name. John Wisden was born in September, 1826, and died April 5th, 1884. Early in his cricketing career he was called the "Little Wonder," a title which, given him by Bob Thoms, he bore through his life. In his time the wickets were not of the "billiard table," or, as I have heard it called, the "bread and butter" type of the present age, consequently the bowlers of the past had a great advantage over those of the present time – but the pitch and precision of Wisden's bowling would have made him difficult even in the present day, and I have but little doubt that his ingenuity would have risen to the occasion as the wickets became easier. Indeed, he lived to see a great improvement in the grounds, but he was a deadly trundler to the end. His bowling, as I remember it, was of a rather fast-medium pace. He sometimes in his later days resorted to underhand slows with which he now and then met with success. Indeed I remember a match at Tunbridge Wells in 1861, when after being rather severely handled, as was thought in those days, he went on with "under-hands" and got five wickets at a very cheap cost. But I must say that I was not greatly impressed with their difficulty as it was owing more to the weakness of the opposition than to the excellence of the bowling that his success on that occasion was due. Still, however, amongst his victims were four excellent batsmen, viz.: Mr W. S. Norton, Willsher, Hopkinson, and H. Fryer.

But he did not shine only as a bowler; for so short a man he was a powerful hitter, and a good bat all-round. The centuries, which in these days are as common as blackberries, were very rare in Wisden's time, but he scored 100 against Kent in 1850 – his innings including four 6s, and these against Willsher, than whom a better or more difficult bowler never lived – and 148 against Yorkshire at Sheffield in 1855, when he met such clever trundlers as Ike Hodgson, Crossland, Wright, and Chatterton, a formidable quartette indeed – a fact which I can personally assert. In the Kent v England Match at Canterbury in 1853 I saw him make a drive for seven all run out, the ball travelling nearly to the entrance gate. The only boundaries then were three or four tents. I have sometimes wondered, when in the present age I see batsmen resting for breath after the very rare four run out, how they would feel after running a hit for seven. Have the Sybaritic luncheons anything to do with this? But it was not only as a cricketer but as a man that the memory of Wisden may be cherished. We have the testimony of the late Mr V. E. Walker, and of Sir Kenelm Digby as to his character when he coached Harrow. Both spoke of him in the highest terms. So much for the past. May John Wisden's memory be kept alive in the cricket world for another 50 years at least, when perhaps one of my great grandchildren may write another In Memoriam in the 100th Edition of *John Wisden's Cricketers' Almanack.*

Sir H. M. Plowden writes: – When I was a junior schoolboy at Harrow, Wisden was the school professional, about 1855 and 1856. I recall him as of short in figure, a little inclined to plumpness, with a beautifully easy, smooth and level delivery as a bowler. I remember that we used to speak of him as "the drawing room player" because he favoured "the draw," a stroke long obsolete but of sufficient importance at that date to form one of the series of drawings by G. F. Watts (No. 86) in the collection of the MCC at Lord's.

# MCC MATCHES

## MCC AND GROUND v YORKSHIRE

Played at Lord's, May 14, 15, 16, 1900

This engagement will be best remembered by its result – the solitary defeat sustained by the Yorkshiremen throughout the season. The MCC were very strongly represented and their first innings of 346 gave them a lead of 159. Warner preferred to go in a second time instead of making Yorkshire follow on, and that his policy was the right one was proved by the fact of the Club playing a second innings of over 300, and setting the county no fewer than 472 to win. Some determined cricket by Brown, senior, and Tunnicliffe yielded 71 runs for the first partnership, and Denton and Hirst added 104 for the fourth, but after Denton was fourth out at 201 the batting broke down and the MCC won by 182 runs. The credit of the triumph was due in the first place to Carpenter, Warner and C. O. H. Sewell (playing under the assumed name of "C. L. Lewes,") and in the second to J. T. Hearne, the last named only just failing to take all ten wickets in the county's first innings. Carpenter's splendid score of 125 was put together in three hours out of 236. Apart from an escape when 47 there were no blemish in a fine display, and his figures included three 6s, five 5s and seven 4s. Sewell and Warner batted splendidly in both innings.

## MCC and Ground

| | | |
|---|---|---|
| H. Carpenter c Denton b Brown sen. | 125 | – b Rhodes ... 23 |
| A. Hearne lbw b Rhodes | 6 | – c Whitehead b Hirst ... 34 |
| Mr C. O. H. Sewell b Haigh | 40 | – b Rhodes ... 87 |
| W. Storer c Washington b Haigh | 11 | – run out ... 4 |
| Mr P. F. Warner b Rhodes | 83 | – c Wainwright b Brown jun. ... 69 |
| A. E. Trott c Wainwright b Brown sen. | 21 | – c Hunter b Whitehend ... 8 |
| W. H. Thompson b Rhodes | 4 | – not out ... 26 |
| Mr A. Page not out | 13 | – lbw b Rhodes ... 2 |
| H. Young c Hunter b Rhodes | 2 | – c Wainwright b Hirst ... 13 |
| J. T. Hearne c Denton b Rhodes | 5 | – c Hunter b Brown jun. ... 6 |
| W. Mead c Brown jun. b Rhodes | 17 | – b Brown jun. ... 24 |
| B 17, l-b 2 | 19 | B 9, l-b 4, w 2, n-b 1 ... 16 |
| | **346** | **312** |

## Yorkshire

| | | |
|---|---|---|
| J. T. Brown sen, b J. T. Hearne | 67 | – b Mead ... 40 |
| J. Tunnicliffe c Storer b J. T. Hearne | 0 | – c Storer b Young ... 41 |
| D. Denton c Carpenter b J. T. Hearne | 12 | – c J. T. Hearne b Young ... 71 |
| E. Wainwright c A. Hearne b J. T. Hearne | 15 | – b Young ... 0 |
| G. H. Hirst b Young | 48 | – b Mead ... 48 |
| J. Washington lbw b J. T. Hearne | 3 | – c Thompson b Young ... 17 |
| S. Haigh b J. T. Hearne | 0 | – c Storer b Mead ... 9 |
| W. Rhodes c Storer b J. T. Hearne | 24 | – b Young ... 16 |
| Whitehead c Trott b J. T. Hearne | 0 | – run out ... 12 |
| J. T. Brown jun. c Sewell b J. T. Hearne | 10 | – b Young ... 21 |
| D. Hunter not out | 3 | – not out ... 5 |
| B 6, l-b 2 | 8 | B 4, l-b 4, n-b 1 ... 9 |
| | **187** | **289** |

**Yorkshire Bowling**

| | Overs | Mdns | Runs | Wkts | Overs | Mdns | Runs | Wkts |
|---|---|---|---|---|---|---|---|---|
| Rhodes . . . . . . . . . . . | 26.5 | 6 | 76 | 6 | 29 | 7 | 85 | 3 |
| Hirst . . . . . . . . . . . . | 14 | 4 | 57 | — | 16 | 4 | 41 | 2 |
| Haigh . . . . . . . . . . . . | 22 | 7 | 69 | 2 | 22 | 7 | 53 | — |
| Brown jun. . . . . . . . . | 14 | 2 | 66 | — | 13.2 | 1 | 55 | 3 |
| Brown sen. . . . . . . . . | 15 | 3 | 34 | 2 | 2 | — | 7 | — |
| Whitehead . . . . . . . . | 11 | 4 | 25 | — | 12 | 5 | 32 | 1 |
| Wainwright . . . . . . . | | | | | 4 | — | 23 | — |

**MCC Bowling**

| | Overs | Mdns | Runs | Wkts | Overs | Mdns | Runs | Wkts |
|---|---|---|---|---|---|---|---|---|
| J. T. Hearne . . . . . . . | 20 | 4 | 71 | 9 | 16 | 2 | 46 | — |
| Trott . . . . . . . . . . . | 14 | — | 70 | — | 14 | 3 | 48 | — |
| Young . . . . . . . . . . | 5 | — | 29 | 1 | 32.2 | 7 | 77 | 6 |
| Mead . . . . . . . . . . . | 2 | — | 9 | — | 23 | 5 | 79 | 3 |
| Thompson . . . . . . . . | | | | | 5 | 1 | 22 | — |
| A. Hearne . . . . . . . . | | | | | 2 | — | 8 | — |

Umpires: J. Phillips and W. A. J. West

## THE LEG-BEFORE-WICKET QUESTION

The ordinary business having been concluded, the meeting was made special to consider the proposed alteration in the Law of leg-before-wicket. The proposal was that, in place of the present rule, Law 24 should read: "If with any part of his person (except the hand) which is between wicket and wicket he intercept a ball which would hit his wicket, 'Leg Before Wicket.'" On the ballot being taken, there were 259 votes in support of the change and 188 against. There was thus a majority of 71 in favour of the change, but as no alteration in the laws of cricket can be carried by less than a two-thirds majority, the proposal fell to the ground. As the discussion was of exceptional interest, some of the best experts in England expressing in detail their views on a very vexed question, it has been thought advisable to print in *Wisden* the full official report.

The chairman, the Right Hon. Spencer Ponsonby-Fane, GCB, said: The meeting will now be made special to take into consideration the alteration of the law of leg-before-wicket, and the Hon. Mr Lyttelton will move a resolution:

The Hon. Alfred Lyttelton: Sir Spencer, my lords, and gentlemen, I have to move that Law 24 as it at present stands, which is that, "If with any part of his person he stops the ball, which in the opinion of the umpire at the bowler's wicket shall have been pitched in a straight line from it to the striker's wicket and would have hit it, 'Leg-before-wicket,'" be altered. I propose to substitute for those words in italics: "If with any part of his person (except the hand) which is between wicket and wicket, he intercept a ball which would hit his wicket, 'Leg before wicket.'" I do not suppose anybody who heard me read those words for the first time would quite understand what they mean. I expect you almost all have heard them; but very briefly I will explain that the proposal is to draw – if I may put it as a sketch – to draw a line from one wicket to another. That, of course, would mean a long thin parallelogram twenty-two yards long, and my proposal is, gentlemen, that that should be the bowler's territory, and that if a leg or any part of a batsman's person occupy that territory, and a ball hit the leg so occupying the territory which would have hit the wicket, then the batsman will be out. (Hear, hear.) And the point of the alteration, as you will readily see, will be to prevent that bowler – the hard-working and admirable functionary – who can produce a break-back upon the ball or a twist upon the ball, and of course does not pitch the ball between wicket and wicket, that when he pitches the ball so, either on the off-side or leg-side off the wicket, and can succeed in baffling that which was intended by Nature and cricketers – the bat – that the grosser article, the leg, or other parts of the person shall intercept the just reward of the bowler who has beaten the bat, and who would hit the wicket. Now, gentlemen, I do not intend to labour the question of the present circumstances of cricket – they are amply familiar to you all. I maintain, subject, of course, to the opinion of others quite as experienced, and quite as sagacious, that the present cricket is somewhat dull. (Hear, hear.) Nothing can make it really dull; it still remains the best game in the world. But, on the other hand, to eliminate leg-hitting, to eliminate on-driving, to eliminate all these strokes on the leg side with which we were familiar twenty years ago is a very serious thing in the game, and it is hoped that if you carry this rule that at any rate the bowler will be encouraged to both twist the ball and break it from the off. But the really important thing is that the game is at present inconclusive. What in any game in the world – what if you went out to play tennis, or went out to play racquets, or went out to play football – what would you think if 50 per cent of the occasions on which you went out it was left undecided whether you were the better man or your opponent? I have not gone into details of statistics this year; but I remember going into them some little time ago – I think two years ago, a fairly typical year – and I remember taking out certain statistics at the time – I won't trouble you with them – which showed that about 50 per cent of the most important matches of the year were drawn. I remember the champion county drew 50 per cent of its matches – half the matches that it played were not concluded. The Australians drew, I think, sixteen out of thirty-five matches, and that though they are the finest bowlers and fieldsmen in the world. And last year, looking as I came up here, I find that out of thirty-three matches Surrey drew sixteen; out of twenty-two Essex drew twelve; out of twenty-one matches Derbyshire drew ten; out of eighteen matches Warwickshire drew thirteen; out of twenty-four Sussex drew nineteen – (laughter) – and I won't trouble you with the rest. But, my lords and gentlemen, may I ask you: Do you wish this state of things to continue unaltered? (Cries of "No" and "Yes.") Do you wish that we should fold our hands in this club and say that such a state of things as that should continue? I do not think I have ever heard anybody dispute that the game is made more tame and monotonous than ever it was. And here are the figures to show that it is inconclusive; that you cannot finish your matches, and cannot prove who is the better side. Then is it your wish that this state of things should continue? I must frankly admit that some persons entitled to great respect do wish no alterations to be made. The committee itself, with a majority in favour of the proposal of eight to five, sent circulars to the Colonies and to the secretaries of the clubs in South Africa, and they seemed against the change. And although I think my friend Mr Warner wrote an article, I have not read it. (Laughter.) I will read it; but I was told that he inserted in the article the statement that the Australians, undoubtedly the persons most competent to judge in this matter after ourselves, were against the proposal. My friend Mr Warner, if he did make that statement, I am sorry, considering the education he had in my chambers; if he did, it is inaccurate, because we have a reply from the Australians, received within the last two days, which is in favour of the proposal which we now make. (Hear, hear.) And, my lords and gentlemen, I am not surprised that they are in favour of it, because the evil in Australia is even greater than the evil here. But, being rich, and men of leisure, and being prepared to play five, six, or seven days if necessary, it does not press upon them quite so much as it does upon a more business-like community. There is the state of things; there is the grievance; there is that which I cannot say all, but which most people wish us to see altered, and can alteration be made in favour of the bowler, can it be made – I ought to say – in a more conservative way? But I ought, before I come to that aspect, just to add one word about second-class matches. I consider the evil to be even greater in second-class matches than it is in first-class. Now it is common for man to go out and play second-class matches, every bit as good as we have here, single day matches, and he is a working man, and he gives, say his Saturday up to cricket. Now, it may well happen to that man that he plays five matches running, and supposing he goes in fifth or sixth, the first four batsmen get 250 or 300 runs, the innings is declared closed, and he gets no innings. Perhaps he is on the other side on another occasion, and has the pleasure of fielding first for this 250 runs, and gets no innings himself, and the result is you may very easily play several Saturday matches and never get an innings at all. What wonder is it, then, that other and inferior games like golf − (laughter) − entice away the disappointed cricketer, and satisfy him with the sedater joys that belong to that game. Well, if that be so − and let me now come to what I was saying before − can you put forward a more conservative proposal than that which the committee now submit to you? It is the least change you can make in the game; it is, I am told by those older than myself, it is a reverting, a return to the old days, that nobody in old days − before I can remember − that nobody ever put his leg in front of the wicket in order to intercept the ball. And for two admirable reasons; one, that he was too good a sportsman, and the other that he had too tender shins. But be that as it may, I have no doubt the question did not press in those days; now it does. I was very much amused with a letter I saw in *The Times* of this morning, and which I read on my way here. I was very much amused to see that certain friends for whom I have a great respect, Lord Hawke, Mr Warner, and others, think that if this rule is carried they would have to abandon the way in which they have been taught to play forward. (Hear, hear.) They say that they have been taught to play forward − and evidently by very sound teachers − to play forward with their left leg close against the bat. Of course they have. I have seen "WG" do that many thousands of times when I was keeping wicket, and the ball has hit his leg. They consider they will have to abandon that practice. Why should they? Why should they not continue to play with their legs alongside their bats? They will have, at any rate, the chance that the umpire won't give them out; but if the bowler has succeeded in beating the bat, why should not he have his reward? (Hear, hear.) And if any of these gentlemen who have learnt forward play in so admirable a way − if they succeed in playing forward in the proper way, and if they fail to hit the ball with the bat, which was intended to hit the ball, and if they intercept the ball with their legs, why should they not be out? And why should they alter their forward style of play because this rule is passed? That is the first point in this letter. Another point in the letter asserts that these gentlemen admitted that this alteration in the rule will do no good on hard wickets. May I say that I don't admit that at all. I utterly deny it, and I quote my friend Mr Steel, whom I remember very well coming back from Australia, where, you know, he played on very hard wickets. Palmer was a great Australian bowler in those days. I remember my friend Mr Steel and Mr Charlie Studd told me that Palmer could break the ball on a hard wicket; and they told me that in order to baffle him they used to put their legs out − ("Shame") − in front alongside the bat, and it was absolutely legitimate, and therefore when he broke a ball which did not pitch straight he beat the bat, and they said "We were safe because the ball hit our legs." Now that is what we want to prevent. That is why no bowlers now will try any enterprise. What is the good of twisting the ball, what is the good of breaking the ball, if the batsmen is able − notwithstanding the fact that you play on these faultless wickets − if the batsman is able to baffle the bowler, whatever device he tries? The plain result is that bowlers are compelled, instead of doing what is amusing, and what is a fine craft, trying to get a break and curl on the ball − and no wonder they are reduced to it, poor fellows! − they are reduced to bowling on the off side in the hope that by dint of mere monotony the batsman will be tempted to do something he ought not do, and be caught in the slips. I ask the meeting whether it is a caricature of the present cricket if I describe it as two bowlers bowling good length balls outside the off stumps, and hoping the batsmen will be tempted to play the ball into the hands of the slips. There is a lot of beautiful play and beautiful hitting; but it is the way on a good wicket which most bowlers are condemned to aim for. Now I think I have said enough, because one ought to be brief. May I just summarise what I have said on the evil existing both in first-class, and still more in second-class matches, of cricket becoming dull and cricket becoming inconclusive, quantities of drawn matches, quantities of occasions in single day matches when batsmen never get an innings at all, and as a result of this, gradual abandonment of second-class matches − (Oh!) − and frequent abandonment of first-class cricket by all gentlemen who are unable to give their whole time to it. That is frequently the result. Do you wish cricket to be monotonous? Do you wish it to be inconclusive? I am sure you do not. Now, if you do not wish the present state of things to continue, can any of you suggest a change more conservative? I am quite prepared to go further, but I think it right first to take the most conservative line, because I think obviously it would be said, if you do not take so moderate a reform as this you will take nothing. Now, therefore, I say you have an admitted evil, and you have a conservative rememdy for it, and I hope you will vote for it. (Cheers.)

Mr John Shuter: Sir Spencer, my lords, and gentlemen, – As a comparatively recent convert to the proposed alteration in this law, I venture to second this proposition which Mr Lyttelton has so ably put before you. I feel that I can add very little indeed to help our cause beyond what he has said, for I so entirely agree with everything he has said, not only as regards first-class cricket, but especially as regards second and third-class cricket. I am quite certain of this, gentlemen, that we all here probably as cricketers have very great respect for the opinions of those gentlemen whose names appear at the bottom of that letter in *The Times* of this morning, to which Mr Lyttelton has referred. But, personally, I cannot help saying that I am beyond measure disappointed in that they have made absolutely no reference to the heavy scoring of the present day, which, to my mind, is the basis of the proposed alteration which is now before us. Personally, speaking with regard to the leg play and the leg glide, which is, of course, a very beautiful and very artistic stroke, I can only say that I was not taught to put the ball where it is put at the present day, and so the batsmen who now play that stroke, and play it so admirably and secure so many runs by it, if they are unable to play that stroke without putting their legs in front of the middle stump or middle and leg, all I can say is that they ought to suffer if anything should occur by way of an appeal to the umpire for lbw. I really add very little beyond that, except to say this, that I am very strongly of opinion that in fine weather the alteration in the rule will have a decided effect. There is one point upon which Mr Lyttelton did not touch, and that is with respect to the umpiring. I feel strongly on that point, because I think that the umpire's position, far from being made more difficult, will, I really think, be made easier – (Hear, hear) – for the simple reason that at the present moment he has to judge in an infinitesimal space of a second as to whether a ball pitches in a space of about that much, whereas under the new law he certainly may have at times, on a slow wicket, rather difficult decisions to give; if so he can give them in favour of the batsman. But in the ordinary case his judgment will be helped, and I think, although I am open to correction – and Mr. Lacey, I believe, can correct me if I am wrong in saying so – that the first-class umpires have expressed the opinion that their position would be made easier instead of more difficult. Gentlemen, I do hope that, though I am sure we all have a very high opinion of all those present-day cricketers who are against this change, I hope that if you are conscientiously in favour of the change, you will not fail to record your vote in favour of it.

Mr A. G. Steel: May I ask that the communication from Australia referred to by Mr Lyttelton be read to this meeting?

Mr – –: May I ask if you received any answer from America?

Mr W. E. Denison: From Philadelphia, yes.

The Secretary: I have a letter from Major Wardill, who writes as secretary of the Melbourne Cricket Club. (Reads letter).

Mr P. F. Warner: I believe there has been no meeting of the Australians, and that is merely a private communication from Major Wardill, and is not official. Just because there are certain cricketers in England who are in favour, therefore you say the whole body are in favour of it.

Mr W. E. Denison: My lords, and gentlemen, – Perhaps, as regards the Australian matter, which I do not think is of particular importance, I may merely comment upon the fact that a most extraordinary number of influential names are conspicuous by their absence. There are only, out of those names that were read out, three of four who would carry any weight in this country, and we do not hear anything from the Hills and Darlings, and all those men who have made themselves conspicuous in the past. That is a matter of comparatively little importance at present, and I will just mention it directly in connection with some of the other countries who have been asked their opinion. Now, Mr Alfred

Lyttelton has told you that this particular alteration which he has mentioned will conduce a very great deal to making the game more lively and more agreeable to the spectators. I myself am of the exact opposite opinion, and I think I may mention one or two points which will, I hope, induce the meeting to take the same view. Now, it would appear that this proposed alteration of the law is faulty in principle. Under the existing law, if a man gets lbw to a ball which is going straight from wicket to wicket, he has placed himself in a false position, from which it is impossible that he can make a correct stroke, and under the proposed law he will be given out, he will be penalised for placing himself in the only position in which he can make a correct stroke, and he will be cramped in consequence. A man's leg must come across on the off-side, and he will be penalised for having assumed the correct position to play the ball. Now, a man's legs must be somewhere, and I cannot think it can conduce to the liveliness of the game to penalise him for placing them in the proper position. Now, something has been said about the umpires, and the comparative ease with which umpires will now perform their duties to what they did before. Well, I really cannot see that the umpire is placed in a more favourable position; he appears to me to be placed in a position of extraordinary difficulty. As it is now, what he has to decide is, did the ball pitch straight and would it go on straight; but now you are going to ask him to decide whether a ball, perhaps with a curl from leg, or a break back, was going to hit the wicket, and whether the exact spot struck on the batsman's leg was in the line of impact between wicket and wicket. I venture to think that is a thing very few umpires will correctly decide, and there are plenty of mistakes made at present, and I think they will be very much multiplied if this law is brought into force. When you make a new law you make it, of course, with a certain object. Now a very distinguished cricketer, Mr MacLaren, said the other day to me, when speaking about this, that you would never have thought of this if it had not been for the long scores. That is to say, it is not an improvement in the game. Mr Lyttleton appears to think the game will be made more lively. My own impression is that given a cautious batsman, you bring before his mind another danger which he is not exposed to now, and that it will make him more cautious, and he will simply stop a good many balls which under the present regime he would have hit. But I do not think myself that on a fast, good, and easy wicket this law will have any effect except that of making the game a little duller than it is now. And although Mr Lyttelton has referred to Palmer, there are not many Palmers about now.

A Voice: There will be, though.

Mr Denison: But where the ball does not beat the bat, these people do not get out lbw; there is no occasion for them to do so – they can find the ball with the bat when they come forward. But if you come to a good ground in a difficult state, or the ordinary ground upon which half-day matches and league matches are played, I think you will find that cricket, which is already too difficult, will become absolutely impossible. I should like to see anybody try to play on one of those grounds on which now 60 or 70 is a good score. I think two curly bowlers upon wickets such as we sometimes see would make the game look rather absurd; but I do not wish to take up all these points on the particular merits and demerits of this proposed law, because I think everybody has been able to make up his mind upon it, one way or the other. But I have to say this as regards the opinions that have been given out – that we have very valuable evidence from Philadelphia. The Philadelphians are, of course, the leading cricket team of the States, and they wrote to us to say that they could not recommend us to adopt this law, for the reason that they had tried it – not for one match or two matches, or for a season, but for several years – and it proved unsuccessful. And they added to that statement that they were very sorry they could not adopt it, because the idea had commended itself to them. Therefore, you have had this scheme thoroughly and sympathetically tried and found to be a failure. But, gentlemen, instead of dwelling upon the particular merits or demerits of this proposal. I should rather ask you to consider the wider question, that is to say, the way in which the laws of cricket are to be brought forward by the Marylebone Club and enforced upon the cricket community. It is a very necessary thing, or a very desirable thing, at all events, that there should be some central law-abiding body, and up to this time the Marylebone Club has filled this position with very great success. And why? Because every alteration made has had the assent and approval of the great body of cricketers; everyone of them has been a success, and they have never been asked to rescind any one. But there is no instance on record of the Marylebone Club endeavouring to pass into law any proposal to which there was a very strong and widespread objection. It has never been done, and I really do not see how you could keep your position as central law givers of cricket if you were to force on new laws which were perhaps strongly and deservedly objected to. Now the process by which this proposed law has come before you is this: It was proposed at a cricket sub-committee, and was looked upon with doubt; as a matter of fact, they were divided, and made no recommendation on the point. It was then taken to a small meeting of the general committee, at which it was adopted and passed into its next stage – that is, the stage when the opinions of certain cricketing bodies were asked upon it. Those bodies were the Counties, the Universities, the Australians (whose opinion you have just heard), the Philadelphians, the West Indians, and the South Africans; the captains I have mentioned. Well, of course, the opinion of the captains came first, and the way in which opinion was asked was by sending letters to the individual captains asking them to state their opinions and that of their eleven. Some the captains did not answer, but the whole of those who did answer were against the proposal; the remainder of them answered at a meeting of the captains, which was a somewhat memorable meeting, which was held at the beginning of this year, and that meeting was reported by Lord Hawke, its chairman – who I am sorry is not here from indisposition – was reported to the Marylebone Club as absolutely unanimous against this proposal.

A Voice: That has since been found out not to be so.

Mr Denison: The meeting was absolutely unanimous against it; but it appears that out of, I think there were twelve out of the fifteen captains present. I think it appears that it is possible – ("Certain") – that four of those who were not present are now in favour of this proposal, but that does not make the meeting of the captains that was held any less unanimous, nor does it in the least weaken what I was going to say, which was this, that on receiving this report from Lord Hawke, we naturally on the cricket sub-committee recommended to the general committee in the mildest terms that in view of the great weight of opinion against this proposal, it was not advisable to proceed with it any further at the present time. We could not have put it more gently than that; we could not have been more soothing to Mr Lyttelton's feelings than we were. One would have thought, perhaps, that an opinion of this sort coming from the committee that you appoint for the purpose might have had some weight; but at another small meeting of the general committee they decided by a small majority, which has been mentioned, of eight to five, to set aside the opinion of their own cricket sub-committee, to treat what was apparently at that time the unanimous opinion of the captains with contempt, and to persevere with their own plans and schemes. Well, since that time they have had also the opinion of the Philadelphians, who have tried this scheme and found it a failure. I do think that it is perfectly impossible that a meeting such as this should enforce upon the cricket world, or endeavour to enforce upon the cricket world, a new law to which such very strong exception has been taken. (Hear, hear.) I do not know really what you keep the cricket sub-committee for if you are not going to take its advice. I have often heard of a proposal made by a sub-committee which has not been accepted by the general committee, but I do not think I ever heard of a general committee insisting upon making an alteration which the sub-committee appointed for the purpose, strongly warned them against. I do not know that I need add any more, except just to summarise and say that I object to this law, first on its merits. I object to it because it is wrong in principle, difficult to carry out, and also on the ground that it will not effect its object, but that it will effect an object which is not desired. But I object to it still more, because I consider that to force on by a general meeting of the Marylebone Club, to force upon a reluctant cricket world a measure to which so many eminent judges are entirely opposed, cannot be anything but injurious to cricket, and, I think, disastrous to the reputation of the Marylebone Club as a cricket law giver. For those reasons, gentlemen, I beg to move the rejection of this proposal. (Cheers.)

Mr A. G. Steel: My lords, and gentlemen, – In the ordinary course of events my friend Lord Hawke would have seconded Mr Denison's proposal this afternoon, but, as you have heard, he is somewhat indisposed, and a few moments ago I was asked if I would second the proposal instead of Lord Hawke, and I at once said that I would be delighted to do so, because I am dead against this proposal. Many years ago I was a bowler, and in spite of that fact I am dead against the proposal, because I do not think it is in the interests of the game. Now, we have heard two – if I may say so – excellent speeches, one from Mr Lyttelton, and the other from Mr Denison, and I am not going to make a speech to-day. My object is to get up and tell you that, personally, I think it would be against the best interests of the game if this proposed alteration is carried to-day. Now, I do not so much object in principle to the off-side of the wicket – that is to the batsman if he puts his leg across the off-stump, and the ball whips back to hit the wicket, he should be out. I do not so much object to that, but I do object to it on the leg-side. I think it is an impossibility as we play the game at present to have this rule altered. It seems to me that you have only to have two medium-paced leg bowlers, under-arm, and no side will get any runs – you will have them all out lbw. As I said before, I am not going to make a speech, but I will ask you, remembering that the captains were against the proposal, and that there is an enormous amount of feeling amongst cricketers against it, I ask you heartily to say that this proposed alteration shall not take effect this afternoon. (Applause.)

Mr R. A. H. Mitchell: Sir Spencer, my lords, and gentlemen, – I hope you will bear with me while I say a few words about the proposed alteration of the lbw rule, because it is one that I have personally supported now for about, at all events, seventeen years; because I was a supporter of it when the great alterations were made in the rules in, I think, the year 1884. I am not perfectly certain about the date. I should like to say a few words first on what appear to me to be the merits of the case. I must go back, I am afraid, to a time when most of those who are now playing first-class cricket had either not appeared on the scene, or were still in their nurse's arms; therefore I may be looked upon almost as an antedeluvian, but at that time the rule was the same; but we were taught, and I have had a good deal of teaching at cricket, and I have always taught players not to put their leg in front more than is absolutely necessary, and in my day there was no one who deliberately stopped the ball with his leg. That may have been stupidity; I cannot say. Someone spoke of "better sportsmen"; but I cannot believe that – I do not believe we were better sportsmen than the cricketers of the present day. But we did not learn to do that, and I totally disagree with Mr Steel, sorry as I am to do so, about balls on the leg side. It would introduce certainly a different style from the present but if I may I will describe the stroke we were taught to play to a good-length ball. Of course, there was a good deal of bowling round the wicket then, and instead of putting your leg in front to a ball that was pitched off the wicket which would take the wicket, we were taught to put the leg a little to the left, and play straight at the ball. That I believe to be the true game. Now people are taught to put their leg in front and tuck it round. Which is the better style I must leave to your own decision. I know which commends itself to me. As to its being impossible, I know it is not impossible, because people in my days had to contend with as much bowling round the wicket as over the wicket. I quite agree it is impossible in the present style. If people will put their legs in front of the wicket, under the proposed alteration they will, of course, very rapidly go back to the pavilion; but you must remember those who support the rule wish to see them go back much quicker than they do now. I think a great deal of the arguments I have seen – I do not pretend to have read all the literature that has appeared upon the subject – but a great deal of what I have seen seems to me to condemn the proposed alteration on the ground that it will get the batsman out. That is what we wish to do. If you are content with the present state of the game which Mr Alfred Lyttelton has described, then, of course, I quite understand your objecting to any change in the law. I have read some of the letters which have appeared, and I think a great many of the people who have written them seem to forget that when the batsman goes to the wicket there is placed in his hands a piece of wood over four inches broad, which is supposed to meet the ball. It is idle to contend that the leg is for the defence of the wicket. I was always taught that the bat was. It seems to me that you can keep your leg clear of that line as long as you like. It is perfectly true that to play a fine ball correctly, pitched outside the off stump, it is necessary to step across the wicket, but then surely the bat is to meet the ball, and if the ball beats the bat, you ought to pay for it. Now I should like to say a few words about umpiring, because, although, of course, I have had nothing like the experience that Mr Steel, for instance, has had in first-class cricket, still I am afraid I must claim to have had more than thirty years' umpiring; I stood umpire at Eton two or three times a week, therefore I cannot say I have no experience. When you are appealed to under the present rule, three things you have to decide. The easiest of all is the question of whether the man's leg is between wicket and wicket: that, I conceive, he has very little difficulty in deciding. The most difficult point is as to whether the ball pitched straight or not; you have to be intent on the game every moment, and even then you cannot tell. That is the real thing we shall get rid of under the proposed alteration. Of course, the umpire may make a mistake as to whether the ball would have hit the wicket or not; so he does under the present rule. He must make some mistakes; that is one of the unfortunate blots in the game. Umpires will makes mistakes, and I do not think they will make more mistakes under the proposed alteration than they do now, because the great difficulty, to my mind, is removed. I should very much prefer, as an umpire, to have to umpire under the proposed alteration than under the rule as it exists now. Well, now, I should like to say a few words – I am afraid I am rather lengthy – but I should like to say a few words about our position as old cricketers in relation to those who are playing cricket now. I cannot follow Mr Denison through the questions about the committee or what they have done; I do not know them, and do not understand them, and there is no necessity to follow them. I remember a gentleman once saying something to me, it was about rather a difficult question, and I said, "Well, I should like to consult a friend upon it," and he said, "If I had not an opinion of my own, I should be sweeping a crossing now." And I think much about the same with regard to the Marylebone Club. We are a representative cricket body, let us do what we think best for the interests of the game. (Hear, hear.) That is my view; but at the same time I have always held this, that those who are playing cricket at the time ought to have the principal say in the question, and that is the great difficulty that I feel. As you know, when a question arises like this, those who are against the game represent – I do not use the words in an invidious sense – represent the noisy party. Those who do not want this change, leave it alone so far as writing goes. I think so far as I can learn there may be, and perhaps is, a large body of the present players against it. But, gentlemen, I should like to say to present players this: That if we grant you that, that we do not want to force a change upon you that is unpalatable even though we think it a good one ourselves, remember, it places on you a strong responsibility, and the responsibility seems to be this: You must either say, "We are content with the game as it is; we don't care twopence whether we finish our matches or not, or whether the game is dull, but we like it as it is; we like long scores, and three days' gate money"; or, if you are not content with that position, then I think it is for you to bring forward some change to shorten the game. It is not enough to say that; you must be prepared to come forward and say what will improve the game, because it is perfectly certain there is a wide discontent amongst a large number with the present state of things, and we are discontented with it because we are afraid it is degenerating from a sport into a profession, and that we do not like. We believe it to be the national game; and we do not want to see it cut out or even impaired by any other games such as are attracting and may attract notice, but we want to see the game a real good sporting game. And with reference to that, I should like to say one word more. I think of a remark which Mr Denison made, that it would make the game slower. Now in my day I consider that, owing to the fact that we had not found out how to defend our wicket with our legs, we were very much on the alert to hit every bad ball, because we knew our time was not likely to be so long as it is now, and we wanted to make use of every opportunity. Under the present system no one wants to make use of any opportunity. They only want to stick there, knowing that the bowler will get tired. Your Palmer cannot go on trying to twist the ball on a good wicket when he finds it is only intercepted by the leg if it beats the batsman. That is what makes it dull, and the batsman plays a slow game, except a few who are most attractive. All I can say is I must apologise for having kept you so long, but my interest in the game must be my excuse.

Mr Denison: I only wish to make an explanatory statement on what Mr Mitchell has said. He has asked why we did not propose any scheme. We did not propose one because there is only one scheme in possession of the house.

Mr Mitchell: Not to-night; I do not mean that. (Cries of "Vote, vote!")

Mr Warner: Mr Lyttelton talked as if one should only play on the off-side, and never by any chance make a stroke on the leg-side. Has he never seen Ranjitsinhji, Fry, or MacLaren? Mr Lyttelton talked about the poor bowler. Such men as Albert Trott and Rhodes are absolutely opposed to any alteration. I do not say this from any selfish motives, because I know I am no bowler. I assure you I have the true interests of the game at heart, and as I have played all over the world I think I am entitled to express an opinion. This has been the finest game in the world for generations, and so I ask you to beware how you tamper with its present laws.

The Chairman: You have all heard the admirable speeches that have been made, and I do not think anybody would be likely to alter his opinion if they spoke on for ever.

Mr Harvey Fellows: My Lords, and Gentlemen, – I should like to say a few words. I should imagine that every fair-minded cricketer would be of opinion that the bowler should always have a free wicket. The batsman has a bat wherewith to defend it, and I think, in common fairness to the bowler, if he bowls a ball which beats the batsman, and would have hit the wicket if the batsman's legs were not in the way, the batsman ought to pay the penalty and be out. But, with reference to the batsman stopping the ball with his legs, if his legs were not before the wicket, of course it would not be out. What can be more unfair towards the bowler than that he should have the ball stopped by the body after having beaten the bat? Now, let me mention one subject about which we ought to be unanimous. Did we not all condemn the mode in which Shrewsbury used to play the ball with his leg? Where is the true cricket if the batsman is not to be confined to using his bat for the protection of his wicket? Now, with reference to the bowler, it is awfully hard upon him. And what is the present state of the law? I am sure you will all agree with me in one illustration. Take a fast bowler who bowls round the wicket. How can he get a leg-before-wicket, except he tosses what you call a yorker? And the idea of a fast bowler's ball pitching in a line between wickets . . . (Cries of "Time" and "Vote.") The eyes of all cricketers are upon this meeting, and they will see whether votes will be given to support the true principle of cricket, namely, that the ball should not be stopped by a man's legs, but by the bat which he has for that purpose. All I can say is, gentlemen, that if you consider what is fair with reference to the bowler, you will alter this law so that a batsman should know that he has to stop the ball with his bat, and not with his leg. (Cries of "Vote, vote.")

Mr C. C. Clarke: I think the writers to the papers based their calculations, if you follow it carefully, on wet wickets. In every paragraph you see "wet wickets," and at the end they recommend you to try a change. (Cries of "Vote, vote.")

The Chairman: I will now take a show of hands upon the question.

After the show of hands the Chairman said: Well, gentlemen, it is quite impossible for us to decide, and I therefore ask you to vote as you leave the room. The result will be announced in the press tomorrow.

I will take this opportunity of informing you that Lord Howe has consented to be President for the ensuing year.

The figures were declared as follows: – For the proposition, 259; against, 188. Majority for, 71. This, however, being less than a two-thirds majority, the proposal was not passed.

## MCC AND GROUND v LEICESTERSHIRE

Played at Lord's, May 16, 17, 18, 1901

The contest with Leicestershire proved to be one of the most interesting of the MCC fixtures, and it was only on the third day that the county, after making a capital start in the fourth innings, failed at just the critical point. A brilliant if lucky display by Gilbert Jessop was the great feature of the first day, the famous hitter, who was badly missed when four, and again when 113, scoring 169 out of 244 in an hour and three-quarters, by means of a 6, a 5, twenty-six 4s, six 3s, ten 2s, and sixteen singles. The position at the end of the first day was slightly against Leicestershire, who, with half their wickets down for 163, were 138 behind, but on the following morning, thanks to a faultless 71 by Geeson, they managed to head the other total by six runs. In the Club's second innings, Jessop was again in dashing form, making 49 out of 83 in thirty-five minutes, but the honours fell to Murdoch, whose 93, obtained in two hours and ten minutes, was without a fault of any kind. His chief hits were twelve 4s. He was sixth out at 197, and with eight wickets down for 205, Leicestershire did not look like being set a heavy task, but as the last two partnerships yielded 95 runs, the county were put in to make 295 on the third day. Their score was 98 before the second wicket fell, and they appeared to be winning, but subsequently Grace and Thompson carried all before them, and the MCC won by 93 runs.

### MCC and Ground

| | | | |
|---|---:|---|---:|
| Mr W. G. Grace b Woodcock | 11 | – b Woodcock | 15 |
| Mr W. I. Murdoch c Whiteside b Wood | 43 | – b Woodcock | 93 |
| A. Hearne c and b King | 2 | – c Whiteside b Woodcock | 0 |
| Mr G. L. Jessop b Geeson | 169 | – c Whitehead b Geeson | 49 |
| J. Thompson b Woodcock | 28 | – c Coe b Wood | 0 |
| A. E. Trott c Knight b Geeson | 5 | – b Woodcock | 12 |
| J. H. Board b Geeson | 19 | – run out | 16 |
| Mr A. M. Miller c Crawford b Woodcock | 0 | – b Coe | 36 |
| Mr T. A. D. Bevington b Geeson | 0 | – c Whitehead b Woodcock | 2 |
| Mr A. Conan Doyle b Woodcock | 1 | – not out | 32 |
| J. T. Hearne not out | 14 | – c Whiteside b King | 30 |
| B 9 | 9 | B 7, l-b 5, w 3 | 15 |
| | **301** | | **300** |

### Leicestershire

| | | | |
|---|---:|---|---:|
| Mr C. J. B. Wood b Trott | 29 | – b Thompson | 55 |
| A. E. Knight b Grace | 16 | – b Grace | 20 |
| A. D. Pougher c and b Thompson | 36 | – b Thompson | 20 |
| S. Coe c Trott b Thompson | 22 | – c A. Hearne b Thompson | 20 |
| H. Whitehead b Trott | 0 | – b Thompson | 0 |
| J. H. King c A. Hearne b Trott | 3 | – b Grace | 7 |
| Mr C. E. de Trafford b J. T. Hearne | 66 | – lbw b Grace | 13 |
| Mr R. T. Crawford c A. Hearne b J. T. Hearne | 8 | – c Thompson b Grace | 21 |
| F. Geeson ht wkt b Grace | 71 | – c Murdoch b Grace | 16 |
| A. Woodcock st Board b J. T. Hearne | 0 | – b Thompson | 17 |
| J. P. Whiteside not out | 17 | – not out | 7 |
| B 19, l-b 20 | 39 | B 2, l-b 3 | 5 |
| | **307** | | **201** |

### Leicestershire Bowling

| | Overs | Mdns | Runs | Wkts | Overs | Mdns | Runs | Wkts |
|---|---|---|---|---|---|---|---|---|
| Woodcock | 22 | 5 | 85 | 4 | 24 | 3 | 82 | 5 |
| King | 10 | 1 | 43 | 1 | 5.3 | — | 35 | 1 |
| Coe | 5 | — | 29 | — | 11 | 2 | 33 | 1 |
| Wood | 6 | 1 | 38 | 1 | 10 | — | 46 | 1 |
| Crawford | 2 | — | 25 | — | | | | |
| Geeson | 10.4 | — | 72 | 4 | 13 | 1 | 81 | 1 |
| Pougher | | | | | 9 | 6 | 8 | — |

## MCC Bowling

| | Overs | Mdns | Runs | Wkts | Overs | Mdns | Runs | Wkts |
|---|---|---|---|---|---|---|---|---|
| J. T. Hearne ....... | 31 | 11 | 71 | 3 | 5 | 1 | 19 | — |
| Grace ............ | 26.3 | 8 | 53 | 2 | 22 | 3 | 68 | 5 |
| Trott ............ | 33 | 5 | 93 | 3 | 8 | 1 | 28 | 0 |
| Thompson ........ | 17 | 5 | 51 | 2 | 12.1 | 1 | 60 | 5 |
| Jessop .......... | | | | | 7 | 1 | 21 | 0 |

Umpires: M. Sherwin and W. Hearn.

# MCC AND GROUND v LONDON COUNTY

## Played at Lord's, June 13, 14, 1901

Bad batting and extremely fine bowling marked the first stage of this match, when no fewer than 24 wickets fell for an aggregate of 306 runs. Grace failed with the bat, but surpassed himself with the ball, dismissing seven of the last eight MCC batsmen for 30 runs. With Grace, Fry, Wood, Vine and Goldie on the side, London County looked likely to gain a big advantage on going in against so poor a total as 94, but, they found Mead and Trott equally as difficult as the Club had found Grace and Vine, and in the end there was only a difference of 15 runs in the respective scores. Aided by escapes in the field, Carpenter and Rawlin gave the home team an advantage, as they only had four wickets down for 103 at the drawing of stumps, and though Grace and Vine again bowled well on the Friday, the London County were set 184 to win. However, with Fry, Goldie, and W. Smith doing themselves full justice, the visitors won by four wickets. Smith played splendidly for his side, but the best thing in the match was Grace's bowling. The veteran actually took thirteen wickets for 110 runs.

### MCC and Ground

| | | | |
|---|---|---|---|
| H. Carpenter c Wood b Vine ................... | 4 | – c Keigwin b Vine ............... | 61 |
| Mr W. L. Murdoch c Goldie b Grace ............. | 24 | – c Gilman b Vine ............... | 5 |
| J. Thompson b Vine .......................... | 4 | – lbw b Grace ................... | 20 |
| Mr G. J. V. Weigall b Vine .................... | 7 | – b Grace ...................... | 0 |
| A. E. Trott c F. E. Smith b Grace ............... | 2 | – b Grace ...................... | 0 |
| J. T. Rawlin c and b Grace .................... | 0 | – c Bompas b Grace ............. | 39 |
| Mr A. Conan Doyle not out .................... | 21 | – c Keigwin b Grace ............ | 10 |
| Mr C. P. Goodden c Gilman b Grace ........... | 2 | – b Vine ...................... | 6 |
| H. R. Murrell lbw b Grace .................... | 2 | – b Grace ..................... | 34 |
| W. Mead c Woods b Grace ................... | 5 | – c Gilman b Vine ............. | 8 |
| W. Smith (Wilts.) c and b Grace ............... | 4 | – not out ..................... | 2 |
| B 14, l-b 4, w 1 ................... | 19 | B 7, l-b 3, w 3 ............ | 13 |
| | **94** | | **198** |

### London County

| | | | |
|---|---|---|---|
| Mr C. J. B. Wood c Murrell b Rawlin ............ | 23 | – b Mead ..................... | 10 |
| Mr P. G. Gale b Trott ....................... | 0 | – b Mead ..................... | 5 |
| J. Vine c Murdoch b Trott .................... | 20 | – not out ..................... | 5 |
| Mr C. B. Fry b Mead ........................ | 2 | – c Murrell b Mead .............. | 32 |
| Mr W. G. Grace b Mead ..................... | 0 | – lbw b Trott ................... | 13 |
| Mr K. O. Goldie b Mead ..................... | 16 | – c Carpenter b Trott ............ | 45 |
| Mr H. S. Keigwin b Mead .................... | 0 | – run out ...................... | 0 |
| Mr. J. Gilman b Mead ....................... | 4 | | |
| Mr W. Smith not out ........................ | 18 | – not out ...................... | 61 |
| Mr H. S. Bompas b Trott .................... | 0 | | |
| F. E. Smith c Murdoch b Trott ................. | 3 | | |
| B 13, l-b 10 ...................... | 23 | B 12, l-b 1 .............. | 13 |
| | **109** | | **184** |

**London County Bowling**

| | Overs | Mdns | Runs | Wkts | Overs | Mdns | Runs | Wkts |
|---|---|---|---|---|---|---|---|---|
| Vine . . . . . . . . . . . . | 18 | 8 | 34 | 3 | 32 | 6 | 101 | 4 |
| F. E. Smith . . . . . . . . | 5 | 2 | 11 | — | 2 | 2 | — | — |
| Grace . . . . . . . . . . . | 12.4 | 2 | 30 | 7 | 32.2 | 11 | 80 | 6 |
| Goldie . . . . . . . . . . | | | | | 2 | 1 | 4 | — |

**MCC Bowling**

| | Overs | Mdns | Runs | Wkts | Overs | Mdns | Runs | Wkts |
|---|---|---|---|---|---|---|---|---|
| Mead . . . . . . . . . . . . | 26 | 14 | 30 | 5 | 24 | 5 | 41 | 3 |
| Trott . . . . . . . . . . . . | 18.2 | 5 | 40 | 4 | 23.1 | 5 | 83 | 2 |
| Rawlin . . . . . . . . . . | 7 | — | 16 | 1 | 4 | — | 12 | — |
| Thompson . . . . . . . . | | | | | 4 | — | 25 | — |
| Smith (Wilts) . . . . . . | | | | | 2 | — | 10 | — |

Umpires: M. Sherwin and A. Pike.

## OXFORD v CAMBRIDGE

Played at Lord's, July 6, 7, 8, 1905

The Oxford and Cambridge elevens had shown such moderate form in their trial games that their meeting was looked forward to with far less interest than usual, but the match itself proved an agreeable surprise, being full of incident and marked on the second day by a change of fortune that was nothing less than astounding. When the sixth wicket fell in their second innings, Cambridge were 24 behind, and it seemed any odds they would be beaten, but in the end they won by 40 runs. Leaving aside the matches of 1870, 1875, and 1896, there have been few finishes more remarkable in the whole series of contests between the two Universities. Oxford had seven old Blues in their eleven, the remaining places being filled by N. R. Udal, a senior from Winchester, F. A. H. Henley, a senior from Forest School, E. L. Wright, a freshman from Winchester, and W. S. Bird, a freshman from Malvern. Cambridge were almost as well off in the way of seasoned players, six members of the team having taken part in the match of 1904. The five new men were L. G. Colbeck (Marlborough), P. R. May (private), A. F. Morcom (Repton), and C. C. Page (Malvern) – all seniors – and the brilliant freshman from Repton, R. A. Young.

The first day's play was, to say the best of it, rather flat. Not more than twelve thousand people were on the ground and the cricket, though always interesting, never rose to any great height of excellence. On winning the toss, Cambridge stayed in till a quarter to four for a total of 218. Up to a certain point a far better score seemed in prospect, but the last five wickets went down for 35 runs. Young bore out the hopes formed of him in the trial matches, Keigwin played with a freedom that contrasted strongly with his over-cautious methods in the previous year, and Payne made a number of fine hits, but, speaking generally, the batting was very ordinary in quality. Oxford lost four wickets for 99, but they had a great deal the best of the game at the drawing of stumps, Raphael and Wright putting on 67 runs together in little more than three-quarters of an hour and being still not out at the close. Wright, after a slow start, hit with great freedom, but he was nearly bowled off his pads by Morcom three times in one over. On the following morning the two batsmen did what they liked with the Cambridge bowling, and so long as they stayed in Oxford looked to have the match well in hand. In eight-five minutes 124 were put on, the partnership for the fifth wicket producing in all 191 runs. Raphael's batting was beyond reproach, but Wright, after getting sixty, gave two of the easiest chances, being missed from skyers at short leg and slip. Over anxiety to get his hundred cost Wright his wicket. He hit all across at a straight ball and was clean bowled. Raphael also missed his hundred, but, as he fell to a perfect length ball that broke back a little, he could not reproach himself. Had he made one more run he would, with exactly the same scores, have rivalled the late William Yardley's feat of getting two hundreds in the University match. In third wicket down at 71 he was out seventh at 297, his innings lasting nearly three hours. Oxford lost their last five wickets in three-quarters of an hour for 29 runs, but nevertheless they finished up with a lead of 101. For the rest of the day the cricket was of absorbing interest. In the course of five minutes batting before lunch Cambridge, on going in for the second time, lost Young to a wonderful catch, low down with the left hand in the slips, and so splendidly did Evans bowl after the interval that half the side were out for 44 and six wickets down for 77. Then came the astonishing change to which reference has already been made. Colbeck who went in with the score at 44, was joined by McDonnell and in the course of eight-five minutes 143 runs were put on. The Oxford bowling became demoralized much sooner than it should have been, and Carlisle did not manage his changes with the best of judgment, but as to the splendid character of the batting there could not be two opinions. In no way affected by the position of the game Colbeck from the first played with rare confidence and freedom, hitting on the off-side in most brilliant fashion. McDonell was not quite so attractive to look at, but he also played a fine game. Still, despite all that the two batsmen did, the innings was over at a quarter to six, Oxford being left with 164 to get to win. All things considered, Colbeck's 107 was one of the most remarkable innings ever seen in the University match. He cut balls off the middle stump and ran all sorts of risks, but so admirable was his timing that he made very few faulty strokes. He was batting for two hours and a quarter and hit thirteen 4s.

With only twenty-five minutes left for play Carlisle altered Oxford's batting order, going in with Bird, and saving the best men for the morning. The policy was a sound one but it turned out disastrously. Three wickets were lost for 4 runs and Henley, who played out time with Udal, had the narrowest escape of being bowled, a ball touching his leg stump without removing the bails. At the close the score was 15. On Saturday 20 runs came from the first three overs, but after that Oxford never looked like winning. Henley was bowled, leg stump out of the ground, at 35 and at 47 a yorker shattered Raphael's wicket. Then a break-back bowled Udal, Morcom having so far, in little more than half-an-hour, taken three wickets at a cost of 6 runs. So long as Evans stayed there was hope for Oxford, but at 76 that batsman was out to a remarkable catch in the slips, McDonell stopping the ball low down with his right hand and securing it with his left at the third attempt. After the eighth wicket had fallen Wright made a great effort for his side, keeping nearly all the bowling to himself for four or five overs. However by ten minutes to one the innings was completed for 123, Cambridge winning by 40 runs. In this last innings Morcom and Napier bowled unchanged. Morcom, who took six wickets – four of them bowled down – was in great form, keeping a good length, coming off the ground very quickly, and again and again breaking back enough to beat the bat. Napier, though not so deadly, was very accurate and difficult to score from. Nothing that they had done in the trial matches suggested the cricket Cambridge showed from half-past three on the second day to the finish and no side could have more fully deserved to win.

## Cambridge

| | | | | |
|---|---|---|---|---|
| Mr R. A. Young lbw b Henley | 51 | – c Branston b Evans | 9 |
| Mr C. H. Eyre b Udal | 13 | – b Evans | 0 |
| Mr E. W. Mann c Henley b Evans | 14 | – c Foster b Evans | 0 |
| Mr C. C. Page c Bird b Martin | 12 | – c Bird b Evans | 4 |
| Mr R. P. Keigwin c Evans b Udal | 50 | – b Udal | 8 |
| Mr M. W. Payne c and b Udal | 36 | – c Foster b Evans | 26 |
| Mr L. G. Colbeck b Udal | 1 | – c Burn b Henley | 107 |
| Mr H. C. McDonell c Branston b Martin | 6 | – c Branston b Udal | 60 |
| Mr P. R. May b Martin | 0 | – c Foster b Henley | 10 |
| Mr A. F. Morcom not out | 1 | – not out | 13 |
| Mr G. G. Napier c and b Udal | 18 | – b Henley | 0 |
| B 9, l-b 2, n-b 5 | 16 | B 14, l-b 5, n-b 8 | 27 |
| | **218** | | **264** |

## Oxford

| | | | |
|---|---|---|---|
| Mr W. H. B. Evans b McDonell | 21 | – c McDonell b Napier | 8 |
| Mr K. M. Carlisle lbw b McDonell | 25 | – run out | 1 |
| Mr G. T. Branston c and b Napier | 28 | – c Payne b Morcom | 0 |
| Mr G. N. Foster b May | 4 | – c Payne b Morcom | 20 |
| Mr J. E. Raphael b Napier | 99 | – b Morcom | 6 |
| Mr E. L. Wright b Morcom | 95 | – b Morcom | 26 |
| Mr W. S. Bird lbw b Napier | 2 | – b Napier | 3 |
| Mr N. R. Udal not out | 16 | – b Morcom | 21 |
| Mr F. A. H. Henley b Payne b Morcom | 1 | – b Morcom | 11 |
| Mr E. G. Martin c Payne b Napier | 4 | – b Napier | 9 |
| Mr R. C. W. Burn b Morcom | 1 | – not out | 4 |
| B 16, l-b 5, n-b 2 | 23 | B 8, l-b 4, n-b 2 | 14 |
| | **319** | | **123** |

### Oxford University Bowling

| | Overs | Mdns | Runs | Wkts | Overs | Mdns | Runs | Wkts |
|---|---|---|---|---|---|---|---|---|
| Burn | 6 | — | 20 | — | 4 | — | 26 | — |
| Udal | 23.4 | 2 | 73 | 5 | 18 | 5 | 54 | 2 |
| Evans | 11 | 1 | 50 | 1 | 14 | 4 | 66 | 5 |
| Martin | 14 | 7 | 19 | 3 | 7 | — | 32 | — |
| Henley | 9 | 1 | 40 | 1 | 6.4 | — | 39 | 3 |
| Branston | | | | | 3 | — | 20 | — |

### Cambridge University Bowling

| | Overs | Mdns | Runs | Wkts | Overs | Mdns | Runs | Wkts |
|---|---|---|---|---|---|---|---|---|
| Napier | 29 | 7 | 92 | 4 | 17.4 | 2 | 68 | 3 |
| Morcom | 25.5 | 4 | 69 | 3 | 17 | 2 | 41 | 6 |
| McDonell | 15 | 1 | 57 | 2 | | | | |
| May | 14 | 1 | 48 | 1 | | | | |
| Keigwin | 6 | — | 17 | — | | | | |
| Mann | 2 | — | 13 | — | | | | |

Umpires: V. A. Titchmarsh and J. Phillips.

# MCC AND GROUND v LEICESTERSHIRE

### Played at Lord's, May 30, 31, June 1, 1907

The feature of the match was the unusual result – a tie. Braund played a great innings for his side on the opening day scoring 137 out of 303 in three hours and twenty minutes. He found useful colleagues in Reeves, who assisted in a first partnership of 57, and Lawton, who made 56 out of 91 in fifty minutes. The cricket was highly attractive on the fast turf, the rate of scoring being between ninety and a hundred runs an hour. Braund gave two very difficult chances and hit twenty 4s. Leicestershire lost three wickets overnight for 69, but, thanks to Coe, who scored exactly 100 in two hours and ten minutes, they got within 132 of the Club's total. There had been heavy rain in the early hours and the wicket, gradually drying, was treacherous when the MCC went in a second time, with the result that they were all dismissed in seventy-five minutes for 69 runs, the county being left with 202 to get to win. Three batsmen were got rid of for 68 on the Friday, and there were five wickets down on the Saturday for 83, but profiting by some blunders in the field King and Coe hit well and the match ended as stated, in a tie.

## MCC and Ground

| | | | |
|---|---|---|---|
| L. C. Braund c and b Crawford | 137 | – c Odell b Jayes | 19 |
| W. Reeves c King b Odell | 39 | – b Odell | 17 |
| Rev. W. P. G. McCormick b King | 17 | – c Crawford b Odell | 0 |
| Mr A. E. Lawton b Coe | 56 | – c Crawford b Jayes | 4 |
| Mr G. J. V. Weigall b King | 19 | – b Odell | 5 |
| Mr H. D. Stratton b King | 5 | – not out | 6 |
| C. P. Buckenham c Payne b Odell | 30 | – b Jayes | 5 |
| Capt. C. Disney Roebuck c Crawford b Whitehead | 7 | – c Crawford b Jayes | 5 |
| W. Overton c Astill b Odell | 19 | – b Jayes | 0 |
| W. Mead c Wood b Odell | 22 | – c Astill b Odell | 0 |
| Mr R. P. Lewis not out | 0 | – lbw b Odell | 3 |
| B 16, l-b 4 | 20 | B 2, l-b 3 | 5 |
| | **371** | | **69** |

## Leicestershire

| | | | |
|---|---|---|---|
| Mr C. J. B. Wood c Lewis b Buckenham | 9 | – c Stratton b Mead | 5 |
| H. Whitehead c Braund b Buckenham | 24 | – b Reeves | 34 |
| J. H. King c Lewis b Buckenham | 21 | – c Braund b Reeves | 51 |
| A. E. Knight b Roebuck b Buckenham | 6 | – c Braund b Reeves | 4 |
| S. Coe c Lewis b Reeves | 100 | – b Overton | 66 |
| Mr V. F. S. Crawford b Reeves | 45 | – c Braund b Overton | 23 |
| Mr W. W. Odell run out | 1 | – c Reeves b Braund | 1 |
| T. Jayes lbw b Mead | 8 | – st Lewis b Overton | 0 |
| Sir A. Hazelrigg c Reeves b Overton | 5 | – c Reeves b Mead | 5 |
| W. E. Astill run out | 2 | – not out | 3 |
| Payne not out | 7 | – c Braund b Reeves | 0 |
| B 6, l-b 3, n-b 2 | 11 | B 7, l-b 1, n-b 1 | 9 |
| | **239** | | **201** |

## Leicestershire Bowling

| | Overs | Mdns | Runs | Wkts | Overs | Mdns | Runs | Wkts |
|---|---|---|---|---|---|---|---|---|
| Jayes | 19 | 4 | 82 | — | 12 | 4 | 31 | 5 |
| Odell | 18 | 3 | 76 | 4 | 11.3 | 1 | 33 | 5 |
| King | 19 | 2 | 58 | 3 | | | | |
| Astill | 16 | 4 | 59 | — | | | | |
| Coe | 9 | 2 | 32 | 1 | | | | |
| Whitehead | 6 | 2 | 20 | 1 | | | | |
| Crawford | 4 | — | 24 | 1 | | | | |

## MCC and Ground Bowling

| | Overs | Mdns | Runs | Wkts | Overs | Mdns | Runs | Wkts |
|---|---|---|---|---|---|---|---|---|
| Buckenham | 16 | 1 | 17 | 4 | 7 | 2 | 24 | — |
| Mead | 29 | 9 | 87 | 1 | 20.1 | 2 | 77 | 2 |
| Reeves | 8.4 | — | 36 | 2 | 19 | 5 | 52 | 4 |
| Overton | 5 | — | 18 | 1 | 8 | 3 | 15 | 3 |
| Braund | 1 | — | 8 | — | 5 | — | 24 | 1 |
| McCormick | 1 | — | 5 | — | | | | |

Umpires: Bean and W. Attewell.

## ETON v HARROW

Played at Lord's, July 8, 9, 1910

Eton and Harrow have been meeting on the cricket field for over a hundred years, but they have never played a match quite so remarkable as that of 1910. Indeed in the whole history of cricket there has been nothing more sensational. After following their innings Eton were only four ahead with nine wickets down, and yet in the end they won the game by 9 runs. The nearest parallel to this finish that one can recall was one between Lancashire and Oxford University in 1888. On that occasion the county followed-on, and managed to win although when their eight wicket fell they were still 17 runs behind. The struggle between the two public schools last season will be known for all time as Fowler's match. Never has a school cricketer risen to the occasion in more astonishing fashion. When Harrow went in with only 55 to get, Fowler took command of the game, secured eight wickets – five of them bowled down – for 23 runs and brought off what might fairly be described as a forty to one chance.

Until the second afternoon was far advanced the match proved one-sided to a degree. On the first day Harrow going in on a soft, but by no means difficult pitch, ran up a total of 232, and when bad light caused stumps to be drawn, five of Eton's best wickets had fallen for 40 runs. By far the best batting for Harrow was shown in different styles by Wilson and Hillyard. In first and out fifth wicket down at 133 Wilson took two hours and a quarter to get his 53, his play all the time being very patient and watchful. Hillyard, more vigorous in his methods, scored 62 in an hour and three-quarters, among his hits being a six to square leg and half-a-dozen 4s. On Saturday morning, Eton's first innings was soon finished off for 67, and a follow-on against a balance of 165 was involved. At first things went so badly that half the wickets were down for 65, no one being able to get the ball away on the slow pitch. The first change in the game came with the partnership between Fowler, and Wigan, 42 runs being added for the sixth wicket in fifty minutes. When Wigan left, Boswell, who had been last man in the first innings, joined Fowler and another good start was made, three-quarters of an hour's play producing 57 runs. Still despite Fowler's heroic efforts – his 64 was the highest innings in the match – the position was reached of Eton being only 4 runs ahead with a wicket to fall. Then began the cricket which will for ever make the match memorable. Kaye joined Manners, and so finely and fearlessly did Manners hit that in less than twenty-five minutes 50 runs were put on, the total being carried from 169 to 219. A remarkable catch in the slips at last brought the innings to an end, Hopley just reaching the ball and turning it to Jameson, who held it a few inches from the ground. There can be no doubt that Earle, the Harrow captain, who had made many changes in the early part of the innings, was at fault in keeping himself and Hillyard on too long. In the case of any ordinary match the ground would have been half empty before the Eton innings closed, but an Eton and Harrow crowd is a law to itself and when Harrow went in with 55 to get about 10,000 people watched the cricket. Whatever their feelings, they must have been glad they stayed as they may never see such a finish again. Probably Harrow made a mistake in having the heavy roller on. At any rate Fowler was able at once to bowl his off-break with deadly effect. He bowled Wilson in the first over; at eight he bowled Hopley; and at the same total, Turnbull, the left-handed hitter was caught in the long field. Earle seemed likely to win the match easily enough for Harrow, but after he had hit up 13 runs, a catch at slip sent him back at 21. Without the addition of a run, Monckton was bowled and Hillyard well caught low down at short mid-on. In this way, as the result of half an hour's cricket, six wickets were down for 21, Fowler having taken them all. Blount was caught and bowled at 26 by Steel, who had just gone on for Kaye, and then Jameson, who had been batting for nearly forty minutes without getting a run, was so badly hurt that for a few minutes the game had to be delayed. With victory in sight, the Eton team played the keenest possible cricket, nothing being thrown away in the field. A yorker bowled Straker at 29, and, after Graham had hit a three, Jameson was bowled by Fowler. It was not to be expected that Graham and

Alexander would get the 23 runs still required, but they made a desperate effort, carrying the score to 45 or only 10 to win. Then a catch low down in the slips got rid of Alexander and a wonderful match was over. The scence of enthusiasm at the finish was quite indescribable. From the time he went on at 21, Steel with his leg breaks gave Fowler excellent support and the Eton fielding all round was magnificent.

### Harrow

| | | |
|---|---|---|
| Mr T. O. Jameson c Lubbock b Fowler | 5 – b Fowler | 2 |
| Mr T. B. Wilson b Kaye | 53 – b Fowler | 0 |
| Mr G. W. V. Hopley b Fowler | 35 – b Fowler | 8 |
| Mr T. L. G. Turnbull lbw b Fowler | 2 – c Boswell b Fowler | 0 |
| Mr G. F. Earle c Wigan b Steel | 20 – c Wigan b Fowler | 13 |
| Mr W. T. Monckton c Lubbock b Stock | 20 – b Fowler | 0 |
| Mr J. M. Hillyard st Lubbock b Fowler | 62 – c Kaye b Fowler | 0 |
| Mr C. H. B. Blount c Holland b Steel | 4 – c and b Steel | 5 |
| Mr A. C. Straker c Holland b Steel | 2 – b Fowler | 1 |
| Mr O. B. Graham c and b Steel | 6 – not out | 7 |
| Hon. R. H. I. G. Alexander not out | 2 – c Holland b Steel | 8 |
| B 18, l-b 2, n-b 1 | 21 | B | 1 |
| | **232** | **45** |

### Eton

| | | |
|---|---|---|
| Mr R. H. Lubbock lbw b Earle | 9 – c Straker b Hillyard | 9 |
| Mr C. W. Tafnell b Hillyard | 5 – lbw b Alexander | 7 |
| Mr W. T. Birchenough c Hopley b Graham | 5 – c Turnball b Jameson | 22 |
| Mr W. T. Holland c Hopley b Hillyard | 2 – st Monckton b Alexander | 5 |
| Mr R. St. L. Fowler c Graham b Jameson | 21 – c Earle b Hillyard | 64 |
| Mr A. I. Steel b Graham | 0 – c Hopley b Hillyard | 6 |
| Mr D. G. Wigan c Turnbull b Jameson | 8 – b Graham | 16 |
| Mr A. B. Stock lbw b Alexander | 2 – lbw b Earle | 0 |
| Hon. J. N. Manners c Graham b Alexander | 4 – not out | 40 |
| Mr K. Lister Kaye c Straker b Alexander | 0 – c Jameson b Earle | 13 |
| Mr W. G. K. Boswell not out | 0 – b Earle | 32 |
| B 10, w 1 | 11 | B 2, w 3 | 5 |
| | **67** | **219** |

### Eton Bowling

| | Overs | Mdns | Runs | Wkts | Overs | Mdns | Runs | Wkts |
|---|---|---|---|---|---|---|---|---|
| Fowler | 37.3 | 9 | 90 | 4 | 10 | 2 | 23 | 8 |
| Steel | 31 | 11 | 69 | 4 | 6.4 | 1 | 12 | 2 |
| Kaye | 12 | 5 | 23 | 1 | 3 | — | 9 | — |
| Stock | 7 | 2 | 12 | 1 | | | | |
| Boswell | 8 | 4 | 17 | — | | | | |

### Harrow Bowling

| | Overs | Mdns | Runs | Wkts | Overs | Mdns | Runs | Wkts |
|---|---|---|---|---|---|---|---|---|
| Earle | 12 | 9 | 4 | 1 | 17.3 | 3 | 57 | 3 |
| Hillyard | 19 | 9 | 28 | 2 | 23 | 7 | 65 | 2 |
| Graham | 9 | 7 | 13 | 2 | 8 | 2 | 33 | 1 |
| Jameson | 4 | 1 | 4 | 2 | 9 | 1 | 26 | 1 |
| Alexander | 4.1 | 1 | 7 | 3 | 14 | 4 | 33 | 2 |
| Wilson | | | | | 2 | 2 | — | — |

Umpires: J. Moss and J. P. Whiteside.

# AUSTRALIANS AND SOUTH AFRICANS IN ENGLAND

## ENGLAND v AUSTRALIA

Played at Birmingham, May 29, 30, 31, 1902

In the first of the five Test matches England experienced a strange mixture of good and bad luck. Up to a certain point fortune, in the shape of dropped catches, and a heavy downpour of rain that spoiled the game after the first day, was all on their side, but at the crucial point there came a complete change, rain by drenching the ground on the last day saving the Australians from a defeat that under ordinary circumstances would have been inevitable. Fourteen players had been picked for England, and all were in readiness at Birmingham, on the morning of the match, the three who had to stand down being J. R. Mason, Llewellyn, and Hayward. The choice had been most carefully made by the selection committee, and by general consent the eleven that went into the field represented English cricket, at this early period of the season, as fully as possible. The Australians had to do the best they could without Hugh Trumble, whose injured thumb was not in a condition to admit of his playing, and they left out Carter and Saunders, the latter of whom had not up to this time shown the bowling form which made him so invaluable in the last three test games. A beautiful wicket had been prepared, and when MacLaren beat Darling in the toss for innings, it was almost taken for granted that England would make a big score. In the end expectation was realised, but success only came after a deplorable start, and after the Australians had discounted their chances by two or three palpable blunders in the field. Fry was caught by the wicket-keeper standing back in the third over; a misunderstanding, for which Ranjitsinhji considered himself somewhat unjustly blamed, led to MacLaren being run out, and then Ranjitsinhji himself quite upset by what had happened, was clean bowled, three of the best English wickets being thus down for 35 runs. The position looked very critical indeed and the Australians, encouraged by success, fielded in their finest form. Happily for England, Jackson and Tyldesley, to some extent, saved the situation. Playing with great judgment and self-restraint against bowling that was changed every few overs, they were still together when at half-past one luncheon was taken, and the score, without further loss, had reached 99. However, soon after the resumption of the game, Jackson ended a beautiful innings by chopping a ball from Jones on to his wicket, and again England were in a bad way. Then came the dropped catches that had such a vital effect on the day's cricket. Tyldesley, with his score at 43, having three escapes. He was missed low down at mid-off by Jones and then, after Lilly had been taken from a skyer, he was palpably missed by Darling at mid-on, and nearly caught and bowled by Armstrong. In this case cricket was as unforgiving as whist, the Australians having to field for the rest of the afternoon, and England's score at the drawing of stumps standing at 351 for nine wickets. The turning point came with the partnership of Tyldesley and Hirst who, in an hour and twenty minutes, put on 94 runs. This was an invaluable stand, but after Hirst left, Jessop, playing very wild cricket, was soon got rid of by a catch at deep cover-point, seven wickets being down for 230. Braund helped to add 34 for the eighth wicket, and the score was up to 295 when Tyldesley was out lbw. The Lancashire batsman's innings of 138, apart from the chances referred to, was a truly magnificent display. He was at the wickets for four hours and twenty minutes, his defence being masterly and his cutting a marvel of power and accurate timing. He made most of his runs on the off-side, his hits including a 5 and twenty 4s. Lockwood and Rhodes played very freely at the end of the afternoon, and took the total from 295 to 351 without being parted.

So much rain fell during Thursday night that it was not until nearly three o'clock that the match was proceeded with. Some people expected that MacLaren would at once declare the English innings closed, but acting, it was understood, on Lilley's advice, he decided to let his own side go on batting for a time, so that his bowlers might not have to start work on a slippery foothold. He declared when the score had been raised to 376, and then followed one of the chief sensations of the cricket season of 1902, the Australians being got rid of in less than an hour and a half for 36, Trumper, who played fine cricket for seventy minutes, alone making a stand. The light was bad, but in the opinion of the umpires the wicket was by no means so difficult as to excuse such an ignominious break-down. Rhodes and Hirst bowled wonderfully well and Braund, in getting rid of Hill, brought off a most dazzling catch at slip. The Australians had of course to follow on, and at the call of time had scored 8 runs without the loss of a wicket. Had Friday night remained fine the Englishmen would have had the match in their hands, but rain fell for twelve hours without cessation, reducing the Edgbaston ground to such a condition that on Saturday morning it was seen at once that cricket would for several hours be out of the question. The afternoon turned out delightfully fine, but nothing was done until a quarter-past five, and but for the fact of thousands of people having been admitted to the ground after four o'clock, the match would no doubt have been abandoned without another ball being bowled. Loosing only two wickets the Australians easily played out time, the game being left drawn at half-past six.

## England

| | | | |
|---|---|---|---|
| Mr A. C. MacLaren run out | 9 | Mr G. L. Jessop c Hopkins b Trumper | 6 |
| Mr C. B. Fry c Kelly b Jones | 0 | L. C. Braund b Jones | 14 |
| K. S. Ranjitsinhji b Armstrong | 13 | W. H. Lockwood not out | 52 |
| Mr F. S. Jackson b Jones | 53 | W. Rhodes not out | 38 |
| J. T. Tyldesley lbw b Howell | 138 | L-b 3 | 3 |
| A. A. Lilley c Jones b Noble | 2 | | |
| G. H. Hirst c Armstrong b Trumper | 48 | (9 wkts dec.) 376 | |

## Australia

| | | | |
|---|---|---|---|
| V. Trumper b Hirst | 18 | – c Braund b Rhodes | 14 |
| R. A. Duff c Jessop b Rhodes | 2 | – c Fry b Braund | 15 |
| C. Hill c Braund b Hirst | 1 | – not out | 10 |
| S. E. Gregory lbw b Hirst | 0 | – not out | 1 |
| J. Darling c Jessop b Rhodes | 3 | | |
| M. A. Noble st Lilley b Rhodes | 3 | | |
| W. W. Armstrong c Lilley b Rhodes | 0 | | |
| A. J. Hopkins c Lilley b Rhodes | 5 | | |
| J. J. Kelly not out | 1 | | |
| E. Jones c Jackson b Rhodes | 0 | | |
| W. P. Howell c Fry b Rhodes | 0 | | |
| W 3 | 3 | L b 4, w 1, n-b 1 | 6 |
| | 36 | | 46 |

## Australian Bowling

| | Overs | Mdns | Runs | Wkts |
|---|---|---|---|---|
| Jones | 28 | 9 | 76 | 3 |
| Noble | 44 | 15 | 112 | 1 |
| Trumper | 13 | 5 | 35 | 2 |
| Armstrong | 25 | 6 | 64 | 1 |
| Howell | 26 | 8 | 58 | 1 |
| Hopkins | 6 | 2 | 28 | — |

## English Bowling

| | Overs | Mdns | Runs | Wkts | Overs | Mdns | Runs | Wkts |
|---|---|---|---|---|---|---|---|---|
| Hirst | 11 | 4 | 15 | 3 | 9 | 6 | 10 | — |
| Rhodes | 11 | 3 | 17 | 7 | 10 | 5 | 9 | 1 |
| Braund | 1 | — | 1 | — | 5 | — | 14 | 1 |
| Jackson | | | | | 4 | 2 | 7 | — |

Umpires: J. Phillips and W. Hearn.

# AUSTRALIANS v YORKSHIRE

Played at Leeds, June 2, 3, 1902

Apart from the test games no match last season excited greater or more widespread interest than the meeting of Yorkshire and the Australians at Leeds, the attendance on both days being enormous. In winning by five wickets on a very treacherous pitch, after being 24 runs behind on the first innings, Yorkshire accomplished a big performance. They clearly owed their victory to Hirst and Jackson, who got the Australians out in about seventy minutes for 23 — with one exception the lowest total ever obtained by a Colonial team in this country. The score was up to 20 with only four men out, but after that there was a dismal collapse, Jackson finishing off the innings by dismissing Hopkins, Kelly, Jones and Howell in five balls. This was an astonishing piece of bowling, but still finer work was done by Hirst, who got rid of the best batsman, bowling Trumper with one of his deadliest swervers. Noble and Howell bowled splendidly in the last innings, and Yorkshire found it very hard work to get the 48 runs required, but they were tolerably safe when their fifth wicket fell at 41. Washington, who showed fine nerve, finished the match with an on-drive to the boundary.

### Australians

| | | | |
|---|---:|---|---:|
| V. Trumper c Denton b Jackson | 38 | – b Hirst | 7 |
| R. A. Duff b Hirst | 12 | – c Jackson b Hirst | 0 |
| C. Hill c Brown b Rhodes | 7 | – st Hunter b Jackson | 1 |
| S. E. Gregory c Jackson b Hirst | 4 | – not out | 10 |
| J. Darling c Washington b Hirst | 3 | – b Hirst | 1 |
| M. A. Noble c Tunnicliffe b Jackson | 0 | – b Hirst | 2 |
| W. W. Armstrong c Denton b Jackson | 3 | – b Hirst | 0 |
| A. J. Hopkins b Jackson | 17 | – lbw b Jackson | 0 |
| J. J. Kelly b Hirst | 23 | – b Jackson | 0 |
| E. Jones c Haigh b Rhodes | 20 | – b Jackson | 0 |
| W. P. Howell not out | 1 | – c Hunter b Jackson | 0 |
| B 1, l-b 1, w 1 | 3 | B 2 | 2 |
| | **131** | | **23** |

### Yorkshire

| | | | |
|---|---:|---|---:|
| J. T. Brown sen. b Noble | 13 | – c Howell b Noble | 9 |
| J. Tunnicliffe c Armstrong b Howell | 1 | – b Howell | 3 |
| D. Denton c Hill b Noble | 32 | – c Gregory b Noble | 5 |
| Mr T. L. Taylor b Noble | 22 | – b Noble | 11 |
| Hon. F. S. Jackson b Howell | 0 | – c Kelly b Howell | 6 |
| G. H. Hirst lbw b Howell | 12 | – not out | 0 |
| I. Washington b Howell | 5 | – not out | 9 |
| S. Haigh c Kelly b Noble | 0 | | |
| Lord Hawke c Armstrong b Howell | 3 | | |
| W. Rhodes c Trumper b Howell | 12 | | |
| D. Hunter not out | 0 | | |
| B 7 | 7 | B 7 | 7 |
| | **107** | | **50** |

### Yorkshire Bowling

| | Overs | Mdns | Runs | Wkts | Overs | Mdns | Runs | Wkts |
|---|---:|---:|---:|---:|---:|---:|---:|---:|
| Hirst | 16.4 | 6 | 35 | 4 | 7 | 4 | 9 | 5 |
| Rhodes | 13 | 1 | 43 | 2 | | | | |
| Jackson | 13 | 2 | 30 | 4 | 7 | 1 | 12 | 5 |
| Haigh | 5 | 1 | 20 | — | | | | |

**Australian Bowling**

| | Overs | Mdns | Runs | Wkts | Overs | Mdns | Runs | Wkts |
|---|---|---|---|---|---|---|---|---|
| Howell .......... | 20 | 4 | 53 | 6 | 10 | 3 | 22 | 2 |
| Jones ........... | 3 | — | 17 | — | | | | |
| Noble .......... | 16.3 | 6 | 30 | 4 | 9.3 | 4 | 21 | 3 |

Umpires: T. Mycroft and J. Moss.

## ENGLAND v AUSTRALIA

Played at Sheffield, July 3, 4, 5, 1902

The third of the Test matches was brought to a definite conclusion and resulted in a severe disaster for England, the Australians winning at a quarter past one on the Saturday, by 143 runs. They played the finer all-round cricket, and fully deserved their victory, but it is no more than the truth to say that all the luck of the game went their way. Bad light towards the close of the first day and a pitch damaged by the rain the following morning told against the Englishmen, and in the closing stage of the match the wicket showed unmistakable signs of wear. An appeal against the light might well have been made earlier than it was on Thursday, and the saving of two wickets thereby involved would possibly have put the elevens on equal terms on the first innings. The match – the first of its kind ever decided at Bramall Lane – naturally proved a strong attraction, but a mistake was made in fixing it for the latter part of the week, Monday being always the best day for public cricket at Sheffield. The Australians played the same eleven that afterwards represented them in the Test games at Manchester and The Oval, the three men left out being Jones, Howell and Carter. The presence of Hugh Trumble in itself made them stronger than they had been either at Birmingham or at Lord's. As regards the England team, Lockwood and Haigh were among the twelve players selected but they were both left out, the final place being given at almost the last moment to Barnes. As the Lancashire bowler took six wickets on the first day at a cost of only 49 runs criticism was disarmed, but in the light of subsequent events there can be no question that a grave mistake was committed in not playing Lockwood. It was not originally intended to play C. B. Fry, who on the day before the match had to take the place of Ranjitsinhji – disabled by a strained leg.

At one point on the first day the Englishmen had much the best of the match as, after getting rid of the Australians for 194, they had 60 on the board when their first wicket went down. When, however, a quarter of an hour before the time for drawing stumps the bad light was successfully appealed against, five wickets had fallen for 102. The cause of this startling change in the game was the bowling of Noble and Saunders, Noble, who had previously shown the best batting for his side, being in wonderful form. Sufficient rain fell in the night to affect the wicket for a time, and the Englishmen on resuming their innings cut such an inglorious figure that by a quarter to twelve the innings was all over for 145, the last seven wickets having actually gone down for 44 runs. The batsmen on the second morning were quite at fault in dealing with Saunders' breakbacks. Holding a useful lead of 49 the Australians went in for the second time, and in the course of the three hours and fifty minutes they ran up a total of 289. This was quite enough to make them pretty sure of the match, but at one time they seemed likely to do a great deal better, their score when the fourth wicket fell standing at 187. Rhodes finished off the innings with a wonderful piece of bowling taking four wickets in nineteen balls. At the start of the innings MacLaren made a mistake in not putting him on at the end from which Saunders had been so successful. Trumper in the course of the season made many bigger scores than his 62 but on no occasion did he play a more marvellous innings. He obtained his runs out of a total of 80 in fifty minutes, doing just what he liked with the English bowling. Hill, who went in first wicket down at 20 and was out at 225 to a wonderful catch – high up at cover slip with one hand – played a great innings on a wicket that was never easy. His cricket was not entirely free from fault as when his score stood between 70 and 80 he might have been caught at slip, and gave a very difficult chance in the long-field, but these were small blemishes in a most brilliant display. He was batting for rather less than two hours and a half. Darling, it should be mentioned, had a very unhappy experience in the match, being in each innings caught at slip off Barnes, without getting a run.

England wanted 339 to win, and it was felt that the task would prove too heavy. However, a good start was made, the experiment of sending Jessop in first with Abel proving a great success. Without being in any way reckless the famour hitter played a brilliant game and, when just before six o'clock, bad light stopped cricket for the day, he was not out 53, the total being 73 for one wicket. Any hopes that the Englishmen might have had were soon destroyed on Saturday morning, Jessop, Tyldesley and Fry being all dismissed in the first half hour for an addition of 25 runs. MacLaren made a great effort to save a lost game, and for nearly an hour found a valuable partner in Jackson, but it was all to no purpose. After Jackson's dismissal at 162 the end soon came, the last five wickets falling for 33 runs. In this closing part of the match Noble bowled magnificently, breaking back again and again in unplayable way. His average from the time he went on for Saunders on Saturday morning came out at five wickets in twelve overs for 22 runs, and in the whole match he took eleven wickets for 103 runs. Trumble who, owing to a blow on his thumb, did not bowl on Friday afternoon, did admirable work at the finish.

## Australia

| | | | |
|---|---|---|---|
| V. Trumper b Braund | 1 | – c Lilley b Jackson | 62 |
| R. A. Duff c Lilley b Barnes | 25 | – c Hirst b Rhodes | 1 |
| C. Hill c Rhodes b Barnes | 18 | – c MacLaren b Jackson | 119 |
| J. Darling c Braund b Barnes | 0 | – c Braund b Barnes | 0 |
| S. E. Gregory c Abel b Barnes | 11 | – run out | 29 |
| M. A. Noble c Braund b Rhodes | 47 | – b Jackson | 8 |
| A. J. Hopkins c Braund b Barnes | 27 | – not out | 40 |
| W. W. Armstrong c and b Braund | 25 | – b Rhodes | 26 |
| J. J. Kelly b Barnes | 0 | – c Hirst b Rhodes | 0 |
| H. Trumble c and b Jackson | 32 | – b Rhodes | 0 |
| J. V. Saunders not out | 0 | – b Rhodes | 1 |
| B 3, l-b 5 | 8 | L-b | 3 |
| | **194** | | **289** |

## England

| | | | |
|---|---|---|---|
| Mr A. C. MacLaren b Noble | 31 | – c Trumper b Noble | 63 |
| R. Abel b Noble | 38 | – c Hill b Noble | 8 |
| J. T. Tyldesley c Armstrong b Noble | 22 | – b Trumble | 14 |
| Hon. F. S. Jackson c Gregory b Saunders | 3 | – b Noble | 14 |
| Mr C. B. Fry st Kelly b Saunders | 1 | – lbw b Trumble | 4 |
| A. A. Lilley b Noble | 8 | – b Noble | 9 |
| L. C. Braund st Kelly b Saunders | 0 | – c Armstrong b Noble | 9 |
| G. H. Hirst c Trumble b Saunders | 8 | – b Noble | 0 |
| Mr G. L. Jessop c Saunders b Noble | 12 | – lbw b Trumble | 55 |
| W. Rhodes not out | 7 | – not out | 7 |
| S. F. Barnes c Darling b Saunders | 7 | – b Trumble | 5 |
| B 4, l-b 3, n-b 1 | 8 | B 4, l-b 1, w 1, n-b 1 | 7 |
| | **145** | | **195** |

## English Bowling

| | Overs | Mdns | Runs | Wkts | Overs | Mdns | Runs | Wkts |
|---|---|---|---|---|---|---|---|---|
| Hirst ........... | 15 | 1 | 59 | — | 10 | 1 | 40 | — |
| Braund .......... | 13 | 4 | 34 | 2 | 12 | — | 58 | — |
| Barnes .......... | 20 | 9 | 49 | 6 | 12 | 4 | 50 | 1 |
| Jackson ......... | 5.1 | 1 | 11 | 1 | 17 | 2 | 60 | 3 |
| Rhodes .......... | 13 | 3 | 33 | 1 | 17.1 | 3 | 63 | 5 |
| Jessop .......... | | | | | 4 | — | 15 | — |

## Australian Bowling

| | Overs | Mdns | Runs | Wkts | Overs | Mdns | Runs | Wkts |
|---|---|---|---|---|---|---|---|---|
| Trumble ......... | 18 | 10 | 21 | — | 21.5 | 3 | 49 | 4 |
| Saunders ........ | 15.3 | 4 | 50 | 5 | 12 | — | 68 | — |
| Trumper ......... | 4 | 1 | 8 | — | 6 | — | 19 | — |
| Noble ........... | 19 | 6 | 51 | 5 | 21 | 4 | 52 | 6 |
| Armstrong ....... | 5 | 2 | 7 | — | | | | |

Umpires: J. Phillips and W. Richards.

## AUSTRALIANS v SURREY

Played at The Oval, July 21, 22, 23, 1902

Although not quite at full strength, Surrey began so well that they had 241 runs on the board with only four men out. They did not maintain this form, but certainly had the worst of the wicket. The draw in which the game ended, was distinctly in favour of the Australians who, with nine wickets in hand, wanted only 84 more runs to gain a victory. Stumps were drawn early in order that the Australians might get away for the Test match at Manchester. Abel played a great innings, showing skill and judgment of the highest class. Rain prevented any cricket on the Tuesday until after four o'clock, and Trumper and Duff hit up 142 in an hour and a quarter. Six Australian wickets were down for 197, but Hill and Darling saved their side from being badly behind on the first innings. When Surrey went in again they fared, thanks to Hayward, extremely well for a time on a difficult wicket, but Saunders brought about an extraordinary collapse.

### Surrey

| | | | |
|---|---|---|---|
| R. Abel c Noble b Trumper ................... 104 | – c and b Howell ................. | 5 |
| T. Hayward c Noble b Saunders .............. 26 | – c Hill b Armstrong ............. | 48 |
| E. G. Hayes lbw b Armstrong ................ 37 | – c Armstrong b Noble ........... | 22 |
| W. H. Lockwood c Armstrong b Howell ........ 16 | – c Darling b Saunders ........... | 18 |
| W. Brockwell b Howell ..................... 39 | – st Carter b Armstrong .......... | 6 |
| Mr H. D. G. Leveson-Gower not out ........... 26 | – c Noble b Saunders ............. | 0 |
| Mr D. L. A. Jephson b Howell ................. 0 | – c Armstrong b Saunders ........ | 7 |
| W. Lees c Trumper b Saunders ................ 6 | – c Duff b Saunders .............. | 0 |
| H. Clode b Saunders ........................ 9 | – c Duff b Saunders .............. | 3 |
| A. Stedman c Armstrong b Howell ............. 6 | – not out ........................ | 0 |
| T. Richardson b Howell ...................... 2 | – c Duff b Saunders .............. | 0 |
| B 22, l-b 2, n-b 1 ................... 25 | B 1, n-b 1 .............. | 2 |
| | 296 | 111 |

## Australians

| | | | |
|---|---|---|---|
| V. Trumper c Stedman b Lockwood ............. 85 | | | |
| R. A. Duff c Abel b Lockwood ................. 57 | | | |
| H. Carter c Hayes b Clode .................... 0 | | | |
| W. W. Armstrong c Richardson b Brockwell ....... 21 | – not out ...................... | 1 | |
| C. Hill lbw b Clode ......................... 90 | | | |
| M. A. Noble lbw b Lees ...................... 0 | | | |
| S. E. Gregory c Hayes b Lees .................. 0 | | | |
| J. Darling b Richardson ...................... 32 | | | |
| A. Hopkins c Leveson-Gower b Clode ............ 6 | | | |
| W. P. Howell not out ........................ 6 | – c Leveson-Gower b Clode ........ | 2 | |
| J. V. Saunders c Leveson-Gower b Clode ......... 0 | – not out ...................... | 8 | |
| B 16 ............................. 16 | | | |
| 313 | | 11 | |

## Australian Bowling

| | Overs | Mdns | Runs | Wkts | Overs | Mdns | Runs | Wkts |
|---|---|---|---|---|---|---|---|---|
| Howell .......... | 28 | 70 | 80 | 5 | 11 | 4 | 34 | 1 |
| Saunders ......... | 34 | 10 | 82 | 3 | 9.1 | 5 | 9 | 6 |
| Armstrong ........ | 34 | 13 | 49 | 1 | 11 | 2 | 34 | 2 |
| Trumper .......... | 14 | 3 | 23 | 1 | | | | |
| Hopkins .......... | 5 | 2 | 21 | — | | | | |
| Noble ........... | 6 | 2 | 16 | — | 12 | 4 | 32 | 1 |

## Surrey Bowling

| | Overs | Mdns | Runs | Wkts | Overs | Mdns | Runs | Wkts |
|---|---|---|---|---|---|---|---|---|
| Clode ........... | 16 | 2 | 65 | 4 | 3 | 1 | 5 | 1 |
| Lees ............ | 20 | 1 | 93 | 2 | | | | |
| Brockwell ........ | 12 | — | 56 | 1 | | | | |
| Richardson ....... | 12 | — | 65 | 1 | 3 | 1 | 6 | — |
| Lockwood ........ | 4 | — | 18 | 2 | | | | |

Umpires: W. Hearn and W. A. J. West.

## ENGLAND v AUSTRALIA

Played at Manchester, July 24, 25, 26, 1902

The fourth of the Test games produced one of the most memorable matches in the whole history of cricket, the Australians, after some extraordinary fluctuations of fortune, winning by three runs. At the end of the first day the looked to have the game in their hands, and at the end of the second it seemed equally certain that they would be beaten. Superb bowling and fielding pulled them through at the finish, but they would probably be the first to admit that fortune was very kind to them, five or six hours' rain during Friday night making the task of the Englishmen in the last innings twice as difficult as it had promised to be. In the opinion of most people England ought, despite the damaged pitch, to have won the match, but defeat by three runs after such a tremendous struggle certainly carried with it no discredit. Nothing that English cricketers did against the Australians last summer – not even the victory at The Oval in the final Test match – was more brilliant than the way in which they recovered themselves on the second day, turning an apparently hopeless position into one that suggested an easy win. In picking twelve men for England the selection committee left out Fry and Jessop, restored Ranjitsinhji to the place he had not been able to take at Sheffield, and brought in L. C. H. Palairet and Tate. As Fry had failed in three matches it was only right to drop him, but it was a mistake not to play Jessop as his absence, apart from all question of run-getting, sadly weakened the fielding on the off-side. On the morning of the match another blunder was committed, Tate being played in preference to Hirst. The condition of the ground – very soft and slow after a lot of rain – offered some excuse for the course adopted, but it meant playing a bowler pure and simple in preference to a first-rate all-round man, and the result proved anything but happy.

The Australians derived great advantage from winning the toss as up to lunch time the ball did nothing at all on the soft turf. Trumper, Duff and Hill, made splendid use of their opportunities, but it must be said that the English bowlers did very poor work, pitching so short that it was often an easy matter to pull them. By magnificent hitting Trumper and Duff scored 135 in an hour and twenty minutes for the first wicket and when lunch time came the total without further loss had reached 173, the Australians seeming already on the high road to victory. After the interval Rhodes got rid of Trumper, Noble and Gregory in quick succession, but Darling punished him tremendously and while in with Hill made an invaluable stand for the fifth wicket. With only five men out for 256 the Australians seemed sure to make considerably over three hundred, but the last few batsmen could do nothing against Lockwood, and the innings ended for 299. It should be stated that owing to the soft ground Lockwood was not tried at all until the score had reached 129. Duff, Hill and Darling all played fine cricket, but the chief batting honours rested with Trumper, who scored his 104 without making a mistake of any kind. His pulling was a marvel of ease and certainty. The wicket had been drying fast since luncheon and the Englishmen on going in to bat could do little or nothing against Trumble and Saunders, five wickets going down in three-quarters of an hour for 44. Jackson and Braund then played out time, the total at the drawing of stumps being 70.

Friday was England's day, the cricket shown by the home side, apart from one lamentable blunder in the field, being magnificent. To begin with Jackson and Braund pulled the game round into quite a respectable position, carrying the overnight score of 70 to 185 before they were separated. Altogether they put on during their partnership 141 runs. It was a splendid performance, for although the wicket had improved a great deal and was in good condition, runs were very hard to get, the Australian bowlers being always able to get break on the ball. Lunch time had nearly arrived, when Braund, in stepping out to drive Noble, turned on to his wicket a ball that would have missed the off stump. A better morning's play all-round was not seen during the whole season. Braund made a wretched stroke with his score at 58 but otherwise his innings was quite beyond reproach, the way in which he punished Armstrong on the leg side being most refreshing. After luncheon Jackson did not get much support, but he played a great game himself, seizing every opportunity of scoring and forcing the hitting in the most skilful way while the last two men were in with him. In fourth wicket down on Thursday, with the score at 30 he was the last man out, England finishing up with a total of 262 or only 37 runs behind. He was at the wickets nearly four hours and a half, playing all the time with superb judgment and skill. When he had made 41 he might have been caught and bowled by Saunders from a very hard return and at 123 he was missed by Gregory at cover-point from the simplest of chances, but these and one or two hits that luckily fell out of harm's way just after luncheon were the only blemishes in his innings.

Excitement was at its highest point when shortly after four o'clock the Australians entered upon their second innings, everyone feeling that the result of the match might depend on the next hour's play. As it happened Lockwood's bowling was even more remarkable in quality than Jackson's batting had been, and the game went entirely in England's favour. Trumper, Hill and Duff were out for 10 runs, Trumper being caught at slip by Braund at the second attempt, and the fourth wicket would have fallen at 16 if Darling had not been missed at square leg off Braund's bowling by Tate. If the catch had been held it is quite likely, as Lockwood was bowling in such wonderful form, that the Australians would have been out for a total of 50 or 60. As it was, Darling and Gregory stayed together for an hour, their partnership producing 54 runs. Gregory was the first to go, and Darling left at 74. Then Lockwood, who had been indulged with a rest, got rid of Hopkins and Noble, and when the time came for drawing stumps eight wickets were down for 85. The Australians were only 122 runs ahead with two wickets to fall, and it is only reasonable to assume that if the weather had kept fine during the night, England would have won the match comfortably enough. Rain poured down for five or six hours however, and on Saturday morning the position had completely changed. Owing to the state of the ground nothing could be done until shortly after twelve, and for the addition of a single run the Australian innings ended, England being left with 124 to get to win. For Lockwood, as a bowler, the match was nothing less than a triumph, his analysis for the two innings coming out at eleven wickets for 76 runs. Finer bowling than his on Friday afternoon can rarely have been seen.

As no one could tell how the wicket would play, the Englishmen entered upon their task under very anxious circumstances. At first, however, everything went well, MacLaren and Palairet scoring 36 runs in fifty minutes, and being still together at lunch time. Still, though they started so well, the difficulty they experienced in playing the bowling made one apprehensive as to what would happen after the interval. Palairet was bowled at 44, and then with MacLaren and Tyldesley together runs for a few overs came so fast that England seemed likely to win hands down. However, at 68 or only 56 to win, Tyldesley was caught in the slips. Another misfortune quickly followed, MacLaren, after playing very fine cricket for an hour and a quarter, hitting out rashly at a ball from Trumble and being caught in the long field at 72. At this point Ranjitsinhji was joined by Abel, and after the latter had been missed by Saunders at mid-on, a slight shower stopped the game for a quarter of an hour. The weather looked very threatening and it was clear, on cricket being again proceeded with, that Abel had received strict injunctions to hit. He played a game quite foreign to his ordinary methods, and for a time got on very well. Ranjitsinhji, however, was altogether at fault and did not seem to have the least confidence in himself. He was always in front of the stumps in trying to play Trumble, and at 92 he was leg-before-wicket to that bowler. With six wickets in hand and only 32 runs wanted, England still seemed sure of victory, but from this point everything changed, Trumble and Saunders, backed up by superb fielding, bowling so finely that in fifty minutes five more wickets went down for 24 runs. Abel was bowled in trying to drive; Jackson was caught at mid-off from a full pitch; Braund beautifully stumped, and Lockwood bowled, the eighth wicket falling at 109. With 15 runs required, Rhodes joined Lilley and in three hits, one of them a big drive over the ring by Rhodes, the score was carried to 116 or only 8 to win. At this point, Lilley, from a fine hit, was splendidly caught by Hill at square-leg, the fieldsman just reaching the ball when running at full speed. Heavy rain then drove the players from the field and there was a delay of three-quarters of an hour before the match could be finished. Tate got a 4 on the leg-side from the first ball he received from Saunders, but the fourth, which came a little with the bowler's arm and kept low, hit the wicket and the match was over, Australia winning by 3 runs. Trumble and Saunders bowled extraordinary well, combining a lot of break with almost perfect length, and the fielding that did so much to win the match was unsurpassable.

## Australia

| | | |
|---|---|---|
| V. Trumper c Lilley b Rhodes | 104 | – c Braund b Lockwood ........... 3 |
| R. A. Duff c Lilley b Lockwood | 54 | – b Lockwood .................. 4 |
| C. Hill c Rhodes b Lockwood | 65 | – b Lockwood .................. 0 |
| M. A. Noble c and b Rhodes | 2 | – c Lilley b Lockwood ........... 4 |
| S. E. Gregory c Lilley b Rhodes | 3 | – lbw b Tate .................... 24 |
| J. Darling c MacLaren b Rhodes | 51 | – c Palairet b Rhodes ............ 37 |
| A. J. Hopkins c Palairet b Lockwood | 0 | – c Tate b Lockwood ............. 2 |
| W. W. Armstrong b Lockwood | 5 | – b Rhodes ..................... 3 |
| J. J. Kelly not out | 4 | – not out ...................... 2 |
| H. Trumble c Tate b Lockwood | 0 | – lbw b Tate ................... 4 |
| J. V. Saunders b Lockwood | 3 | – c Tyldesley b Rhodes .......... 0 |
| B 5, l-b 2, w 1 | 8 | B 1, l-b 1, n-b 1 ......... 3 |
| | **299** | **86** |

## England

| | | | |
|---|---|---|---|
| Mr L. C. H. Palairet c Noble b Saunders | 6 | – b Saunders | 17 |
| R. Abel c Armstrong b Saunders | 6 | – b Trumble | 21 |
| J. T. Tyldesley c Hopkins b Saunders | 22 | – c Armstrong b Saunders | 16 |
| Mr A. C. MacLaren b Trumble | 1 | – c Duff b Trumble | 35 |
| K. S. Ranjitsinhji lbw b Trumble | 2 | – lbw b Trumble | 0 |
| Hon. F. S. Jackson c Duff b Trumble | 128 | – c Gregory b Saunders | 4 |
| L. C. Braund b Noble | 65 | – st Kelly b Trumble | 7 |
| A. A. Lilley b Noble | 7 | – c Hill b Trumble | 3 |
| W. H. Lockwood run out | 7 | – b Trumble | 4 |
| W. Rhodes c and b Trumble | 5 | – not out | 4 |
| F. W. Tate not out | 5 | – b Saunders | 4 |
| B 6, l-b 2 | 8 | B 5 | 5 |
| | **262** | | **120** |

## English Bowling

| | Overs | Mdns | Runs | Wkts | Overs | Mdns | Runs | Wkts |
|---|---|---|---|---|---|---|---|---|
| Rhodes | 25 | 3 | 104 | 4 | 14.4 | 5 | 26 | 3 |
| Jackson | 11 | — | 58 | — | | | | |
| Tate | 11 | 1 | 44 | — | 5 | 3 | 7 | 2 |
| Braund | 9 | — | 37 | — | 11 | 3 | 22 | — |
| Lockwood | 20.1 | 5 | 48 | 6 | 17 | 5 | 28 | 5 |

## Australian Bowling

| | Overs | Mdns | Runs | Wkts | Overs | Mdns | Runs | Wkts |
|---|---|---|---|---|---|---|---|---|
| Trumble | 43 | 16 | 75 | 4 | 25 | 9 | 53 | 6 |
| Saunders | 34 | 5 | 104 | 3 | 19.4 | 4 | 52 | 4 |
| Noble | 24 | 8 | 47 | 2 | 5 | 3 | 10 | — |
| Trumper | 6 | 4 | 6 | — | | | | |
| Armstrong | 5 | 2 | 19 | — | | | | |
| Hopkins | 2 | — | 3 | — | | | | |

Umpires: T. Mycroft and J. Moss.

# ENGLAND v AUSTRALIA

### Played at The Oval, August 11, 12, 13, 1902

Australia having already won the rubber, the fifth and last of the Test matches had not at starting the same importance that would under other circumstances have attached to it, but is produced a never-to-be-forgotten struggle and a more exciting finish, if that were possible, than the one at Manchester. In face of great difficulties and disadvantages England won by one wicket after the odds had been fifty to one on Australia. Some truly wonderful hitting by Jessop made victory possible after all hope had seemed gone, and Hirst and Rhodes got their side home at the close. In its moral results the victory was a very important one indeed, as no one interested in English cricket could have felt other than depressed and low spirited if all the Test matches played out to finish had ended in favour of Darling's team. In making up the English side the Selection Committee restored Jessop and Hirst to the places they ought to have filled at Manchester, and for the first time in the series of games gave a place to Hayward, Ranjitsinhji, Tate and Abel being left out. Hayward had done enough to deserve a trial, but, as it happened, he proved a great failure as a batsman and was by no means lively in the field. The Australians of course kept to the team that had been victorious at Sheffield and Old Trafford. The wicket, through a trifle slow from the effects of recent rain, was in very good condition, and the

Australians, staying in for the whole of the first day, made the highly satisfactory score of 324. At one time they did not seem likely to do nearly so well as this for, though Trumper and Duff scored 47 for the first partnership, there were four wickets down for 82 and five for 126. The change in the game was brought about by Hirst, who for a time bowled in quite his form of 1901. Duff was out to a marvellous catch by the wicket-keeper standing back, Lilley jumping a yard or more on the leg side and holding a ball that would have gone for 4. Noble and Armstrong by putting on 48 runs considerably improved the Australians' position, but with seven wickets down for 175 the outlook was none too promising. However, all these disasters were so well retrieved that the three remaining wickets added 149 runs, an invaluable partnership by Hopkins and Trumble putting on 81. The batting was very painstaking, but an unlucky mistake by Lilley at the wicket when Trumble had made 9 had, from England's point of view, a deplorable effect on the game.

If the weather had kept fine the Englishmen would not on an Oval wicket have been afraid of facing a score of 324, but the bad luck that had handicapped them at Sheffield and Manchester still pursued them, heavy rain during the early hours of Tuesday morning making a great difference in the pitch. Under the circumstances they did not do at all badly to score 183, but apart from some bright hitting by Tyldesley there was nothing remarkable in the efforts of the early batsmen. At lunch time six wickets were down for 83, and it seemed certain that the side would follow on and be beaten. Braund and Hirst made a great effort, the latting hitting with the utmost freedom, but when he left the total had only reached 137, England still wanting 38 runs to avoid going in again. Thanks, however, to a bad blunder by Hill, who palpably missed Lockwood at long-on when that batsman had made 11, the follow-in was saved, the innings ending for 183 or 141 runs behind. Braund was often beaten by balls that missed the wicket, but in staying in for an hour and a half he did invaluable work for his side. Trumble bowled throughout the innings in splendid form and took eight wickets for just over 8 runs apiece. Possessing such a big lead the Australians looked, when they went in for the second time, to have the match in their hands. They opened their innings with a great misfortune, Trumper throwing away his wicket in attempting a foolish run, and for the rest of the afternoon the batting was marked by such extreme care that at the drawing of stumps the score, with eight men out, had only reached 114, two hours and three-quarters being occupied in getting these runs. The wicket was still rather difficult and Lockwood bowled very finely. Hill was out to a magnificent catch low down in the slips in one hand by MacLaren, and Noble bowled off his pads by a ball that he did not attempt to play with his bat.

On Wednesday morning Lockwood quickly obtained the two outstanding wickets, bringing the Australian innings to a close for 121, and then England went in with 263 wanted to win the match. Tuesday's cricket, while the turf was still soft after rain, had damaged the pitch to no small extent, and up to a certain point the batsmen were so helpless against Saunders and Trumble that the easiest of victories for Australia appeared in prospect. Three wickets fell to Saunders for 10 runs and but for Gregory missing Hayward badly at short-leg there would have been four wickets down for 16. Even as it was half the side were out for 48 and the match looked all over. At this point Jackson, who had gone in third wicket down, was joined by Jessop and a stand was made which completely altered the game. At first, however, Jessop's cricket was far from suggesting the wonderful form he afterwards showed. When he had made 22 Kelly missed stumping him and at 27 he gave a rather awkward chance to Trumper at long-off. At lunch time the two batsmen were still together, Jackson, who had played superb cricket, being 39 and Jessop 29. After the interval Jackson was far indeed from keeping up his previous form, being repeatedly in difficulties and giving a palpable chance to Armstrong at slip. Jessop, on the other hand, settled down at once, and hit as he only can. At one point he scored four 4s and a single off successive balls from Saunders. The partnership had added 109 runs in sixty-five minutes when Jackson was easily caught and bowled. Jessop went on hitting for some little time longer, but at 187 he closed his extraordinary innings by placing a ball gently into short-leg's hands. He scored, in just over an hour and a quarter, 104 runs out of 139, his hits being a 5 in the slips, seventeen 4s, two 3s, four 2s, and seventeen singles. All things considered a more astonishing display has never been seen. What he did would have been scarcely possible under the same circumstances to any other living batsman. The rest of the match was simply one crescendo of excitement. Hirst played a great game and, after Lockwood's dismissal at 214, received such help from Lilley that victory gradually came in sight. The score was advanced to 248, or only 15 to win, and then from a good hard drive Lilley was finely caught at deep mid-off. Rhodes as last man had a trying crisis to face, but his nerve did not fail him. Once, however, he nearly lost his wicket, Armstrong at slip getting a catch in his hand, but, being partly overbalanced, dropping the ball. Hirst went on imperturbably, scoring again and again by means of cleverly placed singles, and at last he had the extreme satisfaction of making the score a tie. Then Rhodes sent a ball from Trumble between the bowler and mid-on, and England won the match by one wicket. Hirst's innings was in its way almost as remarkable as Jessop's. So coolly did he play that of his last fourteen hits that scored thirteen were singles, whereas in the early part of his innings he had hit half-a-dozen 4s. Darling is not often at fault in the management of his bowling, but he leaned too heavily on Saunders and did not make enough use of Noble. Trumble, bowling from the Pavilion end, was never changed during the match.

## Australians

| | | | |
|---|---|---|---|
| V. Trumper b Hirst | 42 | – run out | 2 |
| R. A. Duff c Lilley b Hirst | 23 | – b Lockwood | 6 |
| C. Hill b Hirst | 11 | – c MacLaren b Hirst | 34 |
| J. Darling c Lilley b Hirst | 3 | – c MacLaren b Lockwood | 15 |
| M. A. Noble c and b Jackson | 52 | – b Braund | 13 |
| S. E. Gregory b Hirst | 23 | – b Braund | 9 |
| W. W. Armstrong b Jackson | 17 | – b Lockwood | 21 |
| A. Hopkins c MacLaren b Lockwood | 40 | – c Lilley b Lockwood | 3 |
| H. Trumble not out | 64 | – not out | 7 |
| J. J. Kelly c Rhodes b Braund | 39 | – lbw b Lockwood | 0 |
| J. V. Saunders lbw b Braund | 0 | – c Tyldesley b Rhodes | 2 |
| B 5, l-b 3, n-b 2 | 10 | B 7, l-b 2 | 9 |
| | **324** | | **121** |

## England

| | | | |
|---|---|---|---|
| Mr A. C. MacLaren c Armstrong b Trumble | 10 | – b Saunders | 2 |
| Mr L. C. H. Palairet b Trumble | 20 | – b Saunders | 6 |
| J. T. Tyldesley b Trumble | 33 | – b Saunders | 0 |
| T. W. Hayward b Trumble | 0 | – c Keely b Saunders | 7 |
| Hon. F. S. Jackson c Armstrong b Saunders | 2 | – c and b Trumble | 49 |
| L. C. Braund c Hill b Trumble | 22 | – c Kelly b Trumble | 2 |
| Mr G. L. Jessop b Trumble | 13 | – c Noble b Armstrong | 104 |
| G. H. Hirst c and b Trumble | 43 | – not out | 58 |
| W. H. Lockwood c Noble b Saunders | 25 | – lbw b Trumble | 2 |
| A. A. Lilley c Trumper b Trumble | 0 | – c Darling b Trumble | 16 |
| W. Rhodes not out | 0 | – not out | 6 |
| B 13, l-b 2 | 15 | B 5, l-b 6 | 11 |
| | **183** | | **263** |

## English Bowling

| | Overs | Mdns | Runs | Wkts | Overs | Mdns | Runs | Wkts |
|---|---|---|---|---|---|---|---|---|
| Lockwood | 24 | 2 | 85 | 1 | 20 | 6 | 45 | 5 |
| Rhodes | 28 | 9 | 46 | — | 22 | 7 | 38 | 1 |
| Hirst | 29 | 5 | 77 | 5 | 5 | 1 | 7 | 1 |
| Braund | 16.5 | 5 | 29 | 2 | 9 | 1 | 15 | 2 |
| Jackson | 20 | 4 | 66 | 2 | 4 | 3 | 7 | — |
| Jessop | 6 | 2 | 11 | — | | | | |

**Australian Bowling**

| | Overs | Mdns | Runs | Wkts | Overs | Mdns | Runs | Wkts |
|---|---|---|---|---|---|---|---|---|
| Trumble . . . . . . . . . | 31 | 13 | 65 | 8 | 33.5 | 4 | 108 | 4 |
| Saunders . . . . . . . . | 23 | 7 | 79 | 2 | 24 | 3 | 105 | 4 |
| Noble . . . . . . . . . . . | 7 | 3 | 24 | — | 5 | — | 11 | — |
| Armstrong . . . . . . . | | | | | 4 | — | 28 | 1 |

Umpires: C. E. Richardson and A. A. White.

# AUSTRALIANS v SOUTH OF ENGLAND

Played at Bournemouth, September 11, 12, 13, 1902

Not a ball could be bowled on the opening day, rain setting in at six o'clock in the morning and continuing with such persistence that at noon all idea of starting play was given up. The term South of England was stretched a little, Arnold, of Worcestershire, appearing in the English team. Despite the loss of the first day the match was played out, the Australians at half-past four on Saturday winning by 61 runs. On a treacherous pitch the ball completely beat the bat. Trumble fairly won the match for his side, taking in all fifteen wickets for 68 runs, and some almost equally good work was done by Arnold and Tate, who, it will be seen, bowled unchanged through both innings of the Australians. Fry batted well in the last innings, but he alone could cope with the bowling, and after he left the last five wickets fell in half an hour for 20 runs.

**Australians**

| | | | | |
|---|---|---|---|---|
| V. Trumper c and b Arnold . . . . . . . . . . . . . . . . . . . | 10 | – c Woods b Tate . . . . . . . . . . . . . . . | 6 |
| R. A. Duff lbw b Arnold . . . . . . . . . . . . . . . . . . . . . | 7 | – b Tate . . . . . . . . . . . . . . . . . . . . . . | 11 |
| J. Darling b Tate . . . . . . . . . . . . . . . . . . . . . . . . . . | 12 | – c Fry b Arnold . . . . . . . . . . . . . . . . | 3 |
| M. A. Noble c Hayes b Arnold . . . . . . . . . . . . . . | 30 | – lbw b Arnold . . . . . . . . . . . . . . . . . | 20 |
| S. E. Gregory lbw b Arnold . . . . . . . . . . . . . . . . | 12 | – b Tate . . . . . . . . . . . . . . . . . . . . . . | 0 |
| W. W. Armstrong c Bond b Arnold . . . . . . . . . . . | 13 | – b Tate . . . . . . . . . . . . . . . . . . . . . . | 14 |
| A. J. Hopkins lbw b Arnold . . . . . . . . . . . . . . . . . | 0 | – b Tate . . . . . . . . . . . . . . . . . . . . . . | 0 |
| H. Trumble not out . . . . . . . . . . . . . . . . . . . . . . | 17 | – b Arnold . . . . . . . . . . . . . . . . . . . . | 8 |
| J. J. Kelly b Arnold . . . . . . . . . . . . . . . . . . . . . . . | 6 | – c and b Tate . . . . . . . . . . . . . . . . . . | 9 |
| W. P. Howell c Woods b Arnold . . . . . . . . . . . . . . | 2 | – not out . . . . . . . . . . . . . . . . . . . . . . | 3 |
| J. V. Saunders c Hayes b Tate . . . . . . . . . . . . . . . | 9 | – c Vine b Arnold . . . . . . . . . . . . . . . . | 4 |
| B 4, l-b 1 . . . . . . . . . . . . . . . . . . . . . . | 5 | B 10, l-b 3 . . . . . . . . . . . . | 13 |
| | **123** | | **91** |

**South of England**

| | | | | |
|---|---|---|---|---|
| Mr S. M. J. Woods b Trumble . . . . . . . . . . . . . . . | 6 | – run out . . . . . . . . . . . . . . . . . . . . . . | 0 |
| Mr C. B. Fry lbw b Saunders . . . . . . . . . . . . . . . . . | 18 | – b Trumble . . . . . . . . . . . . . . . . . . . | 26 |
| E. G. Hayes b Trumble . . . . . . . . . . . . . . . . . . . . . | 1 | – b Trumble . . . . . . . . . . . . . . . . . . . | 11 |
| Mr E. M. Sprot lbw b Trumble . . . . . . . . . . . . . . . . | 16 | – c Kelly b Trumble . . . . . . . . . . . . . . | 8 |
| J. Vine lbw b Trumble . . . . . . . . . . . . . . . . . . . . . | 5 | – b Trumble . . . . . . . . . . . . . . . . . . . | 0 |
| Mr C. J. B. Wood lbw b Trumble . . . . . . . . . . . . . . | 17 | – c Noble b Saunders . . . . . . . . . . . . | 1 |
| E. Arnold b Trumble . . . . . . . . . . . . . . . . . . . . . | 0 | – st Kelly b Trumble . . . . . . . . . . . . . | 0 |
| W. Brockwell b Trumble . . . . . . . . . . . . . . . . . . . | 2 | – st Kelly b Saunders . . . . . . . . . . . . . | 2 |
| G. Gill b Trumble . . . . . . . . . . . . . . . . . . . . . . . . . | 14 | – b Saunders . . . . . . . . . . . . . . . . . . . | 7 |
| J. H. Board not out . . . . . . . . . . . . . . . . . . . . . . . . | 2 | – c Armstrong b Trumble . . . . . . . . . . | 6 |
| F. W. Tate b Trumble . . . . . . . . . . . . . . . . . . . . . . | 0 | – not out . . . . . . . . . . . . . . . . . . . . . . | 5 |
| B 3, l-b 3 . . . . . . . . . . . . . . . . . . . . . . | 6 | | |
| | **87** | | **66** |

### South of England Bowling

| | Overs | Mdns | Runs | Wkts | Overs | Mdns | Runs | Wkts |
|---|---|---|---|---|---|---|---|---|
| Tate . . . . . . . . . . . . | 27 | 5 | 61 | 2 | 13 | 2 | 48 | 6 |
| Arnold . . . . . . . . . . | 26 | 7 | 57 | 8 | 13.2 | 2 | 30 | 4 |

### Australian Bowling

| | Overs | Mdns | Runs | Wkts | Overs | Mdns | Runs | Wkts |
|---|---|---|---|---|---|---|---|---|
| Trumble . . . . . . . . . . | 16.4 | 3 | 39 | 9 | 11.3 | 2 | 29 | 6 |
| Noble . . . . . . . . . . . | 12 | 3 | 28 | 0 | | | | |
| Saunders . . . . . . . . | 4 | 0 | 14 | 1 | 11 | 1 | 37 | 3 |

Umpires: A. Shaw and W. Richards.

# AUSTRALIANS v GENTLEMEN OF ENGLAND

## Played at Lord's, May 18, 19, 20, 1905

On few occasions were the Australians seen to greater advantage than in this match against the Gentlemen of England. They lost the toss and had to field out for more than four hours and a half, yet at no time was their bowling mastered, and on Saturday morning they gained a wonderful victory by an innings and 189 runs. The performance was the more remarkable from the fact that on going in to bat the Colonials lost their first four wickets for 94. Duff, who played a fine, determined game, helped to add 176 in a hundred minutes, but the feature of the match was the brilliant and resolute hitting of Armstrong and Darling, who put on 273 in two hours and forty minutes. Armstrong, whose 248 is the third highest score ever obtained in a first-class match at Lord's, scored all round the wicket, except that he made no late cuts, and did not give a chance until he had put together 188. His grand innings which extended over four hours and three-quarters included two 5s and thirty-eight 4s. Though overshadowed by his colleague, Darling cut and drove in splendid form. The Englishmen shaped in most unglorious fashion in the final stage of the match, making only 48 runs in an hour and twenty minutes and during that time they lost eight wickets. It should be noted that the Gentlemen were without Jackson, Jones, Jessop, and Bosanquet.

### Gentlemen of England

| | | | | |
|---|---|---|---|---|
| C. B. Fry b Noble . . . . . . . . . . . . . . . . . . . . . . . . . . . . | 25 | – c and b Laver . . . . . . . . . . . . . . . . . | 26 |
| P. F. Warner b Laver . . . . . . . . . . . . . . . . . . . . . . . | 85 | – b Cotter . . . . . . . . . . . . . . . . . . . . | 0 |
| G. W. Beldam run out . . . . . . . . . . . . . . . . . . . . | 26 | – c and b Laver . . . . . . . . . . . . . . . . . | 1 |
| A. C. MacLaren b Cotter . . . . . . . . . . . . . . . . . . . . | 0 | – c Noble b Howell . . . . . . . . . . . . | 10 |
| Capt. E. G. Wynyard b Laver . . . . . . . . . . . . . . . . | 61 | – c Howell b Laver . . . . . . . . . . . . . . | 3 |
| H. K. Foster b Howell . . . . . . . . . . . . . . . . . . . . | 12 | – c Newland b Howell . . . . . . . . . . . | 0 |
| W. H. B. Evans c Newland b McLeod . . . . . . . . . . . | 21 | – not out . . . . . . . . . . . . . . . . . . . . . | 1 |
| H. Martyn c Laver b McLeod . . . . . . . . . . . . . . . . | 12 | – b Laver . . . . . . . . . . . . . . . . . . . . . | 9 |
| H. C. McDonell run out . . . . . . . . . . . . . . . . . . . . | 9 | – b Noble . . . . . . . . . . . . . . . . . . . | 5 |
| Hesketh-Prichard not out . . . . . . . . . . . . . . . . . . . | 10 | – b Noble . . . . . . . . . . . . . . . . . . . . | 5 |
| W. Brearley st Newland b McLeod . . . . . . . . . . . . | 3 | – c Cotter b Howell . . . . . . . . . . . . . | 0 |
| B 27, l-b 6, w 1, n-b 2 . . . . . . . . . . . . . . . | 36 | B 4, l-b 1, n-b 1 . . . . . . . . . . | 6 |
| | **300** | | **66** |

### Australians

| | | | |
|---|---|---|---|
| C. E. McLeod b Brearley . . . . . . . . . . . . . . | 21 | M. A. Noble b Brearley . . . . . . . . . . . . . . . | 4 |
| S. E. Gregory c Martyn b Brearley . . . . . . . | 38 | J. Darling not out . . . . . . . . . . . . . . . . . . . . | 117 |
| W. P. Howell c Warner b Prichard . . . . . . . | 7 | | |
| V. T. Trumper b Brearley . . . . . . . . . . . . . . | 6 | B 14, l-b 2, w 1, n-b 3 . . . . . . . . . . | 20 |
| R. A. Duff b Brearley . . . . . . . . . . . . . . . . | 94 | | |
| W. W. Armstrong not out . . . . . . . . . . . . | 248 | **(6 wkts dec.) 555** | |

F. Laver, A. Cotter and P. M. Newland did not bat.

**Australian Bowling**

| | Overs | Mdns | Runs | Wkts | Overs | Mdns | Runs | Wkts |
|---|---|---|---|---|---|---|---|---|
| Cotter .......... | 11 | 1 | 40 | 1 | 8 | 2 | 23 | 1 |
| Noble ........... | 27 | 5 | 74 | 1 | 14 | 7 | 23 | 2 |
| Laver .......:.... | 21 | 7 | 47 | 2 | 8 | 3 | 13 | 4 |
| McLeod .......... | 20.1 | 6 | 50 | 3 | | | | |
| Howell .......... | 12 | 2 | 30 | 1 | 2 | 1 | 1 | 3 |
| Armstrong ....... | 11 | 5 | 23 | — | | | | |

**Gentlemen of England Bowling**

| | Overs | Mdns | Runs | Wkts |
|---|---|---|---|---|
| Brearley .......... | 34 | 3 | 169 | 5 |
| Beldam ........... | 14 | — | 82 | — |
| Prichard .......... | 23 | 2 | 121 | 1 |
| McDonnell ........ | 7 | — | 62 | — |
| Evans ............ | 14 | — | 74 | — |
| Wynyard ......... | 7 | — | 22 | — |
| Warner .......... | 2 | 1 | 5 | — |

Umpires: T. Mycroft and A. Phillips.

## ENGLAND v AUSTRALIA

### First Test Match

Played at Nottingham, May 29, 30, 31, 1905

In choosing the England Eleven for the first of the five Test matches the selection committee could not secure quite the side they wanted. At this period of the season George Hirst's leg was giving him a great deal of trouble, and as it would have been absurd to play an unsound man in such a game, he was not even included in the thirteen players from among whom the final choice had to be made. In the previous week, C. B. Fry, already in great form, damaged one of his fingers rather badly in practice at Brighton, and though present at Trent Bridge he did not play, the other man who stood down being Walter Lees. Of the eleven that took the field Bosanquet, John Gunn, and Arnold appeared for the first time in a Test match in England. The Australians had their strongest side, and the wicket being hard and the weather fine the match began under conditions that could scarcely have been better. In the end England won by 213 runs, but only after some truly sensational cricket was this result arrived at.

When England won the toss a total of over 300 was regarded as almost a certainty, but to the consternation of the crowd Hayward, A. O. Jones, MacLaren, and Jackson, were so quickly got rid of that four wickets were down for 47 runs. Tyldesley and Bosanquet, and later in the innings Lilley and Rhodes did something to make up for this disastrous start, but by a quarter to four the innings was all over for 196, the advantage of winning the toss being entirely discounted. There was a little moisture in the ground before lunch, but the chief cause of the failure could be found in the demoralising effect of Cotter's bowling. Pitching little more than half-way at a terrific pace he made the ball get up more than shoulder high, and there can be no doubt that the fear of being hit on the head upset the batsmen considerably. Laver, following up some splended work during the previous fortnight, took seven wickets for 64 runs. He kept an irreproachable length, and varied his pace with the nicest skill, but finely as he bowled he would not have met with so much success if the batsmen had not had their confidence shaken at the other end.

Going in against a total of 196 the Australians started their innings with a couple of misfortunes. Duff was caught very low down at short leg in the second over, and Trumper strained his back so badly that after getting three boundary hits and a single he retired from the field, and, as events turned out, played no more cricket for a fortnight. Of course, it was not known at the time that the injury would prove so serious. For these early troubles Hill and Noble made ample amends, and when the hundred went up with only one man out the Australians stood in a most flattering position. It was just after this that Jackson bowled his now famous over. Noble was out to the first ball, Hill to the fourth, and Darling to the last, the game undergoing a change that can only be described as astonishing. Still the Australians left off for the day with much the best of the game, their score standing at 158 for four wickets. Hill and Noble put on 106 runs, playing masterly cricket together for an hour and three-quarters. The attendance all told numbered quite 15,000. It should be mentioned that the wicket had been prepared in a simple way, without any special use of marl.

The second day brought with it an extraordinary change in the fortunes of the match, the Englishmen playing up in a fashion not unworthy of comparison with their never-to-be-forgotten effort on the second day at Manchester three years before. For a little while the Australians got on remarkably well, and when without further loss their over-night score had been carried to 200, they had every reason to feel satisfied, though they knew that Trumper would not be able to bat. There was such a sudden collapse, however, that the last five wickets fell in less than forty minutes, the innings being finished off for 221. The English fielding while these wickets were going down was amazingly brilliant. Indeed, nothing better could be imagined. The best piece of individual work was done by A. O. Jones, who, in getting rid of Laver, brought off a marvellous catch in the slips, throwing himself forward and taking the ball with the left hand close to the ground. It was a catch that recalled George Lohmann's greatest feats. All through the innings Jessop's fielding on the off-side was beyond praise. He stopped everything that came within reasonable distance of him, and such was the moral effect of his presence that a short run was never attempted when the ball went in his direction.

Standing in a far better position than they could possibly have expected after their paltry first innings, the Englishmen went in for the second time before half-past twelve, and at the drawing of stumps they had scored 318 for five wickets. Under ordinary circumstances they would in the same space of time have made a bigger score, but at about three o'clock Armstrong was put on to keep down the runs. He took the ball at 110 and was not changed till the total had reached 301, delivering thirty-five overs for 50 runs. It was something quite new to see the Australians on the second afternoon of a Test Match playing for a draw rather than a win, and the innovation gave rise to endless discussion. In doing so well the Englishmen were mainly indebted to MacLaren and Hayward, who in two hours and a half scored 145 for the first wicket, thus giving their side a splended start. Armstrong's method of keeping the ball wide of the leg stump for over after over irritated the crowd who, quite forgetting their manners, became rather noisy. MacLaren was out second at 222, being finely caught low down at mid-off from a hard drive. His innings of 140, which lasted three hours and forty minutes, was for the most part magnificent. Just after lunch he was inclined to be reckless, but luckily for him the ball always fell out of harm's way, and he soon returned to safer methods. He scarcely cut at all, but he drove and pulled with tremendous power, and nothing could have been more skilful than the way in which he turned the ball on the leg side. Tyldesley played a fine innings, being far more successful than anyone else in scoring from Armstrong, and Jones hit hard at a time when rapid scoring was essential. At the close Jackson and Rhodes were the not-outs. On the following morning these two batsmen gave a splendid display, staying together until a quarter to one, and without being parted carrying the score to 426, Jackson then declaring the innings closed. Altogether he and Rhodes put on 113 runs. Jackson was batting two hours and twenty minutes for his 82 not out. He was not quite happy in the fading light on the second afternoon, but his play in the morning was without a flaw.

The Australians wanted 402 to win, and when they went in at one o'clock four hours and a half remained for cricket. It was not to be supposed, especially with Trumper disabled, that the runs could be obtained, and the only question was whether the

Australians would be able to avoid defeat. In the end, as everyone knows, Bosanquet beat them. Darling opened the innings himself with Duff, and at lunch time the score stood at 21 without loss. Everything pointed to a draw when the total reached 60 with the two batsmen still together, but at 62 Duff was easily caught and bowled, and this as it happened proved the turning point. Forty minutes later there were four wickets down, Noble, Darling, and Hill being got rid of. Hill was out to a remarkable catch. He hit a ball back to Bosanquet so high that only a man standing fully six feet could have got near it. Bosanquet jumped up, got the ball with one hand the kept hold of it, though he stumbled backwards and fell to the ground. It was a great change from 62 for no wicket to 93 for four, and a little later Armstrong was easily caught at cover-point, the Englishmen then looking to have the match in their hands. Bosanquet had taken all the five wickets. Gregory and Cotter added 39 runs together, but at the tea interval seven wickets had fallen for 173. The players were only away ten minutes but during that time the light became very faulty. Gregory, who had played splendid cricket for an hour, was out at 175 – caught at mid-on at the third attempt, and Kelly joined McLeoa. With Trumper unable to bat these were the last two men. The light grew worse and worse with every sign of on-coming rain, and the Englishmen had reason to fear that all their efforts would be thrown away and the match left drawn. For a quarter of an hour play went on in deep gloom, and then McLeod was out leg-before-wicket, England winning a memorable game by 213 runs. In bringing off the victory that MacLaren's hitting had first made possible, the Englishmen owed everything to Bosanquet. He took eight of the nine wickets that fell, completely demoralising the batsmen with his leg-breaks. He gained nothing from the condition of the ground, the pitch remaining firm and true to the end. In the first flush of his triumph his place in the England team seemed secure for the whole season, but he never reproduced his form, and dropped out of the eleven after the match at Leeds. In the course of the three days at Trent Bridge 31,622 people paid for admission.

### England

| | | | |
|---|---|---|---|
| Mr A. O. Jones b Laver | 4 | – b Duff | 30 |
| T. Hayward b Cotter | 5 | – c Darling b Armstrong | 47 |
| J. T. Tyldesley c Duff b Laver | 56 | – c and b Duff | 61 |
| Mr A. C. MacLaren c Kelly b Laver | 2 | – c Duff b Laver | 140 |
| Hon. F. S. Jackson b Cotter | 0 | – not out | 82 |
| Mr B. J. T. Bosanquet b Laver | 27 | – b Cotter | 6 |
| J. Gunn b Cotter | 8 | | |
| Mr G. L. Jessop b Laver | 0 | | |
| A. A. Lilley c and b Laver | 37 | | |
| W. Rhodes c Noble b Laver | 29 | – not out | 39 |
| E. Arnold not out | 2 | | |
| B 21, l-b 5 | 26 | B 11, l-b 9, w 1 | 21 |
| | **196** | **(5 wkts dec.)** | **426** |

### Australia

| | | | |
|---|---|---|---|
| R. A. Duff c Hayward b Gunn | 1 | – c and b Bosanquet | 25 |
| V. T. Trumper retired hurt | 13 | – absent hurt | 0 |
| C. Hill b Jackson | 54 | – c and b Bosanquet | 8 |
| M. A. Noble c Lilley b Jackson | 50 | – st Lilley b Bosanquet | 7 |
| W. W. Armstrong st Lilley b Rhodes | 27 | – c Jackson b Bosanquet | 6 |
| J. Darling c Bosanquet b Jackson | 0 | – b Bosanquet | 40 |
| A. Cotter c and b Jessop | 45 | – b Rhodes | 18 |
| S. E. Gregory c Jones b Jackson | 2 | – c Arnold b Bosanquet | 51 |
| C. E. McLeod b Arnold | 4 | – lbw b Bosanquet | 13 |
| F. Laver c Jones b Jackson | 5 | – st Lilley b Bosanquet | 5 |
| J. J. Kelly not out | 1 | – not out | 6 |
| B 16, l-b 2, w 1 | 19 | B 4, l-b 3, w 2 | 9 |
| | **221** | | **188** |

## Australian Bowling

| | Overs | Mdns | Runs | Wkts | Overs | Mdns | Runs | Wkts |
|---|---|---|---|---|---|---|---|---|
| Cotter .......... | 23 | 2 | 64 | 3 | 17 | 1 | 59 | 1 |
| Laver ........... | 31.3 | 14 | 64 | 7 | 34 | 7 | 121 | 1 |
| McLeod ......... | 8 | 2 | 19 | — | 28 | 9 | 84 | — |
| Armstrong ....... | 6 | 3 | 4 | — | 52 | 24 | 67 | 1 |
| Noble ........... | 3 | — | 19 | — | 7 | 1 | 31 | — |
| Duff ............ | | | | | 15 | 2 | 43 | 2 |

## England Bowling

| | Overs | Mdns | Runs | Wkts | Overs | Mdns | Runs | Wkts |
|---|---|---|---|---|---|---|---|---|
| Arnold .......... | 11 | 2 | 39 | 1 | 4 | 2 | 7 | — |
| J. Gunn ......... | 6 | 2 | 27 | 1 | | | | |
| Jessop .......... | 7 | 2 | 18 | 1 | 1 | — | 1 | — |
| Bosanquet ....... | 7 | — | 29 | — | 32.4 | 2 | 107 | 8 |
| Rhodes.......... | 18 | 6 | 37 | 1 | 30 | 8 | 58 | 1 |
| Jackson ......... | 14.5 | 2 | 52 | 5 | 5 | 3 | 6 | — |

Umpires: J. Phillips and J. Carlin.

## AUSTRALIANS v SOMERSET

Played at Bath, July 13, 14, 15, 1905

So complete was the mastery gained over the Somerset bowling that 609 runs were scored in six hours and a quarter for the loss of four batsmen, 469 of these being obtained for two wickets on the opening day. Armstrong enjoyed the distinction of putting together the highest score ever made by an Australian in this country, beating the 300 obtained by Trumper at Brighton in 1899, which stood as the record. His play on Thursday, when he left off 252 not out, was of a superb description, his driving being almost perfect. Next day, in the endeavour to beat Trumper's record, he was extremely cautious, but his innings as a whole was a masterly achievement, marred only by two chances given just after he had completed 200. His hits included a six and thirty-eight 4s. Trumper helped him to make 145 for the first wicket, while with Noble as his partner 320 runs were obtained for the third wicket in three hours and ten minutes. Noble gave no chance of any kind. Thanks mainly to Braund, Somerset scored 188 for four wickets before the drawing of stumps, and although the innings soon came to an end on Saturday morning the county saved the game in highly creditable fashion. Braund again batted admirably, and with Martyn hit up 146, this being the best first wicket partnership against the Colonials all through the tour. In putting together his first hundred in important cricket Martyn drove to the on magnificently. Altogether 1,151 runs were scored in thirteen hours and ten minutes for the loss of eighteen wickets.

## Australians

V. T. Trumper c Palairet b Robson ....... 86
W. W. Armstrong not out ..............303
C. Hill c Woods b Braund .............. 11
M. A. Noble c Poyntz b Woods .........127
R. A. Duff c Newton b Robson .......... 12

Darling not out ...................... 49

B 16, l-b 4, w 1 ............... 21
—
(4 wkts dec.) 609

D. R. A. Gehrs, C. E. McLeod, A. Cotter, F. Laver and J. J. Kelly did not bat.

## Somerset

| | | | |
|---|---|---|---|
| Mr L. C. H. Palairet b Cotter | 4 | – not out | 2 |
| L. C. Braund c Armstrong b Noble | 117 | – c sub. b Laver | 62 |
| A. Lewis c Darling b Noble | 11 | – b Armstrong | 17 |
| Mr H. S. Poyntz run out | 6 | – c Duff b McLeod | 11 |
| E. Robson c Armstrong b McLeod | 42 | | |
| Mr H. Martyn c Darling b Cotter | 22 | – not out | 130 |
| Mr S. M. J. Woods b Cotter | 1 | | |
| W. Montgomery b Cotter | 1 | – b McLeod | 11 |
| Mr A. E. Newton c Laver b Noble | 4 | | |
| T. Richardson not out | 4 | | |
| Mr J. Thomas b Noble | 0 | | |
| B 10, l-b 2, w 3, n-b 1 | 16 | B 21 | 21 |
| | **228** | | **254** |

## Somerset Bowling

| | Overs | Mdns | Runs | Wkts |
|---|---|---|---|---|
| Braund | 34 | 2 | 142 | 1 |
| Thomas | 14 | 1 | 65 | — |
| Robson | 36 | 6 | 114 | 2 |
| Richardson | 13 | 1 | 65 | — |
| Palairet | 11 | 1 | 48 | — |
| Montgomery | 13 | 1 | 43 | — |
| Woods | 15 | — | 64 | 1 |
| Poyntz | 4 | — | 25 | — |
| Martyn | 3 | — | 22 | — |

## Australian Bowling

| | Overs | Mdns | Runs | Wkts | Overs | Mdns | Runs | Wkts |
|---|---|---|---|---|---|---|---|---|
| Cotter | 24 | 5 | 101 | 4 | 7 | — | 50 | — |
| Noble | 23.4 | 10 | 45 | 4 | 8 | 2 | 21 | — |
| McLeod | 16 | 5 | 31 | 1 | 13 | 4 | 49 | 2 |
| Laver | 12 | 3 | 23 | — | 15 | 2 | 53 | 1 |
| Armstrong | 5 | 1 | 12 | — | 19 | 9 | 39 | 1 |
| Duff | | | | | 4 | — | 21 | — |

Umpires: A. A. White and S. Brown.

# ENGLAND v SOUTH AFRICA

## Second Test Match

### Played at Leeds, July 29, 30, 31, 1907

The second Test Match was the only one of the three that had a definite result, England winning in the end by 53 runs. A less satisfactory Test game has seldom been played. The wicket was soft before the start, and on the second day especially cricket had to be carried on with extreme difficulty between the showers. On the whole the Englishmen had no great reason to congratulate themselves on their victory. They certainly had the best of the luck as regards the ground and, though this is a point on which we would not venture to express an opinion, it was freely stated that the umpiring told against the South Africans in the last innings. With the ground as it was, it was clearly a mistake to play Knox for England in preference to J. N. Crawford. The fast bowler was no more than a passenger on the side, only bowling four overs in the match. There was no particular advantage in winning the toss, but when at lunch time on Monday, 34 runs had been scored in forty minutes for the loss of Fry's wicket, England seemed to have opened well. However, a dismal collapse followed, nine wickets going down after the interval in less than an hour and a quarter for an addition of 42 runs. Faulkner enjoyed his greatest success during the tour. Disguising his break with the utmost skill, he made the ball turn so much both ways that the batsmen were almost hopeless against him, the result being that he took seven wickets in eleven overs at a cost of only 17 runs. Hirst alone showed any capacity to cope with him on the slow pitch. In comparison with most of the batsmen Hayward played exceedingly well. On paper it was not much for him to score 24, but he showed very skilful defence, stopping among other good balls a tremendous break-back from Vogler. Out for such a paltry score as 76 England had of course an uphill task for the rest of the day. Everything depended on Blythe, none of the other bowlers being able to take advantage of the state of the ground. Still if all the catches had been held there would not have been much to choose on the first innings. Four chances were allowed to escape, and though none of them had any serious consequences the blunders naturally proved somewhat demoralizing. As events turned out the South Africans stopped in till ten minutes to six for a total of 110, thus leading on the first innings by 34 runs. They were only twenty behind with half their wickets in hand, but when the seventh wicket fell they were still 17 runs behind the England total. Happily for the Englishmen Blythe did not fail them. He was not quite so accurate in length as he might have been, but he made the ball do a good deal and though two catches were missed off him he took eight wickets for 59 runs. But for him the match might have been irretrievably lost on the first day.

Twenty-five minutes remained for play and R. E. Foster felt much concerned as to what he should do. However, after some consideration, he determined to keep to the previous order and sent in Fry and Hayward. This policy answered admirably, the two batsmen playing with great skill and scoring 25 runs without loss before the call of time. Cricket on the second day was carried on under extreme difficulties. Four times between eleven o'clock and half-past one rain drove the players from the field, but between the showers England's score was carried to 110 for four wickets. After lunch the weather was so bad that nothing further could be done. At half-past two the umpires announced that even in the most favourable circumstances play would be impossible until late in the day and eventually a brief but heavy storm caused stumps to be drawn at ten minutes to five. So far at it went the cricket was full of interest. The South African bowlers were much handicapped by having to use a wet ball, but they triumphed over this disadvantage in a remarkable way, not only keeping their length surprisingly well but getting on a lot of spin. Fry played superbly, his innings of 54 going far to secure England's ultimate victory. He made his 54 out of 100 and was batting altogether for an hour and a quarter. Running no undue risks but seizing every fair opportunity, he made a number of good drives, always picking on the right balls to hit. He gave no chance, but he had a lucky escape on the Monday evening, playing a ball from Faulkner on to his wicket without removing the bails. Tyldesley, though not by any means up to Fry's form, scored an invaluable 30.

So much rain had fallen, the wicket being under water at six o'clock on Tuesday, that everyone thought the start of play would be delayed on the third morning. Thanks, however, to a fine night and a bright windy morning, play was quite practicable at eleven o'clock. Run-getting proved a very hard matter and with the game twice stopped by rain England only increased their overnight score to 162, the innings being all over by a quarter to one. Gordon White and Faulkner bowled uncommonly well, getting on any amount of leg break. Foster made a great effort for his side, his score of 22 being of far more value than it looks on paper. In second wicket down on Tuesday he was out ninth after batting for seventy minutes.

The South Africans wanted 129 to win and the task seemed by no means impossible. However, they made a bad start, losing two wickets for 10 runs before rain came on at twenty past one and stopped play till after luncheon. A third wicket should have fallen, Braund missing Hathorn at slip. Play was not resumed till five minutes to three and then the South Africans soon found themselves in an almost hopeless position, Nourse, Hathorn, and White, being so speedily got rid of that five wickets were down for 18. Sinclair raised the hopes of his side by punishing Blythe for a dozen runs in one over, but at 38 he was caught at slip. After this Faulkner and Snooke made a determined effort to save the game, but though they showed strong defence they could not get the ball away. Faulkner, after exercising the sternest self-restraint for an hour, was tempted at last to hit out at Blythe, and skied the ball to forward point where Foster caught him. From the moment he left the result was never in doubt, the last four wickets falling in less than half-an-hour and the innings ending at a quarter to five for a total of 75. Tyldesley caught Vogler at long off in a wonderful way. He had to run some distance for the catch and fell over, but contrived to keep the ball off the ground. Blythe, who bowled himself almost to a standstill, clearly won the game, taking seven wickets for 40 runs. Altogether he took fifteen wickets, a feat that has only once been equalled in Test matches – by Rhodes for the MCC's England team at Melbourne in 1904.

### England

| | | |
|---|---|---|
| T. Hayward st Sherwell b Faulkner | 24 | – st Sherwell b Vogler ............ 15 |
| Mr C. B. Fry b Vogler | 2 | – lbw b White ................. 54 |
| J. T. Tyldesley b Faulkner | 12 | – c Snooke b Schwarz ........... 30 |
| Mr R. E. Foster b Sinclair | 0 | – lbw b Faulkner .............. 22 |
| L. C. Braund lbw b Faulkner | 1 | – c Schwarz b White ............ 0 |
| G. H. Hirst c Hathorn b Sinclair | 17 | – b White ................... 2 |
| Mr G. I. Jessop c Sherwell b Faulkner | 0 | – c Hathorn b Faulkner .......... 10 |
| E. Arnold b Faulkner | 0 | – c Schwarz b Faulkner .......... 12 |
| A. A. Lilley c Schwarz b Faulkner | 3 | – lbw b White ................. 0 |
| C. Blythe not out | 5 | – not out ................... 4 |
| Mr N. A. Knox c Faulkner b Sinclair | 8 | – run out ................... 5 |
| B 1, l-b 2, n-b 1 | 4 | B 7, l-b 1 ............... 8 |
| | **76** | **162** |

### South Africa

| | | |
|---|---|---|
| Mr P. W. Sherwell lbw b Blythe | 26 | – c Foster b Blythe .............. 1 |
| Mr L. J. Tancred st Lilley b Blythe | 0 | – run out ................... 0 |
| Mr M. Hathorn c Lilley b Hirst | 0 | – b Arnold .................. 7 |
| Mr A. D. Nourse c Arnold b Blythe | 18 | – lbw b Blythe ................ 2 |
| Mr G. C. White c Hirst b Blythe | 3 | – c Arnold b Blythe ............ 7 |
| Mr J. H. Sinclair st Lilley b Blythe | 2 | – c Braund b Blythe ............ 15 |
| Mr G. A. Faulkner c Braund b Blythe | 6 | – c Foster b Blythe ............ 11 |
| Mr S. J. Snooke c Lilley b Knox | 13 | – c Hirst b Blythe ............. 14 |
| Mr W. A. Shalders c Fry b Blythe | 21 | – lbw b Hirst ................. 5 |
| Mr A. E. Vogler c Hayward b Blythe | 11 | – c Tyldesley b Blythe ......... 9 |
| Mr R. O. Schwarz not out | 5 | – not out ................... 0 |
| B 3, l-b 1, n-b 1 | 5 | B 3, n-b 1 ............... 4 |
| | **110** | **75** |

### South African Bowling

| | Overs | Mdns | Runs | Wkts | Overs | Mdns | Runs | Wkts |
|---|---|---|---|---|---|---|---|---|
| Vogler .......... | 8 | 3 | 14 | 1 | 4 | — | 18 | 1 |
| Schwarz ......... | 7 | — | 18 | — | 5.4 | — | 18 | 1 |
| Faulkner ........ | 11 | 4 | 17 | 6 | 20 | 3 | 58 | 3 |
| Sinclair .......... | 10.3 | 2 | 23 | 3 | 4 | — | 13 | — |
| White ........... | | | | | 16 | 3 | 47 | 4 |

**England Bowling**

| | Overs | Mdns | Runs | Wkts | Overs | Mdns | Runs | Wkts |
|---|---|---|---|---|---|---|---|---|
| Hirst ............ | 9 | 3 | 22 | 1 | 9 | 2 | 21 | 1 |
| Blythe .......... | 15.5 | 1 | 59 | 8 | 22.4 | 9 | 40 | 7 |
| Arnold .......... | 4 | 1 | 11 | — | 13 | 7 | 10 | 1 |
| Knox ............ | 4 | — | 13 | 1 | | | | |

Umpires: J. Moss and J. Carlin.

# SOUTH AFRICAN BOWLING, 1907

## By R. E. Foster

The cricket season of 1907 will always be remembered by two distinct features. 1. – The extremely bad weather. 2. – The South Africans' bowling. The less said about the former the better, though the rain and the consequent soft wickets did raise a very interesting question; namely, would the South Africans have fared better in a good dry season? Now, looking at their performances against the counties, it seems difficult to conceive how they could have improved on their magnificent record, however good and fast the wickets might have been. Before their arrival in this country we were told that they must have hard wickets to really suit their particular kind of bowling, but the way they bowled, not only in representative games, but against the counties on sticky wickets, was a revelation to many a good judge of cricket. The feature of their bowling on these wickets was the extraordinary pace the ball came off the pitch. This was to be expected on fast wickets, but no one had foreseen that the same thing would happen on really slow ones. Truly, as one old hand said in the Test match at Leeds, it was like playing Briggs through the air and Tom Richardson off the pitch. Now, the opinion of English cricketers who went to South Africa with the MCC team in 1905 is, that there is all the difference in the world between our fast good wickets and the South African matting wickets, and this lies in the varying height in the bounce of the ball. On the matting the ball nearly always has to be played about chest high, a fact enormously increasing the difficulty of dealing with such bowling. On our fast wickets the ball may turn very quickly and go either one of two ways, but it nearly always comes the same height; and I maintain that the English team would have got any amount of runs under such conditions, and more than that, the South Africans would not have done so well in a dry season. Had the Test matches been played on matting it quite possibly might have been another matter, though it is open to question (their batting being rather a weak point) if the bowling could have carried them to victory in representative games. The South African bowlers could be hit on a good wicket, and it is possible that a little more enterprise might have spelt success. Jessop showed they could be hit, in a magnificent display in the first Test match, on a good wicket; but he also showed, at Leeds and the Oval, that they could not be hit on a bad wicket, for not only did the ball turn too quickly, but it came a different height and pace. The result of a comparison of the dangers presented by the South African attack on fast and slow wickets seems to point to a preference for the latter, and I know this to be the opinion of most of the players who represented England against them.

Now let us turn to a detailed description of the bowling. The interest in the attack of the South Africans is centred round four men – Schwarz, Vogler, Faulkner, and White. These men all bowled with a leg-break action, and could make the ball come in from the off. Though England can claim the 'proud originator' of this style of bowling in Bosanquet, it has been left to South Africa to improve it – I will not say perfect – as I am convinced that this style is capable of still further improvement, which in time will be brought nearly to perfection. Bosanquet taught Schwarz, and Schwarz taught the others, and the others are better than their mentors, as Bosanquet has practically given up bowling in this way, and Schwarz, possibly because he finds he can get as many people out as he wishes, only breaks the ball from the off, but always with a leg-break action. His has been a great achievement this year, of which he and the South Africans may justly be proud, for he is top of the bowling averages, having taken 143 wickets with an average of 11.51 apiece, a performance that speaks for itself. It is rather hard to explain his great success, as, though his bowling is the most difficult to hit of the four bowlers mentioned, it is much the easiest to play, because he only breaks one way, and the batsmen have never got to think of the possibility of the ball breaking the other way. The ball comes very slow through the air, and having hit the ground goes off at the most extraordinary pace. There is nothing very deceptive in the flight, but the break varies from six inches to eighteen inches, and on sticky wickets he is quite capable of breaking a yard. Now, a bowler of this description, you will say, must bowl many loose balls; certainly he does, but the pace the ball comes from the wicket imparted by the spin, makes it very difficult indeed for the batsman to place it accurately between the fielders, six of whom are placed in various parts of the on side, and hitting at random at such bowling courts disaster, and I am sure is one of the causes of his success this year. In addition to this reason, Schwarz is extraordinarily deadly to the last four or five batsmen, and the man who goes in for his county side in rather a humble position seems to have no notion how to play such bowling. He is a great bowler, but I am convinced he gets many more wickets than he should. Play him with your legs – old pavilion critics forgive, but we have to deal with bowling you never had to trouble about – don't hit at him, place him for one's and two's, and wait for the real bad one which you will occasionally get and can score off. Very often a bowler of Schwarz's description will suffer at the umpire's hands, but it must be well nigh impossible to tell if the batsman is out when a ball comes so quickly off the pitch, and knowing how much the bowler is capable of making the ball break; finally, I cannot help think that Schwarz would prove more deadly could he control his break – i.e., break nothing to a foot, and I believe that he would get many good batsmen out with the ball that does not break at all.

Of the remaining three of this interesting quartette, Faulkner and White can be considered together, but Vogler claims our attention all to himself. He was undoubtedly the finest bowler of a very good lot, indeed many good judges consider him the best bowler in the English cricket season of 1907. He has rather a hesitating run up to the wicket, but in the last few steps never gets out of his stride. The ball is well concealed from the batsman before delivery, and the flight and variation of pace are very deceptive indeed. With a new ball, Vogler makes the ball swing quite a lot and often starts bowling fast medium off-break, with a swerve. He then will have two slips and a short leg, and perhaps no man out in the country. With the newness worn off the ball he will settle down to his ordinary slow mediums, in which case his field will be, with the exception of three men, disposed of on the on side of the wicket. Vogler, like Schwarz and other bowlers who have cultivated this particular type of bowling, imparts that spin to the ball which enables it to leave the pitch at such a wonderful pace. His usual ball is the leg-break, but once in two overs perhaps he will bowl what the South Africans have designated "the wrong 'un." Now it is almost impossible to see this ball coming; it seems to the batsman that the ball is delivered in identically the same manner and yet it comes the other way, i.e., from the off. After very careful watching the only difference one can detect, and this is possibly fancy, is that the hand seems to be turned father more over in the action of delivery. The ball seems to come more out of the back of the hand, and the batsman may be able to see almost the palm of the bowler's hand. But it is almost impossible to notice any difference, and I was told Sherwell had said that Vogler was the bowler he found most difficulty in detecting. Vogler's ordinary leg-break will turn from two or three inches up to eighteen inches, but the other one coming from the off rarely breaks more than three or four inches and frequently comes perfectly straight through, and in this case will come even faster off the pitch than the balls that turn. This possibly is due to the bowler intending to bowl the off-break, and, through not quite turning the hand or fingers sufficiently, imparts a top spin. This makes the ball come straight through very quickly and is one of the most difficult balls to deal with – lbw so often resulting. Vogler bowls a slow yorker or well pitched up ball that is very deceptive in the flight and seems more to quiver than swing in the air. He clean bowled C. B. Fry with this ball both at Leeds and at The Oval in the Test matches. As will be seen then, Vogler is a bowler of infinite variation, unbounded resource, and what is better than all, of great natural ability. He can bowl for a long time and does not seem to tire or lose his length. His performances at Lord's this year against a very strong MCC XI and again in the first Test match were as good as anything seen at headquarters for years. Vogler's average for the season works out at 133 wickets for 15 apiece, and in Test matches he was, taken all through, much the best and most consistent bowler on the South African side, though actual figures bring Faulkner out above him, due mainly to a great performance in England's first innings at Leeds. Schwarz does not come out so well, a third of his total number of wickets being obtained in the last innings at The Oval when the English side were risking wickets in order to obtain runs quickly, another instance of the argument that Schwarz cannot be hit recklessly. In Vogler the South Africans possess undoubtedly a bowler of the highest class, and in the writer's humble opinion the greatest bowler playing circket in either hemisphere at the present time, and we may dismiss him with many congratulations on his great performances, and many thanks for the great interest and pleasure his bowling has afforded this summer to all lovers of cricket.

Faulkner and White are to all intents and purposes the same bowler. They deliver the ball from practically the same height, and the flight, pace, and break are almost identical. But Faulkner is certainly the more dangerous bowler, and, if there is any difference, comes through the air and off the pitch a shade faster, and is undoubtedly capable of bowling a more unplayable ball. His performance at Leeds in the first innings against England is surely the greatest that has ever been achieved in this unorthodox style of bowling. Gordon White it is true comes out with a better average, having taken 72 wickets for 13 runs apiece against 73 wickets for 15 runs each, but Faulkner did not get into form till practically July and was hardly ever called upon. These two bowlers in the ordinary way deliver much the same ball as the English batsman is accustomed to expect and receive from a leg-break bowler of the Braund-Vine type with two notable differences – (a) the ball comes from the pitch at a far greater pace; (b) the terrible "wrong 'un." In the first case as has been said above, this characteristic is evident in each of the four bowlers under consideration, and the reason for it is very difficult to explain. A possible cause may be found in the fact that ordinary leg-break bowlers deliver the ball chiefly by the swing of the arm and allowing the ball to come from the back of the hand, whereas the South Africans seem to deliver the ball with a flick, relying entirely on finger and wrist for spin. In the second case both bowlers can effectively bowl the ball that comes from the off with a leg-break action, but again in a measure differ. Faulkner makes the ball break quite a lot from the off and practically always makes it break; White on the other hand makes the ball break comparatively little and very often comes straight through, therefore Faulkner is more likely to clean bowl a batsman and White to get him lbw. Neither has a deceptive flight, and it is possible to see the off break coming in both cases occasionally. Indeed I venture to think that with more practice against such bowling, batsmen would soon find far less difficulty in seeing the break and possibly might never be at fault. In Vogler's case and in future artists of his class that may arise (as this type of bowling and the art of concealing a break will greatly improve), I doubt if the batsmen will ever be impossible to deceive.

Before passing to what must be henceforward termed the ordinary kind of bowlers, it may be interesting just to see if this new type of bowling is likely in the future to improve or deteriorate batting from the spectator's point of view. Personally, I think it will deteriorate batting. For this new kind of bowling is a very great invention, and it is possible it may completely alter cricket, and no one who has not played against it can realize the difference it makes to a batsmen and his shots. It must again be reiterated that this type of bowling is practically in its infancy, and if persevered with – as it surely will be – must improve and become more difficult to deal with. Now a batsmen when he goes in may receive a ball which either breaks from the off, perhaps from the leg, or again may come straight through very quickly. If he survives half-a-dozen overs he ought to be getting set, but such bowling never allows a batsmen to get really set, because he can never make or go for his accustomed shots. The ball just short of a half volley he is accustomed to drive between cover and extra cover fearlessly, now bothers him, and prevents him doing so, owing to his inability to discover which way and how much the ball is going to break. And as this bowling improves the difficulty will become increased, till those beautiful drives we are wont to expect from some of our great batsmen will become a thing of the past. Hayward was stumped in both the first two Test matches, playing that shot through the covers, and after experiences such as these will give up attempting the stroke. No! such bowling will enormously increase defence at the expense of safe scoring shots such as drives and cuts, and scoring will be confined to hitting. Many people may maintain that this will be a good thing, but if Hayward's off-driving and Tyldesley's cutting are to be seen no more and such strokes to be a lost art to future generations, cricket, as far as batting is concerned, must lose a great deal of its attractiveness.

And finally let us turn to the ordinary bowlers. These comprise, Sinclair, Kotze, Nourse, and Snooke. Sinclair is a very fine bowler, and had he played on any other side would have done a great deal better. He never had a chance, and was not put on unless the quartette were unable to get a side out, which was a very rare occurrence. I think he might have been used more, though Sherwell had a very difficult task, having really too much bowling at his command. Sinclair has a nice easy run up to the wicket, and a great command over the flight and pace of the delivery. He uses his great height well, and though bowling quite medium could send down a very fast "Yorker" – a useful and often fatal ball. The members of the English Team had a high opinion of his bowling and were secretly delighted he was not called upon more. His spin enabled him to break the ball on nearly any wicket, and on a pitch that suits him he is very difficult to deal with, as he makes the ball get up very quickly from the pitch, as well as come back sharply.

Kotze had a very unfortunate experience, the wet season rendering him of little value to his side. It is impossible to criticize his bowling as he hardly did any, but he did not seem to be very dangerous and rather to have decreased in pace since his last visit to England in 1904. But he continues to have such great success in South Africa that the cold and wet weather in this country this summer never probably allowed him to get loose or onto form, and had it been a summer of hard wickets he would undoubtedly have been a very useful member of the side. Nourse is a fast-medium left-hand bowler with a big swerve, and occasionally makes the ball break back off the wicket. He bowls absolutely naturally, and might get a wicket any time – but ought not to defeat a batsman who has defied him for three or four overs. Snooke is a fast, right-hand bowler and gets up rather straight from the pitch; but as the two last mentioned were not called upon to any extent, they can hardly be classed among the regular bowlers of the side.

This brings to a close a brief description of the South African bowling, which from its varied nature and novel characteristics affords a most interesting study to the cricket enthusiast. Taken as a whole they were undoubtedly a magnificent bowling side, to be compared with advantage to any Australian side that has visited England in recent years. Had their batting been of the same calibre, England might well have come off second best.

In conclusion, they have won the admiration of everyone with whom they have come in contact, not only for their cricket capabilities but because they have played the game in the right spirit, being led by a man who has only the best interests of cricket at heart. And all will agree that it has been the greatest pleasure to have met and played with the South African Team of 1907.

## THE TRIANGULAR TOURNAMENT, 1912

### The Nine Test Matches

The Triangular Tournament between England, Australia and South Africa – so long expected and so much discussed – duly came off last season. Of the nine matches three were played at Lord's, two at The Oval, two at Manchester, and one each at Leeds and Nottingham. The result was a victory for England, who won four matches out of six –

beating the South Africans three times and the Australians once – and did not suffer a single defeat. From the first the South Africans were obviously outclassed. Owing to rain the matches between England and Australia at Lord's and Manchester had to be left drawn, but in a game which lasted four days England gained a decisive victory at The Oval, and so won the competition.

The results of the nine matches came out as follows: –

|  | Played | Won | Lost | Drawn |
| --- | --- | --- | --- | --- |
| England ........... | 6 | 4 | 0 | 2 |
| Australia .......... | 6 | 2 | 1 | 3 |
| South Africa ....... | 6 | 0 | 5 | 1 |

Bad weather interfered sadly with the success of the Tournament. In the England and Australia match at Lord's play on the second day was only practicable for twenty minutes, and when the teams met five weeks later in Manchester rain caused great delay and not a ball could be bowled on the third day. The experiment of fixing two of the Australia and South Africa matches at Manchester and Nottingham on the Whit-Monday and August Bank Holidays respectively did not turn out well, the attendance at both places falling far below the Test match standard. The full accounts in connection with the Tournament were issued from Lord's by the Board of Control in October, the Test trial games at The Oval and Lord's coming into the general statement. The total receipts amounted to £12,463 4s. 2d. Of this sum, gate-money produced £9,004 8s., and stands and enclosures £3,458 16s. 2d. The Australians received as their share of the gate-money £2,286, and the South Africans £1,878 10s. Deducting these sums and all expenses, there remained for appropriation to English clubs £4,465 16s. 2d.

Taking 60 per cent of this sum, the MCC and the sixteen first-class counties received £157 12s. 4d. each. Thirty per cent going to the grounds where the matches were played, the MCC received £487 3s. 7d., Surrey £365 7s. 8d., Lancashire £243 11s. 9d., Yorkshire £121 15s. 11d., and Nottinghamshire £121 15s. 11d. The remaining 10 per cent yielded £24 16s. 3d. each to be eighteen second-class counties.

By far the most attractive of the Test matches were in the order named: England v Australia, at The Oval; England v Australia, at Lord's; and England v South Africa, at Lord's. These matches produced respectively in gate-money and receipts from stands and enclosures £3,429 8s. 8d., £2,713 15s. 6d., and £1,696 13s. The least attractive match by a long way was Australia v South Africa, at Nottingham, on the August Bank Holiday.

### Summary of Matches

May 27, 28, at Manchester, Australia v South Africa – Australia, 448; South Africa, 265 and 95. Australia won by an innings and 88 runs.

June 10, 11, 12, at Lord's, England v South Africa – South Africa, 58 and 217; England, 337. England won by an innings and 62 runs.

June 24, 25, 26, at Lord's, England v Australia – England, 310 for seven dec.; Australia, 282 for seven wickets. Drawn.

July 8, 9, 10, at Leeds, England v South Africa – England, 242 and 238; South Africa, 147 and 159. England won by 174 runs.

July 15, 16, 17, at Lord's, Australia v South Africa – South Africa, 263 and 173; Australia, 390 and 48 for no wicket. Australia won by ten wickets.

July 29, 30, 31, at Manchester, England v Australia – England 203; Australia, 14 for no wicket. Drawn.

August 5, 6, 7, at Nottingham, Australia v South Africa – South Africa, 329; Australia, 219. Drawn.

August 12, 13, at The Oval, England v South Africa – South Africa, 95 and 93; England, 176 and 14 for no wicket. England won by ten wickets.

August 19, 20, 21, 22, at The Oval, England v Australia – England, 245 and 175; Australia, 111 and 65. England won by 244 runs.

## AUSTRALIA v SOUTH AFRICA

### Played at Manchester, May 27, 28, 1912

In the light of after-events, it was a pity that the Triangular Tournament began with one of the matches between Australia and South Africa. The single innings' victory gained by the Australians in two days convinced the public that the South Africans, whatever their merits, were not up to Test match form. Subsequent play showed, only too plainly, that first impressions were well-founded. The match did not arouse the interest in Manchester that had been hoped for, but on the Bank Holiday, 8,609 people paid for admission. Recent rain had left the ground a trifle soft, but on winning the toss, Gregory had no hesitation in taking first innings. All through the afternoon the wicket proved delightfully easy to bat on, and in something over five hours the Australians ran up a score of 448, thus putting themselves in quite a safe position. In the last twenty minutes or so, the South Africans scored 16 runs for the loss of Taylor's wicket. The Australians started in a way that gave a true forecast of what was to follow, Jennings, who opened the innings with Kelleway, playing so freely, that, when he left, 62 runs had been scored in forty minutes. In the meantime, Kelleway was twice beaten by Pegler with balls that missed the wicket. Macartney began in very lively style, but at 92 he hit across his wicket at a ball from Pegler and was bowled. Then came the stand that, to all intents and purposes, determined the result of the match. Bardsley joined Kelleway, and in two hours and ten minutes 202 runs were added to the score. Kelleway was out at last to a catch at the wicket at 294. His innings of 114, which only included five 4s, was strangely colourless, but his patient, watchful defence was invaluable. Very different was the display given by Bardsley who, even in this early part of the tour, was up to his highest standard of 1909. Out fourth at 314, he scored his 121 in less than two hours and a half, hitting eleven 4s, three 3s, and nine 2s. He was missed at the wicket when he had made 68, and looked to give another chance when 111, but apart from these blemishes no fault could be found with his play. Unfailing in judgment and brilliant in execution, he was master of the bowling from the movement he went in. At the tea interval the Australians' score stood at 359 for five wickets, but on play being continued, the remaining five wickets fell in an hour. Whitty drove with much freedom, his partnership with Matthews adding 63 runs for the last wicket.

Tuesday's cricket was sensational to a degree, Matthews bringing off a double "hat-trick" – a feat quite without precedent in Test matches. Thanks to his bowling the match ended just before half-past six. Australia winning by an innings and 88 runs. In facing a total of 448 in the morning, the South Africans were much handicapped, Gordon White, who had split his hand in trying to make a catch on Monday, batting under great difficulties. Up to a certain point the batsmen made so little headway against very accurate bowling that when the fourth wicket fell the overnight score of 16 for one wicket had only been increased to 54. At this point, White joined Faulkner, and in an hour and forty minutes the two batsmen put on 89 runs, White being out leg-before-wicket soon after luncheon at 143. He could not venture to hit much, but despite his damaged hand, his defence was admirable. In the course of the partnership, a blunder, which cost the Australians no end of trouble, was committed. Faulkner, when 36, gave the easiest of chances at mid-on, but Whitty, trying to make the catch with one hand, dropped the ball. Profiting by this escape, Faulkner went on batting in a style that, on the big ocassions, he never approached during the rest of the season. In the end, he took out his bat for 122, his great innings, which lasted four hours and a quarter and was only marred by the one chance, including thirteen 4s. He made most of his runs by means of skilful cutting and hard drives. At four o'clock, the South Africans, with three wickets to fall, required only 30 runs to avoid the follow-on. Then came the first of Matthews' "hat-tricks." Beaumont was bowled, and to the next two balls Pegler and Ward were out leg-before-wicket. Though his side had been in the field since eleven o'clock, Gregory, holding a lead of 183, was not afraid to make the South Africans bat again. Their second innings began at a quarter to five, and resulted in a dismal collapse. Somewhat unwisely, Faulkner, despite the heavy exertion he had gone through, was sent in first with Hartigan. He was bowled by a break-back without getting a run, and from this disastrous start the South Africans never recovered. Three wickets were down for 22, and five for 70. Matthews then performed his second "hat-trick." He bowled Taylor, and in the cleverest way caught and bowled Schwarz and Ward. Needless to say, the completion of his double feat provoked great enthusiasm. Beaumont made a few hits, but the innings was all over for 95. The match was an all-round triumph for the Australians. Apart from the batting of Bardsley and Kelleway, and Matthews' "hat-tricks," nothing in their cricket was better than the bowling of Whitty in the South Africans' first innings.

### Australia

| | | | |
|---|---:|---|---:|
| C. B. Jennings c Schwarz b Pegler | 32 | S. H. Emery b Schwarz | 1 |
| C. Kelleway c Ward b Pegler | 114 | G. R. Hazlitt lbw b Schwarz | 0 |
| C. G. Macartney b Pegler | 21 | W. Carkeek b Pegler | 4 |
| W. Bardsley c and b White | 121 | W. J. Whitty st Ward b Pegler | 33 |
| S. E. Gregory st Ward b Pegler | 37 | B 14, l-b 9, w 1 | 24 |
| R. B. Minnett c and b Schwarz | 12 | | — |
| T. J. Matthews not out | 49 | | 448 |

### South Africa

| | | | |
|---|---:|---|---:|
| H. W. Taylor c Carkeek b Whitty | 0 | – b Matthews | 21 |
| G. P. D. Hartigan c Carkeek b Emery | 25 | – b Kelleway | 4 |
| A. D. Nourse b Whitty | 17 | – c Bardsley b Whitty | 18 |
| S. J. Snooke b Whitty | 7 | – b Whitty | 9 |
| G. A. Faulkner not out | 122 | – b Kelleway | 0 |
| G. C. White lbw b Whitty | 22 | – c Carkeek b Kelleway | 9 |
| F. Mitchell b Whitty | 11 | – b Kelleway | 0 |
| R. O. Schwarz b Hazlitt | 19 | – c and b Matthews | 0 |
| R. Beaumont b Matthews | 31 | – b Kelleway | 17 |
| S. J. Pegler lbw b Matthews | 0 | – not out | 8 |
| T. A. Ward lbw b Matthews | 0 | – c and b Matthews | 0 |
| B 2, l-b 5, w 1, n-b 3 | 11 | B 5, l-b 1, n-b 3 | 9 |
| | 265 | | 95 |

### South Africa Bowling

| | Overs | Mdns | Runs | Wkts |
|---|---:|---:|---:|---:|
| Faulkner | 16 | 2 | 55 | — |
| Nourse | 14 | 1 | 62 | — |
| Pegler | 45.3 | 9 | 105 | 6 |
| Schwarz | 32 | — | 142 | 3 |
| Hartigan | 9 | — | 31 | — |
| White | 6 | 1 | 29 | 1 |

**Australia Bowling**

| | Overs | Mdns | Runs | Wkts | Overs | Mdns | Runs | Wkts |
|---|---|---|---|---|---|---|---|---|
| Hazlitt . . . . . . . . . . . | 16 | 4 | 46 | 1 | | | | |
| Whitty . . . . . . . . . . . | 34 | 12 | 55 | 5 | 6 | 3 | 15 | 2 |
| Emery . . . . . . . . . . | 37 | 10 | 94 | 1 | | | | |
| Kelleway . . . . . . . . . | 11 | 3 | 27 | — | 14.2 | 4 | 33 | 5 |
| Matthews . . . . . . . . . | 12 | 3 | 16 | 3 | 8 | 1 | 38 | 3 |
| Minnett . . . . . . . . . . | 6 | 2 | 16 | — | | | | |

Umpires: A. A. White and G. Webb.

## ENGLAND v SOUTH AFRICA

### Played at Lord's, June 10, 11, 12, 1912

Losing the second of the Test matches by an innings and 62 runs, the South Africans found themselves out of the running while the season was still young. The first day's play practically decided the game, England, at the drawing of stumps, being 64 runs ahead with nine wickets in hand. Rain, during the previous week and on the Sunday morning, had so saturated Lord's ground that, at half-past eleven, when play should have begun, cricket was out of the question. Quite early in the day it was agreed not to start until after luncheon, and the wicket originally prepared for the match was given up as hopeless. The pitch it was then decided to use, dried more quickly than had been expected, and just after three o'clock, Frank Mitchell having won the toss, the South Africans went in to bat. The result proved disastrous, but in the circumstances, most captains would have acted as Mitchell did, there seeming every likelihood that the wicket would, for a time, be fairly easy. Dean was on the ground in readiness to play for England in place of Brearley, but it was decided to make no change from the first selection. About 12,000 people were present, and the cricket they saw more than compensated them for their long hours of waiting. Batting for rather less than an hour and a half the South Africans were all out at half-past four for a total of 58, Barnes and Foster bowling in irresistible form on the drying ground. At the start, two wickets fell in four overs for 3 runs, Barnes taking them both. Hartigan was neatly caught low down at slip, and Taylor lbw. Then came the only semblance of a stand during the innings, a few hits by Nourse and Llewellyn taking the score to 28 before Foster bowled Nourse with a yorker on the off-stump. Just at this time Foster was especially deadly. At 35, he beat Llewellyn with a shooter, and at 36 he bowled Faulkner's off-stump out of the ground. From these disasters there was no recovery, the remaining batsmen being quite helpless against the splendid bowling. Barnes and Foster divided the wickets equally, Foster hitting the stumps five times. Still, except for the balls that took wickets, he did not look so difficult as Barnes, who broke both ways and kept a perfect length.

In face of a total of 58, England had, of course, nothing to be anxious about, but their innings, which began at ten minutes to five, opened rather ominously, Hobbs, after hitting a full-pitch to the ring, playing on in the first over. From this point, however, everything went well. Spooner joined Rhodes, and when half-past six came, the score had, without further loss, been carried to 122, Rhodes being not out 36, and Spooner not out 67. Both batsmen were beaten by balls that missed the wicket, and Spooner, when 50, gave a chance at mid-on, but considering the condition of the pitch the batting was wonderfully good. Spooner seized every opportunity, but Rhodes did not hit much until Llewellyn was put on to bowl. Spooner was particularly strong in scoring from anything like a short-pitched ball.

The weather was very pleasant on the second day, and over 13,000 people paid for admission. Rhodes was soon bowled, he and Spooner having put on 124 runs together in an hour and forty minutes. Out of this number Rhodes only made 36, but his steady defence was invaluable. After he left, England fared so well that at lunch time the total stood at 303 for four wickets. A huge score seemed in prospect, but after lunch the innings came to an ignominious end, the last six wickets falling – all to Pegler's bowling – for 34 runs. Tried for the first time at the pavilion end, Pegler seemed almost unplayable. He hit the stumps four times, and while finishing the innings in such sensational fashion, had only 16 runs scored from him. Spooner was out, fourth wicket down, at 207, to a brilliant catch close to the ground at mid-off. Batting rather less than three hours, he hit, in his 119, one six and thirteen 4s. After completing his hundred – his first in a Test match – he tried to get runs as quickly as possible. With his score at 93, he would have been caught at mid-on if Frank Mitchell had moved quickly for the ball, but apart from this, he was quite at his best on the second day. The great feature of his innings was his forcing back-play. Fry helped to carry the total from 128 to 183, but never seemed at ease, the amount of break that Faulkner and Schwarz got on the ball cramping his game. Warner and Woolley put on 113 together in an hour and a quarter. Without being seen to any special advantage, Warner, who had a great welcome from the crowd, played steadily. Woolley, on the other hand, was in his happiest vein, hitting with great brilliancy and little or no apparent effort. His 73 included two 6s and seven 4s.

The South Africans had to go in against a balance of 279, and when they had lost Hartigan, Taylor and Nourse for 36, the match seemed almost certain to be over before the end of the afternoon. At this point, Llewellyn, who, before he scored had survived an appeal for a catch by the wicket-keeper off Foster's bowling, was joined by Faulkner. Then, for some reason not easy to understand, Fry tried a change of bowling, putting on Brearley in place of Barnes. Brearley was very steady, but though he sent down half-a-dozen overs for four singles, he could not get a wicket. Feeling that everything depended upon him, Faulkner exercised such extreme self-restraint that when he made his fifth run, he had been at the wickets fifty minutes. In the meantime, however, Llewellyn was hitting finely. The two batsmen sent up the hundred, but at 104, in trying to pull a short ball from Barnes, Faulkner was bowled. With Llewellyn and Snooke batting, the light became very bad, and at twenty minutes to six the game was suspended. After a delay of half-an-hour, the players came out again, but only one more over was bowled, the light being still defective. At the close Llewellyn was not out 60, the score standing at 114, for four wickets.

On the third day the match ended very quietly, the end being reached at twenty minutes to one. The South Africans carried their score to 217, but if all the catches had been held they would not have made 200. Getting a lot of work on the ball, Barnes bowled wonderfully well. Llewellyn was out seventh at 147 – finely caught at the wicket on the leg side off Foster's bowling. In his brilliant 75 – an innings that dwarfted all the rest of the South African batting – he hit eight 4s, most of them powerful drives. Pegler, in scoring ten, might have been out three times. Barnes and Foster took nineteen wickets in the match, Barnes securing eleven for 110, and Foster eight for 70. For some reason Fry did not let Brearley bowl at all on the third morning.

### South Africa

| | | | |
|---|---:|---|---:|
| G. P. D. Hartigan c Foster b Barnes | 0 | – b Foster | 1 |
| H. W. Taylor lbw b Barnes | 1 | – b Barnes | 5 |
| A. D. Nourse b Foster | 13 | – run out | 17 |
| C. B. Llewellyn b Foster | 9 | – c Smith b Foster | 75 |
| G. A. Faulkner b Foster | 7 | – b Barnes | 15 |
| S. J. Snooke b Barnes | 2 | – b Foster | 16 |
| F. Mitchell c and b Barnes | 1 | – b Barnes | 1 |
| R. O. Schwarz c Foster b Barnes | 4 | – b Barnes | 28 |
| S. J. Pegler b Foster | 4 | – b Barnes | 10 |
| C. P. Carter b Foster | 0 | – not out | 27 |
| T. Campbell not out | 0 | – c Jessop b Barnes | 3 |
| B 12, l-b 3, n-b 2 | 17 | B 17, l-b 1, n-b 1 | 19 |
| | **58** | | **217** |

## England

| | | | | |
|---|---|---|---|---|
| J. B. Hobbs b Nourse | 4 | Mr F. R. Foster lbw b Pegler | 11 |
| W. Rhodes b Nourse | 36 | E. J. Smith b Pegler | 2 |
| Mr R. H. Spooner c Llewellyn b Nourse | 119 | S. F. Barnes not out | 0 |
| Mr C. B. Fry b Pegler | 29 | Mr W. Brearley b Pegler | 0 |
| Mr P. F. Warner st Campbell b Pegler | 39 | B 11, l-b 9, w 1 | 21 |
| F. E. Woolley b Pegler | 73 | | — |
| Mr G. L. Jessop b Pegler | 3 | | 337 |

### England Bowling

| | Overs | Mdns | Runs | Wkts | Overs | Mdns | Runs | Wkts |
|---|---|---|---|---|---|---|---|---|
| Foster | 13.1 | 7 | 16 | 5 | 27 | 10 | 45 | 3 |
| Barnes | 13 | 3 | 25 | 5 | 34 | 9 | 85 | 6 |
| Brearley | | | | | 6 | 2 | 4 | — |
| Woolley | | | | | 4 | — | 19 | — |
| Hobbs | | | | | 11 | 2 | 36 | — |

### South Africa Bowling

| | Overs | Mdns | Runs | Wkts |
|---|---|---|---|---|
| Nourse | 16 | 5 | 46 | 3 |
| Pegler | 31 | 8 | 65 | 7 |
| Faulkner | 29 | 6 | 72 | — |
| Carter | 4 | — | 15 | — |
| Llewellyn | 9 | — | 60 | — |
| Schwarz | 20 | 3 | 44 | — |
| Hartigan | 10 | 2 | 14 | — |

Umpires: W. A. J. West and W. Richards.

## ENGLAND v AUSTRALIA

Played at Lord's, June 24, 25, 26, 1912

Under happier circumstances, the England and Australia match at Lord's might well have been the event of the season. There could be no mistake as to the enormous amount of interest it excited. Unfortunately, the weather ruined everything. Play on the first day was limited to about three hours, and on the second to little more than twenty minutes. A delightful Wednesday came too late to save the situation, and the match had, perforce, to be left drawn. Despite all disadvantages, over thirty-five thousand people paid for admission during the three days, the exact numbers being 14,402, 7,300, and 13,500. The prince of Wales was present on the third day. People were flocking up to the ground in such numbers on Tuesday morning that, if the day had turned out fine, it is safe to say there would have been something like a record crowd. In picking the England eleven, the selection committee made two changes from the side that had beaten the South Africans so easily a fortnight before, J. W. Hearne and Dean displacing Jessop and Brearley. The ground being as it was, the absence of a right-handed fast bowler did not matter. Winning the toss, England did so well during the time available on the first day as to secure, on the damaged pitch, what looked like a winning position. Their score at the drawing of stumps stood at 211 with only four wickets down. In doing this they owed nearly everything to Hobbs and Rhodes, who opened the innings by getting 112 together. The value of such a start could scarcely be exaggerated. The two batsmen went in just after half-past eleven, but when they had scored 5 runs each, heavy rain fell, and nothing more could be done until nearly a quarter-past two, lunch having in the meantime been taken. When at last a fresh start became possible, the wicket began to kick, and the batsmen had rather an anxious time. However, with a little luck to help them, they surmounted all difficulties, and when, soon after three o'clock, rain caused another long delay, the total was 77. Up to 34 the batsmen scored evenly, but after that, Rhodes so monopolised the hitting that his share of the 77 runs amounted to 52. The players were out again just before half-past-four, and for a time the wicket was too wet to be difficult. Of this condition of things Hobbs took full advantage, hitting all-round with delightful skill. The hundred went up as the result of about an hour and a quarter's batting, but at 112, Rhodes, from a quick-rising ball, was caught at the wicket. His fine innings of 59 was marked by the strangest contrasts, the latter portion being as cautious as the first part was brilliant. The pitch had become very treacherous when Spooner went in, and through he stayed for over a quarter of an hour, he never looked at all comfortable. In hitting at a ball from Kelleway, he was caught at forward short-leg at 123. With Fry at his next partner, Hobbs hit away splendidly, completing his hundred soon after six o'clock. However, at 197, he was bowled. Very rarely has he shown finer cricket on a difficult wicket. Without being at all rash, he seemed to seize every opportunity of scoring. Batting for two hours and three-quarters, he hit fifteen 4s, one 3, and eight 2s. His 107 – in every respect a great innings – is the fourth hundred obtained for England against Australia at Lord's. Warner left at 211, play then ending for the day with Fry not out 24. The Australians did a lot of smart work in the field, and, generally speaking, their bowling was good. During the afternoon Hazlitt's delivery gave rise to a great deal of discussion, two famous cricketers, who were in the pavilion, condemning it in no measured terms.

On Tuesday, a sharp shower delayed the start until nearly half-past eleven. Fry and Woolley added 30 runs, and then at ten minutes to twelve, rain drove the players from the field. At first little more than a drizzle, the downpour became much heavier, and not another ball could be bowled during the day. Not until a quarter to six, however, was the idea of further cricket given up.

Wednesday produced some remarkable play. Being, of course, quite secure against any risk of defeat, the Englishmen made a desperate effort to force a win, but the Australian batting was too good for them, and, moreover, the wicket rolled out a great deal easier than anyone could have expected. To begin with, England added 69 runs in fifty minutes, Fry declaring at 310 for seven wickets. There was a great deal of excitement when, soon after twelve o'clock, the Australians went in to bat. It soon became evident that England had little hope of winning. Kelleway set himself to play an absolutely defensive game, being at the wickets more than half-an-hour before he made a run. Jennings was caught by the wicket-keeper at 27, but at lunch-time the score was up to 57 for one wicket, Kelleway being then not out 16 and Macartney not out 20. Barnes's bowling had presented no difficulties, and everyone felt that the match would end in a draw. However, there was no lack of interest in the cricket after luncheon. Macartney playing, perhaps, the finest innings seen at Lord's during the season. He showed himself master of nearly every scoring stroke, and though playing rather a daring game he never made a false hit. He missed his hundred by a single run, a catch on the leg-side by the wicket-keeper, standing back to Foster's bowling, getting rid of him at 173. He hit thirteen 4s, one 3, and eight 2s. The rest of the day's cricket was, by comparison, uneventful, much of the Australian batting being marked by more caution than the occasion demanded. However, there was some free hitting towards the cose by Smith and Hazlitt. When stumps were pulled up the score stood at 282 for seven wickets. Far less attractive than Macartney's brilliant display, but even more valuable, in the circumstances, to his side, was Kelleway's innings of 61, which extended over four hours and a half. The English bowlers were powerless against his rigid defence and inexhaustible patience.

## England

| | | |
|---|---|---|
| J. B. Hobbs b Emery | 107 | |
| W. Rhodes c Carkeek b Kelleway | 59 | |
| Mr R. H. Spooner c Bardsley b Kelleway | 1 | |
| Mr C. B. Fry run out | 42 | |
| Mr P. F. Warner b Emery | 4 | |
| F. E. Wooley c Kelleway b Hazlitt | 20 | |
| Mr F. R. Foster c Macartney b Whitty | 20 | |
| J. W. Hearne not out | 21 | |
| E. J. Smith not out | 14 | |
| B 16, l-b 4, n-b 2 | 22 | |
| (7 wkts dec.) | 310 | |

S. F. Barnes and H. Dean did not bat.

## Australia

| | | | | |
|---|---|---|---|---|
| C. B. Jennings c Smith b Foster | 21 | T. J. Matthews b Dean | 0 |
| C. Kelleway b Rhodes | 61 | G. R. Hazlitt b Rhodes | 19 |
| C. G. Macartney c Smith b Foster | 99 | | |
| W. Bardlsey lbw b Rhodes | 21 | B 17, l-b 5, w 1, n-b 1 | 27 |
| S. E. Gregory c Foster b Dean | 10 | | |
| D. Smith not out | 24 | | 282 |

S. H. Emery, W. J. Whitty and W. Carkeek did not bat.

## Australia Bowling

| | Overs | Mdns | Runs | Wkts |
|---|---|---|---|---|
| Whitty | 12 | 2 | 69 | 1 |
| Hazlitt | 25 | 6 | 68 | 1 |
| Matthews | 13 | 4 | 26 | — |
| Kelleway | 21 | 5 | 66 | 2 |
| Emery | 12 | 1 | 46 | 2 |
| Macartney | 7 | 1 | 13 | — |

## England Bowling

| | Overs | Mdns | Runs | Wkts |
|---|---|---|---|---|
| Foster | 36 | 18 | 42 | 2 |
| Barnes | 31 | 10 | 74 | — |
| Dean | 29 | 10 | 49 | 2 |
| Hearne | 12 | 1 | 31 | — |
| Rhodes | 19.2 | 5 | 59 | 3 |

Umpires: J. Moss and A. E. Street.

## ENGLAND v SOUTH AFRICA

### Played at Leeds, July 8, 9, 10, 1912

Already beaten in a single innings at Manchester and Lord's, the South Africans could not have entered upon their third Test match with much hope of victory. Once more they were outplayed at every point, England winning in the easiest fashion on the third morning by 174 runs. The Yorkshire public had evidently come to the conclusion that the South Africans were not equal to the task imposed upon them. The attendance on the opening day would have been considered rather good on an ordinary occasion, but it was far from worthy of a Test match. England made only one change from the side that had met the Australians at Lord's, G. L. Jessop taking the place of P. F. Warner. Fry won the toss, but as the ground had not fully recovered from recent rain, there was no particular advantage in batting first. The ball came along at varying paces and now and then the bowlers could get on a fair amount of break. Allowing for this, however, England's score of 242 was not considered satisfactory. Judged in the light of subsequent events it was more than sufficient, but for the most part the batting was not convincing. The early play suggested that the batsmen were taking things far too easily, and in the course of the first hour four wickets – those of Rhodes, Hobbs, Spooner, and Fry – went down for 68 runs. J. W. Hearne and Woolley saved the situation, playing very finely and putting on 111 runs in an hour and a half. Things might have gone badly, however, if Hearne, with his score at 5, had not been missed at the wicket. This error on the part of Ward proved the turning point of the day's play. Hearne and Woolley had many difficulties to contend against, but they overcame them all, combining clean hitting with very watchful defence – Apart from his one escape, Hearne was never at fault, and Woolley's only bad stroke – a return chance to Pegler – did not affect the game, the batsmen being out immediately afterwards. Except for some capital cricket by Foster and a few hits by Jessop there was nothing in the latter half of England's innings.

The South Africans went in just before four o'clock and soon found themselves in a losing position. Barnes bowled splendidly, and was well supported by Dean after Foster had proved ineffective. Four wickets were down for 43, and seven for 80. Forty minutes being left for play everyone expected to see the innings over before the drawing of stumps, but Snooke and Pegler, with a little luck to help them, put on fifty runs in half-an-hour. At the close the South Africans with two wickets in hand were 101 runs behind. The innings was quickly finished off next morning, England going in for the second time with a lead of 95. The wicket was better than it had been on the first day, but again the English batting as a whole left something to be desired, only three of the trusted run-getters doing themselves justice. Hobbs was very brilliant indeed for just over an hour, scoring 55 out of 78, before a catch at deep mid-off ended his innings. The chief honours, however, rested with Spooner, who in a trifle over two hours and a half scored 82 without giving a chance. He played with such stern self-restraint that his innings was not a characteristic one, but his steadiness was invaluable. In first wicket down at 46, he was out eighth at 207. No one gave him much help except Hearne, who stayed while 70 runs were added for the fourth wicket. England's innings ended for 238, having lasted three hours and fifty minutes. Faulkner bowled in better form than in any match so far during the season.

Wanting 334 to win the South Africans were practically in a hopeless position. Nothing in their form suggested the least likelihood of such a number being obtained against the English bowling. Tancred played a strong defensive game, but except from Nourse and White he could for a long time get no assistance, seven wickets being down for 85. The match looked all over, but Pegler, who ought to have been caught at extra cover point, stayed with Tancred, the score at the close standing at 105. Forty minutes' cricket on Wednesday finished the game. Tancred's plucky innings was closed by a very smart piece of stumping, and though, thanks to Carter's fierce hitting, 49 runs were added in half-an-hour for the ninth wicket, this effort only delayed an end that had long been inevitable. Barnes had a fine record for the match – ten wickets for 115 runs.

## England

| | | |
|---|---|---|
| J. B. Hobbs c Ward b Nourse | 27 | – c Nourse b Faulkner ............ 55 |
| W. Rhodes c and b Pegler | 7 | – b Pegler ..................... 10 |
| Mr R. H. Spooner c Stricker b Nourse | 21 | – b Faulkner .................. 82 |
| Mr C. B. Fry lbw b Pegler | 10 | – c Nourse b Pegler ............. 7 |
| J. W. Hearne b Pegler | 45 | – b Nourse .................. 35 |
| F. E. Woolley b Nourse | 57 | – c Nourse b Pegler ............. 4 |
| Mr G. L. Jessop b Faulkner | 16 | – b Nourse ..................... 1 |
| Mr F. R. Foster c Pegler b Nourse | 30 | – b Nourse ................... 0 |
| E. J. Smith run out | 13 | – c Ward b Faulkner ........... 11 |
| S. F. Barnes b Faulkner | 0 | – not out ..................... 15 |
| H. Dean not out | 2 | – b Faulkner .................. 8 |
| B 12, l-b 2 | 14 | B 5, l-b 5 .............. 10 |
| | **242** | **238** |

## South Africa

| | | |
|---|---|---|
| L. J. Tancred c Spooner b Barnes | 15 | – st Smith b Barnes ........ 39 |
| H. W. Taylor c Hobbs b Dean | 31 | – c Smith b Foster ......... 2 |
| A. D. Nourse b Barnes | 5 | – c Foster b Dean ............. 15 |
| C. B. Llewellyn c Smith b Barnes | 0 | – b Barnes .................... 4 |
| G. A. Faulkner c and b Barnes | 5 | – b Barnes ................... 0 |
| L. A. Stricker b Dean | 10 | – run out ..................... 0 |
| G. C. White c Barnes b Woolley | 6 | – c and b Foster ............. 17 |
| S. J. Snooke b Barnes | 23 | – b Dean ...................... 8 |
| S. J. Pegler not out | 35 | – b Hearne ................... 32 |
| C. P. Carter c Dean b Barnes | 5 | – b Barnes ................... 31 |
| T. A. Ward b Dean | 0 | – not out ..................... 0 |
| B 4, l-b 3, n-b 5 | 12 | B 5, l-b 3, n-b 3 .......... 11 |
| | **147** | **159** |

## South Africa Bowling

|  | Overs | Mdns | Runs | Wkts | Overs | Mdns | Runs | Wkts |
|---|---|---|---|---|---|---|---|---|
| Nourse .......... | 26.1 | 8 | 52 | 4 | 30 | 11 | 52 | 3 |
| Pegler ........... | 35 | 6 | 112 | 3 | 31 | — | 110 | 3 |
| Faulkner ........ | 13 | 2 | 50 | 2 | 24.2 | 2 | 50 | 4 |
| Carter .......... | 4 | — | 14 | — | 5 | 1 | 16 | — |

## England Bowling

|  | Overs | Mdns | Runs | Wkts | Overs | Mdns | Runs | Wkts |
|---|---|---|---|---|---|---|---|---|
| Foster .......... | 16 | 7 | 29 | — | 23 | 4 | 51 | 2 |
| Barnes .......... | 22 | 7 | 52 | 6 | 21.2 | 5 | 63 | 4 |
| Dean ........... | 12.3 | 1 | 41 | 3 | 8 | 3 | 15 | 2 |
| Woolley ......... | 6 | 2 | 13 | 1 |  |  |  |  |
| Rhodes .......... |  |  |  |  | 4 | 1 | 14 | — |
| Hearne .......... |  |  |  |  | 2 | — | 5 | 1 |

Umpires: W. Richards and A. A. White.

## AUSTRALIA v SOUTH AFRICA

Played at Lord's, July 15, 16, 17, 1912

The experience of this match showed clearly enough that the Australians and South Africans should on all three occasions have met in London. Thanks, in some measure, to the presence of the King on the second day, the attendance was better than might have been expected, the South Africans being already, as regards the result of the Tournament, a thoroughly beaten side. Once more the South Africans found themselves quite outclassed, losing the game on the third morning by ten wickets. They had every chance, winning the toss and batting first on a fast wicket, but the simple truth is they were not good enough. Their first innings was a curiosity. After losing five wickets for 74, they ran up a total of 263, but in doing this they were favoured with an extraordinary amount of luck. Never in a Test match in England have the Australians been so sadly at fault in the field. It was calculated that in the course of the innings they allowed nine chances of one kind and another to escape them. Fortunately for them the worst blunder of all – a ridiculously easy catch to Whitty at mid-on –- made no difference to the score, and two other mistakes involved very trifling consequences. Taylor and Stricker saved the situation for the South Africans, putting on 97 runs for the sixth wicket in little more than an hour. Going in when the position was desperate, Stricker hit nine 4s, his innings, though marred by a couple of chances, the second of which profited him nothing, being a remarkable effort. Taylor was missed at third man when 27, and gave a chance at the wicket at 83, but his driving was splendid. Batting for two hours and fifty minutes he hit a dozen 4s and had a single increased to five by an overthrow. Early in the innings Tancred scored 31 out of 71 – the result of an hour and three-quarters' batting.

The Australians started disastrously. In the first over Nourse bowled Jennings and when 14 runs had been scored the same bowler dismissed Macartney with a ball which rose very quickly from the pitch. After such a start Kelleway and Bardsley were bound to be cautious. By means of stubborn defence they gradually mastered the bowling. Some members of the crowd indulged in ironical applause at Kelleway's expense, but the batsman was not in any way disturbed. When half-past six came the score had reached 86. On the second day Kelleway and Bardsley practically won the match for Australia. Playing wonderfully well on a wicket, which, though fast, was far indeed from being at all easy, they took the score from 86 to 256 in something under two hours. In all they put on

242 runs for the third wicket in three hours and a quarter. To look at, there was no possible comparison between the two, Bardsley's free style and brilliant all-round hitting putting Kelleway quite in the shade. Still, in his own quiet methodical way Kelleway played an exceptionally good innings. His patience was limitless, and his defence impregnable. Apart from a difficult chance when 24 to the wicket-keeper standing back, he scarcely made a mistake. Out leg-before-wicket to Faulkner's bowling he hit in his 102 seven 4s, ten 3s and seven 2s.

Bardsley, badly let off by Gordon White at third man when 131, was out fifth wicket down at 316. His 164 was the highest innings hit in the nine Test matches. Leaving aside the one chance at third man his batting was magnificent. He said himself, afterwards, that he had never felt so fatigued at the end of a long innings, the patchy difficult wicket having demanded such ceaseless watchfulness in defence. He hit one 5 (4 from an overthrow) and sixteen 4s. Mayne and Minnett, by fine hitting, sent up 350, but the Australians' innings was all over for 390. After going on at 350 Pegler, at a cost of only 16 runs, took four of the last five wickets.

Wanting 127 to avoid a single inning's defeat the South Africans were in a thankless position. At one point they seemed likely to make a good fight, Llewellyn driving so splendidly that the arrears were hit off with six wickets in hand, but this fine effort was soon discounted. Llewellyn, whose 59 included nine 4s, was bowled by a fine ball at 134, and then Faulkner, Mitchell and Schwarz failed in such quick succession that at the drawing of stumps eight wickets were down for 146. The result being a foregone conclusion, very few people took the trouble to see the end of the match. Taylor could get no one to help him, the South Africans' innings being soon finished off for 173. The Australian slow bowlers had excellent figures, Matthews taking four wickets for 29 runs, and Macartney three at the same cost. Having only 47 to get the Australians won the match by ten wickets, Mayne and Jennings hitting off the runs in less than half-an-hour.

## South Africa

| | | | |
|---|---|---|---|
| G. A. Faulkner b Whitty | 5 | – c and b Matthews | 6 |
| L. J. Tancred lbw b Matthews | 31 | – c Bardsley b Hazlitt | 19 |
| G. C. White c Carkeck b Minnett | 0 | – b Matthews | 18 |
| C. B. Llewellyn c Jennings b Minnett | 8 | – b Macartney | 59 |
| A. D. Nourse b Hazlitt | 11 | – lbw b Kelleway | 10 |
| H. W. Taylor c Kelleway b Hazlitt | 93 | – not out | 10 |
| L. A. Stricker lbw b Kelleway | 48 | – b Hazlitt | 13 |
| F. Mitchell b Whitty | 12 | – b Matthews | 3 |
| R. O. Schwarz b Whitty | 0 | – c Macartney b Matthews | 1 |
| S. J. Pegler c Bardsley b Whitty | 25 | – c Kelleway b Macartney | 14 |
| T. A. Ward not out | 1 | – b Macartney | 7 |
| B 12, l-b 14, w 1, n-b 2 | 29 | B 9, l-b 4 | 13 |
| | **263** | | **173** |

## Australia

| | | | |
|---|---|---|---|
| C. B. Jennings b Nourse | 0 | – not out | 22 |
| C. Kelleway lbw b Faulkner | 102 | | |
| C. G. Macartney b Nourse | 9 | | |
| W. Bardsley lbw b Llewellyn | 164 | | |
| S. E. Gregory b Llewellyn | 5 | | |
| E. R. Mayne st Ward b Pegler | 23 | – not out | 25 |
| R. B. Minnett b Pegler | 39 | | |
| T. J. Matthews c Faulkner b Pegler | 9 | | |
| G. R. Hazlitt b Nourse | 0 | | |
| W. Carkeek not out | 6 | | |
| W. J. Whitty lbw b Pegler | 3 | | |
| B 24, l-b 3, w 2, n-b 1 | 30 | B 1 | 1 |
| | **390** | | **48** |

**Australia Bowling**

|  | Overs | Mdns | Runs | Wkts | Overs | Mdns | Runs | Wkts |
|---|---|---|---|---|---|---|---|---|
| Minnett . . . . . . . . . . | 15 | 6 | 49 | 2 |  |  |  |  |
| Whitty . . . . . . . . . . . | 31 | 9 | 68 | 4 | 9 | — | 41 | — |
| Hazlitt . . . . . . . . . . . | 19 | 9 | 47 | 2 | 13 | 1 | 39 | 2 |
| Matthews . . . . . . . . . | 13 | 5 | 32 | 1 | 13 | 2 | 29 | 4 |
| Kelleway . . . . . . . . . | 11 | 3 | 38 | 1 | 8 | 1 | 22 | 1 |
| Macartney . . . . . . . . |  |  |  |  | 14.1 | 5 | 29 | 3 |

**South Africa Bowling**

|  | Overs | Mdns | Runs | Wkts | Overs | Mdns | Runs | Wkts |
|---|---|---|---|---|---|---|---|---|
| Nourse . . . . . . . . . . . | 36 | 12 | 60 | 3 | 6.1 | 2 | 22 | — |
| Pegler . . . . . . . . . . . . | 29.5 | 7 | 79 | 4 | 4 | 1 | 15 | — |
| Schwarz . . . . . . . . . . | 11 | 1 | 44 | — |  |  |  |  |
| Faulkner . . . . . . . . . | 28 | 3 | 86 | 1 | 2 | — | 10 | — |
| Llewellyn . . . . . . . . . | 19 | 2 | 71 | 2 |  |  |  |  |
| Taylor . . . . . . . . . . . | 2 | — | 12 | — |  |  |  |  |
| Stricker . . . . . . . . . . | 3 | 1 | 8 | — |  |  |  |  |

Umpires: J. Moss and A. E. Street.

# ENGLAND v AUSTRALIA

### Played at Manchester, July 29, 30, 31, 1912

The England and Australia match at Old Trafford proved an even greater disappointment than the meeting of the same sides at Lord's, rain spoiling everything. Play on the first day did not begin until close upon three o'clock; cricket on Tuesday was impossible until five o'clock and on the third day not a ball could be bowled. So far as the game went England played an innings of 203 and Australia scored 14 without loss. Haigh was brought into the England eleven in place of Dean and, though the heavy ground could never have suited his bowling, Hitch was played in preference to Hayes. In getting 203 – by no means a bad total on a dreadfully soft wicket, England owed nearly everything to Rhodes, who played with great skill and self-restraint. Before he had made a run he gave a chance to Hazlitt at point off Whitty's bowling – cutting a long-hop rather hard, but straight to the fieldsman – and when 70 he might have been caught at slip by Jennings, but these were the only real blemishes in a remarkable innings. Rhodes was not out 92 at the close of Monday's play, and everyone hoped when at last cricket became practicable on Tuesday that he would reach his hundred. As it happened, however, he was out without making another run. His chief hits were eight 4s, seven 3s, and seven 2s. Apart from Rhodes's play there was little in the England batting, but Hobbs hit brightly at the start of the innings and Fry, though he never seemed master of the bowling, helped to carry the score from 39 to 83. Hearne was badly missed by Whitty at mid-on when he had made a single 1. For this blunder the Australians had to pay rather dearly, as though Hearne did not personally profit much by his escape, he remained in with Rhodes while the total was being carried from 83 to 140. England lost six wickets for 185 on Monday afternoon, but on the muddy pitch on Tuesday no one could get the ball away, Hazlitt bowling six overs and five balls for 18 runs and three wickets, and Whitty six overs for no runs and one wicket. During the little time the Australians were in the fieldsman crowded round the wicket but nothing happened, the only ball that was put up falling out of reach. The weather kept fine during Tuesday night, and though a little rain fell in the morning there was hope of play at half-past eleven, the wicket being rolled, and the bell rung. However, rain set in again. At first it was only a drizzle, but such a heavy down-fall followed that at quarter-past one the match was abandoned.

### England

| | |
|---|---|
| J. B. Hobbs b Whitty ................. 19 | E. J. Smith c Emery b Hazlitt ........... 4 |
| W. Rhodes b Whitty .................. 92 | S. Haigh c Kelleway b Hazlitt ........... 9 |
| Mr R. H. Spooner b Whitty ............ 1 | S. F. Barnes not out ................... 1 |
| Mr C. B. Fry c sub b Matthews .......... 19 | W. Hitch b Hazlitt .................... 4 |
| J. W. Hearne b Hazlitt ................. 9 | B 9, l-b 9, n-b 1 .............. 19 |
| F. E. Woolley c Kelleway b Whitty ....... 13 | |
| Mr F. R. Foster c and b Matthews ........ 13 | 203 |

### Australia

| | |
|---|---|
| C. B. Jennings not out ................. 9 | |
| C. Kelleway not out ................... 3 | |
| B 2 ....................... 2 | |
| | 14 |

W. Bardsley, S. E. Gregory, C. G. Macartney, E. R. Mayne, T. J. Matthews, S. H. Emery, W. J. Whitty, G. R. Hazlitt and W. Carkeek did not bat.

### Australian Bowling

| | Overs | Mdns | Runs | Wkts |
|---|---|---|---|---|
| Hazlitt ........... | 40.5 | 12 | 77 | 4 |
| Whitty ........... | 27 | 15 | 43 | 4 |
| Kelleway ......... | 6 | 1 | 19 | — |
| Matthews ......... | 12 | 4 | 23 | 2 |
| Emery ........... | 7 | 1 | 22 | — |

### England Bowling

| | Overs | Mdns | Runs | Wkts |
|---|---|---|---|---|
| Foster ........... | 1 | — | 3 | — |
| Haigh ............ | 6 | 4 | 3 | — |
| Woolley .......... | 6 | 3 | 6 | — |

Umpires: G. Webb and W. A. J. West.

## AUSTRALIA v SOUTH AFRICA

### Played at Nottingham, August 5, 6, 7, 1912

Unfortunately for the South Africans the only Test match in which they did themselves justice had to be left drawn, rain reducing the Trent Bridge ground to such a state that not a ball could be bowled on the third day. However, so far as the game went the South Africans had decidedly the best of it, leading on the first innings by 110 runs. The match did not prove attractive, only 2,365 people paying for admission on the Bank Holiday. There was a general complaint that the charges for the reserved seats were too high. Rain during the previous week had soaked Trent Bridge, and had the opening day been bright and sunny, the wicket no doubt, would have been very treacherous. As it was, the day proved rather cloudy, and a couple of showers kept the ground fairly easy. Of this state of things, the South Africans, who won the toss, took excellent advantage. They went in at twelve o'clock, and when half-past six came, they had scored 266 with eight wickets down. The start was discouraging, Taylor being bowled with the score at 2, but Tancred and Nourse, playing a sound game, put on 77 runs together in an hour and forty minutes. Nourse played the highest and best innings of the day. He hit well at times, and gave no chance, but it took him two hours and three-quarters to get 64. He was very cautious indeed when one run short of his 50. Stricker, too, was very careful, but towards the end of the afternoon runs came freely enough. Not one of the seven Australian bowlers could make the ball do much on the rather soft turf. Rain fell for some hours on Tuesday morning, and the ground was quite as dead as on the previous day. So well did Gordon White, Pegler, and Ward hit, that the South Africans' total was carried to 329. The last two wickets added in all 97 runs in an hour and a quarter. For once, Gordon White played in something like his best form of 1907. The Australians found it hard work to get the ball to the boundary on the heavy ground, but up to a certain point, their batting was excellent. The score reached 165 with only four men out, but at this point Bardsley threw his innings away, and in three-quarters of an hour the last five wickets went down for 48 runs, Faulkner and Pegler bowling uncommonly well. Bardsley played by far the best innings of the day. He was at the wickets for over two hours, and never made a mistake. Macartney hit up 34 out of 42 in thirty-five minutes, his batting being in the strongest contrast to that of Kelleway, who took two hours to get 37 out of 101. The light was very bad towards the close of the Australians' innings, and as the clouds did not lift, stumps were drawn at a quarter past six. On Wednesday, not a ball could be bowled. Rain fell heavily for several hours in the night, making the ground so wet that after luncheon the match was given up as a draw.

## South Africa

| | |
|---|---|
| L. J. Tancred c Kelleway b Matthews ..... 30 | G. C. White not out .................... 59 |
| H. W. Taylor b Whitty ................. 2 | R. Beaumont b Hazlitt ................. 2 |
| A. D. Nourse b Whitty ................. 64 | S. J. Pegler b Hazlitt .................... 26 |
| G. A. Faulkner c Kelleway b Emery ...... 15 | T. A. Ward c Emery b Matthews ......... 24 |
| C. B. Llewellyn b Emery ............... 12 | B 30, l-b 7, n-b 1 ............... 38 |
| L. A. Stricker lbw b Macartney .......... 37 | ——— |
| S. J. Snooke b Kelleway ................ 20 | 329 |

## Australia

| | |
|---|---|
| C. B. Jennings run out ................. 9 | S. H. Emery b Faulkner ................ 5 |
| C. Kelleway c Faulkner b Pegler ......... 37 | G. R. Hazlitt not out ................. 2 |
| C. G. Macartney c Faulkner b Llewellyn ... 34 | W. J. Whitty b Pegler .................. 0 |
| W. Bardsley run out .................. 56 | W. Carkeek st Ward b Faulkner ......... 1 |
| S. E. Gregory b Pegler ................. 18 | B 2, l-b 3 .................... 5 |
| R. B. Minnett c Nourse b Faulkner ....... 31 | ——— |
| T. J. Matthews b Pegler ................ 21 | 219 |

## Australia Bowling

| | Overs | Mdns | Runs | Wkts |
|---|---|---|---|---|
| Whitty ........... | 30 | 10 | 64 | 2 |
| Minnett .......... | 8 | 3 | 12 | — |
| Hazlitt ........... | 28 | 10 | 48 | 2 |
| Matthews ........ | 20.5 | 7 | 27 | 2 |
| Emery ........... | 21 | 1 | 87 | 2 |
| Kelleway ........ | 8 | 2 | 18 | 1 |
| Macartney ....... | 13 | 2 | 35 | 1 |

## South Africa Bowling

| | Overs | Mdns | Runs | Wkts |
|---|---|---|---|---|
| Pegler ........... | 36 | 6 | 80 | 4 |
| Faulkner ........ | 20.1 | 2 | 43 | 3 |
| Taylor .......... | 12 | 5 | 19 | — |
| Llewellyn ........ | 22 | 3 | 60 | 1 |
| Nourse .......... | 4 | 1 | 12 | — |

Umpires: W. A. J. West and G. Webb.

# ENGLAND v SOUTH AFRICA

Played at The Oval, August 12, 13, 1912

As in four of their previous Test matches, the South Africans suffered an overwhelming defeat, England winning before lunch time on the second day by ten wickets. Rain on Saturday drenched The Oval, and from start to finish the game was played on a slow and difficult wicket. Had Monday been a bright day, the pitch would have been as nearly as possible unplayable. As it was, with dark clouds hanging over the ground all the afternoon, there was no sunshine to cake the surface of the turf. Still, with light often very bad, the batsmen had much to contend against. Winning the toss, Tancred was bound to take first innings, but the South Africans profited nothing by going in first. In two hours and a quarter they were out for a total of 95. It is likely enough that this score would have been still smaller if Fry had at first put Woolley instead of Foster on to bowl with Barnes. The pitch was far too slow to suit Foster, but before this fact was realised 32 runs had been scored for one wicket. From the moment Woolley took the ball the batsmen were in sad trouble, and no second change of bowling was required. The only man who ventured to hit was Snooke, who went in at 53 and was out in the first over after luncheon to a very smart catch in the slips. Early in the game, Smith, the wicket-keeper, received a severe blow in the mouth, a ball from Barnes getting up straight. Smith had to have his lip stitched, but he was able to return to his post after the luncheon interval, Spooner keeping wicket in the meantime. Barnes and Woolley divided the wickets equally, but Barnes looked by far the more difficult to play. He did not have the least bit of luck to help him, often beating the bat with balls that missed the stumps. Of the 28 runs scored from him, 16 were obtained in four hits. Wooley made the ball turn a good deal, but he was rather slow off the pitch.

England made a bad start, Rhodes playing a ball from Faulkner on to his pads and into the wicket after Hobbs had hit a single and a 3. However, Hobbs and Spooner soon put their side in a flattering position, the batting, while they were together, being very fine indeed. So brilliantly did they hit that the score was up to 41 when the innings had lasted half-an-hour. A little later, Hobbs punished Faulkner for three 4s in one over — all on-drives. Then, at 65, Spooner was caught close to the ground at square leg. The 61 runs put on for the second wicket were made in 21 hits — one 5, ten 4s, a 3, four 2s, and five singles. Considering the state of the ground this was very remarkable batting. Hobbs continued to play a splendid game, but he did not get much help. Out at 127, he scored his 68 in an hour and fifty minutes, hitting eight 4s, three 3s, and six 2s. Few batsmen could have played so well on such a wicket, his driving and pulling being superb. Hearne and Smith put on 28 together for the eighth wicket, but at about twenty minutes to six England's innings was over for 176. Bowling finely, but without luck, Faulkner took seven wickets. At times he made the ball do too much. In the ordinary way, the South Africans would have had fully half-an-hour's batting before time, but the light was too bad to admit of further cricket. England's total was regarded as rather disappointing, but most people thought it big enough to ensure an easy victory, and so it proved.

Thanks to the influence of a strong wind, the wicket was faster on Tuesday than it had been before, but the extra pace made it worse for the batsmen. Going in against a balance of 81, the South Africans were all out for 93. Only once did they look like making anything of a stand. Nourse and Faulkner putting on 44 runs together for the third wicket in less than half-an-hour. Even during this partnership, however, the batting inspired no real confidence, Nourse, though he made some fine hits, being twice completely beaten by breaking balls from Barnes that went to the boundary. Barnes surpassed himself, bowling in even more deadly form than in any of the previous Test matches. He broke both ways and his length was irreproachable. The South Africans thought they had never faced bowling quite so difficult. Nourse was missed from a tremendous skyer when he had made

28, but in the circumstances his 42 – the result of an hour and forty minutes' batting – was a remarkable display. The single innings defeat was saved with three wickets in hand, but only 12 more runs were scored. In first wicket down, Nourse was the ninth man out. Bowling unchanged from the Vauxhall end, Barnes took eight wickets and had only 29 runs hit from him. Considering the amount of work he got on the ball, his accuracy was astonishing. England only wanted 13 to win. Hearne was sent in with Hobbs, and from 27 balls the runs were obtained. The winning hit was a single by Hobbs, increased to 4 by an overthrow.

## South Africa

| | | | |
|---|---:|---|---:|
| L. J. Tancred b Barnes | 0 | – st Smith b Woolley | 0 |
| H. W. Taylor c Foster b Woolley | 23 | – lbw b Barnes | 6 |
| A. D. Nourse lbw b Woolley | 8 | – c and b Foster | 42 |
| G. A. Faulkner c Hayes b Barnes | 9 | – b Barnes | 10 |
| L. A. Stricker b Barnes | 5 | – c Spooner b Barnes | 0 |
| C. B. Llewellyn c Rhodes b Woolley | 0 | – c Hitch b Barnes | 0 |
| G. C. White b Barnes | 4 | – c Smith b Barnes | 1 |
| S. J. Snooke c Foster b Woolley | 23 | – c Hearne b Barnes | 7 |
| R. Beaumont c Hearne b Barnes | 3 | – b Barnes | 6 |
| S. J. Pegler c Hitch b Woolley | 3 | – b Barnes | 0 |
| T. A. Ward not out | 6 | – not out | 0 |
| B 8, l-b 3 | 11 | B 18, l-b 3 | 21 |
| | **95** | | **93** |

## England

| | | | |
|---|---:|---|---:|
| J. B. Hobbs c and b Faulkner | 68 | – not out | 9 |
| W. Rhodes b Faulkner | 0 | | |
| Mr R. H. Spooner c Nourse b Llewellyn | 26 | | |
| Mr C. B. Fry c Snooke b Faulkner | 9 | | |
| E. G. Hayes b Faulkner | 4 | | |
| F. E. Woolley b Pegler | 13 | | |
| J. W. Hearne lbw b Faulkner | 20 | – not out | 5 |
| Mr F. R. Foster st Ward b Faulkner | 8 | | |
| E. J. Smith b Faulkner | 9 | | |
| S. F. Barnes c Taylor b Pegler | 8 | | |
| W. Hitch not out | 0 | | |
| B 10, l-b 1 | 11 | | |
| | **176** | | **14** |

### England Bowling

| | Overs | Mdns | Runs | Wkts | Overs | Mdns | Runs | Wkts |
|---|---|---|---|---|---|---|---|---|
| Foster | 6 | 2 | 15 | — | 7 | 2 | 19 | 1 |
| Barnes | 21 | 10 | 28 | 5 | 16.4 | 4 | 29 | 8 |
| Woolley | 15.3 | 1 | 41 | 5 | 9 | 2 | 24 | 1 |

### South Africa Bowling

| | Overs | Mdns | Runs | Wkts | Overs | Mdns | Runs | Wkts |
|---|---|---|---|---|---|---|---|---|
| Pegler | 19 | 3 | 53 | 2 | | | | |
| Faulkner | 27.1 | 4 | 84 | 7 | 2 | — | 4 | — |
| Llewellyn | 10 | 1 | 28 | 1 | | | | |
| Nourse | | | | | 2.3 | — | 10 | — |

Umpires: A. A. White and W. Richards.

# ENGLAND v AUSTRALIA

### Played at The Oval, August 19, 20, 21, 22, 1912

Whatever might be said about last season's cricket as a whole, the closing Test match at The Oval afforded convincing evidence of the enduring popularity of cricket. The match had much to contend against in the way of unseasonable weather, but in the course of the four days over which it extended, 44,717 paid for admission at the turnstiles. No definite pronouncement had been made at the beginning of the season as to the method of deciding the Triangular Tournament, but almost at the last moment it was stated that the side successful at The Oval would be the winners, the match being played out to a finish even if it lasted a week. As the two previous matches between England and Australia had been left drawn through rain, and both teams had shown an immense superiority over South Africa, the decision was, in a sense, quite just, but it involved some disadvantage to the Englishmen, who had beaten the South Africans three times whereas the Australians had gained two victories, and played a rather unfavourable draw. Thus, if England had been beaten at The Oval, they would have been placed second in the Tournament with the same number of wins to their credit as Australia. However, as events turned out no question arose, England gaining an easy victory at the finish by 244 runs. They had the best of luck as regards the condition of the ground, but theiry victory was gained by splendid all-round cricket. On the morning of the match a change had to be made in the England eleven, Hayes, who was suffering from a cold, giving way to J. W. H. T. Douglas. No place had been found for Douglas in any of the previous Test matches, but he is by temperament so much the man for a big occasion, that he might well have been picked for the whole series. That the public shared this view was proved when he went in to bat, the crowd giving him an overwhelming welcome.

Heavy rain on Sunday night and again in the early hours of the morning had affected The Oval to such an extent that the start of the match had to be delayed until twelve o'clock. At that time the sun was shining, but Fry, on winning the toss, had no hesitation in taking first innings. In such unsettled weather he could not risk putting his opponents in. His policy met with brilliant success, England gaining an advantage on the first day that was never wholly lost. The Australians bowled steadily and well, but they had not on their side any man capable of doing so much on the wicket as Spofforth, Turner, or Hugh Trumble would have done in former years. A couple of very light showers fell during the afternoon, but in neither case was the game delayed for more than a few minutes. At the drawing of stumps England's score stood at 233 for eight wickets – in the circumstances a wonderfully good start. Hobbs and Rhodes once more proved an incomparable pair to open the innings in a big match. Staying together an hour and fifty minutes they scored 107 for the first wicket. This, on a pitch of varying pace and against superb fielding, was a great achievement. Hobbs, who made 66 out of the 107 runs before being caught at the wicket, played just as fine an innings as in the South African match a week before. Though never rash he seized every chance of getting runs, pulling the short balls with absolute certainty. He hit four 4s and seven 3s, and would have made a good many more runs if the outfield had not been so slow. Spooner was out to a wonderful catch at short leg, Hazlitt throwing himself forward and taking a hard hit close to the ground with his left hand, and then things went so badly that at the tea interval five wickets were down for 144. Rhodes and Fry found their task so difficult that it took them three-quarters of an hour to put on 18 runs for the third wicket. Rhodes was batting for three hours, his watchful defence being invaluable. After tea Woolley, with excellent help from Douglas and Foster, more than made up England's lost ground, the sixth and seventh wickets adding 33 runs each. Woolley, who was out just on the call of time, showed the finest hitting of the day, his splendid innings of 62 including eleven 4s.

Cricket on Tuesday was restricted to little more than an hour and a half. Owing to a heavy downpour in the night nothing could be done until just on one o'clock and a drenching shower stopped the game from ten minutes to three till a quarter past five.

England's innings was quickly finished off for 245, and the Australians scored 51 for two wickets, Kelleway and Bardsley playing with great judgment after Gregory and Macartney had failed. On the third day the weather was again very unfavourable, rain causing two stoppages and bad light and further rain cutting the afternoon's cricket short at twenty minutes past five. So long as Kelleway and Bardsley stayed together the Australians got on very well, the score reaching 90 before the third wicket went down. However, an extraordinary change came over the game from the moment the two batsmen were separated. The pitch had become extremely treacherous and the last seven wickets actually went down for 21 runs. The turning point came with a change of bowling, Woolley going on at the Pavilion wicket and Barnes crossing to the other end. Kelleway was out lbw, in Woolley's second over, and thenceforward the batsmen were helpless. Kelleway was in nearly two hours, his defence all that time being impregnable. He and Bardsley put on 71 runs together. Bardsley was bowled by a remarkable ball from Barnes. As it pitched well outside his leg stump he let it alone, but he failed to cover the whole of the wicket, and the ball turning very sharply hit the leg stump. After the eventful change Woolley took five wickets for 22 runs, and Barnes three wickets for 10 runs. Holding a lead of 134, England went in after luncheon. The wicket was very treacherous, the light bad, and rain evidently near at hand. A disastrous start was made, Rhodes being bowled with the score at seven, and Spooner caught at slip from the next ball. Had play gone on without interruption the bowlers would probably have had everything their own way, but when 2 runs had been added down came the rain. When at four o'clock the players came out again the pitch was considerably easier than before, and of the altered conditions Hobbs at first took advantage. So steady was the bowling, however, that at one point eight overs produced only one hit – a snick for 3 by Fry. Then the pace of the run-getting improved again, though Hobbs, spraining a muscle in his thigh, became rather lame. Hobbs fell to a smart catch at point at 51, having as in his first innings played splendid cricket. Woolley was bowled at 56, and when, on a second appeal against the light, play ceased for the day the score, with Fry and Hearne together, was 64 for four wickets. Fry's defence, under trying conditions, was beyond all praise.

As there was no likelihood of the pitch ever being good the Englishmen – leading by 198 runs and having six wickets in hand – entered upon the fourth day's play without much anxiety. To all intents and purposes they had the game in their hands. More rain had fallen in the night, and not until a quarter to twelve was the ground considered fit for play. At first the wicket was easy enough and by free hitting the score was carried from 64 to 91. Then Hazlitt went on and from the first ball he bowled Hearne was caught at short leg. However, Fry found another excellent partner in Douglas, and though the pitch, as it dried, naturally became difficult, the total at lunch time had reached 149. Had the match been limited to four days Fry would have declared at once, but with two more days before him there seemed no need to run the slightest risk. As it happened the innings was quickly finished off for 175, Hazlitt going on in place of Whitty at 167, and taking the last five wickets at the cost of a single run. Subsequent events proved that his astounding success was for England a blessing in disguise, as it led to victory before the end of the day. Out sixth at 170 Fry was batting for three hours and forty minutes. For once in the Test matches he was his true self, his innings of 79 being a masterpiece of skilful defence. No one could have played with finer judgment. The Australians alleged that he was out hit-wicket comparatively early on Thursday morning, but the umpire ruled otherwise. So far as one noticed he gave no chance that went to hand, but when he had scored 41 a quicker fieldsman that Smith might have caught him at short leg. Douglas, proving conclusively his right to a place in the England eleven, helped Fry to put on 79 runs in an hour and fifty minutes.

The Australians wanted 310 to win – practically an impossible task on such a damaged wicket. Jennings and Kelleway went in at half-past three. Barnes and Dean sharing the bowling. In the second over, before a run had been scored, Kelleway was caught at a sort of backward point, Douglas managing to hold the ball at about the sixth attempt. Then came some startling cricket. Jennings punished Barnes for two 4s to leg and Macartney hit so brilliantly that, though Woolley bowled in place of Barnes, runs were put on at an alarming pace. Everyone felt, however, that the pace could not last. At 46 Jennings was caught at extra cover point from a skyer, and at the same total Dean, with a fine ball, clean bowled Macartney. A disaster that followed took all the heart out of the Australians. Bardsley, starting for a short run, seemed to take things easily, and had his wicket thrown down from cover point – an amazing piece of work by Hobbs. There was a lot of discussion about the decision, several famous cricketers in the pavillion expressing a positive opinion that Bardsley was not out. However, Moss, the umpire, when interviewed after the match, said that he had no doubt whatever on the point. Here one may leave a question that will probably be talked about for years to come. Bardsley's downfall meant the end of the game. Though very difficult, the pitch was not so bad as to excuse the utter feebleness of the subsequent batting. Three nore wickets fell with the score at 51, and the innings was over for 65, England winning the match by 244 runs. Playing an innings of 62 and taking ten wickets, Woolley had a big share in a memorable victory. If it had not been finished on the fourth day the match must have ended in a draw, as rain fell incessantly on the Friday and Saturday.

### England

| | | | |
|---|---|---|---|
| J. B. Hobbs c Carkeek b Macartney | 66 | – c Matthews b Whitty | 32 |
| W. Rhodes b Minnett | 49 | – b Whitty | 4 |
| Mr R. H. Spooner c Hazlitt b Macartney | 1 | – c Jennings b Whitty | 0 |
| Mr C. B. Fry c Kelleway b Whitty | 5 | – c Jennings b Hazlitt | 79 |
| F. E. Woolley lbw b Minnett | 62 | – b Hazlitt | 4 |
| J. W. Hearne c Jennings b Whitty | 1 | – c Matthews b Hazlitt | 14 |
| Mr J. W. H. T. Douglas lbw b Whitty | 18 | – lbw b Hazlitt | 24 |
| Mr F. R. Foster b Minnett | 19 | – not out | 3 |
| E. J. Smith b Whitty | 4 | – b Hazlitt | 0 |
| S. F. Barnes c Jennings b Minnett | 7 | – c Whitty b Hazlitt | 0 |
| H. Dean not out | 0 | – b Hazlitt | 0 |
| B 2, l-b 10, n-b 1 | 13 | B 14, n-b 1 | 15 |
| | **245** | | **175** |

### Australia

| | | | |
|---|---|---|---|
| S. E. Gregory c Rhodes b Barnes | 1 | – c Douglas b Dean | 1 |
| C. Kelleway lbw b Woolley | 43 | – c Douglas b Dean | 0 |
| C. G. Macartney b Barnes | 4 | – b Dean | 30 |
| W. Bardsley b Barnes | 30 | – run out | 0 |
| C. B. Jennings c and b Woolley | 0 | – c Fry b Woolley | 14 |
| R. B. Minnett c Rhodes b Woolley | 0 | – lbw b Woolley | 4 |
| D. Smith c Smith b Woolley | 6 | – c Douglas b Dean | 0 |
| T. J. Matthews c Fry b Barnes | 2 | – c and b Woolley | 1 |
| W. J. Whitty c Foster b Barnes | 0 | – b Woolley | 3 |
| G. R. Hazlitt not out | 2 | – c Dean b Woolley | 5 |
| W. Carkeek c Barnes b Woolley | 5 | – not out | 0 |
| B 12, l-b 6 | 18 | B 1, l-b 5, w 1 | 7 |
| | **111** | | **65** |

### Australia Bowling

| | Overs | Mdns | Runs | Wkts | Overs | Mdns | Runs | Wkts |
|---|---|---|---|---|---|---|---|---|
| Whitty | 38 | 12 | 69 | 4 | 33 | 13 | 71 | 3 |
| Matthews | 14 | 5 | 43 | — | 10 | 3 | 21 | — |
| Hazlitt | 26 | 10 | 48 | — | 21.4 | 8 | 25 | 7 |
| Macartney | 19 | 6 | 22 | 2 | 22 | 5 | 43 | — |
| Minnett | 10.1 | 3 | 34 | 4 | | | | |
| Kelleway | 7 | 2 | 16 | — | | | | |

**England Bowling**

| | Overs | Mdns | Runs | Wkts | Overs | Mdns | Runs | Wkts |
|---|---|---|---|---|---|---|---|---|
| Barnes .......... | 27 | 15 | 30 | 5 | 4 | 1 | 18 | — |
| Dean ........... | 16 | 7 | 29 | — | 9 | 2 | 19 | 4 |
| Foster .......... | 2 | — | 5 | — | | | | |
| Woolley ......... | 9.4 | 3 | 29 | 5 | 7.4 | 1 | 20 | 5 |
| Rhodes .......... | | | | | 2 | 1 | 1 | — |

Umpires: J. Moss and A. E. Street.

## AVERAGES FOR THE TRIANGULAR TOURNAMENT

### ENGLISH BATTING AVERAGES

| | Matches | Innings | Not Outs | Runs | Highest Innings | Average |
|---|---|---|---|---|---|---|
| J. B. Hobbs ........ | 6 | 9 | 1 | 387 | 107 | 48.37 |
| W. Rhodes ......... | 6 | 8 | 0 | 257 | 92 | 32.12 |
| Mr R. H. Spooner ... | 6 | 8 | 0 | 251 | 119 | 31.37 |
| F. E. Woolley ...... | 6 | 8 | 0 | 246 | 73 | 30.75 |
| Mr C. B. Fry ....... | 6 | 8 | 0 | 200 | 79 | 25.00 |
| J. W. Hearne ....... | 5 | 8 | 2 | 150 | 45 | 25.00 |
| Mr F. R. Foster ..... | 6 | 8 | 1 | 104 | 30 | 14.85 |
| E. J. Smith ........ | 6 | 8 | 1 | 57 | 14* | 8.14 |
| S. F. Barnes ........ | 6 | 7 | 3 | 31 | 15* | 7.75 |
| Mr G. L. Jessop ..... | 2 | 3 | 0 | 20 | 16 | 6.66 |
| H. Dean .......... | 3 | 4 | 2 | 10 | 8 | 5.00 |

The following also batted: Mr P. F. Warner 39, 4; Mr J. W. H. T. Douglas 18, 24; W. Hitch 4, 0*; S. Haigh 9; E. G. Hayes 4; Mr W. Brearley 0.

* Signifies not out.

### ENGLISH BOWLING AVERAGES

| | Innings | Overs | Maidens | Runs | Wickets | Average |
|---|---|---|---|---|---|---|
| F. E. Woolley ...... | 7 | 57.5 | 12 | 152 | 17 | 8.94 |
| S. F. Barnes ........ | 9 | 190 | 64 | 404 | 39 | 10.35 |
| H. Dean .......... | 5 | 75.3 | 23 | 153 | 11 | 13.90 |
| Mr F. R. Foster ..... | 9 | 131.1 | 50 | 234 | 13 | 18.00 |
| W. Rhodes ......... | 3 | 25.2 | 7 | 74 | 3 | 24.66 |

The following bowled in two innings: J. W. Hearne 14–1–36–1; and in one innings: Mr W. Brearley 6–2–4–0; S. Haigh 6–4–3–0; J. B. Hobbs 11–2–36–0.

The following two three-figure innings were played for England in the Triangular Tournament:

Mr R. H. Spooner (1):
    119 v South Africa, at Lord's.
J. B. Hobbs (1):
    107 v Australia, at Lord's.

## AUSTRALIAN BATTING AVERAGES

|  | Matches | Innings | Not Outs | Runs | Highest Innings | Average |
|---|---|---|---|---|---|---|
| W. Bardsley . . . . . . . . | 6 | 6 | 0 | 392 | 164 | 65.33 |
| C. Kelleway . . . . . . . . | 6 | 7 | 1 | 360 | 114 | 60.00 |
| C. G. Macartney . . . . | 6 | 6 | 0 | 197 | 99 | 32.83 |
| C. B. Jennings . . . . . . | 6 | 8 | 2 | 107 | 32 | 17.85 |
| R. B. Minnett . . . . . . . | 4 | 5 | 0 | 86 | 39 | 17.20 |
| T. J. Matthews . . . . . . | 6 | 6 | 1 | 82 | 49* | 16.40 |
| S. E. Gregory  . . . . . . | 6 | 6 | 0 | 72 | 37 | 12.00 |
| W. J. Whitty  . . . . . . | 6 | 5 | 0 | 39 | 33 | 7.80 |
| G. R. Hazlitt . . . . . . . | 6 | 6 | 2 | 28 | 19 | 7.00 |
| W. Carkeek . . . . . . . . | 6 | 5 | 2 | 16 | 6* | 5.33 |

The following also batted: D. Smith 24*, 6, 0; E. R. Mayne 23, 25*; S. H. Emery 1, 5. J. W. McLaren and H. Webster did not play in any of the Test matches.

* Signifies not out.

## AUSTRALIAN BOWLING AVERAGES

|  | Innings | Overs | Maidens | Runs | Wickets | Average |
|---|---|---|---|---|---|---|
| T. J. Matthews . . . . . . | 9 | 115.5 | 34 | 255 | 15 | 17.00 |
| R. B. Minnett . . . . . . . | 4 | 39.1 | 14 | 111 | 6 | 18.50 |
| W. J. Whitty . . . . . . . | 9 | 220 | 76 | 495 | 25 | 19.80 |
| G. R. Hazlitt . . . . . . . | 8 | 189.3 | 60 | 398 | 19 | 20.94 |
| C. G. Macartney . . . . | 5 | 75.1 | 19 | 142 | 6 | 23.66 |
| C. Kelleway . . . . . . . . | 8 | 86.2 | 21 | 239 | 10 | 23.90 |
| S. M. Emery  . . . . . . . | 4 | 77 | 13 | 249 | 5 | 49.80 |

The following four three-figure innings were played for Australia in the Triangular Tournament:

W. Bardsley (2):
    164 v South Africa, at Lord's.
    121 v South Africa, at Manchester.
C. Kelleway (2):
    114 v South Africa, at Manchester.
    102 v South Africa, at Lord's.

## SOUTH AFRICAN BATTING AVERAGES

|  | Matches | Innings | Not Outs | Runs | Highest Innings | Average |
|---|---|---|---|---|---|---|
| C. P. Carter ........ | 2 | 4 | 1 | 63 | 31 | 21.00 |
| A. D. Nourse ....... | 6 | 11 | 0 | 220 | 64 | 20.00 |
| G. A. Faulkner ..... | 6 | 11 | 1 | 194 | 122* | 19.40 |
| H. W. Taylor ....... | 6 | 11 | 1 | 194 | 93 | 19.40 |
| L. J. Tancred ....... | 4 | 7 | 0 | 134 | 39 | 19.14 |
| C. B. Llewellyn ..... | 5 | 9 | 0 | 167 | 75 | 18.55 |
| S. J. Pegler ......... | 6 | 11 | 2 | 157 | 35* | 17.44 |
| G. C. White ........ | 5 | 9 | 1 | 136 | 59* | 17.00 |
| L. A. Stricker ....... | 4 | 7 | 0 | 113 | 48 | 16.14 |
| S. J. Snooke ........ | 5 | 9 | 0 | 115 | 23 | 12.77 |
| R. Beaumont ....... | 3 | 5 | 0 | 59 | 31 | 11.80 |
| R. O. Schwarz ...... | 3 | 6 | 0 | 52 | 28 | 8.66 |
| T. A. Ward ........ | 5 | 9 | 4 | 38 | 24 | 7.60 |
| G. P. D. Hartigan ... | 2 | 4 | 0 | 30 | 25 | 7.50 |
| F. Mitchell ......... | 3 | 6 | 0 | 28 | 12 | 4.66 |

The following played in one match, T. Campbell 0*, 3. J. L. Cox did not play in the Test series.

* Signifies not out.

## SOUTH AFRICAN BOWLING AVERAGES

|  | Innings | Overs | Maidens | Runs | Wickets | Average |
|---|---|---|---|---|---|---|
| S. J. Pegler ......... | 8 | 231.2 | 40 | 594 | 29 | 20.48 |
| A. D. Nourse ....... | 8 | 134.5 | 40 | 316 | 13 | 24.30 |
| G. A. Faulkner ..... | 9 | 161.4 | 21 | 454 | 17 | 26.70 |
| C. B. Llewellyn ..... | 4 | 60 | 6 | 244 | 4 | 61.00 |
| R. O. Schwarz ...... | 3 | 63 | 4 | 230 | 3 | 76.66 |
| C. P. Carter ........ | 3 | 13 | 1 | 45 | 0 | — |

The following bowled in two innings: G. P. D. Hartigan 19–2–45–0; H. W. Taylor 14–5–31–0; and in one innings: L. A. Stricker 3–1–8–0; G. C. White 6–1–29–1.

Only one three-figure innings was played for South Africa in the Triangular Tournament:

G. A. Faulkner (1):
122* v Australia, at Manchester.

## NOTES BY THE EDITOR IN 1912

The Fates fought against the Triangular Tournament. Such a combination of adverse conditions could hardly have been imagined. To begin with, the Australians, who had been allowed to have everything their own way in choosing the time for the first trial of Sir Abe Bailey's ambitious scheme, quarrelled so bitterly among themselves that half their best players were left at home. In the second place the South Africans, so far from improving, fell a good way below their form of 1907 and, to crown everything, we had one of the most appalling summers ever known, even in England. In the circumstances it was not surprising that the Tournament, as a public attraction, failed to realise the expectations of its supporters. The result is that the experiment is not likely to be repeated for many years to come – perhaps not in this generation. The arrangements provisionally made at the Imperial Conference at Lord's in July for the future inter-change of visits for English, Australian, and South African elevens extend to 1917, and beyond that there is at present no need to look. Personally I could never get up any real enthusiasm for the Triangular scheme. To my mind there always seemed a great danger in crowding so much first-class cricket into a season of little more than four months. Still I am bound to admit that, if we had had a fine summer and the Australians had sent over their best team, the Test matches themselves, despite the weakness of the South Africans, would have proved a substantial success. The objections to the Tournament apply not so much to the big events as to the general run of the season's play. Two visiting elevens must, in the nature of things, stand in each other's way, the fixture list being extended far beyond the limits demanded by the public.

It is no business of mine to go into details with regard to the squabbles and quarrels in Australia. In the special circumstances I think all personal considerations should have been put aside and made subordinate to the prime need of sending over Australia's best men for the Tournament. However, all attempts at compromise failed. The personal differences went too deep to admit of adjustment. The Board of Control carried its point, but as regards the prestige of Australian cricket the victory was dearly won. It says much for the all-round strength of Australia at the present time that with half-a-dozen crack players left behind such a good all-round team could be sent to England, but there was no way of making up for the absence of Trumper, Armstrong, Ransford, Cotter, and Clem Hill. Even Australia cannot manufacture champion players at five minutes' notice. When the wet weather came Bardsley and Macartney, with Kelleway to help them, had in match after match to carry the rest of the side on their shoulders. I venture to predict that when the Australians pay us their next visit they will send over their strongest team. In saying this, I am thinking far less of patriotic considerations than of the stern force of money. The experience of last summer showed that in the matches with the Counties and the Universities an ordinary combination was not good enough to attract the public in any great numbers.

The South Africans were frankly a disappointment – not much above the level of a strong county eleven. They often played well in their less important games, but in five of their six Test matches they failed dismally. Apart from his innings of 122 not out at Manchester, Faulkner – their one great batsman – let them down badly on the big occasions, and their bowling suffered much from lack of variety in pace. One bowler with real speed would have been invaluable as a contrast to Pegler and Faulkner. It was significant that in summing up the play of his side, when the tour was over, Frank Mitchell practically gave up the case for googlie bowling, expressing a hope that the South African bowlers of the future would model themselves on Pegler and not on Faulkner. I doubt if Mr Mitchell will carry public opinion with him. In effect, he asks for nothing less than the abandonment of the individual style of bowling which caused South African cricket to be placed on a level with that of England and Australia. This does not seem quite wise or reasonable. The googlie failed in Australia, but though it has not had the devasting effect on cricket that certain extremists predicted, it is still a power on the matting wickets at Johannesburg, Durban, and Cape Town. To ask South African bowlers to give it up is like telling them to part with their birthright. In judging the South African bowling last season one must remember that Schwarz was a mere shadow of his old self, and that Gordon White scarcely bowled at all. Inasmuch as he only turned the ball one way Schwarz was never in the full sense a googlie bowler, but in the art of bowling the off-break with, to all appearance, a leg-break action, he at his best touched perfection. Had he been able to bowl last summer as he bowled in 1907, the Test matches might not have been quite so one-sided.

Following the triumph of the MCC's team in Australia during the winter, victory in the Triangular Tournament left England unquestionably at the top of the tree. Success did not mean so much as it would have done if Australia had been fully represented, but for that there was no help. I heard disparaging things said by more than one famous cricketer about the England eleven, but in the face of expert opinion I am not afraid to speak up for the side. In my humble opinion we had a first-rate combination – well adapted for all conditions of weather and wicket. We always wanted one more great batsman – a batsman of the class of Hayward, Jackson, and MacLaren at their best – but this was our only weak point. Even as things were our batting came out very well. Not once in the six Test matches did the team have the luck to bat on a plumb wicket – the nearest approach to anything like ideal conditions was in the second innings against the South Africans at Leeds – and yet the run-getting was so consistent that on no occasion was there cause for anxiety. In scoring so well on slow wickets our men, to my thinking, were entitled to far more praise than they received. In some quarters there was a curious tendency to attribute their success not to good play but to the weakness of the opposing sides. So much having been done under difficult conditions, I think it is only a fair assumption that in a summer of sunshine and hard wickets we should have made a heap of runs in the Test matches. The fact that C. B. Fry did not assert himself until the last match with the Australians at The Oval made our batting look far less formidable than it really was.

I would not pretent that we had anything like the batting that we possessed in 1902, but there was nothing to apologise for. Hobbs was magnificent – just as good, allowing for the difference in the wickets, as he had been during his Australian and South African tours – and Woolley proved himself, beyond all question, a Test match batsman. Far more confident and sure of himself than he had ever been before, he was able to play his proper game directly he went in and did not need half-an-hour in which to settle down. Spooner did splendid work against the South Africans, but in the Australian matches he failed as completely as Ranjitsinhji and Fry had failed ten years before. It was a great point in our batting that we had in Hobbs and Rhodes such a splendid pair to go in first. Thanks to constant association in South Africa and Australia the two men understood each other so well that they could with safety attempt short runs that in ordinary circumstances would have savoured of madness. They never seemed to let a chance escape them, and yet they seldom looked to be in any danger. Better running between the wickets has not often been seen.

As regards bowling I think we were better off than in any series of Test matches in England since Lockwood and Rhodes were in their prime. It so happened that our bowlers never had a chance of showing what they could do on fast run-getting wickets, but judging from what F. R. Foster did on perfect wickets in Australia it is very unlikely that the combination would have been found wanting. With the grounds as they were the only failure was when the team, in trying to force a win against the Australians on the third day at Lord's, attempted the impossible. For the rest the bowlers did everything that was asked of them. Barnes surpassed himself, giving conclusive evidence that he is, at the present time, the best bowler in the world. One did not know before that he could, against first-rate batsmen, be quite so deadly on sticky wickets. Bowling that looked more difficult from the ring than his on the second day of the South Africans' match at The Oval I have never seen. The skill with which he broke both ways, while keeping a perfect length all the time, was wonderful. In a fine summer his best supporters, no doubt, would have been F. R. Foster and Hitch, but as it was Woolley and Dean shared the honours with him.

With regard to the selection of the England eleven for the various Test matches there were none of the blunders that caused such irritation and dismay in 1909. As Lord Harris pointed out in a letter to the Board of Control at the end of the season the absence of adverse criticism showed how well the selection committee – Mr Fry, Mr John Shuter, and Mr H. K. Foster – did their work. Keeping clear of fads and prejudices they nearly always made the best choice possible. Only twice, I think, was their judgment open to question. On the form shown in the Test Trial match a fortnight or so before, Hitch instead of Walter Brearley should have been the fast bowler against the South Africans at Lord's, and in the match with the Australians at Manchester it seemed a doubtful policy to weaken the batting on a slow wicket by playing Hitch in preference to Hayes. C. B. Fry was a very zealous captain, but I cannot help thinking that the responsibilities of leadership told on his batting. Once at least his management of the side was rather bewildering. No one, so far as I know, has attempted to explain why he did not let Woolley bowl against the Australians at Lord's. I may add here that, differing from some of our own authorities, Sydney Gregory thought we had a very fine eleven, and that we should have been capable of beating the best Australian side.

S. H. P.

## MCC v SOUTH AFRICANS

Played at Lord's, May 13, 14, 15, 1912

Placing in the field an eleven which included eight fine batsmen and six first-class bowlers, the MCC beat the South Africans by 108 runs. A much more severe defeat than this appeared in prospect when at the tea interval on Tuesday, Marylebone were 313 ahead with seven wickets in hand. On resuming, however, Pegler bowled in such splendid form that in six overs and three balls he took six wickets for 10 runs. Keeping a capital length, he made the ball turn at a great pace. Putting together the first hundred hit against the South Africans, Tarrant enjoyed some luck, but played fine resolute cricket. Snooke batted admirably on Wednesday, when Fry, with a wealth of attack at his command overbowled J. W. Hearne altogether.

### MCC

| | | |
|---|---|---|
| Mr R. H. Spooner c and b Hartigan | 36 – | b Nourse ... 72 |
| F. A. Tarrant b Pegler | 104 – | c Hartigan b Snooke ... 52 |
| J. W. Hearne lbw b Pegler | 12 – | b Hartigan ... 26 |
| J. Hardstaff b Pegler | 1 – | b Pegler ... 12 |
| Mr C. B. Fry b Schwarz | 30 – | c Campbell b Snooke ... 38 |
| Mr A. P. Day lbw b Schwarz | 50 – | b Pegler ... 2 |
| A. E. Relf c Nourse b Pegler | 25 – | c Carter b Pegler ... 1 |
| G. J. Thompson b Hartigan | 17 – | lbw b Pegler ... 0 |
| J. T. Hearne b Hartigan | 0 – | c Snooke b Pegler ... 2 |
| F. H. Huish not out | 6 – | not out ... 3 |
| A. Fielder b Pegler | 2 – | c and b Pegler ... 2 |
| B 5, l-b 5 | 10 | B 8, l-b 3 ... 11 |
| | 293 | 221 |

### South Africans

| | | |
|---|---|---|
| L. J. Tancred b Tarrant | 9 – | c Huish b J. W. Hearne ... 1 |
| L. A. Stricker b Tarrant | 5 – | c Fielder b Relf ... 17 |
| A. D. Nourse lbw b Relf | 35 – | lbw b J. T. Hearne ... 32 |
| S. J. Snooke b Tarrant | 6 – | c Fry b Fielder ... 86 |
| F. Mitchell b J. W. Hearne | 30 – | c J. T. Hearne b J. W. Hearne ... 17 |
| R. O. Schwarz c Thompson b J. W. Hearne | 35 – | b Thompson ... 21 |
| S. J. Pegler b Tarrant | 12 – | run out ... 6 |
| R. Beaumont c Tarrant b Fielder | 13 – | not out ... 0 |
| G. P. D. Hartigan not out | 12 – | b J. W. Hearne ... 16 |
| C. P. Carter b Tarrant | 0 – | c and b Thompson ... 1 |
| T. Campbell b Tarrant | 5 – | c J. T. Hearne b J. W. Hearne ... 23 |
| B 11, l-b 2, n-b 1 | 14 | B 3, l-b 5, w 1, n-b 1 ... 10 |
| | 176 | 230 |

## South African Bowling

| | Overs | Mdns | Runs | Wkts | Overs | Mdns | Runs | Wkts |
|---|---|---|---|---|---|---|---|---|
| Nourse .......... | 10 | — | 40 | — | 12 | 1 | 37 | 1 |
| Pegler ........... | 30.3 | 8 | 75 | 5 | 17.3 | 5 | 44 | 6 |
| Schwarz ......... | 12 | 2 | 54 | 2 | 9 | — | 45 | — |
| Carter .......... | 10 | — | 45 | — | 8 | — | 21 | — |
| Hartigan ........ | 22 | 3 | 69 | 3 | 12 | 1 | 34 | 1 |
| Snooke .......... | | | | | 8 | — | 29 | 2 |

## MCC Bowling

| | Overs | Mdns | Runs | Wkts | Overs | Mdns | Runs | Wkts |
|---|---|---|---|---|---|---|---|---|
| Fielder .......... | 20 | 6 | 45 | 1 | 10 | 2 | 25 | 1 |
| Tarrant ......... | 26.3 | 7 | 55 | 6 | 19 | 5 | 48 | — |
| Relf ............ | 2 | 1 | 3 | 1 | 6 | 2 | 5 | 1 |
| J. W. Hearne ..... | 12 | 3 | 39 | 2 | 25 | 2 | 122 | 4 |
| Thompson ....... | 2 | 1 | 1 | — | 8.2 | 3 | 13 | 2 |
| J. T. Hearne ...... | 5 | 2 | 19 | — | 4 | 2 | 7 | 1 |

Umpires: J. Carlin and A. J. Atfield.

# LEICESTERSHIRE v SOUTH AFRICANS

Played at Leicester, August 8, 9, 1912

Contested on a very treacherous wicket, this match, despite an early stoppage on account of bad light on Thursday, was all over before four o'clock on Friday, the South Africans winning by 60 runs. Leicestershire threw away any chance of victory by mistakes in the field. On the opening day, when the Colonials scored 96 for five wickets before lunch. Faulkner, who as soon as he had once settled down played admirably, was twice missed while making his first 7 runs. After the interval the innings was finished off in little more than half-an-hour. Faulkner followed up his success in batting with some very skilful bowling, he and Pegler disposing of Leicestershire in eighty minutes. Knight, ninth man out, watched the ball, very carefully, and made a few good hits. On Friday the pitch was even more difficult than it had been on the previous day, and King and Bannister – the latter an old Tonbridge boy – disposed of the nine outstanding Colonial wickets in little more than an hour. Bannister, who proved very difficult to hit, had seven wickets in the match for 47 runs and King twelve for 97. Wanting 153 to win, Leicestershire, of course, found the task beyond their powers. Faulkner had a great match.

## South Africans

| | | |
|---|---|---|
| L. J. Tancred lbw b King ...................... | 0 – | st Shields b King .............. 9 |
| H. W. Taylor c and b Bannister ................. | 17 – | st Shields b King .............. 1 |
| A. D. Nourse run out ......................... | 16 – | c Astill b King ................ 4 |
| G. A. Faulkner b Bannister ................... | 33 – | b King ....................... 1 |
| S. J. Snooke b Bannister ...................... | 0 – | b Bannister .................. 5 |
| G. C. White st Shields b King .................. | 20 – | lbw b King ................... 18 |
| L. A. Stricker c Whitehead b King .............. | 15 – | b King ....................... 1 |
| S. J. Pegler c Wood b King ................... | 6 – | c and b King ................. 8 |
| F. Mitchell c Whitehead b King ................. | 1 – | b Bannister .................. 12 |
| C. P. Carter c Whitehead b Bannister ........... | 0 – | lbw b Bannister .............. 4 |
| T. A. Ward not out .......................... | 0 – | not out ...................... 6 |
| B 3, l-b 7, n-b 7 ..................... | 17 | B 2, l-b 2 .............. 4 |
| | 125 | 73 |

## Leicestershire

| | | | |
|---|---|---|---|
| Mr C. J. B. Wood lbw b Pegler | 0 | – b Faulkner | 28 |
| A. E. Knight b Faulkner | 23 | – b Pegler | 6 |
| H. Whitehead b Faulkner | 4 | – c Faulkner b Nourse | 12 |
| A. Mounteney b Faulkner | 0 | – c Ward b Pegler | 1 |
| J. H. King lbw b Faulkner | 1 | – c Carter b Nourse | 0 |
| Mr W. N. Riley lbw b Pegler | 4 | – b Pegler | 3 |
| J. S. Curtis b Pegler | 4 | – lbw b Faulkner | 2 |
| W. Shipman b Faulkner | 0 | – c and b Faulkner | 5 |
| Mr H. M. Bannister b Faulkner | 0 | – b Faulkner | 12 |
| Mr J. Shields not out | 2 | – st Ward b Faulkner | 11 |
| W. E. Astill b Pegler | 3 | – not out | 5 |
| B 4, l-b 1 | 5 | B 4, l-b 2, n-b 1 | 7 |
| | **46** | | **92** |

## Leicestershire Bowling

| | Overs | Mdns | Runs | Wkts | Overs | Mdns | Runs | Wkts |
|---|---|---|---|---|---|---|---|---|
| King | 21 | 4 | 52 | 5 | 12 | 2 | 45 | 7 |
| Astill | 11 | 1 | 22 | — | | | | |
| Curtis | 8 | 2 | 11 | — | | | | |
| Bannister | 11.1 | 3 | 23 | 4 | 11.2 | 2 | 24 | 3 |

## South African Bowling

| | Overs | Mdns | Runs | Wkts | Overs | Mdns | Runs | Wkts |
|---|---|---|---|---|---|---|---|---|
| Pegler | 13.4 | 5 | 20 | 4 | 18 | 7 | 37 | 3 |
| Faulkner | 13 | 4 | 21 | 6 | 11.4 | 1 | 38 | 5 |
| Nourse | | | | | 6 | 2 | 10 | 2 |

Umpires: F. Gutteridge and J. Carlin.

# THE COUNTY MATCHES

## DERBYSHIRE

### DERBYSHIRE v NOTTINGHAMSHIRE

Played at Derby, July 15, 16, 17, 1901

Everything else was completely dwarfed by the personal triumphs of William Gunn and L. G. Wright, each of the famous veterans playing the highest innings of his career in important cricket. Gunn went in at the fall of one wicket for 24, and was not out at the drawing of stumps for 247, with the total at 491 for three wickets. Jones helped to put on 85, John Gunn 174, and Shrewsbury – also not out at the end of the day – 208. Altogether, Gunn was batting five hours and a half, and in a delightful display, free from any blemish, he hit thirty-eight 4s, five 3s, and twenty-three 2s. He was fifth out at 533. Shrewsbury, who just failed to get his 100, also played finely. Derbyshire were set a terrific task, but thanks to Wright they saved the game. Wright took five hours and a half to make his 193, in which his only mistake was a chance when 54. He hit twenty-two 4s, six 3s, and eighteen 2s. Derbyshire followed on against 209, with over two hours to bat, but only lost three wickets before time came to the rescue and enabled them to draw the match.

### Nottinghamshire

| | |
|---|---|
| Mr A. O. Jones b Storer .............. 44 | G. Anthony run out ................. 8 |
| J. Iremonger b Hulme ................ 19 | T. Oates c Hulme b Young ............. 3 |
| W. Gunn c Warren b Hulme .......... 273 | A. Hallam st Chatterton b Storer ........ 34 |
| J. Gunn c Storer b Lawton ............. 84 | T. Wass b Storer .................... 5 |
| A. Shrewsbury c Storer b Hulme ........ 99 | B 13, l-b 6, w 3 .............. 22 |
| J. Carlin not out ..................... 64 | |
| I. Harrison c and b Hulme ............. 6 | 661 |

### Derbyshire

| | | | |
|---|---|---|---|
| Mr L. G. Wright b J. Gunn .................... 193 | – c Wass b Jones ............... | 9 |
| Locker b Hallam .......................... 76 | – run out ...................... | 37 |
| W. Storer c and b Anthony ................. 44 | – not out ...................... | 57 |
| W. Chatterton c W. Gunn b Jones ............... 48 | | |
| E. Needham c W. Gunn b Hallam .............. 0 | | |
| Burton not out ........................... 51 | | |
| Mr A. E. Lawton c Oates b Jones ............. 5 | | |
| Barton c and b Jones ....................... 0 | – c Oates b Carlin ............ | 6 |
| J. H. Young st Oates b Jones ................. 10 | | |
| A. Warren c Hallam b Jones ................. 5 | – not out ..................... | 6 |
| J. Hulme c J. Gunn b Jones .................. 3 | | |
| B 9, l-b 2, w 1, n-b 5 ................. 17 | L-b 1 ................. | 1 |
| 452 | | 116 |

### Derbyshire Bowling

| | Overs | Mdns | Runs | Wkts |
|---|---|---|---|---|
| Hulme ........... | 65 | 15 | 161 | 4 |
| Warren ......... | 34 | 3 | 159 | — |
| Storer ........... | 22.2 | 2 | 105 | 3 |
| Lawton ......... | 17 | — | 78 | 1 |
| Young .......... | 19 | 1 | 86 | 1 |
| Barton .......... | 6 | — | 35 | — |
| Chatterton ........ | 7 | 2 | 15 | — |

## Nottinghamshire Bowling

| | Overs | Mdns | Runs | Wkts | Overs | Mdns | Runs | Wkts |
|---|---|---|---|---|---|---|---|---|
| Wass ............ | 34 | 6 | 108 | — | 7 | — | 13 | — |
| J. Gunn .......... | 32 | 5 | 102 | 1 | | | | |
| Jones ............ | 35.4 | 12 | 93 | 6 | 11 | 4 | 31 | 1 |
| Hallam ........... | 44 | 15 | 97 | 2 | 6 | 2 | 11 | — |
| Anthony ......... | 12 | 1 | 35 | 1 | 13 | 4 | 26 | — |
| Carlin ........... | | | | | 11 | 3 | 34 | 1 |

Umpires: J. Phillips and A. White.

# DERBYSHIRE v ESSEX

## Played at Chesterfield, July 18, 19, 20, 1904

In defeating Essex, Derbyshire accomplished the most phenomenal performance ever recorded in first-class cricket. They went in against a first innings of 597, got within 49, and ultimately won by nine wickets. Such an achievement has no parallel in the history of the game. Two batsmen covered themselves with distinction in the match – P. Perrin whose 343 not out was not only the highest innings of the season, but the fifth best ever made in a great match, and Ollivierre who scored 321 for once out. Perrin obtained his runs in five hours and three quarters, and hit no fewer than sixty-eight 4s.

## Essex

| | | | |
|---|---|---|---|
| Mr F. L. Fane lbw b Curgenven ................. | 63 | – b Warren ..................... | 2 |
| H. Carpenter b Bestwick ...................... | 5 | – c Warren b Bestwick ............ | 2 |
| Mr P. Perrin not out ......................... | 343 | – c and b Warren ................ | 8 |
| Mr C. McGahey b Bestwick ................... | 32 | – c Cadman b Bestwick .......... | 5 |
| Rev. F. H. Gillingham c and b Warren ........... | 43 | – absent ill ..................... | 0 |
| E. H. D. Sewell b Warren ...................... | 10 | – c Cadman b Curgenven .......... | 41 |
| W. Reeves b Warren ......................... | 0 | – b Bestwick .................... | 0 |
| Mr R. P. Keigwin lbw b Ashcroft ............... | 14 | – c Needham b Warren .......... | 0 |
| Mr J. W. H. T. Douglas b Ollivierre ............. | 47 | – not out ...................... | 27 |
| E. Russell c Humphries b Cadman ............. | 23 | – b Curgenven ................. | 0 |
| C. P. Buckenham lbw b Bestwick .............. | 3 | – b Warren ................... | 8 |
| B 2, l-b 5, w 3, n-b 4 ................. | 14 | W 2, n-b 2 .............. | 4 |
| | **597** | | **97** |

## Derbyshire

| | | | |
|---|---|---|---|
| Mr L. G. Wright c Fane b Reeve ............... | 68 | – c Carpenter b Buckenham ........ | 1 |
| Mr C. A. Ollivierre b Reeves ................... | 229 | – not out ..................... | 92 |
| W. Storer b Buckenham ...................... | 44 | – not out ..................... | 48 |
| Mr E. M. Ashcroft b Sewell ................... | 34 | | |
| E. Needham b Reeves ....................... | 47 | | |
| Mr G. Curgenven b Buckenham ............... | 31 | | |
| Morton b Reeves ........................... | 16 | | |
| A. Warren b Douglas ........................ | 18 | | |
| Cadman c Douglas b Reeves ................. | 34 | | |
| J. Humphries not out ....................... | 2 | | |
| W. Bestwick lbw b Douglas .................. | 0 | | |
| B 6, l-b 18, w 1 .................... | 25 | B 4, l-b 2, w 1, n-b 1 ....... | 8 |
| | **548** | | **149** |

## Derbyshire Bowling

| | Overs | Mdns | Runs | Wkts | Overs | Mdns | Runs | Wkts |
|---|---|---|---|---|---|---|---|---|
| Warren .......... | 29 | 3 | 148 | 3 | 16.1 | 5 | 42 | 4 |
| Bestwick ........ | 42.1 | 8 | 160 | 3 | 16 | 4 | 34 | 3 |
| Cadman .......... | 22 | 3 | 65 | 1 | 2 | — | 10 | — |
| Storer ........... | 7 | — | 41 | — | | | | |
| Curgenven ....... | 16 | 1 | 67 | 1 | 5 | 2 | 7 | 2 |
| Ashcroft ......... | 7 | 1 | 38 | 1 | | | | |
| Morton ......... | 8 | 1 | 39 | — | | | | |
| Wright .......... | 4 | — | 15 | — | | | | |
| Ollivierre ........ | 3 | — | 15 | 1 | | | | |

## Essex Bowling

| | Overs | Mdns | Runs | Wkts | Overs | Mdns | Runs | Wkts |
|---|---|---|---|---|---|---|---|---|
| Buckenham ....... | 43 | 5 | 176 | 2 | 13 | — | 78 | 1 |
| Keigwin .......... | 7 | 1 | 36 | — | | | | |
| Reeves ........... | 51 | 7 | 192 | 5 | 13 | 1 | 43 | — |
| Douglas .......... | 15.3 | 1 | 54 | 2 | 2 | — | 14 | — |
| McGahey ......... | 11 | 2 | 34 | — | 2 | 1 | 6 | — |
| Sewell ........... | 7 | — | 31 | 1 | | | | |

Umpires: W. Wright and S. Brown.

## DERBYSHIRE v WARWICKSHIRE

Played at Blackwell, June 18, 20, 21, 1910

In saving the match, after going in against a huge total of 504, and later following-on in face of a majority of 242, Derbyshire accomplished perhaps their best performance of the season. The achievement was made possible by a remarkable ninth wicket stand, which yielded 283 in less than three hours, Warren hitting fourteen 4s and Chapman two 6s and nineteen 4s in their respective scores of 123 and 165. With no possibility of getting the necessary 189 to win in the time available, Warwickshire could, of course, only play for a draw. The feature of the visitors' first innings was the brilliant batting of Charlesworth who, surpassing everything he had previously done, obtained 216 out of 338 in three hours forty minutes.

### Warwickshire

| | | | | |
|---|---|---|---|---|
| A. A. Lilley c Humphries b Warren .............. | 19 | | | |
| S. P. Kinneir st Humphries b Cadman ............ | 87 | | | |
| C. Charlesworth c Warren b Root ............... | 216 | – not out ........................ | 16 |
| W. G. Quaife c Warren b Morton ............... | 88 | | | |
| C. S. Baker lbw b Cadman ..................... | 3 | | | |
| Mr F. E. Tayler c Jelf b Morton ................. | 6 | – c Morton b Higson ............. | 34 |
| S. Santall b Warren .......................... | 37 | | | |
| E. J. Smith not out ......................... | 18 | – st Humphries b Morton .......... | 7 |
| Mr F. R. Foster not out ...................... | 12 | | | |
| B 1, l-b 14, w 1, n-b 2 ................ | 18 | B 1, l-b 5 ............... | 6 |

(7 wkts dec.) 504          63

Mr J. H. Phillips and F. E. Field did not bat.

## Derbyshire

| | | | |
|---|---|---|---|
| F. A. Newton c Foster b Santall | 87 | – lbw b Quaife | 21 |
| E. Needham c Foster b Field | 8 | – c Charlesworth b Foster | 34 |
| J. Handford c Smith b Phillips | 18 | – c Foster b Field | 16 |
| S. Cadman lbw b Foster | 18 | – b Foster | 0 |
| A. Morton c Smith b Field | 22 | – b Santall | 13 |
| Mr T. A. Higson b Foster | 36 | – c Charlesworth b Field | 2 |
| Mr H. F. Jelf c Charlesworth b Foster | 33 | – c Charlesworth b Field | 0 |
| A. R. Warren b Foster | 15 | – c Phillips b Field | 123 |
| F. Root not out | 0 | – run out | 34 |
| Mr J. Chapman c Foster b Santall | 0 | – b Foster | 165 |
| J. Humphries b Foster | 3 | – not out | 8 |
| B 14, l-b 8 | 22 | B 12, w 1, n-b 1 | 14 |
| | **262** | | **430** |

## Derbyshire Bowling

| | Overs | Mdns | Runs | Wkts | Overs | Mdns | Runs | Wkts |
|---|---|---|---|---|---|---|---|---|
| Warren | 41 | 8 | 199 | 2 | | | | |
| Cadman | 30 | 5 | 104 | 2 | 10 | — | 24 | — |
| Morton | 43 | 6 | 137 | 2 | 6 | 1 | 24 | 1 |
| Higson | 5 | — | 33 | — | .2 | — | — | 1 |
| Root | 5 | 1 | 13 | 1 | | | | |
| Needham | | | | | 4 | — | 9 | — |

## Warwickshire Bowling

| | Overs | Mdns | Runs | Wkts | Overs | Mdns | Runs | Wkts |
|---|---|---|---|---|---|---|---|---|
| Foster | 28.1 | 10 | 62 | 5 | 26.4 | 4 | 119 | 3 |
| Field | 23 | 6 | 81 | 2 | 29 | 5 | 124 | 4 |
| Santall | 20 | 5 | 46 | 2 | 22 | 4 | 66 | 1 |
| Quaife | 6 | 1 | 21 | — | 12 | 2 | 47 | 1 |
| Phillips | 8 | — | 30 | 1 | 9 | — | 37 | — |
| Charlesworth | | | | | 4 | — | 16 | — |
| Baker | | | | | 2 | — | 7 | — |

Umpires: A. A. White and J. Moss.

# ESSEX

## ESSEX v YORKSHIRE

Played at Leyton, August 15, 16, 1901

The season at Leyton closed with a genuine sensation, a match of very small scores ending just after twelve o'clock on the second day in a victory for Yorkshire by an innings and 33 runs. As rain had fallen heavily overnight, the bowlers were expected to do well, but for what actually happened no one could have been in the least prepared. Essex promptly lost the game, for on winning the toss and going in at a quarter to one – the state of the ground having prevented an earlier start – they were out in as nearly as possible an hour for a total of 30. Four wickets fell for 1 run, and the only chance of retrieving this disastrous start disappeared when Lucas was run out. Bowling at a great pace, and swerving in an extraordinary way, Hirst was in the opinion of the Essex batsmen quite unplayable. He took seven wickets – six of them bowled down – and only 12 runs were hit from him. Later in the day in the second innings of Essex he was just as deadly, taking five wickets out of six, but there his wonderful success ended, the three wickets that fell the next morning being obtained by Rhodes. The Yorkshiremen found Walter Mead extremely difficult on the damaged pitch, and only Taylor, Tunnicliffe and Frank Mitchell could do anything against him. In a match in which the bowlers had things so entirely their own way, it was a great feat on Taylor's part to score 44, and apart from a couple of lucky snicks he played very finely.

### Essex

| | | | |
|---|---|---|---|
| Mr F. L. Fane b Hirst | 1 | – b Hirst | 3 |
| H. Carpenter b Hirst | 0 | – b Hirst | 0 |
| Mr P. Perrin c Hunter b Hirst | 0 | – c Hawke b Hirst | 9 |
| Mr C. McGahey b Hirst | 11 | – lbw b Rhodes | 1 |
| Mr J. H. Douglas b Hirst | 0 | – b Hirst | 0 |
| Mr A. P. Lucas run out | 3 | – c and b Hirst | 0 |
| Mr G. Tosetti b Hirst | 3 | – c and b Rhodes | 9 |
| W. Reeves c Denton b Rhodes | 10 | – st Hunter b Rhodes | 12 |
| T. M. Russell c Taylor b Rhodes | 0 | – retired hurt | 1 |
| H. Young not out | 1 | – not out | 0 |
| W. Mead b Hirst | 0 | – st Hunter b Rhodes | 2 |
| B 1 | 1 | B 2, n-b 2 | 4 |
| | **30** | | **41** |

### Yorkshire

| | | | |
|---|---|---|---|
| J. T. Brown lbw b Mead | 3 | Mr E. Smith c Fane b Reeves | 8 |
| J. Tunnicliffe b Mead | 10 | Lord Hawke b Mead | 7 |
| D. Denton c Mead b Young | 5 | W. Rhodes not out | 9 |
| Mr T. L. Taylor b Reeves | 44 | D. Hunter lbw b Mead | 4 |
| Mr F. Mitchell b Mead | 10 | | |
| G. H. Hirst c Reeves b Mead | 0 | | **104** |
| E. Wainwright c Young b Reeves | 4 | | |

### Yorkshire Bowling

| | Overs | Mdns | Runs | Wkts | Overs | Mdns | Runs | Wkts |
|---|---|---|---|---|---|---|---|---|
| Hirst | 8.1 | 3 | 12 | 7 | 10 | 6 | 17 | 5 |
| Rhodes | 8 | — | 17 | 2 | 10 | 2 | 20 | 4 |

**Essex Bowling**

|  | Overs | Mdns | Runs | Wkts |
|---|---|---|---|---|
| Young ........... | 12 | 8 | 28 | 1 |
| Mead ........... | 22 | 8 | 40 | 6 |
| Reeves .......... | 10 | 8 | 36 | 3 |

Umpires: R. G. Barlow and H. Wood.

## ESSEX v NOTTINGHAMSHIRE

Played at Leyton, August 6, 7, 8, 1903

Outplayed all through, Essex suffered defeat by an innings and 2 runs, the game ending before half-past twelve on the Saturday morning. Apart from the general excellence of the batting, Nottinghamshire owed their success chiefly to the splendid bowling of John Gunn, who, unchanged through both innings, took fourteen wickets. His length was perfect, and he varied the pace and flight of the ball most cleverly. Taylor, a fast bowler, who played instead of Wass (slightly injured), gave useful help in the first innings, when the pitch was a trifle slow and the visitors secured a commanding lead scoring 236 for the loss of three wickets. Jones and William Gunn both played admirably, adding 121. John Gunn and George Gunn also showed good form, the former batting freely and the latter defending with extreme patience. Late in arriving on the first day, Perrin took his usual place in batting order, when Essex faced their uphill struggle, and played a wonderfully fine innings. Despite his efforts, half the side were out for 147, but then Lucas stayed with Perrin for forty minutes while 58 runs were added, only being dismissed in the last over of the day. Perrin was soon out in the morning, and the last four wickets fell for 44 runs. Perrin gave one chance, but his play was almost perfect. Clean, hard hitting marked the innings after a steady commencement. R. P. Keigwin, the Cambridge Blue, appeared in the Essex eleven for the first time.

### Essex

| | | | |
|---|---|---|---|
| Mr F. L. Fane b J. Gunn ..................... | 13 | – c Oates b Hallam ............... | 26 |
| E. H. D. Sewell c Oates b Taylor ............... | 9 | – b Taylor ..................... | 12 |
| Mr C. McGahey c Oates b J. Gunn ............... | 19 | – b J. Gunn ................... | 11 |
| Mr J. H. Douglas not out ..................... | 40 | – lbw b J. Gunn ................. | 5 |
| C. P. Buckenham lbw b J. Gunn ............... | 10 | – b J. Gunn ................... | 13 |
| Mr A. P. Lucas b J. Gunn ................... | 8 | – b J. Gunn ................... | 20 |
| Mr P. Perrin b Taylor ...................... | 4 | – c and b J. Gunn ............... | 110 |
| Mr R. P. Keigwin b Taylor .................. | 3 | – not out ..................... | 22 |
| H. Young c Oates b J. Gunn ................. | 3 | – c W. Gunn b J. Gunn ........... | 0 |
| T. Russell run out ....................... | 14 | – c W. Gunn b J. Gunn ........... | 11 |
| W. Mead c Iremonger b J. Gunn ............. | 0 | – c Jones b J. Gunn ............. | 5 |
| B 5, n-b 1 ........................ | 6 | B 6, l-b 8 ............... | 14 |
| | **129** | | **249** |

### Nottinghamshire

| | | | |
|---|---|---|---|
| Mr A. O. Jones c Sewell b Douglas ....... | 73 | G. Anthony b Douglas ................ | 5 |
| J. Iremonger c and b Young ............. | 36 | A. Hallam c Sewell b McGahey .......... | 8 |
| W. Gunn b Young .................... | 66 | T. Oates c Russell b Mead ............. | 29 |
| J. Gunn c Russell c Buckenham .......... | 52 | Taylor c Russell b Buckenham .......... | 10 |
| Mr G. T. Branston c Russell b Mead ...... | 16 | B 5, l-b 3, w 1, n-b 3 ........... | 12 |
| G. Gunn not out ..................... | 54 | | |
| Mr E. G. Allen c Perrin b McGahey ...... | 19 | | **380** |

**Nottinghamshire Bowling**

| | Overs | Mdns | Runs | Wkts | Overs | Mdns | Runs | Wkts |
|---|---|---|---|---|---|---|---|---|
| Taylor .......... | 23 | 4 | 58 | 3 | 21 | 1 | 71 | 1 |
| J. Gunn ......... | 26 | 7 | 53 | 6 | 47.4 | 6 | 121 | 8 |
| Hallam .......... | 4 | 1 | 12 | — | 14 | 7 | 15 | 1 |
| Anthony ........ | | | | | 12 | 3 | 28 | — |

**Essex Bowling**

| | Overs | Mdns | Runs | Wkts |
|---|---|---|---|---|
| Mead ........... | 30 | 10 | 67 | 2 |
| Buckenham ...... | 19.3 | 2 | 75 | 2 |
| Young .......... | 13 | — | 42 | 2 |
| McGahey ........ | 27 | 4 | 73 | 2 |
| Douglas ......... | 23 | 3 | 73 | 2 |
| Keigwin ......... | 4 | 1 | 17 | — |
| Sewell .......... | 4 | — | 21 | — |

Umpires: J. Phillips and W. A. J. West.

# ESSEX v LANCASHIRE

Played at Leyton, August 13, 14, 15, 1903

On the opening day, Lancashire secured such a strong position that, although nothing could be done until twenty minutes past four on Saturday, they won by 119 runs. MacLaren hesitated about batting first on winning the toss, the ground remaining very soft from recent rains and the sun shining brightly. That he acted rightly, however, was beyond question. Forcing the game, Lancashire made a fair score. Then, when the pitch gave the bowlers most help, they dismissed Essex cheaply, and finished off the day by hitting up 84 for the loss of one wicket. In the morning, Garnett punished the bowling freely after Tyldesley and Spooner had added a useful 42. MacLaren gave an even finer display when the light was ban and the wicket more treacherous than ever. Splendid bowling by Barnes had given the visitors a big lead on the first innings, and when, at length, play was possible on Saturday, and MacLaren declared, he had chief share in again dismissing the home side. He began by taking five of the first six wickets that fell, and in the match he had the remarkable record of fourteen for 70.

## Lancashire

| | | | |
|---|---|---|---|
| Mr A. C. MacLaren c Lucas b Tremlin .......... | 5 | – not out ..................... | 52 |
| Mr R. H. Spooner b Mead ..................... | 17 | – lbw b Douglas ................ | 27 |
| J. Tyldesley c Sewell b Douglas ................ | 26 | – not out ..................... | 20 |
| Mr H. G. Garnett c Lucas b Mead .............. | 78 | | |
| Mr A. H. Hornby b Mead ..................... | 8 | | |
| J. Sharp b Mead ............................ | 8 | | |
| J. Hallows c and b Tremlin .................... | 6 | | |
| Heap c Russell b Tremlin ..................... | 4 | | |
| W. R. Cuttell st Russell b Mead ................ | 1 | | |
| S. F. Barnes not out ........................ | 5 | | |
| Worsley b Mead ............................ | 0 | | |
| B 10 ............................ | 10 | B 5 ................... | 5 |
| | 168 | (1 wkt dec.) | 84 |

### Essex

| | | | |
|---|---|---|---|
| Mr F. L. Fane c Worsley b Barnes .............. | 0 | – c Spooner b Barnes ........... | 5 |
| E. H. D. Sewell c and b Barnes ................ | 5 | – c Worsley b Barnes ........... | 5 |
| Mr P. Perrin c Heap b Cuttell ................. | 35 | – c Worsley b Cuttell ........... | 3 |
| Mr C. McGahey st Worsley b Barnes ........... | 17 | – c Hornby b Barnes ........... | 0 |
| Mr C. J. Kortright c Hornby b Barnes ........... | 0 | – c Sharp b Barnes ............ | 9 |
| Mr J. H. Douglas c MacLaren b Barnes ......... | 6 | – c Hornby b Hallows ......... | 9 |
| Mr A. P. Lucas b Barnes ..................... | 0 | – c Hornby b Barnes ........... | 0 |
| C. P. Buckenham c and b Cuttell ............... | 4 | – c Barnes b Hallows ......... | 12 |
| Tremlin c Heap b Barnes ..................... | 0 | – lbw b Barnes ................ | 5 |
| T. Russell not out ........................... | 0 | – not out .................... | 3 |
| W. Mead c Hornby b Barnes .................. | 2 | – b Hallows .................. | 11 |
| L-b 2 ........................... | 2 | B 2, n-b 2 .............. | 4 |
| | **71** | | **62** |

### Essex Bowling

| | Overs | Mdns | Runs | Wkts | Overs | Mdns | Runs | Wkts |
|---|---|---|---|---|---|---|---|---|
| Mead ............ | 22.2 | 5 | 55 | 6 | 12 | 3 | 14 | — |
| Tremlin .......... | 16 | 2 | 69 | 3 | 4 | — | 22 | — |
| Douglas .......... | 6 | — | 34 | 1 | 5 | — | 23 | 1 |
| Kortright ......... | | | | | 3 | — | 20 | — |

### Lancashire Bowling

| | Overs | Mdns | Runs | Wkts | Overs | Mdns | Runs | Wkts |
|---|---|---|---|---|---|---|---|---|
| Cuttell ........... | 18 | 4 | 32 | 2 | 11 | 5 | 10 | 1 |
| Barnes ........... | 18 | 5 | 37 | 8 | 20 | 6 | 33 | 6 |
| Hallows .......... | | | | | 8.1 | — | 15 | 3 |

Umpires: G. Bean and C. E. Richardson.

## ESSEX v YORKSHIRE

Played at Leyton, August 24, 25, 26, 1905

Though in the end drawing the match and in so doing making the championship safe, Yorkshire had a humiliating experience, their bowling being completely mastered and the side in the first innings being dismissed in a most ignominious manner. On the opening day Essex scored 404 for six wickets, and on the Friday morning 117 more runs were added. Fane and Carpenter gave the side a good start, scoring 116 for the first wicket, and the former with Gillingham added 132 for the second partnership. Reeves scored 71 out of 90 by fierce hitting and McGahey gave a sound display. Yorkshire's first innings was a remarkable affair, the side losing seven wickets for 42 and being put out in an hour and three-quarters for 98. Douglas did a sensational piece of bowling, sending down his first three overs for 3 runs and five wickets. He bowled Tunnicliffe with the fifth ball of his second over and completed that over after lunch by bowling Hirst, while with the last three balls of his third over he dismissed Rhodes, Haigh, and Myers, accomplishing the hat trick. Douglas actually obtained the five wickets in eight balls without a run being scored from him. Following on 423 behind Yorkshire lost Rothery overnight for 15, but on the third day after a prolonged struggle they succeeded in saving the match. Tunnicliffe and Hirst stayed together for three hours and a quarter, the latter batting for four hours and fifty minutes. Smith was in an hour without scoring.

## Essex

| | | | |
|---|---|---|---|
| Mr F. L. Fane c Myers b Smith | 106 | Benham b Ringrose | 42 |
| H. Carpenter run out | 69 | E. Russell b Rhodes | 17 |
| Rev. F. H. Gillingham st Dolphin b Smith | 82 | C. P. Buckenham b Haigh | 3 |
| Mr C. McGahey b Rhodes | 105 | B. Tremlin not out | 3 |
| Mr S. A. Trick c Hirst b Smith | 0 | B 11, l-b 10 | 21 |
| W. Reeves c Rhodes b Myers | 71 | | |
| Mr J. W. H. T. Douglas b Myers | 2 | | 521 |

## Yorkshire

| | | | |
|---|---|---|---|
| J. Tunnicliffe b Douglas | 11 | – c McGahey b Benham | 59 |
| J. W. Rothery b Buckenham | 0 | – c McGahey b Buckenham | 0 |
| D. Denton c Carpenter b Tremlin | 40 | – b Douglas | 17 |
| G. H. Hirst b Douglas | 0 | – b Reeves | 90 |
| W. Rhodes b Douglas | 2 | – b Buckenham | 6 |
| S. Haigh b Douglas | 0 | – c Russell b Reeves | 12 |
| H. Myers b Douglas | 0 | – lbw b Douglas | 9 |
| Mr E. Smith b Buckenham | 2 | – not out | 0 |
| Lord Hawke b Tremlin | 36 | – not out | 9 |
| W. Ringrose b Tremlin | 5 | | |
| A. Dolphin not out | 0 | | |
| B 1, l-b 1 | 2 | B 10, l-b 10, w 3, n-b 2 | 25 |
| | 98 | | 227 |

### Yorkshire Bowling

| | Overs | Mdns | Runs | Wkts |
|---|---|---|---|---|
| Hirst | 32 | 2 | 111 | — |
| Ringrose | 19 | 1 | 84 | 1 |
| Rhodes | 29.4 | 2 | 107 | 2 |
| Haigh | 23 | 8 | 53 | 1 |
| Myers | 15 | 5 | 38 | 2 |
| Smith | 20 | 1 | 107 | 3 |

### Essex Bowling

| | Overs | Mdns | Runs | Wkts | Overs | Mdns | Runs | Wkts |
|---|---|---|---|---|---|---|---|---|
| Buckenham | 12 | 2 | 47 | 2 | 32 | 15 | 49 | 2 |
| Tremlin | 6.4 | 3 | 16 | 3 | 21 | 10 | 24 | — |
| Douglas | 10 | 1 | 31 | 5 | 26 | 13 | 49 | 2 |
| Reeves | 2 | — | 2 | — | 36 | 24 | 37 | 2 |
| McGahey | | | | | 7 | 2 | 8 | — |
| Benham | | | | | 25 | 14 | 29 | 1 |
| Carpenter | | | | | 8 | 1 | 6 | — |

Umpires: A. Pike and J. Carlin.

# ESSEX IN 1911

*President* – Lord O'Hagan

*Treasurer* – Mr C. R. Higgins

*Secretary* – Mr O. R. Borradaile, Essex County Ground, Leyton

*Captain* – Mr J. W. H. T. Douglas

The Essex eleven played admirable cricket on many occasions, suggesting more than once that they might take a more prominent position in the championship. Figures are notoriously misleading, but a glance at the batting and bowling averages will at once show the reason why Essex did not do better. There was no lack of run-getting power on the side, six members of the side having averages of over 30. The weakness was in bowling, no one having an average of less than 23 runs a wicket. One must take into consideration the exceptionally fine summer, but making due allowance on that score, it must be confessed that the Essex attack was only moderate. It is rather a delicate point to touch upon, but one may be forgiven for questioning the wisdom of starting with two fast bowlers, as this always involved having to fall back later upon two men of medium pace. Better results might possibly have been obtained had the attack been more diversified. Without a left-hander at his disposal, Douglas was limited in his resources, but one cannot help thinking he would have done well at times to open the bowling either with himself or Buckenham and one of the medium-pace bowlers, as a greater contrast in style and pace would from the start have been presented to the batsmen.

## ESSEX IN 1912

The financial position being very unfavourable a special meeting was called in December at which it was unanimously decided to go on with the Club. At this meeting it was formally announced that Mr C. E. Green – the best friend to Essex cricket from the time the county club was formed – had resigned his position as chairman of the committee, and retired altogether from the management. In a letter to the committee, Mr Green, who resigned in August, said he was bitterly disappointed at the lack of support accorded to the club, that country cricket as carried on in these days did not appeal to him, and that, speaking frankly, he was tired of the whole thing. In giving up a task to which he had for years devoted much time and money, Mr Green behaved very generously, paying off the club's debts of £400, and so enabling the committee to start in 1913 with a clean sheet.

## ESSEX v HAMPSHIRE

### Played at Leyton, July 24, 25, 26, 1913

Everything else in this drawn game was dwarfed by a magnificent stand made by Abercrombie and Brown. Early on the Saturday morning Hampshire were apparently in a hopeless position, as with six men out in their second innings they were still 119 behind. At a quarter to twelve Brown joined Abercrombie, and it was not until four o'clock that the two men were parted, they having added 325 in three hours and a half. In this way they placed their side out of all danger. In the three days 1,333 runs were scored.

### Essex

| | | |
|---|---|---|
| Mr C. D. McIver st Stone b Remnant | 134 | – st Johnston b Mead ............ 44 |
| A. C. Russell c Brown b Newman | 102 | – c Brown b Mead ............... 35 |
| J. Freeman c Abercrombie b Kennedy | 54 | – not out ..................... 18 |
| Mr P. Perrin b Newman | 7 | |
| Mr F. L. Fane c Kennedy b Newman | 18 | |
| Rev. F. H. Gillingham c Bowell b Newman | 105 | |
| Mr J. W. H. T. Douglas c Stone b Brown | 18 | |
| Mr O. C. Bristowe c Johnston b Newman | 8 | |
| Mr G. B. Davies not out | 21 | – not out ..................... 0 |
| C. P. Buckenham b Kennedy | 13 | |
| W. Mead b Newman | 4 | |
| B 10, l-b 7, w 6 | 23 | B 4, w 1 ............... 5 |
| | **507** | **102** |

## Hampshire

| | | | |
|---|---|---|---|
| Mr A. C. Johnston b Buckenham | 6 | – b Buckenham | 6 |
| A. Bowell b Douglas | 12 | – c Russell b Douglas | 0 |
| Hon. L. H. Tennyson c Buckenham b Bristowe | 38 | – b Buckenham | 116 |
| C. P. Mead b Mead | 13 | – b Buckenham | 0 |
| Mr E. M. Sprot b Buckenham | 64 | – c Bristowe b Mead | 51 |
| Lieut. C. H. Abercrombie b Bristowe | 5 | – c Russell b Davies | 165 |
| J. Stone c McIver b Davies | 39 | – b Douglas | 15 |
| E. R. Remnant c Davies b Buckenham | 0 | – not out | 1 |
| G. Brown st McIver b Davies | 4 | – not out | 140 |
| J. Newman c Davies b Buckenham | 2 | | |
| A. Kennedy not out | 6 | | |
| B 1 | 1 | B 29, l-b 8, w 3 | 40 |
| | **190** | **(7 wkts dec.)** | **534** |

### Hampshire Bowling

| | Overs | Mdns | Runs | Wkts | Overs | Mdns | Runs | Wkts |
|---|---|---|---|---|---|---|---|---|
| Brown | 21 | 3 | 89 | 1 | | | | |
| Kennedy | 24 | 4 | 71 | 2 | 7 | 1 | 24 | — |
| Newman | 45.4 | 9 | 102 | 6 | 13 | 6 | 28 | — |
| Remnant | 30 | 3 | 78 | 1 | | | | |
| Abercombie | 3 | — | 10 | — | | | | |
| Johnston | 2 | — | 18 | — | | | | |
| Tennyson | 13 | — | 73 | — | | | | |
| Mead | 17 | 3 | 43 | — | 11 | 2 | 25 | 2 |
| Bowell | | | | | 5 | 1 | 10 | — |
| Sprot | | | | | 2 | — | 10 | — |

### Essex Bowling

| | Overs | Mdns | Runs | Wkts | Overs | Mdns | Runs | Wkts |
|---|---|---|---|---|---|---|---|---|
| Douglas | 7 | 1 | 25 | 1 | 16 | 1 | 81 | 2 |
| Buckenham | 14 | 1 | 64 | 4 | 33 | 2 | 97 | 3 |
| Mead | 10 | 2 | 41 | 1 | 26 | 5 | 101 | 1 |
| Bristowe | 8 | 1 | 32 | 2 | 15 | — | 92 | — |
| Davies | 6 | — | 27 | 2 | 23 | 2 | 110 | 1 |
| Perrin | | | | | 4 | 2 | 13 | — |

Umpires: F. G. Roberts and F. Parris.

## ESSEX v MIDDLESEX

### Played at Leyton, May 23, 25, 26, 1914

In one of the most remarkable matches of the season, Essex lost by an innings and 56 runs. Sent in by Douglas, Middlesex actually declared with one wicket down, and did not have to bat again. Soaked by an overnight storm the pitch seemed likely to become difficult, but the sun did not shine, and showers on Saturday and steady rain on the Sunday kept it slow and easy. Tarrant batted in wonderful style. Troubled before getting used to the pace of the turf he settled down to a bold forcing game. Making 140 out of 245 on the first day he was batting altogether five hours twenty minutes for his highest score in first-class cricket, his play being less free on the second morning than when he and Anson put on 235 in three hours and a quarter. J. W. Hearne, who helped to add 229 in the unfinished second partnership of two hours five minutes, had the chief share in winning the game. Taking fourteen wickets for 146 runs he enjoyed a wonderful triumph. His length and break unsettled all the Essex batsmen, and the match ended early on Tuesday afternoon.

## Middlesex

Hon. R. Anson c Fane b Douglas ........ 97
F. A. Tarrant not out .................250
J. W. Hearne not out .................106
             B 9, l-b 2.................... 11
                                        ———
                        (1 wkt dec.) 464

P. Clarke, E. Hendren, Mr F. T. Mann, Mr M. H. C. Doll, Mr A. R. Litteljohn, H. R. Murrell, J. T. Hearne and Mr C. U. Peat did not bat.

## Essex

| | |
|---|---|
| Mr C. D. McIver b Peat ...................... 9 | – st Murrell b J. W. Hearne ........ 23 |
| A. C. Russell c Doll b J. W. Hearne .............. 32 | – c J. T. Hearne b J. W. Hearne ..... 30 |
| J. Freeman b J. W. Hearne ................... 6 | – b J. W. Hearne ................ 4 |
| Mr P. Perrin b J. W. Hearne .................. 32 | – st Murrell b J. W. Hearne ........ 60 |
| Mr F. L. Fane c Murrell b J. W. Hearne .......... 18 | – c Litteljohn b Tarrant .......... 1 |
| Mr J. W. H. T. Douglas b J. W. Hearne ........... 25 | – b J. W. Hearne ............... 63 |
| H. Carpenter b J. W. Hearne ................. 1 | – c Murrell b J. W. Hearne ........ 1 |
| B. Tremlin st Murrell b Tarrant ............... 2 | – b J. W. Hearne ............... 15 |
| H. M. Hills not out ......................... 25 | – not out ..................... 6 |
| B. Strutton c Tarrant b J. W. Hearne ............. 6 | – b Tarrant ................... 11 |
| H. Mayes run out ......................... 2 | – c Litteljohn b Tarrant .......... 0 |
| B 5, l-b 9, w 1 ..................... 15 | B 6, l-b 11, w 2 .......... 19 |

                        173                              235

## Essex Bowling

|            | Overs | Mdns | Runs | Wkts |
|------------|-------|------|------|------|
| Douglas .......... | 12 | 1 | 36 | 1 |
| Tremlin .......... | 39 | 4 | 126 | — |
| Strutton .......... | 28 | 4 | 96 | — |
| Hills ............. | 24 | — | 102 | — |
| Mayes ........... | 14 | — | 69 | — |
| Carpenter ......... | 1 | — | 1 | — |
| Russell .......... | 5 | — | 23 | — |

## Middlesex Bowling

|            | Overs | Mdns | Runs | Wkts | Overs | Mdns | Runs | Wkts |
|------------|-------|------|------|------|-------|------|------|------|
| Peat .............. | 10 | 3 | 15 | 1 | 10 | — | 41 | — |
| Tarrant .......... | 34.2 | 7 | 89 | 1 | 25.5 | 5 | 61 | 3 |
| J. W. Hearne ...... | 25 | 7 | 54 | 7 | 24 | 5 | 92 | 7 |
| Litteljohn ......... | | | | | 3 | 1 | 5 | — |
| J. T. Hearne ....... | | | | | 11 | 4 | 17 | — |

Umpires: J. Blake and A. A. White.

# GLOUCESTERSHIRE

## GLOUCESTERSHIRE v SOMERSET

Played at Bristol, June 26, 27, 28, 1905

Thanks to the successful bowling of Dennett and an exceptional innings by Jessop, Gloucestershire won the return match with their neighbours in a single innings with 65 runs to spare. With the exception of Poyntz, who aided by some luck hit in spirited style, Somerset gave a deplorable display at their first attempt, most of the batsmen being unable to play Dennett, and by scoring 287 for four wickets on the first day Gloucestershire soon had the match in hand. Wrathall and Townsend by their capital batting placed the side in a good position and in the last forty minutes Jessop and Board put on 100 runs. Not out 70 on Monday Jessop next day increased his score to 234, making that number out of 346. He obtained his first hundred in eighty minutes and altogether was only batting for two hours and thirty-five minutes. Though hitting with tremendous vigour and taking many risks Jessop only gave two chances – at 31 and 155. The chief hits in his remarkable innings were forty 4s. In their second innings Somerset did much to retrieve their batting reputation, but they were unable to wipe off the arrears of 352. Martyn hit in determined fashion, his score including thirteen 4s. Woods was compelled to give up his innings owing to an attack of rheumatism.

### Somerset

| | | | |
|---|---|---|---|
| F. P. Hardy st Board b Dennett | 19 | – run out | 38 |
| L. C. Braund b Dennett | 1 | – c Townsend b Dennett | 23 |
| Sellick c Jessop b Dennett | 5 | – b Dennett | 23 |
| E. Robson c Board b Huggins | 1 | – c Godsell b Huggins | 42 |
| Mr H. Martyn b Huggins | 0 | – c Godsell b Dennett | 92 |
| Mr S. M. J. Woods b Dennett | 9 | – retired ill | 13 |
| Mr E. S. M. Poyntz c Jessop b Huggins | 89 | – c Board b Jessop | 42 |
| Mr M. A. S. Sturt c Board b Dennett | 6 | – c Board b Dennett | 0 |
| North c Brownlee b Jessop | 3 | – st Board b Dennett | 7 |
| Mr A. E. Newton lbw b Dennett | 24 | – c Townsend b Dennett | 0 |
| B. Cranfield not out | 6 | – not out | 2 |
| B 2, l-b 4 | 6 | B 1, l-b 3, w 1 | 5 |
| | **169** | | **287** |

### Gloucestershire

| | | | |
|---|---|---|---|
| Mr R. T. Godsell c Braund b Hardy | 21 | T. Langdon b Robson | 11 |
| H. Wrathall c Hardy b North | 55 | Mr L. D. Brownlee lbw b Braund | 18 |
| Mr C. L. Townsend c Cranfield b Braund | 69 | J. H. Huggins c Newton b Cranfield | 11 |
| Mr C. O. H. Sewell c Martyn b Robson | 20 | G. Dennett not out | 0 |
| Mr G. L. Jessop b Braund | 234 | B 15, l-b 3 | 18 |
| J. H. Board c Cranfield b Braund | 49 | | |
| Mr W. S. A. Brown b Sturt | 15 | | **521** |

### Gloucestershire Bowling

| | Overs | Mdns | Runs | Wkts | Overs | Mdns | Runs | Wkts |
|---|---|---|---|---|---|---|---|---|
| Dennett | 28 | 6 | 68 | 6 | 47.4 | 13 | 117 | 6 |
| Huggins | 24.5 | 7 | 70 | 3 | 41 | 17 | 99 | 1 |
| Jessop | 4 | — | 25 | 1 | 1 | — | 2 | 1 |
| Brownlee | 1 | 1 | — | — | | | | |
| Townsend | | | | | 9 | 4 | 24 | — |
| Brown | | | | | 16 | 3 | 40 | — |

## Somerset Bowling

|            | Overs | Mdns | Runs | Wkts |
|------------|-------|------|------|------|
| Hardy      | 3     | —    | 27   | 1    |
| Cranfield  | 13.4  | —    | 94   | 1    |
| Braund     | 31    | 5    | 183  | 4    |
| Robson     | 24    | 1    | 88   | 2    |
| Sturt      | 3     | —    | 15   | 1    |
| North      | 22    | 6    | 96   | 1    |

Umpires: V. A. Titchmarsh and S. Wade.

# GLOUCESTERSHIRE v ESSEX

### Played at Bristol, August 6, 7, 1906

This match furnished the second instance during the season of 1906 of a bowler taking all ten wickets in one innings of a first-class match. The feat was performed by Dennett who disposed of the ten Essex batsmen at a cost of only 40 runs, and followed this up in the second innings by obtaining five more wickets, his record coming out at fifteen wickets for 98 runs. He and Roberts bowled unchanged in the two Essex innings. Dennett's bowling triumph was followed up by some very skilful and judicious batting on the part of Jessop who – at the wickets an hour and a half – gave no chance until he had made 60. Before the first day's cricket came to an end Essex in their second innings had lost four batsmen for 63. Less than two hours' play on Tuesday sufficed to finish off the match, Gloucestershire gaining a brilliant victory by nine wickets. Dennett, it should be added, received splendid support in the field, Brownlee bringing off three brilliant catches in the first innings of Essex.

## Essex

| | | | |
|---|---|---|---|
| Mr F. L. Fane c Jessop b Dennett | 11 | – b Roberts | 2 |
| Mr J. W. H. T. Douglas b Dennett | 14 | – c Townsend b Dennett | 25 |
| Mr P. Perrin c Brownlee b Dennett | 22 | – st Board b Dennett | 1 |
| Mr C. McGahey c Brownlee b Dennett | 17 | – st Board b Dennett | 8 |
| Mr W. M. Turner st Board b Dennett | 0 | – c Goodwin b Dennett | 37 |
| Rev. F. H. Gillingham c Spry b Dennett | 4 | – c Thomas b Dennett | 20 |
| Maj. A. J. Turner c Thomas b Dennett | 3 | – lbw b Roberts | 9 |
| W. Reeves c Brownlee b Dennett | 4 | – b Roberts | 7 |
| C. P. Buckenham lbw b Dennett | 5 | – not out | 4 |
| E. Russell not out | 0 | – b Roberts | 4 |
| W. Mead c Goodwin b Dennett | 2 | – c Sewell b Roberts | 0 |
| L-b 2 | 2 | B 6, l-b 4 | 10 |
| | **84** | | **127** |

## Gloucestershire

| | | | |
|---|---|---|---|
| Mr C. O. H. Sewell st Russell b Mead | 21 | – b Douglas | 14 |
| Mr. E. Barnett b Reeves | 17 | – not out | 20 |
| Mr G. L. Jessop c and b Douglas | 75 | | |
| Mr M. Townsend c Fane b Mead | 23 | | |
| J. H. Board lbw b Douglas | 0 | | |
| Mr F. E. Thomas b Douglas | 4 | | |
| Mr L. D. Brownlee b Mead | 6 | – not out | 5 |
| Mr H. S. Goodwin c McGahey b Douglas | 6 | | |
| Mr F. B. Roberts b Reeves | 10 | | |
| E. Spry c Reeves b Douglas | 6 | | |
| G. Dennett not out | 0 | | |
| B 4, l-b 1 | 5 | | |
| | **173** | | **39** |

## Gloucestershire Bowling

|  | Overs | Mdns | Runs | Wkts | Overs | Mdns | Runs | Wkts |
|---|---|---|---|---|---|---|---|---|
| Dennett ......... | 19.4 | 7 | 40 | 10 | 31 | 12 | 48 | 5 |
| Roberts ......... | 19 | 8 | 42 | — | 30.2 | 7 | 69 | 5 |

## Essex Bowling

|  | Overs | Mdns | Runs | Wkts | Overs | Mdns | Runs | Wkts |
|---|---|---|---|---|---|---|---|---|
| Mead ........... | 19 | 3 | 72 | 3 | 4 | — | 12 | — |
| Douglas ......... | 14 | 3 | 50 | 5 | 3.5 | — | 27 | 1 |
| Reeves .......... | 10 | 1 | 46 | 2 |  |  |  |  |

Umpires: A. E. Clapp and F. W. Marlow.

## GLOUCESTERSHIRE v WORCESTERSHIRE

Played at Cheltenham, August 20, 21, 1906

Giving a splendid display of batting on the opening day when, in just under five hours, they hit up 498 for the loss of eight wickets, Gloucestershire followed this performance up on Tuesday by fielding superbly and, with Dennett bowling in great form, they gained an easy victory by an innings and 230 runs. For their batting triumph they were mainly indebted to Townsend and Sewell who for two hours hit away so brilliantly that they put on 252 runs, taking the score from 63 to 315. Townsend, who was assisting his county for the first time during the season, went in when one run had been obtained and was fifth out at 421. At the wickets for three hours and thirty-five minutes he was rather lucky with a few strokes but gave no absolute chance. The great feature of his play was the tremendous power of his off-driving. Sewell might have been out twice from awkward chances but otherwise batted at his best, and Thomas followed up several previous successes with another admirable innings. The ground remained in fine order next day but Dennett always had the Worcestershire batsmen in difficulties and, bowling unchanged, obtained fifteen wickets for less than 10 runs apiece – an exceptional achievement in the circumstances for a slow bowler. Gloucestershire's total was the second highest ever put together on the Cheltenham ground.

### Gloucestershire

| | |
|---|---|
| Mr E. Barnett b Wilson ................ 0 | Mr F. H. B. Champain c Bowley b Burrows   15 |
| H. Wrathall c Cuffe b Wilson ........... 22 | Mr F. B. Roberts c Burrows b Cuffe ...... 18 |
| Mr C. L. Townsend c Burns b Cuffe ......214 | Mr P. H. Ford not out ................. 18 |
| Mr C. O. H. Sewell b Wilson ...........107 | G. Dennett c Ainley b Burrows .......... 4 |
| Mr G. L. Jessop b Burrows ............. 1 | B 15, l-b 3, w 2, n-b 1 .......... 21 |
| Mr F. E. Thomas st Ainley b Arnold ...... 70 | |
| J. H. Board c Ainley b Burrows .......... 33 | 523 |

### Worcestershire

| | | | |
|---|---|---|---|
| F. Pearson c Barnett b Ford .................... 33 | – c Ford b Dennett ............... 1 |
| F. Bowley c Champain b Dennett ............. 13 | – st Board b Dennett ............ 6 |
| Mr W. B. Burns c Townsend b Ford ............ 0 | – b Dennett .................... 34 |
| E. Arnold not out ........................... 46 | – c Board b Dennett ............ 8 |
| Mr H. K. Foster c Wrathall b Dennett ........... 1 | – b Ford ...................... 20 |
| J. A. Cuffe lbw b Dennett ..................... 13 | – c Thomas b Dennett .......... 32 |
| F. Wheldon c and b Dennett .................. 4 | – st Board b Dennett ........... 1 |
| Mr G. L. Crowe c Thomas b Dennett ........... 4 | – b Roberts .................... 26 |
| G. A. Wilson c Barnett b Dennett ............. 0 | – run out ...................... 3 |
| R. Burrows c Champain b Dennett ............. 30 | – c Thomas b Dennett .......... 4 |
| J. Ainley c Board b Dennett ................... 2 | – not out ...................... 4 |
| B 1 ............................. 1 | B 4, l-b 1, w 2 ............ 7 |
| 147 | 146 |

## Worcestershire Bowling

|              | Overs | Mdns | Runs | Wkts |
| ------------ | ----- | ---- | ---- | ---- |
| Arnold       | 27    | 5    | 119  | 1    |
| Wilson       | 24    | 4    | 108  | 3    |
| Burrows      | 21.5  | 2    | 118  | 4    |
| Cuffe        | 15    | 4    | 56   | 2    |
| Pearson      | 16    | —    | 101  | —    |

## Gloucestershire Bowling

|          | Overs | Mdns | Runs | Wkts | Overs | Mdns | Runs | Wkts |
| -------- | ----- | ---- | ---- | ---- | ----- | ---- | ---- | ---- |
| Ford     | 26    | 7    | 58   | 2    | 8     | —    | 29   | 1    |
| Dennett  | 32.2  | 10   | 69   | 8    | 20.1  | 3    | 71   | 7    |
| Roberts  | 7     | 3    | 19   | —    | 13    | 1    | 39   | 1    |

Umpires: J. E. West and J. Carlin.

# GLOUCESTERSHIRE v NORTHAMPTONSHIRE

Played at Gloucester, June 10, 11, 12, 1907

In this game a fresh record was made by Dennett and Jessop in dismissing Northamptonshire for 12 runs. This is the smallest total for a first-class inter county match, the previous lowest being 13 by Nottinghamshire against Yorkshire at Trent Bridge, in 1901. Play on the first day was restricted to fifty minutes, Gloucestershire losing four wickets for 20 runs, and, despite some hitting by Jessop, being all out next day for 60. The first innings of Northamptonshire only lasted forty minutes, Dennett, who made the ball turn in a remarkable manner, being practically unplayable. Dennett accomplished the "hat trick," in dismissing Hawtin, Beasley and Buswell with successive balls, and should have had four wickets in as many balls, Wrathall dropping a catch offered by East. In Gloucestershire's second innings Jessop and Mackenzie were the only batsmen to overcome the difficulties of the wicket, but Northamptonshire were set 136 to get to win. At their second attempt the visitors again failed before Dennett, who in the course of the day took fifteen wickets for 21 runs. Northamptonshire finished up on the second day in practically a hopeless position, wanting 97 runs to win with only three wickets left, but rain came to their rescue. Not a ball could be bowled on the Wednesday, the game having to be abandoned as a draw.

## Gloucestershire

| | | | |
| --- | ---: | --- | ---: |
| H. Wrathall b Thompson | 4 | – b Thompson | 7 |
| Mr E. Barnett lbw b Thompson | 3 | – b East | 0 |
| J. H. Board b Thompson | 3 | – lbw b Thompson | 5 |
| Mr M. G. Salter c Buswell b East | 3 | – c and b East | 3 |
| Mr G. L. Jessop b East | 22 | – c Hawtin b East | 24 |
| Mr R. T. H. Mackenzie b East | 0 | – c King b East | 21 |
| T. Langdon b East | 4 | – lbw b Thompson | 4 |
| J. H. Huggins c Crosse b East | 8 | – c Buswell b East | 3 |
| E. Spry lbw b Thompson | 6 | – b East | 4 |
| Parker not out | 2 | – not out | 8 |
| G. Dennett c Pool b Thompson | 0 | – b East | 0 |
| B 2, l-b 3 | 5 | B 9 | 9 |
| | **60** | | **88** |

## Northamptonshire

| | | |
|---|---|---|
| Mr E. M. Crosse c Board b Dennett | 4 – c and b Dennett | 0 |
| M. Cox lbw b Dennett | 2 – c Barnett b Dennett | 12 |
| Mr C. J. T. Pool c Spry b Dennett | 4 – st Board b Dennett | 9 |
| W. A. Buswell st Board b Dennett | 1 – c Langdon b Dennett | 0 |
| Mr L. T. Driffield b Dennett | 0 | |
| G. J. Thompson b Dennett | 0 – not out | 5 |
| Mr R. W. R. Hawtin lbw b Dennett | 0 – lbw b Dennett | 8 |
| W. East st Board b Dennett | 0 – lbw b Dennett | 2 |
| Mr R. N. Beasley b Jessop | 1 – b Dennett | 0 |
| Mr S. King not out | 0 – not out | 1 |
| W. Wells c Parker b Jessop | 0 | |
| | B 2, l-b 1 | 3 |
| | 12 | 40 |

## Northamptonshire Bowling

| | Overs | Mdns | Runs | Wkts | Overs | Mdns | Runs | Wkts |
|---|---|---|---|---|---|---|---|---|
| Thompson | 16.5 | 7 | 29 | 5 | 15 | 2 | 43 | 3 |
| East | 16 | 5 | 26 | 5 | 14.2 | 4 | 36 | 7 |

## Gloucestershire Bowling

| | Overs | Mdns | Runs | Wkts | Overs | Mdns | Runs | Wkts |
|---|---|---|---|---|---|---|---|---|
| Dennett | 6 | 1 | 9 | 8 | 15 | 8 | 12 | 7 |
| Jessop | 5.3 | 4 | 3 | 2 | 10 | 3 | 20 | — |
| Parker | | | | | 5 | 2 | 5 | — |

Umpires: A. Millward and J. E. West.

## GLOUCESTERSHIRE v SOMERSET

### Played at Bristol, July 4, 5, 6, 1907

Some curious cricket was witnessed in this game. Owing to rain there was no play on Thursday and on the second day all that was done was the scoring of 59 by Gloucestershire for two wickets, Langdon by strong forcing play making 40 of the number. Owing to the pitch being unfit in consequence of more rain during the night an hour was lost before the game was resumed on Saturday and then Gloucestershire made a great effort to force a win, closing their innings with five wickets down. Somerset lost five wickets for 14, but the later batsmen made something of a stand, Newton and Bailey keeping together for half an hour. In their second innings Gloucestershire again declared, leaving Somerset with 115 to get to win in seventy-five minutes. Six wickets fell for 54 runs and as thirty-five minutes then remained for play Somerset were in grave danger of defeat. However, Bisgood and Deane batted with sound judgment at this critical juncture and after some excitement the game was left drawn, Somerset with two wickets left wanting 13 runs. Thus Jessop's bold policy only just missed being successful.

### Gloucestershire

| | | | | |
|---|---|---|---|---|
| H. Wrathall c Palairet b Lewis | 2 | – b Braund | 11 |
| T. Langdon b Robson | 68 | – b Lewis | 19 |
| J. H. Board b Braund | 8 | – run out | 5 |
| A. Winstone b Braund | 17 | | |
| Mr G. L. Jessop c Lewis b Braund | 5 | – b Braund | 4 |
| Mr F. M. Luce not out | 23 | – not out | 2 |
| Capt. C. E. B. Champain not out | 3 | | |
| B 9, l-b 4 | 13 | B 4, l-b 2 | 6 |

(5 wkts dec.) 139  (4 wkts dec.) 47

Mr E. Barnett, P. Mill, Parker and G. Dennett did not bat.

### Somerset

| | | | | |
|---|---|---|---|---|
| Mr L. C. H. Palairet st Board b Dennett | 4 | – c Mills b Dennett | 4 |
| L. C. Braund c Jessop b Dennett | 2 | – lbw b Dennett | 2 |
| Mr B. L. Bisgood b Parker | 1 | – c Wrathall b Dennett | 17 |
| A. E. Lewis c Board b Dennett | 0 | – b Dennett | 8 |
| Mr C. G. Deane st Board b Dennett | 0 | – not out | 24 |
| Mr G. W. Jupp c Jessop b Dennett | 7 | – b Jessop | 5 |
| Mr S. M. J. Woods b Mills | 18 | – c Langdon b Jessop | 29 |
| E. Robson b Mills | 13 | – b Jessop | 2 |
| Mr E. S. M. Poyntz st Board b Dennett | 4 | – st Board b Dennett | 0 |
| Mr A. E. Newton not out | 3 | | |
| A. E. Bailey c Wrathall b Jessop | 12 | | |
| B 4, l-b 3, w 1 | 8 | B 9, l-b 2 | 11 |
| | 72 | | 102 |

### Somerset Bowling

| | Overs | Mdns | Runs | Wkts | Overs | Mdns | Runs | Wkts |
|---|---|---|---|---|---|---|---|---|
| Lewis | 8 | 3 | 17 | 1 | 0.1 | — | — | 1 |
| Bailey | 4 | 1 | 19 | — | | | | |
| Braund | 20 | 5 | 57 | 3 | 4 | 1 | 14 | 2 |
| Robson | 16 | 5 | 32 | 1 | 3 | — | 27 | — |
| Jupp | 1 | — | 1 | — | | | | |

### Gloucestershire Bowling

| | Overs | Mdns | Runs | Wkts | Overs | Mdns | Runs | Wkts |
|---|---|---|---|---|---|---|---|---|
| Dennett | 16 | 6 | 37 | 6 | 16.5 | 4 | 34 | 5 |
| Parker | 8 | 2 | 15 | 1 | | | | |
| Mills | 6 | 1 | 8 | 2 | 5 | — | 20 | — |
| Jessop | 2 | — | 4 | 1 | 11 | 2 | 37 | 3 |

Umpires: A. A. White and C. E. Dench.

# GLOUCESTERSHIRE v MIDDLESEX

### Played at Bristol, July 30, 31, August 1, 1908

This was a remarkable struggle, the game being a tie on the first innings and Middlesex winning after an exciting tussle by 2 runs. Almost to the last it looked as though Gloucestershire would be successful as, set 120 to get to win, they approached within five of the number with three wickets in hand. Ford and Mills, however, left at 115 and 2 runs later Dennett, who made a plucky effort, was dismissed. Tarrant had an extraordinary share in the victory. On Thursday he played a great innings of 152, which included twenty-eight 4s, and in addition he took twelve wickets for 149 runs. Langdon and Jessop, both of whom played finely in Gloucestershire's first innings, put on 122 runs while together. Dennett bowled uncommonly well in both innings.

### Middlesex

| | | | |
|---|--:|---|--:|
| Mr P. F. Warner c Brownlee b Ford | 22 | – c Roberts b Dennett | 37 |
| F. A. Tarrant c Parker b Dennett | 152 | – b Parker | 11 |
| Mr L. J. Moon c Board b Dennett | 35 | – lbw b Parker | 2 |
| A. E. Trott c Board b Parker | 3 | – c Jessop b Dennett | 12 |
| Mr E. S. Litteljohn b Ford | 14 | – c Mills b Dennett | 0 |
| Mr W. P. Harrison jun. b Dennett | 23 | – b Parker | 19 |
| Mr C. C. Page b Parker | 0 | – c Brownlee b Dennett | 20 |
| Mr L. G. Colbeck b Dennett | 8 | – not out | 7 |
| Mr J. T. Dixon c Board b Dennett | 7 | – c Board b Dennett | 0 |
| D. Hendren c Board b Dennett | 4 | – c Roberts b Dennett | 0 |
| E. Mignon not out | 1 | – c and b Dennett | 6 |
| B 8, l-b 1 | 9 | B 1, l-b 2, n-b 2 | 5 |
| | **278** | | **119** |

### Gloucestershire

| | | | |
|---|--:|---|--:|
| J. H. Board c Harrison b Tarrant | 9 | – b Trott | 29 |
| T. Langdon c Moon b Tarrant | 95 | – c Colbeck b Trott | 15 |
| A. G. Dipper b Tarrant | 0 | – b Tarrant | 0 |
| A. Winstone b Tarrant | 31 | – b Tarrant | 12 |
| Mr L. D. Brownlee c Dixon b Trott | 10 | – c and b Trott | 0 |
| Mr G. L. Jessop run out | 72 | – c Tarrant b Trott | 34 |
| Mr F. B. Roberts c Dixon b Trott | 6 | – c Trott b Tarrant | 1 |
| Mr P. H. Ford b Tarrant | 21 | – b Trott | 3 |
| G. Dennett c and b Tarrant | 14 | – c Warner b Tarrant | 22 |
| P. Mills c Harrison b Tarrant | 0 | – b Tarrant | 0 |
| C. Parker not out | 8 | – not out | 1 |
| B 9, l-b 3 | 12 | | |
| | **278** | | **117** |

### Gloucestershire Bowling

| | Overs | Mdns | Runs | Wkts | Overs | Mdns | Runs | Wkts |
|---|--:|--:|--:|--:|--:|--:|--:|--:|
| Parker | 35 | 12 | 84 | 2 | 23 | 8 | 41 | 3 |
| Dennett | 39.1 | 18 | 59 | 6 | 31.3 | 14 | 61 | 7 |
| Ford | 17 | 5 | 39 | 2 | 6 | 4 | 6 | — |
| Brownlee | 1 | — | 8 | — | | | | |
| Mills | 4 | — | 38 | — | 2 | — | 6 | — |
| Roberts | 8 | — | 28 | — | | | | |
| Dipper | 3 | 1 | 13 | — | | | | |

### Middlesex Bowling

| | Overs | Mdns | Runs | Wkts | Overs | Mdns | Runs | Wkts |
|---|--:|--:|--:|--:|--:|--:|--:|--:|
| Tarrant | 35.1 | 8 | 93 | 7 | 27 | 8 | 56 | 5 |
| Mignon | 6 | 1 | 19 | — | | | | |
| Trott | 35 | 11 | 89 | 2 | 26 | 7 | 61 | 5 |
| Dixon | 5 | — | 22 | — | | | | |
| Hendren | 6 | — | 20 | — | | | | |
| Harrison jun. | 3 | — | 23 | — | | | | |

Umpires: R. G. Barlow and A. Millward.

## GLOUCESTERSHIRE v HAMPSHIRE

Played at Bristol, June 17, 18, 19, 1909

After being in some danger of losing, Hampshire drew the game in good style, staying in the whole of Saturday. The outstanding features of the match were the fine batting performances of Jessop and White. Jessop hit four 6s, one 5, and twenty-one 4s in his first innings, which occupied ninety-five minutes, while his second score, which included thirteen 4s, took him ninety-eight minutes. White was batting for an hour and fifty minutes on the first occasion, and on the third day he played a great game for his side, hitting twenty-two 4s.

### Gloucestershire

| | | | | |
|---|---|---|---|---|
| Mr C. Barnett b Evans | 13 | – b Mead | 6 |
| J. H. Board c Sprot b Evans | 71 | – c Mead b Llewellyn | 48 |
| A. G. Dipper c Sprot b Mead | 1 | – lbw b Evans | 32 |
| Mr P. Barnett b Evans | 5 | – b Llewellyn | 0 |
| Mr G. L. Jessop c and b Newman | 161 | – c Evans b Llewellyn | 129 |
| T. Langdon b Llewellyn | 0 | – c Llewellyn b Mead | 75 |
| Mr R. J. Hewlett c and b Evans | 20 | – c and b Mead | 13 |
| G. Dennett c Llewellyn b Evans | 0 | – b Mead | 0 |
| A. Winstone c and b Evans | 0 | – not out | 9 |
| P. Mills not out | 13 | – not out | 4 |
| C. Parker c Hill b Evans | 3 | | |
| B 1, l-b 2, w 1, n-b 4 | 8 | B 14, l-b 5, w 2, n-b 5 | 26 |
| | **295** | | **342** |

### Hampshire

| | | | | |
|---|---|---|---|---|
| P. Mead c Dennett b Parker | 8 | – st Board b Winstone | 43 |
| A. Bowell b Parker | 0 | – c Jessop b Parker | 70 |
| Capt. W. N. White c Board b Parker | 71 | – not out | 160 |
| C. B. Llewellyn c Board b Parker | 0 | – not out | 15 |
| A. Stone c Board b Parker | 10 | – c Board b Jessop | 20 |
| J. Newman b Parker | 18 | | |
| Mr E. M. Sprot c Board b Dennett | 19 | | |
| Mr W. H. B. Evans c Dennett b Mills | 16 | – b Parker | 17 |
| Mr A. J. L. Hill c Mills b Dennett | 1 | – b Parker | 9 |
| G. Brown not out | 11 | | |
| E. R. Remnant st Board b Dennett | 0 | | |
| B 2, l-b 2 | 4 | B 5, l-b 2, w 4, n-b 4 | 15 |
| | **158** | | **349** |

### Hampshire Bowling

| | Overs | Mdns | Runs | Wkts | Overs | Mdns | Runs | Wkts |
|---|---|---|---|---|---|---|---|---|
| Newman | 18 | 8 | 39 | 1 | 18 | 3 | 60 | — |
| Llewellyn | 23 | 3 | 120 | 1 | 20 | 6 | 61 | 3 |
| Evans | 22.3 | 3 | 59 | 7 | 19 | 6 | 40 | 1 |
| Mead | 13 | 4 | 41 | 1 | 10 | 2 | 38 | 4 |
| Brown | 4 | — | 28 | — | 8 | — | 46 | — |
| Hill | | | | | 8 | 1 | 37 | — |
| Bowell | | | | | 9 | — | 34 | — |

**Gloucestershire Bowling**

|  | Overs | Mdns | Runs | Wkts | Overs | Mdns | Runs | Wkts |
|---|---|---|---|---|---|---|---|---|
| Dennett .......... | 32.2 | 12 | 64 | 3 | 43 | 17 | 82 | — |
| Parker ........... | 31 | 10 | 74 | 6 | 32 | 6 | 137 | 3 |
| Mills ............. | 7 | 3 | 16 | 1 | 18 | 3 | 65 | — |
| Jessop ........... |  |  |  |  | 5 | — | 13 | 1 |
| Dipper ........... |  |  |  |  | 5 | 1 | 20 | — |
| Winstone ........ |  |  |  |  | 7 | 2 | 17 | 1 |
| Langdon ........ |  |  |  |  | 1 | 1 | — | — |

Umpires: J. Blake and J. Carlin.

## GLOUCESTERSHIRE v KENT

### Played at Cheltenham, August 11, 12, 1910

Gloucestershire were hopelessly outplayed in this game, Kent, after declaring, winning by an innings and 242 runs. Kent made their 607 runs on the first day in five hours. Humphreys and Knott put on 93 for the first wicket, Seymour helped the former to add 140 in seventy-five minutes, and Humphreys and Hutchings scored 93 in half an hour. Hooman and Mason scored 85 in forty minutes, and Mason and Huish obtained 134 in fifty-five minutes. Humphreys, who gave one chance – at 137 – hit a 6 and twenty-four 4s. Mason also gave a brilliant display, his score including a 6 and nineteen 4s. Having fielded all day on a splendid wicket, Gloucestershire were unfortunate in having to bat after rain during the night had to some extent affected the pitch. Sewell played with much skill on both occasions, but for the most part the batsmen found Carr too good for them.

### Kent

| | | |
|---|---|---|
| Mr F. H. Knott c Board b Parker ........ 33 | Mr J. R. Mason not out ................121 |
| E. Humphreys c Salter b Sewell ..........162 | F. H. Huish not out ................... 44 |
| James Seymour c Salter b Dennett ........ 90 | |
| Mr K. L. Hutchings c Salter b Brownlee ... 57 | B 17, l-b 5, w 3 ............... 25 |
| F. E. Woolley c F. B. Roberts b Sewell .... 29 | |
| Mr C. V. L. Hooman c Langdon b Parker .. 46 | (6 wkts dec.) 607 |

Mr D. W. Carr, C. Blythe and A. Fielder did not bat.

### Gloucestershire

| | |
|---|---|
| J. H. Board b Carr ........................... 36 | – lbw b Carr .................... 19 |
| T. Langdon c Woolley b Fielder ................. 0 | – c Mason b Fielder ............. 0 |
| Mr M. G. Salter b Fielder ...................... 0 | – c Huish b Carr ................ 27 |
| Mr C. O. H. Sewell c Hooman b Blythe .......... 42 | – b Carr ....................... 62 |
| Mr W. M. Brownlee st Huish b Carr ............. 16 | – b Carr ....................... 3 |
| Mr F. H. B. Champain c Hutchings b Blythe ....... 6 | – c Hooman b Blythe ........... 30 |
| Mr G. L. Jessop st Huish b Carr ................ 35 | – hit wkt b Carr ................ 0 |
| Mr F. B. Roberts b Carr ...................... 10 | – b Carr ....................... 33 |
| Mr A. W. Roberts b Carr ...................... 0 | – c Knott b Blythe .............. 0 |
| C. Parker not out ........................... 14 | – not out ...................... 8 |
| G. Dennett run out .......................... 2 | – st Huish b Blythe ............. 5 |
| B 6, n-b 1 ........................ 7 | B 6, l-b 1, n-b 3 .......... 10 |
| 168 | 197 |

## Gloucestershire Bowling

|               | Overs | Mdns | Runs | Wkts |
|---------------|-------|------|------|------|
| Brownlee ........ | 20    | 1    | 130  | 1    |
| Dennett ......... | 37    | 2    | 149  | 1    |
| A. W. Roberts ..... | 20    | 4    | 108  | —    |
| Parker .......... | 28    | 8    | 83   | 2    |
| F. B. Roberts ...... | 8     | —    | 43   | —    |
| Sewell .......... | 5     | —    | 35   | 2    |
| Langdon ........ | 5     | —    | 34   | —    |

## Kent Bowling

|             | Overs | Mdns | Runs | Wkts | Overs | Mdns | Runs | Wkts |
|-------------|-------|------|------|------|-------|------|------|------|
| Fielder ........... | 11.1  | 4    | 36   | 2    | 12    | 2    | 56   | 1    |
| Blythe ........... | 14    | 2    | 57   | 2    | 10    | —    | 48   | 3    |
| Carr ............. | 15    | 1    | 68   | 5    | 11    | —    | 42   | 6    |
| Mason ........... |       |      |      |      | 3     | —    | 10   | —    |
| Woolley ......... |       |      |      |      | 6     | —    | 31   | —    |

Umpires: T. Brown and H. Wood.

# GLOUCESTERSHIRE v SURREY

## Played at Cheltenham, August 15, 16, 17, 1910

Surrey gained the upper hand on the opening day on a rain-ruined pitch, and in the end won by four wickets. After a wretched first innings, Gloucestershire made a fine effort to recover themselves, but could never quite get on terms. The feature of the match was a superb display by Jessop. Taking half an hour to score his first 10 runs, Jessop reached his hundred in less than two hours. He hit nineteen 4s, he and Sewell putting on 144 together in eighty minutes. Surrey, being set 208 to get to win, had six men out for 125, but at this critical point Hobbs and Hitch hit off the remaining 83 in thirty-five minutes. A splendidly contested game was thus brought to a brilliant conclusion.

## Gloucestershire

| | | | | |
|---|---|---|---|---|
| J. H. Board run out .......................... | 1 | – b Hitch ..................... | 1 |
| Mr M. G. Salter c Hobbs b Platt ............... | 11 | – c Hayes b Smith ............... | 1 |
| Mr W. M. Brownlee b Platt .................... | 5 | – not out ...................... | 13 |
| Mr C. O. H. Sewell b Platt ................... | 2 | – c Smith b Hitch ............... | 46 |
| Mr G. L. Jessop c Smith b Hitch .............. | 32 | – c Abel b Smith ................ | 124 |
| T. Langdon lbw b Smith ...................... | 9 | – b Hitch ...................... | 0 |
| Mr F. B. Roberts c Hayes b Hitch ............. | 1 | – run out ..................... | 10 |
| Mr C. S. Barnett c Smith b Hitch ............. | 0 | – c Hayes b Hitch .............. | 59 |
| P. Mills c Hitch b Smith .................... | 1 | – b Bird ...................... | 54 |
| C. Parker run out .......................... | 9 | – b Hitch...................... | 9 |
| G. Dennett not out ......................... | 0 | – c Hayes b Hitch .............. | 0 |
| B 8, l-b 2 .............................. | 10 | B 15, l-b 3, w 4 .......... | 22 |
| | **81** | | **339** |

## Surrey

| | | | |
|---|---|---|---|
| H. S. Harrison c Board b Parker | 13 | – lbw b Dennett | 1 |
| Mr I. P. F. Campbell run out | 12 | – b Dennett | 11 |
| E. G. Hayes c Brownlee b Dennett | 23 | – c Salter b Dennett | 49 |
| Mr M. C. Bird c Barnett b Dennett | 17 | – b Brownlee | 9 |
| A. Ducat c Dennett b Brownlee | 51 | – b Dennett | 45 |
| J. B. Hobbs lbw b Dennett | 57 | – not out | 40 |
| W. J. Abel c Salter b Brownlee | 22 | – c Mills b Parker | 1 |
| W. Hitch c and b Dennett | 8 | – not out | 48 |
| W. C. Smith not out | 8 | | |
| G. Platt c Brownlee b Dennett | 0 | | |
| H. Strudwick lbw b Dennett | 0 | | |
| W 1, n-b 1 | 2 | B 1, l-b 1, n-b 2 | 4 |
| | **213** | | **208** |

### Surrey Bowling

| | Overs | Mdns | Runs | Wkts | Overs | Mdns | Runs | Wkts |
|---|---|---|---|---|---|---|---|---|
| Smith | 13.1 | 4 | 24 | 2 | 33 | 13 | 62 | 2 |
| Platt | 7 | — | 32 | 3 | 11 | — | 62 | — |
| Hitch | 6 | 1 | 15 | 3 | 34 | 4 | 105 | 6 |
| Abel | | | | | 11 | 2 | 39 | — |
| Hayes | | | | | 9 | 1 | 26 | — |
| Bird | | | | | 6 | 3 | 14 | 1 |
| Hobbs | | | | | 3 | — | 9 | — |

### Gloucestershire Bowling

| | Overs | Mdns | Runs | Wkts | Overs | Mdns | Runs | Wkts |
|---|---|---|---|---|---|---|---|---|
| Dennett | 21.4 | 6 | 69 | 6 | 34.5 | 11 | 94 | 4 |
| Brownlee | 12 | — | 56 | 2 | 18 | 8 | 49 | 1 |
| Parker | 8 | — | 38 | 1 | 15 | 2 | 48 | 1 |
| Mills | 8 | 1 | 37 | — | 2 | — | 13 | — |
| Jessop | 2 | 1 | 11 | — | | | | |

Umpires: W. Flowers and B. W. Mason.

## GLOUCESTERSHIRE v KENT

Played at Cheltenham, August 17, 18, 1911

In this game Gloucestershire were badly beaten, Kent winning by an innings and 94 runs. Winning the toss meant much as the wicket crumbled and Gloucestershire had to bat under difficulties. At the close of the first day's play Gloucestershire were at no great disadvantage, having disposed of Kent for 334 and scored 42 without loss. On the second day, however, their batting went all to pieces, Blythe, and in the second innings, Woolley, proving too much for them. In the Kent innings, the outstanding feature was a fine effort of 148 by Woolley. When 36 he was missed in the long field, but that was his only mistake. Driving with great power he obtained his runs in less than three hours, hitting a 6 and nineteen 4s. He and Prest made a brilliant stand for the sixth wicket, 112 runs being added in sixty-five minutes. Humphreys and Prest were seen to advantage, but Woolley's innings dwarfed everything. On the second day Gloucestershire had to face Blythe on a wicket that suited him admirably. He made the most of his opportunity, keeping a fine length and getting on a good deal of spin. The Gloucestershire batsmen were quite helpless before the Kent left-hander, and following-on 219 behind they did practically no better than before. Blythe bowled superbly, coming sharply off the pitch and being quite the master of the situation. In the match he obtained fourteen wickets for 84 runs. In the two days the gate receipts amounted £279.

### Kent

E. Humphreys c Dipper b Mills . . . . . . . . . . 48
H. T. W. Hardinge c Jessop b Dennett . . . . . 1
James Seymour c F. B. Roberts b Parker . . 12
F. E. Woolley b Mills . . . . . . . . . . . . . . . . . .148
Mr K. L. Hutchings lbw b Dennett . . . . . . . 36
J. C. Hubble run out . . . . . . . . . . . . . . . . . . 1
Mr H. E. W. Prest c Parker b Dennett . . . . . 51

F. H. Huish c Salter b Dennett . . . . . . . . . . 10
Mr D. W. Carr c Brown b Mills . . . . . . . . . 5
C. Blythe not out . . . . . . . . . . . . . . . . . . . . 3
A. Fielder run out . . . . . . . . . . . . . . . . . . . . 0
       B 15, w 4 . . . . . . . . . . . . . . . . . 19
                                       ———
                                       334

### Gloucestershire

J. H. Board c Seymour b Blythe . . . . . . . . . . . . . . . . 23 – c Hardinge b Blythe . . . . . . . . . . . . . 0
A. G. Dipper lbw b Blythe . . . . . . . . . . . . . . . . . . . . 22 – c Fielder b Blythe . . . . . . . . . . . . . . . 12
Mr C. S. Barnett lbw b Blythe . . . . . . . . . . . . . . . . . 0 – c Humphreys b Woolley . . . . . . . . 9
Mr M. G. Salter b Blythe . . . . . . . . . . . . . . . . . . . . . 16 – c and b Blythe . . . . . . . . . . . . . . . . . 22
Mr G. L. Jessop c Seymour b Blythe . . . . . . . . . . . . 21 – c Carr b Woolley . . . . . . . . . . . . . . . 15
Mr A. W. Roberts hit wkt b Carr . . . . . . . . . . . . . . . 2 – c Carr b Blythe . . . . . . . . . . . . . . . 7
Mr F. B. Roberts b Blythe . . . . . . . . . . . . . . . . . . . . 0 – c Prest b Blythe . . . . . . . . . . . . . . . 14
Mr W. S. A. Brown b Blythe . . . . . . . . . . . . . . . . . . 8 – c Huish b Blythe . . . . . . . . . . . . . . . 0
P. Mills c Seymour b Blythe . . . . . . . . . . . . . . . . . . 1 – c Huish b Woolley . . . . . . . . . . . . . 24
C. Parker not out . . . . . . . . . . . . . . . . . . . . . . . . . . . 5 – c Prest b Woolley . . . . . . . . . . . . . . 17
G. Dennett st Huish b Carr . . . . . . . . . . . . . . . . . . . 10 – not out . . . . . . . . . . . . . . . . . . . . . . 0
         B 6, l-b 1 . . . . . . . . . . . . . . . . . . . . . . . . 7               L-b 3, w 2 . . . . . . . . . . . . . 5

                                      ———                          ———
                                      115                          125

### Gloucestershire Bowling

|              | Overs | Mdns | Runs | Wkts |
| ------------ | ----- | ---- | ---- | ---- |
| Dennett . . . . . . . . . | 37.3 | 11 | 97 | 4 |
| Dipper . . . . . . . . . . | 19 | 3 | 67 | — |
| Parker . . . . . . . . . . | 14 | 1 | 67 | 1 |
| Mills . . . . . . . . . . . | 15 | — | 51 | 3 |
| F. B. Roberts . . . . . . | 3 | — | 33 | — |

### Kent Bowling

|            | Overs | Mdns | Runs | Wkts | Overs | Mdns | Runs | Wkts |
| ---------- | ----- | ---- | ---- | ---- | ----- | ---- | ---- | ---- |
| Fielder . . . . . . . . . . | 5 | — | 17 | — | | | | |
| Blythe . . . . . . . . . . | 18 | 5 | 45 | 8 | 19 | 7 | 39 | 6 |
| Carr . . . . . . . . . . . . | 15 | 3 | 46 | 2 | 10 | 2 | 40 | — |
| Woolley . . . . . . . . . | | | | | 11.2 | 3 | 40 | 4 |
| Humphreys . . . . . . . | | | | | 1 | — | 1 | — |

Umpires: W. A. J. West and A. E. Street.

## GLOUCESTERSHIRE v NORTHAMPTONSHIRE

Played at Cheltenham, August 21, 22, 23, 1911

In the third game of the Cheltenham Festival, Gloucestershire proved successful by 79 runs. As a matter of record it should be stated that owing to the railway strike the Northampton cricketers journeyed to Cheltenham by motor cars. The match was commenced on a wicket damaged by rain, and on the opening day batsmen fared badly. Thanks to some steady play by the tail end Northamptonshire secured a small lead on the first innings. On a pitch further affected by rain runs were hard to obtain on the second day, sixteen wickets going down for an aggregate of 149. Gloucestershire, who had gone in a second time overnight, were put out for 141, and in the last eighty minutes Northamptonshire, with 141 to get to win, lost six wickets for 48. With the pitch still difficult the visitors had no real chance on the third day, only 9 more runs being scored.

Dennett made the most of his opportunity, having the fine record of thirteen wickets for 101 runs. Thompson did nearly as well for Northamptonshire with twelve wickets for 111. It was a bowlers' match all through.

### Gloucestershire

| | | | | |
|---|---|---|---|---|
| J. H. Board c Buswell b Thompson | 1 | – c Smith b Thompson | 7 |
| A. G. Dipper c Vials b Thompson | 4 | – b Seymour | 16 |
| Mr M. G. Salter b Thompson | 6 | – b Thompson | 0 |
| T. Langdon c Vials b Smith | 6 | – c Haywood b Seymour | 0 |
| Mr G. L. Jessop b East | 35 | – lbw b Thompson | 3 |
| Mr F. B. Roberts b Thompson | 9 | – c Thompson b Smith | 16 |
| Mr A. W. Roberts b Smith | 35 | – b Thompson | 11 |
| Mr C. S. Barnett b Seymour | 20 | – not out | 18 |
| Mr W. S. A. Brown b Smith | 5 | – b Thompson | 23 |
| C. Parker c Smith b Thompson | 1 | – b Thompson | 5 |
| G. Dennett not out | 10 | – c Ryan b Thompson | 29 |
| L-b 2 | 2 | B 12, l-b 1 | 13 |
| | **134** | | **141** |

### Northamptonshire

| | | | | |
|---|---|---|---|---|
| Mr W. H. Denton c Brown b Dennett | 5 | – not out | 7 |
| John Seymour c Dipper b Dennett | 9 | – run out | 0 |
| R. Haywood b Parker | 30 | – b Parker | 13 |
| Mr S. G. Smith c Dipper b Dennett | 1 | – c Dipper b Dennett | 18 |
| C. J. Thompson b Dennett | 5 | – lbw b Dennett | 7 |
| Mr G. A. T. Vials c Jessop b Dennett | 8 | – c Jessop b Parker | 0 |
| Mr J. S. Denton c F. B. Roberts b Parker | 6 | – c and b Dennett | 3 |
| Mr J. H. Ryan st Board b Dennett | 1 | – c Jessop b Parker | 1 |
| W. East c Board b Dennett | 29 | – c Dipper b Dennett | 5 |
| F. Walden c Jessop b Dennett | 23 | – b Parker | 1 |
| W. A. Buswell not out | 16 | – c Board b Dennett | 0 |
| B 2, l-b 4 | 6 | L-b 2 | 2 |
| | **139** | | **57** |

### Northamptonshire Bowling

| | Overs | Mdns | Runs | Wkts | Overs | Mdns | Runs | Wkts |
|---|---|---|---|---|---|---|---|---|
| Thompson | 22 | 12 | 44 | 5 | 35.1 | 14 | 67 | 7 |
| Smith | 19.5 | 7 | 40 | 3 | 21 | 4 | 38 | 1 |
| East | 6 | — | 31 | 1 | | | | |
| Seymour | 4 | — | 17 | 1 | 14 | 9 | 23 | 2 |

### Gloucestershire Bowling

| | Overs | Mdns | Runs | Wkts | Overs | Mdns | Runs | Wkts |
|---|---|---|---|---|---|---|---|---|
| Dennett | 21 | 7 | 74 | 8 | 21.5 | 8 | 27 | 5 |
| Parker | 23 | 12 | 49 | 2 | 21 | 11 | 28 | 4 |
| Dipper | 5 | 1 | 7 | — | | | | |
| Jessop | 2 | 1 | 3 | — | | | | |

Umpires: W. A. J. West and A. E. Street.

## GLOUCESTERSHIRE v SOMERSET

### Played at Bristol, August 3, 4, 1914

In this match Gloucestershire gained their only victory of the season, beating Somerset by one wicket after a very exciting finish. All the interest centred in the closing stage of the game. Set to get 77 to win, Gloucestershire for a time fared disastrously, J. C. White bowling with great effect on a rain-damaged pitch. Four men were out for 10 and half the side for 22. Barnett and Dennett then put on 25, and with Barnett and Smith taking the total to 74 before the seventh wicket fell, Gloucestershire looked to be winning comfortably. However, Cranfield and Green were both run out through unnecessary anxiety to obtain the remaining 3 runs, and Parker, the last man, was in when Barnett, who played a fine game, made the winning hit.

### Somerset

| | | | |
|---|---|---|---|
| Mr A. D. E. Rippon b Jessop | 19 | – st Smith b Parker | 0 |
| Mr A. E. S. Rippon c Parker b Dennett | 15 | – b Dennett | 6 |
| Mr P. R. Johnson c Jessop b Dennett | 6 | – c Jessop b Dennett | 40 |
| Mr B. L. Bisgood c Langdon b Dennett | 0 | – lbw b Dennett | 8 |
| L. C. Braund not out | 28 | – c Dennett b Cranfield | 6 |
| Mr E. S. M. Poyntz c Roberts b Jessop | 2 | – c Smith b Dennett | 8 |
| E. Robson c Smith b Dennett | 4 | – run out | 0 |
| Mr P. P. Hope c Dipper b Dennett | 0 | – st Smith b Dennett | 0 |
| Mr J. C. White lbw b Dennett | 5 | – c Smith b Jessop | 19 |
| J. F. Bridges b Jessop | 0 | – not out | 0 |
| H. Chidgey b Jessop | 0 | – c Sewell b Parker | 13 |
| L-b 3 | 3 | B 2, l-b 2, n-b 1 | 5 |
| | **82** | | **105** |

### Gloucestershire

| | | | |
|---|---|---|---|
| T. Langdon run out | 7 | – c and b Robson | 12 |
| A. G. Dipper c Braund b White | 5 | – c and b White | 3 |
| Mr C. O. H. Sewell b White | 9 | – c and b White | 2 |
| Mr F. B. Roberts c Bridges b White | 20 | – c Bisgood b White | 0 |
| Mr G. L. Jessop st Chidgey b White | 25 | – st Chidgey b White | 4 |
| Mr C. S. Barnett c Bisgood b White | 1 | – not out | 32 |
| T. J. Smith b White | 10 | – b A. D. E. Rippon | 13 |
| L. Cranfield b White | 0 | – run out | 0 |
| Mr M. A. Green c Braund b White | 17 | – run out | 1 |
| C. Parker c Robson b White | 3 | – not out | 0 |
| G. Dennett not out | 4 | – b White | 5 |
| B 8, l-b 1, n-b 1 | 10 | B 4, l-b 1 | 5 |
| | **111** | | **77** |

### Gloucestershire Bowling

| | Overs | Mdns | Runs | Wkts | Overs | Mdns | Runs | Wkts |
|---|---|---|---|---|---|---|---|---|
| Dennett | 31 | 13 | 36 | 6 | 36 | 23 | 32 | 5 |
| Cranfield | 12 | 7 | 9 | — | 17 | 5 | 35 | 1 |
| Jessop | 19.5 | 5 | 34 | 4 | 7 | 4 | 7 | 1 |
| Parker | | | | | 12 | 5 | 26 | 2 |

### Somerset Bowling

| | Overs | Mdns | Runs | Wkts | Overs | Mdns | Runs | Wkts |
|---|---|---|---|---|---|---|---|---|
| White | 23.4 | 8 | 46 | 9 | 18.1 | 6 | 32 | 5 |
| Robson | 15 | 3 | 38 | — | 9 | 1 | 26 | 1 |
| A. D. E. Rippon | 8 | 4 | 17 | — | 9 | 2 | 14 | 1 |

Umpires: A. E. Street and H. Butt.

# HAMPSHIRE

## HAMPSHIRE v DERBYSHIRE

Played at Southampton, June 12, 13, 14, 1905

Hampshire gained their first, and as it proved, their only victory of the season by 188 runs. Despite an excellent display by Bowell, who played his highest innings for the county, Hampshire fared very moderately on the opening day, but after the first Derbyshire wicket fell in the morning at 149, Hesketh-Prichard caused a collapse, and it was his bowling on the Wednesday that had most to do with his side's success. His record for the match, thirteen wickets for 78, was extraordinary.

### Hampshire

| | | |
|---|---|---|
| Capt. J. G. Greig c Storer b Cadman | 13 – lbw b Curgenven | 11 |
| A. Bowell st Humphries b Bestwick | 101 – c Bestwick b Lawton | 51 |
| Mr E. M. Sprot b Bestwick | 35 – b Bestwick | 26 |
| Mr A. J. L. Hill c Humphries b Storer | 30 – b Warren | 0 |
| G. C. B. Llewellyn c Cadman b Morton | 34 – lbw b Bestwick | 34 |
| Mr W. H. B. Evans c Humphries b Bestwick | 6 – b Storer | 90 |
| Major W. C. Hedley b Bestwick | 0 – b Lawton | 7 |
| A. Stone b Bestwick | 10 – lbw b Bestwick | 4 |
| Mr H. W. Persse b Bestwick | 8 – c Morton b Cadman | 12 |
| Mr H. Hesketh-Prichard c Storer b Morton | 22 – lbw b Storer | 3 |
| H. Baldwin not out | 0 – not out | 5 |
| B 2, l-b 2 | 4        B 12, l-b 5, n-b 1 | 18 |
| | 263 | 261 |

### Derbyshire

| | | |
|---|---|---|
| Mr L. G. Wright c Greig b Llewellyn | 56 – lbw b Hesketh-Prichard | 1 |
| Mr C. A. Olivierre c sub. b Evans | 93 – c Hill b Hesketh-Prichard | 2 |
| Mr A. E. Lawton c Stone b Hesketh-Prichard | 41 – b Hesketh-Prichard | 3 |
| Mr G. Curgenven b Hesketh-Prichard | 19 – b Baldwin | 30 |
| Mr E. M. Ashcroft c and b Hesketh-Prichard | 3 – b Hesketh-Prichard | 10 |
| W. Storer c Persse b Baldwin | 31 – not out | 7 |
| A. R. Warren c Evans b Hesketh-Prichard | 4 – c Hill b Baldwin | 0 |
| S. Cadman b Hedley | 4 – c Stone b Hesketh-Prichard | 0 |
| A. Morton c Llewellyn b Baldwin | 16 – b Hesketh-Prichard | 2 |
| W. Bestwick c Llewellyn b Hesketh-Prichard | 1 – lbw b Hesketh-Prichard | 0 |
| J. Humphries not out | 4 – lbw Hesketh-Prichard | 1 |
| B 4, l-b 1, n-b 1 | 6        L-b 1, w 1 | 2 |
| | 278 | 58 |

### Derbyshire Bowling

| | Overs | Mdns | Runs | Wkts | Overs | Mdns | Runs | Wkts |
|---|---|---|---|---|---|---|---|---|
| Cadman | 16 | 5 | 33 | 1 | 22 | 13 | 26 | 1 |
| Bestwick | 26 | 5 | 74 | 6 | 32 | 11 | 70 | 3 |
| Warren | 11 | — | 48 | — | 11 | 2 | 34 | 1 |
| Storer | 10 | 1 | 31 | 1 | 10.1 | 1 | 27 | 2 |
| Ashcroft | 7 | 1 | 36 | — | | | | |
| Morton | 10.2 | 1 | 37 | 2 | 5 | 2 | 9 | — |
| Curgenven | | | | | 14 | 6 | 34 | 1 |
| Lawton | | | | | 15 | 5 | 43 | 2 |

## Hampshire Bowling

| | Overs | Mdns | Runs | Wkts | Overs | Mdns | Runs | Wkts |
|---|---|---|---|---|---|---|---|---|
| Persse .......... | 3 | — | 18 | — | 4 | 1 | 6 | — |
| Baldwin ......... | 14 | 2 | 50 | 2 | 7 | 2 | 5 | 2 |
| Evans ........... | 19 | 1 | 106 | 1 | 6 | 4 | 13 | — |
| Hesketh-Prichard ... | 15.2 | 3 | 46 | 5 | 17.5 | 6 | 32 | 8 |
| Hedley .......... | 8 | 1 | 23 | 1 | | | | |
| Llewellyn ........ | 5 | — | 29 | 1 | | | | |

Umpires: J. Carlin and A. Shaw.

## HAMPSHIRE v KENT

### Played at Bournemouth, August 30, 31, September 1, 1906

Special interest attached to this match, not from any expectation that Hampshire would beat Kent, but from the fact that Kent had only to escape defeat to be sure of the championship. Some fine bowling by Blythe and Fielder practically determined the result in the first two hours, Hampshire, with the ground in excellent condition, losing eight wickets for 75. By the drawing of stumps Kent were well on the road to victory, Hutchings joining Burnup with two men out for 109 and helping that batsman to put on 189 in ninety-five minutes. Hutchings, hitting the bowling to all parts of the field, brought his score to 100 in sixty-five minutes. Leading by 139 with seven wickets in hand on the first evening, the Kent men next day batted with their customary brilliancy, their total of 610 being scored in six hours. Burnup, after batting in delightful style for nearly five hours, was out to his first really faulty stroke. Hampshire played up pluckily at their second attempt, Johnston doing very well and Llewellyn's vigorous cricket being almost beyond reproach, but Kent won by an innings and 37 runs.

### Hampshire

| | | | |
|---|---|---|---|
| A. Bowell c Seymour b Fielder ................. | 5 | – c Hutchings b Blythe ............. | 24 |
| Mr A. C. Johnston lbw b Blythe ................ | 15 | – b Blythe ..................... | 75 |
| Capt. E. I. M. Barrett b Blythe ................ | 1 | – st Huish b Blythe ............... | 8 |
| P. Mead b Fielder .......................... | 3 | – b Blythe ..................... | 4 |
| Mr A. J. L. Hill b Blythe .................... | 23 | – c Seymour b Humphreys ......... | 14 |
| G. C. B. Llewellyn c Humphreys b Fielder ........ | 18 | – not out ......................... | 158 |
| Capt. J. G. Greig c Burnup b Blythe ............. | 5 | – c Huish b Mason .............. | 29 |
| Mr E. M. Sprot b Blythe .................... | 0 | – b Mason ..................... | 26 |
| T. Langford c Hutchings b Blythe .............. | 30 | – lbw b Blythe .................. | 38 |
| J. R. Badcock c Huish b Mason ............... | 48 | – b Blythe ..................... | 1 |
| Mr F. J. Wyatt not out ...................... | 11 | – run out ...................... | 0 |
| L-b 1, w 2, n-b 1 ................. | 4 | B 14, l-b 7, w 2, n-b 10 ..... | 33 |
| | **163** | | **410** |

### Kent

| | | | |
|---|---|---|---|
| Mr C. J. Burnup c Bowell b Wyatt ........ | 179 | Mr C. H. B. Marsham b Hill ........... | 35 |
| F. E. Woolley c Johnston b Badcock ...... | 22 | F. H. Huish c sub. b Badcock ........... | 11 |
| Jas. Seymour c Bowell b Llewellyn ....... | 21 | C. Blythe c sub. b Hill ................ | 15 |
| Mr K. L. Hutchings c Bowell b Mead ..... | 124 | A. Fielder not out .................... | 3 |
| Mr J. R. Mason c Wyatt b Badcock ...... | 73 | B7, l-b 6, w 3, n-b 4 ........... | 20 |
| E. Humphreys b Wyatt ............... | 50 | | |
| Mr R. N. R. Blaker b Hill ............. | 57 | | **610** |

## Kent Bowling

| | Overs | Mdns | Runs | Wkts | Overs | Mdns | Runs | Wkts |
|---|---|---|---|---|---|---|---|---|
| Fielder ........... | 17 | 1 | 65 | 3 | 30 | 5 | 111 | — |
| Blythe ........... | 17 | 5 | 67 | 6 | 33 | 6 | 123 | 6 |
| Mason ........... | 5 | 1 | 19 | 1 | 15 | 4 | 48 | 2 |
| Humphreys ....... | 3 | — | 8 | — | 13 | 4 | 41 | 1 |
| Woolley .......... | | | | | 5 | 1 | 15 | — |
| Hutchings ........ | | | | | 5 | — | 30 | — |
| Burnup........... | | | | | 2 | — | 3 | — |
| Seymour ......... | | | | | 1 | — | 6 | — |

## Hampshire Bowling

| | Overs | Mdns | Runs | Wkts |
|---|---|---|---|---|
| Badcock .......... | 24 | 1 | 143 | 3 |
| Langford ......... | 19 | 4 | 75 | — |
| Wyatt............. | 28 | 3 | 100 | 2 |
| Llewellyn ......... | 24 | 3 | 119 | 1 |
| Greig ............ | 9 | 1 | 36 | — |
| Hill.............. | 21.2 | 4 | 81 | 3 |
| Mead ............ | 6 | — | 36 | 1 |

Umpires: A. J. Atfield and A. E. Clapp.

# HAMPSHIRE v NORTHAMPTONSHIRE

## Played at Southampton, July 9, 10, 11, 1908

In this match Hampshire created a precedent, and accomplished a unique performance, declaring their first innings when in a minority of 24 runs and winning the match by nine wickets. Rain cut short the first day and prevented anything being done on Friday, so that with the pitch dead, but not difficult in the absence of sunshine, a draw seemed probable. Hampshire had scored only 25 for one wicket and could not make runs fast, but at lunch time Sprot applied the closure. The early trial of Mead in place of Badcock was attended with the happiest results, the left hander carrying all before him, and the visitors being dismissed in an hour and twenty minutes. Hampshire were then left with two hours and a quarter in which to get 85. Johnston was out at three but Sprot hit two 6s and eight 4s, the runs being obtained without further loss in less than an hour.

## Northamptonshire

| | | | |
|---|---|---|---|
| Mr G. A. T. Vials st Stone b Llewellyn .......... | 1 | – c Mead b Badcock ............. | 2 |
| Mr W. H. Kingston c Stone b Wyatt ............. | 27 | – c and b Mead ................ | 18 |
| Mr S. King c Mead b Remnant ................ | 23 | – c Stone b Mead .............. | 0 |
| G. J. Thompson c Sprot b Remnant............. | 0 | – c Stone b Wyatt ............. | 18 |
| M. Cox b Wyatt ............................ | 2 | – st Stone b Wyatt ............. | 0 |
| Mr C. Thorpe c Remnant b Llewellyn ........... | 38 | – c Sprot b Mead .............. | 0 |
| W. Wells run out .......................... | 1 | – c Bowell b Mead ............. | 0 |
| Mr T. E. Manning lbw b Remnant ............... | 6 | – lbw b Mead ................. | 0 |
| W. A. Buswell c Jesson b Badcock............. | 13 | – c Sprot b Mead .............. | 4 |
| Mr L. T. Driffield c Sprot b Mead ............. | 51 | – not out .................. | 14 |
| D. Hardy not out .......................... | 23 | – c Sprot b Mead .............. | 0 |
| B 5, l-b 10, w 3 .................... | 18 | b 4 | 4 |
| | **203** | | **60** |

### Hampshire

| | | | |
|---|---:|---|---:|
| Mr A. C. Johnston b Driffield | 31 | – b Thompson | 1 |
| A. Bowell c Manning b Wells | 12 | – not out | 18 |
| Mr E. M. Sprot c Manning b Thompson | 30 | – not out | 62 |
| C. B. Llewellyn c King b Wells | 13 | | |
| Mr A. J. L. Hill c and b Wells | 21 | | |
| P. Mead not out | 38 | | |
| A. Stone c Thompson b Wells | 6 | | |
| E. R. Remnant b Wells | 0 | | |
| J. R. Badcock st Buswell b Thompson | 20 | | |
| Mr R. W. Jesson b Thompson | 0 | | |
| Mr P. J. Wyatt not out | 3 | | |
| B 1, l-b 1, n-b 3 | 5 | L-b 4, n-b 1 | 5 |
| (9 wkts dec.) | 179 | | 86 |

### Hampshire Bowling

| | Overs | Mdns | Runs | Wkts | Overs | Mdns | Runs | Wkts |
|---|---|---|---|---|---|---|---|---|
| Badcock | 11 | 2 | 27 | 1 | 2 | — | 9 | 1 |
| Llewellyn | 20 | 5 | 46 | 2 | | | | |
| Wyatt | 23 | 6 | 50 | 2 | 12 | 4 | 29 | 2 |
| Remnant | 17 | 5 | 45 | 3 | | | | |
| Jesson | 2 | — | 11 | — | | | | |
| Mead | 2.4 | 1 | 3 | 1 | 10.4 | 4 | 18 | 7 |
| Hill | 2 | — | 3 | — | | | | |

### Northamptonshire Bowling

| | Overs | Mdns | Runs | Wkts | Overs | Mdns | Runs | Wkts |
|---|---|---|---|---|---|---|---|---|
| Thompson | 26 | 7 | 76 | 3 | 9 | 2 | 30 | 1 |
| Wells | 15 | 4 | 56 | 5 | 5 | — | 27 | — |
| Driffield | 11 | 2 | 37 | 1 | 3.3 | — | 24 | — |
| Cox | 1 | — | 5 | — | | | | |

Umpires: F. G. Roberts and J. Moss.

## HAMPSHIRE v SOMERSET

### Played at Southampton, August 10, 11, 12, 1908

Winning by seven wickets Somerset gained a sensational victory. Hampshire scored 425 by consistent batting but in the absence of Sprot did not make their visitors follow on, the difference amounting to 163. The pitch wore badly and the side having last innings seemed to have a poor prospect but, when Hampshire were 243 on, Greswell bowled with such deadly effect as to take seven wickets for 19 runs. Thus on the last day Somerset had a less severe task than had appeared probable. To get 292, however, looked far beyond their powers, and Johnston, Bisgood, and Lewis were out for 93. Then, after mastering the bowling, Braund and Woods hit superbly, and got 199 runs in two hours and a half. When forcing the game each gave a chance, but the performance was in every way astonishing. Both hit thirteen 4s. Woods had not scored a hundred since 1905.

## Hampshire

| | | |
|---|---|---|
| Mr A. C. Johnston b Robson | 40 | – c Chidgey b Lewis ............... 5 |
| A. Bowell c Johnston b Braund | 65 | – c Chidgey b Lewis ............. 32 |
| C. B. Llewellyn b Greswell | 17 | – b Greswell .................... 13 |
| P. Mead c V. T. Hill b Braund | 41 | – b Greswell .................... 23 |
| Mr A. J. L. Hill c Lewis b V. T. Hill | 80 | – b Lewis ....................... 4 |
| Mr A. J. Evans b Robson | 48 | – lbw b Greswell ................ 18 |
| Mr G. N. Bignell c Whittle b Robson | 44 | – b Greswell .................... 0 |
| A. Stone c Chidgey b Robson | 12 | – c Bisgood b Greswell ......... 12 |
| E. R. Remnant b Greswell | 16 | – not out ....................... 7 |
| J. Newman not out | 34 | – c and b Greswell .............. 0 |
| J. R. Badcock c Braund b Lewis | 2 | – b Greswell .................... 8 |
| B 17, l-b 8, n-b 1 | 26 | B 4, w 1, n-b 1 ......... 6 |
| | **425** | **128** |

## Somerset

| | | |
|---|---|---|
| Mr P. R. Johnston c Mead b Newman | 117 | – b Newman .................... 19 |
| A. E. Lewis c Stone b Badcock | 16 | – c Mead b Badcock ............. 3 |
| A. E. Whittle st Stone b Llewellyn | 2 | |
| Mr B. L. Bisgood c Stone b Llewellyn | 17 | – b Mead ....................... 19 |
| L. C. Braund c Evans b Llewellyn | 29 | – not out ......................124 |
| Mr V. T. Hill c Bowell b Newman | 41 | |
| E. Robson b Llewellyn | 0 | |
| Mr S. M. J. Woods c Johnston b Badcock | 18 | – not out ......................105 |
| Mr M. M. Munden c Mead b Badcock | 9 | |
| H. Chidgey b Newman | 1 | |
| Mr W. T. Greswell not out | 0 | |
| B 4, w 4, n-b 4 | 12 | B 11, l-b 6, n-b 4 ......... 22 |
| | **262** | **292** |

### Somerset Bowling

| | Overs | Mdns | Runs | Wkts | Overs | Mdns | Runs | Wkts |
|---|---|---|---|---|---|---|---|---|
| Greswell ......... | 30 | 6 | 89 | 2 | 15.4 | 3 | 42 | 7 |
| Lewis ........... | 35 | 11 | 103 | 1 | 15 | 2 | 61 | 3 |
| Robson ......... | 31 | 7 | 107 | 4 | 4 | 1 | 19 | — |
| V. T. Hill ........ | 7 | 1 | 44 | 1 | | | | |
| Braund .......... | 21 | 5 | 56 | 2 | | | | |

### Hampshire Bowling

| | Overs | Mdns | Runs· | Wkts | Overs | Mdns | Runs | Wkts |
|---|---|---|---|---|---|---|---|---|
| Badcock ......... | 16 | 1 | 79 | 3 | 18.2 | 3 | 93 | 1 |
| Mead ........... | 16 | 3 | 56 | — | 17 | 5 | 40 | 1 |
| Llewellyn ........ | 10 | 1 | 50 | 4 | 11 | 1 | 41 | — |
| Newman ......... | 13.1 | 4 | 30 | 3 | 25 | 6 | 54 | 1 |
| Evans ........... | 3 | — | 18 | — | 3 | 1 | 10 | — |
| Bignell .......... | 2 | — | 10 | — | | | | |
| A. J. L. Hill ....... | 1 | — | 7 | — | 3 | 1 | 6 | — |
| Remnant ........ | | | | | 7 | — | 26 | — |

Umpires: W. A. J. West and F. Parris.

## HAMPSHIRE v KENT

### Played at Southampton, June 5, 6, 7, 1911

Two records were established in the match with Kent at Southampton, the aggregate – 1446 – exceeding that in any previous county engagement, and Hampshire in scoring 463 for eight wickets surpassing Lancashire's 404 for five wickets, made against them a year before. In such a remarkable match many startling things were done, notably Hardinge's two hundreds and the way Hampshire saved the game. Preferring not to enforce the follow-on Kent, by obtaining 359 in three hours and a quarter, were able to put Hampshire in before five o'clock. Day was batting only fifty-five minutes for 100. Fry mastered the bowling, he and Bowell putting on 129. The sensation came when the eight wicket fell with nearly ninety minutes left, Remnant and Newman adding 108 runs and playing out time.

## Kent

| | | |
|---|---|---|
| E. Humphreys c Fry b Newman | 64 – c Newman b Brown | 5 |
| H. T. W. Hardinge c Brown b Newman | 175 – c Remnant b Bowell | 109 |
| James Seymour c Fry b Brown | 0 – lbw b Newman | 12 |
| Mr K. L. Hutchings c Mead b Brown | 6 – c White b Remnant | 51 |
| F. E. Woolley c Kennedy b Remnant | 77 – c Fry b Mead | 65 |
| Mr A. P. Day lbw b Remnant | 5 – not out | 100 |
| Mr C. E. Hatfield c and b Remnant | 32 – not out | 5 |
| F. H. Huish b Bowell | 2 | |
| W. J. Fairservice not out | 22 | |
| C. Blythe b Newman | 5 | |
| A. Fielder c Stone b Newman | 7 | |
| B 14, l-b 1, w 5, n-b 1 | 21 | B 8, l-b 2, w 2 | 12 |

**416**      **(5 wkts dec.) 359**

## Hampshire

| | | |
|---|---|---|
| Mr C. B. Fry c Hatfield b Blythe | 9 – c Hatfield b Woolley | 104 |
| C. P. Mead st Huish b Blythe | 15 – b Fielder | 73 |
| A. Stone b Fielder | 12 – c Hutchings b Fielder | 12 |
| A. Bowell b Fairservice | 62 – lbw b Day | 61 |
| G. Brown c Huish b Fielder | 0 – b Woolley | 4 |
| Capt. W. N. White c Huish b Fielder | 0 – b Blythe | 17 |
| E. R. Remnant st Huish b Woolley | 8 – not out | 115 |
| Mr E. M. Sprot b Fairservice | 68 – c Fielder b Woolley | 5 |
| A. Kennedy run out | 23 – c Humphreys b Fielder | 3 |
| J. Newman c Seymour b Woolley | 0 – not out | 40 |
| V. Luckin not out | 0 | |
| B 8, l-b 1, n-b 2 | 11 | B 13, l-b 5, w 4, n-b 7 | 29 |

**208**      **463**

### Hampshire Bowling

| | Overs | Mdns | Runs | Wkts | Overs | Mdns | Runs | Wkts |
|---|---|---|---|---|---|---|---|---|
| Brown | 15 | 3 | 79 | 2 | 17 | — | 92 | 1 |
| Bowell | 24 | 6 | 76 | 1 | 16 | — | 89 | 1 |
| Newman | 25.5 | 3 | 97 | 4 | 17 | 1 | 71 | 1 |
| Mead | 7 | — | 20 | — | 5 | 1 | 21 | 1 |
| Luckin | 9 | — | 43 | — | 1 | — | 13 | — |
| Kennedy | 3 | — | 18 | — | 2.2 | — | 26 | — |
| Remnant | 17 | 1 | 62 | 3 | 6 | 1 | 35 | 1 |

### Kent Bowling

| | Overs | Mdns | Runs | Wkts | Overs | Mdns | Runs | Wkts |
|---|---|---|---|---|---|---|---|---|
| Fielder | 21 | 3 | 81 | 3 | 32 | 4 | 116 | 3 |
| Blythe | 24 | 7 | 54 | 2 | 42 | 14 | 117 | 1 |
| Woolley | 7 | 2 | 30 | 2 | 25 | 7 | 74 | 3 |
| Fairservice | 10 | 2 | 32 | 2 | 25 | 4 | 68 | — |
| Day | | | | | 13 | 3 | 43 | 1 |
| Humphreys | | | | | 2 | 1 | 4 | — |
| Hutchings | | | | | 3 | 1 | 12 | — |

Umpires: W. Vining and T. Brown.

## HAMPSHIRE v GLOUCESTERSHIRE

Played at Southampton, August 10, 11, 12, 1911

In another match at Southampton, drawn through high scoring, some brilliant batting was seen, Jessop making two hundreds in a game for the fourth time in his career, and Fry playing his third three-figure innings of the week. Both men played in characteristic style. Jessop scored his 153 out of 221 in an hour and fifty minutes, hitting two 6s and twenty-four 4s. He took only an hour and forty minutes over his 123, which included twenty-two 4s. Dipper also batted very well, his sound play being of great value in helping the visitors to avoid defeat. Fry showed such consummate skill that he gave no chance until 220, and, in putting together his highest score in important cricket, he was at the wicket five hours and a quarter. Powerful driving, clever placing to leg, and accurate cutting marked his innings, which included one 5, and thirty-four 4s. The famous batsman exercised considerable caution. Brown obtained 126 in three hours out of 246, the batting during this partnership being perfect.

### Gloucestershire

| | | | |
|---|---:|---|---:|
| J. H. Board run out | 37 | – c Bowell b McDonell | 32 |
| A. G. Dipper lbw b Brown | 8 | – b Mead | 119 |
| Mr A. W. Roberts c Stone b Brown | 2 | – c Forster b Newman | 51 |
| Mr P. H. Bell lbw b McDonell | 10 | | |
| Mr G. L. Jessop c Sprot b McDonell | 153 | – not out | 123 |
| Mr F. B. Roberts b Newman | 17 | – not out | 21 |
| T. Langdon c McDonell b Newman | 21 | – c Mead b McDonell | 22 |
| Mr W. S. A. Brown run out | 21 | – c McDonell b Brown | 16 |
| Mr W. M. Brownlee c and b McDonell | 0 | | |
| G. Dennett c McDonell b Newman | 0 | | |
| C. Parker not out | 19 | | |
| B 12, l-b 7, w 10 | 29 | B 8, l-b 7, w 2, n-b 2 | 19 |
| | **317** | | **403** |

### Hampshire

| | | | |
|---|---:|---|---:|
| C. P. Mead lbw b Dennett | 34 | Mr H. C. McDonell c Parker | |
| A. Bowell b Dipper | 33 | b F. B. Roberts | 68 |
| A. Stone b Dipper | 16 | J. Moore not out | 25 |
| Mr C. B. Fry not out | 258 | L-b 3, n-b 3 | 6 |
| G. Brown c Dipper b Parker | 126 | | |
| Mr E. M. Sprot b F. B. Roberts | 28 | (6 wkts dec.) | **594** |

J. Newman, Mr W. Moorcroft and Col.-Sergt H. Forster did not bat.

### Hampshire Bowling

| | Overs | Mdns | Runs | Wkts | Overs | Mdns | Runs | Wkts |
|---|---|---|---|---|---|---|---|---|
| Brown | 14 | 2 | 67 | 2 | 16 | 3 | 58 | 1 |
| Newman | 20 | — | 79 | 3 | 21 | 5 | 72 | 1 |
| McDonell | 17.5 | 1 | 113 | 3 | 31 | 4 | 110 | 2 |
| Moorcroft | 6 | — | 17 | — | 13 | 1 | 51 | — |
| Bowell | 1 | — | 3 | — | 1 | — | 6 | — |
| Forster | 3 | 1 | 9 | — | 9 | 3 | 18 | — |
| Mead | | | | | 8 | 4 | 32 | 1 |
| Moore | | | | | 6 | — | 37 | — |

**Gloucestershire Bowling**

|               | Overs | Mdns | Runs | Wkts |
|---------------|-------|------|------|------|
| Brownlee ........ | 9  | 1 | 32  | — |
| Parker .......... | 32 | 4 | 107 | 1 |
| Dipper .......... | 33 | 6 | 126 | 2 |
| Dennett ......... | 31 | 5 | 134 | 1 |
| A. W. Roberts ..... | 2 | — | 20  | — |
| F. B. Roberts ...... | 27 | 3 | 110 | 2 |
| Brown .......... | 7 | — | 49  | — |
| Langdon ........ | 5 | — | 10  | — |

Umpires: W. Vining and J. Blake.

## HAMPSHIRE v KENT

Played at Southampton, May 27, 28, 29, 1912

Marked by brilliant batting, the match was drawn. By putting on 346 after the loss of two men for 16, Fry and Mead accomplished a big performance when runs were not easy to get. Together four hours, each had two narrow escapes. Hampshire's innings lasted eight hours. The only men who did not bowl in the match were the wicket-keepers.

### Hampshire

| | | | |
|---|---|---|---|
| A. Bowell c Huish b Fielder .................... | 10 | – b Fairservice .................. | 10 |
| A. Stone c Humphreys ....................... | 5 | – not out ....................... | 17 |
| C. P. Mead run out ........................... | 106 | | |
| Mr C. B. Fry c Jennings b Woolley .............. | 143 | | |
| Mr A. C. Johnston lbw b Woolley ............... | 67 | – b Fairservice .................. | 36 |
| Capt. E. I. M. Barrett c Seymour b Day ......... | 43 | – not out ...................... | 22 |
| Mr G. N. Bignell b Hatfield .................... | 79 | | |
| G. Brown b Huish b Fielder .................... | 22 | | |
| A. Kennedy b Day ........................... | 12 | | |
| J. Newman not out .......................... | 49 | | |
| E. R. Remnant run out ....................... | 31 | | |
| B 10, l-b 11, w 1, n-b 10 .............. | 32 | B 4 .................... | 4 |

|  | |
|---|---|
| 599 | (2 wkts dec.) 89 |

### Kent

| | | | |
|---|---|---|---|
| E. Humphreys c Fry b Kennedy ............. | 83 | | |
| H. T. W. Hardinge c Mead b Brown ............ | 82 | | |
| James Seymour b Newman ................... | 3 | – b Bignell.................... | 14 |
| F. E. Woolley c Stone b Brown ................ | 1 | | |
| Mr A. P. Day b Newman ...................... | 12 | | |
| J. C. Hubble b Newman ...................... | 32 | – b Bignell.................... | 57 |
| D. W. Jennings c Remnant b Mead .............100 | | | |
| Mr C. E. Hatfield c Johnston b Newman .......... | 33 | | |
| F. H. Huish c Bowell b Remnant .............. | 15 | – not out ...................... | 23 |
| W. J. Fairservice c Barrett b Mead .............. | 28 | | |
| A. Fielder not out .......................... | 3 | | |
| B 5, l-b 14, w 6, n-b 1 ................ | 26 | W 1 .................... | 1 |

|  | |
|---|---|
| 418 | 95 |

## Kent Bowling

| | Overs | Mdns | Runs | Wkts | Overs | Mdns | Runs | Wkts |
|---|---|---|---|---|---|---|---|---|
| Fielder ........... | 44 | 8 | 159 | 2 | | | | |
| Humphreys ....... | 15 | 5 | 32 | 1 | | | | |
| Fairservice ........ | 27 | 3 | 89 | — | 11 | 3 | 23 | 2 |
| Day ............. | 28 | 5 | 101 | 2 | 10 | — | 41 | — |
| Woolley .......... | 40 | 7 | 119 | 2 | | | | |
| Hatfield .......... | 6 | — | 28 | 1 | 3 | — | 10 | — |
| Jennings .......... | 7.5 | — | 38 | — | | | | |
| Hardinge ......... | 2 | 1 | 1 | — | | | | |
| Seymour ......... | | | | | 6 | 1 | 10 | — |
| Hubble ........... | | | | | 1 | — | 1 | — |

## Hampshire Bowling

| | Overs | Mdns | Runs | Wkts | Overs | Mdns | Runs | Wkts |
|---|---|---|---|---|---|---|---|---|
| Brown ........... | 34 | 6 | 117 | 2 | | | | |
| Newman ......... | 42 | 10 | 112 | 4 | | | | |
| Kennedy ......... | 22 | 9 | 49 | 1 | | | | |
| Remnant ......... | 16 | 3 | 58 | 1 | 2 | 1 | 9 | — |
| Mead ............ | 7.5 | 1 | 21 | 2 | 12 | 1 | 31 | — |
| Johnston ......... | 2 | — | 17 | — | | | | |
| Bowell ........... | 3 | — | 11 | — | | | | |
| Bignell ........... | 2 | 1 | 7 | — | 13 | 4 | 31 | 2 |
| Fry ............. | | | | | 4 | 1 | 8 | — |
| Barrett ........... | | | | | 2 | — | 15 | — |

Umpires: A. J. Atfield and T. Brown.

# KENT

## KENT v SOMERSET

### Played at Catford, July 29, 30, 1901

Perhaps nothing in Kent's cricket in 1901 was more creditable than their victory in this match by 25 runs. Going in first on a wicket seriously damaged by rain, they were out in less than an hour and a half for 73, Mason alone seeming able to play Braund's leg-breaks, and with an innings completed on each side they found themselves 83 runs to the bad. However, they did well in their second innings, Mason playing superb cricket, and on the third day Somerset had to get 158 in the last innings. With six wickets in hand the score reached 110, but a sudden change then came over the game. Porch and Gill were out at 115 to successive balls, and the remaining four wickets fell for 17 runs. Phillips made a great effort for Somerset, and did not deserve to be on the losing side. Mason was quite the hero of the match, following up his splendid batting by taking five wickets in the last innings for 30 runs.

### Kent

| | | |
|---|---|---|
| Mr C. J. Burnup st Wickham b Braund | 7 – c Robson b Braund | 4 |
| Mr E. W. Dillon st Wickham b Cranfield | 7 – b Braund | 4 |
| Mr P. C. Baker b Braund | 0 – b Braund | 1 |
| Mr S. H. Day b Braund | 1 – b Cranfield | 32 |
| Mr J. R. Mason st Wickham b Braund | 40 – st Wickham b Braund | 81 |
| A. Hearne b Cranfield | 2 – b Gill | 31 |
| Mr R. N. R. Blaker c Lewis b Braund | 0 – b Braund | 48 |
| E. Humphreys b Robson | 0 – st Wickham b Braund | 0 |
| F. H. Huish b Robson | 0 – c Braund b Woods | 15 |
| C. Blythe not out | 0 – b Woods | 0 |
| Mr W. M. Bradley b Robson | 0 – not out | 6 |
| B 15, l-b 1 | 16       B 12, l-b 5, n-b 1 | 18 |
| | | |
| | 73 | 240 |

### Somerset

| | | |
|---|---|---|
| Mr S. M. J. Woods c Blaker b Hearne | 28 – b Blythe | 39 |
| E. Robson c Dillon b Blythe | 18 – c Bradley b Blythe | 23 |
| L. C. Braund c Baker b Hearne | 10 – c Dillon b Hearne | 8 |
| Mr F. A. Phillips run out | 2 – c Blythe b Mason | 45 |
| Lewis b Blythe | 7 – c Huish b Hearne | 1 |
| Mr R. B. Porch c Huish b Mason | 20 – b Mason | 5 |
| Mr O. Samson b Hearne | 21 – b Mason | 1 |
| Mr G. Fowler c Mason b Blythe | 0 – b Mason | 4 |
| G. Gill not out | 30 – c Huish b Mason | 0 |
| B. Cranfield b Hearne | 0 – not out | 4 |
| Rev. A. P. Wickham b Humphreys | 4 – b Hearne | 0 |
| B 15, l-b 1 | 16       N-b 2 | 2 |
| | | |
| | 156 | 132 |

### Somerset Bowling

| | Overs | Mdns | Runs | Wkts | Overs | Mdns | Runs | Wkts |
|---|---|---|---|---|---|---|---|---|
| Cranfield | 14 | 6 | 33 | 2 | 22 | 6 | 34 | 1 |
| Braund | 16 | 7 | 23 | 5 | 35 | 8 | 107 | 6 |
| Robson | 2.3 | 1 | 1 | 3 | 9 | 4 | 19 | — |
| Gill | | | | | 13 | 2 | 41 | 1 |
| Woods | | | | | 8 | 2 | 21 | 2 |

**Kent Bowling**

| | Overs | Mdns | Runs | Wkts | Overs | Mdns | Runs | Wkts |
|---|---|---|---|---|---|---|---|---|
| Blythe .......... | 17 | 3 | 67 | 3 | 17 | 7 | 25 | 2 |
| Hearne .......... | 15 | 5 | 42 | 4 | 21.2 | 6 | 48 | 3 |
| Mason .......... | 10 | 4 | 14 | 1 | 9 | 1 | 30 | 5 |
| Humphreys ....... | 2.3 | — | 17 | 1 | 3 | 1 | 3 | — |
| Bradley ......... | | | | | 2 | — | 24 | — |

Umpires: A. Shaw and J. Phillips.

## KENT v SURREY

Played at Canterbury, August 7, 8, 9, 1902

In no match during the season did the Surrey team render such a miserable account of themselves as in the second game of the Canterbury Week, and they fully deserved their defeat by an innings and 191 runs. They fielded indifferently on the first day and their bowling was lacking in sting. The Kent batsmen took full advantage of their opponents' shortcomings, Burnup and Marsham hitting up 148 runs in eighty minutes, and Mason and Hearne also scoring freely. Marsham, after an indifferent start, batted brilliantly. Burnup's cricket was always excellent, and Hearne, although lucky towards the finish, scored his first 50 runs in most taking fashion. Surrey lost one wicket for 4, and next day when rain caused a long delay, gave, apart from a hard hit 48 by Hayes, a sorry display of batting. Following on, 250 runs in arrear, they lost Abel's wicket for 6 runs before rain and bad light put an end to the day's cricket. The wretched form of Surrey reached its climax on Saturday when, after Hayward and Hayes had raised the score to 55, the last nine wickets went down for the addition of 4 runs. Hayes, Hayward, Bush, Dowson, and Crawford all left at 55. Hayward and Bush were out to exceptionally brilliant catches. After the total had reached 55, Mason took four wickets for 1 run and Blythe five for 3 runs. The contrast in the play of the two sides was extraordinary.

### Kent

| | | |
|---|---|---|
| Mr C. J. Burnup c Clode b Hayes ........ | 60 | Mr R. N. R. Blaker b Clode ............. 5 |
| Mr E. W. Dillon b Lockwood ........... | 5 | F. H. Huish not out .................. 23 |
| Mr C. H. B. Marsham c Hayes b Clode .... | 92 | E. Humphreys st Stedman b Clode ....... 3 |
| Mr S. H. Day c Stedman b Clode ........ | 32 | C. Blythe run out ................... 8 |
| Mr J. R. Mason b Richardson ........... | 45 | B 8, l-b 2, n-b 6 ............. 16 |
| A. Hearne c Stedman b Clode ........... | 73 | ___ |
| Mr F. Marchant b Richardson .......... | 27 | 389 |

### Surrey

| | | | |
|---|---|---|---|
| H. Clode b Mason ......................... | 12 | – c and b Blythe ................. | 0 |
| A. Stedman b Blythe ...................... | 4 | – c Mason b Blythe .............. | 0 |
| T. Hayward c Mason b Blythe .............. | 10 | – c Marchant b Mason ........... | 26 |
| R. Abel b Blythe ......................... | 5 | – b Mason .................... | 5 |
| E. G. Hayes c Marsham b Blythe ........... | 48 | – c Day b Blythe ................ | 22 |
| Mr E. M. Dowson b Humphreys .............. | 12 | – c Huish b Blythe .............. | 0 |
| Mr V. F. S. Crawford b Humphreys .......... | 1 | – c and b Mason ............... | 0 |
| Capt. H. S. Bush c Humphreys b Mason ...... | 24 | – c and b Mason ............... | 0 |
| W. H. Lockwood b Humphreys .............. | 3 | – c and b Mason ............... | 0 |
| Mr H. D. G. Leveson-Gower not out .......... | 13 | – not out ..................... | 3 |
| T. Richardson c Blythe b Mason ............ | 1 | – b Blythe .................... | 1 |
| B 4, l-b 1, w 1 ..................... | 6 | W 1, n-b 1 .............. | 2 |
| | 139 | | 59 |

**Surrey Bowling**

| | Overs | Mdns | Runs | Wkts |
|---|---|---|---|---|
| Lockwood | 23 | 4 | 82 | 1 |
| Clode | 36 | 4 | 130 | 5 |
| Dowson | 10 | — | 40 | — |
| Richardson | 20.2 | 3 | 85 | 2 |
| Hayes | 2 | — | 10 | 1 |
| Hayward | 5 | — | 26 | — |

**Kent Bowling**

| | Overs | Mdns | Runs | Wkts | Overs | Mdns | Runs | Wkts |
|---|---|---|---|---|---|---|---|---|
| Blythe | 23 | 6 | 69 | 4 | 13.5 | 6 | 32 | 5 |
| Burnup | 1 | — | 3 | — | | | | |
| Mason | 16.3 | 8 | 31 | 3 | 13 | 5 | 25 | 5 |
| Humphreys | 8 | 1 | 22 | 3 | | | | |
| Hearne | 3 | — | 8 | — | | | | |

Umpires: H. Shaw and A. White.

# THE TONBRIDGE NURSERY, 1906

## By Capt. W. McCanlis

This, like other institutions, is the outcome of necessity. Kent for many years had been essentially an amateur side; doing great things at times, when at full strength in the latter end of the season. For example, Kent has beaten the Australians on five occasions. Occasional brilliancies, however, are not satisfying when a high position is desired in the County Championship competition. A good side in all matches was required. Hence the establishment, in 1897, of the "Nursery," with the view of training young professionals so as to render them competent to become members of the county team in due course. The arduous practical work in connection with the inaguration and working of the "Nursery" fell largely on Mr T. Pawley, the Kent general manager, who took the matter up with his usual enthusiasm and still retains his keenness for the success of our school.

At first the coaching was undertaken by George Webb, the chief professional at the Tonbridge school. In addition to this teaching, the young players got match practice with local clubs. This is a very important matter. Many and many promising young cricketers have been ruined for the lack of match playing and have become merely mechanical net bowlers, with very little ability to coach. The Metropolitan clubs are specially guilty of the fault of rarely, or never, playing their professionals in matches. In the north of England the practice is otherwise, and to this it is probably due to some extent that the northern counties have been able to fill up vacancies in their county teams with comparative ease. Webb devoted as much time as he could to teaching the youngsters but, of course, his other duties would not permit of his attending as much as was desirable. Consequently in 1900 I, having leisure, undertook to try to teach the lads to the best of my ability. I am fond of the work, and very fond of the lads. They are a nice lot of fellows, and it is a pleasure to deal with them.

There is an element of luck in discovering likely youngsters. The case of C. Blythe is an instance. Kent was playing a match at Blackheath, and the usual preliminary morning practice was proceeding; I noticed a lad, one of the crowd, bowl a few balls to Walter Wright, and was impressed with his delivery. I spoke to him and arranged for him to come and bowl to me one evening. He came; I was pleased with him and recommended him for a trial at Tonbridge – the result of which was that he was engaged for the "Nursery" next season. There he improved rapidly, and is now the great, well-known bowler, C. Blythe.

There was in this "find" a considerable amount of luck. Blythe lived at Deptford, a place one would hardly go to in search of cricketers. The lads of this town have only the roughest parts of Blackheath on which to play their occasional cricket. Of course, under such conditions it is quite impossible for a boy to make any headway in the art of batting; but there is always a chance of finding a boy with natural abilities as a bowler, who may be taught to bat and field. Blythe is not half a bad batsman when he goes in with the intention of staying; and yet, when he came to Tonbridge he had no idea whatever of batting. Blythe, Fielder, Humphreys, Seymour, Hardinge, Fairservice, Hubble, and F. Woolley have all found their way into the county team through the "Nursery." Badcock also passed through it to Hampshire.

This is a record which, I think, justifies the policy of teaching young professionals; a policy which was first adopted by Surrey, I believe, and with considerable success.

The system pursued at Tonbridge may be interesting to officials of other counties who may be thinking of adopting a similar school of instruction. I arrive on the ground at 10.30 a.m., when all is ready to begin at once. One, or two, nets, according to our numbers, the off wing of one being down to give facilities for fielding. All who are not batting or bowling have to field. Each takes his turn of batting and bowling for spells of about fifteen minutes. Long turns of batting practice are, I think, conducive to carelessness. My endeavour is to induce the batsman to try his very best while playing, and to concentrate his thoughts on correcting one fault. In time many faults will be thrown aside. Should a student try to correct all his faults at the same time his progress is likely to be very slow, and confusion and discouragement loom up large.

In bowling I attach the first importance to "length." To attain a command of length requires much practice and perseverance. It is by no means an easy art to acquire. To aid the bowlers in finding the length ball I have a white-wash line drawn across the pitch to aim at. This line is not very frequently hit, but when it is, the batsman always finds the delivery a difficult one to deal with, even without any break; when the ball "does a bit" the batsman is thankful when he finds his wicket intact at the end of the transaction; often it is disturbed, or a catch is given.

The practice continues until about one o'clock – with some special bouts of catching and throwing. All are well tired by this time. In the very early part of the season, when we have the ground to ourselves, I have them out again in the afternoon; but when the members begin to practise, the youngsters have to be ready to bowl at the nets at three o'clock, and consequently I do not call them out for practice again. We are careful to avoid over bowling the young fellows at the nets. Only two are out at a time, and not then for long spells. All have an interval of one hour for tea. In addition to this practice the local clubs are encouraged to apply for the services of the youngsters to assist in their matches, and by this means the lads get a good deal of valuable match playing. A record of their performances in these matches is carefully kept for reference.

Apart from the players who have found a place in the county team we keep but a small staff of about six under tuition. Those who do not make sufficient progress have to go, and others take their place. The results we have achieved ought to encourage other counties to try a similar system. We have had no transcendant cricket genius to deal with, but just ordinary keen young fellows such as are to be found in most counties.

Judgment, of course, is required in selecting the lads, and also in deciding whether to retain or dispense with the services of those you have. Some improve quickly, and others slowly. The slow ones sometimes turn out the best in the long run. Therefore, it is necessary to be patient with the youngsters – always providing they are genuine triers. We must not expect to build up a strong county team in a hurry. Kent has been ten years over the job, and other counties can scarcely hope to make more rapid progress than we have done. Even after a good team has been secured, there must be no slackening of effort to maintain its efficiency and to improve it. There is always room on top. So no lad need despair; he has only to make himself good enough as a player, and a place must be found for him in the team. I say advisedly "make himself," because the success attained by a lad depends mainly upon his own efforts and perseverance. The "coach" can only point out

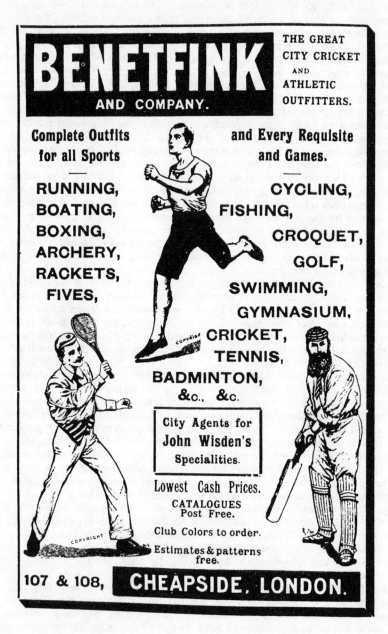

errors and indicate how to overcome them. The actual and necessary work must be done by the player himself.

As regards the financial bearings of the running of a "Nursery," I need hardly say that, of course, it costs money; but in our case the outlay has been remunerative, because our receipts have improved beyond the outlay. A good team is attractive to the lovers of good cricket.

## KENT v MIDDLESEX

### Played at Tonbridge, June 21, 22, 23, 1906

Middlesex had only a moderate side, yet Kent came desperately near being beaten. Indeed the home county must have suffered defeat but for the splendid work of Hutchings. In the first innings this young batsman went in when in face of a Middlesex total of 336 Kent had lost six wickets for 119. A follow-on appeared inevitable, but Hutchings hit the Middlesex bowling to all parts of the field, and made 125 in less than two hours and a quarter. Kent were again in an awkward plight on Saturday, 292 runs being required to win, and four wickets having fallen for 113 when Hutchings went in. With two other batsmen dismissed soon afterwards, Hutchings had to play a game quite foreign to his nature, but he played it so well that he saved his side, Kent, when the game was left drawn, having one wicket to fall and still wanting 39 to win.

### Middlesex

| | | | |
|---|---|---|---|
| Mr P. F. Warner b Fielder | 16 | – c Mason b Humphreys | 122 |
| F. A. Tarrant c Huish b Fielder | 28 | – b Fielder | 0 |
| Mr C. A. L. Payne c Blaker b Mason | 40 | – b Humphreys | 81 |
| Mr H. E. Pearce lbw b Fielder | 17 | – run out | 12 |
| J. T. Rawlin b Woolley | 5 | – c Blaker b Humphreys | 7 |
| A. E. Trott c Seymour b Fairservice | 73 | – c sub. b Humphreys | 8 |
| Mr W. P. Harrison c Marsham b Mason | 93 | – c and b Humphreys | 2 |
| J. T. Hearne b Humphreys | 27 | – c Mason b Humphreys | 4 |
| Mr G. W. Beldam b Fielder | 13 | – c Hubble b Woolley | 16 |
| Mr C. Headlam b Fairservice | 6 | – b Humphreys | 2 |
| E. Mignon not out | 14 | – not out | 0 |
| B 29, l-b 1, n-b 4 | 34 | B 12, l-b 2, n-b 3 | 17 |
| | **366** | | **271** |

### Kent

| | | | |
|---|---|---|---|
| Mr C. H. B. Marsham b Mignon | 7 | – c Tarrant b Mignon | 14 |
| Mr J. R. Mason c Payne b Mignon | 35 | – lbw b Rawlin | 38 |
| E. Humphreys b Mignon | 0 | – b Mignon | 4 |
| James Seymour c Tarrant b Mignon | 4 | – c Headlam b Tarrant | 43 |
| F. E. Woolley c Rawlin b Mignon | 33 | – c Beldam b Trott | 2 |
| Mr R. N. R. Blaker c Tarrant b Mignon | 55 | – b Mignon | 12 |
| J. C. Hubble c Headlam b Hearne | 3 | – b Mignon | 25 |
| Mr K. L. Hutchings b Beldam | 125 | – not out | 97 |
| W. J. Fairservice b Rawlin | 11 | – c Trott b Beldam | 4 |
| F. H. Huish not out | 17 | – not out | 0 |
| A. Fielder st Headlam b Tarrant | 28 | – c Headlam b Mignon | 0 |
| B 22, l-b 6 | 28 | B 6, l-b 6, n-b 2 | 14 |
| | **346** | | **253** |

## Kent Bowling

| | Overs | Mdns | Runs | Wkts | Overs | Mdns | Runs | Wkts |
|---|---|---|---|---|---|---|---|---|
| Fielder ........... | 41 | 6 | 140 | 4 | 25 | 3 | 71 | 1 |
| Woolley .......... | 24 | 9 | 46 | 1 | 22 | 8 | 39 | 1 |
| Mason ........... | 17.1 | 5 | 57 | 2 | 18 | 2 | 68 | — |
| Humphreys ....... | 13 | 2 | 38 | 1 | 13.5 | 4 | 33 | 7 |
| Fairservice ........ | 14 | 4 | 51 | 2 | 13 | 1 | 43 | — |

## Middlesex Bowling

| | Overs | Mdns | Runs | Wkts | Overs | Mdns | Runs | Wkts |
|---|---|---|---|---|---|---|---|---|
| Beldam ........... | 9 | 3 | 27 | 1 | 9 | 1 | 29 | 1 |
| Mignon .......... | 30 | 8 | 108 | 6 | 29 | 5 | 78 | 5 |
| Tarrant .......... | 12.2 | 2 | 60 | 1 | 11 | 2 | 19 | 1 |
| Trott ............ | 11 | 1 | 44 | — | 16 | — | 68 | 1 |
| Hearne ........... | 22 | 5 | 61 | 1 | 4 | 1 | 22 | — |
| Rawlin ........... | 8 | 3 | 18 | 1 | 10 | 1 | 23 | 1 |

Umpires: W. A. J. West and T. Brown.

## KENT v SURREY

Played at Blackheath, July 30, 31, August 1, 1906

Fresh from a brilliant victory over Yorkshire on the previous Saturday, Surrey entered upon the return engagement to that which at The Oval in June had resulted in a win for Kent by one wicket. Kent had 103 on the board at lunch time on the first day with four men out, but on resuming, Knox and Lees finished off the innings in forty minutes for the addition of 33 runs. When Surrey went in, Hayward played a great game, and the score reached 117 before the fourth wicket fell, but late in the day Fielder bowled in deadly form, the close of play finding Surrey 14 ahead with two wickets in hand. Next morning, Hayward, with sturdy assistance from Strudwick, completed his twelfth hundred of the season. Kent, beginning their second innings 83 in arrears, lost Dillon, Seymour, and Burnup for 58, but thenceforward all went well with them. Knox, owing to lameness, had to retire from the field, and Surrey were set 245 to win. There seemed a fair chance of the runs being obtained, but the batting broke down in astounding fashion, and Kent gained a victory by 164 runs. Blythe bowled superbly.

### Kent

| | | | |
|---|---|---|---|
| Mr C. J. Burnup c Dalmeny b Knox | 46 | – b Lees | 20 |
| Mr E. W. Dillon c Strudwick b Lees | 19 | – c Hayes b Lees | 0 |
| James Seymour b Lees | 6 | – c Hobbs b Lees | 27 |
| Mr K. L. Hutchings b Lees | 6 | – c sub. b Lees | 62 |
| F. E. Woolley c Holland b Knox | 15 | – c Lees b Hayes | 68 |
| Mr J. R. Mason c Hayward b Knox | 13 | – b May | 3 |
| E. Humphreys c Crawford b Lees | 23 | – b Crawford | 66 |
| Mr R. N. R. Blaker c Strudwick b Lees | 2 | – c Strudwick b Crawford | 41 |
| F. H. Huish b Knox | 4 | – b Lees | 19 |
| C. Blythe b Knox | 0 | – c Holland b Crawford | 6 |
| A. Fielder not out | 0 | – not out | 7 |
| L-b 2 | 2 | B 6, w 1, n-b 1 | 8 |
| | 136 | | 327 |

**Surrey**

| | | | |
|---|---|---|---|
| T. Hayward b Mason | 124 | – b Blythe | 17 |
| J. B. Hobbs st Huish b Blythe | 5 | – c Seymour b Fielder | 2 |
| E. G. Hayes c Dillon b Fielder | 18 | – c Seymour b Blythe | 1 |
| E. G. Goatly c Blaker b Blythe | 14 | – b Fielder | 16 |
| Mr J. N. Crawford c Blythe b Woolley | 25 | – c Baker b Blythe | 3 |
| F. C. Holland c Dillon b Fielder | 8 | – b Mason | 15 |
| Lord Dalmeny c Seymour b Fielder | 0 | – b Mason | 9 |
| W. Lees c Huish b Fielder | 1 | – not out | 4 |
| Mr P. R. May b Fielder | 0 | – b Blythe | 2 |
| H. Strudwick b Fielder | 15 | – c Seymour b Blythe | 7 |
| Mr N. A. Knox not out | 0 | – b Mason | 0 |
| B 2, l-b 3, w 2, n-b 2 | 9 | W 1, n-b 3 | 4 |
| | **219** | | **80** |

**Surrey Bowling**

| | Overs | Mdns | Runs | Wkts | Overs | Mdns | Runs | Wkts |
|---|---|---|---|---|---|---|---|---|
| Lees | 22 | 7 | 69 | 5 | 30.3 | 6 | 101 | 5 |
| Knox | 12.3 | 1 | 46 | 5 | 8 | — | 38 | — |
| Crawford | 10 | 5 | 14 | — | 17 | 1 | 68 | 3 |
| May | 1 | — | 5 | — | 18 | 2 | 93 | 1 |
| Hayes | | | | | 2 | — | 10 | 1 |
| Hobbs | | | | | 2 | — | 9 | — |

**Kent Bowling**

| | Overs | Mdns | Runs | Wkts | Overs | Mdns | Runs | Wkts |
|---|---|---|---|---|---|---|---|---|
| Fielder | 27.3 | 5 | 108 | 6 | 18 | 5 | 43 | 2 |
| Blythe | 29 | 9 | 59 | 2 | 20 | 12 | 25 | 5 |
| Mason | 13 | 7 | 14 | 1 | 2.5 | — | 8 | 3 |
| Woolley | 9 | 1 | 29 | 1 | | | | |

Umpires: A. Woodcock and C. E. Dench.

## KENT v SURREY

### Played at Blackheath, June 23, 24, 25, 1910

Not only was this match greatly interfered with by rain on the first two days, but on Saturday the downpour proved so heavy that cricket was out of the question, the game being abandoned before one o'clock. Although thus ruined by bad weather, the contest produced a memorable achievement on the part of Blythe, who for the first time in the course of his great career succeeded in performing the "hat trick." Scarcely had the match commenced when rain set in, and prevented anything being done between twenty minutes past twelve and twenty minutes to five. Surrey lost their two amateurs for 36, but then on Hayward and Hobbs forcing the game, the Kent fieldsmen blundered in deplorable fashion, four or five palpable chances being missed. The two famous batsmen made fine use of their luck, putting on 62 in an hour, before Blythe's bowling met with such remarkable success. In one over Blythe disposed of Hayward and Ducat, and in his next Strudwick off the second ball was taken at the wicket, Abel off the third was stumped, and off the fourth, Smith was caught by Humphreys fielding close in on the offside. When he disposed of Smith, Blythe had taken five wickets in ten balls, without a run being scored off him meanwhile. Consequent upon his splendid work, the total, which with Hayward and Hobbs together had reached 98 with only two men out, stood at the drawing of stumps at 105 for eight wickets. Not until after two o'clock was play practicable on Friday, and later on rain caused a further delay of three-quarters of an hour. When Kent went in, Humphreys left at 37, and Dillon at the same total offered the easiest of catches, but the chance being thrown away, the Kent captain and Seymour batting with much skill, put on 90 runs. One run ahead with seven wickets in hand. Kent had much the best of the draw.

### Surrey

| | | | |
|---|---|---|---|
| Capt. H. S. Bush c Huish b Blythe | 6 | W. C. Smith c Humphreys b Blythe | 0 |
| T. Hayward c Huish b Blythe | 42 | W. Hitch c Fairservice b Woolley | 1 |
| Mr M. C. Bird c Day b Blythe | 9 | Mr N. A. Knox not out | 7 |
| J. B. Hobbs c Hubble b Woolley | 55 | W. Lees b Woolley | 0 |
| A. Ducat c Seymour b Blythe | 0 | B 9, n-b 1 | 10 |
| H. Strudwick c Huish b Blythe | 3 | | |
| W. J. Abel st Huish b Blythe | 0 | | 133 |

### Kent

| | | | |
|---|---|---|---|
| Mr E. W. Dillon c Smith b Bird | 65 | C. Blythe not out | 5 |
| E. Humphreys b Smith | 12 | L-b 1, n-b 2 | 3 |
| James Seymour c Strudwick b Smith | 49 | | |
| F. H. Huish not out | 0 | | 134 |

Mr K. L. Hutchings, Mr A. Day, F. E. Woolley, J. C. Hubble, W. J. Fairservice and A. Fielder did not bat.

### Kent Bowling

| | Overs | Mdns | Runs | Wkts |
|---|---|---|---|---|
| Blythe | 27 | 8 | 55 | 7 |
| Fielder | 9 | — | 29 | — |
| Woolley | 14.5 | 3 | 30 | 3 |
| Fairservice | 4 | 1 | 9 | — |

### Surrey Bowling

| | Overs | Mdns | Runs | Wkts |
|---|---|---|---|---|
| Smith | 20 | 4 | 51 | 2 |
| Lees | 12 | 1 | 31 | — |
| Abel | 7 | — | 19 | — |
| Knox | 7 | 1 | 22 | — |
| Bird | 3 | 1 | 8 | 1 |

Umpires: J. Blake and C. E. Dench.

## KENT v HAMPSHIRE

### Played at Canterbury, August 7, 8, 9, 1911

C. B. Fry in this match succeeded for the fifth time in putting together two separate hundreds. On Monday when he scored 123 out of 266 in three hours and a half he was not seen at quite his best, but he gave no actual chance and much of his cricket reached a very high standard. In the second innings, although he stayed at the wickets for four hours, he was repeatedly beaten on Tuesday evening by both Fielder and Carr. Still his 112 included many splendid strokes. In the last over on Tuesday Fry complained that, Blythe bowling full pitches, he lost sight of the ball in the sunshine – an incident which led to considerable discussion. Despite some admirable batting, Kent just failed to reach Hampshire's total. Kent were set 335 to make in two hours and forty minutes, and lost three wickets for 50, but then Humphreys and Hutchings added 173 in a hundred minutes, the match ending in a draw. Hampshire were without Mead.

## Hampshire

| | | | |
|---|---:|---|---:|
| Mr C. B. Fry st Huish b Blythe | 123 | – st Huish b Woolley | 112 |
| A. Bowell c Huish b Blythe | 45 | – c Hardinge b Carr | 19 |
| Mr A. C. Johnston st Huish b Carr | 10 | – b Carr | 14 |
| A. Stone c Humphreys b Carr | 2 | – run out | 17 |
| G. Brown c Seymour b Humphreys | 38 | – st Huish b Humphreys | 5 |
| A. Kennedy b Humphreys | 14 | – absent hurt | 0 |
| Mr D. M. Evans b Fielder | 37 | – c Mason b Woolley | 39 |
| Mr E. M. Sprot not out | 41 | – c Hutchings b Humphreys | 61 |
| Mr H. C. McDonell c Seymour b Fielder | 2 | – b Humphreys | 11 |
| J. Newman b Fielder | 10 | – st Huish b Hardinge | 20 |
| Col.-Sergt H. Forster b Mason | 0 | – not out | 2 |
| B 9, l-b 4, w 1, n-b 3 | 17 | B 4, l-b 12, w 1, n-b 2 | 19 |
| | **339** | | **319** |

## Kent

| | | | |
|---|---:|---|---:|
| E. Humphreys c Stone b Newman | 63 | – not out | 80 |
| H. T. W. Hardinge c Evans b Brown | 7 | – b Brown | 4 |
| James Seymour c Bowell b Brown | 2 | – c Evans b Brown | 8 |
| F. E. Woolley c and b McDonell | 108 | – c Evans b Brown | 26 |
| Mr K. L. Hutchings b Evans | 18 | – not out | 103 |
| Mr E. W. Dillon c sub. b Evans | 73 | | |
| Mr J. R. Mason c Evans b McDonell | 1 | | |
| F. H. Huish b Newman | 27 | | |
| C. Blythe c Bowell b Brown | 14 | | |
| A. Fielder c and b Kennedy | 3 | | |
| Mr D. W. Carr not out | 0 | | |
| B 1, l-b 6, w 1 | 8 | B 2 | 2 |
| | **324** | | **223** |

## Kent Bowling

| | Overs | Mdns | Runs | Wkts | Overs | Mdns | Runs | Wkts |
|---|---|---|---|---|---|---|---|---|
| Fielder | 18 | 1 | 76 | 3 | 15 | 5 | 26 | — |
| Carr | 26 | 2 | 98 | 2 | 20 | 4 | 81 | 2 |
| Mason | 12.2 | 1 | 52 | 1 | 21 | 6 | 39 | — |
| Blythe | 21 | 1 | 69 | 2 | 17 | 5 | 37 | — |
| Humphreys | 8 | — | 23 | 2 | 11 | 3 | 51 | 3 |
| Woolley | 1 | — | 4 | — | 8.4 | 1 | 64 | 2 |
| Hardinge | | | | | 1 | — | 2 | 1 |

## Hampshire Bowling

| | Overs | Mdns | Runs | Wkts | Overs | Mdns | Runs | Wkts |
|---|---|---|---|---|---|---|---|---|
| Brown | 18 | 1 | 93 | 3 | 11 | — | 50 | 3 |
| Evans | 27 | 5 | 84 | 2 | 12.3 | 2 | 70 | — |
| Kennedy | 17.4 | 4 | 46 | 1 | | | | |
| Newman | 13 | 1 | 55 | 2 | 10 | 2 | 28 | — |
| McDonell | 7 | — | 38 | 2 | 7 | — | 42 | — |
| Forster | | | | | 7 | 1 | 31 | — |

Umpires: J. E. West and A. E. Street.

# KENT v GLOUCESTERSHIRE

Played at Gravesend, June 1, 2, 3, 1911

Previous to meeting Gloucestershire in the first of their home matches, Kent had beaten Middlesex, Leicestershire, and Northamptonshire, and, although lacking the services of Humphreys, Seymour, Woolley, Hutchings, and Dillon, they won by 263 runs. A. P. Day, who acted as captain, gave a masterly display, going in first wicket down at 16 and carrying out his bat. Apart from a chance at the wicket when 73, he made no mistake during a stay of two hours and a half. Gloucestershire began badly, and despite some skilful work by Dipper, five wickets were down for 159. The innings was soon finished off by Fielder on Friday morning. When Kent went in again, Hubble and Troughton placed the side in a very strong position, and Hatfeild drove with tremendous power. Gloucestershire, wanting 392 to win, lost four wickets for 63, and an hour's cricket on Saturday morning finished the game. Fielder took thirteen wickets.

## Kent

| | | | |
|---|---:|---|---:|
| G. Collins b Huggins | 12 | – c Dipper b Dennett | 19 |
| H. T. W. Hardinge c Board b Dennett | 28 | – c Board b Mills | 37 |
| Mr A. P. Day not out | 135 | – b Parker | 39 |
| D. W. Jennings b Huggins | 0 | – c Edwards b Parker | 5 |
| J. C. Hubble b Mills | 9 | – c Parker b Dennett | 51 |
| Mr L. H. W. Troughton c Board b Parker | 16 | – c Luce b Levy | 48 |
| Mr C. E. Hatfeild b Huggins | 30 | – c Luce b Huggins | 74 |
| F. H. Huish b Huggins | 4 | – c Luce b Dennett | 25 |
| W. J. Fairservice c Mills b Dennett | 20 | – not out | 4 |
| C. Blythe c Edwards b Dennett | 7 | – c Luce b Dennett | 5 |
| A. Fielder b Dennett | 10 | – st Board b Dennett | 0 |
| B 13 | 13 | N-b 1 | 1 |
| | **284** | | **308** |

## Gloucestershire

| | | | |
|---|---:|---|---:|
| J. H. Board b Fielder | 6 | – c Hardinge b Fielder | 11 |
| T. Langdon b Fielder | 0 | – b Fielder | 1 |
| A. G. Dipper c Jennings b Collins | 53 | – c Hatfeild b Blythe | 52 |
| P. Mills b Blythe | 10 | – b Fielder | 11 |
| Mr F. M. Luce b Collins | 24 | – b Blythe | 19 |
| Mr C. W. Edwards c Jennings b Fielder | 42 | – c Jennings b Fielder | 9 |
| Mr F. E. Tayler b Fielder | 21 | – b Fielder | 6 |
| J. H. Huggins c Huish b Fielder | 4 | – b Blythe | 1 |
| S. Levy not out | 10 | – c Collins b Fielder | 2 |
| C. Parker c Hardinge b Fielder | 8 | – c Hubble b Blythe | 1 |
| G. Dennett b Fielder | 7 | – not out | 1 |
| B 9, l-b 5, n-b 2 | 16 | B 4, w 1, n-b 9 | 14 |
| | **201** | | **128** |

## Gloucestershire Bowling

| | Overs | Mdns | Runs | Wkts | Overs | Mdns | Runs | Wkts |
|---|---|---|---|---|---|---|---|---|
| Huggins | 21 | 1 | 100 | 4 | 24 | 4 | 100 | 1 |
| Dennett | 22 | 4 | 109 | 4 | 20.4 | 2 | 97 | 5 |
| Parker | 8 | 1 | 28 | 1 | 11 | 3 | 32 | 2 |
| Mills | 9 | — | 34 | 1 | 10 | 2 | 28 | 1 |
| Edwards | | | | | 4 | — | 28 | — |
| Levy | | | | | 3 | — | 22 | 1 |
| Dipper | | | | | 1 | 1 | — | — |

## Kent Bowling

|            | Overs | Mdns | Runs | Wkts | Overs | Mdns | Runs | Wkts |
|------------|-------|------|------|------|-------|------|------|------|
| Fielder .......... | 29.3 | 10 | 77 | 7 | 21 | 5 | 58 | 6 |
| Blythe .......... | 30 | 11 | 56 | 1 | 20.3 | 5 | 56 | 4 |
| Fairservice ....... | 10 | 3 | 18 | — | | | | |
| Day ............ | 4 | 1 | 6 | — | | | | |
| Collins .......... | 7 | 2 | 31 | 2 | | | | |

Umpires: H. Wood and W. Richards.

## KENT v ESSEX

### Played at Tonbridge, June 12, 13, 14, 1911

Seen to marked advantage at all points, Essex beat Kent by 256 runs. The visitors laid the foundations of their success by sound and skilful batting on Monday. Perrin played admirably, and Carpenter, after an indifferent start, settled down to fine work. Kent lost Humphreys and Seymour for 18 before the drawing of stumps, and, with one brilliant exception, gave a singularly disappointing display on Tuesday. Hardinge played a great innings, going in first and carrying out his bat. He gave no chance, and hit particularly well on the off-side. Left with a useful lead, Essex again batted finely, Douglas and Gillingham carrying off the honours. Kent were set to score 395 at the rate of more than a hundred an hour. In the endeavour to play a stubborn game, the home side cut a poor figure on a slightly damaged pitch.

### Essex

| | | | |
|---|---|---|---|
| Mr J. W. H. T. Douglas b Fielder ............... | 15 | – c Humphreys b Hatfeild ........ | 98 |
| Mr F. L. Fane c Fielder b Fairservice ........... | 25 | – b Fielder .................... | 21 |
| Mr P. Perrin c Fielder b Woolley .............. | 79 | – c Hutchings b Fairservice ........ | 10 |
| W. Reeves c Dillon b Fairservice ............... | 19 | – c Dillon b Woolley ............. | 0 |
| Rev. F. H. Gillingham lbw b Blythe ............. | 18 | – b Fairservice ................. | 89 |
| Mr C. McGahey b Fielder ..................... | 10 | – not out ...................... | 45 |
| H. Carpenter not out ........................ | 70 | – b Fairservice ................. | 0 |
| Mr K. L. Gibson b Blythe .................... | 15 | – not out ...................... | 12 |
| C. P. Buckenham c Blythe b Fielder ............ | 0 | | |
| B. Tremlin c Blythe b Fielder ................ | 6 | – b Fairservice ................. | 20 |
| W. Mead b Woolley .......................... | 13 | | |
| B 15, l-b 5, w 1, n-b 2 ................ | 23 | B 8, l-b 1 .............. | 9 |
| | **293** | **(7 wkts dec.)** | **304** |

### Kent

| | | | |
|---|---|---|---|
| E. Humphreys c Gibson b Buckenham ........... | 1 | – lbw b Buckenham .............. | 24 |
| H. T. W. Hardinge not out ..................... | 123 | – c Gillingham b Douglas ......... | 4 |
| James Seymour b Douglas ..................... | 3 | – b Douglas ................... | 2 |
| Mr K. L. Hutchings c Carpenter b Douglas ........ | 16 | – b Douglas ................... | 47 |
| F. E. Woolley b Buckenham ................... | 0 | – b Buckenham ................. | 9 |
| Mr E. W. Dillon b Mead ..................... | 24 | – b Buckenham ................. | 12 |
| Mr C. E. Hatfeild c Carpenter b Mead ........... | 4 | – b Buckenham ................. | 12 |
| F. H. Huish c Gibson b Buckenham ............. | 7 | – c Perrin b Buckenham .......... | 7 |
| W. J. Fairservice run out .................... | 14 | – not out ..................... | 9 |
| C. Blythe c and b Douglas ................... | 2 | – c Gibson b Douglas ............ | 1 |
| A. Fielder b Buckenham ..................... | 1 | – b Buckenham ................. | 1 |
| B 7, n-b 1 ........................ | 8 | B 8, l-b 1, w 1 ............ | 10 |
| | **203** | | **138** |

## Kent Bowling

| | Overs | Mdns | Runs | Wkts | Overs | Mdns | Runs | Wkts |
|---|---|---|---|---|---|---|---|---|
| Fielder .......... | 33 | 4 | 95 | 4 | 16 | 3 | 67 | 1 |
| Blythe .......... | 30 | 3 | 70 | 2 | 14 | 3 | 49 | — |
| Fairservice ........ | 19 | 3 | 59 | 2 | 29 | 10 | 76 | 4 |
| Woolley .......... | 16.1 | 2 | 46 | 2 | 27 | 8 | 79 | 1 |
| Humphreys ....... | | | | | 3 | — | 13 | — |
| Hatfeild .......... | | | | | 2 | — | 11 | 1 |

## Essex Bowling

| | Overs | Mdns | Runs | Wkts | Overs | Mdns | Runs | Wkts |
|---|---|---|---|---|---|---|---|---|
| Buckenham ....... | 26.1 | 2 | 93 | 4 | 23.3 | 6 | 55 | 6 |
| Douglas .......... | 16 | — | 46 | 3 | 17 | 6 | 33 | 4 |
| Tremlin .......... | 5 | — | 21 | — | 4 | — | 6 | — |
| Mead ............ | 11 | 3 | 33 | 2 | 13 | 3 | 29 | — |
| McGahey ......... | 1 | — | 2 | — | 2 | 1 | 2 | — |
| Reeves ........... | | | | | 1 | — | 2 | — |

Umpires: A. E. Street and G. P. Harrison.

# KENT v NOTTINGHAMSHIRE

### Played at Canterbury, August 8, 9, 1912

In winning the toss, Kent went a long way towards winning this match, for the pitch, soft but not really difficult at the start on Thursday, had on Friday been reduced to a deplorably treacherous condition. After the heavy rain earlier in the week, much surprise was expressed at a start being practicable at noon, but this was only rendered possible by abandoning the wickets originally selected in favour of that prepared for the match with the Australians. Kent lost Hardinge in the first over, and Humphreys at 24. Seymour and Woolley, however played a great game for their side, putting on 112 in just over an hour and a half. Both batsmen showed splendid skill, and neither gave a chance. The total standing at 159 when the fourth wicket went down, the later batsmen, with a storm threatening, hit out, but without much success, eight wickets having fallen for 201 when at four o'clock rain put an end to the day's play. Following upon half-an-hour's delay on Friday to allow the ground to recover, Kent carried their score to 236. Wass bowled very well for the visitors. With the sun shining, Nottinghamshire, from the time they went in, were in a desperate position. Some of them in the first innings attempted cautious methods, but they were all out in an hour and forty minutes for 58 and in the follow-on, when they all abandoned restraint, an hour and a quarter saw them again dismissed for a total of 58. Kent thus won by an innings and 120 runs. Blythe and Woolley, who, of course, received great assistance from the condition of the ground, bowled unchanged in each innings. Earlier in the season they had dismissed Nottinghamshire for 47.

## Kent

| | | | | |
|---|---|---|---|---|
| E. Humphreys c Riley b Iremonger ....... | 10 | Mr S. H. Day not out .................. | 27 |
| H. T. W. Hardinge c Oates b Wass ....... | 0 | F. H. Huish c J. Gunn b Wass .......... | 2 |
| James Seymour c Carr b Wass .......... | 73 | Mr D. W. Carr lbw b Iremonger ........,. | 1 |
| F. E. Woolley lbw b Wass .............. | 66 | C. Blythe c G. Gunn b Wass ............ | 7 |
| J. C. Hubble lbw b Iremonger ........... | 19 | B 6, l-b 1 .................. | 7 |
| Mr A. P. Day c Hardstaff b Wass ........ | 16 | | |
| Mr E. W. Dillon c J. Gunn b Wass ....... | 8 | | 236 |

## Nottinghamshire

| | | | |
|---|---|---|---|
| Mr A. W. Carr b Blythe | 1 | – c Hardinge b Woolley | 6 |
| G. Gunn b Woolley | 18 | – c Hubble b Blythe | 8 |
| J. Hardstaff c Seymour b Woolley | 3 | – b Woolley | 8 |
| J. Gunn c A. P. Day b Woolley | 0 | – b Blythe | 12 |
| W. Payton c Hubble b Blythe | 5 | – b Woolley | 1 |
| J. Iremonger c Huish b Blythe | 14 | – b Blythe | 0 |
| Mr A. O. Jones c Humphreys b Woolley | 12 | – lbw b Blythe | 2 |
| G. M. Lee c A. P. Day b Woolley | 2 | – lbw b Woolley | 6 |
| T. Oates c A. P. Day b Blythe | 1 | – not out | 6 |
| W. Riley not out | 1 | – lbw b Blythe | 0 |
| T. Wass b Blythe | 0 | – b Blythe | 8 |
| B 1 | 1 | L-b 1 | 1 |
| | **58** | | **58** |

## Nottinghamshire Bowling

| | Overs | Mdns | Runs | Wkts |
|---|---|---|---|---|
| Wass | 33.1 | 6 | 95 | 7 |
| Iremonger | 35 | 11 | 90 | 3 |
| Riley | 6 | 2 | 15 | — |
| J. Gunn | 4 | 1 | 13 | — |
| G. Gunn | 4 | — | 16 | — |

## Kent Bowling

| | Overs | Mdns | Runs | Wkts | Overs | Mdns | Runs | Wkts |
|---|---|---|---|---|---|---|---|---|
| Blythe | 16.1 | 6 | 28 | 5 | 10.3 | 3 | 28 | 6 |
| Woolley | 15 | 4 | 29 | 5 | 10 | 3 | 29 | 4 |

Umpires: J. Hide and A. E. Trott.

## KENT v WARWICKSHIRE

### Played at Tonbridge, June 19, 20, 21, 1913

The resumption of fixtures between Kent and Warwickshire after a lapse of fourteen years yielded the most remarkable day's play during the whole of the season. Kent found themselves in a very awkward position on Saturday morning, for, with the pitch in a terribly treacherous condition, they were 158 runs behind with their four best batsmen out. The six outstanding wickets falling in three-quarters of an hour for 28 runs, Warwickshire were left with a lead which looked certain to decide the match in their favour. Blythe and Woolley, however, making the most of the conditions, actually dismissed Warwickshire in forty-five minutes for 16, the two famous left-handers being quite unplayable, but after this startling achievement, it was impossible to believe Kent would be capable of hitting off 147 runs. Before lunch Humphreys and Seymour were disposed of for 16, eighteen wickets so far having fallen in the day for 60 runs. Afterwards, however, Woolley hit away with such dazzling brilliancy that, under conditions which still placed batsmen at a marked disadvantage, he scored 76 in eighty minutes, Kent gaining a truly memorable victory by six wickets.

## Warwickshire

| | | |
|---|---|---|
| C. Charlesworth c Hatfield b Woolley | 47 – c Seymour b Blythe | 1 |
| J. H. Parsons b Day | 0 – st Huish b Woolley | 5 |
| Mr F. R. Foster b Fielder | 13 – c Hubble b Blythe | 2 |
| W. G. Quaife c Seymour b Blythe | 31 – c Blythe | 0 |
| C. S. Baker c Dillon b Humphreys | 59 – c Humphreys b Woolley | 4 |
| P. Jeeves b Woolley | 30 – c Blythe b Woolley | 0 |
| Mr G. Curle b Woolley | 1 – st Huish b Blythe | 0 |
| Mr W. C. Hands lbw b Blythe | 21 – b Woolley | 0 |
| S. Santall c Dillon b Woolley | 31 – c Huish b Woolley | 3 |
| S. H. Bates lbw b Woolley | 4 – not out | 0 |
| J. Brown not out | 0 – st Huish b Blythe | 1 |
| B 14, l-b 9, n-b 2 | 25 | |
| | **262** | **16** |

## Kent

| | | |
|---|---|---|
| E. Humphreys c Baker b Jeeves | 11 – lbw b Santall | 1 |
| H. T. W. Hardinge c Jeeves b Foster | 15 – b Foster | 27 |
| James Seymour c Hands b Jeeves | 24 – c Jeeves b Foster | 9 |
| F. E. Woolley c Hands b Jeeves | 8 – not out | 76 |
| J. C. Hubble c Bates b Foster | 24 – b Charlesworth | 10 |
| Mr E. W. Dillon c Baker b Foster | 15 – not out | 18 |
| Mr A. P. Day b Foster | 0 | |
| Mr C. E. Hatfeild b Foster | 10 | |
| F. H. Huish not out | 7 | |
| C. Blythe c Quaife b Jeeves | 6 | |
| A. Fielder b Foster | 0 | |
| L-b 8, w 4 | 12 | B 5, l-b 1　6 |
| | **132** | **147** |

### Kent Bowling

| | Overs | Mdns | Runs | Wkts | Overs | Mdns | Runs | Wkts |
|---|---|---|---|---|---|---|---|---|
| Fielder | 21 | 4 | 56 | 1 | | | | |
| Day | 18 | 4 | 61 | 1 | | | | |
| Blythe | 22 | 4 | 50 | 2 | 5.2 | 1 | 8 | 5 |
| Woolley | 16.5 | 4 | 44 | 5 | 5 | 1 | 8 | 5 |
| Humphreys | 10 | 2 | 26 | 1 | | | | |

### Warwickshire Bowling

| | Overs | Mdns | Runs | Wkts | Overs | Mdns | Runs | Wkts |
|---|---|---|---|---|---|---|---|---|
| Foster | 29 | 8 | 62 | 6 | 10 | 1 | 44 | 2 |
| Hands | 8 | 2 | 14 | — | 3.4 | — | 27 | — |
| Jeeves | 12 | 5 | 27 | 4 | 7 | — | 20 | — |
| Santall | 10 | 5 | 17 | — | 11 | — | 27 | 1 |
| Charlesworth | | | | | 6 | — | 23 | 1 |

Umpires: A. J. Atfield and Knott.

# LANCASHIRE

## LANCASHIRE v WORCESTERSHIRE

### Played at Manchester, May 24, 25, 26, 1900

The opening stage of this encounter was rendered memorable by the performance of Briggs, who after twenty years of first-class cricket successed in taking all ten wickets. Worcestershire had seven men out for 45, and Lancashire lost four wickets for 53, but Lancashire left off 85 ahead with three wickets in hand. Worcestershire played up splendidly next day, and at one period possessed a fine chance of winning. They rapidly finished off the Lancashire innings, and then gave a very creditable display of batting, the great feature being the splendid innings of 113 by H. K. Foster. Lancashire were set 155 to get to win, and with the ground drier than it had been at any previous period of the match the result seemed assured. Arnold and Wilson, however, bowled so finely that half the side were out for 82. Eccles then stayed with Tyldesley until the drawing of stumps, and next morning the last 47 runs were hit off in half an hour without further loss, Lancashire winning by five wickets. Tyldesley played superb cricket except for a chance directly after the start on the last day.

## Worcestershire

| | | | |
|---|---|---|---|
| Mr H. K. Foster b Briggs | 0 – | c and b Cuttell | 113 |
| F. Bowley c Eccles b Briggs | 5 – | b Mold | 6 |
| E. Arnold c MacLaren b Briggs | 1 – | b Briggs | 17 |
| F. Wheldon c Radcliffe b Briggs | 25 – | b Cuttell | 25 |
| Mr W. H. Hill b Briggs | 12 – | b Ward | 13 |
| Mr A. W. Issac c MacLaren b Briggs | 3 – | c Tyldesley b Cuttell | 7 |
| A. Bird b Briggs | 32 – | c Radcliffe b Cuttell | 8 |
| G. Wilson lbw b Briggs | 0 – | c Cuttell b Briggs | 31 |
| R. Burrows b Briggs | 17 – | c Sharp b Mold | 8 |
| Bannister c MacLaren b Briggs | 0 – | st Radcliffe b Briggs | 12 |
| T. Straw not out | 7 – | not out | 3 |
| B 3, l-b 1 | 4 | B 8, l-b 2 | 10 |
| | **106** | | **253** |

## Lancashire

| | | | |
|---|---|---|---|
| Mr A. C. MacLaren b Arnold | 12 – | b Arnold | 7 |
| A. Ward b Wilson | 13 – | c Bird b Arnold | 5 |
| J. T. Tyldesley c Issac b Bird | 79 – | not out | 71 |
| Mr C. R. Hartley c Bannister b Wilson | 0 – | b Arnold | 9 |
| W. R. Cuttell b Wilson | 4 – | c Straw b Wilson | 3 |
| J. Briggs b Wilson | 33 – | b Wilson | 14 |
| Mr A. Eccles b Arnold | 10 – | not out | 39 |
| J. Sharp not out | 35 | | |
| J. Hallam b Bird | 2 | | |
| L. Radcliffe b Wilson | 6 | | |
| A. Mold b Wilson | 0 | | |
| B 8, l-b 3 | 11 | B 4, l-b 1, w 1, n-b 2 | 8 |
| | **205** | | **156** |

## Lancashire Bowling

| | Overs | Mdns | Runs | Wkts | Overs | Mdns | Runs | Wkts |
|---|---|---|---|---|---|---|---|---|
| Hallam | 10 | 5 | 16 | — | 2 | — | 10 | — |
| Briggs | 28.5 | 7 | 55 | 10 | 30.3 | 14 | 62 | 3 |
| Cuttell | 9 | 3 | 14 | — | 13 | 11 | 72 | 4 |
| Mold | 10 | 3 | 17 | — | 22 | 7 | 56 | 2 |
| Ward | | | | | 14 | 3 | 43 | 1 |

### Worcestershire Bowling

| | Overs | Mdns | Runs | Wkts | Overs | Mdns | Runs | Wkts |
|---|---|---|---|---|---|---|---|---|
| Wilson .......... | 25.4 | 7 | 63 | 6 | 23 | 3 | 70 | 2 |
| Arnold .......... | 27 | 8 | 80 | 2 | 21.4 | 4 | 76 | 3 |
| Bannister ........ | 3 | — | 15 | — | | | | |
| Burrows ......... | 6 | — | 19 | — | | | | |
| Bird ............ | 3 | — | 17 | 2 | 1 | — | 2 | — |

Umpires: W. Wright and A. A. White.

# LANCASHIRE v SOMERSET

### Played at Manchester, July 11, 12, 1901

There was a great sensation in this match, Mold being no-balled by James Phillips sixteen times in ten overs. The incident naturally gave rise to much excitement, and for the next few days nothing else was talked about in the cricket world. Phillips rested content with what he had done on the opening day, and in the second innings of Somerset, allowed Mold to bowl unchallenged. The excitement of the no-balling dwarfed everything else in the match, and possibly upset some of the players. Lancashire won by ten wickets, this decisive result being largely due to Tyldesley's batting. Apart from a couple of chances, that brilliant cricketer was seen at his very best, scoring 193 in three hours and a quarter, and hitting thirty-five 4s.

### Somerset

| | | | |
|---|---|---|---|
| Mr L. C. H. Palairet c Hallows b Mold | 29 | – c Smith b Steel | 23 |
| L. C. Braund c Tyldesley b Webb | 29 | – c Tyldesley b Steel | 0 |
| Mr G. W. Jupp b Mold | 2 | – absent hurt | 0 |
| Lewis st Smith b Webb | 19 | – c Smith b Steel | 25 |
| Mr S. M. J. Woods b Steel | 40 | – not out | 36 |
| E. Robson b Steel | 24 | – b Mold | 10 |
| Mr V. T. Hill b Steel | 16 | – c Ward b Steel | 8 |
| G. Gill c Tyldesley b Steel | 23 | – c Garnett b Steel | 2 |
| Mr A. E. Newton b Steel | 30 | – c MacLaren b Mold | 3 |
| Mr G. Barrington c Steel b Mold | 14 | – b Mold | 0 |
| B. Cranfield not out | 4 | – c Steel b Mold | 0 |
| B 4, l-b 3, n-b 16 | 23 | L-b 1 | 1 |
| | **253** | | **108** |

### Lancashire

| | | | |
|---|---|---|---|
| Mr E. E. Steel c Cranfield b Gill | 0 | | |
| Mr H. G. Garnett c Gill b Braund | 67 | | |
| J. T. Tyldesley c Newton b Gill | 193 | | |
| A. Ward st Newton b Cranfield | 22 | | |
| J. Hallows c Gill b Cranfield | 26 | | |
| Mr C. R. Hartley c Gill b Cranfield | 0 | | |
| Hibbert not out | 23 | – not out | 4 |
| Mr A. C. MacLaren c Palairet b Cranfield | 2 | – not out | 7 |
| C. Smith b Gill | 0 | | |
| S. Webb b Gill | 2 | | |
| A. Mold c Hill b Braund | 6 | | |
| B 10, l-b 1, n-b 2 | 13 | | |
| | **354** | | **11** |

**Lancashire Bowling**

|  | Overs | Mdns | Runs | Wkts | Overs | Mdns | Runs | Wkts |
|---|---|---|---|---|---|---|---|---|
| Hallows .......... | 7 | 2 | 21 | — | | | | |
| Mold ............ | 23 | 1 | 88 | 3 | 20.4 | 4 | 65 | 4 |
| Webb ............ | 13 | 1 | 64 | 2 | | | | |
| Steel ............ | 13 | — | 57 | 5 | 21 | 6 | 42 | 5 |

**Somerset Bowling**

|  | Overs | Mdns | Runs | Wkts | Overs | Mdns | Runs | Wkts |
|---|---|---|---|---|---|---|---|---|
| Cranfield ......... | 29 | 6 | 76 | 4 | | | | |
| Gill .............. | 32 | 6 | 110 | 4 | | | | |
| Woods ........... | 7 | — | 38 | — | | | | |
| Braund ........... | 11.2 | 1 | 88 | 2 | | | | |
| Robson .......... | 4 | 1 | 28 | — | | | | |
| Palairet .......... | 1 | — | 1 | — | | | | |
| Hill .............. | | | | | 0.5 | — | 11 | — |

Umpires: J. Phillips and C. E. Richardson.

## NOTES BY THE EDITOR, 1900

I had intended to write at considerable length on the subject of unfair bowling and the no-balling of Mold and Tyler by James Phillips, but before I had started on my task the announcement appeared that at the meeting of county captains at Lord's, on December 10, an agreement had been made to take united action in the season of 1901, for the purpose of ridding English cricket of all throwing and dubious bowling. Up to the time of these lines being written – December 14 – full details of the method to be employed have not been officially made public, but I am assured on the highest authority that very strong measures have been determined on. Some bowlers will not be put on at all in county matches and others will receive a significant warning. "Better late then never," but I cannot help thinking what a number of scandals and what an immense amount of grumbling would have been avoided if, in the middle of the "eighties," the county captains had taken concerted action. At that time, however, Lord Harris alone had the courage of his convictions, and really tried to grapple with an admitted evil. It will not be forgotten that in 1885, Kent, at Lord Harris's instigation, dropped their return match with Lancashire on the ground that the Northern county employed unfair bowlers. Things have never since been so bad as they were about that time, when on one occasion three unmistakeable throwers took part in a Gentleman v Players' match at Lord's, but within the last few years there has unquestionably been great laxity. I think that the necessity of doing something was first brought home to the MCC committee and the county authorities when Jones and McKibbin so flagrantly disregarded Law 10, during the Australian tour of 1896. Even the least observant of cricketers must have been struck by the change that had come over Australian bowling since Spofforth, Boyle, Garrett, Palmer, Turner and Ferris earned their laurels on English cricket grounds. The mortifying fact was that the deplorable change was due entirely to our own weakness in not having the laws of the game carried out. The Australians only did against us what we had over and over again done against them. Now that at last English cricketers are taking steps to put their house in order, I think I may, without undue egotism, take some small credit to myself for having tried, year after year to get rid of unfair bowling. I denounced Crossland as a thrower the first time he ever played at Lord's, he being then quite an unknown man; and since that time I have in various newspapers, as well as in "Wisden," urged our cricket authorities to make a firm stand on behalf of fair bowling. To the argument that it is impossible to distinguish between throwing and legitimate bowling, I attach no importance whatever. I wonder what my old friend Bob Thoms would say if anyone told him he could not tell a throw from a fairly bowled ball. A throw may be difficult to define in words, but to the eye of a practical and unbiassed cricketer it is, I think, very obvious. James Phillips holds to the opinion that when a bowler strikes one at first sight as being a thrower, the odds are a hundred to one that he is not bowling fairly. In support of his opinion there is the fact that no bowler with an unimpeachably fair action has ever been accused of throwing. I have heard hard things said of Phillips for having no-balled Jones in Australia, and C. B. Fry, Mold and Tyler in this country, but in my opinion he has done splendid service to the game of cricket. He proved to our formerly timid officials that an umpire could enforce the law without any detriment to his professional position, and his good example was quickly followed by W. A. J. West, Tichmarsh and Sherwin. As to the no-balling of Mold at Trent Bridge, and Tyler at Taunton, I can say nothing at first-hand as I was not present at either match. Mr A. C. MacLaren defended Mold in the columns of the *Manchester Evening News*, but the defence did not really amount to much. Anyway he did not commit himself to the opinion that Mold was a strictly fair bowler. Knowing what I do as to the opinions expressed in private by several of the greatest batsmen in the country, I regard Mold as the luckiest of men to have gone through nearly a dozen seasons before being no-balled. The no-balling of Tyler was valuable in another way, as it emphasised the often neglected truth that a slow ball can be just as much a throw as a fast one.

S. H. P.

## NOTES BY THE EDITOR, 1901

On Tuesday, the 17th of December, the following important circular, addressed to the Secretaries of the various counties, was made public by the MCC:

Lord's Cricket Ground,
St. John's Wood, N.W.
December, 1901.

Dear Sir,

I am directed to inform you that the Captains of the First-class Counties met on September 24th, 1901, and agreed to refer such resolutions and recommendations as were passed then, or may be passed at future meetings, to the MCC Committee for confirmation.

In pursuance of this agreement the following proposals have been approved:

*a That the Bowling Crease shall be widened one foot each way.
 b That it is undesirable, in the interests of Cricket, that the wickets should be prepared artificially (i.e., in any way other than by water and the roller, except when patching is necessary).

### ILLEGAL BOWLING

The MCC Committee have given further careful consideration to the question of illegal bowling, and are of opinion that the decision of the Captains in 1900 has done so much good in discouraging this practice that it is unnecessary to suggest any drastic measure at present.

They hope that the County Cricket Executives will, in future, decline to play bowlers with doubtful deliveries, and thus remove the probability of any further infringement of Law 48.

Should an occasion arise when an Umpire by no-balling a bowler makes it clear that he is protesting against his deliveries, they think the only course open to the Captain is to take such bowler off, otherwise the proper spirit of the game cannot be preserved.

* In accordance with the rules of the MCC this proposal will be brought before a Special General Meeting on May 7th, 1902.

To meet the contingency of any flagrant case of illegal bowling arising, in the future, the following proposal has been made, and the Counties are invited to express an opinion thereon.

The Counties shall authorize their Captains to deal with the question, and, if at any meeting convened, with notice that it will be brought up the Captains shall decide by a majority of 2 to 1 that any bowler has been guilty of illegal bowling, they shall "name" him and recommend his suspension for at least a season, and refer it to the MCC Committee for confirmation.

Yours Faithfully,

F. E. Lacey, Sec., MCC

Dealing first with the latter part of the circular – in some respects the most significant – I rejoice that the MCC committee, though they overruled the decision come to by the county captains in December, 1900 to debar certain bowlers from taking part in county matches, acknowledge that a great deal of good has come from the famous meeting which for a few weeks threw the cricket world into a ferment. At the time I gave the captains what support I could, and, amid all the storm of criticism, I felt perfectly certain that, whether or not they were allowed their own way, nothing but benefit to the game of cricket would result from the action they had resolved on. Never within the last twenty years or more has there been so little unfair or doubtful bowling as in the season of 1901. Indeed the improvement was so marked as to make it clear that, if the captains stick to their guns, we shall soon be entirely free from an evil of which not very long ago it seemed impossible to get rid. The proposal on which the counties have now been invited to express an opinion does not seem to me to be in any way too stringent. There is not the slightest fear that the county captains will by a majority of two to one condemn any bowler unless his delivery is open to serious objection. It has been urged in *The Field* that if the captains put their ban upon a bowler who had passed all the umpires unchallenged, not one of the umpires could with any self-respect consent to stand again, but this argument is not in reality half so strong as might at first sight appear. Bob Thoms told Lord Harris years ago that any steps to get rid of throwing would have to come from those who control the game, and it is generally understood that at one of the private conferences organised at Lord's by Mr Lacey, many of the present umpires asked that in this matter of unfair bowling they might be relieved of responsibility, the necessary action being taken by the county captains and committees. Those who are so extremely sensitive as to the jurisdiction of the umpire being interfered with, even away from the field of play, seem to forget that for many years the law as to fair bowling was flagrantly infringed over and over again without the slightest step being taken by the umpires to put matters right. Personally I do not believe that unless James Phillips had shown the way by pulling up Jones during the tour of Mr Stoddart's second team in Australia, we should have seen any no-balling for throwing in this country. Like most reformers, Phillips has been subjected to a good deal of criticism and many hard words, but he need not trouble himself about anything that has been said against him. To him in the first place is due the present vastly improved condition of things. As to his action in no-balling Mold sixteen times at Old Trafford last July, I can say nothing, as I was not present as the match, but with regard to the agitation that was got up on Mold's behalf I have a very strong opinion indeed. To read some of the comments that appeared one might have supposed that nobody except Phillips had ever called Mold's fairness in question. The fact that the Lancashire fast bowler had been condemned as unfair by the county captains by a majority of eleven to one, at their meeting at Lord's in December, 1900, was systematically ignored. I have not the slightest prejudice against Mold as a man, but, repeating what I said last year, I think he was excessively luck to go through nearly a dozen seasons before being no-balled.

I do not know whether any concerted action will be found possible, but after the expression of opinion I heard from several distinguished cricketers last season, I am not in the least surprised that the question of the preparation of wickets should have been raised.

It is certain that more than three days cannot in this country be given up to a match, and within that limit of time it is, on wickets prepared according to the most modern methods, becoming increasingly difficult in fine weather to play a game out. The climax was reached during the past season at Leyton, the wickets on that ground being so superlatively good that it was almost impossible to get through four innings in three days. Indeed, out of eleven matches seven were left drawn. This was an altogether unsatisfactory state of things, and both Mr C. E. Green and Mr A. P. Lucas made no secret of their opinion that a great mistake had been committed in having the wickets prepared in the modern fashion. Other famous cricketers I could name contend that the use of the sort of liquid manure of which some ground-keepers are now so fond, handicaps the bowler in two ways, first by taking nearly all the life out of the ground, and secondly by rendering the wicket almost impervious to natural wear. No one, I take it, would attempt to lay down any hard and fast rule as to how grounds should be dealt with out of the cricket season, different soils requiring different treatment, but it does not seem to me impossible that the counties should come to an understanding as to what constitutes the legitimate preparation of the individual wicket. The mowing machine, the hose, and the heavy roller have in combination made the task of the modern batsman sufficiently easy, and in the opinion of many good judges of the game he did not need the further help that has lately been accorded him. This question of the preparation of wickets is urgent, as we do not wish to be driven to the necessity of deciding our three day matches on the first innings.

S. H. P.

## NOTES BY THE EDITOR, 1905

It would ill become me to allow the retirement of James Phillips from the post of umpire in first-class cricket to pass without comment. Now that we are almost entirely free from the curse of throwing the value of what Phillips did for the cause of fair bowling is beginning to be realised. He had the courage to act when other umpires were content to express their opinions in private, and for the great improvement that has resulted from the concerted action of the county captains and the present happy condition of things, thanks are chiefly due to him. The concerted action of the captains only came when the question had been fairly brought within the range of cricket politics. It is a little humiliating to think that an Australian umpire undertook a duty that our own men had shirked, but the fact must be borne in mind that Phillips stood in a rather more independent position than most of his colleagues. The courage lay in the initial steps as, the plunge once taken, Phillips soon found that he had authority behind him. As one who in a modest way laboured for many years to rid English cricket of throwing, I have special reason to rejoice at the change that has been brought about, and as I gave Phillips all the support I possibly could at a time when he was subjected to a good deal of criticism and even abuse, I may now congratulate him on his good work. No one could watch first-class cricket last season without being conscious of the great change that had come over the game. There was plenty of very fast bowling, but Cotter, Brearley, Knox, Warren, and others were all so unimpeachably fair in delivery that not the slightest question could be raised with regard to any one of them. I do not think for a moment that there would have been this general fairness of action if Phillips had not stood up for the enforcement of Law 10.

S. H. P.

## LANCASHIRE IN 1903

The deficiency of the side, as in 1902, lay in the bowling. Barnes stood out head and shoulders above his colleagues, and was the only bowler in the team who could be described as first-class. He took 131 wickets in county matches for considerably less than 18 runs each, and got through an enormous amount of work, sending down 1023 overs.

He varied a great deal in form, the difference between his best days and his worst being almost immeasurable, but when he was really himself there could be no two opinions as to his quality. Indeed, some good judges went so far as to say that on his good days he was the most difficult right-handed bowler in England. He enjoyed his greatest success against Essex at Leyton, taking in that match fourteen wickets with a wonderful average. His strength lay in his quickness off the pitch and his power of making the ball go away abruptly with his arm. Had there been another bowler of the same class to support him, Lancashire would no doubt have had a much better season. Before the summer was over, Barnes's connection with the Lancashire Club came to an end. He declined to sign the usual form promising his services for 1904, and in consequence of this step on his part he was left out of the team in the last match. It was stated that he had accepted an offer from the Church Club, and would return to the Lancashire League cricket which first brought him under the notice of the county authorities. His defection caused quite a sensation, and was commented on in rather bitter terms. It is to be hoped that Lancashire will discover some bowler competent to fill his place, but at present, so far as we know, there is no sign of such a prize. Temperament is a great thing in a cricketer, and in this respect Barnes has always been deficient. If he had possessed the enthusiasm for the game that characterised Barlow and Johnny Briggs he might have made a great name for himself, his natural gifts as a bowler being so remarkable.

## LANCASHIRE v WORCESTERSHIRE

### Played at Liverpool, June 22, 23, 24, 1903

Rain on the third day robbed Lancashire of a decisive victory, Worcestershire, when the game was abandoned, having two wickets down in their second innings and being 362 runs behind. MacLaren played a delightful innings on the Monday, and Lancashire got Worcestershire's first four wickets down for 32, but Foster and Gaukrodger hit up 167. The great performance of the match was that of Tyldesley, who, making 248 in less than four hours, gave no chance until he had completed his second hundred. His most brilliant innings included thirty-six 4s. Hornby helped him to put on 242.

### Lancashire

| | | | |
|---|---|---|---|
| Mr H. C. Garnett c Caldwell b Simpson-Hayward | 18 | – c Gaukrodger b Arnold | 24 |
| Mr R. H. Spooner c Simpson-Hayward | 5 | – b Wilson | 23 |
| J. T. Tyldesley c Burrows b Arnold | 41 | – c and b Burrows | 248 |
| Mr A. C. MacLaren b Wilson | 101 | – c Simpson-Hayward b Bird | 29 |
| Mr A. H. Hornby b Simpson-Hayward | 8 | – b Wilson | 74 |
| Mr E. E. Steel c Burrows b Arnold | 15 | – b Wilson | 0 |
| J. Sharp c Foster b Arnold | 1 | – not out | 24 |
| F. S. Barnes run out | 13 | | |
| Mr W. Brearley b Wilson | 7 | – b Arnold | 14 |
| G. Littlewood not out | 5 | | |
| L. Radcliffe b Arnold | 6 | | |
| B 3, l-b 9, w 6 | 18 | B 8, l-b 2, w 3 | 13 |
| | **238** | | **(7 wkts dec.) 449** |

### Worcestershire

| | | | |
|---|---|---|---|
| F. Bowley b Littlewood | 6 | – b Brearley | 17 |
| R. Pearson c MacLaren b Barnes | 2 | | |
| F. Wheldon c Radcliffe b Barnes | 8 | – not out | 0 |
| E. Arnold b Littlewood | 8 | – not out | 10 |
| Mr H. K. Foster lbw b Littlewood | 84 | – c Littlewood b Brearley | 45 |
| G. Gaukrodger b Littlewood | 91 | | |
| Mr W. S. Caldwall c Radcliffe b Barnes | 1 | | |
| Mr G. H. Simpson-Hayward c MacLaren b Barnes | 4 | | |
| A. Bird not out | 6 | | |
| G. A. Wilson c Garnett b Littlewood | 5 | | |
| R. Burrows c Spooner b Barnes | 18 | | |
| B 8, w 1, n-b 3 | 12 | B 8 | 8 |
| | **245** | | **80** |

### Worcestershire Bowling

| | Overs | Mdns | Runs | Wkts | Overs | Mdns | Runs | Wkts |
|---|---|---|---|---|---|---|---|---|
| Simpson Hayward .. | 14 | 1 | 64 | 3 | 10 | 1 | 62 | — |
| Wilson ......... | 19 | 1 | 85 | 2 | 24 | — | 104 | 3 |
| Arnold ......... | 21.2 | 5 | 57 | 4 | 26 | 2 | 118 | 2 |
| Burrows ........ | 4 | — | 14 | — | 17 | 1 | 93 | 1 |
| Bird ........... | | | | | 22 | 3 | 59 | 1 |

### Lancashire Bowling

| | Overs | Mdns | Runs | Wkts | Overs | Mdns | Runs | Wkts |
|---|---|---|---|---|---|---|---|---|
| Littlewood ....... | 33 | 2 | 101 | 5 | 19 | 11 | 20 | — |
| Barnes ......... | 29.5 | 12 | 57 | 5 | 12 | 8 | 11 | — |
| Brearley ........ | 21 | 6 | 50 | — | 12 | 5 | 26 | 2 |
| Steel ........... | 7 | 1 | 25 | — | 7 | 3 | 15 | — |

Umpires: G. Porter and C. E. Richardson.

## LANCASHIRE v GLOUCESTERSHIRE

### Played at Liverpool, July 30, 31, August 1, 1903

For a series of blunders committed in the early stages of the game, Gloucestershire would no doubt have had to pay the price of severe defeat had not the weather come to their assistance. Rain, as it happened, prevented any cricket on the second day until ten minutes past five, and after an hour and a half's play on Saturday late in the afternoon, the game was abandoned as a draw enormously in favour of the home side. MacLaren and Spooner in hitting up 368 for the first wicket established a fresh record for Lancashire cricket. MacLaren drove superbly but he was let off four times in making his first 60 runs two of the chances being very easy. Spooner, who hit splendidly on the off side, also experienced some luck, being missed when 36 and again when 90. After he left at 379 Tyldesley and Garnett added 69, the total, when rain brought a day's cricket on a soft easy pitch to a close, standing at 474 for three wickets. Further progress with the match being so long delayed next day, MacLaren declared and in eighty minutes Gloucestershire lost five batsmen for 49, Wrathall alone being able to cope with the bowling. On the Saturday afternoon Fowler and Jessop were soon dismissed but Brownlee and Thomas ensured a draw. Lancashire tried Heap and Harry, two members of the ground staff at Old Trafford.

## Lancashire

Mr A. C. MacLaren c Board b Huggins ...204
Mr R. H. Spooner c Mills b Huggins ......168
J. T. Tyldesley not out ................. 57
Mr H. G. Garnett c Spry b Mills ........ 23
J. Sharp not out ..................... 13
B 3, l-b 2, w 1, n-b 3 .......... 9
—
(3 wkts dec.) 474

Mr W. Findlay, Mr A. H. Hornby, Harry, Heap, W. R. Cuttell and S. F. Barnes did not bat.

## Gloucestershire

Mr R. W. Rice b Cuttell ................ 1
H. Wrathall c Tyldesley b Cuttell ........ 35
T. Langdon st Findlay b Sharp .......... 6
J. H. Board c Barnes b Heap ............ 6
E. Spry hit wkt b Heap ................ 0
Mr T. H. Fowler b Heap ............... 2
Mr G. L. Jessop c MacLaren b Cuttell ..... 17
Mr F. E. Thomas b Harry ............. 12
Mr L. D. Brownlee c Barnes b Cuttell ..... 43
J. H. Huggins b Sharp ................ 8
Mills not out ...................... 2
L-b 1, n-b 2 ................. 3
—
135

### Gloucestershire Bowling

|  | Overs | Mdns | Runs | Wkts |
|---|---|---|---|---|
| Huggins | 32 | 9 | 79 | 2 |
| Mills | 25 | 2 | 95 | 1 |
| Spry | 26 | — | 128 | — |
| Jessop | 16 | 2 | 64 | — |
| Brownlee | 5 | — | 34 | — |
| Langdon | 4 | — | 25 | — |
| Wrathall | 6 | — | 39 | — |
| Thomas | 2 | 1 | 1 | — |

### Lancashire Bowling

|  | Overs | Mdns | Runs | Wkts |
|---|---|---|---|---|
| Barnes | 5 | 4 | 8 | — |
| Cuttell | 27.3 | 13 | 36 | 4 |
| Sharp | 17 | 5 | 51 | 2 |
| Heap | 11 | 6 | 13 | 3 |
| Harry | 4 | — | 24 | 1 |

Umpires: A. Shaw and W. Richards.

## LANCASHIRE v DERBYSHIRE

Played at Manchester, August 6, 7, 1903

Derbyshire more than held their own on the Thursday, but went all to pieces next day, and had to admit defeat by nine wickets. Thanks to Wright, Storer and Ollivierre, the visitors looked like running up a big score, the first wicket producing 58 runs, and the second 102. Wright, who was fourth out at 213, played a very skilful, if not altogether faultless innings. After he left, Hallows and Brearley met with so little resistance, that the last six wickets fell for 28 runs. MacLaren and Spooner hit up 64 for the first Lancashire wicket, but both were missed, and Tyldesley, Findlay and Eccles all failing, there were four men out for 73 at the drawing of stumps. MacLaren and Hornby added 104 for the fifth wicket, the latter batting very soundly. Derbyshire at their second attempt were all out in two hours. Lancashire had only 98 to get to win, and accomplished the task within an hour, all but one of the number being obtained by MacLaren and Spooner before a wicket fell.

### Derbyshire

| | | | |
|---|---|---|---|
| Mr L. G. Wright b Hallows | 116 | – c Spooner b Brearley | 11 |
| W. Storer b Hallows | 29 | – b Hallows | 11 |
| Mr C. A. Ollivierre c MacLaren b Cuttell | 53 | – c Hallows b Brearley | 8 |
| Mr G. R. Gregory b Brearley | 1 | – not out | 20 |
| Mr A. E. Lawton Findlay b Hallows | 0 | – c Hallows b Barnes | 17 |
| E. Needham b Brearley | 2 | – b Hallows | 8 |
| Mr E. M. Ashcroft c Findlay b Brearley | 13 | – c sub. b Hallows | 1 |
| A. Warren b Brearley | 12 | – b Barnes | 0 |
| Cadman c Findlay b Hallows | 3 | – c MacLaren b Barnes | 1 |
| J. Humphries not out | 0 | – c Tyldesley b Hallows | 6 |
| W. Bestwick lbw b Hallows | 0 | – c Findlay b Barnes | 2 |
| B 4, l-b 3 | 7 | B 3, l-b 2, n-b 1 | 6 |
| | **236** | | **91** |

### Lancashire

| | | | |
|---|---|---|---|
| Mr A. C. MacLaren c Bestwick c Cadman | 88 | – not out | 56 |
| Mr R. H. Spooner b Bestwick | 28 | – c Needham b Lawton | 44 |
| J. T. Tyldesley c Warren b Bestwick | 0 | – not out | 0 |
| Mr W. Findlay lbw b Bestwick | 0 | | |
| Mr A. Eccles lbw b Gregory | 3 | | |
| Mr A. H. Hornby c Bestwick b Warren | 57 | | |
| J. Sharp c Bestwick b Warren | 19 | | |
| W. Hallows not out | 24 | | |
| W. R. Cuttell c Ollivierre b Warren | 8 | | |
| S. F. Barnes lbw b Gregory | 2 | | |
| Mr W. Brearley c Humphries b Gregory | 0 | | |
| B 5, l-b 1 | 6 | W 1 | 1 |
| | **230** | | **101** |

### Lancashire Bowling

| | Overs | Mdns | Runs | Wkts | Overs | Mdns | Runs | Wkts |
|---|---|---|---|---|---|---|---|---|
| Barnes | 8 | 2 | 20 | — | 7.2 | 4 | 3 | 4 |
| Cuttell | 17 | 3 | 49 | 1 | | | | |
| Hallows | 17.2 | 5 | 42 | 5 | 21 | 5 | 38 | 4 |
| Brearley | 23 | 3 | 76 | 4 | 13 | 3 | 44 | 2 |
| Sharp | 5 | 1 | 17 | — | | | | |
| Spooner | 8 | 1 | 25 | — | | | | |

### Derbyshire Bowling

| | Overs | Mdns | Runs | Wkts | Overs | Mdns | Runs | Wkts |
|---|---|---|---|---|---|---|---|---|
| Warren | 26 | 1 | 92 | 3 | 5 | 1 | 23 | — |
| Bestwick | 27 | 6 | 72 | 3 | 6.4 | — | 26 | — |
| Gregory | 8 | 2 | 27 | 3 | 3 | — | 19 | — |
| Cadman | 14 | 3 | 33 | 1 | 3 | — | 18 | — |
| Lawton | | | | | 3 | — | 14 | 1 |

Umpires: F. Martin and J. Carlin.

## LANCASHIRE v NOTTINGHAMSHIRE

### Played at Liverpool, May 28, 29, 1906

A lot of rain having fallen at the end of the previous week, it was expected that the wicket would prove too soft to be really treacherous, but from start to finish batsmen found themselves in the greatest difficulties, and the forty wickets went down in five hours and three-quarters of actual cricket. Wass accomplished a remarkable performance for a fast bowler, dismissing eight batsmen in each innings for an aggregate of 69 runs. Always dangerous on a pitch affected by rain he excelled himself on this occasion. An achievement quite as startling was that of Huddleston, who finished off the first Nottinghamshire innings at a trifling cost and on the Tuesday took the whole of the nine wickets which remained, making his record for the match, thirteen wickets for 41 runs. Spooner rendered his side splendid service, scoring 24 out of 31, and 32 out of 56. Thanks to the brothers Gunn, Nottinghamshire in the first innings obtained 37 before the third wicket fell, but after they were separated the innings was finished off for the addition of 11 runs. Lancashire won by 60 runs, Nottinghamshire, with 110 to get and nine wickets to fall on Tuesday, never looking like accomplishing the task.

### Lancashire

| | | |
|---|---|---|
| Mr A. C. MacLaren c Payton b Wass | 5 | – b Wass | 5 |
| Mr R. H. Spooner c Payton b Wass | 24 | – b J. Gunn | 32 |
| J. T. Tyldesley b Wass | 0 | – c Jones b Wass | 3 |
| Mr L. O. S. Poidevin b J. Gunn | 2 | – c G. Gunn b Wass | 7 |
| J. Sharp b Wass | 1 | – b Wass | 5 |
| F. Harry c Oates b Wass | 0 | – lbw b Wass | 2 |
| Mr A. H. Hornby b J. Gunn | 21 | – c Jones b Wass | 16 |
| W. R. Cuttell c Alletson b Wass | 0 | – not out | 20 |
| W. Huddleston c Jones b Wass | 1 | – c Jones b Wass | 2 |
| Mr W. Findlay c J. Gunn b Wass | 2 | – c Oates b J. Gunn | 2 |
| A. Kermode not out | 0 | – b Wass | 4 |
| L-b 1, n-b 1 | 2 | B 4 | 4 |
| | **58** | | **102** |

### Nottinghamshire

| | | |
|---|---|---|
| Mr A. O. Jones st Findlay b Cuttell | 1 | – c Harry b Huddleston | 6 |
| J. Iremonger b Kermode | 1 | – c Tyldesley b Huddleston | 10 |
| G. Gunn b Huddleston | 11 | – b Cuttell | 0 |
| J. Gunn b Cuttell | 18 | – c Spooner b Huddleston | 0 |
| J. Hardstaff c MacLaren b Cuttell | 5 | – b Huddleston | 1 |
| W. Payton c Hornby b Huddleston | 0 | – lbw b Huddleston | 2 |
| J. W. Day b Huddleston | 0 | – b Huddleston | 18 |
| E. Alletson c Findlay b Huddleston | 2 | – b Huddleston | 0 |
| A. Hallam lbw b Cuttell | 3 | – lbw b Huddleston | 4 |
| T. Wass c Tyldesley b Cuttell | 0 | – b Huddleston | 2 |
| T. Oates not out | 1 | – not out | 7 |
| B 4, n-b 2 | 6 | B 1, n-b 1 | 2 |
| | **48** | | **52** |

### Nottinghamshire Bowling

| | Overs | Mdns | Runs | Wkts | Overs | Mdns | Runs | Wkts |
|---|---|---|---|---|---|---|---|---|
| Wass | 11.4 | 3 | 25 | 8 | 18.3 | 4 | 44 | 8 |
| J. Gunn | 11 | 1 | 31 | 2 | 9 | 2 | 32 | 2 |
| Hallam | | | | | 9 | 1 | 22 | — |

### Lancashire Bowling

| | Overs | Mdns | Runs | Wkts | Overs | Mdns | Runs | Wkts |
|---|---|---|---|---|---|---|---|---|
| Kermode | 8 | 2 | 17 | 1 | | | | |
| Cuttell | 12.4 | 5 | 20 | 5 | 18 | 11 | 14 | 1 |
| Huddleston | 5 | 3 | 5 | 4 | 18 | 3 | 36 | 9 |

Umpires: F. G. Roberts and A. E. Clapp.

## LANCASHIRE v SOMERSET

### Played at Manchester, August 26, 27, 1909

Lancashire brought their season to a close with a victory over Somerset by 93 runs. They enjoyed a big advantage in winning the toss, the pitch at first being too dead to give bowlers any real assistance. Makepeace and Tyldesley, forcing the game in fine style, made 65 in fifty minutes, and Sharp, pulling and driving to great purpose, scored 52 out of 99. These two performances practically determined the result of the match, for afterwards the bowlers carried all before them. Dean, for the second time during the season, achieved the feat of taking nine wickets in an innings. With the Somerset score at 13 he bowled Herbert, and at 20 he dismissed Braund, Sampson, Poyntz, Robson, and Greswell, having at this point taken six wickets for 10 runs, 9 of which came from his first over. The first day's play ended with the completion of an innings on each side. On Friday Greswell and Lewis disposed of Lancashire in an hour and a quarter. Somerset, being set 194 to win, Braund and Herbert, before the effects of the roller wore off, put on 39 in half-an-hour, but afterwards, except for a stand by Samson and Greswell, Dean and Heap met with little resistance.

### Lancashire

| | | | |
|---|---:|---|---:|
| Mr A. H. Hornby b Lewis | 16 | – c Sutton b Lewis | 0 |
| H. Makepeace b Lewis | 38 | – c Sutton b Greswell | 21 |
| J. T. Tyldesley c Lewis b Greswell | 33 | – c Braund b Lewis | 9 |
| J. Sharp b Greswell | 52 | – c Chidgey b Lewis | 0 |
| Mr C. R. Hartley c Herbert b Greswell | 9 | – b Greswell | 7 |
| Mr K. G. MacLeod b Greswell | 1 | – b Greswell | 8 |
| J. S. Heap b Braund | 21 | – c Sutton b Greswell | 5 |
| W. Huddleston c Lewis b Robson | 1 | – c Herbert b Lewis | 0 |
| H. Dean b Robson | 6 | – st Chidgey b Greswell | 3 |
| Ł. Cook b Robson | 2 | – not out | 0 |
| W. Worsley not out | 4 | – c Bisgood b Lewis | 1 |
| B 9, n-b 3 | 12 | B 4, n-b 1 | 5 |
| | **195** | | **59** |

### Somerset

| | | | |
|---|---:|---|---:|
| Hon. M. Herbert b Dean | 7 | – c Huddleston b Dean | 18 |
| L. C. Braund c Cook b Dean | 6 | – b Dean | 27 |
| A. E. Lewis b Dean | 11 | – c Huddleston b Heap | 8 |
| Mr O. M. Samson b Dean | 0 | – st Worsley b Heap | 11 |
| Capt. H. S. Poyntz c Sharp b Dean | 0 | – c and b Heap | 0 |
| E. Robson c MacLeod b Dean | 0 | – c Heap b Dean | 9 |
| Mr W. T. Greswell b Dean | 0 | – not out | 18 |
| Mr B. L. Bisgood not out | 18 | – b Dean | 0 |
| Mr L. C. L. Sutton b Dean | 0 | – b Heap | 0 |
| Mr H. E. Hippisley b Huddleston | 0 | – c Tyldesley b Dean | 5 |
| H. Chidgey b Dean | 13 | – c Hornby b Heap | 0 |
| B 5, l-b 1 | 6 | B 2, n-b 2 | 4 |
| | **61** | | **100** |

### Somerset Bowling

| | Overs | Mdns | Runs | Wkts | Overs | Mdns | Runs | Wkts |
|---|---:|---:|---:|---:|---:|---:|---:|---:|
| Greswell | 25 | 5 | 71 | 4 | 14 | 1 | 28 | 5 |
| Lewis | 26 | 5 | 61 | 2 | 13.1 | 2 | 26 | 5 |
| Robson | 10.4 | 3 | 17 | 3 | | | | |
| Braund | 8 | — | 34 | 1 | | | | |

**Lancashire Bowling**

| | Overs | Mdns | Runs | Wkts | Overs | Mdns | Runs | Wkts |
|---|---|---|---|---|---|---|---|---|
| Dean ........... | 15.1 | 8 | 31 | 9 | 18.2 | 3 | 46 | 5 |
| Huddleston ....... | 15 | 5 | 24 | 1 | 6 | 1 | 15 | — |
| Heap ........... | | | | | 12 | 5 | 35 | 5 |

Umpires: F. G. Roberts and O. Frith.

# LANCASHIRE v HAMPSHIRE

Played at Manchester, June 13, 14, 15, 1910

To quite a number of batting triumphs which he had achieved during the early weeks of the season, John Tyldesley, on the occasion of the first match with Hampshire, added that of making – for the third time in his career – two separate hundreds. He played superbly on Monday, when, scoring 136 out of 242 in two hours thirty-five minutes, he had at first to contend against considerable difficulties, the pitch having been affected by rain in the night. Next day, batting at times with an amount of caution quite unusual with him, he was not seen to such striking advantage. Still in making 101 out of 198 in two hours forty minutes, he brought off some delightful strokes and the only blemish in his play was a hard chance when 27. Whitehead not only hit up 73 in seventy minutes but bowled with much effect. For Hampshire, Llewellyn batted vigorously at a critical time, Bowell played in admirable style and Mead on Wednesday put together a fine innings. Lancashire, however, won very comfortably by 176 runs.

## Lancashire

| | | | | |
|---|---|---|---|---|
| Mr A. H. Hornby b Llewellyn | 1 | – c Brown b Newman | 26 |
| Mr A. Hartley b Llewellyn | 23 | – lbw b Llewellyn | 23 |
| J. T. Tyldesley c Newman b Llewellyn | 136 | – b Llewellyn | 101 |
| J. Sharp c Brown b Llewellyn | 23 | – b Kennedy | 35 |
| W. Tyldesley c Smith b Kennedy | 3 | – b Kennedy | 48 |
| E. Tyldesley c Bowell b Llewellyn | 52 | – b Kennedy | 9 |
| R. Whitehead b Newman | 73 | – c sub. b Llewellyn | 0 |
| W. Huddleston b Llewellyn | 3 | – b Kennedy | 3 |
| L. Cook c Brown b Newman | 25 | | |
| H. Dean b Llewellyn | 0 | – not out | 1 |
| W. Worsley not out | 4 | | |
| B 1, l-b 4, n-b 5 | 10 | B 1, l-b 3, w 1, n-b 2 | 7 |
| | 353 | (8 wkts dec.) | 253 |

## Hampshire

| | | |
|---|---|---|
| Capt. J. G. Greig c E. Tyldesley b Huddleston ..... | 2 – | c Huddleston b Whitehead ....... 1 |
| P. Mead b Dean .......................... | 0 – | b Cook ...................... 90 |
| A. Bowell b Dean .......................... | 50 – | b Dean ...................... 53 |
| C. B. Llewellyn c Cook b Whitehead ............. | 56 – | b Whitehead .............. 17 |
| Mr A. C. Johnston b Sharp .................... | 0 – | not out ..................... 30 |
| G. Brown c Hornby b Whitehead .............. | 5 – | b Dean ..................... 1 |
| A. Stone c Cook b Whitehead ................. | 52 – | b Dean ...................... 0 |
| J. Newman c Worsley b Dean ................. | 0 – | b Dean ..................... 5 |
| Mr H. A. H. Smith b Cook ................. | 0 – | b Whitehead ................ 5 |
| J. Moore not out .......................... | 22 – | b Whitehead .............. 0 |
| A. Kennedy b Whitehead .................... | 2 – | b Sharp ..................... 24 |
| B 4 .......................... | 4 | B 7, l-b 4 .............. 11 |
| | **193** | **237** |

## Hampshire Bowling

| | Overs | Mdns | Runs | Wkts | Overs | Mdns | Runs | Wkts |
|---|---|---|---|---|---|---|---|---|
| Newman ......... | 28.5 | 7 | 87 | 2 | 22 | 1 | 46 | 1 |
| Llewellyn ......... | 34 | — | 136 | 7 | 25 | 2 | 100 | 3 |
| Kennedy ......... | 12 | 1 | 63 | 1 | 18 | 1 | 67 | 4 |
| Mead ............ | 8 | — | 52 | — | 6 | 1 | 16 | — |
| Greig ............ | 1 | — | 5 | — | 3 | — | 17 | — |

## Lancashire Bowling

| | Overs | Mdns | Runs | Wkts | Overs | Mdns | Runs | Wkts |
|---|---|---|---|---|---|---|---|---|
| Dean ............ | 24 | 10 | 45 | 3 | 28 | 4 | 69 | 4 |
| Huddleston ....... | 23 | 4 | 43 | 1 | 19 | 7 | 32 | — |
| Cook ............ | 12 | 3 | 47 | 1 | 10 | 1 | 31 | 1 |
| Whitehead ........ | 17 | 2 | 47 | 4 | 23 | 7 | 62 | 4 |
| Sharp ............ | 3 | — | 7 | 1 | 10 | — | 32 | 1 |

Umpires: F. G. Roberts and J. E. West.

## LANCASHIRE v NOTTINGHAMSHIRE

Played at Manchester, June 16, 17, 18, 1910

Hitting off 400 runs in the last innings, Lancashire achieved a feat altogether unprecedented in county cricket, but, strangely enough, they surpassed it six weeks later at Southampton. For two days Nottinghamshire quite outplayed their opponents, entering upon the concluding stage of the contest no fewer than 352 runs ahead with eight wickets in hand. For the course taken by A. O. Jones in declining – despite a lead of 214 on the first innings – to make Lancashire follow on, there was, no doubt, something to be said, but, in the circumstances, Nottinghamshire could not be excused for pursuing such cautious methods as characterised their play when they went in a second time. As a consequence of this unenterprising work overnight they had, in the endeavour to win, to force the game at all hazards on Saturday morning, and the eight outstanding wickets, falling in three-quarters of an hour, produced only 47 runs. Five hours and a quarter remained for play when Lancashire entered upon their tremendous task. Neither Hartley nor William Tyldesley gave much trouble, but John Tyldesley and Sharp in less than two hours and a half put on 191. Ernest Tyldesley and Whitehead followed up this splendid stand by adding 80 in forty minutes, and so well was the pace maintained that when Whitehead left only 42 runs were required with fifty minutes remaining. Riley disposing of Huddleston and Dean, Lancashire found themselves still wanting 36 with only two wickets to fall. Hornby, though handicapped by lameness and obviously in pain, played with characteristic pluck at this critical time, and Cook rendering him useful assistance the runs were obtained with two minutes to spare, Lancashire winning a wonderful match by two wickets.

## Nottinghamshire

| | | | |
|---|---|---|---|
| Mr A. O. Jones c W. Tyldesley b Cook | 30 | – b Dean | 6 |
| J. Iremonger c sub. b Cook | 35 | – c Whitehead b Cook | 61 |
| G. Gunn c sub. b Cook | 12 | – c and b Huddleston | 41 |
| J. Hardstaff c and b Cook | 106 | – b Dean | 10 |
| W. Payton c Jones b Cook | 22 | – run out | 22 |
| J. Gunn b Whitehead | 15 | – c J. T. Tyldesley b Huddleston | 4 |
| E. Alletson b Dean | 50 | – c E. Tyldesley b Huddleston | 22 |
| T. Oates c Jones b Cook | 57 | – lbw b Huddleston | 0 |
| W. Riley b W. Tyldesley | 5 | – b Dean | 0 |
| C. Clifton c J. T. Tyldesley b Cook | 2 | – c Cook b Huddleston | 0 |
| T. Wass not out | 15 | – not out | 4 |
| B 11, l-b 16 | 27 | B 9, l-b 5, w 1 | 15 |
| | **376** | | **185** |

## Lancashire

| | | | |
|---|---|---|---|
| Mr A. Hartley c Jones b Wass | 22 | – b Wass | 20 |
| W. Tyldesley c and b Clifton | 15 | – c Riley b Wass | 12 |
| J. T. Tyldesley b Clifton | 0 | – c Jones b Wass | 91 |
| J. Sharp b Iremonger | 73 | – b Riley | 102 |
| E. Tyldesley c Payton b Clifton | 2 | – b Clifton | 39 |
| R. Whitehead lbw b Jones | 22 | – b Riley | 48 |
| W. Huddleston c Alletson b Wass | 6 | – b Riley | 2 |
| H. Dean b Clifton | 6 | – c Alletson b Riley | 2 |
| L. Cook b Iremonger | 8 | – not out | 3 |
| Mr J. L. Jones not out | 0 | | |
| Mr A. H. Hornby absent hurt | 0 | – not out | 55 |
| B 5, l-b 3 | 8 | B 16, l-b 11, w 2 | 29 |
| | **162** | | **403** |

## Lancashire Bowling

| | Overs | Mdns | Runs | Wkts | Overs | Mdns | Runs | Wkts |
|---|---|---|---|---|---|---|---|---|
| Whitehead | 26 | 4 | 70 | 1 | 12 | — | 28 | — |
| Dean | 32 | 9 | 88 | 1 | 23 | 8 | 50 | 3 |
| Cook | 35.4 | 4 | 102 | 7 | 15 | 2 | 52 | 1 |
| Sharp | 11 | 1 | 42 | — | | | | |
| Huddleston | 10 | 2 | 29 | — | 16 | 4 | 36 | 5 |
| W. Tyldesley | 8 | 1 | 18 | 1 | 2 | — | 4 | — |

## Nottinghamshire Bowling

| | Overs | Mdns | Runs | Wkts | Overs | Mdns | Runs | Wkts |
|---|---|---|---|---|---|---|---|---|
| Wass | 24 | 3 | 69 | 2 | 36 | 5 | 126 | 3 |
| Clifton | 28 | 5 | 67 | 4 | 22 | 4 | 86 | 1 |
| Iremonger | 7.4 | 4 | 11 | 2 | 22 | — | 90 | — |
| Jones | 3 | — | 7 | 1 | 1 | — | 4 | — |
| Riley | | | | | 19.4 | 2 | 63 | 4 |
| Alletson | | | | | 1 | — | 5 | — |

Umpires: G. P. Harrison and F. G. Roberts.

## LANCASHIRE v SOMERSET

Played at Liverpool, June 1, 2, 3, 1911

Although without Hornby as well as J. T. Tyldesley, and giving a rest to Dean, Lancashire proved far too strong for Somerset who, dismissed in seventy minutes on Saturday morning, had to acknowledge defeat by 423 runs. Rain on Wednesday night had somewhat affected the wicket, but still Lancashire scored creditably at their first attempt, and on Friday the home side had matters all their own way. Spooner played in his most brilliant style for rather less than two hours, scoring at first chiefly on the leg side and afterwards driving grandly. He gave no chance. William Tyldesley, in putting together his first hundred for Lancashire, was badly missed in the slips after scoring 6 but made no other mistake during a stay of two hours and a half. Brearley, bowling in great form, was somewhat flattered by the febbleness of the Somerset batting. In the absence of Dean, Lancashire gave a trial to Fairclough, a left-handed slow bowler.

### Lancashire

| | | |
|---|---|---|
| Mr R. H. Spooner c Chidgey b Lewis | 19 | – c Daniell b Robson .... 117 |
| Mr A. Hartley c Chidgey b Bridges | 43 | – run out .... 1 |
| W. Tyldesley c Chidgey b Lewis | 31 | – c and b Robson .... 108 |
| J. Sharp b Taylor | 45 | – c Braund b Deane .... 8 |
| J. S. Heap b Taylor | 13 | – b Poyntz .... 32 |
| H. Makepeace c Chidgey b Lewis | 65 | – c Deane b Poyntz .... 29 |
| Mr H. G. Garnett c and b Taylor | 2 | – c Chidgey b Hardy .... 5 |
| Mr K. G. McLeod c Poyntz b Taylor | 17 | – c Daniell b Poyntz .... 38 |
| P. M. Fairclough c Braund b Taylor | 19 | – c Hardy b Poyntz .... 19 |
| L. Cook c and b Lewis | 0 | – not out .... 29 |
| Mr W. Brearley not out | 4 | – c Taylor b Poyntz .... 4 |
| B 8, l-b 8, w 3 | 19 | B 13, w 2 .... 15 |
| | **277** | **405** |

### Somerset

| | | |
|---|---|---|
| L. C. Braund b Brearley | 9 | – c Sharp b Brearley .... 18 |
| P. J. Hardy c Garnett b Brearley | 0 | – c Tyldesley b Cook .... 9 |
| A. E. Whittle b Brearley | 15 | – b Fairclough .... 0 |
| Mr E. S. M. Poyntz c McLeod b Sharp | 20 | – c Garnett b Fairclough .... 0 |
| Mr J. Daniell c Garnett b Brearley | 26 | – c Fairclough b Brearley .... 0 |
| E. Robson c Hartley b Brearley | 24 | – b Brearley .... 25 |
| A. E. Lewis c Sharp b Brearley | 27 | – c Garnett b Brearley .... 4 |
| Mr C. G. Deane not out | 31 | – c Spooner b Fairclough .... 0 |
| H. Chidgey b Brearley | 14 | – b Brearley .... 0 |
| W. H. Taylor c Hartley b Brearley | 20 | – c Heap b Brearley .... 0 |
| J. F. Bridges c Garnett b Fairclough | 5 | – not out .... 9 |
| L-b 1, n-b 1 | 2 | L-b 1 .... 1 |
| | **193** | **66** |

### Somerset Bowling

| | Overs | Mdns | Runs | Wkts | Overs | Mdns | Runs | Wkts |
|---|---|---|---|---|---|---|---|---|
| Lewis | 25.3 | 4 | 82 | 4 | 13 | 2 | 46 | — |
| Taylor | 21 | 3 | 65 | 5 | 9 | 2 | 35 | — |
| Bridges | 15 | 1 | 47 | 1 | 6 | — | 51 | — |
| Robson | 6 | — | 29 | — | 23 | 3 | 93 | 2 |
| Deane | 3 | — | 18 | — | 2 | — | 9 | 1 |
| Braund | 4 | — | 17 | — | 10 | 1 | 41 | — |
| Hardy | | | | | 6 | — | 55 | 1 |
| Whittle | | | | | 4 | — | 24 | — |
| Poyntz | | | | | 8.3 | 1 | 36 | 5 |

**Lancashire Bowling**

| | Overs | Mdns | Runs | Wkts | Overs | Mdns | Runs | Wkts |
|---|---|---|---|---|---|---|---|---|
| Brearley . . . . . . . . . | 25 | 2 | 106 | 8 | 10.5 | 2 | 36 | 6 |
| Cook . . . . . . . . . . . | 16 | 4 | 45 | — | 3 | — | 12 | 1 |
| Sharp . . . . . . . . . . . | 5 | 1 | 19 | 1 | | | | |
| Fairclough . . . . . . . | 4.1 | — | 21 | 1 | 7 | 1 | 17 | 3 |

Umpires: H. Bagshaw and W. A. J. West.

## LANCASHIRE v HAMPSHIRE

Played at Manchester, July 3, 4, 1911

Outplaying their opponents at all points, Lancashire declared with seven wickets down and gained the easiest of victories by an innings and 455 runs. Hampshire, in the absence of Fry, Johnston, White, and Sprot were of course weakly represented, but the loss of these amateurs in no way excused the complete failure of the bowlers. Batting for five hours and three-quarters on the opening day, Lancashire scored 621 for six wickets and took three-quarters of an hour next morning to raise their total to 676. Spooner and John Tyldesley made 214 runs in two hours and ten minutes, Hartley and Sharp 136 in seventy minutes and Sharp and McLeod 110 in forty minutes. Spooner's delightful innings, quite without blemish except for a chance at 146, lasted three hours and a half and included twenty-eight 4s. Sharp scored his 135 without a mistake and McLeod obtained his 100 in ninety minutes. Lancashire's total is the second highest ever put together by that county.

### Lancashire

| | |
|---|---|
| Mr R. H. Spooner b Newman . . . . . . . . . . .186 | Mr K. G. McLeod c Kennedy b Remnant . .101 |
| H. Makepeace b Olivier . . . . . . . . . . . . . . . 36 | Mr H. G. Garnett not out . . . . . . . . . . . . . . 28 |
| J. T. Tyldesley c Newman b Bowell . . . . . . . 98 | |
| J. Sharp c Barton b Remnant . . . . . . . . . . .135 | B 6, l-b 6, w 16, n-b 5 . . . . . . . . . . 33 |
| Mr A. Hartley b Bacon . . . . . . . . . . . . . . . 59 | |
| W. Huddleston b Bacon . . . . . . . . . . . . . . . 0 | (7 wkts dec.) 676 |

Mr A. H. Hornby, L. Cook and H. Dean did not bat.

### Hampshire

| | | |
|---|---|---|
| A. Bowell b Dean . . . . . . . . . . . . . . . . . . . . . . . . . | 3 – | c Garnett b Dean . . . . . . . . . . . . . . . 7 |
| A. Kennedy c Hornby b Cook . . . . . . . . . . . . . . . . . . | 46 – | c Dean b Sharp . . . . . . . . . . . . . . . 1 |
| A. Stone c Huddleston b Dean . . . . . . . . . . . . . . . . . | 4 – | c Tyldesley b Dean . . . . . . . . . . . 1 |
| C. P. Mead b Dean . . . . . . . . . . . . . . . . . . . . . . . . . | 10 – | c Tyldesley b Cook . . . . . . . . . . . 46 |
| E. R. Remnant c Garnett b Dean . . . . . . . . . . . . . . . | 6 – | c McLeod b Cook . . . . . . . . . . . . 0 |
| G. Brown c Huddleston b Dean . . . . . . . . . . . . . . . . | 3 – | b Cook . . . . . . . . . . . . . . . . . . . . 6 |
| Mr H. G. M. Barton b Dean . . . . . . . . . . . . . . . . . . | 0 – | c Garnett b Dean . . . . . . . . . . . . . 0 |
| J. Moore c McLeod b Dean . . . . . . . . . . . . . . . . . . . | 10 – | b McLeod . . . . . . . . . . . . . . . . . . 15 |
| J. Newman b Cook . . . . . . . . . . . . . . . . . . . . . . . . . | 8 – | b Huddleston . . . . . . . . . . . . . . . 19 |
| Mr F. H. Bacon not out . . . . . . . . . . . . . . . . . . . . . | 7 – | not out . . . . . . . . . . . . . . . . . . . . 12 |
| Mr E. Olivier c Hornby b Cook . . . . . . . . . . . . . . . | 0 – | st Garnett b Huddleston . . . . . . . . . 2 |
| B 4, w 1 . . . . . . . . . . . . . . . . . . . . . . . . | 5 | B 10 . . . . . . . . . . . . . . . . . . 10 |
| | 102 | 119 |

## Hampshire Bowling

| | Overs | Mdns | Runs | Wkts |
|---|---|---|---|---|
| Brown ........... | 11 | 1 | 66 | — |
| Kennedy ......... | 23 | 3 | 109 | — |
| Newman ......... | 28 | 3 | 139 | 1 |
| Bowell .......... | 23 | 1 | 85 | 1 |
| Olivier .......... | 16 | — | 74 | 1 |
| Remnant ........ | 19.5 | 1 | 99 | 2 |
| Mead ........... | 8 | 1 | 48 | — |
| Bacon .......... | 3 | — | 23 | 2 |

## Lancashire Bowling

| | Overs | Mdns | Runs | Wkts | Overs | Mdns | Runs | Wkts |
|---|---|---|---|---|---|---|---|---|
| Dean ............ | 26 | 13 | 37 | 7 | 17 | 7 | 28 | 3 |
| Cook ........... | 20.3 | 5 | 39 | 3 | 16 | 7 | 29 | 3 |
| Sharp .......... | 6 | 2 | 21 | — | 5 | 1 | 21 | 1 |
| Makepeace ....... | | | | | 3 | — | 14 | — |
| McLeod ......... | | | | | 5 | 2 | 4 | 1 |
| Huddleston ...... | | | | | 3.3 | 1 | 13 | 2 |

Umpires: G. P. Harrison and W. Vining.

## LANCASHIRE v ESSEX

### Played at Manchester, August 21, 22, 1911

Originally fixed for Blackpool, this match was afterwards arranged to be played at Liverpool but owing to the serious labour troubles prevailing in that city it was further transferred to Manchester. Essex suffered defeat by an innings and 64 runs, but for the severity of the reverse they had only themselves to blame, five catches – two of them very easy – being missed on the opening day. Makepeace, who made 54, was let off in the slips before scoring, and John Tyldesley was given a life when 2. The pitch being soft and rather difficult, Lancashire, even allowing for the luck they enjoyed, did very well to get 235 for six wickets in three hours and three-quarters before bad light followed by heavy rain stopped play shortly after five o'clock. John Tyldesley and Makepeace, making excellent use of their good fortune, put on 80 runs in little over an hour. On Tuesday Brearley was compelled to keep to his bed and Lancashire fielded only ten men, the offer of a substitute being declined. As matters went, his absence was not seriously felt. Dean and Fairclough on the ruined pitch doing all that was required. These two men not only got on a lot of break but often made the ball get up awkwardly. Perrin – top scorer in each innings – withstood the Lancashire attack for an hour and fifty minutes and in the follow on for an hour and twenty minutes, but the large majority of his colleagues failed altogether. Play was prolonged for a few minutes beyond the usual hour in order to bring the match to a conclusion on the second day.

### Lancashire

| | | | |
|---|---|---|---|
| Mr A. Hartley c Freeman b Tremlin ...... | 27 | Mr A. H. Hornby c Reeves b Tremlin ..... | 31 |
| H. Makepeace c Perrin b Tremlin ........ | 54 | Mr H. G. Garnett not out ............... | 5 |
| J. T. Tyldesley c Carpenter b Tremlin ..... | 43 | P. M. Fairclough c Carpenter b Mead ..... | 10 |
| H. Dean b Buckenham ................ | 33 | Mr W. Brearley absent ill ............... | 0 |
| J. Sharp c Freeman b Tremlin ........... | 1 | B 18, l-b 4 .................. | 22 |
| E. Tyldesley c Carpenter b Tremlin ....... | 11 | | |
| Mr K. G. McLeod run out ............. | 37 | | **274** |

## Essex

| | | | |
|---|---|---|---|
| Mr J. W. H. T. Douglas c McLeod b Fairclough .... | 10 | – c Hartley b Fairclough ......... | 5 |
| A. C. Russell c McLeod b Sharp ............... | 4 | – c and b Fairclough ............. | 4 |
| Mr P. Perrin lbw b Dean ..................... | 27 | – b Fairclough ................. | 26 |
| J. Freeman c J. T. Tyldesley b Dean ............ | 4 | – b Dean ..................... | 1 |
| H. Carpenter b Dean ....................... | 0 | – c Fairclough b Dean ........... | 17 |
| Mr C. McGahey c Hornby b Fairclough ......... | 7 | – c McLeod b Dean ............. | 11 |
| W. Reeves b Dean ......................... | 24 | – c Dean b Fairclough ........... | 6 |
| Mr K. L. Gibson b Dean ..................... | 10 | – c and b Dean ................. | 10 |
| C. P. Buckenham not out .................... | 1 | – not out ..................... | 14 |
| B. Tremlin c E. Tyldesley b Fairclough .......... | 7 | – c Hartley b Dean ............. | 5 |
| W. Mead c McLeod b Dean ................... | 8 | – c E. Tyldesley b Fairclough ....... | 6 |
| L-b 2 ......................... | 2 | L-b 1 ................. | 1 |
| | **104** | | **106** |

## Essex Bowling

| | Overs | Mdns | Runs | Wkts |
|---|---|---|---|---|
| Douglas .......... | 7 | 1 | 35 | — |
| Buckenham ....... | 8 | 1 | 39 | 1 |
| Tremlin .......... | 33 | 6 | 84 | 6 |
| Mead ........... | 34.3 | 12 | 75 | 1 |
| Reeves .......... | 3 | — | 19 | — |

## Lancashire Bowling

| | Overs | Mdns | Runs | Wkts | Overs | Mdns | Runs | Wkts |
|---|---|---|---|---|---|---|---|---|
| Dean ........... | 27.2 | 10 | 47 | 6 | 23 | 3 | 60 | 5 |
| Sharp ........... | 4 | — | 7 | 1 | | | | |
| Fairclough ....... | 23 | 7 | 48 | 3 | 22.1 | 2 | 45 | 5 |

Umpires: H. Bagshaw and G. P. Harrison.

## LANCASHIRE v KENT

Played at Manchester, May 30, 31, June 1, 1912

There was a desperately exciting finish to this match, Lancashire winning in what, in any case, must have been the last over by an innings and 27 runs. Dean bowled wonderfully well for the home side, and came out with a record of fifteen wickets for just over 7 runs apiece. Fortune, however, greatly favoured the home side. On Thursday, when rain stopped play just after three o'clock, Lancashire scored 138 for three wickets, and on Friday, with progress restricted to an hour and fifty minutes, they increased their total to 227 for the loss of four more batsmen. As in the two previous home Lancashire matches, Sharp put together a three-figure innings. Batting with fine skill and judgment, he withstood the Kent bowling for nearly three hours and a half. Bright sunshine on a drying wicket on Saturday placed the visitors in a desperate position. Humphreys, Hardinge, and Hutchings all played splendid cricket in their endeavours to save the game. In the first innings, Humphreys, seventh man out, batted for an hour and forty minutes, and in the follow-on Hardinge stayed somewhat longer, while Hutchings showed admirable defence for an hour and a quarter. All their endeavours, however, were in vain. There was much question as to whether Blythe, when given out caught and bowled, had not played the ball on to the ground. Owing to a damaged knee, Spooner could not take his place in the Lancashire team.

## Lancashire

| | | |
|---|---|---|
| Mr A. Hartley b Fielder | 3 | Mr A. H. Hornby not out .............. 24 |
| H. Makepeace b Humphreys | 5 | R. Whitehead c Hatfeild b Woolley ....... 4 |
| J. T. Tyldesley c Huish b Fielder | 55 | W. Huddleston c Humphreys b Blythe .... 0 |
| J. Sharp c Hatfeild b Woolley | 106 | H. Dean c Hardinge b Blythe ............ 14 |
| J. S. Heap c Fielder b Blythe | 12 | B 22, l-b 3, w 1, n-b 1 .......... 27 |
| E. Tyldesley b Fairservice | 6 | |
| Mr F. R. R. Brooke b Blythe | 8 | 264 |

## Kent

| | | |
|---|---|---|
| E. Humphreys c J. Tyldesley b Dean ............. 32 | – | c Makepeace b Heap ............ 21 |
| H. T. W. Hardinge c Hartley b Dean ............. 10 | – | st Brooke b Dean .............. 35 |
| James Seymour b Dean ...................... 0 | – | c Huddleston b Dean ........... 0 |
| F. E. Woolley c E. Tyldesley b Dean ............. 7 | – | c Sharp b Huddleston ........... 14 |
| Mr K. L. Hutchings c and b Dean .............. 13 | – | b Huddleston ................. 33 |
| D. W. Jennings b Dean .................... 2 | – | lbw b Dean .................. 1 |
| Mr C. E. Hatfeild c Makepeace b Dean ........... 2 | – | b Dean ..................... 4 |
| F. H. Huish c Makepeace b Dean ............... 3 | – | c Hornby b Dean ............... 6 |
| W. J. Fairservice b Huddleston ................. 3 | – | b Dean ..................... 0 |
| C. Blythe not out ......................... 10 | – | c and b Dean ................. 0 |
| A. Fielder lbw b Huddleston .................. 11 | – | not out ..................... 0 |
| B 14, l-b 3 ........................ 17 | | B 9, l-b 4 .............. 13 |
| 110 | | 127 |

### Kent Bowling

| | Overs | Mdns | Runs | Wkts |
|---|---|---|---|---|
| Fielder .......... | 14 | 2 | 56 | 2 |
| Humphreys ....... | 9 | 5 | 11 | 1 |
| Fairservice ....... | 12 | 3 | 22 | 1 |
| Blythe .......... | 33.5 | 7 | 73 | 4 |
| Woolley ......... | 30 | 3 | 75 | 2 |

### Lancashire Bowling

| | Overs | Mdns | Runs | Wkts | Overs | Mdns | Runs | Wkts |
|---|---|---|---|---|---|---|---|---|
| Dean ............ | 24 | 4 | 59 | 8 | 30.2 | 11 | 49 | 7 |
| Huddleston ....... | 23.3 | 7 | 34 | 2 | 20 | 4 | 31 | 2 |
| Heap ............ | | | | | 20 | 7 | 33 | 1 |
| Whitehead ....... | | | | | 2 | 1 | 1 | — |

Umpires: W. Flowers and H. Bagshaw.

## LANCASHIRE v WORCESTERSHIRE

Played at Manchester, July 1, 2, 3, 1912

As upon the occasion of their match with Kent at Whitsun, Lancashire enjoyed an enormous advantage in winning the toss. Still they were entitled to much credit for making such splendid use of their luck. On Monday, when rain limited play to less than two hours, they obtained 125 for the loss of two wickets. Makepeace and John Tyldesley coming together with the score at 12, hit up 100 runs in eighty minutes. Not a ball could be bowled on Tuesday and on Wednesday the pitch, always soft, became more and more difficult as the day advanced. In the course of two hours Lancashire, before declaring with eight wickets down, increased their total to 269 and then, with Dean in great form, proceeded to dispose of Worcestershire twice for less than a 100 runs. Dean kept an almost perfect length, and made the ball come quickly off the pitch with enough break to beat the bat. He enjoyed a great triumph, taking thirteen wickets for 49 runs. The ground was at its worst when Worcestershire followed on. Lancashire won by an innings and 181 runs.

### Lancashire

| | |
|---|---|
| Mr R. H. Spooner st Bale b Cuffe ........ 7 | Mr A. H. Hornby b Cuffe ............. 20 |
| H. Makepeace run out ................. 69 | R. Whitehead not out ................. 12 |
| J. T. Tyldesley lbw b Pearson ........... 49 | H. Dean not out ..................... 8 |
| J. Sharp c Collier b Arnold ............ 31 | |
| E. Tyldesley c and b Cuffe ............. 1 | B 8, w 4, n-b 1 .............. 13 |
| J. S. Heap b Cuffe .................. 15 | |
| Mr F. R. R. Brooke c Cliff b Pearson ..... 44 | (8 wkts dec.) 269 |

W. Huddleston did not bat.

### Worcestershire

| | | | |
|---|---|---|---|
| F. Bowley c Sharp b Dean .................... | 7 | – lbw b Huddleston .............. | 0 |
| F. Pearson c Dean b Huddleston ............... | 10 | – b Dean ...................... | 0 |
| E. Arnold c Brooke b Dean .................. | 11 | – b Dean ...................... | 8 |
| Mr W. B. Burns b Dean ..................... | 0 | – c Spooner b Huddleston ........ | 0 |
| C. G. A. Collier lbw b Dean .................. | 5 | – c J. T. Tyldesley b Dean ........ | 20 |
| J. A. Cuffe c Hornby b Dean ................. | 1 | – b Dean ...................... | 5 |
| Mr A. T. Cliff run out ..................... | 2 | – c E. Tyldesley b Dean .......... | 2 |
| Mr G. H. Simpson-Hayward c and b Huddleston ... | 0 | – c Sharp b Huddleston .......... | 4 |
| R. Burrows c and b Dean .................... | 5 | – b Dean ...................... | 0 |
| E. Bale c Sharp b Dean ..................... | 0 | – b Huddleston ................. | 2 |
| F. Chester not out ........................ | 0 | – not out ..................... | 0 |
| B 5, n-b 1 ........................ | 6 | | |
| | 47 | | 41 |

### Worcestershire Bowling

| | Overs | Mdns | Runs | Wkts |
|---|---|---|---|---|
| Cuffe ........... | 25 | 4 | 74 | 4 |
| Arnold .......... | 21 | 4 | 63 | 1 |
| Pearson ......... | 15 | 2 | 39 | 2 |
| Cliff ............. | 8 | — | 26 | — |
| Chester ......... | 16 | 4 | 54 | — |

### Lancashire Bowling

| | Overs | Mdns | Runs | Wkts | Overs | Mdns | Runs | Wkts |
|---|---|---|---|---|---|---|---|---|
| Dean ........... | 16.2 | 8 | 24 | 7 | 11 | 4 | 25 | 6 |
| Huddleston ....... | 16 | 7 | 17 | 2 | 10 | 4 | 13 | 4 |
| Heap ........... | | | | | 1 | — | 3 | — |

Umpires: J. Blake and T. Westborough.

## LANCASHIRE IN 1913

*President –* Mr A. N. Hornby

*Hon. Treasurer –* Mr Talbot Fair, Lytham

*Secretary –* Mr T. J. Matthews, 26, Barton Arcade, Manchester

*Captain –* Mr A. H. Hornby

The most unsuccessful season that Lancashire have had for many years ended in a domestic storm. While the last match – the return with Essex – was in progress at Old Trafford, Mr A. H. Hornby, in an interview in the *Manchester Guardian*, expressed great dissatisfaction at the way in which the affairs of the club were being conducted, taking particular exception to the proposal, contemplated at that time, of reducing the fixture list in 1914. He raised various points, but as everything was afterwards amicably settled, it is hardly necessary now to go into details. The Committee did not hesitate to express their opinion that they thought Mr Hornby might well have consulted them privately instead of bringing the matter before the public through the medium of the Press, and it certainly struck the outsider that the various questions in dispute might easily have been put right without the outside world knowing that there had been any friction. The facts having been made known, however, and published all over the country, a public settlement of the quarrel became imperative. Special meetings were held and a special body appointed to go into the whole question and make such suggestions to the Committee as they thought fit for the future guidance of the club. On the whole it was perhaps best that the facts should have come out. There was nothing to conceal, and no discredit attached to anyone concerned, the points raised being only details of management. The air was cleared, and the Committee found their financial position strengthened at once, Lord Derby, Lord Ellesmere, Mr Edward Hulton, and others promising substantial subscriptions for three years to come. In a leading article dealing with the report of the commision of inquiry the *Manchester Guardian* summed up the whole matter as follows:

"The commission of inquiry into Lancashire county cricket has produced a careful and sane review of the situation. The difficulties, as the result of friendly investigation, already begin to look less serious, and the better understanding between all parties of which there are welcome signs should bring an accession of active interest and co-operative effort into the business of the County Club. Already a number of minor practical reforms are promised. The entrance fee is to be suspended, season tickets for the ground side are to be issued, second eleven and colts' matches are to be more seriously treated as means of recruiting the county team, a more intimate relation is likely to be cultivated with the cricket leagues of Lancashire, the curtailment of the programme of county matches has been arrested, and members are to be allowed occasionally to introduce a friend to the pavilion – under a recognised rule instead of as a capricious favour. The Special Committee are not quite satisfied with the County Committee's reply on three points, the most controversial of which is the rule affecting the election of the president. At present the members elect the president annually; they possess an unlimited option to change the president as often as they like, or to re-elect him for as long as they like. The Special Committee wish this option to be restricted by a rule providing for compulsory periodical changes in the presidency. When the point was last raised at a general meeting the feeling was found to be in favour of the continuance of the present unfettered option, under which the members may do exactly what seems best to them at the moment. The Special Committee disapprove, in certain details, of the action both of the Committee and of Mr A. H. Hornby, but they do so with commendable delicacy. The Committee, they think, have made some mistakes, but they recognise, as everyone does, their loyal services to the Club and the difficulties arising from the financial position. As to Mr Hornby, they do not endorse the method he adopted; but here, again, they admit that the result of his action has been beneficial. So the net result of the statement which Mr Hornby communicated to the *Manchester Guardian* of August 23rd is that Lancashire cricket has benefited. The captain's central object, apart from any minor question of procedure, has thus been served. The Committee, the players, and the members have got to understand one another better and the fruit of this will be seen, it is to be hoped, in a revival of prosperity next season."

At the annual meeting, held on December 11th, Mr O. P. Lancashire, the Chairman of the Committee, in moving the adoption of the report and balance sheet, said the Club had to face an adverse balance of £994 10s. Things, however, were not so bad as they looked, as out of this sum they had guaranteed £400 to Paul for his benefit and £100 to Worsley. Lord Derby advocated an appeal to the whole county for increased support, and afterwards moved a resolution, unanimously carried, that the General Committee, together with any members of the club they might co-opt, should be formed into a Committee to consider the best way of raising funds for the Club.

## LANCASHIRE v YORKSHIRE

### Played at Manchester, May 12, 13, 1913

Opening their programme with a victory over Yorkshire by an innings and 3 runs – the first they had secured at the expense of their neighbours since August 1910 – Lancashire raised great expectations of a successful season. Play was only possible for two hours and a half on Monday, the weather turning wet after a pleasant morning, and by twenty minutes to four on Tuesday the game was all over. Yorkshire had rather the worst of the conditions, the ball during the time they were batting coming off the ground at varying paces, while when Lancashire went in light rain had eased the pitch and bowlers were handicapped by a wet ball. Still there can be no question Yorkshire ought to have made considerably more runs and would have done so had their men been in better practice. Scarcely any of the team timed the ball properly. Rhodes and Wilson put on 22 for the first wicket, and Hirst, although often at fault stayed for an hour, but in two hours the Yorkshiremen were all out. Heap, the left-handed slow bowler, kept a remarkable length and took six wickets for 16 runs. Lancashire, for the loss of one batsman, had made 34 runs when rain stopped play for the day. On Tuesday, with the weather bright, the state of the wicket should have enabled the visitors to pull the game round, but the Yorkshire bowlers failed to make the most of the opportunity. Hornby and John Tyldesley brought the score to 51 before the second wicket fell, Sharp defended stubbornly, and Whitehead made some good hits. Yorkshire at their second attempt cut a wretched figure against Heap and Dean. No one showed any confidence in facing Dean, who came out with a record for the match of eleven wickets for 39 runs.

### Yorkshire

| | | |
|---|---|---|
| W. Rhodes c Sharp b Heap | 14 | – lbw b Dean ..... 9 |
| B. B. Wilson b Dean | 8 | – b Dean ..... 1 |
| D. Denton c Hornby b Dean | 10 | – b Heap ..... 11 |
| A. Drake lbw b Huddleston | 2 | – c Hornby b Heap ..... 5 |
| G. H. Hirst c Hornby b Heap | 21 | – b Dean ..... 9 |
| R. Kilner c Huddleston b Heap | 5 | – run out ..... 0 |
| E. Oldroyd st Brooke b Huddleston | 1 | – b Heap ..... 3 |
| M. W. Booth not out | 4 | – lbw b Heap ..... 2 |
| S. Haigh lbw b Heap | 0 | – b Dean ..... 9 |
| Sir A. W. White c Huddleston b Heap | 0 | – b Heap ..... 3 |
| A. Dolphin c Brooke b Heap | 2 | – not out ..... 0 |
| B 7 | 7 | B 1 ..... 1 |
| | **74** | **53** |

### Lancashire

| | |
|---|---|
| Mr A. H. Hornby c Oldroyd b Hirst ...... 28 | Mr F. R. R. Brooke b Hirst ..... 0 |
| H. Makepeace run out ..... 15 | H. Dean c Kilner b Haigh ..... 3 |
| J. T. Tyldesley c Olyroyd b Haigh ..... 12 | R. Whitehead not out ..... 18 |
| J. Sharp c Hirst b Haigh ..... 17 | W. Huddleston st Dolphin b Kilner ..... 10 |
| W. Tyldesley lbw b Hirst ..... 12 | B 10, l-b 2 ..... 12 |
| Mr R. V. Bardsley b Haigh ..... 1 | |
| J. S. Heap b Haigh ..... 2 | **130** |

**Lancashire Bowling**

|            | Overs | Mdns | Runs | Wkts | Overs | Mdns | Runs | Wkts |
|------------|-------|------|------|------|-------|------|------|------|
| Dean . . . . . . . . . . . . | 13 | 6 | 25 | 2 | 11 | 1 | 29 | 4 |
| Huddleston . . . . . . . | 21 | 10 | 26 | 2 | | | | |
| Heap . . . . . . . . . . . | 10.1 | 4 | 16 | 6 | 10 | — | 23 | 5 |

**Yorkshire Bowling**

|            | Overs | Mdns | Runs | Wkts |
|------------|-------|------|------|------|
| Hirst . . . . . . . . . . . . | 20 | 7 | 37 | 3 |
| Drake . . . . . . . . . . . | 5 | — | 22 | — |
| Kilner . . . . . . . . . . . | 7 | — | 17 | 1 |
| Haigh . . . . . . . . . . . | 20 | 5 | 42 | 5 |

Umpires: H. Bagshaw and W. Richards.

# LEICESTERSHIRE

## LEICESTERSHIRE v SUSSEX

Played at Leicester, July 12, 13, 14, 1900

So completely did the bat master the ball throughout this game that not only was it drawn but only 18 wickets fell during three full days, while 1295 runs were scored. Needless to say the pitch could not have been more favourable to batting, and Leicestershire, weakened by the absence of Woodcock and Whiteside never had any chance of winning despite their heavy scoring. They declared their innings closed as early as possible, but on Friday evening had only dismissed two of their visitors for 248, while on Saturday their total was exceeded by 77. Wood helped materially in Leicestershire's excellent start, scoring 92 out of 187 in two hours and a half, but the feature of the innings was the partnership of Knight and Whitehead who added 256 in two hours and three quarters. Knight played brilliantly hitting a 5 and twenty 4s during his stay of four hours. Fry reached his hundred on the second evening, and the last day was remarkable for the superb play of Ranjitsinhji, whose 275 runs was his highest score in important cricket. At the wicket five hours and five minutes he was only once at fault, just before getting out, and he hit twenty-nine 4s, eleven 3s and twenty-seven 2s. He and Fry added 194, and Collins helped his captain to put on 138.

### Leicestershire

| | |
|---|---|
| Mr C. E. de Trafford b Bland | 34 |
| Mr C. J. B. Wood c Butt b Bland | 92 |
| J. H. King c Butt b Bland | 39 |
| A. E. Knight c Marlow b Fry | 182 |
| H. Whitehead c and b Tate | 116 |
| S. Coe c Relf b Ranjitsinhji | 68 |
| L. Brown c Relf b Fry | 21 |
| F. Geeson not out | 8 |
| Mr G. E. Rudd c Collins b Tate | 36 |
| B 5, l-b 2, w 5, n-b 1 | 13 |
| (8 wkts dec.) | 609 |

H. Burgess and T. Marlow did not bat.

### Sussex

| | |
|---|---|
| Mr C. B. Fry b Geeson | 135 |
| A. E. Relf b Wood | 46 |
| E. H. Killick c Coe b Geeson | 21 |
| K. S. Ranjitsinhji c Whitehead b Coe | 275 |
| F. W. Marlow run out | 18 |
| Mr G. Brann c Wood b King | 7 |
| Mr A. Collins c and b Geeson | 98 |
| J. Vine b Geeson | 40 |
| H. R. Butt not out | 8 |
| B 23, l-b 13, w 3, n-b 2 | 38 |
| | 686 |

F. W. Tate and C. H. G. Bland did not bat.

### Sussex Bowling

| | Overs | Mdns | Runs | Wkts |
|---|---|---|---|---|
| Bland | 40 | 5 | 165 | 3 |
| Killick | 17 | 1 | 83 | — |
| Tate | 25.4 | 9 | 47 | 2 |
| Fry | 21 | 3 | 65 | 2 |
| Collins | 9 | 2 | 34 | — |
| Relf | 6 | 1 | 29 | — |
| Ranjitsinhji | 27 | 7 | 99 | 1 |
| Brann | 13 | — | 48 | — |
| Vine | 1 | — | 1 | — |
| Butt | 4 | 1 | 5 | — |
| Marlow | 2 | — | 20 | — |

### Leicestershire Bowling

|          | Overs | Mdns | Runs | Wkts |
|----------|-------|------|------|------|
| Burgess  | 32    | 5    | 116  | —    |
| King     | 43    | 14   | 105  | 1    |
| Wood     | 21    | 4    | 77   | 1    |
| Rudd     | 19    | —    | 105  | —    |
| Geeson   | 39.4  | 8    | 110  | 4    |
| Coe      | 15    | 4    | 35   | 1    |
| Marlow   | 29    | 4    | 91   | —    |
| Brown    | 2     | —    | —    | —    |

Umpires: A. F. Smith and M. Sherwin.

## LEICESTERSHIRE v LANCASHIRE

### Played at Leicester, July 23, 24, 25, 1900

The home county did well to effect a draw after being in serious danger of defeat. By far the best batting for them was shown by Knight, who in the match scored 190 runs. On the first day the Lancashire men bowled admirably despite the great heat and perfect pitch, so that runs always came at quite a moderate pace. Knight took four hours to score his 110. For a long while on Tuesday Lancashire had the worst of matters, but, with seven men out for 125, Hartley hit up 104 out of 150 in two hours, and thanks to him and Ward they led by 67. Losing two wickets for 22 before the drawing of the stumps Leicestershire were left in a bad position. However, King and Knight added 106 for the fourth wicket, and Wood and Geeson later on scored 119 together. All the visitors went on to bowl.

### Leicestershire

| | | | |
|---|---|---|---|
| Mr C. E. de Trafford c Briggs b Sharp | 5 | – c MacLaren b Sharp | 4 |
| Mr C. J. B. Wood c Ward b Cuttell | 27 | – c Briggs b Smith | 55 |
| J. H. King c Hallows b Ward | 15 | – c Smith b Mold | 52 |
| H. Whitehead c Hartley b Ward | 8 | – b Mold | 2 |
| A. E. Knight c and b Ward | 110 | – b Briggs | 80 |
| S. Coe c MacLaren b Sharp | 24 | – b Briggs | 14 |
| L. Brown b Sharp | 33 | – c Mold b Ward | 7 |
| F. Geeson c Smith b Briggs | 18 | – not out | 71 |
| H. Burgess st Smith b Briggs | 20 | – not out | 8 |
| J. P. Whiteside not out | 1 | – c Smith b Sharp | 0 |
| T. Marlow b Ward | 4 | | |
| W 1 | 1 | B 10, l-b 5, w 2 | 17 |
| | **266** | | **310** |

### Lancashire

| | | | |
|---|---|---|---|
| J. Briggs c Whiteside b Burgess | 43 | J. Hallows c Marlow b Geeson | 2 |
| C. Smith b Geeson | 3 | Mr C. R. Hartley c Whitehead b Burgess | 104 |
| Mr A. C. MacLaren b Marlow | 31 | J. Sharp c Brown b Geeson | 4 |
| A. Ward not out | 90 | A. Mold c Whiteside b Coe | 15 |
| J. T. Tyldesley c Geeson b King | 20 | B 8, l-b 12 | 20 |
| Mr A. Eccles b Geeson | 1 | | |
| W. R. Cuttell b Geeson | 0 | | **333** |

## Lancashire Bowling

| | Overs | Mdns | Runs | Wkts | Overs | Mdns | Runs | Wkts |
|---|---|---|---|---|---|---|---|---|
| Mold ............ | 16 | 5 | 32 | — | 18 | 6 | 42 | 2 |
| Sharp ........... | 25 | 6 | 52 | 3 | 22 | 6 | 52 | 2 |
| Cuttell .......... | 16 | 6 | 42 | 1 | 15 | 8 | 21 | — |
| Ward ........... | 25.5 | 3 | 70 | 4 | 22 | 4 | 52 | 1 |
| Briggs .......... | 25 | 13 | 33 | 2 | 25 | 12 | 31 | 2 |
| Hallows ......... | 10 | 3 | 20 | — | 7 | 4 | 13 | — |
| MacLaren ....... | 3 | 1 | 16 | — | 7 | 1 | 27 | — |
| Hartley ......... | | | | | 3 | 1 | 5 | — |
| Eccles .......... | | | | | 3 | — | 16 | — |
| Tyldesley ....... | | | | | 4 | — | 16 | — |
| Smith ........... | | | | | 4 | 1 | 18 | 1 |

## Leicestershire Bowling

| | Overs | Mdns | Runs | Wkts |
|---|---|---|---|---|
| Burgess ......... | 28 | 4 | 83 | 2 |
| Geeson .......... | 46 | 10 | 105 | 5 |
| King ............ | 22 | 6 | 43 | 1 |
| Marlow ......... | 13 | 4 | 45 | 1 |
| Coe ............ | 11.3 | 3 | 31 | 1 |
| Brown .......... | 3 | 1 | 6 | — |

Umpires: H. Pickett and W. Richards.

# LEICESTERSHIRE v NORTHAMPTONSHIRE

### Played at Leicester, August 7, 8, 1905

After some remarkable cricket Leicestershire gained a sensational victory by 8 runs. To such an extent were the bowlers assisted on a pitch ruined by rain that on the first day three innings were completed, and on the next morning Northamptonshire proved unequal to getting the 68 runs wanted to win. Thompson and Simpson bowling unchanged twice dismissed the home county, and Odell and Jayes shared the wickets equally in the visitors' first innings, the amateur having the best record in the match. So finely did the amateur bowl that Northamptonshire lost five wickets for 32 runs in an hour, but, in spite of this startling collapse under conditions even more adverse to batsmen than on the previous day, it seemed probable that the runs would be hit off after Horton and Driffield had added 20. Then, with four batsmen to be dismissed, only 10 runs were wanted, but three more men were disposed of before another run had been scored and Leicestershire just managed to win. King gave Odell useful help at the finish.

## Leicestershire

| | | | |
|---|---|---|---|
| Mr C. J. B. Wood lbw b Simpson ............... | 15 | – c Hawkins b Thompson ......... | 17 |
| J. H. King c Simpson b Thompson ............. | 10 | – b Simpson ................. | 5 |
| A. E. Knight b Thompson .................... | 1 | – lbw b Thompson ............. | 5 |
| T. Jayes b Simpson ........................ | 9 | – b Thompson ................ | 0 |
| S. Coe c Wells b Thompson .................. | 9 | – c Horton b Thompson ......... | 20 |
| H. Whitehead c Thompson b Simpson ........... | 9 | – not out ................... | 10 |
| Mr W. W. Odell b Thompson ................. | 2 | – b Thompson ................ | 6 |
| G. Gill b Thompson ........................ | 0 | – st Smith b Thompson ........... | 0 |
| T. Allsopp run out ........................ | 7 | – b Thompson ................ | 0 |
| J. P. Whiteside c Wells b Simpson ............ | 2 | – c Hawtin b Thompson ......... | 0 |
| Mr C. E. de Trafford not out ................. | 27 | – c Driffield b Simpson ........... | 17 |
| B 4, l-b 3, n-b 2 .................... | 9 | N-b 5 ................. | 5 |
| | 100 | | 85 |

## Northamptonshire

| | | | |
|---|---|---|---|
| Mr C. J. T. Pool b Odell | 18 | – c Jayes b Odell | 0 |
| G. J. Thompson b Odell | 6 | – c Jayes b Odell | 8 |
| Mr E. M. Crosse c and b Odell | 0 | – c Whiteside b Jayes | 5 |
| Mr R. O. Raven b Jayes | 7 | – c Jayes b Odell | 5 |
| Mr R. W. R. Hawtin b Jayes | 2 | – c de Trafford b King | 2 |
| Mr T. Horton b Jayes | 15 | – lbw b Odell | 18 |
| Mr H. B. Simpson b Odell | 2 | – lbw b Odell | 0 |
| Mr L. T. Driffield lbw b Odell | 9 | – c Whiteside b Odell | 14 |
| Mr H. Hawkins c and b Jayes | 31 | – run out | 0 |
| W. Wells c Allsopp b Jayes | 4 | – not out | 1 |
| Mr B. C. Smith not out | 5 | – c Whiteside b King | 0 |
| B 8, l-b 11 | 19 | B 4, l-b 2 | 6 |
| | **118** | | **59** |

### Northamptonshire Bowling

| | Overs | Mdns | Runs | Wkts | Overs | Mdns | Runs | Wkts |
|---|---|---|---|---|---|---|---|---|
| Thompson | 16 | 4 | 62 | 5 | 10 | 1 | 43 | 8 |
| Simpson | 15.2 | 6 | 29 | 4 | 9 | 1 | 37 | 2 |

### Leicestershire Bowling

| | Overs | Mdns | Runs | Wkts | Overs | Mdns | Runs | Wkts |
|---|---|---|---|---|---|---|---|---|
| Odell | 23 | 8 | 42 | 5 | 13 | 3 | 35 | 6 |
| King | 7 | 4 | 10 | — | 6.5 | 4 | 5 | 2 |
| Jayes | 17.3 | 6 | 43 | 5 | 6 | 3 | 13 | 1 |
| Coe | 2 | 1 | 4 | — | | | | |

Umpires: J. Carter and W. Richards.

## LEICESTERSHIRE v SURREY

Played at Leicester, June 7, 8, 9, 1906

Memorable for the fact that Hayward for the second time in the week played two three-figure innings, the match ended in a victory for Surrey by 110 runs. Hayward's batting dwarfed everything else, no one in first-class cricket having previously got two separate hundreds in two successive matches. The famour batsman helped Surrey to a splendid position by scoring 143 on the first day, and on Friday evening he was not out 72. He hit freely in both innings, and with Hobbs opened the game in great style for Surrey, the partnership producing 178 runs. Each of Hayward's innings lasted about three hours, and included fourteen 4s. Leicestershire made a good struggle until they went in with 313 required to win, when, except for Coe, who received some assistance from Knight, their batsmen fared badly.

### Surrey

| | | | |
|---|---|---|---|
| T. Hayward c Coe b King | 143 | – c Coe b Jayes | 125 |
| J. B. Hobbs hit wkt b Coe | 73 | – b Jayes | 14 |
| E. G. Hayes c Whiteside b Jayes | 0 | – c Whiteside b Gill | 26 |
| A. Baker c Odell b Jayes | 47 | – c Whiteside b Gill | 0 |
| Mr J. N. Crawford c Whiteside b Odell | 30 | – run out | 0 |
| Lord Dalmeny c Odell b Coe | 66 | – c Jayes b Odell | 9 |
| J. H. Moulder c Knight b Odell | 6 | – b Odell | 0 |
| W. Lees c Crawford b Coe | 14 | – c Crawford b Jayes | 34 |
| H. Strudwick c Coe b Gill | 29 | – c and b Jayes | 0 |
| W. C. Smith c and b Gill | 4 | – not out | 1 |
| Mr N. A. Knox not out | 8 | – c Wood b Coe | 4 |
| B 2, l-b 2, w 1 | 5 | B 4, l-b 1 | 5 |
| | **425** | | **218** |

## Leicestershire

| | | | |
|---|---|---|---|
| Mr C. E. de Trafford c Strudwick b Knox | 18 | – c Smith b Lees | 0 |
| Mr C. J. B. Wood b Hayes | 50 | – c Hayes b Knox | 7 |
| J. H. King c Dalmeny b Knox | 25 | – c Hayes b Knox | 21 |
| Mr V. F. S. Crawford c Baker b Smith | 73 | – c Hayes b Knox | 7 |
| A. E. Knight c Hayes b Lees | 72 | – c Hayward b Crawford | 37 |
| S. Coe c Moulder b Knox | 34 | – c Moulder b Knox | 76 |
| T. Jayes c Hayes b Lees | 12 | – c and b Crawford | 11 |
| Mr W. W. Odell not out | 22 | – c and b Hayes | 14 |
| G. Gill lbw b Moulder | 14 | – not out | 19 |
| J. P. Whiteside b Crawford | 0 | – b Crawford | 1 |
| H. Whitehead absent hurt | 0 | – absent hurt | 0 |
| B 6, l-b 3, w 2 | 11 | B 7, w 2 | 9 |
| | **331** | | **202** |

### Leicestershire Bowling

| | Overs | Mdns | Runs | Wkts | Overs | Mdns | Runs | Wkts |
|---|---|---|---|---|---|---|---|---|
| Gill | 22.3 | — | 102 | 2 | 18 | 5 | 57 | 2 |
| Odell | 24 | 5 | 103 | 2 | 15 | 3 | 41 | 2 |
| Coe | 20 | 2 | 68 | 3 | 14.2 | 1 | 48 | 1 |
| Jayes | 24 | 1 | 117 | 2 | 19 | 3 | 67 | 4 |
| King | 12 | 6 | 22 | 1 | | | | |
| Crawford | 2 | — | 8 | — | | | | |

### Surrey Bowling

| | Overs | Mdns | Runs | Wkts | Overs | Mdns | Runs | Wkts |
|---|---|---|---|---|---|---|---|---|
| Lees | 28 | 6 | 83 | 2 | 18 | 5 | 34 | 1 |
| Knox | 27 | 2 | 152 | 3 | 18 | 1 | 85 | 4 |
| Crawford | 14.4 | 5 | 42 | 1 | 14.5 | 1 | 68 | 3 |
| Hayes | 5 | — | 22 | 1 | 2 | 9 | 6 | 1 |
| Smith | 2 | — | 18 | 1 | | | | |
| Moulder | 1 | — | 8 | 1 | | | | |

Umpires: A. Millward and F. W. Marlow.

## LEICESTERSHIRE v KENT

### Played at Leicester, May 17, 18, 19, 1909

Completely out-played in their first home match, Leicestershire suffered a severe defeat by an innings and 81 runs. The heavy reverse was the more remarkable as Kent began by losing two men before a run had been scored. Kent recovered, thanks to an admirable innings by Dillon, who received consistent help, Day and Humphreys being seen to special advantage. Rain on Monday had some effect on the pitch, but Leicestershire seemed sure to make plenty of runs when Wood and Knight began steadily. Once they were separated, however, Blythe carried all before him, and after lunch actually took the last nine wickets for 22 runs. If not quite so deadly in the follow-on, Blythe again caused the collapse of the home side, and in the match he had the wonderful record of sixteen wickets for 102 runs. With the idea of concluding the game in two days play was prolonged for a quarter of an hour on Tuesday, but Hazlerigg and Astill could not be parted. However, in the morning, Blythe finished off the match by dismissing the last two men in the first over. Leicestershire should have made a better fight, some costly blunders in the field involving them in serious trouble. The batting of the majority of their men against Blythe's splendid bowling, however, was extremely weak.

### Kent

| | |
|---|---|
| Mr E. W. Dillon c Jayes b Astill ........ 84 | W. J. Fairservice b King ............. 38 |
| H. T. W. Hardinge c Sturman b Jayes ..... 0 | F. H. Huish not out ................. 25 |
| James Seymour c King b Jayes ......... 0 | C. Blythe c Whitehead b King .......... 2 |
| Mr K. L. Hutchings c Wood b Astill ...... 17 | H. Preston c Jayes b King ............. 4 |
| F. E. Woolley c and b King ............. 25 | B 1, l-b 4, n-b 6 ............. 11 |
| Mr A. P. Day c King b Astill ........... 67 | |
| E. Humphreys b King ................. 61 | 334 |

### Leicestershire

| | |
|---|---|
| Mr C. J. B. Wood lbw b Fairservice ............. 26 | – st Huish b Blythe .............. 5 |
| A. E. Knight c Seymour b Blythe ................ 28 | – c Day b Blythe ................ 7 |
| H. Whitehead c Dillon b Blythe ................ 1 | – c and b Blythe ................ 9 |
| J. H. King b Blythe ...................... 0 | – st Huish b Preston ............. 15 |
| S. Coe c Seymour b Blythe .................... 16 | – c Hutchings b Blythe ........... 32 |
| T. Jayes st Huish b Blythe ................... 8 | – b Preston .................... 9 |
| Mr H. Thompson c Huish b Blythe ............. 2 | – c Dillon b Blythe ............. 29 |
| J. Toon c Woolley b Blythe .................. 7 | - run out ...................... 1 |
| Sir A. Hazlerigg not out ..................... 7 | – c Seymour b Blythe ............. 23 |
| W. E. Astill c Day b Blythe .................... 3 | – not out ..................... 12 |
| W. Sturman b Blythe ...................... 1 | – c Seymour b Blythe ............. 0 |
| B 2, l-b 2, n-b 1 .................... 5 | B 4, l-b 3 .............. 7 |
| 104 | 149 |

### Leicestershire Bowling

| | Overs | Mdns | Runs | Wkts |
|---|---|---|---|---|
| Jayes ............ | 35 | 5 | 112 | 2 |
| Astill ............ | 28 | 11 | 79 | 3 |
| King ............. | 29.4 | 3 | 56 | 5 |
| Toon ............ | 23 | 1 | 76 | — |

### Kent Bowling

| | Overs | Mdns | Runs | Wkts | Overs | Mdns | Runs | Wkts |
|---|---|---|---|---|---|---|---|---|
| Blythe ........... | 21.1 | 6 | 42 | 9 | 12 | 2 | 60 | 7 |
| Preston .......... | 6 | — | 18 | — | 15 | 5 | 39 | 2 |
| Fairservice ....... | 13 | 5 | 33 | 1 | 13 | 3 | 43 | — |
| Woolley .......... | 8 | 5 | 6 | — | 1 | 1 | — | — |

Umpires: G. P. Harrison and B. W. Mason.

# LEICESTERSHIRE v YORKSHIRE

### Played at Leicester, July 3, 4, 5, 1913

Preferring to bat a second time Yorkshire were in danger of being robbed of victory by rain on the last day, but they won the match within fifty minutes of time by 190 runs. The pitch was never easy and Rhodes played a masterly game for three hours and three-quarters, making no mistake until 122. He hit fourteen 4s, keeping the ball down in admirable strokes all round the wicket. Wilson helped to put on 180 in two hours twenty minutes, and Hirst played faultlessly for two hours. Riley, the Cambridge blue, gave a remarkable display, hitting up 100 after four Leicestershire wickets had fallen for 27. Following rain during lunch-time he got 60 out of 72 in forty minutes, scoring 24 in one over from Hirst. His catch with the right hand in the long field that dismissed Booth caused almost as much sensation as his hitting. When play was possible on Saturday Leicestershire pluckily strove to stay in all the afternoon, but the batting broke down at the critical time, Yorkshire playing their winning game with great determination.

## Yorkshire

| | | | |
|---|---|---|---|
| W. Rhodes c Shipman b Geary | 152 | – lbw b King | 37 |
| B. B. Wilson c Shields b Shipman | 79 | – c Shields b Astill | 30 |
| D. Denton c Shields b Shipman | 4 | – b Astill | 21 |
| R. Kilner c King b Geary | 7 | – b Astill | 20 |
| M. W. Booth c Riley b King | 17 | – lbw b King | 4 |
| A. Drake c Whitehead b Geary | 26 | – c Shipman b Astill | 5 |
| G. H. Hirst c King b Geary | 55 | – not out | 16 |
| P. Holmes b Astill | 3 | – not out | 5 |
| T. J. Birtles b Shipman | 16 | | |
| Sir A. W. White not out | 19 | | |
| A. Dolphin lbw b Geary | 2 | | |
| B 11, l-b 6, w 1, n-b 7 | 25 | B 2, l-b 2 | 4 |
| | **405** | **(6 wkts dec.)** | **142** |

## Leicestershire

| | | | |
|---|---|---|---|
| Mr C. J. B. Wood b Booth | 14 | – c Kilner b Drake | 25 |
| H. Whitehead b Booth | 5 | – c Rhodes b Hirst | 22 |
| J. H. King c Dolphin b Booth | 1 | – b Hirst | 47 |
| A. Lord b Booth | 3 | – c Rhodes b Drake | 0 |
| S. Coe c Dolphin b Hirst | 4 | – c Holmes b Hirst | 5 |
| Mr W. N. Riley b Rhodes | 100 | – c Holmes b Hirst | 4 |
| A. Mounteney b Hirst | 11 | – c Booth b Rhodes | 17 |
| W. E. Astill b Booth | 0 | – not out | 9 |
| W. Shipman lbw b Booth | 6 | – c Denton b Rhodes | 39 |
| G. Geary b Booth | 17 | – c Kilner b Rhodes | 19 |
| Mr J. Shields not out | 4 | – st Dolphin b Drake | 0 |
| L-b 3 | 3 | L-b 1, n-b 1 | 2 |
| | **168** | | **189** |

### Leicestershire Bowling

| | Overs | Mdns | Runs | Wkts | Overs | Mdns | Runs | Wkts |
|---|---|---|---|---|---|---|---|---|
| Shipman | 37 | 9 | 113 | 3 | 3 | 1 | 20 | — |
| Geary | 38.2 | 11 | 86 | 5 | 8 | — | 32 | — |
| Astill | 21 | 3 | 76 | 1 | 19 | 5 | 48 | 4 |
| King | 18 | 2 | 56 | 1 | 14 | 1 | 38 | 2 |
| Coe | 4 | — | 16 | — | | | | |
| Whitehead | 10 | 1 | 29 | — | | | | |
| Riley | 1 | — | 4 | — | | | | |

### Yorkshire Bowling

| | Overs | Mdns | Runs | Wkts | Overs | Mdns | Runs | Wkts |
|---|---|---|---|---|---|---|---|---|
| Hirst | 21 | 1 | 99 | 2 | 20 | 7 | 46 | 4 |
| Booth | 21 | 3 | 65 | 7 | 10 | 1 | 27 | — |
| Rhodes | 1 | — | 1 | 1 | 24 | 5 | 85 | 3 |
| Drake | | | | | 15 | 3 | 29 | 3 |

Umpires: W. Richards and F. Parris.

# MIDDLESEX

## MIDDLESEX v GLOUCESTERSHIRE

Played at Lord's, June 14, 15, 16, 1900

In this match Middlesex suffered another defeat, Gloucestershire winning in remarkable style by seven wickets. No one expected such a decisive result when Gloucestershire went in to get 224 in the last innings, especially as there was some doubt as to how the wicket would play. However the batsmen made light of their task, the hitting of Jessop and Board and the steady defence of Townsend being equally commendable. With Jessop hitting the bowling all over the field, the last ninety runs were obtained in thirty-seven minutes. Jessop's first innings of 109 was a wonderful display of hitting, and only lasted sixty-five minutes. Trott, in getting his 112, was nothing like so fast as this, but he also hit very brilliantly. In quite a different style Beldam gave two capital displays. Fargus bowled with great effect.

### Middlesex

| | | | |
|---|---|---|---|
| Mr H. B. Hayman c Tagart b Jessop | 16 | – b Jessop | 1 |
| Mr L. J. Moon b Jessop | 48 | – c W. S. A. Brown b Fargus | 46 |
| Mr G. W. Beldam lbw b Townsend | 51 | – b Roberts | 88 |
| Mr E. S. Littlejohn b Jessop | 0 | – lbw b Brown | 16 |
| A. E. Trott b Fargus | 112 | – c Board b Fargus | 24 |
| Mr G. MacGregor c and b Fargus | 18 | – c Townsend b Fargus | 0 |
| Mr G. S. F. Griffin b Roberts | 5 | – c Brown b Fargus | 9 |
| Mr G. E. Winter c Jessop b Fargus | 16 | – b Fargus | 6 |
| Mr W. Williams b Fargus | 0 | – b Fargus | 0 |
| W. Roche not out | 4 | – not out | 1 |
| J. T. Hearne c Board b Fargus | 1 | – c and b Fargus | 0 |
| B 12, l-b 6, w 1, n-b 1 | 20 | B 5, l-b 2, n-b 1 | 8 |
| | **291** | | **199** |

### Gloucestershire

| | | | |
|---|---|---|---|
| Mr C. L. Townsend c Trott b Hearne | 8 | – not out | 66 |
| H. Wrathall c Littlejohn b Trott | 58 | – lbw b Trott | 13 |
| Mr C. O. H. Sewell c Winter b Hearne | 51 | – b Roche | 24 |
| J. H. Board b Hearne | 8 | – b Trott | 50 |
| Mr G. L. Jessop b Roche | 109 | – not out | 58 |
| Mr W. S. A. Brown c MacGregor b Hearne | 5 | | |
| Mr H. J. Hodgkins c Hayman b Roche | 7 | | |
| Mr N. O. Tagart lbw b Williams | 1 | | |
| Mr A. H. C. Fargus st MacGregor b Williams | 2 | | |
| Mr O. E. Wreford-Brown b Roche | 5 | | |
| F. G. Roberts not out | 0 | | |
| B 12, l-b 1 | 13 | B 11, l-b 1, n-b 1 | 13 |
| | **267** | | **224** |

### Gloucestershire Bowling

| | Overs | Mdns | Runs | Wkts | Overs | Mdns | Runs | Wkts |
|---|---|---|---|---|---|---|---|---|
| Jessop | 29 | 5 | 88 | 3 | 12 | 6 | 19 | 1 |
| Roberts | 14 | 5 | 48 | 1 | 24 | 9 | 65 | 1 |
| Brown | 8 | 2 | 33 | — | 14 | 1 | 34 | 1 |
| Hodgkins | 3 | — | 17 | — | | | | |
| Fargus | 12.4 | 5 | 32 | 5 | 19.2 | 4 | 55 | 7 |
| Townsend | 10 | — | 53 | 1 | 6 | 1 | 18 | — |

**Middlesex Bowling**

| | Overs | Mdns | Runs | Wkts | Overs | Mdns | Runs | Wkts |
|---|---|---|---|---|---|---|---|---|
| Hearne . . . . . . . . . . | 23 | 5 | 117 | 4 | 17 | 6 | 46 | — |
| Trott . . . . . . . . . . . | 17 | — | 74 | 1 | 13 | 3 | 57 | 2 |
| Williams . . . . . . . . . | 9 | 1 | 39 | 2 | 10 | 1 | 55 | — |
| Roche . . . . . . . . . . | 7.3 | — | 24 | 3 | 6 | — | 41 | 1 |
| Winter . . . . . . . . . . | | | | | 1.2 | — | 12 | — |

Umpires: J. Lillywhite and R. G. Barlow.

## MIDDLESEX v LEICESTERSHIRE

Played at Lord's, July 19, 20, 21, 1900

This match, which they won in brilliant fashion by five wickets, marked a welcome change in the fortunes of the Middlesex eleven. The victory was badly needed, as out of nine previous matches they had only won one. All the honours were carried off by Bosanquet, who, with scores of 136 and 139, added his name to the list of those who have made two separate hundreds in a first-class match. His second innings was incomparably the better of the two, for though he hit very brilliantly for his 136 he was missed being stumped before he had made a run and had two other escapes with his score respectively at 93 and 99. His 136 lasted an hour and fifty minutes, while for his 139 he was batting two hours and fifty minutes.

### Leicestershire

| | | | |
|---|---|---|---|
| Mr C. E. de Trafford c Hayman b Trott . . . . . . . . . | 7 | – c Bosanquet b Hearne . . . . . . . . . . . | 31 |
| Mr C. J. B. Wood st Robertson b Trott . . . . . . . . . . . | 14 | – b Trott . . . . . . . . . . . . . . . . . . . . . . | 2 |
| Mr J. H. King lbw b Hearne . . . . . . . . . . . . . . . . . . . . | 0 | – c and b Trott . . . . . . . . . . . . . . . . . | 41 |
| A. E. Knight b Trott . . . . . . . . . . . . . . . . . . . . . . . . | 62 | – c Warner b Hearne . . . . . . . . . . . . | 5 |
| H. Whitehead c Rawlin b Hearne . . . . . . . . . . . . . . . | 0 | – c Trott b Hearne . . . . . . . . . . . . . | 38 |
| S. Coe c Bevington b Williams . . . . . . . . . . . . . . . . | 20 | – st Robertson b Bosanquet . . . . . . . . | 98 |
| L. Brown run out . . . . . . . . . . . . . . . . . . . . . . . . . | 10 | – c Bosanquet b Trott . . . . . . . . . . . . | 65 |
| Mr G. E. Rudd c Williams b Hearne . . . . . . . . . . . . . | 36 | – b Trott . . . . . . . . . . . . . . . . . . . . . . | 31 |
| Mr H. Burgess c Robertson b Trott . . . . . . . . . . . . . | 6 | – c Robertson b Trott . . . . . . . . . . . . | 2 |
| F. Geeson not out . . . . . . . . . . . . . . . . . . . . . . . . . . | 16 | – run out . . . . . . . . . . . . . . . . . . . . . . | 12 |
| Jarvis b Hearne . . . . . . . . . . . . . . . . . . . . . . . . . . | 0 | – not out . . . . . . . . . . . . . . . . . . . . . . | 0 |
| B 13 . . . . . . . . . . . . . . . . . . . . . . . . | 13 | B 11, l-b 5, w 1 . . . . . . . . . . . | 17 |
| | **184** | | **342** |

### Middlesex

| | | | |
|---|---|---|---|
| Mr P. F. Warner b Burgess . . . . . . . . . . . . . . . . . . . . | 11 | – lbw b Geeson . . . . . . . . . . . . . . . . . | 61 |
| Mr B. J. T. Bosanquet c Knight b Coe . . . . . . . . . . . . | 136 | – lbw b Geeson . . . . . . . . . . . . . . . . | 139 |
| J. T. Rawlin b King . . . . . . . . . . . . . . . . . . . . . . . | 8 | – b Geeson . . . . . . . . . . . . . . . . . . . . | 39 |
| Mr H. J. Wyld b Burgess . . . . . . . . . . . . . . . . . . . . | 0 | – not out . . . . . . . . . . . . . . . . . . . . . . | 6 |
| A. E. Trott run out . . . . . . . . . . . . . . . . . . . . . . . . | 1 | – not out . . . . . . . . . . . . . . . . . . . . . . | 22 |
| Mr J. C. Bevington st Jarvis b Geeson . . . . . . . . . . . | 6 | – b Geeson . . . . . . . . . . . . . . . . . . . . | 2 |
| Mr W. P. Robertson c Coe b King . . . . . . . . . . . . . . | 31 | – c Jarvis b Burgess . . . . . . . . . . . . . | 22 |
| Mr W. Williams c de Trafford b Geeson . . . . . . . . . . | 0 | | |
| W. Roche not out . . . . . . . . . . . . . . . . . . . . . . . . . | 11 | | |
| J. T. Hearne c Geeson b Burgess . . . . . . . . . . . . . . . | 0 | | |
| Mr H. B. Hayman c Geeson b King . . . . . . . . . . . . . | 10 | | |
| B 6, l-b 4 . . . . . . . . . . . . . . . . . . . . . . . | 10 | B 9, l-b 1, w 3 . . . . . . . . . . . | 13 |
| | **224** | | **304** |

## Middlesex Bowling

| | Overs | Mdns | Runs | Wkts | Overs | Mdns | Runs | Wkts |
|---|---|---|---|---|---|---|---|---|
| Hearne . . . . . . . . . . | 25.2 | 13 | 37 | 4 | 29 | 6 | 83 | 3 |
| Trott . . . . . . . . . . . | 20 | 2 | 67 | 4 | 32 | 5 | 111 | 5 |
| Williams . . . . . . . . . | 9 | 1 | 34 | 1 | 8 | 1 | 45 | — |
| Roche . . . . . . . . . . | 2 | — | 26 | — | | | | |
| Rawlin . . . . . . . . . . | 2 | — | 7 | — | 12 | 3 | 36 | — |
| Bosanquet . . . . . . . | | | | | 12 | — | 47 | 1 |
| Wyld . . . . . . . . . . . | | | | | 3 | 1 | 3 | — |

## Leicestershire Bowling

| | Overs | Mdns | Runs | Wkts | Overs | Mdns | Runs | Wkts |
|---|---|---|---|---|---|---|---|---|
| Burgess . . . . . . . . . | 22 | 3 | 106 | 3 | 16 | 3 | 47 | 1 |
| King . . . . . . . . . . . . | 22.4 | 9 | 49 | 3 | 19 | 5 | 79 | — |
| Geeson . . . . . . . . . . | 14 | 5 | 26 | 2 | 43 | 10 | 108 | 4 |
| Coe . . . . . . . . . . . . | 6 | — | 33 | 1 | 11.3 | 3 | 29 | — |
| Wood . . . . . . . . . . . | | | | | 3 | — | 14 | — |
| Rudd . . . . . . . . . . . | | | | | 4 | — | 14 | — |

Umpires: T. Mycroft and R. G. Barlow.

# MIDDLESEX v SUSSEX

## Played at Lord's, June 19, 20, 21, 1902

So far, Middlesex has lost two county matches and drawn four, and in this fixture they met with an overwhelming defeat, Sussex beating them by an innings and 224 runs. The result, however, did not in any way represent the merits of the two sides, for whereas Sussex had an afternoon's batting on the first day under favourable conditions, Middlesex had to bat on a pitch ruined by rain, cricket on the Friday being quite out of the question. Ranjitsinhji declared the Sussex innings closed the first thing on Saturday morning, and by a quarter to five Middlesex had been twice got rid of, Tate bowling in irresistible form on a wicket that suited him to perfection. Beldam accomplished quite a notable feat in carrying his bat through the first innings, but he was lucky in being missed when he had made a single. The Sussex batting was, up to a certain point, very fine indeed, Fry in particular playing a great innings, and making his first hundred during the season. He was at the wickets for two hours and fifty minutes, and hit fifteen 4s, driving with even more power than usual. He and Vine scored 133 for the first wicket. Killick, who curiously enough was in exactly the same time as Fry, made his 82 without a mistake.

## Sussex

| | | | |
|---|---|---|---|
| Mr C. B. Fry b Bosanquet . . . . . . . . . . . . . . | 122 | F. W. Marlow not out . . . . . . . . . . . . . . . . . | 0 |
| J. Vine b Hearne . . . . . . . . . . . . . . . . . . . . . | 42 | F. W. Tate b Rawlin . . . . . . . . . . . . . . . . . . . | 0 |
| E. H. Killick b Rawlin . . . . . . . . . . . . . . . . | 82 | J. Bean b Rawlin . . . . . . . . . . . . . . . . . . . . . | 0 |
| K. S. Ranjitsinhji b Hearne . . . . . . . . . . . . | 28 | B 5, l-b 8 . . . . . . . . . . . . . . . . . . . | 13 |
| A. E. Relf c MacGregor b Schwarz . . . . . . . | 35 | | |
| Mr G. Brann c Litteljohn b Rawlin . . . . . . . | 32 | (8 wkts dec.) 354 | |

A. Cordingley and H. R. Butt did not bat.

## Middlesex

| | | | | |
|---|---|---|---|---|
| Mr B. J. T. Bosanquet c and b Bean | 9 | – c Butt b Tate | 4 |
| Mr G. W. Baldam not out | 12 | – b Tate | 1 |
| A. E. Trott c sub. b Tate | 11 | – b Bean | 14 |
| Mr W. P. Robertson c Bean b Tate | 2 | – b Tate | 9 |
| Mr R. O. Schwarz b Tate | 0 | – c Fry b Tate | 7 |
| Mr R. W. Nicholls b Relf | 13 | – c and b Tate | 4 |
| Mr E. S. Litteljohn b Tate | 4 | – not out | 13 |
| Mr T. A. D. Bevington c Bean b Relf | 0 | – b Tate | 1 |
| J. T. Rawlin b Tate | 0 | – c Fry b Tate | 8 |
| Mr G. MacGregor b Tate | 0 | – b Bean | 5 |
| J. T. Hearne b Tate | 0 | – c Marlow b Tate | 4 |
| | | B 7, l-b 2 | 9 |
| | **51** | | **79** |

## Middlesex Bowling

| | Overs | Mdns | Runs | Wkts |
|---|---|---|---|---|
| Rawlin | 21.4 | 4 | 51 | 4 |
| Trott | 28 | 3 | 98 | — |
| Hearne | 34 | 10 | 75 | 2 |
| Bosanquet | 20 | 4 | 69 | 1 |
| Schwarz | 14 | 2 | 42 | 1 |
| Bevington | 2 | 1 | 6 | — |

## Sussex Bowling

| | Overs | Mdns | Runs | Wkts | Overs | Mdns | Runs | Wkts |
|---|---|---|---|---|---|---|---|---|
| Tate | 18.8 | 6 | 28 | 7 | 25 | 9 | 40 | 8 |
| Bean | 7 | 6 | 12 | 1 | 13 | 7 | 15 | 2 |
| Relf | 9 | 5 | 11 | 2 | 6 | 5 | 4 | — |
| Killick | | | | | 5 | 1 | 11 | — |

Umpires: T. Mycroft and W. Hearn.

# MIDDLESEX v SUSSEX

### Played at Lord's, May 25, 26, 27, 1905

Played just before the first of the test games this was emphatically Bosanquet's match. Thanks chiefly to his superb batting and highly effective bowling, Middlesex, after declaring their second innings closed, won by 324 runs. For the second time in his life

Bosanquet made two separate hundreds in one match, and in all he took eleven wickets, carrying everything before him in the last innings. He hit up his 103 in an hour and three-quarters and his 100 not out in seventy-five minutes. Field played fine cricket of a far more careful kind and Warner and George Beldam were also seen at their best. Fry was kept out of the Sussex team by a damaged finger and his absence clearly dispirited the Sussex team.

## Middlesex

| | | | |
|---|--:|---|--:|
| Mr P. F. Warner c Goldie b Tate | 49 | – b Leach | 86 |
| Mr E. A. Beldam b Tate | 26 | – lbw b Relf | 10 |
| Mr G. W. Beldam c Butt b Goldie | 3 | – c Butt b Cox | 94 |
| Mr E. Field not out | 107 | | |
| Mr B. J. T. Bosanquet b Goldie | 103 | – not out | 100 |
| Mr G. MacGregor b Goldie | 0 | | |
| Mr J. H. Hunt b Goldie | 1 | | |
| Mr E. S. Litteljohn b Vine | 3 | | |
| Mr H. D. Wyatt c Butt b Cox | 13 | | |
| A. E. Trott c Cox b Goldie | 20 | – not out | 5 |
| J. T. Hearne c Butt b Relf | 17 | | |
| B 4, l-b 11, w 2 | 17 | B 15, l-b 1, w 4, n-b 1 | 21 |
| | **369** | **(3 wkts dec.)** | **316** |

## Sussex

| | | | |
|---|--:|---|--:|
| Mr K. O. Goldie b G. W. Beldam | 19 | – c and b Hunt | 9 |
| J. Vine c Bosanquet b Hunt | 4 | – st MacGregor b Bosanquet | 31 |
| E. H. Killick c Hearne b Hunt | 32 | – c and b Bosanquet | 9 |
| A. E. Relf c Trott b Hunt | 2 | – st MacGregor b Bosanquet | 5 |
| Mr A. L. Gorringe b Hearne | 16 | – b Hunt | 0 |
| G. Cox c MacGregor b Trott | 38 | – b Bosanquet | 8 |
| Mr H. P. Chaplin c G. Beldam b Bosanquet | 42 | – lbw b Bosanquet | 0 |
| Mr C. L. A. Smith b Bosanquet | 41 | – b Bosanquet | 12 |
| G. Leach c Field b Hearne | 35 | – b Bosanquet | 5 |
| H. R. Butt not out | 7 | – c and b Bosanquet | 0 |
| F. W. Tate c sub. b Bosanquet | 4 | – not out | 16 |
| B 13, l-b 6 | 19 | B 4, l-b 2, w 1 | 7 |
| | **259** | | **102** |

## Sussex Bowling

| | Overs | Mdns | Runs | Wkts | Overs | Mdns | Runs | Wkts |
|---|--:|--:|--:|--:|--:|--:|--:|--:|
| Relf | 20 | 4 | 53 | 1 | 17 | 3 | 49 | 1 |
| Cox | 27 | 9 | 60 | 1 | 14 | 5 | 32 | 1 |
| Goldie | 33 | 10 | 80 | 5 | 10 | — | 50 | — |
| Tate | 25 | 5 | 81 | 2 | 11 | 2 | 46 | — |
| Vine | 15 | 4 | 54 | 1 | 10 | — | 42 | — |
| Killick | 6 | 3 | 24 | — | 11 | 1 | 43 | — |
| Leach | | | | | 8 | — | 33 | 1 |

## Middlesex Bowling

| | Overs | Mdns | Runs | Wkts | Overs | Mdns | Runs | Wkts |
|---|--:|--:|--:|--:|--:|--:|--:|--:|
| G. W. Baldam | 8 | 1 | 29 | 1 | | | | |
| Hunt | 19 | 3 | 63 | 3 | 14 | 5 | 42 | 2 |
| Bosanquet | 24.3 | 2 | 75 | 3 | 13.2 | 1 | 53 | 8 |
| Hearne | 18 | 5 | 38 | 2 | | | | |
| Trott | 13 | 3 | 35 | 1 | | | | |

Umpires: W. A. J. West and C. E. Richardson.

## MIDDLESEX IN 1907

*President* – Mr R. D. Walker

*Hon. Secretary* – Mr A. J. Webbe

*Captain* – Mr G. MacGregor

*Deputy Captain* – Mr P. F. Warner

One incident during the season gave rise to a great deal of discussion and not a little ill-feeling. We refer, of course, to the abandonment on the 23rd of July of the match with Lancashire. The details of this most unfortunate affair will be fresh in the memory of everyone who follows cricket at all closely. A lot of rain fell on the first day and in such time as was available Lancashire scored 57 for one wicket. At the ordinary time for resuming the following morning play was quite out of the question, and as events turned out it would have been much better if the umpires, who from time to time inspected the pitch, had early in the day declared cricket impracticable. As it was the people who had paid for admission became very impatient at the long delay, and after stumps had at last been pulled up some of them went so far as to trample on the wicket. A lengthy consultation and discussion by the captains followed, and after six o'clock MacLaren handed the following official statement to the Press:

> Owing to the pitch having been deliberately torn up by the public, I, as captain of the Lancashire eleven, cannot see my way to continue the game, the groundman bearing me out that the wicket could not again be put right.
>
> A. C. MacLaren

Opinion was very much divided as to the action MacLaren took, a letter of indignant protest being addressed to the *Field* by Mr R. D. Walker, the Middlesex president. The actual damage to the pitch did not, it was stated, amount to more than one rather deep heel mark.

## MIDDLESEX v SOMERSET

### Played at Lord's, May 20, 21, 22, 1907

Albert Trott rendered his benefit match memorable by an extraordinary bowling performance in the second innings of Somerset, dismissing Lewis, Poyntz, Woods, and Robson with successive balls, and later on disposing of Mordaunt, Wickham, and Bailey, also with successive balls. Thus he accomplished the unprecedented feat of performing the "hat trick" twice in an innings. Thanks to Trott's bowling, Middlesex won by 166 runs. Rain seriously interfered with cricket on the opening day, the whole time available being occupied by the home team's first innings. Middlesex blundered in the field on Tuesday, but thanks to Tarrant secured a useful lead. Litteljohn followed up his success against Hampshire with two capital displays of batting.

## Middlesex

| | | | |
|---|---|---|---|
| Mr P. F. Warner b Mordaunt | 46 | – b Lewis | 11 |
| F. A. Tarrant c Lee b Lewis | 52 | – c Palairet b Mordaunt | 28 |
| Mr G. W. Beldam lbw b Mordaunt | 12 | – lbw b Lewis | 0 |
| Mr B. J. T. Bosanquet c Johnson b Mordaunt | 32 | – b Bailey | 29 |
| Mr E. S. Litteljohn c Braund b Lewis | 44 | – b Mordaunt | 52 |
| A. E. Trott b Lewis | 1 | – c Wickham b Robson | 35 |
| Mr H. A. Milton b Lewis | 3 | – b Mordaunt | 0 |
| Mr G. MacGregor c Woods b Bailey | 39 | – c Poyntz b Robson | 39 |
| H. R. Murrell b Robson | 33 | – c and b Braund | 9 |
| J. T. Hearne not out | 3 | – not out | 4 |
| E. Mignon b Bailey | 1 | – c Wickham b Braund | 0 |
| B 15, l-b 4, n-b 1 | 20 | B 3, l-b 2, n-b 1 | 6 |
| | **286** | | **213** |

## Somerset

| | | | |
|---|---|---|---|
| Mr L. C. H. Palairet c MacGregor b Mignon | 6 | – c Bosanquet b Tarrant | 35 |
| L. C. Braund c MacGregor b Bosanquet | 59 | – not out | 28 |
| Mr P. R. Johnson b Tarrant | 57 | – c Trott b Tarrant | 14 |
| A. E. Lewis c Tarrant b Mignon | 31 | – lbw b Trott | 1 |
| Mr E. S. M. Poyntz lbw b Tarrant | 9 | – b Trott | 0 |
| Mr S. M. J. Woods c Bosanquet b Tarrant | 17 | – b Trott | 0 |
| E. Robson not out | 20 | – b Trott | 0 |
| Mr F. M. Lee b Hearne | 18 | – c Trott b Tarrant | 7 |
| Mr O. C. Mordaunt c Beldam b Tarrant | 1 | – c Mignon b Trott | 4 |
| Rev. A. P. Wickham c Trott b Tarrant | 0 | – b Trott | 0 |
| A. E. Bailey c Litteljohn b Tarrant | 3 | – c Mignon b Trott | 0 |
| L-b 14, w 1 | 15 | B 4, l-b 4 | 8 |
| | **236** | | **97** |

### Somerset Bowling

| | Overs | Mdns | Runs | Wkts | Overs | Mdns | Runs | Wkts |
|---|---|---|---|---|---|---|---|---|
| Lewis | 32 | 14 | 88 | 4 | 7 | 2 | 17 | 2 |
| Bailey | 16 | 5 | 33 | 2 | 16 | 3 | 58 | 1 |
| Braund | 13 | 1 | 33 | — | 13.4 | 1 | 55 | 2 |
| Mordaunt | 30 | 6 | 97 | 3 | 15 | 1 | 47 | 3 |
| Robson | 7 | 1 | 15 | 1 | 6 | 2 | 30 | 2 |

### Middlesex Bowling

| | Overs | Mdns | Runs | Wkts | Overs | Mdns | Runs | Wkts |
|---|---|---|---|---|---|---|---|---|
| Beldam | 4 | 1 | 15 | — | 3 | 1 | 10 | — |
| Mignon | 24 | 6 | 88 | 2 | 5 | 1 | 24 | — |
| Trott | 5 | 1 | 10 | — | 8 | 2 | 20 | 7 |
| Hearne | 8 | 1 | 22 | 1 | | | | |
| Bosanquet | 8 | — | 39 | 1 | | | | |
| Tarrant | 15 | 4 | 47 | 6 | 14 | 4 | 35 | 3 |

Umpires: F. W. Marlow and S. Brown.

# MIDDLESEX v GLOUCESTERSHIRE

Played at Lord's, May 23, 24, 1907

Thanks mainly to the bowling of Tarrant and Trott, Middlesex beat Gloucestershire by ten wickets. Three innings were got through on the opening day, and forty-five minutes' cricket next morning brought the match to a conclusion. Jessop, alone of the

Gloucestershire batsmen, distinguished himself. In the first innings, on a pitch which rain during the night and early morning had rendered very difficult, he scored 41 out of 42 in half an hour, and later in the day when the visitors were dismissed in eight-five minutes, he made 30 out of 37 in half an hour. Middlesex, despite some steady cricket by Tarrant, lost four men for 55, and Trott should have been run out at 58. The mistake then made proved very costly, Trott hitting up 38 out of 50 before being dismissed by a brilliant catch. Tarrant took thirteen wickets in the match for less than seven runs apiece. Dennett also bowled well.

## Gloucestershire

| | | | |
|---|---|---|---|
| Mr R. T. Godsell b Trott | 5 | – lbw b Trott | 3 |
| H. Wrathall lbw b Trott | 0 | – b Tarrant | 4 |
| J. H. Board b Trott | 9 | – c Stogdon b Tarrant | 10 |
| T. Langdon b Tarrant | 5 | – c Trott b Tarrant | 10 |
| Mr G. L. Jessop c Litteljohn b Tarrant | 41 | – b Mignon | 30 |
| Major A. H. Luard b Trott | 1 | – c Harrison b Tarrant | 1 |
| A. Winstone lbw b Tarrant | 0 | – c and b Tarrant | 2 |
| Mr E. Barnett c Bosanquet b Tarrant | 0 | – not out | 8 |
| J. H. Huggins c Litteljohn b Tarrant | 7 | – st MacGregor b Tarrant | 3 |
| Mr P. H. Ford c Harrison b Tarrant | 2 | – b Trott | 1 |
| G. Dennett not out | 13 | – c Mignon b Tarrant | 1 |
| B 2 | 2 | L-b 1 | 1 |
| | **85** | | **74** |

## Middlesex

| | | | |
|---|---|---|---|
| Mr P. F. Warner c Godsell b Huggins | 15 | – not out | 20 |
| F. A. Tarrant c Board b Dennett | 23 | – not out | 15 |
| Mr E. S. Litteljohn lbw b Huggins | 0 | | |
| Mr B. J. T. Bosanquet c Jessop b Dennett | 10 | | |
| Mr W. P. Harrison b Dennett | 12 | | |
| A. E. Trott c Wrathall b Dennett | 38 | | |
| Mr J. H. Stogdon st Board b Dennett | 5 | | |
| Mr G. MacGregor st Board b Dennett | 5 | | |
| Mr C. V. Baker c Luard b Ford | 0 | | |
| J. T. Hearne run out | 7 | | |
| W. Mignon not out | 0 | | |
| B 1, l-b 2 | 3 | B 5, l-b 2 | 7 |
| | **118** | | **42** |

## Middlesex Bowling

| | Overs | Mdns | Runs | Wkts | Overs | Mdns | Runs | Wkts |
|---|---|---|---|---|---|---|---|---|
| Trott | 14 | 3 | 29 | 4 | 10 | 3 | 32 | 2 |
| Tarrant | 13.5 | 1 | 54 | 6 | 13.5 | 3 | 33 | 7 |
| Mignon | | | | | 4 | 1 | 8 | 1 |

## Gloucestershire Bowling

| | Overs | Mdns | Runs | Wkts | Overs | Mdns | Runs | Wkts |
|---|---|---|---|---|---|---|---|---|
| Dennett | 22.4 | 5 | 64 | 6 | | | | |
| Ford | 9 | 2 | 18 | 1 | 5 | 4 | 5 | — |
| Huggins | 13 | 3 | 33 | 2 | 9 | 4 | 12 | — |
| Winstone | | | | | 1 | — | 6 | — |
| Jessop | | | | | 3 | 1 | 4 | — |
| Langdon | | | | | 1.4 | — | 7 | — |
| Wrathall | | | | | 1 | — | 1 | — |

Umpires: A. Millward and H. Bagshaw.

## MIDDLESEX v LANCASHIRE

### Played at Lord's, July 22, 23, 1907

This match proved an altogether unfortunate affair. So much rain fell during the early hours of Monday that no cricket could be attempted until after lunch. Later on there came a delay of seventy minutes owing to bad light and at five o'clock further rain put an end to play. Spooner turning out for the first time during the season and Worsley resuming his place, Lancashire had their best side for the occasion. MacLaren and Spooner put on 26 for the first wicket and afterwards the former and Tyldesley added 31 without further loss, the Lancashire captain playing particularly well. That evening the pitch was practically under water and, with a wet night, the prospects of play next day were always remote. Unhappily, there came neither sun nor wind to improve the condition of the ground. The spectators, numbering about 600, waited patiently until half-past three, but then began to clamour for the game to be resumed, demonstrating two or three times in front of the pavilion. After several visits to the wicket, the umpires made a final inspection at a quarter to five and, finding the ground still unplayable, pulled up the stumps. Thereupon, some section of the spectators walked right across the pitch and inflicted some damage, noticeably at one end. The crowd having dispersed, a prolonged discussion ensued between the captains and some of their players and the umpires, and eventually MacLaren handed the following statement to the Press: "Owing to the pitch having been deliberately torn up by the public, I, as captain of the Lancashire Eleven, cannot see my way to continue the game, the groundman bearing me out that the wicket could not be again put right. – A. C. MacLaren." The match was accordingly abandoned. Rolled next morning for the regulation ten minutes, the pitch showed little trace of the treatment to which it had been subjected.

### Lancashire

| | |
|---|---:|
| Mr A. C. MacLaren not out | 27 |
| Mr R. H. Spooner c Mignon b Tarrant | 13 |
| J. T. Tyldesley not out | 15 |
| B 2 | 2 |
| | 57 |

Mr L. O. S. Poidevin, J. Sharp, Mr A. H. Hornby, Mr H. D. Stanning, F. Harry, H. Dean, A. Kermode and W. Worsley did not bat.

### Middlesex

Mr G. MacGregor, Mr P. F. Warner, Mr E. S. Litteljohn, Mr C. C. Page, Mr M. W. Payne, F. A. Tarrant, A. E. Trott, D. Hendren, H. R. Murrell, J. T. Hearne, and E. Mignon.

### Middlesex Bowling

| | Overs | Mdns | Runs | Wkts |
|---|---|---|---|---|
| Tarrant | 13 | 4 | 21 | 1 |
| Mignon | 2 | — | 11 | — |
| Hearne | 10 | 4 | 23 | — |

Umpires: W. Flowers and F. W. Marlow.

## MIDDLESEX v KENT

### Played at Lord's, August 24, 25, 26, 1908

Kent snatched a remarkable victory ten minutes before time by 117 runs. Not until nearly four o'clock did Marsham declare, Middlesex to save the game having to stay in less than two hours. Warner failed, yet with only forty-five minutes left there remained six wickets to get down, with Douglas well set. A draw appeared inevitable but Woolley, going on, proved irresistible and in four overs and three balls dismissed six batsmen for 8 runs. No play was possible until half-past three on Monday when Kent, going in, lost six wickets for 131 before the drawing of stumps. For Middlesex on Tuesday Bosanquet forced the game on a slow wicket in grand style. Warner declared directly Kent's total had been equalled but no success attended this course of action.

## Kent

| | | |
|---|---|---|
| Mr C. H. B. Marsham c Etheridge b Hearne | 15 | – c Moon b Wells ............... 8 |
| H. T. W. Hardinge st Moon b Tarrant | 6 | – b Hearne ..................... 33 |
| James Seymour c Trott b Tarrant | 8 | – lbw b Wells .................. 27 |
| Mr S. H. Day st Moon b Tarrant | 11 | – b Bosanquet .................. 40 |
| F. E. Woolley c Douglas b Tarrant | 6 | – b Wells...................... 4 |
| Mr J. R. Mason c Trott b Tarrant | 43 | – b Wells ..................... 2 |
| Mr K. L. Hutchings c Trott b Tarrant | 58 | – c Tarrant b Hearne ........... 27 |
| E. Humphreys c Trott b Hearne | 8 | – not out ..................... 44 |
| F. H. Huish b Wells | 20 | |
| W. J. Fairservice not out | 23 | – not out ..................... 6 |
| C. Blythe c and b Tarrant | 0 | |
| B 8, l-b 1 | 9 | B 13 .................... 13 |

207 (7 wkts dec.) 204

## Middlesex

| | | |
|---|---|---|
| Mr P. F. Warner lbw b Fairservice | 1 | – b Fairservice ................. 3 |
| Mr L. J. Moon b Fairservice | 41 | – c Day b Blythe................ 23 |
| Mr J. Douglas c Mason b Woolley | 28 | – not out ..................... 25 |
| Mr B. J. T. Bosanquet b Hardinge | 50 | – c Hutchings b Fairservice ........ 11 |
| F. A. Tarrant b Hardinge | 13 | – c Seymour b Blythe ............ 0 |
| Mr W. P. Harrison c Mason b Fairservice | 12 | – b Woolley ................... 9 |
| Mr S. G. Etheridge not out | 18 | – c Fairservice b Woolley .......... 2 |
| Mr C. M. Wells b Mason | 27 | – b Woolley ................... 0 |
| A. E. Trott c Woolley b Mason | 7 | – c Mason b Woolley ............ 0 |
| J. T. Hearne did not bat | 0 | – b Woolley ................... 0 |
| E. Mignon did not bat | 0 | – b Woolley ................... 2 |
| B 9, l-b 1 | 10 | B 9, l-b 2, n-b 1 .......... 12 |

(8 wkts dec.) 207 87

## Middlesex Bowling

| | Overs | Mdns | Runs | Wkts | Overs | Mdns | Runs | Wkts |
|---|---|---|---|---|---|---|---|---|
| Tarrant ......... | 44.3 | 12 | 117 | 7 | 33 | 11 | 67 | — |
| Hearne .......... | 40 | 16 | 58 | 2 | 24 | 9 | 43 | 2 |
| Trott ........... | 1 | — | 7 | — | 5 | 2 | 15 | — |
| Wells ........... | 9 | 1 | 16 | 1 | 26 | 7 | 53 | 4 |
| Mignon ......... | | | | | 1 | 1 | — | — |
| Bosanquet ....... | | | | | 6 | 2 | 13 | 1 |

## Kent Bowling

| | Overs | Mdns | Runs | Wkts | Overs | Mdns | Runs | Wkts |
|---|---|---|---|---|---|---|---|---|
| Fairservice ........ | 25 | 10 | 39 | 3 | 13 | 3 | 33 | 2 |
| Blythe .......... | 28 | 7 | 94 | — | 17 | 8 | 34 | 2 |
| Woolley ......... | 10 | 4 | 45 | 1 | 4.3 | 2 | 8 | 6 |
| Hardinge ........ | 5 | — | 18 | 2 | | | | |
| Mason .......... | 2.2 | 1 | 1 | 2 | | | | |

Umpires: A. J. Atfield and H. Bagshaw.

## MIDDLESEX v YORKSHIRE

Played at Lord's, June 16, 17, 18, 1910

There was a wonderful finish to this game, the hit which gave Yorkshire a victory by two wickets being made off the fifth ball of what must in any event have been the last over of the match. Following up two stubborn days' cricket, in which Warner played two fine innings, Rhodes batted admirably, and Tarrant gave a masterly display, Middlesex entered upon the concluding stage of the contest 229 ahead with five wickets in hand. Thanks to Rhodes the innings, despite some capital hitting by Wormald, was soon finished off, but Yorkshire wanting 331 to win lost three wickets for 47. Then came a great stand by Hirst and Denton, who, together for two hours and a half, added 163 runs. Hirst continued to bat splendidly and though badly missed when, with half-an-hour left, 60 runs were still required, his innings could not well be overpraised. His efforts at a most anxious time were ably seconded by Myers. Tremendous enthusiasm prevailed at the close.

### Middlesex

| | | | |
|---|---:|---|---:|
| Mr P. F. Warner c Hirst b Newstead | 60 | – b Haigh | 41 |
| F. A. Tarrant lbw b Hirst | 4 | – c Dolphin b Newstead | 107 |
| E. Hendren b Hirst | 1 | – c Dolphin b Newstead | 14 |
| J. W. Hearne b Hirst | 48 | – c Denton b Rhodes | 9 |
| Mr E. S. Litteljohn b Hirst | 5 | – not out | 35 |
| Mr W. P. Robertson b Myers | 39 | – c Radcliffe b Hirst | 9 |
| Mr J. Wormald b Haigh | 3 | – c Dolphin b Rhodes | 61 |
| H. R. Murrell c Hirst b Myers | 28 | – b Hirst | 15 |
| Mr R. E. More b Drake | 26 | – c Myers b Rhodes | 12 |
| E. Mignon b Drake | 5 | – b Rhodes | 1 |
| J. T. Hearne not out | 13 | – b Rhodes | 2 |
| B 4, l-b 3, w 1 | 8 | Extras | 15 |
| | **240** | | **321** |

### Yorkshire

| | | | |
|---|---:|---|---:|
| W. Rhodes b More | 62 | – b Mignon | 8 |
| J. W. Rothery lbw b Mignon | 2 | – c Warner b Mignon | 11 |
| D. Denton lbw b J. W. Hearne | 25 | – c Hendren b Mignon | 95 |
| W. H. Wilkinson c Tarrant b More | 31 | – c Tarrant b More | 3 |
| G. H. Hirst b J. W. Hearne | 15 | – lbw b More | 137 |
| H. Myers c Tarrant b J. T. Hearne | 23 | – not out | 39 |
| A. Drake b J. T. Hearne | 25 | – c J. W. Hearne b J. T. Hearne | 2 |
| Mr E. J. Radcliffe c Hendren b J. T. Hearne | 15 | – b More | 4 |
| S. Haigh b J. T. Hearne | 6 | – not out | 8 |
| J. T. Newstead not out | 11 | – c sub. b J. T. Hearne | 12 |
| A. Dolphin c Hendren b More | 1 | | |
| B 5, l-b 9, n-b 1 | 15 | B 6, l-b 6 | 12 |
| | **231** | | **331** |

### Yorkshire Bowling

| | Overs | Mdns | Runs | Wkts | Overs | Mdns | Runs | Wkts |
|---|---|---|---|---|---|---|---|---|
| Hirst | 27 | 7 | 74 | 4 | 20 | 1 | 53 | 2 |
| Newstead | 14 | 5 | 28 | 1 | 24 | 5 | 60 | 2 |
| Drake | 12.1 | 4 | 19 | 2 | 10 | 3 | 30 | — |
| Myers | 11 | — | 48 | 2 | 14 | 3 | 49 | — |
| Rhodes | 10 | 1 | 33 | — | 23.1 | 4 | 57 | 5 |
| Haigh | 11 | 3 | 30 | 1 | 19 | 1 | 57 | 1 |

**Middlesex Bowling**

|  | Overs | Mdns | Runs | Wkts | Overs | Mdns | Runs | Wkts |
|---|---|---|---|---|---|---|---|---|
| Mignon | 14 | 1 | 63 | 1 | 15 | — | 82 | 3 |
| Tarrant | 10 | 3 | 34 | — | 22 | 9 | 57 | — |
| J. W. Hearne | 21 | 1 | 67 | 2 | 5 | — | 34 | — |
| More | 24.4 | 16 | 31 | 3 | 31.5 | 8 | 89 | 3 |
| J. T. Hearne | 15 | 5 | 21 | 4 | 24 | 10 | 57 | 2 |

Umpires: F. Parris and A. E. Street.

## MIDDLESEX v ESSEX

### Played at Lord's, August 8, 9, 10, 1910

Among many great finishes during the summer there was none more remarkable than that in this match, Middlesex, when their eighth wicket went down, wanting 100 runs and obtaining that number without further loss. Warner played one of the best innings of his splendid career, but his efforts could not have saved the home side from defeat without the fearless hitting of Saville – a member of the Marlborough eleven of 1907. The two batsmen scored 101 runs in an hour – the last seventy-three in forty minutes. Some sensational cricket also characterised the opening day, J. W. Hearne after lunch, when Essex had 93 on the board with two men out, sending down five overs and a ball for 2 runs and seven wickets. Buckenham, too, bowled in deadly form for a time, the success of two men so unlike in pace and method being very curious. The pitch was rather bad.

### Essex

| | | | |
|---|---|---|---|
| Mr J. W. H. T. Douglas c Douglas b Tarrant | 30 | – c and b Tarrant | 6 |
| Mr P. Perrin c Mignon b Tarrant | 39 | – b Tarrant | 39 |
| Maj. A. J. Turner c Warner b J. W. Hearne | 7 | – c J. W. Hearne b Mignon | 23 |
| Rev. F. H. Gillingham c and b Tarrant | 10 | – c sub. b J. W. Hearne | 18 |
| Mr F. L. Fane c Douglas b J. W. Hearne | 5 | – c Mignon b Tarrant | 51 |
| Mr C. McGahey c Douglas b J. W. Hearne | 1 | – c Murrell b Mignon | 19 |
| Mr A. L. Gibson lbw b J. W. Hearne | 0 | – c Saville b Mignon | 34 |
| C. P. Buckenham c Warner b J. W. Hearne | 0 | – not out | 12 |
| E. Russell lbw b J. W. Hearne | 3 | – b J. W. Hearne | 11 |
| W. Mead c Mignon b J. W. Hearne | 0 | – lbw b J. W. Hearne | 6 |
| B. Tremlin not out | 0 | – b J. W. Hearne | 0 |
| B 8, l-b 5, w 1, n-b 1 | 15 | B 12, l-b 4 | 16 |
| | **110** | | **235** |

### Middlesex

| | | | |
|---|---|---|---|
| Mr J. Douglas c Russell b Buckenham | 3 | – lbw b Buckenham | 0 |
| F. A. Tarrant c Douglas b Buckenham | 12 | – lbw b Buckenham | 42 |
| E. Hendren retired hurt | 29 | – c Douglas b Buckenham | 1 |
| J. W. Hearne not out | 39 | – b Mead | 9 |
| Mr P. F. Warner c Fane b Buckenham | 2 | – not out | 101 |
| Mr K. B. Harper b Buckenham | 0 | – lbw b Mead | 1 |
| Mr C. V. Baker b Buckenham | 2 | – c Gillingham b Mead | 18 |
| Mr S. H. Saville c Russell b Buckenham | 0 | – not out | 56 |
| H. R. Murrell b Douglas | 9 | – b Mead | 0 |
| J. T. Hearne b Douglas | 4 | – b Buckenham | 0 |
| E. Mignon b Douglas | 3 | | |
| L-b 1 | 1 | B 2, l-b 4, n-b 9 | 15 |
| | **104** | | **243** |

**Middlesex Bowling**

| | Overs | Mdns | Runs | Wkts | Overs | Mdns | Runs | Wkts |
|---|---|---|---|---|---|---|---|---|
| Hearne, J. T. ...... | 4 | 1 | 7 | — | 12 | 6 | 16 | — |
| Tarrant ......... | 19 | 7 | 32 | 3 | 35 | 15 | 54 | 3 |
| Mignon ......... | 8 | 2 | 15 | — | 16 | — | 63 | 3 |
| Hearne, J. W. ...... | 22.1 | 9 | 37 | 7 | 34.5 | 7 | 86 | 4 |
| Douglas ......... | 1 | 0 | 4 | 0 | | | | |

**Essex Bowling**

| | Overs | Mdns | Runs | Wkts | Overs | Mdns | Runs | Wkts |
|---|---|---|---|---|---|---|---|---|
| Buckenham ....... | 23 | 6 | 51 | 6 | 33 | 11 | 104 | 4 |
| Tremlin ......... | 6 | 1 | 19 | — | 15 | 6 | 23 | — |
| Mead ........... | 3 | 1 | 11 | — | 23 | 3 | 60 | 4 |
| Douglas ......... | 13.1 | 4 | 22 | 3 | 12 | 3 | 36 | — |
| McGahey ........ | | | | | 2.2 | 1 | 5 | — |

Umpires: W. Richards and W. Vining.

# MIDDLESEX v LANCASHIRE

Played at Lord's, May 25, 26, 27, 1911

In this match A. R. Litteljohn followed up his fine work against Kent with bowling of quite a sensational description. Lancashire, though without J. T. Tyldesley and Hartley, had, thanks to Makepeace and W. Tyldesley who put on 130 for the second wicket, 170 on the board with only one man out, but Litteljohn wrought tremendous havoc, winding up by dismissing eight batsmen in ten overs and four balls for 19 runs. Litteljohn brought about another startling change on Saturday, Lancashire at lunch time having scored 154 for the loss of four wickets and the match being finished off in three-quarters of an hour afterwards. Taking in all fifteen wickets in the match Litteljohn made his aggregate 36 for six consecutive innings. Middlesex, although losing Tarrant and Hendren for 28, kept their opponents in the field for six hours and a quarter. Warner and J. W. Hearne put on 147 in less than two hours. Warner played admirably at a time when upon his personal efforts the success of the side largely depended, and Hearne – at the wickets for two hours and a half – scored particularly well on the on-side. After seven wickets had fallen for 302, E. S. Litteljohn and Anson completely mastered the bowling, adding 120 in an hour and a half. Though freely punished at times, Brearley bowled with splendid energy. Hornby in fielding a ball on the boundary, fell and injured his shoulder so badly that he did not play again for a month. Middlesex won by an innings and 11 runs.

## Lancashire

| | | | |
|---|---|---|---|
| Mr R. H. Spooner b Tarrant ................... | 17 | – b A. Litteljohn ................ | 28 |
| H. Makepeace c Saville b A. Litteljohn ........... | 77 | – c A. Litteljohn b J. W. Hearne ..... | 60 |
| W. Tyldesley lbw b A. Litteljohn ................ | 65 | – b A. Litteljohn ................ | 27 |
| J. Sharp b A. Litteljohn ...................... | 0 | – st Murrell b A. Litteljohn ........ | 45 |
| J. S. Heap not out .......................... | 31 | – c and b A. Litteljohn ........... | 1 |
| Mr H. G. Garnett b A. Litteljohn ................ | 4 | – c Hendren b A. Litteljohn ........ | 33 |
| Mr K. G. McLeod c Baker b A. Litteljohn ........ | 0 | – st Murrell b A. Litteljohn ........ | 35 |
| H. Dean c A. Litteljohn b Tarrant ............... | 0 | – c E. Litteljohn b A. Litteljohn ..... | 1 |
| Mr A. H. Hornby b A. Litteljohn ................ | 2 | – absent hurt .................... | 0 |
| L. Cook b A. Litteljohn....................... | 0 | – not out ...................... | 0 |
| Mr W. Brearley b A. Litteljohn ................ | 0 | – st Murrell b Tarrant ............ | 1 |
| B 8, l-b 6, w 2 ..................... | 16 | L-b 1, n-b 1 ............. | 2 |
| | 212 | | 233 |

## Middlesex

| | |
|---|---|
| Mr P. F. Warner b Brearley ............ 81 | Mr S. H. Saville b Cook ............... 30 |
| F. A. Tarrant c Tyldesley b Dean ........ 14 | Hon. R. Anson b Sharp ............... 70 |
| E. Hendren b Brearley ................ 0 | H. R. Murrell not out ................ 13 |
| J. W. Hearne c Tyldesley b McLeod ...... 77 | J. T. Hearne b Brearley ............... 5 |
| Mr E. S. Litteljohn c Dean b Brearley .....105 | B 21, l-b 12, n-b 6 ............. 39 |
| Mr C. V. Baker c Spooner b Brearley ..... 19 | |
| Mr A. R. Litteljohn b Brearley ........... 3 | 456 |

## Middlesex Bowling

| | Overs | Mdns | Runs | Wkts | Overs | Mdns | Runs | Wkts |
|---|---|---|---|---|---|---|---|---|
| J. T. Hearne ....... | 26 | 13 | 35 | — | 15 | 4 | 23 | — |
| A. R. Litteljohn .... | 27.4 | 5 | 69 | 8 | 34 | 6 | 120 | 7 |
| Tarrant .......... | 24 | 8 | 52 | 2 | 15.3 | 4 | 22 | 1 |
| J. W. Hearne ...... | 15 | 5 | 40 | — | 14 | 2 | 63 | 1 |
| Anson .......... | | | | | 2 | — | 3 | — |

## Lancashire Bowling

| | Overs | Mdns | Runs | Wkts |
|---|---|---|---|---|
| Brearley .......... | 49 | 7 | 162 | 6 |
| Dean ............ | 27 | 8 | 50 | 1 |
| Cook ............ | 28 | 4 | 82 | 1 |
| Heap ............ | 10 | 1 | 43 | — |
| Makepeace ........ | 12 | — | 41 | — |
| McLeod .......... | 8 | 1 | 29 | 1 |
| Sharp ............ | 3 | — | 10 | 1 |

Umpires: F. G. Roberts and W. Richards.

# MIDDLESEX v WORCESTERSHIRE

### Played at Lord's, July 24, 25, 26, 1911

Cheaply dismissed at their first attempt, Worcestershire played more creditably in the second innings but lost by ten wickets. By the drawing of stumps on Monday, Middlesex were 60 runs ahead with nine wickets in hand. J. W. Hearne, sent in first, put together yet another hundred, and in company with Anson added 176 for the second wicket. Hearne played steadily throughout and Anson improved after an indifferent start. Bowley, carrying his bat right through the second innings of Worcestershire, gave no chance. On Wednesday when Middlesex wanted only 62 to win, rain delayed play until after two o'clock.

## Worcestershire

| | | |
|---|---|---|
| F. Bowley lbw b J. T. Hearne ................ | 18 – | not out ..................... 104 |
| F. Pearson run out .......................... | 0 – | c Mann b Mignon ............. 39 |
| Mr G. N. Foster c Hendren b J. T. Hearne ........ | 1 – | c Tarrant b Mignon ............ 0 |
| E. Arnold run out ........................... | 19 – | b J. W. Hearne ............... 32 |
| Mr W. B. Burns c Wormald b J. W. Hearne ....... | 27 – | c Murrell b J. T. Hearne ......... 18 |
| Mr B. S. Foster c Murrell b Mignon ............. | 18 – | c J. W. Hearne b J. T. Hearne ..... 36 |
| J. A. Cuffe b J. W. Hearne ................... | 10 – | lbw b Tarrant ................. 0 |
| Mr G. H. Simpson-Hayward | | |
| c Tarrant b J. W. Hearne . | 14 – | c Hendren b J. T. Hearne ......... 21 |
| R. E. Turner lbw b Mignon ................... | 2 – | lbw b Tarrant ................. 0 |
| E. Bale b Mignon .......................... | 14 – | c Mignon b Tarrant ............ 6 |
| A. J. Conway not out ........................ | 6 – | c Warner b J. T. Hearne ......... 1 |
| B 1, n-b 5 ........................ | 6 | B 6, l-b 1, n-b 3 .......... 10 |
| | 135 | 267 |

## Middlesex

F. A. Tarrant c B. Foster b Simpson-Hayward ..... 22 – not out ...................... 24
J. W. Hearne c Bowley b Conway ..............115
Hon. R. Anson c Burns b Conway .............. 80
Mr P. F. Warner st Bale b Simpson-Hayward ...... 31 – not out ...................... 32
E. Hendren c Turner b Simpson-Hayward ......... 0
H. R. Murrell st Bale b Simpson-Hayward ........ 6
Mr F. T. Mann b Pearson ...................... 24
Mr J. Wormald c G. Foster b Simpson-Hayward ... 28
Mr S. H. Saville b Pearson .................... 11
J. T. Hearne not out ......................... 8
E. Mignon lbw b Pearson ..................... 0
    B 8, l-b 6, w 2 ..................... 16        B 6 ................... 6

                               341                       62

### Middlesex Bowling

|            | Overs | Mdns | Runs | Wkts | Overs | Mdns | Runs | Wkts |
|------------|-------|------|------|------|-------|------|------|------|
| J. T. Hearne ....... | 11 | 4 | 38 | 2 | 23 | 3 | 66 | 4 |
| Mignon .......... | 13.2 | 2 | 43 | 3 | 12 | — | 71 | 2 |
| J. W. Hearne ...... | 13 | 2 | 38 | 3 | 12 | — | 46 | 1 |
| Tarrant .......... | 6 | 1 | 10 | — | 14 | 2 | 53 | 3 |
| Anson .......... | | | | | 6 | 1 | 21 | — |

### Worcestershire Bowling

|            | Overs | Mdns | Runs | Wkts | Overs | Mdns | Runs | Wkts |
|------------|-------|------|------|------|-------|------|------|------|
| Burns ........... | 9 | 2 | 23 | — | | | | |
| Cuffe ........... | 36 | 12 | 87 | — | 7 | — | 17 | — |
| Simpson-Hayward .. | 27 | 4 | 66 | 5 | | | | |
| Pearson .......... | 17 | 2 | 46 | 3 | | | | |
| Conway .......... | 19 | 1 | 86 | 2 | | | | |
| Arnold .......... | 5 | 1 | 17 | — | 7 | — | 20 | — |
| Turner .......... | | | | | 4 | — | 10 | — |
| B. S. Foster ....... | | | | | 3.3 | — | 9 | — |

Umpires: J. Carlin and G. Hutchings.

## MIDDLESEX v ESSEX

Played at Lord's, July 27, 28, 29, 1911

Some wonderful bowling by J. W. Hearne got Essex all out on a good wicket before lunch time on the first day. The visitors had 51 on the board with two men out when Hearne went on at the pavilion end and sent down seven overs for 11 runs and six wickets. Dismissing Carpenter, McGahey, and Gibson with successive balls, Hearne performed the "hat trick." Essex batted feebly but their dismissal was really due to a bowler of exceptional gifts having one of his irresistible days, Hearne mixing up leg-breaks and "googlies" in most disconcerting fashion. Having disposed of their opponents in such startling fashion, Middlesex by the drawing of stumps were 130 ahead with seven wickets in hand. Buckenham soon sent back J. W. Hearne and Anson, but Warner and Tarrant put on 124. Hendren and Tarrant afterwards shared in a quiet partnership of 105, and with Murrell and Tarrant together 104 runs were obtained in an hour. Tarrant during a stay of nearly five hours and a half never departed from a steady method of batting. Essex in their second innings had lost four wickets for 102 when a violent storm burst over the ground, the downpour being the heaviest experienced in London for a couple of months. Next morning, when the pitch was very difficult, Tarrant and J. T. Hearne finished off the match in three-quarters of an hour, Middlesex winning by an innings and 211 runs.

## Essex

| | | | |
|---|---|---|---|
| Mr J. W. H. T. Douglas lbw b J. T. Hearne | 13 | – c J. W. Hearne b Tarrant | 6 |
| Mr F. L. Fane c Murrell b Mignon | 2 | – c Murrell b Mignon | 14 |
| Mr P. Perrin b J. W. Hearne | 20 | – lbw b Tarrant | 22 |
| J. Freeman c Tarrant b J. W. Hearne | 20 | – c J. W. Hearne b J. T. Hearne | 8 |
| Rev. F. H. Gillingham run out | 0 | – lbw b Tarrant | 0 |
| H. Carpenter lbw b J. W. Hearne | 2 | – c Anson b Tarrant | 2 |
| Mr C. McGahey b J. W. Hearne | 0 | – c J. W. Hearne b Tarrant | 49 |
| Mr K. L. Gibson lbw b J. W. Hearne | 0 | – b Tarrant | 24 |
| C. P. Buckenham not out | 3 | – not out | 7 |
| B. Tremlin lbw b J. W. Hearne | 0 | – c Mann b J. T. Hearne | 3 |
| W. Mead c Murrell b Tarrant | 5 | – lbw b J. T. Hearne | 6 |
| B 13 | 13 | B 8, l-b 1, w 1 | 10 |
| | **78** | | **151** |

## Middlesex

| | | | |
|---|---|---|---|
| F. A. Tarrant lbw b Buckenham | 168 | Mr J. Wormald b Buckenham | 21 |
| J. W. Hearne c Fane b Buckenham | 7 | Mr S. H. Saville c Fane b Buckenham | 8 |
| Hon. R. Anson c Gibson b Buckenham | 6 | J. T. Hearne not out | 9 |
| Mr P. F. Warner b Douglas | 61 | | |
| E. Hendren b Mead | 52 | B 10, l-b 8, n-b 1 | 19 |
| H. R. Murrell b Freeman | 62 | | |
| Mr F. T. Mann b Buckenham | 27 | (9 wkts dec.) | 440 |

E. Mignon did not bat.

## Middlesex Bowling

| | Overs | Mdns | Runs | Wkts | Overs | Mdns | Runs | Wkts |
|---|---|---|---|---|---|---|---|---|
| J. T. Hearne | 12 | 6 | 16 | 1 | 20.4 | 4 | 47 | 3 |
| Mignon | 8 | 1 | 23 | 1 | 9 | — | 28 | 1 |
| J. W. Hearne | 10 | 4 | 17 | 6 | 9 | — | 28 | — |
| Tarrant | 8 | 3 | 9 | 1 | 20 | 4. | 38 | 6 |

## Essex Bowling

| | Overs | Mdns | Runs | Wkts |
|---|---|---|---|---|
| Douglas | 28 | 4 | 79 | 1 |
| Buckenham | 30.5 | 3 | 109 | 6 |
| Tremlin | 15 | 1 | 65 | — |
| Mead | 22 | 3 | 67 | 1 |
| McGahey | 19 | 3 | 76 | — |
| Freeman | 7 | — | 25 | 1 |

Umpires: J. Blake and A. F. Bannister.

# NORTHAMPTONSHIRE

## NOTES BY THE EDITOR IN 1904

The promotion of Northamptonshire to a place among the first-class counties is to my mind a very good step and one calculated to increase the harmony of county cricket. If the second-class teams realize that if they show sufficiently marked superiority over their rivals promotion will follow as a matter of course we shall hear no more of proposals to adopt the system of the Football League. I have not a word to say against that body, but the system which answers very well with football would not do at all for cricket. The idea of a county with the traditions of Surrey or Nottinghamshire being relegated to the second-class as the result of one bad season could not be entertained for a moment.

## NORTHAMPTONSHIRE v LEICESTERSHIRE

Played at Northampton, July 2, 3, 4, 1906

Rain had fallen during Sunday night and with the sun shining brightly next morning Crosse, on winning the toss for Northamptonshire, ventured on the risky policy of putting his opponents in first. The action was attended with the happiest results, Northamptonshire gaining a handsome victory by an innings and 40 runs. So difficult a task did the batsmen find run-getting on the damaged pitch that Leicestershire were two hours and three-quarters in putting together their total of 128. G. J. Thompson, on a wicket that just suited him, bowled very finely. When Northamptonshire went in Cox and Crosse laid the foundation of a useful total by scoring 106 in seventy-five minutes for the second partnership. On the following morning G. J. Thompson batted steadily, and his efforts were so well backed up by Kingston, East, and Hawkins that 181 runs were added before the innings came to an end. In Leicestershire's second innings Wood gave a masterly display of defensive cricket, but he could not by himself turn the fortunes of the game. In the whole match G. J. Thompson took fifteen wickets for just over 11 runs apiece.

### Leicestershire

| | | | |
|---|---|---|---|
| Mr C. J. B. Wood c Smith b G. J. Thompson | 9 | – not out | 110 |
| Capt. E. L. Challoner b G. J. Thompson | 3 | – b G. J. Thompson | 16 |
| A. E. Knight c Kingston b G. J. Thompson | 2 | – lbw b G. J. Thompson | 4 |
| H. Whitehead not out | 60 | – c Crosse b G. J. Thompson | 9 |
| S. Coe c Hawkins b G. J. Thompson | 18 | – b G. J. Thompson | 0 |
| Mr V. F. S. Crawford b G. J. Thompson | 10 | – b East | 21 |
| J. H. King lbw b Hawkins | 0 | – c Hawkins b G. J. Thompson | 14 |
| Mr W. W. Odell c G. J. Thompson b East | 15 | – b G. J. Thompson | 0 |
| J. Palmer b East | 4 | – c Pool b Hawkins | 13 |
| J. S. Curtis b G. J. Thompson | 0 | – b G. J. Thompson | 15 |
| A. Hampson b G. J. Thompson | 0 | – b G. J. Thompson | 0 |
| B 3, n-b 4 | 7 | B 8, n-b 10 | 18 |
| | **128** | | **220** |

### Northamptonshire

| | | | |
|---|---|---|---|
| Mr C. J. T. Pool b Odell | 2 | W. East c and b Whitehead | 23 |
| M. Cox b Wood | 51 | G. F. Baldwin b Odell | 6 |
| Mr E. M. Crosse st Hampson b Wood | 60 | Mr H. Hawkins c Coe b Palmer | 29 |
| Mr A. R. Thompson lbw b Wood | 13 | Mr B. C. Smith not out | 9 |
| G. J. Thompson c Odell b Wood | 61 | B 36, l-b 12, w 4, n-b 1 | 53 |
| Mr W. H. Kingston c Palmer b Whitehead | 64 | | |
| Mr G. A. T. Vials st Hampson b Whitehead | 17 | | **388** |

**Northamptonshire Bowling**

|  | Overs | Mdns | Runs | Wkts | Overs | Mdns | Runs | Wkts |
|---|---|---|---|---|---|---|---|---|
| G. J. Thompson .... | 30 | 8 | 72 | 7 | 39.5 | 10 | 95 | 8 |
| East ............ | 22 | 5 | 40 | 2 | 32 | 10 | 71 | 1 |
| Hawkins ........ | 7 | 3 | 9 | 1 | 9 | 2 | 17 | 1 |
| Baldwin ......... |  |  |  |  | 8 | 2 | 18 | — |
| Pool ............ |  |  |  |  | 2 | 1 | 1 | — |

**Leicestershire Bowling**

|  | Overs | Mdns | Runs | Wkts |
|---|---|---|---|---|
| Odell ........... | 48 | 17 | 85 | 2 |
| Coe ............ | 19 | 4 | 43 | — |
| Palmer .......... | 25.3 | 11 | 49 | 1 |
| Curtis ........... | 13 | 2 | 37 | — |
| Wood ........... | 27 | 11 | 43 | 4 |
| Challoner ........ | 5 | — | 15 | — |
| Whitehead ....... | 22 | 6 | 55 | 3 |
| Crawford ........ | 3 | — | 8 | — |

Umpires: A. E. Clapp and J. E. West.

# NORTHAMPTONSHIRE v KENT

## Played at Northampton, May 30, 31, June 1, 1907

Kent were seen at quite the best in this match, and forced a victory in brilliant style. Rain restricted cricket on the opening day to three hours and prevented anything being done on the Friday, but despite this serious loss of time Kent had won at half-past four on the Saturday afternoon by an innings and 155 runs. This was mainly the work of Blythe who, bowling superbly, took all ten wickets in Northamptonshire's first innings, and had a record for the match of seventeen wickets for 48 runs. By consistently good batting, Kent, in the time available on the first afternoon, scored 212 runs for the loss of four wickets, and on the Saturday morning the batsmen hit out in fearless style. Then, on going in, Northamptonshire gave a deplorable display. Against Blythe's bowling seven wickets fell for 4 runs, two of them extras, but Vials, after being missed, hit pluckily, and the innings extended beyond the luncheon interval. In the end, however, the total only reached 60, and following on 194 behind Northamptonshire were dismissed in an hour and a quarter for 39. Kent only just won in time, for no sooner had the players left the field than rain fell heavily.

### Kent

| | |
|---|---|
| F. E. Woolley b Driffield .............. 26 | F. H. Huish not out ................... 19 |
| H. T. W. Hardinge c Cox b East ........ 73 | W. J. Fairservice b East ............... 9 |
| James Seymour b Wells .............. 37 | C. Blythe c Vials b Driffield ........... 6 |
| Mr K. L. Hutchings b Driffield ......... 52 | A. Fielder b East .................... 1 |
| Mr A. P. Day c Kingston b East ........ 23 | B 2, l-b 1, n-b 1 .............. 4 |
| Mr E. W. Dillon b East ............... 4 | |
| E. Humphreys c Pool b Driffield ........ 0 | 254 |

## Northamptonshire

| Batsman | 1st | 2nd |
|---|---|---|
| W. A. Buswell st Huish b Blythe | 0 | c Woolley b Blythe — 7 |
| M. Cox st Huish b Blythe | 0 | st Huish b Blythe — 12 |
| Mr C. J. T. Pool c Fielder b Blythe | 0 | st Huish b Blythe — 5 |
| Mr W. H. Kingston lbw b Blythe | 2 | lbw b Blythe — 0 |
| G. J. Thompson b Blythe | 0 | c Hardinge b Blythe — 1 |
| W. East c Huish b Blythe | 0 | c Huish b Fairservice — 0 |
| Mr E. M. Crosse c Fairservice b Blythe | 0 | c Hardinge b Blythe — 2 |
| Mr A. R. Thompson c Seymour b Blythe | 10 | c Humphreys b Blythe — 7 |
| Mr G. A. T. Vials not out | 33 | b Fairservice — 1 |
| W. Wells c Humphreys b Blythe | 0 | b Humphreys — 0 |
| Mr L. T. Driffield b Blythe | 12 | not out — 1 |
| B 1, l-b 2 | 3 | B 3 — 3 |
| | **60** | **39** |

### Northamptonshire Bowling

| | Overs | Mdns | Runs | Wkts |
|---|---|---|---|---|
| G. J. Thompson | 15 | 1 | 76 | — |
| East | 33.2 | 6 | 77 | 5 |
| Wells | 6 | 1 | 34 | 1 |
| Driffield | 22 | 9 | 50 | 4 |
| Cox | 5 | 1 | 13 | — |

### Kent Bowling

| | Overs | Mdns | Runs | Wkts | Overs | Mdns | Runs | Wkts |
|---|---|---|---|---|---|---|---|---|
| Blythe | 16 | 7 | 30 | 10 | 15.1 | 7 | 18 | 7 |
| Fairservice | 12 | 5 | 17 | — | 9 | 3 | 15 | 2 |
| Fielder | 3 | — | 10 | — | | | | |
| Humphreys | | | | | 6 | 3 | 3 | 1 |

Umpires: W. Attewell and C. E. Dench.

## NORTHAMPTONSHIRE v DERBYSHIRE

Played at Northampton, July 26, 27, 28, 1909

Showing the better form all-round Northamptonshire won by an innings and 95 runs. Having the good fortune to win the toss Northamptonshire gave a fine display of batting, putting together in rather less than five hours a total of 326. This was the outcome of consistent excellence, East's 63 being the best individual score. At one point a much smaller total seemed in prospect, for though Pool and Smith played admirable cricket five men were out for 127. East and Thorpe, however, made a useful stand, and Manning and Buswell put on 84 in an hour for the last partnership. Owing to rain only two overs could be sent down on the Tuesday, and in the time available Derbyshire added 5 runs to their overnight score of 14 for one wicket. On the next day Derbyshire had no chance of making a fight of it, bright sunshine following the downpour of Tuesday making the pitch so difficult that the batsmen were at a serious disadvantage. Newton played steadily for an hour and a quarter, and Wright and Cadman offered some resistance, but Derbyshire had to follow on 175 runs behind. When they went in a second time the pitch was even worse than before, and against the skilful bowling of Smith the batsmen were practically helpless.

## Northamptonshire

| | |
|---|---|
| Mr C. J. T. Pool c Needham b Bestwick ... | 50 |
| Mr W. H. Kingston c Humphries b Warren . | 1 |
| Mr N. F. Norman c Cadman b Bestwick ... | 11 |
| Mr S. G. Smith c Oliver b Bestwick ....... | 51 |
| W. East c Wright b Morton ............. | 63 |
| Mr J. S. Denton b Warren .............. | 2 |
| Mr C. Thorp b Morton ................ | 30 |
| W. Wells c Newton b Morton .......... | 19 |
| Mr T. E. Manning not out ............. | 56 |
| Mr H. Hawkins c Needham b Morton ..... | 0 |
| W. A. Buswell c Newton b Morton ....... | 36 |
| B 4, l-b 2, n-b 1 .............. | 7 |
| | 326 |

## Derbyshire

| | | |
|---|---|---|
| Mr L. G. Wright b Smith ..................... | 27 | – st Buswell b Smith .............. 9 |
| E. Needham b Wells ......................... | 7 | – b East ...................... 15 |
| A. Morton st Buswell b Smith .................. | 8 | – b Smith .................... 13 |
| S. Cadman c Denton b Smith ................... | 34 | – c and b Smith ................. 6 |
| Mr J. Chapman b Smith ...................... | 0 | – b Smith ..................... 2 |
| F. Newton b Smith ......................... | 30 | – b Smith .................... 4 |
| Mr L. Oliver b Smith ....................... | 16 | – c Pool b East ................. 21 |
| A. R. Warren st Buswell b Smith .............. | 13 | – not out ...................... 2 |
| J. Humphries not out ....................... | 12 | – c Kingston b Smith ............. 4 |
| W. Bestwick lbw b East ..................... | 0 | – b Smith .................... 0 |
| Mr R. B. Rickman absent hurt .................. | 0 | – absent hurt ................... 0 |
| B 1, l-b 1, n-b 2 ..................... | 4 | B 4 .................... 4 |
| | 151 | 80 |

## Derbyshire Bowling

| | Overs | Mdns | Runs | Wkts |
|---|---|---|---|---|
| Warren ......... | 37 | 9 | 114 | 2 |
| Bestwick ........ | 35 | 11 | 92 | 3 |
| Cadman ......... | 11 | 3 | 35 | — |
| Morton ......... | 18.4 | 4 | 57 | 5 |
| Rickman ........ | 3 | — | 21 | — |

## Northamptonshire Bowling

| | Overs | Mdns | Runs | Wkts | Overs | Mdns | Runs | Wkts |
|---|---|---|---|---|---|---|---|---|
| Wells ........... | 3 | 2 | 5 | 1 | | | | |
| Smith ........... | 23 | 4 | 87 | 7 | 17.2 | 5 | 36 | 7 |
| East ............ | 13.2 | 3 | 10 | 1 | 17 | 8 | 10 | 2 |
| Hawkins ........ | 7 | 2 | 16 | — | | | | |

Umpires: J. E. West and C. E. Dench.

## NORTHAMPTONSHIRE v GLOUCESTERSHIRE

Played at Northampton, July 14, 15, 16, 1910

Two brilliant displays of batting – one by Jessop and the other by S. G. Smith – stood out above everything else in this drawn game. Seen at his very best Jessop brought off many daring strokes all round the wicket. He obtained 162 out of the 238 put on during his stay of two hours and five minutes, and hit two 6s, one 5, twenty-four 4s, and three 3s. After completing a 100 in an hour and twenty-five minutes he scored his last 62 runs in forty minutes. He gave only one chance, being missed in the long field when 72. On the second day Smith played the highest innings ever hit for Northamptonshire. Going in second wicket down at 65 he was the ninth to leave, having made his runs out of 357 in four hours and a half. When 134 he should have been caught in the slips, but otherwise he made no mistake. His figures included one 6, one 5, and twenty-one 4s. Gloucestershire tried hard to force a win, but without effect.

### Gloucestershire

| | | | |
|---|---|---|---|
| J. H. Board b Wells | 49 | – b Wells | 2 |
| Mr D. C. Robinson b Thompson | 53 | – c Haywood b East | 47 |
| Mr C. S. Barnett b Wells | 0 | – c Seymour b East | 52 |
| T. Langdon b Wells | 48 | – b Seymour | 28 |
| P. Mills st Ellis b East | 20 | – b East | 9 |
| Mr G. L. Jessop b Wells | 162 | – b Wells | 41 |
| Mr E. E. Barnett b Thompson | 19 | – c Vials b Wells | 6 |
| J. H. Huggins b Wells | 33 | – b Thompson | 24 |
| Mr H. Merrick b Wells | 12 | – not out | 46 |
| G. Dennett b Thompson | 15 | | |
| C. Parker not out | 24 | – b Wells | 14 |
| B 18, l-b 3, n-b 10 | 31 | B 15, l-b 2, n-b 1 | 18 |

| | |
|---|---|
| 466 | (8 wkts dec.) 287 |

### Northamptonshire

| | | | |
|---|---|---|---|
| Mr C. J. T. Pool c Parker b Dennett | 32 | – c Jessop b Mills | 82 |
| John Seymour run out | 11 | – c E. E. Barnett b Huggins | 1 |
| Mr G. A. T. Vials c Mills b Dennett | 29 | – c Langdon b Huggins | 5 |
| Mr S. G. Smith b Huggins | 204 | – run out | 60 |
| G. J. Thompson c E. E. Barnett b Dennett | 51 | – b Dennett | 12 |
| W. East b Huggins | 3 | – c Robinson b Parker | 16 |
| R. Haywood b Huggins | 7 | – b Dennett | 17 |
| Mr J. S. Denton lbw b Dennett | 32 | – not out | 2 |
| Mr T. E. Manning c E. E. Barnett b Dennett | 2 | – not out | 5 |
| W. Wells lbw b Dennett | 44 | | |
| H. Ellis not out | 4 | | |
| B 4, l-b 4, w 3 | 11 | B 4, l-b 2, n-b 2 | 8 |

| | |
|---|---|
| 430 | 208 |

### Northamptonshire Bowling

| | Overs | Mdns | Runs | Wkts | Overs | Mdns | Runs | Wkts |
|---|---|---|---|---|---|---|---|---|
| Thompson | 34.1 | 6 | 114 | 3 | 16 | 4 | 45 | 1 |
| Wells | 28 | 5 | 136 | 6 | 23 | 2 | 114 | 4 |
| Smith | 13 | 4 | 30 | — | | | | |
| East | 18 | 2 | 93 | 1 | 19.4 | 2 | 86 | 3 |
| Seymour | 8 | 1 | 29 | — | 6 | 3 | 24 | 1 |
| Denton | 4 | — | 33 | — | | | | |

### Gloucestershire Bowling

| | Overs | Mdns | Runs | Wkts | Overs | Mdns | Runs | Wkts |
|---|---|---|---|---|---|---|---|---|
| Huggins | 33 | 4 | 121 | 3 | 15 | 2 | 42 | 2 |
| Dennett | 45.5 | 8 | 181 | 6 | 12 | 1 | 69 | 2 |
| Mills | 29 | 6 | 70 | — | 16 | 4 | 43 | 1 |
| Parker | 16 | 3 | 47 | — | 16 | 6 | 46 | 1 |

Umpires: R. G. Barlow and C. E. Dench.

## NORTHAMPTONSHIRE v LANCASHIRE

Played at Northampton, August 4, 5, 6, 1910

Though rain limited cricket on the first two days to, roughly, four hours, ample time was found in which to finish this match. Lancashire winning at four o'clock on the Saturday afternoon by an innings and 112 runs. Lancashire made splendid use of the three hours and a half available on the Thursday, scoring 284 runs for the loss of only half their wickets. John Tyldesley hit brilliantly all round the wicket, his play on the off-side being exceptionally good, and made his runs in two hours and three quarters. When 5 he should have been caught in the long field, but this was his only mistake in a sterling innings that included ten 4s. W. Tyldesley assisted him to add 155 in an hour and three-quarters for the second wicket, and Sharp stayed while 77 were put on for the third in forty-five minutes. On the Friday, Lancashire carried their total to 314 without further loss, and first thing on the third morning Hornby applied the closure. The Lancashire bowlers then carried all before them, the resistance offered being generally so feeble that in three hours and three-quarters Northamptonshire were twice dismissed for an aggregate of 202 runs. In the first innings Thompson defended skilfully for seventy minutes, and when Northamptonshire followed on Smith and Haywood batted fairly well, but the result was never in doubt. Heap bowled with great effect, taking fourteen wickets in the match for 93 runs.

## Lancashire

| | | |
|---|---|---|
| H. Makepeace b Thompson | 4 | J. S. Heap not out | 17 |
| W. Tyldesley c Falconer b Wells | 67 | Mr A. H. Hornby not out | 36 |
| J. T. Tyldesley c Smith b Seymour | 124 | B 17, l-b 4, n-b 1 | 22 |
| J. Sharp c Haywood b Seymour | 40 | | |
| E. Tyldelsey c Smith b Wells | 4 | (5 wkts dec.) 314 | |

James Tyldesley, L. Cook, H. Dean and W. Worsley did not bat.

## Northamptonshire

| | | |
|---|---|---|
| Mr G. A. T. Vials lbw b J. Tyldesley | 10 | – c J. T. Tyldesley b Heap | 0 |
| Mr S. G. Smith c Makepeace b J. Tyldesley | 18 | – b Heap | 39 |
| John Seymour c Hornby b Heap | 3 | – c Worsley b Heap | 4 |
| Mr A. P. R. Hawtin b Dean | 18 | – c Worsley b Dean | 0 |
| G. J. Thompson c J. T. Tyldesley b Heap | 53 | – c Sharp b Heap | 0 |
| R. Haywood c J. T. Tyldesley b Heap | 10 | – c E. Tyldesley b Heap | 23 |
| Mr W. H. Denton b Heap | 0 | – b Heap | 2 |
| Mr E. M. Crosse st Worsley b Heap | 1 | – not out | 17 |
| W. Wells c Cook b Dean | 1 | – c Dean b Heap | 2 |
| R. Falconer b Dean | 0 | – c and b Heap | 1 |
| H. Ellis not out | 0 | – b Heap | 0 |
| | 114 | | 88 |

## Northamptonshire

| | Overs | Mdns | Runs | Wkts |
|---|---|---|---|---|
| Thompson | 29 | 4 | 105 | 1 |
| Wells | 20 | 1 | 57 | 2 |
| Smith | 17.2 | 2 | 53 | — |
| Falconer | 8 | — | 26 | — |
| Seymour | 11 | 2 | 51 | 2 |

## Lancashire Bowling

| | Overs | Mdns | Runs | Wkts | Overs | Mdns | Runs | Wkts |
|---|---|---|---|---|---|---|---|---|
| Dean | 18.2 | 1 | 50 | 3 | 18 | 6 | 45 | 1 |
| Cook | 3 | 2 | 8 | — | | | | |
| Heap | 17 | 5 | 50 | 5 | 18 | 6 | 43 | 9 |
| J. Tyldesley | 2 | — | 6 | 2 | | | | |

Umpires: A. J. Atfield and G. P. Harrison.

# NORTHAMPTONSHIRE v YORKSHIRE

## Played at Northampton, July 20, 21, 22, 1911

Playing better than in some previous matches, Northamptonshire defeated Yorkshire by 44 runs. In putting together a total of 316, Northamptonshire were largely indebted to the blunders of their opponents, the Yorkshire fielding being sadly at fault. Haywood, Thompson, Seymour, and Snell were all missed, and by far the best batting was shown by W. H. Denton, who combined admirable placing with sound defence. On the Friday the pitch showed signs of wear, and, with the ball getting up awkwardly and often keeping low, batsmen found run-getting rather a hard matter. Denton and Hirst overcame the difficulties of the wicket in masterly style, but despite their efforts Yorkshire were 66 behind on the first innings. When Northamptonshire went in a second time Smith batted well, but received poor support, and the whole side were dismissed in two hours and a half. Yorkshire were left with 185 to get to win, but on the Saturday, with Thompson, East, and Wells making the most of the damaged wicket, they never looked like accomplishing the task.

## Northamptonshire

| | | |
|---|---|---|
| John Seymour st Dolphin b Rhodes | 34 | – c Hirst b Rhodes ............... 0 |
| Mr W. H. Denton c Booth b Rhodes | 69 | – c Bates b Drake ............... 12 |
| R. Haywood c Booth b Rhodes | 21 | – c Booth b Rhodes .............. 10 |
| Mr S. G. Smith c Dolphin b Haigh | 28 | – not out ...................... 44 |
| G. J. Thompson c Hirst b Rhodes | 40 | – c Hirst b Rhodes ............. 12 |
| Mr H. S. Snell c Hirst b Rhodes | 52 | – lbw b Haigh .................. 6 |
| Mr J. S. Denton c Dolphin b Hartington | 9 | – c Drake b Haigh .............. 5 |
| Mr G. A. T. Vials c Denton b Rhodes | 31 | – c sub. b Rhodes ............. 18 |
| W. East not out | 13 | – hit wkt b Rhodes ............. 1 |
| W. Wells c Booth b Rhodes | 7 | – c Denton b Rhodes ........... 2 |
| W. A. Buswell c Dolphin b Rhodes | 0 | – b Haigh ...................... 3 |
| B 5, l-b 2, w 1, n-b 4 | 12 | B 4, l-b 1 .............. 5 |
| | **316** | **118** |

## Yorkshire

| | | |
|---|---|---|
| B. B. Wilson c Vials b Wells | 10 | – c Buswell b Wells ............. 11 |
| W. E. Bates lbw b Thompson | 19 | – c Buswell b Wells ............. 26 |
| D. Denton b East | 59 | – b East ....................... 17 |
| A. Drake st Buswell b Smith | 24 | – b Thompson ................... 7 |
| W. Rhodes b East | 11 | – c Seymour b Thompson ........ 15 |
| G. H. Hirst c Vials b Wells | 49 | – c Haywood b East ............. 7 |
| R. Kilner b Wells | 6 | – c East b Thompson ............ 2 |
| M. W. Booth b East | 19 | – b East ....................... 8 |
| S. Haigh c Snell b East | 8 | – not out ...................... 19 |
| A. Dolphin not out | 21 | – b Thompson ................... 0 |
| H. E. Hartington c and b Wells | 0 | – c Wells b Thompson ........... 16 |
| B 5, l-b 9, n-b 10 | 24 | B 10, n-b 2 .............. 12 |
| | **250** | **140** |

## Yorkshire Bowling

| | Overs | Mdns | Runs | Wkts | Overs | Mdns | Runs | Wkts |
|---|---|---|---|---|---|---|---|---|
| Hirst ............ | 17 | 5 | 41 | — | 5 | 1 | 16 | — |
| Booth ........... | 14 | 1 | 51 | — | 5 | 1 | 10 | — |
| Hartington ........ | 16 | 2 | 65 | 1 | | | | |
| Drake ............ | 9 | 2 | 29 | — | 5 | 1 | 8 | 1 |
| Rhodes ........... | 38 | 10 | 92 | 8 | 18 | 6 | 47 | 6 |
| Haigh ............ | 14 | 1 | 26 | 1 | 13.1 | 1 | 32 | 3 |

## Northamptonshire Bowling

|  | Overs | Mdns | Runs | Wkts | Overs | Mdns | Runs | Wkts |
|---|---|---|---|---|---|---|---|---|
| Wells ............ | 23 | 3 | 82 | 4 | 10 | 3 | 40 | 2 |
| Thompson ........ | 14 | 2 | 37 | 1 | 19.4 | 8 | 45 | 5 |
| Smith ............ | 11 | 2 | 42 | 1 |  |  |  |  |
| East ............. | 17 | 4 | 53 | 4 | 9 | 1 | 43 | 3 |
| J. S. Denton ....... | 2 | — | 12 | — |  |  |  |  |

Umpires: G. Hutchings and F. G. Roberts.

# NOTTINGHAMSHIRE

## NOTTINGHAMSHIRE v YORKSHIRE

Played at Nottingham, June 20, 21, 1901

This match furnished the sensation of the season at Trent Bridge, the Nottinghamshire eleven finding Rhodes and Haigh unplayable on a sticky wicket, and being got rid of for 13 – the lowest total ever obtained in county cricket, and, with one exception, the lowest on record in first-class matches. One wicket fell for a single run on the Thursday evening, and on the following day, when owing to the state of the pitch cricket did not begin till ten minutes to one, the innings was finished off in fifty-four minutes, the batsmen being absolutely helpless. Counting the few minutes' play overnight, the innings lasted as nearly as possible an hour. A. O. Jones made a leg hit for 4, and Carlin a 2, the other 7 runs being all singles. The innings was so extraordinary in character that it may be of interest to give the fall of the wickets:

     1/1    2/3    3/3    4/4    5/8    6/8    7/10    8/10    9/12    10/13

When Nottinghamshire followed on, A. O. Jones and Iremonger scored 82 in an hour before the first wicket fell, but after that Hirst bowled in form just as wonderful as that of Rhodes and Haigh in the first innings, and soon after six o'clock the match came to an end, Yorkshire winning by an innings and 18 runs. Shrewsbury started playing in the match, but split his hand so badly in fielding a ball at point that he had to retire before play had been in progress an hour, his place in the Nottinghamshire team, thanks to Lord Hawke's courtesy, being taken by Harrison. Denton's batting for Yorkshire was exceptionally good.

### Yorkshire

| | |
|---|---:|
| J. T. Brown c Anthony b Wass | 6 |
| J. Tunnicliffe b Dixon | 31 |
| D. Denton c W. Gunn b J. Gunn | 73 |
| Mr F. Mitchell c and b J. Gunn | 22 |
| E. Wainwright b J. Gunn | 20 |
| G. H. Hirst c Harrison b J. Gunn | 2 |
| L. Whitehead c W. Gunn b Hallam | 27 |
| Lord Hawke c and b Wass | 1 |
| S. Haigh c Carlin b J. Gunn | 5 |
| W. Rhodes c Wass b Hallam | 11 |
| D. Hunter not out | 3 |
| B 1, n-b 1, w 1 | 3 |
| | **204** |

### Nottinghamshire

| | | | |
|---|---:|---|---:|
| A. Hallam c Tunnicliffe b Rhodes | 1 | – b Hirst | 0 |
| C. E. Dench c Wainwright b Haigh | 0 | – c Hunter b Hirst | 0 |
| W. Gunn c Hunter b Rhodes | 2 | – c and b Haigh | 2 |
| Mr A. O. Jones b Haigh | 4 | – c Mitchell b Wainwright | 47 |
| Mr J. A. Dixon c Tunnicliffe b Rhodes | 1 | – b Rhodes | 8 |
| J. Carlin c Tunnicliffe b Rhodes | 2 | – b Wainwright | 8 |
| J. Gunn c Hawke b Haigh | 0 | – c Hunter b Hirst | 35 |
| J. Iremonger not out | 0 | – not out | 55 |
| I. Harrison c Haigh b Rhodes | 0 | – b Hirst | 0 |
| G. Anthony b Haigh | 2 | – b Hirst | 5 |
| T. Wass st Hunter b Rhodes | 1 | – b Hirst | 0 |
| | | B 13 | 13 |
| | **13** | | **173** |

## Nottinghamshire Bowling

|  | Overs | Mdns | Runs | Wkts |
|---|---|---|---|---|
| Wass | 26 | 3 | 84 | 2 |
| Hallam | 16.5 | 6 | 34 | 2 |
| J. Gunn | 33 | 15 | 49 | 5 |
| Dixon | 9 | 2 | 23 | 1 |
| Jones | 3 | 1 | 11 | — |

## Yorkshire Bowling

|  | Overs | Mdns | Runs | Wkts | Overs | Mdns | Runs | Wkts |
|---|---|---|---|---|---|---|---|---|
| Hirst | 1 | — | 1 | — | 12.1 | 2 | 26 | 6 |
| Rhodes | 7.5 | 4 | 4 | 6 | 22 | 4 | 53 | 1 |
| Haigh | 7 | 2 | 8 | 4 | 16 | 3 | 53 | 1 |
| Wainwright | | | | | 13 | 6 | 28 | 2 |

Umpires: G. Porter and W. Hearn.

# NOTTINGHAMSHIRE v LEICESTERSHIRE

## Played at Nottingham, May 25, 26, 27, 1903

John Gunn, whose cricket formed so bright a feature of Nottinghamshire cricket, in scoring 294 – his first hundred for the county – put together the highest innings ever hit for Nottinghamshire. He and William Gunn made 369 – a record for the third wicket – and the total of 739 exceeded the previous highest score obtained for Nottinghamshire. John Gunn was at the wickets only four hours and twenty-five minutes and hit thirty-four 4s. He gave three chances. William Gunn played delightful cricket, and Jones and Iremonger scored 141 for the first wicket. Leicestershire on the last day found themselves 494 behind with all ten wickets in hand. Knight and King saved the game, staying together for four hours and three-quarters. Knight enjoyed some luck, but the performance was a great one.

## Nottinghamshire

| | |
|---|---|
| Mr A. O. Jones c R. T. Crawford b King | 66 |
| J. Iremonger b Woodcock | 94 |
| W. Gunn b Odell | 139 |
| J. Gunn b Whitehead | 294 |
| Rev. H. Staunton c Whitehead b Odell | 2 |
| J. A. Dixon not out | 104 |
| Dexter lbw b R. Crawford | 17 |
| G. Anthony b R. Crawford | 3 |
| T. Oates not out | 9 |
| B 6, l-b 3, w 1, n-b 1 | 11 |
| **(7 wkts dec.)** | **739** |

Hallam and Wass did not bat.

## Leicestershire

| | | | |
|---|---|---|---|
| Mr C. J. B. Wood b Anthony | 30 | – not out | 14 |
| Mr C. E. de Trafford b Hallam | 70 | | |
| A. E. Knight c W. Gunn b Hallam | 10 | – not out | 144 |
| Mr R. T. Crawford b Anthony | 3 | | |
| J. King b Anthony | 14 | – c W. Gunn b Iremonger | 127 |
| Mr V. F. S. Crawford b Anthony | 28 | | |
| H. Whitehead c Jones b Anthony | 62 | – run out | 15 |
| G. Gill Anthony | 0 | | |
| Mr W. W. Odell b Wass | 2 | | |
| A. Woodcock b Wass | 6 | | |
| J. P. Whiteside not out | 1 | | |
| B 2, w 2, n-b 1 | 5 | B 2, l-b 3, w 4, n-b 3 | 12 |
| | **231** | | **312** |

## Leicestershire Bowling

|  | Overs | Mdns | Runs | Wkts |
|---|---|---|---|---|
| Woodcock ........ | 28 | 2 | 113 | 1 |
| King ............ | 30 | 3 | 130 | 1 |
| Odell ........... | 35 | 5 | 142 | 2 |
| R. T. Crawford .... | 19 | 2 | 81 | 2 |
| Whitehead ........ | 28 | — | 131 | 1 |
| Gill ............. | 16 | — | 84 | — |
| Wood ........... | 7 | 1 | 31 | — |
| V. F. S. Crawford .. | 4 | 2 | 16 | — |

## Nottinghamshire Bowling

|  | Overs | Mdns | Runs | Wkts | Overs | Mdns | Runs | Wkts |
|---|---|---|---|---|---|---|---|---|
| J. Gunn .......... | 8 | — | 25 | — | 30 | 13 | 39 | — |
| Wass ............ | 13 | 1 | 64 | 2 | 17 | 2 | 55 | — |
| Anthony ......... | 24 | 8 | 72 | 6 | 20 | 10 | 28 | — |
| Hallam ........... | 18 | 4 | 65 | 2 | 17 | 7 | 25 | — |
| Dixon ............ |  |  |  |  | 29 | 7 | 43 | — |
| Jones ............ |  |  |  |  | 8 | — | 35 | — |
| Dexter ........... |  |  |  |  | 11 | 1 | 33 | — |
| Iremonger ........ |  |  |  |  | 28 | 12 | 42 | 1 |

Umpires: V. A. Titchmarsh and A. A. White.

# NOTTINGHAMSHIRE v LANCASHIRE

Played at Nottingham, July 2, 3, 4, 1903

In heading a total of over 400, Lancashire accomplished a big performance, but the wicket – like several others at Trent Bridge during the summer – was so easy, that bowlers were placed at a tremendous disadvantage, and a draw was almost always certain. Jones for the first time in his career accomplished the feat of making two separate hundreds in a match. He played superb cricket, giving no real chance in either innings. Iremonger helped him to score 205, and the Nottinghamshire total was up to 307 before the second wicket fell. Spooner, whom Tyldesley assisted to put on 206, was not out at 176 when play ceased on Friday. He left at 484, having put together the highest innings ever scored against Nottinghamshire. Batting for seven hours, he gave no chance, and scarcely made a bad hit, his off-driving being delightful. William Gunn played admirably in each innings.

## Nottinghamshire

| | | | |
|---|---|---|---|
| Mr A. O. Jones c Hornby b Barnes ..............137 | – c Spooner b Cuttell ............100 |
| J. Iremonger c MacLaren b Barnes .............. 125 | – c MacLaren b Barnes ........... 0 |
| W. Gunn c Worsley b Littlewood ............... 50 | – c Littlewood b Cuttell .......... 73 |
| J. Gunn c Cuttell b Littlewood ................. 23 | – not out ...................... 50 |
| Mr J. A. Dixon c MacLaren b Littlewood ........ 10 | – not out ...................... 12 |
| G. Gunn c MacLaren b Barnes ................. 3 | |
| Hardstaff b Littlewood ....................... 20 | |
| G. Anthony c Littlewood b Barnes ............. 3 | |
| T. Oates run out ........................... 0 | |
| A. Hallam not out ......................... 38 | |
| T. Wass c Sharp b Barnes ................... 10 | |
| B 2, l-b 3, w 1, n-b 2 ................. 8 | B 8, l-b 2 .............. 10 |
| 427 | 245 |

### Lancashire

| | |
|---|---|
| Mr A. H. Hornby st Oates b J. Gunn . . . . . . | 3 |
| Mr R. H. Spooner st Oates b Iremonger . . .247 | |
| J. T. Tyldesley b Anthony . . . . . . . . . . . . . | 90 |
| Mr A. Eccles b Iremonger . . . . . . . . . . . . . | 47 |
| Mr A. C. MacLaren c Wass b Iremonger . . | 5 |
| J. Sharp c Oates b Hallam . . . . . . . . . . . . . | 8 |
| W. R. Cuttell b Hallam . . . . . . . . . . . . . . . | 0 |

| | |
|---|---|
| S. F. Barnes st Oates b Hallam . . . . . . . . . . | 16 |
| G. Littlewood c Anthony b J. Gunn . . . . . . . | 42 |
| Mr W. Brearley c Dixon b Iremonger . . . . . | 3 |
| Worsley not out . . . . . . . . . . . . . . . . . . . . . | 1 |
| B 11, l-b 10, w 5, n-b 3 . . . . . . . . | 29 |
| | 491 |

### Lancashire Bowling

| | Overs | Mdns | Runs | Wkts | Overs | Mdns | Runs | Wkts |
|---|---|---|---|---|---|---|---|---|
| Littlewood . . . . . . . . | 40 | 12 | 113 | 4 | 18 | 1 | 66 | — |
| Barnes . . . . . . . . . . . | 45.4 | 15 | 114 | 5 | 11 | 4 | 20 | 1 |
| Cuttell . . . . . . . . . . . | 13 | 2 | 34 | — | 24 | 7 | 64 | 2 |
| Brearley . . . . . . . . . . | 23 | 2 | 113 | — | 14 | 3 | 66 | — |
| Spooner . . . . . . . . . . | 8 | — | 45 | — | | | | |
| Sharpe . . . . . . . . . . . | | | | | 3 | 2 | 9 | — |
| Eccles . . . . . . . . . . . | | | | | 1.2 | 1 | 1 | — |
| MacLaren . . . . . . . . | | | | | 1 | — | 9 | — |

### Nottinghamshire Bowling

| | Overs | Mdns | Runs | Wkts |
|---|---|---|---|---|
| J. Gunn . . . . . . . . . . | 53 | 16 | 108 | 2 |
| Wass . . . . . . . . . . . . | 37 | 4 | 127 | — |
| Hallam . . . . . . . . . . . | 41 | 10 | 82 | 3 |
| Dixon . . . . . . . . . . . . | 15 | 2 | 51 | — |
| Anthony . . . . . . . . . | 16 | 3 | 49 | 1 |
| Iremonger . . . . . . . . | 17.4 | 4 | 45 | 4 |

Umpires: F. Martin and A. A. White.

## NOTTINGHAMSHIRE v GLOUCESTERSHIRE

### Played at Nottingham, July 18, 19, 20, 1904

This was a remarkable game, Gloucestershire winning by an innings and 1 run, and fully deserving their victory. Jessop was seen to greater advantage than on any other occasion during the season, scoring in less than two hours and a half 206 runs out of 317. He hit twenty-seven 4s, twenty-six 2s, and forty-six singles, and so far as could be seen gave no chance. He was far from having all the honours to himself, Wrathall and Board scoring 154 in eighty minutes for the first wicket, and Brownlee, who drove with splendid power, obtaining 94 in an hour and a quarter, Nottinghamshire had to follow their innings against a balance of 394, but such a wonderful start was made by Jones and Iremonger, that there seemed every prospect of the game being saved. The two batsmen had scored 122 when stumps were drawn on Tuesday, and it was not till just after the luncheon interval on the third day that they were separated, the total then being 303. Iremonger was out first, and after he left the Nottinghamshire batting broke down badly. Dennett and Spry bowled most perseveringly and towards the finish Dennett had everything his own way.

### Gloucestershire

| | |
|---|---|
| H. Wrathall c J. Gunn b Pennington . . . . . . | 75 |
| J. H. Board b Pennington . . . . . . . . . . . . . . | 80 |
| T. Langdon b J. Gunn . . . . . . . . . . . . . . . . | 10 |
| Mr L. D. Brownlee st Oates b Pennington . . | 94 |
| Mr G. L. Jessop c J. Gunn b Day . . . . . . . .206 |  |
| Mr F. E. Thomas b Jones . . . . . . . . . . . . . . | 24 |
| Mr P. G. Robinson b Pennington . . . . . . . . | 8 |

| | |
|---|---|
| J. H. Huggins c Iremonger b J. Gunn . . . . . . | 53 |
| E. Spry b Day . . . . . . . . . . . . . . . . . . . . . . | 8 |
| A. Sellick not out . . . . . . . . . . . . . . . . . . . . | 29 |
| G. Dennett c Jones b J. Gunn . . . . . . . . . . . | 34 |
| B 8, l-b 4, w 1, n-b 2 . . . . . . . . . . . | 15 |
| | 636 |

## Nottinghamshire

| | | |
|---|---|---|
| Mr A. O. Jones c Langdon b Spry | 71 – c Langdon b Spry | 187 |
| J. Iremonger b Brownlee | 34 – c Spry b Dennett | 138 |
| J. Gunn b Spry | 10 – c and b Spry | 13 |
| G. Gunn c Board b Dennett | 1 – lbw b Spry | 1 |
| J. W. Day c Jessop b Dennett | 48 – c Dennett b Spry | 0 |
| Mr J. A. Dixon c Robinson b Spry | 9 – c Brownlee b Dennett | 22 |
| Hardstaff not out | 26 – c Jessop b Spry | 1 |
| T. Oates c Wrathall b Spry | 13 – c Robinson b Dennett | 0 |
| T. Wass c Jessop b Spry | 7 – c Robinson b Dennett | 1 |
| Pennington b Dennett | 18 – not out | 0 |
| G. Anthony absent ill | 0 – c Sellick b Dennett | 9 |
| B 2, l-b 2, w 1 | 5    B 16, l-b 4, w 1 | 21 |
| | **242** | **393** |

## Nottinghamshire Bowling

| | Overs | Mdns | Runs | Wkts |
|---|---|---|---|---|
| J. Gunn | 34.4 | 7 | 151 | 3 |
| Pennington | 32 | 3 | 135 | 4 |
| Wass | 30 | 4 | 147 | — |
| Dixon | 5 | 1 | 36 | — |
| Iremonger | 5 | 1 | 34 | — |
| Anthony | 8 | 1 | 46 | — |
| Jones | 11 | — | 50 | 1 |
| Day | 9 | 4 | 22 | 2 |

## Gloucestershire Bowling

| | Overs | Mdns | Runs | Wkts | Overs | Mdns | Runs | Wkts |
|---|---|---|---|---|---|---|---|---|
| Huggins | 11 | 2 | 40 | — | 21 | 7 | 57 | |
| Dennett | 26 | 5 | 80 | 3 | 68.2 | 30 | 111 | 5 |
| Wrathall | 6 | 1 | 34 | — | 8 | 1 | 25 | — |
| Spry | 18 | 4 | 72 | 5 | 43 | 11 | 122 | 5 |
| Brownlee | 2 | — | 11 | 1 | 3 | — | 12 | — |
| Langdon | | | | | 8 | 2 | 12 | — |
| Robinson | | | | | 10 | 2 | 19 | — |
| Thomas | | | | | 5 | 2 | 14 | — |

Umpires: R. G. Barlow and C. E. Richardson.

# NOTTINGHAMSHIRE v LANCASHIRE

### Played at Nottingham, June 26, 27, 28, 1905

After fielding out for a day and a half Nottinghamshire had a very narrow escape from defeat, rain setting in eight minutes before time and causing the match to be drawn when with only two wickets to fall they still required 70 runs to avoid being beaten in a single innings. To save the game they had to stay in for the whole of the third day. Two wickets fell for 47, but Jones and Iremonger remained together for two hours and a half and put on 172, Iremonger being altogether at the wickets for nearly four hours. Jones played very attractive cricket but he was somewhat lucky. The Nottinghamshire fielding was at fault at the beginning of the match, both Spooner and Heap being let off. Spooner, hitting very hard, made his hundred before lunch and was afterwards seen at quite his best. Tyldesley enjoyed the satisfaction of playing the highest innings of his career. His performance was a remarkable one, extending over five hours and forty minutes and being free from anything like a palpable chance. The Lancashire total was the second highest ever hit against Nottinghamshire at Trent Bridge.

## Lancashire

| | |
|---|---|
| Mr R. H. Spooner c Jones b Hallam ......164 | Mr A. H. Hornby c Hallam b J. Gunn ..... 42 |
| J. S. Heap b Wass ................... 58 | Mr A. C. MacLaren c Jones b Wass ..... 2 |
| J. T. Tyldesley c J. Gunn b G. Gunn .....250 | A. Kermode st Oates b J. Gunn ......... 2 |
| Mr L. O. S. Poidevin b J. Gunn ......... 3 | W. Worsley not out ................. 37 |
| J. Hallows c Day b J. Gunn ............. 0 | B 15, l-b 2, w 3 ............. 20 |
| J. Sharp b G. Gunn .................. 49 | |
| Mr H. G. Garnett c Hallam b J. Gunn ..... 0 | 627 |

## Nottinghamshire

| | |
|---|---|
| Mr A. O. Jones b Sharp ..................... 23 | – b Kermode .................... 96 |
| J. Iremonger st Worsley b Poidevin ............. 31 | – b Heap ....................... 124 |
| G. Gunn c Tyldesley b Poidevin ................ 44 | – run out ...................... 12 |
| J. W. Day c Worsley b Poidevin .............. 0 | – c MacLaren b Poidevin ......... 15 |
| J. Hardstaff b Sharp ....................... 26 | – c MacLaren b Kermode ......... 56 |
| Mr R. E. Hemingway b Hallows ............... 26 | – b Heap ....................... 4 |
| Rev. H. Staunton c and b Hallows ............. 16 | – b Heap ....................... 0 |
| J. Gunn not out ......................... 15 | – lbw b Poidevin ................. 13 |
| T. Oates run out ........................ 0 | – not out ...................... 26 |
| A. Hallam c Garnett b Poidevin ................ 0 | – not out ...................... 1 |
| T. Wass b Poidevin ...................... 3 | |
| L-b 5, n-b 3 ....................... 8 | B 8, l-b 5, n-b 5 .......... 18 |
| | 192 | | 365 |

## Nottinghamshire Bowling

| | Overs | Mdns | Runs | Wkts |
|---|---|---|---|---|
| Wass ............ | 49 | 3 | 145 | 2 |
| J. Gunn .......... | 61 | 6 | 197 | 5 |
| Day ............. | 11 | 2 | 49 | — |
| Hallam ........... | 30 | 5 | 92 | 1 |
| Jones ............ | 1 | 1 | — | — |
| Iremonger ........ | 10 | — | 39 | — |
| G. Gunn .......... | 9.4 | — | 38 | 2 |
| Hardstaff ......... | 3 | 1 | 10 | — |
| Hemingway ....... | 1 | — | 6 | — |
| Staunton ......... | 2 | — | 11 | — |
| Oates ............ | 3 | — | 20 | — |

## Lancashire Bowling

| | Overs | Mdns | Runs | Wkts | Overs | Mdns | Runs | Wkts |
|---|---|---|---|---|---|---|---|---|
| Sharp ............ | 14 | 1 | 35 | 2 | 16 | 7 | 39 | — |
| Kermode ......... | 5 | 1 | 21 | — | 22.1 | 8 | 56 | 2 |
| Hallows .......... | 24 | 9 | 35 | 2 | 24 | 7 | 45 | — |
| Poidevin ......... | 25.3 | 6 | 93 | 5 | 47 | 7 | 132 | 2 |
| Heap ............ | | | | | 32 | 10 | 75 | 3 |

Umpires: C. E. Richardson and W. Richards.

## NOTTINGHAMSHIRE v NORTHAMPTONSHIRE

Played at Nottingham, July 4, 5, 6, 1910

Having lost three games in succession to Northamptonshire, Nottinghamshire were naturally very anxious to gain a victory. To this end they played such a fine game that at the drawing of stumps on Tuesday a win seemed assured, Northamptonshire, with only three wickets to fall, wanting 189 more runs. Unhappily for Nottinghamshire rain during

Tuesday night and on Wednesday morning so saturated the ground that early in the afternoon the game had to be abandoned as a draw. Winning the toss on a wicket that was practically certain to become difficult as the day advanced, Jones went in and hit up 82 out of 129 in an hour and a half. Payton, too, batted finely. Northamptonshire, despite a life given Thompson when 16, lost nine wickets for 121, Jones gave another resolute display on Tuesday and Payton again played admirably, while Oates hit finely, giving no chance. The visitors were set 329 to win, and Pool and Seymour put on 79 in an hour but, the light turning poor, the Nottinghamshire bowlers afterwards had matters much their own way. Seymour was out in a curious manner. Standing outside his crease, he placed a ball into the hands of the wicket-keeper and was run out.

### Nottinghamshire

| | | | |
|---|---|---|---|
| Mr A. P. Jones c Haywood b Seymour | 82 | – c Vials b Smith | 58 |
| J. Iremonger c Walden b Thompson | 5 | – b Seymour | 16 |
| E. Alletson b Thompson | 7 | – c Vials b Smith | 0 |
| W. Payton lbw b Thompson | 58 | – c Vials b Smith | 47 |
| J. Hardstaff c East b Seymour | 20 | – b Smith | 11 |
| J. Gunn st Ellis b Seymour | 2 | – lbw b Thompson | 0 |
| G. Gunn c Wells b Thompson | 9 | – b East | 15 |
| T. Oates c Denton b Seymour | 0 | – not out | 58 |
| W. Riley c Pool b Seymour | 6 | – c Wells b East | 25 |
| C. Clifton c Denton b Seymour | 1 | – c Pool b East | 2 |
| T. Wass not out | 4 | – c Haywood b Thompson | 9 |
| B 1, l-b 3, w 1, n-b 2 | 7 | B 8, n-b 1 | 9 |
| | **201** | | **250** |

### Northamptonshire

| | | | |
|---|---|---|---|
| Mr C. J. T. Pool b Riley | 15 | – c G. Gunn b J. Gunn | 45 |
| John Seymour c Hardstaff b Wass | 13 | – run out | 22 |
| Mr G. A. T. Vials b Wass | 2 | – c J. Gunn b Wass | 19 |
| Mr S. G. Smith c and b Riley | 7 | – c G. Gunn b Wass | 0 |
| G. J. Thompson not out | 57 | – not out | 16 |
| W. East b Iremonger | 16 | – c and b Riley | 0 |
| R. Haywood b Iremonger | 0 | – c Iremonger b Wass | 14 |
| F. Walden c G. Gunn b Wass | 7 | – lbw b Iremonger | 1 |
| Mr J. S. Denton c Riley b Wass | 1 | – not out | 6 |
| W. Wells b Wass | 0 | | |
| H. Ellis c Jones b Wass | 0 | | |
| B 4, l-b 1 | 5 | L-b 9, n-b 8 | 17 |
| | **123** | | **140** |

### Northamptonshire Bowling

| | Overs | Mdns | Runs | Wkts | Overs | Mdns | Runs | Wkts |
|---|---|---|---|---|---|---|---|---|
| Thompson | 25 | 4 | 71 | 4 | 19.2 | — | 79 | 2 |
| Smith | 9 | 1 | 31 | — | 20 | 1 | 60 | 4 |
| East | 6 | 1 | 26 | — | 15 | 2 | 39 | 3 |
| Seymour | 18.5 | 3 | 58 | 6 | 10 | — | 38 | 1 |
| Haywood | 5 | 1 | 8 | — | 3 | — | 25 | — |

### Nottinghamshire Bowling

| | Overs | Mdns | Runs | Wkts | Overs | Mdns | Runs | Wkts |
|---|---|---|---|---|---|---|---|---|
| Wass | 19.1 | 4 | 44 | 6 | 20 | 1 | 58 | 3 |
| Riley | 23 | 10 | 38 | 2 | 14 | 7 | 25 | 1 |
| Iremonger | 9 | 2 | 22 | 2 | 10 | 2 | 21 | 1 |
| Clifton | 5 | — | 14 | — | 3 | 1 | 5 | — |
| J. Gunn | | | | | 5 | — | 14 | 1 |

Umpires: J. E. West and G. Webb.

## NOTTINGHAMSHIRE v ESSEX

Played at Nottingham, August 15, 16, 17, 1910

Nottinghamshire won this match by 301 runs, Essex, when set 346 to make, failing so dismally against James Iremonger that they were out in an hour and a half for 44. The pitch had worn somewhat at the pavilion end but still Iremonger accomplished a phenomenal performance, sending down fifteen overs for 7 runs and six wickets. McGahey sending Nottinghamshire in to bat, Jones hit up 87 out of 112. The Essex bowling, apart from that of Mead, was very poor. On Tuesday the visitors had five men out for 79, but Turner, although in great difficulties at first and twice missed after scoring 60, played a great game against good length bowling for nearly four hours. On Wednesday morning Nottinghamshire added 136 runs in eighty-five minutes, Oates assisting George Gunn to put on 109.

### Nottinghamshire

| | | | |
|---|---|---|---|
| Mr A. O. Jones c Tremlin b Mead | 87 | – c Gillingham b Tremlin | 45 |
| G. Gunn c Buckenham b Tremlin | 44 | – c Perrin b Read | 98 |
| J. Hardstaff b Tremlin | 27 | – c Mead b Read | 1 |
| W. Payton b Tremlin | 26 | – c Russell b Douglas | 44 |
| J. Gunn not out | 69 | | |
| J. Iremonger c Douglas b Mead | 20 | | |
| E. Alletson lbw b Mead | 0 | – b Buckenham | 20 |
| G. M. Lee b Read | 18 | | |
| A. Iremonger b Mead | 7 | | |
| T. Oates run out | 0 | – not out | 63 |
| T. Wass b Read | 0 | | |
| B 11, l-b 5, n-b 1 | 17 | B 1, l-b 7, w 1 | 9 |
| | **315** | **(5 wkts dec.)** | **280** |

### Essex

| | | | |
|---|---|---|---|
| Mr J. W. H. T. Douglas c Lee b J. Gunn | 11 | – b J. Gunn | 12 |
| Mr P. Perrin lbw b Jones | 10 | – b J. Iremonger | 6 |
| B. Tremlin lbw b J. Iremonger | 42 | – c J. Iremonger b J. Gunn | 1 |
| Maj. A. J. Turner not out | 111 | – b J. Iremonger | 0 |
| Rev. F. H. Gillingham c Jones b J. Iremonger | 0 | – b J. Iremonger | 0 |
| Mr A. L. Gibson run out | 0 | – b J. Iremonger | 1 |
| Mr C. McGahey b J. Gunn | 17 | – c J. Iremonger b J. Gunn | 2 |
| E. Russell lbw b Lee | 17 | – not out | 6 |
| Mr A. H. Read c J. Gunn b Wass | 28 | – c Wass b J. Iremonger | 3 |
| W. Mead c and b Wass | 0 | – b J. Iremonger | 0 |
| C. P. Buckenham c Lee b Wass | 0 | – run out | 9 |
| B 8, l-b 1, w 1, n-b 4 | 14 | B 3, l-b 1 | 4 |
| | **250** | | **44** |

### Essex Bowling

| | Overs | Mdns | Runs | Wkts | Overs | Mdns | Runs | Wkts |
|---|---|---|---|---|---|---|---|---|
| Mead | 40 | 13 | 98 | 4 | 17 | 1 | 85 | — |
| Tremlin | 26 | 4 | 95 | 3 | 10 | 1 | 37 | 1 |
| Read | 8.5 | 2 | 32 | 2 | 7 | — | 43 | 2 |
| Buckenham | 7 | 2 | 29 | — | 17.3 | 3 | 58 | 1 |
| McGahey | 2 | — | 18 | — | | | | |
| Douglas | 8 | 1 | 26 | — | 13 | — | 48 | 1 |

**Nottinghamshire Bowling**

|              | Overs | Mdns | Runs | Wkts | Overs | Mdns | Runs | Wkts |
|--------------|-------|------|------|------|-------|------|------|------|
| Wass ............. | 19.3  | 3    | 43   | 3    |       |      |      |      |
| J. Gunn ......... | 21    | 8    | 41   | 2    | 14.1  | 1    | 33   | 3    |
| J. Iremonger ...... | 31    | 10   | 59   | 2    | 15    | 9    | 7    | 6    |
| Jones ............ | 15    | 5    | 31   | 1    |       |      |      |      |
| A. Iremonger ...... | 15    | 2    | 44   | —    |       |      |      |      |
| Lee ............. | 5     | 1    | 18   | 1    |       |      |      |      |

Umpires: H. Wood and A. A. White.


# NOTTINGHAMSHIRE IN 1911

The disappointment of the team in batting was Alletson. At Brighton in May he played an astounding innings of 189, driving with a power that has perhaps never been surpassed. It seemed for the moment that Nottinghamshire had found a hitter of the stamp of C. I. Thornton and Bonnor, but the early promise was far from being fulfilled. Whether Alletson lost confidence we cannot say, but the fact remains that except for a brilliant half-hour at Bristol in the week following his triumph he never approached his Brighton standard.


# NOTTINGHAMSHIRE v ESSEX

Played at Nottingham, July 13, 14, 15, 1911

This was a very different match to that decided on the same ground a week previously, the visitors, although entering upon the last day's play with a lead of more than a 100 runs, making no attempt to force a victory. Douglas and Perrin on Thursday put on 221 runs. Douglas, batting five hours and three-quarters, gave a chance when 10, but made no other mistake. Perrin for the third time in his career succeeded in scoring two separate hundreds in the same match.

**Essex**

| | | | |
|---|---|---|---|
| Mr J. W. H. T. Douglas b Wass ................ | 176 | – lbw b Jones .................. | 38 |
| J. Freeman b Iremonger ..................... | 8 | – c Oates b Jones ................ | 16 |
| Mr P. Perrin b Wass ........................ | 112 | – not out ..................... | 100 |
| H. Carpenter b Wass ....................... | 0 | – b Iremonger .................. | 33 |
| A. C. Russell c Riley b Iremonger .............. | 8 | – not out ..................... | 63 |
| Mr C. McGahey c Oates b Lee ................ | 7 | | |
| Mr P. Campbell c G. Gunn b Iremonger .......... | 13 | | |
| Mr K. L. Gibson not out ................... | 12 | | |
| C. P. Buckenham c Hardstaff b Wass ........... | 2 | | |
| B. Tremlin b Iremonger ..................... | 5 | | |
| W. Mead c Jones b Wass .................... | 15 | | |
| B 3, l-b 6 ........................ | 9 | B 2, l-b 8 .............. | 10 |
| | 367 | (3 wkts dec.) | 260 |

## Nottinghamshire

| | | | |
|---|--:|---|--:|
| Mr A. O. Jones b Buckenham | 1 | – b Buckenham | 5 |
| G. Gunn st Gibson b Mead | 72 | – c Carpenter b Gibson | 94 |
| J. Hardstaff c Gibson b Buckenham | 49 | – not out | 61 |
| J. Gunn b Buckenham | 11 | | |
| W. Payton c Perrin b McGahey | 27 | | |
| J. Iremonger c and b McGahey | 44 | | |
| E. Alletson b Buckenham | 14 | | |
| G. M. Lee c Carpenter b Mead | 24 | | |
| T. Oates b Buckenham | 9 | | |
| W. Riley not out | 4 | | |
| T. Wass b Buckenham | 2 | | |
| B 1, n-b 3 | 4 | B 4, n-b 4 | 8 |
| | **261** | | **168** |

### Nottinghamshire Bowling

| | Overs | Mdns | Runs | Wkts | Overs | Mdns | Runs | Wkts |
|---|--:|--:|--:|--:|--:|--:|--:|--:|
| Wass | 41.1 | 7 | 130 | 5 | 18 | 3 | 53 | — |
| Iremonger | 55 | 27 | 78 | 4 | 26 | 8 | 46 | 1 |
| J. Gunn | 30 | 7 | 64 | — | 17 | 7 | 29 | — |
| Jones | 6 | — | 19 | — | 14 | 4 | 33 | 2 |
| Riley | 7 | 1 | 16 | — | 6 | 1 | 24 | — |
| Lee | 12 | — | 43 | 1 | 8 | — | 35 | — |
| Alletson | 3 | 1 | 8 | — | | | | |
| Hardstaff | | | | | 5 | — | 25 | — |
| G. Gunn | | | | | 1 | — | 5 | — |

### Essex Bowling

| | Overs | Mdns | Runs | Wkts | Overs | Mdns | Runs | Wkts |
|---|--:|--:|--:|--:|--:|--:|--:|--:|
| Buckenham | 27.4 | 3 | 92 | 6 | 7 | 1 | 13 | 1 |
| Douglas | 12 | 2 | 41 | 1 | 8 | 1 | 22 | — |
| Mead | 19 | 3 | 50 | 2 | 6 | — | 30 | — |
| Tremlin | 10 | 2 | 27 | — | 9 | 1 | 20 | — |
| Carpenter | 1 | 1 | — | — | | | | |
| McGahey | 15 | — | 47 | 2 | 2 | — | 19 | — |
| Campbell | | | | | 3 | — | 26 | — |
| Russell | | | | | 4 | — | 21 | — |
| Gibson | | | | | 1.5 | — | 9 | 1 |

Umpires: R. G. Barlow and G. P. Harrison.

## NOTTINGHAMSHIRE v DERBYSHIRE

Played at Nottingham, August 14, 15, 16, 1911

Making a splendid recovery, Derbyshire not only escaped defeat, but, declaring with nine wickets down, were able to set Nottinghamshire the almost impossible task of getting 282 runs in just over two hours. With the exception of Chapman, Derbyshire gave a poor display on Monday, when Nottinghamshire left off only 77 behind with eight wickets in hand. Hardstaff played an admirable innings, driving particularly well, and on Wednesday followed up his 118 with another three-figure score, being the ninth batsman to accomplish the feat during the summer. Derbyshire, at their second attempt, lost three wickets for 100, but Needham and Morton before play ended on Tuesday carried the total to 229 without further loss. Needham had the great part in saving his side, but Derbyshire would still probably have lost, but for Wood and Forester. Hardstaff scored his 106 not out at the rate of a run a minute and gave no chance.

### Derbyshire

| | | | |
|---|---|---|---|
| Mr L. Oliver b Iremonger | 8 | – b Riley | 24 |
| S. Cadman lbw b Iremonger | 9 | – c G. Gunn b Wass | 18 |
| Mr J. Chapman c Riley b Iremonger | 69 | – c Payton b J. Gunn | 42 |
| A. Morton c Oates b J. Gunn | 13 | – c Riley b Wass | 55 |
| E. Needham b Riley | 11 | – c Hardstuff b Wass | 103 |
| Mr E. C. Moses c Lee b Riley | 4 | – c Lee b Iremonger | 0 |
| Mr A. J. Wood b Iremonger | 14 | – c Hardstaff b Jones | 52 |
| Mr T. Forester c Oates b J. Gunn | 13 | – b Jones | 50 |
| Mr C. J. Corbett b Iremonger | 7 | – b Iremonger | 49 |
| J. Humphries not out | 13 | – not out | 19 |
| A. R. Warren b Iremonger | 5 | – not out | 6 |
| B 4, l-b 6, n-b 2 | 12 | B 10, l-b 7, w 1, n-b 1 | 19 |
| | **178** | **(9 wkts dec.)** | **437** |

### Nottinghamshire

| | | | |
|---|---|---|---|
| Mr A. W. Carr st Humphries b Forester | 47 | – c Moses b Forester | 13 |
| G. Gunn lbw b Warren | 2 | – b Morton | 43 |
| J. Hardstaff c Humphries b Forester | 118 | – not out | 106 |
| W. Payton c Needham b Warren | 10 | | |
| J. Gunn st Humphries b Cadman | 48 | | |
| J. Iremonger not out | 74 | | |
| Mr A. O. Jones b Warren | 1 | | |
| G. M. Lee b Warren | 1 | | |
| W. Riley c Humphries b Warren | 11 | | |
| T. Wass b Forester | 8 | | |
| T. Oates c Humphries b Warren | 10 | | |
| W 1, n-b 3 | 4 | B 12 | 12 |
| | **334** | | **174** |

### Nottinghamshire Bowling

| | Overs | Mdns | Runs | Wkts | Overs | Mdns | Runs | Wkts |
|---|---|---|---|---|---|---|---|---|
| Wass | 11 | 3 | 33 | — | 28 | 7 | 127 | 3 |
| Iremonger | 36.2 | 11 | 67 | 6 | 33 | 8 | 66 | 2 |
| J. Gunn | 30 | 6 | 59 | 2 | 21 | 2 | 89 | 1 |
| Riley | 4 | 1 | 7 | 2 | 23 | 3 | 55 | 1 |
| Lee | | | | | 12 | 2 | 23 | — |
| Jones | | | | | 15 | 1 | 58 | 2 |

### Derbyshire Bowling

| | Overs | Mdns | Runs | Wkts | Overs | Mdns | Runs | Wkts |
|---|---|---|---|---|---|---|---|---|
| Warren | 40.2 | 5 | 131 | 6 | 12 | 1 | 44 | — |
| Forester | 43 | 10 | 115 | 3 | 16 | 2 | 55 | 1 |
| Morton | 6 | 2 | 17 | — | 7 | — | 36 | 1 |
| Cadman | 15 | 3 | 58 | 1 | 12 | 2 | 40 | — |
| Moses | 4 | — | 9 | — | | | | |

Umpires: W. Vining and A. A. White.

## NOTTINGHAMSHIRE v YORKSHIRE

Played at Nottingham, June 5, 6, 7, 1913

Yorkshire, on Thursday, scored 420 for seven wickets, but unable, in face of the dogged tactics pursued by the Nottinghamshire batsmen, to force a win, they had to content themselves with a first innings lead. Denton, making his first hundred of the season, drove and pulled in grand style, his cricket, until he had passed his hundred, being absolutely without blemish. Nottinghamshire on Friday took four hours and forty minutes to make 222, only two wickets falling meanwhile. George Gunn was at the wickets six hours for his 132, but in the second innings, when again he reached three figures, he scored 109 out of 129, by most dazzling cricket, in less than an hour and a half.

## Yorkshire

| | | | |
|---|---|---|---|
| W. Rhodes run out | 19 | – c Oates b Iremonger | 0 |
| B. B. Wilson c Oates b Horsley | 89 | – c Riley b Lee | 34 |
| D. Denton c Riley b Iremonger | 148 | – c Horsley b Iremonger | 16 |
| A. Drake c Oates b Horsley | 34 | – not out | 41 |
| G. H. Hirst lbw b J. Gunn | 0 | – not out | 12 |
| R. Kilner lbw b Iremonger | 76 | | |
| M. W. Booth c G. Gunn b Riley | 25 | | |
| Mr J. Tasker not out | 27 | | |
| E. Oldroyd b Riley | 2 | | |
| S. Haigh c J. Gunn b Riley | 28 | | |
| A. Dolphin c G. Gunn b Iremonger | 0 | | |
| B 9, l-b 10, w 2, n-b 2 | 23 | B 7, w 1, n-b 1 | 9 |
| | **471** | **(3 wkts dec.)** | **112** |

## Nottinghamshire

| | | | |
|---|---|---|---|
| G. Gunn c Hirst b Booth | 132 | – not out | 109 |
| G. M. Lee c Dolphin b Hirst | 4 | – b Haigh | 4 |
| J. Hardstaff c Dolphin b Hirst | 46 | – run out | 3 |
| J. Gunn c Haigh b Hirst | 65 | – not out | 8 |
| W. Payton c Dolphin b Booth | 26 | | |
| W. Whysall c Hirst b Booth | 0 | | |
| E. Alletson b Booth | 6 | – c Booth b Rhodes | 0 |
| J. Iremonger c Rhodes b Booth | 19 | | |
| T. Oates b Hirst | 1 | | |
| W. Riley c Dolphin b Booth | 3 | | |
| J. Horsley not out | 8 | | |
| B 17, l-b 2, n-b 2 | 21 | B 4, n-b 1 | 5 |
| | **331** | | **129** |

## Nottinghamshire Bowling

| | Overs | Mdns | Runs | Wkts | Overs | Mdns | Runs | Wkts |
|---|---|---|---|---|---|---|---|---|
| Iremonger | 36.2 | 1 | 94 | 3 | 12 | 4 | 27 | 2 |
| Horsley | 33 | 1 | 176 | 2 | 11 | 1 | 30 | — |
| J. Gunn | 25 | 6 | 71 | 1 | 3 | 3 | — | — |
| Riley | 41 | 11 | 101 | 3 | 13 | 5 | 17 | — |
| Lee | 4 | 1 | 6 | — | 9 | — | 29 | 1 |

## Yorkshire Bowling

| | Overs | Mdns | Runs | Wkts | Overs | Mdns | Runs | Wkts |
|---|---|---|---|---|---|---|---|---|
| Hirst | 34 | 9 | 69 | 4 | | | | |
| Booth | 40.3 | 5 | 99 | 6 | 3 | 1 | 16 | — |
| Rhodes | 23 | 6 | 55 | — | 5 | — | 18 | 1 |
| Drake | 11 | 5 | 21 | — | 5 | — | 30 | — |
| Haigh | 23 | 10 | 31 | — | 7 | 1 | 34 | 1 |
| Kilner | 14 | 2 | 28 | — | 5 | 2 | 3 | — |
| Oldroyd | 2 | — | 7 | — | 4 | — | 22 | — |
| Denton | | | | | 1 | — | 1 | — |

Umpires: W. Phillips and C. E. Richardson.

## NOTTINGHAMSHIRE v LEICESTERSHIRE

Played at Nottingham, August 11, 12, 13, 1913

Enjoying, thanks to Lee and Carr, a great batting triumph, Nottinghamshire gained a victory by an innings and 126 runs. Less than two hours' cricket proved practicable on Monday, but in that time Lee and Carr, coming together at 38, raised the score to 144 without further loss. So far from being affected by Monday's rain, the pitch rolled out splendidly next morning, and Lee and Carr hit away with such delightful freedom that they carried the total to 371, the second wicket producing 333 runs in little more than three hours. Carr, putting together his first hundred, was missed when 24, but gave a grand display of driving. Lee, at the wickets for just over five hours, gave no chance until 84. He also drove in rare form, and his play on the leg side was very skilful. Leicestershire on Tuesday afternoon had to contend against a bad light, two appeals being allowed and stumps drawn half an hour earlier than usual. On Wednesday Leicestershire had to follow-on before lunch, 364 behind. Yet although four wickets fell for 75, the visitors battled on so well that when the innings closed only forty minutes remained for play.

### Nottinghamshire

| | |
|---|---|
| G. Gunn c Geary b Skelding ............ 11 | W. Payton not out .................... 56 |
| G. M. Lee not out .....................200 | B 42, l-b 5, w 5 .............. 52 |
| Mr A. W. Carr lbw b Coe ..............169 | |
| J. Gunn b Coe ...................... 19 | (3 wkts dec.) 507 |

J. Iremonger, W. Whysall, E. Alletson, Mr G. O. Gauld, T. Oates and T. Wass did not bat.

### Leicestershire

| | | | |
|---|---|---|---|
| Mr C. J. B. Wood run out .................... | 19 | – b Iremonger ................... | 30 |
| H. Whitehead b Iremonger ..................... | 29 | – b Carr ..................... | 2 |
| J. H. King st Oates b Lee ..................... | 0 | – b Carr ..................... | 18 |
| Mr W. N. Riley lbw b J. Gunn ............... | 1 | – c Carr b Lee .................. | 45 |
| S. Coe c Iremonger b Wass ................ | 26 | – not out ..................... | 79 |
| Mr G. F. B. Rudd c Gauld b Wass .............. | 25 | – st Oates b Lee ............... | 0 |
| Mr C. E. de Trafford b Wass .................. | 17 | – c G. Gunn b Carr ........... | 15 |
| Mr G. H. Salmon b Iremonger ............... | 2 | – b J. Gunn .................... | 2 |
| W. E. Astill b Iremonger ..................... | 19 | – lbw b Wass ................. | 28 |
| G. Geary b Iremonger ....................... | 2 | – c Oates b Wass ............... | 0 |
| A. Skelding not out ........................ | 0 | – b Wass .................... | 1 |
| L-b 3 .......................... | 3 | B 8, l-b 8, n-b 2 ......... | 18 |
| | 143 | | 238 |

### Leicestershire Bowling

| | Overs | Mdns | Runs | Wkts |
|---|---|---|---|---|
| Geary ........... | 36 | 6 | 138 | — |
| Skelding ......... | 34 | 7 | 125 | 1 |
| Astill ........... | 14 | 4 | 43 | — |
| Coe ............. | 16 | 2 | 63 | 2 |
| King ............ | 14 | 1 | 52 | — |
| Wood ........... | 4 | — | 27 | — |
| Whitehead ....... | 2 | — | 7 | — |

## Nottinghamshire Bowling

| | Overs | Mdns | Runs | Wkts | Overs | Mdns | Runs | Wkts |
|---|---|---|---|---|---|---|---|---|
| Wass ............ | 28 | 7 | 72 | 3 | 6.5 | 1 | 20 | 3 |
| Iremonger ........ | 24.4 | 11 | 38 | 4 | 15 | 5 | 36 | 1 |
| J. Gunn .......... | 8 | 4 | 23 | 1 | 11 | — | 32 | 1 |
| Lee .............. | 5 | 1 | 7 | 1 | 14 | 2 | 40 | 2 |
| Carr ............. | | | | | 15 | 1 | 73 | 3 |
| Gauld ........... | | | | | 3 | — | 19 | — |

Umpires: G. P. Harrison and R. G. Barlow.

# SOMERSET

## SOMERSET v MIDDLESEX

### Played at Taunton, August 6, 7, 8, 1900

There was a great finish to this match, Middlesex winning by the bare margin of one wicket within seven minutes of time. After a most disastrous first innings Somerset made a splendid fight of it, and were on the whole a little unlucky in not winning. Middlesex owed a great deal to Albert Trott, who not only took all ten wickets in Somerset's first innings, but at the finish of the game played with discretion and nerve. Palairet and Bernard made a big effort for Somerset, scoring 126 for the first wicket in their second innings. On the third day Warner played a fine innings, but at the finish it was a case of touch and go, six runs being wanted to win when Hearne went in.

### Somerset

| | | | |
|---|---|---|---|
| Mr L. C. H. Palairet b Trott | 12 | – b Hearne | 92 |
| Mr C. A. Bernard b Trott | 23 | – c Trott b Bosanquet | 72 |
| Mr E. Robson b Trott | 0 | – b Williams | 50 |
| Mr C. E. Dunlop b Trott | 1 | – b Trott | 0 |
| Mr S. M. J. Woods lbw b Trott | 4 | – b Hearne | 32 |
| Lewis c and b Trott | 8 | – run out | 0 |
| Mr J. Daniell lbw b Trott | 0 | – b Rawlin | 26 |
| Mr V. T. Hill b Trott | 35 | – b Trott | 17 |
| Mr A. E. Newton c Warner b Trott | 0 | – b Rawlin | 18 |
| E. J. Tyler b Trott | 2 | – not out | 7 |
| B. Cranfield not out | 2 | – c Nicholls b Rawlin | 3 |
| L-b 2 | 2 | B 7, l-b 3 | 10 |
| | **89** | | **327** |

### Middlesex

| | | | |
|---|---|---|---|
| Mr P. F. Warner c Tyler b Cranfield | 14 | – lbw b Palairet | 84 |
| J. Douglas b Robson | 7 | – c Newton b Lewis | 29 |
| Mr R. N. Douglas c Bernard b Cranfield | 22 | – b Tyler | 27 |
| Mr C. M. Wells c Bernard b Cranfield | 15 | – b Robson | 35 |
| Mr B. J. T. Bosanquet b Robson | 0 | – c Robson b Cranfield | 19 |
| Mr G. MacGregor b Cranfield | 0 | – c Newton b Robson | 1 |
| Mr R. W. Nicholls b Cranfield | 32 | – st Newton b Cranfield | 15 |
| J. T. Rawlin b Cranfield | 22 | – b Cranfield | 21 |
| A. E. Trott c Robson b Palairet | 13 | – not out | 34 |
| Mr W. Williams b Cranfield | 3 | – c Daniell b Cranfield | 3 |
| J. T. Hearne not out | 3 | – not out | 0 |
| B 6, l-b 1, w 1 | 8 | B 8, l-b 4 | 12 |
| | **139** | | **280** |

### Middlesex Bowling

| | Overs | Mdns | Runs | Wkts | Overs | Mdns | Runs | Wkts |
|---|---|---|---|---|---|---|---|---|
| Hearne | 15 | 4 | 45 | 0 | 22 | 7 | 57 | 2 |
| Trott | 14.2 | 5 | 42 | 10 | 31 | 4 | 116 | 2 |
| Rawlin | | | | | 9.4 | 1 | 29 | 3 |
| Wells | | | | | 7 | 1 | 38 | — |
| Williams | | | | | 12 | 5 | 26 | 1 |
| Bosanquet | | | | | 10 | 1 | 51 | 1 |

## Somerset Bowling

|  | Overs | Mdns | Runs | Wkts | Overs | Mdns | Runs | Wkts |
|---|---|---|---|---|---|---|---|---|
| Robson ......... | 24 | 8 | 50 | 2 | 29 | ·12 | 56 | 2 |
| Cranfield ........ | 25.2 | 5 | 74 | 7 | 39.2 | 7 | 106 | 4 |
| Tyler ........... | 1 | — | 1 | — | 12 | 2 | 48 | 1 |
| Palairet ......... | 2 | — | 6 | 1 | 14 | 3 | 37 | 1 |
| Lewis ........... |  |  |  |  | 1 | 2 | 21 | 1 |

Umpires: W. A. J. West and J. Moss.

## SOMERSET v SUSSEX

### Played at Taunton, August 8, 9, 10, 1901

Some remarkable scoring was witnessed in this match, which was left unfinished, 1,262 runs being scored, and only 19 wickets falling. Apart from an admirable innings by Brann, Sussex quite failed at their first attempt, but when the visitors went in again 324 behind, Charles Fry, Ranjitsinhji and Vine made ample amends. Vine helped Ranjitsinhji to score 174 for the first wicket, and then the two great batsmen added 292 more without being separated. Fry's batting was not worthy of his reputation, but Ranjitsinhji's was magnificent, his score surpassing anything he had previously done in first-class cricket. The Somerset batting was excellent, Palairet and Lewis scoring 258 for the first wicket, while the former and Braund put on 104 for the second partnership. Palairet's innings was without a blemish.

### Sussex

| | | | |
|---|---|---|---|
| Mr C. B. Fry c Daniell b Braund ................ | 20 | – not out ....................... | 119 |
| J. Vine b Cranfield .......................... | 14 | – c Braund b Cranfield ............ | 49 |
| K. S. Ranjitsinhji c Cranfield b Woods .......... | 45 | – not out ....................... | 285 |
| E. H. Killick lbw b Braund .................... | 8 | | |
| Mr G. Brann c Palairet b Cranfield ............. | 107 | | |
| Mr A. M. Sullivan st Wickham b Woods .......... | 0 | | |
| A. E. Relf b Woods .......................... | 6 | | |
| Mr K. R. B. Fry c Palairet b Braund ............ | 15 | | |
| Mr W. Newham not out ....................... | 15 | | |
| F. W. Tate b Braund ........................ | 1 | | |
| J. Bean b Braund ........................... | 0 | | |
| B 4, l-b 1 ........................... | 5 | B 2, l-b 1, w 5, n-b 5 ....... | 13 |
| | **236** | | **466** |

### Somerset

| | | | |
|---|---|---|---|
| Mr L. C. H. Palairet b Bean ............. | 194 | Mr V. T. Hill b Ranjitsinhji ............ | 0 |
| Lewis c Sullivan b Vine ................ | 120 | Mr J. Daniell not out ................ | 9 |
| L. C. Braund run out ................. | 94 | G. Gill b Relf ....................... | 5 |
| Mr F. A. Phillips b Vine ............... | 53 | B 10, l-b 8, n-b 1, w 2 .......... | 21 |
| Mr S. M. J. Woods b Ranjitsinhji ........ | 50 | | |
| E. Robson b Relf .................... | 14 | **(8 wkts dec.) 560** | |

B. Cranfield and Rev. A. P. Wickham did not bat.

## Somerset Bowling

| | Overs | Mdns | Runs | Wkts | Overs | Mdns | Runs | Wkts |
|---|---|---|---|---|---|---|---|---|
| Cranfield ......... | 18 | 4 | 63 | 2 | 29 | 5 | 93 | 1 |
| Braund ........... | 25.3 | 2 | 102 | 5 | 31 | 8 | 106 | — |
| Gill .............. | 5 | 1 | 20 | — | 36 | 6 | 126 | — |
| Woods ........... | 13 | 3 | 46 | 3 | 4 | 1 | 12 | — |
| Hill .............. | | | | | 1 | — | 4 | — |
| Palairet ......... | | | | | 13 | 2 | 60 | — |
| Robson ......... | | | | | 12 | 1 | 40 | — |
| Lewis ............ | | | | | 4 | 1 | 12 | — |

## Sussex Bowling

| | Overs | Mdns | Runs | Wkts |
|---|---|---|---|---|
| Relf ............. | 29.4 | 1 | 71 | 2 |
| Vine ............. | 37 | 6 | 141 | 2 |
| C. B. Fry ......... | 15 | 4 | 89 | — |
| Killick ........... | 25 | 5 | 88 | — |
| Tate ............. | 11 | 3 | 32 | — |
| Bean ............. | 35 | 9 | 130 | 1 |
| Brann ............ | 3 | — | 19 | — |
| Ranjitsinhji ....... | 8 | 1 | 19 | 2 |

Umpires: M. Sherwin and C. E. Richardson.

## SOMERSET v KENT

### Played at Taunton, August 15, 16, 1901

In this match Kent gained quite a remarkable victory, winning in a single innings with 312 runs to spare. On a soft, but very easy wicket, Kent accomplished a fine performance on Thursday, in scoring 435 runs for four wickets. Burnup made 134 out of 243 by almost faultless cricket, in less than three hours, while Mason hit up 145 out of 192 for the fourth partnership in an hour and three-quarters. Mason, who was missed when only a single, batted in brilliant style, his score including 24 fours. At one period while he was in, 100 runs were scored in forty minutes. Hearne played a comparatively steady game, being in over three hours and a half, and he did not give a chance. The cricket on the Friday afforded a striking contrast to that of the previous day. The wicket had become difficult, affording the bowlers considerable help. Mason made remarkable use of his opportunity. In the morning he was hard to play, and when Somerset followed on he looked extremely difficult, frequently at his pace making the ball break the width of the wicket. It was the general opinion that he had never bowled better in his life. Somerset should perhaps have made more runs, but they were in a hopeless position.

### Kent

| | |
|---|---|
| Mr C. J. Burnup st Newton b Cranfield ....134 | E. Humphreys st Palairet b Braund ....... 0 |
| Mr E. W. Dillon b Braund .............. 12 | H. R. Murrell c Braund b Cranfield ....... 4 |
| Mr S. H. Day c Daniell b Cranfield ....... 46 | C. Blythe st Palairet b Cranfield ......... 1 |
| A. Hearne c Daniell b Braund ..........103 | Mr W. M. Bradley not out ............. 1 |
| Mr J. R. Mason c Daniell b Cranfield .....145 | B 5, l-b 6 ................... 11 |
| Mr R. N. R. Blaker c Daniell b Braund .... 7 | |
| Mr P. C. Baker c Daniell b Braund ....... 0 | 464 |

## Somerset

| | | | |
|---|---|---|---|
| Mr L. C. H. Palairet c Murrell b Blythe | 12 | – b Mason | 11 |
| L. C. Braund c Baker b Blythe | 2 | – b Mason | 4 |
| Lewis run out | 15 | – c Blaker b Mason | 0 |
| Mr F. A. Phillips c Blaker b Mason | 1 | – b Blythe | 26 |
| E. Robson run out | 13 | – c Murrell b Mason | 0 |
| Mr J. Daniell b Blythe | 5 | – c Blaker b Mason | 0 |
| Mr V. T. Hill b Mason | 2 | – st Murrell b Mason | 11 |
| G. Gill c Murrell b Mason | 6 | – b Mason | 5 |
| Mr A. E. Newton c Murrell b Mason | 7 | – b Blythe | 10 |
| Mr G. Fowler lbw b Blythe | 0 | – b Mason | 10 |
| B. Cranfield not out | 0 | – not out | 0 |
| B 8, l-b 3 | 11 | N-b 1 | 1 |
| | **74** | | **78** |

## Somerset Bowling

| | Overs | Mdns | Runs | Wkts |
|---|---|---|---|---|
| Cranfield | 36.3 | 9 | 108 | 5 |
| Braund | 37 | 8 | 133 | 5 |
| Robson | 37 | 8 | 115 | — |
| Lewis | 3 | — | 13 | — |
| Gill | 13 | 4 | 41 | — |
| Palairet | 6 | 2 | 21 | — |
| Fowler | 2 | — | 11 | — |
| Hill | 1 | — | 11 | — |

## Kent Bowling

| | Overs | Mdns | Runs | Wkts | Overs | Mdns | Runs | Wkts |
|---|---|---|---|---|---|---|---|---|
| Blythe | 14 | — | 37 | 4 | 13.5 | 2 | 48 | 2 |
| Mason | 13.3 | 7 | 26 | 4 | 13 | 5 | 29 | 8 |

Umpires: A. Hide and A. Shaw.

## SOMERSET v HAMPSHIRE

Played at Taunton, August 22, 23, 24, 1901

In this match Somerset were entirely outplayed, Hampshire winning by an innings and 121 runs. Hampshire's innings was a remarkable affair, runs throughout being obtained at the average rate of 128 an hour. The most rapid piece of scoring was in the making of the third hundred, which only occupied thirty-five minutes. There were three long partnerships, Greig and Sprot adding 148 for the second wicket in an hour, Sprot and Webb 127 for the third in fifty minutes, and Llewellyn and Barton 151 for the fifth in sixty-five minutes. As may be imagined, the Somerset bowling was hit with merciless severity. Lewellyn was quite the hero of the game, as, in addition to playing the highest individual innings, he took ten wickets. Somerset gave a satisfactory display at their first attempt, Braund and Robson both showing fine form, but at their second venture they were very disappointing.

## Somerset

| | | |
|---|---|---|
| Mr L. C. H. Palairet b Llewellyn | 11 | – st Steele b Chignell ............. 5 |
| L. C. Braund c Webb b Llewellyn | 88 | – st Steele b Chignell ............. 4 |
| Lewis lbw b Llewellyn | 18 | – c Webb b Soar ................. 19 |
| Mr F. A. Phillips c Webb b Barton | 23 | – c Steele b Llewellyn ............ 52 |
| Mr S. M. J. Woods lbw b Chignell | 33 | – run out ...................... 44 |
| E. Robson c Steele b Llewellyn | 102 | – c Greig b Llewellyn ............ 7 |
| Mr J. Daniell b Llewellyn | 2 | – b Llewellyn ................... 3 |
| G. Gill b Steele | 48 | – c Sprot b Llewellyn ............ 4 |
| Mr C. E. Dunlop b Steele | 1 | – b Chignell ................... 13 |
| B. Cranfield not out | 12 | – c and b Llewellyn .............. 0 |
| Rev. A. P. Wickham st Robson b Greig | 0 | – not out ...................... 9 |
| B 5, l-b 2 | 7 | B 13, l-b 1, w 2 ........... 16 |
| | **345** | **176** |

## Hampshire

| | | | |
|---|---|---|---|
| Mr C. Robson c Wickham b Gill | 29 | Mr D. A. Steele lbw b Palairet | 6 |
| Capt. J. G. Greig lbw b Robson | 113 | Mr C. G. Ward st Wickham b Braund | 21 |
| Mr E. M. Sprot c Wickham b Gill | 147 | Mr T. A. Chignell b Braund | 5 |
| A. Webb c Wickham b Gill | 56 | T. Soar not out | 12 |
| V. Barton c Gill b Palairet | 47 | B 7, l-b 2, w 1, n-b 4 | 14 |
| G. C. B. Llewellyn b Palairet | 153 | | |
| Mr E. C. Lee not out | 39 | **(9 wkts dec.)** | **642** |

## Hampshire Bowling

| | Overs | Mdns | Runs | Wkts | Overs | Mdns | Runs | Wkts |
|---|---|---|---|---|---|---|---|---|
| Chignell | 19 | 1 | 75 | 1 | 16.5 | — | 80 | 3 |
| Llewellyn | 34 | 5 | 115 | 5 | 27 | 7 | 68 | 5 |
| Soar | 12 | 5 | 29 | — | 4 | 3 | 2 | 1 |
| Barton | 19 | 4 | 61 | 1 | 11 | 7 | 10 | — |
| Greig | 10.4 | 2 | 32 | 1 | | | | |
| Sprot | 1 | — | 2 | — | | | | |
| Steele | 7 | 1 | 24 | 2 | | | | |

## Somerset Bowling

| | Overs | Mdns | Runs | Wkts |
|---|---|---|---|---|
| Cranfield | 14 | 1 | 99 | — |
| Gill | 33 | 1 | 182 | 3 |
| Braund | 19 | — | 144 | 2 |
| Woods | 2 | — | 14 | — |
| Palairet | 24 | 2 | 129 | 3 |
| Robson | 13 | 4 | 60 | 1 |

Umpires: A. Hide and A. Shaw.

# SOMERSET v MIDDLESEX

### Played at Taunton, August 3, 4, 5, 1903

After a great game and a remarkable finish Middlesex defeated Somerset by two wickets. The Metropolitan eleven were set to get 313 runs in three hours and a half and they accomplished their big task with a quarter of an hour to spare, the rate of scoring being roughly a hundred runs an hour. Bosanquet carried off the chief honours, but the brilliant victory was the outcome of collective rather than individual excellence. Bosanquet made 74 out of 106 in sixty-five minutes. The match was played under conditions favourable to batsmen, several of whom met with considerable success, but all that took place in the earlier stages of the match was dwarfed by Middlesex's remarkable victory.

## Somerset

| | | | |
|---|---|---|---|
| L. C. Braund c Douglas b Hunt | 19 | – c Nicholls b Bosanquet | 14 |
| A. Lewis b Hunt | 17 | – c and b Wells | 27 |
| Mr P. R. Johnson c sub. b Hunt | 3 | – c Douglas b Wells | 71 |
| Mr F. A. Phillips b Hearne | 7 | – c Hearne b Beldam | 45 |
| Mr L. C. H. Palairet b Bosanquet | 21 | – c Trott b Hunt | 21 |
| Mr F. M. Lee c MacGregor b Hunt | 4 | – c Douglas b Hearne | 83 |
| Mr S. M. J. Woods run out | 0 | – c Nicholls b Hunt | 28 |
| E. Robson c Bosanquet b Hunt | 35 | – not out | 13 |
| Mr J. Daniell not out | 64 | – b Hunt | 35 |
| Mr A. E. Newton lbw b Bosanquet | 22 | – c and b Hearne | 8 |
| B. Cranfield b Wells | 42 | – c MacGregor b Hunt | 0 |
| B 9, l-b 7, w 3 | 19 | B 14, l-b 12 | 26 |
| | **253** | | **371** |

## Middlesex

| | | | |
|---|---|---|---|
| Mr P. F. Warner c Braund b Cranfield | 36 | – c Newton b Robson | 32 |
| Mr L. J. Moon c Daniell b Cranfield | 42 | – b Cranfield | 1 |
| Mr G. W. Beldam c Palairet b Cranfield | 51 | – c Newton b Cranfield | 52 |
| Mr J. Douglas b Robson | 45 | – b Robson | 17 |
| Mr B. J. T. Bosanquet b Robson | 0 | – c Woods b Palairet | 74 |
| Mr C. M. Wells not out | 65 | – not out | 59 |
| Mr R. W. Nicholls c Robson b Cranfield | 4 | – b Cranfield | 5 |
| Mr J. H. Hunt c and b Braund | 24 | – not out | 3 |
| Mr G. MacGregor c Palairet b Braund | 0 | – st Newton b Cranfield | 39 |
| A. E. Trott c Lewis b Braund | 40 | – c Cranfield b Braund | 20 |
| J. T. Hearne c Daniell b Braund | 0 | | |
| B 1, l-b 4 | 5 | B 8, l-b 5, w 1 | 14 |
| | **312** | | **316** |

### Middlesex Bowling

| | Overs | Mdns | Runs | Wkts | Overs | Mdns | Runs | Wkts |
|---|---|---|---|---|---|---|---|---|
| Beldam | 8 | 4 | 13 | — | 11 | 2 | 33 | 1 |
| Hearne | 28 | 10 | 60 | 1 | 31 | 10 | 71 | 2 |
| Hunt | 29 | 10 | 60 | 5 | 28.4 | 5 | 102 | 4 |
| Bosanquet | 7 | — | 45 | 2 | 11 | 2 | 44 | 1 |
| Trott | 5 | — | 25 | — | 10 | 1 | 42 | — |
| Wells | 14.3 | 3 | 31 | 1 | 15 | 2 | 53 | 2 |

### Somerset Bowling

| | Overs | Mdns | Runs | Wkts | Overs | Mdns | Runs | Wkts |
|---|---|---|---|---|---|---|---|---|
| Cranfield | 39 | 7 | 137 | 4 | 22 | 3 | 114 | 4 |
| Braund | 24.1 | 1 | 91 | 4 | 26 | 4 | 92 | 1 |
| Robson | 18 | — | 68 | 2 | 21 | 3 | 69 | 2 |
| Lewis | 4 | 1 | 11 | — | 4 | 1 | 12 | — |
| Johnson | | | | | 1 | — | 4 | — |
| Palairet | | | | | 2 | — | 11 | 1 |

Umpires: V. A. Titchmarsh and W. Hearn.

# SOMERSET v WARWICKSHIRE

### Played at Taunton, May 17, 18, 1906

Somerset opened their season with a startling victory by eight wickets, the match coming to an end on the second afternoon. When an innings had been completed on each side a close game seemed in prospect, but Warwickshire on going in for the second time collapsed completely, Bailey, well backed up by Lewis at the other end, bowling with such extraordinary effect that six wickets fell to him in fifty-two balls for 6 runs. He made the ball go away a good deal, and the batsmen could do nothing with him. The innings was all over in an hour and five minutes. A heavy storm of rain caused a delay of an hour and a half, and then Somerset quickly obtained the 31 runs they required. Field's elbow gave way while he was bowling on the first day, and he could take no further part in the match.

### Warwickshire

| | | |
|---|---|---|
| S. P. Kinneir b Lewis | 0 | – c Woods b Bailey ............... 2 |
| J. Devey c Braund b Lewis | 0 | – c and b Lewis .................. 0 |
| C. Charlesworth b Bailey | 49 | – c Martyn b Bailey .............. 19 |
| W. G. Quaife b Bailey | 36 | – c Martyn b Lewis ............... 2 |
| Mr T. S. Fishwick c Lee b Lewis | 13 | – c Johnson b Bailey ... 11 |
| A. A. Lilley c Braund b Bailey | 5 | – c Hardy b Bailey .............. 0 |
| S. Santall b Lewis | 0 | – c Braund b Bailey ............. 0 |
| W. George b Maxwell | 60 | – c Martyn b Lewis .............. 0 |
| F. Moorhouse c Robson b Bailey | 2 | – c Woods b Bailey .............. 7 |
| S. Hargreave c Maxwell b Bailey | 12 | – not out ...................... 1 |
| F. E. Field not out | 0 | – absent hurt ................... 0 |
| B 2, l-b 1, n-b 1, w 1 | 5 | N-b 1, w 1 .............. 2 |
| | **182** | **44** |

### Somerset

| | | |
|---|---|---|
| L. C. Braund run out | 17 | – not out ...................... 6 |
| Mr P. R. Johnson c Lilley b Moorhouse | 39 | – c sub. b Charlesworth ... 11 |
| E. Robson run out | 0 | – run out ...................... 4 |
| Mr H. Martyn c Kinneir b Hargreave | 1 | |
| A. E. Lewis b Moorhouse | 35 | – not out ...................... 9 |
| R. P. Hardy c Hargreave b Moorhouse | 52 | |
| Mr S. M. J. Woods b Moorhouse | 2 | |
| Mr F. M. Lee c and b Charlesworth | 23 | |
| L. Cranfield c Santall b Moorhouse | 13 | |
| T. Maxwell c Lilley b Hargreave | 0 | |
| A. E. Bailey not out | 9 | |
| B 4, l-b 1 | 5 | W 1 .................. 1 |
| | **196** | **31** |

### Somerset Bowling

| | Overs | Mdns | Runs | Wkts | Overs | Mdns | Runs | Wkts |
|---|---|---|---|---|---|---|---|---|
| Lewis | 18 | 3 | 45 | 4 | 9 | 2 | 28 | 3 |
| Maxwell | 10.2 | — | 43 | 1 | | | | |
| Braund | 8 | — | 30 | — | 1 | — | 8 | — |
| Bailey | 22 | 4 | 59 | 5 | 8.4 | 5 | 6 | 6 |

### Warwickshire Bowling

| | Overs | Mdns | Runs | Wkts | Overs | Mdns | Runs | Wkts |
|---|---|---|---|---|---|---|---|---|
| Field | 4.1 | — | 34 | — | | | | |
| Hargreave | 25 | 8 | 65 | 2 | 1 | — | 3 | — |
| Moorhouse | 27.2 | 5 | 70 | 5 | 1 | — | 6 | — |
| Santall | 4 | 1 | 9 | — | | | | |
| Charlesworth | 3 | — | 8 | 1 | 3 | 2 | 4 | 1 |
| Quaife | 1 | — | 5 | — | 4 | 1 | 17 | — |

Umpires: F. W. Marlow and T. Brown.

## SOMERSET v YORKSHIRE

Played at Bath, August 27, 28, 29, 1906

As in the match with Kent, Somerset were completely over-matched, Yorkshire winning by 389 runs. Yorkshire led on the first innings by 243 but, with plenty of time to spare, Ernest Smith let his own side bat a second time instead of making Somerset follow on. Having the match in hand he was, no doubt, actuated by a desire to let Hirst complete his 2,000 runs for the season. In this Hirst succeeded, he and Rhodes putting on 202 in an hour and a quarter. In making two separate hundreds in the match Hirst rivalled Denton's achievement at Trent Bridge earlier in the season. These two are the only Yorkshire players who have performed this feat in first-class cricket. It was quite Hirst's match as apart from his batting he took eleven wickets for 115 runs.

### Yorkshire

| | | | |
|---|---|---|---|
| J. Tunnicliffe c and b Braund | 4 | – c Braund b Bailey | 38 |
| W. Rhodes c Johnson b Bailey | 64 | – not out | 115 |
| D. Denton c Martyn b Braund | 67 | | |
| Mr T. L. Taylor c Poyntz b Mordaunt | 41 | | |
| G. H. Hirst c and b Mordaunt | 111 | – not out | 117 |
| H. Rudston c Poyntz b Braund | 21 | | |
| Mr E. Smith c Mordaunt b Braund | 34 | | |
| S. Haigh b Braund | 1 | | |
| H. Myers lbw b Braund | 6 | | |
| D. Hunter b Mordaunt | 8 | | |
| W. Ringrose not out | 2 | | |
| L-b 7, w 1, n-b 1 | 9 | B 2, l-b 6, w 2 | 10 |
| | **368** | **(1 wkt dec.)** | **280** |

### Somerset

| | | | |
|---|---|---|---|
| Mr H. Martyn b Ringrose | 2 | – c Rhodes b Hirst | 23 |
| Mr P. R. Johnson b Rhodes | 29 | – b Hirst | 5 |
| A. E. Lewis b Hirst | 3 | – b Hirst | 0 |
| L. C. Braund b Hirst | 28 | – b Ringrose | 12 |
| Mr L. C. H. Palairet b Hirst | 31 | – c Hunter b Hirst | 42 |
| Mr F. A. Phillips lbw b Rhodes | 2 | – b Hirst | 2 |
| E. Robson c Hunter b Hirst | 3 | – b Haigh | 26 |
| Mr H. S. Poyntz c Hirst b Rhodes | 14 | – b Haigh | 10 |
| Mr F. M. Lee not out | 6 | – not out | 6 |
| Mr O. C. Mordaunt b Hirst | 3 | – lbw b Haigh | 0 |
| A. E. Bailey b Hirst | 0 | – b Haigh | 2 |
| B 3, l-b 1 | 4 | B 2, l-b 1, w 1, n-b 2 | 6 |
| | **125** | | **134** |

### Somerset Bowling

| | Overs | Mdns | Runs | Wkts | Overs | Mdns | Runs | Wkts |
|---|---|---|---|---|---|---|---|---|
| Braund | 38.3 | 3 | 125 | 6 | 6 | — | 44 | — |
| Lewis | 11 | 3 | 43 | — | 10 | 2 | 52 | — |
| Bailey | 19 | 2 | 83 | 1 | 10 | 2 | 36 | 1 |
| Robson | 14 | 2 | 37 | — | 4 | — | 39 | — |
| Mordaunt | 36 | 10 | 71 | 3 | 9 | — | 54 | — |
| Phillips | | | | | 2 | — | 19 | — |
| Palairet | | | | | 2 | — | 9 | — |
| Martin | | | | | 2 | — | 17 | — |

## Yorkshire Bowling

|         | Overs | Mdns | Runs | Wkts | Overs | Mdns | Runs | Wkts |
|---------|-------|------|------|------|-------|------|------|------|
| Hirst ............ | 26 | 3 | 70 | 6 | 15 | 2 | 45 | 5 |
| Ringrose ........ | 12 | 5 | 21 | 1 | 9 | 1 | 38 | 1 |
| Rhodes.......... | 14 | 4 | 28 | 3 | 10 | 1 | 34 | — |
| Haigh........... | 1 | — | 2 | — | 5 | 1 | 11 | 4 |

Umpires: W. A. J. West and A. Millward.

# SOMERSET v LANCASHIRE

## Played at Bath, June 6, 7, 8, 1910

Declaring with only two wickets down, Lancashire forced a win in most brilliant fashion. Hornby sent Somerset in to bat, heavy rain having fallen on the Sunday, but the ball came slowly off the pitch and the home side kept their opponents in the field for two hours and three-quarters. Four wickets had fallen for 41 when Hardy and Hodgkinson made a capital stand, and with six men out for 84 Poyntz, although twice missed, hit in resolute style, making 52 in seventy minutes. Dean took nine wickets in an innings for the fourth time in his career, having previously accomplished that feat against Derbyshire in 1907, and against Warwickshire and Somerset in 1909. The ground had largely recovered when Lancashire went in, and Hornby and Hartley forced the game to such purpose that they scored 100 runs in an hour. Two wickets had fallen for 102 at the drawing of stumps. A severe storm prevented any progress being made with the game next day, but on Wednesday Hartley and John Tyldesley, hitting away in brilliant style, added 184 runs in a couple of hours before lunch. Tyldesley, when 85, had a life given him through a misunderstanding between two of the fieldsmen, but no other chance was given. Hartley batted with fine skill and judgment for more than three hours. At their second attempt Somerset gave a sorry display against Dean, the conditions in no way excusing their complete failure. Lancashire won by an innings and 58 runs.

## Somerset

| | | | | |
|---|---|---|---|---|
| L. C. Braund c J. T. Tyldesley b Dean ............ | 3 | – st Worsley b Heap .............. | 6 |
| P. J. Hardy b Dean ........................... | 40 | – c Hornby b Dean .............. | 25 |
| E. Robson b Dean ......................... | 8 | – c Hartley b Dean .............. | 2 |
| A. E. Lewis c Cook b Dean .................. | 0 | – c Whitehead b Heap ........... | 21 |
| Mr B. L. Bisgood lbw b Heap ................ | 3 | – c Cook b Dean ................ | 0 |
| Mr G. W. Hodgkinson b Dean ................. | 22 | – b Dean ...................... | 1 |
| Mr C. G. Dean st Worsley b Dean .............. | 12 | – run out ..................... | 3 |
| Mr E. S. M. Poyntz not out .................... | 52 | – c J. T. Tyldesley b Dean ........ | 0 |
| Mr L. C. L. Sutton c Sharp b Dean ............. | 0 | – not out ..................... | 0 |
| Mr J. C. White c Heap b Dean................. | 5 | – c J. T. Tyldesley b Dean ........ | 0 |
| H. Chidgey b Dean ......................... | 15 | – c Cook b Dean ................ | 0 |
| B 2, l-b 6 ......................... | 8 | L-b 2 .................. | 2 |
| | **168** | | **60** |

## Lancashire

| | |
|---|---|
| Mr A. H. Hornby c Dean b Hardy ....... | 56 |
| Mr A. Hartley not out ................. | 126 |
| J. S. Heap hit wkt b Braund ............. | 0 |
| J. T. Tyldesley not out ................. | 95 |
| B 5, n-b 4 .................. | 9 |
| **(2 wkts dec.) 286** | |

J. Sharp, H. Makepeace, E. Tyldesley, R. Whitehead, L. Cook, H. Dean and W. Worsley did not bat.

## Lancashire Bowling

| | Overs | Mdns | Runs | Wkts | Overs | Mdns | Runs | Wkts |
|---|---|---|---|---|---|---|---|---|
| Dean ........... | 34 | 6 | 77 | 9 | 14 | 3 | 26 | 7 |
| Heap ........... | 21 | 2 | 56 | 1 | 13 | 3 | 32 | 2 |
| Cook ........... | 12 | 1 | 27 | — | | | | |

## Somerset Bowling

| | Overs | Mdns | Runs | Wkts |
|---|---|---|---|---|
| Lewis ........... | 23 | 3 | 83 | — |
| Robson .......... | 22 | 2 | 86 | — |
| Hardy .......... | 12 | — | 46 | 1 |
| Braund .......... | 10 | 1 | 36 | 1 |
| White ........... | 7 | — | 26 | — |

Umpires: G. P. Harrison and J. Carlin.

# SOMERSET v SUSSEX

### Played at Bath, August 15, 16, 17, 1910

Rain during the night was followed by bright sunshine, yet so little able to make use of these conditions were the Somerset bowlers that Sussex on Monday scored 387 for six wickets. A great personal triumph attended Robert Relf who, batting for four hours and three-quarters, gave only two chances, his driving being of an especially brilliant description. Vine helped to put on 208 for the first wicket. Somerset were beaten by nine wickets but their batting was redeemed by some superb work on the part of Johnson who in neither innings gave a chance, though he always scored rapidly. Cox left his ground to hit a no-ball from Lewis and, the wicket-keeper whipping off the bails, was given run out. This was obviously an incorrect decision.

## Sussex

| | | | |
|---|---|---|---|
| R. Relf lbw b Critchley-Salmonson .............. | 194 | | |
| J. Vine b Taylor ..................... | 78 | | |
| E. H. Killick c Braund b Taylor ................. | 19 | | |
| Mr C. L. Tudor lbw b Taylor .................. | 8 – not out ...................... | 0 |
| A. E. Relf c Joy b Braund .................... | 55 | | |
| J. H. Vincett c Taylor b Lewis .................. | 28 | | |
| Mr H. P. Chaplin c Braund b Critchley-Salmonson .. | 1 | | |
| G. Cox run out ........................... | 11 – c Paul b Joy ................... | 16 |
| V. C. W. Jupp hit wkt b Braund ................. | 20 – not out ...................... | 15 |
| G. Leach b Braund ......................... | 13 | | |
| H. R. Butt not out ......................... | 0 | | |
| B 30, l-b 4, n-b 4 .................... | 38 | W 1 ................... | 1 |
| | 465 | | 32 |

### Somerset

| | | | |
|---|---|---|---|
| Mr E. P. Paul c R. Relf b A. E. Relf | 6 | – b Vine | 12 |
| P. Hardy c R. Relf b A. E. Relf | 8 | – c Cox b A. E. Relf | 23 |
| A. E. Lewis b Leach | 5 | – c and b Leach | 32 |
| E. Robson run out | 9 | – c Butt b R. Relf | 50 |
| Mr O. M. Samson b A. E. Relf | 25 | – b A. E. Relf | 3 |
| L. C. Braund lbw b A. E. Relf | 35 | – b Leach | 0 |
| Mr J. Daniell c A. E. Relf b Vincett | 22 | – b Leach | 5 |
| Mr P. R. Johnson not out | 98 | – not out | 96 |
| Mr H. Critchley-Salmonson b Killick | 10 | – b A. E. Relf | 0 |
| Mr F. H. D. Joy c Cox b Vine | 20 | – c Butt b A. E. Relf | 5 |
| W. H. Taylor c Cox b Vine | 19 | – b A. E. Relf | 0 |
| B 7 | 7 | B 5, l-b 1 | 6 |
| | **264** | | **232** |

### Somerset Bowling

| | Overs | Mdns | Runs | Wkts | Overs | Mdns | Runs | Wkts |
|---|---|---|---|---|---|---|---|---|
| Joy | 30 | 6 | 117 | — | 4.2 | 2 | 7 | 1 |
| Lewis | 38 | 11 | 92 | 1 | | | | |
| Braund | 11.1 | 1 | 48 | 3 | | | | |
| Robson | 8 | 1 | 29 | — | | | | |
| Taylor | 18 | 3 | 59 | 3 | | | | |
| Hardy | 12 | 1 | 51 | — | | | | |
| Critchley-Salmonson | 9 | — | 31 | 2 | 5 | — | 24 | — |

### Sussex Bowling

| | Overs | Mdns | Runs | Wkts | Overs | Mdns | Runs | Wkts |
|---|---|---|---|---|---|---|---|---|
| Leach | 14 | 2 | 56 | 1 | 21 | 2 | 70 | 3 |
| A. E. Relf | 27 | 3 | 96 | 4 | 20.5 | 7 | 42 | 5 |
| Cox | 4 | — | 24 | — | 8 | — | 22 | — |
| Vincett | 8 | — | 24 | 1 | 6 | — | 23 | — |
| Killick | 6 | 1 | 27 | 1 | 1 | — | 8 | — |
| R. Relf | 4 | — | 12 | — | 11 | 2 | 35 | 1 |
| Vine | 3.3 | — | 18 | 2 | 14 | 6 | 26 | 1 |

Umpires: T. Brown and C. E. Dench.

## SOMERSET v HAMPSHIRE

### Played at Bath, June 11, 12, 1914

Outclassed on the first day when the conditions were even, Somerset could do nothing against excellent bowling when rain had ruined the pitch, Hampshire winning by an innings and 192 runs. Both on the opening morning and after rain had prevented a resumption until two o'clock on the Friday, Jaques bowled in irresistible form. His record for the match – fourteen wickets for 54 – might have been still more remarkable, as two catches were missed off him while Somerset were being dismissed in fifty minutes. Kennedy gave useful help, and with Jaques was unchanged throughout the two innings. The professional was in specially good form on the Thursday, at one time bowling thirty-one balls for no runs, and taking three wickets. The Bath pitch was very treacherous when Somerset went in against a margin of 230, but the Hampshire bowlers deserve full credit for their admirable work. Hope, who with Poyntz added 48 in the first innings, scored half the runs from the bat in the second. Hampshire gave a very different display, Mead carrying off the honours by scoring a perfect 126 in two hours and a half. Mead drove hard to the off, and when the bowlers pitched at all short he pulled with great effect. Major Greig and Bowell showed the possibility of making runs, scoring 66 for the first wicket, but Somerset worked with spirit and their bowling was only thoroughly mastered when Mead and Remnant added 118 in seventy minutes, the left-hander getting his second fifty in forty minutes.

## Somerset

| | | | |
|---|---|---|---|
| Mr A. D. E. Rippon b Kennedy | 2 | – c Brown b Jaques | 0 |
| W. Hyman c Livsey b Kennedy | 2 | – c Brown b Jaques | 0 |
| Mr E. C. Ball c Kennedy b Jaques | 3 | – c and b Jaques | 2 |
| L. C. Braund b Kennedy | 1 | – b Jaques | 5 |
| A. H. Beezer b Jaques | 0 | – c Brown b Jaques | 1 |
| Mr E. S. M. Poyntz c Remnant b Jaques | 31 | – c Mead b Kennedy | 8 |
| E. Robson c Newman b Jaques | 2 | – c Brown b Jaques | 2 |
| Mr P. P. Hope b Jaques | 29 | – c Brown b Jaques | 18 |
| Mr A. E. Newton b Kennedy | 5 | – b Kennedy | 0 |
| J. F. Bridges b Jaques | 7 | – not out | 0 |
| Mr J. C. White not out | 0 | – c Stone b Jaques | 0 |
| L-b 1 | 1 | B 2 | 2 |
| | **83** | | **38** |

## Hampshire

| | | | |
|---|---|---|---|
| Maj. J. G. Greig b Robson | 45 | A. Kennedy c Newton b Braund | 0 |
| A. Bowell c Poyntz b Bridges | 32 | Mr A. Jaques b Robson | 1 |
| J. Newman c Beezer b Robson | 26 | Mr H. A. H. Smith not out | 10 |
| C. P. Mead c Poyntz b White | 126 | W. H. Livsey lbw b Robson | 5 |
| G. Brown lbw b Robson | 14 | B 3, l-b 2 | 5 |
| J. Stone c Newton b Bridges | 11 | | |
| E. R. Remnant b Braund | 38 | | **313** |

## Hampshire Bowling

| | Overs | Mdns | Runs | Wkts | Overs | Mdns | Runs | Wkts |
|---|---|---|---|---|---|---|---|---|
| Jaques | 13 | 4 | 33 | 6 | 6 | 2 | 21 | 8 |
| Kennedy | 12.2 | 4 | 49 | 4 | 5 | 2 | 15 | 2 |

## Somerset Bowling

| | Overs | Mdns | Runs | Wkts |
|---|---|---|---|---|
| White | 32 | 10 | 57 | 1 |
| Robson | 32.5 | 4 | 134 | 5 |
| Bridges | 18 | 2 | 50 | 2 |
| Rippon | 8 | — | 43 | — |
| Beezer | 2 | — | 12 | — |
| Hope | 3 | — | 12 | — |
| Braund | 2 | 2 | — | 2 |

Umpires: A. E. Street and R. G. Barlow.

## SOMERSET v YORKSHIRE

Played at Weston-super-Mare, August 27, 28, 1914

Finished in two days, Yorkshire winning by 140 runs, the first match of the Weston-super-Mare festival was chiefly remarkable for the bowling of Drake. Previous to this match no Yorkshireman had in a first-class engagement taken all ten wickets in an innings. Drake did this when Somerset went in requiring 231 for victory. On the first day he dismissed five men and altogether he claimed fifteen wickets at the very small cost of 51 runs. Moreover, Drake was the highest run-getter with 51 and 12 in a small scoring match, his all-round cricket contributing very largely to the success of his side. He and Booth bowled unchanged throughout the two innings of Somerset, having done the same thing at Bristol earlier in the week – a most exceptional feat. The newly laid pitch had suffered from rain and always helped the bowlers materially. In the circumstances Yorkshire were fortunate to bat first, the turf cutting up badly. Denton made 52 in as many minutes, the first hour's play producing 90 runs. Drake played soundly for an hour and a half. Somerset's first innings lasted little more than an hour. The Yorkshiremen faring worse than before, no hope existed of Somerset making a close struggle. Indeed their one stand was for the ninth wicket, Harcombe and Hope putting on 37. Harcombe hit Drake for eleven runs in one over.

## Yorkshire

| | | | |
|---|---|---|---|
| M. W. Booth c Poyntz b Bridges | 1 | – b Bridges | 9 |
| B. B. Wilson c Saunders b Bridges | 20 | – b Bridges | 9 |
| D. Denton c Chidgey b Hylton-Stewart | 52 | – c Saunders b Bridges | 0 |
| R. Kilner c Hylton-Stewart b Bridges | 2 | – c Braund b Bridges | 4 |
| W. Rhodes c and b Hylton-Stewart | 1 | – lbw b Robson | 25 |
| T. J. Birtles lbw b Braund | 16 | – b Robson | 10 |
| A. Drake c Harcombe b Braund | 51 | – c Hope b Robson | 12 |
| P. Holmes b Bridges | 7 | – not out | 3 |
| G. H. Hirst c Bisgood b Bridges | 5 | – c Saunders b Robson | 10 |
| E. Oldroyd not out | 0 | – b Hylton-Stewart | 23 |
| A. Dolphin b Braund | 0 | – b Robson | 0 |
| B 5, n-b 2 | 7 | B 4, l-b 2, w 1 | 7 |
| | **162** | | **112** |

## Somerset

| | | | |
|---|---|---|---|
| Mr B. L. Bisgood c and b Booth | 6 | – c Dolphin b Drake | 11 |
| L. C. Braund b Drake | 1 | – b Drake | 9 |
| E. Robson c Rhodes b Booth | 19 | – c Birtles b Drake | 3 |
| Mr B. D. Hylton-Stewart b Drake | 1 | – st Dolphin b Drake | 3 |
| W. Hyman b Drake | 1 | – st Dolphin b Drake | 4 |
| Mr E. S. M. Poyntz b Drake | 0 | – c Oldroyd b Drake | 5 |
| Mr P. P. Hope b Booth | 3 | – c and b Drake | 19 |
| Mr H. W. Saunders b Drake | 0 | – b Drake | 0 |
| Mr H. D. Harcombe not out | 5 | – b Drake | 26 |
| J. F. Bridges c Drake b Booth | 7 | – not out | 1 |
| H. Chidgey c Holmes b Booth | 0 | – b Drake | 4 |
| B 1 | 1 | B 4, n-b 1 | 5 |
| | **44** | | **90** |

## Somerset Bowling

| | Overs | Mdns | Runs | Wkts | Overs | Mdns | Runs | Wkts |
|---|---|---|---|---|---|---|---|---|
| Robson | 14 | 5 | 45 | — | 14 | 2 | 38 | 5 |
| Bridges | 17 | 1 | 59 | 5 | 14 | 1 | 54 | 4 |
| Hylton-Stewart | 9 | — | 38 | 2 | 2 | — | 6 | 1 |
| Braund | 8.4 | 2 | 13 | 3 | 4 | 2 | 7 | — |

## Yorkshire Bowling

| | Overs | Mdns | Runs | Wkts | Overs | Mdns | Runs | Wkts |
|---|---|---|---|---|---|---|---|---|
| Booth | 8 | — | 27 | 5 | 9 | — | 50 | — |
| Drake | 7 | 1 | 16 | 5 | 8.5 | — | 35 | 10 |

Umpires: A. E. Street and A. Millward.

# SURREY

## SURREY v WORCESTERSHIRE

Played at The Oval, May 21, 22, 23, 1900

The Surrey eleven gave a wonderful display of batting on the first day, but the weather robbed them of the reward fairly earned by their fine cricket. Not a ball could be bowled on Tuesday, and after an hour's play, several times interrupted, on Wednesday, the match was abandoned. Worcestershire had never met Surrey before, having only previously played the second eleven, and the match so far as it went was hardly one of which they would retain pleasant memories, their bowling being so freely knocked about that Surrey scored on the opening day 495 for five wickets. Abel, owing to a badly bruised hand, had been kept out of five matches, and apart from the Easter Monday fixture at The Oval, had had no first-class cricket at all. Loss of practice, however, did not seem to have affected him, for his 221 was in every way a magnificent innings. He was at the wickets for, roughly speaking, five hours, and hit a five and twenty-two 4s. He was stumped at last from a ball that was fully half a yard wide of the off stump. Hayes and Lockwood divided honours with him, 272 runs being added for the second wicket, and 195 in about two hours for the third, the total standing at 469 when Abel left—third wicket down. Hayes hit very brilliantly indeed for his 150, the great majority of his runs being made as usual in front of the wicket. He ought to have been caught at cover point at 140, but this was his only mistake. Lockwood was also seen to extreme advantage, runs coming from nearly every over while he and Abel were together.

## Surrey

| | |
|---|---|
| R. Abel st Straw b Bird | 221 |
| W. Brockwell b Wilson | 2 |
| E. G. Hayes b Bird | 150 |
| W. Lockwood not out | 104 |
| T. Hayward b Arnold | 5 |
| F. C. Holland b Arnold | 0 |
| Mr V. F. S. Crawford not out | 1 |
| B 11, n-b 1 | 12 |
| (5 wkts dec.) | 495 |

Mr. D. L. A. Jephson, W. Lees, H. Wood and T. Richardson did not bat.

## Worcestershire

| | |
|---|---|
| F. Bowley b Brockwell | 6 |
| A. Bird c Holland b Brockwell | 3 |
| E. Arnold not out | 13 |
| Mr H. K. Foster c sub. b Lees | 7 |
| F. Wheldon b Lees | 0 |
| Mr A. Isaak not out | 0 |
| N-b 1 | 1 |
| | 30 |

Mr E. Bromley-Martin, Bannister, G. Wilson, R. Burrows and T. Straw did not bat.

## Worcestershire Bowling

| | Overs | Mdns | Runs | Wkts |
|---|---|---|---|---|
| Wilson | 33 | 5 | 115 | 1 |
| Arnold | 10 | 1 | 36 | 2 |
| Burrows | 17 | 3 | 76 | — |
| Bannister | 26 | 3 | 84 | — |
| Bird | 15 | 2 | 58 | 2 |
| Bromley-Martin | 13 | 1 | 69 | — |
| Foster | 6 | — | 28 | — |
| Bowley | 2 | — | 17 | — |

**Surrey Bowling**

|  | Overs | Mdns | Runs | Wkts |
|---|---|---|---|---|
| Brockwell ......... | 13 | 5 | 18 | 2 |
| Lees ............. | 12 | 7 | 11 | 2 |

Umpires: W. Richards and A. Hide.

## SURREY v ESSEX

Played at The Oval, May 24, 45, 46, 1900

This proved one of the best matches of the season at The Oval, Essex winning on the third morning, after an intensely exciting finish, by five runs. As they had never before beaten Surrey at The Oval the victory naturally afforded them more than ordinary pleasure. The result was unexpected, as at the close of play on the second evening Surrey only wanted 65 to win with seven wickets to go down. However, on the Saturday morning Holland and Abel were soon out to Kortright's bowling, and the Surrey men found themselves with a heavy task before them. Thanks to Brockwell and Lees, they seemed at one point almost certain of victory, only six runs being wanted with two wickets to fall, but Mead, who was in great form, settled the matter by bowling Lees and Wood with successive balls. In the early stages of the match Perrin and Abel batted very finely, Abel's innings—played when the wicket was extremely difficult—being indeed quite a masterpiece of skilful defence.

### Essex

| | | |
|---|---|---|
| Mr F. L. Fane b Lockwood .................... | 2 – b Brockwell .................. | 17 |
| H. Carpenter c Brockwell b Lockwood .......... | 1 – b Lockwood .................. | 4 |
| Mr P. Perrin c Wood b Lockwood ............... | 96 – c and b Brockwell ............. | 22 |
| Mr C. McGahey b Lockwood .................. | 15 – b Brockwell ................. | 2 |
| E. Russell c Crawford b Lockwood ............. | 10 – b Lockwood ................. | 5 |
| Mr C. J. Kortright c Wood b Lockwood .......... | 10 – b Lockwood ................. | 0 |
| Mr H. G. Owen not out ........................ | 29 – b Brockwell ................. | 1 |
| T. Russell c Abel b Lockwood ................. | 0 – c Wood b Brockwell ......... | 7 |
| H. Young b Lockwood ......................... | 7 – b Lockwood ................. | 1 |
| Mr F. G. Bull c Hayward b Lockwood .......... | 10 – b Lockwood ................. | 0 |
| W. Mead c Abel b Smith ..................... | 4 – not out .................... | 7 |
| B 1, n-b 2 ........................ | 3 | N-b 2 .................. | 2 |
| | 187 | 68 |

### Surrey

| | | |
|---|---|---|
| Mr V. F. S. Crawford b Kortright ............... | 10 – c Perrin b Kortright ............ | 5 |
| R. Abel c and b Bull ......................... | 68 – b Kortright ................... | 4 |
| E. G. Hayes c Fane b Mead .................... | 2 – b Mead ..................... | 19 |
| W. Lockwood c Kortright b Mead ............... | 0 – b Kortright ................. | 4 |
| T. Hayward b Mead .......................... | 6 – lbw b Mead ................. | 3 |
| F. C. Holland c Kortright b Young ............. | 17 – c T. Russell b Kortright .......... | 2 |
| W. Brockwell b Mead ........................ | 9 – not out .................... | 28 |
| Mr D. L. A. Jephson c T. Russell b Mead ......... | 25 – b Mead ................. | 0 |
| W. Lees b Mead ............................. | 19 – b Mead ................. | 9 |
| Smith not out ............................... | 0 – b Kortright ................ | 1 |
| H. Wood c T. Russell b Mead ................. | 1 – b Mead ................. | 0 |
| B 12, l-b 2, n-b 1 .................... | 15 | B 2, n-b 1 .............. | 3 |
| | 172 | 78 |

## Surrey Bowling

| | Overs | Mdns | Runs | Wkts | Overs | Mdns | Runs | Wkts |
|---|---|---|---|---|---|---|---|---|
| Lockwood ........ | 40 | 12 | 94 | 9 | 9 | 1 | 33 | 5 |
| Smith ........... | 21 | 6 | 31 | 1 | 5 | — | 20 | — |
| Hayward ........ | 5 | 1 | 14 | — | | | | |
| Brockwell ........ | 1 | 3 | 19 | — | 3.4 | — | 13 | 5 |
| Lees ........... | 6 | — | 26 | — | | | | |

## Essex Bowling

| | Overs | Mdns | Runs | Wkts | Overs | Mdns | Runs | Wkts |
|---|---|---|---|---|---|---|---|---|
| Kortright ........ | 16 | 2 | 64 | 1 | 18 | 6 | 39 | 5 |
| Young .......... | 12 | 3 | 25 | 1 | | | | |
| Mead ........... | 27.1 | 9 | 62 | 7 | 18.4 | 5 | 36 | 5 |
| Bull ........... | 2 | — | 6 | 1 | | | | |

Umpires: A. F. Smith and R. G. Barlow.

# SURREY v WORCESTERSHIRE

Played at The Oval, June 17, 18, 19, 1901

Though Worcestershire started by scoring 309, they left off, on the first day, with the worst of the position, and in the end Surrey won by an innings and four runs, play on the third morning only lasting an hour. For their easy victory, Surrey were indebted, in the first place, to the batting of Abel, Mr Crawford and Hayward, and afterwards to some fine bowling by Richardson and Lockwood. Abel and Crawford were only together for two hours, but in that time 227 runs were put on. Crawford's driving was quite wonderful in its power and certainty. He made his first hundred runs, out of 147, in seventy minutes, and scored, altogether, 159 out of 248 in two hours and a quarter. He gave no chance, but when 143 he played a ball on to his wicket without removing a bail. Abel was naturally far less vigorous than his partner, but he also played splendid cricket, staying in for three hours and forty minutes, and never making a mistake. The game was as good as over when the second day's cricket came to an end, Worcestershire, on going in for the second time against a balance of 164, losing five wickets for 109. R. E. Foster did his best on the third morning, but his play only delayed a result that had become inevitable.

## Worcestershire

| | | | | |
|---|---|---|---|---|
| R. Pearson c Hayes b Brockwell ................ | 27 | – b Brockwell ................... | 1 |
| F. Bowley b Lees ........................... | 38 | – b Richardson ................. | 27 |
| F. Wheldon b Jephson ...................... | 50 | – c Stedman b Richardson ......... | 19 |
| Mr R. E. Foster b Richardson ................. | 21 | – b Richardson ................. | 65 |
| Hunt b Jephson ........................... | 23 | – c Stedman b Richardson ......... | 4 |
| Mr G. Simpson-Hayward run out ............. | 50 | – c Stedman b Richardson ......... | 7 |
| A. Bird c Hayes b Lockwood ................. | 36 | – b Lockwood ................... | 10 |
| T. Straw c Hayes b Lockwood ............... | 5 | – lbw b Lockwood .............. | 7 |
| R. Burrows b Lockwood ..................... | 21 | – b Richardson ................. | 4 |
| G. A. Wilson not out ...................... | 12 | – c Abel b Lockwood ............ | 4 |
| C. Bannister c Hayward b Lockwood ........... | 1 | – not out ..................... | 3 |
| B 8, l-b 10, w 3, n-b 4 ................ | 25 | B 4, l-b 3, w 1, n-b 1 ....... | 9 |
| | 309 | | 160 |

## Surrey

| | | | |
|---|---|---|---|
| R. Abel c Wilson b Bird ................138 | W. Lees b Bird ...................... 2 |
| E. G. Hayes c Bird b Burrows ........... 37 | A. Stedman b Bird ................... 4 |
| Mr L. Walker b Burrows .............. 11 | T. Richardson b Wilson ............... 21 |
| Mr V. F. S. Crawford b Bird ...........159 | Mr D. L. A. Jephson absent injured ....... 0 |
| W. H. Lockwood b Burrows ............ 14 | B 10, l-b 7, w 4 ............... 21 |
| T. Hayward not out .................. 60 | — |
| W.Brockwell b Burrows ............... 6 | 473 |

### Surrey Bowling

| | Overs | Mdns | Runs | Wkts | Overs | Mdns | Runs | Wkts |
|---|---|---|---|---|---|---|---|---|
| Richardson ....... | 18 | 1 | 68 | 1 | 25 | 2 | 77 | 6 |
| Lockwood ........ | 17.1 | — | 78 | 4 | 10.5 | 2 | 29 | 3 |
| Lees ............. | 22 | 8 | 42 | 1 | 7 | 2 | 17 | — |
| Brockwell ........ | 12 | 3 | 30 | 1 | 8 | 3 | 28 | 1 |
| Jephson .......... | 20 | 2 | 50 | 2 | | | | |
| Walker .......... | 5 | 2 | 16 | — | | | | |

### Worcestershire Bowling

| | Overs | Mdns | Runs | Wkts |
|---|---|---|---|---|
| Wilson ........... | 30.1 | 3 | 123 | 1 |
| Pearson .......... | 11 | 1 | 34 | — |
| Burrows .......... | 39 | 9 | 151 | 4 |
| Simpson-Hayward .. | 6 | — | 44 | — |
| Bannister ........ | 5 | — | 39 | — |
| Bird ............. | 23 | 7 | 61 | 4 |

Umpires: A. J. Smith and A. White.

# SURREY v LONDON COUNTY

### Played at The Oval, April 13, 14, 15, 1903

Surrey won their opening match by eight wickets, G. H. Hadfield, a medium pace bowler from Sutton, meeting with some success. Hayward played a delightful innings, marred by only one chance, and Hayes showed that he was in form. For London County, W. G. Grace, who had made his first appearance at The Oval 39 years previously, batted admirably in both innings. Sewell and Board hit up 127 in an hour and a half. In accordance with a recently-issued regulation of the Marylebone Club, the umpires tested the width of the bats with gauges, and more than one player had to get his bat shaved.

## London County

| | | |
|---|---|---|
| Mr W. G. Grace b Lees ...................... | 43 – c Hayward b Hadfield ........... 81 |
| Mr W. L. Murdoch c Strudwick b Hadfield ........ | 9 – b Hadfield ................... 9 |
| B. Jaya Ram c Hayes b Hadfield ............... | 5 – c Hadfield b Lees ............... 3 |
| L. C. Braund c Holland b Davis............... | 11 – absent ill ................. 0 |
| Mr N. F. Norman c Hayes b Davis ............. | 0 – b Hayward................ 7 |
| E. H. D. Sewell c Davis b Hayward ............. | 90 – c Lockwood b Hadfield .......... 18 |
| J. H. Board c Strudwick b Lees ................ | 59 – c Strudwick b Lees ......... 17 |
| J. Vine b Hayward ...................... | 26 – c Hayes b Davis ............. 30 |
| Mr J. G. Hirsch b Hayward ................... | 0 – run out ................. 0 |
| Mr W. W. Odell not out ...................... | 7 – c Lees b Hadfield ............. 0 |
| Mr P. R. May b Hayward ................... | 0 – not out ..................... 7 |
| B 14, l-b 3 ........................ | 17      B 9, l-b 2 .............. 11 |
| | — — |
| | 267                    183 |

## Surrey

| | | |
|---|---|---|
| T. Hayward b Vine | 107 | |
| Mr E. Wiltshire c Hirsch b Braund | 0 | – b Murdoch ... 13 |
| E. G. Hayes c Sewell b Odell | 51 | – not out ... 43 |
| F. Holland b Odell | 17 | |
| W. H. Lockwood b Odell | 36 | – not out ... 1 |
| W. Lees lbw b Odell | 13 | |
| Mr L. Walker c Vine b May | 54 | |
| Davis c and b Odell | 8 | – st Board b Odell ... 1 |
| Mr G. H. Hadfield c Braund b Odell | 10 | |
| Mr D. L. A. Jephson not out | 47 | |
| H. Strudwick c Board b Vine | 12 | |
| B 22, l-b 8 | 30 | B 8, l-b 1 ... 9 |
| | **385** | **67** |

## Surrey Bowling

| | Overs | Mdns | Runs | Wkts | Overs | Mdns | Runs | Wkts |
|---|---|---|---|---|---|---|---|---|
| Lockwood | 7 | — | 27 | — | | | | |
| Hadfield | 19 | 4 | 63 | 2 | 26 | 3 | 61 | 4 |
| Lees | 27 | 3 | 71 | 2 | 29.3 | 10 | 54 | 2 |
| Davis | 15 | 1 | 64 | 2 | 13 | 3 | 27 | 1 |
| Hayes | 1 | — | 8 | — | | | | |
| Hayward | 3.2 | — | 11 | 4 | 10 | 2 | 30 | 1 |
| Holland | 3 | 1 | 6 | — | | | | |

## London County Bowling

| | Overs | Mdns | Runs | Wkts | Overs | Mdns | Runs | Wkts |
|---|---|---|---|---|---|---|---|---|
| Braund | 17 | 1 | 57 | 1 | | | | |
| Odell | 42 | 10 | 117 | 6 | 5 | — | 27 | 1 |
| Vine | 36.4 | 4 | 99 | 2 | | | | |
| May | 15 | 4 | 57 | 1 | 2 | — | 5 | — |
| Hirsch | 3 | — | 20 | — | | | | |
| Grace | 1 | — | 5 | — | | | | |
| Sewell | | | | | 4 | 1 | 10 | — |
| Jaya Ram | | | | | 4 | — | 12 | — |
| Murdoch | | | | | 1.1 | 1 | 4 | 1 |

Umpires: W. Hearn and V. A. Titchmarsh.

## SURREY v WARWICKSHIRE

### Played at The Oval, May 4, 5, 6, 1903

Very fortunately for Warwickshire the ground had been rendered so soft by rain on Sunday that the match could not be commenced until Tuesday. As a result of this delay, the visitors were able to enjoy the assistance of Hargreave, who only arrived from Australia on the Monday evening. What the services of the slow bowler meant to Warwickshire the score shows, no fewer than 15 wickets falling to that player at a cost of 76 runs. An innings on each side was completed on Tuesday, Surrey, who committed a lot of blunders in the field, losing their last eight wickets for 26 runs. Warwickshire's fielding presented a refreshing contrast to that of the home side. Further rain prevented any cricket on Wednesday until after two o'clock but then Byrne soon declared, and the Surrey batsmen being almost helpless against Hargreave on a difficult wicket, Warwickshire won by 126 runs.

## Warwickshire

| | | | |
|---|---|---|---|
| J. Devey c Hayes b Jackson | 2 | – c Lees b Montgomery | 14 |
| S. P. Kinneir c Hayward b Montgomery | 32 | – b Montgomery | 0 |
| Mr J. F. Byrne b Montgomery | 22 | – c Davis b Jackson | 14 |
| W. G. Quaife lbw b Jackson | 6 | | |
| C. Charlesworth c Hayes b Jackson | 64 | – b Jackson | 7 |
| A. A. Lilley c Montgomery b Jackson | 44 | – not out | 14 |
| S. Santall c Walker b Jackson | 0 | | |
| Moorhouse not out | 34 | – not out | 5 |
| Whittle c Lockwood b Jackson | 0 | | |
| S. Hargreave c Lees b Hayward | 9 | | |
| Hopkins c Lockwood b Jackson | 1 | | |
| B 1, l-b 7 | 8 | B 1 | 1 |
| | 222 | (4 wkts dec.) | 55 |

## Surrey

| | | | |
|---|---|---|---|
| T. Hayward c Moorhouse b Santall | 7 | – c Charlesworth b Hargreave | 2 |
| F. Holland c Lilley b Santall | 20 | – c Lilley b Santall | 16 |
| E. G. Hayes c Charlesworth b Hargreave | 27 | – st Lilley b Hargreave | 18 |
| W. H. Lockwood c Devey b Hargreave | 2 | – lbw b Hargreave | 0 |
| Mr E. Wiltshire c and b Hargreave | 0 | – c Santall b Hargreave | 2 |
| Mr L. Walker b Hargreave | 4 | – b Hargreave | 7 |
| Montgomery c Hargreave b Santall | 3 | – c Charlesworth b Hargreave | 0 |
| Davis b Santall | 0 | – not out | 14 |
| W. Lees lbw b Hargreave | 5 | – b Hargreave | 1 |
| A. Stedman not out | 5 | – c Byrne b Hargreave | 8 |
| M. Jackson b Hargreave | 8 | – b Hargreave | 0 |
| B 1 | 1 | B 1 | 1 |
| | 82 | | 69 |

### Surrey Bowling

| | Overs | Mdns | Runs | Wkts | Overs | Mdns | Runs | Wkts |
|---|---|---|---|---|---|---|---|---|
| Jackson | 44.5 | 10 | 96 | 7 | 14 | 3 | 31 | 2 |
| Lees | 9 | 2 | 28 | — | | | | |
| Montgomery | 32 | 7 | 85 | 2 | 13 | 4 | 23 | 2 |
| Hayward | 4 | 2 | 5 | 1 | | | | |

### Warwickshire Bowling

| | Overs | Mdns | Runs | Wkts | Overs | Mdns | Runs | Wkts |
|---|---|---|---|---|---|---|---|---|
| Hargreave | 15.4 | 4 | 41 | 6 | 16.3 | 4 | 35 | 9 |
| Santall | 15 | 7 | 33 | 4 | 16 | 5 | 33 | 1 |

Umpires: J. E. West and A. F. White.

## SURREY v MIDDLESEX

Played at The Oval, August 27, 28, 1903

Middlesex had only to escape defeat in this match – the last on their programme – to be sure of the championship, but they did much more than that, playing fine cricket all round and gaining a splendid victory by an innings and 94 runs. They pursued very cautious tactics on Monday taking, on a somewhat slow but not particularly difficult wicket, nearly five hours to make 230 runs. They lost their first four wickets for 55, but G. W. Beldam, as in the game at Lord's, scored over a hundred, playing the Surrey bowling with marked skill and unfailing patience for four hours and forty minutes. Wells helped to put on 57, and E. A. Beldam to add 70. Rain on Monday evening placed Surrey at a considerable disadvantage. Their first innings proved a sensational affair, Holland and Hayward raising the score to 33 for the first wicket, and the whole side being out in an hour and a quarter for 57. Trott and Hearne – both in great form – were admirably supported by their colleagues. Trott three times disposed of two batsmen in consecutive overs, his analysis reading: w w 1 – 1 – | w – – – w – | – – w – w –. Thanks to Bush and Dowson, Surrey in their second innings had 100 on the board with seven wickets in hand, but then Wells carried all before him.

### Middlesex

| | |
|---|---|
| Mr P. F. Warner lbw b Richardson ....... 3 | A. E. Trott c Holland b Richardson ....... 40 |
| Mr L. J. Moon b Lees ................. 1 | Mr G. MacGregor run out ............. 33 |
| Mr G. W. Beldam c Strudwick b McDonell .112 | Mr F. H. Hunt lbw b McDonell ......... 2 |
| Mr J. Douglas c Strudwick b Richardson .. 9 | J. T. Hearne not out ................. 3 |
| Mr B. J. T. Bosanquet c Strudwick | |
|         b McDonell . 18 |         B 3, n-b 2 .................. 5 |
| Mr C. M. Wells c Hayward b Lees ....... 30 | — |
| Mr E. A. Beldam c Strudwick b Lees ...... 25 | 281 |

### Surrey

| | | |
|---|---|---|
| F. C. Holland c Hunt b Hearne ................. 10 | – b Hearne .................... 11 |
| T. Hayward b Trott ....................... 14 | – b Hearne .................... 5 |
| E. G. Hayes c Wells b Trott ................... 2 | – c Wells b Trott ............... 10 |
| Mr E. M. Dowson c Hunt b Trott .............. 0 | – b Hearne .................... 36 |
| Capt. H. S. Bush c Wells b Hearne ............. 15 | – c Hearne b Wells .......... 42 |
| W. H. Lockwood b Trott .................... 0 | – st MacGregor b Wells ........ 0 |
| Mr L. Walker c MacGregor b Trott ............. 0 | – not out .................... 9 |
| W. Lees lbw b Trott ....................... 0 | – st MacGregor b Wells ........ 0 |
| Mr H. C. McDonell not out ................... 2 | – c MacGregor b Wells ......... 0 |
| H. Strudwick b Hearne ..................... 0 | – c Warner b Wells ............ 0 |
| T. Richardson c Douglas b Hearne ............. 2 | – run out .................... 10 |
| B 10, l-b 2 ........................ 12 | B 7 .................... 7 |
| — | — |
| 57 | 130 |

### Surrey Bowling

| | Overs | Mdns | Runs | Wkts |
|---|---|---|---|---|
| Richardson ....... | 39 | 11 | 93 | 3 |
| Lees ............. | 26 | 6 | 51 | 3 |
| McDonell ......... | 26 | 7 | 72 | 3 |
| Lockwood ........ | 16 | 4 | 45 | — |
| Hayes ........... | 6 | — | 15 | |

### Middlesex Bowling

| | Overs | Mdns | Runs | Wkts | Overs | Mdns | Runs | Wkts |
|---|---|---|---|---|---|---|---|---|
| Hearne .......... | 12.4 | 3 | 26 | 4 | 27 | 13 | 54 | 3 |
| Trott ........... | 12 | 5 | 19 | 6 | 17 | 6 | 27 | 1 |
| G. W. Beldam ..... | | | | | 4 | — | 8 | — |
| Hunt ........... | | | | | 6 | 4 | 8 | — |
| Wells ........... | | | | | 12 | 4 | 26 | 5 |

Umpires: A. Shaw and J. Moss.

## SURREY v LEICESTERSHIRE

Played at The Oval, August 31, September 1, 2, 1903

For two days Leicestershire had the upper hand, but Surrey, set 280 to make in three hours and three-quarters accomplished this task five minutes before time, and so won, after a magnificent finish, by three wickets. Holland and Hayward gave the side a fine start, putting on 108 runs in eighty-five minutes, but the victory was mainly the work of Hayes, who played a most valuable and masterly innings, his driving being superb. Knight would no doubt have earned the distinction of making two separate hundreds could he have found someone to stay with him. He batted with marvellous care and judgment, and gave no actual chance either time. Leicestershire entered upon the concluding stage of the match 182 runs on with seven wickets in hand. Wood sprained his ankle.

### Leicestershire

| | | | |
|---|---:|---|---:|
| Mr C. J. B. Wood b Richardson | 0 | – absent hurt | 0 |
| H. Whitehead c Strudwick b Richardson | 18 | – c Hayward b Lees | 1 |
| A. E. Knight c Hayward b Lees | 144 | – not out | 91 |
| J. H. King c Strudwick b Lockwood | 23 | – c Lockwood b Richardson | 14 |
| Mr V. F. S. Crawford b McDonell | 12 | – c Strudwick b Richardson | 6 |
| Mr C. E. de Trafford c Strudwick b Richardson | 36 | – c and b McDonell | 25 |
| Mr R. T. Crawford b Richardson | 2 | – st Strudwick b McDonell | 6 |
| G. Gill st Strudwick b Hayes | 40 | – b McDonell | 10 |
| Mr W. W. Odell c Bush b Dowson | 9 | – c Strudwick b Lees | 0 |
| Allsopp not out | 4 | – b McDonell | 2 |
| J. P. Whiteside b Lees | 6 | – c Hayes b Lees | 0 |
| B 11, w 2, n-b 5 | 18 | | |
| | **312** | | **155** |

### Surrey

| | | | |
|---|---:|---|---:|
| F. C. Holland lbw b Gill | 6 | – c V. F. S. Crawford b Odell | 66 |
| T. Hayward run out | 16 | – run out | 55 |
| E. G. Hayes c R. T. Crawford b King | 31 | – not out | 105 |
| Capt. H. S. Bush lbw b Odell | 3 | – c Whitehead b Gill | 19 |
| Mr E. M. Dowson lbw b King | 18 | – c King b Gill | 0 |
| W. H. Lockwood not out | 60 | – c and b Gill | 13 |
| Mr L. Walker c King b R. T. Crawford | 36 | – run out | 2 |
| W. Lees b R. T. Crawford | 0 | – c R. T. Crawford b Gill | 10 |
| Mr H. C. McDonell b R. T. Crawford | 3 | – not out | 3 |
| H. Strudwick b King | 1 | | |
| T. Richardson b R. T. Crawford | 4 | | |
| B 3, l-b 3, n-b 4 | 10 | B 3, w 2, n-b 2 | 7 |
| | **188** | | **280** |

### Surrey Bowling

| | Overs | Mdns | Runs | Wkts | Overs | Mdns | Runs | Wkts |
|---|---:|---:|---:|---:|---:|---:|---:|---:|
| Richardson | 25 | 7 | 59 | 4 | 24 | 5 | 62 | 2 |
| Lees | 28.1 | 8 | 57 | 2 | 17 | 3 | 51 | 3 |
| McDonell | 21 | — | 63 | 1 | 24 | 9 | 42 | 4 |
| Lockwood | 18 | 3 | 78 | 1 | | | | |
| Hayes | 6 | 2 | 16 | 1 | | | | |
| Dowson | 5 | — | 21 | 1 | | | | |

## Leicestershire Bowling

| | Overs | Mdns | Runs | Wkts | Overs | Mdns | Runs | Wkts |
|---|---|---|---|---|---|---|---|---|
| R. Crawford ...... | 13.5 | 3 | 43 | 4 | 10 | 2 | 37 | — |
| Gill .............. | 15 | 4 | 42 | 1 | 20 | 2 | 88 | 4 |
| Odell ............ | 15 | 4 | 39 | 1 | 25 | 6 | 73 | 1 |
| King ............ | 15 | 4 | 26 | 3 | 11 | 2 | 44 | — |
| Allsopp ......... | 8 | 2 | 21 | — | 5 | 1 | 18 | — |
| Whitehead ........ | 6 | 2 | 7 | — | 4 | — | 13 | — |

Umpires: A. Pike and G. Bean.

## SURREY v SUSSEX

### Played at The Oval, September 3, 4, 5, 1903

So heavy was the scoring in the concluding county match of the season that 965 runs were obtained for the loss of only 17 wickets, and thus the game terminated in a draw. Sussex, who on the opening day made 332 for the loss of three batsmen, might very well have declared at lunch time on Tuesday with five wickets down for 483, but the innings was allowed to proceed until a quarter to four. Twenty minutes were thrown away by an unnecessary tea interval on Thursday, bad light prevented cricket after twenty minutes past five on Friday, and a storm during the night delayed play on Saturday until one o'clock, when, with the pitch drying slowly, Surrey experienced no great difficulty in saving the game. Fry and Vine laid the foundation of the big total of Sussex by making 153 for the first wicket. Vine's 104 was his first hundred since the season of 1899. Brann helped Ranjitsinhji to add 122, and Newham assisted his captain to put on 141, both batting in capital style. The big feature of the match was, of course, the cricket of Ranjitsinhji, who gave a truly superb display, hitting all round the wicket with equal skill and facility, and giving no chance during a stay of four hours and a half. Sussex made their 600 runs in eight hours and a quarter. The Surrey bowling lacked sting, and their fielding was slack. Bush, apart from a chance at the wicket before he had scored, played excellent cricket. Hayward helped him to make 102. The batting of Surrey generally was very bright.

### Sussex

| | | | |
|---|---|---|---|
| Mr C. B. Fry c Hayward b Lees ......... | 81 | A. E. Relf lbw b McDonell .............. | 11 |
| J. Vine c Bush b McDonell ............. | 104 | Mr R. B. Heygate not out .............. | 39 |
| E. H. Killick run out ................... | 28 | H. R Butt not out .................... | 22 |
| K. S. Ranjitsinhji c Richardson b McDonell | 204 | B 1, l-b 5, n-b 1 .............. | 7 |
| Mr G. Brann c Hayes b Lees ............ | 54 | | |
| Mr W. Newham b Richardson .......... | 50 | (7 wkts dec.) 600 | |

G. Cox and F. W. Tate did not bat.

### Surrey

| | | | |
|---|---|---|---|
| Capt. H. S. Bush c Butt b Killick ......... | 78 | Mr H. C. McDonell st Butt b Relf ........ | 46 |
| Mr E. M. Dowson b Cox ............... | 35 | H. Strudwick b Killick ................ | 4 |
| T. Hayward c and b Killick ............ | 54 | T. Richardson run out ................ | 2 |
| F. C. Holland c Newham b Relf .......... | 39 | Rushby not out ..................... | 3 |
| E. G. Hayes c Newham b Relf .......... | 54 | B 10, l-b 4 .................... | 14 |
| W. H. Lockwood b Relf ............... | 6 | | |
| W. Lees c Heygate b Relf .............. | 29 | | 365 |

**Surrey Bowling**

|  | Overs | Mdns | Runs | Wkts |
|---|---|---|---|---|
| McDonell . . . . . . . . | 37 | 9 | 99 | 3 |
| Rushby . . . . . . . . . | 28 | 1 | 116 | — |
| Richardson . . . . . . . | 47 | 4 | 158 | 1 |
| Lees . . . . . . . . . . . . | 39 | 6 | 109 | 2 |
| Lockwood . . . . . . . . | 14 | — | 62 | — |
| Hayes . . . . . . . . . . | 7 | 1 | 25 | — |
| Dowson . . . . . . . . . | 4 | — | 24 | — |

**Sussex Bowling**

|  | Overs | Mdns | Runs | Wkts |
|---|---|---|---|---|
| Relf . . . . . . . . . . . . | 42 | 12 | 123 | 5 |
| Cox . . . . . . . . . . . . | 30 | 7 | 75 | 1 |
| Tate . . . . . . . . . . . . | 19 | 6 | 59 | — |
| Killick . . . . . . . . . . | 24 | 4 | 90 | 3 |
| Brann . . . . . . . . . . . | 1 | — | 3 | — |

Umpires: W. Hearn and C. E. Richardson.

## SURREY v WARWICKSHIRE

Played at The Oval, May 22, 23, 24, 1905

The wicket was a much better one than that prepared for the Sussex match, and Warwickshire, on winning the toss, ought to have made a larger score than 235. The total was up to 174 with only three men out, but the last six wickets went down in little more than an hour for 61 runs. Byrne played wonderfully well, giving no chance in his 88. Surrey, after a time, found run-getting an easy matter, and at the end of the day they had scored 109 for two wickets. On the second day the bat beat the ball to such an extent that 521 runs were scored in five hours and three-quarters, only ten wickets doing down. Hayes played well, but the feature of Surrey's innings was the hitting of Dalmeny. At one point the Surrey captain scored 31 runs off fourteen balls, and altogether he hit up 116 out of 203 in an hour and forty minutes. Warwickshire had to face a balance of 244, but this did not trouble them. They scored 151 for two wickets on the second afternoon, and were batting all the third day. Quaife played a superb innings, only making two false hits during a stay of six hours and twenty minutes.

### Warwickshire

| | | | |
|---|---|---|---|
| Mr J. F. Byrne c Stedman b Lees . . . . . . . . . . . . . . . 88 | – c Davis b Sheppard . . . . . . . . . . . . | 46 |
| S. P. Kinneir c Holland b Sheppard . . . . . . . . . . . . . . 39 | – c Stedman b Hayes . . . . . . . . . . . . | 99 |
| C. Charlesworth b Davis . . . . . . . . . . . . . . . . . . . . . . 2 | – c Davis b Sheppard . . . . . . . . . . . . | 0 |
| W. G. Quaife lbw b Lees . . . . . . . . . . . . . . . . . . . . . 21 | – not out . . . . . . . . . . . . . . . . . . . . . . .255 |
| C. S. Baker c Baker b Hayes . . . . . . . . . . . . . . . . . . 20 | – c Gooder b Lees . . . . . . . . . . . . | 45 |
| A. A. Lilley lbw b Hayes . . . . . . . . . . . . . . . . . . . . . . 0 | – b Lees . . . . . . . . . . . . . . . . . . . . . | 12 |
| A. E. Whittle c Hobbs b Hayes . . . . . . . . . . . . . . . . . 15 | – c Baker b Gooder . . . . . . . . . . . . . | 17 |
| F. Moorhouse b Lees . . . . . . . . . . . . . . . . . . . . . . . . 3 | – b Hayward . . . . . . . . . . . . . . . . . . . | 29 |
| S. Santall not out . . . . . . . . . . . . . . . . . . . . . . . . . . 24 | – not out . . . . . . . . . . . . . . . . . . . . . . | 56 |
| Lynes lbw b Hayes . . . . . . . . . . . . . . . . . . . . . . . . . . 0 | | |
| S. Hargreave b Lees . . . . . . . . . . . . . . . . . . . . . . . . 9 | | |
| B 11, l-b 3 . . . . . . . . . . . . . . . . . . . . . . . . 14 | B 19, l-b 5, w 2 . . . . . . . . . . | 26 |
| | **235** | | **585** |

## Surrey

| | |
|---|---|
| T. Hayward c Byrne b Hargreave ........ 13 | Mr R. A. Sheppard b Hargreave ......... 24 |
| J. B. Hobbs c and b Hargreave .......... 40 | W. Lees c Quaife b Lynes .............. 18 |
| E. G. Hayes b Quaife .................. 99 | W. Gooder run out .................... 35 |
| A. Baker c Charlesworth b Lynes ........ 28 | A. Stedman not out ................... 7 |
| F. C. Holland c Hargreave b Quaife ...... 47 | B 8, l-b 4, w 4 ................ 16 |
| W. Davis c Hargreave b Quaife .......... 36 | |
| Lord Dalmeny st Lilley b Quaife .........116 | 479 |

## Surrey Bowling

| | Overs | Mdns | Runs | Wkts | Overs | Mdns | Runs | Wkts |
|---|---|---|---|---|---|---|---|---|
| Lees ............. | 32.4 | 8 | 77 | 4 | 44 | 10 | 118 | 2 |
| Gooder .......... | 13 | 3 | 49 | — | 24 | 7 | 72 | 1 |
| Hayes ........... | 18 | 4 | 46 | 4 | 26 | 6 | 83 | 1 |
| Sheppard ......... | 15 | 5 | 25 | 1 | 18 | 7 | 34 | 2 |
| Davis ............ | 5 | — | 24 | 1 | 29 | 5 | 106 | — |
| Hobbs ........... | | | | | 10 | 2 | 29 | — |
| Hayward ......... | | | | | 6 | — | 24 | 1 |
| Holland .......... | | | | | 6 | 1 | 23 | — |
| Baker ............ | | | | | 9 | 1 | 31 | — |
| Dalmeny ......... | | | | | 2 | — | 21 | — |
| Stedman ......... | | | | | 4 | — | 18 | — |

## Warwickshire Bowling

| | Overs | Mdns | Runs | Wkts |
|---|---|---|---|---|
| Hargreave ........ | 38 | 8 | 114 | 3 |
| Santall ........... | 22 | 1 | 98 | — |
| Lynes ............ | 28.5 | 1 | 128 | 2 |
| Quaife ........... | 21 | 1 | 82 | 4 |
| Byrne ............ | 5 | — | 25 | — |
| Moorhouse ....... | 4 | — | 16 | — |

Umpires: A. A. White and J. Phillips.

## SURREY v KENT

### Played at The Oval, August 31, September 1, 2, 1905

For the seventh time in first-class cricket at The Oval there was a tie match. Dalmeny won the toss, but as there seemed every likelihood of the wicket proving difficult, he ventured to put Kent in first. Up to a certain point his policy turned out very badly, and when an innings had been completed on each side Kent held a lead of 77 runs. This looked like a winning advantage, but so splendidly did Lees bowl that Kent's second innings was finished off in two hours and a half. Surrey then went in to get 162, and at the drawing of stumps on Friday they had scored 116 for four wickets. They fully expected to win the next morning, but Blythe bowled wonderfully well, and two wickets were thrown away by sheer impatience. The result was that when Knox, the last man, joined Smith eight runs were still required. Smith made seven of them but then, in hitting a tempting ball a little wide of the off stump, he was caught at third man. By keeping his head and bowling with rare judgment at the finish Blythe clearly saved Kent from defeat.

### Kent

| | | | | |
|---|---|---|---|---|
| Mr E. W. Dillon c Hayward b Smith | 19 | – b Lees | | 9 |
| A. Hearne lbw b Hayes | 28 | – c Baker b Lees | | 20 |
| James Seymour c Hayes b Smith | 3 | – b Knox | | 1 |
| Mr S. H. Day b Crawford | 61 | – b Smith | | 26 |
| Mr J. R. Mason b Knox | 20 | – c Hayward b Lees | | 1 |
| E. Humphreys b Smith | 15 | – c Hayward b Lees | | 10 |
| Mr A. P. Day c and b Smith | 24 | – lbw b Smith | | 6 |
| Mr C. H. B. Marsham c Hayes b Smith | 0 | – b Lees | | 0 |
| H. R. Murrell c and b Knox | 11 | – not out | | 4 |
| F. H. Huish not out | 11 | – b Lees | | 0 |
| C. Blythe c Dalmeny b Knox | 0 | – b Lees | | 1 |
| B 10 | 10 | B 3, w 2, n-b 1 | | 6 |
| | **202** | | | **84** |

### Surrey

| | | | | |
|---|---|---|---|---|
| T. Hayward c and b Blythe | 8 | – c and b Mason | | 40 |
| F. C. Holland c and b Mason | 5 | – c Mason b Humphreys | | 21 |
| E. G. Hayes c Dillon b Mason | 0 | – b Blythe | | 2 |
| A. Baker c Mason b Humphreys | 23 | – st Huish b Hearne | | 28 |
| J. B. Hobbs c Mason b Blythe | 6 | – b Blythe | | 20 |
| Mr J. N. Crawford b Humphreys | 31 | – c Mason b Blythe | | 14 |
| Lord Dalmeny lbw b Hearne | 16 | – c Murrell b Blythe | | 0 |
| W. Lees c Huish b Blythe | 4 | – c Marsham b Hearne | | 0 |
| W. C. Smith b Blythe | 15 | – c Murrell b Blythe | | 21 |
| H. Strudwick c Dillon b Blythe | 2 | – c Mason b Blythe | | 1 |
| Mr N. A. Knox not out | 1 | – not out | | 0 |
| B 14 | 14 | B 11, l-b 2, n-b 1 | | 14 |
| | **125** | | | **161** |

### Surrey Bowling

| | Overs | Mdns | Runs | Wkts | Overs | Mdns | Runs | Wkts |
|---|---|---|---|---|---|---|---|---|
| Crawford | 24 | 7 | 55 | 1 | 3 | — | 15 | — |
| Smith | 22 | 5 | 63 | 5 | 12 | 6 | 17 | 2 |
| Lees | 4 | — | 12 | — | 24.4 | 10 | 29 | 7 |
| Hayes | 6 | 1 | 14 | 1 | | | | |
| Knox | 16.3 | 5 | 48 | 3 | 9 | 1 | 17 | 1 |

### Kent Bowling

| | Overs | Mdns | Runs | Wkts | Overs | Mdns | Runs | Wkts |
|---|---|---|---|---|---|---|---|---|
| Mason | 17 | 8 | 51 | 2 | 11 | 1 | 36 | 1 |
| Blythe | 21.3 | 10 | 45 | 5 | 26.2 | 10 | 47 | 6 |
| Humphreys | 7 | 4 | 11 | 2 | 19 | 9 | 28 | 1 |
| Hearne | 2 | — | 4 | 1 | 19 | 7 | 36 | 2 |

Umpires: T. Mycroft and A. A. White.

## SURREY IN 1906

J. N. Crawford deserves a paragraph all to himself. He was the all-round man of the Surrey eleven just as Hayward, Hayes, and Hobbs were the batsmen and Knox and Lees the bowlers. Confining himself to the county matches he scored 1064 runs and took 111 wickets, and it is worthy of special notice that he is the youngest player who has ever accomplished this double feat in first-class cricket. It was most gratifying to find him in such bowling form as in 1905 there seemed some reason to fear that batting would engage all his attention. At times he bowled astonishingly well, perhaps his best work being done on the second day of the Yorkshire match at Sheffield. On that afternoon he was great, combining a rare amount of spin with extreme accuracy. Only twenty on the first of December, Crawford should be an England cricketer in the immediate future. Few men, except W. G. Grace and A. G. Steel, have won a bigger position in the cricket world at the same age.

## SURREY v SUSSEX

### Played at The Oval, June 11, 12, 13, 1906

Returning home after the memorable week in the Midlands, during which Hayward obtained his four successive hundreds, the Surrey team, despite a delightful innings by their great batsman, found themselves with six wickets down against Sussex for 137 runs. Lees, however, hit away with refreshing vigour and, with Crawford as his partner, made 137 out of 186 in two hours, putting together the highest score of his career. For Sussex, Smith and Albert Relf scored 143 during a partnership of rather more than two hours, but the batting of the side as a whole was rather laborious. In Surrey's second innings, Hayward and Hobbs made 134 in ninety-five minutes, for the first wicket. Sussex, set 354 to get to win, cut up very badly and suffered defeat by 289 runs, Knox bowling at his best.

### Surrey

| | | | |
|---|---|---|---|
| T. Hayward c and b A. E. Relf | 54 | – c Cox b Vine | 69 |
| J. B. Hobbs c Relf b Vine | 19 | – c A. E. Relf b Vine | 61 |
| E. G. Hayes b Vine | 39 | – not out | 52 |
| A. Baker st Butt b Vine | 11 | – not out | 30 |
| F. C. Holland c Cox b A. E. Relf | 11 | | |
| Mr J. N. Crawford not out | 91 | | |
| Lord Dalmeny c R. Relf b A. E. Relf | 1 | – st Butt b Vine | 4 |
| W. Lees lbw b Leach | 137 | | |
| A. W. Spring c Relf b Cox | 19 | | |
| H. Strudwick c Butt b A. E. Relf | 1 | | |
| Mr N. A. Knox c Vine b A. E. Relf | 22 | | |
| B 7, l-b 3 | 10 | B 3, l-b 2, w 1 | 6 |
| | **415** | **(3 wkts dec.)** | **222** |

### Sussex

| | | | |
|---|---|---|---|
| Mr C. L. A. Smith c Spring b Knox | 77 | – b Lees | 9 |
| J. Vine c Holland b Knox | 0 | – b Knox | 3 |
| E. H. Killick b Lees | 11 | – c Crawford b Knox | 0 |
| A. E. Relf c Hayward b Knox | 76 | – b Knox | 12 |
| G. Cox c Knox b Spring | 16 | – b Knox | 5 |
| R. Relf lbw b Spring | 23 | – b Knox | 0 |
| G. Leach b Knox | 29 | – c Strudwick b Lees | 7 |
| John Seymour b Knox | 10 | – c Strudwick b Knox | 0 |
| Mr H. L. Simms c Hayes b Spring | 14 | – c Hayward b Lees | 10 |
| E. B. Dwyer b Knox | 0 | – b Knox | 18 |
| H. R. Butt not out | 12 | – not out | 0 |
| B 14, l-b 1, w 1 | 16 | | |
| | **284** | | **64** |

**Sussex Bowling**

|  | Overs | Mdns | Runs | Wkts | Overs | Mdns | Runs | Wkts |
|---|---|---|---|---|---|---|---|---|
| Dwyer ........... | 15 | 1 | 78 | — | 6 | 1 | 21 | — |
| A. E. Relf ......... | 31.1 | 8 | 75 | 5 | 1 | — | 8 | — |
| Vine ............. | 29 | 9 | 83 | 3 | 21 | 3 | 83 | 3 |
| Leach ............ | 15 | 2 | 70 | 1 | 11 | — | 62 | — |
| Cox ............. | 18 | 4 | 46 | 1 | 14 | 2 | 42 | — |
| Killick ........... | 16 | 2 | 53 | — | | | | |

**Surrey Bowling**

|  | Overs | Mdns | Runs | Wkts | Overs | Mdns | Runs | Wkts |
|---|---|---|---|---|---|---|---|---|
| Lees ............. | 31 | 8 | 87 | 1 | 13.2 | 4 | 38 | 3 |
| Knox ............ | 30 | 7 | 82 | 6 | 13 | 4 | 26 | 7 |
| Crawford ........ | 14 | 1 | 50 | — | | | | |
| Spring ........... | 10.2 | 2 | 35 | 3 | | | | |
| Hayes ........... | 4 | 1 | 14 | — | | | | |

Umpires: J. E. West and J. Carlin.

# SURREY IN 1907

*Patron* – HRH The Prince of Wales

*President* – Lord Alverstone

*Treasurer* – Mr Jeremiah Colman

*Secretary* – Mr W. Findlay, The Oval, SE

*Captain* – Lord Dalmeny

Though they had to be content with fourth place in the championship, Surrey had a very brilliant season. They were never beaten at The Oval, they shared with Nottinghamshire the distinction of beating the South Africans, and by general consent they were, on hard wickets, the best county team of the year. Their fine work was all the more creditable as they had serious disadvantages to contend against. N. A. Knox, who had in 1906 been the most dangerous bowler in England, quite failed to reproduce his form, and at the height of the season a badly bruised foot kept Walter Lees out of the eleven for the best part of a month. If Knox had been his former self and Lees had escaped injury, there would without a doubt have been a still more flattering story to tell. Surrey's weak points were the same as before. They sadly wanted a left-handed bowler, and on two critical occasions, against Lancashire at Old Trafford and Kent at Blackheath, their batting went to pieces on slow wickets. Knox, as it happened, was at his best against the South Africans, his great pace being the chief factor in a memorable victory by 85 runs. In scarcely any other match was he the Knox of 1906. The extent of his falling off may be gathered from the fact that in county matches he took only 44 wickets for over 23 runs apiece, as against 117 for something over 18 runs each. The wet weather was all against him, but even on fine days his bowling lacked the devil that had caused him to be so much feared. He has, it is announced, done with first-class cricket, it being his intention to take up singing as a profession. He has had a brief career, but he has done enough for fame. At his best he was a great fast bowler, and his form in the Gentlemen and Players match at Lord's in 1906 will never be forgotten. There has been no such fast bowling for the Gentlemen within the experience of cricketers now before the public.

## SURREY v GENTLEMEN OF ENGLAND

Played at The Oval, April 20, 21, 22, 1908

Contested in bitterly cold weather, this Easter Monday match possessed a sentimental interest inasmuch as it was the only first-class contest in which W. G. Grace appeared during the season. The famous veteran kept up his wicket for two hours on Tuesday and played very well in the follow-on, but his side suffered defeat by an innings and 41 runs. Although Hobbs and Hayward failed, Surrey occupied the wickets for the whole of the first day, scoring 381 for the loss of eight batsmen. Several members of the team shaped remarkably well considering the early period of the year, and after seven wickets had fallen, Lees, in company with Busher, a Barnes Club amateur, hit up 97 out of 141 in just over an hour, bowlers and fieldsmen being greatly handicapped by the wintry conditions. In addition to scoring 52, Busher bowled in very promising form. Frank Crawford hit with great power in the first innings of the Gentlemen of England. Leveson-Gower – just elected as captain of Surrey – in fielding a ball had the misfortune to injure his thumb. Early on Monday morning The Oval was covered with snow.

### Surrey

| | |
|---|---|
| J. B. Hobbs b Brearley . . . . . . . . . . . . . . . . . 0 | Mr H. D. G. Leveson-Gower c Staples |
| A. Marshal b Cameron . . . . . . . . . . . . . . . 62 | b Cameron . 4 |
| E. G. Hayes c Staples b Brearley . . . . . . . . 56 | W. Lees b Lawton . . . . . . . . . . . . . . . . . . . 97 |
| F. C. Holland c Lawton b Cameron . . . . . . 56 | F. E. Smith c Staples b Brearley . . . . . . . . . 5 |
| Mr J. N. Crawford c V. Crawford | H. Strudwick not out . . . . . . . . . . . . . . . . . 2 |
| b Cameron . 46 | B 6, l-b 2, n-b 2 . . . . . . . . . . . . . . 10 |
| T. Hayward c and b Cameron . . . . . . . . . . 0 | — |
| Mr S. E. Busher c and b Lawton . . . . . . . . 52 | 390 |

### Gentlemen of England

| | | | |
|---|---|---|---|
| Mr H. D. Keigwin b F. E. Smith . . . . . . . . . . . . . . 0 | – b Busher . . . . . . . . . . . . . . . . . . . . . 11 |
| Mr W. G. Grace b Busher . . . . . . . . . . . . . . . . . . . . 15 | – b Busher . . . . . . . . . . . . . . . . . . . . . 25 |
| Mr A. E. Lawton b F. E. Smith . . . . . . . . . . . . . . . 19 | – b Busher . . . . . . . . . . . . . . . . . . . . . 4 |
| Mr C. T. A. Wilkinson b Lees . . . . . . . . . . . . . . . 0 | – b Crawford . . . . . . . . . . . . . . . . . . 39 |
| Mr V. F. S. Crawford c sub. b Lees . . . . . . . . . . . 91 | – c Holland b Busher . . . . . . . . . . . 9 |
| Mr R. T. Crawford b Busher . . . . . . . . . . . . . . . . 55 | – b Crawford . . . . . . . . . . . . . . . . . . 1 |
| Mr J. J. Cameron b Lees . . . . . . . . . . . . . . . . . . . . 0 | – b Crawford . . . . . . . . . . . . . . . . . . 8 |
| Mr R. M. Bell b Busher . . . . . . . . . . . . . . . . . . . . 9 | – c Hobbs b Smith . . . . . . . . . . . . . . 2 |
| Mr C. V. Staples b Marshal . . . . . . . . . . . . . . . . . 1 | – c Busher b Smith . . . . . . . . . . . . . . 14 |
| Mr P. R. May not out . . . . . . . . . . . . . . . . . . . . . . . 17 | – c Smith b Crawford . . . . . . . . . . . 4 |
| Mr W. Brearley c Holland b Marshal . . . . . . . . . . . 5 | – not out . . . . . . . . . . . . . . . . . . . . . . 10 |
| B 4, l-b 3 . . . . . . . . . . . . . . . . . . . . . . . . 7 | B 3 . . . . . . . . . . . . . . . . . . . . . 3 |
| | — | | — |
| | 219 | | 130 |

### Gentlemen of England Bowling

| | Overs | Mdns | Runs | Wkts |
|---|---|---|---|---|
| Brearley . . . . . . . . . . | 35 | 4 | 132 | 3 |
| R. Crawford . . . . . . | 8 | 1 | 46 | — |
| Bell . . . . . . . . . . . . . | 4 | — | 24 | — |
| Keigwin . . . . . . . . . . | 4 | — | 25 | — |
| May . . . . . . . . . . . . . | 10 | 4 | 20 | — |
| Cameron . . . . . . . . . | 1 | 4 | 83 | 5 |
| Grace . . . . . . . . . . . . | 2 | — | 5 | — |
| Wilkinson . . . . . . . . | 4 | — | 18 | — |
| Lawton . . . . . . . . . . | 5 | 1 | 27 | 2 |

**Surrey Bowling**

|              | Overs | Mdns | Runs | Wkts | Overs | Mdns | Runs | Wkts |
| ------------ | ----- | ---- | ---- | ---- | ----- | ---- | ---- | ---- |
| Lees ............. | 21 | 8 | 75 | 3 | 7 | 1 | 32 | — |
| F. E. Smith ....... | 19 | 5 | 35 | 2 | 8.4 | 1 | 33 | 2 |
| Crawford ........ | 7 | 1 | 35 | — | 11 | 3 | 21 | 4 |
| Busher .......... | 12 | 1 | 51 | 3 | 9 | 1 | 41 | 4 |
| Marshal ......... | 4.1 | 1 | 16 | 2 | | | | |

Umpires: A. White and A. Millward.

## SURREY IN 1909

*Patron –* HRH The Prince of Wales

*President –* Lord Alverstone

*Treasurer –* Sir Jeremiah Colman

*Secretary –* Mr W. Findlay, The Oval, SE

*Captain –* Mr H. D. G. Leveson-Gower

If everything had gone well Surrey might have had a very brilliant season in 1909. As it was, however, many misfortunes told against the side, and in the end Surrey had to be content with fifth place in the championship, seven defeats being a heavy set-off against sixteen victories. Still for this disappointing record there was compensation in being the only county to beat the Australians. Surrey won a remarkable game in May by five runs, after the odds had looked to be twenty to one against them, and played a more than creditable draw in the return match at the end of July. Surrey's greatest trouble was Hayward's almost chronic lameness. Hayward has seldom started a season in finer form, his two innings against the Australians at The Oval, and Nottinghamshire at Trent Bridge, being among the best he has ever played. Unfortunately he became very lame towards the finish of the Nottingham match, and thenceforward he was always struggling against difficulties, the mischief being water on the knee. He had to be left out of all the Test matches but one, and even in that one at Lord's he ought not to have played, the advice of his doctors being overruled. Still from time to time he was able to take his place in the Surrey eleven, and altogether in county matches he played twenty-six innings with an average of 42. But for his bad knee it is safe to say that despite the wet weather he would have had one of his greatest years. Another serious misfortune to Surrey was an accident to Hobbs, who, against Lancashire at Old Trafford, in the early days of July, had a nail nearly torn off and could not play cricket again for a month. As if these disasters were not enough, Surrey had trouble with some of their professionals and, as a crowning blow, there came the unhappy quarrel with J. N. Crawford. In the absence of Leveson-Gower, Crawford was picked to captain the side in the return match with the Australians, but he refused to act, his reason being that the committee had left out essential players, among others Rushby whose bowling had done so much to win the first match. The committee were much incensed and passed a resolution that Crawford be not again asked to play for the county. At first great secrecy was preserved over the matter, but when the facts came out the correspondence was published and many other letters appeared in the sporting papers. It seemed to outsiders that the quarrel might have been made up very easily, but bitter feeling was aroused, and in October, Crawford left England to take up an appointment as an assistant master at St. Peter's College, Adelaide. It is sad indeed that at the age of twenty-three such a player should be lost to Surrey cricket. We have been asked not to express an opinion one way or the other, as the matter is to be brought up again at the Annual Meeting of the Surrey Club in May. As to the troubles with the professionals we can say nothing, the committee having kept their own counsel. The fact, however, that the committee took the extreme step of suspending Marshal for a time, at the height of the season, suggests irregularities and insubordination. As the result of the friction with the professionals, Surrey lost Rushby, who at the end of the season gave up county cricket and signed on for Accrington in the Lancashire League.

## SURREY v YORKSHIRE

Played at The Oval, August 19, 20, 21, 1909

While the dismissal of Yorkshire for 26 – the lowest score ever made by the county – constituted the great event of this match, the cricket generally after lunch on the third day proved exciting to a degree. On Thursday when, apart from that of Haigh, the Yorkshire bowling was distinctly poor, Surrey after a bad start put together a satisfactory total and Yorkshire made 97 for two wickets. Only fifteen minutes' cricket took place on Friday, and as at lunch time on Saturday the northern county had scored 205 for the loss of seven batsmen a draw appeared inevitable, but subsequently twenty-three wickets went down for 106 runs. In Surrey's second innings Hayward and Hobbs were out for two runs, but Hayes and Marshal increased the score to 38, Rhodes and Hirst afterwards being irresistible. Eighty minutes remained for play when Yorkshire, wanting 113, went in. Three wickets fell for 12 runs, Denton and Hirst left at 16, and the last five wickets fell at 26. Rushby and Smith bowling superbly on the treacherous pitch, Surrey won with more than half-an-hour to spare by 86 runs. In Surrey's first innings Marshal, batting for two hours, drove superbly.

### Surrey

| | | | | |
|---|---|---|---|---|
| T. Hayward run out | 8 | – lbw b Hirst | 1 |
| J. B. Hobbs c Rothery b Haigh | 8 | – b Hirst | 0 |
| E. G. Hayes lbw b Haigh | 17 | – b Hirst | 19 |
| A. Marshal c Haigh b Rhodes | 110 | – c Drake b Rhodes | 16 |
| Mr M. C. Bird b Haigh | 5 | – b Rhodes | 0 |
| A. Ducat c and b Hirst | 67 | – c Rothery b Hirst | 2 |
| W. Davis lbw b Haigh | 1 | – lbw b Rhodes | 0 |
| W. C. Smith c Hunter b Haigh | 3 | – c Rhodes b Hirst | 6 |
| H. Strudwick lbw b Haigh | 20 | – b Rhodes | 7 |
| W. Lees b Haigh | 5 | – b Hirst | 8 |
| T. Rushby not out | 23 | – not out | 1 |
| B 2, l-b 3, n-b 1 | 6 | L-b 1, n-b 1 | 2 |
| | **273** | | **62** |

### Yorkshire

| | | | | |
|---|---|---|---|---|
| W. Rhodes b Lees | 5 | – b Smith | 0 |
| B. B. Wilson c Marshal b Rushby | 47 | – c Davis b Smith | 2 |
| D. Denton b Lees | 53 | – b Smith | 5 |
| J. W. Rothery lbw b Lees | 43 | – c and b Rushby | 4 |
| G. H. Hirst b Lees | 16 | – c Davis b Rushby | 0 |
| A. Drake c Ducat b Lees | 31 | – b Rushby | 6 |
| W. E. Bates lbw b Smith | 0 | – b Smith | 4 |
| J. T. Newstead c Strudwick b Smith | 4 | – b Smith | 0 |
| S. Haigh b Smith | 1 | – not out | 0 |
| Lord Hawke lbw b Lees | 4 | – b Rushby | 0 |
| D. Hunter not out | 5 | – b Rushby | 0 |
| B 4, l-b 9, n-b 1 | 14 | B 5 | 5 |
| | **223** | | **26** |

## Yorkshire Bowling

| | Overs | Mdns | Runs | Wkts | Overs | Mdns | Runs | Wkts |
|---|---|---|---|---|---|---|---|---|
| Hirst ............ | 23 | 2 | 80 | 1 | 16.1 | 5 | 27 | 6 |
| Newstead ......... | 8 | 2 | 26 | — | | | | |
| Haigh ............ | 29.4 | 5 | 65 | 7 | 6 | 2 | 12 | — |
| Drake ............ | 6 | — | 43 | — | | | | |
| Rhodes ........... | 11 | — | 53 | 1 | 10 | 3 | 21 | 4 |

## Surrey Bowling

| | Overs | Mdns | Runs | Wkts | Overs | Mdns | Runs | Wkts |
|---|---|---|---|---|---|---|---|---|
| Lees ............. | 26 | 3 | 60 | 6 | | | | |
| Rushby .......... | 26 | 9 | 54 | 1 | 8.1 | 4 | 9 | 5 |
| Smith ........... | 27.3 | 6 | 76 | 3 | 8 | 3 | 12 | 5 |
| Marshal ......... | 3 | 1 | 4 | — | | | | |
| Hayes ........... | 3 | — | 15 | — | | | | |

Umpires: G. Webb and W. Richards.

## SURREY IN 1910

The Surrey Committee found it necessary to terminate the engagement of Marshal, who only took part in five county matches and later in the year returned home to Queensland. Marshal had it in him to be a great cricketer, and one may take it for granted that Surrey would not have got rid of him without good reason. The question of the quarrel with J. N. Crawford came up at the Annual Meeting, his father, the Rev. J. C. Crawford, putting a motion on the agenda "That the Committee of the Surrey County Cricket Club be asked to rescind the resolution passed with regard to Mr J. N. Crawford." Lord Alverstone said that the resolution could not be moved as it involved a vote of want of confidence in the committee, but added that if Crawford came forward in a sportsmanlike way he would be proud to give his personal support to the step proposed. This of course meant that an apology was expected. It will be remembered that the quarrel arose out of Crawford's refusal to captain Surrey against the Australians in the second match in 1909 because certain professionals were left out of the team.

## SURREY v NORTHAMPTONSHIRE

### Played at The Oval, July 25, 26, 1910

W. C. Smith had accomplished many brilliant bowling performances before Surrey met Northamptonshire, yet in no previous match had he had batsmen so completely at his mercy. The condition of the ground helped him considerably, but still his achievement in taking fourteen wickets for 29 runs was marvellous. Making the ball get straight up or break away – apparently at will – he finished off the game with the "hat trick," disposing of East, Wells and Haywood with successive balls. He must also have enjoyed that distinction in the first innings if Hayes had not dropped a catch. Some idea of the nature of the cricket will be gathered when it is mentioned that the game did not begin until after lunch on Monday, and was all over shortly after three o'clock on Tuesday, Surrey winning by an innings and 131 runs. Losing Hobbs, Hayes, and Hayward for 33, the home side could cherish no expectations of a decisive victory. Ducat, however, rose to the occasion in masterly fashion, withstanding the Northamptonshire bowling for an hour and a half, and during that time scoring 67 out of 124. Considering the state of the ground, two chances which he gave were small blemishes in his batting. Bush, Bird and Abel in turn all rendered him useful assistance. Nine wickets had fallen and the total stood at 176, when Knight missed Strudwick at long-off, the blunder having such serious consequences that

57 runs were added before the innings came to an end. Altogether Smith and Strudwick hit up 72 runs in just over half-an-hour. Thompson bowled splendidly. Northamptonshire scoring 15 without loss overnight, their twenty wickets went down on Tuesday for 87 runs.

## Surrey

| | | | |
|---|---|---|---|
| T. Hayward c Smith b Thompson | 8 | G. Platt b Thompson | 1 |
| J. B. Hobbs c East b Smith | 17 | W. C. Smith not out | 31 |
| E. G. Hayes c Ellis b Thompson | 0 | W. Hitch st Ellis b Thompson | 3 |
| Capt. H. S. Bush c Wells b Thompson | 19 | H. Strudwick b Smith | 31 |
| A. Ducat st Ellis b Seymour | 67 | B 19, l-b 2, w 4, n-b 3 | 28 |
| Mr M. C. Bird b Thompson | 19 | | |
| W. J. Abel b Seymour | 9 | | 233 |

## Northamptonshire

| | | | |
|---|---|---|---|
| Mr R. F. Knight b Platt | 4 | – c Abel b Smith | 6 |
| John Seymour c Bird b Platt | 8 | – c Hayes b Platt | 1 |
| Mr G. A. T. Vials b Smith | 5 | – c Hayes b Smith | 4 |
| Mr S. G. Smith st Strudwick b Smith | 12 | – b Smith | 2 |
| G. J. Thompson b Platt | 7 | – b Platt | 18 |
| W. East b Smith | 2 | – c Hayes b Smith | 5 |
| Mr A. P. R Hawtin lbw b Smith | 0 | – b Smith | 7 |
| Mr E. M. Crosse c Bird b Platt | 2 | – c Platt b Smith | 0 |
| R. Haywood c Bird b Smith | 0 | – c Ducat b Smith | 2 |
| W. Wells st Strudwick b Smith | 0 | – b Smith | 0 |
| H. Ellis not out | 0 | – not out | 0 |
| B 10, n-b 1 | 11 | B 6 | 6 |
| | 51 | | 51 |

## Northamptonshire Bowling

| | Overs | Mdns | Runs | Wkts |
|---|---|---|---|---|
| Thompson | 26 | 4 | 62 | 6 |
| Smith | 14 | 1 | 69 | 2 |
| East | 8 | 1 | 40 | — |
| Seymour | 8 | — | 34 | 2 |

## Surrey Bowling

| | Overs | Mdns | Runs | Wkts | Overs | Mdns | Runs | Wkts |
|---|---|---|---|---|---|---|---|---|
| Smith | 19 | 9 | 16 | 6 | 9.1 | 3 | 13 | 8 |
| Platt | 17.5 | 7 | 24 | 4 | 9 | 1 | 32 | 2 |
| Hitch | 1 | 1 | — | — | | | | |

Umpires: F. G. Roberts and W. Flowers.

## SURREY v MIDDLESEX

Played at The Oval, August 4, 5, 6, 1910

Although play on the first two days was seriously interfered with by rain, this match produced some truly sensational cricket, Surrey, after looking on two occasions to be a beaten side, gaining a victory by two wickets. On Friday afternoon the home side found themselves with seven men out for 56, Ducat, Abel, and Leveson-Gower having fallen to three successive balls, and on Saturday, when set 79 to win, they lost seven wickets for 39. In the first innings, however, Hayes and Hitch, playing a great game for their side, put on 130 runs for the eighth wicket, and so redeemed the situation, while in the second Leveson-Gower and Smith fairly won the match by taking the score from 39 to 78. Middlesex, however, threw away an almost certain victory by missing Smith twice while that batsman was making his first six runs. In the visitors' second innings when the seventh wicket fell at 24, Smith had taken six wickets for seven runs. K. B. Harper, captain at Uppingham, and S. H. Saville, an old Marlburian – both new to county cricket – assisted Middlesex.

## Middlesex

| | | | |
|---|---|---|---|
| Mr G. E. V. Crutchley run out | 38 | – c and b Hayes | 5 |
| F. A. Tarrant run out | 54 | – st Strudwick b Smith | 1 |
| E. Hendren c Ducat b Smith | 5 | – c and b Smith | 0 |
| H. R. Murrell c Hitch b Hayes | 37 | – c Hayes b Smith | 0 |
| Mr P. F. Warner b Hitch | 31 | – st Strudwick b Smith | 11 |
| Mr K. B. Harper c Abel b Smith | 28 | – b Smith | 0 |
| Mr S. H. Saville st Strudwick b Hayes | 10 | – c Abel b Smith | 5 |
| J. W. Hearne lbw b Smith | 12 | – not out | 11 |
| Mr R. E. More c Ducat b Smith | 15 | – lbw b Hayes | 1 |
| J. T. Hearne c Smith b Hayes | 0 | – b Hayes | 4 |
| E. Mignon not out | 9 | – c Gower b Hayes | 2 |
| B 5, l-b 8, w 1 | 14 | L-b 1 | 1 |
| | **253** | | **41** |

## Surrey

| | | | |
|---|---|---|---|
| T. Hayward c J. W. Hearne b Tarrant | 14 | – b J. T. Hearne | 15 |
| J. B. Hobbs c Mignon b J. T. Hearne | 3 | – c Harper b J. T. Hearne | 5 |
| E. G. Hayes c J. W. Hearne b J. T. Hearne | 88 | – b J. T. Hearne | 1 |
| Capt. H. S. Bush c Hendren b J. T. Hearne | 6 | – b J. T. Hearne | 0 |
| A. Ducat c Warner b Tarrant | 0 | – st Murrell b Tarrant | 14 |
| W. J. Abel b Tarrant | 0 | – c J. W. Hearne b Tarrant | 0 |
| Mr H. D. Leveson-Gower run out | 1 | – not out | 19 |
| W. C. Smith b Tarrant | 11 | – b J. T. Hearne | 19 |
| W. Hitch not out | 74 | – b J. T. Hearne | 0 |
| H. Strudwick c Warner b Tarrant | 6 | – not out | 0 |
| W. Lees c Mignon b More | 5 | | |
| B 6, l-b 2 | 8 | B 5, l-b 1, n-b 1 | 7 |
| | **216** | | **80** |

## Surrey Bowling

| | Overs | Mdns | Runs | Wkts | Overs | Mdns | Runs | Wkts |
|---|---|---|---|---|---|---|---|---|
| Hitch | 14 | 4 | 36 | 1 | | | | |
| Lees | 15 | 2 | 46 | — | | | | |
| Smith | 38.5 | 13 | 75 | 4 | 13 | 5 | 16 | 6 |
| Abel | 4 | — | 17 | — | | | | |
| Bush | 7 | 1 | 27 | — | | | | |
| Hayes | 15 | 2 | 38 | 3 | 12.5 | 1 | 24 | 4 |

## Middlesex Bowling

| | Overs | Mdns | Runs | Wkts | Overs | Mdns | Runs | Wkts |
|---|---|---|---|---|---|---|---|---|
| Tarrant | 30 | 7 | 74 | 5 | 19 | 9 | 39 | 2 |
| J. T. Hearne | 39 | 12 | 90 | 3 | 21.2 | 9 | 30 | 6 |
| More | 11.3 | 2 | 34 | 1 | 2 | 1 | 4 | — |
| J. W. Hearne | 2 | — | 10 | — | | | | |

Umpires: W. A. J. West and G. Webb.

HERBERT STRUDWICK. In one respect he is unique. I cannot remember any wicket-keeper who was so marvellously quick on his feet. One catch that he made last season in the Leicestershire match at The Oval, flinging himself down full length in front of the wicket, was the most remarkable thing of its kind I have ever seen. Strudwick bubbles over with an energy that sometimes carries him too far. I can see no advantage in his habit of leaving his post and chasing the ball to the boundary. The practice is simply the result of over-keenness, but as it does no good it ought to be checked, and I would suggest to the Surrey captain a system of modest fines, the amount being increased for each offence.

S. H. P.

## SURREY v LEICESTERSHIRE

### Played at The Oval, May 11, 12, 13, 1911

Truly astonishing was the change which this game underwent. At twenty minutes to one on Friday, Leicestershire, scoring 162 for one wicket on Thursday, when rain seriously interfered with play, had 255 on the board with only one man out. By eight minutes past four on Saturday they had lost the match by ten wickets. Whitehead and Wood put on 239 in two hours and fifty minutes, but after the dismissal of the former, the last eight wickets fell for 56 runs. Hitch, going on at 289, dismissed five batsmen for ten runs. Hayward and Hobbs, playing very brightly, gave Surrey a capital start, and Ducat helped Hayward to put on 73. Hayward batted admirably and with unusual freedom. Surrey at the drawing of stumps were nine runs behind with nine men out, but in all the last wicket produced 56 runs. With the pitch very treacherous, Smith and Rushby on Saturday disposed of Leicestershire in an hour and a half.

### Leicestershire

| | | | | |
|---|---|---|---|---|
| Mr C. J. B. Wood c Spring b Hitch | 107 | – c Hayes b Rushby | 8 |
| A. E. Knight b Hitch | 6 | – b Smith | 0 |
| H. Whitehead c Hobbs b Spring | 150 | – c Bird b Smith | 6 |
| J. H. King c Bird b Smith | 17 | – c Strudwick b Smith | 6 |
| Mr A. T. Sharp b Bird | 4 | – b Rushby | 5 |
| S. Coe c Hobbs b Hitch | 1 | – not out | 26 |
| Capt. W. W. Jelf c Hayes b Hitch | 0 | – c Hitch b Rushby | 0 |
| T. Jayes c sub. b Smith | 9 | – c Hobbs b Smith | 0 |
| W. Shipman b Hitch | 0 | – run out | 5 |
| Mr J. Shields not out | 2 | – c Hobbs b Rushby | 3 |
| W. E. Astill c Hayes b Hitch | 3 | – b Smith | 0 |
| B 8, l-b 4 | 12 | L-b 1 | 1 |
| | **311** | | **60** |

### Surrey

| | | | |
|---|---|---|---|
| T. Hayward c Shields b Shipman | 84 | – not out | 17 |
| J. B. Hobbs c Wood b King | 43 | – not out | 9 |
| E. G. Hayes b King | 1 | | |
| A. Ducat c Coe b Shipman | 42 | | |
| Mr M. C. Bird c Jelf b Shipman | 1 | | |
| W. Davis c Jelf b Shipman | 49 | | |
| A. W. Spring st Shields b King | 15 | | |
| W. Hitch c Jelf b Shipman | 32 | | |
| W. C. Smith c Astill b Shipman | 10 | | |
| H. Strudwick not out | 21 | | |
| T. Rushby c Shields b Shipman | 33 | | |
| B 1, l-b 4, w 1, n-b 5 | 11 | B 2, n-b 2 | 4 |
| | **342** | | **30** |

## Surrey Bowling

| | Overs | Mdns | Runs | Wkts | Overs | Mdns | Runs | Wkts |
|---|---|---|---|---|---|---|---|---|
| Rushby | 14.2 | 2 | 44 | — | 13 | 5 | 27 | 4 |
| Hitch | 23.3 | 4 | 95 | 6 | | | | |
| Smith | 31 | 6 | 85 | 2 | 14 | 4 | 32 | 5 |
| Spring | 7 | — | 28 | 1 | | | | |
| Hayes | 1 | — | 14 | — | | | | |
| Bird | 9 | 1 | 33 | 1 | | | | |

## Leicestershire Bowling

| | Overs | Mdns | Runs | Wkts | Overs | Mdns | Runs | Wkts |
|---|---|---|---|---|---|---|---|---|
| Jayes | 11 | — | 60 | — | 4 | — | 9 | — |
| Shipman | 27.4 | 2 | 114 | 7 | 0.5 | — | 4 | — |
| Astill | 7 | — | 39 | — | | | | |
| King | 24 | 3 | 85 | 3 | 3 | — | 13 | — |
| Coe | 6 | 3 | 7 | — | | | | |
| Wood | 6 | 1 | 26 | — | | | | |

Umpires: J. Blake and J. Moss.

# SURREY v ESSEX

## Played at The Oval, May 22, 23, 24, 1911

In the course of his splendid career, Hayward has given few finer displays than his not out innings of 170 in this match. Surrey on Wednesday had to go in with five hours and a half left for cricket, and, despite some excellent batting, there remained an hour and forty minutes when the fifth wicket went down. Hayward, however, showed superb skill and judgment throughout, and Goatly rendering him capital assistance, the game came to an end without the fall of another Surrey wicket. From start to finish Hayward was never at fault and, carefully as he played, his cricket was always a delight. Fane on Monday put together a great innings for Essex. Batting for five hours and a quarter and making very few mistakes he was ninth man out. Surrey on Tuesday failed in such extraordinary fashion that, with the ground in splendid order, they actually had eight wickets down for 94.

## Essex

| | | |
|---|---|---|
| Mr J. W. H. T. Douglas b Hitch | 60 | – c Hitch b Rushby .......... 34 |
| Mr F. L. Fane b Smith | 217 | – b Smith .......... 42 |
| J. Freeman b Hobbs | 21 | – b Smith .......... 27 |
| Mr C. McGahey st Strudwick b Hobbs | 0 | – b Smith .......... 10 |
| H. Carpenter b Hitch | 17 | – not out .......... 86 |
| Mr K. L. Gibson b Hitch | 4 | – c Strudwick b Rushby .......... 75 |
| A. C. Russell b Hitch | 0 | |
| W. Reeves c Hobbs b Hayes | 17 | – c sub. b Smith .......... 8 |
| C. P. Buckenham lbw b Hayes | 3 | |
| B. Tremlin c Strudwick b Hitch | 29 | |
| W. Mead not out | 4 | |
| B 4, l-b 1, w 1, n-b 1 | 7 | B 12 .......... 12 |
| | 379 | (6 wkts dec.) 294 |

## Surrey

| | 1st innings | | 2nd innings | |
|---|---|---|---|---|
| T. Hayward c and b Douglas | 17 | – not out | 170 |
| J. B. Hobbs c Buckenham b Douglas | 1 | – b Douglas | 23 |
| E. G. Hayes lbw b Douglas | 9 | – c Carpenter b Douglas | 34 |
| A. Ducat c Douglas b Tremlin | 20 | – b Buckenham | 55 |
| Mr M. C. Bird b Buckenham | 31 | – b Reeves | 5 |
| H. S. Harrison c and b Tremlin | 29 | – lbw b Buckenham | 0 |
| E. G. Goatly c Reeves b Tremlin | 4 | – not out | 36 |
| W. Hitch b Buckenham | 2 | | |
| W. C. Smith b Buckenham | 0 | | |
| H. Strudwick not out | 21 | | |
| T. Rushby run out | 16 | | |
| B 5, l-b 3, n-b 2 | 10 | B 10, l-b 6, n-b 1 | 17 |
| | **160** | | **340** |

### Surrey Bowling

| | Overs | Mdns | Runs | Wkts | Overs | Mdns | Runs | Wkts |
|---|---|---|---|---|---|---|---|---|
| Rushby | 22 | 6 | 69 | — | 14 | 4 | 40 | 2 |
| Hitch | 34.2 | 6 | 124 | 5 | 14 | 3 | 52 | — |
| Smith | 25 | 7 | 64 | 1 | 23.4 | 5 | 90 | 4 |
| Hayes | 15 | 2 | 71 | 2 | 10 | 1 | 46 | — |
| Bird | 3 | — | 11 | — | 5 | 1 | 29 | — |
| Hobbs | 10 | 3 | 27 | 2 | 4 | — | 25 | — |
| Goatly | 1 | — | 6 | — | | | | |

### Essex Bowling

| | Overs | Mdns | Runs | Wkts | Overs | Mdns | Runs | Wkts |
|---|---|---|---|---|---|---|---|---|
| Buckenham | 22 | 4 | 55 | 3 | 29 | 3 | 79 | 2 |
| Douglas | 11 | 1 | 54 | 3 | 24 | 2 | 86 | 2 |
| Tremlin | 15.1 | 2 | 41 | 3 | 16 | 5 | 37 | — |
| McGahey | 1 | 1 | — | — | 19 | 9 | 44 | — |
| Mead | | | | | 21 | 7 | 40 | — |
| Reeves | | | | | 15 | — | 37 | 1 |

Umpires: J. E. West and J. Moss.

## SURREY v LANCASHIRE

Played at The Oval, July 31, August 1, 2, 1911

A great innings by Spooner was the outstanding feature of this match. The famous batsman, against some capital bowling and brilliant fielding, took more than three hours to make his first hundred, but he doubled his score in another hour and a half, and last man out, was altogether at the wickets just over five hours. When 27 he might have been caught at mid-on, and when 126 he gave a chance in the slips, but these were small blemishes in a wonderful display characterised by beautiful off-driving, clever forcing strokes on the on-side, and remarkable skill in getting on the top of balls which rose awkwardly. His innings included thirty 4s, and many other hits which on most grounds must have reached the boundary. On Wednesday, when a draw was soon certain, Hobbs and Hayes put on 200 runs.

### Surrey

| | | | |
|---|---|---|---|
| J. B. Hobbs c Sharp b McLeod | 55 | – lbw b Dean | 117 |
| E. G. Goatly c and b Dean | 22 | – c Garnett b Dean | 17 |
| E. G. Hayes b Whitehead | 18 | – c Spooner b Dean | 123 |
| A. Ducat b Dean | 25 | – c McLeod b Whitehead | 3 |
| A. Sandham c Sharp b Whitehead | 60 | – b Dean | 2 |
| Mr M. C. Bird c Whitehead b Dean | 43 | – not out | 22 |
| H. S. Harrison not out | 38 | | |
| W. C. Smith b Dean | 2 | | |
| W. Hitch c Garnett b Whitehead | 25 | | |
| H. Strudwick c W. Tyldesley b McLeod | 17 | | |
| T. Rushby b McLeod | 0 | | |
| B 1, l-b 8, w 1, n-b 5 | 15 | B 5, l-b 4, w 1, n-b 4 | 14 |
| | **320** | **(5 wkts dec.)** | **298** |

### Lancashire

| | | | |
|---|---|---|---|
| Mr R. H. Spooner b Hitch | 224 | | |
| Mr A. Hartley b Hitch | 0 | – c and b Goatly | 22 |
| W. Tyldesley b Hitch | 6 | – not out | 55 |
| J. T. Tyldesley b Hitch | 11 | | |
| J. Sharp lbw b Rushby | 35 | | |
| Mr K. G. McLeod lbw b Hayes | 18 | | |
| R. Whitehead b Hitch | 11 | – not out | 11 |
| Mr A. H. Hornby b Rushby | 21 | | |
| Mr H. G. Garnett b Bird | 18 | | |
| H. Dean not out | 2 | | |
| J. S. Heap absent hurt | 0 | | |
| B 6, l-b 3, w 1, n-b 4 | 14 | B 4, w 1 | 5 |
| | **360** | | **93** |

### Lancashire Bowling

| | Overs | Mdns | Runs | Wkts | Overs | Mdns | Runs | Wkts |
|---|---|---|---|---|---|---|---|---|
| Dean | 33 | 2 | 108 | 4 | 40.5 | 4 | 98 | 4 |
| Whitehead | 29 | 8 | 88 | 3 | 23 | 2 | 100 | 1 |
| Sharp | 14 | 2 | 47 | — | 14 | 3 | 32 | — |
| Heap | 3 | 2 | 3 | — | | | | |
| McLeod | 20.3 | 4 | 59 | 3 | 6 | — | 54 | — |

### Surrey Bowling

| | Overs | Mdns | Runs | Wkts | Overs | Mdns | Runs | Wkts |
|---|---|---|---|---|---|---|---|---|
| Rushby | 20 | 2 | 96 | 2 | | | | |
| Hitch | 27.3 | 3 | 114 | 5 | 5 | 1 | 11 | — |
| Harrison | 11 | 7 | 20 | — | 8 | 2 | 18 | — |
| Smith | 19 | 2 | 65 | — | | | | |
| Bird | 9 | 1 | 27 | 1 | | | | |
| Hayes | 5 | 1 | 24 | 1 | | | | |
| Goatly | | | | | 7 | — | 19 | 1 |
| Ducat | | | | | 8 | — | 27 | — |
| Strudwick | | | | | 3 | — | 13 | — |

Umpires: J. Blake and A. F. Bannister.

## SURREY v KENT

Played at The Oval, August 21, 22, 23, 1911

Despite the fact that play was found impracticable until after four o'clock on Monday, and on Tuesday until a quarter to three, this match produced a superlatively interesting struggle. Surrey on Monday lost nine wickets for 111, Carr dismissing eight batsmen for 52 runs. Smith and Strudwick next day added 34 for the last wicket – a stand which proved a telling factor in the issue of the match. Kent scored 68 before their third wicket fell, but Smith finished his day's work by getting rid of five batsmen in seven overs and three balls for two runs, eight wickets being down for 92, when play ceased. On Wednesday, Carr disposed of Hobbs and Hayward for eight runs, but Ducat and Hayes took the score to 52. For the moment, Surrey occupied a very strong position. There followed, however, some marvellous bowling by Woolley, who actually took seven wickets for nine runs. Kent wanting 102 to win, 34 runs were hit off by Day and Humphreys, but Smith then became almost unplayable and with seven men out the score was only 60. For all that Kent got to within ten of victory, with two wickets in hand. Kirk, however, then finished off the match, Surrey winning by nine runs. Huish in the two innings stumped nine men – a fresh record in county cricket. The match had been set apart as a benefit to Strudwick. Collections for him on the ground realised over £150.

### Surrey

| | | | |
|---|---|---|---|
| T. Hayward c Prest b Carr | 7 | – st Huish b Carr | 5 |
| J. B. Hobbs st Huish b Carr | 17 | – c Hutchings b Carr | 2 |
| E. G. Hayes c Blythe b Carr | 3 | – b Woolley | 12 |
| A. Ducat st Huish b Carr | 12 | – c Seymour b Woolley | 34 |
| Maj. H. S. Bush st Huish b Carr | 12 | – st Huish b Woolley | 0 |
| Mr M. C. Bird b Blythe | 17 | – st Huish b Woolley | 4 |
| Mr I. P. F. Campbell lbw b Carr | 1 | – st Huish b Woolley | 0 |
| H. Strudwick c Hubble b Blythe | 25 | – b Woolley | 1 |
| Mr E. C. Kirk st Huish b Carr | 2 | – st Huish b Blythe | 0 |
| W. Hitch lbw b Carr | 17 | – c Huish b Woolley | 2 |
| W. C. Smith not out | 20 | – not out | 0 |
| B 6, l-b 3, n-b 3 | 12 | L-b 2, w 1 | 3 |
| | **145** | | **63** |

### Kent

| | | | |
|---|---|---|---|
| Mr A. P. Day b Smith | 3 | – c Strudwick b Smith | 19 |
| E. Humphreys c Bird b Smith | 30 | – run out | 17 |
| James Seymour c Hitch b Kirk | 12 | – c Strudwick b Hayes | 10 |
| F. E. Woolley b Smith | 22 | – st Strudwick b Smith | 8 |
| Mr K. L. Hutchings c and b Smith | 7 | – b Smith | 0 |
| Mr H. E. W. Prest c Campbell b Kirk | 18 | – c Hayes b Smith | 4 |
| J. C Hubble c and b Smith | 2 | – c and b Kirk | 15 |
| F. H. Huish lbw b Smith | 4 | – lbw b Smith | 1 |
| Mr D. W. Carr lbw b Smith | 0 | – not out | 12 |
| C. Blythe st Strudwick b Smith | 1 | – b Kirk | 6 |
| A. Fielder not out | 3 | – c Smith b Kirk | 0 |
| L-b 3, n-b 2 | 5 | | |
| | **107** | | **92** |

### Kent Bowling

| | Overs | Mdns | Runs | Wkts | Overs | Mdns | Runs | Wkts |
|---|---|---|---|---|---|---|---|---|
| Blythe | 25.2 | 7 | 66 | 2 | 13 | 4 | 19 | 1 |
| Carr | 25 | 4 | 67 | 8 | 7 | 0 | 32 | 2 |
| Woolley | | | | | 6.3 | 3 | 9 | 7 |

**Surrey Bowling**

| | Overs | Mdns | Runs | Wkts | Overs | Mdns | Runs | Wkts |
|---|---|---|---|---|---|---|---|---|
| Smith ........... | 31 | 16 | 31 | 8 | 20 | 10 | 33 | 5 |
| Kirk ............. | 30.5 | 9 | 71 | 2 | 8.4 | 1 | 33 | 3 |
| Hayes .......... | | | | | 11 | 1 | 26 | 1 |

Umpires: J. Moss and J. E. West.

## SURREY v LANCASHIRE

Played at the Oval, June 26, 27, 28, 1913

Left drawn, all in favour of Lancashire, this match went so much in the batsmens' way that 1,122 runs were scored for the loss of twenty-six wickets. The game was especially memorable for the achievement of Hayward in putting together his hundredth hundred in first-class cricket – a record which among all other batsmen W. G. Grace alone can claim. Surrey being engaged in a very uphill task all the time he was at the wickets, Hayward took four hours and fifty minutes to make his 139. On Thursday, when Lancashire scored 451 for six wickets J. T. Tyldesley, batting with extraordinary ease and brilliancy, played one of the finest innings of his great career. He gave no chance of any kind during a stay of nearly four hours and a half. Hornby helped him to put on 176, and with the brothers Tyldesley together 177 runs were obtained. The two Tyldesleys had each played a three-figure innings earlier in the week.

### Lancashire

| | |
|---|---|
| Mr A. H. Hornby c Strudwick b Smith .... 86 | Mr R. A. Boddington not out ........... 58 |
| H. Makepeace b Hitch ................. 3 | R. Whitehead b Hitch ................. 0 |
| J. T. Tyldesley c Hayes b Bird ...........210 | W. Huddleston c Strudwick b Smith ...... 16 |
| J. Sharp c Hitch b Smith .............. 11 | H. Dean c Strudwick b Bird ............. 23 |
| E. Tyldesley b Hitch ....................110 | B 5, l-b 5, w 4, n-b 5 ........... 19 |
| Mr K. G. McLeod c Hobbs b Smith ...... 4 | |
| J. S. Heap c Hayes b Hitch ............. 18 | 558 |

### Surrey

| | |
|---|---|
| T. Hayward c Huddleston b Dean ...............139 | – b Huddleston .................. 7 |
| J. B. Hobbs b Dean ......................... 25 | – lbw b Heap ................... 61 |
| E. G. Hayes b Huddleston ................... 13 | – lbw b Sharp .................. 5 |
| E. G. Goatly c J. Tyldesley b Huddleston ........ 28 | – c and b Makepeace ............. 64 |
| Mr M. C. Bird c Boddington b Huddleston ........ 4 | – c E. Tyldesley b Huddleston ...... 23 |
| H. S. Harrison b Huddleston .................. 39 | – c Hornby b McLeod ............ 7 |
| Mr C. T. A. Wilkinson c Sharp b Whitehead ....... 42 | – not out ..................... 30 |
| A. Sandham b Whitehead .................... 33 | – not out ..................... 8 |
| H. Strudwick b Whitehead ................... 5 | |
| W. Hitch b Huddleston ..................... 1 | |
| W. C. Smith not out ....................... 6 | |
| B 5, l-b 5 .......................... 10 | B 11, l-b 2, w 1 .......... 14 |
| 345 | 219 |

## Surrey Bowling

|  | Overs | Mdns | Runs | Wkts |
|---|---|---|---|---|
| Hitch .......... | 43 | 3 | 184 | 4 |
| Smith .......... | 37 | 9 | 116 | 4 |
| Hayes .......... | 13 | 1 | 68 | — |
| Goatly .......... | 10 | — | 34 | — |
| Bird ............. | 23.4 | 5 | 95 | 2 |
| Sandham ........ | 3 | 1 | 10 | — |
| Wilkinson ....... | 1 | — | 6 | — |
| Harrison ........ | 9 | 1 | 26 | — |

## Lancashire Bowling

|  | Overs | Mdns | Runs | Wkts | Overs | Mdns | Runs | Wkts |
|---|---|---|---|---|---|---|---|---|
| Whitehead ....... | 29 | 5 | 93 | 3 | 6 | — | 22 | — |
| Dean ........... | 49 | 13 | 97 | 2 | 4 | — | 17 | — |
| Huddleston ...... | 47 | 18 | 76 | 5 | 16 | 4 | 47 | 2 |
| McLeod ......... | 3 | — | 13 | — | 10 | 1 | 33 | 1 |
| Heap ........... | 19 | 5 | 40 | — | 7 | 2 | 24 | 1 |
| Makepeace ....... | 5 | 2 | 11 | — | 6 | 1 | 22 | 1 |
| Sharp ........... | 1 | — | 5 | — | 12 | — | 40 | 1 |

Umpires: A. J. Atfield and G. P. Harrison.

## HAYWARD'S HUNDRED 100s

In the course of the season of 1913 Tom Hayward had the satisfaction of rivalling W. G. Grace's feat of making a hundred three-figure scores in first-class cricket. He and W. G. are, so far, the only batsmen who have reached the number. Happily the time has not yet come to deal with Hayward's splendid career as a whole. So far as one knows he has no present thought of giving up the game, and while he can bat as he did on many occasions last summer there is assuredly not the least necessity for his retirement. The change that has come over modern cricket in the way of an extended programme of first-class fixtures is brought home to us by the fact that Hayward made his hundredth century in his twenty-first season. W. G. Grace began to play first-class cricket in 1865 – the year following his first appearance at Lord's – and it was not until 1895 that his hundredth 100 was obtained. Between the two batsmen, therefore, there was a difference of just ten years. W. G. made fifty-one of his 100s for Gloucestershire, and Hayward, with many more county matches, no fewer than eighty-six for Surrey. In Gentlemen and Players' matches, on the other hand, W. G. beginning at Lord's in 1865 and finishing at The Oval in 1906, made fifteen 100s, as against Hayward's seven. Hayward, who is, perhaps, not likely to be chosen for the Players again, was first picked against the Gentlemen at Lord's and The Oval in 1895 – two years after he came out for Surrey. Carrying comparison a little further, both batsmen can point to a couple of 100's for England against Australia in this country. W. G. made 152 at The Oval in 1880 – the first test match in England – and 170 on the same ground in 1886. Hayward's two were both obtained in 1899 – 130 at Manchester and 137 at The Oval. It is only a matter of fancy, but if asked to name the finest innings in Hayward's career one would be inclined to select the never-to-be-forgotten 130 at Manchester. The circumstances were quite exceptional. Winning the toss on a fast wicket England made a shocking start, but Hayward saved his side, following up an hour or more of rigid defence by a most brilliant display of hitting. In 1906 Hayward made four 100s for Surrey in one week – 144 not out and 100 against Nottinghamshire at Trent Bridge, and 143 and 125 against Leicestershire at Leicester. In the same year he obtained the record aggregate of runs in first-class cricket in one season, 3,518, and equalled C. B. Fry's feat in 1901 of getting thirteen 100s. As everyone knows, Hayward was preceded, at some considerable distance of time, as the best professional bat in England by the uncle after whom he was named. The first Tom Hayward, who died in 1876, when the present player was only five years old, damaged a great reputation by lingering on in first-class cricket when his day was over, but from 1859 to 1863, and for a few years afterwards, he was right at the top of the tree. The nearest parallel to the position thus won by uncle and nephew is the case of William and George Gunn. Haywards's hundred 100s can be briefly summarised as follows:

**For England** (6):

  v Australia, 137, 130.
  v New South Wales, 174.
  v South Africa, 122.
  v South Australia, 157.
  v Tasmania, 134.

**For An England XI**:

  v South Africans, 105*.

**For Players** (7):

  v Gentlemen, 203, 177, 146*, 134*, 123*, 116*, 111.

**For South** (2):

  v Australians, 106.
  v North, 112.

**For Surrey** (86):

  v Australians, 129*.
  v Cambridge University, 128, 118.
  v Derbyshire, 229*, 202, 158, 144, 120.
  v Essex, 170*, 161, 109.
  v Gloucestershire, 181, 153*, 123, 121, 100.
  v Hampshire, 103*.
  v Kent, 188*, 142, 124 twice, 112, 101.
  v Lancashire, 315*, 139, 122, 114*, 108.
  v Leicestershire, 193, 143, 135, 130, 129, 125, 122, 113.
  v London County, 120*, 108, 107.
  v Middlesex, 148, 119, 111, 110.
  v Northamptonshire, 219.
  v Nottinghamshire, 144*, 131*, 126, 120 twice, 116, 100 twice.
  v Oxford University, 144, 127.
  v Philadelphians, 156*.
  v Somerset, 158 twice, 113.
  v South Africans, 197.
  v Sussex, 175, 164, 146, 144, 126, 125, 115, 112, 106.
  v Warwickshire, 208, 204*, 161*, 137, 131*, 127, 124, 109, 105.
  v Worcestershire, 182, 146, 130, 127.
  v Yorkshire, 273, 177, 164, 115, 108.

  * *Signifies not out.*

## SURREY v KENT

### Played at Lord's, August 10, 11, 1914

Transferred to Lord's – The Oval being in the occupation of the military authorities – and finished off in two days, Hobbs' benefit match did not yield anything like the sum which could have been confidently expected in normal circumstances. Out-playing their opponents at all points, Surrey gained a well-earned victory by eight wickets. In such form did Hitch bowl that the first four Kent wickets fell for eleven runs. Woolley and S. H. Day added 93, but no one else met with success. Thanks to Hayward and Ducat, who added 100 after three wickets had gone down cheaply, Surrey by Monday evening were seven runs ahead with seven wickets in hand. Ninth man out, Hayward enjoyed far more than a fair share of luck, but on the same wicket few men could have played such an innings against Kent's slow bowlers. When Kent went in again Seymour and Woolley put on 44, but only during that partnership did the visitors look like making a fight. Hitch was at his best.

### Kent

| | | | |
|---|---|---|---|
| E. Humphreys b Hitch | 5 | – b Hitch | 4 |
| H. T. W. Hardinge c Hayward b Smith | 2 | – c Ducat b Rushby | 1 |
| James Seymour b Hitch | 0 | – b Hitch | 45 |
| F. E. Woolley b Hitch | 51 | – c Strudwick b Hitch | 14 |
| Mr A. P. Day b Hitch | 0 | – lbw b Fender | 18 |
| Mr S. H. Day c Hayward b Smith | 54 | – c Strudwick b Rushby | 1 |
| Mr L. H. W. Troughton c Fender b Rushby | 5 | – c Hayes b Fender | 15 |
| F. H. Huish b Fender | 10 | – c and b Fender | 7 |
| C. Blythe c Hayward b Smith | 1 | – b Hitch | 7 |
| A. Fielder c and b Fender | 0 | – not out | 5 |
| A. P. Freeman not out | 1 | – b Hitch | 0 |
| B 3, l-b 4, n-b 4 | 11 | B 15, l-b 6, n-b 2 | 23 |
| | **140** | | **140** |

### Surrey

| | | | |
|---|---|---|---|
| T. Hayward lbw b Blythe | 91 | – b Freeman | 7 |
| J. B. Hobbs lbw b Blythe | 16 | – not out | 26 |
| E. G. Hayes c Humphreys b Blythe | 0 | – lbw b A. P. Day | 12 |
| Mr D. J. Knight c Troughton b Blythe | 2 | – not out | 2 |
| A. Ducat c Huish b Blythe | 36 | | |
| Mr P. G. H. Fender c Troughton b Blythe | 48 | | |
| W. J. Abel st Huish b Woolley | 0 | | |
| W. Hitch c Woolley b Blythe | 0 | | |
| H. Strudwick c A. P. Day b Blythe | 2 | | |
| W. C. Smith b Blythe | 12 | | |
| T. Rushby not out | 2 | | |
| B 18, l-b 6, w 1 | 25 | | |
| | **234** | | **47** |

### Surrey Bowling

| | Overs | Mdns | Runs | Wkts | Overs | Mdns | Runs | Wkts |
|---|---|---|---|---|---|---|---|---|
| Smith | 11 | 4 | 20 | 3 | 10 | 2 | 26 | — |
| Hitch | 21 | 7 | 39 | 4 | 19 | 5 | 39 | 5 |
| Rushby | 15 | 3 | 37 | 1 | 17 | 8 | 27 | 2 |
| Fender | 6.4 | — | 27 | 2 | 9 | 5 | 16 | 3 |
| Abel | 1 | — | 6 | — | 1 | — | 9 | — |

**Kent Bowling**

| | Overs | Mdns | Runs | Wkts | Overs | Mdns | Runs | Wkts |
|---|---|---|---|---|---|---|---|---|
| Fielder ........... | 3 | 2 | 3 | — | 4 | 1 | 21 | — |
| Blythe ........... | 25.5 | 3 | 97 | 9 | | | | |
| Woolley .......... | 19 | 1 | 66 | 1 | | | | |
| Freeman ......... | 11 | 1 | 42 | — | 6.3 | 1 | 20 | 1 |
| A. P. Day ......... | 2 | 1 | 1 | — | 3 | 1 | 6 | 1 |

Umpires: F. Parris and H. Butt.

# SUSSEX

## SUSSEX v GLOUCESTERSHIRE

Played at Brighton, June 4, 5, 6, 1900

Batsmen held the upper hand all through this match and at the end of the three full days' cricket 1310 runs had been obtained for the loss of thirty wickets, the game ending in a very even draw. Some brilliant work was done by several of the Sussex batsmen but the great performance of the match was that of Gilbert Jessop, who going in when Gloucestershire had lost three wickets for 105 actually hit up 179 out of 257 in an hour and three quarters. He took forty-five minutes to get his first fifty but twenty minutes later he had made his hundred and he obtained his third fifty in half-an-hour. His innings – the highest he had ever played in a good match – was not marred by any chance until he had passed the hundred. Among his hits were thirty-four 4s. Ranjitsinhji was in great form for Sussex. His 97 – a faultless display of cricket – was closed by a magnificent catch from a hard hit. In the second innings the Sussex captain scored even more heavily but his play was not so free from blemish. Collins by steady cricket scored the first hundred in his career. Soon after the start of the Gloucestershire innings Fry was once more no balled for throwing but going on a second time he bowled with a perfectly fair action.

### Sussex

| | | | |
|---|---:|---|---:|
| Mr A. Collins b Roberts | 22 | – c Board b Townsend | 102 |
| A. E. Relf run out | 3 | – lbw b Wrathall | 0 |
| E. H. Killick c Board b Paish | 94 | – lbw b Townsend | 24 |
| J. Vine b Paish | 16 | – not out | 16 |
| Mr C. B. Fry b Paish | 0 | – c Hodgkins b Roberts | 41 |
| Mr G. Brann c and b Jessop | 23 | – st Board b Townsend | 28 |
| K. S. Ranjitsinhji c Brown b Paish | 97 | – c Board b Wrathall | 127 |
| F. W. Marlow not out | 83 | – b Townsend | 22 |
| H. R. Butt c Paish b Roberts | 31 | – c Goodwin b Wrathall | 19 |
| F. W. Tate c Thomas b Paish | 1 | – c sub. b. Wrathall | 19 |
| C. H. G. Bland c Thomas b Roberts | 4 | – c Wrathall b Townsend | 2 |
| B 10, l-b 2, n-b 4, w 1 | 17 | B 20, l-b 2, n-b 1 | 23 |
| | **391** | | **423** |

### Gloucestershire

| | | | |
|---|---:|---|---:|
| H. Wrathall b Brann | 75 | Mr W. S. A. Brown c Ranjitsinhji b Tate | 89 |
| Mr H. J. Hodgkins b Fry | 3 | Mr E. L. Thomas b Fry | 19 |
| Mr C. L. Townsend b Fry | 0 | A. Paish c Fry b Ranjitsinhji | 4 |
| J. H. Board c Marlow b Relf | 55 | F. G. Roberts not out | 19 |
| Mr G. L. Jessop c Vine b Ranjitsinhji | 179 | B 5, l-b 10, w 1 | 16 |
| Mr W. McG. Hemingway run out | 37 | | |
| Mr H. S. Goodwin c Bland b Ranjitsinhji | 0 | | **496** |

### Gloucestershire Bowling

| | Overs | Mdns | Runs | Wkts | Overs | Mdns | Runs | Wkts |
|---|---:|---:|---:|---:|---:|---:|---:|---:|
| Jessop | 21 | 7 | 43 | 1 | 6 | 3 | 8 | — |
| Paish | 49 | 11 | 151 | 5 | 35 | 9 | 96 | — |
| Roberts | 42 | 18 | 92 | 3 | 34 | 8 | 64 | 1 |
| Hodgkins | 8 | 3 | 13 | — | 6 | 1 | 16 | — |
| Brown | 14 | 5 | 38 | — | 17 | 7 | 60 | — |
| Townsend | 10 | — | 37 | — | 36 | 8 | 119 | 5 |
| Wrathall | | | | | 11 | 1 | 37 | 4 |

**Sussex Bowling**

|           | Overs | Mdns | Runs | Wkts |
|-----------|-------|------|------|------|
| Fry ............. | 16   | 3    | 88   | 3    |
| Tate ............ | 15.2 | 1    | 105  | 1    |
| Bland ........... | 12   | 1    | 66   | —    |
| Relf ............ | 11   | —    | 61   | 1    |
| Brann .......... | 7    | —    | 56   | 1    |
| Killick .......... | 7    | 2    | 41   | —    |
| Ranjitsinhji ...... | 17   | 4    | 63   | 3    |

Umpires: A. White and W. A. J. West.

## SUSSEX v HAMPSHIRE

Played at Brighton, July 16, 17, 18, 1900

Up to a certain point the Hampshire cricketers acquitted themselves with great credit against a much stronger side, but they went all to pieces at the finish and suffered defeat by 232 runs. Against some steady bowling and smart fielding, Sussex who lacked the services of Fry, could not on the first day make more than 282 for six wickets. On Hampshire going in on Tuesday two wickets fell for 10 runs, but then Barton commenced the innings of his life. When play ceased for the day he was 175 not out, and next morning he increased his score to 205. He batted in brilliant style throughout, making his runs in three hours and three-quarters, and giving no chance till 187. Some hard hitting by Relf, Collins, and Ranjitsinhji enabled Sussex to declare, and good bowling did the rest.

### Sussex

| | | | |
|---|---|---|---|
| A. E. Relf c Sprot b Baldwin .............. | 12 | – c Webb b Gravett ............. | 75 |
| Mr A. Collins c Robson b Gravett ............... | 64 | – not out ..................... | 73 |
| E. H. Killick c Webb b Gravett ................. | 67 | – c Robson b English ............ | 15 |
| K. S. Ranjitsinhji b Barton ................... | 41 | – not out ..................... | 88 |
| F. W. Marlow st Gay b Robson ................. | 47 | | |
| J. Vine c and b Barton ...................... | 88 | | |
| Mr G. Brann b Sprot ........................ | 1 | | |
| H. R. Butt c Sprot b Barton ................... | 25 | | |
| W. Humphreys b Baldwin .................... | 2 | | |
| C. H. G. Bland c Sprot b Webb ................ | 30 | | |
| F. W. Tate not out .......................... | 11 | | |
| B 16, l-b 3 ........................ | 19 | B 9, l-b 3, w 2 ............ | 14 |
| | **407** | **(2 wkts dec.)** | **265** |

### Hampshire

| | | | |
|---|---|---|---|
| Mr C. Robson c Vine b Bland ................... | 0 | – c Butt b Bland ................. | 10 |
| A. Webb c Marlow b Humphreys .............. | 27 | – b Tate ..................... | 5 |
| Mr E. M. Sprot c Butt b Bland ................. | 0 | – c Tate b Bland ................. | 9 |
| V. Barton b Killick ...........................205 | | – c Butt b Bland ................. | 7 |
| Mr C. E. Briggs c Brann b Humphreys .......... | 58 | – b Tate ..................... | 2 |
| Mr E. A. English b Humphreys ................. | 35 | – c Tate b Bland ................ | 5 |
| Mr L. H. Gay c and b Bland .................. | 5 | – lbw b Bland ................. | 3 |
| Mr D. A. Steele c Butt b Humphreys ........... | 6 | – c Collins b Tate ............. | 5 |
| E. Light b Killick ........................... | 5 | – not out ..................... | 19 |
| Gravett b Killick .......................... | 3 | – b Tate ..................... | 0 |
| H. Baldwin not out .......................... | 4 | – b Humphreys ................. | 7 |
| B 14, l-b 1, n-b 4 .................. | 19 | N-b 1 ................. | 1 |
| | **367** | | **73** |

## Hampshire Bowling

| | Overs | Mdns | Runs | Wkts | Overs | Mdns | Runs | Wkts |
|---|---|---|---|---|---|---|---|---|
| Baldwin ......... | 46 | 13 | 96 | 2 | 18 | 2 | 79 | — |
| Gravett ......... | 46 | 11 | 100 | 2 | 18 | 1 | 75 | 1 |
| Barton .......... | 40.4 | 17 | 76 | 3 | 10 | 1 | 49 | — |
| Webb ........... | 7 | 1 | 32 | 1 | 7 | — | 25 | — |
| Sprot ........... | 5 | 1 | 17 | 1 | 3 | 1 | 12 | — |
| Steele .......... | 6 | 1 | 27 | — | | | | |
| Robson ......... | 13 | 1 | 40 | 1 | | | | |
| English .......... | | | | | 4 | 1 | 11 | 1 |

## Sussex Bowling

| | Overs | Mdns | Runs | Wkts | Overs | Mdns | Runs | Wkts |
|---|---|---|---|---|---|---|---|---|
| Tate ............ | 16 | 3 | 49 | — | 16 | 2 | 51 | 4 |
| Bland ........... | 21 | 3 | 61 | 3 | 16 | 6 | 20 | 5 |
| Humphreys ....... | 22 | 2 | 96 | 4 | 0.5 | — | 1 | 1 |
| Relf ............ | 7 | 1 | 25 | — | | | | |
| Ranjitsinhji ....... | 7 | 2 | 44 | — | | | | |
| Collins .......... | 3 | 2 | 1 | — | | | | |
| Brann ........... | 7 | 1 | 42 | — | | | | |
| Killick .......... | 5.4 | 3 | 30 | 3 | | | | |

Umpires: W. Hearn and R. Thoms.

## SUSSEX v SURREY

### Played at Brighton, July 19, 20, 21, 1900

Amongst many brilliant triumphs last season, C. B. Fry had particular reason to remember this return game for he not only succeeded in making his highest score in first-class cricket, but for the second time in his life obtained two separate hundreds in one match. In his first innings he started unsteadily but soon ran into splendid form, while in putting his 229 together he not only gave no chance, but scarcely made a bad stroke. Sussex started by getting 121 for the first wicket, but Richardson and Lockwood afterwards bowled very finely, and Surrey, scoring 94 without loss, left off with a big advantage. Next day they carried their total to 493 for seven wickets. Abel's 110 was not one of his best innings. Miller batted with great judgement, and later in the day Lockwood and Crawford hit splendidly. With Sussex 239 in arrear, Fry and Collins put on 133 for the first wicket, while for the third Ranjitsinhji and Fry added 197 in a hundred minutes, the batting despite the great pace, being scarcely marred by the slightest fault. Fry was fifth out at 408, and with a draw inevitable the game was abandoned half an hour before the usual time.

## Sussex

| | | | |
|---|---|---|---|
| Mr C. B. Fry lbw b Richardson ................. | 125 | – c Jephson b Richardson ............... | 229 |
| A. E. Relf b Richardson ....................... | 42 | – c Richardson ................. | 6 |
| E. H. Killick c and b Lockwood ................ | 12 | – c Hayward b Richardson ....... | 0 |
| K. S. Ranjitsinhji c Stedman b Lockwood ......... | 8 | – c Stedman b Richardson ......... | 103 |
| Mr A. Collins b Richardson ................... | 15 | – c Hayward b Richardson ....... | 37 |
| J. Vine b Richardson ......................... | 0 | – b Richardson ................. | 3 |
| F. W. Marlow b Lockwood ..................... | 6 | | |
| H. R. Butt not out .......................... | 35 | – not out ..................... | 32 |
| C. H. G. Bland run out ....................... | 25 | | |
| F. W. Tate b Jephson ........................ | 3 | | |
| W. Humphreys b Richardson .................. | 9 | | |
| B 8, l-b 9, n-b 3 .................... | 20 | B 1, l-b 1, n-b 5 .......... | 7 |
| | 300 | | 417 |

### Surrey

| | | |
|---|---|---|
| R. Abel b Collins | ..................... | 110 |
| W. Brockwell c Butt b Tate | ............. | 64 |
| Mr N. Miller c Collins b Humphreys | ...... | 81 |
| T. Hayward c Vine b Tate | .............. | 52 |
| W. Lockwood c Butt b Ranjitsinhji | ....... | 85 |
| Mr V. F. S. Crawford c Butt b Tate | ....... | 79 |
| W. Lees b Tate | ...................... | 12 |

| | | |
|---|---|---|
| Mr D. L. A. Jephson c Vine b Ranjitsinhji | .. | 0 |
| Mr E. M. Dowson not out | .............. | 4 |
| T. Richardson c and b Tate | ............. | 38 |
| E. Stedman c and b Tate | ............... | 1 |
| B 7, l-b 4, w 1, n-b 1 | ........... | 13 |
| | | **539** |

### Surrey Bowling

| | Overs | Mdns | Runs | Wkts | Overs | Mdns | Runs | Wkts |
|---|---|---|---|---|---|---|---|---|
| Richardson ........ | 18.5 | 2 | 76 | 5 | 26 | 2 | 116 | 6 |
| Brockwell ......... | 5 | — | 21 | — | 16 | 5 | 58 | — |
| Lees ............. | 15 | 1 | 43 | — | 13 | 3 | 48 | — |
| Dowson .......... | 16 | 2 | 72 | — | | | | |
| Lockwood ........ | 16 | 3 | 52 | 3 | 16 | 3 | 69 | — |
| Jephson .......... | 5 | — | 16 | 1 | 7 | 2 | 19 | — |
| Hayward ......... | | | | | 4 | — | 26 | — |
| Miller ............ | | | | | 13 | — | 74 | — |

### Sussex Bowling

| | Overs | Mdns | Runs | Wkts |
|---|---|---|---|---|
| Bland ............ | 28 | 8 | 76 | — |
| Humphreys ....... | 11 | — | 72 | 1 |
| Tate ............. | 48.5 | 16 | 132 | 6 |
| Killick ........... | 17 | 2 | 75 | — |
| Ranjitsinhji ....... | 27 | 7 | 88 | 2 |
| Fry .............. | 16 | 3 | 41 | — |
| Collins .......... | 19 | 3 | 42 | 1 |

Umpires: W. Hearn and H. Pickett.

## SUSSEX v NOTTINGHAMSHIRE

### Played at Brighton, June 17, 18, 19, 1901

At the beginning of the same week in which they were dismissed for 13 by Yorkshire, Nottinghamshire enjoyed the distinction of hitting up 642 runs for the loss of seven wickets against Sussex. The success was the more gratifying, as only ten days previously the majority of the Nottinghamshire batsmen had cut a sorry figure against Vine at Trent Bridge. A. O. Jones was the hero of the match. From the first he hit away most brilliantly, and in less than four hours put together a score of 249. The best features of his play were his on-driving and square-leg hitting. John Gunn helped him to add 128, and then Jones and Shrewsbury hit up 183 in an hour and forty minutes. Sussex looked to be in great danger of defeat on Tuesday evening, but Tate came to the rescue next morning, playing the highest innings of his life. Vine batted with exemplary care in each innings, and had the main share in saving his side from defeat.

### Nottinghamshire

| | | |
|---|---|---|
| Mr A. O. Jones c Smith b Vine | .......... | 249 |
| C. E. Dench c Butt b Relf | ............. | 19 |
| W. Gunn c Butt b Vine | ............... | 17 |
| J. Gunn c and b Goldie | ............... | 48 |
| A. Shrewsbury c Goldie b Tate | .......... | 96 |
| J. Carlin b Vine | ..................... | 85 |

| | | |
|---|---|---|
| J. Iremonger st Butt b Relf | ............. | 85 |
| T. Harrison not out | ................... | 6 |
| G. Anthony not out | ................... | 3 |
| B 25, l-b 3, w 4, n-b 2 | .......... | 34 |
| | (7 wkts dec.) | 642 |

A. Hallam and T. Wass did not bat.

## Sussex

| | | | | |
|---|---|---|---|---|
| Mr C. B. Fry lbw b Wass | 17 | – c J. Gunn b Wass | 62 |
| A. E. Relf b J. Gunn | 13 | – c Hallam b Carlin | 1 |
| E. H. Killick c Wass b Hallam | 24 | – c Hallam b Carlin | 27 |
| Mr K. O. Goldie c Wass b Hallam | 56 | – c Jones b Carlin | 4 |
| J. Vine not out | 55 | – b Hallam | 57 |
| Mr C. L. A. Smith c Carlin b J. Gunn | 1 | – not out | 1 |
| F. W. Marlow c Carlin b Jones | 36 | – not out | 0 |
| J. Bean c Wass b Hallam | 20 | | |
| H. R. Butt c Hallam b Jones | 21 | | |
| F. W. Tate c Carlin b J. Gunn | 84 | | |
| C. H. G. Bland b J. Gunn | 2 | | |
| B 19, l-b 3, w 4, n-b 6 | 32 | – B 5, l-b 1, w 1 | 7 |
| | **361** | | **159** |

### Sussex Bowling

| | Overs | Mdns | Runs | Wkts |
|---|---|---|---|---|
| Bland | 5 | — | 25 | — |
| Vine | 39 | 4 | 175 | 3 |
| Relf | 41 | 15 | 114 | 2 |
| Tate | 49 | 5 | 162 | 1 |
| Goldie | 18 | 3 | 73 | 1 |
| Killick | 19 | 8 | 47 | — |
| Bean | 6 | 3 | 12 | — |

### Nottinghamshire Bowling

| | Overs | Mdns | Runs | Wkts | Overs | Mdns | Runs | Wkts |
|---|---|---|---|---|---|---|---|---|
| Wass | 39 | 8 | 144 | 1 | 9 | 5 | 20 | 1 |
| J. Gunn | 31.1 | 12 | 49 | 4 | 16 | 11 | 13 | — |
| Hallam | 27 | 16 | 34 | 3 | 21 | 11 | 25 | 1 |
| Jones | 23 | 2 | 76 | 2 | 9 | 6 | 11 | — |
| Anthony | 4 | 2 | 11 | — | 4 | 2 | 10 | — |
| Dench | 4 | 1 | 3 | — | | | | |
| Iremonger | 4 | 2 | 12 | — | 14 | 2 | 33 | — |
| W. Gunn | | | | | 7 | 1 | 15 | — |
| Carlin | | | | | 10 | 5 | 25 | 3 |

Umpires: R. G. Barlow and J. E. West.

## SUSSEX v YORKSHIRE

### F. W. Tate's Benefit Match

### Played at Brighton, August 19, 20, 21, 1901

So ineffective did Hirst and Rhodes prove against the Sussex batsmen, that on the opening day only one wicket went down, and 307 runs were scored. Killick and Fry coming together at 66 were not out 111 and 167 respectively at the drawing of stumps, and next day they added 109 more, their partnership in all lasting five hours and ten minutes, and realising 349 runs. Particularly anxious to succeed against the champions, Fry exercised marked care, and his play was scarcely as attractive as usual. Killick, who made the first 200 of his career, enjoyed some luck when he went in, but afterwards, cutting brilliantly, he played a distinctly brighter game than his famous partner. The lack of success which attended the Yorkshire bowlers was followed by an even more pronounced failure on the part of their batsmen, who, fatigued no doubt by their long outing, actually lost eight wickets in an hour and forty minutes for 49 runs. Yorkshire saved the game without much difficulty, but Brown and Tunnicliffe carried caution to such a wearisome extent that in nearly three hours they scored only 77 runs from the bat.

## Sussex

| | |
|---|---|
| Mr C. B. Fry lbw b Brown . . . . . . . . . . . . . .209 | Mr P. H. Latham c Brown b Smith . . . . . . . 7 |
| J. Vine c Hirst b Smith . . . . . . . . . . . . . . . 17 | Mr A. M. Sullivan not out . . . . . . . . . . . . . 2 |
| E. H. Killick c Mitchell b Wainwright . . . . .200 | B 7, l-b 14, w 1, n-b 5 . . . . . . . . . 27 |
| K. S. Ranjitsinhji not out . . . . . . . . . . . . . . 86 | — |
| Mr G. Brann c Taylor b Smith . . . . . . . . . . 12 | (5 wkts dec.) 560 |

Mr F. H. Greeson, A. E. Relf, H. R. Butt and F. W. Tate did not bat.

## Yorkshire

| | | | |
|---|---|---|---|
| J. T. Brown run out . . . . . . . . . . . . . . . . . . . . . . . . . | 6 | – not out . . . . . . . . . . . . . . . . . . . . . . | 53 |
| J. Tunnicliffe c Ranjitsinhji b Vine . . . . . . . . . . . . . . . | 0 | – not out . . . . . . . . . . . . . . . . . . . . . . | 24 |
| D. Denton b Relf . . . . . . . . . . . . . . . . . . . . . . . . . . | 0 | | |
| Mr T. L. Taylor b Vine . . . . . . . . . . . . . . . . . . . . . . | 12 | | |
| Mr F. Mitchell c Latham b Relf . . . . . . . . . . . . . . . | 0 | | |
| J. H. Hirst c Brann b Relf . . . . . . . . . . . . . . . . . . . . | 10 | | |
| E. Wainwright c Butt b Vine . . . . . . . . . . . . . . . . . . | 0 | | |
| Mr E. Smith not out . . . . . . . . . . . . . . . . . . . . . . | 38 | | |
| Lord Hawke c and b Relf . . . . . . . . . . . . . . . . . . . . | 1 | | |
| W. Rhodes b Killick . . . . . . . . . . . . . . . . . . . . . . . . | 7 | | |
| L. Whitehead c and b Greeson . . . . . . . . . . . . . . . . | 6 | | |
| B 7, l-b 2, w 1, n-b 2 . . . . . . . . . . . . . . . . . | 12 | B 25, l-b 1, w 1, n-b 3 . . . . . . | 30 |
| | 92 | | 107 |

### Yorkshire Bowling

| | Overs | Mdns | Runs | Wkts |
|---|---|---|---|---|
| Hirst . . . . . . . . . . . . | 30 | 6 | 76 | — |
| Rhodes . . . . . . . . . . . | 40 | 11 | 97 | — |
| Wainwright . . . . . . . | 38 | 8 | 104 | 1 |
| Smith . . . . . . . . . . . . | 52 | 12 | 152 | 3 |
| Brown . . . . . . . . . . . | 19 | 3 | 54 | 1 |
| Whitehead . . . . . . . . | 7 | 1 | 28 | — |
| Denton . . . . . . . . . . | 6 | — | 22 | — |

### Sussex Bowling

| | Overs | Mdns | Runs | Wkts | Overs | Mdns | Runs | Wkts |
|---|---|---|---|---|---|---|---|---|
| Relf . . . . . . . . . . . . . | 21 | 8 | 32 | 4 | 11 | 8 | 5 | — |
| Vine . . . . . . . . . . . . . | 29 | 20 | 23 | 3 | 26 | 20 | 19 | — |
| Tate . . . . . . . . . . . . . | 15 | 7 | 19 | — | 15 | 10 | 15 | — |
| Killick . . . . . . . . . . . | 7 | 3 | 5 | 1 | 10 | 5 | 9 | — |
| Greeson . . . . . . . . . . | 1 | — | 1 | 1 | 8 | 5 | 9 | — |
| Ranjitsinhji . . . . . . . | | | | | 9 | 5 | 10 | — |
| Brann . . . . . . . . . . . . | | | | | 3 | 1 | 10 | — |

Umpires: J. Phillips and H. Wood.

## SUSSEX v SURREY

### Played at Hastings, July 14, 15, 16, 1902

So completely did the batsmen hold the upper hand from start to finish, that in the course of the three days only 21 wickets went down, and 1,427 runs were scored – a record for a first-class match in England. To begin with, Fry and Vine put on 238 before a wicket fell, and although Newham and Brann, each of whom had made over a hundred on the previous Saturday, were out to following balls, the total stood at 419 for six wickets at the drawing of stumps, Ranjitsinhji being not out 54. Cox helped his captain to add 192 in 100 minutes, and with Tate and Ranjitsinhji together, 160 more runs were obtained in 70 minutes. Ranjitsinhji, whose 234 not out stood as the highest innings of the season until Noble made 284 against Sussex at Brighton, played superb cricket, making runs all round the wicket, giving no chance, and obtaining his score in three hours twenty-five minutes. His hits included thirty-nine 4s. Hayward and Abel playing in brilliant style raised the Surrey total to 246 for the first wicket. At the close of the second day, 980 runs in all had been obtained for nine wickets. On the Wednesday, Bush helped Abel to raise the Surrey total to 443 before the second wicket fell. Bush gave no chance, and Abel, who drove especially well, made no mistake until 137.

## Sussex

| | | | |
|---|---|---|---|
| Mr C. B. Fry c Brockwell b Dowson | 159 | | |
| J. Vine c Dowson b Richardson | 92 | – b Jephson | 7 |
| E. H. Killick lbw b Clode | 41 | – not out | 18 |
| A. E. Relf c and b Dowson | 20 | – c and b Dowson | 77 |
| K. S. Ranjitsinhji not out | 234 | | |
| Mr W. Newham c and b Dowson | 2 | | |
| Mr G. Brann lbw b Dowson | 0 | – b Hayes | 48 |
| G. Cox c Hayes b Clode | 51 | | |
| H. R. Butt c Hayward b Dowson | 6 | | |
| F. W. Tate not out | 61 | | |
| C. H. G. Bland did not bat | 0 | – st Stedman b Hayes | 13 |
| B 25, l-b 9, n-b 5 | 39 | B 5, l-b 1, n-b 1 | 7 |

(8 wkts dec.) 705        170

## Surrey

| | | | |
|---|---|---|---|
| R. Abel c Cox b Bland | 179 | H. Clode c Killick b Tate | 11 |
| T. Hayward c Bland b Tate | 144 | A. Stedman b Bland | 2 |
| Capt. H. S. Bush c Ranjitsinhji b Tate | 122 | T. Richardson b Bland | 0 |
| E. G. Hayes lbw b Cox | 42 | W. H. Lockwood absent ill | 0 |
| W. Brockwell c Butt b Tate | 5 | B 4 | 4 |
| Mr E. M. Dowson b Cox | 0 | | |
| Mr D. L. A. Jephson not out | 43 | | 552 |

## Surrey Bowling

| | Overs | Mdns | Runs | Wkts | Overs | Mdns | Runs | Wkts |
|---|---|---|---|---|---|---|---|---|
| Lockwood | 24 | 5 | 98 | — | | | | |
| Richardson | 30 | 1 | 143 | 1 | | | | |
| Clode | 35 | 3 | 129 | 2 | | | | |
| Brockwell | 21 | 1 | 99 | — | 11 | 2 | 40 | — |
| Dowson | 28 | 4 | 137 | 5 | 7 | 1 | 44 | 1 |
| Jephson | 16 | 1 | 36 | — | 14 | 5 | 59 | 1 |
| Hayes | 8 | 1 | 24 | — | 5.1 | 1 | 11 | 2 |
| Bush | | | | | 1 | — | 9 | — |

## Sussex Bowling

| | Overs | Mdns | Runs | Wkts |
|---|---|---|---|---|
| Vine | 27 | 7 | 77 | — |
| Bland | 29.3 | 4 | 98 | 3 |
| Cox | 40 | 14 | 149 | 2 |
| Relf | 11 | — | 69 | — |
| Tate | 48 | 11 | 155 | 4 |

Umpires: T. Mycroft and F. Martin.

## SUSSEX v MIDDLESEX

Played at Brighton, June 28, 29, 1906

Poorly represented, Middlesex found themselves badly out-played, and suffered defeat by an innings and 101 runs. The game was practically lost within the first two hours, the visitors shaping so wretchedly against Dwyer and Albert Relf that they were all out for 96. Eight wickets, indeed, fell for 54 runs, but Hearne hit with some determination. When Sussex went in, Vine and Smith were out for 6 runs. Killick, however, once again batted in delightful fashion. Going in first wicket down, he was fourth out at 161. He cut and drove admirably, and all that could be urged against his cricket were two awkward chances during a stay of nearly two hours and a half. Albert Relf assisted him to put on 90 in seventy minutes, and with Robert Relf in 65 more runs were obtained. Sussex at the drawing of stumps led by 127 runs and had five wickets in hand. Rain fell during the night and up to noon next day, preventing cricket until nearly three o'clock, the weather then turning quite sunny. Middlesex had no chance, on a treacherous pitch, of retrieving their ground. The Sussex innings was finished off in less than an hour for the addition of 63 runs. Middlesex were 190 in arrear and, after Albert Relf had taken the first wicket, Dwyer carried all before him, the score with seven men out being only 38. Dwyer, keeping an excellent length and varying his pace cleverly, achieved quite a triumph, following up his success in the first innings by taking nine wickets for 44. Altogether he obtained sixteen wickets in the match for 100 runs.

### Middlesex

| | | | |
|---|---|---|---|
| F. A. Tarrant c R. Relf b Dwyer | 13 | – b Dwyer | 13 |
| Mr W. P. Harrison b A. E. Relf | 12 | – b A. E. Relf | 3 |
| Mr J. H. Stogdon b A. E. Relf | 3 | – b Dwyer | 0 |
| J. T. Rawlin c Butt b A. E. Relf | 1 | – b Dwyer | 0 |
| A. E. Trott b Dwyer | 13 | – c Cox b Dwyer | 0 |
| Mr C. P. Foley c Butt b Dwyer | 0 | – b Dwyer | 9 |
| Mr G. MacGregor c R. Relf b Dwyer | 0 | – c A. E. Relf b Dwyer | 11 |
| Mr C. V. Baker b Dwyer | 1 | – not out | 28 |
| Mr C. B. W. Magnay st Butt b Dwyer | 7 | – b Dwyer | 1 |
| J. T. Hearne not out | 28 | – lbw b Dwyer | 4 |
| E. Mignon c Leach b Dwyer | 8 | – b Dwyer | 2 |
| B 4, l-b 5, w 1 | 10 | B 12, l-b 2, n-b 4 | 18 |
| | **96** | | **89** |

### Sussex

| | | | |
|---|---|---|---|
| Mr C. L. A. Smith b Rawlin | 4 | G. Leach run out | 27 |
| J. Vine c MacGregor b Mignon | 0 | Mr H. L. Simms not out | 13 |
| E. H. Killick c Hearne b Trott | 96 | E. B. Dwyer c Stogdon b Trott | 9 |
| A. E. Relf c Trott b Hearne | 40 | H. R. Butt c and b Tarrant | 0 |
| R. Relf c Mignon b Tarrant | 58 | B 4, l-b 3 | 7 |
| Mr E. G. Read b Trott | 0 | | |
| G. Cox b Tarrant | 32 | | **286** |

### Sussex Bowling

| | Overs | Mdns | Runs | Wkts | Overs | Mdns | Runs | Wkts |
|---|---|---|---|---|---|---|---|---|
| Dwyer | 21.3 | 5 | 56 | 7 | 23.3 | 11 | 44 | 9 |
| A. E. Relf | 21 | 8 | 30 | 3 | 15 | 11 | 12 | 1 |
| Killick | | | | | 8 | 4 | 15 | — |

**Middlesex Bowling**

|  | Overs | Mdns | Runs | Wkts |
|---|---|---|---|---|
| Rawlin .......... | 8 | 2 | 24 | 1 |
| Mignon ......... | 13 | — | 65 | 1 |
| Trott ........... | 19 | 5 | 75 | 3 |
| Hearne .......... | 28 | 6 | 63 | 1 |
| Tarrant ........ | 22.2 | 4 | 50 | 3 |
| Magnay ......... | 1 | — | 2 | — |

Umpires: J. Carlin and R. G. Barlow.

# SUSSEX v ESSEX

## Played at Hastings, August 27, 28, 29, 1906

From start to finish batsmen did rather too well to hold out much hope of a definite result. There existed just a chance of Essex winning when – 118 runs on at the drawing of stumps on Tuesday – they forced the game so well in the morning that 229 runs were added in little more than two hours, the innings being declared shortly after half-past one. Sussex, with 348 to get in three hours and a half, had four men out for 92, but Vine and Smith showed strong defence, and ensured a draw. Perrin, on Monday, was seen at his best, batting in most polished fashion for three hours, and making scarcely a single faulty stroke. In the first innings of Sussex, four men played on and Albert Relf was stumped off the wicket-keeper's pads.

### Essex

| | | | |
|---|---|---|---|
| Mr J. W. H. T. Douglas b Cox ................. | 0 | – b Cox ........................ | 8 |
| Mr F. L. Fane b Cox ........................ | 7 | – c Butt b Cox ................. | 82 |
| Mr P. Perrin c Latham b Cox ................. | 150 | – c R. Relf b Cox ............... | 60 |
| Mr C. McGahey c R. Relf b Smith ............. | 21 | – c Latham b A. E. Relf .......... | 58 |
| Rev. F. H. Gillingham run out ................. | 15 | – not out ...................... | 66 |
| Mr W. M. Turner c and b A. E. Relf ........... | 9 | – not out ...................... | 54 |
| H. Carpenter b A. E. Relf ................... | 10 | | |
| C. P. Buckenham lbw b Killick ................ | 22 | | |
| W. Reeves c Butt b Cox ..................... | 20 | | |
| E. Russell not out .......................... | 12 | | |
| W. Mead c Butt b Cox ...................... | 26 | | |
| B 6, l-b 1 ........................ | 7 | B 23, l-b 8, w 4 .......... | 35 |
| | 299 | (4 wkts dec.) | 363 |

### Sussex

| | | | |
|---|---|---|---|
| Mr P. H. Latham b Buckenham ................. | 50 | – c and b Buckenham ........... | 6 |
| J. Vine c Turner b Buckenham ................. | 16 | – not out ...................... | 66 |
| E. H. Killick b Mead ........................ | 53 | – c Turner b Mead ............. | 17 |
| A. E. Relf st Russell b Mead .................. | 42 | – c Russell b McGahey .......... | 18 |
| G. Cox b Buckenham ........................ | 53 | – b Buckenham ................. | 16 |
| Mr C. L. A. Smith b Mead ................... | 3 | – not out ...................... | 66 |
| R. Relf b Perrin .......................... | 16 | | |
| Mr J. W. Nason b McGahey ................... | 18 | | |
| Mr H. L. Simms b Buckenham ................. | 25 | | |
| G. Leach not out .......................... | 16 | | |
| H. R. Butt c Russell b Buckenham ............. | 10 | | |
| B 8, l-b 4, w 1 ...................... | 13 | B 6, l-b 7, n-b 2 .......... | 15 |
| | 315 | | 204 |

## Sussex Bowling

|              | Overs | Mdns | Runs | Wkts | Overs | Mdns | Runs | Wkts |
|--------------|-------|------|------|------|-------|------|------|------|
| Cox          | 27.4  | 2    | 127  | 5    | 29    | 8    | 87   | 3    |
| A. E. Relf   | 26    | 7    | 80   | 2    | 25    | 6    | 82   | 1    |
| Smith        | 7     | 1    | 20   | 1    | 4     | 1    | 13   | —    |
| Killick      | 10    | 1    | 45   | 1    | 8     | —    | 35   | —    |
| Vine         | 3     | 2    | 2    | —    | 13    | —    | 64   | —    |
| Leach        | 5     | 1    | 18   | —    | 9     | —    | 33   | —    |
| Nason        |       |      |      |      | 1     | —    | 5    | —    |
| Simms        |       |      |      |      | 1     | —    | 9    | —    |

## Essex Bowling

|             | Overs | Mdns | Runs | Wkts | Overs | Mdns | Runs | Wkts |
|-------------|-------|------|------|------|-------|------|------|------|
| Buckenham   | 24.5  | 1    | 105  | 5    | 13    | 4    | 33   | 2    |
| Douglas     | 16    | 1    | 67   | —    | 8     | 3    | 15   | —    |
| McGahey     | 21    | 3    | 69   | 1    | 10    | 1    | 25   | 1    |
| Mead        | 15    | 7    | 34   | 3    | 27    | 7    | 85   | 1    |
| Reeves      | 4     | 1    | 17   | —    | 4     | 2    | 10   | —    |
| Perrin      | 3     | 1    | 10   | 1    | 2     | 1    | 2    | —    |
| Turner      |       |      |      |      | 3     | —    | 19   | —    |

Umpires: V. A. Titchmarsh and A. E. Clapp.

## SUSSEX v HAMPSHIRE

Played at Chichester, July 16, 17, 18, 1908

Restricted to one day's cricket which naturally led to no definite result, this match was rendered noteworthy by an altogether unpardonable course of conduct on the part of the Sussex team. Continuous rain precluded any possibility of cricket on Thursday but, although the weather continued very wet during the night, the pitch was fit for play at half-past eleven next morning. At that hour while the Hampshire men were in attendance only two or three members of the Sussex eleven had made their way to the Priory Park. Fry and Vine arrived some time later but the majority of the side did not put in an appearance until between three and four o'clock in the afternoon. Preparations were then made for a start but the weather, always showery, turned wet again and the game was not entered upon until Saturday. Had the Sussex team arrived at the proper hour comparatively little cricket would have been possible but that was no excuse for the non-appearance of the men. The only attempt at explanation urged was that as rain fell heavily twenty miles away where the majority of the Sussex team stayed for the night, the cricketers concluded that no play could take place. On Saturday White hit splendidly all round the wicket, Remnant helping him to put on 74 after six Hampshire wickets had fallen for 78, and for Sussex Ranjitsinhji played in admirable style.

## Hampshire

| | |
|---|---|
| Mr A. C. Johnston b Cox | 3 |
| A. Bowell c and b Vincett | 15 |
| Capt. W. N. White b Vine | 85 |
| C. B. Llewellyn c Butt b Vincett | 0 |
| Mr E. M. Sprot lbw b Cox | 1 |
| P. Mead b Cox | 17 |
| A. Stone st Butt b A. E. Relf | 2 |
| E. R. Remnant lbw b Cox | 26 |
| J. R. Badcock b Cox | 8 |
| A. Kennedy st Butt b Cox | 0 |
| J. Newman not out | 9 |
| B 5, l-b 1, w 1 | 7 |
| | 173 |

## Sussex

| | |
|---|---|
| Mr C. B. Fry b Newman ............... | 4 |
| J. Vine c White b Llewellyn ............. | 21 |
| R. H. Killick b Newman ............... | 10 |
| H. H. Jam Sahib of Nawanager (K. S. Ranjit- | |
| sinhji) not out ...................... | 51 |
| R. Relf lbw b Kennedy ................ | 2 |
| A. E. Relf c Bowell b Llewellyn .......... | 0 |
| Mr J. W. Nason b Kennedy ............. | 10 |
| G. Cox not out ...................... | 8 |
| B 4, l-b 1, w 1 ................ | 6 |
| | 112 |

G. Leach, J. H. Vincett and H. R. Butt did not bat.

## Sussex Bowling

| | Overs | Mdns | Runs | Wkts |
|---|---|---|---|---|
| Killick ........... | 7 | — | 19 | — |
| Cox ............. | 23.4 | 11 | 41 | 6 |
| Vincett ........... | 10 | 1 | 39 | 2 |
| A. E. Relf ........ | 12 | 4 | 32 | 1 |
| Ranjitsinhji ....... | 5 | — | 19 | — |
| Vine ............. | 5 | 1 | 16 | 1 |

## Hampshire Bowling

| | Overs | Mdns | Runs | Wkts |
|---|---|---|---|---|
| Newman ......... | 10 | 4 | 18 | 2 |
| Mead ............ | 5 | 2 | 11 | — |
| Remnant ......... | 5 | 3 | 11 | — |
| Llewellyn ......... | 16 | 6 | 35 | 2 |
| Kennedy ......... | 5 | 4 | 31 | 2 |

Umpires: J. Carlin and W. Flowers.

## SUSSEX v MIDDLESEX

### Played at Eastbourne, August 11, 12, 13, 1910

Fielding out for the whole of the first day, when Middlesex scored 380 for the loss of four wickets, Sussex had to bat on a pitch ruined by rain and suffered defeat by an innings and 165 runs. Warner and Tarrant gave Middlesex a splendid start, putting on 180 runs before the former played on, while after four wickets had fallen for 256 J. W. Hearne and Saville added 124. Owing to rain in the early morning the game on Friday was only in progress for two hours and three quarters, but during that time Middlesex declared and Sussex lost six wickets for 57, the first four batsmen being disposed of for 17 runs. J. W. Hearne played with fine skill and judgment for three hours, making scarcely a single bad stroke. On Saturday, when a further downpour delayed progress with the match until after two o'clock, an easy victory for Middlesex was always a foregone conclusion. In the follow-on, when Vine, Robert Relf, and Heygate had been dismissed for 7 runs. Albert Relf hit up 61 out of 84 in three-quarters of an hour. Cox played admirably in each innings.

## Middlesex

| | |
|---|---|
| Mr P. F. Warner b Killick ............. | 88 |
| F. A. Tarrant c Butt b A. E. Relf ......... | 85 |
| J. W. Hearne c Cartwright b A. E. Relf ....108 | |
| Mr J. Douglas c R. Relf b Leach ......... | 4 |
| Mr C. V. Baker run out ............... | 29 |
| Mr S. H. Saville c Cox b R. Relf ......... | 76 |
| H. R. Murrell c Butt b A. E. Relf ......... | 1 |
| Mr H. S. Weston not out ............... | 15 |
| Mr K. B. Harper c R. Relf b A. E. Relf .... | 2 |
| J. T. Hearne not out .................. | 2 |
| B 13, l-b 3 .................. | 16 |
| (8 wkts dec.) | 426 |

E. Mignon did not bat.

## Sussex

| | | | |
|---|---|---|---|
| R. Relf c Mignon b J. T. Hearne | | 9 – b J. T. Hearne | 1 |
| J. Vine c J. T. Hearne b Tarrant | | 1 – c Baker b J. T. Hearne | 1 |
| Mr R. B. Heygate b Tarrant | | 6 – c J. W. Hearne b Tarrant | 0 |
| Mr P. Cartwright c and b Tarrant | | 1 – c Saville b Tarrant | 0 |
| A. E. Relf c Saville b Tarrant | | 12 – c Baker b Tarrant | 61 |
| Mr H. P. Chaplin run out | | 5 – c Saville b J. T. Hearne | 26 |
| E. H. Killick lbw b Tarrant | | 20 – lbw b Tarrant | 8 |
| G. Cox c and b Tarrant | | 31 – lbw b J. T. Hearne | 30 |
| J. H. Vincett lbw b J. T. Hearne | | 14 – not out | 9 |
| G. Leach c Warner b Tarrant | | 7 – b Tarrant | 8 |
| H. R. Butt not out | | 1 – c J. T. Hearne b Tarrant | 0 |
| L-b 1 | 1 | B 6, l-b 2, n-b 1 | 9 |
| | **108** | | **153** |

### Sussex Bowling

| | Overs | Mdns | Runs | Wkts |
|---|---|---|---|---|
| Leach | 15 | 3 | 62 | 1 |
| A. E. Relf | 31 | 14 | 56 | 4 |
| R. Relf | 18 | 3 | 58 | 1 |
| Cox | 14 | 2 | 41 | — |
| Vincett | 13 | 2 | 36 | — |
| Vine | 15 | 2 | 62 | — |
| Killick | 11 | 2 | 30 | 1 |
| Heygate | 6 | — | 25 | — |
| Chaplin | 3 | 1 | 12 | — |
| Cartwright | 5 | 2 | 12 | — |
| Butt | 4 | — | 16 | — |

### Middlesex Bowling

| | Overs | Mdns | Runs | Wkts | Overs | Mdns | Runs | Wkts |
|---|---|---|---|---|---|---|---|---|
| J. T. Hearne | 23 | 9 | 48 | 2 | 23 | 9 | 43 | 4 |
| Tarrant | 24.3 | 7 | 52 | 7 | 21.5 | 4 | 85 | 6 |
| J. W. Hearne | 2 | — | 7 | — | | | | |
| Weston | | | | | 2 | — | 16 | — |

Umpires: G. P. Harrison and A. E. Street.

# SUSSEX v NOTTINGHAMSHIRE

Played at Brighton, May 18, 19, 20, 1911

A phenomenal display of driving on the part of Edward Alletson rendered this match memorable. Alletson went in when Nottinghamshire in their second innings, with seven men out, were only 9 runs ahead. Before lunch, he took fifty minutes to make 47, but on resuming hit away with such extraordinary power and freedom that he added 142 out of 152 for the last wicket in forty minutes, actually scoring his last 89 runs in fifteen minutes. Twice he sent the ball over the stand, and on six other occasions cleared the ring, while in one over from Killick that included two no-balls, he hit three 6s and four 4s – 34 runs in all. His glorious innings was made up by eight 6s, twenty-three 4s, four 3s, ten 2s and seventeen singles. Sussex, instead of gaining the easy victory which appeared assured before Alletson's tremendous hitting, had 237 to make in three hours and a quarter. Robert Relf and Vine scored 112 in seventy-five minutes, but six men were out for 148 and the eighth wicket fell ten minutes before time.

## Nottinghamshire

| | | | |
|---|---|---|---|
| Mr A. O. Jones b Cox | 57 | – b Leach | 0 |
| J. Iremonger c and b A. E. Relf | 0 | – c Tudor b Killick | 83 |
| G. Gunn st Butt b Cox | 90 | – st Butt b R. Relf | 66 |
| J. Hardstaff b Cox | 8 | – c Butt b A. E. Relf | 7 |
| J. Gunn c R. Relf b Killick | 33 | – b R. Relf | 19 |
| W. Payton c Heygate b Killick | 20 | – lbw b A. E. Relf | 0 |
| W. Whysall b Killick | 1 | – c Butt b A. E. Relf | 3 |
| G. M. Lee c and b Killick | 10 | – c Cox b Leach | 26 |
| E. Alletson c Killick b A. E. Relf | 7 | – c Smith b Cox | 189 |
| T. Oates not out | 3 | – b Leach | 1 |
| W. Riley c Smith b Killick | 3 | – not out | 10 |
| B 5, n-b 1 | 6 | B 3, l-b 2, w 2, n-b 1 | 8 |
| | **238** | | **412** |

## Sussex

| | | | |
|---|---|---|---|
| R. Relf b Jones | 42 | – c Oates b Jones | 71 |
| J. Vine b Jones | 77 | – c Payton b Riley | 54 |
| Mr R. R. Heygate c Lee b Iremonger | 32 | – b J. Gunn | 13 |
| G. Cox c Alletson b Riley | 37 | – st Oates b Riley | 5 |
| A. E. Relf c and b Jones | 4 | – c Oates b Riley | 0 |
| Mr C. L. Tudor c Oates b Riley | 23 | – b J. Gunn | 4 |
| E. H. Killick c Hardstaff b Lee | 81 | – c Lee b Riley | 21 |
| G. Leach b Lee | 52 | – b J. Gunn | 31 |
| Mr C. L. A. Smith not out | 33 | – not out | 12 |
| J. H. Vincett c Iremonger b Lee | 9 | – not out | 1 |
| H. R. Butt b Riley | 13 | | |
| B 4, l-b 3, w 1, n-b 3 | 11 | N-b 1 | 1 |
| | **414** | | **213** |

### Sussex Bowling

| | Overs | Mdns | Runs | Wkts | Overs | Mdns | Runs | Wkts |
|---|---|---|---|---|---|---|---|---|
| A. E. Relf | 19 | 5 | 40 | 2 | 33 | 13 | 92 | 3 |
| Leach | 11 | 2 | 53 | — | 19 | 2 | 91 | 3 |
| Vincett | 4 | — | 31 | — | 3 | 1 | 25 | — |
| R. Relf | 11 | — | 36 | — | 19 | 6 | 39 | 2 |
| Cox | 25 | 4 | 58 | 3 | 9.4 | 2 | 27 | 1 |
| Killick | 10.2 | 4 | 14 | 5 | 20 | 2 | 130 | 1 |

### Nottinghamshire Bowling

| | Overs | Mdns | Runs | Wkts | Overs | Mdns | Runs | Wkts |
|---|---|---|---|---|---|---|---|---|
| Iremonger | 34 | 7 | 97 | 1 | 14 | 2 | 34 | — |
| Riley | 29.4 | 5 | 102 | 3 | 33 | 9 | 82 | 4 |
| J. Gunn | 29 | 2 | 87 | — | 25 | 9 | 41 | 3 |
| Jones | 22 | 2 | 69 | 3 | 5 | 1 | 24 | 1 |
| Alletson | 1 | — | 3 | — | | | | |
| Lee | 14 | 1 | 45 | 3 | 4 | — | 31 | — |

Umpires: H. Wood and A. A. White.

## SUSSEX v LEICESTERSHIRE

Played at Brighton, July 1, 2, 3, 1912

Unsettled weather restricting the opening day's cricket to about three and a half hours, Leicestershire only accomplished a moderate performance in making 168 runs, the features of the afternoon being the patient batting of Wood, the hard driving of King, and the magnificent bowling of Albert Relf. On Tuesday the Sussex batting was excellent, for before rain came on again the side had put together 313 for six wickets, the only real failure, curiously enough, being that of the Jam Sahib, who was out first ball, but it was on the Wednesday that the home cricket reached its greatest height. Albert Relf showed wonderful all-round form. He first increased his not out score of 25 to over 100, and then on his captain applying the closure, he dismissed seven Leicestershire batsmen for 36 runs. In scoring 103 not out and taking fifteen wickets for 77 runs, Relf had an enormous share in the Sussex victory by an innings and 151 runs.

### Leicestershire

| | | |
|---|---|---|
| Mr C. J. B. Wood c Jam Sahib b A. E. Relf | 73 | – lbw b A. E. Relf ... 21 |
| A. Mounteney b A. E. Relf | 0 | – b A. E. Relf ... 5 |
| A. E. Knight c Cox b Simms | 5 | – c Fender b A. E. Relf ... 11 |
| H. Whitehead b A. E. Relf | 2 | – lbw b A. E. Relf ... 0 |
| J. H. King c and b A. E. Relf | 48 | – c and b A. E. Relf ... 34 |
| S. Coe c Cox b A. E. Relf | 4 | – lbw b Cox ... 14 |
| A. Lord c Lang b A. E. Relf | 0 | – c Chaplin b A. E. Relf ... 11 |
| W. Shipman c sub. b A. E. Relf | 18 | – c Vine b Cox ... 3 |
| Mr J. Shields st Lang b A. E. Relf | 7 | – not out ... 3 |
| W. E. Astill c Lang b Cox | 0 | – c Chaplin b A. E. Relf ... 0 |
| A. Skelding not out | 0 | – b Cox ... 0 |
| B 7, l-b 2, n-b 2 | 11 | B 8, l-b 1 ... 9 |
| | **168** | **111** |

### Sussex

| | | |
|---|---|---|
| R. Relf b Shipman | 62 | Mr P. G. H. Fender c Shipman b King .... 2 |
| J. Vine c Shields b Shipman | 90 | Mr H. P. Chaplin c Astill b Wood ........ 33 |
| Mr P. Cartwright c Whitehead b Shipman .. | 75 | Mr A. H. Lang not out ................ 18 |
| Mr H. L. Simms b Shipman | 23 | |
| A. E. Relf not out | 103 | B 14, l-b 7, n-b 3 ............. 24 |
| H. H. the Jam Sahib of Nawanagar c Whitehead b Shipman . | 0 | (7 wkts dec.) 430 |

V. C. W. Jupp and G. Cox did not bat.

### Sussex Bowling

| | Overs | Mdns | Runs | Wkts | Overs | Mdns | Runs | Wkts |
|---|---|---|---|---|---|---|---|---|
| A. E. Relf | 28.1 | 13 | 41 | 8 | 27 | 12 | 36 | 7 |
| Simms | 16 | 1 | 53 | 1 | 3 | — | 16 | — |
| Vine | 11 | 1 | 38 | — | | | | |
| Cox | 18 | 7 | 25 | 1 | 10.5 | 5 | 16 | 3 |
| Fender | | | | | 14 | 3 | 34 | — |

### Leicestershire Bowling

| | Overs | Mdns | Runs | Wkts |
|---|---|---|---|---|
| Shipman | 20 | 2 | 64 | 5 |
| Skelding | 17 | 2 | 56 | — |
| King | 37 | 8 | 117 | 1 |
| Astill | 23 | 3 | 95 | — |
| Wood | 9 | 1 | 36 | 1 |
| Lord | 5 | 1 | 20 | — |
| Coe | 3 | — | 18 | — |

Umpires: F. G. Roberts and W. Richards.

# SUSSEX v OXFORD UNIVERSITY

Played at Brighton, June 19, 20, 21, 1913

Oxford, thanks to Campbell, Bardsley, and Von Melle, recovered from a poor start, and did by no means badly, after losing four wickets for 49, to complete their innings for 240, but they left off with the worst of the game at the end of the first day. Sussex, who made 123 for two wickets, increased their total to 368 on Friday, when wet weather seriously curtailed the play. The county's batting was very uneven, for Vine and Robert Relf, who put on 264 for the third partnership, were responsible for 270 between them. Relf was only in for two hours and three quarters, while Vine stayed a quarter of an hour longer, the former hitting twenty-four 4s and Vine a 5, and six 4s. The University were beaten by an innings and 33 runs, but they were terribly handicapped on the Saturday when, apart from the difficult pitch, Bardsley and White were absent through injuries, and Twining was called away. Chaplin allowed G. G. R. Colman to bat instead of Twining – a very irregular proceeding.

## Oxford University

| | | |
|---|---|---|
| Mr W. G. K. Boswell b Roberts | 6 | – c Roberts b A. E. Relf ............ 5 |
| Mr F. H. Knott c A. E. Relt b Roberts | 0 | – c Vincett b A. E. Relf ........... 26 |
| Mr A. L. Hosie c Cox b Roberts | 14 | – c R. Relf b Roberts ............ 10 |
| Mr I. P. F. Campbell run out | 51 | – c and b Fender .............. 10 |
| Mr A. C. Wilkinson c and b Roberts | 10 | – c A. E. Relf b Fender .......... 18 |
| Mr R. H. Twining b A. E. Relf | 11 | – G. R. R. Colman sub. lbw b Fender 10 |
| Mr R. V. Bardsley lbw b Vincett | 41 | – absent hurt .................... 0 |
| Mr B. G. von Melle b Roberts | 72 | – b Fender ..................... 0 |
| Mr P. H. Davies c Cox b Roberts | 10 | – not out ...................... 8 |
| Mr R. S. M. White not out | 5 | – absent hurt .................. 0 |
| Mr C. U. Peat c Bowley b Vincett | 1 | – c Vine b Fender .............. 2 |
| B 17, l-b 2 | 19 | B 2, l-b 4 .............. 6 |
| | **240** | **95** |

## Sussex

| | |
|---|---|
| J. Vine c Davies b Peat ................ 93 | Mr H. P. Chaplin c sub. b Melle .......... 26 |
| Mr J. L. Wilson lbw b Peat ............ 0 | G. Cox b Melle ....................... 0 |
| A. E. Relf b Peat .................... 0 | J. H. Vincett b Melle .................. 4 |
| R. Relf c Bardsley b Peat ..............177 | H. E. Roberts not out .................. 4 |
| Mr P. G. H. Fender c Knott b Peat ....... 2 | B 16, l-b 3, n-b 1 .............. 20 |
| E. H. Bowley c Twining b Peat .......... 8 | |
| A. Charlwood b Melle ................ 34 | **368** |

## Sussex Bowling

| | Overs | Mdns | Runs | Wkts | Overs | Mdns | Runs | Wkts |
|---|---|---|---|---|---|---|---|---|
| Roberts ......... | 27 | 5 | 80 | 6 | 9 | — | 25 | 1 |
| A. E. Relf ........ | 28 | 8 | 63 | 1 | 17 | 8 | 23 | 2 |
| R. Relf .......... | 6 | 1 | 17 | — | | | | |
| Vincett .......... | 8.2 | — | 27 | 2 | | | | |
| Fender .......... | 4 | — | 34 | — | 10.3 | 4 | 21 | 5 |
| Cox ............. | | | | | 3 | — | 20 | — |

**Oxford University Bowling**

|  | Overs | Mdns | Runs | Wkts |
|---|---|---|---|---|
| Peat .............. | 30 | 1 | 108 | 6 |
| Melle ............ | 33 | 6 | 81 | 4 |
| Davies ........... | 30 | 4 | 86 | — |
| Wilkinson ........ | 8 | 2 | 24 | — |
| Bardsley .......... | 6 | — | 26 | — |
| Hosie ............ | 3 | — | 19 | — |
| Knott ............ | 1 | — | 4 | — |

Umpires: R. G. Barlow and G. Webb.

## SUSSEX v GLOUCESTERSHIRE

### Played at Brighton, August 21, 22, 1913

There was some truly remarkable cricket in this match, four Sussex batsmen scoring hundreds, and only one of the other eighteen men engaged making over 30. H. Wilson and R. Relf were responsible for 222 out of their sides first innings of 309, against which Gloucestershire could only respond with 66. Though leading by 243 Sussex went in again on the Friday, and this time it was Albert Relf and Vine who reached three figures. Chaplin declared his second innings at 307 for five wickets, and Gloucestershire, with Jessop and Gange unable to bat, were set no fewer than 551 to make. Thoroughly disheartened by the position of the game, and their other misfortunes, the visitors actually lost five wickets for 4 runs, and it was only the brilliant hitting of Sewell that saved the side from absolute collapse. Even then Sussex won by 470 runs.

### Sussex

| | | | |
|---|---|---|---|
| Mr H. L. Wilson c Robinson b Dipper ...........109 | – c Langdon b Dennett ........... | 15 |
| J. Vine b Gange ........................... 8 | – c and b Nason ................101 |
| R. Relf c Langdon b Dipper ..................113 | – c Dipper b Dennett ............. | 17 |
| A. E. Relf b Dennett ....................... 28 | – c Robinson b Nason ...........117 |
| V. C. W. Jupp c Dipper b Dennett .............. 5 | – not out ...................... | 3 |
| Mr H. P. Chaplin c Roberts b Dipper ........... 5 | – c Parker b Roberts ............. | 21 |
| Mr P. G. H. Fender c Jessop b Dennett ........... 7 | |
| G. Cox lbw b Dennett ...................... 21 | |
| G. Street c Dennett b Dipper .................. 4 | |
| Mr N. J. Holloway not out .................... 1 | |
| J. H. Vincett b Dipper ...................... 2 | |
| W 2, n-b 4 ........................ 6 | B 23, l-b 5, w 1, n-b 4 ...... 33 |
| | |
| 309 | (5 wkts dec.) 307 |

### Gloucestershire

| | | |
|---|---|---|
| T. Langdon b Holloway ..................... | 1 – b Holloway ................... | 4 |
| A. G. Dipper lbw b A. E. Relf ................. | 3 – b Cox ...................... | 0 |
| Mr F. B. Roberts b Holloway ................. | 5 – c R. Relf b Holloway ............ | 0 |
| Mr J. W. W. Nason c Street b Holloway ........ | 0 – st Street b Cox ................. | 0 |
| Mr G. L. Jessop b Holloway .................. | 0 – absent ill .................... | 0 |
| Mr D. C. Robinson c Cox b A. E. Relf .......... | 17 – c Street b Holloway ............ | 5 |
| Mr C. O. H. Sewell c Jupp b Holloway .......... | 11 – not out ...................... | 63 |
| T. J. Smith run out ........................ | 0 – b Holloway ................... | 0 |
| C. Parker c and b A. E. Relf ................. | 13 – b Cox ...................... | 1 |
| G. Dennett not out ........................ | 13 – b Vincett ................... | 7 |
| T. Gange absent hurt ...................... | 0 – absent hurt .................. | 0 |
| L-b 2, n-b 1 ...................... | 3 | |
| | | |
| | 66 | 80 |

## Gloucestershire Bowling

| | Overs | Mdns | Runs | Wkts | Overs | Mdns | Runs | Wkts |
|---|---|---|---|---|---|---|---|---|
| Gange ........... | 11 | — | 58 | 1 | | | | |
| Dennett .......... | 31 | 7 | 113 | 4 | 23 | 9 | 61 | 2 |
| Dipper ........... | 17.3 | 2 | 77 | 5 | 10 | 4 | 28 | — |
| Parker ........... | 8 | — | 21 | — | 28 | 6 | 56 | — |
| Jessop ........... | 6 | 1 | 29 | — | | | | |
| Roberts .......... | 1 | — | 5 | — | 8 | 1 | 54 | 1 |
| Langdon ......... | | | | | 4 | — | 23 | — |
| Nason ........... | | | | | 7.2 | — | 52 | 2 |

## Sussex Bowling

| | Overs | Mdns | Runs | Wkts | Overs | Mdns | Runs | Wkts |
|---|---|---|---|---|---|---|---|---|
| Holloway ......... | 17 | 7 | 30 | 5 | 11 | 3 | 42 | 4 |
| A. E. Relf ........ | 17 | 9 | 33 | 3 | | | | |
| Cox ............. | | | | | 11 | 4 | 35 | 3 |
| Vincett ........... | | | | | 0.4 | — | 3 | 1 |

Umpires: G. Webb and A. A. White.

# WARWICKSHIRE

## WARWICKSHIRE IN 1911

*President* – The Earl of Craven

*Hon. Secretary* – Mr H. W. Bainbridge, Warwick

*Hon. Treasurer* – Mr F. S. Goodwin, Diddington Hall, Coventry

*Secretary and Treasurer* – Mr R. V. Ryder, County Ground, Edgbaston

*Captain* – Mr F. R. Foster

Never since the County Championship became an organised competition has there been a result half so surprising as the triumph in 1911 of Warwickshire. By comparison, the victory of Middlesex in 1903 was quite an ordinary event. The jump from fourteenth place in 1910 to the top of the tree was nothing less than astonishing. The counties having agreed among themselves to decide the championship on the system brought forward by Somerset, with points allowed on the first innings in drawn matches, it would be both unfair and ungenerous to quarrel with the result arrived at. A more important consideration was that Warwickshire did not meet Kent, Middlesex, Nottinghamshire, or Essex. This, however, was not the fault of the Warwickshire committee. So far as one knows they would have been glad enough to secure a stronger programme. Probably few cricketers would contend that Warwickshire had the best county eleven of the year. Under all conditions Kent, no doubt, had the strongest side, and it was only the accident of a narrow defeat at The Oval on a slow wicket that robbed them of first place. This, however, was only one of the chances of the game. Kent, when in 1906 they carried off the championship for the first time, were also indebted to the misfortunes of their most dangerous rival, Yorkshire being put out of court by a single run defeat at the hands of Gloucestershire at Bristol. At the end of the season Warwickshire tarnished their laurels, cutting an ignominious figure against England at The Oval. Winning the toss on a perfect wicket they might, despite the absence of Kinneir, reasonably have been expected to get three hundred runs, but partly through over-anxiety their batting went all to pieces, the match being as good as lost before lunch time on the first day. To this defeat we must not attach undue weight. Nowadays it seems beyond the power of any county to contend successfully against a team that can fairly be described as England. Since the charity match in September became an annual fixture Kent had made three attempts, but their record comes out at two bad beatings and a draw. To go a little further back, Surrey in 1895, being then at the height of their fame, tried to play England in W. E. Read's testimonial match, but so far from emulating the deeds of F. P. Miller's eleven fifty years ago, they were outplayed from start to finish and beaten in a single innings. It is true that Yorkshire won at The Oval in 1905 by 65 runs, but the match was rather a half-hearted affair.

When the season began nothing could have been more unlikely than that Warwickshire would win the championship. No sooner had F. R. Foster been appointed captain in succession to H. J. Goodwin than he announced his impending retirement from first-class cricket. Dispirited and obviously short of practice, the team opened the season against Surrey at The Oval and were hopelessly beaten in less than a day and a half. The outlook seemed very dismal but, as everyone knows, strong influences were brought to bear upon F. R. Foster, with the result that he agreed to reconsider his decision and, as originally intended, take charge of the side. Nothing very startling occurred for a couple of months, but from the end of June Warwickshire showed wonderful form. Of their last twelve county matches they won nine outright and won the other three on the first innings, scoring in the twelve games 54 points out of a possible 60. So close was the fight, however, with Kent for first place that to secure the championship they needed an actual win in their closing fixture with Northamptonshire. The first day's play, on a Saturday at Northampton, placed them in a winning position, and although delay through rain caused some anxiety, they gained in the end an easy victory.

Their success gave rise to extraordinary enthusiasm. Returning from Northampton immediately after the match the eleven had a formal reception in Birmingham, thousands of people turning out to welcome them. On the 21st of September a dinner was given at the Grand Hotel, Birmingham, to commemorate Warwickshire's triumph, and also the fact that three members of the eleven – F. R. Foster, Kinneir, and Smith – had been given places in the MCC's team for Australia. The Earl of Warwick presided at the dinner and a delightful evening was spent. Lord Cobham proposed the toast of the Warwickshire County Club, and in the course of his speech made a vigorous defence of the competitive system in county cricket. In responding to the toast, Mr G. H. Cartland, the chairman of the committee, said that, in his opinion, Warwickshire had twice before had a side as strong as the one that had now met with such success. Mr G. L. Jessop proposed the Warwickshire Eleven, Mr F. R. Foster of course replying. During the evening many pleasant things were said about the players who, in less prosperous times, had worked so loyally for the county. Success in cricket, as in everything else, is a great stimulus. Never before has cricket made such an appeal to the Birmingham public as it did last summer. From the moment the team began to win matches people flocked to the Edgbaston ground in such numbers as to relieve the committee of all anxiety about money. Such sudden enthusiasm suggests rather too much the spirit of Association football, and is apt to cause misgivings among old-fashioned cricketers. One can only hope that the Birmingham public, having at last taken up county cricket in real earnest, will support their eleven in bad seasons as well as in good ones.

Without in the smallest degree depreciating the splendid work done by Kinneir, Charlesworth, Quaife, and Field, there can be no question that Warwickshire's triumph was mainly due to F. R. Foster. Not since W. G. Grace in the early days of the Gloucestershire eleven has so young a captain been such a match-winning force on a county side. Foster was always getting runs, always taking wickets, and over and above all this, he proved himself a truly inspiring leader. No longer could it be said that Warwickshire played a slow or unenterprising game. they went out on all occasions to win, their cricket being keen and energetic to a degree. Foster himself had a splendid record both as batsman and bowler. He came out top of the averages in both tables, scoring 1,383 runs in county matches, with an average of 44, and taking 116 wickets for a little over 19 runs apiece. He played an innings of 200 against Surrey at Birmingham, but his best match was against Yorkshire on the same ground when he followed up a score of 105 by taking nine wickets in an innings. One feared at times that his success as a batsman would impair his bowling, but much is possible at the age of twenty-two. The Warwickshire players themselves were the first to admit that the abnormally dry season was a main factor in their success. From sheer lack of slow wicket bowlers, they would have had no chance of winning the Championship in an ordinary summer. As it was, Foster and Field bowled day after day on wickets of lightning pace and proved a great combination. It was well for the county that they kept up their form as they did. The change bowling, it must be confessed, did not amount to much. Santall, now almost a veteran, could always be depended on to keep a good length, and Quaife now and then bowled his leg-breaks with success, but except when Foster and Field were on the opposing batsmen had little to be afraid of. In view of the future more bowling of real class is an urgent necessity. W. C. Hands – right hand medium pace with a very easy action – showed distinct promise, but at present he is not capable of any sustained effort. Field, for almost the first time in his career, was able to do himself full justice. As regards accidents, he had up to last summer been the unluckiest fast bowler since Allen Hill, but, except for a damaged finger in one match, he went through four months' cricket unscathed. In the county matches he took six more wickets than F. R. Foster, and was only a fraction below him in average. He bowled at a rare pace all through the summer, and when the wickets became in any way crumbled, his off-break was deadly. He is unquestionably a fine bowler, but he would be better still if his hand were a little higher. In the disastrous match against England he bowled most perseveringly, but it would be flattery to say that he looked difficult on The Oval wicket. Foster's special excellence as in 1910 lay in his pace and spin off the pitch. A medium pace bowler in the air he was very fast off the ground, this quality combined with rather a peculiar flight making him difficult on nearly all occasions.

Warwickshire's batting, as the figures clearly prove, was strong all through the eleven. Foster, Kinneir, Charlesworth, and Quaife stood out far above their colleagues, but much good work was done by other members of the team, Smith, for example, scoring 807 runs with an average of 27. At the end of the season Kinneir was laid aside by an attack of lumbago, but up to a certain point he played, perhaps, better than ever. With an innings of 268 not out against Hampshire at.Birmingham he beat all records for Warwickshire, and against Sussex at Chichester he made two hundreds in the one match. It was not so much, however, his doings for the county at his great innings for the Players against the Gentlemen at The Oval that won him his place in the MCC's team for Australia. Charlesworth, improving on everything he had done before, hit up four hundreds and was not far behind Foster and Kinneir either in aggregate or average. Warwickshire's batting as regards the chief run-getters was well balanced, the steadiness of Kinneir and Quaife blending admirably with the brilliant hitting of Foster and Charlesworth. As he does not play quite straight, one would hesitate to place Foster among the great batsmen of to-day, but he has such confidence and such a wonderful eye that,.at any rate while he remains young, the defect may not tell very much against him.

Shortly before the end of the season Lilley retired from the eleven. He resigned the post of wicket-keeper to Smith in 1910, and, after more than twenty years' service, he thought the time had come to give up first-class cricket. One need not here go into details of Lilley's career. There have been greater wicket-keepers to fast bowling, but season after season he was a marvel of consistency. In Smith, Warwickshire seem to have found a wicket-keeper quite capable of carrying on Lilley's traditions. At any rate the younger man was considered good enough to be chosen for the Players at Lord's last season, and also for the MCC's team in Australia.

Warwickshire played twenty county matches, winning thirteen outright, leading in three on the first innings, and losing four. They beat Lancashire, Sussex, Leicestershire, Northamptonshire, and Derbyshire twice each, and Yorkshire, Hampshire, and Gloucestershire once each. They were beaten once each by Surrey, Yorkshire, Worcestershire, and Gloucestershire, and gained points on the first innings in drawn games with Yorkshire, Surrey, and Worcestershire. Of nothing were they quite so proud as the double win over Lancashire.

## WARWICKSHIRE v HAMPSHIRE

Played at Birmingham, June 29, 30, July 1, 1911

Only moderately represented, Hampshire cut an inglorious figure, missing quite a number of catches, batting feebly, and having to admit defeat by an innings and 296 runs. The match, however, furnished Kinneir with the opportunity of putting together not only the highest innings ever played for Warwickshire, but the highest of the year. At the close of play on Thursday, when the Warwickshire score stood at 476 for seven wickets, he was not out 231 and next morning the declaration was delayed until the left hander had beaten all Warwickshire records. In all, Kinneir was at the wickets for seven hours and ten minutes. Despite the fact that he was missed four times, he gave a wonderfully fine display. Among his hits were twenty-seven 4s, thirteen 3s, and thirty-four 2s. By the time stumps were drawn on Friday, Hampshire had not only been dismissed for 132, but following on, had lost five wickets for 112. There was a sensational finish to the game on

Saturday morning, Hampshire's four outstanding wickets falling in twenty minutes. Field performed the hat trick, dismissing Evans, Newman, and Olivier with following balls. F. R. Foster and Philip Mead were engaged in the Test Trial Match at Lord's.

### Warwickshire

| | |
|---|---|
| Mr F. G. Stephens c Evans b Olivier ...... 29 | Mr J. F. Byrne c Evans b Brown ........ 64 |
| S. P. Kinneir not out .................268 | E. J. Smith c Bowell b Brown ........... 14 |
| C. Charlesworth c Brown b Newman ..... 0 | S. Santall not out .................... 53 |
| W. G. Quaife c Brown b Kennedy ........ 18 | B 28, l-b 5, w 6, n-b 5 ......... 44 |
| J. H. Parsons b Kennedy .............. 58 | |
| A. A. Lilley b Kennedy ............... 6 | (7 wkts dec.) 554 |

Mr A. B. Crawford and F. E. Field did not bat.

### Hampshire

| | | |
|---|---|---|
| A. Bowell b Santall ........................... | 22 – c Stephens b Santall ............ | 30 |
| A. Stone c Parsons b Santall ................... | 11 – absent hurt .................... | 0 |
| E. R. Remnant c and b Santall .................. | 2 – c Kinneir b Santall .............. | 0 |
| G. Brown b Crawford ......................... | 36 – c Crawford b Field ............. | 13 |
| Mr H. G. M. Barton c Smith b Charlesworth ....... | 19 – c and b Quaife ................. | 15 |
| Mr D. M. Evans c Smith b Crawford ............ | 7 – b Field ....................... | 2 |
| Mr E. M. Sprot c Santall b Crawford ............ | 4 – c Stephens b Santall ........... | 9 |
| J. Moore c and b Quaife ...................... | 6 – not out ....................... | 4 |
| A. Kennedy not out .......................... | 8 – lbw b Crawford ............... | 48 |
| J. Newman lbw b Quaife ...................... | 0 – b Field ...................... | 0 |
| Mr E. Olivier c Smith b Charlesworth ............ | 0 – b Field ...................... | 0 |
| B 3, l-b 5, n-b 9 ...................... | 17 | L-b 2, w 1, n-b 2 ......... 5 |
| | 132 | 126 |

### Hampshire Bowling

| | Overs | Mdns | Runs | Wkts |
|---|---|---|---|---|
| Evans ........... | 23 | 1 | 101 | — |
| Kennedy ........ | 40 | 5 | 119 | 3 |
| Olivier .......... | 27 | 2 | 115 | 1 |
| Newman ........ | 26 | 2 | 59 | 1 |
| Remnant ........ | 12 | 2 | 46 | — |
| Brown .......... | 10 | 1 | 53 | 2 |
| Bowell .......... | 5 | — | 17 | — |

### Warwickshire Bowling

| | Overs | Mdns | Runs | Wkts | Overs | Mdns | Runs | Wkts |
|---|---|---|---|---|---|---|---|---|
| Field ............. | 15 | 3 | 36 | — | 14 | 4 | 31 | 4 |
| Santall .......... | 18 | 8 | 38 | 3 | 15 | 3 | 39 | 3 |
| Crawford ........ | 8 | 1 | 24 | 3 | 4 | 1 | 12 | 1 |
| Charlesworth ...... | 4.4 | 1 | 15 | 2 | 3 | — | 17 | — |
| Quaife .......... | 1 | — | 2 | 2 | 12 | 1 | 22 | 1 |

Umpires: A. J. Atfield and G. Webb.

## WARWICKSHIRE v YORKSHIRE

### Played at Birmingham, June 8, 9, 10, 1911

Playing an innings of 105 – his first hundred in county cricket – and taking twelve wickets, Foster was seen to exceptional advantage, but, despite his splendid work, Yorkshire gained a victory by four wickets. Warwickshire made a deplorable start losing half their wickets for 61, notwithstanding that neither Hirst nor Haigh could bowl to any extent, but Foster and Lilley added 96 in less than an hour and Santall and Field hit hard. Yorkshire, after Wilson had been dismissed first ball, carried their score to 99 without further loss. Next day they continued to bat so successfully that only three wickets had fallen, and the total stood at 299, when Foster went on and accomplished a rare piece of bowling, sending down five overs and three balls for 31 runs and seven wickets. In Warwickshire's second innings, Kinneir and Parsons made 130 before a wicket fell, but a poor resistance was offered to the Yorkshire bowling on Saturday morning. Set 216 to win, Yorkshire batted so well on a wicket somewhat below the average at Edgbaston that their success was never in serious doubt.

## Warwickshire

| | | | |
|---|---|---|---|
| S. P. Kinneir lbw b Booth | 13 | – b Haigh | 58 |
| J. H. Parsons b Drake | 1 | – c Haigh b Booth | 67 |
| C. Charlesworth c Hirst b Booth | 17 | – b Bayes | 22 |
| W. G. Quaife c Denton b Bayes | 15 | – c Dolphin b Bayes | 7 |
| C. S. Baker c Hirst b Booth | 0 | – c Dolphin b Drake | 22 |
| A. A. Lilley c Dolphin b Bayes | 70 | – b Bayes | 0 |
| Mr F. R. Foster b Drake | 105 | – st Dolphin b Haigh | 18 |
| Mr G. W. Stephens c Dolphin b Rhodes | 0 | – b Booth | 12 |
| E. J. Smith lbw b Bayes | 0 | – b Booth | 6 |
| S. Santall not out | 48 | – not out | 9 |
| F. E. Field c Rhodes b Booth | 28 | – b Haigh | 5 |
| B 11, l-b 6, w 2, n-b 1 | 20 | B 13, l-b 2, w 3, n-b 1 | 19 |
| | **317** | | **245** |

## Yorkshire

| | | | |
|---|---|---|---|
| W. Rhodes b Field | 47 | – b Foster | 18 |
| B. B. Wilson b Foster | 0 | – lbw b Santall | 45 |
| D. Denton c Lilley b Foster | 83 | – c Charlesworth b Foster | 41 |
| A. Drake b Foster | 83 | – not out | 39 |
| G. H. Hirst b Foster | 85 | – lbw b Foster | 4 |
| M. W. Booth lbw b Foster | 0 | – b Field | 18 |
| A. Turner b Foster | 0 | – b Field | 6 |
| S. Haigh not out | 21 | – not out | 15 |
| Mr E. J. Radcliffe b Foster | 8 | | |
| A. Dolphin b Foster | 2 | | |
| G. Bayes b Foster | 6 | | |
| B 1, l-b 3, w 2, n-b 6 | 12 | B 6, l-b 9, n-b 16 | 31 |
| | **347** | | **217** |

### Yorkshire Bowling

| | Overs | Mdns | Runs | Wkts | Overs | Mdns | Runs | Wkts |
|---|---|---|---|---|---|---|---|---|
| Drake | 32 | 3 | 91 | 2 | 30 | 5 | 66 | 1 |
| Hirst | 4 | 1 | 10 | — | | | | |
| Booth | 21.5 | 5 | 80 | 4 | 16 | 4 | 42 | 3 |
| Bayes | 11 | 1 | 47 | 3 | 16 | — | 53 | 3 |
| Rhodes | 19 | 2 | 58 | 1 | 8 | 1 | 25 | — |
| Haigh | 2 | — | 11 | — | 15 | 2 | 40 | 3 |

### Warwickshire Bowling

| | Overs | Mdns | Runs | Wkts | Overs | Mdns | Runs | Wkts |
|---|---|---|---|---|---|---|---|---|
| Foster | 29.3 | 4 | 118 | 9 | 27 | 4 | 84 | 3 |
| Field | 40 | 5 | 121 | 1 | 27.4 | 10 | 72 | 2 |
| Santall | 17 | 4 | 69 | — | 5 | 2 | 12 | 1 |
| Quaife | 3 | — | 9 | — | 4 | — | 18 | — |
| Charlesworth | 4 | 1 | 18 | — | | | | |

Umpires: F. G. Roberts and G. Hutchings.

# WORCESTERSHIRE

## WORCESTERSHIRE v LEICESTERSHIRE

Played at Worcester, June 21, 22, 23, 1900

In many respects this was a remarkable match, the fortunes of the game, after many fluctuations, turning finally in favour of Worcestershire, who won by the narrow margin of 10 runs. Frequent showers interrupted cricket on the first day, but in the time available Worcestershire scored 160 for nine wickets. At the start Arnold and the brothers Foster played finely but after they had been got rid of, five men were dismissed for 17 runs. The innings was quickly finished the next day, and then Leicestershire fared so badly that seven wickets were down for 35 runs. King and Geeson, however, hit out pluckily, and Leicestershire's total fell only 21 runs behind that of Worcestershire. Some sensational cricket was seen when Worcestershire went in again, and Leicestershire had only 113 runs to get to win. On the last day the score reached 40 with two men out, but half the side were dismissed for 61. Then there was another change, 26 being added before the next wicket fell, but the rest collapsed badly before Wilson, who took the last four wickets for 8 runs.

## Worcestershire

| | | | |
|---|---|---|---|
| F. Bowley c Whitehead b Woodcock | 0 | – b Woodcock | 7 |
| E. Arnold b Woodcock | 63 | – b Woodcock | 5 |
| A. Bird c Whiteside b King | 8 | – c Whiteside b Woodcock | 9 |
| Mr H. K. Foster c J. Brown b Coe | 41 | – b Woodcock | 5 |
| Mr R. E. Foster c J. Brown b King | 20 | – b Woodcock | 7 |
| Mr W. H. Wilkes c Geeson b King | 7 | – b Geeson | 1 |
| M. Bullock c Geeson b King | 4 | – c King b Coe | 27 |
| F. Wheldon c J. Brown b King | 8 | – c Coe b Geeson | 0 |
| G. Wilson c Geeson b Woodcock | 2 | – b Woodcock | 2 |
| Bannister c Whitehead b King | 5 | – not out | 4 |
| T. Straw not out | 1 | – c Knight b Coe | 19 |
| B 4, w 2, n-b 1 | 7 | B 1, l-b 1, n-b 2, w 1 | 5 |
| | **166** | | **91** |

## Leicestershire

| | | | |
|---|---|---|---|
| Mr C. J. B. Wood lbw b Wilson | 2 | – c H. K. Foster b Arnold | 28 |
| A. E. Knight c R. E. Foster b Arnold | 5 | – b Arnold | 5 |
| L. Brown c H. K. Foster b Arnold | 12 | – c Arnold b Bird | 9 |
| H. Whitehead b Wilson | 0 | – c H. K. Foster b Wilson | 22 |
| S. Coe b Wilson | 0 | – c Wheldon b Arnold | 0 |
| Mr C. E. de Trafford c H. K. Foster b Arnold | 7 | – c H. K. Foster b Arnold | 12 |
| J. Brown c Wheldon b Wilson | 8 | – c Wilkes b Wilson | 12 |
| J. H. King not out | 62 | – c R. E. Foster b Arnold | 3 |
| F. Geeson b Wilson | 26 | – not out | 3 |
| A. Woodcock c Bullock b Bird | 1 | – b Wilson | 1 |
| J. P. Whiteside c R. E. Foster b Bird | 12 | – b Wilson | 0 |
| B 7, l-b 3 | 10 | B 6, n-b 1 | 7 |
| | **145** | | **102** |

## Leicestershire Bowling

| | Overs | Mdns | Runs | Wkts | Overs | Mdns | Runs | Wkts |
|---|---|---|---|---|---|---|---|---|
| Woodcock | 23 | 1 | 88 | 3 | 21 | 9 | 27 | 6 |
| King | 18.4 | 5 | 34 | 6 | 4 | — | 8 | — |
| Geeson | 4 | 2 | 6 | — | 22 | 10 | 42 | 2 |
| Coe | 7 | 1 | 31 | 1 | 3.5 | 2 | 9 | 2 |

## Worcestershire Bowling

|  | Overs | Mdns | Runs | Wkts | Overs | Mdns | Runs | Wkts |
|---|---|---|---|---|---|---|---|---|
| Arnold | 20 | 5 | 48 | 3 | 25 | 8 | 44 | 5 |
| Wilson | 22 | 3 | 56 | 5 | 7.5 | 4 | 8 | 4 |
| Bannister | 4 | 1 | 14 | — | 8 | 3 | 11 | — |
| Bird | 10.3 | 3 | 17 | 2 | 10 | 2 | 32 | 1 |

Umpires: W. Richards and A. Hide.

# WORCESTERSHIRE v YORKSHIRE

### Played at Worcester, July 24, 25, 26, 1902

Though deprived of the services of F. S. Jackson, Hirst, and Rhodes, all of whom were away at Manchester, Yorkshire more than held their own against Worcestershire, and would, probably, had circumstances been more favourable, have gained a victory. At the drawing of stumps on Friday evening, Yorkshire, with two wickets to fall in their second innings, were 273 to the good, but rain fell so persistently on Saturday that only two overs could be bowled. The feature of the match was the batting of J. T. Brown, who showed a return to quite his best form. In neither innings did he give anything like a chance, and at times he hit very brilliantly indeed. Arnold, who made his runs at a time when they were sadly needed – Worcestershire having on Thursday lost half their wickets for 96 – batted superbly. For three hours he resisted all the efforts of the Yorkshire bowlers.

### Yorkshire

| | | | |
|---|---|---|---|
| J. Tunnicliffe st Gaukrodger b Simpson-Hayward | 5 | – b Arnold | 19 |
| J. T. Brown b Simpson-Hayward | 76 | – b Simpson-Hayward | 91 |
| I. Washington st Gaukrodger b Simpson-Hayward | 14 | – lbw b Bannister | 50 |
| Mr T. L. Taylor lbw b Wilson | 4 | – c Bowley b Simpson-Hayward | 12 |
| D. Denton b Bird | 37 | – not out | 34 |
| Mr E. R. Wilson c H. K. Foster b Arnold | 63 | – st Gaukrodger b Simpson-Hayward | 6 |
| S. Haigh c R. E. Foster b Arnold | 19 | – c Gaukrodger b Simpson-Hayward | 10 |
| L. Whitehead b Arnold | 8 | – b Simpson-Hayward | 0 |
| Lord Hawke not out | 10 | – b Wilson | 9 |
| D. Hunter c R. E. Foster b Simpson-Hayward | 3 | – not out | 0 |
| Oysten b Arnold | 0 | | |
| B 10, l-b 7, w 1 | 18 | B 9, l-b 6, n-b 2 | 17 |
| | **257** | | **248** |

### Worcestershire

| | | | | |
|---|---|---|---|---|
| Mr H. K. Foster b Haigh | 22 | F. Wheldon c Whitehead b Oysten | 37 |
| F. Bowley run out | 3 | A. Bird b Haigh | 3 |
| E. Arnold c Hunter b Oysten | 92 | G. A. Wilson not out | 36 |
| Mr R. E. Foster c Whitehead b Oysten | 1 | Bannister c Hunter b Haigh | 9 |
| F. Pearson b Haigh | 3 | | |
| G. Gaukrodger c Hunter b Denton | 8 | B 3, l-b 1, n-b 1, w 1 | 6 |
| Mr G. H. Simpson-Hayward | | | |
| c Hunter b Haigh | 10 | | **230** |

### Worcestershire Bowling

|  | Overs | Mdns | Runs | Wkts | Overs | Mdns | Runs | Wkts |
|---|---|---|---|---|---|---|---|---|
| Wilson | 19 | 5 | 65 | 1 | 12 | 3 | 33 | 1 |
| Simpson-Hayward | 17 | — | 78 | 4 | 18 | — | 75 | 5 |
| Arnold | 17.3 | 6 | 61 | 4 | 13 | 4 | 34 | 1 |
| Bird | 13 | 2 | 34 | 1 | 12 | 4 | 34 | — |
| Bannister | 2 | 1 | 1 | — | 13 | 2 | 27 | 1 |
| Pearson | | | | | 7 | — | 28 | — |

**Yorkshire Bowling**

|  | Overs | Mdns | Runs | Wkts |
|---|---|---|---|---|
| Haigh . . . . . . . . . . . | 32.2 | 5 | 90 | 5 |
| Oysten . . . . . . . . . . | 24 | 4 | 70 | 3 |
| Wilson . . . . . . . . . . | 14 | 5 | 20 | — |
| Brown . . . . . . . . . . | 12 | — | 26 | — |
| Denton . . . . . . . . . . | 2 | 1 | 3 | 1 |
| Whitehead . . . . . . . . | 5 | — | 15 | — |

Umpires: A. Pike and W. Wright.

## WORCESTERSHIRE v DERBYSHIRE

Played at Worcester, August 7, 8, 9, 1902

Not a ball could be bowled in this match either on Thursday or Friday, and the time thus lost could not be made up. On the Saturday, however, some batting of a most attractive character was witnessed, Worcestershire staying in the whole of the day and scoring 463 for the loss of only seven wickets, a performance which, though highly creditable, was, of course, to no purpose. The fine total was mainly the work of H. K. Foster; R. E. Foster, and Bowley, who between them made 343 of the number. When 66 R. E. Foster gave a chance to cover-point, but this was the only mistake made by any one of the three batsmen. Of the three H. K. Foster hit the most brilliantly, scoring his 112, out of 147 put on for the first wicket, in an hour and twenty-five minutes. R. E. Foster's innings lasted twenty-five minutes longer than his brother's. Bowley displayed much more care than either of his colleagues and was at the wickets rather over four hours. It will be noticed that all the members of the Derbyshire eleven went on to bowl.

### Worcestershire

| | |
|---|---|
| Mr H. K. Foster st Humphries b Ashcroft . .112 | F. Wheldon c and b Humphries . . . . . . . . . . 1 |
| F. Bowley c Warren b Lawton . . . . . . . . . . .122 | G. Gaukrodger not out . . . . . . . . . . . . . . . 26 |
| Mr R. E. Foster c Ollivierre b Lawton . . . . .109 | A. Bird not out . . . . . . . . . . . . . . . . . . . . . . 0 |
| Mr W. W. Lowe c Ashcroft b Lawton . . . . . 9 | |
| Mr G. H. Simpson-Hayward | B 1, l-b 5, w 1, n-b 2 . . . . . . . . . . 9 |
| c Lawton b Storer . 18 | ____ |
| F. Pearson b Lawton . . . . . . . . . . . . . . . . . 57 | 463 |

G. A. Wilson and E. Arnold did not bat.

### Derbyshire

Mr L. G. Wright, Mr C. A. Ollivierre, Mr E. M. Ashcroft, Mr C. H. Lyon, Mr A. E. Lawton, W. Storer, E. Needham, Humphries, Warren, J. Hulme and W. Bestwick.

### Derbyshire Bowling

|  | Overs | Mdns | Runs | Wkts |
|---|---|---|---|---|
| Bestwick . . . . . . . . | 12 | 1 | 67 | — |
| Hulme . . . . . . . . . | 23 | 6 | 79 | — |
| Ashcroft . . . . . . . . | 18 | — | 68 | 1 |
| Ollivierre . . . . . . . . | 3 | — | 20 | — |
| Warren . . . . . . . . . | 3 | — | 29 | — |
| Storer . . . . . . . . . . | 11 | 1 | 47 | 1 |
| Lawton . . . . . . . . . | 12 | — | 59 | 4 |
| Needham . . . . . . . . | 7 | 1 | 35 | — |
| Wright . . . . . . . . . . | 4 | — | 25 | — |
| Humphries . . . . . . . | 5 | 1 | 19 | 1 |
| Lyon . . . . . . . . . . . | 2 | — | 6 | — |

Umpires: J. Phillips and J. Moss.

# WORCESTERSHIRE v YORKSHIRE

## Played at Worcester, May 25, 26, 27, 1903

Next to the remarkable victory over Sussex at the beginning of August, Worcestershire, in averting defeat at the hands of Yorkshire, accomplished by far their best performance. When play was resumed on the Wednesday they could have had little hope of effecting a draw as with two wickets down in their second innings they still required 231 runs to save an innings defeat. Worcestershire however, set about their task in splendid style and met with a success that was beyond all expectation. Arnold and Wheldon the not-outs of Tuesday, gave the side a fine example, staying together for an hour and forty minutes, and carrying the score from nine to 154. Despite the great effort made by these two batsmen, Worcestershire at a quarter to two had half their wickets down and were still 64 runs behind. Then, however, Foster and Brinton resisted the Yorkshire bowlers for an hour and forty minutes, and added 156 runs. After Foster left, Brinton continued to defend stubbornly, and when the innings closed at five o'clock stumps were pulled up. Brinton batted very patiently for two hours and a half, and rendered his side invaluable service, but Foster's innings of 120 was the feature of the match. Foster batted in his usual free, attractive style, his off-driving being superb. He made no mistake during the two hours and ten minutes he was in, and hit seventeen 4s. In making his 123 on the opening day, Hirst was seen at his very best. He was only at the wickets for two hours and hit twenty 4s.

### Yorkshire

| | |
|---|---|
| J. T. Brown lbw b Bird .................. 27 | Wainwright st Wheldon b Bird .......... 32 |
| J. Tunnicliffe c Binton b Wilson .......... 39 | Lord Hawke b Wilson ................. 76 |
| D. Denton c Foster b Bird .............. 0 | D. Hunter c Foster b Burrows .......... 5 |
| Wilkinson b Hunt .................... 88 | Bedford not out ...................... 30 |
| J. H. Hirst b Hunt ...................123 | B 18, l-b 7, n-b 2 ............. 27 |
| W. Rhodes c Isaac b Burrows .......... 42 | |
| S. Haigh b Burrows ................. 29 | ——— |
| | 518 |

### Worcestershire

| | | |
|---|---|---|
| Nicholls c Hunter b Rhodes ................... | 4 – c Hunter b Haigh ............... | 2 |
| F. Bowley lbw b Rhodes ..................... | 7 – c Wilkinson b Rhodes .......... | 2 |
| E. Arnold b Rhodes ......................... | 35 – c Tunnicliffe b Rhodes ......... | 83 |
| F. Wheldon b Rhodes ....................... | 71 – c and b Rhodes ............... | 71 |
| Mr H. K. Foster not out ..................... | 71 – c Hawke b Wilkinson .......... | 120 |
| Hunt b Rhodes ............................ | 0 – b Haigh ..................... | 2 |
| Mr R. S. Brinton c Hunter b Rhodes ............ | 7 – not out ..................... | 66 |
| Mr A. W. Isaac lbw b Haigh ................. | 55 – c Hunter b Rhodes............. | 3 |
| Bird b Rhodes ............................ | 10 – c Hirst b Haigh ............. | 1 |
| R. Burrows c Wilkinson b Rhodes ............... | 0 – b Rhodes ................... | 15 |
| G. A. Wilson b Haigh ...................... | 1 – c Denton b Rhodes ........... | 8 |
| B 8, l-b 7, n-b 2 .................. | 17      B 1, l-b 5, w 2 ........... | 8 |
| | ——— | ——— |
| | 278 | 381 |

### Worcestershire Bowling

| | Overs | Mdns | Runs | Wkts |
|---|---|---|---|---|
| Arnold .......... | 17 | 3 | 62 | — |
| Burrows ......... | 36 | 8 | 124 | 3 |
| Bird ............ | 39 | 4 | 153 | 3 |
| Wilson .......... | 23.1 | 2 | 94 | 2 |
| Hunt ........... | 16 | 4 | 58 | 2 |

**Yorkshire Bowling**

| | Overs | Mdns | Runs | Wkts | Overs | Mdns | Runs | Wkts |
|---|---|---|---|---|---|---|---|---|
| Rhodes . . . . . . . . . . | 46 | 17 | 87 | 8 | 48.4 | 13 | 124 | 6 |
| Haigh . . . . . . . . . . . | 34.2 | 14 | 80 | 2 | 31 | 8 | 110 | 3 |
| Brown . . . . . . . . . . | 10 | 1 | 38 | — | 6 | — | 21 | — |
| Bedford . . . . . . . . . | 11 | 1 | 35 | — | 15 | 3 | 39 | — |
| Wainwright . . . . . . . | 7 | 1 | 21 | — | 19 | 5 | 46 | — |
| Denton . . . . . . . . . . | | | | | 4 | — | 14 | — |
| Wilkinson . . . . . . . . | | | | | 4 | — | 19 | 1 |

Umpires: J. Carlin and G. Porter.

## WORCESTERSHIRE v KENT

Played at Worcester, July 31, August 1, 2, 1905

Everything else in this match was dwarfed by the superb batting of R. E. Foster, who was making his first appearance for the season for Worcestershire. Not out 47 at the drawing of stumps on Tuesday, he was still unbeaten when, at about half-past three on the third afternoon, the Worcestershire innings was declared closed. Playing all the Kent bowlers with the utmost ease, his mastery was so complete that he did not give a chance of any kind until he had made 225. He might then have been caught close on the boundary by Humphreys. Later on he was again missed in the long-field, but these were small blemishes in a brilliant display that extended over four hours and a half and included two 6s and thirty-four 4s. Pearson also batted well, and the chief honours for Kent were carried off by Dillon, who made some splendid drives and crisp cuts. When Kent went in a second time 195 behind, two hours and forty minutes remained for play. Up to a point everything went well, but after Seymour left – third out at 123 – Humphreys and Marsham were soon got rid of, and as A. P. Day could not bat the situation was rather serious. However, Mason and Blaker played out time and the match was left drawn.

### Kent

| | | | |
|---|---|---|---|
| Mr E. W. Dillon c Wilson b R. E. Foster . . . . . . . . .117 | – b Solly . . . . . . . . . . . . . . . . . . . . . . | 30 |
| A. Hearne b Cuffe . . . . . . . . . . . . . . . . . . . . . . . . . 17 | – c Ainley b Solly . . . . . . . . . . . . . . . | 7 |
| James Seymour b Pearson . . . . . . . . . . . . . . . . . . . 38 | – c Burrows b Cuffe . . . . . . . . . . . . . | 50 |
| Mr A. P. Day c R. E. Foster b Burrows . . . . . . . . . . 64 | |
| E. Humphreys b Burrows . . . . . . . . . . . . . . . . . . . . 12 | – b Solly . . . . . . . . . . . . . . . . . . . . . . | 25 |
| Mr J. R. Mason c R. E. Foster b Pearson . . . . . . . . 27 | – not out . . . . . . . . . . . . . . . . . . . . . . . | 25 |
| Mr C. H. B. Marsham b Solly . . . . . . . . . . . . . . . . . 41 | – b Cuffe . . . . . . . . . . . . . . . . . . . . . . | 0 |
| Mr R. N. R. Blaker b Wilson . . . . . . . . . . . . . . . . . 46 | – not out . . . . . . . . . . . . . . . . . . . . . . | 13 |
| F. H. Huish b Wilson . . . . . . . . . . . . . . . . . . . . . . 18 | |
| W. J. Fairservice not out . . . . . . . . . . . . . . . . . . 19 | |
| C. Blythe c Pearson b Wilson . . . . . . . . . . . . . . . . . 4 | |
| B 21, l-b 6, w 1, n-b 1 . . . . . . . . . . . . . . . . 29 | B 15, l-b 1, w 1 . . . . . . . . . . | 17 |
| | | |
| | 432 | 167 |

### Worcestershire

| | |
|---|---|
| F. Bowley b Mason . . . . . . . . . . . . . . . . . . . 6 | E. W. Solly st Huish b Dillon . . . . . . . . . . . 26 |
| F. Pearson c Mason b Hearne . . . . . . . . . . .104 | R. Burrows b Mason . . . . . . . . . . . . . . . . . 7 |
| J. A. Cuffe b Mason . . . . . . . . . . . . . . . . . . 0 | G. A. Wilson c Fairservice b Blythe . . . . . . . 45 |
| Mr H. K. Foster b Blythe . . . . . . . . . . . . . . 86 | |
| Mr R. E. Foster not out . . . . . . . . . . . . . . .246 | B 6, l-b 4, w 5, n-b 3 . . . . . . . . . . 18 |
| Mr G. N. Foster b Hearne . . . . . . . . . . . . . 54 | |
| Mr W. E. C. Hutchings b Humphreys . . . . . 35 | (9 wkts dec.) 627 |

J. Ainley did not bat.

## Worcestershire Bowling

| | Overs | Mdns | Runs | Wkts | Overs | Mdns | Runs | Wkts |
|---|---|---|---|---|---|---|---|---|
| Wilson . . . . . . . . . . . | 14.4 | 3 | 64 | 3 | 15 | 5 | 25 | — |
| Cuffe . . . . . . . . . . . . | 16 | 4 | 71 | 1 | 12 | 2 | 26 | 2 |
| Solly . . . . . . . . . . . . . | 16 | 1 | 70 | 1 | 21 | 3 | 64 | 3 |
| Burrows . . . . . . . . . . | 21 | 3 | 92 | 2 | 6 | 1 | 18 | — |
| Pearson . . . . . . . . . | 22 | 2 | 77 | 2 | 5 | 2 | 13 | — |
| R. E. Foster . . . . . . . | 4 | 1 | 29 | 1 | | | | |
| G. N. Foster . . . . . . | | | | | 1 | — | 4 | — |

## Kent Bowling

| | Overs | Mdns | Runs | Wkts |
|---|---|---|---|---|
| Mason . . . . . . . . . . . | 38 | 5 | 148 | 3 |
| Blythe . . . . . . . . . . . | 49.4 | 13 | 146 | 2 |
| Fairservice . . . . . . . | 23 | 5 | 106 | — |
| Hearne . . . . . . . . . . . | 26 | 3 | 72 | 2 |
| Humphreys . . . . . . . | 17 | 1 | 53 | 1 |
| Dillon . . . . . . . . . . . | 10 | — | 84 | 1 |

Umpires: A. Pike and W. A. J. West.

## WORCESTERSHIRE v LEICESTERSHIRE

Played at Worcester, July 19, 20, 21, 1906

To such an extent did the bat beat the ball that no fewer than 1,425 runs were scored for the loss of only sixteen wickets, this being the third highest aggregate of runs obtained in a first-class match in this country. As there was never any prospect of the game being finished the cricket was quite uninteresting, but in scoring 701 for four wickets Leicestershire accomplished a remarkable performance, and had the satisfaction of putting together the best total of the season. Wood, who was batting five hours and a half, carried off the chief honours. He hardly made a bad stroke and his innings – the highest he had ever played – included twenty-four 4s. Whitehead, Knight, and V. F. S. Crawford all hit with great vigour and when Worcestershire went in a second time Bowley and Arnold played very finely.

### Worcestershire

| | | | |
|---|---|---|---|
| Mr H. K. Foster b King . . . . . . . . . . . . . . . . . . . . . . | 52 | – c R. T. Crawford b Jayes . . . . . . . . . | 18 |
| F. Bowley b Odell . . . . . . . . . . . . . . . . . . . . . . . . . | 10 | – not out . . . . . . . . . . . . . . . . . . . . . . . | 167 |
| E. Arnold b King . . . . . . . . . . . . . . . . . . . . . . . . . | 18 | – c and b Whitehead . . . . . . . . . . . . . . | 112 |
| Mr W. E. C. Hutchings c Shields b R. T. Crawford . . | 0 | – not out . . . . . . . . . . . . . . . . . . . . . . . | 25 |
| J. A. Cuffe b Jayes . . . . . . . . . . . . . . . . . . . . . . . . | 11 | | |
| Mr W. B. Burns c V. F. S. Crawford b Coe . . . . . . . | 87 | | |
| F. Pearson lbw b Jayes . . . . . . . . . . . . . . . . . . . . . | 95 | | |
| F. Wheldon c Wood b Odell . . . . . . . . . . . . . . . . . | 17 | | |
| G. A. Wilson c Wood b R. T. Crawford . . . . . . . . . | 66 | | |
| R. Burrows b Jayes . . . . . . . . . . . . . . . . . . . . . . . | 15 | | |
| J. Ainley not out . . . . . . . . . . . . . . . . . . . . . . . . . | 0 | | |
| B 9 . . . . . . . . . . . . . . . . . . . . . . . . . . . . . | 9 | B 14, l-b 3, w 5 . . . . . . . . . . | 22 |
| | 380 | | 344 |

### Leicestershire

| | |
|---|---|
| Mr C. J. B. Wood b Wilson . . . . . . . . . . . .225 | J. H. King not out . . . . . . . . . . . . . . . . . . . . 14 |
| H. Whitehead c Foster b Cuffe . . . . . . . . .174 | |
| A. E. Knight c Hutchings b Arnold . . . . . . . 97 | B 25, l-b 4, w 10 . . . . . . . . . . . . . 39 |
| S. Coe b Burrows . . . . . . . . . . . . . . . . . . . . 50 | ——  |
| Mr V. F. S. Crawford not out . . . . . . . . . 102 | (4 wkts dec.) 701 |

Mr C. E. de Trafford, Mr R. T. Crawford, Mr W. W. Odell, Mr J. Shields and T. Jayes did not bat.

### Leicestershire Bowling

| | Overs | Mdns | Runs | Wkts | Overs | Mdns | Runs | Wkts |
|---|---|---|---|---|---|---|---|---|
| Jayes . . . . . . . . . . . . | 30 | 2 | 161 | 3 | 18 | 3 | 57 | 1 |
| Odell . . . . . . . . . . . . | 23 | 5 | 72 | 2 | 9 | 3 | 16 | — |
| King . . . . . . . . . . . . . | 21 | 5 | 58 | 2 | 8 | 1 | 12 | — |
| R. T. Crawford . . . . | 16.3 | 2 | 54 | 2 | 8 | 2 | 24 | — |
| Coe . . . . . . . . . . . . . | 7 | — | 26 | 1 | 9 | 1 | 32 | — |
| Wood . . . . . . . . . . . | | | | | 22 | 2 | 98 | — |
| Whitehead . . . . . . . . | | | | | 22 | 4 | 83 | 1 |

### Worcestershire Bowling

| | Overs | Mdns | Runs | Wkts |
|---|---|---|---|---|
| Wilson . . . . . . . . . . . | 35 | 3 | 162 | 1 |
| Arnold . . . . . . . . . . . | 20 | 3 | 73 | 1 |
| Burrows . . . . . . . . . . | 29 | 2 | 93 | 1 |
| Cuffe . . . . . . . . . . . | 42 | 2 | 165 | 1 |
| Pearson . . . . . . . . . . | 36 | 3 | 148 | — |
| Burns . . . . . . . . . . . . | 1 | — | 6 | — |
| Bowley . . . . . . . . . . . | 2 | — | 15 | — |

Umpires: J. Carlin and W. A. J. West.

## WORCESTERSHIRE v KENT

### Played at Worcester, August 1, 2, 3, 1907

Some dazzling batting was seen in this drawn game. H. K. and R. E. Foster both reaching three figures, and K. L. Hutchings obtaining two sepatate hundreds in the match. H. K. and R. E. Foster hit in such brilliant style that in the three hours and a quarter over which their partnership extended they put on 304 runs. Feeling the effects of a strain in his thigh, sustained in the Surrey match. H. K. Foster had to retire. H. K. Foster hit a 5 and eleven 4s, and R. E. a 5 and fourteen 4s. G. N. Foster hit with tremendous vigour, and amongst them the three brothers scored 375 runs. The feat accomplished by Hutchings was the more remarkable as it was his first appearance for Kent since the accident he met with in the South African match over a month before. The second of his two hundreds was the more brilliant, but in both innings he played magnificent cricket.

### Worcestershire

| | |
|---|---|
| F. Bowley b Fielder . . . . . . . . . . . . . . . . . . 13 | Mr W. B. Burns b Fielder . . . . . . . . . . . . . . 33 |
| F. Pearson b Fielder . . . . . . . . . . . . . . . . . . 11 | R. Burrows c Humphreys b Fairservice . . . . 57 |
| Mr H. K. Foster retired . . . . . . . . . . . . . .123 | A. Bird b Blythe . . . . . . . . . . . . . . . . . . . . . 18 |
| Mr R. E. Foster b Fielder . . . . . . . . . . . . . .174 | T. Straw not out . . . . . . . . . . . . . . . . . . . . . 14 |
| E. Arnold b Fielder . . . . . . . . . . . . . . . . . . 0 | B 22, l-b 9, w 5 . . . . . . . . . . . . . . 36 |
| Mr G. N. Foster b Fairservice . . . . . . . . . . 78 | ——  |
| J. A. Cuffe b Fielder . . . . . . . . . . . . . . . . . . 10 | 567 |

**Kent**

| | | | |
|---|---|---|---|
| Mr E. W. Dillon b Pearson | 45 | – b Burrows | 5 |
| E. Humphreys c R. E. Foster b Cuffe | 15 | – not out | 66 |
| James Seymour c G. N. Foster b Arnold | 23 | – lbw b Arnold | 21 |
| Mr K. L. Hutchings b Bird | 109 | – not out | 109 |
| F. E. Woolley c Straw b Burrows | 13 | | |
| Mr A. P. Day b Burrows | 43 | | |
| Mr L. H. W. Troughton b Burrows | 13 | | |
| F. H. Huish c Straw b Burrows | 0 | | |
| W. J. Fairservice c and b Arnold | 31 | | |
| C. Blythe c Straw b Burrows | 11 | | |
| A. Fielder not out | 1 | | |
| B 12, l-b 1 | 13 | L-b 6, n-b 1 | 7 |
| | **317** | | **208** |

**Kent Bowling**

| | Overs | Mdns | Runs | Wkts |
|---|---|---|---|---|
| Fielder | 52 | 6 | 151 | 6 |
| Blythe | 38.2 | 3 | 143 | 1 |
| Humphreys | 10 | 1 | 35 | — |
| Fairservice | 22 | 2 | 78 | 2 |
| Seymour | 9 | 2 | 30 | — |
| Woolley | 9 | 1 | 41 | — |
| Day | 4 | — | 34 | — |
| Dillon | 2 | — | 19 | — |

**Worcestershire Bowling**

| | Overs | Mdns | Runs | Wkts | Overs | Mdns | Runs | Wkts |
|---|---|---|---|---|---|---|---|---|
| Cuffe | 24 | 4 | 82 | 1 | 13 | 4 | 35 | — |
| Arnold | 31 | 7 | 85 | 2 | 14 | 6 | 26 | 1 |
| Burrows | 17 | 3 | 78 | 5 | 14 | 3 | 55 | 1 |
| Pearson | 6 | — | 32 | 1 | 5 | — | 32 | — |
| Bird | 7 | — | 27 | 1 | 8 | 2 | 29 | — |
| Burns | | | | | 3 | — | 21 | — |
| R. E. Foster | | | | | 2 | 1 | 3 | — |

Umpires: J. Moss and G. P. Harrison.

# WORCESTERSHIRE v SURREY

### Played at Worcester, May 18, 19, 20, 1908

Splendidly contested throughout, this match ended in a victory for Surrey by the narrow margin of 14 runs. The most interesting part of the game came on the last day when Worcestershire made a great effort to score the 307 runs set them to win. At one point it did not seem in the least likely that they would make such a close fight of it, Bowley being out at 3, Pearson at 56, and Arnold at 57. In Cuffe, H. K. Foster, who played a superb innings, found a valuable partner. Everything, however, depended upon Foster, and for a time he proved equal to the occasion, hitting with great power. In the end the long-continued strain told on him, and he could not sustain the effort. He made only one mistake during a stay of four hours, and among his figures were sixteen 4s. In Worcestershire's first innings Bowley gave a splendid display, and when Surrey went in a second time Marshal batted in his finest style.

## Surrey

| | | | |
|---|---:|---|---:|
| T. Hayward c and b Hunt | 79 | – lbw b Cuffe | 3 |
| J. B. Hobbs b Cuffe | 6 | – b Burrows | 7 |
| E. G. Hayes b Cuffe | 7 | – c Cuffe b Simpson-Hayward | 0 |
| A. Marshal st Gaukrodger b Simpson-Hayward | 8 | – lbw b Simpson-Hayward | 176 |
| Mr J. N. Crawford lbw b Pearson | 33 | – b Simpson-Hayward | 76 |
| F. C. Holland c Arnold b Pearson | 1 | – c Arnold b Cuffe | 30 |
| Capt. H. S. Bush c and b Hunt | 47 | – c Pearson b Simpson-Hayward | 25 |
| W. Lees b Hunt | 24 | – c Burns b Burrows | 12 |
| W. C. Smith c Bowley b Cuffe | 5 | – not out | 0 |
| Mr H. D. G. Leveson-Gower not out | 1 | – c Gaukrodger b Cuffe | 0 |
| H. Strudwick b Cuffe | 1 | – b Simpson-Hayward | 0 |
| B 10, l-b 3, w 3, n-b 1 | 17 | B 1, l-b 1, n-b 3 | 5 |
| | **229** | | **334** |

## Worcestershire

| | | | |
|---|---:|---|---:|
| F. Pearson lbw b Smith | 25 | – c Strudwick b Hayes | 18 |
| F. Bowley b Hayes | 123 | – b Crawford | 3 |
| E. Arnold c and b Hayes | 52 | – b Lees | 0 |
| G. Gaukrodger b Hayes | 0 | – not out | 1 |
| J. A. Cuffe lbw b Lees | 8 | – c Strudwick b Hayes | 22 |
| Mr H. K. Foster c Strudwick b Lees | 5 | – b Smith | 174 |
| Mr W. B. Burns c Holland b Lees | 3 | – b Crawford | 7 |
| Mr G. H. Simpson-Hayward b Hayes | 0 | – c Strudwick b Hayes | 2 |
| F. H. Hunt b Lees | 7 | – c Strudwick b Crawford | 7 |
| R. Burrows b Lees | 21 | – b Crawford | 22 |
| Mr R. S. Swalwell not out | 8 | – c Hayes b Smith | 25 |
| B 2, l-b 2, w 1 | 5 | B 10, l-b 1 | 11 |
| | **257** | | **292** |

### Worcestershire Bowling

| | Overs | Mdns | Runs | Wkts | Overs | Mdns | Runs | Wkts |
|---|---|---|---|---|---|---|---|---|
| Burrows | 6 | — | 23 | — | 17 | 1 | 66 | 2 |
| Arnold | 16 | 5 | 38 | — | 13 | 1 | 49 | — |
| Cuffe | 26 | 2 | 72 | 4 | 19.2 | 2 | 59 | 3 |
| Simpson-Hayward | 7 | 1 | 29 | 1 | 13 | 2 | 43 | 5 |
| Pearson | 11 | 3 | 30 | 2 | 19 | 2 | 84 | — |
| Hunt | 7.1 | 1 | 20 | 3 | 5 | — | 28 | — |

### Surrey Bowling

| | Overs | Mdns | Runs | Wkts | Overs | Mdns | Runs | Wkts |
|---|---|---|---|---|---|---|---|---|
| Crawford | 13 | — | 62 | — | 33 | 3 | 104 | 4 |
| Lees | 26.4 | 5 | 83 | 5 | 30 | 6 | 85 | 1 |
| Smith | 9 | 1 | 39 | 1 | 9.3 | 5 | 18 | 2 |
| Marshal | 3 | — | 16 | — | 7 | 1 | 14 | — |
| Hayes | 22 | 5 | 52 | 4 | 20 | 1 | 60 | 3 |

Umpires: T. Brown and H. Baldwin.

## WORCESTERSHIRE v GLOUCESTERSHIRE

Played at Stourbridge, July 7, 8, 1910

Thanks almost entirely to a magnificent display of batting by G. L. Jessop, Gloucestershire gained a victory over Worcestershire by 94 runs. Up to a point, Worcestershire had the best of the game, and on going in a second time 52 behind

Gloucestershire lost three wickets for 45. From this point, however, Jessop by his wonderful hitting brought about a complete change in the fortunes of the match. He scored his 100 in an hour and at the drawing of stumps was not out 106. Gloucestershire were then 126 on with seven wickets in hand – a vivid illustration of how a hard hitter can sometimes transform a match. On the following day Jessop continued to play brilliant cricket, carrying his score to 165. He obtained his runs in two hours out of 205, his superb innings including six 6s and twenty 4s. He hit with characteristic certainty and power in all directions. After Jessop left the last five Gloucestershire wickets fell for 11 runs. Worcestershire were left with 210 to get to win, and on a damaged pitch they did not at any time look like accomplishing the task against the fine bowling of Dennett and Parker.

### Gloucestershire

| | | | |
|---|---|---|---|
| J. H. Board b Burrows | 0 | – b Burrows | 24 |
| T. Langdon b Cuffe | 19 | – c Foster b Burrows | 2 |
| P. Mills c Bale b Taylor | 1 | – b Burrows | 35 |
| A. Nott c Turner b Taylor | 6 | – c Cuffe b Burrows | 4 |
| Mr G. L. Jessop c Turner b Burrows | 6 | – c Taylor b Arnold | 165 |
| Mr D. L. Priestley b Arnold | 13 | – c Turner b Arnold | 7 |
| Mr H. J. Merrick b Cuffe | 4 | – c Bale b Burrows | 0 |
| Mr S. Levy b Cuffe | 0 | – b Burrows | 0 |
| J. H. Huggins c Foster b Cuffe | 10 | – b Burrows | 0 |
| C. Parker c Burrows b Arnold | 0 | – not out | 5 |
| G. Dennett not out | 0 | – b Arnold | 5 |
| B 1, l-b 2, w 1 | 4 | B 10, l-b 3, n-b 1 | 14 |
| | **63** | | **261** |

### Worcestershire

| | | | |
|---|---|---|---|
| F. Bowley c Parker b Mills | 6 | – lbw b Dennett | 6 |
| F. Pearson lbw b Dennett | 27 | – c Langdon b Huggins | 5 |
| E. Arnold c Merrick b Dennett | 6 | – st Board b Dennett | 17 |
| Mr G. N. Foster b Parker | 6 | – b Parker | 46 |
| J. A. Cuffe c and b Parker | 16 | – b Dennett | 11 |
| R. E. Turner st Board b Parker | 16 | – lbw b Dennett | 0 |
| Mr G. H. Simpson-Hayward c Jessop b Parker | 13 | – c Jessop b Parker | 5 |
| R. Burrows c Merrick b Dennett | 0 | – c Dennett b Parker | 7 |
| C. G. A. Collier b Dennett | 14 | – run out | 0 |
| Mr W. H. Taylor not out | 7 | – not out | 6 |
| E. Bale c Mills b Dennett | 0 | – b Dennett | 7 |
| B 3, n-b 1 | 4 | B 2, l-b 3 | 5 |
| | **115** | | **115** |

### Worcestershire Bowling

| | Overs | Mdns | Runs | Wkts | Overs | Mdns | Runs | Wkts |
|---|---|---|---|---|---|---|---|---|
| Burrows | 6 | 1 | 27 | 2 | 26 | 1 | 111 | 7 |
| Taylor | 11 | 4 | 16 | 2 | 8 | 1 | 44 | — |
| Cuffe | 7.5 | 2 | 12 | 4 | 18 | 3 | 69 | — |
| Arnold | 2 | — | 4 | 2 | 4.2 | 2 | 6 | 3 |
| Pearson | | | | | 5 | — | 17 | — |

### Gloucestershire Bowling

| | Overs | Mdns | Runs | Wkts | Overs | Mdns | Runs | Wkts |
|---|---|---|---|---|---|---|---|---|
| Dennett | 20.3 | 10 | 48 | 5 | 20.5 | 7 | 55 | 5 |
| Mills | 8 | 2 | 11 | 1 | | | | |
| Parker | 12 | 1 | 52 | 4 | 11 | 3 | 33 | 3 |
| Huggins | | | | | 9 | 2 | 22 | 1 |

Umpires: W. Flowers and Guttridge.

## WORCESTERSHIRE v YORKSHIRE

Played at Worcester, May 22, 23, 24, 1911

Dismissed in rather less than two hours before lunch, on the first afternoon, Worcestershire, though they batted finely in their second innings, could not recover from a deplorable start, and Yorkshire gained a decisive victory by ten wickets. Remarkable all-round form was shown by Hirst. Bowling with deadly effect, he took in Worcestershire's first innings nine wickets for 41 runs, and followed this up with a fine display of batting. He played in characteristic style, and hit thirteen 4s. The chief batting honours, however, belonged to Booth. Very strong on the off-side, he brought off some delightful drives and square cuts, and hardly made a bad stroke during a stay of four hours. Among his figures were twenty-three 4s. When Worcestershire went in 422 behind, H. K. Foster played splendidly.

### Worcestershire

| | | | |
|---|--:|---|--:|
| F. Bowley b Hirst | 0 | – b Haigh | 81 |
| F. Pearson b Hirst | 1 | – c and b Rhodes | 38 |
| Mr H. K. Foster b Hirst | 39 | – c Newstead b Rhodes | 112 |
| Mr G. N. Foster b Hirst | 13 | – b Haigh | 1 |
| Mr W. B. Burns c Dolphin b Hirst | 31 | – c Booth b Hirst | 28 |
| E. Arnold b Hirst | 9 | – b Hirst | 62 |
| J. A. Cuffe b Hirst | 4 | – b Drake | 52 |
| Mr G. H. Simpson-Hayward b Hirst | 7 | – not out | 51 |
| F. H. Hunt not out | 0 | – c Hirst b Newstead | 0 |
| A. J. Conway b Hirst | 0 | – c Dolphin b Newstead | 1 |
| E. Bale b Newstead | 2 | – b Newstead | 1 |
| B 2, l-b 4, n-b 1 | 7 | B 6, l-b 6, n-b 1 | 13 |
| | **113** | | **440** |

### Yorkshire

| | | | |
|---|--:|---|--:|
| B. B. Wilson c Simpson-Hayward b Arnold | 61 | | |
| W. Rhodes c Bale b Conway | 45 | | |
| D. Denton b Simpson-Hayward | 37 | | |
| A. Drake c Bowley b Cuffe | 33 | – not out | 16 |
| M. W. Booth b Simpson-Hayward | 210 | | |
| R. Kilner b Simpson-Hayward | 12 | – not out | 3 |
| G. H. Hirst b Cuffe | 100 | | |
| S. Haigh b Cuffe | 3 | | |
| Mr E. J. Radcliffe b Pearson | 4 | | |
| J. T. Newstead c Simpson-Hayward b Cuffe | 11 | | |
| A. Dolphin not out | 5 | | |
| B 6, l-b 7, w 1 | 14 | | |
| | **535** | | **19** |

### Yorkshire Bowling

| | Overs | Mdns | Runs | Wkts | Overs | Mdns | Runs | Wkts |
|---|--:|--:|--:|--:|--:|--:|--:|--:|
| Hirst | 15 | 2 | 41 | 9 | 34 | 7 | 89 | 2 |
| Booth | 5 | — | 28 | — | 12 | 1 | 40 | — |
| Newstead | 10 | — | 37 | 1 | 18.1 | 3 | 70 | 3 |
| Haigh | | | | | 24 | 4 | 69 | 2 |
| Drake | | | | | 20 | 4 | 50 | 1 |
| Rhodes | | | | | 47 | 13 | 109 | 2 |

**Worcestershire Bowling**

| | Overs | Mdns | Runs | Wkts | Overs | Mdns | Runs | Wkts |
|---|---|---|---|---|---|---|---|---|
| Hunt ........... | 13 | 3 | 36 | — | 2 | — | 11 | — |
| Arnold .......... | 18 | 2 | 74 | 1 | | | | |
| Burns ........... | 2 | — | 9 | — | | | | |
| Conway .......... | 25 | 2 | 127 | 1 | 2 | — | 8 | — |
| Cuffe ........... | 34 | 3 | 117 | 4 | | | | |
| Pearson ......... | 22 | 5 | 63 | 1 | | | | |
| Simpson-Hayward .. | 25.2 | 1 | 95 | 3 | | | | |

Umpires: G. Webb and B. W. Mason.

# WORCESTERSHIRE v GLOUCESTERSHIRE

### Played at Dudley, August 28, 29, 30, 1911

Worcestershire won a match of small scores by 91 runs. The Dudley ground had not previously been used for first-class cricket and all through batsmen found themselves at a considerable disadvantage. Success came only to those who played a hitting game and took risks. H. K. Foster in Worcestershire's first innings, and Pearson, Burns, and Cuffe in the second, batted well, and for Gloucestershire, Brownlee hit in free, resolute style, but except at rare intervals the bowlers were masters of the situation. On the second day, Board was out in a rather curious fashion. Having run a single he left his crease to pat the turf while the ball was still in the hands of the fieldsman. The ball was returned to Bale, who, seeing that Board was out of his ground, put the wicket down.

### Worcestershire

| | | | |
|---|---|---|---|
| F. Bowley c Parker b Dennett ................. | 17 | – lbw b Parker ................ | 4 |
| F. Pearson b Parker ......................... | 26 | – c Parker b Dennett ........... | 42 |
| E. Arnold b Parker ......................... | 17 | – c and b Dennett ............. | 13 |
| Mr H. K. Foster c Luce b Brownlee ............ | 44 | – c Brownlee b Parker .......... | 12 |
| Mr W. B. Burns b Parker .................... | 6 | – b Jessop .................. | 37 |
| Mr G. N. Foster c Bowles b Parker ........... | 0 | – b Dennett ................. | 0 |
| J. A. Cuffe c Bowles b Dennett .............. | 16 | – b Jessop .................. | 32 |
| Mr G. H. Simpson-Hayward run out ............ | 12 | – b Jessop .................. | 11 |
| Mr H. F. Baker not out ..................... | 8 | – b Jessop .................. | 5 |
| R. Burrows c Board b Parker ................ | 2 | – c Luce b Dennett ........... | 11 |
| E. Bale c Board b Dennett .................. | 9 | – not out ................... | 0 |
| B 3, l-b 4 ......................... | 7 | B 4 .................. | 4 |
| | **164** | | **171** |

### Gloucestershire

| | | | |
|---|---|---|---|
| J. H. Board run out ........................ | 18 | – c Pearson b Cuffe ............. | 6 |
| A. G. Dipper b Arnold ...................... | 0 | – b Arnold .................. | 2 |
| T. Langdon b Cuffe ........................ | 15 | – c G. N. Foster b Cuffe ........ | 13 |
| Mr F. B. Roberts c Burrows b Cuffe ........... | 1 | – c G. N. Foster b Cuffe ......... | 4 |
| Mr G. L. Jessop c Bale b Cuffe ............... | 22 | – c Bale b Cuffe .............. | 8 |
| Mr W. M. Brownlee b Cuffe .................. | 62 | – c Burns b Arnold ............ | 23 |
| Mr F. M. Luce lbw b Cuffe .................. | 0 | – st Bale b Cuffe ............. | 6 |
| J. Bowles b Arnold ........................ | 2 | – st Bale b Cuffe .............. | 2 |
| A. Nott c Baker b Cuffe .................... | 4 | – not out ................... | 13 |
| G. Dennett run out ........................ | 16 | – c H. K. Foster b Cuffe ........ | 14 |
| C. Parker not out ......................... | 1 | – b Cuffe ................... | 5 |
| B 2, l-b 1 ......................... | 3 | B 1, l-b 3 ............... | 4 |
| | **144** | | **100** |

## Gloucestershire Bowling

|  | Overs | Mdns | Runs | Wkts | Overs | Mdns | Runs | Wkts |
|---|---|---|---|---|---|---|---|---|
| Dennett ......... | 37.5 | 16 | 52 | 3 | 20 | 7 | 74 | 4 |
| Parker .......... | 39 | 11 | 92 | 5 | 22 | 4 | 61 | 2 |
| Brownlee | 4 | 2 | 13 | 1 |  |  |  |  |
| Jessop .......... |  |  |  |  | 7.3 | — | 32 | 4 |

## Worcestershire Bowling

|  | Overs | Mdns | Runs | Wkts | Overs | Mdns | Runs | Wkts |
|---|---|---|---|---|---|---|---|---|
| Cuffe ........... | 18.3 | 3 | 74 | 6 | 17.5 | 3 | 41 | 8 |
| Arnold .......... | 15 | 3 | 58 | 2 | 17 | 3 | 55 | 2 |
| Baker ........... | 3 | 1 | 9 | — |  |  |  |  |

Umpires: W. A. J. West and J. E. West.

# WORCESTERSHIRE v SOMERSET

Played at Worcester, June 26, 27, 28, 1913

A magnificent display of hitting by Braund dwarfed everything else in this match. Missed in the slips when 34, Braund afterward held such a complete mastery over the bowling that he did not make another mistake. Batting with remarkable freedom and showing all his old skill in placing the ball, he scored 50 in forty-five minutes, 100 in two hours and ten minutes, doubled his total in the next sixty-five minutes, and altogether obtained 257 out of 370 in three hours and three quarters. He hit a 6 (4 for an overthrow), and thirty-five 4s. In Somerset's second innings Braund again batted finely, but though scoring in all 307 runs he had the misfortune to be on the losing side, Worcestershire winning by eight wickets. In this match Chester, who afterwards did such valuable work for his side, made his first hundred in county cricket.

## Somerset

| | | | |
|---|---:|---|---:|
| Mr M. P. Bajana b Burrows | 7 | – c Pearson b Burns | 32 |
| W. Hyman c Burns b Pearson | 41 | – b Burrows | 6 |
| Mr R. E. Hancock c Bale b Burrows | 2 | – b Burns | 10 |
| L. C. Braund not out | 257 | – b Pearson | 50 |
| Mr E. S. M. Poyntz c Bowley b Burrows | 0 | – c Chester b Burns | 1 |
| Mr H. Southwood c Bale b Burns | 13 | – c Bale b Burns | 0 |
| E. Robson c and b Burrows | 12 | – b Pearson | 1 |
| Mr C. G. Deane c Arnold b Pearson | 23 | – b Pearson | 0 |
| Mr B. D. Hylton-Stewart b Pearson | 9 | – run out | 13 |
| H. Chidgey c Bale b Pearson | 1 | – not out | 0 |
| Mr J. C. White c Bale b Cuffe | 11 | – b Pearson | 0 |
| B 3, l-b 1, w 1, n-b 2 | 7 | B 7 | 7 |
|  | **383** |  | **120** |

### Worcestershire

| | | |
|---|---|---|
| F. Bowley b White | 25 | – c Chidgey b Hylton-Stewart ...... 48 |
| F. Pearson b White | 11 | – not out ........................ 71 |
| Mr H. K. Foster c Chidgey b Hylton-Stewart | 4 | – c Poyntz b Deane .............. 27 |
| Mr W. B. Burns b White | 35 | – not out ....................... 5 |
| E. Arnold b Robson | 18 | |
| J. A. Cuffe c Bajana b Hylton-Stewart | 79 | |
| Mr G. H. Simpson-Hayward b White | 0 | |
| F. Chester c Poyntz b Robson | 115 | |
| F. H. Hunt lbw b Robson | 31 | |
| R. Burrows not out | 12 | |
| E. Bale c Poyntz b Robson | 4 | |
| B 4, l-b 4, w 2 | 10 | B 8, l-b 1 .............. 9 |
| | 344 | 160 |

### Worcestershire Bowling

| | Overs | Mdns | Runs | Wkts | Overs | Mdns | Runs | Wkts |
|---|---|---|---|---|---|---|---|---|
| Burrows .......... | 26 | 2 | 146 | 4 | 9 | — | 39 | 1 |
| Burns ........... | 13 | 2 | 47 | 1 | 15 | 2 | 47 | 4 |
| Hunt ........... | 4 | — | 19 | — | | | | |
| Cuffe .......... | 13.3 | 1 | 48 | 1 | | | | |
| Simpson-Hayward .. | 5 | 2 | 27 | — | | | | |
| Pearson ......... | 20 | 3 | 60 | 4 | 8 | 2 | 27 | 4 |
| Chester ......... | 5 | — | 29 | — | | | | |

### Somerset Bowling

| | Overs | Mdns | Runs | Wkts | Overs | Mdns | Runs | Wkts |
|---|---|---|---|---|---|---|---|---|
| Robson .......... | 35.1 | 3 | 140 | 4 | 7 | 2 | 32 | — |
| White ........... | 54 | 25 | 66 | 4 | 17 | 5 | 37 | — |
| Hylton-Stewart .... | 22 | 2 | 68 | 2 | 9 | 1 | 38 | 1 |
| Deane .......... | 3 | — | 16 | — | 4.5 | — | 21 | 1 |
| Braund .......... | 8 | 1 | 44 | — | | | | |
| Hancock ......... | | | | | 5 | — | 23 | — |

Umpires: A. E. Street and W. Vining.

## WORCESTERSHIRE v WARWICKSHIRE

### Played at Dudley, June 1, 2, 3, 1914

F. R. Foster in this match played the innings of his life. Going in when the third Warwickshire wicket fell at 197, he in four hours and twenty minutes scored 305 out of 448 and was still not out when he declared the innings closed. Tremendous in itself, the performance was invested with a degree of merit truly wonderful by the fact that Foster gave no chance, timing the ball indeed with such exceptional accuracy that he did not make a bad stroke until he had passed 200. Splendid driving and brilliant hitting on the leg side were the outstanding features of a memorable innings in which were one 5, forty-four 4s, fourteen 3s, twenty-one 2s, and forty singles. Prior to Foster's great display, Parsons and Quaife batted admirably in their different styles, adding 116 for the third wicket. The partnership of Foster and Smith yielded 166 in seventy minutes. The match was brought to a startling conclusion on Wednesday, Field going on to bowl when Worcestershire had scored 85 for the loss of four batsmen, and taking the six outstanding wickets at a cost of only 2 runs. Field not only maintained a fine pace, but broke back to a remarkable extent. Warwickshire won by an innings and 321 runs.

## Worcestershire

| | | | |
|---|---|---|---|
| F. Bowley lbw b Field | 34 | – c Parsons b Jeeves | 14 |
| F. Pearson b Field | 11 | – lbw b Jeeves | 19 |
| Mr M. K. Foster lbw b Langley | 12 | – c and b Field | 51 |
| F. Chester c Baker b Langley | 27 | – run out | 11 |
| Mr A. T. Cliff b Langley | 32 | – b Jeeves | 4 |
| Mr B. G. Stevens b Field | 2 | – b Field | 15 |
| Mr W. H. Taylor c Foster b Quaife | 34 | – b Field | 0 |
| Mr N. J. A. Foster b Field | 15 | – not out | 9 |
| R. Burrows c Parsons b Quaife | 4 | – c and b Field | 0 |
| E. Bale lbw b Quaife | 2 | – b Field | 0 |
| A. J. Conway not out | 0 | – lbw b Field | 0 |
| B 7, l-b 2, w 4, n-b 2 | 15 | B 5, l-b 1, w 2, n-b 5 | 13 |
| | **188** | | **136** |

## Warwickshire

| | | | |
|---|---|---|---|
| S. P. Kinneir b Pearson | 12 | Mr G. W. Stephens c Bale b Conway | 10 |
| J. H. Parsons c Bale b Pearson | 102 | E. J. Smith c and b Cliff | 42 |
| C. Charlesworth st Bale b Chester | 26 | P. Jeeves not out | 6 |
| W. G. Quaife c Pearson b Burrows | 85 | B 27, l-b 3, w 2, n-b 5 | 37 |
| Mr F. R. Foster not out | 305 | | |
| C. S. Baker lbw b Burrows | 20 | (7 wkts dec.) | 645 |

Mr C. K. Langley and F. E. Field did not bat.

### Warwickshire Bowling

| | Overs | Mdns | Runs | Wkts | Overs | Mdns | Runs | Wkts |
|---|---|---|---|---|---|---|---|---|
| Foster | 20 | 6 | 40 | — | 16 | 5 | 45 | — |
| Jeeves | 12 | 4 | 27 | — | 16 | 2 | 30 | 3 |
| Field | 22.3 | 6 | 58 | 4 | 8.4 | 6 | 2 | 6 |
| Langley | 12 | — | 37 | 3 | 7 | 1 | 30 | — |
| Quaife | 8 | — | 11 | 3 | | | | |
| Charlesworth | | | | | 2 | — | 16 | — |

### Worcestershire Bowling

| | Overs | Mdns | Runs | Wkts |
|---|---|---|---|---|
| Burrows | 36 | 8 | 140 | 2 |
| Pearson | 24 | 5 | 81 | 2 |
| Conway | 13 | — | 85 | 1 |
| Chester | 26 | 3 | 84 | 1 |
| Taylor | 30 | 2 | 144 | — |
| M. K. Foster | 4 | — | 42 | — |
| Cliff | 9 | 1 | 32 | 1 |

Umpires: A. J. Atfield and G. P. Harrison.

# YORKSHIRE

## YORKSHIRE v HAMPSHIRE

Played at Hull, June 21, 22, 23, 1900

This was quite a holiday match for the Yorkshiremen, their superiority being overwhelming. Rain limited the first day's play to three hours, during which time Hampshire completed their first innings, and Yorkshire scored 16 runs without losing a wicket. On the second day the Yorkshiremen gave a brilliant display of hitting against weak bowling, and made themselves practically sure of a single-innings victory. Brown and Tunnicliffe, by capital cricket, scored 148 for the first wicket, but perhaps the most noteworthy feature of the innings was the success of the left-handed colt Washington, who did far better than in any of his previous trials for the county. Except for a couple of faulty hits that fell out of harm's way his innings of 86 was quite free from blemish. Hirst was in a most vigorous mood, hitting fourteen 4s in his 89, and getting his runs in a little over two hours. He did not give a chance till he had made 84. It seemed likely that rain on the third day would save Hampshire from a beating, it being 20 minutes past three before the game could be proceeded with. Then, however, Rhodes bowled in irresistible form, and at half-past four Yorkshire won the game by an innings and 271 runs.

### Hampshire

| | | |
|---|---|---|
| Mr C. Robson c sub. b Haigh | 0 – b Rhodes | 5 |
| A. Webb c Brown b Rhodes | 31 – c Hunter b Rhodes | 18 |
| Mr E. M. Sprot b Rhodes | 10 – run out | 8 |
| Mr E. J. Newton b Haigh | 19 – c Hunter b Rhodes | 0 |
| Mr E. C. Lee c Tunnicliffe b Rhodes | 34 – st Hunter b Rhodes | 0 |
| V. Barton b Hirst | 15 – c Wainwright b Rhodes | 8 |
| T. Soar c Hirst b Rhodes | 0 – c Hirst b Rhodes | 11 |
| Mr D. A. Steel c Tunnicliffe b Rhodes | 4 – c Hirst b Haigh | 7 |
| Budden b Hirst | 3 – c and b Rhodes | 0 |
| H. Baldwin b Rhodes | 4 – not out | 0 |
| Bull not out | 0 – b Rhodes | 2 |
| B 2, l-b 3, w 2, n-b 1 | 8      W 1, b 1 | 2 |
| | **128** | **61** |

### Yorkshire

| | | | |
|---|---|---|---|
| J. T. Brown sen. b Baldwin | 81 | L. Whitehead c Barton b Baldwin | 50 |
| J. Tunnicliffe c Soar b Budden | 67 | W. Rhodes b Soar | 0 |
| D. Denton lbw b Baldwin | 18 | Riley b Soar | 10 |
| E. Wainwright c Sprot b Baldwin | 2 | D. Hunter not out | 26 |
| G. H. Hirst b Baldwin | 89 | B 10, l-b 2 | 12 |
| J. Washington c Webb b Soar | 86 | | |
| S. Haigh c Newton b Baldwin | 19 | | **460** |

### Yorkshire Bowling

| | Overs | Mdns | Runs | Wkts | Overs | Mdns | Runs | Wkts |
|---|---|---|---|---|---|---|---|---|
| Rhodes | 30.3 | 9 | 43 | 6 | 12.5 | 5 | 23 | 8 |
| Haigh | 19 | 6 | 51 | 2 | 2 | — | 6 | 1 |
| Riley | 4 | — | 6 | — | | | | |
| Hirst | 8 | 2 | 20 | 2 | | | | |
| Wainwright | | | | | 11 | — | 30 | — |

**Hampshire Bowling**

|         | Overs | Mdns | Runs | Wkts |
|---------|-------|------|------|------|
| Soar .............. | 31 | 6 | 100 | 3 |
| Baldwin .......... | 41.2 | 9 | 130 | 6 |
| Bull .............. | 6 | 1 | 25 | — |
| Barton .......... | 20 | 6 | 69 | — |
| Budden .......... | 18 | 5 | 61 | 1 |
| Steele ............ | 7 | 3 | 16 | — |
| Webb ............ | 1 | — | 9 | — |
| Sprot ............ | 6 | — | 25 | — |
| Lee .............. | 3 | — | 8 | — |
| Robson .......... | 1 | — | 5 | — |

Umpires: M. Sherwin and G. Porter.

## YORKSHIRE v SOMERSET

Played at Dewsbury, June 28, 29, 1900

The Yorkshiremen finished up this match in brilliant style, winning before four o'clock on the second afternoon by 140 runs, but it cannot be said they were seen to much advantage on the opening day. With a weak side against them, they were 3 runs behind on the first innings, and on going in for the second time they lost Brown and Tunnicliffe before the drawing of stumps for 37. However, all their shortcomings were atoned for the next day, a superb display of hitting by Hirst being followed up by remarkable bowling on the part of Haigh and Rhodes. Going in third wicket down at 37, Hirst was out ninth, scoring in about two hours 106 runs out of 152. He hit eighteen 4s, and except for a difficult chance when he made 47, his innings was quite free from fault. Somerset only wanted 189 to win, but on a wicket that helped the bowlers they never seemed in the least likely to make such a number, and in about an hour they were all out, most of the batsmen being quite helpless against Rhodes and Haigh.

### Yorkshire

| | | | |
|---|---|---|---|
| J. T. Brown sen. b Robson .................... | 15 | – c Robson b Cranfield ........... | 0 |
| J. Tunnicliffe c Wickham b Bailey ............... | 54 | – c Woods b Cranfield ........... | 0 |
| D. Denton c Bailey b Cranfield .......... | 0 | – c Hyman b Cranfield .......... | 29 |
| E. Wainwright c Wickham b Cranfield .......... | 28 | – b Robson .................... | 12 |
| G. H. Hirst c Woods b Cranfield ............... | 0 | – c Bernard b Cranfield .......... | 106 |
| Mr E. Smith run out ......................... | 0 | – b Cranfield ................... | 3 |
| J. Washington b Cranfield .................... | 10 | – c Woods b Cranfield ........... | 18 |
| Lord Hawke st Wickham b Cranfield ............ | 4 | – b Gill ........................ | 5 |
| S. Haigh c Hyman b Cranfield ................. | 22 | – c Woods b Cranfield .......... | 0 |
| W. Rhodes lbw b Robson ..................... | 0 | – b Lewis ...................... | 14 |
| D. Hunter not out .......................... | 2 | – not out ...................... | 0 |
| N-b 2 .......................... | 2 | L-b 1, n-b 3 ............. | 4 |
| | **137** | | **191** |

### Somerset

| | | | |
|---|---|---|---|
| Mr S. M. J. Woods b Haigh | 49 | – b Haigh | 7 |
| Mr C. A. Bernard c Smith b Rhodes | 7 | – c Hawke b Rhodes | 5 |
| Mr W. Trask lbw b Haigh | 0 | – st Hunter b Rhodes | 7 |
| Mr E. Robson c Washington b Rhodes | 7 | – c Brown b Rhodes | 0 |
| Lewis run out | 7 | – b Haigh | 15 |
| Mr W. Hyman run out | 0 | – c Wainwright b Rhodes | 4 |
| B. Cranfield c Denton b Rhodes | 12 | – c Brown b Haigh | 0 |
| G. Gill c Washington b Rhodes | 8 | – b Haigh | 0 |
| E. J. Tyler c Brown b Haigh | 26 | – not out | 6 |
| Rev. A. P. Wickham c Hawke b Smith | 0 | – run out | 0 |
| Bailey not out | 12 | – b Haigh | 3 |
| B 10, l-b 2 | 12 | L-b 1 | 1 |
| | **140** | | **48** |

### Somerset Bowling

| | Overs | Mdns | Runs | Wkts | Overs | Mdns | Runs | Wkts |
|---|---|---|---|---|---|---|---|---|
| Tyler | 7 | 1 | 20 | — | 6 | — | 27 | — |
| Robson | 25 | 12 | 46 | 2 | 15 | 8 | 25 | 1 |
| Cranfield | 23.3 | 5 | 64 | 6 | 27 | 6 | 95 | 7 |
| Bailey | 5 | 3 | 5 | 1 | 9 | 3 | 29 | — |
| Gill | | | | | 4 | 2 | 11 | 1 |
| Lewis | | | | | 0.2 | — | — | 1 |

### Yorkshire Bowling

| | Overs | Mdns | Runs | Wkts | Overs | Mdns | Runs | Wkts |
|---|---|---|---|---|---|---|---|---|
| Rhodes | 20 | 4 | 52 | 4 | 11 | 3 | 22 | 4 |
| Haigh | 13.1 | 2 | 39 | 3 | 10.1 | 5 | 25 | 5 |
| Smith | 7 | — | 37 | 1 | | | | |

Umpires: R. G. Barlow and J. Moss.

## YORKSHIRE v GLOUCESTERSHIRE

Played at Bradford, July 23, 24, 25, 1900

Of all the Yorkshire matches last season, this was perhaps the most remarkable. The Yorkshiremen proved victorious in the end, but after being 140 ahead on the first innings, they were so hard pressed that they only won by 40 runs. Flattered by the smallness of the Bradford ground, Jessop hit in tremendous form, and had the satisfaction, for the first time in his career, of making two separate hundreds in a first-class match. His 104, though marked by some fine driving, was a very lucky innings, but for his 139 no praise could be too high. He made his runs in less than an hour and a half, and reached his hundred without giving a chance. Seven times he drove Rhodes out of the field for 6. Hirst also showed wonderful cricket, and with 8 more runs on the Tuesday, he also would have made two hundreds. He scored his 111 in an hour and forty minutes, and his 92 in eighty-five minutes. Rhodes suffered severely at Jessop's hands, but nevertheless he took fourteen wickets. The Gloucestershire eleven fielded superbly on the first day, and their defeat did them more credit than many a victory.

## Yorkshire

| | | |
|---|---|---|
| Lord Hawke c Board b Roberts | 32 | – c Roberts b Paish ............... 6 |
| J. Tunnicliffe b Townsend | 25 | – b Roberts ..................... 0 |
| D. Denton c Townsend b Roberts | 85 | – c Wrathall b Roberts .......... 19 |
| Mr T. L. Taylor lbw b Townsend | 64 | – c Townsend b Fargus ........ 35 |
| G. H. Hirst c Jessop b Paish | 111 | – c Townsend b Fargus ........ 92 |
| E. Wainwright c Champain b Fargus | 19 | – run out ..................... 4 |
| J. Washington b Paish | 16 | – c Jessop b Townsend ......... 8 |
| S. Haigh c Paish b Fargus | 2 | – c Paish b Townsend .......... 8 |
| W. Rhodes not out | 23 | – not out ..................... 11 |
| D. Hunter c and b Paish | 11 | – c Paish b Townsend .......... 0 |
| Oyston c Jessop b Paish | 0 | – c Jessop b Townsend ......... 2 |
| B 8, l-b 6, w 1, n-b 6 | 21 | L-b 1, w 1 .............. 2 |
| | **409** | **187** |

## Gloucestershire

| | | |
|---|---|---|
| Mr C. O. H. Sewell c Hawke b Rhodes | 4 | – lbw b Rhodes ................. 10 |
| Mr W. S. A. Brown c Hunter b Rhodes | 0 | – c Tunnicliffe b Rhodes ...... 3 |
| Mr N. O. Tagart c Hunter b Oyston | 25 | – c Hunter b Haigh ............ 4 |
| J. H. Board c Oyston b Rhodes | 4 | – b Haigh ..................... 10 |
| Mr C. L. Townsend b Haigh | 42 | – b Haigh ..................... 22 |
| H. Wrathall c Wainwright b Rhodes | 42 | – c Haigh b Rhodes ............ 31 |
| Mr G. L. Jessop c Hawke b Rhodes | 104 | – c Tunnicliffe b Rhodes ...... 139 |
| Mr F. H. Champain c Hunter b Rhodes | 22 | – c Taylor b Rhodes ........... 53 |
| Mr A. H. C. Fargus st Hunter b Rhodes | 8 | – c Wainwright b Haigh ........ 5 |
| A. Paish c Denton b Rhodes | 8 | – b Rhodes .................... 2 |
| F. G. Roberts not out | 0 | – not out ..................... 2 |
| B 4, l-b 1, w 4, n-b 1 | 10 | B 1, l-b 3, n-b 2 .......... 6 |
| | **269** | **287** |

### Gloucestershire Bowling

| | Overs | Mdns | Runs | Wkts | Overs | Mdns | Runs | Wkts |
|---|---|---|---|---|---|---|---|---|
| Jessop | 13 | 5 | 29 | — | 7 | 2 | 20 | — |
| Paish | 37.3 | 4 | 154 | 4 | 11 | 4 | 27 | 1 |
| Roberts | 20 | 5 | 55 | 2 | 13 | 3 | 44 | 2 |
| Townsend | 10 | — | 39 | 2 | 11 | — | 58 | 4 |
| Brown | 12 | 4 | 30 | — | 5 | — | 20 | — |
| Fargus | 19 | 4 | 81 | 2 | 10 | 5 | 16 | 2 |

### Yorkshire Bowling

| | Overs | Mdns | Runs | Wkts | Overs | Mdns | Runs | Wkts |
|---|---|---|---|---|---|---|---|---|
| Hirst | 17 | 1 | 80 | — | 9 | 1 | 44 | — |
| Rhodes | 20.5 | 6 | 72 | 8 | 24.4 | 5 | 120 | 6 |
| Oyston | 10 | — | 45 | 1 | 2 | — | 3 | — |
| Haigh | 18 | 3 | 62 | 1 | 27 | 4 | 114 | 4 |

Umpires: G. Porter and W. Wright.

## YORKSHIRE v SOMERSET

### Played at Leeds, July 15, 16, 17, 1901

This was the sensational match of the whole season, and the only county fixture in which Yorkshire suffered defeat. To the wonderful victory gained by Somerset, cricket history can furnish few parallels. They started their second innings on the Tuesday morning against a majority of 238, and yet in the end they won the game by 279 runs. Superb batting turned the scale, L. C. H. Palairet and Braund scoring 222 in two hours and twenty minutes for the first wicket. Thanks to this brilliant partnership, the Yorkshire bowling was quite mastered, and for the rest of the afternoon the hitting went on at such a pace that at the drawing of stumps the total stood at 549 with only five men out. Palairet and Braund of course took the chief honours, but Phillips' play was almost equally fine. Palairet was batting three hours and forty minutes. The Yorkshiremen thought that Braund was caught at slip by Tunnicliffe when he had 55. Owing to the bowler being in his way, Mycroft could not give a decision, and Walter Wright on being appealed to decided in the batsman's favour. On the third day the Yorkshiremen collapsed very badly.

### Somerset

| | | |
|---|---|---|
| Mr L. C. H. Palairet b Hirst | 0 | – c and b Brown .................173 |
| L. C. Braund b Rhodes | 0 | – b Haigh .....................107 |
| Lewis c Tunnicliffe b Rhodes | 10 | – b Rhodes ..................... 12 |
| Mr F. A. Phillips b Hirst | 12 | – b Wainwright .................122 |
| Mr S. M. J. Woods c Hunter b Haigh | 46 | – c Tunnicliffe b Hirst ............. 66 |
| Mr V. T. Hill run out | 0 | – c Hirst b Rhodes ............. 53 |
| E. Robson c Hunter b Rhodes | 0 | – c Tunnicliffe b Rhodes ......... 40 |
| G. Gill c Hunter b Rhodes | 4 | – st Hunter b Rhodes ........... 14 |
| Mr A. E. Newton b Haigh | 0 | – c Taylor b Rhodes ..........  4 |
| Mr G. Barrington c Brown b Rhodes | 11 | – st Hunter b Rhodes ........... 15 |
| B. Cranfield not out | 1 | – not out ..................... 5 |
| B 2, l-b 1 | 3 | B 16, n-b 3 .............. 19 |
| | **87** | **630** |

### Yorkshire

| | | |
|---|---|---|
| J. T. Brown c Braund b Cranfield | 24 | – c sub. b Gill ................. 5 |
| J. Tunnicliffe c Newton b Gill | 9 | – c Palairet b Braund ............. 44 |
| D. Denton c Wood b Gill | 12 | – b Braund ................. 16 |
| Mr T. L. Taylor b Cranfield | 1 | – absent hurt ................. 0 |
| Mr F. Mitchell b Gill | 4 | – b Braund ................. 21 |
| G. H. Hirst c Robson b Cranfield | 61 | – lbw b Braund ................. 6 |
| E. Wainwright b Gill | 9 | – c Lewis b Cranfield ......... 1 |
| Lord Hawke b Robson | 37 | – c Barrington b Cranfield ........ 4 |
| S. Haigh c Robson b Cranfield | 96 | – not out ..................... 2 |
| W. Rhodes c Lewis b Robson | 44 | – st Newton b Cranfield ......... 0 |
| D. Hunter not out | 10 | – c Woods b Cranfield ........... 0 |
| B 13, w 5 | 18 | B 12, n-b 2 .............. 14 |
| | **325** | **113** |

### Yorkshire Bowling

| | Overs | Mdns | Runs | Wkts | Overs | Mdns | Runs | Wkts |
|---|---|---|---|---|---|---|---|---|
| Hirst ............ | 12 | 5 | 36 | 2 | 37 | 1 | 189 | 1 |
| Rhodes ........... | 16 | 8 | 39 | 5 | 46.5 | 12 | 145 | 6 |
| Haigh ........... | 4 | — | 9 | 2 | 20 | 4 | 78 | 1 |
| Wainwright ....... | | | | | 34 | 3 | 107 | 1 |
| Brown .......... | | | | | 18 | 1 | 92 | 1 |

### Somerset Bowling

| | Overs | Mdns | Runs | Wkts | Overs | Mdns | Runs | Wkts |
|---|---|---|---|---|---|---|---|---|
| Cranfield ........ | 27 | 5 | 113 | 4 | 18 | 5 | 35 | 4 |
| Gill ............. | 23 | 2 | 105 | 4 | 4 | 1 | 23 | 1 |
| Braund .......... | 5 | — | 33 | — | 15 | 3 | 41 | 4 |
| Robson .......... | 10 | 1 | 35 | 2 | | | | |
| Woods ......... | 5 | 1 | 21 | — | | | | |
| Palairet ......... | 1 | 1 | — | — | | | | |

Umpires: W. Wright and T. Mycroft.

## YORKSHIRE v SOMERSET

Played at Sheffield, June 16, 17, 18, 1902

For the second year in succession Yorkshire's one defeat in the championship was sustained in the home match with Somerset, the western county proving victorious by 34 runs. Somerset enjoyed some advantage in winning the toss, Braund and Palairet making 44 for the first wicket, but after lunch Jackson and Rhodes carried all before them. On Yorkshire going in, the score, thanks to some free hitting by Denton and Brown, reached 50, with only three men out, but Braund and Robson then met with so little resistance that the innings was all over in an hour and a quarter. Not a ball could be bowled on the Tuesday, and it was after one o'clock before play was possible on the last day. Palairet and Braund again batted admirably and, Gill hitting hard, the score reached 100, with five men out, but afterwards Haigh performed the "hat trick," and the innings closed for 106. Haigh took his last five wickets without a run being scored off him. Yorkshire had 119 to get, but never looked like winning. Braund bowled in superb form, getting on a lot of leg-break, keeping an excellent length, and now and then sending down a fine fast ball. In the whole match he obtained fifteen wickets for 71 runs, and played two excellent innings of over thirty.

### Somerset

| | | | |
|---|---:|---|---:|
| Mr L. C. H. Palairet b Jackson | 25 | – c and b Jackson | 24 |
| L. C. Braund c and b Rhodes | 31 | – c Jackson b Haigh | 34 |
| E. Robson b Jackson | 0 | – b Jackson | 0 |
| Mr P. R. Johnson b Jackson | 0 | – run out | 3 |
| Mr S. M. J. Woods lbw b Rhodes | 14 | – c Hirst b Rhodes | 0 |
| A. Lewis c Haigh b Rhodes | 1 | – b Haigh | 4 |
| G. Gill lbw b Jackson | 1 | – b Haigh | 41 |
| Mr F. M. Lee c Denton b Rhodes | 1 | – b Haigh | 0 |
| Mr A. E. Newton b Jackson | 0 | – b Haigh | 0 |
| B. Cranfield b Jackson | 5 | – not out | 0 |
| Mr D. L. Evans not out | 6 | – b Haigh | 0 |
| L-b 1, n-b 1 | 2 | | |
| | **86** | | **106** |

### Yorkshire

| | | | |
|---|---:|---|---:|
| J. T. Brown b Cranfield | 13 | – c Johnson b Cranfield | 8 |
| J. Tunnicliffe b Braund | 4 | – c Robson b Braund | 11 |
| D. Denton b Robson | 20 | – b Braund | 6 |
| Mr T. L. Taylor c Newton b Braund | 8 | – st Newton b Braund | 18 |
| Hon. F. S. Jackson b Braund | 5 | – b Braund | 6 |
| G. H. Hirst c Evans b Braund | 0 | – c Palairet b Braund | 9 |
| I. Washington b Robson | 0 | – b Braund | 3 |
| S. Haigh b Braund | 9 | – b Braund | 6 |
| W. Rhodes b Braund | 5 | – c and b Braund | 5 |
| Lord Hawke lbw b Robson | 1 | – b Braund | 6 |
| D. Hunter not out | 1 | – not out | 0 |
| B 5, l-b 3 | 8 | B 4, l-b 2 | 6 |
| | **74** | | **84** |

### Yorkshire Bowling

| | Overs | Mdns | Runs | Wkts | Overs | Mdns | Runs | Wkts |
|---|---:|---:|---:|---:|---:|---:|---:|---:|
| Hirst | 7 | 3 | 8 | — | 2 | — | 5 | — |
| Rhodes | 26 | 10 | 39 | 4 | 12 | — | 44 | 1 |
| Jackson | 24.2 | 12 | 29 | 6 | 21 | 7 | 38 | 2 |
| Haigh | 4 | 2 | 8 | — | 7.1 | 1 | 19 | 6 |

**Somerset Bowling**

| | Overs | Mdns | Runs | Wkts | Overs | Mdns | Runs | Wkts |
|---|---|---|---|---|---|---|---|---|
| Cranfield ......... | 7 | — | 34 | 1 | 9 | — | 22 | 1 |
| Braund .......... | 13 | 2 | 30 | 6 | 17.3 | 5 | 41 | 9 |
| Robson ......... | 6 | 5 | 2 | 3 | 9 | 3 | 15 | — |

Umpires: G. Porter and W. Wright.

# YORKSHIRE v WORCESTERSHIRE

## Played at Huddersfield, July 16, 17, 18, 1903

Although not a ball could be bowled on the Thursday, and play was limited on Friday to an hour and three-quarters, and on Saturday to two hours, Yorkshire narrowly missed a sensational victory. Worcestershire, when the game had to be abandoned as a draw, being still 25 runs behind with only four wickets to go down. Worcestershire it was thought would profit by batting first, but the wicket proved extremely difficult, and their innings was finished off by Rhodes and Hirst for 24 – the lowest score in a first-class match all the season. Rhodes, who divided the wickets with Hirst, had only four singles scored off him. Further rain then delayed further progress with the game until a quarter to six when, with the wicket so sloppy that the Worcestershire bowlers could scarcely stand, Yorkshire made a capital start, Brown and Tunnicliffe putting on 43, and Denton in company with Tunnicliffe, raising the total to 76 without further loss. There came anothey heavy fall of rain during Friday night, and with neither wind nor sun the wicket was not fit for cricket until half-past four. Hawke at once declared Yorkshire's innings closed, and on Worcestershire going in, Rhodes and Hirst got down four wickets in half-an-hour for 8 runs. Arnold then found a useful partner in Isaac, these two staying together for three-quarters of an hour. Forty minutes from time, however, the visitors had only four wickets to go down but Arnold and Pearson kept up their wickets during this period.

## Worcestershire

| | | | |
|---|---|---|---|
| Mr H. K. Foster c Hirst b Rhodes .............. | 0 | – b Hirst ........................ | 0 |
| F. Bowley c and b Hirst ....................... | 3 | – c Brown b Hirst .............. | 4 |
| E. Arnold st Hunter b Rhodes ................. | 1 | – not out ...................... | 13 |
| F. Wheldon c Brown b Hirst ................... | 4 | – st Hunter b Rhodes ............. | 1 |
| Mr W. S. Caldwell c Hunter b Rhodes ............ | 11 | – c Hunter b Hirst .............. | 0 |
| G. Gaukrodger c Tunnicliffe b Rhodes ........... | 1 | – c Hirst b Rhodes .............. | 0 |
| R. Pearson b Hirst .......................... | 1 | – not out ...................... | 4 |
| A. Bird c Tunnicliffe b Hirst .................... | 0 | | |
| G. A. Wilson c Wilkinson b Rhodes ............. | 0 | | |
| Mr A. W. Isaac b Hirst ...................... | 1 | – c and b Rhodes .............. | 3 |
| J. Keene not out ........................... | 0 | | |
| L-b 1, n-b 1 ...................... | 2 | B 1, n-b 1 .............. | 2 |
| | **24** | | **27** |

## Yorkshire

| | |
|---|---|
| J. T. Brown c Gaukrodger b Arnold ...... | 26 |
| J. Tunnicliffe not out ................. | 38 |
| D. Denton not out .................... | 10 |
| W 2 ...................... | 2 |
| (1 wkt dec.) | **76** |

Lord Hawke, W. Wilkinson, G. H. Hirst, F. Smith, W. Rhodes, S. Haigh, D. Hunter and W. Ringrose did not bat.

**Yorkshire Bowling**

| | Overs | Mdns | Runs | Wkts | Overs | Mdns | Runs | Wkts |
|---|---|---|---|---|---|---|---|---|
| Hirst ............ | 9.3 | 3 | 18 | 5 | 20 | 10 | 16 | 3 |
| Rhodes ........... | 9 | 6 | 4 | 5 | 21 | 16 | 8 | 3 |
| Haigh ............ | | | | | 5 | 5 | — | — |
| Ringrose ......... | | | | | 3 | 2 | 1 | — |
| Denton ........... | | | | | 2 | 2 | — | — |

**Worcestershire Bowling**

| | Overs | Mdns | Runs | Wkts |
|---|---|---|---|---|
| Arnold ........... | 8 | 1 | 44 | 1 |
| Keene ............ | 2 | — | 10 | — |
| Wilson ........... | 2 | — | 14 | — |
| Bird ............. | 4 | 1 | 6 | — |

Umpires: J. Moss and G. Porter.

## YORKSHIRE v KENT

### Played at Harrogate, July 7, 8, 1904

In this match there occurred the unprecedented instance of a game being declared void in consequence of an infringement of Law 9. It was noticed in the course of Thursday's play that the pitch at one end had broken in several places, but when on Friday morning the players turned into the field to proceed with the contest these holes had all disappeared. That the ground had been tampered with after the drawing of stumps on Thursday was agreed by the players as well as the umpires, and, exercising the powers entrusted to them, the latter ruled that the game could not stand. On the opening day Yorkshire, after dismissing Kent for 177 gained a lead of 36 runs and had three wickets in hand. Haigh on the second morning followed up some capital bowling with a fine display of batting and it was very hard luck for him that the match had to be declared void. The decision to abandon the game was come to after the conclusion of the Yorkshire innings, but, in order not to disappoint the crowd, Kent went on batting and were all out before five o'clock at which hour it had been agreed to pull up stumps. Bowling slow leg-breaks Haigh performed the "hat trick."

### Kent

| | | |
|---|---|---|
| A. Hearne b Haigh ......................... | 24 | – c Denton b Rhodes ............. 64 |
| E. Humphreys c Wainwright b Hirst ............. | 0 | – c Hawke b Wainwright .......... 4 |
| James Seymour c Wainwright b Rhodes .......... | 47 | – c and b Wainwright ............ 13 |
| Capt. R. O'H. Livesay b Haigh ................ | 1 | – c Wilkinson b Rhodes .......... 69 |
| Mr R. N. R. Blaker b Haigh ................... | 12 | – b Rhodes ..................... 1 |
| Mr F. Marchant b Haigh ...................... | 26 | – c Wilkinson b Rhodes .......... 10 |
| Mr C. H. B. Marsham b Rhodes ................ | 7 | – not out ...................... 76 |
| Hubble not out ............................. | 33 | – c Tunnicliffe b Haigh ............ 43 |
| Fairservice b Haigh ......................... | 0 | – st Hunter b Haigh ............. 0 |
| C. Blythe c Hunter b Haigh ................... | 11 | – b Haigh ...................... 0 |
| A. Fielder b Rhodes ......................... | 9 | – c Tunnicliffe b Denton .......... 37 |
| B 2, l-b 4, w 1 ...................... | 7 | L-b 4 ................. 4 |
| | 177 | 321 |

### Yorkshire

| | |
|---|---|
| Lord Hawke b Blythe | 14 |
| Mr H. Wilkinson b Fairservice | 40 |
| D. Denton c Hubble b Fairservice | 30 |
| J. Tunnicliffe c Hubble b Blythe | 32 |
| G. H. Hirst c Seymour b Fairservice | 10 |
| W. Wainwright c Seymour b Blythe | 4 |
| W. Rhodes c Hearne b Fairservice | 16 |
| S. Haigh not out | 74 |
| J. W. Rothery b Blythe | 23 |
| H. Myers b Fielder | 9 |
| D. Hunter c Seymour b Blythe | 8 |
| B 10, l-b 5, w 3, n-b 1 | 19 |
| | 279 |

### Yorkshire Bowling

| | Overs | Mdns | Runs | Wkts | Overs | Mdns | Runs | Wkts |
|---|---|---|---|---|---|---|---|---|
| Hirst | 9 | 1 | 34 | 1 | | | | |
| Myers | 8 | 1 | 23 | — | 15 | 3 | 62 | — |
| Rhodes | 23.5 | 2 | 58 | 3 | 15 | — | 61 | 4 |
| Haigh | 23 | 6 | 55 | 6 | 4 | 1 | 30 | 3 |
| Wainwright | | | | | 12 | 1 | 60 | 2 |
| Whitehead | | | | | 19 | 4 | 47 | — |
| Tunnicliffe | | | | | 4 | 2 | 7 | — |
| Denton | | | | | 7 | — | 50 | 1 |

### Kent Bowling

| | Overs | Mdns | Runs | Wkts |
|---|---|---|---|---|
| Fielder | 17 | 1 | 55 | 1 |
| Blythe | 44.4 | 9 | 125 | 5 |
| Fairservice | 28 | 9 | 74 | 4 |
| Humphreys | 1 | — | 6 | — |

Umpires: A. D. Pougher and W. Shrewsbury.

## YORKSHIRE v LEICESTERSHIRE

### Played at Hull, August 1, 2, 1907

On a pitch which placed batsmen at a tremendous disadvantage, Hirst bowled in his finest form, and by the drawing of stumps on the opening day had practically ensured the success of his side. Not only did he in the first innings of Leicestershire dispose of eight batsmen for 25 runs, but in the second he obtained the first four wickets which fell at a cost of 11 runs. Moreover in the second innings he performed the "hat trick," dismissing Wood and King with the last two balls of one over, and Knight with the first of his next. Next morning, when half-an-hour's cricket finished off the Leicestershire innings, 27 runs were obtained from Hirst, but still his fifteen wickets cost little more than 5 runs apiece. Making the ball go with his arm and coming fast off the pitch he always had the opposing batsmen in difficulties. Odell bowled admirably for Leicestershire. Rothery batted steadily and Bates afforded further proof of his value to the side, going in second wicket down and being seventh man out. Yorkshire won the match by ten wickets.

## Leicestershire

| | | | |
|---|---|---|---|
| Mr C. J. B. Wood b Hirst | 0 | – b Hirst | 6 |
| H. Whitehead lbw b Hirst | 16 | – lbw b Rhodes | 8 |
| J. H. King c Wilkinson b Hirst | 0 | – b Hirst | 0 |
| A. E. Knight b Hirst | 13 | – b Hirst | 0 |
| S. Coe b Hirst | 21 | – b Hirst | 6 |
| Mr V. F. S. Crawford c and b Hirst | 1 | – b Hirst | 10 |
| Mr W. W. Odell c Bates b Rhodes | 1 | – b Hirst | 10 |
| Sir A. Hazlerigg b Hirst | 0 | – c Smith b Rhodes | 2 |
| W. E. Benskin b Rhodes | 0 | – c Rothery b Rhodes | 2 |
| Mr J. Shields c and b Hirst | 1 | – not out | 1 |
| W. E. Astill not out | 0 | – b Hirst | 8 |
| B 5, l-b 2 | 7 | N-b 1 | 1 |
| | **60** | | **54** |

## Yorkshire

| | | | |
|---|---|---|---|
| H. Myers c Shields b Odell | 3 | – not out | 1 |
| J. W. Rothery b Odell | 22 | – not out | 0 |
| D. Denton c Crawford b Odell | 5 | | |
| W. E. Bates c Crawford b Benskin | 33 | | |
| G. H. Hirst c Knight b Odell | 11 | | |
| J. Tunnicliffe b Benskin | 2 | | |
| W. Rhodes c Whitehead b Odell | 1 | | |
| Mr E. Smith c Coe b Odell | 5 | | |
| W. H. Wilkinson c Whitehead b Odell | 15 | | |
| Lord Hawke b Odell | 5 | | |
| D. Hunter not out | 5 | | |
| B 6, l-b 1 | 7 | | |
| | **114** | | **1** |

### Yorkshire Bowling

| | Overs | Mdns | Runs | Wkts | Overs | Mdns | Runs | Wkts |
|---|---|---|---|---|---|---|---|---|
| Hirst | 14.4 | 4 | 25 | 8 | 10.2 | 1 | 38 | 7 |
| Myers | 6 | 1 | 18 | — | | | | |
| Rhodes | 8 | 4 | 10 | 2 | 10 | 3 | 15 | 3 |

### Leicestershire Bowling

| | Overs | Mdns | Runs | Wkts | Overs | Mdns | Runs | Wkts |
|---|---|---|---|---|---|---|---|---|
| Odell | 22.5 | 11 | 40 | 8 | | | | |
| Benskin | 22 | 4 | 67 | 2 | | | | |
| Crawford | | | | | 0.2 | — | 1 | — |

Umpires: W. Attewell and S. Brown.

## YORKSHIRE v KENT

### Played at Huddersfield, June 7, 8, 9, 1909

The wicket not having recovered from recent rains, Radcliffe on winning the toss sent Kent in to bat. Had the Yorkshire bowlers been in their best form it is likely enough that the policy would have been justified. As it was, Kent made 119 for four wickets before lunch, and thus got over an anxious time. Day and Hardinge added 100, and Huish hit vigorously. Yorkshire lost two wickets for 5 runs, and next morning, Fielder in his second over disposed of Denton, Hirst, and Rhodes in four balls with the score at 9. Fielder bowled magnificently. In the follow-on Yorkshire lost Wilson, Denton, and Rothery for 61, but Hirst and Rhodes made a great effort for their side, and at the tea interval had raised the score to 201 without further loss. Refreshed by a rest, Fielder on resuming, sent back Hirst, Rhodes, and Myers in quick succession. Bates and Newstead hit well, yet next day Yorkshire only set Kent 115 to win, Humphreys and Seymour decided matters by putting on 80 for the second wicket, Kent gaining a fine victory by seven wickets.

### Kent

| | | |
|---|---|---|
| Mr E. W. Dillon c Hunter b Hirst | 17 | – c Rothery b Newstead ... 0 |
| E. Humphreys c and b Haigh | 22 | – not out ... 59 |
| James Seymour c and b Haigh | 62 | – b Newstead ... 26 |
| Mr K. L. Hutchings c Bates b Newstead | 9 | – c Denton b Rhodes ... 0 |
| F. E. Woolley c Hunter b Hirst | 9 | |
| Mr A. P. Day c Radcliffe b Newstead | 56 | |
| H. T. W. Hardinge b Hirst | 55 | |
| W. J. Fairservice b Hirst | 5 | – not out ... 22 |
| F. H. Huish c Haigh b Newstead | 46 | |
| C. Blythe c Hunter b Rhodes | 4 | |
| A. Fielder not out | 13 | |
| B 12, l-b 9 | 21 | B 4, l-b 4 ... 8 |
| | **319** | **115** |

### Yorkshire

| | | |
|---|---|---|
| B. B. Wilson run out | 1 | – c and b Fielder ... 7 |
| W. Rhodes b Fielder | 11 | – c Dillon b Fielder ... 101 |
| D. Hunter c Hutchings b Fielder | 4 | – b Blythe ... 6 |
| D. Denton c Hutchings b Fielder | 2 | – b Fairservice ... 28 |
| J. W. Rothery c Huish b Fielder | 0 | – c Hutchings b Fielder ... 5 |
| G. H. Hirst c Humphreys b Fielder | 0 | – c Seymour b Fielder ... 61 |
| W. E. Bates b Blythe | 14 | – c Huish b Fielder ... 34 |
| H. Myers b Blythe | 13 | – c Huish b Fielder ... 0 |
| J. T. Newstead c Seymour b Blythe | 11 | – c Woolley b Fielder ... 51 |
| Mr E. J. Radcliffe c Huish b Fielder | 1 | – b Blythe ... 19 |
| S. Haigh not out | 9 | – not out ... 23 |
| L-b 3 | 3 | B 19, l-b 4, w 1, n-b 5 ... 29 |
| | **69** | **364** |

### Yorkshire Bowling

| | Overs | Mdns | Runs | Wkts | Overs | Mdns | Runs | Wkts |
|---|---|---|---|---|---|---|---|---|
| Hirst | 33 | 4 | 104 | 4 | 8 | 5 | 12 | — |
| Rhodes | 20 | 4 | 71 | 1 | 5 | — | 30 | 1 |
| Haigh | 25 | 1 | 66 | 2 | 6 | 2 | 20 | — |
| Newstead | 21.1 | 8 | 45 | 3 | 15.5 | 6 | 28 | 2 |
| Myers | 8 | 4 | 12 | — | 3 | 1 | 17 | — |

### Kent Bowling

| | Overs | Mdns | Runs | Wkts | Overs | Mdns | Runs | Wkts |
|---|---|---|---|---|---|---|---|---|
| Fielder | 15 | 3 | 36 | 6 | 35 | 6 | 128 | 7 |
| Blythe | 14 | 5 | 30 | 3 | 45.4 | 15 | 98 | 2 |
| Fairservice | | | | | 18 | 3 | 60 | 1 |
| Woolley | | | | | 10 | 2 | 20 | — |
| Humphreys | | | | | 4 | — | 13 | — |
| Day | | | | | 5 | — | 16 | — |

Umpires: A. J. Atfield and J. Moss.

## YORKSHIRE v LANCASHIRE

Played at Leeds, May 16, 17, 18, 1910

Rain unfortunately prevented any cricket on the third day, when Yorkshire, with eight wickets to fall, wanted 99 runs to win, and thus a match which held out promise of a most interesting finish had to be abandoned as a draw. So far as it proceeded, the game proved desperately exciting, Lancashire, despite a series of mistakes in the field, securing on what was always a somewhat difficult pitch, a very strong position, and being dislodged from it by George Hirst, who accomplished one of the finest bowling performances of his great career. Almost unplayable, Hirst twice took two wickets with successive balls, hit the stumps eight times, and came out with the wonderful record of nine wickets for 23 runs, his first four wickets being obtained for 5 runs. Tyldesley batted admirably in Lancashire's first innings, but there were six men out for 144. In Yorkshire's innings, though Rhodes, Watson, Hirst, and Rothery were all missed, the ninth wicket fell at 103. Radcliffe being also let off, the last wicket produced 49 runs.

### Lancashire

| | | | |
|---|---|---|---|
| Mr A. H. Hornby b Haigh | 29 | – b Hirst | 6 |
| Mr A. Hartley lbw b Rhodes | 36 | – c Newstead b Hirst | 1 |
| J. T. Tyldesley c Rothery b Hirst | 51 | – b Hirst | 4 |
| J. Sharp b Hirst | 15 | – b Hirst | 0 |
| Mr E. L. Wright lbw b Haigh | 7 | – b Hirst | 4 |
| Mr A. C. MacLaren b Newstead | 1 | – b Haigh | 19 |
| J. S. Heap c Radcliffe b Haigh | 14 | – not out | 9 |
| W. Huddleston c Myers b Hirst | 39 | – b Hirst | 3 |
| H. Dean b Newstead | 25 | – b Hirst | 0 |
| Mr W. Brearley b Hirst | 2 | – b Hirst | 0 |
| W. Worsley not out | 2 | – b Hirst | 6 |
| B 6, l-b 1, n-b 1 | 8 | B 5, l-b 4 | 9 |
| | **229** | | **61** |

### Yorkshire

| | | | |
|---|---|---|---|
| W. Rhodes b Brearley | 15 | – st Worsley b Dean | 7 |
| B. B. Wilson b Dean | 9 | – not out | 20 |
| D. Denton c and b Brearley | 10 | – b Huddleston | 12 |
| A. Drake c Worsley b Dean | 6 | | |
| H. Watson c Wright b Brearley | 0 | | |
| G. H. Hirst c Worsley b Dean | 14 | | |
| J. W. Rothery c and b Brearley | 13 | | |
| H. Myers c and b Huddleston | 14 | | |
| J. T. Newstead c Worsley b Brearley | 10 | | |
| Mr E. J. Radcliffe not out | 24 | | |
| S. Haigh lbw b Dean | 27 | | |
| B 1, l-b 5, w 1, n-b 3 | 10 | N-b 1 | 1 |
| | **152** | | **40** |

### Yorkshire Bowling

| | Overs | Mdns | Runs | Wkts | Overs | Mdns | Runs | Wkts |
|---|---|---|---|---|---|---|---|---|
| Hirst | 18 | 2 | 55 | 4 | 13.2 | 3 | 23 | 9 |
| Newstead | 21.1 | 7 | 38 | 2 | | | | |
| Haigh | 20 | 6 | 44 | 3 | 6 | 2 | 10 | 1 |
| Rhodes | 21 | 1 | 68 | 1 | | | | |
| Drake | 5 | — | 16 | — | | | | |
| Myers | | | | | 8 | 2 | 19 | — |

**Lancashire Bowling**

| | Overs | Mdns | Runs | Wkts | Overs | Mdns | Runs | Wkts |
|---|---|---|---|---|---|---|---|---|
| Brearley ......... | 33 | 8 | 86 | 5 | 3 | — | 12 | — |
| Dean ............ | 36.4 | 19 | 42 | 4 | 10 | 1 | 19 | 1 |
| Huddleston ....... | 11 | 6 | 12 | 1 | 8 | 6 | 8 | 1 |
| Heap ............ | 3 | 1 | 2 | — | | | | |

Umpires: W. Vining and B. W. Mason.

## YORKSHIRE v LEICESTERSHIRE

### Played at Bradford, June 12, 13, 14, 1911

C. J. B. Wood in this contest accomplished the feat – unprecedented in first-class cricket – of carrying his bat right through each innings. Incidentally also he scored two separate hundreds in the same match, batting in all for eight hours and forty minutes, and being, of course, on the field every minute of the game. His achievement was rendered the more wonderful from the fact that in neither innings did he give a chance. On Tuesday, when five Leicestershire wickets had fallen for 46, Mounteney hit up 96 out of 143 in eighty minutes. For Yorkshire, Booth and Rhodes played very finely, and when set 272 to make in three hours and a half the home side batted so freely that the task was accomplished at a cost of five wickets, with three-quarters of an hour to spare.

### Leicestershire

| | | | |
|---|---|---|---|
| Mr C. J. B. Wood not out ..................... | 107 | – not out ..................... | 117 |
| A. E. Knight c Dolphin b Hirst ................ | 12 | – b Hirst ..................... | 14 |
| H. Whitehead c Dolphin b Hirst .............. | 5 | – c Booth b Hirst .............. | 2 |
| A. Lord c Hirst b Booth ...................... | 43 | – b Hirst ..................... | 4 |
| J. H. King b Hirst ........................... | 2 | – b Drake .................... | 1 |
| S. Coe c Hirst b Rhodes ..................... | 49 | – absent hurt ................. | 0 |
| Mr F. M. Joyce b Haigh ...................... | 0 | – b Hirst .................... | 5 |
| A. Mounteney c Booth b Hirst ............... | 21 | – c Denton b Rhodes ........... | 96 |
| W. Shipman c Wilson b Rhodes .............. | 38 | – c Turner b Haigh ............ | 29 |
| Mr J. Shields c Dolphin b Rhodes ........... | 20 | – c Hirst b Bayes ............. | 6 |
| W. Brown run out .......................... | 4 | – b Hirst .................... | 8 |
| B 7, l-b 1 ...................... | 8 | L-b 13, n-b 1 ........... | 14 |
| | **309** | | **296** |

### Yorkshire

| | | | |
|---|---|---|---|
| W. Rhodes c Whitehead b Joyce ............... | 92 | – c Wood b King ............... | 38 |
| B. B. Wilson b Shipman ..................... | 21 | – b Joyce .................... | 16 |
| D. Denton c sub. b Brown ................... | 27 | – not out .................... | 137 |
| A. Drake c Whitehead b Joyce .............. | 19 | – c sub. b Shipman ........... | 25 |
| G. H. Hirst c sub. b Joyce ................ | 20 | – b Shipman .................. | 10 |
| M. W. Booth c King b Joyce ................ | 71 | – c Shields b Joyce .......... | 18 |
| A. Turner c Mounteney b Brown ............ | 12 | – not out .................... | 16 |
| E. Oldroyd c sub. b Whitehead ............ | 17 | | |
| S. Haigh run out ......................... | 39 | | |
| A. Dolphin b Shipman ..................... | 1 | | |
| G. Bayes not out ........................ | 5 | | |
| B 4, l-b 6 ...................... | 10 | B 9, l-b 1, w 1, n-b 1 ...... | 12 |
| | **334** | | **272** |

## Yorkshire Bowling

| | Overs | Mdns | Runs | Wkts | Overs | Mdns | Runs | Wkts |
|---|---|---|---|---|---|---|---|---|
| Hirst | 29 | 7 | 77 | 4 | 29.2 | 8 | 68 | 5 |
| Booth | 24 | 6 | 65 | 1 | 13 | 1 | 50 | — |
| Bayes | 11 | 2 | 50 | — | 7 | — | 29 | 1 |
| Haigh | 9 | 2 | 22 | 1 | 15 | 3 | 40 | 1 |
| Rhodes | 16.3 | 3 | 47 | 3 | 12 | 2 | 58 | 1 |
| Drake | 10 | 1 | 40 | — | 16 | 5 | 37 | 1 |

## Leicestershire Bowling

| | Overs | Mdns | Runs | Wkts | Overs | Mdns | Runs | Wkts |
|---|---|---|---|---|---|---|---|---|
| Shipman | 22 | 3 | 63 | 2 | 16 | — | 93 | 2 |
| King | 15 | 1 | 50 | — | 6 | — | 41 | 1 |
| Brown | 16 | 1 | 64 | 2 | 4.2 | — | 26 | — |
| Wood | 13 | 1 | 39 | — | 3 | — | 22 | — |
| Joyce | 20 | 1 | 70 | 4 | 13 | 2 | 48 | 2 |
| Lord | 1 | — | 1 | — | 2 | 1 | 1 | — |
| Whitehead | 10.4 | — | 37 | 1 | 5 | — | 29 | — |

Umpires: H. Bagshaw and W. Flowers.

# YORKSHIRE v HAMPSHIRE

### Played at Huddersfield, July 13, 14, 15, 1911

Giving a wretched display at their first attempt, Hampshire were practically a beaten side before the first day's play came to an end, and on Saturday suffered defeat by ten wickets. Their reputation, however, was somewhat redeemed by Mead, who put together his third hundred during the week. On Thursday, when Yorkshire passed their opponent's total with nine wickets in hand, Wilson and Denton added 117.

## Hampshire

| | | | |
|---|---|---|---|
| P. Mead lbw b Booth | 5 | – not out | 120 |
| Mr A. J. Evans c Haigh b Hirst | 23 | – c Haigh b Hartington | 3 |
| A. Bowell b Hirst | 0 | – b Hartington | 36 |
| Capt. W. N. White b Hirst | 0 | – b Hirst | 3 |
| A. Stone c Haigh b Booth | 9 | – lbw b Booth | 17 |
| G. Brown b Booth | 7 | – b Haigh | 15 |
| A. Kennedy c Bates b Hirst | 0 | – b Hirst | 0 |
| Mr D. M. Evans b Hirst | 64 | – c Haigh b Hartington | 1 |
| E. R. Remnant c Dolphin b Booth | 9 | – b Hirst | 0 |
| J. Newman c Dolphin b Booth | 17 | – b Hartington | 9 |
| Mr H. A. H. Smith not out | 1 | – c Haigh b Hartington | 13 |
| L-b 6, n-b 1 | 7 | B 7, l-b 8, n-b 2 | 17 |
| | **142** | | **234** |

## Yorkshire

W. Rhodes c Kennedy b D. M. Evans ........... 35
B. B. Wilson c A. J. Evans b Bowell ............. 86
D. Denton b Kennedy ....................... 81
A. Drake b Kennedy ........................ 9
W. E. Bates c Stone b Kennedy ................ 7 – not out ....................... 1
G. H. Hirst c Mead b Newman ................ 23
M. W. Booth c D. M. Evans b Newman .......... 58
S. Haigh c Smith b Mead .................... 11
Mr E. J. Radcliffe c A. J. Evans b Newman ........ 1
A. Dolphin not out ......................... 20 – not out ..................... 21
H. E. Hartington c A. J. Evans b D. M. Evans ..... 7
    B 9, l-b 2, w 3, n-b 3 ................. 17

                355              22

### Yorkshire Bowling

| | Overs | Mdns | Runs | Wkts | Overs | Mdns | Runs | Wkts |
|---|---|---|---|---|---|---|---|---|
| Hirst | 20.1 | 3 | 54 | 5 | 21 | 4 | 41 | 3 |
| Booth | 20 | 4 | 60 | 5 | 6 | — | 24 | 1 |
| Hartington | 2 | — | · 17 | — | 20.2 | 3 | 81 | 5 |
| Haigh | 2 | — | 4 | — | 12 | 3 | 20 | 1 |
| Drake | | | | | 10 | 3 | 31 | — |
| Rhodes | | | | | 12 | 3 | 17 | — |
| Denton | | | | | 2 | — | 3 | — |

### Hampshire Bowling

| | Overs | Mdns | Runs | Wkts | Overs | Mdns | Runs | Wkts |
|---|---|---|---|---|---|---|---|---|
| A. J. Evans | 6 | — | 18 | — | | | | |
| Brown | 16 | — | 58 | — | | | | |
| Newman | 30 | 5 | 98 | 3 | | | | |
| D. M. Evans | 13.2 | 1 | 43 | 2 | | | | |
| Remnant | 6 | — | 22 | — | | | | |
| Smith | 3 | — | 12 | — | | | | |
| Bowell | 9 | 3 | 40 | 1 | | | | |
| Kennedy | 12 | 2 | 32 | 3 | | | | |
| Mead | 5 | — | 15 | 1 | | | | |
| White | | | | | 2 | — | 7 | — |
| Stone | | | | | 1.3 | — | 15 | — |

Umpires: H. Wood and W. Flowers.

## YORKSHIRE v MIDDLESEX

### Played at Bradford, August 14, 15, 16, 1911

There was an exciting finish to this encounter, Yorkshire, when stumps were pulled up, being 141 runs in arrear, and having only one wicket to fall. Going in with four hours and twenty minutes left for play, Yorkshire lost B. Wilson, Rhodes, and Denton in forty minutes, but once again Hirst rose to the occasion. Hirst received excellent support from Drake and Booth, yet when, after batting for three hours, he was sixth out at 187, nearly an hour remained. Haigh, Oldroyd, and White, however, all did their share and Dolphin survived the remainder of the over in which White was dismissed. Tarrant played a magnificent innings, carrying his bat right through, and giving no chance during a stay of five hours. His score – the highest he had made in first-class cricket – included two 6s and twenty-seven 4s, hard driving and clean cutting being the outstanding features of his play.

## Middlesex

| | | | | |
|---|---|---|---|---|
| Mr J. Douglas c Dolphin b Booth | 6 | – lbw b Drake | 46 |
| F. A. Tarrant not out | 207 | – c J. P. Wilson b Booth | 6 |
| J. W. Hearne c White b Booth | 0 | – c and b Hirst | 92 |
| Mr P. F. Warner c Dolphin b Booth | 12 | – not out | 65 |
| E. Hendren b Drake | 57 | – st Dolphin b Haigh | 8 |
| H. R. Murrell b Rhodes | 31 | – c Dolphin b Haigh | 16 |
| Mr F. T. Mann c Drake b Rhodes | 15 | – not out | 17 |
| Mr E. L. Kidd c and b Haigh | 2 | | |
| Mr S. H. Saville b Drake | 24 | | |
| J. T. Hearne lbw b Drake | 0 | | |
| E. Mignon lbw b Rhodes | 14 | | |
| B 4, l-b 6 | 10 | B 1, l-b 9, n-b 1 | 11 |
| | **378** | **(5 wkts dec.)** | **261** |

## Yorkshire

| | | | | |
|---|---|---|---|---|
| W. Rhodes c Tarrant b Mignon | 39 | – lbw b J. W. Hearne | 17 |
| B. B. Wilson c Tarrant b Mignon | 15 | – lbw b J. W. Hearne | 10 |
| D. Denton c Douglas b Mignon | 8 | – c Hendren b Mignon | 0 |
| A. Drake c Murrell b Mignon | 29 | – c Mignon b J. W. Hearne | 33 |
| G. H. Hirst c Saville b Mignon | 4 | – c Kidd b Mignon | 75 |
| M. W. Booth c Murrell b Mignon | 57 | – b J. W. Hearne | 37 |
| E. Oldroyd b Mignon | 0 | – not out | 16 |
| Mr J. P. Wilson c Kidd b Tarrant | 36 | – b J. W. Hearne | 0 |
| S. Haigh st Murrell b Tarrant | 10 | – b Mignon | 32 |
| Sir A. W. White c J. W. Hearne b Tarrant | 2 | – c Kidd b Mignon | 24 |
| A. Dolphin not out | 6 | – not out | 0 |
| B 2, l-b 3, w 5, n-b 1 | 12 | B 24, l-b 7, w 2, n-b 3 | 36 |
| | **218** | | **280** |

### Yorkshire Bowling

| | Overs | Mdns | Runs | Wkts | Overs | Mdns | Runs | Wkts |
|---|---|---|---|---|---|---|---|---|
| Hirst | 24 | 4 | 65 | — | 13 | — | 56 | 1 |
| Booth | 26 | 6 | 102 | 3 | 16 | 3 | 58 | 1 |
| Drake | 25 | 5 | 52 | 3 | 19 | 3 | 50 | 1 |
| Haigh | 16 | 1 | 36 | 1 | 13 | 1 | 62 | 2 |
| Rhodes | 23.5 | 2 | 107 | 3 | 11 | 1 | 24 | — |
| Oldroyd | 3 | — | 6 | — | | | | |

### Middlesex Bowling

| | Overs | Mdns | Runs | Wkts | Overs | Mdns | Runs | Wkts |
|---|---|---|---|---|---|---|---|---|
| J. T. Hearne | 16 | 5 | 24 | — | 11 | 8 | 5 | — |
| Mignon | 22 | 4 | 99 | 7 | 27 | 2 | 100 | 4 |
| J. W. Hearne | 13 | 1 | 55 | — | 36 | 9 | 89 | 5 |
| Tarrant | 13.5 | 6 | 28 | 3 | 14 | 4 | 33 | — |
| Kidd | | | | | 5 | 2 | 17 | — |

Umpires: H. Bagshaw and J. Carlin.

# YORKSHIRE v MCC

Played at Scarborough, August 31, September 1, 2, 1911

Set 339 to get in three hours, the MCC came so desperately near accomplishing the task that when stumps were pulled up they were within 5 runs of victory. Spooner played a delightful innings, making 102 out of 178 in an hour and fifty minutes without a chance and then Jessop hit away in such tremendous fashion that he scored 117 not out in eighty-five minutes. Jessop made no mistake until he had completed his hundred, among his strokes being three 6s, one 5, and seventeen 4s. Rhodes batted in admirable form for Yorkshire, and for the first time in the course of his great career succeeded in putting together two separate hundreds in the same match. The feat had been accomplished by nine other batsmen during the season.

## Yorkshire

| | | | | |
|---|---|---|---|---|
| W. Rhodes c Jessop b Falcon | 128 | – c Bird b Thompson | 115 |
| B. B. Wilson c Spooner b Braddell | 39 | – c Bird b Falcon | 2 |
| D. Denton b Thompson | 94 | – c Jessop b Falcon | 42 |
| A. Drake c Braddell b King | 33 | – run out | 3 |
| G. H. Hirst c Bird b Astill | 17 | – b Braddell | 32 |
| M. W. Booth b Astill | 0 | – c Bird b Falcon | 6 |
| S. Haigh c Astill b Thompson | 34 | – not out | 13 |
| Lord Hawke c Astill | 20 | – not out | 8 |
| Sir A. W. White c Hardstaff b Thompson | 2 | | |
| G. Bayes c Spooner b Astill | 4 | | |
| A. Dolphin not out | 3 | | |
| B 11, l-b 2 | 13 | B 4 | 4 |
| | **387** | **(6 wkts dec.) 225** | |

## MCC

| | | | | |
|---|---|---|---|---|
| Mr W. S. Bird run out | 6 | – c Rhodes b Bayes | 35 |
| J. H. King c Haigh b Bayes | 7 | – b Hirst | 20 |
| J. Hardstaff b Drake | 41 | – c Hirst b Rhodes | 24 |
| Mr R. H. Spooner b Hirst | 8 | – b Drake | 102 |
| Mr M. Falcon b Haigh | 26 | – b Hirst | 4 |
| Mr G. L. Jessop c Wilson b Bayes | 59 | – not out | 117 |
| G. J. Thompson st Dolphin b Rhodes | 52 | – b Drake | 4 |
| Mr R. L. L. Braddell c Bayes b Drake | 8 | | |
| W. E. Bates c Booth b Drake | 9 | – c Dolphin b Booth | 5 |
| Mr H. D. G. Leveson-Gower c Dolphin b Bayes | 35 | | |
| W. E. Astill not out | 13 | | |
| B 1, l-b 8, n-b 1 | 10 | B 11, l-b 10, w 2 | 23 |
| | **274** | **334** | |

## MCC Bowling

| | Overs | Mdns | Runs | Wkts | Overs | Mdns | Runs | Wkts |
|---|---|---|---|---|---|---|---|---|
| Falcon | 20 | 1 | 84 | 1 | 20 | 2 | 56 | 3 |
| Thompson | 30.1 | 2 | 116 | 3 | 24 | 4 | 76 | 1 |
| King | 20 | 4 | 64 | 1 | 8 | 1 | 32 | — |
| Braddell | 9 | 1 | 39 | 1 | 5 | — | 20 | 1 |
| Astill | 15 | 2 | 71 | 4 | 7 | 1 | 37 | — |

## Yorkshire Bowling

| | Overs | Mdns | Runs | Wkts | Overs | Mdns | Runs | Wkts |
|---|---|---|---|---|---|---|---|---|
| Hirst | 20 | 5 | 40 | 1 | 16 | 1 | 64 | 2 |
| Booth | 15 | 6 | 38 | — | 13 | 1 | 59 | 1 |
| Bayes | 17 | — | 78 | 3 | 4 | — | 27 | 1 |
| Haigh | 9 | — | 45 | 1 | | | | |
| Rhodes | 6.2 | 1 | 23 | 1 | 9 | — | 68 | 1 |
| Drake | 14 | 2 | 40 | 3 | 17.5 | — | 93 | 2 |

Umpires: G. P. Harrison and J. Moss.

## YORKSHIRE v GLOUCESTERSHIRE

Played at Sheffield, July 21, 22, 1913

Gilbert Jessop fairly won this match which, after a great finish ended in favour of Gloucestershire by 2 runs. On Monday, when rain prevented anything being done after twenty minutes past four, he had the good fortune to be missed first ball, and turned his luck to such account that he scored 67 out of 83 in an hour, exercising fine judgment in picking out the right ball to hit. On Tuesday he took four wickets in quick succession, knocked up 40 out of 69 in thirty-seven minutes and, going on to bowl when Yorkshire wanted only 13 runs to win, secured the last two wickets. The game, indeed, furnished quite a triumph for the famous cricketer. Despite Jessop's work the fortunes of the game underwent many changes. Yorkshire in their first innings had eight men out for 101, and yet secured a lead, while Gloucestershire at their second attempt lost five wickets for 49. In Yorkshire's second innings, with 110 needed for victory, seven wickets fell for 50, but Drake made a splendid effort to snatch a win for his side and only just failed of success.

### Gloucestershire

| | | | |
|---|---:|---|---:|
| Mr C. S. Barnett b Hirst | 0 | – b Drake | 3 |
| A. G. Dipper c Dolphin b Booth | 22 | – b Drake | 8 |
| T. Langdon c Birtles b Hirst | 25 | – c Holmes b Drake | 7 |
| Mr J. W. W. Nason b Hirst | 0 | – b Rhodes | 5 |
| Mr G. L. Jessop c Denton b Booth | 67 | – c White b Kilner | 40 |
| J. H. Board c Hirst b Booth | 17 | – b Drake | 10 |
| Mr C. O. H. Sewell c White b Booth | 0 | – c Booth b Drake | 23 |
| L. Cranfield b Booth | 5 | – c Wilson b Drake | 7 |
| T. Gange c Denton b Hirst | 5 | – st Dolphin b Drake | 5 |
| C. Parker not out | 5 | – not out | 9 |
| G. Dennett c and b Rhodes | 6 | – c Denton b Drake | 4 |
| B 2, l-b 1, w 1, n-b 1 | 5 | B 1, l-b 1, n-b 1 | 3 |
| | **157** | | **124** |

### Yorkshire

| | | | |
|---|---:|---|---:|
| W. Rhodes b Parker | 2 | – c Board b Gange | 2 |
| T. J. Birtles c Jessop b Gange | 10 | – b Gange | 0 |
| D. Denton c Board b Gange | 21 | – c Jessop b Gange | 0 |
| R. Kilner b Parker | 19 | – c Jessop b Parker | 18 |
| A. Drake c Parker b Jessop | 23 | – not out | 45 |
| B. B. Wilson lbw b Jessop | 1 | – c Langdon b Parker | 11 |
| M W. Booth c Jessop b Gange | 33 | – c Langdon b Gange | 0 |
| G. H. Hirst c Board b Jessop | 0 | – lbw b Gange | 1 |
| P. Holmes b Jessop | 3 | – c Cranfield b Dennett | 16 |
| Sir A. W. White c Nason b Dennett | 22 | – b Jessop | 6 |
| A. Dolphin not out | 17 | – b Jessop | 3 |
| B 10, l-b 6, n-b 5 | 21 | L-b 1, n-b 4 | 5 |
| | **172** | | **107** |

### Yorkshire Bowling

| | Overs | Mdns | Runs | Wkts | Overs | Mdns | Runs | Wkts |
|---|---|---|---|---|---|---|---|---|
| Hirst | 21 | 2 | 69 | 4 | | | | |
| Booth | 21 | 5 | 55 | 5 | | | | |
| Rhodes | 6.4 | 2 | 23 | 1 | 9 | 1 | 41 | 1 |
| Drake | 2 | — | 5 | — | 15.2 | 1 | 59 | 8 |
| Kilner | 1 | 1 | — | — | 6 | — | 21 | 1 |

### Gloucestershire Bowling

| | Overs | Mdns | Runs | Wkts | Overs | Mdns | Runs | Wkts |
|---|---|---|---|---|---|---|---|---|
| Gange .......... | 13.4 | 2 | 39 | 3 | 14 | 3 | 44 | 5 |
| Parker .......... | 25 | 11 | 37 | 2 | 10 | 2 | 35 | 2 |
| Jessop .......... | 21 | 2 | 57 | 4 | 4.1 | 2 | 3 | 2 |
| Dennett .......... | 9 | 3 | 18 | 1 | 8 | 1 | 20 | 1 |

Umpires: R. G. Barlow and W. Phillips.

## YORKSHIRE v SURREY

### Played at Bradford, May 25, 26, 27, 1914

One of the best contested matches of the season was this which ended in favour of Surrey by 28 runs. On a rather soft wicket Hobbs gave a superb display of hitting, making 100 out of 151 in seventy-five minutes. He gave no chance until the over in which he was dismissed, his hits including five 6s and eleven 4s. Although not approaching his colleague in brilliancy, Hayes played with great skill and judgment. Rhodes and Kilner putting on 114, Yorkshire at one point had 191 on the board with only two men out, but the last five wickets fell for 48 runs. When Surrey went in again Hobbs played another delightful innings, scoring 74 out of 107 in seventy-five minutes. The last six wickets fell for 55 runs. Yorkshire on Wednesday had eight men out for 106, but Hirst and Birtles made a splendid effort adding 82 runs before Hirst chopped a ball on to his wicket. Surrey owed much to Rushby and Fender.

### Surrey

| | | | |
|---|---|---|---|
| T. Hayward b Rhodes ........................ | 22 | – lbw b Booth ................... | 7 |
| J. B. Hobbs b Hirst........................... | 100 | – c Denton b Rhodes ............ | 74 |
| E. G. Hayes lbw b Rhodes .................... | 125 | – b Drake ..................... | 16 |
| H. S. Harrison c Dolphin b Rhodes ............. | 0 | – b Rhodes ................... | 21 |
| A. Ducat b Rhodes .......................... | 4 | – lbw b Drake ................. | 20 |
| Mr C. T. A. Wilkinson c Denton b Rhodes ........ | 21 | – b Drake ..................... | 2 |
| Mr P. G. H. Fender lbw b Drake ............... | 2 | – lbw b Rhodes ................ | 9 |
| W. Hitch c Dolphin b Booth .................. | 16 | – c Birtles b Rhodes ............ | 0 |
| H. Strudwick c Burton b Rhodes ............... | 10 | – c Burton b Drake .............. | 13 |
| W. C. Smith c Dolphin b Drake ................ | 6 | – c Denton b Rhodes ............ | 10 |
| T. Rushby not out .......................... | 1 | – not out ..................... | 9 |
| B 5, l-b 5 ......................... | 10 | L-b 7, n-b 1 ............ | 8 |
| | **317** | | **189** |

### Yorkshire

| | | | |
|---|---|---|---|
| W. Rhodes b Hitch.......................... | 89 | – c Fender b Rushby ............. | 0 |
| B. B. Wilson b Rushby ....................... | 9 | – c Fender b Rushby ............. | 51 |
| D. Denton b Fender ......................... | 37 | – b Rushby .................... | 19 |
| R. Kilner b Hitch ........................... | 48 | – c Strudwick b Fender .......... | 17 |
| G. H. Hirst c Hayes b Smith .................. | 48 | – b Fender .................... | 55 |
| Mr D. C. F. Burton b Rushby .................. | 22 | – c Smith b Rushby ............. | 0 |
| A. Drake c Wilkinson b Smith ................. | 1 | – c Hitch b Fender ............. | 5 |
| M. W. Booth b Rushby ....................... | 1 | – lbw b Fender ................. | 0 |
| T. J. Birtles lbw b Smith ..................... | 1 | – run out ..................... | 40 |
| Sir A. W. White lbw b Smith .................. | 4 | – not out ..................... | 0 |
| A. Dolphin not out .......................... | 10 | – b Rushby .................... | 1 |
| B 6, l-b 8 ......................... | 14 | L-b 5, n-b 1 ............ | 6 |
| | **284** | | **194** |

**Yorkshire Bowling**

| | Overs | Mdns | Runs | Wkts | Overs | Mdns | Runs | Wkts |
|---|---|---|---|---|---|---|---|---|
| Hirst . . . . . . . . . . . . | 20 | 1 | 70 | 1 | 7 | 3 | 17 | — |
| Booth . . . . . . . . . . . | 11 | 3 | 43 | 1 | 11 | 1 | 46 | 1 |
| Drake . . . . . . . . . . . | 15 | 4 | 55 | 2 | 26.5 | 9 | 62 | 4 |
| Rhodes . . . . . . . . . . | 24 | — | 109 | 6 | 24 | 3 | 56 | 5 |
| Kilner . . . . . . . . . . . | 7 | — | 30 | — | | | | |

**Surrey Bowling**

| | Overs | Mdns | Runs | Wkts | Overs | Mdns | Runs | Wkts |
|---|---|---|---|---|---|---|---|---|
| Smith . . . . . . . . . . . | 37.5 | 9 | 78 | 4 | 20 | 5 | 37 | — |
| Rushby . . . . . . . . . | 32 | 8 | 73 | 3 | 24 | 7 | 63 | 5 |
| Hitch . . . . . . . . . . . | 19 | 1 | 64 | 2 | 12 | 1 | 41 | — |
| Fender . . . . . . . . . . | 9 | — | 40 | 1 | 21.5 | 9 | 39 | 4 |
| Hayes . . . . . . . . . . | 3 | — | 15 | — | 1 | — | 4 | — |
| Hobbs . . . . . . . . . . | | | | | 3 | — | 4 | — |

Umpires: G. Bagshaw and W. Phillips.

# CAMBRIDGE UNIVERSITY MATCHES

## CAMBRIDGE UNIVERSITY v MCC AND GROUND

Played at Cambridge, May 21, 22, 23, 1900

In this match, with an extremely weak side against them, Cambridge gained a ten wickets victory, the batting of Stanning and the bowling of Driffield bringing about the result. At last asserting himself at Cambridge, Stanning played a capital innings, staying at the wickets for three hours and ten minutes. In the second innings of the MCC, Driffield went on when two wickets had fallen for 64, and actually took seven wickets for 7 runs.

### MCC and Ground

| | | | |
|---|---|---|---|
| Mr T. Horton c Daniell b Scott | 53 | – b Dowson | 11 |
| Thompson c Hind b Scott | 35 | – b Driffield | 29 |
| Mr H. E. Symes-Thompson c Hind b Scott | 31 | – c Wilson b Scott | 11 |
| Mr A. Page c Blaker b Scott | 19 | – c Hind b Driffield | 17 |
| Mr J. Gilman c Taylor b Dowson | 6 | – c Stanning b Dowson | 6 |
| T. Brown c Dowson b Scott | 11 | – lbw b Driffield | 3 |
| Mr C. C. T. Doll c Stanning b Dowson | 27 | – c Stanning b Driffield | 0 |
| Mr G. Howard Smith c Stanning b Dowson | 19 | – c Stanning b Driffield | 18 |
| E. Tate c Stanning b Wilson | 1 | – b Driffield | 0 |
| T. Oates c Hind b Wilson | 0 | – c Stanning b Driffield | 1 |
| W. Overton not out | 0 | – not out | 4 |
| B 8, l-b 1, w 1 | 11 | B 1, l-b 1 | 2 |
| | **213** | | **102** |

### Cambridge University

| | | | |
|---|---|---|---|
| Mr E. R. Wilson c Brown b Thompson | 25 | | |
| Mr J. Stanning c Oates b Thompson | 120 | – not out | 17 |
| Mr S. H. Day c Overton b Thompson | 1 | | |
| Mr J. Daniell b Thompson | 4 | | |
| Mr E. M. Dowson b Brown | 38 | | |
| Mr T. L. Taylor c Gilman b Brown | 9 | | |
| Mr R. N. R. Blaker c Overton b Brown | 0 | – not out | 14 |
| Mr R. P. Johnson c Horton b Brown | 54 | | |
| Mr A. E. Hind c Oates b Brown | 13 | | |
| Mr L. T. Driffield not out | 4 | | |
| Mr G. Scott c Page b Brown | 10 | | |
| B 6, l-b 1 | 7 | B 1 | 1 |
| | **285** | | **32** |

### Cambridge University Bowling

| | Overs | Mdns | Runs | Wkts | Overs | Mdns | Runs | Wkts |
|---|---|---|---|---|---|---|---|---|
| Dowson | 25.3 | 7 | 56 | 3 | 24 | 6 | 63 | 2 |
| Hind | 5 | — | 16 | — | | | | |
| Wilson | 12 | 2 | 28 | 2 | | | | |
| Scott | 23 | 2 | 72 | 5 | 18 | 7 | 30 | 1 |
| Driffield | 7 | 1 | 30 | — | 6.4 | 3 | 7 | 7 |

**MCC and Ground Bowling**

| | Overs | Mdns | Runs | Wkts | Overs | Mdns | Runs | Wkts |
|---|---|---|---|---|---|---|---|---|
| Tate . . . . . . . . . . . . | 21 | 4 | 52 | — | | | | |
| Overton . . . . . . . . . | 11 | 3 | 28 | — | 3.3 | — | 5 | — |
| Thompson . . . . . . . . | 31 | 8 | 107 | 4 | 4 | — | 19 | — |
| Brown . . . . . . . . . . | 33.3 | 11 | 82 | 6 | 4 | 2 | 7 | — |
| Howard Smith . . . . . | 3 | — | 9 | — | | | | |

Umpires: R. Carpenter and H. Richardson.

## FIRST TWELVE v NEXT SIXTEEN

Played at Cambridge, May 12, 13, 14, 1902

In this unimportant trial game, E. R. Wilson, the Cambridge captain, did a wonderful piece of bowling, taking fourteen wickets in the second innings of the Next Sixteen. Thanks to this startling work of his, and the batting of Harris and F. B. Wilson, the First Twelve won very easily by seven wickets.

### Next Sixteen

| | | | |
|---|---|---|---|
| Mr E. W. Mann b E. R. Wilson . . . . . . . . . . . . . . . . | 35 | – c and b E. R. Wilson . . . . . . . . . . . | 68 |
| Mr F. J. Marsh b Penn . . . . . . . . . . . . . . . . . . . . . . | 10 | – lbw b E. R. Wilson . . . . . . . . . . . . . . | 11 |
| Mr H. Chapple st Winter b E. R. Wilson . . . . . . . . . | 6 | – b E. R. Wilson . . . . . . . . . . . . . . . . . | 47 |
| Mr R. T. Godsell c Buxton b E. R. Wilson . . . . . . . . | 48 | – c Haviland b E. R. Wilson . . . . . . . | 5 |
| Mr N. O. Tagart c Morris b E. R. Wilson . . . . . . . . | 12 | – c and b E. R. Wilson . . . . . . . . . . | 4 |
| Mr J. W. Marsh c Ebden b Morris . . . . . . . . . . . . . | 18 | – b E. R. Wilson . . . . . . . . . . . . . . . . . | 0 |
| Mr A. Scott-Murray st Winter b Buxton . . . . . . . . | 12 | – st Winter b E. R. Wilson . . . . . . . . | 18 |
| Mr D. A. Walker c Horne b E. R. Wilson . . . . . . . . | 14 | – c Buxton b E. R. Wilson . . . . . . . . | 23 |
| Mr H. D. Stanning lbw b E. R. Wilson . . . . . . . . . . | 0 | – b F. B. Wilson . . . . . . . . . . . . . . . . | 1 |
| Mr R. S. Lambert b Penn . . . . . . . . . . . . . . . . . . . . | 52 | – b E. R. Wilson . . . . . . . . . . . . . . . . | 0 |
| Mr P. L. Hollins c Ebden b Penn . . . . . . . . . . . . . . | 28 | – b E. R. Wilson . . . . . . . . . . . . . . . . | 9 |
| Mr E. G. McCorquodale b Penn . . . . . . . . . . . . . . | 4 | – c and b E. R. Wilson . . . . . . . . . . | 27 |
| Mr W. H. Sell c and b Penn . . . . . . . . . . . . . . . . . . | 3 | – not out . . . . . . . . . . . . . . . . . . . . . . | 8 |
| Mr P. E. Morris not out . . . . . . . . . . . . . . . . . . . . . | 3 | – c and b E. R. Wilson . . . . . . . . . . | 0 |
| Mr H. G. Driffield c Haviland b F. B. Wilson . . . . . . | 2 | – st Winter b E. R. Wilson . . . . . . . . | 2 |
| Mr T. H. Watson c Haviland b F. B. Wilson . . . . . . | 0 | – c Penn b E. R. Wilson . . . . . . . . . . | 9 |
| B 14, l-b 2, w 1, n-b 4 . . . . . . . . . . . . . . . . | 21 | B 13, l-b 1, w 1, n-b 1 . . . . . . | 16 |
| | **268** | | **248** |

### First Twelve

| | | | |
|---|---|---|---|
| Mr E. R. Wilson b McCorquodale . . . . . . . . . . . . . . | 21 | – not out . . . . . . . . . . . . . . . . . . . . . . | 4 |
| Mr A. Buxton c Scott-Murray b Sell . . . . . . . . . . . . | 4 | | |
| Mr E. F. Penn c Chapple b Lambert . . . . . . . . . . . . | 36 | – b McCorquodale . . . . . . . . . . . . . . | 0 |
| Mr S. S. Harris c F. J. Marsh b Morris . . . . . . . . . . | 149 | | |
| Mr C. H. M. Ebden c Mann b Watson . . . . . . . . . . . | 0 | – b McCorquodale . . . . . . . . . . . . . . | 4 |
| Mr K. R. B. Fry c Watson b Lambert . . . . . . . . . . . | 46 | | |
| Mr F. B. Wilson run out . . . . . . . . . . . . . . . . . . . . . | 108 | | |
| Mr J. W. Horne c Lambert b Morris . . . . . . . . . . . . | 18 | | |
| Mr C. T. Rudd lbw b Hollins . . . . . . . . . . . . . . . . . | 28 | – not out . . . . . . . . . . . . . . . . . . . . . . | 15 |
| Mr J. F. Morris c Lambert b Hollins . . . . . . . . . . . . | 13 | | |
| Mr J. Haviland b Driffield . . . . . . . . . . . . . . . . . . . . | 5 | – b McCorquodale . . . . . . . . . . . . . . | 27 |
| Mr C. E. Winter not out . . . . . . . . . . . . . . . . . . . . . | 10 | – c Scott-Murray b McCorquodale . . | 0 |
| B 14, l-b 8, w 4, n-b 1 . . . . . . . . . . . . . . . . | 27 | B 1, l-b 1 . . . . . . . . . . . . . . | 2 |
| | **465** | | **52** |

**First Twelve's Bowling**

|            | Overs | Mdns | Runs | Wkts | Overs | Mdns | Runs | Wkts |
|------------|-------|------|------|------|-------|------|------|------|
| Penn       | 41    | 9    | 91   | 5    | 20    | 3    | 84   | —    |
| E. R. Wilson | 44  | 18   | 80   | 6    | 40.3  | 16   | 73   | 14   |
| Buxton     | 16    | 3    | 48   | 1    | 9     | 4    | 18   | —    |
| Morris     | 9     | 2    | 22   | 1    | 7     | 1    | 24   | —    |
| F. B. Wilson | 3.5 | 1    | 6    | 2    | 14    | 4    | 33   | 1    |

**Next Sixteen's Bowling**

|             | Overs | Mdns | Runs | Wkts | Overs | Mdns | Runs | Wkts |
|-------------|-------|------|------|------|-------|------|------|------|
| McCorquodale | 24   | 3    | 66   | 1    | 6     | 3    | 5    | 4    |
| Sell        | 25    | 4    | 75   | 1    | 7     | —    | 21   | —    |
| Chapple     | 10    | —    | 36   | —    |       |      |      |      |
| Driffield   | 14    | 1    | 54   | 1    |       |      |      |      |
| Lambert     | 21    | 4    | 80   | 2    | 4.2   | 1    | 17   | —    |
| Watson      | 12    | 2    | 44   | 1    |       |      |      |      |
| Morris      | 13    | 1    | 42   | 2    | 6     | 2    | 7    | —    |
| Hollins     | 6.5   | —    | 41   | 2    |       |      |      |      |

Umpires: G. Watts and A. A. White.

# CAMBRIDGE UNIVERSITY v LANCASHIRE

Played at Cambridge, May 13, 14, 15, 1907

Unable to place anything like their full strength in the field – the absentees including Young, Buchanan, Napier, and Morcom – Cambridge nevertheless defeated Lancashire by an innings and 204 runs. Lancashire, who had not appeared at Cambridge for twenty-five years, took the field without either Hornby or Makepeace. They were decidedly unlucky, fielding out for the whole of the first day when, despite a wet morning, the wicket remained in fair condition and having to go in on Wednesday on a pitch which rain, preventing a ball being bowled on Tuesday, had rendered very soft. For all that the county team played wretched cricket, missing a number of catches and batting very feebly. Payne gave a most brilliant display, scoring 100 out of 155 in two hours and altogether withstanding the Lancashire bowling for two hours and twenty-five minutes. Hitting very hard on the off-side, he made only one really bad stroke. When he left a new ball had to be brought into use.

Against Goodwin's legbreaks, the Lancashire batsmen cut so poor a figure that at their first attempt they were all out in less than two hours, Sharp alone showing any ability to get runs. In the follow-on Stanning and Heap put on 30 for the first wicket, and then Goodwin and Lyttelton – the latter a son of Lord Cobham – carried all before them. The University fielded very finely and Elderton kept wicket in capital style.

## Cambridge University

| | |
|---|---|
| Mr M. W. Payne c Worsley b Kermode ...129 | Mr E. L. Mellin b Harry ............... 13 |
| Mr C. C. G. Wright b Harry ............ 14 | Mr R. T. H. Mackenzie b Huddleston ..... 9 |
| Mr F. H. Mugliston b Kermode .......... 33 | Mr C. S. Rattigan b Dean .............. 28 |
| Mr C. Palmer b Huddleston ............. 52 | Hon. C. F. Lyttelton not out ........... 25 |
| Mr H. J. Goodwin c Worsley b Sharp ..... 47 | B 1, l-b 3, n-b 2 ............... 6 |
| Mr M. B. Elderton c Poidevin b Sharp ..... 9 | ___ |
| Mr B. Meakin c Kermode b Huddleston ... 1 | 366 |

## Lancashire

| | | | | |
|---|---|---|---|---|
| Mr H. D. Stanning b Goodwin | 13 | – lbw b Goodwin | 16 |
| J. S. Heap c Mackenzie b Goodwin | 7 | – c Elderton b Lyttelton | 13 |
| J. T. Tyldesley st Elderton b Goodwin | 3 | – b Lyttelton | 0 |
| Mr L. O. S. Poidevin c Elderton b Rattigan | 11 | – b Goodwin | 4 |
| J. Sharp c and b Lyttelton | 40 | – c and b Goodwin | 2 |
| F. Harry lbw b Goodwin | 0 | – c Mackenzie b Lyttelton | 6 |
| Boden c Payne b Goodwin | 5 | – st Elderton b Goodwin | 3 |
| H. Dean b Goodwin | 5 | – c Wright b Lyttelton | 4 |
| W. Huddleston st Elderton b Goodwin | 10 | – not out | 4 |
| A. Kermode not out | 0 | – c Elderton b Lyttelton | 5 |
| W. Worsley b Lyttelton | 0 | – c Payne b Goodwin | 5 |
| B 2, n-b 1 | 3 | B 3 | 3 |
| | **97** | | **65** |

## Lancashire Bowling

| | Overs | Mdns | Runs | Wkts |
|---|---|---|---|---|
| Kermode | 22 | 2 | 88 | 2 |
| Dean | 24.2 | 2 | 87 | 1 |
| Harry | 23 | 5 | 74 | 2 |
| Huddleston | 18 | 3 | 61 | 3 |
| Heap | 4 | — | 21 | — |
| Sharp | 7 | 1 | 29 | 2 |

## Cambridge University Bowling

| | Overs | Mdns | Runs | Wkts | Overs | Mdns | Runs | Wkts |
|---|---|---|---|---|---|---|---|---|
| Rattigan | 9 | 3 | 35 | 1 | | | | |
| Goodwin | 20 | 5 | 33 | 7 | 12.1 | — | 29 | 5 |
| Lyttelton | 11.5 | 4 | 26 | 2 | 13 | 1 | 33 | 5 |

Umpires: F. W. Marlow and A. Millward.

# OXFORD UNIVERSITY MATCHES

## OXFORD UNIVERSITY v MR A. J. WEBBE'S ELEVEN

Played at Oxford, May 17, 18, 19, 1900

In this the test match of importance at Oxford during the season, the University gained a really brilliant victory of five wickets. Everything else in the game was dwarfed by the magnificent batting of Mr R. E. Foster, who foreshadowed the splendid success that was in store for him at Lord's, and for the second time in first-class cricket made two hundreds in one match. He hit up his 128 in the first innings in two hours' and fifty minutes with only one chance. His second innings, however, was the more remarkable of the two, being played on a wicket that had begun to show decided signs of wear. He batted with perfect judgement and confidence for a little over two hours and a half and never made a mistake.

### Mr A. J. Webbe's Eleven

| | | |
|---|---|--:|
| Mr C. J. Burnup lbw b White | 26 – c Bosanquet b Knox | 10 |
| Mr P. F. Warner c Foster b White | 51 – c Foster b Humphreys | 18 |
| Mr G. J. V. Weigall c Pilkington b White | 5 – c Martyn b Bosanquet | 36 |
| Mr G. F. S. Griffin b Knox | 21 – b Knox | 11 |
| Mr H. B. Chinnery c Foster b Humphreys | 1 – c Foster b Humphreys | 16 |
| Mr G. W. Beldam c and b Knox | 44 – st Martyn b White | 74 |
| Mr H. D. Leveson-Gower c Lee b White | 34 – b Bosanquet | 5 |
| Mr C. E. Cobb c Foster b Humphreys | 17 – c Bosanquet b Knox | 19 |
| M. W. M. Bradley c Humphreys b Williams | 9 – b Humphreys | 8 |
| Mr J. L. Ainsworth c Bosanquet b Humphreys | 4 – not out | 3 |
| F. W. Tate not out | 5 – c Martyn b Knox | 18 |
| B 12, l-b 1 | 13 | B 7, l-b 5 | 12 |
| | **230** | | **230** |

### Oxford University

| | | |
|---|---|--:|
| Mr H. C. Pilkington c Bradley b Ainsworth | 22 – b Bradley | 7 |
| Mr C. H. B. Marsham c Weigall b Tate | 58 – retired hurt | 31 |
| Mr F. P. Knox c Griffin b Tate | 8 – c Cobb b Tate | 2 |
| Mr R. E. Foster b Tate | 128 – not out | 100 |
| Mr R. A. Williams c Griffin b Tate | 8 – b Ainsworth | 2 |
| Mr A. M. Hollins b Leveson-Gower b Bradley | 31 – c Bradley b Ainsworth | 0 |
| Mr E. C. Lee c Weigall b Bradley | 10 – c Leveson-Gower b Tate | 18 |
| Mr B. J. T. Bosanquet c Burnup b Bradley | 12 – not out | 4 |
| Mr H. Martyn c Ainsworth b Bradley | 0 | | |
| Mr F. H. Humphreys c Griffin b Bradley | 0 | | |
| Mr H. White not out | 6 | | |
| B 9, l-b 2 | 11 | B 3 | 3 |
| | **294** | | **167** |

### Oxford University Bowling

| | Overs | Mdns | Runs | Wkts | Overs | Mdns | Runs | Wkts |
|---|---|---|---|---|---|---|---|---|
| Bosanquet | 26 | 5 | 65 | — | 20 | 1 | 51 | 2 |
| White | 27 | 7 | 64 | 4 | 9 | 1 | 27 | 1 |
| Humphreys | 18 | 3 | 60 | 3 | 16.2 | — | 55 | 3 |
| Knox | 10 | 5 | 11 | 2 | 27 | 2 | 85 | 4 |
| Williams | 7 | 4 | 17 | 1 | | | | |

**Mr A. J. Webbe's Eleven's Bowling**

|  | Overs | Mdns | Runs | Wkts | Overs | Mdns | Runs | Wkts |
|---|---|---|---|---|---|---|---|---|
| Bradley .......... | 33 | 7 | 141 | 5 | 26 | 11 | 72 | 1 |
| Ainsworth ........ | 22 | 7 | 47 | 1 | 17 | 5 | 34 | 2 |
| Tate ............. | 27.3 | 6 | 56 | 4 | 30 | 14 | 54 | 2 |
| Beldam ........... | 6 | 1 | 22 | — | | | | |
| Burnup ........... | 3 | — | 17 | — | | | | |
| Leveson-Gower .... | | | | | 0.4 | — | 4 | — |

Umpires: H. B. Daft and J. Moss.

## OXFORD UNIVERSITY v LONDON COUNTY

### Played at Oxford, May 21, 22, 23, 1900

Oxford gained an overwhelming victory by an innings and 330 runs, but fortune was all on their side, rain ruining the wicket after they had on the first day played an innings of 539. Foster gave further evidence of being in exceptional form, and though he gave two or three difficult chances his 169 was a very brilliant display. He hit Grace four times in succession into the shrubbery, and altogether his innings included half-a-dozen 6s, and twenty 4s. Bosanquet also hit finely, obtaining his first hundred runs in an hour and a half. Owing to an injured hand Grace could not bat for the London County, but with the ground as it was he would have had no chance of saving the match.

### Oxford University

| | |
|---|---|
| Mr F. H. Hollins hit wkt b Grace ......... 15 | Mr J. W. Crawfurd c and b Campbell ..... 67 |
| Mr H. C. Pilkington b Grace ............ 3 | Mr H. Martyn run out ................. 16 |
| Mr F. P. Knox c Stedman b Braund ...... 55 | Mr F. H. Humphreys c Stedman b Braund . 12 |
| Mr R. E. Foster c Somerset b Braund .....169 | Mr H. White not out .................. 6 |
| Mr E. C. Lee c Parkes b Smith ........... 20 | B 26, l-b 2, w 4 .............. 32 |
| Mr A. M. Hollins c Robinson b Braund .... 19 | |
| Mr B. J. T. Bosanquet b Braund ........125 | 539 |

### London County

| | | |
|---|---|---|
| S. Tindall b Bosanquet ....................... 10 | – c F. Hollins b Lee .............. 4 |
| Campbell c Pilkington b White ............. 24 | – c Crawfurd b Humphreys ........ 2 |
| L. C. Braund st Martyn b White ............ 0 | – not out ...................... 19 |
| Robinson c Humphreys b Bosanquet ............. 4 | – b Knox .................... 3 |
| H. Parkes c Knox b Bosanquet ............... 1 | –c Lee b Humphreys ............. 6 |
| Mr A. F. Somerset c Knox b White ............ 0 | – st Martyn b Lee ............... 0 |
| Mr W. L. Murdoch b Bosanquet ................ 18 | – c Martyn b Knox ............. 40 |
| Mr L. Walker c Lee b Knox .................... 9 | – st Martyn b Knox ............. 4 |
| Smith not out ............................. 21 | – run out .................... 9 |
| E. Stedman c Crawfurd b White ............. 15 | – b Knox..................... 0 |
| Mr W. G. Grace absent hurt ................ 0 | – absent ..................... 0 |
| B 12, w 2 ........................ 14 | B 5, n-b 1 .............. 6 |
| 116 | 93 |

### Oxford University Bowling

|  | Overs | Mdns | Runs | Wkts | Overs | Mdns | Runs | Wkts |
|---|---|---|---|---|---|---|---|---|
| White ............ | 22 | 5 | 36 | 4 | 4 | 2 | 7 | — |
| Bosanquet ........ | 16 | 1 | 54 | 4 | 6 | 1 | 21 | — |
| Knox ............. | 5 | 2 | 12 | 1 | 8.5 | 4 | 16 | 4 |
| Humphreys ....... | | | | | 9 | 1 | 33 | 2 |
| Crawfurd ......... | | | | | 2 | 1 | 1 | — |
| Lee ............. | | | | | 5 | 2 | 9 | 2 |

## London County Bowling

|  | Overs | Mdns | Runs | Wkts |
|---|---|---|---|---|
| Grace . . . . . . . . . . . . | 34 | 8 | 130 | 2 |
| Smith . . . . . . . . . . . | 25 | 2 | 94 | 1 |
| Simpson . . . . . . . . . | 5 | 1 | 24 | — |
| Walker . . . . . . . . . . | 9 | 1 | 46 | — |
| Braund . . . . . . . . . . | 25 | 5 | 140 | 5 |
| Campbell . . . . . . . . | 8 | — | 57 | 1 |
| Somerset . . . . . . . . | 3 | — | 16 | — |

# OXFORD UNIVERSITY v SUSSEX

## Played at Oxford, May 24, 25, 26, 1900

This match was played on the Christ Church Ground, at which, unlike the University Ground in the Parks, a charge can be made for admission. Rain restricted the first day's play to an hour and twenty minutes, and the wicket never recovered. A hard fought game ended in a victory for Oxford by 11 runs. Bosanquet clearly won the match for his side, taking in the two innings fifteen wickets for 65 runs. In the second innings of Sussex he took at a cost of 31 runs the first nine wickets that fell. Fry did not play for Sussex, and Ranjitsinhji was greatly handicapped by lameness. It was a curious circumstance that at the end of the game the last three Sussex batsmen were all out leg before wicket.

## Oxford University

| | | | |
|---|---|---|---|
| Mr F. H. B. Champain b Tate . . . . . . . . . . . . . . . . . . | 0 | – b Bland . . . . . . . . . . . . . . . . . . . . . . | 9 |
| Mr A. C. Pilkington lbw b Bland . . . . . . . . . . . . . . . . | 23 | – b Tate . . . . . . . . . . . . . . . . . . . . . . . | 10 |
| Mr F. P. Knox b Tate . . . . . . . . . . . . . . . . . . . . . . . | 2 | – b Cox . . . . . . . . . . . . . . . . . . . . . . . | 16 |
| Mr R. E. Foster b Tate . . . . . . . . . . . . . . . . . . . . . . | 0 | – lbw b Cox . . . . . . . . . . . . . . . . . . . . | 39 |
| Mr H. J. Wyld b Tate . . . . . . . . . . . . . . . . . . . . . . . | 4 | – b Cox . . . . . . . . . . . . . . . . . . . . . . . | 0 |
| Mr E. C. Lee b Tate . . . . . . . . . . . . . . . . . . . . . . . | 0 | – b Tate . . . . . . . . . . . . . . . . . . . . . . . | 15 |
| Mr B. J. T. Bosanquet b Tate . . . . . . . . . . . . | 11 | – b Tate . . . . . . . . . . . . . . . . . . . . . . . | 20 |
| Mr J. W. Crawfurd c Ranjitsinhji b Bland . . . . . . . . . | 6 | – b Cox . . . . . . . . . . . . . . . . . . . . . . . | 3 |
| Mr H. Martyn c Fox b Tate . . . . . . . . . . . . . . . . . . . | 0 | – c Vine b Cox . . . . . . . . . . . . . . . . . . | 2 |
| Mr F. H. Humphreys not out . . . . . . . . . . . . . . . . . . | 6 | – c Ranjitsinhji b Cox . . . . . . . . . . . . | 0 |
| Mr H. White b Bland . . . . . . . . . . . . . . . . . . . . . . . | 4 | – not out . . . . . . . . . . . . . . . . . . . . . . . | 0 |
| B 9, l-b 2 . . . . . . . . . . . . . . . . . . . . . . . | 11 | B 6, l-b 3, n-b 1 . . . . . . . . . . | 10 |
| | **67** | | **124** |

## Sussex

| | | | |
|---|---|---|---|
| Mr A. Collins c and b Humphreys . . . . . . . . . . . . . . | 26 | – b Bosanquet . . . . . . . . . . . . . . . . . . . . | 24 |
| A. E. Relf b Bosanquet . . . . . . . . . . . . . . . . . . . . . . | 3 | – lbw b Bosanquet . . . . . . . . . . . . . . . . | 0 |
| E. H. Killick lbw b Bosanquet . . . . . . . . . . . . . . . . | 7 | – c Martyn b Bosanquet . . . . . . . . . . . . | 9 |
| K. S. Ranjitsinhji c Champain b Humphreys . . . . . . . | 31 | – c Foster b Bosanquet . . . . . . . . . . . . | 15 |
| J. Vine c Martyn b Bosanquet . . . . . . . . . . . . . . . . . | 4 | – b Bosanquet . . . . . . . . . . . . . . . . . . . . | 7 |
| Mr C. D. Fisher b Bosanquet . . . . . . . . . . . . . . . . . . | 0 | – lbw b White . . . . . . . . . . . . . . . . . . . | 11 |
| J. Bean b Bosanquet . . . . . . . . . . . . . . . . . . . . . . . . | 0 | – c Champain b Bosanquet . . . . . . . . | 0 |
| G. Cox b Humphreys . . . . . . . . . . . . . . . . . . . . . . . . | 3 | – b Bosanquet . . . . . . . . . . . . . . . . . . . . | 9 |
| Mr R. W. Fox not out . . . . . . . . . . . . . . . . . . . . . . . | 9 | – lbw b Bosanquet . . . . . . . . . . . . . . . | 1 |
| F. W. Tate b Bosanquet . . . . . . . . . . . . . . . . . . . . . . | 6 | – lbw b Bosanquet . . . . . . . . . . . . . . . | 0 |
| C. H. G. Bland b Humphreys . . . . . . . . . . . . . . . . . . | 5 | – not out . . . . . . . . . . . . . . . . . . . . . . . | 0 |
| B 1, n-b 1 . . . . . . . . . . . . . . . . . . . . . . . | 2 | B 5, l-b 3 . . . . . . . . . . . . . . | 8 |
| | **96** | | **84** |

## Sussex Bowling

|  | Overs | Mdns | Runs | Wkts | Overs | Mdns | Runs | Wkts |
|---|---|---|---|---|---|---|---|---|
| Tate .............. | 19 | 8 | 30 | 7 | 26 | 7 | 64 | 3 |
| Bland ............ | 14.2 | 9 | 19 | 3 | 5 | 1 | 17 | 1 |
| Cox .............. | 4 | 1 | 7 | — | 21 | 6 | 33 | 6 |

## Oxford University Bowling

|  | Overs | Mdns | Runs | Wkts | Overs | Mdns | Runs | Wkts |
|---|---|---|---|---|---|---|---|---|
| Bosanquet ........ | 24 | 10 | 34 | 6 | 24 | 12 | 31 | 9 |
| White ............ | 5 | 1 | 11 | — | 19 | 9 | 29 | 1 |
| Champain ........ | 8 | 2 | 18 | — | | | | |
| Knox ............. | 2 | — | 15 | — | | | | |
| Humphreys ....... | 12.2 | 4 | 16 | — | 5 | 1 | 16 | — |

Umpires: H. B. Daft and A. F. Smith.

# GENTLEMEN v PLAYERS

## THE LORD'S MATCH

Played at Lord's, July 16, 17, 18, 1900

The Gentlemen v Players match at Lord's in 1900, was certainly the most remarkable game of the whole season, and in every way worthy of comparison with the memorable match under the same title on the same ground in 1898. It presented two points that were quite without precedent in the long series of Gentlemen v Players matches. R. E. Foster followed up his record innings in the University match by making two separate hundreds, a feat never before performed at Lord's or elsewhere for either Gentlemen or Players, and the Players, though set to make 501 in the last innings, won the game by two wickets. Never before in a match of such importance – and only once indeed in the whole history of first-class cricket – has a total of over five hundred been obtained in the fourth innings. The one previous occasion – also at Lord's ground – was in 1896, when Cambridge were set to make 507 against the MCC and succeeded in accomplishing the task. The performance of the Players was a magnificent one, but they could consider themselves lucky in having sufficient time left them in which to make such a huge score. Under ordinary circumstances the task would have been out of the question. It was in this way that the opportunity of doing an unprecedented thing presented itself. On the second afternoon the Gentlemen already held what was on paper an overwhelming advantage, and Mr Woods, their captain, wishing to have the Players in before the close of the afternoon, instructed his side to play a hitting game, and be out by a certain time. His instructions were loyally obeyed, and though the Gentlemen's score stood at 238 for three wickets when Foster left, the innings was all over for 339. From lunch time till the end of the innings 279 runs were scored in two hours and twenty minutes. No one was disposed to criticise Mr Woods at all severely, some people going so far as to say that if the Gentlemen could not win with a lead of 500 runs they did not deserve to win at all. This was all very well, but the fact remained that there was only one possible way by which the Gentlemen could lose the match, and that their captain adopted it. If he had not been so anxious for his side to be out before the end of the second afternoon he could have made defeat absolutely impossible, and yet have left his side a whole day in which to win. Of course he could not regard it as at all within the range of probability that the Players would make 500 runs in the last innings, but it is a wholesome rule to take nothing for granted at cricket, and to throw nothing away except under stress of absolute necessity. However, though the Gentlemen suffered a defeat to the risk of which they need not have been exposed, the public profited, the cricket on the last day being quite a marvel of sustained interest. Overnight the Players had lost Albert Ward's wicket for 44 runs, so that on Wednesday morning, with nine wickets to go down, they wanted 457 to win. By wonderful batting the task was accomplished, the honours being divided between Brown, Hayward and Abel. Of the three batsmen Abel made the smallest score, but in the opinion of many good judges he played the best cricket. Quite early in the day victory for the Players was seen to be possible, a great stand by Brown and Abel putting them in a flattering position. Abel joined Brown at 81, for two wickets, and when lunch time came the score had reached 242, and the two batsmen were still together. So far Brown had made 106 and Abel 94. On the game being resumed Abel seemed certain of his hundred, but he was a little too anxious, and after getting one boundary hit he attempted a big pull on a short-pitched ball from Jessop, and was easily caught at forward short leg. In this way the third wicket went down at 246, Abel having in a couple of hours scored 98 out of 165. When he left it wanted five minutes to three, and the Players with seven wickets to fall required 255 runs to win. Brown, who had been playing a masterly game all the morning, was then joined by Hayward, and again the good bowling of the Gentlemen was mastered. Hayward had been unwell and away from the ground on the previous day, but having quite shaken off his indisposition, he played superbly. For close upon an hour and a half the two batsmen stayed together, and the total was up to 348 when at last Brown's innings was ended by a catch at cover slip. He had one or two narrow escapes of being bowled and might, with his score at 127, have been caught on the leg-side by Jessop off one of Jephson's lobs, but all the same he played great cricket. He hit one 5 (4 for an overthrow) twenty-nine 4s, two 3s and nine 2s, and was batting for four hours and three-quarters. Brilliant cutting was perhaps the best feature of his game. His 163 is the highest innings ever hit for the Players against the Gentlemen at Lord's, beating by 24 runs the great score made by William Gunn in 1898. When Brown left an interval of a quarter of an hour was taken for tea, the Players with six wickets in hand, wanting 153 to win. A fresh start was made at twenty-five minutes to five, and except that Carpenter failed, things continued to go well for the batting side, victory seeming absolutely certain so long as Hayward and Lilley stayed together. However, Lilley left, sixth wicket down, at 448, and at 469 Hayward's splendid innings was closed by a catch by the wicket-keeper, standing back to Kortright's bowling. In as nearly as possible three hours Hayward had scored 111, his play, though a little unequal in quality, being for the most part admirable. At his dismissal the Players wanted 32 to win with three wickets to fall, and the issue remained in doubt. With 16 added John Gunn was bowled, but on Rhodes joining Trott the end soon came. At half-past six the score stood at a tie, and on Woods taking the ball Rhodes made the winning hit, a wonderful match ending in favour of the Players by two wickets.

We have described the closing stage of the game at considerable length, the cricket being so extraordinary in character. As regards the rest of the match it must suffice to pay proper tribute to the magnificent batting of Foster, and to the excellent services rendered to the Gentlemen in different ways by Fry, Mason, and Jessop. On the second morning Mason and Jessop, with Kortright to help them at the finish, bowled in such capital form that the Players' first innings was finished off for 136, after 66 runs had been scored overnight for two wickets. The performance was the more remarkable as there was nothing the matter with the wicket. Foster's first innings at 102 not out was in many ways a remarkable effort. So keen was he to do well in this, his first Gentlemen and Players' match that, sternly restraining all desire to hit, he was at the wickets nearly half an hour before he made his first run. He was not out 6 at lunch time, but on starting afresh he played a very different game, carrying his score to 102 in less than two hours. As a matter of record, it may be added that he hit fifteen 4s, three 3s, and nine 2s. His second innings was from first to last astonishingly brilliant, but was marred by a palpable chance to John Gunn at mid-off when he had made 40. He completed his first 50 runs in little more than an hour, and then hit away in such tremendous form that when at last Brown caught him in the deep field in front of the pavilion, he had only been at the wickets an hour and three-quarters. In that time he scored 136 out of 195, hitting in his wonderful innings, twenty-four 4s, two 3s, four 2s, and twenty-six singles. Not often, except by such a hitter as Jessop, have first-rate professional bowlers been treated more lightly. Under ordinary circumstances, a batsman who scored 68 and 72 for the Gentlemen at Lord's would stand out very prominently, but Fry on this particular occasion was quite overshadowed by Foster. It should be said for him, however, that in the second innings he played a most unselfish game, caring nothing for his own success when he saw that Foster had a chance of making his second hundred.

### Gentlemen

| | | | |
|---|---|---|---|
| Mr A. O. Jones c Ward b Trott | 9 | – b Rhodes | 5 |
| Mr C. B. Fry b Rhodes | 68 | – hit wkt b Ward | 72 |
| Mr C. L. Townsend run out | 30 | – b Rhodes | 22 |
| Mr R. E. Foster not out | 102 | – c Brown b Trott | 136 |
| Mr J. R. Mason b Trott | 2 | – c Lilley b Trott | 27 |
| Mr D. L. A. Jephson lbw b Rhodes | 9 | – not out | 18 |
| Mr G. L. Jessop c Lilley b Rhodes | 18 | – b Trott | 18 |
| Mr S. M. J. Woods c Lilley b Rhodes | 7 | – c Carpenter b Ward | 0 |
| Mr E. Smith c Rhodes b Gunn | 26 | – c Brown b Trott | 16 |
| Mr C. J. Kortright b Gunn | 4 | – c sub. b Trott | 12 |
| Mr H. Martyn c Brown b Gunn | 3 | – c Quaife b Trott | 4 |
| B 15, l-b 4 | 19 | B 5, l-b 4 | 9 |
| | **297** | | **339** |

### Players

| | | | |
|---|---|---|---|
| R. Abel b Jessop | 30 | – c Jones b Jessop | 98 |
| A. Ward c Jones b Mason | 16 | – c Martyn b Jessop | 4 |
| T. Hayward b Jessop | 8 | – c Martyn b Kortright | 111 |
| W. G. Quaife c Foster b Jessop | 9 | – lbw b Jones | 29 |
| J. T. Brown sen. c Foster b Mason | 18 | – c Jones b Smith | 163 |
| H. Carpenter run out | 14 | – b Woods | 9 |
| A. A. Lilley b Mason | 10 | – b Mason | 30 |
| A. E. Trott c Foster b Mason | 9 | – not out | 22 |
| J. Gunn c Martyn b Kortright | 4 | – b Kortright | 3 |
| W. Rhodes not out | 1 | – not out | 7 |
| W. Mead b Kortright | 4 | | |
| B 9, l-b 4 | 13 | B 13, l-b 8, w 1, n-b 4 | 26 |
| | **136** | | **502** |

### Players' Bowling

| | Overs | Mdns | Runs | Wkts | Overs | Mdns | Runs | Wkts |
|---|---|---|---|---|---|---|---|---|
| Rhodes | 30 | 4 | 93 | 4 | 15 | 2 | 51 | 2 |
| Trott | 27 | 11 | 66 | 2 | 20.2 | — | 142 | 6 |
| Mead | 21 | 5 | 58 | — | 14 | 1 | 57 | — |
| Gunn | 17.3 | 3 | 61 | 3 | 7 | 3 | 23 | — |
| Ward | | | | | 10 | 3 | 39 | 2 |
| Quaife | | | | | 1 | — | 18 | — |

### Gentlemen's Bowling

| | Overs | Mdns | Runs | Wkts | Overs | Mdns | Runs | Wkts |
|---|---|---|---|---|---|---|---|---|
| Kortright | 12.4 | 4 | 30 | 2 | 18 | 4 | 60 | 2 |
| Jephson | 4 | — | 9 | — | 14 | 2 | 46 | — |
| Mason | 17 | 7 | 40 | 4 | 34 | 11 | 92 | 1 |
| Jessop | 14 | 5 | 28 | 3 | 28 | 8 | 74 | 2 |
| Jones | 5 | — | 16 | — | 23 | 4 | 69 | 1 |
| Woods | | | | | 19.5 | 3 | 70 | 1 |
| Smith | | | | | 18 | 3 | 57 | 1 |
| Townsend | | | | | 2 | — | 8 | — |

Umpires: J. Wheeler and J. Phillips.

# THE HASTINGS MATCH

### Played at Hastings, September 9, 10, 11, 1901

The second match of the Hastings week was truly sensational in character, the Players being robbed by rain of almost certain victory after having been 168 behind on the first innings. On the second afternoon, W. G. Grace preferred that the Gentlemen should go in themselves rather than make the Players follow on, but his experiment of altering the order so as to force the pace proved a deplorable failure, the side, with Jephson prevented from batting by an injury, being out in an hour and twenty minutes for 59. Backed up by splendid fielding all round, and brilliant work by Lilley at the wicket, Rhodes enjoyed quite a triumph, six wickets falling to him for 27 runs. The Players only wanted 228 to win, and when after several interruptions rain caused stumps to be pulled up shortly before five o'clock on the third afternoon, they were within 51 runs of victory with seven wickets in hand. Some capital batting was shown during the game, A. O. Jones and Tyldesley taking the honours. Jessop on the first day scored 45 out of 59 in twenty minutes, hitting eight 4s, two 3s, two 2s, and three singles. It will be noticed that Sinclair and Mason were kept on unchanged during the Players innings of 238. Mason's accuracy of pitch was remarkable.

## Gentlemen

| | | | |
|---|---|---|---|
| Mr W. G. Grace b Hayward | 54 | – not out | 0 |
| Mr A. O. Jones c Tyldesley b Rhodes | 105 | – c Lilley b Rhodes | 11 |
| Mr J. R. Mason st Lilley b Vine | 49 | – c Denton b Rhodes | 9 |
| Mr T. L. Taylor c Hirst b Rhodes | 27 | – st Lilley b Rhodes | 10 |
| Mr G. L. Jessop c Hayward b Rhodes | 45 | – st Lilley b Rhodes | 6 |
| Capt. J. G. Greig b Vine | 0 | – b Hirst | 1 |
| Mr E. Smith c Hayward b Rhodes | 9 | – c Killick b Rhodes | 1 |
| Mr J. H. Sinclair b Vine | 11 | – c Brown b Rhodes | 4 |
| Mr D. L. A. Jephson not out | 25 | – absent hurt | 0 |
| Mr K. O. Goldie b Rhodes | 40 | – b Hirst | 6 |
| Mr E. A. Halliwell c Brown b Rhodes | 25 | – b Hirst | 2 |
| B 12, l-b 3, n-b 1 | 16 | B 6, l-b 3 | 9 |
| | **406** | | **59** |

## Players

| | | | |
|---|---|---|---|
| J. Tunnicliffe c Jones b Sinclair | 32 | – c Halliwell b Sinclair | 20 |
| R. Abel b Sinclair | 19 | – c sub. b Mason | 38 |
| J. T. Brown sen. b Sinclair | 31 | – b Greig | 65 |
| T. Hayward b Mason | 0 | – not out | 11 |
| J. T. Tyldesley st Halliwell b Mason | 96 | – not out | 40 |
| G. H. Hirst b Mason | 19 | | |
| D. Denton b Mason | 3 | | |
| A. A. Lilley lbw b Sinclair | 1 | | |
| E. H. Killick b Mason | 2 | | |
| J. Vine c and b Mason | 16 | | |
| W. Rhodes not out | 6 | | |
| B 12, l-b 1 | 13 | L-b 1, n-b 2 | 3 |
| | **238** | | **177** |

### Players' Bowling

| | Overs | Mdns | Runs | Wkts | Overs | Mdns | Runs | Wkts |
|---|---|---|---|---|---|---|---|---|
| Hirst | 18 | 1 | 68 | — | 12.3 | 3 | 23 | 3 |
| Rhodes | 36.2 | 10 | 132 | 6 | 12 | 4 | 27 | 6 |
| Vine | 24 | 1 | 109 | 3 | | | | |
| Killick | 3 | — | 10 | — | | | | |
| Brown | 6 | — | 34 | — | | | | |
| Hayward | 8 | — | 37 | 1 | | | | |

### Gentlemen's Bowling

| | Overs | Mdns | Runs | Wkts | Overs | Mdns | Runs | Wkts |
|---|---|---|---|---|---|---|---|---|
| Sinclair | 31 | 6 | 135 | 4 | 13 | 2 | 58 | 1 |
| Mason | 31 | 8 | 90 | 6 | 20 | 3 | 74 | 1 |
| Jessop | | | | | 5 | — | 17 | — |
| Smith | | | | | 3 | — | 4 | — |
| Greig | | | | | 6 | 1 | 21 | 1 |

Umpires: A. Shaw and J. Lillywhite.

# THE LORD'S MATCH

Played at Lord's, July 6, 7, 8, 1903

For two days the Gentlemen were completely outplayed, following on 293 in arrear, and entering upon the concluding stage of the contest with one wicket down and 219 runs required to escape a single innings defeat. Some truly grand batting by Fry and MacLaren, however, not only saved the amateurs from being beaten, but left them with the honours of the match. These two famous cricketers came together at five minutes past one on the Wednesday with two wickets down for 191, and, on a pitch which had never been perfect, actually hit up 309 runs in rather less than three hours, MacLaren declaring shortly after five o'clock with the total increased to 500 and eight wickets still standing. In mishits which went out of reach and in balls which beat them without hitting the wicket, both Fry and MacLaren enjoyed a liberal share of luck, but considering the position of the game and the conditions which prevailed, the cricket they played was of a truly glorious description. In making 232 not out, Fry established a record for the Gentlemen v Players' match at Lord's, the previous highest scores having been the 169 of W. G. Grace in 1876, and the 163 of J. T. Brown in 1900. Apart from Abel's 247 at The Oval in 1901, Fry's innings was, moreover, the biggest ever played in a Gentlemen v Player's match on any ground. MacLaren's score came, of course, within one of the Lord's record.

On each side there appeared five men who had not previously assisted in a Gentlemen v Players' match at Lord's – Burnup, Bosanquet, Evans, Brearley and Hesketh-Prichard of the amateurs, and Knight, Arnold, Barnes, Hunter and Hargreave of the professionals. F. S. Jackson, G. L. Jessop and Hirst were notable absentees. Hayward winning the toss, he and Braund gave the players a fine start by putting on 114. The wicket, owing to its having been too recently watered, kicked a good deal at times, but not one of the amateurs bowlers proved able to take advantage of its condition. The fielding, too, despite smart work by Burnup and one or two others, lacked cleanness, and three chances were missed, MacLaren letting off Hayward when 24, while Denton was given one life by Brearley at two, and another by Bosanquet at 42. Braund batted admirably for two hours. The score reached 231 before the fourth wicket went down, but there were seven men out for 276. Knight, however, then received unexpectedly strong help from Barnes, these two men adding 111 runs in the last eighty minutes of the day, and being still together at the drawing of stumps. Knight, who had been at the wickets more than three hours, was not out 98. Next morning Barnes soon left, but Hunter helped Knight to put on 57 for the last wicket, the innings in all lasting nearly seven hours. Dowson alone of the Gentlemen bowled at all well. Knight, who had gone in third wicket down at 144, was ninth out at 451, his stay extending over four hours and a half. He gave no chance and made few bad strokes, playing with extreme care for a long time, but hitting very clearly on the off side. His achievement in scoring over 100 in his first Gentlemen v Players' match at Lord's no doubt assisted to get him a place in the team for Australia.

In marked contrast to the bowling of the Gentlemen was that of their opponents, and the latter also fielded the more smartly. Hargreave dismissing Fry at 14 and Ranjitsinhji being grandly caught at square leg by Tyldesley at 39, the professionals quickly gained the upper hand. So repeatedly did the batsmen find themselves in difficulties that they forsook caution and went in for hitting, Warner playing a game quite foreign to him, but playing it very well. In two hours and a half Hargreave and Braund, with assistance from Trott towards the close, had finished off the innings. Barnes went lame after sending down one over, and took no further part in the game. Fry and Warner in the follow-on raised the score to 49, the total at the drawing of stumps standing at 74 for one wicket.

No doubt the pitch was in better condition on the third day than it had been at any previous period of the match, but it never played quite easy. Ranjitsinhji helped Fry to lay the foundation of the big performance, the second wicket, which fell at 191, adding 142 runs. The Sussex captain, handicapped by lameness, took fifty minutes to make 10, but hit in resolute fashion during the last hour he was at the wickets. Some little time before Ranjitsinhji left, Fry had several narrow escapes in playing Arnold, and for a few minutes after Maclaren came in the batting remained somewhat streaky. At lunch time the total had been increased to 263. On resuming the batsmen hit away with tremendous vigour, adding 80 in half an hour and 131 in an hour, MacLaren scoring 75 to Fry's 55. This pace, of course, was not quite maintained, but the batting continued to be of the most brilliant description. By tea-time the total had reached 463, and after another fifteen minutes run-getting MacLaren declared. Fry, who was at the wickets five hours and a half for his 232, played wonderful cricket, the great feature of his batting being his on-driving. He hit thirty-two 4s, six 3s, and fourteen 2s. MacLaren found himself perhaps rather more often in trouble than his colleague, but his batting was of a masterly description. His innings – characterised by especially fine hitting on the off-side and delightful strokes to leg – included twenty-seven 4s, five 3s, and eleven 2s. The Players having 208 to make with only an hour left when they went in, the game ended tamely in a draw. It was a pity Fry and MacLaren did not continue batting to the end. During the day 481 runs were scored, and only two wickets went down.

## Players

| | | | |
|---|---|---|---|
| T. Hayward b Dowson | 51 | – b Dowson | 19 |
| L. C. Braund c MacLaren b Dowson | 69 | – not out | 22 |
| J. T. Tyldesley run out | 6 | – not out | 13 |
| D. Denton c Ranjitsinhji b Bosanquet | 53 | | |
| A. E. Knight b Dowson | 139 | | |
| J. Gunn c Warner b Brearley | 28 | | |
| E. Arnold b Brearley | 1 | | |
| A. E. Trott b Brearley | 0 | | |
| S. F. Barnes c Evans c Brearley | 56 | | |
| D. Hunter b Dowson | 17 | | |
| S. Hargreave not out | 22 | | |
| B 16, l-b 13, w 1, n-b 6 | 36 | N-b 1 | 1 |
| | **478** | | **55** |

## Gentlemen

| | | | |
|---|---|---|---|
| Mr C. B. Fry b Hargreave | 5 | – not out | 232 |
| Mr P. F. Warner c Hunter b Hargreave | 51 | – c Hunter b Hargreave | 27 |
| K. S. Ranjitsinhji c Tyldesley b Braund | 9 | – c Hunter b Gunn | 60 |
| Mr C. J. Burnup lbw b Braund | 11 | | |
| Mr A. C. MacLaren c and b Braund | 9 | – not out | 168 |
| Mr E. M. Dowson c Denton b Braund | 29 | | |
| Mr B. J. T. Bosanquet c Trott b Hargreave | 26 | | |
| Mr W. H. B. Evans c sub. b Trott | 21 | | |
| Mr H. Martyn c Knight b Trott | 7 | | |
| Mr H. Hesketh-Prichard not out | 1 | | |
| Mr W. Brearley b Trott | 0 | | |
| B 13, l-b 3 | 16 | B 8, l-b 2, n-b 3 | 13 |
| | **185** | (2 wkts dec.) | **500** |

## Gentlemen's Bowling

| | Overs | Mdns | Runs | Wkts | Overs | Mdns | Runs | Wkts |
|---|---|---|---|---|---|---|---|---|
| Brearley | 32 | 7 | 93 | 4 | 4 | — | 16 | — |
| Hesketh-Prichard | 34 | 11 | 91 | — | 5 | 2 | 9 | — |
| Evans | 24 | 6 | 52 | — | 8 | 2 | 17 | — |
| Bosanquet | 17 | 2 | 80 | 1 | | | | |
| Burnup | 4 | — | 18 | — | | | | |
| Dowson | 35.2 | 4 | 97 | 4 | 6 | 1 | 12 | 1 |
| Ranjitsinhji | 2 | — | 11 | — | | | | |

**Players' Bowling**

| | Overs | Mdns | Runs | Wkts | Overs | Mdns | Runs | Wkts |
|---|---|---|---|---|---|---|---|---|
| Barnes ........... | 1 | 1 | — | — | | | | |
| Hargreave ........ | 25 | 7 | 59 | 3 | 46 | 12 | 96 | 1 |
| Braund ........... | 26 | 6 | 67 | 4 | 26 | 4 | 107 | — |
| Gunn ............ | 5 | — | 26 | — | 18 | 4 | 68 | 1 |
| Trott ............ | 4 | 1 | 17 | 3 | 20 | 2 | 120 | — |
| Arnold ........... | | | | | 22 | 2 | 74 | — |
| Denton .......... | | | | | 4 | — | 22 | — |

Umpires: J. Phillips and V. A. Titchmarsh.

# THE LORD'S MATCH

### Played at Lord's, July 9, 10, 11, 1906

With no Test games to overshadow it, the Gentlemen v Players match at Lord's had all its old attraction and drew crowds of people, 10,561 paying for admission on the first day, 11,478 on the second, and 5,937 on the third. The full attendance for the three days came to nearly 40,000. Proving in every way worthy of its traditions, the match produced some of the finest cricket of the season, the Gentlemen winning after a strenuous fight by 45 runs. Beyond everything else it will be remembered for the success of the fast bowlers, and especially for the great performance of Fielder, who in the first innings of the Gentlemen took all ten wickets – a feat never performed before in a Gentlemen v Players match. Still, though he in a sense took the chief honours, Fielder was not so fast or deadly as N. A. Knox. The Surrey bowler, who was only just recovering from the effects of a strain, surpassed himself, and by taking twelve wickets clearly won the game for his side. Bowling quite so fast as his has not been seen in the Gentlemen v Players match since C. J. Kortright appeared for the Gentlemen in 1898. Keeping up his full pace in both innings Knox was really intimidating, and only three or four of the professional batsmen faced him with any confidence. Some of them were clearly unnerved by his terrific speed and the way in which even the good length balls got up. In the whole game only one wicket fell to bowling that was not fast, Lees, who met with great success in the Gentlemen's second innings, putting on a lot of extra pace for the occasion. Except for the absence of George Hirst, who declined the MCC's invitation for the reason that he felt obliged to save himself for Yorkshire matches, the sides were nearly as strong as they could be, but A. O. Jones should have been in the Gentlemen's eleven, and for the Players Iremonger might have been given the preference over Bowley. Otherwise there was no room for fault-finding. Yielding to pressure, F. S. Jackson, who up to this time had taken no part in first-class cricket during the season, captained the Gentlemen and played in characteristic form while Fielder was taking all the wickets in the first innings. Both sides have often been stronger in batting, but, as regards all-round skill, there was little reason to be dissatisfied with the display of cricket given. Quite a feature of the game was the magnificent wicket-keeping of Martyn, who, on the first afternoon, stood close up to Knox's bowling, and took it with the ease and certainty of a Blackham or a Pilling. Only five men were new to the match – Perrin, Hutchings, J. N. Crawford, and Knox for the Gentlemen, and Fielder for the Players. Hutchings failed in both innings, but he had fully earned his place by some splendid batting for Kent. In a way the occasion could be regarded as the centenary of the Gentlemen v Players match at Lord's, but the first match under this title in 1806 was played on the old ground situated where Dorest Square now stands, and the Gentlemen were given the services of W. Beldham and W. Lambert – the two most famous professionals of those remote days.

The first day's cricket was very surprising in character. Perhaps the pitch had been rather too recently watered, but whatever the cause the bowlers carried everything before them, seventeen wickets falling for 303 runs. The best compliment to Fielder's bowling could be found in the fact that Jackson took two hours and a half to score 40. Breaking back now and again, but as a rule making the ball go away with his arm, Fielder always looked very difficult. He kept a fine length on or outside the off stump, and the ball left the pitch at a great pace. Bosanquet played a capital innings, but for the most part the Gentlemen's batting was frankly a failure. Martyn, however, who did his best to knock Fielder off, made some fine hits from that bowler. The best batting on the opening day was shown by Hayward, who, after being badly hurt in the first over, resumed his innings when four wickets had fallen to Knox and Brearley for 17 runs, and played the fast bowlers with the utmost skill.

On the second morning, thanks chiefly to Lilley, the Players carried their overnight score of 136 for seven wickets to 199, securing a lead on the first innings of 32 runs. Up to a certain point in their second innings the Gentlemen seemed likely to obtain a big score, Spooner and H. K. Foster making 156 together in two hours and a quarter for the first wicket. However, three wickets were down for 211 and, after a tea interval, four more soon fell to Lees and Fielder, Hutchings, Bosanquet, Jackson, and Crawford being got rid of in less than half an hour. Spooner played one of the finest innings of his life. He gave a chance at the wicket off Lees when he had made 29, but this was his only mistake during a stay of three hours. Batting better worth looking at than his was not seen at Lord's last season. Powerful on-driving and very skilful play on the leg side were the features of his cricket. He had not previously made a hundred at Lord's since his 198 for Marlborough against Rugby in 1899. H. K. Foster's 67 was invaluable, but he took a long time to settle down, and only during the latter part of his innings was he master of the bowling. With nine wickets down for 272 the Gentlemen were in a bad position, but Brearley, who had many narrow escapes of being bowled, managed somehow to stay in, and so fearlessly did Jessop hit that 49 runs were added for the last wicket in half-an-hour. Jessop was only batting for an hour, scoring in that time 73 runs out of 92.

Stumps were drawn at the close of the innings and on the following morning the Players went in with 290 to get to win. Opinion was divided as to their chance, but in a little over half-an-hour they looked a beaten side, Knox in a couple of overs clean bowling Bowley, Tyldesley, and Denton. Not often have three batsmen of equal class looked more helpless, but Bowley and Tyldesley could at least plead that they fell to wonderful balls, Knox combining a deadly off break with his pace. When at 54 a blunder in running cost Hayward's wicket the match seemed all over, but Hayes and John Gunn – Hayes playing incomparably the better cricket – brought about a change, and shortly before half-past three the Players, with four wickets in hand, only wanted 90 to win. Lees made a great effort, and Lilley, who was very lame and had a substitute to run for him, also did well, but by a quarter past four the innings was over for 244, the Gentlemen thus winning by 45 runs.

## Gentlemen

| | | |
|---|---|---|
| Mr R. H. Spooner b Fielder | 5 – | c Fielder b Lees ............114 |
| Mr H. K. Foster b Fielder | 10 – | c Hayward b Lees ............ 67 |
| Mr P. Perrin lbw b Fielder | 2 – | c Hayes b Lees ............ 8 |
| Hon. F. S. Jackson c Lilley b Fielder | 40 – | b Fielder ............ 2 |
| Mr B. J. T. Bosanquet c Lilley b Fielder | 56 – | c Lilley b Lees ............ 7 |
| Mr K. L. Hutchings c Lilley b Fielder | 2 – | b Fielder ............ 10 |
| Mr J. N. Crawford b Fielder | 0 – | c Hayes b Lees ............ 13 |
| Mr G. L. Jessop b Fielder | 12 – | not out ............ 73 |
| Mr H. Martyn c Haigh b Fielder | 26 – | c Bowley b Lees ............ 3 |
| Mr N. A. Knox not out | 6 – | c Rhodes b Fielder ............ 4 |
| Mr W. Brearley b Fielder | 0 – | b Fielder ............ 7 |
| B 6, w 1, n-b 1 | 8 | B 9, l-b 1, n-b 3 .......... 13 |
| | **167** | **321** |

## Players

| | | | |
|---|---|---|---|
| T. Hayward c Foster b Knox | 54 | – run out | 34 |
| F. Bowley b Knox | 1 | – b Knox | 0 |
| J. T. Tyldesley c and b Brearley | 5 | – b Knox | 4 |
| D. Denton b Crawford | 48 | – b Knox | 1 |
| E. G. Hayes lbw b Brearley | 5 | – lbw b Knox | 55 |
| W. Rhodes c Bosanquet b Knox | 1 | – c Bosanquet b Brearley | 19 |
| J. Gunn c Crawford b Knox | 13 | – b Knox | 42 |
| A. A. Lilley b Knox | 31 | – b Knox | 19 |
| W. Lees b Brearley | 13 | – c Foster b Brearley | 51 |
| S. Haigh not out | 2 | – c Jackson b Knox | 2 |
| A. Fielder b Brearley | 2 | – not out | 2 |
| B 16, l-b 2, w 1, n-b 5 | 24 | B 9, l-b 1, n-b 5 | 15 |
| | **199** | | **244** |

## Players' Bowling

| | Overs | Mdns | Runs | Wkts | Overs | Mdns | Runs | Wkts |
|---|---|---|---|---|---|---|---|---|
| Fielder | 24.5 | 1 | 90 | 10 | 32.5 | 3 | 131 | 4 |
| Gunn | 13 | 5 | 15 | — | 15 | 5 | 37 | — |
| Haigh | 5 | 2 | 11 | — | 8 | 1 | 42 | — |
| Lees | 5 | 1 | 15 | — | 27 | 6 | 92 | 6 |
| Rhodes | 11 | 3 | 28 | — | 5 | 2 | 6 | — |

## Gentlemen's Bowling

| | Overs | Mdns | Runs | Wkts | Overs | Mdns | Runs | Wkts |
|---|---|---|---|---|---|---|---|---|
| Brearley | 19.4 | 3 | 63 | 4 | 26 | 4 | 84 | 2 |
| Knox | 20 | 1 | 73 | 5 | 24.1 | 2 | 110 | 7 |
| Crawford | 9 | 2 | 24 | 1 | 4 | 1 | 11 | — |
| Jackson | 4 | — | 15 | — | 9 | 1 | 24 | — |

Umpires: J. E. West and J. Moss.

## THE OVAL MATCH

### Played at The Oval, July 10, 11, 12, 1913

No game more remarkable than the Gentlemen and Players Match at The Oval was seen last season. The only matter for regret was that, after three days of intensely interesting cricket, it had to be left drawn, the Players, when stumps were finally pulled up on Saturday evening being 98 runs behind with two wickets to fall. The Players were without Barnes, but despite the loss of his bowling, and the fact that the extra county match at Liverpool kept all the Yorkshire and Lancashire men away, they put a capital side into the field. In the light of after events, however, it was strange that George Gunn should not have been selected. The Gentlemen were by no means so rich in great names as in former years, the absence from first-class cricket last season of Fry and Spooner leaving the batting somewhat deficient in class, but for all that the Players narrowly escaped defeat. The match proved very attractive, the crowd on Saturday afternoon numbering about 9,000.

On the first day the weather was very gloomy and the wicket, at starting, a trifle soft. Still, finely as Albert Relf and Buckenham bowled, there was no adequate excuse for the deplorable way in which the Gentlemen, on winning the toss, opened their innings. In less than an hour seven wickets actually fell for 38 runs. An utter fiasco seemed in prospect, but Jessop, giving one of the finest displays of his life, saved the side. Out last, he hit up in an hour and ten minutes, 81 runs out of 111, his play, entirely free from fault, being such as, perhaps, no one else could have shown under the same circumstances. Needless to say, his wonderful innings delighted the spectators beyond measure. While Jessop and Falcon were together 58 runs were added for the last wicket in twenty-five minutes. Despite this hitting, however, the total only reached 139. Having got rid of their opponents so cheaply the Players scored 93 for two wickets, Tarrant at the close being not out 57. Play was twice stopped by rain, and just before six o'clock stumps were drawn, the weather being then very damp and gloomy. The Players looked to have the game in their hands when they went on batting on Friday morning, but another sensation was in store, the innings which had opened so well, being finished off for 131, or 8 runs behind. The atmosphere was very heavy, and no doubt Simms and Falcon, who bowled wonderfully well, were able to get on more swerve than usual, but bad batting had much to do with the collapse. Seven men were out to catches behind the wicket. The last eight wickets fell in an hour for 38 runs. In first and out last Tarrant, in his 74, hit eleven 4s. He played a fine game, and was especially strong on the leg side. Falcon had a truly extraordinary average during the morning, going on at 116 and taking five wickets in three overs and two balls, at a cost of only 8 runs.

Standing in a vastly better position than they could possibly have expected, the Gentlemen went in for the second time at a quarter to one, and when, just before half-past six, failing light caused stumps to be pulled up, their score stood at 292 for six wickets. Up to a certain point the batting was very steady, but after the fall of the third wicket Kidd hit away in fine style, he and Warner putting on 90 runs in less than an hour. Kidd quieted down after Warner was out, taking forty minutes to get his last 18 runs. Jessop did not play so well as in his first innings, but he finished up brilliantly and was 77 not out at the close.

Holding a lead of three hundred the Gentlemen, on Saturday morning, were naturally bent on getting runs with the least possible loss of time. They succeeded so well that, in an hour and a quarter, 132 runs were added for the loss of three more wickets, Warner, when he declared the innings closed, leaving his bowlers four hours and a half in which to get the Players out. For the first time in a Gentlemen and Players match, Jessop had the satisfaction of making a hundred. He was at the wickets something under two hours for his 107, scoring this number out of 163, and hitting a dozen 4s. Favoured by mistakes in the field, Simms scored 41 out of 59 in twenty-one minutes, making among other big hits a mighty on drive from Quaife's bowling clean out of The Oval.

Set to get 433 the Players, in order to win the match, would have had to score at the rate of 96 an hour. Tarrant and Hobbs started the innings at this pace, but with four wickets down for 116, the Players were in great danger of defeat. Late in the afternoon the position was again critical, the eighth wicket falling at a quarter past six, but Hardinge and Buckingham played out time. J. W. Hearne and Seymour divided honours in saving their side. While together they put on 146 runs for the fifth wicket. Hearne's great innings of 126, which lasted a little over three hours and a half, was in every way masterly. When 89 he had a narrow escape of being caught at slip, but this was almost his only mistake. He drove and hit to leg splendidly and was rarely or never at fault in defence. Seymour was very brilliant, hitting a 5 and eleven 4s. Warner's management of his bowling did not escape criticism, the afternoon being nearly over before Simms and Falcon were tried at the ends from which they had been so startlingly successful on the previous day. A change in the direction of the wind no doubt accounted for a policy which puzzled the spectators, Falcon, in particular, being largely dependent on his swerve. D. C. Robinson made a most successful first appearance for the Gentlemen, keeping wicket admirably and playing an innings of 58.

## Gentlemen

| | | | |
|---|---|---|---|
| Mr P. F. Warner b Buckenham | 0 | – c Strudwick b Tarrant | 32 |
| Mr M. C. Bird lbw b Relf | 0 | – not out | 34 |
| Mr R. B. Lagden c Strudwick b Relf | 1 | – lbw b Gunn | 0 |
| Mr A. P. Day c Seymour b Buckenham | 0 | – b Buckenham | 25 |
| Mr E. L. Kidd c and b Buckenham | 18 | – b Relf | 69 |
| Mr P. G. H. Fender c Seymour b Relf | 0 | – b Gunn | 10 |
| Mr J. W. H. T. Douglas lbw b Relf | 6 | – c Buckenham b Hearne | 37 |
| Mr G. L. Jessop c Seymour b Gunn | 81 | – c Hobbs b Tarrant | 107 |
| Mr D. C. Robinson c Relf b Hearne | 8 | – Gunn | 58 |
| Mr H. L. Simms c Strudwick b Tarrant | 1 | – c Gunn b Relf | 41 |
| Mr M. Falcon not out | 18 | – not out | 5 |
| B 5, l-b 1 | 6 | B 4, l-b 2 | 6 |
| | **139** | | **(9 wkts dec.) 424** |

## Players

| | | | |
|---|---|---|---|
| J. B. Hobbs lbw b Douglas | 16 | – b Simms | 20 |
| F. A. Tarrant c Bird b Falcon | 74 | – c Falcon b Simms | 41 |
| E. Humphreys c Kidd b Falcon | 8 | – c Robinson b Falcon | 3 |
| J. W. Hearne c Day b Simms | 14 | – c Falcon b Simms | 126 |
| W. G. Quaife c Kidd b Simms | 4 | – b Fender | 14 |
| James Seymour c Robinson b Simms | 0 | – run out | 80 |
| J. Gunn c Robinson b Falcon | 4 | – c Jessop b Simms | 4 |
| A. E. Relf c Robinson b Falcon | 4 | – lbw b Simms | 1 |
| H. T. W. Hardinge c and b Falcon | 0 | – not out | 19 |
| C. P. Buckenham c Day b Falcon | 4 | – not out | 8 |
| H. Strudwick not out | 0 | | |
| B 1, l-b 1, n-b 1 | 3 | B 10, l-b 2, w 5, n-b 1 | 18 |
| | **131** | | **334** |

## Players' Bowling

| | Overs | Mdns | Runs | Wkts | Overs | Mdns | Runs | Wkts |
|---|---|---|---|---|---|---|---|---|
| Buckenham | 11 | 4 | 34 | 3 | 32 | 3 | 136 | 1 |
| Relf | 11 | 2 | 37 | 4 | 44 | 16 | 95 | 2 |
| Tarrant | 7 | 1 | 32 | 1 | 16 | 7 | 32 | 2 |
| Hearne | 6 | 1 | 30 | 1 | 13 | — | 70 | 1 |
| Gunn | 0.3 | — | — | 1 | 25 | 6 | 68 | 3 |
| Humphreys | | | | | 6 | 1 | 17 | — |

## Gentlemen's Bowling

| | Overs | Mdns | Runs | Wkts | Overs | Mdns | Runs | Wkts |
|---|---|---|---|---|---|---|---|---|
| Falcon | 14.2 | 2 | 58 | 6 | 26 | 5 | 87 | 1 |
| Simms | 10 | 2 | 24 | 3 | 22 | 3 | 80 | 5 |
| Douglas | 8 | 2 | 31 | 1 | 14 | 4 | 24 | — |
| Day | 1 | — | 4 | — | 3 | — | 13 | — |
| Bird | 4 | 1 | 11 | — | 4 | 1 | 16 | — |
| Kidd | | | | | 5 | — | 22 | — |
| Fender | | | | | 15 | 1 | 68 | 1 |
| Jessop | | | | | 1 | — | 6 | — |

Umpires: A. E. Trott and A. J. Atfield.

# THE SCARBOROUGH MATCH

### Played at Scarborough, September 4, 5, 6, 1913

The second fixture of the Scarborough Festival produced a memorable fight, the Gentlemen winning in the end by 6 runs. So even was the scoring that the highest of the four totals was 270 and the lowest 245 – in every way an ideal match. On the first day Jessop, by his great hitting, dwarfed everything else in the cricket. In an hour and three-quarters he scored 119 out of 172, among his hits being two 6s and seventeen 4s. He took all sorts of risks, but though the ball was often in the air no catch went to hand. M. C. Bird gave a fine display of driving, and Simms and W. S. Bird helped Jessop to such good purpose that the sixth wicket added 62 runs and the seventh 71. When bad light caused stumps to be drawn at a quarter to six the Players had lost three wickets for 65.

On the second day the game was full of incident. Relf and Hirst batted finely, but the feature of the Players' innings was the tremendous hitting of Hitch, whose 53 not out included three 6s. He and Dolphin put on 67 runs for the last wicket in less than half an hour. The Gentlemen opened their second innings very well, the score being up to 143 when the third wicket went down. Then, however, Rhodes and Hitch bowled in irresistible form and before play ceased five more wickets fell for 11 runs. Faulkner, not out 35, found such a capable partner in Leveson-Gower on Saturday morning that the ninth wicket added 95 runs, the innings ending for 255. Faulkner, who had the satisfaction of getting his hundred, ought to have been stumped with his score at 31, and gave a chance in the slips when 98, but apart from these mistakes he played admirably for about three hours.

The Players required 252 to win, three hours and twenty minutes, roughly speaking, being left for cricket. The early batting was disastrous, and when, soon after four o'clock the sixth wicket fell at 63, an easy victory for the Gentlemen seemed in prospect. Hirst and Booth, however, quite altered the match, putting on 80 runs together. Still with eight men out for 144, the Players again looked a beaten side. At this point Hitch joined Booth, and at once began to hit the bowling all over the field. When six o'clock came – the time for drawing stumps – the score was 225, and it was agreed to play the match out. The hitting continued for two or three overs, but at 240 Booth was caught at the wicket, and Blythe only stayed while 5 runs were being added, the Gentlemen, amid a scene of great excitement, winning the game by 6 runs. Hitch hit four 6s and seven 4s in his 68 not out, he and Booth actually scoring 96 runs together in thirty-five minutes. Hitch was afterwards presented with a souvenir of the match by Lord Londesborough.

## Gentlemen

| | | |
|---|---|---|
| Mr F. L. Fane c Seymour b Booth | 9 | – b Hitch ..... 21 |
| Mr M. C. Bird b Hearne | 56 | – b Hitch ..... 42 |
| Mr G. A. Faulkner c Hirst b Booth | 1 | – c Hirst b Hitch ..... 101 |
| Mr J. R. Mason b Hitch | 23 | – c Hobbs b Rhodes ..... 34 |
| Mr G. L. Jessop b Blythe | 119 | – c Hearne b Rhodes ..... 2 |
| Mr J. W. H. T. Douglas b Hitch | 5 | – c and b Rhodes ..... 2 |
| Mr H. L. Simms b Booth | 20 | – b Hitch ..... 2 |
| Mr W. S. Bird b Blythe | 23 | – c Dolphin b Hitch ..... 0 |
| Mr H. D. G. Leveson-Gower c Seymour b Relf | 3 | – not out ..... 29 |
| Mr D. W. Carr not out | 0 | – c Dolphin b Hitch ..... 0 |
| Mr G. G. Napier b Blythe | 0 | – b Hitch ..... 1 |
| B 2, l-b 5 | 7 | B 20, n-b 1 ..... 21 |
| | **266** | **255** |

## Players

| | | |
|---|---|---|
| J. B. Hobbs b Napier | 26 | – c Douglas b Napier ..... 6 |
| W. Rhodes b Douglas | 11 | – c W. S. Bird b Douglas ..... 22 |
| James Seymour b Napier | 21 | – b Napier ..... 3 |
| J. W. Hearne c W. S. Bird b Simms | 3 | – b Douglas ..... 12 |
| E. Humphreys run out | 1 | – c and b Simms ..... 3 |
| A. E. Relf b Faulkner | 65 | – c Jessop b Simms ..... 6 |
| G. H. Hirst b Faulkner | 51 | – lbw b Napier ..... 49 |
| M. W. Booth c Douglas b Faulkner | 2 | – c W. C. Bird b Douglas ..... 56 |
| W. Hitch not out | 53 | – not out ..... 68 |
| C. Blythe c Leveson-Gower b Faulkner | 0 | – c Napier b Jessop ..... 4 |
| A. Dolphin c M. C. Bird b Faulkner | 21 | – b Douglas ..... 1 |
| B 10, l-b 5, n-b 1 | 16 | B 8, l-b 6, n-b 1 ..... 15 |
| | **270** | **245** |

**Players' Bowling**

| | Overs | Mdns | Runs | Wkts | Overs | Mdns | Runs | Wkts |
|---|---|---|---|---|---|---|---|---|
| Booth ........... | 19 | 3 | 60 | 3 | 10 | 2 | 39 | — |
| Blythe ........... | 15.1 | 3 | 50 | 3 | 15 | 2 | 41 | — |
| Hearne .......... | 8 | — | 34 | 1 | 5 | — | 14 | — |
| Hitch ........... | 8 | 2 | 60 | 2 | 22.1 | 4 | 59 | 7 |
| Hirst ........... | 3 | — | 19 | — | 7 | 1 | 24 | — |
| Relf ............ | 9 | 1 | 36 | 1 | 10 | 3 | 28 | — |
| Rhodes .......... | | | | | 10 | 4 | 29 | 3 |

**Gentlemen's Bowling**

| | Overs | Mdns | Runs | Wkts | Overs | Mdns | Runs | Wkts |
|---|---|---|---|---|---|---|---|---|
| Napier .......... | 17 | 3 | 46 | 2 | 22 | 7 | 64 | 3 |
| Simms .......... | 13 | — | 58 | 1 | 8 | — | 32 | 2 |
| Douglas ......... | 10 | — | 33 | 1 | 19 | 4 | 53 | 4 |
| Carr ............ | 9 | 2 | 39 | — | 3 | — | 30 | — |
| Mason .......... | 5 | 2 | 10 | — | 3 | — | 11 | — |
| Faulkner ........ | 13.2 | 2 | 68 | 5 | 10 | — | 35 | — |
| Jessop .......... | | | | | 1 | — | 5 | 1 |

Umpires: G. P. Harrison and H. Butt.

# LONDON COUNTY MATCHES

## LONDON COUNTY v SURREY

Played at Crystal Palace, May 3, 4, 5, 1900

A magnificent wicket had been prepared at the Palace and so brilliant was the batting that at no time did there seem any prospect of playing the match out. As will be seen from the score below three innings were completed and 1,126 runs scored. Mr Grace had hoped to put a very strong team into the field, but he suffered two or three disappointments, chief among them being the non-appearance of Ranjitsinhji. Under the circumstances the London County did wonderfully well to head Surrey by 105 runs on the first innings. Rain restricted the first day's play to about a couple of hours, but as it turned out, the wicket during the remainder of the game did not suffer. C. L. Townsend played so splendidly for his 141 as to suggest a repetition of the success he had enjoyed in 1899, but for some time afterwards he did not show the same form. The batting of Haward and Lockwood for Surrey, and Fry for the London County was also quite exceptional in quality. Hayward was out in his first innings in a very unlucky way, a ball driven back by Lockwood with great force going off the bowler's hand into the wicket, while Hayward, who had backed up, was outside the crease. On the third day Sir George White, recently back in England after the siege of Ladysmith, drove on to the ground with Lady White and had an enthusiastic reception.

### Surrey

| | | | |
|---|---:|---|---:|
| W. Brockwell c Board b Townsend | 28 | – c Board b Townsend | 19 |
| F. C. Holland st Board b Townsend | 17 | – b Woodcock | 79 |
| E. G. Hayes c Fry b Townsend | 20 | – b Smith | 39 |
| W. H. Lockwood c Townsend b Woodcock | 95 | – b Woodcock | 68 |
| T. Hayward run out | 55 | – c Board b Beldam | 108 |
| Mr V. F. S. Crawford c Braund b Townsend | 11 | – b Woodcock | 0 |
| W. Lees c Beldam b Townsend | 14 | – c Beldam b Woodcock | 27 |
| Mr D. L. A. Jephson not out | 40 | – c Board b Gamble | 39 |
| H. Wood lbw b Townsend | 16 | – c Board b Woodcock | 16 |
| E. H. L. Nice c Fry b Woodcock | 1 | – c Fry b Gamble | 0 |
| T. Richardson c and b Townsend | 3 | – not out | 4 |
| B 2, l-b 2 | 4 | B 5, l-b 3, w 5, n-b 1 | 14 |
| | **304** | | **413** |

### London County

| | | | |
|---|---:|---|---:|
| Mr W. G. Grace c Holland b Richardson | 13 | J. H. Board run out | 16 |
| Mr C. B. Fry c Crawford b Richardson | 97 | Smith b Richardson | 22 |
| L. Braund c Nice b Richardson | 69 | Gamble not out | 4 |
| Mr C. L. Townsend c Wood b Lockwood | 141 | A. Woodcock b Lockwood | 9 |
| Mr G. W. Beldam b Brockwell | 20 | B 2, l-b 2 | 4 |
| H. Wrathall c Wood b Brockwell | 11 | | |
| Mr S. M. Tindall b Lockwood | 3 | | **409** |

### London County Bowling

| | Overs | Mdns | Runs | Wkts | Overs | Mdns | Runs | Wkts |
|---|---|---|---|---|---|---|---|---|
| Woodcock | 24 | 2 | 118 | 2 | 27 | 4 | 121 | 5 |
| Smith | 10 | — | 55 | — | 12 | 1 | 59 | 1 |
| Townsend | 22.5 | — | 99 | 7 | 8 | — | 55 | 1 |
| Gamble | 2 | 1 | 7 | — | 29.2 | 4 | 100 | 2 |
| Grace | 7 | 2 | 21 | — | | | | |
| Braund | | | | | 5 | — | 26 | — |
| Beldam | | | | | 12 | 2 | 38 | 1 |

**Surrey Bowling**

|            | Overs | Mdns | Runs | Wkts |
|------------|-------|------|------|------|
| Richardson | 27    | 2    | 122  | 4    |
| Brockwell  | 16    | —    | 81   | 2    |
| Lockwood   | 23.2  | 3    | 100  | 3    |
| Nice       | 7     | —    | 26   | —    |
| Lees       | 10    | 1    | 46   | —    |
| Hayward    | 7     | —    | 30   | —    |

Umpires: V. A. Titchmarsh and J. Lillywhite.

# LONDON COUNTY v CAMBRIDGE UNIVERSITY

## Played at Crystal Palace, June 17, 18, 19, 1901

With Day and Wilson absent, Cambridge, without accomplishing anything very remarkable, yet did a good performance remaining in the whole of the opening day and scoring 320 for nine wickets. The honours fell to Robertson and Dowson. The Cambridge total, however, was completely eclipsed by London County for whom Grace and Quaife obtained 163 for the first partnership. Quaife hit a five and sixteen 4s, and was batting two hours and fifty minutes. After five wickets had fallen for 236, Smith and Lilley played magnificently. Their stand yielded 241 runs in two hours and five minutes – the professional just failing to reach his 100. Smith, was not out 124 with the figures at 486 for six wickets on Tuesday evening, and on Wednesday he made nineteen more, his only mistake in two hours and forty minutes being a chance when 100. He hit twenty-four 4s. Facing a majority of 231, the Light Blues broke down in batting, and were beaten by an innings and 73 runs. The feature of the last afternoon was the extraordinary success of Ranjitsinhji's bowling.

### Cambridge University

| | | | |
|---|---:|---|---:|
| Mr H. K. Longman c Smith b Braund | 8 | – b Ranjitsinhji | 39 |
| Mr L. V. Harper c Murdoch b Braund | 45 | – b Hampson | 9 |
| Mr P. R. Johnson c Colegrave b Quaife | 18 | – c Hampson b Braund | 48 |
| Mr W. P. Robertson c and b Quaife | 78 | – c Grace b Ranjitsinhji | 4 |
| Mr J. Gilman st Lilley b Quaife | 9 | – st Lilley b Braund | 12 |
| Mr R. N. R. Blaker c Quaife b Braund | 36 | – c Smith b Ranjitsinhji | 14 |
| Mr E. M. Dowson not out | 77 | – c Gale b Braund | 4 |
| Mr A. E. Hind st Lilley b Quaife | 6 | – not out | 5 |
| Mr A. H. C. Fargus b Quaife | 31 | – c and b Ranjitsinhji | 0 |
| Mr L. T. Driffield b Grace | 7 | – b Ranjitsinhji | 4 |
| Mr G. Howard-Smith b Hampson | 11 | – c and b Ranjitsinhji | 13 |
| B 9, l-b 8, w 1, n-b 3 | 21 | B 6 | 6 |
| | **347** | | **158** |

### London County

| | | | |
|---|---:|---|---:|
| Mr W. G. Grace c Blaker b Fargus | 72 | Mr H. Colegrave not out | 36 |
| W. G. Quaife b Johnson | 108 | Mr P. G. Gale b Dowson | 15 |
| K. S. Ranjitsinhji c Blaker b Fargus | 22 | Mr J. Hampson c Harper b Dowson | 17 |
| L. C. Braund c Hind b Fargus | 16 | | |
| Mr W. L. Murdoch c Blaker b Johnson | 0 | B 29, l-b 12, w 2, n-b 9 | 52 |
| A. A. Lilley b Johnson | 97 | | |
| Mr W. Smith b Johnson | 143 | (9 wkts dec.) | 578 |

Mr W. F. L. Frith did not bat.

## London County Bowling

| | Overs | Mdns | Runs | Wkts | Overs | Mdns | Runs | Wkts |
|---|---|---|---|---|---|---|---|---|
| Grace . . . . . . . . . . . | 28 | 8 | 56 | 1 | | | | |
| Braund . . . . . . . . . . | 49 | 4 | 171 | 3 | 26 | 7 | 65 | 3 |
| Quaife . . . . . . . . . | 37 | 8 | 79 | 5 | 6 | 2 | 16 | — |
| Ranjitsinhji . . . . . . . | 4 | — | 19 | — | 13.3 | 2 | 53 | 6 |
| Hampson . . . . . . . . | 0.4 | — | 1 | 1 | 7 | 1 | 18 | 1 |

## Cambridge University Bowling

| | Overs | Mdns | Runs | Wkts |
|---|---|---|---|---|
| Dowson . . . . . . . . . | 28 | 7 | 95 | 2 |
| Fargus . . . . . . . . . . | 30 | 1 | 112 | 3 |
| Howard-Smith . . . . . | 12 | 2 | 48 | — |
| Driffield . . . . . . . . . | 18 | 3 | 92 | — |
| Johnson . . . . . . . . . | 25 | 3 | 99 | 4 |
| Hind . . . . . . . . . . . . | 21 | 6 | 50 | — |
| Longman . . . . . . . . | 5 | — | 30 | — |

Umpires: W. Hearn and J. Phillips.

## LONDON COUNTY v MCC AND GROUND

Played at the Crystal Palace, August 8, 9, 10, 1901

Some remarkable scoring was witnessed in this match, three full days' cricket producing 1,134 runs for the loss of twenty wickets. London County scored 399 for six wickets on the first afternoon, their veteran captain making his first and only hundred in first-class cricket during the season, and Walker, the Surrey amateur, compiling 209 not out. While the pair were together they added 281 in less than three hours. Grace was dismissed at 332, having played faultlessly for three hours and fifty minutes. Walker, who only made two mistakes, increased his figures to 222, a brilliant piece of work occupying four hours and twenty minutes and including thirty-one 4s. When the London County had been got rid of for 633, there was almost equally good work accomplished by the MCC. The visitors had two wickets down for 201 on Friday, and were ultimately dismissed for 501. As it had been agreed to decide on the first innings, victory rested with London County by 132 runs. Hearne was batting three hours and twenty-five minutes, and Doll five hours and three-quarters. It will be noticed that the bowling was absurdly weak on both sides.

### London County

| | |
|---|---|
| Mr W. G. Grace c Hearne b Atfield . . . . . . .132 | Mr J. Gilman c Doll b Fernie . . . . . . . . . . . 64 |
| Mr W. G. Grace jun. c Murrell b Needham . 32 | Mr W. G. Dyas c Fernie b Hearne . . . . . . . . 83 |
| Mr W. L. Murdoch b Needham . . . . . . . . . . 0 | H. W. Murch c Coode b Needham . . . . . . . 58 |
| Mr L. Walker st Murrell b Hearne . . . . . . .222 | F. E. Smith not out . . . . . . . . . . . . . . . . . . . . 6 |
| Mr W. Smith b Atfield . . . . . . . . . . . . . . . . 5 | B 5, l-b 1, w 3, n-b 3 . . . . . . . . . . 12 |
| Mr P. G Gale c Murrell b Atfield . . . . . . . . . 3 | |
| Mr J. E. Raphael run out . . . . . . . . . . . . . . 16 | 633 |

### MCC and Ground

| | |
|---|---|
| Ahsan-ul Hak b F. Smith . . . . . . . . . . . . . . 10 | Mr R. H. Mallett b Grace sen. . . . . . . . . . . . 8 |
| G. G. Hearne b Grace sen . . . . . . . . . . . . .115 | Mr Oliver Marks lbw b Grace sen. . . . . . . . . 1 |
| Mr A. T. Coode c Walker b F. Smith . . . . . . 20 | Mr A. E. Fernie b Grace jun. . . . . . . . . . . . 4 |
| Mr C. C. T. Doll not out . . . . . . . . . . . . . .224 | E. Needham lbw b Grace jun. . . . . . . . . . . . 9 |
| H. R. Murrell c Gale b Grace sen. . . . . . . . . 17 | B 27, l-b 14, n-b 2 . . . . . . . . . . . . 43 |
| Mr N. O. Tagart b Grace sen . . . . . . . . . . . 30 | |
| Atfield c Gilman b F. Smith . . . . . . . . . . . . 20 | 501 |

## MCC Bowling

|            | Overs | Mdns | Runs | Wkts |
|------------|-------|------|------|------|
| Hearne     | 49.1  | 15   | 122  | 2    |
| Fernie     | 20    | 1    | 69   | 1    |
| Needham    | 30    | 2    | 132  | 3    |
| Ahsan-ul Hak | 11  | —    | 71   | —    |
| Murrell    | 11    | 1    | 61   | —    |
| Marks      | 9     | —    | 36   | —    |
| Mallett    | 3     | —    | 28   | —    |
| Atfield    | 28    | 4    | 102  | 3    |

## London County Bowling

|            | Overs | Mdns | Runs | Wkts |
|------------|-------|------|------|------|
| Grace, sen | 64    | 13   | 159  | 5    |
| Raphael    | 6     | 1    | 24   | —    |
| F. Smith   | 45    | 12   | 105  | 3    |
| Grace, jun | 27    | 5    | 74   | 2    |
| Walker     | 28    | 6    | 87   | —    |
| Dyas       | 5     | 2    | 5    | —    |
| Gilman     | 3     | 3    | 4    | —    |

Umpires: V. A. Titchmarsh and W. A. J. West.

# OTHER MATCHES

## WEST INDIANS v GLOUCESTERSHIRE

### Played at Bristol, June 28, 29, 30, 1900

As Gloucestershire in meeting the West Indians put a far more representative team into the field than did most of the counties, their overwhelming victory by an innings and 216 runs was in no way surprising. The hitting of the county on the opening day was brilliant in the extreme, 518 runs being scored for the loss of seven wickets. While Jessop was in 201 runs were actually scored in an hour, the great hitter's share of that number being 157.

## Gloucestershire

| | |
|---|---|
| Mr N. O. Tagart c Burton b Mignon ...... 9 | Mr O. E. Wreford-Brown not out ........ 44 |
| Mr W. S. A. Brown c Mignon b Burton .... 60 | Langdon c Sproston b Burton .......... 50 |
| J. H. Board c Goodman b Burton ........ 3 | A. Paish b Burton .................... 0 |
| Mr H. J. Hodgkins b Burton ............ 0 | Mr F. G. Roberts b Mignon ............ 11 |
| H. Wrathall c Constantine b Mignon ......123 | B 15, l-b 6, n-b 1.............. 22 |
| Mr C. L. Townsend b Mignon ...........140 | ____ |
| Mr G. L. Jessop c Hinds b Mignon .......157 | 619 |

## West Indians

| | | |
|---|---|---|
| Mr S. W. Sproston c Paish b Townsend ........... | 1 – c Townsend b Paish ............. | 36 |
| Mr C. A. Ollivierre c Paish b Roberts ....... | 15 – run out ...................... | 42 |
| Mr G. C. Learmond c Langdon b Townsend ....... | 0 – c Board b Langdon ............. | 17 |
| Mr P. A. Goodman run out ................ | 38 – c Paish b Roberts ............. | 34 |
| Mr F. Hinds lbw b Roberts ................. | 8 – c Board b Townsend ........... | 34 |
| Mr L. Constantine b Roberts ................. | 21 – c sub. b Brown ................ | 65 |
| W. J. Burton b Roberts ................. | 0 – c sub. b Townsend ............. | 11 |
| Mr W. Bowning not out .................... | 5 – c Townsend b Langdon .......... | 21 |
| Mr A. Warner b Roberts .................... | 3 – lbw b Langdon ................. | 24 |
| Mr W. H. Mignon b Townsend ............. | 1 – c Board b Townsend ............ | 10 |
| S. Woods b Townsend ................... | 0 – not out ...................... | 5 |
| B 1, l-b 2, n-b 1.................... | 4          B 7, n-b 1 .............. | 8 |
| | 96 | 307 |

**West Indians' Bowling**

|  | Overs | Mdns | Runs | Wkts |
|---|---|---|---|---|
| Ollivierre ......... | 23 | 2 | 137 | — |
| Burton ........... | 25 | 4 | 68 | 5 |
| Woods ........... | 33 | 5 | 141 | — |
| Mignon .......... | 33.3 | 5 | 162 | 5 |
| Hinds ............ | 3 | — | 72 | — |
| Goodman ......... | 7 | 1 | 17 | — |

**Gloucestershire Bowling**

|  | Overs | Mdns | Runs | Wkts | Overs | Mdns | Runs | Wkts |
|---|---|---|---|---|---|---|---|---|
| Townsend ........ | 16.3 | 1 | 53 | 4 | 17.1 | 1 | 62 | — |
| Roberts .......... | 16 | 8 | 39 | 5 | 18 | 4 | 50 | — |
| Langdon ......... |  |  |  |  | 13 | 3 | 57 | 3 |
| Brown ........... |  |  |  |  | 27 | 10 | 67 | 1 |
| Paish ............ |  |  |  |  | 15 | 2 | 63 | 1 |

## YORKSHIRE v REST OF ENGLAND

### Yardley Benefit Fund

#### Played at Lord's, September 12, 13, 14, 1901

It was originally arranged that the match for the benefit of William Yardley's widow and children should be played under the title of Lord Hawke's Eleven v Mr W. G. Grace's Eleven, but consequent on Yorkshire's brilliant doings it was changed to Yorkshire v The Rest of England. The England team won by an innings and 115 runs, inflicting on Yorkshire the second defeat sustained by the county during the season. C. B. Fry played a beautiful innings – his sixth hundred in succession in first-class matches – but the feature of the game was the astounding batting of Jessop, who has never hit in more wonderful form. At the end of the first afternoon, he was not out 176, and on the following morning he carried his score to 233. His innings -- the highest he has ever played in a first-class match – lasted two hours and a half, and comprised two 5s, thirty-three 4s, four 3s, twenty-four 2s, and thirty-one singles. He gave a very sharp chance to Wainwright at slip when he had made 81, and an absurdly easy one off Rhodes's bowling to Tunnicliffe at slip at 155, but considering the pace at which he scored his faulty strokes were few indeed. Yorkshire never looked like avoiding defeat, and soon after lunch time on Saturday the match was over. Trott bowled splendidly. As a benefit, the match satisfied all reasonable expectations, the proceeds, including subscriptions, amounting to about £350.

### Rest of England

| | |
|---|---|
| Mr A. O. Jones c Tunnicliffe b Smith ...... 65 | Mr H. D. G. Leveson-Gower b Hirst ...... 0 |
| Mr P. F. Warner c Wainwright b Rhodes .. 29 | A. E. Trott b Hirst .................... 0 |
| Mr G. W. Beldam c Tunnicliffe b Rhodes .. 54 | Wilson not out ....................... 4 |
| Mr C. B. Fry c Hirst b Rhodes .........105 | Mr R. B. Brooks b Hirst ............... 4 |
| Mr G. L. Jessop b Hirst ...............233 | B 7, l-b 3 .................... 10 |
| J. Gunn b Whitehead .................. 21 | ——— |
| Mr J. H. Sinclair b Hirst ............... 1 | 526 |

### Yorkshire

| | | | |
|---|---|---|---|
| J. Tunnicliffe b Jones | 27 | – b Trott | 9 |
| J. T. Brown st Brooks b Jones | 12 | – lbw b Trott | 41 |
| D. Denton lbw b Trott | 12 | – c Wilson b Trott | 2 |
| Mr T. L. Taylor lbw b Trott | 1 | – st Brooks b Trott | 0 |
| Lord Hawke b Trott | 28 | – lbw b Trott | 1 |
| G. H. Hirst c Brooks b Sinclair | 48 | – b Trott | 5 |
| Mr E. Smith b Trott | 52 | – not out | 59 |
| W. Rhodes c and b Sinclair | 26 | – c and b Trott | 15 |
| Lees Whitehead not out | 14 | – b Wilson | 6 |
| D. Hunter c Warner b Trott | 1 | – c Warner b Trott | 2 |
| E. Wainwright absent hurt | 0 | – b Sinclair | 30 |
| B 6, l-b 2 | 8 | B 9, l-b 2, w 1 | 12 |
| | **229** | | **182** |

### Yorkshire Bowling

| | Overs | Mdns | Runs | Wkts |
|---|---|---|---|---|
| Hirst | 26.3 | 5 | 92 | 5 |
| Rhodes | 43 | 6 | 179 | 3 |
| Wainwright | 9 | 2 | 49 | — |
| Brown | 9 | — | 53 | — |
| Smith | 19 | 4 | 75 | 1 |
| Whitehead | 14 | 1 | 68 | 1 |

### Rest of England Bowling

| | Overs | Mdns | Runs | Wkts | Overs | Mdns | Runs | Wkts |
|---|---|---|---|---|---|---|---|---|
| Wilson | 18 | 2 | 50 | — | 16 | 5 | 24 | 1 |
| Trott | 27.5 | 4 | 86 | 5 | 29.5 | 8 | 84 | 8 |
| Jones | 6 | 1 | 29 | 2 | | | | |
| Gunn | 6 | 2 | 23 | — | | | | |
| Sinclair | 10 | 2 | 33 | 2 | 13 | 3 | 62 | 1 |

Umpires: V. A. Titchmarsh and W. A. J. West.

## MR BOSANQUET'S TEAM v GENTLEMEN OF PHILADELPHIA

Played at the Mannheim Ground, Philadelphia, October 4, 5, 7, 1901

The Philadelphians had an ample revenge for their previous defeat, winning the match in the easiest fashion by 229 runs. They made a fine start on winning the toss and never lost their advantage. R. D. Brown's 103 – an admirable innings – is the only score of a hundred made by an American cricketer against a visiting team since 1892. The Englishmen did not bat at all well, and found the bowling of King and P. H. Clark far too good for them. King proved that he had not lost the swerve which made his bowling so difficult when he was in England, and Clark at the end of the game took his last five wickets in seven balls.

## Gentlemen of Philadelphia

| | | | | |
|---|---|---|---|---|
| C. C. Morris lbw b Wilson | 55 | – b Dowson | 17 |
| F. H. Bohlen b More | 60 | – b Dowson | 10 |
| J. B. King b Wilson | 2 | – c Mitchell b More | 4 |
| J. A. Lester b More | 0 | – c Wilson b More | 69 |
| A. M. Wood lbw b Moore | 13 | – b More | 2 |
| R. D. Brown c Mitchell b Wilson | 103 | – c Crawford b Wilson | 31 |
| N. Z. Graves b Wilson | 29 | – c Bosanquet b More | 1 |
| E. M. Cregar b Hollins | 4 | – b Dowson | 15 |
| P. H. Clark b More | 12 | – b More | 6 |
| T. C. Jordan c More b Wilson | 16 | – b More | 12 |
| W. Graham not out | 1 | – not out | 4 |
| Extras | 17 | Extras | 15 |
| | **312** | | **186** |

## Mr Bosanquet XI

| | | | | |
|---|---|---|---|---|
| E. R. Wilson c Lester b King | 7 | – c Jordan b Clark | 9 |
| W. E. Harrison c Wood b King | 15 | – b Clark | 0 |
| B. J. T. Bosanquet c Morris b King | 37 | – st Jordan b King | 1 |
| F. Mitchell c Cregar b Clark | 35 | – c Morris b King | 17 |
| A. M. Hollins b Clark | 1 | – not out | 25 |
| V. F. S. Crawford c King b Clark | 5 | – c Cregar b King | 0 |
| E. M. Dowson c and b King | 12 | – b Clark | 10 |
| R. E. More b King | 2 | – st Jordan b Clark | 0 |
| P. R. Johnson c Jordan b King | 4 | – b Clark | 0 |
| R. O. Schwarz not out | 33 | – b Clark | 21 |
| I. U. Parkin c King b Clark | 2 | – b Clark | 0 |
| Extras | 13 | Extras | 20 |
| | **166** | | **103** |

### Mr Bosanquet XI Bowling

| | Overs | Mdns | Runs | Wkts | Overs | Mdns | Runs | Wkts |
|---|---|---|---|---|---|---|---|---|
| More | 34 | 5 | 104 | 4 | 24.1 | 2 | 62 | 6 |
| Bosanquet | 11 | 3 | 44 | — | 9 | 2 | 32 | — |
| Dowson | 12 | 3 | 33 | — | 16 | 3 | 47 | 3 |
| Wilson | 17.3 | 5 | 100 | 5 | 24 | 6 | 30 | 1 |
| Hollins | 4 | — | 19 | 1 | | | | |

### Gentlemen of Philadelphia Bowling

| | Overs | Mdns | Runs | Wkts | Overs | Mdns | Runs | Wkts |
|---|---|---|---|---|---|---|---|---|
| King | 31.2 | 8 | 74 | 6 | 13 | — | 58 | 3 |
| Graham | 9 | 2 | 31 | — | 1 | — | 3 | — |
| Clark | 21 | 3 | 48 | 4 | 11.5 | 4 | 22 | 7 |

## PHILADELPHIANS v LANCASHIRE

### Played at Manchester, July 6, 7, 8, 1903

In beating Lancashire by nine wickets, the Philadelphains enjoyed their greatest triumph.
For their victory they were mainly indebted to some magnificent bowling by King and the
splendid batting of Graves. When on the second morning an innings on each side had been
completed, there was little to choose in the positions, the Philadelphians holding the

comparatively small lead of 29. On Lancashire going in a second time, King bowled with remarkable effect, at one point taking five wickets in three overs for seven runs, and dismissing the last three batsmen in one over. King narrowly missed the distinction of taking all ten wickets in one innings, the fast bowler getting rid of every batsman except Radcliffe, who was run out. As a result of King's fine bowling, the Philadelphians were left with only 143 to get to win, and of this number Graves, who hit with great vigour, made 103. He was only batting for an hour and three-quarters, and among his figures were nineteen 4s.

### Lancashire

| | | |
|---|---:|---:|
| Mr A. C. MacLaren c Jordan b King | 0 – b King | 19 |
| Mr F. H. Hollins c and b King | 3 – b King | 0 |
| J. I'Anson b King | 0 – b King | 1 |
| G. Radcliffe c Wood b King | 34 – run out | 36 |
| Mr A. Eccles b Le Roy | 52 – b King | 0 |
| J. Sharp c Lester b Le Roy | 23 – b King | 3 |
| W. R. Cuttle b King | 0 – b King | 39 |
| Heap c Morris b Le Roy | 7 – not out | 38 |
| G. Littlewood not out | 5 – b King | 13 |
| Worsley run out | 1 – b King | 0 |
| Kermode c Le Roy b Clark | 23 – c Jordan b King | 2 |
| B 2, l-b 8 | 10      B 16, l-b 4 | 20 |
| | **158** | **171** |

### Philadelphians

| | | |
|---|---:|---:|
| Mr N. Z. Graves c Worsley b I'Anson | 19 – not out | 103 |
| Mr F. C. Sharpless run out | 19 – b Littlewood | 23 |
| Mr J. A. Lester lbw b I'Anson | 1 | |
| Mr F. B. King c Littlewood b I'Anson | 3 | |
| Mr F. H. Bohlen c Worsley b Cuttell | 43 | |
| Mr A. M. Wood b Cuttell | 17 | |
| Mr C. C. Morris b Cuttell | 11 | |
| Mr R. D. Brown lbw b Kermode | 26 – not out | 8 |
| Mr P. H. Clark b Kermode | 26 | |
| Mr P. N. Le Roy c I'Anson b Littlewood | 11 | |
| Mr T. C. Jordon not out | 0 | |
| B 4, l-b 7 | 11      B 9 | 9 |
| | **187** | **143** |

### Philadelphians' Bowling

| | Overs | Mdns | Runs | Wkts | Overs | Mdns | Runs | Wkts |
|---|---|---|---|---|---|---|---|---|
| King | 27 | 11 | 46 | 5 | 25.5 | 3 | 62 | 9 |
| Clark | 8.1 | 2 | 27 | 1 | 8 | 2 | 26 | — |
| Lester | 6 | — | 17 | — | 3 | — | 14 | — |
| Sharpless | 4 | — | 20 | — | 8 | 1 | 19 | — |
| Le Roy | 9 | 1 | 38 | 3 | 11 | — | 28 | — |
| Brown | | | | | 1 | — | 2 | — |

### Lancashire Bowling

| | Overs | Mdns | Runs | Wkts | Overs | Mdns | Runs | Wkts |
|---|---|---|---|---|---|---|---|---|
| Littlewood | 10.2 | 4 | 22 | 1 | 12 | 5 | 39 | 1 |
| Kermode | 24 | 4 | 50 | 2 | 16 | 6 | 26 | — |
| I'Anson | 22 | 7 | 42 | 3 | 6 | — | 37 | — |
| Cuttell | 23 | 8 | 49 | 3 | 5 | 2 | 25 | — |
| Heap | 4 | — | 13 | — | | | | |
| MacLaren | | | | | 1 | — | 7 | — |

Umpires: A. Pike and J. E. West.

## MCC TEAM v SEVENTEEN COLTS OF PHILADELPHIA AND A CAPTAIN

Played at St. Martin's, September 24, 25, 1907

In meeting the Colts of Philadelphia the MCC Team had the easiest of tasks. The best features of the match were the batting of Goldie and the bowling of Simpson-Hayward. Goldie, favoured with more than an ordinary share of luck, hit brilliantly, and when the Colts followed on 243 behind, Simpson-Hayward bowled his lobs with great effect.

### MCC Team

| | |
|---|---|
| Mr S. J. Snooke c Melville b L. Lee . . . . . . . 15 | Mr F. H. Browning c Pearce b Goodfellow . 14 |
| Mr K. O. Goldie b Evans . . . . . . . . . . . . . .147 | Mr H. Hesketh-Pritchard c L. Lee b Evans . 1 |
| Mr G. T. Branston b Pearce . . . . . . . . . . . . 29 | Mr J. W. H. T. Douglas not out . . . . . . . . . 2 |
| Mr R. O. Schwarz b Evans . . . . . . . . . . . . 11 | Capt. E. G. Wynyard c Winter b Lee . . . . . . 2 |
| Mr G. MacGregor c Townsend b Keenan . . 27 | |
| Mr G. H. Simpson-Hayward | Extras . . . . . . . . . . . . . . . . . . . . . 22 |
|                  c Evans b Pearce . 20 | |
| Mr L. P. Collins b Evans . . . . . . . . . . . . . . 39 | 329 |

### Philadelphia Colts

| | | | |
|---|---|---|---|
| Mr F. H. Abbot b Hesketh-Prichard . . . . . . . . . . . . . | 1 | – c Snooke b Simpson-Hayward . . . . | 0 |
| Mr M. Hitchen b Simpson-Hayward . . . . . . . . . . . . . | 4 | – c Wynyard b Simpson-Hayward . . . | 4 |
| Mr S. H. Hart c Schwarz b Hesketh-Pritchard . . . . . | 7 | – b Simpson-Hayward . . . . . . . . . . . | 1 |
| Mr W. S. Evans c and b Hesketh-Prichard . . . . . . . . | 3 | – b Simpson-Hayward . . . . . . . . . . . | 0 |
| Mr L. Lee c Wynyard b Snooke . . . . . . . . . . . . . . . . | 2 | – c Branston b Simpson-Hayward . . . | 18 |
| Mr A. N. Goodfellow b Douglas . . . . . . . . . . . . . . . | 8 | – b Simpson-Hayward . . . . . . . . . . . | 0 |
| Mr C. B. Hawley lbw b Simpson-Hayward . . . . . . . . | 2 | – b Simpson-Hayward . . . . . . . . . . . | 5 |
| Mr B. Lee b Schwarz . . . . . . . . . . . . . . . . . . . . . . . | 10 | – st MacGregor b Simpson-Hayward . | 4 |
| Mr A. B. Cartledge c Simpson-Hayward b Douglas . | 2 | – b Snooke . . . . . . . . . . . . . . . . . . . . | 5 |
| Mr E. L. Townsend c Wynyard b Hesketh-Prichard . | 8 | – b Simpson-Hayward . . . . . . . . . . . | 0 |
| Mr H. G. Pearce b Douglas . . . . . . . . . . . . . . . . . . . | 0 | – b Simpson-Hayward . . . . . . . . . . . | 1 |
| Mr E. Thayer hit wkt b Schwarz . . . . . . . . . . . . . . . | 2 | – b Snooke . . . . . . . . . . . . . . . . . . . . | 0 |
| Mr J. M. Shoemaker run out . . . . . . . . . . . . . . . . . . | 9 | – b Simpson-Hayward . . . . . . . . . . . | 0 |
| Mr R. L. Melville b Hesketh-Prichard . . . . . . . . . . . | 1 | – b Snooke . . . . . . . . . . . . . . . . . . . . | 1 |
| Mr C. H. Winter b Douglas . . . . . . . . . . . . . . . . . . . | 12 | – b Branston . . . . . . . . . . . . . . . . . . | 6 |
| Mr W. F. Keenan jun. c Branston b Wynyard . . . . . . | 0 | – not out . . . . . . . . . . . . . . . . . . . . . | 9 |
| Mr G. Priestman b Wynyard . . . . . . . . . . . . . . . . . . | 7 | – st MacGregor b Simpson-Hayward . | 2 |
| Mr S. Young not out . . . . . . . . . . . . . . . . . . . . . . . . | 0 | – b Simpson-Hayward . . . . . . . . . . . | 4 |
|         Extras . . . . . . . . . . . . . . . . . . . . . . . . . . . | 8 |      Extras . . . . . . . . . . . . . . . . | 10 |
| | 86 | | 70 |

### Colts of Philadelphia Bowling

| | Overs | Mdns | Runs | Wkts |
|---|---|---|---|---|
| Goodfellow . . . . . . . | 16 | 4 | 51 | 1 |
| Cartledge . . . . . . . . . | 10 | 2 | 38 | — |
| Pearce . . . . . . . . . . | 18 | 3 | 64 | 2 |
| Hawley . . . . . . . . . | 4 | 1 | 34 | — |
| L. Lee . . . . . . . . . . | 8.4 | 2 | 29 | 2 |
| Keenan . . . . . . . . . | 5 | — | 27 | 1 |
| Melville . . . . . . . . . | 1 | — | 14 | — |
| Evans . . . . . . . . . . . | 14 | 2 | 50 | 4 |

## MCC Team Bowling

| | Overs | Mdns | Runs | Wkts | Overs | Mdns | Runs | Wkts |
|---|---|---|---|---|---|---|---|---|
| Schwarz .......... | 10 | 5 | 11 | 2 | | | | |
| Hesketh-Prichard ... | 15 | 7 | 15 | 5 | | | | |
| Simpson-Hayward .. | 5 | 1 | 10 | 2 | 15 | 2 | 33 | 13 |
| Snooke .......... | 4 | 1 | 7 | 1 | 5 | 1 | 5 | 3 |
| Douglas .......... | 5 | — | 16 | 4 | | | | |
| Branston ........ | 3 | 1 | 3 | — | 9 | 2 | 22 | 1 |
| Wynyard ........ | 6 | — | 14 | 2 | | | | |

# HAMBLEDON v AN ENGLAND TEAM

### Played at Hambledon, September 10, 11, 12, 1908

For the first time for more than a hundred years Broad Half-Penny Down was the scene of a game between elevens styled Hambledon and An England Team. The match proved a great attraction and we have C. B. Fry's enthusiastic testimony to the keenness with which it was played. On the opening day a granite column commemorating the glories of the Hambledon Club was unveiled, the necessary funds having been raised by public subscription. In the absence of W. G. Grace the unveiling ceremony was performed by E. M. Sprot, the Hampshire captain. After being 153 behind on the first innings the England Team pulled the game round but in the end Hambledon won by five wickets, Fry playing in his finest form for 84 not out.

## An England Team

| | | | |
|---|---|---|---|
| A. E. Knight b Llewellyn ...................... | 9 | – c Deer b Newman .............. | 13 |
| Mr A. W. Roberts b Newman ................... | 11 | – b Newman ................... | 69 |
| E. H. Killick b Newman ...................... | 7 | – run out ..................... | 2 |
| J. T. Hearne b Newman ...................... | 4 | – b Newman .................... | 2 |
| Mr F. G. J. Ford c and b Newman ............ | 33 | – c Newman b Llewellyn ....... | 7 |
| Mr G. Wilder b Newman ...................... | 0 | – b Newman ................... | 43 |
| Mr G. L. Jessop b Newman ................... | 19 | – st Stone b Llewellyn ........... | 48 |
| A. E. Trott c Mead b Newman ................ | 4 | – c Mead b Llewellyn ........... | 5 |
| G. Leach lbw b Llewellyn ..................... | 2 | – c Wynyard b Langridge ....... | 80 |
| G. Dennett not out .......................... | 28 | – b Llewellyn .................. | 4 |
| H. R. Butt b Newman ........................ | 3 | – c Fry b Newman .............. | 9 |
| W. E. Astill run out ........................ | 1 | – not out ...................... | 8 |
| L-b 1, n-b 2 ..................... | 3 | B 7, l-b 8, w 2, n-b 2 ....... | 19 |
| | | | |
| | 124 | | 309 |

## Hambledon

| | | | |
|---|---|---|---|
| Mr C. B. Fry b Hearne........................ | 17 | – not out ...................... | 84 |
| Capt. E. G. Wynyard c Hearne b Dennett ......... | 59 | – not out ..................... | 9 |
| Mr E. M. Sprot c Wilder b Astill ............... | 9 | – c Trott b Jessop ............. | 17 |
| C. B. Llewellyn c Trott b Astill ............... | 0 | – b Hearne .................... | 2 |
| Rev. W. V. Jephson not out ................... | 114 | – st Butt b Dennett .............. | 14 |
| Mr G. N. Deer b Roberts ..................... | 10 | | |
| P. Mead b Dennett .......................... | 0 | – c Trott b Hearne .............. | 6 |
| A. Stone c Trott b Killick ................... | 6 | – b Astill ..................... | 2 |
| Mr E. Whalley-Tooker b Killick .............. | 6 | | |
| Mr W. Langridge b Dennett .................... | 2 | | |
| Mr E. M. C. Ede b Killick .................... | 4 | | |
| J. Newman c and b Killick ................... | 23 | – c and b Astill ................. | 5 |
| B 25, l-b 1, n-b 1 ................... | 27 | B 11, l-b 7, n-b 1 ......... | 19 |
| | | | |
| | 277 | | 158 |

## Hambledon Bowling

|  | Overs | Mdns | Runs | Wkts | Overs | Mdns | Runs | Wkts |
|---|---|---|---|---|---|---|---|---|
| Newman | 15.5 | 1 | 54 | 8 | 17.3 | 2 | 66 | 5 |
| Llewellyn | 12 | 1 | 60 | 2 | 26 | 3 | 133 | 4 |
| Deer | 3 | — | 7 | — | 3 | — | 11 | — |
| Mead |  |  |  |  | 10 | 1 | 38 | — |
| Langridge |  |  |  |  | 14 | 2 | 42 | 1 |

## An England Team's Bowling

|  | Overs | Mdns | Runs | Wkts | Overs | Mdns | Runs | Wkts |
|---|---|---|---|---|---|---|---|---|
| Hearne | 9 | — | 31 | 1 | 11 | 1 | 32 | 2 |
| Astill | 5 | — | 23 | 2 | 9 | — | 33 | 2 |
| Leach | 3 | — | 15 | — |  |  |  |  |
| Trott | 10 | 1 | 45 | — | 2 | — | 6 | — |
| Killick | 10.3 | 2 | 44 | 4 | 4.3 | 2 | 13 | — |
| Jessop | 4 | — | 9 | — | 13 | 5 | 30 | 1 |
| Dennett | 17 | — | 74 | 3 | 9 | — | 25 | 1 |
| Roberts | 2 | — | 9 | 1 |  |  |  |  |

Umpires: Tuck and W. Pate.

# GLAMORGAN v WORCESTERSHIRE

### Played at Cardiff, June 6, 7, 8, 1910

With the idea of improving their cricket, Glamorgan played four matches against first-class counties. In the first of the games, Worcestershire beat them very easily by an innings and 33 runs. Play did not begin until three o'clock on the first day, and then, batting first on a wicket that had been protected with tarpaulin, Glamorgan collapsed before the bowling of Cuffe, and were all out for 36. Cuffe hit the stumps eight times in securing nine wickets for five runs. Thanks to Pearson and H. K. Foster, who scored 61 for the second wicket, Worcestershire, after a blank second day owing to rain, led by 134 on the first innings, and with the wicket always difficult Glamorgan never looked like making a fight.

## Glamorgan

| | | | |
|---|---|---|---|
| Mr T. A. L. Whittington b Cuffe | 0 | – c Gaukrodger b Turner | 30 |
| Bancroft b Cuffe | 2 | – c and b Arnold | 6 |
| Mr E. R. Sweet-Escott c Foster b Conway | 4 | – run out | 2 |
| Mr S. Rees b Cuffe | 4 | – c Pearson b Bunting | 6 |
| Mr L. Robotham st Gaukrodger b Cuffe | 4 | – b Turner | 0 |
| Hacker b Cuffe | 1 | – c Conway b Collier | 4 |
| Mr H. G. Symonds b Cuffe | 0 | – c and b Bunting | 1 |
| Mr G. L. Rattenbury b Cuffe | 0 | – st Gaukrodger b Bunting | 36 |
| Smith b Cuffe | 9 | – c Collier b Turner | 2 |
| Nash b Cuffe | 0 | – c Pearson b Bunting | 8 |
| Creber not out | 8 | – not out | 0 |
| Extras | 4 | Extras | 6 |
| | **36** | | **101** |

## Worcestershire

| | |
|---|---|
| F. Pearson c Rattenbury b Creber ........ 69 | J. A. Cuffe c Nash b Creber ............ 0 |
| F. Bowley c Sweet-Escott b Creber ....... 15 | C. G. A. Collier not out ............... 5 |
| Mr H. K. Foster run out .............. 59 | G. Gaukrodger b Creber .............. 0 |
| E. Arnold b Hacker .................. 1 | A. J. Conway st Smith b Creber ........ 5 |
| Dr Bunting c Bancroft b Creber .......... 0 | Extras .................... 9 |
| Mr G. L. Crowe c Nash b Creber ........ 7 | |
| R. E. Turner b Hacker ................ 0 | 170 |

### Worcestershire Bowling

| | Overs | Mdns | Runs | Wkts | Overs | Mdns | Runs | Wkts |
|---|---|---|---|---|---|---|---|---|
| Cuffe ........... | 8.1 | 4 | 5 | 9 | 3 | 1 | 3 | 1 |
| Conway ......... | 8 | — | 27 | — | | | | |
| Arnold .......... | | | | | 5 | 1 | 8 | 1 |
| Turner .......... | | | | | 5 | 1 | 17 | 3 |
| Bunting ......... | | | | | 12.4 | — | 46 | 4 |
| Collier .......... | | | | | 14 | 5 | 21 | 1 |
| Pearson ......... | | | | | 1 | 1 | — | — |

### Glamorgan Bowling

| | Overs | Mdns | Runs | Wkts |
|---|---|---|---|---|
| Nash ........... | 16 | 7 | 32 | — |
| Creber .......... | 26 | 2 | 89 | 7 |
| Hacker .......... | 13 | 4 | 29 | 2 |
| Rattenbury ....... | 4 | 1 | 11 | — |

Umpires: Guttridge and Hutchings.

# GLAMORGAN v SOMERSET

### Played at Cardiff, July 7, 8, 1910

With the batsmen always at a disadvantage this game ended on the second day in a win for Somerset by 172 runs. Twenty-three wickets went down on a drying pitch on the Thursday for 278 runs, Somerset leaving off 80 in front with seven batsmen still to be dismissed. The game was practically won next morning by Braund and Robson, who played splendidly, scoring between them 123 out of 133 runs from the bat. In the last innings of the match, Glamorgan could do little against the bowling of Robson and Lewis, who were unchanged.

## Somerset

| | |
|---|---|
| L. C. Braund lbw b Nash ..................... 14 | – b Nash ..................... 77 |
| P. J. Hardy c Rees b Creber ................... 12 | – lbw b Nash ................... 0 |
| A. E. Lewis c E. R. Sweet-Escott b Creber ........ 12 | – b Nash ..................... 1 |
| E. Robson b Nash ........................ 10 | – c H. Sweet-Escott |
| | b E. R. Sweet-Escott. 46 |
| Dr F. J. Poynton st J. Bancroft b Nash .......... 0 | – not out ..................... 2 |
| Mr N. Napstone b Nash ..................... 22 | – b Nash ..................... 0 |
| Mr L. C. L. Sutton b Rattenbury .............. 62 | – b Nash ..................... 0 |
| B. F. Morgan b Nash ...................... 16 | – b Nash ..................... 0 |
| H. Chidgey b Nash ....................... 0 | – b Nash ..................... 1 |
| Mr J. C. White b Nash ..................... 1 | – b Nash ..................... 0 |
| E. North not out ........................ 16 | – b Nash ..................... 6 |
| Extras ........................... 8 | Extras .............. 7 |
| 173 | 140 |

## Glamorgan

| | | |
|---|---|---|
| Mr T. A. L. Whittington c Napstone b Lewis ...... | 3 | – b Robson ..................... 1 |
| Mr S. Rees b Robson ..................... | 9 | – c Chidgey b Lewis ............. 4 |
| Mr R. A. Gibbs c sub. b Robson ............. | 7 | – b Robson ..................... 0 |
| Mr W. J. Bancroft c Hardley b Lewis ........... | 7 | – c Chidgey b Lewis ............ 2 |
| Mr E. R. Sweet-Escott b Robson ............... | 0 | – b Lewis ...................... 2 |
| Mr H. Sweet-Escott b Robson ................. | 1 | – b Robson ..................... 2 |
| Mr R. L. Rattenbury not out ................. | 32 | – c Lewis b Robson ............. 10 |
| Mr H. G. Symonds b Robson ................. | 4 | – c Robson b Lewis ............ 2 |
| Mr J. Bancroft c Hardy b Robson ............. | 21 | – c Lewis b Robson ............ 4 |
| Nash c Robson b North ..................... | 0 | – c Hardy b Lewis ............ 9 |
| Creber b North .......................... | 7 | – not out ..................... 0 |
| Extras .......................... | 8 | Extras ................. 6 |
| | 99 | 42 |

### Glamorgan Bowling

| | Overs | Mdns | Runs | Wkts | Overs | Mdns | Runs | Wkts |
|---|---|---|---|---|---|---|---|---|
| Nash ........... | 31 | 11 | 74 | 7 | 25 | 7 | 56 | 9 |
| Creber ........... | 28 | 8 | 82 | 2 | 25 | 6 | 47 | — |
| Rattenbury ....... | 2.4 | — | 9 | 1 | 10 | 3 | 26 | — |
| E. R. Sweet-Escott .. | | | | | 3 | — | 4 | 1 |

### Somerset Bowling

| | Overs | Mdns | Runs | Wkts | Overs | Mdns | Runs | Wkts |
|---|---|---|---|---|---|---|---|---|
| Robson .......... | 16 | 5 | 40 | 6 | 10 | 3 | 23 | 5 |
| Lewis ........... | 14 | 6 | 34 | 2 | 10 | 3 | 13 | 5 |
| North ........... | 1.4 | — | 17 | 2 | | | | |

## TEST TRIAL MATCHES

## MR JESSOP'S ELEVEN v MR WARNER'S ELEVEN

### Played at Sheffield, June 1, 2, 3, 1911

The first of the Test Match Trials did not prove an attraction at Bramall Lane, and though it produced some good cricket, fell decidedly flat. The result of the game was a victory for Mr Jessop's side by 162 runs. Jessop himself played a very remarkable and lucky innings on the first day. Going in when six wickets had fallen for 65, he scored in less than an hour and a half 122 not out. He ought to have been caught three times while he was getting his first 25 runs, but his hitting afterwards was terrific. He twice sent Hirst out of the ground, and among his other hits were sixteen 4s. The match was treated quite as a trial game, J. W. Hearne on the second day being allowed to take the place of Shipman, though the latter, who had a slight attack of sunstroke, had both batted and bowled. As it happened, Hearne scored a flawless 74 not out.

## Mr G. L. Jessop's XI

| | | | |
|---|---:|---|---:|
| E. Humphreys c Bale b Hirst | 4 | – c Bale b Buckenham | 0 |
| J. Iremonger c Relf b Hirst | 28 | – c Relf b Buckenham | 15 |
| G. Gunn c Hirst b Buckenham | 9 | – run out | 39 |
| James Seymour b Hitch | 9 | – b Litteljohn | 70 |
| Mr K. L. Hutchings c Mead b Hirst | 2 | – b Litteljohn | 53 |
| F. E. Woolley c Relf b Buckenham | 5 | – b Hobbs | 12 |
| M. W. Booth lbw b Litteljohn | 20 | – c and b Litteljohn | 30 |
| Mr G. L. Jessop not out | 122 | – b Litteljohn | 11 |
| J. Newman c Relf b Hirst | 13 | – b Hitch | 6 |
| W. Shipman c Buckenham b Hobbs | 18 | – (J. W. Hearne) not out | 74 |
| H. Strudwick lbw b Hobbs | 0 | – b Hirst | 74 |
| B 1, l-b 3 | 4 | B 10, l-b 8, n-b 1 | 19 |
| | **234** | | **403** |

## Mr P. F. Warner's XI

| | | | |
|---|---:|---|---:|
| J. B. Hobbs c Gunn b Woolley | 22 | – b Booth | 32 |
| C. P. Mead b Newman | 24 | – c Woolley b Booth | 34 |
| R. Relf b Woolley | 79 | – b Woolley | 6 |
| A. Ducat c Humphreys b Woolley | 33 | – c Iremonger b Woolley | 3 |
| G. H. Hirst c Strudwick b Newman | 19 | – b Newman | 7 |
| Mr P. F. Warner not out | 60 | – b Woolley | 28 |
| Mr A. R. Litteljohn c and b Iremonger | 2 | – c Booth b Woolley | 60 |
| E. Alletson c Seymour b Iremonger | 15 | – b Newman | 8 |
| W. Hitch c Woolley b Iremonger | 0 | – not out | 5 |
| C. P. Buckenham c and b Booth | 21 | – run out | 0 |
| E. Bale st Strudwick b Booth | 0 | – run out | 1 |
| B 2, n-b 2 | 4 | B 4, l-b 5, n-b 3 | 12 |
| | **279** | | **196** |

### Mr P. F. Warner's Eleven Bowling

| | Overs | Mdns | Runs | Wkts | Overs | Mdns | Runs | Wkts |
|---|---:|---:|---:|---:|---:|---:|---:|---:|
| Hirst | 18 | 3 | 74 | 4 | 19.4 | 5 | 71 | 1 |
| Buckenham | 14 | 3 | 43 | 2 | 25 | 5 | 97 | 2 |
| Hitch | 8 | — | 44 | 1 | 18 | 2 | 74 | 1 |
| Litteljohn | 13 | 1 | 48 | 1 | 31 | 4 | 76 | 4 |
| Hobbs | 2.4 | — | 21 | 2 | 9 | 1 | 26 | 1 |
| Relf | | | | | 8 | — | 32 | — |
| Mead | | | | | 2 | — | 8 | — |

### Mr G. L. Jessop's Eleven Bowling

| | Overs | Mdns | Runs | Wkts | Overs | Mdns | Runs | Wkts |
|---|---:|---:|---:|---:|---:|---:|---:|---:|
| Shipman | 5 | — | 16 | — | | | | |
| Woolley | 27 | 5 | 71 | 3 | 22 | 8 | 37 | 4 |
| Booth | 12.5 | 3 | 40 | 2 | 10 | 3 | 12 | 2 |
| Newman | 22 | 2 | 74 | 2 | 19 | 8 | 45 | 2 |
| Iremonger | 33 | 8 | 74 | 3 | 21.5 | 6 | 57 | — |
| Hearne | | | | | 4 | — | 33 | — |

Umpires: G. P. Harrison and J. Carlin.

## ALL INDIAN TEAM v STAFFORDSHIRE

Played at Stoke, June 26, 27, 1911

In this match the Indians had the unenviable experience of having to bat against Barnes in his best form and on a pitch that just suited him. Nothing could be done on the first day, but on the Tuesday the match was commenced and finished, Staffordshire winning by five wickets. Barnes, whose superb bowling proved the outstanding feature of the game, took fourteen wickets at a cost of only 29 runs.

## All Indian Team

| | | | | |
|---|---|---|---|---|
| Dr H. D. Kanga b Deyes | 2 | – lbw b Barnes | 8 |
| M. D. Pai c Meakin b Barnes | 1 | – c and b Barnes | 0 |
| B. Jaya Ram b Barnes | 5 | – b Barnes | 0 |
| R. P. Meherhomji c and b Nichols | 13 | – b Barnes | 0 |
| M. P. Bajana lbw b Barnes | 33 | – c Poole b Deyes | 1 |
| P. Shivram lbw b Barnes | 8 | – b Barnes | 11 |
| J. S. Warden b Nichols | 1 | – st Poole b Barnes | 5 |
| H. F. Mulla c Briggs b Nichols | 1 | – b Barnes | 5 |
| A. Salamudin b Barnes | 9 | – not out | 4 |
| P. Balu b Nichols | 0 | – b Barnes | 18 |
| K. Seshachari not out | 0 | – b Barnes | 0 |
| Extra | 1 | Extras | 5 |
| | **74** | | **57** |

## Staffordshire

| | | | | |
|---|---|---|---|---|
| P. Briggs lbw b Balu | 18 | – c Seshachari b Balu | 0 |
| A. Hollowood b Ward | 30 | – b Balu | 0 |
| Mr H. Hawley c Kanga b Balu | 2 | – b Warden | 13 |
| Rev. W. E. G. Sharp b Balu | 3 | – b Warden | 1 |
| Nichols lbw b Balu | 3 | – not out | 21 |
| Mr B. Meakin c Bajana b Balu | 4 | – c Meherhomji b Kanga | 15 |
| S. F. Barnes not out | 7 | – not out | 1 |
| Mr J. W. Allen c Meherhomji b Warden | 1 | | |
| Deyes b Warden | 0 | | |
| Mr J. Poole b Warden | 1 | | |
| Mr H. Eardley c Shivram b Balu | 2 | | |
| Extras | 6 | Extras | 4 |
| | **77** | | **55** |

### Staffordshire Bowling

| | Overs | Mdns | Runs | Wkts | Overs | Mdns | Runs | Wkts |
|---|---|---|---|---|---|---|---|---|
| Barnes | 15.5 | 9 | 14 | 5 | 12.3 | 6 | 15 | 9 |
| Deyes | 6 | — | 16 | 1 | 10 | 3 | 26 | 1 |
| Eardley | 1 | — | 22 | — | | | | |
| Nichols | 8 | 1 | 21 | 4 | 2 | — | 11 | — |

### All Indian Team Bowling

| | Overs | Mdns | Runs | Wkts | Overs | Mdns | Runs | Wkts |
|---|---|---|---|---|---|---|---|---|
| Balu | 19.4 | 3 | 35 | 6 | 13 | 1 | 23 | 2 |
| Salamudin | 4 | — | 17 | — | 3 | 1 | 4 | — |
| Warden | 15 | 5 | 19 | 4 | 11 | 3 | 22 | 2 |
| Kanga | | | | | 1.4 | — | 2 | 1 |

## MCC'S AUSTRALIAN TEAM v LORD LONDESBOROUGH'S ELEVEN

### Played at Scarborough, September 7, 8, 9, 1911

The last match of the Scarborough Festival ended in a draw, but it produced some remarkable cricket. Inasmuch as F. R. Foster, Kinneir, Woolley, and Iremonger were for various reasons kept away from the MCC's team, there was some talk of changing the name of the match, but in the end it was decided to go on with the original arrangement, the two wicket-keepers, Strudwick and Smith, being included in the side. Lord

Londesborough had a very fine eleven, the team including Le Couteur and the famous South African player, G. A. Faulkner. The first day was occupied by Lord Londesborough's Eleven in playing a first innings of 301. Five wickets were down for 104 before luncheon, but Sharp and Hirst put on 150 runs together. Hirst was missed at long leg when 18 and for this blunder a high price had to be paid. Hitch bowled at a great pace, and took seven wickets. On the second day Hobbs played superbly, but could get no support. Warner was so unwell that he had to put himself in last, and the MCC's side were all out for 190. Going in with a lead of 111, Lord Londesborough's Eleven, when bad light finally stopped play, had scored 208 for three wickets. Spooner was not out 89 and Jessop not out 101, the two batsmen having added 174 in ninety-five minutes. In all, their partnership produced 295 runs in two hours, the innings being declared closed at twelve o'clock on Saturday with seven wickets down. Jessop gave three chances, but his hitting was most brilliant. The MCC's side were left to get 370 in rather less than four hours and a quarter. They did not quite succeed in this tremendous task, but when the match was left drawn they were only 37 runs short of victory, and had five wickets in hand. Hobbs was again seen at his very best and George Gunn and Mead made a great effort to win the game. The match attracted crowds of people, a most successful Festival coming to a brilliant end.

## Lord Londesborough's XI

| | | | | |
|---|---|---|---|---|
| Mr R. H. Spooner c Gunn b Douglas | 41 | – c Hobbs b Barnes | 94 |
| J. T. Tyldesley b Hitch | 11 | – b Hitch | 1 |
| Mr B. J. T. Bosanquet c Strudwick b Hitch | 3 | – b Douglas | 3 |
| Mr G. A. Faulkner c Strudwick b Douglas | 13 | – b Hitch | 5 |
| Mr K. L. Hutchings lbw b Rhodes | 9 | – b Hitch | 3 |
| J. Sharp b Hitch | 76 | – c sub. b Barnes | 6 |
| G. H. Hirst c Rhodes b Hitch | 77 | – not out | 1 |
| Mr G. L. Jessop b Hitch | 45 | – b Hitch | 136 |
| Mr P. R. Le Couteur b Hitch | 2 | | |
| Mr W. S. Bird b Hitch | 5 | | |
| F. E. Field not out | 3 | | |
| B 8, l-b 3, w 3, n-b 2 | 16 | B 4, l-b 2, w 1, n-b 2 | 9 |
| | **301** | **(7 wkts dec.)** | **258** |

## MCC Team for Australia

| | | | | |
|---|---|---|---|---|
| G. Gunn c Bird b Field | 1 | – b Field | 97 |
| J. B. Hobbs not out | 117 | – c Spooner b Le Couteur | 84 |
| C. P. Mead c Spooner b Field | 11 | – b Field | 43 |
| W. Rhodes b Field | 0 | – c Bird b Field | 85 |
| J. Vine c Hutchings b Faulkner | 19 | | |
| Mr J. W. H. T. Douglas lbw b Faulkner | 0 | | |
| E. J. Smith c Bird b Field | 10 | – not out | 0 |
| S. F. Barnes c Hirst b Field | 0 | | |
| H. Strudwick lbw b Faulkner | 2 | | |
| W. Hitch b Faulkner | 12 | – c Hirst b Field | 0 |
| Mr P. F. Warner run out | 5 | | |
| B 2, l-b 3, n-b 8 | 13 | B 1, l-b 8, n-b 15 | 24 |
| | **190** | | **333** |

## MCC Team Bowling

| | Overs | Mdns | Runs | Wkts | Overs | Mdns | Runs | Wkts |
|---|---|---|---|---|---|---|---|---|
| Barnes | 27 | 7 | 82 | — | 13 | — | 50 | 2 |
| Hitch | 25.5 | 2 | 87 | 7 | 13 | 2 | 96 | 4 |
| Douglas | 14 | 2 | 53 | 2 | 6 | — | 39 | 1 |
| Rhodes | 8 | 2 | 35 | 1 | 5 | 1 | 19 | — |
| Hobbs | 5 | — | 10 | — | 1 | — | 11 | — |
| Vine | 6 | 2 | 18 | — | 5 | — | 34 | — |

**Lord Londesborough's Eleven Bowling**

| | Overs | Mdns | Runs | Wkts | Overs | Mdns | Runs | Wkts |
|---|---|---|---|---|---|---|---|---|
| Hirst ........... | 9 | 2 | 31 | — | 19 | 1 | 71 | — |
| Field ............ | 20 | 3 | 96 | 5 | 26.4 | 4 | 113 | 4 |
| Faulkner ........ | 15 | 5 | 36 | 4 | 13 | 3 | 38 | — |
| Sharp ........... | 2 | — | 14 | — | 10 | 2 | 30 | — |
| Le Couteur ...... | | | | | 13 | 1 | 57 | 1 |

Umpires: H. Wood and A. A. White.

## MR L. ROBINSON'S ELEVEN v OXFORD UNIVERSITY

### Played at Attleborough, July 2, 3, 4, 1914

This was the last of Oxford's trial games. Everything else in the match was dwarfed by the splendid play of the veteran batsman, Sir T. C. O'Brien. Thanks to him, Mr Robinson's Eleven escaped defeat after following on against a balance of 192. In his first innings O'Brien saved his side from a collapse, being 74 not out when rain stopped play at lunch time on Friday. On the following morning he increased his score to 90, and in the follow-on he was sent in first. This time he gave, for a man in his fifty-third year, a wonderful display. He was at the wickets three hours and twenty minutes for his 111 and, except for one tremendously hot return, he gave no chance. Among the Oxford batsmen Knight and Howell distinguished themselves by sending up 112 for the first wicket.

### Oxford University

| | |
|---|---|
| Mr D. J. Knight c Schwarz b Pegler ...... 82 | Mr F. C. G. Naumann b Mordaunt ....... 0 |
| Mr M. Howell lbw b Schwarz .......... 50 | Mr E. A. Shaw c MacLaren b Pegler ...... 21 |
| Mr G. R. R. Colman b Pegler .......... 38 | Mr C. E. S. Rucker not out ............. 21 |
| Mr O. C. Bristowe lbw b Pegler ......... 7 | Mr D. C. Johnston b Pegler ............ 6 |
| Mr F. H. Knott c Lang b Crawfurd ....... 26 | B 6, n-b 3 .................. 9 |
| Mr B. G. von B. Melle b Pegler .......... 54 | ___ |
| Mr W. G. K. Boswell b Pegler .......... 25 | 339 |

### Mr L. Robinson's Eleven

| | | |
|---|---|---|
| Mr A. C. MacLaren c Bristowe b Rucker ......... | 0 | |
| Capt. K. R. McCloughlin c Shaw b Rucker ........ | 0 – | b Bristowe .................. 21 |
| Mr J. C. W. McBryan c Knight b Rucker ......... | 15 – | lbw b Naumann ................ 65 |
| Mr J. W. Crawfurd b Bristowe ................ | 9 – | b Boswell .................. 15 |
| Mr B. J. T. Bosanquet c Shaw b Melle ............ | 1 – | st Shaw b Colman .............. 59 |
| Sir T. C. O'Brien c Knott b Rucker .............. | 90 – | b Boswell ....................111 |
| Mr A. H. Lang b Rucker ..................... | 0 – | b Boswell .................. 9 |
| Mr E. J. Fulcher b Melle ...........·....... | 17 – | c Howell b Knott .............. 4 |
| Mr R. O. Schwarz b Bristowe ................. | 8 – | not out .................. 3 |
| Mr O. C. Mordaunt c Howell b Bristowe .......... | 0 – | not out ..................... 1 |
| Mr S. J. Pegler not out ..................... | 2 | |
| B 5 ............................. | 5 | B 11, l-b 3, n-b 6 ......... 23 |
| | ___ | ___ |
| | 147 | 311 |

### Mr L. Robinson's Eleven Bowling

| | Overs | Mdns | Runs | Wkts |
|---|---|---|---|---|
| Schwarz .......... | 20 | 2 | 75 | 1 |
| McCloughin ....... | 10 | 2 | 32 | — |
| Pegler ............ | 36.4 | 5 | 113 | 7 |
| Fulcher .......... | 9 | — | 50 | — |
| Crawfurd ......... | 6 | 1 | 12 | 1 |
| Mordaunt ........ | 12 | — | 48 | 1 |

## Oxford University Bowling

| | Overs | Mdns | Runs | Wkts | Overs | Mdns | Runs | Wkts |
|---|---|---|---|---|---|---|---|---|
| Melle ............ | 17 | 3 | 53 | 2 | 21 | 3 | 86 | — |
| Rucker .......... | 9.3 | 2 | 26 | 5 | 6 | — | 29 | — |
| Bristowe ......... | 12 | 3 | 38 | 3 | 19 | 1 | 63 | 1 |
| Naumann ........ | 4 | — | 25 | — | 8 | — | 27 | 1 |
| Johnston ........ | | | | | 14 | 2 | 39 | — |
| Boswell ......... | | | | | 9 | 2 | 19 | 3 |
| Knott ........... | | | | | 2 | — | 11 | 1 |
| Colman ......... | | | | | 1 | — | 14 | 1 |

Umpires: Rye and Pilch.

One of the most notable feats last season was that of Sir T. C. O'Brien in the match at Attleborough, between Mr Lionel Robinson's Eleven and Oxford University. O'Brien became famous as a batsman in 1884 and yet, after an interval of thirty years, he hit up scores of 90 and 111. For a man of nearly fifty-three this was a big performance. I happen to know that O'Brien has a poor opinion of most modern bowlers, contending that in their craze for the swerve they have lost much in spin and accuracy of length. In the match at Attleborough, as another famous cricketer of the last generation put it, he gave the swervers and slingers of the Oxford eleven a good deal to think about.

# PUBLIC SCHOOLS

## SCHOOLBOYS' BOWLING 1903

### By F. R. Spofforth

Meeting the editor of this interesting Almanack at Lord's during the cricket season he asked how it was the professionals were so much better bowlers than the gentlemen, adding that the latter very rarely produced a really first-class bowler; and in a moment of "mental aberration" I consented to write him a short article on this subject for *Wisden's*, 1904 Edition.

Now in comparing amateurs with professionals from their early start in life all the advantages appear with the former. As children, they are better looked after, clothed and fed (or they ought to be) and have all the advantages of a higher education, are sent to schools and colleges where cricket is taught, and if they show aptitude for a particular department of the game special attention is paid to them. They also have the apparent advantage of playing on good pitches which are looked after by competent caretakers.

And if higher education helps the brain power they should be much superior to the professionals for, in spite of the professionals admitted superiority in bowling, if one were to ask the captains of the last two England teams that visited Australia or the captains of county elevens they would almost all tell you of some really good professional bowler, only he has no headpiece, but one never hears of an amateur who lacks that necessary "the headpiece."

In my opinion no one can ever think of being a first-class bowler without he really works hard and often and starts early, for this is the great secret, because it gives elasticity to the muscles without which it is almost impossible to excel, and this elasticity cannot be got without one starts quite young, and certainly not after twenty-one years of age. This is where the professional has the advantage. He has no one to instruct him, bowls just as he likes on some village green where the pitches are bad and the ground does the breaking for him, and probably the faster he bowls the greater his success. Furthermore he has no one to prevent him practising every day as much as his school hours will allow. This is not so with the amateur. He is to a certain extent taught, but he is not allowed to bowl to his full extent or as long as he likes, because others are waiting for their turn, and above all he is taught to spin a ball which in my opinion is just like trying to teach a child to run before it can walk, because directly you start spinning a ball you check pace and therefore development of elasticity which cannot be gained afterwards. How often one hears of splendid boy bowlers and never hears anything of them afterwards, or only for a short time. As they grow older the work is too hard for them but had they bowled harder and longer when quite young and stretched their arms to the full extent they never would find the work too laborious. One should always bear in mind that no matter how good a bowler is, when he is tired he is comparatively easy to play, and if you bowl with strength alone you cannot be at your best longer than six or eight overs.

In conclusion, I consider the real reason why the sons of gentlemen don't succeed as bowlers is that they don't do the necessary work when young. Their scholastic duties, together with games such as tennis, squash rackets, etc., etc., which they can play at high-class schools, colleges and universities take away a great amount of time which the young professional devotes to the practice of bowling. Also the latter is not called upon to spin the ball because the ground is far from perfect, whereas the young collegian playing on really first-class pitches finds the batting too good and therefore prefers to pay more attention to the latter as he gets more fun out of it and it is not so irksome, so he lets, while young, the opportunity of being a bowler slip at the very time he should work his hardest.

The boy is a creature of the moment, never thinks about the future to any great extent, and therefore cannot be expected to persevere with games without he meets with success.

When he grows up it is too late to repair the evil. Up to a certain age, playing on good wickets has the effect of discouraging a boy to bowl and tends to make him take more to batting or follow some other game.

I might add that most of the Australians who have gained fame have come from country districts where the grounds are comparatively bad, and on coming to the metropolitan grounds had to suffer severe checks in wicket taking and it is owing to this fact that most of them use their "headpiece."

F. E. Allan, E. Evans, C. Turner, H. Trumble, H. Boyle, G. Palmer, W. Howell etc., etc., and the writer all started where there were no really good cricket grounds.

## NOTES BY THE EDITOR

Although the matter does not greatly concern the public I cannot pass over without comment the treatment of the press representatives at Lord's on the occasion of the Oxford and Cambridge, and Eton and Harrow matches. It was an ungracious and uncalled for act to shift them from the grand-stand to the roof of the ground bowlers' house in the corner of the ground. Happily the protest in the newspapers was so loud and unanimous that the MCC bowed before the storm, and at the Gentlemen and Players match – immediately following Eton v Harrow – the unhappy experiment was given up. I cannot see why the MCC should be so reluctant to build a proper Press-box – commanding an end-on view of the game – as a continuation of the new Mound stand. The plans for such a box were, I understand, passed by a subcommittee nearly a twelvemonth ago, but afterwards rejected by the general committee on the ground of expense. The MCC have spent thousands of pounds during the last few years to increase the accommodation for their members and the public and they might surely do for the newspapers what has been done at Manchester, Leeds and Nottingham. At all these three grounds within a comparatively short space of time a commodious Press-box with an end-on view of the cricket has been put up. It is hardly the thing for the first cricket club in the world to thus lag behind the counties in so simple a matter.

## THE REPTON ELEVEN 1904

The Repton XI had a very high standard to maintain in view of the record of the previous year, when only one match was lost, and that by only one run. This year two defeats were suffered, but both school matches were again won, though not each by one innings this time, and the Haverford match, spoilt by rain, was drawn in favour of Repton. It was no mean performance to defeat schools like Malvern and Uppingham, and have the best of the game against our American visitors. Young was captain for the second year, and his average receded by 25 per cent; this however is another illustration of the misleading nature of averages. Young scored nearly a hundred runs more than last year (aggregate this year 630), never made a century and had an average of over 45! As he goes to Cambridge, the Cambridge captain is hardly likely to consider him a "decadent" cricketer. He is a wicket-keeper of more than average excellence, as well as a consistent and reliable bat. As regards Greswell, a spell of want of confidence affected him in the middle of the season, but when a player has an average of 30 and a highest score of 67, he must be a *persona grata* in any team, even though he may have omitted to repeat his century against Malvern. Meyer, who is undoubtedly a good bat, failed to maintain his form of the previous year. Crawford – now we prepare to assimilate our largest strawberry – was throughout the season superb, especially in the two school matches. Against Uppingham he took twelve wickets and against Malvern he secured the unlucky number of thirteen – unlucky indeed for Malvern. Throughout the season, he took seventy-five wickets, just three more than all the other bowlers of the eleven! Though undoubtedly the best public school bowler, with a strong claim to be considered the best amateur bowler of the year, as a bat he was of material assistance, to put it mildly, to his school, his contribution in that department amounting to 759 runs, with an average of 54! As he is staying on at Repton another two years, there is probably trouble in store for Malvern, Uppingham, and other opponents, in the seasons of 1905 and 1906. In the bowling line Halkett and Greswell helped Crawford to take wickets, and Johnson should be included in the category of useful school bowlers. Thwaites was serviceable in all departments, while the fielding of the side can be described as fair, though not brilliant, excepting of course the invincible Crawford.

## THE REPTON ELEVEN 1905

To the Repton eleven let the honour be paid that is due to the best school and an unbeaten side; indeed, during three seasons Repton have only lost three matches, and in 1903 had a balance of two runs been transferred from the debit to the credit side of the score sheet, they would have been undefeated for two seasons out of three. Last year claimed for Winchester the honour due to an unbeaten side, but somewhat tentatively, as they had only won one match, yet that one was against Eton. This year the honour can be claimed for Repton without hesitation, as, with a programme of nine matches, eight victories stand to their credit and one drawn game! It is not often given to a school eleven to win such a remarkable percentage of matches; an unbroken school record being usually attributable to avoidance of defeat. Yet does not a murmur reach me "Oh! we know all about Repton. They were "a one man team; Crawford is a wonderful school cricketer, but "without him, or had he failed as a bowler or bat they would have been out of it?" The reverse is the case, and Repton were far from being Crawford *et praeterea nihil*. In the first four matches Crawford scarcely bowled at all owing to a strained back, and in the drawn game he broke down from the same cause; yet Crawford or no Crawford the highest score made against Repton was 236! Again, to the highest total the school compiled in the year (against the Free Foresters moreover) – a score of 435 for eight wickets – Crawford's contribution was a modest 10! All honour to Crawford as the best public school player of this and many other years, but let us not forget the honour due to the excellent team who supported him. Murdoch – "the torch is handed on from sire to son" – showed himself worthy of his father, the unrivalled W.L. – with an average of 45. Altham proved a really good bat, and most schools would be glad of an all-round player like Johnson, who can make a century, average 33, and take 40 wickets for 14 runs apiece. That the rest of the batsmen supported their leaders is shown by the lowest score for which the team was dismissed being 170! A really good wicket-keeper in Barnardo, backed up by fieldsmen who rarely missed a catch, put the coping stone on the edifice of excellence erected by Crawford and his colleagues. As for Crawford his experience as an all-round school-boy cricketer can only be challenged by two others in the last 40 years, and the names of those two occur readily to all followers of cricket. Time alone can decide whether Crawford will rival A. G. Steel and F. S. Jackson, and captain a victorious English team (or will it be a victorious South African one?) in a test match. It is my portion to deal with the past, and in the past season Crawford, handicapped as he was in the early part of the summer, had an average of 85, and took 51 wickets – practically in five matches – for under 13 runs apiece. In the school matches his double performances set up a record that should long remain unsurpassed. He scored 163 (out of 280) at Uppingham and secured ten wickets for 75, while against Malvern he was slightly less successful, being content with 139, and another ten wickets, this time for 147! My prophecy of last year that there was trouble in store for the Malvern and Uppingham teams in 1905 has indeed been fulfilled. Needless to say both schools succumbed – Uppingham by an innings and 76 runs and Malvern by nine wickets.

## THE REPTON ELEVEN 1914

Repton again had a useful side, with one really fine cricketer, but they fell off a little towards the end of the season. The results of matches were: three won, three lost, and four drawn. In school matches, Repton beat Uppingham by an innings, lost to Malvern, after a very good game and a close finish, and drew with Haverford on the last day of the term. I rather fancy that my informant from Repton, who has done so much for the cricket of the school, is apt to be a rather stern critic. He certainly does not call his geese swans. In John Howell they had certainly the outstanding school cricketer. As a batsman, and in cricket knowledge, he is as matured as was Knight in 1913, and his performances in the matches at Lord's, and in school matches show that he was as a whole very dependable, and not in the least perturbed by a crisis. Defence and back play are his strongest points, but though he is a little dull at times, he can score in a good many ways, and he is a very hard man indeed to get out. The strokes of a MacLaren, the grace of a Palairet, will never be his, but given the opportunity there is no doubt that as a sound and run-getting batsman he must surely take a high place in first-class cricket.

After making 100 in the Surrey trial match, in May, he quite failed to get going in the early part of the term. He only got 127 in seven innings, including a 56 to start with. He then settled down, and finished with an average of 52.76. In 1913 he put up a record at Repton by making two hundreds in a match. This year he made 200 against Uppingham and 200 against the Old Reptonians. No one had made 200 at Repton before, though J. N. Crawford got 196. Next to Howell, Pallett was the most striking bat. He goes for the bowling and hits the ball a long way, but he has not a great defence. Several of the others were by no means bad players.

# ENGLAND IN AUSTRALIA

## ENGLAND v AUSTRALIA

Played at Sydney, December 13, 14, 16, 1901

The first Test match proved to be, from the English point of view, the event of the tour, MacLaren's team gaining a glorious and altogether unexpected victory by an innings and 124 runs. On winning the toss MacLaren went in himself with Hayward as a partner, and by dint of very good but unwontedly steady cricket the two batsmen scored 154 for the first wicket. This splendid start, however, was not by any means well followed up, and at the close of the first day six wickets had fallen for 272. The ground being in perfect order for run-getting, this was not considered nearly good enough, but happily for the Englishmen Lilley and Braund made a great stand on the Saturday morning, their partnership producing in all 124 runs. The last three men all did well, and in the end the total reached 464. The Australians started by losing Trumper very cheaply, but thanks to Gregory and Hill the score at the drawing of stumps had reached 103 with three wickets down. This being the position there seemed every reason on the Monday to expect a protracted match. As things turned out, however, the English bowlers carried all before them, getting seventeen wickets down in the course of the afternoon and finishing the game. Braund, Blythe and Barnes, though the last-named was freely punished in the second innings, bowled very finely indeed, and were backed up by fielding and wicket-keeping of the most brilliant character. There was a regular collapse during the first quarter of an hour in the morning, Hill, Howell, McLeod and Kelly being all out at 112, and from these disasters the Australians, despite strenuous efforts, could never recover. The result of the match caused a great sensation all over the Colonies. It is worthy of note that the Australian team was composed entirely of players who went to England in 1899.

## England

| | |
|---|---|
| Mr A. C. MacLaren lbw b McLeod . . . . . . .116 | L. C. Braund c Jones b McLeod . . . . . . . . . 85 |
| T. Hayward c Hill b Trumble . . . . . . . . . . . . 69 | J. Gunn c and b Jones . . . . . . . . . . . . . . . . . 21 |
| J. T. Tyldesley c McLeod b Laver . . . . . . . . 1 | S. F. Barnes not out . . . . . . . . . . . . . . . . . . 26 |
| W. G. Quaife b Howell . . . . . . . . . . . . . . . . 21 | C. Blythe c Trumble b Laver . . . . . . . . . . . 20 |
| Mr G. L. Jessop b McLeod . . . . . . . . . . . . . 24 | B 6, l-b 7, w 1, n-b 1 . . . . . . . . . . . 15 |
| Mr A. O. Jones c Kelly b Noble . . . . . . . . . . 9 | — |
| A. A. Lilley c Laver b McLeod . . . . . . . . . . 84 | 464 |

## Australia

| | | |
|---|---|---|
| S. E. Gregory (NSW) c Braund b Blythe . . . . . . . . . . | 48 | – c MacLaren b Braund . . . . . . . . . . 43 |
| V. Trumper (NSW) c and b Barnes . . . . . . . . . . . . . . | 2 | – c Lilley b Blythe . . . . . . . . . . . . . . . 34 |
| C. Hill (SA) b Barnes . . . . . . . . . . . . . . . . . . . . . . . | 46 | – b Braund . . . . . . . . . . . . . . . . . . . . . 0 |
| M. A. Noble (NSW) st Lilley b Braund . . . . . . . . . . | 2 | – c Lilley b Blythe . . . . . . . . . . . . . . . 14 |
| W. P. Howell (NSW) c Braund b Blythe . . . . . . . . . | 9 | – not out . . . . . . . . . . . . . . . . . . . . . . . 31 |
| C. McLeod (V) b Barnes . . . . . . . . . . . . . . . . . . . . . | 0 | – b Blythe . . . . . . . . . . . . . . . . . . . . . . 0 |
| J. J. Kelly (NSW) b Blythe . . . . . . . . . . . . . . . . . . . | 0 | – c Barnes b Blythe . . . . . . . . . . . . . . 12 |
| J. Darling (SA) (capt.) c Quaife b Barnes . . . . . . . . | 39 | – c Jessop b Braund . . . . . . . . . . . . . 3 |
| F. Laver (V) c Quaife b Braund . . . . . . . . . . . . . . . . | 6 | – st Lilley b Braund . . . . . . . . . . . . . . 0 |
| H. Trumble (V) not out . . . . . . . . . . . . . . . . . . . . . | 5 | – c Lilley b Barnes . . . . . . . . . . . . . . . 26 |
| E. Jones (SA) c Jessop b Barnes . . . . . . . . . . . . . . . | 5 | – c Jones b Braund . . . . . . . . . . . . . . 2 |
| Extras . . . . . . . . . . . . . . . . . . . . . . . . . . . . | 6 | Extras . . . . . . . . . . . . . . . 7 |
| | — | — |
| | 168 | 172 |

## Australia Bowling

|         | Overs | Mdns | Runs | Wkts |
|---------|-------|------|------|------|
| Jones ............ | 36 | 8 | 98 | 1 |
| Noble ............ | 33 | 17 | 91 | 1 |
| McLeod .......... | 44 | 17 | 84 | 4 |
| Howell ........... | 21 | 8 | 52 | 1 |
| Trumble .......... | 34 | 12 | 85 | 1 |
| Laver ............ | 17 | 6 | 39 | 2 |
| Trumper .......... | 1 | 1 | 0 | 0 |

## England Bowling

|         | Overs | Mdns | Runs | Wkts | Overs | Mdns | Runs | Wkts |
|---------|-------|------|------|------|-------|------|------|------|
| Barnes ........... | 35.1 | 9 | 65 | 5 | 16 | 2 | 74 | 1 |
| Braund ........... | 15 | 4 | 40 | 2 | 18.4 | 8 | 61 | 5 |
| Gunn ............ | 5 | — | 27 | — | | | | |
| Blythe ........... | 16 | 8 | 26 | 3 | 13 | — | 30 | 4 |
| Jessop ........... | 1 | — | 4 | — | | | | |

# ENGLAND v AUSTRALIA

### Played at Melbourne, January 1, 2, 3, 4, 1902

The second Test match was in some respects the most remarkable of the series. Owing to a lot of rain for two or three days the wicket was very difficult on the opening day, but, as is not uncommon in Australia, it had practically recovered on the second morning. MacLaren, on winning the toss, put Australia in first, but his bowlers – Barnes and Blythe – did not serve him so well as he had hoped, and when an innings had been completed on each side the Englishmen found themselves 51 runs behind. When the Australians went in for the second time, Darling, rightly judging that the ground would improve, kept some of his best batsmen in reserve, and at the close of the day five wickets had fallen for 48. On paper the position favoured the Englishmen, but on the second day the cricket changed entirely in character, and the game all the afternoon went in Australia's favour. Hill played a magnificent innings, and at the drawing of stumps the score stood at 300 for nine wickets, Duff being not out 71, with Armstrong as his partner. These two players, who had taken the places filled in the match at Sydney by Charles McLeod and Laver, added 53 on the third morning, their partnership for the last wicket producing in all 120 runs. Duff, who was batting for three hours and a half, had the distinction of making a hundred in his first Test match. Moreover, in getting his 32, he showed by far the best batting while the wicket was difficult. The Englishmen wanted 405 to win, and the task proved far beyond their powers. Tyldesley at last showed his true form, but five wickets fell before the end of the afternoon, and on the fourth morning the end soon came, Australia winning by 229 runs. Noble had a big share in the success of his side, taking in all thirteen wickets for 77 runs. Barnes also took thirteen wickets. He bowled finely, but was over-worked in the second innings of Australia.

## Australia

| | | | |
|---|---:|---|---:|
| V. Trumper c Tyldesley b Barnes | 0 | – c Lilley b Barnes | 16 |
| J. Darling c Lilley b Blythe | 19 | – c Tyldesley b Barnes | 23 |
| C. Hill b Barnes | 15 | – c Jones b Barnes | 99 |
| H. Trumble c Braund b Blythe | 16 | – c Braund b Barnes | 16 |
| M. A. Noble c Lilley b Blythe | 0 | – lbw b Blythe | 16 |
| S. E. Gregory st Lilley b Blythe | 0 | – c Jones b Barnes | 17 |
| R. A. Duff c Braund b Barnes | 32 | – b Braund | 104 |
| J. J. Kelly c Quaife b Barnes | 5 | – run out | 3 |
| W. Armstrong not out | 4 | – not out | 45 |
| W. Howell b Barnes | 1 | – c Hayward b Barnes | 0 |
| E. Jones c MacLaren b Barnes | 14 | – c MacLaren b Barnes | 5 |
| B 6 | 6 | B 7, l-b 1, n-b 1 | 9 |
| | **112** | | **353** |

## England

| | | | |
|---|---:|---|---:|
| Mr A. C. MacLaren c Jones b Trumble | 13 | – c Trumble b Noble | 1 |
| T. Hayward c Darling b Trumble | 0 | – st Kelly b Trumble | 12 |
| J. T. Tyldesley c Gregory b Trumble | 2 | – c Trumble b Noble | 66 |
| W. G. Quaife b Noble | 0 | – b Noble | 25 |
| Mr G. L. Jessop st Kelly b Noble | 27 | – c Gregory b Noble | 32 |
| J. Gunn st Kelly b Noble | 0 | – c Jones b Trumble | 2 |
| A. A. Lilley c Trumper b Noble | 6 | – c Darling b Noble | 0 |
| Mr A. O. Jones c Kelly b Noble | 0 | – c Darling b Trumble | 6 |
| L. C. Braund not out | 2 | – c Darling b Noble | 25 |
| S. F. Barnes c and b Noble | 1 | – c and b Trumble | 0 |
| C. Blythe c Trumper b Noble | 4 | – not out | 0 |
| B 6 | 6 | B 1, l-b 1, n-b 4 | 6 |
| | **61** | | **175** |

### England Bowling

| | Overs | Mdns | Runs | Wkts | Overs | Mdns | Runs | Wkts |
|---|---|---|---|---|---|---|---|---|
| Barnes | 16.1 | 5 | 42 | 6 | 64 | 17 | 121 | 7 |
| Blythe | 16 | 2 | 64 | 4 | 31 | 7 | 85 | 1 |
| Braund | | | | | 53.2 | 17 | 114 | 1 |
| Jessop | | | | | 1 | — | 9 | — |
| Gunn | | | | | 6 | 1 | 13 | — |
| Jones | | | | | 1 | — | 2 | — |

### Australia Bowling

| | Overs | Mdns | Runs | Wkts | Overs | Mdns | Runs | Wkts |
|---|---|---|---|---|---|---|---|---|
| Trumble | 8 | 1 | 38 | 3 | 22.5 | 10 | 49 | 4 |
| Noble | 7.4 | 2 | 17 | 7 | 26 | 5 | 60 | 6 |
| Jones | | | | | 12 | 2 | 33 | — |
| Howell | | | | | 15 | 6 | 23 | — |
| Armstrong | | | | | 2 | 1 | 3 | — |
| Trumper | | | | | 2 | 1 | 1 | — |

## ENGLAND v AUSTRALIA

Played at Adelaide, January 17, 18, 20, 21, 22, 23, 1902

It was in this match – a protracted struggle that lasted into the sixth day – that Barnes's knee gave way. He broke down on the second afternoon and, as events turned out, took no further part in the tour. It is not unreasonable to assume that if he had kept sound, the

Englishmen would have gained a second victory in the Test games. As it was, the Australians, though set to get 315 in the last innings on a pitch somewhat worn at one end, won by four wickets. As at Sydney in the first Test match, MacLaren and Hayward gave their side a splendid start, scoring 149 before they were separated. Something in the nature of a collapse followed, but Quaife and Braund batted very finely, and on the second day the innings ended for 388. Braund in his 103 not out, hit a 5 and twelve 4s. After losing Darling for a single, the Australians showed brilliant form, and at the drawing of stumps on Saturday their score was up to 173 for two wickets. Thanks to some admirable bowling by John Gunn the innings was finished off on Monday for 321, or 67 runs behind. As at Melbourne, Hill just missed his hundred after playing superb cricket. The Englishmen then scored 38 for the loss of MacLaren's wicket and left off for the day in a splendid position, being 165 runs ahead with nine wickets in hand. Tuesday's play was brought to an abrupt conclusion by a dust storm, the English score being then 204 with five wickets down. Barnes could not bat, and on the fifth morning the innings soon ended, Trumble bowling in great form. Quaife took two hours and three-quarters to get his 44. The Australians wanted 315 to win and at the close of the day they were well within sight of victory, having scored 201 for four wickets. Hill again got into the nineties and again played in his finest form. Blythe being handicapped by a damaged finger, the English bowling on the last morning was very weak, but nevertheless the batsmen found it hard work to get runs on the slightly worn pitch. Darling took three hours and a half to score his 69, he and Trumble making the result a certainty before they were separated. It was a fine victory gained by most tenacious cricket.

### England

| | | | |
|---|---|---|---|
| Mr A. C. MacLaren run out | 67 | – b Trumble | 44 |
| T. Hayward run out | 90 | – b Trumble | 47 |
| J. T. Tyldesley c and b Trumble | 0 | – run out | 25 |
| Mr G. L. Jessop c Trumper b Trumble | 1 | – b Trumble | 16 |
| A. A. Lilley lbw b Trumble | 10 | – b McLeod | 21 |
| W. G. Quaife c Kelly b Howell | 68 | – lbw b Trumble | 44 |
| L. C. Braund not out | 103 | – b Howell | 17 |
| Mr A. O. Jones run out | 5 | – c and b Trumble | 11 |
| J. Gunn b Noble | 24 | – lbw b Trumble | 5 |
| S. F. Barnes c Hill b Noble | 5 | – absent | 0 |
| C. Blythe c Hill b Noble | 2 | – not out | 10 |
| B 9, n-b 3, w 1 | 13 | B 7 | 7 |
| | **388** | | **247** |

### Australia

| | | | |
|---|---|---|---|
| J. Darling c MacLaren b Blythe | 1 | – c Hayward b Jessop | 69 |
| V. Trumper run out | 65 | – b Gunn | 25 |
| C. Hill c Tyldesley b Braund | 98 | – b Jessop | 97 |
| R. A. Duff lbw b Braund | 43 | – hit wkt b Gunn | 4 |
| S. Gregory c Blythe b Braund | 55 | – c Braund b Gunn | 23 |
| W. Armstrong c and b Gunn | 9 | – not out | 9 |
| H. Trumble b Gunn | 13 | – not out | 62 |
| W. Howell c Braund b Gunn | 3 | | |
| M. A. Noble b Gunn | 14 | – run out | 13 |
| J. J. Kelly not out | 5 | | |
| C. McLeod b Gunn | 7 | | |
| B 2, l-b 6 | 8 | B 9, l-b 3, n-b 1 | 13 |
| | **321** | | **315** |

## England Bowling

| | Overs | Mdns | Runs | Wkts | Overs | Mdns | Runs | Wkts |
|---|---|---|---|---|---|---|---|---|
| Braund .......... | 46 | 9 | 143 | 3 | 14 | 5 | 79 | — |
| Blythe .......... | 11 | 3 | 54 | 1 | 23 | 16 | 66 | — |
| Barnes .......... | 7 | — | 21 | — | | | | |
| Gunn .......... | 42 | 14 | 76 | 5 | 22 | 14 | 88 | 3 |
| Jessop .......... | 7 | — | 19 | — | 13 | 9 | 41 | 2 |
| Hayward ......... | | | | | 4 | — | 28 | — |

## Australia Bowling

| | Overs | Mdns | Runs | Wkts | Overs | Mdns | Runs | Wkts |
|---|---|---|---|---|---|---|---|---|
| Trumble .......... | 65 | 23 | 124 | 3 | 44 | 18 | 74 | 6 |
| Noble .......... | 26 | 10 | 58 | 3 | 21 | 7 | 72 | — |
| Howell .......... | 36 | 10 | 82 | 1 | 27 | 9 | 54 | 1 |
| Armstrong ........ | 18 | 5 | 45 | — | 5 | — | 9 | — |
| Trumper .......... | 6 | 3 | 17 | — | | | | |
| McLeod .......... | 19 | 5 | 49 | — | 14 | 3 | 31 | 1 |

## ENGLISH TEAM v EIGHTEEN OF WESTERN DISTRICT

### Played at Bathurst, February 7, 8, 1902

W. G. Quaife in this match had one of his many successes in the up country fixtures, going in first and carrying his bat right through the innings. The scoring was much too heavy to admit of a definite result, and the game ended in a draw. MacLaren objected to the Bathurst team playing Marsh, the aboriginal cricketer who had been no-balled for throwing in the Victoria and New South Wales matches in the previous season, and though the matter gave rise to some discussion the local authorities fell in with the English captain's views.

### English Team

| | |
|---|---|
| W. G. Quaife not out ..................159 | Mr S. M. J. Woods lbw b Smith .......... 0 |
| J. Gunn b Allman ..................... 0 | Mr A. C. MacLaren st Rouse b Allman .... 79 |
| L. C. Braund c Lipscombe b Allman ...... 5 | J. T. Tyldesley c Barnes b Allman ........ 14 |
| Mr C. McGahey c Payne b Kerr ......... 71 | T. Hayward b McPhillamy ............. 44 |
| Mr C. Robson b Allman .............. 9 | Extras ..................... 35 |
| Mr G. L. Jessop c Rouse b Allman ....... 0 | |
| Mr H. G. Garnett b Smith .............. 89 | 505 |

Eighteen of Western District scored 177.

## ENGLISH TEAM v SOUTH AUSTRALIA

### Played at Adelaide, March 27, 28, 30, 31, 1903

South Australia placed their full strength in the field for this match, which was not played on the Adelaide Oval, but on the ground of the Sturt CC, called Vuley Oval. The wicket was excellent, but the rest of the field very rough. Lord Hawke's Team made a grand start, their innings, which amounted to 553 – the highest total of the whole tour – lasting until three o'clock on the second afternoon. Warner and Burnup put up 106 for the first wicket. The latter played practically faultless cricket for 103, making his last sixty runs in an hour. An even finer display was that of Taylor, and Bosanquet, Fane, Johnson, and Stanning all made their runs well. Travers (slow left) bowled best, Giffen sending down rather poor stuff. South Australia at the drawing of stumps on Saturday had scored 227 for five wickets, Hill playing delightful cricket. Claxton who drove hard and Jennings who played back very strongly came together at 115, and added 112 without being separated. Thompson's fine bowling soon finished off the home team's innings on Monday. South Australia being 249 behind followed on – the rule being a compulsory one in Australia – and the Englishmen had to field out until three o'clock the next afternoon. Had the rule been optional, the Englishmen would certainly have batted. As it was they fielded out for 758 runs. Hill again played finely, and Hack and Gehrs scored heavily, the latter being lucky not to be given out lbw when 29. The English fielding was rather slack. Lord Hawke's Team had 206 to get to win, and certainly ought to have accomplished the task, but, apart from Dowson, who batted beautifully, they cut a poor figure against Hay's bowling, and were beaten by 97 runs. Hay, a fast right handed bowler with a swinging action, came very fast off the pitch. He took nine wickets for 67 runs and performed the hat trick by dismissing Burnup, Fane, and Taylor with successive balls.

### English Team

| | | | |
|---|---:|---|---:|
| Mr P. F. Warner b Giffen | 47 | – lbw b Hay | 25 |
| Mr C. J. Burnup c and b Giffen | 103 | – b Hay | 3 |
| Mr F. L. Fane c Newland b Travers | 47 | – b Hay | 0 |
| Mr T. L. Taylor c and b Claxton | 105 | – b Hay | 0 |
| Mr E. M. Dowson lbw b Travers | 66 | – run out | 46 |
| Mr J. B. T. Bosanquet c Claxton b Giffen | 57 | – b Hay | 0 |
| G. J. Thompson b Travers | 18 | – not out | 15 |
| Mr J. Stanning c Gehrs b Reidman | 38 | – b Hay | 2 |
| A. E. Trott b Giffen | 4 | – b Hay | 8 |
| Mr P. R. Johnson c Travers b Reidman | 54 | – c and b Hay | 4 |
| S. Hargreave not out | 2 | – c Newland b Hay | 4 |
| Extras | 12 | B 1 | 1 |
| | **553** | | **108** |

### South Australia

| | | | |
|---|---:|---|---:|
| F. T. Hack c Taylor b Thompson | 3 | – b Dowson | 90 |
| A. E. H. Evans b Thompson | 15 | – b Thompson | 1 |
| C. Hill b Thompson | 58 | – st Taylor b Bosanquet | 73 |
| J. C. Reedman b Thompson | 18 | – b Thompson | 41 |
| A. R. Gehrs c Fane b Bosanquet | 6 | – run out | 100 |
| N. Claxton b Thompson | 88 | – b Trott | 32 |
| C. B. Jennings b Thompson | 52 | – b Trott | 0 |
| G. Giffen b Thompson | 14 | – b Thompson | 37 |
| P. M. Newland b Thompson | 0 | – b Dowson | 48 |
| H. Hay not out | 14 | – b Dowson | 0 |
| J. F. Travers c Bosanquet b Thompson | 15 | – not out | 14 |
| B 13, l-b 4, w 3, n-b 1 | 21 | B 13, l-b 4, n-b 1 | 18 |
| | **304** | | **454** |

### South Australian Bowling

| | Overs | Mdns | Runs | Wkts | Overs | Mdns | Runs | Wkts |
|---|---:|---:|---:|---:|---:|---:|---:|---:|
| Giffen | 55 | 9 | 218 | 4 | | | | |
| Travers | 47 | 8 | 145 | 3 | 21 | 10 | 40 | — |
| Hay | 19 | 3 | 70 | — | 21.2 | 4 | 67 | 9 |
| Reedman | 13.5 | 3 | 47 | 2 | | | | |
| Evans | 7 | — | 29 | — | | | | |
| Claxton | 5 | 1 | 32 | 1 | | | | |

**English Team Bowling**

| | Overs | Mdns | Runs | Wkts | Overs | Mdns | Runs | Wkts |
|---|---|---|---|---|---|---|---|---|
| Thompson ........ | 28.3 | 6 | 85 | 9 | 39 | 5 | 113 | 3 |
| Bosanquet ........ | 9 | — | 69 | 1 | 22 | — | 82 | 1 |
| Trott ........... | 21 | 3 | 78 | — | 24.5 | 1 | 101 | 2 |
| Dowson ......... | 3 | — | 14 | — | 20 | 3 | 62 | 3 |
| Hargreave ........ | 6 | — | 30 | — | 9 | 1 | 37 | — |
| Burnup .......... | 3 | — | 7 | — | 8 | 1 | 41 | — |

# ENGLAND v AUSTRALIA
## First Test Match

Played at Sydney, December 11, 12, 14, 15, 16, 17, 1903

The first of the five Test matches was in many ways the best of the series. Indeed a finer game has rarely been seen in Australia. It lasted into the sixth day, and attracted in all about 95,000 people. The Australians, on winning the toss, lost Trumper, Duff, and Hill for a dozen runs, Trumper being out to a wonderful catch at slip. Thanks to Noble these disasters were retrieved, but when at the end of the day the score stood at 259 for six wickets the Australians did not seem to have done anything out of the common. However, rain in the night made their total look far more formidable. Next day the Australian innings ended for 285 and the Englishmen went in under very anxious conditions, as no one could tell how the wicket would play. Tyldesley, batting with the utmost skill, saved his side from a break-down before lunch, and by four o'clock the wicket had practically recovered. At the drawing of stumps the total had reached 243 for four wickets, Foster being not out 73, and Braund not out 67. Noble was at the wickets four hours and three-quarters for his 133, and hardly made a mistake. The third day was marked by the most brilliant and sensational cricket seen during the tour, R. E. Foster, with a magnificent innings of 287, beating all records in Test matches. Altogether he was batting for seven hours, among his hits being thirty-eight 4s. The latter part of his innings was described on all hands as something never surpassed. Foster and Braund added 192 runs together, Braund playing an admirable innings, but with eight men out the Englishmen were only 47 ahead. Then came the startling play, Relf and Rhodes helping Foster to put on respectively 115 and 130 runs for the ninth and tenth wickets. The last wicket partnership set up a new record in Test games. Foster's triumph was the more remarkable as he had never before played in an England and Australia match. He did not begin his great innings at all well, and ought to have been caught when he had made 51, but his batting on the third day was beyond criticism. Going in against a balance of 292 runs, Australia had scored 17 without loss when stumps were pulled up. Next day they did great things, carrying their score to 367 and only losing five wickets. There was a very regrettable and indeed disgraceful demonstration on the part of a large section of the crowd when Hill was given run out, a storm of hooting and booing going on for a long time. On the fifth day the Australian innings ended for 485, Trumper taking out his bat for a faultless 185. His hits included twenty-five 4s, and during a stay of three hours and fifty minutes he gave no chance. Rhodes bowled with the utmost steadiness on the hard ground, and in writing home Mr Warner said he did not know what the side would have done without him. England wanted 194 to win, and found the task a very heavy one. They won on the sixth day by five wickets, but they would very probably have been beaten if, after four wickets had fallen for 83, Laver at short leg had not missed Hirst before that batsman had scored a run. As it was Hayward and Hirst made a great stand, and almost won the game together. Hayward was batting just over four hours for his beautifully-played 91.

## Australia

| | | | |
|---|---|---|---|
| R. A. Duff c Lilley b Arnold | 3 | – c Relf b Rhodes | 84 |
| V. Trumper c Foster b Arnold | 1 | – not out | 185 |
| C. Hill c Lilley b Hirst | 5 | – run out | 51 |
| M. A. Noble c Foster b Arnold | 133 | – st Lilley b Bosanquet | 22 |
| W. W. Armstrong b Bosanquet | 48 | – c Bosanquet b Rhodes | 27 |
| A. J. Hopkins b Hirst | 39 | – c Arnold b Rhodes | 20 |
| W. P. Howell c Relf b Arnold | 5 | – c Lilley b Arnold | 4 |
| S. Gregory b Bosanquet | 23 | – c Lilley b Arnold | 43 |
| F. Laver lbw b Rhodes | 4 | – c Relf b Rhodes | 6 |
| J. J. Kelly c Braund b Rhodes | 10 | – b Arnold | 13 |
| J. V. Saunders not out | 11 | – run out | 2 |
| Extras | 3 | Extras | 28 |
| | **285** | | **485** |

## England

| | | | |
|---|---|---|---|
| P. F. Warner c Kelly b Laver | 0 | – b Howell | 8 |
| T. Hayward b Howell | 15 | – st Kelly b Saunders | 91 |
| J. T. Tyldesley b Noble | 53 | – c Noble b Saunders | 9 |
| E. Arnold c Laver b Armstrong | 27 | | |
| R. E. Foster c Noble b Saunders | 287 | – st Kelly b Armstrong | 19 |
| L. C. Braund b Howell | 102 | – c Noble b Howell | 0 |
| G. H. Hirst b Howell | 0 | – not out | 60 |
| B. J. T. Bosanquet c Howell b Noble | 2 | – not out | 1 |
| A. A. Lilley c Hill b Noble | 4 | | |
| A. E. Relf c Armstrong b Saunders | 31 | | |
| W. R. Rhodes not out | 40 | | |
| Extras | 16 | Extras | 6 |
| | **577** | | **194** |

## England Bowling

| | Overs | Mdns | Runs | Wkts | Overs | Mdns | Runs | Wkts |
|---|---|---|---|---|---|---|---|---|
| Hirst | 24 | 8 | 47 | 2 | 29 | 1 | 79 | — |
| Arnold | 32 | 7 | 76 | 4 | 28 | 3 | 93 | 2 |
| Braund | 26 | 9 | 39 | — | 12 | 2 | 56 | — |
| Bosanquet | 13 | — | 52 | 2 | 24 | 1 | 100 | 1 |
| Rhodes | 17.2 | 3 | 41 | 2 | 40.2 | 10 | 94 | 5 |
| Relf | 6 | 1 | 27 | — | 13 | 5 | 35 | — |

## Australia Bowling

| | Overs | Mdns | Runs | Wkts | Overs | Mdns | Runs | Wkts |
|---|---|---|---|---|---|---|---|---|
| Saunders | 36.2 | 8 | 126 | 2 | 10.5 | 3 | 51 | 2 |
| Laver | 37 | 12 | 116 | 1 | 16 | 4 | 37 | 1 |
| Howell | 31 | 7 | 113 | 3 | 31 | 18 | 35 | 2 |
| Noble | 34 | 8 | 99 | 3 | 12 | 2 | 37 | 0 |
| Armstrong | 23 | 3 | 47 | 1 | 18 | 6 | 28 | 1 |
| Hopkins | 11 | 1 | 40 | — | | | | |
| Trumper | 7 | 1 | 12 | — | | | | |
| Gregory | 2 | — | 8 | — | | | | |

## MCC TEAM v NORTHERN TASMANIA

### Played at Launceston, January 29, 30, 1904

Northern Tasmania saved the game in capital style, after being a long way behind on the first innings, Savigny batting admirably for five hours and taking out his bat for 164. He was badly missed, however, when he had made 33, this blunder perhaps preventing the Englishmen winning the match. Hayward, apart from a chance of stumping when he had scored 113, played a wonderfully good innings.

## MCC Team

| | |
|---|---|
| P. F. Warner b Windsor . . . . . . . . . . . . . . . . 4 | E. Arnold lbw b Smith . . . . . . . . . . . . . . . . 5 |
| T. Hayward c Douglas b Smith . . . . . . . . . .134 | Drummond b Smith . . . . . . . . . . . . . . . . . . 1 |
| J. T. Tyldesley b Smith . . . . . . . . . . . . . . . . 1 | A. Fielder b Windsor . . . . . . . . . . . . . . . . . 23 |
| A. E. Knight b Addison . . . . . . . . . . . . . . . 30 | H. Strudwick b Windsor . . . . . . . . . . . . . . . 21 |
| G. H. Hirst c Cuff b Windsor . . . . . . . . . . . 51 | Extras . . . . . . . . . . . . . . . . . . . . . 7 |
| W. R. Rhodes run out . . . . . . . . . . . . . . . . 39 | |
| A. A. Lilley not out . . . . . . . . . . . . . . . . . . 37 | 353 |

Northern Tasmania scored 141 and 259 for three wickets. (Savigny not out 164.)

## MCC Team's Bowling

| | Overs | Mdns | Runs | Wkts | Overs | Mdns | Runs | Wkts |
|---|---|---|---|---|---|---|---|---|
| Hirst . . . . . . . . . . . . | | | 37 | 5 | | | 32 | 1 |
| Fielder . . . . . . . . . . . | | | 44 | 3 | | | 29 | — |
| Arnold . . . . . . . . . . . | | | 16 | 2 | | | 22 | — |
| Rhodes . . . . . . . . . . . | | | 33 | — | | | 21 | — |
| Knight . . . . . . . . . . . | | | | | | | 34 | 2 |
| Hayward . . . . . . . . . | | | | | | | 17 | — |
| Warner . . . . . . . . . . | | | | | | | 12 | — |
| Drummond . . . . . . . | | | | | | | 21 | — |
| Tyldesley . . . . . . . . . | | | | | | | 22 | — |
| Lilley . . . . . . . . . . . . . | | | | | | | 19 | — |
| Strudwick . . . . . . . . | | | | | | | 6 | — |

## MCC TEAM v VICTORIA

Played at Melbourne, February 5, 7, 8, 9, 1904

This match furnished one of the sensations of the tour, Victoria in their second innings having to face Rhodes and Arnold on a sticky wicket, and being out in three-quarters of an hour for a total of 15. This is the smallest score on record in Australia in first-class cricket, and there have only been two smaller ones in England – 12 by Oxford University against the MCC, and 13 by Nottinghamshire against Yorkshire. Saunders did not go in, having retired from the match through illness. Rhodes and Arnold bowled wonderfully well, but feeble batting rather flattered them. Victoria scored 269 for four wickets on the first day, but they had to finish their innings on a wicket ruined by twenty-four hours' rain and could do nothing against Rhodes. McAlister batted with great skill for four hours and fifty minutes, but was a little deficient in hitting. The Englishmen ought not to have got anything like 248 on such a faulty pitch, but the fieldsmen were very kind to them. Still, Hayward, apart from one chance, played superb cricket. With only 67 to get the Englishmen won by eight wickets, but again the fieldsmen favoured them, both Warner and Tyldesley being missed.

## Victoria

| | | |
|---|---|---|
| P. McAlister b Rhodes . . . . . . . . . . . . . . . . . . . . . . .139 | – st Strudwick b Rhodes . . . . . . . . . . . | 0 |
| C. E. McLeod st Strudwick b Bosanquet . . . . . . . . . . 23 | – c and b Arnold . . . . . . . . . . . . . . . . | 0 |
| W. W. Armstrong lbw b Rhodes . . . . . . . . . . . . . . . 31 | – c Strudwick b Rhodes . . . . . . . . . . . | 0 |
| G. H. S. Trott c Arnold b Bosanquet . . . . . . . . . . . . 13 | – c Arnold b Rhodes . . . . . . . . . . . . . | 9 |
| V. Ransford b Arnold . . . . . . . . . . . . . . . . . . . . . . 26 | – c Rhodes b Arnold . . . . . . . . . . . . . | 0 |
| F. Laver c Foster b Rhodes . . . . . . . . . . . . . . . . . 34 | – b Rhodes . . . . . . . . . . . . . . . . . . . | 1 |
| C. Baker st Strudwick b Arnold . . . . . . . . . . . . . . . 14 | – st Strudwick b Arnold . . . . . . . . . . . | 3 |
| W. Scott c Arnold b Rhodes . . . . . . . . . . . . . . . . . 2 | – not out . . . . . . . . . . . . . . . . . . . . . | 1 |
| W. Carkeek c Hirst b Rhodes . . . . . . . . . . . . . . . . 2 | – c Bosanquet b Arnold . . . . . . . . . . . | 1 |
| H. Fry c Warner b Rhodes . . . . . . . . . . . . . . . . . . 0 | – c Bosanquet b Rhodes . . . . . . . . . . . | 0 |
| J. V. Saunders not out . . . . . . . . . . . . . . . . . . . . . 0 | – absent ill . . . . . . . . . . . . . . . . . . . . | 0 |
| Extras . . . . . . . . . . . . . . . . . . . . . . . . 15 | B 1 . . . . . . . . . . . . . . . . . . . . | 1 |
| | 299 | 15 |

## MCC Team

P. F. Warner c Saunders b McLeod . . . . . . . . . . . . . . 49 – c Trott b Fry . . . . . . . . . . . . . . . . . 16
J. T. Tyldesley b Saunders . . . . . . . . . . . . . . . . . . . . 2 – not out . . . . . . . . . . . . . . . . . . . . . . 23
L. C. Braund run out . . . . . . . . . . . . . . . . . . . . . . . . 6
R. E. Foster st Carkeek b Laver . . . . . . . . . . . . . . . . 7 – not out . . . . . . . . . . . . . . . . . . . . . . 1
T. Hayward c McAlister b Laver . . . . . . . . . . . . . . 77 – run out . . . . . . . . . . . . . . . . . . . . . . 26
A. E. Knight c McAlister b Saunders . . . . . . . . . . . . 6
G. H. Hirst c Laver b Saunders . . . . . . . . . . . . . . . . 21
B. J. T. Bosanquet c Baker b Armstrong . . . . . . . . . . 13
E. Arnold not out . . . . . . . . . . . . . . . . . . . . . . . . . . 17
W. R. Rhodes b Laver . . . . . . . . . . . . . . . . . . . . . . . 5
H. Strudwick c Ransford b Armstrong . . . . . . . . . . 13
         Extras . . . . . . . . . . . . . . . . . . . . . . . . . . . . 32        Extras . . . . . . . . . . . . . . . . . 2

                                                              248                                            68

### MCC Team's Bowling

|            | Overs | Mdns | Runs | Wkts | Overs | Mdns | Runs | Wkts |
|------------|-------|------|------|------|-------|------|------|------|
| Hirst      | 10    | 2    | 26   | —    |       |      |      |      |
| Arnold     | 26.3  | 9    | 61   | 2    | 6     | 2    | 8    | 4    |
| Braund     | 22    | 6    | 50   | —    |       |      |      |      |
| Rhodes     | 30    | 6    | 62   | 6    | 6.1   | 3    | 6    | 5    |
| Bosanquet  | 25    | 3    | 75   | 2    |       |      |      |      |
| Hayward    | 4     | 1    | 10   | —    |       |      |      |      |

### Victoria Bowling

|            | Overs | Mdns | Runs | Wkts | Overs | Mdns | Runs | Wkts |
|------------|-------|------|------|------|-------|------|------|------|
| Saunders   | 15    | 3    | 39   | 3    |       |      |      |      |
| Laver      | 16    | 1    | 64   | 3    | 6     | 1    | 9    | —    |
| Trott      | 3     | —    | 15   | —    |       |      |      |      |
| McLeod     | 9     | —    | 35   | 1    | 8     | —    | 21   | —    |
| Ransford   | 2     | —    | 5    | —    | 3     | —    | 12   | —    |
| Fry        | 5     | 1    | 23   | —    | 10    | 1    | 24   | 1    |
| Armstrong  | 12.2  | 3    | 35   | 2    |       |      |      |      |

## MCC v NEW SOUTH WALES

### Played at Sydney, February 12, 13, 15, 1904

This was emphatically Bosanquet's match. Thanks mainly to his superb all-round cricket the Englishmen won by 278 runs, the victory being one of the most brilliant of the whole tour. At the close of the second day there seemed every reason to expect a close finish, the English team, with six wickets down for 254 in their second innings, being only 212 runs ahead. Next morning New South Wales were without Cotter, who had fallen on his shoulder in fielding, and the English score was increased to 461. Bosanquet, who had made 19 over-night, hit in wonderful form, and was batting altogether for less than an hour and a half, his innings including a straight drive for 5 and seventeen 4s. He and Knight took the score from 235 to 378. Knight, who only played at the last moment instead of Fielder, obtained his 104 in irreproachable style, never giving a chance. When New South Wales went in to get 420, Bosanquet followed up his great innings with some irresistible bowling, sending down nine overs and four balls for 45 runs and six wickets.

## MCC Team

| | | | |
|---|---|---|---|
| P. F. Warner c Noble b Cotter | 0 | – b Bowden | 8 |
| T. Hayward c Kelly b Cotter | 5 | – b Cotter | 46 |
| J. T. Tyldesley c Trumper b Cotter | 17 | – lbw b Cotter | 28 |
| R. E. Foster lbw b Bowden | 19 | – c Bowden b Cotter | 4 |
| L. C. Braund b Hopkins | 5 | – c S. Gregory b Noble | 32 |
| A. E. Knight b Howell | 23 | – c Bowden b Howell | 104 |
| G. H. Hirst c Noble b Cotter | 44 | – c Noble b Hopkins | 40 |
| B. J. T. Bosanquet c Howell b Hopkins | 54 | – c Howell b Noble | 114 |
| A. A. Lilley run out | 8 | – b Bowden | 2 |
| A. E. Relf c Trumper b Cotter | 1 | – c Noble b Hopkins | 21 |
| W. R. Rhodes not out | 2 | – not out | 49 |
| Extras | 12 | Extras | 18 |
| | **190** | | **461** |

## New South Wales

| | | | |
|---|---|---|---|
| C. Gregory b Hirst | 1 | – c Rhodes b Hosanquet | 8 |
| V. Trumper c Hayward b Hirst | 44 | – b Braund | 5 |
| M. A. Noble c Lilley b Bosanquet | 36 | – c Lilley b Hirst | 11 |
| J. R. Mackay b Braund | 2 | – b Bosanquet | 9 |
| S. E. Gregory c Lilley b Bosanquet | 20 | – c Rhodes b Bosanquet | 24 |
| R. A. Duff run out | 10 | – c Relf b Hirst | 18 |
| A. J. Hopkins b Rhodes | 52 | – b Bosanquet | 56 |
| J. J. Kelly not out | 33 | – c and b Bosanquet | 1 |
| Bowden b Rhodes | 0 | – run out | 5 |
| Cotter b Rhodes | 16 | – c Knight b Bosanquet | 3 |
| W. P. Howell c Tyldesley b Hirst | 8 | – not out | 0 |
| Extras | 10 | Extra | 1 |
| | **232** | | **141** |

### New South Wales Bowling

| | Overs | Mdns | Runs | Wkts | Overs | Mdns | Runs | Wkts |
|---|---|---|---|---|---|---|---|---|
| Cotter | 14 | 3 | 44 | 5 | 11 | — | 56 | 3 |
| Hopkins | 18 | 4 | 65 | 2 | 26.1 | 5 | 85 | 2 |
| Bowden | 12 | — | 34 | 1 | 39 | 6 | 135 | 2 |
| Howell | 8 | 2 | 35 | 1 | 23 | 3 | 80 | 1 |
| Noble | | | | | 21 | 1 | 92 | 2 |

### MCC Team's Bowling

| | Overs | Mdns | Runs | Wkts | Overs | Mdns | Runs | Wkts |
|---|---|---|---|---|---|---|---|---|
| Hirst | 16.3 | 3 | 61 | 3 | 11 | — | 37 | 2 |
| Relf | 4 | — | 30 | — | | | | |
| Bosanquet | 14 | 2 | 51 | 2 | 9.4 | — | 45 | 6 |
| Braund | 10 | — | 30 | 1 | 10 | 2 | 38 | 1 |
| Rhodes | 19 | 7 | 50 | 3 | 10 | 3 | 20 | — |

# MCC IN AUSTRALIA 1903-04

## Impressions of the Tour

### By B. J. T. Bosanquet

Our team has been honoured with such a variety of names that it is difficult to select from the number, which range from "An MCC XI" to "England." The one I should prefer is "P. F. Warner's XI," as our captain had so much to do with the success of the year. The above, however, is probably the most popularly known, for which reason I have adopted it. So much has been written about the tour, and all the statistics and scores are already so well known, that it is difficult to know what aspects of the tour to write upon at this distant date. I propose to give a mere outline of the actual cricket and deal chiefly with the incidents of the tour, with individual performances, and, especially with the conditions under which the matches were played, and the influence of weather on their results, concerning which there appears to have been much misapprehension in England, and elsewhere. Even in Australia an enthusiastic lady was good enough to send our captain an urn, labelled "The ashes of Australian Cricket. Won by Captain Warner; assisted by Captain Weather!" I hope to be able to show how unjust this view was, and also to give an idea of the wickets on which we played.

We were favoured with an exceptionally fine passage on the "Orontes," "Captain Weather" being certainly kind to us in this respect. The voyage would have been worth taking if only for a wonderful display of phosphorescent brilliance which we ran into just before Colombo, and also a special performance by the Aurora Australis, which is rarely seen so far north. I refer to the voyage for the reason that, in my opinion, those four weeks of life on board ship, in which we were thrown so much together, were a great factor in our subsequent success. I am sure they went a long way towards helping us all to pull together, in furthering our better acquaintance, and in engendering that feeling of good-comradeship without which it is impossible for any side to do well.

Before touching upon the events in Australia, I wish to refer briefly to the remarkable soil known as "Bulli," of which the wickets at Sydney are composed. Without some knowledge of the extraordinary qualities of this soil, it would be impossible for anyone to follow with any intelligence the course of the matches we played at Sydney. This soil was imported from the "Bulli" Range, laid down to a depth of some six inches, and rolled into a solid mass. In this form it possesses the unique property of being absolutely impermeable to water, which can never penetrate further than half-an-inch from the surface, and can only affect it to this depth owing to the roots of the grass, which break it up to a certain degree, and enable the water to penetrate to this slight extent. Where there is no grass a lump of "Bulli" will remain entirely unaffected by any immersion, however long in water. This being so it is not difficult to understand that the period during which the Sydney wicket remains affected by rain is of the briefest. Once the wicket becomes fit for play, it dries with extraordinary rapidity. The difficulty is to get it fit, for the water, as will be easily understood, being unable to sink through, simply lies on the surface and has to be mopped up, or run off to one side.

The first match v New South Wales is a very good illustration of what I want my readers to understand. The day before the commencement of the match there was a terrific thunderstorm, and at six o'clock in the evening the playing area was a veritable lake. Next day at 12 o'clock one end was quite dry and hard, while the other was only sticky up to lunch time, and had perfectly recovered when we went in. Rhodes was innocuous at one end, and it was not till he changed over that he did any damage. Please, therefore, reader, when you hear of rain at Sydney, do not imagine that the match was played on a sticky wicket; one complete innings is usually the limit of time for which it is affected, and a proper appreciation of this fact will be of great assistance in following the course of these matches.

After the New South Wales match we had a fortnight's rest from serious cricket, and spent the time in a most enjoyable trip to Brisbane, and two matches on the return journey at West Maitland and Newcastle. The journey to Brisbane was remarkable for the great interest in the team that was displayed by the people of the various places at which we stopped. Crowds met the train, and pressed against the saloon, enquiring for Rhodes and Warner, who were the popular heroes. It was quite unsafe to give the real name of anyone, as he would have been promptly mobbed, and those furthest from the windows did duty, as being safest from friendly violence. We did not want a verdict of "killed by kindness" passed on our Yorkshireman.

Queensland gave us a good game, and produced a fast aboriginal bowler. Leonard Braund was selected to open the innings for us and didn't much fancy it. The first ball hit the bat somehow and went to fine leg for two; the second, passed batsman, wicket-keeper, and longstop, and hit the screen about the time Braund finished his shot. The third was slower, and the batsman, retiring gracefully, placed it gently into point's hands. His own account of the proceedings is worth giving, it is as follows:

"I took first ball from the aboriginal, Henry, supposed to be the fastest bowler in the world, and certainly I will say that the first three balls he gave me were indeed the fastest I have ever seen. I got him away for two on the leg side, but the next ball, in cutting him, I was splendidly caught at point!"

Queensland had a most promising cricketer in Evans, who is a very fine natural hitter, and a more than useful wicket-keeper. He should be heard of again.

West Maitland provided an interesting draw. Their fielding and bowling were a bit slack, and Foster remonstrated. Unfortunately when we took the field, I had an off-day, and at the close of the match their captain said quietly to Foster, "Well, I don't think our bowling was much worse than Bosanquet's!"

Newcastle produced another draw, and here George Hirst was insulted. Having adjourned for a drink, he was just in time to hear someone say, "that Hirst is a —— rotten player!" Leaving his drink he retired, being with difficulty restrained from wreaking summary vengeance, and never knew a happy moment till, having persuaded Foster to send him in first, he had taken 50 of the very best in our second innings.

This brings us to the first test match. Of this I will merely say that the luck was evenly distributed and, that we thoroughly deserved our win. I think this will be a good opportunity for me to give a brief summary of the test matches, and the conditions under which they were played.

It is unnecessary to discuss the two matches at Melbourne, which were robbed of all interest by the weather. In the first we had all the luck, and winning the toss meant the match. In the second the conditions were exactly reversed, and they won the toss, and with it the match. These two matches then exactly counter-balanced each other and the real struggle was confined to the two matches at Sydney, and the match at Adelaide. It was, in fact, a series of three matches, in which we won the rubber. In these three matches I venture to say – in spite of many assertions to the contrary, made in the papers, here and elsewhere – that the luck was as evenly distributed as possible, and I hope to be able to make this clear.

In the first match (at Sydney) rain fell on the Friday night, and the wicket did not recover till lunch-time on the second day. In this period (two hours) their last three wickets fell for an addition of twenty-six, and we lost Warner and Hayward. Only a magnificent effort by Tyldesley saved us from further disaster, as the wicket was quite difficult. After lunch it was much easier, though not quite perfect till about 4 o'clock. No one, therefore, can possibly maintain that this rain was to our advantage, and it was the only rain that fell. The rest of the match was fought out under absolutely even conditions, unless the fact of having fourth innings be counted a disadvantage to us, which it was to a certain extent, as the wicket had worn appreciably. At Adelaide no rain fell at all, and conditions were again even, except that again we had to bat last. In the other match at Sydney a great deal of rain fell at various times, and it is somewhat difficult to convey a true notion of how it affected the play.

There had been a good deal before the match started, and the wicket was a bit soft on the first day, though never exactly difficult. Our score of 207 for seven, therefore, was not a bad one, though nothing out of the way. The wicket was much better next day, our three wickets added forty-two runs, and they had thirty-five for one wicket, when a slight drizzle came on, which stopped play for about an hour and a half. After this they had two hours on a fast true wicket, in a slight drizzle, and we got five of them for 114, a good performance on this wicket. There was no more play till the Tuesday at 4 o'clock. The wicket then was quite hard underneath, with water standing on the top. (Remember the "Bulli" soil). Rhodes and Arnold, for some unaccountable reason, got the rest of them out for an addition of 17 runs. Not a ball turned an inch, and why they got out is one of those mysteries that make cricket the game it is. We had an hour on the drying wicket, though it never got difficult, and Hayward and Foster made about 50 without being parted. Next day more rain, and a wicket getting worse right up to the end, which found us with nine men out for 155. Next day a plumb, fast wicket, as was shown by the ease with which Warner and Rhodes added 55 runs. Our opponents thus had to get 329, a task which they were confident of accomplishing in the condition of the wicket.

Well, I don't think there is much in all this that was to our advantage. Personally, I think things were about even. It was a great pity the two matches at Melbourne were robbed of their interest, but the other three were all worthy of the highest traditions of the game. A word is due to our opponents and particularly Noble, for the fine and sportsmanlike spirit in which they met us, which did much to make the games so enjoyable.

Now how was it we managed to win? Of course, as was only to be expected, we are informed that Australia is weaker at the present time than for years past. That is an assertion which I think it is unnecessary to refute, and its fallacy will be sufficiently demonstrated when they are over here next year. I am inclined to think that it was the greater variety we possessed in bowling that carried the day. There was little to choose between the teams as far as batting was concerned. Their famous quartette were, of course, far superior to our four best batsmen, but the rest of our batting was superior to theirs. Trumper was far the best bat on either side, though Noble and Duff have improved enormously since they were seen over here in 1902. They had plenty of bowling, but it was all too much of a kind – nearly all right-hand medium – and it was this lack of variety that let them down.

The introduction of Cotter made a great deal of difference and he should do very well over here. His action is a bit low, but he has plenty of pace, a sure foothold on any wicket, and can generally make the ball get up in a disconcerting fashion. It is strange to Englishmen to see a fast bowler begin the bowling when the wicket is thoroughly wet, but in Australia the ground is so hard underneath that a fast bowler is almost unplayable under such conditions. Cotter certainly was; he got a footing where Rhodes was unable to, and made the ball fly tremendously. It was generally chest high, and frequently over one's head. We made the discovery too late in the tour to take advantage of it, but it looked as if it were always advisable to play a fast bowler on these wet wickets. Hopkins is a greatly improved bowler, and has changed his style. Noble was as good as ever and Trumble not much his inferior. Individually their bowlers were probably quite as good as ours, but they did not form nearly such a strong combination, and that was where we had the pull. In wicket-keeping also we had the advantage. Lilly was magnificent throughout, and hardly missed a catch. Kelly, though bringing off some brilliant catches, was not safe or consistent. (Strudwick, of course, never had a chance.)

Another important factor in our success was the personality of our captain. The keenest of enthusiasts, and, as he would say, a "cheerful optimist" he infected the whole team with his own spirit, and in addition never spared himself if he could do anything for the comfort, or pleasure, of the men under him. His sole thought was for us, and no one of us can ever properly appreciate, or be sufficiently grateful for, all he did for us. A wise, and most successful captain on the field, his tact and kindly influence in less strenuous moments had even more to do with his final triumph. Most of the hard work of the tour, and most of the troubles and worries incidental to such a trip, fell on his shoulders. He never shirked and never complained, and herein performed the greater part of a captain's duty. In his own words the day on which we won the rubber constituted "the happiest moment of his life," and never was happiness more deserved. We could have wished him better luck with the bat, but personal success was the last consideration with him. In other fields he earned distinction, notably as an orator. In this connection we suffered, if I may use the word, from excess of hospitality. Much as we appreciated the kindly feelings which prompted the welcome extended to us on all hands, one *can* have too much of a good thing, and speeches, when one has just arrived after a fatiguing journey, sometimes about 10 pm, can hardly be too short. The kindness and hospitality shown to us by private individuals all over the country could not have been surpassed, and everybody did their best to give us the best of good times, which we certainly had, and we can never be sufficiently grateful for all that was done for us on every hand.

In future tours one would like to see the up country matches omitted. They are no sort of trial, even for one's opponents, and cause slackness, if only from the fact that they can never be finished. They do more harm than good, and in future a team would do far better either to play only first-class matches or, if that would be too great a strain, take six weeks' holiday in the middle to the tour, and visit New Zealand and Tasmania, playing a few matches, which would pay well – "pecunia omnia vincit" – and be of far more interest than those matches in Australia. The trip would be a most enjoyable one, and be a nice rest in the middle of what must always be an arduous undertaking. It was a pity our tour was not financially successful, but on the terms financial success could hardly be looked for, though had we been favoured with finer weather at Melbourne much of the deficit would have been made up. As Warner told Major Wardill, in joke, the Melbourne Club will have to give a guarantee for future matches!

As we are to have a visit next year from our late opponents, a word as to the new men we are likely to see over here. Cotter, for one, Gehrs, Claxton and possibly Newland from S. Australia, and McAlister from Victoria. The last-named is one of the soundest batsmen in Australia and a very fine player. He cuts beautifully, drives well on the off, and seldom lets off a leg ball. He should do extremely well over here if he finds a dry season. Gehrs is the most promising bat in Australia. His forcing strokes both back and forward are splendid. He has tremendous possibilities, and might well be another Trumper. Both these two are magnificent fieldsmen. Claxton is a good bat, and a very much better bowler than he looks. Right-hand, round the wicket, he is much faster than one thinks, and goes away with his arm. He was consistently successful for South Australia last season. Newland is a good wicket-keeper, and a really good bat, though not recognised as such. His on-side play is remarkable. Jennings is also a most promising batsman, and Windsor (of Tasmania) has been mentioned, but, though a good bowler, he is not quite class enough. There is also a probability of Darling being once more seen over here, though not necessarily as captain.

Their chief need is a really good left hand bowler (Saunders being too uncertain), and a right-hand bowler to take the place of Trumble – should the latter adhere to his decision to retire from the game. Personally, I think the odds are about 100 to 1 against his coming here again. In this case his mantle may fall on Hopkins' shoulders. Anyhow they will be a very strong side, equal, I think, to any they have sent over for many years, and probably the best batting side Australia has ever produced.

Let us not underrate them, and let us do our best to beat them. It has been a great pleasure to go over the tour once more, if only in recollection. If I have failed to convey any true impression of it, let the distance of time be my excuse. After the lapse of such a period the tour presents itself to the mental vision as some vast panorama, in which the details are obscured by distance, and it is not easy to provide the telescope wherewith to pick them out clearly. We had the very best of games, and the Goddess of Victory smiled on us. Finis coronat opus, and the tour may be written as successful in every way – except financially.

## ENGLAND v AUSTRALIA
### First Test Match

Played at Sydney, December 13, 14, 16, 17, 18, 19, 1907

A. O. Jones being in hospital at Brisbane, the captaincy of the England team for the First Test match devolved upon Fane. George Gunn was called upon for the first time and with the idea of strengthening the batting, R. A. Young was picked as wicket-keeper, in preference to Humphries. The match proved a great attraction, the takings amounting to £3,000. On the second day the crowd numbered 32,000. Winning the toss, the Englishmen stayed in for four hours and ten minutes for a total of 273. At one time they seemed likely to make a far bigger score, but some of the batsmen found Cotter's pace too much for them. George Gunn's batting was as nearly as possible faultless. Making his runs in two hours and a half, he hit twenty 4s and his only mistake was a hard chance at third man, when 108. At the end of the afternoon the Australians had scored 50 for one wicket, and on the Saturday they exceeded the English total by 27 runs. Clem Hill played a splendid innings, never being at fault till Gunn caught him at third man. In England's second innings all the honours went to the two Nottinghamshire players, Gunn and Hardstaff putting on 113 runs together for the fourth wicket. At one point a big total seemed in prospect but after the tea interval six wickets fell for 34 runs. The innings ended early on the fourth morning for 300. The Australians were left with 274 to get. They lost Trumper, Hill and Macartney for 27 runs, and when at five o'clock rain caused stumps to be drawn, the score stood at 63 for three wickets. On the Wednesday the state of the ground made play impossible, and on the following morning everything pointed to a win for England. The wicket recovered surprisingly well, but it was the general opinion that the English bowlers ought to have done better during the first hour. The finish of the match was exciting to a degree. When their seventh wicket fell the Australians still required 89 runs to win. Carter, who played a fine innings, was out at 218 and then Cotter and Hazlitt amid great enthusiasm hit off the remaining 56 runs in less than forty minutes, Australia gaining a glorious victory by two wickets.

### England

| | | | |
|---|---|---|---|
| F. L. Fane c Trumper b Cotter | 2 | – c Noble b Saunders | 33 |
| R. A. Young c Carter b Cotter | 13 | – b Noble | 3 |
| G. Gunn c Hazlitt b Cotter | 119 | – c Noble b Cotter | 74 |
| K. L. Hutchings c and b Armstrong | 42 | – c Armstrong b Saunders | 17 |
| L. C. Braund b Cotter | 32 | – not out | 32 |
| J. Hardstaff b Armstrong | 12 | – b Noble | 63 |
| W. Rhodes run out | 1 | – c McAlister b Macartney | 29 |
| J. N. Crawford b Armstrong | 31 | – c Hazlitt b Cotter | 5 |
| S. F. Barnes b Cotter | 1 | – b Saunders | 11 |
| C. Blythe b Cotter | 5 | – c Noble b Saunders | 15 |
| A. Fielder not out | 1 | – lbw b Armstrong | 6 |
| B 7, l-b 6, w 1, n-b 2 | 16 | B 2, w 3, n-b 7 | 12 |
| | **273** | | **300** |

### Australia

| | | | |
|---|---|---|---|
| V. Trumper b Fielder | 43 | – b Barnes | 3 |
| P. A. McAlister c Hutchings b Barnes | 3 | – b Crawford | 41 |
| C. Hill c Gunn b Fielder | 87 | – b Fielder | 1 |
| M. A. Noble c Braund b Fielder | 37 | – b Barnes | 27 |
| W. W. Armstrong c Braund b Fielder | 7 | – b Crawford | 44 |
| V. Ransford c Braund b Rhodes | 24 | – c and b Blythe | 13 |
| C. G. Macartney c Young b Fielder | 35 | – c Crawford b Fielder | 9 |
| H. Carter b Braund | 25 | – c Young b Fielder | 61 |
| G. Hazlitt not out | 18 | – not out | 34 |
| A. Cotter b Braund | 2 | – not out | 33 |
| J. V. Saunders c Braund b Fielder | 9 | | |
| B 4, l-b 2, w 2, n-b 2 | 10 | B 6, n-b 3 | 9 |
| | **300** | | **275** |

## Australia Bowling

| | Overs | Mdns | Runs | Wkts | Overs | Mdns | Runs | Wkts |
|---|---|---|---|---|---|---|---|---|
| Cotter .......... | 21.5 | — | 101 | 6 | 26 | 1 | 101 | 2 |
| Saunders ........ | 11 | — | 42 | — | 23 | 6 | 68 | 4 |
| Hazlitt .......... | 9 | 2 | 32 | — | 4 | 2 | 24 | — |
| Armstrong ....... | 26 | 10 | 63 | 3 | 27 | 14 | 33 | 1 |
| Macartney ....... | 3 | — | 5 | — | 14 | 2 | 39 | 1 |
| Noble ........... | 6 | 1 | 14 | — | 15 | 5 | 23 | 2 |

## England Bowling

| | Overs | Mdns | Runs | Wkts | Overs | Mdns | Runs | Wkts |
|---|---|---|---|---|---|---|---|---|
| Fielder .......... | 30.2 | 4 | 82 | 6 | 27.3 | 4 | 88 | 3 |
| Barnes .......... | 22 | 3 | 74 | 1 | 30 | 7 | 63 | 2 |
| Blythe .......... | 12 | 1 | 33 | — | 19 | 5 | 55 | 1 |
| Braund .......... | 17 | 2 | 74 | 2 | 7 | 2 | 14 | — |
| Crawford ........ | 5 | 1 | 14 | — | 8 | 2 | 33 | 2 |
| Rhodes .......... | 5 | 2 | 13 | 1 | 7 | 3 | 13 | — |

# ENGLAND v AUSTRALIA
## Second Test Match

Played at Melbourne, January 1, 2, 3, 4, 6, 7, 1908

In the week previous to the second Test match, five inches of rain had been registered in Melbourne, but the weather cleared up and no fault could be found with the wicket. In fact the ground had dried so rapidly that it was not thought necessary to include Blythe in the England eleven. The mistake of playing Young instead of Humphries was of course not repeated. On the first innings the Englishmen gained a lead of 116 runs and at one time they looked to have the match in their hands, but in the end they only scrambled home by one wicket, the Australians playing a splendid uphill game. Though intensely interesting the cricket was for the most part very slow, the Australians taking the whole of the first afternoon to score 255 for seven wickets. It must be said, however, that Crawford and Fielder bowled extremely well. In England's first innings Hobbs and Hutchings were seen at their best. Hobbs who had never before taken part in a Test Match scored 83 out of 160 in a trifle over three hours, his defence being very strong. Hutchings, after beginning quietly, hit in great form, his 126 including a 6 and twenty-five 4s. At the end of the third day Trumper and Noble scored 96 together without being parted. Next morning Trumper was leg before wicket at 126, and when the fourth wicket fell the total was only 162. The position looked very serious, but Armstrong and Macartney added 106 runs together in two hours and a quarter. Carter afterwards hit finely and the innings did not close until the total had reached 397. The batting all through was admirable, Armstrong showing the best form. England wanted 282 to win, and at the drawing of stumps the score stood at 159 for four wickets. On the sixth and last day the Englishmen began badly and when their eighth wicket fell with 73 runs still required, the match looked all over. However, Humphries and Barnes put on 34 together and then, to the astonishment of everyone concerned, Barnes and Fielder hit off the remaining 39 runs, and won the match. Barnes played with great judgment and coolness for his 38 not uot. The last run was a desperately short one and if Hazlitt, throwing in from cover point, had managed to hit the wicket, the result would have been a tie.

## Australia

| | | | |
|---|---|---|---|
| V. Trumper c Humphries b Crawford | 49 | – lbw b Crawford | 63 |
| C. G. Macartney b Crawford | 37 | – c Humphries b Barnes | 54 |
| C. Hill b Fielder | 16 | – b Fielder | 3 |
| M. A. Noble c Braund b Rhodes | 61 | – b Crawford | 64 |
| W. W. Armstrong c Hutchings b Crawford | 31 | – b Barnes | 77 |
| P. A. McAlister run out | 10 | – run out | 15 |
| A. Cotter b Crawford | 17 | – lbw b Crawford | 27 |
| G. Hazlitt b Crawford | 1 | – b Barnes | 3 |
| V. Ransford run out | 27 | – c Hutchings b Barnes | 18 |
| H. Carter not out | 15 | – c Fane b Barnes | 53 |
| J. V. Saunders b Fielder | 0 | – not out | 0 |
| L-b 1, w 1 | 2 | B 12, l-b 8 | 20 |
| | **266** | | **397** |

## England

| | | | |
|---|---|---|---|
| F. L. Fane b Armstrong | 13 | – b Armstrong | 50 |
| J. B. Hobbs b Carter | 83 | – b Noble | 28 |
| G. Gunn lbw b Cotter | 15 | – lbw b Noble | 0 |
| K. L. Hutchings b Cotter | 126 | – c Cotter b Macartney | 39 |
| L. C. Braund b Cotter | 49 | – b Armstrong | 30 |
| J. Hardstaff b Saunders | 12 | – c Ransford b Cotter | 19 |
| W. Rhodes b Saunders | 32 | – run out | 15 |
| J. N. Crawford c Ransford b Saunders | 16 | – c Armstrong b Saunders | 10 |
| S. F. Barnes c Hill b Armstrong | 14 | – not out | 38 |
| J. Humphries b Cotter | 6 | – lbw b Armstrong | 16 |
| A. Fielder not out | 6 | – not out | 18 |
| B 3, l-b 3, w 1, n-b 3 | 10 | B 9, l-b 7, w 1, n-b 2 | 19 |
| | **382** | | **282** |

## England Bowling

| | Overs | Mdns | Runs | Wkts | Overs | Mdns | Runs | Wkts |
|---|---|---|---|---|---|---|---|---|
| Fielder | 27.5 | 4 | 77 | 2 | 27 | 6 | 74 | 1 |
| Barnes | 17 | 7 | 30 | — | 27.4 | 4 | 72 | 5 |
| Rhodes | 11 | — | 37 | 1 | 16 | 6 | 38 | — |
| Braund | 16 | 5 | 41 | — | 18 | 2 | 68 | — |
| Crawford | 29 | 1 | 79 | 5 | 33 | 6 | 125 | 3 |

## Australia Bowling

| | Overs | Mdns | Runs | Wkts | Overs | Mdns | Runs | Wkts |
|---|---|---|---|---|---|---|---|---|
| Cotter | 33 | 4 | 142 | 5 | 28 | 3 | 82 | 1 |
| Saunders | 34 | 7 | 100 | 3 | 30 | 9 | 58 | 1 |
| Noble | 9 | 3 | 26 | — | 22 | 7 | 41 | 2 |
| Armstrong | 34.2 | 15 | 36 | 2 | 30.4 | 10 | 53 | 3 |
| Hazlitt | 13 | 1 | 34 | — | 2 | 1 | 8 | — |
| Macartney | 12 | 2 | 34 | — | 9 | 3 | 21 | 1 |

## THE MCC TEAM IN AUSTRALIA, 1911-12

As everyone knows, the tour of the MCC's team in Australia in the winter of 1911-12 was, in a cricket sense, a triumphant success. The Englishmen won the rubber of five Test matches by four to one, and except in the first Test game at Sydney, suffered no defeat. The team consisted of the following sixteen players:–

Mr P. F. Warner (Middlesex).
Mr J. W. H. T. Douglas (Essex).
Mr F. R. Foster (Warwickshire).
J. B. Hobbs (Surrey).
W. Rhodes (Yorkshire).
F. E. Woolley (Kent).
S. F. Barnes (Staffordshire).
J. W. Hearne (Middlesex).

George Gunn (Nottinghamshire).
E. J. Smith (Warwickshire).
C. P. Mead (Hampshire).
W. Hitch (Surrey).
H. Strudwick (Surrey).
S. P. Kinneir (Warwickshire).
J. Vine (Sussex), and
J. Iremonger (Nottinghamshire).

Mr P. F. Warner was chosen by the MCC to captain the side, but after scoring 151 in the opening match against South Australia, at Adelaide, he had a serious illness, and could take no further part in the tour, the leadership devolving upon Mr Douglas, who, after the first Test match, proved himself an excellent captain, and had a big share in winning the game that gave the rubber to England. Mr Warner happily recovered in time to see some of the most important matches, and I cannot do better than re-print the general summary of the tour that he sent home to the *Westminster Gazette*. I may add that Mr Tom Pawley of Kent was a most efficient and popular manager.                    S. H. P.

Mr Warner wrote:– Eighteen matches played, twelve won, five drawn, and one lost, is the complete record of the MCC tour, a very great performance. At the present time Australian cricket is honeycombed with an amount of personal feeling and bitterness that is almost incredible, and this fact must, to some extent, have militated against our opponents showing their true form; but it does not explain away our decisive victories. Four of the five Test matches were won, three of them by such large margins as eight wickets, seven wickets, and an innings and 225 runs. South Australia was beaten by an innings and 194 runs, Victoria by 47 runs, and in the return match by eight wickets. Queensland by seven wickets, New South Wales by eight wickets in the return, the first match being drawn, Tasmania by eight wickets and in the return by an innings and 65 runs, while we had rather the better of the undecided XI of Australia game at Brisbane. When I was in Australia eight years ago neither the Queensland nor Tasmanian matches were considered first class, but they are now so reckoned, so that our record for purely first-class matches works out at fourteen played, eleven won, two drawn, and one lost.

The team has had some rare batting triumphs, but the batting of the side never struck me as being relatively so good as the bowling and general out-cricket. I will, therefore, take our bowlers first, and of these Foster and Barnes achieved wonders. Finer bowling than theirs I have never seen on hard, true wickets. In the Test matches alone they took sixty-six wickets (Barnes thirty-four, Foster thirty-two) between them out of the ninety-five that fell, five men being run out, while in all first-class matches Foster took sixty-two wickets and Barnes fifty-nine, the former at a cost of 20.19 and the latter at 20.86 each. Match after match their consistency was extraordinary, and it is impossible to praise them too highly. Barnes is as great a bowler as ever, and that means that he is the finest medium-paced bowler of the day – the Australians have no doubt on this point – while Foster is the best bowler of his type I have ever seen. Bowling round the wicket with a high delivery, his action was the personification of ease. A few short steps, an apparently medium-paced ball through the air, but doubling its speed as it touched the ground, he kept an exceptional length on the leg-stump. He swerved a little with the new ball, but the angle of delivery made the ball swing into the batsman without swerve. Foster at times bowled at the left-handers' legs. He used this form of attack against Hill, Bardsley, and Ransford, and kept them on the defensive. He is not such an artist with the ball as Barnes, but he is a most dangerous bowler, who on his day can "go through" the best side.

It may be interesting to note that the thirty-four wickets Barnes obtained in the Test matches is the largest number obtained by an English bowler in Test matches in Australia, and only equalled by George Giffen in 1894-95; but Barnes averaged 22.88 per wicket as against 24.17 by Giffen. Douglas gave strong support to Foster and Barnes. On Australian wickets he is a better bowler than he has yet proved himself to be in England, but I think he has improved, and, what is more, that he will go on improving. Physically very strong, he bowled with great energy and determination, kept a really excellent length, made pace off the pitch, and all the while was a bit flighty, the ball swinging a little in the air. His bowling in the fourth Test match was up to a high standard. It will be seen that our three stock bowlers had the sovereign merits of length and pace off the pitch. After Foster, Barnes, and Douglas, our bowling was not of great account, though I fancy if Hitch had kept free from strains he would have achieved a fair amount of success. He was bowling well when he broke down at the end of November, and was out of the field for a month. Then just as he had run into form again he broke down once more, and could not play for another three weeks. He bowled well in the first innings of the fifth Test match. His figures for first-class matches are somewhat fallacious, about half of his wickets being taken in Tasmania. The wickets did not suit Woolley, but once or twice he was very useful, and he did far better work than his figures might suggest. Hearne was a great failure – look at his Test match average! He seldom struck a length, and was very expensive; but whenever he did happen to get a length he worried the batsmen. His failure as a bowler was a great disappointment to me, as, remembering what Bosanquet had done in 1903-04, I had thought he would act as a foil to Hordern. He showed no approach to his real form, but I still believe that on his day and in his hour he is nearly as good a bowler as Hordern. He has nothing like Hordern's length, consistency, or persistency, but he comes off the pitch must faster than the great Australian cricketer, and is quicker through the air. He is one who requires very careful supervision. Vine, the other leg-break bowler, was easily got to and driven either on the full-pitch or the half-volley, and Iremonger, though he bowled steadily and well in four or five innings, did not look like taking many wickets. On the other hand, with Barnes in such form, he had few opportunities. Rhodes, who headed the bowling averages in 1903-04, did not take a single wicket in the first-class matches! Eight years ago he used to go in last and bowl the other side out! Finally there was Hobbs, who, in the return with New South Wales, showed that in Australia, as in England, he is a dangerous bowler with a new ball.

Before we left England many critics thought that as a fielding side we should prove weak, but, as a matter of fact, the fielding was excellent. We had no long-field like Ransford, and with such bowlers as Barnes, Foster, and Douglas the want of a really great outfield was not felt, but our catching was very sound and steady, few chances being missed, and in Hobbs we had a cover-point the equal of any fieldsman in that position I have ever seen. Not even G. L. Jessop at his best is his superior. Wonderfully quick in moving to the ball, neat with his feet, and with a pair of hands which were not only always in the right place but which seemed to act as a magnet to the ball, Hobbs has a beautiful and fast return. I have never seen a cover-point hit the wicket so often, his underhand throw-in being particularly deadly in this respect. During the tour he caught seven and ran out no fewer than fifteen men. Surely another record for this record-breaker!

Gunn made a very good first slip, the occasions on which he missed a catch being rare, and Woolley, whenever he was placed in the slips, did fine work, two of his catches in the final Test match being worthy of poor George Lohmann himself. Foster generally fielded second slip, but he does not get down to the ball very quickly, and is not what one would call a good slip. The long-field work was done by Vine, Mead, Hearne, and Woolley. Vine covered a lot of ground, and saved many runs, and was a great favourite with the crowd, who admired his keenness in sprinting; Mead was reliable and caught some good catches. Hearne, too, could be generally depended on to hold a catch. Rhodes was good anywhere; you cannot put him out of place in the field, and Hitch was splendid. He, like Rhodes, seemed to be able to take any position with success, though his throwing-in was sometimes marked by exuberance of spirit.

Barnes is a nonchalant kind of fielder, though he is not so indifferent as he looks. He has long, sinewy fingers, which seem to grasp the ball easily, and he fielded extremely well at point in the first Test match, picking up some hard hits with either hand with marked ease. Iremonger did not field well, and Kinneir, though he tried hard, is very slow. We were very fortunate in possessing two such fine wicket-keepers as Strudwick and Smith. The latter kept in four of the five Test matches, but I should not like to say that he is a better wicket-keeper than Strudwick. His work in the second Test match and in the first innings of the third was magnificent; he kept well in the fourth, but in the final game at Sydney he was distinctly below the standard of what one expects from an England wicket-keeper, and let pass a greater number of byes. Smith is extremely good in taking Foster, who is a difficult bowler to keep wicket to, a thorough understanding appearing to exist between them, and he is extraordinarily clever on the leg-side. He catches his catches, and is, at his best, a great wicket-keeper. If he had not kept so badly at Sydney one would have formed an even higher opinion of his work. In one respect he is certainly not the equal of Strudwick, and that is in getting up to the wicket when standing back to a fast bowler, to take a return. Strudwick kept very well at Sydney, and if he only played in one Test match that does not mean that he has lost anything in reputation. He took his disappointment like the fine manly fellow he is, and never a jealous word passed his lips.

I have long since exhausted my vocabulary of praise in favour of Rhodes and Hobbs, and, thanks in a very large degree to their superlative work, our batting was eminently successful. Too much stress cannot be laid on what they accomplished, for in innings after innings they gave us a wonderful start. They were the backbone of the batting. Gunn batted most consistently. He is quite an original player – a daring, cheeky batsman – who plays in an almost lackadaisical air, but as to his class there can be no two opinions. Hearne was a great success, and the critics thought very highly of him. He made 114 in a Test match before he was twenty-one, and there is no reason why he should not develop into the best batsman in England. I expect him to be that in five or six years' time. He has a faultless method, and is rapidly becoming a powerful driver.

Woolley played a great innings in the final Test, and is a beautiful batsman. I would as soon see him bat as anyone in the world. He drives magnificently, he hits the ball when he plays back, and he is very strong on the leg-side. A natural cricketer, who has very distinctly arrived. Mead was disappointing. He never seemed to hit off the pace of the wickets, and seldom timed the ball really well. He was rather clumsy on his feet, did not play the slow bowlers well, and seemed to lack confidence. There is no reason why on another visit he should not be successful, for after his fine work in England there can be no doubt of his ability.

Douglas did not come off in the Test matches, but he had an average of 34.66 in the first-class matches for fifteen innings and 416 runs, thanks chiefly to a fine innings of 101 not out against an Australia XI at Brisbane and 140 in the return against Victoria. He was more than once of great use in stopping a "rot," and is undoubtedly a batsman of high defensive power, but he is slow on his feet, which is curious for a great boxer, and those powerful arms and shoulders of his should be able to drive the ball harder. If he practised driving in the nets, and worked at it, he would increase his value as a batsman by 30 per cent.

Kinneir would, I am sure, have made a lot of runs had he played regularly, but there was no room for him in the best eleven, his fielding being so moderate. He is a very neat left-handed bat, and by no means the slow scorer he is supposed to be. He played particularly well at Brisbane. Vine could not focus the ball in the bright light for a very long time, but he found his form towards the end of the tour, and in the last Test match played a very good and most invaluable innings of 36. Iremonger, except for one 50 against the weak Toowoomba bowling, showed no form with the bat, and, I fear, became discouraged early in the tour. Strudwick had few opportunities, and Smith did not bat as well as one had expected of a man who goes in first for Warwickshire, while Hitch hit at everything. Our batting had something of a tail, and too much depended on three or four batsmen. A pleasant fact, however, was that in the fifth Test match we made 315 after we had lost five wickets for 125. To Douglas let me offer my best congratulations and most grateful thanks. He was so successful that there is no harm now in saying that at first he did not fulfil expectations. He did not have the side in hand by the time the first Test match was reached, not having any fixed idea as to who were his best batsmen and bowlers, nor were the fielders always in the places to which they are accustomed. The side was somewhat "ragged" to look at, and this should not have been so, for between my falling ill and the first Test match he had command of the side in five matches, time enough to have evolved a more or less definite plan of attack and defence. But the experience gained in the first Test match was invaluable to him, and subsequently he did excellently. As becomes one who has distinguished himself in the ring, Douglas is a great fighting-man. He throws his whole soul into his work, he possesses immense courage and determination, and a calm imperturbability, and he is a man of character. Keenly enthusiastic, good-tempered, modest in success, and cheerful in failure, he deserved, and will continue to deserve all his success.

Lord Roberts once said of the South African Army that they were "heroes on the field of battle and gentlemen off it". I can say the same of my team, and am certain that they left a great name behind them in Australia, for their conduct and bearing both on and off the field. Every man was animated by one thought – the honour of English cricket – and we are proud and happy to think that we have returned victorious. At the same time, we take our success in no boasting or aggressive mood, fully realising that the goddess who presides over the game might have decreed that we should be beaten; and it should be sufficient for every true cricketer to have fought and done his best for the honour of his country. The knock-down blow that I suffered has been to a large extent compensated for by the success of my men, for it is something to have taken two teams to Australia which on both occasions returned unconquered.

## ENGLAND v AUSTRALIA
### Second Test Match

Played at Melbourne, December 30, January 1, 2, 3, 1911

It was in the second Test match that the Englishmen, with a victory by eight wickets, first revealed their full strength. Up to this point they had not impressed the critics that they were anything more than an ordinarily good side and few people in Australia thought they were at all likely to win the rubber. The match was won at the start, some marvellous bowling by Barnes giving England an advantage which, though seriously discounted at one point by weak batting, was never wholly lost. On Australia winning the toss and going in, Barnes led off by bowling five overs, four maidens, for one run and four wickets. Bardsley played a ball on to his wicket, Kelleway was out lbw, Hill clean bowled, and Armstrong was caught at the wicket. In this way, four of the best Australian wickets went down for eleven runs. With six men out for 38, the Australians were in a desperate plight, but Ransford saved the situation by his fine defence, and thanks chiefly to a capital stand by Hordern and Carter, the total in the end reached 184, the innings lasting nearly three hours and three-quarters. At the close of play England had scored 38 runs and lost Hobbs's wicket. On Monday there was a big attendance, over 31,000 people being present. Before play began, Mr Warner, who was getting better after his illness, went out to inspect the wicket, and had a great reception when the crowd recognised him. The Englishmen were batting all day. Rhodes and Hearne took the score to 137 before the second wicket fell, but at a quarter to six the innings was all over for 265. Out fifth at 224, Hearne made his 114 without a mistake of any kind. He hit eleven 4s and was at the wickets three hours and three-quarters. Apart from him and Rhodes, the batting was very disappointing. Going in on Tuesday against a balance of 81, the Australians made a very bad start, losing four wickets for 38 runs. Armstrong, however, played finely and received such good support that at the end of the day, the total, with eight wickets down, had reached 269. Armstrong hit fourteen 4s and gave no chance. On the fourth day England won the match in most brilliant style. The Australians added 30 runs, leaving England 219 to get. Rhodes left at 57, and then Hobbs and Gunn practically won the match, carrying the score to 169 before Gunn was caught by the wicket-keeper. On Hearne going in the remaining runs were hit off without further loss. Hobbs played one of the finest innings of his life. He scored his 126 not out in just under three hours and a half, and did not give a chance of any kind. His hits included eight 4s.

## Australia

| | | | | |
|---|---|---|---|---|
| C. Kelleway lbw b Barnes | 2 | – c Gunn b Foster | 13 |
| W. Bardsley b Barnes | 0 | – run out | 16 |
| C. Hill b Barnes | 4 | – c Gunn b Barnes | 0 |
| W. W. Armstrong c Smith b Barnes | 4 | – b Foster | 90 |
| V. T. Trumper b Foster | 13 | – b Barnes | 2 |
| V. S. Ransford c Smith b Hitch | 43 | – c Smith b Foster | 32 |
| R B. Minnett c Hobbs b Barnes | 2 | – b Foster | 34 |
| H. V. Hordern not out | 49 | – c Mead b Foster | 31 |
| A. Cotter run out | 14 | – c Hobbs b Foster | 41 |
| H. Carter c Smith b Douglas | 29 | – b Barnes | 16 |
| W. J. Whitty b Woolley | 14 | – not out | 0 |
| B 5, l-b 4, n-b 1 | 10 | B 14, l-b 7, w 1, n-b 2 | 24 |
| | **184** | | **299** |

## England

| | | | | |
|---|---|---|---|---|
| J. B. Hobbs c Carter b Cotter | 6 | – not out | 126 |
| W. Rhodes c Trumper b Cotter | 61 | – c Carter b Cotter | 28 |
| J. W. Hearne c Carter b Cotter | 114 | – not out | 12 |
| G. Gunn lbw b Armstrong | 10 | – c Carter b Whitty | 43 |
| C. P. Mead c Armstrong b Whitty | 11 | | |
| Mr F. R. Foster c Hill b Cotter | 9 | | |
| Mr J. W. H. T. Douglas b Hordern | 9 | | |
| F. E. Woolley c Ransford b Hordern | 23 | | |
| E. J. Smith b Hordern | 5 | | |
| S. F. Barnes lbw b Hordern | 1 | | |
| W. Hitch not out | 0 | | |
| B 2, l-b 10, n-b 4 | 16 | B 5, l-b 5 | 10 |
| | **265** | | **219** |

## England Bowling

| | Overs | Mdns | Runs | Wkts | Overs | Mdns | Runs | Wkts |
|---|---|---|---|---|---|---|---|---|
| Barnes | 23 | 9 | 44 | 5 | 32.1 | 7 | 96 | 3 |
| Foster | 15 | 2 | 52 | 1 | 38 | 9 | 91 | 6 |
| Hitch | 7 | — | 37 | 1 | 5 | — | 21 | — |
| Douglas | 15 | 4 | 33 | 1 | 10 | — | 38 | — |
| Hearne | 6 | 4 | 8 | — | 1 | — | 5 | — |
| Woolley | 0.1 | — | — | 1 | 3 | — | 21 | — |
| Rhodes | | | | | 2 | 1 | 3 | — |

**Australia Bowling**

| | Overs | Mdns | Runs | Wkts | Overs | Mdns | Runs | Wkts |
|---|---|---|---|---|---|---|---|---|
| Cotter .......... | 21 | 2 | 73 | 4 | 14 | 5 | 45 | 1 |
| Whitty .......... | 19 | 2 | 47 | 1 | 18 | 3 | 37 | 1 |
| Hordern .......... | 23.1 | 1 | 66 | 4 | 17 | — | 66 | — |
| Kelleway ......... | 15 | 2 | 27 | — | 7 | — | 15 | — |
| Armstrong ........ | 15 | 4 | 20 | 1 | 12 | 1 | 22 | — |
| Minnett .......... | 5 | — | 16 | — | 2 | — | 13 | — |
| Ransford ........ | | | | | 1.1 | — | 11 | — |

# ENGLAND v AUSTRALIA
## Third Test Match

Played at Adelaide, January 12, 13, 15, 16, 17, 1912

England won the third Test match by seven wickets, the game being, in some respects, the most remarkable in the whole tour. To an even greater degree than at Melbourne, the Australians discounted their chances by a disastrous start. Batting first on a perfect wicket, they failed so badly against Foster's bowling that in about three hours and a quarter they were all out for 133. Ransford, with his own score at six and the total at 17, received such a severe blow on the thumb that he had to retire, and did not bat again until the ninth wicket had fallen. This was a piece of very bad luck for Australia. Foster was in his deadliest form. He began by bowling eleven overs, six maidens, for eight runs and one wicket and finished up with the remarkable average of five wickets for 36. Hobbs and Rhodes, not out 29 and 20 at the end of the day, opened England's innings by scoring 147 together, and this time the batting was maintained at a very high standard. Only four wickets fell on Saturday, the score reaching 327, and on the third day the total was carried to 501. Hobbs took the honours with 187. He gave some chances in the latter half of his innings, but for the most part he played splendidly. He hit sixteen 4s and was at the wickets rather more than five hours and a half.

Though they had to face a balance of 368, the Australians made a great fight. Luck was all against them. Trumper, owing to an injured knee, had to go in last, and Ransford, though he made 38, was much hampered by his damaged thumb. Still, the innings, which began on Monday afternoon, did not end until Wednesday, the total reaching 476. The batting was consistently fine, Hill, who gave no chance during a stay of two hours and three-quarters, perhaps showing the best cricket. His cutting and driving were equally good. Barnes's bowling in the long innings was wonderfully steady. Wanting 109 to win, England lost Hobbs with only five runs on the board, but Rhodes and Gunn, by carrying the score to 102, settled the matter. Gunn and Hearne were out, however, before the winning hit was made.

## Australia

| | | | |
|---|---|---|---|
| W. Bardesley c Smith b Barnes ................. | 5 | – b Foster ..................... | 63 |
| C. Kelleway b Foster ......................... | 1 | – b Douglas ................... | 37 |
| H. V. Hordern c Rhodes b Foster .............. | 25 | – c and b Barnes .............. | 5 |
| V. S. Ransford not out ....................... | 8 | – b Hitch...................... | 38 |
| W. W. Armstrong b Foster ................... | 33 | – b Douglas ................... | 25 |
| V. T. Trumper b Hitch ....................... | 26 | – not out ..................... | 1 |
| C. Hill st Smith b Foster ..................... | 0 | – c Hitch b Barnes ........... | 98 |
| R. B. Minnett b Foster ....................... | 0 | – c Hobbs b Barnes ........... | 38 |
| T. J. Matthews c Mead b Barnes ............... | 5 | – b Barnes.................... | 53 |
| A. Cotter b Barnes........................... | 11 | – b Barnes.................... | 15 |
| H. Carter c Gunn b Douglas .................. | 8 | – c Smith b Woolley ........... | 72 |
| B 3, l-b 6, n-b 2..................... | 11 | B 26, l-b 3, n-b 2 ......... | 31 |
| | **133** | | **476** |

## England

| | | | |
|---|---|---|---|
| J. B. Hobbs c Hordern b Minnett | 187 | – lbw b Hordern | 3 |
| W. Rhodes lbw b Cotter | 59 | – not out | 57 |
| G. Gunn c Hill b Cotter | 29 | – c Cotter b Kelleway | 45 |
| J. W. Hearne c Hill b Kelleway | 12 | – c Kelleway b Matthews | 2 |
| C. P. Mead c and b Hordern | 46 | – not out | 2 |
| Mr F. R. Foster b Armstrong | 71 | | |
| Mr J. W. H. T. Douglas b Minnett | 35 | | |
| F. E. Woolley b Cotter | 20 | | |
| E. J. Smith c sub. b Cotter | 22 | | |
| S. F. Barnes not out | 2 | | |
| W. Hitch c sub. b Hordern | 0 | | |
| B 7, l-b 8, n-b 3 | 18 | Extras | 3 |
| | **501** | | **112** |

### England Bowling

| | Overs | Mdns | Runs | Wkts | Overs | Mdns | Runs | Wkts |
|---|---|---|---|---|---|---|---|---|
| Foster | 26 | 9 | 36 | 5 | 49 | 15 | 103 | 1 |
| Barnes | 23 | 4 | 71 | 3 | 46.4 | 7 | 105 | 5 |
| Douglas | 7 | 2 | 7 | 1 | 29 | 10 | 71 | 2 |
| Hearne | 2 | — | 0 | — | 10 | — | 61 | — |
| Hitch | 2 | 1 | 2 | 1 | 11 | — | 69 | 1 |
| Woolley | | | | | 7 | 1 | 30 | 1 |
| Rhodes | | | | | 1 | — | 6 | — |

### Australia Bowling

| | Overs | Mdns | Runs | Wkts | Overs | Mdns | Runs | Wkts |
|---|---|---|---|---|---|---|---|---|
| Cotter | 43 | 11 | 125 | 4 | 5 | — | 21 | — |
| Hordern | 47 | 5 | 143 | 2 | 11 | 3 | 32 | 1 |
| Kelleway | 23 | 3 | 46 | 1 | 7 | 3 | 8 | 1 |
| Matthews | 33 | 8 | 72 | 0 | 9.2 | 3 | 24 | 1 |
| Minnett | 17 | 3 | 54 | 2 | 4 | 1 | 12 | — |
| Armstrong | 14 | — | 43 | 1 | 6 | 1 | 12 | — |

## ENGLAND v AUSTRALIA
### Fourth Test Match

Played at Melbourne, February 9, 10, 12, 13, 1912

In the fourth Test match the Englishmen put the seal on their reputation, giving a most brilliant and convincing display of all-round cricket, and winning by an innings and 225 runs. As they had already won two matches out of three, the victory gave them the rubber. The first day's play went far towards determining the result. Heavy rain had made the ground soft, and Douglas, on winning the toss, put Australia in. At first his policy did not seem likely to answer, the score reaching 53 before the first wicket fell, but Barnes and Foster afterwards bowled splendidly and, despite Minnett's hitting, the innings ended for 191. Hobbs and Rhodes were not out with 30 and 23 respectively at the close of the first day, and on Saturday they set up a test match record, scoring 323 for the first wicket. They were together for just upon four hours and a half. Hobbs, who was first to leave, hit twenty-two 4s in his superb 178. At the drawing of stumps, the total was 370 for one wicket. On Monday, the Englishmen took their total to 589. Rhodes beat Hobbs's score by a single run, and was then caught at the wicket. Though not by any means free from fault, his innings, which lasted nearly seven hours, was a remarkable display of careful batting. The Australians went in for a few minutes at the end of the afternoon, and on Tuesday they failed, being all out just after the tea interval for 173. Douglas bowled in great form. At one point he had sent down fifteen overs for 21 runs and four wickets.

## Australia

| | | | | |
|---|---|---|---|---|
| C. Kelleway c Hearne b Woolley | 29 | – c Smith b Barnes | 5 |
| H. V. Hordern b Barnes | 19 | – c Foster b Douglas | 5 |
| W. Bardsley b Foster | 0 | – b Foster | 3 |
| V. T. Trumper b Foster | 17 | – b Barnes | 28 |
| C. Hill c Hearne b Barnes | 22 | – b Douglas | 11 |
| W. W. Armstrong b Barnes | 7 | – b Douglas | 11 |
| R. B. Minnett c Rhodes b Foster | 56 | – b Douglas | 7 |
| V. S. Ransford c Rhodes b Foster | 4 | – not out | 29 |
| T. J. Matthews c Gunn b Barnes | 3 | – b Foster | 10 |
| A. Cotter b Barnes | 15 | – c Mead b Foster | 8 |
| H. Carter not out | 6 | – c Hearne b Douglas | 38 |
| B 1, l-b 5, n-b 7 | 13 | B 9, l-b 2, n-b 7 | 18 |
| | **191** | | **173** |

## England

J. B. Hobbs c Carter b Hordern ..........178
W. Rhodes c Carter b Minnett ..........179
G. Gunn c Hill b Armstrong ............ 75
J. W. Hearne c Armstrong b Minnett ...... 0
Mr F. R. Foster c Hordern b Armstrong ... 50
Mr J. W. H. T. Douglas
         c Bardsley b Armstrong . 0
F. E. Woolley c Kelleway b Minnett ...... 56

C. P. Mead b Hordern .................. 21
J. Vine not out ...................... 4
E. J. Smith c Matthews b Kelleway ....... 7
S. F. Barnes c Hill b Hordern ........... 0

Extras ..................... 19

**589**

## England Bowling

| | Overs | Mdns | Runs | Wkts | Overs | Mdns | Runs | Wkts |
|---|---|---|---|---|---|---|---|---|
| Foster | 22 | 2 | 77 | 4 | 19 | 3 | 38 | 3 |
| Barnes | 29.1 | 4 | 74 | 5 | 20 | 6 | 47 | 2 |
| Woolley | 11 | 3 | 22 | 1 | 2 | — | 7 | — |
| Rhodes | 2 | 1 | 1 | — | | | | |
| Hearn | 1 | — | 4 | — | 3 | — | 17 | — |
| Douglas | | | | | 17.5 | 6 | 46 | 5 |

## Australia Bowling

| | Overs | Mdns | Runs | Wkts |
|---|---|---|---|---|
| Cotter | 37 | 5 | 125 | — |
| Kelleway | 26 | 2 | 80 | 1 |
| Armstrong | 36 | 12 | 93 | 3 |
| Matthews | 22 | 1 | 68 | — |
| Minnett | 20 | 5 | 59 | 3 |
| Ransford | 2 | 1 | 8 | — |
| Hordern | 47.5 | 5 | 137 | 3 |

# CRICKET IN AUSTRALIA

## SOUTH AUSTRALIA v NEW SOUTH WALES

Played at Adelaide, December 16, 18, 19, 20, 1899

In this match New South Wales made a record score in first-class cricket in the Colonies, their total of 807 beating the 803 obtained by the Non-Smokers against the Smokers, at Melbourne in 1887, and the previous record in Inter-colonial matches, 775 by New South Wales against Victoria, at Sydney, in 1882. Under the circumstances it is not at all surprising that New South Wales won the match by an innings and 392 runs – one of the most decisive victories ever known. In the course of the match 1,222 runs were scored. The South Australian eleven were out-played from the start, the advantage of winning the toss being quite discounted by their inability to play Howell's fine bowling. For New South Wales Trumper, Noble and Gregory did great things, Trumper's innings being the best and most brilliant of the three. Noble was batting for four hours and three-quarters, and Gregory for five hours, Noble giving three chances in the early part of his innings, but making his second hundred without a mistake. George Giffen bowled with wonderful perseverance during the long innings, but Jones was again quite ineffective.

### South Australia

| | | | |
|---|---|---|---|
| J. J. Lyons c and b Noble | 0 | – b Pye | 11 |
| F. Jarvis b Howell | 6 | – b Hopkins | 2 |
| C. Hill c and b Howell | 16 | – b Pye | 53 |
| J. Darling b Noble | 4 | – absent ill | 0 |
| G. Giffen b Howell | 9 | – c Pye b Hopkins | 18 |
| J. C. Reedman c Pye b Howell | 32 | – b Trumper | 88 |
| E. H. Leake not out | 40 | – b Howell | 4 |
| N. Claxton b Pye | 11 | – c Kelly b Pye | 1 |
| H. Chinner run out | 26 | – c Iredale b Pye | 37 |
| A. H. Jarvis run out | 4 | – c Noble b Trumper | 32 |
| E. Jones b Howell | 6 | – not out | 1 |
| L-b 1 | 1 | B 8, l-b 8, n-b 2 | 18 |
| | 155 | | 260 |

### New South Wales

| | | | |
|---|---|---|---|
| A. C. K. Mackenzie run out | 9 | A. J. Hopkins c and b Giffen | 86 |
| H. Donnan b Giffen | 72 | J. J. Kelly b Giffen | 23 |
| V. Trumper lbw b Giffen | 165 | L. W. Pye lbw b Giffen | 27 |
| B. W. Farquhar b Giffen | 0 | W. P. Howell not out | 24 |
| M. A. Noble lbw b Giffen | 200 | B 5, l-b 5, w 3 | 13 |
| S. E. Gregory c sub. b Jones | 176 | | |
| F. A. Iredale c and b Giffen | 12 | | 807 |

### New South Wales Bowling

| | Overs | Mdns | Runs | Wkts | Overs | Mdns | Runs | Wkts |
|---|---|---|---|---|---|---|---|---|
| Noble | 26 | 8 | 71 | 2 | 24 | 7 | 50 | — |
| Howell | 32.5 | 14 | 52 | 5 | 25 | 16 | 66 | 1 |
| Pye | 12 | 5 | 17 | 1 | 34 | 3 | 71 | 4 |
| Trumper | 7 | 4 | 14 | — | 1 | — | 1 | 2 |
| Farquhar | | | | | 4 | — | 9 | — |
| Hopkins | | | | | 17 | 3 | 45 | 2 |

## South Australia Bowling

| | Overs | Mdns | Runs | Wkts |
|---|---|---|---|---|
| Jones .............. | 50 | 6 | 210 | 1 |
| Giffen ............. | 77.1 | 7 | 287 | 8 |
| Reedman ......... | 24 | 3 | 75 | — |
| Lyons ............. | 26 | 4 | 78 | — |
| F. Jarvis .......... | 24 | 2 | 84 | — |
| Claxton .......... | 5 | — | 19 | — |
| Leak ............. | 2 | — | 12 | — |
| Hill .............. | 9 | 1 | 29 | — |

# SOUTH AUSTRALIA v NEW SOUTH WALES

### Played at Adelaide, December 17, 18, 19, 20, 1900

In this match, the South Australians found consolation for their severe defeat a month before at the hands of Victoria, beating New South Wales by an innings and 35 runs. This decisive victory was due to a truly magnificent display of batting by Clement Hill, who, with a score of 365 not out, beat the record in Australia in first-class matches. He was at the wickets eight hours and thirty-five minutes, and his only mistake was a chance when he had made 19. Among his hits were one 8 (4 for an overthrow), and thirty-five 4s. He had a tremendous reception, and was presented to Lord and Lady Tennyson. In the second innings of New South Wales the two young bowlers, Travers and Matthews, did excellent work on a pitch that was beginning to wear.

## New South Wales

| | | | |
|---|---|---|---|
| V. Trumper b F. Jarvis ..................... | 32 | – lbw b Travers ................. | 53 |
| H. Donnan c Matthews b Giffen ............... | 19 | – b Travers .................... | 13 |
| F. A. Iredale c Leak b F. Jarvis ............. | 37 | – b Matthews ................. | 9 |
| M. A. Noble b Travers ..................... | 28 | – b Travers ................. | 46 |
| A. J. Hopkins st A. Jarvis b Travers ............. | 65 | – not out ..................... | 17 |
| S. E. Gregory st A. Jarvis b Reedman ............ | 51 | – lbw b Matthews ............. | 31 |
| R. A. Duff c Stuart b Reedman ................. | 5 | – b Matthews ............. | 16 |
| C. Gregory b Travers ......................... | 16 | – c Hill b Travers ........... | 5 |
| J. J. Kelly c and b Reedman ................... | 11 | – b Travers ................. | 0 |
| W. P. Howell b Reedman ..................... | 5 | – c Leak b Matthews ............. | 19 |
| J. J. Marsh not out .......................... | 3 | – c Reedman b Travers ........... | 1 |
| B 5, l-b 2 ...................... | 7 | L-b 2 ................. | 2 |
| | **279** | | **261** |

## South Australia

| | | | | |
|---|---|---|---|---|
| E. H. Leak b Marsh ................. | 4 | J. Matthews b Marsh ................. | 12 |
| F. T. Hack b Marsh ................. | 12 | A. H. Jarvis b Marsh ................. | 0 |
| C. Hill not out ....................... | 365 | E. Walkley b Marsh ................. | 53 |
| G. Giffen c and b Howell .............. | 7 | J. Travers b Howell ................. | 0 |
| F. Jarvis c Howell b Hopkins ........... | 9 | B 23, l-b 10, w 9 ............. | 42 |
| J. C. Reedman c Howell b Hopkins ....... | 71 | | |
| P. Stuart b Hopkins ................... | 0 | | **575** |

## South Australia Bowling

| | Overs | Mdns | Runs | Wkts | Overs | Mdns | Runs | Wkts |
|---|---|---|---|---|---|---|---|---|
| Travers .......... | 35 | 7 | 85 | 3 | 31.1 | 10 | 74 | 6 |
| Matthews ......... | 9 | 1 | 29 | — | 24 | 6 | 61 | 4 |
| F. Jarvis .......... | 18 | 2 | 50 | 2 | 11 | 1 | 29 | — |
| Giffen ............ | 12 | — | 49 | 1 | 18 | 1 | 67 | — |
| Walkley .......... | 7 | 6 | 27 | — | 5 | — | 18 | — |
| Reedman ......... | 12.3 | 3 | 32 | 4 | 4 | 1 | 10 | — |

**New South Wales Bowling**

|          | Overs | Mdns | Runs | Wkts |
|----------|-------|------|------|------|
| Noble    | 26    | 7    | 57   | —    |
| Marsh    | 53    | 12   | 181  | 5    |
| Howell   | 34    | 3    | 100  | 2    |
| Hopkins  | 34    | 8    | 116  | 3    |
| Trumper  | 15    | 1    | 67   | —    |
| Gregory  | 2     | —    | 12   | —    |

## VICTORIA v NEW SOUTH WALES

### Played at Melbourne, December 24, 26, 27, 1900

The Christmas match at Melbourne was a very curious one. There was nothing the matter with the ground, and yet, except just at the finish, the ball fairly beat the bat, the scores being far smaller than is at all usual nowadays in Australia in fine weather. On the first day, sixteen wickets fell for 257 runs. At the close of the second day Victoria, having gone in to get 135, had five wickets down for 45. Next morning, however, Trumble and Stuckey hit off the remaining runs in an hour and a quarter without being parted. In this last stage of the match, Marsh, the aboriginal bowler, was twice no-balled by Crockett the umpire for doubtful action. Victoria largely owed their success to Trumble and Saunders, the latter of whom was last season the most successful bowler in Australia.

### New South Wales

| | | | |
|---|---|---|---|
| H. Donnan b Trumble | 1 | – c Trumble b Saunders | 2 |
| V. Trumper c Graham b Saunders | 26 | – run out | 26 |
| M. A. Noble c Trumble b Saunders | 0 | – c Stuckey b Trumble | 55 |
| F. A. Iredale c Graham b Sunders | 10 | – lbw b Trumble | 5 |
| A. J. Hopkins b Saunders | 20 | – b Trumble | 1 |
| S. E. Gregory not out | 66 | – c Laver b Saunders | 9 |
| R. A. Duff c McLeod b Trumble | 14 | – b Trumble | 10 |
| J. J. Kelly c Armstrong b Saunders | 0 | – b Trumble | 7 |
| W. P. Howell c Worrall b Saunders | 0 | – c Laver b Trumble | 13 |
| S. McBeth lbw b Laver | 12 | – not out | 5 |
| J. Marsh c Laver b McLeod | 0 | – b Trumble | 0 |
| B 1, l-b 3 | 4 | Extras | 2 |
| | **153** | | **135** |

### Victoria

| | | | |
|---|---|---|---|
| J. Worrall c Gregory b Marsh | 0 | – c Gregory b Marsh | 9 |
| H. Graham lbw b McBeth | 0 | – b Noble | 14 |
| H. Trumble c Kelly b McBeth | 0 | – not out | 45 |
| P. McAlister c Kelly b McBeth | 8 | – c Hopkins b Marsh | 2 |
| W. Armstrong b Hopkins | 50 | – b Marsh | 8 |
| F. Laver b Marsh | 0 | | |
| S. McMichael c Howell b Hopkins | 7 | | |
| C. McLeod c McBeth b Hopkins | 46 | – c Howell b Noble | 8 |
| H. Stuckey not out | 26 | – not out | 32 |
| C. H. Ross b Hopkins | 0 | | |
| J. Saunders b Marsh | 2 | | |
| Extras | 15 | B 7, l-b 2, w 4, n-b 4 | 17 |
| | **154** | | **135** |

**Victoria Bowling**

| | Overs | Mdns | Runs | Wkts | Overs | Mdns | Runs | Wkts |
|---|---|---|---|---|---|---|---|---|
| Trumble ......... | 23 | 5 | 65 | 2 | 26 | 9 | 54 | 7 |
| Saunders ........ | 23 | 5 | 70 | 6 | 15 | 1 | 50 | 2 |
| Laver ........... | 3 | 2 | 4 | 1 | | | | |
| McLeod ......... | 3 | 1 | 10 | 1 | 11 | 4 | 29 | — |

**New South Wales Bowling**

| | Overs | Mdns | Runs | Wkts | Overs | Mdns | Runs | Wkts |
|---|---|---|---|---|---|---|---|---|
| Marsh .......... | 15 | 6 | 39 | 3 | 17 | 3 | 52 | 3 |
| McBeth ......... | 23 | 13 | 38 | 3 | 8 | 2 | 22 | — |
| Howell .......... | 15 | 6 | 24 | — | 8.3 | 1 | 24 | — |
| Hopkins ......... | 16 | 4 | 37 | 4 | | | | |
| Trumper ......... | 1 | 1 | — | — | 1 | — | 9 | — |
| Noble ........... | | | | | 7 | 2 | 11 | 2 |

# NEW SOUTH WALES v VICTORIA

Played at Sydney, February 1, 2, 4, 5, 1901

Of the six Inter-Colonial matches this was by far the most remarkable, Victoria winning by one wicket, after being set to get 344 in the last innings. For their success they were much indebted to Worrall, who, for the only time during the season, played in his old form. The great feature of the match, however, was the batting of Trumper, who scored his 230 without a mistake in four hours and thirty-five minutes. He hit thirty-one 4s. Marsh was no-balled nineteen times by Crockett, for doubtful action. With this match the Victorian eleven wound up a season of brilliant success.

## New South Wales

| | | | |
|---|---|---|---|
| V. Trumper c Saunders b Trumble ............... | 21 | – c Ross b Saunders .............. | .230 |
| F. A. Iredale lbw b Saunders ................... | 10 | – lbw b Trumble ................ | 8 |
| A. J. Hopkins b Saunders ...................... | 3 | – st Ross b Trumble ............. | 0 |
| S. E. Gregory c Ross b Saunders ............... | 6 | – c Worrall b McLeod ........... | 49 |
| M. A. Noble c and b Saunders ................. | 43 | – st Ross b Saunders ........... | 27 |
| R. A. Duff b Trumble ........................ | 29 | – b Saunders ................... | 75 |
| L. O. S. Poidevin b Saunders ................. | 4 | – c Graham b Trumble .......... | 11 |
| J. J. Kelly b Laver .......................... | 17 | – not out ..................... | 28 |
| T. Howard c McMichael b McLeod .............. | 25 | – c Graham b Saunders ......... | 0 |
| J. J. Marsh c Trumble b McLeod .............. | 5 | – b Laver ..................... | 8 |
| A. McBeth not out ......................... | 0 | – c McLeod b Laver ............ | 12 |
| Extras ........................... | 7 | Extras ................ | 4 |
| | 170 | | 452 |

## Victoria

| | | | |
|---|---|---|---|
| W. Armstrong b Marsh ..................... | 5 | – b Trumper .................... | 32 |
| J. Worrall c Poidevin b Noble ................ | 2 | – st Kelly b McBeth ............. | 90 |
| H. Graham run out ........................ | 5 | – c Trumper b Noble ............ | 58 |
| P. McAlister b Marsh ....................... | 0 | – not out ...................... | 22 |
| S. McMichael lbw b Noble ................... | 17 | – c Kelly b Noble ............... | 18 |
| J. H. Stuckey not out .......................| .130 | – c Trumper b McBeth ........... | 16 |
| C. E. McLeod c Iredale b Hopkins ............. | 23 | – b Marsh ..................... | 6 |
| F. Laver c Marsh b McBeth ................... | 56 | – c Kelly b Trumper ............. | 8 |
| H. Trumble lbw b McBeth .................... | 2 | – c Marsh b Trumper ............ | 63 |
| C. H. Ross run out ......................... | 1 | – lbw b McBeth ................. | 2 |
| J. Saunders b McBeth ...................... | 1 | – not out ..................... | 3 |
| Extras ........................... | 37 | Extras ................ | 19 |
| | 279 | | 344 |

## Victoria Bowling

| | Overs | Mdns | Runs | Wkts | Overs | Mdns | Runs | Wkts |
|---|---|---|---|---|---|---|---|---|
| Trumble .......... | 32 | 12 | 71 | 2 | 34 | 5 | 125 | 3 |
| Saunders ........ | 30 | 6 | 78 | 5 | 39 | 5 | 127 | 4 |
| McLeod .......... | 4 | 1 | 9 | 2 | 32 | 8 | 103 | 1 |
| Laver ............ | 3 | 1 | 5 | 1 | 21 | 1 | 81 | 2 |
| Armstrong ....... | | | | | 3 | 1 | 12 | — |

## New South Wales Bowling

| | Overs | Mdns | Runs | Wkts | Overs | Mdns | Runs | Wkts |
|---|---|---|---|---|---|---|---|---|
| Noble ........... | 27 | 8 | 72 | 2 | 40 | 18 | 69 | 2 |
| Marsh ........... | 18 | 3 | 67 | 2 | 23 | 3 | 105 | 1 |
| Howard .......... | 8 | 2 | 32 | — | 1 | 1 | — | — |
| Trumper ......... | 5 | — | 23 | — | 25.3 | 7 | 71 | 3 |
| McBeth ......... | 12.5 | 3 | 26 | 3 | 26 | 7 | 57 | 3 |
| Hopkins ......... | 7 | 3 | 22 | 1 | 7 | 3 | 23 | — |

## SOUTH AUSTRALIA v NEW SOUTH WALES

Played at Adelaide, December 16, 18, 19, 1905

This was a remarkable match, New South Wales winning by an innings and 82 runs, after. South Australia had led off with a score of 359. Diamond had to leave his big innings incomplete owing to the death of his brother. He and Mackay made 139 together for the first wicket. Noble helped to put on 98 for the second wicket, and Waddy 120. Clement Hill and Pellew played finely, carrying South Australia's score from 73 to 242.

### South Australia

| | | | |
|---|---|---|---|
| F. T. Hack run out ............................ | 14 | – run out ...................... | 19 |
| D. R. A. Gehrs b O'Connor .................... | 34 | – not out ...................... | 33 |
| J. H. Pellew b Noble .......................... | 72 | – c Carter b Cotter .............. | 24 |
| C. Hill b Noble ............................. | 146 | – c O'Connor b Garnsey .......... | 0 |
| N. H. Claxton run out ........................ | 0 | – b Garnsey ................... | 9 |
| J. Darling b Cotter ........................... | 26 | – c Carter b Garnsey ........... | 1 |
| L. R. Hill b Cotter .......................... | 0 | – b Garnsey ................... | 0 |
| C. B. Jennings b Garnsey ..................... | 26 | – b Garnsey ................... | 1 |
| A. Wright b Garnsey ......................... | 0 | – b O'Connor .................. | 0 |
| P. Hutton not out ........................... | 22 | – c Redgrave b O'Connor .......... | 8 |
| L. Hansen b Noble .......................... | 10 | – c Mackay b Garnsey .......... | 12 |
| B 7, l-b 1, n-b 1 ..................... | 9 | B 6, l-b 2 .............. | 8 |
| | **359** | | **115** |

### New South Wales

| | | | | |
|---|---|---|---|---|
| J. R. M. Mackay c Pellew b Claxton ...... | 90 | H. Carter b Hansen ................... | 1 |
| A. Diamond retired ................... | 164 | A. Cotter c sub. b Wright .............. | 10 |
| M. A. Noble c Hack b Claxton .......... | 27 | G. L. Garnsey b Wright ............... | 7 |
| Rev. E. F. Waddy b Hansen ............ | 65 | J. O'Connor b Wright ................ | 11 |
| C. Gregory st Gehrs b Wright .......... | 54 | B 26, l-b 4, w 1, n-b 2 .......... | 33 |
| C. G. Macartney not out .............. | 70 | | |
| S. J. Redgrave lbw b Wright ............ | 24 | | **556** |

## New South Wales Bowling

| | Overs | Mdns | Runs | Wkts | Overs | Mdns | Runs | Wkts |
|---|---|---|---|---|---|---|---|---|
| Noble . . . . . . . . . . . . | 22.1 | 5 | 65 | 3 | | | | |
| Garnsey . . . . . . . . . | 14 | 2 | 56 | 2 | 15.2 | 3 | 48 | 6 |
| O'Connor . . . . . . . . | 20 | 3 | 67 | 1 | 6 | 1 | 32 | 2 |
| Macartney . . . . . . . . | 17 | 3 | 57 | — | | | | |
| Cotter . . . . . . . . . . | 26 | 1 | 105 | 2 | 10 | 2 | 27 | 1 |

## South Australia Bowling

| | Overs | Mdns | Runs | Wkts |
|---|---|---|---|---|
| Hansen . . . . . . . . . | 29 | 5 | 102 | 2 |
| Claxton . . . . . . . . . | 36 | 9 | 123 | 2 |
| L. R. Hill . . . . . . . . . | 22 | 2 | 90 | — |
| Wright . . . . . . . . . . . | 40.2 | 7 | 150 | 5 |
| Pellew . . . . . . . . . . | 3 | — | 10 | — |
| Hack . . . . . . . . . . . | 7 | 3 | 15 | — |
| Gehrs . . . . . . . . . . . | 4 | — | 21 | — |
| C. Hill . . . . . . . . . . | 2 | — | 12 | — |

# VICTORIA v NEW SOUTH WALES

### Played at Melbourne, December 23, 26, 27, 28, 1905

The Christmas match at Melbourne afforded convincing evidence of the immense strength of New South Wales. Though they had to play without Trumper and Duff they won by an innings and 253 runs, and this in spite of the fact that at the opening of the game Christian and Warne scored 144 for Victoria's first wicket. Mackay played superb cricket for three hours and three-quarters, hitting twenty-six 4s, and never giving a chance. He and Noble put on 268 for the second wicket. Noble was batting for over six hours, playing wonderfully well, but he had some luck. He and Charles Gregory added 225 for the third wicket.

### Victoria

| | | | |
|---|---|---|---|
| A. Christian c Carter b Redgrave . . . . . . . . . . . . . . | 98 | – b Garnsey . . . . . . . . . . . . . . . . . . . | 6 |
| T. Warne c Macartney b Garnsey . . . . . . . . . . . . . . . | 115 | – b Macartney . . . . . . . . . . . . . . . . . . | 56 |
| P. McAlister c Grounds b Macartney . . . . . . . . . . . | 40 | – hit wkt b Cotter . . . . . . . . . . . . . . . | 3 |
| W. W. Armstrong c Redgrave b O'Connor . . . . . . . . | 43 | – b Cotter . . . . . . . . . . . . . . . . . | 3 |
| J. Horan c Gregory b Garnsey . . . . . . . . . . . . . . . . . | 0 | – run out . . . . . . . . . . . . . . . . . . . . | 2 |
| E. V. Carroll c Noble b Garnsey . . . . . . . . . . . . . . . | 5 | – c Cotter b Macartney . . . . . . . . . . | 48 |
| F. Laver b Cotter . . . . . . . . . . . . . . . . . . . . . . . . . . . | 24 | – c Waddy b Cotter . . . . . . . . . . . . . | 17 |
| V. Ransford not out . . . . . . . . . . . . . . . . . . . . . . . . . | 22 | – st Carter b Garnsey . . . . . . . . . . . . | 0 |
| W. Carkeek b Cotter . . . . . . . . . . . . . . . . . . . . . . . . | 0 | – b Macartney . . . . . . . . . . . . . . . . | 30 |
| F. Collins b Macartney . . . . . . . . . . . . . . . . . . . . . . | 0 | – c Carter b O'Connor . . . . . . . . . . . | 6 |
| J. V. Saunders c Waddy b Cotter . . . . . . . . . . . . . . . | 2 | – not out . . . . . . . . . . . . . . . . . . . . . | 0 |
| B 8, l-b 4, w 2, n-b 4 . . . . . . . . . . . . . . . . . . | 18 | B 9, l-b 1, n-b 3, w 1 . . . . . . . | 14 |
| | **367** | | **185** |

### New South Wales

S. J. Redgrave b Armstrong . . . . . . . . . . . . . 41
J. R. M. Mackay c McAllister b Saunders . .194
C. Gregory c McAlister b Collins . . . . . . . . 73
M. A. Noble b Christian . . . . . . . . . . . . . .281
C. G. Macartney c Armstrong b Christian . 0
Rev. E. F. Waddy b Saunders . . . . . . . . . . . 50
A. Cotter c Ransford b Laver . . . . . . . . . . 68

G. L. Garnsey c Collins b Warne . . . . . . . . . 2
H. Carter b Warne . . . . . . . . . . . . . . . . . . . . 67
J. O'Connor c Armstrong b Laver . . . . . . . . 9
B. Grounds not out . . . . . . . . . . . . . . . . . . 5
B 8, l-b 5, w 2 . . . . . . . . . . . . . . . 15

**805**

## New South Wales Bowling

| | Overs | Mdns | Runs | Wkts | Overs | Mdns | Runs | Wkts |
|---|---|---|---|---|---|---|---|---|
| Cotter .......... | 29 | 4 | 78 | 3 | 17 | 4 | 56 | 3 |
| Garnsey .......... | 22 | 3 | 78 | 3 | 17 | 2 | 51 | 2 |
| Noble ............ | 9 | 2 | 42 | — | | | | |
| Grounds ......... | 9 | 3 | 23 | — | | | | |
| O'Connor ........ | 18 | 5 | 57 | 1 | 7 | 1 | 28 | 2 |
| Redgrave ........ | 12 | 1 | 45 | 1 | | | | |
| Macartney ....... | 12 | 3 | 26 | 2 | 8.2 | 1 | 36 | 2 |

## Victoria Bowling

| | Overs | Mdns | Runs | Wkts |
|---|---|---|---|---|
| Saunders ........ | 37 | 5 | 146 | 2 |
| Armstrong ....... | 56 | 16 | 125 | 1 |
| Laver ........... | 52.3 | 12 | 184 | 2 |
| Collins .......... | 27 | 2 | 138 | 1 |
| Christian ........ | 21 | 1 | 103 | 2 |
| Warne .......... | 21 | 2 | 92 | 2 |
| Ransford ........ | 1 | — | 2 | — |

# QUEENSLAND v NEW SOUTH WALES

### Played at Brisbane, November 10, 12, 13, 1906

Although without Trumper, Noble, and Diamond, New South Wales beat Queensland by an innings and 301 runs. The match was rendered memorable by the fact that Charles Gregory, with his innings of 383, beat the record in Australia in good class cricket. He was batting for five hours and three-quarters, his hits including fifty-five 4s. His play was disfigured by three chances, but when he gave the first of them he had scored 282.

## Queensland

| | | | |
|---|---|---|---|
| R. Hartigan c Waddy b Garnsey ................ | 50 | – c Bardsley b Barnes ............ | 61 |
| G. Brown st Carter b Macartney ................ | 30 | – c Redgrave b Barnes ............ | 32 |
| C. E. Simpson b Macartney .................... | 8 | – st Carter b Barnes .............. | 59 |
| T. B. Faunce b Cotter ........................ | 11 | – c Redgrave b Garnsey .......... | 17 |
| M. F. Dunn b Macartney ...................... | 3 | – c and b Garnesy .............. | 19 |
| W. B. Hayes c and b Cotter ................... | 4 | – run out ...................... | 21 |
| W. T. Evans run out .......................... | 19 | – c Garnsey b Barnes ............ | 43 |
| J. Thomson c Cotter b Garnsey ................ | 3 | – c Blaxland b Garnsey .......... | 43 |
| F. Timbury c Waddy b Garnsey ................ | 5 | – not out ...................... | 2 |
| M. F. McCaffrey c Waddy b Garnsey ............ | 0 | – lbw b Barnes ................. | 5 |
| C. Barstow not out ........................... | 0 | – c Bardsley b Garnsey .......... | 0 |
| B 4, l-b 8 ........................ | 12 | B 9, l-b 4, w 1, n-b 1 ....... | 15 |
| | 145 | | 317 |

## New South Wales

| | | | |
|---|---|---|---|
| W. Bardsley b Barstow ................ | 12 | C. G. Macartney not out ................ | 21 |
| C. Gregory c and b Hayes .............. | 383 | A. Cotter c Hartigan b Hayes ........... | 34 |
| R. N. Hickson run out .................. | 48 | H. Carter c Simpson b Hayes ........... | 1 |
| S. J. Redgrave run out ................. | 32 | G. L. Garnsey c Faunce b Hayes ......... | 10 |
| E. L. Waddy c Hartigan b McCaffrey ..... | 100 | B 10, l-b 4, w 1 ............... | 15 |
| J. C. Barnes c Thomson b Timbury ....... | 13 | | 763 |
| M. H. Blaxland b Barstow .............. | 94 | | |

## New South Wales Bowling

| | Overs | Mdns | Runs | Wkts | Overs | Mdns | Runs | Wkts |
|---|---|---|---|---|---|---|---|---|
| Cotter ........... | 14 | 1 | 53 | 2 | 11 | 3 | 40 | — |
| Garnsey .......... | 17 | 3 | 64 | 4 | 21 | — | 94 | 4 |
| Macartney ........ | 5 | 2 | 14 | 3 | 10 | — | 31 | — |
| Bedgrave ......... | 2 | 1 | 2 | — | 12.5 | — | 105 | 5 |
| Barnes ........... | | | | | 8 | 2 | 32 | — |

## Queensland Bowling

| | Overs | Mdns | Runs | Wkts |
|---|---|---|---|---|
| Hayes ........... | 28.3 | — | 120 | 4 |
| Timbury .......... | 29 | 6 | 123 | 1 |
| McCaffrey ........ | 28 | 2 | 132 | 1 |
| Barstow .......... | 27 | 2 | 115 | 2 |
| Dunn ............ | 10 | — | 59 | — |
| Hartigan ......... | 17 | 3 | 65 | — |
| Brown ........... | 2 | — | 10 | — |
| Simpson .......... | 11 | 1 | 59 | — |
| Thompson ........ | 10 | 3 | 37 | — |
| Evans ............ | 3 | — | 28 | — |

## NEW SOUTH WALES v VICTORIA

Played at Sydney, January 23, 25, 26, 27, 28, 29, 1909

This was a match of huge scoring, 1,911 runs – a record number – being obtained for 34 wickets. Victoria scored 468 and 487, and yet lost the game by six wickets, this being surely a record in first-class cricket. On winning the toss, New South Wales stayed in for nine hours and a half, their total reaching 815. Bardsley and Noble put on 304 runs together in about three hours and three-quarters for the second wicket, and Noble and Gregory 125 for the fifth wicket in an hour and a quarter. Scoring 192 out of 346 in less than four hours and a half, Bardsley played a faultless innings, his cutting and driving being equally fine. He hit twenty-nine 4s. Noble, who hit twenty-four 4s, was slower and less attractive than Bardsley, but all the same he played a fine game. Gregory was very brilliant indeed after giving chances in the slips when 2 and 7. His 129 included twenty-six 4s. Emery and Kelleway added 86 runs for the last wicket. This 815 is New South Wales's record score against Victoria. In face of such a total Victoria could have had no hope of victory, but they made a great fight. Ransford had the distinction of getting two separate hundreds. He was batting six hours for his 182 and only gave one chance, his hits including twenty-four 4s. In his second innings he scored 110 without a mistake in three hours and a quarter. McAlister's 108 was free from fault, and Armstrong's splendid 171, the result of just over four hours' cricket, was only marred by a chance in the deep field with his score at 154.

### New South Wales

| | | | |
|---|---|---|---|
| W. Bardsley c and b Ransford | ....................192 | – c Hazlitt b Saunders ............ | 24 |
| A. J. Hopkins c Horan b Hazlitt | ................ 21 | – b Vernon ..................... | 10 |
| M. A. Noble b Saunders | .......................213 | – not out ...................... | 69 |
| A. Cotter c Smith b Armstrong | ............... 13 | | |
| E. F. Waddy c Vernon b Laver | ................ 14 | – c and b Armstrong ............. | 14 |
| S. E. Gregory b Ransford | .....................179 | – b Hazlitt ..................... | 14 |
| C. G. Macartney c Hazlitt b Vernon | ............. 28 | – not out ...................... | 1 |
| J. C. Barnes run out | ......................... 15 | | |
| H. Carter b Armstrong | ....................... 11 | | |
| S. H. Emery not out | ......................... 58 | | |
| C. Kelleway run out | ......................... 42 | | |
| B 11, l-b 13, w 3, n-b 2 | ............... 29 | B 8, l-b 1 .............. | 9 |
| | 815 | | 141 |

## Victoria

| | | | |
|---|---|---|---|
| E. V. Carroll c Carter b Cotter | 0 | – b Barnes | 7 |
| T. Horan jun. b Cotter | 55 | – b Barnes | 19 |
| V. Ransford b Barnes | 182 | – c Carter b Noble | 110 |
| W. W. Armstrong c Kelleway b Noble | 20 | – lbw b Noble | 171 |
| P. A. McAlister st Carter b Barnes | 108 | – b Emery | 4 |
| D. Smith b Barnes | 11 | – b Barnes | 22 |
| G. Hazlitt b Barnes | 4 | – c Noble b Cotter | 56 |
| L. P. Vernon c Bardsley b Barnes | 2 | – b Cotter | 26 |
| F. Laver c Hopkins b Emery | 22 | – b Barnes | 21 |
| W. Carkeek c Kelleway b Barnes | 15 | – not out | 13 |
| J. V. Saunders not out | 4 | – c Cotter b Barnes | 7 |
| B 22, l-b 12, w 5, n-b 6 | 45 | B 12, l-b 15, w 2, n-b 2 | 31 |
| | **468** | | **487** |

## Victoria Bowling

| | Overs | Mdns | Runs | Wkts | Overs | Mdns | Runs | Wkts |
|---|---|---|---|---|---|---|---|---|
| Vernon | 34 | 3 | 154 | 1 | 4 | — | 28 | 1 |
| Laver | 31 | 5 | 113 | 1 | | | | |
| Hazlitt | 29 | 6 | 129 | 1 | 12 | 5 | 23 | 1 |
| Armstrong | 38 | 5 | 104 | 2 | 12 | 3 | 24 | 1 |
| Saunders | 42.3 | 6 | 178 | 1 | 22 | 5 | 57 | 1 |
| Ransford | 13 | 1 | 61 | 2 | | | | |
| Carroll | 3 | — | 26 | — | | | | |
| McAlister | 3 | — | 21 | — | | | | |

## New South Wales Bowling

| | Overs | Mdns | Runs | Wkts | Overs | Mdns | Runs | Wkts |
|---|---|---|---|---|---|---|---|---|
| Cotter | 38 | 8 | 123 | 2 | 20 | 3 | 52 | 2 |
| Emery | 24 | 3 | 79 | 1 | 24 | 8 | 61 | 1 |
| Kelleway | 20 | 4 | 53 | — | 16 | 3 | 53 | — |
| Hopkins | 24 | 7 | 63 | — | 18 | 2 | 55 | — |
| Noble | 22 | 14 | 28 | 1 | 18 | 5 | 41 | 2 |
| Macartney | 7 | 2 | 18 | — | 12 | 1 | 47 | — |
| Barnes | 14.2 | — | 59 | 6 | 33.5 | 2 | 147 | 5 |

## SOUTH AUSTRALIA v VICTORIA

Played at Adelaide, February 28, March 1, 3, 4, 1913

In winning this match, and with it the Sheffield Shield, South Australia were mainly indebted to J. N. Crawford, who, as an all-round cricketer, played perhaps the game of his life, following up a splendid innings of 163 by taking eight wickets for 66 runs. Thanks to his wonderful cricket South Australia secured a big lead on the first innings, and won the game in the end by 166 runs. Victoria were unlucky in having to play without Ryder, and to make things worse for them the pitch on the last day was much damaged by rain. Still as they had with 381 required to win, lost four wickets overnight for 51, they would no doubt have been beaten in any case.

## South Australia

| | | |
|---|---|---|
| E. R. Mayne st Carkeek b Matthews | 43 | – lbw b McKenzie | 106 |
| G. C. Campbell st Carkeek b Matthews | 27 | – b McNaughton | 9 |
| C. Hill lbw b McNaughton | 16 | – c Matthews b Armstrong | 11 |
| D. R. A. Gehrs b McNaughton | 13 | – b Armstrong | 0 |
| A. G. Moyes b Matthews | 19 | – b Armstrong | 17 |
| R. F. Middleton b Matthews | 20 | – b Cannon | 14 |
| J. N. Crawford c Baring b Cannon | 163 | – b McKenzie | 18 |
| P. D. Rundell c Cannon b McNaughton | 31 | – c Carkeek b Cannon | 13 |
| R. B. Rees b McNaughton | 8 | – not out | 20 |
| W. J. Whitty c Matthews b Cannon | 14 | – b Armstrong | 1 |
| H. J. McKay not out | 0 | – c and b Cannon | 10 |
| Extras | 14 | Extras | 3 |
| | **368** | | **222** |

## Victoria

| | | |
|---|---|---|
| E. L. Carroll b Crawford | 0 | – c McKay b Rees | 17 |
| E. V. Carroll b Crawford | 6 | – b Rundell | 21 |
| F. Baring b Crawford | 22 | – b Rundell | 19 |
| V. S. Ransford b Whitty | 65 | – c Hill b Rundell | 6 |
| W. W. Armstrong b Crawford | 72 | – not out | 17 |
| T. J. Matthews run out | 8 | – b Crawford | 56 |
| M. Hotchin b Crawford | 3 | – b Whitty | 1 |
| C. McKenzie not out | 17 | – b Whitty | 34 |
| W. Carkeek c Gehrs b Crawford | 0 | – run out | 11 |
| L. E. McNaughton b Crawford | 1 | – b Whitty | 1 |
| W. Cannon b Crawford | 0 | – c Gehrs b Whitty | 1 |
| Extras | 15 | Extras | 31 |
| | **209** | | **215** |

### Victoria Bowling

| | Overs | Mdns | Runs | Wkts | Overs | Mdns | Runs | Wkts |
|---|---|---|---|---|---|---|---|---|
| McNaughton | 82 | 6 | 101 | 4 | 21 | 2 | 72 | 1 |
| Cannon | 16.2 | 2 | 67 | 2 | 13.2 | — | 47 | 3 |
| Matthews | 40 | 7 | 111 | 4 | 2 | 1 | 8 | — |
| McKenzie | 20 | 3 | 66 | — | 8 | 2 | 22 | 2 |
| Baring | 3 | — | 9 | — | | | | |
| Armstrong | | | | | 29 | 6 | 70 | 4 |

### South Australian Bowling

| | Overs | Mdns | Runs | Wkts | Overs | Mdns | Runs | Wkts |
|---|---|---|---|---|---|---|---|---|
| Whitty | 21 | 1 | 46 | 1 | 23.4 | 10 | 30 | 4 |
| Crawford | 22.5 | 7 | 66 | 8 | 23 | 5 | 60 | 1 |
| McKay | 7 | 1 | 18 | — | 8 | — | 25 | — |
| Rees | 10 | — | 30 | — | 7 | — | 25 | 1 |
| Rundell | 7 | — | 27 | — | 12 | 4 | 44 | 3 |
| Gehrs | 1 | — | 7 | — | | | | |

# ENGLAND IN SOUTH AFRICA

## ENGLISH TEAM v SOUTH AFRICA

Played at Johannesburg, January 2, 3, 4, 1906

The first of the five Test matches was the most remarkable of the series, the Englishmen being beaten by one wicket after they had seemed to have the game in their hands. South Africa had 284 to get in the last innings, and when their sixth wicket fell before lunch the score was only 134. White played wonderfully well, resisting the bowling for four hours and ten minutes, but despite all his efforts – he was out eighth at 226 – 45 runs were still required when Sherwell, the last man, joined Nourse. Amid ever-increasing excitement the runs were hit off, South Africa thus winning by one wicket. Nourse was batting three hours and forty minutes for his 93 not out – in every way a splendid innings. There was nothing exceptional in the cricket of the English team, but Crawford played two good innings, and Lees bowled finely.

### English Team

| | | | |
|---|---|---|---|
| Mr P. F. Warner c Snooke b Schwarz | 6 | – b Vogler | 51 |
| Mr F. L. Fane c Schwarz b Faulkner | 1 | – b Snooke | 3 |
| D. Denton c Faulkner b Schwarz | 0 | – b Faulkner | 34 |
| Capt. E. G. Wynyard st Sherwell b Schwarz | 29 | – b Vogler | 0 |
| E. G. Hayes c and b Vogler | 20 | – c Schwarz b Snooke | 3 |
| Mr J. N. Crawford c Nourse b Sinclair | 44 | – b Nourse | 43 |
| A. E. Relf b White | 8 | – c Sherwell b Faulkner | 17 |
| S. Haigh b Faulkner | 23 | – lbw b Nourse | 0 |
| J. H. Board not out | 9 | – lbw b Faulkner | 7 |
| W. Lees st Sherwell b White | 11 | – not out | 1 |
| C. Blythe b Sinclair | 17 | – b Faulkner | 0 |
| B 6, l-b 9, n-b 1 | 16 | B 23, l-b 8 | 31 |
| | **184** | | **190** |

### South Africa

| | | | |
|---|---|---|---|
| L. J. Tancred c Board b Lees | 3 | – c Warner b Blythe | 10 |
| W. A. Shalders c Haigh b Blythe | 4 | – run out | 38 |
| M. Hathorn b Lees | 5 | – c Crawford b Lees | 4 |
| G. C. White c Blythe b Lees | 8 | – b Relf | 81 |
| S. J. Snooke c Board b Blythe | 19 | – lbw b Lees | 9 |
| J. H. Sinclair c and b Lees | 0 | – c Fane b Lees | 5 |
| G. A. Faulkner b Blythe | 4 | – run out | 6 |
| A. D. Nourse not out | 18 | – not out | 93 |
| A. E. Vogler b Crawford | 14 | – b Hayes | 2 |
| R. O. Schwarz c Relf b Crawford | 5 | – c and b Relf | 2 |
| P. W. Sherwell lbw b Lees | 1 | – not out | 22 |
| B 9, l-b 1 | 10 | B 6, l-b 2, n-b 7 | 15 |
| | **91** | | **287** |

### South African Bowling

| | Overs | Mdns | Runs | Wkts | Overs | Mdns | Runs | Wkts |
|---|---|---|---|---|---|---|---|---|
| Schwarz | 21 | 5 | 72 | 3 | 8 | 1 | 24 | — |
| Faulkner | 22 | 7 | 35 | 2 | 12.5 | 5 | 26 | 4 |
| Sinclair | 11 | 1 | 36 | 2 | 5 | 1 | 25 | — |
| Vogler | 3 | — | 10 | 1 | 11 | 3 | 24 | 2 |
| White | 5 | 1 | 13 | 2 | 4 | — | 15 | — |
| Nourse | 1 | — | 2 | — | 6 | 4 | 7 | 2 |
| Snooke | | | | | 12 | 4 | 38 | 2 |

### English Team's Bowling

| | Overs | Mdns | Runs | Wkts | Overs | Mdns | Runs | Wkts |
|---|---|---|---|---|---|---|---|---|
| Lees | 23.1 | 10 | 34 | 5 | 33 | 10 | 74 | 3 |
| Blythe | 16 | 5 | 33 | 3 | 28 | 12 | 50 | 1 |
| Crawford | 7 | 1 | 14 | 2 | 17 | 4 | 49 | — |
| Haigh | | | | | 1 | — | 9 | — |
| Relf | | | | | 21.5 | 7 | 47 | 2 |
| Wynyard | | | | | 3 | — | 15 | — |
| Hayes | | | | | 9 | 1 | 28 | 1 |

## MCC TEAM v SOUTH AFRICA

### Second Test Match

Played at Johannesburg, December 26, 27, 29, 30, 1913

For the second Test match South Africa made four changes from the team beaten at Durban, Zulch, Beaumont, Tancred, and Newberry taking the places of Tapscott, Lewis, Cooper, and Baumgartner. The result was not quite so overwhelming as before, but the Englishmen won by an innings and 12 runs. It was Barnes's match. On no occasion during the tour was the great bowler seen to quite such advantage. He took seventeen wickets – eight for 56 and nine for 103 – proving quite irresistible on the last morning. The English batting fell away strangely after a splendid start. Relf and Rhodes put up 141 for the first wicket, and Rhodes and Mead added 152 for the third. Rhodes was too cautious to please the crowd, but his steadiness was invaluable to his side. Batting five hours and ten minutes for his 152, he hit twenty-one 4s. Managing, at last, to get a hundred in a Test match, Mead played extremely well for something over three hours and a half.

### South Africa

| | | | |
|---|---|---|---|
| H. W. Taylor b Barnes | 29 | – c Rhodes b Barnes | 40 |
| J. W. Zulch c Woolley b Barnes | 14 | – c Relf b Barnes | 34 |
| P. A. M. Hands c Rhodes b Barnes | 0 | – c Rhodes b Barnes | 40 |
| R. Beaumont c Strudwick b Barnes | 0 | – c Strudwick b Relf | 5 |
| A. D. Nourse b Barnes | 17 | – c Strudwick b Barnes | 56 |
| L. J. Tancred st Strudwick b Barnes | 13 | – b Barnes | 20 |
| G. P. D. Hartigan c Smith b Rhodes | 51 | – lbw b Barnes | 2 |
| T. A. Ward b Woolley | 19 | – b Barnes | 0 |
| C. J. Newberry st Strudwick b Barnes | 1 | – st Strudwick b Barnes | 5 |
| J. M. Blanckenberg not out | 0 | – not out | 12 |
| J. L. Cox c Strudwick b Barnes | 0 | – b Barnes | 0 |
| B 10, l-b 4, n-b 2 | 16 | B 9, l-b 6, n-b 2 | 17 |
| | **160** | | **231** |

### MCC Team

| | | | |
|---|---|---|---|
| A. E. Relf b Blanckenberg | 63 | Mr M. C. Bird c Ward b Newberry | 1 |
| W. Rhodes c and b Blanckenberg | 152 | E. J. Smith lbw b Cox | 9 |
| J. B. Hobbs lbw b Newberry | 23 | H. Strudwick c Cox b Blanckenberg | 14 |
| C. P. Mead c Beaumont b Blanckenberg | 102 | S. F. Barnes not out | 0 |
| Hon. L. H. Tennyson lbw b Cox | 13 | | |
| Mr J. W. H. T. Douglas c Taylor b Blanckenberg | 3 | B 22, w 1 | 23 |
| F. E. Woolley b Newberry | 0 | | **403** |

**MCC Team Bowling**

| | Overs | Mdns | Runs | Wkts | Overs | Mdns | Runs | Wkts |
|---|---|---|---|---|---|---|---|---|
| Douglas .......... | 2 | — | 11 | — | 6 | — | 27 | — |
| Barnes .......... | 26.5 | 9 | 56 | 8 | 38.4 | 7 | 103 | 9 |
| Relf ............ | 14 | 1 | 34 | — | 9 | 3 | 19 | 1 |
| Woolley .......... | 3 | 1 | 5 | 1 | 21 | 5 | 45 | — |
| Rhodes .......... | 13 | 5 | 23 | 1 | 9 | 2 | 20 | — |
| Bird ............ | 4 | 1 | 15 | — | | | | |

**South Africa Bowling**

| | Overs | Mdns | Runs | Wkts |
|---|---|---|---|---|
| Cox ............ | 30 | 8 | 74 | 2 |
| Nourse .......... | 21 | 2 | 62 | — |
| Blanckenberg ...... | 38 | 13 | 83 | 5 |
| Newberry ........ | 26 | 2 | 93 | 3 |
| Hartigan ........ | 5 | — | 24 | — |
| Taylor .......... | 6 | — | 17 | — |
| Hands .......... | 8 | — | 27 | — |
| Beaumont ........ | 1 | 1 | — | — |

## MCC TEAM v SOUTH AFRICA

### Fourth Test Match

Played at Durban, February 14, 16, 17, 18, 1914

The fourth of the Test games had to be left drawn, rain and bad light cutting play short on the last day. The Englishmen escaped defeat, but except for Barnes's fine bowling and the batting of Hobbs and Rhodes their cricket was not at all up to the mark. When the game was abandoned they required 159 to win with only five wickets to fall. They never recovered from a bad collapse in their first innings, the whole side being out for 163, after Hobbs and Rhodes had scored 92 together for the first wicket. Taylor, in South Africa's second innings, played admirably, but was more cautious than usual. When the Englishmen went in with 313 to get Hobbs and Rhodes put defeat out of the question, taking the score to 133. Hobbs was seen at his best for two hours and a quarter.

**South Africa**

| | | | |
|---|---|---|---|
| H. W. Taylor c Strudwick b Barnes ............. | 16 | – lbw b Barnes ................... | 93 |
| T. A. Ward b Barnes ........................ | 5 | – b Barnes .................... | 1 |
| D. Taylor c Rhodes b Barnes .................. | 36 | – c Strudwick b Barnes ........... | 36 |
| A. D. Nourse b Barnes ...................... | 9 | – c Tennyson b Rhodes ........... | 45 |
| F. Le Roux b Barnes ....................... | 1 | – c and b Barnes ................ | 0 |
| P. A. M. Hands st Strudwick b Rhodes .......... | 51 | – c Rhodes b Barnes ............. | 8 |
| C. J. Newberry b Rhodes .................... | 0 | – c Bird b Barnes ............... | 16 |
| J. M. Blanckenberg c Douglas b Rhodes ......... | 4 | – c Tennyson b Barnes ........... | 13 |
| H. W. Chapman b Barnes .................... | 17 | – not out ..................... | 16 |
| C. P. Carter not out ....................... | 19 | – b Douglas ................... | 45 |
| J. L. Cox c Strudwick b Barnes ............... | 4 | – not out ..................... | 12 |
| Extras ........................ | 8 | Extras ................ | 20 |
| | **170** | **(9 wkts dec.)** | **305** |

## MCC Team

| | | | |
|---|---|---|---|
| J. B. Hobbs c Nourse b Blanckenberg | 64 | – b Blanckenberg | 97 |
| W. Rhodes lbw b Carter | 22 | – lbw b Carter | 35 |
| J. W. Hearne c Newberry b Carter | 2 | – not out | 8 |
| C. P. Mead c Newberry b Blanckenberg | 31 | – c Blanckenberg b Newberry | 1 |
| Hon. L. H. Tennyson c and b Newberry | 1 | – b Blanckenberg | 0 |
| Mr J. W. H. T. Douglas c and b Carter | 0 | – lbw b Blanckenberg | 7 |
| F. E. Woolley c Hands b Newberry | 9 | – not out | 0 |
| Mr M. C. Bird b Carter | 8 | | |
| A. E. Relf b Carter | 11 | | |
| S. F. Barnes not out | 4 | | |
| H. Strudwick b Carter | 0 | | |
| Extras | 11 | Extras | 6 |
| | **163** | | **154** |

## MCC Team Bowling

| | Overs | Mdns | Runs | Wkts | Overs | Mdns | Runs | Wkts |
|---|---|---|---|---|---|---|---|---|
| Barnes | 29.5 | 7 | 56 | 7 | 32 | 10 | 88 | 7 |
| Woolley | 10 | 3 | 27 | — | 13 | 2 | 26 | — |
| Relf | 8 | 3 | 15 | — | | | | |
| Rhodes | 14 | 5 | 33 | 3 | 26 | 6 | 53 | 1 |
| Douglas | 7 | — | 31 | — | 14 | 1 | 51 | 1 |
| Hearne | | | | | 11 | — | 46 | — |
| Bird | | | | | 6 | 1 | 21 | — |

## South African Bowling

| | Overs | Mdns | Runs | Wkts | Overs | Mdns | Runs | Wkts |
|---|---|---|---|---|---|---|---|---|
| Le Roux | 6 | 1 | 19 | — | 3 | 2 | 5 | — |
| Cox | 10 | 1 | 30 | — | 13 | 6 | 18 | — |
| Carter | 28 | 8 | 50 | 6 | 29 | 12 | 27 | 1 |
| Blanckenberg | 20 | 4 | 35 | 2 | 15 | 4 | 43 | 3 |
| Newberry | 11 | 4 | 18 | 2 | 10 | 4 | 22 | 1 |
| Nourse | | | | | 6 | — | 13 | — |
| Chapman | | | | | 4 | — | 20 | — |

# MCC TEAM v WESTERN PROVINCE

Played at Newlands, Cape Town, March 7, 9, 10, 1914

The last match of the tour ended in a draw, the Western Province just managing to avert defeat with one wicket to fall. As they were left to get 289 in three hours and a quarter victory, from the start of the innings, was out of the question. The chief credit for saving the game belonged to P. T. Lewis. Douglas finished up with a characteristic display. At times he was slow, but he drove very hard. His innings of 93 lasted two hours and fifty minutes.

## MCC Team

| | | |
|---|---|---|
| J. B. Hobbs c Budgen b Blanckenberg | 40 | – c Lewis b Blanckenberg ......... 29 |
| W. Rhodes b Blanckenberg | 25 | – not out ...................... 35 |
| J. W. Hearne lbw b Minaar | 20 | |
| C. P. Mead c Lewis b Minaar | 15 | |
| Mr J. W. H. T. Douglas c Blanckenberg b Minaar | 93 | |
| F. E. Woolley hit wkt b Minaar | 16 | – c R. H. M. Hands b Minaar ....... 25 |
| M. W. Booth b Budgen | 27 | – c Short b Budgen ............... 6 |
| Hon. L. H. Tennyson c Minaar b Budgen | 9 | – c Minaar b Blanckenberg......... 42 |
| A. E. Relf c P. A. M. Hands b Blanckenberg | 7 | |
| E. J. Smith not out | 34 | – not out ...................... 35 |
| H. Strudwick c Budgen b Blanckenberg | 6 | |
| Extras | 30 | Extras ................. 5 |
| | **322** | **(4 wkts dec.) 177** |

## Western Province

| | | |
|---|---|---|
| R. Rail c Rhodes b Booth | 8 | – c Hobbs b Booth .............. 5 |
| M. J. Commaille c Woolley b Hearne | 52 | – c Rhodes b Relf .............. 3 |
| P. A. M. Hands c Hobbs b Booth | 24 | – c Strudwick b Booth .......... 0 |
| R. R. Luyt c Hobbs b Hearne | 7 | – c Hearne b Rhodes ........... 18 |
| P. T. Lewis b Hearne | 32 | – b Hearne ................... 59 |
| R. H. M. Hands b Hearne | 8 | – c Relf b Douglas ............. 14 |
| A. V. C. Bisset c Rhodes b Hearne | 27 | – c sub. b Rhodes ............. 25 |
| J. M. Blanckenberg c Smith b Hearne | 22 | – c Douglas b Rhodes........... 29 |
| E. A. Budgen c Relf b Rhodes | 1 | – hit wkt b Rhodes ............. 0 |
| W. H. Short b Hearne | 5 | – not out .................... 0 |
| C. Minaar not out | 0 | – not out .................... 4 |
| Extras | 24 | Extras ................. 21 |
| | **210** | **178** |

### Western Province Bowling

| | Overs | Mdns | Runs | Wkts | Overs | Mdns | Runs | Wkts |
|---|---|---|---|---|---|---|---|---|
| Minaar | 43 | 13 | 95 | 4 | 17 | 3 | 74 | 1 |
| Short | 15 | 3 | 37 | — | 8 | — | 27 | — |
| Blanckenberg | 30.4 | 3 | 102 | 4 | 16 | 1 | 59 | 2 |
| Bugden | 19 | 4 | 58 | 2 | 7 | 1 | 12 | 1 |

### MCC Team Bowling

| | Overs | Mdns | Runs | Wkts | Overs | Mdns | Runs | Wkts |
|---|---|---|---|---|---|---|---|---|
| Booth | 17 | 3 | 65 | 2 | 7 | 1 | 16 | 2 |
| Relf | 6 | 5 | 4 | — | 10 | 5 | 8 | 1 |
| Hearne | 23.2 | 3 | 78 | 7 | 19 | 5 | 48 | 1 |
| Rhodes | 10 | 1 | 30 | 1 | 23 | 8 | 51 | 4 |
| Woolley | 3 | — | 9 | — | 2 | — | 8 | — |
| Tennyson | | | | | 3 | — | 14 | — |
| Douglas | | | | | 6 | 2 | 8 | 1 |
| Hobbs | | | | | 1 | — | 4 | — |

# THE SOUTH AFRICANS IN AUSTRALIA

## AUSTRALIA v SOUTH AFRICA

Played at Melbourne, December 31, January 2, 3, 4, 1910-11

This was the sensational match of the tour, the South Africans suffering defeat by 89 runs when everyone thought they had the game in their hands. Pegler was given a place in their team to the exclusion of Vogler. The Australians led off with a score of 348, their batting being very good but, considering the perfection of the wicket, not exceptionable. Clem Hill was bowled by a ball that he did not attempt to play. Nourse brought off a wonderful catch on the boundary, and was presented with the ball as a memento of his feat. When the South Africans went in, Faulkner played the innings of his life. Batting for five hours and a quarter, he scored 204 runs out of 368 put on while he was in, and hit twenty-six 4s. He might have been caught when 64 and again at 126, but these were his only mistakes. Zulch, Nourse, and Snooke helped him to put on 107, 110, and 90 runs respectively for the second, third, and sixth wickets. In the second innings of Australia Trumper played superbly, scoring 159 out of 237 in less than three hours, but no one else gained any real mastery over Schwarz and Llewellyn. South Africa only required 170 to win, but the occasion proved too much for them. They were soon in a losing position, half the wickets being down for 46, and the innings ended for 80, Australia winning the match by 89 runs. Whitty's bowling was described as beyond praise. No excuse could be offered for the failure but it was thought that Faulkner flattered the bowlers by his extreme caution. Zulch left a sick bed in order to take his innings.

### Australia

| | | | |
|---|---:|---|---:|
| V. T. Trumper b Pegler | 34 | – b Faulkner | 159 |
| W. Bardsley c Snooke b Sinclair | 85 | – st Sherwell b Schwarz | 14 |
| C. Hill b Llewellyn | 39 | – b Schwarz | 0 |
| D. R. A. Gehrs b Llewellyn | 4 | – st Sherwell b Schwarz | 22 |
| C. G. Macartney run out | 7 | – c Snooke b Llewellyn | 5 |
| V. S. Ransford run out | 58 | – c Sinclair b Schwarz | 23 |
| W. W. Armstrong c Sherwell b Faulkner | 75 | – b Llewellyn | 29 |
| C. Kelleway c Faulkner b Stricker | 18 | – b Pegler | 48 |
| H. Carter not out | 15 | – c Sherwell b Llewellyn | 0 |
| A. Cotter c Stricker b Schwarz | 3 | – c sub. b Llewellyn | 15 |
| W. J. Whitty c Nourse b Faulkner | 6 | – not out | 5 |
| L-b 3, n-b 1 | 4 | L-b 6, n-b 1 | 7 |
| | **348** | | **327** |

### South Africa

| | | | |
|---|---:|---|---:|
| P. W. Sherwell c Carter b Cotter | 24 | – b Whitty | 16 |
| J. W. Zulch b Cotter | 42 | – not out | 6 |
| G. A. Faulkner c Armstrong b Whitty | 204 | – c Kelleway b Whitty | 8 |
| A. D. Nourse b Kelleway | 33 | – lbw b Cotter | 2 |
| L. Stricker b Armstrong | 26 | – lbw b Cotter | 0 |
| C. B. Llewellyn b Armstrong | 5 | – b Cotter | 17 |
| S. J. Snooke b Whitty | 77 | – c Armstrong b Whitty | 9 |
| J. H. Sinclair not out | 58 | – lbw b Whitty | 3 |
| R. O. Schwarz b Whitty | 0 | – c Kelleway b Cotter | 7 |
| O. C. Pearse b Armstrong | 6 | – c Kelleway b Whitty | 0 |
| S. J. Pegler lbw b Armstrong | 8 | – lbw b Whitty | 0 |
| B 2, l-b 10, w 2, n-b 9 | 23 | B 6, l-b 3, n-b 3 | 12 |
| | **506** | | **80** |

**South Africa Bowling**

| | Overs | Mdns | Runs | Wkts | Overs | Mdns | Runs | Wkts |
|---|---|---|---|---|---|---|---|---|
| Nourse .......... | 8 | 3 | 24 | — | 5 | 1 | 18 | — |
| Snooke .......... | 5 | 1 | 19 | — | 8 | 1 | 24 | — |
| Pegler ........... | 10 | — | 43 | 1 | 6.3 | 1 | 24 | 1 |
| Schwarz ......... | 13 | — | 66 | 1 | 22 | 2 | 76 | 4 |
| Llewellyn ........ | 10 | — | 69 | 2 | 16 | — | 81 | 4 |
| Sinclair .......... | 13 | 1 | 53 | 1 | 8 | — | 32 | — |
| Stricker ......... | 10 | — | 36 | 1 | 2 | 1 | 10 | — |
| Faulkner ........ | 10.4 | — | 34 | 2 | 12 | 1 | 55 | 1 |

**Australia Bowling**

| | Overs | Mdns | Runs | Wkts | Overs | Mdns | Runs | Wkts |
|---|---|---|---|---|---|---|---|---|
| Cotter ........... | 43 | 5 | 158 | 2 | 15 | 3 | 47 | 4 |
| Whitty ........... | 29 | 6 | 81 | 3 | 16 | 7 | 17 | 6 |
| Kelleway ........ | 17 | 3 | 67 | 1 | | | | |
| Armstrong ....... | 48 | 9 | 134 | 4 | 1 | — | 4 | — |
| Macartney ....... | 16 | 5 | 43 | — | | | | |

# SOUTH AFRICANS v NEW SOUTH WALES

Played at Sydney, February 24, 25, 27, 28, March 1, 1911

This was a match of altogether abnormal scoring. Every total exceeded 400, and the aggregate of runs – 1,744 – was, with one exception, the highest on record in first-class cricket. Playing very brilliantly, Macartney made two separate hundreds, but the most remarkable batting in the match was seen in the last innings. South Africa wanted 487 to win, and when rain stopped play on the fourth afternoon they had scored 232 for two wickets, Faulkner and Nourse being together. On the damaged pitch next morning batting was by no means an easy matter, but New South Wales only won by 44 runs. Faulkner and Nourse put on 318 together, both playing splendidly. Faulkner hit twenty-two 4s.

**New South Wales**

| | | | |
|---|---|---|---|
| V. T. Trumper b Pearse ..................... | 5 | – b Sinclair ..................... | 15 |
| W. Bardsley c Snooke b Pearse ................. | 9 | – b Sinclair ..................... | 73 |
| C. Kelleway lbw b Pegler ................... | 33 | – b Faulkner ................... | 65 |
| E. F. McElhone hit wkt b Sinclair ............. | 94 | – c Schwarz b Faulkner .......... | 2 |
| C. G. Macartney c Pegler b Faulkner ...........119 | | – b Schwarz ...................126 | |
| H. L. Collins c Stricker b Nourse .............. | 83 | – c Snooke b Faulkner .......... | 2 |
| C. J. Tozer c Stricker b Sinclair ................ | 2 | – b Stricker ..................... | 37 |
| L. A. Minnett b Faulkner ...................... | 2 | – c and b Schwarz ............... | 23 |
| S. H. Emery not out ......................... | 58 | – not out ....................... | 80 |
| R. J. A. Massie b Nourse ..................... | 0 | – b Faulkner ................... | 19 |
| G. Harvey b Pegler ......................... | 11 | – c Vogler b Pegler ............. | 7 |
| B 9, l-b 11 ......................... | 20 | B 2, l-b 6, w 1 ............ | 9 |
| | 436 | | 458 |

## South Africans

| | | | |
|---|---|---|---|
| O. C. Pearse c Macartney b Emery | 54 | – b Macartney | 9 |
| M. Commaille c Bardsley b Minnett | 29 | – b Macartney | 1 |
| G. A. Faulkner b Minnett | 2 | – c Kelleway b Macartney | 144 |
| A. D. Nourse b Emery | 81 | – c Collins b Kelleway | 160 |
| S. J. Snooke c Minnett b Kelleway | 13 | – b Kelleway | 4 |
| J. H. Sinclair b Massie | 65 | – b Kelleway | 4 |
| L. Stricker not out | 82 | – b Massie | 18 |
| A. E. Vogler c Macartney b Emery | 0 | – run out | 2 |
| R. O. Schwarz b Macartney | 13 | – not out | 45 |
| S. J. Pegler c Kelleway b Minnett | 16 | – b Kelleway | 16 |
| T. Campbell c McElhone b Kelleway | 32 | – c Minnett b Massie | 3 |
| B 14, l-b 4, n-b 3 | 21 | B 24, l-b 4, w 2, n-b 6 | 36 |
| | **408** | | **442** |

## South Africans Bowling

| | Overs | Mdns | Runs | Wkts | Overs | Mdns | Runs | Wkts |
|---|---|---|---|---|---|---|---|---|
| Vogler | 21 | 6 | 53 | — | 7 | — | 44 | — |
| Pearse | 11 | — | 54 | 2 | 9 | 1 | 36 | — |
| Sinclair | 19 | — | 72 | 2 | 29 | 4 | 92 | 2 |
| Pegler | 15 | 1 | 71 | 2 | 16 | 1 | 61 | 1 |
| Schwarz | 14 | 2 | 68 | — | 12 | — | 77 | 2 |
| Faulkner | 19 | 2 | 61 | 2 | 22 | 3 | 71 | 4 |
| Nourse | 10 | 3 | 24 | 2 | 8 | 2 | 23 | — |
| Stricker | 4 | — | 13 | — | 8 | 1 | 43 | 1 |
| Snooke | | | | | 1 | — | 2 | — |

## New South Wales Bowling

| | Overs | Mdns | Runs | Wkts | Overs | Mdns | Runs | Wkts |
|---|---|---|---|---|---|---|---|---|
| Minnett | 36 | 6 | 140 | 3 | 11 | — | 56 | — |
| Kelleway | 23.5 | 6 | 49 | 2 | 33 | 6 | 120 | 4 |
| Massie | 19 | 3 | 55 | 1 | 20 | 4 | 64 | 2 |
| Emery | 30 | 2 | 101 | 3 | 14 | 2 | 53 | — |
| Macartney | 16 | 2 | 42 | 1 | 35 | 5 | 113 | 3 |
| Collins | | | | | 1 | 1 | — | — |

# NEW ZEALAND

## ENGLISH TEAM v TWENTY-TWO OF MARLBOROUGH

Played at Blenheim, January 23, 24, 1903

A victory by nine wickets rewarded the efforts of the Englishmen at Blenheim. Dowson followed up his 218 not out at Greytown North with a score of 94. He was missed, but on a difficult wicket it was necessary to take risks. Thompson accomplished a remarkable bowling feat in the first innings of the Twenty-two, actually taking fifteen wickets for 11 runs. In the second innings Warner did not let Thompson bowl and the local side succeeded in making their opponents go in again.

### English Team

| | | | | |
|---|---|---|---|---|
| Mr F. L. Fane c Neal b Watty | 5 | | | |
| Mr P. R. Johnson b Greenfield | 28 | | | |
| J. G. Thompson b Watty | 8 | – not out | 4 | |
| S. Hargreave b Watty | 5 | | | |
| Mr A. E. Leatham b Greenfield | 14 | | | |
| Mr E. M. Dowson c Horton b Godfrey | 94 | | | |
| Mr B. J. T. Bosanquet c Bathgate b Greenfield | 22 | | | |
| Mr P. F. Warner c Coleman b Greenfield | 2 | – not out | 11 | |
| Mr T. L. Taylor c Griffiths b Horton | 2 | | | |
| Mr A. D. Whatman c Hortin b Godfrey | 18 | | | |
| Mr C. J. Burnup not out | 1 | – b Greenfield | 3 | |
| Extras | 5 | | | |
| | **204** | | **18** | |

Twenty-two of Marlborough scored 59 and 162.

### English Bowling

| | Overs | Mdns | Runs | Wkts | Overs | Mdns | Runs | Wkts |
|---|---|---|---|---|---|---|---|---|
| Burnup | 17 | 7 | 32 | 5 | | | | |
| Thompson | 16 | 10 | 11 | 15 | | | | |
| Dowson | | | | | 18 | 3 | 39 | 7 |
| Bosanquet | | | | | 15 | 2 | 51 | 7 |
| Hargreaves | | | | | 7 | 1 | 10 | 4 |
| Warner | | | | | 9 | 3 | 20 | 2 |

## THE AUSTRALIAN TEAM IN NEW ZEALAND

At Temuka, March 3, 4, 1914. South Canterbury XV, 180; Australians, 922 for nine wickets (J. N. Crawford 354, V. T. Trumper 135, L. A. Cody 106, M. A. Noble 77 not out, W. McGregor 74, V. S. Ransford 57). Crawford and Trumper added 298 for the eighth wicket in sixty-nine minutes, twice making 50 in ten minutes, and taking the total from 450 to 550 in twenty-three minutes. Crawford and Noble at one period of their partnership put on 50 in nine minutes. Crawford hit fourteen 6s and forty-five 4s, and the innings lasted just over five and a quarter hours. Drawn.

# OBITUARIES

MR CHARLES ABSOLON, the veteran cricketer, died at his residence, Hermitage Road, Finsbury Park, on Saturday, January 4, 1908, having suffered a stroke of paralysis just a week before. Born on May 30, 1817, Mr Absolon was in his 91st year. He had, of course, long ago retired from the active pursuit of cricket, but he continued playing until he had reached a great age. His interest in the game remained unabated to the end, and even as recently as last June he was present at the Middlesex and Surrey match at Lord's. In his day Mr Absolon was the most prominent figure in local cricket in and around London. An under-hand bowler of the type of the famous William Clarke, he was in such request that he has often been known to take part in two matches in the same day, his assistance, while he was at his best, generally meaning victory for the clubs he represented. The full statistics of his career as a bowler, if they had been preserved, would form very interesting reading. At one time his doings used to be published every year in the sporting papers. He took wickets literally by the hundred, some of his records in the seventies being marvellously good. He was much more than an ordinary lob bowler, having a good variety of pace and commanding, when he needed it, a comparatively fast ball. He never aimed at a big break, being content to make the ball do just enough to beat the bat. It is impossible to say how he would have got on in first-class cricket, but the batsmen who met him in club matches had every reason to dread him, his skill in finding out their weak points being so great. A kindly and genial man, Mr Absolon made hosts of friends in the cricket field. Probably no cricketer ever played in so many matches.

Between the ages of 50 and 80 he took 8,500 wickets and made 26,000 runs, and even during the last year he played his bowling accounted for a hundred wickets. Some of his best performances during the latter part of his career were as follows:

In July, 1861, he played at Walham Green for United Master Butchers v XX of the Metropolitan Clubs. The latter were dismissed for 4, Absolon obtaining every wicket except the last. In 1872, playing for W. J. Page's XXII, v UAEE, he dismissed W. H. Iddison, John Smith (of Cambridge), and T. Hayward with consecutive balls, and two deliveries later disposed of Luke Greenwood. Playing for Wood Green v United Willesden at Wood Green in July, 1872, at the age of 55, he had a hand in getting the whole twenty of the Willesden wickets. He bowled down ten, six were caught from his bowling, two hit wicket off his bowling, and he caught out two. He took seventeen wickets (seven in the first innings and all ten in the second) for St Mary's Cray v Shoreham, at St Mary's Cray on June 11, 1873. He obtained seventeen wickets, nine in the first innings and eight in the second, bowling down 16, for Wood Green v Southgate House, at Southgate, August 4, 1873. (One player was run out in each innings). In September, 1873, he took part in a scratch match at Brown's Ground, Nunhead, between Three of All England and A Twelve. The Three made only 6 runs between them:

| | |
|---|---|
| W. G. Grace st Wilson b Absolon | 4 |
| W. R. Gilbert st Wilson b Absolon | 0 |
| H. Charlwood b Absolon | 2 |
| | 6 |

Absolon took the wickets of the three great men in nineteen balls. The Twelve, who were not allowed to hit behind or to leave their ground in striking, scored 15, "W.G." taking nine wickets for 8 runs. In 1878 he took all ten wickets in the first innings and all three which fell in the second for Smithfield Wanderers v Pelham Albert, at Nunhead. In 1882, at the age of 65, he took four wickets with the first four balls he delivered when playing against Page Green, and in a match at Tufnell Park took seven wickets in two overs without being scored from. In 1883, at the age of 66, he obtained all ten wickets in an innings. In 1884, at the age of 67, he played against Bedford Town, carrying his bat through the innings for 40 and obtaining eight of the ten wickets. In the same year, playing against Hatfield, he took five wickets in six balls when they had five wickets in hand and required only 3 runs to win. His side accordingly won by 2 runs. In 1884 also he obtained five wickets in six balls for Cheam v Banstead. In 1885, at the age of 68, he took a team to his native place, Wallingford, and obtained seventeen wickets in the match, including nine for 16 runs in the first innings. In 1888, aged 71, he took four wickets in four balls in a match in Tufnell Park, and three times carried his bat through an innings. He batted over an hour for 2 runs for Westminster Tradesmen v A. Division of Police, on the Westminster School Ground on September 8, 1890, being then 73 years old. During that season he five times carried his bat through an innings. In 1897, at the age of 89, he obtained 100 wickets.

Between 1868 and 1893, when he was 76 years of age, he scored 24,189 runs and took 7,339 wickets, the totals year by year being as follows:

| Year | Runs | Wickets | Year | Runs | Wickets |
|------|------|---------|------|------|---------|
| 1868 | 1,155 | 441 | 1882 | 1,047 | 289 |
| 1869 | 635 | 262 | 1883 | 1,049 | 222 |
| 1870 | 824 | 453 | 1884 | 1,190 | 263 |
| 1871 | 824 | 433 | 1885 | 1,021 | 320 |
| 1872 | 1,109 | 519 | 1886 | 1,075 | 204 |
| 1873 | 1,043 | 420 | 1887 | 1,070 | 222 |
| 1874 | 1,066 | 500 | 1888 | 1,055 | 129 |
| 1875 | 658 | 233 | 1889 | 1,052 | †65 |
| 1876 | 1,151 | 256 | 1890 | 848 | 184 |
| 1877 | 1,179 | 362 | 1891 | 603 | 191 |
| 1878 | 974 | 300 | 1892 | 510 | 200 |
| 1879 | 685 | 178 | 1893 | 532 | 209 |
| 1880 | 910 | 254 | | | |
| 1881 | 924 | 230 | Totals | 24,189 | 7,339 |

† *A small number, owing to an injury sustained.*

Between 1871 and 1893 he did the hat-trick as many as fifty-nine times:

| Year | Times | Year | Times | Year | Times |
|------|-------|------|-------|------|-------|
| 1871 | 9 | 1877 | 1 | 1885 | 2 |
| 1872 | 7 | 1878 | 3 | 1886 | 2 |
| 1873 | 6 | 1880 | 2 | 1887 | 3 |
| 1874 | 5 | 1882 | 3 | 1888 | 2 |
| 1875 | 3 | 1883 | 3 | 1891 | 1 |
| 1876 | 1 | 1884 | 4 | 1893 | 2 |

His easy action allowed him to bowl in matches at a very advanced age. During his last few years he fielded in the slips and when batting always employed the services of a runner. He had been a total abstainer since 1857 and never smoked.

MR CHARLES WILLIAM ALCOCK, JP, who was born at Sunderland on December 2, 1842, died at Brighton on February 26, 1907. He was educated at Harrow, but, not enjoying very good health, did not obtain a place in the eleven. In later years, however, he played occasionally for the Gentlemen of Essex, the Butterflies, Harrow Wanderers, and Incogniti, and once had the curious experience of captaining France against Germany in a match at Hamburg. *Scores and Biographies* describes him as "a steady bat, a fair change fast bowler, and an excellent long stop or long field." On February 6, 1872, on the strong recommendation of Mr V. E. Walker, he was appointed secretary to the Surrey County CC, a position he held until the time of his death. Of his work for Surrey cricket it would be difficult to speak too highly, for he was at all times both willing and anxious to do all in his power to further its welfare. He was a most voluminous writer on the game, and in 1882 founded *Cricket*, of which he was editor from the first until the day of his death. For twenty-nine years he edited *James Lillywhite's Cricketers' Annual*, and was the chief contributor to *Surrey Cricket: Its History and Associations*, published in 1902. For many years he arranged the fixture-list of teams visiting England, and it was due principally to him that the first meeting between England and Australia in this country – at The Oval in 1880 – took place. Mr Alcock's connection with Association Football was so prominent that it is not too much to say that he more than anyone else made the game. He captained England against Scotland in 1875, and it was under his leadership that the Wanderers won the Football Association Cup in 1872 and in four subsequent years. He was hon. secretary of the Football Association from 1867 until 1890, secretary from 1891 until 1896, and a vice-president from the last-mentioned year until his death.

MR EDWARD BANKS, JP, one of the oldest Kent cricketers, died at Sholden Lodge, near Deal, on January 12, 1910, aged 89. He was born in South Wales on August 12, 1820, but moved into Kent before completing his second year. Ill-health limited his appearances in county cricket to ten matches between 1842 and 1846. In the last-mentioned year he appeared for the Gentlemen against the Players at Canterbury, and fielded at Lord's for Alfred Mynn in the first of his single wicket matches with Felix. *Scores and Biographies* (iii – 159) says of him, "Batted in a good free style, and was a most excellent field." Fuller Pilch recalled that "I found him down Sandwich way, where his property lay. He and his youngest brother, Mr William, were the quickest between the wickets I ever did see, and Mr Edward was one of the smartest in the long-field. He was like a thorough-bred horse, for no matter how far the ball was off he would try; and when I sang out 'Go to her, Mr Edward! Go to her!' he would outrun himself almost, and, as sure as ever he got his hands to her, the ball was like a rat in a trap." His younger brother, the late Mr W. J. Banks, played occasionally for Kent in 1846 and 1848. The deceased, who was a grandson of Sir Edward Banks, the builder of London Bridge, rode a tricycle as recently as three months before his death.

WILLIAM BATES passed away on January 8, 1900 at his residence at Lipton. Born on November 19, 1855, he was still a comparatively young man. His career in first-class cricket – exceptionally brilliant while it lasted – was brought to a sudden and very painful close more than a dozen years back. He went out to Australia in the autumn of 1887 as a member of Mr Vernon's team, and while practising at the nets, on the Melbourne ground, met with a sad accident. Several members of the English team were on the ground at the time, and a ball hit by one of them struck Bates in the eye with such terrible force that his sight was permanently injured. Thenceforward county cricket for him was out of the question, and some little time after his return to England he attempted, in a fit of despondency, to commit suicide. He recovered his sight sufficiently to play in local matches and do some coaching, but it was of course, a painful experience for him to drop into obscurity at the age of thirty-three, after having been for over ten seasons one of the most popular cricketers in the country. Coming out in 1877, he quickly took a high position in the Yorkshire eleven, and he was still at the height of his powers when he met with his deplorable accident at Melbourne. He will be remembered as one of the finest of Yorkshire players. As a batsman he was as brilliant as Ulyett, though he did not possess such varied resources, and, especially during his first few seasons, he was a capital slow, round-arm bowler – commanding, as he did, any amount of spin. His one weakness was in fielding, for while a genuine hard-worker, he had a way at times of missing the easiest of catches. It was only this lack of certainty in his catching that prevented him being chosen in this country to play for England against Australia. On Australian cricket fields he was always a great favourite, and during his visits to the Colonies he did many brilliant things. At Melbourne, in January, 1883, playing for the Hon. Ivo Bligh's team against the great

Australian eleven of 1882, he performed the "hat trick", getting rid of Percy McDonnell, George Giffen, and Bonnor with successive balls. The way in which Bonnor's wicket was obtained is amusingly described in the Badminton Book. All the Englishmen were desperately anxious that Bates should get his third wicket, and a council of war resulted in a very neat little plan being devised. It was said that Bonnor was sure to play slowly forward at the first ball he received, whatever its length, and on Bates promising to bowl a short-pitched ball on the leg-stump, Walter Read volunteered to stand short mid-on, and gradually creep in towards the batsman. Everything came off as had been anticipated, and Bonnor, having played the ball into Read's hands, left the wicket lost in amazement that anyone should have ventured to get so near to his bat.

GEORGE JOHN BONNOR, born at Orange (NSW), February 25, 1855; died at Orange (NSW), June 27, 1912. Though he was last seen on an English cricket ground more than twenty years ago, George Bonnor had not in one sense outlived his fame, his doings being constantly recalled and talked about. He was, indeed, far too striking a personality to be forgotten in less than a generation. Australia has sent to England many finer batsmen, but no other hitter of such extraordinary power. During his five visits to this country – he came here with the Australian teams of 1880, 1882, 1884, 1886, and 1888 – Bonnor earned a reputation akin to that of our own C. I. Thornton, the question being often discussed as to which of the two men could make the bigger drives. Whether Bonnor ever equalled Thornton's longest hit at Brighton, or his famous drive over the old racquet court at The Oval, is a moot point, but, be this as it may, the Australian in his own particular line had only one rival. Bonnor was a splendid specimen of manhood. He stood about 6ft 5in, but he was so finely proportioned that there was nothing ungainly in his figure or carriage. His presence contributed almost as much as his wonderful hitting to the popularity that he enjoyed wherever he played. He was not content to be a hitter pure and simple, setting himself at times to play quite an orthodox game. These efforts at steadiness afforded him some satisfaction, but they made his colleagues in various Australian elevens furious. They argued that his business was to hit, and that when he failed to fulfil his proper mission he was no use. Bonnor never met with much success as a batsman in Test matches in England, but in games only less important he played many a fine innings. One remembers in particular his 74 against the Gentlemen of England at The Oval in 1882. In the same season he gave a remarkable display against the Zingari at Scarborough. Nothing in Bonnor's career is more often recalled than the catch with which George Ulyett got him out in the England and Australia match at Lord's in 1884. Bonnor hit a half-volley back with all his force; Ulyett put up his right hand, and the ball stuck. Probably no harder hit was every caught. Members of the England eleven gathered round Ulyett in wonderment at what he had done. All the bowler said was that if the ball had hit his fingers he should have had no more cricket that season. Another famous catch – of quite a different kind – to which Bonnor was out was in the England and Australia match at The Oval in 1880 – the first Test match in England. The ball was hit to such a tremendous height that the batsmen had turned for the third run when Fred Grace caught it. That great cricketer, who died a fortnight after the match, said he was sure his heart stopped beating while he was waiting for the ball to drop. In first-class matches Bonnor scored 4,989 runs with an average of 20.70.

HENRY FREDERICK BOYLE, who more than anyone else, except Spofforth and Blackham, made the fame of the first Australian eleven in England in 1878, died at Bendigo, Victoria, on November 21, 1907. Born on December 10, 1847, he was within three weeks of completing his sixtieth year. He was a Sydney man by birth, but he went to live in Victoria when only three years old, and with Victorian cricket he was always associated. He took to the game when quite a small boy, and at the age of fifteen he played for twenty-two of Sandhurst against Victoria. When in December, 1873, W. G. Grace's eleven played their first match at Melbourne, Boyle appeared for the Eighteen of Victoria, who beat the Englishmen in a single innings, and to the end of his life he recalled with pride the fact that he bowled down W.G.'s wicket. In addition to Boyle, the Victorian team included Frank Allan, Thomas Horan, B. B. Cooper – so well known in England a few years earlier as a batsman – W. Midwinter, John Conway, the manager of the Australian eleven of 1878, and the once famous bowler Sam Cosstick. It is no injustice to Boyle to say that he was a far greater cricketer in England than in Australia. When he came to this country in 1878 he was not regarded as anything like such a good bowler as Allan, but whereas he enjoyed a triumph, Allan gave way before the rigors of a very ungenial summer, and only once or twice did himself justice. It is a very old story now to tell how Spofforth and Boyle on the 27 of May, 1878, dismissed the MCC for totals of 33 and 19, and in one afternoon established for good and all the reputation of Australian cricket. In the eleven-a-side matches of that memorable tour Boyle took 63 wickets, coming out a very respectable second to Spofforth who took 123. Visiting England for the second time in 1880 he did not have many opportunities in first-class matches, the Australian programme that year, owing to the unfortunate incident at Sydney during the tour of Lord Harris's eleven in 1878-79, being largely restricted to games with local eighteens. Boyle however, made the most of such chances as he enjoyed. Indeed, he perhaps never bowled better than when, towards the end of the season, Spofforth's accident threw the whole responsibility upon him and George Palmer. In the England match at The Oval the two bowlers got five wickets down for 31 runs, when England went in with 57 runs to get in the last innings. It was, however, in the great tour of 1882, that Boyle reached his highest point. He bowled down the last wicket when the Australians gained their famous victory by 7 runs against England at The Oval, and in the eleven-a-side matches he took 144 wickets, finishing at the top of the bowling averages with Spofforth, Palmer, and Garrett below him. The tour of 1882 was the climax of his career. From that time his powers as a bowler began to wane. In 1884, when for the first time he experienced a real English summer, he only took 67 wickets as against 216 by Spofforth, and 132 by Palmer, and in 1888, when Turner and Ferris did such wonderful things, he was quite an unimportant member of the team. He paid his last visit to England as manager of the 1890 eleven. Boyle as a bowler relied mainly upon headwork and accuracy of length, and had no very remarkable break. Like Alfred Shaw, though his style did not in any way resemble that of the English bowler, he was satisfied if he could make the ball do just enough to beat the bat. No one was quicker to discover a batsman's weakness, or more persevering in turning his knowledge to account. He could peg away at the wicket for an hour without ever bowling a bad ball, and he was never afraid of pitching one up to be hit. No doubt his very high delivery helped to make him deceptive in the flight and awkward in his quick rise off the pitch. Apart from his bowling, Boyle will be remembered as perhaps the most daring fieldsman Australia has ever produced. The position he made for himself at short mid-on was not of much use on very fast wickets, but on the slow grounds in 1878, 1880 and 1882 he brought off any number of catches. Moreover, the mere fact of his standing so dangerously close in, caused many English batsmen to lose their wickets. Of course he got some ugly knocks at times, but he was quite fearless and did not mind how hard the ball was hit at him. E. M. Grace is proud of the fact that he alone gave him a fright and caused him to stand further back.

JOHN BRIGGS died on January 11, 1902. The last reports as to the condition of Brigg's health had been so discouraging that the news of his death did not cause much surprise. Though he rallied so wonderfully from his seizure at Leeds, during the Test match in 1899, as to bowl with nearly all his old skill and success throughout the season of 1900, it was known that his ailment – a form of epilepsy – admitted of no permanent cure, and was liable to recur at any time. He had another attack sooner than had been expected; was compelled to go back to Cheadle Asylum; and took no part in the cricket of 1901. Five or six weeks before his death it was announced that he had again rallied after a serious relapse, but this time the improvement was of very brief duration. Briggs had a long career, but at the time of his death he was only a little over thirty-nine. Like so many other famous professional cricketers, he was a Nottingham man, being born at

Sutton-in-Ashfield, on October 3, 1862. While still a child, however, he went to live in Lancashire, and all his cricket was learnt in the county for which, during more than twenty years, he did such brilliant work. He must have shown great promise while very young, as he was given a trial in the Lancashire elven before he was seventeen. He played in five matches for the county in 1879, and though he met with little success his aptitude for the game was so obvious that no doubt was felt as to his future. In those early days he was played chiefly for his fielding, his quickness and energy making him from the first a special favourite with the crowds at Old Trafford. The popularity that he thus gained as a lad remained with him to the end, and wherever he went the public took the keenest interest in his doings. For two or three seasons he was not much more than a splendid field, but from 1883 his batting rapidly improved, and a little later, without much warning, he blossomed out as one of the great slow bowlers of his day. In 1885 he headed the bowling averages for Lancashire, with seventy-nine wickets for 10.5 runs each, but, though this was a very fine record, his fame as a bowler really dated from the England and Australia match, at Lord's, in 1886 – the memorable game in which Shrewsbury played his innings of 164. The opening day's cricket was interefered with by rain, and the England eleven, who had won the toss, did not finish their innings till the second day, their total being 353. When the Australians went in against this formidable number, Jones and Scott scored so freely that an even match seemed in prospect. Suddenly, however, the character of the cricket underwent a complete change. Mr A. G. Steel, who captained England, put Briggs on as first change, and the Australians, though their score stood at 45 when the first wicket went down, were all out for 121, Briggs bowling 34 overs, 22 maidens, for 29 runs and five wickets. His success caused great surprise, as he had played for England a fortnight before at Manchester without being called upon to bowl at all. When the Australians followed on, he took six wickets for 45 runs, and England won the match in a single innings. Thenceforward, Briggs's reputation as a left-handed slow bowler was firmly established and, as everyone knows, he remained in the front rank, with, of course, the fluctuations of fortune to which all cricketers are subject, till his unhappy seizure at Leeds in 1899.

He jumped to the top of the tree at a very opportune moment in 1886 – Peate being then almost done with – and for many seasons his only rival in his own particular style was Peel. There is no need to go into details of his work year by year, but it is interesting to note that, according to the figures given in *Bat v Ball*, he took in first-class matches, from 1885 to 1899 inclusive, 2,034 wickets for less than 16 runs each. He had a bad season in 1898, but in 1900, after his first illness, he came out again in such form that 127 wickets fell to him for something over 17.5 runs each. During all his years of success Briggs was much more than a mere bowler. He was always a dangerous bat, likely at any time to get his 50 runs, and in the field he retained all the energy and nearly all the speed of his young days. Though the greater part of his work was done for Lancashire, he was in the truest sense of the word a representative cricketer, being picked over and over again for England and the Players, and being nearly as well known on Australian grounds as in this country. He paid six visits to the Colonies, going out with Shaw and Shrewsbury's teams in 1884-85, 1886-87, and 1887-88; with Lord Sheffield's team in 1891-92, and with Mr Stoddart's elevens in 1894-95, and 1897-98. As it happened, he went once too often, proving a sad failure for Stoddart's second team. In the other trips, however, he did himself full justice. Among all his Australian experiences the most remarkable was the famous 10 runs win at Sydney, in December, 1894, when Australia suffered defeat after playing a first innings of 586. The Australians only had to get 177 in the last innings, and at the close of the fifth day they had scored 113, with two men out. After drenching rain in the night, however, Peel and Briggs secured the eight outstanding wickets for 53 runs, gaining for Stoddart's side perhaps the most sensational victory in the history of cricket. Briggs, as a slow bowler, had nearly every good quality. His beautifully easy action enabled him to stand any amount of work; he had plenty of spin, and no one was more skilful in tempting batsmen to hit on the off-side. For a few seasons he bowled a particularly good fast ball, but in this respect he fell off in later years.

MR CHARLES FRANCIS BULLER, who died at Lyme Regis in October, 1906, will be remembered by cricketers of a past generation as one of the greatest batsmen of the day. Born at Colombo, Ceylon, on the 26 May, 1846, he won his place in the Harrow eleven as a boy of little more than fifteen, taking part in the match against Eton at Lord's in 1861. On the same occasion an almost equally famous batsman, Mr Alfred Lubbock, was seen at Lord's for the first time, but on the opposite side. Buller was in the Harrow team for four seasons, finishing up as captain in 1864. In that year he scored 61 and Harrow beat Eton by an innings and 66 runs. Judged by the standard of these days a score of 61 does not seem anything to make a fuss about, but never did the batting of a public school boy at Lord's earn higher praise. Thanks to his great natural ability and very careful coaching, in which the Surrey player, William Mortlock, had no small share, Buller at eighteen was already a finished batsman, good enough for any eleven. Style in batting was thought a great deal of in the sixties, and Buller's style was as nearly as possible perfect – quite comparable to, though very different from that of Tom Hayward or Richard Daft. In the Canterbury week of 1864 Buller played for England against Thirteen of Kent, and for the MCC against the Gentlemen of Kent, scoring in the latter match 21 and 68. The next season he had an assured position among the leading cricketers of the day, and was picked for Gentlemen against Players both at Lord's and The Oval. His highest and best innings in 1865 was 105 not out for Middlesex against Surrey at The Oval. In 1866 he fully upheld his reputation, but in 1867, having in the meantime entered the 2nd Life Guards, he played very little owing to illness. A year later he was quite himself again, but nothing was seen of him in first-class cricket the following year and in 1870 he played in only a few big matches. Then for nearly three years he dropped out, reappearing at the close of the season of 1873 in George Bennett's benefit match at Gravesend. During 1874, 1875, and 1876 he played for Middlesex, batting in the same perfect style as ever, but his weight had gone up to over fifteen stone and he was not much use in the field. During this latter part of his career two innings that he played are still vividly remembered – 51 for Middlesex against Nottinghamshire on a sticky wicket at Trent Bridge in August 1875, and 67 not out in the North v South match for the late Tom Hearne's benefit at Lord's in 1876. The last match of importance in which he took part was, we believe, Middlesex v Yorkshire at Lord's in 1877. He did not finish up badly, scoring 20 and 25. In *Bat v Ball* only two hundreds and a dozen other scores of over 50 in first-class matches appear against Buller's name, but important fixtures were few in his day and any comparison of his doings with batsmen of our time would be altogether fallacious. Some idea of his merit can be gathered from the fact that the late James Southerton thought he never bowled against a better batsman except, of course, W. G. Grace. Batting was a very exact science when Buller learnt the game, and only E. M. Grace and the left-handers indulged in the pulling by which so many hundreds of runs are nowadays obtained. Buller, however, was a master of all the orthodox strokes, his cut being especially fine. Equally strong in back and forward play he had such wrist power that he could without any apparent effort block a ball to the ring. Quite late in his career he scored 5 runs with a stroke of this kind off a ball that Allan Hill, the bowler, thought good enough to get anyone's wicket. He was very strong indeed in dropping down on a shooter, and the last time the present writer ever met him he was rather humorous at the immunity from shooters enjoyed by modern batsmen. Curiously enough with all his ability Buller met with little success for Gentlemen v Players. In ten matches between 1865 and 1874 he made only 181 runs in eighteen innings, his best score being 41 at The Oval in 1868. Into the scandals that marred Mr Buller's private life and caused his social eclipse, this is obviously not the place to enter. Those whose memories go back thirty to forty years will remember him as one of the most attractive of batsmen and, perhaps, the handsomest man the cricket field has ever known.

THE REV. ARTHUR GRAY BUTLER died at Glenfinnan, Torquay, on January 16, 1909, in his eightieth year. He was in the Rugby eleven in 1847 and 1848, being captain in the latter year, and was above the average as a batsman. For some years he was an assistant-master at Rugby under Dr Temple, and was afterwards appointed first headmaster of Haileybury. He was Butler of "Butler's Leap" at Rugby and winner of the racquet pairs at Oxford in 1855. He is said to have been the only man who ever jumped the river Cherwell, a tributary of the Thames at Oxford.

THE REV. CANON ALFRED MILLARD WILLIAM CHRISTOPHER, who was born at Ealing on August 20, 1820, died at Oxford on March 10, 1913, at the great age of 92. He was in the Cambridge XI of 1843, when he scored 17 and 1. The match, in which there were 82 wides, was played on Bullingdon Green, and was won by Cambridge by 54 runs. Canon Christopher was a sound defensive batsman, but, entering the Church, did not keep up his cricket, although to the last he was interested in the game.

MR JOHN CONWAY, the promoter and manager of the first Australian Team (that of 1878) which visited England, died at Frankston, on August 22, 1909. He was born at Fyansford, near Geelong on February 3, 1843, and was educated at the Melbourne Church of England Grammar School. When only 19 years of age he was chosen to appear for Eighteen of Victoria against H. H. Stephenson's team on the Melbourne ground – the first match ever played by an English side in Australia – and although he made only 1 run in the match he took four wickets for 60. He was then a very fast bowler. In later years he developed into a sound batsmen and an able captain, and his fielding at slip was always of a high order. A week after the match mentioned he played for Victoria against New South Wales and took five wickets for 39 runs, and in the game between the same sides at Sydney in December, 1865, he took eight wickets and scored 33. He took part in a lot of club cricket in Melbourne and for many years was captain of South Melbourne. A good judge of a young cricketer, he was the first to recognise the merits of Horan and Blackham. He was also an interesting and able writer on the game, and, in addition to contributing regularly to Sydney and Melbourne newspapers, edited the *Australian Cricket Annual* which bears his name. Far beyond everything else, however, he will be remembered for his great idea – so fruitful in after results – of sending an Australian Eleven to England.

JOHN CROSSLAND. The death on September 26, 1903, of Crossland – at one time the most talked-of bowler in England – recalled a very lively controversy that disturbed the cricket world in the eighties. A Nottingham man by birth, Crossland qualified for Lancashire by residence, and appeared first for that county in 1878. Three years later, when Lancashire stood at the head of the counties, he began to assert himself, and in 1882 he was beyond doubt the most effective fast bowler in England. His pace was tremendous, and even the best batsmen rather dreaded him. Outside Lancashire, however, his delivery was generally condemned, the majority of experts having no hesitation in describing him as a rank thrower. But for this feeling as to his action he would in all probability have been picked for England in the memorable match at The Oval when the Australians – thanks to Spofforth and Boyle – won by 7 runs. Crossland was passed by the umpires, but all through the season of 1882 his bowling was the subject of discussion, among those who thought him unfair being Thomas Horan and other members of the Australian eleven. At the same time there were other Lancashire bowlers who did not escape criticism, and the upshot was that Middlesex in 1883 and Nottinghamshire in 1884 declined to make fixtures with Lancashire. Naturally, a great deal of ill-feeling was aroused, and on one occasion at The Oval a demonstration against Crossland so enraged Mr Hornby that he was with difficulty persuaded to finish the match. The climax of the controversy was reached in 1885, when Kent, after appearing at Manchester, refused to play their return match with Lancashire on the ground that that county employed unfair bowlers. In taking this step Kent were guided by their captain, Lord Harris, who explained his position in a letter to the Lancashire committee. So far as Crossland was concerned the quarrel suddenly came to an end on a different issue altogether, it being ruled by the MCC – after full inquiry – that by living in Nottinghamshire during the winter he had broken his qualification, and had no longer any right to play for Lancashire. This ended his career in first-class cricket, but he continued to play in small matches, and only gave up the game about four years ago.

RICHARD DAFT, died on July 18, 1900. His death, which took place at Radcliffe-on-Trent, removed from amongst us one of the greatest cricketers of the last generation. As late as the summer of 1899 he seemed to have years of life before him, but some tim afterwards his health completely broke down, and for several weeks before his death he was lying ill without any hope of recovery. He was born on November 2, 1835, and was thus in his sixty-fifth year. Coming out as an amateur, he made his first appearance at Lord's, for North against South, in 1858, and quickly established a reputation as one of the best batsmen of his day. He took to cricket as a professional in 1859, but played again as an amateur when his career in public matches was nearly over. It is a noteworthy fact that he and the Warwickshire cricketer, Diver, are the only men who have played on both sides in the Gentlemen and Players' match. Beginning in 1858, he was a regular member of the Nottinghamshire Eleven for over twenty years, succeeding George Parr as captain, and not retiring until the season of 1881. After he had done with first-class matches he still kept up his cricket, and in 1891 he made so many runs in local matches that for one special occasion he reappeared in the Nottinghamshire Eleven – as a substitute for Shrewsbury – playing against Surrey in the August Bank-holiday match at The Oval. He was at his best as a batsman from perhaps 1861 to 1876. He came before the public at about the same time as Robert Carpenter and the late Thomas Hayward, and for three or four seasons it was a disputed point as to which of the three was the finest bat in England. George Parr was on the wane, and they had no rival until E. M. Grace appeared on the scene. Whether Daft was as good or better than Hayward or Carpenter is purely a matter of opinion, but there can be no question that in their day all three were very great indeed. It is a fair criticism to say that while Daft and Hayward were far ahead of Carpenter in point of style, Carpenter's was, perhaps, the hardest wickets to get. Daft batted in exceptionally fine form, utilising every inch of his height, and being very strong in back play. Like nearly all the batsmen of his time, he learnt most of his cricket against fast bowling, and was, perhaps, never seen to better advantage than when facing such bowlers as Willsher, Emmett, and George Freeman. The finest innings he ever played in his young days was 118 at Lord's for North against South in 1862, and the highest of his whole career in first-class matches was 161 for Nottinghamshire against Yorkshire at Trent Bridge in 1873. His best performance in Gentlemen and Players matches was at Lord's, in 1872, when, against the bowling of Appleby, Powys, and David Buchanan, he scored 102. Scores were far smaller all round in his day than they are now, and grounds by no means so true, and, allowing for these facts, his records were wonderfully good. In the history of Nottinghamshire cricket his name as a batsman will stand with that of George Parr in the past, and those of Arthur Shrewsbury and William Gunn in our own time.

HM KING EDWARD VII died at Buckingham Palace on May 6, 1910. As a small boy he received tuition at Windsor from F. Bell, of Cambridge, but it cannot be said that he ever showed much aptitude for the game. He played occasionally during his Oxford days, however, and, while he was staying at Madingley Hall, a special wicket was reserved for his use at Fenner's. He showed his interest in the game in many ways. When funds were being collected to pay off the pavilion debt at Fenner's, he contributed ten pounds, at the same time promising to make up any amount required at the end of the term, and during one of the critical moments in the history of the MCC was the largest contributor to the fund raised to pay for the freehold of Lord's. Furthermore, as Duke of Cornwall his late Majesty was for many years landlord of The Oval, and in several ways he showed his interest in the Surrey County CC. His Majesty was born at Buckingham Palace on November 9, 1841, and was therefore in his sixty-ninth year at the time of his death.

MR LIONEL H. ELFORD, a well-known umpire in the Hastings district of Sussex, was killed on August 17, 1904, through being thrown out of a brake (the horses, frightened by a traction-engine, having bolted) near Cranbrook, in Kent, whilst on tour with the Hastings Rovers. He was in his sixty-fifth year.

THE REV. WALTER FELLOWS, who was born at Rickmansworth, in Hertford-shire, on February 23, 1834, died at Toorak Parsonage, near Melbourne, July 23, 1902. He was educated at Westminster and Oxford, and is described in *Scores and Biographies* (iv – 471) as "a hard slashing hitter, and a tremendous fast round-armed bowler." He was younger brother of Mr Harvey Fellows, who still, happily, survives. For Westminster against Rugby, at Westminster, in 1852, he obtained nine wickets in the first innings and six in the second, but was on the losing side, Westminster making only 19 and 11, against Rugby's scores of 114 and 129. Although Mr Fellows' bowling was effective, it was certainly expensive, as there were 15 byes in the first innings, and 27 in the second. Moreover, he bowled 30 wides, thereby giving away as many runs as Westminster made in their two innings combined. For four years he assisted Oxford against Cambridge, namely from 1854 to 1857, and made scores of 33, 0 and 5, 35 and 30 (the highest in each innings), 24 and 3. In the 1855 match he bowled twelve overs for 6 runs and two wickets. In 1855 and the two following years he appeared for the Gentlemen against the Players, at Lord's, participating in the match in which Reginald Hankey played his historical innings of 70. Whilst at practice on the Christ Church Ground, at Oxford, in 1856, Mr Fellows hit a ball, bowled by Rogers, a distance of 175 yards from hit to pitch, the length of the drive being carefully measured by E. Martin, the ground-keeper. In 1863 he emigrated to Australia, and joined the Melbourne Club the following year. He was interested in the game to the last. Height, 5ft 11ins, and playing weight as much as 17st 4lbs.

MR J. J. FERRIS, died on November 17, 1900, at Durban, where he was serving with the British forces. Mr Ferris, though only in his thirty-fourth year, had for some time dropped out of first-class cricket, and had to a certain extent outlived his fame. Still, though his career ended early, he will always be remembered as one of the finest left-handed bowlers – either English or Australian – that ever appeared. Having in the two previous winters done great things against English teams in the Colonies, Ferris first came to this country in 1888 as a member of the Australian eleven captained by the late Percy McDonnell. Much was expected of him, and he more than fulfilled the most sanguine anticipations. No one who can recall the cricket season of 1888 – one of the wettest on record – will need to be told what a sensation he and Charles Turner created. They were the mainstays of a team which, after a brilliant start, suffered many defeats, but the shortcomings were not in any way due to the two bowlers, who made their names famous wherever cricket is played. The eleven being deficient in change bowling, they had far too much to do, but they never seemed to tire, keeping up their form in a really wonderful way. Turner was the more successful of the two taking in the whole tour 314 wickets for little more than 11 runs each. Ferris, however, also has a splendid record, 220 wickets falling to him for something over 14 runs apiece. The two men formed a perfect contrast, Turner being right hand, with an off-break perhaps never equalled at his speed, and Ferris left hand, with great accuracy, fine variety of pace, and a lot of spin. The weather flattered them, the wickets day after day giving them immense assistance, but it may be questioned if two finer bowlers ever played on the same side. One would not say that they were better than Spofforth and Palmer in 1882, but by reason of one being right-handed and the other left they were a more effective combination. As to the relative merits of Spofforth and Turner, cricketers have always been divided in opinion, the balance – among English players, at any rate – being in Spofforth's favour on account of his better head and more varied resources. In Ferris's case no question of comparison arose, as he was the first great left-handed bowler produced by Australia since the days on Frank Allan and Tom Kendall. Ferris and Turner came to England for the second time in 1890, and though associated with the least successful of all the Australians elevens, they fully sustained their reputations. This time Turner could only show a fractional superiority over his comrade. In the whole tour each man took 215 wickets, and there was a difference of less than a run a wicket in their averages. The summer was very wet, but there were more hard wickets to bowl on than in 1888, and under conditions favourable to run-getting Ferris perhaps did better work than Turner. That, at least, was the general opinion while the tour was in progress. With the tour of 1890 Ferris's career as a representative Australian cricketer came to an end. He agreed to qualify for Gloucestershire, and when the Australians came here in 1893 he played for the county against his old friends. For Gloucestershire, however, he proved as a bowler – not to mince matters – an utter failure. It was thought that he would be invaluable to the eleven, but he rarely showed a trace of the skill that had made him so famous, and when we last saw him bowl in a Gloucestershire match – in 1895 – he had lost his pace, his spin, his action, and everything. In the autumn of 1895 he returned to Australia, but his efforts to recover his old position in Colonial cricket met with no success, and little was heard of him till it was announced that he had gone to South Africa to try his fortune at the war with the Imperial Light Horse. We must not forget to add that he went out to South Africa with Mr W. W. Read's team in the winter of 1891-2. He had a brilliant tour, taking 235 wickets, but he never bowled in the same form afterwards.

MR THOMAS ARTHUR FISON, a well-known figure in Metropolitan cricket circles about a quarter of a century ago, died at Hampstead, on April 14, 1911. For years he was captain of the Hendon CC, and was in local cricket one of the hardest hitters of his day. Against Highgate School in August, 1879, he scored 264 not out in three hours and a half, hitting a 7, two 5s, nine 4s, twenty-three 3s, and forty 2s. All the hits were run out, and in the score-sheet it was recorded that he "retired to catch a train for the Continent." In a match between the same sides at Hendon in 1884 he made 201. Mr Fison, was 6ft 2ins in height, and was a good wicket-keeper. He was born at Romsey, in Hampshire, on October 7th, 1853, and was educated at Mill Hill School.

MR WILLIAM JUSTICE FORD, the eldest and probably the best-known of the famous brothers, died in London on April 3, 1904. He was in the Repton XI in 1870, 1871 and 1872, and in the following year assisted Cambridge against Oxford, being put into the team at the last moment, and scoring 51 not out and 11. He was a tremendous hitter, a good field at point, a useful wicket-keeper, and a slow round-arm bowler. Height 6ft 3in, and weight (in 1871) 15st 4lbs, which by 1886 had increased to 17st 4lbs. He occasionally appeared for Middlesex, and it was when assisting that side against Kent, at Maidstone, in 1885, that he made 44 in seventeen minutes and 75 out of 90 in three-quarters of an hour. His longest measured hit was 143 yards 2 feet. He hit out of almost all the grounds upon which he played, including Lord's and the Aigburth ground at Liverpool. Playing once for MCC and Ground v Eastbourne, at the Saffrons, he hit J. Bray over the trees, the ball pitching 60 yards beyond them. On another occasion, when playing at Torquay, he hit a ball out of the ground (above the ordinary size), across a road, and so far into another field that it put up a brace of partridges. He made many large scores for the MCC, Nondescripts, and Incogniti, his most productive innings being 250 for MCC v Uxbridge, in 1881. At various times he was a master at Marlborough, Principal of Nelson College, NZ, and head master of Leamington College. Once, in a match at Marlborough, he had made 92 when the last man came in, and, wishing to make sure of his hundred, hit the very next ball with such hearty good will that he and his partner ran 10 for the stroke! Of recent years he had been a prolific writer on the game, his best-known books being the histories of the Middlesex County and Cambridge University Clubs, the latter of which will probably become a classic. His articles on Public School Cricket had for some years been a feature of *Wisden's Almanack*. Mr Ford must be regarded as one of the greatest hitters the world has ever seen, having been equalled by few and surpassed only by Mr C. I. Thornton. He was born in London November 7, 1853.

MR REGINALD ERSKINE FOSTER died at his home in London on the 13th of May, 1914. He was born at Malvern on April 16, 1878. Mr Foster's death from diabetes at the age of thirty-six came as a great shock to the cricket world, but was no surprise to his intimate friends. His health broke down in the summer of 1913, and a visit to South Africa did him no permanent good. He had not reached tha age at which, by means of rigid dieting, diabetes can sometimes be kept in check. He was one of the pre-eminently great batsmen of his day, ranking with MacLaren, Fry, Jackson, Tom Hayward and Tyldesley, among those who stood nearest to Ranjitsinhji. Of all the fine batsmen who learnt the game at Malvern he was incontestably the best and his record for Oxford in 1900 has never been equalled in University cricket. In *Wisden's Almanack* for 1913 Mr Foster's doings in the cricket field were set out in full detail, so one need not in this notice of him go at any length into figures. Three of his feats stand out above all the rest – his 171 against Cambridge at Lord's in 1900, his 102 not out and 136 for the Gentlemen against the Players at Lord's ten days later, and, his 287 for the MCC's England Eleven against Australia at Sydney in December, 1903. This 287 remains the record innings in Test match cricket. Mr Foster was the first batsman to make two separate hundreds in a Gentlemen and Players' match, and the feat has only once been repeated – by J. H. King for the Players at Lord's in 1904. Curiously enough, both Mr Foster and King were playing in the big match for the first time. It is a strange fact that Mr Foster never played for England against Australia in this country. The Australians were not here in either 1900 or 1901 – his two great seasons. This was very unfortunate for him, as in both those years he would have been one of the first men chosen for Test matches. After 1901 he could not, except in 1907, when he captained England against South Africa, spare much time for first-class cricket. When the Australians came here in 1905 he played very little, and in 1909 he was not seen at all. It may not be generally known that Mr Foster had the refusal of the captaincy of the MCC team that visited Australia in the winter of 1907-8. He would have liked above all things to bat again on the Sydney and Melbourne wickets, but he could not arrange to be away from England for the length of time required. His last big match was for Worcestershire against the Australians at Dudley in 1912 when he scored 26. A week before that he had hit up 127 at Lord's for the MCC against the Public Schools, playing, after the first few overs, with undiminished brilliancy. It was characteristic of Mr Foster that, like C. J. Ottaway and W. H. Patterson, he could at any time return to first-class cricket and play as well as if he had been in full practice all the season. A case in point occurred in 1910. He only played once for Worcestershire that year, but he scored 133 against Yorkshire.

A striking parallel can be drawn between Mr Foster's career as a batsman at Oxford and that of F. S. Jackson, at Cambridge. Both were very good bats at school, but in their early days of University cricket there was little suggestion of the heights they were destined to reach. Steadily improving for three seasons, each in his last year – Jackson in 1893 and Foster in 1900 – blossomed out as an England batsman of the first rank. In his position at the wicket – he stood with both eyes turned full on the bowler – and his general style of play, Mr Foster was quite modern but, in adapting himself to swerving bowlers, he did not, like so many batsmen, lose his brilliancy on the off-side. Nothing could have been finer than his hitting past cover-point, and his late cut was a model of safety and clever placing. After his two hundreds for the Gentlemen in 1900, C. B. Fry said of him that no one, except Ranjitsinhji, could wield a bat with greater quickness. One of seven brothers who have been seen in the Malvern School and Worcestershire County Elevens, he was beyond doubt the best of them all. This may be said without in any way disparaging H. K. Foster's skill and commanding style. Apart from his splendid batting, R. E. Foster was one of the finest slip fieldsmen of his day. Tall, slim, and lithe, he brought off catches that would have been impossible to ordinary men. Mr Foster was in the Malvern eleven 1893-96, and in the Oxford eleven 1897-1900. He was on the MCC Committee at the time of his death, having previously served from 1904 to 1907. Without approaching his brother H. K.'s class, he was a good racquet player, and at Association football he won International honours, playing for England three times against Wales, and once each against Scotland and Ireland. He was twice in the Oxford Association team against Cambridge, and did brilliant things for the Old Malvernians.

MR JOHN FURLEY, born at Oakham on March 24, 1847, died suddenly at his native place on June 30, 1909. His first appearance at Lord's (under the assumed name of "A. Yorker, Esq.") was for Northamptonshire v MCC and Ground in July, 1873, when he made 0 and 24 and took eight wickets for 93 runs. In 1877, when he made several very large scores for Burghley Park, he was chosen to play for England against Gloucestershire at The Oval. *Scores and Biographies* (xii – 781) described him as: – "A fair bat, a good and fast round-armed bowler, fielding generally at short slip."

MR GEORGE GILBERT, who died at Summer Hill, NSW, on June 16, 1906, at the age of 78, was a cousin of the Graces, and in his time played no mean part in the cricket field. He was born in Gloucestershire, and appeared several times for the Gentlemen of Surrey, and, in 1851, for the Gentlemen against the Players at Lord's. He went to Australia in 1852, and four years later captained New South Wales in the very first match that State ever played against Victoria. He also played for the New South Wales XXII against the first English team which visited Australia – in 1861-2 – and to the last took a great interest in the game. At The Oval, in 1851, he played a single-wicket match against Mr F. P. Miller, the Surrey captain, in which a curious occurrence took place. The latter cut a ball which went round the boundary stump. Gilbert threw the ball at the wicket but, as it did not pass within bounds, was told to fetch it back and try again. During the argument Mr Miller ran 13 for the hit.

MR EDWARD MILLS GRACE died on May 20, 1911 after a long illness at his residence, Park House, Thornbury, Gloucestershire. But for the accident that his own brother proved greater than himself, E. M. Grace would have lived in cricket history as perhaps the most remarkable player the game has produced. Barring W.G., it would be hard indeed to name a man who was a stronger force on a side or a more remarkable match winner. Primarily, he was a batsman, but his value in an eleven went far beyond his power of getting runs. As a fieldsman at point – at a time when the position was far more important that it is in modern cricket – he never had an equal, and, though he did not pretend to be a first-rate bowler, he took during his career thousands of wickets. In his young days he bowled in the orthodox round-arm style, but his success in club cricket was gained by means of old-fashioned lobs. Fame came to him early in life. Born on November 28, 1841, he made his first appearance at Lord's in 1861, and a year later he was beyond question the most dangerous bat in England. It was in the Canterbury Week in 1862 that, playing as an emergency for the MCC against the Gentlemen of Kent, he scored 192 not out, and took all ten wickets in one innings. This was a 12 a-side and one man was absent in the second innings when he got the ten wickets. He reached his highest point as a batsman in 1863, scoring in all matches that year over 3,000 runs.

After the season was over he went to Australia as a member of George Parr's famous team, but it cannot be said that in the Colonies he did all that was expected of him. He was handicapped by a bad hand, but, as he himself stated, there was another reason for his comparative lack of success. At the start of the tour he fell into rather a reckless style of batting, and, try as he would, he could not get back to his proper method. Still, he did some good things, scoring, for example, 106 not out in a single-wicket match. He had not been back in England more than two years before W.G., as a lad of eighteen, began to put him in the shade. The two brothers were in the Gentlemen's eleven together in 1865 – W.G.'s first year in the representative match – and had a share in gaining for the Gentlemen their first victory at Lord's since 1853. While he was qualifying as a surgeon E. M. Grace to a certain extent dropped out of first-class cricket, but he came very much to the front again on the formation of the Gloucestershire County Club in 1871. He was secretary from the start, and held his post without a break till his resignation in 1909.

In Gloucestershire's early days he renewed the success of his youth, batting especially well in August, 1872, when W.G. was away in Canada with the amateur eleven captained by the late R. A. Fitzgerald. It is matter of common knowledge that chiefly through the efforts of the three Graces – G.F. died in 1880 – Gloucestershire rose to the top of the tree, being champion county in 1876 and again in 1877. Not till the first Australian team played at Clifton in 1878 did the Gloucestershire eleven know what it was to be beaten at home. One of the greatest triumphs of E. M. Grace's career came in 1880, when, strictly on his merits, he was picked to play for England at The Oval in the first Test match with Australia in this country. After an extraordinary game England won by five wickets, the task of getting 57 runs in the last innings against Palmer and Boyle costing the side five of their best batsmen. E.M. and W.G. opened England's first innings, and scored over 90 runs together. W.G. made 152, and in Australia's second innings W. L. Murdoch just beat him by scoring 153 not out. Never has a finer match been seen.

E. M. Grace continued to play for Gloucestershire for many years, dropping out of the eleven after the season of 1894. Thenceforward his energies were devoted to club cricket, chiefly in connection with his own team at Thornbury. Lameness gradually robbed him of his old skill as a run-getter, but even in 1909, 119 wickets fell to his lobs. As a batsman E. M. Grace was unorthodox. Partly, it is thought, through using a full-sized bat while still a small boy, he never played with anything like W.G.'s perfect straightness, but his wonderful eye and no less wonderful nerve enabled him to rise superior to this grave disadvantage. He was perhaps the first right-handed batsman of any celebrity who habitually used the pull. In his young days batting was a very strict science, but he cared little for rules. If an open place in the field suggested runs the ball soon found its way in that direction. Personally, E.M. was the cheeriest of cricketers – the life and soul of the game wherever he played. It was a great misfortune that he could never be induced to write his recollections of the cricket field. His good stories could be numbered by the hundred, and in conversation he told them with immense vivacity.

E. M. Grace's scores of 70 and over in first-class cricket:

192\* MCC v Gentlemen of Kent, at Canterbury, 1862
73 South v North, at Lord's, 1863
75 MCC v Gentlemen of Kent, at Canterbury, 1863
112 XIV Gentlemen of South v XI Players of South, at Southampton, 1863
78 England v Surrey, at The Oval, 1864
111 Gentlemen of England v Gentlemen of Middlesex at Islington, 1865
71 Gentlemen v Players, at The Oval, 1867
115 The World v Surrey, at The Oval, 1867†
108 Gloucestershire v Nottinghamshire, at Clifton, 1872
70 Gloucestershire v Surrey, at The Oval, 1874
76 Gloucestershire v Sussex, at Brighton, 1873
73 Gloucestershire v Sussex, at Cheltenham, 1873
71 Gloucestershire v Sussex, at Cheltenham, 1875
89 Gloucestershire v Nottinghamshire, at Nottingham, 1877
77 Gloucestershire v Surrey, at The Oval, 1881
108 Gloucestershire v Somerset, at Gloucester, 1882
122 Gloucestershire v Lancashire, at Clifton, 1882
71 Gloucestershire v Surrey, at The Oval, 1883
84 Gloucestershire v Lancashire, at Manchester, 1887
70 Gloucestershire v Kent, at Clifton, 1887
96 Gloucestershire v Kent, at Gloucester, 1890
77 Gloucestershire v Surrey, at Bristol, 1890
78 Gloucestershire v Sussex, at Bristol, 1890
70 Gloucestershire v Somerset, at Bristol, 1892

\* *Signifies not out.*
† *This was a scratch match, on the third day of Tom Lockyer's benefit.*

**MR WILLIAM GILBERT GRACE, JUN.**, eldest son of the greatest of cricketers, died suddenly at three o'clock on the morning of March 2, 1905, at East Cowes, after an operation for appendicitis. As he was born on July 6, 1874, he was under thirty-one years of age at the time of his death. He was in the Clifton College XI in 1891-92-93, being captain in his second year, and assisted Cambridge against Oxford in 1895 and 1896. His first pronounced success was gained in the Reigate Festival of 1894, when he played a not out innings of 148 for his father's XI against Mr W. W. Read's XI. At Cambridge on June 1, 1896, he and G. S. Graham-Smith made 337 together for the first wicket of Pembroke College v Caius College, and at the Crystal Palace on September 16, 1901, he and W. L. Murdoch (who carried out his bat for 200) put up 355 for the first wicket of London County v Erratics. In these matches his scores were respectively 213 and 150. As a bowler he frequently did well, and for London County v Bromley Town, at the Crystal Palace, on August 25, 1902, he obtained all ten wickets in an innings. From 1897 until 1903 he was an assistant-master at Oundle, and during the last two years of his life he occupied a similar position at the Royal Naval College, Osborne. He was buried at Elmers End Road Cemetery on March 6.

**MR WILLIAM DRUMMOND HAMILTON**, who died on March 8, 1914, was born at Mellifont, near Drogheda, on May 4, 1859. He was educated at Haileybury, where he was in the Eleven in 1876 and 1877, when he was described as: "A thoroughly good left-handed bat, who always plays the game and hits well to all parts of the field; a capital point." In 1882 he gained his blue at Oxford, but in the match with Cambridge (in which he was so nervous that he once started the wrong way when called for a run) scored only 9 and 0. Earlier in the season he had made 53 v the Gentlemen of England at Oxford, and in 1883 he played an innings of 54 for MCC against University on the same ground.

**MR ARTHUR HAYGARTH.** By the death of Mr Arthur Haygarth at his London residence on the 1st of May, 1903, at the age of seventy-seven, there passed away a famous cricketer, whose name will always be gratefully recalled as long as the game continues to be played. Although a very capable exponent of the game which he loved so much, he will always be chiefly known to fame as the compiler of the *Cricket Scores and Biographies*. In 1842, while still at Harrow School, he commenced his labour of love, being but sixteen years of age at the time, and it says much for his enthusiasm for his work that to the day of his death his interest in the subject remained as great as ever. When he began to collect facts concerning the history of cricket and the chief players, it was merely as an amusement, and with no idea of his notes ever being published. In 1852, however, Mr F. P. Miller, the captain of the famous Surrey team of which Caffyn, H. H. Stephenson, Lockyer, Mortlock, Griffith, and Cæsar were the leading lights, asked Mr Haygarth to lend him his manuscript with a view to publication. To this the latter readily consented, but Vol. I did not appear until ten years later. In 1873, the MCC invited Mr Haygarth to continue his work, with the result that the last ten volumes of the *magnum opus* have been published through the instrumentality of the premier club. Altogether the work consists of fourteen volumes, every line of which was penned by Mr Haygarth, the statement inserted at the commencement of the first volume that the Lillywhites assisted in the compilation being altogether inaccurate, and inserted merely to suit their own ends. It would be impossible to overestimate the value of Mr Haygarth's labours, while to state that his death has left a gap which it will be impossible to fill is a fact of which every student of the game is fully conscious. For a period of over sixty years he worked loyally at his self-imposed task, never losing heart when meeting with a rebuff, nor becoming weary in seeking out unexplored fields that promised to contain any records or novelties connected with the game. With reference to his great work, Mr Haygarth wrote: "There is certainly one great mistake, or rather oversight, which I made during the 50 years and upwards in which I was engaged on the *Cricket Scores and Biographies*, and it is this – I preserved too many matches of an inferior calabre by far. If I had not done this the fourteen volumes already published would have reached a date much further than they do now, namely, to the end of 1878."

The last volume issued was the fourteenth, in 1894, the MCC declining to continue publication owing to the fact that it was not a success financially. This action on the part of the Club caused Mr Haygarth much distress, but did not result in his enthusiasm for the game lessening in the slightest degree. A short time before his death Mr Haygarth said to the writer of this memoir, "I can truly affirm that if, when I began the collection, I had known the trouble and expense I have been put to for so many years, I should never have undertaken the work. I am wise too late." He was a voluminous writer and frequently contributed articles and paragraphs to *Cricket* under the *nom de plume* of "An Old Harrovian".

Mr Haygarth was born at 29, Wellington Square, Hastings, on August 4, 1825, and received his early education at Temple Grove School, East Sheen, Surrey, where he remained from 1833 until 1837, and here it was he first became interested in the game. He entered Harrow in September, 1839, and left in July, 1843. In 1842, and again in the following year, he appeared at Lord's against Eton and Winchester, exhibiting even then defence of a very powerful nature. In 1844 he became a member of the MCC, on the proposal of the Earl of Bessborough (then the Hon. F. Ponsonby) and the Hon. Robert Grinston, who had taught him his cricket whilst at Harrow. He appeared at Lord's, from first to last, for twenty seasons, playing in over 150 matches, and in his last innings – against Hampshire in 1861 – scoring 46 before being bowled off his legs by Holmes. The defence he exhibited on the rough and bumpy wickets which were used at Lord's in his time was remarkable. By his extreme steadiness he frequently wore down the bowling, and so did great service for the side on which he appeared. When asked what his average was, he would reply "One hour," which was about the time he generally stayed at the wicket. Between 1846 and 1859 he assisted the Gentlemen against the Players on sixteen occasions, and one of the incidents of his long life which he was fond of recalling concerned the match between the two sides at Lord's in 1857. In the first innings Mr Reginald Hankey, after stating to the Players that he did not fell very well and probably should not trouble them long, played the innings of his life (70), hitting the bowling of Willsher, Wisden, H. H. Stephenson and Jackson all over the ground – a display to which the veterans are never tired of referring. During all the time Mr Hankey was at the wicket, Mr Haygarth was in with him, and in after years he always spoke with the greatest enthusiasm respecting Hankey's batting upon that occasion. Mr Haygarth, going in first wicket down, carried out his bat for 53, for which he was in over four hours. His chief innings at Lord's in great matches were:

57   Gentlemen of England v Gentlemen of Kent, 1847
71   Viscount Montgarret's XI, v Earl of Winterton's XI, 1849
50   MCC and Ground v Cambridge University, 1851
53   Gentlemen of MCC v Gentlemen of England, 1853
97   MCC and Ground v Surrey Club and Ground, 1855
53*  Gentlemen v Players, 1857
81*  Gentlemen of England v Gentlemen of Kent and Sussex, 1857
71*  MCC and Ground v Cambridge University, 1858

  * *Signifies not out.*

In 1864, on being made a life member of the MCC, he severed his connection with the Surrey Club, which he had joined in 1850. In the field he was very active, and was occasionally of use as a change bowler. His best performance with the ball was for MCC and Ground against Sussex, at Lord's, in 1860, when he and the late J. Grundy bowled unchanged throughout the match.

Mr Arthur Haygarth, who was buried at Brompton on the 5th of May, was the youngest of three brothers, the others being the Rev. Canon Henry William Haygarth, who died on December 31st last, aged eighty-one, having been vicar of Wimbledon since 1859, and Colonel Francis Haygarth, late adjutant of the Scots Fusilier Guards, who was most severely wounded at the battle of the Alma, and who survives. Mr Arthur Haygarth was the only one of the brothers who participated in the game. Three cousins, however, earned distinction on the cricket field, Mr J. W. Haygarth playing for Winchester in 1858, 1858, 1860 and 1861 (being captain the last two years), and for Oxford in 1862, 1863, and 1864; Mr Frederick being in the Winchester elevens of 1864, 1865 and 1866; and Mr E. B. appearing for Lancing College in 1868, 1869, and 1870. The three last-named were brothers, of whom a fourth, Mr G. A. Haygarth, was also a good player, although not known to fame.

**MR GEORGE EDWARD HEMINGWAY**, a brother of Messrs. W. M'G. and R. E. Hemingway, died at Rangoon on March 11, 1907. He was born at Macclesfield in 1872, was in the Uppingham Eleven in 1888, and in 1898 appeared for Gloucestershire against Yorkshire at Sheffield. He was a free batsman and in the field generally stood mid-off or cover-point, but business and weak sight handicapped his play considerably. On one occasion, when playing a single-wicket match against his two brothers, he hit the ball into a bed of nettles; the fieldsmen quarrelled as to who should recover it, and during the argument the batsman ran about 250.

**WILLIAM HICKTON**, who died at Lower Broughton, February 27, 1900, did good service for Lancashire thirty years ago. He was a good batsman and a fast round-armed bowler, being altogether a cricketer above the average, and fielding generally at slip. His first appearance at Lord's was for Lancashire v MCC and Ground, June 3, 4, 5, 1867, and it was a curious fact that none of the Lancashire Eleven (except C. Coward, who appeared as a colt in 1862) had ever before played at Lord's.

**HENRY NORTH HOLROYD**, 3rd Earl of Sheffield, Viscount Pevensey, Baron Sheffield of Dunsmore, Meath, Baron Sheffield of Roscommon, in Ireland, and Baron Sheffield, of Sheffield, Yorkshire, was born in London on January 18, 1832, and died at Beaulieu on April 21, 1909. By his death Sussex lost the best supporter of cricket they ever had. When the fortunes of the county were at a low ebb he engaged Alfred Shaw and William Mycroft to coach Young Sussex players of promise, thereby benefiting the game in the county to a very great extent. His liberality, in fact, was almost unbounded. Unlike Lord Harris he never gained fame as a player, but in 1856, when Viscount Pevensey, was considered good enough to play for the Gentlemen of Sussex against the Gentlemen of Kent. He was President of the County Club from 1879 until 1897, and was re-elected to the position in 1904, when he made an additional donation to the Club of £100. In the winter of 1891-2, entirely at his own expense, he took an English team to Australia, chiefly in order that the Australian public might have another opportunity of seeing W. G. Grace. The visit benefited the game in Australia enormously, and to commemorate the trip Lord Sheffield presented a trophy, known as the Sheffield Shield, for competition between Victoria, South Australia, and New South Wales. His private ground at Sheffield Park was opened in 1846 and no charge was ever made for admission. Five of the Australian teams opened their tours there, as did the South African team of 1894. Lord Sheffield had been a member of the MCC since 1855.

**MR FREDERICK AITKEN LEESTON-SMITH**, who had played for Brecknockshire and Somerset, died during 1903. He was a powerful hitter, a middle-paced round-armed bowler, and generally fielded at point. In 1881 he played an innings of 204 for Weston-super-Mare v Clevedon. He was educated at Malvern, but did not obtain a place in the Eleven, leaving there at the age of fourteen. He afterwards went to Christ College,

Brecon, where he was in the eleven. He was born in London, May 10, 1854, was 5ft 10½in in height and weighed 12st 4lbs. In 1880 he assumed the name of Leeston. In a match between Weston-super-Mare and Thornbury, he once hit E. M. Grace for four 6s from consecutive balls, a performance which the latter has described as follows: – "F. L. Cole made 1 off my first ball, F. A. Leeston-Smith 6 off the second, 6 off third, 6 off fourth, 6 off fifth, when the umpire said, "I am afraid it is over, Doctor." I said, "Shut up, I am going to have another," and off this one he was stumped. Weston-super-Mare had to follow their innings. Leeston-Smith came in first, and the first ball I bowled him he hit for 6. The second also went for 6, but off the third he was stumped again."

THOMAS WILLIAM COKE, 2nd Earl of Leicester, was born at Holkham, in Norfolk, on December 26, 1822, and died there on January 24, 1909, in his eighty-seventh year. He became a member of the MCC in 1847 and in the following year was elected President of the club. He played for Norfolk on several occasions as well as for the Houses of Parliament against I Zingari, and for many years entertained an MCC team at Holkham. In minor matches he made some capital scores and in 1850 was credited with an innings of 123. He was one of the greatest of British agriculturalists and at the time of his death was Father of the House of Lords. He survived the birth of his father by no fewer than 155 years; he had a half-sister who married Viscount Anson as far back as 1794; and he married for the second time in 1875, exactly a century after his father's marriage. His eldest son was born in 1848 and his youngest in 1893.

### R. A. H. MITCHELL

An Appreciation by Lord Harris

Having been asked by the Editor of *Wisden's Almanack* to write a short biography of Mr R. A. H. Mitchell, I gladly embrace the opportunity of recording as much as my memory can compass.

Mr R. D. Walker's intimate acquaintance with Mr Mitchell's cricket, before he accepted a Mastership at Eton, has enabled him to deal with that part of this obituary which I could only have touched on from hearsay; but I had seen dear "Mike" – as he was to every cricketer who played with him – play before then. I lived in London two years before I went to Eton in 1864 and saw many great matches at Lord's, The Oval, and Canterbury; and knew most of the crack players by sight; I saw Mike play for Oxford at Lord's in 1863 and '64 certainly, and possibly in '62, matches which Mr Walker has described, and I also saw him play at Canterbury in 1862 and remember very vividly his being caught at long-leg on the bank by Baker high above his head. It would have been a fourer nowadays for Baker was standing in the crowd, there being no boundaries then.

I believe he came to Eton first as private tutor to a boy at my tutor's; at any rate, one night at Eton, before he took up his Mastership, Mike came down to stay with my tutor, Dr Warre, and slept in one of the boy's rooms; how he managed to stow away his great frame into a boy's bedstead I cannot imagine, it must have been very sound on its fore legs to carry his weight. Haygarth's *Scores and Biographies* (Vol. VI, p. 86) records that at "18 years of age he was 6ft 2ins, and weighed 13st 2lb, afterwards 15st 3lb." I was greatly excited over his visit, for I knew his cricket history far better than most of my schoolmates, and my reverence for him even then was great.

He took up his residence at Eton in 1866, and all cricketers at Eton looked forward with confidence to his making a great improvement in "Upper Club" form; and it was needed, for Eton had fallen on evil days just then, not that she did not turn out some good cricketers, for the Elevens of 1861, '62, and '63 contain some great names, but it is recorded in *Scores and Biographies* in 1862 that Eton had not beaten Harrow since 1850; the '63 match was drawn, and Eton lost in '64, '65, and '66; so that the distinct change that took place in the School's fortune in the "Lord's" match, by which the "form" of Eton and Harrow cricketers must be judged, synchronizes exactly with Mike's advent. I submit that statistics bear this contention out unmistakeably. Out of 63 completed matches Eton has won 30, less than half; but out of 13 completed matches, '67 to '87 inclusive, Eton won eight, and out of the eight completed matches played in his first ten years of "coaching" Eton won six. It may be said that those 21 years do not include the whole of his career as a Master at Eton, which is true; but they were the years in which his physical capacity enabled him to show what his mental capacity could produce; and surely 21 years is a sufficiently long period over which to judge of a man's capacity by results. That Mike fell off after that was a view very generally held, and possibly correctly. I cannot offer an opinion on the point, as I was out of England for a large part of his remaining time at Eton. It is quite possible that, as age crept on, his "steady for the first hour" became intensified, and that he discouraged hitting more than was necessary, but for play on sticky wickets I cannot but think he must still have been as good a coach as ever.

Of his pupils I could not say that in my opinion the style of anyone of them followed Mike's very closely, except in the use of full height. There was no crouching in the style he encouraged. Possibly those who approached nearest to it were Walter Forbes, Alfred Lyttelton, A. W. Ridley, and Charley Studd, but this is a matter where *"quot homines, tot sententiæ"* particularly applies. The above were, of course, four of his most distinguished pupils; but there were others, also distinguished, whose style bore no resemblance to his; and yet their styles were very sound, and in one case, poor C. J. Ottaway, quite as sound as Mike's, but Ottaway was a phenomenon as a school bat.

I am sure that dear Mike would wish it to be put in the forefront of any record of what he did for Eton cricket, that his success could not have been what it was but for the co-operation, I may justly say the daily co-operation, for a long series of years of the Rev. G. R. Dupuis, and the very frequent help of Mr Edward Austen Leigh. Mr Dupuis indeed had commenced giving advice in Upper Club the year before Mike's arrival, at Edgar Lubbock's request. Mr Austen Leigh did not do so much coaching, but he was constantly at the nets bowling to us. The others devoted – really I cannot use too strong an expression for I believe it was – the whole of their spare time to us; after 12, after 4, after 6 there they were either at the nets bowling, advising, teaching, or standing umpire, and giving us equally valuable lessons during games. I am sure I am but voicing the feelings of every Eton cricketer of those times, that everything we acquired, which went to improve natural aptitude, was due to those great cricketers and great masters of the game. Therefore I hope it will be understood that, in describing what Mike did for us, I am not detracting in the slightest degree from Mr Dupuis' deep knowledge of and fine judgment at the game.

He and Mr Dupuis did not take long to get to work, for in the Eastern term of '67 they got down Jemmy Grundy and Tinley (lobs) to bowl to the XI and "choices." W. B. Money had been very successful against us at Lord's, which accounts for the selection of Tinley. The ground was of course dead slow and run-getting except to a big hitter like C. I. Thornton almost impossible, but we youngsters learnt our first important lesson for batting in first-class matches, patience. It is told of Mike that in some match when Mr Voules joined him at the wicket he said, "Now, Rat, steady for the first hour," and that advice was ingrained in our minds in those days.

Mike was a deep student of all that goes to turn out a sure cricketer, that is to say a cricketer who leaves as little as possible to chance: he could turn the most unpromising material into something useful, and from promising material he produced many very perfect cricketers. I do not mean, in saying that, brilliantly successful cricketers, for there are essentials which no tutor can instil; but so far as education is concerned I hold that he turned out many perfectly educated cricketers. He taught us to hit all round, and yet to be careful at off balls until we had got the time of the ground. I see nowadays young batsmen who evidently do not know how to hit correctly on the off side. Caution has been overdone; they not only do not hit to the off, but they also do not know how to. That was not Mike's way: we were taught every possible stroke, and shown by him how it ought to be done: and also in other departments of the game. I have seen a practically certain victory lost by one hand being put out to a catch, which could have been reached with two. "Two hands" in a deep bass voice was dinned so often in our ears that we deemed it criminal to extend only one. He was a master at running between wickets, and had brought it, in his own case at any rate, to as near an exact science as is possible in anything to do with cricket, and woe betide the boy who failed to back up, or to go when he was called. In bowling too, though he was not difficult, notwithstanding that in his earliest days in the Eton XI he had to do a good deal apparently, he could teach certain tricks of the hand or foot which served to improve; and he certainly had an eye for a bowler, witness his unearthing, or would dewatering be a more correct term, of the late Mr S. E. Butler. My poor friend "Sam" Butler used to bowl slows in "aquatics" with a high action; Mike brought him to Upper Club, he got into the XI the following year, and thence passed to the Oxford XI, and in 1871 effected the unrivalled feat of getting all ten wickets in one innings of the Varsity match. It is worth recording that the exact opposite occurred when F. G. (Bunny) Pelham, the late Lord Chichester, was also brought up from aquatics; he was converted from a fast into a slow bowler.

He left no stone unturned to fit us for the "Lord's" wickets, which were very different from the "Upper Club" pitch. I cannot remember Lord's being very fiery in those days, but shooters were constant; I really believe that in '68 we had to play an average of three shooters every eight balls. The slope was supposed to be the cause, and that the slope at Harrow gave the Harrovians an advantage, so we were put to play on a slope. The Upper Club match pitch had been raised some time before '67 from the surrounding level somewhat abruptly, leaving a short slope on two of its sides, and on this we were made to play against a fast low-actioned bowler, in the hope of shooters resulting. If I remember right they did not, but the incident shows how our tutors were constantly thinking how to give us experience of all kinds. And during the Eton v Harrow match too Mike's efforts continued: he sat in "A" Block regularly for some years when Eton was fielding, and signalled to long leg when he wanted to send the captain some advice. I believe my poor friend Donny Walker did the same for Harrow also for some years, and have an idea it was at length, given up by mutual consent.

Then for the nervous ones, when we were in, there was the mysterious bottle of "Pick-me-up" exhibited immediately after a wicket fell.

To some it may seem that all this care was too much "dry nursing" and that boys should be left to look after themselves more. All I can say, and I expect I am speaking for many others, is that I can never be sufficiently grateful to our cricket tutors for the devoted care and attention they lavished upon us. I feel I was learning the whole time, and that there was nothing redundant in their system of teaching.

I saw a good deal of Mike's cricket too away from Eton: in the Rambler matches organized in those days by Alfred Lubbock and his brothers, in IZ matches especially at Woolwich and Chatham, and in the Canterbury Week I played with him frequently. It was at Canterbury that he received the injury to his knee, which brought about his retirement from first-class cricket; he was called for a short run, sent back, and in turning sprained his knee so badly that he was constantly very lame afterwards. It did not matter of what class the match was, he played the game with all his mind, and his strength, and all his heart, and I consider he was the most earnest cricketer I ever met.

He abhorred all sorts of slackness, and everything that tended to throw away a chance of winning; and yet in the matches I am thinking of he was a boy to us boys: there was nothing of the pedagogue about him, he was a kind and jolly friend to us all however junior one might be.

His style of batting was very commanding, more forward than back, for his great reach enabled him to "smother" (as they used to say of Fuller Pilch) a good length ball; and he could and did hit all round. W.G. once said to me he considered he was next best to himself, and there was nothing conceited in the way the "Old Man" put it, for he knew he had far better opportunities of playing first-class cricket then Mike, but that Mike was *facile princeps* amongst the amateurs before W.G. appeared can I think hardly be questioned, and I doubt if there was any professional who would have been ranked above him. He was very proud, and justly so, of the fact that he was invited – when still a boy at Eton – to play for Gentlemen v Players.

It was very sad for us, who remembered his mighty form, to see it slowly shrinking, and to know that he could not be much longer with us: but to the last he could devote some of his time to the great game he loved and admired for its many and its sterling merits. He served on the Committee of the MCC for several years, and though not as vigorous in debate as in earlier days, his advice on the administration of the game was as sound as ever. It is no secret that he would have been nominated to the office of President of MCC if he had lived but a few days longer; it is a matter of regret that he never filled that high position; but it is a consolation to know that he was aware and very proud of the intention, and rejoiced that he thought he had the strength to fill it.

He was a great Etonian, a great cricketer, and a great master of the game; but more than all these he leaves behind him the memory of a great man who, whether on or off "the field," went straight for what was right, and was not afraid to condemn what was wrong, and thereby as well as by his natural geniality and friendliness attracted to himself everyone he met.

## MEMO BY MR R. D. WALKER

On the 19th of April, 1905, the hand of death removed R. A. H. Mitchell, aged 62, who probably was the finest batsman that Eton ever produced. He made his first appearance at Lord's in 1858, which was the year that the match against Harrow was re-established on its present basis. For four years he represented his school, and he began his career at Balliol College, Oxford, in October, 1861, and played v Cambridge from 1862 to 1865 inclusive, being Captain of the Eleven the last three years. In his school matches Eton were twice defeated and twice the game ended in a draw, whilst in his University matches Oxford lost in 1862 but won under his captaincy 1863, 1864 and '65. This last year is rendered memorable for the victory achieved by the Gentlemen against the Players for the first time since 1853, and also from the fact that it was the first appearance of the acknowledged Champion, W. G. Grace, in this annual match. The Oxford Eleven of this year was an exceptionally powerful one, and four of its members were selected for the Gentlemen's team. In addition it had the gratification of defeating the County of Surrey which was then at the top of the tree. During this period of eight years Mitchell played many splendid innings, of which the most notable were perhaps the one v Harrow in 1860 when he made 70 out of 98 in little over an hour, and the one v Cambridge in 1864, when on a treacherous ground and with wickets falling rapidly he succeeded in pulling the match out of the fire and carried his bat for 55.

|  | Innings | Not Outs | Runs | Average |
|---|---|---|---|---|
| His record in the School matches was | 8 | 0 | 168 | 21 |
| And in the University matches | 7 | 1 | 254 | 42.2 |

Those who played with him and against him will always remember his commanding style with admiration. If he had a weakness it was for the first over or two of slow bowling, but when he once got set his driving and leg hitting powers were tremendous, and he was one of those forcing batsmen who "played" the best balls to the boundary. One of his most striking characteristics was his intense keenness for the game, and the pains he took in every department of it, for, though not a brilliant field at first, he always worked hard and eventually became a safe catch, especially at middle wicket off. At Eton he was a fair medium-paced bowler, though he did not keep it up at the University. He was one of those unselfish cricketers who played for his side and not for himself, and those still living who played under his captaincy will readily acknowledge that he invariably inspired his men with the greatest confidence and when things were going adversely that he always rose to the occasion. He was a first-rate judge of the game at all points, and an excellent and judicious captain. For though holding the strongest opinions himself he was ever ready to listen to contrary views and discuss them at length.

The cheeriness of his disposition and the staunchness of his friendship made him beloved by all with whom he came in contact, and many were the regrets when by taking a mastership at Eton in 1866 he was lost to first-class cricket.

Dear Old Mike! as he was familiarly called. His memory will ever be green in the hearts of all who knew him.

MR WILLIAM LLOYD MURDOCH, born at Sandhurst, Victoria, October 18, 1855, died at Melbourne, February 18, 1911. Present at the Test match between Australia and South Africa, he was seized with apoplexy during the luncheon interval and passed away later in the afternoon. Murdoch had a long career as a cricketer, but his fame will rest mainly on what he did for the Australian teams of 1880, 1882, and 1884. He captained the three elevens, and in all three he was incontestably the finest batsman. Within the last ten years his performances have been to some extent eclipsed by Victor Trumper, but comparison between the two men would hardly be fair, their methods being so different. Sufficient that in his own day Murdoch had no serious rival among Australian batsmen, and except W. G. Grace scarcely a superior in England. It is no injustice to him, however, to say that, depending far more than present-day batsmen upon forward play, he did not rise to great heights on wickets spoilt by rain. The daring pulls and hooks by which bowlers are now so often demoralised were not within his range, and when the ball turned a great deal he was reduced to defence. To be seen at his best, he needed sunshine and a lively pitch. Then he could be great indeed, as those who remember his famous 153 not out at The Oval in 1880 in the first Test match in this country, and his 211 on the same ground in 1884 will not need to be told.

Few batsmen have been better worth looking at, his style leaving no loophole for criticism. He was essentially an off-side player, his cut and drive being equally fine. Nothing in his play was more skilful than the quickness of foot by which in getting forward at the ball he made up for a limited reach. It could not be urged against him that he was a slow scorer, but if the occasion demanded caution he had inexhaustible patience. In a word, he was in the domain of orthodox batting a complete master. His method served him well, his perfectly straight bat enabling him even at the end of his career to defy lack of condition and get hundreds. So recently as 1904 he scored 140 in the Gentlemen and Players' match at The Oval.

In his early days in Australia, Murdoch was a first-rate wicket-keeper, and it was chiefly as a wicket-keeper that he secured his place in the Australian team of 1878. He kept wicket in the memorable match against the MCC at Lord's – the match that once for all established the fame of Australian cricket – but he soon found that he could not hold his own with Blackham, and thenceforward batting became his exclusive study. He had to do some wicket-keeping years afterwards for the ill-starred eleven he captained in England in 1890, but little of his old skill remained, and he found the task distasteful. So great was his reputation as a wicket-keeper in his young days that Spofforth declined to play in the first big match against James Lillywhite's team in 1877 because Blackham had been chosen in preference. In the light of after events this scarcely seems credible, but it is strictly true.

Murdoch's career was sharply divided into two parts. Soon after the season of 1884, and following his marriage, he gave up first-class cricket, and little was seen of him in the field till in 1890 he paid his fifth visit to England. It cannot be said that in that year he quite lived up to his reputation, but he played very well, and headed the Australian averages. His doings when he settled in this country, captaining Sussex for several seasons, and afterwards playing for London County, will be fresh in recollection. A man of fine physique and splendid constitution, he ought to have lived to a far greater age than 55. His remains were embalmed, and brought to England for burial at Kensal Green.

W. L. Murdoch in first-class cricket:

|  | Innings | Not Outs | Highest Innings | Runs | Average |
|---|---|---|---|---|---|
| In Australia | 61 | 9 | 321 | 2,249 | 43.25 |
| In England (with Australians) | 223 | 17 | 286* | 5,336 | 25.90 |
| In England (1891-1904) | 411 | 21 | 226 | 9,685 | 24.83 |
| In South Africa (1891-92) | 1 | 0 | 12 | 12 | 12.00 |
| In America (1878) | 2 | 1 | 37 | 37 | 37.00 |
| Totals | 698 | 48 | 321 | 17,319 | 26.64 |

W. L. Murdoch's hundreds in important cricket:

321   New South Wales v Victoria, at Sydney, 1882-83
286*   Australians v Sussex, at Brighton, 1882
279*   Fourth Australian Team v Rest of Australia, at Melbourne, 1883-84
       (He batted on each of the three days for this score)
266   Sussex v Cambridge University, at Brighton, 1895
       (During this innings he took part in three separate stands of over 100)
211   Australia v England, at The Oval, 1884
172   Sussex v Hampshire, at Southampton, 1894
158   New South Wales v Victoria, at Melbourne, 1883-84
158   Australians v Sussex, at Brighton, 1890
155   London County v Lancashire, at Manchester, 1903
153*   Australia v England, at The Oval, 1880
153   First Australian Team v XV of Victoria, at Melbourne, 1878-79
144   Sussex v Somerset, at Brighton, 1896
140   Gentlemen v Players, at The Oval, 1904
132   Australians v Cambridge University, at Cambridge, 1884
132   London County v Leicestershire, at the Crystal Palace, 1902
130   Sussex v Gloucestershire, at Bristol, 1897
129   Australians v Cambridge University Past and Present, at Leyton, 1890
       (He and G. H. S. Trott (186) added 276 for the third wicket)
121*   Sussex v Nottinghamshire, at Nottingham, 1898
107*   Australians v Orleans Club, at Twickenham, 1882
105*   Sussex v Cambridge University, at Cambridge, 1897
104   Gentlemen of South v Players of South, at Lord's, 1894

    * *Signifies not out.*

THE REV. ARTHUR MURSELL, one of the oldest members of the Surrey County CC, and a life-long lover of the game, died at St John's Wood on May 23, 1914, aged 82. When quite a small boy he was included as a substitute in a local XXII against the All-England Eleven, and distinguished himself by hitting the only ball he received from William Clarke for 4 – a feat which so pleased Sir Henry Bromley that he presented him with a half-crown, which was treasured for many years. At the General Meeting of the Middlesex County CC in 1913 he made a delightful speech, in the course of which he said that he had visited Lord's ground for over seventy years.

MR WILLIAM NICHOLSON, DL, JP, of Basing Park, Hampshire, a Trustee of Lord's Cricket Ground, and one of the oldest members of the MCC, died at 2, South Audley Street, London, on July 25, 1909. He was born at Upper Holloway on September 2, 1824, and was in the Harrow Eleven for three seasons, commencing in 1841, and captain in his last. *Scores and Biographies* (iii. – 39) says of him: "Height 5ft 10ins, and weight, 11st 7lbs. Has been a most successful batsman for several years, getting his runs exceedingly fast and well in the best matches, especially about 1852, when he was not to be excelled. Is one of the best wicket-keepers in England, standing up pluckily to the fastest bowling, and has at that important post in the field received many a severe blow. Also an exceedingly fast runner between wickets, a capital judge of a short run, and is altogether an energetic cricketer. Was Captain of the Harrow Eleven in 1843, when, by his strict management and fine play, he helped much to win both against Winchester and Eton. . .. His elder brother, Mr John Nicholson, played for Harrow in 1840 and 1841, and for Cambridge in 1845." Among his contemporaries at Harrow were E. M. Dewing, Arthur Haygarth, and J. Marshall. In the matches with Eton he scored 4 and 9, 7 and 35, 11 and 0, while against Winchester his innings were 4, 1 and 52, 21 and 6. He became a member of the MCC in 1845, and appeared for the Gentlemen against the Players from 1846 to 1858, and in the Canterbury Week from 1847 to 1869. For many years he played for the celebrated Clapton Club, of which Messrs. Craven, Gordon and Key, and the Walker brothers were great supporters. His best scores in matches of note were:

56  MCC and Ground v Sussex, at Lord's, 1849
71  MCC and Ground v Cambridge University, at Cambridge, 1850
69  MCC and Ground v Cambridge University, at Cambridge, 1851
86  Gentlemen of England v Gentlemen of Kent, at Canterbury, 1851
70  England v Kent, at Lord's, 1852
50  Gentlemen of England v Gentlemen of Kent, at Canterbury, 1852
61  MCC and Ground v Cambridge University, at Cambridge, 1854
75  MCC and Ground v Cambridge University, at Cambridge, 1858
63* Gentlemen of South v Gentlemen of North, at Lord's, 1862

   * *Signifies not out.*

His most successful season was that of 1852 when he made the highest score (39 and 70) in each innings for England v Kent at Lord's, and made 86 for Gentlemen of England v Gentlemen of Kent at Canterbury. In the former match his side were set 156 to win and obtained them for three wickets, which was exceptional scoring for those times, especially against such bowlers as Mynn, Martingell and Willsher. Few men attended the Canterbury Week more regularly than did Mr Nicholson, who was an enthusiastic Old Stager and one of the oldest members of I Zingari. As a curiosity it may be mentioned that, when keeping wicket for MCC and Ground v Cambridge University at Fenner's in 1853, he stumped the first three men off Mr F. Walker's bowling.

Great as Mr Nicholson's skill as a player undoubtedly was, it is probable that he will always be best remembered for the unstinted support he was ever ready to accord the game. In *Cricket* of January 1886, it was told how, when the fate of Lord's was almost in the balance, before the sudden increase of wealth from Eton and Harrow and University matches, Mr Nicholson stood in the gap, and after all England had been drawn for subscriptions to save the ground – for few escaped Mr Roger Kynaston and his red book – he advanced the money as mortgage on a security which the outside public would not take. Little was said about it, as men who do such things do not talk about them, but there is no doubt he saved Lord's from the builders. The celebrated Mr William Ward did a similar thing many years before. He drew a cheque for £5,000, and gave it to Lord for the lease, and as it happened this turned out a good investment as indeed did Mr Nicholson's mortgage also, though he ran the risk for the love of cricket, and the sum advanced was a large one – a very long way into five figures. This action on his part should cause his name always to be gratefully remembered, not only by members of the Marylebone Club, but by all English cricketers in whatever part of the world they may be domiciled. His generosity enabled the old Club to purchase the freehold of Lord's: but for him the ground might have been built over and the MCC, the recognised head of the game, have been rendered homeless. In 1879 Mr Nicholson was elected to the Presidency of the Club. Although he led a very busy life his interest in the game and his old School was always of the strongest: in fact fifty years after he had led the Harrow XI he purchased a large piece of ground at Harrow and presented it to the School.

Mr Nicholson became MP for Petersfield, Hampshire, in 1866. He lost his seat at the General Election in 1874, but regained it in 1880, only, however, to be unseated again five years later. At first he was a Liberal in politics, but subsequently a Conservative. His portrait can be seen in the large picture published in 1908 by Messrs Dickinson, of New Bond Street, entitled "Eton v Harrow."

CAPT. LAWRENCE EDWARD GRACE OATES, who died on March 17, 1912, his thirty-second birthday, whilst returning from the South Pole with Capt. Scott's ill-fated party, played cricket for his House as a lower boy at Eton.

THE REV. AUGUSTUS ORLEBAR, the last survivor of the Rugby School v MCC match of June, 1841, immortalised in *Tom Brown's School Days*, died on September 30, 1912, aged 88, at Willington, Bedfordshire, of which place he had been Vicar 54 years. He entered Rugby School in 1838 and was in the Eleven in 1841, 1842, and 1843, being captain the two last seasons. In the match referred to against the MCC he scored only 12 and 1, but in the first innings of his opponents he made a remarkably fine left-handed catch at cover-point which dismissed F. Thackeray, a former Cambridge Blue. His highest score at Rugby was 53 for The School against The Sixth in 1842, but in the following year he did a far better thing in making 23 against Nottingham, who had Redgate to bowl for them. In later years he played occasionally for Bedfordshire. It is of interest to recall that Mr Orlebar was the original of Tom Brown in his fight with "Slogger" Williams, who still survives in the person of the Rev. Bulkeley Owen Jones.

MR THOMAS PAGE, a well-known cricketer in the Windsor district, died at Eton on March 28, 1908, in his fifty-ninth year. In 1888, when playing at Windsor against Ascot, he was hit on the head by a full-pitch delivered by Mr W. A. Tobin. Page ducked down to avoid the ball, as he thought, but instead got into the way of it, and was given out leg-before-wicket by old Tom Hearne's eldest son, who said that the ball would have hit the wicket about four inches from the top. He was born at Apsley Guise, in Bedfordshire, in 1849.

HENRY PICKETT, once so well known as a fast bowler for Essex and the MCC, came to a sad end. He disappeared on the 27th of September, 1907, and his body was discovered on the beach at Aberavon on the 3rd of October. Not till the end of December, however, was his fate known, some articles found in his clothes proving his identity. Born on the 26th March, 1862, he was in his 46th year. For several seasons he was a valuable member of the Essex team. His best piece of work for the county was done in a match against Leicestershire at Leyton in 1895 – the year in which Essex took part for the first time in the championship. At a cost of 32 runs he took all ten wickets in Leicestershire's first innings. Despite his fine performance, however, Essex lost the game by 75 runs. After he retired from first-class cricket he was for some time coach at Clifton College.

EDWARD POOLEY, the once famous Surrey wicket-keeper, died in Lambeth Infirmary on the 18th of July, 1907. He had for a long time been in very poor circumstances and was often compelled to seek the shelter of the workhouse. Born on the 13th of February, 1838, he was in his seventieth year. All through his cricket career it was generally supposed that he was born in 1843 and the real date of his birth was only made known by himself in his interview in *Old English Cricketers*. It seems that when he determined to take up cricket professionally his father thought that he would have a better chance if he knocked a few years off his age. Thus, though regarded at the time as quite a young player, he was over three and twenty when in May, 1861, he played at The Oval for a team of Surrey Colts against the Gentlemen of the Surrey Club with Hayes and Heartfield. At that time his future fame as a wicket-keeper was unthought of, and presumably he was tried for his batting. Playing on the same side were Harry Jupp, and the still surviving J. Bristow. In 1862 Pooley was engaged as one of the bowlers at The Oval, but his regular connection with the Surrey eleven did not begin until about 1865. In the meantime he played for Middlesex, making his first appearance at Lord's for that county against the MCC on July 25, 1864. The match was a memorable one inasmuch as Grundy and Wootton got Middlesex out in the first innings for a total of 20. The story of how he came to succeed Tom Lockyer is graphically told by himself in *Old English Cricketers*. He said "My introduction to wicket-keeping would be about the year 1863. Old Tom Lockyer's hands were bad, and the ground being fiery he could not take his usual place behind the sticks. Mr F. P. Miller, the Surrey captain, was in a quandary as to who should relieve him, so I, saucy-like, as usual, went up to him and said "Mr Miller, let me have a try." "You? What do you know about wicket-keeping? Have you ever kept wicket at all?" was Mr Miller's remark. "No, never, but I should like to try," I replied. "Nonsense" said he, and when just at that moment H. H. Stephenson came up and remarked "Let the young'un have a go, sir," Mr Miller thereupon relented. I donned the gloves, quickly got two or three wickets, and seemed so much at home that Tom Lockyer was delighted, and said I was born to keep wicket and would have to be his successor in the Surrey team. What he said came true."

In 1866, Pooley established his position as one of the leading professionals of the day and thenceforward he remained a member of the Surrey eleven for seventeen years, finally dropping out in 1883. His great days as a wicket-keeper date from the time of the late James Southerton's connection with Surrey in 1867. The two men helped each other enormously. Southerton's slow bowling with a pronounced off break was then something comparatively new and while batsmen were learning to play him the wicket-keeper naturally had great chances. It is safe to say that no wicket-keeper then before the public could have assisted Southerton to the extent that Pooley did. He was quick as lightning and with all his brilliancy very safe. Partly from lack of opportunity he was not quite so good as Pinder or Tom Plumb to very fast bowling, but to slow bowling he was in his day supreme. Two or three pages of *Wisden* could easily be filled with details of his doings, but it is sufficient to say here that the record of the greatest number of wickets obtained in a first-class match still stands to his credit after an interval of nearly forty years. In the Surrey v Sussex match at The Oval in July, 1868, he got rid of twelve batsmen, stumping one and catching five in the first innings and stumping three and catching three in the second. Curiously enough Southerton was in the Sussex team in this match, players in those days being allowed to play for two counties in the same season if qualified by birth for one and by residence for the other. The rule was changed just afterwards and Southerton threw in his lot with Surrey. Apart from his wicket-keeping Pooley was a first-rate bat, free in style, with fine driving power and any amount of confidence. He made many good scores and would without a doubt have been a much greater run-getter if he had not been so constantly troubled by damaged hands. During the Canterbury Week of 1871 he played an innings of 93 when suffering from a broken finger. Of the faults of private character that marred Pooley's career and were the cause of the poverty in which he spent the later years of his life there is no need now to speak. He was in many ways his own enemy, but even to the last he had a geniality and sense of humour that to a certain extent condoned his weaknesses.

MR W. W. READ died on Sunday, January 6, 1906, at his residence, Colworth Road, Addiscombe Park. More than nine years have passed away since Mr Read dropped out of the Surrey eleven and gave up first-class cricket, but his wonderful play during a long career is vividly remembered. Beyond question he was one of the greatest batsmen the game has known, holding a high place among those nearest in merit to W. G. Grace. Born on November 23, 1855, he was in his fifty-second year. He had been in poor health for some little time, but his illness did not assume a dangerous form until a week before his death.

While still quite a lad Mr Read showed extreme promise as a batsman in local cricket at Reigate, and soon came under the notice of the Surrey committee, with the result that he was given his first trial for the county before he was eighteen, playing against Yorkshire at The Oval in the season of 1873. He was put to rather a severe test against the bowling of Hill and Tom Emmett, but, though he only scored 3 and 14, his form was so good that no doubt could be felt as to his ultimate success. At the outset of his career, and for some years afterwards, he assisted his father as a schoolmaster at Reigate, and could only spare time to play for Surrey in the latter part of the summer. Still, though his opportunities were restricted, he steadily improved, and in 1877 he took his place among the best batsmen of his day, playing an innings of 140 against Yorkshire at The Oval, and, with the late Henry Jupp as his partner, sending up 206 for the first wicket.

The turning point of his cricket life came in 1881, when an appointment as assistant secretary at The Oval enabled him to devote all his time to the game. From that year until his powers began to wane he was, as a batsman, the mainstay of the Surrey eleven. In the revival of Surrey cricket, which began in 1883, he and the late George Lohmann had the chief share. They, far more than anyone else, enabled Surrey, under Mr John Shuter's captaincy, to recover in 1887, after an interval of twenty-three years, the first position among the counties. The success was uninterrupted till the breakdown of Lohmann's health after the summer of 1892 and, with only one moderate season, went on until after Mr Read himself had retired, Surrey winning the championship for the last time in 1889. In the meantime, Mr Shuter, compelled by business to give up first-class cricket, was succeeded as captain by Mr K. J. Key.

Mr Read was perhaps at his very best as a batsman during the seasons of 1885, 1886, 1887, and 1888. It was a little earlier, however, that he played the innings of his life – his memorable 117 for England against Australia, at The Oval, in August, 1884. England had a magnificent eleven, and Mr Read, though he ought to have gone in earlier, was tenth on the batting order. In ordinary circumstances he would not have had much chance of distinction, but Scotton, who had gone in first and was firmly set, kept up such an impregnable defence that the ninth wicket added 151 runs, England drawing the game in face of a total by Australia of 551. The way in which Mr Read that afternoon punished the bowling of Spofforth, Palmer, Giffen, and Midwinter, will never be forgotten by those fortunate enough to be present. His innings ranks among the finest ever played in Test matches, and after the lapse of twenty-two years it is still constantly talked about.

His highest score in first-class cricket was 338 for Surrey against Oxford University at The Oval in 1888. In 1887, however, he did something even more remarkable than this, making two scores of over 200 in successive matches – 247 for Surrey against Lancashire at Manchester, and 244 not out for Surrey against Cambridge University at The Oval. After 1888 his play fell off to some extent, but he recovered his form, and in 1892 he was again one of the most successful of batsmen. He remained one of Surrey's chief run-getters for some time longer, but his powers gradually declined, and in 1897, as I have already stated, he dropped out of the eleven. Of his doings for Surrey during his long career it would be an easy matter to write a column. As a match-winner, the county never had a better batsman. He was a wonderfully punishing player, with tremendous power in his off drive.

More forward in style than most of the great batsmen of the present time, he was seen at his best on true, lively wickets, but he came off under all conditions of ground and weather. Among many fine innings that he played, I recall in particular one on a frightfully rough wicket at Derby, when the ball was getting up shoulder high. In his young days Mr Read could be described as an orthodox player, depending as he did on his driving and the perfect straightness of his bat; but as time went on he developed a great fondness for pulling. He carried the pull to a higher pitch than anyone else in his day, but from being a good servant the stroke became, to some extent, his master, and impaired his batting. That, at least, was the opinion of Mr Shuter, than whom he had no warmer admirer.

Mr Read played regularly in the England and Australia matches in this country, from 1884 to 1893, only missing, if I remember rightly, two matches during that period. Next to his 117 in 1884 his best score in the series of games was 94 at The Oval in 1886. He finished up well, making 52 in The Oval match of 1893. In Gentlemen v Players matches he was not so conspicuously successful as some other batsmen of his class, but he made 159 at The Oval in 1885, and had an average of 28 in forty-one innings. He went twice to Australia, first with the eleven captained by the Hon. Ivo Bligh (now Lord Darnley) in the winter of 1882-83, and afterwards with the late Mr G. F. Vernon's team, 1887-88. In the latter tour he was easily first in batting in the eleven-a-side matches, scoring 592 runs, with an average of 65, but he did not play consistently, owing his position entirely to three long innings. Mr Read was pre-eminently a batsman, but he bowled lobs at times with no small amount of success, and was a very good, safe field at point. He had for the last two years acted as coach to the young players at The Oval.

S. H. P.

MR W. L. REES, a cousin of W. G. Grace, died at Gisborne, New Zealand, on May 13, 1912, aged 76. A good all-round cricketer, he played for Victoria v New South Wales in 1857, 1858, and 1865, and later on a few occasions for Auckland. He was chosen captain of the East Melbourne CC upon the formation of that Club over 50 years ago, and in his early days in New Zealand defeated single-handed an eleven in Auckland. He was a member of Parliament in the Dominion, and once made a stone-walling speech of about twenty hours.

COL FRANCIS WILLIAM RHODES, CB, DSO, died of blackwater fever at Groot Schuur, Cape Colony, on September 21, 1905. He was an elder brother of the late Mr Cecil Rhodes, and was born at Bishop Stortford on April 9, 1851. He was educated at Eton and Sandhurst, and in 1869 and 1870 appeared against both Harrow and Winchester. His greatest success in the Public School Matches was gained in the Harrow match of 1870, when his scores of 31 and 18 had a great deal to do with his side's success by 21 runs. Among his contemporaries at Eton were the late C. J. Ottaway, S. E. Butler, G. H. Longman, A. S. Tabor, Lord Clifton, the Hon. G. (now Lord) Harris, and A. W. Ridley. He made many excellent scores in Army matches. He played a leading part in the Jameson Raid, for which, with four others, he was sentenced to death by Judge Gregorowski. He was buried at Dalham Church, near Newmarket, on October 25.

MR JOHN MAUNSELL RICHARDSON, who played for Harrow in 1864 and 1865, and for Cambridge in the three following years, died in London on January 22, 1912, in his 66th year. He was born at Limber, near Caistor, in Lincolnshire, on June 12, 1846, and was an all-round sportsman, excelling at rackets, the long jump and hurdles, fencing, hunting and riding in addition to cricket. *Scores and Biographies* (viii – 391) said of him: – "Is an excellent batsman, a splendid field, generally at a distance from the wicket, and can bowl slow round-armed well. He promised to turn out a first-rate cricketer, had he only continued the game." According to the Hon. Spencer Lyttelton, he anticipated the glide, which is now almost universal. Among Mr Richardson's contemporaries at Harrow were C. F. Buller, W. B. Money, M. H. Stow, and A. N. Hornby. He made 29 and 24 in his two matches with Eton, who were beaten on each occasion by an innings. Proceeding to Cambridge, he obtained his Blue as a freshman, but, although he was on the winning side in two of his three matches with Oxford, he made only 42 runs in six innings. In the field, especially at cover-point, his work was admirable. He played little serious cricket after leaving the University, but his name will occasionally be found in Lincolnshire, Quidnuncs, I Zingari, and Na Shuler matches. Playing once for the Jockeys against the Press he scored 188. Mr W. Richardson, who played for Harrow in 1863, was his brother, and Mr H. G. Southwell, of the School Eleven in 1848 and 1849, his father-in-law. Mr J. M. Richardson, who was one of the best gentlemen jockeys ever seen, rode the winner of the Liverpool Grand National in 1873 and 1874. An excellent portrait of Mr Richardson, whose reminiscences of the Eton v Harrow match appeared in the *Daily Telegraph* in 1908, was published in *Baily's Magazine* of November, 1889.

TOM RICHARDSON, whose tragic end caused such a painful shock to his friends, was born at Byfleet, August 11, 1870: died at St Jean d'Arvey, July 2, 1912. He will live in cricket history as perhaps the greatest of all fast bowlers. Among the only men who can be placed with him are George Freeman, John Jackson, and William Lockwood. Many famous batsmen, among them Ranjitsinhji, contend that on his good days, Lockwood was more difficult to play than Richardson, but for consistent excellence there was no comparison between the two bowlers. While he was at his best – from 1893 to 1897 inclusive – Richardson scarcely knew what it was to be out of form. Allowing for the excellence of the wickets on which he had to bowl, it is quite safe to say that his work during those five years has never been surpassed. Too much was exacted from him, but he ought not to have gone off as soon as he did. He began to lose efficiency before he was twenty-eight, and though for a year or two longer he did brilliant things he was never again his old self. A great increase in weight rather than hard work was responsible for his comparatively early decline. Looking at the matter in the light of after events, it was no doubt a misfortune the he paid a second visit to Australia. When in the autumn of 1897 he went out with Mr Stoddart's second team, he was at the top of his form and the height of his fame, having just completed a wonderful season's bowling. In English first-class cricket in 1897 he took 273 wickets for less than 14.5 runs each. One remembers that when Mr Stoddart's team sailed from Tilbury, Maurice Read was full of forebodings as to the effect the tour might have on Richardson's future, thinking that a winter's rest after his strenuous labours would have been far better for him than Test matches on Australian wickets. After Richardson came home his falling off was plain for everyone to see. He took 161 wickets in first-class matches in 1898, but his bowling had lost its superlative quality, and only in two or three matches at the end of the season – notably against Warwickshire at The Oval was he the Richardson of the previous year. He continued to assist Surrey for several seasons, playing for the county for the last time in 1904. After that he lived for a time at Bath and appeared once at least in the Somerset eleven, but he had become very bulky in figure, and his day for serious cricket was over.

In his prime Richardson had every good quality that a fast bowler can possess. Lithe and supple in figure he combined with his splendid physique an inexhaustible energy. While he kept his weight down to reasonable limits no day was too long for him. There have been faster bowlers – W. N. Powys, forty years ago, and C. K. Kortright and Ernest Jones, the Australian, in our own day – but for sustained pace through a long innings he perhaps never had an equal. Pace, however, was only one of his virtues. It was his pronounced off-break in combination with great speed that made him so irresistible. He took a long run up to the wicket and kept his hand very high at the moment of delivery. Purely a fast bowler, he did nearly all his best work on dry, run-getting wickets. A firm foothold was so essential to him, that he was far less effective after heavy rain than off-break bowlers of less pace, such as Spofforth and Charles Turner. Still, when the ground was dry on the surface and soft underneath he could be very deadly. One recalls a Surrey and Nottinghamshire match at The Oval that began under these conditions. Mr J. A. Dixon won the toss for Nottinghamshire and, as it happened, practically lost the game before luncheon. Richardson on that August Bank Holiday was literally unplayable, fizzing off the pitch and breaking back five or six inches at his full pace.

As regards sustained excellence Richardson never did anything better than his wonderful effort in the last innings of the England v Australia match at Manchester in 1896. After having made England follow on the Australians were left with 125 to get to win. They won the match by three wickets, but it took them three hours to get the runs. It was said at the time that during those three hours Richardson did not send down one really bad ball. He took six wickets and would have won the game if Briggs or Jack Hearne had given him any effective help. In the Test match at Lord's in the same season he did one of his finest performances, he and George Lohmann getting the Australians out on a perfect wicket for a total of 53. Richardson in that innings bowled eleven overs and three balls for 39 runs and six wickets. As contradictory statements have been made on the point, it is only right to say that at the outset of his career the fairness of Richardson's delivery gave rise to a great deal of discussion. When he came out for Surrey in 1892 his action was condemned by, among others, the late W. L. Murdoch, and when in the Whit-Monday match at Trent Bridge in 1893 he gained for Surrey an easy victory over Nottinghamshire, half the Nottinghamshire eleven expressed a positive opinion that he threw his very fast ball. However, he soon learned to straighten his arm, and little or nothing more in the way of adverse criticism was heard. Like a wise man, Richardson in his great days treated himself as a bowler pure and simple. He once scored 60 against Gloucestershire at The Oval, but he never took his batting seriously. His business was to get wickets and, with that end in view, he kept himself fresh, seldom staying in long enough to discount his bowling. He was one of the pre-eminent cricketers of his generation.

Richardson's bowling in first-class cricket:

| Season | Balls | Runs | Wickets | Average |
|--------|-------|------|---------|---------|
| 1892 | 1,173 | 602 | 29 | 20.74 |
| 1893 | 4,969 | 2,680 | 174 | 15.40 |
| 1894 | 4,683 | 2,024 | 196 | 10.33 |
| 1894-95 (in Australia) | 3,554 | 1,616 | 69 | 23.42 |
| 1895 | 8,451 | 4,170 | 290 | 14.37 |
| 1896 | 8,282 | 4,015 | 246 | 16.32 |
| 1897 | 8,019 | 3,945 | 273 | 14.45 |
| 1897-98 (in Australia) | 3,110 | 1,594 | 54 | 29.51 |
| 1898 | 6,119 | 3,147 | 161 | 19.54 |
| 1899 | 5,085 | 2,505 | 98 | 25.56 |
| 1900 | 5,999 | 2,949 | 122 | 24.17 |
| 1901 | 7,810 | 3,697 | 159 | 23.25 |
| 1902 | 5,305 | 2,607 | 106 | 24.59 |
| 1903 | 5,568 | 2,732 | 119 | 22.95 |
| 1904 | 787 | 446 | 9 | 49.55 |
| 1905 | 78 | 65 | 0 | — |
| Totals | 78,992 | 38,794 | 2,105 | 18.42 |

Eight or more wickets in an innings:

10-45   Surrey v Essex, at The Oval, 1894
9-47   Surrey v Yorkshire, at Sheffield, 1893
9-49   Surrey v Sussex, at The Oval, 1895
9-70   Surrey v Hampshire, at The Oval, 1895
8-28   Surrey v Warwickshire, at The Oval, 1898
8-32   Surrey v Cambridge University, at The Oval, 1894
8-36   Surrey v Derbyshire, at Derby, 1893
8-40   Surrey v Cambridge University, at Cambridge, 1894
8-49   Surrey v Kent, at Beckenham, 1897
8-52   Surrey and Sussex v England, at Hastings, 1898
8-52   England v Queensland, at Brisbane, 1894-95
8-54   Surrey v Leicestershire, at Leicester, 1892
8-82   Surrey v Leicestershire, at The Oval, 1896
8-90   Surrey v Essex, at Leyton, 1900
8-91   Surrey v Gloucestershire, at Clifton, 1895
8-94   England v Australia, at Sydney, 1897-98
8-99   Surrey v Yorkshire, at Leeds, 1897
8-108   Surrey v Yorkshire, at The Oval, 1897
8-117   Surrey v Essex, at Leyton, 1892

Thirteen or more wickets in a match:

15-83   Surrey v Warwickshire, at The Oval, 1898
15-95   Surrey v Essex, at The Oval, 1894
15-113  Surrey v Leicestershire, at The Oval, 1896
15-154  Surrey v Yorkshire, at Leeds, 1897
15-155  Surrey v Hampshire, at The Oval, 1895
15-172  Surrey v Essex, at Leyton, 1892
14-102  Surrey v Kent, at Beckenham, 1897
14-145  Surrey v Nottinghamshire, at Nottingham, 1893
14-161  Surrey v Warwickshire, at Edgbaston, 1895
14-185  Surrey v Essex, at Leyton, 1900
13-61   Surrey v Gloucestershire, at Cheltenham, 1894
13-99   Surrey v Nottinghamshire, at Nottingham, 1894
13-131  Surrey v Somerset, at The Oval, 1896
13-134  Surrey v Yorkshire, at Bradford, 1895
13-135  Surrey v Worcestershire, at The Oval, 1903
13-141  Players v Gentlemen, at Hastings, 1897
13-152  Surrey v Somerset, at Taunton, 1895
13-193  Surrey v Middlesex, at Lord's, 1897
13-244  England v Australia, at Manchester, 1896

Bowling unchanged through two completed innings:

with Smith, F. E. for Surrey v Gloucestershire, at The Oval, 1894
with Lohmann for Surrey v Derbyshire, at Derby, 1895
with Hayward for Surrey v Leicestershire, at Leicester, 1897

For Surrey v Leicestershire, at Leicester, in 1897, he took twelve wickets for 20 runs and the match was completed in a day.

In first-class cricket, Richardson took 2,105 wickets for 18.43 runs each. In fourteen Test matches, all against Australia, he obtained 88 for 25.22 runs apiece, and in Gentlemen v Players matches 63 at a cost of 20.71 each.

JOHN SANDS, who died at his residence, The Wickets, Dallington, Sussex, on December 24, 1902, aged 80, was born at Mountfield, Sussex, on November 22, 1822. He had been coach at Stourbridge, in Worcestershire, and Harrow, and for twenty-five years was engaged by the Drumpellier Club, Glasgow. A few years before his death, and when almost an octogenarian, he took six wickets for 3 runs in a village match. When Kent played Sussex, at Tunbridge Wells in 1858, Sands fielded substitute for one of the Kent players, who had met with an accident, and made four brilliant catches during the innings. On September 20 and 21, 1877, the match between XXII of Drumpellier and District and the United South of England Eleven was played for his benefit.

ARTHUR SHREWSBURY. As everyone interested in cricket is aware, Arthur Shrewsbury shot himself on the evening of May 19, 1903. Illness which he could not be induced to believe curable, together with the knowledge that his career in the cricket field was over, had quite unhinged his mind, and those who knew him best – Alfred Shaw among the number – had for some little time before the tragic end came been apprehensive of suicide.

It may fairly be claimed for Shrewsbury that he was the greatest professional batsman of his day. He had strong rivals in William Gunn, Abel, George Ulyett, Barnes, and, more recently, Hayward, but, looking at his career as a whole, he would, by the majority of critics, be given the first place. There was never any doubt about his class, for even when in 1873, as a lad of seventeen, he came up to Lord's to play for the Colts of England against the MCC, it was confidently stated at Nottingham that he was sure to develop into a crack batsman. Like other young Nottinghamshire players of those days, he had, to a certain extent, modelled his style on that of the late Richard Daft, and to this fact can be attributed the ease and finish of his method. He played from the first like one who had little left to learn, and only needed experience. He was given a place in the Nottinghamshire eleven in 1875, and in a season of wet weather and small scores he came out fourth in the county's batting, averaging 17, with an aggregate of 313 runs. His highest innings was only 41, but he played in such fine form as to justify all that had been said in his favour. The following year he made his first great success, scoring 118 against Yorkshire, at Trent Bridge, and in May, 1877, he made 119 at The Oval for the Players of the North against Gentlemen of the South, this being his first big innings on a London ground. Thenceforward he was recognised as one of the leading professional batsmen in England.

The turning point in Shrewsbury's career was his first visit to Australia in the winter of 1881-82. He went out in bad health, but came home, physically speaking, a new man, the sea voyages and the warm climate having done wonders for him. In 1882, in the August Bank Holiday match at The Oval, he played an innings of 207 against Surrey – the first of his many scores of over two hundred in big matches and from that time he met with ever-increasing success, his highest point being reached in 1887, when in first-class cricket he scored 1,653 runs, with the wonderful average of 78. Eight times that season he obtained over a hundred, his highest score being 267 at Trent Bridge against Middlesex. He was absent from English cricket in 1888, being engaged in managing a footbal team in Australia, but he was back again in the Nottinghamshire Eleven in 1889, and played on without interruption until the end of the season of 1893. In 1894, partly by reason of indifferent health, he was not seen in first-class matches, but he reappeared for Nottinghamshire in 1895, and, as everybody knows, went on playing regularly until the close of the season of 1902. In that year his form for a man of forty-six years of age was astonishingly good, and for the first time in his life – against Gloucestershire, at Nottingham – he made two separate hundreds in one match.

Among his many great innings he always thought himself that absolutely the best was his 164 for England against Australia, at Lord's, in 1886. The wicket on the first day varied in pace, owing to rain, in a most puzzling way, and one famous member of the Australian Eleven said frankly that he should not have thought it possible under the conditions that prevailed for any batsman to obtain such a mastery over the bowling. The innings, however, great as it was, could scarcely have been finer than his 106 – also at Lord's – for England against Australia in 1893, when he and F. S. Jackson triumphed over Charles Turner's bowling on a wicket rendered extremely difficult by rain and sun. In Gentlemen and Players matches Shrewsbury was conspicuously successful, scoring over a hundred twice at Lord's and twice at The Oval. As a batsman he had a style of back play peculiarly his own, and his judgment of the length of bowling was almost unequalled. It was said of him that he seemed to see the ball closer up to the bat than any other player. More than that, there was such an easy grace of style and such a suggestion of mastery in everything he did that, whether he scored slowly or fast, his batting, to the true judge of cricket, was always a delight. Excepting of course W. G. Grace, it may be questioned if we have ever produced a more remarkable batsman. On sticky wickets he was, by universal consent, without an equal in his best seasons his defence being so strong and his patience so inexhaustible. Personally, Shrewsbury was a man of quiet, retiring disposition, and while very proud of the place he had won in the cricket-field, always modest when speaking of his own doings.

SIR ARCHIBALD LEVIN SMITH was born at Salt Hill, Chichester, August 27, 1836, and died at Wester Elchies House, Aberlour, Morayshire, October 20, 1901. *Scores and Biographies* (vol. 8, p. 319) says of him, "Plays occasionally for the MCC bats steadily, fields anywhere, and bowls fast underhand, with a curious 'windmill' delivery." He was educated at Trinity College, Cambridge, and became a barrister of the Inner Temple in 1860. In 1879 he was appointed to be a junior Counsel to the Treasury, and in 1883 became a Judge of the High Court. In June, 1892, he became a Lord Justice of

Appeal, and Master of the Rolls at the latter end of 1900, when he succeeded the present Lord Chief Justice (Lord Alverstone). In 1857, 1858, and 1859, he rowed in the Cambridge boat against Oxford. On the last occasion the Light Blues sank; Smith could not swim, being the only member of the two crews ignorant of the art, but was saved by a lifebuoy thrown to him by the umpire. Sir A. L. Smith frequently assisted the Gentlemen of Sussex, and in July, 1862, when appearing for them, played an innings of 95 against the Midland Counties Diamonds, at Brighton. He was above the average as a cricketer, although he did not gain a place either in the Cambridge or the Sussex eleven. There can be no doubt that his death was considerably hastened by the tragic death of his wife, who was drowned in the Spey, near Aberlour, on August 26, 1901, the eve of her husband's sixty-fifth birthday. Sir A. L. Smith was President of the Marylebone Club in 1899, and the author, in *The Walkers of Southgate*, of the chapter entitled: "Reminiscences: by an old friend of the Walkers."

## ALLAN GIBSON STEEL

### A Tribute by the Hon. R. H. Lyttelton

The death of Mr A. G. Steel in the middle of the cricket season of 1914, came with the most painful suddenness. Few, if any, knew that he was ill, and as he was only in his 56th year there was every reason to expect many more years of life for him, but he died after only a few hours' illness at his house in London on the 15th day of June. Mr Steel was captain of the Cambridge Eleven in 1880, President of the MCC in 1902, and for several years was a Barrister with a good practice in Liverpool, and was Recorder of Oldham from 1904 till his death.

Mr Steel's cricket career dates from 1874, when he first got his place in the Marlborough Eleven. He was not much of a bowler in his first year; in fact against Rugby he only went on for a few overs in the second innings, but he carried out his bat for 41 in the first innings, a good performance for a boy not quite sixteen years old. In his second year he only made 1 and 16 against Rugby, but he took four wickets for 52 runs, and against Cheltenham he got six wickets for 30 runs. His first great year was 1876, when as captain he led Marlborough to a great victory by five wickets. Steel's own share in this match was six wickets for 28 runs in Rugby's first innings, which he followed up with an innings of 84; then in Rugby's second innings he got four wickets for 40, and when Marlborough went in, wanting 77 runs to win, Steel got 28 runs out of 32 made while he was batting. In 1877, with the assistance of C. P. Wilson as an all-round player and G. H. Alston as a wicket-keeper, Rugby were beaten by 196 runs, Steel taking twelve wickets for 59 runs and scoring 0 and 128. Steel as a cricketer was always full of confidence, so perhaps the story is true of his saying that it was hard luck for Rugby when he was dismissed without scoring in the first innings, as they would regret it when his second innings came, and it is probable that they did.

The late Mr W. J. Ford, who was a master at Marlborough in Steel's time, and an excellent judge of the game, has left it on record that Steel was never a better bowler than during his last year at school. Mr Ford describes his bowling, that his regular pace was slow, almost slow medium, so it was never easy to get out and take him on the full pitch, and considering he was perpetually breaking the ball both ways, in which respect he was practically the pioneer of slow bowlers, he kept his length with remarkable accuracy, over-pitching rather than under-pitching the ball. Mr Ford adds that he never knew a bowler more difficult to drive than Steel, for among other gifts he could send a ball up at a great pace. This is remarkably high praise for any bowler, and, if what Mr Ford says is true, Steel, in his last year at school was a good enough bowler to play for England, and it is doubtful if this can be said of any other boy bowler in the history of the game.

His first season in first-class cricket was as a member of the celebrated Cambridge Eleven of 1878, which is generally reputed to have been the best University eleven ever seen: this may or may not be the case, but it is certain that no University eleven has ever been so successful either before or since, and the greatest all-round player in it was Steel. They played eight matches, including one against the Australians, and won them all. He headed the batting averages with an average of 37, and his bowling took 75 wickets in 282 overs at an average of 7 runs a wicket. In the whole season he was actually at the head of the bowling averages for All England, taking 164 wickets for an average of 9 runs per wicket. As may be gathered from Mr Ford's criticism, Steel's bowling perhaps, owed its success to a certain trickiness, with the usual result that as batsmen found his tricks out, so did he become rather less effective. He certainly reached his high water mark in his first year at Cambridge and never afterwards was he quite so successful, though of course he was a very fine bowler for several years more, notably in 1879, 1880, and 1881.

In 1878, during the Cambridge season, the wickets were rather soft, and some of his performances were most startling. Against a rather weak Oxford Eleven, he got thirteen wickets for 73 runs; against MCC at Lord's he got fourteen wickets for 80 runs; and against Surrey ten wickets for 50 runs. Yorkshire had on more than one occasion to remember Steel, and at Cambridge he took thirteen wickets for 85 runs. It was said that on one occasion the famous Tom Emmett, when he found that Steel was playing for Lancashire against Yorkshire at Old Trafford, said to the Yorkshire eleven, "Let's go home, lads, Steel's playing, and Yorkshire's beat!" If this was said in 1878, Emmett's fears appear to have been justified, for Lancashire won by an innings and 26 runs, and Steel's bowling took fourteen wickets for 112 runs. He played for the Gentlemen in the great match against the Players at Lord's, and indeed for many years was one of the best players in this match.

It is often the case that if a cricketer develops as a batsman his bowling goes off. Steel was at the top of his bowling form in his last year at Marlborough and his first year at Cambridge. During his four years at Cambridge he was, however, one of the best bowlers in England, but after that there was a decline. But from 1878 to 1881 inclusive he took 474 wickets at an average cost of just under 12 runs a wicket, and for a four years' record this has seldom been equalled by any bowler, professional or amateur. Steel was a bowler who possessed not only a power of varying his methods, but he did not mind being hit, and moreover he made a study of the subject, and his well-known chapter on bowling in the Badminton Library proved what a complete master he was of the art. In his whole career in first-class cricket he took 721 wickets for an average of 14 runs a wicket, but most of his bowling was done in his first five years, and he was never so good as in 1878.

As a batsman Steel was great in every sense of the word. He was a master of every kind of hit. The cut, drive, leg hit, and play off his legs all were alike to Steel, and in addition his driving was equally good on both sides of the wicket. He had not exactly an attractive style as he was short in stature, and he was a trifle short-sighted, and seemed to stoop a little to get a sight of the ball. But he hit at every ball that was off the wicket, and a great many that were straight, and master as he was of every hit he was a very fast scorer, and few cricketers were less troubled by nerves. Against Australia he played some fine innings, and when in Australia with Lord Darnley's Eleven, made 135 not out against Spofforth, Palmer, Boyle, and Midwinter. In all probability his best innings in Australia was one of 76 runs on a difficult wicket, out of a total of 156, against Victoria against the bowling of Palmer, Boyle, and Midwinter. In eleven-a-side matches in this tour Steel headed the averages, and with Barlow got most wickets. His bowling against odds was a triumph, as his 125 wickets only cost 4 runs a wicket. In 1884 for England against Australia, Steel played a superb innings of 148 at Lord's with only one chance. I shall never forget a beautiful innings played in 1878 for Cambridge against the Australians at Lord's. Cambridge had won every match and were out for blood, and though A. P. Lucas could not play the University won by an innings and 72 runs. Alfred Lyttelton, on going in first, played a fine innings, and Steel was run out for 59. Among other batting gifts Steel was very quick-footed, not in the sense of habitually moving in front of the wicket – Steel was never guilty of that – but in jumping out and smothering the ball at the pitch. Spofforth used to bowl a slowish ball every now and then, but Steel constantly was out of his ground and driving any ball that he could get at. In 1884 one of the strongest elevens Australia ever had were playing MCC at Lord's, and the Club on winning the toss made 481 of which W. G. Grace, Steel, Barnes, and T. C. O'Brien made 412. Steel's share was 134. W. G. Grace said of this innings that he should never forget the unceremonious way Steel treated the Australian bowling directly he went in, and Spofforth, Giffen, Palmer, and Cooper had an unenviable time of it.

For England against Australia, A. G. Steel played in thirteen matches, and twice he scored centuries; while for Gentlemen v Players at Lord's he played in twelve matches. At The Oval in 1879 on a soft wicket Steel and A. H. Evans bowled all through both innings against a strong eleven of the Players, Steel's nine wickets costing just under 5 runs a wicket and Evans' ten just under 7. This feat in Gentlemen v Players has for the Gentlemen been performed by Sir F. Bathurst and M. Kempson, A. G. Steel and A. H. Evans, S. M. J. Woods and F. S. Jackson.

A. G. Steel, as has been pointed out, was essentially a tricky bowler, and it is easy to imagine him as developing this side of cricket by a considerable amount of painstaking practice, but as a batsman it is impossible to conceive him as anything but a purely natural cricketer, wanting little practice, and quite capable of playing a fine innings after standing out of first-class or any cricket for weeks. In 1886 he only played twelve innings the whole season, but in the three matches he played for Lancashire his innings were 83, 55, 80 not out, 14, and it was sad for cricket that after seven seasons, from 1878 to 1884, he could only make casual appearances.

What a tower of strength he was for Cambridge may be imagined. His total batting average for all the four years he played was 32 runs per innings, and he got 198 wickets at an average cost of 10 runs. Against Oxford, and the University match is the match for all amateur cricketers, Steel had an average of 30 runs and his bowling took 38 wickets for 9 runs a wicket.[*] It may be truly said that in 1878 Steel's bowling was never really collared the whole season, and as he not only played for Cambridge, but in both Gentlemen and Players matches, and several matches for Lancashire, this is very high praise. I always say that the first batsman who ever really pulverized Steel's bowling was Mr Frank Penn, who playing for MCC against Cambridge in 1879 at Lord's, made 134 in two hours and twenty-five minutes. This was an innings without a chance and was the talk of the season, but though defeated on this occasion this was the year when Steel and A. H. Evans ran through a strong side of Players at The Oval.

Enough has been said to show what a great cricketer A. G. Steel was. If his bowling went off after his first year at Cambridge, still he had a fine record for the whole of his career, but his bowling feats in 1878 were really so remarkable that his analysis is worth considering. Of course in those days visiting elevens to the Universities were not all strong in batting, but there was C. I. Thornton's Eleven with W. G. and G. F. Grace, Gilbert, Midwinter, and Thornton himself, and against this side Steel got eight wickets for 96 runs. There was Yorkshire, one of the leading counties, helpless against Steel, who took thirteen wickets for 85 runs. The whole average of seventy-five wickets for 557 runs under any circumstances is marvellous, and though the season at Cambridge was on the whole in favour of the bowlers, it must be remembered that Fenner's was always a batsman's paradise. For Lancashire against Nottinghamshire he took thirteen wickets for 72 runs, and his great feat against Yorkshire has already been attended to.

As a bat A. G. Steel was great because he had an infinite variety of hits, unbounded confidence, great quickness of feet, and considerable power in judgment of length. He was rather apt to be lbw, from a habit he had of following his bat in playing forward, but he was essentially a batsman by nature, and he did not seem to want to play himself in, but

---

[*] It is interesting to compare Steel's bowling in the University match with that of Mr A. H. Evans, who played for Oxford in the same four years. Evans was practically the only really good bowler Oxford had all the four years, and moreover the Cambridge batting was some way superior to that of Oxford, and Steel had some good bowling colleagues like P. H. Morton and A. F. J. Ford. Steel got thirty-eight wickets for an average of 9 runs a wicket, and Evans thirty-six for an average of 13. Both were very fine performances, and considering the superior quality of the Cambridge batsmen Mr Evans is entitled to an equal share of praise.

scored directly he went to the wicket. He was a rapid scorer and a difficult man to bowl maidens to. A characteristic innings he played was in 1880 against Shaw and Morley at Lord's for Cambridge against MCC. At that time Shaw and Morley were nearly, if not quite, the two best bowlers in England, and Lord's was a favourite ground for both of them. But Steel, on going in first wicket down, made 51 runs out of 75, and it is safe to say that from the moment he went in he seemed to make this celebrated pair of bowlers mere practice bowlers. This was a quality Steel seemed to possess. Most batsmen have one or two bowlers whom they dislike, like the late C. J. Ottaway, who had the strongest defence of his day. But Ottaway once told me that he never felt happy when playing J. C. Shaw, no matter how long he had been batting. Many batsmen on going in first feel this as a rule against good slow bowlers, but Steel's great quickness of foot and power of jumping out to meet such bowling, a lost art in these days, seemed to put slow bowlers off their length, and very few batsmen had this gift. Steel was not a batsman who opened his shoulders and sent a ball over the ropes, but he was a fast scorer because he had such a number of shots in his locker and never left a ball alone unless it got up very high. He was a good field, though not a very safe catch, as he was a quick starter and smart anywhere near the wicket, and he was a good judge of the game. Taken altogether in his prime A. G. Steel as an all-round cricketer had good claims to be considered the best in England, always excepting W. G. Grace.

A speech of A. G. Steel's against changing the lbw rule when the subject was brought up some years ago before the members of the MCC, had a great deal to do in preventing the reform being carried by a sufficient majority. In his later years A. G. Steel completely changed his mind on this subject, and became a whole-hearted supporter of the proposed alteration.

A. G. Steel as a man was always cheery and he never made an enemy. Nothing made him lose his temper, and many a young cricketer was helped by him, and there never existed anybody of whom he was jealous either among his professional brethren at the Bar or in the cricket field. In his later years his financial position was easy, and he gave up active work as a Barrister, but if he had stuck to it he might in Liverpool have made a good practice.

MR HERBERT S. THOMPSON, an old Sydney Grammar School boy, and a great lover of the game, died on March 2, 1907 in his 53rd year. He collapsed suddenly whilst walking towards the pavilion on the conclusion of his innings in a match at Concord Park, and died two hours later.

ROBERT THOMS. For some time before he passed away on June 10, 1903, there had been such very bad accounts of Bob Thoms's health that no one was at all surprised when the announcement of his death appeared in the papers. It had been known for some months there was no chance of his recovery, but less than two months before his death he had so much to say about cricket and his mind was still so bright that it did not seem as if the end were quite so near. He broke up very rapidly at the finish, and died after one final rally. In him there has gone a remarkable and interesting personality. No one had a more thorough knowledge of cricket, or could speak with greater authority about all the leading players of the last sixty years. Ambitious of being a public cricketer himself, he came out at Lord's when Fuller Pilch was the best bat in England, and it was his privilege to watch the triumphs of George Parr, Hayward, Carpenter, Richard Daft, Jupp, Tom Humphrey, E. M. Grace, W. G. Grace, and all the other great run-getters down to Ranjitsinhji and C. B. Fry. Even in the season of 1902 he saw Victor Trumper bat at the Hastings Festival, and complimented him on his splendid innings of 120 against the South of England. Thoms always looked at cricket with the eyes of a young man, and was quite free from the fault – so common among men who live to a great age – thinking that all the good things belonged to the past. This freshness of mind prevented his talk about cricket from ever becoming prosy or flat. In his last years as an umpire – he gave up after the season of 1900 – he was just as enthusiastic in his praise of fine work with bat or ball as he would have been forty years ago. To Middlesex cricket, with which he was closely associated from the formation of the county club in the sixties, he was always devoted, and nothing cheered him up more in his last illness than visits from Mr V. E. Walker and Mr A. J. Webbe. He was never tired of referring to the Middlesex eleven in the days when V. E. Walker was captain, and was very proud of the fact that he stood umpire in every first-class match played on the old Cattle Market ground at Islington. Right up to the end he had a singularly retentive memory, and when in congenial company he would tell numberless stories about the Walkers, C. F. Buller, and A. W. T. Daniel. In those distant days, of course, the modern system had not been adopted, and each county always appointed its own umpire.

The Graces, as cricketers, had no more fervent admirer than Thoms, and he was fond of saying that if W. G. Grace had not been such a marvellous bat he would have been the best slow bowler in England, his head work being so remarkable and his command of length so perfect. Of E. M. Grace's all-round capabilities, too, and especially his fielding at point, Thoms would never weary of talking. Among modern bowlers he, in common with most good judges, placed Spofforth first, while fully recognising the great qualities of Palmer, Turner and George Lohmann. As to the bowlers of his younger days, he thought very highly indeed of Hillyer and John Wisden. Curiously enough the present writer never heard him speak of Buttress, the famous but unfortunately too thirsty leg-breaker, who has been described by more than one distinguished cricketer of the past as absolutely the most difficult bowler England ever produced. Buttress's sovereign gift was his power of bowling a deadly leg-break with a real control over his pitch. He got so much spin on the ball that, according to Mr Henry Perkins, the man who tried to play him without gloves on was almost certain to have the skin knocked off his knuckles.

In dress, manner and appearance Thoms belonged essentially to the sixties, looking exactly like the photographs of some of the players of those days. He had a keen sense of humour, and told his cricket stories in a short, crisp way peculiarly his own. It was to be regretted that he did not, during the throwing controversy, bring the weight of his authority to bear on the side of fair bowling, but the traditions of his youth were too strong for him, and he always shrank from the task. However, in a quiet way he made his influence felt, plainly telling the leading amateurs that if they wanted to rid the game of an evil they all admitted they must act for themselves and not throw the whole onus on the umpires. Moreover, he was the means of some audacious young throwers dropping out of county cricket, his kindly method being to get them employment in other directions. Though cricket was the main interest of his life Thoms was a good all-round sportsman, taking as a young man a keen delight in foot racing and the prize ring. He was a good runner himself, and could, so it is said, do a hundred yards in ten and a half seconds. Of anything he took up he was bound to be a good judge, his perception of excellence amounting to an absolute gift. He often talked about putting into book form his 60 years' experience of the cricket field, but whether he ever seriously commenced the task one cannot say.

ROBERT CRISPIN TINLEY, who died on December 11, 1900, at Burton-on-Trent, was only a name to the present race of players, but he held a very high place among the cricketers of a past generation. He was a very fair bat, often by free hitting getting a few runs when they were most wanted, and as a field at point he divided honours with Robert Carpenter in the days when the annual match between the All England and United All England elevens was the event of the season at Lord's. His fame, however, rested not upon his fielding or batting, but upon his remarkable skill as a lob bowler. His success during a number of seasons for the All England eleven against local twenty-twos was extraordinary, and he took an immense number of wickets when he went out to Australia in 1863 with George Parr's famous team. Alfred Shaw, who came out as a colt for Nottinghamshire while Tinley was still a member of the county eleven, thinks that he never saw so good a lob bowler; but Canon McCormick, whose experiences goes back further, holds a different opinion, ranking Tinley below V. E. Walker and one or two others.

Lob bowling is so little cultivated in these days that since the decline of Walter Humphreys we have had no one of any class except Mr Jephson, but in Tinley's time things were different, and cricketers not very far advanced in middle age can recall the deeds not only of V. E. Walker, but of the Rev. E. T. Drake, the late Mr T. C. Goodrich of the Free Foresters, and, to come down a little later, Mr W. M. Rose and Mr W. B. Money. Prior to the rise of Walter Humphreys, perhaps the last really good lob bowler was Mr A. W. Ridley. Tinley made his first appearance at Lord's for Nottinghamshire against England in 1853. Born on October 25,1830, he was in his seventy-first year at the time of his death. He had, we believe, been for a considerable time an invalid. Tinley played his first match for Nottinghamshire, being than a lad of sixteen, against an England eleven at Nottingham in August, 1847, the match being for T. Barker's benefit, and his last against Surrey at Nottingham in July, 1869. He made his first appearance for the Players against the Gentlemen at Lord's in 1858, and appeared for the Players for the last time at Lord's in 1864. In this latter match he did not have an opportunity of bowling, Willsher and Tarrant being unchanged through both innings of the Gentlemen. He only took part in three Gentlemen and Players matches, scoring 31 runs in four innings, and taking five wickets for 46 runs. Several pages could be filled with details of his performances against twenty-twos, but it must suffice to say that he is said to have taken in all matches – first-class and against odds – 303 wickets in 1860, 186 in 1861, and 351 in 1862. A North v South match was played for his benefit at Nottingham in June, 1875, the profit accruing to him being just over £406. Originally he was a very fast round-arm bowler, but after playing for some few seasons he took to the lob bowling which he carried to such perfection.

ALBERT EDWIN TROTT shot himself at his lodgings, Denbigh Road, Willesden Green, on July 30, 1914. He had been very ill for some time without hope of recovery and, finding the monotony of life in hospital intolerable, he thought a pistol shot the best way out. His death, in his 42nd year, was indeed a tragedy. At his best, Albert Trott was one of the greatest all-round men of his time. The misfortune was that he declined in skill so soon after reaching his highest point. There is nothing unkind in the statement that he ought to have had a much longer career. Born in Melbourne on the 6th of February, 1873, he sprang into fame by reason of his splendid cricket against Mr Stoddart's England Eleven in the winter of 1894-95. At that time he was the most promising young cricketer in Australia. Against the Englishmen in eleven-a-side matches he scored 331 runs in nine innings and took nineteen wickets. His greatest success was gained in the Test match at Adelaide in which he scored 38 and 72, both times not out, and took in the last innings of the game eight wickets for 43 runs. In the fourth Test match of the tour, played at Sydney, he scored 86 not out, but on a bad wicket his bowling was not required. It was taken for granted in this country that Albert Trott would come to England with the team captained by his brother in 1896 but, for some reason which has never been properly explained, he was not selected. Having been thus passed over by his own people, he came to England on his own account, and, as everyone knows, qualified in due course for Middlesex. While qualifying for the county he played for the MCC, and in 1897 he had a record of forty-eight wickets for just over 14 runs each. In 1898 he began to play for Middlesex. Injuring his hand very badly in May, he lost a month's cricket and could not, when he started playing, do himself justice. However, when the injury had healed he lost no time in asserting himself, he and J. T. Hearne bowling in such irresistible form that in August Middlesex won eight matches out of nine and drew the other. In the whole season Trott took for Middlesex 102 wickets.

Following this good beginning, Trott went to the top of the tree, 1899 and 1900 being his greatest years. It would have been hard indeed in those two seasons to find a better all-round man. In first-class matches in 1899 he scored 1,175 runs and took 239 wickets, and in 1900 his figures came out at 1,337 runs and 211 wickets. Thanks to his bowling, his hard hitting, and brilliant fielding, and also his strong personality, he became for the time more popular at Lord's than any other professional. In those days his bowling was extraordinarily good and quite individual. Appreciably lower in delivery than most Australian bowlers, he had plenty of spin, but he depended less on break than upon an endless variety of pace. He rarely bowled two balls alike, and he could whip in his yorker at a tremendous speed. A long and very bright career seemed before him, but unhappily, he soon began to fall off. Even in 1901, though he took 176 wickets, he was not quite the man he had been, and from that time he steadily declined. Becoming heavy and muscle-bound, he could no longer bowl the extra fast ball that had been so deadly, and batsmen ceased to fear him. In 1902-3-4 he still bowled well, but after 1904 he was only a shadow of his former self. In his benefit match against Somerset at Lord's on Whit-Monday, 1907, he came out with a last flash of greatness, taking four wickets in four balls, and finishing the game by doing the "hat trick" a second time in the same innings. This was a feat without precedent in first-class cricket. Trott played for Middlesex for the last time in 1910. His active career as a cricketer over, he became one of the county umpires, giving up the work early last season. His health was then so bad that he could go on no longer. One fact in Trott's career must not be forgotten. He was the only batsman who ever hit a ball over the present pavilion at Lord's. The great hit was made off Noble's bowling in a match between the MCC and the Australians in 1899. Near the wicket, Trott was one of the best fieldsmen of his day, few catches that could be reached escaping his capacious hands. Appended are Trott's records in first-class cricket in England from 1898 to 1907.

| Year | Runs | Average | Wickets | Average |
|------|------|---------|---------|---------|
| 1898 | 482 | 20.08 | 130 | 17.94 |
| 1899 | 1,175 | 22.03 | 239 | 17.09 |
| 1900 | 1,337 | 23.87 | 211 | 23.33 |
| 1901 | 880 | 20.46 | 176 | 21.78 |
| 1902 | 941 | 19.60 | 133 | 21.67 |
| 1903 | 604 | 17.76 | 105 | 19.32 |
| 1904 | 747 | 16.97 | 108 | 23.82 |
| 1905 | 428 | 13.80 | 62 | 27.80 |
| 1906 | 952 | 25.05 | 62 | 25.67 |
| 1907 | 549 | 14.44 | 96 | 16.67 |

His hundreds in first-class cricket were as follows:

101* Lord Hawke's Team v Transvaal, at Johannesburg, 1899
164  Middlesex v Yorkshire, at Lord's, 1899
123  Middlesex v Sussex, at Lord's, 1899
112  Middlesex v Gloucestershire, at Lord's, 1900
102  Rest v Surrey and Sussex, at Hastings, 1900
112  Middlesex v Essex at Lord's, 1901
103  Middlesex v Somerset, at Lord's, 1902
103  Middlesex v Gloucestershire, at Lord's, 1903

   * *Signifies not out.*

Some of his best bowling feats will be found interesting:

Eight or more wickets in an innings

  10-42  Middlesex v Somerset, at Taunton, 1900
   8-43  Australia v England, at Adelaide, 1895
   8-47  Middlesex v Gloucestershire, at Clifton, 1900
   8-53  MCC v Oxford University, at Lord's, 1897
   8-54  Middlesex v Essex, at Lord's, 1901
   8-64  C. I. Thornton's XI v Yorkshire, at Scarborough, 1899
   8-83  Middlesex v Nottinghamshire, at Nottingham, 1898
   8-84  An England XI v Yorkshire, at Lord's, 1901
   8-91  Middlesex v Lancashire, at Lord's, 1899
   8-115  Middlesex v Sussex, at Lord's, 1901

Thirteen or more wickets in a match

15-187  Middlesex v Sussex, at Lord's, 1901
13-88   Middlesex v Gloucestershire, at Lord's, 1900
13-125  Middlesex v Leicestershire, at Lord's, 1899
13-140  Middlesex v Surrey, at Lord's, 1899
13-140  Middlesex v Nottinghamshire, at Lord's, 1901
13-170  MCC v Philadelphians, at Lord's, 1897
13-170  An England XI v Yorkshire, at Lord's, 1901
13-178  Middlesex v Nottinghamshire, at Nottingham, 1898
13-183  C. I. Thornton's XI v Yorkshire, at Scarborough, 1899
13-213  Middlesex v Lancashire, at Lord's, 1900

MR V. E. WALKER. The death at Southgate on January 3, 1906, after a brief illness, of Mr Vyell Edward Walker, removed from among us one of the most famous of cricketers. Mr Walker's career as an active player ended long ago, but his interest in the game remained as keen as ever to the last, and almost daily during the season he was to be seen at Lord's. The fifth of the seven brothers Walker -- all of them cricketers -- he was born on April 20, 1837, and was thus in his sixty-ninth year. He played his first match at Lord's for Harrow against Winchester in 1853, and made such rapid progress that he was picked for Gentlemen against Players when only nineteen years of age. His position as one of the leading cricketers of the day was already secure when in 1859, for England against Surrey, at The Oval, he did the biggest thing of his whole career, scoring 20 not out and 108, and taking with his lobs fourteen wickets -- all ten in the first innings and four in the second. Thenceforward he was quite at the top of the tree as an all-round player, having no rival among amateurs till E. M. and W. G. Grace in turn appeared on the scene. He was at his best, both as batsman and bowler, down to 1866, and went on playing for several years longer, giving up first-class cricket, if we remember rightly, after the season of 1877. Ten years later he returned to the field for one special occasion, captaining the Veterans against the MCC during the MCC's Centenary Week at Lord's in 1887. Mr Walker was in every sense of the word an all-round cricketer, as, apart from his batting, his lob bowling, and his splendid fielding, he was, on the admission of all who played with or against him, the very best captain of his time. No point in the game escaped him, and many stories have been told of his skilful generalship in Middlesex matches.

He was one of the founders of the Middlesex Club early in the sixties, and regularly captained the eleven till, as his powers began to wane, he gave up the post to his youngest brother, Mr I. D. Walker, who died in 1898. In the early days of Middlesex cricket, when the matches were played on the old Cattle Market ground at Islington, the Walkers practically ran the County Club. The support accorded by the public was not great, but the cricket could scarcely have been keener. When the Cattle Market ground had to be given up to the builders, Middlesex, after a tentative experiment at Lillie Bridge, played for some years at Prince's ground. Hans-place, and then, in 1877, came to the arrangement -- still in force -- with the Marylebone Club to play all their home matches at Lord's. County cricket forty years ago was a small thing compared with what it is now, but the Middlesex eleven were very proud of taking the first place in 1866. In that season they played eight county matches, and won six of them, the only defeat being against Cambridgeshire at the Cattle Market. It was one of Mr Walker's best years, and in a couple of single innings' victories over Surrey he had a notable share, scoring 79 at Islington and 74, not out, at The Oval. Encouraged by success, Middlesex ventured to play England at Lord's in 1867, but the result was disastrous, the batting of Alfred Lubbock and W. G. Grace giving the England team an easy victory. Mr Walker became president of the Middlesex County Club in 1898, and retained the post for the rest of his life. He was one of the trustees of the Marlyebone Club, and filled the office of president in 1891.

To Mr Walker's varied gifts as a cricketer many of the men who played side by side with him in his best days bear testimony, all agreeing as to his skill as a captain and the exceptional excellence of his fielding and lob bowling. Writing in Mr Bettesworth's book, *The Walkers of Southgate*, Canon McCormick said, "I think that V. E. was the best slow bowler I ever played after old Clarke, who bowled faster than V. E. as a rule. V. E. and W. B. Money were, perhaps, nearer each other in style than any other two bowlers of the time. I never think that Money had full justice done to him. V. E. was better than he in both judgment and the way in which he fielded his own bowling; they neither of them tossed the ball in the air as much as other bowlers, such as A. W. Ridley and E. T. Drake, who were both very good indeed. V. E.'s difficulty chiefly lay in his deceptive variation of pace. He was a splendid judge of a batsman's abilities, and very quickly found out his weak spots. He did not concern himself with averages; his one leading idea was to get a man out. I have seen all the modern lob-bowlers, including Humphreys, and the only conclusion I can come to is that there is no accurate, well-paced lob-bowling now." Mr Edward Rutter, his companion in many a Middlesex match, was particularly impressed by the catches he made from his own bowling. He said of him, "He was a most formidable customer as a bowler, and he was the most athletic fellow that I ever saw in the cricket field. I have seen him catch a man behind the batsman's wicket near short-leg, which shows as well as anything I can think of what a lot of ground he covered. It did not matter to him how hard the ball was driven back to him; if it was within reach he made a catch of it with either hand." Apart from the Surrey and England match in 1859, Mr Walker twice took all ten wickets in one innings – for Gentlemen of Middlesex against Gentlemen of Kent at Maidstone in 1864, and for Middlesex against Lancashire at Manchester in 1865. He is also said to have performed the feat once in a minor game. With regard to the Surrey and England match, Mr Walker was fond of recalling the fact that the not-out man in Surrey's first innings – Julius Cæsar – was missed off his bowling. As a batsman Mr Walker was more graceful in style than any of his brothers, and was essentially an on-side player. Though very modest when speaking of his own deeds in the cricket field, he remembered with some pride that he made top score against the late George Freeman, when that greatest of purely fast bowlers caused such a sensation in a North and South match at The Oval in 1869.

Of the many famous matches in which Mr Walker took part it would be easy to write several pages without in any way exhausting the subject. Two of the most memorable – Gentlemen v Players and Surrey v England – were played at The Oval in 1862. The Gentlemen and Players match, after a tremendous fight, was left drawn, the Players at the finish having two wickets to fall and wanting 33 runs to win. H. H. Stephenson and George Anderson were the not-outs, and Tom Lockyer had still to go in. Of the Players' eleven on that occasion William Caffyn – now in his seventy-ninth year – is the only survivor, but four or five of the Gentlemen are still living. The late Mr John Walker – eldest of the seven brothers – headed the Gentlemen's score with 98 and 10. The Surrey and England match of 1862 – the last in which Surrey met England's full strength – is, even after the lapse of more than forty-four years, vividly remembered. England scored 503 – a total till then not equalled in first-class matches – and Willsher was no-balled by John Lillywhite for bowling over the shoulder. Lillywhite's action caused a great stir, and led to the alteration of Law 10 in 1864. One of the kindliest of men, Mr Walker had numberless friends in the cricket world, and his death leaves a gap that can never be filled. Of the seven brothers Mr Russell D. Walker, the sixth, is the only one now living.

JOSEPH WELLS, who played for Kent in 1862 and 1863, died at Liss, in Hampshire, on October 20, 1910. He was born at Redleal, Penshurst, in Kent, on July 14, 1828, and was therefore in his eighty-third year at the time of his death. *Scores and Biographies* (vii – 243) says of him: – "Height 5ft 8½ins, and weight about 10st 7lbs (or 11st). Bowls very fast round-armed, with a low delivery; but did not appear for his county till he was about thirty-four years of age. ... As a bat he does not excel, and fields generally at short-slip." He will always be remembered for his great feat in the match between Kent and Sussex on Box's ground at Brighton in June, 1862, when, in the first innings of Sussex he bowled down the wickets of Dean, Mr S. Austin Leigh, Ellis and Fillery with consecutive balls. In 1856 he was responsible for the revival of the Bromley CC, whilst from 1857 to 1869 he was engaged at Chislehurst by the West Kent Club, from 1870 to 1872 by Bickley Park, and afterwards by Norwich Grammar School. He was the father of H. G. Wells, the famous novelist, and a nephew of Timothy Duke, the noted bat and ball maker of Penshurst.

ARTHUR WOODCOCK, the well-known Leicestershire fast bowler, died (as the result of poison self-administered) at Billesdon, on May 14, 1910. He was born at Northampton on September 23, 1865, but when only a few months old was taken into Leicestershire, where he learned the game and spent the greater part of his life. In 1887 he accepted an engagement with the Mitcham CC, of Surrey, and the form he showed whilst there was so good that Mr Alcock, upon being asked to recommend a player as coach at Haverford College, at once mentioned him, the result being that he entered upon the engagement in 1888 and retained it until 1894. The vacation enabled him to play in England from July to September, but it was not until 1889 that he was invited to assist Leicestershire. He played in only one match that year, but appeared more frequently in the following season, when, in consecutive matches against Essex and Warwickshire, he took seventeen wickets for 201 runs. During the next two years he appeared for the side as often as his American engagement permitted and how much Leicestershire's promotion to the first-class was due to his bowling is a matter of history. In 1895 he became a member of the ground-staff at Lord's, and during that season took 102 wickets in first-class matches for a fraction over 19 runs each. That, as it happened, was his most successful year. He continued to appear for Leicestershire regularly for a few more seasons, but knee trouble handicapped him severely and in 1903 he dropped out of the side. Woodcock possessed a splendid physical development, and at one time was, C. J. Kortright alone excepted, the fastest bowler in England. As a batsman he was poor, but he enjoyed one pronounced success, making 62 not out at Old Trafford in 1898 against the bowling of Mold, Cuttell, and Briggs. After dropping out of county cricket he continued to play for the MCC, and, in a match against Lewes Priory on the Dripping Pan, Lewes, as recently as 1908, bowled a bail off the wicket 149 feet 6 inches, sending it over a fourteen feet bank and a wall on the boundary. Among his many good performances with the ball the following were perhaps the best:

| 8-67 7-69 | Leicestershire v Nottinghamshire, at Leicester, 1894 |
| 8-111 | Leicestershire v Warwickshire, at Leicester, 1895 |
| 3-48 6-44 | Leicestershire v Surrey, at The Oval, 1895 |
| 8-66 5-66 | MCC and Ground v Kent, at Lord's, 1897 |
| 13-125 | Leicestershire v MCC and Ground, at Lord's, 1897 |
| 5-44 9-28 | Leicestershire v MCC and Ground, at Lord's, 1899 |

In a minor match at Uppingham in 1894 he bowled down all ten wickets in an innings when playing for Uppingham v The President's Eleven of Past and Present.

ARTHUR WROTTESLEY, third Baron Wrottesley, died at 6 Herbert Crescent, Chelsea, on December 28, 1911. He played in the famous Rugby School v MCC match in June, 1841, immortalised in *Tom Brown's School Days*, taking six wickets in the first innings and four in the second. From this fact he is supposed to be identical with the character Johnson depicted in that book. He was born in London on June 17, 1824, and was educated at Rugby and Oxford.

MR WILLIAM YARDLEY, whose sudden death occurred at Kingston on October 28, 1900, will be remembered as one of the greatest cricketers of his day. After showing brilliant promise at Rugby he was in the Cambridge Eleven from 1869 to 1872, inclusive, and it is safe to say that Cambridge never possessed a more brilliant batsman. It was his distinction to make, in 1870, the first 100 ever hit in the University match. His score was exactly 100 and, as all lovers of cricket will remember, Cambridge in the end won the match by 2 runs, Mr F. C. Cobden performing the "hat trick" after a victory for Oxford had appeared inevitable. In 1872 Mr Yardley scored 130 against Oxford, and his feat of twice getting a 100 in the University match remains to this day unique. He played more or less regularly for Kent between 1868 and 1877, and for Gentlemen against Players at Lord's in every year from 1869 to 1874. At The Oval he played for the Gentlemen twice and at Prince's once. Altogether he scored in nine Gentlemen and Players matches 435 runs, with the fine average of 36. Few batsmen, either of his own day or any other time, have been better worth looking at than Mr Yardley, his style being free and commanding and his hitting brilliant in the extreme. He thought himself that the finest innings he ever played was 73 for South against North at Prince's on a very difficult wicket in May, 1872. It is no flattery to say that in 1870, 1871, and 1872, his only superior as a batsman was Mr W. G. Grace. In those days when he and Mr Grace played on the same side they always had a small wager on their scores and, long after he had retired from first class cricket, Mr Yardley was fond of recalling the fact that in the Gentlemen and Players match at Lord's, in 1871, he beat the great man in both innings. Mr Yardley was in his young days, a good tennis and racquet player. His name was at one time associated with the theatre almost as prominently as it was with cricket. He was part author of *Little Jack Shepherd*, one of the famous Gaiety burlesques, and more recently he helped to write *The Passport*, an amusing farce which still has life in it. He produced other pieces for the stage both alone and in collaboration, and he was for some time a dramatic critic. He was born in Bombay on June 19, 1849.

# MISCELLANY

## NOTES BY THE EDITOR

### 1910

It is a long time since we have had, in the absence of Australian or South African visitors, such as a thoroughly interesting season as that of 1910, but it is equally true that lamentations from the county committees on the score of poverty have seldom been so loud. Since the season ended one has heard little save complaints of diminished receipts and deplorable balance sheets. The natural result is that a good many people have come to the conclusion that first-class cricket is losing its hold on the public. Personally I am far from taking this pessimistic view. There is no getting away from the fact that in several quarters the situation is serious enough, but I do not think that sufficient allowance has been made for the effects of the weather. We may have had wetter summers, but I cannot recall one in which cricket, as a spectacle, was more handicapped. On many days when the rain held off, the temperature was so low that even enthusiasts might have been forgiven for deserting the game. There is, I think, every reason to believe that when we again get a normal summer the present feeling of depression will soon pass away. It was at least encouraging that, even so late as the 13th of September, a sunny afternoon tempted twelve thousand people to watch the second day's play in the Kent and England match at The Oval. In the meantime many of the county clubs are undoubtedly finding it a hard matter to make both ends meet. Still it is a very hopeful sign that when things get to the worst the money required is always forthcoming. For example, there was a grave fear early in the autumn that Derbyshire as a first-class county club would cease to exist. The response to a special appeal, however, was so encouraging that, at a meeting on the 2nd of December, the committee resolved to go on as before, and at Lord's in the following week the usual fixtures were ratified. Of all the counties, Somerset could plead the best excuse for giving up the fight as hopeless, the supply of talent being so inadequate, but whatever may have been contemplated two years ago there is now no idea of winding up the club. Some of the richest counties were hit hard in 1910, both Lancashire and Yorkshire suffering severe losses, but in Lancashire's case the weather was largely responsible and it so happened that the most profitable fixture – the August Bank Holiday match with Yorkshire – had been given to Sharp for his benefit. The weather also told against Yorkshire, but there can be no doubt that the comparative ill-success of the team brought about a regretable apathy on the part of the public, especially in Leeds. Kent, more fortunate than any of their rivals, rose superior to all difficulties, and, after a liberal outlay for ground improvements, left off with a net balance for the season of over seven hundred pounds. Hampshire too, after long years of anxiety made a small profit on their season's working. It is an unpleasant task to write at such length on the purely financial side of cricket, but so many lamentations have been heard during the last three months that the subject could not be passed over. In comparing the present with the past, people are apt to forget that a county club nowadays is a far more expensive business to run that it was years ago. In the old days there was no winter pay for the professionals, and there were not nearly so many matches. I am strongly of opinion that we have now too much county cricket, but there is an obvious danger in cutting down programmes. With the busy agents of the Lancashire League always on the look out for talent, committees cannot hope to retain their professionals unless they ensure them a large amount of remunerative employment. I cannot help thinking that by purely voluntary effort a great deal might be done to avoid the financial difficulties that so frequently crop up. The cry of every committee in trouble is that if they could only get a sufficient number of members to make them more independent of gate money all would be well. Annual subscriptions cannot very well be increased, but a good many people would, I should fancy, if the situation were brought clearly home to them, be willing to pay two guineas a year instead of one. As it is they often pay the extra money, either in supporting bazaars, or in contributing to special funds. Moreover, cricket being one of the cheapest forms of amusement, it ought to be a simple matter for all who have the interest of their county club at heart to get new members. S. H. P.

## 1912

After such a season of financial loss to the Counties one expected to hear all sorts of proposals for altering the game, but except in one direction we have had nothing of the kind. In a letter to the Sportsman in October, Mr F. R. Spofforth made the astounding suggestion that the best way of improving cricket was to give 2 runs to the fielding side for every maiden over bowled. Never, I should think, has such an absurd proposition been put forward by a first-rate expert. The proposal would not bear a moment's examination, and but for the weight that attaches to Spofforth's name the letter would probably have been consigned to the waste-paper basket. I think Spofforth must have rushed into print without realising what his proposal involved. Leaving aside the encouragement to bowlers to adopt the off-theory, or any other expedient to keep down runs, the whole notion is contrary to the true spirit of cricket. Imagine the position of two batsmen coming together, perhaps on a nasty wicket, with the result of a big match entirely dependent on their success. What could be more grossly unjust than to penalise their side, even if they found it necessary to play for half an hour without getting a run? We are not likely to hear any more about Spofforth's suggestion, and I only refer to it here because it came from such a source.

Cricket does not stand in need of alterations. When played in the proper spirit – every match on its own merits – the game is as good as ever it was. It must not be tampered with to please people who vainly think that it can have the concentrated excitement of an hour-and-a-half's football. S. H. P.

## 1914

Writing in the early days of the New Year it is impossible to take other than a gloomy view with regard to the immediate future of cricket. Never before has the game been in such a plight. One may take it for granted that, in any circumstances, county cricket, as we have known it for the last forty years or more, will be out of the question this season, but in the happy event of the War coming to an end at an earlier date than the experts expect, we are sure to see plenty of games of a less competitive character. Indeed, as all the fixtures were provisionally made last summer, the counties might try something in the nature of a modified programme. However, it is idle to speculate in January as to what will happen in May or June. I hope no attempt will be made to close the game down entirely. All the counties are asking their members to keep on with their subscriptions, and in return matches of some kind should from time to time be played on the various grounds. Cricketers have made a splendid response to the call to the colours. They cannot all go to the front; some of them have duties that must keep them at home. To my mind, it would be a great misfortune for any county ground to be closed for the whole summer. I had thought of preparing for *Wisden* a list of the cricketers who have joined the Arny, but the number is so great that I could not be at all sure of accuracy. Any accidental omission might have involved protest and correction. After the War, whenever that may be, cricket will, no doubt, go on as before, but it will naturally take some time for the game to recover completely from the blow it has received.

At The Oval, in August, I was asked to mention in *Wisden* a record which, so far as I know, has escaped the notice of all the statisticians. R. G. Barlow told me that he played first-class cricket for twenty-one years, and that he was then completing his twenty-first season as an umpire. Judging from appearances he is likely to go on for many years to come. He was born on the 28th of May, 1850, and would, I fancy, be very pleased to play a single wicket match with any man of his age in the United Kingdom. In the course of a brief talk he recalled, with some pride, that not long ago he bowled out John Tyldesley and Sharp at the practice nets.

As to the future inter-change of visits between English, Australian, and South African teams, everything for the time being is, of course, in abeyance. The proposed tour of the Australians in South Africa this winter was cancelled soon after the outbreak of the War, and, at a subsequent meeting of the Australian Board of Control, the following resolution was unanimously passed:

"With regard to the proposed visit of an English team to Australia in 1915-16, and to the request of the South African Association that the Imperial programme should be put forward a year, so as to allow Australia to visit South Africa in 1915-16, the Board is of the opinion that, owing to the gravity of the situation in Europe, the matter be left solely to the Marylebone Cricket Club, to decide as to sending a team to Australia in 1915-16, or when they would be prepared to send a team to Australia. Further, that the South African Association be informed that their request cannot be dealt with until the wishes of the MCC are conveyed to the Board."

The most memorable event in the season of 1914 was, to my thinking, the dinner given at the Hotel Cecil by the MCC in June to celebrate the Centenary of the present Lord's ground. Nothing could have illustrated more forcibly the greatness of cricket. On every hand were men whose names are familiar wherever the English language is spoken. No other game or sport could have produced such a company. Half a century of English cricket was fully represented, and in every speech there was a note of unswerving devotion to the game. It was a peculiarly happy circumstance that Lord Hawke, who has played cricket all over the world, should, as president of the MCC for the year, have had the privilege of being in the chair. One may be sure that he appreciated the honour.

S. H. P.

# PERU HOUSE PRIVATE HOTEL,
## 4, 5, & 6, Woburn Place,
### Russell Sq., W.C.

FOR CONVENIENCE, QUIETUDE, COMFORT, AND ECONOMY.

*Telephone :—*
**4462 GERRARD.**

*Telegraphic Address :—*
**FLOWRETRY London.**

Central and pleasantly situated, facing Russell Sq., two doors from Russell Hotel.

Omnibuses pass the door to all parts of London.

Walking distance to most places of amusement, and within an easy distance of Lord's and Kennington Oval, &c., &c.

Bedroom and Meat Breakfast, **4/6.**
Lunch, **1/6.** Dinner, **2/6.** Supper, **1/6.**

### No Charge for Attendance or Lights.

*Electric Light and Bells throughout.*
## J. H. JUDD, Proprietor.

Also for West End—
**Brooklyn,**
**Earl's Court Sq., S.W.**
Telephone—1523 KEN.

Also
**Pier Private Hotel,**
**Folkestone.**
Telephone—110.

# THE GREAT WAR, 1914-18

On the afternoon of 4 August, 1914, Jack Hobbs asserted yet again his primacy among batsmen by scoring a double century, his second of the season, against Nottinghamshire at The Oval; the innings was enjoyed by 15,000 bank holiday celebrants. Up at Derby the home side was being bundled out twice in a day by the Essex bowlers, while at Lord's young Howell of Repton scored 78 not out for The Rest against Lord's Schools, mercifully unaware that this was to be the last half-century of his brief life. Perhaps more precognition clouded the thoughts of the Leicestershire player A. T. Sharp, engaged in the match against Northamptonshire. In the first innings Sharp seemed preoccupied, scoring only 2 runs before being given out LBW. It was a modest performance, but at any rate more effective than what followed. The scorecard for the Leicestershire second innings reads:

A. T. Sharp absent . . . . . . . . . .0

On the evening of the 4th, Sharp had packed his bags in mid-match and left to join his regiment.

In the years since that frightful day, posterity has somewhere gathered the impression that the moment the British ultimatum to Germany expired, so did first-class cricket. In fact the county championship proceeded virtually undisturbed almost to the very end of the season. Two of Surrey's home games had to be removed to Lord's while the military mind performed its mysterious convolutions at The Oval, and the fixture arranged for 10 August between Somerset and Northamptonshire at Taunton was cancelled, although Somerset went on to fulfil three subsequent championship engagements. Dr Grace's muddleheaded command to the sportsmen of England to join the colours did not appear in print until 27 August, and did not effectively ruin the county programme for several days after that. In retrospect it is hard to know what to think of the mentality which announced its discovery that cricket was incompatible with patriotism. "Every cricketer should join the colours immediately", said the elders, without stopping to think who might benefit from this surge of unco-ordinated heroism, and in which way. It is arguable, and has indeed been argued already by more than one historian, the the flood of volunteers unleashed by the kind of fustian of which Dr Grace's letter in *The Sportsman* was typical, did more to embarrass the war effort than to assist it:

Kitchener had expected to get perhaps 100,000 volunteers in the first six months, and maybe 500,000 altogether. This was all, and more than all, that the existing factories could equip with rifles and uniforms. These modest plans were submerged by a wave of patriotic enthusiasm. 500,000 volunteered in the first month. Altogether, Great Britain raised more than three million volunteers. This vast army was not produced by design; it was thrust on a Government and War Office which did not know what to do with it. There were few camps and little equipment. All through the winter of 1914-15, men lived under canvas, and drilled in civilian clothes with walking sticks for rifles. It was the beginning of their disenchantment.

*The First World War* A. J. P. Taylor (1963)

It seems that A. T. Sharp might safely have lingered long enough at Northampton to enjoy his second innings without imperilling the Empire.

At the heart of Grace's invocation was his belief, shared by Englishmen generally, that warfare was a kind of extension of sport, and that the practised athlete must therefore by definition be a deadly soldier. Even Douglas Haig, whose only known sporting accomplishment was pulling strings to improve his own professional situation, finally made football compulsory for the troops, with every platoon issued with a regulation ball. One society lady raised a Sportsman's Battalion of the Royal Fusiliers, "upper and middle classes only, for persons used to shooting, hunting and outdoor sport". This idea that team games and the ritual slaughter of animals was a kind of fortuitous preparation for the Greatest Game of All had long before received its sanction from the philosophers, who, as usual, spoke the greatest nonsense of all. In the light of what was to happen to the young men of Europe in the years between 1914 and 1918, it is interesting to remind ourselves that half a century earlier John Ruskin had written in *The Crown of Wild Olive*:

> I use a test which I have adopted, of the connection of war with other arts. I reflect how, as a sculptor, I should feel if I were asked to design a monument for Westminster Abbey, with a carving of a bat at one end and a ball at the other . . . I had rather carve it with a shield at one end and a sword at the other.

Such was the frame of mind of the White Feather brigade, and such was the mood of the intrepid armchair warriors of the Yorkshire County Committee, who were performing even then their customary appropriation of the moral consciences of their employees by announcing that all their professionals would be engaged on war work – "This was made a strict condition of their continued engagement." But for the moment the county championship went on, simply because no machinery existed to stop it. Not even the approaching thunder of Armageddon had any effect. On 28 August, 1914, Paris came under the authority of the military governor Gallieni; that afternoon at Lord's Kent were being skittled out for 67 by Haig and J. W. Hearne. On the 29th General French displayed his peculiar tactical genius by starting to move the British Expeditionary Force away from the fighting towards the French coast, leaving a spectacular hole between the French fifth and sixth armies; that afternoon at Bournemouth Hampshire romped to an innings victory over Essex. On 1 September, Kitchener, outraged by French's ridiculous antics, took up the mothballed fancy dress of a field marshal's uniform and went over to Paris to browbeat Sir John into doing his duty; meanwhile, still at Bournemouth, Mead scored a century against Kent. That night the French cabinet tried to instil confidence in the residents of Paris by entraining for Bordeaux; the following day the German army was reported to be only thirty miles from Paris, and therefore presumably not much more than a hundred and fifty from Brighton, where Sussex were trying, without success, to bowl out Yorkshire. But George Hirst held out and at the close of play was still there, 18 not out. That night the British army took up its positions on the Marne.

The opening phase of the war was now over, and so, for the duration, was first-class cricket. The Wisden which appeared, deceptively chubby, in the spring of 1915, dealt with events upon which the ironies of circumstance had already bestowed a dim antiquity – except that its obituary columns comprised a curious and pathetic mingling of peace and war. Alongside the ancient reverends who had died that year in bed in slumbrous rectories, and the blue-blooded old bucks who had lived all their lives in the same draughty country house, were the young blades destined never to indulge in the passive pleasure of declaiming that the game had gone to the dogs . . . ". . . who was killed in action near Ypres, was in the Eton eleven of 1901", "... killed in action on the Aisne, was in the Bradfield side of 1895", "... died of wounds received at Mons ... Wellingborough elevens of 1911 and 12". Sometimes the images of peace and war imitated Lear's bowsprit and rudder, and became inextricably tangled, as in the sad case of the Reverend Archibald Hugh Conway Fargus, a Haileybury boy who played twice for Cambridge against Oxford, became a naval chaplain and went down in HMS *Monmouth*, flagship of a long-forgotton admiral, in a long-forgotton action in the Pacific. And so the catalogue droned on, as all over the four kingdoms headmasters addressed the school on the glorious sacrifice of so-and-so whom some of you will remember. At Clifton and at Tonbridge, at Eton and Harrow, Fettes and Marlborough, Highgate and Charterhouse, heads were bared, responses muttered, a scenario later apotheosised in one of the most popular novels of the century:

> Every Sunday night, in the chapel after evening service, Chatteris read out the names of old boys killed, together with short biographies. Very moving, but Chips, in the back pew under the gallery, thought: They are only names to him, he doesn't see their faces as I do.

Not that the death lists in the almanack were confined to public schoolboys; it was simply that the deference paid by Pardon and his team to Gentlemen-cricketers was often excessive, and perhaps inspired by the harmless vanity of self-recognition. That is why so many of the entries have the unconscious humour of what might be called the negative accolade — "did not get into the side at Repton". But the death notices covering the first few months of the war did include one name which, if it evoked recollections of no great deeds in the higher reaches of the game, at least represents a record which still stands all these years later. On 11 November, Lieutenant Arthur Edward Jeune Collins was killed in action, it being his fate to be remembered ever after as the Clifton College schoolboy who, over five days in June 1899, scored 628 not out for his house eleven in an otherwise insignificant match against a local side.

The four editions which followed were reduced to half the usual size. And yet, shrunken though they are, those annuals of the years of the fighting are by far most dramatic in the whole series. Indeed, it is their very emaciation which renders them sensational, like a portly patron suddenly fallen on hard times. But although the contents of the Wisdens dated between 1916-19 are limited they are very nearly unbearably poignant. For instead of being a yearbook devoted to the documentation of cricket, Wisden suddenly became a yearbook devoted to the deaths of cricketers. Indeed, had it not been for the slaughter in the trenches, there would have been nothing to put into those books at all, although ironically the 1916 edition was dominated by news of the peaceful deaths of the two men who might well have been the two greatest batsmen of all time, William Gilbert Grace at Eltham, Kent, and Victor Thomas Trumper in Sydney, Australia.

The only area of English first-class cricket unaffected by the war was hardly first-class at all. The Public Schools section of the almanack was the only one to bear any resemblance to its peacetime predecessors, although even here familiar appearances were deceptive, because now the sixth-formers being honoured were learning to live with the heady stimulus of knowing that before long the bats and pads of summer term might have to be exchanged for a bayonet or a bag of bombs. It was no wonder that the young athletes of 1914-18, plucked from back street or quadrangle and dumped in the mud of Flanders, still clung in their dark extremity to the old sporting images, dreaming of bats and balls. The pathos of their predicament, underlined by what has since been defined as "the ridiculous proximity" of the old life proceeding less than a hundred miles away, was later exploited in a thousand published works, among which Ernest Raymond's *Tell England*, R. C. Sheriff's *Journey's End* and the autobiographical volumes of Siegfried Sassoon can stand for all the rest. This juxtaposition of war and peace, of the old way of life and the new way of death, was almost too much to bear; one officer, confided Arnold Bennett to his diary in 1917, "had breakfasted in the trenches and dined at his club in London". Under such unnatural circumstances, mere truth became distorted. Peace, which might have been a mere season away, or a few miles, was yet worlds distant in terms of experience. Indeed this ironic contrast became so melodramatic as to become a marketable literary device. Stacy Aumonier, a celebrated short story writer of the period almost totally unread today, wrote a tale whose sentimental impact is achieved by the stressing of the faded glories of matches in a distant past, featuring ancient champions long since vanished from the face of the earth; the surprise ending of the the tale consists of the fact that this catalogue of remote deeds is a reference to the cricket of the previous summer. Such was Aumonier's way of defining the difference between the plump Wisden for 1915 and its starveling successors.

Some of the sacrificial victims are more celebrated than others; a few are even celebrated twice over, as in the notorious case of Rupert Brooke, whose obituary stands proudly in the foyer of the national museum of stuffed owls — although to be fair to Pardon and company, there are those who remain convinced that the bathos of the closing line of the Brooke obituary is premeditated high comedy rather than accidental slapstick. Some of the death notices rise to an orotundity reminiscent of a monumental mason, for example that of George Whitehead, one of whose anonymous Clifton contemporaries describes the victim, without a trace of conscious irony, as one "who always stood uncompromisingly for all that was clean", reflecting in that phrase the innocence of August 1914 rather than the disillusions of October 1918, when Whitehead was killed. The obituary of Second Lieutenant John Howell, pitched in a lower key, rightly suggests that a future England batsman had been lost, but neither Brooke, nor Whitehead nor Howell conveys the spirit of noblesse oblige quite as finely as the Reverend Robert Poole, who died at Hove in 1918 in his ninety-second year. The reverend, who receives from the almanack the dubious accolade of having been "considered the best left-hand tennis player of his generation", earns his cricketing immortality for a single act of self-denial which throws into stark relief the rather more predatory morality of succeeding generations.

Among the hired hands, one of the starkest deaths ever recorded by Wisden concerns poor Private Frederick Percy Hardy of the County of London Yeomanry, whose listing in "Other Deaths" in apparent defiance of his military status is explained all too graphically by the nature of that death. The ghost of Charles Pooter appears yet again on the ramparts on the occasion of the death of one Arnell-Thompson, who, on a long-lost day in 1889, suffered the dual ignominies of injury and dismissal simultaneously. Regarding the passing of Frederick Henry Norman, not even the magisterial Pardon can resist a joke, which turns up almost in the final phrase of the paragraph, while the death of John G. Francis preserves a tiny but not inconsiderable fact about the games-playing dottiness of the Victorians, for whom not even a snowfall in summer appeared irrelevant to issues of sport. One death notice which appears in the 1917 edition is a perfect example of those who have greatness posthumously thrust upon him. On 22 July, 1916, Percy Jeeves, of the Royal Warwickshire Regiment, was killed in that military obscenity the Battle of the Somme. Jeeves was a Yorkshireman who, having failed to win over the locals with his bowling skills, migrated to Warwickshire and there developed to such spectacular effect that had the Great War not destroyed him, he would almost certainly have represented his country in a less demanding game than the one played at his expense by Douglas Haig. But Percy Jeeves can claim possession of the most widely-known name of any cricketer except W. G. Grace, not because of technical ability or statistical freakishness, but through the sheer fluke that soon after his death a certain short story writer groping for a suitable name for a gentleman's gentleman, remembered him. That same author did not invent, although he well might have, the occasional cricketer whose passing was lamented in the 1919 edition; the brevity of the last journalistic rites accorded George Tubow, King of Tonga, cannot conceal the fact that this was perhaps the most amazing obituary notice ever to appear in Wisden, or indeed in any almanack.

There are at least two names included in the obituaries whose significance may elude those who believe that everything in a cricket publication has necessarily to allude to cricket. On the Somme there died in action a certain lieutenant called Henry Webber, eighteen months later Brigadier-General Roland Boys Bradford, VC, MC, followed him. Niehter of these two men had been great cricketers. Webber had once played for Tonbridge School and run up some big scores in club cricket, while Bradford had often found a place in the regimental side. So why include among sportsmen as illustrious as Colin Blythe and Kenneth Hutchings these two forgotten soldiers? What can we learn about that terrible war from two such modest men, an obscure lieutenant and an ancient general, a young sprig of 25 and a venerable sport of 68? Nothing, except that it was the general who was 25, the lieutenant who was 68. Perhaps both of them deserved better of that providence which commited them to their sad and shocking fate. Such at least might have been the sentiments of the Reverend Hugh Fargus, who could have been pardoned for concluding, from the evidence available to him, that somebody up there liked him. For the reverend did not after all go down with the *Monmouth* in November 1914 as reported in Wisden. Returning from leave, he missed his train, was unable to rejoin his ship and was appointed to another.

*Benny Green*

## A GREAT BOWLING FEAT

I have been asked to draw attention to a feat by Frank Field, the Warwickshire fast bowler, which owing to the stoppage of the game by the War, has not been given the prominence among cricket records to which it is entitled. Anyway it escaped notice in the cricket records published in *Wisden* for 1916, so it is only right to make up for the omission. In the match between Worcestershire and Warwickshire, played at Dudley on June 1, 2, and 3, 1914. Field, in the second innings of Worcestershire, went on to bowl with the score at 85 for four wickets, and took the six outstanding wickets in eight overs and four balls, seven maidens, at a cost of only 2 runs. The score of the match published at the time credited Field with only six maiden overs, but the detailed analysis which has been sent to me shows that he bowled seven. In fact, the only scoring stroke made off him was a lucky two from the second ball in the second over before he had taken a wicket. While finishing off the Worcestershire innings in this startling fashion, Field delivered five no-balls, with one of which he clean bowled M. K. Foster. In taking his six wickets for 2 runs he received no assistance, three batsmen being bowled, two caught and bowled, and one leg-before-wicket. The feat certainly deserves to be placed in future on the same footing as Pougher's famous five wickets for no runs for MCC and Ground against the Australians at Lord's in 1896, and Peate's eight wickets for 5 runs for Yorkshire against Surrey at Holbeck, in 1883.                                                      S. H. P.

## MCC IN 1916

Throughout the year the War Office has continued to avail itself of the offer made by the MCC and accommodation has been found for units of Territorial Artillery, the ASC (transport), the RAMC Wireless instruction and Military Cooking Classes, No. 2, Grove End Road has been lent as Headquarters to the Old Boys' Volunteer Battalion (London Regiment) which has trained and supplied over 400 Commissioned Officers for the Army.

In the Pavilion the MCC Staff and one or two members and their friends have occupied their spare time in making, at the request of the War Office, hay nets for horses. About eighteen thousand nets have been completed and sent to Woolwich.

At the request of the Canadian Contingent a baseball match was played at Lord's, in September, between Canadians and London Americans for the benefit of a fund raised for the widows and orphans of Canadians who fall in battle. HRH Princess Louise (Duchess of Argyll) graciously gave her patronage to the undertakings and watched the game from the Pavilion. The proceeds exceeded £100.

## MCC IN 1917

The long room in the Pavilion is still being used for making hay-nets for horses for the Army. Owing, however, to a reduction in the staff, the number made (about 12,000) has not been so great as last year (about 18,000).

## ENGLISH ARMY XI v AUSTRALIAN ARMY XI

Played at Lord's, July 14, 1917

It was an excellent idea to arrange two charity matches during the height of the summer, in which well-known players could be seen in the field, and from every point of view the result more than realised expectation. In the bright sunshine on the 14th of July, Lord's ground looked quite its old self. The public mustered in surprisingly large numbers, the pleasure felt in seeing even a one day match of some general interest being very keen. So good was the attendance and sale of tickets beforehand that St Dunstan's Hostel for blinded soldiers and sailors benefited to the extent of about £620. Two capital sides were got together, the English team being composed entirely of men who before the War had taken part in first-class cricket. Several of the Australian names were unfamiliar, but the presence of Macartney, Kelleway, Matthews, and E. P. Barbour – an admirable batsman from New South Wales – lent distinction to the eleven. Some good cricket was seen but the play was too sedate in character to be exciting. The wicket, though in excellent condition, was a trifle slow and the batsmen were perhaps rendered cautious by lack of practice. Winning the toss the Australians began with a disaster, Macartney being out with the score at 7, but after the second wicket had fallen at 26 Kelleway found a most capable partner in Barbour and so long as these two stayed together there seemed every hope of a good total. Sixty-three runs were added and then Kelleway was bowled, his 53, as events turned out, being the highest score of the day. He played very well for an hour and a half. After he left the batting went to pieces. Three more wickets fell before lunch and the innings closed for 130. Lee, who was not tried till the score was up to about a hundred, bowled his slows very skilfully from the nursery end and found some easy victims. On an improving wicket the Englishmen were practically sure of victory, but even in a Test match they could not have set about their light task with greater deliberation. They left nothing to chance, Makepeace and Lee taking forty minutes to get the first 18 runs. Two wickets were down for 24, but Ernest Tyldesley and Warner put on 65 runs in as many minutes. The match was won with five wickets in hand, but little was done after the winning hit had been made and, Franklin being absent, the Englishmen had only a margin of 32 runs in their favour at the end of the innings. Warner, apart from a chance of stumping when 26, played well for eighty minutes, but he became obviously tired and was allowed a man to run for him in the latter part of his innings. Tyldesley's batting was also very sound and steady. An auction sale during the afternoon of cricket bats, balls and pictures proved disappointing.

## Australian Army XI

Lieut C. Kelleway (NSW) b Knox . . . . . . . . 53
W.-O. C. G. Macartney (NSW)
      lbw b Douglas .   0
Sergt W. J. Munday (Adelaide) c Lee
         b Blythe .   8
Capt. E. P. Barbour (capt.) (NSW)
      c Hendren b Lee .   30
Pte P. W. Docker (NSW) lbw b Lee . . . . . .   1
S.-Sergt W. S. Stirling (SA) run out . . . . . . .   7
Corpl T. J. Matthews (Victoria)
      c Franklin b Knox .   1

Lieut C. T. Docker (NSW) st Franklin
         b Lee .   12
Corpl N. G. Dean (Melbourne) b Lee . . . . .   8
Corpl G. B. Inkster (Adelaide) not out . . . . .   4
Pte W. McAndrews (Queensland) b Lee . . .   0

    B 4, l-b 2 . . . . . . . . . . . . . . . . . . .   6
              ——
              130

## England Army XI

Corpl H. Makepeace (Lancashire)
      c Inkster b C. Docker .   13
Pte H. W. Lee (Middlesex) b Macartney . . .   7
Corpl E. Tyldesley (Lancashire) c Docker
         b Andrews .   38
Capt. P. F. Warner (capt.) (Middlesex)
      st Inkster b Macartney .   34
Lient-Col J. W. H. T. Douglas (Essex)
         b C. T. Docker .   20
Pte E. Hendren (Middlesex) c Inkster
         b Macartney .   3
Corpl D. W. Jennings (Kent) c Barbour
         b Matthews .   26

Lieut P. G. H. Fender (Surrey) c Barbour
         b C. Docker .   8
Lieut N. A. Knox (Surrey) c Macartney
         b Barbour .   0
Sergt C. Blythe (Kent) not out . . . . . . . . . . .   2
Capt W. B. Franklin (Buckinghamshire)
           absent .   0

    B 8, l-b 3 . . . . . . . . . . . . . . . . . . .   11
              ——
              162

**England Army XI Bowling**

|  | Overs | Maidens | Runs | Wickets |
|---|---|---|---|---|
| Douglas .......... | 11 | 1 | 39 | 1 |
| Blythe ........... | 8 | 1 | 16 | 1 |
| Fender .......... | 2 | 0 | 12 | 0 |
| Knox ............ | 14 | 3 | 34 | 2 |
| Lee ............. | 10.5 | 1 | 23 | 5 |

**Australian Army XI Bowling**

|  | Overs | Maidens | Runs | Wickets |
|---|---|---|---|---|
| C. T. Docker ...... | 11.5 | 5 | 16 | 3 |
| McAndrews ....... | 12 | 2 | 29 | 1 |
| Macartney ........ | 18 | 5 | 33 | 3 |
| Kelleway ......... | 9 | 2 | 17 | 0 |
| Matthews ......... | 9 | 0 | 32 | 1 |
| Stirling ........... | 4 | 1 | 9 | 0 |
| Barbour .......... | 6 | 0 | 15 | 1 |

Umpires: E. Ball (Worcestershire) and W. Reeves (Essex).

## NOTES BY THE EDITOR IN 1917

There can be no question that as regards the propriety of playing cricket in War time there was a great change of feeling last summer. People realised that with public boxing carried on to an extent never heard of before, and professional billiard matches played in the hottest weather, there was something illogical, not to say absurd, in placing a ban on cricket. The general result was highly satisfactory. Public school cricket attracted more attention than would have been thought possible, interest in the game was kept alive by local matches in all directions, and the two Saturday matches at Lord's, got up by P. F. Warner, received such liberal support that that they produced for War charities a sum of over £1,300. All this was diametrically opposite to the state of mind that prevailed during the first summer of the War. Following closely all that was done I could not help recalling a conversation I had with Mr Findlay in the spring of 1915. I asked him whether the nets would be put up for practice at The Oval, and his reply – I cannot at this distance of time guarantee his exact words – was something like this: "The nets will be up, but I don't expect our fellows will use them much. They will be afraid of being jeered at by the men on the tram cars." Such fears – perhaps rather imaginary even in 1915 – had quite passed away last summer. We had all come to regard the nightmare of War as a normal condition, and cricket was felt to be as legitimate as any other recreation. Cricketers, it must always be remembered, had, unlike our racing friends, no grievance against authority. At the outbreak of War in August, 1914, they shut down the game without coercion of any kind, a speech from Lord Roberts and a letter from W. G. Grace being sufficient to determine them. I am far from thinking that in the first shock of the catastrophe that had befallen the world, they acted unwisely. I have a strong opinion, however, that when – contrary to all expectations – theatres, music halls, and other places of entertainment were found to flourish in War time, more might have been done for cricket in the summers of 1915 and 1916. Without the least detriment to War work it would have been easy to arrange on the Bank Holidays, Gentlemen and Players matches for veteran teams or North and South matches under the same restriction. The two matches at Lord's last summer, to which I have referred, showed clearly enough how pleased people were to get even a glimpse of some of their old favourites. Captain Warner has already arranged – by permission of the MCC – to repeat his experiment at Lord's during the coming season, and I hope his good example will be followed at other grounds. I share to the full the firm faith in the future of cricket expressed by Lord Harris in July at the meeting of the Cricketers' Fund, but when at last the War comes to an end we must all be prepared for at least a temporary falling off in public support. Such a long break in the continuity of public matches is almost bound to have a serious effect. As to the way in which county cricket will be carried on after the War, I will not venture on prediction. These are not days in which the role of prophet should be lightly assumed. It would not be a misfortune if the counties had to be content for a year or two with shorter programmes. Bowlers would keep fresher and every match be more of an event. From the time that the list of first-class counties had to be so largely extended our programme was always too heavy. The suggestion put forward by Mr Ludford Docker, the Warwickshire president, that county matches should be limited to two days does not appeal to me at all. Modern wickets are so good that such a drastic change would, in my opinion, be doomed to certain failure. Unless there was an agreement to decide on the first innings, a two-days' match in fine weather would, nine times out of ten, end in a draw.

## PUBLIC SCHOOL CRICKET IN 1916

### By E. B. Noel

Next to military matches the chief interest in cricket last summer centred in the public schools. As in 1915 the schools adopted various procedure: some played their usual school matches, others played schools which they do not usually play in peace time, in order to make up for the lack of foreign matches.

If as a whole the schools did not have such strong opposition as in an ordinary year a great number of them met one side of exceptional strength. I mean, of course, the Artists' Rifles OTC. Their first eleven with D. J. Knight, A. Hartley, E. C. Kirk, G. G. Dumbleton, etc., was a tough nut indeed for any public school side, and the Schools must have appreciated thoroughly playing against such first-rate batting and bowling.

Another point that may be noticed is that the amount of Public School cricket played in the holidays was probably larger than ever before. The authorities at Lord's very wisely decided to have the Public School match early in August, and at The Oval and Leyton and elsewhere there were a number of matches in which the public schoolboys played as a side. It is a distinctly useful innovation; certainly for several years to come there is not much chance of there being half the amount of country house cricket and games of this kind in which many schoolboys used to take part. In the heyday of country house cricket in the '90's, a boy in the South of England could certainly have played cricket every week and probably every day from August 1 to September 14. Those days are gone, perhaps never to return, and the matches of the kind which were played this year will supply a much-needed want.

A few words must be said of the Rugby and Marlborough match. It was played at Marlborough, and is described as "one of the best school matches ever played. Both sides succeeded in getting themselves into desperate straits, and both sides showed that they could get themselves out again." In the end Rugby won a truly remarkable game by 8 runs. Nearly 1,300 runs were scored; and no innings was under 250 — scoring which a few years back would have been thought quite phenomenal for schoolboys. Rugby won the toss and, helped by a stand of 93 for the eighth wicket by Wright and Kittermaster, made 268 — Wright going in ninth got 94. Marlborough's first innings is described as all head and tail and no middle. 150 for one wicket was up, but six were down for 166; Marlborough like Rugby had a great eighth wicket stand of 88, and in the end Marlborough led on the first innings by 61. They got one Rugby wicket that night for 49. Next morning Rugby, with three for 76 and the bowlers obviously having the upper hand, looked a beaten side; but determination, and it must be admitted some luck, came to their aid. A sixth wicket partnership added 164; the two heroes of this being Patterson, who got 96, and Kittermaster, not out 110. Marlborough were left with 296 to win. Ashfield batted finely for 129, and a very good start at one time gave promise that Marlborough would win. McCarthy's leg breaks changed the situation in favour of Rugby. Then the match veered round once again in favour of Marlborough, and with 260 for six they were in the better position. The seventh wicket fell at 262, the eighth at 283, and the ninth at 287. "Imagine," says the Marlburian, "two small boys out there, last men in, nine runs to get at the end of two whole days' swaying struggle, trying to stave off defeat for a side that a quarter of an hour before seemed to be winning comfortably." They withstood the attack pluckily for several overs, but then Elmhirst was bowled by McCarthy, and this wonderful game ended after so many changes of fortune in a win for Rugby by 8 runs. So remarkable was the game indeed that I make no apology for referring to it at such length.

# W. G. GRACE

## A tribute by LORD HARRIS (1915)

It is thirty years since I ceased to play regularly with "W.G." and a period such as that plays havoc with one's memory of particulars; but as one of the few left who played with him in the great matches of the seventies and eighties I feel that though one's thoughts are concentrated on a far different field, I ought to try, before it is too late, to leave on record my recollections of him and his play.

I suppose it has been difficult for the present generation, who have seen occasionally at Lord's or in some country match his massive form, to realise that in the seventies he was a spare and extremely active man. My old comrade, Mr C. K. Francis, reminded me when we attended his funeral, that in 1872, when Mr Fitzgerald's team of Gentlemen visited Canada and the United States, W.G.'s playing weight was no more than 12 stone 7 lbs.; he was a magnificient field in any position, but more especially in fielding his own bowling he was unsurpassed. For a long time during his career he fielded reguarly at point, and though those who had seen both considered his brother E.M. far the better of the two in that place, he was quite first rate. He was a long thrower in his earliest days, but quite early in his career, when he sometimes went long field, preferred to bowl the ball up to throwing it. He was always when at point on the look-out for a batsman being careless about keeping his ground, and you would see him occasionally face as if about to return the ball to the bowler, and instead sent it under arm to the wicket-keeper, but I never saw him get anyone out that way. He was originally a medium-paced bowler without peculiarity, meeting occasionally with considerable success, but in the seventies he adopted the delivery, slow with a leg break, by which he was known for the rest of his great career, and added to his otherwise extraordinary capacity as a cricketer. He must have been by nature a great bat and field, but he made himself, by ingenuity and assiduity, a successful bowler: and though I never knew anyone keener on having his innings, I am by no means sure he did not prefer the other department of the game; at any rate, it was very difficult to take him off once he had got hold of the ball. It was "Well, just one more over" or "I'll have him in another over or two," when one suggested a change. The chief feature of his bowling was the excellent length which he persistently maintained, for there was very little break on the ball, just enough bias to bring the ball across from the legs to the wicket; not infrequently he bowled for catches at long leg, and when his brother Fred was playing was often successful in trapping the unwary, for with a high flight and a dropping ball it is difficult to avoid skying a hit to leg. Fred Grace was as sure a catch as I ever saw, he caught the celebrated skyer hit by Bonner at The Oval, certainly a very high one. But a better still I thought was one he caught one very cold September day at The Oval in a match played for the benefit of *The Princess Alice* Fund. G.F. was bowling and a tremendous skyer went up, which obviously belonged to mid-off where I was standing. I was not particularly keen about it, and there was plenty of time for me to say "Who's going to have this?" "I will," said G.F., and he held it sure enough.

The success of W.G.'s bowling was largely due to his magnificent fielding to his own bowling. The moment he had delivered the ball he took so much ground to the left as to be himself an extra mid-off, and he never funked a return however hard and low it came. I have seen him make some extraordinary catches thus; he had also the additional chance of the umpire making a mistake over an appeal for lbw. He crossed over to the off so far and so quickly that he could not possibly see whether the ball would have hit the wicket, but he generally felt justified in appealing. On one occasion at Canterbury with a high wind blowing down the hill he was having much success, and asking every time he hit the batsman's legs. He could not get me caught at long leg for I always hit him fine, but he asked every time I missed the ball; I kept remonstrating, and he kept responding indignantly until at last I put my left leg too far to the left, the ball passed through my legs and hit the wicket, upon which he argued that all the previous balls would have done the same, whilst I argued that that and all the others had not pitched straight. He always had his mid-on very straight behind him to make up for his crossing to the off. He seemed quite impervious to fatigue, and after a long innings would gladly, if allowed to, bowl through the opponents' innings. It is right to dwell thus much on his bowling for though not a brilliant he was a decidedly successful bowler, and with a wind to help him actually difficult. But, of course, he will go down to fame as the greatest batsman that ever played, not as the greatest bowler; and I should judge that that description of him is justified. I happen to have seen and played on the average wickets we had to play on before the days of the very heavy roller, and also on the wickets batsmen now enjoy and bowlers groan over. I was too long after his time ever to see Fuller Pilch bat, but I fancy it would be a very fair comparison to pit W.G.'s performances against Fuller's, and great batsman as the latter was, I cannot believe he was as great as W.G.

I have elsewhere dilated, as such length as to prohibit repetition here, on the difference between the wickets of my earlier and of my later experience, the far lower level of batting averages in the seventies, as compared with those of the nineties and subsequently, is ample proof of the improvement of wickets, for tne bowling has certainly not deteriorated, and it should be remembered that W.G. was making as huge scores on the more difficult wickets as his successors have done on the easier.

The great feature of Fuller's batting was his forward play, he used a bat with a short handle and abnormally long pod, so that, whilst he could smother the ball, and drive and play to leg, he could not cut: whereas W.G. could hit all round, he used every known stroke except the draw which had become all but obsolete when he commenced first-class cricket; and he introduced what was then a novel stroke, and one more adaptable to the break-back bowling which he had as a rule to meet, than the leg-break bowling which was common in Pilch's time, viz.: the push to leg with a straight bat off the straight ball, and his mastery of this stroke was so great that he could place the ball with great success clear of short leg and even of two short legs. It was not the glide which that distinguished cricekter Ranjitsinhji developed so successfully, or a hook, but a push and a perfectly orthodox stroke. In his prime he met the ball on the popping crease, neither the orthodox forward nor the backstroke; it was a stroke entirely unique in my opinion needing remarkable clearness of eye and accurate timing: it is easy enough to play thus when one's eye is in, but when at his best he commenced his innings with it. He stood very close to the line from wicket to wicket and made great use of his legs in protecting his wicket, not be it understood, by getting in front of the wicket and leaving the ball alone, for no batsman left fewer balls alone, but bat and legs were so close together that it was difficult for the ball to get past the combination. So much so that the unfortunate umpires of those times were constantly being grumbled at either by the bowlers for not giving him out, or by him for being given out. J. C. Shaw, in particular, who remarked once: "I put the ball where I likes, and that beggar he puts it where he likes" was constantly appealing to heaven – as he had failed in his appeal to the umpire – that he had got him dead leg-before; and W.G. remonstrating in that high-pitched tone of voice "Didn't pitch straight by half-an-inch." I cannot remember his ever – when in his prime – slogging: he seemed to play the same watchful, untiring correct game as carefully towards the close as at the commencement of a long innings: and there was no need for he had so many strokes and could place them so clear of the field, and with such power that when runs had to be made fast his ordinary style was enough to secure all that was wanted.

He was quite untiring during the longest innings, and just as anxious and watchful for every possible run whether he had got to save his duck or had already made 200 and he was very fast between the wickets, and just as reluctant to leave the wicket whatever his score was as was Harry Jupp, but more observant of the rules, practice and etiquette of the game than that stolid player, of whom a story was told that playing in a country match he was bowled first ball. Jupp turned round, replaced the bails, and took guard again; "Ain't you going out, Juppy?" said one of the field. "No," said Jupp, and he didn't. I may repeat another story I have recorded elsewhere how I caught Jupp once at point close under his bat and close to the ground, and he showed no inclination to go and, so it was declared, that I said in a voice so thunderous: "I am not going to ask that Jupp, you've got to go," that he did go.

W.G. was desperately keen for his side to win, and consequently was led, in his excitement, to be occasionally very rigid in demanding his full rights, but he was so popular, and had the game so thoroughly at heart that such slight incidents were readily forgiven him and indeed more often than not added to the fund of humourous stories about him. When the luck of the game went against him his lamentations were deep, and his neighbourhood to be temporarily avoided, except by the most sympathetic. Alfred Lyttelton used to tell a delightful story of how in a Middlesex v Gloucestershire match W.G., having been given out for the second time caught at the wicket for a small score, he retired to the dressing tent with his shoulders so humped up and his whole aspect so ominous that the rest of the Gloucestershire XI were to be seen sneaking out of the back of the tent to avoid an interview. His ability to go on playing in first-class cricket when age and weight had seriously increased was quite remarkable. He was a most experienced and skilful anatomist of his own body, and knew how to save the weak points, but in addition he was always a most plucky cricketer. Standing up as he had to to the fiercest bowling sometimes on most fiery wickets, and putting his hand to everything within reach no matter how hard hit, he had of course at least his share of painful contusions, but I cannot in the years that I was playing with him remember his ever standing out or flinching: and I have seen him playing with badly bruised fingers.

He was so immeasurably above everyone else for many years, that the lines about Alfred Mynn naturally occurred to one as appropriate also to him, substituting batting for bowling and Gloucestershire for Kent:

> "But the Gentlemen of England the match will hardly win
> Till they find another bowler such as glorious Alfred Mynn"

and

> "Till to some old Kent enthusiasts it would almost seem a sin,
> To doubt their country's triumph when led on by Alfred Mynn."

I am sure it seemed to us who played with him in the great matches of the seventies and eighties that with W.G. to start the batting both the Gentlemen and England must be invincible, but Australian bowling took down our pride somewhat and taught us some useful lessons. When the Gentlemen of England were playing in Canada and the States in 1872 we used to grumble because W.G. and Cuthbert Ottaway used generally to put up 100 before a wicket went down, leaving some of us who fancied we could also do well if we had the chance, little to do when our time came. He was then and always a most genial, even-tempered, considerate companion, and of all the many cricketers I have known the *kindest* as well as the best. He was ever ready with an encouraging word for the novice, and a compassionate one for the man who made a mistake.

The soubriquet "Old Man," and it was a very affectionate one, was an abbreviation of "Grand Old Man," copied from that given to Mr Gladstone by his admirers, and indeed he was the Grand Old Man of the Cricket World and the Cricket Field. It is I suppose natural if the present generation who have never seen him play cannot realize what he was to the cricketers of mine. He was a land mark, a figure head, a giant, a master man, and to most of those who are left I imagine it must be as difficult as it is to me to imagine cricket going on without W.G. He devoted his life to it, and was perhaps as well-known by sight to the public as any man in public life; for he played all over England, in his younger days with the United South of England Eleven – managed, if I remember right, by Jim Lillywhite – against odds; later as County Cricket increased the Gloucestershire matches took him to all the great cricketing counties; but I think he would have said that his home in first-class cricket was Lord's; he was a most loyal supporter of MCC cricket, and the admirable likeness of him by Mr Stuart Wortley shows him batting on that historic ground, the combination of man and place surely most appropriate: the greatest cricketer in the history of the game batting on the most celebrated ground in the world.

He has gone and it is difficult to believe that a combination so remarkable of health, activity, power, eye, hand, devotion and opportunity will present itself again; if not then the greatest cricketer of all time has passed away, and we who saw his play, were encouraged by his invariable kindness, and gloried in his overwhelming excellence, may well think ourselves fortunate that a few of our cricketing years fell within his long cricketing life. It was a shock to hear that W.G. was no more; the crowd at his funeral, at a time when many of his greatest admirers were occupied with war work, was the best proof of the respect, admiration and affection he had won. The well-known lines in remembrance of Alfred Mynn pray that the Kentish Turf may lie lightly on him; it now provides a calm and honoured home to the remains of

W. G. Grace.

# W. G. GRACE

William Gilbert Grace, Born at Downend, near Bristol, July 18, 1848;

Died at his home, Fairmount, Eltham, Kent, October 23, 1915

In no branch of sport has anyone ever enjoyed such an unquestioned supremacy as that of W. G. Grace in the cricket field. In his great days he stood alone, without a rival. Not even George Fordham and Fred Archer as jockeys, or John Roberts as a billiard player, had such a marked superiority over the men who were nearest to them in point of ability. Whatever may be in store for the game of cricket in the future it seems safe to say that such a player will never be seen again. A rare combination of qualities went to the making of W. G. Grace. Blessed with great physical advantages, he united to a strength of constitution that defied fatigue a devotion to the game which time was powerless to affect. When he was in his prime no sun was too hot and no day too long for him. It is on record that when, for a cricketer, he was no longer young, he spent the whole night by the bedside of a patient, and on the following day stepped on to the Clifton College ground and scored over 200 runs.

Mr Grace's career in the cricket field – almost unexampled in point of length – can be sharply divided into two portions. His early fame as a batsman culminated in the season of 1876, when in the month of August he scored in three successive innings, 344 against Kent at Canterbury, 177 against Nottinghamshire at Clifton, and 318 not out against Yorkshire at Cheltenham. Soon after that, having passed his examination at Edinburgh as a surgeon, he thought of gradually retiring from cricket and settling down, like his elder brothers, to the busy life of a general practitioner. As a matter of fact, he did for many years hold a parish appointment at Bristol, a locum tenens doing his work in the summer months. There can be little doubt that his change of plans was mainly due to the appearance in England in 1878 of the first Australian eleven. Those whose memories go back to that now somewhat distant time will remember the tremendous sensation caused by the victories of that eleven, and in particular by Spofforth's bowling, and Blackham's wicket-keeping. Englishmen realised, with an excusable shock of surprise, that in the cricket field there were serious rivals to be faced.

Mr Grace had never been in such poor batting form as he was in 1878, and on the few occasions that he met the Australian bowlers he did nothing in the least degree worthy of his reputation. I have no exact knowledge on the point, but I feel tolerably certain that the success of the Australians revived Mr Grace's ambition. At any rate, the fact remains that, though the most brilliant part of his career had ended before the invasion of 1878, the Australians found him for the best part of twenty years the most formidable of their opponents. This second part of his career as a batsman began towards the end of the season of 1880. Following some fine performances for Gloucestershire he played, as everyone will remember, a great innings of 152 at The Oval in the first match in this country between England and Australia. Even then, however, though only in his 33rd year, he laboured under one serious disadvantage. In the four years following his triumphs of 1876, he had put on a lot of weight and was very heavy for so young a man.

He said himself at the time that he was never in better form than in those closing weeks of the season of 1880, and that, but for lack of condition, he would have made many more runs. Against increasing bulk he had to battle for the rest of his cricket life. For a long time he retained his activity to a surprising extent, but as the years went on his once splendid fielding gradually left him. He kept up his batting, however, in a marvellous way, the success of what one may call his second period in the cricket field reaching its climax when in 1895 he scored a thousand runs in first-class cricket in the month of May. His batting at that time has never been approached by a man of the same age; he was nearly 47. In 1896 he was still very good, but after that the years began to tell on him, and in 1899, when he moved from Bristol to the Crystal Palace, he played at Trent Bridge his last match for England against Australia. Still, though he had now done with Test matches, he went on playing first-class cricket for several seasons, his career practically ending with the Gentlemen and Players' match at The Oval in 1906. The finish was worthy of him as, on his 58th birthday, he scored 74, batting up to a certain point with much of the vigour of his younger days.

Of Mr Grace's cricket from the time of his first appearance at Lord's in July, 1864, for the South Wales Club against the MCC down to the end of 1876, columns could be written without exhausting the subject. He was picked for the Gentlemen, as a lad of 17, both at Lord's and The Oval in 1865, the honour being conferred upon him quite as much for his medium-pace bowling as for his batting. A year later, however, he proved himself, beyond all question, the best batsman in England, two wonderful innings at The Oval establishing his fame. He scored 224 not out for England against Surrey and 173 not out for Gentlemen of the South against Players of the South. An attack of scarlet fever interfered with his cricket in 1867, but after that he never looked back. His best seasons as a batsman were, I fancy, 1871, 1873, and 1876. His play in 1871 far surpassed anything that had ever been done before.

In his whole career he scored in Gentlemen and Players' matches 6,008 runs with an average of 42 and took 271 wickets for a trifle under 19 runs each. He made seven hundreds for the Gentlemen at Lord's, four at The Oval, and one each at Brighton, Prince's, Scarborough, and Hastings. The first of his seven hundreds at Lord's was obtained in 1868, and the last, after an interval of twenty-seven years, in 1895. Of these seven innings the first was, perhaps, the most remarkable. Going in first wicket down for a very strong side he took out his bat for 134, the total only reaching 201. As Lord Harris has pointed out the wickets at Lord's in those far-off days were by no means so true and easy as careful attention made them in later years. A score of a hundred at Lord's in the '60's, against the best bowling was an incomparably bigger feat than it is at the present time.

No mention has yet been made of Mr Grace's connection with Gloucestershire cricket. With his two brothers, E.M. and G.F., and other fine, though less gifted, players to help him, he built up a team of remarkable strength in batting and fielding. The county club was established in 1871, and in 1876 and 1877 the eleven stood ahead of all rivals. Until beaten at Clifton by the first Australian Eleven in 1878 the team never lost a match at home. After G. F. Grace's death in 1880, Gloucestershire never seemed quite the same as before, but in 1885, and again in 1898, there was, thanks to W.G.'s batting and C. L. Townsend's bowling, a brief revival of old glories. The Gloucestershire matches at Clifton and Cheltenham in the old days were delightful, the Gloucestershire eleven being quite a family party. Like other families they had their little differences of opinion, but there was a great feeling of comradeship among them, and they played cricket with tremendous zest.

Mr Grace's venture in connection with the London County at the Crystal Palace did not add to his fame. He was in his 51st year when he left Bristol, the experiment being made far too late. Many pleasant matches were played at the Palace, but they were carried through in too leisurely a spirit to appeal to a public brought up on cricket of a much sterner character. If tried fifteen years earlier the project might have proved a success. As it was the London County faded out when Mr Grace's contract with the Crystal Palace Company came to an end.

With Mr Grace's characteristics as a batsman I must deal rather briefly. He was, in the main, quite orthodox in style, his bat being as perfectly straight as Fuller Pilch's, but he greatly enlarged the domain of orthodoxy, playing a far more aggressive and punishing game than any of the classic batsmen who came before him. It should be explained here that E. M. Grace, who first made the family name famous, played a game of his own and was a little outside comparisons. W.G. developed the art of batting to an extraordinary degree, but he was not, like E.M., a revolutionist. There is his own authority for stating that he did not indulge in the pull till he was forty. A splendid all-round hitter, he excelled all his predecessors in his power of placing the ball on the on-side. A story is told of a cricketer who had regarded Fuller Pilch as the last word in batting, being taken in his old age to see Mr Grace bat for the first time. He watched the great man for a quarter of an hour or so and then broke out into expressions of boundless delight. "Why," he said, "this man scores continually from balls that old Fuller would have been thankful to stop." The words conveyed everything. Mr Grace when he went out at the ball did so for the purpose of getting runs. Pilch and his imitators, on the other hand, constantly used forward play for defence alone.

When the wicket was difficult and the ball turning, Mr Grace trusted for defence to that strong back play which, even in his boyhood, convinced his people at home that he would be a greater batsman than his brother, E.M. Mr Grace's batting from 1868 onwards quite overshadowed his bowling, and yet during his career he took many hundreds of wickets. Indeed, old Bob Thoms, the umpire, always contended that if he had not been such a wonderful batsman he would have been the best slow bowler in England. Even as it was he held his own very well with such masters as Alfred Shaw and Southerton. He bowled medium pace with a purely round arm action in his young days, but slackened his speed about 1872.

His superb strength and health enabled him to stand any amount of cricket, but in his best two years as a bowler – 1875 and 1877 – his batting fell off fifty per cent. He did not rely much on break, only turning in a little from leg, but he had great command over his length and very seldom indeed pitched short. His chief strength lay in head work. No one was quicker to find out the weak points of a batsman or more certain to lure an impetuous hitter to his doom. In Gloucestershire's great days he was much helped by brilliant fielding. Fred Grace in particular, at deep square leg, being invaluable to him. When he first appeared for the Gentlemen, Mr Grace was a splendid outfield, capable of throwing the ball a hundred yards, but as time went on he took to fielding near the wicket and for many years he had no superior at point except his brother E.M.

Personally, W.G. struck me as the most natural and unspoiled of men. Whenever and wherever one met him he was always the same. There was not the smallest trace of affectation about him. If anything annoyed him he was quick to show anger, but his little outbursts were soon over. One word I will add. No man who ever won such world-wide fame could have been more modest in speaking of his own doings. Mr Grace was married in 1873 to Miss Agnes Day. His domestic life was unclouded except by the death of his only daughter in 1899 and of his eldest son in 1905. Mrs Grace and two sons – Captain H. E. Grace, RN, and Captain C. B. Grace, KFRE – survive him.

S. H. P.

## W. G. GRACE IN FIRST-CLASS CRICKET

| | Batting | | | | | Bowling | | | |
|---|---|---|---|---|---|---|---|---|---|
| Year | Innings | Not Outs | Runs | Highest Innings | Average | Balls | Runs | Wickets | Average |
| 1865 | 8 | 1 | 189 | 48 | 27.00 | 630 | 268 | 20 | 13.40 |
| 1866 | 13 | 2 | 581 | 224* | 52.81 | 1,215 | 434 | 31 | 14.00 |
| 1867 | 6 | 1 | 154 | 75 | 30.80 | 799 | 292 | 39 | 7.48 |
| 1868 | 13 | 2 | 625 | 134* | 56.81 | 1,384 } | 686 | 48 | 14.29 |
| | | | | | | | — | 1 | — |
| 1869 | 24 | 1 | 1,320 | 180 | 57.39 | 3,138 | 1,255 | 73 | 17.19 |
| 1870 | 38 | 5 | 1,808 | 215 | 54.78 | 1,817 | 782 | 50 | 15.64 |
| 1871 | 39 | 4 | 2,739 | 268 | 78.25 | 3,060 | 1,346 | 79 | 17.03 |
| 1872 | 32 | 3 | 1,561 | 170* | 53.82 | 1,835 } | 736 | 62 | 11.87 |
| | | | | | | | — | 6 | — |
| 1873 | 38 | 8 | 2,139 | 192* | 71.30 | 2,727 } | 1,307 | 101 | 12.94 |
| | | | | | | | — | 5 | — |
| 1874 | 32 | 0 | 1,664 | 179 | 52.00 | 4,101 | 1,780 | 140 | 12.71 |
| 1875 | 48 | 2 | 1,498 | 152 | 32.56 | 6,757 | 2,468 | 191 | 12.92 |
| 1876 | 46 | 4 | 2,622 | 344 | 62.42 | 6,321 | 2,458 | 129 | 19.05 |
| 1877 | 40 | 3 | 1,474 | 261 | 39.83 | 7,170 | 2,291 | 179 | 12.79 |
| 1878 | 42 | 2 | 1,151 | 116 | 28.77 | 6,680 | 2,204 | 152 | 14.50 |
| 1879 | 29 | 3 | 993 | 123 | 38.19 | 4,420 | 1,491 | 113 | 13.19 |
| 1880 | 27 | 3 | 951 | 152 | 39.62 | 4,062 | 1,480 | 84 | 17.61 |
| 1881 | 25 | 1 | 917 | 182 | 38.20 | 2,434 | 1,026 | 57 | 18.00 |
| 1882 | 37 | 0 | 975 | 88 | 26.35 | 3,404 | 1,754 | 101 | 17.36 |
| 1883 | 41 | 2 | 1,352 | 112 | 34.66 | 4,417 | 2,077 | 94 | 22.09 |
| 1884 | 45 | 5 | 1,361 | 116* | 34.02 | 4,150 | 1,762 | 82 | 21.48 |
| 1885 | 42 | 3 | 1,688 | 221* | 43.28 | 5,738 | 2,199 | 117 | 18.79 |
| 1886 | 55 | 3 | 1,846 | 170 | 35.50 | 6,102 | 2,439 | 122 | 19.99 |
| 1887 | 46 | 8 | 2,062 | 183* | 54.26 | 5,094 | 2,078 | 97 | 21.42 |
| 1888 | 59 | 1 | 1,886 | 215 | 32.51 | 4,390 | 1,691 | 93 | 18.18 |
| 1889 | 45 | 2 | 1,396 | 154 | 32.46 | 2,313 | 1,014 | 44 | 23.04 |
| 1890 | 55 | 3 | 1,476 | 109* | 28.38 | 3,048 | 1,183 | 61 | 19.39 |

## W. G. Grace in First Class Cricket – *continued*

| | Batting | | | | | Bowling | | | |
| Year | Innings | Not Outs | Runs | Highest Innings | Average | Balls | Runs | Wickets | Average |
|---|---|---|---|---|---|---|---|---|---|
| 1891 | 40 | 1 | 771 | 72* | 19.76 | 2,364 | 973 | 58 | 16.77 |
| 1891-2 | 11 | 1 | 448 | 159* | 44.80 | 385 | 134 | 5 | 26.80 |
| 1892 | 37 | 3 | 1,055 | 99 | 31.02 | 2,128 | 958 | 31 | 30.90 |
| 1893 | 50 | 5 | 1,609 | 128 | 35.75 | 1,705 | 854 | 22 | 38.81 |
| 1894 | 45 | 1 | 1,293 | 196 | 29.38 | 1,507 | 732 | 29 | 25.28 |
| 1895 | 48 | 2 | 2,346 | 288 | 51.00 | 900 | 527 | 16 | 32.93 |
| 1896 | 54 | 4 | 2,135 | 301 | 42.70 | 2,768 | 1,249 | 52 | 24.01 |
| 1897 | 41 | 2 | 1,532 | 131 | 39.28 | 2,971 | 1,242 | 56 | 22.17 |
| 1898 | 41 | 5 | 1,513 | 168 | 42.02 | 2,378 | 917 | 36 | 25.47 |
| 1899 | 23 | 1 | 515 | 78 | 23.40 | 1,220 | 482 | 20 | 24.10 |
| 1900 | 31 | 1 | 1,277 | 126 | 42.56 | 1,759 | 969 | 32 | 30.28 |
| 1901 | 32 | 1 | 1,007 | 132 | 32.48 | 2,815 | 1,111 | 51 | 21.78 |
| 1902 | 35 | 3 | 1,187 | 131 | 37.09 | 2,917 | 1,074 | 46 | 23.34 |
| 1903 | 27 | 1 | 593 | 150 | 22.80 | 798 | 479 | 10 | 47.90 |
| 1904 | 26 | 1 | 637 | 166 | 25.48 | 1,308 | 687 | 21 | 32.71 |
| 1905 | 13 | 0 | 250 | 71 | 19.23 | 510 | 383 | 7 | 54.71 |
| 1906 | 10 | 1 | 241 | 74 | 26.77 | 506 | 268 | 13 | 20.61 |
| 1907 | 2 | 0 | 19 | 16 | 9.50 | — | — | — | — |
| 1908 | 2 | 0 | 40 | 25 | 20.00 | 12 | 5 | 0 | — |
| Totals | 1,493 | 105 | 54,896 | 344 | 39.55 | { 126,157 <br> — | 51,545 <br> — | 2,864 <br> 12 | 17.99 <br> — |

\* *Signifies not out.*

The above figures, which have been checked most carefully throughout, will be found to differ in several instances from those given in the cricket publications of the sixties and seventies; but, considering that the handbooks of that period frequently contradicted each other, and that the averages given in one seldom, if every, agreed with those tabulated in another, this is not surprising. One instance of the loose manner in which statistics were compiled in those days may be cited. In 1873, when "W.G.'s" scores in the MCC matches v Hertfordshire and Staffordshire, and in the North v South game at The Oval on July 26, were included in his first-class aggregate for the season, his bowling in the same matches was ignored completely.

## MR W. G. GRACE'S PERFORMANCES IN GENTLEMEN v PLAYERS MATCHES, 1865-1906

| Ground and Date of First Appearance | Batting | | | | | | Bowling | | | | |
|---|---|---|---|---|---|---|---|---|---|---|---|
| | Matches | Innings | Not Outs | Runs | Highest Innings | Average | Matches | Balls | Runs | Wickets | Average |
| The Oval, 1865 | 35 | 66 | 5 | 2,582 | 215 | 42.38 | 34 | 5,831 | 2,403 | 110 | 21.84 |
| Lord's, 1865 | 35 | 62 | 3 | 2,398 | 169 | 40.64 | 29 | 4,867 | 1,863 | 108 | 17.25 |
| Brighton, 1871 | 1 | 2 | — | 217 | 217 | 108.50 | 1 | 324 | 123 | 7 | 17.57 |
| Prince's, 1873 | 5 | 8 | — | 281 | 110 | 35.12 | 5 | 1,322 | 473 | 39 | 12.12 |
| Scarborough, 1885 | 1 | 1 | — | 174 | 174 | 174.00 | 1 | 159 | 60 | 3 | 20.00 |
| Hastings, 1889 | 7 | 12 | 2 | 356 | 131 | 35.60 | 5 | 295 | 171 | 4 | 42.75 |
| Totals | 84 | 151 | 10 | 6,008 | 217 | 42.60 | 75 | 12,798 | 5,093 | 271 | 18.78 |

## THE SIDES FOR WHICH W. G. GRACE OBTAINED HIS RUNS

| | Date of First Match | Innings | Not Outs | Runs | Highest Innings | Average |
|---|---|---|---|---|---|---|
| Anglo-American XI | 1873 | 2 | 0 | 157 | 152 | 78.50 |
| England | 1865 | 54 | 5 | 1,930 | 224* | 39.38 |
| England (in Australia) | 1891-2 | 11 | 1 | 448 | 159* | 44.80 |
| England XI's | 1875 | 50 | 2 | 1,267 | 92 | 26.39 |
| Gentlemen v Players | 1865 | 151 | 10 | 6,008 | 217 | 42.60 |
| Gentlemen of England | 1865 | 43 | 2 | 1,595 | 165 | 38.90 |
| Gentlemen of South | 1865 | 37 | 2 | 1,625 | 180 | 46.42 |
| Gloucestershire | 1868 | 618 | 49 | 23,083 | 318* | 40.56 |
| Gloucestershire and Kent | 1874 | 6 | 1 | 346 | 121 | 69.20 |
| Gloucestershire and Yorkshire | 1877 | 2 | — | 162 | 110 | 81.00 |
| Grace's XI, Mr W. G. | 1871 | 15 | 4 | 511 | 81* | 46.45 |
| Kent (with W.G. and A. W. Ridley) | 1877 | 2 | — | 108 | 58 | 54.00 |
| London County | 1900 | 103 | 1 | 3,483 | 166 | 34.14 |
| MCC | 1869 | 12 | 2 | 904 | 344 | 82.18 |
| MCC and Ground | 1869 | 211 | 15 | 6,876 | 196 | 35.08 |
| Non-Smokers | 1884 | 1 | — | 10 | 10 | 10.00 |
| Non-University Gentlemen | 1874 | 1 | — | 12 | 12 | 12.00 |
| Orleans Club | 1882 | 1 | — | 34 | 34 | 34.00 |
| Over 30 | 1879 | 8 | — | 193 | 51 | 24.12 |
| Right-handed | 1870 | 1 | — | 35 | 35 | 35.00 |
| Single | 1871 | 1 | 1 | 189 | 189* | 189.00 |
| South | 1866 | 137 | 8 | 5,130 | 268 | 39.76 |
| South, United | 1870 | 15 | 1 | 492 | 126 | 35.14 |
| South of Thames | 1866 | 7 | 1 | 260 | 130 | 43.33 |
| United XI | 1882 | 3 | — | 38 | 23 | 12.66 |
| Totals | 1865 | 1,493 | 105 | 54,896 | 344 | 39.55 |

* *Signifies not out.*

## THE PREVIOUS TABLE ANALYSED

| For | Date of First Match | Innings | Not Outs | Runs | Highest Innings | Average | Scores of 50 or more |
|---|---|---|---|---|---|---|---|
| **Anglo-American XI** | | | | | | | |
| v XV of MCC (with Rylott) | 1873 | 2 | — | 157 | 152 | 78.50 | 152 |
| **England** | | | | | | | |
| v Australia | 1880 | 36 | 2 | 1,098 | 170 | 32.29 | 152, 170, 75*, 50, 58, 68, 66 |
| v XIII of Kent | 1878 | 4 | 1 | 101 | 63* | 33.66 | 63* |
| v Kent and Sussex | 1902 | 2 | — | 79 | 70 | 39.50 | 70 |
| v Lancashire and Yorkshire | 1903 | 2 | — | 30 | 28 | 15.00 | |
| v MCC and Ground | 1868 | 2 | — | 95 | 66 | 47.50 | 66 |
| v Middlesex | 1867 | 1 | — | 75 | 75 | 75.00 | 75 |
| v New South Wales | 1891-92 | 3 | — | 79 | 45 | 26.33 | |
| v Nottinghamshire and Yorkshire | 1872 | 1 | 1 | 170 | 170* | 170.00 | 170* |
| v South Australia | 1891-92 | 1 | — | 2 | 2 | 2.00 | |
| v Surrey | 1865 | 3 | 1 | 277 | 224* | 138.50 | 224* |
| v Surrey and Middlesex | 1868 | 2 | — | 43 | 24 | 21.50 | |
| v Surrey and Sussex | 1867 | 5 | — | 97 | 40 | 19.40 | |
| v Victoria | 1891-92 | 2 | 1 | 203 | 159* | 203.00 | 159* |
| v Yorkshire | 1902 | 1 | — | 29 | 29 | 29.00 | |
| **England XI's** | | | | | | | |
| v Anglo-Australian XI's | 1885 | 7 | 1 | 161 | 58 | 26.83 | 51, 58 |
| v Australians | 1884 | 26 | — | 679 | 92 | 26.11 | 92, 74, 64, 63 |
| v Cambridge University | 1875 | 11 | — | 282 | 54 | 25.63 | 54, 52 |
| v England XI† | 1892 | 2 | — | 65 | 63 | 32.50 | 63 |
| v Home Counties | 1899 | 2 | 1 | 36 | 21* | 36.00 | |
| v Yorkshire | 1901 | 2 | — | 44 | 24 | 22.00 | |

† *Lord Sheffield's Anglo-Australian XI v Rest of England.*

## The Previous Table Analysed – *continued*

| For | Date of First Match | Innings | Not Outs | Runs | Highest Innings | Average | Scores of 50 or more |
|---|---|---|---|---|---|---|---|
| **Gentlemen** | | | | | | | |
| v Players | 1865 | 151 | 10 | 6,008 | 217 | 42.60 | 134*, 83, 215, 109, 50, 217, 77 and 112, 117, 163, 158, 70, 110, 152, 90, 169, 63, 90, 100, 66, 89, 76, 174, 65 and 50*, 67, 54, 57, and 68, 71, 56, 131, 118, 53*, 54, 66, 50, 60, 78, 58, 57, 54, 82, 74 |
| **Gentlemen of England** | | | | | | | |
| v Australians | 1878 | 13 | — | 656 | 165 | 50.46 | 61, 107, 148, 165 |
| v Cambridge University | 1871 | 3 | — | 181 | 162 | 60.33 | 162 |
| v Gentlemen of Kent | 1879 | 3 | — | 61 | 54 | 20.33 | 54 |
| v Gentlemen of Middlesex | 1865 | 2 | — | 82 | 48 | 41.00 | |
| v I Zingari | 1885 | 9 | 1 | 390 | 101* | 48.75 | 68, 73, 58, 101* |
| v Oxford University | 1866 | 5 | — | 111 | 71 | 22.20 | 71 |
| v Players of South | 1904 | 2 | 1 | 8 | 6* | 8.00 | |
| v Surrey | 1905 | 6 | — | 106 | 32 | 17.66 | |
| **Gentlemen of South** | | | | | | | |
| v Gentlemen of North | 1870 | 5 | 1 | 270 | 118 | 67.50 | 77, 118 |
| v I Zingari | 1866 | 2 | — | 80 | 50 | 40.00 | 50 |
| v Players of North | 1873 | 10 | — | 399 | 145 | 39.90 | 145, 104, 72 |
| v Players of South | 1865 | 20 | 1 | 876 | 180 | 46.10 | 173*, 55, 180, 66, 134, 150 |
| **Gloucestershire** | | | | | | | |
| v Australians | 1878 | 30 | 4 | 856 | 116* | 32.92 | 77, 116*, 110, 51, 92, 66 |
| v Derbyshire | 1886 | 2 | — | 22 | 20 | 11.00 | |
| v England | 1877 | 4 | — | 94 | 31 | 23.50 | |
| v Essex | 1898 | 3 | — | 195 | 126 | 65.00 | 126 |
| v Kent | 1887 | 41 | 6 | 1,680 | 257 | 48.00 | 101 and 103*, 64, 109*, 257 and 73*, 64, 56*, 58, 71 |

| | | | | | | | |
|---|---|---|---|---|---|---|---|
| v Lancashire | 1878 | 75 | 8 | 2,154 | 112 | 32.14 | 58*, 75*, 106, 86, 112, 53, 50, 94, 90, 51 and 102*, 56 |
| v MCC and Ground | 1868 | 5 | 1 | 292 | 172 | 73.00 | 172 |
| v Middlesex | 1879 | 68 | 7 | 2,848 | 221* | 46.68 | 85 and 81*, 69, 64, 80, 89, 85, 94, 69 and 54, 221*, 113, 63, 101, 127*, 57, 72*, 72*, 89, 96, 68, 169, 60 and 56, 51, 55 |
| v Nottinghamshire | 1871 | 84 | 5 | 3,276 | 182 | 41.46 | 78 and 55, 79 and 116, 67, 119, 60, 177, 116, 102, 51 and 182, 55, 92*, 84, 113*, 59, 70*, 61, 119, 55, 126, 131, 63, 168 |
| v Philadelphians | 1897 | 1 | — | 113 | 113 | 113.00 | 113 |
| v Somerset | 1879 | 33 | — | 1,373 | 288 | 41.60 | 113, 80, 75 and 58, 288, 186, 109 |
| v Surrey | 1870 | 97 | 7 | 2,815 | 160* | 31.27 | 143, 83, 160*, 123, 67, 50*, 55, 88 and 51, 66, 55, 104, 58, 94, 54, 64, 61*, 51 |
| v Sussex | 1872 | 73 | 6 | 3,172 | 301 | 47.34 | 51, 179, 53, 77, 104, 78, 52, 56*, 51 and 57, 51, 215, 70, 84, 58, 99, 75, 88, 91, 243*, 301, 116, 93* |
| v Warwickshire | 1894 | 15 | 1 | 392 | 70 | 28.00 | 52, 70 |
| v Yorkshire | 1872 | 87 | 4 | 3,801 | 318* | 45.79 | 150, 79, 167, 127, 111, 57, 318*, 84, 71, 62, 89 and 57*, 56, 51, 54, 132, 92 and 183*, 97, 148 and 153, 50, 52, 98, 53, 61, 54, 70, 55 |
| **Gloucestershire and Kent** | | | | | | | |
| v England | 1874 | 6 | 1 | 346 | 121 | 69.20 | 94 and 121, 91 |
| **Gloucestershire and Yorkshire** | | | | | | | |
| v England | 1877 | 2 | — | 162 | 110 | 81.00 | 52 and 110 |
| **Grace's XI, Mr W. G.** | | | | | | | |
| v Australians | 1899 | 1 | — | 25 | 25 | 25.00 | |
| v Cambridge University | 1906 | 4 | 1 | 109 | 64 | 36.33 | 64 |
| v England XI | 1883 | 2 | — | 132 | 81 | 66.00 | 81 and 51 |

## The Previous Table Analysed – *continued*

| For | Date of First Match | Innings | Not Outs | Runs | Highest Innings | Average | Scores of 50 or more |
|---|---|---|---|---|---|---|---|
| **Grace's XI, Mr W. G.** – *continued* | | | | | | | |
| v Kent | 1871 | 4 | 3 | 194 | 81* | 194.00 | 81*, 69* |
| v Surrey | 1907 | 2 | — | 19 | 16 | 9.50 | |
| v West Indians | 1906 | 2 | — | 32 | 23 | 16.00 | |
| **Kent (with W.G. and A. W. Ridley)** | | | | | | | |
| v England | 1877 | 2 | — | 108 | 58 | 54.00 | 50 and 58 |
| **London County** | | | | | | | |
| v Australians | 1902 | 1 | — | 1 | 1 | 1.00 | |
| v Cambridge University | 1900 | 13 | — | 533 | 93 | 41.00 | 86 and 62, 93, 72, 59 |
| v Derbyshire | 1900 | 16 | — | 307 | 87 | 19.18 | 87 |
| v Gloucestershire | 1903 | 3 | — | 179 | 150 | 59.66 | 150 |
| v Ireland | 1902 | 2 | — | 51 | 32 | 25.50 | |
| v Lancashire | 1903 | 2 | — | 28 | 22 | 14.00 | |
| v Leicestershire | 1901 | 12 | — | 313 | 83 | 26.08 | 83, 73 and 54 |
| v MCC and Ground | 1900 | 15 | — | 674 | 166 | 44.93 | 110, 132, 131, 166 |
| v South Africans | 1901 | 4 | — | 47 | 37 | 11.75 | |
| v Surrey | 1900 | 17 | — | 595 | 97 | 35.00 | 71 and 80, 97, 61, 81, 52 |
| v Warwickshire | 1900 | 14 | — | 523 | 129 | 37.35 | 82, 76, 76, 129 |
| v Worcestershire | 1900 | 4 | 1 | 232 | 110* | 77.33 | 72 and 110* |
| **MCC** | | | | | | | |
| v Kent | 1869 | 11 | 2 | 871 | 344 | 96.77 | 127, 117, 57*, 123, 344 |
| v Yorkshire | 1889 | 2 | — | 33 | 27 | 16.50 | |
| **MCC and Ground** | | | | | | | |
| v Australians | 1878 | 19 | — | 489 | 101 | 25.73 | 101, 75, 50 |
| v Cambridge University | 1869 | 28 | 3 | 993 | 196 | 39.72 | 55, 54*, 116*, 139, 196 |
| v Derbyshire | 1877 | 6 | 1 | 210 | 74* | 42.00 | 74* |
| v England | 1877 | 6 | — | 115 | 47 | 19.16 | |

| | | | | | | | |
|---|---|---|---|---|---|---|---|
| v England XI | 1891 | 2 | — | 21 | 19 | 10.50 | |
| v Hertfordshire | 1872 | 4 | — | 148 | 75 | 37.00 | 75 |
| v Ireland | 1902 | 1 | — | 44 | 44 | 44.00 | |
| v Kent | 1871 | 20 | 2 | 649 | 128 | 36.05 | 51, 80, 128, 125 |
| v Lancashire | 1869 | 17 | 1 | 312 | 73 | 19.50 | 73, 61* |
| v Leicestershire | 1901 | 2 | — | 26 | 15 | 13.00 | |
| v Middlesex | 1871 | 4 | — | 113 | 88 | 28.25 | 88 |
| v North | 1874 | 2 | — | 55 | 43 | 27.50 | |
| v Nottinghamshire | 1869 | 12 | 1 | 492 | 121 | 44.72 | 121, 117*, 52, 63 |
| v Oxford University | 1869 | 23 | 1 | 1,058 | 117 | 48.09 | 117, 54 and 73*, 62, 65, 67, 104, 95, 72, 79 |
| v South | 1869 | 4 | — | 92 | 44 | 23.00 | |
| v South Africans | 1901 | 3 | — | 47 | 27 | 15.66 | |
| v Staffordshire | 1873 | 1 | — | 67 | 67 | 67.00 | 67 |
| v Surrey | 1869 | 14 | 2 | 771 | 181 | 64.25 | 51, 138*, 84, 181, 146 |
| v Sussex | 1871 | 15 | 2 | 516 | 103 | 39.69 | 59, 81*, 73, 103, 65 |
| v Yorkshire | 1870 | 28 | 2 | 658 | 101 | 25.30 | 66, 98, 101, 71 |
| **Non-Smokers** | | | | | | | |
| v Smokers | 1884 | 1 | — | 10 | 10 | 10.00 | |
| **Non-University Gentlemen** | | | | | | | |
| v University Gentlemen | 1874 | 1 | — | 12 | 12 | 12.00 | |
| **Orleans Club** | | | | | | | |
| v Australians | 1882 | 1 | — | 34 | 34 | 34.00 | |
| **Over 30** | | | | | | | |
| v Under 30 | 1879 | 8 | — | 193 | 51 | 24.12 | 51 |
| **Right-handed** | | | | | | | |
| v Left-handed | 1870 | 1 | — | 35 | 35 | 35.00 | |
| **Single** | | | | | | | |
| v Married | 1871 | 1 | 1 | 189 | 189* | 189.90* | 189* |

## The Previous Table Analysed – continued

| For | Date of First Match | Innings | Not Outs | Runs | Highest Innings | Average | Scores of 50 or more |
|---|---|---|---|---|---|---|---|
| **South** | | | | | | | |
| v Australians | 1884 | 19 | 2 | 617 | 84 | 36.29 | 53, 84, 66, 53 |
| v North | 1866 | 118 | 6 | 4,513 | 268 | 40.29 | 122, 96, 178, 268, 87, 114, 68, 192*, 98, 82, 92 and 73, 114*, 69 and 50*, 58, 261, 54, 61, 77, 64, 69, 154, 61, 54, 104, 126 |
| **South, United** | | | | | | | |
| v England | 1876 | 2 | — | 27 | 19 | 13.50 | |
| v North, United | 1871 | 11 | 1 | 435 | 126 | 43.50 | 51*, 65, 126 and 82 |
| v Yorkshire | 1874 | 2 | — | 30 | 15 | 15.00 | |
| **South of Thames** | | | | | | | |
| v North of Thames | 1866 | 7 | 1 | 260 | 130 | 43.33 | 130 and 102* |
| **United XI** | | | | | | | |
| v Australians | 1882 | 3 | — | 38 | 23 | 12.66 | |
| Totals | 1865 | 1,493 | 105 | 54,896 | 344 | 39.55 | |

* *Signifies not out.*

## W.G.'s SCORING ON THE CHIEF LONDON GROUNDS

| | Date of First Match | Matches | Innings | Not Outs | Runs | Highest Innings | Average |
|---|---|---|---|---|---|---|---|
| Lord's | 1865 | 208 | 364 | 19 | 12,690 | 196 | 36.78 |
| The Oval | 1865 | 122 | 209 | 18 | 8,261 | 268 | 43.25 |
| Prince's | 1872 | 17 | 28 | 0 | 1,321 | 261 | 47.17 |
| Crystal Palace | 1899 | 40 | 60 | 1 | 2,535 | 166 | 42.96 |

It should be remembered that the Doctor had completed his 50th year when he appeared at the Crystal Palace for the first time.

## W. G. GRACE'S BATTING AVERAGES FOR GLOUCESTERSHIRE

| Year | Innings | Not Outs | Runs | Highest Innings | Average |
|---|---|---|---|---|---|
| 1868 | 2 | 0 | 37 | 24 | 18.50 |
| 1870 | 4 | 0 | 366 | 172 | 91.50 |
| 1871 | 8 | 1 | 435 | 116 | 62.14 |
| 1872 | 6 | 0 | 284 | 150 | 47.33 |
| 1873 | 11 | 3 | 497 | 160* | 62.12 |
| 1874 | 7 | 0 | 594 | 179 | 84.85 |
| 1875 | 14 | 0 | 541 | 119 | 38.64 |
| 1876 | 12 | 1 | 890 | 318* | 80.90 |
| 1877 | 13 | 1 | 367 | 84 | 30.58 |
| 1878 | 21 | 2 | 605 | 116 | 31.84 |
| 1879 | 15 | 2 | 709 | 123 | 52.53 |
| 1880 | 18 | 2 | 614 | 106 | 38.37 |
| 1881 | 19 | 1 | 720 | 182 | 40.00 |
| 1882 | 22 | 0 | 666 | 88 | 30.27 |
| 1883 | 22 | 0 | 871 | 112 | 39.59 |
| 1884 | 22 | 4 | 672 | 116* | 37.33 |
| 1885 | 26 | 2 | 1,034 | 221* | 43.08 |
| 1886 | 26 | 2 | 714 | 110 | 29.75 |
| 1887 | 27 | 5 | 1,405 | 183* | 63.86 |
| 1888 | 28 | 1 | 1,068 | 215 | 39.55 |
| 1889 | 26 | 2 | 884 | 127* | 36.83 |
| 1890 | 29 | 2 | 930 | 109* | 34.44 |
| 1891 | 22 | 1 | 440 | 72* | 20.95 |
| 1892 | 25 | 3 | 802 | 99 | 36.45 |
| 1893 | 30 | 3 | 747 | 96 | 27.66 |
| 1894 | 33 | 1 | 633 | 88 | 19.78 |
| 1895 | 29 | 1 | 1,424 | 288 | 50.85 |
| 1896 | 36 | 3 | 1,693 | 301 | 51.30 |
| 1897 | 30 | 2 | 1,192 | 131 | 41.84 |
| 1898 | 28 | 4 | 1,141 | 168 | 47.54 |
| 1899 | 7 | 0 | 108 | 33 | 15.42 |
| Totals | 618 | 49 | 23,083 | 318* | 40.56 |

*Signifies not out.*

## W. G. GRACE'S HUNDREDS IN FIRST-CLASS CRICKET

224* England v Surrey at The Oval, 1866
173* Gentlemen of South v Players of South at The Oval, 1866
134* Gentlemen v Players at Lord's, 1868

130
102*⎫ South of Thames v North of Thames at Canterbury, 1868

117  MCC and Ground v Oxford University at Oxford, 1869
138* MCC and Ground v Surrey at The Oval, 1869
121  MCC and Ground v Nottinghamshire at Lord's, 1869
180  Gentlemen of South v Players of South at The Oval, 1869
122  South v North at Sheffield, 1869
127  MCC v Kent at Canterbury, 1869
117* MCC and Ground v Nottinghamshire at Lord's, 1870
215  Gentlemen v Players at The Oval, 1870
109  Gentlemen v Players at Lord's, 1870
143  Gloucestershire v Surrey at The Oval, 1870
172  Gloucestershire v MCC and Ground at Lord's, 1870
181  MCC and Ground v Surrey at Lord's, 1871
118  Gentlemen of South v Gentlemen of North at West Brompton, 1871
178  South v North at Lord's, 1871
162  Gentlemen of South v Cambridge University at Cambridge, 1871
189* Single v Married at Lord's, 1871
146  MCC and Ground v Surrey at The Oval, 1871
268  South v North at The Oval, 1871
117  MCC v Kent at Canterbury, 1871
217  Gentlemen v Players at Brighton, 1871
116  Gloucestershire v Nottinghamshire at Nottingham, 1871
101  MCC and Ground v Yorkshire at Lord's, 1872
112  Gentlemen v Players at Lord's, 1872
117  Gentlemen v Players at The Oval, 1872
170* England v Nottingham and Yorkshire at Lord's, 1872
114  South v North at The Oval, 1872
150  Gloucestershire v Yorkshire at Sheffield, 1872
145  Gentlemen of South v Players of North at Princes's, 1873
134  Gentlemen of South v Players of South at The Oval, 1873
163  Gentlemen v Players at Lord's, 1873
158  Gentlemen v Players at The Oval, 1873
152  Anglo-American XI v XV of MCC (with Rylott) at Lord's, 1873
192* South v North at The Oval, 1873
160* Gloucestershire v Surrey at Clifton, 1873
179  Gloucestershire v Sussex at Brighton, 1874
150  Gentlemen of South v Players of South at The Oval, 1874
104  Gentlemen of South v Players of North at Prince's, 1874
110  Gentlemen v Players at Prince's, 1874
167  Gloucestershire v Yorkshire at Sheffield, 1874
121  Kent and Gloucestershire v England at Canterbury, 1874
123  MCC v Kent at Canterbury, 1874
127  Gloucestershire v Yorkshire at Clifton, 1874
152  Gentlemen v Players at Lord's, 1875
111  Gloucestershire v Yorkshire at Sheffield, 1875
119† Gloucestershire v Nottinghamshire at Clifton, 1875
104  Gloucestershire v Sussex at Brighton, 1876
169  Gentlemen v Players at Lord's, 1876

## W. G. Grace's Hundreds – *continued*

114*  South v North at Nottingham, 1876
126   United South v United North at Hull, 1876
344   MCC v Kent at Canterbury, 1876
177   Gloucestershire v Nottinghamshire at Clifton, 1876
318*  Gloucestershire v Yorkshire at Cheltenham, 1876
261   South v North at Prince's, 1877
110   Gloucestershire and Yorkshire v England at Lord's, 1877
116   Gloucestershire v Nottinghamshire at Nottingham, 1878
123   Gloucestershire v Surrey at The Oval, 1879
102   Gloucestershire v Nottinghamshire at Nottingham, 1879
113   Gloucestershire v Somerset at Clifton, 1879
106   Gloucestershire v Lancashire at Clifton, 1880
152   England v Australia at The Oval, 1880
100   Gentlemen v Players at The Oval, 1881
182   Gloucestershire v Nottinghamshire at Nottingham, 1881
112   Gloucestershire v Lancashire at Clifton, 1883
101   MCC and Ground v Australians at Lord's, 1884
107   Gentlemen of England v Australians at The Oval, 1884
116*  Gloucestershire v Australians at Clifton, 1884
132   Gloucestershire v Yorkshire at Bradford, 1885
104   Gloucestershire v Surrey at Cheltenham, 1885
221*  Gloucestershire v Middlesex at Clifton, 1885
174   Gentlemen v Players at Scarborough, 1885
148   Gentlemen of England v Australians at The Oval, 1886
104   MCC and Ground v Oxford University at Oxford, 1886
110   Gloucestershire v Australians at Clifton, 1886
170   England v Australia at The Oval, 1886
113   Gloucestershire v Middlesex at Lord's, 1887
116*  MCC and Ground v Cambridge University at Lord's, 1887
183*  Gloucestershire v Yorkshire at Gloucester, 1887
113*  Gloucestershire v Nottinghamshire at Clifton, 1887
101 ⎫
103*⎭ Gloucestershire v Kent at Clifton, 1887
215   Gloucestershire v Sussex at Brighton, 1888
165   Gentlemen of England v Australians at Lord's, 1888
148 ⎫
153 ⎭ Gloucestershire v Yorkshire at Clifton, 1888
101   Gloucestershire v Middlesex at Lord's, 1889
127*  Gloucestershire v Middlesex at Cheltenham, 1889
154   South v North at Scarborough, 1889
109*  Gloucestershire v Kent at Maidstone, 1890
159*  England v Victoria at Melbourne, 1891-92
128   MCC and Ground v Kent at Lord's, 1893
139   MCC and Ground v Cambridge University at Cambridge, 1894
196   MCC and Ground v Cambridge University at Lord's, 1894
131   Gentlemen v Players at Hastings, 1894
103   MCC and Ground v Sussex at Lord's, 1895
288‡  Gloucestershire v Somerset at Bristol, 1895
257   Gloucestershire v Kent at Gravesend, 1895
169   Gloucestershire v Middlesex at Lord's, 1895
125   MCC and Ground v Kent at Lord's, 1895
101*  Gentlemen of England v I Zingari at Lord's, 1895

## W. G. Grace's Hundreds – *continued*

| | |
|---|---|
| 118 | Gentlemen v Players at Lord's, 1895 |
| 119 | Gloucestershire v Nottinghamshire at Cheltenham, 1895 |
| 104 | South v North at Hastings, 1895 |
| 243* | Gloucestershire v Sussex at Brighton, 1896 |
| 102* | Gloucestershire v Lancashire at Bristol, 1896 |
| 186 | Gloucestershire v Somerset at Taunton, 1896 |
| 301 | Gloucestershire v Sussex at Bristol, 1896 |
| 113 | Gloucestershire v Philadelphians at Bristol, 1897 |
| 126 | Gloucestershire v Nottinghamshire at Nottingham, 1897 |
| 116 | Gloucestershire v Sussex at Bristol, 1897 |
| 131 | Gloucestershire v Nottinghamshire at Cheltenham, 1897 |
| 126 | Gloucestershire v Essex at Leyton, 1898 |
| 168 | Gloucestershire v Nottinghamshire at Nottingham, 1898 |
| 109 | Gloucestershire v Somerset at Taunton, 1898 |
| 126 | South v North at Lord's, 1900 |
| 110* | London County v Worcestershire at Crystal Palace, 1900 |
| 110 | London County v MCC and Ground at Crystal Palace, 1900 |
| 132 | London County v MCC and Ground at Crystal Palace, 1901 |
| 131 | London County v MCC and Ground at Crystal Palace, 1902 |
| 129 | London County v Warwickshire at Crystal Palace, 1902 |
| 150 | London County v Gloucestershire at Crystal Palace, 1903 |
| 166 | London County v MCC and Ground at Crystal Palace, 1904 |

   * *Signifies not out.*
   † *His 50th century in first-class cricket;*     ‡ *his 100th.*

The above 126 scores were obtained thus:

5 for England; 6 for Gentlemen of England; 15 for Gentlemen (v Players); 51 for Gloucestershire; 1 for Gloucestershire and Kent; 1 for Gloucestershire and Yorkshire; 7 for London County; 4 for MCC; 15 for MCC and Ground; 1 for Single; 10 for South; 7 for Gentlemen of South; 1 for United South; 2 for South of Thames.

## TWO SEPARATE HUNDREDS IN A MATCH

| | |
|---|---|
| 130 and 102* | South of Thames v North of Thames at Canterbury, 1868 |
| 101 and 103* | Gloucestershire v Kent at Clifton, 1887 |
| 148 and 153 | Gloucestershire v Yorkshire at Clifton, 1888 |

The following feats are also noteworthy: –

| | |
|---|---|
| 94 and 121 | Kent and Gloucestershire v England at Canterbury, 1874 |
| 92 and 183* | Gloucestershire v Yorkshire at Gloucester, 1887 |
| 126 and 82 ˜ | United South v United North at Hull, 1876 |

   * *Signifies not out.*

## THREE SEPARATE HUNDREDS IN SUCCESSION

118 Gentlemen of South v Gentlemen of North at West Brompton ⎫
178 South v North at Lord's                                      ⎬ 1871
162 Gentlemen of England v Cambridge University at Cambridge ⎭
112 Gentlemen v Players at Lord's                              ⎫
117 Gentlemen v Players at The Oval                            ⎬ 1872
170* England v Nottingham and Yorkshire at Lord's             ⎭
134 Gentlemen of South v Players of South at The Oval         ⎫
163 Gentlemen v Players at Lord's                              ⎬ 1873
158 Gentlemen v Players at The Oval                            ⎭
121 Kent and Gloucestershire v England at Canterbury          ⎫
123 MCC v Kent at Canterbury                                    ⎬ 1874
127 Gloucestershire v Yorkshire at Clifton                     ⎭
344 MCC v Kent at Canterbury                                    ⎫
177 Gloucestershire v Nottinghamshire v Clifton                ⎬ 1876
318* Gloucestershire v Yorkshire at Cheltenham                 ⎭

*\* Signifies not out.*

For Gloucestershire in 1874 he played consecutive innings of 179 v Sussex at Brighton, 167 v Yorkshire at Sheffield, and 127 v Yorkshire at Clifton.

In consecutive innings for Gentlemen v Players in 1871-72-73 he scored 217, 77 and 112, 117, 163, 158, 70.

In May, 1895, when in his 47th year, he made the following scores in succession for Gloucestershire: 288 v Somerset at Bristol; 257 and 73* (winning the match by nine wickets) v Kent at Gravesend; 169 v Middlesex at Lords; and 91 v Sussex at Brighton.

## CARRYING BAT THROUGH A COMPLETED INNINGS

138 MCC and Ground v Surrey at The Oval, 1869
117 MCC and Ground v Nottinghamshire at Lord's, 1870
189 Single v Married at Lord's, 1871
 81 W. G. Grace's XI v Kent at Maidstone, 1871
170 England v Nottinghamshire and Yorkshire at Lord's, 1872
192 South v North at The Oval, 1873
318 Gloucestershire v Yorkshire at Cheltenham, 1876
221 Gloucestershire v Middlesex at Clifton, 1885
 81 MCC and Ground v Sussex at Lord's, 1887
113 Gloucestershire v Nottinghamshire at Clifton, 1887
 37 Gloucestershire v Lancashire at Bristol, 1889
127 Gloucestershire v Middlesex at Cheltenham, 1889
109 Gloucestershire v Kent at Maidstone, 1890
159 England v Victoria at Melbourne, 1891-92
 61 Gloucestershire v Surrey at The Oval, 1893
243 Gloucestershire v Sussex at Brighton, 1896
102 Gloucestershire v Lancashire at Bristol, 1896

## LARGE FIRST WICKET PARTNERSHIPS SHARED IN BY W. G. GRACE
(69)

283 W.G. (180) and B. B. Cooper (101) for Gentlemen of South v Players of South at The Oval, 1869

238 W.G. (150) and T. G. Matthews (85) for Gloucestershire v Yorkshire at Sheffield, 1872

226 W.G. (154) and Abel, R. (105) for South v North at Scarborough, 1889

203 W.G. (152) and A. J. Webbe (65) for Gentlemen v Players at Lord's, 1875

175 W.G. (73) and C. I. Thornton (107) for Gentlemen of England v I Zingari at Scarborough, 1887

172* W.G. (101*) and A. Sellers (70*) for Gentlemen of England v I Zingari at Lord's, 1895, (Made in 105 minutes, winning the match by ten wickets.)

170 W.G. (170) and Scotton, W. H. (34) for England v Australia at The Oval, 1886

169 W.G. (109) and W. Troup (127) for Gloucestershire v Somerset at Taunton, 1898

168 W.G. (71) and A. Marshal (94) for Gentlemen of England v Oxford University at Oxford, 1905

164 W.G. (215) and J. W. Dale (55) for Gentlemen v Players at The Oval, 1870

163 W.G. (72) and Quaife, W. G. (108) for London County v Cambridge University at the Crystal Palace, 1901

161 W.G. (88) and Smith, John, of Cambridge (81) for MCC and Ground v Middlesex at Lord's, 1871

161 W.G. (85) and W. R. Gilbert (99) for Gloucestershire v Middlesex at Clifton, 1879

160 W.G. (93) and C. J. B. Wood (88) for London County v Cambridge University at the Crystal Palace, 1900

158 W.G. (165) and J. Shuter (71) for Gentlemen of England v Australians at Lord's, 1888

156 W.G. (83) and E. M. Grace (70) for Gloucestershire v Surrey at The Oval, 1873

156 W.G. (92) and Scotton, W. H. (71) for Lord Londesborough's XI v Australians at Scarborough, 1886

154 W.G. (98) and Jupp, H. (80) for South v North at Canterbury, 1873

154 W.G. (73) and W. L. Murdoch (74) for London County v Leicestershire at the Crystal Palace, 1904

151 W.G. (68) and A. E. Stoddart (83) for England v Australia at The Oval, 1893

151 W.G. (118) and A. E. Stoddart (71) for Gentlemen v Players at Lord's, 1895

150 W.G. (104) and A. E. Stoddart (71) for South v North at Hastings, 1895

149 W.G. (123) and I. D. Walker (37) for MCC v Kent at Canterbury, 1874

146 W.G. (64) and Marshal, A. (75) for W. G. Grace's XI v Cambridge University at Cambridge, 1906

142 W.G. (80) and C. J. B. Wood (70) for London County v Surrey at the Crystal Palace, 1901 (second innings.)

140 W.G. (79) and G. J. Mordaunt (55) for MCC and Ground v Oxford University at Lord's, 1897

139 W.G. (172) and C. S. Gordon (53) for Gloucestershire v MCC and Ground at Lord's, 1870

139 W.G. (90) and E. M. Grace (69) for Gloucestershire v Lancashire at Clifton, 1890

137 W.G. (127) and E. M. Grace (51) for Gloucestershire v Yorkshire at Clifton, 1874

134 W.G. (96) and Jupp, H. (63*) for South v North at Canterbury, 1869

134 W.G. (78) and E. M. Grace (65) for Gloucestershire v Nottinghamshire at Clifton, 1871

131 W.G. (71) and C. J. B. Wood (66) for London County v Surrey at the Crystal Palace, 1901 (first innings.)

130 W.G. (52) and A. E. Stoddart (84) for A. J. Webbe's XI v Cambridge University at Cambridge, 1895

## Large Partnerships for First Wicket (69) – *continued*

130   W.G. (61) and C. B.Fry (82) for London County v Surrey at The Oval, 1902

127   W.G. (117*) and I. D. Walker (48) for MCC and Ground v Nottinghamshire at Lord's, 1870

127   W.G. (101) and E. M. Grace (70) for Gloucestershire v Kent at Clifton, 1887

126   W.G. (169) and C. J. Ottaway (42) for Gentlemen v Players at Lord's, 1876

122   W.G. (82) and Arnold, E. G. (58) for London County v Warwickshire at Edgbaston, 1900

121   W.G. (114) and Jupp, H. (40) for South v North at The Oval, 1872

121   W.G. (83) and F. L. Fane (54) for London County v Leicestershire at the Crystal Palace, 1901

120   W.G. (45) and A. E. Stoddart (74) for MCC and Ground v Australians, at Lord's, 1893

120   W.G. (61*) and W. L. Murdoch (68) for MCC and Ground v Lancashire at Lord's 1902

119   W.G. (152) and C. J. Ottaway (52) for Anglo-American XI v XV of MCC (with Rylott) at Lords, 1873

119   W.G. (54) and A. O. Jones (105) for Gentlemen v Players at Hastings, 1901

119   W.G. (82) and G. W. Beldam (57) for Gentlemen v Players at The Oval, 1902

118   W.G. (57) and J. J. Ferris (60) for Gentlemen v Players at The Oval, 1893

118   W.G. (54) and H. H. Burton (59) for London County v Leicestershire at the Crystal Palace, 1904

118   W.G. (166) and W. L. Murdoch (51) for London County v MCC and Ground at the Crystal Palace, 1904

117   W.G. (46) and E. M. Grace (78) for Gloucestershire v Sussex at Bristol, 1890

116   W.G. (67) and C. Booth (78) for MCC and Ground v Oxford University at Lord's 1876

115   W.G. (121) and Lord Harris (33) for Kent and Gloucestershire v England at Canterbury, 1874

114   W.G. (49) and A. E. Stoddart (94) for Shrewsbury's XI v Australians at Nottingham, 1893

113   W.G. (51) and E. M. Grace (73) for Gloucestershire v Sussex at Cheltenham, 1873

113   W.G. (40) and A. C. MacLaren (72) for England v Surrey and Sussex at Hastings, 1898

111   W.G. (29) and A. E. Stoddart (115) for South v North at Lord's, 1890

111   W.G. (76) and W. L. Murdoch (55) for London County v Warwickshire at the Crystal Palace, 1900

107   W.G. (117) and J. W. Dale (36) for MCC v Kent at Canterbury, 1871

106   W.G. (70) and J. J. Ferris (53) for Gloucestershire v Warwickshire at Bristol, 1895

106   W.G. (63) and R. W. Rice (42) for Gloucestershire v Nottinghamshire at Bristol, 1898

106   W.G. (168) and W. Troup (37) for Gloucestershire v Nottinghamshire at Nottingham, 1898

105   W.G. (83) and B. B. Cooper (40) for Gentlemen v Players at The Oval, 1869

105   W.G. (101) and O. G. Radcliffe (55) for Gloucestershire v Middlesex at Lord's, 1889

104   W.G. (80) and E. M. Grace (52) for Gloucestershire v Somerset at Bath, 1881

104   W.G. (148) and W. H. Patterson (44) for Gentlemen of England v Australians at The Oval, 1886

103   W.G. (162) and A. J. A. Wilkinson (19) for Gentlemen of England v Cambridge University at Cambridge, 1871

103   W.G. (73) and Hearne, F.(34) for MCC and Ground v Sussex at Lord's, 1888

101   W.G. (114*) and A. J. Webbe (41) for South v North at Nottingham, 1876

**Large Partnerships for First Wicket** (69) – *continued*

101   W.G. (63) and Shrewsbury, A. (62) for Lord Sheffield's XI v Australians at Sheffield Park, 1893

100   W.G. (36) and A. E. Stoddart (71) for South v North at Hastings, 1891

*\* Denotes an unfinished partnership or not out.*

In three consecutive innings which they opened together against the Australians in 1893, W.G. and A. E. Stoddart made 120, 114 and 151 in partnership.

## LARGE PARTNERSHIPS FOR OTHER WICKETS (12)

281   for 2nd, W.G. (261) and J. M. Cotterill (88) for South v North at Prince's, 1877

281   for 3rd, W.G. (132) and L. Walker (222) for London County v MCC and Ground at the Crystal Palace, 1901

261   for 5th, W.G. (318\*) and W. O. Moberly (103) for Gloucestershire v Yorkshire at Cheltenham, 1876

256   for 2nd, W.G. (139) and Chatterton, W. (113) for MCC and Ground v Cambridge University at Cambridge, 1894

255\*  for 3rd, W.G. (160\*) and E. M. Knapp (90\*) for Gloucestershire v Surrey at Clifton, 1873

248   for 7th, W.G. (243\*) and E. L. Thomas (109) for Gloucestershire v Sussex at Brighton, 1896

241   for 2nd, W.G. (217) and G. F. Grace (98) for Gentlemen v Players at Brighton, 1871

234   for 2nd, W.G. (143) and F. Townsend (89) for Gloucestershire v Surrey at The Oval, 1870

227   for 5th, W.G. (344) and P. C. Crutchley (84) for MCC v Kent at Canterbury, 1876

233   for 3rd, W.G. (288) and C. L. Townsend (95) for Gloucestershire v Somerset at Bristol, 1895

211   for 2nd, W.G. (301) and R. W. Rice (84) for Gloucestershire v Sussex at Bristol, 1896

200   for 3rd, W.G. (196) and K. S. Ranjitsinhji (94) for MCC and Ground v Cambridge University at Lord's, 1894

*\* Denotes an unfinished partnership or not out.*

## MEN WHO HAVE CLEAN-BOWLED W. G. GRACE IN FIRST-CLASS CRICKET

| 20 Times | 9 Times | 6 Times |
|---|---|---|
| Shaw, A. | Peate, E. | Bates, W. |
| | Shaw, J. C. | Hearne, J. T. |
| **14 Times** | | Martin, F. |
| Richardson, T. | | G. E. Palmer |
| | | Peel, R. |
| **13 Times** | **8 Times** | A. G. Steel |
| Barlow, R. G. | Flowers, W. | Wootton, G. |
| | Southerton, J. | |
| **11 Times** | | **5 Times** |
| Morley, F. | | Attewell, W. |
| | | Barnes, W. |
| **10 Times** | **7 Times** | G. Giffen |
| Briggs, J. | Lohmann, G. A. | Lillywhite, Jas., jun. |
| Emmett, T. | F. R. Spofforth | Mold, A. |
| Hill, A. | C. T. B. Turner | Wainwright, E. |

## 4 Times

Hearne, A.
Mycroft, W.
Tate, F. W.
H. Trumble
Watson, A.

## 3 Times

Bean, G.
Cuttell, W. R.
J. J. Ferris
Freeman, G.
Haigh, S.
Hide, A.
Lees, W. S.
Lockwood, W. H.
McIntyre, W.
M. A. Noble
Parris, F.
J. Robertson†
Sharpe, J. W.
Willsher, E.
Young, H.

## Twice

Bland, C. H. G.
Bowley, T.
Burton, G.
S. E. Busher
A. Collins
Crossland, J.
L. T. Driffield
Fairservice, J. W.
Gill, G. C.
Harrison, G. P.
Hide, J. B.
W. P. Howell
Howitt, G.
Humphreys, W. A.
E. Jones
R. W. McLeod
Mead, W.
Quaife, W. G.
T. C. Ross
Santall, S.
Silcock, F.
E. Smith
E. E. Steel
Trott, A. E.
Woodcock, A.
S. M. J. Woods
Wright, W.

## Once

Abel, R.
Adams, (Surrey)
W. W. Armstrong
Arnold, E. G.
L. H. Bacmeister
Barratt, E.
A. R. Bennett
Blake, F.
H. F. Boyle
W. M. Bradley
G. T. Branston
Brockwell, W.
C. A. Brown
W. Bruce
J. Burrough
L. Bury
Buxton, N.
J. F. Byrne
S. T. Callaway
S. Christopherson
Clayton, R. O.
A. H. J. Cochrane
Coe, S.
E. R. de Little
Eastwood, D.
A. H. Evans
Field, F. E.
Fillery, R.
W. Foord-Kelcey
W. F. Forbes
F. G. J. Ford
H. W. Forster
T. W. Garrett
Greenwood, L.
Gunn, J.
Gunn, W.
Handford, A.
J. C. Hartley
Hayward, T. (Cambs.)
Hayward, T. (Surrey)
Hearne, G. G.
Hearne, T.
Hearne, W.
W. C. Hedley
Hicks, J.
Hickton, W.
H. G. Hill
Holland, F. C.
Hughes, J.
Hulme, J.
Iddison, R.
Johnson, F.

N. A. Knox
C. J. Kortright
A. E. Lawton
O. H. Layne
R. Lipscomb
Llewellyn, C. B.
H. T. Luddington
J. McCormick
R. F. Miles
Nash, G.
Needham, F.
Nice, E. H. L.
O'Connor, J.
A. Penn
Potter, J.
W. N. Powys
Read, J. M.
Rhodes, W.
Richardson, H.
Roberts, F. G.
J. J. Robinson
Robson, E.
W. E. Roller
Sewell, T., jun.
V. K. Shaw
Smith, F. E.
Smith, W. C.
Storer, W.
G. Strachan
Street, J.
A. S. Teape
Tester, W. A.
G. Thornton
C. Tillard
G. H. S. Trott
V. T. Trumper
C. F. Tufnell
Tye, J.
Tyler, E. J.
Ulyett, G.
I. D. Walker
A. J. Webbe
W. B. Weighell
Whitehead, H.
Whitehead, L.
Whittle, A. E.
Wild, F.
A. J. A. Wilkinson
C. E. M. Wilson
E. R. Wilson
C. Winter
Wootton, J.
C. Wreford-Brown

† *Now Robertson-Walker.*

## EIGHT OR MORE WICKETS IN AN INNINGS

| | | |
|---|---|---|
| 8-10 | Gentlemen of South v Players of South at The Oval ................. | 1865 |
| 8-25 | Gentlemen v Players at Lord's ................................... | 1867 |
| 8-33 | Gloucestershire v Yorkshire at Sheffield ........................ | 1872 |
| 10-92 | MCC v Kent at Canterbury (12 a-side) ......................... | 1873 |
| 9-48 | South v North at Loughborough ............................... | 1875 |
| 8-69 | Gloucestershire v Nottinghamshire at Clifton ................... | 1876 |
| 8-36 | South v North at Lord's ...................................... | 1877 |
| 8-54 | MCC and Ground v Derbyshire at Lord's ....................... | 1877 |
| 9-55 } 8-34 } | Gloucestershire v Nottinghamshire at Cheltenham ............... | 1877 |
| 8-23 | MCC and Ground v Derbyshire at Lord's ....................... | 1878 |
| 8-81 | Gloucestershire v Surrey at Cirencester ........................ | 1879 |
| 8-31 | Gloucestershire v Somerset at Gloucester ...................... | 1882 |
| 8-93 | Gloucestershire v Australians at Clifton ........................ | 1882 |
| 9-20 | MCC and Ground v Nottinghamshire at Lord's .................. | 1885 |
| 10-49 | MCC and Ground v Oxford University at Oxford ................ | 1886 |
| 8-37 | MCC and Ground v Sussex at Lord's .......................... | 1889 |

## THIRTEEN OR MORE WICKETS IN A MATCH

| | | |
|---|---|---|
| 13-84 | Gentlemen of South v Players of South at The Oval ................ | 1865 |
| 15-79 | Gloucestershire v Yorkshire at Sheffield ........................ | 1872 |
| 15-147 | MCC v Kent at Canterbury (12 a-side) ......................... | 1873 |
| 14-66 | Gloucestershire v Surrey at Cheltenham ........................ | 1874 |
| 13-98 | Gloucestershire v Yorkshire at Clifton ......................... | 1875 |
| 14-108 | South v North at Loughborough ............................... | 1875 |
| 14-109 | MCC and Ground v Derbyshire at Lord's ....................... | 1877 |
| 17-89 | Gloucestershire v Nottinghamshire at Cheltenham ............... | 1877 |
| 13-106 | Gloucestershire v Sussex at Cheltenham ....................... | 1878 |
| 15-116 | Gloucestershire v Surrey at Cirencester ........................ | 1879 |
| 16-60 | MCC and Ground v Nottinghamshire at Lord's .................. | 1885 |
| 13-110 | London County v MCC and Ground at Lord's ................... | 1901 |

## FOUR WICKETS OR MORE FOR THREE RUNS OR LESS EACH

| | | |
|---|---|---|
| 6-10 | MCC and Ground v Lancashire at Lord's ....................... | 1869 |
| 7-19 | MCC and Ground v Hertfordshire at Chorleywood ................ | 1873 |
| 7-18 | Gloucestershire v Surrey at Cheltenham ....................... | 1874 |
| 8-23 | MCC and Ground v Derbyshire at Lord's ....................... | 1878 |
| 6-18 | Gloucestershire v Sussex at Cheltenham ....................... | 1878 |
| 6-16 | Gloucestershire v Middlesex at Lord's .......................... | 1879 |
| 9-20 | MCC and Ground v Nottinghamshire at Lord's .................. | 1885 |

## BOWLING UNCHANGED THROUGH BOTH COMPLETED INNINGS

With I. D. Walker for Gentlemen of South v Players of South at The Oval ....... †1865
With Wootton, G. for MCC and Ground v Staffordshire at Lord's ............. 1873
With W. R. Gilbert for Gloucestershire v Lancashire at Clifton ............... 1878

† *Aged 16.*

## A THREE-FIGURE INNINGS AND TEN WICKETS OR MORE IN ONE MATCH

| | | |
|---|---|---|
| 134* | Gentlemen v Players at Lord's, 1868 | 10-81 |
| 117 | MCC v Kent at Canterbury, 1871 | †12-146 |
| 114 | South v North at The Oval, 1872 | 11-126 |
| 150 | Gloucestershire v Yorkshire at Sheffield, 1872 | 15-79 |
| 179 | Gloucestershire v Sussex at Brighton, 1874 | 12-158 |
| 23 110 } | Gentlemen v Players at Prince's, 1874 | 10-119 |
| 167 | Gloucestershire v Yorkshire at Sheffield, 1874 | 11-101 |
| 94 121 } | Gloucestershire and Kent v England at Canterbury, 1874 | ‡10-160 |
| 123 | MCC v Kent at Canterbury, 1874 | †‡11-129 |
| 127 | Gloucestershire v Yorkshire at Clifton, 1874 | ‡10-124 |
| 7 152 } | Gentlemen v Players at Lord's, 1875 | 12-125 |
| 261 | South v North at Prince's, 1877 | 11-139 |
| 221* | Gloucestershire v Middlesex at Clifton, 1885 | 11-120 |
| 104 | MCC and Ground v Oxford University at Oxford, 1886 | 12-169 |

(Including all ten wickets in second innings.)

*\* Signifies not out. † 12 a-side. ‡ Consecutive matches.*

## FIRST-CLASS CRICKET MEMORABILIA

**1865** – Appeared for the first time, at the age of 16, for Gentlemen v Players, at The Oval. He scored 23 and 12* and took seven wickets for 125 runs.

**1866** – His first match for the South v the North, at Lord's. He made 19, and took one wicket for 33 runs.

Aged 18, he scored 224 not out for England v Surrey, at The Oval, and 173 not out for Gentlemen of South v Players of South on the same ground, thereby earning the title of Champion.

**1868** – His first match for Gloucestershire v MCC and Ground at Lord's. He scored 24 and 13, and took five wickets.

Scored 134 not out, whilst only 57 other runs were made, of a total of 201 for Gentlemen v Players, at Lord's. The runs were obtained on very bad and difficult ground, and the only other double-figure score for the side was 28 by B. B. Cooper, and the next highest in the match 29 not out by Grundy.

For North of Thames v South of Thames, at Canterbury, he scored 130 and 102 not out, this being the first occasion since 1817 on which two separate hundreds had been made by anyone in a match of note. W.G. was then 20 years of age, and he obtained his runs off Wootton, Howitt, Grundy, and Hearne, T.

**1869** – W.G. was elected a member of the MCC, being proposed by T. Burgoyne (Treasurer) and seconded by R. A. FitzGerald (Secretary). In his first innings for the Club v Oxford University, at Oxford – he scored 117.

In making 283 for the first wicket of Gentlemen of South v Players of South, at The Oval, W.G. (180) and B.B. Cooper (101) established a record for first-class cricket.

For North v South, at Sheffield, he scored 122 of the total of 173, the next highest innings for the side being 23 by B. B. Cooper.

**1870** – W.G. scored 117 not out, for MCC and Ground v Nottinghamshire at Lord's, but when he had made about 60 he played-on hard from a ball from Shaw, J. C. without a bail falling.

In his innings of 109 for Gentlemen v Players, at Lord's, were as many as 54 singles, but the fieldsmen were placed deep.

**1871** – In the match between Gentlemen of England and Cambridge University, at Cambridge, W.G. (162) and A. J. A. Wilkinson made 103 runs before the first wicket fell, the latter scoring only 19 of the number, so fast did the Champion obtain his runs.

In first-class cricket this year W.G. scored 2,739 runs, this being the first time that any batsman obtained as many as 2,000 in a single season in such matches.

**1873** – For Gentlemen v Players, at The Oval, W.G. scored 158, but when 44 had his wicket hit by a ball bowled by Emmett without a bail being disturbed.

**1876** – For Gloucestershire v Yorkshire, at Sheffield, the three brothers Grace had a hand in getting out the whole of the Yorkshire Eleven in both innings.

In first innings of United South v United North, at Hull, W.G. scored 126 out of 153 in 165 minutes: the only other score above 4 in the completed innings of 159 (5 extras) was 14 by Pooley.

By making 344 for MCC v Kent, at Canterbury, the Doctor set up a fresh record for first-class cricket, exceeding William Ward's 278 for MCC v Norfolk (with E. H. Budd, T. Vigne, and F. C. Ladbroke) at Lord's in 1820. In his two following innings he made 177 for Gloucestershire v Nottinghamshire at Clifton, and 318 not out for Gloucestershire v Yorkshire at Cheltenham, thus obtaining 839 runs in three innings, once not out, in ten days.

**1877** – In the course of his innings of 261 for South v North, at Prince's, his own score was 202 with the total 300.

For Gloucestershire v Nottinghamshire, at Cheltenham, W.G. obtained 17 wickets, nine in the first innings and eight in the second. With the last forty-one balls he delivered he took seven wickets without a run.

**1878** – As W.G. was running between the wickets in Gloucestershire's match v Surrey, at Clifton, the ball was thrown in and it lodged in his shirt. After running six runs – three with the ball in his possession – he was stopped, and Jupp asked him to give up the ball, but this he wisely declined to do, as he might have been adjudged out for handling the ball.

**1879** – On the second day of the match at Lord's between Over 30 and under 30, W.G. was presented, in front of the pavilion, with a national testimonial in the form of a handsome clock, of the value of 40 guineas, and a cheque for £1,458. The list was headed by the MCC with 100 guineas, and HRH the Prince of Wales was among the subscribers. In the absence in America of the Duke of Beaufort, the presentation was made by Lord Fitzhardinge. It had been arranged that the Over 30 v Under 30 match should be a complimentary one for the Doctor, and the proceeds added to his testimonial fund, but with great liberality he suggested that it should be played for the benefit of Alfred Shaw, whose match earlier in the season – between North and South – had been ruined by the weather.

**1885** – For Gentlemen v Players, at Scarborough, W.G. scored 174 not out of 247 in 235 minutes on a treacherous wicket. The next highet score in the completed innings of 263 (six extras) was 21 by T. C. O'Brien.

For An Eleven of England v Shaw's Australian Team, at Harrogate, he scored 51 of the first 53 runs.

**1886** – For MCC and Ground v Oxford University, at Oxford, W.G. scored 104 and took all ten wickets in the second innings for 49 runs.

For England v Australia at The Oval, W.G. made 170 out of 216 in four hours and a-half. With Scotton, who scored 34, he obtained 170 for the first wicket.

**1888** – For MCC and Ground v Sussex at Lord's, he scored 73 out of 103 in seventy minutes.

**1889** – This year his portrait was painted for the MCC at the cost of £300 by Archibald Stuart Wortley. Private subscriptions for the same were limited to £1. In the following year the portrait was exhibited at the Royal Academy in gallery X, No. 1003.

**1890** – In the second innings of the North v South match, at Lord's, A. E. Stoddart (115) at one period of his innings made 50 runs whilst W.G. was obtaining 3.

**1895** – Aged 46, W.G. scored 1,016 runs during the month of May with an average of 112:

| | |
|---|---|
| 13 and 103 | MCC and Ground v Sussex, at Lord's. |
| 18 and 25 | MCC and Ground v Yorkshire, at Lord's. |
| 288 | Gloucestershire v Somerset, at Bristol. |
| 52 | A. J. Webbe's XI v Cambridge University, at Cambridge. |
| 257 and 73* | Gloucestershire v Kent, at Gravenend. |
| 18 | England v Surrey, at The Oval. |
| 169 | Gloucestershire v Middlesex, at Lord's. |

At lunch-time on the third day of the match at Gravesend only an innings each had been completed, yet Gloucestershire won by nine wickets. W.G. was on the field during every ball of the game. In appreciation of his wonderful rejuvenescence, a National Testimonial was organized, the *Daily Telegraph* collecting £5,000 (by means of a shilling subscription) and the MCC £2,377 2s., less £21 8s. 10d. expenses. He was entertained at banquets both in London and Bristol, that at the latter place being organized by the Gloucestershire County CC.

Gentlemen of England, set 172 to win v I Zingari, at Lord's, made the runs without loss of a wicket in 105 minutes, W.G. scoring 101* and A. Sellers 70*. It was the Zingari Jubilee match.

**1898** – The Gentlemen v Players match at Lord's was commenced on W.G.'s 50th birthday, and every man who took part in it was presented by the MCC, with a medal struck in honour of the occasion. The Champion scored 43 and 31 not out and took a wicket. On the second day of the match he was entertained at dinner by the Sports Club, Sir Richard Webster (Lord Alverstone) presiding.

In the second innings of Gloucestershire's match v Sussex, at Bristol, W.G. declared when he had made 93, thereby crediting himself with having obtained every number 0 to 100 in first-class cricket.

**1899** – In January, W.G. formed the London County CC, with headquarters at the Crystal Palace.

His last match for Gloucestershire v Middlesex, at Lord's. He scored 11 and 33 and bowled 20 balls for 10 runs and one wicket.

His last Test match v Australia, at Nottingham. He made 28 and 1, and delivered 110 balls for 37 runs without obtaining a wicket.

In December he was elected a life-member of the MCC on the suggestion of Lord Harris.

**1900** – In scoring 169 for Oxford University v London County, at Oxford, R. E. Foster made four sixes from consecutive balls from W.G.

Aged 52, he scored 72 and 110 not out for London County v Worcestershire, at the Crystal Palace.

In the first innings of South v North, at Lord's, P. F. Warner drove back to ball to E. Smith, who turned it on to the broad back of W.G., who was batting at the other end. Off the rebound Smith made the catch, Warner thereby being caught and bowled.

**1902** – In the second innings of MCC and Ground v Lancashire, at Lord's, W.G. made a hit to leg off Hallows, the ball going over the grand-stand and out of the ground into an adjoining garden.

For London County v Ireland, at the Crystal Palace, W.G. (32) and W. I. Murdoch (41) made 75 for the first wicket, but the whole side were out for 92.

**1904** – His last match (in first-class cricket) for MCC and Ground v South Africans, at Lord's. He scored 27.

**1905** – Playing for Gentlemen of England v Surrey, at The Oval, W.G. pulled a ball from J. N. Crawford right out of the ground, scoring 6, and sent the next delivery from the same bowler almost as far for 4.

His last match for the South v Australians, at Hastings. He scored 2.

**1906** – A. E. Harragin, for West Indians v W. G. Grace's XI, at the Crystal Palace, scored three 6s and a 2 off an over from W.G.

At the Oval W.G. made his 85th, and last, appearance for Gentlemen v Players. He made 4 and 74, obtaining the latter number on his 58th birthday.

**1908** – His last appearance in first-class cricket – for Gentlemen of England v Surrey, at The Oval. He scored 15 and 25, and bowled twelve balls for 5 runs without taking a wicket.


## SPECTACLES

XXII of Lansdown v The England Eleven, on the Sydenham Field, Bath, May 28, 29, 30, 1863.

c Clarke, A. b Tinley 0; c Anderson b Tinley, 0.


Clifton v Lansdown, on the Sydenham Field, Bath, August 7, 8, 1863.

lbw, b E. M. Grace, 0; b E. M. Grace, 0.


USEE v XXII of the Cadoxton CC (with Howitt), in Knoll Park, Neath, May 21, 22, 23, 1868

c Stuve b Howitt, 0; c and b Howitt, 0.


Bedminster v Great Western Railway (Swindon), at Bedminster, May 7, 1870.

c and b Laverick, 0; c Dormand b Laverick 0.

The Doctor never performed this easy feat in a first-class match.


## AN AGGREGATE OF 3,000 RUNS IN A SEASON

|      |                                    | Average |
|------|------------------------------------|---------|
| 1870 | 3,255 runs in 67 completed innings | 48.58 |
| 1871 | 3,234 runs in 48 completed innings | 67.37 |
| 1872† | 3,030 runs in 63 completed innings | 48.09 |
| 1874‡ | 3,505 runs in 74 completed innings | 47.36 |
| 1876 | 3,908 runs in 72 completed innings | 54.27 |

† *Including the trip to America; and* ‡ *the tour through Australia.*

The runs obtained in first-class matches are included in the above totals.
In 1874, 1875, 1877, and 1878 he took over 300 wickets during the season.

## HUNDREDS IN MINOR MATCHES (91)

170  South Wales v Gentlemen of Sussex, 1864
126  Clifton v Fowne's XI, 1864
157  Clifton v Belmont, 1866
150* Clifton v Clifton College, 1866
101  Bedminster v Lansdown, 1866
118  W. Absolon's XI v Eastern Counties Club, 1866
111  Bedminster v Lansdown, 1868
210  Clifton v Civil Service, 1868
100  Bedminster v Lansdown, 1869
172* Stapleton v Knowle, 1869
111  Stapleton v Swindon, 1869
108  W. G. Grace's XI v Lillington's XI (Bedminster), 1870
197  Gloucestershire v Glamorganshire, 1870
109  Frenchay v Thornbury, 1870
115  United South EE v XXII of Sleaford and District, 1870
112  United South EE v XXII of Glasgow and District, 1872
142  R. A. FitzGerald's Team v XXII of Toronto, 1872
126  England v XXII of Ballarat, 1873-74
126  England v A Victorian XI, 1873-74
259  Thornbury v Clifton, 1874
109  MCC and Ground v Gentlemen of Herefordshire, 1874
153  United South EE v XXII of Leinster, 1874
110  Thornbury v Knole Park, 1875
112  United South EE v XVIII of Trinity College, Dublin, 1875
152  United South EE v XVIII of North Kent, 1875
210  United South EE v XVIII of Hastings and District, 1875
400  United South EE v XVIII of Grimsby and District, 1876
133  United South EE v XVIII of Stockport, 1876
109  United South EE v XVIII of Grange, Edinburgh, 1877
124  United South EE v XXII of Stockport and District, 1877
110  Lord Westmorland's XI v Burghley Park, 1877
126* Married v Single (Clifton), 1880
152  Bedminster v Lansdown, 1880
168* Bristol Medicals v Thornbury, 1880
140  Lansdown v Clifton, 1880
128  Thornbury v Old Sneed Park, 1880
196* Thornbury v Jas. Thorne's XI, 1881
203  Bedminster v St George's, 1881
109  Clifton v Newport, 1881
124  Bedminster v St George's, 1881
144  Thornbury v Baker, Baker & Co., 1882
126  Lansdown v Western Wanderers, 1882
130  Thornbury v Bath Association, 1882
177* Thornbury v Chepstow, 1882
122* United XI v XXII of Market Bosworth, 1882
111  Thornbury v Lansdown, 1883
142  Bedminster v Swindon, 1883
151* Thornbury v Newport, 1883
111  Gloucestershire v XXIV Colts, 1884
131  Clifton v Taunton, 1884
136  Thornbury v Chepstow, 1884
107  East Somerset v Cardiff, 1884

### Hundreds in Minor Matches – *continued*

166   Bedminster v St George's, 1885
100* O. G. Radcliffe's XI v Cardiff, 1885
182   Thornbury v St George's, 1889
174   Thornbury v St George's, 1891
204* Thornbury v Bath Association, 1893
135   W. G. Grace's XI v W. W. Read's XI, 1893
129* Gloucestershire v South Africans, 1894
101* Gloucestershire v XXII Colts, 1895
108   Gloucestershire v XXII Colts, 1896
121   W. G. Grace's XI v Dublin University, 1897
146* Gloucestershire v XXII Colts, 1898
175* London County v Worcestershire, 1899
109   London County v Croydon, 1899
130   Crystal Palace v Beckenham, 1899
100* London County v Ealing, 1899
103* London County v Sydenham, 1899
110* London County v Gravenend, 1900
151* London County v Wanderers, 1900
116* London County v Northern Nomads, 1900
100* London County v Oundle Rovers, 1900
111   London County v HMS *Wildfire*, 1901
114   Worcester Park Beagles v London County, 1901
100   London County v HMS *Wildfire*, 1901
188* London County v Wiltshire, 1901
174   London County v Croydon, 1901
103* London County v XIX of Sydenham Park, 1902
101* London County v Anerley, 1902
137* London County v Heathfield, 1902
127   London County v Wiltshire, 1902
119   London County v Bradford, 1903
104* London County v Belgrave, 1903
103* London County v Clapham, 1904
104* London County v Clare College Rovers, 1905
120   London County v Kensington, 1906
147   London County v Beddington, 1906
140   London County v Forest Hill, 1907
102* London County v Cyphers, 1907
118   London County v Catford, 1907
110* London County v Whitgift Wanderers, 1908

  * *Signifies not out.*

Note – In the match v XXII of Stockport, in 1876, W.G., in his second innings, was bowled by Randon, F. for 13, but later was asked to go in again with the result that he ran up a score of 133.

## MEMORABILIA OF MINOR CRICKET

**1857** – His first match – for West Gloucestershire v Bedminster, at Rodway Hill, July 19. He scored 3 not out.

**1860** – Makes his first half-century – 51 for West Gloucestershire v Clifton, on Durdham Down, July 19, 20.

**1862** – Aged 14. Plays for Gentlemen of Gloucestershire v Gentlemen of Devon, at Teignbridge, and scores 18 and 1.

**1864** – Aged 15, makes 170 and 56 not out for South Wales v Gentlemen of Sussex, at Brighton. He also obtained two wickets.

Made his first appearance at Lord's – for South Wales v MCC and Ground – and scored 50 and 2, and took a wicket.

**1868** – At the athletic sports at The Oval, during the visit of the Australian Aboriginals, W.G., in three successive attempts, threw the cricket ball 116, 117, and 118 yards, and also threw it 109 yards one way and back 105. He once threw it 122 yards at Eastbourne.

W.G. and G. F. Grace, playing for Clifton v Gloucester, at Bristol, obtained all twenty wickets of their opponents, W.G. taking nine of them.

**1870** – In a single-wicket match – for V of the United North EE v XI of Northampton-shire, at Northampton – W.G. made only three singles in a score of 63.

**1872** – Visited the United States and Canada as a member of Mr R. A. FitzGerald's team.

**1873** – In a practice-match, for United South EE v XVIII of Edinburgh, at Raeburn Place, W.G. made a hit of 140 yards.

For United South EE v XXII of Coventry (with Greenwood, L.) he took twenty-five wickets (fourteen and eleven) and made five catches off other bowling, thus claiming thirty wickets in a match.

**1873-74** – Captained a team in Australia, which played fifteen matches (all against odds), winning ten, losing three, and drawing two.

**1874** – In match, W. G. Grace's XI v F. Townsend's XI, at Cheltenham, the arrangement was that W.G. should use a broomstick, each of the other players being allowed a bat. Even so handicapped, he made the second largest score (35) in the game.

**1875** – Col (then Capt.) J. Fellowes, RE, playing at Gravesend for XVIII of North Kent v United South EE, made 20 runs (three 6s – all over the pavilion – and a two) off a four-ball over from W.G.

**1876** – For United South EE v XXII of Grimsby, at Grimsby, he scored 400 not out, batting thirteen and a half hours against fifteen bowlers, hitting four 6s and twenty-one 4s, and offering no chance until 350. This is the record score against odds. *Scores and Biographies* (xiv–cvii) says: "Of this match it was subsequently stated that Mr W. G. Grace's score was 399, not 400, one being added to make the enormous total."

**1879** – For Kingsclere v Newbury, at Kingsclere, he took all ten wickets in an innings.

**1880** – In the XIII a-side match between Thornbury and Lansdown, at Alveston, W.G. took seventeen wickets for the former and E. M. Grace six; the other wicket was run out.

**1881** – For Thornbury v Bath Association, at Bath, W.G. (8) and E.M. (10) again obtained all the wickets between them; one man was absent and another run out.

**1889** – W.G. and E. M. Grace, playing for Thornbury, dismissed Wotton-under-Edge for 35 and 8, each taking ten wickets.

**1899** – Founded the London County CC, of which he was secretary, manager and captain. The Club's first match was v Wiltshire, at Swindon, May 5, 6. W.G. scored 1,092 runs for the Club that season with an average of 84.

**1900** – In all matches for London County, W.G. made 2,273 runs (average 55.43) and took 133 wickets.

**1901** – In all matches for London County, W.G. made 2,457 runs (average 58.50) and took 142 wickets.

**1902** – In minor games for London County, W.G. made 1,200 runs (average 100) and took 100 wickets (average 13.52).

**1904** – For London County v Oundle Rovers, at Crystal Palace, he went in last man and made 86 not out of the 118 added for the wicket with G. R. Ryan (29).

In all matches for London County CC he scored 1,405 runs (average 31.22) and took 121 wickets (average 18.03)

**1905** – When playing for Strutt Cavell's XI v XVII of Twickenham, at Twickenham, W.G. was hit for 28 off six consecutive balls by R. Hiscock.

In all kind of cricket this year, W.G. made 1,038 runs (average 32.43) and took 105 wickets (average 16.97).

**1906** – In all kinds of cricket he made 1,096 runs and took 65 wickets.

**1907** – In all kinds of cricket he scored 1,051 (average 47) and took 104 wickets (average 13).

**1908** – His last hundred – 110 not out for London County v Whitgift Wanderers, at the Crystal Palace, June 26. He made twenty-six hundreds in Minor Matches for London County, 1899-1908, between the ages of 51 and 60.

In all matches this season he made 724 runs (average 33) and took 116 wickets (average 13). On August 19 he injured his foot at Lord's, and played only once or twice afterwards: otherwise he would undoubtedly have made over 1,000 runs as usual.

This was the last season of the London County CC.

**1913** – His last match for MCC v Old Charlton, at Charlton, June 26. He scored 18.

It is estimated that during his career W.G. made about 80,000 runs and took about 7,000 wickets.

# A. E. STODDART

Andrew Ernest Stoddart, one of the greatest of batsmen, died by his own hand on Saturday, the 3rd of April, 1915, shooting himself through the head. A brilliant career thus came to the saddest of ends. Mr Stoddart was born at South Shields on March 11, 1863, and had thus completed his 52nd year. Curiously enough, considering the great fame he won, he did not take to cricket seriously until 22 years of age, when he became associated with the Hampstead Club, and showed such form, scoring no fewer than five separate hundreds for that team, that before the end of the season of 1885 he had been tried for Middlesex. From 1886 to 1898, except for the summer of 1888, when he was engaged playing rugby football in Australia and New Zealand, Mr Stoddart proved a tower of strength to Middlesex in batting, keeping up his skill so well that in 1898 – his last full season in county cricket – he averaged 52. He soon became a popular idol at Lord's, his batting, in conjunction with that of T. C. O'Brien, making the Middlesex matches far more attractive than they had ever been before his day.

He turned out only once for Middlesex in 1899, and twice in the following year, but in his last match for the county – against Somerset at Lord's – he put together a score of 221, the highest of his career in first-class cricket. Among his most famous innings were 215 not out against Lancashire at Manchester in 1891 and 151 for England against the MCC at Lord's in 1887, when he and Arthur Shrewsbury raised the total to 266 for the first wicket. In 1886, for Hampstead against the Stoics, he played an innings of 485 – at that time the highest individual score on record.

On four occasions Mr Stoddart paid visits to Australia, first in 1887, as a member of G. F. Vernon's team, when he averaged 32. Four years later he formed one of the side taken out by Lord Sheffield, his average then amounting to 37. In 1894-95, and again in 1897-98, he himself took a team out to Australia. The first of these undertakings resulted in England winning the rubber after two victories had been gained by each country, but the second proved a big disappointment, no fewer than four of the five Test matches ending in favour of Australia. Still, in the two tours associated with his leadership, Mr Stoddart came out well with averages of 51 and 34. In the fifth match in the tour of 1894-95, which decided the rubber in England's favour, J. T. Brown played a memorable innings of 140, and Albert Ward scored 91. As a Test match player in this country, Mr Stoddart achieved no special distinction. He took no part in those games in 1890, and although he played in all three matches three years later, making 83 at The Oval, his only other appearances for England at home were at Lord's and Manchester in 1896.

A splendid batsman to watch, Mr Stoddart had all strokes at his command, but was especially strong in driving and hitting on the leg side. Again and again he proved his greatness by his ability to make runs under conditions which found other batsmen at fault, his play, both on fiery and on soft wickets, being quite exceptional. As a special instance of his power on fiery wickets one recalls a superb innings of 91 for Middlesex against Surrey at The Oval in 1892. The Oval was not in good order that year, and Lockwood's bowling needed some facing. Stoddart, however, did not mind a bit. Two or three times he hit to the boundary balls that got up as high as his head. Almost equally good was his batting, when in with W. G. Grace, against Richardson and Mold in the Gentlemen and Players match at Lord's in 1895. In the early part of his career he proved a useful change bowler, and anywhere in the field he was both brilliant and safe. In his early seasons for Middlesex he had onerous work to do on the off-side when George Burton was bowling, but he was never known to flinch.

Mr Stoddart was one of the very few men who have represented their country at rugby football as well as at cricket. Between 1886 and 1893 he took part in ten international rugby matches, and would have certainly have played in more but for the fact that in two

of the intermediate seasons England, owing to a dispute with the other Unions, had no
international matches. He appeared twice against Scotland, three times against Ireland,
and four times against Wales, while in 1889 he played against the Maories. A splendid
runner, with plenty of pace and dodging ability, and not above jumping over an opponent
on occasion, he was a great three-quarter – possessed of a very fine pair of hands – a
brilliant kick, and a player full of resource.

It was a memorable drop-kick against a gale of wind he made that, giving Middlesex
victory over Yorkshire by a goal to four tries, led to the rules of the game being altered. At
that time a goal counted more than any number of tries. Mr Stoddart captained England
against Wales in 1890, when, on a muddy swamp at Dewsbury, Wales, scoring a try to
nothing, gained their first victory over England. Another famous match in which he took
part that at Cardiff in 1893, when, after England had established a commanding lead,
Wales finished in great form, and, under the method of scoring then in vogue, succeeded in
snatching a win by one point. It may be questioned whether any two players ever enjoyed
a better understanding than Alan Rotherham, at half, and Andrew Stoddart at
three-quarter. Certainly the combination of these two men formed one of the brightest
features of the rugby game in the "eighties".                                      C. S. C.

## A. E. STODDART IN THE CRICKET FIELD

### BATTING AVERAGES IN FIRST-CLASS MATCHES

| Year | Innings | Not Outs | Runs | Highest Innings | Average |
|------|---------|----------|------|-----------------|---------|
| 1885 | 8 | — | 149 | 79 | 18.62 |
| 1886 | 24 | 1 | 640 | 116 | 27.82 |
| 1887 | 28 | — | 799 | 151 | 28.53 |
| Australia | 15 | — | 459 | 94 | 30.00 |
| 1888 | Absent in Australia | | | | |
| 1889 | 35 | 2 | 817 | 78* | 24.75 |
| 1890 | 45 | 1 | 845 | 115 | 19.20 |
| 1891 | 32 | 1 | 857 | 215* | 27.64 |
| Australia | 12 | — | 450 | 134 | 37.50 |
| 1892 | 47 | 2 | 1,403 | 130 | 31.17 |
| 1893 | 50 | 1 | 2,072 | 195* | 42.28 |
| 1894 | 39 | — | 1,174 | 148 | 30.10 |
| Australia | 18 | 1 | 870 | 173 | 51.17 |
| 1895 | 43 | — | 1,622 | 150 | 37.72 |
| 1896 | 50 | 2 | 1,671 | 127 | 34.81 |
| West Indies | 17 | 2 | 677 | 153* | 45.13 |
| 1897 | 21 | — | 650 | 109 | 30.95 |
| Australia | 11 | — | 205 | 40 | 18.63 |
| 1893 | 26 | 4 | 1,038 | 157 | 47.18 |
| 1899 | 5 | — | 78 | 44 | 15.60 |
| America | 3 | 1 | 193 | 74 | 96.50 |
| 1900 | 11 | 1 | 402 | 221 | 40.20 |
| | | | | | |
| In America | 3 | 1 | 193 | 74 | 96.50 |
| In Australia | 56 | 1 | 1,975 | 173 | 35.90 |
| In England | 464 | 15 | 14,217 | 221 | 31.66 |
| In West Indies | 17 | 2 | 677 | 153* | 45.13 |
| Totals | 540 | 19 | 17,062 | 221 | 32.74 |

* *Signifies not out.*

## HIS SCORING IN TEST MATCHES

| | Date of First Match | Innings | Not Outs | Runs | Highest Innings | Average |
|---|---|---|---|---|---|---|
| In Australia | 1887-88 | 21 | 1 | 731 | 173 | 36.55 |
| In England | 1893 | 9 | 1 | 265 | 83 | 33.12 |
| Totals | 1887-88 | 30 | 2 | 996 | 173 | 35.57 |

## A. E. STODDART'S HUNDREDS IN FIRST-CLASS CRICKET (28)

| | |
|---|---|
| 116 | Middlesex v Kent, at Gravesend, 1886 |
| 151 | England v MCC and Ground, at Lord's, 1887 |
| 116 | Gentlemen of England v I Zingari, at Scarborough, 1887 |
| 115 | South v North, at Lord's, 1890 |
| 215*† | Middlesex v Lancashire, at Manchester, 1891 |
| 134 | England v Australia, at Adelaide, 1891-92 |
| 130 | Middlesex v Nottinghamshire, at Lord's, 1892 |
| 195*† / 124 | Middlesex v Nottinghamshire, at Lord's, 1893 |
| 125 | Middlesex v Surrey, at Lord's, 1893 |
| 127 | C. I. Thornton's XI v Australians, at Scarborough, 1893 |
| 148 | Gentlemen of England v Nottinghamshire, at Nottingham, 1894 |
| 149 | England v Queensland, at Brisbane, 1894-95 |
| 173 | England v Australia, at Melbourn, 1894-95 |
| 150 | Middlesex v Somerset, at Lord's, 1895 |
| 131 | Middlesex v Kent, at Lord's, 1895 |
| 100 | Middlesex v Yorkshire, at Lord's, 1896 |
| 121 | Middlesex v Somerset, at Lord's, 1896 |
| 109 | Middlesex v Lancashire, at Lord's, 1896 |
| 127 | Middlesex v Kent, at Lord's, 1896 |
| 153* | A. Priestley's Team v St Vincent, at Bridgetown, 1896-97 |
| 108* | A. Priestley's Team v Queen's Park, at Port-of-Spain, 1896-97 |
| 100 | A. Priestley's Team v Jamaica, at Lord's, 1896-97 |
| 143 | A. Priestley's Team v Jamaica, at Lord's, 1896-97 |
| 109 | Middlesex v Somerset, at Taunton, 1897 |
| 138 | Middlesex v Nottinghamshire, at Lord's, 1898 |
| 157 | Middlesex v Leicestershire, at Leicester, 1898 |
| 221 | Middlesex v Somerset, at Lord's, 1900 |

* *Signifies not out.* † *Signifies carried bat through completed innings.*

## LARGE PARTNERSHIPS FOR THE FIRST WICKET

266 Stoddart (151) and Shrewsbury (152) for England v MCC and Ground at Lord's, 1887, (Lord's centenary match).

228 Stoddart (125) and T. C. O'Brien (113) for Middlesex v Surrey at Lord's, 1893, (Middlesex followed-on, 179 behind, and won by 79).

218 Stoddart (100) and H. B. Hayman (152) for Middlesex v Yorkshire at Lord's, 1896.

205 Stoddart (116) and A. J. Webbe (103) for Middlesex v Kent t Gravesend, 1886.

In three consecutive innings which they opened together against the Australians in 1893, Stoddart and "W.G." scored 120, 114, and 151 for the first wicket.

In August, 1896, Stoddart and J. Douglas made over 150 for the first wicket of Middlesex three times in a fortnight.

## FIRST-CLASS CRICKET NOTABILIA

**1885** – His début for Middlesex, and his first appearance in first-class cricket v Yorkshire, at Sheffield. Going in first, he scored 3 and 21: he also bowled twelve balls for seven runs and no wickets, and made a catch. Middlesex won by 49 runs.

**1886** – Middlesex v Nottinghamshire, at Nottingham. Stoddart batted three hours twenty minutes on a difficult wicket for 32, the highest score of the match. During the Middlesex innings of 168 as many as 92 maiden overs were bowled.

**1887-88** – Visited Australia as a member of the late G. F. Vernon's team.

**1887-88** – v New South Wales, at Sydney. Of the 74 runs scored for the first wicket with Abel (88) he made 55.

**1890** – On a difficult wicket in second innings of South v North, at Lord's, Stoddart got 115 of the 169 runs scored during the one hundred and forty minutes he was batting, making not the slightest mistake. The runs were obtained off Attewell, Peel, Briggs, and William Barnes. At one period of his innings he scored 50 while "W.G." made 3.

**1891** – Middlesex v Yorkshire, at Lord's. Stoddart obtained spectacles – c Wainwright b Peel, 0; b Peel, 0.

**1891-92** – Visited Australia as a member of the late Earl of Sheffield's team.

**1893** – Middlesex v Nottinghamshire, at Lord's. Stoddart scored 195 not out and 121, carrying his bat through the first innings and being sixth out in the second. This was the first occasion on which a batsman had obtained two separate hundreds in a first-class match at Lord's since 1817.

**1893** – At the end of the season Stoddart was presented with an elegant silver bowl on an ebonised stand thus inscribed:– "Presented to Andrew Ernest Stoddart by the Middlesex County Cricket Club in appreciation of his splendid cricket for the county in 1893". In the bowl itself are recorded his scores – three figures, each of them – against Nottinghamshire, and Surrey, and his total runs and averages for Middlesex in 1893.

**1894-95** – A. E. Stoddart took a team to Australia for the first time.

**1895** – Middlesex v Surrey, at The Oval, Stoddart scored 75 and 67. In his first innings he was given out stumped, but the bail was not dislodged. (His innings was, of course, continued.) In his second innings a ball from Smith, F. E. hit his wicket hard without removing a bail.

**1896-97** – Visited the West Indies with A. Priestley's team.

**1897** – Elected vice-captain of the Middlesex XI, a position he resigned at the end of 1898.

**1897-98** – Took a team to Australia for the second time. This was his fourth, and last, visit to that country.

**1899** – In the autumn visited America as a member of K. S. Ranjitsinhji's team.

**1900** – His last appearance for Middlesex v Somerset, at Lord's, Hearne's (J. T.) benefit match. He made 12 and 221, his highest innings in first-class cricket.

**1900** – South v North, at Lord's. Stoddard made four catches in the second innings of the North, although only seven wickets fell.

## PERFORMANCES FOR THE HAMPSTEAD CC

| Year | Innings | Not Outs | Runs | Highest Innings | Average | Runs | Wickets | Average |
|------|---------|----------|------|---------|---------|------|---------|---------|
| 1885 | 19 | 3 | 1,097 | 185 | 68.56 | † | 51 | † |
| 1886 | 21 | 1 | 1,671 | 485 | 83.55 | † | 72 | † |
| 1887 | 17 | 5 | 1,862 | 275 | 155.16 | 434 | 42 | 10.33 |
| 1888 | Absent in Australia | | | | | | | |
| 1889 | 16 | 2 | 874 | 144 | 62.42 | 587 | 66 | 8.89 |
| 1890 | 12 | 2 | 418 | 97* | 41.80 | 393 | 44 | 8.93 |
| 1891 | 24 | 1 | 979 | 153* | 42.56 | 921 | 105 | 8.77 |
| 1892 | 18 | 2 | 1,053 | 132 | 65.81 | 773 | 80 | 9.66 |
| 1893 | 7 | 2 | 558 | 210 | 111.60 | 90 | 13 | 6.91 |
| 1894 | 11 | 1 | 649 | 226* | 64.90 | 205 | 37 | 5.54 |
| 1895 | 9 | 2 | 310 | 134* | 48.57 | 256 | 26 | 9.81 |
| 1896 | 2 | 1 | 126 | 122 | 126.00 | 43 | 5 | 8.60 |
| 1897 | 9 | 2 | 527 | 127 | 75.28 | 414 | 38 | 10.89 |
| 1898 | 8 | 1 | 336 | 75* | 48.00 | 410 | 32 | 12.81 |
| 1899 | 17 | 4 | 1,363 | 163 | 104.84 | 716 | 60 | 11.90 |
| 1900 | 14 | 2 | 864 | 145 | 72.00 | 493 | 62 | 7.95 |
| 1901 | 12 | 1 | 551 | 109 | 50.09 | 398 | 20 | 19.90 |
| 1902 | 12 | 1 | 535 | 108 | 48.63 | 280 | 16 | 17.56 |
| 1903 | 1 | — | 3 | 3 | 3.00 | 79 | 2 | 39.50 |
| 1907 | 2 | 1 | 106 | 100* | 106.00 | — | — | — |
| | | | | | | — | 123 | — |
| Totals | 231 | 34 | 13,912 | 485 | 70.61 | 6,492 | 648 | 10.01 |

*\* Signifies not out.*     *† No analysis kept.*

## MINOR CRICKET NOTABILIA

**1886** – Playing for Hampstead v Stoics, at Hampstead, on August 4, A. E. Stoddart scored 485 – of 811 obtained whilst in – six hours ten minutes, this being then the highest innings on record. His hits were an 8 (four from an overthrow), three 5s, sixty-three 4s, twenty 3s, thirty-six 2s, and seventy-eight singles, and except for a very difficult chance to mid-on when 421 made no mistake. He was caught eventually from a miss-hit. With J. G. Q. Besch (98) he added 214 for the second wicket, and with E. Swift (92) 383 for the fourth in about three hours. Despite the fact that the bowling was good throughout – only one wide was delivered, and not a single no-ball during the six hours and a-quarter the innings of 813 for nine wickets lasted – the scoring was always fast. At lunch the total was 370 for three wickets, made in two hours and a-half, and runs were obtained throughout at an average rate of 130 an hour.

**1886** – In three consecutive innings in five days Stoddart scored 790 runs, making 485 for Hampstead v Stoics, at Hampstead, on August 4; 207 for Hampstead v Blackheath at Hampstead, on August 7; and 98 for Middlesex v Gloucestershire, at Gloucester, on August 9.

**1887** – In six days, during the Hampstead Week (July 25 to 30) he made 900 runs in six innings, three times not out: – 21 v MCC and Ground, 205 v Ne'er-do-Weels, 275 not out v London Scottish, 55 v Clapham Wanderers, 114 not out v A. D. Slade's XI, and 230 not out v Old Finchleians.

**1887-88** – G. F. Vernon's Team v XVIII Melbourne Juniors, at Melbourne, December 9, 10, 12. Batting just over six and a-quarter hours, and hitting twenty-four 4s. Stoddart contributed 285 to the total of 556, this being then the highest innings obtained for an English team in Australia. He made 125 for the first wicket with Abel (38) and added 215 for the fourth with Peel (95), gave six distinct chances and eventually played-on.

**1892** – In consecutive innings for Hampstead this year he made 126 v Crystal Palace at Hampstead on July 21, 117 v Hendon at Hampstead on July 22, 104 and 17 not out v Bournemouth at Bournemouth on July 25, 26, and 103 and 23 not out v Hampshire Hogs at Southampton on July 27, 28.

**1896-97** – In all matches for A. Priestley's team in the West Indies Stoddart scored 1,079 runs (average 53.95) and took 104 wickets (average 7.85).

**1899** – In consecutive innings for Hampstead he made 154 v South Hampstead on August 7, 126 not out v Gnats on August 9, 130 v London and Westminster Bank on August 12, and 163 v West Hertfordshire County and Ground on August 16. All the scores were made at Hampstead.

In minor cricket Stoddart made sixty-eight scores of a hundred.

# VICTOR THOMAS TRUMPER

Victor Trumper died at Sydney on the 28th of June, 1915. Of all the great Australian batsmen Victor Trumper was by general consent the best and most brilliant. No one else among the famous group, from Charles Bannerman thirty-nine years ago to Bardsley and Macartney at the present time, had quite such remarkable powers. To say this involves no depreciation of Clem Hill, Noble, or the late W. L. Murdoch. Trumper at the zenith of his fame challenged comparison with Ranjitsinhji. He was great under all conditions of weather and ground. He could play quite an orthodox game when he wished to, but it was his ability to make big scores when orthodox methods were unavailing that lifted him above his fellows.

For this reason Trumper was, in proportion, more to be feared on treacherous wickets than on fast, true ones. No matter how bad the pitch might be from the combined effects of rain and sunshine, he was quite likely to get 50 runs, his skill in pulling good-length balls amounting to genius. Of this fact our English bowlers had convincing evidence day after day during the season of 1902. Trumper paid four visits to this country – in 1899, 1902, 1905, and 1909 – but it was in 1902 that he reached his highest point.

In that summer of wretched weather he scored 2,570 runs in thirty-five matches for the Australian team, with the wonderful average, in the circumstances, of 48. He was as consistent as he was brilliant, and did not owe his average to a few exceptional scores. Of eleven innings of over a hundred, the biggest was 128. Trumper did not again touch the same level in this country. He played very well in 1905 and 1909, but he was no longer pre-eminent. He was fifth in the averages in 1905, and in 1909 he was overshadowed by Bardsley and Ransford. In the latter year, however, he was now and then seen at his best, notably against England at The Oval, when he played D. W. Carr's googlies with perfect ease, and in the second match against the MCC at Lord's. When he came here first, in 1899, he jumped at once into the front rank, playing a splendid innings of 135 not out against England at Lord's, and scoring 300 not out against Sussex at Brighton. His innings at Lord's was in itself sufficient to prove that Australia had found a world's batsman. Nothing could have been better.

His career culminated when the South Africans visited Australia in the season of 1910-11. He then recovered his finest form, and on the beautiful wickets at Melbourne, Adelaide, and Sydney the "googly" bowlers had no terrors for him. In the five Test matches he scored 662 runs, with an average of 94. It was agreed on all hands that he had not played so well since his trip to England in 1902. Under all conditions Trumper was a fascinating batsman to watch. His extreme suppleness lent a peculiar grace to everything he did. When he was hitting up a big score batting seemed quite an easy matter. He took so many liberties, however, and scored from so many good balls, that in order to do himself justice he had to be in the best possible health and condition. The strokes with which he drove even the best bowlers to despair demanded a marvellous union of hand and eye. His game at its highest point of excellence could only be played by a young man.

Trumper was the most popular Australian cricketer of his time. A match played for his benefit – between New South Wales and the Rest of Australia – at Sydney in February, 1913 – produced in gate-money and donations nearly £3,000. Born on November 2, 1877, Trumper was in his thirty-eighth year. He had been in bad health for some little time, and the latest accounts of his condition received in this country were so discouraging as to prepare his friends for the worst. He died of Bright's disease. Trumper was never spoilt by success in the cricket field. When his name was in everyone's mouth he remained as a modest and unaffected as on the day he first set foot in England.

S. H. P.

## BATTING AVERAGES IN FIRST-CLASS MATCHES

| Year | Innings | Not Outs | Runs | Highest Innings | Average |
|---|---|---|---|---|---|
| 1894-95 | 4 | 1 | 22 | 11 | 7.33 |
| 1897-98 | 10 | — | 192 | 68 | 19.20 |
| 1898-99 | 15 | 1 | 873 | 292* | 62.35 |
| 1899 | 48 | 3 | 1,556 | 300* | 34.57 |
| 1899-1900 | 10 | — | 721 | 208 | 72.10 |
| 1900-01 | 7 | — | 458 | 230 | 65.42 |
| 1901-02 | 18 | — | 486 | 73 | 27.00 |
| 1902 | 53 | — | 2,570 | 128 | 48.49 |
| 1902-03 in South Africa | 8 | 1 | 307 | 70 | 43.85 |
| 1902-03 | 9 | — | 446 | 178 | 49.55 |
| 1903-04 | 21 | 3 | 990 | 185* | 55.00 |
| 1904-05 | 4 | — | 198 | 81 | 49.50 |
| 1904-05 in New Zealand | 5 | 1 | 436 | 172 | 109.00 |
| 1905 | 47 | 1 | 1,667 | 110 | 36.23 |
| 1905-06 | 6 | — | 250 | 101 | 41.66 |
| 1906-07 | 3 | — | 23 | 11 | 7.66 |
| 1907-08 | 19 | — | 797 | 166 | 41.94 |
| 1908-09 | 1 | — | — | — | — |
| 1909 | 45 | 2 | 1,435 | 150 | 33.37 |
| 1909-10 | 1 | — | 105 | 105 | 105.00 |
| 1910-11 | 20 | 2 | 1,246 | 214* | 69.22 |
| 1911-12 | 20 | 3 | 583 | 113 | 34.29 |
| 1912-13 | 13 | 3 | 843 | 201* | 84.30 |
| 1913-14 | 5 | — | 107 | 32 | 21.40 |
| 1913-14 in New Zealand | 10 | — | 839 | 293 | 83.90 |
| | | | | | |
| In Australia | 186 | 13 | 8,340 | 292* | 48.20 |
| In England | 193 | 6 | 7,228 | 300* | 38.65 |
| In New Zealand | 15 | 1 | 1,275 | 293 | 91.07 |
| In South Africa | 8 | 1 | 307 | 70 | 43.85 |
| | | | | | |
| Totals | 402 | 21 | 17,150 | 300* | 45.01 |

His doings in the very wet season of 1902 were extraordinary, for not once was he dismissed without a run, and he had not even one not-out innings to assist him. Only Shrewsbury, who scored 1,250 runs and was not out seven times, was above him in the averages.

## TRUMPER'S HUNDREDS IN FIRST-CLASS CRICKET

**For Australia** *in Australia* (6)

> v England, 185*, 113, 166, 113
> v South Africa, 159, 214*

**For Australia** *in England* (19)

> v Cambridge University, 128, 133
> v Derbyshire, 113
> v England, 135*, 104
> v XI of England, 113, 150
> v Essex, 109 and 119
> v Gloucestershire, 104, 125, 108

**For Australia** *in England – continued*
  v MCC and Ground, 105
  v Oxford University, 121
  v XI Players, 127
  v South, 120
  v Surrey, 101
  v Sussex, 300*
  v Worcestershire, 110

**For Australia** *in New Zealand* (3)
  v Canterbury, 293
  v New Zealand, 172
  v Southland, 211

**For New South Wales** (15)
  v Australia, 105, 126*
  v New Zealand, 253
  v Queensland, 208
  v South Australia, 165, 178, 135, 201*
  v Tasmania, 292*
  v Victoria, 230, 130, 101, 119, 142, 138

Forty-three such innings in all. His two hundreds against Essex were made in one match in 1902, during which season he obtained eleven centuries. The same year he scored 105 and 86 in a match with MCC and Ground at Lord's. Trumper also made 218 not out for Australia v XV of the Transvaal, at Pretoria in 1902-03.

## TRUMPER'S SCORING IN TEST-MATCH CRICKET

| Year | Innings | Not Outs | Runs | Highest Innings | Average |
|------|---------|----------|------|-----------------|---------|
| 1899 (in England) | 9 | 1 | 280 | 135* | 35.00 |
| 1901-02 (v England) | 10 | — | 219 | 65 | 21.90 |
| 1902 (in England) | 8 | — | 247 | 104 | 30.87 |
| 1902-03 (v South Africa) | 6 | 1 | 239 | 70 | 47.80 |
| 1903-04 (v England) | 10 | 1 | 574 | 185* | 63.77 |
| 1905 (in England) | 8 | 1 | 125 | 31 | 17.85 |
| 1907-08 (v England) | 10 | — | 338 | 166 | 33.80 |
| 1909 (in England) | 9 | 1 | 211 | 73 | 26.37 |
| 1910-11 (v South Africa) | 9 | 2 | 661 | 214* | 94.42 |
| 1911-12 (v England) | 10 | 1 | 269 | 113 | 29.88 |
| | | | | | |
| In Australia | 49 | 4 | 2,061 | 214* | 45.80 |
| In England | 34 | 3 | 863 | 135* | 27.83 |
| In South Africa | 6 | 1 | 239 | 70 | 47.80 |
| | | | | | |
| Against England | 74 | 5 | 2,263 | 185* | 32.79 |
| Against South Africa | 15 | 3 | 900 | 214* | 75.00 |
| | | | | | |
| Totals | 89 | 8 | 3,163 | 214* | 39.04 |

## FIRST-CLASS CRICKET NOTABILIA

Trumper's first century in first-class cricket was 292 not out for New South Wales v Tasmania, at Sydney, in 1898-99. He and F. A. Iredale (196) added 258 for the sixth wicket.

Whilst scoring 300 not out v Sussex, at Brighton, in 1899, he took part in three stands of over 100, adding 178 for the second wicket with J. Worrall (128), 211 for the third with S. E. Gregory (173) and 106, without separation, with J. Darling (56 not out), after the fall of the fourth.

The same season he scored 62 runs out of 80 in fifty minutes in the Test match at Sheffield.

For New South Wales v South Australia, at Sydney, in 1902-03, Trumper (178) and the late R. A. Duff (132) scored 298 for the first wicket.

In the first innings of New South Wales v Victoria on the same ground the same season, the pair obtained 267 ere a wicket fell. In the second innings Trumper, for the first time in 78 innings in first-class cricket, was dismissed without a run.

For New South Wales v Victoria at Sydney, in 1903-04, Trumper and Duff made 113 for the first wicket in the first innings and 119, without being separated, for the first wicket in the second winning the match by ten wickets. Trumper's scores were 53 and 53 not out; Duff's 67 and 62 not out.

For Australia v New Zealand at Wellington in 1904-05, Trumper (172) and C. Hill (129) added 269 for the sixth wicket in 107 minutes. At one period they put on a hundred in thirty-five minutes.

In scoring 108 for Australians v Gloucestershire at Bristol in 1905, Trumper obtained all his runs before lunch on the first day.

On the second afternoon of the Australians' match v Northamptonshire, at Northampton, in 1905, Trumper (68) and W. W. Armstrong (122) added 90 without being parted in thirty-five minutes for the seventh wicket.

In the second innings of Australians v Oxford University, at Oxford, in 1905, Trumper and R. A. Duff scored 30 runs off two consecutive overs, the former obtaining 12 off N. R. Udal and Duff 18 off E. G. Martin.

In making 101 out of 139 in fifty-seven minutes, on a wicket favouring the bowlers, for New South Wales v Victoria, at Sydney, in 1905-06, Trumper gave perhaps the most brilliant display of his career. He hit a 6 and eighteen 4s, and reached 64 out of 78 in thirty-one minutes, and 73 out of 90 in forty minutes.

For New South Wales v Victoria, at Melbourne in 1906-07. Trumper scored 119 out of 150 in 101 minutes. He obtained 62 runs out of 81, and completed his 100 out of 124 in an hour-and-a-half.

He scored 20 runs (five 4s) off an over from G. Hazlitt for New South Wales v Victoria, at Melbourne, in 1907-08.

Whilst making 150 for Australians v An England XI, at Blackpool, in 1909, Trumper added 93 for the sixth wicket in thirty-five minutes with M. A. Noble (36) and 45 for the seventh in ten minutes with A. J. Hopkins (21 not out) for the seventh. Three-quarters of an hour's play thus produced 138 runs.

For New South Wales v South Africans, at Sydney, in 1910-11 Trumper (70 and 78) and W. Bardsley (70 and 45) made over a hundred together in each innings for the first wicket – 122 in the first and 121 in the second.

Trumper made 159 out of 237 in 171 minutes for Australia v South Africa at Melbourne in 1910-11.

In 1911-12 he scored 58 out of 77 in fifty-seven minutes for New South Wales v Victoria, at Melbourne.

For New South Wales v Victoria at Sydney in 1912-13, Trumper (138) and E. P. Barbour (146) added 270 together for the eighth wicket.

Trumper (293) and A. Sims (184 not out) put on 433 for the eighth wicket of Australians v Canterbury, at Christchurch, in 1913-14.

In first-grade cricket in Australia – playing for Paddington from 1896-97 to 1908-09 and for Gordon from 1910-11 to 1914-15, Trumper scored 8,946 runs with an average of 69.

# DEATHS IN THE WAR

SERGT COLIN BLYTHE (Kent Fortress Engineers, attd. KOYLI), born at Deptford May 30, 1879; killed in November, 1917. Went to Australia 1901-02 and 1907-08; to South Africa 1905-06 and 1909-10; to America (with the Kent team) 1903.

The news that Blythe had been killed in France was received everywhere with the keenest regret. Inasmuch as Kenneth Hutchings had practically done with the game before joining the Army, the loss is the most serious that cricket has sustained during the war. It is true that Blythe had announced his intention of playing no more in first-class matches, but quite possibly this decision was not final. He had certainly no need to think of retiring at the age of 38. That Blythe was a great bowler is beyond question. He had no warmer admirers than the many famous batsmen who had the satisfaction of making big scores against him. So far as I know they were unanimous in paying tribute to his remarkable powers. He was one of the five left-handed slow bowlers of the first rank produced by England in the last forty years, the other four being Peate, Peel, Briggs, and Rhodes. To place the five in order of merit is a task I shall not attempt. The best experts, if asked to give an opinion on the point, would vary considerably in their views. For example, W. L. Murdoch thought Peate far ahead of either Peel or Briggs, whereas Arthur Shrewsbury found Peel harder to play than Peate, the fast ball that Peel had at command keeping him always on the alert. Again I have heard Ranjitsinhji say that he considered Blythe a finer bowler than Rhodes, the deceptive flight of the ball making him more difficult to hit. To these views I would only add that judging by the practical test of results a good case could be made out for Rhodes as the best bowler of the five – before he turned his mind to batting. The seasons in which he did such wonderful things for Yorkshire – 1898 to 1901 inclusive – were seasons of fine weather and huge scoring. Peate's great deeds were done chiefly in summers of rain and bad weather.

Blythe had all the good gifts that pertain to the first-rate slow bowler, and a certain imaginative quality that was peculiarly his own. Very rarely did he get to the end of his resources. To see him bowl to a brilliant hitter was a sheer delight. So far from being disturbed by a drive to the ring he would, instead of shortening his length to escape punishment, send up the next ball to be hit, striving of course to put on, if possible, a little extra spin. In this respect he reminded me of David Buchanan in the Gentlemen and Players matches of long ago. Blythe's spin was something quite out of the ordinary. On a sticky wicket or on a dry pitch ever so little crumbled he came off the ground in a way that beat the strongest defence. He had, too, far more pace than most people supposed. The ball that went with his arm often approached the speed of a fast bowler and had of course the advantage of being unsuspected. On this point Fred Huish, the wicket-keeper, can be very illuminating.

Blythe was introduced to Kent cricket by Capt. McCanlis, one of the best coaches the game has known. He was 20 years of age when he first played for Kent, and in 1900 – his second season – he took 114 wickets in county matches alone. Illness during the winter affected his bowling in 1901, but after his visit to Australia with the team captained by A. C. MacLaren in 1901-02 he never looked back. His best season was 1909, when he took in first-class matches 215 wickets, at a cost of 14.5 runs each. A list of Blythe's feats with the ball for Kent would fill a column. Against Northamptonshire, at Northampton, in 1907, he obtained seventeen wickets in one day, taking all ten in the first innings for 30 runs, and seven in the second for 18. Test matches, owing to his tendency to epileptic fits, were very trying to him, and after having had a big share in England's victory over Australia at Birmingham in 1909 he was practically forbidden to play at Lord's. Still he was, out by himself, England's best bowler in the three matches with the famous South African team of 1907, taking twenty-six wickets for less than 10.5 runs a-piece. Only one of the three matches was finished, England winning at Leeds by 53 runs. Blythe on that occasion bowled himself to a standstill, but he had his reward, clearly winning the game for his country. Blythe's reputation will rest on his doings in England. His two visits to Australia scarcely added to his fame, and when he went to South Africa in 1905-06 and again in 1909-10, he did not find the matting wickets altogether to his liking. In the second of his South African tours he had a fairly good record, but as he was only picked for two of the five Test matches, he could not have been at his best. To sum up his career in a phrase, he will live in cricket history as the greatest Kent bowler of modern days. Nearly all his finest work was done for his county. It is pleasant to know that the Kent Committee have decided to put up a suitable memorial to him.

S. H. P.

## EIGHT WICKETS OR MORE IN AN INNINGS

8-42  Kent v Somerset, at Maidstone, 1902
9-67  Kent v Essex, at Canterbury, 1903
9-30  Kent v Hampshire, at Tonbridge, 1904
8-72  Kent v Essex, at Leyton, 1905
10-30  Kent v Northamptonshire, at Northampton,1907
8-59  England v South Africa, at Leeds,1907
8-83  Kent v Hampshire, at Canterbury, 1908
9-42  Kent v Leicestershire, at Leicester,1909
9-44  Kent v Northamptonshire, at Northampton,1909
8-49  Kent v Derbyshire, at Tunbridge Wells, 1909
8-45  Kent v Gloucestershire, at Cheltenham, 1911
8-36  Kent v Leicestershire, at Leicester, 1912
8-55  Kent v Worcestershire, at Dudley, 1912
8-55  Kent v Yorkshire, at Sheffield, 1914
9-97  Kent v Surrey, at Lord's, 1914

## THIRTEEN WICKETS OR MORE IN A MATCH

13-20  Kent v Worcestershire, at Worcester, 1903
13-61  Kent v Yorkshire, at Canterbury, 1903
13-91  Kent v Hampshire, at Southampton, 1904
15-76  Kent v Hampshire, at Tonbridge, 1904
17-48  Kent v Northamptonshire, at Northampton, 1907 (Only two clean bowled. All taken on 3rd day of match.)
15-99  England v South Africa, at Leeds, 1907
13-111  Kent v Northamptonshire, at Gravesend, 1908
13-123  Kent v Leicestershire, at Canterbury, 1908
13-114  MCC's Australian XI v An England XI, at Uttoxeter, 1908
16-102  Kent v Leicestershire, at Leicester, 1909
14-75  Kent v Northamptonshire, at Northampton, 1909
14-84  Kent v Gloucestershire, at Cheltenham, 1911
13-109  Kent v Somerset, at Gravesend, 1912
15-45  Kent v Leicestershire, at Leicester, 1912
13-94  Kent v Leicestershire, at Canterbury, 1913

## FOUR WICKETS OR MORE FOR THREE RUNS OR LESS EACH

10-30*a*⎫
 7-18*b* ⎬Kent v Northamptonshire, at Northampton, 1907
17-46*c* ⎭

 7-20    England v Natal, at Pietermaritzburg, 1909-10
 4-12    England v North-Eastern District, at Queenstown, 1909-10
 6-10    Kent v Leicestershire, at Leicester, 1911

  7-9*a* ⎫
       ⎬Kent v Leicestershire, at Leicester, 1912
15-45*b*⎭

 4-10    Kent v Surrey, at Blackheath, 1912
 7-21    Kent v Worcestershire, at Stourbridge, 1912
 5-8     Kent v Warwickshire, at Tonbridge, 1913
 7-15    Kent v Northamptonshire, at Northampton, 1914
 7-20    Kent v Worcestershire, at Canterbury, 1914

> *a Signifies first innings*          *b second*          *c both.*

The following feats were noteworthy, although the figures do not represent work for the complete innings:

7 wickets for  1 run in 36 balls  Kent v Northamptonshire, at Northampton, 1907
6 wickets for  6 runs in — balls  Kent v Gloucestershire, at Bristol, 1909
5 wickets for 10 runs in 10 balls  Kent v Surrey, at Blackheath, 1910
6 wickets for  7 runs in 48 balls  Kent v Worcestershire, at Sourbridge, 1913

## BOWLING UNCHANGED THROUGH BOTH COMPLETED INNINGS

With J. R. Mason     Kent v Somerset, at Taunton, 1901
With Hearne, A.       Kent v Surrey, at The Oval, 1903
With Woolley, F. E.  Kent v Yorkshire, at Maidstone, 1910
With Woolley, F. E.  Kent v Nottinghamshire, at Canterbury, 1912
With D. W. Carr     Kent v Gloucestershire, at Dover, 1912

## VARIOUS ITEMS OF INTEREST

His first ball for Kent – It bowled F. Mitchell. Kent v Yorkshire, at Tonbridge, 1899
Bowls an hour for 1 run – Kent v Sussex, at Tunbridge Wells, 1904
A good day's work – 17 wickets for 48, v Northanthamtonshire, at Northampton, 1907
A good day's work – 14 wickets for 56, v Leicestershire, at Leicester, 1909
A good day's work – 14 wickets for 84, v Gloucestershire, at Cheltenham, 1911
Bowls nine consecutive maiden overs – Kent v Derbyshire, at Chesterfield, 1909
Bowls 40 overs unchanged – MCC's Australian Team v An England XI, at Scarborough, 1908
3 wickets in 3 balls – Kent v Surrey, at Blackheath, 1910*
3 wickets in 3 balls – Kent v Derbyshire, at Gravesend, 1910
3 wickets in 4 balls – Kent v Worcestershire, at Canterbury, 1914

  * *He took four wickets in five balls.*

## BLYTHE'S BOWLING IN FIRST-CLASS CRICKET

| Year | Balls | Runs | Wickets | Average |
|------|-------|------|---------|---------|
| 1899 | 757 | 310 | 14 | 22.14 |
| 1900 | 5,053 | 2,106 | 114 | 18.47 |
| 1901 | 5,273 | 2,151 | 93 | 21.12 |
| 1901-02 in Australia | 1,792 | 711 | 34 | 20.91 |
| 1902 | 5,082 | 1,965 | 127 | 15.47 |
| 1903 | 5,554 | 1,953 | 142 | 13.75 |
| 1903 in America | 396 | 168 | 13 | 12.92 |
| 1904 | 6,146 | 2,705 | 138 | 19.60 |
| 1905 | 7,170 | 3,142 | 149 | 21.08 |
| 1905-06 in South Africa | 2,889 | 1,046 | 57 | 18.35 |
| 1906 | 5,321 | 2,209 | 111 | 19.90 |
| 1907 | 6,829 | 2,822 | 183 | 15.42 |
| 1907-08 in Australia | 2,360 | 935 | 41 | 22.80 |
| 1908 | 8,200 | 3,326 | 197 | 16.88 |
| 1909 | 7,643 | 3,128 | 215 | 14.54 |
| 1909-10 in South Africa | 2,425 | 820 | 53 | 15.47 |
| 1910 | 6,249 | 2,497 | 175 | 14.26 |
| 1911 | 6,238 | 2,675 | 138 | 19.38 |
| 1912 | 5,517 | 2,183 | 178 | 12.26 |
| 1913 | 6,722 | 2,729 | 167 | 16.34 |
| 1914 | 6,052 | 2,583 | 270 | 15.19 |
| Totals | 103,668 | 42,164 | 2,509 | 16.80 |

**BRIGADIER-GEN. ROLAND BOYS BRADFORD** (Durham Light Infantry), VC, MC. Twice wounded. Born February, 1892; killed first week of December, 1917, aged 25. Played Regimental cricket for Durham Light Infantry. At the outbreak of War he was only a subaltern, and at his death the youngest General in the British Army.

**SUB-LIEUT RUPERT C. BROOKE** (Royal Naval Division), born at Rugby on August 3, 1887, died at Lemnos of sunstroke on April 23, 1917. In 1906 he was in the Rugby Eleven, and although he was unsuccessful in the Marlborough match he headed the School's bowling averages with a record of nineteen wickets for 14.05 runs each. He had gained considerable reputation as a poet.

**LIEUT ARTHUR EDWARD JEUNE COLLINS,** of the Royal Engineers, who was killed in action on November 11, 1914, came suddenly into note by scoring 628 not out for Clarke's House v North Town, in a Junior house match at Clifton College, in June, 1899, when only thirteen years old. During the six hours and fifty minutes he was in he hit a 6, four 5s, thirty-one 4s, thirty-three 3s, and 146 2s, carrying his bat through the innings, and Clarke's, who scored 836, won by an innings and 688 runs. Collins also obtained eleven wickets in the match, seven in the first innings and four in the second, and in partnership with Redfern (13) put on as many as 183 for the last wicket. In 1901 and 1902 he was in the College XI, in the former year scoring 342 runs with an average of 38.00, his highest innings being 112 against Old Cliftonians. He was a free-hitting batsman, but his military duties prevented him from taking cricket seriously: still he made many good scores in Army matches, and for Old Cliftonians v Trojans at Southampton in August, 1913, he and F. G. Robinson made 141 without being parted for the first wicket in thirty-eight minutes, Collins scoring 63 and his partner 77. His best performance at Lord's was to make 58 and 36 for RE v RA in 1913. He was born in India in 1885, gazetted second Lieutenant in 1904 and promoted Lieutenant in 1907.

**ALBERT B. COTTER**, killed at Beersheba, October 20, 1917. New South Wales and Australia.

Albert Cotter was the successor to Ernest Jones as Australia's fast bowler, coming to England with the teams of 1905 and 1909. His first trip was not an unqualified success. It is true that in all matches he took 124 wickets for less than 20 runs apiece, but up to a certain point of the tour he had so little command over his length that his bowling was a quaint mixture of long hops and full pitches. Still, irregular as he was, his extreme pace often made him dangerous. He gained greatly in command over the ball when he shortened his run and in the last Test match, at The Oval, he bowled splendidly on a perfect wicket, his pace being terrific. In 1909 his bowling came out very badly for the whole tour, but he had a big share in winning the Test match at Leeds, taking five wickets in England's second innings at a cost of only 38 runs. For several seasons Cotter was the fast bowler of the New South Wales XI. He will never be ranked among the great Australian bowlers, but on his day he was deadly.

S. H. P.

Some of his best performances were:

Four wickets for 5 runs, NSW v Queensland, at Brisbane, 1903-04.
Seven for 15 and twelve for 34, Australia v Worcestershire, at Worcester, 1905.
Took four wickets in four balls for Glebe v Sydney, at Wentworth Park, April 29, 1911.

**CAPTAIN HAROLD G. GARNETT**, born November 19, 1879, killed on the Italian front at the beginning of December, 1917. Harold Garnett will be remembered as a distinguished member of the Lancashire eleven. Tried twice for his county towards the end of the season of 1900, he jumped into fame the following year, playing so finely that he seemed likely to become the best left-handed bat in England. His style was attractive and his hitting very brilliant. Against Sussex at Manchester he scored 110 and 89, and in two other matches – against Leicestershire at Leicester and Middlesex at Lords – he made over a hundred, his scores being 139 and 114. As the result of his season's work he came out second to Tyldesley in the Lancashire averages. On the strength of this performance he was chosen to go to Australia with Mr MacLaren's team, but he failed, doing next to nothing during the tour. He was so obviously out of form that he was given few chances. For several seasons, till business took him to the Argentine, Garnett batted exceedingly well for Lancashire, but he never quite equalled his efforts in 1901. Returning to England in 1911 and again in 1914 he renewed his connection with the Lancashire eleven. In 1914 he had developed into a first rate wicket-keeper, and strictly on his merits he was picked for Gentlemen v Players at Lords. He proved fully worthy of the distinction, and had no small share in winning the match. The way in which he stumped Hitch in the Players' second innings would have been wonderful even if done by Blackham at his best. Garnett volunteered at the outbreak of the war, and soon obtained a commission.

S. H. P.

**2ND LIEUTENANT JOHN HOWELL** (King's Royal Rifle Corps), was killed in Flanders on September 25, 1915. Among all the young cricketers who have fallen in the war not one of brighter promise than John Howell can be named. Judging from his wonderful record at Repton it is not too much to say that he was potentially an England batsman. But for the war he would have been at Oxford last year and would no doubt have been seen in the Surrey eleven at The Oval. Born on the 5th of July, 1895, he was only twenty when he lost his life. He was in the Repton team for four seasons – 1911 to 1914 – being captain in 1914. From the first he showed great promise as a batsman, his style having obviously been modelled on that of Tom Hayward. He did well in 1911 and 1912, and in the next two years he was probably the best school bat in England. In 1913 he scored 737 runs for Repton, with an average of 56, and in 1914 686 runs with an average of 52. He took some little time to find his form in school cricket in 1914, but he scored 202 not out against the Old Reptonians and 202 against Uppingham. In a trial match at The Oval at the beginning of the season he played an innings of 109. In 1913 he scored 108 and 114 against the Old Reptonians, and 144 for Young Surrey Amateurs against Young Essex Amateurs. Towards the close of the season in 1913 he journeyed up to Walsall with Surrey's second eleven for the express purpose of playing against Barnes's bowling and had the satisfaction of scoring 45.

LIEUT K. L. HUTCHINGS (King's Liverpool Regiment, attached to Welsh Regiment) was killed in action during the first week in September, 1916. He was struck by a shell, death being instantaneous. Of all the cricketers who have fallen in the war he may fairly be described as the most famous.

Kenneth Lotherington Hutchings did not fulfil all the hopes formed of him, but at his best he was one of the most remarkable batsmen seen in this generation. Those who follow cricket will not need to be reminded of the sensation caused by his play in 1906 – the year in which Kent, for the first time in modern days, came out as champion county. To the triumph of the side no one contributed more than Hutchings. It is true that he fell a little below C. J. Burnup in the averages, but he played with amazing brilliancy, getting four hundreds in county matches, and scoring 1,358 runs. His success astonished the public, but it was scarcely a surprise to those who had watched him from his school days. He had a great career at Tonbridge, being in the eleven for five years, and heading the batting for three seasons in succession. The first evidence of his ability in county cricket was given when, in 1903, he scored 106 for Kent against Somerset at Taunton. His batting in 1906 took him at once to the top of the tree, and on all hands he was regarded as an England cricketer. Unfortunately he never again reached quite the level of his great season. From time to time he did brilliant things, playing especially well in 1909 and 1910, but in 1912 he lost his form and dropped out of the Kent eleven.

In 1909 he was chosen twice for England against Australia, scoring 9 at Manchester and 59 at The Oval. He paid one visit to Australia, being a member of the MCC's team in the winter of 1907-08. Taking the tour as a whole, he did not meet with the success expected, but at Melbourne, in the only Test match the Englishmen won, he played a very fine innings of 126. Hutchings was quite individual in his style of batting, recalling no predecessor. His driving power was tremendous, and when at his best he could score from good length balls with wonderful facility. It was said in 1906 that when he played for Kent against Yorkshire, even George Hirst – most fearless of fieldsmen at mid-off – went back several yards for him, so terrific being the force of his hitting. Like most modern batsmen, Hutchings trusted for defence wholly to his back play. When he went forward it was always for the purpose of scoring. Playing the daring game that he did, he could only do himself full justice when physically very fit. His fielding was on a par with his batting. In the slips or in the deep field he was equally brilliant. He was born at Southborough, near Tunbridge Wells, on December 7, 1882.

S. H. P.

The following records of Hutchings' career speak for themselves:

## TONBRIDGE SCHOOL

| Year | Innings | Not Outs | Runs | Highest Innings | Average | |
|------|---------|----------|------|---------|---------|---|
| 1898 | 11 | 2 | 185 | 41 | 20.55 | |
| 1899 | 11 | — | 218 | 60 | 19.81 | |
| 1900 | 15 | 2 | 743 | 127 | 57.15 | – 1st made 127 v Band of Brothers |
| 1901 | 13 | 2 | 522 | 101* | 47.45 | – 1st made 100 v Free Foresters |
| 1902 | 12 | 2 | 633 | 205 | 63.30 | – 1st made 205 v West Kent, 178* v Free Foresters, and 120 v Old Cliftonians. |

## FOR KENT

First played for the County in 1902.

| Year | Innings | Not Outs | Runs | Highest Innings | Average |
|------|---------|----------|------|-----------------|---------|
| 1902 | 2 | — | 11 | 10 | 5.50 |
| 1903 | 17 | 1 | 454 | 106 | 28.37 |
| 1903† | 6 | 1 | 48 | 16 | 9.60 |
| 1904 | 2 | — | 96 | 66 | 48.00 |
| 1905 | 4 | — | 87 | 31 | 21.75 |
| 1906‡ | 28 | 4 | 1,454 | 176 | 60.58 |
| 1907 | 31 | 2 | 955 | 109* | 32.93 |
| 1908 | 36 | — | 953 | 132 | 26.47 |
| 1909‡ | 36 | 1 | 1,368 | 155 | 39.08 |
| 1910‡ | 36 | 2 | 1,461 | 144 | 42.97 |
| 1911 | 34 | 2 | 938 | 103* | 29.31 |
| 1912 | 10 | — | 178 | 53 | 17.80 |
| Totals | 242 | 13 | 8,008 | 176 | 34.94 |

*\* Signifies not out.       † American tour.     ‡ Champion county.*

## HUNDREDS IN FIRST CLASS CRICKET

| | |
|---|---|
| 106 | Kent v Somerset, at Taunton, 1903 |
| 125 | Kent v Middlesex, at Tonbridge, 1906 |
| 131 | Kent v Yorkshire, at Sheffield, 1906 |
| 176 | Kent v Lancashire, at Canterbury, 1906 |
| 124 | Kent v Hampshire, at Bournemouth, 1906 |
| 101 | Kent v Hampshire, at Tonbridge, 1907 |
| 109 109* | Kent v Worcestershire, at Worcester, 1907 |
| 108 | Kent v Lancashire, at Canterbury, 1907 |
| 126 | England v Australia, at Malbourne, 1907-08 |
| 132 | Kent v Northamptonshire, at Gravesend, 1908 |
| 102 | Kent v Derbyshire, at Derby, 1908 |
| 120 | Gentlemen v Players, at Scarborough, 1908 |
| 100 | Kent v Gloucestershire, at Catford, 1909 |
| 155 | Kent v Somerset, at Gravesend, 1909 |
| 116 | Kent v Hampshire, at Bournemouth, 1909 |
| 104 | Kent v Northamptonshire, at Northampton, 1910 |
| 112 | Kent v Derbyshire, at Derby, 1910 |
| 109 | Kent v Leicestershire, at Tonbridge, 1910 |
| 144 | Kent v Sussex, at Hastings, 1910 |
| 114 | MCC and Ground v Yorkshire, at Scarborough, 1910 |
| 103* | Kent v Hampshire, at Canterbury, 1911 |

*\* Signifies not out.*

## IN GENTLEMEN v PLAYERS MATCHES

| Year | Venue | Scores | Innings | Not Outs | Runs | Highest Innings | Average |
|------|-------|--------|---------|----------|------|-----------------|---------|
| 1906 | Lord's | 2 and 10 | 13 | — | 339 | 120 | 26.07 |
| 1906 | Scarborough | 36 and 14* | | | | | |
| 1908 | Scarborough | 3 and 120 | (He made his 120 out of 164 in 100 minutes.) | | | | |
| 1909 | The Oval | 0 and 59 | | | | | |
| 1909 | Scarborough | 11 | | | | | |
| 1910 | Scarborough | 19 and 42 | | | | | |
| 1911 | Scarborough | 18 and 5 | | | | | |

\* *Also took four wickets for 15.*

## IN ENGLAND v AUSTRALIA MATCHES

| Year | Venue | Scores | Innings | Not Outs | Runs | Highest Innings | Average |
|------|-------|--------|---------|----------|------|-----------------|---------|
| 1907-08 | Sydney | 42 and 17 | 12 | — | 341 | 126 | 28.41 |
| 1907-08 | Melbourne | 126 and 39 | | | | | |
| 1907-08 | Adelaide | 23 and 0 | | | | | |
| 1907-08 | Melbourne | 8 and 3 | | | | | |
| 1907-08 | Sydney | 13 and 2 | | | | | |
| 1909 | Manchester | 9 | | | | | |
| 1909 | The Oval | 59 | | | | | |

PERCY JEEVES (Royal Warwickshire Regiment) was killed on July 22, 1916, England losing a cricketer of whom very high hopes had been entertained. Jeeves was born at Earlsheaton, in Yorkshire, on the 5th of March, 1888. He played his first serious cricket for the Goole CC, and became a professional at Hawes. He took part in Yorskhire trial matches in 1910, but presumably failed to attract much attention. Soon afterwards he went to live in Warwickshire, playing for that county, when not fully qualified, against the Australians and South Africans in 1912. No special success rewarded him in those matches, but in 1913 he did brilliant work for Warwickshire, both as bowler and batsman, and firmly established his position. He took 106 wickets in first-class matches that season at a cost of 20.88 each, and scored 765 runs with an average of 20.13. In 1914 he was chosen for Players v Gentlemen at The Oval. Jeeves was a right-handed bowler on the quick side of medium pace. He was very popular among his brother players.

CAPT. JOHN WILLIAM WILLIAM NASON (Royal Flying Corps), born at Corse Grange, Gloucestershire on August 4, 1889, was killed in December, 1916. He was educated at University School, Hastings, and Cambridge, where he obtained his blue in 1909. As a lad he was regarded as a player of unusual promise, but, although he made some useful scores both for the University and Sussex, it cannot be said that he did as well as was expected. In his two matches against Oxford – in 1909 and 1910 – he scored only 32 runs with an average of 10.66. His first appearance for Sussex, against Warwickshire at Hastings in 1906, was marked by a curious incident, for he was allowed to replace Dwyer after that player had bowled five overs, and in his second innings carried out his bat for 53. In 1913 he began to assist Gloucestershire, and in that season played an innings of 139 against Nottinghamshire on the Gloucester ground. This was his highest score in first-class cricket. When playing for University School v Hastings Post Office in 1908, he opened the innings and when he was bowled after batting for half-an-hour the score-sheet read: – J. W. W. Nason b Cox, 97; L. Inskipp not out, 1; bye, 1; total (1 wicket) 99. He obtained all the first 64 runs and hit three 6s and fourteen 4s.

MAJOR R. O. SCHWARZ (8th KRRC) Military Cross. Died of influenza, in France, November 18, 1918.

Major Schwarz, as every one knows, was famous as a slow bowler. Few men did so much to establish the reputation of South African cricket. He learnt the game in England and played for Middlesex before going to South Africa. In those early days, however, he did not make any great mark. His fame began when he returned to this country with the South African team of 1904. Studying very carefully the method of B. J. T. Bosanquet, he acquired, and afterwards carried to a high standard, the art of bowling off breaks with, to all appearance, a leg-break action. He did very well in 1904, but his success that year was only a foretaste of far greater things to come. In the brilliant tour of 1907 he and Vogler and G. A. Faulkner raised South African cricket to the highest pitch it has every reached. He was less successful than his two comrades in the Test matches against England, but for the whole tour he was easily first in bowling, taking 143 wickets at a cost of 11.5 runs each. He proved rather disappointing in Australia, and in the Triangular Tournament in this country in 1912 he failed. Before going to South Africa Schwarz was an international half-back at rugby football, playing against Scotland in 1899 and against Wales and Ireland two seasons later. He also played for Cambridge against Oxford in 1893. He was born on May 4, 1875, and was educated at St Paul's School. Inasmuch as he always made the ball turn from the off and had no leg break Schwarz was not in the strict sense of the word a googly bowler, and was in this respect inferior to his colleagues Vogler and Faulkner. Still, when at his best, he was a truly formidable opponent, his accuracy of length in the season of 1907, in combination with such a big break, being extraordinary.

The writer of the obituary notice in *The Times* said: "Personally 'Reggie' Schwarz was a man of exceptional charm, and his untimely death will bring real sorrow to his hosts of friends in many parts of the world. He had the great gift of absolute modesty and self-effacement. No one meeting him casually would ever have guessed the renown he had won in the world of sport. Quiet, almost retiring, in manner; without the least trace of "side"; and with a peculiarly attractive voice and way of speaking, Schwarz impelled and commanded the affection even of acquaintants. During his years in South Africa he was secretary to Sir Abe Bailey – a post which his social gifts enabled him to fill with remarkable success. Before coming to Europe for service in France, he had won distinction in the campaign in German South-West Africa. All who knew him knew that at the first possible opportunity he would be in the field in France, quietly and unostentatiously devoting all his gifts – gifts that were bound to ensure his success as an officer – to the service of his country. He had been wounded twice."

S. H. P.

LIEUT HENRY WEBBER (South Lancashire Regiment), of Horley, Surrey, and a JP for the County, was killed in action on July 21, 1916, aged 68. He was in the Tonbridge School Eleven fifty years before, among his contemporaries being Mr J. W. Dale, and later played for Pembroke College, Oxford. He had been a member of the MCC since 1872. He made his first hundred in 1863 and as recently as August 6, 1904, when 56 years of age, made 209 not out for Horley v Lowfield Heath, at Horley, in three hours after a full round of golf in the morning. His pluck and patriotism in insisting on being given a commission at his advanced age were much admired.

LIEUT GEORGE WILLIAM EDENDALE WHITEHEAD (RFA, attached RAF), born 1895, killed on October 17, 1918. Among the many public school cricketers lost during the war perhaps none, except John Howell of Repton, had better prospects of winning distinction at the game than George Whitehead. In the Clifton College XI for four years – he was captain in 1913 and 1914 – he had a brilliant record at school. Starting in 1911 he was third in batting with an average of 33, and in the following year he did still better, playing a remarkable innings of 259 not out against Liverpool and averaging 41. Moreover he took fourteen wickets with a fairly good average. Against Cheltenham he played a first innings of 63. In his two years as captain he was conspicuously successful, heading the batting in both seasons with averages of 46 in 1913 and 40 in 1914. He also bowled well, especially in 1914, when he took thirty-six wickets for a trifle over 13 runs apiece. He played three times at Lords for Public Schools against the MCC, and in 1914 he was given a couple of trials for Kent.

An old Cliftonian writes:

George Whitehead was a perfect flower of the public schools. He was not limited to athletics only, great though he was in this respect. Intellectually he was far above the average, and was as happy with a good book as when he was scoring centuries. His ideals were singularly high and though gentle and broad-minded, he always stood uncompromisingly for all that was clean. So modest was he, that strangers sometimes failed to realize his worth. He insisted on being transferred to the Royal Air Force from the RFA, fully appreciating the risks, because he knew of his country's then urgent need of air-men and so he died, greatly patriotic. Clifton has lost more than 500 of her sons in the war. She is proud of every one of them, but of none more than of this very perfect gentleman.

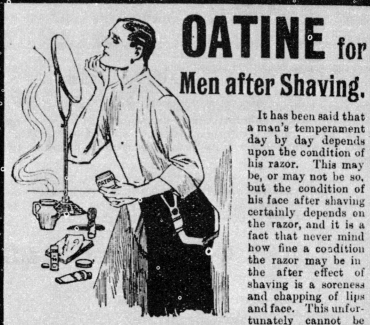

# OATINE for
## Men after Shaving.

It has been said that a man's temperament day by day depends upon the condition of his razor. This may be, or may not be so, but the condition of his face after shaving certainly depends on the razor, and it is a fact that never mind how fine a condition the razor may be in the after effect of shaving is a soreness and chapping of lips and face. This unfortunately cannot be avoided, but it can be minimised to such an extent that it is hardly noticeable by the use of good shaving soap such as either the **Oatine Shaving Cream** (in tubes) or the **Oatine Shaving Stick**, both of which are British made and most carefully prepared for the purpose, the cream giving a heavy, and the stick a lighter, close-lying lather, but being alike in this, that both give a free, smooth, lasting and agreeable lather that will not dry on the face. If you have not tried either of the **Oatine Soaps** for shaving do so without delay.

To relieve the irritation caused by shaving there is nothing so effective as **Oatine Cream**, which possesses special healing properties; it should be applied immediately after shaving and should be gently rubbed into the skin, or, better still, rubbed into the beard over night or before the morning shave, this has the effect of softening the beard in a most astonishing manner.

# FREE SAMPLES

of **Oatine Cream** and **Oatine Soap** will be sent to all applicants together with a copy of our Booklet; or send 3d. in stamps (half-penny stamps preferred) for a box containing samples of eight different preparations.

**The Oatine Co., 465, Denman St., London, S.E.**

# OTHER WARTIME DEATHS

MR FRANK ERSKINE ALLAN ("The Bowler of a Century"), born at Warrambool (Victoria) December 2, 1849. Height 6ft 1in. Died at Melbourne February 9, 1917.

Frank Allan was the first of the long line of great Australian bowlers. There were good men before his day – Sam Cosstick and others – but he was the first to develop those special qualities that made Australian bowling – when the first team came to England in 1878 – the talk of the cricket world. Apart from everything else, the medium-pace bowlers were found capable of getting an amount of work on the ball that in England had only been possible to slow bowlers. Allan, who bowled left-handed and batted right, had abundant spin, but his distinctive gift was a remarkable swerve, or as it was then called a curl in the air. Batsmen who met him for the first time were bewildered by the course of the ball. Allan was a born bowler, if every there was one. He played in his first inter-colonial match at Melbourne on Boxing Day, 1867, within a month of completing his eighteenth year, and became famous at once, taking eight wickets – five for 59 runs and three for 43 – and helping Victoria to beat New South Wales by seven wickets. Thenceforward he was for years the mainstay of the Victorian eleven, and the terror of New South Wales batsmen. Midwinter, who played a great deal with Allan when both were young, said to me once: "When I began to bowl I could scarcely hit a haystack, but Allan was a bowler from the day he first took a ball in his hand."

Allan was at the height of his fame when he came to England with the famous team of 1878 and though he had not done half so well as Spofforth during the preliminary tour in the Colonies he was one of the great hopes of the side. In England, however, he did not do himself justice. Unfortunately for him the summer of 1878 was for the most part extremely cold and wet. At home no day was too hot for him, and he found our climate very trying. The result was that he failed whereas Harry Boyle – immeasurably his inferior in Australia – made a big reputation, and shared with Spofforth the triumph of the tour. Once, however, Allan revealed his powers. In the match with Middlesex at Lord's, played in glorious weather, he took three wickets for 27 runs and six for 76. Bob Thoms, who was umpiring, told me that what he did with the ball was wonderful. It was in that match that Edward Lyttelton got his famous 113 – the innings of his life. Allan never paid a second visit to England, but he continued to play in inter-colonial matches for some time. Soon, however, his old position as Victoria's crack bowler was taken by George Palmer. Like Allan, Palmer came out when very young and jumped at once to the top of the tree, establishing his reputation in a match against Lord Harris's team in March, 1879. In comparing Allan's deeds with those of later Australian bowlers it must be remembered that in his time Australian batting was very far below the standard it has since reached, and that the wickets did not approach their present perfection. Still he was great in his day. As a batsman he played by the light of nature in a style peculiarly his own. His comrades of 1878 used to call him "the crouching panther". He was first-class as a shot, an angler, at bowls, and as a poker player.

S. H. P.

His best performances were:

For Victoria v NSW he took 73 wickets for 10.52 runs each.

### In an innings

9-46   Victoria v XVI of Tasmania, at Hobart, 1867-68
8-20   Victoria v NSW, at Sydney, 1868-69
8-35   Victoria v NSW, at Melbourne, 1871-72
9-26   Australia v XV of Victoria and NSW, at Sydney, 1877-78
11-57  Australia v XVIII of Victoria, at Melbourne, 1877-78

**In a match**

14-70    Victoria v XVI of Tasmania, at Hobart, 1867-68
13-60    Victoria v NSW, at Melbourne, 1871-72
14-84    Australia v XV of NSW and Victoria, at Sydney, 1877-78
18-125   Australia v XVIII of Victoria, at Melbourne, 1877-78

Took all 10 wickets in an innings for 10 runs for Warrambool v Coranderrk Aboriginals, at Warrambool, in January, 1884

For the 1878 team he performed thus:

| | | |
|---|---|---|
| Preliminary Colonial Tour | 68 wickets for 428 runs | |
| In England | 88 wickets for 995 runs | |
| In America | 44 wickets for 131 runs | |
| Final Colonial Tour | 17 wickets for 278 runs | |
| Total | 217 | 1,832 |

MR HARRY THOMPSON ARNALL-THOMPSON, born at Belgrave, Leicestershire, on April 7, 1864, died at Anstey Frith, near Leicester, on December 28, 1916. In 1880 and two following years he was in the Rugby eleven, being captain in 1882, and in his matches v Marlborough took twenty-two wickets for 9.63 runs each and made 36 runs with an average of 12. Originally a fast bowler, it was on the advice of Mr C. F. H Leslie (the Rugby captain of 1880) that he took to slows, a style with which all his subsequent successes were obtained. He was left-handed with a high delivery, a useful batsman and a good field at slip or mid-off. During his last year at Rugby he bowled admirably, taking sixty-three wickets for exactly 12 runs apiece. In his two last matches for the school he took seven wickets in an innings for 67 runs v Marlborough and eight in an innings for 55 v MCC and Ground, both games being played at Lord's. At Oxford he commenced well by taking seven wickets for 47 runs in the Freshmen's match of 1883, but it was not until 1886 (when he had an analysis of seven for 82 v Lancashire at Manchester) that he obtained his blue. On his only appearance against Cambridge he scored 6 and 4 and took four wickets for 52 runs. From 1883 until 1890 he assisted Leicestershire, and in 1888 and 1889 captained the side. Against Yorkshire at Leicester in 1883 he took ten wickets for 112 runs and performed the hat-trick; v Warwickshire a year later he obtained seven wickets for 19; and in 1888 – when, under his leadership, the side beat both the Australians and Surrey – he had analyses of ten for 52 v Essex at Leyton and nine for 65 v the Colonials. In a minor match in 1884 he took all ten wickets in an innings, obtaining five with consecutive balls and six with seven. He had been a member of the MCC since 1886. Whilst playing Shacklock's bowling in the Leicestershire v MCC and Ground match at Lord's in 1889, he had a painful and curious experience. The ball flew off the edge of his bat on to his eyebrow and rebounded to the bowler. Arnall-Thompson was momentarily stunned, and as the blood flowed freely suggested he should retire and finish his innings later. It was then gently broken to him that he was out, caught-and-bowled.

REV. SIR EMILIUS BAYLEY-LAURIE (Eton and Kent), born May 16, 1823, died at Maxweltown, Dumfrieshire, December 3, 1917. Having outlived nearly all his contemporaries, Emilius Bayley, as he was called till he took in 1887 the surname of Laurie, must have been the oldest cricketer of any note in England. He was nearly five years older than the Surrey veteran, William Caffyn. On the strength of one performance he will live in cricket history. For Eton against Harrow at Lord's in 1841 he played an innings of 152, his score remaining unbeaten in the Eton and Harrow matches till D. C. Boles made 183 for Eton in 1904. Except that he got his 152 out of a total of 308 – with the liberal allowance of 63 extras – one can say nothing about Emilius Bayley's great innings. Mr Arthur Haygarth gave no details in *Scores and Biographies*, but in his biographical note attached to the Eton and Harrow match in 1838 he described Bayley as a fine free hitter, especially to leg, and an admirable field either at long leg or cover point. Apart from his big innings Bayley's best score in the matches with Harrow and Winchester during his four years in the Eton eleven was 27 against Harrow in 1838. Still he must have been an excellent bat, as he was considered good enough to play for Kent in the great days of the eleven that included Fuller Pilch, Alfred Mynn, Felix, Wenman, and Hillyer. He took part in two matches for Kent in 1842, five in 1843, and two in 1844. Like many other men in his own time and in later days he gave up serious cricket on entering the Church. In the sensational match between Kent and England at Canterbury in 1842, when Kent, after leading off with a total of 278, went down for 44 in their second innings, and were beaten by nine wickets, Emilius Bayley scored not out 5 and not out 17. The other ten Kent men in the second innings scored only 23 runs.

S. H. P.

COL JAMES FELLOWES, born at the Cape of Good Hope on August 25, 1841, died at Dedham, in Essex, on May 3, 1916. *Scores and Biographies* said of him: "Has been successful in the matches in which his name is found, being a very hard hitter, and a fast round-armed bowler, while in the field he can take any place with effect, except long-stop or wicket-keeper." Between 1873 and 1881 he appeared in nine matches for Kent, and in later years for Hampshire (of which club he was for some seasons co-Secretary with Dr Russell Bencraft) and Devon. The county grounds at Southampton and Exeter were laid down under his supervision, and he was founder of the Hampshire Hogs and Devon Dumplings. His bowling for the Royal Engineers between 1868 and 1877 was noteworthy:

| Year | Overs | Maidens | Runs | Wickets | Average |
|------|-------|---------|------|---------|---------|
| 1868 | 541   | 215     | 813  | 81      | 10.03   |
| 1869 | 863.2 | 339     | 1,237 | 140    | 8.83    |
| 1870 | 619.2 | 218     | 1,250 | 93      | 13.44   |
| 1871 | 604.3 | 235     | 947  | 63      | 15.03   |
| 1872 | 703   | 289     | 1,096 | 88     | 12.45   |
| 1873 | 682   | 263     | 1,068 | 115    | 9.28    |
| 1874 | 675   | 289     | 972  | 111     | 8.75    |
| 1875 | 600   | 270     | 833  | 55      | 15.14   |
| 1876 | 584.1 | 229     | 855  | 72      | 11.87   |
| 1877 | 228.2 | 94      | 382  | 18      | 21.21   |
| Totals | 6,101.2 | 2,441 | 9,453 | 836   | 11.30   |

Against Chatham Garrison, at Chatham in August, 1874, he obtained sixteen wickets.

In strictly first-class cricket his greatest feats were to take seven wickets for 24 runs for Kent against Surrey at Maidstone in 1873, and thirteen for 100 for Kent v Lancashire on the same ground in 1874. He had been a member of the MCC since 1869, and at Lord's in 1887 took part in the Centenary match between XVIII Veteran Gentlemen and XI Gentlemen of the MCC. As a curious occurrence it may be recalled that, when playing for MCC v Woolwich at Lord's in 1871, he hit his foot with his bat in playing the ball and broke one of his toes. When playing for North Kent XVIII v United South of England Eleven, at Gravesend in 1875, he made 20 runs – three 6s (all over the pavilion) and a 2 – off a four-ball over delivered by "W.G." He was father-in-law of Col. W. C. Hedley.

MR JOHN G. FRANCIS, born at Badwell Ash, near Ixworth, Suffolk, February 5, 1834, died at Bury St Edmunds, August 24, 1917, aged 83. Played his first match – for Boys of Drinkstone v Boys of Woolpit – in 1846, at the age of 12, and scored 131. His highest innings was 172 v Garboldisham. His first and last hundreds covered a period of 50 years. Appeared first for the Gentlemen of Suffolk at the age of 19. Was captain of

Suffolk for 12 years. Was selected for Gentlemen v Players in 1863, but declined the honour. During his 49 years' playing he made 38,300 runs in 1,100 completed innings, obtaining 46 hundreds. His son, Mr H. A. Francis, also played for Suffolk. In 1886 Suffolk cricketers presented him with a marble time-piece and a cheque for £56. He played for the Bury and West Suffolk CC as far on as 1903. One of his reminiscences referred to a game at Earl Soham, played late in the month of May when snow had to be cleared off the pitch before play could commence; the game was followed by a snow-balling match.

MR FREDERICK EUSTACE READE FRYER, born at Holbrook, Suffolk, January 7, 1849, died in London, October 1, 1917. Harrow XI, 1867 and 1868; Cambridge XI, 1870 to 1873, captain in 1873; Suffolk 1867-83; Gentlemen v Players, 1873-75; member of MCC since 1878.

F. E. R. Fryer flourished at a time when university cricket was amazingly rich in talent, and when it attracted more public attention than in later days of numberless county matches. Among the Oxford and Cambridge batsmen of his day he was not the best, never reaching the level of Yardley and Ottaway, but he stood very high in the brilliant group that came nearest to those two masters – both so great in their utterly different styles. Upright, easy and graceful, Fryer was a beautiful bat to watch – as attractive to look at as Lionel Palairet in our own time – but he wanted a good wicket. Playing a very forward game he had not the strength of defence demanded by the wickets at Lord's in the '70's. He played finely in his second match for Harrow against Eton, scoring 31 and not out 33 in 1868, but after his school days Lord's was emphatically not his ground. His best score in four University matches was 46 in 1872, and on that occasion Oxford's bowling had been mastered by Longman and Tabor before he went in. In Cambridge's matches with the MCC at Lord's he failed lamentably. On the other hand he could on the true-playing wickets at The Oval and Cambridge hold his own in any company. Of the eleven scores of fifty or more credited to him in *Bat v Ball*, four were obtained at Fenner's and three at The Oval. Brilliant leg hitting was always a feature of his play. I should fancy that the innings of his life was his 76 in the Gentlemen and Players of the South match at The Oval in 1871. That was a wonderful game, the Players winning – ten minutes from time – by 3 runs. The Gentlemen were left to get 249 in the last innings, and their chance seemed gone when they had lost five wickets – those of W. G. Grace, Walter Hadow, Yardley, Fred Grace, and I. D. Walker – for 53 runs. C. I. Thornton, however, gave a display of hitting that was extraordinary even for him, scoring 61 in forty-seven minutes, and finishing up with a 6, a 4, and three 5s. The boundary did not extend all round The Oval in those days. The game underwent such a change that with Fryer and George Strachan well set the Gentlemen had three wickets to fall and required only 15 runs to win. Then for the first time in the innings Southerton was put on at the gas works end. He bowled down the last three wickets and won the match! I gather from the description in *Wisden* for 1872 that of all the magnificent batting in the match nothing surpassed Fryer's innings of 76. In 1870 at The Oval Fryer was concerned in another remarkable game, he and Yardley giving Cambridge a victory over Surrey by eight wickets. Fryer made 69 not out and Yardley 90 not out, the two batsmen scoring 143 runs together after two wickets had fallen for 27. In the University match Fryer was on the winning side against Oxford in 1870 and 1872 and on the losing side in 1871 and 1873. He was captain of the Cambridge eleven in 1873, but he scarcely excelled in leadership. At any rate he took a dark bowler up to Lord's and only allowed him to bowl two overs in a hard-fought match that Oxford won by three wickets.

With regard to the memorable match in 1870, Mr Herbert Troughton, who remembers every incident in the Oxford and Cambridge matches of the last fifty years or more, sends me a very interesting note. He writes: "Playing as he did in the immortal 1870 match, Mr Fryer was responsible for an incident for which he has never received the credit due to him. For without this incident the magnificent batting of Dale and Yardley would have been in vain, and Cobden's sensational "hat trick" would have been impossible. This is the incident to which I refer. Oxford had gone in requiring 178 to win the match, and had scored 160 for four wickets, Ottaway being in and so well set that he looked as if he would never be got out. With the score 160 Ottaway hit a short one from Ward very hard indeed, and very low indeed, to Fryer, who was fielding at short leg, rather deep. Falling on his knees Fryer managed to grip and hold the ball, not more than a couple of inches from the ground. So low down was the catch made, that Ottaway appealed, but the umpire's decision was against the batsman, and Ottaway departed. Of the great merit of the catch there can be no question, and in my opinion it did as much for winning Cambridge the match as Dale and Yardley's batting, or Cobden's phenomenal hat trick." After leaving Cambridge, Fryer kept up his cricket for a good many seasons, dropping out quietly in the '80's. In 1878 he played for C. I. Thornton's Eleven against the Australians at the Orleans Club and, facing the bowling of Spofforth and Frank Allan for the first time, scored 61 in his best style.

GEORGE TUBOW II, King of Tonga. The last of the independent kings in the Pacific. Died April, 1918, aged 46. Very fond of cricket, gaining his love of the game while at school in Auckland. His subjects became so devoted to the game that it was necessary to prohibit it on six days of the week in order to avert famine, the plantations being entirely neglected for the cricket field.

DR ALFRED GRACE, the last of the famous brotherhood, who was born at Downend on May 17, 1840, died in a nursing home in Bristol on May 24, 1916, and was buried at Chipping Sodbury. He never appeared at Lord's, but was a very useful cricketer, his usual post in the field being long-stop. As a player he at no time ranked with his brothers, but in local cricket he scored several hundreds and when only fifteen years of age formed one of the Gloucestershire XXII which met the All England Eleven at Bristol. Although he was not in the front rank of cricketers, he stood out as one of the finest horsemen in England, and for many years followed the Duke of Beaufort's hounds three or four times a week. He was known as "The Hunting Doctor." For many years he practised as a surgeon at Chipping Sodbury, Gloucestershire. He never got over the tragic death of his son, Dr Gerald Grace, in South Africa.

PRIVATE FREDERICK PERCY HARDY (County of London Yeomanry), born at Blandford on June 26, 1881, was found dead on the floor of a lavatory at King's Cross station (GNR) on March 9, 1916. His throat was cut and a blood-stained knife was by his side. He was on The Oval ground-staff in 1900 and 1901 and began to appear for Somerset in 1903. In consecutive innings for the Surrey Colts in 1901 he made 141 v Wandsworth and 144 not out v Mitcham Wanderers. In 1910 he played two excellent innings at Taunton, making 91 v Kent and 79 v Surrey. He was a left-handed batsman and a useful right-handed medium-paced change bowler.

REV. ROBERT POOLE HOOPER died at Hove, September 12, 1918, in the 92nd year of his age. Played for Cambridge University v Harrow in 1848; and was asked to play v Oxford, but "had already made previous promises for matches which I could not honourably throw over." Stroke of the first Trinity boat for two years. Norfolk County Cricket XI. Considered the finest left-hand tennis player of his generation.

JOHN MARSH, the well-known aboriginal fast bowler, died in hospital at Orange (NSW) on May 26, 1916. He played Grade cricket for the South Sydney and Sydney Clubs, and also appeared for New South Wales. In the match with Victoria at Sydney in February, 1901, he was no-balled seventeen times for throwing by R. Crockett, of Melbourne: the other umpire, S. P. Jones, however, allowed his bowling as fair. A few seasons later he had a six months' tour through the Commonwealth with a Hippodrome company, being exhibited in the role of a fast bowler and demonstrating his skill to any countrymen who were anxious to stand up against him.

MR FREDERICK HENRY NORMAN, born at Bromley on January 23, 1839, died in London on October 6, 1916. He belonged altogether to a cricketing family, his father, two brothers and a son having (like himself) all been in the Eton Eleven: he was, too, a nephew of the famous Mr Herbert Jenner-Fust and related by marriage with the Barnard, Bonham-Carter, Dyke, Nepean and Wathen families. He was in the Eton Eleven in 1854 and three following years, being captain in 1857, and in that of Cambridge for three seasons, commencing 1858, and captain in 1860. In his matches against Harrow and Winchester he made no long scores, but against Oxford in 1858, when he obtained his Blue as a Freshman, he played a first innings of 43. He was a free and attractive batsman, hitting well and successfully, and making many large scores. At Cambridge in 1858 he made 100 for the University v Cambridge Town Club, and at Lord's, in 1859, 103 for Gentlemen of Kent v Gentlemen of England. He played in excellent style, perhaps rather too much forward for the rough wickets of his time, when the ground at Lord's was fiery and dangerous. On modern wickets he would doubtless have been a great success. He had been coached by Martingell. In the field he was generally long-leg and cover-point. He was a member of the original Committee of the Kent County CC, formed at Maidstone in 1859, and also one of the original Trustees of the Mynn Memorial Benevolent Institution for Kentish Cricketers. Between 1858 and 1864 he appeared in ten matches for Kent, and at Lord's in 1858 assisted the Gentlemen against the Players. He used sometimes to play for the Home Circuit – he was admitted a barrister, Inns of Court, in 1863 – which had some very good cricketers, Robert Marsham, R. A. Bayford, etc, and some famous men like Sir George Honyman, A. L. Smith and the Hon, A. F. Thesiger, who all became Judges. In one of the Home Circuit's matches, at Maidstone, Mr Norman got over a hundred, and to commemorate the event Honyman (with whom he read law) gave him some law books: a bat would perhaps have been more appropriate. Mr Norman had been a member of the MCC since 1863 and served on the Committee of the Club from 1866 to 1868.

MR GEORGE HENRY ('HARRY') STEVENS TROTT, born August 5, 1866; died at Melbourne, November 12, 1917. Came to England in 1888, 1890, 1893, and 1896.

Australia has produced greater cricketers than Harry Trott, but in his day he held a place in the front rank of the world's famous players. He was a first-rate bat, a fine field at point, and his leg breaks made him a very effective change bowler. Four times he came to England – first in 1888, again in 1890 and 1893, and, finally, in 1896, when he had the honour of captaining the team. As a leader in the field he perhaps gained even more distinction than as an all-round player. Ranjitsinhji considered him a better captain than Darling, and beyond that praise could hardly go. The personal popularity that Harry Trott enjoyed in 1896 wherever he went was remarkable. One is inclined to think that no Australian captain, before or since, was liked so much by his opponents. By sheer force of character he overcame the disadvantages involved in lack of education, and won the warm regard of men with whom, apart from the comradeship of the cricket field, he had nothing in common. In managing his team he owed much to his equable temper and innate tact. Knowing all the little weaknesses and vanities of the men under his command, he believed in a policy of kindly encouragement. Never outwardly disturbed by the state of the game, he could inspire even the most despondent with something of his own cheerfulness. He played cricket in the best possible spirit, taking victory and defeat with the same calm philosophy.

No better loser was ever seen than Harry Trott at the end of the Test match at The Oval in 1896. It was the disappointment of his life, as the result decided the rubber in England's favour, but he was full of praise for the way in which Peel and J. T. Hearne had made the most of a horribly difficult wicket. In the England match at Lord's the same season Trott played his finest innings, he and Sydney Gregory enabling Australia to make a most creditable fight in face of overwhelming odds. Against Tom Richardson's bowling on a wicket of lightning pace Trott trusted to the strength of his back play and was justified by success. His method recalled the way in which Daft and Bob Carpenter used to withstand the fastest bowling at Lord's on the much rougher wickets of the early '60's. Trott made 143 and Gregory 103, the two batsmen putting on 221 runs for the fourth wicket in Australia's second innings. Trott's play was almost flawless, but the Englishmen felt certain that Hayward caught him in the slips with his score at 61. Perhaps next to this 143 the best innings Trott ever played in this country was his 92 against England at The Oval in 1893. Trott, who had been in ill-health for some time before his death, was the elder brother of the late Albert Trott, who for many years played so brilliantly for Middlesex.

S. H. P.

THE REV. A. H. C. FARGUS. He was not lost, as stated in the Press, in Admiral Cradock's flagship, the *Monmouth*, on November 1, 1914. Missing a train, he was prevented from re-joining the ship just before it left for the Pacific and was appointed to another.

## G. H. S. TROTT IN FIRST-CLASS CRICKET

| | BATTING | | | | | BOWLING | | | |
|---|---|---|---|---|---|---|---|---|---|
| Year | Innings | Not Outs | Runs | Highest Innings | Average | Balls | Runs | Wickets | Average |
| **In Australia** | | | | | | | | | |
| 1885-86 | 4 | 2 | 97 | 54* | 48.50 | 414 | 160 | 7 | 23.85 |
| 1886-87 | 11 | 2 | 116 | 29* | 12.88 | 1,038 | 421 | 12 | 35.08 |
| 1887-88 | 14 | 1 | 106 | 30 | 8.15 | 1,367 | 687 | 26 | 26.42 |
| **In England** | | | | | | | | | |
| 1888 | 65 | 2 | 1,212 | 83 | 19.23 | 2,015 | 1,145 | 48 | 23.83 |
| **In Australia** | | | | | | | | | |
| 1888-89 | 13 | — | 507 | 172 | 39.00 | 1,150 | 436 | 25 | 17.44 |
| 1889-90 | 7 | 1 | 228 | 72 | 38.00 | 859 | 379 | 18 | 21.05 |
| **In England** | | | | | | | | | |
| 1890 | 65 | 1 | 1,273 | 186 | 19.89 | 995 | 610 | 23 | 26.52 |
| **In Australia** | | | | | | | | | |
| 1890-91 | 8 | 1 | 161 | 81 | 23.00 | 150 | 98 | 2 | 49.00 |
| 1891-92 | 11 | — | 85 | 23 | 7.72 | 601 | 359 | 11 | 32.63 |
| 1892-93 | 8 | 1 | 304 | 70* | 43.42 | 360 | 179 | 2 | 89.50 |
| **In England** | | | | | | | | | |
| 1893 | 59 | 2 | 1,437 | 145 | 25.21 | 1,906 | 1,141 | 60 | 19.01 |
| **In America** | | | | | | | | | |
| 1893 | 5 | — | 117 | 58 | 23.40 | 200 | 106 | 5 | 21.20 |
| **In Australia** | | | | | | | | | |
| 1893-94 | 8 | — | 132 | 54 | 16.50 | 897 | 395 | 18 | 21.94 |
| 1894-95 | 21 | 1 | 630 | 152 | 31.50 | 1,578 | 806 | 41 | 19.65 |
| 1895-96 | 10 | — | 306 | 66 | 30.60 | 630 | 346 | 7 | 49.42 |
| **In England** | | | | | | | | | |
| 1896 | 54 | 5 | 1,297 | 143 | 26.46 | 1,699 | 928 | 44 | 21.09 |
| **In America** | | | | | | | | | |
| 1896 | 6 | — | 90 | 55 | 15.00 | 398 | 178 | 11 | 16.18 |
| **In Australia** | | | | | | | | | |
| 1896-97 | 8 | — | 323 | 104 | 40.37 | 480 | 285 | 6 | 47.50 |
| 1897-98 | 18 | — | 463 | 92 | 25.72 | 1,678 | 803 | 29 | 27.68 |
| 1900-01 | 2 | — | 39 | 22 | 19.50 | 242 | 177 | 8 | 22.12 |
| 1903-04 | 10 | — | 268 | 59 | 26.80 | 484 | 306 | 13 | 23.53 |
| 1904-05 | 1 | — | 26 | 26 | 26.00 | 48 | 27 | — | — |
| 1907-08 | 2 | — | 34 | 30 | 17.00 | 198 | 155 | 5 | 31.00 |
| **In New Zealand** | | | | | | | | | |
| 1912-13 | 8 | 3 | 188 | 61 | 37.69 | — | 109 | 4 | 27.25 |
| Totals | 418 | 22 | 9,439 | 186 | 23.83 | | 10,236 | 425 | 24.08 |

Note – Only matches on even terms included in the cases of the English and American tours: in New Zealand only the matches with the provinces. Defective bowling analysis in one of these prevents completion of "Balls" column.

Serious illness practically ended Trott's career after the Australian season of 1897-98.

# 1919-1940

When first-class cricket resumed after the war, it did so tentatively, in a flurry of speculation regarding changes in the laws, and with the foolish compromise of the two-day match, a gesture whose uncertainty future historians will no doubt interpret as one of a thousand symptoms of a subconscious fear that although everything was now back to normal, in truth nothing was ever going to be the same again. In the end, societies get the pastimes they deserve, and there was no doubt that by 1919 English society had changed; how would that change be reflected, if at all, on the field of play? Nobody could be sure how many potentially great players had been blown to pieces, like Howell and Jeeves, or how many others had been fortunate enough to be merely maimed, like young Chester of Worcestershire. But certainly the wide breach in the continuity of the first-class game left England's international standing in an uncertain light.

For one thing its preordained leaders were too long in the tooth to lead any longer. Patricians like MacLaren, Perrin and H. K. Foster could hardly be expected to muster their old power. Spooner, offered the England captaincy in 1920, declined on the grounds of physical unfitness; a year later Fry had all but accepted the post when a split finger caused him to stand down, as it proved, forever. Warner contented himself with the lesser prize of the captaincy of Middlesex and the winning of a famous county championship. Jessop might conceivably have mustered a few last dusty thunderbolts to fling at the enemy except that he had fallen a victim to the British, as distinct from the German, army; while serving as a captain with the Lincolnshire Regiment, he was given steam treatment for lumbago, was very nearly boiled alive and survived with a permanently damaged heart. F. S. Jackson was already preoccupied with that political career which was to lead him to a subordinate role in the unedifying black comedy of the Zinoviev Letter.

And so the line of succession passed to Douglas of Essex, whose finest sporting achievement had been, and would remain, his winning of an Olympic Gold Medal at the 1908 Games when he won the Middleweight Boxing Championship. Douglas had already captained England on a pre-war overseas tour, but in 1921 he was replaced by Tennyson of Hampshire, who was followed in turn by others culminating in Chapman of Kent, who finally led the national side into the promised land of victory over the Australians. Posterity cannot help feeling that the arrival of the national side in those hospitable pastures might have been expedited by a committee of selectors which had some constructive idea of what it was supposed to be doing. As Sydney Pardon put it, "The selectors lacked a settled policy, and were inclined to catch at straws and allow themselves to be influenced too much by the latest form".

But Pardon himself contributed to the state of mind which was so exposed to the vacillations of the passing moment. He made the announcement that "during all the years that I have edited Wisden there has never been a season so disheartening as that of 1921". The modern student is frankly bewildered by such arrant pessimism. The three greatest batsmen in the land were Hobbs, Woolley and Mead, with the enigmatic George Gunn never far behind. And, although it is true that Hobbs was dogged in the immediate post-war campaigns by illness, there is no countenancing the incompetence of a team of selectors which could look to the prospect of the fast bowling of Gregory and Macdonald and ignore Mead and Gunn. Admittedly the English attack was weak, but not nearly as weak as selectorial policy made it appear.

Rhodes, after all, was coaxed back in 1926, which suggests that in 1921 he would hardly have needed any coaxing at all. Parkin was a gifted if wayward artist, and Louden of Essex, who never did receive the call, must often have wondered what he had to do to attract attention.

But the most extraordinary oversight by the selectors of the day was of an enormity so overwhelming that it is generally not seen to be an oversight at all so much as a cruel act of nature. The English in 1921 possessed the world's greatest bowler and yet made no attempt to recruit him. It may well be that he was unrecruitable, but that possibility does not explain the failure to make the attempt. In his history of the period, Warner, displaying his consummate mastery of the half-truth, writes that "S. F. Barnes had retired from first-class cricket", which is like saying that after his experience of life in the jungle Tarzan resigned from the House of Lords. Warner's wording conveys the impression of an ageing man who had finally hung up his boots; some idea of how comically inaccurate that impression is may soon be gathered from a glance at what was going on in the Minor County Championship throughout the 1920s. So far from sulking in the tent of middle-age, Barnes was busy making a mockery of all standards in the first-class game; it ought never to be forgotten that he was a year younger than Fry, who had been offered the captaincy of a post-war side, and was in 1921 a year younger that Rhodes was in 1926.

But Barnes, advance scout of a more acrimonious age, was destined never to play representative cricket again, and, if we are to locate the archetypal between-the-wars professional, we must turn neither to him nor to Hobbs nor Woolley nor Mead nor Gunn, all of whom had been prominent in the pre-war game, but to Sutcliffe of Yorkshire, the only batsman to score 1,000 runs in every season between the wars. Sutcliffe's career began in 1919 and ended in 1939, but it is not just the exactitude of his dates which makes him a symbolic figure. Sir Neville Cardus has described the suede shoes and Saville Row suits of the new, post-war professional of whom Sutcliffe may be taken as the exemplar. The old days of the forelock-tugging hired hand were drawing rapidly to a close, from which follows the corollary that there was a sharp decline in the proliferation of the Gentleman-cricketer.

The amateur player soon found that in the less hospitable climate of the post-war world he had to think much more than ever before about earning a living. The number of gifted university and public school players who were now disappearing from the higher reaches of the game while still in their prime showed a dramatic increase on the old days. In the England side which opened the Triangular Tournament in 1912, there were five amateurs, Spooner, Fry, Warner, Jessop and F. R. Foster; in 1926, which was the next occasion when England defeated Australia, there were only two, Chapman and Stevens, of whom the latter is a perfect example of the new-style gifted Gentleman-cricketer unable to devote much time to the game. No more the felicities of a Bernard Bosanquet, who, in the words of his son, was able to while away the Edwardian years by drifting from one country house party to the next, tipping the butler on Monday morning before travelling on to his next social-cum-sporting invitation. (Ironically it was Bosanquet more than any other cricketer who reflected technically the social changes remoulding the new century. His essay in the 1925 Wisden on the genesis of the Googly is remarkable for its disingenuous attempt to absolve its author from any taint of having corrupted the innocence of the days when a ball tended to spin in a predictable direction.)

There was another, far more serious manifestation of the decline of the Gentleman-cricketer, one which spelled out the nemesis waiting in the wings. The days of patronage were numbered. The same iron laws which debarred the amateur cricketer from unlimited indulgence in the game were now dictating that those patrimonies once grasped so eagerly by harassed county secretaries were being diverted into the cellars of the Chancellor of the Exchequer. It is a truism of English cricket in the twentieth century that it has never paid its way; students of Wisden are constantly confronted by reports from the counties bemoaning lost revenues and empty coffers, posing the question-mark of continuing survival, demanding more members and higher subscriptions to offset the mysterious economic tendencies of the new age. The reliance on private contributions was marked and almost always justified, but now that the Gentleman was being dispossessed, what future was there for the first-class game? But the mills of the economic gods grind slow, and the answer to this question was not finally given for another fifty years, when it was couched in tragic terms first of abasement before commercial subsidy and finally of debasement by television.

In the meantime, if the place of the amateur on the field of play grew more uncertain with every dawning season, his position as an administrator and general self-perpetuating panjandrum remained unchallenged. English cricket was still the province of not-so-modern major-generals like my lords Hawke and Harris, and it was the latter who was involved in a small imbroglio illustrating at once the power of the partician in the period under review, and a scepticism regarding his ethical purity on the part of the general public. One of the major factors in the revival of English cricket in the 1920s, and a strong buttress to the argument for a golden age, was the emergence of the Gloucestershire player Walter Hammond. But Hammond had been born in Kent, a technicality which Lord Harris seized upon in a successful attempt to prevent Hammond from participating in the county championship throughout the 1922 season. It might be possible to take the charitable view and assume that Harris, although wrongheaded, was at least righthearted and living by his own code. After all, this was the man who had written, only a year before the Hammond crisis, that to play cricket in the appropriate spirit was "a moral lesson in itself, and the classroom is God's air and sunshine. Foster it, my brothers, so that it may attract all who can find the time to play it, protect it from anything that would sully it, so that it may grow in favour with all men". Let us see how Harris contrived to march abreast of his own precepts.

In a wonderfully indiscreet autobiography entitled with comically unintentional appropriateness *A Few Short Runs*, Harris tells a happy tale of how, in his playing days, an old friend, S. S. Schultz, turned out for Lancashire against Harris's Kent side even though he had "no sort of qualification for Lancashire". Harris then raises this point with the Lancashire captain Hornby, who tells him that Schultz's mother lives at the Port of Liverpool. Harris ends with an endearing chortle: "The audacity of the claim was so astounding that I never said another word". One cannot help reflecting what a pity it was that nobody had given young Hammond Harris's book as a Christmas present in 1921. Naturally the great man was heavily criticised for his act of aggrandisement against so gifted a young player, and defended himself with the following inscrutable remark: "Bolshevism is rampant, and seeks to abolish all laws and rules, and this year cricket has not escaped its attack". That Karl Marx was at the back of Hammond's otherwise inexplicable absence from the 1922 Gloucestershire side, and that God's classroom should teach such interesting double standards, comprises one of cricket's richest jokes. Fortunately, what Harris saw as a thunderous purifying of the game's soul proved no more than a tiny hiccup in Hammond's magisterial procession into cricket history, as the reader will see if he examines the events of August 1928 when, in a spell of six days, Hammond, having scored two centuries and taken ten catches in the game against Surrey, followed it up with fifteen wickets in the Worcestershire match. (Harris's talk of bolshevism might just conceivably have been more justified regarding the 1931-32 Queensland side, which, in the game against Victoria, carried out what appears to have been some sort of uprising of the proletariat, with comically disastrous results.)

There is another example, this time directly involving Wisden, which illustrates the undiminished power of the Gentleman monopoly in the councils of the game, and, more to the point, the totemic inviolability which attached to Gentleman status among the lawgivers. The reader of this volume will find, among the obituaries, the name of one Walter Raleigh Gilbert, a cousinly connection of the Grace family who assisted that prodigious brotherhood in its campaign to establish the Gloucestershire county club. Clearly Gilbert was a considerable performer; he toured Australia with W.G. on the 1873-74 "Honeymoon" tour, and in 1876 stood fifth among all English batsmen with a highest score of 205 not out. Puzzled by Doctor Grace's failure to include so distinguished a close relative in his "Cricketers I Have Met", which includes no fewer than 121 of his contemporaries, I did what all cricket students do in such circumstances, I looked to Wisden. And there, in the 1938 edition, in "Births and Deaths of Cricketers", I found;

Gilbert, Mr W. R. (Middlesex and Gloucestershire)
born September 16, 1853, died July 26, 1924.

This led me to the 1925 edition and the Gilbert obituary which the reader will find towards the end of this volume. In that obituary Gilbert is again defined by that "Mr", which is of course a euphemism to denote "Gentleman". There are one or two striking incongruities about this death notice, especially the place of death, Calgary, Ontario, and the inartistic abruptness with which the notice ends. But most baffling of all is the information "At the beginning of 1886 he became a professional". If so, why grant him his "Mr" in the notice itself? And why persist in retaining that "Mr" in the 1938 edition? Apparently he had forsaken his amateur status forever, so why was he not stripped of all typographical honours? The fog thickens when one turns to the "Births and Deaths" column of that same Wisden where in the obituaries he is buried with full gentlemanly honours. This is what the entry says:

Gilbert, W. R. (Middlesex and Gloucestershire)
born September 16, 1853, died July 26, 1924.

So that the almanack is contradicting itself hopelessly; in one and the same edition it has listed Gilbert as a professional in "Births and Deaths" and as an amateur in the very obituary which says that he turned professional. Curiouser and curiouser. But what about that 1938 edition, where he is restored to his former pristine status? Picking an earlier Wisden at random, I happened upon the 1902 edition, where I found:

Gilbert, W. R. (Middlesex and Gloucestershire).

By now it is quite clear that there is something very peculiar about this man Gilbert, something so disconcerting to his contemporaries that they became literally incapable of knowing who he was. So far as the bewildering changes of status in Wisden are to be trusted, something like the following sequence of events appears to have taken place: In the early 1870s Gilbert begins playing first-class cricket with his cousins the Graces, enjoying considerable success. In 1886 he turns professional only weeks before a sudden mysterious loss of ability ends his career. Wisden dismisses him to the ranks of the hired hands, and W.G. can hardly bring himself to mention the name Gilbert at all, except possibly in reference to himself. In 1924 comes news of Gilbert's death in one of the farflung outposts of empire, at which point Wisden is half-tempted to forgive him, as though by dropping dead a gentleman may expiate his sins. But Wisden, having weakened in the obituary, stiffens its resolve again in "Births and Deaths", and does not finally absolve the poor fellow from his nameless crime until some time in the 1930s, more than half a century after he committed it.

But exactly when did absolution arrive? In the 1934 edition, for the ninth successive year after Gilbert's death, Wisden reads:

Gilbert, W. R.

The following edition, for 1935 carried this apocalyptic vision:

Gilbert, Mr W. R.

The first reaction to this excessive act of charity is to wonder how it might remotely profit a man to lose his own soul and then get it back again ten years after his own death. And is it really possible that there could have existed, as late in the day as 1935, anyone feebleminded enough to bother about restoring a prefix to a corpse? Evidently the editors of Wisden cared enough to take action. At first I wondered if the sudden gesture of forgiveness was due to the fact that in the early-to-mid 1930s, for the first time for half a century, the editorial succession of Wisden moved rapidly. But not even this explains the seesaw fate of Gilbert. The editorship passed in 1934 to Sydney James Southerton, who survived the promotion for only two years; in the first of these years he lists Gilbert as a professional, in the second as an amateur. As is usually the case in this type of muddle, the explanation is really very simple. In 1886 the unfortunate Gilbert, who would surely have been described by Frank Richards as hapless, found himself short of ready money and resolved to embrace the serpent of professionalism. But then, evidently deciding to extend this new philosophy beyond its merely cricketing limits, Gilbert, was, in the words of Roland Bowen, "found in the act of stealing in the dressing room from his fellow-players". He was then subjected to the rough justice of his peers, which comprised colonial exile, the inference being that the Empire, apart from providing a useful safety-valve for the vaulting ambition of thousands of otherwise frustrated bishops, generals and prime ministers, was also a handy receptacle for those who took the principle of self-help in rather the wrong spirit.

Dishonour of a different kind attaches to the lurid events of 1932-33, events that may be said to form the centrepiece of this volume. As to the degree of that dishonour, and to what extent the dogma of my-country-right-or-wrong ought to transcend a sense of fair play, each reader must come to terms with his own conscience, but it is at least interesting that the Bodyline fracas was brought about by those two paragons of the Gentlemen tradition, Warner and Jardine. Wisden's subsequent attempt to tame the beast of intimidation by codifying its excesses makes ironic reading for a later generation cynical enough to believe that no matter what is written into the laws, intimidation will always be practised by sides equipped with a battery of fast bowlers, against opponents who are not.

Statistically the between-wars period is indeed a golden age. Stupefying analyses are returned by Freeman, Tate, Parker, Verity and Richard Tyldesley; treble centuries are rendered very nearly commonplace by the likes of Hammond, Badcock, Kippax and Sandham; even the quadruple hundred is brought into focus by Ponsford and Bradman. Greater and greater become these inflationary feats, until in the end a sort of giantism invades the record books. At Leyton, Sutcliffe and Holmes bat on forever, at The Oval, six years later, young Hutton goes on for over thirteen hours, and that same summer the Kentish opener Fagg goes to Colchester and there finds his own unique kind of immortality. And finally the *reductio ad absurdum* at Durban, where the cricketers of England and South Africa take ten days to settle an argument and still fail to reach a decision.

As in all other periods, umpires prove their fallibility, and in one match between Lancashire and Derbyshire, fail to keep their eye on the bail. In 1931 against Northamptonshire, Turnbull breaks the law and is admonished, not by the umpires but by Wisden. Two years later Dogberry is again in error, over a declaration in the Hampshire v Essex match, while in the 1919 fixture between Somerset and Sussex, the asperities of the new age lose no time in revealing themselves. But officialdom's most alarming fate occurs in the match between Gloucestershire and Yorkshire, where the trials and tribulations of an already handicapped umpire seem excessive. In a 1936 game the Sussex players march off the field in protest at what they take to be a frivolous appeal by Nottinghamshire, while the 1937 Leicestershire v Hampshire game is sabotaged by some remarkable weather.

Sometimes Wisden is frankly baffled by the antics of the cricketers, as in a game between Middlesex and Nottinghamshire in which Carr's declaration provides a riddle for posterity; the same only more so applies to Stephen Fry's declaration in the 1931 Surrey v Hampshire game at The Oval, of which the almanack says, "it will ever remain a puzzle". There are delightful moments when we see performed the dainty dance of the generations, by the Gunns father and son against Warwickshire, and most amazing of all, that moment in a 1922 game between Derbyshire and Warwickshire when Quaife supported by his son, faces the bowling of Bestwick supported by his. Tempers flare in the Roses match in 1922 and again in 1933; when Lancashire play Hampshire in 1920, and again two years later at Gravesend, the crowd takes matters into its own hand and commits spectacular crimes of trespass. Hobbs saunters into history at Taunton in 1926, and Denis Compton serves notice on posterity with a maiden hundred at Northampton; Gimblett hints at a promise never quite fulfilled at Frome in 1935; Constantine shows all-round genius at Lord's in 1928, and in the Sheffield Shield Victoria blithely hit their way to four figures.

But in a sense the most remarkable single event of the 1919-39 period, the one which encapsulates all the humour and pathos of the cricketer's transient grace, besides defining the financial straitjacket into which the first-class game had inexorably wriggled, was neither the Surrey v Gloucestershire match in which Fender and B. H. Lyon strove so ingeniously to reach a conclusion, nor MacLaren's sentimental triumph against Armstrong's Australians at Eastbourne, nor even the staggering fluctuations of the Warwickshire v Hampshire game of the following year. I would instead nominate the fate of a forgotten Leicestershire professional called Shipman, who, in 1934, after long and honourable service, was granted a Benefit match, with results that are at once comic, tragic and downright unbelievable. Perhaps the only writer capable of doing justice to such a theme was the future Nobel Prize-winner who opened the batting one day for Dublin University in an utterly forgettable game against Northamptonshire.

Finally there are the deaths, ranging from the high comedy of Dr Abrahams, who looked so like his own twin that Dr Grace once accused him of batting twice in the same innings, to the ominous instance of tragedy averted in the life of one Charles William Beal, an Australian tour manager burdened with the most deadly secret ever vouchsafed to any sporting functionary. We wonder about the umpire who was buried in his white coat clutching a ball, and hope that the fixtures secretary at the Elysian Fields was suitably prepared for his arrival. We admire the ingenuity with which a Mr Cave snatched greatness by anticipating the stratagems of Liberace. And there are deaths whose circumstances haunt the imagination forever, the deathbed wedding of Archie Jackson, the triumph of James Seymour over the Commissioners of Inland Revenue, the moment in the life of the Reverend Walter Baptist Money when he put sex before cricket; Lord Harris' friend Schultz, who was once out first ball twice in the same innings; a gentleman called Bentinck, bowled out by a swallow.

Wisden registers the feats and follies of such men, only very occasionally lapsing into the orotundity of euphemism. Sydney Southerton did not die at all; life merely "ebbed away at dinner", while in the case of John Mills, who collapsed in mid-match, "life was found to be extinct". The almanack indulges in its customary happy habit of annexing the great for its columns; it is a pleasure to encounter here the creator of Mr Sherlock Holmes, more surprising to find him followed a few years later by the only begetter of Peter Pan. But long after I have put this volume aside, I will live with the recollection of three tiny incidents in its compilation. The first two show how incongruous a man's hold on immortality may sometimes be, and the last rejoices in that ambiguity of terminology which constitutes the Englishman's inexhaustible spring of laughter. I salute Major Edwards, who trotted the globe and once, in Southern Russia, lost everything — except his Wisdens. I salute too that prince of lost causes Mr Edward Ray, "who introduced the game to Russian Lapland". And I cheer for the most heartening escape from certain dismissal in the entire history of cricket. We read of C. I. Thornton that "when war broke out he was in Berlin and was very nearly caught". But soft, what light through yonder Wisden breaks? Cannot posterity be forgiven for inquiring who was the clumsy Prussian who dropped him?

*Benny Green*

## NOTES BY THE EDITOR IN 1919

The season of 1919 proved, beyond all question or dispute, that cricket had lost nothing of its attraction for the public. Indeed, one may go further than that. Despite a break of four years and the fact that at all grounds the charge for admission – in view of the entertainment tax and vastly increased expenses – was doubled, county matches drew far larger crowds than in ordinary seasons before the war. The faint-hearts who, without evidence on the point, had jumped to the conclusion that cricket would never again be its old self, were utterly confuted. Even the hopeful spirits, among whom I include myself, were agreeably surprised, things turning out much better than they had expected. Such being the pleasant state of affairs in the first year of peace, I trust we shall hear no more about the need for drastic alterations in the game. Looking back on the events of the season it is quaint to think that we were asked to shorten the boundaries, to penalise the batting side for every maiden over played, to banish the left-handed batsman, and to limit to three, or at most four, the number of professionals in every county eleven. All these fatuous suggestions and others just as foolish were, it will be remembered, put forward quite seriously. Happily we shall not be worried by them again. It is only right here to pay tribute to the steadfast confidence of Lord Harris. In the darkest days of the war he expressed his conviction that when peace came back cricket would have all its old charm for the English people. Everything he said was amply justified last summer.

I have no wish to pat myself on the back or exult unduly over the abandonment of the two-day scheme in county cricket. I felt sure the experiment – hastily determined on – would not answer, the objections to it being so obvious. It was doomed before the season had run half its course, and in August the Advisory Committee decided unanimously to go back to three-day matches in 1920. Thanks to a fine summer the scheme had every chance, as not till August did the weather do the game any harm. The great trouble lay in the inordinately long hours of play. Hours that even on an exceptional occasion, such as the Eton and Harrow match, are too long for enthusiastic school boys could not suit men of thirty and upwards. On that point I never had the smallest doubt. The players and the umpires hated the long days and the public assuredly did not like them. Only when something quite out of the common was to be seen, as for example the wonderful finish of the Surrey and Kent match at The Oval, did any great number of people wait on the ground till half-past seven. Before that time the craving for food had as a rule become stronger than the passion for cricket. To put the matter in a prosaic way, the advocates of the two-day match overlooked the needs of the human stomach. I have no prejudice against two-day matches as such, but the simple fact is that modern wickets in fine weather are too good for them. At Trent Bridge last summer only one match was played out, and at The Oval, though a miracle of hitting by J. N. Crawford and Hobbs enabled Surrey to beat Kent and the clock, the all-important matches with Nottinghamshire and Yorkshire had to be left drawn. It is often argued, with a good show of reason, that the wickets should not be so easy, but no one has yet solved satisfactorily the problem of preparing a wicket that shall ensure resonable scores and yet not be dangerous. The experiment tried at Old Trafford some years ago of playing on half-rolled wickets was such a failure that it had speedily to be given up.

Though the liberal support given by the public last summer removed many fears, and incidentally had the effect of producing excellent balance sheets, the outlook as regards county cricket is not altogether satisfactory. The menace of the Lancashire and Yorkshire Leagues cannot be ignored. From what I am told leading professionals constantly receive from League clubs offers of better terms than they are getting from the counties, and naturally the temptation of more money for far less work is very strong. I am not sufficiently behind the scenes for my opinion on the subject to be of any value, but one point strikes me. Cricketers who are proud of the positions they have won may, while making the best arrangements they can with their county committees, be willing to sacrifice a little so as to keep in the public eye. Wherever he goes an England player is somebody, but nothing more than local popularity can be won in the Saturday afternoon matches of the Leagues. It is clear that a good deal of anxiety is felt by some of the counties, the resolution proposed by Yorkshire, and carried by the Advisory Committee on the 8th of December, barring from representative matches, tours abroad, and festivals, players who will not pledge themselves to assist their counties when required, being obviously designed to meet the situation. This resolution was confirmed by the MCC a month later.

The death in August of David Gregory set me thinking as to what would have happened if when the first Australian eleven came here in 1878 the season had been dry and sunny and not so miserably cold and wet. My own belief is that the team would not have been so successful. Of course the great bowlers, with their varied gifts and new methods, would have asserted themselves – nothing could have stopped Spofforth – but on fast wickets the comparative weakness of the batting would have been felt far more than it was. More than that our people would have escaped the shock of seeing the MCC out in one afternoon for scores of 33 and 19. The moral effect of that catastrophe was incalculable. As regards the bowling, it is almost certain that in a fine summer we should have thought a great deal more than we did of Frank Allan, and far less of Harry Boyle. Of the twelve men who started a new epoch in cricket there are, now that David Gregory has gone, six survivors – Spofforth, Blackham, Charles Bannerman, Alec Bannerman, George Bailey, and Tom Garrett.

An interesting point in last summer's cricket was the selection for Gentlemen v Players, at Lord's, of G. T. S. Stevens. No cricketer still at school had played in the match since the famous bowler, Alfred Lowth, was picked for Eighteen Gentlemen in 1836. Stevens had thus special reason to feel proud of the distinction conferred on him. He was chosen in the first instance as twelfth man, being given his place on the morning of the match – to the exclusion of J. C. White – owing to the state of the ground. It may not be generally known that N. E. Partridge, who has done such brilliant things at Malvern, was asked to play for the Gentlemen at The Oval. The Surrey Committee did quite the right thing in trying to introduce new talent in the first year after the war, but for some reason the invitation was declined. I cannot see why public school batsmen and bowlers should for so many years have been excluded from the Gentlemen's eleven. R. A. H. Mitchell was asked to play at The Oval while still at Eton, but I know of no other case till last season, though there may have been some that were never made public. Many school batsmen and a few bowlers have, of course, been fully worthy of selection. The batsmen – leaving aside Mitchell – whose names strike me were C. G. Lyttelton (Eton, 1860), F. W. Wright (Rossall, 1862), Alfred Lubbock (Eton, 1863), C. F. Buller (Harrow, 1864), B. Pauncefote (Rugby, 1867), William Yardley (Rugby, 1868), C. J. Ottaway (Eton, 1869), A. J. Webbe (Harrow, 1874), A. P. Lucas (Uppingham, 1874) and, coming to much later years, A. C. MacLaren (Harrow, 1890),. R. H. Spooner (Marlborough, 1899), and that sad disappointment at Oxford, F. H. Knott (Tonbridge, 1910). In contrast to all these instances of brilliant achievement before the age of twenty, A. N. Hornby, Lord Harris, C. T. Studd, F. S. Jackson, C. B. Fry, and R. E. Foster were comparatively slow in getting to their best. Though they did not appear for Gentlemen v Players the year they left school, F. W. Wright and A. P. Lucas got very near to it, both meeting with conspicuous success in representative matches. In 1862 F. W. Wright, in the North and South match at Lord's for Jimmy Grundy's benefit, made 50 against Willsher's bowling – a performance that caused a tremendous sensation – and in 1874 A. P. Lucas, for Gentlemen of the South against Players of the North, at Prince's, scored 48 against Alfred Shaw and Morley at their best.

Of public school bowlers good enough for the Gentlemen I would not in the last fifty years or so suggest more than five – C. K. Francis (Rugby, 1869), A. G. Steel (Marlborough, 1877), S. M. J. Woods (Brighton College, 1886), C. L. Townsend (Clifton, 1895), and J. N. Crawford (Repton, 1904-05). A. G. Steel stood out by himself. Bob Thoms said he was never quite so good as in his last year at school and that what he could do with the ball was marvellous. I have always thought it a misfortune that Townsend did such wonders in the August of 1895. He took a hundred wickets, or very nearly a hundred, in that month for Gloucestershire. He was clearly over-bowled and never again did he have the same spin or the same command over the ball. In happier circumstances he would have stepped into the England eleven against the Australians in 1896.

Considering that we had lost four seasons, the class of English cricket last summer was quite as good as could reasonably have been expected. The weak point was a lack of the highest class bowling, this being emphasised by the fact that Barnes did not take part in the Gentlemen and Players match at Lord's. Whether Barnes has finished with first-class cricket I do not know, but as he will be forty-four in April he can hardly be regarded now as a serious force. Parkin was the best substitute available at Lord's, but, clever and individual bowler as he is, no one would at present venture to place him on anything like Barnes's level. To the best of my belief Barnes was not asked to play at Lord's, it being thought wiser, in view of the future, to give Parkin his chance. The question of bowling apart, there was not, I think, any cause for misgiving. The England team that beat Yorkshire so handsomely at The Oval in September would have done us no discredit in a Test match. I thought our amateur batting would be very weak, but, though a long way below the best pre-war standard, it proved surprisingly good. For this happy state of things we had chiefly to thank D. J. Knight and J. N. Crawford. Knight exceeded the most sanguine hopes entertained of him in 1914, and Crawford, returning to English cricket after an absence of nine years, was a better batsman than ever before. He played a marvellous innings against the Australian eleven at The Oval, and the way in which he and Hobbs won the Surrey and Kent match was the sensation of the season. Knight had nothing less than a triumph for the Gentlemen at Lord's, proving himself a real master on a wicket that varied enormously in pace during the three days, and after that in several Surrey matches he fairly divided honours with Hobbs. Another amateur batsman to whom the season brought distinction was the Hon. C. N. Bruce. He could not play many times, but his innings against Lancashire at Lord's – I unluckily did not see it – was described on all hands as magnificent. Less gifted than Knight and Crawford, he needs a fast wicket, but when the conditions suit him he is brilliant. Before the war Bruce seemed to have dropped out of first-class cricket and his reappearance was very welcome. It will be remembered that when he went up to Oxford from Winchester, with a high reputation, heart trouble stopped his cricket in his first season.

As regards new talent last season, the chief prizes fell to Yorkshire and Lancashire. In finding Sutcliffe and Waddington, Yorkshire received compensation for the loss of Booth in the war and the premature death of Drake. Holmes was not a new man, but his doings in 1914 had hardly suggested that he would jump at once into the front rank of batsmen. As a first wicket pair Holmes and Sutcliffe recalled the feats of Jupp and Tom Humphrey for Surrey in 1864, but their success was more of a surprise to the public than that of the Surrey players. In Hallows Lancashire found a first-season batsman only second to Sutcliffe, and in Norbury a fine hitter. Of Waddington as a bowler we may reasonably expect a great deal. His delivery could scarcely be better. It was a great achievement to take a hundred wickets for Yorkshire, the more so as he was still suffering from the effects of a wound in the leg.

Nothing in the season was more gratifying that the successful revival of the university match. When the fixture was provisionally arranged the outlook seemed very dubious, but watching the game at Lord's one might have imagined there had been no war and that things had gone on without interruption since 1914. Thanks mainly to the batting of Howell and Knight, Oxford won, but Cambridge had, I think, rather the better all-round side, and but for an unhappy run-out in the last innings the result would quite possibly have been different. So many public school cricketers with wonderful records to their credit have gone up to the Universities that the big match this year ought to be something quite out of the common.

The Memorial Biography of W. G. Grace duly appeared during the year, publication having been delayed till after the war. Though the book gives a faithful record of all that W.G. did in the cricket field it would have been all the better if the recollections furnished by many famous players had not had to be so severely condensed, and in some cases left out altogether. Sir Home Gordon tells me he had sufficient material to fill a far larger volume but that the restriction as to size was unavoidable. One omission is much to be regretted. There is no portrait of W.G. in his young days except in a group of the amateur team that went to Canada in 1872. We are in danger of forgetting that W.G. was not always bulky of figure. He put on weight very rapidly before he was thirty but it was not until after 1876 – one of his greatest seasons – that the burden of the flesh began to trouble him. Not the least wonderful thing about him was the way he played when weighing considerably over sixteen stone.

It is to be feared that a good many people who find their pleasure in watching cricket are very ignorant of the game. In no other way can one account for the unseemly "barracking" that sometimes goes on. A particularly bad case occurred in the Middlesex and Yorkshire match at Lord's in August. J. W. Hearne – playing as well as he has ever played in his life – was doing his utmost to save Middlesex from defeat and yet a section of the crowd hooted him. A remedy for this sort of nuisance is not easy to find, as obviously the batsmen cannot leave the wickets. A stoppage of the game, however, with all the players staying on the field, might have the effect of bringing the malcontents to their senses.

I must not forget to mention the dinner given by Messrs. Wisden in September to the Australian Imperial Forces Team. Not since the MCC dinner in 1914, to celebrate the Centenary of the present Lord's ground, had so many famous cricketers gathered together under one roof. Lord Harris took the chair and in all the speeches the one note was confidence in the future of cricket. To the compliments paid to Wisden's Almanack by P. F. Warner and F. S. Jackson I cannot – from motives of modesty – refer in detail, but I need hardly say they were keenly appreciated.

# THE COUNTY MATCHES

## DERBYSHIRE

### DERBYSHIRE v WARWICKSHIRE

Played at Derby, May 22, 24, 1920

Derbyshire were beaten by eight wickets in this match, and deserved to lose. When they won the toss and went in first the wicket was in excellent condition, and there was certainly no excuse for such a paltry total as 80. Most of the batsmen found Howell's pace too much for them, and in two hours and a half the innings was over. Warwickshire's batting was quite moderate, but their score of 164 proved sufficient, Derbyshire having seven wickets down in their second innings before the arrears of 84 were cleared off. Storer is a nephew of the late William Storer, and Bestwick the son of the old Derbyshire fast bowler.

### Derbyshire

| | | | |
|---|---|---|---|
| A. Morton b Hands | 5 | – b Hands | 12 |
| G. Beet c Smith b Hands | 9 | – lbw b Calthorpe | 8 |
| Mr L. Oliver b Howell | 7 | – b Howell | 2 |
| S. Cadman c Smith b Howell | 22 | – c Hands b Calthorpe | 43 |
| Mr J. Chapman b Howell | 0 | – b Howell | 0 |
| Mr G. R. Jackson b Hands | 1 | – c Smith b Howell | 11 |
| T. Revill b Calthorpe | 5 | – b Howell | 5 |
| H. Storer not out | 11 | – b Howell | 0 |
| Mr K. W. C. Dobson c J. Smart b Howell | 0 | – b Howell | 3 |
| A. Woodland b Howell | 1 | – not out | 19 |
| R. J. Bestwick b Howell | 2 | – b Calthorpe | 6 |
| B 5, l-b 8, w 1 | 14 | B 3, l-b 5, n-b 1 | 9 |
| | **80** | | **118** |

### Warwickshire

| | | | |
|---|---|---|---|
| Mr H. Venn b Morton | 19 | – b Cadman | 5 |
| L. A. Bates c Beet b Cadman | 27 | – not out | 19 |
| C. Charlesworth b Morton | 0 | | |
| W. G. Quaife b Cadman | 3 | – not out | 8 |
| R. J. Smith c Beet b Cadman | 1 | | |
| Mr G. W. Stephens c Oliver b Morton | 34 | | |
| Hon. F. S. G. Calthorpe b Morton | 16 | | |
| Mr W. C. Hands lbw b Cadman | 20 | | |
| J. Smart c Bestwick b Cadman | 23 | – c Beet b Morton | 0 |
| C. Smart b Morton | 6 | | |
| H. Howell not out | 4 | | |
| B 4, l-b 1, n-b 6 | 11 | N-b 3 | 3 |
| | **154** | | **35** |

### Warwickshire Bowling

| | Overs | Mdns | Runs | Wkts | Overs | Mdns | Runs | Wkts |
|---|---|---|---|---|---|---|---|---|
| Howell | 19.3 | 7 | 25 | 6 | 24 | 9 | 39 | 6 |
| Hands | 12 | 3 | 19 | 3 | 17 | 4 | 24 | 1 |
| Calthorpe | 12 | 4 | 20 | 1 | 16.3 | 3 | 46 | 3 |
| Quaife | 1 | — | 2 | — | | | | |

## Derbyshire Bowling

| | Overs | Mdns | Runs | Wkts | Overs | Mdns | Runs | Wkts |
|---|---|---|---|---|---|---|---|---|
| Morton .......... | 20.1 | 8 | 44 | 5 | 8 | 1 | 17 | 1 |
| Woodland ....... | 12 | 3 | 47 | — | | | | |
| Cadman .......... | 17 | 5 | 36 | 5 | 7.4 | 3 | 15 | 1 |
| Bestwick ........ | 6 | 1 | 11 | — | | | | |
| Dobson .......... | 3 | — | 15 | — | | | | |

Umpires: T. Brown and T. Flowers.

## DERBYSHIRE v LANCASHIRE

### Played at Chesterfield, May 31, June 1, 1922

The superior side in every respect Lancashire gained an easy victory by an innings and 140 runs. The Chesterfield ground did not favour batsmen, but Makepeace played faultless cricket for four hours and a half. He hit a six and fifteen 4s and was the only batsman to master the bowling until Kenyon forced the game so well that 83 runs came in three-quarters of an hour. The Derbyshire batsmen could not do anything with Parkin. Three of them failed on the Wednesday evening and the whole side were out for 37, no fewer than seven men being dismissed without scoring. Although not quite so deadly in the follow-on, Parkin again took seven wickets and in the match he had the remarkable record of fourteen for 73 runs. Cook was just as difficult to score from and by getting rid of two of the troublesome batsmen, Watson, a slow right-handed bowler, helped to finish the match on the second afternoon. Bestwick and Morton bowled well but Derbyshire batted very poorly.

### Lancashire

| | |
|---|---|
| C. Hallows lbw b Bestwick .............. 5 | R. Tyldesley c and b Morton ........... 33 |
| H. Makepeace b Townsend .............136 | Mr M. N. Kenyon st Elliott b Morton ..... 55 |
| E. Tyldesley run out ................... 6 | L. Cook b Townsend .................. 0 |
| F. Watson b Storer ................... 35 | B. Blomley not out ................... 12 |
| J. Tyldesley c Elliott b Cadman ......... 25 | B 20, l-b 3, n-b 4 .............. 27 |
| W. Ellis c Cadman b A. H. M. Jackson .... 9 | |
| C. Parkin b Bestwick ................. 10 | 353 |

### Derbyshire

| | | |
|---|---|---|
| Mr L. Oliver lbw b Parkin ..................... | 13 – c Ellis b Parkin .............. | 6 |
| H. Storer b Parkin ......................... | 0 – b Parkin .................... | 15 |
| J. Bowden c Cook b Parkin ................. | 0 – b Parkin .................... | 32 |
| L. Townsend c and b Parkin ............... | 0 – b Parkin .................... | 0 |
| J. M. Hutchinson b Parkin .................. | 0 – b Parkin .................... | 36 |
| S. Cadman c Makepeace b Parkin .............. | 4 – b Watson .................... | 34 |
| A. Morton not out ........................ | 9 – b Parkin .................... | 9 |
| Mr G. R. Jackson lbw b Cook ................. | 4 – b Watson .................... | 19 |
| Mr A. H. M. Jackson c E. Tyldesley b Cook ....... | 0 – b Cook ..................... | 7 |
| H. Elliott c Blomley b Cook ................. | 0 – not out ..................... | 3 |
| W. Bestwick c R. Tyldesley b Parkin ............. | 0 – c Hallows b Parkin ........... | 1 |
| B 6, l-b 1 ........................... | 7      B 12, l-b 2 .............. | 14 |
| | 37 | 176 |

## Derbyshire Bowling

|  | Overs | Mdns | Runs | Wkts |
|---|---|---|---|---|
| Bestwick ........ | 30 | 6 | 77 | 2 |
| Morton .......... | 31.3 | 9 | 89 | 2 |
| Storer ............ | 15 | 4 | 53 | 1 |
| Cadman .......... | 15 | 3 | 53 | 1 |
| A. H. M. Jackson ... | 9 | 3 | 30 | 1 |
| Townsend ........ | 4 | — | 24 | 2 |

## Lancashire Bowling

|  | Overs | Mdns | Runs | Wkts | Overs | Mdns | Runs | Wkts |
|---|---|---|---|---|---|---|---|---|
| Parkin ........... | 8 | 3 | 15 | 7 | 24.1 | 10 | 58 | 7 |
| Cook ............ | 7 | 2 | 15 | 3 | 23 | 7 | 56 | 1 |
| R. Tyldesley ....... |  |  |  |  | 14 | 6 | 19 | — |
| Watson .......... |  |  |  |  | 15 | 8 | 29 | 2 |

Umpires: H. Young and W. Reeves.

# DERBYSHIRE v WARWICKSHIRE

Played at Derby, June 3, 5, 1922

Weak batting again brought about Derbyshire's defeat, Warwickshire winning easily on the second afternoon by ten wickets. Cadman and G. R. Jackson made the one stand in the first innings and Bowden alone stayed long on the Monday until Elliott helped him in a partnership which had most to do with clearing off the arrears, the eighth wicket adding 41 runs. A blow on the arm from Howell's bowling compelled Bowden to retire and rest fifty minutes before completing his innings. Warwickshire lost four men for 84 on the Saturday but W. G. Quaife mastered the bowling on Monday and was the one batsman in the match to be seen to much advantage. At the wickets four and a half hours he did not make a mistake until after completing his hundred. At one time the two Quaifes were opposed by the two Bestwicks. For father and son to be batting against bowlers similarly related was a remarkable incident – regarded as unique in county cricket.

## Derbyshire

| | | | |
|---|---|---|---|
| H. Storer b Calthorpe ......................... | 6 | – c Santall b Calthorpe ........... | 1 |
| J. Bowden b Howell ....................... | 6 | – c Smith b Calthorpe ........... | 45 |
| J. M. Hutchinson b Partridge .................. | 2 | – c Venn b Calthorpe ........... | 4 |
| S. Cadman b W. G. Quaife ................. | 42 | – b Howell .................... | 5 |
| Mr G. R. Jackson st Smith b W. G. Quaife ........ | 34 | – c C. Smart b Howell ........... | 7 |
| Mr G. Curgenven c C. Smart b Howell ........... | 1 | – c Santall b Howell ............. | 2 |
| Mr A. H. M. Jackson c Smith b Howell ........... | 10 | – c and b W. G. Quaife ........... | 9 |
| J. Fisher b Howell .......................... | 3 | – b Partridge ................. | 4 |
| H. Elliott not out ........................ | 6 | – c C. Smart b Calthorpe .......... | 30 |
| R. Bestwick b W. G. Quaife .................... | 2 | – b Howell .................... | 10 |
| W. Bestwick c C. Smart b Howell .............. | 6 | – not out ..................... | 1 |
| B 4, l-b 7, n-b 1 .................. | 12 | B 2, l-b 1, n-b 1 .......... | 4 |
| | **130** | | **122** |

## Warwickshire

| | | |
|---|---|---|
| Mr H. Venn c Elliott b W. Bestwick . . . . . . . . . . . . . | 8 | |
| Mr F. R. Santall run out . . . . . . . . . . . . . . . . . . . . . . | 1 | |
| L. A. Bates c Elliott b Cadman . . . . . . . . . . . . . . . . | 11 | |
| W. G. Quaife b R. Bestwick . . . . . . . . . . . . . . . . . . . . | 107 | |
| Hon. F. S. G. Calthorpe b Storer . . . . . . . . . . . . . . . | 14 | |
| E. J. Smith c Elliott b W. Bestwick . . . . . . . . . . . . . . | 22 – not out . . . . . . . . . . . . . . . . . . . . . . | 10 |
| Mr B. W. Quaife b A. H. M. Jackson . . . . . . . . . . . . | 20 | |
| Mr N. E. Partridge c A. H. M. Jackson b R. Bestwick | 31 | |
| J. Smart c Storer b W. Bestwick . . . . . . . . . . . . . . . . | 0 | |
| C. Smart b W. Bestwick . . . . . . . . . . . . . . . . . . . . . . | 1 – not out . . . . . . . . . . . . . . . . . . . . . . | 4 |
| H. Howell not out . . . . . . . . . . . . . . . . . . . . . . . . . . | 1 | |
| B 11, l-b 9, n-b 3 . . . . . . . . . . . . . . . . . . . . | 23 | |
| | **239** | **14** |

## Warwickshire Bowling

| | Overs | Mdns | Runs | Wkts | Overs | Mdns | Runs | Wkts |
|---|---|---|---|---|---|---|---|---|
| Howell . . . . . . . . . . . | 26.2 | 8 | 60 | 5 | 20 | 2 | 50 | 4 |
| Partridge . . . . . . . . . | 9 | 3 | 12 | 1 | 6 | — | 16 | 1 |
| Calthorpe . . . . . . . . . | 12 | 4 | 17 | 1 | 18.5 | 6 | 31 | 4 |
| W. G. Quaife . . . . . . | 9 | 2 | 29 | 3 | 8 | — | 21 | 1 |

## Derbyshire Bowling

| | Overs | Mdns | Runs | Wkts | Overs | Mdns | Runs | Wkts |
|---|---|---|---|---|---|---|---|---|
| W. Bestwick . . . . . . . | 41 | 7 | 66 | 4 | | | | |
| R. Bestwick . . . . . . . | 24.4 | 4 | 47 | 2 | | | | |
| Cadman . . . . . . . . . . | 21 | 7 | 36 | 1 | | | | |
| Storer . . . . . . . . . . . . | 15 | 5 | 37 | 1 | | | | |
| Fisher . . . . . . . . . . . . | 5 | 1 | 15 | — | | | | |
| A. H. M. Jackson . . . | 7 | 1 | 15 | 1 | 1 | — | 2 | — |
| Hutchinson . . . . . . . | | | | | 1.2 | — | 12 | — |

Umpires: A. J. Atfield and J. Moss.

## DERBYSHIRE v GLOUCESTERSHIRE

### Played at Chesterfield, June 21, 22, 23, 1933

Taking fourteen wickets for just over six runs apiece Townsend was largely responsible for Derbyshire's victory by 71 runs. He took all his six wickets for 21 in the first innings and when Gloucestershire went in to get 184 he proved still more deadly, dismissing the first six batsmen for 14 runs. Only Hammond, who drove superbly, and Sinfield batted confidently. Townsend was also Derbyshire's top scorer and Worthington and Pope helped to gain a lead of 60. Goddard bowled most effectively for Gloucestershire. The first day's cricket was limited to forty minutes, but twenty-nine wickets fell on the Friday.

## Derbyshire

| | | | |
|---|---|---|---|
| H. Storer b G. W. Parker | 17 | – b Goddard | 8 |
| Mr A. F. Skinner b Hammond | 22 | – b C. Parker | 17 |
| L. Townsend c and b Goddard | 62 | – lbw b Goddard | 26 |
| D. Smith b Goddard | 6 | – c and b Goddard | 13 |
| G. M. Lee b Sinfield | 5 | – b Goddard | 1 |
| S. Worthington c Stephens b Goddard | 54 | – hit wkt b C. Parker | 0 |
| A. E. Alderman b Goddard | 1 | – b C. Parker | 3 |
| A. V. Pope c and b Goddard | 56 | – b Goddard | 7 |
| H. Elliott lbw b C. Parker | 21 | – run out | 31 |
| T. B. Mitchell run out | 1 | – not out | 5 |
| W. Copson not out | 1 | – c Stephens b Goddard | 0 |
| B 13, l-b 1 | 14 | B 5, l-b 7 | 12 |
| | **260** | | **123** |

## Gloucestershire

| | | | |
|---|---|---|---|
| R. A. Sinfield c Smith b Copson | 69 | – b Townsend | 16 |
| C. J. Barnett b Copson | 33 | – c Skinner b Worthington | 15 |
| E. J. Stephens b Worthington | 11 | – not out | 23 |
| W. R. Hammond c and b Townsend | 67 | – c Worthington b Townsend | 3 |
| C. C. Dacre c Smith b Townsend | 1 | – b Townsend | 12 |
| W. L. Neale lbw b Copson | 2 | – c Worthington b Townsend | 5 |
| Mr G. W. Parker lbw b Townsend | 0 | – lbw b Townsend | 0 |
| Mr B. H. Lyon c Worthington b Townsend | 0 | – b Townsend | 6 |
| Mr P. I. Van der Gucht b Townsend | 0 | – b Townsend | 19 |
| T. W. Goddard c Worthington b Townsend | 3 | – c Elliott b Lee | 9 |
| C. W. L. Parker not out | 0 | – lbw b Townsend | 1 |
| B 9, l-b 4, w 1 | 14 | B 3 | 3 |
| | **200** | | **112** |

## Gloucestershire Bowling

| | Overs | Mdns | Runs | Wkts | Overs | Mdns | Runs | Wkts |
|---|---|---|---|---|---|---|---|---|
| Hammond | 28 | 8 | 65 | 1 | 1 | — | 12 | — |
| Barnett | 13 | 4 | 30 | — | | | | |
| G. W. Parker | 7 | 2 | 8 | 1 | | | | |
| Goddard | 34 | 14 | 49 | 5 | 19 | 5 | 52 | 6 |
| C. Parker | 16 | 2 | 53 | 1 | 20.5 | 8 | 34 | 3 |
| Sinfield | 16 | 7 | 27 | 1 | 1 | — | 13 | — |
| Neale | 2 | — | 14 | — | | | | |

## Derbyshire Bowling

| | Overs | Mdns | Runs | Wkts | Overs | Mdns | Runs | Wkts |
|---|---|---|---|---|---|---|---|---|
| Copson | 16 | 4 | 42 | 3 | 8 | 4 | 26 | — |
| Worthington | 11 | 3 | 35 | 1 | 6 | 1 | 22 | 1 |
| Townsend | 31.5 | 9 | 64 | 6 | 19 | 8 | 26 | 8 |
| Mitchell | 6 | 1 | 12 | — | | | | |
| Storer | 9 | — | 33 | — | 8 | 4 | 8 | — |
| Lee | | | | | 6 | 3 | 12 | 1 |
| Pope | | | | | 2 | — | 15 | — |

Umpires: J. Newman and T. Oates.

# DERBYSHIRE v WARWICKSHIRE

Played at Derby, August 5, 7, 8, 1933

A brilliant victory by 317 runs gave Derbyshire ample revenge for the defeat by eight wickets they suffered at Birmingham. Warwickshire, set to get 410 runs, collapsed before the pace of Copson and the leg-breaks of Mitchell. Derbyshire ran up a big score on the Saturday, lost no time in declaring and, having established a lead of 251, batted so well that they were again able to apply the closure. Townsend, going in first wicket down at 93, stayed four hours and a half. Chances when 121 and 159 were small blemishes on a fine exhibition marked by clean driving which brought two 6s and twenty-six 4s. Worthington and Blaxland shared in productive stands and Skinner batted beautifully in both innings. Wyatt, revealing his usual skill and resolution, prevented a bigger defeat for Warwickshire by putting together, at a crisis, a capital century.

## Derbyshire

| | | | | |
|---|---|---|---|---|
| H. Storer c Smart b Hollies | 39 | – b Collin | | 50 |
| Mr A. F. Skinner c Smart b Paine | 50 | – st Smart b Paine | | 74 |
| L. Townsend not out | 172 | – lbw b Sanders | | 5 |
| S. Worthington c and b Paine | 40 | – not out | | 21 |
| A. V. Pope c Croom b Collin | 23 | | | |
| Mr G. R. Jackson b Sanders | 21 | | | |
| Mr L. B. Blaxland b Paine | 64 | – st Smart b Paine | | 0 |
| H. Elliott b Paine | 9 | | | |
| T. R. Armstrong st Smart b Paine | 6 | | | |
| T. B. Mitchell not out | 6 | | | |
| B 10, l-b 8 | 18 | B 2, l-b 6 | | 8 |
| | **(8 wkts dec.) 448** | | **(4 wkts dec.) 158** | |

W. Copson did not bat.

## Warwickshire

| | | | | |
|---|---|---|---|---|
| N. Kilner lbw b Worthington | 6 | – b Copson | | 2 |
| A. J. Croom b Mitchell | 18 | – b Mitchell | | 28 |
| L. A. Bates b Copson | 2 | – c Storer b Pope | | 8 |
| Mr R. E. S. Wyatt not out | 102 | – lbw b Mitchell | | 4 |
| F. R. Santall c Elliott b Copson | 19 | – lbw b Pope | | 8 |
| T. Collin b Copson | 1 | – lbw b Mitchell | | 8 |
| G. Paine run out | 7 | – b Copson | | 15 |
| W. H. Barber c Elliott b Mitchell | 9 | – b Copson | | 13 |
| J. Smart b Copson | 17 | – c Storer b Copson | | 0 |
| W. Sanders lbw b Mitchell | 12 | – lbw b Mitchell | | 0 |
| E. Hollies lbw b Mitchell | 1 | – not out | | 5 |
| L-b 3 | 3 | L-b 1 | | 1 |
| | **197** | | **92** | |

## Warwickshire Bowling

| | Overs | Mdns | Runs | Wkts | Overs | Mdns | Runs | Wkts |
|---|---|---|---|---|---|---|---|---|
| Wyatt | 11 | 1 | 55 | — | 3 | — | 7 | — |
| Sanders | 18 | 2 | 39 | 1 | 13 | 2 | 38 | 1 |
| Barber | 17 | 2 | 58 | — | 4 | — | 16 | — |
| Hollies | 32 | 10 | 105 | 1 | 9 | 2 | 27 | — |
| Paine | 44 | 11 | 115 | 5 | 15.3 | 6 | 44 | 2 |
| Collin | 16 | 4 | 58 | 1 | 5 | — | 18 | 1 |

## Derbyshire Bowling

| | Overs | Mdns | Runs | Wkts | Overs | Mdns | Runs | Wkts |
|---|---|---|---|---|---|---|---|---|
| Worthington ...... | 6 | 3 | 6 | 1 | 4 | 1 | 12 | — |
| Copson .......... | 24 | 6 | 71 | 4 | 12.5 | 2 | 39 | 4 |
| Mitchell .......... | 32 | 9 | 71 | 4 | 13 | 4 | 28 | 4 |
| Pope ............. | 18 | 7 | 19 | — | 9 | 3 | 12 | 2 |
| Armstrong ........ | 11 | 5 | 10 | — | | | | |
| Skinner .......... | 4 | — | 17 | — | | | | |

Umpires: W. A. Buswell and L. C. Braund.

# DERBYSHIRE v WARWICKSHIRE

### Played at Derby, July 17, 19, 1937

Derbyshire won by five wickets. Put out for the smallest total of the season, Warwickshire made a gallant effort to recover but were beaten during extra time on the second day. Copson, returning after nearly a month's absence through injury, overshadowed everyone else. Bowling probably better than at any other time since his debut in 1932, he maintained great speed and made the ball swing disconcertingly either way. Batsmen compelled to make late defensive strokes were helpless against him. Half the Warwickshire side were out for 18 and Copson sent back Dollery, Mayer, Fantham and Hollies in four deliveries. Derbyshire also fared badly until Townsend and Rhodes put on 85 for the sixth stand. The best batting of the match was seen during a third wicket partnership of 213 between Hill and Dollery, but this admirable play was discounted by a subsequent collapse against Mitchell.

## Warwickshire

| | | | |
|---|---|---|---|
| W. A. Hill c Smith b Copson ................. | 0 | – b Mitchell ................... | 105 |
| N. Kilner c Skinner b Copson ................. | 7 | – b Copson .................... | 0 |
| F. R. Santall b Copson ....................... | 0 | – b Copson .................... | 1 |
| J. Buckingham b A. V. Pope ................. | 9 | – b G. H. Pope ................ | 7 |
| Mr R. E. S. Wyatt b A. V. Pope .............. | 1 | – c Smith b Mitchell ........... | 30 |
| H. E. Dollery b Copson ...................... | 7 | – c Skinner b Copson ........... | 98 |
| J. S. Ord b Copson .......................... | 1 | – c Worthington b Mitchell ....... | 9 |
| Mr P. Cranmer not out ..................... | 2 | – lbw b G. H. Pope ............. | 6 |
| J. H. Mayer b Copson ...................... | 0 | – not out ..................... | 14 |
| W. E. Fantham b Copson .................... | 0 | – c G. H. Pope b Mitchell ......... | 4 |
| E. Hollies b Copson ......................... | 0 | – lbw b Mitchell .............. | 0 |
| L-b 1 ......................... | 1 | B 9, l-b 7, w 1 ........... | 17 |
| | | | |
| | 28 | | 291 |

## Derbyshire

| | | | |
|---|---|---|---|
| D. Smith b Mayer ...................... | 6 | – c Cranmer b Mayer ........... | 32 |
| A. E. Alderman run out ................. | 8 | – lbw b Mayer ................ | 15 |
| T. S. Worthington b Hollies .................... | 5 | – c Buckingham b Mayer ......... | 18 |
| Mr A. F. Skinner lbw b Mayer ............... | 13 | – not out ..................... | 12 |
| L. F. Townsend c Santall b Wyatt ............ | 52 | – b Mayer .................... | 2 |
| G. H. Pope b Mayer ........................ | 8 | – c Dollery b Mayer ............ | 6 |
| A. Rhodes run out .......................... | 58 | – not out ..................... | 7 |
| A. V. Pope b Mayer ........................ | 4 | | |
| H. Elliott b Wyatt .......................... | 9 | | |
| T. B. Mitchell st Buckingham b Mayer .......... | 21 | | |
| W. Copson not out ......................... | 30 | | |
| B 12, l-b 1 ........................ | 13 | L-b 1 ................. | 1 |
| | | | |
| | 227 | | 93 |

**Derbyshire Bowling**

| | Overs | Mdns | Runs | Wkts | Overs | Mdns | Runs | Wkts |
|---|---|---|---|---|---|---|---|---|
| Copson .......... | 8.2 | 2 | 11 | 8 | 32 | 4 | 82 | 3 |
| Rhodes .......... | 4 | — | 11 | — | 5 | 2 | 12 | — |
| A. V. Pope ........ | 4 | 1 | 5 | 2 | 21 | 1 | 56 | — |
| G. H. Pope ........ | | | | | 14 | 5 | 26 | 2 |
| Mitchell .......... | | | | | 31.5 | 5 | 80 | 5 |
| Townsend ........ | | | | | 2 | 1 | 2 | — |
| Worthington ...... | | | | | 5 | — | 16 | — |

**Warwickshire Bowling**

| | Overs | Mdns | Runs | Wkts | Overs | Mdns | Runs | Wkts |
|---|---|---|---|---|---|---|---|---|
| Mayer .......... | 23 | 7 | 83 | 5 | 12.4 | — | 39 | 5 |
| Wyatt .......... | 18.4 | 6 | 48 | 2 | 9 | — | 44 | — |
| Hollies .......... | 11 | 1 | 42 | 1 | 3 | — | 9 | — |
| Fantham ......... | 2 | — | 22 | — | | | | |
| Santall .......... | 5 | — | 19 | — | | | | |

Umpires: E. Robinson and C. W. L. Parker.

# DERBYSHIRE v SUSSEX

### Played at Derby, June 28, 29, 30, 1939

Sussex won by 13 runs. The last day's play was sensational indeed. Leading by 60, Sussex broke down against Mitchell and the brothers Pope in their second innings and Derbyshire began the third stage needing 208 for victory. Thanks to Worthington, who, on a pitch favouring bowlers, pulled and cut splendidly for two hours, the total stood at 185 when he was third out, but the innings ended for a further 9 runs. James Langridge, who did the "hat trick" when dismissing Rhodes, Hounsfield and Alfred Pope, took five wickets without cost in his first eleven deliveries. Nye sent back the last three men in five balls. Cornford, with five catches behind the stumps, helped in the wonderful victory.

## Sussex

| | | | |
|---|---|---|---|
| John Langridge c Smith b Copson .............. | 85 | – c Worthington b Mitchell ......... | 39 |
| J. H. Parks b Copson ....................... | 15 | – lbw b A. V. Pope .............. | 3 |
| H. W. Parks c Elliott b A. C. Pope .............. | 10 | – c Worthington b Copson ........ | 4 |
| G. Cox b Copson ........................... | 0 | – c and b A. V. Pope ............. | 5 |
| Jas. Langridge lbw b Copson ................... | 0 | – lbw b G. H. Pope ............. | 27 |
| Mr H. T. Bartlett c Elliott b Rhodes .............. | 93 | – c and b Mitchell .............. | 39 |
| Mr R. A. A. Holt b Rhodes .................... | 0 | – b G. H. Pope ................. | 9 |
| C. Oakes lbw b Rhodes ...................... | 8 | – b G. H. Pope .................. | 0 |
| W. Cornford c Worthington b Copson .......... | 5 | – lbw b Mitchell ................ | 0 |
| J. Duffield c Elliott b Copson ................. | 33 | – not out .................... | 20 |
| J. Nye not out .............................. | 1 | – b Mitchell ................... | 0 |
| B 5, l-b 3 .......................... | 8 | L-b 1 ................. | 1 |

258          147

### Derbyshire

| | | | |
|---|---|---|---|
| A. E. Alderman c Cornford b Nye | 15 | – c Cornford b Duffield | 30 |
| D. Smith b Nye | 81 | – c Cornford b Duffield | 0 |
| T. S. Worthington b Nye | 0 | – c Cornford b Jas. Langridge | 119 |
| L. F. Townsend c H. Parks b J. Parks | 29 | – c Cornford b Nye | 28 |
| G. H. Pope lbw b Duffield | 37 | – c J. Parks b Jas. Langridge | 1 |
| A. Rhodes c Nye b Jas. Langridge | 8 | – c John Langridge b Jas. Langridge | 0 |
| Mr T. D. Hounsfield b Duffield | 12 | – c J. Parks b Jas. Langridge | 0 |
| A. V. Pope lbw b Duffield | 0 | – c Cornford b Jas. Langridge | 0 |
| H. Elliott lbw b Duffield | 0 | – not out | 0 |
| T. B. Mitchell not out | 0 | – b Nye | 0 |
| W. Copson b Duffield | 0 | – b Nye | 0 |
| B 2, l-b 14 | 16 | B 12, l-b 2, w 1, n-b 1 | 16 |
| | **198** | | **194** |

### Derbyshire Bowling

| | Overs | Mdns | Runs | Wkts | Overs | Mdns | Runs | Wkts |
|---|---|---|---|---|---|---|---|---|
| Copson | 20.4 | 4 | 64 | 6 | 7 | 2 | 16 | 1 |
| A. V. Pope | 18 | 2 | 71 | 1 | 6 | 1 | 19 | 2 |
| G. H. Pope | 12 | — | 55 | — | 12 | 1 | 49 | 3 |
| Mitchell | 4 | — | 22 | — | 9 | 1 | 45 | 4 |
| Rhodes | 10 | — | 38 | 3 | 4 | — | 17 | — |

### Sussex Bowling

| | Overs | Mdns | Runs | Wkts | Overs | Mdns | Runs | Wkts |
|---|---|---|---|---|---|---|---|---|
| Nye | 16 | — | 73 | 3 | 15 | 1 | 69 | 3 |
| Duffield | 10.5 | 1 | 38 | 5 | 14 | — | 78 | 2 |
| J. Parks | 16 | 7 | 33 | 1 | 5 | — | 28 | — |
| Jas. Langridge | 9 | 1 | 36 | 1 | 3 | 1 | 3 | 5 |
| Cox | 1 | — | 2 | — | | | | |

Umpires: A. Dolphin and H. Elliott.

# ESSEX

## ESSEX v SOMERSET

### Played at Chelmsford, June 16, 17, 18, 1926

When Eastman in an attempt to make the winning hit was caught, the umpires removed the bails and although the aggregates were equal declared Somerset entitled to the points for a first innings lead. As half a minute remained, and the last batsman was hurrying to the wickets, Daniell offered to continue, but Perrin, the not out batsman, captain of Essex, accepted the umpires' ruling. However, on reference to the MCC, the match was declared a tie, the full points therefore being divided equally. Apart from the exciting finish the first county match played on the new Chelmsford ground did not present any remarkable features. Bowlers always received some help from the pitch, Nichols and Eastman meeting with such success that they put their side within reach of victory, while Bridges, making the ball turn, almost won the game for Somerset. MacBryan, the one batsman to show to much advantage, played thoroughly well scoring without a mistake 80 out of 142 added during his stay of nearly three hours.

### Somerset

| | | | |
|---|---|---|---|
| Mr J. Daniell b Nichols | 21 | – b Nichols | 2 |
| A. Young c and b Russell | 12 | – b Nichols | 15 |
| Mr M. D. Lyon lbw b Russell | 15 | – b Eastman | 11 |
| Mr J. C. W. MacBryan c Perrin b Russell | 80 | – b Eastman | 12 |
| Mr J. C. White c Ridley b O'Connor | 18 | – c and b Eastman | 0 |
| Mr P. R. Johnson c O'Connor b Morris | 24 | – b Nichols | 0 |
| Mr C. C. Case run out | 4 | – not out | 23 |
| Mr G. F. Earle c Morris b Nichols | 4 | – b Nichols | 15 |
| G. Hunt run out | 0 | – b Eastman | 9 |
| Mr M. L. Hill b Nichols | 9 | – b Eastman | 0 |
| Mr J. J. Bridges not out | 1 | – c Nicholas b Eastman | 17 |
| B 12, l-b 4, w 1, n-b 3 | 20 | B 1, l-b 1, n-b 1 | 3 |
| | **208** | | **107** |

### Essex

| | | | |
|---|---|---|---|
| J. Freeman b Earle | 43 | – c Hunt b Bridges | 37 |
| J. A. Cutmore c Hill b White | 13 | – lbw b White | 26 |
| J. O'Connor c White b Hunt | 10 | – c and b White | 13 |
| A. C. Russell c Lyon b White | 10 | – b Hunt | 4 |
| M. S. Nichols c Johnson b Earle | 0 | – b Bridges | 23 |
| Mr F. W. H. Nicholas c Daniell b White | 9 | – b Bridges | 13 |
| Mr P. Perrin not out | 19 | – not out | 15 |
| Mr H. M. Morris b Hunt | 12 | – b Hunt | 0 |
| Mr G. V. N. Ridley c White b Hunt | 4 | | |
| Mr L. C. Eastman st Hill b White | 0 | – c Earle b Bridges | 0 |
| Sir G. Rowley c Johnson b White | 23 | – b Bridges | 0 |
| B 30, l-b 5 | 35 | B 1, l-b 5 | 6 |
| | **178** | | **137** |

### Essex Bowling

| | Overs | Mdns | Runs | Wkts | Overs | Mdns | Runs | Wkts |
|---|---|---|---|---|---|---|---|---|
| Nichols | 21.5 | 3 | 48 | 3 | 15 | 2 | 45 | 4 |
| Eastman | 26 | 9 | 50 | — | 15 | 4 | 59 | 6 |
| Rowley | 8 | — | 26 | — | | | | |
| Russell | 30 | 13 | 39 | 3 | | | | |
| O'Connor | 8 | 1 | 19 | 1 | | | | |
| Morris | 3 | 1 | 6 | 1 | | | | |

**Somerset Bowling**

| | Overs | Mdns | Runs | Wkts | Overs | Mdns | Runs | Wkts |
|---|---|---|---|---|---|---|---|---|
| Bridges .......... | 15 | 6 | 24 | — | 16 | 4 | 33 | 5 |
| Earle ........... | 7 | 2 | 10 | 2 | 3 | 1 | 13 | — |
| White ........... | 44 | 21 | 57 | 5 | 22 | 5 | 49 | 2 |
| Hunt ........... | 30 | 15 | 42 | 3 | 17 | 6 | 36 | 2 |
| Young .......... | 6 | 2 | 10 | — | | | | |

Umpires: J. Stone and F. Chester.

# ESSEX v MIDDLESEX

## Played at Leyton, May 29, 30, 31, 1929

A struggle on the last afternoon for the first innings lead in which Middlesex proved successful was as interesting as many a close finish. Bray played steadily while Cutmore and O'Connor showed such freedom that each of the first two Essex partnerships produced 127 runs. The total reached 250 with one man out and Russell batted so well that the first day produced 421 runs for seven wickets. Necessarily careful in facing a large total, Middlesex scored 241 for four wickets on the second day when altogether no more than 295 runs were obtained. Hearne, playing an innings that was not exceeded by any batsman during the season, was at the wickets nearly all the eight hours and a half that Middlesex batted. His 285 not out is the highest score ever made for his county. At the top of his form, Hearne made admirable strokes all round the wicket, varying late cuts with leg strokes and straight drives. He hit thirty-three 4s. Guise shared in a stand of 145. When eight wickets had fallen Hart helped to add 100 runs and then Peebles kept up his wicket stubbornly. An overthrow to the boundary and three byes gave Middlesex the lead.

## Essex

| | | | |
|---|---|---|---|
| Mr C. J. Bray c Hendren b Haig ................ | 92 | | |
| J. A. Cutmore st Price b Robins ................. | 79 | – not out ...................... | 35 |
| J. O'Connor lbw b Haig ....................... | 68 | | |
| A. C. Russell not out ........................ | 111 | | |
| M. S. Nichols c Haig b Peebles ................ | 5 | | |
| Mr H. M. Morris c Lee b Peebles ............... | 17 | | |
| L. C. Eastman c Hearne b Peebles .............. | 12 | | |
| A. B. Hipkin c Lee b Haig ..................... | 19 | | |
| Mr M. C. Ralson b Peebles ................... | 38 | | |
| T. H. Wade c Price b Haig .................... | 4 | – st Price b Robins .............. | 9 |
| G. Eastman c Newman b Robins ............... | 4 | – c and b Robins ................ | 4 |
| B 22, l-b 3, w 2, n-b 1 ................ | 28 | B 6 ................... | 6 |
| | 477 | | 54 |

## Middlesex

| | | |
|---|---|---|
| Mr J. L. Guise c Nichols b Hipkin ........ | 55 | Mr R. H. Hill c G. Eastman b O'Connor ... 0 |
| H. W. Lee c and b L. C. Eastman ........ | 1 | W. F. Price lbw b O'Connor ........... 0 |
| J. W. Hearne not out .................. | 285 | G. Hart b Russell .................... 33 |
| E. Hendren lbw b Nichols ............. | 20 | Mr I. A. R. Peebles c and b Hipkin ....... 10 |
| Mr N. Haig b L. C. Eastman ........... | 4 | B 16, l-b 12 ................. 28 |
| Mr G. C. Newman c and b L. C. Eastman .. | 43 | |
| Mr R. W. V. Robins b L. C. Eastman ..... | 7 | 486 |

## Middlesex Bowling

| | Overs | Mdns | Runs | Wkts | Overs | Mdns | Runs | Wkts |
|---|---|---|---|---|---|---|---|---|
| Haig . . . . . . . . . . . . . | 56 | 14 | 110 | 4 | | | | |
| Newman . . . . . . . . | 5 | 1 | 21 | — | | | | |
| Peebles . . . . . . . . . . | 42 | 4 | 142 | 4 | | | | |
| Robins . . . . . . . . . . | 32.4 | 5 | 113 | 2 | 2.2 | 1 | 2 | 2 |
| Hearne . . . . . . . . . . | 8 | — | 19 | — | | | | |
| Lee . . . . . . . . . . . . . | 16 | 1 | 44 | — | | | | |
| Hendren . . . . . . . . . | | | | | 9 | 2 | 37 | — |
| Hart . . . . . . . . . . . . | | | | | 6 | 1 | 9 | — |

## Essex Bowling

| | Overs | Mdns | Runs | Wkts |
|---|---|---|---|---|
| Nichols . . . . . . . . . | 49 | 12 | 114 | 1 |
| L. C. Eastman . . . . . | 51 | 18 | 123 | 4 |
| O'Connor . . . . . . . . | 48 | 12 | 116 | 2 |
| Hipkin . . . . . . . . . . | 26.2 | 6 | 55 | 2 |
| Ralson . . . . . . . . . . | 10 | 1 | 35 | — |
| Russell . . . . . . . . . . | 7 | 3 | 15 | 1 |

Umpires: L. C. Braund and G. Beet.

# ESSEX v KENT

### Played at Southend, August 13, 14, 15, 1930

Taking all ten wickets in the first innings of Essex, Freeman accomplished that feat for the second time in his career and, in gaining this further triumph, equalled a record which previously V. E. Walker alone had achieved. In the visitors' second innings he disposed of six batsmen and for the whole match had sixteen wickets for less than six runs apiece. He thus played the great part in a Kentish victory by 277 runs. Farnes, a Romford amateur, bowling effectively on Wednesday, Essex dismissed Kent cheaply and went ahead with seven wickets in hand before Freeman became so deadly. A. M. Crawley in Kent's second innings drove magnificently and, with two 6s and twenty-six 4s among his strokes, scored 175 out of 257. He reached three figures in eighty minutes. Hardinge helped him to make 186 for the first wicket in two hours and ten minutes.

## Kent

| | | | |
|---|---|---|---|
| Mr A. M. Crawley c Sheffield b Farnes . . . . . . . . . . . | 25 | – b O'Connor . . . . . . . . . . . . . . . . . . | 175 |
| H. T. W. Hardinge not out . . . . . . . . . . . . . . . . . . . . . | 49 | – st Sheffield b Palmer . . . . . . . . . . . . . | 51 |
| F. E. Woolley c Russell b Farnes . . . . . . . . . . . . . . . | 0 | – c Franklin b Nichols . . . . . . . . . . . | 16 |
| L. Ames b Farnes . . . . . . . . . . . . . . . . . . . . . . . . . . . . | 1 | – b Farnes . . . . . . . . . . . . . . . . . . . . . . | 35 |
| W. Ashdown b Palmer . . . . . . . . . . . . . . . . . . . . . . . . | 18 | – c and b Nichols . . . . . . . . . . . . . . . . | 12 |
| Mr. J. L. Bryan b Nichols . . . . . . . . . . . . . . . . . . . | 6 | – c Cutmore b Palmer . . . . . . . . . . . | 37 |
| Mr C. H. Knott c Nichols b Farnes . . . . . . . . . . . . . | 2 | – b O'Connor . . . . . . . . . . . . . . . . . . | 28 |
| L. Todd lbw b Nichols . . . . . . . . . . . . . . . . . . . . . . . . | 10 | – not out . . . . . . . . . . . . . . . . . . . . . . . | 43 |
| C. Wright b Nichols . . . . . . . . . . . . . . . . . . . . . . . . . . | 0 | – st Sheffield b O'Connor . . . . . . . . . . | 3 |
| A. P. Freeman b Farnes . . . . . . . . . . . . . . . . . . . . . . | 2 | – run out . . . . . . . . . . . . . . . . . . . . . . . | 4 |
| C. W. Peach b Nichols . . . . . . . . . . . . . . . . . . . . . . . | 1 | – not out . . . . . . . . . . . . . . . . . . . . . . . | 4 |
| B 5, n-b 3 . . . . . . . . . . . . . . . . . . . . . . . . | 8 | B 8, l-b 4, w 1, n-b 1 . . . . . . . | 14 |

| | |
|---|---|
| 122 | (9 wkts dec.) 422 |

**Essex**

| | | | |
|---|---:|---|---:|
| Mr L. G. Crawley lbw b Freeman | 22 | – b Wright | 8 |
| D. F. Pope c Bryan b Freeman | 38 | – lbw b Freeman | 3 |
| J. O'Connor lbw b Freeman | 19 | – c Woodley b Freeman | 32 |
| A. C. Russell not out | 47 | – c Peach b Freeman | 7 |
| J. A. Cutmore c Knott b Freeman | 6 | – c Knott b Freeman | 9 |
| M. S. Nichols st Ames b Freeman | 0 | – lbw b Peach | 3 |
| Mr. H. W. F. Franklin c Bryan b Freeman | 1 | – c and b Freeman | 38 |
| J. R. Sheffield st Ames b Freeman | 0 | – c Knott b Freeman | 6 |
| Mr K. Farnes b Freeman | 1 | – b Wright | 0 |
| P. Smith c Ashdown b Freeman | 1 | – not out | 8 |
| H. J. Palmer b Freeman | 0 | – b Wright | 2 |
| B 5, l-b 5 | 10 | B 5, l-b 1 | 6 |
| | **145** | | **122** |

**Essex Bowling**

| | Overs | Mdns | Runs | Wkts | Overs | Mdns | Runs | Wkts |
|---|---:|---:|---:|---:|---:|---:|---:|---:|
| Nichols | 15.4 | 5 | 34 | 4 | 18 | 2 | 65 | 2 |
| Smith | 7 | 1 | 19 | — | 13 | — | 76 | — |
| Farnes | 17 | 4 | 36 | 5 | 29 | 4 | 82 | 1 |
| Palmer | 11 | 4 | 14 | 1 | 22 | — | 89 | 2 |
| O'Connor | 2 | — | 11 | — | 29 | 6 | 89 | 3 |
| Franklin | | | | | 1 | — | 7 | — |

**Kent Bowling**

| | Overs | Mdns | Runs | Wkts | Overs | Mdns | Runs | Wkts |
|---|---:|---:|---:|---:|---:|---:|---:|---:|
| Wright | 13 | 2 | 25 | — | 15.3 | 2 | 49 | 3 |
| Ashdown | 9 | 1 | 23 | — | 7 | 2 | 18 | — |
| Freeman | 30.4 | 8 | 53 | 10 | 27 | 11 | 41 | 6 |
| Peach | 6 | 1 | 14 | — | 10 | 8 | 8 | 1 |
| Hardinge | 14 | 6 | 20 | — | | | | |

Umpires: W. Bestwick and W. R. Parry.

## ESSEX v YORKSHIRE

Played at Leyton, June 15, 16, 17, 1932

Holmes and Sutcliffe, Yorkshire's famous opening batsmen, made this match memorable by creating a world's record first wicket stand of 555. They surpassed an achievement that had stood unequalled for 34 years – that of two other Yorkshiremen, J. T. Brown and John Tunnicliffe, who score 554 together for the first wicket against Derbyshire at Chesterfield in 1898. The partnership between Holmes and Sutcliffe was the seventieth of three-figures in which those two men had participated and their 65th for Yorkshire.

While every credit can be given to the two batsmen for their performance, the fact must not be overlooked that Holmes, almost directly he went in, experienced a great piece of luck. He had indeed scored merely three runs when he was missed behind the wicket, low down on the off side where Sheffield got both hands to the ball but failed to hold it. That fault apart, the batting during the big partnership proved wonderfully sound and confident. Rather unusually, Holmes scored more slowly than his colleague but the pair put a hundred runs on the board in an hour and three-quarters and proceeded to maintain their mastery over the bowling for nearly seven hours and a half. The following times indicate the progress of the batsmen:

> 100 in an hour and forty-five minutes.
> 200 in three hours twenty minutes.
> 300 in four hours thirty-five minutes.
> 400 in five hours twenty-five minutes.
> 500 in six hours fifty-five minutes.
> 555 in seven hours twenty-five minutes.

A curious incident occurred immediately after the new record had been made. Sutcliffe – very naturally, since it was obviously Yorkshire's policy to declare as soon as possible – threw away his wicket, playing on with a rather casual stroke, and all the players at once left the field. Then, to everyone's amazement, the total on the score board was altered to read 554. For the moment there seemed reason to fear that the chance of beating the record had been missed but eventually it was discovered that a no ball had not been counted in the total.

Holmes and Sutcliffe, on a perfect Leyton wicket, made their runs in admirable style. They ran singles skilfully and, if neither man took many risks, runs came at an average rate of scoring. Playing the highest innings of his career, Sutcliffe cut, drove and hit to leg with sound judgment. His straight drives, perfectly timed, were particularly good to watch. Holmes, too, showed a lot of skill when off-driving and cutting but in this innings did not properly reveal his strength on the leg side. He hit nineteen 4's while Sutcliffe among his figures had a 6 and thirty-three 4s. The partnership was a magnificent feat in every way and especially of endurance.

The contrast of the Yorkshiremen's batting with that which followed proved truly remarkable. Bowes, with pace off the pitch, and Verity, by cleverly flighted bowling, developed such a mastery that inside two hours Essex were all out for 78. A fourth wicket stand of 29 between O'Connor and Nichols represented the best of the innings. The last five wickets fell for 19 runs, Verity having the striking figures of five wickets in seven overs for eight runs.

From this pronounced collapse, Essex did not recover, and shortly after one o'clock on Friday Yorkshire emerged from an historic match winners by and innings and 313 runs. In the follow-on, with Essex 477 in arrear, Bowes again made the ball get up awkwardly and, although Crawley brought off some powerful drives, Nichols was the only man who really checked Yorkshire's progress towards victory. By the close of play on Thursday Essex had five wickets down for 92. Nichols, who had gone in third wicket down at 50, batted with rare pluck and skill and remained to carry out his bat. He withstood the attack for two hours and a half and hit a 6 and six 4s.

Verity, particularly deadly towards the close of the innings, took five wickets for 45 – a performance which gave him a record for the match of ten for 53. Bowes brought his figures for the two innings to nine for 85.

## Yorkshire

P. Holmes not out . . . . . . . . . . . . . . . . . . . .224
H. Sutcliffe b Eastman . . . . . . . . . . . . . . . .313
       B 13, l-b 2, n-b 2 . . . . . . . . . . . . . 18
                             ——
           (1 wkt dec.) 555

A. Mitchell, M. Leyland, W. Barber, Mr. A. B. Sellers, A. Wood, A. C. Rhodes, G. G. Macaulay, H. Verity and W. E. Bowes did not bat.

## Essex

| | | | |
|---|---|---|---|
| Mr L. G. Crawley b Bowes | 0 | – c Sutcliffe b Bowes | 27 |
| D. F. Pope c Rhodes b Bowes | 6 | – c Mitchell b Bowes | 9 |
| J. O'Connor b Bowes | 20 | – c Rhodes b Bowes | 7 |
| J. A. Cutmore lbw b Bowes | 0 | – b Verity | 1 |
| M. S. Nichols b Verity | 25 | – not out | 59 |
| L. C. Eastman c Sutcliffe b Macaulay | 16 | – c Barber b Verity | 19 |
| Mr C. Bray c and b Verity | 1 | – st Wood b Verity | 6 |
| R. H. Taylor c Macaulay b Verity | 5 | – c Macaulay b Verity | 13 |
| J. R. Sheffield c and b Verity | 0 | – c Sutcliffe b Verity | 5 |
| Mr A. G. Daer c and b Verity | 0 | – c Mitchell b Bowes | 0 |
| P. Smith not out | 2 | – c Rhodes b Bowes | 0 |
| B 3 | 3 | B 15, l-b 1, n-b 2 | 18 |
| | **78** | | **164** |

## Essex Bowling

| | Overs | Mdns | Runs | Wkts |
|---|---|---|---|---|
| Nichols | 31 | 4 | 105 | — |
| Daer | 40 | 5 | 106 | — |
| Smith | 46 | 10 | 128 | — |
| O'Connor | 23 | 5 | 73 | — |
| Eastman | 22.4 | 2 | 97 | 1 |
| Crawley | 3 | — | 7 | — |
| Taylor | 4 | — | 14 | — |
| Bray | 1 | — | 7 | — |

## Yorkshire Bowling

| | Overs | Mdns | Runs | Wkts | Overs | Mdns | Runs | Wkts |
|---|---|---|---|---|---|---|---|---|
| Bowes | 12 | 1 | 38 | 4 | 23.4 | 5 | 47 | 5 |
| Rhodes | 10 | 5 | 15 | — | 9 | 5 | 23 | — |
| Macaulay | 7.1 | 2 | 14 | 1 | 16 | 5 | 31 | — |
| Verity | 7 | 3 | 8 | 5 | 30 | 12 | 45 | 5 |

Umpires: E. J. Smith and F. Field.

## ESSEX v YORKSHIRE

### J. O'Connor's Benefit Match

### Played at Leyton, July 12, 13, 14, 1933

Sent in to bat, Yorkshire, despite the loss owing to rain of the whole of the second day's play, won by an innings and 172 runs. No one had a bigger share in the triumph than Verity, who on Friday equalled the performance standing to the credit of Colin Blythe of taking seventeen wickets in a day. These wickets Verity secured at a cost of 91 runs. Bray's judgment appeared sound when Yorkshire on Wednesday lost Holmes, Sutcliffe and Leyland for 76, and Mitchell was struck on the left temple when he and Barber were batting steadily in an effort to pull round the game. Yorkshire lost half the side for 138, but Barber played extremely well and, helped in turn by Verity and Wood, he reached three figures in three hours and a half. His faultless innings – a remarkable one in the circumstances – and the addition of 202 runs after the fifth wicket fell, enabled Yorkshire to enjoy the best of the day's play, at the end of which Essex had made 13 without loss. On Friday, on a rain-damaged pitch, Essex were dismissed twice before four o'clock for 155 further runs. Verity not only turned the ball quickly but often made it get up awkwardly, and several batsmen were out in attempting to defend. Sellers held seven catches in the two innings and helped in the first to run out Pope, who played with care and resolution for two hours. In the follow-on Essex lost four men while scoring 10, and seven for 34. The batsmen were heavily handicapped by the very difficult wicket.

## Yorkshire

| | | | |
|---|---|---|---|
| P. Holmes c Sheffield b Smith | 15 | H. Verity c Smith b Evans | 28 |
| H. Sutcliffe b Evans | 36 | A. Wood b Nichols | 85 |
| A. Mitchell retired hurt | 43 | G. G. Macaulay c Cutmore b Nichols | 2 |
| M. Leyland lbw b Smith | 3 | A. C. Rhodes not out | 9 |
| W. Barber b Smith | 101 | B 8, l-b 3 | 11 |
| Mr A. B. Sellers c O'Connor b Smith | 1 | | — |
| F. Dennis c Daer b Smith | 6 | | 340 |

## Essex

| | | | |
|---|---|---|---|
| J. A. Cutmore c Sellers b Verity | 3 | – c Dennis b Verity | 6 |
| D. F. Pope run out | 34 | – c Sutcliffe b Verity | 0 |
| R. M. Taylor c Sellers b Verity | 0 | – b Verity | 2 |
| J. O'Connor c Sutcliffe b Verity | 17 | – lbw b Macaulay | 0 |
| M. S. Nichols b Verity | 4 | – c Sellers b Verity | 4 |
| Mr C. Bray lbw b Verity | 2 | – c Barber b Verity | 14 |
| J. R. Sheffield c Barber b Verity | 9 | – b Verity | 7 |
| Mr A. G. Daer c Sellers b Leyland | 3 | – not out | 13 |
| P. Smith c Sellers b Verity | 11 | – c Sellers b Verity | 15 |
| C. S. R. Boswell not out | 2 | – c Dennis b Verity | 0 |
| V. J. Evans c Sellers b Verity | 0 | – st Wood b Verity | 0 |
| B 8, l-b 11 | 19 | L-b 3 | 3 |
| | — | | — |
| | 104 | | 64 |

## Essex Bowling

| | Overs | Mdns | Runs | Wkts |
|---|---|---|---|---|
| Nichols | 20.4 | 3 | 59 | 2 |
| Daer | 15 | 3 | 40 | — |
| Smith | 45 | 9 | 122 | 5 |
| Evans | 31 | 7 | 69 | 2 |
| Boswell | 4 | — | 15 | — |
| O'Connor | 13 | 4 | 24 | — |

## Yorkshire Bowling

| | Overs | Mdns | Runs | Wkts | Overs | Mdns | Runs | Wkts |
|---|---|---|---|---|---|---|---|---|
| Macaulay | 22 | 9 | 25 | — | 11 | 5 | 12 | 1 |
| Sellers | 1 | — | 5 | — | | | | |
| Verity | 27 | 10 | 47 | 8 | 14.1 | 3 | 44 | 9 |
| Rhodes | 5 | 5 | — | — | | | | |
| Leyland | 3 | 1 | 8 | 1 | 3 | 1 | 5 | — |

Umpires: J. Newman and J. Stone.

# ESSEX v MIDDLESEX

## Played at Leyton, August 2, 3, 4, 1933

Winning by seven wickets, Essex gained their eleventh victory and so surpassed any previous season's record. Hendren played a remarkable innings. Going in at 26, he hit twenty-three 4s, scored 222 out of 342 in four hours twenty minutes, and took out his bat.

He defended soundly against good bowling, which earned wickets at regular intervals, and he brought off brilliant strokes all round. By consistent batting Essex in a great struggle gained a lead of ten runs. five wickets falling for 47 runs after tea on the second day. On Friday morning, Middlesex led by 16 with eight wickets in hand, but they collapsed, and Essex, after losing three men for 38, had no further anxiety. Spin bowlers always made the ball turn and on a hard pitch it was apt to rise.

## Middlesex

| | | |
|---|---|---|
| H. W. Lee c Smith b Nichols | 12 | – c Taylor b Smith ... 42 |
| W. F. Price b O'Connor | 28 | – c Sheffield b Farnes ... 18 |
| J. W. Hearne c Taylor b Nichols | 5 | – c Eastman b Farnes ... 0 |
| E. Hendren not out | 222 | – st Sheffield b Eastman ... 5 |
| J. Hulme c Eastman b Nichols | 16 | – st Sheffield b Smith ... 6 |
| Mr. H. E. Carris c Taylor b Smith | 17 | – b Smith ... 9 |
| Mr D. F. Surfleet st Sheffield b Smith | 24 | – c Nichols b Eastman ... 7 |
| J. Sims c Sheffield b Farnes | 8 | – b O'Connor ... 5 |
| Mr N. Haig c Crawley b Nichols | 17 | – st Sheffield b Smith ... 0 |
| W. R. Watkins c Smith b O'Connor | 17 | – c Smith b Farnes ... 5 |
| Mr. J. H. Nevinson c Sheffield b Eastman | 0 | – not out ... 0 |
| B 2 | 2 | |
| | **368** | **97** |

## Essex

| | | |
|---|---|---|
| Mr L. G. Crawley c Hendren b Hulme | 0 | – c Hendren b Sims ... 9 |
| J. A. Cutmore b Sims | 83 | – c Price b Sims ... 15 |
| R. M. Taylor lbw b Hearne | 23 | – c Price b Sims ... 10 |
| J. O'Connor c Hendren b Sims | 74 | – not out ... 40 |
| M. S. Nichols b Sims | 81 | – not out ... 9 |
| L. C. Eastman c Carris b Lee | 38 | |
| Mr D. R. Wilcox b Sims | 28 | |
| D. F. Pope run out | 13 | |
| J. R. Sheffield c Price b Lee | 8 | |
| P. Smith lbw b Lee | 16 | |
| Mr K. Farnes not out | 0 | |
| B 1, l-b 13 | 14 | B 6, l-b 2 ... 8 |
| | **378** | **91** |

## Essex Bowling

| | Overs | Mdns | Runs | Wkts | Overs | Mdns | Runs | Wkts |
|---|---|---|---|---|---|---|---|---|
| Nichols | 14 | 1 | 74 | 4 | 5 | 1 | 19 | — |
| Farnes | 16 | 4 | 40 | 1 | 15 | 4 | 19 | 3 |
| Smith | 33 | 4 | 126 | 2 | 19.2 | 6 | 38 | 4 |
| O'Connor | 29 | 3 | 96 | 2 | 6 | 5 | 3 | 1 |
| Eastman | 13.2 | 3 | 30 | 1 | 15 | 9 | 18 | 2 |

## Middlesex Bowling

| | Overs | Mdns | Runs | Wkts | Overs | Mdns | Runs | Wkts |
|---|---|---|---|---|---|---|---|---|
| Nevinson | 15 | 4 | 39 | — | 2 | — | 15 | — |
| Hulme | 14 | 3 | 42 | 1 | 1 | 1 | — | — |
| Sims | 49 | 13 | 129 | 4 | 15.3 | 6 | 43 | 3 |
| Hearne | 34 | 5 | 99 | 1 | 15 | 6 | 23 | — |
| Lee | 32.1 | 10 | 47 | 3 | | | | |
| Watkins | 5 | 2 | 8 | — | | | | |
| Haig | | | | | 1 | — | 2 | — |

Umpires: A. E. Street and J. Stone.

# ESSEX v SUSSEX

## Played at Leyton, September 2, 4, 5, 1933

The last county match to be played at Leyton provided brilliant cricket and a fine individual performance by Harry Parks. In drawing, Sussex were almost entirely indebted to Parks who scored two separate hundreds and took out his bat in each innings – a feat only four other batsmen have achieved. Sussex without James Langridge, Bowley and Tate, could not prevent Essex building up a huge score before declaring with nine men out. Eastman, exploiting a worn spot, did deadly work with the ball and despite the great effort by Parks, Sussex followed on 158 behind. Parks stayed three hours forth minutes, and in the second innings for two hours and a half. At one point Sussex were 94 behind with four men out. A stand of 133 between Harry Parks and Wensley contributed to an excellent recovery.

## Essex

| | | |
|---|---|---|
| Mr L. G. Crawley c Langridge b Wensley | 8 | |
| J. A. Cutmore st W. Cornford b Wensley | 88 | – not out ... 13 |
| R. M. Taylor lbw b Melville | 37 | |
| J. O'Connor b J. Parks | 93 | |
| M. S. Nichols c W. Cornford b Cook | 28 | |
| L. C. Eastman c Wensley b Pearce | 67 | |
| Mr D. R. Wilcox c H. Parks b Pearce | 74 | |
| D. F. Pope not out | 55 | |
| J. R. Sheffield b Wensley | 34 | – b Wensley ... 17 |
| P. Smith c Greenwood b Langridge | 54 | – c Pearce b Wensley ... 2 |
| B 15, l-b 6, n-b 1 | 22 | L-b 1 ... 1 |

(9 wkts dec.) 560   33

Mr K. Farnes did not bat.

## Sussex

| | | |
|---|---|---|
| John Langridge st Sheffield b Smith | 4 | – c and b Eastman ... 33 |
| J. Parks c Sheffield b Eastman | 74 | – run out ... 14 |
| Mr A. Melville b Eastman | 1 | – not out ... 46 |
| T. Cook b Farnes | 18 | – c and b Eastman ... 1 |
| G. Cox c and b Eastman | 19 | – lbw b Eastman ... 1 |
| H. Parks not out | 114 | – not out ... 105 |
| H. W. Greenwood b O'Connor | 9 | – lbw b Eastman ... 4 |
| A. F. Wensley c Sheffield b Smith | 28 | – c and b Eastman ... 54 |
| W. Cornford c and b Nichols | 26 | |
| G. Pearce c Smith b Farnes | 80 | |
| J. Cornford run out | 1 | |
| B 20, l-b 6, n-b 2 | 28 | B 17, l-b 8, n-b 2 ... 27 |

402   (6 wkts dec.) 285

## Sussex Bowling

| | Overs | Mdns | Runs | Wkts | Overs | Mdns | Runs | Wkts |
|---|---|---|---|---|---|---|---|---|
| Wensley | 47 | 6 | 189 | 3 | 4.2 | — | 15 | 2 |
| J. Cornford | 20 | 1 | 69 | — | 2 | — | 12 | — |
| J. Parks | 50 | 17 | 107 | 1 | 2 | — | 5 | — |
| Cook | 21 | 4 | 66 | 1 | | | | |
| Melville | 10 | 1 | 50 | 1 | | | | |
| Pearce | 19 | 4 | 47 | 2 | | | | |
| Langridge | 3 | — | 10 | 1 | | | | |

**Essex Bowling**

| | Overs | Mdns | Runs | Wkts | Overs | Mdns | Runs | Wkts |
|---|---|---|---|---|---|---|---|---|
| Farnes .......... | 23 | 8 | 60 | 2 | 8 | 1 | 32 | — |
| Nichols ......... | 7 | 1 | 46 | 1 | 8 | 1 | 32 | — |
| Smith ........... | 25 | 2 | 97 | 2 | 28 | 4 | 90 | — |
| Eastman ......... | 37 | 4 | 104 | 3 | 27 | 7 | 69 | 5 |
| O'Connor ....... | 25 | 5 | 67 | 1 | 22 | 8 | 35 | — |

Umpires: J. Stone and D. Hendren.

# ESSEX v WORCESTERSHIRE

Played at Chelmsford, May 19, 21, 22, 1934

On Whit-Monday morning Nichol, the Worcestershire batsman, was found dead in bed – a sad event that marred the enjoyment of the match but did not prevent Worcestershire gaining first innings lead. This performance, in response to an Essex total of 469, was made possible by Walters and Gibbons, who followed their stand of 215 against Northamptonshire by scoring 279 together in three hours ten minutes. Gibbons drove, cut and hit to leg well, his off-side play being excellent. Walters, too, executed all these strokes in perfect style. Batting three hours and a half, he hit twenty-six 4s and fell to a splendid catch, Smith holding a hard, high return one hand. On Saturday, Pearce and Nichols added 210 for the fourth Essex wicket in three hours and a quarter. Pearce hit twelve 4s, Nichols eleven 4s, the driving and leg side strokes of both men being powerful. Brook bowled cleverly when Essex went in again, but time did not allow Worcestershire to get their victory.

## Essex

| | | | |
|---|---|---|---|
| J. A. Cutmore c Perks b Brook .............. | 35 | – c and b Brook ............... | 18 |
| D. F. Pope c Jackson b Brook .............. | 18 | – c and b Brook ............... | 7 |
| Mr T. N. Pearce c Perks b Brook ............. | 111 | | |
| J. O'Connor b Jackson ...................... | 23 | – not out ...................... | 30 |
| M. S. Nichols c and b Howorth ............. | 102 | – c Walters b Brook ............. | 11 |
| R. M. Taylor lbw b Jackson ................. | 28 | – not out ...................... | 34 |
| L. C. Eastman b Perks ...................... | 35 | | |
| Mr C. Bray not out ........................ | 64 | – c Baker b Brook ............... | 7 |
| P. Smith c Martin b Perks .................. | 30 | | |
| J. R. Sheffield c Martin b Perks ........... | 2 | | |
| Mr A. G. Daer lbw b Brook ................. | 7 | | |
| B 8, l-b 3, n-b 3 ..................... | 14 | L-b 2 ................. | 2 |
| | 469 | | 109 |

## Worcestershire

| | | | |
|---|---|---|---|
| Mr. C. F. Walters c and b Smith ......... | 178 | R. T. D. Perks c Smith b Eastman ........ | 5 |
| H. H. Gibbons c Sheffield b Smith ........ | 104 | P. F. Jackson b Smith ................ | 5 |
| Nawab of Pataudi b Cutmore ........... | 97 | Mr E. S. Baker c Eastman b Smith ....... | 0 |
| S. H. Martin c Cutmore b Smith ......... | 72 | M. Nichol (died during match) | |
| C. H. Bull not out .................... | 29 | B 12, l-b 5, w 1 .............. | 18 |
| R. Howorth c Smith b Eastman .......... | 5 | | |
| G. W. Brook c Eastman b Smith ......... | 2 | | 515 |

## Worcestershire Bowling

| | Overs | Mdns | Runs | Wkts | Overs | Mdns | Runs | Wkts |
|---|---|---|---|---|---|---|---|---|
| Perks ........... | 35 | 10 | 92 | 3 | 4 | 1 | 7 | — |
| Jackson ......... | 35 | 7 | 75 | 2 | 12 | 5 | 8 | — |
| Martin .......... | 23 | 4 | 53 | — | | | | |
| Brook ........... | 41 | 6 | 145 | 4 | 19 | 4 | 45 | 4 |
| Howorth ........ | 20 | 2 | 68 | 1 | 15 | 4 | 41 | — |
| Nichol .......... | 2 | — | 7 | — | | | | |
| Pataudi ......... | 4 | — | 15 | — | 2 | 1 | 6 | — |

## Essex Bowling

| | Overs | Mdns | Runs | Wkts |
|---|---|---|---|---|
| Nichols ......... | 15 | 2 | 57 | — |
| Daer ............ | 12 | 3 | 29 | — |
| Eastman ......... | 54 | 7 | 145 | 2 |
| Smith ........... | 45.4 | 5 | 147 | 6 |
| O'Connor ....... | 19 | 3 | 76 | — |
| Pope ............ | 3 | — | 17 | — |
| Cutmore ........ | 6 | 1 | 15 | 1 |
| Taylor .......... | 2 | — | 3 | — |
| Sheffield ........ | 4 | — | 8 | — |

Umpires: J. W. Hitch and A. Morton.

## ESSEX v KENT

### Played at Brentwood, May 30, 31, June 1, 1934

The introduction of modern county cricket to Brentwood was memorable because of the phenomenal scoring of Kent, who, after batting seven hours, declared with four men out for 803. This paved the way to a victory in an innings with 192 runs to spare. Not since 1899, when Surrey hit 811 against Somerset at The Oval, had a first-class match in England produced such a huge total in one innings.

As many as 623 runs were scored on the opening day, when Ashdown and Woolley – the left-hander missed when two – put on 352 for the second wicket in just over three hours. Driving and pulling by sound strokes, Woolley hit a six and twenty-one 4s. Ashdown played a truly remarkable innings – the highest ever made by a Kent player. Nothing resembling a chance occurred during his stay of six and a quarter hours. Hitting well all round the wicket, he scored 332 including a six and forty-five 4s.

Ames, missed when 30, helped him add 245 for the third wicket, and driving in admirably sound style Ames made 202 in two hours fifty minutes, his chief strokes being a six and twenty-nine 4s. Only six maiden overs were bowled during the innings, and the ball never did anything unexpected on a splendidly prepared pitch. A second wicket partnership of 156 by Pope and Pearce suggested Essex might make a good reply, and Pope reached three figures, but Freeman, splendidly supported by Ames at the wicket, caused a breakdown and on Friday Essex, on a wearing pitch, followed on 395 behind. Slow bowling by Freeman and Wright had regular success. Before the first innings closed, O'Connor completed the fifth individual hundred of the match. In the follow-on, however, Essex lost eight men for 115. Then Ashton, who had been out of county cricket for five seasons, hit with such spirit that he got 71 not out in the last eighty minutes, thus proving that the bowling was by no means so deadly as several of his colleagues had made it appear.

The contrasts of cricket were emphasised during the match by the fact that on the first two days eleven wickets fell for 1,169 runs and on the last day thirteen went down while 245 runs were scored.

## Kent

| | |
|---|---|
| W. H. Ashdown c Ashton b Nichols ......332 | Mr I. D. K. Fleming not out ............ 42 |
| A. Fagg lbw b R. Smith ................ 31 | |
| F. E. Woolley b Ashton ................172 | B 8, w 4, n-b 1 .............. 13 |
| L. E. G. Ames not out ................202 | ——— |
| A. E. Watt c R. Smith b Ashton .......... 11 | (4 wkts dec.) 803 |

L. J. Todd, Mr B. H. Valentine, Mr A. P. F. Chapman, D. V. P. Wright and A. P. Freeman did not bat.

## Essex

| | | | |
|---|---|---|---|
| L. C. Eastman c Chapman b Wright ............. | 52 | – c Woolley b Freeman .......... | 4 |
| D. F. Pope c Woolley b Valentine ............... | 100 | – c Ames b Wright ............. | 11 |
| Mr T. N. Pearce c Ames b Valentine ............ | 79 | – c Woolley b Freeman ......... | 17 |
| J. O'Connor not out ......................... | 105 | – lbw b Freeman ............... | 25 |
| M. S. Nichols c Valentine b Wright ............. | 3 | – lbw b Wright ................ | 20 |
| J. A. Cutmore c Ames b Watt .................. | 30 | – c Fleming b Wright .......... | 0 |
| Mr C. T. Ashton st Ames b Freeman ............. | 11 | – not out ..................... | 71 |
| R. M. Taylor st Ames b Freeman ............... | 1 | – st Ames b Freeman .......... | 1 |
| P. Smith c Woolley b Freeman ................. | 11 | – c Ashdown b Freeman ........ | 0 |
| J. R. Sheffield c Woolley b Freeman .......... | 0 | – c Watt b Ashdown ........... | 31 |
| R. Smith b Freeman ......................... | 0 | – st Ames b Freeman .......... | 1 |
| B 7, l-b 8, n-b 1 ...................... | 16 | B 14, l-b 8 ............. | 22 |
| | ——— | | ——— |
| | 408 | | 203 |

## Essex Bowling

| | Overs | Mdns | Runs | Wkts |
|---|---|---|---|---|
| Nichols .......... | 20 | 1 | 93 | 1 |
| R. Smith .......... | 22 | 1 | 115 | 1 |
| Ashton ........... | 31 | 2 | 185 | 2 |
| P. Smith .......... | 36 | 2 | 208 | — |
| O'Connor ........ | 16.2 | — | 83 | — |
| Cutmore ......... | 12 | — | 63 | — |
| Taylor ........... | 7 | — | 36 | — |
| Pope ............. | 2 | — | 7 | — |

## Kent Bowling

| | Overs | Mdns | Runs | Wkts | Overs | Mdns | Runs | Wkts |
|---|---|---|---|---|---|---|---|---|
| Watt ............. | 23 | 4 | 85 | 1 | 9 | — | 20 | — |
| Ashdown ......... | 6 | 2 | 22 | — | 1 | 1 | — | 1 |
| Freeman ......... | 50.5 | 15 | 116 | 5 | 34.2 | 13 | 60 | 6 |
| Wright ........... | 38 | 9 | 117 | 2 | 27 | 12 | 59 | 3 |
| Todd ............ | 6 | — | 11 | — | | | | |
| Woolley .......... | 7 | 2 | 10 | — | 5 | — | 26 | — |
| Valentine ........ | 9 | 2 | 31 | 2 | 5 | 2 | 16 | — |

Umpires: A. E. Street and J. W. Hitch.

## ESSEX v KENT

At Colchester, July 13, 14, 15, 1938

Drawn. The match was notable for the world-record feat achieved by Fagg, of Kent, in scoring two double-hundreds. Essex were without their regular bowlers, engaged in the Gentlemen and Players game at Lord's, but Fagg's performance, nevertheless, was extraordinary. In the first innings he made 244 out of 386 in five hours, and in the second innings he batted two hours and fifty minutes for 202 not out, before Chalk declared. Vigorous on-drives and powerful strokes to leg were his chief means of scoring and he hit thirty-one 4s in the first innings and twenty-seven in the other. On the opening day, Kent kept Essex in the field until six o'clock. Todd helped Fagg in a stand of 133 and Chalk assisted in a partnership of 137. Wright, who in one spell took four wickets for six runs, worried Essex with slow leg-break bowling but Pearce and Smith put on 131 for the ninth wicket. Pearce gave a splendid display of driving and glancing. When Kent batted again leading by 79, Fagg played brilliant cricket. He so dominated the proceedings that he reached three figures out of 134 in 69 minutes, and when stumps were drawn Kent, with three wickets left, led by 221. Play on the last morning was rendered memorable by the completion of Fagg's exploit, and spectators and players alike applauded him all the way to the pavilion. Essex, needing 393 to win, started badly, but rain intervened and prevented a finish.

## Kent

| | | | |
|---|---|---|---|
| A. Fagg lbw b Taylor | 244 | – not out | 202 |
| P. R. Sunnucks c Wade b Smith | 3 | – run out | 82 |
| Mr W. H. V. Levett c Wilcox b Daer | 0 | | |
| L. J. Todd b Smith | 39 | | |
| T. Spencer c Taylor b Vigar | 14 | | |
| Mr F. G. H. Chalk c Lavers b Eastman | 61 | | |
| F. G. Foy c and b Taylor | 25 | | |
| N. W. Harding st Wade b Vigar | 9 | | |
| D. V. P. Wright c Wade b Taylor | 2 | | |
| A. E. Watt not out | 24 | – not out | 24 |
| C. Lewis c Vigar b Taylor | 5 | | |
| L-b 3 | 3 | B 2, l-b 2, n-b 1 | 5 |
| | 429 | (1 wkt dec.) | 313 |

## Essex

| | | | |
|---|---|---|---|
| Mr D. R. Wilcox c Harding b Todd | 5 | – b Watt | 1 |
| L. C. Eastman lbw b Todd | 44 | – c Wright b Todd | 0 |
| R. M. Taylor b Lewis | 37 | – not out | 7 |
| J. O'Connor c Lewis b Wright | 63 | – not out | 0 |
| A. V. Avery b Wright | 1 | | |
| Mr T. N. Pearce not out | 137 | | |
| Mr A. B. Lavers lbw b Wright | 1 | | |
| T. H. Wade b Wright | 4 | | |
| F. Vigar lbw b Wright | 0 | | |
| R. Smith c Fagg b Wright | 37 | | |
| H. Daer lbw b Wright | 4 | | |
| B 5, l-b 6, n-b 6 | 17 | | |
| | 350 | | 8 |

## Essex Bowling

| | Overs | Mdns | Runs | Wkts | Overs | Mdns | Runs | Wkts |
|---|---|---|---|---|---|---|---|---|
| Smith | 22 | 4 | 96 | 2 | 10 | 3 | 46 | — |
| Daer | 10 | 3 | 51 | 1 | 9 | — | 46 | — |
| Eastman | 40 | 15 | 68 | 1 | 17 | 2 | 52 | — |
| Lavers | 9 | 1 | 30 | — | | | | |
| Vigar | 19 | 3 | 91 | 2 | 13 | — | 75 | — |
| O'Connor | 2 | — | 6 | — | 5 | — | 23 | — |
| Pearce | 10 | — | 43 | — | | | | |
| Taylor | 10.1 | 1 | 41 | 4 | 10 | — | 46 | — |
| Wilcox | | | | | 4 | — | 20 | — |

## Kent Bowling

| | Overs | Mdns | Runs | Wkts | Overs | Mdns | Runs | Wkts |
|---|---|---|---|---|---|---|---|---|
| Todd ............. | 19 | 6 | 46 | 2 | 2 | — | 6 | 1 |
| Watt ............. | 22 | 3 | 63 | — | 1.3 | — | 2 | 1 |
| Harding ......... | 5 | 1 | 34 | — | | | | |
| Wright ........... | 31.3 | 7 | 107 | 7 | | | | |
| Lewis ............ | 26 | 7 | 83 | 1 | | | | |

Umpires: J. Newman and C. W. L. Parker.

# ESSEX v WORCESTERSHIRE

### Played at Chelmsford, May 27, 29, 30, 1939

Essex won by 295 runs. Worcestershire had to contend with tragedy. In a car crash on Whit-Sunday evening Bull was killed and Buller injured. Defeat in such circumstances was not surprising. Nichols hit his second successive century, and backed this up with fine fast bowling. O'Connor, with two 6s and nineteen 4s in his hundred, helped to set the unfortunate but plucky visitors too heavy a task. Ray Smith, who helped Nichols put on 83 for the last Essex wicket, bowled with pace and swing on the last day. Jenkins, who bowled leg breaks cleverly, and King were Worcestershire's best players. Yarnold, their twelfth man, kept wicket in place of Buller.

## Essex

| | | | |
|---|---|---|---|
| A. V. Avery lbw b Jenkins .................... | 47 | – c White b Howorth ............ | 77 |
| L. C. Eastman st Buller b Jenkins ............... | 18 | – c Perks b Howorth ............ | 52 |
| T. H. Wade c Buller b Jenkins ................. | 0 | – c sub b Jenkins ................ | 0 |
| J. O'Connor c White b Perks .................. | 4 | – not out ...................... | 118 |
| M. S. Nichols not out ....................... | 116 | – c Martin b Perks .............. | 4 |
| R. M. Taylor c Martin b Jenkins ............... | 9 | – b Perks .................... | 23 |
| Mr D. F. Cock b Jenkins ..................... | 0 | | |
| Capt. J. W. A. Stephenson lbw b Howorth ........ | 24 | | |
| P. Smith b Jenkins .......................... | 3 | – not out ..................... | 1 |
| Mr J. N. Dennis lbw b Jenkins ................. | 0 | | |
| R. Smith c Howorth b Perks .................. | 35 | | |
| B 6, l-b 5, n-b 4 .................... | 15 | B 18, l-b 7 ............. | 22 |
| | **271** | **(5 wkts dec.)** | **285** |

## Worcestershire

| | | | |
|---|---|---|---|
| Mr A. F. T. White b Nichols .................. | 9 | – c Dennis b R. Smith ............ | 9 |
| B. P. King b Nichols ........................ | 54 | – c R. Smith b Stephenson ......... | 61 |
| E. Cooper b Nichols ......................... | 20 | – c Wade b R. Smith ............ | 7 |
| H. H. Gibbons b Nichols ..................... | 0 | – b R. Smith ................. | 0 |
| S. H. Martin c P. Smith b Nichols .............. | 5 | – b R. Smith ................. | 7 |
| P-O. M. Jewell b P. Smith ................... | 2 | – c Wade b R. Smith ............ | 0 |
| R. Howorth not out ........................ | 34 | – c R. Smith b Eastman .......... | 6 |
| R. T. D. Perks b P. Smith ..................... | 23 | – b R. Smith ................. | 5 |
| R. Jenkins c Nichols b Taylor ................. | 2 | – not out ..................... | 9 |
| S. Buller (hurt in car crash) | | | |
| C. H. Bull (killed in car crash) | | | |
| B 1, l-b 5 ........................ | 6 | L-b 1, w 1 ............. | 2 |
| | **155** | | **106** |

## Worcestershire Bowling

| | Overs | Mdns | Runs | Wkts | Overs | Mdns | Runs | Wkts |
|---|---|---|---|---|---|---|---|---|
| Perks ............ | 25.6 | 6 | 74 | 2 | 17 | 2 | 80 | 2 |
| Howorth ......... | 22 | 1 | 83 | 1 | 24 | — | 109 | 2 |
| Jenkins ........... | 33 | 10 | 98 | 7 | 13 | 1 | 64 | 1 |
| Gibbons .......... | 1 | — | 1 | — | 3 | — | 22 | — |

## Essex Bowling

| | Overs | Mdns | Runs | Wkts | Overs | Mdns | Runs | Wkts |
|---|---|---|---|---|---|---|---|---|
| Nichols .......... | 12 | — | 64 | 5 | 7 | 1 | 18 | — |
| R. Smith .......... | 5 | — | 40 | — | 13 | 1 | 46 | 6 |
| P. Smith .......... | 8 | — | 35 | 2 | | | | |
| Taylor ........... | 2.2 | — | 10 | 1 | | | | |
| Eastman .......... | | | | | 7 | — | 32 | 1 |
| Stephenson ....... | | | | | 0.4 | — | 8 | 1 |

Umpires: C. N. Woolley and A. Skelding.

# GLAMORGAN

## GLAMORGAN v DERBYSHIRE

Played at Cardiff, June 18, 20, 1921

In this match – finished off in two days – Derbyshire gained a remarkable victory, winning by two wickets after being 85 runs behind on the first innings. The turning-point came on the second morning, when Bestwick, bowling in great form, took at a cost of 40 runs all ten wickets in Glamorgan's second innings – seven of them bowled down. Despite this big performance, however, Derbyshire had an anxious task when they went in to get 192. The eighth wicket fell at 116, but Elliott played steadily while Carter hit, and the remaining runs were obtained without further loss. From Glamorgan's point of view the best feature of the match was Bates's batting.

### Glamorgan

| | | | |
|---|---|---|---|
| Mr T. A. L. Whittington b Tomlinson | 19 | – b Bestwick | 0 |
| Mr W. N. Gemmill b Bestwick | 11 | – b Bestwick | 2 |
| H. Tomlinson b Bestwick | 0 | – c Storer b Bestwick | 20 |
| W. Bates c and b Tomlinson | 67 | – b Bestwick | 48 |
| Mr G. E. Cording c Storer b Bestwick | 25 | – b Bestwick | 4 |
| Mr H. G. Symonds c Elliott b Bestwick | 6 | – b Bestwick | 1 |
| Mr W. L. Jenkins c Curgenven b Tomlinson | 5 | – c Elliott b Bestwick | 6 |
| Col. A. O'Bree c Curgenven b Blackton | 22 | – c Storer b Bestwick | 16 |
| Mr J. C. Clay b Storer | 3 | – b Bestwick | 5 |
| H. Creber run out | 1 | – b Bestwick | 1 |
| J. Nash not out | 0 | – not out | 0 |
| B 6, l-b 3 | 9 | B 1, n-b 2 | 3 |
| | **168** | | **106** |

### Derbyshire

| | | | |
|---|---|---|---|
| Mr G. M. Buckston c Symonds b Nash | 0 | – c Jenkins b Nash | 0 |
| W. Carter c Cording b Clay | 0 | – not out | 50 |
| Mr G. R. Jackson lbw b Bates | 15 | – b Nash | 4 |
| Mr G. Curgenven b Clay | 0 | – c Jenkins b Bates | 46 |
| S. Cadman b Nash | 25 | – c Gemmill b Creber | 31 |
| H. Storer run out | 13 | – b Clay | 12 |
| J. M. Hutchinson c and b Bates | 19 | – lbw b Nash | 0 |
| Mr W. R. Blackton b Clay | 4 | – b Nash | 0 |
| Mr W. J. V. Tomlinson not out | 3 | – lbw b Nash | 5 |
| H. Elliott b Bates | 0 | – not out | 20 |
| W. Bestwick lbw b Bates | 0 | | |
| B 3, l-b 1 | 4 | B 18, l-b 7 | 25 |
| | **83** | | **193** |

### Derbyshire Bowling

| | Overs | Mdns | Runs | Wkts | Overs | Mdns | Runs | Wkts |
|---|---|---|---|---|---|---|---|---|
| Bestwick | 30 | 9 | 71 | 4 | 19 | 2 | 40 | 10 |
| Storer | 15.2 | 2 | 35 | 1 | 6 | 1 | 24 | — |
| Tomlinson | 16 | 3 | 41 | 3 | 6 | — | 17 | — |
| Blackton | 8 | 2 | 12 | 1 | 6 | 1 | 22 | — |

**Glamorgan Bowling**

| | Overs | Mdns | Runs | Wkts | Overs | Mdns | Runs | Wkts |
|---|---|---|---|---|---|---|---|---|
| Clay ............ | 18 | 6 | 26 | 3 | 16 | 2 | 62 | 1 |
| Creber .......... | 8 | 2 | 17 | — | 3 | — | 19 | 1 |
| Nash ........... | 15 | 6 | 19 | 2 | 29 | 5 | 56 | 5 |
| Bates ........... | 6.5 | 1 | 17 | 4 | 9.2 | 1 | 31 | 1 |

Umpires: G. P. Harrison and J. P. Whiteside.

## GLAMORGAN v HAMPSHIRE

### Played at Swansea, May 20, 22, 23, 1922

In a match in which for the most part the ball beat the bat, Hampshire gained a victory by 178 runs. On the first day the batsmen were so much at fault on the damaged pitch that the third innings began before the drawing of stumps. Glamorgan thought themselves lucky to get Hampshire out for 83, but when their own turn came to go in they were helpless against Newman and Boyes. Newman took four wickets in five overs at a cost of 3 runs. Heavy rain cut the second day's play short, but in the hour and a half available Hampshire increased their score from 6 for no wicket to 71 for three. On Tuesday the match was finished off in very showery weather. Hampshire did not find run-getting at all easy against excellent bowling, and Tennyson, who tried to play a forcing game, was lucky, giving two or three chances. Left with 255 to get, Glamorgan had no chance, Newman and Boyes bowling with a lot of spin on the treacherous pitch. It will be noticed that Creber and Nash divided the Hampshire wickets, Creber taking twelve of them.

### Hampshire

| | | | |
|---|---|---|---|
| G. Brown c Jacobs b Creber ................. | 9 | – c Clay b Nash ................ | 12 |
| A. Bowell c Gemmill b Nash ................... | 4 | – st Bancroft b Creber ........... | 6 |
| A. Kennedy c Nash b Creber .................. | 18 | – c Clay b Creber ............... | 27 |
| C. P. Mead b Creber ........................ | 37 | – c B. L. Morris b Creber ......... | 39 |
| Hon. L. H. Tennyson c B. L. Morris b Creber ...... | 6 | – c Gemmill b Creber ............ | 19 |
| J. Newman b Nash ......................... | 1 | – b Nash ...................... | 25 |
| Capt. R. H. D. Bolton c Whittington b Creber ...... | 0 | – c Whittington b Creber ......... | 6 |
| Mr C. P. Brutton c Whittington b Creber ......... | 0 | – b Nash ...................... | 9 |
| Mr. A. S. McIntyre st Bancroft b Creber .......... | 0 | – b Nash ...................... | 15 |
| W. H. Livsey not out ...................... | 7 | – not out ..................... | 23 |
| G. S. Boyes b Nash ........................ | 1 | – b Nash ...................... | 19 |
| | | B 7 .................... | 7 |
| | **83** | | **207** |

### Glamorgan

| | | | |
|---|---|---|---|
| Mr P. Morris b Newman ..................... | 11 | – c McIntyre b Boyes ............ | 4 |
| Mr W. N. Gemmill c Newman b Kennedy ......... | 15 | – b Newman ................... | 3 |
| W. Bates run out ......................... | 0 | – c Mead b Boyes ............... | 6 |
| Mr T. R. Morgan c and b Newman ............. | 0 | – c Boyes b Newman ............ | 8 |
| Mr B. O. Morris b Boyes .................... | 1 | – c McIntyre b Newman .......... | 19 |
| Mr N. E. Jacobs c Brutton b Boyes ............ | 4 | – lbw b Boyes ................. | 16 |
| Mr T. A. L. Whittington b Boyes ................. | 2 | – c Livsey b Boyes ............. | 1 |
| J. Nash b Newman ......................... | 2 | – b Boyes .................... | 2 |
| Mr J. C. Clay b Newman .................... | 0 | – b Newman ................... | 13 |
| H. Creber not out ......................... | 0 | – not out .................... | 3 |
| J. Bancroft c Bowell b Boyes ................. | 0 | – c McIntyre b Boyes ........... | 1 |
| B 1 ............................ | 1 | | |
| | **36** | | **76** |

**Glamorgan Bowling**

|  | Overs | Mdns | Runs | Wkts | Overs | Mdns | Runs | Wkts |
|---|---|---|---|---|---|---|---|---|
| Nash ............ | 15.3 | 4 | 33 | 3 | 33.5 | 11 | 89 | 5 |
| Creber .......... | 18 | 2 | 47 | 7 | 33 | 7 | 104 | 5 |
| P. Morris ........ | 3 | 1 | 3 | — |  |  |  |  |
| Bates ........... |  |  |  |  | 1 | — | 7 | — |

**Hampshire Bowling**

|  | Overs | Mdns | Runs | Wkts | Overs | Mdns | Runs | Wkts |
|---|---|---|---|---|---|---|---|---|
| Kennedy ........ | 8 | 4 | 13 | 1 | 4 | 2 | 4 | — |
| Newman ........ | 5 | 3 | 3 | 4 | 12 | 4 | 39 | 4 |
| Boyes ........... | 8 | 1 | 19 | 4 | 15.5 | 4 | 33 | 6 |

Umpires: A. McArthur and A. E. Street.

## GLAMORGAN IN 1924

*President* – Lieut-Col Sir Henry Webb

*Hon. Treasurer* – Mr W. Lewis Renwick

*Secretary* – Mr Arthur Gibson, Market Buildings, St Mary Street, Cardiff

*Captain* – Mr J. C. Clay

Bad weather played havoc with Glamorgan's finances in 1924, but as regards cricket there was a very welcome improvement. Indeed, the county at last did something to justify its promotion in 1921 to the front rank. Nothing exceptional was accomplished, but a record of five wins in county matches and eleven defeats was a marked advance upon two matches won and seventeen lost in 1923. Standing out above everything else was the victory over Lancashire at Swansea in August by 38 runs. It was urged that the Lancashire eleven were tired out by travelling all night from Blackpool, but Glamorgan must not on this account be robbed of the credit due to them. A night journey under modern conditions is not a very serious business and, at any rate, the Lancashire players had a Sunday's rest while the game was in progress.

## GLAMORGAN v WORCESTERSHIRE

### Played at Pontypridd, July 18, 20, 1931

To such a pronounced extent did bowlers hold the upper hand in this match that, in the course of two days, thirty-three wickets went down for 11 runs apiece, this eventful cricket resulting in Glamorgan gaining by seven wickets what was only their second victory during the season. Walters on Saturday gave a masterly display for Worcestershire, withstanding for two hours and a half an attack of so deadly a description that no one else reached double figures. Carrying his bat right through the innings, he drove with great power and unfailing judgment. Ryan, spinning the ball a lot and keeping an excellent length, dismissed seven batsmen for 52 runs. Glamorgan lost three wickets for 19 but Turnbull and Dai Davies afterwards added 54 – a partnership which played a big part in determining the issue. Next morning Glamorgan had eight men out for 108 when Howard and Emrys Davies came together and put on 32. Worcestershire at their second attempt fared so disastrously against Clay and Ryan that they lost six wickets in clearing off their small arrears and could set the home side no more than 47 to get. Dyson and Bell failed but Bates and Dai Davies ensured the success of their side.

## Worcestershire

| | | | |
|---|---|---|---|
| Mr C. F. Walters not out | 53 | – lbw b Ryan | 15 |
| J. Fox c D. Davies b Ryan | 3 | – lbw b Ryan | 7 |
| M. Nichol lbw b Ryan | 9 | – c Turnbull b Clay | 3 |
| H. H. Gibbons b Ryan | 5 | – lbw b Clay | 3 |
| Mr. B. W. Quaife lbw b Ryan | 5 | – run out | 18 |
| L. Wright lbw b Clay | 6 | – lbw b Clay | 0 |
| Mr T. L. Winwood run out | 3 | – st Jenkins b Clay | 0 |
| F. Root lbw b D. Davies | 0 | – c Dyson b Clay | 14 |
| G. W. Brook b Ryan | 2 | – c Turnbull b Ryan | 10 |
| R. T. D. Perks b Ryan | 7 | – st Jenkins b Ryan | 3 |
| P. F. Jackson st Jenkins b Ryan | 0 | – not out | 8 |
| B 5, l-b 2 | 7 | B 5 | 5 |
| | **100** | | **86** |

## Glamorgan

| | | | |
|---|---|---|---|
| W. E. Bates lbw b Jackson | 12 | – b Jackson | 19 |
| A. H. Dyson c and b Root | 3 | – b Root | 1 |
| J. T. Bell c Quaife b Root | 4 | – b Brook | 3 |
| D. Davies lbw b Brook | 26 | – not out | 17 |
| R. Duckfield b Brook | 12 | | |
| Mr M. J. Turnbull b Brook | 21 | | |
| A. H. Howard c Quaife b Jackson | 18 | | |
| Mr J. C. Clay c Brook b Root | 3 | | |
| Mr V. G. J. Jenkins lbw b Brook | 0 | | |
| E. Davies not out | 15 | – not out | 1 |
| F. Ryan b Jackson | 0 | | |
| B 22, l-b 4 | 26 | L-b 7 | 7 |
| | **140** | | **48** |

### Glamorgan Bowling

| | Overs | Mdns | Runs | Wkts | Overs | Mdns | Runs | Wkts |
|---|---|---|---|---|---|---|---|---|
| D. Davies | 13 | 6 | 18 | 1 | 9 | 7 | 3 | — |
| E. Davies | 3 | 1 | 5 | — | | | | |
| Clay | 18 | 10 | 18 | 1 | 10 | 3 | 31 | 5 |
| Ryan | 22.2 | 5 | 52 | 7 | 18.4 | 1 | 47 | 4 |

### Worcestershire Bowling

| | Overs | Mdns | Runs | Wkts | Overs | Mdns | Runs | Wkts |
|---|---|---|---|---|---|---|---|---|
| Root | 23 | 10 | 31 | 3 | 6 | 2 | 11 | 1 |
| Perks | 3 | 1 | 12 | — | | | | |
| Jackson | 13.4 | 5 | 13 | 3 | 9 | 3 | 22 | 1 |
| Brook | 29 | 5 | 58 | 4 | 4.2 | 2 | 8 | 1 |

Umpires: D. Hendren and L. C. Braund.

## GLAMORGAN v YORKSHIRE

### Played at Swansea, July 22, 23, 24, 1931

A wonderful bowling performance by Verity was the main factor in a remarkable Yorkshire victory, the young left-hander actually taking fourteen wickets for less than four runs each and the northern county requiring no more than seven hours to beat Glamorgan by an innings and 25 runs. Nothing could be done on Wednesday until half-past two when Greenwood, having won the toss, decided to send Glamorgan in to bat. Startling success attended this course, Verity, when tried, getting four wickets in his first two overs for four runs and seven men being out for 29. Jenkins and Emrys Davies put on 33 but then Verity finished off the innings. Ryan at the start of Yorkshire's innings disposed of Holmes and Sutcliffe cheaply before there came some confident and powerful hitting by Leyland who, in company with Mitchell, put on 51 in forty minutes. Ryan, despite his encouraging start, soon lost his length and at the close Yorkshire with only three men out, had established a lead of 15. Not a ball could be bowled on Thursday, this being the thirteenth experience the Yorkshiremen had had of a blank day. The visitors on Friday added 101 in ninety minutes and then declared with eight men out. Leyland's invaluable display lasted an hour and three-quarters and included ten 4s. Wanting 116 to avert an innings defeat, Glamorgan were dismissed for 91 with an hour to spare. Verity, when put on at 11, sent down his first four overs for 7 runs and five wickets.

### Glamorgan

| | | |
|---|---:|---:|
| A. H. Dyson c Mitchell b Macaulay | 2 – c Macaulay b Verity | 6 |
| A. H. Howard lbw b Bowes | 10 – b Robinson | 35 |
| J. T. Bell c Bowes b Leyland | 7 – st Wood b Verity | 0 |
| D. Davies c Macaulay b Verity | 1 – b Verity | 6 |
| R. Duckfield c Mitchell b Verity | 4 – c Robinson b Verity | 2 |
| Mr M. J. Turnbull st Wood b Verity | 0 – st Wood b Verity | 5 |
| W. E. Bates c Mitchell b Verity | 1 – lbw b Verity | 20 |
| E. Davies c Sutcliffe b Verity | 13 – c Sutcliffe b Robinson | 7 |
| Mr V. G. J. Jenkins c Wood b Bowes | 19 – lbw b Verity | 0 |
| G. Lavis not out | 2 – c Barber b Verity | 4 |
| F. Ryan lbw b Verity | 0 – not out | 0 |
| L-b 3 | 3　　　　B 4, l-b 1, n-b 1 | 6 |
| | **62** | **91** |

### Yorkshire

| | | | | |
|---|---:|---|---|---:|
| P. Holmes c D. Davies b Ryan | 8 | | E. Robinson not out | 5 |
| H. Sutcliffe c Jenkins b Ryan | 9 | | G. G. Macaulay c Bell b Ryan | 0 |
| A. Mitchell b E. Davies | 19 | | H. Verity not out | 10 |
| M. Leyland c Bell b D. Davies | 77 | | | |
| W. Barber c Turnbull b Ryan | 30 | | L-b 2, n-b 2 | 4 |
| A. Wood b D. Davies | 11 | | | |
| Mr F. E. Greenwood b Ryan | 5 | | (8 wkts dec.) | 178 |

W. E. Bowes did not bat.

### Yorkshire Bowling

| | Overs | Mdns | Runs | Wkts | Overs | Mdns | Runs | Wkts |
|---|---:|---:|---:|---:|---:|---:|---:|---:|
| Bowes | 13 | 5 | 20 | 2 | 4 | 1 | 4 | — |
| Robinson | 7 | 4 | 7 | — | 10 | 3 | 32 | 2 |
| Macaulay | 11 | 6 | 11 | 1 | 8 | 3 | 16 | — |
| Verity | 14 | 3 | 21 | 6 | 14.2 | 5 | 33 | 8 |
| Leyland | 2 | 2 | — | 1 | | | | |

### Glamorgan Bowling

| | Overs | Mdns | Runs | Wkts |
|---|---:|---:|---:|---:|
| D. Davies | 17 | 3 | 44 | 2 |
| Ryan | 23 | 2 | 86 | 5 |
| Lavis | 4 | — | 13 | — |
| E. Davies | 11 | 2 | 31 | 1 |

Umpires: D. Hendren and G. Beet.

# GLAMORGAN v NORTHAMPTONSHIRE

Played at Cowbridge, July 25, 27, 28, 1931

The practice of declaring first innings closed at equal scores or at no scores at all – so prevalent during the season of 1931 – underwent a further development on this occasion when, with no cricket practicable until after three o'clock on the second day, the rival captains agreed to declare when a total of 50 had been reached. The particular purpose so served was not obvious and in adhering to the agreement, Turnbull, the Glamorgan captain, broke Law 54 of Cricket which forbids in a two day match a declaration later on the first day than an hour and forty minutes before the time agreed upon for drawing stumps. Northamptonshire, hitting up their runs in three-quarters of an hour, declared at four o'clock but when Glamorgan took a similar action only forty minutes remained for play. Northamptonshire on Tuesday morning had 45 on the board when their second wicket fell. Afterwards Clay and Ryan met with so little resistance that the other eight wickets actually went down for 14 more runs. Set 60 to get, Glamorgan lost three batsmen in half an hour for 24 runs but by three o'clock they had gained a five-wickets victory.

## Northamptonshire

| | | | |
|---|---|---|---|
| A. H. Bakewell not out | 25 | – c Bell b Ryan | 18 |
| J. E. Timms b D. Davies | 8 | – lbw b Clay | 5 |
| A. L. Cox not out | 7 | – b Clay | 20 |
| Mr V. W. C. Jupp (did not bat) | | – b Clay | 2 |
| W. Coverdale (did not bat) | | – c and b Ryan | 0 |
| A. D. Matthews (did not bat) | | – run out | 0 |
| Mr T. B. G. Welch (did not bat) | | – lbw b Clay | 0 |
| Mr E. F. Towell (did not bat) | | – b Ryan | 1 |
| A. E. Thomas (did not bat) | | – c Turnbull b Clay | 3 |
| R. J. Partridge (did not bat) | | – not out | 1 |
| W. Ball (did not bat) | | – b Ryan | 2 |
| B 7, l-b 4 | 11 | L-b 6, n-b 1 | 7 |
| (1 wkt dec.) | 51 | | 59 |

## Glamorgan

| | | | |
|---|---|---|---|
| A. H. Dyson c Cox b Thomas | 3 | – b Matthews | 16 |
| A. H. Howard b Thomas | 9 | – lbw b Matthews | 2 |
| R. Duckfield not out | 17 | – not out | 11 |
| D. Davies not out | 14 | – c Welch b Matthews | 6 |
| Mr M. J. Turnbull (did not bat) | | – b Thomas | 4 |
| J. T. Bell (did not bat) | | – lbw b Matthews | 8 |
| Mr V. G. J. Jenkins (did not bat) | | – not out | 7 |
| B 6, w 2 | 8 | B 4, l-b 1, n-b 1 | 6 |
| (2 wkts dec.) | 51 | | 60 |

Mr J. C. Clay, E. Davies, F. Ryan and J. Mercer did not bat.

## Glamorgan Bowling

| | Overs | Mdns | Runs | Wkts | Overs | Mdns | Runs | Wkts |
|---|---|---|---|---|---|---|---|---|
| Mercer | 4 | 2 | 6 | — | 8 | 3 | 13 | — |
| D. Davies | 9 | 6 | 8 | 1 | 2 | — | 5 | — |
| Ryan | 6 | 1 | 26 | — | 5.4 | — | 12 | 4 |
| Clay | | | | | 11 | 4 | 22 | 5 |

**Northamptonshire Bowling**

| | Overs | Mdns | Runs | Wkts | Overs | Mdns | Runs | Wkts |
|---|---|---|---|---|---|---|---|---|
| Thomas .......... | 13 | 5 | 15 | 2 | 8 | 3 | 10 | 1 |
| Matthews ........ | 5 | 2 | 5 | — | 13.2 | 3 | 25 | 4 |
| Partridge ........ | 1 | 1 | — | — | | | | |
| Jupp ............. | 7.4 | 1 | 23 | — | 7 | — | 19 | — |

Umpires: W. Reeves and H. Watson.

## GLAMORGAN v SURREY

Played at Cardiff, August 5, 6, 7, 1931

Play being impossible on Wednesday or Thursday, Turnbull and Fender decided to follow the practice of declaring first innings closed after bowling one ball. This performance having been duly completed, Surrey went in and in two hours and a half ran up a score of 214, losing meanwhile no more than three wickets, and at that point declaring for the second time during the day. Hobbs, beginning to hit at once, was out at 28 but Sandham and Squires obtained such a complete mastery over the Glamorgan bowling that they put on 142 runs in a hundred minutes. Surrey continued batting until Sandham reached three figures, that player on this occasion making his fifth hundred of the season. Two hours and three-quarters at the outside remained for cricket when Glamorgan started to try and make 215. They lost Howard at 2 yet this failure disturbed Bates and Dyson so little that those two players hit up 74 in fifty-five minutes. A capital display by Turnbull proved a further factor in increasing Glamorgan's prospects. There were six men out for 146 but at that point Jenkins went in and hit so well that twenty minutes before time Glamorgan had gained a most refreshing victory by three wickets.

### Surrey

| | | | |
|---|---|---|---|
| Mr P. G. H. Fender not out ................... | 0 | | |
| E. W. Brooks not out ....................... | 0 | | |
| J. B. Hobbs (did not bat) .................... | | – st Every b Ryan ............... | 21 |
| A. Sandham (did not bat) .................... | | – not out ...................... | 100 |
| H. S. Squires (did not bat) .................. | | – c Ryan b Clay ............... | 69 |
| H. A. Peach (did not bat) ................... | | – lbw b Clay ................... | 9 |
| Mr D. R. Jardine (did not bat) ............... | | – not out ...................... | 12 |
| | | B 2, n-b 1 .............. | 3 |
| | (0 wkts dec.) 0 | (3 wkts dec.) | 214 |

Mr S. A. Block, T. Shepherd, R. J. Gregory and A. R. Gover did not bat.

### Glamorgan

| | | | |
|---|---|---|---|
| Mr M. J. Turnbull not out ................... | 0 | – b Fender ..................... | 44 |
| G. Every not out .......................... | 0 | – st Brooks b Peach ............. | 8 |
| A. H. Dyson (did not bat) ................... | | – lbw b Fender ................. | 38 |
| A. H. Howard (did not bat) .................. | | – lbw b Peach .................. | 2 |
| W. E. Bates (did not bat) ................... | | – c Brooks b Fender ............. | 42 |
| J. Mercer (did not bat) ..................... | | – c Peach b Gregory ............. | 10 |
| Mr J. C. Clay (did not bat) .................. | | – run out ...................... | 13 |
| Mr V. G. J. Jenkins (did not bat) ............. | | – not out ...................... | 40 |
| D. Davies (did not bat) ..................... | | – not out ...................... | 9 |
| | | B 3, l-b 7 .............. | 10 |
| | (0 wkts dec.) 0 | | 216 |

E. Davies and G. Lavis did not bat.

## Glamorgan Bowling

| | Overs | Mdns | Runs | Wkts | Overs | Mdns | Runs | Wkts |
|---|---|---|---|---|---|---|---|---|
| Turnbull . . . . . . . . . . | 0.1 | — | — | — | | | | |
| Mercer . . . . . . . . . . | | | | | 13 | 2 | 42 | — |
| D. Davies . . . . . . . . | | | | | 11 | 1 | 35 | — |
| Clay . . . . . . . . . . . . | | | | | 19.4 | 1 | 60 | 2 |
| Ryan . . . . . . . . . . . | | | | | 17 | 1 | 62 | 1 |
| Bates . . . . . . . . . . . | | | | | 1 | — | 12 | — |

## Surrey Bowling

| | Overs | Mdns | Runs | Wkts | Overs | Mdns | Runs | Wkts |
|---|---|---|---|---|---|---|---|---|
| Fender . . . . . . . . . . | 0.1 | — | — | — | 14 | — | 64 | 3 |
| Gover . . . . . . . . . . . | | | | | 14 | 4 | 42 | — |
| Peach . . . . . . . . . . . | | | | | 15.5 | 3 | 53 | 2 |
| Gregory . . . . . . . . . | | | | | 10 | — | 47 | 1 |

Umpires: A. Skelding and A. Dolphin.

## GLAMORGAN v SOMERSET

### Played at Cowbridge, July 23, 25, 26, 1932

Batting on both Monday and Tuesday on a drying pitch, Somerset suffered defeat by an innings and 153 runs, their total of 40 representing Glamorgan's cheapest dismissal of any first-class county. Glamorgan, for their part, had to face the Somerset attack under conditions far from favourable to run-getting but were placed in a strong position by Turnbull who, missed behind the wicket soon after he went in, hit up 81 out of 112 in less than ninety minutes, with thirteen 4s among his strokes. How completely Turnbull dominated the play – chiefly by jumping in to drive the slow bowlers – was shown by the fact that during a seventy-five minutes' partnership with Dai Davies that produced 95 runs, the professional's share was no more than 19. Emrys Davies and Smart, batting carefully, added 39 but the latter when 25 was twice let off. The day's cricket ended with the score 237 for seven wickets. Not until half past two could the game be resumed on Monday but then, of 36 runs added for the last wicket, Mercer obtained 31 in nine minutes. Somerset had three men out for 9 and six for 31 but Wellard helped White to double the score. White batted a hundred minutes without a mistake. Somerset following on 193 behind lost two wickets for five runs and although on Tuesday play was delayed until one o'clock, the innings was finished in seventy minutes. Clay and Mercer came out with wonderful bowling figures, the latter in the second innings having six wickets for 15 runs.

## Glamorgan

| | |
|---|---|
| A. H. Dyson c and b White . . . . . . . . . . . . . 6 | A. H. Howard c Hazell b White . . . . . . . . . 10 |
| E. Davies c Burrough b Young . . . . . . . . . 41 | Mr J. C. Clay b White . . . . . . . . . . . . . . . . 17 |
| C. Smart c Luckes b Young . . . . . . . . . . . . 21 | G. Lavis not out . . . . . . . . . . . . . . . . . . . . . 8 |
| D. Davies c Wellard b Lee . . . . . . . . . . . . . 28 | J. Mercer c Wellard b White . . . . . . . . . . . 31 |
| Mr M. J. Turnbull c Lee b Hazell . . . . . . . . 81 | B 8, l-b 4 . . . . . . . . . . . . . . . . . . . 12 |
| R. Duckfield b White . . . . . . . . . . . . . . . . . 10 | — |
| G. Every b White . . . . . . . . . . . . . . . . . . . . 16 | 281 |

## Somerset

| | | | |
|---|---|---|---|
| A. Young b Clay | 10 | – c Turnbull b Mercer | 4 |
| J. W. Lee b Clay | 1 | – lbw b Clay | 0 |
| Mr G. M. Bennett b Clay | 0 | – b Clay | 1 |
| Mr R. A. Ingle b E. Davies | 4 | – c Every b Mercer | 9 |
| Mr J. C. White b Mercer | 24 | – b Mercer | 1 |
| Mr C. C. Case lbw b Clay | 0 | – b Clay | 1 |
| Mr H. D. Burrough lbw b E. Davies | 0 | – b Mercer | 4 |
| A. W. Wellard c Clay b E. Davies | 27 | – b Mercer | 0 |
| W. H. Andrews b Mercer | 9 | – b Clay | 5 |
| W. T. Luckes not out | 6 | – not out | 6 |
| H. L. Hazell c Duckfield b Clay | 0 | – c Turnbull b Mercer | 3 |
| B 6, l-b 1 | 7 | L-b 3, n-b 3 | 6 |
| | **88** | | **40** |

### Somerset Bowling

| | Overs | Mdns | Runs | Wkts |
|---|---|---|---|---|
| Andrews | 8 | 3 | 20 | — |
| Wellard | 5 | 2 | 7 | — |
| Lee | 17 | 5 | 73 | 1 |
| White | 54.3 | 24 | 82 | 6 |
| Young | 25 | 13 | 35 | 2 |
| Hazell | 34 | 14 | 52 | 1 |

### Glamorgan Bowling

| | Overs | Mdns | Runs | Wkts | Overs | Mdns | Runs | Wkts |
|---|---|---|---|---|---|---|---|---|
| Mercer | 12 | 6 | 12 | 2 | 9.3 | 4 | 15 | 6 |
| Clay | 22.1 | 7 | 28 | 5 | 9 | 2 | 19 | 4 |
| E. Davies | 11 | 6 | 41 | 3 | | | | |

Umpires: C. N. Woolley and W. Reeves.

# GLAMORGAN v NORTHAMPTONSHIRE

Played at Swansea, June 10, 12, 13, 1933

To such an extent did the bat master the ball that in three days' full play only seventeen wickets fell for an aggregate of 1,071 runs. Glamorgan, in the absence of Clark from the visiting team, seized the opportunity to put together their highest total since being elected a first-class county. Four big partnerships took place during the innings; Dyson assisting E. Davies and Duckfield in adding 112 and 75 for the first and second wickets respectively, while Turnbull put on with Duckfield and Every 110 and 150 for the third and sixth stands. Turnbull gave a brilliant exhibition for Glamorgan, completing his second hundred in eighty-five minutes. Altogether he batted three hours fifty minutes, hitting four 6s and twenty-two 4s. Even more remarkable was the performance of Bakewell, who broke the Northamptonshire individual batting record in his second successive innings, having on the previous Thursday made 246 against Nottinghamshire. Fifth out at 449, he withstood the attack eight and a quarter hours, hit thirty 4s and offered only one real chance, when 155, to mid-on. After he left bowlers met with success for the first time and Northamptonshire collapsed for the addition of 20 runs, Glamorgan thus taking first-innings points for their lead of 78.

## Glamorgan

| | | | | |
|---|---|---|---|---|
| A. H. Dyson c Cox b Thomas | 91 | | | |
| E. Davies lbw b Matthews | 52 | | | |
| R. Duckfield b Cox | 93 | | | |
| Mr M. J. Turnbull not out | 200 | | | |
| D. Davies c Liddell b Cox | 23 | – not out | 13 | |
| Mr E. Bowen lbw b Jupp | 7 | | | |
| T. Every c Cox b Matthews | 65 | | | |
| T. L. Brierley not out | 8 | – c Cox b Liddell | 36 | |
| B 2, l-b 5, n-b 1 | 8 | B 6 | 6 | |
| | | | | |
| **(6 wkts dec.) 547** | | | **55** | |

G. Lavis, W. Jones and J. Mercer did not bat.

## Northamptonshire

| | | | | |
|---|---|---|---|---|
| A. H. Bakewell c E. Davies b Lavis | 257 | Mr W. C. Brown lbw b Mercer | 0 |
| Mr A. W. Snowden c D. Davies b Lavis | 32 | A. D. Matthews not out | 7 |
| B. Bellamy c Lavis b Mercer | 31 | R. J. Partridge b Mercer | 5 |
| J. E. Timms lbw b Lavis | 65 | A. E. Thomas c Turnbull b Mercer | 2 |
| Mr. V. W. C. Jupp b Jones | 35 | B 13, l-b 6, w 4 | 23 |
| A. L. Cox c and b Mercer | 11 | | |
| A. G. Liddell lbw b Lavis | 1 | **469** | |

### Northamptonshire Bowling

| | Overs | Mdns | Runs | Wkts | Overs | Mdns | Runs | Wkts |
|---|---|---|---|---|---|---|---|---|
| Matthews | 36 | 7 | 102 | 2 | 3 | 1 | 6 | — |
| Thomas | 45 | 12 | 101 | 1 | 2 | 1 | 2 | — |
| Cox | 18 | 1 | 108 | 2 | | | | |
| Partridge | 23 | 4 | 67 | — | | | | |
| Jupp | 28 | 4 | 130 | 1 | | | | |
| Bakewell | 2 | — | 14 | — | 3 | — | 32 | — |
| Timms | 2 | — | 17 | — | 4 | 1 | 6 | — |
| Liddell | | | | | 1 | — | 3 | 1 |

### Glamorgan Bowling

| | Overs | Mdns | Runs | Wkts |
|---|---|---|---|---|
| Mercer | 42.2 | 11 | 100 | 5 |
| Lavis | 49 | 11 | 103 | 4 |
| E. Davies | 44 | 9 | 108 | — |
| D. Davies | 29 | 5 | 76 | — |
| Jones | 22 | 6 | 59 | 1 |

Umpires: W. Reeves and D. Hendren.

## GLAMORGAN v NORTHAMPTONSHIRE

### Played at Llanelly, June 1, 3, 1935

J. C. Clay was largely responsible for Glamorgan's easy victory by an innings and 109
runs, and his first day performance of taking nine wickets for 6 runs each was the best of
his career. He was helped by a drying pitch, but by skilful variation of spin, flight and pace
he fairly confused the Northamptonshire batsmen. After the fall of the second wicket he
finished the innings by sending back eight men for 18 runs in less than 15 overs.
Glamorgan batted soundly and wound up 21 ahead with six wickets left. The second and
last day brought a splendid hundred by Lavis – the first of the season for Glamorgan –

and more clever bowling from Clay. Lavis, who reached three figures with Clay, the last man in, drove and pulled in uncommonly good style. Northamptonshire, needing 212 to save an innings defeat, were out in two hours. Clay took six wickets for 32 and fifteen in the match for under 6 runs apiece.

### Northamptonshire

| | | |
|---|---|---|
| A. H. Bakewell c Brierley b Mercer | 43 | – b Mercer ... 16 |
| Mr A. W. Snowden c Brierley b Clay | 18 | – c A. Davies b Clay ... 12 |
| N. Grimshaw not out | 44 | – lbw b Clay ... 1 |
| J. E. Timms lbw b Clay | 8 | – c A. Davies b Clay ... 7 |
| A. L. Cox b Clay | 0 | – c A. Davies b Clay ... 14 |
| R. J. Partridge b Clay | 0 | – lbw b Clay ... 3 |
| D. Brooks lbw b Clay | 0 | – lbw b Clay ... 10 |
| B. Bellamy c Turnbull b Clay | 11 | – b E. Davies ... 5 |
| L. Cullen lbw b Clay | 0 | – b E. Davies ... 4 |
| Mr T. A. Pitt lbw b Clay | 0 | – not out ... 13 |
| E. W. Clark b Clay | 2 | – b E. Davies ... 6 |
| B 4, l-b 7 | 11 | B 5, l-b 7 ... 12 |
| | **137** | **103** |

### Glamorgan

| | | | |
|---|---|---|---|
| A. H. Dyson st Bellamy b Partridge | 36 | T. L. Brierley lbw b Pitt | 5 |
| E. Davies c Bellamy b Pitt | 13 | A. Davies b Partridge | 17 |
| D. Davies c and b Partridge | 21 | J. Mercer c Bakewell b Clark | 18 |
| Mr M. J. Turnbull b Partridge | 0 | Mr J. C. Clay not out | 0 |
| R. Duckfield b Pitt | 54 | B 13, l-b 15 | 28 |
| C. Smart b Clark | 56 | | |
| G. Lavis lbw b Clark | 101 | | **349** |

### Glamorgan Bowling

| | Overs | Mdns | Runs | Wkts | Overs | Mdns | Runs | Wkts |
|---|---|---|---|---|---|---|---|---|
| Mercer | 25 | 3 | 43 | 1 | 13 | 3 | 30 | 1 |
| Lavis | 3 | — | 10 | — | 3 | — | 13 | — |
| Clay | 32.2 | 7 | 54 | 9 | 16 | 1 | 32 | 6 |
| E. Davies | 16 | 8 | 11 | — | 5.2 | — | 16 | 3 |
| Smart | 3 | — | 8 | — | | | | |

### Northamptonshire Bowling

| | Overs | Mdns | Runs | Wkts |
|---|---|---|---|---|
| Clark | 20.4 | 2 | 49 | 3 |
| Pitt | 32 | 9 | 67 | 3 |
| Partridge | 36 | 6 | 106 | 4 |
| Cox | 26 | 7 | 78 | — |
| Cullen | 2 | — | 21 | — |

Umpires: D. Hendren and T. Oates.

## GLAMORGAN v HAMPSHIRE

Played at Cardiff, July 3, 4, 5, 1935

Winning by ten wickets, Glamorgan made history by beating Hampshire for the first time, and Smart set up a probable record when in scoring 109 on the opening day he hit 32 runs

– 6, 6, 4, 6, 6, 4 – off one over from Hill. Duckfield's fifth wicket stand of 181 with Smart equalled the Glamorgan record for that wicket. Although having 426 on the board for four wickets, Glamorgan lost four more batsmen for another 34. Hampshire, however, followed on 234 behind and left their opponents the trifling task of scoring fifteen runs to win.

## Glamorgan

| | | | |
|---|---|---|---|
| A. H. Dyson run out | 28 | | |
| E. Davies c Creese b Herman | 58 | | |
| D. Davies c Lowndes b Hill | 47 | | |
| Mr M. J. Turnbull b Herman | 61 | | |
| R. Duckfield b Hill | 111 | | |
| C. Smart b Hill | 109 | | |
| T. L. Brierley c Herman b Hill | 10 | – not out | 8 |
| Mr J. Cope not out | 14 | | |
| Mr E. R. K. Glover c McCorkell b Herman | 6 | – not out | 8 |
| B 6, l-b 10 | 16 | B 2 | 2 |
| | | | |
| (8 wkts dec.) | 460 | | 18 |

Mr J. C. Clay and J. Mercer did not bat.

## Hampshire

| | | | |
|---|---|---|---|
| J. Arnold lbw (N) b Glover | 42 | – c Brierley b Glover | 1 |
| N. McCorkell b Glover | 2 | – b Glover | 11 |
| A. E. Pothecary c Dyson b Glover | 41 | – c Brierley b E. Davies | 51 |
| C. P. Mead lbw b Clay | 37 | – lbw b Clay | 15 |
| Mr W. G. Lowndes run out | 2 | – c Turnbull b E. Davies | 30 |
| W. L. Creese b Smart | 53 | – c Cope b Mercer | 45 |
| Lord Tennyson c Turnbull b Clay | 9 | – b Glover | 24 |
| G. Hill st Brierley b Smart | 7 | – lbw (N) b Mercer | 19 |
| Mr W. Dodd not out | 6 | – c Turnbull b Clay | 9 |
| W. L. Budd b Clay | 8 | – b Mercer | 29 |
| C. W. Herman run out | 1 | – not out | 0 |
| B 10, l-b 8 | 18 | B 7, l-b 5, w 1, n-b 1 | 14 |
| | | | |
| | 226 | | 248 |

### Hampshire Bowling

| | Overs | Mdns | Runs | Wkts | Overs | Mdns | Runs | Wkts |
|---|---|---|---|---|---|---|---|---|
| Hill | 41 | 10 | 144 | 4 | | | | |
| Herman | 37.1 | 9 | 97 | 3 | | | | |
| Budd | 17 | 1 | 56 | — | | | | |
| Dodd | 20 | 7 | 69 | — | | | | |
| Creese | 22 | 4 | 59 | — | | | | |
| Lowndes | 5 | — | 19 | — | | | | |
| Mead | | | | | 1 | — | 11 | — |
| Arnold | | | | | 0.5 | — | 5 | — |

### Glamorgan Bowlong

| | Overs | Mdns | Runs | Wkts | Overs | Mdns | Runs | Wkts |
|---|---|---|---|---|---|---|---|---|
| Mercer | 13 | 3 | 35 | — | 19.4 | 5 | 48 | 3 |
| Glover | 15 | — | 69 | 3 | 22 | 3 | 66 | 3 |
| Clay | 22 | 5 | 50 | 3 | 27 | 10 | 69 | 2 |
| E. Davies | 6 | 1 | 20 | — | 11 | — | 34 | 2 |
| Smart | 10.3 | 3 | 25 | 2 | 7 | 3 | 17 | — |
| D. Davies | 5 | — | 9 | — | | | | |

Umpires: W. R. Parry and G. Beet.

## GLAMORGAN v ESSEX

### Played at Pontypridd, July 18, 20, 21, 1936

Drawn. The best thing in a rain-spoiled match was a brilliant hundred by L. G. Crawley on his first appearance of the season. When the game began on Monday, he played magnificent cricket while nearly everyone else failed, and invested his drives with such great power that he hit five 6s – two of which sent the ball out of the ground – besides nine 4s. E. Davies bowled cleverly and later with D. Davies added 78 for Glamorgan, but only two other players reached double figures against good bowling by Eastman and P. Smith. Essex, leading by 98, needed to score quickly to win, but the inability of Crawley to bat through a strain handicapped them. When they were in a position to declare only two and a half hours remained and the game ended quietly.

### Essex

| | | |
|---|---|---|
| Mr L. G. Crawley c Turnbull b E. Davies ..........118 | | |
| J. R. Sheffield c Lavis b E. Davies ............... 18 | – c Turnbull b Mercer ............. | 32 |
| M. S. Nichols b Mercer ...................... 7. | – c Clay b Mercer ................ | 0 |
| J. O'Connor lbw (N), b Mercer ............... 3 | – b E. Davies ................... | 25 |
| R. M. Taylor lbw (N) b Mercer ............... 4 | – c Duckfield b D. Davies .......... | 6 |
| P. Smith c Brierley b E. Davies ............... 0 | – b E. Davies ................. | 5 |
| L. C. Eastman lbw b E. Davies ............... 18 | – lbw b E. Davies ............... | 15 |
| Mr J. N. Dennis b E. Davies ................. 14 | – not out ..................... | 24 |
| C. S. R. Boswell b Clay ...................... 8 | | |
| T. H. Wade not out ........................ 12 | | |
| R. Smith c Dyson b E. Davies ............... 15 | – c Duckfield b E. Davies .......... | 18 |
| B 11, l-b 2, n-b 1 ................... 14 | L-b 1 ................ | 1 |
| 231 | (7 wkts dec.) 126 | |

### Glamorgan

| | | |
|---|---|---|
| A. H. Dyson c O'Connor b Nichols ............. 4 | – b Nichols .................... | 7 |
| E. Davies b Eastman ......................... 39 | – not out ..................... | 38 |
| D. Davies c P. Smith b Eastman ............... 43 | – lbw b Eastman ............... | 25 |
| Mr M. J. Turnbull st Wade b Eastman ............ 3 | – lbw b Eastman ............... | 6 |
| R. Duckfield lbw b P. Smith ................... 0 | | |
| C. Smart c R. Smith b P. Smith ............... 22 | — not out ..................... | 2 |
| G. Lavis run out ........................... 1 | | |
| Mr V. G. J. Jenkins b P. Smith ................. 10 | – c sub b Eastman .............. | 19 |
| T. L. Brierley lbw b Eastman ................... 0 | | |
| Mr J. C. Clay not out ....................... 6 | | |
| J. Mercer c O'Connor b P. Smith ................ 0 | | |
| B 4, l-b 1 ........................ 5 | B 5, l-b 3 ............... | 8 |
| 133 | 105 | |

### Glamorgan Bowling

| | Overs | Mdns | Runs | Wkts | Overs | Mdns | Runs | Wkts |
|---|---|---|---|---|---|---|---|---|
| Mercer .......... | 19 | 6 | 60 | 3 | 10 | 1 | 39 | 2 |
| E. Davies ........ | 24.4 | 7 | 62 | 6 | 13.5 | 1 | 57 | 4 |
| Clay ............ | 21 | 3 | 66 | 1 | 8 | 1 | 24 | — |
| D. Davies ........ | 8 | 1 | 24 | — | 4 | — | 5 | 1 |
| Smart ........... | 1 | — | 5 | — | | | | |

**Essex Bowling**

| | Overs | Mdns | Runs | Wkts | Overs | Mdns | Runs | Wkts |
|---|---|---|---|---|---|---|---|---|
| Nichols ......... | 12 | 2 | 29 | 1 | 5 | — | 12 | 1 |
| R. Smith ......... | 4 | 1 | 6 | — | | | | |
| Eastman ......... | 22 | 12 | 29 | 4 | 22 | 6 | 48 | 3 |
| P. Smith ......... | 20 | 4 | 48 | 4 | 8 | 2 | 22 | — |
| Boswell ......... | 5 | — | 16 | — | 10 | 3 | 15 | — |

Umpires: G. Brown and C. W. L. Parker.

## GLAMORGAN v WORCESTERSHIRE

### Played at Swansea, June 23, 24, 25, 1937

Glamorgan won by nine wickets. Clay, with seventeen wickets, surpassed the previous record for Glamorgan of fifteen in a match, jointly held by J. Nash and Clay himself. His remarkable success in the first innings when the pitch gave him no help was earned by skilful flighting and the maintenance of a perfect length. Cooper stayed two hours, but only two other Worcestershire batsmen reached double figures. Turnbull redeemed a poor start by Glamorgan with a brilliant innings lasting four hours which brought him the highest score of his career. He drove, hooked and cut in masterly fashion and besides three 6s hit no fewer than thirty-one 4s. He and Lavis put on 165 for the sixth wicket. Worcestershire, needing 294 to avoid an innings defeat, made a useful start and Martin and Cooper, following a breakdown, added 137, but Glamorgan were set to get no more than 67 for victory.

### Worcestershire

| | | | |
|---|---|---|---|
| C. H. Bull lbw b Clay ..................... | 25 | – lbw b Mercer .................. | 43 |
| F. Warne st Brierley b Mercer .................. | 6 | – b Clay ..................... | 39 |
| E. Cooper b Clay ........................... | 42 | – c Turnbull b Mercer ........... | 47 |
| H. H. Gibbons lbw b Clay ..................... | 2 | – b Clay ..................... | 1 |
| S. H. Martin c Brierley b Clay .............. | 9 | – c Lavis b Clay ............... | 92 |
| Mr B. W. Quaife c Smart b Clay .............. | 2 | – not out ..................... | 55 |
| V. Grimshaw c Dyson b Clay .................. | 15 | – c Lavis b Clay ............... | 2 |
| R. Howorth c Turnbull b Clay .................. | 4 | – b Clay ..................... | 28 |
| S. Buller c and b Clay........................ | 5 | – lbw (N) b Clay ............... | 26 |
| R. T. D. Perks c D. Davies b Clay .............. | 4 | – b Clay ..................... | 9 |
| P. F. Jackson not out ....................... | 7 | – b Clay ..................... | 0 |
| L-b 2 .......................... | 2 | B 15, l-b 2, w 1 .......... | 18 |
| | **123** | | **360** |

### Glamorgan

| | | | |
|---|---|---|---|
| A. H. Dyson c Buller b Perks ................... | 0 | – lbw b Jackson ................ | 25 |
| E. Davies c Buller b Martin .................. | 8 | – not out ..................... | 31 |
| D. Davies lbw b Howorth .................... | 28 | | |
| Mr M. J. Turnbull c Buller b Howorth ...........| 233 | | |
| R. Duckfield b Martin ...................... | 31 | | |
| C. Smart lbw b Howorth ..................... | 0 | | |
| G. Lavis c Warne b Howorth .................. | 63 | | |
| T. L. Brierley c Buller b Howorth ............... | 27 | | |
| Mr J. C. Clay b Jackson ...................... | 5 | | |
| E. C. Jones not out ........................ | 0 | – not out ..................... | 14 |
| J. Mercer c Quaife b Howorth .............. | 12 | | |
| B 2, l-b 8 ......................... | 10 | | |
| | **417** | | **70** |

### Glamorgan Bowling

| | Overs | Mdns | Runs | Wkts | Overs | Mdns | Runs | Wkts |
|---|---|---|---|---|---|---|---|---|
| Mercer ........... | 10 | 1 | 26 | 1 | 27 | 2 | 87 | 2 |
| Lavis ............ | 4 | 1 | 4 | — | 5 | — | 17 | — |
| Clay ............. | 28.5 | 6 | 66 | 9 | 34 | 5 | 146 | 8 |
| E. Davies ........ | 14 | 5 | 17 | — | 22 | 5 | 48 | — |
| Jones ........... | 5 | 1 | 8 | — | 3 | — | 9 | — |
| Smart ........... | 1 | 1 | — | — | 7 | — | 25 | — |
| D. Davies ........ | | | | | 4 | 1 | 10 | — |

### Worcestershire Bowling

| | Overs | Mdns | Runs | Wkts | Overs | Mdns | Runs | Wkts |
|---|---|---|---|---|---|---|---|---|
| Perks ........... | 26 | 5 | 115 | 1 | 5 | — | 14 | — |
| Martin .......... | 25 | 7 | 78 | 2 | 5 | 1 | 22 | — |
| Jackson ......... | 20 | 3 | 102 | 1 | 5 | 1 | 13 | 1 |
| Howorth ........ | 28.2 | 6 | 96 | 6 | 5 | 1 | 12 | — |
| Warne .......... | 2 | — | 16 | — | | | | |
| Quaife .......... | | | | | 1 | — | 5 | — |
| Bull ............ | | | | | 0.4 | — | 4 | — |

Umpires: W. Reeves and E. J. Smith.

## GLAMORGAN v GLOUCESTERSHIRE

Played at Newport, May 31, June 1, 2, 1939

Drawn. Several Glamorgan records were broken in a heartbreaking match for bowlers. Dyson, who batted throughout an innings for the sixth time, lost his last two partners in one over. During the last two days only six wickets fell for 942 runs. Hammond, with 302, equalled the biggest score ever made from Glamorgan bowling. He drove brilliantly, hitting two 6s and thirty-five 4s. Emmett and Crapp helped him in stands of 168 and 214. Emrys Davies and Dyson started Glamorgan's second innings with 255. Davies, in seven and a half hours, made the biggest score by any Glamorgan player. Also the total 557 for four, is the highest in the club's history.

### Glamorgan

| | | | | |
|---|---|---|---|---|
| A. H. Dyson not out ...................... | 99 | – c Wilson b Lambert ............. | 120 |
| E. Davies lbw b Goddard ..................... | 34 | – not out ...................... | 287 |
| T. L. Brierley b Scott ....................... | 9 | – c Hammond b Goddard ......... | 5 |
| Mr M. J. Turnbull c Wilson b Lambert ........... | 18 | – st Wilson b Emmett .......... | 77 |
| D. Davies c Wilson b Scott ................... | 1 | – c Lambert b Sinfield ........... | 48 |
| C. Smart b Scott ........................... | 10 | – not out ...................... | 23 |
| Mr W. Wooller b Goddard ................... | 18 | | |
| E. C. Jones c Wilson b Sinfield ................. | 0 | | |
| H. Davies c Wilson b Sinfield ................. | 0 | | |
| P. F. Judge c Neale b Goddard ............... | 3 | | |
| J. Mercer b Goddard ....................... | 0 | | |
| B 1, l-b 2, n-b 1 .................... | 4 | L-b 17 ................ | 17 |
| | 196 | | 577 |

## Gloucestershire

C. J. Barnett c E. Davies b Mercer . . . . . . . . 15
R. A. Sinfield b E. Davies . . . . . . . . . . . . . . 41
V. Hopkins c Turnbull b Judge . . . . . . . . . . 13
Mr W. R. Hammond c H. Davies
                        b E. Davies .302
G. M. Emmett st H. Davies b Jones . . . . . . . 53

J. F. Crapp not out . . . . . . . . . . . . . . . . . . . . 60
W. L. Neale not out . . . . . . . . . . . . . . . . . . . 5

           B 12, l-b 4 . . . . . . . . . . . . . . . . . . 16

                 (5 wkts dec.) 505

E. A. Wilson, C. J. Scott, G. Lambert and T. W. Goddard did not bat.

## Gloucestershire Bowling

| | Overs | Mdns | Runs | Wkts | Overs | Mdns | Runs | Wkts |
|---|---|---|---|---|---|---|---|---|
| Scott | 13 | — | 52 | 3 | 24 | 1 | 95 | — |
| Barnett | 4 | — | 18 | — | 5 | — | 32 | — |
| Lambert | 14 | 2 | 50 | 1 | 16 | — | 128 | 1 |
| Goddard | 22.6 | 7 | 45 | 4 | 38 | 7 | 123 | 1 |
| Sinfield | 10 | 3 | 16 | 2 | 36 | 5 | 116 | 1 |
| Emmett | 2 | — | 6 | — | 7 | — | 51 | 1 |
| Neale | 1 | — | 5 | — | 1 | — | 11 | — |
| Hammond | | | | | 1 | — | 4 | — |

## Glamorgan Bowling

| | Overs | Mdns | Runs | Wkts |
|---|---|---|---|---|
| Mercer | 21 | — | 105 | 1 |
| Judge | 18 | 1 | 83 | 1 |
| Wooller | 23 | 1 | 124 | — |
| Jones | 9 | — | 41 | 1 |
| E. Davies | 21 | 2 | 91 | 2 |
| D. Davies | 2 | — | 9 | — |
| Smart | 6 | 1 | 36 | — |

Umpires: J. Newman and H. Cruice.

# GLOUCESTERSHIRE

## GLOUCESTERSHIRE v WARWICKSHIRE

Played at Bristol, June 9, 10, 11, 1920

Gloucestershire started this match in capital style, staying in for the greater part of the first day, and in the end they won by 77 runs. They discounted their chance by losing seven wickets in their second innings for 95, but thanks to Robinson's hitting the score with nine men out had been increased to 140 when a storm brought the second day's play to a close. Warwickshire had only 186 to get, but they never looked like winning. At lunch-time on Friday they had lost five wickets for 107, and after the interval Parker took the remaining five wickets in ten balls without having a run hit from him.

### Gloucestershire

| | | |
|---|---:|---:|
| Mr E. Rowlands b H. Howell | 14 | – b H. Howell ... 20 |
| A. G. Dipper c Smith b Santall | 33 | – b W. G. Quaife ... 41 |
| Mr W. H. Rowlands c Stephens b W. G. Quaife | 58 | – b H. Howell ... 5 |
| H. Smith b Illingworth | 2 | – b W. G. Quaife ... 21 |
| Mr P. F. C. Williams c A. Howell b W. G. Quaife | 46 | – b A. Howell ... 2 |
| Mr F. G. Robinson c A. Howell b W. G. Quaife | 78 | – c Santall b H. Howell ... 41 |
| P. Mills c Smith b H. Howell | 32 | – b W. G. Quaife ... 0 |
| C. Parker c Smith b W. G. Quaife | 27 | – st Smith b W. G. Quaife ... 0 |
| J. Bowles b A. Howell | 15 | – b A. Howell ... 3 |
| T. Gange c A. Howell b W. G. Quaife | 0 | – run out ... 2 |
| F. E. Ellis not out | 2 | – not out ... 0 |
| B 5, l-b 4 | 9 | B 6, l-b 5 ... 11 |
| | **316** | **146** |

### Warwickshire

| | | |
|---|---:|---:|
| Mr H. Venn c Robinson b Parker | 40 | – b Mills ... 24 |
| L. A. Bates c and b Dipper | 42 | – lbw b Parker ... 13 |
| C. Charlesworth lbw b Ellis | 80 | – c Bowles b Parker ... 50 |
| W. G. Quaife lbw b Parker | 9 | – b Mills ... 1 |
| E. J. Smith b Parker | 2 | – c Smith b Mills ... 1 |
| Mr G. W. Stephens b Gange | 83 | – c W. H. Rowlands b Mills ... 1 |
| Mr B. W. Quaife b Ellis | 3 | – not out ... 1 |
| Mr F. R. Santall c Smith b Gange | 7 | – c W. H. Rowlands b Parker ... 0 |
| A. Howell b Gange | 0 | – b Parker ... 0 |
| E. A. Illingworth b Parker | 0 | – b Parker ... 0 |
| H. Howell not out | 0 | – st Robinson b Parker ... 0 |
| B 6, l-b 4, n-b 1 | 11 | B 10, l-b 2, n-b 3 ... 17 |
| | **277** | **108** |

### Warwickshire Bowling

| | Overs | Mdns | Runs | Wkts | Overs | Mdns | Runs | Wkts |
|---|---:|---:|---:|---:|---:|---:|---:|---:|
| H. Howell | 28 | 2 | 100 | 2 | 15.5 | 3 | 50 | 3 |
| Illingworth | 22 | 2 | 79 | 1 | 7 | 1 | 15 | — |
| Santall | 8 | 1 | 43 | 1 | | | | |
| W. G. Quaife | 19 | 2 | 70 | 5 | 16 | 5 | 25 | 4 |
| A. Howell | 5.2 | 1 | 15 | 1 | 11 | 3 | 45 | 2 |

**Gloucestershire Bowling**

| | Overs | Mdns | Runs | Wkts | Overs | Mdns | Runs | Wkts |
|---|---|---|---|---|---|---|---|---|
| Ellis .............. | 15 | 2 | 52 | 2 | | | | |
| Parker ........... | 26 | 5 | 86 | 4 | 19.4 | 6 | 48 | 6 |
| Bowles ........... | 2 | — | 10 | — | | | | |
| Gange ........... | 15.3 | 1 | 57 | 3 | 2 | — | 6 | — |
| Dipper ........... | 7 | 1 | 34 | 1 | 7 | 2 | 24 | — |
| Mills ............. | 6 | 1 | 27 | — | 10 | 5 | 13 | 4 |

Umpires: T. Flowers and A. Millward.

## GLOUCESTERSHIRE v SOMERSET

### Played at Bristol, July 31, August 2, 3, 1920

This was a remarkable game, as Gloucestershire after being dismissed for 22 – the smallest total of the season in first-class cricket – gained an astonishing victory by four wickets. In declaring when he did – Gloucestershire had plenty of time to get the 274 runs required – Daniell, the Somerset captain, reckoned without Charles Townsend. That famous batsman played a great innings, hitting with such brilliancy that he scored 84 out of 119 in an hour and a quarter. In the circumstances Gloucestershire's victory was one of the events of the year.

### Somerset

| | | | |
|---|---|---|---|
| Mr A. E. S. Rippon run out .................... | 1 | | |
| Mr J. A. S. Jackson c Williams b Parker .......... | 5 | – b Parker .................... | 10 |
| Mr J. C. W. MacBryan b Parker ............... | 38 | – not out .................... | 29 |
| Mr M. D. Lyon c Mills b Dennett ............... | 12 | – lbw b Parker .................. | 41 |
| Mr F. A. Waldock c Williams b Parker ........... | 45 | – run out .................... | 2 |
| Mr M. L. Hambling c P. G. Robinson b Dennett .... | 3 | – b Parker .................... | 1 |
| Mr J. Daniell c Williams b Parker ............... | 34 | – c F. G. Robinson b Mills ......... | 24 |
| Mr P. A. Foy c and b Dipper .................. | 8 | – b Mills .................... | 2 |
| E. Robson c Rowlands b Dennett .............. | 4 | | |
| Mr J. C. White c F. G. Robinson b Dennett ........ | 8 | – b Mills .................... | 10 |
| Mr J. J. Bridges not out ...................... | 0 | | |
| B 7, l-b 3, n-b 1 .................... | 11 | B 5, l-b 2 .............. | 7 |
| | **169** | **(7 wkts dec.)** | **126** |

### Gloucestershire

| | | | |
|---|---|---|---|
| Mr C. L. Townsend lbw b Robson ............... | 4 | – c Robson b Bridges ............. | 84 |
| A. G. Dipper c Daniell b White ................ | 5 | – b Bridges .................... | 48 |
| Mr W. H. Rowlands b Robson ................. | 0 | – c MacBryan b White ........... | 7 |
| H. Smith c Daniell b White .................. | 1 | – c White b Robson ............. | 1 |
| Mr P. G. Robinson c and b White ............... | 2 | – c Waldock b Robson ........... | 37 |
| Mr M. A. Green c MacBryan b White ............ | 3 | – not out .................... | 32 |
| Mr F. G. Robinson c Daniell b White ............ | 0 | – b Bridges .................. | 28 |
| Mr P. F. C. Williams b Robson ................. | 5 | – not out .................... | 14 |
| P. Mills st Lyon b White ..................... | 0 | | |
| C. Parker c and b White ..................... | 2 | | |
| G. Dennett not out ........................ | 0 | | |
| | | B 18, l-b 7 .............. | 25 |
| | **22** | | **276** |

## Gloucestershire Bowling

|  | Overs | Mdns | Runs | Wkts | Overs | Mdns | Runs | Wkts |
|---|---|---|---|---|---|---|---|---|
| Dennett .......... | 38.5 | 16 | 68 | 4 | 15 | 4 | 43 | — |
| Parker ........... | 39 | 20 | 58 | 4 | 19 | 5 | 41 | 3 |
| Dipper ........... | 7 | 2 | 19 | 1 |  |  |  |  |
| Mills ............. | 6 | 2 | 13 | — | 13.3 | 2 | 35 | 3 |

## Somerset Bowling

|  | Overs | Mdns | Runs | Wkts | Overs | Mdns | Runs | Wkts |
|---|---|---|---|---|---|---|---|---|
| Robson .......... | 9 | 4 | 12 | 3 | 23 | 3 | 68 | 2 |
| White ........... | 9 | 4 | 10 | 7 | 25 | 7 | 65 | 1 |
| Bridges .......... |  |  |  |  | 20 | 4 | 74 | 3 |
| Foy ............. |  |  |  |  | 4 | — | 24 | — |
| Hambling ........ |  |  |  |  | 8 | 3 | 20 | — |

Umpires: A. E. Street and J. Blake.

# GLOUCESTERSHIRE v LEICESTERSHIRE

### Played at Cheltenham, August 21, 23, 1920

Gloucestershire finished off their home matches with an easy victory, beating Leicestershire in two days by an innings and 53 runs. Parker won the match, taking fourteen wickets at a cost of just over 4 runs apiece. Apart from his fine bowling the game presented no special feature except that F. G. Robinson demonstrated the advantage of playing an aggressive rather than a cautious game on the slow ground. Gloucestershire had the match in their hands when at the drawing of stumps on the first day they held a lead of 110 on the first innings.

## Leicestershire

| | | | |
|---|---|---|---|
| Mr. W. F. Curtis b Mills ..................... | 0 | – b Parker ..................... | 9 |
| H. Whitehead lbw b Parker .................... | 0 | – c Green b Mills .............. | 9 |
| Mr G. H. Salmon b Parker ..................... | 2 | – c Dennett b Parker ........... | 3 |
| J. H. King b Mills ........................... | 2 | – c Williams b Parker .......... | 27 |
| Mr A. T. Sharpe c and b Mills ............... | 3 | – b Parker .................... | 16 |
| S. Coe b Parker ......................... | 14 | – lbw b Parker ................ | 0 |
| W. E. Astill b Parker ....................... | 9 | – c Dennett b Parker .......... | 3 |
| Mr H. King b Parker ........................ | 3 | – b Parker .................... | 0 |
| Mr W. C. M. Berridge b Mill ................ | 14 | – c Mills b Parker ............ | 6 |
| W. E. Benskin b Mills ...................... | 3 | – st F. G. Robinson b Parker ....... | 2 |
| T. E. Sidwell not out ...................... | 1 | – not out ..................... | 0 |
| B 2, l-b 1 ......................... | 3 | B 1, l-b 6, n-b 1 .......... | 8 |
| | **54** | | **83** |

## Gloucestershire

| | | | |
|---|---|---|---|
| A. G. Dipper c Sidwell b Benskin ........ | 10 | Mr W. R. Hammond b Benskin .......... | 2 |
| Mr P. G. Robinson b Benskin ........... | 28 | P. Mills b Astill ..................... | 17 |
| Mr M. A. Green hit wkt b J. H. King ...... | 6 | G. Dennett not out ................... | 16 |
| H. Smith b Astill ................... | 7 | C. Parker lbw b J. H. King ............ | 26 |
| Mr P. F. C. Williams c Whitehead | | | |
|               b J. H. King . | 6 | B 6, l-b 3, w 1 ............... | 10 |
| Mr F. G. Robinson b Berridge .......... | 38 | | |
| Mr F. J. Seabrook b Astill ............. | 24 | | **190** |

**Gloucestershire Bowling**

|  | Overs | Mdns | Runs | Wkts | Overs | Mdns | Runs | Wkts |
|---|---|---|---|---|---|---|---|---|
| Parker .......... | 17 | 9 | 22 | 5 | 26.1 | 9 | 35 | 9 |
| Mills ............. | 17 | 8 | 29 | 5 | 20 | 8 | 28 | 1 |
| Dennett .......... |  |  |  |  | 6 | 2 | 12 | — |

**Leicestershire Bowling**

|  | Overs | Mdns | Runs | Wkts |
|---|---|---|---|---|
| Astill ............ | 28 | 11 | 44 | 3 |
| J. H. King ........ | 26.5 | 7 | 51 | 3 |
| Benskin .......... | 21 | 7 | 41 | 3 |
| Berridge .......... | 11 | 3 | 23 | 1 |
| H. King .......... | 3 | — | 21 | — |

Umpires: H. Butt and A. E. Street.

# GLOUCESTERSHIRE v DERBYSHIRE

### Played at Gloucester, June 10, 12, 13, 1922

Showing very good all-round cricket, Derbyshire gained a well-deserved victory by 158 runs. Their early batting did not suggest anything like this, for on winning the toss they had four wickets down for 39. However, Jackson and Hutchinson pulled the game round by putting on 85 together, Curgenven afterwards gave a brilliant display, hitting three 6s and eight 4s and scoring his 65 in a trifle under an hour. Gloucestershire began well by scoring 45 without loss before the drawing of stumps. Their batting failed on the Monday, and during the rest of the day they always looked a beaten side. In Derbyshire's second innings Curgenven, surpassing his previous effort, hit away at such an astonishing pace that he scored 68 runs out of 119 in just under twenty-five minutes. In an innings of 265 Parker did wonders, taking nine wickets – eight of them bowled down. Heavy rain delayed the start of play till a quarter past two on the third day, but Derbyshire won without having to worry about the clock.

## Derbyshire

| | | | |
|---|---|---|---|
| H. Storer b Parker ......................... | 5 | – b Parker ..................... | 25 |
| J. Bowden st Smith b Parker ................. | 11 | – b Parker ..................... | 2 |
| S. Cadman c Dennett b Parker .............. | 7 | – b Parker ..................... | 23 |
| A. Morton c Bessant b Dennett ............... | 8 | – b Parker ..................... | 41 |
| Mr G. R. Jackson c Williams b Parker .......... | 40 | – lbw b Bessant ................ | 10 |
| J. M. Hutchinson b Mills ..................... | 67 | – b Parker ..................... | 41 |
| Mr G. Curgenven b Dennett .................. | 65 | – c Corbett b Parker ............. | 68 |
| W. Carter c Smith b Parker .................. | 7 | – b Parker ..................... | 6 |
| Mr A. H. M. Jackson b Bessant ............... | 22 | – not out ...................... | 28 |
| H. Elliott not out ........................... | 3 | – b Parker ..................... | 11 |
| W. Bestwick c Robathan b Bessant ............. | 4 | – b Parker ..................... | 4 |
| B 7, l-b 1, n-b 1 ..................... | 9 | L-b 5, n-b 1 ............. | 6 |
| | **248** | | **265** |

## Gloucestershire

| | | | |
|---|---|---|---|
| A. G. Dipper lbw b Cadman | 29 | – c Cadman b Bestwick | 20 |
| Mr G. N. Robathan run out | 42 | – c Cadman b Bestwick | 39 |
| H. Smith lbw b Bestwick | 41 | – c Elliott b Morton | 17 |
| P. Mills b Cadman | 1 | – b Morton | 25 |
| Mr L. J. Corbett c Elliott b A. H. M. Jackson | 14 | – b Bestwick | 44 |
| Mr P. F. C. Williams c G. R. Jackson b Morton | 3 | – b Storer | 6 |
| C. Parker c Morton b Bestwick | 9 | – c G. R. Jackson b Bestwick | 0 |
| Mr C. L. Bruton c Elliott b Bestwick | 0 | – b Morton | 0 |
| Mr H. Blagrave c Elliott b Bestwick | 0 | – c Carter b Morton | 12 |
| G. Dennett not out | 10 | – b Bestwick | 0 |
| J. G. Bessant b Morton | 18 | – not out | 4 |
| B 4, l-b 8, n-b 4 | 16 | B 2, l-b 2, n-b 1 | 5 |
| | **183** | | **172** |

## Gloucestershire Bowling

| | Overs | Mdns | Runs | Wkts | Overs | Mdns | Runs | Wkts |
|---|---|---|---|---|---|---|---|---|
| Bessant | 17 | 4 | 39 | 2 | 21 | 4 | 97 | 1 |
| Parker | 40 | 17 | 66 | 5 | 36 | 11 | 87 | 9 |
| Mills | 14 | 4 | 63 | 1 | 3 | — | 31 | — |
| Dennett | 31 | 11 | 71 | 2 | 12 | — | 44 | — |

## Derbyshire Bowling

| | Overs | Mdns | Runs | Wkts | Overs | Mdns | Runs | Wkts |
|---|---|---|---|---|---|---|---|---|
| Bestwick | 27 | 9 | 69 | 4 | 27 | 5 | 59 | 5 |
| Morton | 20.2 | 7 | 45 | 2 | 20.3 | 6 | 73 | 4 |
| Cadman | 19 | 11 | 22 | 2 | 10 | 3 | 15 | — |
| Carter | 4 | — | 17 | — | | | | |
| A. H. M. Jackson | 6 | — | 14 | 1 | | | | |
| Storer | | | | | 6 | 2 | 20 | 1 |

Umpires: F. Parris and H. Young.

## GLOUCESTERSHIRE v LANCASHIRE

Played at Gloucester, July 12, 13, 1922

Following their win earlier in the week Gloucestershire met with a severe reverse, Lancashire beating them in two days by an innings and 11 runs. They practically lost the match when on batting first they were got rid of in two hours and three-quarters for a total of 99. Parkin was at his very best and the batsmen found his break and variety of pace altogether too much for them. He took eight wickets at a cost of 47 runs. Lancashire were at pains not to risk the advantage Parkin had gained for them, and by dint of very careful batting they scored 207 for eight wickets during the rest of the afternoon. The hundred went up just before the second wicket fell, and afterwards Barnes and Watson slowly put on 66 runs together. On the second day the match ended soon after half-past three. Facing a balance of 138, Gloucestershire never seemed in the least likely to escape defeat. Dipper was run out unluckily. He was backing up and the ball, driven back hard by Smith, went off Parkin into the wicket before he could get back to his ground. Mills hit so well that a single innings defeat was not expected, but Richard Tyldesley bowled with such effect that the last three wickets fell for ten runs.

## Gloucestershire

| | | | |
|---|---|---|---|
| Mr C. S. Barnett b Parkin | 18 | – lbw b Parkin | 10 |
| A. G. Dipper c Parkinson b Cook | 0 | – run out | 14 |
| H. Smith lbw b Cook | 19 | – c Rhodes b Cook | 6 |
| Capt. M. A. Green b Parkin | 10 | – b R. Tyldesley | 17 |
| Mr J. Howman hit wkt b Parkin | 1 | – b R. Tyldesley | 12 |
| Mr P. F. C. Williams b Parkin | 4 | – c and b R. Tyldesley | 9 |
| Mr L. Williams b Parkin | 0 | – b R. Tyldesley | 17 |
| P. Mills c Barnes b Parkin | 3 | – b Cook | 35 |
| Mr W. R. Gouldsworthy c and b Parkin | 16 | – b R. Tyldesley | 1 |
| C. Parker c and b Parkin | 23 | – not out | 1 |
| G. Dennett not out | 1 | – c Parkin b R. Tyldesley | 0 |
| B 2, l-b 2 | 4 | B 1, l-b 4 | 5 |
| | **99** | | **127** |

## Lancashire

| | |
|---|---|
| H. Makepeace lbw b Mills | 47 |
| C. Hallows b Gouldsworthy | 22 |
| E. Tyldesley b Mills | 33 |
| Mr J. R. Barnes c and b Gouldsworthy | 42 |
| Mr A. Rhodes b Mills | 0 |
| F. Watson st Smith b Parker | 31 |
| R. Tyldesley c Green b Dennett | 14 |
| C. Parker c Dennett b Parker | 0 |
| Mr M. N. Kenyon c Dipper b Gouldsworthy | 3 |
| L. Cook not out | 20 |
| H. Parkinson b Gouldsworthy | 1 |
| B 7, l-b 2, w 2, n-b 4 | 15 |
| | **237** |

### Lancashire Bowling

| | Overs | Mdns | Runs | Wkts | Overs | Mdns | Runs | Wkts |
|---|---|---|---|---|---|---|---|---|
| Cook | 19 | 2 | 48 | 2 | 15 | 4 | 34 | 2 |
| Parkin | 18.1 | 7 | 47 | 8 | 18 | 5 | 49 | 1 |
| R. Tyldesley | | | | | 13.5 | 4 | 31 | 6 |
| Watson | | | | | 2 | — | 8 | — |

### Gloucestershire Bowling

| | Overs | Mdns | Runs | Wkts |
|---|---|---|---|---|
| Gouldsworthy | 23.5 | 4 | 55 | 4 |
| Parker | 24 | 6 | 76 | 2 |
| Mills | 21 | 2 | 49 | 3 |
| Dennett | 24 | 8 | 42 | 1 |

Umpires: H. Barrett and T. Flowers.

## GLOUCESTERSHIRE v YORKSHIRE

### C. Parker's Benefit Match

#### Played at Bristol, August, 9, 10, 11, 1922

This was a remarkable match, and from Gloucestershire's point of view a very disappointing one. When an innings had been completed on each side they looked to have a splendid chance of beating Yorkshire, but in the end they were defeated by six wickets. Little could be done on the first day, the start being delayed until nearly three o'clock and bad light causing delay later in the afternoon. Gloucestershire scored 92 for four wickets, and on the next morning they carried their total to 172. Then came the sensational cricket, Parker bowling in such form that between ten minutes to three and four o'clock Yorkshire were got rid of for 66. A lead of 106 looked formidable indeed, but Gloucestershire in their turn found run-getting a desperate business, and in two hours their second innings was finished off, Rhodes doing most of the mischief. Left with 165 to get, Yorkshire scored eight without loss and on the following morning fine batting aided by some luck, won the match. The fourth wicket fell at 71, and then Oldroyd and Robinson hit off the remaining runs.

### Gloucestershire

| | | | |
|---|---|---|---|
| Mr C. L. Townsend b Waddington | 19 | – b Rhodes | 3 |
| A. G. Dipper c Waddington b R. Kilner | 54 | – b Rhodes | 16 |
| H. Smith c Dolphin b Macaulay | 4 | – lbw b Rhodes | 7 |
| Mr B. H. Lyon c Oldroyd b Waddington | 2 | – lbw b Waddington | 0 |
| Capt. M. A. Green b R. Kilner | 15 | – run out | 9 |
| Mr P. F. C. Williams b R. Kilner | 19 | – st Dolphin b Rhodes | 7 |
| Mr F. G. Robinson c Oldroyd b Wilson | 8 | – b Rhodes | 4 |
| P. Mills b Rhodes | 17 | – c Robinson b Wilson | 2 |
| C. Parker c Rhodes b Macaulay | 7 | – not out | 2 |
| G. Dennett c Rhodes b Macaulay | 7 | – run out | 1 |
| J. G. Bessant not out | 9 | – c Macaulay b Wilson | 1 |
| B 4, l-b 4, n-b 3 | 11 | B 2, l-b 3, n-b 1 | 6 |
| | **172** | | **58** |

### Yorkshire

| | | | |
|---|---|---|---|
| P. Holmes c Smith b Parker | 0 | – b Mills | 6 |
| H. Sutcliffe lbw b Parker | 11 | – b Mills | 17 |
| E. Oldroyd lbw b Parker | 0 | – not out | 63 |
| R. Kilner b Parker | 14 | – b Parker | 0 |
| W. Rhodes lbw b Mills | 12 | – c Bessant b Parker | 22 |
| E. Robinson b Parker | 1 | – not out | 39 |
| N. Kilner b Parker | 5 | | |
| G. G. Macaulay b Parker | 8 | | |
| A. Dolphin b Parker | 0 | | |
| A. Waddington b Parker | 0 | | |
| Mr E. R. Wilson not out | 13 | | |
| B 1, n-b 1 | 2 | B 12, l-b 8 | 20 |
| | **66** | | **167** |

### Yorkshire Bowling

| | Overs | Mdns | Runs | Wkts | Overs | Mdns | Runs | Wkts |
|---|---|---|---|---|---|---|---|---|
| Waddington | 21 | 6 | 39 | 2 | 5 | 2 | 8 | 1 |
| Robinson | 7 | 3 | 17 | — | | | | |
| R. Kilner | 27 | 14 | 26 | 3 | 3 | — | 13 | — |
| Wilson | 18 | 9 | 16 | 1 | 11.1 | 7 | 7 | 2 |
| Rhodes | 8 | 4 | 15 | 1 | 20 | 11 | 24 | 5 |
| Macaulay | 25 | 7 | 48 | 3 | | | | |

### Gloucestershire Bowling

| | Overs | Mdns | Runs | Wkts | Overs | Mdns | Runs | Wkts |
|---|---|---|---|---|---|---|---|---|
| Parker | 10.2 | 2 | 36 | 9 | 35 | 17 | 46 | 2 |
| Mills | 10 | 2 | 28 | 1 | 38 | 19 | 45 | 2 |
| Dennett | | | | | 11 | 3 | 30 | — |
| Bessant | | | | | 7 | 3 | 26 | — |

Umpires: W. A. J. West and W. Phillips.

## GLOUCESTERSHIRE v WARWICKSHIRE

Played at Cheltenham, August 23, 24, 25, 1922

Owing nearly everything to Parker, Dipper, and Smith. Gloucestershire gained an overwhelming victory by an innings and 163 runs. They practically won the match on the first day when, after Parker had got Warwickshire out in eighty minutes, they scored 238 for four wickets. Barnett failed but Dipper and Smith during their partnership took the score to 155, Smith hitting thirteen 4s in his 92. Play on the second day was cut short at ten minutes to one, rain setting in for the rest of the afternoon. In the little time available Gloucestershire carried their total to 316, and on Friday morning the innings was at once declared. Dipper's 125 not out is the sixth hundred he has obtained during his career against Warwickshire bowling. On a ruined pitch Warwickshire were in a hopeless position, and little more than an hour and a half's cricket proved sufficient to finish off the match. Taking six wickets for 32 runs Parker had the remarkable record in the whole game of fourteen for 61.

### Warwickshire

| | | |
|---|---:|---:|
| L. A. Bates st Smith b Parker | 4 | – c and b Mills ................... 15 |
| E. J. Smith b Parker | 0 | – b Parker ....................... 14 |
| Mr A. L. Murray lbw b Mills | 7 | – b Parker ........................ 0 |
| W. G. Quaife b Parker | 5 | – c Bessant b Mills ............... 10 |
| Mr F. R. Santall c Mills b Parker | 38 | – lbw b Mills ................... 17 |
| Mr J. G. Pugh b Parker | 0 | – b Parker ........................ 6 |
| Mr N. E. Partridge c Green b Parker | 16 | – b Parker ........................ 4 |
| J. Smart lbw b Mills | 0 | – run out ......................... 5 |
| C. Smart c Green b Parker | 8 | – c Bessant b Parker ............. 5 |
| A. Howell b Parker | 0 | – b Parker ........................ 0 |
| H. Howell not out | 0 | – not out ......................... 0 |
| B 2 | 2 | L-b 1, n-b 1 ............. 2 |
| | **80** | **73** |

### Gloucestershire

| | | |
|---|---:|---:|
| Mr C. S. Barnett c Smith b Partridge | 3 | Mr P. F. C. Williams run out ........... 18 |
| A. G. Dipper not out | 125 | Mr C. J. King-Turner c Smith b Quaife .... 8 |
| H. Smith c H. Howell b Quaife | 92 | C. Parker not out ..................... 15 |
| Capt. M. A. Green c Partridge b Quaife | 6 | B 9, l-b 5, n-b 1 ............... 15 |
| Mr F. G. Robinson b Partridge | 15 | |
| Mr B. H. Lyon lbw b Partridge | 19 | (7 wkts dec.) 316 |

P. Mills and J. G. Bessant did not bat.

### Gloucestershire Bowling

| | Overs | Mdns | Runs | Wkts | Overs | Mdns | Runs | Wkts |
|---|---|---|---|---|---|---|---|---|
| Bessant .......... | 1 | — | 4 | — | | | | |
| Parker .......... | 21.2 | 10 | 29 | 8 | 17.4 | 5 | 32 | 6 |
| Mills ............. | 21 | 4 | 45 | 2 | 17 | 4 | 39 | 3 |

### Warwickshire Bowling

| | Overs | Mdns | Runs | Wkts |
|---|---|---|---|---|
| H. Howell ........ | 31 | 1 | 102 | — |
| Partridge ......... | 27 | 4 | 60 | 3 |
| A. Howell ........ | 16.2 | — | 60 | — |
| Quaife .......... | 25 | 3 | 55 | 3 |
| J. Smart .......... | 3 | — | 24 | — |

Umpires: T. Fenwick and H. Bagshaw.

# GLOUCESTERSHIRE v GLAMORGAN

Played at Cheltenham, June 27, 28, 29, 1923

Thanks chiefly to Dipper, who, in taking out his bat for 252, played the highest innings of his life, Gloucestershire gained an easy victory by ten wickets. Dipper took five hours and a half to get his huge score and hit thirty-seven 4s. For the most part his play was beyond reproach, but he gave a chance when he had made 78, and had a further piece of luck when a ball from Clay hit his wicket without removing the bails. Glamorgan's batting was far above its normal form. Bates, in particular, playing fine cricket. On the second evening he scored 54 runs out of 82 in fifty minutes.

## Gloucestershire

| | | | |
|---|---|---|---|
| A. G. Dipper not out | 252 | – not out | 22 |
| W. R. Hammond c Bates b Arnott | 9 | – not out | 19 |
| H. Smith b Clay | 0 | | |
| Major D. C. Robinson c Bates b Ryan | 17 | | |
| Mr C. S. Barnett run out | 27 | | |
| W. T. Bloodworth hit wkt b Bates | 4 | | |
| C. Parker c Tait b Arnott | 44 | | |
| Mr A. E. Waters c Tayler b Clay | 42 | | |
| P. Mills run out | 43 | | |
| G. Dennett c Hill b Arnott | 0 | | |
| J. G. Bessant not out | 6 | | |
| B 27, l-b 10 | 37 | N-b 1 | 1 |
| | **(9 wkts dec.) 481** | | **42** |

## Glamorgan

| | | | |
|---|---|---|---|
| Mr T. R. Morgan c Hammond b Parker | 37 | – c Dennett b Waters | 7 |
| Mr T. A. L. Whittington st Smith b Parker | 43 | – b Parker | 17 |
| W. Bates lbw b Parker | 44 | – c Parker b Mills | 86 |
| Mr J. R. Tait c Parker b Bessant | 4 | – c Smith b Parker | 52 |
| Mr W. Spiller c Smith b Bessant | 4 | – b Hammond | 4 |
| Mr H. W. Tayler lbw b Parker | 10 | – c Hammond b Parker | 31 |
| D. Davies b Dennett | 5 | – b Parker | 0 |
| Mr T. Arnott not out | 59 | – c Robinson b Dennett | 3 |
| F. Ryan c Mills b Parker | 4 | – st Smith b Mills | 28 |
| Mr J. C. Clay b Parker | 22 | – c Bessant b Parker | 0 |
| Mr M. L. Hill b Mills | 30 | – not out | 5 |
| B 15, l-b 4, n-b 1 | 20 | B 2, l-b 1, w 2 | 5 |
| | **282** | | **238** |

## Glamorgan Bowling

| | Overs | Mdns | Runs | Wkts | Overs | Mdns | Runs | Wkts |
|---|---|---|---|---|---|---|---|---|
| Arnott | 21 | 4 | 82 | 3 | 2 | — | 20 | — |
| Clay | 35 | 4 | 116 | 2 | 2 | — | 7 | — |
| Davies | 19 | 1 | 70 | — | | | | |
| Ryan | 24 | 6 | 65 | 1 | 3 | 2 | 4 | — |
| Bates | 14 | — | 71 | 1 | | | | |
| Spiller | 2 | — | 18 | — | | | | |
| Tait | 2 | — | 22 | — | | | | |
| Morgan | | | | | 2.5 | — | 10 | — |

**Gloucestershire Bowling**

| | Overs | Mdns | Runs | Wkts | Overs | Mdns | Runs | Wkts |
|---|---|---|---|---|---|---|---|---|
| Hammond ........ | 7 | 2 | 8 | — | 9 | 3 | 18 | 1 |
| Parker .......... | 54 | 17 | 138 | 6 | 25.4 | 8 | 51 | 5 |
| Mills ............ | 24.4 | 10 | 62 | 1 | 18 | 5 | 63 | 2 |
| Dennett ......... | 22 | 9 | 42 | 1 | 9 | — | 28 | 1 |
| Bessant ......... | 7 | 2 | 12 | 2 | 11 | 1 | 39 | — |
| Waters .......... | | | | | 8 | — | 34 | 1 |

Umpires: W. A. J. West and B. Tremlin.

## GLOUCESTERSHIRE v MIDDLESEX

### Played at Bristol, August 23, 25, 26, 1924

This remarkable match furnished the sensation and the biggest success of Gloucestershire's season. Out in an hour and a quarter for a wretched score of 31, Gloucestershire looked a beaten side, but Parker came to the rescue with some wonderful bowling, and at the end of the day Middlesex held a first innings lead of only 43 runs. All things taken into consideration it may be said that Hammond on Monday gave the batting display of the year. In first wicket down, he hit up his 174 not out in rather less than four hours, and his only mistake was a chance when he had made 137. The character of his cricket may be gathered from the fact that his hits included a six and twenty-one 4s. Left to get 252 on a pitch badly cut up, Middlesex made a bold bid for victory, but Parker did the hat trick for the second time during the match, and Gloucestershire won by 61 runs.

### Gloucestershire

| | | | |
|---|---|---|---|
| A. G. Dipper c Dales b Haig .................. | 6 | – c Durston b Haig .............. | 7 |
| Mr F. J. Seabrook c Murrell b Haig .............. | 7 | – b Durston .................... | 4 |
| W. R. Hammond c Hearne b Haig .............. | 5 | – not out ..................... | 174 |
| Mr B. H. Lyon c Durston b Haig ............... | 4 | – c Hendren b Hearne .......... | 42 |
| H. Smith b Durston ........................ | 3 | – lbw b Hearne ................. | 2 |
| Mr F. G. Rogers c Dales b Haig ............... | 0 | – b Hearne .................... | 0 |
| B. S. Bloodworth not out ..................... | 1 | – run out ..................... | 9 |
| Lieut-Col D. C. Robinson b Durston ............ | 0 | – c Lee b Haig ................. | 24 |
| P. Mills c Murrell b Durston .................. | 0 | – b Allen ...................... | 3 |
| C. Parker b Durston ........................ | 0 | – c Dales b Haig ............... | 13 |
| G. Dennett b Haig .......................... | 3 | – not out ..................... | 5 |
| L-b 1, n-b 1 ....................... | 2 | B 6, l-b 1, n-b 4 .......... | 11 |
| | **31** | **(9 wkts dec.)** | **294** |

### Middlesex

| | | | |
|---|---|---|---|
| Mr. H. L. Dales c Dipper b Hammond .......... | 7 | – lbw b Mills ................. | 42 |
| H. W. Lee c Lyon b Parker .................... | 21 | – b Hammond ................. | 21 |
| J. W. Hearne c Rogers b Parker ................ | 6 | – c Hammond b Parker .......... | 6 |
| E. Hendren c Hammond b Parker .............. | 5 | – lbw b Parker ................. | 23 |
| Mr R. H. Twining c Lyon b Parker ............. | 1 | – b Mills ..................... | 8 |
| Mr G. O. Allen c Dennett b Parker ............ | 0 | – c and b Parker ............... | 31 |
| Mr F. T. Mann st Smith b Parker .............. | 0 | – c Lyon b Parker .............. | 22 |
| Mr J. L. Guise c Lyon b Hammond ............. | 22 | – c Dennett b Parker ........... | 0 |
| Mr N. Haig b Mills ......................... | 8 | – lbw b Parker ................. | 0 |
| H. R. Murrell c Hammond b Parker ............ | 2 | – b Parker .................... | 22 |
| T. J. Durston not out ....................... | 0 | – not out ..................... | 3 |
| B 1, n-b 1 ......................... | 2 | B 2, l-b 8, n-b 2 .......... | 12 |
| | **74** | | **190** |

### Middlesex Bowling

|          | Overs | Mdns | Runs | Wkts | Overs | Mdns | Runs | Wkts |
|----------|-------|------|------|------|-------|------|------|------|
| Haig     | 12    | 7    | 11   | 6    | 33    | 2    | 95   | 3    |
| Durston  | 11    | 4    | 18   | 4    | 16    | 3    | 61   | 1    |
| Allen    |       |      |      |      | 9.2   | 1    | 26   | 1    |
| Hearne   |       |      |      |      | 21    | 1    | 75   | 3    |
| Lee      |       |      |      |      | 5     | 1    | 9    | —    |
| Murrell  |       |      |      |      | 4     | —    | 17   | —    |

### Gloucestershire Bowling

|          | Overs | Mdns | Runs | Wkts | Overs | Mdns | Runs | Wkts |
|----------|-------|------|------|------|-------|------|------|------|
| Hammond  | 9     | 2    | 27   | 2    | 13    | 8    | 22   | 1    |
| Parker   | 10.1  | 3    | 30   | 7    | 31.1  | 5    | 101  | 7    |
| Mills    | 2     | —    | 15   | 1    | 15    | 4    | 45   | 2    |
| Dennett  |       |      |      |      | 8     | 4    | 10   | —    |

Umpires: W. Phillips and W. Reeves.

# GLOUCESTERSHIRE v ESSEX

### Played at Gloucester, July 25, 27, 28, 1925

Won by Gloucestershire by an innings and 109 runs the match proved a veritable triumph for Parker, who in the two innings had the astounding record of seventeen wickets for 56 runs – a very remarkable performance. He took every wicket that fell to the bowlers when Essex, having been put in after losing the toss, were disposed of soon after lunch on the opening day. So well did Gloucestershire follow this up that when stumps were drawn they held a lead of five runs with only two men out. There was no play on the Monday so Gloucestershire forced matters on Tuesday and, declaring with a lead of 172 shortly before three o'clock, finished off the match in dramatic fashion. Parker's eight wickets for 12 runs represented deadly bowling. He was almost unplayable on the treacherous pitch. Dipper carried off the batting honours, being in for three hours and forty minutes. He scarcely made a bad stroke. Hammond helped him to add 83 runs in forty-five minutes.

### Essex

| | | | |
|---|---|---|---|
| Mr L. C. Eastman c Robinson b Parker | 16 | – c Hammond b Parker | 11 |
| J. Freeman c Hammond b Parker | 18 | – lbw b Parker | 2 |
| J. O'Connor b Parker | 18 | – b Parker | 21 |
| A. C. Russell run out | 0 | – c Hammond b Parker | 0 |
| Mr P. Perrin c Hammond b Parker | 2 | – c Hammond b Parker | 2 |
| Mr C. T. Ashton lbw b Parker | 0 | – b Parker | 0 |
| J. A. Cutmore lbw b Parker | 14 | – b Dennett | 0 |
| Mr. R. C. Joy st Smith b Parker | 4 | – b Dennett | 17 |
| Mr H. M. Morris not out | 21 | – c Hammond b Parker | 5 |
| A. B. Hipkin c Dennett b Parker | 9 | – b Parker | 2 |
| M. S. Nichols b Parker | 11 | – not out | 0 |
| B 1, l-b 1 | 2 | B 2, l-b 1 | 3 |
| | **115** | | **63** |

### Gloucestershire

| | |
|---|---|
| Lt-Col D. C. Robinson c Russell b Hipkin . . 22 | Mr R. G. W. Melsome c Joy b Hipkin . . . . . 25 |
| A. G. Dipper b Russell . . . . . . . . . . . . . . . .107 | Mr G. A. Wedel not out . . . . . . . . . . . . . . . 5 |
| H. Smith c O'Connor b Eastman . . . . . . . . 16 | |
| R. A. Sinfield c Morris b Eastman . . . . . . . . 23 | B 7, l-b 7 . . . . . . . . . . . . . . . . . . . 14 |
| W. R. Hammond st Freeman b Eastman . . . 40 | |
| B. S. Bloodworth not out . . . . . . . . . . . . . . 35 | (6 wkts dec.) 287 |

C. Parker, T. W. Goddard and G. Dennett did not bat.

## Gloucestershire Bowling

| | Overs | Mdns | Runs | Wkts | Overs | Mdns | Runs | Wkts |
|---|---|---|---|---|---|---|---|---|
| Parker ........... | 31.3 | 13 | 44 | 9 | 17 | 10 | 12 | 8 |
| Dennett .......... | 27 | 8 | 58 | — | 17 | 5 | 48 | 2 |
| Wedel ............ | 4 | 1 | 11 | — | | | | |

## Essex Bowling

| | Overs | Mdns | Runs | Wkts |
|---|---|---|---|---|
| Nichols .......... | 10 | 4 | 26 | — |
| Eastman .......... | 28 | 5 | 77 | 3 |
| Hipkin ........... | 29 | 8 | 66 | 2 |
| O'Connor ........ | 9 | 1 | 27 | — |
| Ashton ........... | 12 | 2 | 43 | — |
| Russell ........... | 15 | 2 | 32 | 1 |
| Joy .............. | 2 | 1 | 2 | — |

Umpires: A. E. Street and H. Chidgey.

## GLOUCESTERSHIRE v YORKSHIRE

Played at Gloucester, May 7, 9, 10, 1927

Holmes and Sutcliffe sharing in a splendid stand which, extending over three hours and a half, produced 274 runs – their thirty-ninth three-figure first wicket partnership – Yorkshire were able to declare with five men out and win this match by an innings and 21 runs. Sutcliffe's batting, marked by particularly attractive play on the off-side, was quite free from serious blemish. Holmes, who stayed for four hours and a half, also played well, but he gave chances at 20 and at 69. Gloucestershire entered upon Tuesday's play 256 runs behind with Dipper and Lyon out in the second innings. The seventh wicket fell at 115, but Parker assisted Hammond to add 120 in eighty minutes. Hammond, resuming his place in the Gloucestershire team after an absence through illness, of a whole season, put together the first of the wonderful series of splendid innings which enabled him to complete his 1,000 runs in May. Compelled, with his side in a hopeless position, to exercise much restraint, he gave a masterly display which, marred only by a chance at 111, lasted three hours and three-quarters. Parry, an umpire whose leg had been amputated below the knee, fell in getting out of the way of a ball, and fractured the maimed limb.

## Gloucestershire

| | | | |
|---|---|---|---|
| A. E. Dipper c and b Rhodes ................... | 16 | – c Dolphin b Kilner ........... | 9 |
| Mr B. H. Lyon c Macaulay b Rhodes ............ | 39 | – lbw b Rhodes ................... | 10 |
| H. Smith c Lupton b Robinson ................. | 30 | – st Dolphin b Kilner ........... | 4 |
| W. R. Hammond c Leyland b Waddington ........ | 27 | – b Robinson ....................| 135 |
| Mr E. G. Morrison b Waddington ............... | 0 | – c Holmes b Kilner ............ | 8 |
| R. A. Sinfield lbw b Waddington ............... | 22 | – b Kilner ..................... | 4 |
| Mr W. H. Rowlands b Waddington .............. | 6 | – b Waddington ................ | 7 |
| D. F. Pope b Robinson ........................ | 12 | – lbw b Waddington ............. | 13 |
| C. Parker not out ........................... | 18 | – b Robinson .................. | 44 |
| Mr G. Wedel b Waddington .................... | 4 | – c Dolphin b Robinson .......... | 6 |
| P. Mills run out ........................... | 3 | – not out ..................... | 8 |
| B 5, l-b 3, n-b 4 ..................... | 12 | B 5, l-b 3, n-b 2 .......... | 10 |
| | 189 | | 258 |

### Yorkshire

| | | | |
|---|---|---|---|
| P. Holmes c Hammond b Parker | 180 | W. Rhodes c Smith b Mills | 8 |
| H. Sutcliffe b Wedel | 134 | E. Robinson not out | 16 |
| E. Oldroyd c Hammond b Parker | 37 | B 1, l-b 1, n-b 1 | 3 |
| M. Leyland c Sinfield b Parker | 0 | | |
| R. Kilner not out | 90 | (5 wkts dec.) | 468 |

Maj. A. W. Lupton, A. Waddington, G. G. Macaulay and A. Dolphin did not bat.

### Yorkshire Bowling

| | Overs | Mdns | Runs | Wkts | Overs | Mdns | Runs | Wkts |
|---|---|---|---|---|---|---|---|---|
| Macaulay | 20 | 5 | 45 | — | 23 | 5 | 44 | — |
| Kilner | 12 | 1 | 42 | — | 41 | 8 | 70 | 4 |
| Rhodes | 15 | 9 | 24 | 2 | 25 | 12 | 33 | 1 |
| Waddington | 20 | 5 | 51 | 5 | 20 | 2 | 49 | 2 |
| Robinson | 10.1 | 2 | 15 | 2 | 12.2 | 3 | 37 | 3 |
| Oldroyd | | | | | 3 | — | 15 | — |

### Gloucestershire Bowling

| | Overs | Mdns | Runs | Wkts |
|---|---|---|---|---|
| Hammond | 9 | 2 | 25 | — |
| Parker | 54 | 14 | 180 | 3 |
| Wedel | 53 | 17 | 122 | 1 |
| Mills | 32 | 10 | 78 | 1 |
| Sinfield | 19 | 6 | 60 | — |

Umpires: N. R. Parry (A. Paish) and A. Nash.

## GLOUCESTERSHIRE v SURREY

### Played at Cheltenham, August 15, 16, 17, 1928

Beating Surrey by 189 runs Gloucestershire owned almost everything to the magnificent work of Hammond and Parker. Hammond gave a memorable display of all-round cricket. Not only did he perform – for the second time against Surrey – the feat of scoring two separate hundreds in a match, but in the two Surrey innings he brought off ten catches. In this latter way he rendered splendid help to Parker, whose skilful bowling – pronounced spin combined with great accuracy of length – produced a record of thirteen wickets in the match for 197 runs. Hobbs, on Thursday played masterly cricket, but his dismissal and also that of Sandham on the last afternoon for 13 rendered Surrey's task of getting 357 runs practically hopeless. Hammond scored 139 out of 199 in two hours and forty minutes, his second three-figure innings lasting forty-five minutes longer.

### Gloucestershire

| | | | |
|---|---|---|---|
| A. E. Dipper c and b G-Wells | 7 | – c and b Peach | 41 |
| R. A. Sinfield b Peach | 0 | – lbw b Shepherd | 22 |
| W. R. Hammond c Shepherd b Peach | 139 | – c Gregory b Fenley | 143 |
| Mr B. H. Lyon c and b Fender | 6 | – c Hobbs b Shepherd | 27 |
| Mr F. J. Seabrook c Gregory b Fender | 0 | | |
| Mr W. L. Neale c Ducat b G-Wells | 10 | – b Fender | 5 |
| H. Smith c Fender b Shepherd | 56 | – b Shepherd | 0 |
| Mr C. J. Barnett c G-Wells b Peach | 0 | – c Ducat b Fenley | 45 |
| Capt. M. A. Green c Sandham b Fenley | 37 | – not out | 21 |
| C. Parker c Brooks b Fender | 19 | – c Shepherd b Fenley | 11 |
| P. Mills not out | 7 | – b Shepherd | 2 |
| B 12, l-b 10, n-b 1 | 23 | B 2 | 2 |

| | | |
|---|---|---|
| 304 | (9 wkts dec.) | 319 |

## Surrey

| | | | |
|---|--:|---|--:|
| J. B. Hobbs c Seabrook b Hammond | 96 | – c Smith b Parker | 2 |
| A. Sandham c Smith b Sinfield | 0 | – c Hammond b Sinfield | 10 |
| A. Ducat c Dipper b Parker | 6 | – c Hammond b Parker | 55 |
| T. Shepherd c Barnett b Parker | 52 | – c Hammond b Parker | 17 |
| T. H. Barling c Hammond b Parker | 4 | – c Hammond b Parker | 2 |
| R. J. Gregory c Hammond b Parker | 7 | – c Hammond b Parker | 3 |
| Mr P. G. H. Fender c Hammond b Sinfield | 55 | – c Hammond b Parker | 20 |
| Mr H. M. Garland-Wells c Hammond b Parker | 6 | – st Smith b Sinfield | 49 |
| H. A. Peach b Mills | 5 | – c Smith b Parker | 1 |
| E. W. Brooks lbw b Parker | 2 | – run out | 0 |
| S. Fenley not out | 0 | – not out | 0 |
| B 27, l-b 7 | 34 | B 1, l-b 7 | 8 |
| | **267** | | **167** |

## Surrey Bowling

| | Overs | Mdns | Runs | Wkts | Overs | Mdns | Runs | Wkts |
|---|--:|--:|--:|--:|--:|--:|--:|--:|
| Fender | 24.3 | 10 | 57 | 3 | 25 | 6 | 55 | 1 |
| Peach | 27 | 6 | 68 | 3 | 26 | 9 | 71 | 1 |
| Fenley | 12 | 2 | 44 | 1 | 18 | 2 | 83 | 3 |
| Shepherd | 15 | 4 | 43 | 1 | 32.4 | 5 | 74 | 4 |
| Garland-Wells | 22 | 5 | 65 | 2 | 14 | 3 | 34 | — |
| Gregory | 2 | — | 4 | — | | | | |

## Gloucestershire Bowling

| | Overs | Mdns | Runs | Wkts | Overs | Mdns | Runs | Wkts |
|---|--:|--:|--:|--:|--:|--:|--:|--:|
| Hammond | 22 | 3 | 71 | 1 | | | | |
| Sinfield | 9 | 4 | 10 | 2 | 27 | 9 | 59 | 2 |
| Parker | 38.4 | 6 | 117 | 6 | 32 | 10 | 80 | 7 |
| Mills | 24 | 11 | 35 | 1 | 6 | — | 20 | — |

Umpires: W. Bestwick and H. Young.

## GLOUCESTERSHIRE v WORCESTERSHIRE

Played at Cheltenham, August 18, 20, 1928

Hammond, enjoying another personal triumph almost as great as, if of a different description from, that in the Surrey game, Gloucestershire overplayed Worcestershire so completely that they won in two days by an innings and 168 runs. On this occasion bowling brought honours to the famous all-rounder who, proving more effective with the ball than ever before, secured nine Worcestershire wickets in the first innings for 23 runs. As he caught the other batsman off Parker's bowling, he had a hand in disposing of the whole of the side. On a pitch recovering from heavy dew Hammond made the ball turn appreciably as well as swerve through the air and against his deadly attack Worcestershire offered most feeble resistance, their total of 35 being the smallest of the season in county cricket. When Worcestershire faced arrears of 335, Hammond again accomplished fine work with the ball. In the whole match he took fifteen wickets for 128 runs. Parker, too, gave the batsmen a lot of trouble, his left hand slows providing a telling contrast to Hammond's quick right-hand bowling. Worcestershire in their second innings displayed some stubbornness in defence. Higgins remaining until the total reached 73 and Quaife staying an hour. Batting of a very high quality came from Gloucestershire. Dipper and Sinfield showed to advantage in an opening partnership of 116 and Hammond and Lyon added 108 in first-rate style. Gloucestershire finished the first day leading by 246 with five wickets in hand.

## Worcestershire

| | | | | |
|---|---|---|---|---|
| Mr J. B. Higgins b Hammond | 2 | – c Lyon b Parker | 35 |
| L. Wright st Smith b Hammond | 8 | – b Parker | 1 |
| Mr B. W. Quaife c Hammond b Parker | 2 | – c Seabrook b Hammond | 19 |
| W. V. Fox c Lyon b Hammond | 1 | – c Lyon b Hammond | 1 |
| H. H. Gibbons c Stephens b Hammond | 4 | – c Lyon b Parker | 9 |
| F. Root c Seabrook b Hammond | 0 | – lbw b Hammond | 1 |
| C. V. Tarbox b Hammond | 6 | – c Barnett b Hammond | 29 |
| J. W. King not out | 0 | – c Seabrook b Hammond | 4 |
| J. J. Bowles c Lyon b Hammond | 4 | – hit wkt b Parker | 20 |
| Capt. D. V. Hill c Parker b Hammond | 0 | – st Smith b Hammond | 17 |
| F. T. Summers b Hammond | 0 | – not out | 0 |
| B 5, l-b 3 | 8 | B 21, l-b 10 | 31 |
| | **35** | | **167** |

## Gloucestershire

| | | | | |
|---|---|---|---|---|
| A. E. Dipper c Quaife b Wright | 77 | Mr W. L. Neale not out | 51 |
| R. A. Sinfield c Hill b Wright | 30 | Mr C. J. Barnett not out | 34 |
| W. R. Hammond c Summers b Wright | 80 | | |
| Mr B. H. Lyon b Tarbox | 38 | B 15, l-b 9, n-b 1 | 25 |
| Mr F. J. Seabrook b Hill | 29 | | |
| H. Smith lbw b Hill | 6 | (6 wkts dec.) | 370 |

P. H. Stephens, C. Parker and P. Mills did not bat.

## Gloucestershire Bowling

| | Overs | Mdns | Runs | Wkts | Overs | Mdns | Runs | Wkts |
|---|---|---|---|---|---|---|---|---|
| Hammond | 10.2 | 2 | 23 | 9 | 33.3 | 5 | 105 | 6 |
| Sinfield | 2 | 1 | 3 | — | | | | |
| Parker | 8 | 7 | 1 | 1 | 33 | 22 | 31 | 4 |

## Worcestershire Bowling

| | Overs | Mdns | Runs | Wkts |
|---|---|---|---|---|
| Root | 37 | 10 | 82 | — |
| Hill | 20 | 1 | 71 | 2 |
| Bowles | 17 | 3 | 49 | — |
| Tarbox | 30 | 5 | 88 | 1 |
| Wright | 20 | 4 | 55 | 3 |

Umpires: W. Bestwick and H. Young.

# GLOUCESTERSHIRE v SUSSEX

Played at Cheltenham, August 14, 15, 16, 1929

There was a tremendous finish to this match, Sussex winning by a single run. Sussex started by making 128 for two wickets, but afterwards Goddard and Parker bowled with pronounced effect. Gloucestershire, too, fared well for a time, but on Thursday Lyon met with little support and the home side finished 49 in arrear. Bowley had followed up some capital batting by taking with his leg-breaks the first five Gloucestershire wickets, and he played brightly in the visitors' second innings. The other Sussex men could do little with Parker and Goddard. Gloucestershire wanting 166 for victory, Dipper and Sinfield put on 53, but five wickets had fallen for 97 when stumps were drawn. Of the 69 required on Friday, Dipper and Neale obtained 22, and Dipper, batting admirably for three hours, was not dismissed until Gloucestershire were within 21 of victory. Barnett and Parker carried the total to 163 but one run later Langridge disposed of Goddard, and Gloucestershire found themselves defeated. Hammond, who was twice out hit wicket, made four slip catches in the Sussex second innings.

## Sussex

| | | | |
|---|---|---|---|
| E. H. Bowley b Goddard | 49 | – c Lyon b Goddard | 42 |
| Mr A. H. H. Gilligan st Smith b Parker | 31 | – c Hammond b Parker | 8 |
| Mr K. S. Duleepsinhji c Lyon b Parker | 63 | – c Lyon b Parker | 15 |
| T. Cook c Goddard b Parker | 7 | – c Neale b Parker | 4 |
| James Langridge b Goddard | 39 | – b Goddard | 6 |
| A. F. Wensley c Seabrook b Goddard | 13 | – c Barnett b Parker | 4 |
| Mr R. L. Holdsworth c Lyon b Goddard | 2 | – c Hammond b Parker | 2 |
| Mr J. G. Wagener b Parker | 5 | – not out | 23 |
| M. W. Tate lbw b Goddard | 33 | – c Hedges b Goddard | 5 |
| Mr G. S. Grimston not out | 6 | – c Hammond b Parker | 0 |
| W. Cornford c Lyon b Goddard | 3 | – c Hammond b Parker | 0 |
| B 5, l-b 6, w 1 | 12 | L-b 6, n-b 1 | 7 |
| | **263** | | **116** |

## Gloucestershire

| | | | |
|---|---|---|---|
| A. E. Dipper c Langridge b Bowley | 27 | – c Duleepsinhji b Langridge | 69 |
| R. A. Sinfield c Langridge b Bowley | 29 | – c Wensley b Bowley | 26 |
| W. R. Hammond hit wkt b Bowley | 30 | – hit wkt b Langridge | 1 |
| Mr B. H. Lyon c Bowley b Langridge | 62 | – lbw b Wensley | 16 |
| C. J. Barnett c Tate b Bowley | 2 | – not out | 10 |
| Mr F. J. Seabrook c Grimston b Bowley | 8 | – lbw b Langridge | 0 |
| W. L. Neale lbw b Langridge | 10 | – c Cornford b Tate | 8 |
| Mr L. P. Hedges c Grimston b Langridge | 4 | – c Wagener b Langridge | 17 |
| H. Smith b Tate | 14 | – b Wensley | 1 |
| C. Parker not out | 12 | – run out | 8 |
| T. W. Goddard c and b Tate | 0 | – c Cornford b Langridge | 1 |
| B 9, l-b 6, n-b 1 | 16 | B 1, l-b 6 | 7 |
| | **214** | | **164** |

## Gloucestershire Bowling

| | Overs | Mdns | Runs | Wkts | Overs | Mdns | Runs | Wkts |
|---|---|---|---|---|---|---|---|---|
| Sinfield | 11 | 1 | 42 | — | 7 | 1 | 27 | — |
| Barnett | 10 | — | 48 | — | | | | |
| Goddard | 29.4 | 2 | 85 | 6 | 17 | 7 | 33 | 3 |
| Parker | 29 | 6 | 76 | 4 | 24.4 | 6 | 49 | 7 |

## Sussex Bowling

| | Overs | Mdns | Runs | Wkts | Overs | Mdns | Runs | Wkts |
|---|---|---|---|---|---|---|---|---|
| Tate | 17.4 | 6 | 29 | 2 | 19 | 4 | 39 | 1 |
| Wensley | 21 | 4 | 49 | — | 16 | — | 35 | 2 |
| Langridge | 22 | 7 | 34 | 3 | 34.1 | 19 | 72 | 5 |
| Cook | 3 | — | 6 | — | | | | |
| Bowley | 20 | 2 | 64 | 5 | 4 | — | 11 | 1 |
| Grimston | 2 | — | 7 | — | | | | |
| Wagener | 6 | 1 | 9 | — | | | | |

Umpires: W. R. Parry and W. Phillips.

## GLOUCESTERSHIRE v MIDDLESEX

Played at Cheltenham, June 25, 26, 1930

Poorly represented, Middlesex, who on the previous Friday had been beaten by Gloucestershire at Lord's, suffered another defeat at the hands of the west-country team. Once again the great factor in a Gloucestershire victory was the bowling of Parker who, on this occasion, excelled himself, even allowing for the indifferent quality of the Middlesex batting. In the visitors' first innings on a pitch of varying pace he secured eight wickets for 49 runs and in the second, when the ground had become somewhat faster, he again took eight wickets – this time for 60 runs – and so for the whole match had the wonderful record of sixteen wickets for less than 7 runs each. Canning and Hulme alone faced Parker with much confidence. Driving hard, Lyon and Dacre added 59 in forty minutes and Neale and Barnett put on 77 in an hour. Haig on Thursday morning disposed of four batsmen for 9 runs but, set only a very light task, Gloucestershire won by eight wickets.

### Middlesex

| | | | |
|---|---:|---|---:|
| H. W. Lee lbw b Parker | 13 | – c Dacre b Parker | 4 |
| E. G. Canning b Parker | 37 | – c and b Parker | 22 |
| J. W. Hearne c Stephens b Sinfield | 14 | – b Parker | 12 |
| Mr J. L. Guise c Lyon b Parker | 2 | – c Dacre b Parker | 9 |
| Mr N. Haig b Parker | 20 | – c Smith b Parker | 9 |
| G. Hart b Parker | 8 | – c Barnett b Goddard | 8 |
| Mr D. Russell st Smith b Parker | 9 | – lbw b Parker | 12 |
| Mr C. G. Howard b Parker | 0 | – lbw b Parker | 8 |
| J. Hulme not out | 21 | – b Goddard | 31 |
| T. J. Durston c Barnett b Sinfield | 1 | – st Smith b Parker | 7 |
| W. F. Price c Goddard b Parker | 6 | – not out | 8 |
| B 1, l-b 2 | 3 | B 10, l-b 2 | 12 |
| | **134** | | **142** |

### Gloucestershire

| | | | |
|---|---:|---|---:|
| A. E. Dipper c Price b Durston | 11 | – b Haig | 6 |
| R. A. Sinfield b Haig | 13 | – not out | 10 |
| Mr B. H. Lyon lbw b Hearne | 21 | | |
| C. C. Dacre lbw b Haig | 38 | | |
| W. L. Neale b Durston | 47 | – not out | 1 |
| C. J. Barnett c Lee b Hearne | 49 | – b Haig | 21 |
| H. Smith c Guise b Haig | 13 | | |
| P. H. Stephens not out | 4 | | |
| R. G. Ford b Haig | 0 | | |
| C. Parker b Haig | 0 | | |
| T. W. Goddard b Haig | 24 | | |
| B 9, l-b 3, w 1 | 13 | B 3, l-b 3 | 6 |
| | **233** | | **44** |

### Gloucestershire Bowling

| | Overs | Mdns | Runs | Wkts | Overs | Mdns | Runs | Wkts |
|---|---|---|---|---|---|---|---|---|
| Sinfield | 19 | 9 | 35 | 2 | 4 | 2 | 4 | — |
| Barnett | 5 | — | 21 | — | 11 | 2 | 27 | — |
| Goddard | 12 | 3 | 26 | — | 13 | 2 | 39 | 2 |
| Parker | 26 | 11 | 49 | 8 | 22.1 | 5 | 60 | 8 |

**Middlesex Bowling**

| | Overs | Mdns | Runs | Wkts | Overs | Mdns | Runs | Wkts |
|---|---|---|---|---|---|---|---|---|
| Haig . . . . . . . . . . . . . | 28.2 | 12 | 62 | 6 | 9 | 4 | 15 | 2 |
| Durston . . . . . . . . . . | 20 | 5 | 80 | 2 | 5 | 1 | 21 | — |
| Hearne . . . . . . . . . . . | 16 | 2 | 50 | 2 | | | | |
| Russell . . . . . . . . . . | 6 | — | 12 | — | | | | |
| Lee . . . . . . . . . . . . . | 9 | 1 | 16 | — | | | | |
| Hulme . . . . . . . . . . | | | | | 3.5 | 2 | 2 | — |

Umpires: J. Stone and A. E. Street.

## GLOUCESTERSHIRE v SOMERSET

### Played at Bristol, May 27, 28, 29, 1931

Dismissing Somerset for 31, Gloucestershire enjoyed the distinction of disposing of a side for the smallest total recorded in a first-class match all through the season but with that achievement they had to rest content, adverse weather destroying all chance of bringing the contest to a definite issue. Somerset made a capital start, White bowling to such purpose that at lunch time on the opening day, despite a first wicket stand of 48, there were four men out for 81. Afterwards, while Neale batted stolidly, Dacre hit away so brilliantly that by powerful driving, he made 64 in seventy minutes. Backing up, Neale was out in curious fashion, Dacre driving hard back to White a ball which, with Neale out of his ground, White happened to turn on to the stumps. Rain stopped play at four o'clock with the total 207 for seven wickets. Owing to wet weather, nothing could be done on Thursday, but on Friday there came plenty of incident. To begin with Gloucestershire's innings was speedily finished off. Somerset, before a shower held up the game for 15 minutes, lost three wickets for four runs and another brief spell of play produced eight more runs and the loss of one more batsman before heavy rain delayed further progress until a quarter to four. Parker then brought about such an extraordinary collapse that after the score had reached 27 with five wickets to fall these went down for four runs. Parker and Hammond had extra-ordinary figures. Somerset followed on 183 in arrear but this time Young and Lee stayed together for an hour and directly these two men were separated further rain put an end to the match.

### Gloucestershire

| | | | | |
|---|---|---|---|---|
| A. E. Dipper b Lee . . . . . . . . . . . . . . . . . . . . . | 22 | C. J. Barnett c White b Young . . . . . . . . . . . | 38 |
| R. A. Sinfield c Earle b White . . . . . . . . . . . | 21 | E. J. Stephens c Earle b Young . . . . . . . . . . | 4 |
| W. R. Hammond c and b White . . . . . . . . . . | 11 | C. Parker not out . . . . . . . . . . . . . . . . . . . . . | 0 |
| Mr B. H. Lyon c Wellard b White . . . . . . . . | 1 | T. W. Goddard c Earle b Lee . . . . . . . . . . . . | 0 |
| W. L. Neale run out . . . . . . . . . . . . . . . . . . . | 14 | B 6, l-b 5 . . . . . . . . . . . . . . . . . . . | 11 |
| C. C. Dacre c Marshall b White . . . . . . . . . . | 64 | | |
| H. Smith c Burrough b Young . . . . . . . . . . . | 28 | | 214 |

### Somerset

| | | | |
|---|---|---|---|
| A. Young c and b Hammond | 2 | – lbw b Parker | 19 |
| Mr R. A. Ingle c and b Sinfield | 0 | – c Smith b Parker | 2 |
| J. W. Lee c Stephens b Parker | 14 | – not out | 9 |
| Mr L. P. Marshall b Hammond | 0 | | |
| Mr J. C. White c Smith b Hammond | 1 | | |
| Mr C. C. Case c Hammond b Parker | 7 | | |
| Mr G. F. Earle c Sinfield b Parker | 3 | | |
| A. W. Wellard c Goddard b Parker | 0 | | |
| Mr H. D. Burrough c Smith b Parker | 0 | | |
| C. K. Linney b Hammond | 0 | | |
| F. Pratten not out | 0 | | |
| L-b 3, n-b 1 | 4 | L-b 5, n-b 1 | 6 |
| | **31** | | **36** |

### Somerset Bowling

| | Overs | Mdns | Runs | Wkts |
|---|---|---|---|---|
| Wellard | 17 | 3 | 36 | — |
| Lee | 30.1 | 16 | 40 | 2 |
| White | 36 | 9 | 112 | 4 |
| Young | 11 | 4 | 15 | 3 |

### Gloucestershire Bowling

| | Overs | Mdns | Runs | Wkts | Overs | Mdns | Runs | Wkts |
|---|---|---|---|---|---|---|---|---|
| Sinfield | 3 | 1 | 6 | 1 | 1 | — | 1 | — |
| Hammond | 15 | 8 | 10 | 4 | 6 | 2 | 13 | — |
| Parker | 12.2 | 8 | 11 | 5 | 12 | 6 | 8 | 2 |
| Goddard | | | | | 6 | 3 | 6 | — |
| Neale | | | | | 1 | — | 2 | — |

Umpires: F. Walden and G. Beet.

## GLOUCESTERSHIRE v DERBYSHIRE

### Played at Cheltenham (Victoria Ground), May 6, 7, 1931

Victorious over Surrey at The Oval in the first match on their programme, Gloucestershire followed up that rather remarkable success by winning a most exciting match with Derbyshire by four wickets. Deciding, on winning the toss, to bat despite the soft state of the ground, Derbyshire had 80 on the board when their fifth wicket fell but the other five went down in twenty-five minutes for 20 runs. Parker made the most of a favourable opportunity and was ably supported in the field. Lyon helping Hammond to put on 45, Gloucestershire looked like establishing a big advantage but Hammond was seventh out at 98 and Barnett and Parker left at the same total. Next day, despite stubborn work by Alderman and Townsend, Parker enjoyed another triumph, securing for the match a record of fourteen wickets for under 7 runs apiece. Wanting 109 to win, Gloucestershire lost five batsmen for 59 but Hammond again rose to the occasion in grand style and Neale helped him to add 45. Hammond batted for two hours and a quarter without a chance and, by exceptional skill, fairly won the match for his side.

## Derbyshire

| | | |
|---|---|---|
| H. Storer c Goddard b Parker | 24 – b Sinfield | 0 |
| D. Smith b Goddard | 12 – b Parker | 4 |
| A. E. Alderman c and b Parker | 18 – c Hammond b Parker | 29 |
| G. M. Lee c Hammond b Parker | 15 – c Lyon b Parker | 9 |
| L. Townsend b Sinfield | 2 – c Sinfield b Parker | 31 |
| Mr A. W. Richardson b Parker | 4 – lbw b Goddard | 1 |
| S. Worthington run out | 10 – b Parker | 5 |
| J. M. Hutchinson c Stephens b Sinfield | 2 – c Neale b Parker | 3 |
| A. G. Slater b Parker | 0 – lbw b Parker | 3 |
| H. Elliott c Hammond b Parker | 0 – c Sinfield b Parker | 11 |
| T. B. Mitchell not out | 0 – not out | 8 |
| B 8, l-b 5 | 13          B 5, l-b 10, w 1 | 16 |
| | 100 | 120 |

## Gloucestershire

| | | |
|---|---|---|
| A. E. Dipper c Smith b Worthington | 1 – c Elliiott b Worthington | 7 |
| R. A. Sinfield c Smith b Slater | 0 – run out | 11 |
| W. R. Hammond st Elliott b Townsend | 36 – not out | 57 |
| Mr B. H. Lyon lbw b Townsend | 29 – lbw b Mitchell | 4 |
| H. Smith c Lee b Townsend | 0 – st Elliott b Mitchell | 1 |
| C. C. Dacre b Slater | 3 – b Slater | 1 |
| W. L. Neale c Elliott b Slater | 0 – st Elliott b Mitchell | 21 |
| C. J. Barnett b Worthington | 26 – not out | 3 |
| E. J. Stephens not out | 0 | |
| C. Parker b Worthington | 0 | |
| T. W. Goddard b Worthington | 14 | |
| L-b 2, w 1 | 3          B 2, l-b 3, n-b 1 | 6 |
| | 112 | 111 |

### Gloucestershire Bowling

| | Overs | Mdns | Runs | Wkts | Overs | Mdns | Runs | Wkts |
|---|---|---|---|---|---|---|---|---|
| Sinfield | 14.5 | 5 | 14 | 2 | 9 | 2 | 19 | 1 |
| Hammond | 1 | — | 6 | — | 2 | — | 5 | — |
| Goddard | 16 | 7 | 26 | 1 | 33 | 18 | 30 | 1 |
| Parker | 28 | 11 | 41 | 6 | 34.4 | 18 | 50 | 8 |
| Barnett | | | | | 2 | 2 | — | — |

### Derbyshire Bowling

| | Overs | Mdns | Runs | Wkts | Overs | Mdns | Runs | Wkts |
|---|---|---|---|---|---|---|---|---|
| Slater | 15 | 2 | 49 | 3 | 13 | 3 | 19 | 1 |
| Worthington | 10.3 | 3 | 25 | 4 | 13 | 1 | 28 | 1 |
| Mitchell | 3 | — | 16 | — | 16.5 | 3 | 37 | 3 |
| Townsend | 12 | 4 | 19 | 3 | 17 | 9 | 21 | — |

Umpires: F. Field and T. Oates.

## GLOUCESTERSHIRE v NOTTINGHAMSHIRE

Played at Bristol, May 9, 11, 1931

Again in splendid form, Parker and Hammond played a big part in what was Gloucestershire's third victory in six days, the west country team beating Nottinghamshire by an innings and 131 runs. In this way Gloucestershire made such a rare beginning to their Championship programme that at the end of three engagements they had 45 points to their credit. Parker excelled himself. The turf, if a little soft on the top at the start, did not really assist the bowler, the ball coming off the pitch too slowly to place batsmen at a pronounced disadvantage, but, getting on a lot of spin and developing a most deceptive flight, Parker had practically all his opponents in trouble. In the first innings he actually took eight wickets for 39 and following up that achievement with seven for 74 in the second, he came out with the wonderful record of fifteen wickets for 113 runs. At the end of the match he had no fewer than forty wickets to show for his labours in three games, at a cost of less than 9 runs apiece. Hammond, going in first wicket down at 11, assisted Dipper to put on 118 runs and went on to put together his first hundred of the season. The famous batsman gave only one chance – a difficult one when 56 – in a masterly display. Smith and Neale, playing sound cricket, put on 90 for the sixth wicket. Nottinghamshire at their first attempt were all out in less than two hours. In their second innings Arthur Staples hit up 44 out of 56 with six 4s among his strokes.

## Nottinghamshire

| | | | |
|---|---:|---|---:|
| R. Lilley b Goddard | 10 | – c Stephens b Parker | 8 |
| A. Staples b Parker | 9 | – c Stephens b Parker | 44 |
| W. Walker st Smith b Parker | 18 | – b Goddard | 3 |
| H. Larwood b Parker | 0 | – b Goddard | 9 |
| W. Voce c Dacre b Parker | 22 | – c Lyon b Parker | 14 |
| J. Hardstaff c Lyon b Parker | 11 | – b Parker | 7 |
| Mr S. D. Rhodes st Smith b Parker | 2 | – not out | 18 |
| Mr A. W. Carr c Smith b Goddard | 15 | – c Barnett b Goddard | 0 |
| F. W. Shipston not out | 9 | – lbw b Parker | 2 |
| F. Barratt c Barnett b Parker | 5 | – c Neale b Parker | 25 |
| S. J. Staples c Hammond b Parker | 10 | – b Parker | 0 |
| B 2, l-b 1 | 3 | L-b 1 | 1 |
| | **114** | | **131** |

## Gloucestershire

| | | | |
|---|---:|---|---:|
| A. E. Dipper lbw b S. J. Staples | 65 | C. J. Barnett lbw b Larwood | 15 |
| R. A. Sinfield c Lilley b Larwood | 4 | E. J. Stephens not out | 11 |
| W. R. Hammond c Lilley b Larwood | 103 | T. W. Goddard b S. J. Staples | 3 |
| Mr B. H. Lyon c and b S. J. Staples | 7 | C. Parker run out | 14 |
| H. Smith c and b S. J. Staples | 63 | B 9, l-b 6, n-b 6 | 21 |
| C. C. Dacre c Lilley b Barratt | 21 | | |
| W. L. Neale lbw b Barratt | 49 | | **376** |

## Gloucestershire Bowling

| | Overs | Mdns | Runs | Wkts | Overs | Mdns | Runs | Wkts |
|---|---|---|---|---|---|---|---|---|
| Sinfield | 2 | — | 7 | — | 4 | 3 | 4 | — |
| Hammond | 3 | 1 | 10 | — | | | | |
| Parker | 17.2 | 4 | 39 | 8 | 21.1 | 4 | 74 | 7 |
| Goddard | 16 | 5 | 55 | 2 | 20 | 7 | 50 | 3 |
| Barnett | | | | | 2 | — | 2 | — |

## Nottinghamshire Bowling

| | Overs | Mdns | Runs | Wkts |
|---|---|---|---|---|
| Larwood | 22 | 3 | 61 | 3 |
| Barratt | 14 | 1 | 38 | 2 |
| Voce | 32 | 4 | 84 | — |
| S. J. Staples | 46.2 | 9 | 113 | 4 |
| A. Staples | 26 | 5 | 59 | — |

Umpires: F. Field and F. J. Smith.

# GLOUCESTERSHIRE v WARWICKSHIRE

## Played at Bristol, August 23, 24, 25, 1933

Defeat by 180 runs followed five consecutive wins by Gloucestershire. Goddard's absence, owing to illness, weakened their attack and every member of the side bowled during Warwickshire's first innings. Bates, who made a hundred, and Wyatt added 149 for the third wicket. Gloucestershire, thanks to a sound effort by Hammond, saved the follow-on. A free innings by Bates, who in the match scored 204, enabled Warwickshire to declare and set their opponents 293 to get. Injury prevented Sinfield batting, and Hollies and Payne speedily forced a victory.

### Warwickshire

| | | | |
|---|---|---|---|
| A. J. Croom lbw b Sinfield | 13 | – c Barnett b Hammond | 22 |
| N. Kilner c and b Lyon | 60 | – b G. W. Parker | 48 |
| L. A. Bates c Barnett b Sinfield | 124 | – c Hammond b Lyon | 80 |
| Mr R. E. S. Wyatt hit wkt b C. Parker | 72 | – c Neale b C. Parker | 7 |
| F. R. Santall c Allen b Sinfield | 33 | – not out | 9 |
| T. Collin b Sinfield | 5 | – c Dacre b Lyon | 5 |
| J. Smart c Barnett b C. Parker | 10 | – c G. W. Parker b C. Parker | 0 |
| W. A. Hill c Barnett b Sinfield | 15 | | |
| G. Paine b Sinfield | 18 | | |
| J. H. Mayer c Seabrook b Sinfield | 2 | | |
| E. Hollies not out | 0 | | |
| L-b 3 | 3 | B 3, l-b 6, n-b 1 | 10 |
| | **355** | **(6 wkts dec.)** | **181** |

### Gloucestershire

| | | | |
|---|---|---|---|
| C. J. Barnett lbw b Hollies | 37 | – c and b Paine | 8 |
| R. A. Sinfield c Smart b Wyatt | 11 | – absent hurt | 0 |
| W. R. Hammond lbw b Paine | 89 | – c Santall b Hollies | 19 |
| Mr B. H. Lyon b Hollies | 0 | – b Paine | 7 |
| Mr F. J. Seabrook c Smart b Croom | 17 | – b Paine | 0 |
| Mr B. O. Allen c Mayer b Croom | 0 | – b Mayer | 32 |
| C. C. Dacre lbw b Paine | 23 | – lbw b Hollies | 13 |
| Mr G. W. Parker c Bates b Paine | 10 | – c Santall b Hollies | 9 |
| W. L. Neale st Smart b Paine | 12 | – c Santall b Hollies | 0 |
| Mr P. I. Van der Gucht not out | 22 | – not out | 15 |
| C. Parker lbw b Wyatt | 15 | – st Smart b Paine | 3 |
| B 4, l-b 4 | 8 | B 4, l-b 2 | 6 |
| | **244** | | **112** |

### Gloucestershire Bowling

| | Overs | Mdns | Runs | Wkts | Overs | Mdns | Runs | Wkts |
|---|---|---|---|---|---|---|---|---|
| Hammond | 11 | 1 | 42 | — | 12 | — | 62 | 1 |
| Barnett | 2 | 2 | — | — | | | | |
| C. Parker | 58 | 22 | 111 | 2 | 22.2 | 5 | 60 | 2 |
| G. W. Parker | 8 | 3 | 13 | — | 2 | — | 12 | 1 |
| Sinfield | 63.5 | 26 | 98 | 7 | 7 | 3 | 13 | — |
| Neale | 6 | — | 38 | — | | | | |
| Lyon | 8 | 2 | 23 | 1 | 7 | 1 | 24 | 2 |
| Dacre | 5 | 2 | 15 | — | | | | |
| Seabrook | 1 | — | 5 | — | | | | |
| Allen | 1 | — | 2 | — | | | | |
| Van der Gucht | 1 | — | 5 | — | | | | |

**Warwickshire Bowling**

|  | Overs | Mdns | Runs | Wkts | Overs | Mdns | Runs | Wkts |
|---|---|---|---|---|---|---|---|---|
| Mayer ........... | 5 | 1 | 18 | — | 6 | 2 | 14 | 1 |
| Wyatt ........... | 15.5 | 7 | 31 | 2 | 3 | 1 | 9 | — |
| Hollies .......... | 41 | 16 | 78 | 2 | 16 | 3 | 47 | 4 |
| Paine ........... | 31 | 8 | 94 | 4 | 16.5 | 9 | 31 | 4 |
| Croom .......... | 3 | — | 7 | 2 | 2 | — | 5 | — |
| Collin ........... | 2 | 1 | 8 | — |  |  |  |  |

Umpires: H. G. Baldwin and A. Morton.

## GLOUCESTERSHIRE v SOMERSET

### Played at Bristol, May 26, 28, 29, 1934

A remarkable match in which the fortunes of the sides fluctuated to an unusual degree ended in a fine win for Somerset by 39 runs. Following the drought, the pitch was rough in parts and on Saturday Somerset owed much to Wellard and Frank Lee. Lee batted stubbornly and Longrigg helped him in a third wicket stand of 64, while Wellard hit with vigour. That Gloucestershire established a lead of 50 on Monday was largely due to a splendid partnership of 133 for the sixth wicket between Page and Neale. Page, missed when 37, batted brilliantly, making 56 of his runs by boundary strokes. Then, on a crumbling pitch, Parker and Goddard gained such a mastery that Somerset lost seven batsmen for 37, but Case and Bennett pulled the game round in an eighth stand of 125. Case scored readily off good-length bowling, at times hitting very hard. Gloucestershire, against an accurate attack, never seemed likely to score 143 runs to win, especially when they lost half their wickets for 30.

**Somerset**

| | | | |
|---|---|---|---|
| J. W. Lee c Hopkins b Barnett .................. | 0 | – c Dacre b Goddard ............. | 14 |
| F. S. Lee c Hopkins b Goddard .................. | 46 | – b Goddard ................... | 3 |
| Mr R. A. Ingle lbw b Sinfield ................... | 18 | – st Hopkins b Parker ........... | 0 |
| Mr E. F. Longrigg c Goddard b Cranfield ........ | 32 | – c Cranfield b Goddard .......... | 1 |
| Mr C. C. Case b Goddard ...................... | 21 | – not out ...................... | 106 |
| Mr L. Hawkins c Goddard b Cranfield ........... | 23 | – b Goddard ................... | 0 |
| A. W. Wellard c Barnett b Sinfield ............. | 47 | – c Lyon b Parker ............... | 0 |
| Mr J. C. White c Dacre b Goddard ............. | 21 | – c Goddard b Parker ........... | 6 |
| Mr G. M. Bennett b Goddard .................. | 4 | – c Cranfield b Goddard ......... | 54 |
| W. T. Luckes c Neale b Lyon ................. | 5 | – b Goddard ................... | 1 |
| H. T. F. Buse not out ...................... | 3 | – c Allen b Goddard ............. | 0 |
| B 4, l-b 1 ........................ | 5 | L-b 6, n-b 1 ............. | 7 |
| | **225** | | **192** |

**Gloucestershire**

| | | | |
|---|---|---|---|
| C. J. Barnett c Wellard b White ................. | 22 | – c Hawkins b J. W. Lee ......... | 13 |
| R. A. Sinfield c Hawkins b White .............. | 33 | – b J. W. Lee .................. | 10 |
| Mr B. H. Lyon b J. W. Lee .................... | 19 | – c Buse b J. W. Lee ........... | 7 |
| Mr B. O. Allen c Buse b White ................ | 11 | – c and b White ................ | 0 |
| C. C. Dacre c Ingle b J. W. Lee .............. | 9 | – b J. W. Lee ................. | 0 |
| Mr D. A. C. Page lbw b White ................ | 83 | – c and b White ............... | 11 |
| W. L. Neale st Luckes b J. W. Lee ............. | 49 | – b J. W. Lee b White ......... | 39 |
| V. Hopkins c Wellard b White ................. | 8 | – b J. W. Lee ................. | 0 |
| M. Cranfield st Luckes b J. W. Lee ............ | 5 | – not out ..................... | 16 |
| C. W. L. Parker c Bennett b White ............ | 20 | – lbw b White ................. | 2 |
| T. W. Goddard not out ...................... | 6 | – c F. S. Lee b White .......... | 4 |
| B 4, l-b 2, n-b 4 ..................... | 10 | L-b 1 .................. | 1 |
| | **275** | | **103** |

## Gloucestershire Bowling

|            | Overs | Mdns | Runs | Wkts | Overs | Mdns | Runs | Wkts |
|------------|-------|------|------|------|-------|------|------|------|
| Barnett    | 12    | 3    | 21   | 1    |       |      |      |      |
| Sinfield   | 23    | 6    | 48   | 2    | 6     | —    | 22   | —    |
| Parker     | 8     | 2    | 19   | —    | 25    | 5    | 82   | 3    |
| Goddard    | 26.4  | 10   | 54   | 4    | 30    | 6    | 71   | 7    |
| Cranfield  | 16    | 1    | 74   | 2    | 3     | 1    | 10   | —    |
| Lyon       | 2     | —    | 4    | 1    |       |      |      |      |

## Somerset Bowling

|          | Overs | Mdns | Runs | Wkts | Overs | Mdns | Runs | Wkts |
|----------|-------|------|------|------|-------|------|------|------|
| Wellard  | 9     | 1    | 42   | —    |       |      |      |      |
| Buse     | 8     | 1    | 26   | —    |       |      |      |      |
| White    | 40    | 15   | 96   | 6    | 26.1  | 10   | 40   | 5    |
| J. W. Lee| 37    | 10   | 101  | 4    | 27    | 10   | 62   | 5    |

Umpires: H. G. Baldwin and J. Stone.

# GLOUCESTERSHIRE v GLAMORGAN

### Played at Bristol, August 8, 9, 10, 1934

Remarkable forcing cricket by Barnett and a brilliant innings by Hammond overshadowed everything else in this match which, owing to rain, failed to produce even a decision on the first innings. Barnett's display was little short of amazing. He began hitting before he had been in long enough to get a good sight of the ball, and punished the bowlers mercilessly, reaching his fourth hundred of the summer out of 141 in an hour and fifty minutes. He left at 179, having hit six 6s in his 123. This was easily one of the best efforts of his career and, despite the powerful nature of his batting, he rarely misplaced a stroke. Hammond, by contrast, took pains to play himself in but, once set, he brought into use all his skill in off-side strokes and completed his highest score for the county. Lyon helped to add 103 and Page stayed with him while 142 runs came in eighty-five minutes. On Thursday, Hammond, for the fourth time during the summer, reached 200 and he obtained 92 of the last 135 runs added before Lyon declared. His only mistake was at 224 and he hit three 6s and thirty 4s. Davies and Turnbull, both playing well, saved Glamorgan, and on Friday only two hours' cricket was possible.

## Gloucestershire

| | | |
|---|---|---|
| C. J. Barnett c and b Smart | 123 | |
| Mr G. W. Parker b Smart | 15 | |
| W. R. Hammond not out | 302 | |
| Mr B. H. Lyon b Smart | 24 | |
| R. A. Sinfield c and b Smart | 0 | |
| Mr B. O. Allen c Smart b Lavis | 8 | |
| Mr D. A. C. Page b Morgan | 61 | |
| W. I. Neale not out | 41 | |
| B 22, l-b 7 | 29 | |
| (6 wkts dec.) 603 | | |

C. W. L. Parker, T. W. Goddard and V. Hopkins did not bat.

## Glamorgan

| | | |
|---|---|---|
| A. H. Dyson lbw b Goddard | 28 | |
| E. Davies b Goddard | 127 | |
| R. Duckfield st Hopkins b C. Parker | 11 | |
| Mr M. J. Turnbull b Goddard | 97 | |
| G. Lavis hit wkt b Sinfield | 15 | |
| C. Smart not out | 11 | |
| Mr. G. Morgan not out | 10 | |
| B 18, l-b 6, n-b 1 | 25 | |
| 324 | | |

Mr C. V. G. Jenkins, T. L. Brierley, J. Mercer and G. Reed did not bat.

## Glamorgan Bowling

|        | Overs | Mdns | Runs | Wkts |
|--------|-------|------|------|------|
| Mercer | 27    | 3    | 101  | —    |
| Reed   | 19.4  | 1    | 113  | —    |
| Davies | 22    | 1    | 77   | —    |
| Lavis  | 32    | 6    | 81   | 1    |
| Smart  | 30    | 2    | 150  | 4    |
| Morgan | 9     | —    | 52   | 1    |

## Gloucestershire Bowling

|            | Overs | Mdns | Runs | Wkts |
|------------|-------|------|------|------|
| C. Parker  | 35    | 15   | 81   | 1    |
| Goddard    | 46    | 13   | 69   | 3    |
| G. W. Parker | 2   | —    | 6    | —    |
| Sinfield   | 24    | 8    | 42   | 1    |
| Lyon       | 8     | 2    | 25   | —    |
| Neale      | 9     | 1    | 47   | —    |
| Hammond    | 11.4  | 4    | 29   | —    |

Umpires: J. Newman and J. W. Hitch.

# GLOUCESTERSHIRE v NOTTINGHAMSHIRE

## T. W. Goddard's Benefit Match

### Played at Gloucester, August 29, 31, September 1, 1936

Gloucestershire won by an innings and 70 runs. Thanks to Hammond the county finished the season in great style. He was in really wonderful form and putting together an innings of 317 beat his previous best score in England and surpassed the aggregate of 1,278 runs in August set up by W. G. Grace. Hammond's mastery of the Nottinghamshire bowlers and his phenomenal powers of endurance were shown by the fact that after batting five hours for his first two hundred runs he hit the third hundred in just over seventy minutes. In this last stage he cast aside all restraint and exploited his superb off-drive in devastating fashion. Altogether, Hammond batted close on six and a half hours and in all that time made one false stroke. That occurred at 111 when he almost played on. He hit three 6s and thirty-four 4s. Neale, Crapp and Hopkins aided him admirably in stands of 164, 83 and 133 respectively. Staples proved Nottinghamshire's best batsman. Hardstaff in the first innings supported him in a partnership of 76, and Harris and Staples scored 71 together on the last day when Hammond, owing to a badly bruised instep, could not play. The second day's attendance of 7,000 was the largest ever seen on the ground.

## Nottinghamshire

| | | | |
|---|---|---|---|
| W. W. Keeton b Stephens | 35 | – lbw b Cranfield | 20 |
| C. B. Harris b Hammond | 6 | – c sub b Stephens | 50 |
| W. Walker c Barnett b Goddard | 6 | – b Cranfield | 9 |
| J. Hardstaff c Hopkins b Stephens | 46 | – b Cranfield | 0 |
| G. V. Gunn b Goddard | 5 | – b Goddard | 12 |
| A. Staples c Goddard b Cranfield | 58 | – c Allen b Cranfield | 52 |
| Mr G. F. Heane c Page b Cranfield | 11 | – c Barnett b Stephens | 18 |
| W. Voce b Cranfield | 25 | – b Barnett | 23 |
| F. G. Woodhead not out | 6 | – c Stephens b Barnett | 0 |
| A. B. Wheat c Stephens b Goddard | 1 | – c Page b Barnett | 24 |
| H. J. Butler lbw b Goddard | 0 | – not out | 3 |
| L-b 1 | 1 | B 3, l-b 1 | 4 |
| | **200** | | **215** |

## Gloucestershire

| | |
|---|---|
| C. J. Barnett b Voce | 2 |
| R. W. Haynes c Staples b Voce | 18 |
| Mr B. O. Allen c Staples b Butler | 18 |
| W. R. Hammond b Woodhead | 317 |
| W. L. Neale c Heane b Butler | 66 |
| J. F. Crapp c Woodhead b Gunn | 22 |
| Mr D. A. C. Page lbw b Heane | 8 |
| E. J. Stephens b Voce | 0 |
| T. W. Goddard b Heane | 1 |
| V. J. Hopkins not out | 25 |
| M. Cranfield c Wheat b Staples | 0 |
| B 6, l-b 1, n-b 1 | 8 |
| | 485 |

### Gloucestershire Bowling

| | Overs | Mdns | Runs | Wkts | Overs | Mdns | Runs | Wkts |
|---|---|---|---|---|---|---|---|---|
| Hammond | 7 | — | 21 | 1 | | | | |
| Barnett | 13 | 3 | 51 | — | 11.3 | 2 | 25 | 3 |
| Goddard | 28.1 | 9 | 49 | 4 | 25 | 6 | 71 | 1 |
| Stephens | 11 | — | 27 | 2 | 8 | 1 | 32 | 2 |
| Cranfield | 23 | 6 | 51 | 3 | 33 | 11 | 71 | 4 |
| Haynes | | | | | 6 | 1 | 12 | — |

### Nottinghamshire Bowling

| | Overs | Mdns | Runs | Wkts |
|---|---|---|---|---|
| Voce | 31 | 2 | 117 | 3 |
| Butler | 31 | 5 | 79 | 2 |
| Woodhead | 24 | 3 | 86 | 1 |
| Staples | 17.4 | 2 | 69 | 1 |
| Gunn | 19 | 3 | 53 | 1 |
| Heane | 28 | 5 | 73 | 2 |

Umpires: W. A. Buswell and G. Brown.

## GLOUCESTERSHIRE v WORCESTERSHIRE

Played at Cheltenham, August 7, 9, 10, 1937

Gloucestershire won by three wickets. The match was notable for the feat of Goddard, who took all ten wickets in an innings for the first time in his career, and some brilliant batting on a wearing pitch by Hammond and Allen. Goddard perplexed the Worcestershire men with his cleverly flighted off-spin bowling, and only Bull, Kimpton and Gibbons appeared to have his measure. The magnificent stand between Hammond and his captain lasted over four hours and assured their side of success. They came together on the second evening when Gloucestershire, needing 317 for victory, had lost two wickets for 15, and were not separated until the score stood at 284. Their batting was the more remarkable seeing that spin bowlers were able to turn the ball sharply. Hammond's thirteenth three-figure score of the season included nineteen 4s.

## Worcestershire

| | | | |
|---|---|---|---|
| C. H. Bull st Watkins b Goddard | 81 | – st Watkins b Goddard | 24 |
| S. Buller b Lyon | 26 | – c Hammond b Goddard | 12 |
| E. Cooper c Lyon b Neale | 32 | – b Goddard | 18 |
| H. H. Gibbons b Goddard | 36 | – not out | 72 |
| Mr R. H. C. Human c Barnett b Goddard | 10 | – c Allen b Goddard | 9 |
| S. H. Martin hit wkt b Scott | 8 | – c Hammond b Goddard | 4 |
| Mr B. W. Quaife b Goddard | 7 | – b Goddard | 4 |
| Mr R. C. M. Kimpton b Sinfield | 92 | – c Parker b Goddard | 6 |
| R. Howorth c Parker b Goddard | 6 | – c Parker b Goddard | 4 |
| R. T. D. Perks b Goddard | 6 | – c Crapp b Goddard | 33 |
| P. F. Jackson not out | 2 | – c Crapp b Goddard | 3 |
| B 3, l-b 1 | 4 | B 6, l-b 7 | 13 |
| | 310 | | 202 |

## Gloucestershire

| | | | | | |
|---|---|---|---|---|---|
| C. J. Barnett lbw (N) b Jackson | 35 | – c Human b Perks | 9 |
| Mr G. W. Parker b Howorth | 24 | – lbw b Jackson | 5 |
| Mr B. O. Allen c Buller b Martin | 33 | – st Buller b Jackson | 78 |
| W. R. Hammond c and b Howorth | 5 | – c Martin b Howorth | 178 |
| J. F. Crapp b Jackson | 31 | – b Jackson | 13 |
| Mr E. K. Scott c Kimpton b Howorth | 0 | | |
| R. A. Sinfield c Kimpton b Martin | 19 | – not out | 6 |
| Mr B. H. Lyon c Gibbons b Howorth | 3 | – b Perks | 2 |
| W. L. Neale not out | 27 | – b Jackson | 1 |
| T. W. Goddard c Perks b Martin | 4 | – not out | 0 |
| B. L. Watkins b Jackson | 2 | | |
| B 8, l-b 5 | 13 | B 11, l-b 12, n-b 2 | 25 |
| | **196** | | **317** |

### Gloucestershire Bowling

| | Overs | Mdns | Runs | Wkts | Overs | Mdns | Runs | Wkts |
|---|---|---|---|---|---|---|---|---|
| Barnett | 5 | 1 | 16 | — | 2 | 1 | 5 | — |
| Parker | 6 | 1 | 21 | — | | | | |
| Lyon | 8 | 3 | 24 | 1 | 2 | — | 9 | — |
| Scott | 19 | 5 | 42 | 1 | 3 | — | 8 | — |
| Sinfield | 24.2 | 5 | 82 | 1 | 25 | 7 | 54 | — |
| Neale | 11 | 2 | 53 | 1 | | | | |
| Goddard | 18 | 4 | 68 | 6 | 28.4 | 4 | 113 | 10 |

### Worcestershire Bowling

| | Overs | Mdns | Runs | Wkts | Overs | Mdns | Runs | Wkts |
|---|---|---|---|---|---|---|---|---|
| Perks | 6 | 1 | 14 | — | 19 | 4 | 52 | 2 |
| Martin | 7 | 1 | 24 | 3 | 25 | 4 | 67 | — |
| Human | 3 | — | 5 | — | | | | |
| Howorth | 22 | 4 | 70 | 4 | 26.4 | 4 | 76 | 1 |
| Jackson | 24.5 | 5 | 70 | 3 | 30 | 4 | 92 | 4 |
| Kimpton | | | | | 1 | — | 5 | — |

Umpires: G. M. Lee and F. Walden.

# GLOUCESTERSHIRE v ESSEX

Played at Gloucester, August 31, September 1, 2, 1938

Essex won by an innings and 65 runs. The game was a triumph for Nichols, who besides scoring 159 took fifteen wickets for 11 runs apiece. Avery and O'Connor by sound and enterprising batting laid the foundations of a big Essex total and Nichols and Pearce consolidated the position by hard accurate driving. Nichols's fast bowling was more impressive than his batting. Even Hammond could not properly time him off the pitch and was out twice on the second afternoon to Nichols who took nine wickets in the first innings for 37 runs – five in five overs for 6 runs. Barnett stood up manfully to the fast attack, and when Gloucestershire followed on 456 behind he gave another grand exhibition of powerful driving. He made light of an injury which caused his retirement for a time and reached the century in two hours. Crapp also hit splendidly and helped Barnett in a fifth wicket stand of 159 but the bowling of Nichols eventually earned reward.

## Essex

| | | |
|---|---|---|
| L. C. Eastman c Goddard b Emmett | ...... | 22 |
| A. V. Avery c Allen b Barnett | .......... | 138 |
| R. M. Taylor c Hammond b Sinfield | ...... | 9 |
| J. O'Connor lbw b Barnett | .............. | 83 |
| M. S. Nichols b Sinfield | ................ | 159 |
| Mr T. N. Pearce c Wilson b Barnett | ....... | 71 |
| P. Smith c Hammond b Goddard | ........ | 34 |
| Dr N. Vere Hodge c Wilson b Goddard | .... | 8 |
| R. Smith c Allen b Goddard | ............. | 4 |
| T. H. Wade not out | ................... | 10 |
| Mr K. Farnes c Crapp b Goddard | ........ | 0 |
| B 5, l-b 10 | ................... | 15 |
| | | — |
| | | 553 |

## Gloucestershire

| | | |
|---|---|---|
| C. J. Barnett c Taylor b Nichols | ................. | 43 – lbw b Nichols ................. 151 |
| V. Hopkins lbw b Nichols | .................... | 5 – c P. Smith b Nichols ............ 1 |
| Mr B. O. Allen c Wade b Farnes | ................. | 0 – c Pearce b Eastman ............. 28 |
| Mr W. R. Hammond b Nichols | ................. | 4 – lbw b Nichols ................. 2 |
| W. L. Neale b Nichols | ..................... | 5 – c Taylor b Nichols ............. 2 |
| J. F. Crapp b Nichols | ...................... | 5 – c Wade b Farnes .............. 89 |
| G. M. Emmett b Nichols | ................... | 15 – c Pearce b Nichols ........... 39 |
| E. A. Wilson lbw b Nichols | ................. | 0 – c Wade b Farnes ............. 48 |
| R. A. Sinfield not out | ..................... | 11 – c Taylor b Farnes ............. 6 |
| T. W. Goddard c and b Nichols | ............. | 2 – not out .................... 8 |
| C. J. Scott b Nichols | ...................... | 0 – b Nichols .................... 2 |
| B 4, l-b 2, n-b 1 | ..................... | 7       B 2, l-b 12, n-b 1 ......... 15 |
| | | — — |
| | | 97       391 |

## Gloucestershire Bowling

| | Overs | Mdns | Runs | Wkts |
|---|---|---|---|---|
| Hammond ........ | 7 | 2 | 22 | — |
| Barnett ........... | 19 | — | 71 | 3 |
| Scott ............ | 20 | — | 106 | — |
| Sinfield ........... | 40 | 9 | 96 | 2 |
| Goddard ......... | 43.3 | 9 | 127 | 4 |
| Emmett .......... | 28 | 2 | 99 | 1 |
| Neale ............ | 3 | — | 17 | — |

## Essex Bowling

| | Overs | Mdns | Runs | Wkts | Overs | Mdns | Runs | Wkts |
|---|---|---|---|---|---|---|---|---|
| Farnes ........... | 12 | 1 | 44 | 1 | 27 | 2 | 90 | 3 |
| Nichols .......... | 15.2 | 3 | 37 | 9 | 30.1 | 2 | 128 | 6 |
| R. Smith .......... | 4 | — | 9 | — | 5 | — | 39 | — |
| P. Smith .......... | | | | | 13 | 1 | 62 | — |
| Eastman .......... | | | | | 12 | 2 | 27 | 1 |
| Taylor ........... | | | | | 3 | — | 30 | — |
| Pearce ........... | | | | | 1 | 1 | — | — |

Umpires: J. Smart and N. Kilner.

## GLOUCESTERSHIRE v SUSSEX

### R. A. Sinfield's Benefit Match

### Played at Gloucester, September 3, 5, 6, 1938

Sussex won by seven wickets. Their success was the more meritorious seeing they avoided the follow-on by only three runs. Hammond punished their bowling severely on the first day when he recorded his 100th century for Gloucestershire during an innings notable for its graceful strokes and perfection of timing. Barnett, Neale, Crapp and Emmett were others to show to advantage. A third wicket stand of 186 by J. H. Parks and Cox saved Sussex from cheap dismissal in their first innings but Gloucestershire led by 147 and after brisk hitting on the last morning they declared. Allen's challenge left Sussex the task of making 304 runs in four hours, and this they accomplished in first-rate fashion. They were chiefly indebted to H. W. Parks and A. J. Holmes who hit so freely that in an unfinished fourth wicket partnership of less than an hour and a half they knocked off the last 152 runs. Holmes played an especially creditable innings for owing to a strained leg he was forced to employ a runner.

### Gloucestershire

| | | |
|---|---|---|
| C. J. Barnett c Holmes b Jas. Langridge | 63 | – c Nye b J. Cornford ............ 47 |
| V. Hopkins c W. Cornford b Wood | 28 | – lbw b J. Cornford ............. 15 |
| Mr B. O. Allen lbw b Oakes | 32 | – c John Langridge b Nye ........ 47 |
| Mr W. R. Hammond lbw b J. Cornford | 116 | – c J. Parks b Jas. Langridge .... 31 |
| W. L. Neale b Jas. Langridge | 54 | – not out ..................... 11 |
| J. F. Crapp b Nye | 65 | – c J. Parks b Nye ............. 0 |
| G. M. Emmett c Jas. Langridge b J. Parks | 88 | – not out ..................... 0 |
| E. A. Wilson lbw b Holmes | 4 | |
| R. A. Sinfield lbw b J. Cornford | 16 | |
| T. W. Goddard b J. Cornford | 4 | |
| C. J. Scott not out | 4 | |
| L-b 10, w 2, n-b 2 | 14 | B 4, l-b 1 ............... 5 |
| | **488** | **(5 wkts dec.) 156** |

### Sussex

| | | |
|---|---|---|
| John Langridge b Scott | 0 | – lbw b Goddard ................ 69 |
| J. H. Parks c sub b Hammond | 118 | – lbw b Goddard ................ 28 |
| H. W. Parks c Scott b Sinfield | 18 | – not out ..................... 119 |
| G. Cox b Goddard | 102 | – b Goddard ................... 0 |
| Ft-Lt A. J. Holmes b Goddard | 36 | – not out ..................... 78 |
| C. Oakes b Barnett | 10 | |
| W. Cornford b Scott | 20 | |
| J. Nye b Scott | 13 | |
| D. J. Wood c Hopkins b Scott | 4 | |
| Jas. Langridge not out | 5 | |
| J. Cornford b Goddard | 0 | |
| B 6, l-b 5, n-b 4 | 15 | B 6, l-b 4, n-b 2 .......... 12 |
| | **341** | **306** |

### Sussex Bowling

| | Overs | Mdns | Runs | Wkts | Overs | Mdns | Runs | Wkts |
|---|---|---|---|---|---|---|---|---|
| J. Cornford | 36 | 8 | 83 | 3 | 11 | 1 | 40 | 2 |
| Nye | 29 | 3 | 101 | 1 | 4.5 | — | 30 | 2 |
| J. H. Parks | 30.5 | 12 | 94 | 1 | 4 | — | 33 | — |
| Wood | 14 | 2 | 49 | 1 | | | | |
| Jas. Langridge | 23 | 4 | 59 | 2 | 5 | — | 48 | 1 |
| Oakes | 11 | 1 | 69 | 1 | | | | |
| John Langridge | 3 | 1 | 10 | — | | | | |
| Holmes | 2 | — | 9 | 1 | | | | |

### Gloucestershire Bowling

| | Overs | Mdns | Runs | Wkts | Overs | Mdns | Runs | Wkts |
|---|---|---|---|---|---|---|---|---|
| Scott | 28 | 3 | 88 | 4 | 13 | — | 61 | — |
| Barnett | 8 | 2 | 17 | 1 | 6 | — | 20 | — |
| Hammond | 9 | — | 39 | 1 | 3 | — | 22 | — |
| Goddard | 26 | 6 | 60 | 3 | 27 | 4 | 98 | 3 |
| Sinfield | 25 | 3 | 67 | 1 | 18 | 5 | 39 | — |
| Emmett | 7 | 1 | 23 | — | 3 | — | 22 | — |
| Neale | 5 | — | 32 | — | 3 | — | 26 | — |
| Allen | | | | | 1 | — | 6 | — |

Umpires: E. Cooke and G. M. Lee

## GLOUCESTERSHIRE v KENT

### Played at Bristol, July 1, 3, 1939

Gloucestershire won by an innings and 40 runs in a match of individual triumphs. Goddard equalled a world's record by taking 17 wickets in a day, a feat previously performed only by the left-handers, Verity (Yorkshire) against Essex in 1933 and Blythe (Kent) against Northamptonshire in 1907. Counting the previous match at Bristol, against Yorkshire, Goddard claimed 30 wickets for 205 runs within six days. Even this magnificent achievement did not monopolise the honours for in the Gloucestershire innings Wright dismissed nine men for little over five runs each, finishing with a hat-trick. Hammond scored more than half the total. After a partnership of 125 with Barnett, he shielded his partners from Wright and took out his bat, having hit a 6 and nineteen 4s. He also won the toss for the thirteenth time.

### Gloucestershire

| | |
|---|---|
| C. J. Barnett lbw b Wright .............. 66 | E. A. Wilson b Wright ................. 10 |
| R. A. Sinfield c and b Longfield .......... 15 | R. W. Haynes b Wright ................ 16 |
| V. Hopkins c and b Wright ............. 2 | G. Lambert b Wright ................... 0 |
| Mr W. R. Hammond not out ............153 | T. W. Goddard lbw b Wright ........... 0 |
| J. F. Crapp c Levett b Wright ........... 4 | B 7, l-b 10, n-b 1.............. 18 |
| G. M. Emmett lbw b Wright ............ 0 | |
| W. L. Neale lbw b Wright ............. 0 | 284 |

### Kent

| | |
|---|---|
| A. Fagg b Goddard .......................... 8 | – c Hammond b Goddard ......... 33 |
| Mr F. G. H. Chalk c Neale b Goddard .......... 40 | – lbw b Sinfield ................. 21 |
| L. E. G. Ames lbw b Lambert .......... 12 | – c Haynes b Goddard ............ 16 |
| Mr B. H. Valentine c Crapp b Goddard ........... 14 | – c Hopkins b Sinfield ........... 0 |
| L. J. Todd b Goddard ................... 15 | – c Barnett b Goddard .......... 2 |
| T. Spencer b Goddard ................... 0 | – lbw b Goddard ................ 15 |
| Mr T. C. Longfield b Goddard ................... 0 | – c Emmett b Goddard ........... 14 |
| D. V. P. Wright b Goddard ................. 0 | – st Wilson b Goddard .......... 2 |
| N. W. Harding not out ................... 19 | – c Emmett b Goddard ........... 13 |
| Mr W. H. V. Levett b Goddard ................. 8 | – not out ....................... 3 |
| C. Lewis b Goddard ..................... 0 | – c Haynes b Goddard .......... 5 |
| B 2, l-b 2.......................... 4 | |
| 120 | 124 |

### Kent Bowling

| | Overs | Mdns | Runs | Wkts |
|---|---|---|---|---|
| Harding .......... | 12 | 3 | 39 | — |
| Todd ............ | 25 | 2 | 111 | — |
| Longfield ........ | 14 | 3 | 40 | 1 |
| Wright .......... | 21.5 | 8 | 47 | 9 |
| Lewis ........... | 8 | — | 29 | — |

### Gloucestershire Bowling

| | Overs | Mdns | Runs | Wkts | Overs | Mdns | Runs | Wkts |
|---|---|---|---|---|---|---|---|---|
| Barnett .......... | 2 | — | 9 | — | 1 | — | 6 | — |
| Lambert ......... | 8 | 1 | 40 | 1 | 6 | 1 | 19 | — |
| Goddard ........ | 15.4 | 2 | 38 | 9 | 16.2 | 1 | 68 | 8 |
| Sinfield ......... | 9 | 2 | 29 | — | 12 | 3 | 31 | 2 |

Umpires: H. G. Baldwin and H. Cruice.

# GLOUCESTERSHIRE v HAMPSHIRE

Played at Bristol, July 19, 20, 21, 1939

Gloucestershire won by five wickets. Hammond's astute captaincy and more great bowling by Goddard won an amazing match. Only an hour's play was possible during the first two days but on the third morning Scott and Goddard dismissed the remaining eight Hampshire batsmen for 55 runs. Gloucestershire found batting just as difficult but Hammond carried them through and declared with a lead of one run. Then Goddard set to work again and Hampshire were shot out in an hour and a quarter, leaving Gloucestershire 66 to get in 70 minutes. This was not easy against the clever spin bowling of Creese and Boyes. Hammond with 30 was top scorer in the match.

## Hampshire

| | | | | |
|---|---|---|---|---|
| N. McCorkell c Scott b Goddard | 6 | – b Goddard | 11 |
| J. Bailey c Hopkins b Goddard | 7 | – b Goddard | 10 |
| Mr J. P. Blake c Crapp b Sinfield | 28 | – b Goddard | 5 |
| J. Arnold lbw b Scott | 18 | – c Emmett b Goddard | 20 |
| D. F. Walker b Scott | 1 | – lbw b Goddard | 5 |
| W. L. Creese lbw b Sinfield | 22 | – c Eagar b Sinfield | 9 |
| A. E. Pothecary c Scott b Goddard | 0 | – st Wilson b Goddard | 0 |
| A. Mackenzie not out | 14 | – lbw b Goddard | 0 |
| Mr G. R. Taylor b Scott | 4 | – c Haynes b Goddard | 4 |
| G. S. Boyes b Scott | 0 | – c Goddard b Sinfield | 2 |
| G. E. M. Heath b Goddard | 3 | – not out | 0 |
| | **103** | | **66** |

## Gloucestershire

| | | | | |
|---|---|---|---|---|
| R. A. Sinfield c Mackenzie b Bailey | 2 | | |
| V. Hopkins b Heath | 0 | – lbw b Creese | 16 |
| G. M. Emmett b Bailey | 19 | – c Creese b Boyes | 7 |
| Mr W. R. Hammond b Bailey | 30 | – b Creese | 3 |
| J. F. Crapp c Blake b Heath | 21 | – not out | 7 |
| Mr E. D. R. Eagar c Walker b Boyes | 6 | – c Pothecary b Boyes | 8 |
| C. J. Scott not out | 15 | – not out | 5 |
| W. L. Neale not out | 8 | | |
| R. W. Haynes (did not bat) | | – b Creese | 12 |
| B 3 | 3 | B 2, l-b 6 | 8 |
| (6 wkts dec.) | **104** | | **66** |

E. A. Wilson and T. W. Goddard did not bat.

## Gloucestershire Bowling

| | Overs | Mdns | Runs | Wkts | Overs | Mdns | Runs | Wkts |
|---|---|---|---|---|---|---|---|---|
| Scott | 11 | 3 | 18 | 4 | 6 | — | 22 | — |
| Hammond | 1 | — | 6 | — | | | | |
| Goddard | 19.5 | 7 | 36 | 4 | 9 | 2 | 36 | 8 |
| Sinfield | 14 | 3 | 43 | 2 | 3.5 | — | 8 | 2 |

## Hampshire Bowling

| | Overs | Mdns | Runs | Wkts | Overs | Mdns | Runs | Wkts |
|---|---|---|---|---|---|---|---|---|
| Heath | 8.1 | — | 33 | 2 | 3 | — | 12 | — |
| Bailey | 11 | 1 | 36 | 3 | 4 | 1 | 11 | — |
| Boyes | 6 | — | 25 | 1 | 2 | — | 18 | 2 |
| Creese | 2 | — | 7 | — | 3.6 | 2 | 17 | 3 |

Umpires: H. Elliott and F. Walden

# HAMPSHIRE

## HAMPSHIRE v WARWICKSHIRE

Played at Portsmouth, August 25, 26, 27, 1920

Seen at their best at all points Hampshire gained an overwhelming victory by an innings and 159 runs. They made themselves perfectly secure on the first day, scoring 405 with only five men out. Brown and Captain Barrett divided the honours, putting on 280 runs for the second wicket. Out at 309 Barrett gave only one chance in getting his 148. Brown was batting for over four hours, and so far as could be seen did not make a mistake of any kind. The hitting was kept up next morning, Tennyson declaring immediately Mead had completed his 100. Warwickshire showed excellent batting in their first innings, but failed badly against Kennedy's bowling when they followed on.

### Hampshire

| | |
|---|---|
| G. Brown b Charlesworth | 151 |
| A. Bowell b Calthorpe | 20 |
| Capt. E. I. M. Barrett b Rotherham | 148 |
| Maj. Hon. L. H. Tennyson b Rotherham | 15 |
| Comdr. G. C. Harrison c Holdsworth b Howell | 82 |
| Mr R. Aird b Quaife | 5 |
| C. P. Mead not out | 102 |
| Mr H. C. McDonell c Holdsworth b Rotherham | 51 |
| J. Newman not out | 17 |
| B 16, l-b 6, w 3 | 25 |
| (7 wkts dec.) | 616 |

A. Kennedy and W. H. Livsey did not bat.

### Warwickshire

| | | | |
|---|---|---|---|
| Comdr. C. F. Cowan c Livsey b Mead | 78 | – c sub b Tennyson | 0 |
| L. A. Bates lbw b Kennedy | 61 | – c Brown b Kennedy | 1 |
| C. Charlesworth b Kennedy | 11 | – c Aird b Kennedy | 11 |
| W. G. Quaife b Kennedy | 1 | – b Kennedy | 33 |
| Mr R. L. Holdsworth run out | 73 | – lbw b Kennedy | 0 |
| Rev. E. F. Waddy c Brown b McDonell | 33 | – b Kennedy | 15 |
| Mr C. A. Fiddian-Green c Mead b Kennedy | 0 | – not out | 19 |
| E. J. Smith c Tennyson b Kennedy | 4 | – c Livsey b McDonell | 7 |
| Mr G. A. Rotherham lbw b Kennedy | 45 | – st Livsey b McDonell | 0 |
| Hon. F. S. G. Calthorpe not out | 14 | – c Brown b Tennyson | 13 |
| H. Howell b Tennyson | 0 | – c Aird b Kennedy | 12 |
| B 4, l-b 4, w 1 | 9 | B 12, l-b 4, w 1 | 17 |
| | 329 | | 128 |

### Warwickshire Bowling

| | Overs | Mdns | Runs | Wkts |
|---|---|---|---|---|
| Calthorpe | 34 | 4 | 133 | 1 |
| Howell | 31.1 | 3 | 141 | 1 |
| Quaife | 24 | — | 110 | 1 |
| Rotherham | 33 | 3 | 152 | 3 |
| Charlesworth | 18 | 5 | 55 | 1 |

**Hampshire Bowling**

| | Overs | Mdns | Runs | Wkts | Overs | Mdns | Runs | Wkts |
|---|---|---|---|---|---|---|---|---|
| Brown ........... | 5 | — | 19 | — | | | | |
| Kennedy ......... | 37 | 6 | 113 | 6 | 17.1 | 4 | 34 | 6 |
| McDonell ........ | 18 | 2 | 75 | 1 | 7 | — | 38 | 2 |
| Newman ......... | 11 | 1 | 49 | — | | | | |
| Mead ........... | 17 | 3 | 52 | 1 | | | | |
| Tennyson ........ | 4 | — | 12 | 1 | 10 | 1 | 39 | 2 |

Umpires: J. Blake and C. Marshall.

# HAMPSHIRE v YORKSHIRE

Played at Portsmouth, August 28, 30, 31, 1920

In some respects this match resembled the previous one, but with the important difference that Hampshire, instead of winning, lost by an innings and 235 runs. Yorkshire did wonders on the first day. Holmes and Sutcliffe scored 347 together in four hours and a half, and at the close the total for the loss of Sutcliffe's wicket was 400, Holmes being not out 230. On the following day Holmes, in carrying his score to 302 before Burton declared, had the satisfaction of making the highest score of the season in first-class cricket. He was batting for seven hours and a quarter, and gave only two chances – at 209 and 271. Hampshire failed dismally in their first innings, and their improved batting when they followed-on was of no avail. Rhodes had a great match as a bowler and batsman, and for the eleventh time in his career completed the double feat of making 1,000 runs and taking 100 wickets in a season.

## Yorkshire

| | |
|---|---|
| P. Holmes not out .....................302 | W. Rhodes not out .................... 63 |
| H. Sutcliffe st Livsey b McDonell ........131 | B 10, l-b 5, w 4, n-b 2 .......... 21 |
| D. Denton b Newman ................. 68 | ——— |
| N. Kilner c Livsey b McDonell .......... 0 | (3 wkts dec.) 585 |

R. Kilner, G. H. Hirst, Mr D. C. F. Burton, E. Robinson, A. Dolphin and Mr E. R. Wilson did not bat.

## Hampshire

| | | | |
|---|---|---|---|
| G. Brown c Hirst b Wilson ..................... | 32 | – c Rhodes b Wilson ............. | 29 |
| A. Bowell st Dolphin b Wilson ................. | 17 | – c Wilson b Rhodes ............. | 36 |
| Capt. E. I. M. Barrett b Rhodes ................. | 12 | – st Dolphin b Rhodes ........... | 12 |
| C. P. Mead c and b Wilson .................... | 10 | – b Rhodes .................... | 1 |
| Maj. Hon. L. H. Tennyson c Holmes b Wilson ..... | 22 | – c Holmes b Rhodes ........... | 0 |
| J. Newman lbw b Rhodes ...................... | 0 | – st Dolphin b Rhodes .......... | 14 |
| Dr B. G. Melle b Rhodes ...................... | 0 | – st Dolphin b Hirst .............. | 26 |
| Comdr. G. C. Harrison c Sutcliffe b Wilson ....... | 28 | – c Holmes b Rhodes .......... | 25 |
| Mr H. C. McDonell c Hirst b Rhodes ............ | 4 | – c Robinson b Hirst ........... | 64 |
| A. Kennedy b Rhodes ....................... | 0 | – c Robinson b R. Kilner .......... | 0 |
| W. H. Livsey not out ........................ | 1 | – not out ..................... | 12 |
| B 5 ............................ | 5 | | |
| | ——— | | ——— |
| | 131 | | 219 |

## Hampshire Bowling

|  | Overs | Mdns | Runs | Wkts |
|---|---|---|---|---|
| Kennedy ........ | 37 | 6 | 110 | — |
| Melle ........... | 21 | 7 | 56 | — |
| Newman ........ | 44 | 6 | 146 | 1 |
| McDonell ........ | 36 | 3 | 148 | 2 |
| Tennyson ........ | 13 | — | 61 | — |
| Mead ........... | 7 | 1 | 22 | — |
| Brown .......... | 4 | — | 21 | — |

## Yorkshire Bowling

|  | Overs | Mdns | Runs | Wkts | Overs | Mdns | Runs | Wkts |
|---|---|---|---|---|---|---|---|---|
| Hirst ........... | 12 | 2 | 15 | — | 11.3 | 2 | 31 | 2 |
| Robinson ........ | 8 | 2 | 23 | — | 10 | 2 | 29 | — |
| Wilson .......... | 25.1 | 18 | 20 | 5 | 23 | 9 | 42 | 1 |
| R. Kilner ........ | 6 | 2 | 12 | — | 15 | — | 44 | 1 |
| Rhodes .......... | 16 | 4 | 56 | 5 | 25 | 3 | 73 | 6 |

Umpires: A. Millward and F. Parris.

# HAMPSHIRE v SUSSEX

### Played at Southampton, May 6, 8, 9, 1922

Dramatic to a degree were the changes which Hampshire's first match underwent. On the opening day, with the Hampshire batting breaking down badly before the fast bowling of A. E. R. Gilligan, Sussex left off 162 ahead with eight wickets to fall. On the Monday, however, Hampshire at the drawing of stumps had apparently a certain victory in prospect. Of the 319 set them to win, Kennedy and Bowell had put on 151 for the second wicket and afterwards Mead and Bowell had added a further 90, only 63 runs being required on the last day with eight wickets in hand. A brilliant catch, however, disposed of Mead and, the remaining seven wickets falling for 42, Sussex gained a sensational victory by ten runs.

## Sussex

| | | | |
|---|---|---|---|
| E. H. Bowley b Kennedy ..................... | 0 | – c Mead b Kennedy ............. | 0 |
| M. W. Tate b Kennedy ..................... | 31 | – b Kennedy .................... | 71 |
| Mr A. H. H. Gilligan c Fry b Remnant .......... | 0 | – b Kennedy .................... | 74 |
| G. Street not out ......................... | 71 | – lbw b Kennedy ................ | 5 |
| W. Cornford run out ....................... | 0 | – c Brown b Remnant ............. | 11 |
| Lieut-Col A. C. Watson c Brown b Remnant ...... | 18 | – b Newman .................... | 3 |
| H. E. Roberts b Kennedy .................... | 2 | – b Kennedy .................... | 1 |
| Mr A. E. R. Gilligan c Bowell b Boyes ........... | 16 | – b Kennedy .................... | 42 |
| G. Cox b Newman ......................... | 0 | – st Livsey b Newman ............ | 6 |
| G. Stannard b Newman ..................... | 11 | – lbw b Kennedy ................ | 2 |
| Mr A. A. Saunders c Newman b Tennyson ........ | 14 | – not out ...................... | 0 |
| B 5, l-b 5 ......................... | 10 | B 1, l-b 2 .............. | 3 |
| | 173 | | 218 |

## Hampshire

| | | | | |
|---|---|---|---|---|
| A. Kennedy lbw b Roberts | 8 | – b Cox | 70 |
| A. Bowell b Roberts | 0 | – run out | 140 |
| G. Brown b Cox | 9 | – st Street b Tate | 5 |
| C. P. Mead b A. E. R. Gilligan | 8 | – c Saunders b A. E. R. Gilligan | 50 |
| Hon. L. H. Tennyson c and b Bowley | 30 | – lbw b Cox | 2 |
| Mr S. Fry b A. E. R. Gilligan | 0 | – b Cox | 0 |
| J. Newman c Street b A. E. R. Gilligan | 3 | – b Cox | 3 |
| Mr A. E. L. Hill b A. E. R. Gilligan | 4 | – b Roberts | 7 |
| W. H. Livsey b A. E. R. Gilligan | 0 | – b Roberts | 0 |
| G. S. Boyes b A. E. R. Gilligan | 0 | – not out | 4 |
| E. R. Remnant not out | 6 | – c Roberts b A. E. R. Gilligan | 10 |
| B 1, l-b 4 | 5 | B 11, l-b 4, w 1, n-b 1 | 17 |
| | **73** | | **308** |

### Hampshire Bowling

| | Overs | Mdns | Runs | Wkts | Overs | Mdns | Runs | Wkts |
|---|---|---|---|---|---|---|---|---|
| Kennedy | 24 | 6 | 55 | 3 | 22.1 | 3 | 71 | 7 |
| Newman | 20 | 6 | 66 | 2 | 19 | 1 | 70 | 2 |
| Remnant | 18 | 8 | 25 | 2 | 9 | 1 | 38 | 1 |
| Boyes | 7 | 1 | 16 | 1 | 2 | — | 13 | — |
| Tennyson | 1 | — | 1 | 1 | 2 | — | 9 | — |
| Brown | | | | | 4 | 1 | 14 | — |

### Sussex Bowling

| | Overs | Mdns | Runs | Wkts | Overs | Mdns | Runs | Wkts |
|---|---|---|---|---|---|---|---|---|
| Roberts | 7 | 2 | 22 | 2 | 13 | 4 | 35 | 2 |
| Tate | 4 | 3 | 5 | — | 14 | 3 | 39 | 1 |
| Cox | 8 | 2 | 18 | 1 | 40 | 9 | 90 | 4 |
| A. E. R. Gilligan | 8 | 3 | 18 | 6 | 23.2 | 2 | 66 | 2 |
| Bowley | 2 | — | 5 | 1 | 11 | — | 35 | — |
| A. H. H. Gilligan | | | | | 3 | — | 12 | — |
| Stannard | | | | | 6 | — | 14 | — |

Umpires: T. Flowers and J. H. Board.

## HAMPSHIRE v MIDDLESEX

### Played at Portsmouth, July 22, 24, 1922

Unbeaten since their great fight with Kent at the beginning of June, Hampshire came badly to grief in their return contest with Middlesex, suffering defeat by an innings and 160 runs. Indeed, even taking into account the severe defeats inflicted towards the end of the season by Yorkshire and Nottinghamshire, it may be questioned whether in any match during the whole summer they were seen to so little advantage. The wickets on the United Services ground are admittedly vastly inferior to those which were provided on that enclosure in years gone by, but making every allowance Hampshire's batting was deplorable. Taking the adverse conditions into consideration, Dales and Hendren accomplished a truly grand performance, coming together when two Middlesex wickets had fallen for 33, withstanding the Hampshire bowling for three hours and twenty minutes, and putting on 230. After they left four more batsmen were disposed of for 46 runs. Hampshire on Monday had 48 runs on the board with one man out when Stevens was put on to bowl and carried everything before him, showing such remarkable skill that he secured eight wickets for 38 runs. Badly as they had shaped at their first attempt, Hampshire did infinitely worse in the follow-on, crumpling up so completely on the awkward pitch before Durston and Haig that they were all out in an hour and a quarter for 35. The two bowlers shared the wickets, 15 runs being hit off Haig and 18 off Durston. Mead, it will be noted, had a terrible match. Several weeks had elapsed since Middlesex contested a game.

### Middlesex

| | |
|---|---|
| Mr H. L. Dales c Newman b Tennyson . . . .112 | Mr C. H. L. Skeet not out . . . . . . . . . . . . . . 20 |
| H. W. Lee c Kennedy b Newman . . . . . . . . 1 | Mr G. O. Allen c Brown b Kennedy . . . . . . 3 |
| J. W. Hearne c Livsey b Kennedy . . . . . . . . 10 | H. R. Murrell b Kennedy . . . . . . . . . . . . . . 1 |
| E. Hendren b Boyes . . . . . . . . . . . . . . . . . .137 | T. J. Durston c and b Kennedy . . . . . . . . . . 1 |
| Mr F. T. Mann c Mead b Boyes . . . . . . . . . . 13 | B 13, l-b 3 . . . . . . . . . . . . . . . . . . 16 |
| Mr N. Haig b Kennedy . . . . . . . . . . . . . . . 10 | ___ |
| Mr G. T. S. Stevens run out . . . . . . . . . . . . 4 | 328 |

### Hampshire

| | | | |
|---|---|---|---|
| A. Kennedy c Durston b Haig . . . . . . . . . . . . . . . . . . | 9 | – c Hearne b Durston . . . . . . . . . . . . | 1 |
| A. Bowell c Hendren b Stevens . . . . . . . . . . . . . . . . | 30 | – c Stevens b Haig . . . . . . . . . . . . . . | 2 |
| Mr R. Aird st Murrell b Stevens . . . . . . . . . . . . . . . . | 10 | – not out . . . . . . . . . . . . . . . . . . . . . | 4 |
| C. P. Mead c Haig b Hearne . . . . . . . . . . . . . . . . . . | 1 | – c Stevens b Durston . . . . . . . . . . . | 0 |
| Mr H. L. V. Day c Skeet b Stevens . . . . . . . . . . . . . | 36 | – c Hearne b Durston . . . . . . . . . . . | 6 |
| G. Brown c Mann b Stevens . . . . . . . . . . . . . . . . . . . | 8 | – b Durston . . . . . . . . . . . . . . . . . . . | 0 |
| Hon. L. H. Tennyson c Durston b Stevens . . . . . . . . | 4 | – c Stevens b Durston . . . . . . . . . . . | 4 |
| J. Newman hit wkt b Stevens . . . . . . . . . . . . . . . . . . | 10 | – b Haig . . . . . . . . . . . . . . . . . . . . . . | 4 |
| Mr W. R. Shirley st Murrell b Stevens . . . . . . . . . . . | 0 | – c Murrell b Haig . . . . . . . . . . . . . . | 7 |
| W. H. Livsey b Stevens . . . . . . . . . . . . . . . . . . . . . . | 8 | – b Haig . . . . . . . . . . . . . . . . . . . . . . | 3 |
| G. S. Boyes not out . . . . . . . . . . . . . . . . . . . . . . . . | 3 | – c Stevens b Haig . . . . . . . . . . . . . . | 2 |
| B 14 . . . . . . . . . . . . . . . . . . . . . . . . . . . | 14 | B 1, l-b 1 . . . . . . . . . . . . . . | 2 |
| | ___ | | ___ |
| | 133 | | 35 |

### Hampshire Bowling

| | Overs | Mdns | Runs | Wkts |
|---|---|---|---|---|
| Kennedy . . . . . . . . . | 38 | 8 | 108 | 5 |
| Newman . . . . . . . . . | 32 | 10 | 95 | 1 |
| Boyes . . . . . . . . . . . . | 23 | 6 | 66 | 2 |
| Tennyson . . . . . . . . . | 9 | — | 36 | 1 |
| Shirley . . . . . . . . . . | 4 | 1 | 7 | — |

### Middlesex Bowling

| | Overs | Mdns | Runs | Wkts | Overs | Mdns | Runs | Wkts |
|---|---|---|---|---|---|---|---|---|
| Haig . . . . . . . . . . . . . | 7 | — | 26 | 1 | 11 | 5 | 15 | 5 |
| Durston . . . . . . . . . . | 4 | 3 | 2 | — | 10 | 3 | 18 | 5 |
| Allen . . . . . . . . . . . . | 3 | — | 20 | — | | | | |
| Stevens . . . . . . . . . . | 17.2 | 7 | 38 | 8 | | | | |
| Hearne . . . . . . . . . . | 17 | 8 | 33 | 1 | | | | |

Umpires: B. Brown and T. M. Russell.

## HAMPSHIRE v MIDDLESEX

### Played at Southampton, June 13, 14, 15, 1923

In this match the weather proved very unkind to Middlesex, depriving them of their chance of victory after they had shown, perhaps, the most remarkable batting of the season. Rain set in at a quarter past one on the third day and as it was still falling heavily at three o'clock, the game was abandoned as a draw. It is safe to say that no better wicket had ever been prepared on the Southampton ground. Only once before in England – by Middlesex against Sussex at Lord's in 1920 – had hundreds been scored by the first four batsmen on a side. Dales and Lee scored 174 together for the first Middlesex wicket, and Hearne and Hendren set up a new record in first-class cricket by putting on 375 for the third. Another record was the total of 642 with only three men out. Hearne and Hendren, in their different styles, played equally fine cricket. Hearne, who hit thirty 4s, was batting five hours for his 232, and Hendren three hours and fifty minutes for his 177 not out. Hendren pulled and drove with great freedom, but his timing was so perfect that he did not make a single bad stroke. Tennyson and Jameson batted finely for Hampshire on the first day, but their efforts were completely dwarfed by what followed.

### Hampshire

| | | |
|---|---|---|
| A. Bowell c Hendren b Durston | 67 – not out | 13 |
| A. Kennedy b Fowler | 34 – not out | 8 |
| J. Newman b Durston | 3 | |
| C. P. Mead b Fowler | 13 | |
| Hon. L. H. Tennyson c Lee b Durston | 85 | |
| Capt. T. O. Jameson b Fowler | 95 | |
| Mr W. R. Shirley b Durston | 0 | |
| Mr W. K. Pearce b Hendren | 1 | |
| W. H. Livsey b Hearne | 23 | |
| Mr A. S. McIntyre lbw b Hearne | 13 | |
| G. S. Boyes not out | 0 | |
| B 6, l-b 2 | 8 | B 1    1 |
| | **342** | **22** |

### Middlesex

| | |
|---|---|
| Mr H. L. Dales c Shirley b Kennedy ......103 | S. Beton not out ..................... 3 |
| H. W. Lee b Boyes ....................107 | B 13, l-b 5, w 1, n-b 1 .......... 20 |
| J. W. Hearne c and b Shirley ............232 | |
| E. Hendren not out ....................177 | (3 wkts dec.) 642 |

Mr F. T. Mann, Mr P. N. Durlacher, Mr R. H. Hill, H. R. Murrell, A. Fowler and T. J. Durston did not bat.

### Middlesex Bowling

| | Overs | Mdns | Runs | Wkts | Overs | Mdns | Runs | Wkts |
|---|---|---|---|---|---|---|---|---|
| Durston | 25 | 1 | 112 | 4 | 3 | — | 10 | — |
| Lee | 10 | — | 65 | — | 3 | — | 11 | — |
| Fowler | 21.2 | 4 | 44 | 3 | | | | |
| Hearne | 20 | 3 | 68 | 2 | | | | |
| Hendren | 13 | 1 | 45 | 1 | | | | |

### Hampshire Bowling

| | Overs | Mdns | Runs | Wkts |
|---|---|---|---|---|
| Kennedy | 34 | 5 | 115 | 1 |
| Newman | 42 | 7 | 115 | — |
| Boyes | 30 | 6 | 94 | 1 |
| Jameson | 25 | 7 | 78 | — |
| Mead | 5 | 1 | 21 | — |
| Shirley | 18 | 1 | 104 | 1 |
| Tennyson | 3 | — | 30 | — |
| McIntyre | 4 | — | 16 | — |
| Bowell | 12 | — | 49 | — |

Umpires: H. Wrathall and A. E. Street.

# HAMPSHIRE v GLOUCESTERSHIRE

Played at Southampton, May 31, June 2, 3, 1924

Rain set in on the third afternoon and caused a most interesting match to be left unfinished. When, after waiting over an hour in the hope of better weather it was agreed to pull up stumps, Hampshire, with five wickets to fall, required only 23 runs to win. Brown, not out 50 on Monday evening, played wonderfully well for his 107. He and Mead put on 138 together in exactly two hours. In Gloucestershire's second innings Kennedy, with the last two balls of one over and the first of his next, did the hat trick. Rogers, against bowling far too good for anyone else, gave a remarkable display on Tuesday, actually scoring 50 runs out of 60 in three-quarters of an hour.

### Gloucestershire

| | | | |
|---|---:|---|---:|
| W. R. Hammond c Livsey b Boyes | 13 | – c Livsey b Newman | 0 |
| A. G. Dipper st Livsey b Boyes | 23 | – c and b Kennedy | 0 |
| Mr F. G. Rogers lbw b Boyes | 28 | – c and b Kennedy | 69 |
| B. S. Bloodworth c Gross b Newman | 54 | – c Boyes b Newman | 0 |
| H. Smith c Boyes b Kennedy | 5 | – c Livsey b Kennedy | 3 |
| Lieut-Col D. C. Robinson b Kennedy | 8 | – b Kennedy | 0 |
| Mr B. H. Lyon lbw b Boyes | 31 | – c and b Kennedy | 2 |
| Mr A. E. Waters b Kennedy | 11 | – b Kennedy | 2 |
| C. Parker c and b Newman | 0 | – c Livsey b Kennedy | 3 |
| P. Mills lbw b Kennedy | 26 | – not out | 9 |
| G. Dennett not out | 4 | – lbw b Kennedy | 3 |
| B 1, l-b 5 | 6 | B 1 | 1 |
| | **209** | | **92** |

### Hampshire

| | | | |
|---|---:|---|---:|
| A. Kennedy c Smith b Dennett | 21 | – b Hammond | 1 |
| Mr H. L. V. Day c Smith b Parker | 7 | – b Hammond | 1 |
| Mr R. Aird c Dennett b Mills | 2 | – b Mills | 29 |
| Mr T. M. Smith b Parker | 0 | | |
| C. P. Mead lbw b Parker | 59 | – c Mills b Parker | 26 |
| G. Brown run out | 107 | – c Smith b Mills | 6 |
| J. Newman c Mills b Waters | 1 | – not out | 9 |
| Mr A. Kneller c Smith b Waters | 0 | – not out | 0 |
| W. H. Livsey c Hammond b Parker | 6 | | |
| Mr F. Gross c Mills b Dennett | 0 | | |
| G. S. Boyes not out | 0 | | |
| B 4 | 4 | | |
| | **207** | | **72** |

### Hampshire Bowling

| | Overs | Mdns | Runs | Wkts | Overs | Mdns | Runs | Wkts |
|---|---|---|---|---|---|---|---|---|
| Kennedy | 28.4 | 12 | 46 | 4 | 13 | 7 | 24 | 8 |
| Newman | 30 | 6 | 83 | 2 | 7 | 2 | 35 | 2 |
| Boyes | 33 | 11 | 59 | 4 | 5 | — | 32 | — |
| Gross | 3 | — | 15 | — | | | | |

### Gloucestershire Bowling

| | Overs | Mdns | Runs | Wkts | Overs | Mdns | Runs | Wkts |
|---|---|---|---|---|---|---|---|---|
| Hammond | 15 | 3 | 33 | — | 5 | — | 22 | 2 |
| Parker | 32 | 12 | 66 | 4 | 13 | 3 | 31 | 1 |
| Mills | 20 | 7 | 53 | 1 | 5 | 2 | 8 | 2 |
| Dennett | 17 | 3 | 38 | 2 | | | | |
| Waters | 5 | — | 13 | 2 | 3 | — | 11 | — |

Umpires: T. M. Russell and A. E. Street.

# HAMPSHIRE v MIDDLESEX

Played at Bournemouth, August 11, 12, 13, 1926

When on Friday, with his side leading by 159, Tennyson did not enforce the follow-on, a draw became inevitable. Middlesex lost Hearne, who had to retire owing to an old injury proving troublesome and, in different circumstances, the lack of that famous player's services might have brought disaster. In a curious match there were some fine batting performances and many failures. Unable to make headway at the start against accurate bowling, Hampshire lost three wickets cheaply and Mead and Day, after rain, had to exercise great restraint. These men, however, by determined batting raised the total to 227 before the close and, in all, their splendid partnership realised 210 in three hours. In the 92nd 100 of his career, Mead scored with perfect strokes all round the wicket and like Day, who batted stubbornly for over four hours, hit fifteen 4s. But for Hendren, Middlesex must have been in serious difficulties. Half the side were out for 146, and Hearne could not bat, but Hendren, displaying watchful defence, stayed three hours and with Crutchley put on 123 runs. Brown enlivened the concluding stages of the game by vigorous hitting. He scored 103 out of 188, his innings including twelve 4s.

## Hampshire

| | | |
|---|---|---:|
| G. Brown c Hendren b Haig | 27 – not out | 103 |
| J. Newman lbw b Haig | 12 – lbw b Stevens | 26 |
| A. Bowell lbw b Stevens | 11 – st Murrell b Stevens | 0 |
| C. P. Mead run out | 117 – c and b Lee | 4 |
| Mr H. L. V. Day c Mann b Haig | 103 – b Lee | 7 |
| A. Kennedy b Lee | 29 – c Haig b Enthoven | 7 |
| Hon. L. H. Tennyson b Stevens | 29 – run out | 21 |
| Mr J. P. Parker c Mann b Haig | 1 – b Crutchley | 3 |
| Mr W. N. McBride c sub b Haig | 7 – not out | 9 |
| W. H. Livsey not out | 14 – lbw b Lee | 2 |
| G. S. Boyes c Murrell b Enthoven | 31 – c Enthoven b Crutchley | 0 |
| B 24, l-b 5, w 4, n-b 2 | 35      B 5, n-b 1 | 6 |
| | **416** | **188** |

## Middlesex

| | | |
|---|---|---:|
| Mr H. L. Dales b Newman | | 6 |
| H. W. Lee c Mead b Kennedy | | 19 |
| Mr G. T. S. Stevens run out | | 44 |
| E. Hendren c Mead b Newman | | 104 |
| Mr H. J. Enthoven run out | | 4 |
| Mr F. T. Mann c Brown b Boyes | | 10 |
| Mr G. E. V. Crutchley c Brown b Kennedy | | 56 |
| Mr N. Haig b Newman | | 0 |
| G. Hart b Kennedy | | 2 |
| H. R. Murrell not out | | 7 |
| J. W. Hearne absent hurt | | 0 |
| B 3, l-b 1, n-b 1 | | 5 |
| | | **257** |

## Middlesex Bowling

| | Overs | Mdns | Runs | Wkts | Overs | Mdns | Runs | Wkts |
|---|---|---|---|---|---|---|---|---|
| Haig | 53 | 16 | 115 | 5 | 7 | — | 24 | — |
| Enthoven | 18 | 3 | 71 | 1 | 15 | 3 | 61 | 1 |
| Stevens | 45 | 8 | 125 | 2 | 11 | 1 | 32 | 2 |
| Crutchley | 2 | 1 | 4 | — | 9 | 1 | 43 | 2 |
| Lee | 18 | 2 | 41 | 1 | 11 | 3 | 22 | 3 |
| Hendren | 10 | 2 | 25 | — | | | | |

**Hampshire Bowling**

|  | Overs | Mdns | Runs | Wkts |
|---|---|---|---|---|
| Kennedy ......... | 29.5 | 4 | 87 | 3 |
| Newman ......... | 35 | 7 | 97 | 3 |
| Boyes ........... | 16 | 6 | 32 | 1 |
| McBride ......... | 6 | 1 | 28 | — |
| Mead ........... | 4 | 1 | 8 | — |

Umpires: F. Chester and J. H. King.

## HAMPSHIRE v WARWICKSHIRE

Played at Portsmouth, August 27, 29, 30, 1927

Rain during Monday night brought about such a remarkable change in the character of the cricket that, whereas the first two days had been occupied in each side completing an innings for an aggregate of 716 runs, the match was all over by half-past two on Tuesday, Hampshire gaining a sensational victory by nine wickets. Finding Kennedy in almost irresistible form on a drying pitch Warwickshire, who led by 12 runs on the first innings, were quickly in a desperate position, seventy-five minutes sufficing to dismiss the side for the smallest total of the season. Kennedy actually captured the last six wickets in the course of three overs for only four runs. On Monday Kennedy batted in resolute fashion in a partnership of 112 with Newman, who combined a sound defence with powerful leg hitting. Wyatt's first hundred of the season was a faultless effort.

### Warwickshire

| | | |
|---|---|---|
| E. J. Smith st Brown b Boyes ................... 36 | – c Mead b Newman ............. | 6 |
| N. Kilner b Newman ........................ 34 | – lbw b Kennedy ................. | 3 |
| L. A. Bates lbw b Boyes ...................... 1 | – lbw b Newman ................. | 11 |
| W. G. Quaife c Boyes b Newman ............. 2 | – b Kennedy .................... | 6 |
| J. H. Parsons c Brown b Boyes .............. 26 | – c Day b Kennedy ............... | 4 |
| Mr R. E. S. Wyatt c Brown b McBride .........117 | – not out ...................... | 1 |
| A. J. Croom b McBride ...................... 29 | – c Boyes b Kennedy ............. | 1 |
| F. R. Santall c Kennedy b Newman ............ 59 | – b Kennedy .................... | 0 |
| Hon. F. S. G. Calthorpe c Tennyson b Newman .... 8 | – b Kennedy .................... | 3 |
| J. Fox not out ............................. 13 | – lbw b Kennedy ................. | 0 |
| Mr A. W. Speed c Tennyson b Cadell .......... 8 | – run out ...................... | 0 |
| B 27, l-b 1, n-b 3 ................... 31 | N-b 1 .................. | 1 |
| **364** | | **36** |

### Hampshire

| | | |
|---|---|---|
| G. Brown lbw b Calthorpe .................... 26 | – b Speed ..................... | 16 |
| J. Newman c Smith b Speed ................... 90 | – not out ..................... | 15 |
| A. Kennedy lbw b Fox ....................... 52 | | |
| C. P. Mead c Smith b Speed .................. 28 | | |
| Mr H. L. V. Day c Santall b Quaife ........... 30 | | |
| Hon. L. H. Tennyson b Quaife ................. 38 | | |
| Mr J. P. Parker c Santall b Quaife ............. 4 | | |
| Lieut A. R. Cadell b Quaife .................... 6 | | |
| Mr W. N. McBride not out .................... 26 | – not out ..................... | 10 |
| G. S. Boyes c Smith b Speed ................. 12 | | |
| Mr R. P. H. Utley b Speed ................... 4 | | |
| B 20, l-b 15, w 1 ................... 36 | B 8, l-b 1, w 1 ............ | 10 |
| **352** | | **51** |

### Hampshire Bowling

| | Overs | Mdns | Runs | Wkts | Overs | Mdns | Runs | Wkts |
|---|---|---|---|---|---|---|---|---|
| Utley ............. | 21 | 2 | 69 | — | | | | |
| Kennedy ......... | 14 | 2 | 67 | — | 10 | 7 | 8 | 7 |
| Boyes ............. | 37 | 12 | 78 | 3 | | | | |
| Newman ......... | 22 | 3 | 72 | 4 | 9.3 | — | 27 | 2 |
| Cadell ........... | 7.2 | 1 | 18 | 1 | | | | |
| McBride .......... | 11 | 3 | 29 | 2 | | | | |

### Warwickshire Bowling

| | Overs | Mdns | Runs | Wkts | Overs | Mdns | Runs | Wkts |
|---|---|---|---|---|---|---|---|---|
| Calthorpe ........ | 31 | 11 | 48 | 1 | 6 | — | 14 | — |
| Speed ............ | 21 | 4 | 63 | 4 | 6 | 1 | 12 | 1 |
| Wyatt ............. | 30 | 4 | 78 | — | 11.2 | 5 | 15 | — |
| Quaife ........... | 24 | 3 | 64 | 4 | | | | |
| Santall ........... | 19 | — | 35 | — | | | | |
| Fox ............. | 25 | 12 | 28 | 1 | | | | |

Umpires: F. Parris and J. H. King.

## HAMPSHIRE v LEICESTERSHIRE

Played at Bournemouth, August 22, 24, 25, 1931

Some splendid bowling by Kennedy so completely dominated the play in this match that Leicestershire had to admit defeat by nine wickets. Kennedy in the visitors' first innings disposed of seven batsmen for 40 runs and in the second sent back six for 15 so that he actually secured thirteen wickets for little more than four runs apiece. Leicestershire on Saturday were only saved from complete disaster by Berry and Sidwell, the former hitting up 33 out of 41 added for the third wicket and Sidwell making 35 of the last 43 runs. Hampshire began by losing three batsmen for 32 but Mead and Harfield put on 40 and at the drawing of stumps the home side stood seven runs ahead with half their wickets in hand. Rain prevented play on Monday but on Tuesday when the state of the ground delayed the resumption for an hour, the game was speedily finished. Hampshire's five wickets went down for 35 more runs. Ninth man out, Mead rendered his side invaluable service but he had been missed three times on Saturday and was given another life on Tuesday. Leicestershire's second innings was all over in ninety minutes.

### Leicestershire

| | | | |
|---|---|---|---|
| A. Shipman c Arnold b Kennedy ................ | 5 | – run out ................... | 11 |
| L. G. Berry c Boyes b Kennedy ................ | 33 | – c Baring b Kennedy ........... | 3 |
| N. F. Armstrong b Kennedy .................... | 0 | – c Harfield b Boyes ............. | 0 |
| J. C. Bradshaw b Kennedy ..................... | 10 | – c Harfield b Kennedy ........... | 4 |
| Mr E. W. Dawson st Brown b Kennedy .......... | 1 | – c Boyes b Kennedy ............. | 0 |
| W. E. Astill lbw b Kennedy .................... | 9 | – c Bailey b Kennedy ............. | 7 |
| H. Riley c and b Boyes ....................... | 6 | – run out ...................... | 9 |
| G. Geary run out ........................... | 0 | – lbw b Kennedy ................. | 3 |
| T. E. Sidwell b Kennedy ...................... | 35 | – not out ...,.................. | 5 |
| H. C. Snary lbw b Bailey ..................... | 9 | – b Kennedy .................... | 1 |
| H. A. Smith not out ......................... | 1 | – b Boyes ...................... | 2 |
| | | B 4, l-b 3 .............. | 7 |
| | 109 | | 52 |

## Hampshire

| | | | |
|---|---|---|---|
| J. Arnold b Snary | 9 | – not out | 2 |
| J. Bailey b Astill | 9 | – b Snary | 6 |
| G. Brown lbw b Snary | 8 | – not out | 4 |
| C. P. Mead b Snary | 65 | | |
| L. Harfield c Smith b Astill | 19 | | |
| Mr H. L. V. Day c Sidwell b Smith | 11 | | |
| Mr R. H. Moore c Sidwell b Geary | 5 | | |
| A. Kennedy c Berry b Geary | 0 | | |
| Lord Tennyson c and b Geary | 16 | | |
| G. S. Boyes c Astill b Geary | 0 | | |
| Mr A. E. G. Baring not out | 0 | | |
| B 8, l-b 1 | 9 | | |
| | **151** | | **12** |

### Hampshire Bowling

| | Overs | Mdns | Runs | Wkts | Overs | Mdns | Runs | Wkts |
|---|---|---|---|---|---|---|---|---|
| Baring | 5 | — | 15 | — | | | | |
| Kennedy | 30.3 | 13 | 40 | 7 | 16.4 | 11 | 15 | 6 |
| Bailey | 8 | 3 | 23 | 1 | | | | |
| Boyes | 18 | 7 | 31 | 1 | 16 | 4 | 30 | 2 |

### Leicestershire Bowling

| | Overs | Mdns | Runs | Wkts | Overs | Mdns | Runs | Wkts |
|---|---|---|---|---|---|---|---|---|
| Geary | 25.2 | 8 | 49 | 4 | 2 | 2 | — | — |
| Snary | 32 | 16 | 33 | 3 | 2.5 | — | 12 | 1 |
| Astill | 22 | 9 | 47 | 2 | | | | |
| Smith | 10 | 5 | 13 | 1 | | | | |

Umpires: F. Walden and H. Watson.

## HAMPSHIRE v SURREY

Played at Bournemouth, July 22, 23, 24, 1931

Taking the field without either Hobbs or Ducat, Surrey found themselves in arrear on the first innings, but they had no difficulty in effecting a draw. Sandham rose to the occasion in great style, carrying his bat right through the visitors' first innings when he batted more than four hours without a chance, and giving in the second innings an equally faultless display. He was on the field every minute of the match. Mead in Hampshire's second innings, when the first five wickets fell for 84 runs, withstood the Surrey bowling for more than four hours, the only real blemish in his play being a catch offered to short leg when 123. Following upon a very careful start, he hit to leg and drove in great style, and included in what was his 128th hundred were twenty-one 4s.

## Hampshire

| | | | | |
|---|---|---|---|---|
| J. Bailey c Fender b Gover | 43 | – c Fender b Gover | 6 |
| J. Arnold b Gregory | 15 | – b Gover | 0 |
| G. Brown c and b Gregory | 47 | – lbw b Sheffield | 17 |
| C. P. Mead st Brooks b Gregory | 26 | – not out | 169 |
| L. Harfield c Brooks b Gregory | 22 | – c Sandham b Gregory | 12 |
| A. Kennedy c Brooks b Sheffield | 27 | – c Brooks b Gover | 5 |
| A. E. Pothecary c Brooks b Gregory | 0 | – lbw b Sheffield | 31 |
| W. L. Creese c Jardine b Wellings | 2 | – lbw b Sheffield | 26 |
| G. S. Boyes lbw b Fender | 22 | – not out | 11 |
| Mr A. E. G. Baring b Gregory | 35 | – c Shepherd b Fender | 0 |
| O. W. Herman not out | 18 | – run out | 3 |
| B 3, l-b 5, n-b 9 | 17 | B 4, l-b 4, w 2, n-b 7 | 17 |

274                    (9 wkts dec.) 297

## Surrey

| | | | | |
|---|---|---|---|---|
| A. Sandham not out | 113 | – not out | 77 |
| T. H. Barling c Boyes b Baring | 1 | | |
| Mr E. M. Wellings c and b Kennedy | 9 | | |
| T. Shepherd b Kennedy | 28 | – lbw b Creese | 15 |
| Mr D. R. Jardine b Kennedy | 0 | – not out | 2 |
| Mr P. G. H. Fender b Baring | 21 | | |
| H. S. Squires b Kennedy | 7 | – c Brown b Creese | 62 |
| R. J. Gregory c Pothecary b Baring | 4 | – c Brown b Baring | 6 |
| E. J. Sheffield b Baring | 6 | | |
| E. W. Brooks c Kennedy b Boyes | 14 | | |
| A. R. Gover lbw b Herman | 3 | | |
| B 1, l-b 8, n-b 6 | 15 | L-b 3, n-b 2 | 5 |

221                                        167

### Surrey Bowling

| | Overs | Mdns | Runs | Wkts | Overs | Mdns | Runs | Wkts |
|---|---|---|---|---|---|---|---|---|
| Gover | 18 | 1 | 45 | 1 | 22 | — | 81 | 3 |
| Sheffield | 26 | 7 | 63 | 1 | 26 | 5 | 60 | 3 |
| Gregory | 49.5 | 25 | 69 | 6 | 24 | 8 | 52 | 1 |
| Wellings | 21 | 9 | 31 | 1 | 10 | 1 | 43 | — |
| Fender | 11 | — | 49 | 1 | 8 | 1 | 31 | 1 |
| Jardine | | | | | 3 | — | 13 | — |

### Hampshire Bowling

| | Overs | Mdns | Runs | Wkts | Overs | Mdns | Runs | Wkts |
|---|---|---|---|---|---|---|---|---|
| Kennedy | 33 | 9 | 65 | 4 | 10 | 4 | 12 | — |
| Baring | 24 | 1 | 68 | 4 | 12 | 3 | 29 | 1 |
| Herman | 13.5 | 1 | 43 | 1 | 13 | 1 | 22 | — |
| Boyes | 13 | 4 | 30 | 1 | | | | |
| Bailey | | | | | 8 | — | 26 | — |
| Harfield | | | | | 4 | 1 | 18 | — |
| Creese | | | | | 16 | 6 | 35 | 2 |
| Arnold | | | | | 5 | — | 20 | — |

Umpires: A. Morton and W. R. Parry.

## HAMPSHIRE v NOTTINGHAMSHIRE

Played at Southampton, May 18, 19, 20, 1932

Nottinghamshire won this match by 161 runs, bowlers dominating matters so completely after the completion of the visitors' first innings, that thirty wickets fell for little more than 4 runs apiece. Nottinghamshire on Wednesday made 87 for the loss of three batsmen, rain preventing anything being done after half-past two. On Thursday twenty-five wickets went down for an aggregate of 217 and Friday's play, lasting eighty-five minutes, resulted in twelve wickets falling for 31 runs. Harris showed skilful defence and Carr, with Arthur Staples as his partner, put on 58 for the fourth Nottinghamshire wicket. McCorkell assisted in the dismissal of four batsmen and did not give a single bye. Hampshire took forty-five minutes to make 10 runs and were all out in two hours twenty minutes for 57, Sam Staples getting six wickets for 17. Bailey, bowling left-arm slow, disposed, in Nottinghamshire's second innings, of seven batsmen for seven runs – five in his last two overs for five runs. Hampshire, wanting 192 for victory, were all out for 30, Voce taking five wickets for 21 and Sam Staples making his record for the match ten wickets for 21.

## Nottinghamshire

| | | |
|---|---|---|
| W. W. Keeton c Dodd b Kennedy | 7 | – c Moore b Bailey ............... 10 |
| C. B. Harris st McCorkell b Bailey | 31 | – c Moore b Kennedy ........... 8 |
| W. Walker c McCorkell b Herman | 5 | – st McCorkell b Bailey ......... 6 |
| Mr A. W. Carr st McCorkell b Boyes | 46 | – c Moore b Boyes ............... 0 |
| A. Staples c Kennedy b Bailey | 31 | – c Dodd b Boyes ................ 0 |
| G. V. Gunn c Boyes b Bailey | 8 | – c Boyes b Bailey .............. 0 |
| J. Hardstaff c McCorkell b Boyes | 24 | – c Herman b Bailey ............ 12 |
| B. Lilley c Mead b Boyes | 15 | – c Boyes b Bailey .............. 4 |
| H. Larwood c Moore b Bailey | 15 | – c Brown b Bailey ............. 1 |
| W. Voce c Herman b Boyes | 14 | – st McCorkell b Bailey ......... 0 |
| S. J. Staples not out | 5 | – not out ...................... 1 |
| L-b 4, n-b 1 | 5 | |
| | **206** | **42** |

## Hampshire

| | | |
|---|---|---|
| G. Brown lbw b Voce | 4 | – b S. J. Staples ................ 5 |
| J. Bailey c Larwood b S. J. Staples | 8 | – b Larwood ................... 3 |
| A. Kennedy c Gunn b S. J. Staples | 13 | – c Larwood b Voce ............ 2 |
| C. P. Mead c Harris b Voce | 0 | – c Larwood b S. J. Staples ..... 5 |
| Mr R. H. Moore lbw b S. J. Staples | 8 | – b S. J. Staples ................ 9 |
| N. McCorkell c Hardstaff b Voce | 1 | – lbw b S. J. Staples ........... 1 |
| G. S. Boyes hit wkt b S. J. Staples | 0 | – c Walker b Voce ............. 0 |
| A. E. Pothecary not out | 5 | – b Voce ...................... 1 |
| O. W. Herman c Gunn b S. J. Staples | 4 | – st Lilley b Voce .............. 2 |
| W. Dodd st Lilley b S. J. Staples | 5 | – c A. Staples b Voce ........... 0 |
| G. Hill st Lilley b Voce | 0 | – not out ...................... 0 |
| B 8, n-b 1 | 9 | N-b 2 ................... 2 |
| | **57** | **30** |

## Hampshire Bowling

| | Overs | Mdns | Runs | Wkts | Overs | Mdns | Runs | Wkts |
|---|---|---|---|---|---|---|---|---|
| Kennedy ......... | 26 | 8 | 60 | 1 | 6 | 1 | 11 | 1 |
| Herman .......... | 9 | — | 21 | 1 | 3 | — | 10 | — |
| Boyes ............ | 36 | 9 | 63 | 4 | 4 | — | 14 | 2 |
| Hill ............. | 8 | — | 17 | — | | | | |
| Bailey ........... | 19 | 4 | 40 | 4 | 7 | 3 | 7 | 7 |

## Nottinghamshire Bowling

| | Overs | Mdns | Runs | Wkts | Overs | Mdns | Runs | Wkts |
|---|---|---|---|---|---|---|---|---|
| Larwood ......... | 2 | 1 | 2 | — | 3 | 1 | 3 | 1 |
| Voce ............ | 26.3 | 13 | 29 | 4 | 13.3 | 2 | 21 | 5 |
| S. J. Staples ....... | 25 | 16 | 17 | 6 | 11 | 8 | 4 | 4 |

Umpires: J. H. King and W. Hitch.

# HAMPSHIRE v ESSEX

Played at Bournemouth, August 30, 31, September 1, 1933

The umpires committed an extraordinary mistake over their instructions regarding the declaration in this drawn match, for when Wilcox closed his innings as the teams went to lunch on the last day, insistence was made on the interval being extended fifteen minutes for rolling. As it happened, this action did not influence the result. Throughout the contest the bat mastered the ball. Hitting his first hundred for Hampshire, Moore drove brilliantly for three and three-quarter hours, his figures including twenty 4s. Cutmore, O'Connor and Eastman batted finely for Essex, the first two adding 203 together in two and a half hours, O'Connor's share being 130 with one six and eighteen 4s as the chief strokes. Eastman, who batted the same time as Moore, punished the bowling severely, getting one six and twenty 4s. Sheffield helped him to add 90 in an unbroken stand. Facing arrears of 141, Hampshire lost four men for 88, but Pothecary and Creese, putting on 90, staved off disaster and Creese went on to reach three figures in the last over of the match.

## Hampshire

| | | |
|---|---|---|
| G. Brown c Smith b Nichols | 0 – c Smith b Farnes | 33 |
| J. Bailey c Sheffield b Farnes | 48 – c Nichols b Farnes | 3 |
| N. McCorkell b O'Connor | 34 – c Sheffield b Farnes | 3 |
| A. E. Pothecary c O'Connor b Farnes | 17 – c Sheffield b Smith | 65 |
| J. Arnold b Farnes | 11 – c Wilcox b Smith | 11 |
| W. L. Creese c and b Smith | 48 – not out | 101 |
| Mr R. H. Moore c Sheffield b Farnes | 159 – b Smith | 0 |
| A. Kennedy b Eastman | 38 – run out | 0 |
| G. S. Boyes b Nichols | 42 – not out | 19 |
| O. W. Herman not out | 14 | |
| G. Hill b Nichols | 2 | |
| B 5, l-b 4, n-b 1 | 10 | L-b 6, w 1 ............ 7 |
| | 423 | 242 |

## Essex

| | | |
|---|---|---|
| Mr L. G. Crawley c Kennedy b Herman | 0 | D. F. Pope c Arnold b Boyes ........... 3 |
| J. A. Cutmore c Moore b Bailey | 87 | P. Smith b Kennedy ................... 23 |
| R. M. Taylor lbw b Boyes | 35 | J. R. Sheffield not out ................ 54 |
| J. O'Connor c Arnold b Brown | 130 | |
| M. S. Nichols c Brown b Hill | 46 | B 1, l-b 13, w 1 .............. 15 |
| L. C. Eastman not out | 157 | |
| Mr D. R. Wilcox c Moore b Hill | 14 | (8 wkts dec.) 564 |

Mr K. Farnes did not bat.

## Essex Bowling

| | Overs | Mdns | Runs | Wkts | Overs | Mdns | Runs | Wkts |
|---|---|---|---|---|---|---|---|---|
| Nichols | 30 | 5 | 99 | 3 | 11 | — | 73 | — |
| Farnes | 35 | 7 | 114 | 4 | 11 | 1 | 42 | 3 |
| Smith | 19 | 4 | 57 | 1 | 21 | 4 | 84 | 3 |
| O'Connor | 50 | 12 | 114 | 1 | 15 | 4 | 36 | — |
| Eastman | 11 | 2 | 29 | 1 | | | | |

**Hampshire Bowling**

|  | Overs | Mdns | Runs | Wkts |
|---|---|---|---|---|
| Kennedy | 26 | 8 | 60 | 1 |
| Herman | 25 | 1 | 122 | 1 |
| Boyes | 44 | 8 | 158 | 2 |
| Hill | 32 | 8 | 83 | 2 |
| Creese | 12 | 1 | 59 | — |
| Brown | 8 | 2 | 14 | 1 |
| Bailey | 10 | 2 | 27 | 1 |
| Moore | 4 | — | 11 | — |
| Pothecary | 3 | — | 12 | — |
| Arnold | 2 | 1 | 3 | — |

Umpires: L. C. Braund and J. Hardstaff.


# HAMPSHIRE v SURREY

### Played at Basingstoke, June 26, 27, 1935

In the first match to be played at Basingstoke for twenty-one years, Surrey won readily by an innings and seven runs. The home county in both innings had the worst of the wicket. Following storms on Tuesday night, Lowndes decided, with disastrous consequences, to take first innings, and in an hour and three-quarters Hampshire were all out, the one stand coming from Mead and Lowndes, who added 33. Sandham and Gregory driving and pulling admirably during an opening partnership of 84, Surrey took the lead without loss, and Sandham went on to complete his 100th century in first-class cricket. Batting three hours and a half, he offered one chance and hit a 6 and eleven 4s. Fishlock drove with marked skill and next day, on a pitch affected by rain during the night, Surrey finished their innings 195 ahead. Arnold, in Hampshire's second innings, showed his best form for an hour and three-quarters, but after he left, Gover and Fender disposed of the remaining seven wickets for 91.

### Hampshire

| | | | |
|---|---|---|---|
| J. Arnold c Brooks b Gover | 0 | – b Gover | 56 |
| N. McCorkell b Gover | 0 | – c Gover b G. Wells | 4 |
| Mr A. L. Hosie c Brooks b Watts | 4 | – c Brooks b Watts | 16 |
| C. P. Mead run out | 23 | – c Brooks b Gover | 32 |
| Mr W. G. Lowndes c Brooks b Gover | 13 | – b Gover | 2 |
| W. L. Creese b Fender | 0 | – b Fender | 10 |
| Lord Tennyson b Gover | 1 | – run out | 14 |
| G. S. Boyes c Barling b Fender | 20 | – b Fender | 12 |
| G. Hill c Brooks b Watts | 3 | – c Sandham b Fender | 7 |
| Mr A. E. G. Baring not out | 8 | – b Fender | 0 |
| O. W. Herman b Fender | 5 | – not out | 22 |
| L-b 1, n-b 1 | 2 | B 8, l-b 3, n-b 2 | 13 |
| | **79** | | **188** |

### Surrey

| | | | |
|---|---|---|---|
| A. Sandham c Herman b Hill | 103 | E. W. Whitfield b Creese | 2 |
| R. J. Gregory lbw (N), b Hill | 51 | E. A. Watts b Hill | 2 |
| H. S. Squires b Baring | 8 | E. W. Brooks b Baring | 16 |
| T. H. Barling lbw b Hill | 12 | A. R. Gover not out | 3 |
| L. B. Fishlock c Boyes b Creese | 56 | B 1, l-b 3, n-b 1 | 5 |
| Mr H. M. Garland-Wells c Arnold b Creese | 1 | | |
| Mr P. G. H. Fender c Tennyson b Hill | 15 | | **274** |

## Surrey Bowling

| | Overs | Mdns | Runs | Wkts | Overs | Mdns | Runs | Wkts |
|---|---|---|---|---|---|---|---|---|
| Gover . . . . . . . . . . . | 11 | 4 | 21 | 4 | 21 | 5 | 51 | 3 |
| Watts . . . . . . . . . . . | 9 | 1 | 29 | 2 | 11 | 2 | 30 | 1 |
| Fender . . . . . . . . . . | 11.1 | 4 | 27 | 3 | 16.2 | 1 | 64 | 4 |
| Garland-Wells . . . . . | | | | | 10 | 2 | 30 | 1 |

## Hampshire Bowling

| | Overs | Mdns | Runs | Wkts |
|---|---|---|---|---|
| Baring . . . . . . . . . . | 16.3 | 4 | 45 | 2 |
| Lowndes . . . . . . . . | 8 | — | 27 | — |
| Herman . . . . . . . . . | 13 | 1 | 73 | — |
| Boyes . . . . . . . . . . . | 13 | 4 | 35 | — |
| Creese . . . . . . . . . . | 14 | 3 | 43 | 3 |
| Hill . . . . . . . . . . . . . | 18 | — | 46 | 5 |

Umpires: J. Hardstaff and W. Reeves.

# HAMPSHIRE v WARWICKSHIRE

### At Bournemouth, July 28, 29, 1937

Hampshire won by an innings and 143 runs. With the highest score ever made for Hampshire, beating by 12 R. M. Poore's 304 against Somerset in 1899, Moore helped materially in his side's most emphatic victory of the season. Moore was last out, after batting six hours and twenty minutes. He drove with customary power, and cut with facility, hitting forty-three 4s, besides three 6s, one of which completed his first century of the season. He did not give a chance to hand. Paris shared in a fourth wicket stand of 207 in two hours and Creese also attacked the bowling vigorously. An injured knee caused the retirement of Boyes, but Hampshire disposed of Warwickshire twice on the second day, only Santall and Kilner offering a bold front. Herman's deliveries often "kicked" and few of the batsmen were comfortable. In the follow-on Creese flighted and spun his left arm slows to fine purpose.

## Hampshire

| | |
|---|---|
| Mr R. H. Moore lbw b Hollies . . . . . . . . . . .316 | D. F. Walker c Kilner b Hollies . . . . . . . . . . 2 |
| N. McCorkell lbw (N) b Mayer . . . . . . . . . 33 | G. Hill st Buckingham b Paine . . . . . . . . . . 0 |
| W. L. Creese b Paine . . . . . . . . . . . . . . . . . 45 | G. S. Boyes retired hurt . . . . . . . . . . . . . . . 8 |
| J. Arnold lbw b paine . . . . . . . . . . . . . . . . 13 | G. E. M. Heath not out . . . . . . . . . . . . . . . . 2 |
| Mr C. G. A. Paris b Hollies . . . . . . . . . . . . . 75 | B 8, l-b 2 . . . . . . . . . . . . . . . . . . 10 |
| A. E. Pothecary c Wyatt b Santall . . . . . . . . 2 | |
| O. W. Herman c Croom b Hollies . . . . . . . . 3 | 509 |

## Warwickshire

| | |
|---|---|
| N. Kilner c sub b Creese . . . . . . . . . . . . . . . . . . . . . . 64 | – c Paris b Moore . . . . . . . . . . . . . . . 7 |
| A. J. Croom b Herman . . . . . . . . . . . . . . . . . . . . . . . 15 | – c Paris b Creese . . . . . . . . . . . . . . . 22 |
| W. A. Hill run out . . . . . . . . . . . . . . . . . . . . . . . . . . 7 | – lbw b Creese . . . . . . . . . . . . . . . 22 |
| Mr R. E. S. Wyatt run out . . . . . . . . . . . . . . . . . . . . 13 | – c McCorkell b Creese . . . . . . . . . . 0 |
| H. E. Dollery b Creese . . . . . . . . . . . . . . . . . . . . . . . 0 | – c McCorkell b Creese . . . . . . . . . . 0 |
| F. R. Santall c McCorkell b Herman . . . . . . . . . . . . 32 | – c and b Heath . . . . . . . . . . . . . . . 69 |
| J. S. Ord c Moore b Creese . . . . . . . . . . . . . . . . . . . . 8 | – c McCorkell b Heath . . . . . . . . . . 36 |
| J. Buckingham b Herman . . . . . . . . . . . . . . . . . . . . . 12 | – c Walker b Creese . . . . . . . . . . . . . . 0 |
| G. E. Paine b Herman . . . . . . . . . . . . . . . . . . . . . . . . 2 | – c McCorkell b Creese . . . . . . . . . 4 |
| J. H. Mayer c Paris b Herman . . . . . . . . . . . . . . . . . 16 | – not out . . . . . . . . . . . . . . . . . . . . . 6 |
| E. Hollies not out . . . . . . . . . . . . . . . . . . . . . . . . . . . 1 | – b Creese . . . . . . . . . . . . . . . . . . . . . 2 |
| B 10, l-b 5 . . . . . . . . . . . . . . . . . . . . . . . 15 | B 9, l-b 4 . . . . . . . . . . . . . . . 13 |
| 185 | 181 |

**Warwickshire Bowling**

| | Overs | Mdns | Runs | Wkts |
|---|---|---|---|---|
| Mayer ........... | 23 | 4 | 90 | 1 |
| Wyatt ........... | 11 | 2 | 51 | — |
| Hollies .......... | 49.5 | 9 | 205 | 4 |
| Santall .......... | 11 | — | 56 | 1 |
| Paine ........... | 32 | 7 | 97 | 3 |

**Hampshire Bowling**

| | Overs | Mdns | Runs | Wkts | Overs | Mdns | Runs | Wkts |
|---|---|---|---|---|---|---|---|---|
| Herman ......... | 17.4 | 5 | 42 | 5 | 8 | 2 | 12 | — |
| Heath ........... | 10 | 4 | 19 | — | 15 | — | 40 | 2 |
| Creese .......... | 23 | 4 | 74 | 3 | 22.3 | 3 | 85 | 7 |
| Hill ............. | 16 | 4 | 35 | — | 5 | — | 22 | — |
| Moore .......... | | | | | 7 | 5 | 9 | 1 |

Umpires: W. Bestwick and A. Skelding.

# HAMPSHIRE v LANCASHIRE

## At Southampton, May 7, 9, 10, 1938

Lancashire won by an innings and 160 runs. With a stand of 306, which eclipsed everything else in the match, Paynter and Oldfield wrote a new page in Lancashire's cricket history. The previous highest partnership for the third Lancashire wicket stood to Spooner and Hallows, with 296 against Essex in 1904. Paynter and Oldfield were together for three hours forty minutes during which time Oldfield, driving tremendously hard, hit a 6 and nineteen 4s. He gave three chances before reaching 50 and his display could not be compared with that of Paynter who made not a single mistake. Even more fierce in power of stroke, Paynter obtained seven 6s and twenty-five 4s in the second highest score of his career. Six of the major hits sent the ball out of the ground. In a deadly spell on the opening day Nutter dismissed Walker, Pothecary and Arnold for five runs but McCorkell batted attractively and Paris showed strength on the leg-side. Five Hampshire wickets fell in the second innings for 29 and Lancashire's victory was then inevitable.

## Hampshire

| | | | | |
|---|---|---|---|---|
| N. McCorkell b Nutter ....................... | 83 | – lbw b Pollard ................... | 2 |
| D. F. Walker c Pollard b Nutter ................. | 9 | – b Phillipson .................... | 10 |
| A. E. Pothecary c and b Nutter ................. | 5 | – b Phillipson .................... | 1 |
| J. Arnold st Farrimond b Nutter .............. | 0 | – c Lister b Phillipson ............. | 10 |
| Mr C. G. A. Paris b Nutter ................... | 76 | – c Farrimond b Pollard .......... | 2 |
| W. L. Creese c Hopwood b Wilkinson ........... | 33 | – not out ...................... | 61 |
| Rev. J. W. J. Steele b Pollard ................. | 35 | – c Farrimond b Pollard .......... | 13 |
| G. S. Boyes c Nutter b Pollard ................. | 6 | – b Nutter ...................... | 21 |
| G. Hill lbw b Nutter ......................... | 6 | – c and b Wilkinson ............. | 12 |
| O. W. Herman c Farrimond b Pollard .......... | 17 | – c Phillipson b Nutter ........... | 8 |
| G. E. M. Heath not out ...................... | 0 | – st Farrimond b Wilkinson ........ | 0 |
| L-b 5, n-b 2 ...................... | 7 | L-b 1 ................. | 1 |
| | **277** | | **141** |

## Lancashire

| | | | | |
|---|---|---|---|---|
| C. Washbrook b Heath | 4 | Mr W. H. L. Lister b Steele | 0 |
| E. Paynter c Walker b Hill | 291 | R. Pollard not out | 19 |
| J. Iddon c Boyes b Herman | 52 | | |
| N. Oldfield c Walker b Herman | 135 | B 3, l-b 5 | 8 |
| J. L. Hopwood c Paris b Heath | 34 | | |
| A. Nutter not out | 35 | (6 wkts dec.) | 578 |

W. E. Phillipson, W. Farrimond and L. L. Wilkinson did not bat.

## Lancashire Bowling

| | Overs | Mdns | Runs | Wkts | Overs | Mdns | Runs | Wkts |
|---|---|---|---|---|---|---|---|---|
| Phillipson | 19 | 3 | 88 | — | 16 | 5 | 36 | 3 |
| Pollard | 24.1 | 6 | 52 | 3 | 19 | 7 | 48 | 3 |
| Wilkinson | 25 | 5 | 64 | 1 | 10.2 | 2 | 28 | 2 |
| Nutter | 27 | 5 | 66 | 6 | 7 | 1 | 28 | 2 |

## Hampshire Bowling

| | Overs | Mdns | Runs | Wkts |
|---|---|---|---|---|
| Herman | 25 | 2 | 113 | 2 |
| Heath | 34 | 7 | 119 | 2 |
| Steele | 33 | 4 | 104 | 1 |
| Boyes | 27 | 6 | 118 | — |
| Hill | 20 | 4 | 94 | 1 |
| Creese | 2 | — | 22 | — |

Umpires: J. Hardstaff and H. W. Lee.

# KENT

## KENT v MIDDLESEX

Played at Canterbury, August 4, 5, 6, 1920

Middlesex won the second match of the week by 5 runs. Rain stopped play on Thursday when Kent, with four wickets in hand, wanted 29 runs for victory. Wet grass and a light drizzle seemed to favour Kent, who would probably have won had not a return by Hendren run out Humphreys, who responded to Fairservice's call for a short single. Freeman fell a run later, and Middlesex snatched a win, thanks mainly to Hearne, who took eight wickets for 26. A few hundred people went to the St Lawrence ground expecting a great struggle, and there was much excitement. In the visitors' second innings Freeman did the hat trick. Hendren was the most successful batsman, and Stevens helped him pull the game round when Middlesex, with six out the second time, led by only 42. Haig in Kent's first innings actually took his seven wickets in thirty-seven balls for 14 runs after Hardinge and Seymour had made the one big stand in the match.

### Middlesex

| | | | |
|---|---|---|---|
| H. W. Lee c and b Woolley | 4 | – c Freeman b Woolley | 12 |
| Mr H. L. Dales lbw b Freeman | 8 | – b Woolley | 11 |
| J. W. Hearne b Woolley | 20 | – lbw b Freeman | 10 |
| E. Hendren not out | 77 | – b Freeman | 45 |
| Mr P. F. Warner b Freeman | 1 | – c Hubble b Woolley | 0 |
| Mr F. T. Mann lbw b Freeman | 11 | – c Seymour b Freeman | 0 |
| Mr N. Haig c Woolley b Fairservice | 57 | – b Freeman | 0 |
| Mr G. T. S. Stevens lbw b Fairservice | 23 | – lbw b Fairservice | 26 |
| H. R. Murrell c Freeman b Woolley | 4 | – b Freeman | 16 |
| Dr C. H. Gunasekara run out | 0 | – not out | 4 |
| T. J. Durston b Woolley | 1 | – b Freeman | 1 |
| B 1, l-b 5 | 6 | L-b 1, n-b 1 | 2 |
| | **212** | | **127** |

### Kent

| | | | |
|---|---|---|---|
| H. T. W. Hardinge c Dales b Haig | 82 | – lbw b Hearne | 16 |
| Mr A. F. Bickmore c Murrell b Dales | 8 | – b Hearne | 51 |
| James Seymour c Hearne b Stevens | 73 | – c Gunasekara b Stevens | 7 |
| F. E. Woolley st Murrell b Haig | 18 | – b Hearne | 0 |
| J. C. Hubble b Haig | 11 | – b Hearne | 0 |
| Mr L. P. Hedges b Haig | 10 | – lbw b Hearne | 4 |
| E. Humphreys c Gunasekara b Haig | 0 | – run out | 13 |
| Mr L. H. W. Troughton st Murrell b Haig | 3 | – c and b Hearne | 12 |
| Mr G. E. C. Wood c and b Hearne | 0 | – b Hearne | 3 |
| W. J. Fairservice c Gunasekara b Haig | 3 | – not out | 2 |
| A. P. Freeman not out | 1 | – b Hearne | 0 |
| B 5, l-b 2, n-b 1 | 8 | B 4, l-b 2, n-b 3 | 9 |
| | **217** | | **117** |

### Kent Bowling

| | Overs | Mdns | Runs | Wkts | Overs | Mdns | Runs | Wkts |
|---|---|---|---|---|---|---|---|---|
| Fairservice | 22 | 7 | 54 | 2 | 11 | 2 | 35 | 1 |
| Woolley | 27 | 9 | 62 | 4 | 18 | 6 | 42 | 3 |
| Freeman | 14 | 2 | 55 | 3 | 11.3 | 3 | 36 | 6 |
| Hardinge | 7 | 1 | 28 | — | 4 | 1 | 12 | — |
| Humphreys | 2 | — | 7 | — | | | | |

**Middlesex Bowling**

| | Overs | Mdns | Runs | Wkts | Overs | Mdns | Runs | Wkts |
|---|---|---|---|---|---|---|---|---|
| Durston .......... | 17 | 6 | 35 | — | 7 | 1 | 30 | — |
| Gunasekara ....... | 9 | 6 | 11 | — | | | | |
| Hearne ........... | 22 | 2 | 70 | 1 | 16.5 | 3 | 26 | 8 |
| Dales ............ | 5 | 1 | 20 | 1 | | | | |
| Stevens .......... | 8 | 1 | 31 | 1 | 4 | — | 16 | 1 |
| Lee .............. | 3 | — | 9 | 1 | 4 | 1 | 10 | — |
| Haig ............. | 16.1 | 8 | 33 | 7 | 7 | — | 26 | — |

Umpires: A. Millward and F. Parris.

# KENT v LEICESTERSHIRE

Played at Gravesend, June 28, 29, 30, 1922

Beating Leicestershire by an innings and 162 runs, Kent practically won the game on the first day. Play was curtailed by rain before lunch, but, after the interval, runs were put on at such a pace that, when further rain cut the afternoon's cricket short just after six o'clock, Kent's score stood at 393 for six wickets. Hardinge played admirably, but the most attractive batting was shown with Woolley and Hurst together, 126 runs being added for the fifth wicket. Woolley, who hit sixteen 4s in his 123, was quite at his best, but Hurst had the good luck to be missed twice – quite easy chances. Troughton naturally declared first thing on Thursday morning. Drenching rain during luncheon caused a long delay and a section of the crowd became very impatient. Some of them got quite out of hand, even making their way into the pavilion. After a fresh start had been made rain came down again. In the time available Leicestershire lost six wickets for 143, King being not out 75. On Friday the Leicestershire batsmen were helpless on a very treacherous pitch, and could do nothing against Woolley and Freeman. King was batting about two hours and a quarter for his 79 and hit twelve 4s.

## Kent

| | |
|---|---|
| H. T. W. Hardinge b Benskin ............ 83 | Mr G. N. Foster b Shipman ............. 6 |
| G. C. Collins lbw b Astill ............... 13 | Mr L. H. W. Troughton not out .......... 11 |
| J. C. Hubble c Fowke b Benskin ......... 28 | |
| F. E. Woolley st Sidwell b Astill .........123 | B 8, l-b 9, n-b 1 .............. 18 |
| W. Ashdown b Benskin ................ 7 | |
| Mr C. S. Hurst not out .................104 | (6 wkts dec.) 393 |

S. G. Hearn, A. P. Freeman and Capt. W. S. Cornwallis did not bat.

## Leicestershire

| | | |
|---|---|---|
| A. Mounteney b Collins ....................... 2 | – c Freeman b Woolley ............ | 6 |
| W. E. Astill lbw b Woolley .................... 3 | – c Collins b Freeman ............. | 20 |
| J. H. King c Foster b Cornwallis ................ 79 | – b Woolley ..................... | 0 |
| Major G. H. S. Fowke lbw b Freeman ............ 26 | – st Hubble b Woolley ............. | 4 |
| T. E. Sidwell c Ashdown b Freeman ............. 13 | – c Freeman b Woolley ............ | 2 |
| S. Coe b Woolley .......................... 0 | – b Woolley .................... | 0 |
| A. Shipman lbw b Woolley .................. 12 | – lbw b Freeman ................. | 0 |
| W. E. Benskin b Cornwallis .................. 4 | – not out ..................... | 7 |
| N. B. Lee not out .......................... 16 | – c Hubble b Collins ............. | 4 |
| F. Bale b Woolley .......................... 0 | – b Freeman .................... | 15 |
| A. Skelding b Freeman ....................... 5 | – b Freeman .................... | 0 |
| B 2, l-b 7, n-b 2 ..................... 11 | L-b 2 ................. | 2 |
| | | |
| 171 | | 60 |

## Leicestershire Bowling

| | Overs | Mdns | Runs | Wkts |
|---|---|---|---|---|
| Skelding ......... | 17 | 3 | 50 | — |
| Benskin .......... | 18 | 2 | 61 | 3 |
| Shipman ......... | 10 | 1 | 48 | 1 |
| Astill ........... | 24 | 3 | 104 | 2 |
| Bale ............. | 14 | — | 79 | — |
| King ............. | 9 | 2 | 33 | — |

## Kent Bowling

| | Overs | Mdns | Runs | Wkts | Overs | Mdns | Runs | Wkts |
|---|---|---|---|---|---|---|---|---|
| Collins ........... | 4 | 1 | 5 | 1 | 5 | 1 | 14 | 1 |
| Woolley .......... | 30 | 9 | 59 | 4 | 11 | 6 | 23 | 5 |
| Freeman ........ | 24.5 | 7 | 55 | 3 | 17.5 | 2 | 20 | 4 |
| Ashdown ........ | 4 | — | 13 | — | 1 | — | 1 | — |
| Hardinge ........ | 7 | 3 | 16 | — | | | | |
| Cornwallis ....... | 5 | 1 | 12 | 2 | | | | |

Umpires: T. Flowers and H. Barrett.

# KENT v NOTTINGHAMSHIRE

### Played at Dover, August 16, 17, 18, 1922

Kent had a great triumph in the first of the Dover fixtures, beating Nottinghamshire by an innings and 69 runs. With a score of 351 they went a long way towards victory on the first day. J. L. Bryan and Hardinge opened the innings in brilliant style by getting 158 together. Bryan hit a six and nine 4s in his 84, and Hardinge played flawless cricket for over three hours and a half. The sensation of the match came in the later stages, Collins bowling as he had never bowled in his life. Twelve wickets fell to him in the course of the second day, and in the end he had the satisfaction of adding his name to the list of bowlers who have taken all ten wickets in one innings. He kept a capital length and came off the ground with plenty of life, but it was not easy to understand why he left all his previous form so far behind. For once last season the Nottinghamshire batting was decidedly poor.

## Kent

| | |
|---|---|
| Mr J. L. Bryan b Richmond ............. | 84 |
| H. T. W. Hardinge c Oates b Richmond ... | 90 |
| J. Seymour b Staples .................. | 21 |
| F. E. Woolley b Richmond ............. | 31 |
| Mr A. F. Bickmore lbw b J. Gunn ........ | 26 |
| Mr G. J. Bryan b Staples .............. | 28 |
| W. Ashdown b Staples ................. | 7 |
| G. C. Collins lbw b Staples ............. | 5 |
| J. C. Hubble b Barratt ................. | 30 |
| Mr L. H. W. Troughton b Barratt ........ | 15 |
| A. P. Freeman not out ................. | 1 |
| L-b 10, w 1, n-b 2 ............. | 13 |
| | **351** |

## Nottinghamshire

| | | | |
|---|---|---|---|
| G. Gunn lbw b Collins ...................... | 6 | – b Collins ..................... | 6 |
| W. Whysall c G. J. Bryan b Collins ............ | 4 | – lbw b Collins ................. | 2 |
| J. Gunn c Ashdown b Collins................... | 15 | – b Collins ..................... | 4 |
| Mr A. W. Carr b Collins ..................... | 22 | – c Freeman b Collins ........... | 0 |
| J. Hardstaff not out ....................... | 18 | – lbw b Collins ................. | 49 |
| W. Payton c Woolley b Freeman ............... | 2 | – c Hubble b Collins ............ | 42 |
| G. M. Lee c Woolley b Collins ................ | 1 | – c and b Collins ............... | 1 |
| S. J. Staples b Collins ...................... | 5 | – b Collins ..................... | 19 |
| T. Oates lbw b Freeman ..................... | 1 | – c Ashdown b Collins ........... | 8 |
| F. Barratt b Freeman ....................... | 11 | – c Freeman b Collins ........... | 19 |
| L. Richmond b Woolley ...................... | 19 | – not out ...................... | 7 |
| B 4, l-b 10, n-b 2 .................... | 16 | B 2, l-b 1, w 1, n-b 1 ....... | 5 |
| | **120** | | **162** |

### Nottinghamshire Bowling

|  | Overs | Mdns | Runs | Wkts |
|---|---|---|---|---|
| Barratt ........... | 27.5 | 5 | 81 | 2 |
| Staples ........... | 40 | 11 | 92 | 4 |
| Richmond ........ | 23 | 10 | 87 | 3 |
| J. Gunn .......... | 33 | 7 | 78 | 1 |

### Kent Bowling

|  | Overs | Mdns | Runs | Wkts | Overs | Mdns | Runs | Wkts |
|---|---|---|---|---|---|---|---|---|
| Collins ........... | 17 | 6 | 18 | 6 | 19.3 | 4 | 65 | 10 |
| Woolley .......... | 13.4 | 2 | 47 | 1 | 7 | 2 | 15 | — |
| Freeman ......... | 14 | 4 | 21 | 3 | 20 | 7 | 55 | — |
| G. J. Bryan ....... | 7 | — | 18 | — | 3 | — | 14 | — |
| Ashdown ......... |  |  |  |  | 5 | — | 8 | — |

Umpires: B. Brown and G. A. Fuller.

## KENT v LANCASHIRE

Played at Dover, June 30, July 1, 2, 1926

A fine match ended in Lancashire's favour by 33 runs. Consistent batting, followed by effective bowling from Macdonald, enabled Lancashire to lead by 182 and later on thanks to a brilliant display by Ernest Tyldesley the visitors declared, Kent being set 426 to get. Two wickets fell for 41, but Hardinge and Woolley added no fewer than 253 in two hours and fifty minutes. Woolley hit fifteen 4s in a characteristic innings and Hardinge thirteen 4s during a stay of three hours fifty minutes. Kent with five wickets in hand wanted only another 65 runs when Macdonald accomplished the hat trick, dismissing Chapman, Deed, and Wright, and that proved the turning point.

### Lancashire

| | | | |
|---|---|---|---|
| H. Makepeace b Collins ........................ | 71 | – c Hubble b Ashdown ............ | 37 |
| C. Hallows c Freeman b Ashdown ............. | 12 | – lbw b Wright .................. | 2 |
| E. Tyldesley c Ashdown b Freeman ............. | 69 | – not out ...................... | 144 |
| F. Watson st Hubble b Freeman ................ | 78 | – b Freeman .................... | 3 |
| J. Iddon lbw b Wright ........................ | 18 | – b Chapman ................... | 39 |
| T. M. Halliday b Cornwallis .................... | 13 | – not out ....................... | 1 |
| Mr L. Green c Hubble b Collins ................. | 18 | | |
| F. M. Sibbles c Hubble b Wright ............... | 17 | | |
| E. A. Macdonald c Chapman b Freeman ......... | 0 | – c Woolley b Chapman ........... | 13 |
| G. Duckworth b Wright ....................... | 10 | | |
| R. Tyldesley not out ......................... | 15 | | |
| B 1, l-b 12, w 1, n-b 1 ................ | 15 | B 1, l-b 3 .............. | 4 |
| | 336 | (5 wkts dec.) | 243 |

## Kent

| | | | |
|---|---|---|---|
| H. T. W. Hardinge c Duckworth b Macdonald | 27 | – run out | 132 |
| W. Ashdown c Duckworth b Macdonald | 19 | – b Sibbles | 6 |
| J. Seymour c R. Tyldesley b Macdonald | 1 | – c Halliday b Macdonald | 24 |
| F. E. Woolley b Watson | 24 | – lbw b Watson | 137 |
| Mr A. P. F. Chapman c Duckworth b Macdonald | 3 | – c Makepeace b Macdonald | 49 |
| Mr J. A. Deed b Watson | 8 | – b Macdonald | 0 |
| G. C. Collins c Duckworth b Macdonald | 17 | – b R. Tyldesley | 0 |
| J. C. Hubble c Duckworth b Macdonald | 20 | – st Duckworth b R. Tyldesley | 17 |
| C. Wright st Duckworth b R. Tyldesley | 19 | – b Macdonald | 0 |
| A. P. Freeman b Macdonald | 14 | – b Macdonald | 13 |
| Capt. W. S. Cornwallis not out | 1 | – not out | 1 |
| N-b 1 | 1 | B 8, l-b 1, n-b 4 | 13 |
| | **154** | | **392** |

## Kent Bowling

| | Overs | Mdns | Runs | Wkts | Overs | Mdns | Runs | Wkts |
|---|---|---|---|---|---|---|---|---|
| Wright | 38.2 | 9 | 81 | 3 | 16 | 2 | 51 | 1 |
| Cornwallis | 7 | — | 26 | 1 | | | | |
| Ashdown | 24 | 4 | 69 | 1 | 16 | 2 | 46 | 1 |
| Freeman | 50 | 4 | 96 | 3 | 12 | 4 | 34 | 1 |
| Woolley | 8 | 2 | 23 | — | 11 | 1 | 42 | — |
| Collins | 14 | 3 | 25 | 2 | 5 | — | 24 | — |
| Hardinge | 2 | 1 | 1 | — | 7 | 1 | 18 | — |
| Chapman | | | | | 4 | — | 24 | 2 |

## Lancashire Bowling

| | Overs | Mdns | Runs | Wkts | Overs | Mdns | Runs | Wkts |
|---|---|---|---|---|---|---|---|---|
| Macdonald | 17.3 | — | 81 | 7 | 30 | 2 | 106 | 5 |
| Sibbles | 9 | 3 | 27 | — | 16 | 1 | 75 | 1 |
| R. Tyldesley | 10 | 3 | 35 | 1 | 22.4 | 1 | 93 | 2 |
| Watson | 2 | 1 | 10 | 2 | 16 | 2 | 58 | 1 |
| Iddon | | | | | 9 | — | 47 | — |

Umpires: F. Chester and H. Butt.

# KENT v HAMPSHIRE

## Played at Canterbury, July 31, August 2, 3, 1926

A remarkable match ended in a victory for Kent by nine wickets. Left with 172 to get in a little over two hours, Kent lost Hardinge at 17, and 20 runs later Ashdown retired. Then Chapman, who, on the previous day, had helped Hardinge in a partnership of 118, joined Woolley and, in an hour, the rest of the runs were hit off. Hampshire looked like being beaten on the second afternoon, for, going in 268 in arrear, they had by the tea interval lost six wickets for 59 runs. Parker and Mead, however, put on 194 before stumps were drawn and, on the following morning, raised the total to 327, their partnership altogether producing 270 runs in two hours and fifty minutes.

## Hampshire

| | | | |
|---|---:|---|---:|
| G. Brown b Wright | 24 | – c Hubble b Wright | 17 |
| J. Newman run out | 27 | – st Hubble b Ashdown | 9 |
| A. Kennedy c Ashdown b Wright | 0 | – b Wright | 6 |
| C. P. Mead lbw b Freeman | 27 | – not out | 175 |
| Mr H. L. V. Day b Freeman | 5 | – c Ashdown b Wright | 5 |
| Hon. L. H. Tennyson c Hubble b Freeman | 1 | – c Hubble b Wright | 1 |
| Mr A. K. Judd b Freeman | 0 | – lbw b Freeman | 1 |
| Mr W. N. McBride st Hubble b Marriott | 3 | – c Hubble b Marriott | 2 |
| Mr J. P. Parker run out | 16 | – c Freeman b Marriott | 156 |
| W. H. Livsey not out | 26 | – c Hardinge b Collins | 31 |
| G. S. Boyes st Hubble b Freeman | 8 | – b Freeman | 1 |
| L-b 6, n-b 1 | 7 | B 25, l-b 6, w 1, n-b 3 | 35 |
| | **144** | | **439** |

## Kent

| | | | |
|---|---:|---|---:|
| H. T. W. Hardinge c Tennyson b Newman | 117 | – c Kennedy b Newman | 9 |
| W. Ashdown run out | 6 | – retired hurt | 14 |
| Mr J. L. Bryan c Boyes b Kennedy | 0 | | |
| F. E. Woolley c and b Newman | 67 | – not out | 62 |
| Mr A. P. F. Chapman run out | 136 | – not out | 81 |
| J. C. Hubble b Kennedy | 3 | | |
| G. C. Collins b Boyes | 26 | | |
| C. Wright c Parker b Newman | 19 | | |
| A. P. Freeman c Tennyson b Newman | 20 | | |
| Capt. W. S. Cornwallis not out | 3 | | |
| Mr C. S. Marriott c McBride b Newman | 4 | | |
| B 3, l-b 6, w 2 | 11 | B 6 | 6 |
| | **412** | | **172** |

## Kent Bowling

| | Overs | Mdns | Runs | Wkts | Overs | Mdns | Runs | Wkts |
|---|---:|---:|---:|---:|---:|---:|---:|---:|
| Wright | 20 | 5 | 43 | 2 | 28 | 6 | 93 | 4 |
| Ashdown | 5 | 1 | 13 | — | 19 | 3 | 44 | 1 |
| Marriott | 13 | 2 | 38 | 1 | 24 | 4 | 67 | 2 |
| Freeman | 18 | 7 | 43 | 5 | 33.2 | 7 | 135 | 2 |
| Cornwallis | | | | | 4 | — | 12 | — |
| Woolley | | | | | 6 | 2 | 19 | — |
| Collins | | | | | 8 | 3 | 16 | 1 |
| Hardinge | | | | | 7 | 1 | 18 | — |

## Hampshire Bowling

| | Overs | Mdns | Runs | Wkts | Overs | Mdns | Runs | Wkts |
|---|---:|---:|---:|---:|---:|---:|---:|---:|
| Kennedy | 42 | 10 | 137 | 2 | 10 | — | 42 | — |
| Newman | 37.4 | 9 | 156 | 5 | 8 | — | 52 | 1 |
| Boyes | 17 | 3 | 52 | 1 | 5 | — | 30 | — |
| McBride | 17 | 2 | 56 | — | 2.5 | — | 14 | — |
| Brown | | | | | 6 | — | 28 | — |

Umpires: H. Young and L. C. Braund.

# KENT v HAMPSHIRE

Played at Canterbury, July 30, August 1, 2, 1927

Kent played very good all-round cricket in the opening match of the Canterbury Week, and beat Hampshire by an innings and 92 runs. The home side were seen to great advantage on the first day, when, after staying in for five hours and a quarter, they got rid of two of their opponents for 2 runs. Freeman and Wright bowling splendidly on the Monday, Hampshire were all out for 81. Rain then came on, and stopped cricket until the next morning, when Hampshire, following on, lost three wickets for 62. Mead made a great effort to save his side from defeat, batting for over four hours, but off what must have been the last ball of the match he was caught at slip, Kent's victory thus being obtained in a very exciting finish. Mead gave no chance at all in a remarkable exhibition which included fourteen 4s. Freeman, in the whole game, took fourteen wickets for just over 9 runs apiece. Kent's batting on the opening day was consistent and extremely skilful. Bryan and Ashdown put on 134 in less than two hours, and Woolley and Evans added 110 in eighty minutes, while Chapman hit up 64 in an hour, with ten 4s as his chief strokes. Ames also showed good form.

### Kent

| | |
|---|---|
| Mr J. L. Bryan c Tennyson b Newman .... 59 | L. Ames st Livsey b Brown ............. 46 |
| W. Ashdown c Tennyson b Newman ...... 54 | C. Wright lbw b Brown ................ 13 |
| F. E. Woolley lbw b Kennedy ........... 88 | A. P. Freeman c Mead b Brown .......... 1 |
| Mr A. J. Evans b Newman .............. 46 | Mr C. S. Marriott not out .............. 5 |
| Mr A. P. F. Chapman c Brutton b Boyes ... 64 | B 6, l-b 8, w 1 ................ 15 |
| H. T. W. Hardinge b Newman .......... 0 | |
| Mr G. B. Legge b Boyes ............... 16 | 407 |

### Hampshire

| | |
|---|---|
| G. Brown c Ashdown b Wright ................. | 1 – st Ames b Freeman ............ 0 |
| Mr C. P. Brutton b Wright .................... | 0 – lbw b Freeman ................ 5 |
| Mr R. Aird c Evans b Freeman ................ | 6 – lbw b Wright ................. 37 |
| C. P. Mead c Woolley b Freeman .............. | 5 – c Woolley b Freeman .........128 |
| J. Newman c Bryan b Freeman ................ | 32 – c Ashdown b Freeman ......... 12 |
| Hon. L. H. Tennyson c Ames b Freeman ......... | 7 – c Bryan b Marriott ........... 28 |
| Mr A. K. Judd b Freeman .................... | 1 – c Legge b Freeman .......... 10 |
| Mr H. L. V. Day c Ames b Freeman ............ | 4 – c Evans b Freeman .......... 0 |
| A. Kennedy c Ames b Wright ................. | 14 – c and b Freeman ............. 2 |
| W. H. Livsey c Ames b Wright ................ | 0 – c Wright b Freeman .......... 0 |
| G. S. Boyes not out ........................ | 7 – not out ..................... 0 |
| B 2, l-b 1, n-b 1 .................... 4 | B 6, l-b 4, n-b 2 .......... 12 |
| 81 | 234 |

### Hampshire Bowling

| | Overs | Mdns | Runs | Wkts |
|---|---|---|---|---|
| Kennedy ........ | 35 | 10 | 113 | 1 |
| Newman ........ | 38 | 5 | 115 | 4 |
| Brown .......... | 24.5 | 4 | 72 | 3 |
| Boyes .......... | 22 | 2 | 92 | 2 |

### Kent Bowling

| | Overs | Mdns | Runs | Wkts | Overs | Mdns | Runs | Wkts |
|---|---|---|---|---|---|---|---|---|
| Wright ......... | 15 | 4 | 25 | 4 | 13 | 2 | 40 | 1 |
| Freeman ........ | 17.3 | 5 | 38 | 6 | 40.1 | 10 | 91 | 8 |
| Marriott ......... | 7 | 2 | 11 | — | 28 | 8 | 44 | 1 |
| Ashdown ........ | 3 | 1 | 3 | — | 3 | 1 | 4 | — |
| Woolley ......... | | | | | 10 | 2 | 29 | — |
| Hardinge ........ | | | | | 6 | — | 14 | — |

Umpires: F. Sugg and H. Butt.

## KENT v MCC

Played at Folkestone, September 7, 8, 9, 1927

In a game marked by much brilliant batting, MCC defeated Kent by 188 runs. Hendren, for the first time in his career, enjoyed the distinction of making two separate 100s in a match. His form in each innings was magnificent. On the first day he batted two hours and ten minutes, and hit two 6s and thirteen 4s. In his second innings, he had two 6s and eleven 4s during a stay of eighty minutes, he and Hearne in that time adding 158 runs. Against a lot of good bowling, Woolley, on the second day, gave a dazzling exhibition, making 141 in two hours and three-quarters, and at no time being in the slightest difficulty. He hit a 6 and seventeen 4s.

### MCC

| | | |
|---|---|---|
| G. Brown lbw b Wright | 37 | – b Wright ... 4 |
| J. Newman lbw b Freeman | 49 | – b Freeman ... 13 |
| J. W. Hearne c Woolley b Freeman | 21 | – c Legge b Chapman ... 100 |
| E. Hendren c Ames b Freeman | 119 | – b Freeman ... 102 |
| Mr H. Ashton lbw b Freeman | 8 | – run out ... 4 |
| Hon. L. H. Tennyson c Hubble b Wright | 18 | – b Freeman ... 9 |
| Hon. F. S. G. Calthorpe c Freeman b Wright | 13 | – not out ... 15 |
| Mr A. H. H. Gilligan c Hilder b Wright | 31 | – lbw b Legge ... 1 |
| Mr F. T. Mann b Wright | 22 | – c Chapman b Hilder ... 13 |
| G. Cox not out | 8 | |
| T. J. Durston b Wright | 0 | |
| B 8, l-b 9 | 17 | B 10, l-b 4 ... 14 |

343      (8 wkts dec.) 275

### Kent

| | | |
|---|---|---|
| H. T. W. Hardinge b Durston | 0 | – st Brown b Newman ... 19 |
| W. Ashdown b Durston | 1 | – b Durston ... 0 |
| F. E. Woolley not out | 141 | – c Brown b Durston ... 5 |
| L. Ames c Ashton b Durston | 18 | – lbw b Newman ... 55 |
| Mr A. P. F. Chapman c Brown b Durston | 0 | – c Brown b Newman ... 60 |
| Mr G. B. Legge c Ashton b Durston | 38 | – st Brown b Hearne ... 24 |
| J. C. Hubble c Hearne b Durston | 6 | – c Ashton b Durston ... 9 |
| Mr A. L. Hilder b Durston | 5 | – c Gilligan b Durston ... 5 |
| Mr G. E. C. Wood b Hearne | 0 | – c and b Hearne ... 2 |
| A. P. Freeman b Hearne | 7 | – b Durston ... 6 |
| C. Wright b Durston | 0 | – not out ... 14 |
| B 3, l-b 2, w 1, n-b 1 | 7 | L-b 1, w 4, n-b 3 ... 8 |

223      207

### Kent Bowling

| | Overs | Mdns | Runs | Wkts | Overs | Mdns | Runs | Wkts |
|---|---|---|---|---|---|---|---|---|
| Wright | 29.4 | 3 | 116 | 6 | 16 | 1 | 57 | 1 |
| Chapman | 5 | 1 | 13 | — | 5 | — | 22 | 1 |
| Freeman | 35 | 4 | 153 | 4 | 16 | — | 92 | 3 |
| Hilder | 12 | 4 | 35 | — | 9 | 1 | 37 | 1 |
| Hardinge | 2 | — | 9 | — | 3 | — | 16 | — |
| Ames | | | | | 4 | 1 | 21 | — |
| Legge | | | | | 2 | — | 16 | 1 |

**MCC Bowling**

| | Overs | Mdns | Runs | Wkts | Overs | Mdns | Runs | Wkts |
|---|---|---|---|---|---|---|---|---|
| Durston .......... | 23 | 3 | 110 | 8 | 17 | 4 | 64 | 5 |
| Calthorpe ........ | 9 | 1 | 29 | — | 5 | — | 18 | — |
| Hearne ........... | 15 | 3 | 46 | 2 | 15 | 1 | 59 | 2 |
| Newman ......... | 6 | — | 19 | — | 11 | — | 45 | 3 |
| Cox ............. | 4 | — | 12 | — | 4 | 1 | 13 | — |

Umpires: F. Chester and A. E. Street.

## KENT v LANCASHIRE

### Played at Maidstone, July 24, 25, 26, 1929

Lancashire beat Kent – leaders at the time in the championship – by 189 runs. Freeman made the match memorable by taking all ten wickets in the first innings of Lancashire, but Kent were outplayed. A shower and bad light handicapped the home batsmen when they went in, and on the second day the follow-on was not saved until Freeman and Todd, by hard hitting, put on 63. Lancashire, declaring before noon on Friday, always looked like winning with plenty of time to spare. They worked consistently well in the field, R. Tyldesley and Iddon, the slow bowlers, who met with most success, receiving capable support. Lancashire also showed superiority in batting. Ernest Tyldesley played two fine innings. He helped Watson put on 146 and on the second day obtained 97 out of 181. His cricket was practically faultless besides being most stylish. Watson did not give a chance, but Hallows, in scoring the second hundred of the match, had three escapes – the first when 21. Ames and Duckworth both kept wicket splendidly.

### Lancashire

| | | | |
|---|---|---|---|
| F. Watson lbw b Freeman .................... | 126 | – lbw b Woolley ................. | 25 |
| C. Hallows c Ames b Freeman ................ | 13 | – c Valentine b Wright ........... | 114 |
| E. Tyldesley st Ames b Freeman ............. | 66 | – c Legge b Wright ............. | 97 |
| J. Iddon st Ames b Freeman ................. | 30 | – st Ames b Woolley ........... | 41 |
| C. Hopwood lbw b Freeman ................. | 1 | – not out ...................... | 9 |
| T. M. Halliday b Freeman .................. | 5 | – b Freeman ................... | 4 |
| Mr L. Warburton c Todd b Freeman ............. | 14 | | |
| G. Duckworth c Ashdown b Freeman ........... | 4 | | |
| Mr P. T. Eckersley b Freeman ............... | 27 | – st Ames b Woolley ........... | 0 |
| R. Tyldesley not out ........................ | 27 | | |
| E. A. McDonald c Watson b Freeman ........... | 18 | | |
| L-b 15, n-b 1 ...................... | 16 | B 8, l-b 5, w 1, n-b 1 ....... | 15 |
| | 347 | (6 wkts dec.) | 305 |

### Kent

| | | | |
|---|---|---|---|
| H. T. W. Hardinge b Warburton ................ | 12 | – c E. Tyldesley b McDonald ....... | 57 |
| Mr G. S. Watson c Duckworth b McDonald ....... | 0 | – b Hopwood .................. | 2 |
| F. E. Woolley c Duckworth b Watson ........... | 61 | – b McDonald ................. | 16 |
| L. Ames c and b R. Tyldesley ................ | 33 | – st Duckworth b Hopwood ........ | 24 |
| W. Ashdown lbw b R. Tyldesley .............. | 1 | – not out ..................... | 52 |
| Mr B. H. Valentine c McDonald b Iddon ......... | 20 | – b R. Tyldesley ............... | 14 |
| L. Todd not out ......................... | 52 | – c Hopwood b R. Tyldesley ....... | 4 |
| Mr I. Akers-Douglas lbw b R. Tyldesley .......... | 4 | – b R. Tyldesley ............... | 0 |
| Mr G. B. Legge c Duckworth b Iddon ........... | 8 | – st Duckworth b Iddon ......... | 21 |
| A. P. Freeman b McDonald ................... | 28 | – c Halliday b Iddon ............. | 11 |
| C. Wright c Iddon b McDonald ................ | 6 | – c Eckersley b Iddon ............ | 23 |
| B 4, l-b 5, n-b 1 .................... | 10 | B 1, l-b 2, n-b 1 .......... | 4 |
| | 235 | | 228 |

## Kent Bowling

|  | Overs | Mdns | Runs | Wkts | Overs | Mdns | Runs | Wkts |
|---|---|---|---|---|---|---|---|---|
| Wright . . . . . . . . . . . | 21 | 3 | 81 | — | 19 | 1 | 73 | 2 |
| Ashdown . . . . . . . . | 17 | 5 | 43 | — | 14 | 1 | 61 | — |
| Freeman . . . . . . . . | 42 | 9 | 131 | 10 | 23 | 6 | 96 | 1 |
| Woolley . . . . . . . . . | 13 | 6 | 35 | — | 13.3 | — | 31 | 3 |
| Hardinge . . . . . . . . | 14 | 5 | 41 | — | 5 | — | 29 | — |

## Lancashire Bowling

|  | Overs | Mdns | Runs | Wkts | Overs | Mdns | Runs | Wkts |
|---|---|---|---|---|---|---|---|---|
| McDonald . . . . . . . . | 16 | 2 | 81 | 3 | 15 | — | 73 | 2 |
| Warburton . . . . . . . . | 17 | 2 | 53 | 1 | 3 | — | 19 | — |
| R. Tyldesley . . . . . . | 13 | 1 | 55 | 3 | 17 | 5 | 46 | 3 |
| Watson . . . . . . . . . . | 4 | — | 17 | 1 | 1 | 1 | — | — |
| Iddon . . . . . . . . . . . . | 8 | 3 | 19 | 2 | 9.4 | — | 38 | 3 |
| Hopwood . . . . . . . . |  |  |  |  | 28 | 8 | 48 | 2 |

Umpires: J. Stone and A. Morton.

## KENT v ESSEX

### Played at Gravesend, May 2, 4, 5, 1931

In opening the season with a victory by an innings and 47 runs, Kent were indebted mainly to two of their veterans. Freeman, first on a perfect pitch and then after rain, bowled in a way that bewildered all the Essex batsmen except O'Connor and Bray. Flight and varied spin as usual brought the slow bowler his many successes. Freeman started his work on the last day by dismissing three of the best Essex batsmen in four overs for three runs and in the match took fifteen wickets for 142 runs. Hardinge on Saturday afternoon played fine cricket and when on Monday the state of the pitch – drying after a week-end downpour – allowed of a resumption at half-past two, he again drove, pulled and cut so brilliantly that his 128 – made out of 218 – included seventeen 4s. Ashdown helped to score 178, Todd batted soundly and Valentine drove in vigorous attractive style. O'Connor played at the top of his form, and, despite poor support, always scored freely. Using the pull with special effect, he also drove well and, hitting nineteen 4s, he obtained his 100 runs in two hours and a quarter. Bray on Saturday showed to advantage while 60 runs came, and he alone offered any serious resistance during the second innings. He cut and drove in fine style.

## Essex

| | | | |
|---|---|---|---|
| J. A. Cutmore b Ashdown . . . . . . . . . . . . . . . . . . . . | 4 | – b Ashdown . . . . . . . . . . . . . . . . . . | 20 |
| D. F. Pope b Watt . . . . . . . . . . . . . . . . . . . . . . . . . | 9 | – b Ashdown . . . . . . . . . . . . . . . . . . | 1 |
| J. O'Connor lbw b Freeman . . . . . . . . . . . . . . . . . . . | 100 | – c Watt b Freeman . . . . . . . . . . . | 8 |
| L. C. Eastman c and b Freeman . . . . . . . . . . . . . . . | 4 | – c Wright b Freeman . . . . . . . . . | 2 |
| M. S. Nichols b Freeman . . . . . . . . . . . . . . . . . . . . | 6 | – c Ames b Freeman . . . . . . . . . . . | 1 |
| J. R. Sheffield b Freeman . . . . . . . . . . . . . . . . . . . . | 0 | – run out . . . . . . . . . . . . . . . . . . . . . | 8 |
| Mr C. Bray lbw b Freeman . . . . . . . . . . . . | 22 | – b Freeman . . . . . . . . . . . . . . . . . . | 40 |
| Mr H. M. Morris st Ames b Freeman . . . . . . . . . . . | 4 | – st Ames b Freeman . . . . . . . . . . . | 5 |
| A. B. Hipkin b Freeman . . . . . . . . . . . . . . . . . . . . . | 20 | – c Watt b Freeman . . . . . . . . . . . . | 15 |
| Mr A. G. Daer st Ames b Freeman . . . . . . . . . . . . . | 27 | – c Peach b Freeman . . . . . . . . . . . | 18 |
| P. Smith not out . . . . . . . . . . . . . . . . . . . . . . . . . | 6 | – not out . . . . . . . . . . . . . . . . . . . . . . | 0 |
| B 18, l-b 3, n-b 1 . . . . . . . . . . . . . . . . . . . . | 22 | B 2, l-b 6 . . . . . . . . . . . . . . | 8 |
| | **224** | | **126** |

## Kent

| | |
|---|---|
| H. T. W. Hardinge b Eastman . . . . . . . . . . .128 | A. E. Watt b Nichols . . . . . . . . . . . . . . . . . 21 |
| W. Ashdown c Hipkin b Smith . . . . . . . . . . 63 | C. Wright b Nichols . . . . . . . . . . . . . . . . . . 1 |
| F. E. Woolley c Hipkin b Eastman . . . . . . . 16 | A. P. Freeman lbw b Eastman . . . . . . . . . . . 18 |
| L. Ames lbw b O'Connor . . . . . . . . . . . . . . 6 | C. W. Peach not out . . . . . . . . . . . . . . . . . . 3 |
| L. Todd b Nichols . . . . . . . . . . . . . . . . . . . 48 | B 5, l-b 9, n-b 5 . . . . . . . . . . . . . . 19 |
| Mr B. H. Valentine c Cutmore b Eastman . . 54 | ___ |
| Mr T. A. Pearce st Sheffield b Smith . . . . . . 20 | 397 |

## Kent Bowling

| | Overs | Mdns | Runs | Wkts | Overs | Mdns | Runs | Wkts |
|---|---|---|---|---|---|---|---|---|
| Wright . . . . . . . . . . | 15 | 7 | 22 | — | 3 | — | 19 | — |
| Ashdown . . . . . . . . . | 8 | 1 | 25 | 1 | 13 | 2 | 33 | 2 |
| Freeman . . . . . . . . | 33.5 | 7 | 109 | 8 | 23.3 | 6 | 33 | 7 |
| Watt . . . . . . . . . . . . | 14 | 5 | 37 | 1 | 4 | — | 9 | — |
| Peach . . . . . . . . . . . | 9 | 5 | 9 | — | | | | |
| Hardinge . . . . . . . . | | | | | 9 | 3 | 24 | — |

## Essex Bowling

| | Overs | Mdns | Runs | Wkts |
|---|---|---|---|---|
| Nichols . . . . . . . . . . | 22 | 6 | 53 | 3 |
| Daer . . . . . . . . . . . . . | 16 | 4 | 29 | — |
| Smith . . . . . . . . . . . | 33 | 8 | 119 | 2 |
| O'Connor . . . . . . . . | 22 | 3 | 71 | 1 |
| Hipkin . . . . . . . . . . | 19 | 6 | 36 | — |
| Eastman . . . . . . . . . | 22.4 | 7 | 70 | 4 |

Umpires: J. Stone and A. E. Street.

## KENT v WARWICKSHIRE

### Played at Folkestone, June 24, 25, 1931

Although rain prevented a start until three o'clock on Wednesday, this match ended on the second evening just after half-past six, Warwickshire winning by eight wickets. The faster bowlers always made the ball rise nastily, but, whereas Warwickshire had in Foster and Mayer two men capable of troubling batsmen in this disconcerting fashion, Kent once more were dependent almost entirely upon Freeman, who bowled his slows cleverly but needed assistance. Warwickshire, after dismissing Kent for 134, lost four wickets for 41 before play ceased on Wednesday but on Thursday they showed superior all-round cricket. Woolley, however, gave a display that, even for him, was remarkable and saved Kent from utter collapse. Making 51 out of 67 and altogether 103 out of 144 in little more than two hours, Woolley drove, pulled and cut with delightful ease while his colleagues were practically helpless. By faultless cricket he mastered Mayer, who at the beginning of Kent's second innings dismissed four men for 14 runs. Warwickshire fielded smartly. Kilner batted well and Bates shaped well when helping to finish off the match.

## Kent

| | | | |
|---|---|---|---|
| Mr B. H. Valentine c Smart b Mayer | 1 | – c Smart b Foster | 0 |
| W. Ashdown b Foster | 54 | – b Mayer | 2 |
| F. E. Woolley c Paine b Wyatt | 17 | – not out | 103 |
| L. Ames c Kilner b Wyatt | 12 | – b Mayer | 9 |
| L. Todd c Smart b Foster | 5 | – b Mayer | 0 |
| Mr A. P. F. Chapman c Bates b Foster | 4 | – c Foster b Mayer | 0 |
| Mr T. C. Longfield c Wyatt b Foster | 7 | – c Wyatt b Mayer | 5 |
| C. Fairservice c Kilner b Foster | 0 | – run out | 1 |
| A. E. Watt c Smart b Foster | 24 | – c Smart b Mayer | 5 |
| C. Wright not out | 9 | – lbw b Foster | 14 |
| A. P. Freeman c and b Foster | 0 | – c Wyatt b Mayer | 3 |
| W 1 | 1 | L-b 1, n-b 1 | 2 |
| | 134 | | 144 |

## Warwickshire

| | | | |
|---|---|---|---|
| N. Kilner c Ames b Watt | 54 | – lbw b Freeman | 29 |
| A. J. Croom c Chapman b Freeman | 8 | – b Freeman | 6 |
| L. A. Bates run out | 4 | – not out | 33 |
| G. Paine b Freeman | 1 | | |
| W. Sanders run out | 1 | | |
| Mr R. E. S. Wyatt lbw b Freeman | 12 | – not out | 9 |
| Rev. J. H. Parsons b Watt | 38 | | |
| F. R. Santall b Ashdown | 33 | | |
| J. Smart c Woolley b Freeman | 28 | | |
| Mr D. G. Foster b Freeman | 1 | | |
| J. H. Mayer not out | 13 | | |
| B 4, l-b 4 | 8 | L-b 1 | 1 |
| | 201 | | 78 |

### Warwickshire Bowling

| | Overs | Mdns | Runs | Wkts | Overs | Mdns | Runs | Wkts |
|---|---|---|---|---|---|---|---|---|
| Mayer | 8 | — | 18 | 1 | 18.5 | 2 | 61 | 7 |
| Foster | 17 | 2 | 68 | 7 | 10 | — | 57 | 2 |
| Wyatt | 13 | — | 44 | 2 | 4 | — | 15 | — |
| Paine | 1 | — | 3 | — | | | | |
| Sanders | | | | | 4 | — | 9 | — |

### Kent Bowling

| | Overs | Mdns | Runs | Wkts | Overs | Mdns | Runs | Wkts |
|---|---|---|---|---|---|---|---|---|
| Wright | 13 | 1 | 42 | — | | | | |
| Watt | 18 | 2 | 49 | 2 | 2 | — | 8 | — |
| Freeman | 24 | 7 | 59 | 5 | 10 | 1 | 27 | 2 |
| Longfield | 8 | 1 | 26 | — | | | | |
| Ashdown | 6.4 | 2 | 17 | 1 | 11 | 1 | 33 | — |
| Valentine | | | | | 1 | — | 9 | — |

Umpires: J. Stone and W. A. Buswell.

# KENT v SUSSEX

Played at Tunbridge Wells, July 4, 6, 7, 1931

The outcome of a great struggle was a splendid victory for Sussex who, set 314 to make, accomplished that formidable task for the loss of only three batsmen and so won by seven wickets. In gaining so notable a success, Sussex were enormously indebted to Duleepsinhji who, after putting together 91 in faultless style on Monday, shared on Tuesday in such a brilliant display of batting that 316 runs were obtained inside three hours. Bowley and John Langridge hit up 78 and the former and Duleepsinhji followed with a stand of 124, only 31 runs being required when the Sussex captain's 127 – put together in an hour and three-quarters – came to an end. Kent on Saturday had 200 on the board with five wickets to fall when Tate took four of these at the same total. In the home team's second innings Ames batted admirably on both Monday evening and Tuesday morning. A number of brilliant catches were brought off in the course of a memorable match.

## Kent

| | | |
|---|---|---|
| H. T. W. Hardinge b Wensley | 17 | – c Tate b Wensley ............... 28 |
| W. Ashdown run out | 35 | – b Tate ....................... 7 |
| F. E. Woolley c Wensley b J. Cornford | 35 | – c Cook b J. Cornford ........... 62 |
| L. Ames c Bowley b Tate | 39 | – st W. Cornford b Bowley ........112 |
| Mr A. P. F. Chapman b J. Cornford | 43 | – b Tate ...................... 19 |
| Mr B. H. Valentine b Tate | 12 | – b Tate ...................... 35 |
| Mr T. C. Longfield st W. Cornford b Tate | 4 | – c Duleepsinhji b Jas. Langridge .... 12 |
| C. Fairservice not out | 42 | – c and b Bowley ............... 2 |
| J. C. Hubble lbw b Tate | 0 | – c and b Bowley ............... 39 |
| A. E. Watt b Tate | 1 | – st W. Cornford b Bowley ....... 0 |
| A. P. Freeman c Bowley b J. Cornford | 20 | – not out ..................... 0 |
| B 9, l-b 1 | 10 | B 6, l-b 4 ............... 10 |
| | **258** | **326** |

## Sussex

| | | |
|---|---|---|
| Jas. Langridge hit wkt b Freeman | 2 | |
| John Langridge lbw b Freeman | 75 | – lbw b Freeman ................. 40• |
| Mr G. A. K. Collins c Woolley b Freeman | 44 | |
| E. H. Bowley lbw b Freeman | 0 | – c Longfield b Freeman .......... 78 |
| K. S. Duleepsinhji b Freeman | 91 | – b Longfield ..................127 |
| T. Cook c Ashdown b Hardinge | 11 | – not out ..................... 44 |
| H. Parks lbw b Freeman | 11 | – not out ..................... 16 |
| A. F. Wensley c Hardinge b Freeman | 14 | |
| M. W. Tate c Chapman b Hardinge | 9 | |
| W. Cornford not out | 2 | |
| J. Cornford lbw b Freeman | 0 | |
| L-b 10, w 1, n-b 1 | 12 | B 6, l-b 5 ............... 11 |
| | **271** | **316** |

## Sussex Bowling

| | Overs | Mdns | Runs | Wkts | Overs | Mdns | Runs | Wkts |
|---|---|---|---|---|---|---|---|---|
| Tate ............. | 36 | 6 | 77 | 5 | 30 | 5 | 87 | 3 |
| Wensley .......... | 34 | 3 | 84 | 1 | 26 | 3 | 82 | 1 |
| Cook ............ | 9 | 2 | 19 | — | | | | |
| J. Cornford ....... | 13.5 | 3 | 34 | 3 | 18 | 1 | 70 | 1 |
| Jas. Langridge ..... | 5 | — | 31 | — | 12.3 | 2 | 41 | 1 |
| Bowley .......... | 1 | — | 3 | — | 6 | — | 36 | 4 |

## Kent Bowling

| | Overs | Mdns | Runs | Wkts | Overs | Mdns | Runs | Wkts |
|---|---|---|---|---|---|---|---|---|
| Watt ............. | 14 | 6 | 19 | — | 13 | 3 | 58 | — |
| Freeman ......... | 48.4 | 10 | 150 | 8 | 19 | 1 | 81 | 2 |
| Ashdown ......... | 6 | 1 | 22 | — | 16 | 2 | 86 | — |
| Hardinge ......... | 32 | 14 | 68 | 2 | 9 | — | 37 | — |
| Longfield ........ | | | | | 11 | 2 | 36 | 1 |
| Fairservice ........ | | | | | 1.1 | — | 7 | — |

Umpires: L. C. Braund and W. Reeves.

## KENT v LEICESTERSHIRE

### Played at Maidstone, July 22, 23, 24, 1931

Freeman's bowling was the deciding factor in a splendid struggle which Kent won by 25 runs. Although lacking the assistance of Marriott, Freeman almost atoned for his side's moderate display on what was certainly a bowler's pitch but Astill pulling and driving finely made 56 out of Leicestershire's last 77 runs and in doing so helped largely to bring about a lead of eleven for the visitors. When on Thursday morning, Ashdown – batting altogether two hours and a quarter – and Woolley put on 62, Kent held a strong position, yet despite consistent batting they were only able to set a task which at one point Leicestershire appeared certain to accomplish. Indeed, of the 244 required for victory, Dawson and Shipman obtained 107 together. However, those two men and Berry all fell on the second evening and next morning Freeman lured to destruction all the batsmen except Sidwell. That player, unhappily for Leicestershire, misjudged a run just as he and Geary looked like winning the match. Two great bowling performances were accomplished, Freeman securing fifteen wickets for 144 and Geary eleven for 127. Snary, keeping a fine length with considerable spin, also put in excellent work.

### Kent

| | | | | |
|---|---:|---|---:|
| W. Ashdown c Sidwell b Shipman | 10 | – b Snary | 58 |
| Mr A. M. Crawley lbw b Snary | 3 | – c Berry b Geary | 17 |
| F. E. Woolley c Sidwell b Geary | 33 | – c Sidwell b Armstrong | 68 |
| L. Ames b Geary | 7 | – b Geary | 4 |
| Mr B. H. Valentine c Bowley b Geary | 0 | – b Snary | 17 |
| H. T. W. Hardinge not out | 33 | – b Geary | 19 |
| Mr A. P. F. Chapman c Astill b Geary | 14 | – c Bradshaw b Geary | 22 |
| C. Fairservice b Snary | 12 | – lbw b Geary | 23 |
| H. J. Hubble b Geary | 3 | – not out | 16 |
| A. E. Watt c Astill b Geary | 2 | – b Snary | 0 |
| A. P. Freeman b Shipman | 3 | – b Snary | 2 |
| B 2, l-b 1 | 3 | B 6, l-b 2 | 8 |
| | **123** | | **254** |

### Leicestershire

| | | | | |
|---|---:|---|---:|
| A. Shipman c Chapman b Freeman | 2 | – b Ashdown | 66 |
| Mr E. W. Dawson c Hubble b Freeman | 28 | – b Freeman | 41 |
| L. G. Berry c Valentine b Freeman | 27 | – c Hardinge b Ashdown | 2 |
| N. F. Armstrong c Chapman b Hardinge | 5 | – c Ashdown b Freeman | 16 |
| W. E. Astill c Valentine b Freeman | 56 | – c Watt b Freeman | 1 |
| J. C. Bradshaw b Freeman | 1 | – lbw b Freeman | 0 |
| H. Riley c Watt b Freeman | 0 | – c Woolley b Freeman | 15 |
| G. Geary c Watt b Freeman | 0 | – st Ames b Freeman | 30 |
| T. E. Sidwell b Freeman | 1 | – run out | 20 |
| H. C. Snary c Chapman b Hardinge | 10 | – c Valentine b Freeman | 7 |
| F. G. Bowley not out | 0 | – not out | 4 |
| B 2, l-b 2 | 4 | B 7, l-b 7, w 1, n-b 1 | 16 |
| | **134** | | **218** |

### Leicestershire Bowling

| | Overs | Mdns | Runs | Wkts | Overs | Mdns | Runs | Wkts |
|---|---:|---:|---:|---:|---:|---:|---:|---:|
| Shipman | 7.1 | 1 | 22 | 2 | 7 | 1 | 25 | — |
| Snary | 19 | 7 | 23 | 2 | 23.4 | 6 | 55 | 4 |
| Geary | 28 | 9 | 45 | 6 | 29 | 3 | 77 | 5 |
| Astill | 9 | 1 | 23 | — | 14 | — | 54 | — |
| Bowley | 7 | 4 | 7 | — | 8 | 1 | 20 | — |
| Armstrong | | | | | 8 | 1 | 15 | 1 |

**Kent Bowling**

| | Overs | Mdns | Runs | Wkts | Overs | Mdns | Runs | Wkts |
|---|---|---|---|---|---|---|---|---|
| Ashdown ......... | 20 | 4 | 56 | — | 25 | 12 | 34 | 2 |
| Freeman ......... | 28.1 | 10 | 52 | 8 | 47.2 | 16 | 92 | 7 |
| Watt ............. | 3 | — | 12 | — | 2 | — | 9 | — |
| Hardinge ......... | 6 | 3 | 10 | 2 | 28 | 12 | 48 | — |
| Woolley ......... | | | | | 7 | — | 19 | — |

Umpires: R. D. Burrows and F. Field.

## KENT v SOMERSET

### Played at Canterbury, August 1, 3, 1931

Helped by faulty Somerset fielding on Saturday, Kent gained a very easy victory by eight wickets, so much progress being made that day that the first match of the festival ended at half-past three on Bank Holiday. The wicket-keeping of Frank Lee, who held five catches, assisted Wellard and Andrews on Saturday to bowl with almost as much effect as Freeman but the Kent man on Monday with five wickets for 10 runs and the first eight wickets while only 30 runs were hit from him, excelled himself. For the third time in the season Freeman in a match dismissed fifteen men – and on this occasion, at no greater cost than 94 runs. On Saturday, for the fourth consecutive season, he brought his aggregate of wickets to over 200. A strong cross wind caused him to open the second innings with two wides but after that he bewildered all the batsmen. A brilliant long-field catch and a smart piece of stumping off successive balls gave Marriott the last two wickets.

### Somerset

| | | |
|---|---|---|
| J. W. Lee st Ames b Freeman ................ | 14 – c Ames b Freeman ............ | 5 |
| Mr E. F. Longrigg b Marriott .................. | 24 – c and b Freeman .............. | 0 |
| F. S. Lee lbw b Marriott ..................... | 0 – c Todd b Freeman ............ | 29 |
| Mr R. A. Ingle st Ames b Freeman ............ | 3 – c Ames b Freeman ............ | 3 |
| Mr J. C. White lbw b Freeman ................ | 1 – st Ames b Marriott ........... | 7 |
| Mr C. C. Case b Freeman ..................... | 34 – c Ashdown b Freeman .......... | 0 |
| Mr G. F. Earle b Freeman .................... | 19 – b Freeman .................. | 8 |
| Mr H. D. Burrough c Ashdown b Freeman ........ | 3 – c Woolley b Freeman .......... | 2 |
| A. W. Wellard c Valentine b Freeman ........... | 4 – c Ames b Freeman ............ | 0 |
| G. Hunt run out ........................... | 13 – c Valentine b Marriott ........ | 7 |
| W. Andrews not out ........................ | 2 – not out .................. | 0 |
| B 1, 1-b 4 ........................ | 5 | B 2, 1-b 2, w 2 ............. | 6 |
| | **122** | | **67** |

### Kent

| | | |
|---|---|---|
| H. T. W. Hardinge b Andrews ................ | 11 – b Hunt ................... | 26 |
| W. Ashdown c F. S. Lee b Wellard ............ | 3 – c J. W. Lee b Hunt .......... | 4 |
| F. E. Woolley c Hunt b Andrews .............. | 6 – not out .................. | 12 |
| L. Ames c F. S. Lee b Wellard .............. | 28 – not out .................. | 6 |
| L. Todd c White b Andrews .................. | 0 | | |
| C. Fairservice b Wellard ................... | 6 | | |
| Mr J. L. Bryan c F. S. Lee b Andrews .......... | 10 | | |
| Mr B. H. Valentine c F. S. Lee b Hunt .......... | 38 | | |
| Mr A. P. F. Chapman c F. S. Lee b Wellard ....... | 24 | | |
| A. P. Freeman b Andrews ................... | 13 | | |
| Mr C. S. Marriott not out ................... | 0 | | |
| B 1, 1-b 5 ........................ | 6 | | |
| | **145** | | **48** |

## Kent Bowling

|              | Overs | Mdns | Runs | Wkts | Overs | Mdns | Runs | Wkts |
|--------------|-------|------|------|------|-------|------|------|------|
| Ashdown      | 7     | 4    | 5    | —    |       |      |      |      |
| Marriott     | 27    | 9    | 52   | 2    | 14.5  | 4    | 26   | 2    |
| Freeman      | 22.1  | 6    | 59   | 7    | 15    | 5    | 35   | 8    |
| Hardinge     | 2     | 1    | 1    | —    |       |      |      |      |

## Somerset Bowling

|              | Overs | Mdns | Runs | Wkts | Overs | Mdns | Runs | Wkts |
|--------------|-------|------|------|------|-------|------|------|------|
| Wellard      | 29    | 5    | 65   | 4    | 9     | 2    | 12   | —    |
| Andrews      | 24.5  | 6    | 52   | 5    | 4     | —    | 16   | —    |
| White        | 5     | —    | 10   | —    |       |      |      |      |
| Hunt         | 3     | 1    | 7    | 1    | 7     | 3    | 11   | 2    |
| J. W. Lee    | 2     | 1    | 5    | —    | 2.1   | —    | 9    | —    |

Umpires: H. Young and F. Chester.

# KENT v WARWICKSHIRE

## Played at Folkestone, June 29, 30, 1932

While Mayer and Foster accomplished splendid work, Freeman, in one of the best performances of his career, met with such remarkable success that Kent won a low scoring match by 74 runs. Bowling throughout both innings, Freeman took seventeen wickets at a cost of 92 runs. The game underwent some startling changes. On Wednesday the pitch soon began to wear and, except when Woolley and Ashdown put on 83 runs, bowlers had matters very much their own way. Woolley, hitting a 6 and thirteen 4s, scored 92 out of 139 and, following his dismissal, six wickets fell for 30 runs. Still more startling was the collapse at the same point in Warwickshire's innings, six batsmen being sent back for 15 runs. Hardinge subsequently prevented a Kent break-down but no one else did much. Wyatt was the one Warwickshire batsman to withstand Freeman's bowling. Warwickshire wanting 215 for victory, five wickets fell for 58. Wyatt and Santall added 46 but only 36 more runs were obtained.

## Kent

| | | | |
|---|---|---|---|
| Mr A. M. Crawley b Foster | 5 | – lbw b Mayer | 2 |
| W. Ashdown c Santall b Foster | 30 | – b Foster | 5 |
| F. E. Woolley c Wyatt b Mayer | 92 | – c Foster b Mayer | 25 |
| L. Ames c Croom b Mayer | 12 | – lbw b Foster | 16 |
| H. T. W. Hardinge c Kilner b Mayer | 18 | – not out | 66 |
| Mr A. P. F. Chapman c Kilner b Mayer | 3 | – c Smart b Mayer | 1 |
| Mr I. Akers-Douglas b Mayer | 1 | – c Smart b Foster | 20 |
| Mr B. H. Valentine c Wyatt b Foster | 3 | – c Wyatt b Foster | 3 |
| L. Todd b Foster | 2 | – c Roberts b Foster | 13 |
| A. E. Watt not out | 1 | – b Foster | 4 |
| A. P. Freeman b Foster | 4 | – b Mayer | 4 |
| W 1, n-b 2 | 3 | B 2, l-b 8 | 10 |
| | **174** | | **169** |

## Warwickshire

| | | | |
|---|---|---|---|
| Mr G. D. Kemp-Welch run out | 9 | – st Ames b Freeman | 3 |
| A. J. Croom lbw b Freeman | 12 | – lbw b Freeman | 28 |
| L. A. Bates st Ames b Freeman | 18 | – c Valentine b Watt | 14 |
| Mr R. E. S. Wyatt not out | 59 | – not out | 49 |
| Rev. J. H. Parsons c Ashdown b Freeman | 11 | – c Hardinge b Freeman | 1 |
| N. Kilner lbw b Freeman | 13 | – lbw b Freeman | 1 |
| F. R. Santall st Ames b Freeman | 1 | – b Freeman | 21 |
| H. J. Roberts st Ames b Freeman | 0 | – c Ashdown b Freeman | 0 |
| J. Smart st Ames b Freeman | 1 | – b Freeman | 6 |
| Mr D. G. Foster b Freeman | 0 | – b Freeman | 6 |
| J. H. Mayer c Ames b Watt | 0 | – lbw b Freeman | 3 |
| B 4, l-b 1 | 5 | B 3, l-b 3, n-b 2 | 8 |
| | **129** | | **140** |

### Warwickshire Bowling

| | Overs | Mdns | Runs | Wkts | Overs | Mdns | Runs | Wkts |
|---|---|---|---|---|---|---|---|---|
| Mayer | 13 | 2 | 25 | 5 | 21.2 | 4 | 48 | 4 |
| Foster | 18.3 | 1 | 81 | 5 | 24 | 5 | 82 | 6 |
| Wyatt | 5 | 1 | 23 | — | 5 | — | 15 | — |
| Roberts | 3 | — | 28 | — | | | | |
| Santall | 3 | — | 14 | — | 5 | 2 | 5 | — |
| Croom | | | | | 3 | — | 9 | — |

### Kent Bowling

| | Overs | Mdns | Runs | Wkts | Overs | Mdns | Runs | Wkts |
|---|---|---|---|---|---|---|---|---|
| Ashdown | 14 | 3 | 63 | — | | | | |
| Freeman | 19 | 7 | 31 | 8 | 22.4 | 5 | 61 | 9 |
| Hardinge | 2 | — | 19 | — | | | | |
| Watt | 3.3 | 1 | 11 | 1 | 23 | 3 | 71 | 1 |

Umpires: F. Chester and T. Oates.

## KENT v NORTHAMPTONSHIRE

### Played at Tunbridge Wells, July 6, 7, 8, 1932

Remarkable for three individual performances of exceptional merit, this match ended before lunch on the third day in a victory for Kent by an innings and 188 runs. Jupp for the first time in his career took all ten wickets and Freeman, unchanged in Northamptonshire's two innings, met with even more pronounced success, his record for the match being sixteen wickets for 82 runs. Both Freeman and Jupp flighted the ball cleverly and made it turn quickly. As a set-off to the triumph of the two bowlers, Ames gave another great display of batting. Directly after lunch he saw Jupp dispose of three men in the course of twenty-two balls for 6 runs, and he was himself the first of four men dismissed in one over which yielded two runs to Freeman before the last ball finished the innings. Batting just four hours, Ames, who had gone in second wicket down at 81, scored 149 out of 277. He hit fourteen 4s and fell to a catch in the long field. Pearce, who had helped to put on 194 by brilliant cricket, was clean bowled next ball. While Ames pulled, drove and cut with effect, Pearce excelled in off-driving. Ashdown and Woolley also got their runs well but the other seven batsmen scored only 18 between them. Jupp alone of the Northamptonshire batsmen showed ability to deal with Freeman who began by taking six wickets for 33. Hardinge completed the collapse. In the whole match only one batsman fell to a bowler not absolutely slow. Northamptonshire played their second innings on a drying pitch.

## Kent

| | |
|---|---|
| W. Ashdown c Bakewell b Jupp .......... 43 | Mr T. A. Pearce b Jupp ................ 83 |
| L. Todd lbw b Jupp .................... 7 | Mr B. H. Valentine not out ............. 0 |
| F. E. Woolley lbw b Jupp ............... 52 | A. E. Watt b Jupp ..................... 0 |
| L. Ames c M. Cox b Jupp .............149 | A. P. Freeman st Bellamy b Jupp ........ 2 |
| Mr A. M. Crawley b Jupp ............. 7 | B 13, l-b 2 ................... 15 |
| H. T. W. Hardinge c Bakewell b Jupp ..... 0 | — |
| Mr I. Akers-Douglas b Jupp ............ 2 | 360 |

## Northamptonshire

| | | | |
|---|---|---|---|
| A. H. Bakewell st Ames b Freeman .............. | 2 | – lbw b Freeman ................. | 7 |
| Mr A. W. Snowden st Ames b Freeman .......... | 18 | – lbw b Freeman ................. | 0 |
| A. L. Cox lbw b Freeman ...................... | 14 | – st Ames b Freeman ............. | 5 |
| J. E. Timms c Ashdown b Freeman ............. | 2 | – c Valentine b Ashdown .......... | 0 |
| Mr V. W. C. Jupp c Hardinge b Freeman ......... | 34 | – b Freeman ................... | 32 |
| K. J. Rymill c Ashdown b Freeman ............. | 0 | – st Ames b Freeman ............. | 0 |
| M. Cox b Hardinge ......................... | 0 | – st Ames b Freeman ............. | 5 |
| Mr W. C. Brown not out ...................... | 6 | – not out ..................... | 12 |
| A. D. Matthews b Freeman .................... | 9 | – c Hardinge b Freeman .......... | 11 |
| B. Bellamy c Todd b Hardinge ................. | 0 | – run out ..................... | 0 |
| R. J. Partridge c Todd b Freeman .............. | 2 | – c Hardinge b Freeman .......... | 0 |
| B 9, l-b 1 ...................... | 10 | B 3 ................... | 3 |
| | 97 | | 75 |

## Northamptonshire Bowling

| | Overs | Mdns | Runs | Wkts |
|---|---|---|---|---|
| Matthews ........ | 28 | 6 | 80 | — |
| Partridge ......... | 33 | 9 | 81 | — |
| Jupp ............. | 39 | 6 | 127 | 10 |
| A. L. Cox ......... | 13 | 4 | 39 | — |
| M. Cox .......... | 6 | 1 | 17 | — |
| Timms ........... | 2 | 1 | 1 | — |

## Kent Bowling

| | Overs | Mdns | Runs | Wkts | Overs | Mdns | Runs | Wkts |
|---|---|---|---|---|---|---|---|---|
| Freeman ......... | 21.1 | 5 | 44 | 8 | 14.3 | 4 | 38 | 8 |
| Ashdown ......... | 15 | 6 | 28 | — | 6 | — | 13 | 1 |
| Hardinge ......... | 6 | — | 15 | 2 | 9 | 4 | 21 | — |

Umpires: E. J. Smith and F. Field.

## KENT v SURREY

Played at Blackheath, July 15, 17, 18, 1933

Declaring their second innings closed with six wickets down Kent won the match by 215 runs. Except that of Hobbs, who made his 194th century in two hours, and Sandham, in a stand for 159 – their sixty-third of three figures for Surrey – the batting lacked distinction until Ames and Todd put on 230 in two hours fifty minutes. Cutting, driving to the off, and pulling specially well, Todd hit eighteen 4s. So freely did he play after completing fifty that his last 71 runs came in sixty-five minutes while 136 were added. Ames finished as brilliantly and hit twelve 4s, mostly drives, during three hours and a half. On a pitch worn outside the leg stump at each end, affected by rain, and becoming more difficult under sunshine, Surrey gave a disappointing display, but Barling and Brooks held their own for fifty minutes, and it was nearly six o'clock when Fender and Gover fell to successive balls from Freeman.

## Kent

| | | | |
|---|---|---|---|
| Mr F. G. H. Chalk b Gamble | 11 | – b Gamble | 1 |
| W. H. Ashdown c Gregory b Gover | 11 | – c Sandham b Brown | 35 |
| L. E. G. Ames c Gregory b Gover | 2 | – c Gamble b Brown | 137 |
| L. J. Todd lbw b Gover | 2 | – c Gamble b Brown | 121 |
| F. E. Woolley b Brown | 38 | – lbw b Brown | 53 |
| Mr B. H. Valentine c Gregory b Gover | 52 | – b Gamble | 11 |
| Mr H. P. Dinwiddy b Gover | 45 | – not out | 5 |
| H. T. W. Hardinge c Gover b Gamble | 45 | | |
| A. E. Watt b Gamble | 16 | | |
| A. P. Freeman b Gover | 13 | | |
| D. V. P. Wright not out | 1 | | |
| B 6, l-b 1, w 1, n-b 7 | 15 | B 5, l-b 5, n-b 4 | 14 |
| | **251** | **(6 wkts dec.)** | **377** |

## Surrey

| | | | |
|---|---|---|---|
| J. B. Hobbs lbw b Freeman | 101 | – st Ames b Ashdown | 6 |
| A. Sandham b Freeman | 70 | – c Valentine b Freeman | 12 |
| H. S. Squires lbw b Watt | 38 | – lbw b Ashdown | 5 |
| T. H. Barling lbw b Freeman | 8 | – lbw b Freeman | 61 |
| R. J. Gregory c and b Wright | 1 | – c Valentine b Freeman | 9 |
| Mr F. R. Brown b Freeman | 7 | – c Valentine b Wright | 26 |
| E. F. Wilson st Ames b Freeman | 9 | – lbw b Watt | 3 |
| Mr P. G. H. Fender c Ames b Watt | 23 | – lbw b Freeman | 14 |
| F. Gamble lbw b Freeman | 0 | – b Watt | 0 |
| E. W. Brooks c Woolley b Watt | 0 | – not out | 5 |
| A. R. Gover not out | 1 | – lbw b Freeman | 0 |
| B 1, n-b 2 | 3 | B 2, l-b 7, n-b 2 | 11 |
| | **261** | | **152** |

### Surrey Bowling

| | Overs | Mdns | Runs | Wkts | Overs | Mdns | Runs | Wkts |
|---|---|---|---|---|---|---|---|---|
| Gover | 29.3 | 8 | 82 | 6 | 14 | 1 | 51 | — |
| Gamble | 22 | 6 | 52 | 3 | 20 | 2 | 84 | 2 |
| Brown | 14 | — | 51 | 1 | 31.5 | 5 | 104 | 4 |
| Fender | 10 | 2 | 37 | — | 21 | 5 | 69 | — |
| Gregory | 7 | 3 | 14 | — | 8 | 2 | 33 | — |
| Squires | | | | | 6 | 1 | 22 | — |

### Kent Bowling

| | Overs | Mdns | Runs | Wkts | Overs | Mdns | Runs | Wkts |
|---|---|---|---|---|---|---|---|---|
| Watt | 18.4 | 1 | 56 | 3 | 13 | 3 | 28 | 2 |
| Ashdown | 16 | 5 | 39 | — | 9 | 3 | 22 | 2 |
| Freeman | 42 | 14 | 110 | 6 | 30.2 | 13 | 56 | 5 |
| Wright | 21 | 7 | 53 | 1 | 19 | 9 | 35 | 1 |

Umpires: J. Newman and W. Reeves.

# KENT v NORTHAMPTONSHIRE

### Played at Dover, August 16, 17, 1933

Sent in on a drying pitch Kent lost five wickets for 52, but recovered so well that they won the match before six o'clock on the second afternoon by 429 runs. Clark, after two early successes, strained himself, and his loss completely upset Jupp's anticipations. Ames, playing two splendid innings, scored separate hundreds in a match for the first time. When eight men were out for 119 Freeman stayed while Ames hit so brilliantly that 101 runs came in an hour before tea. Then Freeman and Marriott disposed of the opposition in an hour and a half. Leading by 132 Kent batted on Tuesday until four o'clock when Valentine declared. Ames, going in second wicket down at 29, again saved his side from fear of collapse and after a stand with Todd for 109 runs at one a minute, Valentine hit just as freely as his partner, 205 runs coming by grand cricket in ninety-five minutes. Both men drove, pulled and cut in superb style. Valentine's 104 included a six and fourteen 4s; Ames, batting altogether three hours and a quarter, hit seventeen 4s.

### Kent

| | | |
|---|---|---|
| W. H. Ashdown c Bakewell b Clark | 6 | – c Liddell b Thomas ............ 2 |
| L. J. Todd c Bakewell b Clark | 2 | – c Partridge b Thomas .......... 67 |
| F. E. Woolley c Liddell b Thomas | 19 | – c Partridge b Thomas .......... 19 |
| L. E. G. Ames c Bellamy b Partridge | 132 | – not out ...................... 145 |
| Mr B. H. Valentine c Liddell b Thomas | 0 | – st Bellamy b Jupp ............ 104 |
| Mr F. G. H. Chalk c Bakewell b Partridge | 3 | |
| Mr C. H. Knott c Jupp b Thomas | 24 | |
| H. T. W. Hardinge st Bellamy b Jupp | 8 | |
| A. E. Watt c Knight b Jupp | 6 | |
| A. P. Freeman not out | 14 | |
| Mr C. S. Marriott c Bakewell b Thomas | 0 | |
| B 5, l-b 5 | 10 | B 5, l-b 1 ............... 6 |
| | **224** | **(4 wkts dec.) 343** |

### Northamptonshire

| | | |
|---|---|---|
| A. H. Bakewell st Ames b Marriott | 31 | – lbw b Freeman ................ 2 |
| Mr A. W. Snowden c Watt b Freeman | 2 | – b Watt ...................... 6 |
| B. Bellamy lbw b Freeman | 0 | – lbw b Freeman ............... 10 |
| J. E. Timms lbw b Marriott | 39 | – st Ames b Freeman ........... 7 |
| A. G. Liddell run out | 5 | – b Freeman ................... 0 |
| Mr V. W. C. Jupp c Woolley b Freeman | 1 | – st Ames b Freeman ........... 3 |
| A. L. Cox st Ames b Marriott | 1 | – c Ashdown b Watt ............ 0 |
| R. Knight b Freeman | 6 | – st Ames b Freeman ........... 4 |
| A. E. Thomas lbw b Marriott | 2 | – b Freeman ................... 5 |
| R. J. Partridge not out | 1 | – not out ..................... 4 |
| E. W. Clark absent hurt | 0 | – absent hurt ................. 0 |
| L-b 4 | 4 | B 4, l-b 1 ............... 5 |
| | **92** | **46** |

### Northamptonshire Bowling

| | Overs | Mdns | Runs | Wkts | Overs | Mdns | Runs | Wkts |
|---|---|---|---|---|---|---|---|---|
| Clark ............ | 10 | 1 | 23 | 2 | | | | |
| Thomas .......... | 29.4 | 12 | 50 | 4 | 25 | 5 | 64 | 3 |
| Jupp ............. | 18 | 1 | 85 | 2 | 23.4 | 6 | 94 | 1 |
| Partridge ........ | 25 | 7 | 48 | 2 | 21 | 2 | 67 | — |
| Cox ............. | 1 | — | 8 | — | 16 | — | 112 | — |

### Kent Bowling

| | Overs | Mdns | Runs | Wkts | Overs | Mdns | Runs | Wkts |
|---|---|---|---|---|---|---|---|---|
| Freeman ......... | 16 | 5 | 40 | 4 | 12.2 | 7 | 19 | 7 |
| Marriott .......... | 15.3 | 2 | 48 | 4 | 1 | — | 3 | — |
| Watt ............. | | | | | 11 | 2 | 19 | 2 |

Umpires: J. Hardstaff and J. Stone.

## KENT v DERBYSHIRE

Played at Dover, August 21, 22, 23, 1935

Rain saved Derbyshire from the danger of defeat after following-on 180 behind in a match made memorable by a remarkable performance by Ashdown. On Wednesday Ashdown scored 282 out of 518 and when the Kent innings closed he carried his bat after a wonderful display. Following a disastrous start, runs came so freely that Kent's 560 occupied no more than six hours forty minutes. Ashdown always claimed a good share of the runs. He got 102 out of 188; 200 out of 380; and his practically faultless 305 included forty-seven 4s mostly off-drives and cuts. Not until Valentine hit up 62 out of 137 in 85 minutes was the attack really mastered; then Ashdown became so brilliant that even Chapman, with two 6s and five 4s, claimed no more than 49 out of 124 put on in an hour. Derbyshire faced their uphill fight courageously. Richardson and Smith made 111 together; a ninth wicket stand by George Pope and Harry Elliott yielded 105, and Derbyshire were almost safe when the weather intervened. Richardson this time played carefully.

### Kent

| | |
|---|---|
| W. H. Ashdown not out .................305 | Mr A. P. F. Chapman b G. H. Pope ...... 49 |
| F. E. Woolley lbw b G. H. Pope .......... 6 | C. Cole lbw (N) b A. V. Pope ........... 11 |
| L. E. G. Ames c A. V. Pope b Mitchell .... 12 | A. P. Freeman b G. H. Pope ............ 27 |
| L. J. Todd lbw b A. V. Pope ............. 28 | C. Lewis b G. H. Pope ................. 9 |
| Mr B. H. Valentine b G. H. Pope ........ 62 | B 2, l-b 6, w 4 ............... 12 |
| Mr F. G. H. Chalk c Smith b Mitchell ..... 23 | |
| Mr C. H. Knott c H. Elliott b A. V. Pope .. 16 | 560 |

### Derbyshire

| | | |
|---|---|---|
| Mr A. W. Richardson st Ames b Freeman ......... 59 | – not out ...................... | 28 |
| D. Smith st Ames b Freeman ................... 48 | – c Ames b Cole ................. | 11 |
| C. Elliott lbw (N) b Lewis .................... 31 | – c Woolley b Freeman .......... | 52 |
| L. F. Townsend c Ames b Todd ................ 5 | – not out ..................... | 29 |
| E. Carrington c Woolley b Cole ................ 47 | | |
| A. E. Alderman b Todd ...................... 17 | | |
| Mr L. B. Blaxland c Todd b Lewis .............. 28 | | |
| G. H. Pope b Freeman ....................... 67 | | |
| A. V. Pope b Freeman ....................... 0 | | |
| H. Elliott lbw b Ashdown .................... 46 | | |
| T. B. Mitchell not out ....................... 2 | | |
| B 11, l-b 16, n-b 3 ................... 30 | B 1 ................... | 1 |
| | 380 | 121 |

### Derbyshire Bowling

| | Overs | Mdns | Runs | Wkts |
|---|---|---|---|---|
| A. V. Pope ........ | 45 | 8 | 120 | 3 |
| G. H. Pope ........ | 32.5 | 2 | 126 | 5 |
| Blaxland .......... | 3 | 2 | 1 | — |
| Mitchell .......... | 23 | 1 | 156 | 2 |
| L. F. Townsend .... | 27 | 2 | 125 | — |
| Smith ............ | 4 | — | 20 | — |

**Kent Bowling**

| | Overs | Mdns | Runs | Wkts | Overs | Mdns | Runs | Wkts |
|---|---|---|---|---|---|---|---|---|
| Cole . . . . . . . . . . . . . | 31 | 5 | 79 | 1 | 15 | 2 | 33 | 1 |
| Todd . . . . . . . . . . . | 40 | 13 | 84 | 2 | 13 | 5 | 24 | — |
| Freeman . . . . . . . . | 50.4 | 18 | 104 | 4 | 18 | 5 | 63 | 1 |
| Lewis . . . . . . . . . . . | 27 | — | 80 | 2 | | | | |
| Ashdown . . . . . . . . | 3 | 1 | 3 | 1 | | | | |

Umpires: J. Newman and W. R. Parry.

## A. P. FREEMAN IN THE CRICKET FIELD

After the close of the 1936 season, the engagement of A. P. Freeman with the Kent County Club was not renewed. The acceptance of an offer from Walsall, a Birmingham and District League club, suggests that Freeman will not play any more county cricket; so an epitome of his career is opportune. One of the smallest first-class players, he became a great slow bowler by the diverse ways he found to spin and flight the ball with his strong right hand.

Born on May 17, 1889, at Lewisham, Freeman played first for Kent in 1914 when 25 years of age, and the break in county cricket until 1919 delayed the development of his full powers until the completion of his 30th year. This prolonged hindrance makes his aggregate of 3,775 wickets taken in first-class cricket all the more remarkable. Wilfred Rhodes, with 4,184 wickets, alone has surpassed this figure, and the Yorkshire slow left-hander, starting when 20, accomplished this from 1898 to 1930 – 29 seasons, compared with Freeman's 19.

Freeman's record is specially noteworthy because all but 29 of his wickets – his measure of success in 1914 – were taken after he had passed his 30th year. Nearly all his best work has been accomplished for Kent, and his bowling in the six seasons 1928-1933, when 1,673 wickets fell to him, was little short of astounding. As he continued to dismiss 200 or more batsmen in each season, his aggregate number of "victims" during the eight seasons ending 1935 was 2,090, no fewer than 1,754 in county matches. In 1928 he began this period of phenomenal success by taking 304 wickets, beating the record of 290 set up by Tom Richardson, of Surrey, in 1895. In 1933 Freeman claimed 298 wickets and, besides these two best achievements by an English bowler, these figures stand to his name – 276, 275, 267 and 253 in a season. In County Championship matches he took over 200 wickets six times, including 252 in 1933, and once his figure was 199.

Of the twelve times that 250 or more wickets have fallen to a bowler in a season, Freeman is credited with exactly half; Richardson and Rhodes accomplished the feat twice; J. T. Hearne and C. T. B. Turner, the Australian, once each.

Freeman is the only bowler who has taken ten wickets in an innings three times – all these instances occurring after he had turned forty.

It must be admitted that Freeman proved disappointing when tried in cricket of the very highest class. He never appeared in a Test match against Australia at home and only twice in Australia, in 1924-25, when he was exceedingly expensive. Freeman did well in the three tests with West Indies in 1928, taking 22 wickets at 13.72 each, but he fared moderately against South Africa in 1927-28 and in 1929. He appeared for the Players at Lord's in five matches from 1924 to 1932.

As a batsman he rarely accomplished much and seldom had a double-figure batting average for the season, but strangely enough he played one of his highest innings – 50 not out – in a Test match at Sydney. His best scores in England were 66 for Kent v Lancashire at Manchester in 1925, and 51 not out for Kent against Sussex at Hastings in 1926. He always fielded well, and sometimes brilliantly, at cover point.

## ALL FIRST-CLASS MATCHES

| Year | Runs | Wickets | Average | Year | Runs | Wickets | Average |
|------|------|---------|---------|------|------|---------|---------|
| 1914 | 799 | 29 | 27.55 | 1927-28 | | | |
| 1919 | 1,209 | 60 | 20.15 | in S. Africa | 963 | 49 | 19.65 |
| 1920 | 1,790 | 102 | 17.54 | 1928 | 5,489 | 304 | 18.05 |
| 1921 | 3,086 | 166 | 18.59 | 1928-29 | | | |
| 1922 | 2,839 | 194 | 14.63 | in Australia | 1,136 | 25 | 32.45 |
| 1922-23 | | | | 1929 | 4,879 | 267 | 18.27 |
| in Australia | 989 | 30 | 32.96 | 1930 | 4,632 | 275 | 16.84 |
| 1922-23 | | | | 1931 | 4,307 | 276 | 15.60 |
| in N. Zealand | 667 | 39 | 17.10 | 1932 | 4,149 | 253 | 16.39 |
| 1923 | 2,642 | 157 | 16.82 | 1933 | 4,549 | 298 | 15.26 |
| 1924 | 2,518 | 167 | 15.07 | 1934 | 4,753 | 205 | 23.18 |
| 1924-25 | | | | 1935 | 4,562 | 212 | 21.51 |
| in Australia | 1,209 | 40 | 30.22 | 1936 | 2,796 | 110 | 25.41 |
| 1925 | 2,544 | 146 | 17.42 | | | | |
| 1926 | 3,740 | 180 | 20.77 | Total | 69,577 | 3,775 | 18.43 |
| 1927 | 3,330 | 181 | 18.39 | | | | |

## COUNTY CHAMPIONSHIP MATCHES

| Years | Runs | Wickets | Average | Years | Runs | Wickets | Average |
|-------|------|---------|---------|-------|------|---------|---------|
| 1914 | 602 | 26 | 23.15 | 1929 | 3,244 | 199 | 16.30 |
| 1919 | 1,068 | 55 | 19.41 | 1930 | 3,850 | 249 | 15.46 |
| 1920 | 1,722 | 102 | 16.88 | 1931 | 3,667 | 241 | 15.21 |
| 1921 | 2,667 | 156 | 17.09 | 1932 | 3,205 | 209 | 15.33 |
| 1922 | 2,839 | 194 | 14.60 | 1933 | 3,740 | 252 | 14.84 |
| 1923 | 2,538 | 148 | 17.14 | 1934 | 4,090 | 187 | 21.87 |
| 1924 | 2,244 | 146 | 15.36 | 1935 | 4,385 | 201 | 21.81 |
| 1925 | 2,544 | 146 | 17.42 | 1936 | 2,431 | 103 | 23.60 |
| 1926 | 3,308 | 163 | 20.29 | | | | |
| 1927 | 2,718 | 158 | 17.20 | Total | 54,543 | 3,151 | 17.30 |
| 1928 | 3,681 | 216 | 17.04 | | | | |

## BOWLING SUMMARY

| | Runs | Wickets | Average |
|------|------|---------|---------|
| **In England** | | | |
| Kent (county championship) | 54,543 | 3,151 | 17.30 |
| Kent (other matches) | 4,401 | 189 | 23.28 |
| Tests (v South Africa) | 547 | 22 | 24.86 |
| Tests (v West Indies) | 302 | 22 | 13.72 |
| Players v Gentlemen, at Lord's | 701 | 33 | 21.24 |
| Other first-class matches | 4,119 | 165 | 26.06 |
| **In Australia** | | | |
| Tests | 459 | 8 | 57.37 |
| Other first-class matches | 2,875 | 97 | 29.63 |
| **In South Africa** | | | |
| Tests | 399 | 14 | 28.50 |
| Other first-class matches | 564 | 35 | 16.11 |
| **In New Zealand** | 667 | 39 | 17.10 |
| Total | 69,577 | 3,775 | 18.43 |

## 10 WICKETS IN AN INNINGS

10-131  Kent v Lancashire, at Maidstone, 1929
10-53   Kent v Essex, at Southend, 1930
10-79   Kent v Lancashire, at Manchester, 1931

## 9 WICKETS IN AN INNINGS

9-87    Kent v Sussex, at Hastings, 1920 (The innings was declared at the fall of the 9th
        wicket.)
9-11†   Kent v Sussex, at Hove, 1922
9-104   Kent v West Indies, at Canterbury, 1928
9-50    Kent v Derbyshire, at Ilkeston, 1930
9-61*   Kent v Warwickshire, at Folkestone, 1932

## 8 WICKETS IN AN INNINGS

8-22    Kent v Northamptonshire, at Northampton, 1921
8-78    Kent v Worcestershire, at Worcester, 1921
8-56†   Kent v Sussex, at Hove, 1922
8-127   Kent v Yorkshire, at Maidstone, 1922
8-80    Kent v Essex, at Dover, 1925
8-91    Kent v Hampshire, at Canterbury, 1927
8-48    England v Border, at East London, 1927-28
8-64    Kent v Leicestershire, at Tonbridge, 1928
8-94    Kent v Essex, at Canterbury, 1928
8-41    Players v Gentlemen, at Lord's, 1929
8-74    Kent v Nottinghamshire, at Canterbury, 1929
8-43    Kent v Middlesex, at Lord's, 1930
8-70    Kent v Derbyshire, at Tonbridge, 1930
8-71    Kent v Warwickshire, at Tonbridge, 1930
8-101   Kent v Gloucestershire, at Bristol, 1930
8-35    Kent v Somerset, at Canterbury, 1931
8-52    Kent v Leicestershire, at Maidstone, 1931
8-99    Kent v Oxford University, at Oxford, 1931
8-109   Kent v Essex, at Gravesend, 1931
8-150   Kent v Sussex, at Tunbridge Wells, 1931
8-31*   Kent v Warwickshire, at Folkestone, 1932
8-38‡   Kent v Northamptonshire, at Tunbridge Wells, 1932
8-44‡   Kent v Northamptonshire, at Tunbridge Wells, 1932
8-56    Kent v Lancashire, at Folkestone, 1932
8-105   Kent v Yorkshire, at Tonbridge, 1932
8-22    South of England v MCC, at Folkestone, 1933
8-48    Kent v Gloucestershire, at Bristol, 1933
8-57    Kent v Sussex, at Hastings, 1933
8-64    Kent v Middlesex, at Lord's, 1933
8-110   Kent v Worcestershire, at Gravesend, 1933
8-103   Kent v Northamptonshire, at Northampton, 1934
8-136   Kent v Surrey, at Blackheath, 1934
8-170   Kent v Warwickshire, at Tonbridge, 1934
8-40    Kent v Leicestershire, at Gravesend, 1935
8-123   Kent v Leicestershire, at Oakham, 1935

*Same match.*          *† Same match.*          *‡ Same match.*

## 15 OR MORE WICKETS IN A MATCH

17-67   Kent v Sussex, at Hove, 1922
17-92   Kent v Warwickshire, at Folkestone, 1932
16-94   Kent v Essex, at Southend, 1930
16-82   Kent v Northamptonshire, at Tunbridge Wells, 1932
15-224  Kent v Leicestershire, at Tonbridge, 1928
15-94   Kent v Somerset, at Canterbury, 1931
15-142  Kent v Essex, at Gravesend, 1931
15-144  Kent v Leicestershire, at Maidstone, 1931
15-122  Kent v Middlesex, at Lord's, 1933
15-122  Kent v Middlesex, at Lord's, 1933

## 14 WICKETS IN A MATCH

14-161  Kent v Warwickshire, at Dover, 1923
14-129  Kent v Hampshire, at Canterbury, 1927
14-181  Kent v Essex, at Canterbury, 1928
14-180  Kent v Derbyshire, at Chesterfield, 1929
14-131  Kent v Nottinghamshire, at Canterbury, 1929
14-143  Kent v Warwickshire, at Tonbridge, 1930
14-198  Kent v Gloucestershire, at Bristol, 1930
14-149  Kent v Sussex, at Hastings, 1933
14-206  Kent v Northamptonshire, at Dover, 1934
14-115  Kent v Essex, at Gravesend, 1935

## 13 WICKETS IN A MATCH

13-127  Kent v Hampshire, at Bournemouth, 1919
13-67   Kent v Northamptonshire, at Northampton, 1921
13-193  Kent v Warwickshire, at Birmingham, 1926
13-182  Kent v Gloucestershire, at Dover, 1927
13-168  Kent v Northamptonshire, at Northampton, 1928
13-105  Kent v Sussex, at Maidstone, 1929
13-144  Players v Gentlemen, at Lord's, 1929
13-110  Kent v Derbyshire, at Tonbridge, 1930
13-154  Kent v Middlesex, at Lord's, 1931
13-184  Kent v Oxford University, at Oxford, 1931
13-83   Kent v Leicestershire, at Leicester, 1932
13-84   Kent v Glamorgan, at Canterbury, 1932
13-96   Kent v Gloucestershire, at Bristol, 1932
13-144  Kent v Lancashire, at Folkestone, 1932
13-128  Kent v Leicestershire, at Maidstone, 1933
13-152  South of England v MCC, at Folkestone, 1933
13-158  Kent v Worcestershire, at Gravesend, 1933
13-171  Kent v Lancashire, at Tonbridge, 1933
13-187  Kent v Northamptonshire, at Northampton, 1934
13-245  Kent v Glamorgan, at Gravesend, 1934
13-155  Kent v Yorkshire, at Bradford, 1935

In the course of four days' cricket at Folkestone in 1932, against Lancashire and Warwickshire, Freeman took 30 wickets for 236 runs. During three consecutive maches in 1929 – against Derbyshire at Chesterfield, Somerset and Yorkshire, both at Tonbridge – 38 batsmen fell to him for 457. In 1930, four matches in succession, against Hampshire at Southampton, Gloucestershire at Bristol, Derbyshire and Warwickshire, both at Tonbridge, yielded him 53 wickets at a cost of 582 runs. All these performances were for Kent.

F. J. C. G.

## KENT v NOTTINGHAMSHIRE

At Canterbury, August 4, 5, 6, 1937

Nottinghamshire won by five wickets. Set to get 310, Nottinghamshire hit off the runs in three hours with forty-five minutes to spare. Keeton and Knowles, by adding 118 in an hour and a quarter, started the fast-scoring and Hardstaff, in a phenomenal display, hit up 117 out of 134 put on by the third wicket in an hour. This stand assured Nottinghamshire of success but half the side were out for 279, and, as the last four wickets had fallen for 23 in the first innings, Kent persevered until the very end which came through the agency of four byes. Hardstaff, in his most easy, graceful style, scored largely in front of the wicket and, no matter what the pace or length of the ball, always used the right stroke. He actually completed his 100 in fifty-one minutes, and hit a 6 and seventeen 4s. His first innings was as good, though not so wonderfully free. Both he and Todd scored over 200 runs in the match. Wright, by taking three wickets in four balls, secured Kent their first innings lead. The visitors owed their triumph largely to superior running between the wickets. In this connection it is noteworthy that Todd batted four hours and a half for 135, which contained 58 singles; he hit three 6s in his last 24 runs after the eighth wicket fell and was himself last out to a long-on catch. Hardstaff, also last out in Nottinghamshire's first innings, batted three hours for his 97, which included 44 singles, and comparison with this effort made his second effort all the more dazzling.

### Kent

| | | |
|---|---:|---:|
| W. H. Ashdown b Woodhead | 25 | – c Harris b Heane ............... 13 |
| P. R. Sunnucks c Wheat b Staples | 16 | – c Staples b Heane ............. 5 |
| F. E. Woolley b Woodhead | 2 | – c Bradford b Woodhead ......... 5 |
| L. E. G. Ames c and b Bradley | 93 | – c Heane b Bradley ............. 44 |
| L. J. Todd c Harris b Woodhead | 135 | – b Woodhead ................... 72 |
| Mr F. G. H. Chalk c Butler b Bradley | 6 | – b Woodhead ................... 7 |
| Mr J. G. W. Davies c Gunn b Butler | 17 | – c Harris b Heane ............. 49 |
| Mr B. H. Valentine b Woodhead | 7 | – c Wheat b Woodhead ........... 37 |
| D. V. P. Wright c Wheat b Bradley | 22 | – not out ..................... 4 |
| C. Cole st Wheat b Bradley | 1 | – c Hardstaff b Butler ......... 5 |
| C. Lewis not out | 0 | |
| B 2, l-b 5, w 1 | 8 | W 1 ................... 1 |
| | **332** | **(9 wkts dec.) 242** |

### Nottinghamshire

| | | |
|---|---:|---:|
| W. Keeton b Wright | 27 | – c and b Lewis ................. 51 |
| C. B. Harris b Wright | 21 | – c Valentine b Todd ............ 8 |
| J. Knowles lbw b Todd | 41 | – lbw b Davies ................. 84 |
| J. Hardstaff c Woolley b Davies | 97 | – c Cole b Davies .............. 126 |
| G. V. Gunn c Woolley b Wright | 5 | – not out ..................... 16 |
| A. Staples c Ashdown b Wright | 29 | – lbw b Wright ................. 0 |
| Mr G. F. H. Heane c Ames b Davies | 22 | – not out ..................... 12 |
| H. J. Butler lbw b Wright | 2 | |
| F. G. Woodhead lbw b Wright | 0 | |
| A. B. Wheat c and b Wright | 0 | |
| J. Bradley not out | 5 | |
| B 1, l-b 10, n-b 5 | 16 | B 4, l-b 8, w 1, n-b 1 ....... 14 |
| | **265** | **311** |

## Nottinghamshire Bowling

| | Overs | Mdns | Runs | Wkts | Overs | Mdns | Runs | Wkts |
|---|---|---|---|---|---|---|---|---|
| Butler ............ | 28 | 6 | 89 | 1 | 10 | 1 | 35 | 1 |
| Woodhead ........ | 31.2 | 6 | 60 | 4 | 24 | 6 | 50 | 4 |
| Staples .......... | 20 | 5 | 48 | 1 | 14 | — | 52 | — |
| Bradley .......... | 22 | — | 116 | 4 | 10 | — | 50 | 1 |
| Harris .......... | 6 | 1 | 11 | — | | | | |
| Heane .......... | | | | | 11 | — | 54 | 3 |

## Kent Bowling

| | Overs | Mdns | Runs | Wkts | Overs | Mdns | Runs | Wkts |
|---|---|---|---|---|---|---|---|---|
| Todd ............ | 21 | 4 | 66 | 1 | 7 | — | 44 | 1 |
| Cole ............ | 15 | 4 | 41 | — | 7 | 1 | 28 | — |
| Wright .......... | 28 | 1 | 94 | 7 | 25 | 2 | 104 | 1 |
| Davies .......... | 12.1 | — | 41 | 2 | 22 | 3 | 74 | 2 |
| Lewis ............ | 6 | 2 | 7 | — | 5 | — | 29 | 1 |
| Woolley ......... | | | | | 2 | — | 18 | — |

Umpires: W. Bestwick and A. Skelding.

# KENT v GLOUCESTERSHIRE

## At Dover, August 18, 19, 20, 1937

Kent won by eight wickets. Set to get 218 in less than two hours, they actually hit off the runs in seventy-one minutes. History contains no mention of a faster scoring feat in first-class cricket. Faulty slip-fielding at first involved Kent in serious trouble but they recovered in wonderful style. Parker, missed four times, scored his second consecutive century and the highest innings of his career. He hit three 6s and twenty 4s during four hours at the wicket. Barnett began the match with 70 out of 90 in 35 minutes, and Sinfield helped Parker add 214 but the last five wickets fell for 45 and Woolley followed up clever bowling by scoring a hundred. He got his runs in two hours. Pearce and Spencer put on 100 in sixty-five minutes but this was nothing to the rate of scoring that occurred in the fourth innings. Woolley made 44 out of 68 in twenty-five minutes; Ames hit up 70 out of 100 in thirty-six minutes and then Watt gave such an amazing display that the last 51 runs came in ten minutes. From the moment that Woolley hit nine runs off the first over that average rate of scoring was maintained. Ashdown played a second admirable innings.

## Gloucestershire

| | | | | |
|---|---|---|---|---|
| C. J. Barnett b Watt .......................... | 70 | – c Valentine b Harding ........... | 0 |
| Mr G. W. Parker b Watt .................... | 210 | – b Watt ...................... | 20 |
| Mr B. O. Allen c Spencer b Watt ................ | 21 | – c Woolley b Todd ............. | 9 |
| W. R. Hammond c Ashdown b Woolley .......... | 3 | – c Woolley b Wright ............. | 52 |
| J. F. Crapp c Ashdown b Watt ................. | 2 | – b Watt ...................... | 1 |
| R. A. Sinfield not out .......'............... | 74 | – b Watt ...................... | 26 |
| Mr B. H. Lyon c Pearce b Watt ................. | 0 | – b Watt ...................... | 21 |
| W. L. Neale lbw b Watt ...................... | 0 | – c Chalk b Todd ............... | 3 |
| E. J. Stephens c Ashdown b Woolley ............ | 4 | – run out .................... | 15 |
| T. W. Goddard c Ames b Woolley .............. | 6 | – b Harding ................. | 9 |
| B. L. Watkins b Harding ..................... | 25 | – not out ................... | 11 |
| B 9, l-b 9, w 1 ..................... | 19 | B 7, l-b 4, n-b 4 .......... | 15 |
| | 434 | | 182 |

## Kent

| | | | |
|---|---|---|---|
| W. H. Ashdown c Hammond b Parker | 45 | – not out | 62 |
| F. E. Woolley c and b Sinfield | 100 | – c Barnett b Sinfield | 44 |
| Mr F. G. H. Chalk b Neale | 34 | | |
| L. E. G. Ames b Neale | 1 | – c Barnett b Sinfield | 70 |
| L. J. Todd b Parker | 12 | | |
| Mr B. H. Valentine c Hammond b Parker | 30 | | |
| Mr T. A. Pearce b Sinfield | 59 | | |
| T. Spencer b Sinfield | 53 | | |
| D. V. P. Wright c Watkins b Goddard | 29 | | |
| A. E. Watt c Barnett b Sinfield | 0 | – not out | 39 |
| N. W. Harding not out | 14 | | |
| B 22 | 22 | B 2, l-b 2 | 4 |
| | **399** | | **219** |

### Kent Bowling

| | Overs | Mdns | Runs | Wkts | Overs | Mdns | Runs | Wkts |
|---|---|---|---|---|---|---|---|---|
| Harding | 24.1 | 2 | 104 | 1 | 14.1 | 2 | 43 | 2 |
| Watt | 29 | 2 | 129 | 6 | 26 | 7 | 69 | 4 |
| Todd | 8 | — | 22 | — | 18 | 8 | 26 | 2 |
| Wright | 25 | 7 | 78 | — | 12 | 4 | 29 | 1 |
| Woolley | 24 | 6 | 82 | 3 | | | | |

### Gloucestershire Bowling

| | Overs | Mdns | Runs | Wkts | Overs | Mdns | Runs | Wkts |
|---|---|---|---|---|---|---|---|---|
| Barnett | 16 | 2 | 45 | — | 3 | — | 23 | — |
| Lyon | 8 | — | 39 | — | | | | |
| Sinfield | 31 | 5 | 83 | 4 | 9 | — | 69 | 2 |
| Goddard | 23.1 | 2 | 77 | 1 | 8.2 | — | 98 | — |
| Parker | 24 | 5 | 78 | 3 | 3 | — | 25 | — |
| Neale | 11 | — | 55 | 2 | | | | |

Umpires: W. Reeves and F. Chester.

# MY HAPPY CRICKET LIFE [1938]

## By Frank E. Woolley

The time has come for me to say farewell to cricket as a player, and I readily acquiesce to the invitation of the Editor of *Wisden* to record some of the greatest moments of my career. It is a severe wrench leaving the game which I have enjoyed so much. My whole life in cricket from beginning to end has been 32 years of happiness, apart from 1915–1918. I have a lot for which to be thankful, having always enjoyed good health, and I have no regrets at all.

Even my last season in first-class cricket brought me memorable days when I touched my best form, but I do think it is best to say good-bye before I fail to satisfy my admirers. I believe I could have gone on for another season or two, but I might have struck a bad patch and then many people would have said, "Why doesn't he retire?"

I will not say that I will never turn out again, because Kent, who have always treated me kindly, might – when short of players – invite me to play and in that event I could not refuse. There were occasions last summer, however, when I felt the strain of a long day in the field, especially after I had made a big score.

### DEBUT AS A BOWLER

It is delving into the dim and distant past when I made my first acquaintance with the game, but it all stands out very clearly in my memory. I never played serious cricket at school, but I was born close to the Angel ground at Tonbridge and I always took a keen

interest in the game. In those days I used to wander into the ground and, after leaving school at 14, never missed an opportunity of bowling at the nets.

My heart and soul were in cricket. I was fortunate enough to bowl to Colin Blythe and he mentioned my name to the Kent manager, Mr Tom Pawley. That was in 1902, but as I had rather outgrown my strength at that age, being very tall and thin, they allowed me to attend the ground on mornings only. In 1903 I became a regular member of the staff. Colin Blythe was without doubt one of the greatest left-hand bowlers I have ever seen. He had a perfect action and run-up. I do not think I copied him. His style was so different from mine.

Curiously enough, my first match for Kent, which was against Lancashire at Old Trafford in 1906, came about through an accident to Blythe at Brighton. Kent wired for me. I was reckoned purely a left-arm slow bowler and I shall never forget my debut. The great John Tyldesley hit 295 not out, the highest innings of his career, and some funny things happened. We lost the toss and I was put at third man. Tyldesley cut one very hard, but misjudging it altogether the ball hit me on the chest. Our captain, Mr C. H. B. Marsham, feeling sorry for me, moved me to mid-off and to mid-on; in each place I dropped a skier, although one was off a no-ball.

Johnny Tyldesley was hitting us all over the place when he was joined by the last man, W. Worsley, the wicket-keeper, who was reckoned the worst batsman in the world. We all wanted to see Tyldesley get 300. I was bowling at one end and our captain called us together and said, "Who can we put on the other end to bowl a maiden over to Worsley so that Tyldesley can get his 300?" The cry went up "Put 'Punter' on," and he was told to bowl away from the stumps. His first four balls were well over to the off, but to everyone's amazement, including "Punter" Humphries, the fifth swung in viciously and knocked down Worsley's leg stump. So Tyldesley did not realise his ambition. My analysis was one for 103 and Humphries had one for 101. He came in for some rare "chipping" in the dressing room for having to be satisfied with only Worsley's wicket. In our first innings I was bowled third ball for a "duck", but after a rather bad beginning I had a satisfactory last day when I made 64.

My part in the next match against Somerset at Gravesend can be best described by quoting *Wisden* of 1907 which says: "Somerset in their second innings began well, but collapsed before the bowling of Woolley." My bag was six wickets for 39. The following game, against Surrey at The Oval, which we won was probably the deciding factor that season in Kent winning the championship for the first time. Again we lost the toss and I opened the bowling with Fielder. I had never seen Tom Hayward. I imagined he was a tall athletic looking man and when five wickets were down I said to Fielder, "When does Tom Hayward come in?" He replied, "That was the first chap you bowled out." Actually in that innings I bowled Hayward, Hayes and Goatly. It was a comparatively low scoring match and I could do little wrong. I went in number eight, made Kent's top score, 72: then took five more wickets; Kent wanted 131 and I was in at the death. I remember being dropped by Jack Crawford when one, but I got 23 not out and we scrambled home with one wicket to spare.

Those were the great days when plenty of amateurs could spare time for cricket. I do not think there are so many good players in the game now as before the war. In the old days we were probably educated in cricket in a far more serious way than now. For the purpose of giving the younger people my idea of the difference I will put up Walter Hammond, England's captain, as an example. Before 1914 there were something like 30 players up to his standard and he would have been in the England team only if at the top of his form. I make these remarks without casting the slightest reflection on Hammond. He is a grand player and one of the greatest all-round cricketers since the war – in fact, the greatest.

I doubt whether English cricket has really recovered from the effects of the war. You see, we missed half a generation, and since then young men have found many other ways of occupying their leisure hours. Still, I believe it is only a passing phase and cricket will one day produce an abundance of great players.

## TWO-DAY COUNTY MATCHES

There is little wrong with the game itself. Just a question of the way it is played. It is amazing how the public steadfastly refuse to attend the third day of a match when so often the last day produces the best and most exciting cricket. Certain sides are to blame for batting too long and leaving the chance of a sporting finish impossible. The time may arrive when the third day will be abolished. I am fully aware that in 1919, the first season after the war, two-day matches proved a failure, but then we played three matches a week and stumps were not drawn until 7 p.m. or 7.30 p.m. and everyone became weary of the experiment. I think if the counties played matches of two days' duration with a day's rest between each for travelling, it would be a step towards better cricket. We have been suffering from a surfeit of cricket. There are too many match days and the players get jaded.

Touching on another personal subject I have been asked if I can explain why I was dismissed so many times in the "nineties". The statisticians inform me that I was out 35 times between 90 and 99 and I am also told I am credited with 89 "ducks". With regard to those "nineties", I can honestly say that with me it was never a question of the "nervous nineties." Lots of time I was out through forcing the game. We were never allowed to play for averages in the Kent side or take half-an-hour or more to get the last ten runs under normal conditions. We always had to play the game and play for the team. It is a Kent tradition.

## TWO "90's" IN A TEST

As a matter of fact I consider the two finest innings I ever played were in the second test against Australia at Lord's in 1921 when I was out for 95 and 93. I do not think I ever worked harder at any match during my career to get runs as I did then, nor did I ever have to face in one game such consistently fast bowlers as the Australian pair, Gregory and MacDonald. Square cuts which ordinarily would have flashed to the boundary earned only two and I believe that those two innings would have been worth 150 apiece in a county match.

I was not depressed when they got me out. I have always taken my dismissals as part of the game. In the first innings I was in the "eighties" when I was joined by the last man, Jack Durston. It was my own fault completely that I lost my wicket. Mailey bowled me a full toss to the off, I walked down the pitch and, stepping to the on to force the ball past extra cover, I missed it and that fine wicket-keeper, H. Carter, eagerly accepted the opportunity to stump me. I was rather unlucky in the second innings when again I fell to Mailey. The ball stuck in his hand and dropped half-way on the leg side. I hit it pretty plumb between square leg and mid-on and just there was standing "Stalky" Hendry. As I made the shot he jumped in the air and up went his right hand. The ball hit him, I think, on the wrist, and he lost his balance. The ball went up ten feet and as he was lying on the ground it fell in his lap and he caught it. He was the only man on the leg side and I think the shot would have carried for six. It was a marvellous catch.

In 1934 I was the first winner of the "Lawrence Trophy" which Sir Walter Lawrence offers each year. As it tends to encourage brighter cricket I cannot see that it does any harm to the game, although there was no idea of the trophy in my mind when I won it. We were playing Northamptonshire at Dover and were pushed for time. I seized every chance and reached the hundred in 63 minutes.

It is often argued that left-handed batsmen have an advantage compared with the right-handers. I do not agree with this contention. When the turf is worn the right-hand leg-break bowlers and left-arm slow bowlers are able to pitch the ball into the footholes of the bowlers who have operated at the other end. Right-handed batsmen can let these balls hit their pads, but the left-handers must use their bats. Perhaps the new lbw rule has not helped us there, but the amended law does not worry me though in my opinion it has not improved the game. As for further extending the lbw rule I think it would make a farce of the game.

In many quarters surprise was expressed last season that at the age of 51 I went in number one. Until then I had never been in first regularly, though I have always preferred that place. Beginning as a bowler made Kent place me four or five in the order and moreover the county were always rich in opening batsmen. Consequently my wish to start the innings was denied until 1938. Because Kent have experienced their bad times against fast bowling the cry has gone round that we cannot play the fast men, but I think if you search the records you will also find that Kent have hit a tremendous lot of runs off fast bowling. Perhaps our opponents, encouraged with the idea that we did not fancy ourselves against pace, have bowled with their tails up. Again I must emphasise that Kent always endeavour to play sporting cricket, and trying to make runs off that type of bowling must sometimes have contributed to our downfall. It was never a policy of the Kent team that the pitch *must* be occupied all day after winning the toss.

I cannot let this opportunity pass without placing on record how much I have enjoyed my cricket with Kent. If I was a youngster starting as a batsman I think I should like to play always at The Oval, but the Kent grounds, with their natural decorations of beautiful trees, members' tents flying their own colours and bedecked with flowers, lend the right tone to cricket. I am devoting most of this coming summer to coaching the boys at King's School, Canterbury, and look forward to the experience, especially as it is a Kent school.

## F. E. WOOLLEY IN FIRST-CLASS CRICKET 1906-1938

### Career at a Glance

|  | Runs | 100's | Average | Wickets | Average | Catches |
|---|---|---|---|---|---|---|
| Test matches | 3,283 | 5 | 36.07 | 83 | 33.91 | 61 |
| Gentlemen v Players | 1,510 | 1 | 33.55 | 60 | 23.61 | 39 |
| County matches | 43,603 | 112 | 41.17 | 1,581 | 18.58 | 641 |
| Other matches | 10,573 | 27 | 41.95 | 344 | 21.71 | 172 |
| Total | 58,969 | 145 | 40.75 | 2,068 | 19.86 | 913 |

### Where His Cricket was Played

|  | Runs | 100's | Average | Wickets | Average | Catches |
|---|---|---|---|---|---|---|
| In England | 54,553 | 135 | 41.67 | 1,898 | 19.22 | 800 |
| In Australia | 2,562 | 7 | 45.75 | 68 | 35.02 | 44 |
| In South Africa | 1,499 | 2 | 25.40 | 73 | 22.34 | 65 |
| In New Zealand | 355 | 1 | 35.50 | 29 | 20.00 | 4 |
| Total | 58,969 | 145 | 40.75 | 2,068 | 19.86 | 913 |

### Test Cricket

|  | Tests | Runs | 100's | Average | Wickets | Average | Catches |
|---|---|---|---|---|---|---|---|
| v Australia | 32 | 1,664 | 2 | 33.28 | 43 | 36.16 | 34 |
| v South Africa | 26 | 1,354 | 3 | 42.56 | 27 | 37.00 | 27 |
| v New Zealand | 5 | 235 | — | 33.57 | 13 | 20.09 | — |
| v India | 1 | 30 | — | 15.00 | — | — | — |
| Total | 64 | 3,283 | 5 | 36.07 | 83 | 33.91 | 61 |

**1,000 runs in a season** (15):
1907, 1908, 1909, 1910, 1911, 1912, 1913, 1919, 1920, 1927, 1932, 1933, 1936, 1937, 1938

**2,000 runs in a season** (12):
1914, 1921, 1922, 1923, 1924, 1925, 1926, 1929, 1930, 1931, 1934, 1935

**3,000 runs in a season** (1):
1928

**100 wickets in a season** (8):
1910, 1912, 1914, 1919, 1920, 1921, 1922, 1923

**50 wickets in a season** (7):
1908, 1909, 1911, 1913, 1924, 1925, 1929

**2,000 runs and 100 wickets** (4):
1914, 1921, 1922, 1923

**1,000 runs and 100 wickets** (4):
1910, 1912, 1919, 1920

**Batting**

| Innings | Not Outs | Runs | 100's | 50's | Highest Innings | Average |
|---------|----------|--------|-------|------|-----------------|---------|
| 1,532   | 85       | 58,969 | 145   | 274  | 305*            | 40.75   |

**Bowling**

| †Overs | Maidens | Wickets | Runs | 10 wickets in a Match | Average |
|--------|---------|---------|--------|-----------------------|---------|
| 15,711.1 | 4,142 | 2,068 | 41,075 | 28 | 19.86 |

*† For one match in Australia and one in South Africa no details of the overs are available.*

**Hundreds** (145)

Woolley made 122 hundreds for Kent

| | | |
|---|---|---|
| v Sussex . . . . . . . . . . . 14 | v Worcestershire . . . . . 7 | v Warwickshire . . . . . 4 |
| v Somerset . . . . . . . . 12 | v Essex . . . . . . . . . . . . 6 | v Nottinghamshire . . . 3 |
| v Gloucestershire . . . . 10 | v Lancashire . . . . . . . . 6 | v Oxford University . . 3 |
| v Hampshire . . . . . . . . 10 | v Middlesex . . . . . . . . 5 | v New Zealanders . . . . 2 |
| v Leicestershire . . . . . . 10 | v Yorkshire . . . . . . . . . 5 | v Glamorgan . . . . . . . 1 |
| v Surrey . . . . . . . . . . 8 | v Derbyshire . . . . . . . . 4 | v South Africans . . . . . 1 |
| v Northamptonshire . . 7 | v MCC . . . . . . . . . . . . 4 | |

**Other Matches** (23)

England v South Africa 3; v Australia 2
MCC v New South Wales 3; v South Australia 1; v Tasmania 1; v Otago 1; v Transvaal 1
Players v Gentlemen 1
Rest of England v Yorkshire 3; v Lancashire 1; v Nottinghamshire 1
MCC Australian Team v Rest of England 1; v C. I. Thornton's XI 1
An England XI v West Indies 1; v South Africans 1

Woolley made 135 hundreds in England and 10 abroad.

## Double Hundreds

305* MCC v Tasmania at Hobart, 1912
270  Kent v Middlesex at Canterbury, 1932
229  Kent v Surrey at The Oval, 1935
224* Kent v Oxford University at Oxford, 1913
224  Kent v New Zealanders at Canterbury, 1931
219  MCC v New South Wales at Sydney, 1929
217  Kent v Northamptonshire at Northampton, 1926
215  Kent v Somerset at Gravesend, 1925
202* Rest of England v Yorkshire at The Oval, 1924

In addition to scoring 145 hundreds, Woolley was dismissed after reaching the nineties on 35 occasions.

## Two Hundreds in a Match

104 and 185* for Kent v Somerset at Tunbridge Wells, 1911

Woolley scored a hundred and fifty in the same match eleven times – eight times for Kent; and for MCC v New South Wales, Rest of England v Yorkshire, and an England XI v West Indies.

On 21 occasions Woolley scored two fifties in a match – twice for England v South Africa, once for England v Australia, once for the Players v Gentlemen, once for MCC v Transvaal, and sixteen times for Kent.

## A Hundred and Ten Wickets in a Match

111* and 12-122 for Kent v Gloucestershire at Gloucester, 1914
139* and 10-132 for Kent v Sussex at Horsham, 1920
174  and 11-66  for Kent v Gloucestershire at Maidstone, 1921
109  and 10-116 for Kent v Nottinghamshire at Nottingham, 1921
156  and 10-78  for Kent v Warwickshire at Tunbridge Wells, 1928
132  and 10-88  for Kent v MCC v Otago at Dunedin, 1930

On 28 occasions Woolley took ten or more wickets in a match – 14 wickets, once; 13, once; 12, six times; 11, nine times; 10, eleven times.

## Notes

Woolley has registered the second highest aggregate in first-class cricket, and the second highest aggregate for a single season (1928).

He scored 95 and 93 for England v Australia at Lords in 1921.

In 1929 he scored four hundreds in consecutive innings – v Derbyshire, Somerset, Yorkshire and Hampshire.

His 305 not out for MCC v Tasmania at Hobart in 1912 is the highest innings scored by an English batsman in Australia.

For the Rest of England v Champion County at The Oval, Woolley scored 701 runs, including hundreds in three successive seasons (1924-25-26), and averaged 100.85.

In Test matches at Lord's (1912-1926) he scored 502 runs and averaged 100.40.

Against Northamptonshire at Dover in 1934, Woolley won the Lawrence Trophy for the quickest hundred of the season, his time being 63 minutes.

## Records

1. A thousand or more runs in 28 consecutive seasons.

2. Woolley played in 52 consecutive Test matches – 29 v Australia; 23 v South Africa.

3. In four seasons – three in succession – he scored 2,000 runs and took 100 wickets.

4. He has the best bowling analysis for an England v Australia Test match – ten wickets for 49 runs at The Oval in 1912.

5. Most catches in first-class cricket – 913.

6. In 1909 at Stourbridge, Woolley and Fielder scored 235 for Kent's last wicket v Worcestershire (an English record).

E. L. R.

## KENT v WORCESTERSHIRE

### At Gillingham, May 17, 18, 19, 1939

Worcestershire won by 83 runs. Saturated turf delayed the start and the conditions always helped bowlers. Lewis, with spin and flight, was specially effective with his left-hand slows; Martin did still better and the South African practically won the match. Making most of his height Martin swung the ball into the batsmen and got lift from a worn spot. Howorth helped in the first Kent collapse, the last five wickets falling for 17 runs, and two early successes by Perks marred Kent's prospects of hitting off the runs. Gibbons batted best, his second innings of ninety minutes including many brilliant off-side strokes.

### Worcestershire

| | | | |
|---|---|---|---|
| C. H. Bull c Levett b Todd | 4 | – b Todd | 4 |
| Mr A. F. T. White c Levett b Lewis | 27 | – c Dovey b Lewis | 29 |
| B. P. King c Foster b Dovey | 21 | – c Foster b Todd | 5 |
| E. Cooper c Levett b Lewis | 1 | – lbw b Lewis | 13 |
| H. H. Gibbons b Dovey | 36 | – hit wkt b Watt | 63 |
| S. H. Martin run out | 25 | – b Lewis | 0 |
| Hon. C. J. Lyttelton st Levett b Lewis | 6 | – b Dovey | 4 |
| R. Howorth st Levett b Lewis | 20 | – c Ames b Lewis | 1 |
| S. Buller c Ames b Lewis | 3 | – b Dovey | 7 |
| R. T. D. Perks b Lewis | 0 | – c Fagg b Lewis | 29 |
| P. F. Jackson not out | 1 | – not out | 1 |
| L-b 2 | 2 | B 1, l-b 1 | 2 |
| | **146** | | **158** |

### Kent

| | | | |
|---|---|---|---|
| A. Fagg c and b Martin | 1 | – lbw b Perks | 1 |
| P. R. Sunnucks lbw b Howorth | 5 | – c Lyttelton b Martin | 1 |
| L. E. G. Ames c Buller b Martin | 22 | – lbw b Martin | 19 |
| Mr F. G. H. Chalk c Bull b Howorth | 26 | – c Buller b Perks | 2 |
| Mr B. H. Valentine c Lyttelton b Martin | 4 | – b Martin | 48 |
| L. J. Todd c King b Martin | 4 | – st Buller b Martin | 28 |
| Mr P. G. Foster c Martin b Howorth | 5 | – b Martin | 4 |
| Mr W. H. V. Levett c Perks b Martin | 0 | – c White b Martin | 2 |
| A. E. Watt b Howorth | 0 | – c Howorth b Martin | 34 |
| C. Lewis c Howorth b Martin | 0 | – not out | 3 |
| R. Dovey not out | 0 | – b Martin | 0 |
| B 4, l-b 1 | 5 | B 3, l-b 3, n-b 1 | 7 |
| | **72** | | **149** |

## Kent Bowling

| | Overs | Mdns | Runs | Wkts | Overs | Mdns | Runs | Wkts |
|---|---|---|---|---|---|---|---|---|
| Todd ............ | 13 | 3 | 34 | 1 | 8 | — | 30 | 2 |
| Watt ............. | 10 | 3 | 26 | — | 4 | 1 | 17 | 1 |
| Lewis ........... | 16.3 | 4 | 46 | 6 | 14 | 3 | 57 | 5 |
| Dovey .......... | 14 | 2 | 38 | 2 | 10 | 1 | 52 | 2 |

## Worcestershire Bowling

| | Overs | Mdns | Runs | Wkts | Overs | Mdns | Runs | Wkts |
|---|---|---|---|---|---|---|---|---|
| Perks ........... | 4 | 1 | 13 | — | 13 | 1 | 34 | 2 |
| Martin .......... | 13 | 5 | 23 | 6 | 18 | 2 | 84 | 8 |
| Howorth ........ | 9.2 | 1 | 31 | 4 | 1 | — | 5 | — |
| Jackson ......... | | | | | 4 | — | 19 | — |

Umpires: J. Durston and J. Newman.

# LANCASHIRE

## LANCASHIRE v DERBYSHIRE

### Played at Manchester, June 23, 24, 25, 1920

With the conditions against them Derbyshire suffered defeat by an innings and 228 runs after Lancashire had declared with six men out. Oliver played very good cricket for two hours and a quarter on a rain-affected pitch at the start of the game and Cadman helped to add 120. Cook then caused a collapse, and, after scoring 28 on Wednesday evening Lancashire batted all the next day to secure an overwhelming advantage. Rain fell in the night and the visitors, when put in, could make nothing of a fight against James Tyldesley and Dean, the whole side being dismissed in an hour and a half on the ruined pitch. Makepeace and Hallows scored 130 together, giving Lancashire the upper hand, while after Sharp had helped Ernest Tyldesley add 74 the bowling was mastered. Tyldesley and Pewtress, formerly of Christ's Hospital, put on 141 for the fourth wicket, and Richard Tyldesley punished the bowling freely. In playing his first three-figure innings of the season Ernest Tyldesley batted admirably. He took over three hours to complete his hundred, but afterwards scored more readily, being altogether at the wickets four hours and a half for his 169 not out. At the opening of Derbyshire's second innings James Tyldesley took four wickets for 13 runs. Dismissing Cadman with the last ball of one over and Morton and Elliott with the first two balls of the next over, he did the hat trick.

## Derbyshire

| | | | |
|---|---|---|---|
| Mr L. Oliver c sub. b R. Tyldesley | 73 | – c E. Tyldesley b J. Tyldesley | 3 |
| H. Wild b J. Tyldesley | 1 | – b J. Tyldesley | 17 |
| S. Cadman lbw b Cook | 47 | – c Cook b J. Tyldesley | 14 |
| A. Severn st Blomley b R. Tyldesley | 2 | – c R. Tyldesley b Dean | 3 |
| H. Elliott c R. Tyldesley b Cook | 6 | – b J. Tyldesley | 0 |
| H. Storer b Cook | 25 | – b Dean | 2 |
| Mr G. R. Jackson lbw b Cook | 11 | – b Dean | 0 |
| W. N. Malthouse st Blomley b R. Tyldesley | 9 | – not out | 26 |
| A. Morton not out | 30 | – lbw b J. Tyldesley | 1 |
| Mr J. Chapman c J. Tyldesley b Dean | 3 | – c Blomley b Dean | 0 |
| Mr A. H. M. Jackson c Hallows b Cook | 2 | – c J. Tyldesley b Dean | 0 |
| B 13, l-b 1, n-b 2 | 16 | B 1, l-b 7, n-b 1 | 9 |
| | **225** | | **75** |

## Lancashire

| | | | |
|---|---|---|---|
| H. Makepeace c Elliott b Storer | 89 | R. Tyldesley b Storer | 63 |
| J. Hallows c Wild b Storer | 57 | H. Dean not out | 5 |
| E. Tyldesley not out | 169 | | |
| Mr J. Sharp b Cadman | 41 | B 20, l-b 7, w 1, n-b 2 | 30 |
| Mr A. W. Pewtress b Morton | 68 | | |
| James Tyldesley b Morton | 6 | (6 wkts dec.) | 528 |

J. S. Heap, L. Cook and B. Blomley did not bat.

## Lancashire Bowling

| | Overs | Mdns | Runs | Wkts | Overs | Mdns | Runs | Wkts |
|---|---|---|---|---|---|---|---|---|
| J. Tyldesley | 21 | 4 | 53 | 1 | 13 | 1 | 40 | 5 |
| Dean | 28 | 5 | 61 | 1 | 12.1 | 1 | 26 | 5 |
| Cook | 34.1 | 13 | 50 | 5 | | | | |
| Heap | 4 | 2 | 5 | — | | | | |
| R. Tyldesley | 17 | 4 | 40 | 3 | | | | |

### Derbyshire Bowling

| | Overs | Mdns | Runs | Wkts |
|---|---|---|---|---|
| Morton .......... | 48 | 9 | 150 | 2 |
| A. H. M. Jackson ... | 20 | 2 | 91 | — |
| Malthouse ........ | 16 | — | 60 | — |
| Cadman .......... | 40 | 5 | 107 | 1 |
| Storer ............ | 24 | 3 | 90 | 3 |

Umpires: J. Blake and J. Carlin.

# LANCASHIRE v HAMPSHIRE

Played at Liverpool, July 3, 5, 6, 1920

A remarkable match on the Aigburth ground ended in a win for Lancashire by one run. Play was impossible on the Saturday until two o'clock and the game began on a freshly prepared pitch. A crowd of 7,000 people then invaded the ground, enclosure and pavilion, causing considerable damage, without interfering with the cricket or giving serious trouble. Fourth out at 133 after batting two hours, Makepeace completed his 1,000 runs. Following his dismissal Newman carried all before him, and when Tennyson hit up 50 out of 63 in thirty-five minutes Hampshire held an advantage. Greig, at the wickets seventy minutes, played soundly against difficult bowling, and, after he left, Dean took the last four wickets for 14 runs leaving Lancashire with a lead which just enabled them to win the match. The batsmen could do nothing with Kennedy late in the afternoon, and on the Tuesday, after heavy rain, Hampshire had a great chance of victory. The pitch was not fit for cricket until two o'clock, and Evans, who with Newman had scored six over-night, stayed an hour and five minutes, all but twelve of the 66 wanted for victory being obtained for five wickets. But batsmen were so helpless that the last five wickets produced only ten runs, Lancashire snatching a victory amid great enthusiasm. Cook and Dean bowled splendidly in both innings.

### Lancashire

| | | | | |
|---|---|---|---|---|
| H. Makepeace c Mead b Newman | 65 | – c Mead b Kennedy | 7 |
| J. Hallows b Kennedy | 19 | – st Livsey b Kennedy | 10 |
| E. Tyldesley c Evans b Kennedy | 37 | – b Newman | 1 |
| Mr J. Sharp c Barrett b Newman | 9 | – b Kennedy | 4 |
| Mr J. R. Barnes b Newman | 6 | – lbw b Kennedy | 4 |
| Mr A. W. Pewtress lbw b Newman | 3 | – b Kennedy | 12 |
| James Tyldesley b Newman | 8 | – c Evans b Kennedy | 6 |
| R. Tyldesley b Mead | 13 | – b Kennedy | 0 |
| H. Dean b Kennedy | 5 | – c Brown b Kennedy | 0 |
| Mr R. A. Boddington c Mead b Newman | 0 | – b Kennedy | 0 |
| L. Cook not out | 12 | – not out | 12 |
| B 2, 1-b 3 | 5 | N-b 1 | 1 |
| | **182** | | **57** |

## Hampshire

| | | | | |
|---|---|---|---|---|
| G. Brown c E. Tyldesley b Dean | 0 | – b Dean | | 1 |
| A. Bowell c Hallows b Cook | 17 | – lbw b Cook | | 12 |
| Capt. E. I. M. Barrett b Cook | 29 | – c Hallows b Cook | | 11 |
| C. P. Mead c Cook b Dean | 15 | – c and b Dean | | 0 |
| Maj. Hon. L. H. Tennyson c and b R. Tyldesley | 55 | – b Cook | | 0 |
| Col J. G. Greig c R. Tyldesley b Cook | 35 | – b Cook | | 3 |
| J. Newman b Dean | 4 | – c E. Tyldesley b Cook | | 8 |
| A. Kennedy b Dean | 0 | – c Boddington b Dean | | 1 |
| W. H. Livsey lbw b Dean | 6 | – b Cook | | 2 |
| J. Evans b Dean | 9 | – b Cook | | 21 |
| F. Ryan not out | 0 | – not out | | 4 |
| B 4 | 4 | B 1 | | 1 |

|  |  |
|---|---|
| 174 | 64 |

### Hampshire Bowling

| | Overs | Mdns | Runs | Wkts | Overs | Mdns | Runs | Wkts |
|---|---|---|---|---|---|---|---|---|
| Kennedy | 20.1 | 3 | 74 | 3 | 13.3 | 6 | 33 | 9 |
| Newman | 24 | 7 | 68 | 6 | 13 | 5 | 23 | 1 |
| Bowell | 1 | — | 10 | — | | | | |
| Ryan | 5 | 1 | 22 | — | | | | |
| Mead | 4 | 3 | 3 | 1 | | | | |

### Lancashire Bowling

| | Overs | Mdns | Runs | Wkts | Overs | Mdns | Runs | Wkts |
|---|---|---|---|---|---|---|---|---|
| Dean | 25.5 | 5 | 85 | 6 | 16.3 | 5 | 41 | 3 |
| Cook | 29 | 9 | 65 | 3 | 16 | 9 | 22 | 7 |
| R. Tyldesley | 4 | 1 | 20 | 1 | | | | |

Umpires: J. Blake and G. P. Harrison.

## LANCASHIRE v YORKSHIRE

### Played at Manchester, July 31, August 2, 3, 1920

The weather proved less unkind than during some matches at Old Trafford, but rain at five minutes to six caused a draw. The game was remarkable for the great crowds during the three days, 58,399 people paying for admission and there being 9,000 ticket holders. The receipts were £3,321 15s. 3d. after deducting entertainment tax. Holmes distinguished himself by scoring a hundred in each Yorkshire innings – 237 runs for once out. He took five and a half hours over his 126, but only three hours and a quarter to get 111 when his side had the best of the match. Apart from a chance when 70 on the third day his batting was practically faultless. Only Spooner among the other famous batsmen playing was seen to advantage. Twice he was at the wickets nearly two hours. First he removed all anxiety about the follow-on, and then he saved his side from serious danger of defeat. He was at his best in both innings.

## Yorkshire

| | | | |
|---|---|---|---|
| P. Holmes c Musson b Heap | 126 | – not out | 111 |
| H. Sutcliffe c Musson b Parkin | 26 | – lbw b Parkin | 8 |
| D. Denton b Parkin | 0 | – b Heap | 21 |
| R. Kilner c J. Tyldesley b Parkin | 3 | – c Spooner b Cook | 6 |
| W. Rhodes lbw b Cook | 15 | – b Parkin | 35 |
| G. H. Hirst lbw b R. Tyldesley | 31 | – b Parkin | 2 |
| E. Robinson b Parkin | 8 | – not out | 15 |
| Mr D. C. F. Burton b Dean | 10 | | |
| Mr E. R. Wilson b Parkin | 4 | | |
| A. Dolphin st Musson b Cook | 16 | | |
| A. Waddington not out | 3 | | |
| B 8, l-b 2, n-b 1 | 11 | B 6, l-b 12 | 18 |
| | **253** | **(5 wkts dec.) 216** | |

## Lancashire

| | | | |
|---|---|---|---|
| Mr R. H. Spooner c Kilner b Waddington | 62 | – st Dolphin b Rhodes | 63 |
| J. S. Heap b Waddington | 5 | – b Waddington | 2 |
| E. Tyldesley c Dolphin b Kilner | 23 | – c Sutcliffe b Rhodes | 22 |
| Mr J. Sharp b Waddington | 15 | – st Dolphin b Rhodes | 0 |
| Mr A. W. Pewtress lbw b Rhodes | 10 | – not out | 8 |
| Mr F. W. Musson c and b Rhodes | 26 | – not out | 13 |
| James Tyldesley c Robinson b Rhodes | 6 | | |
| R. Tyldesley b Waddington | 3 | | |
| C. Parkin st Dolphin b Rhodes | 6 | | |
| H. Dean not out | 11 | | |
| L. Cook run out | 2 | | |
| B 2, l-b 8 | 10 | B 7, l-b 1 | 8 |
| | **179** | | **116** |

### Lancashire Bowling

| | Overs | Mdns | Runs | Wkts | Overs | Mdns | Runs | Wkts |
|---|---|---|---|---|---|---|---|---|
| Dean | 28 | 8 | 43 | 1 | 6 | — | 20 | — |
| Cook | 35.4 | 11 | 54 | 2 | 24 | 9 | 44 | 1 |
| Heap | 26 | 13 | 30 | 1 | 13 | — | 49 | 1 |
| Parkin | 45 | 16 | 86 | 5 | 29 | 8 | 65 | 3 |
| R. Tyldesley | 17 | 4 | 29 | 1 | 4 | — | 20 | — |

### Yorkshire Bowling

| | Overs | Mdns | Runs | Wkts | Overs | Mdns | Runs | Wkts |
|---|---|---|---|---|---|---|---|---|
| Waddington | 27 | 8 | 64 | 4 | 11 | 5 | 22 | 1 |
| Robinson | 2 | — | 5 | — | 4 | — | 12 | — |
| Rhodes | 22.3 | 3 | 60 | 4 | 24 | 7 | 49 | 3 |
| Wilson | 16 | 6 | 16 | — | 9 | 2 | 17 | — |
| Kilner | 9 | 4 | 17 | 1 | 11 | 5 | 8 | — |
| Hirst | 6 | 2 | 7 | — | | | | |

Umpires: J. Carlin and J. Moss.

## LANCASHIRE v WORCESTERSHIRE

### Played at Manchester, July 19, 20, 21, 1922

Rain saved Worcestershire from defeat, permitting barely half-an-hour's play on the last day, which began with the visitors wanting 243 runs for victory with three wickets to fall. Lancashire seemed sure to win when they had dismissed six of their visitors a second time for 27. This was due to J. Tyldesley, who did the hat trick, dismissing H. Higgins, Preece and Tarbox at that total, with successive balls. Maclean and Root stopped the collapse by carrying the game into the third day. They put on 67 on Thursday evening after J. B. Higgins had been dismissed at 60. Root hit freely and did most towards saving his side. R. Tyldesley again showed his all-round ability and Hallows and Makepeace opened the second innings by scoring 151 together. Hallows hit twelve 4s in an admirable display, and Norbury did so well that Lancashire declared at the tea interval, only to be robbed of victory by the weather.

## Lancashire

| | | | |
|---|---|---|---|
| H. Makepeace b Gilbert | 2 | – run out | 69 |
| C. Hallows lbw b Gilbert | 24 | – c Taylor b Gilbert | 100 |
| V. Norbury run out | 17 | – b Tarbox | 71 |
| W. Ellis c H. L. Higgins b Gilbert | 1 | – c Hopkins b Gilbert | 0 |
| F. Watson c Maclean b Root | 20 | – lbw b Tarbox | 37 |
| W. Brown b Gilbert | 0 | – c Taylor b Gilbert | 22 |
| J. Tyldesley b Root | 4 | – not out | 5 |
| R. Tyldesley b Pearson | 58 | – not out | 3 |
| Mr M. N. Kenyon run out | 0 | | |
| L. Cook not out | 11 | | |
| H. Parkinson lbw b Pearson | 8 | | |
| B 9, l-b 4 | 13 | B 2, l-b 7, n-b 2 | 11 |
| | **158** | **(6 wkts dec.)** | **318** |

## Worcestershire

| | | | |
|---|---|---|---|
| F. Bowley b Cook | 3 | – b J. Tyldesley | 9 |
| F. Pearson b J. Tyldesley | 3 | – lbw b Cook | 8 |
| Mr H. O. Hopkins c R. Tyldesley b J. Tyldesley | 8 | – b J. Tyldesley | 2 |
| Mr H. L. Higgins lbw b J. Tyldesley | 9 | – b J. Tyldesley | 1 |
| Mr J. B. Higgins lbw b R. Tyldesley | 36 | – c Norbury b R. Tyldesley | 30 |
| C. A. Preece lbw b R. Tyldesley | 32 | – lbw b J. Tyldesley | 0 |
| C. V. Tarbox b Cook | 2 | – b J. Tyldesley | 0 |
| F. Root b Cook | 0 | – c Makepeace b Cook | 81 |
| Mr H. A. Gilbert b Cook | 3 | | |
| Mr W. H. Taylor b R. Tyldesley | 0 | – not out | 9 |
| Mr J. F. Maclean not out | 6 | – not out | 43 |
| L-b 5 | 5 | L-b 4 | 4 |
| | **107** | | **187** |

## Worcestershire Bowling

| | Overs | Mdns | Runs | Wkts | Overs | Mdns | Runs | Wkts |
|---|---|---|---|---|---|---|---|---|
| Root | 27 | 12 | 36 | 2 | 28 | 4 | 96 | — |
| Gilbert | 24 | 7 | 77 | 4 | 33 | 10 | 81 | 3 |
| Preece | 5 | — | 23 | — | 5 | — | 21 | — |
| Pearson | 2.3 | 1 | 9 | 2 | 11 | 2 | 26 | — |
| J. B. Higgins | | | | | 15 | — | 62 | — |
| Tarbox | | | | | 10 | 3 | 21 | 2 |

## Lancashire Bowling

| | Overs | Mdns | Runs | Wkts | Overs | Mdns | Runs | Wkts |
|---|---|---|---|---|---|---|---|---|
| Cook | 17 | 2 | 39 | 4 | 23.2 | 2 | 100 | 2 |
| J. Tyldesley | 12 | 2 | 34 | 3 | 13 | 1 | 44 | 5 |
| Brown | 2 | — | 15 | — | | | | |
| R. Tyldesley | 6.5 | 1 | 14 | 3 | 9 | — | 39 | 1 |

Umpires: T. Flowers and T. Fenwick.

# LANCASHIRE v GLAMORGAN

## Played at Blackpool, June 20, 21, 1923

Batting all Wednesday, Lancashire declared in the morning and, dismissing Glamorgan twice during the day, they won the match by an innings and 220 runs. It was regrettable that the visitors gave such a poor display, as otherwise the first county match at Blackpool since 1910 proved fairly successful. Ernest Tyldesley batted admirably for three hours after Makepeace had lost Green at 46, the two batsmen adding 128. Tyldesley and Barnes afterwards put on 123. Watson and Richard Tyldesley also batted well against very moderate bowling. Vastly different cricket was seen on the Thursday, Parkin having nearly all the batsmen at his mercy and taking fifteen wickets for 95 runs. He became more and more difficult as the pitch dried and, after one stand by Morgan and Bates, the batting broke down. Parkin got a lot of work on the ball.

## Lancashire

| | |
|---|---:|
| H. Makepeace c Whittington b Moss | 79 |
| Mr L. Green b Moss | 29 |
| E. Tyldesley c Moss b Clay | 125 |
| Mr J. R. Barnes b Ryan | 49 |
| F. Watson b Davies | 47 |
| W. Ellis c sub. b Ryan | 11 |
| R. Tyldesley c Tomlinson b Bates | 47 |
| G. Duckworth not out | 19 |
| C. Parkin run out | 4 |
| W. E. Hickmott not out | 5 |
| B 16, l-b 7, n-b 3 | 26 |
| **(8 wkts dec.)** | **441** |

L. Cook did not bat.

## Glamorgan

| | | | |
|---|---:|---|---:|
| Mr T. R. Morgan c Hickmott b Parkin | 33 | – c Cook b Parkin | 3 |
| D. Davies b Parkin | 0 | – b R. Tyldesley | 10 |
| W. Bates c E. Tyldesley b Parkin | 56 | – c Duckworth b Parkin | 21 |
| Mr W. N. Gemmill b Parkin | 1 | – b Parkin | 0 |
| H. Tomlinson run out | 1 | – b Parkin | 0 |
| Mr F. W. Matthias b Parkin | 1 | – c E. Tyldesley b R. Tyldesley | 0 |
| Mr T. A. L. Whittington c Duckworth b Cook | 37 | – b Parkin | 12 |
| Mr J. C. Clay st Duckworth b Parkin | 6 | – b Parkin | 4 |
| S. Hacker b Parkin | 1 | – not out | 1 |
| E. Moss c Barnes b Cook | 5 | – c and b Parkin | 10 |
| F. Ryan not out | 6 | – b Parkin | 2 |
| B 4, l-b 2, n-b 1 | 7 | B 2, l-b 2 | 4 |
| | **154** | | **67** |

## Glamorgan Bowling

| | Overs | Mdns | Runs | Wkts |
|---|---:|---:|---:|---:|
| Clay | 17 | 3 | 78 | 1 |
| Hacker | 12 | — | 34 | — |
| Ryan | 36 | 8 | 130 | 2 |
| Moss | 25 | 4 | 70 | 2 |
| Tomlinson | 7 | 1 | 24 | — |
| Bates | 6 | — | 36 | 1 |
| Davies | 12 | 1 | 43 | 1 |

**Lancashire Bowling**

| | Overs | Mdns | Runs | Wkts | Overs | Mdns | Runs | Wkts |
|---|---|---|---|---|---|---|---|---|
| Parkin .......... | 24 | 5 | 54 | 7 | 18 | 7 | 41 | 8 |
| Cook ............ | 19.4 | 3 | 50 | 2 | 11 | 4 | 14 | — |
| Hickmott ........ | 7 | — | 21 | — | | | | |
| R. Tyldesley ....... | 10 | 3 | 22 | — | 6 | 3 | 8 | 2 |

Umpires: J. H. Board and J. Moss.

# LANCASHIRE v LEICESTERSHIRE

### Played at Manchester, July 2, 3, 4, 1924

Completely outplaying Leicestershire and winning by an innings and 194 runs, Lancashire were fortunate in having the best of the wicket and also in the extension of time beyond the usual luncheon hour, when only one man had to be dismissed, as a thunderstorm with heavy rain broke over the ground soon after the match ended. On a dead pitch Lancashire batted consistently well, Hallows and Ernest Tyldesley doing best in a partnership of 110 runs. When the innings had been closed on the second day, Richard Tyldesley accomplished a bowling performance similar to those of Pougher for MCC at Lord's in 1896 against the Australians and Cox for Sussex against Somerset at Weston-super-Mare in 1921. After lunch he bowled five maiden overs and dismissed five batsmen, bringing his wickets during the season up to a hundred. The weather interfered with the game, but in the follow-on Leicestershire lost Berry for 19 runs. Parkin had most to do with finishing off the match on Friday. Richard Tyldesley gave useful help and in the whole match he had the wonderful analysis of eight wickets for 16 runs, besides scoring 65 not out.

### Lancashire

| | | | |
|---|---|---|---|
| C. Hallows c Sidwell b Geary | 51 | J. Iddon b Skelding | 13 |
| J. L. Hopwood run out | 7 | R. Tyldesley not out | 65 |
| E. Tyldesley c Sidwell b Skelding | 70 | G. Duckworth not out | 29 |
| F. Watson lbw b Geary | 45 | B 17, l-b 4, w 1, n-b 1 | 23 |
| H. Makepeace b Skelding | 41 | | |
| Mr J. Sharp b Geary | 35 | (7 wkts dec.) | 379 |

C. Parkin and E. A. McDonald did not bat.

### Leicestershire

| | | | |
|---|---|---|---|
| L. G. Berry lbw b Parkin | 0 | – c Duckworth b Parkin | 7 |
| S. S. Coulson c Hopwood b McDonald | 22 | – b Parkin | 18 |
| G. Geary lbw b R. Tyldesley | 39 | – c Watson b Parkin | 1 |
| J. H. King b McDonald | 0 | – c Iddon b Parkin | 13 |
| T. E. Sidwell lbw b R. Tyldesley | 22 | – b R. Tyldesley | 25 |
| Major G. H. S. Fowke b R. Tyldesley | 0 | – b Parkin | 0 |
| A. Shipman lbw b McDonald | 0 | – b Parkin | 1 |
| W. Berridge b R. Tyldesley | 0 | – b Parkin | 0 |
| W. E. Benskin c Watson b McDonald | 4 | – st Duckworth b R. Tyldesley | 19 |
| F. Bale b R. Tyldesley | 0 | – c Hallows b R. Tyldesley | 6 |
| A. Skelding not out | 0 | – not out | 6 |
| B 1, l-b 1 | 2 | | |
| | 89 | | 96 |

## Leicestershire Bowling

| | Overs | Mdns | Runs | Wkts |
|---|---|---|---|---|
| Skelding .......... | 29 | 4 | 80 | 3 |
| Geary ............ | 35 | 7 | 104 | 3 |
| Bale ............. | 33 | 6 | 83 | — |
| Shipman .......... | 11 | 1 | 35 | — |
| Benskin .......... | 14 | 3 | 54 | — |

## Lancashire Bowling

| | Overs | Mdns | Runs | Wkts | Overs | Mdns | Runs | Wkts |
|---|---|---|---|---|---|---|---|---|
| Parkin .......... | 14 | 2 | 38 | 1 | 20 | 9 | 51 | 7 |
| McDonald ........ | 18 | 4 | 45 | 4 | 9 | 2 | 29 | — |
| Watson .......... | 1 | — | 4 | — | | | | |
| R. Tyldesley ....... | 5 | 5 | — | 5 | 10.4 | 3 | 16 | 3 |

Umpires: W. Reeves and A. R. Warren.

# LANCASHIRE v NORTHAMPTONSHIRE

Played at Liverpool, August 6, 7, 8, 1924

On a soaked pitch, kept favourable to bowlers by rain that prevented play after lunch on the first day, Lancashire had an easy task, and won the match by an innings and one run. R. Tyldesley bowled irresistibly when put on with the total at 57 for one wicket, five men falling to him for 6 runs in six overs and a ball. Losing seven wickets for 71 before the weather broke once more, Northamptonshire made nothing of a fight on the Thursday. Ernest Tyldesley and Watson put on 79 in an hour to place Lancashire in a very strong position, and the fall of the last six wickets for 43 preceded a second collapse of the visitors. McDonald took, at a cost of 11 runs, four of the five wickets that went down for 47 on Thursday and his full analysis for the second innings was seven for five runs apiece – figures that were eclipsed in the whole match by R. Tyldesley with ten for 37.

## Northamptonshire

| | | | |
|---|---|---|---|
| Mr A. P. R. Hawtin c Duckworth b McDonald ..... | 1 | – c Parkin b McDonald .......... | 0 |
| C. N. Woolley st Duckworth b R. Tyldesley ....... | 33 | – b McDonald ................. | 28 |
| Mr V. W. C. Jupp c Watson b R. Tyldesley ........ | 26 | – b McDonald ................. | 0 |
| R. Haywood st Duckworth b R. Tyldesley ........ | 6 | – b McDonald ................. | 1 |
| B. Bellamy c and b R. Tyldesley ............... | 0 | – b McDonald ................. | 2 |
| F. Walden c Ritchie b R. Tyldesley .............. | 0 | – b McDonald ................. | 0 |
| W. Wells c Ritchie b R. Tyldesley .............. | 14 | – c Duckworth b R. Tyldesley ...... | 29 |
| Mr R. L. Wright b Parkin .................... | 5 | – b R. Tyldesley ............... | 27 |
| A. E. Thomas b R. Tyldesley .................. | 5 | – b McDonald ................. | 0 |
| E. Tyler c Duckworth b Parkin ................ | 0 | – not out .................... | 5 |
| V. Murdin not out ........................ | 1 | – b R. Tyldesley ............... | 0 |
| B 3, l-b 1, w 1, n-b 1 ................. | 6 | B 7, l-b 8, n-b 1 .......... | 16 |
| | **97** | | **108** |

## Lancashire

| | | | |
|---|---|---|---|
| H. Makepeace b Thomas ............... | 1 | R. Tyldesley b Thomas ................ | 23 |
| C. Hallows c Bellamy b Wells .......... | 21 | G. Duckworth b Thomas .............. | 0 |
| E. Tyldesley b Murdin ................ | 42 | C. Parkin not out .................... | 13 |
| F. Watson lbw b Walden ............... | 60 | E. A. McDonald b Thomas ............. | 2 |
| Mr A. W. Pewtress c Haywood b Wells .... | 32 | B 6, l-b 2.................... | 8 |
| Mr D. M. Ritchie b Wells .............. | 3 | | —— |
| Mr J. Sharp c Tyler b Thomas .......... | 1 | | 206 |

**Lancashire Bowling**

| | Overs | Mdns | Runs | Wkts | Overs | Mdns | Runs | Wkts |
|---|---|---|---|---|---|---|---|---|
| Parkin .......... | 20 | 3 | 51 | 2 | 9 | 2 | 26 | — |
| McDonald ........ | 9 | — | 32 | 1 | 20 | 9 | 35 | 7 |
| R. Tyldesley ....... | 14 | 12 | 6 | 7 | 11.1 | 3 | 31 | 3 |
| Watson .......... | 4 | 2 | 2 | — | | | | |

**Northamptonshire Bowling**

| | Overs | Mdns | Runs | Wkts |
|---|---|---|---|---|
| Wells ............ | 18 | 3 | 52 | 3 |
| Thomas .......... | 19.4 | 10 | 24 | 5 |
| Tyler ............ | 10 | 2 | 49 | — |
| Woolley .......... | 12 | 3 | 34 | — |
| Murdin ........... | 8 | 2 | 25 | 1 |
| Walden .......... | 4 | — | 14 | 1 |

Umpires: F. Parris and B. Tremlin.

## LANCASHIRE IN 1926

*President –* Sir Edwin F. Stockton, JP

*Hon. Treasurer –* Mr T. A. Higson

*Secretary –* Mr H. Rylance, 26, Barton Arcade, Manchester

*Captain –* Major L. Green

For the first time since 1904 Lancashire are champion county. Their success was popular throughout the country, partly because cricketers felt that the best interests of the game would be served by a change, at long last, in the leadership. Lancashire's supremacy over Yorkshire could be challenged easily enough: Yorkshire were undefeated and amongst the teams they severely thrashed was Lancashire. Moreover, Lancashire had to bow the knee to so modest a county as Leicestershire. Invincibility ought to be one of the attributes of the conqueror; Yorkshire throughout the summer was certainly a harder side to beat than Lancashire. On the other hand, it must be admitted that towards the summer's end, Yorkshire lost much of match-winning ability, even at the same time that Lancashire went forward, match after match, in destroying vein. During August any team placed in a bad corner would have found it easier to force a draw against Yorkshire than against Lancashire.

Lancashire invariably begin a season in ambitious spirit – with eyes on the championship. But last summer there were periods during which it was a positive virtue to practice optimism at Old Trafford. Yorkshire won at Bradford in an innings, and Lancashire's batting in the game was deplorable. Then followed the débâcle at Ashby-de-la-Zouch. Leicestershire won by 144; and there were not wanting pessimists in the Lancashire Eleven itself, who prophesied that at the end of the season Lancashire would be amongst the lower half of the championship table. The match at Ashby-de-la-Zouch has been called a blessing in disguise. The team thenceforward was new in temper and ability alike. Ernest Tyldesley ran into one of the richest veins ever struck by batsman in this country. Of their last eleven matches Lancashire won nine outright; the other two were won on the first innings and one of these was against Yorkshire. At Old Trafford, on August Bank Holiday, the biggest crowd that has ever witnessed a single day's cricket in this country saw Lancashire make 500 against Yorkshire. In that handsome total, compiled in such a match, is perhaps Lancashire's strongest justification of their present lofty position. A thunderstorm at night, followed by an impossible wicket and some clever bowling by Iddon, saved Lancashire from defeat at Bournemouth. Had that game been lost, the championship could scarcely have come again to Old Trafford.

Lancashire's success was the more remarkable because it might be argued that the side was not as strong in bowling as in 1925. Parkin ceased to play for Lancashire after the fourteenth match, and, of course, Parkin had always been a 100 wickets bowler. Sibbles did not fulfil his promise of twelve-months previously; and Richard Tyldesley, though consistently steady, was rarely making the ball come from the pitch with his old keenness. Iddon and Woolley were merely useful change-bowlers. Watson could not bowl during August, owing to a strain. The side therefore must be described as short, on the whole, of the bowling strength we commonly get from a champion county. It was Macdonald, more than any other one player in the eleven who won the matches at the season's end, and so took advantage of those chances which came Lancashire's way – partly as a result of the ultra-cautiousness which hindered Yorkshire. McDonald was rarely as fast as he was in 1921. None the less, he was far faster than the average English fast bowler. His temperament seemed to thrive on any situation which gave his side a sporting chance; he won more than one game against time in a manner that did credit both to his imagination and opportunism. He is a bowler of varying moods – and varying paces. But, at a pinch, he can achieve true greatness, both of technique and temperament.

The batting was more reliable all-round than in recent Lancashire sides. The young players, Iddon, Sibbles and Woolley imparted some substance to the innings at its latter end, and even Macdonald made a century against Middlesex. But it was from Makepeace, Hallows and Ernest Tyldesley that authentic batsmanship came. Watson was again useful, but he is not exactly a stylist. Ernest Tyldesley had a wonderful summer. At one stage his consistency recalled the C. B. Fry of 1901. In nine innings from June 26, Tyldesley scored 1,128 runs with an average of 141. He scored seven centuries in consecutive matches – and four in successive innings. He was, at his best, as stylish as he was prolific. A big innings by Tyldesley will exhibit every stroke excepting the cut, all done with infinite grace and mastery. He had bad luck to play in only one of the Test matches. Makepeace was his true dependable self; on a bad pitch he still has few superiors in cricket to-day as a defensive batsman. Against Nottinghamshire in the last crucial match of Lancashire's season, he transformed himself with the adaptability of genius into the quick scorer demanded by the situation. Hallows fell away a little in aggregate, and dependability. He often got out when apparently set, by sheer thoughtlessness. With more concentration, ball by ball, he would be one of our best left-handed batsmen. Major Green led his men with much tactical instinct, and better still, with understanding of character. He played many useful innings and is a cleverer batsman than he himself would seem to think.

Duckworth had many brilliant days behind the wicket, and, but for an inexplicable untidiness that sometimes comes over his work, he would be in the running for the position of Strudwick's successor. Sibbles ought to learn to spin the ball. Iddon advanced as a dashing maker of runs; he showed also much aptitude to exploit spin on a bowler's wicket. Other young cricketers likely to do well for Lancashire in the near future are Farrimond, a wicket-keeper with some utility as a bat; P. T. Eckersley, and Woolley – a useful right-handed batsman and bowler, though like Sibbles he depends over-much on the new ball. A young player, named M. L. Taylor, a left-hander, may easily develop into a beautiful batsman; already he has style.

The season at Old Trafford was admirably managed and proved very prosperous. The balance sheet showed a surplus of over £10,000. A successful benefit was given to Mr W. E. Howard, who for many years has done good work on the Old Trafford pavilion staff.

Neville Cardus

# LANCASHIRE v SURREY

## C. Hallows' Benefit Match

### Played at Manchester, June 2, 4, 5, 1928

Favoured on the first two days with pleasant weather, Lancashire's match with Surrey proved a big success as a benefit for Hallows, but to such an extent did the bat beat the ball, that 1,155 runs were registered and only thirteen wickets went down, the average per wicket thus coming out at more than 88. Going in against a total of 567, Lancashire accomplished an extraordinary performance in heading that score for the loss of four batsmen. Watson seized upon the occasion to put together an innings of 300 not out. This score, beating J. T. Tyldesley's 295 in 1902, was the highest ever played at Old Trafford. A further record was the partnership of Watson and Ernest Tyldesley who, adding 371 for the second wicket, shared in the biggest stand ever made for Lancashire. Batting for eight hours and a half, Watson gave only two chances – one at 119 and the other at 204 – in a memorable display, and he hit thirty-seven 4s. Surrey on Saturday lost Hobbs at 34, but Sandham and Ducat mastered the fast bowling so completely that they obtained 299 runs in three hours and a half. Ducat, when 46, gave a chance behind the wicket, but otherwise his batting was nearly as masterly as that of Sandham. Surrey left off on the first evening with 483 on the board and five men out, Sandham's score being 277. Scarcely had the game been resumed when Sandham was attacked with severe pain, and had to abandon his splendid innings which, quite free from blemish, lasted nearly six hours, and included thirty-six 4s.

## Surrey

| | | | |
|---|---|---|---|
| J. B. Hobbs c Duckworth b McDonald | 22 | R. J. Gregory c E. Tyldesley b McDonald | 15 |
| A. Sandham retired ill | 282 | H. A. Peach b McDonald | 6 |
| A. Ducat c Watson b R. Tyldesley | 119 | A. Geary b Iddon | 25 |
| T. Shepherd b Watson | 11 | E. W. Brooks not out | 19 |
| Mr D. R. Jardine c Duckworth b Watson | 4 | B 6, l-b 10, w 1 | 17 |
| T. H. Barling c Duckworth b McDonald | 22 | | |
| Mr P. G. H. Fender b Hodgson | 25 | | 567 |

## Lancashire

| | | | |
|---|---|---|---|
| F. Watson not out | 300 | J. Iddon not out | 39 |
| C. Hallows c Shepherd b Gregory | 36 | | |
| E. Tyldesley c Geary b Fender | 187 | B 4, l-b 3, w 1, n-b 2 | 10 |
| H. Makepeace run out | 9 | | |
| M. L. Taylor lbw b Fender | 7 | | 588 |

Mr L. Green, E. A. McDonald, R. Tyldesley, G. Duckworth and G. Hodgson did not bat.

## Lancashire Bowling

| | Overs | Mdns | Runs | Wkts |
|---|---|---|---|---|
| McDonald | 32 | 3 | 140 | 4 |
| Hodgson | 29 | 2 | 142 | 1 |
| Watson | 35 | 4 | 88 | 2 |
| R. Tyldesley | 33 | 5 | 89 | 1 |
| Iddon | 29.3 | 3 | 74 | 1 |
| Green | 3 | — | 17 | — |

**Surrey Bowling**

|  | Overs | Mdns | Runs | Wkts |
|---|---|---|---|---|
| Geary . . . . . . . . . . . | 25 | 8 | 43 | — |
| Peach . . . . . . . . . . . | 42 | 17 | 86 | — |
| Fender . . . . . . . . . . | 45 | 3 | 161 | 2 |
| Shepherd . . . . . . . . | 45 | 15 | 128 | — |
| Gregory . . . . . . . . . | 44 | 15 | 98 | 1 |
| Jardine . . . . . . . . . . | 17 | 3 | 52 | — |
| Ducat . . . . . . . . . . . | 3.1 | 1 | 10 | — |

Umpires: R. D. Burrows and T. Oates.

## LANCASHIRE v KENT

### Played at Manchester, August 15, 16, 17, 1928

This was one of the most dramatic, as well as important, matches of the season, Kent making 262 for their first four wickets, and yet meeting with defeat by an innings and 88 runs. Kent, in doing so well up to a point, owed nearly everything to Woolley who, assisted in a partnership of 128 by Ames, hit up in just over three hours 151 out of 248 with only one chance. After Woolley left, McDonald and Sibbles obtained the last six wickets for 15 runs. Hallows and Watson replied with 98 for no wicket in seventy minutes, and on Thursday, when rain caused several interruptions, the home side raised their score to 391 for two wickets. The first partnership produced 155 runs, and then Hallows and Ernest Tyldesley put on 207. Hallows obtained a complete mastery over the Kent attack and Tyldesley played practically faultless cricket. Lancashire declaring after an hour's cricket on Friday, Kent lost five wickets in making 95 and the other five for 18 more runs. Admirable as was much of the Lancashire batting, the chief factor in a splendid victory was the bowling of McDonald who took fifteen wickets for just over 10 runs apiece.

### Kent

| | | | |
|---|---|---|---|
| H. T. W. Hardinge c Duckworth b McDonald . . . . . | 8 | – c Duckworth b McDonald . . . . . . . . | 17 |
| W. Ashdown c Duckworth b McDonald . . . . . . . . . . | 17 | – c Barnes b McDonald . . . . . . . . . . | 17 |
| F. E. Woolley c Iddon b McDonald . . . . . . . . . . . . .151 | | – c Sibbles b McDonald . . . . . . . . . . | 31 |
| L. Ames b McDonald . . . . . . . . . . . . . . . . . . . . | 48 | – c Duckworth b Sibbles . . . . . . . . . . | 14 |
| Mr J. L. Bryan lbw b Sibbles . . . . . . . . . . . . . . . . . | 28 | – not out . . . . . . . . . . . . . . . . . . . . | 16 |
| Mr C. H. Knott b McDonald . . . . . . . . . . . . . . . . . | 0 | – b McDonald . . . . . . . . . . . . . . . . | 3 |
| Mr G. B. Legge b Sibbles . . . . . . . . . . . . . . . . . . . | 8 | – b McDonald . . . . . . . . . . . . . . . . | 4 |
| A. P. Freeman b McDonald . . . . . . . . . . . . . . . . . . . | 4 | – b McDonald . . . . . . . . . . . . . . . . | 0 |
| Mr B. Howlett c Watson b Sibbles . . . . . . . . . . . . . . | 0 | – b Iddon . . . . . . . . . . . . . . . . . . | 0 |
| C. Wright c Barnes b McDonald . . . . . . . . . . . . . . . | 1 | – c Iddon b McDonald . . . . . . . . . . . | 1 |
| Mr C. S. Marriott not out . . . . . . . . . . . . . . . . . . . | 0 | – c Iddon b McDonald . . . . . . . . . . . | 0 |
| B 5, l-b 7 . . . . . . . . . . . . . . . . . . . . . . . . . | 12 | B 7, l-b 3 . . . . . . . . . . . . . . | 10 |
| | **277** | | **113** |

### Lancashire

| | | | |
|---|---|---|---|
| F. Watson c Legge b Wright . . . . . . . . . . . | 56 | C. Hopwood not out . . . . . . . . . . . . . . . . . . | 13 |
| C. Hallows lbw b Freeman . . . . . . . . . . . . . .184 | | Mr J. R. Barnes not out . . . . . . . . . . . . . . . . | 12 |
| E. Tyldesley st Ames b Freeman . . . . . . . . .159 | | B 2, l-b 5, n-b 1 . . . . . . . . . . . . | 8 |
| H. Makepeace run out . . . . . . . . . . . . . . . . . | 46 | | |
| J. Iddon st Ames b Freeman . . . . . . . . . . . . | 0 | (5 wkts dec.) 478 | |

F. M. Sibbles, G. Duckworth, R. Tyldesley and E. A. McDonald did not bat.

## Lancashire Bowling

| | Overs | Mdns | Runs | Wkts | Overs | Mdns | Runs | Wkts |
|---|---|---|---|---|---|---|---|---|
| McDonald ........ | 25.1 | 4 | 101 | 7 | 22.2 | 6 | 53 | 8 |
| Sibbles ........... | 25 | 1 | 59 | 3 | 16 | 3 | 33 | 1 |
| Hopwood ......... | 9 | 1 | 34 | — | | | | |
| Iddon ............ | 8 | 1 | 34 | — | 6 | 1 | 17 | 1 |
| Watson .......... | 9 | — | 10 | — | | | | |
| R. Tyldesley ....... | 8 | 1 | 27 | — | | | | |

## Kent Bowling

| | Overs | Mdns | Runs | Wkts |
|---|---|---|---|---|
| Wright ........... | 36 | 7 | 118 | 1 |
| Ashdown ......... | 21 | 1 | 89 | — |
| Freeman·......... | 42 | 6 | 137 | 3 |
| Howlett .......... | 14 | — | 52 | — |
| Marriott .......... | 21 | 4 | 74 | — |

Umpires: H. Young and F. Chester.

# LANCASHIRE v ESSEX

### Played at Liverpool, July 18, 19, 20, 1928

Essex, despite a great batting performance on the part of Russell, who for the third time in his career put together two separate 100s in the same match, suffered defeat by ten wickets. In each innings Russell gave a chance when in the 60s, but his cricket, marked by particularly strong play on the leg-side, and much fine driving, reached a very high standard. Watson and Hallows, although the pitch was fast and the Essex attack, in the absence of Nichols and L. C. Eastman, not particularly formidable, took two hours to make 85. Altogether the first wicket produced 142. Hallows batted three hours and a half. Iddon and Hopwood – the latter missed when 69 – added 161, both playing with much skill. O'Connor rendered Russell useful support, especially in a second innings partnership of 145.

## Lancashire

| | | |
|---|---|---|
| F. Watson c Russell b Thompson ............... | 86 | – not out ...................... 36 |
| C. Hallows lbw b Martin ...................... | 74 | – not out ...................... 20 |
| J. Iddon c and b O'Connor ..................... | 112 | |
| H. Makepeace b Douglas ...................... | 19 | |
| C. Hopwood c and b Hipkin ................... | 140 | |
| E. A. McDonald c Treglown b Lockes ............ | 6 | |
| T. M. Halliday not out ....................... | 10 | |
| Mr L. Green not out ......................... | 4 | |
| B 2, l-b 2, w 1 ...................... | 5 | |

(6 wkts dec.) 456            56

F. M. Sibbles, W. Farrimond and G. Hodgson did not bat.

## Essex

| | | | |
|---|---|---|---|
| J. A. Cutmore lbw b McDonald | 15 | – b Hodgson | 1 |
| A. B. Hipkin b Hodgson | 8 | – b McDonald | 4 |
| J. O'Connor b Iddon | 37 | – c Hallows b McDonald | 41 |
| A. C. Russell c Hopwood b Sibbles | 131 | – c Hopwood b Hodgson | 104 |
| Mr E. G. Martin c Hodgson b Iddon | 0 | – b McDonald | 13 |
| Mr J. W. H. T. Douglas c Sibbles b McDonald | 3 | – c Farrimond b Green | 38 |
| Capt. C. J. Treglown b McDonald | 0 | – b Hodgson | 2 |
| G. W. Hockey c Farrimond b Hodgson | 4 | – c Makepeace b McDonald | 11 |
| E. C. Thompson c Farrimond b McDonald | 16 | – c Farrimond b McDonald | 34 |
| G. Eastman not out | 4 | – st Farrimond b Iddon | 7 |
| Mr G. K. Lockes b McDonald | 0 | – not out | 2 |
| B 2, l-b 10, n-b 3 | 15 | B 7, l-b 8, n-b 5 | 20 |
| | **233** | | **277** |

### Essex Bowling

| | Overs | Mdns | Runs | Wkts | Overs | Mdns | Runs | Wkts |
|---|---|---|---|---|---|---|---|---|
| Lockes | 32 | 6 | 123 | 1 | 10 | 2 | 18 | — |
| Douglas | 32 | 3 | 79 | 1 | | | | |
| Hipkin | 33 | 6 | 81 | 1 | 7.5 | 2 | 25 | — |
| Martin | 22 | 1 | 63 | 1 | 6 | 1 | 13 | — |
| Thompson | 14 | 1 | 50 | 1 | | | | |
| O'Connor | 25 | 4 | 55 | 1 | | | | |

### Lancashire Bowling

| | Overs | Mdns | Runs | Wkts | Overs | Mdns | Runs | Wkts |
|---|---|---|---|---|---|---|---|---|
| McDonald | 21.3 | 5 | 55 | 5 | 35.1 | 3 | 72 | 5 |
| Hodgson | 16 | 2 | 49 | 2 | 15 | 4 | 65 | 3 |
| Sibbles | 15 | 7 | 40 | 1 | 13 | 2 | 30 | — |
| Iddon | 15 | 2 | 41 | 2 | 18 | 1 | 52 | 1 |
| Watson | 3 | — | 20 | — | | | | |
| Hopwood | 3 | — | 13 | — | 11 | 2 | 27 | — |
| Green | | | | | 4 | — | 11 | 1 |

Umpires: W. R. Parry and A. Nash.

## LANCASHIRE v KENT

Played at Manchester, June 28, 30, July 1, 1930

Lancashire outplayed Kent so completely that after thirty-five minutes' cricket on Tuesday the southern county – occupying at the time first place in the championship – had to admit defeat by an innings and 49 runs. There were three big factors in Lancashire's handsome victory – the bowling of McDonald, the batting of Watson and Ernest Tyldesley, and the wicket-keeping of Farrimond. McDonald, temporarily recovered from the trouble which had overtaken him in the Surrey match, was in great form and took eleven wickets for 160 runs. Watson and Tyldesley put on 206 runs in little more than three hours and Farrimond helped in the second innings of Kent to dispose of seven batsmen, so equalling the performance of E. J. Smith of Warwickshire in 1926. Kent batted brightly on Saturday, Todd hitting up 50 in an hour but at the drawing of stumps Lancashire stood only 23 behind with nine wickets in hand. Watson and Ernest Tyldesley took the home score from 7 to 213. Tyldesley played in quite his best form, giving no chance and driving with fine power. Watson, too, made no mistake and showed pleasing variety of stroke. There were seven men out for less than 300 but Farrimond hit hard and received useful support. Rain twice interrupted play when Kent entered upon their second innings. Four wickets fell for 112 and next morning the other six went down for 35 runs.

## Kent

| | | | |
|---|---|---|---|
| H. T. W. Hardinge c Hallows b McDonald | 16 | – c Hopwood b R. Tyldesley | 47 |
| W. Ashdown b McDonald | 16 | – c Farrimond b McDonald | 6 |
| L. Todd b Hodgson | 50 | – c Farrimond b McDonald | 33 |
| L. Ames b Hodgson | 31 | – c Farrimond b McDonald | 5 |
| Mr J. A. Deed c R. Tyldesley b McDonald | 22 | – c Farrimond b McDonald | 28 |
| Mr T. A. Crawford b R. Tyldesley | 1 | – c Farrimond b McDonald | 0 |
| Mr G. B. Legge b R. Tyldesley | 0 | – c Farrimond b McDonald | 0 |
| C. Fairservice lbw b R. Tyldesley | 10 | – st Farrimond b R. Tyldesley | 0 |
| A. P. Freeman c Hodgson b McDonald | 2 | – c Sibbles b R. Tyldesley | 7 |
| C. Wright not out | 34 | – c Sibbles b R. Tyldesley | 19 |
| C. W. Peach b McDonald | 11 | – not out | 1 |
| L-b 1 | 1 | L-b 1 | 1 |
| | **194** | | **147** |

## Lancashire

| | | | | |
|---|---|---|---|---|
| F. Watson c Hardinge b Freeman | 134 | W. Farrimond not out | 46 |
| C. Hallows lbw b Ashdown | 2 | R.Tyldesley b Freeman | 22 |
| E. Tyldesley c Wright b Ashdown | 117 | E. A. McDonald b Freeman | 28 |
| J. Iddon c Ames b Hardinge | 10 | G. Hodgson b Wright | 7 |
| C. Hopwood st Ames b Freeman | 4 | B 5, 1-b 3 | 8 |
| Mr P. T. Eckersley b Hardinge | 5 | | |
| F. M. Sibbles b Wright | 7 | | **390** |

## Lancashire Bowling

| | Overs | Mdns | Runs | Wkts | Overs | Mdns | Runs | Wkts |
|---|---|---|---|---|---|---|---|---|
| McDonald | 21.1 | — | 77 | 5 | 20 | 1 | 83 | 6 |
| Sibbles | 5 | — | 21 | — | 2 | — | 9 | — |
| R. Tyldesley | 19 | 6 | 61 | 3 | 9.4 | 1 | 25 | 4 |
| Hodgson | 7 | — | 21 | 2 | 10 | 1 | 29 | — |
| Hopwood | 4 | 1 | 13 | — | | | | |

## Kent Bowling

| | Overs | Mdns | Runs | Wkts |
|---|---|---|---|---|
| Wright | 20.3 | 2 | 60 | 2 |
| Ashdown | 20 | 5 | 48 | 2 |
| Freeman | 55 | 9 | 129 | 4 |
| Hardinge | 22 | 4 | 70 | 2 |
| Peach | 18 | 1 | 51 | — |
| Fairservice | 5 | 1 | 24 | — |

Umpires: D. Denton and G. Beet.

## LANCASHIRE v KENT

Played at Manchester, May 27, 28, 29, 1931

Freeman rendered this match memorable by his achievement in taking for the third time in his career all ten wickets in an innings. In the previous summer, accomplishing the feat for the second time, he had equalled the record of V. E. Walker and in doing it on a third occasion, he could boast a performance which stood to the credit of no other player in the long history of the game of cricket. In the early stages of the contest he obtained four wickets but before any further success attended his efforts there came a stand of 80 runs. This partnership, however, he eventually broke up and then proceeded to take the other five wickets. Ably as he bowled he ought not to have had all ten wickets as McDonald gave a chance off Hardinge. Ernest Tyldesley and Paynter were the batsmen who made the one stand, coming together at 66 and raising the score to 146. Kent, following upon Freeman's triumph, batted so successfully that they left off on Wednesday evening only 41 behind with eight wickets in hand. Rain so affected the pitch that nothing could be done on Thursday. On Friday, following upon half an hour's delay at the start, the weather turned wet at four o'clock and prevented any further cricket. Woolley and Ames put on 102 in ninety minutes, the former batting in delightful style if not quite so brilliantly as usual.

### Lancashire

| | | |
|---|---|---|
| C. Hallows b Freeman | 9 | |
| F. Watson c Woolley b Freeman | 19 – not out | 41 |
| E. Tyldesley lbw b Freeman | 70 – not out | 42 |
| J. Iddon st Ames b Freeman | 4 | |
| C. Hopwood b Freeman | 2 | |
| E. Paynter c and b Freeman | 39 | |
| Mr P. T. Eckersley b Freeman | 1 | |
| F. M. Sibbles c Crawley b Freeman | 8 | |
| G. Duckworth not out | 7 | |
| R. Tyldesley c Valentine b Freeman | 1 | |
| E. A. McDonald b Freeman | 20 | |
| B 1, l-b 1, w 1, n-b 1 | 4 | L-b 1 ... 1 |
| | **184** | **84** |

### Kent

| | | | | |
|---|---|---|---|---|
| H. T. W. Hardinge b Hopwood | 30 | L. Todd b Hopwood | 18 | |
| Mr A. M. Crawley b Hopwood | 50 | A. E. Watt b McDonald | 1 | |
| F. E. Woolley c R. Tyldesley b McDonald | .108 | W. Ashdown c Duckworth b Hopwood | 8 | |
| L. Ames c R. Tyldesley b Hopwood | 42 | Mr T. A. Pearce not out | 2 | |
| Mr A. P. F. Chapman c Duckworth | | B 5, l-b 8 | 13 | |
| b McDonald | 9 | | | |
| Mr B. H. Valentine b Hopwood | 4 | (9 wkts dec.) | 285 | |

A. P. Freeman did not bat.

### Kent Bowling

| | Overs | Mdns | Runs | Wkts | Overs | Mdns | Runs | Wkts |
|---|---|---|---|---|---|---|---|---|
| Watt | 11 | 3 | 19 | — | 2 | — | 4 | — |
| Ashdown | 18 | 7 | 37 | — | 4 | — | 12 | — |
| Freeman | 36.1 | 9 | 79 | 10 | 15 | 2 | 30 | — |
| Hardinge | 23 | 6 | 45 | — | 4 | 1 | 16 | — |
| Woolley | | | | | 5 | — | 16 | — |
| Todd | | | | | 3 | 1 | 5 | — |

### Lancashire Bowling

| | Overs | Mdns | Runs | Wkts |
|---|---|---|---|---|
| McDonald | 26 | 3 | 82 | 3 |
| Sibbles | 18 | 2 | 56 | — |
| R. Tyldesley | 23 | 3 | 79 | — |
| Hopwood | 21 | 4 | 55 | 6 |

Umpires: A. Morton and W. A. Buswell.

# LANCASHIRE v GLOUCESTERSHIRE

Played at Manchester, June 20, 22, 1931

A glorious triumph awaited Lancashire in the first of their encounters with Gloucestershire, the north-countrymen showing such complete mastery over their opponents that, declaring with only four men out, they won in the course of less than two days' cricket by an innings and 147 runs. Gloucestershire certainly laboured under a big handicap through the inability of Goddard to take the field; indeed had the services of that bowler been available, Hammond, on winning the toss, might quite possibly have taken the risk of sending Lancashire in to bat. For all that Lancashire fully deserved their overwhelming victory. On the tricky pitch no Gloucestershire player, except Dipper, who withstood the attack for nearly three hours and a half, going in first and being eighth out, met with any success against Hopwood and Richard Tyldesley and although at lunch time the visitors had 66 on the board with three men out, afterwards they cut so sorry a figure that ninety minutes' further cricket saw seven wickets go down for the addition of 35 runs. Tyldesley obtained seven wickets for less than six runs apiece. Lancashire, thanks to Hallows and Ernest Tyldesley, scored 100 for one wicket on Saturday evening and on Monday, when the game could not be resumed until after lunch, the home side batted with such refreshing freedom that they added 207 runs in two hours. Altogether Hallows and Ernest Tyldesley put on 183 in two hours and a half, both of them driving particularly well. Tyldesley, more vigorous than his partner, obtained his 127 runs in two hours and forty minutes and hit fifteen 4s. Gloucestershire at their second attempt collapsed completely, losing half their wickets for 14 runs and being all out in a hundred minutes. Sibbles disposed of four batsmen for 18 and Hopwood in four overs took the last four wickets, only a single run being hit off him meanwhile.

## Gloucestershire

| | | | |
|---|---:|---|---:|
| A. E. Dipper st Duckworth b R. Tyldesley | 59 | – b Hodgson | 6 |
| R. A. Sinfield c Duckworth b R. Tyldesley | 4 | – c Duckworth b Sibbles | 1 |
| W. R. Hammond c E. Tyldesley b R. Tyldesley | 14 | – b Sibbles | 0 |
| W. L. Neale c Duckworth b Hopwood | 4 | – lbw b Sibbles | 1 |
| C. C. Dacre lbw b R. Tyldesley | 1 | – b Hodgson | 4 |
| H. Smith c Paynter b R. Tyldesley | 7 | – c Iddon b Hopwood | 18 |
| C. J. Barnett st Duckworth b R. Tyldesley | 9 | – c E. Tyldesley b Sibbles | 17 |
| E. J. Stephens b Hopwood | 2 | – b Hopwood | 7 |
| F. A. Harris c Hodgson b R. Tyldesley | 1 | – c Paynter b Hopwood | 0 |
| R. G. Ford c Hodgson b Hopwood | 0 | – st Duckworth b Hopwood | 2 |
| C. Parker not out | 0 | – not out | 0 |
| | | B 1, l-b 2, n-b 2 | 5 |
| | **101** | | **61** |

## Lancashire

| | | | |
|---|---:|---|---:|
| C. Hallows c Barnett b Sinfield | 100 | M. L. Taylor not out | 22 |
| F. M. Sibbles c Smith b Parker | 18 | | |
| E. Tyldesley c Barnett b Parker | 127 | L-b 2 | 2 |
| J. Iddon c Hammond b Parker | 15 | | |
| E. Paynter not out | 25 | (4 wkts dec.) | 309 |

C. Hopwood, Mr P. T. Eckersley, G. Duckworth, R. Tyldesley and G. Hodgson did not bat.

## Lancashire Bowling

|              | Overs | Mdns | Runs | Wkts | Overs | Mdns | Runs | Wkts |
|--------------|-------|------|------|------|-------|------|------|------|
| Hodgson ........ | 5 | 2 | 6 | — | 11 | 3 | 24 | 2 |
| Sibbles .......... | 3 | — | 12 | — | 12 | 2 | 18 | 4 |
| Hopwood ........ | 36 | 13 | 36 | 3 | 4 | 3 | 1 | 4 |
| R. Tyldesley ...... | 40 | 21 | 39 | 7 | 5 | 1 | 13 | — |
| Iddon ........... | 5 | 1 | 8 | — | | | | |

## Gloucestershire Bowling

|              | Overs | Mdns | Runs | Wkts |
|--------------|-------|------|------|------|
| Sinfield .......... | 46 | 13 | 131 | 1 |
| Hammond ........ | 25 | 3 | 81 | — |
| Parker ......... | 33 | 12 | 68 | 3 |
| Harris .......... | 3 | — | 27 | — |

Umpires: D. Hendren and A. Morton.

# LANCASHIRE v DERBYSHIRE

### Played at Blackpool, August 26, 27, 1931

Lancashire concluded their season with a most exciting game against Derbyshire, being 107 behind on the first innings and yet winning by three wickets. Alderman on the opening day, going in after Derbyshire's first wicket had fallen at 48, played most skilful cricket for two hours and a half. Lancashire shaped so wretchedly against Slater and Worthington that half the side were out for 19 and the innings closed for 66. Next day, however, Derbyshire at their second attempt fared even worse yet Lancashire – so heavily in arrear on the first innings – were set 173 to make. Three wickets fell for 31 but Hallows rose to the occasion, putting on 53 with Ernest Tyldesley and 59 with Horrocks. With the total at 69 Elliott, believing that Hallows had been bowled – the bails had been dislodged – appealed for the wicket but Dolphin at the bowler's end was unsighted and Buswell could not say definitely what had happened, so Hallows was given the benefit of the doubt.

## Derbyshire

| | | | |
|---|---|---|---|
| Mr A. W. Richardson b R. Tyldesley ............ | 13 | – b Sibbles .................... | 1 |
| D. Smith st Duckworth b Hopwood ............ | 33 | – lbw b Sibbles ................. | 3 |
| A. E. Alderman not out ...................... | 62 | – c Duckworth b R. Tyldesley ...... | 6 |
| G. M. Lee c Duckworth b McDonald ........... | 23 | – b R. Tyldesley ................ | 25 |
| Mr C. C. Clarke c Duckworth b Iddon .......... | 0 | – lbw b R. Tyldesley ............. | 0 |
| L. Townsend b R. Tyldesley ................... | 5 | – c Hopwood b R. Tyldesley ....... | 7 |
| S. Worthington b R. Tyldesley ................ | 3 | – st Duckworth b R. Tyldesley ...... | 11 |
| A. G. Slater lbw b R. Tyldesley ................ | 16 | – c R. Tyldesley b Hopwood ....... | 5 |
| H. Elliott lbw b Sibbles ..................... | 16 | – b Hopwood ................. | 4 |
| T. B. Mitchell c and b Sibbles ................ | 0 | – b R. Tyldesley ............... | 1 |
| T. R. Armstrong run out .................... | 0 | – not out .................... | 0 |
| B 2 ...................... | 2 | B 1, l-b 1 .............. | 2 |
| | 173 | | 65 |

## Lancashire

| | | | |
|---|---|---|---|
| C. Hopwood b Worthington | 5 | – run out | 6 |
| E. Paynter lbw b Slater | 1 | – lbw b Slater | 7 |
| E. Tyldesley c Slater b Worthington | 0 | – c Worthington b Townsend | 29 |
| J. Iddon b Slater | 9 | – lbw b Slater | 6 |
| C. Hallows lbw b Slater | 3 | – lbw b Armstrong | 74 |
| W. Horrocks not out | 21 | – c Elliott b Armstrong | 30 |
| Mr P. T. Eckersley b Worthington | 0 | – lbw b Mitchell | 10 |
| F. M. Sibbles b Slater | 3 | – not out | 8 |
| G. Duckworth c Richardson b Worthington | 4 | – not out | 5 |
| R. Tyldesley b Slater | 1 | | |
| E. A. McDonald b Armstrong | 12 | | |
| B 4, l-b 3 | 7 | L-b 1 | 1 |
| | **66** | | **176** |

### Lancashire Bowling

| | Overs | Mdns | Runs | Wkts | Overs | Mdns | Runs | Wkts |
|---|---|---|---|---|---|---|---|---|
| McDonald | 24 | 2 | 62 | 1 | 7 | 2 | 9 | — |
| Sibbles | 13 | 3 | 18 | 2 | 10 | 4 | 16 | 2 |
| R. Tyldesley | 28 | 5 | 66 | 4 | 12.2 | 5 | 21 | 6 |
| Hopwood | 11 | 5 | 16 | 1 | 9 | 3 | 17 | 2 |
| Iddon | 4 | — | 9 | 1 | | | | |

### Derbyshire Bowling

| | Overs | Mdns | Runs | Wkts | Overs | Mdns | Runs | Wkts |
|---|---|---|---|---|---|---|---|---|
| Slater | 22 | 11 | 22 | 5 | 19 | 6 | 39 | 2 |
| Worthington | 22 | 4 | 30 | 4 | 12 | 1 | 38 | — |
| Mitchell | 2 | — | 3 | — | 22.3 | 6 | 51 | 1 |
| Armstrong | 1.5 | — | 4 | 1 | 12 | 4 | 9 | 2 |
| Townsend | | | | | 14 | 4 | 38 | 1 |

Umpires: W. A. Buswell and A. Dolphin.

## LANCASHIRE v YORKSHIRE

Played at Manchester, June 3, 5, 1933

Beaten on the Monday afternoon by an innings and 156 runs, Lancashire went through an unpleasant experience. Complaints that Hodgson tore up the turf opposite the leg stump caused his withdrawal from the attack and the pitch, otherwise the cause of a special investigation as to the state of the Old Trafford ground, became so favourable to bowlers that the Bank Holiday crowd of some 25,000 people saw twenty-four wickets fall for 239 runs. Considering the help that bowlers received from the start of the match when Sutcliffe, Holmes and Leyland were out for 61 runs, Yorkshire did well to raise their score to 287 for the further loss of Barber and Sellers on Saturday evening. For the addition of 120 and 78 in which these batsmen assisted, Mitchell claimed chief honours, and altogether he batted for more than six hours in a grim struggle for runs on a pitch described as dusty almost all through the game. Accurate slow bowling, notably by Iddon, whose left-hand deliveries often broke back quickly from the worn patch, compelled defence for long periods, but Mitchell never blundered. No one approached his skill when Lancashire batted. In the follow-on a ball from Bowes hit Watson on the head and a second collapse ensued. Macaulay enjoyed a great triumph taking twelve wickets for 49 runs. His leg breaks troubled everyone and Lancashire, whose previous smallest total was 336, were twice dismissed for 185. So deadly was Macaulay in finishing off the first innings that he took four wickets, including the hat trick, in five balls, the second half of the side, following two steady partnerships, actually falling for three runs. Verity completed Lancashire's discomfiture.

### Yorkshire

| | | | |
|---|---|---|---|
| P. Holmes c Booth b Iddon | 22 | A. Wood b Iddon | 6 |
| H. Sutcliffe b Booth | 7 | A. C. Rhodes b Iddon | 3 |
| A. Mitchell c Hodgson b Parkinson | 123 | G. G. Macaulay b Iddon | 5 |
| M. Leyland lbw b Parkinson | 3 | W. E. Bowes not out | 13 |
| W. Barber c Eckersley b Bennett | 62 | B 11, l-b 23, n-b 5 | 39 |
| Mr A. B. Sellers lbw b Bennett | 31 | | |
| H. Verity lbw b Parkinson | 27 | | 341 |

### Lancashire

| | | | |
|---|---|---|---|
| F. Watson c Leyland b Macaulay | 5 | – retired hurt | 11 |
| J. L. Hopwood b Macaulay | 13 | – c Macaulay b Verity | 12 |
| E. Tyldesley b Bowes | 15 | – lbw b Macaulay | 13 |
| J. Iddon b Macaulay | 1 | – b Verity | 0 |
| E. Paynter c Verity b Macaulay | 17 | – not out | 29 |
| L. W. Parkinson c Holmes b Verity | 24 | – b Macaulay | 4 |
| A. Bennett b Macaulay | 0 | – lbw b Macaulay | 2 |
| Mr P. T Eckersley c Macaulay b Verity | 0 | – b Verity | 0 |
| F. S. Booth b Macaulay | 1 | – c Sutcliffe b Verity | 0 |
| G. Duckworth lbw b Macaulay | 0 | – c Rhodes b Macaulay | 3 |
| G. Hodgson not out | 1 | – c Sellers b Macaulay | 18 |
| B 8, l-b 8 | 16 | | |
| | 93 | | 92 |

### Lancashire Bowling

| | Overs | Mdns | Runs | Wkts |
|---|---|---|---|---|
| Booth | 34 | 9 | 48 | 1 |
| Hodgson | 13 | 4 | 30 | — |
| Parkinson | 47 | 9 | 105 | 3 |
| Iddon | 43.3 | 19 | 60 | 4 |
| Hopwood | 11 | 5 | 16 | — |
| Bennett | 12 | — | 43 | 2 |

### Yorkshire Bowling

| | Overs | Mdns | Runs | Wkts | Overs | Mdns | Runs | Wkts |
|---|---|---|---|---|---|---|---|---|
| Bowes | 10 | 3 | 22 | 1 | 5 | — | 27 | — |
| Macaulay | 19.3 | 10 | 28 | 7 | 10.4 | 5 | 21 | 5 |
| Verity | 11 | 2 | 27 | 2 | 12 | 3 | 41 | 4 |
| Rhodes | | | | | 3 | 2 | 3 | — |

Umpires: W. A. Buswell and J. Humphries.

## LANCASHIRE IN 1934

Perhaps the best, certainly the most dramatic performance by Lancashire was the victory over Nottinghamshire at Trent Bridge by 101 runs after being 147 behind on the first innings. Before the game announcements, whether imaginary or exaggerated by irresponsible busybodies it is impossible to say, suggested that trouble would occur. So many unpleasant statements were made in a season notorious for scandals, mostly without foundation in fact, that nothing definite can be placed on record as to the attitude of the officials of the two clubs when entering upon the encounter. Lancashire might well have considered that they had ample satisfaction as they declared their second innings closed with seven men out for 394, dismissed Nottinghamshire for 146 and won as stated. But their great triumph failed to clear the air. It remained obvious that Lancashire and Nottinghamshire did not meet under the happiest auspices and they have not arranged fixtures for next season.

# LANCASHIRE v HAMPSHIRE

Played at Manchester, June 20, 21, 22, 1934

Play on the second day was limited to an hour and a half owing to rain and generally the conditions during a drawn game were adverse to good cricket. Lancashire, on hard turf that was softened on top by morning showers, gave a poor account of themselves, Watson alone causing much trouble and he took nearly three hours and a quarter to score 60 out of 143 before being eighth out. The best stand, by him and Parkinson, realised no more than 37. Hampshire began just as indifferently, losing six wickets for 93 on the first afternoon but Mead and McCorkell, in a partnership which was spread over all three days, put on 89 and secured the lead with still four wickets in hand. McCorkell played very good defensive cricket for two hours and twenty minutes and Mead, favoured by two escapes on the second afternoon, was altogether at the wickets three hours and a quarter. During most of the last day the wind was so troublesome that bails were dispensed with for long periods. Between the innings on the first day the motor roller broke down and had to be hauled away from the middle of the ground. Also a sight-screen was blown down and broken so that the match was notable for several unusual occurrences. In fielding Hampshire proved the superior side. Arnold in dismissing Paynter brought off a brilliant running catch at square leg.

## Lancashire

| | | | |
|---|--:|---|--:|
| F. Watson c McCorkell b Kennedy | 60 | – c Pothecary b Boyes | 4 |
| J. L. Hopwood b Kennedy | 13 | – run out | 13 |
| J. Iddon b Boyes | 5 | – c Moore b Boyes | 13 |
| E. Tyldesley c Paris b Boyes | 1 | – not out | 2 |
| E. Paynter c Arnold b Creese | 16 | – not out | 0 |
| Mr W. H. L. Lister c Pothecary b Boyes | 1 | | |
| L. W. Parkinson b Boyes | 27 | | |
| Mr P. T. Eckersley st McCorkell b Kennedy | 7 | | |
| F. M. Sibbles b Kennedy | 5 | | |
| G. Duckworth not out | 12 | | |
| F. S. Booth st McCorkell b Kennedy | 0 | | |
| B 9, l-b 1, n-b 1 | 11 | B 2, l-b 4 | 6 |
| | **158** | | **38** |

## Hampshire

| | | | |
|---|--:|---|--:|
| J. Arnold c Tyldesley b Booth | 15 | N. McCorkell c Duckworth b Booth | 50 |
| Mr R. H. Moore c Watson b Sibbles | 4 | G. S. Boyes c Eckersley b Sibbles | 20 |
| A. E. Pothecary c Booth b Sibbles | 22 | G. Hill not out | 12 |
| C. P. Mead st Duckworth b Sibbles | 63 | O. W. Herman c Hopwood b Booth | 14 |
| Mr C. G. A. Paris b Sibbles | 5 | B 1, l-b 7, n-b 1 | 9 |
| W. L. Creese c Duckworth b Sibbles | 5 | | |
| A. Kennedy c Watson b Hopwood | 6 | | **225** |

## Hampshire Bowling

| | Overs | Mdns | Runs | Wkts | Overs | Mdns | Runs | Wkts |
|---|--:|--:|--:|--:|--:|--:|--:|--:|
| Kennedy | 23.5 | 10 | 43 | 5 | 17 | 8 | 18 | — |
| Herman | 11 | 1 | 43 | — | | | | |
| Boyes | 29 | 16 | 28 | 4 | 16 | 10 | 14 | 2 |
| Hill | 4 | — | 14 | — | | | | |
| Creese | 4 | — | 19 | 1 | | | | |

## Lancashire Bowling

|  | Overs | Mdns | Runs | Wkts |
|---|---|---|---|---|
| Sibbles ........... | 49 | 16 | 90 | 6 |
| Booth ............. | 36.3 | 8 | 74 | 3 |
| Hopwood ......... | 20 | 10 | 27 | 1 |
| Iddon ............. | 3 | — | 16 | — |
| Parkinson ........ | 3 | — | 9 | — |

Umpires: G. Beet and A. E. Dipper.

# LANCASHIRE v SOMERSET

## Played at Manchester, August 24, 26, 27, 1935

Rain and the state of the pitch interfered with cricket on each day, and the match, limited to an innings apiece, ended when Somerset were out for 12 runs less than Lancashire made. When play was possible after lunch on Saturday, Ingle sent in his opponents but Washbrook and Iddon, by making 119 in ninety minutes for the second wicket, removed fear of a collapse until Hazell bowled his left-hand slows effectively. An attack of tonsillitis prevented Pollard from taking the field on Monday when the weather precluded cricket after lunch, but next morning half Somerset were out for 109. Then a great display of hitting by Wellard made the fight for the lead most exciting. So freely did Wellard pull and drive that he made 50 out of 67 in thirty-five minutes, but then he got less of the bowling and, as he avoided risks, his rate of scoring decreased so much that he took 85 minutes over his hundred and batted altogether an hour and a half for 112 out of 145 added before he was last out. One of his five 6s landed near the railway station and another hit a tower on the pavilion roof; there were also ten 4s in his remarkable exhibition of forcing cricket. Burrough played in good, free style for an hour.

## Lancashire

| | |
|---|---|
| J. L. Hopwood c Seamer b Wellard ....... 6 | R. Pollard st Luckes b Hazell ........... 9 |
| C. Washbrook c Andrews b Hazell ....... 75 | Mr P. T. Eckersley c Hazell b Andrews .... 4 |
| J. Iddon c and b Hazell ................ 64 | F. M. Sibbles c Ingle b Andrews ......... 0 |
| E. Paynter c and b Hazell ............. 22 | G. Duckworth c J. W. Lee b Wellard ...... 3 |
| N. Oldfield lbw b J. W. Lee ............. 31 | B 3, l-b 5, n-b 1 .............. 9 |
| W. E. Phillipson not out ................ 33 | |
| E. Greenhalgh c Ingle b Hazell .......... 10 | 266 |

## Somerset

| | |
|---|---|
| J. W. Lee c sub. b Hopwood ............. 30 | Mr R. A. Ingle lbw b Iddon ............. 12 |
| F. S. Lee lbw (N), b Phillipson ........... 22 | W. H. R. Andrews c Washbrook b Sibbles . 7 |
| Mr N. S. Mitchell-Innes lbw b Sibbles ..... 3 | W. T. Luckes c Paynter b Phillipson ...... 0 |
| Mr J. W. Seamer b Hopwood ........... 3 | H. L. Hazell not out ................... 1 |
| Mr J. H. Cameron b Iddon ............. 13 | B 3, l-b 8 ................... 11 |
| Mr H. D. Burrough b Phillipson ......... 40 | |
| A. W. Wellard lbw b Sibbles ............112 | 254 |

## Somerset Bowling

|  | Overs | Mdns | Runs | Wkts |
|---|---|---|---|---|
| Wellard .......... | 16 | 4 | 26 | 2 |
| Andrews ......... | 15 | 3 | 53 | 2 |
| J. W. Lee ......... | 24 | 6 | 58 | 1 |
| Hazell ........... | 33 | 9 | 94 | 5 |
| Cameron ......... | 4 | — | 26 | — |

**Lancashire Bowling**

| | Overs | Mdns | Runs | Wkts |
|---|---|---|---|---|
| Sibbles ........... | 26 | 5 | 68 | 3 |
| Phillipson ........ | 22 | 7 | 47 | 3 |
| Hopwood ......... | 20 | 2 | 86 | 2 |
| Greenhalgh ....... | 6 | 2 | 9 | — |
| Iddon ............ | 8 | 1 | 33 | 2 |

Umpires: F. E. Woolley and W. A. Buswell.

# LEICESTERSHIRE

## LEICESTERSHIRE v SURREY

### Played at Leicester, June 9, 10, 1920

An easy victory by an innings and 105 runs was gained by Surrey on the second afternoon. The match was remarkable for the fact that five men were unable to play on the Thursday. Salmon, Mounteney, and Benskin were injured by severe blows when batting on the previous day; Rushby strained his side when bowling, and Fender, called away on urgent business, did not return until the match was over. Hobbs captained Surrey during the home side's second innings. Hobbs played a wonderful innings of 134. Getting his runs in ninety-five minutes.without a mistake, he hit a 6 and nineteen 4s, his cutting, driving, and pulling being equally brilliant. Sandham helped in a first partnership of 177 runs, and Hitch and Harrison put on 58 in twenty-five minutes. Rushby took five wickets at the start of Leicestershire's innings, and when he had to retire, Reay proved almost as effective. Coe once more batted resolutely, but in the unfortunate circumstances Leicestershire made nothing of a fight against their powerful visitors.

### Surrey

| | |
|---|---|
| J. B. Hobbs c Shingler b Mounteney ......134 | W. Hitch b Astill ..................... 41 |
| A. Sandham c Sidwell b Benskin ......... 49 | Mr G. M. Reay lbw b Shipman .......... 0 |
| A. Ducat c Shingler b Mounteney ........ 11 | H. Strudwick c and b Shipman .......... 5 |
| T. Shepherd c Sidwell b Benskin ......... 8 | T. Rushby not out .................... 3 |
| H. A Peach c Whitehead b Benskin ....... 1 | B 1, l-b 5 .................... 6 |
| H. S. Harrison c and b Astill ............ 34 | |
| Mr P. G. H. Fender c Whitehead b Benskin . 17 | 309 |

### Leicestershire

| | | | |
|---|---|---|---|
| Mr C. J. B. Wood b Rushby.................. | 1 | – c Shepherd b Hitch ............. | 17 |
| H. Whitehead b Rushby....................... | 33 | – b Ducat ...................... | 19 |
| W. E. Astill c Strudwick b Rushby.............. | 0 | – b Reay ....................... | 1 |
| A. Mounteney c Harrison b Rushby ........... | 3 | – absent hurt.................... | 0 |
| S. Coe b Rushby ........................... | 21 | – b Shepherd.................... | 40 |
| Mr G. H. Salmon retired hurt.................. | 13 | – absent hurt ................... | 0 |
| G. Shingler b Fender ....................... | 13 | – b Reay ....................... | 4 |
| A. Shipman not out ........................ | 10 | – b Reay ....................... | 0 |
| F. Bale b Rushby .......................... | 2 | – b Reay ....................... | 0 |
| W. E. Benskin b Rushby .................... | 0 | – absent hurt................... | 0 |
| T. E. Sidwell c Ducat b Hitch.................. | 5 | – not out ...................... | 1 |
| B 13, l-b 3 ........................ | 16 | B 5 .................... | 5 |
| | **117** | | **87** |

### Leicestershire Bowling

| | Overs | Mdns | Runs | Wkts |
|---|---|---|---|---|
| Benskin .......... | 20 | 3 | 83 | 4 |
| Astill ............ | 13 | 1 | 56 | 2 |
| Shipman.......... | 10.5 | — | 60 | 2 |
| Bale ............. | 5 | — | 37 | — |
| Shingler .......... | 4 | — | 28 | — |
| Mounteney ........ | 11 | 3 | 39 | 2 |

**Surrey Bowling**

|  | Overs | Mdns | Runs | Wkts | Overs | Mdns | Runs | Wkts |
|---|---|---|---|---|---|---|---|---|
| Hitch ........... | 16.1 | 4 | 34 | 1 | 9 | 1 | 25 | 1 |
| Rushby ......... | 21 | 9 | 32 | 7 | 2 | 1 | 6 | — |
| Reay ........... | 5 | 1 | 13 | — | 9 | 2 | 32 | 4 |
| Fender .......... | 8 | 1 | 22 | 1 |  |  |  |  |
| Ducat ........... |  |  |  |  | 5 | — | 16 | 1 |
| Shepherd ........ |  |  |  |  | 2 | — | 3 | 1 |

Umpires: G. P. Harrison and J. Moss.

# LEICESTERSHIRE v SUSSEX

## Played at Leicester, May 21, 23, 24, 1921

In this match Leicestershire gained an astonishing victory by three wickets after being 141 runs behind on the first innings. Nothing more sensational was seen during the season, Jupp and Bowley, when Sussex won the toss, scoring 235 together for the first wicket and apparently putting defeat out of the question. The turning-point of the game came on the third morning, when Sussex went to pieces against some fine bowling. Leicestershire had seven wickets down for 172 in the last innings, but King and Pratt hit off the remaining 82 runs, King playing superbly. Sharp on the second day played the innings of his life.

## Sussex

| | | | |
|---|---|---|---|
| Mr V. W. C. Jupp c Coe b Benskin ..............179 | – b Benskin ..................... | 9 |
| E. H. Bowley b Bale ...........................127 | – c Sharp b Astill ............... | 0 |
| Mr K. A. Higgs b King ........................ 21 | – c Sidwell b Benskin ........... | 12 |
| Major W. G. M. Sarel b Benskin ................ 74 | – b Benskin .................... | 14 |
| M. W. Tate c Coe b Astill ..................... 2 | – c King b Benskin .............. | 4 |
| G. Street b Astill.............................. 2 | – b King ....................... | 5 |
| Mr A. E. R. Gilligan b King ................... 12 | – c Coe b King ................. | 12 |
| G. Stannard b Benskin ........................ 29 | – b Astill ..................... | 28 |
| G. Cox not out ............................... 8 | – not out ...................... | 10 |
| Mr A. H. H. Gilligan c and b Astill ............. 5 | – c Sidwell b King .............. | 18 |
| H. E. Roberts (did not bat)..................... | – b Astill ..................... | 0 |
| B 12, l-b 7, n-b 1 ................... 20 | B 4, n-b 1 .............. | 5 |

(9 wkts dec.) 479                                               117

## Leicestershire

| | | | |
|---|---|---|---|
| Mr G. H. Salmon b Cox........................ 26 | – b Cox ........................ | 32 |
| A. Lord b Roberts ........................... 4 | – b Cox ........................ | 34 |
| J. H. King b Tate ........................... 3 | – not out ......................110 |
| W. E. Astill c Jupp b A. E. R. Gilligan ........... 50 | – b Cox ........................ | 27 |
| Mr A. T. Sharp b Jupp .......................150 | – b Cox ........................ | 4 |
| S. Coe b Higgs .............................. 27 | – b Cox ........................ | 1 |
| Mr G. B. F. Rudd c Cox b Tate ................ 13 | – lbw b Cox ................... | 5 |
| Mr W. E. Pratt b Cox ........................ 18 | – not out ...................... | 29 |
| W. E. Benskin not out ....................... 12 | | |
| T. E. Sidwell c Street b Jupp .................. 6 | – b Jupp ...................... | 0 |
| F. Bale b Jupp .............................. 0 | | |
| B 20, l-b 7, n-b 2 ................... 29 | B 11, l-b 5, n-b 1 ........ | 17 |

338                                               259

**Leicestershire Bowling**

| | Overs | Mdns | Runs | Wkts | Overs | Mdns | Runs | Wkts |
|---|---|---|---|---|---|---|---|---|
| Benskin ......... | 31 | 2 | 148 | 3 | 12 | 3 | 30 | 4 |
| Astill ........... | 40.1 | 6 | 139 | 3 | 20 | 6 | 42 | 3 |
| Bale ............. | 14 | — | 58 | 1 | | | | |
| King ............. | 22 | 2 | 75 | 2 | 9.4 | 1 | 40 | 3 |
| Lord ............. | 7 | 2 | 19 | — | | | | |
| Pratt ............ | 3 | — | 20 | — | | | | |

**Sussex Bowling**

| | Overs | Mdns | Runs | Wkts | Overs | Mdns | Runs | Wkts |
|---|---|---|---|---|---|---|---|---|
| Roberts ......... | 19 | 5 | 55 | 1 | 4 | — | 10 | — |
| Tate ............. | 25 | 8 | 50 | 2 | 10 | 4 | 24 | — |
| Jupp ............. | 17.4 | 2 | 71 | 3 | 19 | 1 | 74 | 1 |
| Cox ............. | 24 | 8 | 35 | 2 | 34.5 | 8 | 73 | 6 |
| A. H. H. Gilligan ... | 5 | — | 15 | — | 2 | — | 12 | — |
| A. E. R. Gilligan ... | 21 | 4 | 68 | 1 | 10 | 1 | 49 | — |
| Higgs ........... | 3 | 1 | 15 | 1 | | | | |

Umpires: J. Blake and J. Carlin.

# LEICESTERSHIRE v GLOUCESTERSHIRE

## Played at Ashby-de-la-Zouch, July 22, 24, 25, 1922

Despite the loss of Monday owing to rain and the state of the Ashby-de-la-Zouch ground the match ended early on Tuesday in a win for Leicestershire by two wickets. Batsmen generally failed to stay long, but Dipper carried his bat through Gloucestershire's first innings which lasted two hours and twenty minutes. Leicestershire fared rather better and their first innings' lead enabled them to win. So helpless were batsmen on the third morning that eighteen wickets fell for 112 runs in two hours and a quarter. Victory seemed easy when only 37 were required but Mills and Parker bowled with such deadly effect that eight men were out for 18. Leg-byes helped Geary and Shipman to get the runs in a most exciting finish. Phenomenal bowling figures were credited to Astill, eleven wickets for 68, and Geary, eight for 31, for Leicestershire. Parker, bowling unchanged with Mills, did still better, his eleven wickets costing 66 runs. His second innings' analysis was quite exceptional and he took his first five wickets for eight runs before lunch. Mills was more difficult to hit, but no so effective as the left-hander. Leicestershire actually lost five men for five runs in half-an-hour, and their seventh wicket fell at eight before Geary and Sidwell managed to do something with the bowling.

## Gloucestershire

| | | |
|---|---|---|
| Capt. M. A. Green c sub. b Geary .............. | 4 | – b Geary ...................... 10 |
| A. G. Dipper not out ..................... | 22 | – lbw b Astill ................... 13 |
| H. Smith c and b Astill .................... | 4 | – c sub. b Astill ................. 7 |
| Mr B. H. Lyon st Sidwell b Benskin .............. | 9 | – c Shipman b Astill ............. 14 |
| Mr J. Howman b Astill .................... | 1 | – b Geary ..................... 0 |
| Mr L. Williams b Astill ................... | 1 | – b Astill ..................... 4 |
| P. Mills c Sidwell b Geary .................. | 10 | – b Geary ..................... 1 |
| Mr P. F. C. Williams c Coe b Geary ............. | 10 | – b Astill ..................... 3 |
| C. Parker lbw b Astill .................... | 2 | – not out ..................... 1 |
| G. Dennett b Geary ...................... | 1 | – c Benskin b Geary ............. 20 |
| J. G. Bessant b Astill .................... | 1 | – b Astill ..................... 0 |
| L-b 6, n-b 1 ...................... | 7 | B 1, l-b 1 .............. 2 |
| | **72** | **75** |

## Leicestershire

| | | | |
|---|---|---|---|
| A. Mounteney b Parker | 23 | – lbw b Mills | 1 |
| A. Lord lbw b Mills | 12 | – b Parker | 4 |
| W. E. Astill c Green b Mills | 2 | – b Mills | 0 |
| J. H. King b Mills | 2 | – b Parker | 0 |
| Maj. G. H. S. Fowke c Green b Parker | 10 | – b Parker | 2 |
| H. Whitehead c Dipper b Mills | 8 | – b Parker | 0 |
| S. Coe lbw b Parker | 7 | – b Parker | 1 |
| G. Geary b Mills | 12 | – not out | 9 |
| T. E. Sidwell c P. F. C. Williams b Parker | 10 | – c Bessant b Parker | 10 |
| A. Shipman b Parker | 0 | – not out | 4 |
| W. E. Benskin not out | 6 | | |
| B 16, l-b 1, n-b 2 | 19 | L-b 6 | 6 |
| | **111** | | **37** |

### Leicestershire Bowling

| | Overs | Mdns | Runs | Wkts | Overs | Mdns | Runs | Wkts |
|---|---|---|---|---|---|---|---|---|
| Astill | 26.2 | 11 | 38 | 5 | 18 | 8 | 30 | 6 |
| Geary | 18 | 9 | 13 | 4 | 12 | 5 | 18 | 4 |
| Benskin | 6 | 2 | 11 | 1 | 5 | 1 | 25 | — |
| Shipman | 2 | — | 3 | — | | | | |

### Gloucestershire Bowling

| | Overs | Mdns | Runs | Wkts | Overs | Mdns | Runs | Wkts |
|---|---|---|---|---|---|---|---|---|
| Mills | 25.3 | 8 | 44 | 5 | 9.4 | 4 | 13 | 2 |
| Parker | 25 | 12 | 48 | 5 | 9 | 3 | 18 | 6 |

Umpires: W. Reeves and W. Phillips.

# LEICESTERSHIRE v LANCASHIRE

### Played at Ashby-de-la-Zouch, June 21, 23, 24, 1922

Weakly represented, Leicestershire were outplayed, and Lancashire, declaring with one man out a second time, won easily by 270 runs. Hallows enjoyed the rare distinction of playing two three figure innings in the match, and was not dismissed. He excelled all the other batsmen until Ernest Tyldesley joined him – on Hopwood's dismissal on the Tuesday afternoon – when they carried the score from 57 to 224 and in the morning completed their hundreds in a partnership producing in all 185 in two hours. Neither batsman gave a chance. Hallows was batting nearly five hours and a half during the match, scoring 215 out of 401 runs made while he was at the wickets. Richard Tyldesley bowled best in Leicestershire's first innings, but failed when Parkin brought the match to a summary close by taking nine wickets for 32, a run out spoiling his chance of getting rid of the whole side.

## Lancashire

| | | | |
|---|---|---|---|
| H. Makepeace lbw b Skelding | 3 | | |
| J. L. Hopwood b Benskin | 38 | – b Benskin | 23 |
| E. Tyldesley c Hutchinson b Shipman | 12 | – not out | 101 |
| F. Watson run out | 6 | | |
| C. Hallows not out | 112 | – not out | 103 |
| Mr J. Sharp c Berridge b Hutchinson | 36 | | |
| J. Iddon c Astill b Skelding | 16 | | |
| R. Tyldesley b Bale | 0 | | |
| C. Parkin b Astill | 5 | | |
| G. Duckworth c Astill b Shipman | 0 | | |
| W. E. Hickmott b Benskin | 7 | | |
| B 19, l-b 5 | 24 | B 7, l-b 8 | 15 |
| | —— | | —— |
| | 259 | (1 wkt dec.) | 242 |

## Leicestershire

| | | | |
|---|---|---|---|
| T. E. Sidwell c Watson b R. Tyldesley | 3 | – c Duckworth b Parkin | 0 |
| Major G. H. S. Fowke b Parkin | 5 | – b Parkin | 4 |
| W. E. Astill lbw b R. Tyldesley | 61 | – c Hallows b Parkin | 20 |
| W. Berridge lbw b Hickmott | 10 | – run out | 0 |
| L. G. Berry b Hickmott | 0 | – lbw b Parkin | 6 |
| S. S. Coulson b Parkin | 25 | – st Duckworth b Parkin | 22 |
| A. Shipman c Makepeace b R. Tyldesley | 8 | – b Parkin | 0 |
| L. S. Hutchinson b R. Tyldesley | 0 | – c Sharp b Parkin | 3 |
| W. E. Benskin b R. Tyldesley | 8 | – not out | 25 |
| F. Bale not out | 1 | – c Duckworth b Parkin | 0 |
| A. Skelding b Parkin | 0 | – b Parkin | 11 |
| B 14, l-b 1 | 15 | B 4 | 4 |
| | —— | | —— |
| | 136 | | 95 |

### Leicestershire Bowling

| | Overs | Mdns | Runs | Wkts | Overs | Mdns | Runs | Wkts |
|---|---|---|---|---|---|---|---|---|
| Skelding | 19 | 7 | 32 | 2 | 13 | 2 | 39 | — |
| Astill | 34 | 14 | 80 | 1 | 14 | 4 | 46 | — |
| Shipman | 18 | 6 | 42 | 2 | 9 | 2 | 16 | — |
| Bale | 15 | 3 | 44 | 1 | 13 | 2 | 53 | — |
| Benskin | 7.3 | 1 | 28 | 2 | 14 | 1 | 49 | 1 |
| Hutchinson | 5 | — | 9 | 1 | 9 | 1 | 24 | — |

### Lancashire Bowling

| | Overs | Mdns | Runs | Wkts | Overs | Mdns | Runs | Wkts |
|---|---|---|---|---|---|---|---|---|
| Parkin | 26 | 3 | 68 | 3 | 11.4 | 3 | 32 | 9 |
| R. Tyldesley | 25 | 14 | 46 | 5 | 11 | 2 | 59 | — |
| Hickmott | 10 | 7 | 7 | 2 | | | | |

Umpires: A. E. Street and B. Tremlin.

## LEICESTERSHIRE v SUSSEX

### Played at Ashby-de-la-Zouch, August 2, 3, 1933

This match provided one of the sensations of the season, Leicestershire defeating Sussex by six wickets. Except in one or two cases where batsmen mastered the difficulties of the pitch and the good bowling, the ball always beat the bat, twenty-six wickets falling on the opening day for 287 runs. Winning the toss, Sussex were all out soon after lunch, their last eight wickets going down for 49 runs. Leicestershire batted more aggressively and at tea time led by 13 with four wickets in hand, but in the end they finished only 39 ahead. Then came the most startling cricket of the day, Sussex losing six wickets for 36 runs. When, at one point, half the side were out for 17, Geary had taken four wickets for 6 runs. The next day Leicestershire were left wanting only 34 runs for victory, but this task, easy as it appeared, occupied them forty minutes and involved the loss of four batsmen.

## Sussex

| | | |
|---|---|---|
| E. H. Bowley b Marlow | 4 | – b Smith ............ 4 |
| J. Parks c Astill b Geary | 36 | – st Sidwell b Geary ....... 0 |
| Mr A. Melville c Smith b Astill | 24 | – lbw b Geary ......... 1 |
| T. Cook lbw b Geary | 0 | – b Geary ............. 1 |
| Jas. Langridge c Armstrong b Astill | 7 | – b Astill ............. 31 |
| H. Parks c Packe b Geary | 0 | – b Geary ............. 3 |
| Mr R. S. G. Scott st Sidwell b Marlow | 11 | – st Sidwell b Astill ...... 4 |
| A. F. Wensley c Wigginton b Astill | 2 | – st Sidwell b Marlow ...... 24 |
| H. E. Hammond b Geary | 3 | – b Marlow ............ 0 |
| J. Eaton not out | 0 | – lbw b Astill .......... 1 |
| J. Cornford st Sidwell b Marlow | 6 | – not out ............. 1 |
| B 11, l-b 2 | 13 | B 2 ............... 2 |
| | **106** | **72** |

## Leicestershire

| | | |
|---|---|---|
| A. Shipman c Scott b Wensley | 1 | – c Hammond b Langridge ..... 6 |
| L. G. Berry run out | 50 | – c Bowley b Langridge ...... 5 |
| N. F. Armstrong c Cook b Cornford | 37 | – lbw b Langridge ......... 12 |
| S. H. Wigginton c Scott b Bowley | 0 | – not out ............. 5 |
| Mr E. W. Dawson b Cornford | 12 | |
| G. Geary lbw b Cornford | 0 | |
| T. E. Sidwell lbw b Langridge | 16 | |
| W. E. Astill c Cornford b Wensley | 5 | |
| Mr R. J. Packe not out | 2 | – c and b Langridge ........ 0 |
| W. H. Marlow b Langridge | 0 | |
| H. A. Smith b Wensley | 15 | – not out ............. 9 |
| B 7 | 7 | N-b 1 ............... 1 |
| | **145** | **38** |

## Leicestershire Bowling

| | Overs | Mdns | Runs | Wkts | Overs | Mdns | Runs | Wkts |
|---|---|---|---|---|---|---|---|---|
| Smith | 8 | 1 | 21 | — | 16 | 3 | 27 | 1 |
| Marlow | 11.3 | — | 36 | 3 | 1.1 | — | 2 | 2 |
| Geary | 15 | 6 | 20 | 4 | 21 | 9 | 26 | 4 |
| Astill | 12 | 3 | 16 | 3 | 8 | 3 | 15 | 3 |

## Sussex Bowling

| | Overs | Mdns | Runs | Wkts | Overs | Mdns | Runs | Wkts |
|---|---|---|---|---|---|---|---|---|
| Langridge | 19 | 6 | 31 | 2 | 6 | 1 | 12 | 4 |
| Wensley | 12.5 | 3 | 55 | 3 | 6.1 | 2 | 17 | — |
| Melville | 5 | — | 14 | — | | | | |
| Bowley | 7 | 1 | 22 | 1 | | | | |
| Cornford | 8 | 2 | 16 | 3 | 2 | 1 | 4 | — |
| Hammond | | | | | 2 | 1 | 4 | — |

Umpires: W. A. Buswell and C. N. Woolley.

## LEICESTERSHIRE v NORTHAMPTONSHIRE

Played at Leicester, August 5, 7, 8, 1933

A bold declaration by Jupp, the Northamptonshire captain, enabled Leicestershire to gain an unexpected, yet exciting victory by four wickets. No doubt influenced by the poor display of the Leicestershire batsmen in the first innings and the fact that the pitch showed signs of wear, Jupp allowed his side to bat for only half an hour on the last day, setting Leicestershire 283 to win. Thanks largely to Shipman and Berry scoring 141 in an opening stand, they accomplished the task with ten minutes of the extra half-hour remaining. Above everything else in the match stood out the brilliant batting on Saturday of Bakewell, who, hitting three 6s and twenty-two 4s, was last to leave. He alone saved Northamptonshire from a collapse.

### Northamptonshire

| | | | |
|---|---|---|---|
| A. H. Bakewell c Dawson b Smith | 192 | – b Smith | 2 |
| A. G. Liddell c Smith b Shipman | 1 | – c Dawson b Smith | 9 |
| B. Bellamy lbw b Smith | 7 | – c Astill b Marlow | 34 |
| J. E. Timms c Geary b Shipman | 2 | – c Dawson b Geary | 15 |
| Mr V. W. C. Jupp c Sidwell b Packe | 6 | – not out | 36 |
| Mr A. W. Snowden c Marlow b Smith | 25 | – b Marlow | 11 |
| A. D. Matthews c Wigginton b Astill | 1 | – c Dawson b Marlow | 12 |
| A. L. Cox c and b Astill | 24 | – not out | 7 |
| Mr E. F. Towell c Smith b Astill | 2 | | |
| A. E. Thomas st Sidwell b Smith | 8 | – b Marlow | 10 |
| R. J. Partridge not out | 7 | | |
| B 19, l-b 3, n-b 2 | 24 | B 9, l-b 6, n-b 1 | 16 |
| | **299** | **(7 wkts dec.)** | **152** |

### Leicestershire

| | | | |
|---|---|---|---|
| A. Shipman c Bellamy b Matthews | 12 | – st Bellamy b Cox | 59 |
| L. G. Berry c Bellamy b Matthews | 63 | – b Jupp | 76 |
| N. F. Armstrong run out | 4 | – not out | 45 |
| S. H. Wigginton b Partridge | 3 | – lbw b Cox | 0 |
| Mr E. W. Dawson b Jupp | 5 | – c Matthews b Thomas | 46 |
| G. Geary b Jupp | 5 | – not out | 15 |
| T. E. Sidwell lbw b Matthews | 11 | | |
| W. E. Astill b Jupp | 48 | – lbw b Matthews | 19 |
| Mr R. J. Packe c Bakewell b Jupp | 12 | | |
| W. H. Marlow lbw b Thomas | 0 | | |
| H. A. Smith not out | 0 | – c Thomas b Matthews | 0 |
| L-b 6 | 6 | B 12, l-b 11 | 23 |
| | **169** | | **283** |

### Leicestershire Bowling

| | Overs | Mdns | Runs | Wkts | Overs | Mdns | Runs | Wkts |
|---|---|---|---|---|---|---|---|---|
| Shipman | 12 | 3 | 36 | 2 | 3 | — | 4 | — |
| Smith | 29.1 | 7 | 55 | 4 | 18 | 4 | 61 | 2 |
| Geary | 21 | 7 | 30 | — | 7 | 3 | 6 | 1 |
| Astill | 36 | 14 | 72 | 3 | 12 | 1 | 26 | — |
| Packe | 8 | 2 | 31 | 1 | | | | |
| Marlow | 18 | 6 | 34 | — | 9 | — | 39 | 4 |
| Armstrong | 3 | — | 17 | — | | | | |

**Northamptonshire Bowling**

| | Overs | Mdns | Runs | Wkts | Overs | Mdns | Runs | Wkts |
|---|---|---|---|---|---|---|---|---|
| Matthews ......... | 23 | 8 | 38 | 3 | 26 | 6 | 58 | 2 |
| Partridge ......... | 16 | 5 | 43 | 1 | 4 | 1 | 16 | — |
| Thomas .......... | 17 | 10 | 16 | 1 | 18 | 7 | 28 | 1 |
| Towell ........... | 16 | 3 | 28 | — | 19 | 5 | 45 | — |
| Jupp ............. | 15.5 | 5 | 36 | 4 | 25 | 4 | 68 | 1 |
| Cox ............. | 2 | 1 | 2 | — | 17 | 3 | 45 | 2 |

Umpires: D. Hendren and J. Stone.

# LEICESTERSHIRE v HAMPSHIRE

### Played at Leicester, August 16, 17, 18, 1933

Even if they could not force a victory, Hampshire carried off the honours, for Leicestershire, who were 159 behind on the first innings, finished six runs in arrear with both their opening batsmen dismissed. The game might have taken a very different course, but for a mishap to Geary, who, when Hampshire had made 76, in running to deliver the ball, pulled a muscle and had to retire. Against a depleted attack Hampshire batted consistently, but with little enterprise. They occupied the whole of Wednesday scoring 330 for seven wickets. The next morning Bailey completed his only three-figure innings of the season. Like many left-handers, he showed to particular advantage when hitting to leg. He also drove well. Altogether he batted three hours and did not offer a chance until the over in which he was dismissed. Upon Leicestershire going in, a strong wind gave much assistance to Herman, who bowled extremely fast, but Shipman and Berry scored 102 together for the first wicket. Clouds of dust caused much discomfort to the batsmen, and the game was frequently interrupted owing to the bails falling off the stumps. After tea, much time having been wasted in trying to keep the bails in position, the umpires agreed to do without them. Consequently when the ball appeared to touch the stumps both Dawson and Shipman got the benefit of the doubt. Dawson, however, obviously playing on, a united appeal was upheld.

## Hampshire

| | | |
|---|---|---|
| G. Brown c Sidwell b Smith ............. | 14 | J. Bailey b Armstrong .................106 |
| J. Arnold lbw b Astill .................. | 14 | G. S. Boyes c Sidwell b Marlow .......... 39 |
| N. McCorkell c Smith b Marlow ......... | 35 | O. W. Herman c Astill b Smith .......... 12 |
| C. P. Mead c Smith b Astill ............. | 44 | G. Hill not out ....................... 1 |
| A. E. Pothecary c and b Astill ........... | 18 | B 16, l-b 10, w 1, n-b 2 ......... 29 |
| W. L. Creese c sub. b Smith ............. | 48 | ——— |
| A. Kennedy lbw b Smith ............... | 77 | 437 |

## Leicestershire

| | | | |
|---|---|---|---|
| A. Shipman b Boyes ...................... | 80 | – st Brown b Boyes ............... | 13 |
| L. G. Berry c Herman b Hill .................... | 58 | – c and b Creese ................. | 54 |
| N. F. Armstrong hit wkt b Boyes ................. | 11 | – not out ....................... | 42 |
| A. Riddington b Herman ...................... | 1 | – not out ....................... | 37 |
| Mr E. W. Dawson b Herman .................... | 22 | | |
| W. E. Astill b Herman ........................ | 19 | | |
| H. Bowley b Boyes ........................... | 16 | | |
| T. E. Sidwell lbw b Hill ....................... | 21 | | |
| H. A. Smith lbw b Hill ........................ | 30 | | |
| W. H. Marlow not out ........................ | 8 | | |
| G. Geary absent hurt ......................... | 0 | | |
| B 3, l-b 9 ........................ | 12 | | |

| | | |
|---|---|---|
| | 278 | 153 |

## Leicestershire Bowling

| | Overs | Mdns | Runs | Wkts |
|---|---|---|---|---|
| Shipman . . . . . . . . . | 19 | 3 | 54 | — |
| Smith . . . . . . . . . . . | 43 | 9 | 92 | 4 |
| Astill . . . . . . . . . . . | 58 | 15 | 141 | 3 |
| Marlow . . . . . . . . . | 25 | 5 | 81 | 2 |
| Geary . . . . . . . . . . . | 4 | 2 | 3 | — |
| Armstrong . . . . . . . . | 10 | 2 | 23 | 1 |
| Riddington . . . . . . . . | 5 | 2 | 14 | — |

## Hampshire Bowling

| | Overs | Mdns | Runs | Wkts | Overs | Mdns | Runs | Wkts |
|---|---|---|---|---|---|---|---|---|
| Kennedy . . . . . . . . . | 8 | 3 | 15 | — | 14 | 8 | 15 | — |
| Herman . . . . . . . . . . | 36 | 9 | 84 | 3 | 9 | 1 | 23 | — |
| Boyes . . . . . . . . . . . | 56 | 18 | 108 | 3 | 7 | 1 | 13 | 1 |
| Hill . . . . . . . . . . . . . . | 21.1 | 6 | 52 | 3 | 17 | 10 | 24 | — |
| Creese . . . . . . . . . . | 6 | 2 | 7 | — | 19 | 1 | 49 | 1 |
| Pothecary . . . . . . . . | | | | | 4 | — | 22 | — |
| Arnold . . . . . . . . . . | | | | | 3 | 3 | — | — |

Umpires: A. Morton and A. E. Dipper.

## LEICESTERSHIRE IN 1934

The one distressing feature of the season was in the matter of finance. The public demanded brighter cricket and their desires were certainly complied with, but even so the "gates" were extremely disappointing. Indeed, on the occasion of Shipman's benefit the attendances were so poor that the player found himself some £60 out of pocket as a result of the match. Happily this was cleared off by the proceeds of the "Sportsmen's" match. Other subscriptions came in later. During the season a suggestion was made that Leicestershire should amalgamate with Lincolnshire, but naturally nothing came of the proposal and the Leicestershire authorities decided to carry on in the hope of better support in the future. Special incentive for this came in January, when a few county enthusiasts cleared off at the club's debt of over £5,000. This generous act should arouse keener local interest in Leicestershire cricket with resulting larger membership of the club and far better attendances at Aylestone Road.

## LEICESTERSHIRE v YORKSHIRE

### Played at Leicester, August 8, 9, 10, 1934

For the first time in twenty-three years Leicestershire defeated Yorkshire. Their victory – by 58 runs – proved to be one of the most sensational of the season, for not only were they outplayed for the first two days, but Sellers, the Yorkshire captain, declared his first innings closed with a lead of 102 when five men were out. On Wednesday Leicestershire fared disastrously against Bowes and Smailes, who made the best use of a difficult wicket, and were dismissed in just over two hours. Yorkshire, too, found run-getting no easy matter, but Leyland and Sellers, by hard driving, put on 125 for the fifth partnership. Sellers declared first thing on Thursday. Then Leicestershire, thanks chiefly to Armstrong and Astill, made a good recovery and set Yorkshire to get 149. Smith, making the ball lift awkwardly, proved extremely difficult and Yorkshire gave a poor account of themselves.

## Leicestershire

| | | | |
|---|---|---|---|
| A. Shipman c Wood b Smailes | 1 | – b Bowes | 23 |
| S. H. Wigginton c Sutcliffe b Smailes | 11 | – lbw b Verity | 16 |
| N. F. Armstrong c Macaulay b Bowes | 0 | – not out | 98 |
| L. G. Berry c Wood b Smailes | 1 | – c Bowes b Leyland | 16 |
| Flt-Lieut W. K. Beisiegel b Bowes | 5 | – c Leyland b Macaulay | 13 |
| Mr G. A. Ball lbw b Smailes | 0 | – c Sellers b Leyland | 12 |
| W. E. Astill c Macaulay b Bowes | 5 | – c Wood b Macaulay | 40 |
| G. Geary not out | 24 | – c Verity b Bowes | 0 |
| P. Corrall c Verity b Bowes | 11 | – run out | 3 |
| H. A. Smith c Mitchell b Verity | 32 | – c sub. b Bowes | 6 |
| W. H. Marlow b Macaulay | 1 | – b Bowes | 0 |
| L-b 3 | 3 | B 13, l-b 9, n-b 1 | 23 |
| | **94** | | **250** |

## Yorkshire

| | | | |
|---|---|---|---|
| H. Sutcliffe c Armstrong b Marlow | 26 | – lbw b Smith | 5 |
| A. Mitchell lbw b Geary | 14 | – b Smith | 14 |
| W. Barber c Ball b Marlow | 1 | – b Shipman | 5 |
| M. Leyland b Marlow | 90 | – c Corrall b Smith | 8 |
| K. R. Davidson c Smith b Geary | 8 | – b Astill | 3 |
| Mr A. B. Sellers not out | 53 | – b Astill | 18 |
| H. Verity not out | 0 | – c Corrall b Smith | 16 |
| T. F. Smailes (did not bat) | | – c Marlow b Smith | 4 |
| A. Wood (did not bat) | | – c Astill b Geary | 8 |
| G. G. Macaulay (did not bat) | | – c Astill b Smith | 0 |
| W. E. Bowes (did not bat) | | – not out | 2 |
| L-b 4 | 4 | B 3, l-b 4 | 7 |
| (5 wkts dec.) | **196** | | **90** |

### Yorkshire Bowling

| | Overs | Mdns | Runs | Wkts | Overs | Mdns | Runs | Wkts |
|---|---|---|---|---|---|---|---|---|
| Bowes | 12 | 4 | 17 | 4 | 28 | 4 | 87 | 4 |
| Smailes | 11 | 2 | 30 | 4 | 7 | 3 | 26 | — |
| Verity | 9 | 2 | 28 | 1 | 27 | 13 | 47 | 1 |
| Macaulay | 8.2 | 3 | 16 | 1 | 26 | 8 | 51 | 2 |
| Leyland | | | | | 6 | 1 | 16 | 2 |

### Leicestershire Bowling

| | Overs | Mdns | Runs | Wkts | Overs | Mdns | Runs | Wkts |
|---|---|---|---|---|---|---|---|---|
| Shipman | 8 | 2 | 16 | — | 5 | 2 | 8 | 1 |
| Smith | 17 | 3 | 40 | — | 25 | 8 | 39 | 6 |
| Marlow | 23 | 7 | 59 | 3 | 3 | 1 | 6 | — |
| Geary | 18 | 7 | 26 | 2 | 14.4 | 7 | 19 | 1 |
| Astill | 14 | 2 | 51 | — | 9 | 4 | 11 | 2 |

Umpires: W. Bestwick and W. A. Buswell.

# LEICESTERSHIRE v DERBYSHIRE

### Played at Leicester, June 15, 17, 18, 1935

T. B. Mitchell, the Derbyshire slow bowler, achieved the rare distinction of taking all ten wickets in an innings, but rain on the last day spoiled what promised to be an interesting finish. Derbyshire secured the major points for first-innings' lead. Sent in to bat on a difficult wicket, Derbyshire could not cope with the bowling of Smith and Geary. Leicestershire were even less successful. They lost six batsmen for 68 runs and on Monday Mitchell took the remaining four wickets for the addition of 29 and Derbyshire led by 17. Flighting the ball with considerable skill and varying his spin, Mitchell tempted the batsmen to hit, but his ten wickets cost only 64 runs. Alderman and Storer gave Derbyshire a good start and, Townsend and Worthington hitting hard, Leicestershire had to get 245 to win. On Tuesday play could not begin until half-past three and with Leicestershire 133 behind with three men out rain stopped the game for good.

### Derbyshire

| | | | |
|---|---|---|---|
| A. E. Alderman b Geary | 0 | – b Marlow | 29 |
| H. Storer lbw b Geary | 5 | – lbw b Geary | 33 |
| T. S. Worthington b Geary | 44 | – c Berry b Marlow | 37 |
| L. F. Townsend b Geary | 5 | – c Marlow b Smith | 35 |
| E. Carrington c Astill b Smith | 40 | – c Geary b Smith | 24 |
| Mr G. F. Hodgkinson b Geary | 0 | – c Corrall b Smith | 0 |
| A. Townsend not out | 24 | – c Smith b Marlow | 9 |
| A. V. Pope c Corrall b Smith | 0 | – c Prentice b Marlow | 21 |
| H. Elliott b Smith | 2 | – not out | 9 |
| T. B. Mitchell c Prentice b Smith | 6 | – b Smith | 1 |
| W. Copson c Prentice b Smith | 9 | – c Corrall b Marlow | 9 |
| B 1, l-b 3, n-b 1 | 5 | B 16, l-b 1, w 1, n-b 2 | 20 |
| | **140** | | **227** |

### Leicestershire

| | | | |
|---|---|---|---|
| A. Shipman c Worthington b Mitchell | 10 | – not out | 60 |
| L. G. Berry b Mitchell | 11 | – c Storer b L. F. Townsend | 18 |
| N. F. Armstrong c Worthington b Mitchell | 13 | – c Copson b Mitchell | 5 |
| F. Prentice lbw (N) b Mitchell | 10 | – hit wkt b Mitchell | 4 |
| G. Watson b Mitchell | 0 | – not out | 16 |
| C. A. Coleman b Mitchell | 8 | | |
| W. E. Astill b Mitchell | 18 | | |
| G. Geary b Mitchell | 16 | | |
| H. A. Smith c Worthington b Mitchell | 8 | | |
| W. H. Marlow st Elliott b Mitchell | 14 | | |
| P. Corrall not out | 6 | | |
| B 5, l-b 4 | 9 | L-b 7, w 1 | 8 |
| | **123** | | **111** |

### Leicestershire Bowling

| | Overs | Mdns | Runs | Wkts | Overs | Mdns | Runs | Wkts |
|---|---|---|---|---|---|---|---|---|
| Smith | 20.5 | 7 | 51 | 5 | 23 | 5 | 57 | 4 |
| Geary | 29 | 13 | 46 | 5 | 26 | 8 | 57 | 1 |
| Marlow | 18 | 5 | 23 | — | 16.2 | 3 | 69 | 5 |
| Astill | 8 | 2 | 15 | — | 8 | — | 24 | — |

### Derbyshire Bowling

| | Overs | Mdns | Runs | Wkts | Overs | Mdns | Runs | Wkts |
|---|---|---|---|---|---|---|---|---|
| Copson | 16 | 3 | 30 | — | 4 | — | 20 | — |
| Worthington | 2 | — | 6 | — | 3 | 1 | 7 | — |
| Mitchell | 19.1 | 4 | 64 | 10 | 17 | 4 | 39 | 2 |
| L. F. Townsend | 6 | 2 | 14 | — | 15 | 5 | 35 | 1 |
| A. V. Pope | | | | | 4 | 3 | 2 | — |

Umpires: E. J. Smith and W. R. Parry.

## LEICESTERSHIRE v KENT

Played at Oakham, August 31, September 2, 3, 1935

On Tuesday Kent collapsed in sensational fashion and Leicestershire, playing for the first time at Oakham, gained a surprisingly easy win by ten wickets. By this success they set up a record number of victories for the county in one season. Facing arrears of 37, Kent, on Monday evening, lost two wickets for 24 and next morning the remaining seven – Chapman was unable to bat – fell for 32. Even allowing for the accuracy with which Smith and Geary bowled on a slightly worn pitch, Kent gave a sorry display. On Saturday Kent did well on a wicket which always helped bowlers. Six men were out for 149, however, before Ames and Chapman added 97. Leicestershire owed much to Berry, who drove and hooked vigorously for two and a half hours. Edgson and Geary also batted attractively, but seven men were out before Kent's total was passed.

### Kent

| | | | |
|---|---|---|---|
| W. H. Ashdown c Marlow b Smith | 28 | – b Smith | 36 |
| A. Fagg c Corrall b Astill | 26 | – b Smith | 6 |
| F. E. Woolley c Edgson b Marlow | 21 | – b Smith | 0 |
| L. E. G. Ames c Berry b Geary | 86 | – b Geary | 0 |
| L. J. Todd run out | 7 | – b Geary | 0 |
| Mr B. H. Valentine c Armstrong b Marlow | 15 | – not out | 1 |
| Mr F. G. H. Chalk b Geary | 2 | – b Smith | 1 |
| Mr A. P F. Chapman c Astill b Smith | 47 | – absent hurt | 0 |
| A. E. Watt b Smith | 3 | – lbw b Geary | 5 |
| A. P. Freeman not out | 4 | – c Watson b Geary | 0 |
| C. Lewis b Geary | 0 | – c Armstrong b Smith | 7 |
| B 18, l-b 7, n-b 1 | 26 | B 4 | 4 |
| | **265** | | **56** |

### Leicestershire

| | | | |
|---|---|---|---|
| A. Shipman lbw b Freeman | 4 | – not out | 11 |
| L. G. Berry b Freeman | 88 | – not out | 9 |
| N. F. Armstrong lbw (N), b Watt | 32 | | |
| G. Watson c and b Freeman | 3 | | |
| F. Prentice lbw (N) b Todd | 30 | | |
| Mr C. L. Edgson lbw b Freeman | 48 | | |
| G. Geary c Valentine b Freeman | 52 | | |
| W. E. Astill b Freeman | 2 | | |
| P. Corrall c Watt b Freeman | 5 | | |
| H. A. Smith c Valentine b Freeman | 18 | | |
| W. H. Marlow not out | 3 | | |
| B 11, l-b 6 | 17 | B 1 | 1 |
| | **302** | | **21** |

### Leicestershire Bowling

| | Overs | Mdns | Runs | Wkts | Overs | Mdns | Runs | Wkts |
|---|---|---|---|---|---|---|---|---|
| Smith | 33 | 5 | 96 | 3 | 16 | 7 | 25 | 5 |
| Shipman | 8 | — | 24 | — | | | | |
| Geary | 26.2 | 8 | 55 | 3 | 15.5 | 7 | 22 | 4 |
| Astill | 11 | 3 | 25 | 1 | | | | |
| Marlow | 21 | 6 | 39 | 2 | 1 | — | 5 | — |

**Kent Bowling**

| | Overs | Mdns | Runs | Wkts | Overs | Mdns | Runs | Wkts |
|---|---|---|---|---|---|---|---|---|
| Freeman ......... | 57.1 | 15 | 123 | 8 | 3 | — | 13 | — |
| Lewis ........... | 18 | 4 | 39 | — | | | | |
| Todd ........... | 20 | 3 | 53 | 1 | | | | |
| Watt ........... | 24 | 9 | 51 | 1 | | | | |
| Woolley ......... | 5 | 3 | 10 | — | | | | |
| Ashdown ........ | 3 | — | 9 | — | | | | |
| Ames ........... | | | | | 2.5 | 1 | 7 | — |

Umpires: J. Newman and W. A. Buswell.

# MIDDLESEX

## MIDDLESEX IN 1920

*President* – Mr. R. D. Walker

*Hon. Secretaries* – Mr A. J. Webbe and Mr P. F. Warner

*Hon. Treasurer* – Mr S. S. Pawling

*Captain* – Mr P. F. Warner

*Deputy-Captain* – Mr F. T. Mann

Never in the history of the County Championship has there been anything so dramatic as the triumph of Middlesex last summer. When on the 27th of July they lost their return game with Essex by 4 runs, nothing seemed more unlikely than that they would finish at the head of the list. From that time forward, however, they met with nothing but success, actually winning their last nine matches. On two occasions they had a desperately narrow margin in their favour, beating Kent at Canterbury by 5 runs and Yorkshire at Bradford by 4 runs. Not till the last moment were they secure of their prize, as if they had drawn instead of actually winning their final match with Surrey at Lord's they would, according to the method of scoring points, have finished fractionally below Lancashire. That final match was the event of the year, P. F. Warner, who had previously announced his intention of retiring, winding up his career as Middlesex captain amid a scene of enthusiasm which no one fortunate enough to be present will ever forget. It would have been a misfortune if, after doing such brilliant things, Middlesex had missed the Championship, as they had a far better record than any of their rivals. Taking part in twenty county fixtures and meeting only the strongest opponents, they won fifteen matches, drew three, and lost only two. In the drawn games they won once on the first innings and lost twice. Their fifteen victories consisted of two each against Surrey, Kent, Sussex, Hampshire, Somerset and Warwickshire, and one each against Yorkshire, Lancashire and Nottinghamshire. They were beaten by Nottinghamshire at Trent Bridge and Essex at Leyton. In the latter case it is not unfair to suggest that, as things turned out, the result might have been different if Warner had not had to leave his first innings unfinished. He had to be at Lord's for the meeting at which the English team for Australia was selected.

When the season began there was no suggestion of what was in store. Even the most sanguine of the county's supporters would have smiled at the idea of winning the Championship. There was no fear as to the strength of the batting, but in the light of what had happened in 1919 the prospect as regards bowling seemed rather hopeless. The doleful expectations, however, were entirely falsified. J. W. Hearne, apart from the fact that he seemed mistrustful of his leg-break, recovered his pre-war form, Durston as a fast bowler improved out of knowledge, and in G. T. S. Stevens, the side had a bowler who, though often expensive, could now and then, even on the best wickets, send down a more or less unplayable ball. The other bowlers in the eleven were Lee and Nigel Haig, the former of whom did some brilliant work at Lord's during the first half of the season. Still though the bowling proved so much stronger than anyone had dared to hope it was the batting that made Middlesex in 1920 so remarkable. The run-getting of the side at Lord's must have been almost without precedent. In the ten matches Middlesex obtained two totals of over 500, four of over 400, and three of over 300. In doing all these things they were mainly indebted to Hendren, Hearne and Lee. These three batsmen had a wonderful season. They found their form in the opening match against Warwickshire in May, and they never looked back. Lee finished a modest third to his more gifted colleagues, but for most counties he would on his record have been easily first. Eighteen hundreds were hit for

Middlesex, and for fifteen of them the three batsmen were responsible, making curiously enough five each. It may be questioned whether in the history of Lord's any batsmen has had such a season at the ground as Hendren. He made 232 against Nottinghamshire, 183 not out against Hampshire, 183 not out against Lancashire, 170 against Kent, and 158 against Warwickshire. More than that, when playing for the MCC against Oxford University, he scored 160. Of all these big innings the 232 against Nottinghamshire was the most brilliant. Whereas all Hendren's hundreds were at Lord's, Hearne reached three figures at The Oval and Birmingham, and Lee at Southampton and Brighton. Taken as a whole the batting of the three professionals deserves a chapter to itself in cricket history. Scoring 1,552 runs with an average of 59 and taking 119 wickets Hearne was the great all-round man of the eleven, having indeed no rival in any county, except Woolley. Hendren, apart from his marvellous batting was, as in seasons before the war, the best out-field in England, never knowing the meaning of the word fatigue. G. T. S. Stevens as an all-round man was of far more value than would be guessed from his figures. He nearly always made scores when runs were most wanted, and his bowling often told well on the fastest wickets. A famous cricketer said of him as a batsman that, whatever the position, he could always go in and play his natural game. The great batsmen of the team were backed up by fine hitters in Haig and F. T. Mann, and C. H. L. Skeet – an almost incomparable field on the off-side – made 106 in the all-important match with Surrey at Lord's. Warner could not keep up the run-getting form in which he started the season, but he saved his side against Surrey when things were going very badly. As a captain he finished his career in triumph. It is safe to say that but for his generalship in the hand-fought matches in August, Middlesex would not have won the Championship. In Murrell, Middlesex had one of the best of wicket-keepers – never estimated at quite his real value.

In honour of Middlesex having won the Championship a dinner was given to the team at the Cafe Royal on the 12th of October, Mr. A. J. Webbe presiding in the absence – on account of age and health – of Mr. R. D. Walker. Many famous cricketers who assisted Middlesex in years gone by were present, among them Messrs J. G. Walker, James Douglas, C. M. Wells, F. G. J. Ford, P. J. de Paravicini, George Beldam, J. T. Hearne and George Burton. Unfortunately the three players who did most for Middlesex last season could not be with their colleagues. Hendren and J. W. Hearne were on their way to Australia and Lee had left England to fulfil a winter engagement as coach in South Africa. In the course of his speech – a very happy one – the chairman paid high compliments to P. F. Warner as cricketer and captain, and specially mentioned G. T. S. Stevens as, in his opinion, one of the England players of the future. Middlesex enjoyed in a financial sense a season of unprecedented success. The surplus on the year came to £3,270 9s. 2d., about £1,100 out of this sum being due, under agreement, to the Marylebone Club.

## MIDDLESEX v SUSSEX

### Played at Lord's, May 22, 24, 1920

In beating Sussex by an innings and 130 runs Middlesex did, to the best of one's knowledge, something without precedent in first-class cricket, their first four batsmen all scoring over a hundred. Though 956 runs were obtained the match was finished off in two days, play being prolonged on Whit Monday till a quarter to seven. There was a huge crowd on the Bank Holiday, 14,129 people paying for admission. Lee had a great match, as in addition to playing an innings of 119, he took eleven wickets at a cost of only 68 runs. His bowling was the more remarkable as the ground did not give him the least assistance. The match was played for the benefit of Whiteside, of the MCC ground staff, who was fortunate in receiving a substantial sum of money. On the Saturday Warner and Lee opened the Middlesex innings at a quarter-past four, and at the drawing of stumps the score was 156 for no wicket. On Monday Lee was out at 241 and Warner at 284. Then followed some extraordinary cricket, Haig hitting up 131 runs out of 228 for the third wicket in an hour and fifty minutes, his figures including twenty 4s, most of them drives. Hearne played finely for two hours and three quarters. Sussex on batting for the second time went all to pieces against Lee and Durston.

### Sussex

| | | |
|---|---|---|
| E. H. Bowley c Lee b Durston | 0 – b Durston | 14 |
| F. D. Jenner c Durston b Prentice | 18 – b Lee | 24 |
| Mr V. W. C. Jupp c Murrell b Prentice | 20 – lbw b Lee | 3 |
| Mr H. L. Wilson c Murrell b Prentice | 11 – c Murrell b Durston | 0 |
| M. W. Tate b Lee | 37 – c Hendren b Lee | 5 |
| Mr A. K. Wilson b Hearne | 4 – b Lee | 0 |
| Mr A. H. H. Gilligan c Hearne b Lee | 47 – c Dales b Lee | 4 |
| G. Cox c Prentice b Lee | 0 – lbw b Lee | 38 |
| G. Stannard b Lee | 53 – c Murrell b Durston | 37 |
| G. Street lbw b Lee | 27 – c Murrell b Kent | 2 |
| H. E. Roberts not out | 4 – not out | 33 |
| B 4, l-b 6, w 1 | 11     B 9, l-b 8, n-b 4 | 21 |
| | **232** | **181** |

### Middlesex

| | |
|---|---|
| Mr P. F. Warner c Street b Gilligan | 139 |
| H. W. Lee c Roberts b Gilligan | 119 |
| J. W. Hearne not out | 116 |
| Mr N. Haig c H. L. Wilson b Tate | 131 |
| E. Hendren c Gilligan b Tate | 17 |
| B 10, l-b 8, n-b 3 | 21 |
| (4 wkts dec.) | 543 |

Mr H. L. Dales, Mr. F. T. Mann, H. R. Murrell, Mr H. N. Kent, Mr L. V. Prentice and T. J. Durston did not bat.

### Middlesex Bowling

| | Overs | Mdns | Runs | Wkts | Overs | Mdns | Runs | Wkts |
|---|---|---|---|---|---|---|---|---|
| Durston | 14 | 3 | 47 | 1 | 16.2 | 3 | 42 | 3 |
| Prentice | 22 | 6 | 92 | 3 | 8 | — | 37 | — |
| Kent | 1 | 1 | — | — | 4 | — | 13 | 1 |
| Hearne | 15 | 3 | 50 | 1 | 4 | — | 21 | — |
| Lee | 11.2 | 4 | 21 | 5 | 17 | 7 | 47 | 6 |
| Haig | 3 | 1 | 11 | — | | | | |

### Sussex Bowling

| | Overs | Mdns | Runs | Wkts |
|---|---|---|---|---|
| Roberts | 25 | 5 | 103 | — |
| Cox | 40 | 9 | 110 | — |
| Jupp | 19 | 1 | 67 | — |
| Gilligan | 30 | 7 | 95 | 2 |
| Tate | 28.3 | 5 | 86 | 2 |
| A. K. Wilson | 2 | — | 10 | — |
| Stannard | 7 | — | 41 | — |
| H. L. Wilson | 1 | — | 10 | — |

Umpires: J. Blake and C. Marshall.

## MIDDLESEX v NOTTINGHAMSHIRE

### Played at Lord's, August 11, 12, 13, 1920

In beating Nottinghamshire by nine wickets Middlesex were mainly indebted to Hendren who played, perhaps, the most brilliant of all his great innings last summer. He began with extreme care, taking an hour and three-quarters to get his first fifty runs, but after that his hitting was so terrific that in the same space of time he added 182. Ignoring the pull to some extent he drove as perhaps he has never driven before, his hits including a six and thirty-three 4s. Getting 232, he had the satisfaction of making his biggest score in first-class cricket. While he and Stevens were together 157 runs were put on in a little over an hour, and then Hendren and Murrell added 110 in forty minutes. Nottinghamshire made a feeble fight on the third morning, Hearne's bowling being much too good for them.

### Nottinghamshire

| | | | |
|---|---:|---|---:|
| G. Gunn b Durston | 1 | – st Murrell b Hearne | 27 |
| W. Whysall c Hendren b Hearne | 96 | – b Stevens | 37 |
| J. Gunn c Hendren b Durston | 7 | – c Murrell b Durston | 22 |
| Mr A. W. Carr c Hearne b Durston | 61 | – c Murrell b Durston | 23 |
| J. Hardstaff c Hendren b Lee | 47 | – not out | 34 |
| W. Payton c Stevens b Durston | 12 | – c Hendren b Hearne | 12 |
| S. J. Staples c Murrell b Durston | 15 | – b Lee | 3 |
| F. Barratt b Lee | 11 | – b Lee | 7 |
| T. Oates c Haig b Durston | 6 | – lbw b Hearne | 14 |
| F. C. Matthews b Durston | 4 | – st Murrell b Hearne | 13 |
| L. Richmond not out | 4 | – c Stevens b Hearne | 4 |
| B 8, l-b 5, n-b 1 | 14 | B 4, l-b 2, n-b 1 | 7 |
| | **278** | | **203** |

### Middlesex

| | | | |
|---|---:|---|---:|
| Mr C. H. L. Skeet c Barratt b Matthews | 40 | – b Carr | 0 |
| H. W. Lee c G. Gunn b Matthews | 41 | | |
| J. W. Hearne b Staples | 29 | | |
| E. Hendren lbw b Richmond | 232 | | |
| Mr P. F. Warner b Richmond | 15 | | |
| Mr F. T. Mann c Oates b Barratt | 6 | | |
| Mr N. Haig b Barratt | 2 | | |
| Mr G. T. S. Stevens c Barratt b J. Gunn | 61 | – not out | 10 |
| H. R. Murrell not out | 23 | | |
| Dr C. H. Gunasekara did not bat | | – not out | 6 |
| B 3, l-b 10, w 2, n-b 1 | 16 | N-b 1 | 1 |
| (8 wkts dec.) | **465** | | **17** |

T. J. Durston did not bat.

### Middlesex Bowling

| | Overs | Mdns | Runs | Wkts | Overs | Mdns | Runs | Wkts |
|---|---:|---:|---:|---:|---:|---:|---:|---:|
| Durston | 36.2 | 14 | 79 | 7 | 17 | 3 | 59 | 2 |
| Haig | 14 | 5 | 24 | — | 8 | 3 | 17 | — |
| Stevens | 13 | 2 | 40 | — | 5 | 1 | 15 | 1 |
| Hearne | 17 | 2 | 56 | 1 | 27.3 | 7 | 59 | 5 |
| Lee | 16 | 4 | 47 | 2 | 19 | 4 | 46 | 2 |
| Gunasekara | 8 | 2 | 18 | — | | | | |

**Nottinghamshire Bowling**

| | Overs | Mdns | Runs | Wkts | Overs | Mdns | Runs | Wkts |
|---|---|---|---|---|---|---|---|---|
| Barratt .......... | 34 | 8 | 98 | 2 | | | | |
| Richmond ....... | 35.4 | 4 | 125 | 2 | | | | |
| Matthews ........ | 21 | 4 | 98 | 2 | | | | |
| Staples .......... | 20 | 2 | 92 | 1 | | | | |
| J. Gunn .......... | 9 | 1 | 36 | 1 | | | | |
| Carr ............. | | | | | 3 | 1 | 7 | 1 |
| Whysall ......... | | | | | 2.1 | — | 9 | — |

Umpires: W. Phillips and A. Millward.

## MIDDLESEX v SURREY

### Played at Lord's, August 28, 30, 31, 1920

This was the match of the season. Middlesex and Lancashire were running neck and neck for the Championship, and as Lancashire on the same days had the simplest of tasks against Worcestershire, Middlesex knew that nothing less than an actual victory would be of real value to them. Never before has a county match proved such an attraction at Lord's. On the Saturday there must have been nearly 25,000 people on the ground, 20,700 paying for admission at the gates. A great fight was looked forward to, and as it happened all expectations were exceeded. It was a game never to be forgotten, Middlesex in the end winning by 55 runs, and so securing the Championship. Winning the toss Middlesex had the advantage of batting first on a hard wicket, but nothing could have been less promising than their start. For once Lee and Hearne failed them, and in less than an hour three wickets were down for 35 runs. After these disasters nothing was risked, and at the end of the afternoon the Middlesex score with eight men out had only reached 253. Warner was blamed in some quarters for over-caution, but he saved his side. In getting 79 he was batting for nearly four hours and a half. On the Monday there was again an enormous attendance, the number paying at the gates this time being 20,021. Owing nearly everything to Sandham, Surrey had the best of the day's cricket. Sandham had some luck – a chance of stumping at 40 and a chance at slip at 77 – but for the most part he played superbly, combining an ever-watchful defence with his clean hitting. For his 167 not out he was batting four hours and twenty minutes, his figures including seventeen 4s. With the object of getting Middlesex in before the end of the afternoon Fender declared with nine wickets down, but his policy met with no reward, Skeet and Lee batting for forty minutes and taking the score to 27. For sustained excitement the third day beat everything seen in London last season. Skeet and Lee made victory for Middlesex possible, staying in until after lunch and sending up 208 for the first wicket. Lee was splendid, and Skeet, though not so certain in timing the ball, played better than he had ever played before in a first-class match. Warner declared at twenty minutes to four, leaving Surrey to get 244 in a trifle over three hours. The downfall of Hobbs – caught in the slips at 22 – was discouraging, but Surrey went for the runs and, with Sandham playing even more finely than on the previous day, the 100 was up in an hour and a quarter for two wickets. However, Hendren got rid of Shepherd by means of a wonderful catch in the deep field – just in front of the screen with his hands above his head – this being really the turning-point of the game. Surrey's great hope departed when Sandham – the sixth man out – was caught and bowled from a full pitch. In the end Middlesex won with ten minutes to spare. Warner was carried off the field shoulder high, and before the crowd dispersed he and Fender had to make speeches.

## Middlesex

| | | |
|---|---|---|
| Mr C. H. L. Skeet c Ducat b Rushby | 2 | – c Fender b Hitch ............106 |
| H. W. Lee c Hitch b Fender | 12 | – b Hitch ....................108 |
| J. W. Hearne c and b Hitch | 15 | – lbw b Rushby ................ 26 |
| E. Hendren b Reay | 41 | – c Sandham b Rushby ........... 5 |
| Mr P. F. Warner b Rushby | 79 | – not out ..................... 14 |
| Mr F. T. Mann c and b Fender | 12 | – c Peach b Fender ............. 22 |
| Mr N. Haig b Reay | 18 | – b Rushby .................... 1 |
| Mr G. T. S. Stevens b Fender | 53 | – not out ..................... 21 |
| Mr H. K. Longman b Fender | 0 | |
| H. R. Murrell c Ducat b Hitch | 9 | – b Reay ...................... 0 |
| T. J. Durston not out | 0 | |
| B 12, l-b 12, n-b 3 | 27 | B 8, l-b 4, w 1 ........... 13 |
| | **268** | **(7 wkts dec.) 316** |

## Surrey

| | | |
|---|---|---|
| J. B. Hobbs c Mann b Hearne | 24 | – c Lee b Haig ................. 10 |
| A. Sandham not out | 167 | – c and b Hearne ............... 68 |
| Mr M. Howell c Murrell b Durston | 7 | – st Murrell b Stevens ............ 25 |
| T. Shepherd c Murrell b Durston | 0 | – c Hendren b Stevens ............ 26 |
| H. A. Peach hit wkt b Stevens | 18 | – b Stevens ................... 11 |
| A. Ducat st Murrell b Lee | 49 | – lbw b Hearne ................. 7 |
| Mr P. G. H. Fender c Haig b Durston | 30 | – b Durston ................... 1 |
| W. Hitch b Durston | 1 | – b Hearne .................... 6 |
| Mr G. M. Reay c Haig b Lee | 6 | – b Hearne .................... 5 |
| H. Strudwick b Hearne | 9 | – b Stevens ................... 10 |
| T. Rushby not out | 6 | – not out .................... 7 |
| B 17, l-b 5, n-b 2 | 24 | B 11, l-b 1 .............. 12 |
| | **(9 wkts dec.) 341** | **188** |

## Surrey Bowling

| | Overs | Mdns | Runs | Wkts | Overs | Mdns | Runs | Wkts |
|---|---|---|---|---|---|---|---|---|
| Hitch ............ | 32.1 | 10 | 66 | 2 | 20 | 5 | 71 | 2 |
| Rushby .......... | 23 | 9 | 48 | 2 | 22 | 7 | 73 | 3 |
| Fender .......... | 28 | 4 | 76 | 4 | 16.5 | 2 | 70 | 1 |
| Reay ........... | 26 | 17 | 31 | 2 | 18 | 1 | 61 | 1 |
| Ducat........... | 3 | 1 | 10 | — | 3 | — | 12 | — |
| Shepherd ........ | 6 | 3 | 10 | — | 4 | — | 16 | — |

## Middlesex Bowling

| | Overs | Mdns | Runs | Wkts | Overs | Mdns | Runs | Wkts |
|---|---|---|---|---|---|---|---|---|
| Durston ......... | 30 | 9 | 97 | 4 | 14 | 1 | 42 | 1 |
| Haig ............ | 10 | 4 | 25 | — | 8 | — | 19 | 1 |
| Stevens ......... | 16 | — | 72 | 1 | 13.4 | — | 61 | 5 |
| Hearne .......... | 24 | 8 | 57 | 2 | 11 | — | 37 | 3 |
| Lee ............. | 15 | 2 | 66 | 2 | 4 | — | 17 | — |

Umpires: J. Blake and G. P. Harrison.

# MIDDLESEX v SURREY

Played at Lord's, August 27, 29, 30, 1921

As in 1920, the Championship hinged on the return match with Surrey. Middlesex entered upon the all-important fixture with a good deal in their favour, as nothing short of an actual victory would have given Surrey the honours in the competition. As things turned out Middlesex, after more than once looking to be a beaten side, gained a wonderful victory, going in to get 322 in the last innings, and actually hitting off the runs for the loss of four wickets. The match excited enormous interest, 15,945 people paying for admission on the first day, 17,663 on the second, and 14,311 on the third. Surrey won the toss, but their advantage was quickly discounted, Knight, Sandham, and Ducat being out when only 56 runs had been scored. Knight was bowled by a deadly break-back. Shepherd and Jardine made ample amends for the disastrous start and, taking infinite pains, put on 144 runs together in two hours and twenty minutes before Jardine was bowled. When he left Surrey had done very well, but two more wickets fell for 10 runs, and the innings was finished off for 269. Shepherd took out his bat for perhaps the best of all the fine innings he played last summer. The importance of the occasion made him at times unusually cautious, but he hit with splendid power, and was rarely at fault. His 128 not out included a dozen 4s. Middlesex lost one wicket before the call of time, and on Monday morning they broke down so badly that soon after the luncheon interval they were all out for 132. Surrey's bowling was excellent, Reay being at his best, and Strudwick in getting rid of Hendren brought off a wonderful catch on the leg side. Going in with a lead of 137, Surrey were in a most flattering position, and when their score stood at 115 with only two men out they looked to have the game in their hands. A startling collapse followed the dismissal of Shepherd, however, the last seven wickets going down for 69 runs. D. J. Knight was for once last season seen in his form of 1919. His innings of 74 was perfect. Haig brought about Surrey's collapse. He bowled very finely, and caught and bowled Shepherd in a wonderful way, running up the pitch and taking the ball low down with his left hand. Middlesex had rather more than a quarter of an hour's batting before stumps were drawn, and, taking no risks, Twining and Lee hit up 19 without being separated. The third day's cricket was unforgettable. A sterner fight no one could wish to see. The great point in favour of Middlesex was that they were free from anxiety as to the clock. There was always ample time in which to get the runs. Lee was out at 48, and then came the batting that won the match. Hearne joined Twining at five minutes past twelve, and not until twenty minutes past five did the second wicket fall, 277 runs being added in four hours and ten minutes of actual play. The only mistake, so far as could be seen, was a chance offered by Twining when he had made 59 to Knight in the slips. Apart from this the batting of both men was flawless. Surrey fielded untiringly, trying their hardest until at five minutes past six Hendren made the winning hit.

## Surrey

| | | | |
|---|---|---|---|
| Mr D. J. Knight b Durston | 1 | – b Durston | 74 |
| A. Sandham b Durston | 13 | – b Durston | 17 |
| A. Ducat c Hearne b Lee | 21 | – b Durston | 7 |
| T. Shepherd not out | 128 | – c and b Haig | 24 |
| Mr D. R. Jardine b Durston | 55 | – c Tanner b Lee | 8 |
| Mr M. Howell b Haig | 0 | – c Hendren b Haig | 21 |
| W. Hitch c Murrell b Durston | 0 | – b Haig | 25 |
| Mr P. G. H. Fender c Tanner b Haig | 10 | – c Murrell b Hearne | 2 |
| H. A. Peach c Murrell b Lee | 1 | – not out | 2 |
| Mr G. M. Reay b Hearne | 21 | – b Haig | 0 |
| H. Strudwick b Lee | 0 | – lbw b Haig | 0 |
| B 11, l-b 6, n-b 2 | 19 | L-b 4 | 4 |
| | **269** | | **184** |

## Middlesex

| | | | |
|---|---|---|---|
| Mr R. H. Twining b Hitch | 10 | – b Peach | 135 |
| H. W. Lee lbw b Reay | 7 | – lbw b Reay | 20 |
| Mr H. L. Dales lbw b Hitch | 18 | | |
| J. W. Hearne c Strudwick b Peach | 22 | – c Jardine b Reay | 106 |
| E. Hendren c Strudwick b Reay | 22 | – not out | 17 |
| Hon. C. N. Bruce b Reay | 0 | – b Peach | 0 |
| Mr F. T. Mann b Reay | 29 | – not out | 22 |
| Mr N. Haig lbw b Peach | 2 | | |
| H. R. Murrell b Fender | 16 | | |
| Mr A. R. Tanner b Fender | 0 | | |
| T. J. Durston not out | 0 | | |
| B 4, l-b 1, n-b 1 | 6 | B 5, l-b 6, n-b 11 | 22 |
| | **132** | | **322** |

## Middlesex Bowling

| | Overs | Mdns | Runs | Wkts | Overs | Mdns | Runs | Wkts |
|---|---|---|---|---|---|---|---|---|
| Haig | 36 | 8 | 93 | 2 | 23.2 | 4 | 62 | 5 |
| Durston | 26 | 7 | 47 | 4 | 17 | 2 | 56 | 3 |
| Tanner | 8 | 1 | 14 | — | | | | |
| Hearne | 16 | 3 | 47 | 1 | 3 | 1 | 2 | 1 |
| Lee | 15.2 | 3 | 49 | 3 | 14 | 3 | 60 | 1 |

## Surrey Bowling

| | Overs | Mdns | Runs | Wkts | Overs | Mdns | Runs | Wkts |
|---|---|---|---|---|---|---|---|---|
| Hitch | 14 | 6 | 17 | 2 | 26 | 4 | 69 | — |
| Reay | 18.4 | 3 | 44 | 4 | 27 | 6 | 77 | 2 |
| Fender | 12 | 2 | 41 | 2 | 33 | 10 | 73 | — |
| Peach | 14 | 4 | 24 | 2 | 27 | 14 | 44 | 2 |
| Jardine | | | | | 4 | — | 16 | — |
| Shepherd | | | | | 3 | — | 7 | — |
| Ducat | | | | | 11 | 3 | 14 | — |

Umpires: T. Flowers and F. Harry.

# MIDDLESEX v KENT

### Played at Lord's, August 23, 24, 25, 1922

Middlesex, returning to Lord's after an absence of two months, had to take the field against Kent without J. W. Hearne. A drawn match was made memorable by the wonderful batting of Hendren, who, with a not out innings of 277, fell only one run short of Mr Ward's record score at Lord's in 1820. Going in second wicket down with the total at 21 for two wickets, he made, during a stay of just over six hours, 277 runs out of 435. He hit thirty-seven 4s, and, so far as could be seen, his only mistake was a chance to Woolley in the slips when he had scored 118. On no other occasion during the season, perhaps, was he so much the Hendren of 1920, cutting, pulling and hooking the Kent bowling in dazzling style. While in with Hendren, Merrell had the misfortune to edge a full pitch from G. J. Bryan on to his nose and could take no further part in the match. Rain cut the second day's cricket short before half-past three, and on Friday, with an early drawing of stumps arranged for, the game ended in the quietest way. A curious incident was that on the second afternoon Collins bowled four wides in succession.

## Middlesex

| | |
|---|---|
| Mr R. H. Twining lbw b Woolley . . . . . . . . . 24 | Mr C. H. L. Skeet b Woolley . . . . . . . . . . . . 18 |
| H. W. Lee run out . . . . . . . . . . . . . . . . . . . . 1 | Mr G. O. Allen c and b Freeman . . . . . . . . . 12 |
| Mr G. T. S. Stevens c Hedges b Collins . . . . 2 | H. R. Murrell retired hurt . . . . . . . . . . . . . . 44 |
| E. Hendren not out . . . . . . . . . . . . . . . . . . . .277 | T. J. Durston c Ashdown b Hardinge . . . . . 15 |
| Mr F. T. Mann c G. J. Bryan b Hardinge . . 37 | B 9, l-b 7, w 4, n-b 5 . . . . . . . . . . 25 |
| Mr N. Haig lbw b Freeman . . . . . . . . . . . . . 1 | — |
| Mr J. L. Guise b Freeman . . . . . . . . . . . . . . 0 | 456 |

## Kent

| | |
|---|---|
| Mr J. L. Bryan c Twining b Allen . . . . . . . . . . . . . . . 58 | – not out . . . . . . . . . . . . . . . . . . . . . . 16 |
| H. T. W. Hardinge b Haig . . . . . . . . . . . . . . . . . . . . 24 | – c and b Durston . . . . . . . . . . . . . . 15 |
| J. Seymour b Stevens . . . . . . . . . . . . . . . . . . . . . . . 31 | – not out . . . . . . . . . . . . . . . . . . . . . . 4 |
| F. E. Woolley c Guise b Lee . . . . . . . . . . . . . . . . . . . 69 | |
| Mr L. P. Hedges b Stevens . . . . . . . . . . . . . . . . . . . . 23 | |
| Mr G. J. Bryan b Durston . . . . . . . . . . . . . . . . . . . . 1 | |
| J. C. Hubble b Durston . . . . . . . . . . . . . . . . . . . . . . 0 | |
| G. C. Collins b Durston . . . . . . . . . . . . . . . . . . . . . 0 | |
| W. Ashdown not out . . . . . . . . . . . . . . . . . . . . . . . 32 | |
| Mr L. H. W. Troughton c and b Haig . . . . . . . . . . . 5 | |
| A. P. Freeman b Allen . . . . . . . . . . . . . . . . . . . . . . 30 | |
| B 11, l-b 7, w 2 . . . . . . . . . . . . . . . . . . . . 20 | L-b 1, n-b 2 . . . . . . . . . . . . . 3 |
| — | — |
| 293 | 38 |

## Kent Bowling

| | Overs | Mdns | Runs | Wkts |
|---|---|---|---|---|
| Collins . . . . . . . . . . | 30 | 1 | 85 | 1 |
| G. J. Bryan . . . . . . . | 16 | 4 | 62 | — |
| Freeman . . . . . . . . . | 49 | 14 | 105 | 3 |
| Woolley . . . . . . . . . | 33 | 7 | 104 | 2 |
| Ashdown . . . . . . . . . | 15 | 2 | 58 | — |
| Hardinge . . . . . . . . . | 3.5 | — | 17 | 2 |

## Middlesex Bowling

| | Overs | Mdns | Runs | Wkts | Overs | Mdns | Runs | Wkts |
|---|---|---|---|---|---|---|---|---|
| Haig . . . . . . . . . . . . . | 32 | 9 | 83 | 2 | 8 | 3 | 12 | — |
| Durston . . . . . . . . . . | 30 | 11 | 66 | 3 | 4 | 1 | 8 | 1 |
| Stevens . . . . . . . . . . | 20 | 4 | 57 | 2 | 2 | — | 9 | — |
| Allen . . . . . . . . . . . . | 13.4 | 6 | 32 | 2 | 6 | 5 | 1 | — |
| Lee . . . . . . . . . . . . . | 8 | 1 | 35 | 1 | 1 | — | 5 | — |

Umpires: T. Flowers and H. Barrett.

# MIDDLESEX v SURREY

Played at Lord's, August 26, 28, 29, 1922

Middlesex cricket for the season ended quietly, the match with Surrey – always looked forward to with such keen interest – having to be left drawn. Before lunch on Saturday, on a pitch affected by heavy dew, the Surrey bowling was rather deadly, but after that the bat always beat the ball. Hobbs played one of his finest innings, though it is true he gave a couple of possible chances. As usual with him last season he tired after getting his hundred and became rather reckless. Middlesex were in danger on Tuesday, with five wickets down for 105, but Haig, who had played spendidly in his first innings, was quite equal to the occasion. In the course of the match 116 extras were given away.

## Middlesex

| | | | |
|---|---|---|---|
| Mr R. H. Twining b Fender | 23 | – b Lockton | 5 |
| H. W. Lee lbw b Lockton | 6 | – c Knight b Lockton | 25 |
| J. W. Hearne c Howell b Fender | 36 | – c Lockton b Fender | 10 |
| E. Hendren c Abel b Fender | 10 | – c Shepherd b Fender | 62 |
| Mr F. T. Mann c Strudwick b Lockton | 14 | – c Peach b Fender | 61 |
| Mr G. T. S. Stevens c Strudwick b Lockton | 31 | – c Lockton b Fender | 5 |
| Mr N. Haig c Howell b Fender | 85 | – b Shepherd | 41 |
| Mr J. L. Guise b Lockton | 4 | – not out | 10 |
| Mr C. H. L. Skeet c Howell b Fender | 45 | – b Fender | 22 |
| Mr G. O. Allen not out | 4 | – not out | 4 |
| T. J. Durston b Abel | 6 | | |
| B 25, l-b 10 | 35 | B 29, l-b 3, n-b 1 | 33 |
| | **299** | **(8 wkts dec.)** | **278** |

## Surrey

| | | | |
|---|---|---|---|
| J. B. Hobbs b Durston | 126 | | |
| A. Sandham b Hearne | 35 | | |
| A. Ducat c Durston b Haig | 84 | | |
| T. Shepherd c Twining b Durston | 17 | | |
| Mr P. G. H. Fender c Skeet b Durston | 25 | | |
| Mr D. J. Knight b Allen | 12 | – b Haig | 0 |
| Mr M. Howell b Allen | 5 | – not out | 12 |
| W. J. Abel not out | 8 | – not out | 29 |
| H. A. Peach not out | 8 | | |
| H. Strudwick (did not bat) | | – b Haig | 0 |
| B 34, l-b 6 | 40 | B 8 | 8 |
| | **(7 wkts dec.) 360** | | **49** |

Mr J. H. Lockton did not bat.

## Surrey Bowling

| | Overs | Mdns | Runs | Wkts | Overs | Mdns | Runs | Wkts |
|---|---|---|---|---|---|---|---|---|
| Peach | 13 | 7 | 22 | — | 9 | 4 | 12 | — |
| Lockton | 30 | 5 | 69 | 4 | 29 | 9 | 43 | 2 |
| Fender | 34 | 5 | 87 | 5 | 35 | 9 | 99 | 5 |
| Abel | 16.3 | 6 | 37 | 1 | 15 | 4 | 23 | — |
| Shepherd | 25 | 8 | 49 | — | 29 | 6 | 62 | 1 |
| Ducat | | | | | 5 | 2 | 6 | — |

## Middlesex Bowling

| | Overs | Mdns | Runs | Wkts | Overs | Mdns | Runs | Wkts |
|---|---|---|---|---|---|---|---|---|
| Durston | 27 | 5 | 81 | 3 | 5 | 2 | 13 | |
| Allen | 13 | 4 | 35 | 2 | | | | |
| Haig | 20 | 3 | 70 | 1 | 8 | 3 | 14 | 2 |
| Stevens | 21 | 3 | 59 | — | | | | |
| Hearne | 14 | 1 | 52 | 1 | | | | |
| Lee | 4 | — | 23 | — | | | | |
| Hendren | | | | | 2 | — | 14 | — |

Umpires: T. Fenwick and F. Chester.

# MIDDLESEX v YORKSHIRE

Played at Lord's, June 6, 8, 9, 1925

Brilliantly as they performed on many occasions last summer, the Yorkshiremen excelled themselves in this match, dismissing Middlesex on a good wicket for 118, hitting up 538 for the loss of six batsmen and gaining a glorious victory by an innings and 149 runs. The game was rendered especially memorable by the batting of Holmes, who, in putting together an innings of 315, not out, beat the famous 278 by William Ward, which had stood as the record score at Lord's for 105 years. Holmes' batting was superb. On Saturday, when he left off with 121 runs to his credit, he depended mainly upon cuts and skilful strokes on the leg side, but on Monday he drove splendidly on both sides of the wicket, displaying his varied resources as a batsman in a manner that compelled general admiration. Altogether, he was at the wickets for six hours and fifty minutes, giving no chance, making very few faulty strokes and hitting thirty-eight 4s, twelve 3s and twenty-one 2s. The collapse of Middlesex was due primarily to Robinson, who made the ball swing a lot and come fast off the pitch. Macaulay, too, although handicapped by an injury did fine work. Holmes and Sutcliffe had brought the Yorkshire score to 140 when the latter had to retire owing to a damaged thumb, but by the drawing of stumps the total had reached 209 with only Oldroyd out. Leyland helped Holmes to add 166. Stevens and Hearne played admirably in the Middlesex second innings.

## Middlesex

| | | |
|---|---|---|
| Mr G. T. S. Stevens c Sutcliffe b Robinson | 10 | – b Macaulay ... 65 |
| Mr H. L. Dales b Robinson | 27 | – b Macaulay ... 0 |
| J. W. Hearne b Macaulay | 1 | – b Macaulay ... 91 |
| E. Hendren lbw b Robinson | 15 | – c Robinson b Macaulay ... 7 |
| Hon. C. N. Bruce b Robinson | 25 | – not out ... 42 |
| Mr G. O. Allen c Kilner b Macaulay | 7 | – c and b Kilner ... 2 |
| Mr F. T. Mann b Robinson | 5 | – c sub. b Robinson ... 7 |
| Mr N. Haig b Macaulay | 5 | – b Waddington ... 32 |
| H. W. Lee c Macaulay b Waddington | 5 | – b Kilner ... 0 |
| H. R. Murrell not out | 8 | – b Robinson ... 4 |
| T. J. Durston c Robinson b Waddington | 2 | – lbw b Robinson ... 4 |
| B 5, l-b 1, w 1, n-b 1 | 8 | B 11, l-b 2, n-b 4 ... 17 |

|  |  |
|---|---|
| 118 | 271 |

## Yorkshire

| | |
|---|---|
| P. Holmes not out | 315 |
| H. Sutcliffe c Murrell b Stevens | 58 |
| E. Oldroyd b Allen | 8 |
| M. Leyland c Mann b Haig | 61 |
| W. Rhodes c Murrell b Durston | 0 |
| R. Kilner c Hendren b Stevens | 37 |
| E. Robinson c Murrell b Allen | 6 |
| G. G. Macaulay not out | 21 |
| B 19, l-b 7, w 1, n-b 5 | 32 |
| (6 wkts dec.) | 538 |

A. Waddington, Maj. A. W. Lupton and A. Dolphin did not bat.

## Yorkshire Bowling

| | Overs | Mdns | Runs | Wkts | Overs | Mdns | Runs | Wkts |
|---|---|---|---|---|---|---|---|---|
| Robinson | 27 | 6 | 52 | 5 | 21 | 1 | 64 | 3 |
| Macaulay | 24 | 7 | 54 | 3 | 27 | 3 | 94 | 4 |
| Waddington | 2.5 | — | 4 | 2 | 11 | 2 | 33 | 1 |
| Kilner | | | | | 33 | 15 | 56 | 2 |
| Rhodes | | | | | 5 | 1 | 7 | — |

**Middlesex Bowling**

|         | Overs | Mdns | Runs | Wkts |
|---------|-------|------|------|------|
| Haig    | 43    | 11   | 93   | 1    |
| Durston | 30    | 6    | 97   | 1    |
| Allen   | 23    | 2    | 106  | 2    |
| Stevens | 26    | 3    | 89   | 2    |
| Hearne  | 31    | 3    | 100  | —    |
| Lee     | 2     | —    | 21   | —    |

Umpires: F. Chester and J. A. Cuffe.

## MIDDLESEX v SURREY

### Played at Lord's, August 28, 30, 31, 1926

Hobbs seized upon this occasion to make what was at once the highest score of his wonderful career, and the highest ever made at Lord's, beating his own 266, not out, for Players against Gentlemen at Scarborough in 1925, and Holmes' 315, not out, for Yorkshire against Middlesex – also put together in the previous summer. The great batsman, who obtained his runs mainly on the on side, placed the ball with marvellous skill and did not appear to give a chance. He was at the wickets six hours and fifty-five minutes, scoring forty-one 4s, six 3s, twenty 2s, and ninety-four singles. Sandham helped to raise the total to 115 – the two Surrey men's thirty-sixth three-figure first wicket stand. Ducat shared in the partnership of 101, and Jardine in one of 270. Hendren, in the first innings of Middlesex, withstood the Surrey attack for three hours and a half, and put together his seventh hundred of the season, but the home side had to follow on 304 in arrear, and Surrey, fielding brilliantly, won the match by an innings and 63 runs.

### Surrey

| | |
|---|---|
| J. B. Hobbs not out .................316 | Mr A. Jeacocke run out ............... 26 |
| A. Sandham c Hendren b Haig .......... 58 | Mr P. G. H. Fender not out ............ 1 |
| A. Ducat b Durston ................... 41 | B 12, l-b 7.................. 19 |
| T. Shepherd c and b Stevens ........... 15 | — |
| Mr D. R. Jardine c and b Powell ........103 | (5 wkts dec.) 579 |

Mr E. R. T. Holmes, H. A. Peach, H. Strudwick and S. Fenley did not bat.

### Middlesex

| | | | |
|---|---|---|---|
| Mr G. T. S. Stevens c Strudwick b Holmes ........ | 2 | – c Fender b Peach .............. | 63 |
| Mr H. L. Dales b Jardine ...................... | 52 | – c Fender b Holmes ........... | 4 |
| Mr G. O. Allen c Shepherd b Peach ............. | 21 | – c Jardine b Fenley ........... | 17 |
| E. Hendren not out ...........................| 101 | – c Fenley b Jardine ............ | 37 |
| Mr H. J. Enthoven run out .................... | 1 | – b Fenley .................... | 5 |
| Mr F. T. Mann c Peach b Jardine .............. | 3 | – not out .................... | 37 |
| Mr N. Haig c Strudwick b Fender .............. | 12 | – c Shepherd b Fender ......... | 18 |
| H. W. Lee run out ........................... | 42 | – c Strudwick b Holmes ......... | 31 |
| H. R. Murrell c Peach b Fenley ............... | 20 | – c Fenley b Peach ............ | 7 |
| T. J. Durston b Fender ...................... | 0 | – b Holmes ................... | 1 |
| J. A. Powell c and b Fender ................. | 0 | – c Strudwick b Holmes ......... | 4 |
| B 15, l-b 6 ........................ | 21 | B 11, l-b 3, w 2, n-b 1 ...... | 17 |
| | 275 | | 241 |

**Middlesex Bowling**

|            | Overs | Mdns | Runs | Wkts |
|------------|-------|------|------|------|
| Haig ............. | 37 | 7 | 118 | 1 |
| Durston .......... | 31 | 12 | 69 | 1 |
| Allen ............ | 19 | 3 | 88 | — |
| Stevens .......... | 22.3 | 1 | 95 | 1 |
| Lee .............. | 8 | 1 | 44 | — |
| Powell ........... | 27 | 4 | 109 | 1 |
| Enthoven ........ | 10 | 1 | 37 | — |

**Surrey Bowling**

|            | Overs | Mdns | Runs | Wkts | Overs | Mdns | Runs | Wkts |
|------------|-------|------|------|------|-------|------|------|------|
| Holmes ......... | 14 | 2 | 41 | 1 | 15.4 | 2 | 49 | 4 |
| Peach ........... | 18 | 7 | 26 | 1 | 23 | 5 | 41 | 2 |
| Fenley .......... | 24 | 4 | 76 | 1 | 23 | 4 | 66 | 2 |
| Fender .......... | 23 | 5 | 76 | 3 | 14 | 2 | 38 | 1 |
| Shepherd ........ | 9 | 5 | 22 | — | 8 | 3 | 12 | — |
| Jardine .......... | 8 | 2 | 13 | 2 | 6 | 1 | 18 | 1 |

Umpires: R. D. Burrows and H. Chidgey.

# MIDDLESEX v SURREY

## Played at Lord's, August 27, 29, 30, 1927

Wonderful bowling by Fender was the big factor in a Surrey victory by five wickets. Fender, hitting the stumps six times and getting J. A. Powell leg before, took seven wickets for 10 runs. He obtained the last six in the course of eleven balls, with only one run scored off him meanwhile, and the first five of these six in seven balls without a run. Twice in his fifth over he secured two wickets with following balls. On the same day Hearne took eight Surrey wickets for 39 runs, but Sandham defended skilfully for two hours, and Fender hit with fine judgment. Hearne on Monday played a masterly innings, withstanding the Surrey bowling for five hours and three quarters and giving no chance. Seven wickets were down for 199, but Durston helped Hearne to add 99, Mann, declaring on Monday, sent Surrey in for ten minutes but to no purpose and next day Hobbs and Sandham, raising the score to 116 – their forty-first three-figure partnership – practically ensured Surrey's success.

## Middlesex

| | | | |
|---|---|---|---|
| Mr. N. Haig b Allom ........................ | 8 | – c Shepherd b Geary ............. | 11 |
| H. W. Lee lbw b Geary ....................... | 0 | – c Ducat b Shepherd ............. | 20 |
| J. W. Hearne c Peach b Geary .................. | 0 | – not out ...................... | 167 |
| E. Hendren b Fender ........................ | 22 | – c Fender b Holmes .............. | 46 |
| Mr H. J. Enthoven b Fender ................. | 16 | – lbw b Holmes.................. | 0 |
| Mr F. T. Mann b Fender ..................... | 5 | – b Fender .................... | 7 |
| Mr W. H. F. K. Horton b Fender ................ | 0 | – b Fender .................... | 8 |
| Mr A. P. Powell b Fender .................... | 0 | – c Strudwick b Fender ........... | 0 |
| T. J. Durston b Fender ...................... | 0 | – c Knight b Shepherd ........... | 37 |
| J. A. Powell lbw b Fender ................... | 0 | – lbw b Fender ................. | 0 |
| W. F. Price not out ......................... | 1 | – not out ..................... | 1 |
| B 2 ........................... | 2 | B 20, l-b 5 .............. | 25 |
| | **54** | | **(9 wkts dec.) 322** |

## Surrey

| | | | |
|---|---|---|---|
| J. B. Hobbs b Haig | 11 | – b Durston | 54 |
| A. Sandham lbw b Hearne | 39 | – c A. P. Powell b Durston | 55 |
| A. Ducat b Hearne | 4 | – c Durston b Hearne | 51 |
| T. Shepherd b Hearne | 11 | – b J. A. Powell | 8 |
| Mr D. J. Knight lbw b Hearne | 4 | – lbw b J. A. Powell | 17 |
| Mr P. G. H. Fender c Price b Haig | 42 | – not out | 20 |
| Mr E. R. T. Holmes st Price b Hearne | 4 | – not out | 11 |
| H. A. Peach b Hearne | 6 | | |
| A. Geary b Hearne | 4 | | |
| H. Strudwick not out | 13 | | |
| Mr M. J. C. Allom b Hearne | 0 | | |
| B 6, l-b 5 | 11 | B 9, l-b 2, n-b 2 | 13 |
| | **149** | | **229** |

## Surrey Bowling

| | Overs | Mdns | Runs | Wkts | Overs | Mdns | Runs | Wkts |
|---|---|---|---|---|---|---|---|---|
| Allom | 12 | 6 | 18 | 1 | | | | |
| Geary | 11 | 7 | 10 | 2 | 24 | 3 | 62 | 1 |
| Peach | 5 | 2 | 14 | — | 35 | 11 | 61 | — |
| Fender | 5.3 | 2 | 10 | 7 | 44 | 14 | 71 | 4 |
| Holmes | | | | | 22 | 8 | 35 | 2 |
| Shepherd | | | | | 39 | 9 | 68 | 2 |

## Middlesex Bowling

| | Overs | Mdns | Runs | Wkts | Overs | Mdns | Runs | Wkts |
|---|---|---|---|---|---|---|---|---|
| Haig | 23 | 9 | 42 | 2 | 19 | 7 | 49 | — |
| Durston | 8 | 3 | 12 | — | 19 | 3 | 59 | 2 |
| Hearne | 26.2 | 8 | 39 | 8 | 11 | 2 | 35 | 1 |
| Enthoven | 4 | — | 16 | — | 9 | 1 | 22 | — |
| J. A. Powell | 8 | 1 | 29 | — | 13.1 | 1 | 51 | 2 |

Umpires: J. Stone and D. Denton.

# MIDDLESEX v SUSSEX

Played at Lord's, June 7, 9, 10, 1930

A match, rendered memorable through a batsman on each side scoring two separate hundreds, was left drawn, Sussex, after Middlesex had declared, being within 72 of victory when thirty-five minutes before time the game, owing to bad light, was abandoned. Duleepsinhji not only played delightful cricket for 116 but in the second innings, after two wickets had fallen for 17 runs, helped to add 169 in two hours. Enthoven on Saturday batted eighty minutes for 21 and then, with the last man in, hit up 102 out of 107 in seventy-five minutes. His 115, if not marked by such contrasts, was a faultless display.

## Middlesex

| | | | |
|---|---|---|---|
| Mr N. Haig b Tate | 17 | – c J. Parks b Wensley | 21 |
| Mr G. T. S. Stevens lbw b Tate | 18 | – b Tate | 1 |
| J. W. Hearne c Cornford b Cook | 20 | – not out | 12 |
| E. Hendren c Duleepsinhji b Tate | 49 | – b Wensley | 14 |
| H. W. Lee c Duleepsinhji b Tate | 48 | – c Cook b Tate | 21 |
| Mr G. O. Allen c J. Parks b Tate | 11 | – b Bowley | 1 |
| Mr H. J. Enthoven c Duleepsinhji b Bowley | 123 | – c Duleepsinhji b Langridge | 115 |
| Mr R. W. V. Robins lbw b Tate | 2 | – not out | 51 |
| Mr G. C. Newman lbw b Wensley | 17 | – c Cornford b Langridge | 24 |
| E. G. Canning c Cornford b Wensley | 8 | | |
| W. F. Price not out | 3 | | |
| B 5, l-b 4, w 1, n-b 1 | 11 | B 12, l-b 10, w 2 | 24 |
| | **327** | **(7 wkts dec.)** | **284** |

## Sussex

| | | | |
|---|---|---|---|
| Mr A. H. H. Gilligan c Canning b Stevens | 37 | – c Hendren b Allen | 4 |
| E. H. Bowley c Stevens b Allen | 23 | – c Robins b Allen | 0 |
| K. S. Duleepsinhji st Price b Lee | 116 | – not out | 102 |
| T. Cook lbw b Stevens | 0 | – not out | 62 |
| James Langridge lbw b Allen | 18 | | |
| J. Parks run out | 6 | | |
| M. W. Tate b Robins | 18 | | |
| H. Parks b Stevens | 47 | | |
| A. F. Wensley not out | 59 | | |
| R. A. Hollingdale lbw b Hearne | 5 | | |
| W. Cornford b Allen | 3 | | |
| B 8, l-b 12, w 1, n-b 1 | 22 | | |
| | **354** | | **186** |

### Sussex Bowling

| | Overs | Mdns | Runs | Wkts | Overs | Mdns | Runs | Wkts |
|---|---|---|---|---|---|---|---|---|
| Tate | 44 | 15 | 92 | 6 | 26 | 5 | 60 | 2 |
| Wensley | 29 | 5 | 72 | 2 | 25 | 5 | 69 | 2 |
| J. Parks | 8 | 3 | 28 | — | | | | |
| Hollingdale | 9 | 3 | 25 | — | 12 | 3 | 27 | — |
| Cook | 16 | 2 | 49 | 1 | 7 | 1 | 14 | — |
| Langridge | 7 | 1 | 22 | — | 21 | 4 | 55 | 2 |
| Bowley | 5.4 | — | 28 | 1 | 8 | — | 35 | 1 |

### Middlesex Bowling

| | Overs | Mdns | Runs | Wkts | Overs | Mdns | Runs | Wkts |
|---|---|---|---|---|---|---|---|---|
| Allen | 26.5 | 3 | 90 | 3 | 14 | 2 | 41 | 2 |
| Haig | 22 | 3 | 52 | — | 15 | 3 | 51 | — |
| Robins | 23 | 2 | 83 | 1 | 7 | 1 | 36 | — |
| Stevens | 21 | 2 | 72 | 3 | 7 | — | 26 | — |
| Lee | 5 | 1 | 16 | 1 | 3 | 1 | 5 | — |
| Hearne | 6 | — | 19 | 1 | | | | |
| Enthoven | | | | | 4 | 1 | 9 | — |

Umpires: W. R. Parry and A. Nash.

## MIDDLESEX v KENT

### Played at Lord's, August 22, 24, 25, 1931

Kent concluded their championship programme in brilliant style, declaring with five wickets down and beating Middlesex by 200 runs. In accomplishing this fine performance they were enormously indebted to Ashdown and Freeman. Ashdown, who during the season had not previously put together a three-figure score, seized upon the occasion to register two separate hundreds. On Saturday he made 121 out of 254 in rather more than three hours, and in the second innings 103 out of 167 in two hours and a quarter. He hit all round the wicket and, despite the pace at which he obtained his runs, gave no absolute chance. Freeman, scarcely ever dropping the ball short and varying his spin cleverly, took thirteen wickets for just under 12 runs each. On Saturday when the start was delayed an hour Ashdown and Woolley put on 155 in ninety-five minutes. After Ashdown left eight wickets fell for 92 runs. Hendren played a great game for Middlesex who, when going in with 343 to get, lost seven wickets for 63.

### Kent

| | | | |
|---|---|---|---|
| H. T. W. Hardinge lbw b Durston | 50 | – b Hearne | 19 |
| W. Ashdown c Hendren b Stevens | 121 | – b Hearne | 103 |
| F. E. Woolley b Stevens | 74 | – lbw b Stevens | 1 |
| L. Ames lbw b Durston | 1 | – lbw b Durston | 34 |
| Mr A. P. F. Chapman c Haig b Durston | 14 | – not out | 15 |
| Mr B. H. Valentine c Peebles b Stevens | 2 | – lbw b Durston | 0 |
| Mr J. L. Bryan c Durston b Peebles | 25 | – not out | 16 |
| C. Fairservice st Price b Durston | 3 | | |
| L. Todd b Peebles | 26 | | |
| A. P. Freeman lbw b Peebles | 2 | | |
| Mr C. S. Marriott not out | 8 | | |
| B 15, l-b 5 | 20 | B 10, l-b 2 | 12 |
| | **346** | **(5 wkts dec.)** | **200** |

### Middlesex

| | | | |
|---|---|---|---|
| Mr G. T. S. Stevens st Ames b Freeman | 0 | – lbw b Marriott | 6 |
| J. W. Hearne c Ashdown b Freeman | 18 | – c Ashdown b Freeman | 7 |
| H. W. Lee st Ames b Freeman | 7 | – b Marriott | 3 |
| E. Hendren c Ashdown b Hardinge | 82 | – st Ames b Freeman | 69 |
| Mr J. L. Guise c and b Freeman | 40 | – lbw b Freeman | 7 |
| Mr N. Haig c Bryan b Freeman | 32 | – lbw b Marriott | 7 |
| Mr F. T. Mann b Freeman | 2 | – b Freeman | 1 |
| Mr D. F. Surfleet lbw b Marriott | 0 | – b Freeman | 0 |
| T. J. Durston c and b Freeman | 6 | – b Ashdown | 12 |
| W. F. Price c Ames b Marriott | 2 | – b Freeman | 13 |
| Mr I. A. R. Peebles not out | 4 | – not out | 1 |
| B 6, l-b 5 | 11 | B 11, l-b 5 | 16 |
| | **204** | | **142** |

### Middlesex Bowling

| | Overs | Mdns | Runs | Wkts | Overs | Mdns | Runs | Wkts |
|---|---|---|---|---|---|---|---|---|
| Durston | 34 | 6 | 82 | 4 | 15 | 3 | 30 | 2 |
| Haig | 10 | 3 | 28 | — | 10 | — | 28 | — |
| Stevens | 29 | 8 | 84 | 3 | 15 | 2 | 49 | 1 |
| Peebles | 19 | 1 | 56 | 3 | 5 | — | 23 | — |
| Hearne | 18 | 4 | 40 | — | 15 | 4 | 52 | 2 |
| Lee | 9 | — | 36 | — | 1 | — | 6 | — |

**Kent Bowling**

| | Overs | Mdns | Runs | Wkts | Overs | Mdns | Runs | Wkts |
|---|---|---|---|---|---|---|---|---|
| Ashdown ........ | 3 | — | 8 | — | 7 | 3 | 19 | 1 |
| Freeman ........ | 41 | 6 | 88 | 7 | 32.1 | 10 | 66 | 6 |
| Marriott ......... | 33.1 | 8 | 81 | 2 | 25 | 7 | 41 | 3 |
| Hardinge ........ | 5 | 2 | 16 | 1 | | | | |

Umpires: R. D. Burrows and J. H. King.

# MIDDLESEX v GLAMORGAN

## Played at Lord's, May 9, 11, 12, 1931

Making their first appearance at Lord's as competitors in the county championship, Glamorgan showed poor form and Middlesex, declaring with only two wickets down in their second innings, won by 135 runs. Hearne, batting with all his well-known skill and judgment, seized upon the occasion to put together for the first time in his career two separate hundreds. On Saturday, he and Lee made 211 for the first Middlesex wicket. He scored chiefly on the leg side. Middlesex on Saturday had 299 on the board with only three men out when Clay, on being tried for the fifth time, dismissed five batsmen in nine overs for 18 runs. Bates and Dyson made 85 for Glamorgan's opening partnership on Monday and 109 for that of Tuesday, but most of their colleagues shaped indifferently against Peebles who secured eleven wickets for less than 12 runs each.

### Middlesex

| | | | | |
|---|---|---|---|---|
| H. W. Lee b Clay ............................ | 107 | – c Every b Ryan ............... | 21 |
| J. W. Hearne c D. Davies b Clay ............. | 104 | – not out ...................... | 101 |
| E. Hendren c and b Clay .................... | 49 | – c Mercer b D. Davies .......... | 43 |
| J. Hulme c Dyson b Bates .................... | 25 | – not out ...................... | 26 |
| Mr G. C. Newman c and b Mercer ............. | 9 | | |
| Mr N. M. McCaskie b Mercer ................. | 4 | | |
| A. Howard b Clay .......................... | 9 | | |
| T. J. Durston c Ryan b Clay .................. | 13 | | |
| W. F. Price c Hills b Clay ................... | 0 | | |
| Mr I. A. R. Peebles c E. Davies b Clay ........... | 1 | | |
| R. Beveridge not out ......................... | 1 | | |
| B 7, l-b 7, w 1 ...................... | 15 | B 7, l-b 4 .............. | 11 |
| | 337 | (2 wkts dec.) | 202 |

### Glamorgan

| | | | | |
|---|---|---|---|---|
| W. E. Bates st Price b Hearne .................. | 50 | – c Howard b Lee ............... | 70 |
| A. H. Dyson c Newman b Peebles .............. | 34 | – lbw b Peebles ................ | 35 |
| Mr M. J. Turnbull b Peebles .................. | 1 | – c Price b Peebles ............. | 36 |
| J. T. Bell b Peebles ......................... | 0 | – b Beveridge ................. | 35 |
| J. Hills b Peebles ......................... | 24 | – b Durston ................... | 2 |
| D. Davies c Hearne b Peebles ................. | 1 | – c Howard b Hearne ........... | 8 |
| G. Every b Peebles ......................... | 7 | – not out .................... | 20 |
| E. Davies not out .......................... | 27 | – b Hearne ................... | 4 |
| Mr J. C. Clay lbw b Peebles .................. | 4 | – absent hurt .................. | 0 |
| J. Mercer c Beveridge b Hearne ............... | 24 | – b Peebles .................. | 12 |
| F. Ryan c Price b Hearne .................... | 0 | – c and b Peebles ............. | 0 |
| B 1, l-b 2, w 1 ...................... | 4 | B 3, l-b 2, w 1 ........... | 6 |
| | 176 | | 228 |

## Glamorgan Bowling

| | Overs | Mdns | Runs | Wkts | Overs | Mdns | Runs | Wkts |
|---|---|---|---|---|---|---|---|---|
| Mercer . . . . . . . . . . | 38 | 9 | 75 | 2 | 13 | 1 | 40 | — |
| D. Davies . . . . . . . . | 15 | 2 | 39 | — | 18 | 5 | 32 | 1 |
| Clay . . . . . . . . . . . . | 30.5 | 2 | 90 | 7 | 13 | 1 | 29 | — |
| Ryan . . . . . . . . . . . | 15 | 1 | 62 | — | 14 | 1 | 39 | 1 |
| Bates . . . . . . . . . . | 8 | — | 42 | 1 | 7 | 2 | 27 | — |
| E. Davies . . . . . . . . | 9 | 2 | 14 | — | 6 | — | 14 | — |
| Turnbull . . . . . . . . . | | | | | 2 | — | 10 | — |

## Middlesex Bowling

| | Overs | Mdns | Runs | Wkts | Overs | Mdns | Runs | Wkts |
|---|---|---|---|---|---|---|---|---|
| Durston . . . . . . . . . | 9 | 2 | 33 | — | 13 | 1 | 38 | 1 |
| Hulme . . . . . . . . . . | 2 | — | 9 | — | 6 | 1 | 24 | — |
| Peebles . . . . . . . . . | 29 | 8 | 58 | 7 | 27.2 | 5 | 72 | 4 |
| Hearne . . . . . . . . . . | 27.5 | 3 | 62 | 3 | 13 | 2 | 33 | 2 |
| Beveridge . . . . . . . . | 5 | 2 | 10 | — | 6 | 4 | 17 | 1 |
| Lee . . . . . . . . . . . . . | | | | | 14 | 2 | 38 | 1 |

Umpires: L. C. Braund and A. E. Street.

# MIDDLESEX v NOTTINGHAMSHIRE

### Played at Lord's, May 28, 30, 31, 1932

The Saturday, which should have seen the opening of this match, proved to be the twelfth day since the opening of the season when cricket was impossible at Lord's. The weather showed little improvement on Monday, the light, always uncertain, turning so poor that the umpires stopped play before one o'clock and rain, which set in soon afterwards, destroying any further progress with the game that day. Limited as it was to about eighty-five minutes the play proved full of incident. Haig winning the toss, sent Nottinghamshire in to bat and, although the score reached 30 before the second wicket fell, there were seven men out for 37. Then came some spirited batting by Larwood who, with two 6s among his strokes, made 32 out of 49 in twenty-five minutes before the umpires stopped play. Next morning came the extraordinary announcement that Carr had declared at Monday's score of 86 for seven wickets. What purpose he considered would be served by taking such a course it is impossible to understand. Lee and Stevens putting on 37 and the latter in company with Hearne adding 64 more, the Nottinghamshire total was passed with nine wickets in hand. Both Stevens and Hearne lost their wickets in endeavours to force the game while Robins hit up 34 out of 48 in eighteen minutes. After Hearne left six wickets fell for 25 runs. Entering upon their second innings 100 runs in arrear, Nottinghamshire lost Keeting and Walker for 35 but Arthur Staples batted vigorously and Harris defended soundly for more than two hours.

### Nottinghamshire

| | | | | |
|---|---|---|---|---|
| W. W. Keeton c Durston b Haig | 9 | – st Price b Robins | 15 |
| J. Hardstaff lbw b Haig | 7 | | |
| W. Walker c Robins b Durston | 8 | – lbw b Robins | 7 |
| Mr A. W. Carr b Durston | 0 | – c Hearne b Robins | 14 |
| A. Staples run out | 4 | – c Robins b Haig | 27 |
| G. V. Gunn c Robins b Durston | 0 | – not out | 4 |
| C. B. Harris not out | 14 | – not out | 33 |
| B. Lilley lbw b Stevens | 0 | | |
| H. Larwood not out | 32 | | |
| B 7, l-b 4, w 1 | 12 | B 5, l-b 3, n-b 1 | 9 |

(7 wkts dec.) 86                    109

W. Voce and S. J. Staples did not bat.

### Middlesex

| | | | |
|---|---|---|---|
| Mr G. T. S. Stevens c Walker b Voce | 56 | W. F. Price c and b S. J. Staples | 0 |
| H. W. Lee b S. J. Staples | 25 | Mr I. A. R. Peebles c Hardstaff | |
| J. W. Hearne c and b Voce | 39 | b S. J. Staples | 4 |
| Mr R. W. V. Robins b S. J. Staples | 34 | Mr H. J. Enthoven absent ill | 0 |
| J. Hulme c Larwood b S. J. Staples | 6 | | |
| Mr N. Haig c Lilley b A. Staples | 11 | L-b 5, n-b 2 | 7 |
| T. J. Durston run out | 3 | | |
| J. Sims not out | 1 | | 186 |

### Middlesex Bowling

| | Overs | Mdns | Runs | Wkts | Overs | Mdns | Runs | Wkts |
|---|---|---|---|---|---|---|---|---|
| Durston | 14 | 6 | 22 | 3 | 15 | 4 | 19 | — |
| Haig | 6 | 2 | 13 | 2 | 6 | 2 | 6 | 1 |
| Stevens | 6 | 3 | 21 | 1 | 4 | — | 20 | — |
| Robins | 3 | — | 12 | — | 15 | 3 | 32 | 3 |
| Peebles | 1 | — | 6 | — | 10 | 2 | 16 | — |
| Hearne | | | | | 9 | 4 | 7 | — |

### Nottinghamshire Bowling

| | Overs | Mdns | Runs | Wkts |
|---|---|---|---|---|
| S. J. Staples | 36 | 6 | 86 | 5 |
| Voce | 27 | 7 | 75 | 2 |
| A. Staples | 8 | 1 | 18 | 1 |

Umpires: W. Reeves and F. Chester.

## MIDDLESEX IN 1933

In view of the great traditions of Middlesex cricket, it is a little disturbing to note their inability at the present time to command the services of players who could, in normal circumstances, enable the team seriously to challenge their most powerful opponents. Like most other counties, Middlesex have been hard hit because their leading amateurs cannot devote as much time to the game as did their predecessors during the palmy days of the county. The news that a strong effort is to be made to bring club cricket in the county more closely to the attention of the authorities is therefore indeed welcome. High hopes are entertained of the success of this scheme, which may result in the discovery of outstanding talent among the numerous cricketers participating in a less distinguished sphere of the game.

# MIDDLESEX v HAMPSHIRE

### Played at Lord's, May 10, 11, 12, 1933

Middlesex won a remarkable game by two wickets. Hampshire occupied practically all Wednesday over their first innings. Mead batting steadily while Creese gave a dashing display. A stand of 90 by Hendren and Hulme enabled Middlesex to recover from a poor start, and when by the close on Thursday Hampshire had increased a first-innings' lead of 31 to 54 with nine wickets standing, a draw appeared likely. Sunshine following rain, however, seventeen wickets fell for an aggregate of 185 runs. Robins, taking seven wickets for just over five runs each, did most to finish off Hampshire's innings for a further 65. Set to get 120, Middlesex lost four men for 37 and then occurred an incident that had a big influence on the result. Enthoven, before scoring, was run out, but following a consultation between the umpires, was allowed to stay because Boyes, the bowler, had unintentionally obstructed him. Enthoven and Hulme put on 60, placing their side on the road to success, though the issue remained in doubt to the very end. No fewer than fourteen batsmen were out leg-before-wicket.

## Hampshire

| | | | |
|---|---|---|---|
| G. Brown st Price b Robins | 27 | – b Robins | 17 |
| J. Arnold c Hart b Durston | 14 | – st Price b Enthoven | 3 |
| J. Bailey lbw b Hearne | 45 | – lbw b Durston | 8 |
| C. P. Mead b Durston | 70 | – c and b Robins | 2 |
| A. Kennedy lbw b Peebles | 17 | – hit wkt b Robins | 24 |
| A. E. Pothecary b Robins | 9 | – c Hulme b Robins | 2 |
| Mr A. K. Judd b Peebles | 3 | – lbw b Durston | 0 |
| W. L. Creese b Hearne | 48 | – c Hulme b Robins | 6 |
| N. McCorkell c Durston b Hearne | 0 | – lbw b Robins | 2 |
| G. S. Boyes c Hendren b Durston | 12 | – not out | 1 |
| O. W. Herman not out | 0 | – b Robins | 14 |
| B 12, l-b 4 | 16 | B 4, l-b 5 | 9 |
| | **261** | | **88** |

## Middlesex

| | | | |
|---|---|---|---|
| H. W. Lee c Arnold b Herman | 14 | – c Mead b Boyes | 2 |
| J. Sims b Kennedy | 2 | – lbw b Boyes | 24 |
| J. W. Hearne lbw b Kennedy | 3 | – lbw b Kennedy | 8 |
| E. Hendren lbw b Brown | 76 | – lbw b Kennedy | 3 |
| J. Hulme lbw b Boyes | 60 | – lbw b Boyes | 39 |
| Mr H. J. Enthoven lbw b Boyes | 8 | – b Bailey | 18 |
| Mr R. W. V. Robins run out | 21 | – run out | 0 |
| G. E. Hart b Brown | 16 | – not out | 14 |
| T. J. Durston c Arnold b Brown | 18 | – b Boyes | 1 |
| W. F. Price lbw b Kennedy | 0 | – not out | 7 |
| Mr I. A. R. Peebles not out | 1 | | |
| B 5, l-b 6 | 11 | B 2, l-b 1, n-b 1 | 4 |
| | **230** | | **120** |

## Middlesex Bowling

| | Overs | Mdns | Runs | Wkts | Overs | Mdns | Runs | Wkts |
|---|---|---|---|---|---|---|---|---|
| Durston | 42.3 | 16 | 82 | 3 | 25 | 13 | 33 | 2 |
| Peebles | 31 | 13 | 59 | 2 | | | | |
| Robins | 23 | 2 | 56 | 2 | 18.2 | 4 | 36 | 7 |
| Hearne | 27 | 6 | 48 | 3 | | | | |
| Enthoven | | | | | 6 | 1 | 10 | 1 |

**Hampshire Bowling**

| | Overs | Mdns | Runs | Wkts | Overs | Mdns | Runs | Wkts |
|---|---|---|---|---|---|---|---|---|
| Kennedy ......... | 24.4 | 7 | 55 | 3 | 25 | 8 | 36 | 2 |
| Herman .......... | 18 | 6 | 55 | 1 | 2 | 1 | 4 | — |
| Boyes ............ | 28 | 8 | 67 | 2 | 28 | 11 | 57 | 4 |
| Bailey ............ | 5 | — | 21 | — | 6.4 | 1 | 19 | 1 |
| Brown .......... | 5 | — | 21 | 3 | | | | |

Umpires: W. Reeves and F. Walden.

## MIDDLESEX v SOMERSET

### Played at Lord's, June 14, 15, 16, 1933

Enthoven's policy in giving Somerset first innings turned out satisfactorily and Middlesex won the match by eight wickets. From the start bowlers made the ball rise and turn from a pitch drying under hot sunshine, but batsmen fared unexpectely well until the third morning. Then from turf that had become hard, but was softened on the surface by more rain, the Middlesex bowling flew about in disconcerting fashion. Except when Longrigg and Young put on 50 for the fifth wicket, the batsmen offered little resistance. Somerset were unlucky to play their second innings under such difficult conditions and the absence of Hazell, the slow left-handed bowler, owing to the death of his father, handicapped them, especially in the field. Among some remarkable incidents was a right-handed catch by which Robins, at short-leg dismissed Young. Frank Lee and Luckes were both struck in the face by the ball going off the bat.

### Somerset

| | | | |
|---|---|---|---|
| J. W. Lee c Taylor b Durston .................. | 0 | – b Durston ................... | 1 |
| F. S. Lee lbw b Robins ....................... | 18 | – b Robins ..................... | 17 |
| Mr C. C. Case c Taylor b Hearne .............. | 55 | – c Price b Durston .............. | 1 |
| Mr E. F. Longrigg b Hearne ................. | 30 | – b Hearne ................... | 20 |
| A. Young lbw b Robins ...................... | 16 | – c Robins b Hearne ............. | 43 |
| Mr R. A. Ingle lbw b Robins ................. | 36 | – b Sims ..................... | 0 |
| Mr H. D. Burrough b Durston ................ | 12 | – not out .................... | 3 |
| A. W. Wellard c Price b Robins ............. | 41 | – c Hearne b Sims ............... | 1 |
| W. T. Luckes retired hurt ................... | 11 | – c Durston b Taylor ........... | 2 |
| Mr R. C. Robertson-Glasgow st Price b Robins .... | 4 | – lbw b Sims ................... | 1 |
| H. L. Hazell not out ......................... | 0 | – absent ...................... | 0 |
| B 23, l-b 7 ......................... | 30 | B 4, l-b 1 .............. | 5 |
| | 253 | | 94 |

### Middlesex

| | | | |
|---|---|---|---|
| H. W. Lee c F. S. Lee b J. W. Lee .............. | 82 | – run out ...................... | 14 |
| W. F. Price b Robertson-Glasgow .............. | 8 | – c and b Robertson-Glasgow ...... | 5 |
| J. W. Hearne c Luckes b Robertson-Glasgow ...... | 8 | | |
| E. Hendren b J. W. Lee ...................... | 4 | | |
| Mr R. W. V. Robins c Young b J. W. Lee ......... | 1 | | |
| J. Hulme c Ingle b Wellard ................... | 4 | – not out ..................... | 23 |
| Mr H. J. Enthoven c Burrough b Wellard ......... | 38 | | |
| J. Sims c Young b J. W. Lee ................... | 24 | – not out ..................... | 38 |
| G. E. Hart not out ........................ | 49 | | |
| T. J. Durston lbw b J. W. Lee.................. | 30 | | |
| Mr H. Taylor b Robertson-Glasgow ............. | 4 | | |
| B 3, l-b 8, w 2, n-b 1 ................. | 14 | L-b 1, n-b 1 ............. | 2 |
| | 266 | | 82 |

## Middlesex Bowling

| | Overs | Mdns | Runs | Wkts | Overs | Mdns | Runs | Wkts |
|---|---|---|---|---|---|---|---|---|
| Durston .......... | 29 | 8 | 57 | 2 | 16 | 11 | 15 | 2 |
| Taylor ........... | 7 | 3 | 14 | — | 10 | 4 | 17 | 1 |
| Robins ........... | 39.1 | 8 | 102 | 5 | 10 | 1 | 30 | 1 |
| Hearne .......... | 20 | 3 | 42 | 2 | 8 | 4 | 12 | 2 |
| Sims ............. | 2 | — | 8 | — | 8.1 | 3 | 15 | 3 |

## Somerset Bowling

| | Overs | Mdns | Runs | Wkts | Overs | Mdns | Runs | Wkts |
|---|---|---|---|---|---|---|---|---|
| Robertson-Glasgow . | 29.5 | 9 | 63 | 3 | 13 | 4 | 23 | 1 |
| Wellard .......... | 24 | 4 | 72 | 2 | 4 | 1 | 10 | — |
| J. W. Lee ......... | 45 | 19 | 69 | 5 | 9 | 1 | 23 | — |
| Young ........... | 24 | 7 | 48 | — | | | | |
| F. S. Lee ......... | | | | | 3 | 1 | 4 | — |
| Case ............. | | | | | 2.1 | — | 20 | — |

Umpires: C. N. Woolley and F. Chester.

# MIDDLESEX v KENT

### Played at Lord's, August 30, 31, 1933

Remarkable performances by Hendren and Freeman brought distinction to this game, which Kent won without much trouble at ten minutes to seven on Thursday by six wickets. Freeman did astonishingly fine work in taking fifteen wickets for 122 runs. He began on Wednesday by obtaining all the seven wickets which fell before lunch for 163, but Watt broke the sequence by dismissing Hendren. When Middlesex went in again 153 behind, Freeman once more bowled splendidly on a good pitch. Hendren, scoring 101 in each innings, alone played Freeman confidently. He used his feet to get to the pitch of the ball and drove powerfully. Ames batted faultlessly for Kent.

## Middlesex

| | | | |
|---|---|---|---|
| W. F. Price lbw b Freeman .................. | 35 | – lbw b Freeman ................ | 6 |
| G. E. Hart b Freeman ....................... | 32 | – c Woolley b Todd ............. | 1 |
| W. R. Watkins lbw b Freeman ................. | 3 | – b Todd ...................... | 7 |
| E. Hendren c Valentine b Watt ................ | 101 | – lbw b Freeman ................ | 101 |
| Mr B. G. W. Atkinson lbw b Freeman ........... | 4 | – lbw b Freeman ................ | 0 |
| H. W. Lee b Freeman ........................ | 8 | – lbw b Freeman ................ | 10 |
| Mr N. Haig b Freeman ....................... | 1 | – b Freeman ................... | 28 |
| Mr M. Tindall c Levett b Freeman .............. | 5 | – c Watt b Freeman ............. | 4 |
| Mr A. W. Childs-Clarke c Watt b Freeman ........ | 34 | – b Todd ...................... | 8 |
| L. Muncer b Watt .......................... | 4 | – c and b Freeman .............. | 2 |
| Mr P. F. Judge not out ...................... | 0 | – not out ..................... | 8 |
| B 3, l-b 2, n-b 1 ..................... | 6 | B 1, l-b 4, w 1 ........... | 6 |
| | **233** | | **181** |

## Kent

Mr A. P. F. Chapman c Price b Haig . . . . . . . . . . . . . 13
W. H. Ashdown b Judge . . . . . . . . . . . . . . . . . . . . . . 33 – not out . . . . . . . . . . . . . . . . . . . . . . . 13
F. E. Woolley c Watkins b Judge . . . . . . . . . . . . . . . . 11 – c Hart b Muncer . . . . . . . . . . . . . . 0
L. E. G. Ames c Hart b Judge . . . . . . . . . . . . . . . . . .125 – c Atkinson b Tindall . . . . . . . . . . . 0
L. J. Todd c Watkins b Lee . . . . . . . . . . . . . . . . . . . 74 – c and b Tindall . . . . . . . . . . . . . . . . . 6
Mr B. H. Valentine b Childs-Clarke . . . . . . . . . . . . . . 21 – not out . . . . . . . . . . . . . . . . . . . . . . . 4
Mr C. H. Knott st Price b Childs-Clarke . . . . . . . . . . 63
Mr F. G. H. Chalk b Haig . . . . . . . . . . . . . . . . . . . . 32
A. E. Watt lbw b Haig . . . . . . . . . . . . . . . . . . . . . . . 0 – c Tindall b Muncer . . . . . . . . . . . . . 7
Mr W. H. V. Levett not out . . . . . . . . . . . . . . . . . . . 12
       L-b 2 . . . . . . . . . . . . . . . . . . . . . . . . . . . 2        B 2 . . . . . . . . . . . . . . . . . . . . . 2

(9 wkts dec.) 386             32

A. P. Freeman did not bat.

### Kent Bowling

|  | Overs | Mdns | Runs | Wkts | Overs | Mdns | Runs | Wkts |
|---|---|---|---|---|---|---|---|---|
| Watt . . . . . . . . . . . . | 13 | 1 | 47 | 2 | 10 | 1 | 36 | — |
| Ashdown . . . . . . . . . | 9 | — | 42 | — | 2 | — | 10 | — |
| Freeman . . . . . . . . | 37.4 | 10 | 64 | 8 | 32.2 | 11 | 58 | 7 |
| Todd . . . . . . . . . . . | 23 | 2 | 74 | — | 21 | 5 | 71 | 3 |

### Middlesex Bowling

|  | Overs | Mdns | Runs | Wkts | Overs | Mdns | Runs | Wkts |
|---|---|---|---|---|---|---|---|---|
| Atkinson . . . . . . . . . | 7 | — | 27 | — |  |  |  |  |
| Haig . . . . . . . . . . . . | 24 | 2 | 72 | 3 |  |  |  |  |
| Lee . . . . . . . . . . . . . | 27 | 3 | 69 | 1 |  |  |  |  |
| Judge . . . . . . . . . . . | 28 | 3 | 65 | 3 |  |  |  |  |
| Childs-Clarke . . . . . | 32.2 | 8 | 90 | 2 |  |  |  |  |
| Watkins . . . . . . . . . | 8 | — | 31 | — |  |  |  |  |
| Hart . . . . . . . . . . . . | 9 | — | 30 | — |  |  |  |  |
| Muncer . . . . . . . . . |  |  |  |  | 2 | — | 9 | 2 |
| Tindall . . . . . . . . . . |  |  |  |  | 2 | — | 21 | 2 |

Umpires: A. E. Street and W. Reeves.

# REFLECTIONS [1937]

By E. (Patsy) Hendren (Middlesex and England)

In an Interview

It is a big pull leaving the stage, as they call it: leaving the people I have played with and the camaraderie of the game, but we all have to come to it at some time, and I thought it as well to give up while I was doing well.

You know what they say about cards: bad beginning, good ending. Well, my first county match was one in which I did not get an innings! That was in 1907 against Lancashire at Lord's, the game being abandoned before lunch on the second day. There were naturally unusual circumstances. After heavy rain, a drizzle set in, but the crowd – allowed, as they were then, on the playing-area – gathered in front of the Pavilion and clamoured for cricket. In the middle of all the rumpus, somebody got on to the pitch itself and, accidentally or not, stuck the ferrule of an umbrella into the turf. When this was discovered by Mr. Archie MacLaren, the Lancashire captain, he refused to play, even if a fresh wicket were cut out. So there was nothing for it but to pack up and go home.

The fight for the Championship in my last season, 1937, provided a great struggle, but it was not the closest in which I have been concerned. I remember in 1920, when

Middlesex were under the captaincy of Mr. P. F. Warner (as he was then) for the last time, Lancashire, in celebration of winning the Championship, split a bottle or two of champagne before the result of the Middlesex and Surrey match at Lord's reached them. As a matter of fact, I started the turn of that game by catching Tom Shepherd in the deep – I can see myself now running from long-off to long-on to take the ball – and, with a win by 55 runs, Middlesex gained the title.

It has been suggested that cricket at the present time does not attract spectators as it used to do. All I can say is that the kind of game Middlesex played in 1937 most certainly does not fail to attract. Many times we made 350 or more before tea, and that is a lot of runs. Then, too, we had a skipper who was always out to win. That in itself must make the game interesting and worth watching, particularly when the skipper concerned is a great fielder and one who studies the viewpoint of the spectator.

## TO HELP YOUNG CRICKETERS

Anyway, I have said good-bye to all that, and I take up with confidence my new task as coach at Harrow School. I have done a good bit of coaching: I was the first to start indoor cricket schools in London. A big mistake often made in coaching is that of trying to teach the youngsters too much. No two batsmen play alike, and it is no use one trying to copy another. It cannot be done.

My advice to budding batsmen if they want to keep the game alive is to play off the left foot a little more, ready to hit the half volley. The average cricketer is apt to play a bit too "safe". That is all very well till you have made 20 or 30, but then you must be ready to hit the ball. Otherwise what should be hundreds are only seventies.

I consider that a batsman should make a good coach for bowlers – as good, indeed, as a bowler. The bowler can show the pupil how to hold the ball, how to spin it and how to flight it: but the man towards whom the ball is coming is the one who can say whether or not the bowler is bowling well. I am in favour of indoor cricket schools. Lots of people improve their game there. They have, of course, to adapt themselves from matting wickets to turf, but winter practice cannot fail to do a lot of good to club cricketers, who in this way get the necessary exercise to commence a cricket season already loosened-up.

There is, at the moment, a scarcity of outstanding bowlers. I cannot give a reason: they run in cycles, and this is one of the "off-periods". Wickets, too, do not help them nowadays. We want another Maurice Tate or another F. R. Foster. We cannot expect to get another Barnes; that is too much to ask.

## IMPORTANCE OF FIELDING

I must say a word about fielding, to my mind the most interesting part of the game. Good fielders make a fair bowler very good. There is nothing more pleasant for a bowler than to see people dashing about trying to save runs and improve his analysis; it puts heart into him. It is a great mistake for fieldsmen to stop chasing the ball. Too many men slacken off when a four seems a certainty. Spectators like to see the ball chased to the very end, with the resultant thrill in the point of whether the man or the ball will win the race to the boundary. Sir Pelham Warner once said he would never, if he could help it, play anybody who could not field. There is a lot in that idea.

In connection with fielding, a funny thing once happened to me when on an MCC tour in Australia. Between fixtures, I was journeying into the Bush by motor-car with a colleague when we stopped to watch a cricket match. One of the players, unaware of our identity, approached and asked if, as his team was a man short, one of us would play. I had already been in the field for two and half days, but I yielded to persuasion and, rigged out in borrowed gear, was put in the deep field at the bottom of a pronounced slope, from where I could see nothing at all of the cricket. For hour after hour I fielded there, throwing the ball back at intervals until, at long last, I caught one. I ran to the top of the hill and announced with some satisfaction that I had made a catch. To my consternation, I was informed that the other team's innings had closed and that I had caught one of my own side!

## VIEWS ON LBW

Some important changes in the Laws of the game have been made during my thirty years in first-class cricket. As regards the larger stumps, I do not think they have made a big difference to the real class player. Certainly the increased size of the wicket has helped the bowler a little, but when a good batsman is in, it does not really matter. The smaller ball, too, has been of assistance to the bowler, though strangely enough, while this was supposed to help in spinning the ball, there are fewer people bowling "spinners". Now about "LBW, N"; I am in favour of the rule being applied to the ball turning from leg as well as that breaking from the off. After all, the leg-break is the most difficult ball to bowl, and the additional reward to this type of attack would bring the spin-bowler back into the game.

Personally, however, I thought the "snick" experiment with the LBW Law better than the "N" rule. It put a stop to those batsmen who, given out leg before, so often returned to the pavilion declaring: "I played it." The new rule is not fulfilling expectations as regards improvement in off-side strokes; maybe it makes batsmen afraid to get across as they should. One thing I do think, and that is that a batsman should not be given out under the "N" rule when playing a forward stroke to an off-break. After all, the rule was directed chiefly against the men who merely raised their bats and stepped across to play the ball with their pads. It was not intended to penalise the player employing an attacking stroke, and I am pleased to say that, so far as I have noticed, not many umpires give a man out in these circumstances.

## A NOTE ON WICKETS

My opinion is that, if all wickets were the same as at Lord's, we should have more of a fight for runs. Men are too often picked for a Test match on the strength of a hundred on a "doped" pitch. Another mistake we in England make is in preparing special wickets for touring teams. As early as the autumn of the year preceding an Australian visit, for instance, some of the ground-staffs get to work on wickets for their county's game with the touring team, who in consequence are able to play in England on something like their own wickets. If visiting sides had to bat, especially in Test matches, on the same pitches as those upon which ordinary county games are played, there would not be so many big scores.

## A DREAM COME TRUE

So much has happened during my career that I find it no easy matter to single out the happiest incident. Probably my proudest moment was when, in 1926, I completed my first hundred in a Test match against Australia. That was a dream come true: a century at Lord's, where I had been a ground-boy! A certain incident concerning a hose, which by some strange manner of means was left running all night on the pitch, nearly spoiled it all for me.

Among the players with or against whom I have played, I shall never forget the famous "W.G." I first played in a charity match with him and also for MCC at Charlton, and very proud I was to be in the same side with him. In one of these games, I got a hundred and the Doctor 50 odd – he was past his best at that time – and I well remember him clapping me on the back and saying in that high-pitched voice of his: "You'll play for England one day, young'un". I am glad he was right. Then there was Albert Trott, one of the grandest cricketers of all time and the only man ever to hit a ball clean over the Pavilion at Lord's. In his benefit match against Somerset at Lord's in 1907, he performed the "hat trick" twice in one innings. He took four wickets with four balls and with the fifth dislodged a bail with a ball that went for four byes. In those days, the bail had to be removed before a batsmen was out. Next over, he sent back three men with following deliveries, making his analysis for the innings seven for 20. At the end of the innings, Albert punched his own head and called himself names for finishing his benefit match early on the third day! Sammy Woods, captain of Somerset, and one of the "victims", gave him a straw hat with a hand-painted picture on the band of seven rabbits bolting into the Pavilion. Albert wore it at a good many matches during the rest of the season – to the wonderment of everyone not "in the know".

I cannot fail to mention J. T. Hearne, my great hero on and off the field. He was a very dear man and an outstanding example to young cricketers. I have never seen a bowler with a prettier action. he did the "hat trick" against the Australians in the Test match at Leeds in 1899, the batsmen concerned being Clem Hill, S. E. Gregory and M. A. Noble.

## STRAIN OF OVERSEAS TOURS

I have made a good number of tours abroad, and I must confess that one gets extremely tired in the course of them. It is a big strain, especially in Australia, where there are very few easy matches. In most of the State sides there are four or five Test players, and in the up-country matches, where the cricket is less arduous, there is much travelling to do. You have to be very strong to stand it. I had five continuous seasons of it, and as I fielded in the long field at that time, it demanded the highest standard of physical fitness. In one match at Melbourne, by the way, I once occupied every position in the field – except that of wicket-keeper, of course. My football training did me the world of good as a cricketer, and among other things it helped me to keep my pace in the deep. Personally, I do not consider the absence of a cricketer-footballer from a Soccer season when on tour is a handicap to him; it does him more good than harm.

On these tours, about seventeen players are generally taken. One can never tell if that number is going to be sufficient. As it is, four or five players sometimes do not get a game for perhaps three weeks at a time. It would, of course, be very nice if you could take enough to rest the whole of the Test team now and again, but I am afraid it would cost too much money. When on tour, amateurs and professionals "mix" splendidly. They are all part of one team: all live together, all change together.

A lot has been said and written from time to time about separate exits on grounds for amateurs and professionals. So far as Lord's is concerned, the professionals have the option of going through the centre-gate on to the field if they care, but they probably think it too much trouble to walk along there from the dressing-room.

## MIDDLESEX v NOTTINGHAMSHIRE

### At The Oval, July 15, 17, 18, 1939

Nottinghamshire won by an innings and 190 runs. Keeton, missed four times, put together a record innings for Nottinghamshire and what proved to be the highest of the season. Carrying his bat after seven hours and a quarter at the crease, he hit a 5 and twenty-eight 4s, mainly off-drives. Harris shared in an opening stand of 104 and Heane helped to add 167. Rain altered the conditions when Middlesex batted and Voce caused the ball to rise awkwardly. The loss of seven wickets for 84 made a follow-on certain and, despite a rally, arrears of 441 were clearly insuperable. Surrey lent The Oval because Lord's was engaged by Eton and Harrow on the Saturday.

### Nottinghamshire

| | | | |
|---|---|---|---|
| W. W. Keeton not out | 312 | W. Voce lbw b Smith | 0 |
| C. B. Harris c Sims b Peebles | 33 | A. B. Wheat lbw b Smith | 1 |
| Mr G. F. H. Heane lbw b Sims | 88 | H. J. Butler c Peebles b Sims | 10 |
| J. Hardstaff c Price b Edrich | 30 | A. Jepson not out | 15 |
| G. V. Gunn c Smith b Peebles | 43 | B 3, l-b 4, w 2 | 9 |
| J. Knowles c Gray b Peebles | 3 | | — |
| R. Giles b Smith | 16 | (9 wkts dec.) | 560 |

## Middlesex

| | | | |
|---|---|---|---|
| J. Robertson c Wheat b Jepson | 14 | – c Jepson b Voce | 21 |
| S. M. Brown c Giles b Voce | 37 | – lbw b Voce | 21 |
| W. J. Edrich c Heane b Voce | 5 | – c Wheat b Heane | 51 |
| D. Compton c Heane b Voce | 17 | – b Heane | 65 |
| Mr N. S. Hotchkin c Knowles b Butler | 0 | – not out | 41 |
| L. Compton b Butler | 2 | – b Jepson | 4 |
| J. Sims c Hardstaff b Voce | 7 | – c Jepson b Heane | 0 |
| J. Smith c Keeton b Voce | 25 | – c and b Voce | 40 |
| Mr I. A. R. Peebles c Harris b Voce | 2 | – c Voce b Butler | 4 |
| W. F. Price not out | 7 | – absent hurt | 0 |
| L. H. Gray c Gunn b Voce | 1 | – run out | 7 |
| B 2 | 2 | B 4, l-b 6, n-b 3 | 13 |
| | **119** | | **251** |

## Middlesex Bowling

| | Overs | Mdns | Runs | Wkts |
|---|---|---|---|---|
| Smith | 26 | 2 | 102 | 3 |
| Gray | 12 | — | 74 | — |
| Edrich | 16 | — | 74 | 1 |
| Sims | 18 | — | 116 | 2 |
| Peebles | 20 | — | 95 | 3 |
| D. Compton | 16 | 2 | 59 | — |
| Robertson | 6 | — | 31 | — |

## Nottinghamshire Bowling

| | Overs | Mdns | Runs | Wkts | Overs | Mdns | Runs | Wkts |
|---|---|---|---|---|---|---|---|---|
| Voce | 19.4 | 3 | 70 | 7 | 25 | 6 | 69 | 3 |
| Butler | 15 | 4 | 31 | 2 | 15 | 2 | 50 | 1 |
| Jepson | 4 | — | 16 | 1 | 16 | 1 | 55 | 1 |
| Giles | | | | | 3 | — | 9 | — |
| Heane | | | | | 8.1 | 1 | 55 | 3 |

Umpires: H. G. Baldwin and A. Dolphin.

# NORTHAMPTONSHIRE

## NORTHAMPTONSHIRE v YORKSHIRE

Played at Northampton, July 14, 15, 1920

Northamptonshire had no chance in this match. Yorkshire winning by an innings and 173 runs. The end came in a little over an hour on the second morning. Holmes took the batting honours of the game, playing right through Yorkshire's innings. He scored his 145 not out in three hours and a half, hit twenty 4s, and gave no chance. In making such a big score he owed much to Waddington, who helped him to put on 83 runs for the ninth wicket. The Northamptonshire batsmen could do nothing against Waddington, who enjoyed one of his biggest successes. At one point of the game he not only did the hat trick, but took four wickets in five balls. It will be seen that he and Robinson bowled unchanged through the two innings. Waddington had the remarkable record of 13 wickets for 48 runs.

### Yorkshire

| | |
|---|---|
| P. Holmes not out ..................145 | E. Robinson lbw b Thomas .............. 20 |
| H. Sutcliffe b Wells .................... 0 | N. Kilner b Wells ..................... 9 |
| D. Denton b Wells ................... 28 | A. Dolphin lbw b Wells ............... 2 |
| R. Kilner c Buswell b Thomas ........... 14 | A. Waddington b Thomas .............. 21 |
| E. Oldroyd b Wells................... 4 | L-b 5, n-b 1 ................. 6 |
| G. H. Hirst b Woolley ................ 16 | |
| Mr D. C. F. Burton b Murdin .......... 5 | 270 |

### Northamptonshire

| | | | |
|---|---|---|---|
| F. Walden c Robinson b Waddington ............ | 16 | – b Waddington ................. | 0 |
| Mr W. Adams b Robinson ..................... | 7 | – not out ..................... | 14 |
| Mr P. Walker b Waddington ................... | 0 | – c and b Robinson.............. | 0 |
| C. N. Woolley b Waddington.................... | 6 | – lbw b Robinson ............. | 1 |
| R. Haywood st Dolphin b Waddington ........... | 11 | – st Dolphin b Waddington ........ | 2 |
| W. Wells run out .......................... | 6 | – c Burton b Waddington ......... | 0 |
| Mr H. G. Beers c Dolphin b Waddington ......... | 0 | – c and b Waddington ........... | 0 |
| Mr R. O. Raven b Robinson ................... | 0 | – b Waddington ............... | 0 |
| W. A. Buswell b Robinson ................... | 5 | – b Robinson ................. | 8 |
| V. Murdin lbw b Waddington ................. | 0 | – b Waddington ............... | 0 |
| A. E. Thomas not out........................ | 0 | – st Dolphin b Waddington ....... | 6 |
| B 4, l-b 2.......................... | 6 | B 5, l-b 4 .............. | 9 |
| | 57 | | 40 |

### Northamptonshire Bowling

| | Overs | Mdns | Runs | Wkts |
|---|---|---|---|---|
| Wells ............ | 26 | 4 | 91 | 5 |
| Woolley .......... | 16 | 1 | 52 | 1 |
| Thomas .......... | 23 | 4 | 57 | 3 |
| Murdin ........... | 16 | 3 | 47 | 1 |
| Walden .......... | 3 | — | 17 | — |

**Yorkshire Bowling**

|              | Overs | Mdns | Runs | Wkts | Overs | Mdns | Runs | Wkts |
|--------------|-------|------|------|------|-------|------|------|------|
| Waddington . . . . . . . | 17 | 7 | 30 | 6 | 15.5 | 9 | 18 | 7 |
| Robinson . . . . . . . . | 16.3 | 9 | 21 | 3 | 15 | 10 | 13 | 3 |

Umpires: H. Butt and F. Parris.

## NORTHAMPTONSHIRE v SURREY

Played at Northampton, August 25, 26, 27, 1920

Though beaten by eight wickets in a match which produced 1,475 runs – a record in county cricket – the Northamptonshire players had good reason to be pleased with themselves. Scores of 306 and 430 against Surrey were immeasurably above their ordinary form. Surrey's huge total was the more remarkable as Hobbs contributed only 3 runs to it. The hitting on the second afternoon was some of the fiercest of the season. Fender actually getting his hundred in thirty-five minutes. Peach and Ducat also played in dazzling style.

### Northamptonshire

| | | |
|---|---|---|
| Mr W. Adams b Rushby . . . . . . . . . . . . . . . . . . . . . | 3 | – c Hobbs b Fender . . . . . . . . . . . . . 31 |
| Mr A. P. R. Hawtin c and b Fender . . . . . . . . . . . . | 34 | – b Rushby . . . . . . . . . . . . . . . . . . 5 |
| R. Haywood c sub. b Hitch . . . . . . . . . . . . . . . . . | 15 | – c Peach b Fender . . . . . . . . . . . . . 96 |
| C. N. Woolley c Wilkinson b Fender . . . . . . . . . . . | 58 | – lbw b Hitch . . . . . . . . . . . . . . . . . 42 |
| F. Walden c Hitch b Lockton . . . . . . . . . . . . . . . .128 | | – b Rushby . . . . . . . . . . . . . . . . . . 63 |
| Mr S. G. H. Humphrey b Ducat . . . . . . . . . . . . . . | 24 | – b Hitch . . . . . . . . . . . . . . . . . . . . 31 |
| W. Wells c Strudwick b Hitch . . . . . . . . . . . . . . . | 4 | – c Rushby b Shepherd . . . . . . . . . . . 71 |
| Mr R. O. Raven b Ducat . . . . . . . . . . . . . . . . . . . | 4 | – lbw b Shepherd . . . . . . . . . . . . . . 28 |
| V. Murdin b Shepherd . . . . . . . . . . . . . . . . . . . . | 15 | – c Strudwick b Shepherd . . . . . . . . . 4 |
| A. E. Thomas not out . . . . . . . . . . . . . . . . . . . . . | 8 | – c Ducat b Hitch . . . . . . . . . . . . . . . 30 |
| B. Bellamy c Hitch b Fender . . . . . . . . . . . . . . . . | 11 | – not out . . . . . . . . . . . . . . . . . . . . . 13 |
| L-b 2 . . . . . . . . . . . . . . . . . . . . . . . . . . | 2 | B 9, l-b 6, n-b 1 . . . . . . . . . . 16 |

306                    430

### Surrey

| | | |
|---|---|---|
| J. B. Hobbs c Bellamy b Murdin . . . . . . . . . . . . . . . | 3 | – b Walden . . . . . . . . . . . . . . . . . . . . 54 |
| A. Sandham c Hawtin b Woolley . . . . . . . . . . . . . . | 92 | – b Thomas . . . . . . . . . . . . . . . . . . . . 6 |
| Mr C. T. A. Wilkinson b Woolley . . . . . . . . . . . . . . | 43 | |
| T. Shepherd c Bellamy b Woolley . . . . . . . . . . . | 9 | – not out . . . . . . . . . . . . . . . . . . . . . . 42 |
| H. A. Peach not out . . . . . . . . . . . . . . . . . . . . . . .200 | | |
| A. Ducat c Bellamy b Thomas . . . . . . . . . . . . . . . .149 | | – not out . . . . . . . . . . . . . . . . . . . . . . 11 |
| Mr P. G. H. Fender not out . . . . . . . . . . . . . . . . . .113 | | |
| B 9, l-b 1 . . . . . . . . . . . . . . . . . . . . . . . | 10 | B 2, l-b 5 . . . . . . . . . . . . . . . 7 |

(5 wkts dec.) 619                    120

W. Hitch, Mr. J. H. Lockton, H. Strudwick and T. Rushby did not bat.

### Surrey Bowling

|              | Overs | Mdns | Runs | Wkts | Overs | Mdns | Runs | Wkts |
|--------------|-------|------|------|------|-------|------|------|------|
| Hitch . . . . . . . . . . . | 24 | 6 | 90 | 2 | 28.2 | 2 | 137 | 3 |
| Rushby . . . . . . . . . | 25 | 10 | 66 | 1 | 27 | 5 | 68 | 2 |
| Lockton . . . . . . . . . | 20 | 5 | 53 | 1 | 10 | — | 34 | — |
| Shepherd . . . . . . . . | 6 | 1 | 17 | 1 | 13 | 5 | 27 | 3 |
| Fender . . . . . . . . . . | 21.5 | 1 | 69 | 3 | 29 | 1 | 118 | 2 |
| Ducat . . . . . . . . . . | 9 | 4 | 9 | 2 | 8 | 1 | 23 | — |
| Peach . . . . . . . . . . | | | | | 4 | 2 | 7 | — |

**Northamptonshire Bowling**

| | Overs | Mdns | Runs | Wkts | Overs | Mdns | Runs | Wkts |
|---|---|---|---|---|---|---|---|---|
| Wells ............ | 31 | 6 | 133 | — | | | | |
| Murdin ........... | 22.4 | — | 162 | 1 | 9 | 1 | 37 | — |
| Thomas .......... | 23 | — | 142 | 1 | 14 | 3 | 24 | 1 |
| Woolley .......... | 26 | 3 | 116 | 3 | 9.3 | 2 | 26 | — |
| Humphrey ........ | 4 | — | 36 | — | | | | |
| Haywood ......... | 4 | — | 20 | — | | | | |
| Walden .......... | | | | | 4 | — | 26 | 1 |

Umpires: J. Moss and T. M. Russell.

## NORTHAMPTONSHIRE v YORKSHIRE

Played at Northampton, May 6, 8, 1922

On a rain-damaged pitch bowlers had matters so much their own way that soon after one o'clock on the Monday Yorkshire had won by ten wickets. Winning the toss for Yorkshire, Geoffrey Wilson decided to put Northamptonshire in and the happiest results attended his policy. Woolley offered some resistance, but no one else could make much headway, the whole side being dismissed before lunch. Macaulay bowled with remarkable effect, only three of his deliveries being scored from. Yorkshire quickly lost Holmes and Sutcliffe, but Oldroyd, R. Kilner and Rhodes batted so well on the difficult pitch that the Northamptonshire total was passed with five wickets in hand. A collapse followed the tea interval, the innings being finished off for the addition of 30 runs. Murdin took the last four wickets for 10 runs. In their second innings, Northamptonshire again found the bowling of Macaulay and Rhodes far beyond them, Yorkshire being left with the simple task of getting 12 runs to win.

### Northamptonshire

| | | | |
|---|---|---|---|
| C. N. Woolley b Rhodes ..................... | 34 | – b Macaulay ................... | 4 |
| Mr N. P. Andrews lbw b Robinson ............. | 1 | – c Waddington b R. Kilner ........ | 4 |
| Mr C. Baker st Dolphin b Waddington .......... | 0 | – c R. Kilner b Rhodes ........... | 7 |
| F. Walden c Rhodes b Macaulay ................ | 12 | – b Macaulay ................. | 5 |
| W. Wells c Rhodes b Macaulay ................. | 0 | – st Dolphin b Rhodes .......... | 7 |
| Mr J. Wright b Macaulay ..................... | 1 | – b Rhodes .................... | 0 |
| B. Bellamy lbw b Macaulay ................... | 6 | – b Macaulay ................. | 0 |
| Mr T. E. Manning b Macaulay ................. | 1 | – lbw b Rhodes ................ | 1 |
| A. E. Thomas not out ........................ | 15 | – b Macaulay ................. | 3 |
| V. Murdin c Sutcliffe b Rhodes .............. | 8 | – not out .................... | 3 |
| Mr R. S. Venes lbw b Macaulay ............... | 0 | – b Macaulay ................. | 0 |
| B 1, l-b 2 ................................. | 3 | B 6, w 2 ................ | 8 |
| | **81** | | **42** |

### Yorkshire

| | | | |
|---|---|---|---|
| P. Holmes b Murdin ......................... | 2 | – not out ..................... | 6 |
| H. Sutcliffe c and b Murdin ................. | 12 | – not out ..................... | 6 |
| E. Oldroyd c and b Wells .................... | 34 | | |
| R. Kilner b Woolley ......................... | 12 | | |
| W. Rhodes c Bellamy b Wells ................. | 14 | | |
| E. Robinson b Thomas ....................... | 1 | | |
| N. Kilner b Murdin ......................... | 16 | | |
| Mr G. Wilson b Murdin ...................... | 7 | | |
| G. G. Macaulay b Murdin .................... | 3 | | |
| A. Dolphin b Murdin ........................ | 4 | | |
| A. Waddington not out ...................... | 0 | | |
| B 5, l-b 2 ................................. | 7 | | |
| | **112** | | **12** |

## Yorkshire Bowling

| | Overs | Mdns | Runs | Wkts | Overs | Mdns | Runs | Wkts |
|---|---|---|---|---|---|---|---|---|
| Robinson ......... | 8 | 5 | 12 | 1 | | | | |
| Waddington ...... | 7 | — | 19 | 1 | 2 | 2 | — | — |
| Macaulay ......... | 11.3 | 8 | 8 | 6 | 16.5 | 8 | 23 | 5 |
| Rhodes ........... | 11 | 2 | 39 | 2 | 12 | 7 | 6 | 4 |
| R. Kilner ......... | | | | | 6 | 4 | 5 | 1 |

## Northamptonshire Bowling

| | Overs | Mdns | Runs | Wkts | Overs | Mdns | Runs | Wkts |
|---|---|---|---|---|---|---|---|---|
| Wells ........... | 9 | 2 | 22 | 2 | | | | |
| Murdin .......... | 21.1 | 9 | 38 | 6 | 3 | 1 | 6 | — |
| Thomas ......... | 11 | 3 | 27 | 1 | 0.4 | — | 3 | — |
| Woolley ......... | 15 | 8 | 18 | 1 | | | | |
| Venes ........... | | | | | 4 | 1 | 3 | — |

Umpires: H. Young and J. P. Whiteside.

# NORTHAMPTONSHIRE v DERBYSHIRE

### Played at Northampton, May 13, 15, 1922

After a very close finish Derbyshire beat Northamptonshire by two wickets. Set 168 to get, Derbyshire seemed to have an easy task, but they had to fight very hard to win. The finish was even closer that the score would suggest, for Bestwick had had to leave the ground with neuralgia, so that actually the last two men were together when a leg-bye gave Derbyshire the victory. Hutchinson gave a fine batting display when his side were battling hard, but Derbyshire owed their win in the main to Morton, who bowled with splendid effect. The only batsman to obtain a real mastery over him was Woolley. At the wickets for just over three hours for his 111, Woolley played almost perfect cricket, his defensive work reaching a very high standard. Hard driving and clever hitting on the leg-side were the features of his innings, which included eight 4s.

## Northamptonshire

| | | | |
|---|---|---|---|
| C. N. Woolley c Cadman b Bestwick ............. | 35 | – lbw b Morton ................. | 111 |
| Mr N. P. Andrews b Morton ................. | 0 | – b Morton ..................... | 2 |
| F. Walden c G. R. Jackson b Morton ........... | 7 | – b Morton ..................... | 42 |
| Mr B. Wright c Townend b Morton .............. | 4 | – b Bestwick ................... | 2 |
| W. Wells c Cadman b Morton ................. | 1 | – lbw b Bestwick ............... | 0 |
| Mr N. E. Wright lbw b Morton ................. | 0 | – b Cadman .................... | 6 |
| Mr G. H. Drummond run out .................. | 1 | – b Morton .................... | 11 |
| B. Bellamy b Morton ....................... | 0 | – not out ...................... | 14 |
| A. E. Thomas lbw b Morton .................. | 4 | – b Cadman .................... | 0 |
| V. Murdin lbw b Bestwick ................... | 5 | – lbw b Morton ................. | 0 |
| Mr R. S. Venes not out ..................... | 2 | – b Cadman .................... | 1 |
| B 1, w 1, n-b 2 ................. | 4 | B 11, l-b 5 .............. | 16 |
| | **63** | | **205** |

## Derbyshire

| | | | |
|---|---|---|---|
| J. Bowden lbw b Venes | 4 | – b Thomas | 15 |
| L. Townsend b Murdin | 6 | – b Murdin | 8 |
| J. M. Hutchinson c Thomas b Wells | 28 | – lbw b Wells | 53 |
| S. Cadman b Wells | 25 | – b Murdin | 38 |
| Mr A. H. M. Jackson lbw b Thomas | 1 | – c Bellamy b Wells | 4 |
| A. Morton b Thomas | 2 | – b Murdin | 0 |
| H. Storer c Bellamy b Wells | 7 | – b Murdin | 25 |
| Mr G. Curgenven b Wells | 4 | – b Wells | 6 |
| Mr G. R. Jackson b Wells | 7 | – not out | 2 |
| H. Elliott b Wells | 0 | – not out | 1 |
| W. Bestwick not out | 0 | | |
| B 4, l-b 13 | 17 | B 4, l-b 9, n-b 3 | 16 |
| | **101** | | **168** |

### Derbyshire Bowling

| | Overs | Mdns | Runs | Wkts | Overs | Mdns | Runs | Wkts |
|---|---|---|---|---|---|---|---|---|
| Bestwick | 13.1 | 8 | 21 | 2 | 18 | 3 | 45 | 2 |
| Morton | 13 | 4 | 38 | 7 | 23 | 4 | 65 | 5 |
| Cadman | | | | | 18.1 | 5 | 46 | 3 |
| Storer | | | | | 10 | 3 | 18 | — |
| Townsend | | | | | 2 | 1 | 4 | — |
| A. H. M. Jackson | | | | | 4 | — | 11 | — |

### Northamptonshire Bowling

| | Overs | Mdns | Runs | Wkts | Overs | Mdns | Runs | Wkts |
|---|---|---|---|---|---|---|---|---|
| Wells | 12.1 | 3 | 25 | 6 | 23 | 4 | 52 | 3 |
| Murdin | 12 | 4 | 11 | 1 | 20.4 | 4 | 44 | 4 |
| Venes | 9 | 1 | 28 | 1 | 5 | 1 | 8 | — |
| Thomas | 12 | 4 | 20 | 2 | 12 | 6 | 12 | 1 |
| Woolley | | | | | 6 | — | 15 | — |
| N. E. Wright | | | | | 3 | 1 | 8 | — |
| Walden | | | | | 4 | — | 13 | — |

Umpires: J. P. Whiteside and H. Barrett.

## NORTHAMPTONSHIRE v HAMPSHIRE

Played at Northampton, May 15, 17, 1926

Failing completely in batting, Northamptonshire were beaten early on the second day by an innings and 79 runs. In the whole match only three home players succeeded in reaching double-figures. Chief honours were carried off by Newman, the Hampshire all-rounder, who besides playing the highest individual innings on either side, took eleven wickets for 31 runs. Owing to rain, play did not begin until three o'clock on Saturday, and on the damaged pitch, Boyes ably assisted by Livsey at the wicket, disposed of six batsmen for less than 3 runs each. An especially clever piece of stumping dismissed Jupp when that player was hitting confidently. Going on at 48, Newman got rid of three men in three overs for one run. Brown and Newman, scoring 21 together in the last half hour, hit hard on Monday, and the first Hampshire wicket realised 67. Jupp, by clever change of pace, troubled the majority of the batsmen, but Newman played soundly for over two hours. In arrears of 154, Northamptonshire made 23 without loss before Newman came on to bowl, and then the home side collapsed. Fitzroy, their captain, hit with power, but otherwise the bowlers held complete sway.

## Northamptonshire

| | | | |
|---|---|---|---|
| C. N. Woolley c Livsey b Boyes | 6 | – b Boyes | 8 |
| Mr A. P. R. Hawtin lbw b Brown | 8 | – lbw b Boyes | 14 |
| Mr R. L. Wright b Boyes | 0 | – b Newman | 0 |
| Mr V. W. C. Jupp st Livsey b Boyes | 17 | – b Newman | 2 |
| Mr J. E. Timms c Brown b Boyes | 5 | – b Newman | 0 |
| B. Bellamy b Newman | 8 | – c Brown b Newman | 6 |
| F. Walden not out | 3 | – c Brutton b Newman | 5 |
| Mr J. M. Fitzroy b Boyes | 1 | – not out | 26 |
| A. E. Thomas b Boyes | 0 | – c and b Newman | 4 |
| V. Murdin b Newman | 1 | – b Newman | 0 |
| E. C. Clark b Newman | 0 | – b Newman | 2 |
| B 1 | 1 | B 7, l-b 1 | 8 |
| | **50** | | **75** |

## Hampshire

| | | | |
|---|---|---|---|
| G. Brown b Clark | 41 | Mr F. Gross b Jupp | 1 |
| J. Newman b Thomas | 47 | B. Harfield lbw b Jupp | 2 |
| Mr C. P. Brutton b Jupp | 26 | A. Hayward c Timms b Jupp | 0 |
| C. P. Mead b Jupp | 33 | 1G. S. Boyes not out | 7 |
| A. Bowell c Murdin b Thomas | 8 | L-b 2, n-b 1 | 3 |
| Mr W. K. Pearse run out | 0 | | |
| W. H. Livsey b Thomas | 36 | | **204** |

### Hampshire Bowling

| | Overs | Mdns | Runs | Wkts | Overs | Mdns | Runs | Wkts |
|---|---|---|---|---|---|---|---|---|
| Brown | 16 | 8 | 31 | 1 | 6 | 2 | 7 | — |
| Boyes | 18 | 8 | 17 | 6 | 14 | 5 | 30 | 2 |
| Newman | 3 | 2 | 1 | 3 | 8.1 | 3 | 30 | 8 |

### Northamptonshire Bowling

| | Overs | Mdns | Runs | Wkts |
|---|---|---|---|---|
| Clark | 19 | 3 | 60 | 1 |
| Thomas | 24.1 | 6 | 52 | 3 |
| Jupp | 23 | 3 | 79 | 5 |
| Murdin | 3 | 2 | 10 | — |

Umpires: J. W. Day and H. Young.

# NORTHAMPTONSHIRE v DUBLIN UNIVERSITY

### Played at Northampton, July 7, 8, 1926

Not fully represented, Dublin University were completely outclassed. Only four members of the regular eleven turned out for Northamptonshire, but less known players acquitted themselves with credit, and early on the second afternoon the county won in an innings, with 241 runs to spare. W. E. Adams and Timms each made his first three-figure score in big cricket. First in and third out, Adams played a stylish game for three hours, obtaining 101 out of 246, while Timms, showing more freedom, scored 102 out of 165 in an hour and three-quarters. S. C. Adams also batted confidently. When Northamptonshire declared on Thursday with seven wickets down, the University, apart from Dickson and Forsythe, cut a poor figure on the good wicket. In the follow-on, the mastery of the bowlers was so complete, that seventy minutes sufficed to finish of the match. S. C. Adams had successes with his first two balls, dismissed another batsman in the same over, and altogether took six wickets for just over five runs apiece.

## Northamptonshire

| | |
|---|---|
| Mr W. E. Adams st Forsythe b Jeffares ....101 | Mr E. F. Powell c and b Radcliffe ........ 32 |
| Mr W. C. Brown c Forsythe | A. I. Cox not out ..................... 25 |
| b T. H. Dickson . 9 | Mr G. H. Johnson not out ............. 43 |
| Mr J. E. Timms c Beckett b Jeffares ......115 | |
| Mr S. C. Adams c Beckett b T. H. Dickson . 87 | B 9, l-b 8, w 5 ............... 22 |
| F. Walden lbw b T. H. Dickson .......... 18 | |
| Mr K. Rymill c Forsythe b T. H. Dickson .. 2 | (7 wkts dec.) 454 |

Mr J. M. Fitzroy and Mr T. Addis did not bat.

## Dublin University

| | | |
|---|---|---|
| Mr S. V. Beckett b Powell ..................... | 4 – b S. C. Adams ................. | 1 |
| Mr C. M. Deverill b Powell ..................... | 2 – b Powell ..................... | 1 |
| Mr T. H. Dickson b Addis ..................... | 13 – c Rymill b S. C. Adams .......... | 7 |
| Mr P. M. Dickson c and b Walden .............. | 47 – b S. C. Adams ............... | 0 |
| Mr H. C. Forsythe b Powell ..................... | 43 – c and b Walden ............... | 6 |
| Mr J. R. Wills b Powell ..................... | 0 – lbw b S. C. Adams ............. | 10 |
| Mr A. F. Jeffares b Fitzroy ..................... | 13 – b Walden ................... | 2 |
| Mr W. J. McMahon b Fitzroy ..................... | 4 – b Walden ................... | 0 |
| Mr F. T. Radcliffe b Fitzroy ..................... | 2 – b S. C. Adams ................. | 14 |
| Mr H. T. Baker not out ..................... | 0 – st Johnson b S. C. Adams ....... | 2 |
| Mr J. D. Groynne b Fitzroy ..................... | 0 – not out ..................... | 11 |
| B 20, l-b 5, w 2 ..................... | 27 | B 3, n-b 1 ............... 4 |
| | 155 | 58 |

## Dublin University Bowling

| | Overs | Mdns | Runs | Wkts |
|---|---|---|---|---|
| T. H. Dickson ..... | 54 | 15 | 118 | 4 |
| Beckett ........... | 15 | — | 47 | — |
| McMahon ........ | 21 | 3 | 74 | — |
| Jeffares .......... | 27 | 3 | 72 | 2 |
| Wills ............ | 13 | — | 80 | — |
| P. M. Dickson ..... | 3 | — | 30 | — |
| Radcliffe ........ | 7 | 2 | 11 | 1 |

## Northamptonshire Bowling

| | Overs | Mdns | Runs | Wkts | Overs | Mdns | Runs | Wkts |
|---|---|---|---|---|---|---|---|---|
| Powell ........... | 16 | 3 | 42 | 4 | 5 | 3 | 8 | 1 |
| Addis ........... | 14 | 4 | 25 | 1 | 4 | 3 | 1 | — |
| Timms ........... | 4 | — | 12 | — | | | | |
| Walden .......... | 8 | — | 35 | 1 | 6 | 1 | 13 | 3 |
| Fitzroy .......... | 5.4 | 1 | 14 | 4 | | | | |
| S. C. Adams ..... | | | | | 7 | — | 32 | 6 |

Umpires: East and Stockwin.

## NORTHAMPTONSHIRE v NOTTINGHAMSHIRE

Played at Northampton, June 7, 8, 9, 1933

Everything else in this drawn game was dwarfed by the brilliant batting of Bakewell, who scoring 246 out of 428 in five minutes under five hours, set up a record for his county. He hit magnificently all round the wicket, his cover drives and leg strokes being especially fine. Despite the rapid pace he made his runs, he did not offer a chance. He hit twenty-nine 4s. Jupp, Cox and Liddell assisted Bakewell in stands that realised 50, 131 and 163 respectively. Scoring the second hundred of his career, Liddell hit fifteen 4s. On Wednesday, Nottinghamshire, thanks mainly to Carr and Keeton, who added 111 for the third wicket, scored 378 for the loss of eight wickets. Carr, driving vigorously, batted two and three-quarter hours for his 125 made out of 211. Although without Clark, who strained a thigh, Northamptonshire bowled very well on the last day, Jupp turning the ball cleverly and Nottinghamshire seemed in some danger of defeat when, with six men out they were only 18 in front. Gunn and Hardstaff, however, stayed together until the end, adding 86.

### Nottinghamshire

| | | | |
|---|---:|---|---:|
| W. W. Keeton lbw b Cox | 94 | – st Bellamy b Jupp | 43 |
| C. B. Harris lbw b Jupp | 24 | – lbw b Matthews | 5 |
| W. Walker c Bellamy b Matthews | 48 | – c Bellamy b Jupp | 53 |
| Mr A. W. Carr b Jupp | 125 | – c Matthews b Jupp | 1 |
| A. Staples b Cox | 10 | – c Bellamy b Matthews | 0 |
| W. Voce c Snowden b Jupp | 28 | | |
| F. W. Shipston c Partridge b Timms | 6 | – c Snowden b Jupp | 6 |
| G. V. Gunn not out | 39 | – not out | 43 |
| J. Hardstaff b Jupp | 4 | – not out | 41 |
| B. Lilley c Bellamy b Matthews | 8 | | |
| S. J. Staples b Partridge | 29 | | |
| B 8, l-b 6 | 14 | B 4 | 4 |
| | **429** | | **196** |

### Northamptonshire

| | | | |
|---|---:|---|---:|
| A. H. Bakewell c Harris b Gunn | 246 | A. D. Matthews b A. Staples | 37 |
| Mr A. W. Snowden c Lilley b Gunn | 16 | Mr W. C. Brown not out | 13 |
| B. Bellamy c Voce b S. J. Staples | 7 | R. J. Partridge b A. Staples | 5 |
| J. E. Timms lbw b S. J. Staples | 0 | E. W. Clark absent hurt | 0 |
| Mr V. C. W. Jupp c Harris b S. J. Staples | 31 | B 14, l-b 6, w 1, n-b 1 | 22 |
| A. L. Cox lbw b Gunn | 43 | | |
| A. G. Liddell c and b Gunn | 101 | | **521** |

### Northamptonshire Bowling

| | Overs | Mdns | Runs | Wkts | Overs | Mdns | Runs | Wkts |
|---|---|---|---|---|---|---|---|---|
| Clark | 20 | 1 | 87 | — | | | | |
| Matthews | 34 | 8 | 70 | 2 | 22 | 4 | 60 | 2 |
| Partridge | 15.3 | 1 | 32 | 1 | 13 | 3 | 34 | — |
| Cox | 21 | 1 | 71 | 2 | 12 | — | 38 | — |
| Jupp | 31 | 5 | 116 | 4 | 15 | 3 | 39 | 4 |
| Timms | 11 | 2 | 39 | 1 | 6 | — | 21 | — |

### Nottinghamshire Bowling

| | Overs | Mdns | Runs | Wkts |
|---|---|---|---|---|
| Voce | 32 | 6 | 100 | — |
| A. Staples | 35.4 | 7 | 67 | 2 |
| S. J. Staples | 30 | 1 | 177 | 3 |
| Gunn | 33 | 7 | 99 | 4 |
| Harris | 11 | 1 | 35 | — |
| Hardstaff | 2 | — | 7 | — |
| Keeton | 2 | — | 14 | — |

Umpires: J. Stone and A. Skelding.

## NORTHAMPTONSHIRE v YORKSHIRE

Played at Kettering, June 14, 15, 1933

Lacking the services of Clark, Northamptonshire on winning the toss, batted first in brilliant sunshine on a pitch which had previous been subjected to heavy rain. Collapsing twice in sensational fashion for 27 and 68 they left Yorkshire easy winners before lunch-time on Thursday by an innings and 206 runs. In the first innings Bowes and Macaulay began the bowling, but after sending down one over Bowes gave way to Verity, and Snowden at once hit the new man for two 4s. The first wicket, however, went down at 12, and the remainder fell for the addition of 15 runs. Macaulay and Verity did the damage, the former, after 4 runs had been scored from him, taking seven wickets for 9 runs, and eleven in the match for 34. Yorkshire fared none too well at first, losing Holmes and Mitchell for 4, while Leyland was missed at slip next ball. Then Sutcliffe and Leyland batted carefully for a time, but upon Jupp bowling, Sutcliffe hit freely and when caught at the wicket, claimed 113 out of 181 in two hours. He hit no fewer than ten 6s over the very short boundary on the leg side. With Barber and Sellers also batting effectively, Yorkshire, despite the fact that Jupp took the last five wickets for 12, gained a lead of 274. Going in again Northamptonshire lost six wickets for 23 runs, but Bellamy, Partridge and Matthews spared them the indignity of another such complete breakdown as in the first innings.

### Northamptonshire

| | | | |
|---|---|---|---|
| A. H. Bakewell lbw b Verity | 4 | – c Verity b Bowes | 6 |
| Mr A. W. Snowden b Macaulay | 10 | – b Bowes | 0 |
| B. Bellamy c Macaulay b Verity | 0 | – c Verity b Macaulay | 12 |
| J. E. Timms st Wood b Verity | 1 | – c Barber b Macaulay | 1 |
| Mr V. W. C. Jupp b Macaulay | 0 | – c Rhodes b Bowes | 3 |
| A. L. Cox lbw b Macaulay | 1 | – c Wood b Macaulay | 4 |
| A. G. Liddell b Macaulay | 6 | – run out | 0 |
| A. D. Matthews c Rhodes b Macaulay | 0 | – lbw b Macaulay | 8 |
| Mr W. C. Brown c Verity b Macaulay | 0 | – c Rhodes b Bowes | 1 |
| R. J. Partridge b Macaulay | 0 | – not out | 14 |
| A. E. Thomas not out | 3 | – b Verity | 10 |
| L-b 2 | 2 | B 1, l-b 2, w 1, n-b 5 | 9 |
| | **27** | | **68** |

### Yorkshire

| | | | |
|---|---|---|---|
| H. Sutcliffe c Bellamy b Thomas | 113 | A. Wood lbw b Jupp | 6 |
| P. Holmes run out | 0 | A. C. Rhodes lbw b Jupp | 14 |
| A. Mitchell c Partridge b Matthews | 1 | G. G. Macaulay not out | 4 |
| M. Leyland c Partridge b Jupp | 36 | W. E. Bowes c Matthews b Jupp | 0 |
| W. Barber c Bakewell b Partridge | 69 | B 4, l-b 5 | 9 |
| Mr A. B. Sellers c Brown b Jupp | 49 | | |
| H. Verity c Brown b Jupp | 0 | | **301** |

### Yorkshire Bowling

| | Overs | Mdns | Runs | Wkts | Overs | Mdns | Runs | Wkts |
|---|---|---|---|---|---|---|---|---|
| Bowes | 1 | — | 1 | — | 18 | 8 | 20 | 4 |
| Macaulay | 14 | 7 | 9 | 7 | 23 | 10 | 25 | 4 |
| Verity | 13 | 8 | 15 | 3 | 5.3 | 2 | 14 | 1 |

## Northamptonshire Bowling

|  | Overs | Mdns | Runs | Wkts |
|---|---|---|---|---|
| Matthews ......... | 23 | 5 | 67 | 1 |
| Thomas .......... | 18 | 2 | 38 | 1 |
| Jupp ............. | 17 | — | 99 | 6 |
| Partridge ........ | 19 | 4 | 54 | 1 |
| Cox ............. | 9 | — | 34 | — |

Umpires: E. J. Smith and A. Skelding.

# NORTHAMPTONSHIRE v WARWICKSHIRE

### Played at Northampton, July 19, 20, 21, 1933

No fewer than five players scored hundreds in this drawn match, which became memorable for the prodigious display of hitting by Santall on the last day. In less than two hours before lunch Santall scored 173. He reached 50 out of 66 in forty-five minutes: 100 out of 132 in eighty minutes; 150 out of 201 in an hour and fifty minutes, and 200 out of 297 in two and three-quarter hours. His 201 was the highest score of his career, and apart from a difficult chance when 173, he made no mistake, hitting four 6s and twenty-five 4s. In the absence of Clark, playing at Lord's, the Northamptonshire attack proved most ineffective. On Thursday Kilner and Croom seized the opportunity to put together 219 for the opening Warwickshire partnership before Kilner, who was very strong on the leg side, skied a ball to mid-off. Croom stayed until the total reached 259. The next day came Santall's magnificent exhibition. Bakewell and Timms both batted faultlessly for Northamptonshire while Jupp and Matthews hit freely.

## Northamptonshire

| | | |
|---|---|---|
| A. H. Bakewell b Hollies ..................... | 116 | – c Smart b Brown ............... 10 |
| A. G. Liddell c Parsons b Mayer ............. | 0 | – b Paine ..................... 29 |
| B. Bellamy c Santall b Paine ................ | 26 | – not out ..................... 28 |
| J. E. Timms hit wkt b Brown ................. | 113 | |
| Mr V. W. C. Jupp c Smart b Mayer ............. | 47 | |
| Mr A. W. Snowden b Hollies .................. | 1 | |
| A. L. Cox c Paine b Hollies ................. | 29 | – not out ..................... 5 |
| A. D. Matthews c Croom b Hollies ............. | 50 | |
| Mr W. C. Brown b Mayer .................... | 0 | |
| R. J. Partridge b Hollies ..................... | 0 | |
| A. E. Thomas not out ....................... | 6 | |
| B 4, l-b 4, w 1, n-b 2 ................. | 11 | B 4 ................. 4 |

399                     76

## Warwickshire

| | | |
|---|---|---|
| N. Kilner c Matthews b Jupp ............ 114 | Rev. J. H. Parsons c and b Partridge ...... 65 |
| A. J. Croom b Matthews ................ 116 | E. Brown b Partridge .................. 1 |
| L. A. Bates b Matthews ................ 15 | J. H. Mayer not out ................... 3 |
| G. Paine b Matthews ................. 7 | |
| J. Smart lbw b Matthews ............... 2 | B 10, l-b 4, n-b 1 ............. 15 |
| F. R. Santall not out ................... 201 | |
| W. A. Hill b Matthews ................ 26 | (8 wkts dec.) 565 |

E. Hollies did not bat.

## Warwickshire Bowling

| | Overs | Mdns | Runs | Wkts | Overs | Mdns | Runs | Wkts |
|---|---|---|---|---|---|---|---|---|
| Mayer .......... | 41 | 7 | 90 | 3 | 7 | 3 | 9 | — |
| Brown .......... | 28 | 7 | 71 | 1 | 10 | 4 | 19 | 1 |
| Santall .......... | 8 | 1 | 18 | — | | | | |
| Paine ........... | 27 | 3 | 95 | 1 | 13 | 7 | 14 | 1 |
| Hollies .......... | 42.2 | 6 | 114 | 5 | 6 | 1 | 21 | — |
| Croom .......... | | | | | 3 | — | 9 | — |

## Northamptonshire Bowling

| | Overs | Mdns | Runs | Wkts |
|---|---|---|---|---|
| Matthews ........ | 42 | 17 | 86 | 5 |
| Thomas .......... | 44 | 14 | 123 | — |
| Cox ............. | 17 | 5 | 37 | — |
| Partridge ........ | 30 | 3 | 110 | 2 |
| Jupp ............. | 32 | 5 | 153 | 1 |
| Liddell .......... | 3 | — | 24 | — |
| Timms .......... | 4 | 1 | 17 | — |

Umpires: A. Skelding and T. Oates.

# NORTHAMPTONSHIRE v MIDDLESEX

Played at Northampton, June 17, 18, 19, 1936

Drawn. When Middlesex appeared within sight of victory, bad light, followed by a thunderstorm, caused the game to be given up; Northamptonshire were in a hopeless position, for with only two wickets to fall they wanted 25 to avert an innings defeat. G. O. Allen, who had been appointed captain of England, led the visitors, whose bowling suffered much punishment before tea on Wednesday. Bakewell touched his best form, excelling with the cut and drive. Northway and Timms helped him in stands of 91 and 114 respectively, and by tea the total reached 283 for four wickets. Afterwards, six wickets fell for 15, Bakewell being caught after batting four hours and hitting thirteen 4s. Middlesex lost three men for 36, but on Thursday, Hendren, twice missed early in his innings, scored freely all round the wicket and, with Allen and Hulme rendering excellent support, Middlesex finished three runs ahead with half their wickets in hand. Friday was memorable for a brilliant display by Compton, who hit his first hundred in first-class cricket after Matthews had disposed of Hendren, Hulme and Smith for 13. Altogether Hendren batted fours hours, hitting thirteen 4s. By perfect timing Compton drove, pulled and cut with remarkable power, and took out his bat with fourteen 4s as his best strokes, in one and three-quarter hours. He and Sims put on 76 for the ninth wicket and there followed a remarkable last partnership of 74 with Peebles, who by sound defence stayed while Compton scored his last 60 runs.

## Northamptonshire

| | | | |
|---|---|---|---|
| Mr R. P. Northway b Allen .................... | 31 | – c Allen b Smith ............... | 6 |
| D. Brookes lbw (N) b Smith ................... | 2 | – b Allen ...................... | 13 |
| A. H. Bakewell c Peebles b Smith .............. | 144 | – b Sims ...................... | 15 |
| J. E. Timms c Peebles b Allen ................. | 53 | – lbw b Sims .................. | 35 |
| Mr V. W. C. Jupp c Fairservice b Smith ......... | 8 | – b Sims ...................... | 7 |
| A. L. Cox lbw b Sims ........................ | 22 | – c and b Allen ............... | 33 |
| K. C. James b Smith ........................ | 0 | – st Price b Peebles ............... | 2 |
| C. Perkins b Sims .......................... | 0 | – lbw b Allen ................... | 9 |
| Mr H. J. H. Lamb b Sims ..................... | 5 | – not out ..................... | 17 |
| A. D. Matthews c Fairservice b Sims ........... | 0 | – not out ..................... | 0 |
| E. W. Clark not out ........................ | 1 | | |
| B 9, l-b 23 ........................ | 32 | B 2, l-b 1, n-b 1 .......... | 4 |
| | 298 | | 141 |

## Middlesex

| | | |
|---|---|---:|
| G. E. Hart b Matthews | | 16 |
| C. Fairservice b Matthews | | 0 |
| W. F. Price lbw (N) b Jupp | | 25 |
| Mr F. F. Covington b Jupp | | 3 |
| E. Hendren b Matthews | | 145 |
| Mr G. O. Allen c James b Perkins | | 47 |
| J. Hulme c James b Matthews | | 55 |
| D. Compton not out | | 100 |
| J. Smith c Timms b Matthews | | 2 |
| J. Sims c Jupp b Clark | | 31 |
| Mr I. A. R. Peebles b Timms | | 18 |
| B 13, l-b 8, n-b 1 | | 22 |
| | | 464 |

## Middlesex Bowling

| | Overs | Mdns | Runs | Wkts | Overs | Mdns | Runs | Wkts |
|---|---|---|---|---|---|---|---|---|
| Smith | 27 | 8 | 49 | 4 | 13 | 2 | 26 | 1 |
| Allen | 20 | 2 | 91 | 2 | 13 | 1 | 39 | 3 |
| Hulme | 4 | — | 15 | — | | | | |
| Sims | 20.5 | 3 | 69 | 4 | 16 | 1 | 50 | 3 |
| Peebles | 8 | 2 | 21 | — | 12 | 3 | 22 | 1 |
| Compton | 3 | — | 21 | — | | | | |

## Northamptonshire Bowling

| | Overs | Mdns | Runs | Wkts |
|---|---|---|---|---|
| Clark | 32 | 5 | 95 | 1 |
| Matthews | 36 | 5 | 116 | 5 |
| Jupp | 16 | 3 | 89 | 2 |
| Perkins | 29 | 5 | 79 | 1 |
| Cox | 12 | — | 57 | — |
| Timms | 1.2 | — | 6 | 1 |

Umpires: T. Oates and H. G. Baldwin.

# NORTHAMPTONSHIRE v SUSSEX

## Played at Northampton, July 20, 21, 22, 1938

Drawn. Consistent batting brought Northamptonshire their best score of the season, but their bowlers went through an exceptional experience while four Sussex men scored hundreds in their county's highest total. Nelson was out unluckily. He cut a ball hard on to the wicket-keeper's foot and from the rebound first slip held the catch. Sussex secured a lead of 122 on the second day thanks chiefly to John Langridge, who, missed when 91 and 222, scored nearly half the 464 runs made during his stay of five hours and a half. Perfectly timed drives brought most of his four 6s and twenty-two 4s. The opening stand produced 192 and the third wicket put on 213. James Parks hit well with a variety of strokes and Cox got his runs at one a minute while John Langridge was just as free during a dashing partnership. Bartlett and Stainton, in an hour, made 132 on the third morning. Brookes and Timms repeated their good form and Nasiruddin, a young Indian, gave a second promising display in saving the match.

## Northamptonshire

| | | | |
|---|---|---|---|
| H. W. Greenwood c Holmes b Hammond | 1 | – lbw b Hammond | 5 |
| R. J. Partridge b J. Cornford | 40 | – lbw b J. Cornford | 20 |
| D. Brookes c Holmes b J. Parks | 56 | – run out | 72 |
| I. E. Timms c W. Cornford b Wood | 45 | – c Holmes b Cox | 86 |
| K. C. James c W. Cornford b Langridge | 29 | – b J. Cornford | 3 |
| M, R. P. Nelson c Hammond b J. Cornford | 64 | – b J. Parks | 15 |
| F. P. O'Brien lbw b J. Parks | 44 | – st W. Cornford b Hammond | 0 |
| S. M. Nasiruddin c Holmes b J. Parks | 24 | – not out | 42 |
| M. Dunkley b Wood | 50 | – c H. Parks b Hammond | 9 |
| E. J. Herbert b J. Parks | 1 | – not out | 16 |
| J. Buswell not out | 9 | | |
| B 9, l-b 4, n-b 1 | 14 | B 16, l-b 9 | 25 |
| | **377** | | **293** |

## Sussex

| | | | |
|---|---|---|---|
| John Langridge c Dunkley b Buswell | 227 | Mr R. G. Stainton not out | 67 |
| J. H. Parks lbw b Nelson | 106 | | |
| H. W. Parks c Greenwood b Buswell | 1 | B 17, l-b 8, n-b 3 | 28 |
| G. Cox c Nelson b Partridge | 101 | | |
| Mr H. T. Bartlett not out | 101 | (4 wkts dec.) | 631 |

Mr. A. J. Holmes, W. Cornford, H. E. Hammond, J. Cornford and D. J. Wood did not bat.

### Sussex Bowling

| | Overs | Mdns | Runs | Wkts | Overs | Mdns | Runs | Wkts |
|---|---|---|---|---|---|---|---|---|
| J. Cornford | 35 | 7 | 110 | 2 | 28 | 8 | 77 | 2 |
| Hammond | 28 | 7 | 68 | 1 | 23 | 3 | 61 | 3 |
| Wood | 24.5 | 2 | 81 | 2 | 11 | 4 | 20 | — |
| J. H. Parks | 35 | 8 | 72 | 4 | 21 | 8 | 42 | 1 |
| Holmes | 8 | 2 | 19 | — | 4 | — | 15 | — |
| Langridge | 4 | — | 13 | 1 | 13 | 5 | 34 | — |
| Cox | | | | | 3 | — | 19 | 1 |

### Northamptonshire Bowling

| | Overs | Mdns | Runs | Wkts |
|---|---|---|---|---|
| Buswell | 32 | 2 | 127 | 2 |
| Partridge | 34 | 2 | 115 | 1 |
| Herbert | 23 | 2 | 109 | — |
| Timms | 26 | 3 | 106 | — |
| O'Brien | 11 | — | 61 | — |
| Nelson | 13 | 1 | 63 | 1 |
| Greenwood | 2 | — | 22 | — |

Umpires: J. Smart and N. Kilner.

## NORTHAMPTONSHIRE v SUSSEX

Played at Kettering, July 1, 3, 4, 1939

Sussex won by five wickets. Two batsmen shared chief honours in a remarkable game. Although fifteen wickets fell on Saturday for 318 runs, Timms scored 101 perfectly and, after a second innings stand of 136 by Greenwood and Brookes, he became the first

Northamptonshire batsman ever to make two centuries in a match. Merritt, with three 6s and ten 4s, scored 87 in fifty-seven minutes. When Nelson declared Sussex lost two wickets for 40 runs, the order having been altered, but John Langridge and Cox added 219 in two hours. Cox went to 232, his highest innings. He hit four 6s and thirty-two 4s, his drives, cuts and leg strokes being equally good.

## Northamptonshire

| | | | |
|---|---:|---|---:|
| H. W. Greenwood c Jas. Langridge b J. Parks | 16 | – b Nye | 94 |
| P. Davis lbw b J. Parks | 12 | – c H. Parks b J. Parks | 5 |
| D. Brookes run out | 0 | – lbw b Oakes | 67 |
| J. E. Timms c Jas. Langridge b J. Parks | 101 | – not out | 114 |
| L. P. O'Brien c Nye b Cox | 40 | – b Nye | 0 |
| Mr R. P. Nelson c Bartlett b Jas. Langridge | 7 | – c H. Parks b Oakes | 11 |
| W. E. Merritt c Bartlett b J. Parks | 8 | – c J. Parks b Duffield | 87 |
| W. Kemmey c Cornford b Jas. Langridge | 3 | – not out | 8 |
| P. Dunkley b J. Parks | 8 | | |
| R. J. Partridge not out | 0 | | |
| A. Robinson run out | 0 | | |
| L-b 3, n-b 2 | 5 | B 4, l-b 8, n-b 1 | 13 |
| | **200** | **(6 wkts dec.)** | **399** |

## Sussex

| | | | |
|---|---:|---|---:|
| John Langridge b Partridge | 4 | – b Nelson | 93 |
| J. H. Parks c Kemmey b Partridge | 13 | – not out | 50 |
| H. W. Parks b Nelson | 25 | – c Kemmey b Partridge | 8 |
| G. Cox c Merritt b Partridge | 58 | – st Kemmey b Merritt | 232 |
| Jas. Langridge lbw b Merritt | 6 | – c Dunkley b Nelson | 4 |
| Mr H. T. Bartlett c Greenwood b Partridge | 3 | – not out | 14 |
| W. Cornford not out | 41 | | |
| Mr R. A. A. Holt b Robinson | 4 | | |
| C. Oakes c Dunkley b Merritt | 0 | – lbw b Robinson | 9 |
| J. Duffield b Nelson | 7 | | |
| J. Nye c Merritt b Nelson | 2 | | |
| B 4, l-b 4, w 1 | 9 | B 16, l-b 2 | 18 |
| | **172** | | **428** |

## Sussex Bowling

| | Overs | Mdns | Runs | Wkts | Overs | Mdns | Runs | Wkts |
|---|---|---|---|---|---|---|---|---|
| Nye | 16 | 1 | 55 | — | 24 | — | 116 | 2 |
| Duffield | 6 | — | 14 | — | 16 | — | 76 | 1 |
| J. Parks | 19.6 | 1 | 55 | 5 | 22 | 6 | 78 | 1 |
| Jas Langridge | 12 | 1 | 48 | 2 | 3 | — | 16 | — |
| Cox | 6 | — | 23 | 1 | 3 | — | 16 | — |
| John Langridge | | | | | 5 | — | 16 | — |
| Oakes | | | | | 9 | 1 | 68 | 2 |

## Northamptonshire Bowling

| | Overs | Mdns | Runs | Wkts | Overs | Mdns | Runs | Wkts |
|---|---|---|---|---|---|---|---|---|
| Partridge | 16 | — | 51 | 4 | 18 | 2 | 84 | 1 |
| Timms | 4 | — | 27 | — | 13 | — | 88 | — |
| Robinson | 11 | 1 | 32 | 1 | 16 | — | 77 | 1 |
| Nelson | 6.4 | 3 | 7 | 3 | 17 | 2 | 79 | 2 |
| Merritt | 10 | 1 | 46 | 2 | 10 | — | 75 | 1 |
| O'Brien | | | | | 2 | — | 7 | — |

Umpires: F. Chester and H. W. Lee.

# NOTTINGHAMSHIRE

## NOTTINGHAMSHIRE v MIDDLESEX

Played at Nottingham, July 12, 14, 15, 1924

This was the most remarkable match of the season at Trent Bridge, Nottinghamshire, after hitting up a score of 462 in their first innings, suffering an astonishing defeat by 27 runs. On the first day John Gunn and Carr had a great partnership, putting on 196 runs before Gunn, owing to a strained leg, had for a time to retire. The exciting cricket of the match came on the last day. Middlesex, who had to follow on, looked hopelessly beaten, but Guise batted as he had never batted before for his county and Bruce, on coming back after being off the field with a bruised hand, hit away in dashing fashion. Despite all this fine batting Nottinghamshire, left with only 150 to get, looked certain of victory when George Gunn and Whysall had scored 72 runs together, but after that Allen's fast bowling was irresistible.

### Nottinghamshire

| | | | |
|---|---|---|---|
| G. Gunn b Durston | 55 | – b Haig | 38 |
| W. Whysall lbw b Haig | 36 | – c Lee b Allen | 32 |
| J. Gunn st Murrell b Haig | 113 | – b Allen | 1 |
| Mr A. W. Carr c Guise b Lee | 134 | – b Haig | 2 |
| W. Payton c Moffat b Durston | 65 | – c Durston b Allen | 1 |
| B. Lilley c Murrell b Guise | 19 | – b Allen | 0 |
| W. Flint c Guise b Haig | 13 | – lbw b Durston | 23 |
| S. J. Staples c Murrell b Durston | 4 | – c Durston b Haig | 1 |
| F. Barratt b Haig | 2 | – b Allen | 1 |
| F. C. Matthews run out | 2 | – b Allen | 0 |
| L. Richmond not out | 0 | – not out | 14 |
| B 9, l-b 8, w 2 | 19 | B 4, l-b 5 | 9 |
| | **462** | | **122** |

### Middlesex

| | | | |
|---|---|---|---|
| Mr H. L. Dales b Staples | 13 | – c Carr b Matthews | 5 |
| H. W. Lee lbw b Richmond | 38 | – c Flint b Matthews | 51 |
| Mr G. O. Allen lbw b Barratt | 21 | – c and b Staples | 22 |
| Hon. C. N. Bruce c G. Gunn b Flint | 26 | – st Whysall b Richmond | 58 |
| Mr F. T. Mann lbw b Barratt | 0 | – b Barratt | 0 |
| Mr J. L. Guise c Flint b Barratt | 1 | – c Carr b Flint | 100 |
| Mr N. Haig b Matthews | 17 | – b Matthews | 29 |
| Mr N. J. D. Moffat not out | 55 | – lbw b Matthews | 6 |
| H. R. Murrell b Matthews | 2 | – c Whysall b Flint | 44 |
| T. J. Durston c and b Flint | 45 | – lbw b Richmond | 28 |
| A. Fowler b Richmond | 4 | – not out | 4 |
| B 16, l-b 11, w 2, n-b 2 | 31 | B 2, l-b 4, w 1, n-b 4 | 11 |
| | **253** | | **358** |

### Middlesex Bowling

| | Overs | Mdns | Runs | Wkts | Overs | Mdns | Runs | Wkts |
|---|---|---|---|---|---|---|---|---|
| Haig | 42 | 5 | 134 | 4 | 19 | 5 | 49 | 3 |
| Durston | 25.4 | 2 | 83 | 3 | 5.5 | — | 33 | 1 |
| Allen | 16 | 2 | 68 | — | 13 | 1 | 31 | 6 |
| Lee | 15 | — | 61 | 1 | | | | |
| Guise | 15 | 1 | 64 | 1 | | | | |
| Fowler | 7 | — | 33 | — | | | | |

**Nottinghamshire Bowling**

| | Overs | Mdns | Runs | Wkts | Overs | Mdns | Runs | Wkts |
|---|---|---|---|---|---|---|---|---|
| Barratt .......... | 22 | 4 | 61 | 3 | 22 | 6 | 62 | 1 |
| Matthews ........ | 10 | 3 | 33 | 2 | 24 | 3 | 98 | 4 |
| Staples .......... | 14 | 3 | 49 | 1 | 9 | — | 45 | 1 |
| Flint ............. | 13 | 3 | 26 | 2 | 22 | 4 | 80 | 2 |
| Richmond ....... | 16.5 | 4 | 53 | 2 | 17.2 | 1 | 48 | 2 |
| J. Gunn .......... | | | | | 3 | — | 14 | — |

Umpires: W. A. Buswell and W. Phillips.

# NOTTINGHAMSHIRE v MIDDLESEX

Played at Nottingham, June 20, 22, 23, 1925

Middlesex established a world's record by getting 502 runs to win by four wickets. They lost Stevens, Lee, Hearne and North for 66, but Hendren and Bruce added 154 in ninety-five minutes, while after lunch Mann and Hendren hit off the remaining 271 runs in three hours and a quarter. Hendren played his third innings of over two hundred in a fortnight. At the wickets five hours and a quarter he hit two 5s and nineteen 4s. Apart from one hard chance at slip when 161 Hendren played perfectly, but Bruce enjoyed two early escapes, and Mann was missed when 4 at backward point, those blunders costing Nottinghamshire the match. Mann played a restrained game, but, awaiting the loose ball, hit fourteen 4s. Middlesex scored their 502 in six hours and a quarter. Carr and Payton made 155 in ninety minutes.

## Nottinghamshire

| | | | |
|---|---|---|---|
| B. Lilley b Haig ............................ | 12 | – c Kidd b Hearne .............. | 34 |
| W. Whysall b Haig .......................... | 11 | – lbw b Stevens ................. | 82 |
| W. Walker c Hendren b North ................. | 25 | – c Stevens b Durston ........... | 6 |
| Mr A. W. Carr b Haig ....................... | 4 | – c Kidd b Hearne .............. | 123 |
| W. Payton c North b Durston ................. | 78 | – not out ...................... | 126 |
| W. Flint lbw b Durston ..................... | 0 | – b North ...................... | 8 |
| S. J. Staples c Hendren b North ............. | 3 | – b Stevens .................... | 19 |
| L. Richmond b Durston ...................... | 1 | – c Lee b Stevens .............. | 8 |
| F. Barratt c Stevens b North ............... | 1 | – b North ...................... | 16 |
| F. C. Matthews b Durston ................... | 7 | – c Durston b Stevens .......... | 10 |
| H. Larwood not out ........................ | 5 | – not out ..................... | 8 |
| B 12, l-b 8 ........................ | 20 | B 13, l-b 8 ............... | 21 |

                       167             (9 wkts dec.) 461

## Middlesex

| | | | |
|---|---|---|---|
| Mr G. T. S. Stevens run out .................. | 18 | – lbw b Matthews ............... | 28 |
| H. W. Lee c Whysall b Barratt ................ | 0 | – b Flint ...................... | 19 |
| J. W. Hearne c Carr b Barratt ............... | 16 | – c Matthews b Barratt ......... | 5 |
| E. Hendren c Flint b Staples ................ | 10 | – not out ...................... | 206 |
| Hon. C. N. Bruce c Payton b Staples .......... | 21 | – c Payton b Staples ........... | 103 |
| Mr E. L. Kidd b Barratt ..................... | 28 | – b Matthews ................... | 7 |
| Mr F. T. Mann c Barratt b Staples ........... | 6 | – not out ...................... | 101 |
| Mr N. Haig c Whysall b Staples .............. | 18 | | |
| H. R. Murrell b Barratt .................... | 0 | | |
| E. J. North c Matthews b Barratt ............ | 6 | – c Flint b Matthews ........... | 3 |
| T. J. Durston not out ...................... | 2 | | |
| L-b 2 ........................... | 2 | B 14, l-b 7, w 5, n-b 4 ...... | 30 |

                       127                       502

## Middlesex Bowling

| | Overs | Mdns | Runs | Wkts | Overs | Mdns | Runs | Wkts |
|---|---|---|---|---|---|---|---|---|
| Haig . . . . . . . . . . . . | 14 | 3 | 37 | 3 | 25 | 4 | 86 | — |
| Durston . . . . . . . . . | 18.1 | 7 | 46 | 4 | 22 | 5 | 76 | 1 |
| Hearne . . . . . . . . . . | 5 | 2 | 8 | — | 20 | 4 | 68 | 2 |
| Stevens . . . . . . . . . . | 5 | 1 | 16 | — | 19 | 2 | 83 | 4 |
| North . . . . . . . . . . . | 10 | 1 | 40 | 3 | 26 | 4 | 127 | 2 |

## Nottinghamshire Bowling

| | Overs | Mdns | Runs | Wkts | Overs | Mdns | Runs | Wkts |
|---|---|---|---|---|---|---|---|---|
| Barratt . . . . . . . . . . | 19.4 | 2 | 44 | 5 | 28 | 3 | 87 | 1 |
| Matthews . . . . . . . . | 5 | 1 | 25 | — | 25 | 2 | 97 | 3 |
| Larwood . . . . . . . . | 12 | 5 | 23 | — | 24 | 4 | 76 | — |
| Staples . . . . . . . . . . | 15 | 3 | 33 | 4 | 31 | 5 | 109 | 1 |
| Flint . . . . . . . . . . . . | | | | | 18 | 2 | 60 | 1 |
| Richmond . . . . . . . . | | | | | 14.5 | 3 | 43 | — |

Umpires: W. A. Buswell and A. R. Warren.

# NOTTINGHAMSHIRE v KENT

### Played at Nottingham, July 29, 30, 31, 1925

Set to get 327 Kent gained a great victory by four wickets, obtaining the runs in four hours and thirty-five minutes, within a quarter of an hour of time. Hardinge, Ashdown and Woolley fell for 20 runs and half the side were out for 157, Knott having helped to add 137 in two hours ten minutes for the fourth partnership. The Collins forced the game, and, when joined by Hubble, Bryan hit so brilliantly that the last 100 runs came in sixty-five minutes. Missed twice, Bryan, who went in first, hit twenty-three 4s. Fifteen wickets fell for 223 before Knott and Collins gave Kent the upper hand by adding 116, and when on Wednesday Nottinghamshire lost three men a second time for 61 Carr and Lilley put on 152 in a hundred minutes. Carr hit six 6s and nine 4s.

## Nottinghamshire

| | | | |
|---|---|---|---|
| G. Gunn c Wright b Collins . . . . . . . . . . . . . . . . . . . . | 2 | – c Woolley b Marriott . . . . . . . . . . . | 32 |
| W. Whysall b Wright . . . . . . . . . . . . . . . . . . . . . . . . | 4 | – run out . . . . . . . . . . . . . . . . . . . . . . | 4 |
| W. Walker c Woolley b Freeman . . . . . . . . . . . . . . . | 45 | – c Hubble b Freeman . . . . . . . . . . . | 21 |
| Mr A. W. Carr c Hubble b Collins . . . . . . . . . . . . . . | 0 | – c Johnstone b Collins . . . . . . . . . . . | 103 |
| W. Payton lbw b Freeman . . . . . . . . . . . . . . . . . . . | 27 | – run out . . . . . . . . . . . . . . . . . . . . . . | 69 |
| B. Lilley c Hubble b Wright . . . . . . . . . . . . . . . . . . | 3 | – b Collins . . . . . . . . . . . . . . . . . . . . | 44 |
| W. Flint lbw b Freeman . . . . . . . . . . . . . . . . . . . . . | 1 | – lbw b Freeman . . . . . . . . . . . . . . . | 10 |
| S. J. Staples b Wright . . . . . . . . . . . . . . . . . . . . . . | 18 | – c Bryan b Woolley . . . . . . . . . . . . | 19 |
| H. Larwood not out . . . . . . . . . . . . . . . . . . . . . . . . | 21 | – c Wright b Collins . . . . . . . . . . . . . | 18 |
| F. Barratt c Johnstone b Freeman . . . . . . . . . . . . . . | 15 | – c Johnstone b Freeman . . . . . . . . . | 41 |
| L. Richmond c Woolley b Freeman . . . . . . . . . . . . . | 8 | – not out . . . . . . . . . . . . . . . . . . . . . . | 0 |
| B 8, l-b 2 . . . . . . . . . . . . . . . . . . . . . . . . . | 10 | B 10, l-b 5, n-b 1 . . . . . . . . . | 16 |

154

377

## Kent

| | | | | |
|---|---|---|---|---|
| Mr C. P. Johnstone b Barratt | 5 | – c Staples b Richmond | 0 |
| H. T. W. Hardinge b Staples | 24 | – c Gunn b Barratt | 0 |
| W. Ashdown c Gunn b Barratt | 8 | – b Larwood | 1 |
| F. E. Woolley b Barratt | 16 | – c Lilley b Flint | 13 |
| Mr J. L. Bryan c Lilley b Barratt | 9 | – not out | 172 |
| Mr C. H. Knott c Lilley b Flint | 47 | – c Carr b Richmond | 57 |
| G. C. Collins c Flint b Staples | 67 | – b Barratt | 22 |
| J. C. Hubble st Lilley b Staples | 0 | – not out | 46 |
| C. Wright c Whysall b Staples | 12 | | |
| A. P. Freeman c Walker b Staples | 5 | | |
| Mr C. S. Marriott not out | 4 | | |
| B 2, l-b 6 | 8 | B 12, l-b 5, n-b 1 | 18 |
| | **205** | | **329** |

### Kent Bowling

| | Overs | Mdns | Runs | Wkts | Overs | Mdns | Runs | Wkts |
|---|---|---|---|---|---|---|---|---|
| Wright | 21 | 9 | 29 | 3 | 20 | 3 | 67 | — |
| Collins | 8 | 2 | 18 | 2 | 25 | 6 | 80 | 3 |
| Freeman | 23.4 | 6 | 65 | 5 | 21.1 | 5 | 71 | 3 |
| Marriott | 10 | 6 | 13 | — | 27 | 9 | 61 | 1 |
| Woolley | 5 | 1 | 19 | — | 16 | 3 | 70 | 1 |
| Hardinge | | | | | 2 | — | 12 | — |

### Nottinghamshire Bowling

| | Overs | Mdns | Runs | Wkts | Overs | Mdns | Runs | Wkts |
|---|---|---|---|---|---|---|---|---|
| Barratt | 22 | 6 | 56 | 4 | 23 | 7 | 73 | 2 |
| Larwood | 12 | 3 | 28 | — | 21 | 3 | 67 | 1 |
| Staples | 16 | 3 | 56 | 5 | 17 | 4 | 58 | — |
| Richmond | 5 | 1 | 29 | — | 15 | 3 | 46 | 2 |
| Flint | 7 | — | 28 | 1 | 23.1 | 4 | 67 | 1 |

Umpires: H. Young and C. Charlesworth.

## NOTTINGHAMSHIRE v WARWICKSHIRE

### Played at Nottingham, May 28, 30, 31, 1927

George Gunn in this encounter put together, for the third time in his career, two separate hundreds. On Saturday, when sixth man out at 197, he batted for over three hours without a mistake, and on Monday, when second out at 214, he again gave no chance, playing so brightly, that he obtained his runs in less than two hours and a half. Whysall and he shared in a partnership of 124, but the other nine wickets fell for 125 more runs. Warwickshire lost four men for 23, Larwood bowling in great form, but as Parsons drove finely and secured useful help from Croom, they ran the home side very close. Warwickshire batted very poorly at their second attempt, and Nottinghamshire, who had declared, with five men out, won by 252 runs. Walker, making the highest score of his career, helped Gunn to add 165.

## Nottinghamshire

| | | | | |
|---|---|---|---|---|
| G. Gunn c Smith b Santall | 100 | – b Calthorpe | 110 |
| W. Whysall lbw b Mayer | 48 | – lbw b Calthorpe | 27 |
| W. Walker b Mayer | 6 | – not out | 144 |
| Mr A. W. Carr c Santall b Mayer | 2 | – c Croom b Calthorpe | 0 |
| W. Payton c Mayer b Calthorpe | 10 | – b Santall | 22 |
| B. Lilley lbw b Santall | 8 | – c and b Santall | 59 |
| W. Flint c Smith b Mayer | 14 | – not out | 8 |
| A. Staples c Smith b Mayer | 9 | | |
| S. J. Staples c Calthorpe b Quaife | 22 | | |
| H. Larwood b Mayer | 17 | | |
| L. Richmond not out | 1 | | |
| B 6, l-b 6 | 12 | B 2, l-b 3, w 2 | 7 |

**249**  **(5 wkts dec.) 377**

## Warwickshire

| | | | | |
|---|---|---|---|---|
| E. J. Smith c S. J. Staples b Larwood | 8 | – b Larwood | 2 |
| N. Kilner b Larwood | 0 | – c A. Staples b Richmond | 29 |
| L. A. Bates b Larwood | 4 | – c Lilley b S. J. Staples | 21 |
| W. G. Quaife c Lilley b S. J. Staples | 11 | – b Larwood | 2 |
| J. H. Parsons b A. Staples | 87 | – lbw b S. J. Staples | 48 |
| A. J. Croom c Lilley b Larwood | 25 | – c Lilley b Flint | 12 |
| Hon. F. S. G. Calthorpe b Larwood | 20 | – c Gunn b Richmond | 4 |
| Mr R. E. S. Wyatt c S. J. Staples b Larwood | 20 | – c Larwood b Richmond | 0 |
| F. R. Santall c Payton b S. J. Staples | 31 | – c Lilley b Larwood | 13 |
| J. Fox not out | 7 | – not out | 0 |
| J. H. Mayer b Richmond | 10 | – b S. J. Staples | 1 |
| B 4, l-b 4 | 8 | B 4, l-b 6, n-b 1 | 11 |

**231**  **143**

### Warwickshire Bowling

| | Overs | Mdns | Runs | Wkts | Overs | Mdns | Runs | Wkts |
|---|---|---|---|---|---|---|---|---|
| Calthorpe | 23 | 1 | 75 | 1 | 23 | 5 | 63 | 3 |
| Mayer | 26 | 4 | 66 | 6 | 29 | 6 | 98 | — |
| Santall | 17 | 1 | 45 | 2 | 20 | 2 | 74 | 2 |
| Quaife | 16.1 | — | 44 | 1 | 18 | — | 71 | — |
| Wyatt | 4 | 1 | 7 | — | 8 | 2 | 20 | — |
| Fox | | | | | 5 | — | 30 | — |
| Croom | | | | | 5 | 1 | 14 | — |

### Nottinghamshire Bowling

| | Overs | Mdns | Runs | Wkts | Overs | Mdns | Runs | Wkts |
|---|---|---|---|---|---|---|---|---|
| Larwood | 22 | 1 | 87 | 6 | 14 | 4 | 39 | 3 |
| S. J. Staples | 22 | 10 | 58 | 2 | 18.5 | 7 | 33 | 3 |
| Richmond | 13.2 | 2 | 37 | 1 | 18 | 4 | 43 | 3 |
| A. Staples | 12 | 4 | 35 | 1 | 1 | — | 1 | — |
| Flint | 1 | — | 6 | — | 8 | 1 | 16 | 1 |

Umpires: F. Parris and W. A. Buswell.

## NOTTINGHAMSHIRE v SURREY

### Played at Nottingham, May 26, 28, 29, 1928

This was one of the most remarkable matches of the season. Nottinghamshire, after leading by 169 runs on the first innings, losing by seven wickets. Nottinghamshire batted all the first day and part of the second to score 457 in six hours and a quarter, George

Gunn, Barratt, Arthur Staples and Walker all meeting with pronounced success. Surrey, during their long spell of fielding missed only one catch. Hobbs, when the visitors went in, made his 150th century in first-class cricket, but beyond Ducat, nobody else did much. Carr should have compelled his opponents to follow-on in the failing light of the second evening. This error of policy proved fatal. Nottinghamshire lost four wickets for 15 runs in thirty-five minutes, and were all out early on the third morning for 50. Thanks to Sandham, Shepherd and Jardine, Surrey knocked off the 220 required for victory in two hours and three-quarters.

## Nottinghamshire

| | | | |
|---|---|---|---|
| G. Gunn b Shepherd | 122 | – c Brooks b Peach | 4 |
| W. Whysall c and b Peach | 10 | – c and b Fender | 4 |
| W. Walker c Brooks b Fenley | 51 | – c Jardine b Fender | 5 |
| Mr A. W. Carr b Shepherd | 1 | – c Brooks b Fender | 22 |
| W. Payton lbw b Fender | 4 | – c Ducat b Peach | 0 |
| B. Lilley b Fender | 12 | – b Fender | 2 |
| H. Larwood b Peach | 20 | – b Peach | 0 |
| A. Staples c Jardine b Fender | 94 | – c Jardine b Peach | 0 |
| F. Barratt c Fender b Peach | 96 | – not out | 0 |
| S. J. Staples c Peach b Fender | 28 | – c Jardine b Peach | 7 |
| L. Richmond not out | 6 | – b Peach | 1 |
| B 10, l-b 1, w 2 | 13 | B 4, l-b 1 | 5 |
| | **457** | | **50** |

## Surrey

| | | | |
|---|---|---|---|
| J. B. Hobbs c Whysall b A. Staples | 114 | – c S. J. Staples b Larwood | 0 |
| A. Sandham b S. J. Staples | 9 | – not out | 92 |
| A. Ducat lbw b Richmond | 45 | – b S. J. Staples | 2 |
| T. Shepherd c S. J. Staples b Larwood | 26 | – st Lilley b Richmond | 68 |
| Mr D. R. Jardine lbw b Richmond | 22 | – not out | 36 |
| T. H. Barling b S. J. Staples | 10 | | |
| R. J. Gregory lbw b Barratt | 13 | | |
| Mr P. G. H. Fender c S. J. Staples b Larwood | 3 | | |
| H. A. Peach c and b S. J. Staples | 25 | | |
| S. Fenley b Larwood | 5 | | |
| E. W. Brooks not out | 0 | | |
| B 9, l-b 4, w 1, n-b 2 | 16 | B 14, l-b 8 | 22 |
| | **288** | | **220** |

### Surrey Bowling

| | Overs | Mdns | Runs | Wkts | Overs | Mdns | Runs | Wkts |
|---|---|---|---|---|---|---|---|---|
| Fender | 38 | 11 | 92 | 4 | 13 | 4 | 21 | 4 |
| Peach | 44 | 7 | 143 | 3 | 12.2 | 6 | 24 | 6 |
| Fenley | 28 | 2 | 83 | 1 | | | | |
| Shepherd | 32 | 8 | 63 | 2 | | | | |
| Gregory | 16 | 2 | 61 | — | | | | |
| Jardine | 1 | — | 2 | — | | | | |

### Nottinghamshire Bowling

| | Overs | Mdns | Runs | Wkts | Overs | Mdns | Runs | Wkts |
|---|---|---|---|---|---|---|---|---|
| Larwood | 25.1 | 7 | 47 | 3 | 13 | 2 | 35 | 1 |
| Barratt | 18 | 4 | 37 | 1 | 8 | 3 | 15 | — |
| S. J. Staples | 23 | 5 | 56 | 3 | 20 | 3 | 63 | 1 |
| A. Staples | 14 | 1 | 43 | 1 | 10.1 | 1 | 30 | — |
| Richmond | 23 | 4 | 89 | 2 | 17 | 1 | 50 | 1 |
| Gunn | | | | | 1 | — | 5 | — |

Umpires: J. H. King and W. Phillips.

## NOTTINGHAMSHIRE v KENT

Played at Nottingham, August 1, 2, 3, 1928

Two performances stood out in a match limited by rain to two days, and won brilliantly by Nottinghamshire by nine wickets. Despite wet weather on Wednesday which prevented a start being made until the next morning the pitch was in quite good order when Kent went in, but in the course of four overs Larwood bowled Hardinge, Ashdown, Ames and Deed at a cost of 2 runs. Larwood did not do anything more, but Kent were all out for 118. Carr declared with a lead of 111 runs, and following Kent's second dismissal, Nottinghamshire were set 157 to get to win in two hours and a quarter. George Gunn seized upon the occasion for a demonstration of his exceptional batting skill, and the runs were actually knocked off in an hour and thirty-five minutes. Whysall helped to put on 148 for the first wicket, at which point Gunn had reached his sixth century of the season.

### Kent

| | | | |
|---|---|---|---|
| H. T. W. Hardinge b Larwood | 4 | – b Voce | 12 |
| W. Ashdown b Larwood | 1 | – run out | 84 |
| F. E. Woolley not out | 66 | – c Whysall b S. J. Staples | 66 |
| L. Ames b Larwood | 1 | – c S. J. Staples b Barratt | 24 |
| Mr J. A. Deed b Larwood | 0 | – c S. J. Staples b Larwood | 6 |
| Mr J. L. Bryan lbw b S. J. Staples | 7 | – c Lilley b Barratt | 10 |
| Mr G. B. Legge b Barratt | 3 | – c Carr b Voce | 11 |
| Mr T. C. Longfield c Lilley b Barratt | 4 | – not out | 29 |
| A. P. Freeman b S. J. Staples | 8 | – b Voce | 2 |
| C. Wright b Barratt | 15 | – b Voce | 0 |
| Mr C. S. Marriott b Barratt | 0 | – b Larwood | 3 |
| B 4, l-b 5 | 9 | B 8, l-b 8, w 4 | 20 |
| | **118** | | **267** |

### Nottinghamshire

| | | | |
|---|---|---|---|
| G. Gunn b Marriott | 16 | – not out | 100 |
| W. Whysall st Ames b Freeman | 15 | – c Bryan b Woolley | 46 |
| W. Walker c and b Freeman | 56 | | |
| Mr A. W. Carr c Woolley b Freeman | 19 | – not out | 9 |
| W. Payton c Legge b Wright | 30 | | |
| B. Lilley lbw b Freeman | 1 | | |
| A. Staples c Legge b Freeman | 16 | | |
| F. Barratt c Legge b Marriott | 5 | | |
| H. Larwood not out | 36 | | |
| S. J. Staples not out | 30 | | |
| B 2, l-b 1, n-b 2 | 5 | B 2, l-b 1 | 3 |
| | (8 wkts dec.) **229** | | **158** |

W. Voce did not bat.

### Nottinghamshire Bowling

| | Overs | Mdns | Runs | Wkts | Overs | Mdns | Runs | Wkts |
|---|---|---|---|---|---|---|---|---|
| Larwood | 12 | 2 | 28 | 4 | 16.2 | 2 | 62 | 2 |
| Barratt | 18 | 2 | 47 | 4 | 13 | 2 | 58 | 2 |
| S. J. Staples | 11 | — | 28 | 2 | 18 | 4 | 47 | 1 |
| Voce | 1 | — | 6 | — | 14 | 3 | 45 | 4 |
| A. Staples | | | | | 7 | — | 35 | — |

**Kent Bowling**

| | Overs | Mdns | Runs | Wkts | Overs | Mdns | Runs | Wkts |
|---|---|---|---|---|---|---|---|---|
| Wright .......... | 15 | 3 | 31 | 1 | 7 | 1 | 20 | — |
| Ashdown ........ | 6 | — | 20 | — | 4 | — | 10 | — |
| Freeman ........ | 33 | 9 | 98 | 5 | 14 | 2 | 51 | — |
| Marriott ......... | 24 | 5 | 75 | 2 | 8 | 1 | 31 | — |
| Longfield ........ | | | | | 2 | — | 15 | — |
| Woolley .......... | | | | | 2.4 | — | 28 | 1 |

Umpires: W. R. Parry and L. C. Braund.

## NOTTINGHAMSHIRE v HAMPSHIRE

Played at Nottingham, July 2, 3, 4, 1930

Defeated by Hampshire at Southampton, Nottinghamshire in the return encounter secured first innings points. Whysall and Walker put on 256 in about three hours, the latter hitting a 6 and twenty 4s. Whysall for the second time in his career obtained two separate hundreds in the same match. He drove particularly well and gave no chance in either innings. Rhodes, an amateur from the second eleven, showed capital form and Barratt scored 57 out of 71 in twenty-five minutes. For Hampshire, Mead and Tennyson hit up 195 in two hours and a half.

### Nottinghamshire

| | | | |
|---|---|---|---|
| G. Gunn b Kennedy | 6 | – c Mead b Kennedy | 3 |
| W. Whysall c Baring b Newman | 117 | – not out | 101 |
| W. Walker c Adams b Creese | 140 | – run out | 21 |
| W. Payton c and b Arnold | 39 | – lbw b Kennedy | 11 |
| B. Lilley c Newman b Baring | 8 | – c Creese b Kennedy | 6 |
| A. Staples lbw b Kennedy | 53 | – not out | 40 |
| Mr S. D. Rhodes not out | 68 | | |
| F. Barratt c Creese b Tennyson | 57 | | |
| S. J. Staples b Newman | 8 | | |
| W. Voce not out | 5 | | |
| B 4, l-b 6 | 10 | L-b 3, w 1 | 4 |

(8 wkts dec.) 511    (4 wkts dec.) 186

Mr R. D. F. Bland did not bat.

### Hampshire

| | | | |
|---|---|---|---|
| G. Brown b S. J. Staples | 26 | – not out | 58 |
| J. Arnold lbw b S. J. Staples | 5 | – lbw b Bland | 13 |
| A. Kennedy c S. J. Staples b Barratt | 6 | | |
| C. P. Mead c S. J. Staples b A. Staples | 143 | | |
| J. Newman c A. Staples b Voce | 0 | | |
| Lord Tennyson lbw b Bland | 97 | | |
| Mr G. C. A. Adams lbw b Barratt | 31 | | |
| W. L. Creese lbw b Barratt | 16 | – c Gunn b Bland | 7 |
| A. E. Pothecary not out | 14 | – not out | 3 |
| Mr. A. E. G. Baring c S. J. Staples b A. Staples | 16 | | |
| G. S. Boyes absent hurt | 0 | | |
| B 7, l-b 18, n-b 4 | 29 | L-b 1 | 1 |

383    82

**Hampshire Bowling**

| | Overs | Mdns | Runs | Wkts | Overs | Mdns | Runs | Wkts |
|---|---|---|---|---|---|---|---|---|
| Kennedy ......... | 40 | 8 | 95 | 2 | 18 | 5 | 38 | 3 |
| Baring ........... | 22 | 2 | 140 | 1 | 9 | 2 | 33 | — |
| Newman ......... | 27 | 3 | 101 | 2 | 12 | 1 | 34 | — |
| Boyes ............ | 15 | 4 | 27 | — | | | | |
| Arnold ........... | 13 | 1 | 51 | 1 | 2 | — | 20 | — |
| Creese ........... | 9 | 1 | 47 | 1 | 6 | — | 29 | — |
| Adams ........... | 4 | — | 21 | — | 1 | — | 13 | — |
| Pothecary ........ | 6 | 1 | 19 | — | 2 | — | 15 | — |
| Tennyson ......... | 1 | 1 | — | 1 | | | | |

**Nottinghamshire Bowling**

| | Overs | Mdns | Runs | Wkts | Overs | Mdns | Runs | Wkts |
|---|---|---|---|---|---|---|---|---|
| Barratt ........... | 28 | 8 | 87 | 3 | 3 | 1 | 2 | — |
| S. J. Staples ....... | 31 | 10 | 75 | 2 | | | | |
| Voce ............. | 18 | 5 | 50 | 1 | | | | |
| A. Staples ........ | 26.3 | 3 | 82 | 2 | 6 | — | 12 | — |
| Bland ............ | 20 | 2 | 60 | 1 | 12 | 1 | 42 | 2 |
| Rhodes ........... | | | | | 4 | — | 18 | — |
| Gunn ............ | | | | | 1 | — | 2 | — |
| Whysall .......... | | | | | 1 | — | 5 | — |

Umpires: W. R. Parry and W. Reeves.

## NOTTINGHAMSHIRE IN 1933

Important events in the history of Nottinghamshire cricket during the season were the retirement of George Gunn after a most distinguished career extending from 1902 until 1932, when he received a blow from the ball and did not venture to play at all last summer: a presentation to Larwood and Voce to commemorate their splendid work in helping England to beat Australia during the previous winter, and the opening of the gates erected at the pavilion entrance to the Trent Bridge ground as a memorial to John Auger Dixon – a member of the county eleven 1882-1905; captain 1889-1899; member of the committee 1895-1910, when he was elected life honorary member of the committee. The gates make a handsome structure, worthy of one of our leading counties. When performing the opening ceremony, Sir Francis Stanley Jackson, a former president of the MCC, Cambridge University and England captain, famous in Yorkshire cricket, said "Throughout the whole of his life John Dixon played the game and did his best to help others to do likewise".

## NOTTINGHAMSHIRE IN 1934

*President* – The Duke of Portland

*Hon. Treasurer* – Mr C. W. Wright, JP

*Hon. Secretary* – Dr G. O. Gauld

*Secretary* – Mr H. A. Brown, 26 Park Row, Nottingham

*Captain* – Mr A. W. Carr

At the end of a season, described as "unhappy" by a regular follower and intimate friend of the team, Nottinghamshire found themselves ninth in the championship – a further decline from their fall of the previous year. Various causes accounted for Nottinghamshire again failing to reach the high standard of cricket usually associated with them.

Throughout the previous summer Larwood and Voce suffered from the effects of their exertions during the tour in Australia. An operation put Larwood's damaged foot in order, but strains troubled him so much that he required considerable rest and, well as he bowled on occasions, he scarcely ever attempted his fastest pace. Far worse than this individual physical experience was the loss of three very important members of the side owing to illness. S. J. Staples made but one appearance; Walker, stricken with appendicitis during the first game, could not appear regularly until the middle of June, and then came the crowning catastrophe – the breakdown of A. W. Carr. Upon Lilley devolved the duties of captain. The wicket-keeper came through the ordeal with considerable credit, but the want of the regular leader when controversy raged round the bowling methods exploited by Larwood and Voce affected the form of the whole side. Lancashire and Middlesex threatened to abandon the game if this system of direct attack were waged against their batsmen. The dispute did not come to such an open rupture as this and Lancashire, after being 147 behind, declared with seven men out and won by 101 runs in the last over of the match; yet fixtures with Nottinghamshire have not been arranged for the coming season. Then, the strong opinion that Voce if not Larwood should play for England but were never asked added further fuel to the flames of unpleasantness. This much debated subject is dealt with elsewhere in the *Almanack*, and it is necessary merely to assert here that the unfortunate business seriously unsettled Nottinghamshire cricket – as if the incapacity of members of the side were not sufficient handicap.

Still more extraordinary was the retirement of Voce from the match with the Australians under the plea that he was suffering from sore shins after he had taken eight wickets for 66 runs. Then too, the pitches at Trent Bridge – hitherto renowned for their excellence – failed to last three days. Supporters of the county became annoyed; the cup of bitterness overflowed.

Club members and regular spectators at Trent Bridge naturally enough felt aggrieved at the criticisms levelled against their famous bowlers and, most unfortunately, they allowed their resentment to express itself. Some teams were not received in a sporting spirit. The Australians were regarded as responsible for the trouble over Larwood and Voce; "scenes" during their visit had for a climax considerable unpleasantness at the end of the match. As a corollary to all the trouble came the decision of the club committee in December to appoint G. F. Heane and S. D. Rhodes joint captains. And finally, feeling in certain quarters in Nottinghamshire reached such a height that at a special meeting called to discuss the attitude of the committee a motion of "no confidence" in that body was carried and the committee resigned "en bloc".

## NOTTINGHAMSHIRE v LANCASHIRE

### Played at Nottingham, June 16, 18, 19, 1934

Although Larwood began by taking six wickets in 29 balls for 1 run and on the second morning hit six 6s and eight 4s while scoring 80 out of 105 in forty-five minutes, Lancashire – 147 behind on the first innings – won the match just on time by 101 runs. Keeping up his fastest pace, Larwood varied his field but always bowled an accurate length and would have had a wonderful analysis had not five slip catches off him been dropped. Tyldesley, hitting fifteen 4s in a splendid innings, and Lister, missed when 21, by adding 182 in two hours, pulled the game round. Larwood and Voce failed to repeat their deadly form and when, after rain, Eckersley declared, Hopwood enjoyed the chief share in gaining Lancashire's remarkable victory.

## Lancashire

| | | | |
|---|---|---|---|
| F. Watson c Lilley b Voce | 11 | – c Keeton b Staples | 63 |
| J. L. Hopwood c Lilley b Voce | 2 | – c Carr b Larwood | 1 |
| J. Iddon b Larwood | 21 | – c Lilley b Staples | 18 |
| E. Tyldesley b Larwood | 23 | – c and b Voce | 109 |
| E. Paynter c Larwood b Voce | 31 | – b Larwood | 8 |
| Mr W. H. L. Lister c Staples b Larwood | 0 | – c Butler b Harris | 86 |
| I. W. Parkinson c Voce b Larwood | 0 | – c Carr b Larwood | 30 |
| Mr P. T. Eckersley c Staples b Larwood | 0 | – not out | 40 |
| F. M. Sibbles b Larwood | 1 | | |
| G. Duckworth c Larwood b Voce | 15 | – not out | 26 |
| F. S. Booth not out | 12 | | |
| B 1, l-b 1, n-b 1 | 3 | B 3, l-b 5, n-b 5 | 13 |
| | **119** | **(7 wkts dec.)** | **394** |

## Nottinghamshire

| | | | |
|---|---|---|---|
| W. W. Keeton c Tyldesley b Iddon | 42 | – c Duckworth b Hopwood | 61 |
| C. B. Harris c Duckworth b Booth | 4 | – c Parkinson b Iddon | 10 |
| J. Hardstaff lbw b Iddon | 42 | – lbw b Hopwood | 3 |
| Mr P. Vaulkhard c Eckersley b Iddon | 3 | – c and b Parkinson | 17 |
| A. Staples c Sibbles b Hopwood | 37 | – c Parkinson b Watson | 6 |
| G. V. Gunn c Watson b Hopwood | 5 | – c Tyldesley b Hopwood | 0 |
| Mr A. W. Carr st Duckworth b Iddon | 0 | – b Watson | 5 |
| B. Lilley c Booth b Hopwood | 40 | – not out | 24 |
| W. Voce c Duckworth b Iddon | 8 | – c Iddon b Hopwood | 0 |
| H. Larwood c Duckworth b Hopwood | 80 | – c Parkinson b Hopwood | 18 |
| H. J. Butler not out | 2 | – lbw b Hopwood | 0 |
| L-b 3 | 3 | L-b 2 | 2 |
| | **266** | | **146** |

### Nottinghamshire Bowling

| | Overs | Mdns | Runs | Wkts | Overs | Mdns | Runs | Wkts |
|---|---|---|---|---|---|---|---|---|
| Larwood | 17 | 4 | 51 | 6 | 18 | 3 | 85 | 3 |
| Voce | 15.3 | 3 | 49 | 4 | 30 | 5 | 98 | 1 |
| Butler | 5 | — | 13 | — | 8 | — | 35 | — |
| Staples | 3 | 1 | 3 | — | 21 | 6 | 72 | 2 |
| Gunn | | | | | 13 | 1 | 50 | — |
| Harris | | | | | 8 | — | 41 | 1 |

### Lancashire Bowling

| | Overs | Mdns | Runs | Wkts | Overs | Mdns | Runs | Wkts |
|---|---|---|---|---|---|---|---|---|
| Sibbles | 6 | 2 | 11 | — | 12 | 3 | 23 | — |
| Booth | 10 | 1 | 55 | 1 | 2 | — | 2 | — |
| Hopwood | 42.2 | 14 | 99 | 4 | 21.1 | 5 | 58 | 6 |
| Parkinson | 9 | — | 28 | — | 6 | 1 | 23 | 1 |
| Iddon | 29 | 11 | 70 | 5 | 14 | 10 | 12 | 1 |
| Watson | | | | | 7 | 1 | 26 | 2 |

Umpires: G. Beet and E. J. Smith.

# SOMERSET

## SOMERSET v SUSSEX

### Played at Taunton, May 21, 22, 1919

An extraordinary and in some respects very regrettable incident marked the first of the Taunton matches last season. On the second afternoon Sussex, with the score at a tie, had a wicket to fall, the remaining batsman being Heygate who was crippled by rheumatism. It was understood when the innings began that he would not be able to bat and as there was some doubt as to whether he would come in, one of the Somerset players – not J. C. White, the acting captain – appealed to Street, the umpire, on the ground that the limit of two minutes had been exceeded. Street pulled up the stumps and the match was officially recorded as a tie. The matter gave rise to much discussion and the MCC committee, when the question was referred to them, upheld the umpire's decision. Whether or not Heygate would have been able to crawl to the wicket, it was very unsportsmanlike that such a point should have been raised when there remained ample time to finish the match. Up to the time of the incident the game was a very good one, the ball beating the bat on the second day.

### Somerset

| | | | |
|---|--:|---|--:|
| Mr A. E. S. Rippon c Miller b Stannard | 26 | – b Cox | 8 |
| Mr A. D. E. Rippon c Miller b Vincett | 60 | – b Cox | 8 |
| Mr J. C. W. MacBryan lbw b Cox | 18 | – b Cox | 0 |
| E. Robson b Cox | 14 | – b Roberts | 11 |
| L. C. Braund b Roberts | 3 | – b Roberts | 11 |
| Mr J. D. Harcombe c H. Wilson b Cox | 0 | – run out | 5 |
| Mr P. P. Hope c Tate b Vincett | 48 | – c Stannard b Vincett | 6 |
| J. F. Bridges c Miller b Vincett | 34 | – st Miller b Vincett | 14 |
| Capt. Amor b Cox | 14 | – c Cox b Tate | 13 |
| Mr J. C. White b Cox | 12 | – not out | 11 |
| H. Chidgey not out | 1 | – c Vincett b Cox | 10 |
| B 8, l-b 4, w 1 | 13 | B 5, w 1 | 6 |
| | **243** | | **103** |

### Sussex

| | | | |
|---|--:|---|--:|
| Mr H. L. Wilson b Bridges | 56 | – not out | 42 |
| Mr A. K. Wilson c Braund b Bridges | 4 | – c Braund b Robson | 4 |
| Mr T. E. Bourdillon b Bridges | 21 | – c Bridges b Robson | 7 |
| Mr A. C. Somerset b Robson | 33 | – c Braund b Robson | 0 |
| Mr R. A. T. Miller b Bridges | 2 | – c Bridges b White | 0 |
| Mr J. H. Vincett b Bridges | 14 | – b Bridges | 6 |
| H. E. Roberts b Robson | 5 | – b D. Rippon | 28 |
| M. W. Tate c Braund b Robson | 69 | – c Chidgey b Bridges | 11 |
| G. Stannard b A. D. E. Rippon | 3 | – c McBryan b D. Rippon | 0 |
| G. Cox not out | 24 | – b Bridges | 0 |
| Mr H. J. Heygate b White | 0 | – absent | 0 |
| B 5, l-b 6 | 11 | B 1, l-b 5 | 6 |
| | **242** | | **104** |

## Sussex Bowling

|  | Overs | Mdns | Runs | Wkts | Overs | Mdns | Runs | Wkts |
|---|---|---|---|---|---|---|---|---|
| Roberts ......... | 17 | 4 | 51 | 1 | 16 | 1 | 40 | 2 |
| Vincett .......... | 31 | 4 | 69 | 3 | 9 | — | 20 | 2 |
| Stannard ........ | 8 | — | 27 | 1 | | | | |
| Tate ............ | 12 | 3 | 32 | — | 6 | 1 | 11 | 1 |
| Cox ............ | 15.4 | 4 | 51 | 5 | 18.4 | 6 | 26 | 4 |

## Somerset Bowling

|  | Overs | Mdns | Runs | Wkts | Overs | Mdns | Runs | Wkts |
|---|---|---|---|---|---|---|---|---|
| White ........... | 18.4 | 1 | 76 | 1 | 33 | — | 14 | 1 |
| Robson ......... | 15 | 3 | 49 | 3 | 14 | 2 | 51 | 3 |
| Bridges .......... | 22 | 4 | 84 | 5 | 12 | 2 | 32 | 3 |
| D. Rippon ....... | 9 | 2 | 22 | 1 | 2 | 1 | 1 | 2 |

Umpires: F. G. Roberts and A. E. Street.

## SOMERSET v HAMPSHIRE

### Played at Bath, May 27, 29, 30, 1922

Somerset suffered defeat, Hampshire winning the match by seven wickets. In Somerset's second innings Considine made a great effort, withstanding the Hampshire bowling for three hours and a half, but except from Daniell he did not get much support. Left with 174 to get Hampshire lost two wickets for 63 before the call of time on Monday. The third wicket fell at 74, and then Bowell and Mead steadily hit off the last hundred runs.

### Somerset

| | | | |
|---|---|---|---|
| Mr J. C. W. MacBryan c Livsey b Kennedy ....... | 2 | – lbw b Kennedy ................. | 0 |
| Mr A. E. S. Rippon c Mead b Boyes ............. | 35 | – b Newman .................... | 11 |
| A. Young b Kennedy ......................... | 2 | – b Kennedy ................... | 14 |
| Mr S. G. U. Considine b Kennedy ............... | 9 | – lbw b Kennedy ............... | 77 |
| Mr J. Daniell c Bolton b Kennedy .............. | 7 | – c Brown b Kennedy ........... | 43 |
| Mr J. C. White c Livsey b Kennedy ............. | 0 | – c Livsey b Kennedy .......... | 0 |
| Mr W. T. Greswell c Brown b Newman .......... | 27 | – c McIntyre b Newman ......... | 21 |
| G. Hunt b Kennedy ......................... | 0 | – c Mead b Kennedy ............ | 4 |
| F. Robson c Bowell b Newman ................. | 7 | – b Kennedy ................... | 0 |
| Mr J. J. Bridges st Livsey b Kennedy ............. | 6 | – not out ..................... | 25 |
| Mr S. L. Amor not out ....................... | 5 | – b Kennedy ................... | 2 |
| B 9, l-b 4 ......................... | 13 | B 12, l-b 8 .............. | 20 |
| | **113** | | **217** |

### Hampshire

| | | | |
|---|---|---|---|
| G. Brown c and b Bridges .................... | 23 | – c MacBryan b White ........... | 26 |
| A. Bowell b Bridges ......................... | 12 | – not out ..................... | 76 |
| A. Kennedy b Bridges ....................... | 10 | | |
| C. P. Mead run out ......................... | 19 | – not out ..................... | 57 |
| Lt-Col J. G. Greig c Amor b Robson ............. | 2 | – c and b White ............... | 11 |
| J. Newman c Bridges b Robson ................. | 55 | – lbw b Young ................. | 3 |
| Capt. R. H. D. Bolton b Bridges ............... | 1 | | |
| Mr C. P. Brutton c Amor b Robson ............. | 6 | | |
| Mr A. S. McIntyre b White ................... | 22 | | |
| W. H. Livsey c Amor b Robson ................. | 2 | | |
| G. S. Boyes not out ........................ | 1 | | |
| B 3, l-b 1 ......................... | 4 | L-b 1 ................. | 1 |
| | **157** | | **174** |

**Hampshire Bowling**

| | Overs | Mdns | Runs | Wkts | Overs | Mdns | Runs | Wkts |
|---|---|---|---|---|---|---|---|---|
| Kennedy ......... | 24 | 11 | 37 | 7 | 37.3 | 10 | 79 | 8 |
| Newman ......... | 14 | 4 | 36 | 2 | 25 | 5 | 78 | 2 |
| Boyes ........... | 10 | 2 | 27 | 1 | 16 | 4 | 40 | — |

**Somerset Bowling**

| | Overs | Mdns | Runs | Wkts | Overs | Mdns | Runs | Wkts |
|---|---|---|---|---|---|---|---|---|
| Bridges .......... | 25 | 3 | 83 | 4 | 16 | 1 | 50 | — |
| Robson ......... | 25.5 | 7 | 52 | 4 | 14 | 2 | 45 | — |
| White ........... | 7 | 4 | 18 | 1 | 25 | 10 | 49 | 2 |
| Young .......... | | | | | 4 | — | 10 | 1 |
| Greswell ......... | | | | | 9 | 2 | 19 | — |

Umpires: A. E. Street and J. P. Whiteside.

## SOMERSET v MIDDLESEX

Played at Weston-super-Mare, July 26, 27, 28, 1922

This match proved the event of the Somerset season. Steady rain cut the first day's play short at the tea interval, and when on Thursday Mann declared at lunch time with six wickets down for 346, the defeat of his side seemed out of the question. However, Somerset played up finely, and in the second innings of Middlesex the last five wickets fell for 35 runs. It thus came about that Somerset had to get 244 against time. They just managed to beat the clock, winning the match at exactly seven o'clock by two wickets. The winning hit was a 6 by Robson clean out of the ground.

### Middlesex

| | | |
|---|---|---|
| Mr H. L. Dales b Robson ..................... | 9 – | c Robson b Bridges ........... 9 |
| H. W. Lee run out ......................... | 66 – | b Robson ................... 24 |
| J. W. Hearne c Lyon b Bridges ............... | 84 – | c Lowry b White ............. 61 |
| E. Hendren not out ....................... | 100 – | c White b Greswell ........... 12 |
| Mr F. T. Mann c Daniell b White ............. | 45 – | b Greswell ................. 49 |
| Mr N. Haig c Young b White ............... | 17 – | b Greswell ................. 10 |
| Mr G. T. S. Stevens st Lyon b White ............. | 4 – | b Greswell ................. 0 |
| Mr C. H. L. Skeet not out ................. | 6 – | st Lyon b White ............. 3 |
| H. R. Murrell (did not bat) ................. | – | b White ................... 0 |
| Mr G. O. Allen (did not bat) ................. | – | lbw b Bridges ............... 0 |
| T. J. Durston (did not bat) ................. | – | not out ................... 12 |
| B 6, l-b 8, w 1 ..................... | 15 | B 3, l-b 2 .............. 5 |

(6 wkts dec.) 346        185

### Somerset

| | | |
|---|---|---|
| Mr P. R. Johnson c Murrell b Durston ........... | 74 – | b Haig ..................... 28 |
| Mr J. C. W. MacBryan st Murrell b Hearne ....... | 23 – | c Skeet b Stevens ........... 65 |
| A. Young hit wkt b Hearne ................. | 34 – | c Hearne b Haig ........... 16 |
| Mr S. G. U. Considine c Stevens b Durston ........ | 0 – | c Stevens b Hearne ........... 40 |
| Mr J. Daniell b Allen ..................... | 23 – | b Hearne ................. 22 |
| Mr T. C. Lowry st Murrell b Hearne ............. | 40 – | c Murrell b Haig ........... 15 |
| Mr M. D. Lyon b Allen ................... | 34 – | st Murrell b Haig ........... 11 |
| Mr J. C. White lbw b Stevens ................. | 8 – | st Murrell b Hearne ........... 13 |
| Mr W. T. Greswell c Allen b Durston ............. | 35 – | not out ..................... 20 |
| E. Robson c Murrell b Stevens ................. | 9 – | not out ................... 12 |
| Mr J. J. Bridges not out ................. | 0 | |
| B 3, l-b 5 ......................... | 8 | B 4, l-b 2, w 1 ........... 7 |

288        249

## Somerset Bowling

|            | Overs | Mdns | Runs | Wkts | Overs | Mdns | Runs | Wkts |
|------------|-------|------|------|------|-------|------|------|------|
| Robson .......... | 22 | 7 | 44 | 1 | 8 | 3 | 15 | 1 |
| Bridges .......... | 25 | 3 | 76 | 1 | 8 | 1 | 42 | 2 |
| White ........... | 38 | 10 | 89 | 3 | 26.4 | 7 | 57 | 3 |
| Greswell ......... | 22 | 6 | 70 | — | 27 | 7 | 66 | 4 |
| Young .......... | 13 | 1 | 52 | — | | | | |

## Middlesex Bowling

|            | Overs | Mdns | Runs | Wkts | Overs | Mdns | Runs | Wkts |
|------------|-------|------|------|------|-------|------|------|------|
| Haig ............ | 13 | 3 | 24 | — | 22 | 6 | 54 | 4 |
| Durston ......... | 17 | 3 | 73 | 3 | 8 | — | 44 | — |
| Hearne .......... | 22 | 1 | 93 | 3 | 9.2 | — | 47 | 3 |
| Stevens .......... | 15.4 | 1 | 71 | 2 | 13 | — | 59 | 1 |
| Allen ........... | 9 | 1 | 19 | 2 | 8 | 1 | 38 | — |

Umpires: T. Brown and A. E. Street.

# SOMERSET v ESSEX

### Played at Taunton, June 6, 8, 9, 1925

Somerset, despite the great performance of Daniell in playing two three-figure innings, could not force a win, Essex staying in for the whole of the third day for 251 runs and so averting defeat. Daniell batted splendidly in carrying his bat right through the first innings for 174, and in the second, although missed five times, hit finely. Unhappily he twisted his knee so badly that several weeks elapsed before he could turn out again. Essex, at their first attempt, cut a sorry figure against White. Case, when Somerset went in again, helped his captain to make 117 for the first wicket and Bligh played well. Set 481 to win, Essex lost three batsmen rather cheaply but then came stubborn opposition from Russell and Perrin who stayed together for more than two hours and a half and added 137. Russell, in putting together his second hundred of the season, withstood the Somerset attack for three hours and a half and Perrin, as in the visitors' first innings, defended with great skill.

## Somerset

| | | |
|---|---|---|
| Mr J. Daniell not out ........................ | 174 | – c Hipkin b Nichols ............... 108 |
| Mr C. C. Case b Douglas ...................... | 2 | – c O'Connor b Nichols ........... 59 |
| Mr S. G. U. Considine c Hipkin b Nichols ......... | 1 | – b Nichols ..................... 0 |
| Mr J. C. White c Nichols b Douglas ............. | 15 | – c Russell b Sharp .............. 0 |
| Mr A. S. Bligh lbw b Douglas .................. | 24 | – b Hipkin...................... 71 |
| Mr C. A. Winter c Douglas b Hipkin ............. | 13 | – c Nichols b Sharp .............. 11 |
| Mr G. F. Earle c Sharp b Russell ............... | 2 | – c Hipkin b Sharp .............. 15 |
| G. Hunt b O'Connor .......................... | 8 | – st Freeman b Hipkin ........... 13 |
| Mr P. P. Hope c Hipkin b O'Connor ............. | 19 | – c Douglas b Sharpe ............ 0 |
| Mr J. J. Bridges c Cutmore b O'Connor ......... | 20 | – c Hipkin b Sharp .............. 3 |
| Mr M. L. Hill b Russell ....................... | 29 | – not out ...................... 3 |
| B 6, l-b 5 ......................... | 11 | B 8, l-b 1, w 2 ........... 11 |
| | **318** | **294** |

## Essex

| | | | |
|---|---|---|---|
| J. Freeman c Considine b Bridges | 11 | – b Bridges | 17 |
| J. A. Cutmore c Hill b White | 10 | – b White | 5 |
| J. O'Connor c and b Hunt | 27 | – c sub. b Hunt | 27 |
| A. B. Hipkin c Bligh b White | 11 | | |
| A. C. Russell st Hill b White | 11 | – c Hill b Bridges | 111 |
| Mr P. Perrin not out | 32 | – not out | 48 |
| Mr J. W. H. T. Douglas c Bridges b Hunt | 1 | – not out | 10 |
| M. S. Nichols c Winter b White | 0 | | |
| Mr H. M. Morris c and b Hunt | 10 | | |
| Capt. R. H. Sharp b White | 4 | | |
| A. S. Grimwood c Bligh b White | 4 | | |
| B 10, l-b 1 | 11 | B 28, l-b 5 | 33 |
| | **132** | | **251** |

### Essex Bowling

| | Overs | Mdns | Runs | Wkts | Overs | Mdns | Runs | Wkts |
|---|---|---|---|---|---|---|---|---|
| Douglas | 24 | 8 | 70 | 3 | 6 | — | 18 | — |
| Nichols | 14 | 1 | 57 | 1 | 16 | 2 | 55 | 3 |
| Sharp | 8 | 3 | 16 | — | 13 | — | 66 | 5 |
| O'Connor | 24 | 3 | 83 | 3 | 9 | 1 | 41 | — |
| Hipkin | 18 | 4 | 46 | 1 | 23 | 2 | 80 | 2 |
| Russell | 16.4 | 4 | 35 | 2 | 13 | 2 | 23 | — |

### Somerset Bowling

| | Overs | Mdns | Runs | Wkts | Overs | Mdns | Runs | Wkts |
|---|---|---|---|---|---|---|---|---|
| Bridges | 14 | 4 | 33 | 1 | 26 | 3 | 61 | 2 |
| Hunt | 22 | 7 | 52 | 3 | 27 | 11 | 63 | 1 |
| White | 32 | 17 | 36 | 6 | 43 | 25 | 47 | 1 |
| Winter | | | | | 6 | — | 21 | — |
| Bligh | | | | | 6 | 1 | 14 | — |
| Earle | | | | | 3 | — | 12 | — |

Umpires: J. Bedford and B. Brown.

## SOMERSET v SURREY

### Played at Taunton, August 15, 17, 18, 1925

This was the match rendered for ever memorable by the triumph of Hobbs who, playing innings of 101 and 101 not out, equalled on the Monday morning W. G. Grace's aggregate of 126 centuries in first-class cricket, and on the Tuesday afternoon beat the "Grand Old Man's" record. Circumstances generally combined to invest the occasion with exceptional excitement. During the early part of the season Hobbs had been so phenomenally successful that by July 20, when he completed a score of 105 at Blackheath, there were a dozen hundreds standing to his credit and the three-figure innings of his career numbered 125. There, as it happened, his extraordinary run of triumphs temporarily ended. He made many substantial scores but in match after match the century needed to bring his total up to that of W. G. Grace eluded his efforts. Thus it came about that when Surrey entered upon their contest with Somerset on August 15, Hobbs was still one short of the coveted number of hundreds. That the Taunton ground, with its rather short boundaries, might furnish Hobbs with the opportunity he wanted, was very generally expected and a big crowd gathered in the hope of assisting at his triumph. No such gratification was vouchsafed for those present on the Saturday, but the play was of absorbing interest, Hobbs batting for two hours and twenty minutes and leaving off not out 91. Those spectators who did not hear "no ball" called had an anxious moment when in the first over Hobbs gave a catch to cover point, and there came another thrill shortly afterwards, the famous batsman with his score at seven making on the leg-side a stroke which might have brought about his dismissal, had MacBryan moved more smartly. Thenceforward he played masterly cricket, exercising great care when facing White, but making a number of fine drives and leg hits off Bridges and Robertson-Glasgow. Towards the close, however, he was content to score mainly by singles. Wanting only nine for his hundred on Monday morning Hobbs did not keep the large company long in suspense. Three singles, a four off a no-ball and another single brought him to 99, and then placing a ball from Bridges to square leg for a further single, he attained the object of his great ambition, the total then standing at 167. Tremendous cheering, of course, greeted the accomplishment of the feat; indeed so pronounced was the enthusiasm that the progress of the game was delayed some minutes while at the end of the over all the players in the field shook hands with Hobbs, and the Surrey captain brought out a drink for the hero of the occasion, who raised the glass high and bowed to the crowd before partaking of the refreshment. The memorable innings – put together exactly four weeks after Hobbs' 105 at Blackheath – came to an end shortly afterwards through a catch at the wicket. The total at that point was 177 and Hobbs, batting two hours and thirty-five minutes, had hit nine 4s.

Fortunately for Hobbs, Somerset played up so well at the second attempt that Surrey were set a task substantial enough to furnish that batsman with the chance of making a second hundred. Of that opportunity he duly availed himself, and so less than thirty hours after equalling W. G. Grace's record, he surpassed it. Surrey had 183 to make to win and Hobbs and Sandham obtained that number in two hours and twenty-five minutes without being separated. Hobbs, who reached three figures with the total at 174, hit fourteen 4s and gave no chance. As in the first innings he treated White with great respect, but otherwise played a game as bold as it was skilful and attractive. In putting together this further hundred, Hobbs not only beat Grace's record but, bringing his three-figure innings for 1925 up to fourteen, he created a new record, the previous largest number of centuries in a season having been thirteen – made by C. B. Fry in 1901, Tom Hayward in 1906 and Hendren in 1923. On two previous occasions Hobbs had obtained two separate hundreds in the same match.

Somerset made a most disastrous start on Saturday, but were saved from complete failure by Young and Johnson. As it was, with Sandham afterwards helping Hobbs to bring the score to 50 and Knight sharing in a partnership of 100, Surrey left off only 16 behind with seven wickets in hand. On Monday after Hobbs' dismissal, Jardine and Holmes put on 51 and Fender, let off when seven, hit up 59 in less than an hour, Surrey, although batting one short, establishing a lead of 192. In Somerset's second innings MacBryan batted in splendid form, scoring 109 out of 184 in two hours and a quarter with sixteen 4s as his chief strokes. Young was also seen to advantage but gave two chances. The home side entered upon the third day's cricket 64 ahead with seven wickets in hand, but there was little in their batting except some hard hitting by Hunt. Still, when Surrey went in to knock off the runs the home team fielded admirably. Sandham played truly admirable and most unselfish cricket for his 74 not out.

### Somerset

| | | |
|---|---|---|
| Mr J. C. W. MacBryan b Holmes | 6 | – b Fender ...... 109 |
| A. Young c Sadler b Lockton | 58 | – c Strudwick b Sadler ...... 71 |
| Mr T. E. S. Francis b Sadler | 0 | – c Strudwick b Lockton ...... 12 |
| Mr J. C. White b Sadler | 1 | – c Strudwick b Sadler ...... 30 |
| Mr P. R. Johnson c and b Lockton | 30 | – c Peach b Fender ...... 16 |
| Mr E. F. Longrigg b Sadler | 5 | – run out ...... 4 |
| Mr R. A. Ingle b Fender | 22 | – c Shepherd b Peach ...... 23 |
| G. Hunt b Lockton | 4 | – b Fender ...... 59 |
| Mr R. C. Robertson-Glasgow c Jardine b Lockton | 4 | – c Sadler b Fender ...... 5 |
| Mr J. J. Bridges c and b Shepherd | 25 | – b Fender ...... 26 |
| Mr M. L. Hill not out | 0 | – not out ...... 1 |
| L-b 8, w 4 | 12 | B 9, l-b 5, n-b 4 ...... 18 |
| | **167** | **374** |

## Surrey

| | | | |
|---|---|---|---|
| J. B. Hobbs c Hill b Bridges | 101 | – not out | 101 |
| A. Sandham c Longrigg b Bridges | 13 | – not out | 74 |
| Mr D. J. Knight run out | 34 | | |
| T. Shepherd b White | 0 | | |
| Mr D. R. Jardine run out | 47 | | |
| Mr E. R. T. Holmes c Hill b R-Glasgow | 24 | | |
| Mr P. G. H. Fender st Hill b Young | 59 | | |
| H. A. Peach b Young | 20 | | |
| W. Sadler c Johnson b Young | 25 | | |
| H. Strudwick not out | 10 | | |
| Mr J. H. Lockton absent | 0 | | |
| B 15, l-b 8, n-b 3 | 26 | B 6, l-b 1, n-b 1 | 8 |
| | **359** | | **183** |

## Surrey Bowling

| | Overs | Mdns | Runs | Wkts | Overs | Mdns | Runs | Wkts |
|---|---|---|---|---|---|---|---|---|
| Sadler | 16 | 4 | 28 | 3 | 21 | 5 | 59 | 2 |
| Holmes | 6 | 2 | 12 | 1 | 17 | — | 56 | — |
| Fender | 13 | 3 | 39 | 1 | 35.5 | 8 | 120 | 5 |
| Lockton | 16 | 4 | 36 | 4 | 9 | 2 | 15 | 1 |
| Peach | 9 | 2 | 21 | — | 20 | 7 | 46 | 1 |
| Shepherd | 6.3 | 1 | 19 | 1 | 21 | 5 | 60 | — |

## Somerset Bowling

| | Overs | Mdns | Runs | Wkts | Overs | Mdns | Runs | Wkts |
|---|---|---|---|---|---|---|---|---|
| Robertson-Glasgow | 26 | 1 | 144 | 1 | 6 | — | 42 | — |
| Bridges | 37 | 5 | 115 | 2 | 11 | 3 | 27 | — |
| White | 29 | 13 | 51 | 1 | 14 | 6 | 34 | — |
| Hunt | 4 | 1 | 14 | — | 8 | 4 | 15 | — |
| Young | 5.3 | 1 | 9 | 3 | 15.5 | 1 | 39 | — |
| Longrigg | | | | | 3 | — | 18 | — |

Umpires: H. Draper and H. Young.

## SOMERSET v HAMPSHIRE

### Played at Weston-super-Mare, August 3, 4, 5, 1927

In the first match of the Weston festival, Somerset suffered defeat by 236 runs. Their good bowling prevented the Hampshire batsmen from scoring freely, but their steadiness was completely eclipsed by the deadly work of Newman who took eight wickets in each innings at a total cost of 88 runs. On the first evening Newman dismissed four men for as many runs, and next morning Somerset actually had six wickets down for 18. Some hitting by Earle saved the danger of a follow-on, and the last stand realised 55. Hampshire in their second innings, lost Kennedy without a run, but Brown and Livsey put on 115. Brown, playing in restrained style, received little further help but Newman, going in late, put his side in a safe position and went on to win the match on the last morning. Again Newman took four of the first five wickets, this time at a cost of 6 runs, and the last three fell to him at one total. Length, spin, and life from the pitch earned Newman his wonderful success.

### Hampshire

| | | | |
|---|---|---|---|
| G. Brown c R-Glasgow b Greswell | 18 | – c Earle b R-Glasgow | 127 |
| J. Newman b R-Glasgow | 5 | – c MacBryan b Greswell | 58 |
| A. Kennedy c Lee b R-Glasgow | 77 | – b R-Glasgow | 0 |
| C. P. Mead b White | 40 | – c Longrigg b White | 0 |
| Mr H. L. V. Day b Greswell | 15 | – b R-Glasgow | 6 |
| Hon. L. H. Tennyson lbw b White | 10 | – b R-Glasgow | 18 |
| Mr A. K. Judd b Greswell | 1 | – c Luckes b White | 0 |
| Mr J. P. Parker lbw b Greswell | 0 | – not out | 8 |
| W. H. Livsey not out | 12 | – b Lee | 41 |
| G. S. Boyes c Young b Greswell | 0 | – absent hurt | 0 |
| J. Bailey run out | 0 | – c Young b White | 8 |
| B 4, l-b 2 | 6 | L-b 2 | 2 |
| | **184** | | **268** |

### Somerset

| | | | |
|---|---|---|---|
| Mr J. C. W. MacBryan b Newman | 2 | – lbw b Newman | 0 |
| A. Young c Kennedy b Newman | 0 | – b Newman | 17 |
| J. W. Lee c Mead b Kennedy | 5 | – b Newman | 8 |
| Mr R. A. Ingle b Newman | 0 | – lbw b Newman | 7 |
| W. T. Luckes b Newman | 0 | – c sub. b Newman | 0 |
| Mr C. C. Case lbw b Newman | 15 | – c Judd b Kennedy | 0 |
| Mr J. C. White b Newman | 1 | – b Kennedy | 4 |
| Mr E. F. Longrigg b Newman | 17 | – not out | 15 |
| Mr G. F. Earle c Brown b Newman | 33 | – c Mead b Newman | 18 |
| Mr R. C. Robertson-Glasgow not out | 31 | – c Bailey b Newman | 4 |
| Mr W. T. Greswell b Bailey | 29 | – b Newman | 0 |
| L-b 1, n-b 1 | 2 | B 5, l-b 3 | 8 |
| | **135** | | **81** |

### Somerset Bowling

| | Overs | Mdns | Runs | Wkts | Overs | Mdns | Runs | Wkts |
|---|---|---|---|---|---|---|---|---|
| Robertson-Glasgow . | 33 | 9 | 57 | 2 | 27 | 6 | 66 | 4 |
| Greswell | 26 | 11 | 47 | 5 | 17 | 3 | 61 | 1 |
| White | 32.5 | 13 | 56 | 2 | 34 | 8 | 77 | 3 |
| Lee | 15 | 5 | 18 | — | 22 | 5 | 50 | 1 |
| Young | | | | | 3 | — | 12 | — |

### Hampshire Bowling

| | Overs | Mdns | Runs | Wkts | Overs | Mdns | Runs | Wkts |
|---|---|---|---|---|---|---|---|---|
| Kennedy | 21 | 7 | 52 | 1 | 19 | 3 | 50 | 2 |
| Newman | 21 | 9 | 65 | 8 | 19 | 7 | 23 | 8 |
| Bailey | 4.2 | — | 10 | 1 | | | | |
| Brown | 4 | 1 | 6 | — | | | | |

Umpires: F. Field and F. Chester.

## SOMERSET v DERBYSHIRE

Played at Taunton, August 27, 28, 29, 1930

Following upon a desperately close fight for first innings points – Derbyshire were only two runs behind with two wickets to fall when White settled matters – Somerset gained a great victory by 203 runs. Declaring with six men out, the home side set their opponents

311 to get in four hours. Young then bowled in wonderful form, delivering at one point twenty-two balls for 20 runs and five wickets and altogether taking eight wickets for 30. Previously he had batted in excellent form. Lyon gave two fine displays of hitting and Longrigg put together – with two chances – his fourth hundred of the season.

## Somerset

| | | | |
|---|---|---|---|
| A. Young c Elliott b Worthington | 63 | – lbw b Smith | 70 |
| Mr E. F. Longrigg c Hutchinson b Mitchell | 25 | – st Elliott b Mitchell | 108 |
| Mr R. A. Ingle lbw b Mitchell | 2 | – run out | 16 |
| Mr M. D. Lyon c Mitchell b Worthington | 80 | – st Elliott b Mitchell | 73 |
| Mr J. C. White b Worthington | 27 | – c Elliott b Mitchell | 9 |
| Mr C. C. Case b Townsend | 1 | – not out | 6 |
| A. W. Wellard c Worthington b Mitchell | 12 | – c Hutchinson b Lee | 9 |
| Mr R. C. Robertson-Glasgow b Mitchell | 8 | | |
| Mr P. H. F. Mermagen b Mitchell | 9 | | |
| Mr A. G. Marshall lbw b Mitchell | 2 | | |
| G. Hunt not out | 0 | – not out | 2 |
| B 5, l-b 11 | 16 | B 13, l-b 1, n-b 1 | 15 |
| | **245** | **(6 wkts dec.)** | **308** |

## Derbyshire

| | | | |
|---|---|---|---|
| J. Bowden c Wellard b White | 12 | – b R-Glasgow | 16 |
| D. Smith c Marshall b R-Glasgow | 56 | – b R-Glasgow | 0 |
| G. M. Lee b White | 5 | – c Hunt b Young | 18 |
| Mr G. R. Jackson c Marshall b Wellard | 11 | – lbw b Young | 22 |
| L. Townsend c White b Young | 48 | – c Lyon b Young | 0 |
| Mr A. W. Richardson c R-Glasgow b White | 16 | – c White b Young | 8 |
| S. Worthington lbw b Young | 3 | – c Mermagen b Young | 0 |
| J. M. Hutchinson lbw b Young | 41 | – c White b Young | 0 |
| A. G. Slater not out | 34 | – c Hunt b Young | 28 |
| H. Elliott c Mermagen b White | 6 | – not out | 6 |
| T. B. Mitchell lbw b White | 0 | – c Marshall b Young | 0 |
| B 1, l-b 4, w 1, n-b 5 | 11 | B 4, l-b 3, n-b 2 | 9 |
| | **243** | | **107** |

## Derbyshire Bowling

| | Overs | Mdns | Runs | Wkts | Overs | Mdns | Runs | Wkts |
|---|---|---|---|---|---|---|---|---|
| Worthington | 24 | 7 | 45 | 3 | 15 | 1 | 65 | — |
| Slater | 14 | 2 | 48 | — | 16 | 2 | 58 | — |
| Mitchell | 29.2 | 8 | 79 | 6 | 30 | 4 | 77 | 3 |
| Townsend | 22 | 4 | 45 | 1 | 10 | 4 | 33 | — |
| Lee | 4 | — | 12 | — | 8 | — | 39 | 1 |
| Smith | | | | | 5 | 1 | 21 | 1 |

## Somerset Bowling

| | Overs | Mdns | Runs | Wkts | Overs | Mdns | Runs | Wkts |
|---|---|---|---|---|---|---|---|---|
| Wellard | 16 | 5 | 46 | 1 | 7 | 1 | 21 | — |
| Robertson-Glasgow | 24 | 6 | 57 | 1 | 10 | 4 | 13 | 2 |
| White | 46 | 15 | 69 | 5 | 16 | 8 | 29 | — |
| Hunt | 4 | 2 | 13 | — | | | | |
| Young | 26 | 6 | 47 | 3 | 14 | 6 | 30 | 8 |
| Lyon | | | | | 2 | 1 | 5 | — |

Umpires: W. A. Buswell and W. R. Parry.

# SOMERSET v DERBYSHIRE

Played at Weston-super-Mare, August 11, 13, 14, 1934

A great all-round performance – his best of the season – by Townsend stood out above everything else in this match, which Derbyshire won easily by an innings and 69 runs. Not only did Townsend take out his bat for 106, but claimed in the two Somerset innings eleven wickets for less than 12 runs apiece. Smith drove and pulled hard, scoring all but 20 of the 104 realised by the opening Derbyshire partnership. Townsend, too, after a cautious start, hit in brilliant style all round the wicket, though, like Smith, he offered a chance. Worthington and Blaxland also brought off some fine forcing strokes. With the exception of Longrigg and Wellard, the Somerset batsmen could make little of Townsend's bowling. Wellard twice drove Townsend out of the ground, and Longrigg, twice let off, drove and hit to leg splendidly. Still, at one point five wickets fell for 14 runs, and Somerset had to follow on against a deficit of 192. This time they fared even worse than before, Copson commencing a collapse that Townsend continued. Ingle and Wellard added 58 for the sixth wicket, but that was the only stand of note in the innings. Certainly the turf helped bowlers all through, but Somerset batting generally was woefully irresolute.

## Derbyshire

| | |
|---|---|
| A. E. Alderman b Hazell ............... 18 | A. V. Pope b J. W. Lee ................. 3 |
| D. Smith b J. W. Lee .................. 84 | E. Carrington st Luckes b Hazell ......... 4 |
| L. F. Townsend not out ...............106 | H. Elliott c Luckes b Hazell ............. 2 |
| Mr A. F. Skinner c Hawkins b Hazell ..... 24 | |
| T. S. Worthington c Hawkins | |
| b Mitchell-Innes . 66 | B 4, l-b 7, n-b 3 ............... 14 |
| Mr L. B. Blaxland c Mitchell-Innes | —— |
| b Wellard . 30 | (8 wkts dec.) 351 |

T. R. Armstrong and W. Copson did not bat.

## Somerset

| | | | |
|---|---|---|---|
| J. W. Lee c Alderman b Armstrong .............. 19 | – c Worthington b Copson ........... | 2 |
| F. S. Lee c Pope b Townsend ................... 16 | – c Elliott b Copson ............... | 12 |
| Mr N. S. Mitchell-Innes c Alderman b Townsend ... 6 | – c Smith b Townsend ............. | 20 |
| Mr E. F. Longrigg not out ..................... 57 | – c Townsend b Copson ........... | 17 |
| Mr J. W. Seamer c Alderman b Townsend ........ 2 | – c Copson b Townsend ........... | 1 |
| A. W. Wellard c Smith b Armstrong ............. 31 | – c Blaxland b Townsend .......... | 34 |
| Mr R. A. Ingle st Elliott b Armstrong ............ 9 | – c Copson b Townsend ........... | 21 |
| Mr L. Hawkins lbw b Townsend ............... 10 | – c Skinner b Townsend ........... | 1 |
| Mr G. M. Bennett lbw b Townsend .............. 6 | – b Armstrong ................. | 4 |
| W. T. Luckes lbw b Townsend .................. 0 | – c Smith b Armstrong ........... | 2 |
| H. L. Hazell run out ......................... 3 | – not out ..................... | 2 |
| | B 3, l-b 3, n-b 1 .......... | 7 |
| 159 | | 123 |

## Somerset Bowling

| | Overs | Mdns | Runs | Wkts |
|---|---|---|---|---|
| Wellard .......... | 28 | 8 | 84 | 1 |
| Mitchell-Innes ..... | 15 | 2 | 52 | 1 |
| J. W. Lee ......... | 47 | 20 | 86 | 2 |
| Hazell ........... | 39.2 | 12 | 115 | 4 |

**Derbyshire Bowling**

|  | Overs | Mdns | Runs | Wkts | Overs | Mdns | Runs | Wkts |
|---|---|---|---|---|---|---|---|---|
| Copson .......... | 9 | 1 | 20 | — | 13 | 5 | 17 | 3 |
| Worthington ...... | 8 | 4 | 6 | — | 3 | 1 | 12 | — |
| Pope.............. | 5 | — | 12 | — |  |  |  |  |
| Townsend ........ | 23 | 7 | 66 | 6 | 17 | 2 | 64 | 5 |
| Armstrong ........ | 20 | 5 | 55 | 3 | 8 | 2 | 23 | 2 |

Umpires: J. Newman and A. E. Dipper.

## SOMERSET v ESSEX

### Played at Frome, May 18, 20, 21, 1935

A remarkable century by Gimblett, playing in his first match for Somerset, completely overshadowed everything else at Frome, where Essex were beaten by an innings and 49 runs. Full of confidence from the start of his innings, Gimblett, whose previous experience had largely been confined to club cricket at Watchet, reached three figures in sixty-three minutes – the fastest hundred of the season. He completed his first fifty in twenty-eight minutes, and altogether scored 123 out of 175 in eighty minutes, his principal scoring strokes being three 6s and seventeen 4s. When Gimblett went in Somerset had lost six wickets for 107 runs; he attacked the bowling like a seasoned player and ninth out at 282 placed his side in what proved to be a winning position. Possessing a very upright stance, Gimblett cut, drove, pulled and hooked in a manner that set cricket circles talking for weeks of his audacious batting. Without scoring so fast as Gimblett, Andrews also gave a grand display of hard hitting, and with the aid of three 6s and five 4s obtained 71 in fifty minutes. Owing to rain, play was impossible on the second day and on Tuesday, Essex, who resumed with half their wickets down for 87, were overwhelmed. Although O'Connor batted with great stubbornness on both occasions, especially in the follow-on 196 behind, he, like most of his colleagues, did not face the slow bowling of J. W. Lee with very much confidence. That bowler in the match took nine wickets for 93 runs.

### Somerset

| | |
|---|---|
| J. W. Lee c Pearce b Nichols ............ 3 | H. Gimblett c and b Eastman ............123 |
| F. S. Lee lbw b Nichols ................ 41 | W. T. Luckes b Nichols ................ 7 |
| Mr R. A. Ingle c Eastman b Nichols ...... 12 | W. H. R. Andrews c O'Connor b Evans ... 71 |
| Mr J. C. White c Eastman b Nichols ...... 4 | H. L. Hazell not out ................... 7 |
| Mr C. C. Case b P. Smith .............. 35 | B 5, l-b 5, w 1 ................ 11 |
| Mr H. D. Burrough b Nichols ........... 2 | |
| A. W. Wellard st Wade b Evans ......... 21 | 337 |

### Essex

| | | |
|---|---|---|
| J. A. Cutmore lbw b Wellard .................. 24 | – b J. W. Lee.................... 26 |
| F. Rist c J. W. Lee b Wellard .................. 41 | – c Wellard b Hazell ............ 21 |
| Mr T. N. Pearce b Wellard.................... 1 | – st Luckes b Hazell ............ 0 |
| J. O'Connor not out ........................ 30 | – c Burrough b Wellard .......... 25 |
| M. S. Nichols c J. W. Lee b Wellard ............ 0 | – st Luckes b White ............. 31 |
| Mr T. P. Lawrence b Wellard.................. 4 | – b J. W. Lee.................... 6 |
| L. C. Eastman b J. W. Lee ................... 35 | – lbw b White ................... 1 |
| P. Smith b J. W. Lee....................... 0 | – c Ingle b J. W. Lee ............. 22 |
| T. H. Wade c Wellard b Hazell ................ 1 | – lbw b J. W. Lee................ 9 |
| V. J. Evans c Wellard b J. W. Lee ............. 2 | – st Luckes b J. W. Lee........... 1 |
| R. Smith lbw (N) b J. W. Lee ................. 0 | – not out ...................... 0 |
| L-b 2, n-b 1 ...................... 3 | B 2, l-b 3 .............. 5 |
| 141 | 147 |

## Essex Bowling

| | Overs | Mdns | Runs | Wkts |
|---|---|---|---|---|
| Nichols .......... | 23 | 3 | 87 | 6 |
| R. Smith ....... | 13 | 2 | 43 | — |
| Eastman ......... | 13 | 4 | 38 | 1 |
| Evans ............ | 14.5 | 1 | 69 | 2 |
| P. Smith .......... | 13 | 1 | 89 | 1 |

## Somerset Bowling

| | Overs | Mdns | Runs | Wkts | Overs | Mdns | Runs | Wkts |
|---|---|---|---|---|---|---|---|---|
| Wellard .......... | 23 | 6 | 66 | 5 | 9 | 2 | 18 | 1 |
| Andrews ......... | 7 | 1 | 20 | — | 1 | — | 5 | — |
| White ............ | 16 | 8 | 16 | — | 15 | 4 | 31 | 2 |
| J. W. Lee ......... | 10 | 1 | 26 | 4 | 21.5 | 5 | 67 | 5 |
| Hazell ........... | 11 | 8 | 10 | 1 | 10 | 4 | 21 | 2 |

Umpires: A. E. Dipper and F. Chester.

## SOMERSET v DERBYSHIRE

Played at Wells, August, 26, 27, 28, 1936

Somerset won by one wicket. In a great finish, they beat Derbyshire for the second time in the season. Needing 271 to win, Somerset lost half their side for 140, but Wellard scored tremendously fast. Missed when one off Armstrong, he drove that bowler for five successive 6s, a feat considered a record. Of the 88 he scored out of 102 in 62 minutes, Wellard made 74 in fifteen strokes: seven 6s and eight 4s. As he took nine wickets and scored 103 runs, Wellard bore a leading part in the triumph. Despite his batting effort, 6 runs were wanted when the ninth wicket fell, but Hazell settled matters with two boundaries. McRae, who played a fine defensive innings at a crisis, was carried shoulder-high from the field. For Derbyshire, Smith on Wednesday and Richardson on Thursday carried off batting honours, both driving and pulling admirably. Copson, bowling well all through, made a great effort to pull the game round.

## Derbyshire

| | | | | |
|---|---|---|---|---|
| A. E. Alderman b Wellard ..................... | 9 | – c and b Meyer ................. | 17 |
| D. Smith b Andrews ........................... | 93 | – b Wellard ..................... | 2 |
| T. S. Worthington lbw (N) b Wellard ............. | 35 | – lbw b Wellard ................. | 9 |
| L. F. Townsend b Andrews .................... | 7 | – b Wellard ..................... | 5 |
| Mr A. F. Skinner c Meyer b Andrews ........... | 9 | – st Luckes b Meyer ............. | 38 |
| C. Elliott not out ........................... | 29 | – b Andrews .................... | 8 |
| H. Elliott b Meyer .......................... | 11 | – b Andrews .................... | 10 |
| Mr A. W. Richardson b Wellard ................ | 8 | – c Meyer b Wellard ............. | 50 |
| A. V. Pope b Andrews ....................... | 0 | – c Meyer b Gimblett ............ | 30 |
| T. R. Armstrong b Andrews ................... | 1 | – not out ...................... | 8 |
| W. Copson b Wellard ........................ | 1 | – c Luckes b Wellard ............ | 1 |
| B 4, l-b 7, n-b 2 ..................... | 13 | B 6, l-b 14, n-b 3 .........23 |

216                                    200

## Somerset

| | | | |
|---|---|---|---|
| F. S. Lee b Pope | 35 | – c H. Elliott b Copson | 27 |
| H. Gimblett b Worthington | 4 | – b Copson | 41 |
| Mr F. M. McRae c H. Elliott b Pope | 2 | – not out | 14 |
| Mr R. J. O. Meyer b Copson | 2 | – b Copson | 14 |
| Mr E. F. Longrigg b Pope | 44 | – c Smith b Armstrong | 38 |
| Mr J. H. Cameron lbw b Worthington | 23 | – run out | 8 |
| Mr R. A. Ingle lbw (N) b Copson | 8 | – c Smith b Copson | 16 |
| A. W. Wellard c C. Elliott b Pope | 17 | – c Townsend b Copson | 88 |
| W. H. R. Andrews c H. Elliott b Pope | 4 | – c Alderman b Townsend | 12 |
| W. T. Luckes b Copson | 1 | – b Copson | 6 |
| H. L. Hazell not out | 0 | – not out | 8 |
| L-b 6 | 6 | L-b 9, n-b 1 | 10 |

146    (9 wkts) 272

## Somerset Bowling

| | Overs | Mdns | Runs | Wkts | Overs | Mdns | Runs | Wkts |
|---|---|---|---|---|---|---|---|---|
| Wellard | 15.1 | 2 | 52 | 4 | 22.1 | 4 | 47 | 5 |
| Meyer | 24 | 6 | 53 | 1 | 17 | 3 | 46 | 2 |
| Andrews | 16 | 4 | 42 | 5 | 16 | 2 | 56 | 2 |
| Gimblett | 3 | — | 15 | — | 8 | 4 | 14 | 1 |
| Hazell | 9 | 1 | 41 | — | 7 | 4 | 14 | — |

## Derbyshire Bowling

| | Overs | Mdns | Runs | Wkts | Overs | Mdns | Runs | Wkts |
|---|---|---|---|---|---|---|---|---|
| Copson | 21 | 3 | 55 | 3 | 30 | 6 | 81 | 6 |
| Pope | 20.1 | 3 | 35 | 5 | 34 | 13 | 64 | — |
| Worthington | 7 | 1 | 34 | 2 | 5 | — | 20 | — |
| Townsend | 4 | — | 16 | — | 17.5 | 5 | 35 | 1 |
| Armstrong | | | | | 8 | 1 | 64 | 1 |

Umpires: C. W. L. Parker and T. Oates.

# SOMERSET v GLOUCESTERSHIRE

### Played at Taunton, June 4, 6, 7, 1938

Somerset won by one wicket. Gloucestershire were beaten after one of the most thrilling finishes witnessed at Taunton for many years. Throughout a remarkable game the fortunes of both sides frequently changed. Each in turn seemed set for a big first innings score, but collapse followed. Somerset gained a first innings lead of 55 and then the real struggle began. Gloucestershire, with half their second innings wickets down, led by no more than 64, but a masterly effort by Hammond placed them in a strong position. Summing up the exact length of each ball with consummate ease and skill, he held out for four and a half hours and hit eighteen 4s. Following an eighth stand of 161 by Hammond and Lyon, Gloucestershire declared 283 ahead. Somerset took up the challenge in spirited style, but when their seventh wicket fell they needed 112 for victory. This situation suited Wellard's temperament, and making a vigorous attack on the bowling he scored 68 in forty minutes with the aid of six 6s and five 4s. Buse, sound in defence, stayed over three hours, and in the last over of the day, Luckes hit two 4s to win the match for his side.

## Gloucestershire

| | | | |
|---|---|---|---|
| Mr B. O. Allen c Lyon b Hazell | 52 | – run out | 28 |
| C. J. Barnett lbw b Wellard | 41 | – c and b Wellard | 0 |
| G. M. Emmett b Wellard | 18 | – lbw b Wellard | 6 |
| Mr W. R. Hammond c Luckes b Hazell | 6 | – not out | 140 |
| J. F. Crapp b Buse | 33 | – b Wellard | 29 |
| W. L. Neale c Luckes b Hazell | 13 | – c Luckes b Wellard | 6 |
| Mr B. H. Lyon c Gimblett b Hazell | 0 | – c Longrigg b Hazell | 88 |
| R. A. Sinfield b Wellard | 0 | – not out | 0 |
| E. A. Wilson b Andrews | 38 | – c Andrews b Kinnersley | 32 |
| C. J. Scott lbw b Andrews | 9 | | |
| M. Cranfield not out | 5 | | |
| B 1, l-b 3, w 1, n-b 1 | 6 | B 4, l-b 3, n-b 2 | 9 |
| | **221** | **(7 wkts dec.)** | **338** |

## Somerset

| | | | |
|---|---|---|---|
| H. Gimblett c Wilson b Emmett | 67 | – c Allen b Sinfield | 7 |
| F. S. Lee lbw b Sinfield | 56 | – c Allen b Barnett | 18 |
| Mr M. D. Lyon b Hammond | 48 | – lbw b Barnett | 19 |
| H. T. F. Buse c Wilson b Scott | 27 | – c Emmett b Hammond | 79 |
| Mr E. F. Longrigg c Hammond b Sinfield | 7 | – b Sinfield | 24 |
| Mr J. W. Seamer c Allen b Scott | 23 | – run out | 34 |
| W. H. R. Andrews c Wilson b Barnett | 6 | – c Barnett b Emmett | 2 |
| Mr K. C. Kinnersley c Allen b Scott | 12 | – c and b Emmett | 7 |
| A. W. Wellard b Hammond | 21 | – c Barnett b Scott | 68 |
| W. T. Luckes lbw b Scott | 2 | – not out | 18 |
| H. L. Hazell not out | 0 | – not out | 0 |
| B 1, l-b 4, w 1, n-b 1 | 7 | B 7, l-b 1 | 8 |
| | **276** | | **284** |

### Somerset Bowling

| | Overs | Mdns | Runs | Wkts | Overs | Mdns | Runs | Wkts |
|---|---|---|---|---|---|---|---|---|
| Wellard | 30 | 6 | 77 | 3 | 32 | 7 | 85 | 4 |
| Andrews | 15.1 | — | 48 | 2 | 13 | 1 | 76 | — |
| Buse | 17 | 4 | 48 | 1 | 27 | 6 | 86 | — |
| Hazell | 16 | 2 | 42 | 4 | 27 | 6 | 72 | 1 |
| Kinnersley | | | | | 5 | 2 | 10 | 1 |

### Gloucestershire Bowling

| | Overs | Mdns | Runs | Wkts | Overs | Mdns | Runs | Wkts |
|---|---|---|---|---|---|---|---|---|
| Hammond | 33.2 | 8 | 64 | 2 | 17 | 3 | 57 | 1 |
| Scott | 19 | 2 | 42 | 4 | 15 | 3 | 51 | 1 |
| Sinfield | 39 | 20 | 57 | 2 | 29.4 | 10 | 68 | 2 |
| Barnett | 10 | 1 | 21 | 1 | 17 | 5 | 50 | 2 |
| Cranfield | 6 | — | 33 | — | 2 | — | 5 | — |
| Emmett | 9 | 1 | 52 | 1 | 6 | — | 36 | 2 |
| Neale | | | | | 2 | — | 9 | — |

Umpires: A. Dolphin and E. Robinson

## SOMERSET v KENT

Played at Wells, August 24, 25, 1938

Somerset won by 27 runs. The match provided a personal triumph for Wellard, a Kent-born player, who dismissed thirteen batsmen for 115 runs, and gave a magnificent display of hard, clean driving. On a small ground, which favoured forcing tactics, Wellard, in Somerset's first innings, included seven 6s in his 57 made in thirty-seven minutes. So fiercely did he attack one over from Woolley that five 6s and a single obtained through a dropped catch enabled him to surpass his 30 in an over by means of five consecutive 6s off Derbyshire's bowling on the same ground two seasons before. After losing three wickets without a run scored, Kent rallied, Valentine and Knott adding 180 for the fifth partnership in less than two hours. During a faultless innings marked by powerful hooks and drives Valentine hit four 6s and fourteen 4s. Wellard, taking three of the last four wickets for 1 run, dashed Kent's hopes of a lead. More free batting characterised the rest of the game. Kent were set to get 188 to win, and after a typical effort by Woolley, the clever spin bowling of Wellard and Hazell turned the scale in Somerset's favour.

## Somerset

| | | | | |
|---|---|---|---|---|
| F. S. Lee lbw b Lewis | 35 | – c Levett b Todd | 3 |
| H. Gimblett c Chalk b Todd | 14 | – c Woolley b Harding | 5 |
| W. H. R. Andrews b Watt | 30 | – lbw b Lewis | 54 |
| H. T. F. Buse c Levett b Lewis | 11 | – b Harding | 25 |
| Mr E. F. Longrigg c Levett b Lewis | 6 | – b Lewis | 18 |
| Mr M. D. Lyon not out | 50 | – st Levett b Woolley | 8 |
| Mr G. M. Bennett b Harding | 1 | – b Harding | 9 |
| W. T. Luckes c Spencer b Lewis | 2 | – lbw b Lewis | 4 |
| A. W. Wellard c Harding b Todd | 57 | – b Harding | 37 |
| Mr A. M. T. Jones c Spencer b Lewis | 1 | – c Levett b Harding | 2 |
| H. L. Hazell c Watt b Lewis | 2 | – not out | 0 |
| B 12, w 1, n-b 3 | 16 | B 8, l-b 4 | 12 |
| | **225** | | **177** |

## Kent

| | | | | |
|---|---|---|---|---|
| F. E. Woolley lbw b Wellard | 0 | – lbw b Wellard | 34 |
| Mr F. G. H. Chalk b Andrews | 0 | – c Andrews b Hazell | 33 |
| L. J. Todd lbw b Wellard | 0 | – c Jones b Wellard | 13 |
| Mr B. H. Valentine st Luckes b Hazell | 114 | – st Luckes b Hazell | 13 |
| P. R. Sunnucks c Luckes b Wellard | 8 | – b Wellard | 0 |
| Mr C. H. Knott c Lyon b Wellard | 65 | – b Wellard | 19 |
| T. Spencer c Luckes b Wellard | 14 | – st Luckes b Wellard | 12 |
| Mr W. H. V. Levett b Wellard | 0 | – not out | 12 |
| N. W. Harding not out | 9 | – c Jones b Wellard | 6 |
| A. E. Watt b Andrews | 0 | – c Wellard b Hazell | 8 |
| C. Lewis b Wellard | 1 | – b Hazell | 1 |
| B 3, l-b 1 | 4 | L-b 9 | 9 |
| | **215** | | **160** |

## Kent Bowling

| | Overs | Mdns | Runs | Wkts | Overs | Mdns | Runs | Wkts |
|---|---|---|---|---|---|---|---|---|
| Todd | 15 | 4 | 46 | 2 | 11 | 5 | 11 | 1 |
| Harding | 12 | 4 | 25 | 1 | 15.3 | 3 | 51 | 5 |
| Watt | 16 | 6 | 22 | 1 | 12 | 2 | 40 | — |
| Lewis | 25.3 | 4 | 76 | 6 | 21 | 6 | 57 | 3 |
| Woolley | 2 | — | 40 | — | 5 | 1 | 6 | 1 |

## Somerset Bowling

| | Overs | Mdns | Runs | Wkts | Overs | Mdns | Runs | Wkts |
|---|---|---|---|---|---|---|---|---|
| Wellard | 25.3 | 8 | 65 | 7 | 27 | 7 | 50 | 6 |
| Andrews | 14 | 1 | 49 | 2 | 4 | — | 35 | — |
| Hazell | 17 | 3 | 67 | 1 | 22.2 | 2 | 60 | 4 |
| Buse | 6 | 1 | 30 | — | 1 | — | 6 | — |

Umpires: A. Skelding and H. G. Baldwin.

# SOMERSET v KENT

Played at Bath, June 21, 22, 23, 1939

Drawn. Gimblett and Lee started by making 66 together, but Wright wrought such havoc that the last nine wickets realised only 79 runs. Staying two and a half hours, Spencer checked a breakdown against Andrews, and Kent led by 31. Apart from Wellard, missed four times in the course of five balls from Wright, the Somerset batsmen did little in their second innings. Wright made his match record 16 wickets for 80 runs and Kent needed 99 on the last day. Unluckily for them rain and sodden turf prevented play until quarter past four and changed batting order, in the effort to get the runs in seventy-five minutes, was partly responsible for a collapse.

## Somerset

| | | | |
|---|---|---|---|
| F. S. Lee c Watt b Wright | 23 | – c Foster b Watt | 29 |
| H. Gimblett c Harding b Wright | 52 | – c Spender b Todd | 14 |
| H. T. F. Buse c Fagg b Wright | 3 | – c Spencer b Wright | 0 |
| Mr C. J. P. Barnwell st Levett b Wright | 4 | – c Fagg b Wright | 0 |
| Mr H. D. Burrough b Wright | 25 | – c Todd b Wright | 4 |
| Mr R. A. Ingle b Wright | 7 | – st Levett b Wright | 3 |
| W. T. Luckes c Fagg b Watt | 0 | – c and b Wright | 5 |
| W. H. R. Andrews c Harding b Wright | 2 | – c Fagg b Wright | 2 |
| Mr G. M. Bennett b Wright | 0 | – st Levett b Wright | 9 |
| A. W. Wellard b Watt | 6 | – c Watt b Wright | 48 |
| H. L. Hazell not out | 10 | – not out | 0 |
| B 3, l-b 10 | 13 | B 8, l-b 7 | 15 |
| | **145** | | **129** |

## Kent

| | | | |
|---|---|---|---|
| A. Fagg b Andrews | 39 | – lbw b Wellard | 6 |
| Mr F. G. H. Chalk c Wellard b Andrews | 23 | – c Buse b Wellard | 3 |
| Mr P. G. Foster c Gimblett b Andrews | 1 | – b Andrews | 29 |
| Mr B. H. Valentine b Andrews | 4 | – c Luckes b Andrews | 4 |
| L. J. Todd lbw b Andrews | 15 | – not out | 8 |
| P. R. Spencer c Wellard b Buse | 33 | – b Wellard | 0 |
| D. V. P. Wright c Gimblett b Andrews | 7 | – not out | 4 |
| N. W. Harding c Bennett b Andrews | 12 | – run out | 4 |
| Mr W. H. V. Levett b Buse | 23 | | |
| A. E. Watt not out | 11 | – c Lee b Andrews | 10 |
| C. Lewis c Gimblett b Buse | 0 | | |
| L-b 8 | 8 | B 2, l-b 2 | 4 |
| | **176** | | **72** |

## Kent Bowling

| | Overs | Mdns | Runs | Wkts | Overs | Mdns | Runs | Wkts |
|---|---|---|---|---|---|---|---|---|
| Todd | 10 | 2 | 30 | — | 10 | 1 | 31 | 1 |
| Harding | 4 | — | 22 | — | 3 | — | 10 | — |
| Watt | 11.6 | — | 45 | 2 | 11 | 1 | 28 | 1 |
| Wright | 11 | 3 | 35 | 8 | 17.4 | 6 | 45 | 8 |

## Somerset Bowling

| | Overs | Mdns | Runs | Wkts | Overs | Mdns | Runs | Wkts |
|---|---|---|---|---|---|---|---|---|
| Wellard | 22 | 3 | 53 | — | 8 | 1 | 32 | 3 |
| Andrews | 31 | 7 | 56 | 7 | 8 | 1 | 36 | 3 |
| Buse | 16.6 | 1 | 46 | 3 | | | | |
| Hazell | 4 | — | 13 | — | | | | |

Umpires: H. Smith and H. Cruice.

# SURREY

## SURREY v KENT

### Played at The Oval, August 18, 19, 1922

Hobbs's benefit match brought county cricket at The Oval to an end for the season and a glorious end it proved. Nothing quite equal to the cricket at the finish can be recalled. Surrey had 95 to get in less than three-quarters of an hour, and in thirty-two minutes, despite the disadvantage of bad light, Hobbs and Crawford hit off the runs, accomplishing in dazzling style a task that had seemed impossible. Crawford set the pace at first and put his side on good terms with the clock, Hobbs for an over or two being content with a few singles. Once set, however, Hobbs went even faster than his partner and to him fell the honour of making the winning hit. Naturally with such cricket in progress the crowd waited till the end, and when all was over there was a great scene in front of the pavilion.

### Kent

| | | | |
|---|---|---|---|
| E. Humphreys c Ducat b Hitch | 59 | – c Knight b Hitch | 1 |
| H. T. W. Hardinge run out | 31 | – c Strudwick b Rushby | 25 |
| James Seymour b Hitch | 0 | – b Hitch | 0 |
| F. E. Woolley b Crawford | 55 | – c Hobbs b Crawford | 29 |
| Mr L. P. Hedges b Hitch | 1 | – c Strudwick b Rushby | 12 |
| J. C. Hubble b Rushby | 1 | – c Peach b Lockton | 40 |
| Mr G. E. C. Wood b Rushby | 0 | – lbw b Rushby | 5 |
| Mr L. H. W. Troughton c Rushby b Crawford | 15 | – b Lockton | 41 |
| Mr C. P. Johnstone b Hitch | 21 | – not out | 9 |
| W. J. Fairservice not out | 24 | – b Hitch | 0 |
| A. P. Freeman run out | 0 | – c Strudwick b Hitch | 5 |
| B 8, l-b 3 | 11 | B 13, l-b 3, w 1 | 17 |
| | **218** | | **184** |

### Surrey

| | | | |
|---|---|---|---|
| J. B. Hobbs c and b Fairservice | 17 | – not out | 47 |
| Mr D. J. Knight c Hubble b Woolley | 14 | | |
| A. Ducat b Johnstone | 76 | | |
| A. Sandham lbw b Freeman | 11 | | |
| H. S. Harrison c Hubble b Woolley | 66 | | |
| Mr J. N. Crawford c Hedges b Fairservice | 28 | – not out | 48 |
| H. A. Peach b Freeman | 17 | | |
| W. Hitch b Fairservice | 42 | | |
| Mr J. H. Lockton c Johnstone b Woolley | 13 | | |
| H. Strudwick not out | 3 | | |
| T. Rushby b Fairservice | 1 | | |
| B 15, l-b 5 | 20 | B 1 | 1 |
| | **308** | | **96** |

### Surrey Bowling

| | Overs | Mdns | Runs | Wkts | Overs | Mdns | Runs | Wkts |
|---|---|---|---|---|---|---|---|---|
| Hitch | 20 | 6 | 58 | 4 | 26.3 | 4 | 64 | 4 |
| Rushby | 23.5 | 7 | 81 | 2 | 24 | 10 | 39 | 3 |
| Crawford | 15 | 3 | 29 | 2 | 16 | 3 | 37 | 1 |
| Lockton | 11 | 2 | 39 | — | 13 | 4 | 21 | 2 |
| Peach | | | | | 3 | 1 | 6 | — |

**Kent Bowling**

| | Overs | Mdns | Runs | Wkts | Overs | Mdns | Runs | Wkts |
|---|---|---|---|---|---|---|---|---|
| Fairservice ........ | 33.2 | 8 | 96 | 4 | 5 | — | 26 | — |
| Woolley .......... | 46 | 15 | 101 | 3 | 6 | — | 54 | — |
| Freeman ......... | 23 | 5 | 62 | 2 | 1.1 | — | 15 | — |
| Humphreys ....... | 7 | 1 | 20 | — | | | | |
| Johnstone ........ | 3 | — | 9 | 1 | | | | |

Umpires: H. Butt and T. M. Russell.

# SURREY v HAMPSHIRE

Played at The Oval, May 13, 15, 16, 1922

A wonderful display of hitting by Fender on the first day put Surrey in an unbeatable position, and in the end they won the match by an innings and 28 runs. Going in at the fall of the fourth wicket at 164 Fender was lucky in being missed at extra cover point when he had made 22, the fieldsman having the sun in his eyes. Profiting by this escape Fender proceeded to do very much as he liked with the bowling. He gave a second chance in the long field with his score at 92, and after completing his hundred hit in such wonderful form that at one time he actually scored 52 runs off fourteen consecutive balls bowled to him. He was batting only two hours and ten minutes for his 185, his hits including three 6s, three 5s, and twenty-five 4s. When he left the score was 455 for nine wickets. His play naturally overshadowed everything else in the day's cricket, but Sandham, Shepherd and Abel were all in form, and Strudwick, towards the close, hit the tired bowlers freely. Hampshire lost one wicket before the drawing of stumps, and on Monday they were batting all day. When they followed on Bowell played wonderfully well. He was not out 97 at the finish and with five wickets down for 218 there seemed a good chance of escaping a single innings defeat. On Tuesday morning, however, the remaining wickets fell in little more than half an hour. Bowell's innings – almost flawless – lasted three hours and three quarters.

## Surrey

| | | | |
|---|---|---|---|
| J. B. Hobbs c Livsey b Brown .......... 15 | | W. Hitch lbw b Kennedy .............. 11 |
| A. Sandham b Kennedy ................ 73 | | H. A. Peach b Jameson ................ 5 |
| A. Ducat c and b Jameson ............. 19 | | H. Strudwick c Tennyson b Brown ....... 34 |
| T. Shepherd b Kennedy ............... 45 | | A. Geary not out .................... 3 |
| Mr A. Jeacocke c Mead b Kennedy ....... 8 | | B 6, l-b 3 .................... 9 |
| Mr P. G. H. Fender c Fry b Newman .....185 | | |
| W. J. Abel b Newman ................. 63 | | 470 |

## Hampshire

| | | |
|---|---|---|
| G. Brown b Fender .......................... 47 | – c and b Fender ................ 35 |
| A. Bowell b Peach .......................... 0 | – c Strudwick b Hitch ............114 |
| A. Kennedy b Peach ......................... 27 | – c Fender b Shepherd ........... 10 |
| C. P. Mead st Strudwick b Peach ................ 7 | – b Abel ........................ 21 |
| Hon. L. H. Tennyson b Hitch ................. 49 | – c Strudwick b Abel ............. 31 |
| Capt. T. O. Jameson b Abel .................... 9 | – b Fender ...................... 1 |
| J. Newman b Fender ......................... 17 | – c Abel b Peach ................. 0 |
| Mr A. E. L. Hill c Abel b Fender ............... 3 | – c Strudwick b Hitch ............ 1 |
| Mr S. Fry run out ........................... 2 | – b Peach ....................... 4 |
| W. H. Livsey lbw b Hitch .................... 8 | – not out ....................... 11 |
| E. R. Remnant not out ...................... 5 | – b Peach ....................... 4 |
| B 4, l-b 2, n-b 7 ..................... 13 | B 12, l-b 5, n-b 6 ......... 23 |
| 187 | 255 |

## Hampshire Bowling

| | Overs | Mdns | Runs | Wkts |
|---|---|---|---|---|
| Kennedy ......... | 31 | 7 | 147 | 4 |
| Brown ........... | 19.4 | 2 | 91 | 2 |
| Jameson ......... | 13 | 2 | 79 | 2 |
| Newman ........ | 17 | 3 | 99 | 2 |
| Remnant ........ | 6 | 1 | 26 | — |
| Tennyson ........ | 2 | — | 19 | — |

## Surrey Bowling

| | Overs | Mdns | Runs | Wkts | Overs | Mdns | Runs | Wkts |
|---|---|---|---|---|---|---|---|---|
| Hitch ........... | 16.2 | 6 | 37 | 2 | 17 | 4 | 59 | 2 |
| Peach ........... | 16 | 6 | 51 | 3 | 13.4 | 3 | 34 | 3 |
| Geary ........... | 7 | — | 24 | — | 5 | — | 14 | — |
| Fender .......... | 12 | 1 | 43 | 3 | 20 | 4 | 46 | 2 |
| Abel ............ | 4 | — | 19 | 1 | 17 | 1 | 52 | 2 |
| Shepherd ........ | | | | | 10 | 3 | 27 | 1 |

Umpires: A. J. Atfield and T. Brown.

# SURREY v ESSEX

### Played at The Oval, May 20, 22, 23, 1922

Never perhaps did the Essex match prove quite so attractive. After Essex had just secured a lead on the first innings the bat beat the ball, and in the end the game had to be left drawn. For Russell and G. M. Louden the match was nothing less than a triumph. Russell had the distinction of getting two hundreds, and in Surrey's first innings Louden, with nothing in the condition of the ground to help him, took seven wickets – four of them bowled down – at a cost of only 84 runs. This was certainly one of the best pieces of bowling seen in London last summer. Russell was batting two hours and fifty minutes for his 115 and ten minutes less for his 118. He had two escapes in his first innings but the second was fautless. Douglas was slow in declaring on Tuesday, leaving Surrey only three hours and a half to get 410 runs.

## Essex

| | | | |
|---|---|---|---|
| Rev. F. H. Gillingham c Strudwick b Shepherd ..... | 46 | – lbw b Abel .................... | 65 |
| A. C. Russell c Hitch b Fender ................ | 115 | – c Fender b Shepherd ........... | 118 |
| J. Freeman run out ......................... | 17 | – c and b Fender ................ | 43 |
| Mr J. G. Dixon b Hitch ..................... | 0 | – c Strudwick b Fender .......... | 9 |
| Mr J. W. H. T. Douglas c Hitch b Fender ........ | 23 | – c Strudwick b Hitch ........... | 7 |
| Capt. F. W. H. Nicholas lbw b Fender ........... | 13 | – c Fender b Peach .............. | 24 |
| Mr H. M. Morris c Hitch b Shepherd ........... | 18 | – b Fender .................... | 44 |
| Mr H. W. F. Franklin b Shepherd .............. | 13 | – b Peach ..................... | 12 |
| Mr P. E. Morris c and b Shepherd ............. | 4 | – not out ..................... | 55 |
| Mr G. M. Louden b Shepherd ................. | 0 | – b Fender .................... | 5 |
| J. P. Herringshaw not out ................... | 1 | – not out ..................... | 8 |
| B 6, l-b 5, w 1, n-b 3 ................. | 15 | B 10, l-b 3, n-b 4 ........ | 17 |
| | 265 | (9 wkts dec.) | 407 |

## Surrey

| | | | | |
|---|---|---|---|---|
| J. B. Hobbs b Dixon | 102 | – c P. E. Morris b Dixon | 43 |
| A. Sandham lbw b Louden | 15 | – c Nicholas b Douglas | 13 |
| A. Ducat c Franklin b Douglas | 47 | – not out | 108 |
| T. Shepherd c Nicholas b Louden | 28 | – b Louden | 4 |
| H. S. Harrison st Nicholas b Dixon | 8 | – not out | 32 |
| Mr P. G. H. Fender b Louden | 3 | | |
| W. J. Abel b Louden | 35 | | |
| W. Hitch lbw b Louden | 3 | | |
| H. A. Peach b Louden | 10 | | |
| H. Strudwick b Louden | 1 | | |
| T. Watts not out | 4 | | |
| B 5, l-b 1, n-b 1 | 7 | L-b 3 | 3 |
| | **263** | | **203** |

### Surrey Bowling

| | Overs | Mdns | Runs | Wkts | Overs | Mdns | Runs | Wkts |
|---|---|---|---|---|---|---|---|---|
| Hitch | 14 | 1 | 61 | 1 | 19 | 4 | 65 | 1 |
| Watts | 17 | 3 | 28 | — | 22 | 3 | 68 | — |
| Peach | 14 | 3 | 53 | — | 17 | 2 | 73 | 2 |
| Fender | 34 | 5 | 58 | 3 | 37 | 8 | 105 | 4 |
| Abel | 5 | 1 | 26 | — | 5 | — | 24 | 1 |
| Shepherd | 11.5 | 1 | 24 | 5 | 28 | 11 | 55 | 1 |

### Essex Bowling

| | Overs | Mdns | Runs | Wkts | Overs | Mdns | Runs | Wkts |
|---|---|---|---|---|---|---|---|---|
| Douglas | 21 | 2 | 75 | 1 | 10 | — | 44 | 1 |
| Louden | 27.1 | 3 | 84 | 7 | 16 | 4 | 49 | 1 |
| Dixon | 10 | — | 38 | 2 | 8 | — | 37 | 1 |
| P. E. Morris | 10 | — | 50 | — | 10 | 2 | 33 | — |
| Herringshaw | 2 | — | 9 | — | 6 | 2 | 18 | — |
| Russell | | | | | 8 | 2 | 19 | — |

Umpires: T. Flowers and T. Brown.

## SURREY v KENT

### Played at The Oval, July 29, 31, August 1, 1922

Rushby's match was the sensation of the season at The Oval. Up to a point Surrey did wonders, and when, on the second afternoon, they finished their innings with a lead of 329 their victory seemed assured. Fender followed up some capital bowling on the first day by giving a truly marvellous display of hitting, scoring 137 out of 217 in an hour and a half. His figures were three 6s, one 5, eighteen 4s, three 3s, nine 2s and fifteen singles. His extreme brilliancy quite overshadowed Sandham's admirable 129. Rain stopped play on Monday when Kent had scored 82 for one wicket, but the pitch rolled out in perfect condition the following morning and Surrey's bowling was completely mastered. Hardinge and Seymour put on 205 in two hours and a quarter for the second wicket, and long before the early drawing of stumps which had been agreed to a draw had become inevitable. Kent's batting was superb, Seymour playing the most brilliant cricket. The match was such an attraction that over fifty-three thousand people paid for admission, but of this huge number only 5,603 passed through the turnstiles on the third day.

## Kent

| | | | |
|---|---|---|---|
| Mr J. L. Bryan lbw b Shepherd | 70 | – b Gentry | 7 |
| H. T. W. Hardinge c Strudwick b Gentry | 21 | – b Gentry | 119 |
| J. Seymour lbw b Fender | 1 | – b Peach | 129 |
| F. E. Woolley c Strudwick b Fender | 0 | – lbw b Shepherd | 100 |
| W. Ashdown b Gentry | 11 | – lbw b Gentry | 3 |
| Mr G. J. Bryan b Fender | 14 | – b Abel | 54 |
| Mr L. P. Hedges c Gentry b Shepherd | 14 | – lbw b Gentry | 39 |
| J. C. Hubble b Gentry | 0 | – not out | 11 |
| G. C. Collins not out | 36 | – not out | 50 |
| Mr L. H. W. Troughton c Fender b Gentry | 11 | | |
| A. P. Freeman b Fender | 1 | | |
| B 7, n-b 2 | 9 | B 31, l-b 12, n-b 2 | 45 |
| | **188** | | **557** |

## Surrey

| | |
|---|---|
| J. B. Hobbs st Hubble b Woolley | 8 |
| A. Sandham lbw b Woolley | 129 |
| A. Ducat st Hubble b Freeman | 61 |
| T. Shepherd c J. L. Bryan b Freeman | 3 |
| Mr A. Jeacocke c Collins b Woolley | 26 |
| Mr M. Howell c Woolley b Freeman | 46 |
| Mr P. G. H. Fender b Woolley | 137 |
| H. A. Peach c Ashdown b Hardinge | 61 |
| W. J. Abel c Hardinge b Freeman | 30 |
| Mr J. S. B. Gentry not out | 4 |
| H. Strudwick c Hubble b Hardinge | 1 |
| B 1, l-b 7, n-b 3 | 11 |
| | **517** |

### Surrey Bowling

| | Overs | Mdns | Runs | Wkts | Overs | Mdns | Runs | Wkts |
|---|---|---|---|---|---|---|---|---|
| Peach | 15 | 6 | 37 | — | 36 | 5 | 137 | 1 |
| Gentry | 39 | 19 | 53 | 4 | 47 | 12 | 91 | 4 |
| Fender | 29.1 | 6 | 75 | 4 | 28 | — | 131 | — |
| Shepherd | 9 | 3 | 14 | 2 | 22 | 4 | 83 | 1 |
| Abel | | | | | 21 | 4 | 57 | 1 |
| Ducat | | | | | 3 | — | 13 | — |

### Kent Bowling

| | Overs | Mdns | Runs | Wkts |
|---|---|---|---|---|
| Collins | 13 | — | 72 | — |
| Woolley | 40 | 11 | 128 | 4 |
| Freeman | 36 | 10 | 117 | 4 |
| Ashdown | 14 | 1 | 80 | — |
| G. J. Bryan | 22 | 2 | 80 | — |
| J. L. Bryan | 1 | — | 11 | — |
| Hardinge | 3.2 | — | 18 | 2 |

Umpires: F. Parris and G. A. Fuller.

## SURREY v LANCASHIRE

Played at The Oval, July 14, 16, 17, 1923

Hobbs made a hundred at The Oval for the first time during the season, and, at the close of Monday's cricket, Surrey looked to have an assured victory in prospect, Lancashire, with four wickets down, after having followed on, still requiring 117 runs to avoid a single innings defeat. There was, however, a surprise in store. Ernest Tyldesley, not out 81, played one of the finest innings of his life. At the wickets five hours for his 236, he did not, so far as could be seen, give a chance of any kind. He hooked and pulled with astonishing certainty, and his off-driving was scarcely less remarkable. Set to get 194 in two hours and ten minutes – including the extra half-hour – Surrey intended going for the runs, but rain soon caused a delay of twenty-five minutes and after that a draw was inevitable. In the end, further rain caused stumps to be pulled up.

### Surrey

| | | | |
|---|---:|---|---:|
| J. B. Hobbs c Sharp b R. Tyldesley | 104 | – c Duckworth b Cook | 23 |
| A. Sandham lbw b Parkin | 21 | – not out | 29 |
| A. Ducat b R. Tyldesley | 26 | – c R. Tyldesley b Parkin | 19 |
| T. Shepherd st Duckworth b R. Tyldesley | 55 | | |
| Mr A. Jeacocke lbw b R. Tyldesley | 5 | | |
| W. J. Abel st Duckworth b R. Tyldesley | 88 | | |
| Mr P. G. H. Fender c and b Parkin | 69 | – b Parkin | 8 |
| W. Hitch b Cook | 28 | – not out | 5 |
| H. A. Peach not out | 17 | | |
| Mr G. M. Reay not out | 4 | | |
| B 13, l-b 5, n-b 1 | 19 | | |
| | (8 wkts dec.) 436 | | 84 |

H. Strudwick did not bat.

### Lancashire

| | | | |
|---|---:|---|---:|
| H. Makepeace lbw b Fender | 61 | – lbw b Fender | 21 |
| F. Watson c Jeacocke b Hitch | 0 | – c Strudwick b Fender | 10 |
| E. Tyldesley c Shepherd b Hitch | 6 | – c Shepherd b Peach | 236 |
| C. Hallows b Hitch | 6 | – run out | 7 |
| Mr L. Green c Strudwick b Fender | 44 | – lbw b Abel | 12 |
| Mr A. Rhodes b Hitch | 1 | – b Fender | 43 |
| Mr J. Sharp c Peach b Fender | 8 | – lbw b Jeacocke | 30 |
| R. Tyldesley c Hobbs b Fender | 22 | – c and b Peach | 23 |
| C. Parkin c Sandham b Fender | 25 | – run out | 7 |
| G. Duckworth c and b Fender | 0 | – not out | 21 |
| L. Cook not out | 0 | – lbw b Fender | 17 |
| B 8, l-b 1, n-b 3 | 12 | B 13, l-b 3, w 1 | 17 |
| | 185 | | 444 |

### Lancashire Bowling

| | Overs | Mdns | Runs | Wkts | Overs | Mdns | Runs | Wkts |
|---|---:|---:|---:|---:|---:|---:|---:|---:|
| Parkin | 33 | 5 | 131 | 2 | 13.1 | 1 | 48 | 2 |
| Rhodes | 11 | — | 41 | — | | | | |
| R. Tyldesley | 36 | 7 | 112 | 5 | | | | |
| Cook | 26 | 4 | 81 | 1 | 13 | 2 | 36 | 1 |
| Watson | 9 | 1 | 30 | — | | | | |
| Green | 2 | — | 22 | — | | | | |

### Surrey Bowling

| | Overs | Mdns | Runs | Wkts | Overs | Mdns | Runs | Wkts |
|---|---:|---:|---:|---:|---:|---:|---:|---:|
| Hitch | 18 | 2 | 39 | 4 | 21 | 2 | 98 | — |
| Peach | 11 | 5 | 21 | — | 31 | 8 | 75 | 2 |
| Fender | 27.3 | 3 | 60 | 6 | 36.1 | 6 | 118 | 4 |
| Reay | 15 | 4 | 32 | — | 12 | 2 | 50 | — |
| Abel | 5 | 1 | 14 | — | 17 | 4 | 39 | 1 |
| Shepherd | 3 | — | 7 | — | 11 | — | 39 | — |
| Jeacocke | | | | | 2 | 1 | 8 | 1 |

Umpires: J. H. Board and H. Butt.

## JACK HOBBS IN 1925

Great as his successes had been since he first appeared for Surrey in 1905 when, with scores in his first two matches of 18 and 88 against the Gentlemen of England and 28 and 155 against Essex, he showed himself at once a batsman of remarkable ability, John Berry Hobbs surpassed himself in the summer of 1925. Never previously had he made 3,000 runs in one season or headed the batting averages, but he accomplished both those feats, his aggregate amounting to 3,024 and an average of 70.32 placing him above all his rivals. He seized the occasion, too, of the Gentlemen and Players match at Scarborough to put together the highest innings of his career, beating his previous best – 226 for Surrey against Nottinghamshire at The Oval in 1914 – with 266 not out. Furthermore, whereas until last summer the largest number of hundreds he had obtained in one season was eleven – his total in 1914 and again in 1920 – and the record for any batsman was thirteen – made by C. B. Fry in 1901 and equalled by Tom Hayward in 1906 and by Hendren in 1923 – he eclipsed those performances by reaching three figures on no fewer than sixteen occasions.

These achievements, however, notable as they were, counted for little compared with Hobbs' triumph in first equalling and then heading the number of centuries which stand to the credit of W. G. Grace. That the "Grand Old Man's" record of 126 hundreds was likely to go, Hobbs speedily demonstrated. So far from the strain of the Australian tour having any ill effects upon his powers, he jumped into form at once, playing such wonderful cricket that at the end of a dozen matches he had ten centuries to his name. A few small scores ensued but an innings of 140 for the Players at Lord's being immediately followed by one of 105 against Kent at Blackheath, Hobbs by July 20 was within one of Grace's total. Then came what must have been a nerve-wracking time even for one so well-balanced as Hobbs. He found himself the most talked of man in England, pursued by interviewers and photographers, and day after day, while the coveted century eluded his powers, he was referred to – whatever score he made – as having "failed again". For the time being the performances of one individual were, in many quarters, actually allowed to overshadow the game as a whole. Hobbs managed to survive all the embarrassing attentions showered upon him but, according to those watching him closely, he became rather wear y-looking during the four weeks which elapsed before August 16 when with an innings of 101 against Somerset at Taunton he at last equalled Grace's record and on the following day beat it with 101 not out.

Grandly as Hobbs batted in 1925 there yet were times when something seemed to have gone out of his game. He who had often in the past shaped in the first over as though he had batted for an hour, generally found it necessary to play himself in with some care, as, perhaps, was not surprising now that he is in the "forties". Yet, whatever might be noticed at the start of one of his innings, once he had settled down, he was usually as adventurous as of old. Certainly he had not to drop any of his special strokes, although many of these demand supreme quickness of foot and wrist.

That Hobbs, during the forthcoming season, may show himself in something like the form of last summer will be the fervent prayer of all followers of the game. The great occasion is at hand and we look to him to "speak with the enemy at the gate". It would be a glorious climax to an historic career were he, by his batting, to play the outstanding part in so long-delayed a triumph of England over Australia. Curiously enough while more than 2,000 runs (including nine centuries) stand to his credit in Test matches with Australia, he has played only ten innings for England against Australia in this country. He did quite well in 1912, scoring 224 runs in four innings, but in 1921 he figured in only one of the five encounters and, attacked with appendicitis during the progress of the struggle, he did not bat.

In view of that disappointment a real triumph for him next summer would be singularly appropriate. Certainly it will not be his fault if he cannot give of his best for he has been at much pains during the winter to keep himself in condition. Still, whatever the next few months may have in store – whether success or failure attends his efforts – Hobbs will go down to posterity as one of the greatest figures in cricket history. A masterly batsman under all conditions, possessed of exceptional grace of style, remarkable in the variety of his strokes, ready to run any risk for his side, and a superb field, he has been at once the wonder and delight of all cricketers of his generation.

## SURREY v LEICESTERSHIRE

### Played at The Oval, August 25, 26, 27, 1926

Declaring twice in the course of the game, Surrey beat Leicestershire by 119 runs, but not until ten minutes to six on Friday did the contest come to an end. Curiously enough, Hobbs and Sandham did little, but Shepherd, on Wednesday, helped Ducat to put on 261 in three hours, and with the closure delayed a few minutes on Friday morning, he enjoyed the satisfaction for the first time in his career of making two separate hundreds – both admirable displays of batting – in the same match. Fourth out at 438, Ducat, missed when 33 and again when 218, batted brilliantly for nearly four hours and a half, and hit thirty-three 4s. The last hour and fifty-five minutes on Wednesday produced 280 runs. Holmes bowled so finely that Leicestershire had seven men out for 110, but Geary and Sidwell added 150, and on Friday, Geary and Astill put on 114.

### Surrey

| | | | |
|---|---|---|---|
| J. B. Hobbs c Bale b Rudd | 10 | – c Armstrong b Astill | 23 |
| A. Sandham c Armstrong b Astill | 22 | – c Geary b Snary | 2 |
| A. Ducat c Taylor b Astill | 235 | – c Armstrong b Rudd | 14 |
| T. Shepherd b Snary | 121 | – not out | 101 |
| Mr D. R. Jardine not out | 69 | – b Snary | 23 |
| Mr A. Jeacocke c Armstrong b Astill | 62 | – c Armstrong b Bale | 13 |
| Mr P. G. H. Fender not out | 7 | – c Rudd b Armstrong | 10 |
| Mr E. R. T. Holmes (did not bat) | | – not out | 11 |
| B 10, l-b 2, n-b 3 | 15 | | |

(5 wkts dec.) 541         (6 wkts dec.) 197

H. A. Peach, H. Strudwick and S. Fenley did not bat.

### Leicestershire

| | | | |
|---|---|---|---|
| Mr E. W. Dawson b Holmes | 7 | – lbw b Fenley | 19 |
| L. G. Berry lbw b Fender | 18 | – c Jardine b Fender | 12 |
| N. F. Armstrong c Shepherd b Holmes | 0 | – lbw b Jardine | 30 |
| Mr C. H. Taylor c Strudwick b Holmes | 1 | – c Fenley b Fender | 20 |
| W. E. Astill b Holmes | 6 | – c Holmes b Fender | 85 |
| Mr G. B. F. Rudd lbw b Fenley | 7 | – c Fender b Shepherd | 32 |
| G. Geary c Peach b Fenley | 100 | – lbw b Fender | 55 |
| Maj. G. H. S. Fowke b Holmes | 13 | – b Fender | 6 |
| T. E. Sidwell b Fender | 105 | – lbw b Fenley | 39 |
| F. Bale not out | 4 | – lbw b Fender | 21 |
| H. C. Snary lbw b Fender | 0 | – not out | 5 |
| B 25 | 25 | B 6, l-b 1, w 2 | 9 |

286             333

## Leicestershire Bowling

| | Overs | Mdns | Runs | Wkts | Overs | Mdns | Runs | Wkts |
|---|---|---|---|---|---|---|---|---|
| Geary ............ | 26 | 5 | 79 | — | 9.4 | 2 | 41 | — |
| Snary ............ | 38 | 8 | 149 | 1 | 10 | — | 63 | 2 |
| Rudd ............ | 9 | 1 | 50 | 1 | 3 | — | 26 | 1 |
| Astill ............ | 29 | 4 | 138 | 3 | 9 | 3 | 12 | 1 |
| Bale ............. | 17 | 1 | 53 | — | 7 | — | 31 | 1 |
| Armstrong ........ | 7 | 2 | 22 | — | 4 | — | 24 | 1 |
| Taylor ........... | 3 | — | 13 | — | | | | |
| Fowke ........... | 2 | — | 22 | — | | | | |

## Surrey Bowling

| | Overs | Mdns | Runs | Wkts | Overs | Mdns | Runs | Wkts |
|---|---|---|---|---|---|---|---|---|
| Peach ............ | 13 | 6 | 30 | — | 20 | 3 | 64 | — |
| Fender ........... | 23.5 | 8 | 67 | 3 | 30.2 | 8 | 67 | 6 |
| Holmes .......... | 20 | 5 | 58 | 5 | 16 | 3 | 66 | — |
| Fenley ........... | 26 | 5 | 70 | 2 | 29 | 6 | 82 | 2 |
| Shepherd ......... | 11 | 4 | 28 | — | 12 | 2 | 22 | 1 |
| Jardine .......... | 2 | — | 8 | — | 9 | 4 | 23 | 1 |

Umpires: W. Reeves and J. Bedford.

# SURREY v HAMPSHIRE

## Played at The Oval, May 7, 9, 10, 1927

Surrey's opening home match was rendered memorable by Hobbs and Newman each of whom made two separate hundreds. Only once before had that feat been achieved, the brothers R. E. and W. L. Foster accomplishing it for Worcestershire against Hampshire in 1899. Hobbs' 112 was a masterly display of batting on a pitch which had not recovered from the previous day's rain. In the second innings when he and Sandham put on 152 for the first wicket, Hobbs gave no chance and obtained his score in less than two hours and a half. Newman on Monday, when Hampshire found themselves in a position of some anxiety, gave a chance in the slips with his score at 5 and then settled down to withstand the Surrey attack for three hours and a half. When Fender declared – after lunch on Tuesday – Newman went in first and stayed to the end.

## Surrey

| | | | |
|---|---|---|---|
| J. B. Hobbs c Livsey b Newman ............... | 112 | – c sub. b Pothecary ................ | 104 |
| A. Sandham c Livsey b Newman ................ | 0 | – c Livsey b Pothecary ............ | 58 |
| Mr A. Jeacocke c Kennedy b Newman .......... | 55 | – c Livsey b Pothecary ............ | 0 |
| T. Shepherd lbw b Kennedy ................... | 120 | – st Livsey b Pothecary ......... | 22 |
| A. Ducat c Livsey b Newman ................. | 0 | – c Newman b Kennedy .......... | 25 |
| H. Baldwin b Newman ....................... | 0 | – c Gross b Kennedy ........... | 22 |
| Mr P. G. H. Fender c Mead b Gross ............ | 53 | – not out ..................... | 27 |
| H. A. Peach c and b Kennedy ................. | 77 | | |
| H. Strudwick c Brown b Pothecary ............. | 12 | – not out ..................... | 15 |
| A. Geary b Gross .......................... | 2 | | |
| S. Fenley not out .......................... | 1 | | |
| B 4, l-b 3 ......................... | 7 | B 4, l-b 4 .............. | 8 |
| | **439** | | **(6 wkts dec.) 281** |

## Hampshire

| | | |
|---|---|---|
| A. Kennedy b Fender | 33 | – c Fender b Shepherd ............10 |
| G. Brown lbw b Fender | 22 | – lbw b Geary ................. 6 |
| A. Bowell b Peach | 0 | – lbw b Fender ............... 19 |
| C. P. Mead lbw b Shepherd | 57 | |
| J. Newman b Fender | 102 | – not out .....................102 |
| Hon. L. H. Tennyson run out | 16 | – c Sandham b Jeacocke ......... 36 |
| W. H. Livsey b Geary | 48 | – c and b Jeacocke ............. 1 |
| Mr J. P. Parker not out | 46 | – not out ..................... 46 |
| G. S. Boyes b Geary | 1 | |
| Mr F. Gross b Geary | 1 | |
| E. Pothecary run out | 24 | |
| B 14, l-b 5, n-b 1 | 20 | B 23, l-b 6 .............. 29 |
| | **370** | **249** |

### Hampshire Bowling

| | Overs | Mdns | Runs | Wkts | Overs | Mdns | Runs | Wkts |
|---|---|---|---|---|---|---|---|---|
| Kennedy | 29.1 | 5 | 87 | 2 | 18 | 4 | 43 | 2 |
| Newman | 30 | 3 | 123 | 5 | 11 | 1 | 39 | — |
| Boyes | 20 | 5 | 54 | — | 14 | — | 37 | — |
| Brown | 5 | — | 22 | — | 11 | 1 | 36 | — |
| Pothecary | 16 | 1 | 80 | 1 | 8 | 1 | 47 | 4 |
| Gross | 12 | — | 66 | 2 | 17 | — | 71 | — |

### Surrey Bowling

| | Overs | Mdns | Runs | Wkts | Overs | Mdns | Runs | Wkts |
|---|---|---|---|---|---|---|---|---|
| Geary | 26 | 5 | 75 | 3 | 15 | 8 | 14 | 1 |
| Peach | 24 | 9 | 38 | 1 | | | | |
| Fenley | 18.5 | 3 | 59 | — | 17 | 4 | 47 | — |
| Fender | 38 | 9 | 106 | 3 | 12 | 2 | 42 | 1 |
| Shepherd | 17 | 2 | 66 | 1 | 18 | 6 | 47 | 1 |
| Baldwin | 3 | 1 | 6 | — | 8 | 5 | 3 | — |
| Jeacocke | | | | | 9 | — | 67 | 2 |

Umpires: H. Young and F. Parris.

## SURREY v GLAMORGAN

### Played at The Oval, June 12, 13, 1929

Dismissed in their first innings for 37 – the lowest score registered in any first-class county match during the season – Glamorgan had, early on the second afternoon, to admit defeat by an innings and 75 runs. Half the wickets fell for 11 runs, the five batsmen disposed of up to that point having all failed to score. The innings was all over in eighty minutes, Allom and A. Geary dividing the wickets. Surrey fielded very accurately, Shepherd and Brooks each bringing off three catches. When Surrey went in Sandham and Ducat, coming together at 23, added 167 in less than two hours. Out in the last over of the day, Sandham gave two chances, but still played admirably with a 5 and twenty-four 4s as his chief strokes. Of the six Surrey wickets down at the drawing of stumps all had fallen to Mercer's bowling. Fender declared next morning, and had the fielding been up to the standard of the previous day, Glamorgan, under the awkward conditions which prevailed, must again have been cheaply dismissed. Bell, making 87 out of 134 brought off some fine hits, but was missed three times.

## Glamorgan

| | | | |
|---|---|---|---|
| W. Bates c Lock b Allom | 18 | – c Gregory b Geary | 12 |
| J. T. Bell c Shepherd b Geary | 0 | – c Gregory b Shepherd | 87 |
| D. Davies c Shepherd b Geary | 0 | – c Ducat b Fender | 2 |
| Mr T. Arnott c Brooks b Geary | 0 | – c and b Lock | 8 |
| Mr F. W. Matthias b Allom | 0 | – c Shepherd b Lock | 20 |
| A. H. Dyson c Brooks b Allom | 0 | – c Shepherd b Geary | 0 |
| Mr W. G. Morgan c Brooks b Geary | 1 | – c Geary b Shepherd | 4 |
| E. Davies c Shepherd b Geary | 7 | – lbw b Geary | 15 |
| J. Mercer c Sandham b Allom | 6 | – c sub. b Geary | 3 |
| G. Every c Gregory b Allom | 0 | – b Geary | 10 |
| W. Jones not out | 4 | – not out | 0 |
| B 1 | 1 | B 14, l-b 4, n-b 4 | 22 |
| | 37 | | 183 |

## Surrey

| | | | | |
|---|---|---|---|---|
| A. Sandham lbw b Mercer | 187 | Mr P. G. H. Fender c Bates b Mercer | 0 |
| T. H. Barling b Mercer | 8 | R. J. Gregory not out | 13 |
| A. Ducat lbw b Mercer | 70 | B 1, l-b 5, w 1, n-b 2 | 9 |
| T. Shepherd lbw b Mercer | 5 | | |
| E. F. Wilson c Bates b Mercer | 3 | (6 wkts dec.) | 295 |

Mr M. J. C. Allom, E. W. Brooks, A. Geary and H. Lock did not bat.

### Surrey Bowling

| | Overs | Mdns | Runs | Wkts | Overs | Mdns | Runs | Wkts |
|---|---|---|---|---|---|---|---|---|
| Allom | 15 | 10 | 14 | 5 | 5 | 1 | 10 | — |
| Geary | 14 | 7 | 22 | 5 | 19.3 | 2 | 48 | 5 |
| Fender | | | | | 12 | — | 43 | 1 |
| Lock | | | | | 15 | 3 | 47 | 2 |
| Shepherd | | | | | 5 | 2 | 13 | 2 |

### Glamorgan Bowling

| | Overs | Mdns | Runs | Wkts |
|---|---|---|---|---|
| Mercer | 24.5 | 6 | 76 | 6 |
| Arnott | 18 | 4 | 67 | — |
| E. Davies | 5 | 1 | 10 | — |
| Bates | 5 | — | 24 | — |
| Jones | 13 | 3 | 40 | — |
| D. Davies | 16 | 2 | 64 | — |
| Morgan | 1 | — | 5 | — |

Umpires: T. Oates and W. R. Parry.

## SURREY v GLAMORGAN

Played at The Oval, April 30, May 1, 2, 1930

Hobbs rendered Surrey's opening engagement notable by putting together for the fifth time two separate hundreds. Going in on Thursday against the Glamorgan total of 474, he took three hours and three-quarters to make 137 but played a very strong game on the leg side and gave no chance. In his second innings he was missed when 62 but otherwise batted in his most attractive form. Despite Hobbs' performance Glamorgan, for whom

Bates and Hills made 217 for the fourth wicket, carried off first innings' points. Bates played admirable cricket, but had an escape when 42 while Hills, after a shaky start, settled down to a fine game. Stroud, a medium-paced bowler, made a promising appearance in Surrey's first eleven.

## Glamorgan

| | | | |
|---|---:|---|---:|
| W. E. Bates c Fender b Stroud | 168 | – c Barling b Allom | 2 |
| A. H. Dyson c and b Fender | 28 | – b Allom | 7 |
| E. Davies c Ducat b Peach | 10 | – b Gregory | 7 |
| J. T. Bell lbw b Allom | 9 | – lbw b Allom | 5 |
| J. Hills c Brooks b Stroud | 100 | – c Shepherd b Stroud | 53 |
| Mr M. J. Turnbull c Peach b Stroud | 29 | – c and b Gregory | 61 |
| D. Davies b Allom | 30 | – c Shepherd b Stroud | 31 |
| G. Lavis c Fender b Peach | 27 | – c Shepherd b Stroud | 10 |
| G. Every c Brooks b Peach | 11 | – lbw b Allom | 11 |
| J. Mercer b Allom | 39 | – c Ducat b Gregory | 0 |
| F. Ryan not out | 0 | – not out | 1 |
| B 20, l-b 3 | 23 | B 11, l-b 6 | 17 |
| | **474** | | **205** |

## Surrey

| | | | |
|---|---:|---|---:|
| J. B. Hobbs b Bates | 137 | – not out | 111 |
| A. Sandham c Turnbull b Mercer | 41 | – b Mercer | 25 |
| A. Ducat st Every b Bates | 30 | – c E. Davies b Mercer | 0 |
| T. Shepherd c Every b Mercer | 20 | – not out | 52 |
| T. H. Barling b Ryan | 45 | | |
| Mr P. G. H. Fender lbw b Ryan | 1 | | |
| R. J. Gregory lbw b Mercer | 11 | | |
| H. A. Peach b Ryan | 0 | | |
| Mr E. G. Stroud b Mercer | 22 | | |
| Mr M. J. C. Allom c Every b Mercer | 3 | | |
| E. W. Brooks not out | 12 | | |
| B 6, l-b 5 | 11 | B 1, l-b 1 | 2 |
| | **333** | | **190** |

## Surrey Bowling

| | Overs | Mdns | Runs | Wkts | Overs | Mdns | Runs | Wkts |
|---|---|---|---|---|---|---|---|---|
| Allom | 36 | 12 | 81 | 3 | 25 | 5 | 50 | 4 |
| Peach | 26.3 | 4 | 117 | 3 | 13 | 4 | 19 | — |
| Shepherd | 22 | 6 | 76 | — | 11 | 3 | 33 | — |
| Stroud | 30 | 9 | 76 | 3 | 13.5 | 3 | 29 | 3 |
| Fender | 19 | 3 | 73 | 1 | 11 | 6 | 16 | — |
| Gregory | 6 | 1 | 28 | — | 13 | 3 | 41 | 3 |

## Glamorgan Bowling

| | Overs | Mdns | Runs | Wkts | Overs | Mdns | Runs | Wkts |
|---|---|---|---|---|---|---|---|---|
| Mercer | 31.2 | 10 | 61 | 5 | 12 | 2 | 41 | 2 |
| Lavis | 13 | 1 | 58 | — | 6 | — | 32 | — |
| Ryan | 28 | 5 | 96 | 3 | 11 | — | 55 | — |
| E. Davies | 18 | 2 | 56 | — | 10 | 2 | 16 | — |
| D. Davies | 7 | — | 20 | — | — | — | 17 | — |
| Bates | 9 | — | 31 | 2 | — | — | 19 | — |
| Turnbull | | | | | — | — | 2 | — |
| Bell | | | | | — | — | 6 | — |

Umpires: G. Beet and H. Young.

## SURREY v GLOUCESTERSHIRE

Played at The Oval, May 2, 4, 5, 1931

Gloucestershire, after a truly memorable day's cricket in the concluding stage of this encounter, defeated Surrey by three wickets. When the final day's play was entered upon, Gloucestershire, against Surrey's total of 258, had made only 69 for one wicket and consequently a draw appeared inevitable. Lyon, however, declared when with seven men out the visitors stood 83 in arrear. Fender, not to be outdone in enterprise, closed Surrey's innings after six wickets had fallen for 60 and then Gloucestershire, set 144 to get in an hour and fifty minutes, accomplished that task for the loss of seven batsmen in what must in any case have been the last over of the match. Notable as was the performance of Gloucestershire in hitting off the runs at such a pace, success should not have attended the endeavour, seeing that not only was Dacre let off once and Hammond missed upon two occasions but the latter should have been run out. Hammond and Dacre hit up 77 in forty-five minutes. Parker at a most critical stage of the game sent back Hobbs, Shepherd, Ducat and Fender for 25 runs.

### Surrey

| | | | | |
|---|---|---|---|---|
| J. B. Hobbs run out | 65 | – c Hammond b Parker | 0 |
| A. Sandham run out | 7 | – c Smith b Goddard | 6 |
| A. Ducat lbw b Parker | 1 | – c Hammond b Parker | 22 |
| T. Shepherd b Parker | 27 | – c Barnett b Parker | 6 |
| T. H. Barling c Lyon b Goddard | 45 | – run out | 0 |
| Mr P. G. H. Fender lbw b Parker | 4 | – lbw b Parker | 20 |
| R. J. Gregory lbw b Parker | 68 | – not out | 5 |
| Mr M. J. C. Allom c Sinfield b Parker | 17 | | |
| E. W. Brooks c Neale b Parker | 9 | | |
| A. Geary not out | 2 | | |
| A. R. Gover b Parker | 6 | | |
| B 6, l-b 1 | 7 | L-b 1 | 1 |
| | **258** | **(6 wkts dec.)** | **60** |

### Gloucestershire

| | | | | |
|---|---|---|---|---|
| A. E. Dipper b Geary | 40 | – lbw b Allom | 9 |
| R. A. Sinfield not out | 71 | – c and b Gover | 8 |
| H. Smith b Geary | 12 | – lbw b Allom | 2 |
| W. R. Hammond c and b Fender | 8 | – not out | 58 |
| Mr B. H. Lyon c and b Fender | 2 | – b Gover | 2 |
| C. C. Dacre c Brooks b Gover | 25 | – b Allom | 46 |
| W. L. Neale c Fender b Gover | 0 | – c Brooks b Gover | 3 |
| C. J. Barnett lbw b Fender | 6 | – b Fender | 9 |
| C. Parker (did not bat) | | – not out | 2 |
| L-b 5, w 1, n-b 5 | 11 | L-b 3, n-b 3 | 6 |
| | **(7 wkts dec.) 175** | | **145** |

T. W. Goddard and A. Rogers did not bat.

### Gloucestershire Bowling

| | Overs | Mdns | Runs | Wkts | Overs | Mdns | Runs | Wkts |
|---|---|---|---|---|---|---|---|---|
| Sinfield | 23 | 9 | 45 | — | | | | |
| Rogers | 3 | 2 | 3 | — | | | | |
| Goddard | 55 | 27 | 75 | 1 | 10 | 2 | 34 | 1 |
| Parker | 44.4 | 13 | 128 | 7 | 10.1 | 3 | 25 | 4 |

**Surrey Bowling**

| | Overs | Mdns | Runs | Wkts | Overs | Mdns | Runs | Wkts |
|---|---|---|---|---|---|---|---|---|
| Allom . . . . . . . . . . . | 17 | 6 | 40 | — | 14.3 | 2 | 43 | 3 |
| Gover . . . . . . . . . . . | 19 | 5 | 43 | 2 | 7 | 1 | 22 | 3 |
| Geary . . . . . . . . . . . | 22 | 6 | 38 | 2 | 3 | — | 21 | — |
| Gregory . . . . . . . . . | 26 | 10 | 27 | — | 3 | — | 12 | — |
| Fender . . . . . . . . . . | 6.1 | 1 | 16 | 3 | 7 | — | 41 | 1 |

Umpires: F. Chester and W. Reeves.

## SURREY v SOMERSET

### Played at The Oval, May 13, 14, 15, 1931

A sensational piece of bowling on the part of E. J. Sheffield at the start of this match resulted in Somerset losing four batsmen for 35 but during the remainder of Wednesday and on Thursday the bat beat the ball so completely that 882 runs were obtained and only ten wickets went down. On Friday, owing to rain, no cricket was possible so the game ended in a draw. Sheffield, taking part in his second contest for Surrey, bowled fast medium and made the ball swing a lot to begin with, sending down six overs and three balls for four wickets and 4 runs and altogether obtaining the first six wickets. Case came to Somerset's rescue, withstanding Surrey's attack for three hours and a half, giving no real chance and putting together the highest innings of his career. He had three useful partners, White helping to add 95, Earle scoring 55 out of 79 and Linney assisting in a stand of 95. On Thursday evening Hobbs – missed when three – and Sandham put on 67 runs and next day they shared for the fifty-first time in a three-figure partnership. Raising the score to 231 before Hobbs was out, the two batsmen withstood Somerset's attack for three hours and a half. In addition to his early chance Hobbs should have been caught when 79, but his strokes on the leg side and his pulls were made in delightful style. Sandham, employing the cut in masterly fashion, made no mistake until his score reached 128. Ducat and Jardine added 109 and then Fender actually hit up 139 out of 181 in eighty minutes with three 6s and seventeen 4s as his chief strokes. The Surrey captain was missed when 10 and enjoyed considerable luck in the ball falling out of harm's way but still gave a wonderful display. Jardine, although overshadowed, scored cleverly on the leg side.

### Somerset

| | |
|---|---|
| A. Young c Ducat b Sheffield . . . . . . . . . . . 20 | Mr G. F. Earle b Gover . . . . . . . . . . . . . . . 55 |
| Mr R. A. Ingle b Sheffield . . . . . . . . . . . . . 0 | Mr L. Hawkins b Gover . . . . . . . . . . . . . . . 10 |
| J. W. Lee b Sheffield . . . . . . . . . . . . . . . . . 0 | C. K. Linney not out . . . . . . . . . . . . . . . . . 35 |
| Mr H. D. Burrough b Sheffield . . . . . . . . . . 8 | F. Pratten c Shepherd b Sheffield . . . . . . . . 0 |
| Mr J. C. White c Fender b Sheffield . . . . . . . 41 | B 9, l-b 3, w 1, n-b 1 . . . . . . . . . . 14 |
| Mr C. C. Case c Brooks b Gover . . . . . . . . .155 | |
| A. W. Wellard b Sheffield . . . . . . . . . . . . . 0 | 338 |

### Surrey

| | |
|---|---|
| J. B. Hobbs c Pratten b Wellard . . . . . . . . . .128 | Mr P. G. H. Fender not out . . . . . . . . . . . . .139 |
| A. Sandham c Young b Wellard . . . . . . . . .131 | B 11, w 1, n-b 1 . . . . . . . . . . . . . . 13 |
| A. Ducat c Hawkins b White . . . . . . . . . . . 83 | |
| T. Shepherd b White . . . . . . . . . . . . . . . . . 5 | (4 wkts dec.) 579 |
| Mr D. R. Jardine not out . . . . . . . . . . . . . . 80 | |

R. J. Gregory, H. A. Peach, E. W. Brooks, A. R. Gover and E. J. Sheffield did not bat.

**Surrey Bowling**

|              | Overs | Mdns | Runs | Wkts |
|--------------|-------|------|------|------|
| Gover .......... | 23 | 2 | 99 | 3 |
| Sheffield ........ | 34.4 | 3 | 123 | 7 |
| Gregory ........ | 15 | 5 | 38 | — |
| Peach .......... | 11 | 4 | 31 | — |
| Fender ......... | 10 | — | 33 | — |

**Somerset Bowling**

|              | Overs | Mdns | Runs | Wkts |
|--------------|-------|------|------|------|
| Wellard ......... | 45 | 7 | 189 | 2 |
| Lee ............. | 42 | 6 | 148 | — |
| White .......... | 44 | 17 | 110 | 2 |
| Young .......... | 17 | 2 | 54 | — |
| Hawkins ....... | 8 | 1 | 30 | — |
| Linney ......... | 9 | 2 | 35 | — |

Umpires: A. Morton and H. Young.

## SURREY v HAMPSHIRE

Played at The Oval, May 16, 18, 19, 1931

Among a number of strange actions taken by county captains during the summer of 1931, there was nothing quite so extraordinary as that of Stephen Fry in this match. Rain having interfered considerably with play on Saturday and Monday, the progress made when the third day's play began was limited to the completion of an innings by Surrey. Arnold and Bailey batting admirably on a slightly slow but by no means difficult wicket put on 127 runs and were still together at the luncheon interval. Everything then suggested that Hampshire in the course of the afternoon would most deservedly obtain first innings points. There came, however, the amazing announcement that Fry, with Hampshire 118 in arrear, the pitch likely to play well and the visitors commanding scarcely anyone capable of forcing the game, had declared. Surrey subsequently contented themselves with seventy-five minutes batting while Hampshire, set 222 to get in two hours and three-quarters, survived some anxious moments but what purpose could possibly have been served by Hampshire declaring will ever remain a puzzle.

### Surrey

| | | | |
|---|---|---|---|
| J. B. Hobbs c Bailey b Kennedy ................ | 41 | – c Herman b Boyes .............. | 25 |
| A. Sandham c Arnold b Kennedy .............. | 7 | | |
| A. Ducat c Mead b Judd ..................... | 45 | – not out ....................... | 34 |
| Mr P. G. H. Fender c Fry b Judd .............. | 57 | – c Judd b Bailey ............... | 19 |
| T. Shepherd st Fry b Boyes ................... | 49 | – not out ....................... | 17 |
| H. S. Squires b Kennedy ..................... | 19 | | |
| R. J. Gregory c Mead b Judd ................. | 6 | | |
| E. J. Sheffield c Herman b Kennedy ........... | 0 | | |
| E. W. Brooks b Kennedy ..................... | 4 | | |
| A. Geary not out ........................... | 6 | | |
| A. R. Gover b Kennedy ...................... | 8 | | |
| B 3 ............................. | 3 | B 4, l-b 4 .............. | 8 |
| | **245** | | **(2 wkts dec.) 103** |

## Hampshire

| | | |
|---|---|---|
| J. Arnold not out .......................... 51 | – c Fender b Sheffield ............. | 1 |
| J. Bailey not out ........................... 69 | – c Shepherd b Fender ........... | 12 |
| L. Harfield (did not bat) ...................... | – b Gover ...................... | 34 |
| C. P. Mead (did not bat) .................... | – not out ...................... | 56 |
| Mr A. K. Judd (did not bat) .................. | – c Sheffield b Gover ............ | 0 |
| A. E. Pothecary (did not bat) ................. | – c Brooks b Gover ............. | 0 |
| A. Kennedy (did not bat) ..................... | – not out ...................... | 13 |
| B 1, l-b 3, n-b 3 .................... 7 | B 2, l-b 5, n-b 2 .......... | 9 |

(0 wkt dec.) 127 125

Mr S. Fry, W. L. Creese, G. S. Boyes and O. W. Herman did not bat.

## Hampshire Bowling

| | Overs | Mdns | Runs | Wkts | Overs | Mdns | Runs | Wkts |
|---|---|---|---|---|---|---|---|---|
| Kennedy ......... | 22.4 | 9 | 86 | 6 | 8 | 3 | 18 | — |
| Herman .......... | 9 | — | 28 | — | 2 | — | 7 | — |
| Boyes ............ | 20 | 5 | 43 | 1 | 8 | 1 | 32 | 1 |
| Creese ........... | 18 | 6 | 33 | — | | | | |
| Bailey ............ | 10 | 2 | 20 | — | 6 | 2 | 24 | 1 |
| Judd ............. | 10 | 1 | 32 | 3 | 1 | — | 14 | — |

## Surrey Bowling

| | Overs | Mdns | Runs | Wkts | Overs | Mdns | Runs | Wkts |
|---|---|---|---|---|---|---|---|---|
| Gover ............ | 9 | 1 | 20 | — | 14 | 3 | 22 | 3 |
| Sheffield ......... | 9 | 1 | 23 | — | 13 | 3 | 18 | 1 |
| Gregory .......... | 12 | 4 | 25 | — | 2 | 1 | 6 | — |
| Geary ............ | 6 | 2 | 16 | — | 11 | 2 | 32 | — |
| Squires .......... | 4 | — | 8 | — | 3 | 1 | 5 | — |
| Fender .......... | 5 | — | 28 | — | 10 | — | 33 | 1 |

Umpires: W. Reeves and A. Dolphin.

## SURREY v OXFORD UNIVERSITY

Played at The Oval, June 24, 25, 26, 1931

The Nawab of Pataudi invested this match with special interest by his achievement in putting together two separate hundreds. The two displays presented strong contrasts. On Wednesday Pataudi took half an hour to reach double figures and had other spells of quiet play intermingled with a lot of polished all-round run-getting. Altogether he scored 165 out of 301 in four hours and three-quarters, the only real blemish being a difficult chance at the wicket when 142. On Friday he hit up 100 out of 158 in just over two hours without a real mistake. Evans and Wellings in the first innings and Hone in the second shared with him in three-figure partnerships. Six of Surrey's regular eleven were absent from the home side. Play on Wednesday was not possible until half-past two.

### Oxford University

| | | |
|---|---|---|
| Mr B. W. Hone c Fender b Sheffield | 2 | – c Sheffield b Allom ........ 48 |
| Mr E. N. Evans b Lock | 48 | – c Mobey b Allom ........... 3 |
| Nawab of Pataudi c and b Lock | 165 | – c Whitfield b Lock ........ 100 |
| Mr A. Melville b Allom | 21 | – c Mobey b Lock ............ 9 |
| Mr F. G. H. Chalk b Allom | 6 | – not out ................... 18 |
| Mr E. M. Wellings b Lock | 55 | |
| Mr R. S. G. Scott c Gregory b Fender | 8 | – not out ................... 15 |
| Mr T. M. Hart not out | 6 | – b Lock ..................... 0 |
| Mr R. H. J. Brooke c Mobey b Lock | 5 | |
| Mr W. H. Bradshaw not out | 6 | |
| B 5, l-b 1 | 6 | L-b 5, w 1 ............... 6 |

                (8 wkts dec.) 328                 (5 wkts dec.) 199

Mr D. C. G. Raikes did not bat.

### Surrey

| | | |
|---|---|---|
| T. H. Barling c Brooke b Bradshaw | 3 | – c Chalk b Bradshaw ........... 3 |
| R. J. Gregory c Brooke b Bradshaw | 28 | – not out ..................... 69 |
| E. F. Wilson c Melville b Bradshaw | 59 | – c and b Scott ................ 8 |
| L. B. Fishlock run out | 5 | – not out ..................... 41 |
| H. S. Squires c Melville b Bradshaw | 31 | |
| Mr P. G. H. Fender b Scott | 52 | |
| E. W. Whitfield c and b Wellings | 60 | |
| G. S. Mobey c Melville b Scott | 0 | |
| E. J. Sheffield b Scott | 5 | |
| Mr M. J. C. Allom b Wellings | 37 | |
| H. Lock not out | 5 | |
| B 7, l-b 6 | 13 | B 12, l-b 1 ............... 13 |

                298                 134

### Surrey Bowling

| | Overs | Mdns | Runs | Wkts | Overs | Mdns | Runs | Wkts |
|---|---|---|---|---|---|---|---|---|
| Allom | 26 | 6 | 78 | 2 | 16 | 5 | 31 | 2 |
| Sheffield | 34 | 7 | 68 | 1 | 12 | 4 | 21 | — |
| Lock | 39 | 15 | 57 | 4 | 18 | 1 | 54 | 3 |
| Fender | 15 | — | 51 | 1 | 6 | 1 | 29 | — |
| Gregory | 10 | — | 40 | — | 8 | 1 | 18 | — |
| Squires | 9 | 2 | 28 | — | 5 | — | 19 | — |
| Whitfield | | | | | 5 | 1 | 21 | — |

### Oxford University Bowling

| | Overs | Mdns | Runs | Wkts | Overs | Mdns | Runs | Wkts |
|---|---|---|---|---|---|---|---|---|
| Bradshaw | 32 | 6 | 82 | 4 | 12 | — | 29 | 1 |
| Wellings | 25.2 | 7 | 61 | 2 | 9 | 2 | 38 | — |
| Scott | 30 | 11 | 83 | 3 | 11 | — | 31 | 1 |
| Hart | 4 | 1 | 7 | — | 3 | 1 | 14 | — |
| Melville | 7 | 1 | 36 | — | 1 | — | 9 | — |
| Brooke | 7 | 2 | 16 | — | | | | |

Umpires: F. Chester and J. Hardstaff.

# SURREY v YORKSHIRE

Played at The Oval, August 22, 24, 25, 1931

A curious occurrence marked the opening stage of this contest, the players after cricket had been in progress for about ten minutes leaving the field and nothing further being done until eighty minutes later. It transpired that when Greenwood having won the toss decided to bat, Fender, without having inspected the conditions, accepted the situation but found when play began – Greenwood meanwhile having had the heavy roller put over the pitch – his bowlers could not obtain a satisfactory footing. The umpires being appealed to at once removed the bails and, but for pressure brought upon them, the resumption might have been further delayed than it was. Surrey on Monday had three men out for 51 but then Hobbs and Block, after a most careful start, hit out and added 118 in an hour and three-quarters. Next day, following rain during the night Surrey had eight wickets down for 195 but Hobbs rose to great heights and Allom helped to put on 82. Carrying his bat right through the innings, Hobbs, in making his eighth hundred of the season, batted for just over five hours. He gave a masterly display. Holmes and Sutcliffe afterwards batted in excellent form, the latter putting together his twelfth hundred of the season.

## Yorkshire

| | | | |
|---|---:|---|---:|
| P. Holmes c Brooks b Allom | 51 | – b Brown | 37 |
| H. Sutcliffe b Allom | 26 | – not out | 101 |
| E. Oldroyd b Fender | 15 | – hit wkt b Brown | 24 |
| M. Leyland c Brooks b Allom | 15 | | |
| Mr F. E. Greenwood b Peach | 40 | | |
| W. Barber c Gregory b Peach | 14 | | |
| E. Robinson b Fender | 21 | | |
| A. Wood c Gregory b Fender | 3 | – c Brooks b Block | 4 |
| G. G. Macaulay lbw b Allom | 0 | | |
| H. Verity c Sandham b Fender | 24 | – c Allom b Gregory | 0 |
| W. E. Bowes not out | 5 | | |
| B 12, l-b 7 | 19 | B 3, l-b 7, w 1, n-b 1 | 12 |
| | **233** | | **178** |

## Surrey

| | | | |
|---|---:|---|---:|
| J. B. Hobbs not out | 133 | Mr F. R. Brown c Robinson b Bowes | 4 |
| A. Sandham lbw b Bowes | 0 | H. A. Peach b Macaulay | 0 |
| H. S. Squires b Verity | 14 | Mr M. J. C. Allom c Oldroyd b Robinson | 38 |
| T. Shepherd c Greenwood b Verity | 3 | E. W. Brooks st Wood b Verity | 18 |
| Mr S. A. Block b Macaulay | 70 | B 4, l-b 5, n-b 2 | 11 |
| R. J. Gregory c Wood b Bowes | 7 | | **300** |
| Mr P. G. H. Fender b Bowes | 2 | | |

## Surrey Bowling

| | Overs | Mdns | Runs | Wkts | Overs | Mdns | Runs | Wkts |
|---|---:|---:|---:|---:|---:|---:|---:|---:|
| Allom | 30 | 10 | 48 | 4 | 12 | 5 | 11 | — |
| Peach | 15 | 7 | 28 | 2 | 4 | 1 | 8 | — |
| Brown | 28 | 6 | 62 | — | 27 | 5 | 69 | 2 |
| Gregory | 24 | 12 | 25 | — | 24 | 9 | 30 | 1 |
| Fender | 28 | 8 | 51 | 4 | 8 | — | 17 | — |
| Squires | | | | | 11 | 2 | 31 | — |
| Block | | | | | 0.2 | — | — | 1 |

**Yorkshire Bowling**

|              | Overs | Mdns | Runs | Wkts |
|--------------|-------|------|------|------|
| Bowes ........... | 42 | 8 | 92 | 4 |
| Robinson ......... | 14 | 2 | 46 | 1 |
| Verity ............ | 30 | 5 | 81 | 3 |
| Macaulay ......... | 19 | 5 | 63 | 2 |
| Leyland .......... | 1 | — | 7 | — |

Umpires: F. Chester and D. Hendren.

## SURREY v MIDDLESEX

Played at The Oval, August 6, 8, 9, 1932

A truly memorable match was this, interest in which reached its climax on Tuesday evening when Surrey, set 57 to win, knocked off that number in twenty minutes for the loss of four batsmen and so gained a six wicket victory. With only three balls left of what, in any event, must have been the last over, Surrey still required 10 runs. Off the first of these Jardine gave a chance to deep mid-off but, Enthoven missing the catch, 2 runs resulted. The next – a rather wide half-volley – Jardine chopped through the slips for 4 and the sixth he drove to the pavilion rails, so deciding the issue of the game off the last ball the umpires could have allowed to be delivered.

Surrey's start in going for the runs was not promising for, although Killick missed Shepherd from a skyer, Brown off the last ball of Durston's first over was caught at slip and the second ball sent down by Haig, Fender "skied" to mid-on. In this way, with five minutes gone, there were two wickets down and only 9 runs registered. Shepherd and Block, however, made victory possible by hitting up 36 runs off practically four overs but again the chances veered round when in Haig's third over both batsmen were run out. Indeed the position when Jardine joined Ratcliffe was: – One over to be sent down and 11 runs required for a win while, of course, the fall of a wicket to any of the six balls would have ended the match. Off the first ball Ratcliffe obtained a single and then Jardine, if unable to get either of the next two past the fieldsmen, brought the contest to so remarkable a conclusion by scoring off the last three balls the requisite 10 runs. The detailed bowling analysis was:

Durston * . 2 1 . 4 w   2 1 1 4 . 2   1 . 1 1 1 .   1 . . 2 4 4.
Haig       1 w 1 . 4 1   . 1 . 1 4 4   4 1 1 1 . .

   * *A wide.*

The rate of scoring – 171 an hour – was very nearly equal to that recorded at The Oval in 1919 when for Surrey against Kent Hobbs and J. N. Crawford knocked off 96 runs needed for victory in thirty-two minutes – a rate of 180 an hour. On that occasion the match was won with ten minutes to spare.

While the great excitement came at the end, the game was always full of interest. Middlesex, winning the toss and getting first innings, had, despite the fact of the pitch being rather on the slow side, a good chance of putting together a reasonably large score and at lunch time on the first day, if nothing of special note had been accomplished, a score of 103 for three wickets held out considerable possibilities. On resuming, however, Brown and Parker bowled to such purpose that the seven wickets then remaining fell for 38 runs – the last four for 5 runs. Surrey began disastrously, losing three batsmen for 59, but then Jardine joined Hobbs and those two batsmen put on 125 runs. Caught at mid-off just at the close, Hobbs played masterly cricket for two hours and forty minutes. Surrey, when stumps were drawn on Saturday, had for the loss of four wickets, established a lead of 43. On Monday when the home side increased their score of 184 for four wickets to 540 for nine, batting in all for six hours, Jardine played practically faultless cricket. Having gone in third wicket down at 59, he was sixth out at 338, making his 126 in little more than three hours.

Following upon the fall of Surrey's fifth wicket at 195, Brown joined Jardine and helped to add 143 in eighty-five minutes. Hitting in great form he completed his hundred in as many minutes and when, with the fall of the eighth wicket at 385, the Surrey innings looked like soon coming to an end, he found an invaluable partner in Allom who shared in an exhilarating stand that realised 155 in sixty-five minutes. At the wickets for three hours and twenty minutes, Brown gave a glorious display of fearless hitting. Out of 345 runs added during his stay he obtained 212 with seven 6s – two of these strokes which sent the ball out of the ground – and fifteen 4s included in his score. While driving stood out as the great feature of his play, he scored practically all round the wicket and, apart from a sharp high return to Hearne when 66, there was little fault to find with a remarkable piece of batting.

Middlesex, entering upon their second innings 399 in arrear, scored 134 for the loss of one wicket before the drawing of stumps on Monday and next day, keeping their opponents in the field until six o'clock, put together a total of 455. Hearne, missed off the last ball on Monday, shared with Sims in a partnership of 113. Sims not only kept up his end for four hours and forty minutes but, in putting together an innings of 103, made his highest score for Middlesex. Hendren also played a great game for four hours and a half. Apart from an easy chance when 64 to Parker, his batting was of the highest class. After the fall of the eighth wicket he found an invaluable partner in Price who helped to add 105. Brown, in addition to giving such a splendid display of hitting, took eight wickets in the match for just under 15 runs apiece.

## Middlesex

| | | | |
|---|---:|---|---:|
| H. W. Lee c Parker b Fender | 40 | – c Jardine b Fender | 25 |
| J. Sims lbw b Allom | 6 | – b Parker | 103 |
| J. W. Hearne c Brooks b Parker | 57 | – c Fender b Brown | 61 |
| E. Hendren c Brown b Owen | 4 | – run out | 145 |
| Rev. E. T. Killick b Brown | 11 | – lbw b Brown | 10 |
| J. Hulme b Brown | 0 | – b Brown | 24 |
| Mr H. J. Enthoven b Parker | 13 | – b Brown | 8 |
| Mr N. Haig c Ratcliffe b Parker | 2 | – c Allom b Brown | 0 |
| G. Hart b Parker | 0 | – c Block b Fender | 1 |
| W. F. Price b Brown | 0 | – not out | 35 |
| T. J. Durston not out | 0 | – c Parker b Fender | 10 |
| B 4, l-b 2, w 2 | 8 | B 19, l-b 8, w 5, n-b 1 | 33 |
| | **141** | | **455** |

## Surrey

| | | | |
|---|---:|---|---:|
| J. B. Hobbs c Enthoven b Lee | 92 | | |
| Mr A. Ratcliffe c Price b Durston | 12 | – not out | 1 |
| T. Shepherd c Hearne b Durston | 1 | – run out | 22 |
| Mr P. G. H. Fender b Hulme | 12 | – c Lee b Haig | 0 |
| Mr D. R. Jardine c Durston b Lee | 126 | – not out | 10 |
| Mr S. A. Block b Durston | 3 | – run out | 19 |
| Mr F. R. Brown c Killick b Haig | 212 | – c Lee b Durston | 4 |
| J. F. Parker st Price b Sims | 8 | | |
| E. W. Brooks lbw b Sims | 3 | | |
| Mr M. J. C. Allom not out | 57 | | |
| B 1, l-b 9, w 3, n-b 1 | 14 | W 1 | 1 |
| | **(9 wkts dec.) 540** | | **57** |

J. G. Owen did not bat.

## Surrey Bowling

|              | Overs | Mdns | Runs | Wkts | Overs | Mdns | Runs | Wkts |
|--------------|-------|------|------|------|-------|------|------|------|
| Allom ............ | 12    | 2    | 23   | 1    | 42    | 6    | 82   | —    |
| Parker .......... | 20    | 7    | 36   | 4    | 40    | 6    | 104  | 1    |
| Brown .......... | 20.5  | 7    | 38   | 3    | 48    | 14   | 81   | 5    |
| Fender .......... | 6     | —    | 26   | 1    | 40    | 8    | 123  | 3    |
| Owen ........... | 8     | 4    | 10   | 1    | 9     | 4    | 19   | —    |
| Jardine .......... |       |      |      |      | 3     | 1    | 13   | —    |

## Middlesex Bowling

|              | Overs | Mdns | Runs | Wkts | Overs | Mdns | Runs | Wkts |
|--------------|-------|------|------|------|-------|------|------|------|
| Durston ......... | 42    | 6    | 122  | 3    | 4     | —    | 32   | 1    |
| Hulme .......... | 23    | 2    | 93   | 1    |       |      |      |      |
| Lee ............. | 30    | 5    | 115  | 2    |       |      |      |      |
| Sims ............ | 12    | 1    | 54   | 2    |       |      |      |      |
| Hearne ......... | 20    | 3    | 86   | —    |       |      |      |      |
| Haig ........... | 8.4   | —    | 56   | 1    | 3     | —    | 24   | 1    |

Umpires: W. Bestwick and C. N. Woolley.

## SURREY v CAMBRIDGE UNIVERSITY

### Played at The Oval, June 21, 22, 23, 1933

Though Surrey won by six wickets, chief distinction in the game fell to Human who, in scoring two separate hundreds in a match, became the third Cambridge batsman to accomplish that feat. Apart from that of Human, the University batting was rather ordinary. Human drove and cut with power and gave no actual chance in either innings. Hobbs showed his best form for Surrey, he and Squires putting on 143 for the second stand, but Human bowled his slows cleverly and the last eight wickets fell for 80 runs. Facing arrears of 18, Cambridge lost four men for 42, but Human averted a complete collapse by hitting up 122 out of 190. So in the end Surrey needed 223 to win with two and a half hours remaining for play and, thanks to brisk play by Gregory and Jeacocke, they completed the task with five minutes to spare.

### Cambridge University

| | | | |
|---|---|---|---|
| Mr A. W. Allen b Gover ..................... | 41 | – c Brown b Gover .............. | 1 |
| Mr A. S. Lawrence c Read b Gover ............. | 2 | – c Mobey b Read .............. | 7 |
| Mr D. R. Wilcox c Mobey b Gregory ........... | 5 | – c Jeacocke b Brown ............ | 36 |
| Mr B. O. Allen lbw b Gover ................... | 0 | – c Read b Gover ............... | 0 |
| Mr R. de W. K. Winlaw c Gregory b Brown ....... | 45 | – c Jeacocke b Brown ............ | 14 |
| Mr J. H. Human c Gover b Brown .............. | 110 | – c Hobbs b Read ............... | 122 |
| M. Jahangir Khan c Hobbs b Brown ............ | 10 | – b Gover ..................... | 22 |
| Mr J. G. W. Davies b Brown ................. | 12 | – lbw b Gregory ................ | 16 |
| Mr E. Cawston c Gregory b Brown ............. | 1 | – b Read ...................... | 13 |
| Mr R. S. Grant b Read ....................... | 13 | – not out ..................... | 3 |
| Mr J. T. H. Comber not out .................. | 25 | – b Read ...................... | 0 |
| B 4, l-b 5 ......................... | 9 | B 2, l-b 3, n-b 1 .......... | 6 |
| | **273** | | **240** |

## Surrey

| | | | |
|---|---|---|---|
| J. B. Hobbs c B. O. Allen b Cawston | 118 | | |
| R. J. Gregory c Cawston b Human | 30 | – not out | 89 |
| H. S. Squires lbw b J. Khan | 69 | – c Cawston b Lawrence | 16 |
| E. F. Wilson c Lawrence b Human | 24 | – not out | 11 |
| Mr A. Jeacocke st Comber b Human | 5 | – b Grant | 76 |
| Mr W. T. Cook c Cawston b Grant | 3 | – c Comber b Grant | 10 |
| Mr F. R. Brown c Comber b Human | 24 | – c Davies b Grant | 17 |
| G. S. Mobey c Comber b J. Khan | 3 | | |
| Mr D. Weeks c B. O. Allen b Human | 1 | | |
| Mr H. D. Read b J. Khan | 0 | | |
| A. R. Gover not out | 1 | | |
| B 12, l-b 1 | 13 | B 2, l-b 3 | 5 |
| | 291 | | 224 |

### Surrey Bowling

| | Overs | Mdns | Runs | Wkts | Overs | Mdns | Runs | Wkts |
|---|---|---|---|---|---|---|---|---|
| Gover | 21 | 3 | 84 | 3 | 19 | 2 | 59 | 3 |
| Read | 17 | 2 | 69 | 1 | 11 | 3 | 26 | 4 |
| Gregory | 14 | 6 | 37 | 1 | 4 | — | 16 | 1 |
| Brown | 19.4 | 2 | 62 | 5 | 19 | 2 | 87 | 2 |
| Weeks | 5 | 1 | 12 | — | 11 | 1 | 46 | — |

### Cambridge University Bowling

| | Overs | Mdns | Runs | Wkts | Overs | Mdns | Runs | Wkts |
|---|---|---|---|---|---|---|---|---|
| Lawrence | 11 | 6 | 18 | — | 6 | 2 | 18 | 1 |
| Cawston | 25 | 7 | 55 | 1 | 1.2 | — | 11 | — |
| Jahangir Khan | 31 | 15 | 41 | 3 | 21 | 3 | 84 | — |
| Human | 33.1 | 8 | 73 | 5 | 8 | 1 | 38 | — |
| Grant | 30 | 9 | 53 | 1 | 25 | 5 | 68 | 3 |
| Davies | 9 | 2 | 38 | — | | | | |

Umpires: J. Stone and J. Humphries.

## SURREY v MIDDLESEX

Played at The Oval, August 8, 9, 10, 1934

In a thrilling finish Surrey won by one wicket. They set Middlesex to score 175 to save an innings defeat and seemed in a comfortable position when stumps were drawn on Thursday with the visitors still 13 behind and six wickets to fall. The next day nine men were out for 242 before Smith made 45 out of 50. Thus Surrey wanted 118 to win, but six wickets fell for 43 and Winlaw retired hurt. Garland-Wells came to the rescue by scoring 45 out of 67, being eighth out at 102. Gover left at 104 and then Winlaw resumed his innings. So that Brooks could face the bowling a bye was run at the end of an over while the ball travelled to the wicket-keeper, standing back. The following delivery laid out Brooks but he recovered and, driving the next two balls to the boundary, he snatched a narrow win for Surrey. Fender and Smith bowled splendidly.

## Middlesex

| | | | |
|---|---|---|---|
| G. E. Hart c Gover b Fender | 18 | – c and b Fender | 30 |
| W. F. Price b Watts | 5 | – c Watts b Holmes | 87 |
| J. W. Hearne c Watts b Garland-Wells | 13 | – b Gover | 4 |
| E. Hendren b Fender | 15 | – b Fender | 11 |
| J. Hulme c Watts b Fender | 62 | – b Watts | 49 |
| Mr G. O. Allen c Brooks b Gover | 13 | – lbw b Fender | 11 |
| Mr J. L. Guise c Brooks b Gover | 5 | – c Brooks b Gover | 4 |
| J. Sims b Fender | 8 | – b Watts | 7 |
| Mr N. Haig b Holmes | 25 | – b Fender | 23 |
| L. Muncer c Holmes b Fender | 8 | – not out | 9 |
| J. Smith not out | 4 | – c Gregory b Fender | 45 |
| L-b 2, w 1, n-b 5 | 8 | L-b 6, n-b 6 | 12 |
| | **184** | | **292** |

## Surrey

| | | | |
|---|---|---|---|
| A. Sandham c Hearne b Smith | 5 | – c Allen b Smith | 12 |
| R. J. Gregory c and b Hearne | 121 | – b Allen | 6 |
| H. S. Squires c Price b Smith | 3 | – c Price b Smith | 1 |
| Mr R. de W. K. Winlaw c Sims b Smith | 69 | – not out | 4 |
| T. H. Barling c Sims b Smith | 4 | – c Guise b Smith | 2 |
| Mr E. R. T. Holmes c Smith b Hulme | 37 | – b Allen | 9 |
| E. A. Watts run out | 48 | – c Hendren b Allen | 2 |
| Mr H. M. Garland-Wells c Hulme b Hearne | 43 | – c Sims b Smith | 45 |
| Mr P. G. H. Fender b Smith | 9 | – b Allen | 9 |
| A. R. Gover lbw b Smith | 5 | – b Smith | 1 |
| E. W. Brooks not out | 3 | – not out | 9 |
| B 6, l-b 5, n-b 1 | 12 | B 9, l-b 8, n-b 1 | 18 |
| | **359** | | **118** |

## Surrey Bowling

| | Overs | Mdns | Runs | Wkts | Overs | Mdns | Runs | Wkts |
|---|---|---|---|---|---|---|---|---|
| Gover | 16 | 4 | 34 | 2 | 28 | 5 | 101 | 2 |
| Watts | 9 | 2 | 34 | 1 | 15 | 3 | 58 | 2 |
| Fender | 21.4 | 4 | 84 | 5 | 23.3 | 2 | 94 | 5 |
| Holmes | 4 | — | 12 | 1 | 9 | 1 | 27 | 1 |
| Garland-Wells | 7 | 1 | 12 | 1 | | | | |

## Middlesex Bowling

| | Overs | Mdns | Runs | Wkts | Overs | Mdns | Runs | Wkts |
|---|---|---|---|---|---|---|---|---|
| Allen | 24 | 6 | 85 | — | 16 | 2 | 42 | 4 |
| Smith | 42.3 | 6 | 98 | 6 | 15.3 | 3 | 58 | 5 |
| Sims | 20 | 2 | 63 | — | | | | |
| Hulme | 8 | 2 | 20 | 1 | | | | |
| Hearne | 19 | — | 81 | 2 | | | | |

Umpires: W. Reeves and A. Dolphin.

# THE HOBBS ERA, 1903-1933

### By Jack Hobbs

My career in first-class cricket having, after a very happy period, reached its end, I gladly comply with the request of the Editor of *Wisden's Almanack* to jot down some personal impressions which may be of interest to present and future readers of the book.

The honour has been done me of referring to the period of my active participation in important cricket as "The Hobbs Era", and I should like to say at once how mindful I am of this distinction. Roughly thirty years have gone by since I first played for Surrey under the residential qualification, and nothing has ever occurred to cause me the slightest regret that I took the advice of Tom Hayward and migrated from Cambridge to London. Without blowing my own trumpet I can say that when I went to The Oval I knew pretty well my own capabilities; it was just a question as to how great I should find the difference between first-class and Minor Counties cricket. The feeling was strong within me that I could make good, but I little thought then that I should achieve the success in an even higher sphere of cricket than that to which I was then aspiring, or that I should be the first man to beat the record of that wonderful batsman, W. G. Grace, in the matter of making centuries. However, this article is not meant to be a statement of what I myself have accomplished; the purport of it is to give in some slight degree my ideas on the changes that have come about in the game – whether of improvement or otherwise – and the points that have struck me as being worthy of mention.

## THIRTY YEARS IN CRICKET

The era to which my name has been given by you, Mr Editor, covers first-class cricket from 1903 to 1933. The war came to rob all of us of four solid years of the game, and although I played a little last summer I think that I really finished in 1933 when at 50 years of age after, roughly, 30 seasons at The Oval, I was beginning to feel that the strain of the game day after day was getting just a little too much for me. There was also the fact that younger players were knocking at the door, and that it did not become me, having had a longer innings than most cricketers of modern days, to stand in the way of promising recruits who wanted to feel that their positions in a county eleven were secure. So even though I scored one century last season I still fall short by three of the two hundred I had fondly hoped to obtain. Records after all are ephemeral; they are only made to be beaten by somebody else, and while it is nice to think that one has accomplished something out of the common there are other and more important considerations to bear in mind. The new leg-before-wicket rule, which is being tried experimentally may, if adopted, have a far-reaching effect on batsmen, but at the back of my mind there is the impression that someone will come along one of these days and surpass the 197 hundreds which now stand to my credit.

Before my time there were other epochs in our great game. The days of top-hats, when Alfred Mynn, the "Lion of Kent" and other famous men were in their prime, are now far distant. Then came the Grace period when that marvellous batsman stood out head and shoulders above everybody else; the Hon. F. S. Jackson, Ranjitsinhji, G. L. Jessop, Tom Hayward, C. B. Fry, A. C. MacLaren, George Hirst, J. T. Tyldesley, Victor Trumper, M. A. Noble and others too numerous to mention were contemporaries in what has been described as the "Golden Age" of cricket. It will be seen therefore that my own follows in a natural sequence in this recurring cycle.

## IS CRICKET BETTER?

As to whether during the past thirty years cricket generally has been better or worse than those periods to which I have referred is not perhaps for me to say. Cricket was at its very best in that Golden Age when almost every county had one, if not two or three outstanding personalities either as batsmen or bowlers.

I do not agree, however, with the oft-repeated statement that cricket nowadays is not what it used to be, and I would ask why, when in the ordinary affairs of every-day life as well as in most other games we have gone ahead, cricket should be singled out as an example of deterioration in all-round form and skill? We know that, in a broad sense, wickets are more favourable to run-getting, and while I do not hold with the over-preparation of pitches and the use of various forms of "dope" to achieve perfection and make the batsman's task easier, it must always be remembered that, with a heavier programme now necessary owing to the increase of first-class counties since the days shortly before my advent, cricket grounds are subjected to far harder wear.

But it should not be overlooked that there were several county enclosures before say 1900 where the wickets were really good, and one has only to look up the records to find that big scores were made at The Oval before swerve bowlers came into existence, and when length, allied to spin, was the first consideration. All wickets were not bad, as many people seem to think. The one important difference between those of my early times and those of the present is that you very, very rarely see a real "sticky" wicket nowadays. Over-preparation is the cause of this, and probably the system in use at certain centres of covering the pitch completely before the match has also had something to do with it. That, however, brings you to another consideration, that of finance. Many county clubs are often hard put to it to make both ends meet. If rain not only prevents play for a long time but in the end hastens the completion of a match, measures have to be adopted to mitigate undue loss of time.

Efforts have been made more than once, because of the heavy programmes and constant play day after day, to limit first-class matches to two days. I am not altogether opposed to this; in fact I would ask: why not two-day matches of one innings each? That would give a lot of our professionals a much needed rest and, as far as I can see, the main argument against this would come from professionals themselves because they would not be able to earn quite as much as they do now. Possibly, however, that is a question which time will solve.

## SOME CHANGES

I have always regarded it as curious that while most of the changes in cricket in my thirty years have been in favour of the bowler, such as the smaller ball and the wider wicket, bowling generally, in my opinion, has deteriorated. There are very few outstanding bowlers of real class to-day, and I remember that just after the war, when admittedly things had changed a good deal, bowlers opened for their sides who weren't considered prior to 1914. Everyone nowadays seems to want to bowl the in-swinger. This is absurd, for my experience is that this particular ball is not so dangerous as the one which goes away from you. It has led to what I should call "negative cricket". Bowlers adopting this method try rather to keep the batsman quiet than to get him out. The result of this is that back-play has developed to a large extent and on-side play has increased out of all proportion, to the detriment of off-side batting. But then it must be remembered that it is very difficult indeed to drive an in-swinging ball on the off-side, and with bowlers keeping just short of a length, as modern bowlers do, the natural tendency of a batsman, at any rate since the war, has been to step back and play the ball to the on.

In regard to this it would seem that the new leg-before-wicket rule is going to make things difficult for opening batsmen, and the in-swinging ball is more dangerous under this rule than the off-spinner. You can see and, to a degree, anticipate off-spinners better, and an in-swinger seems to come off dry ground much quicker. That, therefore, is one of the big changes I have noticed in the style of batting during my era. In my early days youngsters were taught to play forward, and it was the accepted theory that one only played back when the wicket was soft and the ball was turning. Now, batsmen play back on a hard wicket largely because, as I have said, of the preponderance of in-swinging bowlers who keep just short of a length. Consequently, young bowlers, seeing that this type of attack cannot be driven to the off, very rarely try to make themselves spin bowlers pure and simple. I know, of course, that it is not given to everyone to keep such a perfect length as J. T. Hearne or Albert Relf used to. They would bowl all the afternoon and scarcely give you six balls that you could hit with safety.

While bowling, particularly as regards length, has gone back, batting in a certain way has advanced. The means have been found to contend with the swing, but at the expense of many of those glorious off-side strokes for which our predecessors were famous, and it is only when an over-pitched ball comes along that you can drive it to the off. Even then, when it does come, your feet may be wrong and you are too late to get into position.

There is one point about the improvement in batting to which I should like to draw attention, and that is that it is not confined to those in the first half of the order. Even in my early days we seldom expected or saw the last four men stay very long. Nowadays Numbers 8, 9, 10 and 11 all come in, not so much to have a wild swipe, but to play for runs; and they very often obtain them. This, of course, may be considered to be partly due to the difference in bowling. Back-play, too, has been the means of driving the off-spinner largely out of the game, and figures clearly show that batsmen, even when allowances is made for a great deal of extra cricket which they play, generally get far more runs now than they used to do.

## ON FIELDING

It is a little difficult to say definitely if fielding has improved. Individually it may not have done, but collectively I think it has. Thirty years ago, the positions of mid-on and short-leg were both known as "Mugs' Corner". The captain looked round and almost invariably put his two incompetent fieldsmen in those places. I have never agreed that mid-on's was an easy job. You have to watch the batsman and anticipate his stroke, and you have to be quick off the mark when you field there. Only in recent years have we awakened to this fact, while men like "Bill" Hitch made short-leg an honourable position in which to field. Hammond is my ideal fieldsman. He would be great anywhere, and Mitchell of Yorkshire runs him very close. No matter where they are put these two men can be right at the top, and it has often struck me that Hammond's fielding would very likely have been far more extensively talked-of had he been an outfielder, while it is certain he would do wonderful work at cover-point. With regard to the placing of the field there can be no question at all that this has engaged the attention of captains to a far greater degree than it used to and consequently it is better. The Australians, for instance, have developed the study of this to such an extent that they are now much better than we in England at placing their fieldsmen to stop runs, and the increase in on-side strokes by batsmen has led to two or three men being placed on the leg-side when in my early days there was only one. This is not meant as a reference to "body-line" bowling. My views on that are well known. I deplore its introduction. I think it has done great harm to the game, because it fosters a spirit foreign to the traditions of cricket and which certainly never existed when I first came on the scene.

I think the development of the county championship in regard to the number of counties now competing is rather to be regretted. There are too many counties – some of them, I am afraid, not quite up to the best standard – and we in England have got a false opinion of the strength of our cricket. The trouble is that, against the weaker counties, players get plenty of runs and wickets and they are thought at once to be Test match cricketers. It is much harder now to pick a team for a Test match than it was thirty years ago. The field of choice is so much wider and the all-round standard consequently more on a level – especially in the county averages.

## HAMMOND AND HENDREN

Since I started, the hook and the leg-glide have become common strokes, and I always had the idea too, that before my time it was considered rather *infra dig* to hook a ball round to the leg-side. Nowadays, batsmen will step right across and hook a ball from wide of the off-stump round to square-leg. Hammond is the great exception. He won't hook. He considers it a dangerous stroke and I remember once, the first time I saw him, he persisted in playing balls which the ordinary batsmen would have hooked, hard back either to mid-on or mid-off. But then Hammond, as a batsman, is a law unto himself. He can step right back and force the short ball to the off, but not many men possess such power of wrist and forearm, and quickness on the feet, to be able to do that. Pat Hendren is my ideal batsman, for I think he has every stroke for all sorts of wicket against all types of bowling. Had he played thirty or forty years ago he would, I think, have been equally effective.

We saw last season one noticeable feature about the batting of the Australians in the power they put into their strokes. When young, they are taught first to hit the ball; we in England are taught defence. The wickets in Australia are, of course, easier as a general rule than ours. They are the same pace and the ball comes along at a uniform height. Because of this Australian batsmen are for the most part more confident.

## "SWINGERS" AND "GOOGLIES"

I have already said that one of the most notable changes in cricket with regard to bowling has been the introduction of "swing" or "swerve". No doubt long before my time bowlers were able to, and probably often did, make the ball swing, but it was not known then how this was brought about and quite likely when it occurred bowlers put in down to an extra strong current of air or some outside influence of a similar kind. The secret of being able to make a ball move about in the air was acquired during my era and at the present time almost anybody with any knowledge of bowling can send down swingers of one sort or the other. It is all a question of how the ball is held in the hand at the moment of delivery and bowlers of this description now come under the general heading of "seam-up bowlers". Shortly after I began to play first-class cricket came the googly, known in Australia as the "bosie" because it was first discovered by B. J. T. Bosanquet. The South Africans were quick to realise the deadliness of this ball once a command of length had been gained. On the matting wickets in their country they soon perfected it and in G. A. Faulkner, A. E. Vogler, Gordon White and R. O. Schwarz they produced the finest array of googly bowlers ever seen together in one team. W. G. Grace did not, I think, play in an important match against googly bowling but obviously he must have been so very good that he, like many of us later on, would have mastered it. He would have played every ball on its merits.

While on the question of bowling I am definitely of the opinion that during my career the art of flighting the ball has steadily deteriorated. We have nobody now so good at this as Colin Blythe. He was one of the world's greatest bowlers of his type, and, unlike most of the present-day exponents, was never afraid of being hit. Of fast bowlers the only ones of recent years at all comparable with those giants of the past have been Larwood and McDonald. Being a member of the same county side I only played against N. A. Knox in Gentlemen and Players matches and games of a similar description, when he was probably past his best, but I think he was the best fast bowler I ever saw. He brought the ball down from such a great height that he could often make good length deliveries rear up straight.

The widening of the wicket, which previously had often been advocated, did not, when it came into general use, help bowlers to the extent that had been anticipated and, although a batsman, I personally am all for still wider wickets. When the alteration was made I thought at the time that the decision had not gone quite far enough – not far enough, at any rate, to achieve its main object of putting the bowler on more level terms with the batsman. Events have, I think, proved me to be right.

## CHEAP ENGLAND CAPS

The past thirty years have brought with them a remarkable increase in tours to this country and visits abroad of English teams. As the mother country of cricket, England, as represented by the MCC, have naturally considered it politic to foster the game overseas but I am of opinion that, on the question of elevating countries like South Africa, West Indies, New Zealand and India to the same rank as Australia in the matter of Test matches, we have been premature. The vast host of cricket followers throughout the world know in their own minds that there are only two really top-class cricketing countries – England and Australia. Far be from me any idea of throwing cold water on those countries who aspire to the highest status in cricket but when we think that of the numerous teams which have come from South Africa not one has ever won a Test match in England it makes me wonder why they are put on the same plane as Australia in being allotted five "Tests". I am not forgetting that they, as well as the West Indies, have beaten England in their own countries. I should not be averse to them having three and I would give the others I have mentioned one each. The honour of wearing the England cap with the three silver lions on it has, I am afraid, become rather cheap since its inception. These caps should have been awarded only to cricketers who have appeared in England against Australia.

During my years of first-class cricket I do not think captaincy has improved. With one or two exceptions there has been too much chopping and changing about but, of course, other considerations have to be remembered, for amateurs do not find it so easy to spare the time for first-class cricket as their predecessors did. I have often thought that it was a mistake for counties to put an amateur into the team merely to act as captain when he has had little or no experience of county cricket. We had an example last season in Maurice Tate, of how well a professional could acquit himself as leader of a side, but I definitely always prefer to see an amateur rather than a professional captaining England if his cricket ability entitles him to a place in the eleven.

The umpiring has improved all-round, and I should say the two best umpires I have known are "Bob" Crockett of Australia, and Frank Chester. Umpires nowadays are younger than most of those who officiated when I started, and naturally their eyesight and hearing are better.

In the last quarter of a century – and perhaps during a longer time – there has come about a great change for the better in the relations existing between amateurs and professionals. County committees have realised that both on and off the field their players are all members of the same team and professionals are not, as was largely the case some years ago, relegated to incommodious dressing-rooms with no amenities, while, as a general rule, amateurs and professionals now take their luncheon and tea together in the same room. The natural consequence of this, of course, has been a pronounced improvement in the bearing of professional cricketers off the field. The average professional nowadays can, I think, hold his own as a man in any company.

## HOBBS' TWENTY-FIVE YEARS OF TRIUMPH (1905-1934)

|  | Innings | Not Outs | Runs | Highest Innings | Average |
|---|---|---|---|---|---|
| In England | 1,179 | 98 | 53,968 | 316* | 49.93 |
| In Australia | 94 | 5 | 4,570 | 187 | 51.34 |
| In South Africa | 42 | 3 | 2,683 | 187 | 68.79 |
| Totals | 1,315 | 106 | 61,221 | 316* | 50.63 |

### FOR SURREY

|  | Innings | Not Outs | Runs | Highest Innings | Average |
|---|---|---|---|---|---|
| All First-Class matches | 958 | 80 | 43,703 | 316* | 49.77 |

| Overs | Maidens | Runs | Wickets | Average |
|---|---|---|---|---|
| 640.4 | 130 | 1,948 | 86 | 22.65 |

## IN TEST MATCHES

**v Australia**

| | Innings | Not Outs | Runs | Highest Innings | Average |
|---|---|---|---|---|---|
| In England | 26 | 2 | 1,143 | 119 | 47.62 |
| In Australia | 45 | 2 | 2,493 | 187 | 57.97 |
| Totals | 71 | 4 | 3,636 | 187 | 54.26 |

**v South Africa**

| | Innings | Not Outs | Runs | Highest Innings | Average |
|---|---|---|---|---|---|
| In England | 12 | 1 | 580 | 211 | 52.72 |
| In South Africa | 17 | 2 | 982 | 187 | 65.46 |
| Totals | 29 | 3 | 1,562 | 211 | 60.76 |

**v West Indies**

| | Innings | Not Outs | Runs | Highest Innings | Average |
|---|---|---|---|---|---|
| In England | 2 | — | 212 | 159 | 106.00 |

| | Innings | Not Outs | Runs | Highest Innings | Average |
|---|---|---|---|---|---|
| Grand Totals | 102 | 7 | 5,410 | 211 | 56.94 |

## GENTLEMEN v PLAYERS

| | Innings | Not Outs | Runs | Highest Innings | Average |
|---|---|---|---|---|---|
| Lord's | 28 | 3 | 1,545 | 163 | 61.80 |
| The Oval | 31 | 1 | 1,240 | 156 | 41.33 |
| Scarborough | 17 | 1 | 1,188 | 266* | 74.25 |
| Totals | 76 | 5 | 3,973 | 266* | 55.95 |

Hobbs was only once dismissed without scoring for the Players.

## HUNDREDS AT A GLANCE

### County Championship (130)

**For Surrey**

v Derbyshire (3): 133 (1910); 118* (1924); 105 (1931).
v Essex (10): 155, 102 (1905); 130 (1906); 215* (1914); 102 (1922); 129, 107 (1925); 102* (1929); 113, 119* (1932).
v Glamorgan (5): 109 (1925); 128 (1929); 137 and 111* (1930); 106 (1931).
v Gloucestershire (10): 133 (1909); 113, 107 (1913); 141 (1914); 139, 143 (1922); 105 (1924); 104 (1925); 112 (1926); 124 (1928).

v Hampshire (12): 135, 161 (1907); 205, 162 (1909); 109 (1913); 163 (1914); 169
    (1920); 189 (1925); 200 (1926); 112 and 104 (1927); 154 (1929).
v Kent (12): 106, 155 (1908); 115 (1913); 122 (1914); 102 (1919); 132 (1920); 105
    (1925); 121 (1927); 109 (1928); 150*, 118 (1929); 101 (1933).
v Lancashire (7): 117 (1911); 111 (1912); 142 (1914); 106, 102 (1919); 104 (1923); 116
    (1934).
v Leicestershire (7): 116 (1910); 127 (1911); 134 (1920); 145 (1922); 101 (1928); 115*
    (1929); 100 (1930).
v Middlesex (9): 103 (1906); 144* (1913), 112, 126 (1922); 136 (1923); 176*, 316*
    (1926); 11i (1929); 111 (1932).
v Northamptonshire (4): 125 (1908); 136* (1913); 114 (1920); 117 (1928).
v Nottinghamshire (10): 117* (1908); 104 (1912); 226 (1914); 151* (1922); 105
    (1923); 203*, 105 (1924); 131 (1927); 114 (1928); 133 (1933).
v Somerset (10): 116* (1923); 111, 101 and 101* (1925); 204, 134 (1929); 128, 101*
    (1931); 123 (1932); 117 (1933).
v Sussex (3): 110 (1920); 106 (1930); 117 (1931).
v Warwickshire (14): 150* (1907); 159, 160 and 100 (1909); 122 (1913); 183 (1914);
    122, 101 (1920); 168 (1922); 120, 215 (1925); 200* (1928); 147 (1931); 100 (1933).
v Worcestershire (6): 125, 162* (1906); 166*, 110 (1907); 184 (1913); 126 (1914).
v Yorkshire (8): 100, 202 (1914); 112 (1920); 172* (1921); 102 (1926); 150 (1927); 105
    (1928); 133 (1931).

## Test Matches (15)

### For England

v Australia 126*, 187, 178 (1911-12); 107 (1912); 122, 123 (1920-21); 115, 154, 119
    (1924-25); 119, 100 (1926); 142 (1928-29).
v South Africa (2): 187 (1909-10); 211 (1924).
v West Indies (1): 159 (1928).

## Against Empire Teams; Home and Abroad (20)

### v Australians (7)

104    v Tasmania, 1907-08
115    v Victoria, 1907-08
205*   v Australian I F, 1919
131    v Victoria, 1920-21
112    v New South Wales, 1920-21
101    v South Australia, 1928-29
146    v Australians, 1930.

### v South Africans (8)

114    v Western Province, 1909-10
163    v Natal, 1909-10
170    v Cape Province, 1913-14
102    v Transvaal, 1913-14
137    v Transvaal XI, 1913-14
141    v Griqualand West, 1913-14
131    v Transvaal, 1913-14
151    v South Africans, 1929.

### v West Indies (3)

123* 119* (1928); 221 (1933).

### v New Zealand (2)

146 (1927); 153 (1931).

## Players v Gentlemen (16)

154* (1911); 156 (1914); 120*, 113, 116 (1919); 138 (1920); 140 (1922); 105 (1923); 118 (1924); 140, 266* (1925); 163 (1926); 119 (1927); 110, 141 (1931); 161* (1932).

## Rest of England v Champion County (5)

101 v Yorkshire, 1919
215 v Middlesex, 1920
100 v Yorkshire, 1920
106 v Yorkshire, 1925
150 v Lancashire, 1928.

## Surrey v University Teams (7)

102   v Oxford, 1908
119   v Oxford, 1910
104
143* } v Cambridge, 1925
118   v Cambridge, 1933
108   v Cambridge, 1926
261   v Oxford, 1926.

## Various Matches (4)

117*  for MCC Australia XI v Lord Londesborough's XI, 1911
150   for Surrey v Scotland, 1913
115   for Players of South v Gentlemen of South, 1920
100*  for Surrey v MCC, 1928.

Of the 130 hundreds in county championship matches, 45 were scored before the European War and 85 after peace was restored. That is to say after his thirty-sixth birthday.

No fewer than 175 of these 197 were made in England and 90 at The Oval.

In 1925 he obtained sixteen three-figure innings. This number in one season is unsurpassed.

Hobbs completed his fiftieth hundred – 170 v Cape Province at Port Elizabeth, on November 21, 1913, his hundredth hundred 116* v Somerset at Bath, on May 8, 1923, his 150th, 114 v Nottinghamshire, at Trent Bridge on May 28, 1928, and his 197th v Lancashire at Old Trafford, on May 28, 1934.

On August 28, 1926. Hobbs scored 316* for Surrey v Middlesex, the highest individual innings ever made in a first-class match in the long history of Lord's ground. On September 3 and 4, 1925, he made 266* for the Players against the Gentlemen, at Scarborough – the highest ever made on either side in the long history of these matches.

Hobbs hit his fiftieth hundred on The Oval ground on September 12, 1925, for the Rest of England v Yorkshire – this being his sixteenth and last century of a season when he finished six runs short of 3,000, twenty years after his first appearance for Surrey.

Hobbs' one-hundredth hundred at Bath was his first against Somerset. Two years later (1925) against the same county at Taunton, he obtained 101 and 101 not out on successive days – August 17 and 18 – by the first equalling Grace's record of 126 hundreds and by the second realising a deferred ambition. Probably this is the most cherished of his series of hundreds in each innings of six first-class matches.

A score of 121 for Surrey v Kent at Blackheath on July 12, 1927, was his hundredth three-figure score for Surrey. This innings was very rightly described in the sixty-fifth edition of *Wisden* as "one of his best".

Early in his career Hobbs fielded at third man, and in the long field, but he became a cover-point of universal renown for accuracy and speed in every respect. In eleven matches of the tour in Australia (1911-12) his returns to the wicket brought about the dismissal of 15 batsmen.

Hobbs has made more centuries and more runs than any other player on either side in Tests between England and Australia.

## FIRST WICKET SUCCESSES

In no fewer than 166 innings Hobbs has shared in a partnership that brought 100 runs and upwards on the score-board before the fall of the first wicket. His partners on such occasions were T. Hayward 40 times, A. Sandham 66, H. Sutcliffe 26, W. Rhodes 13, Mr D. J. Knight 6, A. Russell 5, G. Gunn and Percy Holmes each 2, and Mr C. B. Fry, A. Baker, E. Hayes, Mr M. Howell, A. Ducat and R. Gregory each 1.

Particulars of these performances which produced upwards of 200 runs are appended, with the name of each partner:

428† with A. Sandham for Surrey v Oxford University at The Oval, 1926
352  with T. Hayward for Surrey v Warwickshire at The Oval, 1909
323§ with W. Rhodes for England v Australia at Melbourne, 1911-12
313  with T. Hayward for Surrey v Worcestershire at Worcester, 1913
290  with T. Hayward for Surrey v Yorkshire at Lord's, 1914
283  with H. Sutcliffe for England v Australia at Melbourne, 1924-25
268‡ with H. Sutcliffe for England v South Africa at Lord's, 1924
264  with A. Sandham for Surrey v Somerset at Taunton, 1932
253  with A. Sandham for Surrey v West Indies at The Oval, 1928
244  with A. Sandham for Surrey v Middlesex at The Oval, 1923
243  with H. Sutcliffe, H. D. G. Leveson-Gower's XI v New Zealand at Scarborough, 1931
242  with E. G. Hayes for Surrey v Lancashire at The Oval, 1911
234  with T. Hayward for Surrey v Kent at Blackheath, 1914
233  with A. Sandham for Surrey v Gloucestershire at The Oval, 1922
232  with A. Sandham for Surrey v Warwickshire, at The Oval, 1925
231  with A. Sandham for Surrey v Somerset at The Oval, 1931
227  with H. Sutcliffe for Players v Gentlemen at Scarborough, 1931
221  with W. Rhodes for England v South Africa at Cape Town, 1909-10
219  with T. Hayward for Surrey v Worcestershire at Worcester, 1907
216  with A. Sandham for Surrey v Essex at Leyton, 1925
212  with H. Sutcliffe for The Rest v Lancashire at The Oval, 1928
211* with W. Rhodes for MCC v Transvaal at Johannesburg, 1913-14
210  with A. Sandham for Surrey v Glamorgan at Cardiff, 1929
209  with A. Sandham for Surrey v Glamorgan at The Oval, 1931
207  with W. Rhodes for MCC v Natal at Durban, 1909-10

203   with A. Sandham for Surrey v Nottinghamshire at The Oval, 1927
203   with H. Sutcliffe for Players v Gentlemen at The Oval, 1931
203   with A. Sandham for Surrey v Middlesex at Lord's, 1932.

\* *Partnership unfinished.*
† *Record for first wicket of Surrey.*
‡ *Record for any wicket, England v South Africa.*
§ *Record for first wicket of England v Australia.*

J. A. H. C.

## SURREY v MIDDLESEX

### Played at The Oval, August 7, 9, 10, 1937

Middlesex won by three wickets. The visit of the Middlesex team to The Oval when they were running neck and neck with Yorkshire for the Championship aroused enormous interest and the cricket was worthy of the occasion. One reason for the exceptional nature of the struggle was forthcoming in the explanation that the original pitch reserved for the game was torn up during a Minor county fixture, and there was no alternative but to use the strip of turf intended for the Test the following week. Before lunch on the first day Surrey scored 123 for the loss of Sandham and Fishlock, but the under-prepared wicket soon became powdery and thereafter batsmen had to fight hard for runs. Surrey collapsed against Owen-Smith, who turned the ball prodigiously and in the course of eleven deliveries dismissed five men without conceding a run. Though Surrey committed shocking blunders in the slips, Gover experiencing wretched luck, Parker changed the aspect of the match by disposing of Hendren, Edrich and Compton in two overs, and Middlesex finished on Saturday 32 behind with one wicket left. The honours of the second day went to Surrey, but the fight was hard. Gregory, showing unerring skill in dealing with the three Middlesex spin bowlers, played one of the finest innings of his career, but no-one else could score freely. In order to win, Middlesex needed to put together in the fourth innings the highest total of the match. They began their task in disastrous fashion and though Human and Robins made a stand, the Middlesex captain was out in the last over of the day when his side still required 137 with only four wickets left. Next day the Surrey fielding was again faulty, for at 107 both Owen-Smith and Human were dropped in the slips off Gover. Human received some severe blows on the body, but he played a wise and restrained game while at the critical period of the match Sims gave an amazing display of hitting. Few better innings have been played for Middlesex than that of Human, who batted in superb style until the match was decided. During the three days 30,000 people were present.

### Surrey

| | | | |
|---|---|---|---|
| A. Sandham c Sims b J. Smith | 13 | – c Human b Robins | 17 |
| L. B. Fishlock c Sims b Gray | 21 | – lbw (N) b Robins | 29 |
| R. J. Gregory c Robins b Owen-Smith | 52 | – lbw (N) b Sims | 72 |
| H. S. Squires c Price b Gray | 51 | – b Sims | 18 |
| T. H. Barling c Robins b Owen-Smith | 0 | – b Sims | 0 |
| Mr E. R. T. Holmes st Price b Owen-Smith | 1 | – b Sims | 11 |
| J. F. Parker b Owen-Smith | 0 | – c Owen-Smith b Robins | 8 |
| E. A. Watts b Sims | 11 | – not out | 24 |
| L. G. Berry b Owen-Smith | 0 | – c Robins b Sims | 2 |
| E. W. Brooks not out | 15 | – b Robins | 9 |
| A. R. Gover lbw b Sims | 2 | – run out | 0 |
| L-b 4 | 4 | B 7, l-b 9, n-b 3 | 19 |
| | 170 | | 209 |

## Middlesex

| | | |
|---|---|---|
| W. F. Price c Brooks b Gover | 16 – c Parker b Gover | 0 |
| Mr B. D. Carris c Brooks b Gover | 0 – b Watts | 8 |
| W. J. Edrich c Gover b Parker | 30 – c Parker b Gover | 3 |
| E. Hendren b Parker | 18 – b Parker | 18 |
| D. Compton c Brooks b Parker | 2 – run out | 15 |
| Mr J. H. Human b Gover | 1 – not out | 74 |
| Mr R. W. V. Robins b Squires | 15 – lbw b Gover | 26 |
| Mr H. G. Owen-Smith b Watts | 27 – c Gregory b Gover | 33 |
| J. Sims run out | 21 – not out | 44 |
| J. Smith b Watts | 0 | |
| L. Gray not out | 9 | |
| B 4, l-b 1, n-b 7 | 12 | B 1, l-b 6, n-b 2 ......... 9 |
| | **151** | **230** |

### Middlesex Bowling

| | Overs | Mdns | Runs | Wkts | Overs | Mdns | Runs | Wkts |
|---|---|---|---|---|---|---|---|---|
| J. Smith | 11 | 1 | 26 | 1 | 9 | 2 | 12 | — |
| Gray | 16 | 2 | 48 | 2 | 13 | 3 | 30 | — |
| Edrich | 4 | 2 | 2 | — | 1 | — | 3 | — |
| Owen-Smith | 20 | 3 | 52 | 5 | 13 | 1 | 39 | — |
| Robins | 3 | — | 8 | — | 25.5 | 3 | 71 | 4 |
| Sims | 6.4 | 1 | 30 | 2 | 18 | 3 | 35 | 5 |

### Surrey Bowling

| | Overs | Mdns | Runs | Wkts | Overs | Mdns | Runs | Wkts |
|---|---|---|---|---|---|---|---|---|
| Gover | 16.1 | 5 | 53 | 3 | 20 | 2 | 86 | 4 |
| Watts | 9 | — | 33 | 2 | 13 | 1 | 47 | 1 |
| Parker | 13 | 2 | 44 | 3 | 12 | 1 | 58 | 1 |
| Berry | 2 | — | 2 | — | | | | |
| Squires | 2 | — | 7 | 1 | 11 | 1 | 23 | — |
| Gregory | | | | | 1 | — | 7 | — |

Umpires: T. Oates and F. Chester.

## SURREY v YORKSHIRE

Played at The Oval, August 21, 23, 24, 1937

Drawn. Surrey's last match at The Oval also had an important bearing on the championship as Yorkshire were still being closely challenged by Middlesex. It proved a triumph for Fishlock, who enjoyed the distinction of being the eighth cricketer to hit two separate hundreds in one game against Yorkshire, and curiously, the only other case since the war was also furnished by a Surrey man – Donald Knight in 1919. Fishlock stood between Yorkshire and victory. He played two faultless innings in which driving and pulling brought him most runs. On the last day Gregory, who helped the left-hander to put on 201 for the second wicket, scored 109 with a fine variety of strokes. By consistent batting over seven hours Yorkshire built up a big total and Hutton so overshadowed Sutcliffe that he made 73 of an opening stand of 106. A wonderful running catch by Whittaker at long leg disposed of Mitchell, but until Yardley began to force the pace Yorkshire's batting lacked enterprise. Hitting his first hundred for the county, Yardley drove magnificently and Barber, timing his cutting perfectly, helped the amateur to add 157 for the fifth wicket.

## Yorkshire

| | |
|---|---|
| H. Sutcliffe b Gover . . . . . . . . . . . . . . . . . . . 33 | T. F. Smailes c Fishlock b Gover . . . . . . . . . 1 |
| L. Hutton c Gover b Squires . . . . . . . . . . . . 73 | A. Wood c and b Gover . . . . . . . . . . . . . . . 14 |
| A. Mitchell c Whittaker b Holmes . . . . . . . . 39 | W. E. Bowes not out . . . . . . . . . . . . . . . . . 5 |
| M. Leyland b Gover . . . . . . . . . . . . . . . . . . 77 | H. Verity b Gover . . . . . . . . . . . . . . . . . . . 0 |
| W. Barber c Brooks b Watts . . . . . . . . . . . . 87 | B 5, l-b 10, w 1 . . . . . . . . . . . . . . 16 |
| Mr N. W. D. Yardley c Brooks b Gover . . .101 | |
| Mr A. B. Sellers c Brooks b Watts . . . . . . . . 17 | 463 |

## Surrey

| | | | |
|---|---|---|---|
| A. Sandham c Smailes b Bowes . . . . . . . . . . . . . . . . . 20 | – lbw b Smailes . . . . . . . . . . . . . . . . . . 2 |
| L. B. Fishlock b Bowes . . . . . . . . . . . . . . . . . . . . . . .113 | – c Yardley b Verity . . . . . . . . . . . . . . .105 |
| R. J. Gregory c Hutton b Smailes . . . . . . . . . . 17 | – c Wood b Sutcliffe . . . . . . . . . . . . . . .109 |
| H. S. Squires lbw (N) b Smailes . . . . . . . . . . . . . . . 2 | – c Mitchell b Bowes . . . . . . . . . . . . . 5 |
| T. H. Barling st Wood b Hutton . . . . . . . . . . . . . . . . . 48 | – c Wood b Sutcliffe . . . . . . . . . . . . . . 22 |
| Mr E. R. T. Holmes b Verity . . . . . . . . . . . . . . . . . . 1 | |
| J. F. Parker c Hutton b Bowes . . . . . . . . . . . . . . . . 10 | – not out . . . . . . . . . . . . . . . . . . . . . . 8 |
| G. J. Whittaker b Bowes . . . . . . . . . . . . . . . . . . . . . 2 | – b Leyland . . . . . . . . . . . . . . . . . . . . 1 |
| E. A. Watts c Hutton b Verity . . . . . . . . . . . . . . . . 20 | – not out . . . . . . . . . . . . . . . . . . . . . . 9 |
| E. W. Brooks c Mitchell b Verity . . . . . . . . . . . . . . 21 | |
| A. R. Gover not out . . . . . . . . . . . . . . . . . . . . . . . . 4 | |
| B 3, l-b 12 . . . . . . . . . . . . . . . . . . . . . . . . 15 | B 15, l-b 18, n-b 1 . . . . . . . . 34 |
| 273 | 295 |

## Surrey Bowling

| | Overs | Mdns | Runs | Wkts |
|---|---|---|---|---|
| Gover . . . . . . . . . . . . | 34.5 | 4 | 130 | 6 |
| Watts . . . . . . . . . . . . | 26 | 3 | 95 | 2 |
| Parker . . . . . . . . . . | 27 | 4 | 62 | — |
| Squires . . . . . . . . . . | 29 | 4 | 92 | 1 |
| Gregory . . . . . . . . . | 19 | 4 | 52 | — |
| Holmes . . . . . . . . . . | 3 | — | 16 | 1 |

## Yorkshire Bowling

| | Overs | Mdns | Runs | Wkts | Overs | Mdns | Runs | Wkts |
|---|---|---|---|---|---|---|---|---|
| Bowes . . . . . . . . . . | 26 | 7 | 58 | 4 | 17 | — | 57 | 1 |
| Smailes . . . . . . . . . | 17 | 4 | 45 | 2 | 13 | 2 | 30 | 1 |
| Yardley . . . . . . . . . | 5 | 1 | 14 | — | 11 | 2 | 27 | — |
| Verity . . . . . . . . . . . | 27.5 | 4 | 89 | 3 | 17 | 5 | 31 | 1 |
| Hutton . . . . . . . . . . | 13 | 3 | 40 | 1 | 11 | — | 57 | — |
| Leyland . . . . . . . . . | 5 | — | 12 | — | 12 | 3 | 31 | 1 |
| Barber . . . . . . . . . . | | | | | 6 | 1 | 12 | — |
| Sutcliffe . . . . . . . . . | | | | | 6 | 2 | 16 | 2 |

Umpires: W. Bestwick and C. V. Tarbox.

# SUSSEX

## SUSSEX v MIDDLESEX

### Played at Brighton, July 31, August 2, 1920

In this match Sussex found themselves completely outplayed, Middlesex winning in two days by an innings and 123 runs. Sussex never recovered from a disastrous start. As the weather looked threatening Wilson, on winning the toss, decided to bat first on a soft wicket, but the sun came out, and on the treacherous pitch Stevens's bowling proved irresistible. The wicket rolled out well for Middlesex, and at the drawing of stumps they had the game in their hands. Lee was missed at long-on when 47, and had another escape at 106, but he hit very finely, his 132 including a 6 and thirteen 4s. He and Hearne put on 144 runs in two hours. On Monday Hendren played admirably, and Mann at one point hit three 6s off successive balls from Tate. Sussex in their second innings were all out in less than two hours and a quarter. Stevens as a bowler had his best match of the whole season, taking thirteen wickets for 60 runs.

### Sussex

| | | | |
|---|---|---|---|
| Mr V. W. C. Jupp c Warner b Durston | 11 | – b Durston | 12 |
| J. Vine c Haig b Stevens | 28 | – c Hendren b Stevens | 11 |
| E. H. Bowley c Stevens b Durston | 2 | – c Hendred b Durston | 17 |
| R. Relf c Durston b Hearne | 6 | – b Stevens | 11 |
| Mr H. L. Wilson b Stevens | 19 | – c Hearne b Stevens | 2 |
| M. W. Tate c Durston b Stevens | 9 | – c Murrell b Stevens | 21 |
| A. E. Relf c Hendren b Stevens | 0 | – c Murrell b Stevens | 2 |
| Mr A. E. R. Gilligan c Murrell b Stevens | 6 | – c Skeet b Stevens | 2 |
| Mr A. H. H. Gilligan b Stevens | 0 | – b Durston | 33 |
| G. Cox c Haig b Stevens | 1 | – b Hearne | 21 |
| G. Street not out | 1 | – not out | 0 |
| B 6, l-b 3 | 9 | B 16, l-b 4, n-b 2 | 22 |
| | **92** | | **154** |

### Middlesex

| | | | |
|---|---|---|---|
| Mr P. F. Warner b A. E. R. Gilligan | 0 | Mr F. T. Mann b Cox | 44 |
| H. W. Lee c Vine b A. E. Relf | 132 | Mr G. T. S. Stevens lbw b Cox | 22 |
| J. W. Hearne lbw b Jupp | 54 | Mr C. H. L. Skeet c Vine b Cox | 0 |
| E. Hendren c A. E. Relf b Tate | 88 | H. R. Murrell not out | 1 |
| Mr N. Haig c and b A. E. Relf | 1 | B 22 | 22 |
| Dr C. H. Gunasekara c A. E. R. Gilligan b A. E. Relf | 5 | (9 wkts dec.) | 369 |

T. J. Durston did not bat.

### Middlesex Bowling

| | Overs | Mdns | Runs | Wkts | Overs | Mdns | Runs | Wkts |
|---|---|---|---|---|---|---|---|---|
| Durston | 13 | 3 | 30 | 2 | 10.2 | 1 | 54 | 3 |
| Lee | 7 | 1 | 17 | — | 7 | 2 | 14 | — |
| Hearne | 5 | 1 | 19 | 1 | 8 | 2 | 15 | 1 |
| Stevens | 7.5 | 2 | 17 | 7 | 13 | 3 | 43 | 6 |
| Gunasekara | | | | | 8 | 7 | 6 | — |

**Sussex Bowling**

| | Overs | Mdns | Runs | Wkts |
|---|---|---|---|---|
| A. E. Relf ........ | 20 | 7 | 51 | 3 |
| A. E. R. Gilligan ... | 28 | 10 | 57 | 1 |
| Tate ............ | 25.4 | 9 | 90 | 1 |
| Cox ............ | 36 | 9 | 82 | 3 |
| Jupp ............ | 10 | 4 | 27 | 1 |
| Wilson .......... | 1 | — | 3 | — |
| A. H. H. Gilligan ... | 6 | — | 30 | — |
| R. Relf .......... | 2 | 1 | 7 | — |

Umpires: A. J. Atfield and W. Smith.

## SUSSEX v LEICESTERSHIRE

Played at Horsham, June 29, 30, July 1, 1921

Getting the best of the game on the first day, when they left off with a score of 196 for five wickets, Sussex won by an innings and 27 runs. They would have gained a still easier victory if they had held all the catches offered them. The great turning-point of the game was the partnership on Thursday of Albert Relf and the Indian batsman Malik, who put on 175 runs together, scoring at a tremendous pace. A curious incident occurred on the first afternoon, Just after the tea interval Jupp had an appeal for leg-before-wicket answered in his favour, but the ball, unnoticed by him, rolled on to the stumps and dislodged a bail. With his score of 64, obtained in less than an hour out of 103, he completed his 1,000 runs for the season.

### Leicestershire

| | | |
|---|---|---|
| W. E. Astill c Street b Gilligan .................. | 0 | – c and b Cox .................. 63 |
| A. Mounteney b Gilligan ...................... | 22 | – c Higgs b Gilligan .............. 0 |
| J. Middleton b Gilligan ...................... | 33 | – c Gilligan b Bowley ............ 9 |
| J. H. King c Street b Cox .................. | 30 | – c and b Wilson .................. 73 |
| Mr C. Gimson b Cox ...................... | 8 | – run out ...................... 0 |
| Mr G. B. F. Rudd lbw b Cox .............. | 0 | – b Cox ...................... 30 |
| S. Coe b Bowley ............................ | 33 | – c Higgs b Bowley .......... 59 |
| Mr W. C. M. Berridge b Bowley ............... | 18 | – c Street b Gilligan .............. 14 |
| Mr A. Howard b Bowley .................... | 27 | – b Tate ...................... 9 |
| W. E. Benskin not out ...................... | 0 | – absent hurt .................... 0 |
| T. E. Sidwell b Bowley .................... | 1 | – not out .................... 34 |
| B 10, l-b 7 ...................... | 17 | B 10, l-b 2 .............. 12 |
| | **189** | **303** |

### Sussex

| | | |
|---|---|---|
| Mr V. W. C. Jupp b Astill .............. 64 | Mr H. S. Malik st Sidwell b Astill .........106 |
| Mr H. L. Wilson c Astill b Berridge ....... 4 | G. Cox c Astill b Rudd ................ 11 |
| E. H. Bowley b Berridge ................ 57 | Mr W. J. Malden b Astill .............. 9 |
| M. W. Tate lbw b Astill ................ 14 | G. Street not out ...................... 33 |
| Mr K. A. Higgs b Rudd ................ 12 | B 18, l-b 4, w 1, n-b 6 .......... 29 |
| A. E. Relf c Middleton b Astill ..........153 | |
| Mr A. E. R. Gilligan b Astill ............ 27 | **519** |

## Sussex Bowling

| | Overs | Mdns | Runs | Wkts | Overs | Mdns | Runs | Wkts |
|---|---|---|---|---|---|---|---|---|
| Gilligan .......... | 15 | 2 | 72 | 3 | 19 | 2 | 100 | 2 |
| Relf ............. | 10 | — | 44 | — | | | | |
| Tate ............. | 10 | 3 | 14 | — | 13 | 4 | 34 | 1 |
| Cox ............. | 12 | 4 | 22 | 3 | 14.5 | 5 | 40 | 2 |
| Bowley .......... | 6.3 | 1 | 20 | 4 | 24 | 8 | 70 | 2 |
| Higgs ............ | | | | | 2 | 1 | 6 | — |
| Wilson .......... | | | | | 5 | 1 | 24 | 1 |
| Jupp ............. | | | | | 5 | 1 | 17 | — |

## Leicestershire Bowling

| | Overs | Mdns | Runs | Wkts |
|---|---|---|---|---|
| Astill ............ | 39.3 | 2 | 187 | 6 |
| Berridge .......... | 21 | 2 | 117 | 2 |
| King ............. | 3 | — | 18 | — |
| Rudd ............ | 29 | 4 | 124 | 2 |
| Gimson .......... | 4 | — | 21 | — |
| Coe ............. | 4 | — | 23 | — |

Umpires: J. Blake and T. Flowers.

# SUSSEX v NORTHAMPTONSHIRE

## Played at Brighton, July 13, 14, 15, 1921

Giving an extraordinary display of hitting on the first day, when they scored 563 for eight wickets, Sussex beat Northamptonshire by an innings and 291 runs, the match finishing early on the third afternoon. All the batting honours for Sussex went to Bowley and Tate, who put on 385 runs together for the second wicket. This was only 13 short of the record set up by Arthur Shrewsbury and William Gunn for Nottinghamshire against Sussex at Trent Bridge in 1890. Tate hit two 6s and thirty 4s and Bowley a 5 and thirty-five 4s. Not often last season was bowling more mercilessly punished. Haywood played a splendid innings on the second day, but apart from him and Hawtin the Northamptonshire batting was dreadfully weak. Carrying his bat right through the first innings, Haywood was at the wickets for three hours and three-quarters. He hit fifteen 4s, his cutting and driving being equally fine.

## Sussex

| | | | |
|---|---|---|---|
| Mr H. L. Wilson c Adams b Murdin ...... 25 | | G. Street b Ball ..................... 6 |
| E. H. Bowley c Walden b Wells ..........228 | | G. Cox b Murdin .................... 70 |
| M. W. Tate b Wells ...................203 | | W. Cronford not out ................. 30 |
| Mr W. J. Malden b Thomas ............. 41 | | |
| Mr A. E. R. Gilligan b Woolley .......... 3 | | B 13, l-b 8, w 4, n-b 2 ......... 27 |
| Mr A. H. H. Gilligan c Bellamy b Wells ... 4 | | — |
| Mr J. E. Fraser c Adams b Ball .......... 33 | | (9 wkts dec.) 670 |

H. E. Roberts did not bat.

### Northamptonshire

| | | | | |
|---|---|---|---|---|
| C. N. Woolley c Wilson b Roberts | 21 | – b Roberts | | 3 |
| R. Haywood not out | 131 | – b Roberts | | 2 |
| Mr A. P. R. Hawtin c A. H. H. Gilligan b A. E. R. Gilligan | 32 | – b Bowley | | 59 |
| F. Walden c Cox b Bowley | 25 | – c and b Roberts | | 0 |
| W. Wells c Roberts b Bowley | 0 | – c Roberts b Bowley | | 0 |
| G. J. Thompson b Cox | 4 | – b Bowley | | 10 |
| Mr W. Adams b Cox | 1 | – c Cox b A. E. R. Gilligan | | 3 |
| K. G. Ball c Wilson b Cox | 0 | – b Bowley | | 7 |
| B. Bellamy c Bowley b A. E. R. Gilligan | 2 | – b A. E. R. Gilligan | | 14 |
| V. Murdin c A. H. H. Gilligan b Cox | 19 | – c Wilson b Bowley | | 22 |
| A. E. Thomas c A. H. H. Gilligan b Cox | 9 | – not out | | 2 |
| B 4, l-b 1, w 2 | 7 | L-b 6 | | 6 |
| | **251** | | | **128** |

### Northamptonshire Bowling

| | Overs | Mdns | Runs | Wkts |
|---|---|---|---|---|
| Wells | 27 | — | 114 | 3 |
| Woolley | 32 | 3 | 129 | 1 |
| Murdin | 16.4 | 1 | 95 | 2 |
| Walden | 10 | — | 75 | — |
| Thomas | 19 | 4 | 54 | 1 |
| Ball | 15 | 3 | 82 | 2 |
| Haywood | 9 | — | 81 | — |
| Adams | 2 | — | 13 | — |

### Sussex Bowling

| | Overs | Mdns | Runs | Wkts | Overs | Mdns | Runs | Wkts |
|---|---|---|---|---|---|---|---|---|
| A. E. R. Gilligan | 15 | 1 | 59 | 2 | 10 | 1 | 41 | 2 |
| Tate | 22 | 7 | 46 | — | 7 | 4 | 8 | — |
| Roberts | 6 | 1 | 27 | 1 | 10 | 3 | 27 | 3 |
| Bowley | 16 | 7 | 31 | 2 | 14.5 | 4 | 33 | 5 |
| Cox | 22.3 | 10 | 53 | 5 | 5 | 2 | 10 | — |
| A. H. H. Gilligan | 6 | — | 28 | — | | | | |
| Wilson | | | | | 3 | 1 | 3 | — |

Umpires: J. Blake and H. Young.

## SUSSEX v GLOUCESTERSHIRE

### Played at Horsham, June 21, 22, 23, 1922

For their victory by 137 runs Gloucestershire had chiefly to thank Dipper who for the first time in his career made two hundreds in a match. Sussex, with showers falling when they went in to get 293 on the last day, should have saved the game easily, but they threw it away by reckless batting. Gloucestershire batted all the first day for their total of 320, the last four wickets adding 163 runs. Dipper out seventh, at 238, batted stolidly, scoring chiefly on the off side. Corbett and Mills both played well. Gloucestershire fielded badly, otherwise Sussex, despite useful innings by Bowley and Roberts, would have been out for a small total. Dipper batted for three hours and twenty minutes in his second innings against steady bowling.

### Gloucestershire

| | | | |
|---|---|---|---|
| Capt. M. A. Green c Street b Roberts | 7 | – b Tate | 0 |
| A. G. Dipper c Street b A. E. R. Gilligan | 117 | – c A. H. H. Gilligan b Roberts | 103 |
| H. Smith b A. H. H. Gilligan | 4 | – c Higgs b Tate | 2 |
| Mr E. C. J. Sheppard b Roberts | 5 | – b Tate | 12 |
| Mr L. J. Corbett c Street b A. E. R. Gilligan | 48 | – b Bowley | 34 |
| Mr P. F. C. Williams c Street b Bowley | 13 | – c Bowley b Roberts | 8 |
| Mr L. Williams st Street b Bowley | 2 | – c A. E. R. Gilligan b Roberts | 33 |
| P. Mills b Roberts | 92 | – b Roberts | 3 |
| C. Parker b A. H. H. Gilligan | 1 | – c A. H. H. Gilligan b Tate | 0 |
| G. Dennett not out | 21 | – not out | 11 |
| J. G. Bessant b Tate | 1 | – c Street b Roberts | 20 |
| B 4, l-b 2, n-b 3 | 9 | B 10, l-b 5, w 1, n-b 3 | 19 |
| | **320** | | **245** |

### Sussex

| | | | |
|---|---|---|---|
| E. H. Bowley c Corbett b Dennett | 65 | – c Corbett b Dennett | 0 |
| G. Street c Sheppard b Dennett | 27 | – c Dipper b Parker | 48 |
| Mr E. L. Harris c Smith b Bessant | 2 | – b Dennett | 41 |
| Mr K. A. Higgs lbw b Bessant | 1 | – b Parker | 0 |
| Mr A. H. H. Gilligan c Corbett b Dennett | 9 | – c Sheppard b Parker | 11 |
| M. W. Tate c P. F. C. Williams b Parker | 19 | – b Parker | 31 |
| H. E. Roberts b Parker | 62 | – not out | 4 |
| Mr A. E. R. Gilligan c and b Mills | 39 | – b Parker | 0 |
| G. Stannard c Dennett b Mills | 3 | – c Green b Parker | 5 |
| Lieut-Col A. C. Watson b Parker | 27 | – c L. Williams b Dennett | 6 |
| A. F. Wensley not out | 0 | – c Corbett b Dennett | 4 |
| B 10, l-b 5, w 1, n-b 3 | 19 | B 3, n-b 2 | 5 |
| | **273** | | **155** |

### Sussex Bowling

| | Overs | Mdns | Runs | Wkts | Overs | Mdns | Runs | Wkts |
|---|---|---|---|---|---|---|---|---|
| Roberts | 28 | 3 | 65 | 3 | 25 | 4 | 66 | 5 |
| Tate | 17.1 | 5 | 31 | 1 | 35 | 9 | 88 | 4 |
| A. H. H. Gilligan | 25 | 3 | 61 | 2 | 6 | 1 | 15 | — |
| A. E. R. Gilligan | 20 | 4 | 63 | 2 | 13 | 5 | 39 | — |
| Bowley | 18 | 4 | 58 | 2 | 11 | 3 | 18 | 1 |
| Wensley | 9 | — | 33 | — | | | | |

### Gloucestershire Bowling

| | Overs | Mdns | Runs | Wkts | Overs | Mdns | Runs | Wkts |
|---|---|---|---|---|---|---|---|---|
| Bessant | 12 | 1 | 37 | 2 | 4 | 2 | 3 | — |
| Parker | 36.4 | 7 | 97 | 3 | 25 | 7 | 81 | 6 |
| Dennett | 36 | 9 | 85 | 3 | 28.2 | 7 | 66 | 4 |
| Mills | 6 | 1 | 35 | 2 | | | | |

Umpires: T. Brown and J. Blake.

## SUSSEX v KENT

Played at Brighton, August 30, 31, September 1, 1922

Sussex wound up their season in dismal fashion, Kent beating them in an innings with 23 runs to spare. Beyond everything else the bowling of Freeman stood out by itself. In the whole match he took seventeen wickets for 67 runs – an astounding performance, much as rain had affected the pitch. His nine wickets for 11 runs in the first innings was altogether out of the common even among the many feats of bowlers getting rid of nine or ten men in one innings. Kent had four men out for 69 after dismissing Sussex in seventy minutes, but Hardinge and G. J. Bryan added 81 in seventy minutes. Hardinge batted two hours while Bryan hit seven 4s in a splendid display lasting ninety minutes. Kent gained a lead of 149 runs and declaring first thing on Friday again got rid of Sussex cheaply. Roberts hit freely and Bowley showed good form before being bowled by a googly he made no attempt to play. On the first day there was little more than fifty minutes cricket.

## Sussex

| | | | |
|---|---|---|---|
| J. Vine c Collins b Freeman | 4 | – c G. J. Bryan b Freeman | 0 |
| E. H. Bowley c G. J. Bryan b Freeman | 24 | – b Freeman | 31 |
| Mr R. A. Young st Hubble b Freeman | 0 | – c J. L. Bryan b Freeman | 8 |
| Mr V. W. C. Jupp c J. L. Bryan b Freeman | 2 | – c Ashdown b Woolley | 0 |
| T. Cook c Troughton b Freeman | 0 | – c Seymour b Freeman | 4 |
| H. E. Roberts c Hedges b Freeman | 9 | – c G. J. Bryan b Freeman | 31 |
| G. Cox c Ashdown b Freeman | 4 | – c Troughton b Hardinge | 4 |
| M. W. Tate b Freeman | 0 | – b Freeman | 0 |
| Mr A. E. R. Gilligan c Hedges b Freeman | 3 | – b Freeman | 10 |
| G. Street c Ashdown b Woolley | 0 | – c Ashdown b Freeman | 21 |
| Mr A. H. H. Gilligan not out | 0 | – not out | 12 |
| N-b 1 | 1 | B 1, l-b 4 | 5 |
| | **47** | | **126** |

## Kent

| | | | |
|---|---|---|---|
| Mr J. L. Bryan c Street b Bowley | 0 | G. C. Collins run out | 5 |
| H. T. W. Hardinge c Young b Cox | 44 | J. C. Hubble not out | 6 |
| J. Seymour b Cox | 23 | Mr L. H. W. Troughton b Jupp | 11 |
| F. E. Woolley b Jupp | 14 | | |
| Mr L. P. Hedges b Cox | 20 | B 5, l-b 3, w 1 | 9 |
| Mr G. J. Bryan c Roberts b Cox | 64 | | |
| W. Ashdown st Street b Cox | 0 | (9 wkts dec.) | 196 |

A. P. Freeman did not bat.

## Kent Bowling

| | Overs | Mdns | Runs | Wkts | Overs | Mdns | Runs | Wkts |
|---|---|---|---|---|---|---|---|---|
| Collins | 1 | — | 6 | — | | | | |
| Woolley | 10.1 | 3 | 29 | 1 | 20 | 5 | 61 | 1 |
| Freeman | 10 | 4 | 11 | 9 | 23.5 | 6 | 56 | 8 |
| Hardinge | | | | | 4 | 3 | 4 | 1 |

## Sussex Bowling

| | Overs | Mdns | Runs | Wkts |
|---|---|---|---|---|
| Bowley | 19 | 3 | 46 | 1 |
| Tate | 8 | 2 | 26 | — |
| Cox | 19 | 2 | 43 | 5 |
| Jupp | 11.1 | — | 58 | 2 |
| A. H. H. Gilligan | 4 | 1 | 14 | — |

Umpires: T. Flowers and F. Chester.

## SUSSEX v HAMPSHIRE

### Played at Brighton, July 11, 12, 13, 1923

In this match – quite a remarkable one – Hampshire gained a well-deserved victory by five wickets. The wicket being soft after a thunderstorm on Monday night, Tennyson, on winning the toss, put Sussex in, and though at lunch time the score stood at 94 for two wickets, his policy was fully justified by events. Before stumps were drawn, Mead and Tennyson put on 105 runs together in seventy minutes. Tennyson had some luck but he hit finely. Mead, not out 78, carried his score next day to 147. Batting with great skill for nearly four hours, he hit sixteen 4s. There was a sensation at the end of the match, Hampshire, with only 64 to get, having five wickets down for 51. For the most part the Sussex batting was weak, but Bowley played splendidly in both innings.

### Sussex

| | | |
|---|---|---|
| Mr A. H. H. Gilligan c Love b Newman | 24 | – b Newman ... 9 |
| E. H. Bowley b Kennedy | 55 | – not out ... 93 |
| Mr A. J. Holmes lbw b Mead | 9 | – b Newman ... 8 |
| G. Street not out | 47 | – run out ... 1 |
| Mr J. E. Frazer c Bowell b Newman | 2 | – c Mead b Newman ... 33 |
| Mr A. E. R. Gilligan b Kennedy | 0 | – b Newman ... 9 |
| T. Cook c Mead b Newman | 2 | – c Livsey b Newman ... 18 |
| M. W. Tate b Newman | 0 | – b Kennedy ... 6 |
| A. F. Wensley b Newman | 4 | – b Newman ... 1 |
| H. E. Roberts st Livsey b Newman | 5 | – c Livsey b Shirley ... 0 |
| G. Cox lbw b Newman | 0 | – c Livsey b Shirley ... 0 |
| B 8, l-b 2, w 2 | 12 | B 7, l-b 3 ... 10 |
| | 160 | 188 |

### Hampshire

| | | |
|---|---|---|
| A. Kennedy lbw b A. E. R. Gilligan | 7 | – c Wensley b A. E. R. Gilligan ... 8 |
| A. Bowell b Tate | 13 | – c Wensley b A. E. R. Gilligan ... 2 |
| Mr P. E. Lawrie b A. E. R. Gilligan | 16 | – b A. H. H. Gilligan ... 5 |
| C. P. Mead b Tate | 147 | – not out ... 41 |
| Hon. L. H. Tennyson lbw b Tate | 53 | – b A. E. R. Gilligan ... 1 |
| Maj. R. A. H. D. Love b A. E. R. Gilligan | 2 | – c Wensley b A. E. R. Gilligan ... 0 |
| J. Newman b Roberts | 3 | |
| G. Brown c Street b Roberts | 18 | |
| Mr C. P. Brutton b Tate | 3 | |
| Mr W. R. Shirley not out | 7 | – not out ... 2 |
| W. H. Livsey b Tate | 0 | |
| B 13, l-b 2, n-b 1 | 16 | B 4, l-b 1 ... 5 |
| | 285 | 64 |

### Hampshire Bowling

| | Overs | Mdns | Runs | Wkts | Overs | Mdns | Runs | Wkts |
|---|---|---|---|---|---|---|---|---|
| Kennedy | 18 | 5 | 46 | 2 | 21 | 6 | 49 | 1 |
| Newman | 22.5 | 2 | 59 | 7 | 21 | 5 | 79 | 6 |
| Shirley | 4 | 1 | 17 | — | 1 | — | 1 | 2 |
| Mead | 7 | — | 20 | 1 | 3 | — | 22 | — |
| Love | 2 | — | 6 | — | | | | |
| Brown | | | | | 3 | — | 27 | — |

### Sussex Bowling

| | Overs | Mdns | Runs | Wkts | Overs | Mdns | Runs | Wkts |
|---|---|---|---|---|---|---|---|---|
| Tate | 32 | 8 | 64 | 5 | 9 | 2 | 16 | — |
| Roberts | 16 | 3 | 52 | 2 | | | | |
| A. E. R. Gilligan | 22 | 4 | 86 | 3 | 11 | 2 | 34 | 4 |
| Cox | 13 | 3 | 38 | — | | | | |
| Bowley | 12 | 3 | 28 | — | | | | |
| A. H. H. Gilligan | 1 | — | 1 | — | 2.1 | — | 9 | 1 |

Umpires: J. H. Board and A. J. Atfield.

# SUSSEX v SOMERSET

### Played at Eastbourne, July 21, 23, 1923

On a pitch that proved unexpectedly difficult, Sussex cut up very badly, Somerset winning the game on the second afternoon by ten wickets. As things turned out, Arthur Gilligan, on winning the toss, would perhaps have done well to put Somerset in, but there was nothing in the appearance of the wicket to suggest such a risky policy. Bright sunshine, however, after a little rain in the night and a heavy dew in the morning helped Robertson-Glasgow, who has perhaps never bowled better. His quick break was too much for most of the Sussex batsmen. In the second innings, he was just as deadly as before, his record for the match coming out at fourteen wickets for 106 runs. There was a startling change in the character of the cricket when Somerset went in with 60 to get, Lowry hitting up a dazzling 50 not out in half an hour.

## Sussex

| | | | |
|---|---|---|---|
| Mr A. H. H. Gilligan c Lowry b Robertson-Glasgow | 0 | – b Robertson-Glasgow | 0 |
| E. H. Bowley c White b Robertson-Glasgow | 25 | – b Robertson-Glasgow | 7 |
| Mr A. J. Holmes b White | 11 | – lbw b White | 28 |
| Mr J. E. Frazer b White | 24 | – b Robertson-Glasgow | 1 |
| T. Cook b Robertson-Glasgow | 0 | – b White | 0 |
| Mr A. E. R. Gilligan c Jones b Robertson-Glasgow | 5 | – c Lowry b Robertson-Glasgow | 4 |
| M. W. Tate lbw b White | 23 | – c White b Robertson-Glasgow | 36 |
| G. Street b Robertson-Glasgow | 0 | – b Robertson-Glasgow | 0 |
| H. E. Roberts b Robertson-Glasgow | 0 | – not out | 10 |
| A. F. Wensley c MacBryan b Robertson-Glasgow | 6 | – c White b Robertson-Glasgow | 1 |
| G. Cox not out | 8 | – b White | 2 |
| B 8, l-b 4, n-b 5 | 17 | B 8, n-b 3 | 11 |
| | **119** | | **100** |

## Somerset

| | | | |
|---|---|---|---|
| Mr J. Daniell run out | 0 | – not out | 11 |
| Mr J. C. W. MacBryan st Street b Cox | 55 | | |
| Mr M. D. Lyon b Tate | 22 | | |
| Mr T. C. Lowry run out | 0 | – not out | 50 |
| A. Young c Holmes b A. E. R. Gilligan | 35 | | |
| J. Jones c and b A. E. R. Gilligan | 0 | | |
| Mr J. C. White c Street b A. E. R. Gilligan | 16 | | |
| Mr G. F. Earle b Cox | 0 | | |
| G. Hunt b Cox | 4 | | |
| Mr R. C. Robertson-Glasgow b Tate | 22 | | |
| Mr J. J. Bridges not out | 2 | | |
| B 2, l-b 1, w 1 | 4 | | |
| | **160** | | **61** |

## Somerset Bowling

| | Overs | Mdns | Runs | Wkts | Overs | Mdns | Runs | Wkts |
|---|---|---|---|---|---|---|---|---|
| Robertson-Glasgow | 20 | 3 | 56 | 7 | 20 | 5 | 50 | 7 |
| Bridges | 10 | 1 | 19 | — | 5 | 1 | 14 | — |
| White | 15.1 | 5 | 27 | 3 | 18 | 7 | 25 | 3 |

**Sussex Bowling**

| | Overs | Mdns | Runs | Wkts | Overs | Mdns | Runs | Wkts |
|---|---|---|---|---|---|---|---|---|
| Tate ............ | 14.4 | 4 | 28 | 2 | 1 | — | 9 | — |
| A. E. R. Gilligan ... | 24 | 9 | 39 | 3 | 2 | — | 17 | — |
| Cox ............ | 14 | 2 | 51 | 3 | 3 | — | 13 | — |
| Roberts .......... | 6 | 2 | 14 | — | | | | |
| A. H. H. Gilligan ... | 6 | 1 | 19 | — | 2.4 | — | 22 | — |
| Bowley .......... | 4 | 1 | 5 | — | | | | |

Umpires: W. Reeves and F. Chester.

# SUSSEX v WORCESTERSHIRE

## Played at Horsham, June 18, 19, 1924

Thanks chiefly to Tate and Bowley, Sussex gained rather an astonishing victory by five wickets. Play went on till ten minutes to seven on Thursday to avoid running the game into the third day. Though he had a little luck M. K. Foster played a magnificent innings on Wednesday, taking out his bat after a stay of nearly four hours and a quarter. He hit a 6 and fourteen 4s. Opening their second innings with a lead of 125 Worcestershire looked to be in a winning position, but they found Tate unplayable. In winning the match Bowley batted delightfully.

### Worcestershire

| | | | |
|---|---|---|---|
| C. V. Tarbox b A. E. R. Gilligan ............... | 22 | – lbw b Tate .................... | 12 |
| F. Pearson c Bowley b A. E. R. Gilligan .......... | 0 | – b Tate .................... | 2 |
| Mr M. K. Foster not out ..................... | 157 | – c Cook b Tate ................. | 8 |
| Lord Somers c Bowley b Tate ................. | 1 | – b A. E. R. Gilligan ............. | 7 |
| Mr H. E. Bryant b Tate ...................... | 0 | – c and b A. E. R. Gilligan ........ | 0 |
| Hon. J. Coventry b Tate...................... | 29 | – c A. H. H. Gilligan b Tate ........ | 16 |
| F. Root b Tate ........................... | 22 | – b Tate .................... | 6 |
| Mr M. F. S. Jewell lbw b Cox ................. | 5 | – b Tate .................... | 2 |
| C. A. Preece b A. E. R. Gilligan ................ | 16 | – c and b Tate ................. | 0 |
| C. J. Wilson c Parks b Bowley ................. | 14 | – not out .................... | 2 |
| H. O. Rogers c Watson b A. E. R. Gilligan ........ | 0 | – b Tate .................... | 0 |
| B 8, l-b 5, n-b 1 ..................... | 14 | L-b 2 .................... | 2 |
| | **280** | | **57** |

### Sussex

| | | | |
|---|---|---|---|
| Mr A. H. H. Gilligan b Root ................... | 17 | – c Root b Pearson ............. | 29 |
| E. H. Bowley b Root ......................... | 9 | – c Rogers b Wilson ............. | 78 |
| W. Cornford b Root ......................... | 6 | – c Foster b Jewell ............. | 30 |
| Mr A. J. Holmes c and b Root ................. | 0 | – b Rogers .................... | 16 |
| T. Cook c Bryant b Root ..................... | 0 | – lbw b Rogers ................. | 2 |
| M. W. Tate b Pearson ....................... | 16 | – not out .................... | 9 |
| Mr A. E. R. Gilligan b Pearson ................. | 34 | | |
| G. Cox b Preece ........................... | 24 | | |
| A. F. Wensley c Rogers b Preece ............... | 40 | – not out .................... | 7 |
| Col. A. C. Watson c Somers b Pearson ........... | 1 | | |
| J. H. Parks not out ......................... | 0 | | |
| L-b 8 ..................... | 8 | B 11, l-b 2 ............. | 13 |
| | **155** | | **184** |

## Sussex Bowling

|  | Overs | Mdns | Runs | Wkts | Overs | Mdns | Runs | Wkts |
|---|---|---|---|---|---|---|---|---|
| A. E. R. Gilligan ... | 20.1 | 3 | 64 | 4 | 14 | 2 | 37 | 2 |
| Tate ............. | 33 | 6 | 96 | 4 | 14.3 | 7 | 18 | 8 |
| Cox ............. | 12 | 2 | 31 | 1 | | | | |
| Parks ........... | 8 | 1 | 15 | — | | | | |
| Bowley .......... | 10 | — | 33 | 1 | | | | |
| Wensley ......... | 3 | — | 16 | — | | | | |
| A. H. H. Gilligan ... | 4 | 1 | 11 | — | | | | |
| Watson ......... | 1 | 1 | — | — | | | | |

## Worcestershire Bowling

|  | Overs | Mdns | Runs | Wkts | Overs | Mdns | Runs | Wkts |
|---|---|---|---|---|---|---|---|---|
| Root ............. | 21 | 3 | 71 | 5 | 14 | 2 | 37 | — |
| Pearson ......... | 25 | 5 | 59 | 3 | 14 | 1 | 40 | 1 |
| Preece .......... | 4.1 | — | 17 | 2 | 8 | 4 | 12 | — |
| Wilson .......... | | | | | 14 | 1 | 53 | 1 |
| Coventry ........ | | | | | 2 | 1 | 1 | — |
| Rogers .......... | | | | | 6 | — | 15 | 2 |
| Jewell ........... | | | | | 3.5 | — | 13 | 1 |

Umpires: W. A. J. West and T. M. Russell.

# SUSSEX v GLAMORGAN

## Played at Brighton, May, 20, 21, 22, 1925

Beating Glamorgan by 326 runs, Sussex gained their first success of the season. They owed it largely to Tate who, bowling in wonderful fashion, had a record for the match of fourteen wickets for 58 runs. His spin and pace off the ground made him very difficult to play, and smart fielding completed the discomfiture of the opposing batsmen. Harold Gilligan and Bowley for Sussex scored 54 together and Isherwood and Cook batted well, but the Glamorgan bowling was never loose and those who attempted hitting soon lost their wickets. Glamorgan collapsed deplorably and Sussex, declaring their second innings with seven men out, set the visitors to get 406 to win. Langridge, a young left-hander, showed fine defence and many good scoring strokes. He and Naumann added 82 in seventy-five minutes. Before play ceased Glamorgan lost eight wickets for 25 runs, but Spencer, Ryan and Sullivan delayed the inevitable issue by some plucky batting on the last morning.

## Sussex

| | | | |
|---|---|---|---|
| Mr A. H. H. Gilligan c Arnott b Mercer .......... | 26 | – b Mercer .................... | 4 |
| E. H. Bowley c Clay b Arnott ................... | 44 | – lbw b Mercer ............... | 32 |
| Capt. L. C. R. Isherwood c Mercer b Clay ........ | 27 | – b Spencer ................... | 12 |
| T. Cook c Sullivan b Mercer ................... | 49 | – b Spencer ................... | 0 |
| J. Langridge lbw b Ryan ..................... | 14 | – not out .................... | 58 |
| M. W. Tate c Clay b Mercer ................... | 10 | – c Ryan b Davies ............ | 38 |
| A. F. Wensley b Mercer ...................... | 4 | – b Mercer ................... | 5 |
| Mr J. H. Naumann lbw b Ryan ................. | 3 | – c Arnott b Mercer ........... | 45 |
| Col. A. C. Watson c Harrison b Ryan ........... | 5 | – not out .................... | 13 |
| G. Cox b Spencer ........................... | 15 | | |
| W. Cornford not out ........................ | 17 | | |
| B 3, l-b 9, n-b 1 ..................... | 13 | B 7, l-b 5 .............. | 12 |
| | 227 | (7 wkts dec.) | 219 |

## Glamorgan

| | | | | |
|---|---|---|---|---|
| Mr N. V. H. Riches b Tate | 9 | – b Tate | | 6 |
| W. Bates c and b Tate | 4 | – c and b Wensley | | 3 |
| G. B. Harrison run out | 12 | – c Cornford b Wensley | | 0 |
| Mr C. F. Walters b Tate | 1 | – b Tate | | 2 |
| Mr T. Arnott b Wensley | 2 | – c Wensley b Tate | | 0 |
| D. Davies b Tate | 0 | – b Tate | | 4 |
| Mr J. C. Clay b Tate | 3 | – c Bowley b Wensley | | 0 |
| J. Mercer lbw b Tate | 0 | – b Tate | | 1 |
| H. Spencer b Tate | 0 | – b Tate | | 22 |
| F. Ryan run out | 1 | – b Tate | | 23 |
| D. Sullivan not out | 4 | – not out | | 13 |
| B 4, l-b 1 | 5 | B 3, l-b 2 | | 5 |
| | **41** | | | **79** |

## Glamorgan Bowling

| | Overs | Mdns | Runs | Wkts | Overs | Mdns | Runs | Wkts |
|---|---|---|---|---|---|---|---|---|
| Arnott | 12 | 4 | 16 | 1 | 5 | 1 | 10 | — |
| Mercer | 37 | 10 | 60 | 4 | 20 | 6 | 58 | 4 |
| Ryan | 33 | 8 | 63 | 3 | 16 | 2 | 38 | — |
| Clay | 15 | 1 | 33 | 1 | 5 | 1 | 17 | — |
| Spencer | 9.1 | 1 | 24 | 1 | 19 | 6 | 43 | 2 |
| Bates | 4 | — | 9 | — | 3 | — | 8 | — |
| Davies | 3 | — | 9 | — | 4 | — | 16 | 1 |
| Riches | | | | | 4 | — | 17 | — |

## Sussex Bowling

| | Overs | Mdns | Runs | Wkts | Overs | Mdns | Runs | Wkts |
|---|---|---|---|---|---|---|---|---|
| Tate | 17.4 | 6 | 23 | 7 | 18.1 | 2 | 35 | 7 |
| Wensley | 17 | 10 | 13 | 1 | 18 | 5 | 39 | 3 |

Umpires: W. Reeves and A. E. Street.

## SUSSEX v WARWICKSHIRE

### Played at Horsham, June 5, 7, 8, 1926

Without Arthur Gilligan and Tate, Sussex defeated Warwickshire by five wickets, the winning hit being made in what must have been the last over of the game. For their success, Sussex were chiefly indebted to Cox and Holmes, the veteran professional taking seventeen wickets for 106 – a feat which, accomplished in his 53rd year, enabled him to join a very select band of bowlers. Only on fifteen previous occasions has such a performance been accomplished in first-class cricket. To Holmes and Bowley, and to Bates of Warwickshire, fell the batting honours. Holmes, when Sussex were struggling to avert the follow-on, stayed for two hours and a half, and eventually the Warwickshire total was just headed. Bates gave a delightful display on Saturday while Bowley's effort on the last day was invaluable. Sussex had three hours in which to score 174, but delays through rain made the task difficult.

## Warwickshire

| | | | |
|---|---|---|---|
| Mr R. E. S. Wyatt c Watson b Cox | 33 | – c Cornford b Cox | 35 |
| J. H. Parsons b Bowley | 20 | – b Cox | 50 |
| L. A. Bates b Cox | 77 | – c Wensley b Cox | 30 |
| W. G. Quaife b Cox | 43 | – c Bowley b Cox | 1 |
| F. R. Santall c Cook b Langridge | 5 | – st Cornford b Cox | 7 |
| Mr N. E. Partridge b Cox | 12 | – b Wensley | 3 |
| A. J. Croom c Bowley b Cox | 15 | – not out | 23 |
| N. Kilner st Cornford b Cox | 28 | – b Cox | 0 |
| J. Smart st Cornford b Cox | 15 | – b Cox | 23 |
| W. G. Peare b Cox | 0 | – b Cox | 0 |
| J. H. Mayer not out | 2 | – b Cox | 1 |
| B 6, l-b 1 | 7 | B 2, l-b 1, w 1 | 4 |
| | **257** | | **177** |

## Sussex

| | | | |
|---|---|---|---|
| E. H. Bowley b Mayer | 8 | – b Wyatt | 53 |
| J. H. Parks c Bates b Quaife | 48 | – c Partridge b Quaife | 22 |
| A. F. Wensley b Santall | 5 | – c Mayer b Wyatt | 40 |
| T. Cook c Wyatt b Quaife | 20 | – not out | 9 |
| J. Langridge b Partridge | 5 | | |
| G. Cox c Bates b Quaife | 0 | | |
| Mr A. J. Holmes b Partridge | 87 | – not out | 8 |
| Mr A. H. H. Gilligan c Partridge b Parsons | 20 | – run out | 15 |
| Col. A. C. Watson b Partridge | 11 | – run out | 19 |
| H. Parks b Mayer | 14 | | |
| W. Cornford not out | 12 | | |
| B 21, l-b 6, w 3, n-b 1 | 31 | B 3, l-b 4, w 1 | 8 |
| | **261** | | **174** |

### Sussex Bowling

| | Overs | Mdns | Runs | Wkts | Overs | Mdns | Runs | Wkts |
|---|---|---|---|---|---|---|---|---|
| Wensley | 33 | 17 | 48 | — | 35 | 17 | 62 | 1 |
| J. Parks | 14 | 4 | 36 | — | 5 | 2 | 11 | — |
| H. Parks | 4 | 2 | 6 | — | | | | |
| Bowley | 22 | 4 | 71 | 1 | 14 | 2 | 50 | — |
| Cox | 38.4 | 19 | 56 | 8 | 36.5 | 17 | 50 | 9 |
| Langridge | 7 | 1 | 33 | 1 | | | | |

### Warwickshire Bowling

| | Overs | Mdns | Runs | Wkts | Overs | Mdns | Runs | Wkts |
|---|---|---|---|---|---|---|---|---|
| Partridge | 39.5 | 12 | 91 | 3 | 18.1 | 2 | 59 | — |
| Wyatt | 28 | 14 | 44 | — | 17 | 2 | 56 | 2 |
| Santall | 11 | 4 | 27 | 1 | 2 | — | 14 | — |
| Peare | 10 | 2 | 11 | — | | | | |
| Mayer | 13 | 6 | 15 | 2 | 2 | — | 5 | — |
| Quaife | 15 | 4 | 34 | 3 | 12 | — | 32 | 1 |
| Parsons | 3 | — | 8 | 1 | | | | |

Umpires: A. E. Street and H. Young.

## SUSSEX v KENT

Played at Hastings, August 10, 12, 13, 1929

Beaten in an innings when they met Kent at Maidstone in July, Sussex atoned so brilliantly for that failure that as the outcome of a truly memorable struggle in which they declared with eight wickets down, they won by 167 runs. In the course of the three days no fewer than 1,451 runs were registered for the loss of thirty-six wickets – an average of 40 runs a wicket – the aggregate being the second largest ever recorded in a county championship match. On the one occasion that this number had been exceeded, Surrey and Northamptonshire, meeting at Northampton in 1920, scored between them 1,475 runs for twenty-seven wickets. A performance yielded by this contest between Sussex and Kent even more notable than the huge total was the individual achievement of Duleepsinhji in making 115 in the first innings of Sussex and 246 in the second. The only four other instances of this feat of scoring a hundred in one innings and two hundred in the other being accomplished in first-class cricket are:

157* and 245   W. W. Armstrong for Victoria v South Australia at Melbourne, 1921
125   and 229   C. B. Fry for Sussex v Surrey at Brighton, 1900
207   and 102*  H. T. W. Hardinge for Kent v Surrey at Blackheath, 1921
113   and 224   C. P. Mead for Hampshire v Sussex at Horsham, 1921

The one matter for real regret during this great struggle was the disablement of A. P. F. Chapman who, when only 22 runs had been scored, fell in the endeavour to field a ball and injured his knee so badly that he could take no further part in the contest. In this circumstance J. L. Bryan captained the Kent team.

The key-note of the match was set from the start, Sussex, before lunch on the first day, making 201 runs for the loss of four wickets. Following upon the speedy dismissal of Bowley, Gilligan and Duleepsinhji put on 121 in fifty-five minutes, the score indeed being increased from 52 to 104 in a quarter of an hour. Duleepsinhji hit away so brilliantly that he put together his 115 in a hundred minutes, and despite the pace at which he travelled and the variety of his strokes, he gave nothing like a chance. His delightful innings included a six and fourteen 4s. Gilligan also played finely and afterwards came further severe punishment of the Kent bowling by Langridge and Wensley, the latter of whom obtained 61 out of 97 in fifty minutes. Less fierce hitting but still very bright cricket was shown by Langridge and by Holdsworth, the old Oxford Blue, who until the previous week had been out of first-class cricket for two years. Sussex ran up their total of 428 in four hours and forty minutes, Freeman bowling with much effect towards the close of the innings.

Kent lost Bryan with only 19 runs on the board and on Monday, despite some fine cricket by Woolley, had half their wickets down for 129. For the moment the prospects of the visitors getting anywhere near the Sussex total appeared, of course, remote in the extreme, yet so finely did Knott, Ashdown and Wright play up that, batting ten minutes longer than Sussex, Kent fell only 30 short of their opponents' big score. Ashdown kept his wicket up for two hours and Wright showed much freedom, but the recovery was mainly the work of Knott who, missed at long-off when 20 and next over at the wicket, proceeded to hit so brilliantly that, given a third life when 94, he scored 140 in little more than two hours and a half. Despite the three chances, he played a great game and had two 6s and sixteen 4s among his strokes.

Sussex at their second attempt soon lost Gilligan, but Duleepsinhji at once settled down and gained such a complete mastery over the Kent attack that he made 50 in under the hour, doubled his score in the next half-hour and altogether registered 149 runs in little more than two hours, the total at the drawing of stumps on Monday being 215 for three wickets. Next morning Duleepsinhji resumed with such complete confidence, that hitting away with delightful freedom, he added 97 in seventy minutes before falling to a catch at long-on. He did not play quite as well as he had done on the previous day, giving indeed, two hard chances, but for the most part he was completely master of the Kent bowling and considering the pace at which he scored – his innings of 246 lasted no more than three hours and a quarter – the excellence and brilliancy of his execution were marvellous. Getting most of his runs by strokes on the leg side and by drives, he had among his hits five 6s and thirty-one 4s. Thanks so largely to his wonderful display Sussex obtained 381 runs in three hours forty minutes and were able to declare soon after half-past twelve.

Set 412 to make in three hours forty minutes, Kent lost Hardinge and Woolley to catches by Duleepsinhji in the slips with 20 on the board, and soon after lunch there were four wickets down for 66. Ames and Todd then played up so freely and well that they added 128 in seventy-five minutes. After the tea interval, however, Tate with the new ball dismissed Ames, Kent's four wickets remaining at the adjournment going down in less than half an hour. Apart from a chance when 56 Ames batted admirably for two hours and a quarter, hitting two 6s and sixteen 4s. In such an exceptionally heavy scoring game. Tate accomplished a very fine performance in taking thirteen wickets for just under 15 runs apiece.

## Sussex

| | | | |
|---|---|---|---|
| E. H. Bowley b Ashdown | 3 | – lbw b Freeman | 30 |
| Mr A. H. H. Gilligan c Hardinge b Freeman | 56 | – c Ashdown b Wright | 4 |
| Mr K. S. Duleepsinhji c Bryan b Marriott | 115 | – c sub. b Freeman | 246 |
| T. Cook c Wright b Freeman | 7 | | |
| James Langridge lbw b Woolley | 80 | – c Ames b Ashdown | 32 |
| A. F. Wensley c Marriott b Freeman | 61 | – c Ashdown b Freeman | 33 |
| Mr R. L. Holdsworth not out | 69 | – lbw b Marriott | 8 |
| M. W. Tate c Ames b Freeman | 5 | – b Marriott | 9 |
| Mr G. S. Grimston b Freeman | 4 | – b Marriott | 6 |
| W. Cornford b Marriott | 6 | – not out | 6 |
| R. A. Hollingdale b Freeman | 3 | | |
| B 13, l-b 5, n-b 1 | 19 | B 5, l-b 2 | 7 |
| | **428** | **(8 wkts dec.)** | **381** |

## Kent

| | | | |
|---|---|---|---|
| H. T. W. Hardinge b Tate | 22 | – c Duleepsinhji b Tate | 5 |
| Mr J. L. Bryan c Duleepsinhji b Tate | 3 | – c Hollingdale b Tate | 17 |
| F. E. Woolley c Hollingdale b Tate | 58 | – c Duleepsinhji b Tate | 4 |
| L. Ames c Duleepsinhji b Cook | 14 | – b Tate | 118 |
| W. Ashdown c Cornford b Tate | 63 | – b Tate | 21 |
| L. Todd c Wensley b Hollingdale | 6 | – c sub. b Wensley | 43 |
| Mr C. H. Knott not out | 140 | – not out | 26 |
| C. Wright c Duleepsinhji b Wensley | 69 | – c Duleepsinhji b Tate | 0 |
| A. P. Freeman b Tate | 0 | – c Gilligan b Wensley | 0 |
| Mr C. S. Marriott c Cornford b Tate | 0 | – c Langridge b Tate | 3 |
| Mr A. P. F. Chapman absent hurt | 0 | – absent hurt | 0 |
| B 6, l-b 15, n-b 2 | 23 | B 5, l-b 1, n-b 1 | 7 |
| | **398** | | **244** |

### Kent Bowling

| | Overs | Mdns | Runs | Wkts | Overs | Mdns | Runs | Wkts |
|---|---|---|---|---|---|---|---|---|
| Wright | 16 | 2 | 61 | — | 18 | 1 | 73 | 1 |
| Ashdown | 15 | 5 | 62 | 1 | 19 | 1 | 97 | 1 |
| Freeman | 32.1 | 3 | 131 | 6 | 23 | 4 | 106 | 3 |
| Marriott | 17 | 1 | 91 | 2 | 15.2 | 2 | 69 | 3 |
| Woolley | 16 | 3 | 40 | 1 | 6 | — | 29 | — |
| Hardinge | 7 | 1 | 21 | — | | | | |
| Todd | 2 | — | 3 | — | | | | |

### Sussex Bowling

| | Overs | Mdns | Runs | Wkts | Overs | Mdns | Runs | Wkts |
|---|---|---|---|---|---|---|---|---|
| Tate | 41 | 5 | 136 | 6 | 23.3 | 6 | 58 | 7 |
| Wensley | 30 | 6 | 80 | 1 | 23 | 3 | 85 | 2 |
| Cook | 11 | 4 | 30 | 1 | | | | |
| Hollingdale | 9 | 1 | 32 | 1 | 10 | 4 | 24 | — |
| Langridge | 8 | 3 | 36 | — | 5 | — | 34 | — |
| Bowley | 8 | — | 37 | — | 5 | — | 16 | — |
| Grimston | 9 | 1 | 24 | — | 2 | — | 20 | — |

Umpires: J. W. Day and J. Hardstaff.

## SUSSEX v NORTHAMPTONSHIRE

Played at Brighton, May 7, 8, 9, 1930

To Duleepsinhji this match brought the great distinction of beating the Sussex record made by his uncle, K. S. Ranjitsinhji, At Taunton in 1901. Going in with one run on the board, Duleepsinhji scored 333 out of 520 and, when seventh out was taking many risks. Batting for five hours and a half, he hit a 6 and thirty-four 4s, his stroke play all round the wicket being magnificent. Three steady partners helped him to master the bowling and then Tate, chiefly by powerful drives and pulls, hit up 111 out of 255 in an hour and three-quarters. Gilligan having declared first thing on the second morning, Wensley, on a pitch which, slow and easy on the first day, proved rather treacherous as it became faster, bowled swingers cleverly. Tate in the follow-on took four of the first five wickets for 22 runs. Bellamy did not concede a bye and he showed the soundest defence for the visitors, who in the end had to admit defeat by an innings and 209 runs.

### Sussex

| | |
|---|---|
| E. H. Bowley c Bellamy b Thomas ....... 1 | M. W. Tate b Partridge ................111 |
| J. Parks c Liddell b Thomas ............ 9 | Mr A. H. H. Gilligan not out ............ 8 |
| K. S. Duleepsinhji st Bellamy b Matthews . .333 | A. F. Wensley not out ............ 0 |
| T. Cook c Liddell b Clark .............. 19 | L-b 6, n-b 6 ................. 12 |
| James Langridge b Cox ................. 17 | |
| H. Parks b Clark ..................... 11 | (7 wkts dec.) 521 |

R. A. Hollingdale and W. Cornford did not bat.

### Northamptonshire

| | | | |
|---|---|---|---|
| C. N. Woolley b Wensley .................... | 18 | – c Duleepsinhji b Wensley ......... | 4 |
| A. H. Bakewell lbw b J. Parks .................. | 12 | – b Tate ..................... | 7 |
| J. E. Timms c J. Parks b Langridge .............. | 19 | – lbw b Tate ................... | 20 |
| Mr V. W. C. Jupp c Duleepsinhji b Wensley ....... | 0 | – lbw b Tate ................... | 11 |
| B. Bellamy b Wensley ...................... | 21 | – c Cornford b Tate ............. | 35 |
| A. D. Matthews lbw b J. Parks .............. | 13 | – c Duleepsinhji b Tate ............ | 0 |
| A. G. Liddell c Gilligan b Bowley .............. | 18 | – c Cook b Tate ................. | 28 |
| A. L. Cox lbw b Tate ........................ | 40 | – c Cornford b Cook ............ | 4 |
| A. E. Thomas lbw b Wensley .................. | 29 | – b Hollingdale ................. | 11 |
| R. J. Partridge not out ...................... | 3 | – b Tate ..................... | 2 |
| E. C. Clark b Tate .......................... | 1 | – not out ..................... | 0 |
| B 9, l-b 4 ........................ | 13 | B 2, l-b 1 .............. | 3 |
| | 187 | | 125 |

### Northamptonshire Bowling

| | Overs | Mdns | Runs | Wkts |
|---|---|---|---|---|
| Clark ............ | 27 | 1 | 75 | 2 |
| Thomas .......... | 29 | 11 | 69 | 2 |
| Partridge ......... | 12 | — | 80 | 1 |
| Matthews ......... | 22 | 2 | 101 | 1 |
| Jupp ............. | 20 | 3 | 92 | — |
| Cox ............. | 11 | 2 | 50 | 1 |
| Liddell ........... | 2 | — | 16 | — |
| Timms ........... | 3 | — | 26 | — |

**Sussex Bowling**

| | Overs | Mdns | Runs | Wkts | Overs | Mdns | Runs | Wkts |
|---|---|---|---|---|---|---|---|---|
| Tate ............ | 9.5 | 1 | 18 | 2 | 20.2 | 3 | 45 | 7 |
| Wensley ......... | 28 | 10 | 45 | 4 | 14 | 5 | 41 | 1 |
| J. Parks ......... | 22 | 11 | 37 | 2 | 2 | — | 12 | — |
| Langridge ....... | 14 | 7 | 21 | 1 | | | | |
| Hollingdale ...... | 10 | 2 | 21 | — | 8 | 3 | 14 | 1 |
| Bowley .......... | 13 | 2 | 32 | 1 | 4 | 2 | 6 | — |
| Cook ........... | | | | | 1 | — | 4 | 1 |

Umpires: P. Toone and F. Chester.


# SUSSEX v MIDDLESEX

## Played at Hove, July 30, August 1, 1932

In a Sussex victory over Middlesex by an innings and 37 runs, Tate played the part of a great cricketer. On Saturday, when seven Middlesex wickets fell to him for 28 runs, he sent down after lunch seven overs and three balls for 13 runs and five wickets while on Monday, after hitting up in fifty minutes 50 out of 73 for the ninth wicket, he disposed of six batsmen for 30 runs, thus obtaining a bowling record of thirteen wickets for 4.5 runs apiece. On a pitch affected by rain and sunshine, Middlesex had lost half their wickets for 61 when Hearne and Hulme came together and added 50 in forty-five minutes. Sussex gave nothing away in the field, the sun being in the fieldsman's eyes in the solitary instance of a catch being dropped. Bowley and James Parks opened the Sussex innings with a stand of 51 yet runs were always hard to get, Bowley batting ninety minutes for 25 and Duleepsinhji experiencing much difficulty in getting the ball away. Play ceased with five men out for 137 and the eighth wicket fell at 191. Langridge batted three hours and a quarter for 57 not out. Hulme and Hendren in the Middlesex second innings put on 48 runs but the latter found his skill so severely tested that his 32 occupied him two hours.


### Middlesex

| | | |
|---|---|---|
| Rev. E. T. Killick lbw b Tate ................... | 3 | – lbw b Tate ................... 5 |
| Mr J. L. Guise c Wensley b Tate ............... | 17 | – c J. Parks b Tate ............... 7 |
| J. W. Hearne c Wensley b Tate ................. | 44 | – c J. Parks b Scott ............. 3 |
| E. Hendren run out ......................... | 0 | – c Duleepsinhji b Tate ........... 32 |
| Mr G. O. Allen st Cornford b Langridge .......... | 3 | – lbw b Tate ................... 11 |
| Mr H. J. Enthoven b Langridge ................. | 6 | – b Wensley ................... 1 |
| J. Hulme b Tate ............................ | 25 | – b Wensley ................... 19 |
| Mr N. Haig c Melville b Tate ................. | 17 | – b Wensley ................... 0 |
| W. F. Price c Melville b Tate ................ | 3 | – b Tate ...................... 2 |
| T. J. Durston c Duleepsinhji b Tate ............ | 6 | – not out ..................... 10 |
| Mr I. A. R. Peebles not out .................. | 0 | – c Bowley b Tate .............. 0 |
| B 12, l-b 3, w 1 .................... | 16 | B 5, l-b 2, w 1 ........... 8 |
| | **140** | **98** |


### Sussex

| | | |
|---|---|---|
| E. H. Bowley b Allen ................. 25 | Mr R. S. G. Scott c Hulme b Peebles ...... 9 |
| J. Parks b Allen ...................... 23 | A. F. Wensley c Hulme b Durston ........ 7 |
| K. S. Duleepsinhji c Guise b Durston ..... 29 | M. W. Tate lbw b Peebles .............. 50 |
| T. Cook c Price b Peebles ............. 3 | W. Cornford c Hearne b Peebles ......... 4 |
| Jas. Langridge not out ................. 57 | B 18, l-b 10, w 2, n-b 5 ......... 35 |
| H. Parks run out .................... 9 | |
| Mr A. Melville b Haig ................ 24 | **275** |

## Sussex Bowling

|  | Overs | Mdns | Runs | Wkts | Overs | Mdns | Runs | Wkts |
|---|---|---|---|---|---|---|---|---|
| Tate ............. | 21.3 | 6 | 28 | 7 | 25 | 11 | 30 | 6 |
| Scott ............ | 10 | 1 | 32 | — | 9 | 4 | 13 | 1 |
| Wensley .......... | 11 | 6 | 19 | — | 18 | 6 | 31 | 3 |
| Langridge ........ | 15 | 3 | 36 | 2 | 7 | 2 | 11 | — |
| Bowley ........... | 3 | — | 9 | — | 1 | — | 3 | — |
| Melville .......... |  |  |  |  | 1 | — | 2 | — |

## Middlesex Bowling

|  | Overs | Mdns | Runs | Wkts |
|---|---|---|---|---|
| Allen ............ | 34 | 10 | 72 | 2 |
| Durston .......... | 22 | 7 | 37 | 2 |
| Haig ............. | 17 | 9 | 29 | 1 |
| Peebles ........... | 41.4 | 12 | 86 | 4 |
| Hearne ........... | 6 | 1 | 16 | — |

Umpires: W. Hitch and W. A. Buswell.

# SUSSEX IN 1933

*President* – The Duke of Norfolk

*Chairman* – Rev. E. D. L. Harvey, DL, JP

*Hon. Treasurer* – Mr B. Y. Bevan

*Secretary* – Mr W. L. Knowles, County Ground, Hove

*Captain* – K. S. Duleepsinhji (retired)

Mr R. S. G. Scott

Sussex began under something of a cloud, for before the campaign opened it was known that they would not enjoy the assistance or be again under the leadership of K. S. Duleepsinhji. Unhappily the visit he paid to Switzerland, in the hope of bringing about an improvement in his health, did not have the desired effect and he was told that it would be better for him to give up all ideas of cricket for the summer in order to have a better chance of complete recovery later on. As it happened the pulmonary disease from which he was suffering, took, if anything, a more firm grip of his system. Duleepsinhji had to content himself with reading and listening about the manner in which his side were acquitting themselves and, towards the end of the season, he knew definitely that he had played his last ball in county cricket. In a letter which breathed a spirit of hope, but in which it was clear he felt that his career was ended, he wrote definitely resigning the captaincy of the Sussex eleven. Thus, after an all too brief sojourn among us there passed from the game he had adorned with such conspicuous grace and success, one of the most beautiful batsmen of recent years. English cricket in general and that of Sussex in particular will be all the poorer for his enforced absence. A young man of singular charm of character; extremely modest of his own wonderful ability; and with a love for the game which transcended his joy in all other pastimes, Duleepsinhji will always be remembered as one of the outstanding personalities during his period in first-class cricket.

## SUSSEX v MIDDLESEX

Played at Hove, August 5, 7, 8, 1933

Sussex overwhelmed Middlesex and declaring with three men out, won the match by an innings and 65 runs. Bowley and John Langridge placed their side in an impregnable position by scoring 490 together in five hours fifty minutes – a first-wicket record for Sussex. Bowley, batting six hours without fault for the highest score of his career, hit two 6s, a 5, and twenty-three 4s. Langridge also did not give a chance. Despite some missed catches and good batting by Hendren, with useful support from Haig, Sims and Watkins, Middlesex had to follow on 222 behind. Then, after a bad start, Allen drove strongly, but, he and Hulme having added 65, the last five wickets fell before Tate and James Langridge for 47, the match ending early on Tuesday.

### Sussex

| | |
|---|---|
| E. H. Bowley c Hulme b Lee ............283 | Jas. Langridge not out ................. 10 |
| John Langridge lbw b Sims .............195 | B 6, l-b 11................... 17 |
| J. Parks c Enthoven b Sims ............ 5 | |
| T. Cook not out ...................... 2 | (3 wkts dec.) 512 |

H. Parks, Mr R. S. G. Scott, A. F. Wensley, M. W. Tate, W. Cornford and J. Cornford did not bat.

### Middlesex

| | | |
|---|---|---|
| H. W. Lee b Tate ........................... 10 | – b Tate ...................... | 0 |
| W. F. Price c John Langridge b J. Parks .......... 15 | – b Tate ...................... | 4 |
| J. W. Hearne lbw b Wensley ................. 12 | – lbw b Tate .................... | 0 |
| E. Hendren b Wensley .................. 79 | – b J. Cornford ............... | 17 |
| Mr G. O. Allen c W. Cornford b Tate ........... 23 | – b Jas. Langridge ............. | 80 |
| J. Hulme st W. Cornford b Jas. Langridge ........ 19 | – c J. Cornford b Tate .......... | 35 |
| Mr H. J. Enthoven lbw b Jas. Langridge ......... 8 | – st W. Cornford b Jas. Langridge ... | 4 |
| Mr N. Haig c Cook b Jas. Langridge ............ 41 | – b Jas. Langridge ............. | 2 |
| J. Sims not out ......................... 36 | – st W. Cornford b Jas. Langridge ... | 0 |
| W. R. Watkins run out ...................... 25 | – c Scott b Jas. Langridge ......... | 1 |
| Mr J. H. Nevinson b Tate ..................... 0 | – not out ...................... | 0 |
| B 8, l-b 12, n-b 2 ................... 22 | L-b 14 ................. | 14 |
| 290 | | 157 |

### Middlesex Bowling

| | Overs | Mdns | Runs | Wkts |
|---|---|---|---|---|
| Nevinson ......... | 25 | 4 | 84 | — |
| Hulme ........... | 8 | 1 | 33 | — |
| Sims ............. | 31 | 2 | 122 | 2 |
| Enthoven ......... | 13 | 2 | 42 | — |
| Hearne .......... | 10 | — | 53 | — |
| Haig ............. | 20 | 1 | 63 | — |
| Allen ............ | 7 | 1 | 8 | — |
| Lee .............. | 27 | 2 | 90 | 1 |

### Sussex Bowling

| | Overs | Mdns | Runs | Wkts | Overs | Mdns | Runs | Wkts |
|---|---|---|---|---|---|---|---|---|
| Tate ............. | 28 | 10 | 41 | 3 | 15 | 5 | 20 | 4 |
| J. Cornford ....... | 20 | 4 | 61 | — | 16 | 6 | 34 | 1 |
| J. Parks .......... | 10 | 1 | 25 | 1 | | | | |
| Jas. Langridge ..... | 30 | 10 | 68 | 3 | 20.3 | 7 | 33 | 5 |
| Wensley .......... | 26 | 6 | 53 | 2 | 17 | 2 | 42 | — |
| Bowley .......... | 5 | — | 20 | — | 2 | — | 14 | — |

Umpires: W. Reeves and H. G. Baldwin.

## SUSSEX v KENT

### Played at Hastings, August 12, 14, 15, 1933

Kent, winning by 149 runs, took ample revenge for a ten wickets beating in July. The match proved a triumph for Freeman who, dismissing fourteen batsmen for less than 11 runs each, raised his aggregate of wickets for the season above 200. Wensley and J. Cornford bowling well on Saturday, Kent lost four wickets for 82, but Valentine drove, pulled and hit to leg with such skill and vigour that he obtained 103 out of 132 at the rate of one a minute, scoring 64 of his runs in fourteen strokes – four 6s and ten 4s. Knott helped in a fifth stand that realised 80 runs. When Sussex batted, Freeman and Ashdown met with marked success, seven wickets falling for 73, and though a courageous innings by W. Cornford resulted in a recovery, Kent led by 61 runs. Ashdown, Knott and Todd playing well, Sussex were left to get 278 to win with the whole of Tuesday at their disposal. Two wickets fell for 45 and, following rain that left the turf favourable to spin bowlers, Freeman finished off the innings for the addition of 83 runs.

### Kent

| | | |
|---|---|---|
| W. H. Ashdown c J. Parks b Wensley | 10 – b J. Parks | 59 |
| L. J. Todd b Wensley | 23 – c J. Parks b Bowley | 39 |
| F. E. Woolley c Melville b Wensley | 26 – c W. Cornford b Tate | 3 |
| Mr F. G. H. Chalk c and b Wensley | 8 – b Wensley | 12 |
| Mr B. H. Valentine b J. Cornford | 103 – c Bowley b J. Cornford | 7 |
| Mr C. H. Knott lbw b J. Cornford | 14 – st W. Cornford b Bowley | 52 |
| Mr A. P. F. Chapman c Tate b Wensley | 5 – c Scott b J. Parks | 15 |
| H. T. W. Hardinge lbw b J. Cornford | 5 – c W. Cornford b Wensley | 17 |
| Mr W. H. V. Levett b Wensley | 4 – c W. Cornford b Wensley | 4 |
| A. E. Watt c W. Cornford b J. Cornford | 12 – b Tate | 0 |
| A. P. Freeman not out | 5 – not out | 0 |
| B 12, l-b 3 | 15      B 5, l-b 3 | 8 |
| | 230 | 216 |

### Sussex

| | | |
|---|---|---|
| E. H. Bowley lbw b Freeman | 26 – c Levett b Watt | 4 |
| John Langridge st Levett b Freeman | 12 – c Ashdown b Freeman | 8 |
| J. Parks b Ashdown | 1 – c J. Parks b Freeman | 40 |
| T. Cook b Ashdown | 20 – c Ashdown b Freeman | 22 |
| Mr A. Melville hit wkt b Freeman | 2 – lbw b Freeman | 17 |
| H. Parks b Freeman | 1 – c Woolley b Freeman | 0 |
| Mr R. S. G. Scott st Levett b Freeman | 21 – lbw b Freeman | 13 |
| A. F. Wensley lbw b Ashdown | 6 – st Levett b Freeman | 11 |
| W. Cornford not out | 50 – st Levett b Freeman | 8 |
| M. W. Tate b Ashdown | 25 – b Ashdown | 0 |
| J. Cornford b Freeman | 0 – not out | 0 |
| B 4, l-b 1 | 5      L-b 4, n-b 1 | 5 |
| | 169 | 128 |

### Sussex Bowling

| | Overs | Mdns | Runs | Wkts | Overs | Mdns | Runs | Wkts |
|---|---|---|---|---|---|---|---|---|
| Tate | 18 | 7 | 29 | — | 27 | 8 | 39 | 2 |
| J. Cornford | 17 | 5 | 32 | 4 | 20 | 2 | 53 | 1 |
| Wensley | 25.5 | 3 | 101 | 6 | 17.1 | 3 | 28 | 3 |
| J. Parks | 7 | 2 | 17 | — | 25 | 8 | 37 | 2 |
| Melville | 3 | — | 16 | — | 8 | — | 31 | — |
| Bowley | 4 | — | 20 | — | 6 | — | 17 | 2 |
| Scott | | | | | 4 | 2 | 3 | — |

**Kent Bowling**

|  | Overs | Mdns | Runs | Wkts | Overs | Mdns | Runs | Wkts |
|---|---|---|---|---|---|---|---|---|
| Watt . . . . . . . . . . . . | 15 | 3 | 30 | — | 17 | 1 | 43 | 1 |
| Ashdown . . . . . . . . | 24 | 9 | 42 | 4 | 19 | 9 | 23 | 1 |
| Freeman . . . . . . . . | 32.3 | 5 | 92 | 6 | 32.3 | 11 | 57 | 8 |

Umpires: J. Stone and H. G. Baldwin.

## SUSSEX v NORTHAMPTONSHIRE

### Played at Hove, July 11, 12, 13, 1934

Captaining the side again, Tate not only bowled with amazing success, but made a wise declaration which led to Sussex winning by 163 runs. At first Sussex did not have matters all their own way. They lost four men for 63 runs, James Parks having retired hurt. Then James Langridge, chiefly by cuts and drives, and Harry Parks, with powerful drives, added 146 before the fourth wicket fell. The next day rain prevented any play before four o'clock and then Tate, contrary to expectations, declared at the overnight total. His judgment proved correct, for on a tricky pitch Northamptonshire fared badly. With the second ball of the innings Tate bowled Bakewell and though Snowden and Timms put on 72, only Cox was really certain in defence. Going in again Sussex boldly went for the runs before Tate declared a second time, leaving Northamptonshire to get 221 runs in two and a half hours. The visitors were soon in trouble once more, Tate with swing, and pace from the pitch, bowling in such form that he took six wickets for 7 runs, bringing his record for the match to ten wickets for 58 runs.

### Sussex

| | | | |
|---|---|---|---|
| John Langridge lbw b Pitt . . . . . . . . . . . . . . . . . . . . . | 2 | – c Timms b Partridge . . . . . . . . . . . . | 36 |
| J. H. Parks retired hurt . . . . . . . . . . . . . . . . . . . . . . . | 13 | | |
| G. Pearce c Clark b Partridge . . . . . . . . . . . . . . . | 23 | – lbw b Matthews . . . . . . . . . . . . . . . | 0 |
| T. Cook b Pitt . . . . . . . . . . . . . . . . . . . . . . . . . . . . . | 19 | – b Partridge . . . . . . . . . . . . . . . . . . . | 44 |
| Jas. Langridge c Cox b Partridge . . . . . . . . . . . . . . . | 109 | | |
| H. W. Parks c Matthews b Clark . . . . . . . . . . . . . . | 77 | – not out . . . . . . . . . . . . . . . . . . . . . . | 15 |
| G. Cox b Clark . . . . . . . . . . . . . . . . . . . . . . . . . . . . | 3 | – b Pitt . . . . . . . . . . . . . . . . . . . . . . . . | 1 |
| H. E. Hammond not out . . . . . . . . . . . . . . . . . . . . | 24 | – b Matthews . . . . . . . . . . . . . . . . . . . | 2 |
| J. Eaton b Matthews . . . . . . . . . . . . . . . . . . . . . . . | 5 | – not out . . . . . . . . . . . . . . . . . . . . . . | 8 |
| B 3, l-b 6, w 1, n-b 2 . . . . . . . . . . . . . . . . . . | 12 | B 4, l-b 5 . . . . . . . . . . . . . . | 9 |

(7 wkts dec.) 287                          (5 wkts dec.) 115

M. W. Tate and J. Cornford did not bat.

### Northamptonshire

| | | | |
|---|---|---|---|
| A. H. Bakewell b Tate . . . . . . . . . . . . . . . . . . . . . . . | 0 | – c Cornford b Pearce . . . . . . . . . . . | 3 |
| Mr A. W. Snowden c and b Pearce . . . . . . . . . . . . . . | 33 | – st Eaton b Tate . . . . . . . . . . . . . . . | 4 |
| J. E. Timms c sub. b Pearce . . . . . . . . . . . . . . . . . . | 35 | – b Tate . . . . . . . . . . . . . . . . . . . . . . . | 2 |
| Mr G. G. Tebbitt c H. Parks b Tate . . . . . . . . . . . . . . | 1 | – b Hammond . . . . . . . . . . . . . . . . . | 13 |
| A. L. Cox c Hammond b Jas. Langridge . . . . . . . . . . | 64 | – c Cook b Tate . . . . . . . . . . . . . . . . | 22 |
| B. Bellamy lbw b Tate . . . . . . . . . . . . . . . . . . . . . . | 7 | – b Tate . . . . . . . . . . . . . . . . . . . . . . . | 0 |
| A. D. Matthews c Eaton b Tate . . . . . . . . . . . . . . . . | 8 | – b Hammond . . . . . . . . . . . . . . . . . | 4 |
| Mr W. C. Brown b Jas. Langridge . . . . . . . . . . . . . . | 5 | – c John Langridge b Hammond . . . . | 0 |
| R. J. Partridge c Hammond b Pearce . . . . . . . . . . . . | 8 | – lbw b Tate . . . . . . . . . . . . . . . . . . . | 0 |
| Mr T. A. Pitt not out . . . . . . . . . . . . . . . . . . . . . . . | 2 | – not out . . . . . . . . . . . . . . . . . . . . . . | 0 |
| E. W. Clark c Eaton b Jas. Langridge . . . . . . . . . . . . | 2 | – b Tate . . . . . . . . . . . . . . . . . . . . . . . | 2 |
| B 11, l-b 6 . . . . . . . . . . . . . . . . . . . . . . . | 17 | B 4, l-b 3 . . . . . . . . . . . . . . | 7 |

182                                                    57

## Northamptonshire Bowling

| | Overs | Mdns | Runs | Wkts | Overs | Mdns | Runs | Wkts |
|---|---|---|---|---|---|---|---|---|
| Clark ............ | 20 | 5 | 54 | 2 | 5 | 2 | 9 | — |
| Matthews ........ | 29.5 | 8 | 58 | 1 | 7 | 1 | 33 | 2 |
| Pitt ............. | 20 | 3 | 60 | 2 | 5 | — | 24 | 1 |
| Partridge ........ | 26 | 6 | 57 | 2 | 8 | 1 | 40 | 2 |
| Bakewell ........ | 3 | — | 16 | — | | | | |
| Cox ............ | 9 | 1 | 30 | — | | | | |

## Sussex Bowling

| | Overs | Mdns | Runs | Wkts | Overs | Mdns | Runs | Wkts |
|---|---|---|---|---|---|---|---|---|
| Tate ............ | 28 | 7 | 51 | 4 | 10.4 | 7 | 7 | 6 |
| Cornford ........ | 19 | 5 | 38 | — | 7 | 1 | 16 | — |
| Hammond ........ | 5 | 1 | 12 | — | 8 | 3 | 12 | 3 |
| Pearce .......... | 22 | 9 | 34 | 3 | 6 | — | 10 | 1 |
| Jas. Langridge ..... | 20.4 | 8 | 30 | 3 | 7 | 3 | 5 | — |

Umpires: A. E. Street and T. Oates.

# SUSSEX v NOTTINGHAMSHIRE

### A. F. Wensley's Benefit Match

### Played at Hove, June 27, 29, 30, 1936

Drawn. Sussex had all the best of the match. With five minutes of the extra half-hour remaining, they went in to get 9 runs for victory. The first over yielded 7 runs; then slight rain began and Heane, having appealed to the umpires, led his team from the field. A threat by Sussex to cancel fixtures arose out of this incident but the trouble was smoothed over. Nottinghamshire broke down badly on Saturday and Sussex followed brilliant fielding by gaining a lead of 253. They owed nearly everything to Melville and Holmes. Though suffering from a damaged leg, Melville hit in delightful fashion, and Holmes, who helped him add 91, drove and cut well in playing his highest innings in county cricket. Keeton and Walker batted soundly in the visitors' second innings and put on 108.

## Nottinghamshire

| | | | |
|---|---|---|---|
| W. W. Keeton c W. Cornford b J. Cornford ....... | 7 | – lbw b Tate ................... | 77 |
| C. B. Harris lbw b J. Cornford ................. | 5 | – c Holmes b J. Parks ........... | 17 |
| W. Walker lbw (N) b J. Cornford .............. | 0 | – c W. Cornford b Hammond ...... | 71 |
| G. V. Gunn c and b J. Parks ................. | 34 | – c and b J. Cornford ........... | 47 |
| J. Knowles c W. Cornford b J. Cornford ......... | 0 | – c Langridge b J. Cornford ....... | 1 |
| A. Staples c Holmes b Hammond .............. | 12 | – b Tate ...................... | 0 |
| Mr G. F. H. Heane c Hammond b J. Parks ........ | 2 | – lbw (N) b J. Cornford .......... | 9 |
| B. Lilley c Hammond b J. Parks ............... | 6 | – c Hammond b J. Cornford ....... | 5 |
| W. Voce c Holmes b Hammond ................ | 0 | – not out ..................... | 18 |
| F. G. Woodhead c H. Parks b Hammond ......... | 0 | – c Langridge b Hammond ......... | 0 |
| H. J. Butler not out ........................ | 4 | – b Hammond .................. | 0 |
| B 3, l-b 1 ...................... | 4 | B 15, l-b 1 ............. | 16 |
| | **74** | | **261** |

## Sussex

| | | | | |
|---|---|---|---|---|
| John Langridge c Voce b Butler | 21 | | | |
| J. H. Parks b Butler | 9 | – not out | | 2 |
| Mr A. Melville b Voce | 125 | | | |
| T. Cook c Lilley b Butler | 11 | – not out | | 0 |
| H. E. Hammond lbw b Butler | 0 | | | |
| H. W. Parks run out | 7 | | | |
| Flt-Lt A. J. Holmes c Staples b Hearne | 107 | | | |
| A. F. Wensley c Harris b Heane | 28 | | | |
| M. W. Tate b Voce | 9 | | | |
| W. Cornford not out | 2 | | | |
| B 4, l-b 3, w 1 | 8 | B 4, l-b 1 | | 5 |
| | | | | |
| (9 wkts dec.) | 327 | | | 7 |

J. Cornford did not bat.

## Sussex Bowling

| | Overs | Mdns | Runs | Wkts | Overs | Mdns | Runs | Wkts |
|---|---|---|---|---|---|---|---|---|
| Tate | 10 | 5 | 13 | — | 45 | 12 | 73 | 2 |
| J. Cornford | 11 | 3 | 31 | 4 | 32 | 8 | 70 | 4 |
| Hammond | 8 | 2 | 16 | 3 | 22.3 | 6 | 55 | 3 |
| J. H. Parks | 6.1 | 3 | 10 | 3 | 29 | 11 | 43 | 1 |
| Wensley | | | | | 2 | 1 | 4 | — |

## Nottinghamshire Bowling

| | Overs | Mdns | Runs | Wkts | Overs | Mdns | Runs | Wkts |
|---|---|---|---|---|---|---|---|---|
| Voce | 34 | 6 | 66 | 2 | 1 | — | 2 | — |
| Butler | 26 | 5 | 69 | 4 | | | | |
| Woodhead | 17 | 2 | 42 | — | | | | |
| Staples | 17 | 2 | 45 | — | | | | |
| Knowles | 6 | — | 25 | — | | | | |
| Heane | 14.4 | — | 72 | 2 | | | | |

Umpires: C. N. Woolley and J. Newman.

## SUSSEX v LANCASHIRE

### Played at Hove, July 23, 25, 1936

Lancashire won by an innings and 5 runs. They were immeasurably superior at all points. Pollard began a Sussex batting breakdown and Wilkinson, sending back Bartlett, W. Cornford and Nye, accomplished the "hat trick". Wilkinson's spin proved puzzling to everybody. Bartlett, suiting his methods to the needs of the occasion, stayed nearly two hours, but his unusual restraint could not pull round the game. There followed an excellent innings by Washbrook who, taking advantage of two early escapes, brought his figures for three consecutive innings to 405 for once out. Iddon helped him add 204 for the second wicket. When Sussex went in again requiring 217 to avert an innings reverse, the brothers Parks shared in a stand of 64 and Bartlett made top score, but otherwise the batting disappointed.

## Sussex

| | | | |
|---|---|---|---|
| John Langridge b Pollard | 8 | – lbw b Nutter | 16 |
| J. H. Parks c Farrimond b Nutter | 27 | – c Farrimond b Edge | 43 |
| H. W. Parks b Pollard | 8 | – c Edge b Wilkinson | 28 |
| G. Cox c Hopwood b Pollard | 0 | – lbw b Wilkinson | 0 |
| Jas. Langridge c Nutter b Pollard | 43 | – c Farrimond b Pollard | 6 |
| Mr H. T. Bartlett c Pollard b Wilkinson | 72 | – c Washbrook b Wilkinson | 63 |
| Flt-Lt A. J. Holmes run out | 11 | – st Farrimond b Nutter | 0 |
| H. E. Hammond not out | 10 | – c Oldfield b Greenhalgh | 18 |
| W. Cornford b Wilkinson | 0 | – c Nutter b Wilkinson | 2 |
| J. Nye b Wilkinson | 0 | – not out | 16 |
| J. Cornford b Wilkinson | 1 | – b Pollard | 9 |
| B 5, l-b 6, w 1, n-b 3 | 15 | B 4, l-b 5, w 1, n-b 1 | 11 |
| | **195** | | **212** |

## Lancashire

| | | | |
|---|---|---|---|
| C. Washbrook c sub. b J. Cornford | 135 | W. Farrimond not out | 16 |
| J. L. Hopwood lbw b J. Cornford | 11 | R. Pollard b Jas. Langridge | 0 |
| J. Iddon c J. Parks b Nye | 95 | L. L. Wilkinson b J. Cornford | 2 |
| Ň. Oldfield b Hammond | 47 | C. Edge not out | 0 |
| A. Nutter b J. Parks | 42 | | |
| E. Greenhalgh c W. Cornford b Jas. Langridge | 38 | B 12, l-b 10, w 2 | 24 |
| Mr W. H. L. Lister b J. Parks | 2 | **(9 wkts dec.) 412** | |

### Lancashire Bowling

| | Overs | Mdns | Runs | Wkts | Overs | Mdns | Runs | Wkts |
|---|---|---|---|---|---|---|---|---|
| Edge | 14 | 1 | 35 | — | 14 | — | 54 | 1 |
| Pollard | 16 | 2 | 63 | 4 | 16.1 | 6 | 41 | 2 |
| Nutter | 13 | 3 | 39 | 1 | 15 | 2 | 44 | 2 |
| Wilkinson | 9.4 | 2 | 18 | 4 | 19 | 3 | 51 | 4 |
| Greenhalgh | 9 | 1 | 25 | — | 6 | 2 | 11 | 1 |

### Sussex Bowling

| | Overs | Mdns | Runs | Wkts |
|---|---|---|---|---|
| J. Cornford | 28 | 3 | 89 | 3 |
| Nye | 35 | 4 | 136 | 1 |
| J. H. Parks | 25 | 7 | 63 | 2 |
| Hammond | 19 | 3 | 47 | 1 |
| Jas. Langridge | 14 | 2 | 42 | 2 |
| John Langridge | 2 | — | 11 | — |
| Holmes | 1 | 1 | — | — |

Umpires: H. G. Baldwin and W. Reeves.

## SUSSEX v MIDDLESEX

Played at Hove, July 30, August 1, 2, 1936

Middlesex won by three wickets. When four men were out with 90 runs required for victory, Robins, possibly fearing a repetition of a first innings collapse, promoted Smith in the batting order. So well did this policy succeed that the giant hitter in thirty-five minutes obtained 57, including two 6s and six 4s, and virtually settled the issue. Sussex began well enough; the board showed 248 when the fifth wicket fell. John Langridge, freer than usual, and H. Parks put on 100 for the second stand and Stainton batted well, but Allen took the last five wickets for 17 runs. After free scoring by Edrich and Compton, eight Middlesex wickets fell for 59, Nye, in one spell, claiming five for 11 runs. Gray followed with even more remarkable bowling, dismissing five men in eleven deliveries for a single – four of them in six balls. Edrich batted brilliantly when Middlesex began the task of scoring 300 to win, and Robertson assisted him in an opening partnership of 125.

## Sussex

| | | | |
|---|---|---|---|
| John Langridge b Peebles | 63 | – lbw b Smith | 48 |
| J. H. Parks lbw b Smith | 19 | – c Gray b Allen | 0 |
| H. W. Parks lbw b Smith | 66 | – hit wkt b Allen | 15 |
| Mr R. G. Stainton b Smith | 58 | – c Sims b Allen | 52 |
| Jas. Langridge c and b Peebles | 10 | – st Price b Peebles | 28 |
| Mr H. T. Bartlett c Gray b Allen | 27 | – b Gray | 16 |
| Flt-Lt A. J. Holmes b Allen | 5 | – b Gray | 2 |
| H. E. Hammond not out | 14 | – not out | 11 |
| W. Cornford b Allen | 0 | – b Gray | 0 |
| J. Nye b Allen | 11 | – c Compton b Gray | 0 |
| J. Cornford b Allen | 6 | – lbw b Gray | 1 |
| B 2, l-b 6, w 4, n-b 5 | 17 | L-b 4, n-b 4 | 8 |
| | **296** | | **181** |

## Middlesex

| | | | |
|---|---|---|---|
| W. J. Edrich b Nye | 50 | – c John Langridge b Nye | 95 |
| J. Robertson c Holmes b J. Cornford | 21 | – b J. Cornford | 46 |
| W. F. Price c Holmes b J. Parks | 16 | – not out | 52 |
| D. Compton c W. Cornford b Hammond | 31 | – c Hammond b Nye | 4 |
| J. Hulme c John Langridge b Nye | 1 | – c John Langridge b Nye | 18 |
| Mr R. W. V. Robins b J. Cornford | 24 | – not out | 4 |
| Mr G. O. Allen c Hammond b Nye | 0 | – c Nye b Holmes | 2 |
| J. Simms c W. Cornford b Nye | 0 | – lbw b Nye | 2 |
| J. Smith c J. Cornford b Nye | 5 | – b J. Parks | 57 |
| Mr I. A. R. Peebles b J. Cornford | 17 | | |
| L. H. Gray not out | 2 | | |
| B 8, l-b 3 | 11 | B 14, l-b 6, w 1 | 21 |
| | **178** | | **301** |

## Middlesex Bowling

| | Overs | Mdns | Runs | Wkts | Overs | Mdns | Runs | Wkts |
|---|---|---|---|---|---|---|---|---|
| Allen | 22.5 | 6 | 68 | 5 | 9 | — | 45 | 3 |
| Smith | 25 | 4 | 80 | 3 | 11 | 2 | 45 | 1 |
| Gray | 10 | 1 | 37 | — | 6.1 | 1 | 22 | 5 |
| Edrich | 2 | — | 8 | — | | | | |
| Sims | 11 | 1 | 37 | — | 4 | 1 | 16 | — |
| Robins | 6 | 2 | 12 | — | 3 | — | 12 | — |
| Peebles | 10 | 1 | 37 | 2 | 11 | 3 | 33 | 1 |

## Sussex Bowling

| | Overs | Mdns | Runs | Wkts | Overs | Mdns | Runs | Wkts |
|---|---|---|---|---|---|---|---|---|
| Nye | 17 | 2 | 55 | 5 | 27 | 2 | 105 | 4 |
| J. Cornford | 15.2 | 5 | 32 | 3 | 19 | 1 | 77 | 1 |
| Hammond | 13 | 2 | 47 | 1 | 11 | — | 40 | — |
| J. H. Parks | 5 | — | 33 | 1 | 13 | 2 | 36 | 1 |
| Jas. Langridge | | | | | 6 | 1 | 18 | — |
| Holmes | | | | | 0.4 | — | 4 | 1 |

Umpires: A. Dolphin and N. Kilner.

# WARWICKSHIRE

## WARWICKSHIRE v SURREY

### Played at Birmingham, June 12, 14, 15, 1920

In this match the weather saved Warwickshire from an overwhelming defeat. When on the third afternoon a thunderstorm burst over the ground, followed by more rain, and made further cricket impossible, the home side, with a wicket to fall, still required 29 runs to avoid being beaten in a single innings. On Saturday the game could not be started till ten minutes past five, and in the little time available Hobbs, for 21 runs, took five of the six wickets that fell. This unexpected success as a bowler he supplemented by getting a brilliant 101, but he might twice have been out when his score was 85. Ducat was batting very finely when rain caused stumps to be drawn at six o'clock on the second day. Though the season was so young Hobbs's score was his fifth hundred for Surrey, and his third in succession.

### Warwickshire

| | | |
|---|---|---|
| L. A. Bates c and b Hobbs | 23 | – b Hitch .................... 44 |
| Mr H. Venn b Hobbs | 1 | – b Hobbs .................... 4 |
| C. Charlesworth b Hobbs | 6 | – b Hitch .................... 20 |
| W. G. Quaife lbw b Hobbs | 0 | – c Shepherd b Hitch .......... 10 |
| E. J. Smith c Ducat b Abel | 20 | – c Harrison b Abel .......... 26 |
| Mr A. J. Bostock-Hill b Fender | 0 | – b Fender .................... 4 |
| C. Smart b Hobbs | 0 | – run out .................... 23 |
| Mr W. C. Hands c and b Fender | 10 | – not out .................... 18 |
| H. Howell not out | 5 | – c Fender b Abel .......... 6 |
| A. Howell b Abel | 2 | – lbw b Fender .............. 2 |
| E. A. Illingworth run out | 0 | – not out .................... 0 |
| L-b 1, n-b 2 | 3 | L-b 2 .................... 2 |
| | **70** | **159** |

### Surrey

| | | | |
|---|---|---|---|
| J. B. Hobbs c Bates b Hands | 101 | T. Shepherd not out ............... | 2 |
| A. Sandham b A. Howell | 28 | | |
| A. Ducat not out | 104 | B 5, w 1, n-b 1 .............. | 7 |
| Mr F. C. W. Newman lbw b A. Howell | 0 | | |
| W. Hitch b A. Howell | 16 | (4 wkts dec.) | **258** |

Mr P. G. H. Fender, H. A. Peach, H. S. Harrison, T. Abel and H. Strudwick did not bat.

### Surrey Bowling

| | Overs | Mdns | Runs | Wkts | Overs | Mdns | Runs | Wkts |
|---|---|---|---|---|---|---|---|---|
| Hitch ............. | 7 | — | 17 | — | 16 | 3 | 42 | 3 |
| Hobbs ........... | 14 | 7 | 21 | 5 | 6 | 2 | 4 | 1 |
| Fender ........... | 11.2 | 2 | 26 | 2 | 23.3 | 6 | 65 | 2 |
| Abel ............. | 4 | 2 | 3 | 2 | 11 | 2 | 33 | 2 |
| Peach ........... | | | | | 8 | 3 | 13 | — |

**Warwickshire Bowling**

| | Overs | Mdns | Runs | Wkts |
|---|---|---|---|---|
| H. Howell . . . . . . . | 17 | 7 | 34 | — |
| Hands . . . . . . . . . . . | 15 | 3 | 50 | 1 |
| Illingworth . . . . . . . . | 11 | 2 | 40 | — |
| Quaife . . . . . . . . . . | 15 | 1 | 56 | — |
| A. Howell . . . . . . . | 13 | 1 | 49 | 3 |
| Bostock-Hill . . . . . . . | 4 | — | 22 | — |

Umpires: J. Moss and A. J. Atfield.

## WARWICKSHIRE v WORCESTERSHIRE

Played at Birmingham, August 4, 5, 6, 1920

In this match Warwickshire had naturally the easiest of tasks. Scoring on the first day 525 for seven wickets, they won in the end by an innings and 340 runs. The early play gave no suggestion of the tremendous run-getting that followed, Warwickshire having three wickets down for 58. Calthorpe and Stephens, however, hit at such a pace that they added 143 runs in sixty-five minutes, and later in the afternoon Holdsworth and Waddy put on 187 together in an hour and forty minutes. In getting his first 100 for his county Holdsworth hit a five and seventeen 4s.

### Warwickshire

| | |
|---|---|
| L. A. Bates st A. N. Jewell b Pearson . . . . . 4 | E. J. Smith c Turner b Foster . . . . . . . . . . . . 80 |
| Hon. F. S. G. Calthorpe c Taylor b Preece . 87 | Mr C. A. Fiddian-Green not out . . . . . . . . . 53 |
| Comdr C. F. Cowan b Preece . . . . . . . . . . . 4 | Mr G. A. Rotherham b Preece . . . . . . . . . . 4 |
| W. G. Quaife lbw b Preece . . . . . . . . . . . . . 3 | H. Howell not out . . . . . . . . . . . . . . . . . . . . 21 |
| Mr G. W. Stephens b Pearson . . . . . . . . . . .111 | B 10, l-b 12, w 2 . . . . . . . . . . . . . 24 |
| Mr R. L. Holdsworth c Bowley b Preece . . .141 | ___ |
| Rev. E. F. Waddy b Taylor . . . . . . . . . . . . . 71 | (9 wkts dec.) 603 |

### Worcestershire

| | | | |
|---|---|---|---|
| Mr A. N. Jewell b Calthorpe . . . . . . . . . . . . . . . . . . . | 15 | – b Calthorpe . . . . . . . . . . . . . . . . . . . | 4 |
| F. Bowley c and b Calthorpe . . . . . . . . . . . . . . . . . . . | 14 | – b Calthorpe . . . . . . . . . . . . . . . . . . . | 0 |
| F. Pearson c and b Calthorpe . . . . . . . . . . . . . . . . . . | 5 | – absent hurt . . . . . . . . . . . . . . . . . . | 0 |
| Mr H. L. Higgins c Stephens b Rotherham . . . . . . . | 0 | – c Smith b Quaife . . . . . . . . . . . . . | 25 |
| Mr M. K. Foster c Howell b Rotherham . . . . . . . . . | 4 | – c Waddy b Howell . . . . . . . . . . . . . | 56 |
| Mr J. W. C. Turner lbw b Quaife . . . . . . . . . . . . . . . | 14 | – c Smith b Rotherham . . . . . . . . . . . | 24 |
| Mr J. D. Abbott c Fiddian-Green b Howell . . . . . . . . | 11 | – b Howell . . . . . . . . . . . . . . . . . . . . | 7 |
| Mr W. H. Taylor b Howell . . . . . . . . . . . . . . | 7 | – not out . . . . . . . . . . . . . . . . . . . . . | 5 |
| Mr M. F. S. Jewell c Holdsworth b Calthorpe . . . . . . | 24 | – b Howell . . . . . . . . . . . . . . . . . . . . | 31 |
| C. A. Preece c Calthorpe b Howell . . . . . . . . . . . . . . | 0 | – b Howell . . . . . . . . . . . . . . . . . . . . | 3 |
| Mr W. E. Richardson not out . . . . . . . . . . . . . . . . . . | 4 | – run out . . . . . . . . . . . . . . . . . . . . . | 2 |
| B 4 . . . . . . . . . . . . . . . . . . . . . . . . . . . | 4 | B 4 . . . . . . . . . . . . . . . . . . . . | 4 |
| | 102 | | 161 |

**Worcestershire Bowling**

| | Overs | Mdns | Runs | Wkts |
|---|---|---|---|---|
| Richardson . . . . . . . | 8 | — | 41 | — |
| Pearson . . . . . . . . . . | 31 | 3 | 155 | 2 |
| Preece . . . . . . . . . . . | 37 | 5 | 176 | 5 |
| Taylor . . . . . . . . . . . | 14 | — | 97 | 1 |
| M. F. S. Jewell . . . . . | 4 | — | 29 | — |
| Foster . . . . . . . . . . . | 16 | 1 | 81 | 1 |

**Warwickshire Bowling**

| | Overs | Mdns | Runs | Wkts | Overs | Mdns | Runs | Wkts |
|---|---|---|---|---|---|---|---|---|
| Howell . . . . . . . . . . | 11 | 2 | 29 | 3 | 11.5 | 4 | 35 | 4 |
| Rotherham . . . . . . . . | 13 | 4 | 19 | 2 | 19 | 7 | 40 | 1 |
| Calthorpe . . . . . . . . | 16.4 | 3 | 34 | 4 | 22 | 9 | 50 | 2 |
| Quaife . . . . . . . . . . | 7 | — | 16 | 1 | 14 | 3 | 32 | 1 |

Umpires: H. Butt and A. J. Atfield.

# WARWICKSHIRE v YORKSHIRE

Played at Birmingham, June 7, 8, 9, 1922

Yorkshire simply overwhelmed Warwickshire, declaring with only two wickets down, and yet winning the match by an innings and 152 runs. They put themselves in an impregnable position on the first day, scoring 360 for the loss of Sutcliffe's wicket. Warwickshire had to pay a high price for a blunder in the field, Oldroyd being badly missed at square leg by B. W. Quaife when he had made 14. After that the batting was almost flawless. In all, Holmes and Oldroyd put on 333 runs together – a record partnership for Yorkshire's second wicket. Batting six hours and ten minutes for his 209, and giving no chance, Holmes hit twenty-six 4s. Apart from his one piece of luck, Oldroyd, whose 138 not out, included thirteen 4s, was rarely or never at fault. Warwickshire, when at last their turn came to go in, could make little headway against first-rate bowling, and during the rest of the afternoon they lost sixteen wickets, being, of course, in an absolutely hopeless position at the drawing of stumps. On the third morning Partridge hit brilliantly, but less than an hour's play proved sufficient to finish off the match. It will be noticed that Rhodes bowled with astonishing success, taking five wickets at a cost of only twelve runs in Warwickshire's first innings and having a full record of nine wickets for 59.

## Yorkshire

| | |
|---|---|
| P. Holmes lbw b Calthorpe . . . . . . . . . . . . .209 | |
| H. Sutcliffe b Partridge . . . . . . . . . . . . . . . 40 | |
| E. Oldroyd not out . . . . . . . . . . . . . . . . . . . .138 | |
| R. Kilner not out . . . . . . . . . . . . . . . . . . . . . 29 | |
| B 15, l-b 16, w 1, n-b 5 . . . . . . . . . 37 | |

(2 wkts dec.) 453

Mr G. Wilson, W. Rhodes, E. Robinson, N. Kilner, G. G. Macaulay, A. Dolphin and A. Waddington did not bat.

## Warwickshire

| | | | |
|---|---|---|---|
| L. A. Bates run out . . . . . . . . . . . . . . . . . . . . . . . . . . . . . . | 30 | – lbw b Robinson . . . . . . . . . . . . . . . . | 0 |
| E. J. Smith b Macaulay . . . . . . . . . . . . . . . . . . . . . . . | 8 | – c Robinson b R. Kilner . . . . . . . . . . | 47 |
| Mr F. R. Santall st Dolphin b Macaulay . . . . . . . . . . | 4 | – c Macaulay b Waddington . . . . . . . | 5 |
| W. G. Quaife b Rhodes . . . . . . . . . . . . . . . . . . . . . . | 13 | – b Macaulay . . . . . . . . . . . . . . . . . . . | 14 |
| Hon. F. S. G. Calthorpe c and b Macaulay . . . . . . . . | 18 | – c Dolphin b Rhodes . . . . . . . . . . . . | 28 |
| Mr H. L. Simms c Sutcliffe b Rhodes . . . . . . . . . . . . | 26 | – b Rhodes . . . . . . . . . . . . . . . . . . . . | 2 |
| Mr B. W. Quaife b Macaulay . . . . . . . . . . . . . . . . . . . | 6 | – c Dolphin b Rhodes . . . . . . . . . . . . | 9 |
| Mr N. E. Partridge c R. Kilner b Rhodes . . . . . . . . . . | 1 | – not out . . . . . . . . . . . . . . . . . . . . . . | 64 |
| J. Smart not out . . . . . . . . . . . . . . . . . . . . . . . . . . . . . | 7 | – b Macaulay . . . . . . . . . . . . . . . . . . . | 0 |
| C. Smart c R. Kilner b Rhodes . . . . . . . . . . . . . . . . . | 1 | – b Rhodes . . . . . . . . . . . . . . . . . . . . | 3 |
| H. Howell st Dolphin b Rhodes . . . . . . . . . . . . . . . . | 4 | – b Macaulay . . . . . . . . . . . . . . . . . . . | 1 |
| L-b 2, w 1, n-b 2 . . . . . . . . . . . . . . . . . . . | 5 | L-b 1, w 1, n-b 3 . . . . . . . . . | 5 |

123                                                                   178

**Warwickshire Bowling**

| | Overs | Mdns | Runs | Wkts |
|---|---|---|---|---|
| Howell .......... | 35 | 3 | 104 | — |
| Calthorpe ........ | 33 | 15 | 61 | 1 |
| Partridge ........ | 31 | 5 | 90 | 1 |
| Simms .......... | 19 | 4 | 71 | — |
| W. G. Quaife ...... | 11 | — | 45 | — |
| J. Smart ......... | 11 | 4 | 24 | — |
| C. Smart ........ | 2 | — | 9 | — |
| Santall .......... | 2 | — | 10 | — |
| Bates ........... | 1 | — | 2 | — |

**Yorkshire Bowling**

| | Overs | Mdns | Runs | Wkts | Overs | Mdns | Runs | Wkts |
|---|---|---|---|---|---|---|---|---|
| Robinson ......... | 5 | 1 | 9 | — | 5 | — | 16 | 1 |
| Waddington ....... | 13 | 4 | 29 | — | 8 | 1 | 21 | 1 |
| Macaulay ......... | 20 | 3 | 50 | 4 | 16.1 | 1 | 53 | 3 |
| R. Kilner ........ | 14 | 6 | 18 | — | 14 | 5 | 36 | 1 |
| Rhodes .......... | 10.2 | 4 | 12 | 5 | 22 | 7 | 47 | 4 |

Umpires: G. A. Fuller and J. H. Board.

# WARWICKSHIRE v HAMPSHIRE

## Played at Birmingham, June 14, 15, 16, 1922

This was the sensational match of the whole season, at Birmingham or anywhere else, Hampshire actually winning by 155 runs after being out for a total of 15. That their astounding failure in the first innings was just one of the accidents of cricket, and not due in any way to the condition of the ground, was proved by their getting 521 when they followed on. The victory, taken as a whole, must surely be without precedent in first-class cricket. Hampshire looked in a hopeless position when the sixth wicket in their second innings went down at 186, but Shirley helped Brown to put on 85 runs, and then, with Livsey in after McIntyre had failed, the score was carried to 451. Brown batted splendidly for four hours and three-quarters and Livsey made his first hundred without a mistake.

## Warwickshire

| | | | |
|---|---|---|---|
| L. A. Bates c Shirley b Newman ................ | 3 | – c Mead b Kennedy ............. | 1 |
| E. J. Smith c Mead b Newman .................. | 24 | – c Shirley b Kennedy ........... | 41 |
| Mr F. R. Santall c McIntyre b Boyes ....... | 84 | – b Newman .................... | 0 |
| W. G. Quaife b Newman ...................... | 1 | – not out ...................... | 40 |
| Hon. F. S. G. Calthorpe c Boyes b Kennedy ....... | 70 | – b Newman .................... | 30 |
| Rev. E. F. Waddy c Mead b Boyes ............. | 0 | – b Newman .................... | 0 |
| Mr B. W. Quaife b Boyes ...................... | 0 | – c and b Kennedy ............. | 7 |
| J. Fox b Kennedy ........................... | 4 | – b Kennedy ................... | 0 |
| J. Smart b Newman .......................... | 20 | – b Newman ................... | 3 |
| C. Smart c Mead b Boyes .................. | 14 | – c and b Boyes .............. | 15 |
| H. Howell not out........................... | 1 | – c Kennedy b Newman ........ | 11 |
| L-b 2 .......................... | 2 | B 6, l-b 4 .............. | 10 |

| | | |
|---|---|---|
| | 223 | 158 |

## Hampshire

| | | | |
|---|---|---|---|
| A. Bowell b Howell | 0 | – c Howell b W. G. Quaife | 45 |
| A. Kennedy c Smith b Calthorpe | 0 | – b Calthorpe | 7 |
| Mr H. L. V. Day b Calthorpe | 0 | – c Bates b W. G. Quaife | 15 |
| C. P. Mead not out | 6 | – b Howell | 24 |
| Hon. L. H. Tennyson c Calthorpe b Howell | 4 | – c C. Smart b Calthorpe | 45 |
| G. Brown b Howell | 0 | – b C. Smart | 172 |
| J. Newman c C. Smart b Howell | 0 | – c and b W. G. Quaife | 12 |
| Mr W. R. Shirley c J. Smart b Calthorpe | 1 | – lbw b Fox | 30 |
| Mr A. S. McIntyre lbw b Calthorpe | 0 | – lbw b Howell | 5 |
| W. H. Livsey b Howell | 0 | – not out | 110 |
| G. S. Boyes lbw b Howell | 0 | – b Howell | 29 |
| B 4 | 4 | B 14, l-b 11, w 1, n-b 1 | 27 |
| | 15 | | 521 |

## Hampshire Bowling

| | Overs | Mdns | Runs | Wkts | Overs | Mdns | Runs | Wkts |
|---|---|---|---|---|---|---|---|---|
| Kennedy | 24 | 7 | 74 | 2 | 26 | 12 | 47 | 4 |
| Newman | 12.3 | — | 70 | 4 | 26.3 | 12 | 53 | 5 |
| Boyes | 16 | 5 | 56 | 4 | 11 | 4 | 34 | 1 |
| Shirley | 3 | — | 21 | — | | | | |
| Brown | | | | | 5 | — | 14 | — |

## Warwickshire Bowling

| | Overs | Mdns | Runs | Wkts | Overs | Mdns | Runs | Wkts |
|---|---|---|---|---|---|---|---|---|
| Howell | 4.5 | 2 | 7 | 6 | 63 | 10 | 156 | 3 |
| Calthorpe | 4 | 3 | 4 | 4 | 33 | 7 | 97 | 2 |
| W. G. Quaife | | | | | 49 | 8 | 154 | 3 |
| Fox | | | | | 7 | — | 30 | 1 |
| J. Smart | | | | | 13 | 2 | 37 | — |
| Santall | | | | | 5 | — | 15 | — |
| C. Smart | | | | | 1 | — | 5 | 1 |

A. J. Atfield and B. Brown.

## WARWICKSHIRE v YORKSHIRE

### Played at Birmingham, May 23, 24, 25, 1923

Though beaten in the end by 84 runs Warwickshire up to a point made a great fight against the champion county. Nothing could be done on the first day till after half-past four and in the time that remained five Yorkshire wickets fell – all to Howell's bowling – for 67 runs. The next morning Howell was just as deadly as before and had the satisfaction of taking all ten wickets in the innings. Only once before against Yorkshire – in 1865 by the still-surviving Nottinghamshire veteran George Wootton – had this feat been accomplished. Yorkshire were in a critical position with five wickets down in their second innings for 59, but Kilner and Leyland came to the rescue. Not until twenty minutes past three could a ball be bowled on the third day, but thanks to splendid bowling Yorkshire forced a win before half-past six.

## Yorkshire

| | | | | | |
|---|---|---|---|---|---|
| P. Holmes c Smart b Howell | 1 | – c Smart b Calthorpe | 23 |
| H. Sutcliffe c Smart b Howell | 8 | – c Smith b Calthorpe | 1 |
| E. Oldroyd c Smith b Howell | 44 | – c White b Calthorpe | 26 |
| E. Robinson c Partridge b Howell | 4 | – b Howell | 2 |
| W. Rhodes c Smart b Howell | 12 | – lbw b Howell | 0 |
| R. Kilner b Howell | 6 | – c Wyatt b Calthorpe | 60 |
| M. Leyland lbw b Howell | 3 | – not out | 34 |
| Mr G. Wilson c Smith b Howell | 14 | – not out | 4 |
| G. G. Macaulay b Howell | 0 | | |
| A. Dolphin c Smith b Howell | 6 | | |
| A. Waddington not out | 7 | | |
| B 8 | 8 | B 10, l-b 2 | 12 |
| | 113 | (6 wkts dec.) | 162 |

## Warwickshire

| | | | | | |
|---|---|---|---|---|---|
| L. A. Bates c Robinson b Macaulay | 20 | – c Robinson b Macaulay | 9 |
| E. J. Smith c Kilner b Robinson | 14 | – c Waddington b Robinson | 1 |
| Hon. F. S. G. Calthorpe b Kilner | 9 | – c Rhodes b Macaulay | 7 |
| W. G. Quaife c Kilner b Macaulay | 18 | – c Wilson b Macaulay | 22 |
| Mr G. W. Stephens b Macaulay | 12 | – c Dolphin b Kilner | 5 |
| J. Smart c Robinson b Macaulay | 0 | – run out | 20 |
| F. R. Santall c Robinson b Macaulay | 0 | – lbw b Macaulay | 6 |
| Mr R. E. S. Wyatt c Rhodes b Kilner | 8 | – not out | 5 |
| Mr N. E. Partridge c Wilson b Rodes | 17 | – c Dolphin b Robinson | 3 |
| H. A. White not out | 2 | – st Dolphin b Kilner | 2 |
| H. Howell b Kilner | 4 | – c Waddington b Kilner | 0 |
| B 3, l-b 2, n-b 1 | 6 | B 1 | 1 |
| | 110 | | 81 |

### Warwickshire Bowling

| | Overs | Mdns | Runs | Wkts | Overs | Mdns | Runs | Wkts |
|---|---|---|---|---|---|---|---|---|
| Howell | 25.1 | 5 | 51 | 10 | 24 | 2 | 54 | 2 |
| Partridge | 19 | 4 | 41 | — | 13 | 3 | 44 | — |
| Calthorpe | 6 | 1 | 13 | — | 25 | 8 | 52 | 4 |

### Yorkshire Bowling

| | Overs | Mdns | Runs | Wkts | Overs | Mdns | Runs | Wkts |
|---|---|---|---|---|---|---|---|---|
| Waddington | 5 | 1 | 13 | — | | | | |
| Robinson | 7 | 2 | 12 | 1 | 9 | 2 | 21 | 2 |
| Macaulay | 22 | 7 | 42 | 5 | 17 | 1 | 51 | 4 |
| Rhodes | 4 | 1 | 7 | 1 | | | | |
| Kilner | 24 | 12 | 30 | 3 | 8 | 5 | 8 | 3 |

Umpires: T. M. Russell and W. A. Buswell.

## WARWICKSHIRE v KENT

Played at Birmingham, June 20, 22, 1925

Kent gained a remarkable victory on the second day by seven wickets. On Saturday fast bowlers met with extraordinary success. Wright, at one stage, had five wickets for nine runs and Howell and Calthorpe were so deadly that the Kent innings lasted only seventy minutes. Bright cricket by Smith, Croom and Santall then established what appeared to be a winning position for Warwickshire, but Woolley was brilliant to a degree. He drove with tremendous power, a faultless innings including seventeen 4s. Hardinge, too, gained a full mastery over the bowling, his invaluable partnership with Woolley realising 175 runs in rather less than two hours.

### Warwickshire

| | | | |
|---|---|---|---|
| E. J. Smith c Beslee b Wright | 24 | – c Collins b Woolley | 51 |
| L. A. Bates c Woolley b Wright | 0 | – c Woolley b Wright | 1 |
| J. H. Parsons c Woolley b Wright | 9 | – run out | 1 |
| W. G. Quaife hit wkt b Freeman | 7 | – b Freeman | 25 |
| Hon. F. S. G. Calthorpe c Hubble b Woolley | 69 | – c Hubble b Wright | 0 |
| Mr B. W. Quaife c Hearn b Wright | 0 | – c Hubble b Freeman | 16 |
| Mr N. E. Partridge c and b Wright | 0 | – b Wright | 6 |
| A. J. Croom c Woolley b Wright | 3 | – b Hearn | 51 |
| F. R. Santall c and b Freeman | 13 | – lbw b Cornwallis | 71 |
| Mr R. E. S. Wyatt not out | 6 | – not out | 2 |
| H. Howell c Seymour b Woolley | 0 | – c Beslee b Hearn | 0 |
| B 4, l-b 1, w 1 | 6 | B 13, l-b 7, w 1, n-b 1 | 22 |
| | **137** | | **246** |

### Kent

| | | | |
|---|---|---|---|
| H. T. W. Hardinge c Smith b Howell | 0 | – lbw b Wyatt | 114 |
| W. Ashdown c Smith b Calthorpe | 3 | – retired hurt | 1 |
| J. Seymour c Partridge b Howell | 6 | – c Calthorpe b Partridge | 20 |
| F. E. Woolley b Calthorpe | 10 | – c Smith b Calthorpe | 136 |
| G. C. Collins b Calthorpe | 2 | – not out | 33 |
| J. C. Hubble c Calthorpe b Howell | 1 | – not out | 5 |
| S. G. Hearn b Howell | 7 | | |
| C. Wright c Howell b Calthorpe | 8 | | |
| A. P. Freeman not out | 1 | | |
| Capt. W. S. Cornwallis c Parsons b Calthorpe | 3 | | |
| G. Beslee c Parsons b Calthorpe | 0 | | |
| B 1 | 1 | B 27, l-b 5, w 1, n-b 1 | 34 |
| | **42** | | **343** |

### Kent Bowling

| | Overs | Mdns | Runs | Wkts | Overs | Mdns | Runs | Wkts |
|---|---|---|---|---|---|---|---|---|
| Wright | 26 | 10 | 62 | 6 | 26 | 10 | 70 | 3 |
| Beslee | 8 | 1 | 37 | — | 3 | — | 20 | — |
| Freeman | 20 | 7 | 32 | 2 | 16 | 3 | 53 | 2 |
| Woolley | 1.4 | 1 | — | 2 | 12 | 5 | 21 | 1 |
| Ashdown | | | | | 4 | 2 | 7 | — |
| Cornwallis | | | | | 9 | 1 | 34 | 1 |
| Collins | | | | | 4 | — | 14 | — |
| Hearn | | | | | 1.4 | — | 5 | 2 |

### Warwickshire Bowling

| | Overs | Mdns | Runs | Wkts | Overs | Mdns | Runs | Wkts |
|---|---|---|---|---|---|---|---|---|
| Calthorpe | 10.2 | 3 | 17 | 6 | 16 | 2 | 41 | 1 |
| Howell | 10 | 2 | 24 | 4 | 20 | 2 | 87 | — |
| Partridge | | | | | 10 | 1 | 55 | 1 |
| Wyatt | | | | | 14 | 2 | 43 | 1 |
| Santall | | | | | 10 | — | 45 | — |
| W. G. Quaife | | | | | 11 | — | 38 | — |

Umpires: D. Denton and F. Chester.

## WARWICKSHIRE v SUSSEX

Played at Birmingham, June 27, 29, 30, 1925

By scoring 392 to win the match by nine wickets Warwickshire established a record. The three men who batted each obtained a hundred. In their different styles Smith, Parsons and Calthorpe played fine, free cricket and Warwickshire had three-quarters of an hour to spare. Smith and Parsons put up 176. The game proved a veritable triumph for batsmen. Sound cricket brought hundreds to Bowley and Holmes, making five altogether in the match, while Cox failed by five to reach three-figures after an innings of great merit.

### Sussex

| | | | |
|---|---|---|---|
| E. H. Bowley b Howell | 14 | – c Howell b Partridge | 133 |
| J. H. Parks c Smith b Partridge | 18 | – b Calthorpe | 9 |
| W. Cornford c Parsons b Partridge | 3 | | |
| T. Cook c Calthorpe b Quaife | 20 | – b Howell | 0 |
| Mr A. J. Holmes c and b Quaife | 38 | – not out | 100 |
| G. Cox c Bates b Partridge | 95 | – b Croom | 18 |
| J. Langridge c Parsons b Howell | 4 | – c Smith b Howell | 8 |
| Mr A. H. H. Gilligan b Howell | 5 | – b Quaife | 7 |
| Capt. L. C. R. Isherwood run out | 18 | – b Howell | 53 |
| A. F. Wensley not out | 7 | – not out | 17 |
| G. Stannard c Partridge b Quaife | 7 | – c Smith b Quaife | 10 |
| B 4, l-b 10 | 14 | B 9, l-b 6 | 15 |
| | **243** | **(8 wkts dec.)** | **370** |

### Warwickshire

| | | | |
|---|---|---|---|
| E. J. Smith c Cox b Parks | 3 | – not out | 139 |
| J. H. Parsons c Cornford b Wensley | 38 | – c Cook b Cox | 124 |
| A. J. Croom b Cox | 8 | | |
| W. G. Quaife c Cornford b Wensley | 18 | | |
| Mr G. W. Stephens c and b Bowley | 0 | | |
| Hon. F. S. G. Calthorpe c Cook b Bowley | 25 | – not out | 109 |
| Mr R. E. S. Wyatt c Gilligan b Langridge | 55 | | |
| F. R. Santall c Langridge b Bowley | 20 | | |
| L. A. Bates b Bowley | 16 | | |
| Mr N. E. Partridge not out | 29 | | |
| H. Howell b Wensley | 1 | | |
| B 1, l-b 8 | 9 | B 9, l-b 9, w 2 | 20 |
| | **222** | | **392** |

### Warwickshire Bowling

| | Overs | Mdns | Runs | Wkts | Overs | Mdns | Runs | Wkts |
|---|---|---|---|---|---|---|---|---|
| Calthorpe | 8 | 2 | 24 | — | 15 | 2 | 66 | 1 |
| Howell | 27 | 8 | 62 | 3 | 22 | 4 | 60 | 3 |
| Partridge | 27 | 7 | 64 | 3 | 19.2 | 3 | 67 | 1 |
| Quaife | 13.4 | 2 | 41 | 3 | 18 | 2 | 57 | 2 |
| Santall | 7 | 1 | 12 | — | 9 | — | 36 | — |
| Wyatt | 13 | 2 | 26 | — | 17 | 1 | 62 | — |
| Croom | | | | | 1 | — | 7 | 1 |

## Sussex Bowling

| | Overs | Mdns | Runs | Wkts | Overs | Mdns | Runs | Wkts |
|---|---|---|---|---|---|---|---|---|
| Wensley | 34.5 | 10 | 67 | 3 | 15 | — | 71 | — |
| Parks | 8 | 2 | 12 | 1 | 10 | 2 | 28 | — |
| Bowley | 34 | 8 | 99 | 4 | 18 | 1 | 68 | — |
| Cox | 18 | 7 | 32 | 1 | 20 | 1 | 89 | 1 |
| Gilligan | 1 | — | 3 | — | 5 | — | 19 | — |
| Langridge | 1 | 1 | — | 1 | 7 | 1 | 20 | — |
| Stannard | | | | | 13 | 1 | 49 | — |
| Cook | | | | | 5 | — | 22 | — |
| Holmes | | | | | 1 | — | 3 | — |
| Isherwood | | | | | 5 | — | 3 | — |

Umpires: B. Brown and R. D. Burrows.

# WARWICKSHIRE v KENT

## Played at Coventry, June 11, 13, 14, 1927

The great performance of Bates in playing two three-figure innings was the outstanding feature of a drawn match with Kent. When on Saturday – rain having delayed the start until three o'clock – Warwickshire were sent in and lost two wickets for 27, Bates played an uphill game with much skill and determination, and on the third day, in different circumstances, he gave a magnificent display. Sharing with Smith in a remarkable stand of 296 – the outcome of two and a half hours' attractive cricket – he hit four 6s and fourteen 4s and gave only one chance – just before he was out. Smith, on the other hand, was missed several times. In helping Kent to gain a lead of 43, Hardinge showed his best form. He timed his on side strokes perfectly during a brilliant partnership of 125 with Evans.

## Warwickshire

| | | | | |
|---|---|---|---|---|
| E. J. Smith c Ashdown b Wright | 3 | – c Wright b Woolley | 132 |
| N. Kilner c Legge b Wright | 4 | – c Wright b Ashdown | 28 |
| L. A. Bates c Ames b Capes | 116 | – c Evans b Wright | 144 |
| W. G. Quaife b Woolley | 21 | | |
| J. H. Parsons b Capes | 35 | – not out | 4 |
| A. J. Croom b Capes | 38 | | |
| F. R. Santall c Beslee b Capes | 45 | | |
| Mr R. E. S. Wyatt st Ames b Freeman | 7 | | |
| Hon. F. S. G. Calthorpe c Legge b Capes | 5 | – not out | 6 |
| Mr N. E Partridge not out | 1 | | |
| J. H. Mayer run out | 0 | | |
| B 3, l-b 6, w 1 | 10 | B 27, l-b 4 | 31 |
| | **285** | **(3 wkts dec.)** | **345** |

## Kent

| | | | | |
|---|---|---|---|---|
| H. T. W. Hardinge c Calthorpe b Wyatt | 134 | – b Mayer | 42 |
| W. Ashdown lbw b Calthorpe | 7 | – not out | 34 |
| Mr A. J. Evans b Wyatt | 68 | | |
| F. E. Woolley c Croom b Quaife | 10 | | |
| L. Ames lbw b Wyatt | 6 | | |
| Mr G. B. Legge not out | 46 | | |
| L. Todd b Partridge | 2 | | |
| Mr C. J. Capes c Croom b Wyatt | 19 | | |
| C. Wright c Calthorpe b Mayer | 9 | | |
| A. P. Freeman c Parsons b Santall | 17 | | |
| G. Beslee b Santall | 0 | | |
| B 4, l-b 5, w 1 | 10 | B 1, l-b 3 | 4 |
| | **328** | | **80** |

**Kent Bowling**

| | Overs | Mdns | Runs | Wkts | Overs | Mdns | Runs | Wkts |
|---|---|---|---|---|---|---|---|---|
| Wright ........... | 23 | 10 | 49 | 2 | 12 | 3 | 33 | 1 |
| Ashdown ......... | 18 | 3 | 57 | — | 17 | 4 | 64 | 1 |
| Beslee ............ | 3 | 1 | 8 | — | 22 | 1 | 68 | — |
| Freeman ......... | 23 | 5 | 78 | 1 | 4 | — | 37 | — |
| Woolley .......... | 7 | — | 25 | 1 | 5 | — | 14 | 1 |
| Capes ............ | 27.3 | 12 | 45 | 5 | 14 | 1 | 68 | — |
| Hardinge ........ | 7 | 3 | 13 | — | 4 | — | 30 | — |

**Warwickshire Bowling**

| | Overs | Mdns | Runs | Wkts | Overs | Mdns | Runs | Wkts |
|---|---|---|---|---|---|---|---|---|
| Calthorpe ........ | 14 | 4 | 37 | 1 | 5 | — | 18 | — |
| Partridge ........ | 14 | 1 | 54 | 1 | 5 | — | 21 | — |
| Mayer ........... | 18 | 1 | 63 | 1 | 5.4 | — | 12 | 1 |
| Santall .......... | 6.1 | 2 | 18 | 2 | | | | |
| Quaife .......... | 20 | — | 66 | 1 | | | | |
| Wyatt ........... | 25 | 6 | 80 | 4 | 6 | 2 | 25 | — |

H. Young and J. W. Day.

## WARWICKSHIRE v NOTTINGHAMSHIRE

Played at Coventry, June 23, 25, 26, 1928

Rain preventing a ball being bowled on Tuesday, brought to an end a match which during the first two days produced, for the loss of twelve wickets, 1,027 runs, and incidentally six individual innings of over a hundred. Flattered by the short boundaries and the weakness of the Warwickshire bowling, the Nottinghamshire batsmen excelled at every point, and in registering a total of 656 for three wickets, set up a new record for first-class cricket in England. Of the five men who went to the wicket Carr alone failed to reach three-figures and even he scored over fifty and hit four 6s. Gunn and Whysall, staying together for three hours, wore down the bowling during a brilliant first-wicket stand of 245. Subsequently the hitting became so fierce that in successive partnerships, Walker added 117 in seventy minutes with Gunn, 98 in fifty minutes with Carr and 196 in eighty-four minutes with Barratt. The last-named gave a remarkable display of powerful driving, his hits including no fewer than seven 6s and eighteen 4s. The innings lasting six hours and forty minutes, Nottinghamshire made their runs at roughly 100 an hour. Undaunted by the formidable nature of Warwickshire's task, Smith and Kilner at the start hit with refreshing freedom. The total had reached 200 with three men out at tea, and there remained one wicket to fall at the close. Further cricket being impossible, not even a first innings result was reached. Smith played finely and Wyatt, in the course of a skilful innings, became the first amateur to complete 1,000 runs for the season.

**Nottinghamshire**

| | | | |
|---|---|---|---|
| G. Gunn c Parsons b Sanders ...........148 | F. Barratt not out .....................139 |
| W. Whysall c and b Wyatt ..............132 | B 27, l-b 3, w 2, n-b 1 .......... 33 |
| W. Walker not out ....................146 | |
| Mr A. W. Carr c Santall b Parsons ....... 58 | (3 wkts dec.) 656 |

W. W. Keeton, B. Lilley, A. Staples, S. J. Staples, Mr G. F. H. Heane and L. Richmond did not bat.

### Warwickshire

| | | | | |
|---|---|---|---|---|
| N. Kilner c Lilley b Barratt | 23 | D. L. Clugston c and b S. J. Staples | 17 |
| E. J. Smith b Barratt | 108 | L. A. Bates b S. J. Staples | 0 |
| Hon. F. S. G. Calthorpe b Richmond | 17 | W. Sanders lbw b Richmond | 6 |
| Mr R. E. S. Wyatt not out | 134 | J. H. Mayer not out | 4 |
| J. H. Parsons lbw b Richmond | 2 | B 14, l-b 17, w 1 | 32 |
| A. J. Croom b A. Staples | 28 | | |
| F. R. Santall b A. Staples | 0 | | 371 |

### Warwickshire Bowling

| | Overs | Mdns | Runs | Wkts |
|---|---|---|---|---|
| Mayer | 20 | 3 | 68 | — |
| Calthorpe | 24 | 7 | 71 | — |
| Wyatt | 28 | 3 | 96 | 1 |
| Sanders | 21 | 2 | 81 | 1 |
| Santall | 16 | 2 | 34 | — |
| Clugston | 26 | — | 137 | — |
| Parsons | 17 | 1 | 60 | 1 |
| Croom | 9 | 1 | 76 | — |

### Nottinghamshire Bowling

| | Overs | Mdns | Runs | Wkts |
|---|---|---|---|---|
| Barratt | 26 | 8 | 69 | 2 |
| S. J. Staples | 32 | 5 | 84 | 2 |
| A. Staples | 20 | 5 | 52 | 2 |
| Richmond | 36 | 8 | 94 | 3 |
| Heane | 12 | 1 | 39 | — |
| Carr | 2 | 1 | 1 | — |

Umpires: W. Bestwick and R. D. Burrows.

## WARWICKSHIRE v DERBYSHIRE

Played at Birmingham, August 4, 6, 7, 1928

W. G. Quaife, the famous Warwickshire veteran, could not have wished for a more fitting close to his long career than in playing an innings of 115 on his last appearance for the county. Notwithstanding his 56 years and the fact that it was his first and only county match of the season, he batted with all his old-time steadiness and skill for four hours and twenty minutes, offering no chance and making his runs with nice variety of stroke. His performance coincided with Warwickshire's highest score of the summer. An innings of vastly different character was that of Parsons who attacked the bowling with great vigour. Santall, Calthorpe and Smart also forced the game with excellent results. Although compelled to follow-on 309 in arrear, Derbyshire were never in a position of much anxiety, the Warwickshire bowling, as in many other matches, lacking the strength necessary to drive home an advantage gained by good batting. Storer and Bowden shared in opening partnerships of 63 and 104 for Derbyshire, who were only 87 behind when the match was given up as a draw.

### Warwickshire

| | | | | |
|---|---|---|---|---|
| N. Kilner c Townsend b Worthington | 11 | F. R. Santall c Elliott b Slater | 49 |
| Mr R. E. S. Wyatt lbw b Lee | 47 | Hon. F. S. G. Calthorpe not out | 71 |
| L. A. Bates b Storer | 90 | J. Smart not out | 40 |
| W. G. Quaife c Townsend b Lee | 115 | B 2, l-b 6, w 1 | 9 |
| J. H. Parsons c Jackson b Storer | 114 | | |
| A. J. Croom lbw b Worthington | 18 | (7 wkts dec.) | 564 |

Mr A. W. Speed and Mr T. W. Durnell did not bat.

## Derbyshire

| | | | | |
|---|---|---|---|---|
| H. Storer lbw b Durnell | 34 | – run out | 61 |
| J. Bowden c Durnell b Quaife | 28 | – c Smart b Speed | 92 |
| G. M. Lee c Croom b Durnell | 24 | – not out | 52 |
| J. M. Hutchinson c Smart b Quaife | 29 | – c Croom b Santall | 2 |
| L. Townsend b Santall | 49 | – not out | 12 |
| S. Worthington c Calthorpe b Santall | 12 | | |
| Mr A. W. Richardson c Bates b Speed | 20 | | |
| A. G. Slater c Wyatt b Durnell | 21 | | |
| Mr G. R. Jackson b Durnell | 26 | | |
| H. Elliott b Durnell | 2 | | |
| T. B. Mitchell not out | 2 | | |
| L-b 6, w 1, n-b 1 | 8 | B 1, l-b 1, w 1 | 3 |
| | **255** | | **222** |

## Derbyshire Bowling

| | Overs | Mdns | Runs | Wkts |
|---|---|---|---|---|
| Worthington | 36 | 8 | 85 | 2 |
| Slater | 22 | 4 | 53 | 1 |
| Townsend | 40 | 9 | 78 | — |
| Lee | 41 | 5 | 156 | 2 |
| Mitchell | 25 | 3 | 87 | — |
| Storer | 32 | 6 | 83 | 2 |
| Hutchinson | 3 | — | 13 | — |

## Warwickshire Bowling

| | Overs | Mdns | Runs | Wkts | Overs | Mdns | Runs | Wkts |
|---|---|---|---|---|---|---|---|---|
| Durnell | 31.2 | 6 | 63 | 5 | 12 | 2 | 29 | — |
| Calthorpe | 4 | 1 | 9 | — | 7 | 2 | 18 | — |
| Wyatt | 9 | 3 | 26 | — | 6 | 3 | 8 | — |
| Speed | 20 | 5 | 58 | 1 | 13 | 2 | 47 | 1 |
| Quaife | 34 | 9 | 56 | 2 | 6 | — | 22 | — |
| Santall | 14 | 7 | 21 | 2 | 15 | 3 | 50 | 1 |
| Croom | 2 | — | 14 | — | 7 | 1 | 25 | — |
| Parsons | | | | | 9 | 1 | 20 | — |

Umpires: J. Stone and A. E. Street.

## WARWICKSHIRE v SURREY

### Played at Birmingham, August 8, 9, 10, 1928

Pace off the pitch, combined with accurate length, made Mayer's fast bowling very deadly on the first morning and from the loss of Hobbs, Ducat and Sandham for 30 runs Surrey did not recover until their second innings, when Hobbs, batting with characteristic skill and much care for nearly six hours, made the game safe. Mayer's eight wickets for 62 was the best performance of his career. Warwickshire followed up his excellent work by uniformly good batting, amid which Wyatt and Bates scored freely in a partnership which produced 145. In knocking off Surrey's arrears of 112, Hobbs received great assistance in stands of 68 and 136 respectively from Sandham and Ducat, both of whom batted with commendable steadiness.

## Surrey

| | | | |
|---|---|---|---|
| J. B. Hobbs lbw b Mayer | 2 | – not out | 200 |
| A. Sandham b Mayer | 18 | – b Santall | 23 |
| A. Ducat b Mayer | 2 | – b Mayer | 71 |
| T. Shepherd c Smith b Mayer | 60 | – c Parsons b Mayer | 25 |
| T. H. Barling b Mayer | 31 | – c Croom b Santall | 24 |
| H. A. Peach c Wyatt b Mayer | 28 | – b Fiddian-Green | 4 |
| Mr P. G. H. Fender b Mayer | 11 | – c Fiddian-Green b Croom | 24 |
| R. J. Gregory lbw b Foster | 42 | – not out | 1 |
| Mr H. M. Garland-Wells b Santall | 19 | | |
| E. W. Brooks not out | 11 | | |
| A. R. Gover lbw b Mayer | 0 | | |
| B 7, l-b 7, w 1 | 15 | B 12, l-b 8, n-b 1 | 21 |
| | **239** | **(6 wkts dec.)** | **393** |

## Warwickshire

| | | | |
|---|---|---|---|
| N. Kilner lbw b Shepherd | 23 | – c Brooks b Gover | 2 |
| Mr C. A. Fiddian-Green c Brooks b Shepherd | 15 | – not out | 41 |
| L. A. Bates c Fender b Garland-Wells | 73 | – not out | 22 |
| Mr R. E. S. Wyatt c Ducat b Gover | 74 | | |
| J. H. Parsons c Brooks b Gover | 18 | | |
| A. J. Croom not out | 60 | | |
| E. J. Smith c Fender b Gover | 21 | | |
| F. R. Santall c Garland-Wells b Peach | 17 | | |
| Mr G. D. Foster c Garland-Wells b Fender | 2 | | |
| J. H. Mayer c Garland-Wells b Gregory | 36 | | |
| Mr T. W. Durnell absent hurt | 0 | | |
| B 4, l-b 2, w 1, n-b 5 | 12 | B 4, l-b 3, n-b 3 | 10 |
| | **351** | | **75** |

### Warwickshire Bowling

| | Overs | Mdns | Runs | Wkts | Overs | Mdns | Runs | Wkts |
|---|---|---|---|---|---|---|---|---|
| Durnell | 15 | 1 | 47 | — | | | | |
| Mayer | 21.2 | 5 | 62 | 8 | 34 | 6 | 85 | 2 |
| Santall | 13 | 2 | 54 | 1 | 27 | 2 | 85 | 2 |
| Croom | 10 | — | 39 | — | 16 | 3 | 57 | 1 |
| Foster | 10 | 2 | 22 | 1 | 31.1 | 9 | 83 | — |
| Fiddian-Green | | | | | 17 | 3 | 62 | 1 |

### Surrey Bowling

| | Overs | Mdns | Runs | Wkts | Overs | Mdns | Runs | Wkts |
|---|---|---|---|---|---|---|---|---|
| Fender | 32 | 6 | 86 | 1 | 5 | — | 14 | — |
| Peach | 29 | 9 | 67 | 1 | | | | |
| Gover | 28 | 4 | 71 | 3 | 8 | 3 | 12 | 1 |
| Garland-Wells | 24 | 6 | 50 | 1 | 6 | 2 | 19 | — |
| Shepherd | 26 | 7 | 65 | 2 | 4 | 1 | 10 | — |
| Gregory | 0.2 | — | — | 1 | 7 | 2 | 10 | — |

Umpires: J. W. Day and W. Cuttell.

## WARWICKSHIRE v MIDDLESEX

Played at Birmingham, July 1, 2, 3, 1931

If there never existed much likelihood of this match being brought to a definite issue, Hendren rendered the contest memorable by making, for the first time in a championship game, two separate hundreds. His performance on Wednesday was particularly meritorious as Middlesex began by losing three wickets for eleven runs. He and Lee put on 201 in less than three hours. Hendren gave no chance until 151. Last man out he batted for four hours and forty minutes. Warwickshire had lost three wickets for 88 when Parsons, before he scored, offered a return to Peebles. After this escape Parsons settled down and batted admirably. Middlesex in their second innings had two men out for 94 when Hendren joined Stevens, these two adding 218 runs and being still together when Haig declared, Hendren raised his score from 21 to 100 in an hour.

## Middlesex

| | | | |
|---|---|---|---|
| Mr G. T. S. Stevens c Croom b Partridge | 6 | – not out | 170 |
| J. W. Hearne lbw b Wyatt | 2 | – c Partridge b Paine | 38 |
| Mr N. Haig lbw b Wyatt | 2 | – b Partridge | 1 |
| E. Hendren c Sanders b Paine | 189 | – not out | 100 |
| H. W. Lee c Kilner b Partridge | 94 | | |
| Mr D. F. Surfleet c Partridge b Wyatt | 5 | | |
| J. Hulme c Kent b Wyatt | 0 | | |
| A. Howard lbw b Partridge | 20 | | |
| T. J. Durston b Partridge | 11 | | |
| W. F. Price b Partridge | 0 | | |
| Mr I. A. R. Peebles not out | 0 | | |
| B 1 | 1 | B 1, l-b 1, w 1 | 3 |
| | **330** | **(2 wkts dec.)** | **312** |

## Warwickshire

| | | | |
|---|---|---|---|
| A. J. Croom b Hearne | 46 | – lbw b Hulme | 89 |
| N. Kilner c Hendren b Durston | 29 | – lbw b Durston | 46 |
| L. A. Bates run out | 0 | – c Price b Haig | 27 |
| Mr R. E. S. Wyatt c Price b Durston | 21 | – c Peebles b Hulme | 13 |
| Rev. J. H. Parsons not out | 83 | – not out | 14 |
| F. R. Santall c Durston b Peebles | 15 | – not out | 17 |
| Mr N. E. Partridge c Surfleet b Peebles | 15 | | |
| J. Smart b Stevens | 12 | | |
| W. Sanders b Stevens | 0 | | |
| G. Paine c Price b Hearne | 6 | | |
| Mr K. G. Kent b Durston | 0 | | |
| B 2, l-b 12 | 14 | B 11, l-b 1 | 12 |
| | **241** | | **218** |

### Warwickshire Bowling

| | Overs | Mdns | Runs | Wkts | Overs | Mdns | Runs | Wkts |
|---|---|---|---|---|---|---|---|---|
| Partridge | 33 | 3 | 92 | 5 | 24 | 1 | 85 | 1 |
| Wyatt | 23 | 9 | 45 | 4 | 14 | 2 | 69 | — |
| Sanders | 22 | 4 | 54 | — | 8 | — | 32 | — |
| Kent | 12 | — | 56 | — | 7 | — | 37 | — |
| Paine | 21.2 | 3 | 64 | 1 | 24.4 | 2 | 86 | 1 |
| Santall | 5 | — | 18 | — | | | | |

### Middlesex Bowling

| | Overs | Mdns | Runs | Wkts | Overs | Mdns | Runs | Wkts |
|---|---|---|---|---|---|---|---|---|
| Haig | 20 | 5 | 47 | — | 18 | 8 | 33 | 1 |
| Durston | 14.3 | 4 | 30 | 3 | 16 | 4 | 30 | 1 |
| Peebles | 24 | 3 | 70 | 2 | 17 | 1 | 61 | — |
| Stevens | 10 | 2 | 37 | 2 | | | | |
| Hearne | 12 | 2 | 29 | 2 | 15 | 1 | 43 | — |
| Hulme | 3 | — | 14 | — | 13 | 5 | 17 | 2 |
| Lee | | | | | 15 | 8 | 22 | — |

Umpires: A. Dolphin and A. E. Street.

# WARWICKSHIRE v NOTTINGHAMSHIRE

Played at Birmingham, July 22, 23, 24, 1931

Truly phenomenal scoring characterised this match which saw Nottinghamshire – after Warwickshire had declared at 511 for three wickets – head that huge total for the loss of seven batsmen. The aggregate for the three days was 1,032 and, as no more than ten wickets went down, the average per wicket reached more than a hundred runs. Formidable as it was the Warwickshire run-getting scarcely furnished matter for great surprise, seeing that Nottinghamshire had to take the field without Larwood, Voce or Sam Staples. Against an attack thus weakened Kemp-Welch and Croom opened Warwickshire's innings with a stand which, lasting nearly two hours and a half, realised 158 runs. Croom and Bates followed with a partnership of 174 and, after the fall of the third wicket, Parsons and Kilner hit up 164 in rather less than two hours. Croom's 159 was his third consecutive hundred and his sixth of the season. While he shaped finely, he gave three chances. Bates reached three figures for the first time during the season. George Gunn and Keeton opened the Nottinghamshire innings with extreme caution, taking over three hours to bring the score to 123. Altogether George Gunn batted for seven hours and ten minutes. Sixth out with the total at 367, he was missed two or three times but he certainly gave a remarkable display for a man in his 53rd year. Another very interesting feature of the game was the success of G. V. Gunn, the son of George Gunn, who seized the occasion to put together his first hundred in first-class cricket and after the fall of the seventh wicket at 383, added, in company with Harris, 138 inside two hours.

### Warwickshire

| | |
|---|---|
| Mr G. D. Kemp-Welch c and b Harris .... 60 | N. Kilner not out ..................... 81 |
| A. J. Croom c Staples b Oates ..........159 | B 10, l-b 9, w 1, n-b 2 .......... 22 |
| L. A. Bates c Lilley b Oates .............105 | |
| Rev. J. H. Parsons not out .............. 84 | (3 wkts dec.) 511 |

Mr R. E. S. Wyatt, F. R. Santall, J. Smart, W. Sanders, J. H. Mayer and G. Paine did not bat.

### Nottinghamshire

| | |
|---|---|
| G. Gunn c Paine b Santall .............183 | B. Lilley b Paine ..................... 30 |
| W. W. Keeton c Sanders b Paine ......... 72 | G. V. Gunn not out ...................100 |
| W. Walker b Mayer ................... 29 | C. B. Harris not out ................... 41 |
| Mr A. W. Carr c Parsons b Sanders ...... 38 | B 10, l-b 3, w 1 .............. 14 |
| W. Payton lbw b Wyatt ................ 6 | |
| A. Staples c Mayer b Wyatt ............. 8 | 521 |

T. A. W. Oates and F. Barratt did not bat.

### Nottinghamshire Bowling

| | Overs | Mdns | Runs | Wkts |
|---|---|---|---|---|
| Barratt .......... | 35 | 6 | 76 | — |
| Carr ............. | 16 | 2 | 71 | — |
| Harris .......... | 33 | 5 | 99 | 1 |
| G. V. Gunn ....... | 34 | 4 | 115 | — |
| G. Gunn .......... | 8 | 1 | 39 | — |
| Oates ........... | 28 | 3 | 89 | 2 |

**Warwickshire Bowling**

| | Overs | Mdns | Runs | Wkts |
|---|---|---|---|---|
| Mayer ........... | 46 | 18 | 106 | 1 |
| Wyatt ........... | 51 | 12 | 134 | 2 |
| Paine ........... | 74 | 24 | 125 | 2 |
| Sanders ......... | 34 | 11 | 62 | 1 |
| Santall .......... | 24 | 4 | 72 | 1 |
| Parsons ......... | 4 | 2 | 5 | — |
| Bates ........... | 1 | — | 3 | — |

Umpires: L. C. Braund and A. Skelding.

## WARWICKSHIRE v YORKSHIRE

### Played at Birmingham, May 23, 24, 25, 1934

Rain and tedious batting by the Yorkshiremen prevented even a first-innings decision, each side taking four points. Barber and Mitchell putting on 95 for the second wicket, Yorkshire scored 135 for two while play was possible on Wednesday and next day batted most of the time, the innings lasting altogether six and a half hours. Hutton, of Pudsey, making his first appearance in county cricket, showed sound form, and Turner helped him add 85 for the fifth wicket, but, apart from Leyland who hit well during a stay of ninety minutes, the Champions displayed little enterprise. Hutton obtained two valuable wickets while Warwickshire scored 47, but on the last day a stubborn innings by Hill baulked Yorkshire, Warwickshire, despite the claiming of extra time by their opponents, holding out. Hill outplayed Yorkshire at their own game, staying three and a quarter hours for 70. He scored a single in his second over, then went forty minutes before getting another run. Still, he never failed to punish anything loose, and once hit Leyland for three 4s in an over. With Kilner hurt, and N. E. Partridge and D. G. Foster unavailable, Warwickshire brought in F. A. Gross, who, appearing for Warwickshire for the first time, formerly assisted Hampshire.

### Yorkshire

| | |
|---|---|
| H. Sutcliffe b Mayer .................. 25 | A. Wood lbw b Paine ................. 0 |
| A. Mitchell c Smart b Santall ........... 48 | H. Verity c Collin b Paine ........... 19 |
| W. Barber c Mayer b Paine ............. 67 | T. F. Smailes b Mayer ............... 14 |
| M. Leyland c Collin b Wyatt ........... 75 | W. E. Bowes not out ................. 0 |
| L. Hutton c and b Gross .............. 50 | L-b 16 .................... 16 |
| C. Turner st Smart b Paine ............. 53 | |
| Mr A. B. Sellers c Croom b Paine ........ 3 | 370 |

### Warwickshire

| | |
|---|---|
| A. J. Croom c and b Hutton ........... 16 | T. Collin not out ..................... 49 |
| W. A. Hill st Wood b Hutton ........... 70 | Mr F. A. Gross not out .............. 0 |
| L. A. Bates c and b Hutton ............ 1 | B 6, l-b 9, n-b 1 ............... 16 |
| Mr R. E. S. Wyatt c Bowes b Verity ...... 21 | |
| F. R. Santall c Hutton b Turner ......... 32 | 205 |

G. E. Paine, J. Smart, J. H. Mayer and E. Brown did not bat.

**Warwickshire Bowling**

|  | Overs | Mdns | Runs | Wkts |
|---|---|---|---|---|
| Mayer ........... | 37 | 9 | 90 | 2 |
| Brown ........... | 13 | — | 51 | — |
| Wyatt............ | 11 | 2 | 35 | 1 |
| Paine ............ | 46.5 | 20 | 67 | 5 |
| Gross ............ | 25 | 4 | 76 | 1 |
| Collin ............ | 2 | 1 | 8 | — |
| Santall .......... | 8 | 2 | 27 | 1 |

**Yorkshire Bowling**

|  | Overs | Mdns | Runs | Wkts |
|---|---|---|---|---|
| Bowes ........... | 25 | 9 | 47 | — |
| Smailes .......... | 10 | 7 | 6 | — |
| Turner ........... | 6 | 3 | 3 | 1 |
| Hutton ........... | 15 | 2 | 65 | 3 |
| Verity ........... | 19 | 12 | 15 | 1 |
| Leyland .......... | 18 | 5 | 53 | — |

Umpires: W. Bestwick and G. Beet.

# TRIALS OF A COUNTY SECRETARY [1935]

## FORTY YEARS OF CRICKET MANAGEMENT

### By R. V. Ryder (Secretary, Warwickshire County Cricket Club)

I am attempting, at the request of the Editor, to give the reader an insight into county cricket organisation from the management point of view together with impressions of change during the past 40 years, the period I have acted as Secretary to Warwickshire.

Unhurried leisure was the keynote of the game, and, for most of the time, of its organisation in my early days. Cricket had fewer rivals; there were plenty of interested people to enjoy this popular pastime. A county secretary, with the programme comprising no more than 18 to 20 first-class matches, really had time to take a deep breath in between games and devote a little quiet thought to his many problems.

Fixture-making, for one thing, was an unhurried business, commencing in September, through the agency of the penny post, and culminating in a visit to Lord's in December where the silk hat and frock coat were *de rigueur*. Most matches started on Monday, and I may say many of my Sundays were far from days of rest.

One of the outstanding changes in cricket organisation during my time was the decision to begin matches on Saturday, and in this connection it is interesting to me to recall that I drafted the motion which was first submitted to the Advisory County Cricket Committee on January 13, 1913. Seven years later, Saturday starts were introduced to the great advantage of first-class cricket.

In the days when Monday starts were the rule our ground-staff was smaller, so we frequently had to scout round for the occasional player engaged perhaps with a local club, and persuasion was often needed to get a business man or a schoolmaster to fill a gap. The need of persuasion many times found me spending Sunday in a hansom cab trying first this man and then another. The telephone had no place then in team collection. I imagine my Committee regarded it as a luxury!

We even worked a Test match — and our first too — without the help of this sometimes blessed invention. And thereby hangs a story which will tell eloquently of the trials which beset a county secretary.

## TEST MATCH PLAYED ON "A SWAMP"

It was in 1902 that a Test match – England v Australia – was allocated to Birmingham for the first time. This meant fitting up the ground to accommodate more people than had ever before patronised a cricket match at Edgbaston. It meant many other things and I was to find out that they mainly concerned the club secretary. Quickly we got to work – many months in advance of the date. New stands were erected, and thousands of seats carted to the ground. Committees of all kinds were hard at work for months. There were, indeed, 36 meetings of the General Committee that year!

It was an anxious time as the day drew near. Had we thought of everything? (Events were to prove we hadn't.) Details had been carefully thought out. Sixty gatemen were required. Sixty police were ordered for duty. There were 90 pressmen to accommodate. The catering staff approached 200. As I recall the occasion it astonishes me to realise that my clerical staff then consisted of myself only, and that besides the non-possession of a telephone a typewriter was something else we did not have. But to continue.

It was our custom at the time to await payment of membership subscription before issuing the member's card. The Test match started on May 29. You can perhaps imagine what happened. Crowds of members delayed payment until they arrived at the match on the first day. At the end of the day I solicited the help of a friend, and eight hours after stumps were drawn I balanced up and as I crawled home between 2 and 3 am thanked my lucky stars I lived near the ground.

But worse was to come. The last day of the match was Saturday, May 31st. Torrents of rain fell overnight, and at 9 am the ground was a complete lake. Not a square yard of turf was visible and play was, of course, out of the question that day. The head groundman agreed; I paid off half my gatemen and dispensed with the services of half the police. It proved a "penny wise, pound foolish" action. The umpires arrived; the players arrived – the captains were there. I have never known any men more patient, more hopeful than those umpires and captains. They just sat still and said nothing most effectively. At two o'clock the sun came out and a great crowd assembled outside the ground. What I hadn't thought of was that two umpires and two captains would sit and wait so long without making a decision. The crowd broke in, and to save our skins we started play at 5.20 on a swamp. The main result of our promotion to Test match rank was that at the end of the season we had to appeal to the public for £3,000 to repair our finances!

## THE DAYS OF THE HORSE

And apropos of the changes cricket has undergone in the past forty years let us turn to the following account of the scene outside the ground during that memorable Test.

"At the corner of the road it was amusing to come across an imposing but obviously excited coachman (with a pair of restive horses) trying to ascertain from a humble pedestrian the whereabouts of the county cricket ground, the while a lady, cool, composed and statuesque reclined in a tandem. Every minute a hansom dashed up, carriages and pairs were as common as blackberries in autumn, and bicycles crept in and out everywhere."

Yes, I remember it all very well. Not a single motor vehicle reached the scene of *that* cricket encounter. Horse transport was the thing in those days. What quaint reading is afforded now by the perusal of this extract from the Warwickshire Committee Minutes of April 26, 1897: "A member wrote suggesting that accommodation should be provided for horses as many members had to travel long distances."

## WARWICKSHIRE LOST WILFRED RHODES

And while my thoughts are on those old minutes let me quote another recorded in 1897, one which will probably bring a sigh of regret as well as a smile to Warwickshire members whose eyes may fall upon it. This entry, dated October 4, reads: "It was decided that on account of the heavy expenses already incurred in connection with next year's ground staff an engagement could not be offered W. Rhodes of Huddersfield." If we had only known!

When I took up my work in Warwickshire forty years ago, the team under the captaincy of Mr H. W. Bainbridge had just won promotion to first-class rank. It was well equipped for the struggle on which it was entering and was a force with which to be reckoned for ten or twelve years until the temporary deterioration in 1909 and 1910 which was blotted from the memory by winning the Championship in 1911.

From the start budget balancing was a difficult business. At first I don't think I fully realised my responsibilities. In this connection there was a Finance Committee! Little did I know then how much of my life was to be spent in staring at figures, and adding them up again. However, if the reader will pardon the digression, I frequently found time for a knock at the nets and I played a great deal of club and ground cricket. Once or twice I was included in the county side – in matches outside the championship competition.

## CRICKET FINANCE

Cricket finance to some of us, has always been "a thing of shreds and patches", varying a little perhaps in texture and colouring but failing generally to provide that protection and comfort which is the lot of the well-breeched. We shiver at the thought of rain – especially at Whitsuntide and on August Bank holiday. A wet holiday week may make the difference between making ends meet or heavily increasing a bank overdraft. There are one or two counties which never have to meet trouble of this kind; playing success has earned them this exemption from anxiety. The problems of the counties differ. There are clubs which have several good grounds within their boundaries. Matches can therefore be allocated to towns wide apart. The county exchequer is not dependent on one public. The fact that Birmingham has never quite risen to the needs of Warwickshire cricket remains something of a mystery.

For one thing we are awkwardly situated geographically. Birmingham's giant strides have taken her into three counties. A condition of my appointment was that I "must live near the ground", with the result that for most of the time I have lived in Worcestershire! From Warwickshire's point of view, with so many Birmingham people living in Worcestershire and Staffordshire, the position as it bears on county qualification is a nightmare. The value of Lancashire's membership has risen as high as £10,000 in a season. We in Warwickshire have never exceeded £4,500 and a very large proportion of that comes, of course, from the Birmingham area. The smaller Warwickshire towns contribute very little. Coventry, thriving and pulsating with energy, produces crowds of active cricketers but not a single ground equipped to accommodate a county match. Many Warwickshire matches have been played in Coventry during the past 25 years but the cost of providing temporary equipment is a very heavy extra charge and this has led to a suspension of the fixtures in that city.

In 1906 cricket interest fell away in Warwickshire. There was a heavy slump in membership. It was clear something must be done to repair the damage, so I spent the winter months in a personal canvass of the city and suburbs and secured 600 new members.

## PLAYERS AND PITCHES

Two hundred players have represented Warwickshire in first-class cricket during the past forty years. Thousands have been tried out at the nets and in club and ground matches. Many indeed have been called but few chosen. We could have done with Wilfrid Rhodes.

When I came to Edgbaston in 1895 the wicket was a marl prepared pitch. W. G. Grace and A. C. MacLaren were at the top of the batting averages, 51 each. Not all county grounds were "doped" with marl. The only two Yorkshiremen who scored a thousand runs that season – Tunnicliffe and Brown – averaged 27 and 26 respectively. By 1904

C. B. Fry's average was 79 and there were quite a number of 60s. In 1932 Sutcliffe and Leyland headed the Yorkshire list with 87 and 60. Marl had found its way into Yorkshire.

So the procession of happy successful batsmen continued. Well, at last something has been done through the new lbw experiment to make the conditions of the cricket fight more equal, and we may surely look forward to a further growth in cricket interest.

## WARWICKSHIRE v LANCASHIRE

### At Birmingham, August 13, 15, 16, 1938

Lancashire won by seven wickets. They owed a great deal to Paynter, who for the first time in his career, scored a hundred in each innings. Apart from Wyatt, the Warwickshire batsmen could do little against Wilkinson's leg-breaks. Lancashire also were forced to struggle, but Paynter, batting more cautiously than usual, held out for four hours and scored more than half his side's total. Warwickshire, 25 behind, again failed against spin bowling, but set their opponents to get 205. Then Paynter gave another fine display and he was the one outstanding batsman in the match. During seven hours twenty minutes' almost faultless cricket, he scored 238 for once out. Smart fielding closed his first innings.

### Warwickshire

| | | | |
|---|---|---|---|
| A. J. Croom c Farrimond b Iddon | 18 | – c Oldfield b Phillipson | 0 |
| F. R. Santall c Wilkinson b Nutter | 20 | – b Nutter | 35 |
| J. Buckingham b Wilkinson | 38 | – c Pollard b Wilkinson | 28 |
| Mr R. E. S. Wyatt not out | 81 | – c Farrimond b Wilkinson | 3 |
| H. E. Dollery c Nutter b Iddon | 11 | – lbw b Wilkinson | 10 |
| J. S. Ord hit wkt b Wilkinson | 7 | – lbw b Wilkinson | 22 |
| Mr P. Cranmer lbw b Wilkinson | 2 | – c Farrimond b Wilkinson | 38 |
| W. E. Fantham run out | 0 | – not out | 27 |
| G. E. Paine lbw b Pollard | 5 | – st Farrimond b Nutter | 21 |
| K. Wilmot lbw b Wilkinson | 1 | – c Farrimond b Phillipson | 21 |
| J. H. Mayer b Wilkinson | 1 | – c Farrimond b Pollard | 3 |
| B 6, l-b 10, n-b 1 | 17 | B 11, l-b 9, n-b 1 | 21 |
| | **201** | | **229** |

### Lancashire

| | | | |
|---|---|---|---|
| E. Paynter run out | 125 | – not out | 113 |
| C. Washbrook c Mayer b Fantham | 24 | – c Wilmot b Mayer | 7 |
| J. Iddon c Mayer b Fantham | 9 | – c Croom b Fantham | 11 |
| N. Oldfield b Mayer | 9 | – lbw b Paine | 22 |
| J. L. Hopwood c Dollery b Mayer | 5 | – not out | 29 |
| A. Nutter b Fantham | 20 | | |
| W. E. Phillipson b Wilmot | 17 | | |
| Mr W. H. L. Lister b Mayer | 11 | | |
| W. Farrimond c Santall b Mayer | 0 | | |
| R. Pollard not out | 0 | | |
| L. L. Wilkinson c Buckingham b Wilmot | 0 | | |
| B 4, l-b 2 | 6 | B 21, l-b 4 | 25 |
| | **226** | | **207** |

### Lancashire Bowling

| | Overs | Mdns | Runs | Wkts | Overs | Mdns | Runs | Wkts |
|---|---|---|---|---|---|---|---|---|
| Phillipson | 19 | 10 | 18 | — | 10 | 1 | 40 | 2 |
| Pollard | 23 | 4 | 37 | 1 | 20.4 | 4 | 59 | 1 |
| Nutter | 11 | 2 | 21 | 1 | 12 | 1 | 39 | 2 |
| Iddon | 22 | 6 | 50 | 2 | | | | |
| Wilkinson | 33 | 10 | 58 | 5 | 28 | 6 | 70 | 5 |

## Warwickshire Bowling

|          | Overs | Mdns | Runs | Wkts | Overs | Mdns | Runs | Wkts |
|----------|-------|------|------|------|-------|------|------|------|
| Mayer .......... | 25 | 8 | 43 | 4 | 12 | 2 | 31 | 1 |
| Wilmot .......... | 19.1 | 1 | 57 | 2 | 9 | 1 | 24 | — |
| Paine ............ | 25 | 7 | 55 | — | 19 | 5 | 31 | 1 |
| Croom .......... | 6 | — | 21 | — | 13 | 3 | 35 | — |
| Fantham ......... | 14 | 3 | 44 | 3 | 15.2 | 2 | 50 | 1 |
| Cranmer ........ | | | | | 3 | — | 11 | — |

Umpires: J. Hardstaff and E. Cooke.

# WARWICKSHIRE v SURREY

### At Birmingham, August 19, 21, 22, 1939

Surrey won by an innings and one run. Consistent batting enabled Surrey to build up a score which just sufficed for victory. Fishlock mixed perfect defence with powerful strokes. Brown followed some hard hitting by clever bowling on the second day when rain caused delay, after which seven wickets went down for 71. Watts finished the day by dismissing three men and he went on to take all ten wickets in an innings for the first time. Not since 1921 had a Surrey man accomplished this feat. Watts made the ball swing in heavy atmosphere. So deadly was he at one time that he dismissed six men for four runs. In neither Warwickshire innings was a batsman clean bowled; Shortland played on.

## Surrey

| | |
|---|---|
| R. J. Gregory c Croom b Wyatt ......... 30 | Mr P. J. Dickinson c Croom b Hollies ..... 2 |
| L. B. Fishlock c Buckingham b Croom .... 91 | E. A. Watts st Buckingham b Croom ..... 21 |
| E. W. Whitfield c Wyatt b Hollies ........ 7 | A. R. Gover b Croom ................. 0 |
| H. S. Squires lbw b Hollies .............. 29 | |
| J. F. Parker b Hollies ................... 28 | |
| Mr F. R. Brown lbw b Mayer ........... 46 | |
| G. S. Mobey not out ................... 55 | B 3, l-b 7 .................... 10 |
| Mr H. M. Garland-Wells | |
| c Cranmer b Wyatt . 17 | 336 |

## Warwickshire

| | | |
|---|---|---|
| A. J. Croom c Fishlock b Gover ................. 13 | – c Gregory b Watts ............... 12 |
| W. A. Hill c Gregory b Gover ................... 10 | – c Gregory b Watts ............... 31 |
| F. R. Santall c Gover b Brown ................... 13 | – c Squires b Watts ............... 2 |
| Mr R. E. S. Wyatt c Gregory b Brown ........... 12 | – c Mobey b Watts ............... 59 |
| H. E. Dollery c Garland-Wells b Parker .......... 25 | – c Garland-Wells b Watts ......... 41 |
| Mr P. Cranmer c Garland-Wells b Brown ......... 3 | – c Dickinson b Watts ............ 3 |
| N. A. Shortland b Brown ...................... 4 | – c Fishlock b Watts .............. 3 |
| J. Buckingham c Mobey b Parker ............... 5 | – lbw b Watts ................... 22 |
| E. Hollies c Parker b Brown ................... 3 | – c Mobey b Watts ............... 1 |
| J. H. Mayer c Gover b Brown .................. 7 | – lbw b Watts ................... 13 |
| C. Grove not out .......................... 11 | – not out ....................... 13 |
| B 5, n-b 4 ......................... 9 | B 12, l-b 3, w 2, n-b 3 ...... 20 |
| 115 | 220 |

## Warwickshire Bowling

|        | Overs | Mdns | Runs | Wkts |
|--------|-------|------|------|------|
| Mayer  | 16    | 2    | 65   | 1    |
| Grove  | 16    | —    | 65   | —    |
| Wyatt  | 20    | 7    | 49   | 2    |
| Hollies| 32    | 2    | 118  | 4    |
| Santall| 4     | —    | 7    | —    |
| Croom  | 3.4   | —    | 22   | 3    |

## Surrey Bowling

|         | Overs | Mdns | Runs | Wkts | Overs | Mdns | Runs | Wkts |
|---------|-------|------|------|------|-------|------|------|------|
| Gover   | 11    | —    | 32   | 2    | 12    | —    | 36   | —    |
| Watts   | 4     | —    | 15   | —    | 24.1  | 8    | 67   | 10   |
| Brown   | 13.6  | 1    | 46   | 6    | 17    | 2    | 78   | —    |
| Parker  | 7     | 2    | 13   | 2    | 5     | 2    | 7    | —    |
| Squires |       |      |      |      | 4     | 1    | 12   | —    |

Umpires: J. Hardstaff and C. W. L. Parker.

# WORCESTERSHIRE

## WORCESTERSHIRE v SOMERSET

### Played at Worcester, June 18, 20, 21, 1920

After a first-rate game Somerset beat Worcestershire by 83 runs, play going on till a quarter to seven on the third day. J. C. White had a great triumph, taking all ten wickets in Worcestershire's first innings. When Somerset went in for the second time Johnson and Daniell took the score to 154, and Johnson played brilliantly till the end of the afternoon. Left to get 365 in less than four hours and three-quarters, Worcestershire had 210 on the board with three men out, but after that the batting failed.

### Somerset

| | | |
|---|---|---|
| M. P. R. Johnson c Ponsonby b Richardson | 4 | – b Tarbox ......... 163 |
| Mr J. Daniell c Ponsonby b Humpherson | 24 | – lbw b Richardson ......... 38 |
| Mr F. E. Spurway c Higgins b Richardson | 0 | – c Turner b Tarbox ......... 31 |
| Mr T. C. Lowry b Humpherson | 22 | – b Richardson ......... 18 |
| Mr L. E. Wharton lbw b Gilbert | 38 | – c Ponsonby b Tarbox ......... 36 |
| E. Robson c Tarbox b Pearson | 111 | – b Tarbox ......... 8 |
| Mr P. P. Hope b Gilbert | 13 | – b Tarbox ......... 8 |
| Mr J. C. White b Gilbert | 6 | – b Tarbox ......... 29 |
| Mr L. H. Key b Pearson | 5 | – c Bowley b Richardson ......... 3 |
| G. Hunt b Pearson | 3 | – b Tarbox ......... 10 |
| H. Chidgey not out | 6 | – not out ......... 0 |
| B 3, l-b 2 | 5 | B 14, l-b 3, w 1, n-b 2 ...... 20 |
| | **237** | **364** |

### Worcestershire

| | | |
|---|---|---|
| F. Bowley c Lowry b White | 1 | – b Robson ......... 99 |
| F. Pearson c and b White | 74 | – b Robson ......... 80 |
| R. E. Turner b White | 12 | – b Robson ......... 24 |
| Mr H. L. Higgins lbw b White | 16 | – b Robson ......... 3 |
| Mr M. F. S. Jewell st Chidgey b White | 66 | – lbw b White ......... 2 |
| Mr W. E. Richardson b White | 7 | – c Daniell b White ......... 0 |
| C. A. Preece c Daniell b White | 27 | – b White ......... 0 |
| C. V. Tarbox b White | 13 | – c Spurway b White ......... 17 |
| Mr C. B. Ponsonby lbw b White | 0 | – c Lowry b White ......... 15 |
| Mr V. W. Humpherson not out | 2 | – b Robson ......... 13 |
| Mr H. A. Gilbert c Hope b White | 0 | – not out ......... 0 |
| B 14, l-b 5 | 19 | B 20, l-b 7, w 1 ......... 28 |
| | **237** | **281** |

### Worcestershire Bowling

| | Overs | Mdns | Runs | Wkts | Overs | Mdns | Runs | Wkts |
|---|---|---|---|---|---|---|---|---|
| Gilbert | 32 | 6 | 99 | 3 | 28 | 2 | 100 | — |
| Richardson | 18 | 4 | 60 | 2 | 16 | 3 | 59 | 3 |
| Humpherson | 9 | 1 | 36 | 2 | 9 | 2 | 38 | — |
| Pearson | 10.4 | 3 | 32 | 3 | 12 | — | 48 | — |
| Preece | 2 | — | 5 | — | 6 | — | 36 | — |
| Jewell | | | | | 4 | — | 8 | — |
| Tarbox | | | | | 14.5 | 3 | 55 | 7 |

## Somerset Bowling

| | Overs | Mdns | Runs | Wkts | Overs | Mdns | Runs | Wkts |
|---|---|---|---|---|---|---|---|---|
| Robson ......... | 25 | 4 | 71 | — | 39.5 | 15 | 83 | 5 |
| White .......... | 42.2 | 11 | 76 | 10 | 47 | 17 | 99 | 5 |
| Hunt .......... | 18 | 4 | 55 | — | 15 | 4 | 42 | — |
| Wharton ........ | 6 | 2 | 16 | — | 9 | 1 | 29 | — |

Umpires: J. Moss and J. Carlin.

# WORCESTERSHIRE v GLOUCESTERSHIRE

### Played at Dudley, June 11, 12, 13, 1924

In a match in which for the most part the ball completely beat the bat, Gloucestershire won by 102 runs. The finish was rather startling. Left with 151 to get Worcestershire lost three wickets – all to Parker's bowling – for ten runs before the drawing of stumps on Thursday, and on the following day the game was over soon after one o'clock. The pitch was very difficult and Parker more or less unplayable. In Worcestreshire's first innings M. K. Foster saved his side from collapse in wonderful style. Going in when six wickets were down for 14 he scored 73 runs out of 93 in less than an hour and a half.

## Gloucestershire

| | | | | |
|---|---|---|---|---|
| Lieut-Col D. C. Robinson b Root ............. | 6 | – c and b Preece ............... | 6 |
| A. G. Dipper b Preece .................. | 33 | – c Preece b Root ............... | 10 |
| H. Smith c Wilson b Lang .................. | 15 | – b Pearson .................... | 8 |
| B. S. Bloodworth c Tarbox b Root ........... | 22 | – c Lang b Root ............... | 5 |
| Mr F. G. Rogers not out .................. | 50 | – b Preece ................... | 1 |
| W. R. Hammond b Preece .................. | 4 | – st Foster b Lang ............. | 25 |
| Mr B. H. Lyon c Jeavons b Root ........... | 0 | – c Jeavons b Preece ........... | 31 |
| G. Dennett b Preece .................... | 8 | – c and b Lang ............... | 16 |
| N. F. Hobbs c Foster b Root ............ | 2 | – not out .................... | 0 |
| P. Mills b Root ....................... | 0 | – b Preece ................... | 3 |
| C. Parker b Root ...................... | 4 | – hit wkt b Preece ............ | 0 |
| B 8, l-b 2 ........................ | 10 | B 6 ................ | 6 |
| | **154** | | **111** |

## Worcestershire

| | | | | |
|---|---|---|---|---|
| F. Pearson b Parker ..................... | 2 | – c Bloodworth b Parker .......... | 7 |
| C. V. Tarbox lbw b Parker .................. | 0 | – b Hammond ................ | 5 |
| J. M. Lang b Mills ..................... | 0 | – c Mills b Parker ............. | 4 |
| Mr H. L. Higgins b Mills .................. | 0 | – lbw b Parker ................ | 0 |
| Mr E. P. Jeavons b Mills .................. | 0 | – not out .................... | 1 |
| C. J. Wilson st Smith b Hammond ............... | 4 | – b Parker ................... | 5 |
| C. A. Preece b Parker ................... | 18 | – b Parker ................... | 4 |
| Mr M. K. Foster b Parker ................. | 73 | – c Smith b Hammond .......... | 20 |
| Hon. J. Coventry c Smith b Parker ........... | 2 | – b Mills .................... | 0 |
| F. Root c Hobbs b Mills ................. | 11 | – b Parker ................... | 0 |
| E. Suckling not out ..................... | 0 | – c Hobbs b Mills ............. | 0 |
| B 2, l-b 3 ........................ | 5 | L-b 2 ................. | 2 |
| | **115** | | **48** |

## Worcestershire Bowling

|  | Overs | Mdns | Runs | Wkts | Overs | Mdns | Runs | Wkts |
|---|---|---|---|---|---|---|---|---|
| Root . . . . . . . . . . . . | 26.5 | 9 | 69 | 6 | 11 | 2 | 18 | 2 |
| Pearson . . . . . . . . . | 10 | 3 | 14 | — | 9 | 2 | 20 | 1 |
| Preece . . . . . . . . . | 20 | 8 | 37 | 3 | 16.3 | 4 | 32 | 5 |
| Lang . . . . . . . . | 12 | 3 | 24 | 1 | 12 | 1 | 34 | 2 |
| Wilson . . . . . . . . . . | | | | | 1 | — | 1 | — |

## Gloucestershire Bowling

|  | Overs | Mdns | Runs | Wkts | Overs | Mdns | Runs | Wkts |
|---|---|---|---|---|---|---|---|---|
| Parker . . . . . . . . . . | 21 | 7 | 50 | 5 | 21.5 | 10 | 24 | 6 |
| Mills . . . . . . . . . . . . | 18 | 3 | 45 | 4 | 8 | 5 | 8 | 2 |
| Hammond . . . . . . . . | 6 | 1 | 7 | 1 | 13 | 7 | 14 | 2 |
| Dennett . . . . . . . . . | 3 | — | 8 | — | | | | |

Umpires: G. P. Harrison and B. Brown.

# WORCESTERSHIRE v WARWICKSHIRE

### Played at Kidderminster, June 21, 23, 1924

In some respects this was a remarkable game, Warwickshire winning in two days by six wickets, after being 63 runs behind on the first innings. In order to prevent the game running into the third day play was continued till a quarter to seven on Monday. On winning the toss Worcestershire but for an unfortunate accident would, no doubt, have made a far better score than 182. Tarbox, when nicely set, received such a severe blow on the shoulder that he could not resume batting till after the fall of the ninth wicket. Rain cut Saturday's play short, but on Monday the cricket went on without interruption and was full of incident. Root and Pearson gave their side a fine chance, but the Worcestershire batting broke down hopelessly. Thanks to the fine batting of Parsons, Warwickshire had no anxiety in the last innings.

## Worcestershire

| | | | |
|---|---|---|---|
| F. Pearson b Howell . . . . . . . . . . . . . . . . . . . . . . . . . | 34 | – c Partridge b Howell . . . . . . . . . . . . | 9 |
| C. V. Tarbox not out . . . . . . . . . . . . . . . . . . . . . . . | 26 | – c sub. b Partridge . . . . . . . . . . . . . . | 0 |
| Mr M. K. Foster b Wyatt . . . . . . . . . . . . . . . . . . . . . . | 29 | – c Smith b Howell . . . . . . . . . . . . . . | 12 |
| C. J. Wilson b Partridge . . . . . . . . . . . . . . . . . . . . . | 1 | – c Stephens b Wyatt . . . . . . . . . . . . . | 11 |
| Lord Somers b Calthorpe . . . . . . . . . . . . . . . . . . . . | 17 | – b Howell . . . . . . . . . . . . . . . . . . . | 5 |
| J. C. Smith b Howell . . . . . . . . . . . . . . . . . . . . . . | 25 | – b Howell . . . . . . . . . . . . . . . . . . . | 8 |
| F. Root b Calthorpe . . . . . . . . . . . . . . . . . . . . . . . | 0 | – c Wyatt b Howell . . . . . . . . . . . . . . | 5 |
| C. A. Preece b Howell . . . . . . . . . . . . . . . . . . . . . | 26 | – c Parsons b Wyatt . . . . . . . . . . . . . | 7 |
| Mr R. L. Brinton b Wyatt . . . . . . . . . . . . . . . . . . . | 1 | – run out . . . . . . . . . . . . . . . . . . . . . | 7 |
| F. T. Summers run out . . . . . . . . . . . . . . . . . . . . . | 4 | – lbw b Wyatt . . . . . . . . . . . . . . . . . . | 1 |
| H. O. Rogers run out . . . . . . . . . . . . . . . . . . . . . . | 8 | – not out . . . . . . . . . . . . . . . . . . . . . | 2 |
| B 9, l-b 2 . . . . . . . . . . . . . . . . . . . . . . . . | 11 | B 7 . . . . . . . . . . . . . . . . . . . | 7 |
| | **182** | | **74** |

## Warwickshire

| | | | |
|---|---|---|---|
| J. H. Parsons lbw b Root | 37 | – not out | 81 |
| E. J. Smith c Foster b Root | 12 | – c Summers b Root | 16 |
| L. A. Bates lbw b Root | 19 | – c Foster b Preece | 19 |
| W. G. Quaife b Pearson | 1 | – b Pearson | 8 |
| Mr G. W. Stephens c Summers b Pearson | 14 | – c Somers b Root | 11 |
| Mr B. W. Quaife b Pearson | 0 | – not out | 0 |
| Mr N. E. Partridge b Root | 5 | | |
| F. R. Santall b Pearson | 9 | | |
| Mr R. E. S. Wyatt not out | 4 | | |
| H. Howell c Foster b Root | 6 | | |
| Hon. F. S. G. Calthorpe absent | 0 | | |
| B 5, l-b 7 | 12 | B 5, l-b 1 | 6 |
| | **119** | | **141** |

### Warwickshire Bowling

| | Overs | Mdns | Runs | Wkts | Overs | Mdns | Runs | Wkts |
|---|---|---|---|---|---|---|---|---|
| Howell | 18 | — | 77 | 3 | 13 | 2 | 37 | 5 |
| Calthorpe | 9 | — | 34 | 2 | | | | |
| Partridge | 8.4 | — | 31 | 1 | 7 | 2 | 8 | 1 |
| Wyatt | 12 | 3 | 29 | 2 | 5.4 | — | 22 | 3 |

### Worcestershire Bowling

| | Overs | Mdns | Runs | Wkts | Overs | Mdns | Runs | Wkts |
|---|---|---|---|---|---|---|---|---|
| Root | 24.3 | 7 | 33 | 5 | 15.3 | 3 | 53 | 2 |
| Pearson | 20 | 3 | 63 | 4 | 17 | 3 | 40 | 1 |
| Rogers | 4 | 2 | 11 | — | | | | |
| Wilson | | | | | 7 | 2 | 17 | — |
| Preece | | | | | 9 | 2 | 25 | 1 |

Umpires: W. A. Buswell and W. Reeves.

## WORCESTERSHIRE v HAMPSHIRE

### Played at Worcester, August 25, 26, 27, 1926

Worcestershire's last home fixture was drawn after some exceptionally high scoring. Foster distinguished himself by making two separate 100s, and Jewell played his highest innings in first-class cricket. The latter preferred his side to bat a second time although Worcestershire led by 200. Root had gained this advantage. Afterwards only eight wickets fell, and 731 runs were scored. Requiring 508 for victory, Hampshire lost Judd and Brown for 62 on the second evening, and Livsey left at 92, but only one other wicket fell on the last day. Bowell and Mead, staying together three hours fifty minutes, added 248.

## Worcestershire

| | | | |
|---|---|---|---|
| Mr M. F. S. Jewell b Newman | 12 | – c Brown b Newman | 125 |
| Mr R. H. Williams b Brown | 3 | – lbw b Boyes | 14 |
| L. Wright c Mead b McBride | 13 | – c Livsey b Newman | 25 |
| Mr M. K. Foster c and b Mead | 141 | – c Parker b Newman | 106 |
| Mr H. L. Higgins run out | 14 | – not out | 17 |
| C. V. Tarbox c Brown b Newman | 6 | – not out | 4 |
| J. J. Bowles c Judd b Newman | 14 | | |
| F. Pearson c Brown b Boyes | 58 | | |
| F. Root not out | 47 | | |
| H. O. Rogers b Newman | 6 | | |
| C. J. Wilson b Boyes | 0 | | |
| B 16, l-b 5 | 21 | B 11, l-b 5 | 16 |
| | **335** | | **(4 wkts dec.) 307** |

## Hampshire

| | | | |
|---|---|---|---|
| G. Brown c Jewell b Root | 69 | – b Root | 20 |
| Mr A. K. Judd c Bowles b Root | 0 | – b Pearson | 0 |
| A. Bowell c Bowles b Root | 19 | – lbw b Tarbox | 132 |
| Mr J. P. Parker c Wilson b Root | 3 | | |
| C. P. Mead b Root | 0 | – not out | 177 |
| W. H. Livsey lbw b Root | 5 | – c Root b Pearson | 43 |
| A. Kennedy b Root | 14 | | |
| J. Newman run out | 5 | – not out | 32 |
| Mr W. N. McBride lbw b Wilson | 0 | | |
| Mr H. L. V. Day lbw b Root | 9 | | |
| G. S. Boyes not out | 1 | | |
| B 3, l-b 7 | 10 | B 8, l-b 9, w 1, n-b 2 | 20 |
| | **135** | | **424** |

### Hampshire Bowling

| | Overs | Mdns | Runs | Wkts | Overs | Mdns | Runs | Wkts |
|---|---|---|---|---|---|---|---|---|
| Kennedy | 24 | 5 | 69 | — | 6 | 1 | 22 | — |
| Brown | 3 | 1 | 2 | 1 | | | | |
| Newman | 29 | 6 | 102 | 4 | 29 | 10 | 92 | 3 |
| McBride | 11 | 1 | 33 | 1 | 14 | 2 | 35 | — |
| Boyes | 15.4 | 3 | 63 | 2 | 17 | 2 | 43 | 1 |
| Mead | 10 | 1 | 45 | 1 | 7 | 2 | 26 | — |
| Parker | | | | | 8 | — | 48 | — |
| Judd | | | | | 6 | — | 25 | — |

### Worcestershire Bowling

| | Overs | Mdns | Runs | Wkts | Overs | Mdns | Runs | Wkts |
|---|---|---|---|---|---|---|---|---|
| Root | 24.5 | 10 | 46 | 8 | 38 | 9 | 91 | 1 |
| Pearson | 12 | 3 | 43 | — | 27 | 12 | 55 | 2 |
| Wilson | 11 | 1 | 35 | 1 | 23 | 2 | 89 | — |
| Jewell | 1 | — | 1 | — | 12 | 4 | 33 | — |
| Wright | | | | | 6 | 1 | 25 | — |
| Rogers | | | | | 13 | 2 | 44 | — |
| Bowles | | | | | 10 | 2 | 36 | — |
| Tarbox | | | | | 6 | — | 31 | 1 |

Umpires: F. Sugg and W. A. Buswell.

## WORCESTERSHIRE v NORTHAMPTONSHIRE

### Played at Dudley, May 12, 14, 1928

The all-round form of Jupp proved the deciding factor in this match which, played in bitterly cold weather, ended in a victory for Northamptonshire by five wickets. On a pitch apparently fast and true, batsmen fared so badly on Saturday that twenty wickets fell for an aggregate of 258 runs. Jupp, making the ball turn quickly, so troubled the Worcestershire batsmen that, at one point in Worcestershire's first innings, he took five wickets in nine balls without being scored from, and he came out with a record of eight wickets for less than four runs apiece. He owed much to Nicholson who, fielding at short-leg, made five catches. Northamptonshire found difficulty in scoring against Tarbox, but resolute batting by Jupp, who hit up 40 out of 62, turned the game in favour of the visitors. Worcestershire, losing three wickets before they cleared off their arrears, set Northamptonshire no more than 97 to make, but Root, on a pitch that gave him some help, bowled so finely that there were four men out for 30. Jupp had a great match, taking twelve wickets for 88 and scoring 50 runs.

## Worcestershire

| | | | |
|---|---|---|---|
| Mr J. B. Higgins c Timms b Thomas | 11 | – b Thomas | 29 |
| L. Wright c Nicholson b Jupp | 24 | – b Jupp | 26 |
| H. H. Gibbons c Nicholson b Jupp | 10 | – lbw b Jupp | 12 |
| W. V. Fox not out | 20 | – c Matthews b Clark | 33 |
| J. W. King lbw b Jupp | 0 | – b Thomas | 6 |
| C. V. Tarbox c Nicholson b Jupp | 0 | – c Clark b Jupp | 28 |
| Mr L. Gale c Nicholson b Jupp | 0 | – lbw b Jupp | 13 |
| F. Root c Walden b Nicholson | 5 | – c Walden b Nicholson | 26 |
| J. J. Bowles b Jupp | 0 | – b Nicholson | 0 |
| Mr W. E. Richardson c Nicholson b Jupp | 0 | – lbw b Nicholson | 5 |
| F. T. Summers lbw b Jupp | 6 | – not out | 5 |
| B 1, l-b 5, n-b 1 | 7 | B 3, l-b 2 | 5 |
| | **83** | | **188** |

## Northamptonshire

| | | | |
|---|---|---|---|
| C. N. Woolley b Root | 4 | – b Tarbox | 7 |
| A. G. Liddell c Bowles b Tarbox | 10 | – b Root | 5 |
| B. Bellamy b Tarbox | 6 | – b Root | 4 |
| Mr V. W. C. Jupp c Higgins b Tarbox | 40 | – c Bowles b Root | 10 |
| J. E. Timms lbw b Richardson | 19 | – not out | 45 |
| F. Walden run out | 29 | – c Richardson b Root | 1 |
| Mr W. C. Brown b Tarbox | 13 | – not out | 18 |
| A. D. Matthews not out | 23 | | |
| A. E. Thomas c Gibbons b Tarbox | 11 | | |
| J. H. Nicholson b Root | 5 | | |
| E. C. Clark b Tarbox | 11 | | |
| B 1, l-b 3 | 4 | B 6, l-b 1 | 7 |
| | **175** | | **97** |

### Northamptonshire Bowling

| | Overs | Mdns | Runs | Wkts | Overs | Mdns | Runs | Wkts |
|---|---|---|---|---|---|---|---|---|
| Clark | 8 | 2 | 17 | — | 15 | 1 | 57 | 1 |
| Thomas | 15 | 10 | 14 | 1 | 24 | 10 | 46 | 2 |
| Jupp | 14.1 | 4 | 29 | 8 | 20 | 3 | 59 | 4 |
| Nicholson | 7 | 3 | 16 | 1 | 10.2 | 3 | 21 | 3 |

### Worcestershire Bowling

| | Overs | Mdns | Runs | Wkts | Overs | Mdns | Runs | Wkts |
|---|---|---|---|---|---|---|---|---|
| Root | 23 | 3 | 77 | 2 | 18 | 9 | 37 | 4 |
| Tarbox | 23.5 | 4 | 52 | 6 | 17.5 | 2 | 53 | 1 |
| Richardson | 5 | — | 20 | 1 | | | | |
| Bowles | 6 | 1 | 22 | — | | | | |

Umpires: A. Nash and J. W. Day.

## WORCESTERSHIRE v KENT

Played at Worcester, May 16, 17, 18, 1928

Everything else in this drawn match was overshadowed by the batting of Gibbons, the young Worcestershire professional, who, making his first hundred in county cricket, saved his side from what at one time, appeared almost inevitable defeat. On the second day, when rain restricted cricket to less than an hour, Worcestershire followed on 202 behind, and with nine wickets standing they began the last day needing 174 to escape an innings defeat. Gibbons, scoring his runs in delightful style, played all the bowling, and especially that of Freeman and Woolley, with consummate ease, driving with immense power and occasionally employing a skilful late cut. To such a degree did he master the Kent attack that he actually scored 100 out of 129 in seventy-five minutes and altogether 140 out of 176 in an hour and forty minutes. His great and faultless innings, which contained twenty-seven 4s, took all the sting out of the Kent bowling and, after luncheon, Fox and Root made Worcestershire safe from defeat by putting on 129 for the seventh wicket. Root, like Gibbons, made his first hundred for the county and, in addition, took seven wickets for 125 runs. On Friday, Higgins broke one of his thumbs in three places and had to retire.

### Kent

| | | | |
|---|---:|---|---:|
| H. T. W. Hardinge c Rogers b Root | 52 | L. Todd not out | 20 |
| W. Ashdown c Williams b Root | 22 | A. P. Freeman c Williams b Root | 13 |
| F. E. Woolley b Bowles | 68 | Mr B. Howlett b Rogers | 6 |
| L. Ames b Root | 80 | C. Wright c Bowles b Root | 3 |
| G. C. Collins c Bowles b Tarbox | 3 | B 9, l-b 2, n-b 1 | 12 |
| Mr G. B. Legge b Root | 11 | | — |
| Mr L. W. Recordon lbw b Root | 0 | | 290 |

### Worcestershire

| | | | |
|---|---:|---|---:|
| Mr J. B. Higgins b Wright | 17 | – retired hurt | 0 |
| L. Wright b Wright | 6 | – b Wright | 27 |
| H. H. Gibbons b Wright | 12 | – b Howlett | 140 |
| W. V. Fox c Ames b Ashdown | 4 | – c Todd b Collins | 82 |
| J. W. King not out | 25 | – c Ames b Ashdown | 16 |
| C. V. Tarbox c Ames b Ashdown | 1 | – b Ashdown | 5 |
| Mr R. H. Williams b Ashdown | 2 | – c Ames b Wright | 0 |
| F. Root c Wright b Ashdown | 2 | – st Ames b Woolley | 107 |
| H. O. Rogers lbw b Ashdown | 1 | – lbw b Freeman | 10 |
| J. J. Bowles b Wright | 10 | – b Freeman | 1 |
| F. T. Summers b Wright | 4 | – not out | 11 |
| B 3, l-b 1 | 4 | B 4, l-b 3, n-b 2 | 9 |
| | — | | — |
| | 88 | | 408 |

### Worcestershire Bowling

| | Overs | Mdns | Runs | Wkts |
|---|---:|---:|---:|---:|
| Root | 31.2 | 5 | 125 | 7 |
| Tarbox | 25 | 5 | 89 | 1 |
| Rogers | 10 | — | 51 | 1 |
| Bowles | 4 | 1 | 13 | 1 |

### Kent Bowling

| | Overs | Mdns | Runs | Wkts | Overs | Mdns | Runs | Wkts |
|---|---:|---:|---:|---:|---:|---:|---:|---:|
| Wright | 13.5 | 3 | 28 | 5 | 31 | 4 | 79 | 2 |
| Ashdown | 15 | 1 | 50 | 5 | 19 | 2 | 48 | 2 |
| Howlett | 4 | 1 | 6 | — | 12 | — | 42 | 1 |
| Collins | | | | | 6 | — | 23 | 1 |
| Woolley | | | | | 16 | 2 | 50 | 1 |
| Recordon | | | | | 2 | — | 22 | — |
| Freeman | | | | | 28 | 4 | 124 | 2 |
| Todd | | | | | 3 | 1 | 11 | — |

Umpires: F. Field and J. H. King.

# WORCESTERSHIRE v DERBYSHIRE

Played at Stourbridge, June 8, 10, 11, 1929

About this time Derbyshire were playing fine cricket and, beating Worcestershire by 116 runs, they not only registered their sixth victory in nine games, but regained first place in the county championship. To such an extent were bowlers masters of the situation on the Saturday that on a rain-affected pitch sixteen wickets fell for an aggregate of 154 runs. Derbyshire lost half their wickets for 42, only plucky hitting by Townsend averting complete collapse, and at the drawing of stumps, Worcestershire had six men out for 39. On Monday Derbyshire, having secured a lead on the first innings, steadily consolidated their position on batting a second time. Worcestershire, set to get 286 to win, never looked· like accomplishing the task. Quaife and Gibbons batted in resolute fashion without ever gaining a real mastery over the Derbyshire attack. Slater bowled uncommonly well on a pitch that gave him little help.

## Derbyshire

| | | | |
|---|---:|---|---:|
| J. Bowden lbw b Root | 11 | – b Jackson | 45 |
| H. Storer c and b Root | 11 | – c Quaife b Tarbox | 5 |
| S. Worthington lbw b Tarbox | 11 | – lbw b Jackson | 21 |
| Mr G. R. Jackson c Nichol b Tarbox | 2 | – b Jackson | 35 |
| A. G. Slater c Tarbox b Root | 4 | – c Gilbert b Jackson | 36 |
| D. Smith run out | 0 | – b Tarbox | 1 |
| L. Townsend c Gibbons b Tarbox | 33 | – c V. Fox b Tarbox | 26 |
| J. M. Hutchinson c Nichol b Gilbert | 11 | – b Tarbox | 40 |
| Mr A. W. Richardson c V. Fox b Gilbert | 0 | – lbw b Root | 2 |
| H. Elliott not out | 17 | – lbw b Root | 0 |
| T. R. Armstrong b Tarbox | 1 | – not out | 1 |
| B 6, l-b 7, w 1 | 14 | B 21, l-b 6, w 1 | 28 |
| | **115** | | **240** |

## Worcestershire

| | | | |
|---|---:|---|---:|
| Mr M. F. S. Jewell c Townsend b Worthington | 2 | – lbw b Storer | 6 |
| Mr B. W. Quaife c Elliott b Slater | 1 | – b Townsend | 40 |
| M. Nichol c Bowden b Worthington | 9 | – b Slater | 15 |
| H. H. Gibbons c Elliott b Townsend | 6 | – run out | 27 |
| W. V. Fox c Elliott b Townsend | 1 | – c Elliott b Worthington | 20 |
| L. Wright b Worthington | 14 | – not out | 33 |
| J. Fox b Townsend | 4 | – lbw b Slater | 1 |
| C. V. Tarbox b Worthington | 8 | – c Elliott b Storer | 12 |
| F. Root not out | 19 | – run out | 0 |
| Mr H. A. Gilbert run out | 3 | – b Slater | 6 |
| P. Jackson c Elliott b Worthington | 0 | – b Slater | 0 |
| B 2, w 1 | 3 | L-b 8, n-b 1 | 9 |
| | **70** | | **169** |

## Worcestershire Bowling

| | Overs | Mdns | Runs | Wkts | Overs | Mdns | Runs | Wkts |
|---|---:|---:|---:|---:|---:|---:|---:|---:|
| Root | 35 | 18 | 38 | 3 | 30 | 10 | 53 | 2 |
| Tarbox | 22.5 | 9 | 36 | 4 | 24.1 | 5 | 57 | 4 |
| Jackson | 3 | 1 | 6 | — | 19 | 3 | 50 | 4 |
| Gilbert | 13 | 6 | 17 | 2 | 14 | — | 52 | — |
| J. Fox | 3 | — | 4 | — | | | | |
| Jewell | 1 | 1 | — | — | | | | |

**Derbyshire Bowling**

| | Overs | Mdns | Runs | Wkts | Overs | Mdns | Runs | Wkts |
|---|---|---|---|---|---|---|---|---|
| Slater ............ | 8 | 2 | 12 | 1 | 26.5 | 10 | 29 | 4 |
| Worthington ...... | 17.3 | 7 | 21 | 5 | 25 | 5 | 44 | 1 |
| Townsend ........ | 16 | 8 | 24 | 3 | 26 | 13 | 32 | 1 |
| Armstrong ........ | 6 | 4 | 10 | — | 15 | 8 | 20 | — |
| Storer ........... | | | | | 16 | 4 | 35 | 2 |

Umpires: A. Sellick and L. Benwell.

# WORCESTERSHIRE v NOTTINGHAMSHIRE

Played at Worcester, June 12, 13, 14, 1929

What in the ordinary way would have proved one of Worcestershire's most attractive matches was largely ruined by rain. Cricket was limited to fifty minutes on the opening day and not a ball could be bowled on Friday. Still, a drawn match, in which there being no decision on the first innings, each side took four points, produced a memorable performance, George Gunn, the Nottinghamshire veteran, seizing the occasion of his fiftieth birthday – the Thursday – to play a characteristic innings of 164 not out. He and Whysall in fifty minutes on the opening day scored 49 together and the following day they remained partners until 176 runs were on the board, this being their thirty-fifth stand of three figures. Gunn, in making his second hundred of the season and the fifty-fourth of his career, showed much of the supreme skill which marked his greatest days. He batted for over five hours and a half and only once during his long innings did he make anything like a really bad stroke. This, moreover, did not occur until 135 runs stood to his credit and then Fox failed to hold a catch at slip. Nottinghamshire declared, after batting for more than five hours and a half, and Worcestershire in the hour remaining for play that day failed so utterly before the bowling of Arthur Staples that at the drawing of stumps seven men were out for 44. Arthur Staples actually took five wickets at a cost of 9 runs. In all probability Friday's rain saved Worcestershire from a crushing defeat.

**Nottinghamshire**

| | | |
|---|---|---|
| G. Gunn not out ..................... | 164 | W. Payton not out ................... 3 |
| W. Whysall c Root b Nichol ........... | 72 | |
| W. Walker c Quaife b Tarbox .......... | 50 | B 21, l-b 7, w 1, n-b 1 ......... 30 |
| Mr A. W. Carr b Root ................ | 28 | |
| F. Barratt c sub. b Root .............. | 3 | (4 wkts dec.) 350 |

A. Staples, B. Lilley, H. Larwood, S. J. Staples and W. Voce did not bat.

**Worcestershire**

| | | |
|---|---|---|
| Mr B. W. Quaife b Barratt ............. | 9 | Mr M. F. S. Jewell c S. J. Staples |
| L. Wright b Larwood ................. | 1 | b A. Staples . 3 |
| M. Nichol lbw b A. Staples ............ | 8 | F. Root c Carr b A. Staples ............. 7 |
| H. H. Gibbons b A. Staples ............ | 1 | B 4, l-b 3, n-b 1 .............. 8 |
| W. V. Fox not out ................... | 7 | |
| C. V. Tarbox c Lilley b A. Staples ....... | 0 | 44 |

Mr A. F. Lane, Mr H. A. Gilbert and J. Price did not bat.

## Worcestershire Bowling

|            | Overs | Mdns | Runs | Wkts |
|------------|-------|------|------|------|
| Root ............ | 47    | 14   | 88   | 2    |
| Tarbox .......... | 26    | 2    | 87   | 1    |
| Gilbert .......... | 28.4  | 9    | 64   | —    |
| Price .......... | 9     | —    | 29   | —    |
| Lane ............ | 5     | —    | 13   | —    |
| Jewell .......... | 8     | 1    | 11   | —    |
| Nichol .......... | 7     | 1    | 25   | 1    |
| Wright .......... | 2     | —    | 3    | —    |

## Nottinghamshire Bowling

|            | Overs | Mdns | Runs | Wkts |
|------------|-------|------|------|------|
| Larwood ......... | 4     | 1    | 12   | 1    |
| Barratt .......... | 6     | —    | 15   | 1    |
| A. Staples ....... | 5     | 2    | 9    | 5    |

Umpires: A. Nash and W. Phillips.

# WORCESTERSHIRE v KENT

## Played at Stourbridge, June 3, 4, 1931

Worcestershire followed up their notable successes in overcoming Lancashire and Gloucestershire with a five wickets victory over Kent. Nothing sensational marked the start of the game which owing to the flooded state of the Worcester ground had been transferred to Stourbridge. Hardinge and Ashdown batting with considerable care opened Kent's innings with a partnership which, extending over an hour, produced 41 runs. There followed such a startling collapse before the bowling of Jackson, that the last nine wickets went down in sixty-five minutes for the addition of 35 runs. On Worcestershire going in Quaife and Nichol brought the score to 41 before the second wicket fell and although half the side were out for 52, the home side at the tea adjournment stood only two runs behind with five wickets in hand. Freeman, however, afterwards proved so deadly that those wickets fell while 38 runs were obtained. Hardinge and Ashdown made 50 in Kent's second innings for the first wicket, the visitors entering upon Thursday's play 20 ahead with one man out. Perks, however, disposing of Todd, Valentine and Pearce with following balls, performed the "hat trick," the nine wickets going down for 54 runs. Worcestershire wanting 75 to win, lost three men for 15 but Walters afterwards hit up 40 out of 62 and so determined the issue.

## Kent

| | | |
|---|---|---|
| H. T. W. Hardinge b Jackson .................... | 32 – c Jackson b Brook ............. | 36 |
| W. Ashdown c Quaife b Jackson ............... | 11 – b Perks ...................... | 15 |
| F. E. Woolley c Walters b Root ................ | 1 – b Root ...................... | 12 |
| L. Ames b Jackson ........................ | 0 – b Perks ..................... | 6 |
| L. Todd not out .......................... | 13 – b Perks ..................... | 9 |
| Mr B. H. Valentine b Jackson ............... | 4 – c Nichol b Perks ........... | 0 |
| Mr T. A. Pearce b Jackson .................... | 0 – c Quaife b Perks ............ | 0 |
| C. Fairservice b Brook ...................... | 1 – c Quaife b Root ............. | 6 |
| A. E. Watt run out ....................... | 7 – c Ahl b Root ............... | 3 |
| C. Wright b Jackson ..................... | 0 – c and b Perks .............. | 7 |
| A. P. Freeman b Root ...................... | 3 – not out ................... | 4 |
| B 2, l-b 2 ...................... | 4          B 5, l-b 7 .............. | 12 |
| | **76** | **110** |

## Worcestershire

| | | | |
|---|---|---|---|
| Mr B. W. Quaife not out | 31 | – lbw b Freeman | 0 |
| J. Fox lbw b Watt | 2 | – lbw b Ashdown | 4 |
| M. Nichol c Todd b Freeman | 26 | – c Ames b Ashdown | 11 |
| H. H. Gibbons lbw b Freeman | 1 | – c Watt b Freeman | 13 |
| Mr C. F. Walters c Valentine b Ashdown | 0 | – not out | 40 |
| L. Wright b Ashdown | 5 | – c Todd b Freeman | 1 |
| F. D. Ahl c Wright b Freeman | 11 | – not out | 7 |
| F. Root c Pearce b Freeman | 20 | | |
| G. W. Brook c Todd b Freeman | 4 | | |
| R. T. D. Perks c Valentine b Freeman | 1 | | |
| P. F. Jackson st Ames b Freeman | 1 | | |
| B 9, l-b 1 | 10 | | |
| | **112** | | **76** |

### Worcestershire Bowling

| | Overs | Mdns | Runs | Wkts | Overs | Mdns | Runs | Wkts |
|---|---|---|---|---|---|---|---|---|
| Root | 14.3 | 8 | 21 | 2 | 19 | 6 | 31 | 3 |
| Perks | 8 | 2 | 12 | — | 20 | 6 | 40 | 6 |
| Jackson | 13 | 3 | 25 | 6 | 5 | — | 11 | — |
| Brook | 7 | — | 14 | 1 | 6 | 2 | 16 | 1 |

### Kent Bowling

| | Overs | Mdns | Runs | Wkts | Overs | Mdns | Runs | Wkts |
|---|---|---|---|---|---|---|---|---|
| Watt | 12 | 3 | 28 | 1 | | | | |
| Wright | 4 | — | 7 | — | | | | |
| Freeman | 24 | 7 | 44 | 7 | 12.2 | 3 | 42 | 3 |
| Ashdown | 16 | 2 | 23 | 2 | 13 | 3 | 34 | 2 |

Umpires: J. Stone and H. Young.

## WORCESTERSHIRE v WARWICKSHIRE

Played at Worcester, August 15, 17, 18, 1931

Warwickshire, half an hour before time, defeated Worcestershire by 84 runs. Play on Saturday could not begin until one o'clock and had lasted only seventy-five minutes when rain put an end to the day's cricket. Warwickshire who had scored 52 for two wickets, resumed under strange conditions on Monday, a belt of flood water covering part of the playing field which had to be curtailed in this particular direction by some twenty-five yards. Warwickshire's innings was finished off – mainly through Brook – for 71 more runs. Parsons, discovering he had left his spectacles at home, went to fetch them, expecting his county's innings would last until after lunch and, consequent upon the collapse, he had no chance of batting. Worcestershire scored 68 for the loss of two batsmen but Wyatt bowled so effectively that the last eight wickets fell for 61 more runs. On the last day Warwickshire batted to useful purpose. Worcestershire, set 195 to win, showed pronounced lack of restraint and were only saved by Fiddian-Green from utter failure.

## Warwickshire

| | | | |
|---|---|---|---|
| Mr G. D. Kemp-Welch c Hopkins b Brook | 20 | – b Jackson | 9 |
| A. J. Croom lbw b Brook | 28 | – lbw b Fox | 33 |
| L. A. Bates lbw b Jackson | 21 | – b Perks | 20 |
| Mr R. E. S. Wyatt c Quaife b Root | 5 | – c Ahl b Brook | 2 |
| N. Kilner lbw b Root | 9 | – run out | 34 |
| J. Smart c Fox b Jackson | 16 | – lbw b Brook | 36 |
| W. Sanders b Brook | 0 | – lbw b Jackson | 0 |
| Mr D. G. Foster b Brook | 2 | – b Jackson | 11 |
| J. H. Mayer lbw b Brook | 5 | – b Perks | 13 |
| G. Paine not out | 2 | – not out | 0 |
| Rev J. H. Parsons absent | 0 | – b Root | 16 |
| B 5, l-b 8, n-b 2 | 15 | B 4, l-b 10, w 1, n-b 11 | 26 |
| | **123** | | **200** |

## Worcestershire

| | | | |
|---|---|---|---|
| Mr C. F. Walters c Smart b Paine | 27 | – c and b Foster | 4 |
| Mr B. W. Quaife lbw b Wyatt | 14 | – lbw b Mayer | 5 |
| Mr C. A. Fiddian-Green b Paine | 21 | – c Kilner b Wyatt | 60 |
| H. H. Gibbons c Croom b Wyatt | 20 | – c Smart b Foster | 0 |
| Mr H. O. Hopkins st Smart b Wyatt | 8 | – b Wyatt | 17 |
| J. Fox b Paine | 9 | – c Kemp-Welch b Paine | 1 |
| F. D. Ahl b Paine | 16 | – b Mayer | 2 |
| F. Root c Foster b Wyatt | 3 | – c Wyatt b Paine | 2 |
| G. W. Brook b Wyatt | 1 | – c Croom b Paine | 4 |
| R. T. D. Perks lbw b Wyatt | 3 | – not out | 4 |
| P. F. Jackson not out | 0 | – b Paine | 6 |
| L-b 7 | 7 | B 4, l-b 1 | 5 |
| | **129** | | **110** |

## Worcestershire Bowling

| | Overs | Mdns | Runs | Wkts | Overs | Mdns | Runs | Wkts |
|---|---|---|---|---|---|---|---|---|
| Root | 24 | 9 | 46 | 2 | 19 | 11 | 26 | 1 |
| Perks | 15 | 4 | 22 | — | 18.2 | 4 | 50 | 2 |
| Jackson | 13 | 6 | 19 | 2 | 18 | 5 | 36 | 3 |
| Brook | 9.1 | 1 | 21 | 5 | 23 | 5 | 56 | 2 |
| Fox | | | | | 8 | 3 | 6 | 1 |

## Warwickshire Bowling

| | Overs | Mdns | Runs | Wkts | Overs | Mdns | Runs | Wkts |
|---|---|---|---|---|---|---|---|---|
| Mayer | 10 | 3 | 15 | — | 12 | 2 | 32 | 2 |
| Foster | 6 | 1 | 12 | — | 5 | — | 17 | 2 |
| Paine | 26 | 8 | 33 | 4 | 17 | 5 | 27 | 4 |
| Wyatt | 23.4 | 7 | 52 | 6 | 10 | — | 29 | 2 |
| Sanders | 6 | 1 | 10 | — | | | | |

Umpires: W. A. Buswell and W. R. Parry.

## WORCESTERSHIRE v GLOUCESTERSHIRE

Played at Worcester, July 1, 3, 4, 1933

Outstanding performances of the past were equalled during this remarkable match which produced 1,330 runs for the loss of twenty-five wickets. Heavy scoring at the start of each innings precluded any likelihood of a definite result, and Gloucestershire had to fight hard for a first innings lead of 93.

As many as six hundreds were scored – five for Gloucestershire – and Hammond and Dacre both enjoyed the distinction of putting together a century in each innings. The two Gloucestershire batsmen thus equalled the feat of R. E. Foster and W. L. Foster in the match against Hampshire at Worcester in 1899. Cricket history provides only two other instances of six three-figure innings being played in a match. As long ago as 1898 at Derby four Derbyshire and two Hampshire players reached three-figures, and in 1928 at Coventry four Nottinghamshire and two Warwickshire men were credited with centuries.

B. H. Lyon's experiment of sending in Dacre to open the Gloucestershire innings with Barnett proved an unqualified success, the partnership realising 206 runs in little more than two hours. The bowling was treated with such scant respect that, prior to tea, runs came at the rate of 100 an hour, but the later men could not maintain this ascendancy, the last six wickets falling for 109. Barnett, first to leave, offered a chance just before being bowled, but, driving and cutting with special skill, he otherwise batted in sound as well as brilliant style. He hit fourteen 4s. Dacre played in his usual daring fashion and, with powerful drives predominating, made his first hundred of the season. Hammond was masterly. Reaching 50 in an hour, he doubled his score in another thirty-five minutes and, with two 6s and twelve 4s among his hits, he made 122 out of 205 in a trifle over two hours. After Dacre and Hammond had added 64, Lyon was quite overshadowed in the third partnership which produced 141 runs in ninety minutes.

Worcestershire made a courageous response, and accomplished an excellent performance. After Gibbons left with three scored, Lyon tried seven bowlers in an endeavour to dislodge Walters and Nichol, whose association realised 117 in less than a hundred minutes before the professional was run out. Walters, driving with power and precision, played flawless cricket for three hours and a half. Martin offered stubborn resistance; Brook hit fiercely and Jackson also played freely, while Quaife defended and the follow-on was avoided. On the third morning the last two wickets fell for 19 runs and then Gloucestershire scored 195 in an hour and three-quarters before lunch-time, but the declaration was not made until ten minutes to three. Dacre's 125, scored in two hours and a quarter, included sixteen 4s, while Hammond took only a hundred minutes over his century. Needing 364 to win, Worcestershire lost four men for 44, but Quaife and Martin averted any fear of defeat.

### Gloucestershire

| | | | |
|---|---|---|---|
| C. C. Dacre c Brook b White | 119 | – not out | 125 |
| C. J. Barnett b Jackson | 107 | – c Ahl b Jackson | 18 |
| W. R. Hammond c Walters b Jackson | 122 | – not out | 111 |
| Mr B. H. Lyon c Quaife b Perks | 58 | | |
| R. A. Sinfield c Jackson b White | 9 | | |
| W. L. Neale b Martin | 20 | | |
| Mr P. I. Van der Gucht b Ahl | 5 | | |
| E. J. Stephens not out | 8 | | |
| T. W. Goddard c Jackson b Martin | 16 | | |
| C. Parker b Ahl | 0 | | |
| Mr G. W. Parker c White b Brook | 49 | | |
| B 20, l-b 4, w 2, n-b 2 | 28 | B 9, l-b 7 | 16 |
| | 541 | (1 wkt dec.) | 279 |

## Worcestershire

| | | | |
|---|---|---|---|
| Mr C. F. Walters c Van der Gucht b Barnett | 114 | – b Stephens | 11 |
| H. H. Gibbons c Lyon b Barnett | 0 | – c Van der Gucht b Stephens | 10 |
| M. Nichol run out | 66 | – c and b Lyon | 6 |
| L. Wright b Goddard | 28 | – c Lyon b Goddard | 11 |
| S. H. Martin lbw b C. Parker | 29 | – not out | 20 |
| Mr B. W. Quaife b C. Parker | 81 | – not out | 5 |
| F. D. Ahl b Goddard | 10 | | |
| M. E. White b Goddard | 6 | | |
| G. W. Brook c Goddard b Sinfield | 56 | | |
| P. F. Jackson c Van der Gucht b Neale | 40 | | |
| R. T. D. Perks not out | 0 | | |
| B 11, l-b 7 | 18 | L-b 6, w 1, n-b 1 | 8 |
| | **448** | | **71** |

## Worcestershire Bowling

| | Overs | Mdns | Runs | Wkts | Overs | Mdns | Runs | Wkts |
|---|---|---|---|---|---|---|---|---|
| Perks | 56 | 2 | 122 | 1 | 8 | — | 40 | — |
| White | 12 | 1 | 60 | 2 | 4 | 1 | 22 | — |
| Jackson | 30 | 2 | 119 | 2 | 12 | — | 77 | 1 |
| Martin | 22 | 3 | 86 | 2 | 6 | — | 43 | — |
| Brook | 7.4 | — | 49 | 1 | 4 | — | 31 | — |
| Wright | 10 | — | 36 | — | 8 | — | 27 | — |
| Nichol | 4 | — | 25 | — | | | | |
| Ahl | 6 | 1 | 16 | 2 | | | | |
| Gibbons | | | | | 2 | — | 9 | — |
| Walters | | | | | 1 | — | 5 | — |

## Gloucestershire Bowling

| | Overs | Mdns | Runs | Wkts | Overs | Mdns | Runs | Wkts |
|---|---|---|---|---|---|---|---|---|
| Barnett | 21 | 5 | 58 | 2 | | | | |
| Hammond | 12 | 1 | 37 | — | | | | |
| Sinfield | 19 | 3 | 47 | 1 | 2 | 1 | 1 | — |
| Lyon | 3 | — | 21 | — | 8 | 2 | 21 | 1 |
| C. Parker | 47.1 | 10 | 115 | 2 | 7 | 3 | 7 | — |
| Goddard | 46 | 14 | 114 | 3 | 9 | 5 | 10 | 1 |
| Neale | 5 | 2 | 14 | 1 | 2 | — | 8 | — |
| Stephens | 5 | 1 | 15 | — | 9 | 3 | 15 | 2 |
| Dacre | 4 | 2 | 9 | — | | | | |
| G. W. Parker | | | | | 3 | 2 | 1 | — |

Umpires: L. C. Braund and D. Hendren.


# WORCESTERSHIRE v CAMBRIDGE UNIVERSITY

### Played at Worcester, June 27, 28, 29, 1934

J. H. Human, the Cambridge captain, was the dominant personality in the University's brilliant win by three wickets. On Wednesday, Worcestershire, apart from R. H. C. Human, a brother of the Cambridge player, who was making his début for the county, fared moderately, but they led by 101 on the first innings. Human batted well a second time, and Worcestershire declared, setting the University to get 353 to win in under six hours. Cambridge lost three men for 63, but J. H. Human turned impending defeat into triumph. Batting four hours, he drove and hit to leg in refreshing fashion and, giving only one chance, hit sixteen 4s in his fourth hundred of the season. With an hour left for play 82 runs were wanted but Pelham helped to obtain these readily.

### Worcestershire

| | | | |
|---|---|---|---|
| H. H. Gibbons b King | 54 | – c Powell b Jahangir Khan | 11 |
| C. H. Bull lbw b Grimshaw | 19 | – b Jahangir Khan | 23 |
| Mr C. A. Fiddian-Green run out | 5 | – c Powell b Jahangir Khan | 45 |
| S. H. Martin b King | 4 | – b Davies | 11 |
| Mr R. H. C. Human lbw b King | 75 | – c Human b King | 45 |
| Mr C. A. Humphries b King | 13 | – run out | 44 |
| Mr B. W. Quaife not out | 26 | – b Grimshaw | 30 |
| F. Warne c Powell b King | 2 | – b Jahangir Khan | 5 |
| Mr C. S. Harrison b King | 3 | – c and b Jahangir Khan | 13 |
| R. T. D. Perks lbw b Jahangir Khan | 7 | – not out | 12 |
| P. F. Jackson b Jahangir Khan | 0 | | |
| B 6, l-b 2, n-b 1 | 9 | B 8, l-b 4 | 12 |
| | **217** | **(9 wkts dec.)** | **251** |

### Cambridge University

| | | | |
|---|---|---|---|
| Mr A. W. Allen c Quaife b Perks | 6 | – b Jackson | 17 |
| Mr G. W. Parker lbw b Warne | 24 | – b Perks | 18 |
| Mr R. de W. K. Winlaw b Jackson | 18 | – c Martin b Harrison | 44 |
| Mr H. T. Bartlett c Human b Jackson | 2 | – c Human b Jackson | 11 |
| Mr J. H. Human c Harrison b Perks | 20 | – not out | 146 |
| Mr J. G. W. Davies b Warne | 12 | – c Quaife b Jackson | 47 |
| Mr A. G. Powell lbw b Jackson | 8 | – lbw b Jackson | 2 |
| M. Jahangir Khan c Bull b Jackson | 12 | – lbw b Warne | 19 |
| Mr A. G. Pelham c Martin b Jackson | 5 | – not out | 40 |
| Mr F. King st Quaife b Warne | 1 | | |
| Mr J. W. T. Grimshaw not out | 0 | | |
| B 1, l-b 6, n-b 1 | 8 | B 5, l-b 4 | 9 |
| | **116** | | **353** |

### Cambridge University Bowling

| | Overs | Mdns | Runs | Wkts | Overs | Mdns | Runs | Wkts |
|---|---|---|---|---|---|---|---|---|
| Pelham | 12 | 4 | 26 | — | 15 | 6 | 26 | — |
| Jahangir Khan | 16.5 | 3 | 39 | 2 | 41.1 | 13 | 90 | 5 |
| Davies | 16 | 10 | 6 | — | 17 | 3 | 38 | 1 |
| Grimshaw | 25 | 12 | 48 | 1 | 6 | 4 | 4 | 1 |
| Human | 4 | 1 | 8 | — | | | | |
| King | 20 | 3 | 64 | 6 | 23 | 5 | 55 | 1 |
| Parker | 10 | 3 | 17 | — | 7 | 2 | 26 | — |

### Worcestershire Bowling

| | Overs | Mdns | Runs | Wkts | Overs | Mdns | Runs | Wkts |
|---|---|---|---|---|---|---|---|---|
| Perks | 13 | 5 | 24 | 2 | 27 | 3 | 87 | 1 |
| Jackson | 14.1 | 3 | 31 | 5 | 27 | 7 | 71 | 4 |
| Harrison | 4 | — | 18 | — | 12 | 2 | 30 | 1 |
| Martin | 4 | 2 | 2 | — | 9.4 | 1 | 38 | — |
| Warne | 14 | 3 | 33 | 3 | 33 | 2 | 109 | 1 |
| Human | | | | | 4 | — | 9 | — |

Umpires: Major M. F. S. Jewell and H. R. Cox.

## WORCESTERSHIRE v DERBYSHIRE

Played at Stourbridge, July 7, 9, 1934

Put out in their first innings for 48 – the second lowest total recorded the whole summer – and forced to follow on 258 runs behind, Worcestershire, by one o'clock on Monday, lost by an innings and 115 runs. Derbyshire, helped by errors in the field, gave a fairly consistent display of batting, but they could never take any liberties with accurate bowling. Storer and Alderman began quietly with a partnership of 78, but the best innings of the day came from Carrington who, going in at the fall of the fourth wicket at 146, remained unbeaten for a faultless 70 which occupied him two hours. Carrington's defence was superb and, by means of delightful strokes to the off, he hit ten 4s. The cricket after the tea interval proved sensational indeed, for on a good pitch Worcestershire were disposed of in just over an hour. Mitchell, with his slow leg-breaks and "googlies," carried everything before him, obtaining his eight wickets in six overs, one of which was a maiden, for 22 runs – a wonderful piece of work. Worcestershire made a better fight of it on Monday but Mitchell again bowled finely, bringing his record for the match to thirteen wickets for less than seven runs apiece. Townsend also bowled skilfully. Only Gibbons and Bull offered much resistance.

### Derbyshire

| | |
|---|---|
| H. Storer c Harrison b Brook | 38 |
| A. E. Alderman lbw b Brook | 53 |
| D. Smith lbw b Jackson | 10 |
| L. F. Townsend c and b Perks | 17 |
| T. S. Worthington c Howorth b Brook | 24 |
| E. Carrington not out | 70 |
| A. V. Pope b Perks | 38 |
| H. Elliott lbw b Martin | 6 |
| G. H. Pope c and b Howorth | 25 |
| T. B. Mitchell st Baker b Brook | 0 |
| W. Copson b Jackson | 8 |
| B 16, l-b 1 | 17 |
| | 306 |

### Worcestershire

| | | | |
|---|---|---|---|
| H. H. Gibbons b Worthington | 6 | – st Elliott b Mitchell | 41 |
| C. H. Bull lbw b Townsend | 7 | – c A. V. Pope b Townsend | 41 |
| Mr B. W. Quaife lbw b Mitchell | 2 | – c Elliott b Townsend | 12 |
| S. H. Martin b Mitchell | 5 | – st Elliott b Mitchell | 4 |
| Mr C. A. Humphries b Mitchell | 3 | – lbw b Townsend | 0 |
| R. Howorth c Worthington b Mitchell | 4 | – b Mitchell | 5 |
| Mr C. S. Harrison c and b Mitchell | 10 | – c Worthington b Mitchell | 0 |
| G. W. Brook c Worthington b Mitchell | 0 | – b Mitchell | 1 |
| R. T. D. Perks not out | 6 | – c G. H. Pope b Townsend | 24 |
| Mr E. S. Baker b Mitchell | 0 | – b Townsend | 0 |
| P. F. Jackson st Elliott b Mitchell | 4 | – not out | 11 |
| W 1 | 1 | L-b 4 | 4 |
| | 48 | | 143 |

### Worcestershire Bowling

| | Overs | Mdns | Runs | Wkts |
|---|---|---|---|---|
| Perks | 20 | 6 | 59 | 2 |
| Jackson | 17.3 | 4 | 40 | 2 |
| Martin | 13 | 2 | 24 | 1 |
| Brook | 21 | 3 | 84 | 4 |
| Harrison | 8 | — | 50 | — |
| Howorth | 9 | 2 | 32 | 1 |

**Derbyshire Bowling**

|              | Overs | Mdns | Runs | Wkts | Overs | Mdns | Runs | Wkts |
|--------------|-------|------|------|------|-------|------|------|------|
| Worthington  | 6     | 3    | 6    | 1    | 3     | —    | 20   | —    |
| Copson       | 4     | 3    | 5    | —    | 3     | 2    | 5    | —    |
| Mitchell     | 6     | 1    | 22   | 8    | 14    | 2    | 66   | 5    |
| Townsend     | 4     | 1    | 14   | 1    | 14.2  | 2    | 48   | 5    |

Umpires: E. J. Smith and T. Oates.

# WORCESTERSHIRE v GLAMORGAN

Played at Worcester, July 29, 30, 31, 1935

Drawn. Mercer made history by becoming the first Glamorgan player to take all ten wickets in an innings. Although the pitch on Wednesday gave him little assistance, he kept an immaculate length, turned the ball sharply either way and, before lunch, took six wickets for 15 runs. Brilliant fielding helped in the triumph. Human, the only batsman really to master Mercer, put on 54 with Singleton for Worcestershire's sixth stand. Next day, Glamorgan recovered splendidly and, thanks to an eighth wicket partnership of 63 by Lavis and Brierley, they secured a lead of eight. Howorth and Jackson, aided by the conditions, turned the ball considerably. Worcestershire began badly. They found Reed (fast left-hand) difficult to play. As rain delayed the resumption until half-past three on Friday, Glamorgan had little chance of getting 156 runs in ninety-five minutes and made no bid for success.

## Worcestershire

| | | |
|---|---|---|
| Mr R. D. Evers c Smart b Mercer | 3 | – lbw b Reed ... 18 |
| C. H. Bull c Brierley b Mercer | 22 | – c Turnbull b Reed ... 66 |
| S. H. Martin c Turnbull b Mercer | 4 | – b Reed ... 0 |
| H. H. Gibbons c Turnbull b Mercer | 2 | – lbw (N) b Mercer ... 8 |
| Mr B. W. Quaife c D. Davies b Mercer | 2 | |
| J. Horton b Mercer | 0 | |
| Mr R. H. C. Human not out | 59 | – c Smart b Reed ... 42 |
| Mr A. P. Singleton st Brierley b Mercer | 29 | |
| R. Howorth b Mercer | 3 | – not out ... 14 |
| R. T. D. Perks lbw b Mercer | 0 | – not out ... 8 |
| P. F. Jackson c Lavis b Mercer | 1 | |
| B 6, l-b 9, w 3 | 18 | B 3, l-b 3, w 1 ... 7 |
| | **143** | **(5 wkts dec.) 163** |

## Glamorgan

| | | |
|---|---|---|
| A. H. Dyson c Howorth b Martin | 14 | – c Evers b Martin ... 6 |
| E. Davies run out | 8 | – not out ... 6 |
| D. Davies b Perks | 1 | |
| Mr V. G. J. Jenkins lbw b Jackson | 13 | |
| R. Duckfield c Human b Howarth | 5 | |
| C. Smart c and b Howorth | 1 | – b Perks ... 0 |
| Mr M. J. Turnbull c Horton b Howorth | 14 | – c Jackson b Perks ... 29 |
| G. Lavis b Perks | 34 | – not out ... 14 |
| T. L. Brierley b Howorth | 37 | |
| J. Mercer c Horton b Perks | 12 | – b Martin ... 1 |
| G. Reed not out | 0 | |
| B 7, l-b 5 | 12 | |
| | **151** | **56** |

**Glamorgan Bowling**

| | Overs | Mdns | Runs | Wkts | Overs | Mdns | Runs | Wkts |
|---|---|---|---|---|---|---|---|---|
| Mercer ........... | 26 | 10 | 51 | 10 | 21 | 2 | 52 | 1 |
| Reed ........... | 12 | 2 | 38 | — | 22 | 3 | 55 | 4 |
| D. Davies ......... | 6 | 1 | 9 | — | 6 | 1 | 15 | — |
| E. Davies ......... | 7 | — | 27 | — | 8 | 3 | 23 | — |
| Smart ........... | | | | | 7 | 1 | 11 | — |

**Worcestershire Bowling**

| | Overs | Mdns | Runs | Wkts | Overs | Mdns | Runs | Wkts |
|---|---|---|---|---|---|---|---|---|
| Perks ........... | 15 | 2 | 38 | 3 | 9 | 1 | 24 | 2 |
| Human ........... | 1 | — | 4 | — | | | | |
| Jackson ......... | 21 | 6 | 38 | 1 | 4 | — | 10 | — |
| Martin .......... | 9 | 2 | 28 | 1 | 6 | 1 | 17 | 2 |
| Howorth ........ | 18.1 | 8 | 31 | 4 | 2 | — | 5 | — |

Umpires: J. Newman and E. Cooke.

# WORCESTERSHIRE v YORKSHIRE

Played at Stourbridge, May 16, 18, 19, 1936

Worcestershire won by 11 runs. A memorable match ended in Worcestershire's first victory over Yorkshire since 1909. On Saturday, when cricket was restricted to under four hours, Lyttelton, despite sunshine following a thunderstorm, took first innings, and Worcestershire attacked the bowling with such spirit that eleven 6s were registered. Lyttelton hit four of these, as well as four 4s, but Verity, although conceding four 6s, claimed half the wickets for 48. On Monday, 20 batsmen were dismissed for 217. In turn, Jackson and Verity bowled irresistibly, and Yorkshire left off wanting 55 runs to win with eight wickets intact. Verity, securing eight wickets for five runs apiece, made his match record 13 for 88. On a crumbling pitch Yorkshire, with the exception of Leyland, who batted courageously for an hour, were routed by Jackson and Howorth, and these two spin bowlers equally shared the wickets.

### Worcestershire

| | | | | |
|---|---|---|---|---|
| H. H. Gibbons c Hutton b Verity ............... | 13 | – lbw b Verity ................... | 10 |
| C. H. Bull c and b Turner ..................... | 1 | – c Mitchell b Leyland ........... | 24 |
| S. H. Martin hit wkt b Robinson ............. | 20 | – lbw b Verity .................. | 2 |
| Hon. C. J. Lyttelton c and b Verity ............. | 48 | – c Leyland b Verity ............. | 2 |
| Mr B. W. Quaife c Sellers b Verity ............... | 0 | – not out ....................... | 28 |
| R. Howorth c Sellers b Verity ............. | 14 | – c Hutton b Leyland ........... | 4 |
| B. P. King st Wood b Verity ................. | 13 | – c Mitchell b Verity ........... | 4 |
| F. Warne c Leyland b Robinson ................ | 8 | – c Mitchell b Verity ........... | 0 |
| S. Shepherd lbw b Robinson ................. | 9 | – c Barber b Verity ............. | 0 |
| R. T. D. Perks st Wood b Robinson ............ | 12 | – lbw (N) b Verity ............. | 8 |
| P. F. Jackson not out ...................... | 0 | – st Wood b Verity ............. | 0 |
| B 9, l-b 1 ......................... | 10 | B 9, n-b 1 .............. | 10 |
| | **148** | | **92** |

## Yorkshire

| | | | |
|---|---|---|---|
| H. Sutcliffe c Lyttelton b Perks | 7 | – lbw (N) b Jackson | 29 |
| A. Mitchell c Warne b Martin | 34 | – lbw b Jackson | 17 |
| W. Barber c Quaife b Jackson | 9 | – st Quaife b Howorth | 5 |
| M. Leyland c Warne b Martin | 20 | – lbw b Howorth | 35 |
| L. Hutton run out | 0 | – lbw (N) b Jackson | 0 |
| C. Turner c Martin b Jackson | 27 | – b Jackson | 0 |
| A. Wood c Warne b Martin | 3 | – lbw b Howorth | 8 |
| Mr A. B. Sellers c and b Martin | 4 | – c Martin b Howorth | 2 |
| H. Verity not out | 11 | – not out | 6 |
| E. P. Robinson c Lyttelton b Jackson | 0 | – c Lyttelton b Howorth | 0 |
| E. Rawlin b Jackson | 1 | – lbw b Jackson | 4 |
| B 2, l-b 5 | 7 | | |
| | **123** | | **106** |

## Yorkshire Bowling

| | Overs | Mdns | Runs | Wkts | Overs | Mdns | Runs | Wkts |
|---|---|---|---|---|---|---|---|---|
| Rawlin | 1 | — | 2 | — | 4 | — | 9 | — |
| Turner | 3 | 2 | 7 | 1 | 3 | 1 | 2 | — |
| Verity | 14 | 4 | 48 | 5 | 26.4 | 15 | 40 | 8 |
| Robinson | 11.3 | 1 | 81 | 4 | 6 | 2 | 12 | — |
| Leyland | | | | | 15 | 6 | 19 | 2 |

## Worcestershire Bowling

| | Overs | Mdns | Runs | Wkts | Overs | Mdns | Runs | Wkts |
|---|---|---|---|---|---|---|---|---|
| Perks | 19 | 6 | 35 | 1 | 6 | 2 | 15 | — |
| Shepherd | 2 | 1 | 4 | — | | | | |
| Howorth | 9 | 1 | 25 | — | 15 | 7 | 21 | 5 |
| Jackson | 16 | 6 | 18 | 4 | 18.3 | 3 | 66 | 5 |
| Martin | 13 | 4 | 34 | 4 | 2 | — | 4 | — |

Umpires: A. Skelding and C. N. Woolley.

# WORCESTERSHIRE v SURREY

### At Kidderminster, May 28, 30, 31, 1938

Drawn. Gover, the Surrey fast bowler, was the outstanding figure in a match spoiled by the weather. He took fourteen wickets including all seven which fell in Worcestershire's second innings before rain prevented any cricket on the last day. With the pitch soft on top and hard underneath Surrey had to struggle hard, and Worcestershire began disastrously, losing three wickets for nine runs before Lyttelton, hitting out, and Martin put on 53. The second day's play went so overwhelmingly in favour of bowlers that twenty-one wickets went down for 193 runs, ten to Gover for 46 runs. Nine batsmen were leg before. Sunshine after rain made the turf very treacherous, the ball coming along at different heights and turning quickly. Fishlock alone played Perks well and Surrey's last five wickets yielded only 18 runs. Worcestershire were helpless until bad light stopped the game when Surrey had claimed the extra half hour in the hope of a victory in two days.

## Surrey

| | | | |
|---|---|---|---|
| L. B. Fishlock c Gibbons b Perks | 0 | – b Howorth | 32 |
| T. McMurray c Martin b Perks | 3 | – lbw b Jackson | 2 |
| R. J. Gregory c Howorth b Perks | 25 | – lbw b Perks | 20 |
| H. S. Squires b Jackson | 34 | – lbw b Perks | 16 |
| T. H. Barling b Perks | 14 | – lbw b Perks | 1 |
| Mr E. R. T. Holmes c Lyttelton b Howorth | 43 | – lbw b Martin | 0 |
| F. Berry run out | 14 | – b Perks | 4 |
| E. A. Watts b Jackson | 0 | – lbw b Perks | 4 |
| K. King c Martin b Jackson | 22 | – b Martin | 1 |
| E. W. Brooks b Jackson | 22 | – b Perks | 4 |
| A. R. Gover not out | 9 | – not out | 4 |
| B 4, l-b 2 | 6 | B 8, l-b 4, n-b 1 | 13 |
| | **192** | | **101** |

## Worcestershire

| | | | |
|---|---|---|---|
| B. P. King c and b Watts | 6 | – lbw b Gover | 15 |
| V. Grimshaw c Gregory b Gover | 3 | – lbw b Gover | 2 |
| E. Cooper c Brooks b Gover | 0 | – c McMurray b Gover | 7 |
| H. H. Gibbons b Gover | 9 | – b Gover | 10 |
| S. H. Martin lbw b Berry | 52 | – c and b Gover | 0 |
| Hon. C. J. Lyttelton b Berry | 28 | – b Gover | 0 |
| J. Horton c Brooks b Gover | 5 | – not out | 8 |
| S. Buller not out | 22 | – lbw b Gover | 0 |
| R. Howorth b Gover | 0 | – not out | 12 |
| R. T. D. Perks b Gover | 0 | | |
| P. F. Jackson b Gover | 1 | | |
| B 5, l-b 1 | 6 | B 4, l-b 4, n-b 1 | 9 |
| | **132** | | **63** |

### Worcestershire Bowling

| | Overs | Mdns | Runs | Wkts | Overs | Mdns | Runs | Wkts |
|---|---|---|---|---|---|---|---|---|
| Perks | 15 | 3 | 47 | 4 | 17.1 | 4 | 38 | 6 |
| Martin | 17 | 6 | 43 | — | 10 | 7 | 11 | 2 |
| Howorth | 13 | 1 | 57 | 1 | 6 | — | 12 | 1 |
| Jackson | 10.2 | 1 | 39 | 4 | 13 | 2 | 27 | 1 |

### Surrey Bowling

| | Overs | Mdns | Runs | Wkts | Overs | Mdns | Runs | Wkts |
|---|---|---|---|---|---|---|---|---|
| Gover | 25.1 | 7 | 50 | 7 | 14 | 2 | 35 | 7 |
| Watts | 6 | 2 | 9 | 1 | 4 | 1 | 8 | — |
| King | 5 | 3 | 21 | — | | | | |
| Berry | 14 | 4 | 46 | 2 | 9 | 5 | 11 | — |
| Squires | | | | | 0.1 | — | — | — |

Umpires: A. Skelding and A. C. Russell.

## WORCESTERSHIRE v LANCASHIRE

At Dudley, June 22, 23, 24, 1938

Drawn. For the first time in their history Worcestershire fielded an entirely professional eleven. A strange incident occurred on the first day. Phillipson, foolishly going for a short run off a no-ball, collided with Jackson, who was trying to throw down the wicket. Phillipson dislocated his left collar-bone and Jackson hurt his back; neither took further part in the match. Hopwood and Iddon batted well in a stand of 113 but Nutter was missed three times off Perks. Lister helped to add 81. Although six men reached double figures, Worcestershire had to follow on 207 behind. Then King and Cooper made 84 together while Gibbons, the acting captain, played at the top of his form in a stand which turned a deficit of 102 into a lead of 105. Gibbons cut and drove beautifully, and Cooper maintained a sound defence for four hours and forty minutes. Wilkinson took five wickets for 27 in his last twelve overs. Rain came soon after Worcestershire's declaration.

### Lancashire

| | | | |
|---|---|---|---|
| J. L. Hopwood c Jackson b Martin | 67 | | |
| C. Washbrook b Perks | 4 | – not out | 8 |
| J. Iddon c and b Martin | 60 | | |
| N. Oldfield c Howorth b Perks | 1 | | |
| A. Nutter not out | 89 | | |
| Mr D. M. Matthews c Gibbons b Jackson | 22 | | |
| Mr W. H. L. Lister lbw b Howorth | 46 | | |
| W. E. Phillipson retired hurt | 15 | | |
| W. Farrimond c Gibbons b Martin | 0 | – not out | 16 |
| R. Pollard b Martin | 1 | | |
| L. L. Wilkinson b Perks | 0 | | |
| L-b 2 | 2 | L-b 1, w 1 | 2 |
| | **307** | | **26** |

### Worcestershire

| | | | |
|---|---|---|---|
| C. H. Bull lbw b Nutter | 0 | – c Farrimond b Pollard | 17 |
| B. P. King c Wilkinson b Pollard | 0 | – b Pollard | 56 |
| E. Cooper c Farrimond b Pollard | 13 | – c Farrimond b Wilkinson | 111 |
| H. H. Gibbons b Pollard | 11 | – lbw b Wilkinson | 123 |
| S. H. Martin c Farrimond b Pollard | 5 | – not out | 42 |
| F. Warne b Nutter | 17 | – b Pollard | 6 |
| J. Horton not out | 15 | – b Wilkinson | 9 |
| S. Buller c Nutter b Wilkinson | 15 | – c Nutter b Wilkinson | 0 |
| R. Howorth c and b Wilkinson | 16 | – c Pollard b Wilkinson | 0 |
| R. T. D. Perks st Farrimond b Wilkinson | 4 | – not out | 1 |
| P. F. Jackson absent hurt | 0 | | |
| L-b 3, n-b 1 | 4 | L-b 6, n-b 1 | 7 |
| | **100** | **(8 wkts dec.)** | **372** |

### Worcestershire Bowling

| | Overs | Mdns | Runs | Wkts | Overs | Mdns | Runs | Wkts |
|---|---|---|---|---|---|---|---|---|
| Perks | 30.2 | 4 | 91 | 3 | | | | |
| Martin | 32 | 6 | 90 | 4 | | | | |
| Howorth | 13 | 3 | 47 | 1 | | | | |
| Jackson | 10 | 1 | 36 | 1 | | | | |
| Warne | 12 | — | 41 | — | 3 | — | 7 | — |
| Horton | | | | | 4 | — | 17 | — |

### Lancashire Bowling

| | Overs | Mdns | Runs | Wkts | Overs | Mdns | Runs | Wkts |
|---|---|---|---|---|---|---|---|---|
| Pollard | 19 | 6 | 42 | 4 | 28 | 5 | 79 | 3 |
| Nutter | 10 | 4 | 12 | 3 | 32 | 7 | 71 | — |
| Wilkinson | 18.2 | 2 | 42 | 3 | 37 | 4 | 118 | 5 |
| Iddon | | | | | 31 | 7 | 85 | — |
| Hopwood | | | | | 3 | — | 12 | — |

Umpires: T. Oates and H. G. Baldwin.

## WORCESTERSHIRE v GLOUCESTERSHIRE

At Stourbridge, July 9, 11, 12, 1938

Gloucestershire won by 34 runs. Sinfield, bowling off-breaks in deadly fashion, took chief part in a victory gained with only ten minutes of extra time remaining. Rain spoiled the opening day when during two and a half hours' cricket Gloucestershire lost four wickets while scoring 122, three falling to Howorth at the start for 19 runs. On the Monday 23 fell for 305 runs. Allen drove and cut well, good left-handed strokes bringing half his runs by boundaries. The last seven Worcestershire wickets fell for 45, Sinfield and Tyler carrying all before them. Gloucestershire, in turn, had to struggle, and Howorth, flighting the ball and mixing his pace, finished with a match record of thirteen wickets for 133 runs. Worcestershire lost five men for 83, before rain eased the pitch. Then Cooper and Palmer put on 94, but Sinfield, unchanged, and Tyler disposed of the last four men for 30 runs. Sinfield's match record showed fourteen wickets for 110.

### Gloucestershire

| | | | |
|---|---|---|---|
| Mr B. O. Allen c Bull b Howorth | 72 | – c King b Howorth | 15 |
| V. Hopkins b Howorth | 9 | – c Buller b Howorth | 16 |
| W. L. Neale st Buller b Howorth | 9 | – lbw b Jackson | 3 |
| G. M. Emmett lbw b Howorth | 11 | – c Palmer b Howorth | 11 |
| Mr E. D. R. Eagar b Jackson | 6 | – c Howorth b Jackson | 0 |
| E. A. Wilson c Jackson b Perks | 52 | – c Palmer b Perks | 10 |
| R. W. Haynes lbw b Howorth | 9 | – c Palmer b Howorth | 6 |
| C. J. Scott c Perks b Howorth | 2 | – c Cooper b Howorth | 5 |
| R. A. Sinfield not out | 22 | – lbw b Jackson | 7 |
| M. Cranfield st Buller b Jackson | 20 | – not out | 10 |
| Mr C. Tyler st Buller b Howorth | 14 | – lbw b Howorth | 16 |
| B 5, l-b 3, n-b 3 | 11 | B 2, l-b 4, n-b 1 | 7 |
| | **237** | | **106** |

### Worcestershire

| | | | |
|---|---|---|---|
| C. H. Bull c Hopkins b Sinfield | 26 | – b Sinfield | 0 |
| B. P. King c Eagar b Tyler | 15 | – b Tyler | 14 |
| E. Cooper c Wilson b Sinfield | 28 | – b Sinfield | 84 |
| H. H. Gibbons b Tyler | 14 | – c Hopkins b Sinfield | 26 |
| Mr C. H. Palmer b Sinfield | 2 | – not out | 51 |
| Mr C. D. A. Pullan c Wilson b Tyler | 0 | – b Sinfield | 0 |
| Hon. C. J. Lyttelton b Sinfield | 2 | – b Sinfield | 4 |
| S. Buller not out | 14 | – c Hopkins b Sinfield | 0 |
| R. Howorth c Scott b Sinfield | 0 | – b Sinfield | 7 |
| R. T. D. Perks c Scott b Tyler | 6 | – c Allen b Sinfield | 7 |
| P. F. Jackson c and b Sinfield | 0 | – b Tyler | 1 |
| B 6 | 6 | B 2 | 2 |
| | **113** | | **196** |

### Worcestershire Bowling

| | Overs | Mdns | Runs | Wkts | Overs | Mdns | Runs | Wkts |
|---|---|---|---|---|---|---|---|---|
| Perks | 9 | 1 | 34 | 1 | 7 | 2 | 10 | 1 |
| Howorth | 43.2 | 13 | 85 | 7 | 19.2 | 4 | 48 | 6 |
| Jackson | 38 | 6 | 102 | 2 | 14 | 4 | 41 | 3 |
| Palmer | 2 | 1 | 5 | — | | | | |

**Gloucestershire Bowling**

|          | Overs | Mdns | Runs | Wkts | Overs | Mdns | Runs | Wkts |
|----------|-------|------|------|------|-------|------|------|------|
| Scott    | 4     | —    | 16   | —    |       |      |      |      |
| Cranfield| 3     | 1    | 14   | —    | 3     | —    | 16   | —    |
| Sinfield | 16.1  | 3    | 45   | 6    | 33    | 12   | 65   | 8    |
| Tyler    | 16    | 4    | 32   | 4    | 26.5  | 3    | 100  | 2    |
| Emmett   |       |      |      |      | 3     | —    | 13   | —    |

Umpires: F. Walden and G. M. Lee.

# WORCESTERSHIRE v ESSEX

At Worcester, July 30, August 1, 2, 1938

Essex won by four wickets. Superb fast bowling by Farnes accounted for the result in a most interesting struggle. Helped by moisture in the pitch and a cross wind, the Essex fast bowlers were checked only by Pataudi, who batted stylishly for nearly two hours and placed the ball skilfully. Eastman, eighth to leave, was also a solitary batting success in Essex securing the lead. He drove and pulled admirably, hitting thirteen 4s. A stand of 135 by Human and Gibbons altered the state of the game but Farnes caused another collapse, and made his match figures fourteen wickets for 119 runs. Human excelled in driving with eleven 4s among his strokes. The pitch played easily on the third morning and, after the dismissal of O'Connor, Dennis and Peter Smith hit off the last 40 runs.

## Worcestershire

| | | |
|---|---|---|
| E. Cooper lbw b Nichols | 3 | – b Farnes ............ 6 |
| B. P. King c Taylor b Farnes | 16 | – lbw b Farnes ........ 1 |
| Mr C. D. A. Pullan b Farnes | 5 | – b Farnes ............ 8 |
| Nawab of Pataudi b Farnes | 61 | – b Farnes ............ 37 |
| H. H. Gibbons b Farnes | 0 | – c Taylor b Nichols ... 58 |
| Mr R. H. C. Human b Stephenson | 10 | – b Nichols ........... 81 |
| Mr C. H. Palmer b Nichols | 5 | – lbw b Farnes ........ 0 |
| R. Howorth c Wade b Nichols | 11 | – b Farnes ............ 21 |
| S. Buller lbw b Farnes | 4 | – lbw b Farnes ........ 4 |
| R. Jenkins b Farnes | 21 | – not out ............ 11 |
| R. T. D. Perks not out | 1 | – c Wade b Farnes ..... 0 |
| B 10, l-b 4 | 14 | B 14, l-b 7 ........... 21 |
| | **151** | **248** |

## Essex

| | | |
|---|---|---|
| L. C. Eastman c Perks b Jenkins | 90 | – b Howorth .......... 19 |
| A. V. Avery b Human | 9 | – lbw b Perks ......... 21 |
| R. M. Taylor lbw b Howorth | 19 | – c Howorth b Perks ... 29 |
| J. O'Connor c King b Howorth | 3 | – lbw b Howorth ...... 46 |
| M. S. Nichols b Perks | 14 | – c Buller b Perks ..... 6 |
| Mr T. N. Pearce c Gibbons b Howorth | 20 | – b Parks ............ 12 |
| Mr J. N. Dennis c Buller b Human | 5 | – not out ............ 37 |
| P. Smith c Human b Howorth | 12 | – not out ............ 21 |
| T. H. Wade not out | 18 | |
| Capt. J. W. A. Stephenson b Perks | 2 | |
| Mr K. Farnes b Perks | 0 | |
| L-b 8 | 8 | B 5, l-b 4 ........... 9 |
| | **200** | **200** |

**Essex Bowling**

|  | Overs | Mdns | Runs | Wkts | Overs | Mdns | Runs | Wkts |
|---|---|---|---|---|---|---|---|---|
| Farnes .......... | 16.1 | 2 | 43 | 6 | 24.1 | 5 | 76 | 8 |
| Nichols ......... | 14 | 5 | 31 | 3 | 24 | 8 | 65 | 2 |
| Stephenson ....... | 9 | 2 | 30 | 1 | 11 | 1 | 40 | — |
| Smith ........... | 9 | — | 33 | — | 11 | — | 46 | — |

**Worcestershire Bowling**

|  | Overs | Mdns | Runs | Wkts | Overs | Mdns | Runs | Wkts |
|---|---|---|---|---|---|---|---|---|
| Perks ........... | 15.5 | 2 | 66 | 3 | 31 | 5 | 111 | 4 |
| Human .......... | 15 | 4 | 51 | 2 | 1 | — | 5 | — |
| Howorth ........ | 19 | 3 | 58 | 4 | 30 | 11 | 43 | 2 |
| Jenkins .......... | 5 | — | 17 | 1 | 3 | 2 | 5 | — |
| Pullan .......... |  |  |  |  | 3 | — | 15 | — |
| Palmer .......... |  |  |  |  | 6 | 2 | 12 | — |

Umpires: C. N. Woolley and H. G. Baldwin.

## WORCESTERSHIRE v SOMERSET

### At Worcester, August 17, 18, 19, 1938

Worcestershire won by 45 runs. Lee, the Somerset left-hand batsman, nearly equalled the world record of C. J. B. Wood (Leicestershire) who against Yorkshire at Bradford in 1911, scored two separate hundreds and carried his bat through each innings. Not out in the first innings, Lee was last to leave in the second. Wellard took the first six Worcestershire wickets which fell during a spell lasting a hundred minutes. Somerset, too, were worried by swing bowling and only Lee and Andrews, in a stand of 95, offered much resistance. Worcestershire steadily cleared off arrears and Lyttelton, going in fourth wicket down, hit two 6s and thirteen 4s while scoring 75 out of 97 in fifty minutes. Afterwards, on a pitch drying under sunshine Lee received little help against the admirable bowling of Howorth and Martin, but the innings lasted four hours. Lee hit ten 4s, his cuts and leg strokes being excellent.

### Worcestershire

| | | |
|---|---|---|
| Hon. C. J. Lyttelton b Wellard .................. | 18 – | c Hazell b Andrews .............. 75 |
| R. Howorth lbw b Wellard ..................... | 20 – | c Gimblett b Wellard ............ 52 |
| E. Cooper b Wellard ......................... | 2 – | b Hazell ...................... 16 |
| Nawab of Pataudi b Wellard ................... | 0 – | c Wellard b Andrews ............ 14 |
| H. H. Gibbons c Gimblett b Wellard ............ | 21 – | c Gimblett b Wellard ............ 69 |
| S. H. Martin c Luckes b Andrews .............. | 32 – | c Gimblett b Wellard ............ 22 |
| Mr C. D. A. Pullan b Wellard ................. | 16 – | b Hazell ...................... 11 |
| Mr A. P. Singleton c Wellard b Buse .......... | 11 – | not out ....................... 24 |
| S. Buller b Wellard ......................... | 19 – | c Lyon b Hazell ................ 1 |
| R. Jenkins b Andrews ....................... | 4 – | b Hazell ...................... 0 |
| R. T. D. Perks not out ...................... | 1 – | b Hazell ...................... 3 |
| L-b 2 .......................... | 2 | B 4, l-b 3, w 2, n-b 4 ....... 13 |
| | 146 | 300 |

## Somerset

| | | | | |
|---|---|---|---|---|
| F. S. Lee not out | 109 | – c Singleton b Martin | 107 |
| H. Gimblett c Buller b Perks | 0 | – c Gibbons b Howorth | 20 |
| W. H. R. Andrews run out | 49 | – c Buller b Howorth | 12 |
| H. T. F. Buse b Jenkins | 1 | – c Pataudi b Howorth | 3 |
| Mr A. M. T. Jones lbw b Martin | 0 | – c and b Jenkins | 0 |
| Mr M. D. Lyon c Perks b Jenkins | 9 | – c and b Howorth | 3 |
| Mr C. J. P. Barnwell c Cooper b Perks | 18 | – c Perks b Howorth | 0 |
| W. T. Luckes b Perks | 6 | – b Martin | 15 |
| A. W. Wellard c Pullan b Martin | 0 | – c Pataudi b Howorth | 27 |
| Mr A. A. Pearse b Martin | 0 | – c Singleton b Martin | 0 |
| H. L. Hazell b Martin | 2 | – not out | 5 |
| W 1, n-b 1 | 2 | B 4, l-b 9 | 13 |
| | **196** | | **205** |

## Somerset Bowling

| | Overs | Mdns | Runs | Wkts | Overs | Mdns | Runs | Wkts |
|---|---|---|---|---|---|---|---|---|
| Wellard | 18.1 | 4 | 59 | 7 | 27 | 4 | 106 | 3 |
| Andrews | 10 | 2 | 35 | 2 | 26 | 4 | 81 | 2 |
| Buse | 8 | 2 | 25 | 1 | 8 | 2 | 29 | — |
| Hazell | 6 | — | 17 | — | 16.2 | 2 | 50 | 5 |
| Lyon | 2 | — | 8 | — | 1 | — | 5 | — |
| Gimblett | | | | | 3 | 1 | 8 | — |
| Jones | | | | | 1 | — | 8 | — |

## Worcestershire Bowling

| | Overs | Mdns | Runs | Wkts | Overs | Mdns | Runs | Wkts |
|---|---|---|---|---|---|---|---|---|
| Perks | 24 | 3 | 83 | 3 | 16 | 7 | 35 | — |
| Martin | 24.3 | 3 | 49 | 4 | 15.4 | 4 | 48 | 3 |
| Howorth | 7 | 2 | 13 | — | 25 | 6 | 51 | 6 |
| Singleton | 10 | 2 | 33 | — | 7 | 2 | 16 | — |
| Jenkins | 11 | 3 | 16 | 2 | 11 | — | 42 | 1 |

Umpires: A. Dolphin and E. Robinson.

# WORCESTERSHIRE v HAMPSHIRE

### At Worcester, May 20, 22, 23, 1939

Worcestershire won by six wickets. An injured man played a great part in a memorable victory. A torn thigh muscle prevented Martin bowling or fielding in Hampshire's second innings but, when Worcestershire lost four men for 48 after being set to get 255, Martin changed his decision not to carry on. With his side strapped and in obvious pain, Martin defied the bowling while he and Gibbons knocked off the remaining 207 runs. The winning hit gave Martin his hundred. Gibbons, with a not out century in each innings, Arnold, whose highest score since 1932 contained a 6 and twenty-one 4s, and Perks also performed noteworthy feats.

## Hampshire

| | | | |
|---|---|---|---|
| N. McCorkell c Buller b Martin | 7 | – b Perks | 0 |
| J. Bailey b Martin | 5 | – c Howorth b Perks | 21 |
| G. Hill c White b Martin | 3 | – b Perks | 2 |
| W. L. Creese b Perks | 11 | – c and b Jenkins | 20 |
| J. Arnold not out | 179 | – lbw b Perks | 34 |
| A. E. Pothecary c Gibbons b Jenkins | 25 | – b Perks | 2 |
| D. F. Walker b Perks | 1 | – b Howorth | 62 |
| A. Holt st Buller b Howorth | 28 | – c Buller b Perks | 4 |
| G. S. Boyes b Howorth | 47 | – c Bull b Perks | 6 |
| Mr G. R. Taylor b Jenkins | 1 | – c Buller b Perks | 27 |
| G. E. M. Heath c Martin b Jenkins | 0 | – not out | 3 |
| B 8, l-b 1, n-b 3 | 12 | B 10, l-b 3, w 1, n-b 2 | 16 |

319         197

## Worcestershire

| | | | |
|---|---|---|---|
| C. H. Bull c McCorkell b Heath | 0 | – c McCorkell b Heath | 22 |
| Mr A. F. T. White c McCorkell b Heath | 6 | – b Heath | 9 |
| B. P. King c Arnold b Heath | 16 | – lbw b Bailey | 3 |
| E. Cooper lbw b Heath | 8 | – lbw b Bailey | 8 |
| H. H. Gibbons not out | 111 | – not out | 100 |
| Hon. C. J. Lyttelton c and b Bailey | 5 | | |
| S. H. Martin b Hill | 39 | – not out | 102 |
| R. Howorth b Boyes | 0 | | |
| S. Buller lbw b Creese | 33 | | |
| R. T. D. Perks b Boyes | 35 | | |
| R. Jenkins run out | 0 | | |
| B 3, l-b 6 | 9 | B 1, l-b 11 | 12 |

262         256

### Worcestershire Bowling

| | Overs | Mdns | Runs | Wkts | Overs | Mdns | Runs | Wkts |
|---|---|---|---|---|---|---|---|---|
| Perks | 18 | — | 91 | 2 | 13.7 | 5 | 59 | 8 |
| Martin | 18 | 3 | 55 | 3 | | | | |
| Howorth | 14 | — | 73 | 2 | 16 | 4 | 46 | 1 |
| Lyttelton | 8 | 1 | 48 | — | 4 | 1 | 10 | — |
| Jenkins | 10.4 | — | 40 | 3 | 17 | 3 | 66 | 1 |

### Hampshire Bowling

| | Overs | Mdns | Runs | Wkts | Overs | Mdns | Runs | Wkts |
|---|---|---|---|---|---|---|---|---|
| Heath | 20 | 1 | 86 | 4 | 21 | 2 | 104 | 2 |
| Bailey | 12 | — | 58 | 1 | 12.1 | 1 | 77 | 2 |
| Hill | 14.3 | 2 | 46 | 1 | 4 | 2 | 12 | — |
| Boyes | 13 | 1 | 45 | 2 | 10 | 1 | 40 | — |
| Creese | 3 | — | 18 | 1 | 5 | 1 | 11 | — |

Umpires: D. Hendren and H. Cruice.

## WORCESTERSHIRE v SOMERSET

### At Kidderminster, July 8, 10, 11, 1939

A tie. Such a result to a county championship match had not occurred for thirteen years. Somerset needed six to win when the last pair, Weaver and Hazell, came together. With the scores level Howorth got through Hazell's defence with the fourth ball of the last over of extra time and the game ended in a tie. After a blank first day the wicket was responsive to spin and bowlers were always on top. Cooper batted stylishly but Wellard, changing to off-breaks, took six wickets for 15, Worcestershire's last seven men going in for 18 runs. Somerset just got the lead, and in Worcestershire's second innings Hazell tumbled out five of the last six batsmen. Then came the fourth feverish innings. This time the odd run favoured Worcestershire and each side received six points.

## Worcestershire

| | | | |
|---|---:|---|---:|
| R. Howorth c Luckes b Wellard | 16 | – b Buse | 45 |
| E. Cooper lbw b Wellard | 69 | – c Hazell b Buse | 21 |
| B. P. King c Weaver b Buse | 3 | – lbw b Buse | 17 |
| H. H. Gibbons c Priddy b Hazell | 29 | – b Wellard | 0 |
| S. H. Martin b Wellard | 0 | – c Bennett b Hazell | 25 |
| Mr C. H. Palmer b Wellard | 2 | – c and b Hazell | 11 |
| Mr J. Stanning c Priddy b Wellard | 4 | – b Hazell | 0 |
| Hon. C. J. Lyttelton c Lee b Wellard | 1 | – c Gimblett b Hazell | 0 |
| Mr E. H. Perry st Lee b Wellard | 0 | – run out | 1 |
| R. Jenkins not out | 1 | – not out | 0 |
| R. T. D. Perks c Lee b Hazell | 0 | – c Gimblett b Hazell | 16 |
| B 5 | 5 | B 5, l-b 1 | 6 |
| | **130** | | **142** |

## Somerset

| | | | |
|---|---:|---|---:|
| F. S. Lee b Perks | 5 | – c Jenkins b Howorth | 23 |
| H. Gimblett b Perks | 0 | – b Perry | 5 |
| H. T. F. Buse c King b Martin | 26 | – b Perks | 11 |
| Mr F. M. McRae c King b Perry | 1 | – st King b Jenkins | 28 |
| Mr E. F. Longrigg c Howorth b Martin | 13 | – c and b Howorth | 1 |
| Mr J. Priddy c Perks b Palmer | 15 | – b Jenkins | 13 |
| W. T. Luckes b Perks | 24 | – c Perks b Howorth | 22 |
| Mr G. M. Bennett b Perry | 10 | – c Martin b Perks | 16 |
| A. W. Wellard b Perks | 0 | – b Perry | 12 |
| Mr S. Weaver b Jenkins | 19 | – not out | 3 |
| H. L. Hazell not out | 13 | – b Howorth | 4 |
| L-b 2, n-b 3 | 5 | L-b 3 | 3 |
| | **131** | | **141** |

## Somerset Bowling

| | Overs | Mdns | Runs | Wkts | Overs | Mdns | Runs | Wkts |
|---|---|---|---|---|---|---|---|---|
| Wellard | 16 | 1 | 45 | 7 | 16 | 1 | 62 | 1 |
| Weaver | 3 | — | 16 | — | 1 | — | 13 | — |
| Buse | 10 | 2 | 24 | 1 | 21 | 5 | 55 | 3 |
| Hazell | 11.7 | 2 | 40 | 2 | 5.7 | 1 | 6 | 5 |

## Worcestershire Bowling

| | Overs | Mdns | Runs | Wkts | Overs | Mdns | Runs | Wkts |
|---|---|---|---|---|---|---|---|---|
| Perks | 13 | 1 | 40 | 4 | 10 | 2 | 34 | 2 |
| Perry | 12 | 2 | 31 | 2 | 10 | 1 | 43 | 2 |
| Martin | 11 | 1 | 26 | 2 | | | | |
| Howorth | 4 | 1 | 18 | — | 9.4 | 1 | 27 | 4 |
| Palmer | 1 | — | 6 | 1 | | | | |
| Jenkins | 2.5 | — | 5 | 1 | 10 | 1 | 34 | 2 |

Umpires: J. Smart and E. Cooke.

# YORKSHIRE

## YORKSHIRE v HAMPSHIRE

Played at Leeds, June 26, 28, 29, 1920

This match produced a genuine sensation, Hampshire declaring with two wickets down and beating Yorkshire by an innings and 72 runs. It should be said, however, that Yorkshire had to bowl on a perfect wicket and bat on one more or less ruined by rain. Still Hampshire placed themselves in an impregnable position on the first day when they gave a marvellous display of batting. Brown and Bowell sent up 183 for the first wicket, and after Capt. Barrett had failed Brown and Mead took the score to 456. They had no need to do any more, as rain fell for several hours on Sunday night, and on Monday morning Tennyson at once declared. Brown in getting his highest score in first-class cricket, hit twenty-nine 4s, and Mead's 122 included fifteen 4s. Seldom in English cricket have two left-handed batsmen enjoyed such a triumph. On the damaged pitch Yorkshire had a hopeless task, and, with bright sunshine following more rain, the end came at a quarter-past one on the third day. Holmes made a great effort, batting three hours for his 78.

### Hampshire

| | |
|---|---:|
| G. Brown not out . . . . . . . . . . . . . . . . . . . . . | .232 |
| A. Bowell lbw b Whiting . . . . . . . . . . . . . . | 95 |
| Capt. E. I. M. Barratt b Whiting . . . . . . . . | 2 |
| C. P. Mead not out . . . . . . . . . . . . . . . . . . . | .122 |
| B 2, l-b 3 . . . . . . . . . . . . . . . . . . . | 5 |

(2 wkts dec.) 456

Maj. Hon. L. H. Tennyson, Mr H. D. Hake, J. Newman, A. Kennedy, W. H. Livsey, J. Evans and F. Ryan did not bat.

### Yorkshire

| | | | |
|---|---:|---|---:|
| P. Holmes c Evans b Mead . . . . . . . . . . . . . . . . . . . . | 15 | – c Ryan b Newman . . . . . . . . . . . . . . | 78 |
| H. Sutcliffe b Kennedy . . . . . . . . . . . . . . . . . . . . . . . | 58 | – lbw b Ryan . . . . . . . . . . . . . . . . . . | 25 |
| D. Denton b Kennedy . . . . . . . . . . . . . . . . . . . . | 13 | – b Newman . . . . . . . . . . . . . . . . . . | 8 |
| R. Kilner c Livsey b Kennedy . . . . . . . . . . . . . . . . . | 2 | – c Mead b Kennedy . . . . . . . . . . . | 4 |
| W. Rhodes c and b Newman . . . . . . . . . . . . . . . . . | 2 | – run out . . . . . . . . . . . . . . . . . . . . . . . | 64 |
| E. Robinson lbw b Kennedy . . . . . . . . . . . . . . . . . . . | 1 | – c Mead b Kennedy . . . . . . . . . . . | 0 |
| Mr D. C. F. Barton run out . . . . . . . . . . . . . . . . . . . | 9 | – lbw b Kennedy . . . . . . . . . . . . . . . | 3 |
| N. Kilner not out . . . . . . . . . . . . . . . . . . . . . . . . . . | 35 | – c Barrett b Kennedy . . . . . . . . . . . | 0 |
| A. Dolphin b Newman . . . . . . . . . . . . . . . . . . . . . . | 12 | – b Newman . . . . . . . . . . . . . . . . . . | 37 |
| C. P. Whiting c Tennyson b Kennedy . . . . . . . . . . . . | 5 | – b Newman . . . . . . . . . . . . . . . . . . | 1 |
| A. Waddington c Newman b Kennedy . . . . . . . . . . | 0 | – not out . . . . . . . . . . . . . . . . . . . . . . | 1 |
| B 4, l-b 3 . . . . . . . . . . . . . . . . . . . . . . . . . | 7 | L-b 4 . . . . . . . . . . . . . . . . . | 4 |

| | | |
|---|---:|---:|
| | 159 | 225 |

### Yorkshire Bowling

| | Overs | Mdns | Runs | Wkts |
|---|---|---|---|---|
| Waddington . . . . . . . | 28 | 4 | 96 | — |
| Robinson . . . . . . . . . | 16 | — | 59 | — |
| Whiting . . . . . . . . . . | 22 | — | 124 | 2 |
| Rhodes . . . . . . . . . . | 29 | 6 | 69 | — |
| R. Kilner . . . . . . . . . | 35 | 8 | 103 | — |

## Hampshire Bowling

| | Overs | Mdns | Runs | Wkts | Overs | Mdns | Runs | Wkts |
|---|---|---|---|---|---|---|---|---|
| Kennedy ......... | 29 | 8 | 69 | 6 | 31 | 10 | 66 | 4 |
| Ryan ............ | 9 | 1 | 35 | — | 9 | 1 | 41 | 1 |
| Mead ............ | 7 | 4 | 7 | 1 | 6 | 1 | 13 | — |
| Newman ......... | 20 | 5 | 41 | 2 | 25.4 | 5 | 69 | 4 |
| Brown ........... | | | | | 2 | — | 6 | — |
| Evans ............ | | | | | 4 | 1 | 16 | — |
| Tennyson ........ | | | | | 2 | — | 10 | — |

Umpires: H. Bagshaw and C. Marshall.

# YORKSHIRE v MIDDLESEX

## Played at Bradford, August 14, 16, 17, 1920

The last of Yorkshire's county matches at home provided a genuine sensation, Middlesex winning after a tremendous finish by four runs. It was unfortunate for Yorkshire that illness kept Kilner away in the last innings. Yorkshire had 198 to get, and although Rhodes batted with great skill for nearly an hour and a half 58 runs were still required with a wicket to fall. The match, of course, seemed all over, but Wilson and Waddington, amid growing excitement, added 53 in an hour. Then with victory in sight Waddington was bowled by Stevens. Middlesex owed much to Haig's splendid hitting on the second afternoon.

## Middlesex

| | | | | |
|---|---|---|---|---|
| Mr C. H. L. Skeet c Waddington b Rhodes ........ | 1 | – not out ...................... | 0 |
| H. W. Lee c and b Rhodes .................... | 21 | – c and b Rhodes .............. | 48 |
| J. W. Hearne lbw b Rhodes ................... | 26 | – c Hirst b Wilson ............. | 9 |
| E. Hendren b Rhodes ........................ | 12 | – c Waddington b Wilson ........ | 56 |
| Mr P. F. Warner not out ..................... | 8 | – lbw b Wilson ................ | 15 |
| Mr F. T. Mann c Burton b Wilson ............. | 0 | – c Waddington b Wilson ........ | 0 |
| Mr N. Haig b Wilson ........................ | 25 | – b Rhodes ................... | 86 |
| Mr G. T. S. Stevens lbw b Rhodes ............ | 5 | – b Wilson ................... | 21 |
| Mr H. K. Longman c Burton b Wilson .......... | 1 | – b Waddington ............... | 3 |
| H. R. Murrell c Robinson b Rhodes ........... | 2 | – c Rhodes b Wilson ........... | 13 |
| T. J. Durston c Waddington b Rhodes ........... | 2 | – lbw b Rhodes ............... | 0 |
| B 2 ........................... | 2 | B 4, l-b 5, w 1 ........... | 10 |

105　　　　　　　　　　　　　　　　　261

## Yorkshire

| | | | | |
|---|---|---|---|---|
| P. Holmes c Hearne b Stevens ................. | 22 | – c Murrell b Durston ......... | 13 |
| H. Sutcliffe c Hearne b Stevens .............. | 23 | – c Hendren b Durston ......... | 2 |
| D. Denton b Hearne ........................ | 1 | – lbw b Hearne ............... | 21 |
| R. Kilner c Durston b Stevens ............... | 7 | – absent ill ................. | 0 |
| W. Rhodes c Hendren b Hearne .............. | 0 | – b Durston ................. | 26 |
| G. H. Hirst b Hearne ...................... | 0 | – c Mann b Stevens ........... | 11 |
| E. Robinson st Murrell b Hearne .............. | 2 | – c Hendren b Haig ........... | 10 |
| Mr D. C. F. Burton b Hearne .................. | 36 | – b Durston ................. | 19 |
| A. Dolphin b Durston ...................... | 52 | – c Warner b Hearne .......... | 15 |
| Mr E. R. Wilson lbw b Hearne ............... | 4 | – not out ................... | 39 |
| A. Waddington not out ..................... | 1 | – b Stevens ................. | 25 |
| B 16, l-b 2, w 1, n-b 2 ............. | 21 | B 3, l-b 4, w 3, n-b 2 ....... | 12 |

169　　　　　　　　　　　　　　　　　193

**Yorkshire Bowling**

| | Overs | Mdns | Runs | Wkts | Overs | Mdns | Runs | Wkts |
|---|---|---|---|---|---|---|---|---|
| Waddington . . . . . . . | 11 | 6 | 11 | — | 26 | 8 | 61 | 1 |
| Robinson . . . . . . . . | 5 | 2 | 9 | — | 7 | — | 28 | — |
| Rhodes . . . . . . . . . . | 23.4 | 6 | 53 | 7 | 41.5 | 9 | 98 | 3 |
| Wilson . . . . . . . . . . | 20 | 11 | 30 | 3 | 44 | 22 | 62 | 6 |
| Kilner . . . . . . . . . . . | 2 | 2 | — | — | | | | |
| `Tirst . . . . . . . . . . . | | | | | 5 | 3 | 2 | — |

**Middlesex Bowling**

| | Overs | Mdns | Runs | Wkts | Overs | Mdns | Runs | Wkts |
|---|---|---|---|---|---|---|---|---|
| Hearne . . . . . . . . . . | 32.4 | 13 | 52 | 6 | 26 | 6 | 48 | 2 |
| Lee . . . . . . . . . . . . . | 4 | — | 20 | — | | | | |
| Stevens . . . . . . . . . . | 19 | 2 | 43 | 3. | 6.5 | 2 | 17 | 2 |
| Haig . . . . . . . . . . . . | 5 | 2 | 8 | — | 9 | 2 | 30 | 1 |
| Durston . . . . . . . . . | 13 | 5 | 25 | 1 | 32 | 8 | 86 | 4 |

Umpires: W. A. J. West and J. Moss.

# YORKSHIRE v LANCASHIRE

Played at Sheffield, June 3, 5, 6, 1922

Yorkshire had the satisfaction of beating Lancashire by six wickets and fully deserved their victory, but the match was not altogether a satisfactory one. The spirit of partisanship ran very high, and the over-keenness of the spectators affected some of the players, no little ill-feeling being provoked. In one respect the game was astonishing. Nothing seemed less likely than a defeat for Lancashire when, on winning the toss, they had 165 on the board with only Makepeace out. Ernest Tyldesley played his finest innings of the season. At the wickets for four hours and a quarter he hit twenty-one 4s. Lancashire clung far too closely to their first innings lead of a single run, the batting in their second innings being sadly deficient in enterprise. When Yorkshire went in to get 146 Sutcliffe and Roy Kilner practically settled the matter, putting on 73 runs in three-quarters of an hour after the second wicket had fallen at 32. The match proved an enormous attraction.

## Lancashire

| | | | |
|---|---|---|---|
| H. Makepeace run out . . . . . . . . . . . . . . . . . . . . . . . | 19 | – lbw b Robinson . . . . . . . . . . . . . . . . | 20 |
| C. Hallows lbw b Macaulay . . . . . . . . . . . . . . . . . . . | 66 | – lbw b R. Kilner . . . . . . . . . . . . . . . . . . | 47 |
| E. Tyldesley c N. Kilner b Robinson . . . . . . . . . . . . | 178 | – c Robinson b Macaulay . . . . . . . . . | 4 |
| Mr J. Sharp c Dolphin b Robinson . . . . . . . . . . . . . | 1 | – b Robinson . . . . . . . . . . . . . . . . . . . | 1 |
| Mr J. R. Barnes lbw b Robinson . . . . . . . . . . . . . . | 3 | – b Rhodes . . . . . . . . . . . . . . . . . . . . . | 43 |
| J. Tyldesley st Dolphin b Macaulay . . . . . . . . . . . . . | 4 | – c Robinson b Rhodes . . . . . . . . . . . | 12 |
| C. Parkin b Robinson . . . . . . . . . . . . . . . . . . . . . . . | 1 | – c Robinson b R. Kilner . . . . . . . . . . | 5 |
| R. Tyldesley c R. Kilner b Waddington . . . . . . . . . . | 6 | – b Rhodes . . . . . . . . . . . . . . . . . . . . . | 0 |
| Mr M. N. Kenyon c R. Kilner b Macaulay . . . . . . . . | 4 | – c Macaulay b R. Kilner . . . . . . . . . . | 3 |
| L. Cook lbw b Rhodes . . . . . . . . . . . . . . . . . . . . . . | 4 | – lbw b Rhodes . . . . . . . . . . . . . . . . . | 0 |
| B. Blomley not out . . . . . . . . . . . . . . . . . . . . . . . . | 0 | – not out . . . . . . . . . . . . . . . . . . . . . . . | 0 |
| B 15, l-b 2, n-b 4 . . . . . . . . . . . . . . . . . . . . | 21 | B 3, l-b 5, n-b 1 . . . . . . . . . . | 9 |
| | **307** | | **144** |

### Yorkshire

| | | | |
|---|---|---|---|
| P. Holmes c R. Tyldesley b Cook | 19 | – b Cook | 5 |
| H. Sutcliffe run out | 65 | – not out | 73 |
| E. Oldroyd c Hallows b R. Tyldesley | 77 | – c Blomley b R. Tyldesley | 8 |
| R. Kilner lbw b R. Tyldesley | 1 | – st Blomley b Parkin | 47 |
| W. Rhodes c R. Tyldesley b Cook | 13 | – not out | 8 |
| N. Kilner c Hallows b R. Tyldesley | 36 | – lbw b Parkin | 0 |
| E. Robinson lbw b R. Tyldesley | 0 | | |
| Mr G. Wilson not out | 49 | | |
| G. G. Macaulay c Barnes b Cook | 15 | | |
| A. Dolphin lbw b R. Tyldesley | 5 | | |
| A. Waddington st Blomley b R. Tyldesley | 3 | | |
| B 9, l-b 12, n-b 2 | 23 | B 4, l-b 3 | 7 |
| | **306** | | **148** |

### Yorkshire Bowling

| | Overs | Mdns | Runs | Wkts | Overs | Mdns | Runs | Wkts |
|---|---|---|---|---|---|---|---|---|
| Robinson | 25.1 | 7 | 68 | 4 | 22 | 12 | 32 | 2 |
| Waddington | 22 | 4 | 54 | 1 | 5 | 6 | 21 | — |
| R. Kilner | 19 | 7 | 37 | — | 22.5 | 10 | 25 | 3 |
| Macaulay | 28 | 5 | 79 | 3 | 22 | 9 | 29 | 1 |
| Rhodes | 21 | 2 | 48 | 1 | 20 | 8 | 28 | 4 |

### Lancashire Bowling

| | Overs | Mdns | Runs | Wkts | Overs | Mdns | Runs | Wkts |
|---|---|---|---|---|---|---|---|---|
| Parkin | 28 | 5 | 74 | — | 15 | 4 | 41 | 2 |
| Cook | 46 | 16 | 80 | 3 | 19 | 7 | 41 | 1 |
| J. Tyldesley | 14 | — | 59 | — | 1 | — | 7 | — |
| R. Tyldesley | 36.1 | 11 | 70 | 6 | 16 | 5 | 46 | 1 |
| E. Tyldesley | | | | | 0.4 | — | 6 | — |

Umpires: H. Butt and T. Fenwick.

## YORKSHIRE v WARWICKSHIRE

Played at Huddersfield, June 21, 22, 1922

Quickly recovering the all-round form that had deserted them against Nottinghamshire, Yorkshire inflicted a crushing defeat on Warwickshire, winning the game in two days by an innings and 271 runs. Warwickshire were completely outplayed but they had bad luck in batting two men short in their second innings. Still more serious for them was the absence of Calthorpe, their captain, and H. Howell, their fast bowler. On the first afternoon Yorkshire scored 495 for five wickets and on the following morning Wilson at once declared. Getting his fourth hundred during the season Holmes was at his very best. He gave no chance and was especially strong on the leg side. He and Sutcliffe sent up the hundred for the first wicket and, with Roy Kilner in, 98 runs were put on in three quarters of an hour. Handicapped by a damaged pitch and bad light and very much dispirited, Warwickshire on the second day offered little resistance to the fine bowling of Waddington and Macaulay.

## Yorkshire

| | | | |
|---|---|---|---|
| P. Holmes not out | 220 | E. Robinson st Smith b Quaife | 23 |
| H. Sutcliffe c Quaife b Bates | 61 | N. Kilner not out | 57 |
| E. Oldroyd c Smart b Partridge | 7 | B 32, l-b 6, w 8, n-b 7 | 53 |
| R. Kilner c Scorer b Howell | 59 | | |
| W. Rhodes b Howell | 15 | (5 wkts dec.) | 495 |

Mr G. Wilson, G. G. Macaulay, A. Dolphin and A. Waddington did not bat.

## Warwickshire

| | | | |
|---|---|---|---|
| L. A. Bates c Macaulay b Waddington | 19 | – not out | 50 |
| E. J. Smith b Waddington | 10 | – b Waddington | 2 |
| Mr F. R. Santall c Macaulay b Robinson | 6 | – c Waddington b Macaulay | 39 |
| W. G. Quaife c Rhodes b Waddington | 8 | – absent hurt | 0 |
| Mr R. I. Scorer c Waddington b Robinson | 8 | – c Wilson b Waddington | 12 |
| Mr N. E. Partridge c Sutcliffe b Macaulay | 26 | – c Sutcliffe b Macaulay | 2 |
| C. Smart c Robinson b Waddington | 2 | – c Robinson b Waddington | 0 |
| A. Howell not out | 10 | – c Waddington b Macaulay | 1 |
| Mr F. W. Morter c Waddington b Macaulay | 4 | – b Waddington | 8 |
| Mr G. M. Nelson b Macaulay | 0 | – b Macaulay | 2 |
| J. Smart absent hurt | 0 | – absent hurt | 0 |
| B 4, l-b 2 | 6 | B 8, l-b 1 | 9 |
| | **99** | | **125** |

### Warwickshire Bowling

| | Overs | Mdns | Runs | Wkts |
|---|---|---|---|---|
| Morter | 23 | 2 | 76 | — |
| Partridge | 29 | 2 | 114 | 1 |
| Nelson | 10 | 2 | 33 | — |
| J. Smart | 5 | — | 29 | — |
| Quaife | 17 | 1 | 62 | 1 |
| Howell | 10 | 2 | 59 | 2 |
| Bates | 5 | — | 25 | 1 |
| C. Smart | 2 | — | 12 | — |
| Santall | 3 | — | 9 | — |
| Scorer | 4 | 1 | 12 | — |
| Smith | 3 | — | 11 | — |

### Yorkshire Bowling

| | Overs | Mdns | Runs | Wkts | Overs | Mdns | Runs | Wkts |
|---|---|---|---|---|---|---|---|---|
| Robinson | 16 | 4 | 34 | 2 | 5 | 2 | 9 | — |
| Waddington | 17 | 4 | 49 | 4 | 16 | 2 | 47 | 4 |
| R. Kilner | 2 | — | 6 | — | 6 | 2 | 13 | — |
| Macaulay | 1 | — | 4 | 3 | 17 | 4 | 47 | 4 |

Umpires: W. Phillips and W. Reeves.

# YORKSHIRE v LANCASHIRE

Played at Leeds, June 7, 9, 10, 1924

The Whitsuntide match furnished the sensation of Yorkshire's season. On Saturday the cricket, twice interrupted by rain, was dreary in the extreme, Lancashire taking three hours and three-quarters to hit up a score of 113. Such extremely cautious play naturally flattered the excellent bowling. At the close Yorkshire lost Sutcliffe's wicket for three runs. Yorkshire had much the best of the struggle on Monday, and left of with the game, to all appearance, in their hands, as with all ten wickets to fall they required only 57 runs to win.

On Tuesday morning, however, there came, perhaps, the most startling collapse of the year. Bowling on a wicket that gave them a good deal of help Parkin and Richard Tyldesley proved so irresistible that in sixty-five minutes they rattled Yorkshire out for 33. Lancashire winning the match by 24 runs.

## Lancashire

| | | | |
|---|---|---|---|
| H. Makepeace b Rhodes | 17 | – c Robinson b Kilner | 9 |
| C. Hallows lbw b Macaulay | 5 | – lbw b Rhodes | 0 |
| E. Tyldesley lbw b Macaulay | 29 | – c Waddington b Kilner | 2 |
| F. Watson c Waddington b Rhodes | 13 | – lbw b Kilner | 21 |
| Mr A. W. Pewtress b Macaulay | 20 | – b Macaulay | 5 |
| Mr J. Sharp b Kilner | 12 | – c and b Kilner | 14 |
| J. Iddon b Macaulay | 6 | – b Rhodes | 4 |
| Mr A. Rhodes c Oldroyd b Macaulay | 1 | – b Macaulay | 6 |
| C. Parkin lbw b Macaulay | 0 | – not out | 2 |
| R. Tyldesley c Holmes b Kilner | 3 | – b Macaulay | 0 |
| G. Duckworth not out | 0 | – c Robinson b Macaulay | 0 |
| B 3, l-b 2, n-b 2 | 7 | B 5, l-b 4, n-b 2 | 11 |
| | **113** | | **74** |

## Yorkshire

| | | | |
|---|---|---|---|
| P. Holmes b Parkin | 10 | – lbw b R. Tyldesley | 0 |
| H. Sutcliffe c R. Tyldesley b Parkin | 0 | – lbw b Parkin | 3 |
| E. Oldroyd b R. Tyldesley | 37 | – b Parkin | 3 |
| M. Leyland run out | 21 | – c and b R. Tyldesley | 0 |
| W. Rhodes lbw b Parkin | 18 | – c Makepeace b R. Tyldesley | 7 |
| R. Kilner b Parkin | 35 | – not out | 13 |
| E. Robinson c and b Parkin | 1 | – run out | 2 |
| I. Turner lbw b R. Tyldesley | 2 | – b R. Tyldesley | 1 |
| G. G. Macaulay c and b R. Tyldesley | 0 | – b Parkin | 4 |
| A. Waddington b R. Tyldesley | 0 | – b R. Tyldesley | 0 |
| A. Dolphin not out | 0 | – st Duckworth b R. Tyldesley | 0 |
| B 4, l-b 2 | 6 | | |
| | **130** | | **33** |

### Yorkshire Bowling

| | Overs | Mdns | Runs | Wkts | Overs | Mdns | Runs | Wkts |
|---|---|---|---|---|---|---|---|---|
| Robinson | 11 | 7 | 10 | — | 2 | 1 | 3 | — |
| Macaulay | 33 | 14 | 40 | 6 | 16.2 | 7 | 19 | 4 |
| Kilner | 26.2 | 12 | 28 | 2 | 23 | 16 | 13 | 4 |
| Rhodes | 20 | 7 | 28 | 2 | 15 | 5 | 28 | 2 |

### Lancashire Bowling

| | Overs | Mdns | Runs | Wkts | Overs | Mdns | Runs | Wkts |
|---|---|---|---|---|---|---|---|---|
| Parkin | 27.2 | 9 | 46 | 5 | 12 | 7 | 15 | 3 |
| R. Tyldesley | 27 | 9 | 69 | 4 | 11.5 | 6 | 18 | 6 |
| Watson | 7 | 2 | 9 | — | | | | |

Umpires: F. Chester and A. R. Warren.

## YORKSHIRE v SUSSEX

### Played at Bradford, August 15, 17, 18, 1925

The last of Yorkshire's county matches at home produced a genuine sensation. For the only time during the season, Yorkshire stood face to face with what looked like certain defeat. At lunchtime on the third day, Sussex had six wickets in hand and required only 40 runs to win. The result looked inevitable, but by dint of magnificent bowling Macaulay pulled the game out of the fire and gave Yorkshire a victory by 23 runs. In doing this he had these astonishing figures, five overs and three balls, one maiden, eight runs, and five wickets. He took a wicket in each of his first three overs, one in his fifth and the last in his sixth, expending so much nervous energy that, with the match won, he was exhausted. It was Bowley who afforded Sussex their chance of upsetting Yorkshire's unbeaten record for the season. Playing with admirable skill for just over four hours, he made only one mistake – a chance to the wicket-keeper when he had scored 94. Oldroyd maintained an impregnable defence for three hours and fifty minutes.

## Yorkshire

| | | | |
|---|---:|---|---:|
| P. Holmes b Wensley | 10 | – c Cox b Wensley | 7 |
| H. Sutcliffe c Wensley b Tate | 9 | – c Cox b Browne | 38 |
| E. Oldroyd c Cook b Wensley | 19 | – c Wensley b Cox | 77 |
| M. Leyland lbw b Browne | 18 | – c Bowley b Browne | 1 |
| W. Rhodes c Bowley b Wensley | 15 | – b Browne | 3 |
| R. Kilner c Bowley b Cox | 3 | – c Bowley b Browne | 0 |
| E. Robinson b Browne | 17 | – c Gilligan b Bowley | 54 |
| G. G. Macaulay c Cornford b Tate | 0 | – c Parks b Browne | 39 |
| A. Waddington not out | 19 | – b Browne | 2 |
| Maj. A. W. Lupton c Cox b Browne | 0 | – not out | 0 |
| A. Dolphin b Wensley | 0 | – b Browne | 0 |
| B 2, l-b 5, n-b 2 | 9 | B 6, l-b 2, w 1 | 9 |
| | **119** | | **230** |

## Sussex

| | | | |
|---|---:|---|---:|
| E. H. Bowley lbw b Robinson | 8 | – c Dolphin b Macaulay | 105 |
| M. W. Tate c Dolphin b Robinson | 9 | – b Kilner | 39 |
| Mr R. A. Young c Holmes b Robinson | 26 | – c Oldroyd b Macaulay | 11 |
| T. Cook run out | 1 | – b Waddington | 42 |
| G. Cox lbw b Kilner | 4 | – b Macaulay | 16 |
| Mr R. L. Holdsworth c Oldroyd b Kilner | 11 | – b Macaulay | 2 |
| J. H. Parks c Holmes b Kilner | 7 | – b Macaulay | 3 |
| Mr A. E. R. Gilligan c Waddington b Kilner | 7 | – c Robinson b Macaulay | 3 |
| A. F. Wensley lbw b Macaulay | 6 | – lbw b Kilner | 2 |
| W. Cornford not out | 1 | – c Waddington b Macaulay | 0 |
| Rev. F. B. R. Browne b Kilner | 0 | – not out | 0 |
| B 6, n-b 1 | 7 | B 8, l-b 4, n-b 4 | 16 |
| | **87** | | **239** |

## Sussex Bowling

| | Overs | Mdns | Runs | Wkts | Overs | Mdns | Runs | Wkts |
|---|---:|---:|---:|---:|---:|---:|---:|---:|
| Tate | 24 | 8 | 36 | 2 | 23 | 6 | 55 | — |
| Wensley | 20.1 | 6 | 44 | 4 | 22 | 3 | 52 | 1 |
| Cox | 11 | 6 | 13 | 1 | 17 | 9 | 25 | 1 |
| Browne | 8 | 3 | 17 | 3 | 27.5 | 4 | 62 | 7 |
| Bowley | | | | | 5 | 2 | 17 | 1 |
| Parks | | | | | 2 | — | 10 | — |

## Yorkshire Bowling

| | Overs | Mdns | Runs | Wkts | Overs | Mdns | Runs | Wkts |
|---|---:|---:|---:|---:|---:|---:|---:|---:|
| Robinson | 18 | 5 | 38 | 3 | 22 | 9 | 59 | — |
| Macaulay | 12 | 7 | 21 | 1 | 22.3 | 1 | 67 | 7 |
| Kilner | 15.2 | 9 | 14 | 5 | 32 | 13 | 35 | 2 |
| Waddington | 3 | 1 | 7 | — | 15 | 3 | 42 | 1 |
| Rhodes | | | | | 11 | 3 | 20 | — |

Umpires: W. Reeves and J. Stone.

## YORKSHIRE v SOMERSET

Played at Huddersfield, June 2, 3, 4, 1926

Fortunate in winning the toss, Yorkshire, despite the absence of Holmes and Sutcliffe – playing for North of England against the Australians – beat Somerset by an innings and 39 runs. Some splendid bowling by Rhodes was the big factor in this success, the famous veteran, in the course of the match, securing fourteen wickets at a cost of $5\frac{1}{2}$ runs apiece. In the first innings of the visitors, after Daniell and Young had raised the score to 52 for the first wicket, he disposed of six batsmen for 29, and in the second, in which at one time there were 58 runs on the board with only one wicket down, he proved so deadly that eight batsmen fell before him for 48 runs. Accurate length, deceptive flight, varied pace, and pronounced spin formed a combination that would, under the conditions which prevailed, have had most sides in great trouble. Little more than two hours play proved practicable on Wednesday, and next day Yorkshire appeared likely to be out for a decidedly moderate score, when Macaulay came in and gave a most brilliant display, hitting up 108 in just over two hours with seventeen 4s – mostly drives – as his chief strokes. Robinson, who previously had had a dismal batting season, withstood the Somerset attack for four hours and a quarter. Wanting 153 to escape a follow-on, the visitors for a long time looked fairly sure to reach that number, but then came the deadly bowling of Rhodes, and on Friday morning they fell short of that figure by 9 runs.

### Yorkshire

| | |
|---|---|
| M. Leyland c Earle b Lee .............. 37 | G. G. Macaulay c Earle b White .........108 |
| A. Mitchell run out .................... 2 | A. Waddington c Case b Hunt ........... 12 |
| E. Oldroyd c Daniell b White ........... 10 | Maj. A. W. Lupton c and b Young ....... 10 |
| E. Robinson c Daniell b Hunt ........... 85 | A. Dolphin not out .................... 0 |
| R. Kilner run out .................... 13 | B 1, l-b 2.................... 3 |
| W. Rhodes c Hunt b White ............. 21 | |
| C. Turner lbw b White ................ 1 | 302 |

### Somerset

| | | |
|---|---|---|
| Mr J. Daniell b Waddington .................... | 35 – b Waddington ................ | 11 |
| A. Young run out ........................... | 17 – c Macaulay b Rhodes ........... | 27 |
| Mr M. D. Lyon st Dolphin b Rhodes ............. | 34 – st Dolphin b Rhodes ........... | 31 |
| Mr C. C. Case b Rhodes ...................... | 19 – c Waddington b Rhodes ......... | 2 |
| Mr J. C. White b Rhodes ..................... | 3 – not out ....................... | 26 |
| Mr G. E. Northway c Waddington b Rhodes ...... | 2 – lbw b Kilner .................... | 1 |
| Mr G. F. Earle c Leyland b Rhodes ............. | 3 – c Oldroyd b Rhodes ............ | 0 |
| G. Hunt b Waddington ...................... | 12 – st Dolphin b Rhodes ........... | 2 |
| Mr C. P. Ewens not out ....................... | 3 – c Mitchell b Rhodes ............ | 7 |
| Mr G. H. Pruett run out ...................... | 5 – c Kilner b Rhodes ............. | 2 |
| F. Lee c Robinson b Rhodes ................... | 0 – c Robinson b Rhodes ........... | 0 |
| B 5, l-b 2, n-b 4 ..................... | 11      B 2, l-b 8 .............. | 10 |
| | 144 | 119 |

### Somerset Bowling

| | Overs | Mdns | Runs | Wkts |
|---|---|---|---|---|
| Hunt ........... | 34 | 8 | 86 | 2 |
| White ........... | 63.3 | 34 | 79 | 4 |
| Young .......... | 8 | 1 | 24 | 1 |
| Pruett ........... | 9 | — | 49 | — |
| Lee ............. | 23 | 8 | 61 | 1 |

**Yorkshire Bowling**

| | Overs | Mdns | Runs | Wkts | Overs | Mdns | Runs | Wkts |
|---|---|---|---|---|---|---|---|---|
| Robinson ......... | 5 | 3 | 2 | — | | | | |
| Macaulay ......... | 8 | 1 | 23 | — | 11 | 3 | 18 | — |
| Kilner ............ | 12 | 1 | 35 | — | 21 | 9 | 30 | 1 |
| Rhodes ........... | 21 | 8 | 29 | 6 | 20.5 | 4 | 48 | 8 |
| Waddington ....... | 21 | 5 | 44 | 2 | 10 | 3 | 13 | 1 |

Umpires: J. H. King and J. A. Cuffe.

# WILFRED RHODES, 1930

Wilfred Rhodes now 53 years of age has announced that, although he obtained more than seventy wickets for less than 20 runs apiece last summer and had a batting average of nearly 23, he will take no further part in first-class cricket. So comes to an end a splendid career which, including the years of war, extended over thirty-three seasons. The distinction peculiar to Rhodes consists in his achievement – after gaining great fame as the leading bowler in the country for a dozen years or more – of developing his batting to such an extent that for a time in Test matches he regularly opened England's innings in company with Hobbs. That attainment would of itself have invested Rhodes' career with special quality but, as it happened, his prowess did not end with his advance to such high rank as a batsman. After the war, with Yorkshire's attack enormously weakened owing to the deaths of Booth and Drake, Rhodes was once again called upon for a huge amount of work with the ball and, as happily his skill had not deserted him, he found himself able to respond so handsomely to the demands of his county that, when over 40, he took in the course of six seasons 828 wickets for 13 runs each. The extraordinary nature of his transition from bowler to batsman and then – while not losing his batting – back to bowler again may be better realised when it is mentioned that when he went out to Australia in 1903-04, P. F. Warner meant him to devote his energies so entirely to bowling that, to begin with, he was sent in last and rarely earlier than ninth. Incidentally, Rhodes seized the occasion of the first Test match to put on in company with R. E. Foster 130 for the tenth wicket – a record which still obtains to-day. Eight years later, when again P. F. Warner was chosen to captain a side in Australia, Rhodes – then a leading batsman – shared in another record stand – 323 for the first wicket in company with Hobbs. He appeared to have finished with international contests in 1921, being picked for only one of the five games in that season so disastrous for the reputation of English cricket but there came five years later, when he was 48, the opportunity for his "swan-song" at The Oval where, taking six wickets for 79 runs, he had a big share in regaining "The Ashes" for England.

From the figures which, furnished by Mr J. N. Pentelow, are given below it will be seen that Rhodes in the course of his career obtained 4,184 wickets at a cost of less than 17 runs each and that he scored nearly 40,000 runs with an average of 30. During his first six seasons – he came out for Yorkshire in 1898 – Rhodes obtained 1,251 wickets for 14 runs each. His highest aggregate was 261 wickets in 1900 but in the next two years also his total of wickets exceeded 200. Twice in 1899 – against Essex and against the Australians – he secured nine wickets in an innings and he repeated that performance against Essex thirty years later. In the Essex contest of 1899 he obtained fifteen wickets in all and in a Test match at Melbourne in 1903-04 he again had fifteen wickets to his credit. So recently as 1923 he took 134 wickets in a season and these at a cost of about eleven runs and a half apiece.

Altogether he made fifty-eight hundreds, forty-seven in all in England (forty-six for Yorkshire), eight in Australia, two in India and one in South Africa. Two of his three-figure innings were played in Test matches – one at Melbourne and one at Johannesburg. His highest score was 267 not out against Leicestershire at Leeds in 1921 and he also obtained 210 against South Australia at Adelaide, 201 against Somerset at Taunton, 199 against Sussex at Brighton, and 196 against Worcestershire at Worcester.

Twice he made two centuries in a match – 128 and 115 for Yorkshire against MCC at Scarborough and 119 and 109 for England against New South Wales at Sydney in 1911-12. His highest aggregates were 2,261 in 1911 and 2,094 in 1909, and his highest average in England 40 – a figure he reached in 1909 and also in 1925.

It should be mentioned that Mr Pentelow favours the inclusion in this record of a match for Patiala against the MCC's team in India in 1926-27 when Rhodes scored 13 not out, and bowled 144 balls for 73 runs and three wickets. These figures do not appear in the list appended.

## BATTING

| | Season | Innings | Not Outs | Runs | Highest Innings | Average |
|---|---|---|---|---|---|---|
| | 1898 | 41 | 9 | 557 | 78 | 17.40 |
| | 1899 | 49 | 12 | 432 | 81* | 11.67 |
| | 1900 | 42 | 11 | 655 | 79 | 21.12 |
| | 1901 | 45 | 13 | 854 | 105 | 26.68 |
| | 1902 | 46 | 14 | 490 | 92* | 15.31 |
| | 1903 | 51 | 9 | 1,137 | 98* | 27.07 |
| In Australia | 1903-04 | 18 | 7 | 239 | 49 | 21.72 |
| | 1904 | 47 | 4 | 1,537 | 196 | 35.74 |
| | 1905 | 52 | 8 | 1,581 | 201 | 35.93 |
| | 1906 | 62 | 3 | 1,721 | 119 | 29.16 |
| | 1907 | 47 | 1 | 1,055 | 112 | 22.93 |
| In Australia | 1907-08 | 27 | 8 | 929 | 119 | 48.78 |
| | 1908 | 57 | 4 | 1,673 | 146 | 31.56 |
| | 1909 | 59 | 7 | 2,094 | 199 | 40.26 |
| In S. Africa | 1909-10 | 22 | 2 | 579 | 77 | 28.95 |
| | 1910 | 59 | 4 | 1,465 | 111 | 26.63 |
| | 1911 | 64 | 5 | 2,261 | 128 | 38.32 |
| In Australia | 1911-12 | 24 | 4 | 1,098 | 179 | 54.90 |
| | 1912 | 58 | 5 | 1,597 | 176 | 30.13 |
| | 1913 | 64 | 4 | 1,963 | 152 | 32.71 |
| In S. Africa | 1913-14 | 24 | 3 | 731 | 152 | 34.80 |
| | 1914 | 49 | 2 | 1,377 | 113 | 29.29 |
| | 1919 | 46 | 10 | 1,237 | 135 | 34.36 |
| | 1920 | 45 | 5 | 1,123 | 167* | 28.07 |
| In Australia | 1920-21 | 19 | — | 713 | 210 | 37.52 |
| | 1921 | 47 | 10 | 1,474 | 267* | 39.83 |
| In India | 1921 | 2 | — | 339 | 183 | 169.50 |
| | 1922 | 46 | 8 | 1,511 | 110 | 39.76 |
| | 1923 | 48 | 8 | 1,321 | 126 | 33.02 |
| | 1924 | 50 | 7 | 1,126 | 100 | 26.18 |
| | 1925 | 43 | 9 | 1,391 | 157 | 40.91 |
| | 1926 | 36 | 3 | 1,132 | 132 | 34.30 |
| | 1927 | 37 | 7 | 577 | 73 | 19.23 |
| | 1928 | 28 | 6 | 579 | 100* | 26.31 |
| | 1929 | 32 | 9 | 617 | 79 | 26.82 |
| In W. Indies | 1929-30 | 12 | 7 | 129 | 36 | 25.80 |
| | 1930 | 29 | 8 | 478 | 80* | 22.76 |
| | Totals | 1,527 | 236 | 39,772 | 267* | 30.80 |

* *Signifies not out.*

## BOWLING

| Season | | Balls | Runs | Wickets | Average |
|---|---|---|---|---|---|
| | 1898 | 6,200 | 2,249 | 154 | 14.60 |
| | 1899 | 7,594 | 3,062 | 179 | 17.10 |
| | 1900 | 9,318 | 3,606 | 261 | 13.81 |
| | 1901 | 9,390 | 3,797 | 251 | 15.12 |
| | 1902 | 7,839 | 2,801 | 213 | 13.15 |
| | 1903 | 8,268 | 2,813 | 193 | 14.57 |
| In Australia | 1903-04 | 2,667 | 1,055 | 65 | 16.23 |
| | 1904 | 7,184 | 2,829 | 131 | 21.59 |
| | 1905 | 7,449 | 3,085 | 182 | 16.95 |
| | 1906 | 5,876 | 3,018 | 128 | 23.57 |
| | 1907 | 6,403 | 2,757 | 177 | 15.57 |
| In Australia | 1907-08 | 2,564 | 1,069 | 31 | 34.48 |
| | 1908 | 4,827 | 1,855 | 115 | 16.13 |
| | 1909 | 5,239 | 2,241 | 141 | 15.89 |
| In S. Africa | 1909-10 | 1,229 | 526 | 21 | 25.04 |
| | 1910 | 3,678 | 1,671 | 88 | 18.98 |
| | 1911 | 5,485 | 2,817 | 117 | 24.07 |
| In Australia | 1911-12 | 372 | 234 | — | — |
| | 1912 | 2,387 | 1,165 | 53 | 21.98 |
| | 1913 | 4,338 | 1,882 | 86 | 21.88 |
| In S. Africa | 1913-14 | 1,449 | 662 | 31 | 21.35 |
| | 1914 | 5,044 | 2,157 | 118 | 18.27 |
| | 1919 | 6,291 | 2,365 | 164 | 14.42 |
| | 1920 | 6,172 | 2,123 | 161 | 13.18 |
| In Australia | 1920-21 | 1,107 | 479 | 18 | 26.61 |
| | 1921 | 5,778 | 1,872 | 141 | 13.27 |
| In India | 1921 | 432 | 103 | 19 | 5.42 |
| | 1922 | 4,885 | 1,451 | 119 | 12.19 |
| | 1923 | 5,574 | 1,547 | 134 | 11.54 |
| | 1924 | 4,479 | 1,576 | 109 | 14.46 |
| | 1925 | 3,220 | 1,134 | 57 | 19.89 |
| | 1926 | 5,356 | 1,709 | 115 | 14.86 |
| | 1927 | 5,442 | 1,731 | 85 | 20.36 |
| | 1928 | 6,980 | 2,258 | 115 | 19.63 |
| | 1929 | 6,105 | 1,870 | 100 | 18.70 |
| In W. Indies | 1920-30 | 3,007 | 947 | 39 | 24.28 |
| | 1930 | 4,661 | 1,395 | 73 | 19.10 |
| | Totals | 184,289 | 69,911 | 4,184 | 16.70 |

## YORKSHIRE v WARWICKSHIRE

Played at Leeds, May 16, 18, 1931

After fulfilling four out-engagements, Yorkshire took the field against Warwickshire at Headingley and Verity seized upon the occasion to accomplish a memorable bowling performance, the young left hander in the visitors' second innings taking all ten wickets for

36 runs. Only once previously had a Yorkshire bowler enjoyed so exceptional a measure of success, Drake at Weston-super-Mare in 1914 obtaining all ten wickets in the second innings of Somerset. Up to the time Verity bowled in such deadly form, and by so doing finished off the contest on Monday evening in a victory for Yorkshire by an innings and 25 runs, the match had proceeded on somewhat uneventful lines. Croom and Bates made a stand of 67 for Warwickshire and Parsons drove with power but, Holmes and Sutcliffe settling down in determined fashion, the home side replied with 83 for no wicket. The famous Yorkshire pair stayed together on Monday until the score reached 120 and so registered their fifty-ninth three-figure partnership for the county. Oldroyd and Robinson showing the brightest cricket of the match, Warwickshire's total was headed with six wickets in hand. Later on Wood batted freely and Yorkshire gained a lead of 97. Subsequent to the tea interval came the startling bowling of Verity who at one point disposed of four batsmen in one over, getting Smart caught at backward point off the first ball and Foster stumped off the second, while Tate was leg-before to the fifth and Paine taken left hand from a return to the bowler off the sixth.

### Warwickshire

| | | | | |
|---|---|---|---|---|
| Mr R. E. S. Wyatt b Macaulay | 13 | – c Holmes b Verity | 23 |
| A. J. Croom c Wood b Robinson | 46 | – c Greenwood b Verity | 7 |
| L. A. Bates c Mitchell b Bowes | 54 | – c Mitchell b Verity | 19 |
| N. Kilner lbw b Macaulay | 9 | – c Mitchell b Verity | 0 |
| Rev. J. H. Parsons lbw b Macaulay | 48 | – c Leyland b Verity | 9 |
| A. W. Hill lbw b Bowes | 0 | – c Wood b Verity | 8 |
| J. Smart b Verity | 6 | – c Mitchell b Verity | 0 |
| Mr D. G. Foster b Macaulay | 5 | – st Wood b Verity | 0 |
| C. F. Tate lbw b Verity | 8 | – lbw b Verity | 0 |
| G. Paine b Verity | 6 | – c and b Verity | 0 |
| J. H. Mayer not out | 2 | – not out | 6 |
| L-b 3, w 1 | 4 | | |
| | **201** | | **72** |

### Yorkshire

| | | | |
|---|---|---|---|
| P. Holmes b Mayer | 58 | A. Wood not out | 40 |
| H. Sutcliffe c Croom b Tate | 67 | G. G. Macaulay b Mayer | 0 |
| M. Leyland c Kilner b Mayer | 2 | H. Verity b Mayer | 7 |
| E. Oldroyd lbw b Mayer | 67 | W. E. Bowes c Kilner b Paine | 0 |
| A. Mitchell b Wyatt | 12 | B 2, l-b 10, n-b 1 | 13 |
| Mr F. E. Greenwood c Smart b Mayer | 30 | | |
| E. Robinson run out | 2 | | **298** |

### Yorkshire Bowling

| | Overs | Mdns | Runs | Wkts | Overs | Mdns | Runs | Wkts |
|---|---|---|---|---|---|---|---|---|
| Bowes | 14 | 5 | 25 | 2 | 5 | 1 | 7 | — |
| Robinson | 20 | 8 | 50 | 1 | 4 | 1 | 9 | — |
| Macaulay | 35 | 14 | 61 | 4 | 18 | 11 | 20 | — |
| Verity | 32.3 | 11 | 61 | 3 | 18.4 | 6 | 36 | 10 |

### Warwickshire Bowling

| | Overs | Mdns | Runs | Wkts |
|---|---|---|---|---|
| Mayer | 30 | 8 | 76 | 6 |
| Foster | 17 | 2 | 58 | — |
| Wyatt | 8 | 3 | 12 | 1 |
| Paine | 17.3 | 3 | 45 | 1 |
| Tate | 25 | 6 | 94 | 1 |

Umpires: J. H. King and W. Bestwick.

## YORKSHIRE v GLOUCESTERSHIRE

Played at Sheffield, June 3, 4, 5, 1931

Following upon the two idle days in which the contest with Kent ended, came two days at Bramall Lane where, instead of Yorkshire engaging in their home fixture with Gloucestershire, not a ball could be bowled. These were the depressing circumstances in which B. H. Lyon and F. E. Greenwood decided to take a course which, if certainly not contemplated by the authorities when drawing up the county championship rules for 1931, produced what was practically a one-innings contest for 15 points. In order that the points at stake should not be reduced from 15 to 8, the first innings of each side was declared after a ball had been bowled to register four byes. Thereupon Gloucestershire – sent in by Greenwood – entered upon their second innings which, extending over three hours, produced 171 runs. Barnett and Sinfield gave the side a useful start in putting on 45 runs and Lyon and Dacre scored at a fair pace but latterly the batting against some skilful bowling on the part of Verity met with comparatively little success, except that Smith played an innings of 30. To gain a victory Yorkshire had to hit off 172 runs in two hours and a half and so laboured under some considerable handicap on essaying that task. Sutcliffe and Leyland batted freely and with some success but soon Yorkshire found themselves in a losing position and, although Greenwood showed plenty of enterprise, Goddard bowled to such effective purpose that the innings was all over by twenty minutes to six for 124, Gloucestershire being left winners by 47 runs.

### Gloucestershire

| | | | |
|---|---|---|---|
| R. A. Sinfield not out | 0 | – c Verity b Macaulay | 24 |
| C. J. Barnett (did not bat) | | – st Wood b Verity | 26 |
| W. R. Hammond (did not bat) | | – c Robinson b Verity | 6 |
| Mr B. H. Lyon (did not bat) | | – c Bowes b Verity | 31 |
| C. C. Dacre (did not bat) | | – b Verity | 21 |
| A. E. Dipper not out | 0 | – c Leyland b Bowes | 0 |
| W. L. Neale (did not bat) | | – c Macaulay b Verity | 9 |
| H. Smith (did not bat) | | – b Verity | 30 |
| A. Rogers (did not bat) | | – b Verity | 0 |
| C. Parker (did not bat) | | – not out | 6 |
| T. W. Goddard (did not bat) | | – c Greenwood b Leyland | 13 |
| B 4 | 4 | B 3, n-b 2 | 5 |
| (no wkt dec.) | 4 | | 171 |

### Yorkshire

| | | | |
|---|---|---|---|
| P. Holmes not out | 0 | – c Smith b Hammond | 2 |
| H. Sutcliffe (did not bat) | | – lbw b Goddard | 27 |
| M. Leyland (did not bat) | | – c Dacre b Goddard | 35 |
| A. Wood not out | 0 | – run out | 1 |
| E. Oldroyd (did not bat) | | – b Goddard | 1 |
| Mr F. E. Greenwood (did not bat) | | – not out | 33 |
| A. Mitchell (did not bat) | | – lbw b Goddard | 6 |
| E. Robinson (did not bat) | | – lbw b Goddard | 0 |
| G. G. Macaulay (did not bat) | | – c Lyon b Parker | 4 |
| H. Verity (did not bat) | | – c Hammond b Parker | 0 |
| W. E. Bowes (did not bat) | | – run out | 0 |
| B 4 | 4 | B 13, l-b 2 | 15 |
| (no wkt dec.) | 4 | | 124 |

**Yorkshire Bowling**

| | Overs | Mdns | Runs | Wkts | Overs | Mdns | Runs | Wkts |
|---|---|---|---|---|---|---|---|---|
| Robinson ......... | 0.1 | — | — | — | 6 | 1 | 19 | — |
| Bowes .......... | | | | | 15 | 5 | 38 | 1 |
| Verity ............ | | | | | 25 | 5 | 64 | 7 |
| Macaulay ........ | | | | | 13 | 3 | 28 | 1 |
| Leyland ......... | | | | | 4.5 | 3 | 17 | 1 |

**Gloucestershire Bowling**

| | Overs | Mdns | Runs | Wkts | Overs | Mdns | Runs | Wkts |
|---|---|---|---|---|---|---|---|---|
| Hammond ........ | 0.1 | — | — | — | 6 | 2 | 18 | 1 |
| Rogers .......... | | | | | 4 | — | 18 | — |
| Goddard ........ | | | | | 13 | 4 | 21 | 5 |
| Parker .......... | | | | | 11 | — | 52 | 2 |

Umpires: J. Hardstaff and L. C. Braund.

# YORKSHIRE v LANCASHIRE

### Played at Sheffield, August 1, 3, 4, 1931

Holmes and Sutcliffe seized upon the occasion of Yorkshire's return match with Lancashire to put together the second highest of 68 three-figure first wicket partnerships in which they have shared, the two batsmen withstanding Lancashire's attack for four hours and a half and raising the score to 323. Neither player gave a chance until he had passed his hundred. Sutcliffe, showing the brighter cricket, drove particularly well to the off and had twenty-one 4s in his 195. If somewhat overshadowed by his colleague, Holmes batted very soundly. The total at the drawing of stumps on Saturday stood at 391 for three wickets. On Monday, when the spectators numbered about 25,000, Greenwood declared with seven men out. Lancashire batted very doggedly, Hallows staying ninety-five minutes for 18, Iddon two hours for 30, and only 180 runs (for seven wickets) being obtained in more than four hours and a half. When on Tuesday Lancashire followed on, there existed some likelihood of a Yorkshire victory but Ernest Tyldesley and Paynter averted all real danger by resisting the Yorkshire bowling successfully for two hours.

## Yorkshire

| | |
|---|---|
| P. Holmes c Eckersley b McDonald ......125 | A. Wood c McDonald b Sibbles ......... 12 |
| H. Sutcliffe c Paynter b Hopwood ........195 | E. Oldroyd c Duckworth b Paynter ....... 17 |
| M. Leyland b Iddon .................. 28 | E. Robinson not out .................. 5 |
| A. Mitchell b Sibbles ................ 58 | B 3, l-b 12, w 2, n-b 5 .......... 22 |
| Mr F. E. Greenwood c Duckworth | |
| b McDonald . 22 | (7 wkts dec.) 484 |

G. G. Macaulay, W. E. Bowes and H. Verity did not bat.

## Lancashire

| | | | |
|---|---|---|---|
| C. Hallows lbw b Bowes | 18 | – c and b Leyland | 14 |
| C. Hopwood c Wood b Bowes | 20 | | |
| E. Tyldesley c and b Verity | 22 | – c Holmes b Verity | 41 |
| J. Iddon c Wood b Verity | 30 | – not out | 14 |
| W. Horrocks lbw b Robinson | 18 | | |
| E. Paynter not out | 45 | – not out | 87 |
| Mr P. T. Eckersley b Verity | 0 | | |
| F. M. Sibbles b Macaulay | 14 | | |
| G. Duckworth b Robinson | 14 | | |
| R. Tyldesley c Wood b Bowes | 12 | | |
| E. A. McDonald b Verity | 0 | | |
| B 8, l-b 18, w 1, n-b 1 | 28 | B 6, l-b 3 | 9 |
| | **221** | | **165** |

### Lancashire Bowling

| | Overs | Mdns | Runs | Wkts |
|---|---|---|---|---|
| McDonald | 31 | 2 | 142 | 2 |
| Sibbles | 51 | 5 | 136 | 2 |
| R. Tyldesley | 33 | 5 | 79 | — |
| Hopwood | 20 | 12 | 55 | 1 |
| Paynter | 10.2 | 3 | 34 | 1 |
| Iddon | 7 | 2 | 16 | i |

### Yorkshire Bowling

| | Overs | Mdns | Runs | Wkts | Overs | Mdns | Runs | Wkts |
|---|---|---|---|---|---|---|---|---|
| Bowes | 36 | 16 | 45 | 3 | 12 | 4 | 18 | — |
| Robinson | 40 | 16 | 41 | 2 | 5 | — | 8 | — |
| Macaulay | 35 | 18 | 36 | 1 | 5 | 1 | 14 | — |
| Verity | 25.4 | 7 | 57 | 4 | 24 | 8 | 31 | 1 |
| Leyland | 4 | 1 | 14 | — | 24 | 5 | 49 | 1 |
| Mitchell | | | | | 3 | — | 9 | — |
| Holmes | | | | | 3 | 1 | 6 | — |
| Greenwood | | | | | 4 | 1 | 14 | — |
| Oldroyd | | | | | 7 | 2 | 7 | — |

Umpires: W. Bestwick and F. Walden.

## YORKSHIRE v NORTHAMPTONSHIRE

### Played at Bradford, August 8, 10, 11, 1931

Conditions proving so adverse that not a ball could be bowled on Saturday or Monday, Greenwood and Jupp in order to try and reach a definite issue decided to follow the plan adopted two months previously in Yorkshire's match with Gloucestershire, under which each side, after a ball had registered four byes, declared their first innings closed. While agreeing to that course of action, the rival captains differed as to the fitness of the pitch for play and there occurred a delay of an hour before the umpires decided that cricket was practicable. As it happened four hours and a quarter sufficed to give Yorkshire a five wickets victory – and incidentally 15 points. Northamptonshire began by losing half their wickets for 15 and although Welch scored 36 out of 45 in half an hour, the visitors' innings was all over in two hours, Verity getting seven wickets for less than nine runs apiece. Yorkshire wanting 87 runs for a win, Holmes and Sutcliffe knocked off 43 so the success of the home team was never in doubt. Missed at short leg off the first ball he received Sutcliffe, who hit nine 4s, afterwards played great cricket. The game was all over before half-past five.

### Northamptonshire

| | | | |
|---|---|---|---|
| A. H. Bakewell not out | 0 | – c Wood b Bowes | 0 |
| Mr G. H. Johnson not out | 0 | – b Verity | 13 |
| J. E. Timms (did not bat) | | – c Greenwood b Bowes | 6 |
| A. L. Cox (did not bat) | | – lbw b Verity | 3 |
| Mr V. W. C. Jupp (did not bat) | | – c Holmes b Bowes | 0 |
| A. D. Matthews (did not bat) | | – c Greenwood b Verity | 6 |
| Mr T. B. G. Welch (did not bat) | | – c Wood b Verity | 36 |
| W. Coverdale (did not bat) | | – c sub. b Verity | 0 |
| Mr E. F. Towell (did not bat) | | – not out | 12 |
| A. E. Thomas (did not bat) | | – st Wood b Verity | 6 |
| R. J. Partridge (did not bat) | | – c Sutcliffe b Verity | 2 |
| B 4 | 4 | L-b 2 | 2 |
| (no wkt dec.) | 4 | | 86 |

### Yorkshire

| | | | |
|---|---|---|---|
| W. E. Bowes not out | 0 | | |
| Mr F. E. Greenwood not out | 0 | – c Thomas b Jupp | 0 |
| P. Holmes (did not bat) | | – c and b Jupp | 11 |
| H. Sutcliffe (did not bat) | | – b Towell | 62 |
| M. Leyland (did not bat) | | – c Matthews b Thomas | 5 |
| W. Barber (did not bat) | | – c Cox b Jupp | 0 |
| E. Robinson (did not bat) | | – not out | 6 |
| A. Wood (did not bat) | | – not out | 3 |
| B 4 | 4 | B 1 | 1 |
| (no wkt dec.) | 4 | | 88 |

A. Mitchell, G. G. Macaulay and H. Verity did not bat.

### Yorkshire Bowling

| | Overs | Mdns | Runs | Wkts | Overs | Mdns | Runs | Wkts |
|---|---|---|---|---|---|---|---|---|
| Robinson | 0.1 | — | — | — | 6 | 2 | 8 | — |
| Bowes | | | | | 10 | 7 | 5 | 3 |
| Verity | | | | | 16.5 | 4 | 62 | 7 |
| Macaulay | | | | | 9 | 5 | 9 | — |

### Northamptonshire Bowling

| | Overs | Mdns | Runs | Wkts | Overs | Mdns | Runs | Wkts |
|---|---|---|---|---|---|---|---|---|
| Jupp | 0.1 | — | — | — | 12 | 1 | 42 | 3 |
| Thomas | | | | | 13 | 6 | 22 | 1 |
| Matthews | | | | | 3 | — | 15 | — |
| Towell | | | | | 2.2 | — | 8 | 1 |

Umpires: A. Morton and F. Field.

## YORKSHIRE v LANCASHIRE

### Played at Bradford, May 14, 16, 17, 1932

Yorkshire opened their championship programme with a defeat from Lancashire by an innings and 50 runs, this being the first match between the counties brought to a definite issue since 1927. On Saturday when the wet state of the ground delayed the start, Paynter gave a great display of driving and pulling which lasted three hours and a half and included five 6s – four off Verity – and seventeen 4s. He registered his last fifty runs in half an hour. Watson helped to put on 67 and Parkinson. making a first appearance. batted in capital form. Yorkshire fielded very keenly and Verity. although. on a pitch much too slow for him, severely punished at times by Paynter, took eight wickets for less than 14 runs each.

Heavy rain on Sunday night drenched the ground and might possibly have prevented any cricket on Monday but the application of an absorbent roller allowed of Yorkshire commencing their innings at half-past two. Startling play proved to be in store on the drying pitch, Sibbles bowling in such deadly form that he and Hopwood actually dismissed the Yorkshire eleven in an hour and fifty minutes for 46. Sibbles. often making the ball come very quickly off the ground and certainly bowling with remarkable skill. actually sent down twenty overs and four balls for 10 runs and seven wickets. Sutcliffe batted for eighty minutes but after he left – fourth out at 38 – three wickets fell at 42 and the remaining three at 46. In the follow on – 217 in arrear – Holmes helped to raise the score to 34 and then Sutcliffe and Mitchell played out time and meanwhile brought the total to 81, Sutcliffe showing masterly cricket and Mitchell defending stubbornly.

Next day, however, when conditions, if not at all what could have been desired. suggested that Yorkshire might put up a big fight to avert defeat. Sutcliffe was out in the first over and, apart from Leyland, no one offered any real resistance. Leyland hit up 43 out of 57 in forty-five minutes but so completely did the home batsmen fail to realise expectations that the nine wickets remaining when the last day's cricket began went down in an hour and three-quarters for 86 runs. Sibbles, if accomplishing no such startling performance as on the previous day, was again the most effective bowler and came out with a record for the match of twelve wickets for less than six runs each.

### Lancashire

| | | |
|---|---|---|
| F. Watson c Holmes b Verity | ........... | 19 |
| E. Paynter st Wood b Verity | ........... | 152 |
| E. Tyldesley lbw b Verity | ............... | 20 |
| J. Iddon c Sutcliffe b Verity | ............ | 2 |
| C. Hallows c Smailes b Verity | ........... | 0 |
| J. L. Hopwood c Mitchell b Verity | ........ | 2 |
| L. Parkinson c and b Bowes | ............ | 39 |
| R. Parkin c Mitchell b Verity | ........... | 13 |
| Mr P. T. Eckersley b Verity | ............. | 5 |
| F. M. Sibbles not out | ................. | 3 |
| G. Duckworth c Sutcliffe b Bowes | ........ | 2 |
| L-b 4, n-b 2 | ................. | 6 |
| | | 263 |

### Yorkshire

| | | | |
|---|---|---|---|
| P. Holmes c Tyldesley b Sibbles | ................. | 0 | – lbw b Parkin ................. 7 |
| H. Sutcliffe c Sibbles b Hopwood | ................ | 27 | – c Tyldesley b Sibbles ............. 61 |
| A. Mitchell b Sibbles | ........................ | 1 | – lbw b Hopwood ................. 13 |
| M. Leyland c Parkin b Sibbles | ................ | 6 | – c Eckersley b Hopwood .......... 43 |
| W. Barber c Hallows b Sibbles | ................ | 3 | – b Hopwood ................... 2 |
| Mr F. E. Greenwood c Watson b Hopwood | ....... | 3 | – st Duckworth b Sibbles ........... 9 |
| F. Smailes b Hopwood | ........................ | 0 | – b Parkin ..................... 7 |
| A. Wood lbw b Sibbles | ..................... | 0 | – b Sibbles .................... 11 |
| H. Verity not out | .......................... | 4 | – c Iddon b Sibbles .............. 8 |
| G. G. Macaulay c Watson b Sibbles | ............ | 0 | – not out ...................... 1 |
| W. E. Bowes c Watson b Sibbles | ................ | 0 | – c Watson b Sibbles ............. 0 |
| B 2 | ............................. | 2 | B 1, l-b 4 .............. 5 |
| | | 46 | 167 |

### Yorkshire Bowling

| | Overs | Mdns | Runs | Wkts |
|---|---|---|---|---|
| Bowes .......... | 10.5 | 5 | 16 | 2 |
| Smailes ......... | 13 | 4 | 30 | — |
| Macaulay ........ | 20 | 10 | 65 | — |
| Verity .......... | 39 | 13 | 107 | 8 |
| Leyland ......... | 11 | 3 | 39 | — |

## Lancashire Bowling

| | Overs | Mdns | Runs | Wkts | Overs | Mdns | Runs | Wkts |
|---|---|---|---|---|---|---|---|---|
| Sibbles . . . . . . . . . . . | 20.4 | 13 | 10 | 7 | 27 | 8 | 58 | 5 |
| Hopwood . . . . . . . . | 20 | 6 | 34 | 3 | 25 | 3 | 52 | 3 |
| Iddon . . . . . . . . . . . . | | | | | 10 | 2 | 18 | — |
| Parkin . . . . . . . . . . . | | | | | 12 | 4 | 32 | 2 |
| Parkinson . . . . . . . . | | | | | 1 | — | 2 | — |

Umpires: W. Bestwick and T. Oates.

# YORKSHIRE v NOTTINGHAMSHIRE

Played at Leeds, July 9, 11, 12, 1932

Verity in this match took – for the second time in his career – all ten wickets in an innings. Prior to lunch on the last day Nottinghamshire scored 38 without loss but on resuming, their ten wickets went down for 29 runs. Verity not only performed the "hat trick" in sending back Walker, Harris and Gunn, but got rid of Arthur Staples and Larwood with the last two balls of his next over and then, disposing of Voce and Sam Staples with the third and fourth balls of his following over, brought the innings to a close. This splendid bowling feat Sutcliffe and Holmes followed up by hitting off in about an hour and a half the 139 runs required for victory. Thus, Yorkshire gained a glorious win by ten wickets although, when on Monday afternoon a thunderstorm burst over the ground, they had stood 71 behind with only one wicket to fall.

## Nottinghamshire

| | | | | |
|---|---|---|---|---|
| W. W. Keeton b Rhodes . . . . . . . . . . . . . . . . . . . . . | 9 | – c Macaulay b Verity . . . . . . . . . . . . | 21 |
| F. W. Shipston b Macaulay . . . . . . . . . . . . . . . . . . . . | 8 | – c Wood b Verity . . . . . . . . . . . . . . | 21 |
| W. Walker c Barber b Bowes . . . . . . . . . . . . . . . . . . | 36 | – c Macaulay b Verity . . . . . . . . . . . . | 11 |
| Mr A. W. Carr c Barber b Verity . . . . . . . . . . . . . . . . | 0 | – c Barber b Verity . . . . . . . . . . . . . | 0 |
| A. Staples b Macaulay . . . . . . . . . . . . . . . . . . . . . . . . | .3 | – c Macaulay b Verity . . . . . . . . . . . . | 7 |
| C. B. Harris lbw b Leyland . . . . . . . . . . . . | 35 | – c Holmes b Verity . . . . . . . . . . . . . | 0 |
| G. V. Gunn b Verity . . . . . . . . . . . . . . . . . . . . . . . . . | 31 | – lbw b Verity . . . . . . . . . . . . . . . . . | 0 |
| B. Lilley not out . . . . . . . . . . . . . . . . . . . . . . . . . . . | 46 | – not out . . . . . . . . . . . . . . . . . . . . | 3 |
| H. Larwood b Leyland . . . . . . . . . . . . . . . . . . . . . . . | 48 | – c Sutcliffe b Verity . . . . . . . . . . . . | 0 |
| W. Voce b Leyland . . . . . . . . . . . . . . . . . . . . . . . . . | 0 | – c Holmes b Verity . . . . . . . . . . . . . | 0 |
| S. J. Staples b Leyland . . . . . . . . . . . . . . . . . . . . . . | 0 | – st Wood b Verity . . . . . . . . . . . . . | 0 |
| B 8, l-b 6, w 2, n-b 2 . . . . . . . . . . . . . . . . . | 18 | B 3, n-b 1 . . . . . . . . . . . . . . | 4 |
| | **234** | | **67** |

## Yorkshire

| | | | | |
|---|---|---|---|---|
| P. Holmes b Larwood . . . . . . . . . . . . . . . . . . . . . . . | 65 | – not out . . . . . . . . . . . . . . . . . . . . . . | 77 |
| H. Sutcliffe c Voce b Larwood . . . . . . . . . . . . . . . . . | 0 | – not out . . . . . . . . . . . . . . . . . . . . . . | 54 |
| A. Mitchell run out . . . . . . . . . . . . . . . . . . . . . . . . . | 24 | | |
| M. Leyland b Voce . . . . . . . . . . . . . . . . . . . . . . . . . | 5 | | |
| W. Barber c and b Larwood . . . . . . . . . . . . . . . . . . . | 34 | | |
| Mr A. B. Sellers b A. Staples . . . . . . . . . . . . . . . . . . | 0 | | |
| A. Wood b Larwood . . . . . . . . . . . . . . . . . . . . . . . | 1 | | |
| A. C. Rhodes c A. Staples b Voce . . . . . . . . . . . . . . . | 3 | | |
| H. Verity b Larwood . . . . . . . . . . . . . . . . . . . . . . . | 12 | | |
| G. G. Macaulay not out . . . . . . . . . . . . . . . . . . . . . . | 8 | | |
| W. E. Bowes not out . . . . . . . . . . . . . . . . . . . . . . . | 1 | | |
| B 5, l-b 5 . . . . . . . . . . . . . . . . . . . . . . . . . | 10 | B 4, l-b 4 . . . . . . . . . . . . . . | 8 |
| | **(9 wkts dec.) 163** | | **139** |

## Yorkshire Bowling

| | Overs | Mdns | Runs | Wkts | Overs | Mdns | Runs | Wkts |
|---|---|---|---|---|---|---|---|---|
| Bowes .......... | 31 | 9 | 55 | 1 | 5 | — | 19 | — |
| Rhodes .......... | 28 | 8 | 49 | 1 | | | | |
| Verity .......... | 41 | 13 | 64 | 2 | 19.4 | 16 | 10 | 10 |
| Macaulay ........ | 24 | 10 | 34 | 2 | 23 | 9 | 34 | — |
| Leyland .......... | 8.2 | 3 | 14 | 4 | | | | |

## Nottinghamshire Bowling

| | Overs | Mdns | Runs | Wkts | Overs | Mdns | Runs | Wkts |
|---|---|---|---|---|---|---|---|---|
| Larwood ........ | 22 | 4 | 73 | 5 | 3 | — | 14 | — |
| Voce ........... | 22 | 2 | 52 | 2 | 10 | — | 43 | — |
| S. J. Staples ...... | 7 | 2 | 8 | — | 18.4 | 5 | 37 | — |
| A. Staples ....... | 11 | 3 | 20 | 1 | 6 | 1 | 25 | — |
| Harris .......... | | | | | 3 | — | 12 | — |

Umpires: H. G. Baldwin and W. Reeves.

# YORKSHIRE v WARWICKSHIRE

## Played at Scarborough, July 18, 19, 20, 1934

After being dismissed for 45, the lowest score of the season, Warwickshire gained a remarkable victory by one wicket. Rain affected the pitch and though the match did not start until twenty minutes to three, eighteen wickets fell on Wednesday for 126. Sent in by Parsons, Yorkshire began by losing three men for 12 runs and were all out in two and a half hours, but before stumps were drawn Warwickshire had eight wickets down for 25. On going in again Yorkshire made very slow progress and might have been got rid of quite cheaply had not five chances been missed. The pitch was in better condition than at any previous time in the match when Warwickshire went in to get 216. Parsons rose to the occasion and by superb driving he dominated the cricket to such an extent that in less than two hours he made 94 out of 121, hitting three 6s and twelve 4s. Only 12 runs were wanted when he left.

## Yorkshire

| | | | |
|---|---|---|---|
| A. Mitchell c Kilner b Paine .................... | 5 | – b Hollies .............. | 15 |
| L. Hutton c Hollies b Mayer ................... | 3 | – lbw b Paine .............. | 9 |
| W. Barber c Santall b Paine .................... | 4 | – lbw b Hollies .............. | 15 |
| K. R. Davidson st Buckingham b Paine ........... | 3 | – c and b Hollies .............. | 38 |
| C. Turner c Mayer b Hollies ................... | 51 | – lbw b Mayer .............. | 9 |
| T. F. Smailes c Kilner b Paine .................. | 7 | – b Mayer .............. | 20 |
| Mr A. B. Sellers lbw b Paine ................... | 10 | – b Paine .............. | 23 |
| G. G. Macaulay st Buckingham b Paine .......... | 6 | – c Mayer b Paine .............. | 13 |
| A. Wood not out ........................... | 11 | – st Buckingham b Paine .......... | 5 |
| S. Douglas lbw b Paine ...................... | 0 | – not out .............. | 3 |
| H. Hargreaves st Buckingham b Paine ........... | 0 | – b Mayer .............. | 0 |
| W 1 ..................................... | 1 | B 4, l-b 5 .............. | 9 |
| | **101** | | **159** |

## Warwickshire

| | | | |
|---|---|---|---|
| N. Kilner run out | | 2 – lbw b Macaulay | 58 |
| A. J. Croom c Sellers b Macaulay | | 5 – c Wood b Douglas | 20 |
| L. A. Bates c Davidson b Macaulay | | 0 – c Macaulay b Douglas | 1 |
| F. R. Santall c Mitchell b Hargreaves | | 8 – c Turner b Hutton | 17 |
| Rev. J. H. Parsons c Hutton b Hargreaves | | 3 – b Hargreaves | 94 |
| H. E. Dollery c Davidson b Hargreaves | | 1 – c Wood b Macaulay | 0 |
| Mr P. Cranmer c Barber b Hargreaves | | 3 – c and b Macaulay | 0 |
| J. Buckingham not out | | 14 – c Sellers b Macaulay | 1 |
| G. E. Paine c Smailes b Macaulay | | 0 – c Sellers b Hutton | 2 |
| J. H. Mayer c Davidson b Smailes | | 2 – not out | 11 |
| E. Hollies c Barber b Smailes | | 6 – not out | 0 |
| B 1 | | 1  B 2, l-b 9, n-b 1 | 12 |
| | | **45** | **216** |

### Warwickshire Bowling

| | Overs | Mdns | Runs | Wkts | Overs | Mdns | Runs | Wkts |
|---|---|---|---|---|---|---|---|---|
| Mayer | 19 | 11 | 25 | 1 | 26.2 | 13 | 37 | 3 |
| Santall | 5 | 3 | 3 | — | | | | |
| Paine | 20.1 | 5 | 62 | 8 | 29 | 10 | 59 | 4 |
| Hollies | 3 | 1 | 10 | 1 | 25 | 5 | 50 | 3 |
| Cranmer | | | | | 2 | — | 4 | — |

### Yorkshire Bowling

| | Overs | Mdns | Runs | Wkts | Overs | Mdns | Runs | Wkts |
|---|---|---|---|---|---|---|---|---|
| Hargreaves | 9 | 2 | 19 | 4 | 13 | 2 | 34 | 1 |
| Macaulay | 10 | 1 | 19 | 3 | 34.2 | 14 | 67 | 4 |
| Smailes | 3 | — | 6 | 2 | 9 | 2 | 22 | — |
| Turner | | | | | 5 | 1 | 13 | — |
| Douglas | | | | | 27 | 17 | 34 | 2 |
| Hutton | | | | | 8 | 1 | 34 | 2 |

Umpires: W. R. Parry and A. Skelding.

# YORKSHIRE v ESSEX

### Played at Huddersfield, July 31, August 1, 1935

This was the match that produced the sensation of the season. Unbeaten up to that point, Yorkshire collapsed twice in two days before the Essex fast bowlers and suffered defeat by an innings and 204 runs. Before half-past twelve on the first day, Yorkshire were put out for 31 – their lowest total in an innings for 26 years – and when they went in a second time 303 runs in arrear their batting again broke down completely. Their two innings lasted altogether less than three hours. Nichols, accomplishing fine performances with both ball and bat, enjoyed the greatest triumph of his career. After taking four wickets for 17, he played an innings of 146 and then dismissed seven Yorkshire batsmen for 37 runs. Read's pace was also devastating and in Yorkshire's first innings six wickets fell for a mere nine runs. Essex lost five wickets for 65, but Nichols and Belle came along with a magnificent partnership of 174 in just over three hours and Nichols, driving and pulling superbly, hit two 6s and sixteen 4s. The contrast to what had gone before was amazing. The Essex innings closing on Wednesday, Yorkshire had to bat first thing next morning and then Nichols and Read again paralysed the batsmen by sheer pace off the ground. Except for three overs by Eastman, those two fast bowlers were on unchanged in each innings. During the match, which was decided by one o'clock on the Thursday, Nichols secured his hundredth wicket of the season.

## Yorkshire

| | | | |
|---|---|---|---|
| H. Sutcliffe c Sheffield b Nichols | 4 | – c Eastman b Nichols | 1 |
| W. Barber c Wilcox b Read | 1 | – b Nichols | 18 |
| Mr A. B. Sellers c Wilcox b Read | 2 | – lbw b Nichols | 2 |
| M. Leyland b Read | 0 | – b Read | 2 |
| Mr P. A. Gibb c Rist b Read | 0 | – lbw (N) b Nichols | 11 |
| C. Turner c Sheffield b Read | 4 | – b Nichols | 13 |
| L. Hutton b Nichols | 0 | – lbw b Nichols | 0 |
| A. Wood c Read b Nichols | 13 | – b Nichols | 24 |
| H. Fisher b Read | 0 | – c Rist b Read | 2 |
| H. Verity not out | 0 | – c P. Smith b Read | 6 |
| W. E. Bowes c Rist b Nichols | 4 | – not out | 19 |
| B 1, l-b 1, n-b 1 | 3 | L-b 1 | 1 |
| | **31** | | **99** |

## Essex

| | | | |
|---|---|---|---|
| J. R. Sheffield b Verity | 5 | L. C. Eastman c Gibb b Bowes | 23 |
| F. Rist c Gibb b Verity | 35 | P. Smith b Bowes | 5 |
| Mr D. R. Wilcox c Wood b Turner | 2 | R. Smith not out | 16 |
| J. A. Cutmore c Wood b Fisher | 2 | Mr H. D. Read st Wood b Verity | 0 |
| J. O'Connor b Fisher | 0 | B 24, l-b 13 | 37 |
| M. S. Nichols c Hutton b Bowes | 146 | | |
| Mr B. H. Belle c Verity b Leyland | 63 | | **334** |

### Essex Bowling

| | Overs | Mdns | Runs | Wkts | Overs | Mdns | Runs | Wkts |
|---|---|---|---|---|---|---|---|---|
| Nichols | 6.4 | 2 | 17 | 4 | 15 | 3 | 37 | 7 |
| Read | 6 | 1 | 11 | 6 | 11.4 | 2 | 51 | 3 |
| Eastman | | | | | 3 | — | 10 | — |

### Yorkshire Bowling

| | Overs | Mdns | Runs | Wkts |
|---|---|---|---|---|
| Bowes | 37 | 8 | 77 | 3 |
| Turner | 16 | 2 | 41 | 1 |
| Verity | 24.2 | 4 | 79 | 3 |
| Fisher | 25 | 5 | 62 | 2 |
| Leyland | 5 | 1 | 38 | 1 |

Umpires: F. Walden and F. Chester.

## YORKSHIRE v KENT

### Played at Sheffield, May 23, 25, 1936

Yorkshire won by an innings and 153 runs. The match was a wonderful triumph for Verity, who had a record of fifteen wickets for 38 runs. In the Kent second innings he had a hand in dismissing the whole side, for after he caught Fagg he took all the other nine wickets. Kent, who at the time were leaders of the county competition, were completely outplayed from the start. Showers and poor light may have formed some handicap to batsmen on Saturday, but the resistance offered to Verity was dreadfully weak. Although Watt hit a six and three 4s off him, Verity secured six wickets for 26 runs. A century by Barber served to show there was nothing seriously wrong with the wicket. By sound stroke play, Barber hit 158 out of 289 in considerably less than four hours. His chief scoring strokes were seventeen 4s. By the end of the day Yorkshire led by 78 with only three men out, and when, after heavy week-end rain, the wicket showed signs of becoming difficult Sellers declared. No one could have been prepared for what followed. Verity made the ball rise and turn either way, and in an hour and a quarter Kent were out for a paltry 39 runs. Half the side fell for 30, and after a few hits by the early batsmen, Sunnucks alone contrived to keep up his wicket. The conditions undoubtedly placed batsmen at a great disadvantage, but Verity showed splendid control of flight, length and pace, and made the batsmen play at every ball. He could scarcely have received better support in the field, where Mitchell often did brilliant things.

### Kent

| | | |
|---|---|---|
| W. H. Ashdown c Mitchell b Turner | 21 | – lbw b Verity ................... 12 |
| A. Fagg b Bowes | 7 | – c Verity b Smailes ............. 6 |
| F. E. Woolley c Sutcliffe b Smailes | 26 | – c Hutton b Verity ............. 5 |
| Mr B. H. Valentine st Wood b Verity | 11 | – c Mitchell b Verity .......... 0 |
| L. J. Todd c Sellers b Verity | 20 | – c Mitchell b Verity .......... 2 |
| P. R. Sunnucks b Verity | 7 | – not out ...................... 7 |
| D. V. P. Wright lbw b Verity | 0 | – st Wood b Verity ............. 0 |
| Mr W. H. V. Levett c Wood b Verity | 3 | – b Verity ..................... 0 |
| A. E. Watt c Sellers b Verity | 10 | – c Barber b Verity ............ 4 |
| A. P. Freeman not out | 0 | – c Mitchell b Verity .......... 3 |
| C. Lewis b Bowes | 0 | – c Mitchell b Verity .......... 0 |
| L-b 2 | 2 | |
| | **107** | **39** |

### Yorkshire

| | | | |
|---|---|---|---|
| A. Mitchell lbw b Wright | 43 | A. Wood c Freeman b Wright | 34 |
| L. Hutton b Todd | 6 | Mr A. B. Sellers not out | 2 |
| W. Barber c Ashdown b Wright | 158 | H. Verity not out | 0 |
| M. Leyland c Levett b Wright | 8 | B 9, l-b 10 | 19 |
| H. Sutcliffe b Freeman | 29 | | |
| C. Turner b Freeman | 0 | (7 wkts dec.) | **299** |

T. F. Smailes and W. E. Bowes did not bat.

### Yorkshire Bowling

| | Overs | Mdns | Runs | Wkts | Overs | Mdns | Runs | Wkts |
|---|---|---|---|---|---|---|---|---|
| Bowes | 18.1 | 4 | 36 | 2 | 5 | 2 | 8 | — |
| Smailes | 12 | 2 | 29 | 1 | 11 | 3 | 19 | 1 |
| Turner | 10 | 4 | 14 | 1 | | | | |
| Verity | 13 | 5 | 26 | 6 | 6.3 | 3 | 12 | 9 |

### Kent Bowling

| | Overs | Mdns | Runs | Wkts |
|---|---|---|---|---|
| Todd | 14 | 5 | 36 | 1 |
| Watt | 13 | 1 | 41 | — |
| Freeman | 34 | 8 | 97 | 2 |
| Wright | 13 | 2 | 25 | 4 |
| Lewis | 27 | 6 | 81 | — |

Umpires: H. G. Baldwin and F. Walden.

## YORKSHIRE v SURREY

At Sheffield, June 18, 20, 1938

Yorkshire won by an innings and 202 runs. The pitch at no time helped bowlers, but Surrey's batting failed badly. Yorkshire stayed in all the first day when Barber, after an uncertain start, hit well all round. Mitchell helped him in a stand of 140 and he and Smailes put on 134, Smailes driving splendidly and hitting a 6 and fifteen 4s. Surrey were twice put out in the course of four hours for an aggregate of 214 runs. Bowes and Smailes, bowling unchanged, routed them completely in the first innings, and when Surrey followed on against arrears of 364, Fishlock alone showed his normal form. The left-hander, with some fine off-drives among his strokes, hit two 6s and eleven 4s, but he received little support. Hutton, with leg-breaks and an occasional googly, this time brought about the collapse.

## Yorkshire

| | | | |
|---|---|---|---|
| L. Hutton lbw b Parker | 23 | A. Wood b Parker | 29 |
| W. Barber c Holmes b Gregory | 157 | H. Verity lbw b Squires | 6 |
| A. Mitchell c Watts b Parker | 56 | E. P. Robinson c Brooks b Parker | 1 |
| M. Leyland b Brown | 10 | W. E. Bowes not out | 7 |
| Mr A. B. Sellers b Brown | 0 | L-b 9, n-b 2 | 11 |
| T. F. Smailes c Brown b Squires | 116 | | |
| H. Halliday lbw b Brown | 0 | | **416** |

## Surrey

| | | | |
|---|---|---|---|
| L. B. Fishlock lbw b Bowes | 9 | – st Wood b Hutton | 74 |
| R. J. Gregory lbw b Smailes | 0 | – c Wood b Hutton | 14 |
| H. S. Squires b Bowes | 4 | – lbw b Verity | 8 |
| T. H. Barling c Robinson b Bowes | 7 | – run out | 1 |
| J. F. Parker b Bowes | 7 | – lbw b Robinson | 6 |
| Mr E. R. T. Holmes b Smailes | 9 | – c Wood b Hutton | 15 |
| Mr F. R. Brown b Bowes | 11 | – b Hutton | 6 |
| F. Berry b Smailes | 0 | – b Leyland | 6 |
| E. A. Watts not out | 1 | – not out | 14 |
| E. W. Brooks lbw b Bowes | 0 | – b Leyland | 4 |
| A. R. Gover b Smailes | 0 | – lbw b Hutton | 5 |
| B 1, l-b 2, n-b 1 | 4 | B 1, l-b 8 | 9 |
| | **52** | | **162** |

## Surrey Bowling

| | Overs | Mdns | Runs | Wkts |
|---|---|---|---|---|
| Gover | 12 | 1 | 43 | — |
| Watts | 15 | 1 | 70 | — |
| Berry | 11 | — | 48 | — |
| Parker | 26 | 4 | 92 | 4 |
| Brown | 25 | 3 | 107 | 3 |
| Squires | 15.1 | 3 | 37 | 2 |
| Gregory | 4 | 2 | 8 | 1 |

## Yorkshire Bowling

| | Overs | Mdns | Runs | Wkts | Overs | Mdns | Runs | Wkts |
|---|---|---|---|---|---|---|---|---|
| Bowes | 11 | 3 | 32 | 6 | 9 | 1 | 34 | — |
| Smailes | 10.2 | 3 | 16 | 4 | 9 | 6 | 17 | — |
| Verity | | | | | 10 | 2 | 45 | 1 |
| Robinson | | | | | 1 | — | 1 | 1 |
| Hutton | | | | | 14.2 | 3 | 45 | 5 |
| Leyland | | | | | 5 | 1 | 11 | 2 |

Umpires: C. V. Tarbox and G. Beet.

## YORKSHIRE v GLAMORGAN

### At Hull, June 22, 23, 24, 1938

Yorkshire won by 12 runs. Fine bowling by Smailes and a bold declaration by Sellers made the victory possible in a thrilling finish. An opening stand of 148 by Mitchell and Barber occupied most of a first day cut short by rain that left the pitch treacherous. Next day Emrys Davies and Jones got down the last eight wickets for 109, Leyland alone putting up much resistance. Dyson and Emrys Davies gave Glamorgan a good start with a partnership of 88 and Brierley batted so well that at the end of the second day the Welsh county stood within 133 of their opponents' total with nine wickets to fall. So well did Smailes bowl on the following morning, however, that the innings ended for the addition of 39. Smailes, in 37 deliveries, dismissed six men for 17 runs. Leading by 94, Yorkshire went all out for runs, and Sellers soon declared. Fierce hitting by Brierley and enterprising batting on the part of Dai Davies and H. Davies kept the issue open to the very end, but Smailes, with the best bowling performance of his career, turned the scale in favour of Yorkshire. Relying mainly upon off-breaks round the wicket he caused trouble to all the batsmen.

### Yorkshire

| | | | |
|---|---|---|---|
| A. Mitchell c H. Davies b Smart | 69 | – b Mercer | 0 |
| W. Barber c and b E. Davies | 90 | – c Dyson b E. Davies | 10 |
| Mr A. B. Sellers b Jones | 7 | – b Mercer | 3 |
| M. Leyland c and b Jones | 39 | – c E. Davies b Mercer | 21 |
| Mr J. Brumfitt c Dyson b E. Davies | 9 | | |
| T. F. Smailes c Turnbull b E. Davies | 1 | – c Turnbull b Jones | 7 |
| H. Halliday b E. Davies | 17 | | |
| A. Wood c H. Davies b Jones | 18 | – not out | 1 |
| E. P. Robinson b E. Davies | 11 | – not out | 24 |
| F. Wilkinson b Jones | 2 | | |
| W. E. Bowes not out | 0 | | |
| B 7, l-b 3 | 10 | B 2 | 2 |
| | **273** | **(5 wkts dec.)** | **68** |

### Glamorgan

| | | | |
|---|---|---|---|
| A. H. Dyson lbw b Bowes | 34 | – lbw b Smailes | 15 |
| E. Davies b Smailes | 64 | – b Smailes | 13 |
| T. L. Brierley c and b Smailes | 40 | – b Smailes | 36 |
| D. Davies b Robinson | 0 | – c and b Smailes | 23 |
| R. Duckfield c and b Smailes | 7 | – b Smailes | 13 |
| C. Smart c Robinson b Smailes | 0 | – lbw b Smailes | 9 |
| Mr M. J. Turnbull c Bowes b Smailes | 2 | – b Leyland | 6 |
| E. C. Jones c Wilkinson b Robinson | 0 | – b Leyland | 0 |
| H. Davies c Wilkinson b Robinson | 4 | – not out | 19 |
| A. Davies b Smailes | 3 | – b Smailes | 0 |
| J. Mercer not out | 6 | – b Smailes | 4 |
| B 8, l-b 9, n-b 2 | 19 | B 9, l-b 3 | 12 |
| | **179** | | **150** |

### Glamorgan Bowling

| | Overs | Mdns | Runs | Wkts | Overs | Mdns | Runs | Wkts |
|---|---|---|---|---|---|---|---|---|
| Mercer | 25 | 7 | 48 | — | 7 | — | 31 | 3 |
| Smart | 16 | 3 | 31 | 1 | | | | |
| E. Davies | 34.1 | 5 | 83 | 5 | 5 | — | 31 | 1 |
| A. Davies | 3 | — | 10 | — | | | | |
| Jones | 26 | 3 | 75 | 4 | 2 | 1 | 4 | 1 |
| D. Davies | 4 | — | 16 | — | | | | |

### Yorkshire Bowling

| | Overs | Mdns | Runs | Wkts | Overs | Mdns | Runs | Wkts |
|---|---|---|---|---|---|---|---|---|
| Bowes | 22 | 5 | 43 | 1 | 1 | 1 | — | — |
| Smailes | 14.1 | 4 | 35 | 6 | 22.5 | 3 | 68 | 8 |
| Wilkinson | 11 | 3 | 27 | — | | | | |
| Robinson | 18 | 5 | 49 | 3 | 11 | 2 | 51 | — |
| Leyland | 2 | 1 | 6 | — | 10 | 5 | 19 | 2 |

Umpires: C. N. Woolley and J. Smart.

# YORKSHIRE v GLAMORGAN

At Bradford, June 21, 22, 1939

Yorkshire won by an innings and 93 runs. The match provided another triumph for Verity, on a rain-damaged pitch, only Dyson, who batted resolutely for two hours, offering real resistance. Against the medium-pace swing bowling of Judge, Yorkshire began indifferently, but Hutton and Barber, in a partnership of 90, pulled the game round. Hutton, staying four hours and a half, hit a 6 and eleven 4s, being last to leave. Robinson, during twenty-five minutes forcing play, hit three 6s and four 4s. Verity then carried everything before him and Glamorgan were all out in 100 minutes.

## Glamorgan

| | | | |
|---|---|---|---|
| A. H. Dyson c Robinson b Verity | 59 | – c Mitchell b Bowes | 8 |
| E. Davies c Sutcliffe b Robinson | 13 | – b Verity | 4 |
| T. L. Brierley c Robinson b Verity | 17 | – lbw b Verity | 15 |
| D. Davies c Yardley b Verity | 5 | – c Barber b Verity | 0 |
| Mr M. J. Turnbull c Mitchell b Verity | 0 | – st Wood b Verity | 10 |
| C. Smart st Wood b Robinson | 20 | – c Hutton b Verity | 12 |
| E. C. Jones lbw b Verity | 11 | – c Barber b Verity | 0 |
| H. Davies run out | 4 | – st Wood b Verity | 4 |
| D. Thomas not out | 14 | – b Robinson | 0 |
| P. F. Judge c Sutcliffe b Verity | 4 | – st Wood b Robinson | 5 |
| J. Mercer b Verity | 10 | – not out | 3 |
| B 8, l-b 3 | 11 | L-b 4 | 4 |
| | **168** | | **65** |

## Yorkshire

| | | | |
|---|---|---|---|
| H. Sutcliffe c Smart b Judge | 11 | A. Wood b E. Davies | 9 |
| L. Hutton b Judge | 144 | E. P. Robinson c Brierley b Judge | 48 |
| A. Mitchell c D. Davies b Judge | 3 | H. Verity c Turnbull b Judge | 4 |
| M. Leyland c Dyson b Judge | 6 | W. E. Bowes not out | 16 |
| W. Barber c Judge b E. Davies | 37 | B 8, l-b 5, w 1 | 14 |
| Mr N. W. D. Yardley c Thomas b Judge | 6 | | |
| Mr A. B. Sellers c and b Judge | 30 | | **328** |

## Yorkshire Bowling

| | Overs | Mdns | Runs | Wkts | Overs | Mdns | Runs | Wkts |
|---|---|---|---|---|---|---|---|---|
| Bowes | 11 | 1 | 27 | — | 10 | 2 | 32 | 1 |
| Yardley | 4 | 2 | 9 | — | | | | |
| Robinson | 14 | 2 | 73 | 2 | 3.4 | 1 | 9 | 2 |
| Verity | 16.3 | 3 | 48 | 7 | 12 | 6 | 20 | 7 |

## Glamorgan Bowling

| | Overs | Mdns | Runs | Wkts |
|---|---|---|---|---|
| Mercer | 10 | — | 62 | — |
| Judge | 25.4 | 6 | 75 | 8 |
| E. Davies | 23 | 3 | 106 | 2 |
| Thomas | 6 | 1 | 28 | — |
| Jones | 4 | — | 32 | — |
| Smart | 2 | — | 11 | — |

Umpires: H. G. Baldwin and D. Hendren.

# YORKSHIRE v DERBYSHIRE

## At Sheffield, June 24, 26, 27, 1939

Yorkshire won by 276 runs. Derbyshire fell for their smallest total since Lancashire dismissed them for 17 at Old Trafford in 1888. Before the swerve bowling of Smurthwaite and Smailes they were all out in forty minutes. Yorkshire, helped by faulty fielding, did well in their second innings. Barber, while putting together his first century of the summer, received such help from Yardley, Wilson and Sellers that three following stands realised 160. Specially strong in driving, Barber hit fourteen 4s. Smailes finished the match by dismissing the whole Derbyshire side; and with 14 wickets for 58 runs in the game, did his best performance in county cricket. He kept a perfect length with his medium paced swingers.

## Yorkshire

| | | | |
|---|---|---|---|
| H. Sutcliffe c Worthington b A. V. Pope | 9 | – b G. H. Pope | 18 |
| A. Mitchell c Rhodes b G. H. Pope | 14 | – c Smith b A. V. Pope | 40 |
| W. Barber c Elliott b A. V. Pope | 2 | – c Smith b A. V. Pope | 100 |
| M. Leyland b G. H. Pope | 0 | – c Elliott b G. H. Pope | 1 |
| Mr N. W. D. Yardley c Gladwin b A. V. Pope | 21 | – c and b Rhodes | 34 |
| Mr G. A. Wilson b A. V. Pope | 0 | – b Mitchell | 21 |
| Mr A. B. Sellers c Elliott b G. H. Pope | 31 | – run out | 43 |
| T. F. Smailes c A. V. Pope b G. H. Pope | 4 | – b A. V. Pope | 8 |
| E. P. Robinson b G. H. Pope | 0 | – c Hounsfield b G. H. Pope | 23 |
| J. Smurthwaite b G. H. Pope | 0 | – b A. V. Pope | 1 |
| K. Fiddling not out | 0 | – not out | 5 |
| L-b 2 | 2 | B 8, l-b 8 | 16 |
| | **83** | | **310** |

## Derbyshire

| | | | |
|---|---|---|---|
| D. Smith b Smurthwaite | 5 | – b Smailes | 8 |
| A. E. Alderman c Fiddling b Smailes | 1 | – c Smurthwaite b Smailes | 0 |
| T. S. Worthington run out | 0 | – c Mitchell b Smailes | 32 |
| L. F. Townsend c Robinson b Smurthwaite | 2 | – b Smailes | 0 |
| G. H. Pope c Robinson b Smailes | 0 | – lbw b Smailes | 1 |
| A. Rhodes c Robinson b Smurthwaite | 0 | – b Smailes | 18 |
| Mr T. D. Hounsfield c Sutcliffe b Smailes | 2 | – not out | 21 |
| A. V. Pope b Smurthwaite | 6 | – b Smailes | 4 |
| Gladwin c Smailes b Smurthwaite | 0 | – b Smailes | 0 |
| H. Elliott not out | 2 | – b Smailes | 6 |
| T. B. Mitchell c Leyland b Smailes | 0 | – st Fiddling b Smailes | 6 |
| L-b 2 | 2 | B 1 | 1 |
| | **20** | | **97** |

## Derbyshire Bowling

| | Overs | Mdns | Runs | Wkts | Overs | Mdns | Runs | Wkts |
|---|---|---|---|---|---|---|---|---|
| A. V. Pope | 18 | 4 | 37 | 4 | 25 | 5 | 72 | 4 |
| G. H. Pope | 17.3 | 2 | 44 | 6 | 24.5 | 3 | 90 | 3 |
| Mitchell | | | | | 9 | — | 52 | 1 |
| Gladwin | | | | | 8 | 2 | 36 | — |
| Rhodes | | | | | 4 | — | 16 | 1 |
| Townsend | | | | | 5 | — | 28 | — |

**Yorkshire Bowling**

| | Overs | Mdns | Runs | Wkts | Overs | Mdns | Runs | Wkts |
|---|---|---|---|---|---|---|---|---|
| Smailes .......... | 4.3 | — | 11 | 4 | 17.1 | 5 | 47 | 10 |
| Smurthwaite ...... | 4 | 2 | 7 | 5 | 14 | 5 | 43 | — |
| Yardley .......... | | | | | 2 | — | 5 | — |
| Robinson ......... | | | | | 1 | — | 1 | — |

Umpires: H. G. Baldwin and H. Elliott.

# MCC MATCHES

## OLD ETONIANS v OLD HARROVIANS

Played at Lord's, July 12, 13, 1920

This was an interesting revival, two excellent sides being got together. The Old Etonians had the worst of the opening day, but they showed splendid all-round cricket on Tuesday, and won the game in dazzling fashion by 162 runs. Longman and Wilkinson, by scoring 126 together, turned the game in their favour, and, when holding a lead of 230, they declared. P. W. Cobbold did the rest, bowling his leg-breaks in such irresistible form that he took six wickets for eight runs. Cobbold is seldom seen in public matches, but he has for years past done wonders in amateur cricket of a less important kind. A member of the Cambridge XI of 1896 he is now something of a veteran.

### Old Etonians

| | | | |
|---|---|---|---|
| Mr H. K. Longman c Bird b Falcon | 4 | – c Jessopp b Falcon | 107 |
| Mr A. C. Wilkinson b Falcon | 7 | – b Jessopp | 72 |
| Mr N. Haig b Falcon | 0 | – c Wilson b Jessopp | 16 |
| Mr R. H. Twining c Falcon b Mann | 3 | – st Brooke b Jameson | 10 |
| Maj. Hon. L. H. Tennyson c Bird b Jessopp | 48 | – not out | 56 |
| Mr P. F. C. Williams c Blount b Falcon | 8 | | |
| Capt. M. B. Burrows b Jessopp | 6 | – not out | 9 |
| Capt. R. St L. Fowler not out | 50 | | |
| Mr G. H. M. Cartwright b Jessopp | 0 | | |
| Mr C. H. Gibson b Falcon | 0 | | |
| Mr P. W. Cobbold c Wilson b Mann | 22 | | |
| B 6, l-b 1, n-b 4 | 11 | B 23, l-b 5, n-b 3 | 31 |
| | **159** | **(4 wkts dec.)** | **301** |

### Old Harrovians

| | | | |
|---|---|---|---|
| Mr W. P. Robertson c Cartwright b Gibson | 0 | – b Haig | 0 |
| Mr G. E. V. Crutchley b Haig | 5 | – c Twining b Burrows | 0 |
| Mr G. Wilson c Wilkinson b Cartwright | 98 | – b Cobbold | 0 |
| Capt. F. R. R. Brooke c Longman b Gibson | 41 | – lbw b Cobbold | 22 |
| Mr C. H. Blount b Fowler | 11 | – b Fowler | 14 |
| Mr M. C. Bird c Cobbold b Haig | 10 | – c Fowler b Cobbold | 5 |
| Hon. R. Anson c Twining b Haig | 0 | – not out | 5 |
| Capt. T. O. Jameson b Gibson | 24 | – c Cartwright b Fowler | 7 |
| Mr N. A. Jessopp c Cobbold b Gibson | 18 | – c Twining b Cobbold | 3 |
| Mr M. Falcon b Cartwright | 0 | – b Cobbold | 0 |
| Mr E. W. Mann not out | 7 | – b Cobbold | 0 |
| B 15, n-b 1 | 16 | B 8, l-b 3, w 1 | 12 |
| | **230** | | **68** |

### Old Harrovians' Bowling

| | Overs | Mdns | Runs | Wkts | Overs | Mdns | Runs | Wkts |
|---|---|---|---|---|---|---|---|---|
| Mann | 12.1 | 5 | 16 | 2 | 7 | 2 | 30 | — |
| Falcon | 20 | 4 | 61 | 5 | 19 | 3 | 79 | 1 |
| Jessopp | 13 | 3 | 54 | 3 | 18 | 6 | 55 | 2 |
| Crutchley | 3 | — | 17 | — | 5 | — | 35 | — |
| Anson | | | | | 11 | 2 | 33 | — |
| Jameson | | | | | 9 | — | 38 | 1 |

## Old Etonians' Bowling

| | Overs | Mdns | Runs | Wkts | Overs | Mdns | Runs | Wkts |
|---|---|---|---|---|---|---|---|---|
| Gibson .......... | 26 | 9 | 53 | 4 | 4 | 1 | 13 | — |
| Haig ............. | 19 | 5 | 49 | 3 | 7 | 4 | 6 | 1 |
| Fowler .......... | 19 | 6 | 49 | 1 | 8 | 3 | 22 | 2 |
| Cobbold ......... | 7 | — | 31 | — | 9.1 | 4 | 8 | 6 |
| Cartwright ....... | 12.5 | 4 | 31 | 2 | | | | |
| Burrows ......... | 2 | 1 | 1 | — | 4 | 2 | 7 | 1 |

Umpires: G. Bean and W. Wainwright.

# CLIFTON v TONBRIDGE

## Played at Lord's, July 26, 27, 1920

Though they had lost Hedges, Tonbridge, as in 1919, were too strong for Clifton, winning the game by nine wickets. Nothing in the first day's play suggested such a result, but on Tuesday the Clifton batting went all to pieces against Knott's slow bowling, and Tonbridge were left with only 97 to get. They began their task with extreme caution, but Solbe, when he had settled down, hit finely.

## Clifton

| | | | |
|---|---|---|---|
| Mr R. C. M. King c Holton b Webster ............ | 0 | – c Gaunt b Knott .............. | 8 |
| Mr C. W. Tosh run out ...................... | 7 | – b Knott ..................... | 2 |
| Mr J. J. Lyons c Sherwell b Webster ............. | 11 | – c Knott b Holton ............. | 15 |
| Mr E. W. Thomas c Sherwell b Knott ............ | 2 | – c Gaunt b Holton ............. | 9 |
| Mr W. M. Hampton not out ................... | 81 | – not out ..................... | 6 |
| Mr O. H. Bonham-Carter c Hubbard b Knott ...... | 19 | – lbw b Knott ................. | 1 |
| Mr C. J. Burton c Amistead b Knott ............. | 9 | – c Knott b Holton ............. | 1 |
| Mr F. J. Weeks c and b Knott ................. | 21 | – c Gilbert b Knott ............ | 1 |
| Mr O. M. Meares b Knott .................... | 5 | – lbw b Knott ................. | 0 |
| Mr J. T. Webster run out .................... | 13 | – b Knott .................... | 2 |
| Mr J. M. Craster lbw b Knott ................. | 0 | – c Hancock b Knott ........... | 2 |
| B 16, l-b 1 ........................ | 17 | B 7, l-b 1, w 1 ............ | 9 |
| | **185** | | **56** |

## Tonbridge

| | | | |
|---|---|---|---|
| Mr E. P. Solbe c Hampton b Craster ............. | 7 | – not out ...................... | 66 |
| Mr H. C. A. Gaunt c Thomas b Meares ......... | 53 | – run out ..................... | 5 |
| Mr T. E. S. Francis b Craster .................. | 0 | – not out ..................... | 26 |
| Mr C. H. Knott b Craster ................... | 45 | | |
| Mr J. C. Hubbard st Webster b Meares .......... | 0 | | |
| Mr V. Armistead b Meares .................. | 0 | | |
| Mr N. B. Sherwell c and b Meares .............. | 7 | | |
| Mr H. P. Holton run out ................... | 0 | | |
| Mr H. T. Gilbert not out ................... | 9 | | |
| Mr G. M. Hancock c Bonham-Carter b Weeks ..... | 3 | | |
| Mr A. S. Webster c Meares b Weeks ............ | 7 | | |
| B 13, l-b 1 ........................ | 14 | B 1, w 2 ............... | 3 |
| | **145** | | **100** |

## Tonbridge Bowling

|  | Overs | Mdns | Runs | Wkts | Overs | Mdns | Runs | Wkts |
|---|---|---|---|---|---|---|---|---|
| Webster .......... | 15 | 6 | 24 | 2 | 5 | — | 15 | — |
| Knott ............ | 23.3 | — | 83 | 6 | 11.1 | 1 | 27 | 7 |
| Holton .......... | 9 | 2 | 10 | — | 7 | 4 | 5 | 3 |
| Gilbert .......... | 7 | 2 | 20 | — |  |  |  |  |
| Hancock ......... | 5 | — | 16 | — |  |  |  |  |
| Francis .......... | 2 | — | 6 | — |  |  |  |  |
| Solbe ........... | 1 | — | 9 | — |  |  |  |  |

## Clifton Bowling

|  | Overs | Mdns | Runs | Wkts | Overs | Mdns | Runs | Wkts |
|---|---|---|---|---|---|---|---|---|
| Lyons ........... | 7 | 3 | 14 | — | 12 | 3 | 46 | — |
| Craster .......... | 12 | 2 | 44 | 3 | 14 | 12 | 3 | — |
| Meares .......... | 11 | — | 52 | 4 | 8.5 | — | 43 | — |
| Thomas .......... | 2 | — | 9 | — |  |  |  |  |
| Bonham-Carter .... | 2 | — | 4 | — |  |  |  |  |
| Weeks .......... | 5 | 3 | 8 | 2 | 3 | 1 | 5 | — |

Umpires: J. H. Board and T. M. Russell.

## MCC IN 1922

The committee after consideration of several designs have decided as authorised by the general meeting of May 5, 1920, that the memorial to Dr W. G. Grace shall take the form of a gateway with handsome iron gates, at the members' entrance, to be adapted to harmonise with certain improvements at that entrance. Originally intended to be erected exclusively by the MCC, it was afterwards determined, as members may remember, to guarantee the cost of the memorial but to accept donations up to a moiety of the cost, in the belief that cricket clubs and admirers of the late Dr Grace would like to be associated with it. A tender has been accepted amounting to £2,268 and it is hoped that the work will be completed early in May.

Sixteen candidates incapacitated by wounds received on active service and who would otherwise have been brought forward for election as cricketers have been elected.

Wounded soldiers were again entertained by the club during the season.

## THE MARYLEBONE CLUB AND THE WAR

At the beginning of August 1922 the MCC issued the following statement:

During the war the committee of the MCC wrote to 5,100 candidates entered in the books between 1889 and 1896 in order to ascertain if they were still desirous of becoming members of the club. Of these 1,360 decided to take up their election, 268 asked for their election to be postponed, 158 desired to take up their election but have not since applied, while from 1,650 no replies were received. In the case of 760 the letters were returned by the Post Office, 290 declined election, and the committee are informed that 614 were killed in action or are deceased. The committee are most desirous that no hardship should occur to those candidates who were written to during the war.

In the case of those who replied, they are communicating by letter with each individual except those who have declined, but in the case of the remainder they feel that the best course they can pursue is to notify them through the Press that if they wish to be considered for election in due course and in order of entry as candidates, they should at once notify the secretary of their desire.

## MCC IN 1923

Members will have had an opportunity of inspecting the "Dr. W. G. Grace" Memorial Gateway completed in July last. Mrs Grace was asked to open it formally but did not feel able to accept the invitation.

## LORD'S AND THE MCC [1930]

### THIRTY YEARS OF HISTORY

By Sir Francis Lacey

Changes are frequent in these days but it is doubtful if any place has changed more completely than Lord's cricket ground in the last thirty years or any institution grown more in administration than the MCC which owns it. Taking the physical condition first, the only part remaining of the earliest history of Lord's is the match ground. Its turf was brought from Dorset Square and North Bank over 100 years ago and, except for a complete system of drainage supplied about 20 years ago, the usual operations of upkeep, the addition of two tanks for conserving rain water and the work of earthworms, it is the same. The tanks were made on the north and south sides to catch the rain water falling on the large stands. The value of these additions was soon shown. They provide suitable water for preparing wickets and an opportunity of reducing water rates. It is almost imperative, especially in a large town, to have an independent water supply in case of drought.

All else has undergone improvements and additions to meet the requirements of the public and the members. Outwardly the hotel (in early days called "The Tavern"), the members' luncheon room and the pavilion appear to be unchanged. Internally these buildings have been brought up to date. The hotel is the centre of the refreshment department and from it are dispensed refreshments to different parts of the ground. Its excavations extend from the hotel proper to the members' entrance. When the refreshment business was taken over in 1898, the hotel and its accommodation were found to be unsuitable and inadequate for the business it was required to carry on and bakeries, cold storage and other facilities were provided and now, although it is impossible to serve every individual in a large crowd at the same time, the conduct of the business compares favourably with any ground that has the same problems to solve. The shop adjoining the hotel was built some years later for the purpose of finding employment for some of the staff in the "off season" and in order to reduce the loss which, owing to overhead charges, has to be faced during that period. The addition to the pavilion, on the north side, was made so as to give the Press the best position from which to watch the game in progress and in order to improve and extend the professionals' quarters below.

### ADDITIONS AND FINANCES

All the present stands and seating accommodation were built within the time under review. The large mound stand followed a decision of the committee in 1898 to give more spectators an opportunity of seeing Test matches. This involved removing the tennis and racket courts to a site behind the pavilion. Many mourned the loss of the ivy-mantled wall of this old building and the large clock it held, which offered an invitation to ambitious batsmen to reach its face with a square-leg hit. Owing to the growing popularity of Test matches these familiar and attractive features were sacrificed out of consideration for the public. The stand has answered its purpose. It is only when it is unoccupied that it offends the artistic eye. As the popularity of the big matches grew an increased demand for accommodation for entertaining arose. This was, to a great extent, satisfied by building luncheon arbours on the north, south and east sides of the practice ground. The erection of the members' extension and its south-west tower followed and all the covered seating on the ground floor was replaced subsequently by buildings of a more permanent and less dusty character. The new grand stand (replacing one built in the middle of the last century) and the cantilever stands on the east side of the match ground, recently erected, were constructed from the plans of Sir Herbert Baker and have made a substantial addition to the seating capacity of the ground.

On the death of Dr W. G. Grace, the champion cricketer, in 1915, the committee decided to erect a memorial in his honour. This took the form of memorial gates at the members' entrance on the south-west side of the ground.

Finance is not usually regarded as a matter of general interest; but those who are under the impression that the MCC has always been a rich club will be surprised to learn that in 1898 there was an overdraft at one bank, a loan from another bank and the balance of the purchase money of the freehold of the match ground, bought in the middle of the last century, still owing. The purchase money had been advanced by Mr W. Nicholson, a member of the committee and in his day a famous wicket-keeper. These liabilities had to be faced in spite of the fact that £40,000 had been raised by the election of 200 life members to meet, in part, the erection of the large mound stand and the removal and building of the tennis and racket courts. In the year above-mentioned the property of the club consisted, besides the match and practice ground, of two leasehold houses in Grove End Road, two freeholds and one leasehold in Elm Tree Road and a leasehold in Cavendish Road West. Now the MCC owns as freeholds all the houses abutting on the ground from St John's Wood Road to 22, Elm Tree Road, the Secretary's official residence. Flats for housing several of the club staff, whose services may be required at short notice, have recently been built on the north side of the practice ground.

The improvement in the financial position has enabled the club to set aside a sum of money for financing, or helping to finance, tours in different parts of the Empire, thereby enlarging its responsibilities towards Empire cricket and increasing its opportunities of strengthening family ties. Cricket finance, however, has always its problems and difficulties owing to increasing expenses and rates and taxes. Although stronger financially than it has ever been, MCC, after a few bad seasons or a decrease in the popularity of the game, might easily find, unless a large reserve is provided, that its work in promoting cricket in this country and elsewhere in the Empire would have to be curtailed. Exchanges of visits have done much to give birth to an Empire sense and it is to be hoped that a sufficiently large reserve may be secured to enable MCC's work to be continued and even increased.

## THE PROFESSIONAL STAFF

MCC professionals, 30 years ago, were recruited from the county cricket clubs which then needed help. These clubs often sent up promising but inexperienced youths. If these youngsters turned out well they were claimed for county matches, except when representative MCC matches such as those against Australia or South Africa, were played. If they did not come up to expectations they were left under the parental influence of MCC. When the counties played only eight home and away matches, this arrangement could be tolerated. As the counties increased their matches, however, MCC found itself left with elderly or second-rate players only. In these circumstances it was found necessary to train young players at Lord's conditionally on MCC having first claim on their services. The members of the professional staff used to be given a "benefit" match in rotation, subject to an agreement to retire on receipt and to the approval of the MCC Committee with regard to the investment of the proceeds of the match. The fixture allotted was the Whitsuntide match at Lord's and the money taken fluctuated with the weather, the game more than once producing nothing. It was accordingly decided to give on retirement £500 in lieu of a match and this is always granted now on the old conditions, even when the professional has given all, or nearly all, his services to his county.

Most of the professional staff are taught the principles of coaching so that they may be available for the Easter classes. These Easter classes are held during three weeks of the

Easter holidays when the MCC gives instruction in every department of the game to the sons of members and to boys introduced by them. The classes were first held 25 years ago for about ten sons of members. They are now attended by nearly 200 boys a day and Lord's, for this purpose, cannot take more.

The Middlesex CCC has for many years used Lord's for its home matches. As, however, other county clubs thought that Middlesex was unduly favoured, a carefully considered agreement was drawn up dealing with the equities of the case and creating a situation to the mutual advantage of the MCC and the Middlesex CCC. Under this agreement Middlesex pays a fair rent and its proportion of expenses and its members are granted facilities in Middlesex and other matches.

## A COURT OF APPEAL

Membership of the MCC, limited to 6,000, has naturally increased by slow degrees. It is now, roughly speaking, about 1,000 more than it was 30 years ago and, owing to wastage, it may be many years before the limit will be reached. The increased membership and the fact that the MCC is regarded as the Court of Appeal throughout the cricket world, entail a very large and wide range of correspondence. Enquiries and requests for decisions in disputes and difficulties, often couched in quaint language, are received even from remote parts of the Empire. These show a loyalty to the club such as cannot be enjoyed by many institutions. Correspondence connected with the laws of cricket and interpretations thereon became so voluminous that a pamphlet giving decisions and interpretations on all the laws and rules in cricket and its conduct, about which there can be reasonable doubt, was published by the MCC. This has a large circulation.

When the war came in 1914 the committee felt that any tendency towards scare or morbidity should be resisted and an outward show of "carrying on" was allowed. But the ground and its buildings were, at once, placed at the disposal of the War Office and, the offer having been accepted, were used until the end of the war as accommodation and a training ground for the military. The policy of the committee was directed towards providing games for soldiers and sailors in training and on leave and for boys too young to serve. Contrary to the usual custom of changing the president each year, Lord Hawke remained President until after the war, and he and the treasurer (Lord Harris), although doing everything possible to serve their country in other ways, helped and directed in the administration of the changed conditions of the club.

## TOURS AND THEIR CONTROL

While the physical outlook at Lord's was altering a less conspicuous though more valuable and potent growth was taking place in the influence and responsibility of the MCC. Tours abroad became frequent and on them, especially on those to Australia, public interest was focused. It was generally felt that tours of such importance should be controlled and conducted by some responsible body. Under pressure, the MCC, somewhat reluctantly, accepted responsibility. These tours involved money liability as well as administrative responsibility and for these reasons there was no competition for the honour. Of recent years tours to Australia have given a satisfactory return and the county clubs have shared in the profits. For some time previously MCC was out of pocket; but the deficit was honourably made good by the Australian Board of Control. There can be no doubt that Australian cricket has benefited considerably by visits from home.

Other Empire tours, financed, or partly financed, by MCC, have visited India, Egypt, Canada, the West Indies, New Zealand, Ceylon and South Africa. The South African Cricket Association has been particularly helpful as it has generally guaranteed all, or nearly all, the expenses of a tour to that country. Only those in close touch with the network of interest created by these visits can fully appreciate their value in making friendly relations and understanding.

## NEW GOVERNING BODIES

In proportion as interest in imperial cricket increased, responsibility in selecting sides and organising Test matches, in England, also increased. In order to secure the best advice and the willing co-operation of the country clubs, the MCC convened a meeting composed of representatives of these clubs and the constitution of a Board of Control of Test Matches at Home was established. This was in 1898. Besides passing rules as to the conduct of Test Matches and selecting grounds on which they should be played, it was agreed that there should be an apportionment of profits, if any. One of the leading counties moved that MCC owing to its position and the work it did for cricket, should not contribute to the pool from profits from a match at Lord's. This proposal would have been passed had not the Rt Hon. Alfred Lyttelton, MP (the President of the MCC) intervened and stated that MCC wished to share equally with the county clubs. The equality arrangement was passed and has held good ever since.

Cricket legislation and control had been in the hands of the MCC for over 100 years. The idea of a more democratic form of government had already taken root in the minds of the MCC committee and another meeting of the county clubs was called and an Advisory County Cricket Committee brought into being. This Committee, on which all the first class counties are represented, with three nominees appointed by the Minor Counties' Cricket Association, is consulted on cricket matters of importance and meetings can be called by the counties themselves.

Arrangements, so far, enlarged the duties and advantages of clubs at home only. The MCC, owing to its close connection with clubs and cricketers throughout the Empire, realised the importance of bringing these forces within the network of cricket organisation and invited the largest clubs outside England to form governing bodies and to send delegates to an Imperial Cricket Conference. At least one meeting of this conference is held yearly. The above-mentioned consultative bodies, with the MCC, now control and manage home and Empire cricket and the organisation thus created has proved its value in many ways. The MCC still remains the parliament of cricket, holding its position by general consent, and the county clubs in framing their rules have invited it to accept the responsibility of a Court of Appeal. The MCC, apparently, assumed the position of head of cricket at the end of the eighteenth century and it is significant that through such a long time of change and criticism it has been free from any serious attack. This is, no doubt, due to the constitution of the MCC committee on which can be found famous cricketers and men of the highest repute in business and in other activities. The committee has been trusted and has never failed to aim at securing the best interests of the game as a whole and to preserve the spirit in which it should be played.

## OXFORD v CAMBRIDGE

### Played at Lord's, July 7, 8, 9, 1930

Oxford in the ninety-second match between the universities not only threw away by mistakes in the field a great chance of beating Cambridge but, collapsing so completely in the fourth innings that they were dismissed in two hours for 101, suffered twenty minutes before time an extraordinary defeat by 205 runs. Soon after twelve o'clock on the third day, Cambridge found themselves, with six men out, no more than 110 runs ahead. For the moment victory for Oxford appeared practically certain but two or three catches were dropped and, so far from the Light Blues' innings ending for the moderate total the position suggested, Cambridge batted for three hours and twenty minutes longer and added 196 runs for the loss of three more wickets before Morgan declared. In this way Oxford – set 307 to make in less than two hours and a half – had to realise that all possibility of a win had disappeared. Still, no strong reason existed why they should lose and if the early batsmen achieved nothing of much note, a draw seemed assured when, with only seventy minutes left for play, the Dark Blues had seven wickets to fall. A little stubbornness at that point would, no doubt, have led to stumps being pulled up at half-past six. In such remarkable fashion, however, did the batting crumple up that fifty minutes later the seven wickets had gone down for the addition of only 23 runs and Cambridge could rejoice in a surprising triumph.

While the weakness of Oxford in the concluding stage of the contest was essentially the determining factor in the issue of the struggle, Cambridge in gaining so substantial a victory owed much to Killick who not only shared on Monday in a first-wicket stand of 139 but in the second innings, putting together a score of 136, withstood the Oxford attack for five hours and a quarter. His 136 – the ninth highest score in the annals of the university match – was especially meritorious seeing that nearly all his leading colleagues failed him. In making 211 runs in the course of the match he accomplished a performance which must give him high rank among the famous players who have distinguished themselves in the great battle between Oxford and Cambridge. Much of the Cambridge batting was disappointing but Kemp-Welch helped Killick to give the side a fine start and Brown put together two useful scores at critical times. Of the bowlers Hazlerigg (right-hand slow) carried off the honours with seven wickets for less than ten runs apiece, doing peculiarly deadly work on Wednesday evening, but in the second innings of Oxford, Kemp-Welch, Rought-Rought and Brown also bowled cleverly and were ably backed up in the field, the whole Cambridge side, when they saw the possibility of victory, playing up with splendid keenness.

Oxford, in heading the Cambridge score after three of their crack batsmen had failed them, had good reason to be satisfied with the position at the end of an innings on each side and there can be no question that they ought to have registered what would have been their first success in seven years. They had only themselves to blame that this happiness was denied them. Curiously enough Crawley and Pataudi, who in the match of the previous year had been responsible for more than three hundred runs, scored only 38 runs between them. The mistakes in the field on Wednesday, too, were surprising, seeing the example set by Melville who took four catches off Peebles' bowling – one very high up and one very low down. Peebles, much the best bowler in the match, secured thirteen wickets and might well have gained his side a victory but he was called upon for too much work. Hill-Wood was the bowler to suffer from the blunders of his colleagues. Reasonably supported in the field, he must in the second innings have come out with an excellent analysis.

Included in the Cambridge eleven were five old blues, three seniors in Carris, Ratcliffe and Human and three freshmen in Brown, Hazlerigg and Rought-Rought. Of the Oxford team six were old blues, two seniors (Bradshaw and Mayhew) and three freshmen (Peebles, Melville and Moore). Fine weather favoured the game but the attendance falling below the average, the scene during the intervals while, of course, bright and animated, lacked something of the brilliancy of former years.

Fortunate – for the fifth time in succession – in winning the toss, Cambridge took first innings. Killick and Kemp-Welch gave them a splendid start, withstanding the Oxford attack for nearly two hours and raising the score to 139 before Peebles dismissed Killick who, obtaining most of his runs on the off-side, showed both skill and judgment and gave no chance. After lunch, when 24 runs had been added, Ratcliffe, Grant and Kemp-Welch all left with the total at 163. Ratcliffe was bowled round his legs and Grant dismissed in the same over. Kemp-Welch played thoroughly sound cricket for two hours and a half. Human batted freely yet both he and Carris were soon got rid of with the result that there were six men out for 192, five wickets having fallen in less than an hour after lunch for 53 runs. For the moment the success of the opening partnership had been largely discounted. Morgan and Brown, however, if they found themselves in difficulties at first, rose to the occasion manfully and in little more than an hour put on 66 runs before a leg-break sent back Brown. Getting Hazlerigg leg-before first ball Peebles again secured two wickets in an over and after the tea interval the innings, which had extended over four hours and a half, closed for 286.

Having disposed of their opponents more cheaply than they could reasonably have expected, Oxford proceeded to prejudice their prospects in pitiful fashion. Crawley ran himself out, Pataudi played-on and Kingsley hit a ball into mid-on's hands, three of the leading batsmen being dismissed – in every case through bad cricket – for 57 runs. The drawing of stumps found the score increased to 68 without further loss.

Despite the disastrous start overnight, the Dark Blues accomplished a highly creditable performance next day when, as the result of some five hours' batting, they headed the Cambridge total by 26 runs. Not, however, until they had passed through periods of considerable anxiety did the Oxonians complete so fine a reply. They were indebted in the first place to Moore and Ford who, if by no means masters of the Cambridge attack at a time when the Light Blue bowlers presented considerable difficulties, offered a stout if somewhat lucky opposition which lasted an hour and a half and yielded 83 runs. During this period Brown kept a capital length. Hazlerigg, bowling steadily, got in considerable off-break and Rought-Rought occasionally flew up in awkward fashion. Hazlerigg broke up the partnership by dismissing Moore who had batted soundly for nearly two hours and a half and, Melville and Ford both leaving shortly afterwards, Oxford with six men out for 160 again found themselves in serious trouble. Again, however, there came an excellent stand, Hill-Wood, after a narrow escape when four, rendering such useful support to Garland-Wells that the seventh wicket produced 83 runs in little more than an hour. Garland-Wells hit finely and Hill-Wood showed capital judgment. Still, when the ninth wicket fell Oxford stood eight runs in arrear. Peebles, however, batted freely and 34 runs were added before the innings closed.

The opening of the Cambridge second innings saw Kemp-Welch out to a foolish stroke, Ratcliffe again bowled round his legs and Grant caught and bowled. In this way the Light Blues found themselves with three men out leading by only 40 runs. Happily for the side, Killick, while his colleagues failed, batted in masterly fashion and, with Carris, raised the score from 66 to 102 before play ceased.

Next morning Killick who, when 49, had given a chance at the wicket overnight, again settled down in excellent form but, catches by Melville disposing of Carris, Human and Morgan, three batsmen were got rid of in forty-five minutes for the addition of only 34 runs. This was the point at which, Cambridge having lost six wickets and being no more than 110 ahead, Oxford looked to have a won game. Then came the remarkable succession of partnerships, the seventh wicket adding 57, the eighth 54 and the ninth 38, while finally 47 runs were obtained without the last two batsmen being separated. Killick, ninth out with the total at 285, had the big share in all these stands except the last. He should, when 122, have been caught in the slips but, apart from the chance at the wicket overnight, this was the only serious blemish in a memorable display of exemplary restraint and unfailing skill. At no time could he risk batting with freedom but hooking, pulling and driving to fine purpose he had fifteen 4s among his strokes. While Killick played such a great game, the seventh wicket should have produced only 29 runs, Brown being let off when 18 and enjoying other good fortune. Still, Brown made some fine drives and Hazlerigg batted steadily for over an hour, the latter helping to raise the total to 247, but just after Hazlerigg's departure came two mistakes, Crawley missing Fabian before that batsman had scored and Bradshaw letting off Killick at slip. The first of these two blunders cost 31 runs and following upon Killick's departure, Fabian and Rought-Rought hit up 47 in thirty-five minutes before Morgan declared. Cambridge at that point, after losing six wickets for 136, had made 332 for nine wickets.

Oxford's sorry collapse began with Kingsley, who went in with Crawley, being finely caught at short leg at 22 and Crawley was out in similar fashion at 37. Still, as Pataudi and Moore stayed together for more than half an hour, increasing the score meanwhile to 78, the game looked like ending tamely. Directly after Hazlerigg had bowled Pataudi however, Brown, off successive balls, had Moore and Melville caught at slip. Next over Garland-Wells was bowled middle stump, six men being out for 87 at five minutes past six. Hill-Wood stayed with Ford for twenty-five minutes but Rought-Rought going on to bowl disposed of Hill-Wood and Peebles in his first over. The fieldsmen crowding in round the batsmen, catches at forward short leg off Hazlerigg got rid of Mayhew and Bradshaw and so by twenty minutes to seven Oxford, after batting for two hours and five minutes, were all out for 101. Following upon Pataudi's departure at 78, the last seven wickets went down in fifty minutes for 23 runs.

## Cambridge

| | | | |
|---|---|---|---|
| Mr G. D. Kemp-Welch c Mayhew b Hill-Wood..... | 61 | – c Kingsley b Bradshaw........... | 8 |
| Mr E. T. Killick b Peebles ..................... | 75 | – b Bradshaw................... | 136 |
| Mr A. T. Ratcliffe b Peebles.................... | 11 | – b Peebles.................... | 9 |
| Mr G. C. Grant b Peebles...................... | 0 | – c and b Garland-Wells........... | 11 |
| Mr H. E. Carris b Hill-Wood .................. | 4 | – c Melville b Peebles............. | 25 |
| Mr R. H. C. Human c Peebles b Hill-Wood........ | 21 | – c Melville b Peebles............. | 8 |
| Mr J. T. Morgan c Hill-Wood b Peebles........... | 39 | – c Melville b Peebles............. | 1 |
| Mr F. R. Brown b Peebles...................... | 42 | – c and b Peebles................. | 29 |
| Mr A. G. Hazlerigg lbw b Peebles............... | 0 | – c Melville b Peebles............. | 17 |
| Mr A. H. Fabian not out...................... | 12 | – not out ...................... | 33 |
| Mr R. C. Rought-Rought lbw b Peebles........... | 5 | – not out ...................... | 18 |
| B 10, l-b 1, w 1, n-b 6 ................. | 18 | B 15, l-b 8, n-b 14......... | 37 |
| | **288** | | **(9 wkts dec.) 332** |

## Oxford

| | | | |
|---|---|---|---|
| Mr A. M. Crawley run out ..................... | 0 | – c Ratcliffe b Kemp-Welch ........ | 13 |
| Mr D. N. Moore c Rought-Rought b Hazlerigg ..... | 59 | – c Hazlerigg b Brown............. | 29 |
| Nawab of Pataudi b Human.................... | 5 | – b Hazlerigg.................... | 20 |
| Mr P. G. T. Kingsley c Rought-Rought b Hazlerigg.. | 13 | – c Ratcliffe b Kemp-Welch ........ | 13 |
| Mr N. M. Ford c Human b Rought-Rought ........ | 53 | – not out ...................... | 9 |
| Mr A. Melville c and b Brown.................. | 3 | – c Hazlerigg b Brown ........... | 0 |
| Mr H. M. Garland-Wells lbw b Hazlerigg.......... | 53 | – b Hazlerigg................... | 1 |
| Mr C. K. Hill-Wood c Fabian b Rought-Rought .... | 47 | – c Hazlerigg b Rought-Rought ..... | 0 |
| Mr W. H. Bradshaw c Hazlerigg b Rought-Rought .. | 7 | – c Kemp-Welch b Hazlerigg ....... | 0 |
| Mr I. A. R. Peebles not out..................... | 26 | – lbw b Rought-Rought............ | 0 |
| Mr J. F. N. Mayhew c Fabian b Brown ........... | 6 | – c Kemp-Welch b Hazlerigg ....... | 1 |
| B 26, l-b 13, w 1, n-b 2 ................. | 42 | B 12, l-b 2, n-b 1 ......... | 15 |
| | **314** | | **101** |

## Oxford Bowling

| | Overs | Mdns | Runs | Wkts | Overs | Mdns | Runs | Wkts |
|---|---|---|---|---|---|---|---|---|
| Hill-Wood ........ | 31 | 5 | 102 | 3 | 36 | 8 | 79 | 0 |
| Bradshaw......... | 11 | 3 | 37 | 0 | 14 | 2 | 25 | 2 |
| Peebles ........... | 31.1 | 6 | 75 | 7 | 50 | 6 | 162 | 6 |
| Garland-Wells ..... | 14 | 4 | 37 | 0 | 20 | 6 | 29 | 1 |
| Melville .......... | 2 | 0 | 19 | 0 | | | | |

## Cambridge Bowling

| | Overs | Mdns | Runs | Wkts | Overs | Mdns | Runs | Wkts |
|---|---|---|---|---|---|---|---|---|
| Rought-Rought .... | 26 | 6 | 64 | 3 | 7 | 3 | 10 | 2 |
| Human........... | 19 | 3 | 62 | 1 | 2 | 0 | 13 | 0 |
| Hazlerigg ......... | 24 | 5 | 49 | 3 | 11 | 7 | 17 | 4 |
| Brown .......... | 33.5 | 6 | 81 | 2 | 14 | 2 | 36 | 2 |
| Fabian .......... | 11 | 4 | 16 | 0 | 2 | 2 | 0 | 0 |
| Kemp-Welch ...... | | | | | 6 | 2 | 10 | 2 |

Umpires: J. H. King and A. Morton.

## OXFORD v CAMBRIDGE

Played at Lord's, July 6, 7, 8, 1931

Beating Cambridge by eight wickets, Oxford not only registered their first victory over the Light Blues for eight years but, considering the circumstances in which the win was gained, accomplished by far the finest performance credited to either university since the war. Fielding out for the whole of the first day they had to go in against a total of 385. For the loss of eight wickets they headed that score by 68 and in registering 453 runs, they put together the second highest innings on record in the long history of games between Oxford and Cambridge. Furthermore, although when the concluding day's cricket was entered upon the Light Blues had all ten wickets in the second innings standing, the Oxonians followed up their batting triumph with such a workmanlike display of bowling and fielding that the match was all over by a quarter to four. Indeed, however regarded, the performance of the Dark Blues attained to exceptional excellence and so more than atoned for the disappointments of recent years.

Oxford entered into the struggle with considerable prospects of success for the eleven could show four victories as compared with two gained by Cambridge and they had met with no reverse since the middle of May. For the sixth consecutive year, however, the spin of the coin gave the Light Blues choice of innings and when Cambridge turned the opportunity of batting first to such good purpose that their joint efforts resulted in a total of nearly 400, Oxford's prospects of victory seemed to have disappeared. The great piece of luck enjoyed by Cambridge, however, consisted not in the advantage conferred by choice of innings but rather in an accident which affected the composition of their eleven. In making up the side, Kemp-Welch had given a place to J. G. W. Davies, a freshman from Tonbridge, and had dropped A. T. Ratcliffe, a member of the 1930 team, who in the course of a dozen innings at Cambridge had scored only 109 runs. A few days prior to the big match Davies sprained his ankle and Ratcliffe, called on to complete the team at Eastbourne, showed himself in such fine form that when, on the morning of the match, Davies was still unable to take the field, the vacant place naturally fell to Ratcliffe.

Such wonderful success attended this alteration in the Cambridge team that Ratcliffe, selected by Kemp-Welch to assist in the opening of the innings, not only helped his captain to put on 149 for the first wicket but went on to complete his hundred, then to beat the record innings of the match – 172 not out, by J. F. Marsh in 1904 – and finally to bring his score to 201. Steady, confident and skilful from start to finish, Ratcliffe played a truly admirable innings, his triumph being so well deserved that he gave no chance until he had brought his figures to 179. The extent to which Ratcliffe's batting dominated the first day's play is suggested by the score. Latterly, no doubt, there appeared to exist no strong reason for restraint on the part of the Cambridge batsmen, but there remained the fact that, apart from Ratcliffe and Kemp-Welch, no one put together an innings of five-and-twenty.

While Ratcliffe's big innings of itself would, in the special circumstances in which he came to play, have rendered the match memorable, that batsman's score was not allowed to stand as a record for the university match for twenty-four hours. Next day the Nawab of Pataudi not only equalled Ratcliffe's total in eight minutes less than that player had been at the wickets but went on to raise his figures to 238, and was still unbeaten when Melville declared. Batting altogether for nearly five hours, without giving an absolute chance, Pataudi made runs all round the wicket in masterly fashion. His 238 not out, it may be added, was his fifth hundred in the course of the last six innings he had played and – for those innings – brought his aggregate to 802 and his average to 223. In addition to making the record score in the University match, Pataudi joined that very select band of cricketers who have put together two separate hundreds in that encounter, the other members being William Yardley who scored 130 in 1872 and 100 in 1870 and H. J. Enthoven who made 104 in 1924 and 129 in the following season's contest.

Favoured with fine and at times bright weather, the match attracted large crowds each day, the number paying for admission in the course of the contest being 30,558. D. N. Moore, the Gloucestershire amateur should have led the Oxford team in what was the ninety-third encounter of the series, but illness kept him out of the field after the first few weeks of the season and the responsibility of captaining the Dark Blues fell to A. Melville, a South African.

Some showers had fallen during Monday morning without seriously affecting the pitch, and Kemp-Welch on winning the toss, did not hesitate in deciding that Cambridge should bat. Fortune favoured the Cambridge captain not only in the spin of the coin and in the selection of Ratcliffe as his partner, but in two escapes off Wellings' bowling while making his first thirty runs. Incidentally the first of these mistakes – a bad one by Hone – proved terribly expensive, the first wicket, which should have fallen at 26, not going down until there were 149 runs on the board. Once set, Kemp-Welch dominated the game, for while Ratcliffe brought off some capital pulls and drives at intervals, Kemp-Welch, in addition to scoring finely on the leg-side, brought off well-executed strokes in other directions. Melville tried five bowlers but none of these troubled the batsmen seriously. Still, in what must have been in any case the last over before lunch, a good catch at short leg disposed of Kemp-Welch who, playing skilful and attractive cricket after his early luck, had made 87 out of 149 in two hours. Ratcliffe at that point was 59.

Joined by Hazlerigg who was restrained to a degree, Ratcliffe, inside three hours, completed a thoroughly sound and creditable hundred. Hazlerigg stayed for nearly an hour and a half and helped to increase the total by 71, but his share of that number was only 20. Thenceforward, although Parry shared in a partnership of 61, interest centred almost entirely in what Ratcliffe might do. Marsh's record was passed when Ratcliffe had batted for five hours and shortly afterwards came that batsman's one blunder – a chance when 179 to forward short leg. With Fabian as his partner, Ratcliffe proceeded to bring his score to 200 but he was out directly afterwards to a catch at slip – the total then standing at 349. Batting for five hours and forty minutes, Ratcliffe had played a great innings singularly free from fault, marked by particularly fine pulling and off-driving and including twenty-four 4s, six 3s and twelve 2s. Ratcliffe's triumph recalled the successes in 1887 of two other last choices, Lord George Scott on that occasion making 100 and 66 for Oxford and Eustace Crawley 35 and 103 not out for Cambridge. Extending over six hours, the Cambridge innings came to an end just at half-past six.

Wanting 236 to avoid a follow-on, Oxford lost Hone and Lindsay for 37 runs so their position was an anxious one when Melville joined Pataudi. Moreover, Pataudi did not at once settle down, and as the Cambridge bowling, with Farnes commanding some pace and Brown able to bowl not only a leg break but a fairly speedy googly, presented more variety than that of Oxford, the Dark Blues had to go very warily. Brown, flighting the ball cleverly, had Melville in great trouble for a time. Gradually the Oxford prospects improved and in less than an hour the total had been raised from 37 to 100. Pataudi, after batting with marked skill for eighty minutes, brought his score to 50 but the invaluable partnership came to an end on Hazlerigg being tried, the third wicket having produced 104 runs in eighty minutes.

Following upon the luncheon interval – taken with the score at 147 for three wickets – Chalk was fourth out at 185 and then from Pataudi and Owen-Smith came the most brilliant batting of the match, these two men hitting away with such freedom that 174 runs were actually registered in ninety-five minutes. This splendid scoring was essentially the work of Owen-Smith, who hit in delightful fashion on the off-side. Pataudi, after a narrow escape when 97, the ball falling just short of first slip, completed his first hundred in rather less than two hours and a half with the total at 221. Then came such fine off-driving and cutting by Owen-Smith that that batsman reached his 50 in forty-five minutes. For the moment indeed Pataudi was somewhat overshadowed by his colleague, so the Cambridge attack found itself in a truly awkward plight. Pataudi took his score from 100 to 150 in fifty minutes but at 359 a smart catch at second slip brought about the dismissal of Owen-Smith whose 78 – put together in little more than an hour and a half – included some most refreshing strokes on the off side.

Scott left at 381 but, with Wellings in, the Cambridge total was headed in rather more than four hours and a half with four wickets in hand. A little later Pataudi after batting for four hours and twenty minutes passed Ratcliffe's score, and then proceeded to hit away with refreshing freedom until, on Hart's dismissal at 453, Melville declared. Enthusiastically cheered on retiring, Pataudi played splendid cricket for nearly five hours, scoring all round the wicket with delightful ease and freedom and, if in trouble three or four times, giving no absolute chance. The hits of his 238 not out – his sixth hundred during the season – included nineteen 4s, twelve 3s and twenty-two 2s. While he pulled, hit to leg, and cut in brilliant fashion, he did not drive a great deal but for all that he made some delightful strokes of that description on the off side.

Batting for twenty-five minutes before the drawing of the stumps on Tuesday, Cambridge scored 23 runs without loss and next morning Kemp-Welch and Hazlerigg raised the score to 45. For the moment, although the pitch showed some signs of wear, a draw appeared almost certain to be the outcome of the struggle but after the opening pair had been separated the last nine wickets actually went down in less than two hours for 77 runs, the collapse subsequent to the luncheon interval being so pronounced that on the resumption four batsmen were dismissed for 30 runs. The issue was practically assured at the adjournment when, with six men out, Cambridge found themselves no more than 24 runs ahead. In disposing of Kemp-Welch and Hazlerigg – the only batsmen who gave any trouble – Owen-Smith rendered his side useful service but the big factor in the cheap dismissal of the Light Blues was the medium-pace bowling of Wellings who, sending down with a curious delivery off-breaks outside the leg stump, took five wickets for 25 runs. Scott did not on Wednesday repeat his success of Monday yet, if bowling less steadily, he in securing eight wickets for eleven runs each in the course of the match played no small part in the victory of his side. The Dark Blues on the last day supported their bowlers well in the field until after seven wickets had fallen but then damaged their reputation by letting off Human three times. Fabian was again not out. He has batted five times against Oxford, scored 86 runs and has never lost his wicket on any of those occasions.

Oxford had no more than 55 to make for victory and, although losing Lindsay and Pataudi cheaply to Brown's bowling, were of course never in a position of any anxiety. Hone and Melville finished off the match in brilliant style.

Oxford's Eleven was made up of four old "Blues", three seniors in Lindsay, Scott and Raikes – and four freshmen in Hone, Owen-Smith, Chalk and Hart. Cambridge had six old "Blues", three seniors – Wilcox, Parry and Christopherson – and two freshmen – Comber and Farnes. Neither side included a left-handed player.

### Cambridge

| | | |
|---|---|---|
| Mr G. D. Kemp-Welch (Charterhouse) c Scott b Owen-Smith . 87 | – b Owen-Smith. | 28 |
| Mr A. T. Ratcliffe (Rydal Mount) c Melville b Scott .201 | – b Scott | 9 |
| Mr A. G. Hazlerigg (Eton) c Raikes b Wellings . . . . . 20 | – c Melville b Owen-Smith. | 29 |
| Mr J. C. Christopherson (Uppingham) b Scott. . . . . . 9 | – c Lindsay b Wellings | 7 |
| Mr D. R. Wilcox (Dulwich) lbw b Scott . . . . . . . . . . 0 | – c Melville b Scott | 4 |
| Mr D. M. Parry (Merchant Taylors') c Hone b Wellings . 13 | – c Bradshaw b Wellings | 2 |
| Mr F. R. Brown (Leys) c Hone b Owen-Smith . . . . . . 3 | – c Pataudi b Wellings. | 1 |
| Mr R. H. C. Human (Repton) b Scott . . . . . . . . . . . 8 | – b Owen-Smith. | 17 |
| Mr A. H. Fabian (Highgate) not out. . . . . . . . . . . . . 14 | – not out | 11 |
| Mr J. T. H. Comber (Marlborough) b Scott . . . . . . . . 22 | – c Raikes b Wellings | 1 |
| Mr K. Farnes (Royal Liberty School, Romford) b Scott . 1 | – b Wellings | 0 |
| B 5, l-b 2 . . . . . . . . . . . . . . . . . . . . . . . . 7 | B 7, l-b 6. . . . . . . . . . . . . . | 13 |
| | **385** | **122** |

## Oxford

| | | | | |
|---|---|---|---|---|
| Mr B. W. Hone (Adelaide University) b Farnes | 6 | – not out | | 25 |
| Mr W. O'B. Lindsay (Harrow) c Fabian b Brown | 13 | – c Human b Brown | | 2 |
| Nawab of Pataudi (Chief's College, Lahore) not out | .238 | – c Comber b Brown | | 4 |

Mr B. W. Hone (Adelaide University) b Farnes ..... 6 – not out ........................ 25
Mr W. O'B. Lindsay (Harrow) c Fabian b Brown ... 13 – c Human b Brown ............. 2
Nawab of Pataudi (Chief's College, Lahore) not out .238 – c Comber b Brown............. 4
Mr A. Melville (Michaelhouse, South Africa)
                          b Hazlerigg . 47 – not out ...................... 14
Mr F. G. H. Chalk (Uppingham) c Comber
                          b Hazlerigg . 10
Mr H. G. Owen-Smith (Diocesan College,
          South Africa) c Christopherson b Brown . 78
Mr R. S. G. Scott (Winchester) c Hazlerigg b Brown . 6
Mr E. M. Wellings (Cheltenham) b Brown ......... 2
Mr T. M. Hart (Strathallan) c Ratcliffe b Brown .... 14
         B 32, l-b 5, w2...................... 39           B 4, l-b 5, n-b 1........... 10

                      (8 wkts dec.) 453                55

Mr W. H. Bradshaw (Malvern) and Mr D. C. G. Raikes (Shrewsbury) did not bat.

### Oxford Bowling

| | Overs | Mdns | Runs | Wkts | Overs | Mdns | Runs | Wkts |
|---|---|---|---|---|---|---|---|---|
| Bradshaw ......... | 12 | 5 | 26 | — | 3 | 1 | 2 | — |
| Scott.............. | 33.2 | 11 | 64 | 6 | 20 | 10 | 23 | 2 |
| Wellings .......... | 40 | 11 | 106 | 2 | 23.4 | 11 | 25 | 5 |
| Owen-Smith ....... | 51 | 12 | 141 | 2 | 20 | 5 | 59 | 3 |
| Melville........... | 12 | 1 | 41 | — | | | | |

### Cambridge Bowling

| | Overs | Mdns | Runs | Wkts | Overs | Mdns | Runs | Wkts |
|---|---|---|---|---|---|---|---|---|
| Farnes............ | 28 | 5 | 79 | 1 | 8 | 2 | 18 | — |
| Human ........... | 17 | 2 | 59 | — | | | | |
| Brown............ | 43.5 | 4 | 153 | 5 | 10.2 | 4 | 18 | 2 |
| Hazlerigg ......... | 28 | 3 | 86 | 2 | 3 | — | 9 | — |
| Fabian ........... | 7 | 1 | 37 | — | | | | |

Umpires: A. Morton and H. Young.

# MCC v CAMBRIDGE UNIVERSITY

## Played at Lord's, July 1, 3, 4, 1933

All things considered, Cambridge put up a very good show, and at one time looked to have an excellent chance of winning, but, handicapped by the absence of Farnes after the first day and the retirement on Monday afternoon of Comber, they suffered defeat by seven wickets. The University batting proved consistent. MCC, however, thanks largely to a stubborn innings by Hearne, who batted two and three-quarter hours, and a dashing exhibition by Robertson-Glasgow, gained a lead of 29. When the Club went in to get 208 to win, three wickets fell for 49, but then the Nawab of Pataudi and Hendren hit off the remaining runs in a brilliant unfinished partnership that realised 164 in an hour and three-quarters. The Indian revealed his best form, getting his runs with effortless ease. Hendren was missed at 65, but otherwise showed very sound defence, in addition to treating the slow bowlers severely. A misunderstanding between the scorer and the umpires resulted in the game continuing after the winning hit had been made, Pataudi adding 5 runs to his score.

## Cambridge University

| | | | |
|---|---|---|---|
| Mr A. W. Allen c Hearne b R.-Glasgow | 34 | – b Smith | 8 |
| Mr A. S. Lawrence c Pataudi b Brown | 21 | – not out | 41 |
| Mr D. R. Wilcox c Jeacocke b Brown | 17 | – b Robertson-Glasgow | 8 |
| Mr B. O. Allen c R.-Glasgow b Smith | 32 | – c and b Rutter | 40 |
| Mr. R. de W. K. Winlaw c Smith b R.-Glasgow | 46 | – b Brown | 39 |
| Mr J. H. Human b Smith | 0 | – c and b Brown | 13 |
| Mr J. G. W. Davies b Smith | 33 | – b Rutter | 31 |
| Mr Jahangir Khan c Hendren b Smith | 0 | – c Sweetland b Rutter | 11 |
| Mr E. Cawston c Sweetland b Rutter | 31 | – b Brown | 17 |
| Mr J. T. H. Comber not out | 17 | – absent hurt | 0 |
| Mr K. Farnes b Rutter | 0 | – b Hearne | 15 |
| B 14, l-b 6, w 2, n-b 1 | 23 | B 6, l-b 3, n-b 4 | 13 |
| | **254** | | **236** |

## MCC

| | | | |
|---|---|---|---|
| Mr S. A. Blook c Comber b Khan | 44 | – lbw b Human | 17 |
| Mr A. Jeacocke b Jahangir Khan | 3 | – b Jahangir Khan | 6 |
| J. W. Hearne c Lawrence b Khan | 84 | – c sub. b Davies | 7 |
| E. H. Sweetland b Davies | 4 | | |
| E. Hendren b Jahangir Khan | 1 | – not out | 70 |
| Nawab of Pataudi lbw b Davies | 42 | – not out | 99 |
| Mr F. R. Brown run out | 9 | | |
| Mr C. P. Johnstone not out | 26 | | |
| J. Smith lbw b Davies | 0 | | |
| Mr R. C. Robertson-Glasgow lbw b Human | 48 | | |
| Mr R. H. Rutter b Human | 0 | | |
| B 15, l-b 5, w 1, n-b 1 | 22 | B 11, l-b 2, w 1 | 14 |
| | **283** | | **213** |

### MCC Bowling

| | Overs | Mdns | Runs | Wkts | Overs | Mdns | Runs | Wkts |
|---|---|---|---|---|---|---|---|---|
| R.-Glasgow | 21 | 6 | 55 | 2 | 18 | 7 | 35 | 1 |
| Smith | 21 | 3 | 50 | 4 | 24 | 5 | 62 | 1 |
| Rutter | 12.5 | 1 | 36 | 2 | 13 | 5 | 27 | 3 |
| Hearne | 13 | 3 | 46 | — | 10.5 | 2 | 25 | 1 |
| Brown | 16 | 6 | 44 | 2 | 20 | 4 | 74 | 3 |

### Cambridge University Bowling

| | Overs | Mdns | Runs | Wkts | Overs | Mdns | Runs | Wkts |
|---|---|---|---|---|---|---|---|---|
| Farnes | 9 | 1 | 24 | — | | | | |
| Jahangir Khan | 36 | 10 | 78 | 4 | 10 | 1 | 30 | 1 |
| Lawrence | 15 | 2 | 24 | — | 10 | 5 | 13 | — |
| Davies | 39 | 8 | 83 | 3 | 24.4 | 7 | 55 | 1 |
| Human | 10.5 | — | 39 | 2 | 21 | 4 | 64 | 1 |
| Cawston | 7 | 1 | 13 | — | 10 | 2 | 37 | — |

Umpires: A. Morton and J. Newman.

# AUSTRALIANS IN ENGLAND

## GENTLEMEN OF ENGLAND v AUSTRALIANS

Played at Lord's, June 23, 24, 25, 1919

In this match, the most important of the whole programme, the Australians at last met with defeat, the Gentlemen beating them in uncompromising fashion by an innings and 133 runs. Though a little rain fell late on the first afternoon there was nothing in the condition of the ground to account for the one-sided result. One may safely say that the Gentlemen were the better side, but whereas they were at the top of their form at every point, the Australians for once lost all their fighting spirit. The Gentlemen's victory was made certain on the second day when Douglas and Falcon, by means of really wonderful bowling, got the Australians out in two hours. Falcon made the ball swerve in deadly fashion, and Douglas had a little swerve to help his irreproachable length. Against the two the Australians were helpless, and though their batting was better in the follow-on there never seemed the slightest chance of avoiding defeat. The Gentlemen's batting on the first day was consistently good; Gillingham was at his best, Douglas's defence was impregnable, and Carr, after a rather shaky start, drove Gregory's fast bowling with refreshing vigour.

### Gentlemen of England

| | |
|---|---|
| Rev. F. B. Gillingham c Gregory b Lampard 83 | Capt. D. C. Robinson c Pellew b Stirling ... 14 |
| Mr D. J. Knight lbw b Winning .......... 42 | Mr M. Falcon c Lampard b Collins ....... 11 |
| Mr A. J. Evans c Pellew b Stirling ........ 68 | Mr J. C. White st Long b Stirling ......... 5 |
| Mr P. F. Warner b Gregory ............. 43 | Mr C. S. Marriott not out .............. 1 |
| Hon. C. N. Bruce b Gregory ............ 11 | B 14, l-b 3 ................... 17 |
| Mr J. W. H. T. Douglas c Stirling b Collins . 56 | |
| Mr A. W. Carr st Long b Collins ......... 51 | 402 |

### Australians

| | | |
|---|---|---|
| Mr H. L. Collins c Carr b Douglas............... | 11 – c Evans b Douglas .............. | 1 |
| Mr W. L. Trennery lbw b Douglas ............... | 1 – c Carr b Evans ................. | 40 |
| Mr C. B. Willis c Gillingham b Falcon ............ | 6 – b Douglas .................... | 6 |
| Mr J. M. Taylor c Carr b Falcon ................ | 9 – c Bruce b Falcon ............... | 35 |
| Mr A. W. Lampard b Falcon ................... | 9 – c Gillingham b Douglas .......... | 23 |
| Mr C. E. Pellew c Knight b Douglas.............. | 14 – c Douglas b White ............. | 15 |
| Mr E. Bull c Gillingham b Falcon................ | 5 – b White.................... | 14 |
| Mr J. M. Gregory c Robinson b Falcon ........... | 16 – c Robinson b Douglas ........... | 12 |
| Mr W. S. Stirling b Falcon ..................... | 2 – c Gillingham b White ........... | 1 |
| Mr C. Winning not out ...................... | 3 – c Evans b White............... | 17 |
| Mr E. J. Long c Carr b Douglas ................. | 4 – not out ................... | 6 |
| L-b 5 ............................. | 5 | B 8, l-b 1, n-b 5 .......... 14 |
| | 85 | 184 |

### Australians Bowling

| | Overs | Mdns | Runs | Wkts |
|---|---|---|---|---|
| Gregory .......... | 23 | 2 | 110 | 2 |
| Collins ........... | 27 | 7 | 63 | 3 |
| Lampard.......... | 33 | 1 | 121 | 1 |
| Winning .......... | 17 | 2 | 48 | 1 |
| Stirling ........... | 14 | — | 38 | 3 |

**Gentlemen Bowling**

| | Overs | Mdns | Runs | Wkts | Overs | Mdns | Runs | Wkts |
|---|---|---|---|---|---|---|---|---|
| Douglas .......... | 17.4 | 3 | 34 | 4 | 17 | 4 | 40 | 4 |
| White ............ | 3 | — | 5 | — | 18 | 7 | 38 | 4 |
| Falcon ........... | 14 | 3 | 41 | 6 | 11 | 1 | 33 | 1 |
| Marriott ......... | | | | | 14 | 5 | 30 | — |
| Evans ............ | | | | | 9 | 2 | 29 | 1 |

Umpires: W. A. J. West and W. Smith.

# THE AUSTRALIANS IN ENGLAND [1922]

The Australians had a wonderful tour, and narrowly missed setting up a record that might have stood for all time. When on the 27th of August, they stepped on to the field at Eastbourne to play the England eleven that A. C. MacLaren had got together it seemed any odds that, surpassing the doings of all previous teams in this country, they would go home unbeaten. As everyone knows, they met with an astounding reverse, and after that, in their last match, they were defeated for the second time. No doubt they were much disappointed at the change that came over their fortunes, but they had done more than enough for fame. Their final record was almost exactly the same as that of the great team of 1902, the only difference being that they won 22 matches out of 38, and Darling's famous side 23 out of 39. Both teams lost two matches and left 14 unfinished. A comparison between the two records, however, would be very delusive. Last year the summer was one of almost unprecedented sunshine, whereas in 1902 we had an enormous rainfall, and the really fine days were comparatively few. Thus the conditions of play were utterly dissimilar. Whether the team of 1902 would have been quite so formidable in a dry season is a question difficult to answer, and one can only conjecture as to how Armstrong's side would have got on in a wet summer. On one point, however, there can be no dispute. In the tour of nearly twenty years ago the Australians were put to a far more searching test, English cricket in 1902 being overwhelmingly strong, and last summer lamentably weak. Allowing for all this, however, one need not hesitate to say that Armstrong had a great side. Their record speaks for itself, but the statistics on the printed page give a poor idea of the consummate ease with which for four months they crumpled up nearly all the teams that opposed them. Only twice did they look at all likely to be beaten, and on one of those occasions they were without Warren Bardsley and Macartney. I cannot think that they were estimated at quite their true value. Even when they were winning match after match there was a tendency in many quarters to underrate them and explain away their victories. One critic – usually the soundest of judges – went so far as to say that their bowling was weaker than that of almost any previous team from Australia. This, in face of the repeated failures of our batting, was rather an astonishing pronouncement. I am inclined, personally, to take perhaps too flattering a view of them. They seemed to me to be fully equipped at every point for matches on fast wickets, and even if English cricket had been up to its pre-war standard I think they would have been terribly hard to beat. It was, of course, a strong testimony in their favour that with exactly the same body of players, barring Kelleway, they won all the Test matches at home against the MCC's team. That remarkable series of victories told us pretty plainly what we should have to face.

Given fine weather the Australians as a side had not a weak point of any kind. They could all get runs, even the last man being capable on occasion of hitting up 20 or 30; their fielding was magnificent; and, above all, they possessed in Gregory and McDonald two very fast bowlers of the highest class. It was the fast bowling more than anything else that brought about our undoing. Never before have England batsmen been so demoralised by great pace. The Test matches at Nottingham and Lord's were both practically lost in the first half-hour, Gregory in one and McDonald in the other neutralising all the advantage we had gained by winning the toss. The two bowlers had fine records for the whole tour, but their value to the side was far greater than their figures, good as they are, would suggest. I am sure that some of our batsmen, knowing they would have to face Gregory, were out before they went in. Since Knox bowled his fastest in 1906 I have never seen batsmen so obviously intimidated. McDonald struck one as being really the finer bowler of the two, but Gregory was by far the more alarming. Gregory was apt when he pitched at all short to get up dangerously high, but old cricketers were inclined to be sarcastic when they saw batsmen frightened by long hops. They perhaps remembered Mr R. D. Walker's dictum years ago that the batsman who could not take care of himself ought not to play cricket. Finding the effect of the rising ball so great Gregory would have been almost more than human if he had not now and then dropped one short with intention. To back up McDonald and Gregory the Australians had in Armstrong himself and Mailey two right-handed slow bowlers as strongly contrasted in method as two men could be. Armstrong had an almost miraculous accuracy of pitch, combined at times with enough break to beat the bat, whereas Mailey, varying very much in length and constantly asking to be hit to the ring, relied to an enormous extent on his finger spin. Armstrong headed the bowling averages of the whole tour with 106 wickets for just over fourteen and a half runs apiece – remarkable figures for a slow bowler in such a summer – and Mailey, though more expensive, took 146 wickets. Except that Hendry sent down 52 overs the four leading bowlers, though Mailey was left out at Nottingham and Manchester, carried the side through the Test matches. Few critics seemed to think much of Mailey, but he was always getting wickets, and it was a strong proof of his excellence that batsmen who tried to make light of him always came to grief, his spin resulting at once in false hits and easy catches. A striking instance of this occurred in the final match at Scarborough. Apart from the leading men and Hendry there was another bowler of good reputation in Ryder, but he was not given much chance, only bowling 229 overs during the tour. Apparently Armstrong had not much faith in him. In view of his tremendous value as a batsman Macartney was put on as little as possible, but as a left-handed bowler he would have had to do more work in a wet summer. It puzzles me that anyone should have thought the Australian bowling other than first-rate. The strongest evidence of its high quality could be found in the meagre scores obtained in a season of huge run-getting by most of the opposing sides. Still, I think that our batsmen flattered Armstrong by playing him with such exaggerated caution. In old days a Hornby or a C. I. Thornton would have knocked him off his length or perished in the attempt.

As to the collective excellence of the Australian batting the figures speak for themselves. Of the fifteen players all but two could show an average for the whole tour of over 20, the records ranging from Macartney's 58 to Carter's 21, and even Mailey and McDonald, with a liberal allowance of not outs to their credit, managed to reach double figures. This run-getting power shows what a task it was for any team to beat the Australians in three days on a hard wicket. Macartney and Bardsley stood right out above their fellows, and were the only batsmen who could be described as great, Armstrong, though he hit up three hundreds in the last few weeks of the tour, failing for a long time to approach the wonderful form he had shown at home against the MCC's team. For this, however, there was an easy explanation, as, apart from the anxieties of captaincy, he had to do a great deal more bowling than he had expected. Of Macartney and Bardsley it would be impossible to say too much. Each in his way was magnificent. Playing from the 30th of April to the 10th of September, with very few intervals for rest, neither batsman seemed to know what it was to be even temporarily out of form. Both, of course, had occasional failures, but they were so much at the top of their game all through the summer that whenever they went in one looked for a big score. Such almost unvaried success says as much for their stamina and condition as for their superlative skill. Bardsley hit up nine hundreds and Macartney eight, the latter's 345 against Nottinghamshire being the highest score of the season and the highest ever obtained by an Australian batsman in this country. There is a reluctance among English critics to place Bardsley among left-handed batsmen on a level with Clem Hill. This, I confess, I cannot understand. He seems to me quite as good as ever Hill was, with the advantage of having a little more freedom and variety in his hitting. More than that, of all Australian batsmen who have come to England, left-handed or right, he has proved himself the most consistent. He has now gone through three tours in England, and in every one of them he has scored over 2,000 runs – a marvellous record, indeed. I am not so well acquainted with his doings at home, but so far as I know he has never had a set-back except when he found Frank Foster's bowling unplayable during the tour of the English team in 1911-12. He is the ideal batsman for a big occasion, starting an innings with the same supreme confidence in a Test match as in an ordinary game. He did not happen to get a hundred against England last summer, but he made 66 at Trent Bridge, 88 and not out 63 at Lord's, and headed the averages in the five matches. For the whole tour Macartney beat him both in aggregate of runs and average, but only by a trifle. In point of efficiency the two men stood absolutely on an equality. Macartney was a law to himself – an individual genius but not in any way a model to be copied. He constantly did things that would be quite wrong for an ordinary batsman, but by success justified all his audacities. Except Victor Trumper at his best no Australian batsman has ever demoralised our bowlers to the same extent. Macartney scored the only hundred against England in the Test matches, but, curiously enough it was not one of his really characteristic innings. Taking nearly three hours and a quarter to get 115, he was at times, for him, unusually restrained. In his various hundreds against the counties he reached almost the extreme limit of brilliancy. Of the Australian batsmen other than Bardsley and Macartney, and at the end of the tour Armstrong, I should be inclined, from what I saw, to place Andrews distinctly first, but judged by results he was no better than Collins, who was kept out of the team for some little time by a broken thumb. Still, by reason of his straighter bat and finer play on the off-side, Andrews, who narrowly missed his hundred against England both at Leeds and The Oval, struck one as the higher class batsmen of the two. Collins made five hundreds, but two of them were in holiday games in Scotland. His great triumph was in the Test match at Manchester, when there was nothing to play for but a draw. He withstood the English bowling for four hours and fifty minutes on a slow wicket, and averted all possibility of defeat. His inexhaustible patience recalled memories of Noble's play on the same ground in 1899. Taylor, who did not have the best of health, scarcely lived up to the reputation he enjoys at Sydney, but he often played well, and was at his best against England at The Oval. Ryder, Pellew and Mayne did not impress one as being batsmen of high class, but they were all capable of getting big scores. Mayne could not be fairly judged, as he was kept so much in the background. Ryder, considering the position he holds in Victoria, was certainly not given the prominence to which he felt entitled, being left out of all the Test matches. Gregory, for a crack fast bowler, had an extraordinary season as a batsman, scoring 1,171 runs with an average of 35. There was no style in his batting, but he hit very hard, and on several occasions pulled the game round when a small score seemed in prospect. He was emphatically the match winner of the side, and apart from his value as bowler and batsman, he was an almost incomparable field at slip.

People might argue that the Australian bowling and batting were not really quite so good as the figures make them out to be, but as to the fielding of the side there could not be two opinions. Never day after day on hard wickets has one seen such run-saving. The work of Andrews, Pellew, Taylor and Macartney, in their several positions on the off side, Bardsley in the deep field and Gregory and Hendry in the slips, was a revelation and beyond all praise. Within my experience there has never been a combination so perfect. Pellew was generally the most conspicuous figure on the field, his speed in chasing the ball being exceptional. The placing of the field was reduced as nearly as possible to an exact science. Neither of the wicket-keepers was a Blackham, but Carter more than upheld his old reputation, and Oldfield – the youngest player in the team – got on wonderfully well. It was quite a fitting compliment to give him his place against England at The Oval.

In a sense the record of the tour was, as it always must be when the Australians come to England in full strength, very flattering. More than half the matches were without significance, the English sides having no chance of success. People would laugh at the idea of any of our weaker counties playing England on even terms. Against the conquerors of England such elevens as Essex, Leicestershire, Warwickshire and Northamptonshire, to mention no others, were attempting the impossible. Still, the hopelessness of the task did not in any instance keep the public away, the Australians attracting big crowds wherever they went. In a financial as well as in a cricket sense the tour was a huge success, and on reaching home in December the players were given a bonus of £200 apiece. The team enjoyed an extraordinary immunity from illness, and no one except Collins met with a bad accident.                                                                                   S.H.P.

## NOTTINGHAMSHIRE v AUSTRALIANS

Played at Nottingham, June 25, 27, 1921

In the long history of Nottinghamshire cricket there has perhaps never been such a deplorable match as this. The county began well when Richmond clean bowled Bardsley, but for the rest of the game they were hopelessly outplayed, and in the end they suffered defeat by an innings and 517 runs. On the admission of the Nottinghamshire batsmen themselves nothing in the condition of the ground offered the least excuse for such miserable scores as 58 and 100. Indeed, the pitch was so good that even Gregory could not make the ball get up. Despite Bardsley's failure the Australians on the first day scored 608 for seven wickets. Nottinghamshire had to pay a terribly high price for one blunder, Macartney being missed in the slips when he had made 9. Never afterwards at fault, he went on to play the highest innings of the season, scoring his 345 in rather less then four hours. He simply did as he liked with the bowling, hitting four 6s and forty-seven 4s. One of the 6s – off John Gunn – went clean out of the ground. Pellew was also very brilliant, getting his 100 in an hour and three quarters. While he was in with Macartney 291 runs were put on. After lunch the Nottinghamshire bowling was weakened by the absence of Barratt, who had injured his hand. Though batting a man short, Oates having damaged his thumb, Nottinghamshire ought to have saved the game, but the batting was dreadfully feeble. When they followed on George Gunn shewed good defence for an hour and a quarter, and Carr made a few fine hits, but that was all.

### Australians

| | |
|---|---|
| W. Bardsley b Richmond .............. 0 | H. L. Hendry st Oates b Hardstaff ........ 51 |
| T. J. E. Andrews c Oates b Barratt ........ 29 | W. A. Oldfield b Staples ............... 40 |
| C. G. Macartney lbw b Hardstaff .......345 | E. A. McDonald b Hardstaff ............ 1 |
| J. M. Taylor c Whysall b Barratt ......... 50 | A. A. Mailey not out................... 0 |
| C. E. Pellew c Oates b Staples ..........100 | B 8, l-b 10, w 1, n-b 1 .......... 20 |
| J. M. Gregory c G. Gunn b Hardstaff...... 19 | ——— |
| J. Ryder b Hardstaff.................. 20 | 675 |

### Nottinghamshire

| | | | |
|---|---|---|---|
| G. Gunn b McDonald....................... | 4 | – c Oldfield b Mailey ............. | 20 |
| G. M. Lee c Pellew b Gregory................... | 1 | – run out ..................... | 9 |
| J. Gunn c McDonald b Gregory................. | 0 | – b Gregory.................... | 1 |
| J. Hardstaff b Gregory ........................ | 16 | – b McDonald................... | 6 |
| Mr A. W. Carr b McDonald.................... | 15 | – c Oldfield b Mailey ............ | 31 |
| W. Payton lbw b McDonald................... | 2 | – lbw b Gregory ............... | 14 |
| W. Whysall b Gregory ....................... | 15 | – b Gregory.................... | 9 |
| S. J. Staples b Mailey ........................ | 2 | – c Andrews b Mailey ............ | 3 |
| F. Barratt not out ........................... | 2 | – c Gregory b Mailey ............ | 4 |
| L. Richmond st Oldfield b Mailey................ | 0 | – not out :.................... | 1 |
| T. Oates absent hurt ......................... | 0 | – absent hurt ................... | 0 |
| L-b 1............................ | 1 | B 1, n-b 1 .............. | 2 |
| | 58 | | 100 |

**Nottinghamshire Bowling**

|              | Overs | Mdns | Runs | Wkts |
|--------------|-------|------|------|------|
| Barratt      | 23    | 4    | 89   | 2    |
| Richmond     | 36    | 1    | 193  | 1    |
| Staples      | 27    | 3    | 131  | 2    |
| J. Gunn      | 9     | 1    | 71   | —    |
| Lee          | 2     | —    | 14   | —    |
| Carr         | 1     | —    | 24   | —    |
| Hardstaff    | 28.2  | 3    | 133  | 5    |
| Whysall      | 1     | 1    | —    | —    |

**Australian Bowling**

|           | Overs | Mdns | Runs | Wkts | Overs | Mdns | Runs | Wkts |
|-----------|-------|------|------|------|-------|------|------|------|
| Gregory   | 8     | 1    | 23   | 4    | 11    | 1    | 26   | 3    |
| McDonald  | 10    | —    | 24   | 3    | 13    | 6    | 25   | 1    |
| Ryder     | 7     | 2    | 9    | —    | 1     | 1    | —    | —    |
| Mailey    | 1.4   | 1    | 1    | 2    | 13.5  | 1    | 36   | 4    |
| Hendry    |       |      |      |      | 3     | —    | 11   | —    |

Umpires: G. P. Harison and W. A. J. West.

# GLOUCESTERSHIRE v AUSTRALIANS

Played at Cheltenham, August 20, 22, 23, 1921

The Australians were bound to beat Gloucestershire, and their victory by an innings and 136 runs was in no way surprising. Still, they might not have won quite so easily if the wicket on the second day had not helped their bowlers. Winning the toss, the Australians were batting the whole of Saturday afternoon, and scored 425 for eight wickets. Bardsley and Macartney were seen at their very best, putting on 218 runs during their partnership. Macartney, who hit twenty-three 4s, was at the wickets for two hours and five minutes and Bardsley half-an-hour longer. No other batting in the innings was of the same class, but Gregory hit well, scoring at the rate of just over a run a minute. On Monday morning the Australian innings soon ended, and then on a pitch damaged by rain Gloucestershire had a very bad time. Keigwin showed fine defence, withstanding the bowlers for two hours, but that was all. In the follow-on Keigwin again took the honours, being 48 not out at the drawing of stumps. Mailey took the six wickets that fell, and on the following morning he obtained the other four, he being the fifth bowler in the season to take all ten wickets in an innings. The Australians proved a big attraction at Cheltenham, the gate receipts beating all records.

**Australians**

| | |
|---|---|
| H. L. Collins c Barnett b Bessant ......... 15 | J. Ryder not out ...................... 39 |
| W. Bardsley lbw b Bessant .............127 | H. L. Hendry b Mills.................. 0 |
| C. G. Macartney b Parker .............121 | H. Carter b Mills..................... 9 |
| C. E. Pellew c Mills b Parker ............ 1 | A. A. Mailey c Dipper b Parker .......... 3 |
| J. M. Gregory b Mills .................. 78 | B 12, l-b 3, n-b 1 .............. 16 |
| W. W. Armstrong lbw b Parker .......... 22 | |
| E. R. Mayne b Parker.................. 7 | **438** |

## Gloucestershire

| | | | |
|---|---|---|---|
| Mr C. S. Barnett b Armstrong | 3 | – b Mailey | 25 |
| A. G. Dipper b Gregory | 7 | – b Mailey | 4 |
| Mr R. P. Keigwin c Carter b Hendry | 47 | – c Mayne b Mailey | 65 |
| H. Smith lbw b Armstrong | 2 | – c and b Mailey | 0 |
| W. R. Hammond b Gregory | 0 | – b Mailey | 1 |
| Mr F. G. Robinson b Hendry | 18 | – b Mailey | 4 |
| Mr W. H. Rowlands c Mayne b Hendry | 19 | – b Mailey | 23 |
| Mr F. J. Seabrook b Mailey | 6 | – c and b Mailey | 30 |
| P. Mills not out | 18 | – c Pellew b Mailey | 3 |
| C. Parker st Carter b Mailey | 2 | – not out | 8 |
| J. G. Bessant b Mailey | 2 | – b Mailey | 0 |
| B 1, l-b 2 | 3 | B 5, l-b 6, n-b 1 | 12 |
| | **127** | | **175** |

### Gloucestershire Bowling

| | Overs | Mdns | Runs | Wkts |
|---|---|---|---|---|
| Parker | 50.2 | 9 | 148 | 5 |
| Bessant | 19 | 2 | 106 | 2 |
| Mills | 37 | 4 | 129 | 3 |
| Keigwin | 3 | — | 16 | — |
| Hammond | 3 | — | 23 | — |

### Australian Bowling

| | Overs | Mdns | Runs | Wkts | Overs | Mdns | Runs | Wkts |
|---|---|---|---|---|---|---|---|---|
| Gregory | 19 | 6 | 37 | 2 | 12 | 2 | 38 | — |
| Armstrong | 21 | 5 | 53 | 2 | 12 | 1 | 54 | — |
| Hendry | 11 | 4 | 13 | 3 | | | | |
| Mailey | 8.3 | 1 | 21 | 3 | 28.4 | 5 | 66 | 10 |
| Ryder | | | | | 5 | 3 | 5 | — |

Umpires: R. Brown and A. Millward.

## AN ENGLAND XI v AUSTRALIANS

Played at Eastbourne, August 27, 29, 30, 1921

This was the match that produced the sensation of the season. Unbeaten up the the closing days of August, it seemed certain that the Australians, surpassing the records of all the previous teams, would go through their tour without suffering defeat, but, as events turned out, the side selected by MacLaren won the game after a tremendous struggle by 28 runs. MacLaren all through the summer had maintained that he could pick a side good enough to overcome the Australians, but all hope of victory seemed gone when on winning the toss, and taking first innings on a perfect wicket, the Englishmen went down in an hour and a quarter for a score of 43. Probably the strong wind that was blowing accounted in some measure for the failure, but be that as it may, McDonald and Armstrong were irresistible. Gregory started the bowling with McDonald, but he hurt the thumb of his bowling hand after sending down two overs and had to retire. With the match to all appearance in their hands the Australians possibly regarded their task too lightly. Thanks to Bardsley and Macartney the score was up to 80 with only one man out, but the last eight wickets went down for 91 runs, Falcon bowling finely. Still, though the total only reached 174 there did not seem the least cause for apprehension, especially as the Englishmen lost a wicket for 8 runs before the drawing of stumps. Bardsley played a beautiful innings, making 70 in two hours without giving a chance. On the Monday Faulkner and Hubert Ashton brought about a marvellous change in the game. Becoming partners with the score at 60 for four wickets, they put on 154 runs together, both playing superbly. Ashton was out lbw at 214, and Faulkner left, eighth wicket down, at 307. Not since the first match of the Triangular Tournament in 1912 had Faulkner played such an innings as his 153. He hit a 6 and twenty 4s, and was at the wickets for three hours and a half without making a mistake. Ashton did not hit so hard, but his innings was also flawless. The Australians were left with only 196 to get, and at the close of play they had scored 21 for the loss of Collins' wicket. Most people took it for granted that the Australians would win readily enough, nothing in their record suggesting failure in the last innings. If what happened could in any way have been foreseen the Eastbourne ground would hardly have accommodated the crowd. Bardsley was bowled at 52, and at the same total Carter was caught at point. Then at 73 a fine ball clean bowled Macartney, this being perhaps the turning point of the game. Andrews and Pellew added 30 runs together, but at lunch time the Australians had five wickets down, and still required 87 runs to win. For some little time after resuming things went well for them, Andrews and Ryder taking the score to 143 before Ryder left. Gregory, who followed, was out leg-before-wicket to the second ball he received, and the chances veered round. Andrews was out at 153, and amidst intense excitement Amstrong was lbw. Mailey, the last man, joined McDonald with 42 runs still wanted. Thirteen runs were added, and then Gibson clean bowled Mailey and won the match. When it was all over there was a scene of wild enthusiasm, MacLaren, in particular, coming in for endless congratulations. For once last season the English fielding was magnificent, and it was said that Gibson, in taking six wickets for 64 runs, scarcely sent down a bad length ball. So fine was the fielding of both sides that no catch which went to hand was dropped.

## An England XI

| | | | |
|---|---|---|---|
| Mr G. N. Foster c Gregory b McDonald | 5 | – c and b McDonald | 11 |
| Mr G. A. Faulkner b Armstrong | 3 | – c Mailey b Armstrong | 153 |
| Mr G. Ashton lbw b Armstrong | 6 | – lbw b Armstrong | 36 |
| Mr H. Ashton b McDonald | 0 | – lbw b Armstrong | 75 |
| Mr A. P. F. Chapman b McDonald | 16 | – b McDonald | 11 |
| Mr C. T. Ashton c Ryder b Armstrong | 1 | – b McDonald | 0 |
| Mr M. Falcon b McDonald | 8 | – c and b McDonald | 17 |
| Mr G. E. C. Wood lbw b Armstrong | 1 | – b McDonald | 2 |
| Mr A. C. MacLaren b McDonald | 0 | – b McDonald | 5 |
| Mr C. H. Gibson not out | 1 | – not out | 0 |
| Mr W. Brearley b Armstrong | 1 | – run out | 0 |
| N-b 1 | 1 | B 10, l-b 1, n-b 5 | 16 |
| | 43 | | 326 |

## Australians

| | | | |
|---|---|---|---|
| H. L. Collins b Falcon | 19 | – c H. Ashton b Gibson | 12 |
| W. Bardsley lbw b Faulkner | 70 | – b Gibson | 22 |
| C. G. Macartney b Faulkner | 24 | – b Falcon | 14 |
| T. J. E. Andrews b Faulkner | 0 | – b Faulkner | 31 |
| C. E. Pellew c H. Ashton b Falcon | 1 | – c H. Ashton b Gibson | 16 |
| J. Ryder b Falcon | 10 | – c G. Ashton b Gibson | 28 |
| W. W. Armstrong b Falcon | 13 | – lbw b Faulkner | 11 |
| H. Carter c H. Ashton b Faulkner | 10 | – c C. T. Ashton b Falcon | 16 |
| J. M. Gregory not out | 16 | – lbw b Gibson | 0 |
| E. A. McDonald b Falcon | 4 | – not out | 9 |
| A. A. Mailey b Falcon | 4 | – b Gibson | 0 |
| B 1, l-b 2 | 3 | L-b 3, n-b 5 | 8 |
| | 174 | | 167 |

## Australian Bowling

| | Overs | Mdns | Runs | Wkts | Overs | Mdns | Runs | Wkts |
|---|---|---|---|---|---|---|---|---|
| Gregory .......... | 2 | — | 6 | — | 9 | — | 51 | — |
| McDonald ....... | 10 | 2 | 21 | 5 | 31 | 3 | 98 | 6 |
| Armstrong ........ | ˋ8.1 | 4 | 15 | 5 | 24.5 | 6 | 74 | 3 |
| Ryder ........... | | | | | 5 | 1 | 11 | — |
| Mailey .......... | | | | | 22 | 3 | 76 | — |

## An England XI's Bowling

| | Overs | Mdns | Runs | Wkts | Overs | Mdns | Runs | Wkts |
|---|---|---|---|---|---|---|---|---|
| Falcon ........... | 18.4 | 2 | 67 | 6 | 18 | 2 | 82 | 2 |
| Gibson .......... | 14 | 2 | 54 | — | 22.4 | 6 | 64 | 6 |
| Faulkner ........ | 16 | 1 | 50 | 4 | 5 | 1 | 13 | 2 |

Umpires: H. Butt and J. P. Whiteside.

# NOTES BY THE EDITOR [1922]

During all the years I have edited *Wisden* there has never been a season so disheartening as that of 1921. England was not merely beaten, but overwhelmed. The drawn games at Manchester and The Oval did something to restore our self-respect, but at the best they afforded small consolation for the crushing defeats at Nottingham, Lord's and Leeds. We had, of course, wretched luck in having to play without Hobbs – when at last he took the field at Leeds he was suddenly attacked by serious illness – but the loss of his invaluable batting, though a tremendous handicap, did not wholly account for our failure. We had no Test match bowlers of the pre-war standard, Parkin being by far the best of the various men tried, and our fielding compared with the brilliant work of the Australians was very second rate. At Lord's the contrast was humiliating. Never before was an England side so slow and slovenly. I cannot help thinking that if when the fixtures were arranged in December 1920, our authorities had had any idea of the Australian's strength, something in the nature of systematic preparation of the Test matches would have been decided on. The five defeats in Australia of the MCC's team showed us plainly enough what we should have to face, but the revelation came too late. Everything had been left to chance, and we paid the penalty. It seems to me that there is a good deal of misapprehension as to the real meaning and value of trial games. No sensible people, I take it, imagine that cricketers of the first rank would, in any literal sense, have to play for their places. That is an absurd idea, but there cannot surely be two opinions as to the desirability of giving the selected players a little preliminary work together. Even one game would be very helpful in accustoming men to unfamiliar positions in the field and giving the wicket-keeper a chance of studying bowlers to whom he may never have stood up before. The fact that thirty players appeared for England in the Test matches last summer is in itself proof that we had not a real eleven, but a series of scratch sides. Even at The Oval, when our fielding as a whole was better than in the previous matches, we could not boast a cover-point worthy the name. In saying all this I have no wish or intention to depreciate the Australians. Far from that, I was among those who regarded them, at any rate on hard wickets, as one of the finest all-round teams that ever went into the field. All I contend is that our cricket authorities played into their hands by treating the Test matches from the first so casually. I do not think that in any circumstances, with our weak bowling and Hobbs disabled, we could have won the rubber, but, given reasonable preparation, we might have made a much better fight than we did.

The members of the selection committee had a difficult task and it would be ungracious to find fault with them. Still I have a feeling amounting to conviction that they lacked a settled policy. They were inclined to catch at straws, and allowed themselves to be influenced too much by the latest form. An example of what I mean was the preference given to Dipper over Holmes in the match at Lord's. Dipper batted uncommonly well in his second innings but, perhaps because he could not be put in his proper position, he was a long way below England form in the field. I regard Holmes as having been the least fortunate of out Test match players. He stayed in for an hour and a half at Trent Bridge when Gregory and McDonald were at their deadliest, and yet he never played again. Certainly he was as much entitled to a second trial as Donald Knight and he would have helped the fielding – our weakest point. It is easy to be wise after the event but, as Mr Spofforth pointed out, it would perhaps have been better from the first not to lean so much on the players who went to Australia. The fact of having been on the losing side five times was not calculated to inspire confidence. I must admit, however, that the position was very awkward. As the first Test match came so early in the season – far too soon in my opinion – there was no form to go on in picking new men. The great experiment that the committee ventured on – the choice of Tennyson to play at Lord's – turned out, by happy chance, a triumph. If early in his second innings Tennyson had not been missed by the wicket-keeper – quite an ordinary catch – we should have seen no more of him in the Test matches. As it was he scored 74 not out and made himself indispensable. His success at Lord's, Leeds and The Oval was a severe indictment of modern methods of batting. He played the fast bowlers in the old-fashioned way, trusting to honest driving and not trying to pull balls that came along at sixty miles an hour. Modern batting is far from being the tame unaggressive thing some critics represent it – the high scores prove that – but the experience of last summer revealed it as dismally ineffective against bowling of great pace. While watching the feeble efforts to play Gregory and McDonald, my thoughts often went back to the Gentlemen and Players match at Lord's in 1895. I recalled the way in which W. G. Grace and Stoddart, on a rather fiery wicket, treated Tom Richardson and Mold. One more word about out Test match teams and I have done. I could not, holding firmly to the belief that in any circumstances the best wicket-keeper should be played, reconcile myself to the policy, after the match at Lord's, of substituting Brown for Strudwick. Brown might very well have been picked for his batting and his fearless fielding at mid-off. His selection was a success, one good effect being that we so constantly had a left-handed batsman in at one end to worry the bowlers. The transfer of the captaincy to Tennyson after the second defeat could not be regarded as an affront to Douglas. In the hope of changing the luck something had to be done.

It is quite clear that when the Australians come here again the programme will have to be very differently arranged. A day must be kept clear in advance of each Test match. We do not want a repetition of the farcical cricket seen in the match with Kent at Canterbury or of the squabble that preceded the second game with Yorkshire. I cannot imagine why, as the Australians were so insistent on the point, Mr Latham was not advised before he drew up the fixture list. A brief cable message would have solved all difficulties. The Australians were so immeasurably superior to nearly all the sides they met that the trouble threatened by restricting the hours of play in all games other than the Test matches came to nothing. Still, Armstrong and Mr Sydney Smith – an admirably efficient manager – might well have given way in the case of the match with the MCC at Lord's. It was neither wise nor tactful to force the MCC to issue an apology to the public.

In one respect things turned out exactly as I ventured to predict a year ago. The Australians, even more than in previous tours, made everything subordinate to the Test matches, Armstrong seeing to it that Gregory and McDonald should be fresh and able to keep up their full pace on the big occasions. We unfortunately had no one of the same type to trouble about, but our teams suffered a good deal from the casual and unsystematic way in which things were managed. Men ought not to be in doubt twenty-four hours beforehand as to whether or not they are going to play in a Test match. I think the side should always be definitely chosen well in advance of the day, an extra bowler being held in reserve in view of a sudden change in the weather. I notice that on reaching home Armstrong paid a well-deserved compliment to his two fast bowlers for the splendid way in which they stuck to their work till the rubber was won. Of course, it is a comparatively easy task to lead a team when all the men can get runs and nearly everyone is a star fieldsman, but Armstrong struck me as being in every way a first-rate captain. Leading off with a run of success, only checked by the drawn game at Attleborough, he was never faced by the troubles and difficulties that Noble surmounted so triumphantly in 1909, but he always seemed to do the right thing at the right time. In particular he managed his bowling changes with the nicest skill. In retiring from the game he will leave behind him a record that is never likely to be approached. Under him Australia won eight Test matches in succession – five at home and three in this country.

On the vexed question as to whether or not Test matches in England should be played to a finish, no matter how many days they last, opinion here is a good deal divided. At their meeting at Lord's in December the advisory committee of the counties were strongly in favour of continuing to restrict the matches to three days with, of course, unlimited time in the final match when the rubber depends on it, but some prominent cricketers take the opposite view, and agree fully with the Australians. Personally I am inclined to think that if we in the future give up the three-day system the Test matches should, as in the tours from 1884 to 1896, be limited to three. I do not see how in our short season the counties could be asked to let their players off for five weeks. Looking at the matter in its purely financial aspect, the share of profits from the Test matches would not compensate for such an upset of the ordinary programme. There is no real analogy between the state of things in this country and Australia. We have first-class cricket at a great number of centres, whereas in Australia all the cricket that counts is played at Sydney, Melbourne and Adelaide. When we send a team to Australia there is no difficulty involved in playing the Test matches to a finish, as apart from the English fixtures only half a dozen inter-state matches have to be provided for. Happily there is plenty of time to discuss the subject in all its bearings before the Australians come here again. It is hardly likely to be a burning question when the South Africans visit us in 1924.

As regards our county cricket I have a strong feeling that the time has come when the admission of a county to the first-class should not be determined wholly by the ability to secure the requisite number of fixtures. There ought surely to be some clear proof of first-rate form. Far be it from me to discourage ambition, but as a matter of fact there was not sufficient justification for the promotion last year of Glamorgan. They had done nothing out of the common in 1920 in the second division competition, winning four matches out of eight, losing two, and winning twice on the first innings. As the result of their modest efforts they finished up with a worse percentage than five of their rivals. The county championship must not be a close borough, but there is an obvious danger in treating teams as first-class when they are really nothing of the kind. English cricket has not gained in quality by the huge increase in county fixtures. The reason, as I pointed out in *Wisden* last year, is obvious enough. The best sides have too many easy tasks and as a natural result batsmen and bowlers get false reputations. What we want is more cricket of the highest class but, with the pressure of county matches, it is difficult to see how we can get it.

While the last pages of *Wisden* were passing through the press two items of news came to hand from Australia. One was that the bonus to the members of the Australia team was £300 each, not £200 as at first cabled, and the other that McDonald had decided not to return to England to play for Nelson in the Lancashire League. The non-fulfilment of the contract he had signed will, it seems, involve on his part a forfeit of £200. I confess to feeling extremely glad he is not coming back. To me there was something very distasteful in the idea of a Test match bowler of the highest class going into league cricket, and more than that, I object strongly to the importation of Australian players. Clubs with money to spend should encourage native talent and not buy cricketers of established reputation. Partly for the reason that it would open to door to financial dealings. I was glad that the registration scheme, drawn up at the request of the counties by Lord Harris and brought forward in December, was rejected by the advisory committee. I quite see the hardship of keeping out of county cricket young amateurs with no qualification either by birth or residence, and only a few years to spare for the game, but the welfare of cricket far outweighs occasional cases of this kind. It was impossible to confine the scheme to amateurs, and the absence of restriction with regard to professionals would at once have increased the power of the purse. Even at the risk of being described, as I have been before now, as a hide-bound Tory, I must affirm my belief that the two years' residential qualification is a great safeguard in preserving the true spirit of county cricket.

Reading much that is written about our great game I am struck by the tendency to regard English cricket as having been more or less negligible till the first visit of the Australians. Young people not versed in cricket history might very well gather from what they are told that nothing of real importance happened prior to 1878. This, of course, is an utterly fallacious view. The absurdity of it is proved by the fact that W. G. Grace had passed his best before the Australians came here. They gave a fresh spur to his ambition but, though he did brilliant things against them and was their most formidable opponent in many tours, he was never, by reason of increased weight, in the same physical condition as in his younger days. In comparing the past with the present Lord Harris, with his long experience and undiminished interest in the game, is a safe guide, and in his book "A Few Short Runs", he maintains strongly that the great batsmen of a past generation – R. A. H. Mitchell, Yardley, Ottaway and A. P. Lucas among others – would on the wickets of to-day have easily held their own, with W. G. Grace as unrivalled as he always was. One point I cannot pass over. I was frankly astounded to read one day last summer that Blackham taught Englishmen to keep wicket. To those of us who could recall Pinder, Pooley and Pilling in their prime this was too much. Pilling came out for Lancashire in 1877 – the year before Blackham was seen here – and was potentially great in his first match. Blackham was by general consent the best of all wicket-keepers, but he did not discover a new art. The whole science of wicket-keeping does not consist in dispensing with the long stop and as a matter of fact Pinder was the first to do that in a North and South match at Prince's. One can say without much risk of contradiction that Tom Lockyer during the tour of George Parr's team in 1863-64 taught the Australians to keep wicket. It is quite possible that Blackham as a child saw him at Melbourne. By the way it may not be generally known that when Tom Lockyer died in 1869 a leading article in *The Daily Telegraph* was written in his honour by W. J. Prowse – author of the immortal verses on Alfred Mynn. Even in those far-off days cricket played an important part in English life.

## ENGLAND v AUSTRALIA

### Fifth Test Match

Played at The Oval, August 14, 16, 17, 18, 1926

After a wonderfully interesting struggle, the fifth Test match – arranged, however long it might last, to be played to a finish – ended shortly after six o'clock on the fourth day in a splendid victory for England by 289 runs. Winning in this handsome fashion, the only one of the five Test games in which a definite issue was reached, the old country regained possession of the mythical "ashes" that Australia had held since the wholesale triumph over the English team led by John Douglas in the commonwealth during the winter of 1920-21. Looked forward to with extraordinary interest, the contest underwent some truly dramatic changes. England, on the opening day, appeared to have jeopardised their chances by some strangely reckless batting, and yet left off on the first evening in distinctly the stronger position. On Monday, Australia played an uphill game to such good purpose, that they gained a slight lead. Tuesday brought with it some superb batting on a difficult wicket by Hobbs and Sutcliffe, and to wind up, came the collapse of Australia, who, when set 415 to win, failed so completely, that they were all out for 125 – their second lowest total during the whole tour.

England's eleven underwent no fewer than four changes from that which had met Australia three weeks earlier at Manchester. Chapman succeeded Carr in the captaincy of the side, and Geary, Larwood and Rhodes displaced Earnest Tyldesley, Kilner and Root. The inclusion of Rhodes, a man nearly 49 years of age, naturally occasioned a good deal of surprise, but it was crowned with complete success, the bowling of the veteran Yorkshireman proving no small factor in determining the issue of the struggle. Chapman, too, despite lack of experience in leading a first-class team in the field, turned out a very happy nomination for the post of captain, the young amateur, for the most part, managing his bowling with excellent judgment, and in two or three things he did, showing distinct imagination. Anxious to strengthen the batting, the selection committee decided that George Brown of Hampshire should keep wicket instead of Strudwick, but circumstances intervened to prevent this alteration in the constitution of the side. Brown damaged his thumb, and so the authorities once again called upon Strudwick, who giving away only 5 byes, making two catches and running out Ponsford, rendered England excellent service. Collins, having recovered from the illness which prevented him playing at Leeds and Manchester, resumed the captaincy of the Australians, Ryder making way for him.

Chapman, winning the toss, secured first innings for England on a wicket which varied in pace at times, but otherwise played well. The start was full of hope, Hobbs and Sutcliffe settling down in excellent style, and in rather less than an hour, putting on 53 runs. Then, to the general amazement, Hobbs, who appeared to be in particularly fine form, was bowled by a full pitch. A googly dismissing Woolley, and Hendren pulling an off ball on to the wicket, there were three men out for 108 at lunch time. This poor beginning, notwithstanding, Chapman, on resuming, hit out in vigorous fashion. Possibly he considered the position called for an endeavour to knock Mailey off his length. At any rate, he made 49 out of 87 in an hour and a quarter, but, following upon his departure, Mailey and Grimmett met with such poor resistance, that the last six wickets went down in an hour for the addition of 91 runs. Sixth out at 214, Sutcliffe batted admirably for three hours and a half, his clean off-driving and the certainty of his strokes on the leg side being the chief features of his play. His innings had an unfortunate termination, a ball rising off his pad and striking him on the tip of the nose, and the next, a leg-break which he did not appear to see, taking his wicket. Tate – missed when 12 – hit up 23 out of 35 in a quarter of an hour, and Rhodes batted thoroughly well for three-quarters of an hour, but the innings was all over in four hours and a quarter for 280. In a match unlimited as to time, the lack of restraint shown by several of the batsmen was difficult to understand. Mailey met with a good deal of punishment, but he mixed his break and pace in a way very difficult to judge.

Having disappointed so considerably in batting, the England team proceeded to atone for their shortcomings in that department by the excellence of their out cricket. Australia's score was only 9 when a catch behind the wicket sent back Bardsley and Macartney, having scored 25 out of 35 in half an hour, played on in attempting to hit a long hop to leg. Shortly afterwards, Ponsford, starting for a foolish run, could not regain his crease before a smart gather, and return by Larwood had enabled Strudwick to whip off the bails, while at 59, a fine break-back knocked Andrews' off stump out of the ground. Collins had just joined Woodfull when stumps were drawn for the day, Australia, with four men out for 60, being 220 behind and having six wickets to fall.

While on Saturday the attendance did not exceed that of a popular county match – the public having been frightened away by prophecies of over-crowding and tales of all night vigils outside the ground – the crowd on Monday was so large that the gates had to be closed shortly after noon. Collins and Woodfull, with Australia in so anxious a position, naturally batted stubbornly, but the former had only added 7 when a fieldsman, quicker on his feet than Stevens, might have caught him. Australia's captain proceeded to make a great effort for his side, but he lost his partner at 90. Only once previously had Woodfull faced Rhodes and on that occasion the second ball from the left-hander brought about his dismissal. Now he encountered Rhodes a second time, and the veteran, after sending down two maidens, led the famous Australian to play on and so ended a watchful innings of more than two hours. With Richardson in, Collins was guilty of a strangely foolish action. A ball from Tate bounced back off Strudwick's gloves. Collins caught it and threw it back to the wicket-keeper. Had an appeal been made against Collins for handling the ball when in play, the umpire could scarcely have avoided giving the batsman out under Rule 29. Richardson tried hard to bat as cautiously as his captain, but his patience at length deserted him, and lashing out, he fell to a beautiful catch low and wide by Geary at mid-off. At this point Australia, with six men out, were 158 runs behind, but Collins then found a splendid partner in Gregory. While his captain continued to bat with extreme caution, Gregory hit up 73 out of 107 in an hour and three-quarters, with ten 4s as his chief strokes. Not only did Gregory bat so freely, but he showed rare judgment in picking the ball to hit. The stand completely altered the aspect of the game. Collins, who left directly after Gregory, withstood the England attack for three hours and forty minutes. It was gratifying to notice that the excellence of the skill he displayed in trying to save his side was thoroughly appreciated by the crowd. Following Collins' departure, came some capital batting by Oldfield and Grimmett, who not only headed the England total, but altogether added 67 for the ninth wicket in an hour and a quarter. Out at last for 302, Australia, at the wickets two hours longer than England, secured a lead of 22. Tate bowled with remarkable steadiness: indeed, except just before the tea interval, when Oldfield and Grimmett were together, the English attack always looked as though it wanted a lot of playing.

Exactly an hour remained for play when Hobbs and Sutcliffe entered upon England's second innings. As no object was to be served by forcing the runs, they proceeded quietly and if Hobbs took a little time to settle down, he and Sutcliffe at the close had raised the total to 49. This hour's steady cricket had, unquestionably, a big influence upon the later stages of the struggle.

The crux of the match came before lunch on Tuesday, when Hobbs and Sutcliffe excelled themselves. A thunderstorm, accompanied by a good deal of rain had broken over south London on Monday evening, rendering the pitch slow and dead to begin with, and afterwards very difficult. The two batsmen, it is true, enjoyed the advantage of playing themselves in before conditions became distinctly awkward for them, but, admitting this, their performance during the last hour before lunch in withstanding all endeavours to separate them, was an achievement of the highest order. While giving Hobbs and Sutcliffe all praise, those two famous men were fortunate in the fact that Richardson, while making the ball turn and rise quickly, stuck doggedly to the "leg theory". He was awkward enough pursuing that method. He would probably have been deadly had he bowled over the wicket with something like a normally placed field, and point of course close in. As it was, Hobbs and Sutcliffe added 112 runs in rather less than two hours and a half before lunch, but directly afterwards Hobbs, having just completed his 100, was at 172 bowled by a ball that came back a little and touched the top of the off stump. He and his partner batted superbly for three hours and forty minutes; indeed, his innings which included ten 4s, must be regarded as one of the most masterly displays of his great career. His 100 was his eleventh three-figure innings for England against Australia, while the stand was the seventh of three-figures he and Sutcliffe had made in Test matches with Australia. Woolley helped to put on 48, Hendren stayed while 57 runs were obtained. Chapman shared in a partnership of 39, and Stevens remained to add 57, but all the time interest of course, centred chiefly on Sutcliffe. The Yorkshireman withstood Australia's bowling for rather more than seven hours and then in the last over of the day was bowled by a fine ball from Mailey. He gave no real chance, hit fifteen 4s and shared with Hobbs in a memorable piece of work. England left off 353 ahead with four wickets to fall, and thus in a very strong position. On this day the Prince of Wales was present, and on the concluding afternoon the visitors included Prince Arthur of Connaught and the Prime Minister.

On Wednesday there was a slight shower before play started, and further rain setting in at a quarter past one, there was no more cricket until ten minutes past three. While never heavy, the rain, being followed by sunshine, of course affected the pitch, but it is doubtful whether the conditions when Australia batted were ever as difficult as during the hour before lunch on Tuesday. To begin with, on the last day sixty-five minutes of actual cricket sufficed to finish off England's innings for the addition of 61 runs. Rhodes – missed when 12 by Gregory at slip – helped in a partnership of 43 for the eighth wicket, but the best batting was that of Tate, who hit up his 33 in fifty minutes. In all, England's innings lasted eight hours and ten minutes.

Under the conditions which obtained, there never existed the slightest likelihood of Australia making the 415 runs required for victory, but no one could have been prepared to see a famous batting side collapse so badly. As matters went, an easy win for England was assured in fifty minutes, the first four wickets falling for 35 runs. The heavy roller brought up litle moisture but Larwood made the ball fly, and Rhodes, directly he was tried, made it turn. Woodfull putting a ball up in the slips, Chapman brought Rhodes up from deep fine leg to the "gully", and moved Geary to third slip. The effect was instantaneous, Woodfull with only 1 run registered, edging the next ball straight into Geary's hands. Macartney joining Ponsford, the score was carried to 31 before he also gave a catch to Geary, and then in quick succession, Rhodes got Ponsford taken low down at second slip, and Collins – cheered all the way to the wicket – at first slip. Andrews and Bardsley made something of a stand, but at 63, Andrews, hitting a little too soon at a long hop, was finely caught one hand at short leg by Tate. Twenty runs later, Bardsley, after a stay of sixty-five minutes, gave the simplest of catches to slip, and Gregory, lashing out at Tate, placed the ball in the hands of mid off. Eight wickets were down for 87, and although Oldfield and Grimmett remained together half an hour to add 27, the side were all out for 125. Rhodes, with four wickets for 44, and Larwood with three for 34, had the chief share in the cheap dismissal of Australia, but all round, the bowling was excellent. Moreover, not a catch was missed nor was a run given away, the whole England side rising gallantly to the occasion. Naturally a scene of tremendous enthusiasm occurred at the end, the crowd swarming in thousands in front of the pavilion, and loudly cheering the players, both English and Australian.

The number of people paying for admission during the four days was 76,472. This, with members and holders of privilege tickets, brought the full total to nearly 103,000. The amount taken at the gates was about £11,470.

## England

| | | | |
|---|---|---|---|
| J. B. Hobbs b Mailey | 37 | – b Gregory | 100 |
| H. Sutcliffe b Mailey | 76 | – b Mailey | 161 |
| F. E. Woolley b Mailey | 18 | – lbw b Richardson | 27 |
| E. Hendren b Gregory | 8 | – c Oldfield b Grimmett | 15 |
| Mr A. P. F. Chapman st Oldfield b Mailey | 49 | – b Richardson | 19 |
| Mr G. T. S. Stevens c Andrews b Mailey | 17 | – c Mailey b Grimmett | 22 |
| W. Rhodes c Oldfield b Mailey | 28 | – lbw b Grimmett | 14 |
| G. Geary run out | 9 | – c Oldfield b Gregory | 1 |
| M. W. Tate b Grimmett | 23 | – not out | 33 |
| H. Larwood c Andrews b Grimmett | 0 | – b Mailey | 5 |
| H. Strudwick not out | 4 | – c Andrews b Mailey | 2 |
| B 6, l-b 5 | 11 | B 19, l-b 18 | 37 |
| | **280** | | **436** |

## Australia

| | | |
|---|---|---|
| W. M. Woodfull b Rhodes | 35 – c Geary b Larwood | 0 |
| W. Bardsley c Strudwick b Larwood | 2 – c Woolley b Rhodes | 21 |
| C. G. Macartney b Stevens | 25 – c Geary b Larwood | 16 |
| W. H. Ponsford run out | 2 – c Larwood b Rhodes | 12 |
| T. J. E. Andrews b Larwood | 3 – c Tate b Larwood | 15 |
| H. L. Collins c Stevens b Larwood | 61 – c Woolley b Rhodes | 4 |
| A. J. Richardson c Geary b Rhodes | 16 – b Rhodes | 4 |
| J. M. Gregory c Stevens b Tate | 73 – c Sutcliffe b Tate | 9 |
| W. A. Oldfield not out | 33 – b Stevens | 23 |
| C. V. Grimmett b Tate | 35 – not out | 8 |
| A. A. Mailey c Strudwick b Tate | 0 – b Geary | 6 |
| B 5, l-b 12 | 17    L-b 7 | 7 |
| | **302** | **125** |

## Australia Bowling

| | Overs | Mdns | Runs | Wkts | Overs | Mdns | Runs | Wkts |
|---|---|---|---|---|---|---|---|---|
| Gregory | 15 | 4 | 31 | 1 | 18 | 1 | 58 | 2 |
| Grimmett | 33 | 12 | 74 | 2 | 55 | 17 | 108 | 3 |
| Mailey | 33.5 | 3 | 138 | 6 | 42.5 | 6 | 128 | 3 |
| Macartney | 6 | 3 | 16 | — | 26 | 16 | 24 | — |
| Richardson | 7 | 2 | 10 | — | 41 | 21 | 81 | 2 |

## England Bowling

| | Overs | Mdns | Runs | Wkts | Overs | Mdns | Runs | Wkts |
|---|---|---|---|---|---|---|---|---|
| Tate | 37.1 | 17 | 40 | 3 | 9 | 4 | 12 | 1 |
| Larwood | 34 | 11 | 82 | 3 | 14 | 3 | 34 | 3 |
| Geary | 27 | 8 | 43 | — | 6.3 | 2 | 15 | 1 |
| Stevens | 29 | 3 | 85 | 1 | 3 | 1 | 13 | 1 |
| Rhodes | 25 | 15 | 35 | 2 | 20 | 9 | 44 | 4 |

Umpires: F. Chester and H. Young.

# AUSTRALIAN TOURS AND THEIR MANAGEMENT [1929]

### By Sir Frederick Toone

It is but natural that when for the first time one is entrusted by the MCC with the management of a tour to Australia, he should feel impressed with the sense of responsibility and be anxious to justify the confidence placed in him by the rulers of the game. The success of a tour depends, to a very large extent, upon the preliminary arrangements at headquarters, and, of course, it is the manager's duty faithfully to carry out the intentions of the authorities he represents. As manager of the three tours in which I have had the privilege of representing the MCC, I have, naturally, appreciated the great work done beforehand by Lord Harris, the selection committee, and those indefatigable secretaries, Sir Francis Lacey and Mr W. Findlay. They have done everything possible in advance to ensure the smooth working of the undertakings and, although I have had no experience beyond the tours in Australia, I think the work and foresight of those at home have been of the greatest value in all tours, not only from a cricket point of view but also from the imperial standpoint. So far as I am personally concerned, I have from the very outset regarded these tours primarily as imperial enterprises, tending to cement friendship between the mother country and her dominions. Players, therefore, selected to take part in them – and this has always been borne in mind by the MCC – should not be chosen for their cricket qualities alone. They must be men of good character, high principle, easy of address, and in every personal sense worthy ᴼf representing their country in all circumstances, irrespective of their work on the field.

The tours it has been my privilege to manage were those of 1920-21, 1924-25 and 1928-29. The three captains who have shared the responsibilities of the visits are Mr J. W. H. T. Douglas, Mr A. E. R. Gilligan and Mr A. P. F. Chapman. And here let me say that with all three I had the most happy relations. Nothing but absolutely good sportsmanship was the keynote of all our proceedings. Not a wrong word was spoken on any of the tours; nothing but the greatest good feeling prevailed among all the players. Sunshine is lovely in Australia but it was never more lovely than the feeling which prevailed in defeat as well as in victory. Australia is a happy country and the cricketers privileged to visit and to play there are assured of five and a half happy months. They make very many friends whom they leave with regret. The travelling arrangements for these tours, including the selection of the hotels at which the team will stay, are made on the other side but they have to be ratified by the MCC. The carrying out of these arrangements, of course, devolves upon the manager, who makes it his first duty to see that the comfort of the players is properly provided for. This, indeed, is the constant consideration of the manager and it necessarily involves some degree of tact and not a little patience. No trouble must be spared; no little detail overlooked. The health of the players, too, must be a special managerial care. No illness, or mishap however slight, can be neglected. An expert masseur always accompanies the team, and is constant in his attentions. The need of such services can be judged when it is said that, apart from the strains of continuous match play, we had on the last tour to spend between twenty and thirty nights in the train, the longest journeys being from Perth to Adelaide which occupied about four days – i.e., three nights on the train – and, after the last Test, from Melbourne to Perth. The whole tour means a round journey of between 40,000 and 50,000 miles.

Though one does not like to stress it, managing an Australian cricket tour is hard work. An avalanche of letters has to be dealt with, a mountain of data about plans and itinerary removed. Not the least of this work has reference to the social side of the tour. A very great deal of tact is required in this connection for the offers of hospitality are innumerable and one has to be very careful that the comfort, the convenience and personal wishes and health of the players are properly considered without giving the least cause to any host to feel slighted. I must say here that the Governor General and state governors have always been extremely cordial and eager in welcoming the teams I have accompanied. Lord Foster during my first and second tours took a very great personal interest in the progress of the team and their individual and collective performances. The spirit of imperialism which animated the party had a very ready response from their Excellencies and the Australian public at large.

From what one could gather there can be no doubt that the Australian Board of Control is the constituted authority to which the Australians as a body look to guide the game in the proper channel. The board has the finger on the pulse of Australian cricket. Its authority is recognised throughout the states. There may be differences of opinion. There always will be. We have them at home. But the great thing recognised is that the members of the board do their best for the game and its exponents. The trustees of the various grounds have done wonderful work in building up some of the finest enclosures in the world. The arrangements for the accommodation of members and the public and for getting them to and from the grounds are on a scale not to be beaten for efficiency anywhere. During the last tour I was asked to give my definition of cricket, and as it roused considerable interest, and I believe was received with approval, I may be forgiven for including it in this, I fear somewhat sketchy, contribution to "Wisden's" immortal pages.

"It is a science, the study of a lifetime, in which you may exhaust yourself, but never your subject. It is a contest, a duel or melee, calling for courage, skill, strategy and self-control. It is a contest of temper, a trial of honour, a revealer of character. It affords a chance to play the man and act the gentleman. It means going into God's out-of-doors, getting close to nature, fresh air, exercise, a sweeping away of mental cobwebs, genuine recreation of the tired tissues. It is a cure for care, an antidote to worry. It includes companionship with friends, social intercourse, opportunities for courtesy, kindliness, and generosity to an opponent. It promotes not only physical health but mental force."

It would be remiss on my part if I did not state how deeply I have felt the confidence which the MCC reposed in me in offering me the appointment of manager of three consecutive Australian tours. As I have mentioned, the success of those tours, so far as a manager can make them, has been due in the first place to the care and foresight by which the ground was prepared in advance. My work has been to carry out the wishes of the MCC, and to cultivate the real spirit of cricket, and this I have endeavoured to do to the best of my powers. My grateful thanks are also due to Lord Hawke and to the members of the Yorkshire County Cricket Committee for giving me the necessary leave of absence which the management of the tours made necessary.

## WORCESTERSHIRE v AUSTRALIANS

Played at Worcester, April 30, May 1, 2, 1930

The Australians opened their tour in most successful fashion, outplaying Worcestershire so completely that they won early on the third day by an innings and 165 runs. To no particularly high standard did the fielding attain and the bowling, apart from that of Grimmett, was not impressive, but rather chilly weather handicapped the tourists who, moreover, had enjoyed little practice. Still on the opening day the visitors, after disposing of Worcestershire for 131, put on 199 for the loss of one wicket. This was essentially the work of Woodfull and Bradman. Altogether the second wicket partnership lasted two hours and ten minutes and produced 208 runs. Woodfull, batting very soundly and with much more freedom than expected, drove and cut particularly well. Bradman put together the first of the many big scores he obtained during the summer. Batting for just over four hours and a half, he drove, hit to leg and hooked with wonderful power and certainty and apart from a hard return when 215 gave no chance. Altogether he made 236 out of 423, among his strokes being twenty-eight 4s. The Australians registered their 492 runs in five hours and forty minutes. Finding his skill at once, Gimmett took nine wickets for less than 10 runs apiece. On Friday morning Root and Walters hit up 84 for Worcestershire's sixth wicket.

### Worcestershire

| | | | |
|---|---|---|---|
| Mr M. F. S. Jewell c Fairfax b Grimmett | 7 | – hit wkt b Hornibrook | 10 |
| L. Wright lbw b Grimmett | 28 | – run out | 18 |
| M. Nichol run out | 8 | – c Hornibrook b Grimmett | 1 |
| H. H. Gibbons not out | 31 | – b Hornibrook | 22 |
| W. V. Fox lbw b Grimmett | 0 | – c Oldfield b Grimmett | 28 |
| Mr C. F. Walters st Oldfield b Grimmett | 21 | – c and b Grimmett | 44 |
| F. Root st Oldfield b Fairfax | 9 | – b Grimmett | 48 |
| G. Brook b Fairfax | 2 | – b Grimmett | 0 |
| S. W. Styler run out | 13 | – lbw b Hornibrook | 1 |
| Mr H. A. Gilbert b Fairfax | 0 | – absent ill | 0 |
| P. Jackson lbw b Fairfax | 0 | – not out | 4 |
| B 7, l-b 4, n-b 1 | 12 | B 8, l-b 10, w 1, n-b 1 | 20 |
| | **131** | | **196** |

## Australians

| | |
|---|---|
| W. M. Woodfull b Brook . . . . . . . . . . . . . .133 | W. A. Oldfield c Jackson b Root . . . . . . . . . 4 |
| A. Jackson c Walters b Brook . . . . . . . . . . 24 | C. V. Grimmett not out . . . . . . . . . . . . . . . 15 |
| D. G. Bradman c Walters b Brook . . . . . . . .236 | T. W. Wall not out . . . . . . . . . . . . . . . . . . . 9 |
| S. McCabe c Root b Brook . . . . . . . . . . . . 15 | |
| V. Y. Richardson run out . . . . . . . . . . . . . . 24 | B 4, l-b 2, w 1, n-b 1 . . . . . . . . . . . 8 |
| A. Fairfax c Root b Jackson . . . . . . . . . . . . 0 | — |
| E. L. A Beckett c Gilbert b Root . . . . . . . . . 24 | (8 wkts dec.) 492 |

P. M. Hornibrook did not bat.

### Australians Bowling

| | Overs | Mdns | Runs | Wkts | Overs | Mdns | Runs | Wkts |
|---|---|---|---|---|---|---|---|---|
| Wall . . . . . . . . . . . . . | 8 | 1 | 21 | — | 11 | 5 | 22 | — |
| A'Beckett . . . . . . . . . | 6 | 4 | 2 | — | 11 | 3 | 25 | — |
| Grimmett . . . . . . . . . | 24 | 12 | 38 | 4 | 28.3 | 13 | 46 | 5 |
| Hornibrook . . . . . . . | 7 | 1 | 22 | — | 17 | 5 | 30 | 3 |
| Fairfax . . . . . . . . . . . | 12.3 | 2 | 36 | 4 | 21 | 8 | 45 | — |
| McCabe . . . . . . . . . . | | | | | 3 | 1 | 8 | — |

### Worcestershire Bowling

| | Overs | Mdns | Runs | Wkts |
|---|---|---|---|---|
| Root . . . . . . . . . . . . . | 43 | 9 | 112 | 2 |
| Jackson . . . . . . . . . . . | 25 | 1 | 105 | 1 |
| Gilbert . . . . . . . . . . . | 4 | — | 30 | — |
| Brook . . . . . . . . . . . . | 36 | 1 | 148 | 4 |
| Wright . . . . . . . . . . . | 18 | 1 | 68 | — |
| Gibbons . . . . . . . . . . | 2 | — | 21 | — |

Umpires: J. Hardstaff and T. Oates.

# YORKSHIRE v AUSTRALIANS

Played at Sheffield, May 10, 12, 13, 1930

A splendid bowling performance on the part of Grimmett, who took all ten Yorkshire wickets for 37 runs, was the outstanding feature of a match in which rain, after interfering considerably with play on the first two days, ruined the pitch so completely that on the Tuesday no cricket could be attempted. Grimmett's triumph was the more remarkable as Yorkshire commenced in distinctly promising fashion. Holmes and Sutcliffe put on 59 runs and the score had reached 120 when Sutcliffe, who batted admirably for two hours, was third man out. Then came such devastating work by Grimmett that the seven remaining wickets went down for 35 more runs. From the time he went on at 46, Grimmett bowled with wonderful accuracy and varied his break and flight with delightful ingenuity. He received excellent assistance from Walker who caught one batsman and stumped three. On two previous occasions all ten wickets in an innings had been taken in England by an Australian, Howell performing the feat in 1899 and Mailey in 1921. When the tourists went in, rain and bad light prevented much progress being made but 69 runs were scored for one wicket. So much rain fell on Sunday that on Monday the game could not be resumed until after two o'clcok. Woodfull and Bradman, who had come together at 35 then played so well on the soft pitch that they raised the total to 142, Bradman by brilliant cricket making 78 out of 107 in a hundred minutes. Woodfull, while always sound and watchful, employed the drive and the hook shot to good purpose. Batting for four hours, he hit twelve 4s and helped to raise the score to 243. Leyland and Rhodes afterwards bowled effectively but still the Australians secured a lead of 165.

### Yorkshire

| | | | |
|---|---:|---|---:|
| P. Holmes b Grimmett | 31 | A. Wood c Richardson b Grimmett | 17 |
| H. Sutcliffe c Walker b Grimmett | 69 | G. G. Macaulay st Walker b Grimmett | 1 |
| E. Oldroyd lbw b Grimmett | 2 | W. Rhodes not out | 6 |
| M. Leyland st Walker b Grimmett | 9 | W. E. Bowes b Grimmett | 0 |
| Mr A. T. Barber st Walker b Grimmett | 1 | B 4, l-b 9, n-b 1 | 14 |
| A. Mitchell b Grimmett | 3 | | |
| E. Robinson c Bradman b Grimmett | 2 | | 155 |

### Australians

| | | | |
|---|---:|---|---:|
| W. M. Woodfull c Barber b Macaulay | 121 | C. V. Grimmett not out | 23 |
| W. H. Ponsford lbw b Robinson | 6 | C. W. Walker c Macaulay b Leyland | 3 |
| D. G. Bradman c and b Macaulay | 78 | T. W. Wall c Robinson b Leyland | 1 |
| A. F. Kippax lbw b Leyland | 3 | P. M. Hornibrook st Wood b Rhodes | 6 |
| S. McCabe c Oldroyd b Robinson | 16 | L-b 4 | 4 |
| V. Y. Richardson c Wood b Rhodes | 45 | | |
| E. L. A'Beckett st Wood b Rhodes | 14 | | 320 |

### Australians Bowling

| | Overs | Mdns | Runs | Wkts |
|---|---:|---:|---:|---:|
| Wall | 16 | 3 | 42 | — |
| A'Beckett | 12 | 6 | 11 | — |
| Hornibrook | 12 | 4 | 49 | — |
| Grimmett | 22.3 | 8 | 37 | 10 |
| McCabe | 3 | 2 | 2 | — |

### Yorkshire Bowling

| | Overs | Mdns | Runs | Wkts |
|---|---:|---:|---:|---:|
| Robinson | 28 | 8 | 60 | 2 |
| Bowes | 26 | 7 | 63 | — |
| Macaulay | 28 | 2 | 80 | 2 |
| Rhodes | 31.5 | 5 | 95 | 3 |
| Leyland | 8 | 3 | 18 | 3 |

Umpires: T. Oates and G. Beet.

## ENGLAND v AUSTRALIA

### Second Test Match

Played at Lord's, June 27, 28, 30, July 1, 1930

Beating England, after a memorable struggle, by seven wickets Australia took an ample revenge for their overthrow a fortnight previously at Trent Bridge. The batting of the Australians and particularly that of Bradman will assuredly live long in the minds of those who saw it but, while giving the visitors the fullest praise for winning so handsomely after having to face a first innings total of 425, it is only proper to observe that to a large extent England played right into the hands of their opponents. Briefly, the Englishmen lost a match, which, with a little discretion on the last day, they could probably have saved. The result of this encounter had a strong bearing on the rubber for, if England had made a draw and the Leeds and Manchester games ended as they did, the final match at the Oval would have been limited to four days. It can with truth be said however, that the England bowling in no other game not only looked but actually was so entirely lacking in sting and effect.

Records went by the board. Australia, in putting together a total of 729 before declaring with only six wickets down, broke four – the highest score by Australia in England, 551 at The Oval in 1884; the highest score by England in this country, 576 at The Oval in 1899; the highest score by Australia, 600 at Melbourne in 1924; and the highest score in the whole series of Test Matches, 636 by England at Sydney in December 1928. Bradman himself, with a score of 254, played the second highest individual innings in the whole series of Test matches between England and Australia, while Duleepsinhji, not only made a hundred on the occasion of his first appearance in a Test match against Australia but scored the highest number of runs ever obtained by an England player in these matches at Lord's. There was one other notable point, A. P. F. Chapman, after leading England to victory six times, captaining the losing side. As some set off against that he enjoyed, for the first time in his career, the distinction of making a hundred in a Test match. In addition to Duleepsinhji, J. C. White and G. O. Allen came into the home team, Sutcliffe – owing to injury – Larwood and Richard Tyldesley standing down.

Chapman again won the toss and England, batting for five hours and fifty minutes, scored on the first day 405 runs for nine wickets. This, seeing that with the score only 13 Hobbs was out and that despite some delightful driving by Woolley and Hammond three wickets were down for 105, was a distinctly fine performance. Duleepsinhji and Hendren obtained the first real mastery over the attack, adding 104 runs in ninety minutes. The batting of these two after lunch was delightful, Duleepsinhji driving with fine power and Hendren scoring by cleverly executed strokes to the on. Chapman and Allen failing, the game took a strong turn in favour of Australia and, while the 200 had gone up with only three wickets down, six men were out for 239. Duleepsinhji, however, found a valuable partner in Tate who hit so hard as to make 54 out of 98 in seventy minutes with eight 4s – chiefly drives – as his most important strokes. Duleepsinhji seemed certain to play out time after he had lost Robins at 363 but at quarter past six, with the score at 387, he was caught at long-off. It seems ungracious to say it, but Duleepsinhji was guilty of a bad error of judgment. He had twice driven Grimmett to the boundary in glorious fashion and in the same over lashed out wildly. Batting for four hours and three-quarters he gave a magnificent display. When the occasion demanded it he exercised restraint and at other times hit beautifully all round the wicket, having twenty-one 4s among his strokes. His innings was not faultless, for at 65 he was missed at short leg by Woodfull from a very simple chance, while at 98 he was let off by Wall at third slip. Had Duleepsinhji been patient and stayed in until the close of play there is no telling what would have been the subsequent course of events.

The next morning another 20 runs were added and then Australia, by skilful and judicious batting, remained in for the rest of the day and scoring 404 for the loss of only two batsmen left off no more than 21 runs behind – a very great performance. Tate bowled with great pluck and determination but, generally, the England attack was indifferent, Allen especially being innocuous and expensive. The Australians batted to a set plan, Woodfull and Ponsford steadily wearing down the bowling for Bradman later on to flog it. Nearly three hours were occupied over the first 162 runs, but in another two hours and three-quarters no fewer than 242 came. While in the end Bradman made most runs very great credit was due to Woodfull and Ponsford who, when England's bowling was fresh, put on 162 for the first wicket. Curiously enough the partnership terminated almost directly after a break in the play while the members of both teams were presented to the King in front of the pavilion, Ponsford, who had batted very soundly, being caught at slip. Woodfull, who was always restrained but who showed rare judgment, stayed in until twenty minutes past six, having withstood the attack for five hours and a half. His defence was remarkable and he scarcely ever lifted the ball but he enjoyed one great stroke of fortune. Just before the King arrived, Woodfull, with his score at 52, playing forward to Robins, dragged his foot over the crease. Duckworth gathered the ball and swept it back to the stumps but omitted to remove the bails. That little error cost England dear. Bradman, who went in when Ponsford was out and the bowling had been mastered, seized his opportunity in rare style and, hitting all round the wicket with power and accuracy, scored in two hours and forty minutes 155 runs and was not out at the close. The Englishmen fielded well and often brilliantly.

On the Monday, Australia kept England in the field for another four hours and a half and added 325 runs for the loss of four more batsmen before declaring their innings closed at the tea interval. The partnership between Bradman and Kippax which did not end until ten minutes to three when Bradman was caught right-hand at extra-mid-off, produced 192 runs in less than three hours. In obtaining his 254, the famous Australian gave nothing approaching a chance. He nearly played on at 111 and, at 191, in trying to turn the ball to leg he edged it deep into the slips but, apart from those trifling errors, no real fault could be found with his display. Like Woodfull, he scarcely ever lifted the ball and, while his defence generally was perfect, he hit very hard in front of the wicket. Altogether he batted five and a half hours, his chief strokes being twenty-five 4s, three 3s, and twenty-six 2s. Kippax, who was in for three hours, left three runs later at 588, but England's troubles were not over, Richardson and McCabe adding 55, and Oldfield and Fairfax 57 in the last forty-five minutes before the closure was put into force. For their huge total Australia batted ten hours and ten minutes.

England thus found themselves requiring 304 runs to escape an innings defeat. At their second attempt they lost Hobbs at 45 and Woolley at 58 but in the last forty minutes Hammond and Duleepsinhji added 40 runs. The score was up to 129 the next morning before Hammond left but when, shortly before twelve o'clock, the fifth wicket fell at 147 England looked like losing in an innings. Indeed, but for an unaccountable misunderstanding between Richardson and Ponsford, this would probably have happened. Chapman, before he had scored, mishit a ball and the two fieldsmen mentioned stood and watched it fall to the ground between them. Eventually settling down, Chapman hit in rare style, being especially severe on Grimmett. Allen, too, batted with marked skill and aggression and 125 runs were added before he was out. It was about this time that, with a little care and thoughtfulness, England might have saved the game for at the luncheon interval, with five men out, they had cleared off all but 42 of the arrears. So far from devoting their energies to defence they continued hitting away, adding another 113 runs in an hour and a quarter afterwards but losing their last five wickets. Chapman, eighth to leave at 354, obtained his runs in just over two hours and a half. Four 6s and twelve 4s were among his strokes. He drove and pulled with tremendous power in a very wonderful display. A foolish call by Robins cost a valuable wicket when White was run out and the innings closed just before half-past three for 375.

Australia thus had to make only 72 to win but in twenty minutes there was much excitement. Ponsford was bowled at 16, Bradman caught low down at backward point at 17, and Kippax taken at the wicket at 22. Visions of a remarkable collapse arose but Woodfull, exercising sound generalship by taking most of Robins' bowling himself, tided over an anxious period and by five o'clock he and McCabe had obtained the remaining runs.

In the course of the four days, 110,000 people watched the cricket, the takings being roughly £14,500.

## England

| | | | |
|---|---|---|---|
| J. B. Hobbs c Oldfield b Fairfax | 1 | – b Grimmett | 19 |
| F. E. Woolley c Wall b Fairfax | 41 | – hit wkt b Grimmett | 28 |
| W. R. Hammond b Grimmett | 38 | – c Fairfax b Grimmett | 32 |
| K. S. Duleepsinhji c Bradman b Grimmett | 173 | – c Oldfield b Hornibrook | 48 |
| E. Hendren c McCabe b Fairfax | 48 | – c Richardson b Grimmett | 9 |
| Mr A. P. F. Chapman c Oldfield b Wall | 11 | – c Oldfield b Fairfax | 121 |
| Mr G. O. Allen b Fairfax | 3 | – lbw b Grimmett | 57 |
| M. W. Tate c McCabe b Wall | 54 | – c Ponsford b Grimmett | 10 |
| Mr R. W. V. Robins c Oldfield b Hornibrook | 5 | – not out | 11 |
| Mr J. C. White not out | 23 | – run out | 10 |
| G. Duckworth c Oldfield b Wall | 18 | – lbw b Fairfax | 0 |
| B 2, l-b 7, n-b 1 | 10 | B 16, l-b 13, w 1 | 30 |
| | **425** | | **375** |

## Australia

| | | | |
|---|---|---|---|
| W. M. Woodfull st Duckworth b Robins | 155 | – not out | 26 |
| W. H. Ponsford c Hammond b White | 81 | – b Robins | 14 |
| D. G. Bradman c Chapman b White | 254 | – c Chapman b Tate | 1 |
| A. F. Kippax b White | 83 | – c Duckworth b Robins | 3 |
| S. McCabe c Woolley b Hammond | 44 | – not out | 25 |
| V. Y. Richardson c Hobbs b Tate | 30 | | |
| W. A. Oldfield not out | 43 | | |
| A. Fairfax not out | 20 | | |
| B 6, l-b 8, w 5 | 19 | B 1, l-b 2 | 3 |
| | **(6 wkts dec.) 729** | | **72** |

C. V. Grimmett, P. M. Hornibrook and T. W. Wall did not bat.

### Australia Bowling

| | Overs | Mdns | Runs | Wkts | Overs | Mdns | Runs | Wkts |
|---|---|---|---|---|---|---|---|---|
| Wall | 29.4 | 2 | 118 | 3 | 25 | 2 | 80 | — |
| Fairfax | 31 | 6 | 101 | 4 | 12.4 | 2 | 37 | 2 |
| Grimmett | 33 | 4 | 105 | 2 | 53 | 13 | 167 | 6 |
| Hornibrook | 26 | 6 | 62 | 1 | 22 | 6 | 49 | 1 |
| McCabe | 9 | 1 | 29 | — | 3 | 1 | 11 | — |
| Bradman | | | | | 1 | — | 1 | — |

### England Bowling

| | Overs | Mdns | Runs | Wkts | Overs | Mdns | Runs | Wkts |
|---|---|---|---|---|---|---|---|---|
| Allen | 34 | 7 | 115 | — | | | | |
| Tate | 64 | 16 | 148 | 1 | 13 | 6 | 21 | 1 |
| White | 51 | 7 | 158 | 3 | 2 | — | 8 | — |
| Robins | 42 | 1 | 172 | 1 | 9 | 1 | 34 | 2 |
| Hammond | 35 | 8 | 82 | 1 | 4.2 | 1 | 6 | — |
| Woolley | 6 | — | 35 | — | | | | |

Umpires: F. Chester and T. Oates.

# ENGLAND v AUSTRALIA

## Third Test Match

### Played at Leeds, July 11, 12, 14, 15, 1930

The third Test match, while it afforded that remarkable young batsman, Bradman, the opportunity of leaving all individual batting records in representative matches far behind, was in many respects an unsatisfactory affair. England had the worst of it from start to finish but escaped with a draw, a heavy storm on Sunday night, followed by further rain on the Monday restricting the third day's play to forty-five minutes while, on the Tuesday, further delay occurred owing to defective light.

The game will go down to history on account of the wonderful batting performance accomplished by Bradman who, with an innings of 334, beat the previous highest – 287 by R. E. Foster for England at Sydney – which had stood since December, 1903. In the course of this, Bradman achieved fame in other directions. Like C. G. Macartney on the same ground four years previously, he reached three-figures before lunch-time on the first day. Not out 309 at the close he had then exceeded a total of a thousand runs in Test cricket and reached an aggregate of exactly 2,000 runs for the season. In playing two consecutive innings of over 200 in Test Matches he equalled the performance of Hammond during the previous tour in Australia. He also equalled Macartney's performance of 1926 in scoring three separate hundreds in successive Test matches. Truly could it be called "Bradman's Match". Bigger though it was and characterised by splendid stroke play, Bradman's innings did not quite approach his 254 at Lord's in freedom from fault but as to its extraordinary merit there could be no two opinions. As usual, he rarely lifted the ball and when making two or more consecutive scoring strokes seldom sent it in the same direction. His footwork was admirable as was the manner in which he played his defensive strokes to balls just short of a length.

Australia, who had played the same eleven in the previous two games, had to make two changes. Suffering from gastritis, Ponsford stood down and Fairfax had not completely recovered from an operation he had had to undergo at Nottingham. Jackson and A'Beckett, therefore, played in their first Test match in England.

England also had alterations. Woolley, Hendren, Allen, Robins and White were all dropped, Sutcliffe, Larwood and Richard Tyldesley coming back and Leyland and Geary being included. As events proved, some of these changes might just as well have not been made. For one thing, the English fielding compared most unfavourably with that in the earlier matches. Tyldesley, avowedly brought in with the idea of keeping the Australian batsmen quiet, again failed in his mission. Geary's bowling had no terrors at all while Larwood, still looking very drawn as the result of his illness, had not the stamina to bowl at his full pace and was terribly expensive. Tate, as usual, bore the brunt of the attack and bowled as pluckily as ever but, taken all round, the Englishmen lacked the attributes of a great side and Hammond alone made over fifty runs.

This time, Woodful won the toss and Australia led off so brilliantly that, when the first day's play ended, they had 458 runs on the board with only three wickets down. The pitch, like those at Nottingham and Lord's, was, on the first day at any rate, lacking in life and pace and all in favour of batsmen. Opening the innings with Woodfull, Jackson off the fifth ball of the second over was caught at forward short leg but England had to wait until five minutes past three before they took another wicket, Woodfull and Bradman, in the meantime, putting on 192 runs in two hours and thirty-five minutes. This was very largely the work of Bradman who, quick to settle down, completed 102 out of the first 127 in ninety-five minutes. All the same, Woodfull, by another great display of defensive cricket, rendered his side invaluable assistance. After Woodfull left, bowled in trying to hook a shortish ball, Bradman found another admirable partner in Kippax who, if overshadowed by his colleague, played uncommonly well in helping to add 229 in rather less than two and three-quarter hours. The next day McCabe, who had batted twenty minutes overnight, stayed until 63 runs had been put on but nothing of any consequence was accomplished by the rest, the last seven wickets falling in a hundred minutes for 108 runs. Bradman, sixth out at 508, obtained his 334 in six hours and a quarter, his score being made up of    ty-six 4s, six 3s, twenty-six 2s, and eighty singles. When he had made 141 he put up a ball towards mid wicket and at 202 he skied a ball over Tate's head at mid-on. Indeed, a man a little quicker on his feet than Tate might have made a catch of it. Actually, Bradman gave only one chance, being missed at the wicket off Geary at 273 when the total was 385. He hit very hard in front of the wicket, scored splendidly on the leg side and very often cut in dazzling fashion. Nobody could have had a better reception than that accorded to Bradman on his return to the pavilion.

Before lunch Hobbs and Sutcliffe scored 17 runs for England but the total was only 53 when Hobbs was out in a manner which provoked considerable discussion. A'Beckett, fielding very close in on the on-side to Grimmett's bowling, took the ball from a gentle stroke very low down, turning a complete somersault but retaining possession. Hobbs was about to walk away but stepped back into his crease on overhearing a remark by Oldfield and an appeal from other members of the side. An appeal having been made, Hobbs was perfectly justified in waiting for the decision. Oates, the umpire at the bowler's end, was unable to give one. A'Beckett in falling over obscuring his view, so he referred to Bestwick standing at square leg. Unhappily, Bestwick hesitated before holding up his finger, and the great majority of the crowd took the view that A'Beckett had not properly made the catch.

Soon afterwards Sutcliffe was out but Hammond and Duleepsinhji added 59 and then Leyland helped to put on 83, Hammond, when 52, having just previously been missed by Oldfield standing back to Wall. Geary was run out at 206 and England at the close of play, with five wickets down for 212, found themselves 354 behind and requiring 205 to save the follow-on. On the Monday the weather following a storm in the night, which resulted in water lying in patches on the ground, was very bad. So long a delay occurred that not until half past five was play proceeded with. From the manner in which the pitch rolled out it was quite obvious that cricket would have been possible at least an hour earlier. 30 runs were scored before an appeal against the light at a quarter past six was upheld.

On Tuesday morning Duckworth, who had gone in for ten minutes on Saturday evening, batted so well that the score was up to 289 before he was caught at the wicket, 83 runs having been added in rather more than two hours. Hammond stayed until the score was 319, after resisting the bowling for five hours and twenty minutes. He hit only fourteen 4s but gave a splendid display of skilful batting, neglecting very few opportunities of scoring off anything in the nature of a punishable ball. Chapman, hitting hard, put on 51 runs with Tate but England were all out at a quarter to three for 391, their innings lasting nearly eight hours. The last three wickets fell in half an hour for 36 runs.

England followed on 179 behind and, as over three hours remained for cricket, there was always a possibility of them losing. Hobbs and Sutcliffe opened the innings in a very poor light. After a quarter of an hour, they appealed against it and the players went in. For some extraordinary reason the crowd took this in very bad part, booing the batsmen and cheering the Australians, while on the game being resumed there was a continuance of this unseemly behaviour. With 24 scored, Hobbs was brilliantly thrown out by Bradman from deep mid-off but Sutcliffe and Hammond stayed nearly an hour to add 50. After Duleepsinhji had been caught at point off a ball which he afterwards confessed he did not see, another appeal against the light was made at ten minutes to six and no further cricket took place.

The total attendance reached 77,500, and the gate receipts £8,597.

## Australia

| | | | |
|---|---:|---|---:|
| W. M. Woodfull b Hammond | 50 | W. A. Oldfield c Hobbs b Tate | 2 |
| A. Jackson c Larwood b Tate | 1 | C. V. Grimmett c Duckworth b Tyldesley | 24 |
| D. G. Bradman c Duckworth b Tate | 334 | T. W. Wall b Tyldesley | 3 |
| A. F. Kippax c Chapman b Tate | 77 | P. M. Hornibrook not out | 1 |
| S. McCabe b Larwood | 30 | B 5, l-b 8, w 1 | 14 |
| V. Y. Richardson c Larwood b Tate | 1 | | |
| E. L. A'Beckett c Chapman b Geary | 29 | | 566 |

## England

J. B. Hobbs c A'Beckett b Grimmett . . . . . . . . . . . . . 29 – run out . . . . . . . . . . . . . . . . . . . . . . . 13
H. Sutcliffe c Hornibrook b Grimmett . . . . . . . . . . . 32 – not out . . . . . . . . . . . . . . . . . . . . . . . 28
W. R. Hammond c Oldfield b McCabe . . . . . . . . . . .113 – c Oldfield b Grimmett . . . . . . . . . . . 35
K. S. Duleepsinhji b Hornibrook . . . . . . . . . . . . . . . . 35 – c Grimmett b Hornibrook . . . . . . . . 10
M. Leyland c Kippax b Wall . . . . . . . . . . . . . . . . . . . 44 – not out . . . . . . . . . . . . . . . . . . . . . 1
G. Geary run out . . . . . . . . . . . . . . . . . . . . . . . . . . . 0
G. Duckworth c Oldfield b A'Beckett . . . . . . . . . . . 33
Mr A. P. F. Chapman b Grimmett . . . . . . . . . . . . . . 45
M. W. Tate c Jackson b Grimmett . . . . . . . . . . . . . . 22
H. Larwood not out . . . . . . . . . . . . . . . . . . . . . . . . 10
R. Tyldesley c Hornibrook b Grimmett . . . . . . . . . . 6
         B 9, l-b 10, n-b 3 . . . . . . . . . . . . . . . . . . . 22          L-b 8 . . . . . . . . . . . . . . . . . 8

                                    391                      95

## England Bowling

|  | Overs | Mdns | Runs | Wkts |
|---|---|---|---|---|
| Larwood | 33 | 3 | 139 | 1 |
| Tate | 39 | 9 | 124 | 5 |
| Geary | 35 | 10 | 95 | 1 |
| Tyldesley | 33 | 5 | 104 | 2 |
| Hammond | 17 | 3 | 46 | 1 |
| Leyland | 11 | — | 44 | — |

## Australia Bowling

|  | Overs | Mdns | Runs | Wkts | Overs | Mdns | Runs | Wkts |
|---|---|---|---|---|---|---|---|---|
| Wall | 40 | 12 | 70 | 1 | 10 | 3 | 20 | — |
| A'Beckett | 28 | 8 | 47 | 1 | 11 | 4 | 19 | — |
| Grimmett | 56.2 | 16 | 135 | 5 | 17 | 3 | 33 | 1 |
| Hornibrook | 41 | 7 | 94 | 1 | 11.5 | 5 | 14 | 1 |
| McCabe | 10 | 4 | 23 | 1 | 2 | 1 | 1 | — |

Umpires: W. Bestwick and T. Oates.

## GLOUCESTERSHIRE v AUSTRALIANS

Played at Bristol, August 23, 25, 26, 1930

There was a memorable finish to this match, the Australians, who had been set 118 to make a win, being all dismissed for 117 and the contest thus ending in a tie. Never before in England had a first-class match, in which an Australian team figured, terminated in this way. For a long time after the Australians entered upon their second innings the contest held out no promise of excitement. Indeed, of the 118 runs needed for victory no fewer than 59 – exactly half the number – were put on by Jackson and McCabe for the opening partnership. The pitch was obviously in a condition to assist the bowlers but to begin with Parker proved so erratic that the score reached 50 in forty minutes. Gradually, however,

Parker found not only his length but a worn spot and thenceforward he was deadly in the extreme. Before he sent back McCabe at 59, he twice beat that batsman completely. Goddard, after two unsuccessful appeals for leg before, disposed of Jackson in that manner and, with Richardson stumped, there were three men out for 67 at the luncheon interval.

Despite the fall of these three wickets in such quick succession, the chances of Gloucestershire still appeared remote but on play being resumed the game took a most dramatic turn. Six runs were added and then, with the total at 73, not only did Parker get Kippax leg before but Sinfield, picking up smartly and getting in a splendid return, threw out Ponsford from mid-on. Bradman still remained but neither he nor à Beckett, against skilful bowling and most brilliant fielding, could get the ball away. Roused to tremendous excitement, the spectators cheered everything and their enthusiasm knew no bounds when at 81 Parker bowled Bradman. They had still further occasion for joy 5 runs later when a catch in the slips disposed of A'Beckett. By this time the Australians found themselves in a truly awkward plight for, with their seven leading batsmen out, they still required 32 more runs. For the moment, indeed, everything pointed to the probability of a win for the county.

Unhappily for the home side, there came just afterwards a blemish on what up to that point had been a superb display of fielding, Lyon, when Grimmett had made 7, getting his hand to a ball put up by that batsman but failing to effect the catch. As matters turned out, this mistake no doubt robbed Gloucestershire of victory, for Grimmett and Hurwood offered such a determined resistance to Parker and Goddard that they added 22 for the eighth wicket before Hurwood was leg before. Thus only 10 runs were wanted when Hornibrook joined Grimmett. The newcomer surviving two appeals for lbw, the score had been advanced to 115 – 3 to win – when Parker dismissed Grimmett who had withstood the attack for an hour. Walker followed in and two singles brought the total to 117. With the scores level, there came three maidens in succession and then on a further appeal against Hornibrook being answered in the bowler's favour, the Australians were all out and the match had ended in a tie. In bringing about this remarkable finish, Parker, taking seven wickets for 54, had the big share but Goddard bowled much better than his figures would suggest.

Following upon their triumph over England at The Oval on the day before the match with Gloucestershire, the Australians asked that the start of their game against the western county might be delayed until two o'clock. As matters turned out, the ground had been so saturated that, despite a drying wind and some sunshine, nothing could be done for two hours after that time. Richardson, winning the toss, decided to send Gloucestershire in to bat and such pronounced success attended that course that the home side were all out in two hours and a quarter for 72. Hornibrook, making the ball turn in bewildering fashion, took four wickets for 5 runs apiece and Grimmett and Hurwood also met with little resistance. Hammond kept up his end for an hour and Seabrook stayed for forty minutes but no one else escaped failure.

On Monday the pitch, while still on the soft side, was, in the absence of sunshine, too slow to be really difficult. Ponsford, second out at 78, batted in attractive fashion for an hour and a half but Bradman, although staying for an hour and three-quarters, never mastered the attack. Subsequent to lunch seven wickets fell for 64 runs. Goddard, after the score had been raised to 129, disposed of Richardson, A'Beckett and Hurwood in five balls. Altogether he obtained five wickets for just over 10 runs apiece.

No more than 85 runs in arrear, Gloucestershire, at their second attempt played up so well that at the drawing of stumps they had scored 147 for the loss of three batsmen and so left off 62 ahead with seven wickets in hand. This was mainly the work of Hammond who, batting in splendid form, completed his 50 in less than an hour. Hammond received such excellent support from Dipper that the second wicket yielded 80 runs in sixty-five minutes.

Next morning Hammond and Smith brought the score to 166 before the former lost his wicket. Altogether Hammond gave a splendid display, batting in faultless fashion for two hours and having a 6 and thirteen 4s among his strokes. After he left, Hornibrook bowled to such purpose that the last six wickets fell for 36 runs. Disposing of four batsmen on Tuesday for 17 runs, Hornibrook brought his record for the match to nine wickets for 69. Following upon the close of Gloucestershire's innings for 202, came the desperately exciting and unsuccessful endeavour of the Australians to hit off the 118 runs required for victory.

## Gloucestershire

| | | | |
|---|---|---|---|
| R. A. Sinfield c Walker b Hurwood | 1 | – c A'Beckett b Hornibrook | 16 |
| A. E. Dipper c Richardson b Hurwood | 1 | – c A'Beckett b McCabe | 26 |
| W. R. Hammond c A'Beckett b Hornibrook | 17 | – bHornibrook | 89 |
| Mr B. H. Lyon b Hurwood | 5 | – b McCabe | 8 |
| H. Smith c Richardson b Hornibrook | 16 | – b Hornibrook | 23 |
| C. C. Dacre c A'Beckett b Grimmett | 4 | – c McCabe b Grimmett | 17 |
| Mr F. J. Seabrook c and b Grimmett | 19 | – lbw b Hornibrook | 2 |
| W. L. Neale c Walker b Hornibrook | 2 | – b Hornibrook | 0 |
| C. J. Barnett b Grimmett | 2 | – c Walker b Grimmett | 6 |
| C. Parker not out | 0 | – not out | 3 |
| T. W. Goddard c Kippax b Hornibrook | 3 | – run out | 0 |
| L-b 2 | 2 | B 6, l-b 6 | 12 |
| | **72** | | **202** |

## Australia

| | | | |
|---|---|---|---|
| W. H. Ponsford b Sinfield | 51 | – run out | 0 |
| A. Jackson b Goddard | 8 | – lbw b Goddard | 25 |
| D. G. Bradman c Sinfield b Parker | 42 | – b Parker | 14 |
| A. F. Kippax lbw b Sinfield | 3 | – lbw b Parker | 0 |
| S. McCabe c Smith b Parker | 5 | – b Parker | 34 |
| V. Y. Richardson lbw b Goddard | 12 | – st Smith b Parker | 3 |
| E. L. A'Beckett c Sinfield b Goddard | 1 | – c Lyon b Parker | 2 |
| A. Hurwood b Goddard | 0 | – lbw b Parker | 14 |
| C. V. Grimmett not out | 7 | – c Seabrook b Parker | 12 |
| P. M. Hornibrook b Goddard | 9 | – lbw b Goddard | 4 |
| C. W. Walker c Seabrook b Parker | 7 | – not out | 0 |
| B 5, l-b 7 | 12 | B 2, l-b 7 | 9 |
| | **157** | | **117** |

## Australia Bowling

| | Overs | Mdns | Runs | Wkts | Overs | Mdns | Runs | Wkts |
|---|---|---|---|---|---|---|---|---|
| A'Beckett | 8 | 4 | 9 | — | 9 | 4 | 16 | — |
| Hurwood | 11 | 5 | 13 | 3 | 11 | 4 | 29 | — |
| Grimmett | 19 | 3 | 28 | 3 | 28.2 | 4 | 83 | 2 |
| Hornibrook | 14.3 | 6 | 20 | 4 | 25 | 5 | 49 | 5 |
| McCabe | | | | | 10 | 3 | 13 | 2 |

## Gloucestershire Bowling

| | Overs | Mdns | Runs | Wkts | Overs | Mdns | Runs | Wkts |
|---|---|---|---|---|---|---|---|---|
| Sinfield | 14 | 5 | 18 | 2 | | | | |
| Barnett | 4 | 3 | 3 | — | | | | |
| Goddard | 26 | 7 | 52 | 5 | 34.1 | 10 | 54 | 2 |
| Parker | 30.5 | 9 | 72 | 3 | 35 | 14 | 54 | 7 |

Umpires: W. A. Buswell and W. Huddleston.

# ENGLAND v AUSTRALIA

## Second Test Match

Played at Lord's, June 22, 23, 25, 1934

For their defeat at Trent Bridge, England took an ample revenge at Lord's, winning the match in three days in an innings with 38 runs to spare. This was England's first success in a Test match against Australia at Lord's since 1896 when Lohmann and Tom Richardson in a memorable struggle swept the Australians off their feet. While everyone in England naturally was jubilant over the triumph of the Englishmen it could not be denied that they were helped in a pronounced degree by the weather.

Winning the toss England stayed in until nearly three o'clock on the Saturday and put together a total of 440, but before the end of the day Australia had 192 runs on the board with only two men out. In view of this splendid start by the visitors there existed no sound reason why they should not have closely approached if not even passed the England total, but the suffered the cruellest luck, rain falling during the week-end and rendering their chances almost hopeless. Fortunately England had in the team a bowler capable of taking full advantage of the conditions that prevailed, and Verity, obtaining seven wickets in the first innings for 61 runs, followed this up with eight in the second for 43, to be the chief factor in giving England such a pronounced success. With his full record for the match, fifteen wickets for 104 runs, he excelled Rhodes's performance at Melbourne in 1904 when that even more famous left-hander, took fifteen wickets for 124 runs. By a singular coincidence Rhodes was present at Lord's to see his brother Yorkshireman accomplish his wonderful performance. Verity had taken one of the Australian wickets which fell on Saturday, and on the Monday he dismissed fourteen men for 80 runs, six of them after tea at a cost of 15. This amazing achievement would probably have been only possible to a man possessed of such length and finger-spin as Verity, because although the wicket certainly helped him considerably it could scarcely be described as genuinely "sticky" except for one period after lunch. Verity's length was impeccable and he made the ball come back and lift so abruptly that most of the Australians were helpless. The majority of them had had no experience in England of such a pitch, and they showed no ability or skill in dealing with bowling like that of Verity under these conditions. Those who tried to play forward did not get far enough, and their efforts at playing back were, to say the least, immature.

Dealing with the earlier part of the match, Walters and Sutcliffe made 70 together for the opening England wicket in just under an hour and three-quarters, but then came that series of dreadful failures which at this point of the proceedings characterised England's batting throughout the series. Hammond was out at 78 Hendren at 99, and Walters, after playing admirably for two hours and fifty minutes, at 130. In the course of his display, he showed marked skill in driving both Grimmett and O'Reilly, and altogether batted extremely well. When Walters left, Leyland went in and began what was to be a very fine exhibition. He and Wyatt put on 52 to effect a partial recovery which was consolidated by Leyland and Ames. By the time stumps were drawn these two had raised the score to 293, and next morning they carried it to 311, their partnership realising 129 runs in two and a half hours. Leyland, who batted three hours and a half, drove superbly in his great innings of 109, hitting a six and fourteen 4s. In the end he was bowled by what is known in Yorkshire as a "long half-volley", hitting a little too late and over the ball. Ames and Geary next added 48, Ames, missed by Oldfield standing back at 96, being eighth out at 409. He hit fourteen 4s during his stay of four hours and twenty minutes, powerful driving being the outstanding feature of an inspiring display. Verity helped him to add 50 and the last wicket produced 30 runs. Neither Grimmett nor O'Reilly looked nearly as difficult as they had at Nottingham, but except when Leyland and Ames were in they bowled well.

Woodfull, who took Brown in first with him, score 22 out of the first 68, and then Bradman, with seven 4s, hit up 36 of the next 73, but actually he never looked like staying very long, making many of his strokes without restraint. The England bowlers met with no further success that day, Brown and McCabe adding 51 and carrying the score to 192. McCabe brought off some wonderful hooks, while Brown with admirable drives and cuts completed 100 out of 184 in two hours and three-quarters. On the Monday, the light was very bad, an appeal being made against it directly the batsmen reached the wickets, but soon after the game had been resumed Brown was out at 203. He and McCabe added 62 in about an hour. Brown batted in first-rate style for three hours and twenty minutes and in his century on the occasion of his first appearance in a Test match at Lord's he hit fourteen 4s. He drove beautifully and placed the ball cleverly on the on side. His dismissal was the beginning of the end. Darling left at 204, McCabe one hour later, and Bromley at 218. Then soon afterwards came a short break while the players on both sides were presented to His Majesty the King. Chipperfield and Oldfield put on 40, but by half-past two Australia were all out for 284, the last eight wickets having gone down in two hours and twenty minutes for 92 runs. Verity took six of them for 37.

The follow-on not having been saved – Australia finishing 156 behind – the visitors had to go in again, and with only 10 on the board Brown was out to a fine catch at long leg, the ball travelling down wind at terrific speed. Verity, coming on at 17, quickly got to work again, dismissing McCabe and Bradman at 43 and 57, while after tea Woodfull, who had defended stubbornly for two hours, was fourth to leave at 94. The rest of the innings was a mere procession, for by this time the wicket had become even more difficult. There seemed a chance of Verity doing the hat-trick when he dismissed Oldfield and Grimmett with consecutive balls but he was denied this distinction. Still he took the last six wickets, and at ten minutes to six the match was all over, seven men having left in an hour for 44 runs. He was supported by brilliant fielding close to the wicket.

Ponsford being ill, Bromley came into the Australian team in his place, while England had Wyatt and Bowes for Pataudi and Mitchell. Farnes, however, was nothing like the success he had been at Nottingham, an injury to his heel preventing him from bowling in anything like his usual form. Hammond, too, was not in his best health, his back all through the match being very painful.

## England

| | |
|---|---|
| Mr C. F. Walters c Bromley b O'Reilly .... 82 | H. Verity st Oldfield b Grimmett ......... 29 |
| H. Sutcliffe lbw b Chipperfield ........... 20 | Mr K. Farnes b Wall .................. 1 |
| W. R. Hammond c and b Chipperfield ..... 2 | W. E. Bowes not out .................. 10 |
| E. Hendren c McCabe b Wall .......... 13 | |
| Mr R. E. S. Wyatt c Oldfield b Chipperfield . 33 | L-b 12 .................. 12 |
| M. Leyland b Wall ...................109 | |
| L. E. G. Ames c Oldfield b McCabe .....120 | 1/70 2/78 3/99 4/130 5/182     440 |
| G. Geary c Chipperfield b Wall .......... 9 | 6/311 7/359 8/409 9/410 |

## Australia

| | | |
|---|---|---|
| W. M. Woodfull b Bowes ..................... 22 | – c Hammond b Verity ............ 43 |
| W. A. Brown c Ames b Bowes ..................105 | – c Walters b Bowes ............. 2 |
| D. G. Bradman c and b Verity ................. 36 | – c Ames b Verity .............. 13 |
| S. J. McCabe c Hammond b Verity ............. 34 | – c Hendren b Verity ............ 19 |
| L. S. Darling c Sutcliffe b Verity ............. 0 | – b Hammond ................. 10 |
| A. G. Chipperfield not out .................... 37 | – c Geary b Verity .............. 14 |
| E. H. Bromley c Geary b Verity ................ 4 | – c and b Verity ............... 1 |
| W. A. Oldfield c Sutcliffe b Verity ............. 23 | – lbw b Verity ................ 0 |
| C. V. Grimmett b Bowes ...................... 9 | – c Hammond b Verity ........... 0 |
| W. J. O'Reilly b Verity ....................... 4 | – not out ................... 8 |
| T. W. Wall lbw b Verity ...................... 0 | – c Hendren b Verity ............ 1 |
| B 1, l-b 9 ......................... 10 | B 6, n-b 1 .............. 7 |

1/68 2/141 3/203 4/204 5/205 6/218     284     1/10 2/43 3/57 4/94 5/94 6/95     118
7/258 8/273 9/284                                     7/95 8/95 9/112

**Australia Bowling**

| | Overs | Mdns | Runs | Wkts |
|---|---|---|---|---|
| Wall .............. | 49 | 7 | 108 | 4 |
| McCabe .......... | 18 | 3 | 38 | 1 |
| Grimmett ......... | 53.3 | 13 | 102 | 1 |
| O'Reilly .......... | 38 | 15 | 70 | 1 |
| Chipperfield ....... | 34 | 10 | 91 | 3 |
| Darling .......... | 6 | 2 | 19 | — |

**England Bowling**

| | Overs | Mdns | Runs | Wkts | Overs | Mdns | Runs | Wkts |
|---|---|---|---|---|---|---|---|---|
| Farnes ........... | 12 | 3 | 43 | — | 4 | 2 | 6 | — |
| Bowes ........... | 31 | 5 | 98 | 3 | 14 | 4 | 24 | 1 |
| Geary ............ | 22 | 4 | 56 | — | | | | |
| Verity ............ | 36 | 15 | 61 | 7 | 22.3 | 8 | 43 | 8 |
| Hammond ........ | 4 | 1 | 6 | — | 13 | — | 38 | 1 |
| Leyland .......... | 4 | 1 | 10 | — | | | | |

Umpires: F. Chester and J. Hardstaff.

# ENGLAND v AUSTRALIA

## Fourth Test Match

Played at Leeds, July 20, 21, 23, 24, 1934

Just as at Lord's rain came to damage the wicket and ruin Australia's chance of making an even fight of it, so in the fourth Test match on the Headingly ground at Leeds did one of the shortest but heaviest rainstorms seen at a cricket match for years arrive just in time to rob Australia of victory and enable England to draw a game in which they were completely outplayed. Escaping defeat in the luckiest manner possible, the England team accomplished nothing in the match on which they could congratulate themselves. In their unavailing efforts to get together a side which "balanced" the selectors made further changes from those who had represented England at Manchester. A strained leg compelled Sutcliffe to stand down, Keeton of Nottinghamshire thus getting the opportunity of making his first appearance for his country; G. O. Allen and Clark were left out and Bowes and Mitchell of Derbyshire reintroduced. James Langridge and Nichols attended and it was decided not to include Langridge and to make Nichols – for the third time – twelfth man.

His good fortune in the matter of winning the toss again attended Wyatt and for the third consecutive game England enjoyed the advantage of batting first. Wyatt himself described the wicket as being "like a feather-bed", whatever that may have meant. The assumption at the time was that it would be slow and easy. There was nothing in the way it played during the first day to suggest that it was otherwise, yet England, giving one of the worst displays of batting probably ever seen under similar conditions were all dismissed between twenty-five minutes to twelve and twenty-five minutes past five for a paltry total of 200. It can be said that O'Reilly, Grimmett and Chipperfield bowled very well, but nothing they accomplished with the ball was quite sufficient to account for the shocking exhibition of weak and hesitant batting given by the Englishmen. Even Walters, who with 44 made top score, did not, after Wall had been taken off at 30, show anything of the brilliance that characterised many of his strokes at Lord's and Manchester. Keeton made two good cuts and a square drive in scoring 25 out of 43 in fifty minutes and although, after Walters' dismissal at 85, Hammond and Hendren put on 50 in an hour none of the rest, equally with those who had gone before, played in form worthy of the occasion.

Before cricket ended, however, further surprises were in store for the crowd. Bowes and Hammond started the bowling for England and both Ponsford and Brown played them so easily that there seemed no reason to expect any pronounced success for the England attack up to half-past six. Bowes, however, changed ends and, coming on again at 37 from the pavilion wicket, bowled Brown at 37 and two runs later sent back Oldfield and Woodfull in one over. Stumps were then pulled up, Bowes having sent down ten balls from the pavilion end and dismissed three batsmen without conceding a run. Australia, therefore, finished the day 161 runs behind with seven men to be disposed of and the situation had thus completely changed. Those, however, were the last crumbs of comfort England were destined to enjoy in this disastrous match. Bradman joined Ponsford the next morning and not until ten minutes to six on Saturday evening did another wicket fall. Giving a great display of batting, the two famous Australian run-getters beat all previous partnership records in Test matches. They carried the score in five and a half hours to 427 before Ponsford, hooking a short ball from Verity, trod on his wicket, knocked the leg bail off and was out. Altogether their stand realised no fewer than 388 runs. They always scored at a good rate but, as usual with Australians, unless the bowling is exceptionally steady, pushed along very quickly after tea when, in an hour, 98 runs were put on. Up to lunch time they scored 129 in two hours and twenty-five minutes and between lunch and tea 161 in two hours and five minutes.

Ponsford's innings was very good indeed. In the course of the partnership each batsman gave a chance, for Ponsford when 70 should have been caught by Mitchell at cover-point while Bradman at 71 was let off by Hopwood. Ponsford obtained many of his runs by late cuts and turning the ball to leg and all through his innings, which lasted six and a quarter hours and included nineteen 4s, he hit the ball hard and placed it well when scoring in front of the wicket. Moreover, his defence was rocklike in its steadiness and accuracy. For the greater part of the day Bradman, who unlike Ponsford obtained most of his runs in front of the stumps batted with the utmost certainty but during the last thirty-five minutes when he and McCabe were raising the score to 494 he played in a more light-hearted spirit. Twice he lifted the ball over the ring for six, and hit Hopwood for 15 runs in one over.

Australia, therefore, began the third day in a most comfortable position being 294 runs on with six wickets to fall and altogether Bradman and McCabe added 90 in an hour before McCabe was out. Thanks to some most effective bowling by Bowes Australia's innings was finished off in a hundred minutes, the last six wickets falling on Monday morning for 90 runs. Bradman, sixth out at 550, made his 304 in six hours and fifty-five minutes. Going in third wicket down, he took the leading part in adding 511 runs while as many more wickets fell. Not out on Saturday with 271 he was perhaps lucky in reaching 300 because when 280 he was missed at third slip by Verity. He did not play so well during the fifty minutes he was in on Monday morning as he had done previously but all the same his innings was a masterly affair. He hit the ball very hard and placed his strokes beautifully while until joined by McCabe on Saturday evening he rarely sent the ball into the air. He hit two 6s, forty-three 4s, one 3, fifteen 2s and eighty-seven singles.

Bowes was responsible for the Australian innings being wound up so quickly and in the end he came out with what was a really good record of six wickets for 142 runs. Yet on the Saturday when Ponsford and Bradman were scoring so readily Bowes, like the rest of the England bowlers, looked quite innocuous. His analysis was interesting enough to bear dissection. After going on at 37 on Friday, he took three wickets for no runs. On Saturday he bowled over twenty-eight overs, did not take a wicket and had 81 runs hit from him while up to the time he dismissed Darling at 551 he took three wickets on Monday morning in nine overs and four balls for 25 runs. Verity was the only other man to get a wicket but his three cost him 113.

England went in again at one o'clock 384 runs behind so that the most they could hope for was a draw. Keeton fell just before lunch at 28 and afterwards Hammond played better than in any other Test match during the season. He was seeing the ball well, hitting it hard and accurately and seemed likely to put together an innings in his best style. With the total up to 70, however, a dreadful disaster occurred, for Hammond, responding to the call of Walters for a foolish run and then checking himself, lost his wicket. From that blow England did not recover. Walters left at 87 but by dint of very hard work and much watchful batting Hendren and Wyatt added 65 in rather less than two hours. During this stand Bradman, trying to stop the ball in the long field with his foot, strained his leg and had to retire. Hendren and Leyland, both entirely on the defensive, stayed together for the last fifty-five minutes and added 36, Hendren having been in for three hours and a quarter when stumps were pulled up. Coupled with the rain which fell on Tuesday this stand saved England but they began the last day with only 188 on the board and still wanting 196 to save the innings defeat. Heavy rain fell in the night and the wicket was very wet, while a further shower caused a delay soon after cricket had been resumed. Then Hendren was out at 190 and when Ames left at 213 the end seemed very near. Just before one o'clock a thunderstorm broke over the ground and, although it lasted only ten minutes, the downpour was so severe that no further cricket was possible. Not until six o'clock, however, was the decision to abandon the match arrived at. Not only the pitch but parts of the outfield and especially that in front of the pavilion was, even then, far too wet for cricket to be proceeded with.

## England

| | | | |
|---|---|---|---|
| Mr C. F. Walters c and b Chipperfield | 44 | – b O'Reilly | 45 |
| W. W. Keeton c Oldfield b O'Reilly | 25 | – b Grimmett | 12 |
| W. R. Hammond b Wall | 37 | – run out | 20 |
| E. Hendren b Chipperfield | 29 | – lbw b O'Reilly | 42 |
| Mr R. E. S. Wyatt st Oldfield b Grimmett | 19 | – b Grimmett | 44 |
| M. Leyland lbw b O'Reilly | 16 | – not out | 49 |
| L. E. G. Ames c Oldfield b Grimmett | 9 | – c Brown b Grimmett | 8 |
| J. L. Hopwood lbw b O'Reilly | 8 | – not out | 2 |
| H. Verity not out | 2 | | |
| T. B. Mitchell st Oldfield b Grimmett | 9 | | |
| W. E. Bowes c Ponsford b Grimmett | 0 | | |
| L-b 2 | 2 | B 1, l-b 6 | 7 |
| | **200** | | **229** |

1/43 2/85 3/135 4/135 5/168 6/170
7/189 8/189 9/200

1/28 2/70 3/87 4/152
5/190 6/213

## Australia

| | | | |
|---|---|---|---|
| W. A. Brown b Bowes | 15 | C. V. Grimmett run out | 15 |
| W. H. Ponsford hit wkt b Verity | 181 | W. J. O'Reilly not out | 11 |
| W. A. Oldfield c Ames b Bowes | 0 | T. W. Wall lbw b Verity | 1 |
| W. M. Woodfull b Bowes | 0 | | |
| D. G. Bradman b Bowes | 304 | B 8, l-b 9 | 17 |
| S. J. McCabe b Bowes | 27 | | |
| L. S. Darling b Bowes | 12 | | **584** |
| A. G. Chipperfield c Wyatt b Verity | 1 | | |

1/37 2/39 3/39 4/427 5/517
6/550 7/551 8/557 9/574

## Australia Bowling

| | Overs | Mdns | Runs | Wkts | Overs | Mdns | Runs | Wkts |
|---|---|---|---|---|---|---|---|---|
| Wall | 18 | 1 | 57 | 1 | 14 | 5 | 36 | — |
| McCabe | 4 | 2 | 3 | — | 5 | 4 | 5 | — |
| Grimmett | 30.4 | 11 | 57 | 4 | 56.5 | 24 | 72 | 3 |
| O'Reilly | 35 | 16 | 46 | 3 | 51 | 25 | 88 | 2 |
| Chipperfield | 18 | 6 | 35 | 2 | 9 | 2 | 21 | — |

## England Bowling

| | Overs | Mdns | Runs | Wkts |
|---|---|---|---|---|
| Bowes | 59 | 13 | 142 | 6 |
| Hammond | 29 | 5 | 82 | — |
| Mitchell | 23 | 1 | 117 | — |
| Verity | 46.5 | 15 | 113 | 3 |
| Hopwood | 30 | 7 | 93 | — |
| Leyland | 5 | — | 20 | — |

Umpires: J. Hardstaff and A. Dolphin.

# NOTTINGHAMSHIRE v AUSTRALIANS

Played at Nottingham, August 11, 13, 14, 1934

A match rendered unpleasant by the antagonistic attitude of the spectators towards the visitors ended in a draw. The Australians, encountering "direct attack" bowling for the first time during the tour, fared none too well. Woodfull and Brown began with a stand of 70, but afterwards only Woodfull and Chipperfield gave much trouble. During Voce's various spells of bowling, the Australian batsmen were obviously uncomfortable with short-pitched deliveries, and found themselves subjected to considerable barracking. Voce placed five men on the leg side, four of them close to the batsman, and of his eight victims, five fell to catches in this "leg trap". Although Wall, suffering from leg strain, retired from the game early in Nottinghamshire's innings, the county batted indifferently, the tourists gaining a lead of 54. The absence of Voce – stated to be suffering from sore shins – on Tuesday began a series of rumours, the crowd apparently attributing his withdrawal from the match to an Australian protest. Consequently, the atmosphere grew increasingly hostile, and when the Australians took the field for the last innings, they were greeted by a storm of booing. A fine partnership of 164 between Brown and Kippax enabled the tourists to declare, and Nottinghamshire, set 285 to get, never looked like succeeding.

## Australians

| | | |
|---|---:|---:|
| W. M. Woodfull c Harris b Voce | 81 – b Butler | 1 |
| W. A. Brown c Gunn b Voce | 27 – not out | 100 |
| S. J. McCabe c Harris b Voce | 10 – b Butler | 43 |
| A. F. Kippax c Hardstaff b Voce | 7 – not out | 75 |
| L. S. Darling c Lilley b Voce | 11 | |
| A. G. Chipperfield c Harris b Voce | 57 | |
| E. H. Bromley b Butler | 13 | |
| B. A. Barnett c Lilley b Voce | 1 | |
| C. V. Grimmett c Hardstaff b Butler | 0 | |
| T. W. Wall c and b Voce | 13 | |
| L. O'B. Fleetwood-Smith not out | 7 | |
| B 6, l-b 3, n-b 1 | 10 | B 5, w 2, n-b 4 ........... 11 |
| | **237** | **(2 wkts dec.) 230** |

## Nottinghamshire

| | | |
|---|---:|---:|
| W. W. Keeton c Bromley b Wall | 24 – b Fleetwood-Smith | 17 |
| C. B. Harris lbw b Fleetwood-Smith | 14 – c Darling b Grimmett | 9 |
| W. Walker lbw b Grimmett | 25 – c Grimmett b Fleetwood-Smith | 8 |
| J. Hardstaff lbw b Grimmett | 38 – c and b Grimmett | 13 |
| A. Staples lbw b Grimmett | 0 – c Bromley b Grimmett | 9 |
| R. Taylor b McCabe | 1 – not out | 16 |
| G. V. Gunn run out | 26 – c Grimmett b Fleetwood-Smith | 29 |
| B. Lilley b Grimmett | 25 – not out | 18 |
| W. Voce c Bromley b McCabe | 22 | |
| F. G. Woodhead b McCabe | 1 | |
| H. J. Butler not out | 1 | |
| B 3, l-b 3 | 6 | B 8, l-b 1 ............... 9 |
| | **183** | **128** |

## Nottinghamshire Bowling

| | Overs | Mdns | Runs | Wkts | Overs | Mdns | Runs | Wkts |
|---|---:|---:|---:|---:|---:|---:|---:|---:|
| Voce | 23 | 6 | 66 | 8 | 2 | — | 2 | — |
| Butler | 16 | 4 | 43 | 2 | 15 | 3 | 50 | 2 |
| Woodhead | 7 | 3 | 23 | — | 7 | 1 | 31 | — |
| Staples | 10 | — | 43 | — | 17 | 2 | 54 | — |
| Gunn | 12 | 3 | 38 | — | 11 | — | 44 | — |
| Harris | 3 | — | 14 | — | 6 | — | 38 | — |

**Australians Bowling**

| | Overs | Mdns | Runs | Wkts | Overs | Mdns | Runs | Wkts |
|---|---|---|---|---|---|---|---|---|
| Wall . . . . . . . . . . . . | 9 | — | 31 | 1 | | | | |
| McCabe . . . . . . . . . . | 19.3 | 2 | 42 | 3 | 4 | 1 | 6 | — |
| Grimmett . . . . . . . . | 36 | 16 | 70 | 4 | 14 | 5 | 35 | 3 |
| Fleetwood-Smith . . . | 14 | 6 | 34 | 1 | 20 | — | 47 | 3 |
| Darling . . . . . . . . . | | | | | 6 | 2 | 8 | — |
| Chipperfield . . . . . . | | | | | 5 | — | 21 | — |
| Bromley . . . . . . . . . | | | | | 3 | 1 | 2 | — |

Umpires: W. A. Buswell and J. W. Hitch.

# ENGLAND v AUSTRALIA

## Fifth Test Match

### Played at The Oval, August 18, 20, 21, 22, 1934

Each side having won once with two games left drawn, the fifth and concluding Test match was entered upon without any restrictions as to the time involved in reaching a definite result. As it happened four days proved sufficient for Australia to win by 562 runs. Thus they regained the Ashes. Being successful in the rubber by two victories to one, they brought their number of wins in the whole series of encounters between the two countries to 52 as against 51 by England. Under conditions which, apart from the winning of the toss, favoured neither side unduly the result was a fitting tribute to the superior all-round skill of Australia. They batted, bowled and fielded better than England and in every way thoroughly deserved what was, after all, a notable achievement. England in the course of the match laboured under a disadvantage when Ames, on the third day, had to retire with a strained back and took no further part in the game and Bowes was compelled to undergo a slight operation which prevented him batting but was not sufficiently serious to hinder his return and bowl on the fourth morning. Still, making every allowance for these incidents, there can be no doubt that everyone who saw the match from beginning to end must have been convinced of the all-round superiority of Australia. They made two changes, Kippax and Ebeling were brought in for Darling and Wall and thus made their first appearances of the tour in Test matches. The England team also was altered. Sutcliffe returned to the exclusion of Keeton; Hopwood and Mitchell, both having been twice tried and found wanting, gave way to G. O. Allen and Clark; while in the other case a daring experiment was tried, Frank Woolley, the famous left-hander, taking the place of Hendren, when it became known that Hendren did not feel justified in accepting an invitation owing to an injury he had sustained just previously. Gover of Surrey and I. A. R. Peebles – the latter an extraordinary choice having regard to the comparatively little cricket in which he had taken part – were both in the list of names from whom the team was to be chosen but neither was selected. Woolley was brought in on the strength of his wonderful batting for Kent, but as events proved it was a sad error of judgment on the part of the selectors to fall back on a man, no matter what his county record may have been, who had not played in a Test match against Australia for four years and who, moreover was 47 years of age. Dismissed for 4 and 0, Woolley failed in both innings at the very part of the order which previous experience during the summer had proved to be England's most vulnerable point in batting.

The law of averages suggested that it was Woodfull's turn to win the toss. This he did and when Clark, coming on at 20, bowled Brown at 21 with the best ball send down all day long, it seemed as though the England attack on a hard wicket was about to come into its own. Never were hopeful anticipations more rudely dispelled. Between them Ponsford and Bradman gave another glorious display of batting, staying together until nearly half-past six and engaging in a partnership which left that of Leeds far behind and produced 451 runs in five hours and a quarter. This time Bradman was the first to leave, hitting over his head at a bouncing ball and being caught behind the wicket at 472. McCabe went in and played out time, Australia, as the result of the first day's cricket, having 475 runs on the board with only two men out. It would be hard to speak in too high terms of praise of the magnificent displays of batting given by Ponsford and Bradman. Before Bradman joined him Ponsford had shown an inclination to draw away from the bowling of Bowes but he received inspiration afterwards from the example of his partner, who from the very moment he reached the centre and took up his stance was coolness and mastery personified. The pitch did not help bowlers at all. Those with a command of spin found it extremely difficult to make the ball turn in the slightest and only by dropping it short could the fast bowlers make the ball rise above stump high. Clark tried leg theory with a packed leg-side field but as, for the most part, he maintained a good length, his bowling, even if he now and again dropped the ball short, scarcely came under the category of what is known as "body-line". Incidentally Clark and the others tried all sort of theories but they had no effect on Bradman who, as the afternoon wore on, invested his batting with increasing daring. He drove, and cut with the utmost certainty and power and when the ball did bounce he just stepped back and hooked it. Included in his hits were a six and thirty-two 4s and, having regard to the rate at which he, as well as Ponsford scored, a better display has rarely been seen. Ponsford was not quite so sure as Bradman and he frequently turned his back to the ball to receive blows on the thigh. All the same, he drove with great power and was clever in getting the ball away between the fieldsmen placed close in. Just after the new ball was brought into use at 200 the England bowling was at its best but generally speaking it never looked quite good enough for the task at hand and it was noticeable that scarcely a single yorker was sent down all day long while the bowlers of pace failed to keep their deliveries just that little bit short of a length to compel batsmen to play the forward defensive stroke. As during the day about 80 runs an hour were obtained it can be realised that too many long-hops and half-volleys were sent down. This great partnership meant that in consecutive representative encounters Bradman and Ponsford in two stands scored 839 runs in ten hours and three-quarters. Ponsford offered three very difficult chances and one when 115 comparatively easy; Bradman's batting, as far as was seen, was flawless.

On Monday England had further trouble before the innings which lasted nearly ten hours closed at twenty minutes to five for 701 runs – the second highest in the history of Test matches between England and Australia. On this day 226 runs were made in four and a quarter hours for eight wickets – evidence of an improvement in the England attack. Of the fast bowlers Clark was the best from the point of sustained effort and real class but he had no luck. Allen was faster and more virile and Bowes had an inspired period when, going on at 605, he took three wickets in five overs and a ball for 19 runs. McCabe was out early at 488 and Ponsford gave another chance before once more hitting his wicket in drawing back to Allen. Fourth out at 574, he batted seven hours and thirty-five minutes for his workmanlike innings of 266 and he hit a five and twenty-seven 4s. Woodfull gave a plodding display which lasted two hours and a half, Kippax was in for just over fifty minutes and none of the batting approached in class that of the opening afternoon. It was curious that six of the Australians were clean bowled and in this connection it is proper to observe that Bowes, who started the day trying to bounce the ball, met with success directly he bowled normally. The England fielding fell much below the standard demanded in Test cricket. On the dry ground the ball sometimes shot off at an awkward angle but the catching was poor.

An hour and a half remained for cricket when England went in and anything might have happened, but Walters and Sutcliffe, scoring at a fine pace, made 90 together without being separated. Walters once nearly played on; he looked to give a chance at 36, and at

41 was nearly caught at mid-on. Just about six o'clock the pace of the run-getting decreased which, in the circumstances, was a wise policy. Still, England were still 611 runs behind at the end of the day.

Tuesday was a black day for England and except for a superbly aggressive display by Maurice Leyland the batting proved deplorable. Sutcliffe and Walters were separated at 104, Sutcliffe being out to a good catch at the wicket on the leg side when the partnership had lasted an hour and fifty minutes and then followed a series of disasters. Walters and Woolley left in one over at 108 and 111; Wyatt playing on at 136 gave Grimmett his 100th wicket in Test cricket and Hammond went at 142. Leyland and Ames put a better appearance on affairs but when they had added 85 in less than an hour, Ames retired with a strained back. After that Leyland dominated the proceedings. He drove spendidly and when at length bowled at 321 he had made 110 out of 185 in two hours and forty minutes. He hit a six and fifteen 4s, nearly all drives. Bowes being absent, the innings closed with Leyland's dismissal at four o'clock, the last three wickets having put on 179 runs. The Australian bowling was always good and their fielding accurate.

Australia, 380 ahead, scored 186 for two wickets before the end of the day, Brown leaving at 13 and Ponsford at 42. Woolley kept wicket and Gregory and McMurray of Surrey acted as substitute fielders. Incidentally, the work of these two men was brilliantly accurate. Nobody on the England side, except Leyland, did so well in the outfield in any of the Test matches. Bradman and McCabe scored at a fine pace, making 144 together in ninety minutes. Light rain fell during the night but the wicket the next morning was not greatly affected. Ames was still away but Bowes returned and went on to bowl. He soon dismissed Bradman who, with McCabe, had added 150 in ninety-five minutes and then for the first time England's bowling got really on top so that, although the last partnership between Ebeling and O'Reilly produced 55 in forty minutes, Australia were all out by half-past two for 327, the last eight wickets having produced 141 in two hours and ten minutes. Clark and Bowes shared the wickets, both bowling extremely well. Woolley kept wicket and made a catch standing back.

England were thus left with no fewer than 708 to get to win – only 34 short of the number England had set Australia in the first Test match at Brisbane during the 1928 29 tour. England made a shocking start, Walters leaving at one and Woolley at three but Sutcliffe and Hammond added 64 in sixty-five minutes. Hammond was fourth to leave after tea at 89 and following that it only became a question as to whether the match would be over or not before half-past six. Apart from an easy chance of stumping, Hammond certainly played very well but the tea interval proved his undoing. Leyland left at 109 and Wyatt at 122 and shortly before six o'clock with Allen stumped the innings was all over for 145 and as was the case four years previously Australis won the rubber on the anniversary of Woodfull's birthday. Grimmett bowled superbly.

## Australia

| | | |
|---|---|---|
| W. A. Brown b Clark | 10 | – c Allen b Clark .... 1 |
| W. H. Ponsford hit wkt b Allen | 266 | – c Hammond b Clark .... 22 |
| D. G. Bradman c Ames b Bowes | 244 | – b Bowes .... 77 |
| S. J. McCabe b Allen | 10 | – c Walters b Clark .... 70 |
| W. M. Woodfull b Bowes | 49 | – b Bowes .... 13 |
| A. F. Kippax lbw b Bowes | 28 | – c Walters b Clark .... 8 |
| A. G. Chipperfield b Bowes | 3 | – c Woolley b Clark .... 16 |
| W. A. Oldfield not out | 42 | – c Hammond b Bowes .... 0 |
| C. V. Grimmett c Ames b Allen | 7 | – c Hammond b Bowes .... 14 |
| H. I. Ebeling b Allen | 2 | – c Allen b Bowes .... 41 |
| W. J. O'Reilly b Clark | 7 | – not out .... 15 |
| B 4, l-b 14, w 2, n-b 13 .... 33 | | B 37, l-b 8, w 1, n-b 4 .... 50 |

1/21 2/472 3/488 4/574 5/626       701   1/13 2/42 3/192 4/213 5/224   327
6/631 7/638 8/676 9/682             6/236 7/236 8/256 9/272

## England

| | | | |
|---|---|---|---|
| Mr C. F. Walters c Kippax b O'Reilly | 64 | – b McCabe | 1 |
| H. Sutcliffe c Oldfield b Grimmett | 38 | – c McCabe b Grimmett | 28 |
| F. E. Woolley c McCabe b O'Reilly | 4 | – c Ponsford b McCabe | 0 |
| W. R. Hammond c Oldfield b Ebeling | 15 | – c and b O'Reilly | 43 |
| Mr R. E. S. Wyatt b Grimmett | 17 | – c Ponsford b Grimmett | 22 |
| M. Leyland b Grimmett | 110 | – c Brown b Grimmett | 17 |
| L. E. G. Ames retired hurt | 33 | – absent ill | 0 |
| Mr G. O. Allen b Ebeling | 19 | – st Oldfield b Grimmett | 26 |
| H. Verity b Ebeling | 11 | – c McCabe b Grimmett | 1 |
| E. W. Clark not out | 2 | – not out | 2 |
| W. E. Bowes absent ill | 0 | – c Bradman b O'Reilly | 2 |
| B 4, l-b 3, n-b 1 | 8 | L-b 1, n-b 2 | 3 |

1/104 2/108 3/111 4/136 5/142     321   1/1 2/3 3/67 4/89 5/109    145
6/263 7/311 8/321                    6/122 7/138 8/141 9/145

## England Bowling

| | Overs | Mdns | Runs | Wkts | Overs | Mdns | Runs | Wkts |
|---|---|---|---|---|---|---|---|---|
| Bowes | 38 | 2 | 164 | 4 | 11.3 | 3 | 55 | 5 |
| Allen | 34 | 5 | 170 | 4 | 16 | 2 | 63 | — |
| Clark | 37.2 | 4 | 110 | 2 | 20 | 1 | 98 | 5 |
| Hammond | 12 | — | 53 | — | 7 | 1 | 18 | — |
| Verity | 43 | 7 | 123 | — | 14 | 3 | 43 | — |
| Wyatt | 4 | — | 28 | — | | | | |
| Leyland | 3 | — | 20 | — | | | | |

## Australia Bowling

| | Overs | Mdns | Runs | Wkts | Overs | Mdns | Runs | Wkts |
|---|---|---|---|---|---|---|---|---|
| Ebeling | 21 | 4 | 74 | 3 | 10 | 5 | 15 | — |
| McCabe | 6 | 1 | 21 | — | 5 | 3 | 5 | 2 |
| Grimmett | 49.3 | 13 | 103 | 3 | 26.3 | 10 | 64 | 5 |
| O'Reilly | 37 | 10 | 93 | 2 | 22 | 9 | 58 | 2 |
| Chipperfield | 4 | — | 22 | — | | | | |

Umpires: F. Chester and F. Walden.

# WORCESTERSHIRE v AUSTRALIANS

## Played at Worcester, April 30, May 2, 3, 1938

Australians won by an innings and 77 runs. Lyttelton caused astonishment when after winning the toss he sent in the touring team to bat on a true and easy wicket. By the end of the first day 474 runs had been scored for the loss of six wickets and in the end the Australians made their highest total against Worcestershire. Batting in biting, wintry weather, Bradman, as on his two previous matches on the ground, began the tour with a double hundred. Starting in a cautious way, he developed capital form and during an innings lasting four hours fifty minutes, offered no semblance of a chance. Pulling, driving, cutting and placing the ball with skill, he hit thirty-three 4s. Badcock, on his first appearance in England, created a big impression and he helped Bradman to put on 277 for the fourth wicket. Crisp, by pace and swing, looked the best of the bowlers and he and Perks both bowled steadily. Monday's play furnished a most remarkable happening. McCormick, the fast bowler, repeatedly went over the crease and during his first three overs was no-balled nineteen times by umpire Baldwin. His first over actually comprised fourteen balls and the second over fifteen. Trying to hook one of the no-balls, Bull turned it against his face and received a terrific blow over the right eye, causing him to retire. Lyttelton drove O'Reilly and Fleetwood-Smith with vigour and Cooper gave a stylish display, their stand for the county producing 103, but apart from Bull, who resumed his innings, the remaining batsmen shaped poorly, and Fleetwood-Smith took eight wickets for 98. On Worcestershire following on, Lyttelton and Bull scored 65 together but the tourists did not encounter really formidable opposition afterwards. In the match, McCormick was no-balled 35 times.

### Australians

| | |
|---|---|
| J. H. Fingleton c Crisp b Howorth ........ 41 | E. S. White b Crisp ................... 26 |
| W. A. Brown lbw b Crisp ............... 2 | W. J. O'Reilly b Perks ................ 11 |
| D. G. Bradman c Martin b Howorth .....258 | E. L. McCormick b Crisp ............. 5 |
| S. J. McCabe b Perks .................. 34 | L. O'B. Fleetwood-Smith not out ......... 6 |
| C. L. Badcock c Singleton b Perks ........ 67 | B 13, l-b 15, w 2, n-b 2 ........ 32 |
| A. L. Hassett c Howorth b Perks ......... 43 | |
| B. A. Barnett b Crisp ................. 16 | 541 |

### Worcestershire

| | |
|---|---|
| Hon. C. J. Lyttelton b Fleetwood-Smith .......... 50 | – c Badcock b White ............ 35 |
| C. H. Bull not out .......................... 37 | – c McCormick b Fleetwood-Smith .. 69 |
| E. Cooper c Hassett b Fleetwood-Smith .......... 61 | – lbw b White ................... 16 |
| H. H. Gibbons b Fleetwood-Smith ............... 29 | – c Brown b O'Reilly ............ 9 |
| S. H. Martin b White ...................... 1 | – c Fingleton b O'Reilly .......... 5 |
| Mr R. H. C. Human c Fingleton b Fleetwood-Smith . 10 | – lbw b Fleetwood-Smith .......... 26 |
| R. Howorth c Hassett b Fleetwood-Smith ........ 12 | – c McCabe b O'Reilly ........... 0 |
| Mr A. P. Singleton st Barnett b Fleetwood-Smith ... 5 | – run out ..................... 14 |
| S. Buller lbw b O'Reilly ...................... 5 | – c Fleetwood-Smith b McCormick .. 10 |
| R. T. D. Perks c McCabe b Fleetwood-Smith ...... 21 | – c McCabe b Fleetwood-Smith ..... 4 |
| Mr R. J. Crisp c Hassett b Fleetwood-Smith ....... 11 | – not out ..................... 0 |
| B 4, l-b 5, w 1, n-b 16 ................. 26 | B 5, n-b 3 .............. 8 |
| 268 | 196 |

### Worcestershire Bowling

| | Overs | Mdns | Runs | Wkts |
|---|---|---|---|---|
| Crisp ............ | 37.3 | 5 | 170 | 4 |
| Perks ............ | 34 | 3 | 147 | 4 |
| Martin ........... | 29 | 8 | 70 | — |
| Howorth ......... | 21 | 1 | 85 | 2 |
| Singleton ......... | 3 | — | 37 | — |

### Australians Bowling

| | Overs | Mdns | Runs | Wkts | Overs | Mdns | Runs | Wkts |
|---|---|---|---|---|---|---|---|---|
| McCormick ....... | 8 | — | 44 | — | 12 | 2 | 51 | 1 |
| McCabe .......... | 4 | — | 16 | — | 5 | 1 | 13 | — |
| O'Reilly .......... | 14 | 2 | 77 | 1 | 23 | 9 | 56 | 3 |
| Fleetwood-Smith ... | 29 | 8 | 98 | 8 | 13.1 | — | 38 | 3 |
| White ........... | 11 | 7 | 7 | 1 | 10 | 1 | 30 | 2 |

Umpires: J. Smart and H. G. Baldwin.

## ENGLAND v AUSTRALIA

### First Test Match

Played at Trent Bridge, June 10, 11, 13, 14, 1938

Drawn. England, in a match memorable for the setting-up of many new records including seven individual hundreds, put together the highest innings total ever hit against Australia. Not until half past three on the second day did Australia have an opportunity of batting and with 151 scored half their wickets had fallen. McCabe then played an innings the equal of which has probably never been seen in the history of Test cricket; for the best part of four hours he maintained a merciless punishment of the bowling. Although his phenomenal effort did not save his side from the indignity of having to follow on, it broke the control of the play which England had held from the outset and by concentrating upon defence in their second innings Australia saved the game.

In a magnificent contest of skill, the excellence of the wicket always counted heavily in favour of batsmen. First innings conferred upon England a very important advantage. Australia put their faith in spin bowlers, but hardly ever did a ball turn and the bowlers who had so confused county sides came in for harsh treatment. On the opening day Barnett shared with Hutton in a first-wicket partnership of 219 which surpassed the previous best against Australia in England by the Hon. F. S. Jackson and Tom Hayward, who made 185 for England's first wicket at The Oval in 1899. The full value of Barnett's dashing attack on Australia's bowling was probably not appreciated at the time. Besides easing the task of the batsmen who followed, it provided a heartening influence on the play of Hutton, who together with Compton, had the distinction of hitting a century on a first appearance against Australia. For the first time in a Test match, four individual hundreds were registered in one innings for, following the successes of Barnett, Hutton and Compton, Paynter made the highest score against Australia in England and also shared with Compton in a record fifth wicket partnership of 206. The previous best figure for this wicket was 192 by R. E. Foster and Braund (L. C.) at Sydney in 1903.

As the result of two hours' batting by Barnett and Hutton before lunch on Friday 169 runs were scored. The Gloucestershire man drove and cut in magnificent style and was particularly severe on Fleetwood-Smith. In view of the kind of innings he played, it was not surprising that he made false strokes; he was almost caught in the gulley when 3, when 51 he hit a ball back hard towards Fleetwood-Smith and next over offered a difficult chance to Bradman, running from deep mid-off. The satisfaction of making a hundred before lunch-time was denied to Barnett, but off the first ball bowled after the interval he completed three-figures and altogether he made 126, batting nearly three hours and hitting eighteen 4s. Some of his drives off the back foot were splendidly executed. Hutton batted about half an hour longer and if, compared with Barnett, he looked slow, he was very sure of himself. An incident that occured soon after the match began, when the ball rolled against the middle and leg stumps without displacing a bail, did not disturb him. He summed up the length of every delivery to a nicety, and three fieldsmen close to the bat did not have the least chance to snap up. Hutton placed his strokes particularly well and his hitting to the on side and to leg and his late-cutting was admirably done. He hit fourteen 4s.

The next ball after the completion of his hundred ended Hutton's innings and then Australia made better progress; Edrich played on and Hammond, after a few forcing shots, was bowled neck and crop, but England finished the day with a score of 422 for four wickets, the last hour and a half producing 141 runs from Paynter and Compton. Some fine running between wickets featured this stand. Compton's stylish and confident play created a big impression and Paynter by quick footwork mastered the spin bowling.

When on Saturday, Compton was fifth out, England had 487 runs on the board. In a stand with Paynter lasting two hours twenty minutes Compton hit finely on the leg side, also excelling with the drive and square cut, and in scoring 102, including fifteen 4s, he batted without a mistake. Owing to the ball lodging in the wicket-keeper's pads, Paynter escaped being stumped when 88 and the one other opportunity Australia had of getting him out occurred with his score 163, Fleetwood-Smith at fine leg making a creditable but unavailing effort to hold a hard hit. Some good cover driving by Ames featured a sixth wicket stand of 90 and with Wright batting steadily after the eighth wicket fell, Paynter completed 200. When Hammond declared England's innings and Paynter left the crease about quarter-past three on Saturday, 30,000 spectators rose to their feet, cheering the Lancashire left-hander all the way to the pavilion. Just as the effort of Barnett was the foundation of England's batting triumph after an innings lasting ten minutes less than nine hours, so Paynter during five hours twenty minutes' batting most efficiently consolidated the work of the early batsmen. Often jumping in to drive he forced runs well, hit Ward for a 6 and also included a 5 and twenty-six 4s among his figures. During the innings four of Australia's bowlers each had a hundred runs hit off him.

No such inspiring start as had been given to England by the first wicket pair was enjoyed by Australia. Going on at 29, Wright, with his fourth ball in a Test match, dismissed Fingleton who played a long hop on to his wicket. By subdued and not altogether certain batting, Brown and Bradman raised the score to 111 and then Bradman, deceived in the flight of a ball, played it against his pads from which it glanced into the wicket-keeper's hands. Two appeals against the light were unsuccessful and before time Australia also lost Brown, who batted extremely well for two hours and a half. Ward went in as "stop-gap" and played through the last two overs despite the intimidating effect of an arc of nine fieldsmen within nine yards of his bat and Farnes bowling at top speed.

As a result of this most successful day for England, Monday's play began with Australia's score 138 for three, McCabe being 19 not out, made in 35 minutes. A record of these facts is a necessary preliminary to a description of the amazing batting which followed from McCabe and gave such an epic turn to the game. Six wickets were down for 194 and then McCabe, assisted in turn by three left-hand batsmen – Barnett, O'Reilly and McCormick – altered the whole aspect of affairs. In a little less than four hours, McCabe scored 232 out of 300 – his highest score in a Test match. His driving was tremendously hard, he hooked short balls with certainty and power, one off Farnes yielding a six, and he showed real genius in beating Hammond's efforts to keep him away from the bowling. While McCabe was running riot, the England captain delayed calling for the new ball and took other measures in his hope of keeping down runs, but the Australian, having completed his first hundred in two hours twenty minutes, proceeded to score 4s much more readily. Wright was hit for 44 runs off three successive overs. Although he travelled so fast, McCabe did not offer a real chance, but once Edrich made a plucky effort to hold a ball hooked with terrific power. In the last ten overs bowled to him, McCabe took the strike in eight and hit sixteen of his thirty-four 4s and in a last wicket stand of 77 with Fleetwood-Smith he scored 72 in 28 minutes. His glorious innings ended in a fitting way for in attempting a big hit off Verity he skied the ball to cover.

The probability that he would be in a position to enforce a follow-on influenced Hammond to conserve Verity's energies and the Yorkshireman bowled no more than 45 balls during the innings. England's fielding remained sure and enthusiastic all the time and although McCabe's rate of scoring might suggest the attack was demoralised that was not the case. When Australia followed on 247 behind, batting of a much different character was seen. Brown and Fingleton adopted "stone-walling" tactics which called forth mild "barracking" from some of the spectators and Fingleton followed the extraordinary procedure of stepping away from his wicket, taking off his gloves and laying down his bat. A good left-hand slip catch by Hammond disposed of Fingleton after an opening partnership of 89 in two and a quarter hours and Tuesday's play was notable for a dour resistance by Brown and Bradman who, making a hundred apiece, batted with grim patience and admirable skill. In view of the position of Australia they were of course justified in playing this type of game and by adding 170 in three hours ten minutes they robbed England of practically all chance of winning. Brown stayed nearly five hours and a half and hit thirteen 4s – a splendid performance for his side. He played Verity admirably. Troubled by a leg strain, Bradman was never seen as an attacking batsman, but he amazed everyone by the power of his concentration while batting the whole day. His second innings, begun twenty minutes before Monday's play closed, lasted six hours and there were only five 4s in his not out 144 which, being his thirteenth hundred in England v Australia matches, allowed him to take the record from Jack Hobbs, who hit twelve hundreds in the series. Verity bowled with precision and Wright sometimes made a ball turn, but the pitch was too good for England to force a win. Shortly after the tea interval Australia stood only 114 ahead with half their wickets gone and they saved the match, although the Englishmen stuck gamely to their task. Annoyed by the wearisome cricket.

spectators late in the day indulged in ironical cheering, whereupon Bradman showed disapproval of this slight demonstration by standing clear of his wicket until the noise subsided. The total attendance was 89,681 and the receipts £15,293 2*s.* 9*d.*

## England

| | | |
|---|---|---:|
| L. Hutton lbw b Fleetwood-Smith | | 100 |
| C. J. Barnett b McCormick | | 126 |
| W. J. Edrich b O'Reilly | | 5 |
| Mr W. R. Hammond (Capt.) b O'Reilly | | 26 |
| E. Paynter not out | | 216 |
| D. Compton c Badcock b Fleetwood-Smith | | 102 |
| L. E. G. Ames b Fleetwood-Smith | | 46 |
| H. Verity b Fleetwood-Smith | | 3 |
| R. A. Sinfield lbw b O'Reilly | | 6 |
| D. V. P. Wright not out | | 1 |
| B 1, l-b 22, n-b 4 | | 27 |

1/219 2/240 3/244 4/281     (8 wkts dec.) 658
5/487 6/577 7/597 8/626

Mr. K. Farnes did not bat.

## Australia

| | | |
|---|---:|---:|
| J. H. Fingleton b Wright | 9 | – c Hammond b Edrich ............ 40 |
| W. A. Brown c Ames b Farnes | 48 | – c Paynter b Verity ............. 133 |
| D. G. Bradman (Capt.) c Ames b Sinfield | 51 | – not out ...................... 144 |
| S. J. McCabe c Compton b Verity | 232 | – c Hammond b Verity .......... 39 |
| F. Ward b Farnes | 2 | – not out ...................... 7 |
| A. L. Hassett c Hammond b Wright | 1 | – c Compton b Verity ........... 2 |
| C. L. Badcock b Wright | 9 | – b Wright .................... 5 |
| B. A. Barnett c Wright b Farnes | 22 | – lbw b Sinfield ............... 31 |
| W. J. O'Reilly c Paynter b Farnes | 9 | |
| E. L. McCormick b Wright | 2 | |
| L. O'B. Fleetwood-Smith not out | 5 | |
| B 10, l-b 10, w 1 | 21 | B 5, l-b 16, n-b 5 ........ 26 |

1/34 2/111 3/134 4/144 5/151 6/194          411
7/263 8/319 9/334

1/89 2/259 3/331 4/337          427
5/369 6/417

### Australia Bowling

| | Overs | Mdns | Runs | Wkts |
|---|---|---|---|---|
| McCormick ....... | 32 | 4 | 108 | 1 |
| O'Reilly ................ | 56 | 11 | 164 | 3 |
| McCabe .......... | 21 | 5 | 64 | — |
| Fleetwood-Smith ... | 49 | 9 | 153 | 4 |
| Ward ............ | 30 | 2 | 142 | — |

### England Bowling

| | Overs | Mdns | Runs | Wkts | Overs | Mdns | Runs | Wkts |
|---|---|---|---|---|---|---|---|---|
| Farnes .......... | 37 | 11 | 106 | 4 | 24 | 2 | 78 | — |
| Hammond ........ | 19 | 6 | 44 | — | 12 | 6 | 15 | — |
| Sinfield .......... | 28 | 8 | 51 | 1 | 35 | 8 | 72 | 1 |
| Wright .......... | 39 | 6 | 153 | 4 | 37 | 8 | 85 | 1 |
| Verity ........... | 7.3 | — | 36 | 1 | 62 | 27 | 102 | 3 |
| Edrich .......... | | | | | 13 | 2 | 39 | 1 |
| Barnett .......... | | | | | 1 | — | 10 | — |

Umpires: F. Chester and E. Robinson.

# ENGLAND v AUSTRALIA

## Second Test Match

Played at Lord's, June 24, 25, 27, 28, 1938

Drawn. A match of many fluctuations and fine personal achievements ended with Australia needing 111 runs to win and with four wickets to fall. In the Nottingham game, the scoring of a double hundred on each side had been unprecedented and yet in the very next Test match the same thing was done again. Hammond, who with able assistance from Paynter and Ames rescued England from a deplorable start, played an innings of 240 – the highest in England against Australia. Brown batted through the whole of Australia's first innings, scoring 206 not out and equalling the performances of Dr J. E. Barrett, Warren Bardsley and W. M. Woodfull by carrying his bat through a Test innings against England.

The danger of losing faced the Englishmen at one time on Tuesday when, after taking their second innings on a rain-affected pitch, they led by no more than 148 with half the side out. Then Compton once again met Australia's bowling with admirable nerve and coolness for so young a player and from the inspiration of his effort and that of Paynter England recovered their grip on the match and, declaring, set Australia a task of 315 runs in two and three-quarter hours. On the last day Bradman, as in each of his four previous Tests against England, hit a three-figure score and in doing so exceeded the highest individual aggregate in the series – the 3,636 runs made by Hobbs.

Only in one respect did England's eleven differ from that which appeared at Trent Bridge, Wellard, the Somerset fast bowler, replacing Sinfield. Australia brought in Chipperfield for Ward. After England's wonderful start in the previous Test, the events that followed success in the toss came as a rude shock. McCormick made the ball swing in to the batsmen and caused it to "lift" awkwardly; in half an hour he had Hutton and Barnett caught at short leg and Edrich, in between these successes, played on in trying to hook. Actually, excluding no-balls, McCormick in twenty-five deliveries took all three wickets for 15 runs; he bowled more accurately than at any previous time during the tour. With England in this sorry position Hammond joined Paynter, the resolute cricket of the left-hander gave Hammond confidence to play his natural game, and this fourth wicket pair set up a new record by adding 222. The previous best stand for England's fourth wicket against Australia was 151 by C. B. Fry and F. S. Jackson (now Sir Stanley) at The Oval in 1905.

The partnership lasted over three hours. McCormick lost his pace and lapsed into inaccuracy; O'Reilly, although not difficult, alone kept a steady length; Fleetwood-Smith worried neither batsman. Hammond went to his hundred after two hours and twenty-five minutes' masterly batting and gradually Paynter, bringing into play the off-drive, cut and hit to leg, scored more freely. It was Paynter's misfortune to miss a three-figure innings by one run, but his competent display was made at a very opportune time for England. Besides a 6 off Fleetwood-Smith, he hit thirteen 4s. Compton was soon out but that was Australia's last success before stumps were drawn with a total of 409 for five wickets to show a very fine recovery. O'Reilly, towards the close of play, bowled grandly, but Ames batted with sound judgment and it was altogether a day of triumph for the experienced batsmen on England's side. So large was the crowd that the gates were closed before noon. Part of the record partnership between Hammond and Paynter was watched by His Majesty the King.

On Saturday, the cricket was seen by the largest crowd ever to assemble at headquarters – the attendance was officially returned as 33,800. The gates were closed before the start and, after hurried consultations between officials, spectators were permitted to retain positions they had taken up on the grass, the boundary ropes being moved forward a few yards, thus reducing the playing area. England definitely gained the upper hand before the close. First of all, Hammond and Ames established a new sixth wicket record by putting on 186 and surpassing the 170 made in the Oval Test of 1930 by Sutcliffe and R. E. S. Wyatt. They had been together two hours and a half when Hammond, playing late for a good length in-swinger, was bowled leg stump. Making the highest score for England in any home Test match, and hitting thirty-two 4s, Hammond batted over six hours. His straight, off and cover-driving was magnificent; he moved to meet the ball with the ease of a master. The only semblance of a mistake occurred when a sizzling drive speed towards Chipperfield who, in trying to stop it, split a finger and did not afterwards field.

Just before his dismissal, Hammond received a nasty blow on the left elbow and the injury and also a pulled leg muscle prevented him bowling in this match and for some time afterwards. Either by instruction or on their own inclination, the other batsmen attempted to force the game but not with much success. Ames, ninth to leave, played a splendid innings at a pinch, batting three and a quarter hours without a chance to hand and hitting ten 4s. It must be added that through an innings lasting seven hours and producing England's highest total at Lord's, the Australian fielding was maintained at a high standard.

By the call of time, Australia had lost half their wickets, but a fine, fighting innings by Brown checked England's progress. Bradman played on and when McCabe's audacious hooks and hard cuts threatened another punishing effort from his bat Verity dismissed him with a brilliant catch in the gully, holding on to a hard-hit ball as he lost his balance. A longer partnership followed, Hassett batting with style and confidence but Wellard, resuming, disposed of Hassett and Badcock in one over. Barnett stayed through the last half hour with Brown, who left off with his score 140 not out, and that of Australia 299 for five.

On Monday, the Englishmen lost little time in strengthening their grip on the game. Verity, put on first thing, disposed of Barnett and Chipperfield in eight deliveries and when O'Reilly went in seventh wicket down Australia needed 37 more runs to avoid a follow-on. O'Reilly promptly hit out at the slow bowling and a serious mistake occurred in the field. It is not too much to say that had Paynter held the ball when O'Reilly skied it to long-on after scoring 11, England would have been in a position to make Australia follow their innings, and thereby secure a better chance to force a win. The fieldsman, however, misjudged the flight of the ball and came too far forward so that although he leaped up for it he could not complete a catch. Australia at this point required seventeen more runs to save the follow-on and O'Reilly, pulling two successive deliveries from Verity for 6 and taking 16 off the over, soon settled that question.

Meanwhile Brown, keeping up his strong back play and scoring with stylish drives and well timed cuts and hits to leg, had reached 150 in ten minutes under five hours and before England got down the eighth wicket, 85 runs were added in 42 minutes. Soon after Farnes was brought back into the attack he not only bowled O'Reilly and had McCormick caught at short leg off successive balls but was deprived of a "hat trick" owing to Compton missing a slip catch offered by Fleetwood-Smith. In his highest score against England, O'Reilly, besides his two 6s, hit five 4s.

After three hours had been lost owing to rain Brown, at 184, was also missed by Paynter, this time at mid-on, and with Fleetwood-Smith showing surprisingly good defence, Brown was able to complete a double hundred before the innings ended with a difference of 72 runs in England's favour. As already stressed, Australia's fine fight was almost entirely the work of Brown, who from start to finish of an innings lasting six and a quarter hours, played with a beautifully straight bat, kept an almost impregnable defence and, without ever appearing to make real effort to punish the bowling, hit a five and twenty-two 4s. Some of his glides and pushes towards the on side were made with remarkable accuracy.

The rain transformed an easy wicket into one soft on top and hard underneath, and England's opening pair fell for 28 so that when the last day was entered upon the match was in a fairly even position. Not even O'Reilly proved such a nuisance to batsmen as did McCormick at this juncture. After taking the wicket of Edrich in his first over, McCormick bowled Verity, who had been sent in overnight, and half the England side were out for 76 when Hammond, who owing to his injury had a runner, tried a one-hand stroke at a ball outside his leg stump and skied it. Paynter and Compton added 52 but Ames did not stay long after a blow from the ball fractured a finger. In the hour of great need, however, Compton batted superbly for England, playing fast rising balls from McCormick very coolly, driving grandly on either side of the wicket and relishing short-pitched balls from McCormick. Some hard hitting by Wellard helped to carry

England clear of anxiety, the eighth partnership realising 74, including a mighty pull by Wellard which sent a ball from McCabe on to the grand stand balcony.

Hammond declared, with Compton not out after making 56 of his runs from boundaries, and left Australia an impossible task in the time available. Any thought of a failure was soon dispelled by Bradman. After the tea interval the Australian captain batted in brisk style and he and Hassett added 64, short bowling by Farnes receiving instant punishment. It had long since become evident that the Test would be another case of stalemate and Bradman kept life in the cricket by hitting his fourteenth hundred against England as the outcome of less than two hours twenty minutes' batting; his 102 included fifteen 4s. During this innings, Paynter kept wicket in place of Ames and did the job well. An interesting point of the match was that Brown was on the field from the start of play until five o'clock on the fourth day; another was that Badcock failed to score in either innings. The total number of spectators admitted to the ground on payment was 100,933 – a record for Lord's – and the receipts were £28,164 11s. 9d.

### England

| | | |
|---|---|---|
| L. Hutton c Brown b McCormick | 4 | – c McCormick b O'Reilly ......... 5 |
| C. J. Barnett c Brown b McCormick | 18 | – c McCabe b McCormick ......... 12 |
| W. J. Edrich b McCormick | 0 | – c McCabe b McCormick ......... 10 |
| Mr W. R. Hammond (Capt.) b McCormick | 240 | – c sub. b McCabe ............. 2 |
| E. Paynter lbw b O'Reilly | 99 | – run out ..................... 43 |
| D. Compton lbw b O'Reilly | 6 | – not out ..................... 76 |
| L. E. G. Ames c McCormick b Fleetwood-Smith | 83 | – c McCabe b O'Reilly ........... 6 |
| H. Verity b O'Reilly | 5 | – b McCormick .................. 11 |
| A. W. Wellard c McCormick b O'Reilly | 4 | – b McCabe .................... 38 |
| D. V. P. Wright b Fleetwood-Smith | 6 | – not out ..................... 10 |
| Mr. K. Farnes not out | 5 | |
| B 1, l-b 12, w 1, n-b 10 | 24 | B 12, l-b 12, w 1, n-b 4 ..... 29 |

1/12 2/20 3/31 4/253 5/271 6/457          494     1/25 2/28 3/43 4/64   (8 wkts dec.) 242
7/472 8/476 9/483                                 5/76 6/128 7/142 8/216

### Australia

| | | |
|---|---|---|
| J. H. Fingleton c Hammond b Wright | 31 | – c Hammond b Wellard .......... 4 |
| W. A. Brown not out | 206 | – b Verity ..................... 10 |
| D. G. Bradman (Capt.) b Verity | 18 | – not out ..................... 102 |
| S. J. McCabe c Verity b Farnes | 38 | – c Hutton b Verity ............. 21 |
| A. L. Hassett lbw b Wellard | 56 | – b Wright .................... 42 |
| C. L. Badcock b Wellard | 0 | – c Wright b Edrich ............. 0 |
| B. A. Barnett c Compton b Verity | 8 | – c Paynter b Edrich ............. 14 |
| A. G. Chipperfield lbw b Verity | 1 | |
| W. J. O'Reilly b Farnes | 42 | |
| E. L. McCormick c Barnett b Farnes | 0 | |
| L. O'B. Fleetwood-Smith c Barnett b Verity | 7 | |
| B 1, l-b 8, n-b 6 | 15 | B 5, l-b 3, w 2, n-b 1 ....... 11 |

1/69 2/101 3/152 4/276 5/276 6/307          422     1/8 2/71 3/111 4/175           204
7/308 8/393 9/393                                   5/180 6/204

### Australia Bowling

| | Overs | Mdns | Runs | Wkts | Overs | Mdns | Runs | Wkts |
|---|---|---|---|---|---|---|---|---|
| McCormick ....... | 27 | 1 | 101 | 4 | 24 | 5 | 72 | 3 |
| McCabe .......... | 31 | 4 | 86 | — | 12 | 1 | 58 | 2 |
| Fleetwood-Smith ... | 33.5 | 2 | 139 | 2 | 7 | 1 | 30 | — |
| O'Reilly ......... | 37 | 6 | 93 | 4 | 29 | 10 | 53 | 2 |
| Chipperfield ....... | 9 | — | 51 | — | | | | |

**England Bowling**

| | Overs | Mdns | Runs | Wkts | Overs | Mdns | Runs | Wkts |
|---|---|---|---|---|---|---|---|---|
| Farnes ........... | 43 | 6 | 135 | 3 | 13 | 3 | 51 | — |
| Wellard .......... | 23 | 2 | 96 | 2 | 9 | 1 | 30 | 1 |
| Wright ........... | 16 | 2 | 68 | 1 | 8 | — | 56 | 1 |
| Verity ............ | 35.4 | 9 | 103 | 4 | 13 | 5 | 29 | 2 |
| Edrich ........... | 4 | 2 | 5 | — | 5.2 | — | 27 | 2 |

Umpires: E. J. Smith and F. Walden.

## ENGLAND v AUSTRALIA

### Fifth Test Match

Played at The Oval, August 20, 22, 23, 24, 1938

England won by an innings and 579 runs and each country having gained one victory the rubber was drawn. No more remarkable exhibition of concentration and endurance has ever been seen on the cricket field than that of Leonard Hutton, the Yorkshire opening batsman, in a match which culminated in the defeat of Australia by a margin more substantial than any associated with the series of matches between the two countries. Record after record went by the board as Hutton mastered the bowling in calm, methodical fashion for the best part of two and a half days. At the end of an innings which extended over thirteen hours twenty minutes, this batsman of only 22 years had placed the highest score in Test cricket to his name, and shared in two partnerships which surpassed previous figures. Adding 382 with Leyland, he took part in a stand which was a record not only for England's second wicket but for any wicket for England, and his stand of 215 with Hardstaff established a new record for England's sixth wicket. As a boy of fourteen, Hutton, at Leeds in 1930, had seen Bradman hit 334 – the record individual score in Test matches between England and Australia. Now on his third appearance in the series the Yorkshireman left that figure behind by playing an innings of 364.

This Test will always be remembered as "Hutton's Match", and also for the calamity which befell Australia while their opponents were putting together a mammoth total of 903. First of all Fingleton strained a muscle and Bradman injured his ankle so badly that he retired from the match and did not play again during the tour. Before this accident, England had established a supremacy which left little doubt about the result; indeed, Hammond probably would not have closed the innings during the tea interval on the third day but for the mishap to the opposing captain.

The moral effect of the loss of Bradman and Fingleton upon the other Australians was, of course, very great. After fielding out an innings lasting fifteen hours and a quarter, several of them batted – to all appearances – with very poor heart but Brown, going in first, was last man out before a follow-on 702 runs in arrear. He played an heroic innings under the shadow of impending defeat and Barnes, in his first Test match, well justified his choice, but from a depressing start in each innings there was no real recovery. This came as an anti-climax after the batting mastery which obtained until the tea interval on Monday. It was not a case of England driving home the advantage but rather of Australia losing inspiration to make a braver struggle to put a better face on defeat.

Hammond's fourth consecutive success in the toss was, of course, one factor influencing the result. Another was the way in which the Australian team was chosen. The risks taken by Bradman in going into the match with only O'Reilly, Fleetwood-Smith and

Waite to bowl seemed to be inviting trouble. Neuritis was given as the reason for the omission of McCormick, who in any case had done nothing to suggest he was likely to trouble England's batsmen on a good Oval wicket. It came to a question of choosing either White or Ward, or omitting both those bowlers and so making the batting as strong as possible. Whether Bradman, as was suggested, gambled upon winning the toss after three failures and so being in a position tò call upon his spin bowlers when the pitch had become worn will probably never be known. Although deprived through injuries of both Ames and Wright, England, with more all-round strength, were able to include six players who were recognised bowlers. The inclusion once again of Leyland was a move which yielded splendid results. As Wood, in his fortieth year, at last gained the honour of keeping wicket for England, there were five Yorkshiremen in England's eleven, and every one of them excelled. Between them they scored 612 of the runs and took ten of the sixteen wickets that fell, and Wood held three catches.

Compared with the England side beaten at Leeds, there were three changes, Hutton, Wood and Leyland replacing Barnett, Price and Wright; the last-named together with Ames, met with injury after being selected. The first day's cricket brought about the overwhelming success of batsmen which, with the wicket easy-paced and true, it was natural to expect. Waite and McCabe, the opening pair of bowlers, were innocuous and although O'Reilly, soon after he went on, got rid of Edrich and so took his 100th wicket in Tests against England, that was the one success for Australia before stumps were drawn with 347 runs scored. Coming together at 29, Hutton and Leyland settled down to a partnership which surpassed all previous records for England. Each of them enjoyed one escape. Hutton, when 40, jumping in to hit an off-break from Fleetwood-Smith, missed the ball which, with the batsman well out of his ground, Barnett failed to gather. Leyland, having scored 140, would have been run out had not Waite, the bowler, after a fast throw-in by Badcock, knocked the bails off before the ball was in his hands.

With few bowlers of class at his call, Bradman had to conserve the energies of O'Reilly as much as possible. The field was set carefully for the saving of runs and although both the England batsmen scored numerous singles on the off side Australia gave a superb display in the field, Bradman inspiring the team with his fast running and clean picking-up. If the bowling lacked venom it was mainly accurate in length, particularly before lunch-time when 89 runs were scored. In a match with no time limit, Hutton and Leyland very wisely refused to take risks until after the interval; Hutton, in fact, never altered his cautious game. That the scoring rate quickened was due mainly to the powerful driving and neat cutting of Leyland. Hutton used similar types of strokes in correct and fluent style and all the time his defence never faltered. At the close on Saturday, Hutton had scored 160 and Leyland 156 – the former having batted nearly six hours and Leyland fifty minutes less time. A curiosity of the day's cricket was that four times a no-ball led either to the wicket being hit or the ball being caught.

A heavy shower which fell shortly before Monday's play was due to begin caused twenty-five minutes' delay but this improved rather than spoiled the wicket. The first event of note was the passing of the record stand against Australia made by Hobbs and Rhodes, who in 1911-12 at Melbourne shared a first-wicket partnership of 323. Following the same steady lines as before, Hutton and Leyland carried on this magnificent batting until England had 411 runs up when the stand ended through a wonderful piece of fielding. Hutton drove a ball from O'Reilly hard to the off side and Hassett fumbled it. Then he slung in a very fast return to the bowler's end and Bradman sizing up the situation in an instant, dashed towards the wicket from mid-on, caught the throw-in and broke the wicket before Leyland could complete a second run. Out for 187 – his highest of seven three-figure innings against Australia – Leyland batted nearly six and a half hours and hit seventeen 4s.

Hammond was at the wicket to see his personal record of highest score for England in a home Test match surpassed by Hutton. It was a remarkable feature of the season's Test games that the 182 not out by Philip Mead at The Oval in 1921 which stood as the record for England against Australia in any home Test was beaten four times during the current series. At Nottingham Paynter made 216 not out, at Lord's Hammond excelled this with 240, Leyland followed with 187 and Hutton not only eclipsed these achievements but surpassed all individual records in Test cricket. Hammond stayed two hours twenty minutes and helped to add 135 for the third wicket. He was much more defensive than usual, and although taking 12 off one over by Fleetwood-Smith, hit no more than one boundary stroke during his last two hours at the wicket. Paynter's dismissal with one more run scored after Hammond left was a surprise. Misjudgment of a leg-break was the reason. Rain extended the tea interval to half an hour and Compton left immediately afterwards. By this time Hutton had entered upon the tenth hour of his innings and he remained full of confidence even if becoming a little monotonous by reason of his grim, determined dominance of the bowling. Hardstaff, no. 7 in the order, batted very surely and after an ovation to Hutton when he passed the 287 made at Sydney in 1903-4 by R. E. Foster – before this match the highest innings hit against Australia – an appeal against the light led to stumps being drawn early. England at the end of two days had put together a total of 634 and only half their wickets had fallen.

Hutton claimed exactly 300 of the runs scored at this point and the 30,000 people who assembled at The Oval on Tuesday saw fresh cricket history made. The bowling and fielding of Australia looked more formidable than at any other time in the game and as Hutton carried his score nearer to the record Test innings, Bradman, the holder of it, brought several fieldsmen close in to the wicket for O'Reilly's bowling. Every run had to be fought for. As might be supposed, Hutton showed an occasional sign of strain and he completely missed the ball when with his total 331 he had an opportunity of beating the record by hitting a no-ball from O'Reilly. However, with a perfect cut off Fleetwood-Smith, Hutton duly reached his objective and the scene at the ground, with the whole assembly rising to its feet, and every Australian player, as well as Hardstaff, congratulating Hutton will be remembered for a long time by those who saw it. Hutton took nearly twice as long as Bradman did over as many runs eight years previously, but the Australian's big innings came during a Test limited in duration whereas Hutton played his innings on an occasion when time did not matter.

Before this memorable incident, Hardstaff hit with judgment without departing from the policy of all his preeessors in avoiding risks. The whole of the batting seemed to be inspired by a desire to build up a stupendous total. Hardstaff reached three figures in three hours ten minutes and a little later Hutton lifted a stroke towards cover and Hassett held the ball easily low down. So a phenomenal innings, lasting from half-past eleven on the Saturday until half-past two on the Tuesday – the longest ever played in first-class cricket – came to an end. Only A. C. MacLaren, who hit 424 for Lancashire v Somerset at Taunton in 1895, has made a higher individual score in England. In addition to thirty-five 4s, Hutton hit fifteen 3s, eighteen 2s and 143 singles.

England's total had reached 770 for the loss of six wickets and some spirited hitting by Wood came as a refreshing contrast to the stern batting which had gone before. Another three-figure stand resulted, Wood adding 106 in an hour and a half with Hardstaff, and shortly after these batsmen were separated there occurred the tragic accident to Bradman, who when bowling caught his foot in a worn foot-hole, fell prone and was carried off the field by two of his colleagues. During the tea interval, England's innings, which was the longest on record and produced the highest total for any Test match innings and the highest for any first-class match in England, was declared closed. It was said that O'Reilly, who bowled 85 overs, wore the skin off a finger in imparting spin to the ball.

Before Australia scored a run, Badcock fell to a catch at short leg and McCabe left at 19. Hassett made some excellent strokes on the leg side; afterwards Barnes and Brown raised the total from 70 to 117 before stumps were drawn and altogether added 75. Bowes on Wednesday twice took two wickets in an over but neither pace nor spin bowling could disturb the equanimity of Brown. An unusual incident happened during the eighth and last stand in which Fleetwood-Smith participated. When Brown cut the last ball of an over, intending to run a single, Hutton, with the idea of trying to give the less experienced batsmen the strike, kicked the ball to the boundary.

Instructions to umpires, however, provide for four runs to be added to the runs already made should a fieldsman wilfully cause the ball to reach the boundary, and as this meant the award to Brown of five runs, he kept the bowling. In the end, Brown missed the distinction of carrying his bat, for Hammond, running from slip, knocked up the ball and caught it at the second attempt, so disposing of Brown and bringing Australia's first innings to a close.

Brown was in for two and three-quarter hours and in the follow-on, when he was fourth out, he again revealed better defence than any of his colleagues. In the most satisfactory batting of this second innings, Barnes and Barnett made some capital strokes while putting on 74. Verity took the wickets of Barnes and Waite with the last two balls of an over and although Barnett stayed for an hour and hooked and drove Farnes with power and certainty Australia were out for 123. They were actually dismissed twice in four and three-quarter hours' cricket. On the fourth day, the proceedings were so one-sided as to be almost farcical. The fact that Australia batted only nine men removed some of the honour and glory from England's triumph but there was nothing in the condition of the wicket to excuse the poor resistance of so many Test batsmen. Bowes, by sustained pace and skilful swerve, made himself England's best bowler and in the two innings he took seven wickets for 74.

The number of people who saw the game was 94,212, including 81,336 who paid for admission. The takings of £19,176 3s. 0d. are a record for a Test match at The Oval.

## England

| | |
|---|---|
| L. Hutton c Hassett b O'Reilly .........364 | J. Hardstaff not out ...................169 |
| W. J. Edrich c Hassett b O'Reilly ........ 12 | A. Wood c and b Barnes ............... 53 |
| M. Leyland run out ...................187 | H. Verity not out ..................... 8 |
| Mr W. R. Hammond (Capt.) | B 22, l-b 19, w 1, n-b 8 ......... 50 |
|     lbw b Fleetwood-Smith . 59 | |
| E. Paynter lbw b O'Reilly .............. 0 | 1/29 2/411 3/546 4/547    (7 wkts dec.) 903 |
| D. Compton b Waite ................. 1 | 5/555 6/770 7/876 |

Mr K. Farnes and W. E. Bowes did not bat.

## Australia

| | |
|---|---|
| C. L. Badcock c Hardstaff b Bowes .............. 0 | – b Bowes ..................... 9 |
| W. A. Brown c Hammond b Leyland ............ 69 | – c Edrich b Farnes .............. 15 |
| S. J. McCabe c Edrich b Farnes ................. 14 | – c Wood b Farnes ................ 2 |
| A. L. Hassett c Compton b Edrich .............. 42 | – lbw b Bowes ................... 10 |
| S. Barnes b Bowes ......................... 41 | – lbw b Verity .................. 33 |
| B. A. Barnett c Wood b Bowes ................. 2 | – b Farnes..................... 46 |
| M. G. Waite b Bowes ....................... 8 | – c Edrich b Verity .............. 0 |
| W. J. O'Reilly c Wood b Bowes ................. 0 | – not out ..................... 7 |
| L. O'B. Fleetwood-Smith not out ............... 16 | – c Leyland b Farnes ............. 0 |
| D. G. Bradman (Capt.) absent hurt .............. 0 | – absent hurt .................... 0 |
| J. H. Fingleton absent hurt ..................... 0 | – absent hurt .................... 0 |
|     B 4, l-b 2, n-b 3 ..................... 9 |     B 1 ................... 1 |

1/0 2/19 3/70 4/145 5/147           201    1/15 2/18 3/35 4/41          123
6/160 7/160 8/201                      5/115 6/115 7/117 8/123

## Australia Bowling

| | Overs | Mdns | Runs | Wkts |
|---|---|---|---|---|
| Waite ........... | 72 | 16 | 150 | 1 |
| McCabe .......... | 38 | 8 | 85 | — |
| O'Reilly ......... | 85 | 26 | 178 | 3 |
| Fleetwood-Smith ... | 87 | 11 | 298 | 1 |
| Barnes ........... | 38 | 3 | 84 | 1 |
| Hassett .......... | 13 | 2 | 52 | — |
| Bradman ......... | 3 | 2 | 6 | — |

**England Bowling**

| | Overs | Mdns | Runs | Wkts | Overs | Mdns | Runs | Wkts |
|---|---|---|---|---|---|---|---|---|
| Farnes .......... | 13 | 2 | 54 | 1 | 12.1 | 1 | 63 | 4 |
| Bowes .......... | 19 | 3 | 49 | 5 | 10 | 3 | 25 | 2 |
| Edrich .......... | 10 | 2 | 55 | 1 | | | | |
| Verity ........... | 5 | 1 | 15 | — | 7 | 3 | 15 | 2 |
| Leyland ......... | 3.1 | — | 11 | 1 | 5 | — | 19 | — |
| Hammond ........ | 2 | — | 8 | — | | | | |

Umpires: F. Chester and F. Walden.

# SUSSEX v AUSTRALIANS

## Played at Hove, August 27, 29, 30, 1938

Drawn. At one time the Australians stood in danger of defeat, but in the end they easily saved the game. Brisk hitting by Hassett and White and a stand of 71 by Brown and Waite were the best features of the Australian first innings, when batsmen contributed largely to their own downfall. The best thing in the match however, was a brilliant innings by Bartlett, who put together the fastest century of the summer. Playing confidently from the start, Bartlett reached three figures in 57 minutes and altogether batted no more than two hours for his 157. He offered only one actual chance and, by powerful strokes in front of the wicket, hit six 6s and eighteen 4s. In one over he hit Ward for 21. James Langridge helped him in a fourth partnership of 195, and Sussex went in front with six wickets standing. Cox, driving and pulling hard, and Stainton also played valuable innings, and Sussex led by 117. Badcock, suffering from lumbago, and Hassett and Walker, both labouring under the handicap of injury, helped the visitors out of an awkward situation, and Barnes and Barnett played well, so that Sussex were left with only 50 minutes batting and a task of 184 to win.

## Australians

| | | | |
|---|---|---|---|
| C. W. Walker b Hammond .................... | 7 | – not out ...................... | 2 |
| C. L. Badcock c Jas. Langridge b Wood .......... | 22 | – c Holmes b Wood ............ | 58 |
| A. L. Hassett b Hammond ..................... | 74 | – c J. Cornford b Wood ........... | 56 |
| S. Barnes lbw b Jas. Langridge .................. | 24 | – b Wood ...................... | 44 |
| S. J. McCabe b Wood ......................... | 3 | – b Hammond ................. | 16 |
| W. A. Brown b Wood ......................... | 75 | – c W. Cornford b Hammond ...... | 23 |
| B. A. Barnett c Hammond b John Langridge ....... | 17 | – lbw b Hammond .............. | 53 |
| M. G. Waite c Stainton b J. Cornford ............ | 46 | – b Hammond ................. | 9 |
| E. S. White c Stainton b Wood .................. | 44 | – b Hammond ................. | 15 |
| F. Ward c Hammond b J. Cornford .............. | 2 | – c W. Cornford b J. Cornford ...... | 0 |
| E. L. McCormick not out ...................... | 8 | – lbw b Jas. Langridge ............ | 2 |
| B 6, 1-b 5, w 3 ...................... | 14 | B 13, 1-b 8, w 1 ........... | 22 |

| | |
|---|---|
| 336 | 300 |

## Sussex

| | | | |
|---|---|---|---|
| John Langridge st Walker b Ward | 32 | – st Barnett b Ward | 13 |
| Mr R. G. Stainton lbw b Ward | 58 | – b McCormick | 10 |
| H. W. Parks lbw b White | 12 | – not out | 29 |
| Mr H. T. Bartlett c Barnes b Ward | 157 | | |
| Jas. Langridge st Barnett b Barnes | 68 | | |
| G. Cox b Ward | 76 | | |
| Ft-Lt A. J. Holmes c Barnes b White | 13 | | |
| H. E. Hammond c McCormick b White | 8 | | |
| D. J. Wood st Barnett b Ward | 1 | | |
| W. Cornford not out | 12 | | |
| J. Cornford st Barnett b Ward | 1 | | |
| B 4, l-b 10, n-b 1 | 15 | W 1 | 1 |
| | **453** | | **53** |

## Sussex Bowling

| | Overs | Mdns | Runs | Wkts | Overs | Mdns | Runs | Wkts |
|---|---|---|---|---|---|---|---|---|
| J. Cornford | 29 | 4 | 84 | 2 | 26 | 6 | 55 | 1 |
| Hammond | 32 | 6 | 86 | 2 | 34 | 4 | 107 | 5 |
| Wood | 25.4 | 1 | 96 | 4 | 25.4 | 3 | 81 | 3 |
| Jas. Langridge | 18 | 4 | 49 | 1 | 19 | 7 | 35 | 1 |
| John Langridge | 2 | — | 7 | 1 | | | | |

## Australians Bowling

| | Overs | Mdns | Runs | Wkts | Overs | Mdns | Runs | Wkts |
|---|---|---|---|---|---|---|---|---|
| McCormick | 24 | 1 | 86 | — | 6 | — | 18 | 1 |
| Waite | 17 | 4 | 55 | — | 4 | 2 | 5 | — |
| McCabe | 2 | — | 6 | — | | | | |
| Ward | 36.1 | 6 | 184 | 6 | 4.4 | — | 19 | 1 |
| White | 33 | 13 | 75 | 3 | | | | |
| Barnes | 6 | 1 | 32 | 1 | | | | |
| Brown | | | | | 3 | — | 10 | — |

Umpires: A. C. Russell and H. W. Lee.

# SOUTH AFRICANS IN ENGLAND

## ENGLAND v SOUTH AFRICA

### First Test Match

Played at Birmingham, June 14, 16, 17, 1924

The first of the Test matches, taken in conjunction with the startling failure against Lancashire at Old Trafford, went far to prove that the South Africans had no chance of beating England. It is true that, when in a hopeless position, they made a great effort to save a lost game but the fact that, with nothing in the condition of the wicket to excuse such a collapse, they went down before Arthur Gilligan and Tate for a score of 30 told heavily against them in public estimation. On the form shown so far during the season, the England side could hardly have been strengthened except by playing Strudwick in preference to George Wood as wicket-keeper. The last place on the side was left between A. P. F. Chapman and Ernest Tyldesley, and Chapman was chosen. A lot of rain had fallen in Birmingham and Taylor, on winning the toss for South Africa, decided to put England in. The temptation to take this venturesome course was certainly strong, as with the sun shining there seemed good reason to think that the pitch would, for a time at least, be treacherous, but as things turned out the result of the policy was disastrous. The Englishmen found run-getting a comparatively easy matter and at half-past six the score stood at 398 with seven wickets down. Chief credit for a fine performance belonged to Hobbs and Sutcliffe, who gave their side a splendid start, putting up 136 runs together in two hours and ten minutes. Sutcliffe's first appearance in a Test match was nothing less than a triumph. Bowled by a yorker just after luncheon, he played flawless cricket, being especially strong on the leg side. Hobbs was out second wicket down at 164 and then followed some brilliant cricket, Woolley and Hendren adding 83 runs in sixty-five minutes. In a delightful innings, Woolley hit eight 4s. Naturally anxious, after his failures in 1921, to do himself justice in a Test match Hendren played a very restrained game, being at the wickets nearly two hours and three-quarters for his 74. In second wicket down, he was out sixth at 356. Of the seven wickets that fell Parker, the Bradford League player who was brought into the South African eleven, took five. He bowled himself to a standstill and became so exhausted that he had to leave the field shortly before the drawing of stumps, the South Africans finishing the day with ten men. The half-crown charge for admission kept many people away, the full attendance numbering scarcely more than 10,000.

The sensation of the match came on the second day. England's innings soon ended for 438 and then in three-quarters of an hour Arthur Gilligan and Tate rattled the South Africans out for 30 – the lowest total in any Test match in England. The lowest before this match – also curiously enough on the Edgbaston ground – was 36 by Australia in 1902. There was another record, Gilligan's figures of six wickets for 7 runs never having been equalled. He bowled, very fast and with any amount of fire. Three times during the innings, he took a wicket immediately after sending down a no-ball. Tate, though he did not look quite so deadly, was also at the top of his form. Nothing during their tour did the South Africans more credit than the way in which, on following on, they battled against overwhelming odds. Taylor and Commaille started well by scoring 54 before Taylor was cleverly caught and bowled by Tate, close to the ground, and at the end of the afternoon the score stood at 274 for four wickets – a remarkable recovery indeed – Catterall 52 and Blanckenberg 56, the not outs at the close, having added 113 runs together in an hour and a quarter. They were in dire trouble when their partnership began but hit brilliantly when they had become set. With a single run added on Tuesday morning, Blanckenberg was out to an amazing catch by Chapman in the slips. Catterall, however, went on playing in far finer form than he had shown on the previous day and was the last man out – caught at extra mid-off when he was hitting at everything in the hope of saving his side from a single innings defeat. The total was 390, England winning the match by an innings and 18 runs. Few Test match hundreds have been so uneven in quality as Catterall's 120, but in the circumstances it was a very great effort – marked by magnificent driving. In third wicket down at 152, Catterall was batting for three hours and a quarter, his hits including two 6s and fifteen 4s. Arthur Gilligan will never forget his first experience as a Test match captain. He took in all eleven wickets for 90 runs. Tate, to whom fortune was unkind in the last innings, had a record for the match of eight wickets for 115 runs. The other England bowlers did not look at all difficult.

### England

| | | | | |
|---|---|---|---|---|
| J. B. Hobbs lbw b Blanckenberg | 76 | M. W. Tate c Taylor b Parker | 19 |
| H. Sutcliffe b Parker | 64 | Mr A. E. R. Gilligan b Pegler | 13 |
| F. E. Woolley c Ward b Parker | 64 | Mr G. E. C. Wood b Parker | 1 |
| E. Hendren c Nourse b Parker | 74 | C. Parkin not out | 8 |
| Mr A. P. F. Chapman b Parker | 8 | | |
| Mr P. G. H. Fender c Taylor b Blanckenberg | 36 | B 4, l-b 11, n-b 1 | 16 |
| R. Kilner c and b Pegler | 59 | | **438** |

### South Africa

| | | | | |
|---|---|---|---|---|
| H. W. Taylor b Tate | 7 | – c and b Tate | 34 |
| R. H. Catterall b Gilligan | 0 | – c Hobbs b Tate | 120 |
| M. J. Susskind c Kilner b Tate | 3 | – b Gilligan | 51 |
| A. D. Nourse lbw b Gilligan | 1 | – c Wood b Gilligan | 34 |
| J. M. M. Commaille not out | 1 | – c Hendren b Tate | 29 |
| J. M. Blanckenberg b Tate | 4 | – c Chapman b Gilligan | 56 |
| H. G. Deane b Gilligan | 2 | – run out | 5 |
| E. P. Nupen b Gilligan | 0 | – lbw b Tate | 5 |
| S. J. Pegler b Tate | 0 | – c Hobbs b Gilligan | 6 |
| T. A. Ward b Gilligan | 1 | – b Gilligan | 19 |
| G. M. Parker lbw b Gilligan | 0 | – not out | 2 |
| B 1, l-b 7, n-b 3 | 11 | B 4, l-b 18, w 1, n-b 6 | 29 |
| | **30** | | **390** |

### South Africa Bowling

| | Overs | Mdns | Runs | Wkts |
|---|---|---|---|---|
| Parker | 37 | 2 | 152 | 6 |
| Pegler | 36 | 8 | 106 | 2 |
| Blanckenberg | 32 | 5 | 95 | 2 |
| Nupen | 18 | 2 | 66 | — |
| Nourse | 1 | — | 3 | — |

### England Bowling

| | Overs | Mdns | Runs | Wkts | Overs | Mdns | Runs | Wkts |
|---|---|---|---|---|---|---|---|---|
| Gilligan | 6.3 | 4 | 7 | 6 | 28 | 6 | 83 | 5 |
| Tate | 6 | 1 | 12 | 4 | 54.4 | 19 | 103 | 4 |
| Parkin | | | | | 16 | 5 | 38 | — |
| Kilner | | | | | 22 | 10 | 40 | — |
| Fender | | | | | 17 | 5 | 56 | — |
| Woolley | | | | | 10 | 2 | 41 | — |

Umpires: H. Butt and W. Reeves.

## YORKSHIRE v SOUTH AFRICANS

Played at Sheffield, June 22, 24, 25, 1935

A convincing proof of the all-round strength of the South Africans was afforded by their victory by 128 runs over the unbeaten Yorkshire eleven. Yorkshire had to pay a heavy price for two fielding errors on Saturday when Siedle was twice let off before reaching double figures. Four wickets were down for 144, but Cameron hit up 45 out of 53 in forty minutes. Yorkshire scored 123 for the loss of four batsmen, but Bell and Balaskas finished off the innings for a further 78 runs. On Monday Siedle became the first batsman during the season to reach a thousand runs, and Cameron made 81 in just over an hour, hitting Verity for 30 – 4,4,4,6,6,6 – off one over and altogether registering five 6s and eleven 4s in his second hundred of the tour. Balaskas, quickly finding a worn spot, made it clear Yorkshire would not get the 364 runs required for victory and turning the ball sharply from leg he came out with full figures of twelve wickets for 154 runs.

### South Africans

| | | | |
|---|---|---|---|
| I. J. Siedle b Bowes | 51 | – c Smailes b Leyland | 48 |
| B. Mitchell c Sellers b Fisher | 39 | – c Verity b Bowes | 15 |
| E. A. Rowan c Verity b Bowes | 31 | – b Bowes | 76 |
| A. D. Nourse b Bowes | 12 | – b Leyland | 9 |
| H. F. Wade c Verity b Fisher | 7 | – b Smailes | 0 |
| H. B. Cameron c Barber b Fisher | 45 | – not out | 103 |
| E. L. Dalton b Smailes | 23 | – c Turner b Bowes | 23 |
| C. L. Vincent b Smailes | 14 | – not out | 1 |
| X. Balaskas not out | 12 | – c Wood b Smailes | 17 |
| R. J. Crisp b Smailes | 14 | | |
| A. J. Bell lbw (N) b Fisher | 4 | | |
| B 9, l-b 2 | 11 | B 1, l-b 4, n-b 4 | 9 |
| | **263** | **(7 wkts dec.)** | **301** |

### Yorkshire

| | | | |
|---|---|---|---|
| H. Sutcliffe lbw (N) b Bell | 1 | – b Bell | 17 |
| A. Mitchell c Cameron b Bell | 61 | – c Bell b Balaskas | 41 |
| M. Leyland c Vincent b Bell | 13 | – b Balaskas | 22 |
| W. Barber lbw b Balaskas | 28 | – c Cameron b Balaskas | 10 |
| C. Turner lbw (N) b Balaskas | 22 | – lbw (N) b Balaskas | 35 |
| A. Wood c Cameron b Balaskas | 20 | – b Balaskas | 17 |
| H. Fisher run out | 9 | – b Balaskas | 4 |
| Mr A. B. Sellers c Cameron b Bell | 9 | – c Cameron b Bell | 19 |
| T. F. Smailes b Balaskas | 3 | – c Crisp b Balaskas | 27 |
| H. Verity not out | 12 | – b Balaskas | 19 |
| W. E. Bowes run out | 10 | – not out | 4 |
| B 8, l-b 3, w 1, n-b 1 | 13 | B 15, l-b 5 | 20 |
| | **201** | | **235** |

### Yorkshire Bowling

| | Overs | Mdns | Runs | Wkts | Overs | Mdns | Runs | Wkts |
|---|---|---|---|---|---|---|---|---|
| Bowes | 26 | 10 | 58 | 3 | 29 | 9 | 70 | 3 |
| Smailes | 21 | — | 96 | 3 | 19 | 5 | 42 | 2 |
| Turner | 8 | 4 | 16 | — | 5 | — | 11 | — |
| Fisher | 27.3 | 12 | 52 | 4 | 15 | 5 | 33 | — |
| Verity | 9 | 5 | 20 | — | 14 | 2 | 87 | — |
| Leyland | 2 | — | 10 | — | 11 | — | 49 | 2 |

**South Africans Bowling**

| | Overs | Mdns | Runs | Wkts | Overs | Mdns | Runs | Wkts |
|---|---|---|---|---|---|---|---|---|
| Crisp ............ | 12 | 1 | 45 | — | 13 | 3 | 37 | — |
| Bell .............. | 19.5 | 5 | 65 | 4 | 20 | 2 | 64 | 2 |
| Vincent .......... | 10 | 2 | 23 | — | | | | |
| Balaskas ......... | 20 | 3 | 55 | 4 | 29.2 | 2 | 99 | 8 |
| Mitchell .......... | | | | | 4 | — | 15 | — |

Umpires: A. Skelding and E. J. Smith.

# WEST INDIES IN ENGLAND

## LORD HARRIS'S XI v WEST INDIES

Played at Belmont, July 20, 21, 1923

A very pleasant holiday game resulted in a win for the West Indies by three wickets. Lord Harris's eleven – a side that included some well-known names – got on remarkably well up to a certain point on the first afternoon, but on batting for the second time they lost five wickets for 36 before the drawing of stumps, only G. J. Bryan being able to cope with John's fine bowling. For some time on Saturday the finish promised to be exciting, the West Indies, with 164 to get, having six men out for 87. However, Small and Austin put on 59 runs together in just over half an hour, and practically settled the matter. Small hit a 6 and eight 4s in his 65 not out.

### Lord Harris's XI

| | | | |
|---|---|---|---|
| Mr A. F. Bickmore b Browne | 6 | – b John | 5 |
| Mr G. J. Bryan b John | 31 | – b John | 21 |
| Mr R. L. Kay b John | 15 | – c Pascall b John | 1 |
| Mr A. J. Evans c Ince b John | 20 | – b John | 0 |
| Mr C. J. Capes b John | 0 | – b Browne | 1 |
| Mr H. L. Cremer b John | 20 | – c Challenor b John | 22 |
| Mr J. R. Tylden b Pascall | 8 | – c Pascall b John | 10 |
| Mr J. R. Mason b Pascall | 0 | – c Holt b John | 10 |
| Mr J. A. Deed c Small b John | 8 | – c Austin b Browne | 7 |
| Mr A. Leach-Lewis b John | 0 | – not out | 27 |
| Mr B. Howlett not out | 1 | – c Holt b Constantine | 13 |
| B 5, l-b 3 | 8 | B 7, l-b 2 | 9 |
| | **117** | | **126** |

### West Indies

| | | | |
|---|---|---|---|
| P. H. Tarilton c Mason b Capes | 6 | – c Capes b Howlett | 4 |
| G. Challenor lbw b Capes | 18 | – c Evans b Capes | 8 |
| C. R. Browne lbw b Howlett | 11 | – b Bryan | 26 |
| H. W. Ince c Evans b Howlett | 5 | – c Bryan b Howlett | 16 |
| J. Small c Leach-Lewis b Howlett | 0 | – not out | 65 |
| J. K. Holt run out | 15 | – b Howlett | 3 |
| C. V. Hunter b Evans | 4 | – c Evans b Capes | 2 |
| H. B. G. Austin b Capes | 6 | – c Bickmore b Mason | 21 |
| L. Constantine b Capes | 2 | – not out | 5 |
| V. Pascall c Capes b Evans | 6 | | |
| G. John not out | 4 | | |
| B 1, l-b 1, n-b 1 | 3 | B 9, l-b 2, n-b 3 | 14 |
| | **80** | | **164** |

### West Indies Bowling

| | Overs | Mdns | Runs | Wkts | Overs | Mdns | Runs | Wkts |
|---|---|---|---|---|---|---|---|---|
| John | 18.3 | — | 45 | 7 | 18 | 2 | 55 | 7 |
| Browne | 11 | 3 | 30 | 1 | 15 | 3 | 32 | 2 |
| Constantine | 2 | — | 8 | — | 2 | — | 6 | 1 |
| Pascall | 8 | 1 | 26 | 2 | 4 | — | 24 | — |

## Lord Harris's XI Bowling

| | Overs | Mdns | Runs | Wkts | Overs | Mdns | Runs | Wkts |
|---|---|---|---|---|---|---|---|---|
| Howlett .......... | 14 | 5 | 28 | 3 | 13.3 | 1 | 43 | 3 |
| Capes ............ | 15 | 2 | 48 | 4 | 13 | 2 | 44 | 2 |
| Evans ............ | 1.4 | — | 1 | 2 | 3 | — | 14 | — |
| Bryan ............ | | | | | 6 | 1 | 29 | 1 |
| Mason ........... | | | | | 3 | — | 15 | 1 |
| Kay ............. | | | | | 2 | 1 | 5 | — |

## MIDDLESEX v WEST INDIES

### Played at Lord's, June 9, 11, 12, 1928

A splendid all-round performance on the part of Constantine enabled West Indies to gain a memorable victory by three wickets. When that player went in on Monday the tourists, as the result of more than two hours' laborious batting, had lost half their wickets for 79, and stood in no small danger of having to follow on. In such a brilliant manner did he deal with the situation that, driving with great power, and pulling in daring fashion, he made 86 out of 107 in less than an hour. Despite this fine effort, the visitors fell 122 short of the total at which, with six men out, Middlesex had declared, but in the county's second innings, Constantine, hitting the stumps five times, proceeded to take seven wickets for little more than 8 runs apiece. On going on to bowl for the second time, Constantine sent down six overs and three balls for 11 runs and six wickets. Even after this deadly piece of bowling, West Indies – set 259 to win and losing five batsmen for 121 – looked sure to be beaten. Coming once again to the rescue of his side, however, Constantine crowned a wonderful display by hitting up 103 out of 133 in an hour, with two 6s and twelve 4s as his chief strokes. Martin shared in his success on Monday, and in the further triumph, Fernandes was his partner. Haig, whom Hearne assisted to add 153, settled down after a moderate start to the making of a capital 100, and Hendren, who also reached three figures, was seen to advantage. In stopping a drive from Constantine, Hearne had a finger so badly damaged that he could play no more cricket last season.

## Middlesex

| | | | |
|---|---|---|---|
| Mr N. Haig b Small ........................ | 119 | – b Constantine ................. | 5 |
| H. W. Lee c Martin b Constantine ............... | 7 | – b Constantine ................. | 15 |
| J. W. Hearne c Nunes b Roach ................. | 75 | – lbw b Small ................... | 28 |
| E. Hendren not out ........................ | 100 | – c Francis b Constantine .......... | 52 |
| Mr E. T. Killick b Francis .................... | 6 | – c Francis b Constantine .......... | 4 |
| Mr G. O. Allen run out ..................... | 4 | – c and b Francis ................ | 7 |
| Mr F. T. Mann b Francis .................... | 32 | – b Small...................... | 4 |
| Mr I. A. R. Peebles not out .................. | 0 | – b Constantine ................. | 0 |
| T. J. Durston (did not bat) ................... | | – not out ...................... | 9 |
| W. F. Price (did not bat) .................... | | – b Constantine ................. | 3 |
| J. A. Powell (did not bat) ................... | | – b Constantine ................. | 1 |
| B 2, l-b 4, n-b 3 .............. | 9 | B 3, l-b 2, n-b 3 .......... | 8 |

| (6 wkts dec.) 352 | 136 |
|---|---|

## West Indies

| | | | |
|---|---|---|---|
| G. Challenor c Hendren b Durston | 23 | – b Haig | 33 |
| C. A. Roach c Lee b Durston | 0 | – run out | 10 |
| M. P. Fernandes c Hearne b Allen | 29 | – c Allen b Haig | 54 |
| W. H. St Hill c Hendren b Peebles | 5 | – b Durston | 5 |
| E. L. Bartlett st Price b Powell | 13 | – lbw b Hearne | 26 |
| F. R. Martin not out | 26 | – not out | 1 |
| L. N. Constantine b Peebles | 86 | – c Haig b Lee | 103 |
| J. A. Small c Hendren b Haig | 7 | – c and b Peebles | 5 |
| R. K. Nunes b Durston | 17 | | |
| C. R. Browne c Allen b Durston | 0 | – not out | 4 |
| G. N. Francis lbw b Haig | 1 | | |
| B 18, l-b 3, n-b 2 | 23 | B 18 | 18 |
| | **230** | | **259** |

## West Indies Bowling

| | Overs | Mdns | Runs | Wkts | Overs | Mdns | Runs | Wkts |
|---|---|---|---|---|---|---|---|---|
| Francis | 35.5 | 4 | 107 | 2 | 10 | 3 | 30 | 1 |
| Constantine | 20 | 1 | 77 | 1 | 14.3 | 1 | 57 | 7 |
| Browne | 11 | 2 | 21 | — | | | | |
| Small | 29 | 5 | 72 | 1 | 11 | 3 | 36 | 2 |
| Martin | 13 | — | 30 | — | 3 | — | 5 | — |
| Roach | 7 | — | 36 | 1 | | | | |

## Middlesex Bowling

| | Overs | Mdns | Runs | Wkts | Overs | Mdns | Runs | Wkts |
|---|---|---|---|---|---|---|---|---|
| Durston | 21 | 10 | 16 | 4 | 15 | 3 | 32 | 1 |
| Haig | 24.4 | 7 | 32 | 2 | 22 | 5 | 80 | 2 |
| Hearne | 11 | 4 | 25 | — | 15 | 3 | 51 | 1 |
| Peebles | 18 | 2 | 51 | 2 | 11 | 2 | 45 | 1 |
| Allen | 8 | 2 | 43 | 1 | | | | |
| Powell | 7 | 1 | 40 | 1 | 1 | — | 6 | — |
| Lee | | | | | 4.4 | — | 27 | 1 |

Umpires: J. W. Day and W. R. Parry.

# SURREY v WEST INDIES

### Played at The Oval, May 27, 29, 30, 1933

There never existed much chance of a definite result, but a drawn match was notable for brilliant batting by Roach and Hobbs. Roach performed the rare feat of reaching three figures before lunch. Driving splendidly, besides cutting crisply and hooking with power, he hit twenty-five 4s, and after batting two hours fifty minutes he was second to leave at 285. Barrow helped in an opening partnership of 187, and with Wiles playing freely 98 runs came in fifty-five minutes. Roach gave four difficult chances, but they were small blemishes in a magnificent display. Hobbs was masterly. For a man playing in his first match of the season at 50 years of age, his display was not only a triumph of skill, but no mean feat of physical endurance. Fifth out at 418, he withstood the bowling for six and a half hours. Although his innings contained only seventeen 4s it was abundant in beautiful strokes all round the wicket. His opening stand with Gregory yielded 117; Squires, Barling and Brown also rendered useful assistance. Owing to injury Sandham did not bat.

## West Indies

| | | | |
|---|---|---|---|
| C. A. Roach c Brooks b Brown | 180 | – b Gover | 29 |
| I. Barrow c Gregory b Gover | 62 | – lbw b Parker | 0 |
| C. A. Wiles run out | 51 | – c Ratcliffe b Parker | 4 |
| F. R. Martin c Brooks b Gregory | 33 | – lbw b Gover | 2 |
| G. C. Grant run out | 8 | – not out | 35 |
| O. C. Da Costa c Fender b Parker | 38 | – not out | 58 |
| C. A. Merry st Brooks b Brown | 14 | – lbw b Fender | 18 |
| V. A. Valentine b Gover | 28 | | |
| E. A. Martindale c Brooks b Gover | 0 | | |
| H. C. Griffith c Brooks b Gover | 13 | | |
| E. Achong not out | 8 | | |
| B 7, l-b 13, n-b 5 | 25 | B 10, l-b 3, n-b 1 | 14 |
| | **460** | | **160** |

## Surrey

| | | | |
|---|---|---|---|
| J. B. Hobbs b Valentine | 221 | J. F. Parker b Martin | 0 |
| R. J. Gregory b Da Costa | 55 | E. W. Brooks run out | 0 |
| H. S. Squires c Grant b Griffith | 42 | A. R. Gover not out | 10 |
| T. H. Barling c and b Martin | 28 | A. Sandham absent hurt | 0 |
| Mr F. R. Brown c and b Valentine | 26 | B 10, l-b 15, w 2, n-b 3 | 30 |
| Mr A. Ratcliffe b Martin | 34 | | |
| Mr P. G. H. Fender c Valentine b Martin | 24 | | **470** |

### Surrey Bowling

| | Overs | Mdns | Runs | Wkts | Overs | Mdns | Runs | Wkts |
|---|---|---|---|---|---|---|---|---|
| Gover | 33.1 | 4 | 108 | 4 | 11 | 6 | 23 | 2 |
| Parker | 15 | 2 | 78 | 1 | 18 | 7 | 57 | 2 |
| Brown | 34 | 3 | 134 | 2 | 9 | 4 | 18 | — |
| Gregory | 22 | 5 | 62 | 1 | | | | |
| Fender | 17 | 2 | 53 | — | 12 | 1 | 27 | 1 |
| Squires | | | | | 3 | — | 21 | — |

### West Indies Bowling

| | Overs | Mdns | Runs | Wkts |
|---|---|---|---|---|
| Martindale | 9 | — | 28 | — |
| Griffith | 35 | 7 | 93 | 1 |
| Achong | 30 | 1 | 108 | — |
| Da Costa | 24 | 4 | 50 | 1 |
| Valentine | 33 | 5 | 89 | 2 |
| Merry | 9 | 1 | 15 | — |
| Martin | 18.2 | 4 | 53 | 4 |
| Grant | 1 | — | 4 | — |

Umpires: J. Newman and D. Hendren.

## WORCESTERSHIRE v WEST INDIES

Played at Worcester, May 31, June 1, 2, 1933

In a thrilling finish the county, after being 24 runs behind on the first innings, won by one wicket. The match proved a triumph for the Nawab of Pataudi who, revealing his best form, hit his first hundred for Worcestershire and took out his bat when the match ended. His display was not free from fault, for he was missed when 29 and 51, but apart from these chances he gave a superb exhibition. Batting four hours ten minutes, he made his 162 out of 247. Gibbons helped him to put on 107, and Nichol stayed until lunch time, when Worcestershire with eight wickets in hand still required 136. Subsequently wickets fell steadily and when Jackson, the last man, went in 16 were needed. These runs the Nawab obtained. Earlier in the match, Hoad and Sealy batted well. Sealy, cutting and driving finely for two hours, made his first hundred of the tour.

### West Indies

| | | | | |
|---|---:|---|---|---:|
| C. A. Roach b White | 8 | – b White | | 7 |
| E. L. G. Hoad not out | 80 | – lbw b White | | 11 |
| C. A. Wiles b White | 5 | – c Martin b Jackson | | 1 |
| F. R. Martin lbw b Brook | 39 | – c Brook b Howarth | | 7 |
| O. C. Da Costa c Nichol b Brook | 16 | – b Jackson | | 9 |
| C. A. Merry c Quaife b White | 5 | – st Quaife b Howarth | | 18 |
| B. J. Sealy b Howarth | 21 | – c and b Martin | | 103 |
| C. M. Christiani b Jackson | 1 | – b White | | 25 |
| V. A. Valentine b Howarth | 2 | – c Martin b Jackson | | 36 |
| H. C. Griffith b White | 34 | – c Brook b Martin | | 24 |
| E. Achong b Brook | 9 | – not out | | 4 |
| B 14, l-b 2, w 1, n-b 2 | 19 | B 4, l-b 3, w 5 | | 12 |
| | **239** | | | **257** |

### Worcestershire

| | | | | |
|---|---:|---|---|---:|
| Maj. M. F. S. Jewell run out | 3 | – run out | | 16 |
| H. H. Gibbons c Christiani b Achong | 61 | – lbw b Martin | | 64 |
| Nawab of Pataudi c Sealy b Da Costa | 5 | – not out | | 162 |
| M. Nichol c Christiani b Da Costa | 2 | – c Christiani b Sealy | | 2 |
| C. H. Bull b Da Costa | 3 | – c Da Costa b Sealy | | 0 |
| S. H. Martin c Merry b Valentine | 16 | – b Martin | | 7 |
| Mr B. W. Quaife c Christiani b Valentine | 11 | – lbw b Martin | | 10 |
| R. Howarth lbw b Griffith | 68 | – c Griffith b Merry | | 10 |
| G. W. Brook b Griffith | 10 | – c Merry b Griffith | | 11 |
| M. E. White run out | 23 | – b Sealy | | 0 |
| P. F. Jackson not out | 4 | – not out | | 0 |
| B 6, n-b 3 | 9 | L-b 2 | | 2 |
| | **215** | | | **284** |

### Worcestershire Bowling

| | Overs | Mdns | Runs | Wkts | Overs | Mdns | Runs | Wkts |
|---|---|---|---|---|---|---|---|---|
| White | 20 | 1 | 73 | 4 | 17 | 3 | 61 | 3 |
| Jackson | 24 | 9 | 40 | 1 | 18 | 2 | 62 | 3 |
| Martin | 8 | — | 27 | — | 8.5 | 1 | 32 | 2 |
| Howarth | 16 | 1 | 52 | 2 | 9 | 1 | 50 | 2 |
| Brook | 16.1 | 5 | 28 | 3 | 5 | — | 40 | — |

### West Indies Bowling

| | Overs | Mdns | Runs | Wkts | Overs | Mdns | Runs | Wkts |
|---|---|---|---|---|---|---|---|---|
| Griffith | 19.4 | 4 | 49 | 2 | 26.3 | 5 | 69 | 1 |
| Valentine | 19 | 7 | 55 | 2 | 10 | 2 | 26 | — |
| Da Costa | 18 | 5 | 32 | 3 | 17 | 3 | 41 | — |
| Martin | 9 | 1 | 33 | — | 25 | 5 | 56 | 3 |
| Achong | 9 | 1 | 37 | 1 | 14 | 3 | 30 | — |
| Merry | | | | | 10 | — | 24 | 1 |
| Sealy | | | | | 17 | 2 | 36 | 3 |

Umpires: J. Humphries and F. Walden.

## DERBYSHIRE v WEST INDIES

Played at Derby, June 14, 15, 16, 1933

Headley dominated the cricket in this drawn game. Making 258 for once out, he put together his fourth hundred of the tour, his second double century, and became the first of the tourists to complete 1,000 runs. In the second innings he resisted the attack for four hours and forty minutes. Grant, who, in a stand of 110, helped to avert a threatened collapse, declared when Headley left, setting Derbyshire to get 309. Da Costa and Sealy batted brightly in each innings. With two hours remaining, Derbyshire played to save the game. A stand of 124 by Lee and Smith when two wickets had fallen for 9 runs laid the foundation of Derbyshire's first innings lead of 38.

### West Indies

| | | | |
|---|---:|---|---:|
| C. A. Roach lbw b Pope | 14 | – c Elliott b Armstrong | 0 |
| I. Barrow c Smith b Mitchell | 18 | – b Mitchell | 18 |
| G. Headley lbw b Lee | 58 | – not out | 200 |
| E. L. G. Hoad st Elliott b Armstrong | 2 | – b Storer | 0 |
| C. A. Wiles b Lee | 26 | – c and b Townsend | 7 |
| O. C. Da Costa st Elliott b Armstrong | 43 | – c Pope b Townsend | 33 |
| G. C. Grant c Elliott b Mitchell | 16 | – c Mitchell b Townsend | 34 |
| B. J. Sealy c Smith b Armstrong | 58 | – c sub. b Lee | 34 |
| V. A. Valentine st Elliott b Mitchell | 33 | – c Townsend b Mitchell | 1 |
| E. A. Martindale c Worthington b Mitchell | 8 | – not out | 13 |
| E. Achong not out | 0 | | |
| B 1, l-b 4 | 5 | L-b 6 | 6 |
| | **281** | **(8 wkts dec.)** | **346** |

### Derbyshire

| | | | |
|---|---:|---|---:|
| H. Storer b Martindale | 0 | | |
| G. M. Lee c Barrow b Achong | 78 | – c Sealy b Achong | 21 |
| L. Townsend b Valentine | 3 | – b Sealy | 9 |
| D. Smith c Grant b Achong | 67 | – not out | 15 |
| S. Worthington c and b Da Costa | 22 | | |
| A. E. Alderman lbw b Valentine | 12 | – b Da Costa | 1 |
| A. V. Pope b Valentine | 28 | – b Da Costa | 2 |
| Mr A. F. Skinner lbw b Valentine | 24 | – b Achong | 68 |
| H. Elliott c Valentine b Achong | 43 | | |
| T. B. Mitchell st Barrow b Headley | 28 | | |
| T. R. Armstrong not out | 1 | | |
| B 9, l-b 2, n-b 2 | 13 | B 5, l-b 4 | 9 |
| | **319** | | **125** |

### Derbyshire Bowling

| | Overs | Mdns | Runs | Wkts | Overs | Mdns | Runs | Wkts |
|---|---|---|---|---|---|---|---|---|
| Worthington | 12 | 2 | 27 | — | | | | |
| Pope | 11 | 3 | 33 | 1 | 13 | 1 | 59 | — |
| Mitchell | 29 | 5 | 93 | 4 | 35 | 11 | 81 | 2 |
| Armstrong | 19.3 | 4 | 48 | 3 | 31 | 3 | 86 | 1 |
| Townsend | 21 | 6 | 41 | — | 17 | 3 | 34 | 3 |
| Lee | 9 | — | 34 | 2 | 8 | 1 | 36 | 1 |
| Storer | | | | | 10 | — | 44 | 1 |

## West Indies Bowling

| | Overs | Mdns | Runs | Wkts | Overs | Mdns | Runs | Wkts |
|---|---|---|---|---|---|---|---|---|
| Martindale ........ | 18 | 5 | 66 | 1 | 5 | — | 21 | — |
| Valentine ........ | 32 | 6 | 83 | 4 | 6 | — | 19 | — |
| Achong .......... | 45 | 11 | 108 | 3 | 16 | 4 | 33 | 2 |
| Headley .......... | 13 | 6 | 21 | 1 | | | | |
| Da Costa ........ | 16 | 7 | 23 | 1 | 3.5 | 1 | 3 | 2 |
| Sealy ........... | 1 | — | 5 | — | 11 | 1 | 37 | 1 |
| Grant ........... | | | | | 1 | — | 3 | — |

Umpires: A. Dolphin and J. Stone.

# YORKSHIRE v WEST INDIES

## Played at Harrogate, July 5, 6, 7, 1933

Though the West Indies enjoyed the assistance of Constantine, whereas Yorkshire were without Bowes and Macaulay, the visitors suffered defeat by 200 runs. The steady batting of Mitchell, who took out his bat in each innings, and the clever bowling of Verity, who dismissed fourteen batsmen for 83, were almost solely responsible for the county's success. Constantine did fine work with the ball, and on Wednesday half the Yorkshire side were out at lunch time for 66, but Verity and Wood helped Mitchell to improve the position. In the second innings Sutcliffe offered three chances, but made many good strokes. When things were going badly Grant revealed capital defence for the visitors.

## Yorkshire

| | | | |
|---|---|---|---|
| H. Sutcliffe c Grant b Constantine ............... | 2 | – c Da Costa b Sealy ............. | 86 |
| W. Barber st Barrow b Achong ................. | 37 | – c Headley b Constantine ......... | 6 |
| P. Holmes lbw b Constantine ................... | 0 | – c Headley b Sealy ............. | 27 |
| A. Mitchell not out .......................... | 94 | – not out ...................... | 67 |
| M. Leyland c Barrow b Constantine ............. | 9 | – c Barrow b Constantine ......... | 10 |
| Mr A. B. Sellers c Sealy b Constantine ........... | 0 | – run out ...................... | 4 |
| H. Verity c Griffith b Achong ................. | 22 | – lbw b Sealy ................. | 0 |
| F. Dennis lbw b Sealy ....................... | 12 | – c Grant b Constantine ......... | 1 |
| A. Wood lbw b Achong ..................... | 24 | – lbw b Da Costa ............. | 31 |
| T. F. Smailes c Da Costa b Valentine ........... | 4 | – b Da Costa ................. | 0 |
| A. C. Rhodes c Sealy b Constantine ............. | 16 | – c Grant b Constantine ......... | 3 |
| B 8, l-b 10, w 1, n-b 1 ............. | 20 | B 2, l-b 7, w 3, n-b 1 ....... | 13 |
| | **240** | | **248** |

## West Indies

| | | | |
|---|---|---|---|
| C. A. Roach c Barber b Rhodes ................. | 25 | – lbw b Smailes .................. | 30 |
| I. Barrow c Wood b Smailes ................... | 16 | – c Rhodes b Smailes ............. | 13 |
| G. Headley c Rhodes b Verity ................. | 25 | – b Verity ..................... | 1 |
| E. L. G. Hoad c Mitchell b Verity .............. | 6 | – c and b Verity ............... | 22 |
| G. C. Grant st Wood b Verity ................. | 16 | – not out ..................... | 37 |
| O. C. Da Costa st Wood b Verity .............. | 1 | – c Wood b Verity ............. | 19 |
| L. N. Constantine c Dennis b Verity ............. | 0 | – c Wood b Verity ............. | 2 |
| B. J. Sealy c Mitchell b Verity ................. | 13 | – c Verity b Smailes ............. | 5 |
| V. A. Valentine b Rhodes .................... | 0 | – c Smailes b Verity ............. | 9 |
| E. Achong not out ......................... | 1 | – c Mitchell b Verity ............. | 17 |
| H. C. Griffith c Dennis b Verity ................ | 0 | – c Sellers b Verity ............. | 9 |
| B 3, l-b 6, w 1, n-b 2 ................. | 12 | B 3, l-b 5, n-b 1 .......... | 9 |
| | **115** | | **173** |

## West Indies Bowling

| | Overs | Mdns | Runs | Wkts | Overs | Mdns | Runs | Wkts |
|---|---|---|---|---|---|---|---|---|
| Constantine . . . . . . . | 22.5 | 8 | 44 | 5 | 18.4 | 4 | 50 | 4 |
| Griffith . . . . . . . . . . | 15 | 3 | 40 | — | 8 | — | 45 | — |
| Achong . . . . . . . . . | 29 | 3 | 55 | 3 | 4 | — | 13 | — |
| Valentine . . . . . . . . | 16 | 6 | 42 | 1 | 11 | 2 | 37 | — |
| Da Costa . . . . . . . . | 3 | — | 8 | — | 7 | 2 | 15 | 2 |
| Headley . . . . . . . . . | 7 | 1 | 14 | — | 2 | — | 2 | — |
| Sealy . . . . . . . . . . . | 5 | 2 | 12 | 1 | 16 | 2 | 73 | 3 |
| Grant . . . . . . . . . . . | 1 | — | 5 | — | | | | |

## Yorkshire Bowling

| | Overs | Mdns | Runs | Wkts | Overs | Mdns | Runs | Wkts |
|---|---|---|---|---|---|---|---|---|
| Smailes . . . . . . . . . | 10 | 2 | 25 | 1 | 15 | 5 | 38 | 3 |
| Rhodes . . . . . . . . . . | 20 | 5 | 42 | 2 | 12 | 6 | 25 | — |
| Verity . . . . . . . . . . . | 15.2 | 6 | 29 | 7 | 26.3 | 12 | 54 | 7 |
| Leyland . . . . . . . . . | 3 | — | 5 | — | 8 | 1 | 27 | — |
| Sellers . . . . . . . . . . | 1 | — | 2 | — | 3 | 1 | 11 | — |
| Dennis . . . . . . . . . . | | | | | 5 | 1 | 9 | — |

Umpires: W. Reeves and A. E. Dipper.

# OXFORD AND CAMBRIDGE UNIVERSITIES

## OXFORD v CAMBRIDGE [1927]

### CENTENARY DINNER

Many notable cricketers, famous in the history of the university match, and in that of international encounters, gathered on Wednesday, July 6 at the Savoy Hotel, to celebrate, under the chairmanship of Lord Harris, the Centenary year of the Oxford and Cambridge match.

Lord Harris had around him a company which included Viscount Chelmsford, who, as the Hon. F. J. N. Thesiger, captained Oxford in 1890, Hon. Edward Lyttelton, captain of Cambridge in 1878, G. H. Longman, captain of Cambridge in 1874 and 1875, E. F. S. Tylecote, Oxford captain of 1871 and 1872, and the only surviving member of the England team against the Australians at Lord's in 1886, S. M. J. Woods, one of the most famous of Cambridge captains, and a very remarkable Rugby footballer, P. F. Warner, who did not captain Oxford, but led an England team which recovered "The Ashes" from Australia, A. J. Webbe, M. C. Kemp, L. C. H. Palairet, H. D. G. Leveson Gower – all Oxford captains – W. H. Patterson, Sir Timothy O'Brien, Sir K. J. Key, Canon Douglas Hamilton, A. H. Evans, and W. W. Pulman (Oxford), and Sir J. E. Kynaston Studd, the Cambridge captain of 1884.

None but Old Blues were present. Sitting together were M. R. Jardine, who made his great hundred for Oxford in 1892, and his son, D. R. Jardine, vice-captain of Surrey. A. P. F. Chapman, England's captain in the Test match which saw England regain the "Ashes" at The Oval in 1926 was at the same table as A. E. R. Gilligan who took out the last MCC team to Australia. Frank Mitchell, the Cambridge batsman and international rugger forward, was with F. B. Wilson, and E. W. Dawson and E. R. T. Holmes, the rival captains in this year's match, sat opposite each other. B. S. Cumberlege, another English international rugger player, was with F. T. Mann, E. I. Kidd, J. N. Buchanan and the Hon. C. N. Bruce. By a very happy idea the tables were, as far as possible, so arranged that Blues of the same year or years sat together.

In proposing the toast of the evening, Lord Harris said he regarded himself as a connecting link in university cricket inasmuch as he had known one or more of the players in every match from the first in 1827. In conclusion Lord Harris said "In meeting here to-night we are celebrating a great occasion in our splendid game. Each man perhaps looks back on his own particular years. But we are all united in one sense – our devotion to the game of cricket. It has enabled many of us to bear a great part in public events. In itself the varsity match is a public event and our cricket at the universities has been the means of forming great friendships. It leaves in our memories something that is a joy and a happiness for the rest of our lives. Divided though we are in years, we are all united in affection for the game, and the memories of those who have passed away."

In the speeches in reply by E. F. S. Tylecote and G. H. Longman, enthusiastic reference was made to two famous players of long ago – C. J. Ottaway and W. Yardley.

## CAMBRIDGE UNIVERSITY v FREE FORESTERS

### Played at Cambridge, June 10, 12, 13, 1922

It was in this match, the last of the Cambridge season, that the incident occurred which brought down such a sharp reproof from Lord's. J. N. Buchanan was not well enough to play on the second day, and G. B. Cuthbertson, was allowed to bat in his place. Cuthbertson scored 25 before the drawing of stumps, and on Tuesday he was 76 not out when rain set in and caused the game to be left drawn. For Cambridge Fiddian-Green played one of his best innings and Wright bowled very well.

## Free Foresters

| | | | |
|---|---|---|---|
| Mr C. D. McIver b Doggart | 12 | – b Allen | 17 |
| Mr M. W. Payne c Doggart b Wright | 6 | – lbw b Doggart | 7 |
| Mr G. Ashton c Chapman b Allen | 7 | – b Allen | 0 |
| Mr E. L. Kidd c Hill-Wood b Wright | 2 | – c C. T. Ashton b Wright | 2 |
| Mr R. V. Bardsley c C. T. Ashton b Tomlinson | 14 | – b Allen | 55 |
| Mr J. N. Buchanan c Doggart b Tomlinson | 0 | – Mr G. B. Cuthbertson not out | 76 |
| Mr B. Meakin c Lowry b Tomlinson | 8 | – b Wright | 60 |
| Mr M. Falcon c Allen b Wright | 43 | – b Wright | 9 |
| Mr R. G. Evans c and b Hill-Wood | 1 | – b Wright | 15 |
| Mr W. R. Shirley not out | 24 | – b Doggart | 11 |
| Mr P. W. Cobbold c Lowry b Wright | 13 | – not out | 1 |
| B 11, l-b 1, n-b 3 | 15 | B 17, l-b 3, n-b 1 | 21 |
| | **145** | | **274** |

## Cambridge University

| | | | | |
|---|---|---|---|---|
| Mr C. A. Fiddian-Green b Evans | 83 | Mr T. C. Lowry b Falcon | | 18 |
| Mr W. W. Hill-Wood c G. Ashton b Falcon | 49 | Mr G. O. Allen c McIver b Kidd | | 6 |
| Mr A. G. Doggart st Payne b Kidd | 23 | Mr W. J. V. Tomlinson b Falcon | | 8 |
| Mr H. Ashton lbw b Kidd | 9 | Mr P. A. Wright not out | | 4 |
| Mr G. O. Shelmerdine retired hurt | 15 | B 16, l-b 9, n-b 4 | | 29 |
| Mr A. P. F. Chapman c Kidd b Falcon | 46 | | | |
| Mr C. T. Ashton b Kidd | 12 | | | **302** |

### Cambridge University Bowling

| | Overs | Mdns | Runs | Wkts | Overs | Mdns | Runs | Wkts |
|---|---|---|---|---|---|---|---|---|
| Allen | 17 | 6 | 41 | 1 | 21 | 4 | 70 | 3 |
| Wright | 19.1 | 5 | 38 | 4 | 25 | 4 | 82 | 4 |
| Doggart | 8 | 2 | 30 | 1 | 17 | 5 | 48 | 2 |
| Tomlinson | 6 | 2 | 20 | 3 | 4 | — | 15 | — |
| Hill-Wood | 1 | — | 1 | 1 | 3 | — | 21 | — |
| C. T. Ashton | | | | | 5 | — | 17 | — |

### Free Foresters' Bowling

| | Overs | Mdns | Runs | Wkts |
|---|---|---|---|---|
| Falcon | 26 | 4 | 107 | 4 |
| Evans | 17 | 3 | 40 | 1 |
| Cobbold | 17 | 7 | 30 | — |
| Shirley | 4 | 1 | 16 | — |
| Kidd | 19 | 1 | 80 | 4 |

Umpires: G. H. Watts and Hayward.

# MY YEARS AT CAMBRIDGE [1928]

### By George H. Longman

My recollection of Cambridge cricket, which commences as far back as 1872, must of necessity be somewhat dim, and this dimness is immensely increased by the loss of my old friend, Mr A. S. Tabor, with whom my cricket career, both at Eton and Cambridge, was so closely connected, and whose powers of memory would have been of immense assistance.

One thing which has impressed itself on my memory very particularly is the extreme cold of certain early May days at Fenner's, with a strong NE wind blowing, and I particularly recollect having a catch from Mr C. I. Thornton's bat out in the country on such a day, which mercifully stuck in my hands.

Another recollection concerns college examinations. In those days there were certain so-called "May" examinations, and in 1872 the days of those examinations clashed with those fixed for one of the university matches. Mr Thornton, who was then captain of the Cambridge eleven, was very anxious that I should play for the university, and informed me that when he was in the same position he went to his tutor, Mr Blore, told him that he knew nothing about the subjects, and that Mr Blore had excused him from sitting for the examinations. In the innocence of my heart I called upon Mr Blore and the interview was as follows:

Mr Blore: "Good morning, Mr Longman, what can I do for you?"

Mr Longman: "Well, sir, the fact is that the May examinations take place on the same days as those fixed for one of the university cricket matches, and I thought perhaps I might be excused from sitting. The fact is, I don't know much about the subjects."

Mr Blore: "Mr Longman, if you do not know much about the subjects, all I can say is you ought to. Such a request never was made before and I trust it never may be again. Good morning."

Such is life!

Well, in process of time my old friend and companion in arms, Mr A. S. Tabor (now, alas, no longer with us) and I – both freshmen – were given our Blues, and, Cambridge having won the toss, we were selected to go in first for Cambridge in the Oxford match. I took the first ball – a fast yorker on the off stump – which I just managed to stop. The Reverend G. R. Dupuis, who for many years, together with Mr R. A. H. Mitchell, looked after the cricket at Eton, remarked at the time that if he had wanted to bowl me out that was the ball he would have bowled. The wicket was good, runs came steadily, and we were so successful that the hundred was hoisted on the telegraph board without the loss of a wicket – an achievement which had never before been accomplished in the history of the match. As the hundred went up I caught Mr Tabor's eye, and I have always felt that that was the supreme moment of my cricket career.

One cannot give an account of this match without saying one word of admiration for the extraordinarily masterly innings of Mr Yardley, who made 130. He ran me out, but I think he was justified, as I was tired and getting runs very slowly.

The other individual performance which I would like to mention is that of Mr Powys, who obtained six wickets in the first innings and seven in the second; in both Oxford innings my cousin, Sir Edward Bray, the late county court judge, and Mr Powys shared the wickets.

In my judgment Mr Powys was in 1872 the fastest and one of the best left-handed bowlers in England, but he never again bowled with the pace and spin he achieved in that year.

There is an incident which showed supreme captaincy. In the second innings, when Mr Powys was bowling to Mr Ottaway from the nursery end, Mr C. I. Thornton placed himself in a then very unusual place, about level with the long-stop and about three yards on the leg side, where, sure enough, he caught out Mr Ottaway, off quite a good stroke from a ball of Mr Powys's, which, but for Mr Thornton's intervention, would have gone to the boundary.

One recollection of this match might be of interest, viz: that Mr R. A. H. Mitchell, who as everyone knows, was a tower of strength to the Oxford side during his Oxford career, was heard to say at the beginning of the match that he hoped those boys would get a few before they were out. When 20 and 30 went up without a wicket he began to get a little uneasy, and I think that his love for his two Etonian cricket pupils soon became overwhelmed by his loyal partisanship for Oxford – and quite right too.

The one other recollection to which I shall refer only came to the knowledge of Mr Tabor and me two years ago, and was as follows: An ardent Oxonian was sitting in the pavilion at about one o'clock on the first day of the match, and up to him came another Oxonian with the eager question: "Well – how is it going?" "Going!" replied his friend, "there are two . . . little freshmen in, and they've got the hundred up without a wicket."

This match is ancient history, and all cricketers know that we won in one innings. In spite of that, however, I cannot help feeling that Oxford were quite as strong a side as Cambridge, if not stronger. Anyone looking through the list of names of the Oxford eleven will see that it contains those of Mr C. J. Ottaway, Mr W. H. Hadow, Mr W. Law, Mr E. F. S. Tylecote, Mr C. A. Wallroth (an extremely good batsman), Lord Harris (then the Hon. G. Harris), Mr C. K. Francis, Mr A. W. Ridley, and last, not least, Mr S. E. Butler, at that time an extremely good fast bowler. All of these gentlemen, with the exception of Mr C. A. Wallroth, represented the Gentlemen at Lord's in the Gentlemen v Players match at some time during their cricket career.

The 1873 match was won by Oxford by three wickets and was chiefly remarkable for the extreme value of Mr Ottaway's batting for Oxford, but there occurred one hitherto unrecorded incident which, to my mind, immensely emphasised his value. In the second innings, during the stand made by Mr Ottaway and Mr C. E. B. Nepean (which certainly decided the match) the following incident occurred: − A ball from, I think, Mr Tillard, pitched on Mr Ottaway's toe, causing him excruciating pain, but his bat was so close to his foot that all we fieldsmen, with the exception of Mr Tabor, thought he had played the ball. Mr Tabor, fielding at mid-off, did not like to appeal, but after the over he asked the umpire what decision he would have given if he had been appealed to on the question of Mr Ottaway's being out lbw, and the reply came quickly: "I should have given him out, sir!" Mr Ottaway did not wince in the slightest degree until the next ball had been bowled in spite of being in great pain. This was heroic, and I have little doubt was the turning point of the match. Had Mr Ottaway been given out, I think we might have won.

With regard to the Cambridge side, I think it should be mentioned that Mr Goldney, who was given a place in the eleven as a fast bowler, only bowled two overs during the entire match.

In the 1874 match we were entirely out-played, and so far as the Cambridge side is concerned, Mr Tabor's score of 52 in the first innings was the one redeeming feature. He certainly played extremely well.

No picture of Cambridge cricket in the '70's would be complete without some reference to the Rev. A. R. Ward. He was president of the CUCC during the whole of my Cambridge career and was, I believe, chiefly instrumental in preserving Fenner's ground for the university, though this was completed before I went up. He was very anxious to eliminate the word "Fenner's", and took a great deal of trouble to establish the name of the ground as "The University Ground". This desire of his had so great an effect on me that I always write and speak of it as "The University Ground" even now. I believe, however, that to-day the ground is usually described as "Fenner's".

He took an immense interest in Cambridge cricket and at his house in Jesus Lane dispensed hospitality to cricketers with no grudging hand. He was also a well-known figure at Lord's, could always during Oxford and Cambridge matches be found on the top of the pavilion watching every ball bowled, and during hot days was provided with a basin, a large towel and a sponge for the purposes of mitigating the effects of the heat which were bound to be great in the case of a man of his very large build.

One season we were rather short of bowlers and the following conversation took place between Mr Ward and J. C. Shaw who was engaged that May term to bowl at the nets on the university ground.

> Rev. A. R. Ward: "We are a bit short of bowling this year and I think we shall have to enrol you as an undergraduate. Do you know your Greek Testament?"
> J. C. Shaw: "Wort's thot?"

The 1875 match was, to my thinking, one of the best contested games ever played. Oxford won the toss and made 86 runs before a wicket fell. I believe this start was chiefly due to the fact that while the wicket where the ball pitched had been covered, the run-up to the wicket had not, so that whereas Cambridge bowlers had to bowl on a wet run-up the ball pitched on a perfectly dry wicket. This start practically won the match.

In the last innings the two incidents which, I think, sealed the fate of Cambridge were: one, the magnificent catch by Mr A. J. Webbe, which brought Mr Edward Lyttelton's innings to an end, and the other, the catch by Mr Pulman which disposed of Mr Sims. Mr Pulman judged the catch extremely well and held it in spite of the ball being wet. When it came to the last wicket I was anxious to give Mr A. F. Smith a little sal volatile before he went in, but he declined it, saying that he was all right. When he came back to the pavilion he confessed to me that though he did feel all right until he got outside the pavilion, he then felt sick. Poor old fellow, he has departed this life and on the principle of *de mortuis* we will make no further remark about his innings. I feel firmly convinced that, if Mr Macan could only have got to the other end, he would have made the 7 runs off Mr Ridley's lobs.

May I end on another personal note? The Rev. Hon. Edward Lyttelton wrote an article two years ago describing this match, and his last sentence was this: "Has George Longman ever got over it?" I will reply to that question, even at this distance of time, by telling him that considering the match only occurred 53 years ago, he must be patient, but that I am going on as well as can be expected.

## CAMBRIDGE IN 1929

In his very interesting article on "My Years at Cambridge", published in last year's issue of the Almanack, Mr G. H. Longman referred to an old colleague, Mr A. F. Smith, a member of the Cambridge eleven led by Mr Longman, as having departed this life. It is gratifying to learn from Mr Reginald Smith that his brother is not only alive but able to play golf.

## OXFORD MEMORIES [1927]

### By Lord Harris

My first recollection of the Oxford and Cambridge match at Lord's was in 1863 and 1864 when I saw Mr R. A. H. Mitchell play one of his finest innings on a difficult wicket. The story was told that when Voules, better known as Rat Voules, came in Mitchell said to him, "Now, Rat, steady for the first hour", and that, during my career in first-class cricket, was a maxim that I always kept in mind. After that, for six years, being at Eton, I saw no varsity matches though some of my comrades in the Eton eleven had the luck to go to Lord's in 1869 and saw the finish of the celebrated Cobden match, when Frank Cobden in three balls disposed of the last three Oxford wickets with only 3 runs to get. I found at Christ Church several of my old comrades and throughout my residence at Oxford I enjoyed my Christ Church cricket a great deal more than the university cricket. I have elsewhere recorded how I got into the Oxford eleven by a piece of luck. I happened to be a member of the Marylebone Cricket Club and Mitchell, who was then our coach at Eton, wrote to the secretary of MCC, Bob FitzGerald, to give me a place – and to me, that I must play. I had to face some very good bowling, Sam Butler, a very fast and very terrifying bowler, and C. K. Francis. I scored a duck in my first innings but got over a hundred in the second – rather a rarity in those days – and made them sufficiently well to get me a place against the Gentlemen of England in the next match when I scored 67 not out and 64, got three wickets, and fielded well. That secured me a place in the eleven for that year, but I was not successful in the Lord's match. W. N. Powys, one of the fastest bowlers I have ever played, was in great form. However, we had very much the best of it for Sam Butler was quite irresistible, getting fifteen wickets for 95 runs – all ten in the first innings.

Cricket on the Magdalen ground at Oxford was not an exhilarating occupation. The weather at Oxford in May is generally pretty detestable and the ground being close to Cowley Marsh was, I always thought, a dreary place. What remains more distinct than anything perhaps about varsity matches was my re-introduction to Russy Walker whom I had seen playing at Lord's when I was some years younger. He had got on a pair of very wide flannel trousers (one turned up at the bottom) with a harlequin stripe, a harlequin shirt, and a wide-brimmed hat turned up on one side! David Buchanan in those days was a celebrated slow left-hand bowler. He was about the height of "Tich" Freeman, very bald, and of no use at all either with the bat or in the field but a really good bowler. However, I had been so well instructed by Mitchell and Dupuis at Eton in the correct way of playing a slow bowler breaking away to the off – either run out and take the ball full pitch or play back – that he caused me no trouble.

In my third year I was very unlucky. I was a very good long-field catch and used to practise long-field catches assiduously, but doing so that spring in the cold weather I bruised the bones in the palm of my right hand and it hurt me so much to bat that I had to give up my place in the eleven. That contributed to my not being selected for the captaincy of 1874. My father had died and I was down at the time of the annual meeting when the officers were selected. It is quite possible that under any circumstances Billy Law would have been selected captain, but, anyhow, I being absent and it not being known whether I was coming up again, he was elected captain and I, treasurer. We worked together most harmoniously the following term with an eleven which had no distinct merits about it, but developed into one of the finest fielding sides I have ever seen, with some useful bats and bowling.

We played the England eleven that year on the Christ Church ground where one ball from Allen Hill flew up within an inch of my nose and over the wicket-keeper's head to long stop, and Tom Emmett, as he passed me at the end of the over said to me "I reckon you smelt her". Tom Hayward, the Cambridgeshire, not the Surrey, crack, had a fit in the match, and I think never played again. In the match at Lord's that year my father-in-law having asked me to put something on Oxford for him, I was haggling about the odds with Charlie Thornton during lunch, standing out for 6 to 4. Cambridge had made a very good start on a dry wicket. It came on to rain and we went in to lunch. Just before the first ball was bowled when we resumed, Thornton ran down to me as I was fielding close to the rails and laid me the odds I asked for. The first ball got a wicket and we won in one innings. I caught the last man out at long leg and Billy Law gave me the ball with the scores engraved on a silver band.

I remember being full of enthusiasm and zeal that last year, but I cannot remember that I enjoyed 'Varsity matches as I did Christ Church matches on our own ground. There I was playing with the friends of my youth and of The House on a really good ground. For Bullingdon cricket I cared not a jot: it was not business-like enough for my temperament: to start cricket at one o'clock and go to lunch – and a very elaborate one – at a quarter past one did not appeal to me.

Of those with whom I played I suppose not many will be recognised now as players of distinction; but then we thought much of the following: – I have alluded to Sam Butler. At Eton, Mitchell brought him up from Aquatics where he was bowling slows to Upper Club, and taught him to bowl fast. He was a very fierce bowler, drew himself up on his toes, rushed at the wickets, and flung the ball at you – a fling is not an inappropriate expression, for his great feat in the 1871 match spoilt him. He thought pace was all in all, and to keep it up resorted, in the few years of cricket left to him, to a very doubtful action.

C. K. Francis, my comrade in the Gentlemen of England eleven to Canada, 1872, had a beautiful action (tho' it was sometimes questioned) with much spin, and was a very good cricketer all round, but a little lazy.

E. F. S. Tylecote was of the highest class as a bat and wicket-keeper, and after our Oxford days we played together for Kent. He was a most courageous and hardy wicket-keeper in days when gloves were little better than the bare hand. He told me recently that what he suffered from far more than blows, was cold hands. The wicket-keeping gloves in his days were very hard and dry, and keeping them wet improved the chance of holding the ball. Sometimes a piece of ice could be seen at the foot of and behind the wicket for that purpose.

Walter Hadow distinguished himself by scoring over 200 in a Middlesex county match in 1871 – a very rare feat in those days. He was, or thought he was, pursued by a malicious fate; one example of this occurring on our trip to Canada when his brand new dressing bag was dropped in the St Lawrence.

Another fine fast bowler was Cecil Boyle. He did not keep up cricket for long; he went out to South Africa with the Imperial Yeomanry, and was almost the first man killed. But the tower of strength in the Eton and Oxford elevens of my time was C. J. Ottaway. He was a genius at all games, and of great mental ability; a very correct and patient bat, with no brilliant strokes, but all made with great care. He died soon after leaving the university – leaving a marked blank in the athletic world.

Although Oxford cricket has not remained to me as an entirely joyous reminiscence, Oxford itself and its life there have. There one made the friends of one's life and I subscribe loyally and wholeheartedly to the lines:

> "And thro' all the strife and turmoil of life
> 　　Be he Parson, Lord or Squire,
> He's as well known to all in the Cottage and the Hall,
> 　　As the Vane on the old Church spire.
> You may search the whole batch you'll ne'er find his match
> 　　That have been since the world began,
> Be he sober, be he mellow, you'll ne'er find a better fellow
> 　　Than the thoroughbred Oxford Man."

## OXFORD UNIVERSITY v MINOR COUNTIES

Played at Oxford, May 30, 31, June 1, 1934

In a match remarkable for free scoring and dropped catches 1,137 runs were made and only 22 wickets fell. Lord Remnant and Ord took ninety-five minutes over 60 runs but then Rawlins, of Bedfordshire, hitting with extraordinary power, particularly to leg, scored 74 out of 124 in seventy minutes with four 6s and ten 4s among his figures. Farrimond, very fortunate to have three escapes, the first when 64, then punished the bowling with such ease that, hitting a 6 and twenty-two 4s, he got his 174 in three hours forty minutes. The Lancashire reserve wicket-keeper drove, pulled and hit to leg equally well. He had two capable partners, Edrich helping to add 152 in eighty minutes and Sime seeing 119 put on before the innings was closed. Seamer gave a still sounder and more prolonged display. Going in first wicket down at 12 Seamer held out for six hours and three-quarters. Until 168, when he gave his one chance, he did nothing wrong and hit twenty 4s. His sure defence saved Oxford from fear of collapse and he played all his varied strokes with certainty while surpassing his previous admirable effort. Mitchell-Innes, let off behind the wicket when 29, and giving a second chance when 82, stayed with Seamer two hours and fifty minutes while 219 were added. He hit two 6s and nineteen 4s in a most attractive innings. Two unusual incidents occurred on the second morning. When the batsmen were running a three for a hit by Farrimond, each umpire signalled "one short" so reducing the value of the stroke to a single. Then during lunchtime a turf was laid to fill a hole worn by the bowlers and considered dangerous by causing an insecure foothold. The captains agreed with the umpires that this course should be adopted in order to avoid the possibility of accident to a batsman or a bowler.

## Minor Counties

| | | | |
|---|---|---|---|
| Mr C. L. Adamson c Knight b Cohen | 15 | – c Badham b Mitchell-Innes | 0 |
| Lord Remnant b Jackson | 47 | | |
| Mr J. D. Ord b Badham | 35 | – c and b Walker | 7 |
| Mr F. Rawlins b Jackson | 74 | – c Walker b Seamer | 36 |
| Mr T. K. Dobson lbw b Cohen | 18 | – not out | 19 |
| Mr J. G. Halliday c Knight b Badham | 49 | – not out | 33 |
| W. Farrimond b Mitchell-Innes | 174 | | |
| Mr W. J. Edrich c Knight b Jackson | 55 | | |
| Mr W. A. Sime not out | 41 | – c sub. b Walker | 28 |
| B 17, l-b 11, n-b 3 | 31 | B 5, w 1 | 6 |

(8 wkts dec.) 539                     (4 wkts dec.) 129

C. Walters and Mr J. E. Merrall did not bat.

## Oxford University

| | | | | |
|---|---|---|---|---|
| Mr D. F. Walker b Edrich | 38 | Mr P. C. H. Badham b Walters | 2 |
| Mr L. T. Burrowes run out | 3 | Mr N. Cohen b Halliday | 6 |
| Mr J. W. Seamer c Farrimond b Sime | 194 | Mr N. S. Knight b Halliday | 20 |
| Mr N. S. Mitchell-Innes c Merrall b Sime | 140 | Mr J. H. Dyson not out | 4 |
| Mr A. M. Lee c Merrall b Sime | 24 | L-b 7, n-b 1 | 8 |
| Mr A. Benn st Farrimond b Halliday | 5 | | |
| Mr K. L. T. Jackson c Farrimond b Walters | 25 | | 469 |

## Oxford University Bowling

| | Overs | Mdns | Runs | Wkts | Overs | Mdns | Runs | Wkts |
|---|---|---|---|---|---|---|---|---|
| Jackson | 37 | 5 | 109 | 3 | | | | |
| Badham | 36 | 7 | 91 | 2 | | | | |
| Dyson | 21 | 4 | 83 | — | | | | |
| Cohen | 21 | 2 | 89 | 2 | | | | |
| Mitchell-Innes | 17 | — | 88 | 1 | 4 | 3 | 4 | 1 |
| Burrowes | 5 | — | 27 | — | 3 | — | 10 | — |
| Benn | 4 | — | 21 | — | 6 | 2 | 30 | — |
| Walker | | | | | 8 | — | 36 | 2 |
| Seamer | | | | | 10 | 1 | 43 | 1 |

## Minor Counties Bowling

| | Overs | Mdns | Runs | Wkts |
|---|---|---|---|---|
| Merrall | 13 | 3 | 49 | — |
| Remnant | 12 | 6 | 25 | — |
| Dobson | 31 | 13 | 52 | — |
| Edrich | 46 | 8 | 110 | 1 |
| Walters | 28 | 5 | 72 | 2 |
| Halliday | 29 | 8 | 69 | 3 |
| Sime | 40.2 | 8 | 84 | 3 |

Umpires: J. H. King and A. Stoner.

# RECOLLECTIONS OF OXFORD CRICKET [1936]

## Some Memorable 'Varsity Matches

### By H. D. G. Leveson Gower

The editor of *Wisden* has paid me the compliment of asking me to give some reminiscences of Oxford cricket – a compliment that I naturally appreciate very much and an invitation that I readily accept. Perhaps my chief qualification to do this is that, since the beginning of this century, I have had the pleasure of getting up "teams" against the universities, both at Oxford and Cambridge, for over twenty years at Eastbourne, and the last three years at Reigate. While there is always a certain amount of responsibility and at times anxiety in collecting sides, the reward is great, for it has enabled me year after year, not only to keep in touch with the different generations of 'varsity cricketers, but also to retain the friendship of those who were good enough to play for my "elevens". I would like to thank most sincerely the members of the Eastbourne Cricket Club and Sir Jeremiah Colman, the president, and members of the Reigate Priory Club for the use of their famous and picturesque grounds.

My reminiscences of Oxford cricket date back to 1893 for although, before I "went up", I had with keen and boyish delight followed the fortunes of the university matches at Lord's since the early 1880's, it was when I got my "Blue" in 1893 that I may be said to have become intimately connected with Oxford cricket. As now, so in the past, I think every boy had his cricket heroes. My two heroes, funnily enough, were "Cambridge" – A. G. Steel and C. T. Studd, two great cricketers. If at any time they failed – and it was seldom they did – I took their temporary lapses as a personal matter! I had the good fortune to get into the Oxford eleven as a freshman; and here I may say what I think is the general opinion that luck plays a very important part in getting one's "Blue", particularly as a batsman, as a "fresher".

The summer term is so short – a bare eight weeks – that unless one strikes form almost immediately, one is up against very strong opposition. I make mention of this from my own personal experience, for this fortune was on my side. I have before me a list of some of those who played in the freshmen's match of 1893: – G. O. Smith, G. B. Raikes, M. J. Barlow, P. F. Warner, B. N. Bosworth Smith, H. K. Foster, F. G. H. Clayton, G. J. Mordaunt, H. A. Arkwright – and myself. Of these only Mordaunt and I succeeded that year in getting into the eleven; we had the luck of a good start in the trial matches.

Of the four university matches in which I took part, those of 1893 and 1896 provided "incidents". In 1893 C. M. Wells and in 1896 E. B. Shine gave away 8 runs while bowling to prevent Oxford following-on. Being captain at Oxford in 1896 I was naturally very interested in the decision reached by Frank Mitchell in giving orders to E. B. Shine to bowl "no balls" to the boundary in order to prevent my side from going in again. In my opinion the reception he and his team received from the members of MCC and when his team went in to bat from the "spectators", was quite unjustifiable. His motive, no doubt, was to do what he thought was best to ensure victory; whether his policy was sound or not was entirely a matter for him as captain to decide. Personally, I should not have done it; I do not say this because we won. The moral effect of following-on in a university match is great, and the Cambridge eleven had not had an over-strenuous time in the field. Of all the players on both sides only G. J. Mordaunt and myself took part in both these "incident matches".

## TRIUMPH OF THE "LAST CHOICE"

I may perhaps be excused for going rather fully into the match of 1896. Naturally it is the ambition of a captain to win his 'varsity match, and once again Dame Fortune did not forsake me. I had the luck at the last moment of making the right choice for the last place in my side. I left the selection till the morning of the match. G. O. Smith and G. B. Raikes, both old "Blues", were the candidates. I had practically made up my mind to play Raikes. He was a good all-round cricketer – useful bowler, very good slip and a sound bat. What made me alter my mind was this: when I inspected the wicket I did not think that another bowler, unless an exceptional one, would make the difference, and I decided to play the better bat of the two, G. O. Smith. Experience had taught me that you can never have too much batting in a 'varsity match. I took the risk of going into the field against a powerful Cambridge batting side with only four bowlers. It meant that I should have to work these extremely hard. F. H. E. Cunliffe and J. C. Hartley, my two chief bowlers, sent down no fewer than 88 and 92 overs in the match respectively. The last choice won me the match by a superb 132 when we were set 330 runs to win. Thus, G. O. Smith followed the example of Lord George Scott in 1887, for Oxford, and Eustace Crawley, of the Cambridge Eleven, in the same year. The former contributed 100 and 66; the latter 33 and 103 not out; both were last choices. P. F. Warner had a most unusual experience in this 1896 match, being run out in both innings.

Another incident during this game that I recall is a personal talk I had with an onlooker, who apparently came to watch the 'varsity match like one might "The Derby", to spot the winner with advantage to himself. During the lunch interval on the last day, when I was none too happy of our prospects of victory – three good wickets were down for just over 70 – this spectator approached me and said, "I'm afraid Oxford's prospects of victory are very poor. What do you think?" My answer, given rather abruptly, was "We shall win all right". "What?" said my interrogator, "are you sure? I have been laid 8 to 1 against Oxford, shall I take it?" "Certainly", I said, anxious to get away from this rather adhesive person. Ten days afterwards I received a registered envelope with a sapphire pin enclosed – and the following letter: – "Thank you so much for your very valuable information. I collected a very nice sum but I knew it was a certainty as it came from 'The Horse's Mouth'."

With the conclusion of this match my cricket career at Oxford came to an end. Of the four Oxford teams that I played with, I think the 1895 one was the strongest; although we lost this 'varsity match, H. K. Foster played a magnificent 121 out of 196. It was during this match that I received a rather doubtful compliment from an uncle of mine, Sir Edward Chandos Leigh, who was president of MCC in the Jubilee year of 1887. I had made 73 runs in Oxford's first innings, and on my return to the pavilion my uncle, who was seated near the entrance gate, greeted me with these words: "Well done, Schwimp (he could not pronounce his R's). Capital, capital, you played just like I used to." I was somewhat ignorant of his ability as a cricketer beyond what he had from time to time told me so I proceeded to look up his record in 'Varsity matches. It was: 8 in 1852, 0 in 1853, 0 in 1854. A certain limited success!

Knowing that anything written for *Wisden* is handed down to posterity I was anxious to refresh my memory on some subjects and A. H. J. Cochrane, the Oxford Blue of the 'eighties, placed at my disposal helpful and interesting information for which I am much indebted. With regard to facilities for cricket at the universities, the wickets at Fenner's and at Oxford are easy. "The Parks" wicket has improved enormously since the war and has the reputation of being almost the easiest-paced in England. It has been said that despite its loveliness "The Parks" is the only first-class ground in England where it is impossible to get a bath in the pavilion, that the woodwork of the pavilion has not been painted for 25 years; also the practice wickets are very moderate, surrounded by children and perambulators and with a very difficult background to the bowler's arm. In these respects Fenner's has a distinct advantage and another is that a "gate" can be taken there, which is not the case in "The Parks."

## A MATCH PLAYED ON TWO GROUNDS

The Oxford University ground was first used for cricket in 1881. The second fixture of that season – against the Gentlemen of England – was transferred at the last moment to the Christ Church ground where entrance fees could be demanded. The Gentlemen went in on a wicket described as having been hastily prepared. The Oxford fast bowler was E. Peake, whose efforts were marked by pace rather than precision. He got out three batsmen who were no doubt relieved to escape alive, and finally he laid out a prominent amateur with a severe blow on the side of the head. The game was then stopped and about three o'clock in the afternoon another start was made in "The Parks". This time Oxford won the toss and in the course of a drawn match 1,064 runs were scored for 36 wickets.

The Christ Church ground can provide an admirable wicket and the engagement with the Australians has taken place there since 1882. Here it was that in 1884 Oxford for the first and last time beat an Australian eleven. Fifty years ago one joined the OUCC and paid, if I remember right, thirty shillings subscription. The annual grant from the MCC to the University Cricket Club dates from 1881. I think at first it was £150 and has been for the last few years £500. In addition to this each university has received for 1936 the equivalent of a half share of the sum given to each first-class county from the profits of Test matches.

## INTERESTING UNIVERSITY MATCHES

It is a long time since a 'varsity match yielded a close finish. The 2 runs win by Cambridge in 1870 and the 6 runs success of Oxford in 1875 are now very distant memories. In the last decade the only thrill that one remembers was when, a few years ago, the last two Oxford men managed to stay in until the finish and had the minor satisfaction of annoying their opponents though they could not defeat them. During the present century the nearest approaches to a level result were the matches of 1908 and 1926. In the former game Oxford got home by only two wickets, while in the other, the margin in favour of Cambridge was 34 runs.

Often enough we have seen reversal of public form. The side supposed to be the weaker nearly always confounded the prophets not only by winning, but by winning easily. In 1881 Cambridge, with A. G. Steel, Ivo Bligh, the three brothers Studd and other great players had what looked like an invincible side. Steel, practically on his own one may say, had already beaten Oxford three times and was confidently expected to do so a fourth time. But the side failed completely against the fast bowling of Evans, the Oxford captain, and were beaten by 135 runs. In 1895 Oxford, with a splendid eleven, were never in it from start to finish and lost by 134 runs.

Almost every boy who has gone up to Oxford or Cambridge with a big cricket reputation has established himself in university cricket. When the famous Harrovian, F. S. Jackson, appeared depressed by doing badly in the trial matches, S. M. J. Woods, the Cambridge captain, told him that if he was worrying about his "Blue", he could have it at once. Whether such bold policy would always pay may be an open question; it certainly paid in the case of Jackson.

## A MATCH OF FOUR DAYS

Like so many historic engagements, the university match is more difficult to finish than used to be the case. From 1827, the year of the first match played, until 1898, there were 64 matches, and of these only two were drawn. In 1888 on the Monday the weather was so bad, with thick darkness and continuous rain that there was never the remotest possibility of play, and on the two following days, though cricket was possible, progress in the mud was so slow as to make it soon evident that a draw was inevitable. In these circumstances it was pointed out by a strong body of outside opinion that there had not been a draw for over 40 years, and perhaps in order to obviate such a novelty the MCC agreed to allot a fourth day to the match. As it happened there came a further downpour and the game had to be abandoned unfinished, after all.

The university match probably has lost something of its old interest and popularity, but this idea may be more apparent than real. Before the Mound stand was built a ring of ten or fifteen thousand people was about as many as Lord's could hold. Given fine weather you might get ten thousand spectators a day at the university match, but with the accommodation at Lord's increased to Test match requirements, this is a mere sprinkling and the ground looks somewhat empty. But, while this contrast is not much to go by, it remains true that there are not the coaches and carriages, the arbours and the luncheons, at the match that there once were. It is curious that the attraction of matches like Eton and Harrow, or Eton and Winchester, seems to increase as the years go by; as opportunities for social gatherings they become more patronised every season. But, if as a cricket spectacle it holds its own, as a society function the university match is not what it used to be.

## SOME COMPARISONS

How cricketers of to-day compare with the generations of thirty or forty years ago is a subject always likely to provide plenty of argument – I personally can see very little difference. Many able critics of the game deplore the decadence of modern cricket, and sigh for the glories of the past when bowlers bowled a length, and batsmen hit sixers instead of pottering about and stopping the ball with their pads. Have there not always been hitters and slow players, stylists and pad-players, steady bowlers and erratic bowlers? One must allow that shortly after the war a style of batting came into fashion which seemed to most of us far from an improvement on methods of the older school. The player moved in front of the stumps, facing the bowler, and with a short lift of the bat pushed the ball to either side of the wicket. The style was quite distinctive and many batsmen exploited it with much skill. Its advantage was that it involved close watching of the ball, but the limited swing of the bat meant a loss of power, while against fast bowling the "two-eyed stance", as it was then and is still called, was less effective than the usual position with the left shoulder forward. All this was fifteen years ago, but in 1936 the two-eyed stance or anything approaching it was less in evidence. Men like Mitchell-Innes and Yardley are typical high-class university batsmen, playing in what surely should be the correct style – the style handed down by tradition and coaching.

The status of the university player in relation to other first-class cricket has not changed much in the last half century. The universities meet the first-class counties as equals, and most Blues would be worth a place, or at any rate a trial, in all but the strongest county teams. This, it may be contended, has always been the case, but what is more curious is that the proportion of Blues who, after their undergraduate days are over, have the inclination and the opportunity of taking a prominent part in public cricket has also hardly altered at all. If you look at the score of any Oxford and Cambridge match, whether in 1885 or 1895 or 1925, you will find four or five names familiar in county or other first-class cricket. Hawke, Key, O'Brien, Bainbridge, Marchant, Fry, Woods, Jackson, Jessop, Warner, the Fosters, Ranjitsinhji and A. O. Jones, of the earlier decades have their counterparts in Allen, Jardine, Chapman, Robins, Holmes, Duleepsinhji, Turnbull and others of our own time. It is pleasant to notice that the longer first-class programme, with its exhausting calls upon a young man's leisure, and the economic conditions, with their even more exacting demands on his resources, have not stopped this valuable supply of test-match captains and county captains and players. Space will not permit of my trying to describe what I might think were the best teams that played for Oxford and Cambridge during the time I was connected with university cricket and afterwards. But I would say that the best Cambridge side that I played against was that of 1893. Of individual players, there are obviously many that I would like to mention but again space will not allow me to do so. Are they not to be found in *Wisden*?

Let us examine finally university cricket as a stepping-stone to Test cricket. If we restrict our enquiry to matches against Australia and South Africa, as being contests in which for many years we have in this country chosen absolutely our best teams, we find that since 1880, when we first played Australia over here, 63 amateur cricketers have appeared in England elevens. Of these, 33 have been Oxford or Cambridge Blues. The distinction of being selected while still in residence at the university is uncommon, and only seven of the 33 have enjoyed it. And yet four of the five English teams sent out to Australia since the war have been under the leadership of university players, A. E. R. Gilligan, A. P. F. Chapman, D. R. Jardine and G. O. Allen. If I had to choose a combined university eleven of Blues since 1919 – and what a difficult task! – my nominations would be the following twelve: – G. O. Allen, H. Ashton, A. P. F. Chapman, K. S. Duleepsinhji, A. E. R. Gilligan, E. R. T. Holmes, D. R. Jardine, D. J. Knight, C. S. Marriott, Nawab of Pataudi, G. T. S. Stevens and G. E. C. Wood.

The older one gets, more precious must be one's memories. Very precious to me are the memories of my Oxford days and my connection with Oxford cricket – happiest of cricket days. Never shall I forget the kindness shown to my by one to whom Oxford owes more than she can ever repay with regard to university cricket. That is A. J. Webbe, who for so many years brought teams to play against the universities. It was the example he set that I tried to follow and if in any way I was successful it is to him that I give my grateful thanks.

Long may the universities continue to be the stepping stone of "Cricket" – long may university cricketers continue to keep up the high tradition handed down to them by famous cricketers of the past.

# GENTLEMEN v PLAYERS

## THE LORD'S MATCH

Played at Lord's, July 14, 15, 16, 1919

As at The Oval, though not to the same extent, cricket on the first day was seriously curtailed by rain. The start was delayed till close upon three o'clock, and the game was only in progress for about two hours and a quarter. During that time the Gentlemen scored 138 and lost five wickets. Thanks to Knight and Warner the hundred went up with only two men out, but the last half-hour was disastrous. Knight played flawless cricket on the slow pitch, and did not seem at all troubled by Parkin's clever variations of pace. Tuesday was cold but dry, and the Gentlemen had a great day, fairly outplaying their powerful opponents. The sensation of the match came at the start of the Players' innings, four wickets going down – the first three to Douglas and the fourth to Falcon – for 17 runs. After this dreadful collapse the Players had an uphill battle to fight and despite a great effort by George Hirst they found themselves 49 runs to the bad at the end of the innings. For the third time in his career Douglas did great things at Lord's for the Gentlemen. Swerving a little and keeping an irreproachable length he was at his very best, and he had his reward in the shape of eight wickets for 49 runs. At the end of the afternoon the Gentlemen pushed home their advantage. Knight played beautifully on the improving pitch, and for the loss of Gillingham's wicket 71 runs were scored. On Wednesday the match ended in a draw but the cricket was in many respects so splendid that the inconclusive result did not spoil anyone's pleasure. The wicket had become quite fast, and the batting on both sides asserted itself. To begin with the Gentlemen carried their score to 322 for eight wickets, Warner declaring at three o'clock, and leaving the Players with 372 to get to win. Knight had the extreme satisfaction of making a hundred in his first Gentlemen v Players match at Lord's. Not till he began to force the pace in view of an early closure was there the slightest blemish in his cricket. As a matter of record it may be added that he hit thirteen 4s and was batting for three hours and ten minutes. He was a master in everything that he did and especially in the skill with which he detected and duly punished the very slow ball of which Parkin is so fond. When the Players went in the Gentlemen, with no fear of being beaten, made heroic efforts to win. At the opening of the innings Hobbs and George Gunn, the latter of whom was tired out by fielding, had to withstand a tremendous onslaught from Falcon and Douglas. Nothing happened, but during the first half-hour or so Gunn had many anxious moments. Surmounting all difficulties the two batsmen scored 134 together and a draw became inevitable. Hobbs played a great innings, hitting up his 113, without a chance, in a little over two hours and a half. The last incident of the game was a wonderful catch at short leg, Stevens stopping the ball with his left hand and holding it at the second attempt. A point in connection with Hobbs's batting must not be forgotten. Except W. G. Grace, who performed the feat in 1870, 1872, and 1873, no one had ever before made a hundred both at The Oval and Lord's in Gentlemen and Players matches in the same year.

## Gentlemen

| | | | |
|---|---|---|---|
| Rev. F. H. Gillingham lbw b Parkin | 10 | – lbw b Parkin | 29 |
| Mr D. J. Knight c Kennedy b Parkin | 71 | – c Hearne b Parkin | 124 |
| Mr A. J. Evans c Woolley b Parkin | 0 | – b Parkin | 63 |
| Mr P. F. Warner c Woolley b Parkin | 34 | – b Woolley | 0 |
| Hon. C. N. Bruce b Parkin | 9 | – hit wkt b Woolley | 37 |
| Mr J. W. H. T. Douglas c Gunn b Kennedy | 30 | – not out | 11 |
| Mr M. Falcon lbw b Kennedy | 11 | | |
| Mr A. W. Carr c Woolley b Kennedy | 2 | – b Woolley | 40 |
| Maj. D. C. Robinson c Woolley b Kennedy | 9 | – c Hobbs b Woolley | 0 |
| Mr G. T. S. Stevens c Hearne b Parkin | 24 | – b Bestwick | 11 |
| Mr G. M. Louden not out | 4 | | |
| B 4, l-b 6 | 10 | B 1, l-b 1, n-b 5 | 7 |
| | **214** | **(8 wkts dec.)** | **322** |

## Players

| | | | |
|---|---|---|---|
| J. B. Hobbs c and b Douglas | 2 | – c Louden b Falcon | 113 |
| G. Gunn c Louden b Douglas | 1 | – b Louden | 57 |
| J. W. Hearne b Douglas | 5 | – not out | 32 |
| P. Mead c Bruce b Falcon | 9 | – c Stevens b Falcon | 2 |
| E. Hendren c Gillingham b Douglas | 42 | | |
| F. E. Woolley b Douglas | 22 | | |
| G. H. Hirst not out | 50 | | |
| A. S. Kennedy lbw b Stevens | 12 | | |
| C. Parkin b Douglas | 9 | | |
| A. Dolphin c Louden b Douglas | 2 | | |
| W. Bestwick b Douglas | 0 | | |
| B 6, l-b 3, n-b 2 | 11 | B 8, l-b 3 | 11 |
| | **165** | | **215** |

## Players' Bowling

| | Overs | Mdns | Runs | Wkts | Overs | Mdns | Runs | Wkts |
|---|---|---|---|---|---|---|---|---|
| Kennedy | 19 | 5 | 36 | 4 | 13 | 2 | 38 | — |
| Bestwick | 3 | — | 7 | — | 13.3 | 2 | 55 | 1 |
| Parkin | 39.5 | 9 | 85 | 6 | 24 | 2 | 109 | 3 |
| Woolley | 31 | 12 | 45 | — | 25 | 7 | 71 | 4 |
| Hirst | 7 | 1 | 18 | — | 5 | — | 22 | — |
| Hearne | 4 | — | 13 | — | 6 | — | 20 | — |

## Gentlemen's Bowling

| | Overs | Mdns | Runs | Wkts | Overs | Mdns | Runs | Wkts |
|---|---|---|---|---|---|---|---|---|
| Falcon | 12 | 2 | 44 | 1 | 12.1 | 2 | 55 | 2 |
| Douglas | 20.5 | 3 | 49 | 8 | 16 | — | 59 | — |
| Stevens | 6 | 2 | 28 | 1 | 14 | 3 | 34 | — |
| Louden | 9 | 1 | 33 | — | 15 | 3 | 45 | 1 |
| Evans | | | | | 4 | — | 11 | — |

Umpires: Atfield and Moss.

# THE OVAL MATCH

Played at The Oval, June 30, July 1, 1920

The weak point of English cricket in 1920 was clearly revealed in the representative match at The Oval, the Gentlemen's batting being so immeasurably below the standard of pre-war days. There was plenty of run-getting power of an ordinary kind on the side, but at the same time a sad lack of class. J. N. Crawford on his best form stood out above his colleagues, but he had not had much practice. This indeed was with one exception, his only first-class match during the season. The Players, on the other hand, had overwhelming strength in batting, and it is not surprising that they won the game by an innings and 87 runs. The result, however, should not have been quite so bad as this. The Gentlemen had to play their second innings on a wicket that kicked in the most disconcerting fashion after rain, and to add to this ill-luck P. R. Johnson was badly hurt and F. T. Mann kept at home by influenza. Johnson had a bone in his wrist broken by a ball from Howell, and could not play cricket again till nearly the end of August.

The match had a sensational opening, the Gentlemen, batting first on a good wicket, being so demoralised by Parkin's variety of pace that they were all out for 184, a total that against such opponents was almost equivalent to defeat. Encouraged by early success Parkin bowled in a form he had never approached in his other matches in London. He tried all his experiments, and they all answered. He bowled Carr with the very slow ball of which he is so fond, and beat Fender, who was hitting away in fine style, with a yorker of lightning pace. It was a big performance to take as he did nine of the ten wickets – six of them bowled down – but one could not help speculating as to how he would have got on against a Gentlemen's team of years ago. The Players wound up on the first day in a winning position, their score standing at 215 for three wickets with Hearne not out 76. Hobbs, when firmly set, was out to a wonderful catch with the right hand by Tennyson at mid-on. On the following morning Hearne was a little too anxious to get his hundred, and missed it by 5 runs. Still, he played a very fine innings, and Woolley hit splendidly. Rain had taken the pace out of the ground and the wicket had become very nasty indeed when the Gentlemen went in for the second time. Bowling at a great pace Howell got up so much that very little could be done against him.

## Gentlemen

| | | | |
|---|---|---|---|
| Mr P. R. Johnson b Parkin | 9 | – retired hurt | 4 |
| Mr A. N. Jewell b Parkin | 3 | – b Howell | 0 |
| Mr A. W. Carr b Parkin | 23 | – c Strudwick b Howell | 18 |
| Mr H. L. Wilson c Strudwick b Howell | 7 | – c Holmes b Parkin | 25 |
| Mr J. N. Crawford c Woolley b Parkin | 37 | – b Howell | 5 |
| Mr F. T. Mann c Rhodes b Parkin | 0 | – absent ill | 0 |
| Maj. Hon. L. H. Tennyson c Russell b Parkin | 54 | – c Parkin b Hearne | 35 |
| Mr P. G. H. Fender b Parkin | 38 | – c Strudwick b Howell | 0 |
| Hon. F. S. G. Calthorpe b Parkin | 0 | – c Hobbs b Howell | 3 |
| Mr M. Falcon b Parkin | 0 | – b Howell | 0 |
| Mr J. C. White not out | 4 | – not out | 15 |
| B 4, l-b 5 | 9 | B 7, l-b 1 | 8 |
| | **184** | | **113** |

## Players

| | | | |
|---|---|---|---|
| J. B. Hobbs c Tennyson b Falcon | 63 | A. Kennedy c White b Falcon | 17 |
| P. Holmes b Falcon | 0 | H. Strudwick c and b Fender | 6 |
| A. C. Russell b White | 35 | C. Parkin c White b Falcon | 9 |
| J. W. Hearne c Fender b Crawford | 95 | H. Howell not out | 3 |
| E. Hendren c Jewell b Crawford | 54 | B 10, l-b 3, w 1 | 14 |
| F. E. Woolley c and b Fender | 60 | | |
| W. Rhodes c Carr b Falcon | 28 | | **384** |

## Players' Bowling

| | Overs | Mdns | Runs | Wkts | Overs | Mdns | Runs | Wkts |
|---|---|---|---|---|---|---|---|---|
| Howell | 19 | 6 | 54 | 1 | 16 | 5 | 40 | 6 |
| Parkin | 24.1 | 1 | 85 | 9 | 14 | 2 | 52 | 1 |
| Kennedy | 8 | 1 | 26 | — | 1 | — | 4 | — |
| Woolley | 2 | — | 10 | — | | | | |
| Hearne | | | | | 2.3 | — | 9 | 1 |

**Gentlemen's Bowling**

|  | Overs | Mdns | Runs | Wkts |
|---|---|---|---|---|
| Falcon | 26.5 | 2 | 157 | 5 |
| Calthorpe | 6 | 1 | 13 | — |
| White | 30 | 4 | 83 | 1 |
| Crawford | 17 | — | 65 | 2 |
| Fender | 9 | 1 | 51 | 2 |
| Tennyson | 2 | 1 | 1 | — |

Umpires: W. A. J. West and A. Millward.

## THE OVAL MATCH

Played at The Oval, July 8, 9, 10, 1925

Giving a wonderful display of hitting on Friday evening, the Gentlemen beat the Players by four wickets, the winning stroke being made in what must, in any circumstances, have been the last over of the match. The performance of the amateurs in thus snatching a victory was truly extraordinary for they were set 198 to make in an hour and three-quarters against some of the best bowling in the country. From the time they went in, however, it at once became obvious they meant to go for the runs. Three wickets fell for 59 and although a fine pace was maintained, the task looked almost impossible of achievement, when, with only thirty-five minutes left, 87 runs were still required. For all that, Haig hit out at everything and after Fender's dismissal ten minutes later with the total at 141, nothing could stop Haig and Aird who, finishing with 30 runs in the last ten minutes, gained for their side a memorable triumph. The remarkable nature of the amateurs' play, moreover, was not confined to the fierce hitting at the close. After losing eight wickets in the first innings for 217, they brought their total to 458. The aggregate of runs – 1,313 for the loss of 31 wickets – was the highest ever recorded in a match between Gentlemen and Players.

The Players occupied the wickets for the whole of the opening day, scoring 403 for the loss of eight batsmen. To the dismay of the spectators, Hobbs was bowled in trying to pull the first ball he received from Calthorpe. For any further success, however, the Gentlemen had to wait nearly an hour and a half, Sandham and Hearne, meanwhile, raising the score to 101. Sandham played particularly stylish cricket and if Hearne was not so happy, the latter went on to complete a three-figure innings in about three hours and shared in a partnership of 115 with Hendren, who batted in his finest form. Well as the game was going for their side, Bowley and Parsons batted very cautiously but there came a refreshing change when the latter was joined by Kennedy. Haig met with little success but he seemed to cause the batsmen more trouble than anyone else.

Hobbs next morning declared the Players' innings closed at the overnight total and on the Gentlemen going in, Calthorpe hit so finely through the covers that the first wicket produced 81 runs. To break up the partnership, Tate crossed over and found himself so well suited by the change of ends that, coming very fast off the pitch, he sent down fourteen overs for 37 runs and five wickets. In this way half the side were out for 113 and although Tennyson drove finely, if enjoying some luck in several strokes in the slips not going to hand, there came the time when eight wickets had fallen for 217. Thus when Haig joined Allen, the Gentlemen required 37 runs to escape a follow-on. A great partnership ensued, the two Middlesex amateurs gradually obtaining a mastery over the bowling and then hitting with such freedom that well inside three hours they put on 193 runs. Haig drove with great power on either side of the wicket and Allen, more varied in his strokes, was seen to remarkable advantage. Thanks to these two men, so far from the question of a follow-on arising, the Gentlemen left off 9 runs ahead with a wicket to fall, and next morning increased their lead to 55. If a little uncertain at times, Allen offered no actual chance and in the circumstances gave a famous display. He batted altogether about four hours and had sixteen 4s in his 130.

Hobbs in the Players' second innings was seen quite at his best, scoring 51 out of 90 in less than an hour but then starting for a run Bowley, his partner, would not have, threw away his wicket. The rest of the professionals' batting, although Bowley and Hendren enjoyed some success, rather lacked distinction, except that Hearne maintained a skilful and untiring defence. With 252 runs on the board, Hobbs for the second time in the match declared and then came the marvellous hitting of the amateurs that won the match just on time. The Players, it should be noted, enjoyed the assistance of none of the Yorkshiremen and they were also without the help of Woolley. Carr and Stevens were the most prominent amateurs missing from the other side. An interesting appearance was that of C. H. Titchmarsh who has made numerous hundreds for Hertfordshire. Edwards, a left-handed bowler, included in the Players' team, takes a lot of wickets for Buckinghamshire.

## Players

| | | | |
|---|---|---|---|
| J. B. Hobbs b Calthorpe | 5 | – run out | 51 |
| A. Sandham c Hill b Fender | 50 | | |
| J. W. Hearne b Allen | 103 | – not out | 65 |
| E. Hendren b Haig | 59 | – c Tennyson b Calthorpe | 31 |
| E. H. Bowley lbw b Bettington | 12 | – b Bettington | 39 |
| J. H. Parsons c Hill b Fender | 72 | – lbw b Calthorpe | 14 |
| A. Kennedy not out | 59 | – c Fender b Tennyson | 15 |
| M. W. Tate b Allen | 7 | – lbw b Calthorpe | 5 |
| F. Edwards b Fender | 8 | – c Bettington b Tennyson | 10 |
| H. Strudwick not out | 4 | – not out | 7 |
| B 5, l-b 17, n-b 2 | 24 | B 12, n-b 3 | 15 |
| | (8 wkts dec.) 403 | | (7 wkts dec.) 252 |

H. Howell did not bat.

## Gentlemen

| | | | |
|---|---|---|---|
| Hon. F. S. G. Calthorpe c Parsons b Tate | 63 | – b Tate | 11 |
| Mr C. H. Titchmarsh c Strudwick b Tate | 21 | – run out | 15 |
| Mr R. Aird c Strudwick b Tate | 8 | – not out | 31 |
| Mr G. R. Jackson b Tate | 5 | – c Hobbs b Kennedy | 14 |
| Hon. C. N. Bruce lbw b Tate | 7 | – b Kennedy | 36 |
| Hon. L. H. Tennyson c Strudwick b Tate | 69 | – st Strudwick b Tate | 28 |
| Mr P. G. H. Fender b Edwards | 21 | – b Tate | 12 |
| Mr G. O. Allen b Howell | 130 | | |
| Mr R. H. Bettington b Kennedy | 8 | | |
| Mr N. Haig c Strudwick b Tate | 98 | – not out | 51 |
| Mr M. L. Hill not out | 6 | | |
| B 15, l-b 6, n-b 1 | 22 | L-b 2 | 2 |
| | 458 | | 200 |

### Gentlemen's Bowling

| | Overs | Mdns | Runs | Wkts | Overs | Mdns | Runs | Wkts |
|---|---|---|---|---|---|---|---|---|
| Allen | 23 | 4 | 81 | 2 | 3 | 1 | 9 | — |
| Calthorpe | 27 | 6 | 71 | 1 | 17 | — | 59 | 3 |
| Haig | 26 | 5 | 56 | 1 | 18 | 3 | 64 | — |
| Bettington | 17 | 1 | 86 | 1 | 17 | 1 | 64 | 1 |
| Fender | 27 | 4 | 85 | 3 | 9 | 3 | 19 | — |
| Tennyson | | | | | 4 | — | 22 | 2 |

**Players' Bowling**

|  | Overs | Mdns | Runs | Wkts | Overs | Mdns | Runs | Wkts |
|---|---|---|---|---|---|---|---|---|
| Tate .............. | 42 | 9 | 148 | 7 | 12 | — | 80 | 3 |
| Howell ........... | 28 | — | 119 | 1 | 6 | — | 31 | — |
| Kennedy ......... | 23 | 4 | 64 | 1 | 9.3 | — | 59 | 2 |
| Hearne ........... | 10 | 2 | 31 | — | | | | |
| Edwards .......... | 23 | 3 | 55 | 1 | | | | |
| Bowley ........... | 11 | 2 | 19 | — | 5 | — | 28 | — |

Umpires: F. Parris and W. Phillips.

## THE OVAL MATCH

Played at The Oval, July 6, 7, 8, 1927

All the northern counties having engagements, the teams for this match had necessarily to be chosen exclusively from the south and consequently were not representative. Still the Players had a powerful side and, had time allowed, would have won by a large margin, the Gentlemen, when stumps were pulled up, wanting 163 runs to avoid an innings defeat and having only two wickets to fall. Rain, preventing any cricket on Thursday, altered the conditions so completely that the Gentlemen laboured under a tremendous disadvantage, but, in any circumstances, they could not have been expected to make a close fight with opponents obviously so much the stronger in every respect.

Hobbs turned out for the first time since the Surrey and Yorkshire match at Leeds at the end of May. Despite over a month's absence from the field, he played soundly for an hour and a half, though lacking something of his customary ease and freedom. Following upon Hobbs' dismissal at 93, Hendren began the innings of the match. In mastering the bowling the Middlesex batsman enjoyed the assistance of three good partners. Mead scored 54 out of 99 in seventy minutes, Parsons shared in a stand of 74 and, with Hendren and Shepherd together 100 runs were added in sixty-five minutes. The hitting all round the wicket was of the most brilliant description. Hendren had started in somewhat restrained fashion, taking nearly an hour and a half over his first 50 runs, but he reached three figures in two hours and a half and when eventually out to a catch near the pavilion rails, he had made 150 in three hours and a half. Although taking considerable risks latterly, he did not give a chance and among his strokes were sixteen 4s.

The Gentlemen had 424 runs hit from their bowling in five hours and a half but they secured nine wickets during that time – no small achievement considering the formidable nature of the batting they had to face. Falcon, going on when Hendren and Shepherd were scoring fast, actually disposed not only of those two batsmen, but of Newman and Kennedy as well, in the course of fourteen balls at a cost of 5 runs. Durston, hitting up 25 out of the last 33 runs, showed himself a much improved batsman. Utley of the Royal Air Force, a bowler of considerable pace, did not cause any trouble but Peebles, who had never before figured in a first-class match, kept Hobbs watchful for a long time and beat Sandham who, playing forward, turned a ball onto the stumps.

The great feature of the match came on Friday, when Hobbs having declared, Kennedy proceeded to dismiss the whole of the Gentlemen's team. On a drying pitch that showed signs of wear in places, Kennedy found a spot in line with the leg stump and, making the ball get up as well as turn a lot, he compelled eight batsmen to give catches while another was stumped, the ball on only one occasion hitting the stumps. In taking all ten wickets, the Hampshire medium paced bowler recalled the still more remarkable achievement of Arthur Fielder in the Centenary Match at Lord's – memorable for the wonderful success of fast bowlers on each side.

Despite the soaking it had received on Thursday, the pitch improved appreciably when rolled a second time and Falcon and Franklin withstanding the bowling during the last half hour, the Gentlemen managed to avoid defeat. Some dropped catches when the follow-on began early in the afternoon contributed however to the amateurs' escape. Peebles, going in third wicket down at 91, showed very good form and helped Tennyson to add 40 for the fifth partnership. He was the first of four batsmen who, after the tea interval, fell to Shepherd in the course of ten overs at a cost of 16 runs. Kennedy made his record for the match, twelve wickets for 58.

### Players

| | |
|---|---|
| J. B. Hobbs c Franklin b Wyatt .......... 43 | J. Newman lbw b Falcon ............... 0 |
| A. Sandham b Peebles ................. 27 | A. Kennedy c Franklin b Falcon ......... 2 |
| J. W. Hearne c Utley b Haig ............ 19 | W. H. Livsey not out .................. 9 |
| E. Hendren c Jeacocke b Falcon .........150 | T. J. Durston not out ................. 25 |
| C. P. Mead b Haig ................... 54 | B 16, l-b 6, n-b 3 .............. 25 |
| J. H. Parsons st Franklin b Wyatt ........ 29 | |
| T. Shepherd b Falcon ................. 41 | (9 wkts dec.) 424 |

### Gentlemen

| | |
|---|---|
| Mr N. V. H. Riches c Durston b Kennedy ........ 0 | – c Shepherd b Hearne ............ 26 |
| Mr R. E. S. Wyatt c Shepherd b Kennedy ......... 18 | – c Newman b Kennedy .......... 15 |
| Mr A. Jeacocke c Sandham b Kennedy .......... 7 | – c Shepherd b Kennedy ......... 19 |
| Mr N. Haig c Hendren b Kennedy ............... 19 | – c Kennedy b Durston ........... 23 |
| Mr C. P. Brutton b Kennedy ................... 0 | – c Hendren b Shepherd .......... 3 |
| Hon. L. H. Tennyson c Hendren b Kennedy ....... 4 | – lbw b Shepherd ............... 29 |
| Mr J. P. Parker c Durston b Kennedy ............ 2 | – c Kennedy b Shepherd .......... 1 |
| Mr M. Falcon c Hendren b Kennedy ............. 16 | – not out ...................... 11 |
| Mr W. B. Franklin c Mead b Kennedy ............ 2 | – not out ...................... 20 |
| Mr I. A. R. Peebles not out .................... 3 | – c Livsey b Shepherd ........... 17 |
| Mr R. P. H. Utley st Livsey b Kennedy .......... 7 | |
| L-b 2 ........................... 2 | B 10, l-b 5, w 1, n-b 1 ...... 17 |
| **80** | **181** |

### Gentlemen's Bowling

| | Overs | Mdns | Runs | Wkts |
|---|---|---|---|---|
| Haig ............. | 36 | 6 | 117 | 2 |
| Utley ............ | 13 | 3 | 57 | — |
| Peebles .......... | 25 | 4 | 95 | 1 |
| Wyatt ............ | 24 | 4 | 70 | 2 |
| Falcon ........... | 22 | 1 | 60 | 4 |

### Players' Bowling

| | Overs | Mdns | Runs | Wkts | Overs | Mdns | Runs | Wkts |
|---|---|---|---|---|---|---|---|---|
| Kennedy ......... | 22.4 | 10 | 37 | 10 | 15 | 8 | 21 | 2 |
| Newman ......... | 7 | 3 | 8 | — | 14 | 5 | 27 | — |
| Hearne ........... | 15 | 5 | 33 | — | 19 | 1 | 61 | 1 |
| Durston ......... | | | | | 18 | 3 | 35 | 1 |
| Shepherd ......... | | | | | 14 | 7 | 20 | 4 |

Umpires: L. C. Braund and J. Stone.

## THE LORD'S MATCH

Played at Lord's, July 15, 16, 17, 1936

Drawn. The match will long be remembered for its stirring finish. G. O. Allen, who led the Gentlemen, declared his innings closed at five o'clock on the third day when eight wickets were down for 195 runs, and set the Players 132 to get in roughly seventy-five minutes, including the extra half-hour. Extraordinary cricket followed. By six o'clock the Players had four men out for 33 runs. The breakdown was caused by Kenneth Farnes, the Essex fast bowler, who, taking a little longer run than usual and making the fullest use of his height, sent the ball down at a pace unequalled at headquarters since the days of C. J.

Kortright. When Farnes bowled Gimblett, Hammond and Hardstaff, he sent a stump in each case catapulting head high to drop at the feet of Levett, who stood back more than a dozen yards. It is extremely probable that by this wonderful bowling Farnes won his place in the team for Australia.

Allen, when Farnes tired, bowled with tremendous zeal and he sent away Leyland's middle stump with a ball almost as fast as his colleague produced. Allen claimed the extra half-hour, an unusual thing in these matches, but Fishlock, the leading left-hander of the year, and Sinfield played out time, the Players, who were a particularly strong side, finishing 68 behind with half their wickets in hand. J. W. A. Stephenson, Army and Essex, played a leading part in the match, for in the Players' first innings he bowled his medium-fast swinging deliveries with such deadly effect that he accomplished his best performance in first-class cricket. T. N. Pearce, another Essex player, made the highest score in the game and was the one Gentleman who mastered exceptionally good bowling. Disappointments on the Gentlemen's side ware R. E. S. Wyatt, G. O. Allen and N. S. Mitchell-Innes, and Gimblett, Barnett and Leyland did little for the Players. McCorkell, however, kept wicket splendidly, conceding only four byes while 325 runs were scored.

Not a ball could be bowled on Wednesday, eight hours' continuous rain leaving the turf so saturated that at five o'clock it was decided to give up all hope of play for the day. Winning the toss on Thursday, Allen decided to take a chance and bat, but the Gentlemen were put out for 130. The collapse was so complete at the start that at the end of an hour six men were out for 22, and had it not been for the Surrey players, E. R. T. Holmes and F. R. Brown, who came to the rescue by adding 70 runs in just over an hour, the side would have been in sorry plight. Brown hit hard in front of the wicket and claimed six 4s while scoring 55 in seventy-five minutes. Alan Melville was caught off a ball that struck his forehead after going off the edge of his bat, and he did not field. Gover and Copson, who were both striving for a place in the MCC Australian side, shared the wickets, Gover taking six for 41 runs and Copson, in seventeen overs and a ball, securing four for 29. Each man made many deliveries keep unexpectedly low, and Gover found his length and best pace so quickly that in his first seven overs he disposed of four men for 10 runs.

The Players began in hardly more promising fashion, losing Barnett, Gimblett and Leyland for 21 runs, and it was left to Hammond and Hardstaff to effect a recovery. They put on 95 in seventy minutes, Hammond, with the help of a 6 and six 4s, making 72 in a hundred minutes. In one dramatic spell Stephenson took three wickets in four balls, and, going on a second time, he took six more wickets for 27 runs in the course of ten overs. Altogether, Stephenson claimed the last nine wickets for 46 runs, a feat ranking as one of the best by an amateur in a Gentlemen v Players match.

Beginning their second innings 64 runs in arrear, the Gentlemen experienced a bad time between noon and half past one, but Holmes and Pearce pulled the game round. Pearce withstood a keen attack for nearly three hours and he hit splendidly on the leg side. Allen's declaration and the exciting conclusion of the match followed.

### Gentlemen

| | | | |
|---|--:|---|--:|
| Mr R. E. S. Wyatt b Gover | 0 | – c Hammond b Sinfield | 4 |
| Mr N. S. Mitchell-Innes lbw b Gover | 3 | – c Copson b Sinfield | 19 |
| Mr A. Melville c Verity b Copson | 1 | – b Verity | 13 |
| Mr M. J. Turnbull c Gimblett b Gover | 4 | – lbw (N) b Verity | 1 |
| Mr T. N. Pearce b Gover | 1 | – st McCorkell b Verity | 85 |
| Mr E. R. T. Holmes b Gover | 30 | – c Fishlock b Hammond | 37 |
| Mr G. O. Allen lbw (N) b Copson | 3 | – c Copson b Hammond | 13 |
| Mr F. R. Brown c Copson b Gover | 55 | – c Hammond b Sinfield | 4 |
| Mr W. H. V. Levett not out | 9 | – not out | 15 |
| Mr J. W. A. Stephenson b Copson | 9 | | |
| Mr K. Farnes b Copson | 5 | | |
| B 4, l-b 6 | 10 | L-b 3, n-b 1 | 4 |
| | **130** | **(8 wkts dec.)** | **195** |

## Players

| | | | |
|---|---|---|---|
| H. Gimblett c and b Stephenson | 3 | – b Farnes | 1 |
| C. J. Barnett c Levett b Allen | 0 | – lbw b Stephenson | 2 |
| W. R. Hammond b Stephenson | 72 | – b Farnes | 7 |
| M. Leyland b Stephenson | 0 | – b Allen | 11 |
| J. Hardstaff c Pearce b Stephenson | 69 | – b Farnes | 4 |
| L. B. Fishlock not out | 21 | – not out | 26 |
| R. A. Sinfield lbw b Stephenson | 0 | – not out | 12 |
| N. McCorkell b Stephenson | 0 | | |
| H. Verity b Stephenson | 2 | | |
| A. R. Gover c Levett b Stephenson | 3 | | |
| W. Copson b Stephenson | 8 | | |
| B 14, l-b 2 | 16 | | |
| | **194** | | **63** |

## Players' Bowling

| | Overs | Mdns | Runs | Wkts | Overs | Mdns | Runs | Wkts |
|---|---|---|---|---|---|---|---|---|
| Gover | 15 | 3 | 41 | 6 | 12 | 2 | 46 | — |
| Copson | 17.1 | 6 | 29 | 4 | 13 | 1 | 25 | — |
| Verity | 15 | 5 | 35 | — | 26.3 | 13 | 33 | 3 |
| Sinfield | 6 | 3 | 15 | — | 23 | 7 | 39 | 3 |
| Hammond | | | | | 8 | 2 | 32 | 2 |
| Leyland | | | | | 4 | 1 | 16 | — |

## Gentlemen's Bowling

| | Overs | Mdns | Runs | Wkts | Overs | Mdns | Runs | Wkts |
|---|---|---|---|---|---|---|---|---|
| Allen | 14 | 3 | 46 | 1 | 2 | — | 16 | 1 |
| Farnes | 16 | 3 | 43 | — | 9 | 3 | 22 | 3 |
| Stephenson | 16.5 | 6 | 46 | 9 | 9 | 3 | 20 | 1 |
| Brown | 7 | — | 37 | — | 2 | — | 5 | — |
| Wyatt | 1 | — | 6 | — | | | | |

Umpires: J. Hardstaff and J. Newman.

# OTHER MATCHES

## MIDDLESEX (Champion County) v THE REST OF ENGLAND

### Played at The Oval, September 13, 14, 15, 1920

Middlesex having won the championship in such dramatic fashion by beating Surrey at Lord's, their match with the Rest of England naturally proved a big attraction at The Oval, the fixture bringing a memorable season to an end. The profits were divided between Earl Haig's Fund and the Cricketers' Fund. Middlesex did themselves no discredit and escaped defeat, a break-up in the weather limiting play on the third day to three hours, but against a side which included nine of the men chosen to go to Australia they were completely over-matched. Up to a certain point the county quite failed on winning the toss, but after seven wickets had gone down for 162 Stevens and Longman pulled the game round, putting on, by really fine cricket, 129 runs. The total at the drawing of stumps was 302 for eight wickets. The sensational cricket of the match came on the second day. Never, perhaps, has the bowling of a champion county been so mercilessly knocked about. The Rest of England went in soon after twelve o'clock, and when the time came to draw stumps they had actually scored 603 for five wickets, runs coming at the rate, roughly speaking, of 115 an hour. Hobbs and Russell opened the innings by hitting up 185 together in an hour and a half, and after Russell left Ernest Tyldesley helped Hobbs to put on 152 in an hour and a quarter. No such hitting, against a good side, was seen at The Oval or anywhere else during the season. Making his biggest score of the year, Hobbs was for the most part astonishingly brilliant. At one point of his innings he became reckless, and seemed as if he wanted to get out, but the hope of making 200 steadied him, and he played as well as ever. Except for a possible chance in the slips there was no flaw in his cricket during his first 100 runs. Batting for three hours and twenty minutes, he hit a 6, two 5s, and twenty-five 4s. The condition of the ground did not admit of play on Wednesday till just upon two o'clock and as the match, owing to the departure of the team for Australia, had been restricted to three days, a draw was always probable. Middlesex did well on the soft wicket, and only four men were out when at six o'clock the game was given up. Despite the disappointment of the third day the financial result was eminently satisfactory, each Fund receiving the sum of £493 11s. 11d.

### Middlesex

| | | | |
|---|---|---|---|
| Mr C. H. L. Skeet b Douglas | 9 | – c Strudwick b Douglas | 7 |
| H. W. Lee c Strudwick b Parkin | 21 | – c Tyldesley b Woolley | 36 |
| J. W. Hearne b Wilson | 22 | – c Woolley b Wilson | 26 |
| E. Hendren b Woolley | 65 | – c and b Woolley | 67 |
| Mr P. F. Warner c Hitch b Douglas | 20 | – not out | 19 |
| Mr F. T. Mann lbw b Wilson | 8 | – not out | 30 |
| Mr N. Haig c Tyldesley b Douglas | 4 | | |
| Mr G. T. S. Stevens not out | 69 | | |
| Mr H. K. Longman c Russell b Rhodes | 66 | | |
| H. R. Murrell c Woolley b Wilson | 13 | | |
| T. J. Durston b Wilson | 5 | | |
| B 10, l-b 4, n-b 2 | 16 | B 3, l-b 3, n-b 1 | 7 |
| | **318** | | **192** |

## Rest of England

| | |
|---|---|
| J. B. Hobbs c Hendren b Stevens . . . . . . . . .215 | Mr J. W. H. T. Douglas not out . . . . . . . . . 69 |
| A. C. Russell c Hendren b Durston . . . . . . . 84 | W. Rhodes not out . . . . . . . . . . . . . . . . . . . . 29 |
| E. Tyldesley c Lee b Durston . . . . . . . . . . . . 66 |     B 16, l-b 1, w 6, n-b 2 . . . . . . . . . . 25 |
| P. Holmes c Hendren b Durston . . . . . . . . 44 | |
| F. E. Woolley c Skeet b Stevens . . . . . . . . . 71 | (5 wkts dec.) 603 |

W. Hitch, Mr E. R. Wilson, C. Parkin and H. Strudwick did not bat.

## Rest of England Bowling

| | Overs | Mdns | Runs | Wkts | Overs | Mdns | Runs | Wkts |
|---|---|---|---|---|---|---|---|---|
| Hitch . . . . . . . . . . . . | 18 | 3 | 67 | — | 4 | — | 20 | — |
| Douglas . . . . . . . . . . | 20 | 6 | 61 | 3 | 8 | 1 | 31 | 1 |
| Woolley . . . . . . . . . . | 20 | 7 | 46 | 1 | 18 | 6 | 67 | 2 |
| Parkin . . . . . . . . . . | 18 | 2 | 57 | 1 | 13 | 2 | 42 | — |
| Wilson . . . . . . . . . . | 26.4 | 9 | 44 | 4 | 13 | 4 | 23 | 1 |
| Rhodes . . . . . . . . . . | 10 | 2 | 27 | 1 | 6 | 4 | 2 | — |

## Middlesex Bowling

| | Overs | Mdns | Runs | Wkts |
|---|---|---|---|---|
| Durston . . . . . . . . . . | 34 | 2 | 174 | 3 |
| Haig . . . . . . . . . . . . . | 12 | — | 71 | — |
| Stevens . . . . . . . . . . | 29 | 2 | 153 | 2 |
| Hearne . . . . . . . . . . | 20 | 1 | 116 | — |
| Lee . . . . . . . . . . . . . | 15 | 3 | 64 | — |

Umpires: A. J. Atfield and W. A. J. West.

## LANCASHIRE (Champion County) v THE REST OF ENGLAND

Played at The Oval, September 11, 13, 14, 1926

A truly extraordinary game was this between Lancashire and the Rest of England, the champion county accomplishing a splendid performance on Saturday, but in the subsequent stages of the contest going to pieces so completely, that on the third afternoon England – having declared with only two wickets down – gained a victory by 374 runs. Rarely indeed does cricket, with all its uncertainty, furnish such a complete transformation. To meet the champions, Mr H. D. G. Leveson Gower had succeeded in getting together the identical eleven that on the same ground only a few weeks earlier had beaten Australia in the final Test match. No higher compliment could have been paid any side, and on the opening day Lancashire gave every suggestion that they would justify the flattering estimate of their powers. In little more than three hours they disposed of the England team for 217, and then proceeded to make 84 without loss, thus leaving off on Saturday evening only 133 behind with all their wickets in hand.

Possibly the pitch was a trifle damp at the start. At any rate Macdonald made the ball get up in awkward fashion, and his work seemed to have a very disconcerting effect upon the batsmen, Hobbs and Sutcliffe were both out by the time the score reached 9, and Woolley left at 36. Chapman made a brilliant attempt to knock the bowlers off their length, hitting up 43 out of 64 in forty minutes, but Stevens failed, and at lunch time there were actually five wickets down for 115. It was left to Hendren to come to the rescue of the side. The Middlesex professional going in on Sutcliffe's dismissal at 9, was ninth man out at 206. For two hours and a half he played superlatively good cricket and, apart from a mis-hit when 31, he scarcely made a single faulty stroke. He drove particularly well to the off, and his hooking of the short ball was most skilful. His hits included two 5s – all run – and ten 4s. Sibbles, in disposing of him held a very hard return, and another fine catch was that by which Watson got rid of Geary, the fieldsman taking the ball high up one hand at long-on. All round, Lancashire's work in dismissing England for so moderate a score was admirable. On the champions going in, Makepeace and Hallows set to work carefully and skilfully. They took seventy minutes to bring the score to 50, but added 34 runs in another half hour, and so placed their side in what appeared to be a commanding position.

Monday brought such an astonishing collapse that in about two hours the ten Lancashire wickets went down for the addition of 93 runs. Makepeace and Hallows – together for rather more than two hours in all – were separated at 106, and although Hallows left at 145, Lancashire – at that point only 72 behind with eight wickets in hand – still appeared to have much the best of the game. Those eight wickets however, produced only 32 runs, and so the county, instead of gaining a handsome lead, found themselves at the end of an innings on each side 40 runs in arrear. Yorkers from Larwood sent back Ernest Tyldesley and Watson, and with the dismissal of those two men all resistance vanished. Once Makepeace and Hallows had gone, Larwood bowled splendidly, and Tate accomplished an admirable piece of work.

Having broken down in batting, Lancashire proceeded to lose their skill in bowling, and to such purpose did Hobbs and Sutcliffe turn the many opportunities afforded them that these two men hit up 157 in ninety-five minutes. Not only did the county bowlers become demoralised, but Richard Tyldesley missed Hobbs twice. Following upon Hobbs' departure, Sutcliffe hit out in most brilliant fashion. In one over from Sibbles he scored two 4s, a 2, a 6, and a 4, and was bowled by the last ball of the over – but that happened to be a no ball. Altogether Sutcliffe made 136 out of 225 in two hours and five minutes, with a 6 and twenty-three 4s among his strokes. Despite the pace at which he travelled, he gave no chance, and made only one false hit. Never has he given a more dazzling display. During the last twenty-five minutes of the day, Woolley and Hendren added 66, England leaving off 331 ahead with eight wickets in hand. The 291 runs were made in a hundred and fifty-five minutes.

Next day the Lancashire bowlers fared even worse than on Monday, Woolley and Hendren hitting up 177 runs in seventy minutes, and the full partnership of ninety-five minutes producing 243 runs. This tremendous scoring was chiefly the work of Woolley, who, a little uncertain in his timing to begin with, and giving chances at 76 and 93, actually made 172 in two hours and five minutes. Once over early troubles he gave an amazing display – one which even he in his brilliant career can rarely have surpassed. He had two 6s and seventeen 4s among his figures, and Hendren hit twelve 4s, the latter, although over-shadowed by his colleague, also playing fine cricket. Thanks to this wonderful partnership, England by ten minutes past one were 508 runs on, and Hobbs thereupon declared.

Lancashire, after the tremendous "towelling" their bowlers had met with, proceeded to bat so wretchedly, that they were all out in two hours for 134. In the course of twenty minutes before lunch Makepeace and Ernest Tyldesley were got rid of for 12 and immediately on resuming Hallows left. Iddon and Watson made something of a stand, but Stevens broke up the partnership, and, flattered by the reckless batting of the Lancastrians, the Middlesex amateur secured six wickets for 52 runs.

## Rest of England

| | | | |
|---|---|---|---|
| J. B. Hobbs b Sibbles | 1 | – c Makepeace b Sibbles | 62 |
| H. Sutcliffe c Duckworth b Macdonald | 6 | – c Macdonald b Iddon | 136 |
| F. E. Woolley lbw b R. Tyldesley | 21 | – not out | 172 |
| E. Hendren c and b Sibbles | 100 | – not out | 77 |
| Mr A. P. F. Chapman b Macdonald | 43 | | |
| Mr G. T. S. Stevens b Sibbles | 2 | | |
| W. Rhodes c Woolley b Macdonald | 10 | | |
| G. Geary c Watson b R. Tyldesley | 9 | | |
| M. W. Tate c Sibbles b R. Tyldesley | 1 | | |
| H. Larwood b Macdonald | 8 | | |
| H. Strudwick not out | 4 | | |
| B 8, l-b 2, n-b 2 | 12 | B 15, l-b 5, n-b 1 | 21 |
| | **217** | **(2 wkts dec.)** | **468** |

## Lancashire

| | | | |
|---|---|---|---|
| H. Makepeace b Larwood | 43 | – c Strudwick b Larwood | 2 |
| C. Hallows lbw b Rhodes | 73 | – c Woolley b Tate | 7 |
| E. Tyldesley b Larwood | 17 | – lbw b Tate | 1 |
| F. Watson b Larwood | 0 | – b Stevens | 15 |
| J. Iddon st Strudwick b Rhodes | 6 | – st Strudwick b Stevens | 34 |
| F. M. Sibbles c Strudwick b Geary | 3 | – not out | 25 |
| Mr L. Green not out | 4 | – c Woolley b Stevens | 11 |
| E. A. Macdonald b Tate | 0 | – c Geary b Stevens | 0 |
| R. Tyldesley b Tate | 3 | – b Stevens | 10 |
| A. Woolley b Tate | 10 | – c Hendren b Stevens | 4 |
| G. Duckworth lbw b Tate | 0 | – b Tate | 19 |
| B 14, l-b 4 | 18 | B 5, n-b 1 | 6 |
| | **177** | | **134** |

### Lancashire Bowling

| | Overs | Mdns | Runs | Wkts | Overs | Mdns | Runs | Wkts |
|---|---|---|---|---|---|---|---|---|
| Macdonald | 19.5 | 3 | 73 | 4 | 19 | — | 113 | — |
| Sibbles | 17 | 4 | 48 | 3 | 20 | 3 | 87 | 1 |
| R. Tyldesley | 13 | 2 | 54 | 3 | 6 | — | 53 | — |
| Woolley | 7 | 2 | 16 | — | 18 | — | 99 | — |
| Iddon | 8 | 2 | 14 | — | 13 | — | 95 | 1 |

### Rest of England Bowling

| | Overs | Mdns | Runs | Wkts | Overs | Mdns | Runs | Wkts |
|---|---|---|---|---|---|---|---|---|
| Larwood | 24 | 5 | 61 | 3 | 3 | — | 7 | 1 |
| Tate | 27.3 | 7 | 40 | 4 | 18.4 | 4 | 49 | 3 |
| Geary | 18 | 6 | 27 | 1 | | | | |
| Stevens | 5 | — | 14 | — | 12 | 4 | 52 | 6 |
| Rhodes | 7 | 2 | 17 | 2 | 10 | 2 | 20 | — |

Umpires: H. Chidgey and H. Butt.

# NOTTINGHAMSHIRE (Champion County) v THE REST OF ENGLAND

Played at The Oval, September 14, 16, 17, 18, 1929

Pitted against the very powerful team chosen to represent the Rest of England, Nottinghamshire gave a display full worthy of the champion county of the year. Victory, as it happened, did not attend their efforts but the margin against them in the end amounted to no more than 8 runs and in driving their formidable antagonists so close they gave the best performance of any county similarly engaged since Yorkshire beat The Rest twenty-four years ago. Neither Hammond nor Sutcliffe took part in the game, but otherwise the team Nottinghamshire were called upon to oppose, even if it did not include J. C. White or Freeman, was thoroughly representative. Wyatt winning the toss, The Rest enjoyed the advantage of first innings and, keeping the Nottinghamshire men in the field for the whole of Saturday, ran up in four hours and forty minutes a score of 399. Only 5 runs had been registered when a clever catch at fine leg sent back Hobbs but this early success on the part of the county was immediately followed by a glorious display of hitting on the part of Woolley who in the course of a hundred minutes scored 106 out of 154. Settling down at once in his brightest form, Woolley seemed to experience no difficulty in dealing with any of the bowling brought against him and, while not omitting other strokes, drove with that particular ease and power that render his batting such a delight. Not only did he hit the ball to the boundary twelve times, but on three occasions he sent it out of the ground and, despite the pace at which he obtained his runs, made not the semblance of a mistake. In marked contrast to the brilliant exhibition given by Woolley was the quiet work of Sandham who, if quite vigorous after the luncheon interval, exercised, to begin with, such pronounced caution that when his score reached 50, he had been at the wicket nearly two hours. Still, Sandham played exceedingly good cricket and gave no chance. He was out from a hard drive, George Gunn at mid-off just reaching the ball with his left hand, knocking it on to his body and holding it with his right hand. Nottinghamshire worked very keenly, their fielding being maintained at a high standard of excellence, but they experienced further trouble from Wyatt who, while giving when 13 a hard chance to short leg, played in fine form for two hours and three-quarters yet, after showing so much judgment, lost his wicket hitting out wildly. Later on came some very bright batting from Robins and Tate, both of whom were out to Bland, the Shrewsbury boy, so successful at school in 1928. Larwood, called upon to send down only eighteen overs, came out with much the best bowling figures.

Facing so considerable a total as 399, Nottinghamshire, no doubt, would in any circumstances have set to work with no small measure of deliberation and, as it happened, two early disasters, George Gunn leaving at 21 and Walker at 35, compelled pronounced caution. Whysall and Carr set themselves to retrieve the position and deserved great praise for the way in which they pulled the game round. At the same time the cricket prior to the luncheon interval – justified as it was – proved rather trying for the spectators. Afterwards came a marked change. Carr repeatedly drove with much power, and Whysall, encouraged by the example of his captain, investing his play with some freedom, an admirable partnership of two hours and a quarter in all produced no fewer than 169 runs. Dismissed at last by Woolley, Carr, when at length he allowed himself to play his usual game, intermingled drives with fine pulls and, giving no chance, had fifteen 4s among his strokes. Equally free from fault was the batting of Whysall who, if slow at times, placed his strokes with much skill, and maintained a flawless defence during a stay which lasted three hours and a quarter. After five wickets had fallen, Barratt gave a characteristic display. Taking many risks, he gave chances – almost on the pavilion rails – when 36 and 41, but, with three 6s among his hits, scored 54 in forty minutes. The Nottinghamshire batting never really broke down but no large measure of success attended anyone else and the close of the innings which lasted four hours and three-quarters found the county 35 runs in arrear. Clark, occasionally making the ball rise awkwardly, was the leading figure in an attack admirably supported in the field.

Hobbs on Tuesday atoned for his failure in the first innings by a masterly piece of batting. With such ease did he score from the Nottinghamshire bowlers that he appeared assured of yet another hundred when, playing outside a ball from Bland, he lost his wicket. Among his strokes – many of them through the covers – were ten 4s. Woolley, Sandham and Wyatt failing to repeat their successes of Saturday, The Rest found themselves in a distinctly anxious position – six men out and only 135 runs on the board – but relief came from Leyland and Robins who, despite skilful bowling backed up by admirable work in the field, hit to such purpose that they added 107 in sixty-five minutes. Both batsmen drove especially well and, if Robins began in somewhat uncertain fashion, Leyland played splendidly all through, varying his powerful drives with some well-timed cuts. Thanks largely to these two men the total, which at one time had threatened to leave

Nottinghamshire only a moderate task, amounted to 282. Sam Staples came out with the best figures of four skilful bowlers.

Set 318 runs to get, Nottinghamshire made on Tuesday evening a capital start to that formidable task. George Gunn and Whysall, of course, were at pains to play themselves in but while Gunn continued to exercise much restraint right up to the drawing of stumps, Whysall, after a while, batted with considerable freedom, scoring with particular skill on the leg side and putting together a score of 50 out of 88 in sixty-five minutes. G. V. Gunn, being sent in to play out time with his father, did so, the day's cricket ending with the score 99 for one wicket.

In this way Nottinghamshire, when they enetered upon the concluding stage of the contest, wanted 219 more runs for victory, and had nine wickets to fall. The county thus possessed no mean chance of success, and, had the support accorded George Gunn been really good, the runs must have been knocked off. As it was Carr stayed until the score reached 141, and Payton helped to add 59, but this was not enough. Certainly Gunn did his part, displaying such superb defence and unlimited patience that a win for his side and a personal triumph in the shape of a three-figure innings would have been a fitting reward for his skill. At times it is true, with the bowling excellent and the light indifferent, he seemed quite content to keep up his wicket, and he had batted two hours and forty minutes when his score reached 50. Still he accomplished a great performance in withstanding the attack for nearly four hours and a half and in assisting to bring the total to 279. To such an extent did he hold himself in hand that only five of his strokes reached the boundary. Barratt again made a spirited effort, hitting up 45 in less than an hour with eight 4s among his figures. When Bland the last man came in 20 runs were still required for victory. Sam Staples scoring cleverly and keeping the bowling as far as possible, 11 of the 20 were obtained but then Robins disposed of Bland and a very fine struggle ended in a desperately narrow win for The Rest. Robins, making the ball turn considerably on occasion, took six wickets and thus had a big share in the success of his side.

## Rest of England

| | | | |
|---|---|---|---|
| J. B. Hobbs c Larwood b Barratt | 2 | – b Bland | 68 |
| A. Sandham c G. Gunn b Larwood | 82 | – lbw b Larwood | 15 |
| F. E. Woolley b Barratt | 106 | – c Whysall b S. J. Staples | 15 |
| J. O'Connor c Bland b Larwood | 6 | – c G. V. Gunn b Bland | 10 |
| Mr R. E. S. Wyatt c Barratt b S. J. Staples | 85 | – b Barratt | 11 |
| M. Leyland c Whysall b Bland | 17 | – c and b Bland | 75 |
| L. Ames c Whysall b S. J. Staples | 15 | – b Barratt | 0 |
| Mr R. W. V. Robins b Bland | 37 | – st Lilley b S. J. Staples | 45 |
| M. W. Tate c Carr b Bland | 32 | – c Whysall b S. J. Staples | 7 |
| T. W. Goddard b Larwood | 13 | – not out | 13 |
| E. C. Clark not out | 1 | – c Lilley b S. J. Staples | 16 |
| B 1, l-b 2 | 3 | B 2, l-b 5 | 7 |
| | **399** | | **282** |

## Nottinghamshire

| | | | |
|---|---|---|---|
| G. Gunn b Tate | 8 | – b Robins | 96 |
| W. Whysall b Clark | 97 | – c O'Connor b Goddard | 50 |
| W. Walker c Tate b Clark | 1 | – c Sandham b Robins | 0 |
| Mr A. W. Carr b Woolley | 91 | – b Goddard | 6 |
| W. Payton c Ames b Clark | 21 | – c Hobbs b Robins | 32 |
| B. Lilley c Tate b Clark | 10 | – b Goddard | 5 |
| F. Barratt c Wyatt b Woolley | 54 | – c Sandham b Clark | 45 |
| G. V. Gunn st Ames b Robins | 6 | – lbw b Robins | 17 |
| S. J. Staples lbw b Robins | 21 | – not out | 18 |
| H. Larwood st Ames b Robins | 11 | – c Woolley b Robins | 11 |
| Mr R. D. F. Bland not out | 15 | – c Woolley b Robins | 1 |
| B 17, l-b 10, n-b 2 | 29 | B 14, l-b 13, n-b 1 | 28 |
| | **364** | | **309** |

## Nottinghamshire Bowling

| | Overs | Mdns | Runs | Wkts | Overs | Mdns | Runs | Wkts |
|---|---|---|---|---|---|---|---|---|
| Larwood ......... | 18 | 3 | 54 | 3 | 15 | 1 | 73 | 1 |
| Barratt .......... | 21 | 1 | 83 | 2 | 18 | 2 | 50 | 2 |
| S. J. Staples ....... | 36.1 | 7 | 146 | 2 | 18.5 | 2 | 63 | 4 |
| Bland ........... | 24 | 2 | 106 | 3 | 13 | — | 75 | 3 |
| G. V. Gunn ....... | 2 | — | 7 | — | 2 | — | 14 | — |

## Rest of England Bowling

| | Overs | Mdns | Runs | Wkts | Overs | Mdns | Runs | Wkts |
|---|---|---|---|---|---|---|---|---|
| Clark ........... | 25 | 5 | 69 | 4 | 25 | 5 | 73 | 1 |
| Robins .......... | 26.1 | 6 | 108 | 3 | 27.3 | 3 | 89 | 6 |
| Tate ............ | 21 | 2 | 64 | 1 | 13 | 4 | 38 | — |
| Goddard ........ | 14 | 2 | 52 | — | 23 | 5 | 56 | 3 |
| Woolley .......... | 9 | — | 42 | 2 | 4 | — | 12 | — |
| Wyatt ........... | | | | | 4 | — | 13 | — |

Umpires: J. Hardstaff and J. Stone.

# MR H. D. G. LEVESON GOWER'S XI v MCC AUSTRALIAN TEAM

### Played at Scarborough, September 6, 7, 8, 1933

In this drawn game Mitchell emulated the rare feat performed three days previously by Harry Parks of Sussex, of scoring two separate not out hundreds. His first, occupying nearly four hours, was characterised by sound defensive cricket, but he hit gaily in the last innings when, however, play could not be regarded seriously. For MCC Hendren, who with Macaulay completed the side as illness and other engagements kept away eight of the seventeen members of the original party, batted magnificently. His century, the fifth in six innings, included two 6s and twenty-three 4s. Wyatt, despite injury, showed good form as did Sutcliffe, whose hundred took him less than two and a half hours.

## MCC Australian Team

| | | |
|---|---|---|
| H. Sutcliffe c Mitchell b Townsend ............. | 41 – not out ...................... | 119 |
| Mr R. E. S. Wyatt not out .................... | 70 – not out ...................... | 44 |
| M. Leyland c Dobson b Jupp ................... | 11 – c Mitchell b Jupp .............. | 82 |
| E. Hendren c Dobson b Human ................ | 154 – c Langridge b Jupp ............ | 7 |
| E. Paynter b Jupp ........................... | 7 | |
| Mr F. R. Brown c Farnes b Jupp ................ | 8 – st Gilligan b Jupp .............. | 10 |
| H. Verity c Gilligan b Farnes .................. | 12 | |
| W. Voce c Gilligan b Farnes ................... | 10 | |
| G. Duckworth c Langridge b Townsend ......... | 20 | |
| G. G. Macaulay c Gilligan b Langridge .......... | 3 | |
| W. E. Bowes c Farnes b Langridge .............. | 4 | |
| B 2, l-b 5, n-b 2 .................... | 9 | B 2, l-b 4, w 1 ............ 7 |
| | 349 | (3 wkts dec.) 269 |

## Mr H. D. G. Leveson Gower's XI

| | | |
|---|---|---|
| A. H. Bakewell b Macaulay | 51 | – b Bowes ........................ 0 |
| W. W. Keeton lbw b Voce | 10 | – c Paynter b Brown ............. 41 |
| Jas. Langridge b Voce | 2 | – Paynter b Brown ............... 45 |
| A. Mitchell not out | 100 | – not out ....................... 100 |
| Mr T. K. Dobson c Wyatt b Bowes | 21 | – b Brown ...................... 0 |
| L. Townsend c Duckworth b Bowes | 56 | – c sub. b Brown ................. 34 |
| Mr J. H. Human c Voce b Bowes | 2 | – c Voce b Leyland .............. 16 |
| Mr V. W. C. Jupp c Wyatt b Bowes | 0 | |
| Mr G. T. S. Stevens c Duckworth b Brown | 39 | – not out ....................... 29 |
| Mr F. W. Gilligan b Macaulay | 0 | |
| Mr K. Farnes b Bowes | 0 | |
| B 10, l-b 4, w 8, n-b 6 | 28 | B 12, l-b 8, n-b 1 ......... 21 |
| | **309** | **286** |

## Mr H. D. G. Leveson Gower's XI Bowling

| | Overs | Mdns | Runs | Wkts | Overs | Mdns | Runs | Wkts |
|---|---|---|---|---|---|---|---|---|
| Farnes ........... | 23 | 3 | 119 | 1 | 11 | — | 83 | — |
| Townsend ........ | 27 | 14 | 37 | 3 | 13 | 1 | 40 | — |
| Jupp ............. | 18 | 2 | 91 | 3 | 8 | — | 43 | 3 |
| Langridge ........ | 16.4 | 4 | 34 | 2 | 5 | 1 | 14 | — |
| Stevens ........... | 7 | — | 31 | — | 3 | — | 16 | — |
| Human........... | 4 | — | 28 | 1 | 3 | — | 16 | — |
| Dobson .......... | | | | | 8 | — | 50 | — |

## MCC Australian Team Bowling

| | Overs | Mdns | Runs | Wkts | Overs | Mdns | Runs | Wkts |
|---|---|---|---|---|---|---|---|---|
| Bowes .......... | 25 | 3 | 94 | 5 | 12 | 1 | 46 | 1 |
| Voce ........... | 18 | 5 | 49 | 2 | 7 | 2 | 23 | — |
| Brown .......... | 20 | 3 | 58 | 1 | 16 | 2 | 81 | 4 |
| Macaulay ........ | 22 | 5 | 63 | 2 | 6 | — | 23 | — |
| Leyland ......... | 4 | 2 | 3 | — | 5 | — | 11 | 1 |
| Verity ........... | 9 | 3 | 14 | — | 15 | 1 | 80 | — |
| Paynter ......... | | | | | 1 | — | 1 | — |

Umpires: J. Newman and A. Dolphin.

## STAFFORDSHIRE IN 1924

*Joint Hon. Secretaries* – Mr J. S. Heath, "Ryecroft", Wolstanton, Stoke-on-Trent, and Mr G. A. F. Bagguley, Newcastle, Staffordshire

Easily the outstanding feature of Staffordshire cricket last summer was the splendid bowling of Sidney Barnes. Taking as many as seventy-three wickets, the England bowler, at the age of forty-eight, wound up with the truly remarkable average of 7.17. A. Lockett fell away considerably but Sedgwick was deadly at times and altogether Staffordshire possessed a formidable attack. As regards the batting, however, there was a sad weakness. In the home games with Cheshire and Norfolk, the side went down for very small scores and there was another failure against Lancashire's Second Eleven. Although not playing very often, H. W. Homer and W. H. Fitchford were fairly consistent bats and the latter had one brilliant innings of 100 not out. Playing ten games, Staffordshire won the first two – against Lincolnshire and Nottinghamshire Second Eleven – and also succeeded in the return engagements with these counties. An unusual happening was that three times during the season Staffordshire's opponents saved the follow-on by 1 run.

## STAFFORDSHIRE IN 1926

*Hon. Secretary* – Mr G. A. F. Bagguley, Newcastle-under Lyme, Staffordshire

Bad weather spoiled several of Staffordshire's matches, but despite this misfortune the county made some progress. The feature of the seasons's work was the wonderful success of Barnes, who, heading the bowling averages once again, despite his 50 years, brought his total of wickets in the course of fourteen seasons to 1,050 for 7.98 runs each. His best performance was in taking fourteen wickets for 31 runs in the second match with Lincolnshire. Without Barnes the side must have been in a sad plight, for only A. Lockett and Sedgwick of the other bowlers rendered anything like valuable help. While, however the attack was more effective than before, the batting frequently disappointed. The main trouble lay in the inability of the county to find a really capable opening pair – a difficulty in no way lessened by the fact that no fewer than twenty-five players were called upon during the season. Most of the regular members of the side met with little success, but H. W. Homer was consistently good, with an average of 27 for ten innings.

## THE SECOND-CLASS COUNTIES IN 1933

An unfortunate oversight in the notification of the result of the match between Yorkshire Second Eleven and Staffordshire in the Minor Counties' competition of 1933 led to a serious blunder coming to light. As originally made up, the final table of results showed that Norfolk, with a percentage of 72.00, and Yorkshire Second Eleven, with a percentage of 71.66 finished first and second in the competition. Exercising their right to participate in a challenge match with the leaders, Yorkshire Second Eleven duly met Norfolk and defeated them. Some seven weeks later, when the table was being checked for insertion in *Wisden's Cricketers' Almanack*, it was discovered that certain of the columns of figures did not agree. Closer investigation, followed by correspondence with Maj. R. C. Campbell, the Hon. Secretary of the Minor Counties' Cricket Association, elicited the fact that mistakes had occurred in calculating the points of Yorkshire Second Eleven and Straffordshire.

It was then found that, as the outcome of the match between these elevens at Sheffield in July when cricket did not take place on the second day, Yorkshire, owing to a late and ambiguous report being sent to the secretary of the Minor Counties, had been credited with points for a win in a one-day match instead of points for a win on the first innings. This revelation meant that Yorkshire's percentage was reduced from 71.66 to 68.33, and that in consequence, their position in the table was third, Wiltshire being second with a percentage of 70.00.

An extraordinary situation was thus created. Yorkshire had played Norfolk in the challenge match when actually they possessed no right to an honour which should have fallen to Wiltshire but, the cricket season being closed (it was then towards the end of October), no opportunity presented itself, should Wiltshire have claimed to play the leaders, for a meeting between Norfolk and Wiltshire in a challenge match. Yorkshire Second Eleven obviously had no standing in the matter and could not be regarded as champions of the Minor Counties' competition because their position as third in the list precluded then from taking part in a challenge match. Meanwhile, Major Campbell placed his resignation as Hon. Secretary in the hands of the committee, but at the Annual Meeting of the Minor Counties' Cricket Association at Lord's on December 5th, he withdrew this and was re-elected, a resolution exonerating him from all blame in connection with the incorrect table of percentages being passed unanimously. It was also agreed to regard the Championship of 1933 as "not decided" and to ignore the so-called challenge match between Yorkshire Second Eleven and Norfolk. As the match took place, the batting and bowling figures are included in the averages of the counties concerned.

## STAFFORDSHIRE IN 1934

*Hon. Secretary* – Mr L. W. Hancock, 4 Kingsland Avenue, Oakhill, Stoke-on-Trent

Due largely to their inability to place in the field a regular eleven – 34 players were called upon in eight matches – Staffordshire, as in 1933, fared very moderately. In addition, several batsmen of experience often failed unaccountably while Sydney Barnes, the famous bowler, concluded his career with the county after the first two matches. A. Smith, E. Perry, E. Mayer, S. Crump, Lockett and Backhouse did most of the run-getting, but unfortunately neither Smith nor Perry was able to play regularly. The bulk of the attack fell upon Lockett, Backhouse and Crump, and they were splendidly supported in the field. A feature of the season was the high standard of wicket-keeping shown by C. C. Goodway. In twenty-two seasons covering a period of 31 years with Staffordshire, his native county, Barnes had the following figures:

| Overs | Maidens | Runs | Wickets | Average |
|-------|---------|--------|---------|---------|
| 5367.1 | 1,629 | 11,500 | 1,432 | 8.03 |

# ENGLAND IN AUSTRALASIA

## MCC TEAM v WESTERN AUSTRALIA

Played at Perth, October 18, 19, 20, 1928

Two days after landing at Fremantle, the team began their tour with the match against Western Australia at Perth. Arthur Richardson, having been appointed coach to the Western Australian Cricket Association, captained the home side. The game had to be left drawn, the Englishmen having the best of matters. Ernest Tyldesley played beautifully in his first match in Australia. Jardine in a splendid innings of 109 gave promise of what was to come. Driving well, he made his runs in less than two hours and a half. Hendren also hit finely, having two 6s in his 90. Bryant and Horrocks showed capital form for Western Australia. Unfortunately the close of the match was marked by a serious accident to Geary who, struck on the nose by a rising ball from Halcombe, had to be taken to hospital and did not play again for nearly a month.

### MCC Team

| | | | |
|---|---|---|---|
| H. Sutcliffe lbw b Halcombe | 28 | | |
| M. Leyland c Halcombe b Evans | 15 | – not out | 6 |
| E. Tyldesley b Halcombe | 66 | | |
| W. R. Hammond b Evans | 14 | | |
| C. P. Mead lbw b Inverarity | 1 | – not out | 1 |
| Mr D. R. Jardine c Richardson b Halcombe | 109 | | |
| E. Hendren c Taaffe b Richardson | 90 | | |
| L. Ames c Stokes b Richardson | 36 | | |
| Mr A. P. F. Chapman c Richardson b Evans | 26 | | |
| G. Geary run out | 1 | – retired hurt | 15 |
| Mr J. C. White not out | 1 | | |
| B 7, l-b 9, n-b 3 | 19 | B 2, l-b 2 | 4 |
| | **406** | | **26** |

### Western Australia

| | | | |
|---|---|---|---|
| A. J. Richardson c Chapman b White | 44 | M. Inverarity b Hammond | 2 |
| F. Quinlan c Chapman b White | 14 | A. Evans c Ames b Geary | 2 |
| F. Taaffe c Hammond b White | 0 | W. Stokes c Leyland b Hammond | 5 |
| F. Bryant run out | 61 | R. A. Halcombe b Hammond | 0 |
| W. M. McRae c Ames b Jardine | 34 | B 13, l-b 4, w 1 | 18 |
| W. Horrocks not out | 75 | | |
| R. Bryant c Sutcliffe b Leyland | 2 | | **257** |

### Western Australia Bowling

| | Overs | Mdns | Runs | Wkts | Overs | Mdns | Runs | Wkts |
|---|---|---|---|---|---|---|---|---|
| Halcombe | 21 | — | 114 | 3 | 4 | 1 | 10 | — |
| Evans | 24 | 3 | 82 | 3 | 3 | 2 | 5 | — |
| Richardson | 19.2 | 4 | 58 | 2 | | | | |
| Inverarity | 23 | 1 | 92 | 1 | 2 | — | 7 | — |
| R. Bryant | 3 | — | 25 | — | | | | |
| Taaffe | 1 | — | 7 | — | | | | |
| Quinlan | 3 | — | 9 | — | | | | |

## MCC Team Bowling

|          | Overs | Mdns | Runs | Wkts |
|----------|-------|------|------|------|
| Hammond  | 33.6  | 12   | 67   | 3    |
| Leyland  | 13    | 3    | 47   | 1    |
| Geary    | 24    | 4    | 55   | 1    |
| White    | 34    | 8    | 59   | 3    |
| Mead     | 11    | —    | 11   | —    |
| Jardine  | 2     | 2    | —    | 1    |

# MCC TEAM v VICTORIA

### Played at Melbourne, November 1, 2, 3, 5, 1928

The run-getting powers of the eleven were further illustrated in the first match against Victoria, and the previously entertained ideas of the bowling being weak, definitely dispelled. The match was drawn, rain interfering a good deal with the progress of the game, but England established a big advantage over their opponents. Batting first, Victoria were all out early on the second morning for 164 runs, their innings having lasted just over three hours. Light rain falling at intervals, the pitch, with the ball often getting up awkwardly, was entirely suited to Larwood's bowling, and he accomplished a great performance by taking the first seven wickets off the reel. Ponsford played on to him at 19 and, apart from Ryder who brought off one or two hooks in clever fashion, only Woodfull offered any real resistance. With the score at 85, Larwood nearly did the hat trick, getting Hartkopf and Seaife with following balls and, after almost bowling Ellis with his third, had him caught at second slip off the next. Larwood, who had one short rest, was taken off at 105 and did not go on again in the innings, but, judging by the tremendous way in which he was bowling, he might well, had he been persevered with, have taken all ten wickets. Woodfull carried his bat through the innings and gave a remarkable display. When only one, he was nearly bowled by Tate and near the end of the day he might have been run out; otherwise he made no mistake under conditions definitely against the batsman. Having disposed of their opponents so cheaply, the MCC proceeded to score runs with the utmost readiness and batting until ten minutes to five on Saturday, put together in less than seven hours and a half a total of 486. Hobbs and Jardine made 93 together for the first wicket, but Hobbs was not quite at his best. Then Jardine and Mead added 71, Jardine being third out at 233. His second hundred in succession was a model innings and an object lesson to all who saw it in its revelation of strong back-play and skilfully applied strokes to every kind of ball. Hendren drove and hooked with great certainty during his stay of less than two hours and a quarter; Chapman hit with tremendous power on the off-side while he and Larwood were adding 93 in forty-eight minutes, and Larwood himself, last out, displayed batting powers of which Australian people seemed quite unaware. Victoria went in a second time, Hendry and Ponsford scoring 135 together, but the cricket was without much point, bowlers being greatly handicapped by drizzling rain which fell all the time.

## Victoria

| | | | |
|---|---|---|---|
| W. H. Ponsford b Larwood | 14 | – not out | 60 |
| W. M. Woodfull not out | 67 | | |
| H. L. Hendry b Larwood | 8 | – not out | 74 |
| J. Ryder b Larwood | 25 | | |
| Dr A. E. V. Hartkopf b Larwood | 13 | | |
| J. Scaife c White b Larwood | 0 | | |
| J. L. Ellis c Chapman b Larwood | 0 | | |
| D. J. Blackie c Chapman b Larwood | 3 | | |
| H. Ebeling st Duckworth b White | 4 | | |
| F. L. Morton c Duckworth b Tate | 14 | | |
| H. Ironmonger c Hendren b White | 16 | | |
| | | N-b 1 | 1 |
| | **164** | | **135** |

## MCC Team

| | | | |
|---|---|---|---|
| J. B. Hobbs st Ellis b Hartkopf | 51 | M. W. Tate lbw b Blackie | 1 |
| Mr D. R. Jardine c and b Morton | 104 | H. Larwood run out | 79 |
| C. P. Mead lbw b Hartkopf | 37 | A. P. Freeman c Blackie b Ebeling | 6 |
| E. Hendren run out | 100 | G. Duckworth not out | 4 |
| Mr J. C. White b Ironmonger | 20 | B 5, l-b 7, w 1 | 13 |
| M. Leyland b Ironmonger | 0 | | |
| Mr A. P. F. Chapman c sub. b Ebeling | 71 | | **486** |

### MCC Team Bowling

| | Overs | Mdns | Runs | Wkts | Overs | Mdns | Runs | Wkts |
|---|---|---|---|---|---|---|---|---|
| Larwood | 13 | 2 | 51 | 7 | 3 | — | 16 | — |
| Tate | 19 | 6 | 45 | 1 | 4 | — | 30 | — |
| Freeman | 7 | — | 25 | — | | | | |
| White | 15 | 1 | 43 | 2 | 10 | — | 35 | — |
| Leyland | | | | | 6 | — | 37 | — |
| Jardine | | | | | 3 | — | 16 | — |

### Victoria Bowling

| | Overs | Mdns | Runs | Wkts |
|---|---|---|---|---|
| Morton | 14 | 2 | 51 | 1 |
| Ebeling | 20 | 1 | 89 | 2 |
| Ironmonger | 36 | 10 | 116 | 2 |
| Blackie | 29 | 2 | 120 | 1 |
| Hartkopf | 11 | 1 | 76 | 2 |
| Ryder | 5 | 1 | 21 | — |

# ENGLAND v AUSTRALIA

## First Test Match

### Played at Brisbane, November 30, December 1, 3, 4, 5, 1928

Having by now run into first-rate all-round form, England entered upon the opening Test match with feelings of confidence, but not even the most sanguine member of the team could have anticipated that they would gain a victory by such an astounding margin as that of 675 runs – easily the most pronounced success by runs in the history of Test matches. In picking the side, the selection committee of the team – Chapman, White, Jardine, Hobbs, and Tyldesley – spent many hours overnight before arriving at their decision and when the names were announced next morning, Englishmen in Australia, and no doubt in England as well, were rather perturbed to find that, in order to strengthen the batting, the attack was limited to four bowlers, Larwood, Tate, White and Hammond. It had been generally expected that a place would be found for Geary, who in previous games had shown that he was bowling very well. Freeman, too, had claims to be included. However, the risk was taken and, aided by the weather, the breakdown of Gregory and the illness of Kelleway, England triumphed in such a startling manner as to cause real consternation in Australia cricket circles. All the same, England, after a none too promising start, played magnificent cricket in which brilliant and accurate fielding bore a very prominent part. Australia relied largely upon tried men, Bradman being the one youngster to secure inclusion. On paper, their eleven appeared quite formidable, with Gregory, Grimmett, Ironmonger and Kelleway, backed up by Hendry and Ryder, as bowlers, while ten of the side could, in the ordinary way, be relied upon to make runs. All ideas on this point were upset by the damage to Gregory and Kelleway's indisposition.

Chapman did his side a good turn by winning the toss, Hobbs and Sutcliffe beginning so well as to score 85 runs between twelve o'clock and lunch-time. Then, in the last over before the interval, Sutcliffe was tempted to hit a short-pitched ball from Gregory round to leg and fell to a very fine running catch by Ponsford. For this error of judgment, Sutcliffe received probably more than his fair share of blame, for he hit the ball well and the catch was, after all, brilliantly made almost in front of the sight-screen. Soon after lunch, Hobbs was run out, this being largely his own fault for not running a second run quickly enough. A fine return by Bradman to the opposite end, supplemented by brilliant work from Oldfield, did the rest. Mead being leg-before at 108, England were doing badly. Hammond should have gone at 155, Oldfield, with the ball dropping into the top of his pad, missing a chance of stumping. Hammond and Jardine made 53 together, and although Jardine and Hendren subsequently added 56, England, with five wickets down for 217, had not made such a good start as expected. Ryder frequently changed his bowling to give the batsmen less chance of settling down and soon after Chapman went in there had been no fewer than fourteen alterations in the attack. Hendren and Chapman raised the score to 272 before an appeal against the light was upheld. Next morning the score was carried to 291, 74 runs having been added in fifty-eight minutes, and then Tate went in and hit up 26 out of the next 28. Even then, England, with seven men out, did not seem to have made enough runs but Larwood gave Hendren such magnificent assistance that the eighth partnership realised 124 runs in less than two hours, Larwood hitting a 6, a 5 and seven 4s in an invaluable innings. All this time, Hendren has been batting superbly, neglecting few opportunities of scoring, running no risk, and driving, cutting and hooking with the utmost certainty. When Larwood got out, Hendren hit away in great style; White stayed while 52 were added and in the end Hendren was the last to leave. Hendren batted nearly five hours, made no mistake and hit sixteen 4s. England, with a total of 521 had effected a great recovery. Before this day ended, great things were to happen, for between five minutes to five and ten minutes to six when bad light again stopped play, Australia lost four wickets for 44 runs. Before a run had been scored Woodfull, off the fourth ball of Larwood's first over, fell to a magnificent left-handed catch by Chapman standing rather fine in the gully. It is safe to say that few other men could have made the ground and held the ball. With the second ball of his third over Larwood bowled Ponsford with a yorker and, Tate changing ends, Kippax was caught and bowled, while Larwood, coming on again at 29, bowled down Kelleway's off-stump at 40. Larwood's three wickets to this point cost 9 runs. Next morning, Hendry and Ryder carried the score to 71, but nobody else did anything and on the fall of the ninth wicket the innings ended, Gregory being unable to go in. Australia batted less than two hours and a half, Larwood earning great fame by taking six wickets for just over 5 runs apiece.

England found themselves 399 ahead and, very wisely, Chapman took no risk but went in again. Oxenham and Thompson fielded as substitutes for Gregory and Kelleway. By tea-time both Hobbs and Sutcliffe were out and there were only 74 runs on the board. Afterwards there came defective light and a slight shower of rain, so that at twenty minutes to six stumps were pulled up with the score at 103 for two wickets. Next morning Hammond, after being missed, was out to a brilliant catch by Thompson at 117 while Mead left at 165. Mead took three hours and a half over his runs and, valuable though his score was, he seldom seemed really at home. For the second time in the match he was leg-before. Just afterwards, Hendren, when 6, was missed by Bradman at long-on but then proceeded to hook and drive so well as to make 45 out of 63 in less than an hour, hitting two 6s, one of them a huge drive on to the top of the stand. Jardine, batting splendidly, received further valuable help from Chapman, Tate and Larwood, the Australian attack, so considerably weakened by the absence of Gregory and Kelleway, being, by this time, thoroughly mastered. On the fall of Larwood's wickets at 342, Chapman declared at twenty minutes to five in order to get Australia in at a very anxious time. Jardine was at the wickets over three hours and made only one false hit.

Australia were thus set the tremendous task of getting 742 runs to win. With only 6 scored, Ponsford, off the third ball of the second over from Larwood, was caught by Duckworth standing back and at ten minutes past five bad light ended play for the day with the score at 17 for one wicket. Australia's wretched position was made hopeless by heavy rain during the night followed in the morning by bright sunshine. Kippax left at 33 and then, White going on at 43 and Tate changing ends, the issue was quickly settled. The last six wickets – the two invalids being still unable to bat – went down in fifty minutes. Australia being all out for 66. Woodfull, batting splendidly, received no support at all, nearly everyone who joined him hitting out wildly immediately on going in. The English fielding was again magnificent, and White had the astounding record of four wickets for 7 runs.

## England

| | | | |
|---|---|---|---|
| J. B. Hobbs run out | 49 | – lbw b Grimmett | 11 |
| H. Sutcliffe c Ponsford b Gregory | 38 | – c sub. b Ironmonger | 32 |
| C. P. Mead lbw b Grimmett | 8 | – lbw b Grimmett | 73 |
| W. R. Hammond c Woodfull b Gregory | 44 | – c sub. b Ironmonger | 28 |
| Mr D. R. Jardine c Woodfull b Ironmonger | 35 | – not out | 65 |
| E. Hendren c Ponsford b Ironmonger | 169 | – c Ponsford b Grimmett | 45 |
| Mr A. P. F. Chapman c Kelleway b Gregory | 50 | – c Oldfield b Grimmett | 27 |
| M. W. Tate c Ryder b Grimmett | 26 | – c Bradman b Grimmett | 20 |
| H. Larwood lbw b Hendry | 70 | – c Ponsford b Grimmett | 37 |
| Mr J. C. White lbw b Grimmett | 14 | | |
| G. Duckworth not out | 5 | | |
| L-b 10, n-b 3 | 13 | L-b 3, n-b 1 | 4 |
| | **521** | **(8 wkts dec.)** | **342** |

## Australia

| | | | |
|---|---|---|---|
| W. M. Woodfull c Chapman b Larwood | 0 | – not out | 30 |
| W. H. Ponsford b Larwood | 2 | – c Duckworth b Larwood | 6 |
| A. F. Kippax c and b Tate | 16 | – c and b Larwood | 15 |
| H. L. Hendry lbw b Larwood | 30 | – c Larwood b White | 6 |
| C. E. Kelleway b Larwood | 8 | – absent ill | 0 |
| J. Ryder c Jardine b Larwood | 33 | – c Larwood b Tate | 1 |
| D. G. Bradman lbw b Tate | 18 | – c Chapman b White | 1 |
| W. A. Oldfield lbw b Tate | 2 | – c Larwood b Tate | 5 |
| C. V. Grimmett not out | 7 | – c Chapman b White | 1 |
| H. Ironmonger b Larwood | 4 | – c Chapman b White | 0 |
| J. M. Gregory absent hurt | 0 | – absent hurt | 0 |
| B 1, l-b 1 | 2 | N-b 1 | 1 |
| | **122** | | **66** |

## Australia Bowling

|  | Overs | Mdns | Runs | Wkts | Overs | Mdns | Runs | Wkts |
|---|---|---|---|---|---|---|---|---|
| Gregory .......... | 41 | 2 | 142 | 3 |  |  |  |  |
| Kelleway ......... | 34 | 9 | 77 | — |  |  |  |  |
| Grimmett ......... | 40 | 2 | 167 | 3 | 44.1 | 9 | 131 | 6 |
| Ironmonger ....... | 44.3 | 18 | 79 | 2 | 50 | 20 | 85 | 2 |
| Ryder ............ | 6 | 2 | 23 | — | 14 | 3 | 43 | — |
| Hendry .......... | 10 | 1 | 20 | 1 | 27 | 6 | 79 | — |

## England Bowling

|  | Overs | Mdns | Runs | Wkts | Overs | Mdns | Runs | Wkts |
|---|---|---|---|---|---|---|---|---|
| Larwood ......... | 14.4 | 4 | 32 | 6 | 7 | — | 30 | 2 |
| Tate ............. | 21 | 6 | 50 | 3 | 11 | 3 | 26 | 2 |
| Hammond ........ | 15 | 5 | 38 | — | 1 | — | 2 | — |
| White ........... |  |  |  |  | 6.3 | 2 | 7 | 4 |

Umpires: D. Elder and G. Hele.

# ENGLAND v AUSTRALIA
## Fourth Test Match

Played at Adelaide, February 1, 2, 4, 5, 6, 7, 8, 1929

The rubber having been won, the English team had no cause for anxiety beyond the desire to preserve their unbeaten record. Still they did not exhibit any lack of keenness in the fourth Test match which, characterised by very even scoring throughout, had a most exciting finish, England gaining a victory by 12 runs. This success atoned for the defeat on the same ground in the previous tour, when Australia won by 11 runs. England had no reason for changing their eleven, but Australia brought in Jackson for Richardson, the young New South Wales batsman enjoyed the distinction of playing a three-figure innings in his first Test match. Before going further, it is only right to pay a great tribute to his performance. Accomplished, as will be told later, in circumstances calculated to daunt a player of mature experience, it was, in point of style and beauty of execution and stroke play, the best innings played against the Englishmen during the whole tour. Other achievements made the match memorable. Hammond followed his innings of 251 and 200 at Sydney and Melbourne respectively by making two separate hundreds; Hobbs and Sutcliffe once more gave the side a good start; Jardine played an invaluable innings in partnership with Hammond and, above all, White, sending down over 124 overs, obtained thirteen wickets for 256 runs, eight of them in the second innings. Well as he had bowled in all his previous games, White, in this match, was really wonderful in his stamina, clever flighting and remarkable accuracy of pitch.

England's first innings lasted until after three o'clock on the second day yet, excellent as was a total of 334, there existed reason for anticipating when Hobbs and Sutcliffe had made 143 in two hours and three-quarters that the final score would be considerably higher. Both these men left at the same total, Grimmett going on when Hobbs was out and getting Sutcliffe second ball. To show the character of Hobb's innings, his hits may be given in detail. These were two 4s, two 3s, eleven 2s and thirty-eight singles. Still, each man batted wonderfully well. Hammond, who had gone in at the fall of the first wicket, saw Jardine and Hendren quickly dismissed, and although Chapman helped to add 67, nobody else did anything. Taking out his bat, Hammond scored 72 of the last 88 runs, batting altogether for nearly four hours and a half. He hit nine 4s, his driving all through being splendid. Grimmett in this innings bowled better than in any other match against the Englishmen.

Going in on the second day just before half-past three, Australia made a deplorable start, three wickets falling for 19 runs. Off the fourth ball from Tate, Woodfull was magnificently caught at the wicket on the leg-side, Hendry left at six and White, going on at 16, bowled Kippax. It was then that Jackson revealed his great powers. The position did not seem to trouble him in the slightest, and he drove, cut and hit to leg with the utmost certainty and confidence. Ryder helped him to add 126, Bradman stayed while 82 were put on, and then 60 more came in fifty minutes before his superb innings ended at 287. Jackson batted for five hours and twenty minutes, gave no chance, and hit fifteen 4s, seven 3s and twenty-three 2s. In the end Australia, after being in over seven hours and a half, led by 35 runs. A word of praise is due to Tate for some fine bowling.

Going in on the fourth day just before half-past twelve, England lost Hobbs and Sutcliffe for 21, Hobbs, like Woodfull, being splendidly caught on the leg-side at the wicket with only 1 run scored. The position was serious, but Hammond and Jardine rose to the occasion in wonderful style. Both men forced the ball to the on-side with clever strokes, and were together at the close of play with the score at 206. They were not separated until a quarter to three on Wednesday afternoon, and by adding 262 runs established a record for the third wicket partnership in Test matches. The stand lasted nearly five hours and fifty minutes, Jardine, when he looked certain to reach his hundred, being caught at silly mid-off. In a masterly exhibition he hit ten 4s. England had then pulled the game round but they proceeded to throw away their advantage, Hendren, Chapman and Larwood all leaving while the score was being raised to 302. Hammond was at length seventh out at 327, just before four o'clock. Batting seven hours and twenty minutes, he hit seventeen 4s and, in the circumstances in which it was played, this was probably his best innings of the tour. He was master of the bowling all the time. After tea, Tate, hitting a 6 and five 4s, played an invaluable innings and England, all out for 383, set their opponents 349 to get. Before play ceased 24 runs were scored without loss, and on Thursday and Friday there came a fight which will long be remembered by those who saw it. The first wicket fell at 65, and soon after lunch on the Thursday three men were out for 74. A little later occurred an incident which looked like losing the game for England, Ryder, with his score at 26, offering the simplest of catches to White who, to everyone's surprise and his own obvious annoyance, dropped the ball. Kippax and Ryder added 137, Australian then being on top, but soon afterwards White made amends for his previous blunder by holding a hard return from Ryder high up with the left hand. The Australian captain had made a great effort for his side in a fine display of hard hitting. A'Beckett stayed for thirty-five minutes, Hammond making a sensational catch at second slip to dismiss him, and when play ceased for the day Australia, with six men out for 260, required 89 to win. When, next morning, Bradman and Oxenham carried the score to 308, victory for Australia appeared more than likely. These two had added 50 in sixty-five minutes. At 320, with Bradman run out, fortunes changed again. Oldfield hit a ball to cover point, both batsmen dashing for the run, but Hobbs returned like lightning for Duckworth to put down the wicket. Grimmett stayed for half an hour, but left at 336, Tate at short leg knocking up the ball from a hard hit and bringing off a great catch. Blackie went in amidst tense excitement and carefully played four balls from White. Then came one pitched just a little shorter; Blackie hooked it high into the long field in front of square leg where Larwood, running a few yards, brought off a fine catch and finished a wonderful struggle.

## England

| | | | | |
|---|---|---|---|---|
| J. B. Hobbs c Ryder b Hendry | 74 | – c Oldfield b Hendry | 1 |
| H. Sutcliffe st Oldfield b Grimmett | 64 | – c Oldfield b A'Beckett | 17 |
| W. R. Hammond not out | 119 | – c and b Ryder | 177 |
| Mr D. R. Jardine lbw b Grimmett | 1 | – c Woodfull b Oxenham | 98 |
| E. Hendren b Blackie | 13 | – c Bradman b Blackie | 11 |
| Mr A. P. F. Chapman c A'Beckett b Ryder | 39 | – c Woodfull b Blackie | 0 |
| G. Duckworth c Ryder b Grimmett | 5 | – lbw b Oxenham | 1 |
| H. Larwood b Hendry | 3 | – lbw b Oxenham | 5 |
| G. Geary run out | 3 | – c and b Grimmett | 6 |
| M. W. Tate b Grimmett | 2 | – lbw b Oxenham | 47 |
| Mr J. C. White c Ryder b Grimmett | 0 | – not out | 4 |
| B 3, l-b 7, w 1 | 11 | B 6, l-b 10 | 16 |
| | **334** | | **383** |

## Australia

| | | | | |
|---|---|---|---|---|
| W. M. Woodfull c Duckworth b Tate | 1 | – c Geary b White | 30 |
| A. Jackson lbw b White | 164 | – c Duckworth b Geary | 36 |
| H. L. Hendry c Duckworth b Larwood | 2 | – c Tate b White | 5 |
| A. F. Kippax b White | 3 | – c Hendren b White | 51 |
| J. Ryder lbw b White | 63 | – c and b White | 87 |
| D. G. Bradman c Larwood b Tate | 40 | – run out | 58 |
| E. L. A'Beckett b White | 36 | – c Hammond b White | 21 |
| R. K. Oxenham c Chapman b White | 15 | – c Chapman b White | 12 |
| W. A. Oldfield b Tate | 32 | – not out | 15 |
| C. V. Grimmett b Tate | 4 | – c Tate b White | 9 |
| D. J. Blackie not out | 3 | – c Larwood b White | 0 |
| L-b 5, w 1 | 6 | B 9, l-b 3 | 12 |
| | **369** | | **336** |

### Australia Bowling

| | Overs | Mdns | Runs | Wkts | Overs | Mdns | Runs | Wkts |
|---|---|---|---|---|---|---|---|---|
| A'Beckett | 31 | 8 | 44 | — | 27 | 9 | 41 | 1 |
| Hendry | 31 | 14 | 49 | 2 | 28 | 11 | 56 | 1 |
| Grimmett | 52.1 | 12 | 102 | 5 | 52 | 15 | 117 | 1 |
| Oxenham | 34 | 14 | 51 | — | 47.4 | 21 | 67 | 4 |
| Blackie | 29 | 6 | 57 | 1 | 39 | 11 | 70 | 2 |
| Ryder | 5 | 1 | 20 | 1 | 5 | 1 | 13 | 1 |
| Kippax | | | | | 2 | — | 3 | |

### England Bowling

| | Overs | Mdns | Runs | Wkts | Overs | Mdns | Runs | Wkts |
|---|---|---|---|---|---|---|---|---|
| Larwood | 37 | 6 | 92 | 1 | 20 | 4 | 60 | — |
| Tate | 42 | 10 | 77 | 4 | 37 | 9 | 75 | — |
| White | 60 | 16 | 130 | 5 | 64.5 | 21 | 126 | 8 |
| Geary | 12 | 3 | 32 | — | 16 | 2 | 42 | 1 |
| Hammond | 9 | 1 | 32 | — | 14 | 3 | 21 | — |

Umpires: D. Elder and G. Hele.

## ENGLAND v AUSTRALIA

### Third Test Match

Played at Adelaide, January 13, 14, 16, 17, 18, 19, 1933

The third Test match of the tour, in which England – well on top when an innings had been completed on each side – were victorious by no fewer than 338 runs, will go down to history as probably the most unpleasant ever played. So hostile was the feeling of the

Australian public against Jardine that on the days before the game started people were excluded from the ground when the Englishmen were practising. As Jardine won the toss and England batted first nothing out of the common occurred to begin with, but later on, when Australian went in and Woodfull was hit over the heart again while Oldfield had to retire owing to a blow he received on the head, the majority of the spectators completely lost all hold on their feelings. Insulting remarks were hurled at Jardine, and when Larwood started to bowl his leg-theory he came in for his share of the storm of abuse. Not to put too fine a point on it, pandemonium reigned. A passage of words between P. F. Warner and Woodfull in the dressing-room increased the bitter feeling prevalent in the crowd, and the dispatch of the cablegram protesting against "body-line" bowling served no purpose in whatever endeavours were made to appease tempers already badly frayed by the various happenings.

Altogether the whole atmosphere was a disgrace to cricket. One must pay a tribute to Jardine. He did not shrink from the line of action he had taken up; he showed great pluck in often fielding near to the boundary where he became an easy target for offensive and sometimes filthy remarks; and above all he captained his team in this particular match like a genius. Much as they disliked the method of attack he controlled, all the leading Australian critics were unanimous in their praise of his skill as a leader.

England made a dreadful start, four wickets going down in an hour for 30 runs and the score being 37 at lunch, but then came a stand which turned the course of the game and put England on the road to ultimate success. Leyland and Wyatt, if enjoying a certain amount of luck, batted, in the circumstances, uncommonly well while adding 156 in about two and a half hours. Leyland, who in the end played on, hit thirteen 4s, in an innings which included many fine off-drives. Wyatt, whose hitting to square-leg brought him two or three 6s, left soon afterwards, but Paynter – included in the side for Pataudi – and Allen added a useful 32 runs, so that at the end of the day England had 236 on the board with seven men out. On the next morning Paynter continued to bat marvellously well, and Verity, who took Bowes's place in the England team, defended so manfully that the stand for the eighth wicket realised 96 runs in about two and a quarter hours. Paynter pulled and drove well, while his cutting and leg-glancing were almost as good. England were all out soon after three o'clock for 341 and followed this up by getting down the first four Australian wickets for 51. It was during this time that Woodfull, ducking to avoid what he thought would be a rising ball, was hit on the body. Later, Ponsford and Richardson added 58 in the last seventy minutes, but Australian wound up 232 behind with six wickets to fall. Ponsford played a fine fighting innings, cutting very well and meeting the leg-theory form of attack in able style. He and Richardson put on 80 runs and Oldfield stayed for just over two hours when his active participation in the match was closed by a blow on the head by a ball from Larwood. Australia finished their innings 119 behind, and although with one wicket down for 85 England lost Sutcliffe cheaply they stood, at the close of play, 204 runs ahead. On the fourth day, England placed themselves in such a position that they could not very well lose, and realising that their team was going to be beaten the Adelaide public who went to the ground were not nearly so noisy and insulting. Both Leyland and Wyatt again made useful scores; Verity supplemented his 45 in the first innings with 40, while Jardine, Hammond and Ames by first-rate cricket all played important parts in carrying England towards victory. England wound up with six men out for 296 and were thus 415 runs ahead.

As the wicket showed definite signs of wear, the outlook for Australia was very gloomy. Jardine batted four hours and a quarter and did great work in wearing down the bowling. Hammond and Leyland accomplished some bright and fearless hitting, and altogether it was a very good day for the Englishmen. Ames and Verity adding 98 runs in just over two hours England in the end put together a total of 412 so that Australia were left to get 532 to win. Before the fifth day's play ended, the home side lost four of their best batsmen for 120 runs and to all intents and purposes the game was as good as over. Australia in their last innings had Fingleton and Ponsford out with only 12 runs on the board, but then came an excellent stand by Woodfall and Bradman, 88 being put on in an hour and a quarter. Bradman was in first-rate form, hitting a six and ten 4s, but just when he was becoming dangerous Verity caught him from a hard return. On the last day of the match Richardson and Woodfull defended stubbornly for a time, but they were separated at 171, and then Allen and Larwood quickly finished off the innings for 193. The greatest praise is due to Woodfull who for the second time in his career in a Test match carried his bat through the innings. He was in for nearly four hours, making most of his runs from strokes on the leg-side. Throughout the match the Englishmen fielded well, while Allen bowled splendidly.

## England

| | | | |
|---|---|---|---|
| H. Sutcliffe c Wall b O'Reilly | 9 | – c sub. b Wall | 7 |
| Mr D. R. Jardine b Wall | 3 | – lbw b Ironmonger | 56 |
| W. R. Hammond c Oldfield b Wall | 2 | – b Bradman | 85 |
| L. E. G. Ames b Ironmonger | 3 | – b O'Reilly | 69 |
| M. Leyland b O'Reilly | 83 | – c Wall b Ironmonger | 42 |
| Mr R. E. S. Wyatt c Richardson b Grimmett | 78 | – c Wall b O'Reilly | 49 |
| E. Paynter c Fingleton b Wall | 77 | – not out | 1 |
| Mr G. O. Allen lbw b Grimmett | 15 | – lbw b Grimmett | 15 |
| H. Verity c Richardson b Wall | 45 | – lbw b O'Reilly | 40 |
| W. Voce b Wall | 8 | – b O'Reilly | 8 |
| H. Larwood not out | 3 | – c Bradman b Ironmonger | 8 |
| B 1, l-b 7, n-b 7 | 15 | B 17, l-b 11, n-b 4 | 32 |
| | **341** | | **412** |

## Australia

| | | | |
|---|---|---|---|
| J. H. Fingleton c Ames b Allen | 0 | – b Larwood | 0 |
| W. M. Woodfull b Allen | 22 | – not out | 73 |
| D. G. Bradman c Allen b Larwood | 8 | – c and b Verity | 66 |
| S. J. McCabe c Jardine b Larwood | 8 | – c Leyland b Allen | 7 |
| W. H. Ponsford b Voce | 85 | – c Jardine b Larwood | 3 |
| V. Y. Richardson b Allen | 28 | – c Allen b Larwood | 21 |
| W. A. Oldfield retired hurt | 41 | – absent hurt | 0 |
| C. V. Grimmett c Voce b Allen | 10 | – b Allen | 6 |
| T. W. Wall b Hammond | 6 | – b Allen | 0 |
| W. J. O'Reilly b Larwood | 0 | – b Larwood | 5 |
| H. Ironmonger not out | 0 | – b Allen | 0 |
| B 2, l-b 11, n-b 1 | 14 | B 4, l-b 2, w 1, n-b 5 | 12 |
| | **222** | | **193** |

## Australia Bowling

| | Overs | Mdns | Runs | Wkts | Overs | Mdns | Runs | Wkts |
|---|---|---|---|---|---|---|---|---|
| Wall | 34.1 | 10 | 72 | 5 | 29 | 6 | 75 | 1 |
| O'Reilly | 50 | 19 | 82 | 2 | 50.3 | 21 | 79 | 4 |
| Ironmonger | 20 | 6 | 50 | 1 | 57 | 21 | 87 | 3 |
| Grimmett | 28 | 6 | 94 | 2 | 35 | 9 | 74 | 1 |
| McCabe | 14 | 3 | 28 | — | 16 | — | 42 | — |
| Bradman | | | | | 4 | — | 23 | 1 |

## England Bowling

| | Overs | Mdns | Runs | Wkts | Overs | Mdns | Runs | Wkts |
|---|---|---|---|---|---|---|---|---|
| Larwood | 25 | 6 | 55 | 3 | 19 | 3 | 71 | 4 |
| Allen | 23 | 4 | 71 | 4 | 17.2 | 5 | 50 | 4 |
| Hammond | 17.4 | 4 | 30 | 1 | 9 | 3 | 27 | — |
| Voce | 14 | 5 | 21 | 1 | 4 | 1 | 7 | — |
| Verity | 16 | 7 | 31 | — | 20 | 12 | 26 | 1 |

Umpires: G. Hele and G. Borwick.

## ENGLAND v NEW ZEALAND

### Second Test Match

Played at Auckland, March 31, April 1, 2, 1933

Drawn, like the other Test because of the weather, the second match against New Zealand was made memorable by the record score of Hammond, whose 336 not out surpassed Bradman's 334 obtained at Leeds in 1930. The great performance was the more remarkable as it came after a poor batting display by New Zealand. Dempster, at the wickets while all the home team's 158 runs were scored, alone showed real ability to cope with Bowes. The Yorkshire fast bowler beat Mills and Weir with consecutive balls without a run on the board and a notable feature of his work was that in dismissing six men for 34 runs he hit the stumps each time. Hammond went in when Sutcliffe left at 56 and got his runs out of 492 – a wonderful proportion. Hitting freely from the start Hammond completed 50 in seventy-two minutes, and his hundred came less than an hour later. His third fifty occupied only thirty-eight minutes, and, after reaching 200 in four hours, he actually added a hundred in forty-seven minutes while when Wyatt declared he had been at the wickets no more than five hours and a quarter. Hammond when 134 gave the one real chance in his great innings, but Dempster was hurt in trying to make a catch that he found too hot to hold. Showing to the utmost advantage in driving, pulling and cutting Hammond placed strokes with astonishing accuracy no matter how the bowlers positioned their fieldsmen. Throughout he treated the moderate attack with unflagging freedom. By clever footwork he took the bowling at the length he desired and aroused the spectators to enthusiasm. Of ten 6s three were off successive deliveries from Newman and he hit thirty-three 4s. New Zealand scored eight without loss before stumps were pulled up and as many more runs were added on a soaked pitch before a recurrence of rain caused the match to be abandoned.

### New Zealand

| | | |
|---|---|---|
| J. E. Mills b Bowes | 0 | – not out ... 11 |
| D. Whitelaw b Bowes | 12 | – not out ... 5 |
| G. L. Weir b Bowes | 0 | |
| C. S. Dempster not out | 83 | |
| J. L. Kerr lbw b Voce | 10 | |
| M. L. Page st Duckworth b Mitchell | 20 | |
| F. T. Badcock b Bowes | 1 | |
| K. C. James b Bowes | 0 | |
| J. A. Dunning b Bowes | 12 | |
| J. Newman b Voce | 5 | |
| D. L. Freeman run out | 1 | |
| B 9, l-b 4, n-b 1 | 14 | |
| | **158** | **16** |

### England

| | |
|---|---|
| H. Sutcliffe c Weir b Freeman | 24 |
| Mr R. E. S. Wyatt b Dunning | 60 |
| W. R. Hammond not out | 336 |
| E. Paynter b Dunning | 36 |
| L. E. G. Ames b Badcock | 26 |
| Mr G. O. Allen b Badcock | 12 |
| Mr F. R. Brown c Page b Weir | 13 |
| W. Voce b Weir | 16 |
| G. Duckworth not out | 6 |
| B 7, l-b 6, w 1, n-b 5 | 19 |
| **(7 wkts. dec.) 548** | |

W. E. Bowes and T. B. Mitchell did not bat.

**England Bowling**

| | Overs | Mdns | Runs | Wkts | Overs | Mdns | Runs | Wkts |
|---|---|---|---|---|---|---|---|---|
| Allen ............ | 5 | 2 | 11 | — | 3 | 1 | 4 | — |
| Bowes .......... | 19 | 5 | 34 | 6 | 2 | — | 4 | — |
| Mitchell ......... | 18 | 1 | 49 | 1 | | | | |
| Voce ............ | 9.5 | 3 | 20 | 2 | 1.3 | — | 2 | — |
| Brown .......... | 2 | — | 19 | — | | | | |
| Hammond ........ | 3 | — | 11 | — | 2 | — | 6 | — |

**New Zealand Bowling**

| | Overs | Mdns | Runs | Wkts |
|---|---|---|---|---|
| Badcock .......... | 59 | 16 | 126 | 2 |
| Dunning .......... | 43 | 5 | 156 | 2 |
| Freeman ......... | 20 | 1 | 91 | 1 |
| Newman ......... | 17 | 2 | 87 | — |
| Page ............. | 6 | 2 | 30 | — |
| Weir ............. | 11 | 2 | 39 | 2 |

# THE BOWLING CONTROVERSY

## TEXT OF THE CABLES

During the tour of the MCC team in Australia in 1932-33, exception was taken in that country to the methods adopted by certain of the visiting bowlers, and long correspondence by cable between the MCC and the Australian Board of Control followed. Below will be found, in chronological order, the text of these cables, together with – in proper sequence – a short report of meetings bearing upon the subject.

### From Australian Board of Control to MCC, January 18, 1933

"Body-line bowling has assumed such proportions as to menace the best interests of the game, making protection of the body by the batsmen the main consideration.

This is causing intensely bitter feeling between the players as well as injury. In our opinion it is unsportsmanlike.

Unless stopped at once it is likely to upset the friendly relations existing between Australia and England."

### From MCC to Australian Board of Control, January 23, 1933

"We, Marylebone Cricket Club, deplore your cable. We deprecate your opinion that there has been unsportsmanlike play. We have fullest confidence in captain, team and managers and are convinced that they would do nothing to infringe either the Laws of Cricket or the spirit of the game. We have no evidence that our confidence has been misplaced. Much as we regret accidents to Woodfull and Oldfield, we understand that in neither case was the bowler to blame. If the Australian Board of Control wish to propose a new Law or Rule, it shall receive our careful consideration in due course.

We hope the situation is not now as serious as your cable would seem to indicate, but if it is such as to jeopardize the good relations between English and Australian cricketers and you consider it desirable to cancel remainder of programme we would consent, but with great reluctance."

### From Australian Board of Control to MCC, January 30, 1933

"We, Australian Board of Control, appreciate your difficulty in dealing with the matter raised in our cable without having seen the actual play. We unanimously regard body-line bowling, as adopted in some of the games in the present tour, as being opposed to the spirit of cricket, and unnecessarily dangerous to the players.

We are deeply concerned that the ideals of the game shall be protected and have, therefore, appointed a committee to report on the action necessary to eliminate such bowling from Australian cricket as from beginning of the 1933-34 season.

We will forward a copy of the Committee's recommendations for your consideration, and it is hoped co-operation as to its application to all cricket. We do not consider it necessary to cancel remainder of programme."

The Committee appointed consisted of Messrs. R. J. Hartigan (Queensland) representing the Board of Control; W. M. Woodfull, V. Y. Richardson and M. A. Noble.

### From MCC to Australian Board of Control, February 2, 1933

"We, the Committee of the Marylebone Cricket Club note with pleasure that you do not consider it necessary to cancel the remainder of programme, and that you are postponing the whole issue involved until after the present tour is completed. May we accept this as a clear indication that the good sportsmanship of our team is not in question?

We are sure you will appreciate how impossible it would be to play any Test Match in the spirit we all desire unless both sides were satisfied there was no reflection upon their sportsmanship.

When your recommendation reaches us it shall receive our most careful consideration and will be submitted to the Imperial Cricket Conference."

### From Australian Board of Control to MCC, February 8, 1933

"We do not regard the sportsmanship of your team as being in question.

Our position was fully considered at the recent meeting in Sydney and is as indicated in our cable of January 30.

It is the particular class of bowling referred to therein which we consider is not in the best interests of cricket, and in this view we understand we are supported by many eminent English cricketers.

We join heartily with you in hoping that the remaining Tests will be played with the traditional good feeling."

The Australian Board of Control, meeting on April 21, 1933, considered a proposal submitted to them by the special sub-committee set up to consider the question of "body-line" bowling and cabled MCC asking that body to give the proposal their consideration. The cable read as follows:

"Australian Board adopted following addition to Laws of Cricket in Australia, namely:

Any ball delivered which, in the opinion of the umpire at the bowler's end is bowled at the batsman with the intent to intimidate or injure him shall be considered unfair and 'No-ball' shall be called. The bowler shall be notified of the reason. If the offence be repeated by the same bowler in the same innings he shall be immediately instructed by the umpire to cease bowling and the over shall be regarded as completed. Such bowler shall not again be permitted to bowl during the course of the innings then in progress.

Law 48a shall not apply to this Law. Foregoing submitted for your consideration and it is hoped co-operation by application to all cricket."

## From MCC to Australian Board of Control, June 12, 1933

"The MCC Committee have received and carefully considered the cable of the Australian Board of Control of April 28th last. They have also received and considered the reports of the Captain and Managers of the cricket team which visited Australia 1932-33.

With regard to the cable of the Australian Board of Control of April 28th last, the Committee presume that the class of bowling to which the proposed new law would apply is that referred to as 'body-line' bowling in the Australian Board of Control's cable of January 18th. The Committee consider that the term 'body-line' bowling is misleading and improper. It has led to much inaccuracy of thought by confusing the short bumping ball, whether directed on the off, middle or leg stump, with what is known as 'leg-theory.'

The term 'body-line' would appear to imply a direct attack by the bowler on the batsman. The Committee consider that such an implication applied to any English Bowling in Australian is improper and incorrect. Such action on the part of any bowler would be an offence against the spirit of the game and would be immediately condemned. The practice of bowling on the leg stump with a field placed on the leg side necessary for such bowling is legitimate, and has been in force for many years. It has generally been referred to as 'leg-theory.' The present habit of batsmen who move in front of their wicket with the object of gliding straight balls to leg tends to give the impression that the bowler is bowling at the batsman, especially in the case of a fast bowler when the batsman mistimes the ball and is hit.

The new Law recommended by the Australian Board of Control does not appear to the Committee to be practicable. Firstly, it would place an impossible task on the umpire, and secondly, it would place in the hands of the umpire a power over the game which would be more than dangerous, and which any umpire might well fear to exercise.

The Committee have had no reason to give special attention to 'leg-theory' as practised by fast bowlers. They will, however, watch carefully during the present season for anything which might be regarded as unfair or prejudicial to the best interests of the game. They propose to invite opinions and suggestions from County Clubs and Captains at the end of the season, with a view to enabling them to express an opinion on this matter at a Special Meeting of the Imperial Cricket Conference.

With regard to the reports of the Captain and Managers, the Committee, while deeply appreciative of the private and public hospitality shown to the English Team, are much concerned with regard to barracking, which is referred to in all the reports, and against which there is unanimous deprecation. Barracking has, unfortunately, always been indulged in by spectators in Australia to a degree quite unknown in this Country. During the late tour, however, it would appear to have exceeded all previous experience, and on occasions to have become thoroughly objectionable. There appears to have been little or no effort on the part of those responsible for the administration of the game in Australia to interfere, or to control this exhibition. This was naturally regarded by members of the team as a serious lack of consideration for them. The Committee are of opinion that cricket played under such conditions is robbed of much of its value as a game, and that unless barracking is stopped, or is greatly moderated in Australia, it is difficult to see how the continuance of representatives matches can serve the best interest of the game.

The Committee regret that these matters have to be dealt with by correspondence and not by personal conference. If at any time duly accredited representatives of Australian Cricket could meet the Committee in conference, such conference would be welcomed by MCC."

### From Australian Board of Control to MCC, September 22, 1933

"We note that you consider that a form of bowling which amounted to a direct attack by the bowler on the batsman would be against the spirit of the game. We agree with you that Leg-theory bowling as it has been generally practised for many years is not open to objection. On these matters there does not appear to be any real difference between our respective views.

We feel that while the type of bowling to which exception was taken in Australia, strictly was not in conflict with the Laws of Cricket, yet its continued practice would not be in the best interests of the game. May we assume that you concur in this point of view and that the teams may thus take the field in 1934 with that knowledge?

We are giving consideration to the question of barracking and you may rely upon our using our best endeavours to have it controlled in future tours.

We are most anxious that the cordial relations which have so long existed between English and Australian cricket shall continue."

### From MCC to Australian Board of Control, October 9, 1933

"The MCC Committee appreciate the friendly tone of your cable and they heartily reciprocate your desire for the continuance of cordial relations.

In their view the difference between us seems to be rather on the question of fact than on any point of interpretation of the Laws of Cricket or of the spirit of the game. They agree and have always agreed that a form of bowling which is obviously a direct attack by the bowler upon the batsman would be an offence against the spirit of the game.

Your team can certainly take the field with the knowledge and with the full assurance that cricket will be played here in the same spirit as in the past and with the single desire to promote the best interests of the game in both countries.

The Committee much appreciate your promise to take the question of barracking into consideration with a view to ensuring that it shall be kept within reasonable bounds.

Your team can rely on a warm welcome from MCC, and every effort will be made to make their visit enjoyable."

### From Australian Board of Control to MCC, November 16, 1933

"We appreciate the terms of your cablegram of October 9 and assume that such cable is intended to give the assurance asked for in our cablegram of September 22.

It is on this understanding that we are sending a team in 1934."

A joint meeting of the Advisory County Cricket Committee and the Board of Control of Test Matches at Home, at which the county captains were present, was held at Lord's on Thursday, November 23, 1933, to consider the replies received from the counties to the MCC's circular letter in regard to fast leg-theory bowling.

A decision was reached that no alteration of the Law was desirable. It was agreed that any form of bowling which is obviously a direct attack by the bowler upon the batsman would be an offence against the spirit of the game.

It was decided to leave the matter to the captains in complete confidence that they would not permit or countenance bowling of such type.

### From MCC to Australian Board of Control, December 12, 1933

"Reference your cable of November 16th, you must please accept our cable of October 9th, which speaks for itself, as final.

We cannot go beyond the assurance therein given. We shall welcome Australian cricketers who come to play cricket with us next year. If, however, your Board of Control decide that such games should be deferred, we shall regret their decision.

Please let us know your Board's final decision as soon as possible and in any event before the end of the year."

From Australian Board of Control to MCC, December 14, 1933

"With further reference to your cable of October 9 and your confirmatory cable of December 12 in reply to ours of November 16, we too, now regard the position finalised. Our team will leave Australia on March 9."

From MCC to Australian Board of Control, December 14, 1933

"Thank you for your cable. We are very glad to know we may look forward to welcoming the Australians next summer. We shall do all in our power to make their visit enjoyable."

## NOTES BY THE EDITOR

Had the foregoing cables been the medical history sheets of a person suddenly affected by some mental or physical trouble a doctor would have experienced little difficulty in tracing and analysing the disease from its onset to its cure. In like manner cricketers can gather from the cables almost the whole course of the disturbance brought about between the MCC and the Australian Board of Control over the question of fast leg-theory bowling. I have purposely omitted to use the expression "body-line bowling". It may have conveyed to those to whom it was presented at the outset the meaning the inventor of it wished to infer, but to my mind it was an objectionable term, utterly foreign to cricket, and calculated to stir up strife when the obvious aim of everybody should have been directed towards the prevention of any breach.

Happily the controversy is now at an end, and little reason exists, therefore, to flog what we can regard as a "dead horse". But, obviously from the historical point of view, something on the subject must be said. I hope and believe that the ventilation of their grievances by the Australians, and the placatory replies of the MCC will have done much towards imparting a better spirit to Test matches which of recent years have become battles rather than pleasurable struggles. A false atmosphere has pervaded them. During the last few tours of MCC teams in Australia, and the visits of the Australians to this country one could not fail to detect a subtle change taking place in the conduct of Test matches – reflected unfortunately in the style of play of the cricketers themselves. The result of the contests was given a prominence out of keeping with the importance of Test matches, and the true sense of perspective stood in danger of disappearing altogether.

There is no need to enter into some of the reasons for the hostility with which D. R. Jardine in particular and certain of his team were received by the huge crowds in Australia. Animosity existed and was fanned into flame largely by the use of the term "body-line" when Larwood and others met with such success against the leading Australian batsmen. To such an extent had real bitterness grown that the storm burst during the third Test match at Adelaide. The dispatch of the petulant cablegram by the Australian Board of Control even placed the completion of the tour in jeopardy. Saner counsels prevailed, and, although tension existed for months afterwards, the MCC for their part never lost their grip of the situation and, what was even more important, refused to be stampeded into any panic legislation. Whatever individual opinions were held at the time the MCC committee, as a whole, naturally stood by the captain of their team in Australia. They had heard only one side of the question.

And now, what of this fast leg-theory method of bowling to which not only the Australian players themselves, but a vast majority of the people of Australia took such grave exception? With the dictum of the MCC that any form of bowling which constitutes a direct attack by the bowler on the batsman is contrary to the spirit of the game everyone must unquestionably concur. D. R. Jardine, on his return to England, stated definitely in his book that the bowling against which the Australians demurred was not of this description, and Larwood, the chief exponent of it, said with equal directness that he had never intentionally bowled at a man. On the other hand, there are numerous statements by responsible Australians to the effect that the type of bowling adopted was calculated to intimidate batsmen, pitched as the ball was so short as to cause it to fly shoulder and head high and make batsmen, with the leg-side studded with fieldsmen, use the bat as a protection for their bodies or their heads rather than in defence of the wicket or to make a scoring stroke. Victor Richardson, the South Australian batsman, has said that when he took his ordinary stance at the wicket he found the ball coming on to his body; when he took guard slightly more to the leg-side he still had the ball coming at him; and with a still wider guard the ball continued to follow him. I hold no brief either for Jardine or Larwood or for Richardson, Woodfull or Bradman; but while some of the Australians may have exaggerated the supposed danger of this form of bowling I cling to the opinion that they cannot all be wrong. When the first mutterings of the storm were heard many people in this country were inclined to the belief that the Australians, seeing themselves in danger of losing the rubber, were not taking defeat in the proper spirit always expected from honourable opponents. I will confess that I thought they did not relish what seemed to me at that stage to be a continuous good length bombardment by our fast bowlers on to their leg-stump. This idea I afterwards found was not quite correct.

There is nothing new in leg-theory bowling. The most notable exponent of it in recent years was Root, of Worcestershire; to go back to just before the war A. Jacques, of Hampshire, often exploited it with success; and to delve deeper into the past an Australian – no less than the famous Spofforth himself – would at times bowl on the leg-stump with an off-break and two fieldsmen close in on the leg-side. Root and Jacques were, however, medium-paced bowlers while Spofforth, even if he had a very destructive fast ball always at command, could not truthfully be classified as a fast bowler consistent in the pace of say Larwood, Knox, Richardson, Lockwood, or Kortright. Moreover, Root, Jaques and Spofforth almost invariably bowled a good length, so that the ball could be played either in a defensive manner or with the idea of turning it to leg, and when the batsman made a mistake in timing or in placing he usually paid the penalty by being caught.

That type of bowling, however, is very different from the kind sent down at top-speed with the ball flying past the shoulders or head of the batsman who has only a split second in which to make up his mind as to whether he will duck, move away, or attempt to play it with the bat high in the air. Against one sort a perfectly legitimate and reasonable stroke could be played without any apprehension of physical damage; against the other it seems to me that by touching the ball in defence of the upper part of his body or his head a batsman would be almost bound to be out. One would not accuse Hammond or Hendren of being slow on their feet, yet Hendren at Lord's on one occasion was not quick enough to get out of the way and received a crashing blow on his head, while last season at Manchester Hammond, in the Test match against the West Indies, had his chin laid open, and on resuming his innings was caught off a similar kind of ball. We saw in that particular match at Old Trafford what I should conceive to be a somewhat pale – but no less disturbing – imitation of Larwood in Australia, when Martindale and Constantine on the one hand, and Clark, of Northamptonshire, on the other were giving a demonstration of fast leg-theory bowling. Not one of the three had the pace, accuracy of pitch, or deadliness of Larwood, but what they did was sufficient to convince many people with open minds on the subject that it was a noxious form of attack not to be encouraged in any way.

Cricketers whose memories go back to the days of the bad wickets at Lord's, are I think a little too prone to emphasise the fact that W. G. Grace and other famous batsmen of that era were often struck so frequently on the body that after their innings they were covered with bruises, but I should like to suggest that the blows they received were to a large extent caused by good-length balls getting up quickly off the rough turf. I certainly can find no trace in the course of a good deal of research among old reports and comments on these matches that the fast bowlers of those days like Tarrant and Jackson continually dropped the ball short with the idea of making it bounce.

Fast bowlers of all periods have delivered the ball short of a length on occasions – sometimes by accident, and sometimes by intention to keep batsmen on the *qui-vive* – but in modern days some of our bowlers of pace have become obsessed with the idea that it is necessary to do this three or four times in an over. I desire none of my readers to get the impression that I am against fast bowling. Nothing is further from by thoughts. I like to see fast bowling, the faster the better, but I do like to see it of good length and directed at the stumps.

The Australians without any doubt thought that during the last tour they were being bowled at, and small wonder that edging away as some of them unquestionably did they found themselves bowled when, instead of the expected short-pitched "bouncer," occasional good-length straight balls came along and beat them before they were in a proper position to defend their wickets. It is, to say the least, significant that G. O. Allen, whom nobody would place quite in the same class as Larwood, enjoyed many successes and for the most part obtained his wickets by bowling with which we in England are familiar. Surely, with his extra pace, Larwood could have done as well as Allen and so have prevented that bitter ill-feeling which led a good many people in this country to the belief that the winning of The Ashes had been gained at too great a cost to the relations hitherto existing between England and Australia.

For myself, I hope that we shall never see fast leg-theory bowling as used during the last tour in Australia exploited in this country. I think that (1) it is definitely dangerous; (2) it creates ill-feeling between the rival teams; (3) it invites reprisals; (4) it has a bad influence on our great game of cricket; and (5) it eliminates practically all the best strokes in batting. Mainly because it makes cricket a battle instead of a game I deplore its introduction and pray for its abolition, not by any legislative measures, but by the influence which our captains can bring to bear and by avoiding use of the objectionable form of attack take a great part in wiping away a blot. Early last season I heard Mr Weigall, the Recorder of Gravesend, deliver a great speech at a dinner to the West Indies team, in which in beautifully chosen phrases he exhorted them always to look upon cricket with the idea that the game is of far greater importance than the result. If that lesson is driven home to all our cricketers we shall hear no more of the kind of bowling which so nearly brought about a severance of the cricket relations between England and Australia.

## THE SETTLEMENT OF THE BOWLING CONTROVERSY

The following communication was issued by the MCC Committee from Lord's cricket ground on Wednesday, November 21, 1934, after the meetings of the Advisory County Cricket Committee and the Board of Control of Test Matches at Home:

### FAST SHORT BOWLING ON THE LEG SIDE

In 1933 the MCC Committee passed the following resolution:

"That any form of bowling which is obviously a direct attack by the bowler upon the batsman would be an offence against the spirit of the game."

On November 23, 1933, at a joint meeting of the Board of Control of Test Matches at Home and the Advisory County Cricket Committee, at which fourteen of the seventeen captains of the first-class cricketing counties were present and the remaining three represented, this resolution was accepted and an "understanding" was arrived at to the effect that the county captains would not permit or countenance bowling of such type.

This principle was also affirmed by the Imperial Cricket Conference on July 25, 1934, and it was urged that the controlling bodies of cricket should not permit or countenance such form of bowling.

In June 1933 the MCC Committee cabled to the Australian Board of Control to say that they would watch carefully for anything which might be regarded as unfair or prejudicial to the best interests of the game.

As a result of their own observations and from the reports received the MCC Committee consider that there is evidence that cases of the bowler making a direct attack upon the batsman have on occasions taken place during the past cricket season. Bowling of this kind was not unknown in the past, but has developed and may continue to develop it left unchecked.

In order to eliminate this type of bowling from the game and to ensure in future that there shall be no misunderstanding as to what exactly constitutes "a direct attack by the bowler upon the batsman," the MCC Committee have ruled:

"That the type of bowling regarded as a direct attack by the bowler upon the batsman and therefore unfair consists in persistent and systematic bowling of fast short-pitched balls at the batsman standing clear of his wicket."

The MCC Committee have further ruled that umpires in the 1st and 2nd class county competitions be instructed that they will be strongly supported by the MCC Committee in any action which they may take under Law 43 to prevent this type of bowling as now defined being practised.

At a meeting of the Advisory County Cricket Committee held to-day the counties represented endorsed the above definition of "a direct attack by the bowler on the batsman" and it was resolved that the county committees and the county captains would take the strongest possible steps to see that the type of bowling as now defined be in future eliminated from the game.

The MCC Committee hope that these steps will suffice and that it will not be found necessary to take further action.

## THE LEG-BEFORE-WICKET LAW

In conjunction with the foregoing, the MCC Committee on the same day issued the following statement:

It has been decided by a very large majority that throughout the season 1935 a trial be given in the 1st and 2nd class county competitions to an amended lbw Law reading as follows:

"The striker is out lbw if with any part of his person (except his hand) which is between wicket and wicket he intercept a ball which, in the opinion of the umpire at the bowler's wicket, shall have been pitched in a straight line from the bowlers' wicket to the striker's wicket or shall have been pitched on the off-side of the striker's wicket and would have hit it."

## NOTES BY THE EDITOR

No matter the angle from which it may be viewed it is next to impossible to regard the cricket season of 1934 as other than unpleasant. In using this word I am not referring to the fact that England lost the rubber in the Test matches with Australia. That, after we had won four matches out of five in Australia in the winter of 1932-33, was a hard enough blow to our self-esteem; but the whole atmosphere of cricket in England was utterly foreign to the great traditions of the game. As a journalist, born and bred in cricket and in mature years coming under the influence of that great lover and writer of the game, Sydney Pardon, I deplored the attitude of a certain section of the Press in what seemed to me an insane desire constantly to stir up strife.

One can only assume that the modern idea of being always in search of a "stunt" – horrible word – was the dominating influence which caused them to see trouble where none existed and, as the Hon. Mr Justice Evatt says in his article in another part of the book, to magnify an "incident" into a "dispute" and subsequently into an "international episode". All sense of proportion was lost and we constantly read during the Test matches, not so much how the game was going or how certain players acquitted themselves, but rather, tittle-tattle of a mischievous character which, in the long run, prompted the inevitable question: "Are Test matches really worth while?" One outcome of this was the Australians themselves, who had come here perfectly prepared and hoping to go through the season without any bother or recurrence of the arguments surging around "direct attack" bowling, proceeded through their programme of matches constantly on the look out for something which might occur to give them just cause for complaint. Happily the season was nearing its close before anything happened to rouse their feelings, but at Nottingham in August they were subjected to a form of attack in bowling which not only they themselves, but the majority of people in England, fondly imagined had been "scotched".

While, therefore, fourteen of the seventeen first-class county captains – the other three being represented – at a joint meeting of the Board of Control and the Advisory County Cricket Committee in November, 1933, came to an "understanding" that they would not permit or countenance any form of bowling which was obviously a direct attack on the batsman, Mr A. W. Carr, the Nottinghamshire captain, whether he agreed with the "understanding" or not, stated that not only was he opposed to "direct attack" bowling but that neither Larwood nor Voce practised it. Consequently it was not in the least degree surprising that, influenced by his opinions, so often freely and openly expressed, Voce and Larwood felt that they were justified in continuing to bowl on many occasions during the summer fast bumping leg-theory deliveries with the leg-side packed with fieldsmen. Larwood escaped censure; Voce, on the definite evidence of the umpires, exploited direct attack methods against both the Australians at Trent Bridge and Middlesex at Lord's, but it is important to note that Carr did not captain Nottinghamshire in either of these games. In each case complaint was made; the allegation was found proved and the Nottinghamshire committee, as they were bound to do, apologised. Later on this committee appointed two young amateurs G. F. Heane and S. D. Rhodes joint captains of the Nottinghamshire eleven for next season in place of A. W. Carr. This sequence of events led to a storm of protest in Nottingham and the county. A special general meeting was held at which a resolution of "no confidence" in the committee was passed. The committee thereupon resigned en bloc.

I do not intend here to go into the question of what may happen – or by the time these lines appear in print what has happened – if the new Nottinghamshire committee disavows the action of their predecessors, first in apologising and later on dispensing with the services of A. W. Carr. The effects may be far-reaching but, in any case, Nottinghamshire, unless they conform strictly to the agreement arrived at during the meeting in November, 1933, will have fewer friends among the other counties than they now possess. The thought of the glorious traditions of Nottinghamshire cricket, the history of which extends back for so many years, makes it hard to believe that such a state of affairs could have been brought about by a few men who placed their own individual conception of what they imagined was right and above-board in the spirit of cricket, against the considered opinion of practically the whole of the cricketers of England.

At the same time I do not hold the former Nottinghamshire committee entirely blameless for the position in which they found themselves. With some feeling of confidence in their members I fell sure a statement could have been put forward, which, without betraying any secrets that should not have been made known generally, would have convinced those who clamoured for the heads of the committee on a charger that the course taken was in the best interests of the county club. I would even go as far as to commend this paragraph with my suggestion to the attention of other county clubs and even to the MCC. They perhaps may not know it but they have many friends besides myself on the Press and a little well-judged confidence at times has before now smoothed over difficult situations. Even statesmen and politicians do not forever remain silent on important questions. Secrecy carried to excess begets mistrust.

The Test matches last season dominated everything and there can be no doubt that sharp feelings of disappointment were felt when England were defeated in the first and the last of the five great fixtures and could claim only the one victory at Lord's where rain and Verity proved altogether too much for our opponents. Exceptionally strong in batting, the **Australians really possessed in Grimmett and O'Reilly only two bowlers to carry them** through. Woodfull and his fellow selectors probably thought that Fleetwood-Smith, if making a remarkable advance in the latter half of the season, might be rather too expensive if he were included in a Test team. The pinning down of the England batsmen was too important an advantage lightly to be thrown away. After his return to Australia Fleetwood-Smith jumped right to the top of the tree with a number of splendid performances, thus fulfilling the prophecies made on his behalf by Arthur Mailey, who never ceased to sing his praises. Although of very different types, Grimmett and O'Reilly were, in their work, almost comparable with Gregory and McDonald of the 1921 team, while the figures of Woodfull, Ponsford, Bradman, Brown and McCabe suggested that, man for man, they were better than our first five batsmen. The two bowlers, however, in addition to all-round superiority in team-work, carried Australia through. Here I cannot refrain from criticising adversely some of the Australian batsmen. The MCC and the general body of cricketers in England gave a patient hearing to, and acted with forbearance towards, the protest condemning the method of bowling adopted, particularly by Larwood, in Australia during the last MCC tour there. Consequently it was, to say the least, an ungenerous and misleading gesture when some of the visiting batsmen, as we all saw in several matches, ducked or turned their backs to balls which got up, not head high, but about a foot above the stumps. If that was meant as a sign of silent resentment, it carried no conviction whatever, even to those who abhor short bowling that bumps.

England suffered all through the series of Tests from the fact that the selectors could never get together a team which, in all respects, "balanced". In C. F. Walters they certainly found an excellent successor to Hobbs as opening partner for Sutcliffe but, unfortunately, Hammond, though like Woolley, simply superb as a county batsman, failed badly. Only once did he look the master and then, in the second innings at Leeds, he was run out. In nearly every match either Hendren, Leyland or Ames, instead of being able to go in and play a free, confident game, had to save or remedy a position seriously damaged by the quick fall of two or three wickets. But in bowling and fielding the weakness just referred to was accentuated. The form of Nichols, from whom so much had been expected, was only a shadow of that of 1933; Farnes broke down after the first Test match and should not have played in the second; Bowes, if increasingly successful from Lord's to Leeds and on to The Oval, failed us when he was most urgently required to be at his best – during the partnerships of Ponsford and Bradman at Leeds and The Oval. Mitchell, a Triton among the minnows in many of his county matches, like Hopwood, emerged from two Tests with his reputation sadly tarnished and even Verity, apart from his one amazing performance at Lord's, could be complimented upon his steadiness rather than upon his effectiveness on hard wickets. Allen did not realise expectations – he was a very tired bowler at Manchester, where his first over consisted of thirteen balls in which were four no-balls and three wides, while Brown hit two boundaries off the others. This overstepping the crease was a common fault with many of our fast bowlers whose work must have suffered by their being frequently "no-balled". Clark, if trying hard, found none of his theories successful and received scarcely adequate support in the field. Hammond only occasionally bowled with real "fire". Clark, by the way, when he had several men close in on the leg side, kept, for the most part, a good length – left-hand round the wicket, be it remembered – and the suggestion that his occasional short ball constituted "direct attack" bowling, as was put forward at the time, did not hold water.

Nobody envied the selection committee their thankless task, but, admitting all their difficulties, we could have wished that they might have had just a little wider vision and when they found that some of those men selected did not come up to scratch, have taken a chance and introduced new blood. Unlike the Australians, they did not set sufficient store on youth and all that it meant as a revivifying influence. No better illustration of the unbalanced nature of the team, particularly with regard to fielding, could have been presented than at The Oval. Scarcely a man apart from the wicket-keeper knew where he was to go and Wyatt himself had to field in the deep. He did brilliant work there, but as captain a more advantageous position for him would have been much nearer the wicket. Without committing any pronounced blunder either in tactics or strategy, Wyatt, I am afraid, was not the ideal leader. It is difficult definitely to point out where he failed to fill the bill, but if a great trier himself, both as batsman and fielder, in what, after all, was never a well-balanced eleven, he did not possess the essential attribute of a great captain in being able to inspire the men under him to a big effort.

No greater disservice was ever done to English cricket than when Larwood was induced to dash into print and become responsible for statements which put him beyond the pale of being selected for England. I think I am right in saying that he would have been chosen for the Test Match at Lord's – to mention only one – but for the article under his name which appeared shortly before that game. No selection committee worthy of the name could possibly have considered him after that and the backing which unfortunately he received in the Press from certain quarters merely added fuel to the flames of controversy about this unhappy incident. Jardine as I have explained elsewhere, ruled himself out of selection by his communications from India and subsequent decision to write for the Press on the Test matches; thus two cricketers, whose services England greatly needed, were absent from the big games.

Perhaps, after all, it was as well. Possibly greater complications than those which arose in Nottinghamshire were avoided. After deep consideration, and carefully weighing up the effects of the disruption in English cricket together with contributory causes, I incline to the opinion that it would in the long run have been better if the Australians had postponed their visit until the echoes of the cable fencing between the MCC and the Australian Board of Control died away. Test cricket then could have been resumed when both sides were in the mood to meet in the traditional sporting spirit which characterised the struggles of thirty or forty years ago. One little sentence more: let us get back to cricket as a game; compose our internal differences and, above all, go on to the field against Australia with the knowledge that we intend to "play the game".

And now I have to draw attention to two very important decisions that occurred when the season was over. At a meeting of the Advisory County Cricket Committee last November a ruling by the MCC Committee that the type of bowling regarded as a direct attack by the bowler upon the batsman is unfair was endorsed. A year ago I had occasion to express the opinion that this bowling was scarcely such as could be prevented by the passing of any law, but that it could be stamped out if county committees would, through the medium of their captains, drastically discountenance it. I thought then that the agreement reached at the joint meeting of county captains and the Advisory Committee would effect its purpose. Not for a moment did I imagine that any captain would go behind the agreement and, in effect, repudiate it. All the same I still believe that it would have been better to have left the matter to the captains, who in time would have worked out their own salvation, always, of course, if backed up by their committees. It is a subject requiring a lot of thought. Even a definition of this type of bowling is difficult. However, I will quote and paraphrase a saying of a very famous Blackheath and England rugby footballer, the late Arthur Budd. Asked one day if there was any difference between hard and rough play at rugby he replied: – "There is a very great difference, Sir, between hard and rough play, and a gentleman knows the difference." I would say in regard to this bowling which has caused such trouble that, "There is a great difference between fast bowling and direct attack bowling, and a cricketer knows the difference." There, I think, we can for the time leave it.

There is just one other small, but I think important point to which I should like to draw the attention of the MCC. Everyone will remember that last season an incident which did not sound nice occurred at Eastbourne in the match between Sussex and Lancashire. James Parks of Sussex, not hearing the umpire and under the impression that he had been given out for a catch at the wicket made by Duckworth standing back, walked away and when he was out of his ground Duckworth ran up and put down the wicket; Parks was thereupon given out by the other umpire. We will admit that Parks, before walking away, should have made certain if the umpire put up his finger or not, but that does not really concern the point I wish to raise. It has been the custom – in my opinion a very bad one – for some years now for umpires when answering an appeal in the negative to turn their heads away; look towards the sight-screen and say nothing, or else tell the bowler or wicket-keeper to "get on with it". In its simplest interpretation this gesture has always appeared to me to be of a contemptuous nature and unnecessary on the cricket field. I would urge the MCC to issue an instruction that when an answer to an appeal is in the negative the umpire must clearly and audibly say: – "Not out". There ought never to be any misunderstanding over the affirmative reply, which is the raising of the index finger above the head; equally there should be none when the answer to the appeal is in the batsman's favour.

## BARRACKING

When English critics speak of Australian barracking, they are apt to overlook the crowds' very generous treatment of nearly all of our English visitors. Hobbs' reception from the Sydney crowd, first in December 1924 when he beat Victor Trumper's record of six Test centuries, and later in December 1928, when he was given a presentation, was quite wonderful. Players like Hobbs, Douglas, Gilligan, Kilner, Chapman, Parkin, Hendren and Tate, were idols of Australian crowds. It is a great mistake to judge the Australian spectators by the reaction of some of them when many of their players were repeatedly hit in 1932-33 as a result of an entirely novel method of fast bowling. Unfortunately a section of the press exaggerates every trifle. It becomes an "incident", then a "dispute", and it ends in an "international episode", In February 1920 for instance, in the Fifth Test at Sydney, Hobbs, who had a bad leg, was fielding at cover when Macartney drove a ball for 4. Hobbs was allowed by two other English players (at mid-off and extra-cover) to limp to the boundary in order to return the ball. Some of the crowd chaffed, not Hobbs, but his two, apparently, inconsiderate colleagues. One of two English papers misunderstood what had happened and asserted that Hobbs himself had been barracked about his injury. It is all very well to counsel silence, but nothing in the world will prevent occasional comment by some of the spectators.

## DIRECT ATTACK AND LBW

### Instructions to Umpires

In March, 1935, MCC issued the following provisional instructions (for 1935 only) to umpires, county committees and county captains, with regard to "direct attack" bowling and the new LBW rule:

### DIRECT ATTACK

1. During the cricket season of 1934 there was evidence that cases of the bowler making a "direct attack" upon the batsman occurred. The MCC Committee have defined a "direct attack" as "persistent and systematic bowling of fast short-pitched balls at the batsman standing clear of his wicket".

2. The MCC Committee have always considered this type of bowling to be unfair and that it must be eliminated from the game. Umpires are the sole judges of fair and unfair play (*vide* Law 43) and are therefore empowered to deal with "direct attack".

3. If in the opinion of the umpire at the bowler's end unfair bowling of this type takes place he shall adopt the following procedure:

   (a) As soon as he decides that such bowling is becoming persistent he shall forthwith "caution" the bowler.
   (b) If this "caution" is ineffective he shall inform the captain of the fielding side and the other umpire of what has occurred.

(*c*) Should the above prove ineffective the umpire at the bowler's end shall:

(1) At the first repetition call "dead ball" and the over shall be regarded as completed.
(2) Request the captain of the fielding side to take the bowler "off" forthwith.
(3) Report the occurrence to the captain of the batting side, as soon as an interval of play takes place.
(4) At the end of the day make a report to the secretary of the MCC and also to the secretary of the county club to which the offending bowler belongs.

4. A bowler who has been "taken off" as above shall not bowl again during the same innings.

5. Umpires should note that they will be strongly supported by the MCC Committee in any action which they may take under Law 43 to prevent this type of bowling from being practised. The Advisory County Cricket Committee on November 21, 1934, confirmed the recommendation of the MCC Committee "that the county committees and the county captains shall take all steps in their power to eliminate from the game the type of bowling as now defined, i.e., direct attack".

6. Umpires appointed to stand in first and second-class county matches are reminded that it is their duty to report forthwith to the secretary of the MCC any case on or off the field of a captain or a player criticising or showing resentment to the decision of an umpire. The umpires, are, however, required to give notice to the captains during the match that it is their intention to make such a report.

## LBW

In regard to LBW, umpires must note that in all inter-county matches in the first and second-class county competitions, in all universities' matches whether played at the universities or away, and in all South African matches they are to read Law 24 as follows:

"The striker shall be out LBW if with any part of his person (except his hand) which is between wicket and wicket he intercept a ball which, in the opinion of the umpire at the bowler's wicket, shall have been pitched in a straight line from the bowler's wicket to the striker's wicket or shall have been pitched on the off side of the striker's wicket and would have hit it."

Umpires will observe that the only new instruction is that the striker is out to a ball which pitching on the off side of the striker's wicket would have hit the wicket had it not been intercepted by part of the striker's person which was between wicket and wicket at the moment of impact.

## ENGLAND v AUSTRALIA

### Second Test Match

Played at Sydney, December 18, 19, 21, 22, 1936

England won by an innings and 22 runs. Possibly even more than in the first Test, the winning of the toss was of paramount importance. Owing to the long drought, the groundman feared the wicket would not last as well as is usual in Test matches at Sydney. The prospect of unsettled weather contributed to uncertainty about the way the wicket would play after the first day or two.

Allen beating Bradman in the toss, England were presented with a flying start and they occupied the wicket for the whole of the first day but scored no more than 279 for the loss of three wickets. Worthington was left out of the eleven and Sims brought in so that the tourists had to rely on Barnett and Fagg as first wicket batsmen. Again England quickly suffered a reverse for Fagg left at 27 but Hammond came in at this point and graced the match with a hundred.

A much-discussed feature of play before lunch, when 100 runs were scored for one wicket, concerned five overs sent down by McCormick, who was not only erratic but pitched short, so that the ball flew all over the place. It should be made clear, however, that suggestions of "body-line" bowling were uncalled for. McCormick merely used the recognised methods of the fast bowler and did not set an exaggerated leg field. Batsmen experienced little trouble in playing him during the later stages of the match; he had not fully recovered from his attack of lumbago and never again attained any real speed.

Barnett lost his wicket immediately after lunch when he played outside a ball that came through faster than anticipated. Then Leyland came on the scene to dash the hopes of the Australians. This was not one of the Yorkshire left-hander's most attractive displays but it was obvious that he and Hammond played to a set plan. Leyland was criticised even more than Hammond for his slow play by Australian experts who neglected to give their own bowlers and captain full credit for limiting the batsmen's scoring scope by the nature of their attack and the setting of the field. Nevertheless O'Reilly rather wasted time with leg theory while Ward bowled on or just outside the leg stump, and so prevented Leyland from going all out for a shot without taking a risk.

The tea interval found England's total 209 with two men out: a much different state of things from some of the previous matches. During the period between lunch and tea the Australians' fielding was surprisingly, ragged, returns to the wicket-keeper being very loose. It improved afterwards when the England batsmen, instead of putting on runs fast against a tired attack, proceeded even more slowly. The idea was for Hammond and Leyland to play for "close" but this they failed to do for Leyland was given out, leg-before-wicket under the new rule.

The third wicket stand realised 129. Ames joined Hammond, who was unbeaten at the end of the first day with 147, and batted throughout the second day, curtailed owing to rain by ninety minutes, for an addition of 84. England lost only three more wickets, raising the total to 426 for six. There was a curious incident when Hardstaff had scored 11. Robinson, the twelfth man, was fielding behind the square leg umpire and Hardstaff hit a ball from O'Reilly hard into his hands. A shower had rendered the ball as slippery as wet soap and the catch was missed. Apparently both umpires were watching the fieldsman for when Bradman called attention to the fact that the Nottinghamshire man had stepped on to his wicket sufficiently to dislodge a bail when making the stroke, Hardstaff was given the benefit of the doubt.

Heavy rain in the night created a problem for Allen next morning, and as events proved, he was right in declaring straightaway. Australia, as at Brisbane, were caught on a wet wicket, and figured in an inglorious collapse – all out for 80.

Nothing more sensational can be imagined than their first dreadful quarter of an hour, when O'Brien, Bradman and McCabe were all sent back without scoring. Voce dismissed them with his seventh, eight and tenth balls and equalled the feat of F. S. Jackson (at Nottingham in 1905) and of W. J. O'Reilly (at Manchester in 1934), who both took three Test wickets in four balls. Seven wickets were down for 31 but with lunch-time approaching, O'Reilly played a desperate innings, and hit three 6s, one off Verity and two off Sims. Allen, though not perhaps relishing such prolific scoring, was no doubt secretly glad Austral were not all out before lunch, a happening which would have necessitated an immediate decision as to whether to enforce a follow on or bat a second time. During lunch Allen decided to put Australia in again. Already the wicket had shown signs of recovery, and it rolled out a perfect batting wicket, so that he took a risk which might have cost him the match.

The general opinion was that Australia's batsmen had exaggerated the dangers of the wicket, which was damp, not sticky. They did much better on going in again, and at the close of the third day Fingleton (67) and Bradman (57) were together with the score 145 for one wicket.

The English victory was said by Australian critics to have been registered at five minutes to one on the fourth day, when Bradman, having surpassed Clem Hill's aggregate of 2,660 runs in Test matches for Australia v England, was bowled by Verity for 82. McCabe alone refused to be unnerved. He proceeded after lunch to give the brightest batting exhibition of the whole match and mastered all the English bowling, which was made to look suspiciously weak. Fortunately, Hammond kept the attack together with his perfect length and his speed off the pitch.

Tea-time came with the score 309 for five wickets and odds on England having to bat again. The interval gave England's bowlers fresh heart; Voce once more found top form, and he and Hammond, bringing about another sensational Australian collapse, won the match. McCabe tried to hit a ball from Voce to leg but it kept low and he was out lbw – the only ball that beat him in an heroic innings of 93. The whole side were out for 324.

Though it was Hammond's steadiness as a bowler that clinched England's superiority, which he himself had established with his great innings of 231 not out, Voce again came out with fine figures – seven wickets in the match for 76 runs. England enjoyed all the luck that was going – winning the toss and getting rain just when it was wanted – while Australia were hard hit by Badcock being ill; he could not bat in the first innings and although he left a sick bed to bat in the second, he made only 2. No one could dispute the fact that England, as at Brisbane, looked the better side. The details of Hammond's wonderful innings are worth recording. He batted for four hundred and sixty minutes and hit twenty-seven 4s, seven 3s, nineteen 2s and sixty-four single.

### England

| | |
|---|---|
| A. Fagg c Sievers b McCormick ......... 11 | J. Hardstaff b McCormick ............. 26 |
| C. J. Barnett b Ward .................. 57 | H. Verity not out ..................... 0 |
| W. R. Hammond not out ...............231 | B 8, l-b 8, w 1, n-b 4 ........... 21 |
| M. Leyland lbw (N) b McCabe .......... 42 | |
| L. E. G. Ames c sub. b Ward ........... 29 | 1/27 2/118      (6 wkts dec.) 426 |
| Mr G. O. Allen lbw b O'Reilly .......... 9 | 3/247 4/351 5/368 6/424 |

Mr R. W. V. Robins, W. Voce and J. Sims did not bat.

### Australia

| | |
|---|---|
| J. H. Fingleton c Verity b Voce ................. 12 | – b Sims ....................... 73 |
| L. P. O'Brien c Sims b Voce .................... 0 | – c Allen b Hammond ........... 17 |
| D. G. Bradman c Allen b Voce ................. 0 | – b Verity ..................... 82 |
| S. J. McCabe c Sims b Voce .................... 0 | – lbw b Voce ................. 93 |
| A. G. Chipperfield c Sims b Allen ............. 13 | – b Voce ..................... 21 |
| M. W. Sievers c Voce b Verity ................. 4 | – run out ..................... 24 |
| W. A. Oldfield b Verity ....................... 1 | – c Ames b Voce ................ 1 |
| W. J. O'Reilly not out ....................... 37 | – b Hammond ................. 3 |
| E. L. McCormick b Allen ..................... 10 | – lbw b Hammond ............. 0 |
| F. Ward b Allen ............................ 0 | – not out ..................... 1 |
| C. L. Badcock absent ill ..................... 0 | – lbw (N) b Allen ............. 2 |
| B 1, l-b 1, n-b 1 .................... 3 | L-b 3, n-b 4 ............. 7 |

1/1 2/1 3/1 4/16 5/28                          80   1/38 2/162 3/186 4/220              324
6/30 7/31 8/80 9/80                                 5/226 6/318 7/319 8/323 9/323

### Australia Bowling

| | Overs | Mdns | Runs | Wkts |
|---|---|---|---|---|
| McCormick ....... | 20 | 1 | 79 | 2 |
| Sievers .......... | 16.2 | 4 | 30 | — |
| Ward .......... | 42 | 8 | 132 | 2 |
| O'Reilly .......... | 41 | 17 | 86 | 1 |
| Chipperfield ....... | 13 | 2 | 47 | — |
| McCabe .......... | 9 | 1 | 31 | 1 |

**England Bowling**

| | Overs | Mdns | Runs | Wkts | Overs | Mdns | Runs | Wkts |
|---|---|---|---|---|---|---|---|---|
| Voce ............ | 8 | 1 | 10 | 4 | 19 | 4 | 66 | 3 |
| Allen ............ | 5.7 | 1 | 19 | 3 | 19 | 4 | 61 | 1 |
| Verity ........... | 3 | — | 17 | 2 | 19 | 7 | 55 | 1 |
| Hammond ........ | 4 | — | 6 | — | 15.7 | 3 | 29 | 3 |
| Sims ............ | 2 | — | 20 | — | 17 | — | 80 | 1 |
| Robins .......... | 1 | — | 5 | — | 7 | — | 26 | — |

Umpires: G. Borwick and J. D. Scott.

## ENGLAND v AUSTRALIA

## Third Test Match

Played at Melbourne, January 1, 2, 4, 5, 6, 7, 1937

Australia won by 365 runs. England were not disgraced even though the margin was a large one; outside influences had much to do with the result. The faith of Australians that their side, in which Brown, Darling, Rigg and Fleetwood-Smith appeared, in place of Chipperfield, O'Brien, Badcock and McCormick, would atone for the two previous disappointments was reflected in the attendances. All records for attendances and receipts at a cricket match were broken. On the third day alone they were 87,798 people present – the takings were £7,405 – and the aggregate attendance for the match was 350,534 and the full receipts £30,124.

As things turned out Bradman won the match for Australia when he won the toss and his tactics influenced the result. On the second day he took the unusual procedure in a played-to-a-finish Test match of declaring his first innings closed and sent England in to bat on a pitch from which the ball often reared up almost straight and at other times kept low. It is important to mention that on the first day, when Australia were batting, the wicket was lifeless and unhelpful to spin bowling and yet England got down six wickets for 130 and would probably have done still better had not rain set in and led to the bowlers being handicapped by the wet ball. Next day rain held up a resumption of the match until after lunch. The difficulties of the wicket quickly became apparent, and batsman experienced such an unhappy time that in about three hours thirteen wickets fell.

England, after losing nine wickets for 76, also declared so that for the first time in Test cricket each side closed its first innings.

It is possible England would have done better had Allen's declaration been made earlier but, as one authority put it, the England captain could not be expected to possess second sight. At the close of play on the second day, one Australian – O'Reilly – had been dismissed for 3 runs and a Sunday without rain enabled the wicket to recover so that when Australia took up their second innings again the conditions were more favourable for batting than at any previous time in the match.

Following the dismissal of Fingleton from a weak stroke after he had promised great things, McCabe was Australia's hero on the first day. Towards the end of the afternoon, with six wickets down, McCabe suddenly found his best form and revelled in a hectic ten minutes of big hitting, in which he was joined enthusiastically by Oldfield. The England bowlers were steady all day and the field gave nothing away.

Play on the second day, Saturday, was sensational throughout. On the "glue-pot wicket" Australia's apparently feeble total of 200 assumed formidable proportions. Leyland was the one real success for England. Hammond scored more runs, and made some daring if desperate shots with a close ring of fieldsmen almost within touch of his bat; Leyland never seemed in difficulties. Both men were out to extraordinary catches by

Darling at short-leg; just as Rigg had fallen to Verity on the first day – catches that would have been missed ninety-nine times out of a hundred.

Australia batted all the third day. It was inevitable that Bradman should find his form soon, and he chose the moment of his country's greatest need to do so. Rain fell in the afternoon and between – and during – the showers the England bowlers were handicapped by a wet ball which they wiped with a towel between each delivery. Bradman took full advantage of this and, though not quite his old scintillating self, and eschewing the off-drive, he thrilled the crowd and subdued the bowlers. Scoring 270 he played his highest innings against England in Australia. Not until the evening was it revealed that Bradman was suffering from a severe chill. That explained his sedateness. In Rigg he found a splendid partner; a man who had been on the fringe of the Australia XI for a long time and looked good enough a cricketer to have gained a place earlier. Rigg, reputed a poor starter, showed none of this failing, and the free use of his arms and wrists proved his class. Hereabouts came the first glimpse during the tour of the Bradman known in England. It was after a stoppage for rain and he faced Voce. He took 13 off the over (of eight balls) and 2 and 3 off the first two balls of Allen's next over. Another shower cut short the burst of hitting.

The fact that, on the fourth day, Bradman and Fingleton put up a sixth wicket record of 346 – actually the highest stand for any wicket in a Test match in Australia – was due to Bradman sending in his tail-end batsmen first. Usually those two players would have been associated for the second wicket. The pitch had become as perfect as any batsman could wish, and though the England bowlers remained steady they had little chance of beating Bradman or Fingleton. One admired the brilliant fielding of the Englishmen all day. Hammond, Worthington, Allen and others were top-class, while Robins was magnificent, constantly winning applause from the huge crowd. Only when Robins and Sims were bowling did the batsmen show real mastery.

Bradman, still suffering from mild influenza, was quickly dismissed on the morning of the fifth day, and immediately after lunch England opened their second innings wanting 689 runs to win. Such a task had never before been achieved in Test history but the wicket was still very easy and a dour fight was anticipated. However, Leyland alone of the earlier batsmen, and Robins, towards the end of the day, batted really well. Hammond made a splendid 50 and then was out to a rather careless stroke. The scoring was certainly fast and delighted the spectators, but this was not quite the type of cricket the situation demanded.

On the sixth morning Leyland and Robins rose to their greatest heights. Previously, Leyland had carried such responsibility that he had repressed many of his most spectacular shots, but this time he exploited them all, his hitting through the covers being reminiscent of his finest innings in England. With Robins out England virtually were all out, and Leyland remained undefeated with a noteworthy 111.

The Australian team looked better balanced than in the first two Tests. Batting for six and a half hours, Fingleton not only scored his second century of the series – like Leyland – but also saved something like 60 more runs with his fine fielding close to the wicket. Sievers bowled very well, but Fleetwood-Smith's figures, five for 124 in the second innings, were flattered by his dismissing Voce and Sims with the last two balls of the match. Against Hammond, he seemed incapable of bowling a length. Ward failed with the ball and Darling, though fielding well, did not justify his being brought back into the team.

The Australians never allowed their initial advantage of winning the toss to slip from their grasp. Allen's captaincy was above criticism, for the chance he might have taken in an earlier declaration when the wicket was bad would have looked ludicrous if the weather had changed. He had his men on their toes the whole time, and neither he nor they lost heart through the defeat. Voce and Verity were outstanding England bowlers. The latter kept an immaculate length and allowed no batsman to take liberties with him. It can be recorded with truth that Voce never bowled quite as well as in the first three Tests of this tour. He was untiring in his work and maintained his concentration and deadlines right through each innings.

## Australia

| | | | |
|---|---|---|---|
| J. H. Fingleton c Sims b Robins | 38 | – c Ames b Sims | 136 |
| W. A. Brown c Ames b Voce | 1 | – c Barnett b Voce | 20 |
| D. G. Bradman c Robins b Verity | 13 | – c Allen b Verity | 270 |
| K. E. Rigg c Verity b Allen | 16 | – lbw (N) b Sims | 47 |
| S. J. McCabe c Worthington b Voce | 63 | – lbw (N) b Allen | 22 |
| L. S. Darling c Allen b Verity | 20 | – b Allen | 0 |
| M. Sievers st Ames b Robins | 1 | – not out | 25 |
| W. A. Oldfield not out | 27 | – lbw b Verity | 7 |
| W. J. O'Reilly c Sims b Hammond | 4 | – c and b Voce | 0 |
| F. Ward st Ames b Hammond | 7 | – c Hardstaff b Verity | 18 |
| L. O'B. Fleetwood-Smith (did not bat) | – | – c Verity b Voce | 0 |
| B 2, l-b 6, n-b 2 | 10 | B 6, l-b 2, w 1, n-b 10 | 19 |

1/7 2/33 3/69       (9 wkts dec.) 200     1/0 2/3 3/38 4/74 5/97       564
4/79 5/122 6/130 7/183                    6/443 7/511 8/511
8/190 9/200                                     9/549

## England

| | | | |
|---|---|---|---|
| T. S. Worthington c Bradman b McCabe | 0 | – c Sievers b Ward | 16 |
| C. J. Barnett c Darling b Sievers | 11 | – lbw b O'Reilly | 23 |
| W. R. Hammond c Darling b Sievers | 32 | – b Sievers | 51 |
| M. Leyland c Darling b O'Reilly | 17 | – not out | 111 |
| J. Sims c Brown b Sievers | 3 | – lbw (N) Fleetwood-Smith | 0 |
| L. E. G. Ames b Sievers | 3 | – b Fleetwood-Smith | 19 |
| Mr R. W. V. Robins c O'Reilly b Sievers | 0 | – b O'Reilly | 61 |
| J. Hardstaff b O'Reilly | 3 | – c Ward b Fleetwood-Smith | 17 |
| Mr G. O. Allen not out | 0 | – c Sievers b Fleetwood-Smith | 11 |
| H. Verity c Brown b O'Reilly | 0 | – c McCabe b O'Reilly | 11 |
| W. Voce not out | 0 | – c Bradman b Fleetwood-Smith | 0 |
| B 5, l-b 1, n-b 1 | 7 | L-b 3 | 3 |

1/0 2/14 3/56       (9 wkts dec.) 76     1/29 2/65 3/117       323
4/68 5/71 6/71 7/76                   4/155 5/179 6/195 7/306
8/76 9/76                                  8/322 9/323

## England Bowling

| | Overs | Mdns | Runs | Wkts | Overs | Mdns | Runs | Wkts |
|---|---|---|---|---|---|---|---|---|
| Voce | 18 | 3 | 49 | 2 | 29 | 2 | 120 | 3 |
| Allen | 12 | 2 | 35 | 1 | 23 | 2 | 84 | 2 |
| Sims | 9 | 1 | 35 | — | 23 | 1 | 109 | 2 |
| Verity | 14 | 4 | 24 | 2 | 37.7 | 9 | 79 | 3 |
| Robins | 7 | — | 31 | 2 | 11 | 2 | 46 | — |
| Hammond | 5.3 | — | 16 | 2 | 22 | 3 | 89 | — |
| Worthington | | | | | 4 | — | 18 | — |

## Australia Bowling

| | Overs | Mdns | Runs | Wkts | Overs | Mdns | Runs | Wkts |
|---|---|---|---|---|---|---|---|---|
| McCabe | 2 | 1 | 7 | 1 | 8 | — | 32 | — |
| Sieves | 11.2 | 5 | 21 | 5 | 12 | 2 | 39 | 1 |
| O'Reilly | 12 | 5 | 28 | 3 | 21 | 6 | 65 | 3 |
| Fleetwood-Smith | 3 | 1 | 13 | — | 25.6 | 2 | 124 | 5 |
| Ward | | | | | 12 | 1 | 60 | 1 |

Umpires: G. Borwick and J. D. Scott.

## ENGLAND v AUSTRALIA

### Fifth Test Match

Played at Melbourne, February 26, 27, March 1, 2, 3, 1937

Australia won by an innings and 200 runs and thereby retained the "Ashes". The weather was glorious for the first two days but was less settled on the third, and a thunderstorm during the early hours of the fourth day denied England the chance of making a closer match of it, though by then their position was precarious, to say the least. Again Bradman showed the way, after winning the toss for the third successive time, and his brilliant display – one of the finest of his career – made it easy for his colleagues to help build up the mammoth total of 604 in the first innings. This was the highest total Australia have ever amassed against England in their own country, though England still hold the record, 636 made at Sydney in 1928-29.

All the bright, attacking, stroke-making batting came from Australia. On the first day, Bradman and McCabe broke another record by putting on 249 for the third wicket, and Bradman, reaching three figures, equalled Hobbs' record of twelve hundreds in England v Australia Tests. At close of play Australia were 342 for three, a total that should never have been achieved, as four important catches were dropped, all at short leg behind the umpire. Allen, who had been taking far harder catches during the tour, dropped two, and Farnes was the other delinquent. There was a patch of bad ground-fielding, too, but the bowlers stuck to their gruelling task in a humid temperature of 99 degrees with notable courage and stamina. Farnes was the best bowler – indeed throughout this match he bowled in his finest form.

This first day's play was a tragic one for England. Fingleton was dropped twice, when 1 and 2, while McCabe was missed early in his innings and again when 86. The fillip the fast bowlers would have gained had all the catches been taken was incalculable. Despite his chances, McCabe gave a classic display, with delightful crisp cutting the feature of aggressive hitting all round the wicket. Right through his innings Bradman did not once put the ball into the air; nor did he give the semblance of a chance. The heat had its effect and next morning he seemed unable to concentrate; he added only 4 more runs. Bradman batted over three and a half hours and hit fifteen 4s.

The Englishmen were on their toes for fresh successes but the wicket was a batsman's paradise – it was not fast even on the first morning – and Gregory joined Badcock in another great stand for the fifth wicket that realised 161. Badcock hit with great power and scored fluently in the manner of Hendren. His 118 – his first Test century – took 205 minutes and contained fifteen 4s. Australia were 593 for nine at the close and raised the total to 604 on the third morning. Farnes came out with the magnificent figures of six wickets for 96 runs.

As the pitch was still perfect, giving no assistance to any bowler, England had a wonderful chance to make a telling reply but, after a dazzling start by Barnett and Worthington there was a disastrous collapse.

In the first seventeen minutes, 33 runs were scored, and then Barnett fell, caught at the wicket high up in trying to cut a ball. Had he not been seeing the ball perfectly from the start Barnett would not have tried such a stroke early in his innings. Worthington, who had been selected in place of Robins, was also in an aggresive mood but he had bad luck all through the series and his ill-fortune still pursued him. Soon after lunch when, with Hardstaff in, Worthington made a hook shot, he caught his heel against his wicket and knocked a bail off before completing his stroke. Hardstaff went on to play his best innings of the tour but Hammond was pegged down by O'Reilly's leg-theory and never looked like making progress. Trying a wristy flick at a leg ball from O'Reilly that had proved his undoing in the Adelaide Test, Hammond was caught at short-leg. Leyland also failed, so England had four wickets down for 140 and the game looked as good as over. Wyatt played out time with Hardstaff, the score being increased to 184 at the close of the third day.

The fourth day clinched matters, for England had to bat on a wet wicket that O'Reilly was able to exploit. Faulty timing was the cause of Hardstaff's early dismissal and accounted for the failure of most of the other batsmen, but Wyatt met a ball from O'Reilly that turned and popped up suddenly. The last four wickets fell for 3 runs and at the lunch interval England were all out and had to follow on 365 behind.

O'Reilly was the chief agent of destruction while Nash, whose inclusion in Australia's eleven came as a surprise, bowled fast and well in his first Test. The wicket was too slow for Fleetwood-Smith.

Though Barnett and Hammond added 60, England that night had lost eight second innings wickets for 165, and two balls by Fleetwood-Smith on the following morning accounted for Voce and Farnes. Again O'Reilly bowled a perfect length but was too fond of defensive tactics. On such a wicket S. F. Barnes would have attacked all the time instead of flirting with leg-theory. On England's side, Allen's bowling was disappointing. The misfortune of losing the toss and then missing two catches possibly upset him. However, Allen again worked like a Trojan and handled his side well, though there was a little criticism because he opened the bowling himself with Farnes instead of using Voce. Verity came out with poor figures, on paper, but he put up a remarkable feat of endurance. Voce was not as dangerous as in previous Tests and Farnes stood alone as a destructive bowler. A notable point about the match was that only one bye was conceded.

## Australia

| | | |
|---|---|---|
| J. H. Fingleton c Voce b Farnes | 17 | |
| K. E. Rigg c Ames b Farnes | 28 | |
| D. G. Bradman b Farnes | 169 | |
| S. J. McCabe c Farnes b Verity | 112 | |
| C. L. Badcock c Worthington b Voce | 118 | |
| R. Gregory c Verity b Farnes | 80 | |
| W. A. Oldfield c Ames b Voce | 21 | |
| L. J. Nash c Ames b Farnes | 17 | |
| W. J. O'Reilly b Voce | 1 | |
| E. L. McCormick not out | 17 | |
| L. O'B. Fleetwood-Smith b Farnes | 13 | |
| B 1, l-b 5, w 1, n-b 4 | 11 | |

1/42 2/54 3/303 4/346 5/507     604
6/544 7/563 8/571 9/576

## England

| | | | |
|---|---|---|---|
| C. J. Barnett c Oldfield b Nash | 18 | – lbw b O'Reilly | 41 |
| T. S. Worthington hit wkt b Fleetwood-Smith | 44 | – c Bradman b McCormick | 6 |
| J. Hardstaff c McCormick b O'Reilly | 83 | – b Nash | 1 |
| W. R. Hammond c Nash b O'Reilly | 14 | – c Bradman b O'Reilly | 56 |
| M. Leyland b O'Reilly | 7 | – c McCormick b Fleetwood-Smith | 28 |
| Mr R. E. S. Wyatt c Bradman b O'Reilly | 38 | – run out | 9 |
| L. E. G. Ames b Nash | 19 | – c McCabe b McCormick | 11 |
| Mr G. O. Allen c Oldfield b Nash | 0 | – c Nash b O'Reilly | 7 |
| H. Verity c Rigg b Nash | 0 | – not out | 2 |
| W. Voce st Oldfield b O'Reilly | 3 | – c Badcock b Fleetwood-Smith | 1 |
| Mr K. Farnes not out | 0 | – c Nash b Fleetwood-Smith | 0 |
| L-b 12, n-b 1 | 13 | L-b 3 | 3 |

1/33 2/96 3/130 4/140 5/202     239     1/9 2/10 3/70 4/121 5/142     165
6/236 7/236 8/236 9/239            6/142 7/153 8/162 9/165

## England Bowling

| | Overs | Mdns | Runs | Wkts |
|---|---|---|---|---|
| Allen | 17 | — | 99 | — |
| Farnes | 28.5 | 5 | 96 | 6 |
| Voce | 29 | 3 | 123 | 3 |
| Hammond | 16 | 1 | 62 | — |
| Verity | 41 | 5 | 127 | 1 |
| Worthington | 6 | — | 60 | — |
| Leyland | 3 | — | 26 | — |

**Australia Bowling**

| | Overs | Mdns | Runs | Wkts | Overs | Mdns | Runs | Wkts |
|---|---|---|---|---|---|---|---|---|
| McCormick ....... | 13 | 1 | 54 | — | 9 | — | 33 | 2 |
| Nash ............ | 17.5 | 1 | 70 | 4 | 7 | 1 | 34 | 1 |
| O'Reilly .......... | 23 | 7 | 51 | 5 | 19 | 6 | 58 | 3 |
| Fleetwood-Smith ... | 18 | 3 | 51 | 1 | 13.2 | 3 | 36 | 3 |
| McCabe .......... | | | | | 1 | — | 1 | — |

Umpires: G. Borwick and J. D. Scott.

# ENGLAND IN THE WEST INDIES

## MCC TEAM v WEST INDIES
### Third Representative Match

Played at Georgetown, February 21, 22, 24, 25, 26, 1930

The third meeting with the full strength of the West Indies ended in defeat for MCC by 289 runs. In achieving a noteworthy victory, West Indies owed a great deal to the batting of Headley – who created a record by scoring a hundred in each innings in a representative engagement – and to that of Roach and also to some effective fast bowling by Constantine and Francis. MCC's fielding was badly at fault when West Indies opened their first innings with a stand of 144, Hunte being missed four times. Roach, however, played brilliantly for rather less than five hours, hitting three 6s and twenty-two 4s, and in partnership with Headley he added 196. The total stood at 425 on the fall of the fifth wicket but the remaining batsmen were dismissed for 46. The only real resistance in the MCC's first innings came from Hendren and Ames and the West Indies went in again leading by 326. Slow methods at their second attempt almost deprived the home team of success for MCC, when facing the task of getting 617 runs, set themselves to save the game and held out until within a quarter of an hour of time. Hendren carefully waiting for the right ball to hit, had twenty-one 4s in his sixth century of the tour.

### West Indies

| | | | | |
|---|---|---|---|---|
| C. A. Roach c Haig b Townsend | 209 | – st Ames b Astill | 22 |
| E. Hunte c Wyatt b Townsend | 53 | – b Townsend | 14 |
| G. Headley run out | 114 | – c Townsend b Haig | 112 |
| M. P. Fernandes c Ames b Rhodes | 22 | – c Calthorpe b Rhodes | 19 |
| J. D. Sealy c and b Rhodes | 0 | – c Hendren b Rhodes | 10 |
| C. V. Wight b Wyatt | 10 | – b Haig | 22 |
| L. N. Constantine st Ames b Wyatt | 13 | – b Astill | 0 |
| C. R. Browne b Voce | 22 | – not out | 70 |
| C. Jones c Ames b Voce | 6 | – b Townsend | 2 |
| E. St Hill st Ames b Haig | 3 | – b Astill | 3 |
| G. N. Francis not out | 5 | – lbw b Astill | 2 |
| Extras | 14 | Extras | 14 |
| | **471** | | **290** |

### MCC Team

| | | | | |
|---|---|---|---|---|
| G. Gunn hit wkt b Francis | 11 | – c Hunte b Francis | 45 |
| A. Sandham c Hunte b Browne | 9 | – c and b Constantine | 0 |
| Mr R. E. S. Wyatt c Francis b Constantine | 0 | – c Jones b Constantine | 28 |
| E. Hendren b Constantine | 56 | – lbw b St Hill | 123 |
| L. E. G. Ames c Hunte b Francis | 31 | – c Francis b Constantine | 3 |
| L. Townsend c Hunte b Francis | 3 | – b Constantine | 21 |
| W. E. Astill run out | 0 | – hit wkt b Constantine | 5 |
| Mr N. Haig b Constantine | 4 | – b Browne | 0 |
| Hon. F. S. G. Calthorpe c Headley b Constantine | 15 | – c Jones b Roach | 49 |
| W. Rhodes b Francis | 0 | – not out | 10 |
| W. Voce not out | 1 | – lbw b Francis | 2 |
| Extras | 15 | Extras | 41 |
| | **145** | | **327** |

## MCC Team Bowling

| | Overs | Mdns | Runs | Wkts | Overs | Mdns | Runs | Wkts |
|---|---|---|---|---|---|---|---|---|
| Voce ............ | 26 | 4 | 81 | 2 | 16 | 4 | 44 | — |
| Haig ............ | 23 | 7 | 61 | 1 | 10 | 1 | 44 | 2 |
| Townsend ....... | 16 | 6 | 48 | 2 | 7.3 | 2 | 25 | 2 |
| Rhodes .......... | 40 | 8 | 96 | 2 | 51 | 23 | 93 | 2 |
| Astill .......... | 28 | 3 | 92 | — | 43 | 17 | 70 | 4 |
| Calthorpe ........ | 6 | — | 23 | — | | | | |
| Wyatt ........... | 9 | — | 56 | 2 | | | | |

## West Indies Bowling

| | Overs | Mdns | Runs | Wkts | Overs | Mdns | Runs | Wkts |
|---|---|---|---|---|---|---|---|---|
| Francis .......... | 21 | 5 | 40 | 4 | 26.5 | 11 | 69 | 2 |
| Constantine ....... | 16.3 | 6 | 35 | 4 | 40 | 17 | 87 | 5 |
| Browne .......... | 10 | 2 | 29 | 1 | 33 | 15 | 32 | 1 |
| St Hill .......... | 14 | 4 | 26 | — | 33 | 15 | 61 | 1 |
| Roach .......... | | | | | 9 | 2 | 18 | 1 |
| Headley ......... | | | | | 2 | — | 8 | — |
| Jones ........... | | | | | 10 | 7 | 5 | — |
| Wight ........... | | | | | 5 | 1 | 6 | — |

# MCC v WEST INDIES

## Fourth Representative Match

Played at Kingston, April 3, 4, 5, 7, 8, 9, 10, 11, 12, 1930

Each side having won once and one game having been drawn, it was decided to play to a finish the fourth representative match, but rain prevented cricket on the eighth and ninth days. By that time the MCC team were due to return home so no result could be reached. Had MCC, after gaining a first innings lead of 563, enforced the follow on, they might have won, but Calthorpe decided to bat again and the weather destroyed the possibility of victory. MCC placed themselves in a practically impregnable position during the first three days when they put together the tremendous total of 849. While the run-getting was very consistent and Ames registered a capital hundred, Sandham carried off the honours with an innings of 325 which, occupying ten hours, included a 7, a 5 and twenty-seven 4s. Nunes gave the West Indies a fair start but nobody stayed long afterwards. Although when batting again MCC failed to repeat their huge success of the first innings, they set their opponents the appalling task of getting 836 runs. Headley made a great effort for his side, staying six hours and a half and hitting twenty-eight 4s. He and Nunes put on 228, the West Indies at the end being 427 behind with half their wickets in hand.

## MCC Team

G. Gunn st Barrow b Martin ................... 85 – run out ...................... 47
A. Sandham b Griffith ....................... 325 – lbw b Griffith .................. 50
Mr R. E. S. Wyatt c Barrow b Da Costa .......... 58 – c Passalique b Da Costa ......... 10
E. Hendren c Passalique b Scott ................ 61 – b Roach ...................... 55
L. E. G. Ames b Griffith .................... 149 – c Nunes b Scott ................ 27
J. O'Connor c Da Costa b Scott ................ 51 – c Headley b Scott ............... 3
Hon. F. S. G. Calthorpe c Griffith b Scott ......... 5 – st Barrow b Scott ............... 8
Mr N. Haig c Da Costa b Gladstone ............. 32 – c Passalique b Scott ............ 34
W. E. Astill b Scott ........................ 34 – b Griffith .................... 10
W. Rhodes not out ......................... 8 – not out ..................... 11
W. Voce c Da Costa b Scott .................. 20 – not out ...................... 6
     Extras ............................ 21       Extras ................. 11

           849          (9 wkts dec.) 272

## West Indies

| | | | |
|---|---|---|---|
| R. K. Nunes c Ames b Voce | 63 | – b Astill | 92 |
| C. A. Roach lbw b Haig | 15 | – c Gunn b Rhodes | 22 |
| G. Headley c Haig b Voce | 10 | – st Ames b Wyatt | 223 |
| F. R. Martin lbw b Haig | 33 | – c Sandham b Wyatt | 24 |
| F. I. de Caires run out | 21 | – b Haig | 16 |
| I. Barrow b Astill | 0 | | |
| C. Passalique b Haig | 44 | – not out | 2 |
| O. C. Scott c and b Astill | 8 | | |
| O. Da Costa c Haig b Astill | 39 | | |
| H. C. Griffith c Hendren b Rhodes | 7 | | |
| G. Gladstone not out | 12 | | |
| Extras | 31 | Extras | 29 |
| | **283** | | **408** |

### West Indies Bowling

| | Overs | Mdns | Runs | Wkts | Overs | Mdns | Runs | Wkts |
|---|---|---|---|---|---|---|---|---|
| Griffith | 58 | 6 | 155 | 2 | 21.1 | 5 | 52 | 2 |
| Da Costa | 21 | — | 81 | 1 | 6 | 2 | 14 | 1 |
| Gladstone | 42 | 5 | 139 | 1 | 8 | — | 50 | — |
| Scott | 80.2 | 13 | 266 | 5 | 25 | — | 108 | 4 |
| Martin | 45 | 6 | 128 | 1 | 9 | 1 | 12 | — |
| Headley | 5 | — | 23 | — | | | | |
| Roach | 5 | — | 21 | — | 10 | 1 | 25 | 1 |
| Passalique | 2 | — | 15 | — | | | | |

### MCC Team Bowling

| | Overs | Mdns | Runs | Wkts | Overs | Mdns | Runs | Wkts |
|---|---|---|---|---|---|---|---|---|
| Voce | 22 | 3 | 81 | 2 | — | — | 94 | — |
| Haig | 30 | 10 | 73 | 3 | — | — | 49 | 1 |
| Rhodes | 20.5 | 12 | 17 | 1 | — | — | 22 | 1 |
| Astill | 33 | 12 | 73 | 3 | — | — | 108 | 1 |
| Wyatt | 4 | — | 11 | — | — | — | 58 | 2 |
| O'Connor | 2 | 2 | — | — | — | — | 32 | — |
| Calthorpe | | | | | — | — | 16 | — |

Details of the overs and maidens in the second innings of the West Indies were not available.

## ENGLAND v WEST INDIES

### First Test Match

Played at Barbados, January 8, 9, 10, 1935

The first Test match ended in a remarkable victory for England by four wickets. The ball, on a pitch affected by rain, nearly always mastered the bat. Sensations began at the start, for Wyatt, upon winning the toss, sent his opponents in to bat. Thanks to begin with to the fast bowling of Farnes, and later to the slow deliveries of Paine and Hollies, considerable success attended the venture. Farnes, making the ball lift awkwardly, dismissed four West Indies batsmen at a personal cost of 15 runs, and half the side were out for 31. Headley alone offered real resistance, and he gave two chances. Still, he defied the attack for two hours and lost his wicket when Christiani refused a run. England fared no better than their opponents and, although Hammond saved the side from complete collapse, half the wickets were down for 81 when the first day ended. The wicket being saturated by overnight rain, the game could not be resumed until after tea on Wednesday. Then two disasters swiftly overtook England, for in the first over Hylton disposed of Hammond and Holmes, and Wyatt, realising the treacherous state of the wicket, declared with his side still 21 runs in arrear. In the hope that conditions might improve, G. C. Grant altered his batting order, but Smith sent back R. S. Grant, Martindale and Achong with 4 runs on the board. Hylton and Christiani carefully played out time, raising the total to 33. More heavy rain fell during the night leaving the pitch waterlogged, and not till half past three could cricket be attempted next day. A strong breeze and bright sunshine then rendered the wicket difficult, and bowlers took command to such an extent that three batsmen left for the addition of 18 runs before tea. During the interval, G. C. Grant, in turn, adopted the bold policy of declaring, leaving England 73 runs to get for victory. That the conditions remained helpful to the attack was soon demonstrated. Martindale and Hylton making the ball rise in disconcerting fashion. With a view to knocking the bowlers off their length, Wyatt sent in Farnes and Smith to open the innings, but England met with a series of reverses, six wickets falling – five of them to Martindale, who bowled at a tremendous pace – for 49 runs. Fortunately for England, Hammond, at a critical period, revealed his best form. Content to wait for scoring opportunities, Hammond steadily gained something of a mastery over the bowling and, Wyatt defending stoutly, the end came without further success to bowlers. Hammond enjoyed the satisfaction fo bringing off the winning hit – a huge drive for 6 at the expense of Martindale. All the same, Martindale's five wickets cost him only 22 runs and his match record of eight for 61 constituted a noteworthy achievement.

### West Indies

| | | | |
|---|---|---|---|
| C. A. Roach c Paine b Farnes | 9 | – not out | 10 |
| G. Carew c Holmes b Farnes | 0 | | |
| G. Headley run out | 44 | – c Paine b Farnes | 0 |
| C. Jones c Leyland b Farnes | 3 | | |
| J. E. D. Sealey c Paine b Farnes | 0 | | |
| G. C. Grant c Hendren b Hollies | 4 | | |
| R. S. Grant c Hammond b Hollies | 5 | – c Paine b Smith | 0 |
| L. G. Hylton st Ames b Paine | 15 | – lbw b Smith | 19 |
| C. M. Christiani not out | 9 | – b Smith | 11 |
| E. Achong st Ames b Paine | 0 | – b Smith | 0 |
| E. A. Martindale c Leyland b Paine | 9 | – lbw b Smith | 0 |
| Extras | 4 | Extras | 11 |
| | **102** | **(6 wkts dec.)** | **51** |

### England

| | | | |
|---|---|---|---|
| Mr R. E. S. Wyatt c R. Grant b Martindale | 8 | – not out | 6 |
| M. Leyland b Martindale | 3 | – c R. Grant b Martindale | 2 |
| W. R. Hammond c R. Grant b Hylton | 43 | – not out | 29 |
| E. Hendren c R. Grant b Martindale | 3 | – b Martindale | 20 |
| L. E. G. Ames lbw b R. S. Grant | 8 | | |
| J. Smith c Jones b Hylton | 0 | – c Christiani b Martindale | 0 |
| J. Iddon not out | 14 | | |
| Mr E. R. T. Holmes c Achong b Hylton | 0 | – c G. Grant b Martindale | 6 |
| Mr K. Farnes | | – c G. Grant b Hylton | 5 |
| G. E. Paine | | – c R. Grant b Martindale | 2 |
| Extras | 2 | Extras | 5 |
| | **(7 wkts dec.) 81** | | **75** |

E. Hollies did not bat.

### England Bowling

| | Overs | Mdns | Runs | Wkts | Overs | Mdns | Runs | Wkts |
|---|---|---|---|---|---|---|---|---|
| Farnes | 15 | 4 | 40 | 4 | 9 | 2 | 22 | 1 |
| Smith | 7 | 3 | 8 | — | 8 | 4 | 15 | 5 |
| Hollies | 16 | 1 | 36 | 2 | | | | |
| Paine | 9 | 3 | 14 | 3 | 1 | 1 | — | — |
| Hammond | | | | | 1 | — | 3 | — |

**West Indies Bowling**

| | Overs | Mdns | Runs | Wkts | Overs | Mdns | Runs | Wkts |
|---|---|---|---|---|---|---|---|---|
| Martindale ........ | 9 | — | 39 | 3 | 8.3 | 1 | 22 | 5 |
| Hylton .......... | 7.3 | 3 | 8 | 3 | 8 | — | 48 | 1 |
| Achong ......... | 6 | 1 | 14 | — | | | | |
| R. S. Grant ....... | 7 | — | 18 | 1 | | | | |

# ENGLAND v WEST INDIES
## Second Test Match

Played at Trinidad, January 24, 25, 26, 28, 1935

Winning the toss for the sixth time in succession, Wyatt, as in the opening Test, gave his opponents first innings; but on this occasion the gamble failed. West Indies winning by 217 runs. The match ended in dramatic circumstances, England's final stand being broken by the last ball but one of the game. A great all-round display by Constantine who, in the match, scored 121 runs and took five wickets for 52, played no small part in the victory. England were undoubtedly handicapped by the inability of Farnes, owing to a strained neck muscle, to turn out; having regard to the success achieved by the West Indies pace bowlers, the absence of the Essex man probably represented a greater loss than most people realised.

Wyatt's venture may have been engendered by the belief that the wicket would be fiery, but events proved the reverse to be the case. Yet the West Indies made none too promising a start, two men being dismissed for 38. Headley and Sealey added 64, but G. C. Grant fell at 115, and not until Constantine came in were the bowlers mastered. Constantine's daring methods thrilled the crowd of 11,000 – a record attendance for a match in the West Indies. As usual, Constantine did not hesitate to take risks, and he timed the ball perfectly in vigorous drives, pulls and hits to leg. Sealey played polished cricket, scoring readily all round, and, with thirteen 4s as his chief figures, he helped Constantine to put on 118. He made no mistake during nearly three hours at the crease. Next day, Constantine obtained all 18 runs added to the overnight 284 for nine wickets. Wyatt, who kept an excellent length, returned the best bowling figures for England. When England went in, Constantine, Martindale and Hylton, the fast bowlers, disposed of half the side for 23. Fine fielding contributed to the collapse, Wyatt, Hammond and Ames being out to capital catches by R. S. Grant close in on the leg-side. Hendren and Iddon effected an improvement by putting on 71 and Iddon, using his feet well to bring off powerful drives, found another able partner in Holmes, who joined in a seventh stand of 74. After Iddon's departure, Holmes, sound in defence yet neglecting few scoring opportunities, added 62 with Farrimond and in the end England stood only 44 runs behind. Holmes's innings at a crisis deserved the highest praise.

In their second innings the West Indies were scarcely so enterprising as on the opening day. Headley batted quietly for nearly three hours and three-quarters, and Constantine and R. S. Grant were the only players who adopted aggressive tactics. Still, the methods paid, and, declaring at lunch on the fourth day, West Indies set their opponents 325 to get. Wyatt followed the amazing and inexplicable course of almost completely reversing his batting order. The efforts of the early men met with such little success that by tea five were out for 75. England's hopes of saving the game virtually disappeared when Wyatt left without addition and Hendren at 79 were easily run out. Ames and Iddon gave no trouble and though Leyland and Holmes, the last pair, defended stubbornly for a while, the innings and the match ended almost on the stroke of time.

## West Indies

| | | | | |
|---|---|---|---|---|
| C. M. Christiani c Farrimond b Smith | 11 | – c Farrimond b Smith | 8 |
| C. Jones c Farrimond b Paine | 19 | – c Wyatt b Paine | 19 |
| G. Headley c Holmes b Paine | 25 | – lbw b Smith | 93 |
| J. E. D. Sealey b Wyatt | 92 | – c Hammond b Leyland | 35 |
| G. C. Grant b Smith | 8 | – c Hammond b Paine | 23 |
| O. Da Costa b Holmes | 25 | – not out | 19 |
| L. N. Constantine c Hendren b Smith | 90 | – c Ames b Paine | 31 |
| R. S. Grant b Wyatt | 0 | – not out | 38 |
| L. G. Hylton c Hendren b Smith | 8 | | |
| E. Achong lbw b Wyatt | 9 | | |
| E. A. Martindale not out | 0 | | |
| Extras | 15 | Extras | 14 |
| | **302** | **(6 wkts dec.)** | **280** |

## England

| | | | | |
|---|---|---|---|---|
| Mr R. E. S. Wyatt c R. Grant b Hylton | 15 | – c Headley b Constantine | 2 |
| Mr D. C. H. Townsend lbw b Constantine | 5 | – c Da Costa b Achong | 36 |
| W. R. Hammond c R. Grant b Hylton | 1 | – b Constantine | 9 |
| L. E. G. Ames c R. Grant b Martindale | 2 | – c Achong b Hylton | 6 |
| M. Leyland lbw b Constantine | 0 | – lbw b Constantine | 18 |
| E. Hendren c G. Grant b R. Grant | 41 | – run out | 11 |
| J. Iddon c Headley b R. Grant | 73 | – c Christiani b Hylton | 0 |
| Mr E. R. T. Holmes not out | 85 | – not out | 0 |
| J. Smith b R. Grant | 8 | – run out | 3 |
| W. Farrimond c Constantine b Sealey | 16 | – c Headley b Hylton | 2 |
| G. E. Paine lbw b Sealey | 4 | – b R. Grant | 14 |
| Extras | 8 | Extras | 6 |
| | **258** | | **107** |

## England Bowling

| | Overs | Mdns | Runs | Wkts | Overs | Mdns | Runs | Wkts |
|---|---|---|---|---|---|---|---|---|
| Smith | 26 | 2 | 100 | 4 | 30 | 9 | 73 | 2 |
| Wyatt | 17 | 7 | 33 | 3 | 8 | 2 | 26 | — |
| Hammond | 14 | 5 | 28 | — | 10 | — | 17 | — |
| Paine | 26 | 6 | 85 | 2 | 42 | 10 | 109 | 3 |
| Leyland | 9 | 1 | 31 | — | 13 | 3 | 41 | 1 |
| Holmes | 3 | 1 | 10 | 1 | | | | |

## West Indies Bowling

| | Overs | Mdns | Runs | Wkts | Overs | Mdns | Runs | Wkts |
|---|---|---|---|---|---|---|---|---|
| Martindale | 17 | 5 | 26 | 1 | 5 | 1 | 5 | — |
| Hylton | 23 | 6 | 55 | 2 | 14 | 4 | 25 | 3 |
| Constantine | 19 | 5 | 41 | 2 | 14.5 | 9 | 11 | 3 |
| Achong | 16 | 4 | 27 | — | 12 | 5 | 24 | 1 |
| R. S. Grant | 28 | 7 | 68 | 3 | 12 | 4 | 18 | 1 |
| Da Costa | 8 | 2 | 23 | — | 1 | 1 | — | — |
| Sealey | 6 | 2 | 7 | 2 | 5 | — | 16 | — |
| Headley | 4 | 2 | 3 | — | | | | |
| Jones | | | | | 2 | — | 2 | — |

# ENGLAND IN SOUTH AFRICA

## MCC TEAM v ORANGE FREE STATE

Played at Bloemfontein, November 25, 26, 28, 1927

Batting in most brilliant fashion the MCC team actually hit up 592 – the biggest total ever put together by an English side in South Africa – in rather less than five hours and three quarters and again declaring – on this occasion with seven men out – won by an innings and 164 runs. A great personal triumph was enjoyed by Holmes who, opening the visitors' innings in company with Sutcliffe on what was the birthday of both of them, carried out his bat for 279 – the largest individual score on record in an Anglo-South African match. Holmes did not give a chance, hit thirty-eight 4s and shared in two stands of over two hundred runs, making 203 in company with Sutcliffe in a hundred minutes and 224 with Legge as his partner in just over two hours. Legge had a 6 and thirteen 4s in his 120, but gave chances when 63 and 76. Commaille scored well in each innings of the Free State but was indifferently supported. Peebles, particularly successful as a bowler in the home team's first innings, secured ten wickets in the match for 8 runs apiece.

### Orange Free State

| | | | |
|---|---|---|---|
| J. M. M. Commaille b Peebles | 77 | – c Geary b Peebles | 54 |
| S. Coen b Hammond | 2 | – c Stevens b Geary | 10 |
| R. Dick lbw b Stevens | 20 | – b Astill | 12 |
| M. Francis st Elliott b Peelbes | 2 | – c Stevens b Peebles | 3 |
| A. J. Minogue c Geary b Peebles | 30 | – c Sutcliffe b Peebles | 32 |
| C. W. Travers b Peebles | 2 | – lbw b Astill | 14 |
| T. E. Holmes c Legge b Stevens | 6 | – not out | 61 |
| L. G. Fuller lbw b Peebles | 0 | – c and b Geary | 8 |
| C. Reynolds b Peebles | 0 | – lbw b Geary | 4 |
| G. Vels not out | 6 | – run out | 0 |
| A. Newton c Elliott b Peebles | 27 | – b Stevens | 7 |
| Extras | 20 | Extras | 31 |
| | **192** | | **236** |

### MCC Team

| | | | |
|---|---|---|---|
| H. Sutcliffe lbw b Travers | 73 | G. Geary lbw b Coen | 0 |
| P. Holmes not out | 279 | Capt. R. T. Stanyforth c Commaille b Coen | 3 |
| Mr G. T. S. Stevens st Holmes b Travers | 51 | Mr I. A. R. Peebles not out | 1 |
| W. R. Hammond st Holmes b Coen | 26 | Extras | 22 |
| Mr G. B. Legge c Holmes b Fuller | 120 | | |
| W. E. Astill c and b Fuller | 17 | **(7 wkts dec.) 592** | |

R. E. S. Wyatt and H. Elliott did not bat.

### MCC Bowling

| | Overs | Mdns | Runs | Wkts | Overs | Mdns | Runs | Wkts |
|---|---|---|---|---|---|---|---|---|
| Hammond | 5 | — | 7 | 1 | 7 | 1 | 25 | — |
| Geary | 13 | 3 | 23 | — | 23 | 4 | 71 | 3 |
| Astill | 10 | 2 | 30 | — | 19 | 5 | 38 | 2 |
| Peebles | 13.4 | 3 | 54 | 7 | 16 | 8 | 26 | 3 |
| Stevens | 15 | 2 | 43 | 2 | 16 | 1 | 45 | 1 |
| Wyatt | 4 | 1 | 15 | — | | | | |

**Orange Free State Bowling**

|            | Overs | Mdns | Runs | Wkts |
|------------|-------|------|------|------|
| Coen       | 22    | 4    | 80   | 3    |
| Vels       | 21    | 2    | 106  | —    |
| Travers    | 19    | 1    | 67   | 2    |
| Dick       | 2     | —    | 9    | —    |
| Reynolds   | 10    | —    | 40   | —    |
| Newton     | 26    | 2    | 135  | —    |
| Fuller     | 23    | 1    | 97   | 2    |
| Francis    | 5     | —    | 36   | —    |

# ENGLAND v SOUTH AFRICA

## Fifth Test Match

### Played at Durban, February 21, 23, 24, 25, 1931

England required to win the last Test match in order to avoid defeat in the rubber and, the result being a draw, honours went to South Africa. A piece of forgetfulness delayed the start of the game and prejudiced England's chance of gaining a victory. The state of the pitch and the weather influenced Chapman, on winning the toss, to put South Africa in to bat. A difficult pitch was certain and obviously the sooner the bowlers got to work the better for England but bails of the size to fit the larger stumps could not be found and the umpires had to make a set before the game could begin. Chapman protested strongly against this loss of time – inexcusable from his point of view – and he led the England team on to the field. Siedle and Mitchell followed while the umpires completed their task. Following upon the preposterous situation, rain limited play to seventy minutes during which 32 runs were scored without a wicket falling. As South Africa occupied all Monday in completing their innings for 252, five hours being spent over 220 runs, the prospect of a good match depended upon England's ability to put together a big score at a rapid rate. So far from accomplishing this, the visiting batsmen found the pitch by no means easy. Vincent with a cross wind to help his left-hand deliveries, caused particular trouble. Five wickets fell for 101 and except when Farrimond and Tate put on 62 there was no suggestion of a mastery over the bowling. South Africa led by 22 and scored 3 without loss before bad light stopped play for the day. Practically all interest had then gone from the game and another display of slow batting yielded only 216 runs in three hours and forty minutes. Cameron's declaration was purposeless, barely an hour remaining for England to bat. Wyatt fell to the last ball of the first over but, as Chapman changed his batting order and Cameron did not call upon his best bowlers, the match ended tamely. White replaced Lee in the England eleven and South Africa made four changes, Christy, Dalton, Bell and Cochrane coming in for Catterall, Curnow, Nupen and Hall.

### South Africa

| | | |
|---|---|---|
| I. J. Siedle c and b White | 57 | – c Chapman b White ............ 30 |
| B. Mitchell b Hammond | 73 | – c Hammond b Voce ............ 21 |
| J. A. J. Christy b Peebles | 16 | – st Farrimond b Peebles .......... 37 |
| H. W. Taylor c and b Peebles | 16 | – lbw b Peebles ................. 14 |
| K. F. Viljoen c Hammond b Tate | 16 | – c Chapman b Voce ............ 18 |
| H. B. Cameron b Voce | 4 | – not out ...................... 41 |
| E. L. Dalton c Farrimond b Hammond | 31 | – st Farrimond b Peebles .......... 11 |
| Q. McMillan not out | 29 | – c Chapman b Wyatt ............ 28 |
| C. L. Vincent c Chapman b Peebles | 6 | – not out ...................... 5 |
| A. J. Bell b Voce | 0 | |
| J. Cochrane b Peebles | 4 | |
| | | Extras ................. 14 |
| | **252** | **(7 wkts dec.) 219** |

## England

| | | | | |
|---|---|---|---|---|
| Mr R. E. S. Wyatt c Cameron b Bell | 24 | – c Mitchell b Christy | 1 |
| W. R. Hammond c Mitchell b Vincent | 29 | – c Vincent b Bell | 28 |
| M. Leyland lbw b Bell | 8 | | |
| E. Hendren c McMillan b Vincent | 30 | | |
| Mr M. J. Turnbull b McMillan | 6 | – c and b Siedle | 7 |
| W. Farrimond c Taylor b Vincent | 35 | – c Cameron b Taylor | 9 |
| Mr A. P. F. Chapman c McMillan b Vincent | 24 | | |
| M. W. Tate b Vincent | 50 | – not out | 24 |
| W. Voce c Bell b McMillan | 0 | | |
| Mr J. C. White c and b Vincent | 10 | | |
| Mr I. A. R. Peebles not out | 2 | | |
| Extras | 12 | Extras | 3 |
| | 230 | | 72 |

### England Bowling

| | Overs | Mdns | Runs | Wkts | Overs | Mdns | Runs | Wkts |
|---|---|---|---|---|---|---|---|---|
| Tate | 22 | 4 | 35 | 1 | 9 | 2 | 17 | — |
| Hammond | 19 | 6 | 36 | 2 | 5 | — | 28 | — |
| Voce | 27 | 10 | 51 | 2 | 22 | 1 | 46 | 2 |
| Peebles | 27.4 | 3 | 67 | 4 | 25 | 4 | 71 | 3 |
| White | 35 | 9 | 63 | 1 | 17 | 6 | 37 | 1 |
| Wyatt | | | | | 4 | 2 | 6 | 1 |

### South Africa Bowling

| | Overs | Mdns | Runs | Wkts | Overs | Mdns | Runs | Wkts |
|---|---|---|---|---|---|---|---|---|
| Bell | 30 | 4 | 63 | 2 | 3 | — | 14 | 1 |
| Cochrane | 23 | 5 | 47 | — | | | | |
| Vincent | 31.2 | 9 | 51 | 6 | | | | |
| McMillan | 17 | 3 | 57 | 2 | | | | |
| Christy | | | | | 4 | 1 | 17 | 1 |
| Taylor | | | | | 3 | — | 13 | 1 |
| Siedle | | | | | 3.1 | 1 | 7 | 1 |
| Mitchell | | | | | 1 | — | 18 | — |

# SOUTH AFRICA v ENGLAND

## Fifth Test Match

Played at Durban, March 3, 4, 6, 7, 8, 9, 10, 11, 13, 14, 1939

Drawn. Unparalleled in the history of the game this was in many ways an extraordinary match, emphasising that there are no limits to the possibilities of what may occur in cricket: but it ended farcically, for insufficient time remained to finish the "time-less" Test. Although undecided, the final Test left the rubber with England after a magnificent and unequalled performance by W. R. Hammond and his men. Stopped by rain on the tenth day, the longest match ever played produced amazing records and brought personal triumph to Edrich who, after most heart-breaking experiences in Test cricket, established his reputation by hitting a double century at a time when England needed an almost superhuman effort to avoid disaster.

South Africa set England to make 696 to win and few people imagined the team had a ghost of a chance of averting defeat, much less of scoring such a colossal total. Instead of going in with their tails down the batsmen set about their task in a magnificent manner and proved what can be done when the wicket remains unimpaired. It was an astonishing achievement to get within 42 runs of their objective with five wickets in hand, but, like The Oval Test between England and Australia the previous August, the game developed into a test of endurance. For one thing the pitch was much too good and many batsmen discarded their natural methods and adopted unnecessary caution.

When heavy rain prevented any more cricket after tea on the tenth day the South African Board of Control and the two captains went into conference before issuing a statement that the game had been abandoned because the England team had to catch the five minutes past eight train that night (Tuesday) from Durban in order to reach Cape Town in time to make the necessary arrangements for their departure on the *Athlone Castle* on Friday. The date of sailing for England could not be postponed.

### Records

During the course of the match the following cricket records were established. (1) The match lasted until tea time on the tenth day and was the longest ever played in first-class cricket. (2) Biggest aggregate of runs in any first-class match, 1,981. (3) England's 654 for five wickets, the highest fourth innings score in a first-class match. (4) South Africa's first innings total of 530 was their highest in Test cricket, and the longest in England v South Africa Tests, lasting 13 hours. (5) Verity bowled 766 balls in the two South African innings – 17 more than J. C. White against Australia at Adelaide in 1929. (6) P. A. Gibb and Paynter, in putting on 280 for the second wicket, set up a record partnership for any wicket in England v South Africa Tests. (7) On eight consecutive days when cricket took place stumps were drawn before time – on seven occasions through bad light and once through rain. (8) A. D. Nourse's 103 in six hours four minutes was the slowest hundred scored for South Africa in Test cricket. (9) P. G. Van der Byl's innings was the longest played by a South African in a Test. It occupied seven hours eighteen minutes. (10) R. E. Grieveson's 75 was the highest first innings in Test cricket by a player chosen to keep wicket. (11) P. G. Van der Byl was the first South African to score a hundred and a ninety in the same Test. Only P. A. Gibb had previously accomplished the feat – in the first Test of the same series. (12) A South African Test record of nine fifties was set up in the two innings. No previous Test had ever produced as many – sixteen fifties by both teams. (13) Each side in the Test scored over 900 runs – South Africa 1,011, England 970. (14) P. A. Gibb's 100 in seven hours thirty-one minutes – the slowest Test century scored for England, rate being 15.96 runs per hour. (15) In the match a record number of balls was bowled – 5,463. (16) W. R. Hammond hit his twenty-first hundred in Test cricket, equalling the record of D. G. Bradman.

### First Day (*Friday*)

After Hammond had won the toss for England eight consecutive times his luck changed, and Melville gained first innings for South Africa. Whereas England made two changes compared with the fourth Test, Perks and Wright replacing Goddard and Wilkinson, South Africa chose the team which shaped so well at Johannesburg. The opening batsmen gave their side a splendid start by scoring 131 together in three hours ten minutes. Against the fast bowling of Farnes and Perks, who frequently made the ball rise awkwardly, they exercised much caution and the total reached only 49 at lunch. Van der Byl spent forty-five minutes before opening his score and three hours elapsed before he hit a boundary. Melville, who brought off some attractive strokes, was more restrained than usual and the innings had lasted two hours ten minutes before he claimed the first boundary by hooking a no-ball. He batted faultlessly until, playing back to Wright, he stepped on his wicket. Van der Byl offered a very hard catch when 71 to Wright, otherwise he did not take the slightest risk though he astonished everyone when he punished Wright for twenty-two in one over, including five boundaries. Next he pulled a ball into the grand stand for 6; Rowan stayed while 88 were added and the total reached 229 for two wickets at the end of the day. Van der Byl being 105 not out after batting four hours forty-seven minutes.

*Second Day (Saturday)*

Encouraged by their success on the opening day, South Africa went on "Digging for Victory" and another spell of dour cricket was witnessed. Van der Byl was several times hit on the body by the bowling of Farnes but he maintained his unperturbed attitude. Mitchell was bowled off his pads at 236 and, with Nourse and Van der Byl together, the scoring became so slow that the first hour produced only 17 runs. Van der Byl, who hit one 6 and eight 4s, was disposed of after a stay of seven hours eighteen minutes when he was bowled by a ball which swung late. It was his first century in a Test. His dismissal occurred shortly after lunch and with the addition of 4 runs Viljoen also lost his wicket. Another valuable stand for South Africa followed, as Dalton played beautiful cricket while helping Nourse to add 90 for the sixth wicket. Nourse displayed unlimited patience, taking three and a half hours to make 50 and at the close of play South Africa's total was 423 for six wickets.

*Third Day (Monday)*

Rain on Sunday did not affect the pitch adversely and Nourse and Grieveson carried their unfinished stand of 55 to 107 before Nourse, after batting six hours, was yorked by Perks. He hit six 4s. When Grieveson punished Verity for 4 and sent up 500, it was the first boundary hit off the Yorkshireman since the opening day. At length, Grieveson, having played soundly for three and a half hours, was bowled middle stump, and the innings ended with Langton being caught at long-off. The English bowling analysis made sorry reading, though Perks could be satisfied with his first Test effort in taking five wickets for 100. By his perfect length, Verity kept the runs down, but he did not meet with success until he accounted for Newson and Langton in the final over. England followed their opponents' methods and opened cautiously, making only 10 runs in three-quarters of an hour, and when heavy rain ended play for the day shortly after tea the total stood at 35 for the loss of Gibb.

*Fourth Day (Tuesday)*

On this day South Africa appeared to gain a real mastery, as accurate bowling, supported by brilliant fielding – only one chance was missed – left them well on top. Misfortune soon overtook England; a misunderstanding with Paynter led to Hutton being run out. Hammond survived a shaky start against Gordon, but at 125 was well stumped trying to drive. Meanwhile, Paynter was completely tied down, and when dismissed he had batted four hours twenty minutes and hit only three 4s. As Edrich promptly fell to an easy catch at short leg, half the side were out for 171. Then the Kent pair, Ames and Valentine, introduced some enterprise to the batting, each driving splendidly until Dalton broke the partnership by getting Valentine stumped. All day the sun never shone and the light became inferior. Dalton bowled Verity at 245 but Ames, joined by another county colleague, Wright, maintained his grand form, the total being raised to 268, with Ames 82 not out and Wright 5 not out, before an appeal against the light was upheld.

*Fifth Day (Wednesday)*

England suffered an early set-back, as with 8 more scored Ames fell to a smart running catch by Dalton after Melville had tried to hold the ball. Ames made his 84, including seven 4s, in two hours fifty-two minutes. Wright and Farnes each hit vigorously but England were all out for 316, the innings having lasted seven hours thirty-eight minutes. South Africa enjoyed a lead of 214 runs but probably did not consider enforcing the follow-on, and, so well did they drive home the advantage that their opening pair, Mitchell and Van der Byl, were not separated until the score realised 191 in three and three quarter hours. Then Mitchell hit his wicket and England recovered some ground, for, in the same over Rowan was magnificently caught by Edrich, while in the following over – the last of the day – Van der Byl gave an easy catch to short leg. In this way South Africa lost their first three wickets at the same total, and Nourse might have left immediately, but

Hammond at mid-off could not hold a very hard drive. At the close South Africa were 193 for three wickets – 407 ahead. Van der Byl failed by only 3 runs to become the first South African to score a hundred in each innings of a Test against England.

*Sixth Day (Thursday)*
   On a pitch that improved, following showers during the night, South Africa took their second innings score to 481. First thing, Nourse and Viljoen showed the utmost confidence but at 242 Nourse mistimed a hook and fell to a good running catch. Although never really aggressive Melville and Viljoen relentlessly strengthened their side's strong position, and the stand produced 124 before Viljoen played on. Batting just over three hours he made some strong forcing strokes, hitting seven 4s. Dalton decided to attack the bowling and punished Wright for a 6 and three 4s. The Kent bowler, however, had revenge by taking a grand return catch. An injured thigh prevented Melville opening the innings, but now, despite lameness, he displayed his best form, making many delightful strokes in front of the wicket. Grieveson, who batted forty minutes before getting a run, gave his captain excellent support, but having completed his first Test century in three hours nineteen minutes, Melville was bowled. His 103 contained ten 4s. A characteristic slip catch by Hammond in his best manner disposed of Langton; Wright bowled Newson and Grieveson was the last to leave. Until the tea interval when the score was 387 for six, Ames kept wicket magnificently, having conceded only six byes while 917 runs were scored altogether, but after the interval Gibb went behind the stumps. England faced the tremendous task of scoring 696 to win and the newspapers everywhere were practically unanimous that it was hopeless. The light was extremely poor when Hutton and Gibb began the last innings and only one ball was bowled before stumps were pulled up on appeal.

*Seventh Day (Friday)*
   After being out-played England at last asserted themselves. Hutton and Gibb were never at fault until, by a timing error, Hutton, after driving and hitting to leg freely, played the ball on to his wicket at 78. Here Hammond revealed a masterly stroke of leadership in promoting Edrich to first wicket down. The young Middlesex batsman lost no time in seizing this opportunity to silence his critics and, hitting cleanly, he claimed eight 4s in his first 50. Gibb pursued his usual placid game and, though handicapped by slight intermittent rain which smeared his spectacles, he offered an impregnable defence. There was a remarkable scene when Edrich completed his first Test hundred (twelve boundaries). The crowd gave him an ovation, the South Africans congratulated him and high up on the balcony shouts of triumph came from his comrades. He and Gibb remained together until bad light stopped cricket ten minutes before time. England's total stood at 253 for one wicket, Gibb 78 and Edrich 107.

*Eighth Day (Saturday)*
   Not a ball could be bowled owing to rain.

*Ninth Day (Monday)*
   The wicket rolled out well after the week-end rain and Edrich and Gibb were still together at lunch time when the score was 331. Altogether the stand produced 280 before Gibb, whose innings lasted nine hours, was bowled. He hit only two 4s. Then Hammond joined Edrich and the score was taken to 447 before Edrich was third out. Very strong on the leg side and driving magnificently, he hit twenty-five 4s, making his 219 in seven hours forty minutes. Hammond and Paynter then took command until again poor light put an early end to the day's play when England were 496 for three wickets, with Hammond 58 and Paynter 24.

*Tenth Day (Tuesday)*
   South Africa put forth a great effort to check the flow of runs and keen fielding, coupled with particularly accurate bowling by Gordon, who aimed at the leg stump, tied England down to 39 runs in the first hour. By this time rain threatened to stop play. Hammond and

Paynter, realising that they were now engaged in a race against the weather and the clock, attacked the bowling. A smart catch near the ground by the wicket-keeper off Gordon ended the partnership which put on 164, at 611. Paynter batted three and a half hours but had to be satisfied with five 4s. Soon two interruptions occurred through rain and Hammond, when endeavouring to force the pace, was stumped. The England captain, in one of the finest innings of his career, excelled with masterly drives and powerful leg hits. His stay lasted six hours, yet his 4s numbered only seven. No sooner had Valentine joined Ames than the threatened downpour broke over the ground and nothing more could be done.

N. P.

### South Africa

| | | |
|---|---|--:|
| P. G. Van der Byl b Perks | 125 – c Paynter b Wright | 97 |
| A. Melville hit wkt b Wright | 78 – b Farnes | 103 |
| E. A. Rowan lbw b Perks | 33 – c Edrich b Verity | 0 |
| B. Mitchell b Wright | 11 – hit wkt b Verity | 89 |
| A. D. Nourse b Perks | 103 – c Hutton b Farnes | 25 |
| K. Viljoen c Ames b Perks | 0 – b Perks | 74 |
| E. L. Dalton c Ames b Farnes | 57 – c and b Wright | 21 |
| R. E. Grieveson b Perks | 75 – b Farnes | 39 |
| A. B. C. Langton c Paynter b Verity | 27 – c Hammond b Farnes | 6 |
| E. S. Newson c and b Verity | 1 – b Wright | 3 |
| N. Gordon not out | 0 – not out | 7 |
| B 2, l-b 12, n-b 6 | 20    B 5, l-b 8, n-b 4 | 17 |
| | 530 | 481 |

### England

| | | |
|---|---|--:|
| L. Hutton run out | 38 – b Mitchell | 55 |
| Mr P. A. Gibb c Grieveson b Newson | 4 – b Dalton | 120 |
| E. Paynter lbw b Langton | 62 – c Grieveson b Gordon | 75 |
| Mr W. R. Hammond st Grieveson b Dalton | 24 – st Grieveson b Dalton | 140 |
| L. E. G. Ames c Dalton b Langton | 84 – not out | 17 |
| W. J. Edrich c Rowan b Langton | 1 – c Gordon b Langton | 219 |
| Mr B. H. Valentine c Grieveson b Dalton | 26 – not out | 4 |
| H. Verity b Dalton | 3 | |
| D. V. P. Wright c Langton b Dalton | 26 | |
| Mr K. Farnes b Newson | 20 | |
| R. T. D. Perks not out | 2 | |
| B 7, l-b 17, w 1, n-b 1 | 26    B 8, l-b 12, w 1, n-b 3 | 24 |
| | 316 | 654 |

### England Bowling

| | Overs | Mdns | Runs | Wkts | Overs | Mdns | Runs | Wkts |
|---|---|---|---|---|---|---|---|---|
| Farnes | 46 | 9 | 108 | 1 | 22.1 | 2 | 74 | 4 |
| Perks | 41 | 5 | 100 | 5 | 32 | 6 | 99 | 1 |
| Wright | 37 | 6 | 142 | 2 | 32 | 7 | 146 | 3 |
| Verity | 55.6 | 14 | 97 | 2 | 40 | 9 | 87 | 2 |
| Hammond | 14 | 4 | 34 | — | 9 | 1 | 30 | — |
| Edrich | 9 | 2 | 29 | — | 6 | 1 | 18 | — |
| Hutton | | | | | 1 | — | 10 | — |

### South Africa Bowling

| | Overs | Mdns | Runs | Wkts | Overs | Mdns | Runs | Wkts |
|---|---|---|---|---|---|---|---|---|
| Newson | 25.6 | 5 | 58 | 2 | 43 | 4 | 91 | — |
| Langton | 35 | 12 | 71 | 3 | 56 | 12 | 132 | 1 |
| Gordon | 37 | 7 | 82 | — | 55.2 | 10 | 174 | 1 |
| Mitchell | 7 | — | 20 | — | 37 | 4 | 133 | 1 |
| Dalton | 13 | 1 | 59 | 4 | 27 | 3 | 100 | 2 |

## CHOSEN TO VISIT INDIA

MCC made full preparations and chose their team to visit India in 1939-40, but the tour was cancelled owing to the war. Three Tests were arranged to be played at Bombay, Calcutta and Madras. The following were selected to represent MCC:

Flight-Lieut A. J. Holmes (Sussex) *captain*, Mr H. T. Bartlett (Sussex), Mr J. M. Brocklebank (Lancashire), Mr S. C. Griffith (Sussex), Mr R. H. C. Human (Worcestershire), Mr R. E. S. Wyatt (Warwickshire), E. Davies (Glamorgan), H. E. Dollery (Warwickshire), H. Gimblett (Somerset), G. H. Pope (Derbyshire), John Langridge (Sussex), G. Mobey (Surrey), M. S. Nichols (Essex), J. F. Parker (Surrey), P. Smith (Essex), A. W. Wellard (Somerset). *Manager*: Lieut-Col C. B. Rubie.

# CRICKET IN AUSTRALIA

## VICTORIA v SOUTH AUSTRALIA

Played at Melbourne, January 2, 3, 5, 6, 1920

Victoria won by ten wickets. Park and Armstrong added 215 for the eighth wicket, Park batting altogether six hours and forty minutes. For South Australia, Rundell batted admirably in the first innings, and in the second Richardson and Pritchard put on exactly 200 for the third wicket. McDonald and Armstrong were the most successful bowlers.

### South Australia

| | | | |
|---|---|---|---|
| D. E. Pritchard b McNaughton | 4 | – lbw b Ryder | 91 |
| D. R. A. Gehrs b McDonald | 13 | – b McDonald | 5 |
| P. D. Rundell not out | 122 | – b McDonald | 0 |
| V. Richardson b Park | 20 | – b Park | 134 |
| D. M. Steele c Armstrong b McNaughton | 17 | – c Hartkopf b Ryder | 73 |
| R. J. B. Townsend b Armstrong | 46 | – c Park b Armstrong | 4 |
| N. Williams b McDonald | 4 | – not out | 20 |
| A. Richardson b McDonald | 0 | – c Park b Armstrong | 29 |
| E. Schultz c Armstrong b McDonald | 0 | – b Ryder | 0 |
| W. J. Whitty c Armstrong b McNaughton | 3 | – c Ellis b Armstrong | 5 |
| F. R. Lucas b Armstrong | 10 | – run out | 0 |
| Extras | 8 | Extras | 17 |
| | 247 | | 378 |

### Victoria

| | | | |
|---|---|---|---|
| L. Cody b Whitty | 15 | – not out | 8 |
| E. R. Mayne c Shultz b A. Richardson | 70 | – not out | 13 |
| L. McNaughton c Whitty b Lucas | 5 | | |
| L. Keating c Steele b Rundell | 3 | | |
| J. Ryder c Townsend b Rundell | 18 | | |
| L. W. Ferguson b Whitty | 29 | | |
| A. E. V. Hartkopf b Rundell | 49 | | |
| Dr R. L. Park c Pritchard b Lucas | 228 | | |
| W. W. Armstrong b Williams | 143 | | |
| J. Ellis b Williams | 17 | | |
| E. A. McDonald not out | 11 | | |
| Extras | 17 | | |
| | 605 | | 21 |

### Victoria Bowling

| | Overs | Mdns | Runs | Wkts | Overs | Mdns | Runs | Wkts |
|---|---|---|---|---|---|---|---|---|
| McNaughton | 23 | 6 | 88 | 3 | 16 | 4 | 58 | — |
| McDonald | 18 | 1 | 71 | 4 | 20 | 2 | 84 | 2 |
| Ryder | 9 | 1 | 39 | — | 11.1 | — | 54 | 3 |
| Park | 3 | — | 15 | 1 | 5 | — | 17 | 1 |
| Hartkopf | 3 | — | 20 | — | 10 | 1 | 57 | — |
| Armstrong | 4.2 | — | 6 | 2 | 17 | 1 | 69 | 3 |
| Keating | | | | | 2 | — | 16 | — |
| Mayne | | | | | 1 | — | 6 | — |

## South Australia Bowling

| | Overs | Mdns | Runs | Wkts | Overs | Mdns | Runs | Wkts |
|---|---|---|---|---|---|---|---|---|
| Whitty .......... | 36 | 4 | 104 | 2 | | | | |
| Lucas ........... | 18 | 1 | 88 | 2 | | | | |
| Townsend ........ | 14 | — | 50 | — | | | | |
| Rundell ......... | 27 | 1 | 147 | 3 | | | | |
| A. Richardson ..... | 26 | 3 | 92 | 1 | | | | |
| Williams ......... | 15.5 | — | 87 | 2 | | | | |
| V. Richardson ..... | 3 | — | 15 | — | 1 | — | 13 | — |
| Pritchard ........ | 1 | — | 5 | — | | | | |
| Gehrs ........... | | | | | 1 | — | 8 | — |

Umpires: R. Crockett and W. Bowes.

## AIF TEAM v NEW SOUTH WALES

Played at Sydney, January 31, February 2, 3, 1920

The Imperial Forces team winning easily by 203 runs. The match was specially noteworthy for the wonderful all-round cricket of Gregory. In addition to scoring a century in each innings, he secured eight wickets for 130 runs, and caught three men out. His 102 occupied him only an hour and a half. He then deliberately threw his wicket away. Collins also shewed exceptional skill in getting his 129. Mailey took ten wickets in the game for 167 runs, and greatly impressed the critics as a googly bowler. The AIF team, and Gregory in particular, had a tremendous reception at the finish.

### AIF Team

| | | | |
|---|---|---|---|
| H. L. Collins b Norman ...................... | 0 | – c and b Mailey ................ | 129 |
| J. M. Gregory c Carter b Norman .............. | 122 | – st Carter b Mailey ............. | 102 |
| C. E. Pellew c E. Trennery b Hendry ............. | 1 | – c Carter b Mailey ............. | 10 |
| A. W. Lampard c Mailey b E. Trennery .......... | 45 | – c E. Trennery b Mailey .......... | 18 |
| J. M. Taylor c Mailey b E. Trennery ............. | 7 | – b Mailey ..................... | 32 |
| W. L. Trennery st Carter b Mailey ............... | 31 | – b E. Trennery ................. | 26 |
| J. T. Murray lbw b Mailey .................... | 0 | – c Trennery b Mailey ........... | 29 |
| W. A. Oldfield c Mailey b Hendry ............... | 12 | – b Hendry .................... | 2 |
| W. S. Stirling lbw b Hendry ................... | 0 | – c Carter b Mailey ............. | 12 |
| C. T. Docker c Carter b Mailey ................ | 38 | – lbw b Mailey ................. | 1 |
| C. S. Winning not out ....................... | 2 | – not out ..................... | 13 |
| Extras ........................... | 7 | Extras ................. | 21 |
| | **265** | | **395** |

### New South Wales

| | | | |
|---|---|---|---|
| H. Carter b Gregory ........................ | 17 | – c Oldfield b Gregory ......... | 15 |
| H. L. Hendry b Gregory ..................... | 85 | – c Gregory b Collins ......... | 3 |
| W. Bardsley c Oldfied b Collins ............... | 60 | – b Gregory ................. | 2 |
| T. J. E. Andrews c Docker b Gregory ........... | 39 | – b Winning ................. | 65 |
| A. Kippax c Winning b Gregory ............... | 17 | – run out ................... | 2 |
| K. B. Docker lbw b Lampard ................... | 0 | – c Lampard b C. T. Docker ..... | 27 |
| A. Punch b Docker ........................ | 30 | – c Oldfield b C. T. Docker ...... | 6 |
| A. A. Ratcliffe c Oldfield b Gregory ........... | 22 | – c Winning b Gregory ......... | 12 |
| R. Norman c Gregory b Winning .............. | 3 | – c Gregory b Lampard ......... | 24 |
| E. Trennery run out ........................ | 0 | – not out ................... | 15 |
| A. A. Mailey not out ....................... | 0 | – c Taylor b Winning ........... | 1 |
| Extras ........................... | 6 | Extras ................. | 6 |
| | **279** | | **178** |

### New South Wales Bowling

| | Overs | Mdns | Runs | Wkts | Overs | Mdns | Runs | Wkts |
|---|---|---|---|---|---|---|---|---|
| Norman | 16 | 3 | 66 | 2 | 15 | — | 81 | 1 |
| Hendry | 10 | 2 | 62 | 3 | 20 | 3 | 85 | 1 |
| E. Trennery | 14 | 1 | 85 | 2 | 9 | — | 69 | 1 |
| Mailey | 10.4 | 1 | 45 | 3 | 26.7 | — | 122 | 7 |
| Andrews | | | | | 2 | — | 17 | — |

### AIF Team Bowling

| | Overs | Mdns | Runs | Wkts | Overs | Mdns | Runs | Wkts |
|---|---|---|---|---|---|---|---|---|
| Lampard | 12 | — | 70 | 1 | 2 | — | 8 | 1 |
| Gregory | 5.3 | 1 | 65 | 5 | 15 | 3 | 65 | 3 |
| Collins | 11 | — | 59 | 1 | 20 | 1 | 52 | 1 |
| C. T. Docker | 9 | — | 34 | 1 | 8 | 1 | 28 | 2 |
| Winning | 10 | — | 45 | 1 | 4.7 | 1 | 19 | 2 |

## SOUTH AUSTRALIA v NEW SOUTH WALES

Played at Adelaide, December 15, 16, 18, 19, 20, 1922

New South Wales won by an innings and 310 runs. Winning the toss and batting on a perfect wicket, New South Wales hit up the huge score of 786, four batsmen getting hundreds. Kippax played the finest innings, showing all the skill that made him the batsman of the season. The fifth wicket put on 263 runs, the sixth 114 and the seventh 180. South Australia batted about as well as could have been expected after their tremendous spell of work in the field. Owing to a strain Everett, who had met with marked success, could bowl only two overs when South Australia followed-on.

### New South Wales

| | |
|---|---|
| H. L. Collins c Bennett b A. Richardson ... 64 | W. A. Oldfield st Bennett b Williams ......118 |
| W. Bardsley run out .................... 40 | C. R. Campling c A. Richardson b Williams 10 |
| C. G. Macartney c Williams b Morton .... 6 | A. A. Mailey not out ................. 38 |
| T. J. Andrews lbw b A. Richardson ....... 14 | S. Everett hit wkt b Williams ........... 4 |
| J. M. Taylor c Townsend b Morton .......159 | Extras ..................... 17 |
| A. Kippax b Williams ................170 | — |
| H. L. Hendry st Bennett b A. Richardson ..146 | 786 |

### South Australia

| | | |
|---|---|---|
| F. K. Gould run out ..................... 24 | – c Oldfield b Hendry ....... | 0 |
| C. E. Dolling c Oldfield b Everett ............. 54 | – c Collins b Mailey ....... | 17 |
| V. Richardson c Collins b Mailey .......... 47 | – c Bardsley b Hendry ....... | 6 |
| R. J. Townsend b Everett ................. 4 | – c Andrews b Mailey ........... | 24 |
| L. V. Pellew st Oldfield b Mailey ......... 14 | – b Mailey ..................... | 31 |
| A. Richardson not out .................. 60 | – lbw b Mailey ............. | 29 |
| D. E. Pritchard c Collins b Everett ......... 2 | – st Oldfield b Mailey ......... | 14 |
| R. Grey c Campling b Everett ............ 18 | – c Oldfield b Hendry ............. | 0 |
| N. L. Williams c Macartney b Mailey ....... 37 | – not out ................. | 51 |
| R. L. Bennett lbw b Everett ............. 6 | – b Mailey ................. | 5 |
| F. L. Morton c Everett ................. 3 | – b Campling ............. | 19 |
| Extras ......................... 5 | Extras ............... | 6 |
| 274 | | 202 |

## South Australia Bowling

| | Overs | Mdns | Runs | Wkts |
|---|---|---|---|---|
| Morton .......... | 23 | — | 134 | 2 |
| A. Richardson ..... | 33 | 2 | 135 | 3 |
| Townsend ....... | 29 | 1 | 176 | — |
| Williams .......... | 23.5 | — | 206 | 4 |
| V. Richardson ..... | 3 | — | 13 | — |
| Grey ............ | 11 | — | 78 | — |
| Pellew .......... | 4 | — | 27 | — |

## New South Wales Bowling

| | Overs | Mdns | Runs | Wkts | Overs | Mdns | Runs | Wkts |
|---|---|---|---|---|---|---|---|---|
| Everett ........... | 20.6 | 2 | 59 | 6 | 2 | 1 | 5 | — |
| Campling ........ | 9 | 1 | 41 | — | 16.4 | 1 | 62 | 1 |
| Mailey ........... | 29 | 1 | 106 | 3 | 20 | 1 | 77 | 6 |
| Hendry .......... | 9 | 2 | 27 | — | 13 | 4 | 52 | 3 |
| Macartney ........ | 9 | 3 | 28 | — | | | | |
| Andrews ......... | 1 | — | 8 | — | | | | |

# NEW SOUTH WALES v SOUTH AUSTRALIA

Played at Sydney, January 11, 12, 14, 1924

New South Wales won by an innings and 104 runs. On batting first, South Australia did wonders up to a point, but after their fourth wicket had fallen at 360 the batting went to pieces against Mailey and Hendry. V. Y. Richardson scored his 135 out of 296 in three hours and a quarter. For their huge total of 685, New South Wales were at the wickets just eight hours. Kippax, playing superbly, made so far the highest score of his career. In getting 248 runs out of 497 in five hours and a quarter, he hit thirty-two 4s. Warren Bardsley, though overshadowed by Kippax, was also seen at his very best.

## South Australia

| | | |
|---|---|---|
| E. L. Bowley c Oldfield b Mailey ................ | 33 – b Everett ..................... | 0 |
| A. J. Richardson st Oldfield b Mailey ............ | 90 – b Everett ..................... | 41 |
| V. Y. Richardson b Mailey ..................... | 135 – c Hendry b Punch .............. | 67 |
| D. M. Pritchard st Oldfield b Punch ............. | 62 – b Hendry ..................... | 20 |
| F. K. Gould st Oldfield b Mailey ................ | 24 – b Everett ..................... | 23 |
| J. W. Rymill b Mailey ........................ | 0 – st Oldfield b Mailey ........... | 13 |
| R. J. B. Townsend c Mailey b Hendry ............ | 0 – b Punch ...................... | 1 |
| W. J. Whitty c Collins b Mailey ................. | 3 – not out ...................... | 9 |
| N. L. Williams not out ...................... | 9 – b Everett ..................... | 2 |
| H. M. Fisher c Everett b Hendry ............... | 0 – b Everett ..................... | 1 |
| A. Ambler c Hendry b Mailey ................. | 8 – lbw b Everett ................. | 4 |
| Extras .......................... | 19     Extras ................ | 16 |
| | **383** | **197** |

## New South Wales

| | | | |
|---|---|---|---|
| H. L. Collins c Ambler b Whitty ......... | 19 | A. Gray b Townsend ................. | 8 |
| W. Bardsley c Ambler b Williams ........ | 144 | W. A. Oldfield b Whitty .............. | 36 |
| T. J. E. Andrews b A. J. Richardson ...... | 47 | A A. Mailey st Ambler b Williams ....... | 0 |
| J. M. Taylor st Ambler b Williams ........ | 29 | S. Everett not out ................... | 2 |
| A. F. Kippax c Whitty b Williams ........ | 248 | Extras .................. | 20 |
| A. Punch b A. J. Richardson ............ | 84 | | |
| H. L. Hendry c Bowley b Whitty ........ | 47 | | **684** |

## New South Wales Bowling

| | Overs | Mdns | Runs | Wkts | Overs | Mdns | Runs | Wkts |
|---|---|---|---|---|---|---|---|---|
| Everett ........... | 11 | — | 64 | — | 14 | — | 54 | 6 |
| Gray ............. | 7 | — | 45 | — | 1 | — | 3 | — |
| Hendry .......... | 22 | 2 | 68 | 2 | 12 | 1 | 35 | 1 |
| Mailey .......... | 28.4 | 1 | 133 | 7 | 15 | — | 60 | 1 |
| Punch .......... | 7 | — | 42 | 1 | 7 | — | 29 | 2 |
| Kippax .......... | 2 | — | 12 | — | | | | |

## South Australia Bowling

| | Overs | Mdns | Runs | Wkts |
|---|---|---|---|---|
| Whitty .......... | 37 | 2 | 153 | 3 |
| Williams .......... | 24.4 | — | 196 | 4 |
| Townsend ....... | 25 | 2 | 97 | 1 |
| Fisher ........... | 15 | 1 | 113 | — |
| A. J. Richardson ... | 20 | — | 105 | 2 |

# NEW SOUTH WALES v VICTORIA

Played at Sydney, January 25, 26, 28, 29, 30, 1924

As there had been a good deal of rain Victoria, on winning the toss, put New South Wales in. Their policy could scarcely have answered better. They had the advantage of playing their first innings on a firm pitch and in the end they won by eight wickets. Scoring 110 and 110 not out, Ponsford enjoyed the culminating success of his wonderful season. In his first innings he made his runs out of 186 in two hours and three-quarters, and in his second out of 195 in just over three hours. Batting of a very different kind was shown by Mayne, whose innings of 154 not out began towards the end of the first day, and lasted into the third. In all he was at the wickets just seven hours. Andrews played splendidly for New South Wales in the first innings when the wicket was far from easy. New South Wales had a piece of very bad luck, Scott, their fast bowler, falling lame after he had sent down four overs. However, balancing this to some extent, Victoria were without Ryder and Ellis in the New South Wales second innings. Ryder had hurt his back and Ellis was ill in bed.

## New South Wales

| | | | |
|---|---|---|---|
| H. L. Collins c Ryder b Liddicut ................ | 16 | – c Woodfull b Liddicut ........... | 81 |
| W. Bardsley c Ellis b Wallace .................. | 4 | – b Wallace ..................... | 0 |
| C. G. Macartney b Wallace ................... | 30 | – c Love b Wallace ............. | 35 |
| T. J. E. Andrews c Woodfull b Hartkopf .......... | 96 | – c Wallace b Hartkopf ........... | 44 |
| A. F. Kippax c Ellis b Wallace ................. | 1 | – c Ponsford b Wallace ........... | 65 |
| A. Punch c Ellis b Liddicut ................... | 10 | – b Hartkopf .................... | 6 |
| H. L. Hendry b Carlton ..................... | 6 | – b Hartkopf .................... | 73 |
| W. A. Oldfield c and b Hartkopf ............... | 4 | – c Love b Wallace ............. | 0 |
| J. D. Scott c sub. b Hartkopf .................. | 6 | – not out ...................... | 2 |
| A. A. Mailey not out ..................... | 22 | – b Wallace ..................... | 0 |
| L. Wall c Ransford b Hartkopf ............... | 9 | – b Hartkopf .................... | 9 |
| Extras ......................... | 13 | Extras ................ | 6 |
| | **217** | | **321** |

## Victoria

| | | | |
|---|---:|---|---:|
| E. R. Mayne not out | 154 | – c Mailey b Hendry | 10 |
| W. M. Woodfull c Mailey b Hendry | 0 | – c Hendry b Wall | 30 |
| H. S. Love lbw b Mailey | 31 | – not out | 43 |
| W. H. Ponsford b Macartney | 110 | – not out | 110 |
| J. S. Ryder b Hendry | 3 | | |
| A. E. V. Hartkopf c Kippax b Macartney | 2 | | |
| V. S. Ransford b Hendry | 10 | | |
| A. E. Liddicut c Mailey b Wall | 14 | | |
| T. Carlton st Oldfield b Mailey | 1 | | |
| J. L. Ellis b Punch | 2 | | |
| P. L. Wallace b Macartney | 4 | | |
| Extras | 14 | Extras | 2 |
| | **345** | | **195** |

### New South Wales Bowling

| | Overs | Mdns | Runs | Wkts | Overs | Mdns | Runs | Wkts |
|---|---|---|---|---|---|---|---|---|
| Wallace | 16 | 3 | 47 | 3 | 27 | 4 | 99 | 5 |
| Carlton | 16 | 2 | 37 | 1 | 12 | 2 | 37 | — |
| Liddicut | 17 | 1 | 49 | 2 | 20 | 5 | 50 | 1 |
| Ryder | 6 | — | 22 | — | | | | |
| Hartkopf | 14.1 | — | 49 | 4 | 28.4 | — | 129 | 4 |

### Victoria Bowling

| | Overs | Mdns | Runs | Wkts | Overs | Mdns | Runs | Wkts |
|---|---|---|---|---|---|---|---|---|
| Scott | 4 | — | 11 | — | | | | |
| Hendry | 35 | 4 | 81 | 3 | — | — | 35 | 1 |
| Wall | 14 | — | 35 | 1 | 17.3 | 1 | 55 | 1 |
| Mailey | 37 | 6 | 125 | 2 | 10 | — | 47 | — |
| Punch | 7 | 1 | 26 | 1 | 7 | — | 21 | — |
| Andrews | 3 | — | 17 | — | | | | |
| Macartney | 29.7 | 12 | 36 | 3 | 12 | 3 | 35 | — |

## VICTORIA v NEW SOUTH WALES

Played at Melbourne, December 26, 28, 29, 30, 1924

Although starting with a total of 413 Victoria lost by an innings and 162 runs. Love, coming in for Ellis – injured – made his runs in good style and kept wicket excellently, giving away only nine byes while New South Wales ran up the huge score of 705. A ninth wicket stand of 226 between Kelleway and Oldfield, who each got a hundred, was the feature of this great batting display. Victoria when they went in 292 behind, collapsed badly against a well-varied attack. Half the side were out for 71, no recovery being made from this early breakdown.

### Victoria

| | | | |
|---|---:|---|---:|
| E. R. Mayne c Gregory b Kelleway | 25 | – b Gregory | 7 |
| W. M. Woodfull c Gregory b Macartney | 53 | – lbw b Macartney | 13 |
| J. S. Ryder b Macartney | 5 | – c and b Mailey | 18 |
| H. L. Hendry b Macartney | 5 | – b Kelleway | 5 |
| W. H. Ponsford c and b Macartney | 68 | – not out | 25 |
| F. A. Tarrant b Macartney | 9 | – b Macartney | 2 |
| H. S. Love lbw b Macartney | 115 | – lbw b Mailey | 11 |
| F. Baring lbw b Macartney | 57 | – b Gregory | 30 |
| Dr A. E. V. Hartkopf not out | 54 | – c Oldfield b Kelleway | 1 |
| A. E. Liddicut b Gregory | 18 | – lbw b Mailey | 4 |
| D. D. J. Blackie b Gregory | 0 | – b Kelleway | 3 |
| Extras | 4 | Extras | 11 |
| | **413** | | **130** |

## New South Wales

| | | |
|---|---|---|
| H. L. Collins run out | 45 | |
| W. Bardsley b Hartkopf | 45 | |
| T. J. E. Andrews b Blackie | 61 | |
| J. M. Taylor c Tarrant b Hendry | 66 | |
| C. G. Macartney lbw b Hartkopf | 59 | |
| A. F. Kippax c Love b Ryder | 29 | |
| H. O. Rock lbw b Blackie | 81 | |
| C. E. Kelleway lbw b Ryder | 145 | |
| J. M. Gregory c Love b Blackie | 32 | |
| W. A. Oldfield c sub. b Blackie | 129 | |
| A. A. Mailey not out | 1 | |
| Extras | 12 | |
| | **705** | |

## New South Wales Bowling

| | Overs | Mdns | Runs | Wkts | Overs | Mdns | Runs | Wkts |
|---|---|---|---|---|---|---|---|---|
| Gregory | 31.5 | 3 | 102 | 2 | 11 | 1 | 57 | 2 |
| Kelleway | 27 | 4 | 74 | 1 | 6 | — | 12 | 3 |
| Mailey | 33 | — | 148 | — | 8 | 1 | 34 | 3 |
| Macartney | 37 | 6 | 85 | 7 | 8 | 3 | 16 | 2 |

## Victoria Bowling

| | Overs | Mdns | Runs | Wkts |
|---|---|---|---|---|
| Hendry | 39 | 4 | 159 | 1 |
| Blackie | 38.6 | — | 153 | 4 |
| Tarrant | 27 | 6 | 76 | — |
| Ryder | 35 | 5 | 121 | 2 |
| Hartkopf | 22 | 2 | 122 | 2 |
| Liddicut | 16 | 2 | 62 | — |

## NEW SOUTH WALES v SOUTH AUSTRALIA

Played at Sydney, January 8, 9, 11, 12, 13, 14, 15, 16, 1925

Extending over eight days and characterised by abnormal scoring which produced an aggregate of 1,929 runs – a record in first-class cricket – this match ended in a hollow victory for New South Wales by 541 runs. After their arduous experience in the match at Melbourne and the long railway journey, the South Australians, on losing the toss, went into the field very tired. Collins and Bardsley gave New South Wales a great start by making 203 together for the opening partnership and Andrews and Kelleway put on 196 for the sixth wicket. South Australia after fielding out for nearly ten hours made a good reply, and thanks to the two Richardsons, were only 167 behind when each side had completed an innings. Arthur Richardson was troubled by a bandaged foot but both he and Victor dominated the proceedings while the visitors were batting. At their second attempt New South Wales again scored heavily, Macartney batting finely and five others making over 70 each. South Australia had to get 761 to win, but Rundell and Rymill alone batted with confidence. The side were handicapped owing to the sudden illness of Alexander.

## New South Wales

| | | |
|---|---|---|
| H. L. Collins st Parry b Grimmett | 108 | – b Grimmett | 84 |
| W. Bardsley b A. J. Richardson | 159 | – c V. Y. Richardson b Whitty | 13 |
| C. G. Macartney c Whitty b Scott | 20 | – c Parry b Grimmett | 113 |
| A. F. Kippax c Scott b A. J. Richardson | 21 | – b Whitty | 71 |
| C. E. Kelleway b Grimmett | 111 | – c Scott b Grimmett | 75 |
| J. M. Taylor c V. Y. Richardson b Scott | 5 | – c and b A. J. Richardson | 82 |
| T. J. E. Andrews run out | 98 | – b A. J. Richardson | 72 |
| W. A. Oldfield b Grimmett | 17 | – b Grimmett | 19 |
| A. Punch not out | 47 | – c A. J. Richardson b Grimmett | 26 |
| A. A. Mailey st Parry b Grimmett | 6 | – not out | 15 |
| S. C. Everett b Scott | 19 | – b Grimmett | 11 |
| Extras | 31 | Extras | 12 |
| | **642** | | **593** |

## South Australia

| | | |
|---|---|---|
| C. E. Parry c Oldfield b Everett | 13 | – b Everett | 1 |
| P. D. Rundell c Everett b Kelleway | 25 | – b Mailey | 52 |
| J. W. Rymill c Collins b Everett | 23 | – not out | 52 |
| V. Y. Richardson b Kelleway | 107 | – c Everett b Kelleway | 27 |
| D. E. Pritchard c Punch b Macartney | 10 | – c Macartney b Mailey | 27 |
| A. J. Richardson c Punch b Macartney | 153 | – b Macartney | 7 |
| W. C. Alexander c Kelleway b Kippax | 59 | – absent ill | 0 |
| J. T. Murray st Oldfield b Andrews | 29 | – c Oldfield b Everett | 31 |
| C. V. Grimmett c Kelleway b Andrews | 32 | – c Collins b Mailey | 0 |
| J. D. Scott c Bardsley b Andrews | 1 | – c Macartney b Mailey | 1 |
| W. J. Whitty not out | 12 | – run out | 11 |
| Extras | 11 | Extras | 10 |
| | **475** | | **219** |

## South Australia Bowling

| | Overs | Mdns | Runs | Wkts | Overs | Mdns | Runs | Wkts |
|---|---|---|---|---|---|---|---|---|
| Scott | 34.1 | 2 | 190 | 3 | 30 | 3 | 155 | — |
| Whitty | 26 | 6 | 88 | — | 20 | 1 | 99 | 2 |
| A. J. Richardson | 34 | 2 | 113 | 2 | 29 | 11 | 35 | 2 |
| Grimmett | 51 | 7 | 192 | 4 | 55 | 7 | 202 | 6 |
| Murray | 8 | — | 24 | — | 12 | — | 80 | — |
| Rundell | 1 | — | 4 | — | 1 | — | 10 | — |

## New South Wales Bowling

| | Overs | Mdns | Runs | Wkts | Overs | Mdns | Runs | Wkts |
|---|---|---|---|---|---|---|---|---|
| Everett | 19 | 1 | 101 | 2 | 10 | 3 | 32 | 2 |
| Kelleway | 20 | 1 | 83 | 2 | 10 | 1 | 41 | 1 |
| Macartney | 24 | 4 | 83 | 2 | 7.1 | 1 | 40 | 1 |
| Mailey | 23 | 1 | 103 | — | 22 | 4 | 96 | 4 |
| Punch | 2 | — | 16 | — | | | | |
| Kippax | 7 | — | 44 | 1 | | | | |
| Andrews | 4.1 | — | 34 | 3 | | | | |

# NEW SOUTH WALES v VICTORIA

Played at Sydney, January 24, 26, 27, 28, 1925

In an extraordinary match New South Wales, with only a moderate side, lost by seven wickets after putting together the huge total of 614 in the first innings. Both Rock, who shared with Morgan in an opening partnership of 202, and Kippax gave brilliant displays of batting. Victoria made a capital response to the great total, and then skilful bowling by Hartkopf and Hendry brought about such a collapse of the New South Wales batsmen that the visitors had a fairly light task in the last innings.

## New South Wales

| | | | |
|---|---|---|---|
| H. O. Rock c Tarrant b Hartkopf | 235 | – c Hartkopf b Blackie | 51 |
| G. Morgan b Hendry | 87 | – c Hartkopf b Wallace | 3 |
| A. Ratcliffe lbw b Blackie | 1 | – c Hartkopf b Hendry | 8 |
| B. M. Salmon run out | 31 | – c Liddicut b Blackie | 9 |
| A. P. Wells st Ellis b Hartkopf | 9 | – run out | 14 |
| A. Kippax not out | 212 | – st Ellis b Hartkopf | 40 |
| C. V. Morrissey c Ellis b Hartkopf | 4 | – b Hendry | 0 |
| C. Lawes b Hartkopf | 0 | – st Ellis b Hartkopf | 1 |
| A. D. Mayes run out | 6 | – not out | 5 |
| J. D. Scott b Wallace | 1 | – c Schneider b Hartkopf | 4 |
| N. Bosley st Ellis b Hartkopf | 1 | – c Mayne b Hendry | 9 |
| Extras | 27 | Extras | 8 |
| | **614** | | **152** |

## Victoria

| | | | |
|---|---|---|---|
| E. R. Mayne b Scott | 12 | – lbw b Scott | 1 |
| W. M. Woodfull run out | 81 | – not out | 120 |
| H. L. Hendry c Mayes b Lawes | 19 | – c Scott b Morrissey | 85 |
| F. A. Tarrant c Ratcliffe b Scott | 23 | – not out | 18 |
| A. E. Liddicut b Scott | 132 | – c Ratcliffe b Morgan | 28 |
| A. E. V. Hartkopf c Wells b Morrissey | 56 | | |
| K. J. Schneider b Scott | 1 | | |
| J. L. Ellis run out | 20 | | |
| C. B. Willis c Rock b Scott | 100 | | |
| D. Blackie c Kippax b Lawes | 23 | | |
| P. H. Wallace not out | 0 | | |
| Extras | 35 | Extras | 13 |
| | **502** | | **265** |

## Victoria Bowling

| | Overs | Mdns | Runs | Wkts | Overs | Mdns | Runs | Wkts |
|---|---|---|---|---|---|---|---|---|
| Wallace | 24 | — | 103 | 1 | 5 | — | 16 | 1 |
| Blackie | 31 | 1 | 108 | 1 | 12 | 2 | 29 | 2 |
| Hendry | 33 | 2 | 129 | 1 | 9 | — | 23 | 3 |
| Hartkopf | 23.1 | — | 121 | 5 | 8 | — | 45 | 3 |
| Tarrant | 20 | 1 | 69 | — | 6 | 1 | 13 | — |
| Liddicut | 14 | 1 | 42 | — | 2 | — | 9 | — |
| Schneider | 3 | — | 15 | — | 2 | — | 9 | — |

## New South Wales Bowling

| | Overs | Mdns | Runs | Wkts | Overs | Mdns | Runs | Wkts |
|---|---|---|---|---|---|---|---|---|
| Scott | 33.1 | 3 | 149 | 5 | 11 | — | 44 | 1 |
| Lawes | 33 | 9 | 82 | 2 | 16 | 1 | 47 | — |
| Morrissey | 26 | 4 | 91 | 1 | 11 | — | 36 | 1 |
| Kippax | 14 | 3 | 58 | — | 9 | — | 47 | — |
| Bosley | 12 | 2 | 36 | — | 15.4 | 1 | 46 | — |
| Mayes | 16 | 3 | 51 | — | 10 | 3 | 15 | — |
| Morgan | | | | | 6 | — | 17 | 1 |

## NEW SOUTH WALES v VICTORIA

Played at Sydney, January 23, 25, 26, 27, 1926

New South Wales concluded a highly successful season with a victory by an innings and 96 runs. Dismissing Victoria for 290, they proved their collective batting strength by putting together 708, the chief honours resting with Kippax. Scoring 271 not out, out of 548, Kippax played faultlessly for over seven hours, and mainly by powerful driving hit thirty 4s. Collins also reached three figures, while Ponsford and Woodfull, when Victoria batted again, added 178 for the fourth wicket and, between them, obtained 264 of the 322 runs scored by the whole side. Everett's bowling, in fierce sunshine, was distinctly creditable.

### Victoria

| | | | | |
|---|---|---|---|---|
| W. M. Woodfull b Everett | 15 | – b Everett | 126 |
| W. H. Ponsford b Kelleway | 79 | – b Everett | 138 |
| H. L. Hendry c Oldfield b Everett | 9 | – st Oldfield b Mailey | 1 |
| J. S. Ryder run out | 49 | – b Kelleway | 5 |
| H. S. Love b Everett | 16 | – lbw b Everett | 22 |
| F. Baring b Mailey | 70 | – c Oldfield b Everett | 0 |
| V. S. Ransford b Everett | 3 | – run out | 0 |
| A. E. Liddicut lbw b Macartney | 28 | – st Oldfield b Mailey | 6 |
| J. L. Ellis b Mailey | 9 | – b Gregory | 7 |
| W. H. Rayson b Macartney | 7 | – not out | 3 |
| D. J. J. Blackie not out | 0 | – b Everett | 8 |
| Extras | 5 | Extras | 6 |
| | **290** | | **322** |

### New South Wales

| | |
|---|---|
| W. Bardsley c Blackie b Rayson | 28 |
| H. L. Collins c Love b Baring | 143 |
| C. G. Macartney c Ransford b Rayson | 36 |
| A. F. Kippax not out | 271 |
| C. E. Kelleway c Ellis b Blackie | 68 |
| T. J. E. Andrews b Rayson | 22 |
| H. O. Rock c Hendry b Rayson | 39 |
| J. M. Gregory c Woodfull b Hendry | 21 |
| W. A. Oldfield run out | 49 |
| A. A. Mailey b Hendry | 0 |
| S. C. Everett st Ellis b Hendry | 0 |
| Extras | 31 |
| | **708** |

### New South Wales Bowling

| | Overs | Mdns | Runs | Wkts | Overs | Mdns | Runs | Wkts |
|---|---|---|---|---|---|---|---|---|
| Gregory | 13 | — | 50 | — | 12 | — | 67 | 1 |
| Kelleway | 19 | 5 | 40 | 1 | 13 | 1 | 42 | 1 |
| Mailey | 21 | 1 | 95 | 2 | 17 | 1 | 94 | 2 |
| Everett | 15 | 3 | 57 | 4 | 16.6 | 1 | 91 | 5 |
| Macartney | 14.3 | — | 43 | 2 | 8 | — | 22 | — |

### Victoria Bowling

| | Overs | Mdns | Runs | Wkts |
|---|---|---|---|---|
| Ryder | 25 | 1 | 117 | 1 |
| Blackie | 34 | 4 | 144 | — |
| Hendry | 30.5 | 1 | 122 | 3 |
| Rayson | 30 | — | 148 | 4 |
| Baring | 9 | — | 41 | 1 |
| Ransford | 6 | — | 28 | — |
| Liddicut | 22 | 3 | 77 | — |

# VICTORIA v NEW SOUTH WALES

Played at Melbourne, December 24, 27, 28, 29, 1926

In this match Victoria set up a new record in first-class cricket, their total of 1,107 beating that of 1,059 obtained by the same State against Tasmania in the 1922-23 season. Throughout the innings which lasted ten hours and a half, runs came at a great pace. A brilliant opening partnership between Ponsford and Woodfull produced 375 runs in three hours and three-quarters and the former player and Hendry added a further 219 for the second wicket in just under two hours. Ponsford hit thirty-six 4s in a memorable display. The brightest of some wonderful batting was that of Ryder, who, by powerful driving, obtained six 6s and thirty-three 4s and scored 295 out of 449 in rather more than four hours. New South Wales, with a weak team, were outplayed from the start and suffered defeat by an innings and 656 runs.

## New South Wales

| | | |
|---|---|---|
| N. E. Phillips c Blackie b Liddicut | 52 | – lbw b Hartkopf ............... 36 |
| G. Morgan c Love b Liddicut | 13 | – c King b Liddicut .............. 26 |
| T. J. E. Andrews st Ellis b Hartkopf | 42 | – b Liddicut .................... 0 |
| A. F. Kippax b Liddicut | 36 | – b Hartkopf ................... 26 |
| A. D. Ratcliffe c Ryder b Liddicut | 2 | – c Morton b Hartkopf .......... 44 |
| A. Jackson c Ellis b Blackie | 4 | – not out ...................... 59 |
| J. R. Hogg not out | 40 | – c Hendry b Liddicut .......... 13 |
| A. A. Mailey b Ryder | 20 | – c Morton b Hartkopf .......... 3 |
| N. Campbell lbw b Blackie | 0 | – c Ryder b Hartkopf ........... 8 |
| R. McNamee b Ryder | 8 | – b Liddicut ................... 7 |
| H. McGuirk b Ryder | 0 | – b Hartkopf ................... 0 |
| Extras | 4 | Extras ................. 8 |
| | **221** | **230** |

## Victoria

| | |
|---|---|
| W. M. Woodfull c Ratcliffe b Andrews ....133 | A. E. V. Hartkopf c McGuirk b Mailey .... 61 |
| W. H. Ponsford b Morgan ..............352 | A. E. Liddicut b McGuirk .............. 36 |
| H. L. Hendry c Morgan b Mailey ........100 | J. L. Ellis run out ..................... 63 |
| J. Ryder c Kippax b Andrews ...........295 | D. D. J. Blackie not out ............... 27 |
| F. L. Morton run out .............. 0 | Extras...................... 27 |
| H. S. B. Love st Ratcliffe b Mailey ........ 6 | |
| S. King st Ratcliffe b Mailey ............ 7 | **1107** |

## Victoria Bowling

| | Overs | Mdns | Runs | Wkts | Overs | Mdns | Runs | Wkts |
|---|---|---|---|---|---|---|---|---|
| Morton .......... | 15 | 4 | 45 | — | 11 | — | 42 | — |
| Liddicut .......... | 21 | 7 | 50 | 4 | 19 | 2 | 66 | 4 |
| Ryder ............ | 9 | 1 | 32 | 3 | | | | |
| Blackie ........... | 16 | 3 | 34 | 2 | 5 | 1 | 16 | — |
| Hendry .......... | 3 | 2 | 1 | — | | | | |
| Hartkopf ......... | 17 | 1 | 57 | 1 | 16.3 | — | 98 | 6 |

## New South Wales Bowling

| | Overs | Mdns | Runs | Wkts |
|---|---|---|---|---|
| McNamee ........ | 24 | 2 | 124 | — |
| McGuirk ......... | 26 | 1 | 130 | 1 |
| Mailey .......... | 64 | — | 362 | 4 |
| Campbell ......... | 11 | — | 89 | — |
| Phillips ........... | 11.7 | — | 64 | — |
| Morgan .......... | 26 | — | 137 | 1 |
| Andrews ......... | 21 | 2 | 148 | 2 |
| Kippax .......... | 7 | — | 26 | — |

## SOUTH AUSTRALIA v VICTORIA

Played at Adelaide, December 2, 3, 5, 6, 1927

Overwhelmingly superior, Victoria won in an innings with 310 runs to spare. They were fortunate in having perfect conditions under which to bat, whereas South Australia had to struggle for runs on a damaged pitch. The visitors had 361 on the board when their second wicket fell, and maintained such a mastery over the bowling that Woodfull closed the innings with eight wickets down. Ponsford, Hendry and Hartkopf each made a three-figure score and, while Hendry enjoyed some luck, the play of the other two batsmen was faultless. Rain affecting the wicket, the South Australian batsmen were quickly in trouble with the bowling of Morton and Ironmonger. Whitfield in his first Shield game, showed watchful defence, but the side were 469 in arrear, and did even worse in the follow-on. Harris and Schneider scored 68 for the opening partnership, but the remaining wickets went down for 91, Blackie in this innings varying his bowling with remarkable skill.

### Victoria

| | |
|---|---|
| W. M. Woodfull c Williams b Grimmett ... 43 | D. D. J. Blackie c Richardson b Schneider . 55 |
| W. H. Ponsford c Whitfield b Halcombe ...133 | J. L. Ellis lbw b Williams ............... 3 |
| H. L. Hendry c Halcombe b Williams .....168 | F. L. Morton not out .................. 1 |
| J. Ryder lbw b Grimmett .............. 70 | |
| B. A. Onyons b Grimmett ............. 2 | B 15, l-b 10, n-b 7............. 32 |
| J. Scaife st Inkster b Whitfield .......... 28 | |
| A. E. V. Hartkopf not out .............111 | (8 wkts dec.) 646 |

H. Ironmonger did not bat.

### South Australia

| | | | |
|---|---|---|---|
| G. W. Harris c Ryder b Morton ................. | 1 | – c Ellis b Ironmonger ........... | 61 |
| K. J. Schneider lbw b Ironmonger ............... | 21 | – run out ...................... | 6 |
| V. Y. Richardson c Hendry b Ironmonger ......... | 21 | – st Ellis b Ironmonger ........... | 25 |
| W. C. Alexander c Blackie b Ironmonger ......... | 5 | – c Ponsford b Blackie ........... | 4 |
| H. E. P. Whitfield c Ellis b Morton ............... | 48 | – c Hartkopf b Blackie .......... | 4 |
| E. A. Johnson run out ...................... | 16 | – b Morton .................... | 27 |
| P. K. Lee c Morton b Ironmonger ............... | 12 | – b Morton .................... | 11 |
| C. V. Grimmett st Ellis b Ironmonger ............ | 13 | – not out ..................... | 10 |
| N. L. Williams c Blackie b Morton ............. | 0 | – c Scaife b Morton ............ | 2 |
| G. B. Inkster b Morton ....................... | 10 | – b Blackie ................... | 1 |
| R. A. Halcombe not out ...................... | 3 | – b Blackie ................... | 0 |
| B 22, l-b 3, n-b 2 .................... | 27 | B 5, n-b 3 .............. | 8 |
| | 177 | | 159 |

### South Australia Bowling

| | Overs | Mdns | Runs | Wkts |
|---|---|---|---|---|
| Halcombe ........ | 26 | 1 | 119 | 1 |
| Whitfield ........ | 26 | 2 | 100 | 1 |
| Grimmett ........ | 56 | 7 | 175 | 3 |
| Lee ............. | 18 | 3 | 62 | — |
| Williams ......... | 27 | 1 | 119 | 2 |
| Alexander ........ | 4 | — | 16 | — |
| Schneider ........ | 7 | — | 23 | 1 |

**Victoria Bowling**

| | Overs | Mdns | Runs | Wkts | Overs | Mdns | Runs | Wkts |
|---|---|---|---|---|---|---|---|---|
| Morton .......... | 11.5 | — | 35 | 4 | 14 | 3 | 47 | 3 |
| Ironmonger ....... | 32 | 11 | 50 | 5 | 23 | 6 | 52 | 2 |
| Hendry .......... | 3 | — | 11 | — | | | | |
| Blackie .......... | 20 | 7 | 54 | — | 20.5 | 4 | 45 | 4 |
| Ryder ........... | | | | | 3 | — | 7 | — |

Umpires: G. A. Hele and J. J. Quinn.

## VICTORIA v QUEENSLAND

### Played at Melbourne, December 16, 17, 19, 20, 1927

This match, which Victoria won by an innings and 197 runs, was the most noteworthy of the series. O'Connor, the Queensland captain, won the toss and sent Victoria in but at the end of the first day's play only two men were out with 400 runs on the board and ultimately Victoria completed their innings for the huge total of 793. Scoring 437, Ponsford established a new world's record, beating his 420 against Tasmania in 1922 – the previous record for an individual innings in first-class cricket. At the crease for ten hours and twenty-one minutes, Ponsford gave two chances – both difficult ones. He might have been caught off a return to Bensted when 162 and offered a chance of stumping with his score 239. Using a bat weighing 2lb 10oz, he placed his shots with rare judgment, and was practically always master of the situation throughout his long stay. Victoria forced their opponents to follow-on in a minority of 604. Oxenham, although making only 19, kept his end up for an hour and a half, but Nothling alone showed real ability to cope with the slow deliveries of Blackie, who took six wickets for less than 8 runs each. In the Queensland second innings, Blackie and Ryder, owing to injury, could not bowl, and Thompson took advantage of the weakened attack to score a faultless hundred but occupied more than four hours in so doing.

### Victoria

| | | | |
|---|---|---|---|
| W. M. Woodfull run out ................. | 31 | J. L. Ellis c Nothling b Thompson ........ | 15 |
| W. H. Ponsford c and b Amos .......... | .437 | D. D. J. Blackie b Amos .............. | 35 |
| H. L. Hendry b Gough ................ | .129 | F. L. Morton c O'Connor b Amos ........ | 0 |
| J. Ryder c Rowe b Nothling ............ | 70 | H. Ironmonger not out ................ | 1 |
| J. Scaife b Amos ..................... | 18 | B 6, l-b 3, w 6 ................ | 15 |
| A. E. V. Hartkopf b Amos .............. | 15 | | |
| C. Sindrey c Bensted b Rowe ........... | 27 | | 793 |

### Queensland

| | | | |
|---|---|---|---|
| L. P. D. O'Connor c Ellis b Blackie ............. | 11 | – c sub. b Ironmonger ............ | 66 |
| L. E. Oxenham lbw b Ryder .................... | 19 | – lbw b Morton ................. | 3 |
| F. Gough b Blackie ......................... | 0 | – b Ironmonger ................. | 54 |
| F. C. Thompson lbw b Blackie ................ | 8 | – c Ellis b Ironmonger ............ | 118 |
| W. Rowe b Morton ........................ | 34 | – b Ryder ................... | 9 |
| O. E. Nothling lbw b Ironmonger ................ | 66 | – b Morton ................... | 18 |
| L. Litster c Hendry b Ironmonger ............. | 10 | – b Ironmonger ................. | 43 |
| E. Bensted not out ........................ | 11 | – run out ................... | 14 |
| L. L. Gill b Blackie ........................ | 0 | – c Ellis b Ironmonger ............ | 27 |
| A. C. Hurwood lbw b Blackie ................. | 1 | – b Morton ................... | 1 |
| G. S. Amos st Ellis b Blackie ................. | 0 | – not out .................... | 27 |
| B 15, l-b 9, w 2, n-b 3 ................ | 29 | B 16, l-b 8, n-b 3 ......... | 27 |
| | 189 | | 407 |

## Queensland Bowling

|  | Overs | Mdns | Runs | Wkts |
|---|---|---|---|---|
| Amos . . . . . . . . . . . . | 29 | — | 148 | 5 |
| Hurwood . . . . . . . . . | 28 | 3 | 133 | — |
| Gill . . . . . . . . . . . . . . | 19 | — | 91 | — |
| Nothling . . . . . . . . . . | 26 | 6 | 101 | 1 |
| Bensted . . . . . . . . . . | 20 | — | 95 | — |
| Rowe . . . . . . . . . . . | 13 | 1 | 65 | 1 |
| Thompson . . . . . . . . | 22 | 2 | 74 | 1 |
| Gough . . . . . . . . . . | 10 | 1 | 56 | 1 |
| Litster . . . . . . . . . . | 2 | — | 15 | — |

## Victoria Bowling

|  | Overs | Mdns | Runs | Wkts | Overs | Mdns | Runs | Wkts |
|---|---|---|---|---|---|---|---|---|
| Morton . . . . . . . . . . | 13 | 3 | 34 | 1 | 32 | 6 | 103 | 3 |
| Ironmonger . . . . . . . | 17 | 5 | 26 | 2 | 40.6 | 12 | 88 | 5 |
| Blackie . . . . . . . . . . | 23.5 | 5 | 46 | 6 | 3 | 2 | 2 | — |
| Ryder . . . . . . . . . . . | 5 | 1 | 17 | 1 | 5.6 | — | 12 | 1 |
| Hartkopf . . . . . . . . . | 7 | — | 37 | — | 22 | 1 | 128 | — |
| Hendry . . . . . . . . . |  |  |  |  | 16 | 4 | 47 | — |

Umpires: J. Richards and P. E. Smith.

# VICTORIA v SOUTH AUSTRALIA

Played at Melbourne, December 30, 31, 1927, January 2, 3, 1928

The outstanding feature of this match – won by Victoria by an innings and 35 runs – was the batting of Ponsford, who scored 336 out of 582 in just over six hours. Ponsford gave a chance when 90 but otherwise played without mistake and hit thirty-three 4s. He and Woodfull, who got the ball to the boundary only twice, put on 236 for Victoria's first wicket and subsequently Ryder helped to add 140 for the third and Scaife 104 for the sixth partnership. Well though Harris, Grimmett and Lee batted, South Australia never looked like escaping a follow-on and, in the second innings, only Schneider and Harris saved them from complete failure. These two put on 138 for the opening partnership and Schneider – one of the best left-handers in Australia – stayed to score 143 in five hours and a quarter. After Schneider and Harris had been parted, South Australia collapsed in dismal fashion before the bowling of Morton and Ironmonger, the innings closing for a total of 283, of which the opening pair between them made no fewer than 217.

## Victoria

| | |
|---|---|
| W. M. Woodfull c Richardson b Wall . . . . .106 | J. L. Ellis c Lee b Grimmett . . . . . . . . . . . . . 0 |
| W. H. Ponsford st Hack b Grimmett . . . . . .336 | F. L. Morton st Hack b Grimmett . . . . . . . . 13 |
| H. L. Hendry lbw b Grimmett . . . . . . . . . . 35 | D. D. J. Blackie not out . . . . . . . . . . . . . . . 28 |
| J. Ryder c Wall b Ryan . . . . . . . . . . . . . . . 52 | H. Ironmonger c Hack b Wall . . . . . . . . . . 8 |
| C. Sindrey b Grimmett . . . . . . . . . . . . . . . . 5 | B 10, l-b 6, n-b 1 . . . . . . . . . . . . . 17 |
| A. E. V. Hartkopf c Scott b Wall . . . . . . . . . 4 |  |
| J. Scaife c Richardson b Scott . . . . . . . . . . 33 | 637 |

## South Australia

| | | | |
|---|---|---|---|
| K. J. Schneider b Blackie | 38 | – st Ellis b Hendry | 143 |
| G. W. Harris b Morton | 69 | – b Blackie | 74 |
| V. Y. Richardson c Woodfull b Blackie | 5 | – b Morton | 0 |
| W. C. Alexander c and b Ironmonger | 1 | – b Ironmonger | 8 |
| A. J. Ryan c Morton b Ironmonger | 34 | – c Ryder b Morton | 11 |
| A. Hack st Ellis b Blackie | 5 | – not out | 13 |
| C. V. Grimmett not out | 61 | – c Hendry b Ironmonger | 17 |
| P. K. Lee c Ryder b Morton | 66 | – b Hendry | 7 |
| J. D. Scott c Hendry b Morton | 0 | – b Ironmonger | 1 |
| N. L. Williams b Morton | 1 | – b Morton | 2 |
| T. Wall b Hartkopf | 18 | – run out | 2 |
| B 16, l-b 3, n-b 2 | 21 | L-b 3, n-b 2 | 5 |
| | **319** | | **283** |

## South Australia Bowling

| | Overs | Mdns | Runs | Wkts |
|---|---|---|---|---|
| Scott | 28 | 3 | 114 | 1 |
| Wall | 16.6 | — | 83 | 3 |
| Grimmett | 41 | 2 | 170 | 5 |
| Lee | 18 | — | 135 | — |
| Williams | 9 | — | 78 | — |
| Ryan | 8 | 1 | 28 | 1 |
| Schneider | 1 | — | 12 | — |

## Victoria Bowling

| | Overs | Mdns | Runs | Wkts | Overs | Mdns | Runs | Wkts |
|---|---|---|---|---|---|---|---|---|
| Morton | 24 | 2 | 111 | 4 | 18.2 | 2 | 57 | 3 |
| Ironmonger | 25 | 2 | 68 | 2 | 27 | 7 | 67 | 3 |
| Blackie | 33 | 9 | 68 | 3 | 26 | 6 | 59 | 1 |
| Hendry | 3 | — | 24 | — | 15 | 2 | 50 | 2 |
| Hartkopf | 7 | 1 | 27 | 1 | 7 | — | 45 | — |

Umpires: J. Richards and P. E. Smith.

# NEW SOUTH WALES v QUEENSLAND

Played at Sydney, December 31, 1927, January 2, 3, 4, 5, 1928

Recovering splendidly after following on 417 in arrear, Queensland went very near to victory, New South Wales, with eight second innings wickets down, being 127 behind at the finish. Kippax played his highest innings in first-class cricket and with Morgan put on 253 after New South Wales had lost five wickets for 214. Batting for six and a half hours without real fault, Kippax hit forty-one 4s. In pulling the match round, Queensland owed nearly everything to Rowe and Higgins. The last five wickets put on 255. When New South Wales had to bat again on a pitch damaged by rain Nothling made a great effort to force a win against time, and took five wickets for less than 8 runs each.

## New South Wales

| | | | |
|---|---|---|---|
| N. E. Phillips c Hurwood b Bensted | 17 | – lbw b Nothling | 29 |
| J. M Gregory c and b Nothling | 63 | – run out | 0 |
| T. J. E. Andrews b Hurwood | 41 | – b Nothling | 11 |
| A. F. Kippax not out | 315 | – c O'Connor b Nothling | 9 |
| A. Ratcliffe c O'Connor b Nothling | 25 | – b Nothling | 0 |
| A. Jackson c O'Connor b Bensted | 19 | – c O'Connor b Hurwood | 9 |
| G. Morgan c O'Connor b Bensted | 121 | – c Gough b Thompson | 12 |
| D. Bradman b Gough | 0 | – c O'Connor b Nothling | 13 |
| H. S. Love b Rowe | 26 | – not out | 13 |
| E. O'Brien b Gough | 6 | – not out | 0 |
| R. L. A. McNamee st O'Connor b Gough | 1 | | |
| B 2, w 1, n-b 2 | 5 | B 2, l-b 1, n-b 1 | 4 |
| | 639 | | 100 |

## Queensland

| | | | |
|---|---|---|---|
| L. L. Gill lbw b O'Brien | 29 | – b McNamee | 3 |
| L. E. Oxenham b Gregory | 1 | – st Love b Bradman | 50 |
| W. Rowe b Gregory | 0 | – c O'Brien b Bradman | 147 |
| F. C. Thompson lbw b Phillips | 18 | – c Kippax b Phillips | 68 |
| L. Litster st Love b McNamee | 82 | – b Gregory | 0 |
| O. E. Nothling b Phillips | 74 | – c Gregory b Morgan | 5 |
| L. P. D. O'Connor run out | 37 | – b Morgan | 32 |
| F. J. Gough c Love b Phillips | 17 | – b McNamee | 42 |
| R. L. Higgins c Gregory b Phillips | 0 | – run out | 179 |
| E. Bensted c Jackson b O'Brien | 6 | – run out | 38 |
| A. C. Hurwood not out | 1 | – not out | 5 |
| B 1, l-b 7, w 3 | 11 | B 7, l-b 13, w 1 | 21 |
| | 276 | | 590 |

## Queensland Bowling

| | Overs | Mdns | Runs | Wkts | Overs | Mdns | Runs | Wkts |
|---|---|---|---|---|---|---|---|---|
| Bensted | 27 | 1 | 126 | 3 | 2 | — | 4 | — |
| Hurwood | 27 | 4 | 118 | 1 | 18 | 4 | 40 | 1 |
| Nothling | 28 | 3 | 109 | 2 | 21 | 7 | 39 | 5 |
| Gill | 8 | — | 57 | — | 1 | — | 1 | — |
| Thompson | 17 | 1 | 68 | — | 4 | 1 | 5 | 1 |
| Gough | 16.5 | — | 100 | 3 | 2 | 1 | 3 | — |
| Rowe | 13 | 1 | 56 | 1 | 2 | — | 4 | — |

## New South Wales Bowling

| | Overs | Mdns | Runs | Wkts | Overs | Mdns | Runs | Wkts |
|---|---|---|---|---|---|---|---|---|
| Gregory | 17 | 1 | 63 | 2 | 16 | — | 99 | 1 |
| McNamee | 19 | 6 | 50 | 1 | 33.6 | 5 | 110 | 2 |
| Phillips | 11 | 3 | 26 | 4 | 22 | 2 | 85 | 1 |
| O'Brien | 16.3 | 1 | 73 | 2 | 15 | — | 88 | — |
| Andrews | 8 | — | 45 | — | 4 | — | 30 | — |
| Morgan | 4 | 2 | 8 | — | 22 | 1 | 95 | 2 |
| Kippax | | | | | 6 | — | 21 | — |
| Bradman | | | | | 10 | — | 41 | 2 |

Umpires: A. Williams and S. Parsons.

## VICTORIA v NEW SOUTH WALES

Played at Melbourne, December 22, 24, 25, 26, 27, 1928

Putting on 307 for the last wicket – a world's record – Kippax and Hooker resisted the Victoria attack for more than five hours and were clearly responsible for New South Wales gaining a first innings lead. Victoria had lost five wickets for 117 when Ryder and A'Beckett came together and retrieved the position admirably. Naturally the home state seemed sure of a formidable advantage when the ninth New South Wales wicket fell with the side 263 behind. Then, however, Hooker played fine, defensive cricket while Kippax – at the wickets from late Monday afternoon until after mid-day on Wednesday – batted with such delightful ease and effect that the whole aspect of the game was altered. A'Beckett, scoring 208 in his two innings, received prompt recognition in an invitation to play in the third Test match. Neither Woodfull nor Ponsford turned out for Victoria.

### Victoria

| | | | |
|---|---|---|---|
| H. L. Hendry c Kelleway b Nicholls | 8 | – not out | 69 |
| F. Baring c Love b Hooker | 12 | – lbw b Fairfax | 30 |
| J. Ryder c and b Andrews | 175 | | |
| K. Rigg c Hooker b Nicholls | 3 | – b Nicholls | 0 |
| R. Ellis c Love b Kelleway | 20 | – c Love b Fairfax | 4 |
| J. Scaife b Hooker | 0 | – b Fairfax | 6 |
| E. A'Beckett c Jackson b Andrews | 113 | – c Kippax b Hooker | 95 |
| J. L. Ellis not out | 19 | – c and b Andrews | 23 |
| H. I. Ebeling lbw b Fairfax | 1 | | |
| W. J. Rayson b Everett | 10 | – not out | 4 |
| H. Ironmonger c Jackson b Hooker | 3 | | |
| B 7, l-b 2, n-b 3 | 12 | B 1, l-b 7, w 1, n-b 11 | 20 |
| | **376** | **(6 wkts dec.)** | **251** |

### New South Wales

| | | | |
|---|---|---|---|
| A. Jackson c J. Ellis b Ironmonger | 19 | | |
| A. Fairfax c Ironmonger b A'Beckett | 2 | – b R. Ellis | 30 |
| T. J. E. Andrews b Hendry | 33 | | |
| A. F. Kippax not out | 260 | | |
| D. G. Bradman b Hendry | 1 | – not out | 71 |
| C. Kelleway b Hendry | 0 | – c A'Beckett b Ironmonger | 13 |
| D. Seddon lbw b Ironmonger | 0 | – not out | 38 |
| H. S. B. Love lbw b Ebeling | 0 | | |
| C. O. Nicholls b Ebeling | 10 | | |
| S. Everett lbw b Ironmonger | 20 | | |
| H. Hooker c Ryder b A'Beckett | 62 | | |
| B 5, l-b 6, n-b 2 | 13 | L-b 3, w 1 | 4 |
| | **420** | | **156** |

### New South Wales Bowling

| | Overs | Mdns | Runs | Wkts | Overs | Mdns | Runs | Wkts |
|---|---|---|---|---|---|---|---|---|
| Everett | 26 | 2 | 91 | 1 | 8 | — | 28 | — |
| Kelleway | 24 | 5 | 53 | 1 | 14 | 3 | 39 | — |
| Nicholls | 17 | 2 | 41 | 2 | 12 | 2 | 35 | 1 |
| Hooker | 23.7 | 5 | 100 | 3 | 8 | — | 38 | 1 |
| Andrews | 10 | 1 | 49 | 2 | 8 | — | 46 | 1 |
| Fairfax | 8 | — | 30 | 1 | 18 | 6 | 45 | 3 |

## Victoria Bowling

| | Overs | Mdns | Runs | Wkts | Overs | Mdns | Runs | Wkts |
|---|---|---|---|---|---|---|---|---|
| A'Beckett ......... | 29.1 | 2 | 92 | 2 | 10 | 3 | 19 | — |
| Ebeling .......... | 25 | 1 | 81 | 2 | 4 | 1 | 10 | — |
| Ironmonger ....... | 33 | 4 | 95 | 3 | 8 | 2 | 12 | 1 |
| Hendry .......... | 18 | 5 | 58 | 3 | | | | |
| Rayson ......... | 7 | — | 42 | — | 5 | — | 41 | — |
| R. Ellis ........... | 10 | 1 | 31 | — | 6 | 1 | 29 | 1 |
| Baring .......... | 5 | 1 | 8 | — | 5 | — | 22 | — |
| Rigg ............ | | | | | 2 | — | 19 | — |

Umpires: J. Richards and P. E. Smith.

# NEW SOUTH WALES v VICTORIA

## Played at Sydney, January 24, 25, 26, 28, 29, 1929

This proved to be the key match of the competition and New South Wales, taking first innings points, made sure of the Sheffield Shield. Of absorbing interest, the cricket was especially notable for the feat of Bradman who made 340 not out – the highest score by a New South Wales player in Sheffield Shield games and the highest in a first-class match on the Sydney ground. Bradman batted for roughly eight hours and did not give a chance. Fairfax also making a hundred, New South Wales, having established themselves in an impregnable position, were able to declare with six wickets down. Hooker and Bettington – the latter recently returned from England – bowled with such success that Victoria had to follow on 448 behind. Hooker actually took four wickets with four balls, his victims being Ebeling, Gamble and Ironmonger in one over, and Austen, with his next ball – his first in the second innings. Onyons in the follow-on batted with skill for four hours and a half. Scaife assisted him to add 187 and Darling, a left-hander, hit hard in a third wicket stand realising 143. Lansdown and Bird also showed confidence at the crisis of the game, and New South Wales had to be content with the honours of a drawn match.

## New South Wales

| | |
|---|---|
| A. Jackson b Ironmonger .............. 41 | R. H. Bettington c Austen b Darling ...... 40 |
| A. Fairfax b Gamble ....,.......... 104 | J. Fingleton not out ................... 25 |
| D. G. Bradman not out .............. 340 | |
| T. J. E. Andrews lbw b Ironmonger ....... 19 | B 11, l-b 15, n-b 2 ............. 28 |
| S. McCabe b Gamble .................. 60 | |
| A. Marks c Lansdown b Darling ......... 56 | (6 wkts dec.) 713 |

L. Davidson, C. O. Nicholls and H. Hooker did not bat.

## Victoria

| | |
|---|---|
| B. A. Onyons st Davidson b Bettington ........... 61 | – c Fingleton b Hooker ............ 131 |
| E. T. Austen b Hooker ........................ 19 | – b Hooker ..................... 5 |
| J. Scaife c Fingleton b Bettington ................ 42 | – run out ...................... 91 |
| L. Darling c Davidson b Hooker ................ 37 | – c McCabe b Fairfax ............ 96 |
| W. Reddrop b Hooker ........................ 33 | – b McCabe ................... 14 |
| H. C. Lansdown b Bettington ................. 4 | – not out ..................... 48 |
| T. Bird c and b Nicholls ...................... 22 | – c Fingleton b Marks ........... 63 |
| J. L. Ellis not out ........................... 19 | – not out ..................... 7 |
| H. I. Ebeling b Hooker ...................... 4 | – b Fairfax ................... 14 |
| H. S. Gamble b Hooker ...................... 0 | |
| H. Ironmonger c and b Hooker ................. 0 | |
| B 14, l-b 2, n-b 8 .................... 24 | B 27, l-b 7, w 1, n-b 6 ...... 41 |
| 265 | 510 |

**Victoria Bowling**

| | Overs | Mdns | Runs | Wkts |
|---|---|---|---|---|
| Gamble . . . . . . . . . | 29 | 1 | 193 | 2 |
| Ebeling . . . . . . . . . . | 39 | 3 | 142 | — |
| Ironmonger . . . . . . . | 56 | 7 | 220 | 2 |
| Darling . . . . . . . . . | 18 | 1 | 77 | 2 |
| Scaife . . . . . . . . . . . | 2 | — | 14 | — |
| Austen . . . . . . . . . . | 1 | — | 17 | — |
| Onyons . . . . . . . . . | 1 | — | 22 | — |

**New South Wales Bowling**

| | Overs | Mdns | Runs | Wkts | Overs | Mdns | Runs | Wkts |
|---|---|---|---|---|---|---|---|---|
| Nicholls . . . . . . . . . | 23 | 7 | 52 | 1 | 18 | 3 | 88 | — |
| Hooker . . . . . . . . . | 28 | 11 | 42 | 6 | 27 | 3 | 94 | 2 |
| Bettington . . . . . . . | 27 | 3 | 92 | 3 | 25 | 3 | 96 | — |
| Fairfax . . . . . . . . . . | 19 | 4 | 35 | — | 19 | 4 | 54 | 2 |
| McCabe . . . . . . . . . | 5 | 3 | 10 | — | 16 | 2 | 44 | 1 |
| Andrews . . . . . . . . | 1 | — | 10 | — | 6 | — | 33 | — |
| Fingleton . . . . . . . . | | | | | 2 | 1 | 1 | — |
| Marks . . . . . . . . . . | | | | | 15 | 4 | 59 | 1 |

Umpires: A. C. Jones and W. H. Bayfield.

## TEST TRIAL MATCH

### Played at Sydney, December 6, 7, 9, 10, 11, 1929

The performance of Bradman in scoring two centuries in a match – the second time he had achieved the distinction – constituted the chief feature of some remarkable cricket in the trial arranged by the Australian selectors with a view to choosing the team to tour England in 1930. Ryder's XI had so much the best of the game to begin with that the follow-on was enforced with Woodfull's side 354 in arrear. That policy, however, nearly brought about the defeat of Ryder's XI, who, left to get 188 to win, experienced such difficulty in playing Hornibrook and Blackie on a rain-damaged pitch that ultimately they only struggled home by one wicket. Jackson and Ponsford with a partnership of 278 laid the foundation of a huge score by Ryder's team. Jackson drove superbly through the covers and his partner played sound, skilful cricket. Bradman, however, overshadowed these successes by scoring 349 in his two innings. Rigg in the first innings and Kippax, who in the second made a splendid three-figure score, shared with Bradman in important stands and the three players between them were responsible for 592 of the 850 runs scored for Woodfull's XI. The cleverly-flighted good length deliveries of Oxenham, coupled with Grimmett's power of spin, led, despite the huge aggregate, to many batting failures. Eleven of the players taking part in the match afterwards made the trip to England.

### J. Ryder's XI

| | | | |
|---|---|---|---|
| A. Jackson c Kippax b Hornibrook . . . . . . . . . . . . . . .182 | – c Ellis b Hornibrook . . . . . . . . . . . . | 15 |
| W. H. Ponsford c Rigg b Blackie . . . . . . . . . . . . . . . .131 | – c Fairfax b Hornibrook . . . . . . . . . | 25 |
| A. Marks c Kippax b Blackie . . . . . . . . . . . . . . . . . . . 83 | – run out . . . . . . . . . . . . . . . . . . . . . . | 14 |
| J. Ryder c Rigg b Hornibrook . . . . . . . . . . . . . . . . . . 6 | – not out . . . . . . . . . . . . . . . . . . . . . . . | 18 |
| S. McCabe c Kippax b Burrows . . . . . . . . . . . . . . . . . 35 | – c Fairfax b Blackie . . . . . . . . . . . . . . | 46 |
| W. Horrocks lbw b Blackie . . . . . . . . . . . . . . . . . . . . 25 | – c Burrows b Blackie . . . . . . . . . . . . . | 5 |
| H. E. P. Whitfield c Bradman b Hornibrook . . . . . . . 68 | – lbw b Blackie . . . . . . . . . . . . . . . . . . | 20 |
| R. K. Oxenham not out . . . . . . . . . . . . . . . . . . . . . . . 84 | – c and b Hornibrook . . . . . . . . . . . . . | 4 |
| C. W. Walker c Wall b Bradman . . . . . . . . . . . . . . . . 12 | – run out . . . . . . . . . . . . . . . . . . . . . . . | 9 |
| C. V. Grimmett c Blackie b Wall . . . . . . . . . . . . . . . . 13 | – not out . . . . . . . . . . . . . . . . . . . . . . . | 7 |
| H. H. Alexander c Allsopp b Wall . . . . . . . . . . . . . . . 6 | – b Hornibrook . . . . . . . . . . . . . . . . . . | 8 |
| B 8, l-b 8, w 1, n-b 1 . . . . . . . . . . . . . . . . 18 | B 8, l-b 12 . . . . . . . . . . . . . . | 20 |

663                    191

## W. M. Woodfull's XI

| | | | |
|---|---|---|---|
| A. Fairfax c and b Alexander | 27 | – st Walker b Grimmett | 26 |
| W. M. Woodfull st Walker b Oxenham | 36 | – c and b Grimmett | 43 |
| A. F. Kippax st Walker b Grimmett | 17 | – c Walker b Oxenham | 170 |
| D. G. Bradman c Jackson b Oxenham | 124 | – lbw b Grimmett | 225 |
| A. Allsopp b Oxenham | 4 | – c McCabe b Grimmett | 5 |
| K. Rigg b Whitfield | 73 | – c Ponsford b McCabe | 9 |
| A. O. Burrows b Oxenham | 7 | – c and b Grimmett | 0 |
| J. L. Ellis lbw b Oxenham | 4 | – b Oxenham | 24 |
| D. J. Blackie c McCabe b Grimmett | 0 | – b Grimmett | 11 |
| P. M. Hornibrook st Walker b Grimmett | 2 | – c Alexander b Grimmett | 1 |
| T. W. Wall not out | 0 | – not out | 2 |
| B 2, l-b 9, w 3, n-b 1 | 15 | B 14, l-b 7, w 3, n-b 1 | 25 |
| | **309** | | **541** |

## W. M. Woodfull's XI Bowling

| | Overs | Mdns | Runs | Wkts | Overs | Mdns | Runs | Wkts |
|---|---|---|---|---|---|---|---|---|
| Wall | 27.7 | — | 131 | 2 | 5 | — | 20 | — |
| Hornibrook | 22 | 4 | 102 | 3 | 22 | 4 | 67 | 4 |
| Fairfax | 27 | — | 116 | — | 2 | — | 19 | — |
| Blackie | 29 | — | 163 | 3 | 20 | 3 | 65 | 3 |
| Burrows | 14 | 1 | 77 | 1 | | | | |
| Bradman | 11 | — | 56 | 1 | | | | |

## J. Ryder's XI Bowling

| | Overs | Mdns | Runs | Wkts | Overs | Mdns | Runs | Wkts |
|---|---|---|---|---|---|---|---|---|
| Alexander | 11 | 1 | 73 | 1 | 11 | — | 73 | — |
| Whitfield | 12 | 2 | 46 | 1 | 14 | — | 71 | — |
| Oxenham | 14.6 | 3 | 42 | 5 | 30.5 | 7 | 97 | 2 |
| Grimmett | 15 | 2 | 68 | 3 | 33 | 3 | 173 | 7 |
| McCabe | 3 | — | 26 | — | 7 | 1 | 42 | 1 |
| Marks | 5 | — | 39 | — | 6 | — | 45 | — |
| Ryder | | | | | 5 | — | 15 | — |

Umpires: A. C. Jones and M. Carney.

## NEW SOUTH WALES v QUEENSLAND

Played at Sydney, January 3, 4, 6, 7, 1930

Everything else in this game paled before the phenomenal performance of Bradman, who, in scoring 452 not out – a feat that occupied him 415 minutes – played the highest individual innings recorded in first-class cricket. That splendid exhibition led the way to a victory for New South Wales by 685 runs. Displaying a wider range of strokes than usual, Bradman batted without a trace of error during his long stay and hit no fewer than 49 4's. His prolific scoring followed upon comparatively low totals in the first innings of each side. Against Hurwood, who kept an admirable length, New South Wales found run getting hard and Queensland fared no better, only Bensted and Goodwin appearing to advantage. New South Wales going in again eight runs ahead, gained a complete mastery over the bowling. Bradman, batting with such brilliancy, made matters easy for his colleagues. Kippax put together a hundred, and McCabe and Allsopp also scored readily. Faced with the appalling task of getting 770 runs, Queensland offered scarcely any resistance. Half the wickets actually fell for 23, and on the last morning Everett finished off the innings. In the two spells of bowling he disposed of six batsmen at a cost of less than four runs each.

## New South Wales

| | | | |
|---|---|---|---|
| C. Andrews st Leeson b Hurwood | 56 | – c Levy b Hurwood | 16 |
| D. G. Bradman c Leeson b Hurwood | 3 | – not out | 452 |
| A. Marks c Hurwood b Thurlow | 40 | – c Bensted b Hurwood | 5 |
| A. F. Kippax lbw b Thurlow | 15 | – lbw b Rowe | 115 |
| S. McCabe c Leeson b Thurlow | 15 | – c Leeson b Hurwood | 60 |
| A. Allsopp c Thurlow b Hurwood | 9 | – b Hurwood | 66 |
| A. Fairfax b Brew | 20 | – st Leeson b Hurwood | 10 |
| S. C. Everett c Bensted b Brew | 41 | – c Goodwin b Hurwood | 4 |
| H. L. Davidson lbw b Hurwood | 14 | – c and b Goodwin | 22 |
| S. Burt b Thurlow | 10 | | |
| H. Chilvers not out | 6 | | |
| B 3, l-b 3 | 6 | B 6, l-b 1, w 2, n-b 2 | 11 |
| | **235** | **(8 wkts dec.)** | **761** |

## Queensland

| | | | |
|---|---|---|---|
| R. M. Levy c Everett b Fairfax | 6 | – b Everett | 0 |
| L. P. O'Connor c Andrews b Fairfax | 21 | – b McCabe | 17 |
| P. C. Thompson lbw b Chilvers | 1 | – lbw b Everett | 0 |
| W. Rose b McCabe | 11 | – c Bradman b Chilvers | 1 |
| F. J. Gough c Marks b McCabe | 14 | – c Allsopp b Chilvers | 20 |
| E. C. Bensted c Davidson b McCabe | 51 | – b Everett | 5 |
| V. Goodwin c Marks b Fairfax | 67 | – run out | 4 |
| A. Hurwood b Chilvers | 4 | – b Everett | 6 |
| F. M. Brew b McCabe | 20 | – c Davidson b Everett | 26 |
| H. Leeson c Davidson b McCabe | 14 | – not out | 2 |
| H. M. Thurlow not out | 3 | – b Everett | 0 |
| B 9, l-b 3, n-b 3 | 15 | B 1, l-b 1, w 1, n-b 2 | 5 |
| | **227** | | **84** |

### Queensland Bowling

| | Overs | Mdns | Runs | Wkts | Overs | Mdns | Runs | Wkts |
|---|---|---|---|---|---|---|---|---|
| Thurlow | 18.1 | — | 83 | 4 | 25 | — | 147 | — |
| Hurwood | 22 | 6 | 57 | 4 | 34 | 1 | 179 | 6 |
| Bensted | 6 | — | 39 | — | 12 | — | 70 | — |
| Brew | 8 | — | 50 | 2 | 6 | — | 61 | — |
| Rowe | | | | | 19 | — | 143 | 1 |
| Thompson | | | | | 15 | — | 90 | — |
| Gough | | | | | 4 | — | 40 | — |
| Levy | | | | | 2 | — | 20 | — |
| Goodwin | | | | | 0.1 | — | — | 1 |

### New South Wales Bowling

| | Overs | Mdns | Runs | Wkts | Overs | Mdns | Runs | Wkts |
|---|---|---|---|---|---|---|---|---|
| Everett | 10 | 1 | 46 | — | 8.5 | 1 | 23 | 6 |
| Fairfax | 15 | 1 | 53 | 3 | 7 | 3 | 12 | — |
| Chilvers | 20 | 5 | 52 | 2 | 8 | — | 22 | 2 |
| McCabe | 15.1 | 5 | 36 | 5 | 5 | 3 | 15 | 1 |
| Burt | 8 | 1 | 25 | — | 2 | — | 7 | — |

Umpires: G. Borwick and E. J. Shaw.

## VICTORIA v QUEENSLAND

### Played at Melbourne, December 18, 19, 20, 1930

Flouting the authority of their selectors, and themselves choosing the team, the Queensland players, after putting Victoria in to bat, fared so disastrously against the bowling of Ironmonger and Blackie that, dismissed twice for small scores, they were beaten by an innings and 242 runs. Thanks mainly to Rigg and Ryder, Victoria on the opening day, placed themselves well on the way to victory, scoring 303 for half their wickets. When Queensland went in, none of their batsmen played confidently against Ironmonger who, maintaining excellent length and making the ball come in quickly, took five wickets for less than 6 runs apiece. Blackie also bowled well and as these two men repeated their good work when Queensland followed on 371 in arrear Victoria gained a brilliant success. In the whole match, Ironmonger had eleven wickets for 70 runs and Blackie seven for 94.

## Victoria

| | |
|---|---|
| H. L. Hendry b Oxenham | 15 |
| E. K. Tolhurst b Oxenham | 22 |
| K. E. Rigg c Oxenham b Bensted | 124 |
| J. Ryder c Bensted b Hurwood | 114 |
| L. Darling c Leeson b Gilbert | 0 |
| E. L. A'Beckett c and b Oxenham | 92 |
| L. P. O'Brien lbw b Oxenham | 65 |
| B. J. Barnett b Oxenham | 7 |
| D. J. Blackie c Leeson b Hurwood | 15 |
| H. Alexander not out | 0 |
| H. Ironmonger b Oxenham | 0 |
| B 12, l-b 6, n-b 2 | 20 |
| | **474** |

## Queensland

| | | |
|---|---|---|
| F. J. Gough b Alexander | 19 | – c and b Blackie | 27 |
| M. Briggs lbw b A'Beckett | 0 | – c Rigg b Ironmonger | 6 |
| E. C. Bensted lbw b Blackie | 20 | – c Rigg b Blackie | 40 |
| F. C. Thompson st Love b Ironmonger | 13 | – c Hendry b Ironmonger | 6 |
| V. H. Goodwin c Rigg b Ironmonger | 5 | – c Barnett b Ironmonger | 4 |
| R. K. Oxenham lbw b Ironmonger | 18 | – c Alexander b Blackie | 1 |
| G. Bourne c O'Brien b Blackie | 4 | – not out | 6 |
| A. Hurwood lbw b Ironmonger | 3 | – b Ironmonger | 6 |
| H. Leeson not out | 10 | – lbw b Blackie | 14 |
| E. Gilbert c Ryder b Blackie | 5 | – c A'Beckett b Ironmonger | 0 |
| H. M. Thurlow b Ironmonger | 0 | – b Ironmonger | 11 |
| B 4, l-b 2 | 6 | B 4, l-b 4 | 8 |
| | **103** | | **129** |

### Queensland Bowling

| | Overs | Mdns | Runs | Wkts |
|---|---|---|---|---|
| Gilbert | 25 | 4 | 78 | 1 |
| Thurlow | 18 | 2 | 70 | — |
| Oxenham | 43.4 | 15 | 92 | 6 |
| Hurwood | 33 | 4 | 115 | 2 |
| Thompson | 14 | 3 | 38 | — |
| Bensted | 10 | — | 48 | 1 |
| Goodwin | 2 | — | 13 | — |

### Victoria Bowling

| | Overs | Mdns | Runs | Wkts | Overs | Mdns | Runs | Wkts |
|---|---|---|---|---|---|---|---|---|
| Alexander | 6 | 1 | 17 | 1 | 14 | 1 | 10 | — |
| A'Beckett | 3 | — | 14 | 1 | 3 | — | 13 | — |
| Blackie | 13 | 1 | 37 | 3 | 14 | 1 | 57 | 4 |
| Ironmonger | 10.6 | 4 | 29 | 5 | 14.2 | 3 | 41 | 6 |

Umpires: E. C. Ramsden and W. R. Wetenhall.

## NEW SOUTH WALES v SOUTH AUSTRALIA

### Played at Sydney, February 3, 4, 6, 1933

Despite a great bowling feat by Wall, South Australia lost this return match by 98 runs. On the opening day New South Wales had 87 on the board for two wickets, but after lunch Wall's fast bowling was almost unplayable. Fingleton, McCabe, Rowe and

Cummins were sent back in one over without a run being scored, and Wall took all ten wickets for 36 runs – nine for 5 runs after the interval and six clean-bowled. The pitch gave him little assistance, but a stiff breeze helped him swing the ball. South Australia lost eight men for 77 before Wall and Shepherd gave their side a single run lead, the last two wickets falling at the same total. When New South Wales went in again, Brown, Bradman and McCabe batted freely, and South Australia were set 356 for victory. Scoring 143 for the loss of two wickets, they looked to have a chance, but Nitschke, after making an excellent hundred, hit out rashly, and after his dismissal O'Reilly and Hill soon finished the match. The win of New South Wales enabled them to retain the Shield.

### New South Wales

| | | |
|---|---|---:|
| J. H. Fingleton b Wall | 43 – c Tobin b Wall | 0 |
| W. Brown c Whitington b Wall | 0 – c Walker b Wall | 79 |
| D. G. Bradman b Wall | 56 – b Lee | 97 |
| S. J. McCabe c Walker b Wall | 0 – lbw b Grimmett | 67 |
| R. Rowe b Wall | 0 – c Tobin b Lee | 19 |
| F. S. Cummins c Walker b Wall | 0 – b Grimmett | 36 |
| H. S. Love b Wall | 1 – lbw b Ryan | 31 |
| C. Hill b Wall | 0 – not out | 9 |
| W. Howell b Wall | 0 – b Ryan | 8 |
| W. J. O'Reilly b Wall | 4 – c Walker b Lee | 5 |
| G. L. Stewart not out | 2 – b Lee | 0 |
| L-b 1, w 1, n-b 5 | 7     B 1, l-b 2, n-b 2 | 5 |
| | **113** | **356** |

### South Australia

| | | |
|---|---|---:|
| V. Y. Richardson b McCabe | 5 – b O'Reilly | 35 |
| H. C. Nitschke c O'Reilly b Howell | 12 – c Rowe b O'Reilly | 105 |
| A. R. Lonergan lbw b O'Reilly | 22 – lbw b Hill | 20 |
| A. J. Ryan c Stewart b Howell | 4 – c Rowe b Hill | 33 |
| R. S. Whitington c Love b Howell | 1 – c sub. b O'Reilly | 2 |
| B. J. Tobin b Howell | 8 – b O'Reilly | 1 |
| A. G. Shepherd c Brown b Bradman | 32 – c sub. b O'Reilly | 0 |
| P. K. Lee c Brown b McCabe | 8 – b Hill | 11 |
| C. V. Grimmett run out | 1 – b Hill | 10 |
| T. W. Wall c Cummins b Howell | 13 – st Love b Bradman | 19 |
| C. W. Walker not out | 0 – not out | 6 |
| B 5, w 1, n-b 2 | 8     B 11, l-b 1, w 1, n-b 2 | 15 |
| | **114** | **257** |

### South Australia Bowling

| | Overs | Mdns | Runs | Wkts | Overs | Mdns | Runs | Wkts |
|---|---|---|---|---|---|---|---|---|
| Wall | 12.4 | 2 | 36 | 10 | 22 | 1 | 91 | 2 |
| Tobin | 5 | — | 23 | — | 12 | — | 69 | — |
| Grimmett | 11 | — | 47 | — | 20 | 2 | 84 | 2 |
| Ryan | | | | | 17 | 3 | 38 | 2 |
| Lee | | | | | 16.5 | 2 | 69 | 4 |

### New South Wales Bowling

| | Overs | Mdns | Runs | Wkts | Overs | Mdns | Runs | Wkts |
|---|---|---|---|---|---|---|---|---|
| Stewart | 3 | 1 | 8 | — | 6 | — | 32 | — |
| McCabe | 6 | 1 | 18 | 2 | | | | |
| Howell | 15 | 5 | 31 | 5 | 9 | 1 | 57 | — |
| O'Reilly | 13 | 2 | 34 | 1 | 25 | 8 | 56 | 5 |
| Hill | 4 | 2 | 11 | — | 22 | 2 | 61 | 4 |
| Bradman | 1.2 | — | 4 | 1 | 5.4 | — | 36 | 1 |

## NEW SOUTH WALES v QUEENSLAND

Played at Sydney, December 30, 1933, January 1, 2, 3, 1934

Another great double century by Bradman against Queensland featured the victory of New South Wales by an innings and 84 runs. On the opening day Thompson batted patiently for four hours, and Allen and Oxenham drove strongly, but Bradman surpassed everyone. Exploiting all the strokes, he dealt unmercifully with the bowling, actually scoring his 253 in less than three and a half hours. His execution of the cut, drive, pull and leg-glance was perfect. Kippax was by no means overshadowed. Batting with his usual grace he reached his hundred in two hours. His record third-wicket stand of 363 with Bradman occupied only two and a quarter hours. Chipperfield placed his strokes cleverly in a hard-hitting effort, and at tea-time, when the innings had lasted seven hours, Kippax declared. Needing 242 runs to save the innings defeat, Queensland lost four men while scoring 70. Tait and Oxenham put on 56 in the one real stand, but few batsmen did much against the slow bowling of Chivers, who took six wickets for just over 10 runs apiece.

### Queensland

| | | | | |
|---|---|---|---|---|
| G. G. Cook lbw b Chivers | 24 | – c Chipperfield b Chilvers | 2 |
| F. M. Brew run out | 14 | – c Bradman b Howell | 21 |
| C. W. Andrews c Bradman b Chipperfield | 38 | – lbw b Hill | 6 |
| F. C. Thompson st Easton b Chipperfield | 92 | – st Easton b Chilvers | 10 |
| R. M. Levy b Chilvers | 45 | – c and b Chilvers | 16 |
| E. C. Bensted c Easton b Howell | 0 | – st Easton b Chilvers | 29 |
| T. Allen run out | 86 | – c Chipperfield b McGilvray | 6 |
| R. K. Oxenham st Easton b Hill | 51 | – st Easton b Chilvers | 24 |
| A. Tait not out | 3 | – c Easton b Chilvers | 35 |
| H. Leeson c Chipperfield b Hill | 14 | – not out | 0 |
| H. S. Gamble c Easton b Hill | 0 | – run out | 0 |
| L-b 4, w 1 | 5 | B 8, l-b 1, w 2 | 11 |
| | **372** | | **158** |

### New South Wales

| | |
|---|---|
| J. H. Fingleton c Bensted b Brew | 42 |
| W. A. Brown c Levy b Oxenham | 50 |
| D. G. Bradman b Brew | 253 |
| A. F. Kippax c sub. b Oxenham | 125 |
| R. Rowe c Leeson b Oxenham | 7 |
| A. G. Chipperfield c Leeson b Andrews | 84 |
| A. McGilvray not out | 34 |
| C. J. Hill not out | 2 |
| B 8, l-b 2, w 5, n-b 2 | 17 |
| **(6 wkts dec.)** | **614** |

A. Easton, H. C. Chilvers and W. Howell did not bat.

### New South Wales Bowling

| | Overs | Mdns | Runs | Wkts | Overs | Mdns | Runs | Wkts |
|---|---|---|---|---|---|---|---|---|
| McGilvray | 14 | 3 | 36 | — | 8 | 1 | 18 | 1 |
| Hill | 30.4 | 12 | 51 | 3 | 13 | 8 | 13 | 1 |
| Chilvers | 48 | 17 | 95 | 2 | 22.3 | 5 | 62 | 6 |
| Howell | 43 | 16 | 79 | 1 | 15 | 3 | 35 | 1 |
| Chipperfield | 25 | 3 | 88 | 2 | 5 | 1 | 19 | — |
| Kippax | 5 | — | 16 | — | | | | |
| Bradman | 1 | — | 2 | — | | | | |

**Queensland Bowling**

|            | Overs | Mdns | Runs | Wkts |
| ---------- | ----- | ---- | ---- | ---- |
| Gamble     | 6     | —    | 17   | —    |
| Bensted    | 19    | 2    | 97   | —    |
| Brew       | 25    | 1    | 176  | 2    |
| Oxenham    | 42    | 9    | 116  | 3    |
| Tait       | 10    | 1    | 77   | —    |
| Cook       | 4     | —    | 32   | —    |
| Andrews    | 3     | —    | 19   | 1    |
| Levy       | 5     | —    | 63   | —    |

Umpires: G. Borwick and H. Armstrong.

# SOUTH AUSTRALIA v QUEENSLAND

## Played at Adelaide, December 22, 24, 26, 1934

Queensland, after scoring 430, lost by eight wickets. South Australia were indebted to four men for their huge total and Grimmett accomplished a splendid feat by taking nine wickets in Queensland's first innings and sixteen for 289 in the match. Levy, Christy, Oxenham, and Tallon batted well in Queensland's first innings, but only Andrews and Tallon did anything afterwards. Richardson, Nitschke, Lonergan and Badcock all scored hundreds for South Australia, Richardson and Nitschke, with a partnership of 255, making the highest opening stand for their state against Queensland. Richardson batted brilliantly for four hours and hit a 6, a 5, and twenty 4s.

### Queensland

| | | | |
|---|---|---|---|
| J. A. Christy lbw b Lee | 80 | – b Grimmett | 29 |
| T. Allen c Moyle b Grimmett | 24 | – run out | 14 |
| D. Hansen c and b Grimmett | 28 | – c Wade b Grimmett | 9 |
| C. W. Andrews c Moyle b Grimmett | 5 | – b Lee | 68 |
| R. M. Levy b Grimmett | 90 | – b Lee | 8 |
| E. C. Bensted lbw b Grimmett | 16 | – c and b Grimmett | 4 |
| R. K. Oxenham not out | 74 | – b Grimmett | 15 |
| D. Tallon b Grimmett | 58 | – c Nitschke b Grimmett | 86 |
| B. O'Connor lbw b Grimmett | 18 | – not out | 4 |
| H. Leeson c Moyle b Grimmett | 14 | – st Edwards b Grimmett | 0 |
| E. R. Wyeth st Edwards b Grimmett | 4 | – lbw b Grimmett | 5 |
| B 13, l-b 2, n-b 4 | 19 | B 3, l-b 4 | 7 |
| | **430** | | **249** |

### South Australia

| | | | |
|---|---|---|---|
| V. Y. Richardson b Wyeth | 185 | | |
| H. C. Nitschke c Bensted b Wyeth | 116 | | |
| A. R. Lonergan c Oxenham b Christy | 137 | | |
| C. L. Badcock run out | 137 | – not out | 10 |
| M. G. Waite b Oxenham | 10 | – lbw b Wyeth | 8 |
| E. J. Moyle c Andrews b Wyeth | 0 | | |
| P. K. Lee hit wkt b Oxenham | 25 | | |
| F. H. Collins not out | 28 | – b O'Connor | 9 |
| F. R. Edwards(did not bat) | | – not out | 10 |
| B 4, n-b 2 | 6 | | |
| | **(7 wkts dec.) 644** | | **37** |

C. V. Grimmett and T. W. Wall did not bat.

**South Australia Bowling**

|  | Overs | Mdns | Runs | Wkts | Overs | Mdns | Runs | Wkts |
|---|---|---|---|---|---|---|---|---|
| Wall | 24 | 1 | 85 | — | 14 | — | 59 | — |
| Collins | 22 | 2 | 72 | — | 10 | 2 | 33 | — |
| Grimmett | 33.2 | 1 | 180 | 9 | 27.3 | 3 | 109 | 7 |
| Lee | 16 | 2 | 49 | 1 | 12 | 1 | 41 | 2 |
| Waite | 5 | — | 25 | — | | | | |

**Queensland Bowling**

|  | Overs | Mdns | Runs | Wkts | Overs | Mdns | Runs | Wkts |
|---|---|---|---|---|---|---|---|---|
| Oxenham | 40 | 8 | 121 | 2 | | | | |
| O'Connor | 17 | — | 120 | — | 4 | — | 17 | 1 |
| Bensted | 16 | — | 72 | — | | | | |
| Wyeth | 48 | 8 | 169 | 3 | 3.3 | — | 20 | 1 |
| Levy | 16 | — | 105 | — | | | | |
| Christy | 7 | — | 22 | 1 | | | | |
| Andrews | 1 | — | 4 | — | | | | |
| Allen | 3 | — | 25 | — | | | | |

Umpires: J. D. Scott and A. G. Jenkins.

# NEW SOUTH WALES v VICTORIA

Played at Sydney, January 25, 26, 28, 29, 1935

More fine bowling by Fleetwood-Smith, who took fifteen wickets for 226, brought Victoria victory by 213 runs. O'Brien played a sound innings of 173, but it occupied him nearly seven hours; a bright 84 by Lee, a young player, was an equally noteworthy effort. McCabe, on his reappearance after injury, contributed a valuable 92 and he and Robinson alone did much with Fleetwood-Smith. Chilvers troubled the Victorian batsmen in their second innings to almost the same extent.

## Victoria

| | | | |
|---|---|---|---|
| L. P. O'Brien st Oldfield b O'Reilly | 173 | – c Oldfield b Theak | 12 |
| K. E. Rigg run out | 22 | – c O'Reilly b Chilvers | 33 |
| L. S. Darling b Chipperfield | 17 | – c Fingleton b White | 12 |
| J. W. Scaife c Chilvers b O'Reilly | 12 | – c and b Theak | 44 |
| E. H. Bromley b White | 16 | – b Chilvers | 4 |
| M. W. Sievers b O'Reilly | 44 | – lbw b Chilvers | 29 |
| I. S. Lee c and b Chilvers | 84 | – c White b Robinson | 54 |
| B. A. Barnett not out | 28 | – c White b Chilvers | 0 |
| H. I. Ebeling st Oldfield b Chilvers | 7 | – c and b Chilvers | 19 |
| E. L. McCormick c and b O'Reilly | 3 | – st Oldfield b Chilvers | 9 |
| L. O'B. Fleetwood-Smith st Oldfield b Chilvers | 3 | – not out | 1 |
| B 4, l-b 5, n-b 2 | 11 | B 2, l-b 7 | 9 |
| | **420** | | **226** |

## New South Wales

| | | | |
|---|---|---|---|
| J. H. Fingleton c Barnett b Ebeling | 3 | – c Sievers b Fleetwood-Smith | 49 |
| W. A. Brown c Barnett b Ebeling | 19 | – c Barnett b McCormick | 0 |
| S. J. McCabe c Sievers b Fleetwood-Smith | 92 | – c Lee b Fleetwood-Smith | 53 |
| A. F. Kippax b McCormick | 7 | – c and b Fleetwood-Smith | 17 |
| A. G. Chipperfield c O'Brien b Fleetwood-Smith | 10 | – b Fleetwood-Smith | 1 |
| R. Robinson hit wkt b Fleetwood-Smith | 57 | – not out | 28 |
| W. A. Oldfield lbw b Fleetwood-Smith | 12 | – c O'Brien b Fleetwood-Smith | 0 |
| E. S. White c and b Fleetwood-Smith | 8 | – st Barnett b Fleetwood-Smith | 21 |
| W. J. O'Reilly not out | 20 | – c McCormick b Fleetwood-Smith | 1 |
| H. C. Chilvers st Barnett b Fleetwood-Smith | 10 | – run out | 2 |
| H. J. Theak c Lee b Fleetwood-Smith | 4 | – c Sievers b Fleetwood-Smith | 0 |
| B 12, l-b 1 | 13 | B 2, l-b 3, n-b 1 | 6 |
| | **255** | | **178** |

## New South Wales Bowling

| | Overs | Mdns | Runs | Wkts | Overs | Mdns | Runs | Wkts |
|---|---|---|---|---|---|---|---|---|
| Theak | 14 | 1 | 43 | — | 8 | — | 32 | 2 |
| McCabe | 14 | 3 | 36 | — | 5 | 2 | 11 | — |
| O'Reilly | 43 | 14 | 85 | 4 | 21 | 7 | 56 | — |
| Chilvers | 38.7 | 3 | 120 | 3 | 23.7 | 3 | 76 | 6 |
| Chipperfield | 15 | 2 | 47 | 1 | 6 | — | 19 | — |
| White | 16 | 3 | 46 | 1 | 8 | 2 | 17 | 1 |
| Robinson | 3 | — | 16 | — | 1 | — | 6 | 1 |
| Kippax | 3 | — | 16 | — | | | | |

## Victoria Bowling

| | Overs | Mdns | Runs | Wkts | Overs | Mdns | Runs | Wkts |
|---|---|---|---|---|---|---|---|---|
| McCormick | 17 | 1 | 73 | 1 | 10 | 1 | 33 | 1 |
| Ebeling | 14 | 4 | 43 | 2 | 16 | 7 | 26 | — |
| Sievers | 6 | 1 | 13 | — | | | | |
| Fleetwood-Smith | 20.6 | 3 | 113 | 7 | 17.6 | — | 113 | 8 |

Umpires: G. Borwick and H. Armstrong.

# VICTORIA v SOUTH AUSTRALIA

### Played at Melbourne, January 1, 2, 3, 4, 1936

South Australia won on the first innings. Big crowds enjoyed a feast of interesting cricket between two unbeaten sides. Bradman overshadowed everyone else. His 357 which followed innings of 233 and 117 in the two previous Shield matches, was his fifth score of 300 and his twenty-third of 200. Bradman, when 18, passed his 5,000 runs in Shield cricket. Picking out the loose ball with unhurried but masterly decision, Bradman made 229 before the close of the first day and, next morning, he gave a scintillating display, hitting up 128 in less than two hours. In all he batted just over seven hours, gave no chance and hit forty 4s; he scored his runs out of 502 and used every stroke with equal facility. Gregory made a gallant 80 when Victoria badly wanted runs and in the follow-on a fine fighting innings by Rigg was primarily resonsible for his side saving the game.

## South Australia

| | | | | |
|---|---|---|---|---|
| A. J. Ryan run out | 7 | C. W. Walker lbw b Welch | 8 |
| R. Parker c Rigg b Welch | 63 | F. H. Collins not out | 37 |
| D. G. Bradman c Quin b Bromley | 357 | F. Ward st Quin b Welch | 29 |
| E. J. Moyle c Quin b Welch | 9 | T. W. Wall lbw b Smith | 0 |
| M. G. Waite b Gregory | 24 | L-b 4, n-b 2 | 6 |
| A. F. Richter c Smith b Welch | 7 | | — |
| T. O'Connell c Quin b Plant | 22 | | 569 |

## Victoria

| | | | |
|---|---|---|---|
| K. E. Rigg lbw b Wall | 0 | – c Ryan b O'Connell | 124 |
| S. Quin b Ryan | 52 | – c Bradman b O'Connell | 47 |
| I. S. Lee c and b Waite | 50 | – run out | 14 |
| J. W. Scaife b Wall | 48 | – c Wall b O'Connell | 25 |
| V. Nagel st Walker b Ward | 0 | | |
| E. H. Bromley c Waite b Ryan | 1 | – c Walker b Wall | 2 |
| R. Gregory lbw b Ward | 80 | – not out | 18 |
| H. J. Plant c Ryan b Waite | 42 | – not out | 16 |
| S. Smith c Walker b Wall | 22 | | |
| H. I. Ebeling not out | 1 | | |
| C. Welch c Ryan b Wall | 1 | | |
| B 3, l-b 13 | 16 | B 1, l-b 3 | 4 |
| | 313 | | 250 |

### Victoria Bowling

| | Overs | Mdns | Runs | Wkts |
|---|---|---|---|---|
| Ebeling | 4 | 1 | 9 | — |
| Nagel | 25 | 5 | 85 | — |
| Plant | 27 | 2 | 86 | 1 |
| Smith | 14.1 | 2 | 56 | 1 |
| Welch | 25 | 1 | 155 | 5 |
| Gregory | 19 | 1 | 101 | 1 |
| Bromley | 14 | 2 | 71 | 1 |

### South Australia Bowling

| | Overs | Mdns | Runs | Wkts | Overs | Mdns | Runs | Wkts |
|---|---|---|---|---|---|---|---|---|
| Wall | 25.2 | 4 | 77 | 4 | 9 | — | 15 | 1 |
| O'Connell | 11 | 1 | 33 | — | 15 | 2 | 42 | 3 |
| Collins | 13 | 2 | 24 | — | 28 | 2 | 66 | — |
| Waite | 14 | 3 | 45 | 2 | 9 | 1 | 30 | — |
| Ryan | 18 | 8 | 26 | 2 | 4 | 1 | 6 | — |
| Ward | 25 | 6 | 77 | 2 | 5 | — | 29 | — |
| Richter | 3 | — | 15 | — | 13 | — | 58 | — |
| Bradman | | | | | 1 | 1 | — | — |

Umpires: A. N. Barlow and C. Dwyer.

## SOUTH AUSTRALIA v VICTORIA

Played at Adelaide, February 21, 22, 24, 25, 1936

South Australian won by an innings and 190 runs. Despite the failure of Bradman – caught at second slip off an out-swinger – Victoria were outplayed in every department. Ward's slow bowling was always too clever for their batsmen non of whom, with the exception of Hassett in the first innings, managed to pass fifty, and Badcock overwhelmed the Victoria bowling. The young Tasmanian, in making the highest score of his career, gave a great exhibition. Solid rather than brilliant, he did not force the pace, but produced the right stroke for nearly every ball he received during his long stay of nine and a quarter hours. His hands were blistered in the latter stages of his innings but his drives, cuts, hooks and hits to leg lost little power in consequence. He hit thirty-four 4s. Badcock took part in three century stands. He and Parker set up a new South Australia record by scoring 210 for the first wicket, Ryan helped Badcock put on 198 for the fourth wicket and Walker and Badcock added 119 for the sixth stand.

## Victoria

| | | |
|---|---|---|
| K. E. Rigg st Walker b Ward | 6 | – c Walker b Ward ............... 21 |
| S. Quinn c Ryan b Ward | 30 | – c Collins b Ward ............. 26 |
| I. S. Lee st Walker b Ward | 12 | – b Ward ...................... 0 |
| J. W. Scaife c Walker b Wall | 4 | – c Waite b Ward ............... 33 |
| R. Gregory b Wall | 2 | – lbw b Williams .............. 4 |
| J. Ledward b Ward | 19 | – st Walker b Waite ........... 47 |
| A. Hassett c Collins b Wall | 73 | – st Walker b Ward ........... 2 |
| H. J. Plant c Bradman b Ward | 26 | – c Parker b Waite ........... 25 |
| W. Y. Wilson c Bradman b Waite | 13 | – c Ward b Waite ............ 5 |
| H. I. Ebeling st Walker b Waite | 5 | – b Waite ................... 0 |
| R. B. Scott not out | 2 | – not out ................... 0 |
| B 3, l-b 5, w 1 | 9 | B 8, l-b 3 ............... 11 |
| | **201** | **174** |

## South Australia

| | | | |
|---|---|---|---|
| R. Parker c Scott b Wilson | 88 | M. G. Waite c Rigg b Wilson | 8 |
| C. L. Badcock c Rigg b Gregory | 325 | C. W. Walker not out | 33 |
| D. G. Bradman c Ledward b Ebeling | 1 | B 6, l-b 12, w 1, n-b 9 | 28 |
| E. J. Moyle b Ebeling | 5 | | |
| A. J. Ryan b Wilson | 77 | (6 wkts dec.) | 565 |

F. H. Collins, F. Ward, T. W. Wall and R. G. Williams did not bat.

## South Australia Bowling

| | Overs | Mdns | Runs | Wkts | Overs | Mdns | Runs | Wkts |
|---|---|---|---|---|---|---|---|---|
| Wall | 14 | 3 | 21 | 3 | 9 | 1 | 32 | 1 |
| Williams | 9 | 2 | 15 | — | 11 | 4 | 12 | 1 |
| Ward | 23 | 2 | 74 | 5 | 15 | 1 | 72 | 4 |
| Ryan | 17 | 5 | 31 | — | 4 | 3 | 1 | — |
| Waite | 12.4 | 4 | 35 | 2 | 9.6 | 1 | 29 | 4 |
| Collins | 11 | 4 | 16 | — | 9 | 4 | 17 | — |

## Victoria Bowling

| | Overs | Mdns | Runs | Wkts |
|---|---|---|---|---|
| Scott | 30 | 3 | 110 | — |
| Ebeling | 41 | 6 | 97 | 2 |
| Wilson | 30 | 4 | 122 | 3 |
| Gregory | 22.6 | 1 | 99 | 1 |
| Plant | 36 | 11 | 109 | — |

Umpires: J. D. Scott and R. A. Nelson.

# VICTORIA v QUEENSLAND

Played at Melbourne, December 18, 19, 21, 22, 1936

Victoria won by an innings and 85 runs. Fleetwood-Smith's wonderful bowling overshadowed everything. Ebeling's confidence in the left-arm bowler was not misplaced when he put Queensland in on a soft wicket. Keeping a tantalising length and spinning the ball disconcertingly, Fleetwood-Smith proved practically unplayable. Although more expensive in the second innings, he was generally the master and so puzzled the batsmen that four were leg-before. Allen deserved praise for withstanding him so long. Darling returned to form with a century, strong off-side play bringing him most of his runs.

## Queensland

| | | | |
|---|---|---|---|
| R. Rogers b Fleetwood-Smith | 14 | – c Barnett b Pearson | 7 |
| T. Allen c Plant b Ebeling | 0 | – c Plant b Fleetwood-Smith | 101 |
| C. W. Andrews lbw b Fleetwood-Smith | 16 | – lbw b Fleetwood-Smith | 1 |
| D. Tallon c Barnett b Fleetwood-Smith | 3 | – c Ledward b Fleetwood-Smith | 11 |
| G. Baker lbw b Fleetwood-Smith | 0 | – lbw b Pearson | 18 |
| D. Hansen c Rigg b Fleetwood-Smith | 0 | – c Lee b Fleetwood-Smith | 2 |
| G. G. Cook not out | 8 | – lbw b Fleetwood-Smith | 7 |
| R. K. Oxenham c Ebeling b Pearson | 1 | – lbw b Fleetwood-Smith | 15 |
| G. Amos c Hassett b Fleetwood-Smith | 1 | – b Fleetwood-Smith | 4 |
| E. R. H. Wyeth lbw b Fleetwood-Smith | 3 | – lbw b Fleetwood-Smith | 4 |
| P. L. Dixon c Darling b Pearson | 1 | – not out | 0 |
| B 2 | 2 | B 2, l-b 2, w 1 | 5 |
| | **49** | | **157** |

## Victoria

| | | | |
|---|---|---|---|
| K. E. Rigg c Tallon b Dixon | 11 | B. A. Barnett not out | 9 |
| I. S. Lee c Wyeth b Amos | 13 | H. J. Plant lbw b Cook | 10 |
| L. S. Darling b Cook | 111 | H. I. Ebeling lbw b Cook | 6 |
| R. G. Gregory c Hansen b Amos | 46 | L. O'B. Fleetwood-Smith c sub. b Cook | 0 |
| A. L. Hassett c Wyeth b Amos | 5 | B 1, l-b 1, w 1, n-b 2 | 5 |
| J. D. Ledward c Rogers b Dixon | 57 | | |
| W. E. Pearson b Dixon | 36 | | **309** |

## Victoria Bowling

| | Overs | Mdns | Runs | Wkts | Overs | Mdns | Runs | Wkts |
|---|---|---|---|---|---|---|---|---|
| Ebeling | 13 | 2 | 21 | 1 | 11 | 1 | 24 | — |
| Pearson | 9.6 | 3 | 9 | 2 | 12 | 2 | 25 | 2 |
| Fleetwood-Smith | 10 | 2 | 17 | 7 | 23.1 | 3 | 79 | 8 |
| Gregory | | | | | 10 | — | 36 | — |
| Plant | | | | | 3 | — | 6 | — |

## Queensland Bowling

| | Overs | Mdns | Runs | Wkts |
|---|---|---|---|---|
| Dixon | 21 | 3 | 87 | 3 |
| Amos | 16 | 3 | 67 | 3 |
| Oxenham | 12 | 3 | 28 | — |
| Cook | 15.7 | 1 | 60 | 4 |
| Wyeth | 10 | 2 | 30 | — |
| Allen | 5 | — | 32 | — |

Umpires: A. N. Barlow and C. Dwyer.

## NEW SOUTH WALES v QUEENSLAND

Played at Sydney, December 31, January 2, 3, 4, 1938-39

Queensland won by eight wickets. Don Tallon, Queensland's wicket-keeper and Brown, the captain, were the men of the match. Tallon gave his finest performance behind the stumps and equalled a world record by dismissing twelve batsmen – six in each innings. Brown narrowly missed a century in the first innings which Queensland finished 14 behind, but his grand stroke-play earned full reward in the second. With an opening stand of 265 – a State record – he and Cook made the task of getting 279 for victory a simple one. The New South Wales captain sportingly carried on while his opponents scored the last 20 runs in pouring rain.

### New South Wales

| | | | |
|---|---|---|---|
| J. H. Fitzpatrick st D. Tallon b Christ | 26 | – c D. Tallon b Ellis | 0 |
| A. G. Cheetham c D. Tallon b Dixon | 20 | – c Christ b Ellis | 10 |
| S. G. Barnes c D. Tallon b Christ | 21 | – c sub. b Christ | 51 |
| C. M. Solomon b Ellis | 4 | – c Baker b Ellis | 31 |
| V. McCaffrey c D. Tallon b Ellis | 4 | – st D. Tallon b W. Tallon | 40 |
| C. Pepper b Dixon | 39 | – c D. Tallon b Dixon | 17 |
| K. Gulliver c D. Tallon b Dixon | 31 | – c D. Tallon b Dixon | 40 |
| R. James st D. Tallon b Christ | 11 | – c Christ b W. Tallon | 42 |
| F. A. Easton b Dixon | 0 | – c D. Tallon b Ellis | 0 |
| E. S. White c and b Ellis | 44 | – c D. Tallon b Ellis | 17 |
| J. Murphy not out | 3 | – not out | 5 |
| B 2, l-b 4, n-b 5 | 11 | L-b 9, n-b 2 | 11 |
| | **214** | | **264** |

### Queensland

| | | | |
|---|---|---|---|
| W. A. Brown c Pepper b Cheetham | 95 | – c Cheetham b Murphy | 168 |
| R. Rogers lbw b Cheetham | 2 | | |
| G. G. Cook lbw b Barnes | 19 | – run out | 93 |
| T. Allen b Cheetham | 5 | – not out | 3 |
| D. Hansen c sub. b Fitzpatrick | 7 | | |
| D. Tallon b Gulliver | 28 | – not out | 9 |
| G. Baker c Gulliver b Murphy | 0 | | |
| W. Tallon b Barnes | 13 | | |
| P. L. Dixon lbw b Barnes | 10 | | |
| C. Christ run out | 0 | | |
| J. Ellis not out | 7 | | |
| B 10, l-b 1, w 3 | 14 | B 3, l-b 3 | 6 |
| | **200** | | **279** |

### Queensland Bowling

| | Overs | Mdns | Runs | Wkts | Overs | Mdns | Runs | Wkts |
|---|---|---|---|---|---|---|---|---|
| Ellis | 13 | 1 | 42 | 3 | 21 | 2 | 67 | 5 |
| Cook | 9 | 1 | 27 | — | 9 | — | 41 | — |
| Dixon | 15 | 1 | 61 | 4 | 14 | 1 | 59 | 2 |
| Christ | 18 | 3 | 60 | 3 | 15 | 1 | 51 | 1 |
| W. Tallon | 2 | — | 13 | — | 8 | 1 | 32 | 2 |
| Baker | | | | | 1 | — | 3 | — |

**New South Wales Bowling**

| | Overs | Mdns | Runs | Wkts | Overs | Mdns | Runs | Wkts |
|---|---|---|---|---|---|---|---|---|
| Murphy .......... | 18 | 5 | 31 | 1 | 16 | 2 | 54 | 1 |
| Cheetham ........ | 18 | 1 | 52 | 3 | 20 | 4 | 71 | — |
| White ............ | 12 | 5 | 18 | — | 8 | 3 | 18 | — |
| Fitzpatrick ........ | 9 | 2 | 22 | 1 | 9 | 2 | 18 | — |
| Pepper ........... | 3 | — | 16 | — | 8 | — | 38 | — |
| Barnes .......... | 10.2 | 6 | 20 | 3 | 8 | — | 46 | — |
| Gulliver .......... | 8 | 2 | 27 | 1 | 2 | — | 14 | — |
| James ............ | | | | | 1 | — | 5 | — |
| McCaffrey ....... | | | | | 1 | — | 9 | — |

Umpires: G. Borwick and F. Lyons.

## SOUTH AUSTRALIA v NEW SOUTH WALES

Played at Adelaide, December 17, 18, 20, 21, 1938

New South Wales won by 33 runs. The craft of O'Reilly turned the fortune of an exciting game. The Test bowler narrowly missed taking all ten wickets in South Australia's first innings – at one point he sent back five men for 1 run – and when the home side batted a second time, needing 225 to win, his skilful control of length, flight and spin proved the winning factor. South Australia were 153 for four but O'Reilly dashed their hopes of success. For a good first innings total, New South Wales were indebted mainly to Fingleton and McCabe who added 163 for the second wicket. Bradman, who shared with Whitington and Badcock in partnerships of 141 and 121, was South Australia's most effective batsman, and Grimmett bowled extremely well.

### New South Wales

| | | |
|---|---|---|
| J. H. Fingleton c Badcock b Ward ............... | 81 | – b Cotton ..................... 10 |
| A. G. Cheetham c and b Grimmett .............. | 4 | – run out ...................... 18 |
| S. J. McCabe c Grimmett b Waite .............. | 106 | – c Badcock b Grimmett .......... 10 |
| S. G. Barnes lbw b Grimmett ................... | 79 | – lbw b Cotton ................. 5 |
| A. G. Chipperfield run out .................... | 21 | – c Waite b Cotton ............. 20 |
| V. Jackson c Hamence b Grimmett ............. | 4 | – c Badcock b Grimmett ......... 2 |
| L. C. Hynes lbw b Ward ..................... | 7 | – not out ...................... 11 |
| W. A. Oldfield b Grimmett.................... | 15 | – c Whitington c Grimmett ........ 0 |
| E. S. White not out ......................... | 7 | – b Waite ..................... 5 |
| W. J. O'Reilly lbw b Grimmett................. | 2 | – b Grimmett ................. 0 |
| L. J. O'Brien b Williams ..................... | 4 | – b Ward ..................... 21 |
| L-b 4, w 1, n-b 2 ................... | 7 | B 1, l-b 1 ............... 2 |
| | **337** | **104** |

### South Australia

| | | |
|---|---|---|
| C. L. Badcock lbw b O'Brien .................. | 2 | – b O'Brien .................... 77 |
| R. S. Whitington c Fingleton b O'Reilly .......... | 54 | – lbw b O'Brien................. 1 |
| D. G. Bradman c O'Brien b O'Reilly ........... | 91 | – c Chipperfield b O'Reilly ........ 62 |
| R. H. Robinson b O'Reilly .................... | 0 | – c O'Brien b O'Reilly ............ 16 |
| R. A. Hamence c Oldfield b O'Reilly ............ | 17 | – b O'Brien .................... 4 |
| M. G. Waite c Oldfield b O'Reilly .............. | 3 | – c Oldfield b McCabe ........... 7 |
| C. W. Walker b O'Reilly ..................... | 1 | – lbw b O'Reilly ................. 9 |
| F. A. Ward c Chipperfield b O'Reilly ............ | 23 | – run out ...................... 0 |
| R. G. Williams c Chipperfield b O'Reilly .......... | 6 | – c and b O'Reilly ................ 0 |
| C. V. Grimmett lbw b O'Reilly................. | 4 | – c Fingleton b O'Reilly .......... 3 |
| H. J. Cotton not out ........................ | 10 | – not out ..................... 10 |
| L-b 2, n-b 4 ................... | 6 | L-b 1, n-b 1 ............. 2 |
| | **217** | **191** |

### South Australia Bowling

|            | Overs | Mdns | Runs | Wkts | Overs | Mdns | Runs | Wkts |
|------------|-------|------|------|------|-------|------|------|------|
| Cotton     | 20    | 1    | 60   | —    | 12    | 5    | 22   | 3    |
| Williams   | 23.4  | 6    | 46   | 1    | 8     | 3    | 14   | —    |
| Grimmett   | 32    | 5    | 103  | 5    | 19    | 5    | 51   | 4    |
| Waite      | 18    | 5    | 35   | 1    | 8     | 3    | 15   | 1    |
| Ward       | 17    | 2    | 86   | 2    | 1     | 1    | —    | 1    |

### New South Wales Bowling

|            | Overs | Mdns | Runs | Wkts | Overs | Mdns | Runs | Wkts |
|------------|-------|------|------|------|-------|------|------|------|
| O'Brien    | 19    | 1    | 67   | 1    | 12    | —    | 58   | 3    |
| Hynes      | 11    | 1    | 34   | —    | 6     | —    | 24   | —    |
| O'Reilly   | 33.6  | 12   | 41   | 9    | 20    | 8    | 57   | 5    |
| Jackson    | 8     | 3    | 14   | —    | 5     | 2    | 7    | —    |
| Cheetham   | 6     | 1    | 20   | —    | 2     | —    | 17   | —    |
| White      | 11    | 3    | 35   | —    | 7     | —    | 17   | —    |
| McCabe     |       |      |      |      | 2.1   | —    | 9    | 1    |

Umpires: J. D. Scott and A. G. Jenkins.

## SOUTH AUSTRALIA v QUEENSLAND

### Played at Adelaide, December 25, 27, 28, 29, 1938

South Australia won by eight wickets. Queensland recovered finely, but they lacked a bowler who could trouble Bradman. Williams, making the ball swing appreciably in the heavy atmosphere, was responsible for Queensland's poor show at the start, and when South Australia lost three men for 50 it seemed there might be a keen struggle. Bradman, however, soon dominated affairs and with all the strokes at his command in a magnificent exhibition lasting six hours he hit twenty 4s. In Queensland's second innings, Brown and Rogers hit the South Australian bowling all over the field. Rogers was especially brilliant, often scoring at nearly 2 runs a minute, and he found the boundary twenty-three times. Ward came in for heavy punishment after taking three wickets for only 1 run. Despite the Queensland rally, South Australia needed only 91 for victory, and in helping to knock off the runs Bradman brought his match aggregate to 285 for once out.

### Queensland

| | | | |
|---|---|---|---|
| W. A. Brown c Walker b Williams | 10 | – c Williams b Grimmett | 132 |
| G. G. Cook b Williams | 0 | – b Ward | 11 |
| J. Coats st Walker b Ward | 21 | – lbw b Waite | 13 |
| C. A. Loxton c Robinson b Ward | 2 | – st Walker b Ward | 1 |
| R. E. Rogers b Williams | 19 | – c Walker b Williams | 181 |
| D. Tallon c Walker b Williams | 3 | – st Walker b Waite | 24 |
| T. Allen c Cotton b Grimmett | 6 | – run out | 26 |
| G. Baker c and b Williams | 13 | – lbw b Ward | 1 |
| E. R. Wyeth lbw b Grimmett | 4 | – c Badcock b Ward | 7 |
| J. Govan not out | 7 | – c Walker b Grimmett | 9 |
| P. L. Dixon c Hamence b Williams | 2 | – not out | 5 |
| B 2, w 1, n-b 3 | 6 | B 5, l-b 10, n-b 2 | 17 |
| | **93** | | **426** |

## South Australia

C. L. Badcock c Dixon b Cook ................. 10 – st Tallon b Govan ............. 45
C. W. Walker run out ......................... 11 – c Loxton b Dixon ............. 0
D. G. Bradman c Baker b Dixon ................ .246 – not out ...................... 39
F. A. Ward c Tallon b Loxton .................. 0
R. G. Williams c Baker b Govan ............... 34
R. H. Robinson c Loxton b Dixon ............... 49
R. A. Hamence c Tallon b Dixon ................ 5 – not out ...................... 9
R. S. Whitington run out ..................... 3
M. G. Waite not out .......................... 52
C. V. Grimmett not out ....................... 5
    B 3, l-b 8, n-b 3 ..................... 14

             (8 wkts dec.) 429               93

H. J. Cotton did not bat.

## South Australia Bowling

|              | Overs | Mdns | Runs | Wkts | Overs | Mdns | Runs | Wkts |
|--------------|-------|------|------|------|-------|------|------|------|
| Cotton ...........| 8 | — | 27 | — | 20 | 3 | 62 | — |
| Williams ..........| 11.1 | 4 | 21 | 6 | 16 | 2 | 57 | 1 |
| Waite ............| 3 | — | 12 | — | 24 | 10 | 31 | 2 |
| Ward ............| 6 | 1 | 16 | 2 | 30 | 2 | 152 | 4 |
| Grimmett .........| 6 | 2 | 11 | 2 | 33.3 | 3 | 107 | 2 |

## Queensland Bowling

|              | Overs | Mdns | Runs | Wkts | Overs | Mdns | Runs | Wkts |
|--------------|-------|------|------|------|-------|------|------|------|
| Dixon ...........| 24 | — | 130 | 3 | 4 | — | 22 | 1 |
| Cook ...........| 23 | 1 | 87 | 1 | 10 | 1 | 30 | — |
| Loxton ...........| 11 | — | 41 | 1 | 4 | 1 | 11 | — |
| Govan ...........| 12 | — | 72 | 1 | 1.2 | — | 9 | 1 |
| Wyeth ...........| 24 | 3 | 70 | — | 3 | — | 12 | — |
| Baker ...........| 3 | 1 | 15 | — | 1 | — | 9 | — |

Umpires: J. D. Scott and A. G. Jenkins.

# OTHER MATCHES

## AUSTRALIA v SOUTH AFRICA
### Fourth Test Match

Played at Adelaide, January 29, 30, February 1, 2, 1932

Up to a point South Africa rendered a fairly good account of themselves but, as in previous matches, the combination of Bradman and Grimmett as batsman and bowler proved too much for them and Australia won the fourth Test match by ten wickets. Bradman played a great innings of 299 not out, while Grimmett took fourteen wickets – seven in each innings – for 199 runs. Rarely in a Test match can two men have contributed so materially to the defeat of the opposing side. Having won the rubber, Australia, with a view to the future, introduced two or three young players into their team, but except that O'Reilly took four wickets, it was left to the two men mentioned above to carry off chief honours.

Grimmett bowled very steadily on the opening day when South Africa scored 265 for seven wickets. After two men had left for 45, Mitchell and Taylor put on 120 runs in about ninety-five minutes, Mitchell batting solidly, while Taylor showed his best form of the tour in an innings of 78. Grimmett bowled with great effect after tea, but the next day South Africa carried their score to 308 before the last wicket fell. In reply to that Australia made 302 for four wickets. This was almost entirely the work of Woodfull and Bradman, who added 176 for the second wicket. Rigg, later, gave Bradman useful assistance, the latter at the close being 170 not out.

On Monday the Australian total amounted to 513, Bradman remaining undefeated until the end. In his attempt to reach his 300th run, however, he ran Thurlow out. Bradman's score of 299 was the highest ever made by one man in a Test match in Australia, but it fell short by 35 of his record made against England at Leeds in 1930. He dominated the proceedings on this day after he and Rigg had increased their overnight partnership to 114. There were times, however, when he was not at all comfortable. During one particular hour he scored only 25 runs and survived several appeals for leg-before and catches at the wicket. Oldfield and Grimmett gave valuable help and with O'Reilly in 78 runs were added. The innings closed just before tea, South Africa being left to get 205 to save the innings defeat.

Mitchell again played well and Christy batted brightly, these two putting on 81 in an hour and a quarter after Curnow had left at 22. Before play ceased the visitors made 124 for two wickets and on the last day they ran their total to 274. Taylor and Mitchell made a brave effort to get on top of the bowling with a partnership which produced 121 in just over two hours, but after the dismissal of Taylor, very little real resistance was offered. When there were two wickets to fall Mitchell wanted only 9 runs for his hundred, but he was caught at cover-point and the innings closed a little later. Actually the last seven South African wickets wend down for 70 runs. The wicket had worn slightly at one end, but that was no real excuse for such a bad collapse.

Australia had to get only 70 runs, these being hit off by Ponsford and Woodfull in less than an hour.

## South Africa

| | | | |
|---|---|---|---|
| S. H. Curnow c Ponsford b Grimmett | 20 | – b McCabe | 3 |
| B. Mitchell c and b McCabe | 75 | – c Thurlow b Grimmett | 95 |
| J. A. J. Christy b O'Reilly | 7 | – b Grimmett | 51 |
| H. W. Taylor c Rigg b Grimmett | 78 | – b O'Reilly | 84 |
| H. B. Cameron lbw b Grimmett | 52 | – b O'Reilly | 4 |
| D. P. B. Morkel c and b Grimmett | 0 | – b Grimmett | 15 |
| K. F. Viljoen c and b Grimmett | 0 | – b Grimmett | 1 |
| C. L. Vincent lbw b O'Reilly | 48 | – b Grimmett | 5 |
| Q. McMillan b Grimmett | 19 | – c Hunt b Grimmett | 3 |
| N. A. Quinn c Ponsford b Grimmett | 1 | – b Grimmett | 1 |
| A. J. Bell not out | 2 | – not out | 0 |
| L-b 2, n-b 4 | 6 | B 4, l-b 3, n-b 5 | 12 |
| | **308** | | **274** |

## Australia

| | |
|---|---|
| W. M. Woodfull c Morkel b Bell | 82 – not out ... 37 |
| W. H. Ponsford b Quinn | 5 – not out ... 27 |
| D. G. Bradman not out | 299 |
| A. F. Kippax run out | 0 |
| S. J. McCabe c Vincent b Bell | 2 |
| K. E. Rigg c Taylor b Bell | 35 |
| W. A. Oldfield lbw b Vincent | 23 |
| C. V. Grimmett b Bell | 21 |
| W. A. Hunt c Vincent b Quinn | 0 |
| W. J. O'Reilly b Bell | 23 |
| H. M. Thurlow run out | 0 |
| B 18, l-b 3, w 1, n-b 1 | 23     B 4, l-b 5 ... 9 |
| | **513**      **73** |

### Australia Bowling

| | Overs | Mdns | Runs | Wkts | Overs | Mdns | Runs | Wkts |
|---|---|---|---|---|---|---|---|---|
| Thurlow | 27 | 6 | 53 | — | 12 | 1 | 33 | — |
| McCabe | 17 | 6 | 34 | 1 | 14 | 1 | 51 | 1 |
| O'Reilly | 39.4 | 10 | 74 | 2 | 42 | 13 | 81 | 2 |
| Grimmett | 47 | 11 | 116 | 7 | 49.2 | 17 | 83 | 7 |
| Hunt | 10 | 1 | 25 | — | 6 | 1 | 14 | — |

### South Africa Bowling

| | Overs | Mdns | Runs | Wkts | Overs | Mdns | Runs | Wkts |
|---|---|---|---|---|---|---|---|---|
| Bell | 40 | 2 | 142 | 5 | | | | |
| Quinn | 37 | 5 | 114 | 2 | 3 | — | 5 | — |
| Vincent | 34 | 5 | 110 | 1 | 7 | — | 31 | — |
| McMillan | 9 | — | 53 | — | 7.2 | — | 23 | — |
| Morkel | 18 | 1 | 71 | — | 2 | — | 5 | — |

Umpires: G. A. Hele and G. Borwick.

# AUSTRALIA v SOUTH AFRICA

## Fifth Test Match

### Played at Melbourne, February 12, 13, 15, 1932

Before proceeding to New Zealand, South Africa engaged in their concluding Test match with Australia and for the fifth time were defeated, Australia, although scoring only 153, winning in an innings with 72 runs to spare. For this game Australia brought in L. Nash, a Tasmanian fast bowler who jumped into prominence by taking seven wickets for 50 runs when the tourists played Tasmania. Short, but of powerful build, Nash made the ball rise in very awkward fashion, several of them getting head high. He and Ironmonger proved so effective on a pitch slightly on the soft side that in a little more than ninety minutes South Africa were dismissed for the sorry total of 36. This was not their lowest total in Test cricket for they had twice been got rid of previously by England for 30 – at Port Elizabeth in 1895-96 and at Birmingham in 1924. Their lowest score before this in Test matches against Australia was 80 at Melbourne in 1910-11. Cameron alone reached double figures and Ironmonger had the remarkable analysis of five wickets for 6 runs.

Before the day was over there were further surprises, Australia being got rid of for 153. The wicket appeared a little easier, but Bell, Quinn and McMillan were all able to get considerable work on the ball. Woodfull was out first ball, but Fingleton and Rigg put on 51, the only other stand being that between Kippax and Nash which produced 37. Australia's total was their smallest against South Africa, the previous lowest being 175 at Johannesburg in 1902-03. South Africa, 117 behind, lost one wicket for 5 runs before play ceased for the day, and on Saturday no cricket took place, heavy rain during the night and a further downfall soon after two o'clock preventing any chance of resumption. On the Monday, however, there came more sensational play.

The game was not proceeded with until quarter past two and then in less than an hour and a half the last nine South African wickets went down for another 40 runs. Thus South Africa were twice dismissed for an aggregate of 81, the lowest total for two innings ever recorded in the history of Test match cricket. The wicket was very difficult and Ironmonger once more proved practically unplayable. He dismissed six men for 18 runs, thus having a record in the match of eleven wickets for 24. Five batsmen failed to score and only Curnow reached double figures.

The third wicket fell at 25 and then, with the sun coming out, the wicket became terribly treacherous, the last seven batsmen being dismissed for another 20 runs.

### South Africa

| | | | |
|---|---|---|---|
| B. Mitchell c Rigg b McCabe | 2 | – c Oldfield b Ironmonger | 4 |
| S. H. Curnow c Oldfield b Nash | 3 | – c Fingleton b Ironmonger | 16 |
| J. A. J. Christy c Grimmett b Nash | 4 | – c and b Nash | 0 |
| H. W. Taylor c Kippax b Nash | 0 | – c Bradman b Ironmonger | 2 |
| K. F. Viljoen c sub. b Ironmonger | 1 | – c Oldfield b O'Reilly | 0 |
| H. B. Cameron c McCabe b Nash | 11 | – c McCabe b O'Reilly | 0 |
| D. P. B. Morkel c Nash b Ironmonger | 1 | – c Rigg b Ironmonger | 0 |
| C. L. Vincent c Nash b Ironmonger | 1 | – not out | 8 |
| Q. McMillan st Oldfield b Ironmonger | 0 | – c Oldfield b Ironmonger | 0 |
| N. A. Quinn not out | 5 | – c Fingleton b Ironmonger | 5 |
| A. J. Bell st Oldfield b Ironmonger | 0 | – c McCabe b O'Reilly | 6 |
| B 2, l-b 3, n-b 3 | 8 | B 3, l-b 1 | 4 |
| | **36** | | **45** |

### Australia

| | | | |
|---|---|---|---|
| W. M. Woodfull b Bell | 0 | C. V. Grimmett c Cameron b Quinn | 9 |
| J. H. Fingleton c Vincent b Bell | 40 | W. J. O'Reilly c Curnow b McMillan | 13 |
| K. E. Rigg c Vincent b Quinn | 22 | H. Ironmonger not out | 0 |
| A. F. Kippax c Curnow b McMillan | 42 | D. G. Bradman absent hurt | 0 |
| S. J. McCabe c Cameron b Bell | 0 | L-b 3 | 3 |
| L. J. Nash b Quinn | 13 | | |
| W. A. Oldfield c Curnow b McMillan | 11 | | **153** |

### Australia Bowling

| | Overs | Mdns | Runs | Wkts | Overs | Mdns | Runs | Wkts |
|---|---|---|---|---|---|---|---|---|
| Ironmonger | 7.2 | 5 | 6 | 5 | 15.3 | 7 | 18 | 6 |
| Nash | 12 | 6 | 18 | 4 | 7 | 4 | 4 | 1 |
| McCabe | 4 | 1 | 4 | 1 | | | | |
| O'Reilly | | | | | 9 | 5 | 19 | 3 |

## South Africa Bowling

|  | Overs | Mdns | Runs | Wkts |
|---|---|---|---|---|
| Bell . . . . . . . . . . . . . . | 16 | — | 52 | 3 |
| Quinn . . . . . . . . . . . | 19.3 | 4 | 29 | 3 |
| Vincent . . . . . . . . . | 11 | 2 | 40 | — |
| McMillan . . . . . . . . | 8 | — | 29 | 3 |

Umpires: G. A. Hele and G. Borwick.

# CRICKET IN SOUTH AFRICA

## WESTERN PROVINCE v GRIQUALAND WEST

Played at Cape Town, December 17, 19, 1921

Griqualand West, 135 and 270 (W. V. Ling, 43 and 83, top scorer in each innings); Western Province, 203 and 204 for four (M. J. Commaille 98 not out. Commaille had another ball or two bowled to him after the winning hit was made, to let him complete his century, and his score was returned at 102 not out in some quarters. But it is difficult to justify this procedure, though a similar thing was done in the case of R. H. Bettington at Eastbourne last year, and the century was allowed to rank). V. Veal had four wickets for 18 in the first innings of Griqualand West, and L. G. Tapscott five for 47 in the first of Western Province. Western Province won by six wickets.

# DEATHS IN 1919-1940

ROBERT ABEL, the old Surrey and England cricketer, died at his home near The Oval on December 10, 1936, in his eightieth year. A great favourite at The Oval, Bobby Abel, popularly known as "The Guv'nor", began his career with Surrey in 1881, and played his last match for the county in 1904, failing eyesight causing him to drop out of the eleven earlier than otherwise he need have done. Born on November 30, 1857, he was 23 when first appearing for his county. Found in club cricket in Southwark Park, he took some time to accustom himself to new surroundings and his early efforts in first-class cricket gave no idea of the skill which he steadily attained. Very keen, he overcame the handicap of being short and, while maturing his form with the bat, he attracted attention by smart fielding, especially at slip.

In his third season with Surrey he advanced rapidly as a batsman and in 1886 against the Australians at The Oval he played a remarkable innings of 144. In 1888 – one of the wettest summers ever experienced – he came out first among the professional batsmen of the year, scoring in first-class matches 1,323 runs with an average of 31. Thenceforward his successful career was interrupted only in 1893 when a serious affection of the eyes interfered with his play. If late in reaching his best, he was right at the top of the tree from 1895 to 1902, scoring over 2,000 runs in first-class matches in eight successive seasons. His highest aggregate of runs, 3,309, was obtained in 1901 and his average in these eight years of conspicuous ability ranged from 56 to 41. In 1903 his eyes troubled him again, and though playing in glasses helped him to some extent next year his first-class career then closed.

His highest innings was 357 not out against Somerset at The Oval in May, 1899; it remains a Surrey record and is second best for any county, A. C. MacLaren's 424, also off Somerset bowlers, at Taunton in 1895, still being unapproached. Besides this great score, Abel played eight innings of more than 200, and nine times in first-class matches he carried his bat through an innings. Among Surrey batsmen he ranks with Hobbs, Hayward, W. W. Read and Harry Jupp.

Extraordinarily successful in Gentlemen and Players matches at The Oval, he scored 168 not out in 1894, 195 in 1899, 153 not out in 1900, and 247 in 1901. This 247 was the biggest score ever obtained in a Gentlemen and Players match until 1925, when Hobbs made 266 at Scarborough. For Players against Gentlemen at Lord's, his highest score was 98 in a memorable match in 1900. Playing first for England against Australia in 1888, he took part in eight Test matches in this country, his best score being 94 at Lord's in 1896.

In the winter of 1887-88 when, owing to what may have been a misunderstanding between Sydney and Melbourne, but at the time was generally regarded as rivalry between the cricket authorities, two English teams visited Australia. Abel went with G. F. Vernon's side and scored 320 runs in eleven-a-side matches, average 24. He was not chosen when the two bands joined forces on the occasion when Peel and Lohmann disposed of Australia for totals of 42 and 82. Abel went to Australia again in 1891-92 when W. G. Grace captained Lord Sheffield's side, and he averaged 38 for the eleven-a-side games. At Sydney, in the second of the three Test matches, he accomplished the remarkable performance of carrying his bat through the first innings for 132 but Australia won the contest in which Alex Bannerman, who batted seven hours and a half for 91, received 204 balls from Attewell and scored off only five. Abel visited South Africa with Major Wharton's team in 1888-89 and scored 1,075, average 48 – more than twice the aggregate and average of any other member of the side.

A batsman of great resource and patience, he rarely if ever carried caution to an extreme and for a man of his small stature he was quite a punishing player. Once at The Oval he performed the rare feat of scoring a hundred runs between twelve o'clock and lunch-time. He and Brockwell enjoyed many big partnerships together for the Surrey first wicket, and against Hampshire at The Oval in August 1897, scored 379 – a record for an opening stand at that time – 265 against Warwickshire at The Oval in September, 1898, 231 against Sussex at The Oval in May, 1897 and 270 (unbroken) against Kent at The Oval in 1900. Other great first-wicket stands in which he shared were 364 with D. L. A. Jephson against Derbyshire at The Oval in 1900, 246 with Tom Hayward against Sussex at Hastings in 1902, and 226 with W. G. Grace for South against North at Scarborough in 1889. The biggest partnership of all in which he participated was one of 448 with Hayward for Surrey's fourth wicket against Yorkshire at The Oval in 1899, Abel scoring 193 and Hayward 273. This is the world's record for the fourth wicket.

Abel drove hard and cut well, but his special strength came in ability to get runs on the on-side. Very few batsmen have excelled him in scoring in front of short leg with brilliant and safe forcing strokes off his legs. Like many little men, he did not keep his bat perfectly straight, but accurate judgment of length of bowling and quickness on his feet compensated for this defect. A very sure field, notably at slip, Abel also bowled slow off breaks skilfully but was not often wanted in the very powerful Surrey attack. Quiet and unassuming in manner, Abel was never spoiled by success. After one of his great days at The Oval, hundreds of his admirers would gather in front of the pavilion and chant "Bob, Bob, Bob," again and again until the "Gov'nor" bowed his acknowledgements.

DR ARTHUR ABRAHAM who died at Whitley Bay, on June 1, 1922, aged 69, was at one time a well-known cricketer in Ireland, playing for Leinster against the South of England, when his resemblance to his twin brother led W. G. Grace to protest against him taking a second innings. He developed into a good wicket-keeper and batsman, and played county cricket for both Durham and Northumberland. In two seasons, also, he took part in the Scarborough Festival.

MR FREDERICK SAMUEL ASHLEY-COOPER, unrivalled as an authority on cricket history, died on January 31, 1932, at his home at Milford, Surrey. He was born in London on March 2, 1877, and so had not quite completed his 55th year.

From his earliest days he was troubled with poor health and consequently did not follow any profession and yet his unvarying researches and his literary output involved an amount of labour which might well have deterred the most robust of men. His enthusiasm, however, carried him through from these early days when, helped by his friend H. T. Waghorn, an officer of the Reading Room at the British Museum, he spent several years going through, in his search for cricket matter, the newspapers and magazines printed up to the year of 1830.

In this devotion to the history of the game, he was in the succession of the Rev. James Pycroft who, born in 1813, was author of *The Cricket Field* and of Mr Arthur Haygarth (born in 1825) the compiler of that wonderful work *Scores and Biographies*.

Such was Ashley-Cooper's amazing energy that altogether he brought out 103 books and pamphlets on the game dealing with cricket in England, Australia, South Africa, New Zealand, India and other places, besides a very large amount of matter including 40,000 biographical and obituary notices, every production of his pen, moreover, being characterised by phenomenal accuracy to secure which he spared neither time nor trouble.

Among his works were two brought out in conjunction with Lord Harris, *Lord's and the MCC* (dedicated to King George) and *Kent Cricket Matches 1719-1880* and one with P. F. Warner *Oxford and Cambridge at the Wicket*. Other products of his pen were *Cricket Highways and Byways, Curiosities of First-Class Cricket, Eton and Harrow at the Wicket, Gentlemen v Players, E. M. Grace, Cricketer. W. G. Grace, Cricketer, Hambledon Cricket Chronicle*, a new edition of Pycroft's *Cricket Field*, and *Scores and Biographies, Volume 15*, this last being a monumental piece of biography based in the first place upon notes left by Mr Arthur Haygarth and by innumerable additions brought up to date.

Mr Ashley-Cooper edited the newspaper, *Cricket* for five years and in 1920 he held the Secretaryship of the Nottinghamshire County Cricket Club.

He was responsible for more than thirty years for "Births and Deaths" and "Cricket Records" in *Wisden*, which latter section of the Almanack had grown from two pages in 1887 to sixty-one pages in last year's edition.

In the course of his career he had gathered a unique collection of cricket books and pictures. For this fortunately he found in Sir Julien Cahn a purchaser a month or two before he died so the splendid library was not dispersed.

Early in 1931, Ashley-Cooper took a trip to the West Indies but derived no benefit from the voyage. Indeed, his health became worse and his sight failed so badly that in the autumn he had to abandon all work. A most modest and kindly man, he was always ready to give from his wonderful store of cricket history to anyone who asked his help and grudged no time spent in satisfying such requests.

To those associated in the production of *Wisden's Almanack* the passing of Ashley-Cooper is naturally felt as a personal loss. Year by year he had spared no endeavour to make the list of "Births and Deaths" as complete as possible, conducting an enormous correspondence on the subject and searching the columns of practically every paper he could obtain to bring his information up to date and to eliminate any error. Equally zealous was he in his pursuit of any happening in the game of sufficient importance to be included in "Cricket Records". All this labour he performed with a measure of enthusiasm which never flagged even when the shadows were gathering and he knew his days were numbered. Such devotion as his to the game of cricket could not have been surpassed. It should be recognised by the powers that be in the making of arrangements such as will ensure the enlightened continuance of his life's work.

HENRY ("HARRY") BAGSHAW, born at Foolow, Tideswell, Derbyshire, on September 1, 1861, died at Crowden, near Glossop, on January 31, 1927, aged 65, and was buried in his umpire's coat and with a cricket ball in his hand. He was a free-hitting batsman well above the average, a medium-paced bowler and a hard-working field in the slips: in batting he was left-handed, but in the other departments of the game right-handed. His first match for Derbyshire, though he had appeared for the colts seven years earlier, was in 1887, and his last in 1902. Among his many good scores may be mentioned 96 and 90 not out v Essex at Derby in 1893; 127 not out v Yorkshire on the same ground in 1895; 121 v Leicestershire and 115 v Yorkshire, both at Derby, in 1896; 124 v Leicestershire at Derby, 114 not out v Surrey at The Oval, and 105 v Hampshire at Southampton, all in 1897; and 100 not out v Yorkshire at Harrogate in 1898. In 1900 he took five wickets for 27 runs v Hampshire at Southampton and four for 16 v Warwickshire at Glossop. For many years – until the end of 1923 – he was an umpire in great matches. Whilst engaged by the Barnsley CC he scored 220 against Crofton Wanderers in August, 1888, and took all ten wickets in an innings against Wakefield in 1891.

RICHARD BARBER, who was found dead in a railway-carriage at Cookham Station on June 13, 1924, whilst on his way to umpire in a match at Shoeburyness, was born at Hedsor, Buckinghamshire, on August 2.

SIR JAMES MATTHEW BARRIE, Bart., OM, who died on June 19, 1937, constantly referred in his writings and speeches to cricket. He was in the eleven of the Authors Club who met the Press Club at Lord's in September 1896. In the Press Club eleven were H. Vincent Jones, Hubert Preston and S. J. Southerton, all associated for many years with the production of *Wisden*.

MR CHARLES WILLIAM BEAL, who died at Randwick, Sydney, on February 5, 1921, aged 65, was manager of the Australian teams of 1882 and 1888. He was captain of the eleven whilst at Sydney Grammar School, and nephew of Mr J. Beal who played in

1856, in the first of the long series of matches between New South Wales and Victoria. Mr Beal made many friends during his two trips to England, being genial and sociable to a degree. He was extremely proud of being associated with the great team of 1882. As manager in 1888 he had to face a very awkward crisis. It was largely due to his tact that the nature of S. P. Jones's illness was so carefully kept secret. Had it become known that Jones was suffering from small-pox the tour might have been nearly ruined.

MR BERNHARD W. BENTINCK, who died on June 27, 1931, aged 53, appeared for Hampshire in 1900 and for some time was President of the Hampshire Hogs CC. Educated at Winchester, he possessed fine driving powers. Playing for Alton in August 1921, he had the unusual experience of being bowled by a ball (delivered by H. E. Roberts, the Sussex professional) which was deflected on to the wicket through striking and killing a swallow. Mr Bentinck had been a member of MCC for thirty years.

MR SAM BIRCHAM, who died at Yarrowfield, Mayford, Surrey, on June 4, 1923, aged 84, had been Auditor to the MCC for many years, and a member of the Club since 1869. His intimate acquaintance with Parliamentary and Private Bill procedure enabled him, with the late Lord James of Hereford, to procure for the MCC immense and lasting advantages when it seemed possible that Lord's ground might be encroached upon by covetous railway promoters.

MR WILLIAM HENRY BRAIN, a sound batsman and first-class wicket-keeper, died on November 20, 1934. Born at Clifton, near Bristol, on July 21, 1870, he played in the Clifton College eleven of 1887 and two following years, being captain in 1889. He got his Oxford Blue in 1891, and in 1893 distinguished himself in the Lord's match by catching five Cambridge men at the wicket. Mr Brain turned out for Gloucestershire in that year but the following season he appeared for Glamorgan under the residential qualification. In 1893, when Somerset's second innings was finished with a hat trick by C. L. Townsend, he accomplished the rare feat of stumping three men off consecutive balls. His highest score in an important match was 65 not out for MCC and Ground against Somerset at Taunton in 1891. He did much to help promote Glamorgan to first-class status, and one of his sons. Capt. J. H. P. Brain, played for them. W. H. Brain kept goal for Oxford at Association football.

MR ARTHUR JAMES BUSH, born July 28, 1850, died on September 21, 1924. Mr Bush, who had been in failing health for some little time before his death, will always have a distinct place in cricket history. He was the Gloucestershire wicket-keeper in those far-off days in the 1870's, when the county had its golden time and for two seasons at least – 1876 and 1877 – stood far ahead of all rivals. I often wonder what the class of club cricket in and around Bristol must have been that the Graces, immediately after the formation of the county club, could find such first rate material ready to their hands. Mr Bush was only one of many who at once enrolled themselves under W.G.'s banner. He went right through the great days – Gloucestershire never lost a match at home till the first Australian eleven beat them at Clifton in 1878 – and held his post for long afterwards, playing less and less as time went on and finally dropping out of the team after the season of 1890. He went to Australia with W. G. Grace's eleven in 1873-74 and, quoting W.G. "It was the general opinion of the team that no wicket-keeper alive could have done better or stood the wear and tear of the task so well." In 1874 and 1875 Mr Bush kept wicket for Gentlemen v Players at Lord's and would very likely have been picked in later years but in 1876 Alfred Lyttelton appeared on the scene. In this connection it is interesting to recall the fact that Mr Bush was the wicket-keeper when the Gentlemen beat the Australians at Prince's in 1878. He was a wonderfully safe catch whatever the pace of the bowling. Though originally chosen for Gloucestershire on account of his batting and fielding Mr Bush – at any rate in first class company – had no pretensions as a batsman. Still, if he had not struck in against Yorkshire at Cheltenham in 1876 W.G.'s famous innings would have fallen short of 318 not out. In his young days Mr Bush was a rugby international.

S. H. P.

WILLIAM CAFFYN. Many cricket memories were revived by the announcement that the veteran Surrey player, William Caffyn, died at his home, at Reigate, on Thursday, August 28, 1919. Born on February 2, 1828, he had lived to the great age of 91. His fame rests mainly on the fact that he was the best all-round man in the Surrey eleven that, with the late F. P. Miller as captain, used to meet – and twice beat – the full strength of England at The Oval. Of that brilliant band the one survivor now left is Mr E. Dowson – only ten years Caffyn's junior, but quite hale and hearty. Many other amateurs who played with Caffyn in his prime are still living, but of the great professionals who used to make the match at Lord's between the All England and United Elevens one of the events of the season, only George Wootton, the Nottinghamshire bowler, remains with us.

Caffyn played his first match for Surrey in 1849, and in the following year – there were very few county fixtures in those days – he headed the batting. From that time he never looked back, becoming more and more prominent as the fame of Surrey cricket grew. He was the leading bowler in the team, as well as the finest batsman. About 1857 he reached his highest point, and right on to 1863 his powers showed no decline. Then came the end of his real career in English cricket. In the autumn of 1863 he paid his second visit to Australia as a member of George Parr's team – he had gone out two years before with H. H. Stephenson's side – and at the close of the tour he stayed behind in the colonies, accepting a position as coach. While in Australia he played in inter-colonial matches, but though he did much to develop young talent he scarcely, judging from the scores, added to his own reputation. He was back in England in 1872, and played several times for Surrey that year and in 1873, but it was too late to start over again. His day was done, and, though Surrey were far from strong, he could not keep his place in the eleven. His long stay in Australia lost him the chance of a benefit match at The Oval, but to the end of his life the Surrey club paid him an annuity of £39.

On the evidence of all who played side by side with him in his great days, Caffyn was a very fine batsman, free and attractive in style and master of a cut that only Tom Humphrey surpassed in brilliancy. Had he lived in these days he would no doubt have made big scores, for he needed a good wicket. The Oval and Fenner's at Cambridge were the grounds that suited him best. On the rough wickets at Lord's he was admittedly far inferior to George Parr, Carpenter, Richard Daft, and the first Tom Hayward. Still even at Lord's against Jackson he was on two occasions seen at his best. As regards his bowling, one is rather doubtful. Right hand medium pace, he belonged to the purely round arm school – he had just settled in Australia when the law was altered – and modern wickets would very likely have been too good for him. Still on the best wickets of his own time he did wonderful things for Surrey and the United All-England Eleven. As an all-round fieldsman he had scarcely a superior.

S. H. P.

Lord Cobham – the Hon. C. G. Lyttelton in his cricket days, and incidentally one of the most brilliant batsmen in England – who played several times against Caffyn in Gentlemen v Players matches, and also in matches between Cambridge University and Surrey, has very kindly sent the following notes on the veteran as he knew him:

"My recollections of Caffyn date back sixty years, when I was captain of the Eton Eleven and Caffyn was our "coach" for a few weeks. He was rather a small man, well and compactly built and very active. I do not think he was a born coach, or that he troubled himself to give much oral instruction, but his bowling, which was slow to medium, straight, and of a good length gave us excellent practice, and much could be learnt from watching his batting which was sound, graceful, and often brilliant.

Until he left England in 1863, Caffyn was always a good man on a side. He never ceased to be a dangerous bat and he was as consistent a scorer as most of his contemporaries. He could hit hard all round, but his most notable hit was his cut, which denoted great strength and flexibility of wrist. I well remember, in a country match, his cutting an over-pitched ball of mine through a big drum, supposed to be at a safe distance from the wicket. It was said that when facing the great Jackson at Lord's, he was apt to show some "softness" and want of nerve, but then Jackson on a characteristic Lord's wicket was a "terror" such as is never seen in these days. Once, at all events, in the 1857 North and South match at Lord's, Caffyn made 90 against Jackson, which long ranked amongst historical innings, with those of R. Hankey, C. G. Lane and others.

Caffyn was a good bowler, but never I think quite in the first rank. His bowling had no cunning or "devil" in it and on present day wickets it could probably be "pulled" or "hooked" without much difficulty. Nevertheless he took plenty of wickets, and runs did not come easily or rapidly from him, as his analysis shows. He was a good and active field.

At Eton, and as long as I played cricket with him, I always thought of Caffyn as a well-mannered man and pleasant to deal with, and this impression seems to me to be borne out by his book – *71 Not Out* – which is written in a modest and kindly spirit, free from jealousy or depreciation of others."

Mr E. Dowson, now, as already stated, the only survivor of F. P. Miller's famous Surrey eleven, writes:

"He was a neat, good-looking, dapper little man. As regards his bowling he bowled a medium pace ball, not difficult to look at, but he nearly always obtained his share of wickets. Curiously enough we were always glad when he had a good innings, as the more runs he made the better he bowled. His batting was always worth watching as he could hit all round, and his cutting was brilliant, expecially balls off the bails. He used to get hundreds, which were very few in those days. In my opinion he would have been one of the first chosen in a Test match. He also was a good field. I must relate one case when he was really frightened. In a match v Yorkshire at Sheffield a storm came on which deluged the ground. The captains, Mr F. P. Miller and Mr W. Prest, both agreed that there could be no more cricket. Poor Caffyn had dressed and got out of the ground when some of the roughs brought him back with his bag, swearing they were not going to be done out of seeing more cricket as they had paid their 3d. Chaffing then commenced and we said we were not afraid to go on. They gathered round Mr Prest, saying "Are you not ashamed of yourself?" He replied "Yes, that I was born here and amongst such a lot!" The wickets were again pitched and I should imagine never on a wetter ground. The water spluttered in your face as you fielded the ball. However, Mr Prest was so angry that he came in and won the match himself, hitting the bowling all over the place."

Mr Herbert C. Troughton writes:

"I saw Caffyn pretty frequently during the years 1859-1863. I thought him an extremely brilliant bat. He had not the defence of Carpenter or Hayward, but he was, in my opinion, far more interesting to watch, as when he made runs, he always made them quickly; he – at least whenever I saw him – acted upon what is supposed to have been the immortal Yardley's maxim – "Get runs or get out". He was rather impetuous and was apt to get himself out by adopting hitting tactics before he had got set. Caffyn had many strokes, and all of them stylish. With perhaps the exception of Lord Cobham, better known as the Hon. C. G. Lyttelton, he was the hardest cutter I have ever seen, and his hitting to deep square leg was brilliant in the extreme. His driving powers, too, especially to the on were quite out of the common, and he had one stroke which he and W. Mortlock alone, so far as I remember, have ever regularly put in force – a huge hit between deep square leg and long on, rather nearer long-on than square leg, a stroke that earned him hundreds of runs. As a bowler he was most excellent and did many brilliant things. He seemed to love bowling, and when he did not go on first, his joy, when he was put on, was unmistakable. He had an easy and very graceful delivery, and could bowl equally well, either round or over the wicket. If the wicket gave him ever so little help he could be deadly in the extreme. He generally failed at Lord's, where Jackson's expresses were not to his liking. Indeed though I saw him at Lord's in some eight matches I can only remember his coming off in one match and that was for South v North in 1861 when he played a beautiful first innings of 65, and supplemented this with an excellent 25 in his second innings, Jackson's bowling, for once at Lord's, having no terrors for him."

## WILLIAM CAFFYN'S CAREER FIGURES

| For | BATTING | | | | | BOWLING | | |
|-----|---------|------|------|---------|---------|------|---------|---------|
| | Innings | Not Outs | Runs | Highest Innings | Average | Runs | Wickets | Average |
| Surrey | 180 | 16 | 3,656 | 157 | 23.18 | { 5,230 | 422 | 12.39 |
| | | | | | | — | 15 | — |
| Players | 27 | 1 | 288 | 48 | 11.07 | 464 | 25 | 18.56 |
| AEE | 191 | 13 | 2,125 | 88 | 11.93 | — | 208 | — |
| UAEE | 191 | 7 | 2,585 | 124 | 14.04 | — | 671 | — |
| NSW (v Victoria) | 9 | — | 114 | 38 | 12.66 | 77 | 2 | 38.50 |

## CHIEF SCORES

73   Surrey v Sussex, at The Oval, 1850
55   England v Kent, at Canterbury, 1853
52   Surrey v Sussex, at Brighton, 1854
57   Surrey v Nottinghamshire, at Nottingham, 1854
52   Surrey v England, at The Oval, 1855
60   Kent and Surrey v England, at Canterbury, 1855
88   Surrey v Sussex, at The Oval, 1856
50   United England XI v Earl of Stamford's XXII, at Enville Hall, 1856
87   Players Engaged at Oxford v Oxford University, at Oxford, 1857
66*   MCC and Ground v Sussex, at Lord's, 1857
60   Surrey v The North, at The Oval, 1857
90   South v The North, at Lord's, 1857
81   Surrey v Kent and Sussex, at Brighton, 1858
59   Surrey v Kent and Sussex, at The Oval, 1858
102   Surrey v England, at The Oval, 1858
157   Surrey v Cambridge University XVI, at Cambridge, 1859
76   Surrey v Nottinghamshire, at The Oval, 1859
124   United England XI v John Walker's Southgate XVI (with Slinn) at Southgate, 1859
73   Surrey v Sussex, at The Oval, 1860
91   Surrey v Nottinghamshire, at Nottingham, 1860
55   South v North, at Rochdale, 1860
103   Surrey v Cambridgeshire, at Cambridge, 1861
65   South v North, at Lord's, 1861
98   Surrey v North, at The Oval, 1861
58   Surrey v England, at The Oval, 1861
63   United England XI v All England XI, at The Oval, 1861
79   England v Victoria XVIII, Melbourne, 1861-62
75*   Surrey v The World, at Melbourne, 1861-62
57*   Surrey v Kent, at The Oval, 1862

50　Surrey v Cambridgeshire, at The Oval, 1862
63　England v Kent XIV, at Canterbury, 1862
70　Surrey v Kent, at Tunbridge Wells, 1863

Also made 104 for United England XI v XXII of Bedfordshire, at Luton in 1856.

　\* *Signifies not out.*

## BOWLING PERFORMANCES

### Eight or More Wickets in an Innings

8-24　　United England XI v Cambridge University XVI, at Lord's, 1857
9-29　　Surrey and Sussex v England, at The Oval, 1857
16-24　England v United States XXII, at Hoboken, 1859
9-31　　Surrey v Cambridge University XVI, at The Oval, 1860
8-30　　England v Oxford University XVI, at Lord's, 1860
8-28　　United England XI v J. Walker's Southgate XVI, at Southgate, 1860
8-33　　Players v Oxford and Cambridge XVI, at Lord's, 1861
8-38　　England v Kent XIV, at Canterbury, 1861
8-72　　Surrey v Oxford University XV, at The Oval, 1862
8-25　　Surrey v Yorkshire, at Sheffield, 1862
$\left.\begin{array}{l} 9\text{-}43a \\ 12\text{-}83b \end{array}\right\}$ United England XI v Hampshire XXII, at Winchester, 1862
8-44　　Surrey v Hampshire XIV, at Southampton, 1863.

### Thirteen or More Wickets in a Match

15-54　Surrey v Cambridge University XVI, at The Oval, 1860
13-52　England v NSW and Victoria XXII, at Sydney, 1861-62
13-49　Surrey v Kent, at Canterbury, 1862.

### Four Wickets or More for Three Runs or Less Each

$\left.\begin{array}{l} 7\text{-}1b \\ 9\text{-}25c \end{array}\right\}$ United England XI v XVIII of Ireland, at Phoenix Park, 1856
$\left.\begin{array}{l} 7\text{-}19b \\ 9\text{-}25c \end{array}\right\}$ Surrey v Cambridgeshire, at Cambridge, 1857
8-24　　United England XI v Cambridge University XVI, at Lord's, 1857
5-14　　Surrey v Sussex, at The Oval, 1857
16-24　England v United States XXII, at Hoboken, 1859
7-21　　Surrey v Nottinghamshire, at Nottingham, 1861
6-16　　England v NSW and Victoria XXII, at Sydney, 1861-62
5-15　　Surrey v Yorkshire, at The Oval, 1862
7-7　　Surrey v Kent, at Canterbury, 1862
5-11　　England v NSW XXII, at Sydney, 1863-64.

　　　　　　　*a* signifies first innings.　　　*b* second.　　　*c* both.

### Bowling Unchanged Through Both Completed Innings

with Griffith, for Surrey v Sussex, at The Oval, 1857
with Griffith, for Surrey v The North, at Sheffield, 1857
with Stephenson (H. H.), Surrey County and Ground v MCC and Ground, at The Oval, 1859
with Atkinson, for United England XI v The England XI, at Lord's, 1859
with Hayward, for Anderson's XI v Parr's XI, at Christchurch, 1863-64.

**Various Performances**

Three wickets in 4 balls, Surrey v Oxford University XVI, at The Oval, 1860
For the United England XI Caffyn took 119 wickets in 1857 and 124 in 1858
For the All England XI he obtained 102 wickets in 1854.

Caffyn visited America in 1859 and Australia in 1861-62, and 1863-64.

Whilst engaged at Winchester in 1860 he played a single-wicket match, on June 25, single-handed against eleven of the Town of Winchester. He had two men to field for him and won by 28 runs. The scores were 35 and 1 against 4 and 4. The match is recorded in *Scores and Biographies*, VI, 399.

During his residence in Australia he took part in two great single-wicket matches for New South Wales against Victoria – at Melbourne, in December, 1865, and on the Albert Ground, Sydney, in April, 1869 – but was on the losing side each time, Victoria winning the first game by 19 runs and the second by a wicket.

MR WALTER FREDERICK CAVE, who died on January 7, 1939, aged 75, was in the Eton eleven of 1880 and two following seasons. He played his best innings, 49, on his last appearance against Harrow. In 1883 he appeared a few times in the Gloucestershire eleven, his highest score being 42 against Surrey at The Oval. A good defensive batsman he was strong in off-side strokes. In the field he showed special smartness at long-leg. An architect of distinction, he designed many notable buildings, especially some for music, and was credited with the idea of placing candle holders on pianos. A good athlete, he won the hundred yards race and other events at Eton.

MR TOM COLLINS, the oldest living cricket Blue, died on March 16, 1934, at his home at Newport, Salop, in his 94th year. Born on January 31, 1841, at Warwick, for which constituency his grandfather was Member of Parliament, Tom Collins went at an early age to Bury St Edmunds, and from King Edward the Sixth School he gained an open scholarship at Christ College, Cambridge in 1859. He became Headmaster of Newport Grammar School, Salop, in 1871 and occupied the position for thirty-two years until his retirement. When an assistant master at King Edward School, Birmingham, Mr Collins became a barrister of the Middle Temple in 1866 but he did not practise at the Bar.

In the cricket field Mr Collins was remembered best for the part he took, inadvertently, in bringing about the alteration in Law Ten, which until June, 1864, prevented a bowler from delivering the ball from above the height of his shoulder. In 1862 Edgar Willsher, when playing for England against Surrey at The Oval, was no-balled six times consecutively by John Lillywhite for having his hand above the shoulder at the moment of delivery. On the same ground a year later Tom Collins and Mr H. M. Plowden, who subsequently became a famous metropolitan magistrate, disposed of Surrey for 99 runs, and so took a prominent part in Cambridge beating the very powerful Surrey eleven.

Directly after this came the university match at Lord's and on a wet pitch Cambridge, thanks to Plowden and Collins, gained a lead on the first innings of 6 runs with a total of 65. Collins disposed of such famous batsmen as R. D. Walker and R. A. H. Mitchell early in the innings, and then, to everyone's astonishment, he was no-balled five times in succession. The occurrence was influenced by an instruction just issued directing umpires to attend particularly to the height of the bowler's hand. Collins was so upset that he did not get another wicket and failed with the bat, being dismissed for nought and one. Oxford, set to get 68, won comfortably by eight wickets. Collins regarded his bad luck on his only appearance for Cambridge against Oxford as a distinct misfortune which he did not deserve to undergo. Still, his experience helped to make cricket history; his being "called" went a long way towards the removal of all restrictions as to the height from which a bowler delivered the ball.

Tom Collins played for Suffolk county from 1862 to 1869. Over six feet in height, of powerful build and dark complexion, he was a conspicuous figure on the field. About medium pace, with swerve and spin from leg, he accomplished many notable performances in those days of low scoring. In addition to his ability as an all-round cricketer he was a fine player at billiards, representing Cambridge against Oxford both in the singles and doubles matches.

Early in 1933, he received the very rare distinction of being elected to honorary membership of the MCC in recognition of his being the oldest living cricket Blue. This seniority now belongs to the Rev. A. H. Winter of Westminster School and Cambridge who was born on December 4, 1844 and played against Oxford in 1865, 1866 and 1867.

MR CHARLES FREDERICK CARLOS CLARKE, born at Welton, Northampton-shire, on April 26, 1853, died at Sunninghill on January 29, 1931. He was one of the oldest members of I Zingari, the Free Foresters and MCC. He started the Silwood Park Cricket Club which numbered among its players R. E. Foster, H. K. Foster, B. J. T. Bosanquet and Aubrey Faulkner and was one of the very few cricket clubs which always used white stumps. Mr Clarke played for Surrey between 1873 and 1882 and for Berkshire but he was more attracted by the brighter atmosphere of country house and club cricket. Closely associated with the Canterbury week and the famous band of amateur actors – the Old Stagers – he was an accomplished actor and musician. A good batsman, wicket-keeper and a first-rate field, he scored 65 for Gentlemen of England v Oxford University at Oxford in 1883 and in the same season 63 for MCC v Kent at Canterbury. A keen all-round sportsman, he had hunted with 33 different packs of hounds.

MR FRANK CARROLL COBDEN, who died at Capel Curig, North Wales, on December 7, 1932, was the hero of perhaps the most sensational piece of bowling in the history of cricket.

In the Oxford and Cambridge match of 1870, Oxford, set 179 runs to win, had made 175 for the loss of seven batsmen and thus, with three wickets to fall, wanted only 4 runs for victory when Cobden began the over which will be for ever memorable. The first ball was hit by F. H. Hill for a single, the stroke being one which would certainly have sent the ball to the boundary had it not been brilliantly fielded by mid-wicket – as to whether this was mid-off or mid-on even those taking part in the match differ. S. E. Butler was caught off the second ball, T. H. Belcher bowled by the third, and W. A. Stewart by the fourth, with the result that Cambridge snatched an extraordinary victory by 2 runs.

Born at Lambley, Nottinghamshire, on October 14, 1849, Mr Cobden was in the Harrow XI in 1866, and in the match against Eton, which Harrow won by an innings and 136 runs, he took five wickets for 37 and three for 10, or eight wickets in all for 47 runs. In the same match, W. B. Money (Harrow), afterwards captain at Cambridge, in the year Cobden accomplished his memorable bowling feat, performed the "hat trick". Included in the Eton eleven on that occasion was C. I. Thornton, the famous hitter, who in the first innings scored 46 not out. Before going to Harrow in 1864, Cobden was at Brighton College (1860-1863) and at Highgate School (1863-1864). He left school early, and going up to Trinity College, Cambridge, was given his Blue in 1870 and in the two following years taking, on the occasion of his great triumph, eight wickets for 76 runs. He was an excellent fast round-arm bowler and very straight, spoken of 60 years ago as "one of the best who has appeared in any eleven" and described as being a better bowler at school than at any time afterwards. He stood nearly 6ft high, and weighed 12st. He generally fielded at mid-on, and was a free and powerful hitter.

REV. JOHN CHARLES CRAWFORD, MA, died at Wimbledon on February 21, 1935, aged 85. Born on May 29, 1849 at Hastings, he was the oldest surviving member of a remarkable cricketing and athletic family. "Parson" Crawford, as he was always called when well known as a cricketer, played occasionally for Kent from 1872 to 1877 and for Leicestershire in 1878; also for Gentlemen of Sussex and Gentlemen of Surrey, and for Surrey second eleven; but he never appeared for the county. Large-framed and powerfully built, he could bowl very fast right hand or slow left. It is on record that Willsher, the famous umpire, said that Crawford was the fastest bowler he had ever seen. In a match at Dunkirk in 1867 he sent one bail 51 yards and the other 49 yards. He hit very hard and against weak bowling would sometimes bat left-handed, particularly in club cricket in which he was a familiar figure around London for many years. He loved the game so much that all his children played from an early age. More than once a team of eleven Crawfords, including grandfather, his two sons, the Parson's two sons, daughters and a nephew took the field. One of the oldest and most respected members both of the MCC and of the Surrey club, he had numberless friends both at Lord's and The Oval, where he was constantly in the pavilion watching cricket very late in life.

His father, who lived to the age of 101, played for Gentlemen of England in the days when cricketers wore top hats. His brother, Major F. F. Crawford, who died in the South African War, captained Kent in the early seventies and played for MCC in South Africa, India and elsewhere. Parson Crawford was the father of R. T., J. N. and the late V. F. S. Crawford, all of whom played first-class cricket with distinction. J. C. Crawford took his degree from University College, Oxford, and for 36 years was chaplain to Cane Hill Mental Hospital in Surrey.

**MR VIVIAN FRANK SHERGOLD CRAWFORD**, died on August 21, 1922, at the age of forty-three. He was born on April 11, 1879. Coming out for Surrey in 1898 he took part in twelve matches, his best scores being 73 against Gloucestershire and 83 against Oxford University – both at The Oval. His first hundred for Surrey was 129 against Somerset at The Oval in 1899. In June that year he put his knee out at Chesterfield and could play no more for Surrey during the season. He was appointed secretary to Leicestershire in 1903 and having a birth qualification for the county was able to step into the eleven at once. At The Oval in 1909 he hit up a score of 172 against Surrey, and in the following season he finished with county cricket. For some years before the war he was living in Ceylon. He died, after two or three days' illness, from pneumonia, the war having left him with a much-impaired constitution.

Mr D. L. A. Jephson has written the following tribute to his old colleague in the Surrey eleven: To those of us who love the clean, straight bat, the full-faced drive, the low, clean, golf-tinged shot, or the shoulder swing that cleared the ground, minimum of effort, maximum of accomplishment, his passing in the very prime of manhood, came as a blow delivered in the face. From his earliest school days he showed a wonderful aptitude for the game, in all its branches, though as quite a youngster his bowling overshadowed his batting – he was always a splendid field. Educated at Whitgift Grammar School he was for years the brain and backbone of their cricket side. It is impossible here for me to give a full list of his astonishing performances. These can be found in *Wisden's Note Book* for 1900, and strangely pleasant is the reading of them to those of us who knew him. To those who did not, their perusal must be a continual source of surprise at the startling success of so young a player.

In 1895 he made 1,780 runs and took 200 wickets. Playing for Richmond and District v Surrey he took eight wickets for 35 in seventeen overs, his victims being Abel, Lockwood, Holland, Ayres, Thompson, Mills, Clarke, and Richardson. In his second innings he made 25 out of 48 for eight wickets down. In 1896 he scored 218 before lunch, for the Young Amateurs v Young Professionals at The Oval – 218 out of a total of 296, the sort of innings many of us would tramp long, weary miles to see. For years I had the privilege of playing on his side; I played with him in club games and I played with him for Surrey. As a batsman Frank Crawford possessed many strokes, he was strictly orthodox in all his methods of attack or defence, and the straightness of his bat was a thing to marvel at, considering the wonderful power behind what seemed, and was, an effortless stroke. He will go down to posterity as one of the greatest straight-drivers the game has known: at any rate this is the opinion of players like Ranjitsinhji, C. B. Fry and G. W. Beldam. He was esentially a scientific hitter not a slogger. Here are a few of the many memories that are always with me of Frank Crawford at his best.

In his prime he was the personification of athleticism at its zenith. I shall never forget at Bradford once when Surrey had lost five wickets for 30, he made a lightning hundred against Hirst and Rhodes, then in the heyday of their fame. The football pavilion at Bradford is opposite the cricket pavilion; its two ends are ornamented with flagstaffs and it has a slate roof. Crawford hit six 6s – the right-hand flagstaff was struck, and the ball rebounded twenty yards into play. An over afterwards, and the left-hand staff returned the compliment, and on two occasions the slates went upwards in a cloud of dust. And there was one fierce low drive, off Wilfred Rhodes, that Denton, great outfield that he was, would not touch; it laid out a parson first hop.

Again, at Bristol I saw him carry the pavilion. We were all seated on the top of the old-time structure – Paish was bowling, Champain, the old Oxford Blue, was in the outfield on the edge of the cinder track. Crawford took one step and the ball soared upwards. "He's out", I cried, and we watched Champain; there was so little fuss about the shot. Out, not a bit of it – it cleared Champain, it cleared the track, it sailed twenty yards over our heads on the top of the pavilion, to fall nearly 170 yards from the crease. It was the greatest drive I have ever seen. I watched him make a hundred against Lancashire at The Oval, in less than an hour: at fifty he was caught by E. M. Dowson on the top of the ladies' pavilion, and before he was out he had planted Mold, at his fastest, into the football stand from a wicket well to the right of the members' enclosure. Space forbids me to tell many an anecdote I should love to tell, many an innings of his that would well bear allusion, but in conclusion I will say this, that I have seen and appreciated the punching of C. I. Thornton, the firm-footed fireworks of J. J. Lyons, and the wonderful hitting of Gilbert Jessop, whirling a leviathan weapon; but I have never seen a drive to the rails, a drive over the rails, or a drive that cleared the pavilion equal to the driving of Frank Crawford; he never "drove furiously", but he drove uncommonly straight! His physical equipment was magnificent, his heart was in the right place and he played the game in the great spirit – the spirit that strives not for itself but for the side.

MR ARTHUR CAPEL MOLYNEUX CROOME, born at Stroud, Gloucestershire, on February 21, 1866, died in a nursing-home at Maidenhead on September 11, 1930, aged 64. A good hard-hitting batsman and an energetic field at mid-off, he was in the Wellington eleven in 1883 and 1884, played for Oxford against Cambridge in 1888 and 1889, and appeared for Gloucestershire between 1885 and 1892, and for Berkshire from 1895 until 1901, being captain of the last-mentioned side 1895-1900. Among his good innings in first-class cricket were 81 for Oxford v MCC at Lord's in 1889, 71 for Gloucestershire v Lancashire at Clifton in 1890, and 66 for Past and Present of Oxford v Australians at Leyton in 1888. Whilst fielding against Lancashire at Manchester in 1887, he impaled himself on the railings; one of the points entered his neck, and for some time his life hung in the balance, but after a severe illness he regained his health. His highest score for Berkshire was 158 v Hertfordshire at St Albans in 1897. In September, 1890, he made 120 in thirty-seven minutes for A. S. Winterbotham's XI at Thornbury. As a golfer, hurdler and skater he gained many honours, and he took part in the inter-university sports from 1886 to 1889 inclusive, winning the hurdle race in 16.4 seconds in 1886 and being second in the same event two years later. For many years, from 1889 onwards, he was an assistant-master at Radley College but later on became an author and journalist by profession.

MR JOHN WILLIAM HENRY TYLER DOUGLAS, born at Clapton, Middlesex on September 3, 1882, was drowned on December 18, 1930, in a collision which occurred in the Cattegat between the steamships "Oberon" and "Arcturus". Together with his father, Mr J. H. Douglas, Mr Douglas, when the accident occurred, was a passenger on the "Oberon" returning to England from a business trip.

Johnny Douglas, as he was known in nearly every country where cricket is played, had a remarkable career. He was not only a fine cricketer but an even greater boxer and he attained some fame at Association football, appearing for the Corinthians and the Casuals and gaining an AFA international cap. While it was as a cricketer that he made his name a household word in so many parts of the world, he came to the front as a boxer when still at Felsted by his doings in the public schools' championship. Later on, as he developed physically, he reached the highest class as a middle-weight and in 1905 won the amateur championship while in 1908 he carried off the Olympic middle-weight championship by beating in a memorable encounter the Australian "Snowy" Baker. So level were the men at the end of three rounds that neither judges nor referee could arrive at a decision and after an extra round the margin was of the narrowest.

Douglas learned his early cricket at Moulton Grammar School, Lincolnshire. He was in the Felsted eleven in 1898, 1899, 1900 and 1901 and captain in the last of these years. It is curious, in view of the stolid batsman Douglas became, that when at Felsted he was coached by T. N. Perkins, a notable hitter in his Cambridge days. Douglas first appeared for Essex in 1901 – the year he left school – and had a most disheartening experience in his opening match being bowled in each innings by George Hirst's "swerver" without making a run either time. He saw little of county cricket during the next year or two and for some time afterwards was merely a useful all-round player. By 1908, however, he had thoroughly established his position in the Essex eleven and three years later he showed he had about him the possibilities of an international player. He became captain of Essex in 1911 and continued to hold that post until the close of the season of 1928. In that summer of 1911, he enjoyed a great personal triumph in the Gentlemen and Players match at Lord's, scoring 72 and 22, not out, and taking seven wickets. This performance suggested he was the man for the big occasion and that he often proved in subsequent years. He had been out to New Zealand as a member of the MCC's team in the winter of 1906-07, distinguishing himself there with both bat and ball, and in the autumn of 1907 he had formed one of the side Marylebone sent out to the United States and Canada.

Heavy responsibility was soon thrust upon his shoulders for P. F. Warner, who had been appointed captain of the team which went out to Australia in 1911-12, falling ill after the opening contest, the duties of leadership devolved upon Douglas. The first Test match was lost but, the side enjoying the services of those exceptionally fine bowlers, S. F. Barnes and F. R. Foster, the other four were won and so Douglas returned home with his reputation as a captain established. Strangely enough in the following summer – the season of the Triangular Tournament – when he might well have played for England in all six Tests, Douglas did not get a chance until the last match with Australia. For all that further honours soon fell to him as he was chosen to captain the MCC team in South Africa in 1913-14 when four Test games were won by England and the other drawn. After the war, in the course of which, getting a commission in the Bedfordshire Regiment, he reached the rank of Lieutenant-Colonel, Douglas was appointed captain of the MCC side that visited Australia in 1920-21 and lost all five Test matches. He played for England against Australia in the five Test contests of 1921 – in the first two as captain and in the remainder under the leadership of Tennyson. Finally he accompanied to Australia the team sent out under A. E. R. Gilligan in 1924-25 but played a very small part in that tour. His record in Test match cricket was as follows:

| | Innings | Not Outs | Runs | Highest Innings | Average |
|---|---|---|---|---|---|
| v Australia | 28 | 2 | 696 | 75 | 26.76 |
| v South Africa | 7 | — | 266 | 119 | 38.00 |

Possessed of exceptional defensive skill and inexhaustible patience, Douglas was a batsman very hard to dismiss. Sometimes, so intent was he upon keeping up his wicket, that he carried caution to excess and became tiresome to watch. Indeed, with his rather cramped style and limited number of strokes, he could never be described as an attractive player. Still there could be no question about his ability to face an awkward situation or about the soundness of his methods and, although so chary of investing his play with enterprise, he was able to hit with plenty of power on either side of the wicket. As a bowler he was a much more interesting figure. Distinctly above medium pace, he could keep at work for hours without losing either speed or length and to a new ball he imparted, late in its flight, a very awkward swerve to leg. Always extremely fit, Douglas, even at the end of the hottest and longest day, scarcely knew what fatigue was and, if – strangely enough for a first-rate boxer – by no means quick on his feet in the cricket field, and therefore apt to miss the chance of making a catch, he never spared himself. As to his abilities as a captain on the field, opinions differed and he certainly was more brusque of manner than might be wished in a leader, but eloquent testimony in his favour was always forthcoming from players, professional as well as amateur, who had served under him on tours in other lands. To balance any lack of restraint in expressing his views about a blunder, he possessed that saving grace of humour which enjoyed tales against himself. How thoroughly he realised his limitations was shown by his remark "An optimist is a man who batting with Johnny Douglas, backs up for a run". On one occasion Douglas batted an hour and a half for 8, not out, against Kent at Canterbury but, in so doing, he saved his side from defeat. His highest score was 210, not out, for Essex against Derbyshire at Leyton in 1921. In company with A. E. Knight of Leicestershire, he put on for an England eleven against the Australians at Blackpool in 1909 no fewer than 284 for the first wicket.

Among his many achievements in taking wickets, the following were the most striking:

5 bowled in 8 balls for 0 runs, including hat trick, Essex v Yorkshire, Leyton, 1905
 8-83    Essex v Leicestershire, Southend, 1906
13-155  Essex v Kent, Leyton, 1907
3 in 4 balls, Gentlemen of South v Players of South, Hastings, 1909
13-172  (including 9 for 105), Gentlemen v Players, Lord's, 1914
 6-18    Essex v Sussex, Southend, 1914
Unchanged through both innings with Tremlin for Essex in 1914 v Surrey, Oval, and v Derbyshire, Derby
 8-49    Gentlemen v Players, Lord's, 1919
 8-39    Essex v Derbyshire, Derby, 1920
Hat trick, England v New South Wales, Sydney, 1920-21
14-156  Essex v Worcestershire, Leyton, 1921
14-91   (including 7 for 17), Essex v Hampshire, Bournemouth, 1921
 9-47    Essex v Derbyshire, Leyton, 1921
 8-45    Essex v Gloucestershire, Cheltenham, 1922
4 in 6 balls (including hat trick), Essex v Sussex, Leyton, 1923
13-150  Essex v Somerset, Colchester, 1923
 6-14    Essex v Northamptonshire, Southend, 1923

SIR ARTHUR CONAN DOYLE, MD (Edin.), the well-known author, born at Edinburgh on May 22, 1859, died at Crowborough, Sussex on July 7, 1930, aged 71. Although never a famous cricketer, he could hit hard and bowl slows with a puzzling flight. For MCC v Cambridgeshire at Lord's, in 1899, he took seven wickets for 61 runs, and on the same ground two years later carried out his bat for 32 against Leicestershire, who had Woodcock, Geeson and King to bowl for them. In *The Times* of October 27, 1915, he was the author of an article on "The Greatest of Cricketers. An Appreciation of Dr Grace". (It is said that Shacklock, the former Nottinghamshire player, inspired him with the Christian name of his famous character, Sherlock Holmes, and that of the latter's brother Mycroft was suggested by the Derbyshire cricketers.)

MAJOR REGINALD OWEN EDWARDS, born on October 17, 1881, died at Bishop's Stortford, on November 16, 1925. A great cricket enthusiast Major Edwards went to big matches in any part of the country whenever possible, and had a large circle of intimate friends among county cricketers. A Yorkshireman, he supported the champions zealously without undue prejudice; his chief interests for many years were largely in the south. He played occasionally for Norfolk and Cambridgeshire, and in 1921 for Rest of England v Royal Air Force at Eastbourne. He played for the MCC in Germany in 1922; for Incogniti in Holland, and often captained Surrey Club and Ground in recent seasons. He spent a considerable time in Africa, and years ago found solace during solitary days up country reading *Wisden* to which he frequently contributed. During the war he was gassed badly, and in a later expedition to Southern Russia he lost all his baggage except his set of *Wisden*, which accompanied him on all his travels. Major Edwards never tired of retailing stories of first-class cricketers.

MR DONALD ELIGON, died at Port of Spain, Trinidad, on June 4, 1937, aged 28. After playing for Shannon Cricket Club he joined the Trinidad inter-colonial team in 1934 and quickly became one of the outstanding bowlers in West Indies. Last season he took seven wickets for 63 runs in the second innings against British Guiana, and five for 39 against Grenada. His death was due to blood poisoning caused by a nail in his cricket boot.

MR F. HADFIELD FARTHING, a very capable club cricketer, died from heart failure while taking part in a match at East Dulwich on September 1, 1929. After sending down two overs, in each of which he obtained a wicket, he moved to his place in the slips and there collapsed. Born in Yorkshire on July 30, 1875, he was a well-known and popular journalist, and at the time of his death occupied the post of night editor of the *Daily Express*, to which paper he contributed a weekly article on cricket.

MAJOR GEORGE AUBREY FAULKNER, born at Port Elizabeth on December 17, 1881, died of gas poisoning at the Faulkner School of Cricket, Ltd, on September 10, 1930, at the age of 48. During the South African War and whilst living in Cape Town, he received some coaching from Walter Richards, of Warwickshire, then engaged by Western Province, and later became not only one of the dominating figures in South African cricket but also one of the finest of all-round players. One of the earliest exponents of the googly, he differed from other bowlers of that type because of his ability to send down quite a fast ball, almost a yorker, and when at his best, with faultless length, skill in turning the ball either way and puzzling variation of flight, he proved too much for some of the world's greatest batsmen.

Many will remember his fine bowling at Leeds in 1907 when, playing for South Africa in the second Test match of that series against England, he dismissed six men in the course of eleven overs for 17 runs. His career was full of remarkable performances. In that same season of 1907 he, in all matches for the South Africans, scored 1,288 runs and took 73 wickets. He was probably at his best in 1909-10 when his doings with both bat and ball against the English team were magnificent. When South Africa visited Australia in the season of 1910-11, Faulkner headed the Test match batting averages with 732 runs and an average of 73.20. In all matches during that tour he scored 2,080 runs, taking 60 wickets, and in the Test match at Melbourne he hit a splendid 204. For the team of 1912 he made 1,075 runs and obtained 163 wickets. Although at the beginning of his career, particularly at the time when he first became prominent in South African inter-state cricket in 1906, he was of little value as a batsman, he became as the years passed, almost as great a batsman as he was a bowler. His style rather conveyed the impression of awkwardness and he could not, at any time, be described as a free, forcible bat. Nevertheless, very few men made runs with more assurance than Faulkner, and he was a most difficult batsman to get out. After settling down in England he had a great season in club cricket in Nottinghamshire, making twelve hundreds in scoring 2,868 runs with an average of 84.35, besides taking 218 wickets, including all ten in an innings on two occasions. Still, his finest innings in this country was at Eastbourne in 1921 when by a wonderful 153 against the Australians – up to that point an unbeaten side – he virtually gave victory to A. C. MacLaren's XI. Faulkner was also a first-rate field.

When the time came for him to retire from the game, he gained much distinction as a coach. He followed a theory entirely his own when he established the first cricket school known in London and at the time of his death the school had earned world-wide fame. Faulkner devoted the greater part of his time to the school, though he found opportunity to write many articles on the game. During the European War he served with distinction in Salonika, Egypt and Palestine, gaining the DSO in 1918 and the Order of the Nile.

MR CHARLES RODEN FILGATE, born at Cheltenham on October 16, 1849, died at Northwood, Middlesex, after a prolonged period of ill-health, on September 1, 1930, in his eighty-first year. *Scores and Biographies* said of him: "Has a strong defence, combined with fine hitting powers, besides being a brilliant field anywhere (though generally at long-leg or cover-point) with a quick return". At Cheltenham College, where H. W. Renny-Tailyour and George Strachan were among his contemporaries, he was coached by James Lillywhite, senior and junior, and was in the eleven four years, 1865 to 1868 inclusive. In each of his last two seasons there he made over a 1,000 runs, his aggregate in 1868 being 1,027 with an average of 54. Beginning his county cricket in 1870, he took part in many Gloucestershire triumphs. Against Surrey at The Oval in 1873 he carried out his bat for 58, and in the match with Sussex at Clifton three years later he scored 93. He also took part in much cricket in Ireland and, for County Louth in 1868, at the age of eighteen, he made 158 v Navan. For the long period of sixty-two years – since 1869 – he had been a member of the MCC. When playing for the Club against Yorkshire at Lord's, in 1870, he had the unusual experience of seeing all his three stumps sent out of the ground when bowled by Freeman.

FRANK E. FIELD, died on August 25, 1934, at his home in Droitwich. Born near Alcester on September 23, 1875, he played first for Warwickshire in 1897 and steadily improved as a fast bowler, but not until 1908, at the age of 32 did he accomplish anything out of the ordinary. In that season Field took 106 wickets in county matches at a cost of 20 runs apiece, and three years later, in company with his captain, F. R. Foster, he played a leading part in carrying off the county championship – the only time that this honour has come to Warwickshire. That was Frank Foster's first year as captain, and his fast left-hand bowling round the wicket, coupled with Field's extra pace, with good easy right-hand delivery and off-break, caused many sides to collapse. Proving slightly more effective than did Foster, Field took 122 wickets at 19 runs apiece in championship matches. He met with special success against Yorkshire at Harrogate, where in the second innings he dismissed seven men for 20 runs. He was unchanged with Foster, Yorkshire, on a worn pitch, failing so completely before the two fast bowlers, that they were all out for 58, and suffered defeat by 198 runs. Rather above medium height, Field did not always deliver the ball at the full extent of his arm above his head, but ability to impart spin made him very fast off the pitch, and in the hot season of 1911 the dry turf suited his style perfectly. He and Foster kept up their form with remarkable energy day after day in the heat and never seemed to tire. Each sent down more than 700 overs, and as a combination they were invariably effective.

Field accomplished a remarkable feat in the match between Worcestershire and Warwickshire at Dudley on June 1, 2 and 3, 1914. In the second innings of Worcestershire he went on to bowl with the score at 85 for four, and took the six remaining wickets in eight overs and four balls, seven maidens, at a cost of 2 runs, the only scoring stroke made off him being lucky from the second ball of the second over before he had taken a wicket. While finishing off the Worcestershire innings in this startling fashion Field delivered five no-balls, with one of which he clean-bowled M. K. Foster. In taking these six wickets Field received no assistance, three batsmen being bowled, two caught and bowled, and one leg-before wicket.

For the Players at Scarborough in 1911 he dismissed eight of a powerful side of Gentlemen in the first innings for 94 runs. Field was very smart in stopping hard return strokes from his own bowling. When he ceased to play for Warwickshire in 1920 he had taken in first-class cricket 1,024 wickets at a cost of 23 runs each. He made no pretensions to being a batsman. In recent years he acted as a first-class umpire, until chronic rheumatism ruined his health.

CAPT. ROBERT ST LEGER FOWLER, MC, born on April 7, 1891, died at Rahinston, Enfield, County Meath, on June 13, 1925, aged 34. Owing to his profession, he was not very well-known to the general cricket public, but he was the hero of a match which may, without exaggeration, be described as the most extraordinary ever played. The story of the Eton and Harrow match in 1910 has been told over and over again, but it can never grow stale. No victory in a match of widespread interest was ever snatched in such a marvellous way. As captain of the Eton eleven Fowler – it was his third year in the big match – found his side for about a day and a half overwhelmed. On the first day Harrow scored 232, and Eton, before bad light caused stumps to be drawn, lost five wickets for 40 runs. This was bad enough, but worse was to come. Eton's innings ended on the Saturday morning for 67, and in the follow-on five wickets were lost for 65. Fowler, scoring 64, played splendidly and received valuable help, but, in spite of all his efforts, the game reached a point at which the odds on Harrow could not have been named. With one wicket to fall Eton were only 4 runs ahead. But the Hon. J. N. Manners – killed in the war in 1914 – hit so fearlessly and had such a cool-headed partner in Lister-Kaye that the last wicket put on 50 runs. Honour was in a measure saved, no one imagined that Harrow would fail to get the 55 runs required. Then came the crowning sensation. Fowler bowled his off-breaks with such deadly accuracy that he took eight wickets – five of them bowled down – and won the match for Eton by 9 runs. No one who was at Lord's on that eventful Saturday evening will ever forget the scene at the finish. Old Harrovians, bearing their sorrow with as much fortitude as could have been expected, said sadly that a grievous blunder had been committed in putting the heavy roller on the rather soft pitch, and there was a good deal in their contention. Still, nothing could detract from Fowler's achievement. Something heroic was demanded of him, and he rose to the height of his opportunity. From one point of view it was a pity he went into the Army. In Oxford or Cambridge cricket he would assuredly have played a great part.

In his three matches against Winchester he scored 113 runs for twice out and took fifteen wickets for 136 runs: altogether in his six big public school matches he made 238 runs with an average of 29.75 and obtained 39 wickets for 10.10 runs each. For Eton he was first in bowling in 1909, and first in both batting and bowling the following year. For Sandhurst v Woolwich in 1911 he carried out his bat for 137 and took seven wickets for 9 runs in a total of 63, and in a small game at the RMC that year, for CCo v ECo, he scored 112 in his first innings and 132 in his second. When he made 92 not out for Army v MCC at Lord's in 1920 he and Capt. W. V. D. Dickinson (150) put on 237 together for the eighth wicket in ninety minutes, and on the same ground four years later he took seven wickets for 22 runs for Army v Royal Navy. With the Incogniti he toured America in 1920, making 142 v All Philadelphia at Haverford, and with the Free Foresters he visited Germany the same year and Canada in 1923. When it was contemplated sending an MCC team to the West Indies in 1924-25 he was offered, and accepted, the captaincy. In 1924 he appeared in two matches for Hampshire. In the Great War he served as Captain in the 17th Lancers and gained the Military Cross.

S. H. P.

LIEUT COL CYRIL PELHAM FOLEY, born on November 1, 1868, died on March 9, 1936, aged 67. He enjoyed the very special distinction of being in the Eton elevens of 1886-87 when both matches with Winchester and Harrow were won, and then helping Cambridge beat Oxford three times – 1889 to 1891. Patient and sound in defence he scored freely to the off side. Usually going in first he seldom failed. Against Harrow in 1886 he made 114 and 36. His scores next year were 37 and 8 while against Winchester he played innings of 38 and 23 and 23 and 7. For Cambridge he was equally consistent with 22, 26 and 1 not out, 12 and 41.

He appeared for Worcestershire in 1888, played for Middlesex from 1893 till 1906, and in the winter of 1904-05 toured the West Indies as a member of Lord Brackley's team. At Lord's in 1893 he was the centre of an unusual incident. In the match between Middlesex and Sussex he picked up a bail which had fallen and, on appeal, Henty, the umpire, gave him out; but, at the request of W. L. Murdoch, the Sussex captain, Mr Foley continued his innings. As a soldier, he had much experience abroad and his exploits in the Jameson raid of 1895 earned for him the nickname of "The Raider".

He served with distinction in the Boer War and came home in temporary command of the 3rd Royal Scots. During the European War he commanded the 9th East Lancashire Regiment.

**EDWARD CHARLES FREEMAN**, died at Sherborne in his 79th year on October 16, 1939. He played occasionally when Essex were promoted to first-class rank in 1895, but became prominent in the cricket world for making the Leyton ground suitable for important cricket. In the effort to improve the pitches and prolong the matches, he asked Sam Apted, the Surrey expert, how he kept The Oval turf so impervious to wear. Freeman was advised to apply a liquid mixture "three days before the match". Surrey were the next visitors to Leyton, and Essex winning the toss, expected a perfect pitch, but on a real "sticky dog", their powerful batting side fell for 37 before Lockwood and Brockwell. The most attractive match of the Essex season ended on the second afternoon. Freeman had applied the mixture on each of the three days, instead of only on the third day before the match! Afterwards he produced pitches equal to any in the country and Essex prospered. Several of his family were players of repute, the chief being his nephew, A. P., "Tich", whose slow bowling for Kent earned records season after season – notably 304 wickets in 1928. He was succeeded as coach and groundsman at Sherborne School by one of his six sons, E. J. Freeman.

**MR WILLIAM FULLER-MAITLAND**, at the time of his death the oldest surviving Oxford Blue, was born at Stansted, Bishop's Stortford on May 6, 1844, and so, when he passed away at Brighton on November 15, 1932 had completed his 88th year. A hard-hitting batsman, an excellent field and a remarkable fine slow bowler, he stood out among the leading amateurs of the day in the later "sixties". Going up to Oxford after four years in the Harrow eleven, he, as a freshman in 1864, obtained a place in the university team. In that same season he appeared for the Gentlemen against the Players at The Oval and in the following summer he assisted the Gentlemen at Lord's. Indeed for some six years he was a fairly regular participant in the great match of the season, but after the summer of 1869, when he once again figured in the Gentlemen's team at The Oval, the cricket field saw him no more. Thus his career was almost as brief as it was brilliant. In answer to an enquiry early last year as to the cause of retirement from the game when, with his fame solidly established, he was at the height of his powers, Mr Fuller-Maitland wrote "One reason was that I always suffered badly from hay-fever in the months of June and July. Another reason – that I had a great wish to see as much of the world as I could. In my travels I spent three years in America, India and Spain and had no hay-fever at all. When three years more were over, I went into Parliament."

At Harrow, where he first secured a place in the eleven in 1860, he had among his colleagues I. D. Walker, for so many years captain of Middlesex, and in the opposing Eton team of that year was James Round, the best amateur wicket-keeper of his day, who, when up at Oxford, was not given his Blue and yet in the same year appeared for Gentlemen against Players at Lord's. Fuller-Maitland apparently developed his bowling only towards the close of his school-days, four wickets for 52 runs rewarding his efforts in the first innings of his last match against Eton, but in 1862, although on the losing side, he put together a score of 73. Strangely enough, considering the fame he afterwards obtained as a bowler, Fuller-Maitland's association with the Harrow eleven was identified with the first three unfinished Eton and Harrow matches.

Fuller-Maitland had a happy experience of the university match as, with eight wickets for 53 in 1864 and eight wickets for 76 in 1865, he took more wickets than anyone else on his side and in the two subsequent years, with scores of 51 and 45, he proved to be the most successful run-getter. In all he obtained 21 wickets for Oxford against Cambridge at a cost of 10 runs apiece and in six completed innings registered 157 runs with an average of 26. His personal success, however, was discounted to some extent by the fact that while during his first three years in residence – the first two under R. A. H. Mitchell – Oxford gained the victory, Cambridge won when Fuller-Maitland was captain in 1867. In 1864 against Surrey – a most formidable combination at that time – he secured twelve wickets for 138 runs and in the following summer twelve wickets for 135 runs.

He first appeared for Gentlemen v Players at The Oval in 1864 and at Lord's in that contest a year later. The match in which he assisted the Gentlemen at Lord's in 1865 was that in which W. G. Grace first appeared for the Gentlemen. E. M. Grace taking eleven wickets and F. R. Evans seven, Fuller-Maitland enjoyed little opportunity on that occasion of displaying his abilities as a bowler.

A very slow bowler, Fuller-Maitland added to a fine command of length and skill in "flighting" the ball – what *Scores and Biographies* described as a "great curve, getting many wickets" – a fine leg-break and, at times, according to a famous old enthusiast, a phenomenal one. This admirer of Fuller-Maitland remembered that in the university match of 1867 J. S. E. Hood was bowled by a ball which came right round his legs. The ball pitched so wide that Hood left it alone, only, much to his chagrin, to find himself bowled. The enthusiast used to say that in the course of half a century, he had seen only three other balls which did so much. According to the same authority, Fuller-Maitland was the best slow bowler that had ever appeared in the university match except A. G. Steel as that great cricketer was in 1878. He further insisted that, with the exception of V. E. Walker, there was no one so clever in making a catch off his own bowling. Mr Fuller-Maitland had been a member of the MCC since his days at Harrow – nearly 70 years ago.

An all-round athlete, Fuller-Maitland showed great ability at the high jump as well as at the long jump and took part in the university sports from 1865 to 1867. In 1866 he appeared for Oxford at racquets in both the singles and doubles. He entered Parliament as member for Breconshire in 1875 and held the seat until 1895 when he retired.

MR HARRY FURNISS, the well-known artist and caricaturist, was born at Wexford on March 26, 1854, and died at Hastings on January 14, 1925. He contributed the preface and a hundred sketches of W. G. Grace to "How's That?" published by Messrs Arrowsmith, of Bristol.

MR WALTER RALEIGH GILBERT, was born in London on September 16, 1853, and died at Calgary, in Alberta, Canada, on July 26, 1924, aged 70. A steady batsman, a very useful slow round-armed bowler, and a very good field at long leg and cover point, he played for Middlesex by birth in 1873 and 1874, for Gloucestershire by residence 1876 to 1886, and four times for the Gentlemen v Players between 1874 and 1877. He also appeared in a few stray matches for Worcestershire and Northamptonshire. In 1873-74 he toured Australia under the captaincy of his cousin, W. G. Grace, and he took part in a very large number of minor matches, especially for the United South of England eleven, which he "managed" after the death of G. F. Grace in 1880. His fielding at deep leg to W. G. Grace's bowling was always excellent, for he covered much ground and was a sure catch. Although overshadowed by his famous cricketing cousins, he played a prominent part in the victories gained during Gloucestershire's greatest years. For Thornbury v Sneyd Park in 1874 he made 254 not out, but in a match of note his highest innings was 205 not out for An England Eleven at Cambridge against the university in 1876, when he batted for about seven hours without a mistake and carried his bat through; he hit a 5, nine 4s and as many as 66 singles, and batted on each of the three days. At Canterbury later in the same season he scored 143 for Kent and Gloucestershire against England, and at Gloucester in 1885 made 102 v Yorkshire. In the match with Nottinghamshire at Clifton in the last-mentioned year he took seventy minutes to obtain 4 runs in his first innings, and two hours and three-quarters to score 21 in his second. Against Sussex at Brighton in 1878 he took four wickets for 12 runs and in the return, at Cheltenham, four for 8, while in the match with Lancashire at Clifton in 1878 he and W. G. Grace bowled unchanged through both innings. At the beginning of 1886 he became a professional, and the season was not far advanced before his career in first-class cricket ended abruptly. He then left England for Canada. He kept up the game in the Dominion and made hundreds in both Halifax and Montreal.

MRS AGNES NICHOLLS GRACE, widow of "W.G.", died at Hawkhurst, Kent, on March 23, 1930, aged 76. Mrs Grace possessed a rare fund of reminiscences of the game. Her memory will be cherished by many cricketers.

DR ALFRED HENRY GRACE, born at Chipping Sodbury on March 10, 1866, died at Iron Acton, near that town, on September 16, 1929, aged 63. He was son of Dr Alfred Grace and, therefore, nephew of W. G., E. M., and G. F. Grace. His appearances for Gloucestershire were very few, although in good-class club cricket he was a free and successful bat, often going in without pads against all types of bowling and playing a dashing innings. He was also a good change bowler, similar in style to "W.G.", and an excellent field. For Thornbury, Chipping Sodbury and British Medicals he made many hundreds. He was educated at Epsom College, where he gained a place in the eleven.

MR CHARLES BUTLER GRACE, the last surviving son of W. G. Grace, died while playing in a cricket match at Hawkhurst, on June 6, 1938, aged 56.

WILLIAM GUNN. After a long illness, the nature of which left no hope of recovery, William Gunn died at his home at Nottingham on January 29, 1921. Born on December 4, 1858, he was in his 63rd year. Few batsmen of his own or any other day were so well worth looking at as William Gunn. He carried his great height – he must have been nearly if not quite 6ft 3in – without the least stoop, and there was a natural grace in his every movement. Wherever he played he was the most striking figure in the field. As a batsman he represented the orthodox – one might even say the classic – school at its best. With his perfectly straight bat and beautifully finished style, he was a model to be copied.

During his long career William Gunn played many innings that have become historical. His 228 for the Players at Lord's in 1890 is the highest score ever made against the Australians in this country. The Australians as a team were not strong in 1890, but they had Charles Turner and Ferris to bowl for them. With regard to this particular match rather a good story has been told. Asked in an interview whether he had ever felt tired of cricket, Sydney Gregory said he thought not, except, perhaps, when he heard Billy Gunn say "No" at Lord's for seven hours and a half. Another great innings that Gunn played was his 139 for the Players against the Gentlemen at Lord's in W. G. Grace's jubilee match in 1898. Just after he went in Gunn was beaten and all but bowled by one of Kortright's fastest. Then he played magnificently, till at last, deceived in the pace, he lunged forward at a slow ball from Woods and was bowled all over his wicket.

Between 1888 and 1899, Gunn played in nine matches for England against Australia. He did best in 1893 – when, incidentally, he just beat Stoddart in the season's averages – scoring 77 at Lord's and 102 not out at Manchester. Though he made bigger scores without number, Gunn never played finer cricket than in the memorable match between Nottinghamshire and Surrey at The Oval in 1892. His 58 against the superb bowling of George Lohmann and Lockwood on a far from easy wicket was a veritable masterpiece of batting. For an hour and a quarter on the second afternoon he and William Barnes withstood a tremendous onslaught. It was cricket that no one who saw it could ever forget.

In his young days Gunn was a famous forward at Association Football, combining skill with great speed. He was a mainstay of Notts County and played for England in 1884 against Scotland and Wales. – This notice of Gunn appeared, almost as it stands, in *The Times.*

S. H. P.

In strictly first-class cricket Gunn made forty-eight centuries:

**For England** (1)
   v Australia, 102*

**For England XI** (1)
   v Yorkshire, 137

**For MCC and Ground** (6)
   v Australians, 118
   v Somerset, 188
   v Sussex, 124, 138
   v Worcestershire, 110
   v Yorkshire, 203

**For Non-Smokers** (1)
   v Smokers, 150

**For North** (1)
   v South, 125*

**For Nottinghamshire** (34)
   v Derbyshire, 135, 207*, 152, 230, 273, 120, 101
   v Essex, 127
   v Gloucestershire, 119
   v Kent, 109, 129, 137
   v Lancashire, 116
   v Leicestershire, 111, 139
   v Middlesex, 138, 120
   v Somerset, 121*, 101
   v Surrey, 118, 125, 236*, 112
   v Sussex 122, 205*, 196, 161, 109, 156, 219, 125, 150
   v Yorkshire, 150, 110

**For Players** (4):
   v Australians, 228
   v Gentlemen, 169, 103, 139

For Nottinghamshire he also made 161 v West Indians, in 1900, in a match not counted first-class.

His eight scores of over 200 were obtained thus:

273   Nottinghamshire v Derbyshire, at Derby, 1901
236*  Nottinghamshire v Surrey, at The Oval, 1898
230   Nottinghamshire v Derbyshire, at Trent Bridge, 1897
228   Players v Australians, at Lord's, 1890
219   Nottinghamshire v Sussex, at Trent Bridge, 1893
207*  Nottinghamshire v Derbyshire, at Derby, 1896
205*  Nottinghamshire v Sussex, at Trent Bridge, 1887
203   MCC and Ground v Yorkshire, at Lord's, 1885

His longest partnerships:

398 for 2nd, Gunn (196) and Shrewsbury (267) for Nottinghamshire v Sussex at Trent Bridge, 1890

367 for 3rd, Gunn (139) and Gunn, J. (294) for Nottinghamshire v Leicestershire, at Trent Bridge, 1903

330 for 4th, Gunn (203) and Barnes (140*) for MCC and Ground v Yorkshire at Lord's, 1885

312 for 2nd, Gunn (161) and Shrewsbury (165) for Nottinghamshire v Sussex at Brighton, 1891

310 for 3rd, Gunn (150) and Shrewsbury (236) for Non-Smokers v Smokers, at East Melbourne, 1886-87

At Lord's in 1889, for MCC and Ground v Northumberland, he carried out his bat for 219, and, in partnership with Attewell (200), put on 419 for the second wicket. On the same ground against the same county in the following year he scored 196 and Flowers 99 not out.

## AVERAGES IN ALL NOTTINGHAMSHIRE MATCHES

| Year | Innings | Not Outs | Runs | Highest Innings | Average |
|------|---------|----------|------|-----------------|---------|
| 1880 | 20 | 4 | 162 | 29* | 10.12 |
| 1881 | 20 | 2 | 435 | 91 | 24.16 |
| 1882 | 19 | 4 | 176 | 39 | 11.73 |
| 1883 | 19 | 1 | 455 | 77 | 25.27 |
| 1884 | 20 | 1 | 537 | 138 | 28.26 |
| 1885 | 21 | 2 | 627 | 88 | 33.00 |
| 1886 | 24 | 3 | 655 | 83 | 31.19 |
| 1887 | 23 | 2 | 791 | 205* | 37.66 |
| 1888 | 28 | 2 | 614 | 91 | 23.61 |
| 1889 | 21 | 1 | 832 | 118 | 41.60 |
| 1890 | 29 | 2 | 939 | 196 | 34.77 |
| 1891 | 24 | 2 | 938 | 161 | 42.63 |
| 1892 | 26 | 2 | 764 | 98* | 31.83 |
| 1893 | 33 | 1 | 1,450 | 156 | 45.31 |
| 1894 | 29 | 1 | 933 | 121* | 33.32 |
| 1895 | 27 | — | 843 | 219 | 31.22 |
| 1896 | 25 | 4 | 933 | 207* | 44.42 |
| 1897 | 30 | 4 | 1,154 | 230 | 44.38 |
| 1898 | 32 | 6 | 1,239 | 236* | 47.65 |
| 1899 | 28 | 1 | 1,230 | 150 | 45.55 |
| 1900 | 27 | 2 | 892 | 161 | 35.68 |
| 1901 | 20 | 1 | 751 | 273 | 39.52 |
| 1902 | 24 | 1 | 807 | 120 | 35.08 |
| 1903 | 29 | 1 | 1,011 | 139 | 36.10 |
| 1904 | 7 | — | 121 | 39 | 17.28 |
| | 605 | 50 | 19,289 | 273 | 34.75 |

Bowling lobs for Nottinghamshire in sixteen seasons during his career, Gunn took 49 wickets for 1,324 runs, average 27.02

In Gentlemen v Players matches he scored 1,666 runs with an average of 32.66 and in Test matches with Australia 392 with an average of 21.77

* *Signifies not out.*

MR HERBERT B. HAYMAN, born on October 5, 1873, died on July 31, 1930, at the age of 56. A capital hard-hitting bat and an excellent outfield, he began to assist Middlesex in 1893, and in all matches for the county made 3,518 runs with an average of 25. His highest scores for the side were 152 v Yorkshire at Lord's in 1896 and 110 v Gloucestershire on the same ground in 1901: in the former game he made 218 for the first wicket with A. E. Stoddart and in the latter 200 with P. F. Warner. Against Kent at Catford in 1898 he carried his bat through the innings for 104, and twice at The Oval – in 1896 and 1901 – took part in the Gentlemen v Players match. For the Hampstead CC, for whom he played with Stoddart, Spofforth and other first-class cricketers, he did some remarkable things. When the club made 273 for two wickets in ninety-five minutes v Eltham, at Hampstead in 1901, he and B. Everett took the total from 100 to 178 in twenty minutes: on that occasion he carried out his bat for 164, at one period of his innings making eight 4s and a 6 in successive scoring hits. Four years later, also on the Hampstead ground, he made 201, run out, after Upper Tooting had declared at 377 for seven, leaving the home side two and a half hours in which to bat. In that time 348 were made for the loss of four men, Hayman, hitting three 6s and 30 4s, and obtaining his runs in eighty minutes.

COLONEL ARTHUR HOWARD HEATH, born at Newcastle-under-Lyme, Staffordshire, on May 29, 1856, died in London on April 21, 1930, in his 74th year. He was summed-up as "A free-hitting bat, strong on the off-side, fielded well at long-leg or cover-point, bowled fast-round and lobs". In 1873 and two next years he was in the Clifton eleven, making 120 not out v Sherborne in 1874 and a faultless 164 v Cheltenham in 1875 – in each case on his opponents' ground. He also played for Gloucestershire in 1875. Going up to Oxford, he played in the XI in 1876-77-78-79, but hardly did himself justice against Cambridge, though in 1878 he took two wickets for 4 runs with five deliveries and in 1879 played an innings of 45. Among his notable scores for Oxford were: 1876, 71 against Middlesex and 50 against MCC; 1879, 61 against Middlesex. He played for Middlesex in 1878 against Yorkshire at Sheffield, and against Nottinghamshire at Trent Bridge. Colonel Heath had a long active and official association with the Staffordshire Cricket Club. He played for the county from 1879 to 1898 and was captain from 1884 to 1893, hon. secretary from 1886 to 1888, and for many years hon. treasurer. He was chiefly a bat and a safe field but could bowl on occasion. His highest scores for the county were 217 v Lincolnshire at Stoke in 1889 – made in four hours – and 155 not out v Cheshire in 1882. Whilst bowling for MCC in Surrey's second innings at Lord's in 1876, he sent down a curious over. The first ball was a wide, the second jumped over long-stop's head and five byes resulted, the third knocked Elliott's middle stump out of the ground, the fourth nearly bowled R. Humphrey, the fifth was a wide for which two were run, and the sixth was played. Col Heath was also well known as a Rugby footballer in the seventies. He was in the Oxford University XV v Cambridge in 1875, 1877, 1879, and 1880, and appeared for England against Scotland in 1876, the last occasion on which twenty-a-side was played in international games. He represented Hanley and, later, Leek in Parliament in the Conservative interest.

ROBERT HENDERSON, a member of the Surrey eleven during the great years of the side when led by Mr John Shuter, first played for the county in 1883 at the age of eighteen. He was an excellent batsman, generally able to give of his best when most was required of him, a useful slow bowler in his early years of first-class cricket and a thoroughly sound, if scarcely brilliant, fieldsman. In his first season with Surrey he scored 581 with an average of 15 and took 35 wickets at a cost of 18 runs apiece. Against Gloucestershire that summer, in a match which W. W. Read and Maurice Read finished off by hitting up 141 runs in sixty-five minutes, Henderson took six wickets in the second innings for 17 runs.

Bad health prevented Henderson from playing regularly until the season of 1887 and, though he was occasionally called upon in 1896, his last season before losing his form was that of 1893. Altogether during the period that Henderson was a member of the county eleven Surrey won the championship seven times, and in 1889 tied with Lancashire and Nottinghamshire for first place, this being the only break of uninterrupted headship of the tournament during six consecutive seasons. So powerful were Surrey at that time that it was a great distinction to belong to the side. Henderson kept his place because of his consistent scoring and splendid nerve. As an example of his ability to do himself full justice at a crisis may be mentioned his innings of 59 not out against Yorkshire at The Oval, in what is still known as the "Gaslight Match", the gas-lamps in the road circling The Oval having been lighted for some time before the end was reached. Thanks to Henderson's determined batting, Surrey won by two wickets, Henderson finishing the match with a cut to the boundary when it was difficult to see the ball. Again, in 1893, when Surrey twice beat the Australians at The Oval, Henderson scored 28 and 15 in a small scoring game which the county won by 58 runs, and in the return match he made 60 not out and 14 not out.

Altogether, between 1883 and 1896, he made 5,061 runs for Surrey with an average of 19, among his scores being three separate hundreds at The Oval – 106 v Somerset, 105 v Hampshire and 133 v Scotland. During one winter he went to India to coach the Parsees, was paid great honours on his departure, and on his return was given – by his Surrey colleagues – the name of "Framjee." Born at Newport, in Monmouthshire on March 30, 1865, Robert Henderson went to live at Beddington as a boy, and in local cricket for his choir he scored many runs and took wickets very cheaply. Always maintaining his association with church work, Henderson for many years was warden of Beddington Parish Church, and chorister and churchwarden over a period of 56 years. He died on January 28, 1931, at Wallington.

MR ALBERT NEILSON HORNBY, the famous batsman who captained Lancashire for nearly twenty seasons, and whose association with that county as a player extended over a period of 33 years, was born at Blackburn on February 10, 1847, and died at Parkfield, Nantwich, on December 17, 1925. Going up to Harrow in 1862, he played against Eton at Lord's in 1864 and 1865, his first appearance there taking place thirteen days before that of W. G. Grace. At that time, Hornby was of such slight physique that he weighed ("bat and all", according to one account) less than six stone. He took part in a match between Lancashire and Yorkshire at Whalley in 1867, but two more years elapsed before that close and active connection with the Lancashire eleven, that only ceased in 1899, really commenced.

For many seasons one of the leading English batsmen, Hornby had an attractive forward style, and possessed splendid punishing powers which he used freely. In addition, he was a magnificent field, and as a captain so firm, keen and genial that he could always get the best out of the men under his charge. His dashing methods, coupled with his obvious enthusiasm – he appeared thoroughly to enjoy every moment he was on the field – made him a general favourite wherever he went.

The extent to which he dominated matters as a run-getter during his prime may be gauged from the fact that during the twelve years, 1870 to 1881 inclusive, he was the only batsman to reach three figures for Lancashire, and that during that period he did so on seven occasions – three times in 1881, in which season he was credited with the largest aggregate and highest average of any player in the country, his figures being respectively, 1,531 and 41.38. Of the hundreds he made for Lancashire the highest was his 188 v Derbyshire at Old Trafford in 1881, but of more merit was his 161 against Surrey at Liverpool in 1886. He and R. G. Barlow formed perhaps the most famous first-wicket pair of their time, and although Hornby's impulsiveness often led to Barlow being run out, they enjoyed many memorable successes. Among these were the putting on of 191 against Oxford University at Manchester in 1886, 180 against Middlesex at Lord's in 1882 and 157 against Derbyshire at Manchester in 1881. Their greatest triumph, however, was achieved in the match with Yorkshire at Manchester in 1875, when Lancashire, set 146 to win, scored 148 without loss, Hornby making 78 of the number and his partner 50. The performance, which would have been a noteworthy one even on the smoother grounds of more recent years, made quite a sensation at the time, such a feat being without parallel.

In the course of his career, Hornby put together seventeen hundreds in first-class matches – ten of these being for Lancashire, and two for the MCC – while in 1873 he made 104 for Gentlemen against Players at Prince's and four years later 144 for Gentlemen against the Players at The Oval. Between 1869 and 1885 he represented the Gentlemen against the Players on 31 occasions, scoring 1,221 runs in those matches and, only once not out, having an average of 24.42. Hornby played twice for England against Australia, captaining the side that at The Oval in 1882 lost by 7 runs, and also figuring in the Test match at Manchester in 1884. He went out to America in August, 1872 with the side got together by Mr R. A. Fitzgerald, at that time the secretary of the MCC, and also formed one of the team that Lord Harris took to Australia in the winter of 1878-79. For many years he was president of the Lancashire County Club and also a member of the MCC committee.

Hornby figured in that memorable match at Lord's in May, 1878, when a very powerful MCC eleven lost to the Australians by nine wickets, 31 wickets going down for an aggregate of 105 runs and the game being all over in a day. In the second innings of the MCC Hornby in playing Spofforth met with an injury of so severe a description that it compelled his retirement and would certainly have kept most men out of the field for a week or so, but such was his indomitable pluck that with his side faring disastrously – they were all out for 19 – he came out to resume his innings. The painful experience, however, probably shook even his splendid nerve, for, although he remained one of England's leading batsmen for several years afterwards, his only notable score against Spofforth was one of 94 for the North in 1884.

Another incident in Hornby's career was that on the Sydney ground when Lord Harris's team played there in February, 1879. Annoyed with an umpire's decision the crowd burst on to the field and a "larrikin" struck Lord Harris with a stick. Hornby seized the offender and although hit in the face and having his shirt nearly torn off his back he conveyed his prisoner to the pavilion.

A characteristic tale of the famous batsman concerned the Gentlemen and Players match at The Oval in 1881. Hornby and W. G. Grace had given the amateurs a capital start when, from a powerful drive, Hornby was magnificently caught high up in the long field by William Gunn, who stood some six feet three inches in height. "Bad luck, Monkey" said a friend as Hornby passed into the pavilion. "Yes", answered Hornby, "no one but a damned giraffe would have got near it".

In addition to being one of the most famous cricketers of his day, A. N. Hornby took high rank as a Rugby football player in the late 70's and early 80's. He appeared five times for North v South, and nine times for England – on four occasions against Scotland and on five against Ireland. All through his life he was a keen rider to hounds, and after his football days he spent most of the winter in the hunting field, but of late years lameness prevented him from enjoying any form of activity.

MR HENRY MAYERS HYNDMAN, died at his home in Hampstead on the morning of November 22, 1921. Mr Hyndman, so well known as a Socialist leader, had some claim to be remembered for his powers in the cricket field. While up at Cambridge he only just missed getting his Blue in 1864. In his first book of recollections he admitted that in later life many things of greater moment caused him far less disappointment. He was very pleased one night at his club to hear the opinion expressed that he ought to have been chosen. Still, Cambridge were rich in run-getters in 1864, and Mr Hyndman's best score in the three trial matches in which he took part was 35 against the Free Foresters. He was one of the Thirteen of Cambridge who played against Surrey at The Oval, a drawn game producing 1,104 runs – a huge aggregate in those days. Mr Hyndman kept up his cricket for several years, playing a good deal for Sussex and the Gentlemen of Sussex. He was clearly at his best in 1864. In August that year he scored at Brighton 58 against Hampshire and 62 against Middlesex, the latter innings enabling Sussex to gain a hard-won victory by three wickets. In his first book of recollections Mr Hyndman had a good deal to say about cricket, paying a high tribute to Buttress, the famous slow bowler. Born on March 7, 1842, he was in his eightieth year at the time of his death.

MR ARCHIBALD JACKSON, the New South Wales and Australian Test cricketer, died at Brisbane on February 16, 1933, the day that England defeated Australia and regained the "Ashes", at the early age of 23. His passing was not only a very sad loss to Australian cricket in particular but to the cricket world in general. A native of Scotland, where he was born on September 5, 1909, he was hailed as a second Victor Trumper – a comparison made alike for his youthful success, elegant style and superb stroke play. Well set up, very active on his feet, and not afraid to jump in to the slow bowlers and hit the ball hard, he accomplished far more in big cricket than Trumper had done at his age. He first attracted attention when at school at Balmain, Sydney, and later at the Roselle School. So quickly did he mature that, at the age of seventeen, he gained an assured place in the New South Wales team. In his first season of Sheffield Shield cricket he scored 464 runs at an average of 58; next year he achieved a feat no other batsman of his age had performed, by making two centuries in a match – 131 and 122 against South Australia. For a time Jackson had something of a reputation of being a second innings batsman, for often he failed at his first attempt and then made a good score in the second innings. This weakness, however, he overcame and he soon established himself as an opening batsman for New South Wales. Given his place in the Australian team when the MCC side, under the captaincy of Mr A. P. F. Chapman, toured Australia in 1928-29, Jackson, on his first appearance in Test cricket against England, made a hundred – the youngest player to do so. This was at Adelaide where in the fourth Test match, which England won by 12 runs, he scored 164. For sheer brilliance of execution his strokes during this delightful display could scarcely have been exceeded. He reached three figures with a glorious square drive off Larwood in the first over after lunch and was one of the very few Australian batsmen who during that tour could successfully jump in and drive J. C. White. An innings of 182 in the Australian test trial – regarded as the finest he ever played – made certain of his inclusion in the team which visited England in 1930. Unfortunately, English cricket lovers did not in that tour see Jackson at his best, for although he scored over 1,000 runs he failed to reveal his true form until towards the end of the summer. Then, in the final Test match at The Oval, he put together a score of 73 and helped Bradman in a partnership of 243 for the fourth wicket which still stands as a record in a Test match between Australia and England. Jackson, of course, never saw Trumper play, but Kippax, in style and stance and in some strokes, was not unlike Trumper; and Jackson, consciously or unconsciously, and while giving full play to his natural tendencies, took Kippax as his model. He had a splendid return from the deep field and, if not so fast a runner as Bradman, covered ground very quickly. His later years were marred by continued ill-health and his untimely end was not unexpected. While lying in hospital on what was to prove his death-bed he was married.

MR DIGBY LODER ARMROID JEPHSON, born at Clapham, in Surrey, on February 23, 1871, died at Cambridge on January 19, 1926, in his 55th year. For many seasons a familiar and popular figure in the game, Jephson was a most useful all-round cricketer, fit, when at the height of his powers, for inclusion in any team except those of an international character. He learned the game whilst at Manor House School, Clapham, and, with more opportunities, developed his skill at Cambridge. As a batsman he possessed many strokes and could hit very hard indeed, while in the field he always worked hard. He will, however, always be best remembered for his lob bowling, a style he cultivated after employing fast over-arm for some years. In 1890 he obtained his Blue for Cambridge, but in his three matches against Oxford he scored only 31 runs in three completed innings. It was for Surrey that most of his best feats in first-class cricket were performed. He assisted that county from 1891 until 1904, and in two seasons, 1901 and 1902, captained the side. His highest of the nine three-figure innings he played for Surrey was 213 against Derbyshire at The Oval in 1900, when he and R. Abel (193), going in against a total of 325, made 364 together for the first wicket. In the match with Sussex at Hove a year later the same pair twice made over a hundred together for the opening partnership – 114 in the first innings and 109 in the second, Jephson's scores being 95 and 85. In 1900 he had an excellent all-round record, for, besides making 1,952 runs with an average of 41.53, he took 66 wickets for 23.40 runs each. In the Gentlemen v Players match at Lord's in 1899 his lobs gained him an analysis of six for 21 – a splendid performance against a strong batting side. For Surrey he took five wickets for 12 runs against Derbyshire at Chesterfield in 1899, and performed the hat trick v Middlesex at The Oval in 1904. In club cricket he did many remarkable things, especially for the Wanderers. For Crystal Palace v Seaton in 1894 he and Stanley Colman made 300 together for the first wicket, and for Wanderers v Tonbridge in 1900 the same pair put up 349 together, his own contribution on the latter occasion being 226. Other large innings played by him were 261 for Crystal Palace v Eastbourne in 1893 and 301 not out – made in three hours and a quarter – for Wanderers against Norwood two years later. With his fast bowling he took five wickets in eight balls for Crystal Palace v Eastbourne in 1888, and twice his lobs accounted for all ten wickets in an innings – for Wanderers v Chiswick Park in 1894 and for G. E. Bicknell's Eleven v Streatham in 1902. For some time he was on the London Stock Exchange, but later he took to journalism and coaching on the Cambridge University cricket ground. He was the author of a book of verse entitled *A Few Overs*.

MR GEORGE MORTIMER KELSON, died on the 29th of March, 1920, in his 85th year. He was born on December 8, 1835. Mr Kelson retired from first-class cricket so long ago that to the present generation he was not even a name, but in his day he held a prominent place, being at one time beyond question the best bat in the Kent eleven. Kent cricket in the '60's was in a very depressed condition, but Mr Kelson took part in many a hard-fought game side by side with Willsher and George Bennett. The irony of the position at the end of the '60's was that Kent, with their full strength in the field, would have had about the strongest batting side in England. Some of the amateurs avoided county matches, but were seen during the Canterbury week. Mr Kelson played his first match for Kent in 1859 and his last in 1873. He was at his best in the seasons of 1863-64-65. In 1863 he played at The Oval the innings of his life – 122 against Surrey. He was on the losing side in an extraordinary match, Surrey with 192 to get in the last innings hitting off the runs for one wicket. To the best of my knowledge the feat was, at that time, without parallel in first-class cricket. H. H. Stephenson made 78 not out, and Jupp, then just coming to the front, 74 not out. There used to be a little harmless betting on cricket in those days and the task looked so formidable that Caffyn who had backed Surrey hedged all his money. Mr Kelson did not do a great deal outside Kent cricket, but he was picked for Gentlemen against Players at The Oval in 1864 and 1866, and when, after 1862, the notorious schism kept Hayward, Carpenter, and George Parr away from The Oval he played two or three times for England against Surrey, scoring 26 and 40 in 1864 and 40 in 1865. Appearing for the Gentlemen in 1866 when, for a very strong side, he was put in last, he had the satisfaction of taking part in a game in which the Players were beaten at The Oval for the first time, the match dating from 1857. I cannot recall Mr Kelson's batting, though I saw him play, but from all accounts he was a fine punishing player with a free attractive style. Mr Kelson was a great fisherman and wrote much on the gentle art, being at one time fishing editor of "Land and Water".

S. H. P.

ALEXANDER KERMODE, died at Sydney on July 17, 1934, aged 58. Discovered by M. A. Noble when playing junior cricket, Kermode was chosen for New South Wales in 1901 and during the same season A. C. MacLaren, captain of the English touring team, was so impressed with his form that he induced him to come to England and qualify for Lancashire. From 1904 to 1908 Kermode remained with Lancashire but his fast bowling against first-class batsmen never reached the standard expected. He met with most success in 1905 when 107 wickets fell to him at 21.43 runs apiece as compared with Walter Brearley's 121 at 18.64. Of tall and ungainly build Kermode ended his term with Lancashire as his ability suddenly deteriorated. When in league cricket moderate batsmen fell ready victims to his speed and off-break. The importation of Kermode to qualify for Lancashire received severe criticism in many quarters. The case of Albert Trott – one of the best all-round cricketers ever produced by Australia or England – coming to Middlesex, was cited as a precedent, but the example of Yorkshire and Nottinghamshire relying entirely upon native talent was urged as desirable to be copied by all counties.

MAJOR NEVILLE ALEXANDER KNOX, died at Surbiton, Surrey on March 3, 1935, at the age of 50. His cricketing career was brief but brilliant. Born on October 10, 1884, he played both cricket and Rugby football for Dulwich College. He appeared for Surrey against Lancashire in 1904 and took four wickets. Next season he rose to fame in remarkable fashion and had a big share in winning back for Surrey, after a year of extreme depression, a high position among the counties. For the county he took 121 wickets, and in all matches dismissed 129 batsmen at an average of less than 22 runs apiece. In the following year he did even better, taking 144 wickets for 19.63 runs each and achieving a notable triumph for the Gentlemen against the Players at Lord's. By taking twelve wickets for 183, he had a large share in a victory for the Gentlemen by 45 runs; seven of his victims were clean bowled. It was astonishing how H. Martyn, the Oxford and Somerset wicket-keeper, stood up to his tremendously fast bowling. In the same game Arthur Fielder, the Kent fast bowler, performed the feat – never previously accomplished in this fixture – of taking, at a cost of 90 runs, all ten wickets in the Gentlemen's first innings.

The first-class career of Knox ended in 1910. He developed an acute form of shin soreness, and had to struggle against chronic lameness. He often played when he ought to have been resting, and only sheer pluck and resolution enabled him to get through the work he did. Loose-limbed and standing well over six feet, Knox made full use of his physical advantage. His long and peculiar run, starting from near deep mid-off, made the length and direction of the ball difficult to judge. He bowled at a great pace with undeniable off-break, and his good length deliveries often reared up straight.

In 1907 he played for England against South Africa in the second and third Test matches at Leeds and The Oval, without, however, achieving much success. In last year's Almanack Hobbs, referring to fast bowlers, said: – "Being a member of the same county side, I only played against N. A. Knox in Gentlemen and Players matches and games of a similar description, when he was probably past his best, but I think he was the best fast bowler I ever saw."

Knox joined the RAOC as a lieutenant in 1915 and was promoted captain in 1919.

SIR WALTER LAWRENCE, founder of the Lawrence Trophy for cricket, died on November 15, 1939, at his home at Hyde Hall, Sawbridgeworth, Herts, aged 67. An enthusiastic sportsman, who kept his own cricket field at Hyde Hall, Sir Walter in 1934 introduced his trophy and a 100 guineas order on a London store for the cricketer who hit the fastest hundred in a first-class match. It discouraged senseless stonewalling and was an inducement to enterprising players to try for the annual prize. The winners have been: Woolley, Gimblett in his first match for Somerset, Ames, Hardstaff, H. T. Bartlett and again Ames, who in 1939 scored the fastest hundred of the season for the second time. Hardstaff made his hundred at Canterbury in fifty-one minutes.

MR JOSEPH CLEMENT LAWTON, who died on January 20, 1934, at the age of 76, played regularly for the Blackpool club until 65. A native of Moseley, Birmingham, he appeared occasionally for Warwickshire, in company with three of his brothers, before going to New Zealand whence he returned in 1906. On his 57th birthday, playing for Blackpool against Fylde, he took seven wickets for 1 run, five men falling to consecutive balls. Against Burnley Crusaders he dismissed the whole side by taking nine wickets and catching the other bastman. As a professional for Otago in a New Zealand interprovincial match all ten wickets fell to him at a cost of 71 runs. He was also a good free batsman.

WILLIAM HENRY LOCKWOOD, the famous fast bowler, died at his home, Radford, Nottingham, on April 26, 1932, at the age of 64. He had been in failing health for about five years. On his day one of the finest fast bowlers the game of cricket has ever known, Lockwood had a somewhat chequered career. Born at Old Radford, Nottingham, on March 25, 1868, he was given a trial for Nottinghamshire in 1886, but accomplished nothing of note and in the following year he accepted an engagement on the ground staff at The Oval. He duly qualified for Surrey and although Nottinghamshire were anxious to secure his services in 1889, he preferred to stay with his adopted county, and that season signalised his association with Surrey by an innings of 83 against Nottinghamshire in the August bank holiday match at The Oval.

Not until two years later did he make his mark as a bowler, his great performance that summer being eleven wickets for 40 runs against Kent at The Oval, but in 1892 when Surrey had George Lohmann and Tom Richardson as well as Lockwood, the last-named headed the averages for all matches, taking 168 wickets for less than twelve and a half runs apiece. Lockwood continued a great bowler during the next two seasons but, going out to Australia in 1894-95, he failed deplorably and, on his return home, went down the hill so steadily that in 1897 he lost his place in the Surrey team.

Happily in the ensuing winter he was at great pains to get himself fit, and in 1898 obtained 134 wickets and scored nearly a 1,000 runs in first-class matches. He remained a splendid bowler for several years after this, but finally dropped out of the Surrey team in 1904.

In 1902 he appeared for England against Australia in four of the five Test matches, and in the contest at Manchester, securing eleven wickets for 76 runs, accomplished one of the greatest bowling performances ever witnessed. To begin with, the pitch proved so soft that not until the score reached 129 was Lockwood given a trial but still, in an innings of 299, he disposed of six batsmen for 48, the last five wickets falling for 43 runs. In Australia's second innings Lockwood got rid of Trumper, Hill and Duff while the score was reaching 10. Fred Tate, at deep square leg, missing Darling off Braund the fourth wicket, which should have gone down at 16, did not fall until 64. For all that Lockwood dominated the game, taking five wickets for 28 and the tourists were all out for 86. England had only 124 to make but a night's heavy rain placed batsmen at a big disadvantage and Australia, despite Lockwood's magnificent work, won by 3 runs.

Lockwood took no such long run as his famous colleague, Tom Richardson, and did not appear quite so fast through the air, but when he was at the top of his form, no one ever came off the pitch much faster than he or – with his off-break also a distinguishing quality of his bowling – was more difficult to play under conditions favourable to batting. He had, too, at his command a slow ball which in his early days he sent down without any perceptible change of delivery. After he "came back" in 1898 he did not bowl this ball quite as well as before but it was still a very useful part of his equipment.

In addition to being one of the most famous bowlers of his generation, Lockwood was also a first-rate batsman and, had he not been compelled to concentrate his energies upon the taking of wickets would, no doubt, have gained high rank as a run-getter. Among his many triumphs was one for the Players against the Gentlemen at Lord's in 1902, when in addition to taking nine wickets for less than 12 runs apiece, he put together an innings of 100.

MR GEORGE HENRY LONGMAN, died on August 19, 1938, aged 86. An enthusiastic cricketer, he retained a close interest in the game until the end of his life. At Eton he was in the XI for four years, 1868 to 1871; captain in his last year. At Cambridge, Longman got his Blue as a freshman and played against Oxford four times from 1872 to 1875. With a score of 80 he helped to beat Oxford by an innings and 166 runs in his first university match. Longman and A. S. Tabor, another Eton freshman, put up the hundred for the first wicket, then a record for this engagement.

Mr Longman writing about "My Years at Cambridge" in the 1929 *Wisden* said regarding that match — "An ardent Oxonian was sitting in the pavilion and up to him came another Oxonian with the eager question: 'Well, how is it going?' 'Going', replied his friend, 'there are two — little freshmen in, and they've got the hundred up without a wicket.'"

Oxford were very strong at that time and in the three following years, twice as Cambridge captain, Longman was on the losing side.

Longman played for the Gentlemen at Lord's in 1875 and on subsequent occasions. He was an excellent batsman, possessing beautiful style. Very keen on fielding, he enjoyed the reputation of having greatly improved this important part of the game at Cambridge. No doubt he was influenced in this effort by the fact that in his first match for Eton at Lord's he was run out twice, while his big performances for Cambridge came to a similar end. How good he was in the field may be imagined from the following description given in *Wisden* of the catch which dismissed Allan Hill, the Yorkshire fast bowler, in the Gentlemen and Players match at Prince's in 1876. "The innings was ended at long-field-on by 'the catch of the season' made by Mr Longman, who was then fielding at deep long off, close up to the people in front of the new road in course of formation. With body bent back over some of the visitors, and right arm extended still farther over, he caught and held the ball with that right hand in such grand style that a roar of admiring cheers rang out, and all who witnessed it agreed it was the finest catch they had seen that season. It was hard lines for Hill to suffer defeat from so fine a drive but his consolation must be he suffered from a catch in a thousand." Longman himself described how "A. P. Lucas and I both went for it. I called out 'Mine' just in time to prevent a collision. The ball came fairly into my right hand."

After leaving the university he played cricket for Hampshire for some years. He joined the Surrey club in 1894, became president in 1926, a position he held for three years, after which he exchanged offices with Mr H. D. G. Leveson Gower, and remained honorary treasurer until his death, which came in his sleep. He played golf on the previous day.

THE HON. ROBERT HENRY LYTTELTON, died at North Berwick on November 7, 1939, aged 85. Educated at Eton and Cambridge, he excelled as a student and critic of the game rather than as a player. With A. G. Steel he edited the *Badminton Library* volume in 1887, and in particular he was a foremost advocate of reform of the leg-before-wicket rule. Trained in the earlier school, which regarded putting the legs in front of the wicket for the purpose of defence as not only bad play but unsportsmanlike, he strove hard for over 30 years to bring about such alteration in the law as would penalise batsmen backing up with their pads. He went so far as to urge that a batsman should be given out "if the ball hit any part of his person (except his hand) that is between wicket and wicket". In *Crisis in Cricket in the "Leg-Before" Rule*, he expounded his views on the subject and also on the artificial preparation of wickets. His dramatic account in the *Badminton* volume of the university match at Lord's in 1870 ("Cobden's match") was honoured by inclusion in *The Oxford Book of English Prose*. "Bob" Lyttelton, sixth son of the fourth Lord Lyttelton, and one of eight brothers, seven of whom played for Eton between the years 1857 and 1872, was nearly 6 feet 3 inches tall. A useful bat for Eton he failed to get his Blue at Cambridge but represented the university in the doubles tennis match of 1874.

## GREGOR MACGREGOR

### Born 1869 – Died 1919

### A Tribute by D. L. A. Jephson

To many, who like myself were at Lord's last year during the 'varsity match and saw and chatted with Gregor MacGregor, the news of his sudden death in a nursing home came almost with the force of a physical blow.

I have known MacGregor and played cricket with him for more years than the average man cares to count. I have played with him in games which men label 'first class' – in games of the country house, or 'brown sherry' variety, as they are often derisively called, and I have played against him in college and county cricket, and whether with him or against him or under him, he was always the same, – even-tempered – imperturbable – at times perhaps bordering on the cynical; rarely if ever depressed by fear of disaster, or over-elated with the joy of success.

As a captain he never bustled or hustled his side – he was silent, determined, full of supreme self-confidence, but not with that aggressive, assertive confidence that lessens the value of many, who otherwise would make excellent leaders of a side. His knowledge and sound judgment of the thousand and one aspects of the game were almost unrivalled.

He was a pessimist at the start of a day – he was an optimist all through it!

I' played with him at Cambridge in 1890 and under him there in 1891. I played against him in that fine, clean, keen cricket the Surrey v Middlesex matches, and this I will say, speaking with that truth that is only given to 'babes' and fools to utter, that he never asked: "How's That?" unless the man were out. And there is no finer compliment – no finer praise – no finer tributer to say of one of the greatest wicket-keepers that ever lived than to say that he never asked in vain.

Some men behind the 'sticks' led away by the excitement of a close finish – the rapid advance of defeat or the approach of victory – snatch at an appeal – but MacGregor never did – he was a grand clean stumper – clean in every sense of the word – a stumper, absolutely 'frillless.'

He never gesticulated – he never jumped about like a jack-in-the-box or as a badly regulated monkey on a stick – he was the personification of quietude.

In the world of sport there have been pairs, P. M. and A. M. Walters, the great Corinthians for example, and hosts of others in their different games, but in all my forty years I have never seen that machine-like precision – that foreshadowing of the possible – that existed between MacGregor and Sammy Woods. The faster Sam bowled, the nearer the sticks stood Mac, and he took the five and a half ounces of leather, cork and string, as if it were a ping-pong ball! He took it on the off or on the on-side with equal facility, and he would throw the ball back, time in and time out, with the suggestion that he was a little tired at the simplicity of it all!

One of the most wonderful things connected with MacGregor's wicket-keeping is the fact that he never hurt his fingers. Now, I have looked with keen interest at the hands of many of our great stumpers, and some of them are as the gnarled roots of trees – twisted – curved, – battered joints protrude everywhere. I looked at MacGregor's hands – and they were untouched – unmarked. "Why?" I asked him one day at The Oval – and this was his answer: "As a boy I learnt to bend my wrists backwards, so that I take the ball with my fingers pointing down – the result being that if I do not take it clean, my fingers are simply bent backwards – not driven in at the tips." In other words the front of his hand faced the ball – not his finger tips, and this is the reason why he never broke down.

Even-tempered as MacGregor invariably was, I well remember one occasion on which this usual tranquility broke down – the reason I have forgotten. Cambridge were playing Surrey at The Oval in June 1891. As a rule he was chary of tendering advice to his bowlers, but in the second innings of Surrey, on a none too easy wicket, he remarked in his quiet way to our great fast bowler: "Let 'em go, Sam." And then for the first time I saw MacGregor stand back – and he was right, for on his day and in the right mood, Sammy Woods was a real fast bowler. Surrey required 122 to win. Sam 'let 'em go'! As he started to bowl the majority of the famous eleven developed a strange desire for the company of the square leg umpire and 'edged' in his direction, and the stumps, unguarded, were hurled with fierce velocity to MacGregor who carried them back, with never a smile, and silently placed them, re-bailed, in their original position. Surrey were out for 103, of which number Jack Shuter made 51 – he was one of the few who stood up – he faced the bowling, as that parallelogram of a man, George Hirst, would have done. As we walked back to the pavilion, a faint, very faint smile illuminated for a moment the dark features of MacGregor – "Well bowled, Sam," was all he said.

But silent, imperturable as MacGregor usually was, occasionally his splendid keenness broke through his cold reserve. Surrey, as was often the case, were hard pressed by our old rivals Middlesex, and on the morning of the third day at The Oval, seemed certain to lose the match. There had been some rain and the wicket was slow and easy, and with all their side to bat, Middlesex required only 150 or so to win. From the very start the game swung in their favour – the ball cut through and runs were as plentiful as fallen autumn leaves. At the interval they had made 120 odd for three. At lunch I noticed that several of the amateurs had not even changed, so certain were they of the runs. I whispered to MacGregor: "Mac, I should like to make those fellows change." And he smiled. After lunch, forty-five minutes of a hot sun, a wonderful change came 'o'er the spirit of their dream.' Hayward and Lockwood and the sticky wicket caused a rapid search for garments – wicket after wicket fell and MacGregor arrived only to be run out by Turkey Rawlin in his first over! As he passed Rawlin in the middle of the pitch, seeing he had no earthly chance to get in – he shouted in a voice literally broken with emotion: "Great Scott, Turkey, what have you done?"

His whole thought was for his side. No man could stop a rot better than he, and this he knew. But on this occasion his openly expressed fear was groundless, as Billy Williams, that rough and ready cricketer, made 17! and Middlesex won by one wicket.

The last time I had the pleasure of playing against MacGregor, the last time I ever played in a first-class match, was for Surrey v Middlesex at The Oval in June, 1904. For the first and only time in my life I did the 'hat trick' and Gregor MacGregor gave it me. Bosanquet had been stumped by Strudwick, and Nicholl bowled, and then MacGregor arrived – he took guard and then he slowly scraped forward, a thing I very rarely saw him do – the ball pitched on the leg stump and did just enough to beat the bat.

In the end Middlesex won by seven wickets, and in Surrey's second innings MacGregor stumped three and caught two. I was one of the two – c MacGregor b Bosanquet, 0 – So my old captain and I were quits. It was our last meeting in the cricket field, and the last cricket match that a man plays in is the one he never forgets. I shall never forget my last duck! I shall never forget MacGregor – for indeed he was, because of his great knowledge of the game – his persistency of purpose – his very silence, a terribly hard nut to crack.

Wishing for another opinion than my own as to MacGregor's captaincy, I wrote to an old friend of mine who played under MacGregor for Middlesex for many years. This is his reply:

"As a captain, MacGregor required a lot of knowing – he was dour – he said very little, but he had the gift of getting the very best out of those who understood him – those who did not understand him mistook his attempt to disguise his own keenness to win, for pessimism. MacGregor was a curious study in character. When a big effort was needed and it depended on the effort of one man, he would say just the right word to that man to make him feel his responsibility, at the same time conveying his own belief in the fact that he would not fail. As to words he was parsimonious, but he always said the right thing at the right moment. In this way MacGregor was a better skipper than many gave him credit for – it was all done so quietly, and few knew of it except those who played under him in the field.

When I first played with him he asked me where I was in the habit of fielding. I replied slip or mid-off or mid-on, anywhere close in. That was enough! I was generally put in the out-field after that! No doubt he thought it was good for my training and discipline. Then one day there was a vacancy at short slip, a left-hander was coming in, and as more than one regular member of the side refused the position, Mac beckoned to me: "I think you like short slip?" I jumped at the chance, being only too delighted to get out of the long-field which I detested. I beamed all over: "Yes, I do like short slip"; and as I went to my place I saw the old hands grin and among them was Stoddart (this was his last match for Middlesex). Stoddart was among those who had refused, remarking: "that his life was not insured!" I wondered why they smiled – I was not left wondering long! Trott was bowling to Tyler of Somerset. I took up my position, preferring to fall forward, than to be too near for my focus, then I was pulled up by Mac and Trott two or three yards, till I could almost shake hands with the batsman. Trott bowled three slow ones, and of the fourth all I knew was that my right hand was touching my ear, and the ball was in it. It was Trott's fast ball!

I turned round to meet laughter everywhere.

In the pavilion the voice of Sammy Woods greeted me: 'I say, old chap, do you always catch 'em like that?'

'No, Sammy – and I don't want to again.' And looking at MacGregor I saw a rare sight, I saw him smile."

As a batsman MacGregor was of the useful, not ornamental type – a splendid stop-gap – a fine breakwater against a sea of adversity – he was a 'no-stroke' player, but he made as many runs as he wanted to. He always played back in preference to pushing forward – he watched the ball when he was batting, almost as closely as when he was behind the stumps, and he once made 73 not out against the greatest pair of bowlers in the world, Turner and Ferris, who were backed up by a man who could also bowl a little, Hughie Trumble!

Rest in peace, old friend. You were a great stumper – you were a great cricketer, and you saw in the grand old game more than a circus show on which men may find it worth while to spend sixpence – you saw in it, as C. B. Fry says "a physical fine art full of plot-interest, enlivened by difficulties," difficulties that through the long, long years you successfully overcame.

MR HUGH HAMON MASSIE, died at Point Piper, Sydney, on October 12, 1928, at the advanced age of 83. A remarkably free and attractive batsman, he took a prominent part in the seven runs victory gained by Australia at The Oval in 1882 – the first defeat of England in this country which caused such a sensation that it inspired "The Ashes" memorial. Bowlers always held the upper hand in the match except when Australia batted a second time 38 behind. Then Massie, by hitting up 55 out of 66 for the first wicket on wet turf paved the way for the ultimate triumph brought about by the bowling of Spofforth and Boyle. Between showers Australia made only 56 runs after Massie was bowled by A. G. Steel, but England, wanting 85 to win, were dismissed for 77 on the drying pitch.

Nearly six feet in height and very active, Massie was a wonderful forcing batsman with drives and cuts his most effective strokes in hitting bowlers off their length. He went to the pitch of the ball whenever possible and did not mind lifting his drives – he was invaluable on treacherous turf. He fielded brilliantly anywhere, and held the most difficult catches in amazing style. He began his England experience by scoring 206 out of 265 against Oxford University, getting his second hundred while his partners contributed 12 runs between them. Altogether in first-class matches during the tour, Massie scored 1,403 runs, average 24. He played many fine innings for New South Wales, but his position in a Sydney bank prevented him from accepting invitations for other tours to England. When on a private visit in 1895 Massie was made an honorary member of MCC. He then played for the Club against Kent, and in the match celebrating the Jubilee of I Zingari he was in the Gentlemen of England eleven.

MR JOHN MAUDE, died on November 17, 1934, aged 84, having been born on March 17, 1850. Going to Eton when ten as a colleger he was there for nine years under three headmasters – Goodford, Balston, and Hornby. His tutor was the Rev. J. E. Yonge. In his time he had three future Bishops as fags – Welldon (Calcutta), Ryle (Liverpool) and Harmer (Rochester).

He played in the Eton eleven at Lord's as a medium left-hand bowler in 1868 and 1869. In the former year, when Harrow won, he took three wickets for 20 runs. Lord Harris, who was also a member of the team, wrote in his recollections of the match, "Our best bowler was John Maude, who probably did not bowl nearly enough." In 1869 Maude, by taking seven wickets for 36 in the second innings, contributed largely to Eton's victory by an innings and 19 runs. Of that famous match Mr H. S. Salt, in his *Memories of Bygone Eton*, wrote: – "C. J. Ottaway made a century. Thanks mainly to his patient and skilful batting and to some fine left-hand bowling by John Maude, the match ended in a single innings victory for Eton. Old Stephen Hawtrey is said to have stopped Maude in the street and asked to be allowed to shake 'that noble hand', which by a wonderful 'caught and bowled' had disposed of Harrow's most formidable batsman. We all believed the story. It seemed exactly what Stephen Hawtrey would have done. But 57 years later I was told by Maude that he had no recollection of the incident. It ought to have happened, anyhow." Maude also played in the Mixed Wall and Field elevens in 1868, and won the school fives in 1869. He went up to Oxford, and got his cricket Blue in 1873. At Lord's he took six Cambridge wickets for 39 runs in the second innings. On the first day he caught F. E. R. Fryer, the Light Blue captain, in sensational fashion. He was a member of the Harlequins, and played for the Gentlemen of Warwickshire in 1874.

MR JOHN MILLS, born at Coddington, near Newark, on January 28, 1855, collapsed in his seat during an interval in the match between Derbyshire and Nottinghamshire at Ilkeston on June 27, 1932, and when carried into the pavilion life was found to be extinct. He and Arthur Shrewsbury appeared at Trent Bridge for the first time for the Colts on Easter Monday 1873 and were top scores against the County XI with 24 and 35 respectively. A couple of seasons later both were introduced into the county side, for which Mills played occasionally for eight years. He made the record hit on the Wollaton ground and assisted Lenton United until an accident caused his retirement from active participation in the game.

THE REV. WALTER BAPTIST MONEY, who was born at Sternfield in Suffolk on the 27th of July, 1848, died suddenly at Edgbaston on the 1st of March, 1924. As Walter Money retired from first-class cricket directly he entered the Church, only people whose memories go back more than fifty years will recall him in the field, but for a few seasons he was in the first flight of amateur cricketers – a dominating figure at Harrow and Cambridge. Few men have ever had a pleasanter experience of Lord's ground. In the matches there that specially appealed to him, he was never on the losing side till in 1871, Butler – taking all ten wickets in the first innings – brought about the downfall of the Cambridge eleven. Money was in the very strong Harrow teams that beat Eton in one innings in 1865 and 1866 and was captain in the drawn game of 1867. In those days he was essentially an all-round player and more to be feared for his lob bowling than his batting. He took in the three matches 21 Eton wickets, doing the hat trick in 1866. By the way Canon McCormick, who saw all the lob bowlers from William Clarke to Walter Humphreys, thought that Money in his prime was always rather underrated.

Going up from Harrow with a big reputation, Money stepped straight into the Cambridge eleven as a Freshman in 1868 and played the regulation four years. He does not seem to have been in residence in 1871, as he only took part in the London matches, and to judge from his scores he could scarcely have been in full practice. Cambridge beat Oxford by 168 runs in 1868 and by 58 runs in 1869. Then came the 2 runs victory in 1870 – Cobden's match – when Money was captain. In 1871 Oxford won by eight wickets. Of the many stories that have enshrouded the Cobden match – the Balaclava Charge of the cricket field – Money himself contributed one of the best, telling how Jack Dale, when reproached for allowing a simple catch at point to go unheeded, apologised by saying "I'm awfully sorry, Walter, I was looking at a lady getting out of a drag".

SAM MOSS, reputed to have been at one time the fastest bowler in England, was killed on the railway line whilst walking to a match at Featherstone on August 7, 1923. He was in his fifty-sixth year. He was very successful for Bacup in the Lancashire League in 1899 and at least twice during his career he obtained all ten wickets in an innings – for 19 runs for Padiham in 1908 and for 32 runs for Barnsley v Huddersfield. At various times he was also on the Old Trafford ground-staff and with the Batley CC.

MAJOR E. G. MURDOCK, born on November 14, 1864, died in his flannels in the Bristol pavilion in the third week of May, 1926. A good wicket-keeper, he played for both Somerset and Gloucestershire, and was associated prominently with the Bedminster CC.


MAURICE NICHOL, the Worcestershire cricketer, died suddenly at Chelmsford, where Essex were playing Worcestershire on May 21, 1934. Born at Hetton, Durham, on September 10, 1905, Nichol was in his 29th year. He played as an amateur for Durham in the Minor counties competition and had a trial at The Oval for Surrey before qualifying for Worcestershire in 1929. During his period of qualification Nichol had the distinction of making a hundred on his first appearance in first-class cricket – 104 for Worcestershire against West Indies in 1928. Playing regularly for the county in 1929 he scored 1,442 runs and the following season he registered the highest innings of his career, 262 not out against Hampshire at Bournemouth. Nichol possessed a neat style and, as he proved himself a consistent run-getter, hopes were entertained that he would become an England cricketer. In 1931 he acted as twelfth man for England in the Test match against New Zealand at Lord's, and after faring moderately the following season, he jumped into his best form in 1933 when he concluded the summer with three successive hundreds: – 116, against Hampshire at Bournemouth; 165 not out against Glamorgan at Worcester and 154 against Yorkshire at Worcester, he and Martin adding 243.


MR LIONEL CHARLES HAMILTON PALAIRET, a famous batsman with a singularly graceful style who played for Oxford University, Somerset and England, died on March 27, 1933. Somerset by close association – he received his early education at a school at Clevedon – he was born on May 27, 1870 at Grange-over-sands in Lancashire. It was rather curious that, while above all remembered for his graceful and virile batting, he achieved a remarkable bowling performance at the age of ten when in a school match he took seven wickets with consecutive balls. Proceeding to Repton, he was in the eleven there in 1886 and the three following seasons, being captain in 1888 and 1889. In his last year he had a batting average of 29 and took fifty-six wickets for little more than 12 runs apiece. Going up to Oxford in the autumn of 1889 he sprang into prominence as soon as he appeared by his strikingly beautiful and effortless batting. He played four times in the Varsity match (1890-1893) and was captain in the last two years. The most interesting part of Lionel Palairet's history, however, consisted in his career with Somerset, for whom he first played in 1890. The county had not attained first-class rank at that time, but the following season they were admitted to the county championship. Palairet that season scored 560 runs, with an average of 31, and in 1892 he ranked as one of the great batsmen of the day by scoring 1,343 runs with an average of 31 and appearing for Gentlemen against Players at Lord's. Late in August he and H. T. Hewett – a formidable opening pair – put up a record opening partnership of 346 runs against Yorkshire at Taunton. The two batsmen were together only three hours and a half. Right up to 1907 Palairet – if not always able to play a great deal – remained a leading member of the Somerset eleven. He never went to Australia but played twice for England in 1902. Those games were two of the most thrilling Test matches in history, Australia winning at Manchester by 3 runs and England getting home at The Oval by one wicket. In first-class games Palairet hit twenty-seven centuries, his highest innings being 292 against Hampshire in 1896. His best season was that of 1901 when he scored 1,906 runs with an average of 57; he and L. C. Braund made 222 for the first Somerset wicket in the second innings against Yorkshire at Leeds, Palairet obtaining 173. That was a remarkable match, Somerset, going in a second time 238 behind, hitting up a score of 630 and beating Yorkshire by 279 runs. Palairet's cricket for Somerset will never be forgotten. His drives into the river and the churchyard at Taunton are still remembered by those who had the good fortune to see him in such form. He had almost every good quality as a batsman; combining strong defence with fine cutting and driving on either side of the wicket he always shaped in classic style.

Essentially a forward player he was handicapped on a soft pitch, but under any conditions he made the off drive in a manner few have approached and no one has surpassed. He represented Oxford in the three miles, and played Association football for Combined Universities, London, and Corinthians. In addition he was at one period an ardent follower of hounds. He was president of the Somerset County Cricket Club in 1929.

JAMES PHILLIPS, who was born at Port Adelaide in South Australia on September 1, 1860, and died at Burnaby, Vancouver, on April 21, 1930, will be remembered more for his work as an umpire than for anything he accomplished as a player. To Phillips more than anyone else is due the credit for stamping out throwing in first-class cricket. Going out to Australia to act as umpire with A. E. Stoddart's team in 1897-98, he twice no-balled Ernest Jones, the fast bowler, whose delivery when visiting this country with Harry Trott's team in 1896 was condemned as unfair, and the courageous action of Phillips found many imitators. Throwing on English cricket grounds had for a long time been allowed to go on unchecked but in 1898 C. B. Fry was no-balled by West at Trent Bridge, by Phillips himself at Brighton and by Sherwin at Lord's while a new Warwickshire bowler, Hopkins, came under the ban of Titchmarsh at Tonbridge. A storm of controversy was aroused after F. R. Spofforth, in a letter to the *Sporting Life* in 1897, suggested that the best way would be to legalise throwing and in one season it would bring about its own cure. However, as a result of Phillips' example, speedy and satisfactory action was taken by the captains of the first-class counties who at a meeting at Lord's in December, 1900 arrived at an agreement to deal strongly with the matter in the following summer. Then, in a match between Lancashire and Somerset at Old Trafford, Phillips no-balled Mold sixteen times. A strong agitation was got up on Mold's behalf but owing to the fact that the Lancashire fast bowler had been condemned as unfair by the county captains at their famous meeting – by a majority of eleven to one – this was systematically ignored. The MCC Committee in the following December issued a circular to all the county secretaries in which was expressed the hope that the County Cricket Executives would, in future, decline to play bowlers with doubtful deliveries. Thereafter English bowling was more uniformly fair and above suspicion than in any season during the previous twenty-five years and, eventually, throwing practically disappeared.

Phillips was a good medium-pace bowler, a fairly useful batsman and a smart field at cover-point. He came to England in 1888 and joined the ground staff at Lord's, appearing for Middlesex between 1890 and 1898 and for many years journeying between England and Australia. For a time he was engaged as coach at Christchurch, in New Zealand, and whilst there played an innings of 110 not out for Canterbury v Wellington in 1898-99. In the course of his career with Middlesex, Phillips made 1,091 runs and took 216 wickets for just over 22 runs each. Among his bowling feats were: seven wickets for 20 runs (Victoria v New South Wales at Melbourne in 1890-91); thirteen for 117 (Middlesex v Sussex at Lord's in 1895), and thirteen for 187 (Middlesex v Gloucestershire on the same ground in 1896). In the course of a week's cricket for MCC at Lord's in 1888 he took sixteen of Scarborough's twenty wickets and dismissed four Nottinghamshire Castle men in four balls. His benefit match was Middlesex v Australians at Lord's in 1899.

BRIGADIER-GENERAL ROBERT MONTAGU POORE, who during one season was the most prolific scorer in England, died on July 14, 1938, aged 72. He used to relate that he did not take seriously to cricket before going to India as a lieutenant in the 7th Hussars. Then he studied text books on the game while playing in Army matches. From 1892 to 1895 when ADC to Lord Harris, then Governor of Bombay, he averaged 80 for Government House. Going to South Africa, better opportunities came for finding his true ability when facing the formidable bowlers under the command of Lord Hawke. He hit up 112 at Pietermaritzburg and at Durban, when fifteen of Natal were set to get 228, he scored 107, being mainly responsible for the local side winning by five wickets; these were the only hundreds scored against the touring team of 1895-96. He also appeared for South

Africa in the three Test matches without distinguishing himself more than did some others in badly beaten elevens.

In the course of a few months in Natal he scored 1,600 runs, including nine separate hundreds, so that when returning to England in 1898 at the age of 32, Major Poore was ready for first-class cricket. On a soft wicket at Lord's he scored 51 and helped appreciably in an innings victory for MCC over Lancashire. He averaged 34 for eleven Hampshire matches and next season he became the most sensational batsman in the country, his doings being described as phenomenal. Making a late start he scored in two months – June 12 to August 12 – 1,399 runs for Hampshire with an average of 116.58. Major Poore hit seven centuries, two against Somerset at Portsmouth, and in his next innings another off the Lancashire bowlers at Southampton; he also scored exactly 100 runs in two innings against the Australians. In 21 first-class innings he made 1,551 runs, average 91.23 – a figure not exceeded until Herbert Sutcliffe averaged 96.96 in 1931. The return with Somerset at Taunton was specially noteworthy, Major Poore scoring 304 and with Captain E. G. Wynyard (225) adding 411 in four hours twenty minutes – the English record for the sixth wicket. Chosen for the Gentlemen against the Players at both The Oval and Lord's, Poore did little. Military duty took him back to South Africa before the end of the season, and after occasional appearances his county cricket ceased in 1906, but so well did he retain his form and activity that in 1923, when 57 years old, he hit three consecutive centuries during a tour of MCC in the west country. His 304 stood as a Hampshire record for 38 years, being surpassed in 1937 by R. H. Moore with 316 against Warwickshire at Bournemouth.

Six feet four inches in height, of massive frame with powerful limbs, Major Poore when at the top of his form used his long reach with great effect in driving, his strokes between the bowler and cover point going with such speed over the turf that fieldsmen, no matter how placed, could not prevent him from scoring freely. Before becoming accustomed to English wickets, he played forward more in defence for smothering the ball than as a hitter, but his drive ripened to one of the most powerful ever known.

A versatile sportsman, Major Poore was one of the finest swordsmen in the Army, taking the highest honours at the military tournament. A first-rate polo player he also twice won the West of India lawn tennis championship, a feat he repeated in Matabeleland and was in his regimental shooting team. His exceptional physical powers were demonstrated in his wonderful 1899 season; during a fortnight in June he played in the winning team of the inter-regimental polo tournament, won the best-man-at-arms mounted event at the Royal naval and military tournament and scored three consecutive centuries for Hampshire, 104 and 119 not out against Somerset and 111 against Lancashire.

MR REGINALD WILLIAM RICE, died at Bedford on February 11, 1938, in his 70th year. Born at Tewkesbury, he played for Gloucestershire in 1890, three years before being given his Oxford Blue by L. C. H. Palairet.

Both universities were very strong at that time. C. B. Fry, G. J. Mordaunt and H. D. G. Leveson Gower were in the Oxford eleven besides the brothers Lionel and R. C. N. Palairet, while Cambridge, captained by F. S. Jackson, now Sir Stanley, included K. S. Ranjitsinhji, A. O. Jones, James Douglas, A. J. L. Hill, E. C. Streatfeild, C. M. Wells and L. H. Gay. Cambridge won by 266 runs.

This was the match in which C. M. Wells gave away 8 runs by bowling wides in order to frustrate the apparent desire of Oxford to follow-on so that Cambridge would have to bat last. This incident and a repetition three years later brought about the change in the law placing the question of the follow-on at the option of the side who, having batted first, held a lead authorising them to enforce the law.

A steady batsman with admirable defence, Rice played for Gloucestershire until 1903 and when at his best he often opened the innings with W. G. Grace. He made some centuries, but never played a more valuable innings than his 82 not out at Bath in 1900. Going in first with 210 runs wanted for victory, Rice was missed in the slips when the game was a tie, the ball went to the boundary and Gloucestershire won by one wicket six minutes from time. The next highest score in the match was 66 by Lionel Palairet for Somerset, Rice's captain at Oxford.

After being a master at Forest School, Rice continued his scholastic career at Bedford and played for the county. He had a curious experience at Bury St Edmunds in 1909 against Suffolk. The game was a tie with three Bedfordshire wickets to fall. Rice was indisposed and, though coming from his hotel, he did not have an opportunity to make the winning hit. All three wickets fell at one total and the match was a tie.

**MAJOR HESKETH-VERNON HESKETH PRICHARD, DSO, MC, FRGS, FZS,** born in India on November 17, 1876, died at Gorhambury, near St Albans, on June 14, 1922. He learned his cricket at Fettes and afterwards played successfully for Hampshire, MCC, the Gentlemen and other prominent teams. As a fast bowler he was most useful, his deliveries getting up very quickly from the pitch. For Hampshire he obtained 222 wickets for 23.11 runs each, and he was probably at his best in 1904 when, in all first-class matches, he took 106 wickets for an average of 21.92. He assisted the Gentlemen in 1903 and two following seasons, and took part in a couple of tours, visiting the West Indies with Lord Brackley in 1904-05 and America as a member of the MCC team in 1907. When Kent were set 131 to win v MCC at Lord's in 1904, Hesketh Prichard took six wickets for 23 runs, the innings closing for 97. Half the side were out for 12, and he dismissed C. H. B. Marsham, Hardinge and Murrell without a run between them. For Hampshire he claimed thirteen wickets for 78 runs v Derbyshire at Southampton in 1905, and six for 18 v Worcestershire at Worcester in 1912. For MCC v Gentlemen of Philadelphia at Haverford in 1907 he did the hat trick. He was well-known as a traveller and author, and during the war carried out responsible duties and was twice mentioned in despatches.

**ARTHUR DICK POUGHER,** born at Leicester, on April 19, 1865, died at his native place on May 20, 1926, aged 61. An excellent all-round cricketer, he will be recalled chiefly as a capital medium-pace bowler with a high delivery and a break-back, combined with skilful variation of pace. His most memorable feat was in taking five wickets without a run in fifteen balls for MCC against the Australians at Lord's in June, 1896, the latter being dismissed for 18: one man was absent ill, and the last six wickets went down with the total unchanged. Among many other good performances with the ball by Pougher the following are worthy of mention:

13-54   (including 6-10), Leicestershire v Surrey, at Leicester, 1886 (he and Rylott bowled unchanged)

  7-8   Leicestershire v Warwickshire, at Edgbaston, 1886

Hat trick MCC v Cambridge University, at Lord's, 1887

  8-81   Leicestershire v Essex, at Leicester, 1887

  6-14   Shrewsbury's Team v Queensland XVIII, at Brisbane, 1887-88

10-71   Leicestershire v Australians, at Leicester, 1888 (the county won by 20 runs)

  6-15   Leicestershire v Derbyshire, at Leicester, 1888

  6-13   Leicestershire v Essex, at Leyton, 1888

13-104 Leicestershire v Surrey, at Leicester, 1888 (he and Rylott bowled unchanged)

  8-115 Leicestershire v Warwickshire, at Leicester, 1890 (The other two men were run out)

13-41   (including 8 for 18), Leicestershire v MCC, at Lord's, 1890

  8-52   Leicestershire v MCC, at Lord's, 1891 (he did the hat trick)

  8-48   Leicestershire v Essex, at Leyton, 1892

  5-15   Leicestershire v Surrey, at Leicester, 1893

13-86   Leicestershire v Hampshire, at Leicester, 1893

14-84   Leicestershire v Hampshire, at Southampton, 1893

Unchanged with J. T. Hearne, MCC v Kent, at Lord's, 1894

  7-17   Leicestershire v South Africans, at Leicester, 1894

14-89   (including 8-60), Leicestershire v Essex, at Leyton, 1894

8-40   Leicestershire v Surrey, at Leicester, 1894
9-34   England v Surrey, at The Oval, 1895
8-85   Leicestershire v Yorkshire, at Leicester, 1895
Unchanged with J. T. Hearne, Earl de la Warr's XI v Australians at Bexhill, 1896
8-151  MCC v Worcestershire, at Lord's, 1900

In games of less note he took eleven wickets for 18 runs for R. G. Barlow's XI v XXII of Blackpool and District in 1889, and (in conjunction with F. Martin, of Kent) obtained eight wickets in nine balls for Mr W. W. Read's Team v XXII of the Country Clubs at Cape Town in 1891-92, each player taking four in succession. In a twelve-a-side match, too, at Streatham in July, 1892, whilst playing for MCC v Streatham he took all eleven wickets for 37 runs.

For Leicestershire he made many good scores, including 109 v Essex at Leyton in 1894, 102 not out v Warwickshire at Leicester and 114 v Derbyshire at Derby in 1896, and 104 v Surrey and 106 v Yorkshire, both at Leicester, in 1899. From 1887 until 1909 he was a member of the MCC ground-staff at Lord's, and he took part in two tours overseas, visiting Australia with Shrewsbury's Team in 1887-88 and South Africa with Mr W. W. Read's in 1891-92. His only appearance for the Players was at The Oval in 1895. He received reward for his service to the game in two benefit matches – Leicestershire v Yorkshire at Leicester in 1900 and Middlesex v Kent at Lord's in 1910. For many years he had kept the Old Cricket Ground Hotel, Aylestone Park, Leicester.

MR EDWARD RAE, who introduced the game into Russian Lapland, died at Birkenhead on June 26, 1923, aged 76.

## RANJITSINHJI

### By Sir Stanley Jackson

The news of the death in India in April, 1933, of His Highness the Jam Saheb of Nawanagar, better known to the cricket public throughout the world as K. S. Ranjitsinhji, was received with profound regret by his innumerable friends in this country. It seems but natural that an appreciation of His Highness and his remarkable career upon the cricket field should appear in *Wisden* in the volumes of which his achievements are chronicled and provide a lasting testimony to his skill. There must be many who knew Ranji better than I did during the last period of his cricket career in this country, but for some years after we first met at Cambridge in 1892 I had the pleasure of his close friendship, and many indications of a confidence and goodwill which in later years I realised was but a natural return of a high caste Indian gentleman for what he regarded as some special act of friendship or service. I have, therefore, readily responded to an invitation from the editor to write a few lines about Ranji as I knew him.

The first time I can remember seeing him play cricket was early in the summer term at Cambridge in 1892. I had heard of an Indian playing occasionally for Trinity in 1891, but only as one who with coaching and practice and less resort to unorthodox methods might become a useful cricketer. One day in 1892 on my way up to Fenner's I noticed a match in progress on Parker's Piece, and seeing a rather unusually large crowd of spectators I stopped to watch. As luck would have it Ranji was at the wicket. After a short exhibition of brilliant and certainly unorthodox strokes I thought Ranji was stumped, but much to the satisfaction of the crowd the umpire decided in his favour. I left the scene not particularly impressed.

I spent the winter months of 1892-93 playing cricket with Lord Hawke's team in India and I have no doubt now that my experience in India during that tour awakened in me a sympathetic interest for Indians which perhaps in 1892 I did not possess to the same degree. At Fenner's in the early part of the summer term of 1893 I saw Ranji at the nets, being bowled to by two fast bowlers whom I recognised as Lockwood and Richardson of

Surrey, who with other county professionals came in those days to Cambridge to get fit for the county season. When I had finished my practice Ranji was still at it, but with two fresh bowlers. I mentioned to C. M. Wells that I thought Ranji seemed to be overdoing the practice; and when Wells made this suggestion, Ranji replied "I find I am all right for half an hour but I cannot last. I must now master endurance".

In later days I had many opportunities of remembering this remark when consistent centuries appeared to demonstrate that he had succeeded in his object and justified his efforts at practice. Ranjitsinhji had a passion for cricket and was determined to excel. He had that confidence in himself which springs from natural ability. That he possessed capacity for application and perseverance was further shown by his skill as a shot and as a fisherman, and later in the more serious walks of life, by his success as a ruler and administrator in his State. Mention of application and perseverance inevitably brings to my mind C. B. Fry – a great personal friend of mine, as he was also Ranji's friend and partner in countless triumphs in the cricket field for Sussex. With such a colleague it would not have been surprising had Fry been completely overshadowed; but this he certainly was not; on the contrary his place in the annals of cricket comes but very little short of that of the famous Indian himself. But what an interesting contrast! If ever there was an example of the natural and the created in cricket, here it was. Ranji playing with an ease and grace as though to the manner born; Fry with a skill and technique obviously the product of a wonderful physique, indomitable determination and perseverance, and backed by the brain of a genius and a master of applied science.

I had the pleasure of giving Ranjitsinhji his Blue in 1893. He was a brilliant slip and played several good innings in the university matches at Cambridge. The university match tried him highly. He received an ovation on going in to bat, which, meant at an encouragement, proved, I know, an embarrassment. He made only a few runs. He quickly became a great favourite with the public, a position he gained not only by his skill as a cricketer but in no small degree through a personality made additionally attractive by a modest demeanour and invariable courtesy which is a natural attribute of a Rajput. The disappointment at his failure, which was rare, was almost as great as the pleasure enjoyed from his success, even amongst the most enthusiastic of the supporters of his opponents. I am reminded of an occasion during a Test match at Manchester when, staying with friends, I sat next to a lady at dinner who bemoaned her fate at having come a long way only to be disappointed by Ranji's failure. I, personally, felt duly subdued as I had myself made 128 that day!

A figure so prominent in the cricket life of this country for so many years must necessarily have had an influence upon the game one way or another. Ranji certainly played the game as all would wish to see it played. Perhaps he was fortunate to have placed at a time when many have declared cricket in this country was at its best. My friend Gilbert Jessop has referred to him as "The most brilliant figure during cricket's most brilliant period", and "It was during the nineties that cricket reached its pinnacle as a national game and Ranji was one of those who helped to put it there". Ranjitsinhji had no desire to be placed upon a pinnacle. He was happiest when singing the praises of others. The names of three of his contemporaries occur to me, who for brilliance and attractiveness could possibly claim a seat alongside him – Trumper, R. E. Foster and A. C. MacLaren. His example was an inspiration to his own people in India, and his main desire to feel that the part he had played in the game was for its good.

"When I have finished", he once said, "I hope I may be remembered not only for the success it has been my fortune to enjoy as a player, but rather as one who tried his best to popularise the game for the game's sake."

When an unfortunate stroke of fate deprived him of that priceless possession to which he owed so much – the sight of one of his eyes – he showed a fortitude in adversity which none could help but admire; but if this meant the end of his cricket it did not prevent him from seeing his way along the difficult path of statesmanship when called upon to undertake the high responsibility of Chancellor of the Chamber of Princes at a time of crisis in India's future – a position he filled with success.

I think it will be generally agreed that the game of cricket gained by Ranji's association with it, as also can his innumerable friends feel that they gained much by their association with so good a sportsman.

## BY THE EDITOR

Almost the greatest tribute to the memory of HH. The Jam Saheb of Nawanagar, whose sudden death at Delhi, on April 2, came as such a shock to the whole world of cricket, is the fact that everywhere he was referred to as "Ranji". It is scarcely necessary to add that this contraction of his name was used with true affection early in his career and remained to the end.

Born at Sarodar, Kathiawar, India, on September 10, 1872. Kumar Shri Ranjitsinhji came of ancient Rajput stock. He received his earliest lessons in cricket while at school at Rajkumar College, Rajkote, and when in 1888 he paid a visit to England he was, thanks to the coaching he had received from Mr Chester Macnaghten, a Cambridge man but not a "Blue", a batsman of some skill but very unorthodox in his methods. Actually he played no cricket of any note in England until he went into residence at Trinity College, Cambridge where he secured a place in the college eleven. Probably because he was an Indian he attracted a certain amount of attention but nobody who watched him playing for Cambridgeshire in 1892-93, and for Cambridge University when he was given his "Blue" by F. S. Jackson in 1893, had the least idea that they were looking at a man who, in a few years, was to dazzle the world and bring about such an alteration in the methods of batting as definitely to mark a turning point in the history of the game. It is not too much to say that by his extraordinary skill Ranjitsinhji revolutionised cricket, the effects of his wonderful play on the leg-side being seen day after day down to the present time.

If a little crude and most certainly unreliable at the outset, Ranjitsinhji was blessed with a most versatile brain and the capacity for application which in course of time made him one of the most brilliant batsmen ever seen. Quite individual and distinctive in style, he possessed exceptional keenness of eye, besides such power and flexibility of wrist, that on a fast wicket he could do almost anything in the way of scoring. Admitting the use of the word in connection with cricket, genius could with the greatest truth be applied to him. Thanks to his special gifts he could – and did – take the good length ball off the middle-stump and glance it to leg with a measure of certainty no one else has ever equalled or even approached. In this way he was no safe model for any player of average skill, for the attempt to bring off many of his strokes must have been fatal to most people.

Ranjitsinhji did not attain to this pitch of perfection without much hard work. For two or three seasons before he got his "Blue" he put in hours of practice at the nets with Lockwood, Richardson, J. T. Hearne and Tom Hayward bowling at him. The first two, then almost at their zenith in regard to pace and accuracy, had definite instructions from him always to try and bowl at their fastest when he was having practice, and the value of this intensive training was seen a few years later when he blossomed forth as a batsman able to bring off the most daring strokes. To begin with he was not player at all on soft wickets, but he steadily increased his ability to make runs under adverse conditions and put together some remarkable innings on bowlers' pitches. Primarily, however, he was a fast-wicket batsman because, for the successful exploitation of his own particular strokes, hard turf was essential. When he first came out he appeared to lack the strength necessary for driving, making nearly all his runs behind or square with the wicket, and mainly on the leg-side. But before long he employed the drive a lot and invested that stroke with plenty of power. In many of his displays he gave full proof that he could score with readiness in front of the wicket, but by those who watched him throughout his great days he will be remembered best for the extraordinary skill with which he glanced the ball to leg.

In the only university match in which he took part he did nothing of any consequence, but in that season at Cambridge he played some good innings and against the Australians scored 58 and not out 37 in splendid style. I was present at that match and never forgot the impression he created on my mind. I knew that I was watching an accomplished batsman, but little thought that the lithe, supple figure then playing such bowlers as George Giffen, C. T. B. Turner, and Hugh Trumble, to mention nothing of Bob McLeod, Harry Trott and Billy Bruce, with consummate ease and confidence was to become and to remain from 1895 until 1912 – with two breaks of four years each – the most talked-of man in cricket.

Deciding to stay in England after leaving Cambridge, Ranjitsinhji duly qualified for Sussex, and in 1895 commenced a memorable association with that county which continued unbroken up to 1904. No happier augury for his future success could have occurred than when on the occasion of his first appearance for Sussex, against the MCC at Lord's, he scored 77 not out and 150. That summer he obtained 1,775 runs and averaged nearly 50. A year later this performance was completely eclipsed. His average went up to nearly 58 and he registered no fewer than 2,780 runs. This was the highest aggregate obtained by any one up to that date and, what was of greatest importance, bigger than that of W. G. Grace – 2,739 in 1871 – which had stood as the record for a quarter of a century. The seasons of 1901 and 1904 also brought Ranjitsinhji aggregates of over 2,000 runs, while in 1899 and 1900 he exceeded 3,000, his totals respectively for these years being 3,159 and 3,065. In 1900 he had the remarkable average of 87. Altogether in the course of his career he scored 24,567 runs with an average of 45, and played 72 three-figure innings – ten during the summer of 1896. On fourteen occasions he reached 200, obtaining all these scores for Sussex and five of them in 1900. In that year he twice obtained three hundreds in succession – 127 against Gloucestershire, 222 against Somerset, and 215 not out against Cambridge University, and, later in the season, his scores were 103 against Surrey, 202 against Middlesex, and 109 against Gloucestershire. It must be mentioned too that in 1896 he accomplished the feat of making three consecutive hundreds, getting 100 and 125 not out against Yorkshire immediately following 165 against Lancashire. In the match with Yorkshire he went in on the second evening, but had not scored at the drawing of stumps, so that he really made two separate hundreds on the same day.

Among the many big partnerships in which he was concerned were two of over 300; he and W. Newham scored 344 for the seventh wicket in the Sussex and Essex match of 1902, and 325 for the second wicket came with George Brann in the game between Sussex and Surrey in 1899. Taunton, always one of his favourite grounds, was in 1901 the scene of his highest individual score – 285 not out against Somerset. In county cricket probably his most masterly display was that at Hove in 1900 when against Middlesex he got 202 in three hours. The pitch helped the bowlers considerably, but Ranjitsinhji triumphed over all the difficulties and actually hit thirty-five 4s. He was, however, always insistent that the best innings he played on a hard wicket was his 234 not out at Hastings in 1902 when in the match between Sussex and Surrey 1,427 runs were scored and only twenty-one wickets went down. Richardson and Lockwood were among the Surrey bowlers, but Ranjitsinhji batted so superbly that he made both of them look just ordinary. His driving was wonderful. Some years afterwards he said to me, apropos of this innings and without any trace of boasting in his remarks, "I think I could have stayed there for ever, for the ball looked as big as a balloon the whole time I was in". By a sad coincidence, Hastings was the ground on which in 1920 he played in his last match in England – Sussex v Northamptonshire. He had then grown very stout and suffered from the grave disability of having lost one of his eyes, through an accident when out shooting. I saw both these matches and well remember the feeling of sorrow which came over me when I realised the inevitable change which the passage of years had wrought in his wonderful powers of execution. It is of interest to know, however, that his one idea in coming back and playing cricket after the War was prompted by his desire to write another book on cricket, with special emphasis on the art of batting with only one eye. As he said at the time, he could deal with good-length balls almost as well as formerly, but the long-hop or half-volley caused him real trouble in properly focussing his sight.

Ranjitsinhji was captain of Sussex for five years – 1899 to 1903. Returning to India after the summer of 1904 he did not play again until 1908 when he turned out and obtained over 1,100 runs. There came a similar interval after that, and in 1912 returning once more to first-class cricket, he made more than eleven hundred runs.

Taking part in fourteen Test matches – five in Australia – he scored in the course of those games 989 runs with an average of nearly 45. When, in the winter of 1897-98, he formed one of A. E. Stoddart's second team to Australia, he played an innings of 175 at Sydney but as an England cricketer his great triumph was that at Manchester in 1896 when he scored 154 not out in superb style, being so completely master of the Australian bowling that, could he have got anybody to stay with him, he might have saved England from defeat. As it was, the Australians wanted only 125 to win, but Ranjitsinhji's splendid batting was followed by some of the most magnificent bowling ever seen, on the part of Tom Richardson, and seven wickets went down before the runs were obtained, Richardson being on for three hours without sending down one really loose ball.

While his general record in Test matches against Australia came out quite well, Ranjitsinhji finished his career in those games ingloriously in 1902 when, curiously enough he had as his companion in misfortune C. B. Fry. Here were two of the greatest batsmen in the world, but a more deplorable failure than that of both could not well be imagined. Ranjitsinhji, in the course of three matches, scored 13, 0, 2, and 0, and Fry 0, 0, 1, and 4. Still, those particular contests furnished the only serious blot on a wonderful career. Ranjitsinhji figured prominently in Gentlemen v Players matches. He made his first appearance in 1893 and his last in 1912, his score of 121 at Lord's in 1904 being his best.

In 1897 he wrote the "Jubilee Book of Cricket" and two years later he took a team to America.

So has passed a great character in the history of the game. We may never see his like again, for he burst on the circket horizon at the start of what has been described as its most brilliant era, when there existed scope for introducing new ideas and methods.

I count myself unusually fortunate to have been a witness of many of his great performances, and even more privileged to have enjoyed his friendship. To me Ranjitsinhji was the embodiment of all that a cricketer should be – generous in defeat, modest in success and genuinely enthusiastic regarding the achievements of either colleagues or opponents.

S. J. S.

LIEUTENANT-COLONEL ARTHUR CAREW RICHARDS, was born on February 2, 1865, and died at Nottingham on November 9, 1930, aged 65. He was in the Eton Eleven in 1881 and two following years, and in his matches against Harrow and Winchester scored 118 runs besides taking sixteen wickets. He became quite a good batsman of vigorous methods and he could also bowl a useful slow ball and field well at short-slip. He played occasionally for Hampshire and took part in much military cricket. In an inter-company game of the 2nd Hampshire Regiment at Barberton, South Africa, in October 1901, he made 101 not out and 185, scoring altogether 286 out of 311 from the bat. No-one else could make more than two in the first innings, (through which he carried his bat), nor more than six in the second. He also took eight wickets in his opponents' first innings.

MR WILLIAM NICHOLS ROE, died in a London nursing home after an operation on October 11, 1937. A very well-known figure in the world of cricket from the time that he played with great success for the Clergy Orphan School, Canterbury, until last summer, when at the age of 76 he regularly attended Lord's and The Oval, W. N. Roe maintained his close connexion with the game unbroken.

For his school in 1878 he scored 1,095 runs, including four hundreds, with an average of 57. Next year he took all ten Chartham Asylum wickets for 16 runs, and in three seasons for the school 292 wickets fell to him at 8 runs each. Going to Magdalene College, Cambridge, he received his Blue in 1883 from C. T. Studd, but, though on the winning side, he did not get a run and the Oxford wickets were shared by his captain and C. Aubrey Smith. He was famous already for the highest score then on record, having made

415 not out when, on invitation, he completed the Emmanual Long Vacation Club eleven in a game against Caius Long Vacation Club in 1881. W. N. Roe got these runs out of 708 for four wickets in five hours. This was in reply to a score of 100 and Caius gave up the match rather than continue on the third day. So close was his concentration on the game that he counted all his runs and on this occasion he challenged the scorer with having given him one less than his total!

MR JOHN HARVEY TORRENS ROUPELL, who was born in Madras on July 15, 1845, died at Hurst, Berkshire, on May 15, 1920. He was educated at Harrow and Uppingham, and was in the latter XI in 1863. He was a tremendous hitter, a very fast round-armed bowler and a good field at long-on. In an innings of 97 for Trinity Hall v Emmanuel College in June, 1865, he made clear hits for 10, 9, and 8, without any overthrows. "The tenner travelled about 240 yards".

MR SANDFORD SPENCE SCHULTZ, who died on December 17, 1937, aged 80, was in the Uppingham eleven of 1873 and four years later was given his Cambridge Blue by W. S. Patterson. From 1877 to 1882 he appeared occasionally for Lancashire. He went to Australia in 1878-79 under Lord Harris for the tour which originated in an invitation from the Melbourne club to the Gentlemen of England. By arrangement, Tom Emmett and George Ulyett, the two Yorkshire fast bowlers, were included because suitable amateurs were not available, but the team lacked slow bowling. The one match played against Australia, represented by David Gregory's Eleven who were in England during the previous summer, was lost by ten wickets, F. R. Spofforth taking thirteen wickets for 110 runs. Schultz, scoring 20, helped to save the innings defeat.

A fast round-arm bowler, good bat and smart slip fieldsman, Schultz was very prominent in club cricket. He took nine wickets, one man being run out, in an innings for Orleans Club against Bexley in 1882 and for Uppingham Rovers against United Services at Portsmouth in 1887 he scored 286 – a noteworthy performance 50 years ago. Mr Schultz, who changed his name to Storey late in life, was concerned in one exceptional incident. Mr Leveson Gower, in *Recollections of Oxford Cricket* in last year's *Wisden*, mentioned a match with Gentlemen of England in 1881 begun on the Christchurch ground, and, because of the bumpy state of the pitch, re-started a few hours later in The Parks. Mr Edmund Peake, in a letter to *The Times* last July, explained: "The fast bowler (I blush to say it) committed such havoc as would have made him famous in these days. The Gentlemen refused to continue and the match was begun all over again in The Parks. One batsman – S. S. Schultz – was out first ball each time. Twice first ball in one innings – a record". Mr A. J. Webbe will remember the match.

JAMES SEYMOUR, an indispensable member of the great Kent elevens before the War, was born at Brightling, in Sussex, on October 25, 1879, and died at Marden on September 30, 1930, aged 50. He played for Kent through long residence at Pembury. Like Humphreys, whose name is inevitably associated with his own, he never rose to the highest standard of representative cricket for in his day that standard was very high but as a county player he was in the highest class. In August during any of Kent's halcyon years, when room had to be found for so many great amateur players, it must have been almost impossible to decide on what actually was Kent's best team, but Seymour could never be left out. He was not a classic batsman – even in those days his stance was too modern – but he possessed many strokes both skilful and attractive. His flash past cover-point was a thing of special delight, and if he did not always appear sure of himself in playing fast bowling, he was a wonderfully watchful player of the ball on a turning wicket. As a slip fieldsman he ranked with the greatest in that position, the combination of Huish, Seymour, J. R. Mason, R. N. R. Blaker, and K. L. Hutchings behind the wicket being one difficult to surpass. Whilst fielding there he caught six South Africans in an innings at Canterbury in 1904. He never took part in a Test and appeared in only three Gentlemen v Players matches, in the first of which – at The Oval in 1913 – he made 80 in his second innings. In

1900 he was engaged to play for the London County Cricket Club and an innings of 66 not out which he made in that year for Kent Club and Ground against Gravesend gained for him the offer of a place on the ground staff at Tonbridge. There he developed his skill considerably through the coaching of the late Capt. W. McCanlis. His first season as a regular member of the Kent team was in 1902 and from then until 1927 he was a regular member of the side. When in 1906 Kent won the county championship, he scored 1,096 runs and was the leading professional batsman of the eleven and in 1913 he had a great season, finishing up with an aggregate of 2,088 runs and an average of 38. He scored fifty-three centuries during his career and twice made a three-figure innings in each innings of a match – against Worcestershire at Maidstone in 1904 and against Essex at Leyton in 1923. He played a great innings against Hampshire at Tonbridge in 1907, his 204 setting up a new record for Kent, and twice subsequently again exceeded the second hundred, scoring 218 not out v Essex at Leyton in 1911 and 214 against the same county at Tunbridge Wells three years later. Only Woolley and Hardinge have played more three-figure innings for Kent and in all matches for the county, including those in the American tour of 1903, he scored 27,064 runs with an average of 32. His benefit was against Hampshire at Canterbury in 1920, and arising from it was the case – brought to the House of Lord's – that established the right of the cricket benefit, unless guaranteed by contract, to be free from tax. After he had dropped out of first-class cricket he accepted an engagement as coach at Epsom College. He was brother of John Seymour who played for Sussex.

MR JOHN SHARP, who died on January 27, 1938, enjoyed an unparalleled career in cricket and football. As a professional with Everton, he took part in two final ties for the Football Association Cup and was on the winning side in 1906. He helped England beat Ireland in 1903, in 1905 was in the eleven victorious over Scotland and he became a director of the Everton Club. When still in his football prime as an outside right, he played in three cricket Tests against the Australian team of 1909, scoring 105 at The Oval, the only century for England in that series. The Oval match was made historic by Warren Bardsley getting 136 and 130 – the first batsman credited with two centuries in a Test and the only Australian who has met with such success. From 1899 to 1914 Sharp was a regular member of the Lancashire eleven and played in all matches of 1904 when the championship was won without defeat being suffered. After the war he appeared as an amateur and captained the side from 1923 to 1925 when he retired. In 1924 he was on the England Test selection committee with H. D. G. Leveson Gower and John Daniell – so completing a unique set of honours.

Born at Hereford on February 15, 1878, John Sharp showed exceptional batting ability when 14 years of age by scoring 208 not out against Ledbury, but for Lancashire he did best as a bowler for some time. Short and thick-set he put a lot of power behind the ball and, if not very fast, he kept up a good pace with off-break and lift. In 1901 he took 112 wickets at 22.43 each, and with 883 runs, average 25.22, he was the one notable all-rounder in his county eleven. Nine batsmen fell to him in an innings at Worcester and ten years later at Derby he took five wickets for 14 runs. Another good performance with the ball was seven Middlesex wickets for 25 at Lord's in 1909, six men being dismissed by him in the course of four overs and two balls. Altogether for Lancashire Sharp took 448 wickets at 26.22 runs apiece. His batting figures are much more impressive – 20,829 runs for the county and 22,715 all told, average nearly 32 in each case, while his first-class centuries numbered 38, the highest being 211 against Leicestershire at Old Trafford in 1912. On that occasion A. H. Hornby, then the Lancashire captain, helped Sharp add 245 for the eighth wickets in two hours and a half.

Always good to watch, Sharp scored freely to the off by hard drives and cuts, while, like most short batsmen, he pulled with plenty of power. Brilliant fielding, usually at cover point, completed John Sharp's cricket equipment and a bright cheerful disposition helped him as captain; yet an error in judging a catch influenced his retirement from first-class cricket. This happened when Cecil Parkin was taking his benefit at Old Trafford in 1925.

Middlesex won the toss and John Sharp, fielding at short-leg, missed H. W. Lee off the first ball. An opening partnership of 121 between Lee and J. W. Hearne ensued and Middlesex won decisively. Sharp was greatly upset by the attitude of some of the crowd over the dropped catch, and he threatened never again to play at Old Trafford. The Lancashire Committee persuaded him to change his decision, but at the end of the season Sharp sent in his resignation.

In 1913 John Sharp was given a benefit which realised £1,679 and in 1936 he was made an honorary life member of the Lancashire County Club.

MR JOHN SHUTER. The sudden death on July 5, 1920, at his home at Blackheath, of John Shuter came as a shock to the general body of cricketers. On the previous Friday he was at The Oval and to all appearances in good health. His intimate friends knew, however, that the attack of haemorrhage that killed him was not the first of the kind from which he had suffered. It was in September 1919, when Mr Findlay went to Lord's, that he took up the post of secretary to the Surrey Club. He was, perhaps, a little too old for such an onerous position, but everyone hoped he had several years of work before him. Any way it was only fitting that he should to the end have been closely associated with Surrey cricket. His name will be remembered as long as the Surrey Club exists, as it was under his leadership that Surrey won back the first place among the counties in 1887, and enjoyed for the next five seasons a period of unexampled success. John Shuter belonged to Surrey by birth – he was born at Thornton Heath on February 9, 1855 – but living at Bexley he was in his young days connected with club cricket in Kent. He was in the Winchester eleven in 1871, 1872, and 1873 being captain and the best bat in the team in his last year. In 1873 he played a fine innings of 52 but it was only in 1871 that he had the good fortune to be on the winning side. It was in that year and 1870 that G. S. Raynor – anticipating modern bowlers – demoralised the Eton batsmen by his bewildering swerve. After leaving Winchester John Shuter played in a county match for Kent – against Lancashire at Maidstone – in 1874, and in the following year he played for the county eleven against the Kent Colts at Catford Bridge. However, his potential value as a batsman was not realised, and after a time he threw in his lot with Surrey, playing in three matches for his native county in 1877. No success rewarded him that year, but in 1878 he took a very decided step to the front, and left no doubt as to his class.

To the end of his life Mr Shuter recalled with some pride – he was talking about the matter last summer – that when the Australians were seen for the first time at The Oval he scored 39 against Spofforth. I remember the occasion very well for some of the Australians – flushed with the triumph over the MCC at Lord's – said in their innocence that Shuter was the best bat in England! I am not quite sure when Mr Shuter became permanently captain of Surrey – the books are rather vague on the point, but he was, I think firmly installed when the great revival began in 1883. From that time the improvement went on almost without check. The season of 1886, marked by a double victory over the Australians, saw Surrey practically as good a side as Nottinghamshire, and in 1887 came the full reward of long-continued effort. For the first time since 1864 Surrey stood at the top of the tree. Mr Shuter had long before this made himself a first-rate captain and he had a splendid eleven under his command, George Lohmann's bowling and W. W. Read's batting being of course the main elements of strength. Once on top Surrey did not look back till 1893. They were first in 1888, tied with Lancashire and Nottinghamshire in 1889, and were first in 1890, 1891 and 1892. Then came a change of fortune in 1893, but as some compensation for falling behind in purely county cricket, Surrey won both their matches with the Australians. After the season of 1893, Mr Shuter, to everyone's regret, was compelled by stress of business to resign the captaincy of the eleven. He was succeeded by Mr K. J. Key and as all lovers of cricket will remember Surrey under their new leader won the championship in 1894, 1895 and 1899.

In thinking of John Shuter as the Surrey captain one is apt to forget what a fine batsman he was – good enough for any eleven. For so short a man – he stood only 5ft 6ins – he had a singularly graceful style, and his punishing power on the off side was remarkable. He did not care for averages or personal glory. His one idea was to win the match for his side. Among all his doings in the cricket field there was nothing he recalled with keener pleasure than a fight against time in a match between the MCC and the Australians at Lord's in 1890. The MCC were left with only 111 to get, but they had to beat the clock as well as the Australians, eight-five minutes remaining for play. W. G. Grace took Shuter in with him and, with Turner and Ferris bowling, 32 runs were scored in a quarter of an hour. In an hour the match was over, the MCC winning by seven wickets. Mr Shuter played nine times for Gentlemen v Players, but little or no success rewarded him, his best score being 41, and his aggregate of runs in fifteen innings only 182. All his best work was done for Surrey. He played once for England against Australia – at The Oval in 1888. In the long years between his resignation of the captaincy and his appointment in 1919 as secretary of the club Mr Shuter was always in closest touch with Surrey cricket. I find from *Bat v Ball* that he made nine scores of over a hundred for Surrey. The first was 110 against Sussex at Brighton in 1879, and the last 117 against Essex at The Oval in 1890. His best score against the Australians was 71 for the Gentlemen of England at Lord's in 1888.

S. H. P.

MR G. H. SIMPSON-HAYWARD, who died on October 2, 1936, aged 61, was one of the last underhand bowlers in first-class cricket. He seldom flighted the ball like the ordinary lob bowler and did not often use spin from leg. In fact he was quite unusual with the speed at which he could make the ball, delivered with low trajectory, break from the off. Going from Malvern to Cambridge, he did not get his Blue and not until 1902 did he play much for Worcestershire. He met with most success in 1908 when sixty-eight wickets fell to him at an average cost of 18.61. Also a very useful forcing batsman, he hit up 105 out of 140 in eighty minutes against the University at Oxford and then took six wickets for 13 runs. He played for the Gentlemen at Lord's that summer without emulating the success of D. L. A. Jephson, who with his lobs in 1899 dismissed six of the Players for 21. One big performance in the best class cricket stands to Simpson-Hayward's name. Going to South Africa with Mr H. D. G. Leveson Gower's team in 1909, he took twenty-three wickets at 18.26 runs each in the five Tests, and in the first at Johannesburg his first innings analysis was 6 for 43. The matting wickets just suited his exceptional power of spinning the ball. His all-round ability stood out against the Australians at Worcester in 1909, when he was highest scorer for the county with 51 and took six wickets for 132 in a total of 389. A very good Association football full back, before adding Hayward to his name, he played against Oxford from 1896 to 1898.

WILLIAM H. SLATTER, born September 12, 1851, died in Harrow Hospital on August 16, 1929, aged 77. Son of the better-known "Steevie" Slatter, he was engaged at Lord's for 57 years, originally as a pavilion dressing-room attendant in 1863, and working his way up to become clerk of works. His reminiscences were published in a private circulation pamphlet, in 1914, entitled "Recollections of Lord's and the Marylebone Cricket Club". Some idea of the changes which time wrought during his long association with the ground can be gauged from the fact that he could recall seeing wild rabbits there. He designed and built the luncheon arbours surrounding the practice-ground.

HARRY SMITH, the Gloucestershire professional, died on November 12, 1937, aged 46. He succeeded Jack Board as wicket-keeper in 1914, and did good service until illness checked his career in 1932. After an unexpected return to the side in 1935 he retired and was for a time coach to the county colts. Besides being a reliable wicket-keeper he was a sound batsman and in 1928 played for England against West Indies at Lord's. Against Hampshire at Southampton in 1919 he made 120 and 102 not out. A noteworthy incident occurred in that match. Pothecary, the last Hampshire batsman, played a ball from Parker into the top of his pad, shook it into Smith's hands, and was given out "caught" contrary to law 33 B which declares in such a case that the ball becomes "dead".

# SYDNEY JAMES SOUTHERTON

The third Editor of *Wisden's Almanack* to die in the course of less than ten years Sydney James Southerton passed away on March 12, 1935. His end came even more suddenly than that of each of his predecessors. Sydney H. Pardon collapsed in his office and died the next morning, November 20, 1925; Charles Stewart Caine, after fighting the trouble of a weak heart for many months, went to sleep in his chair at home and did not wake again; Southerton having proposed the toast of "Cricket" at the dinner of "The Ferrets" Club at The Oval, sank down and a few minutes later his life ebbed away.

He had just seen the fruits of his labours in bringing out the 72nd issue of *Wisden* and died in circumstances such as he might have wished. Surrounded by cricketers, many of them close friends and leading players, he surrendered his innings when in the full glow of success. Though his health had shown signs of flagging, there did not seem any reason to suppose that he would succumb without any warning from serious illness. For only two years did he act as Editor of the *Almanack* but from 1894, when as statistician, he enjoyed the nick-name of "Figure Fiend" in the office of the Cricket Reporting Agency, he had assisted in the production of the book, except during the period of the war when he held a commission in the Royal West Kent Regiment.

Born at Mitcham, the younger son of James Southerton, the famous slow bowler, who played for England, Sussex, Hampshire and Surrey, Sydney was reared in cricket air, and the game became the idol of his life. Taken to The Oval on the occasion of his father's benefit match when a very small boy, he got to know at an early age all about the bat, the ball and the stumps. Until manhood his home was at "The Cricketers" overlooking the green where many Surrey professionals grew proficient and young Southerton himself became a useful all-round player. He often found a place in a Mitcham eleven and he did the "hat trick" for Press Club against Authors Club at Lord's in 1895.

Australian teams used to practise on Mitcham Green before the serious business of their tour and in 1893 Southerton, who was in service in the boat which brought over the side captained by J. McC. Blackham – one of the greatest wicket-keepers of all time – became scorer for the tour. In this way began the association with first class cricket, severed only by death in his sixty-second year – for Sydney Southerton was born on July 7, 1874.

His practical knowledge of cricket naturally gave him a close insight into the character and ability of players. He had sound judgment on real merit and was prompt to note errors in method or execution by either batsman or bowler. The acquaintance and even close friendship with many cricketers of all grades helped towards this general mastery of the intricacies in every phase of cricket. As instances of his keen observation it may be recalled that when Lord Tennyson declared in the 1921 Test match at Old Trafford, Southerton was the first, if not the only, man in the press box to remember that such action could not be taken later than an hour and forty minutes before time if rain had reduced the fixture to two days. Again, during the Test match at The Oval in 1926 he said, "Rhodes soon got Woodfull at Sheffield". Thought transference might have been at work, for A. P. F. Chapman promptly put on Rhodes with the same result. Used more in Australia's second innings Rhodes took a large share in gaining a victory by 289 runs and so winning the rubber for England.

Such perception made itself felt when discussing the game with leading authorities and, influenced by constant company with Pardon and Caine, Southerton was ripe for the work of special correspondent for the *Press Association* and *Reuter's* with the MCC team that toured Australia under the captaincy of A. P. F. Chapman during the winter of 1928-29. His cables brought more life into the game than ever previously had appeared in reports of cricket played out of England. James Southerton went to Australia with Lillywhite's team in 1876 and played for England in the first representative matches. Consequently Sydney found special interest in retracing his father's footsteps under conditions very different from those that prevailed 52 years before; and he delighted in having seen England victorious at Brisbane, Sydney, Melbourne and Adelaide.

How he dealt with the "direct attack" episode in his second and last term as Editor of *Wisden* earned general commendation and brought one eulogistic remark from an old friend, a member of a county club committee, who in a letter of condolence on Southerton's death wrote – "just as Sydney Pardon helped to stamp out throwing, so did Southerton help to put an end to the unfair attack on the batsman by the bowler with the bumping ball".

Besides his ability to describe a game in graphic style Southerton enjoyed the confidence of all cricket officials and his great store of anecdotes of all kinds made him the best of "company". Constantly in demand for dinners and social functions he made a large circle of friends with whom he was always welcome wherever called by his cricket or football duties – for he was known almost as well on our winter as on our summer playing fields. Of all the tales he told in most racy style one appealed specially, because it helped to portray Southerton's inherited instinct to adapt himself to any situation. His maternal grandfather, living at Merton – the home of Nelson at the beginning of the last century – went out to buy a leg of mutton for the Sunday dinner. The wife waited in vain for the husband to return; he had just vanished; no trace; no tidings. Some four years later a bronzed and bearded sailor walked into the house, dumped a leg of mutton on the table and said, "Here's tomorrow's dinner, my dear!" Sydney's ancestor, Pratt, had been the victim of a "press gang" and served in the Navy during the war that had for its climax Trafalgar.

An ardent freemason, Sydney Southerton was a past master of the Somersetshire Lodge, a member of the Alfred Robbins Lodge and of the Temple Chapter. He succeeded Stewart Caine on the Newspaper Press Fund Council.

When unable to play much cricket Southerton took up golf with such success that he won press competitions from a low handicap. Quite good at billiards and snooker he held his own at most card games and in recent years bridge and gardening were his hobbies. At one time he was captain of the press rifle club.

H. P.

Following are a few of the many tributes received after Mr Southerton's death:

## Mr A. P. F. Chapman

"I was very fond of him. He was always trustworthy. You could tell him the facts of a matter and he never exaggerated. When he went out to Australia with us he never let us down once and was universally popular with the members of the England team and the Australians. He was made a member of the team and came into our dressing room. We knew he would use his discretion in his reports. We trusted him implicitly. I thought he maintained the fine standard always associated with *Wisden*."

## Mr H. D. G. Leveson Gower

"The death of Mr Southerton removed a great personality from the cricket world. I first knew him over 40 years ago, and have always entertained a great friendship for him. While his criticisms were often severe, they never gave offence. His judgment was sound."

## Mr W. Findlay (Secretary, MCC)

"When Mr Southerton became Editor of *Wisden's Cricketers' Almanack*, on the death of Mr Stewart Caine in 1933, it was felt that considerable responsibility rested with him, if the high traditions of the *Almanack* were to be maintained. Cricketers did not have to wait long for an assurance on this point. It was clear to all who read his articles in the *Almanack* that he kept uppermost in his mind all that was best for the game.

He was well-known to cricketers in this country and in Australia, and was always a welcome guest at any cricket function, being of a bright personality and blessed with a sense of humour. As in the case of his predecessors, it was often expedient to confide in him – that confidence was never misplaced."

Mr J. B. Hobbs

> "The judgment of Mr Southerton on cricket was absolutely sound. We always took notice of what he said. He was popular wherever he went."

MR FREDERICK ROBERT SPOFFORTH, one of the most remarkable players the game has ever known, was born at Balmain, Sydney, on September 9, 1853, and died at Ditton Hill Lodge, Ditton Hill, Surbiton, Surrey, on June 4, 1926, aged 72. As in another part of the *Almanack*, Lord Harris, Lord Darnley, and Mr C. I. Thornton have given their recollections of Mr Spofforth and his wonderful bowling, it will suffice here to deal with the chief facts of a memorable career. From his earliest days cricket had the greatest possible fascination for him, and whilst still quite a small boy at Eglington College, Sydney, he determined, through seeing the success met with by George Tarrant, of Cambridge, to become as fast a bowler as possible. Later he studied the methods of Southerton and Alfred Shaw, and resolved, if possible, to combine the styles of all three men. He had played with success in good class matches before he ever bowled a ball in England, but his great days may be said to date from May 27, 1878, when he had so much to do with the wonderful victory gained, in the course of a single day, by D. W. Gregory's team over a very strong MCC side at Lord's. From that day forward, Spofforth was always regarded as a man to be feared, even by the strongest teams. He probably never did anything better than to take fourteen wickets for 90 runs in the Test match at The Oval in 1882, when Australia gained their first success – by 7 runs – in an international game on English soil. It is to be regretted that when he came over with the teams of 1878 and 1880 so few eleven a side matches were played, for he was presumably then at about his best, and his energies were expended for the most part in mowing down wickets in games against odds. For the former side he obtained 764 wickets at a cost of 6.08 runs each, and for the latter 763 for 5.49 apiece. These figures include his doings in the colonies and (in 1878) in America.

Spofforth was a member of the Australian teams of 1878, 1880, 1882, 1884, and 1886, and for them he performed the following feats:

19-108  v 15 of New South Wales, at Sydney, 1877-78
17-125  v 18 of South Australia, at Adelaide, 1877-78
14-25   v 22 of Southland, at Invercargill, 1877-78
15-41   v 22 of Wellington, at Wellington, 1877-78
22-59   v 22 of Hawke's Bay, at Napier, 1877-78
22-68   v 22 of Auckland, at Auckland, 1877-78
10-20   v MCC, at Lord's. (Including the hat trick), 1878
13-134  (including 9 for 53), v Lancashire, at Manchester, 1878
20-64   v 18 of New York, at Hoboken, 1878
17-66   v 22 of Ontario, at Toronto, 1878
19-84   v 18 of South Australia, at Adelaide, 1878-79
13-110  v England, at Melbourne. (Including the hat-trick), 1878-79
16-112  v 15 of Victoria, at Melbourne, 1879-80
13-85   v Derbyshire, at Derby, 1880
17-77   v 18 of Northamptonshire (with given men), at Northampton, 1880
17-96   v 15 of South Australia, at Adelaide, 1880-1
10-19   v 22 of Southland, at Invercargill, 1880-81
20-65   v 22 of Wellington, at Wellington, 1880-81
22-60   v 22 of Hawke's Bay, at Napier, 1880-81
13-113  (including 9 for 51), v Somerset, at Taunton, 1882
14-90   v England at The Oval, 1882
14-58   (including 8 for 11), v Scotland, at Glasgow, 1882
5-15    v Shaw's XI, at Holbeck, 1882
10-12   v 18 of New York, at Hoboken, 1882

14-37  (including 7 for 3), v An England XI, at Aston, 1884
13-123 v Players, at Sheffield, 1884
 7-16  v Middlesex, at Lord's, 1884
14-96  v Players, at The Oval, 1884
13-85  v Cambridge University Past and Present, at Hove, 1884
Hat trick v South, at The Oval, 1884
15-36  v Oxford University, at Oxford, 1886
 7-19  v North, at Manchester, 1886

    After settling in England:

15-81  Derbyshire v Yorkshire, at Derby, 1889
14-114 (including 9 for 56), Derbyshire v Leicestershire, at Derby, 1890
 8-74  MCC v Yorkshire, at Scarborough, 1896

In tests against England he obtained 94 wickets for 18.41 runs each. In his own country he represented both New South Wales and Victoria, the former by birth and the latter by residence, and in really big cricket, both at home and abroad, took 1,146 wickets with an average of 13.55.

Below are the records of his most noteworthy seasons:

|                    | Balls | Runs  | Wickets | Average |
|--------------------|-------|-------|---------|---------|
| Australia 1877-78  | 1,379 | 449   | 58      | 7.74    |
| England 1878       | 3,018 | 1,259 | 109     | 11.55   |
| Australia 1878-79  | 1,274 | 634   | 52      | 12.18   |
| Australia 1879-80  | 1,546 | 688   | 49      | 14.04   |
| England 1880       | 968   | 396   | 46      | 8.60    |
| Australia 1880-81  | 2,075 | 852   | 84      | 10.14   |
| England 1882       | 6,395 | 2,282 | 188     | 12.13   |
| Australia 1882-83  | 1,766 | 700   | 33      | 21.21   |
| England 1884       | 6,364 | 2,732 | 218     | 12.53   |
| Australia 1884-85  | 1,216 | 469   | 25      | 18.76   |
| Australia 1885-86  | 741   | 274   | 18      | 15.22   |
| England 1886       | 3,726 | 1,528 | 89      | 17.16   |

The summary of his bowling in good matches during the whole of his career was:

|             | Balls  | Runs   | Wickets | Average |
|-------------|--------|--------|---------|---------|
| In Australia| 13,140 | 5,515  | 385     | 14.32   |
| In England  | 24,101 | 9,917  | 750     | 13.22   |
| In America  | 259    | 107    | 11      | 9.72    |
|             |        |        |         |         |
| Totals      | 37,500 | 15,539 | 1,146   | 13.55   |

In eleven a-side games he bowled unchanged throughout as follows:

With E. Evans, New South Wales v Victoria, at Sydney, 1875-76
With G. E. Palmer, Australia v Rest, at Melbourne, 1880-81
With H. F. Boyle, Australians v Somerset, at Taunton, 1882
With H. F. Boyle, Australians v Scotland, at Glasgow, 1882
With G. E. Palmer, Australians v Yorkshire, at Bradford, 1884
With G. E. Palmer, Australians v Middlesex, at Lord's, 1884
With T. W. Garrett, Australians v Oxford University, at Oxford, 1886

In minor matches he naturally did many very remarkable things. Thus, in an up-country game in Australia, in 1881-82, he bowled down all twenty wickets of his opponents; for the Australian team of 1878 he took nine wickets in twenty balls against XVIII of Hastings, and for that of 1880, twelve in eighteen against XVIII of Burnley; while twice for Hampstead he obtained all ten wickets in an innings of Marlow on his opponents' ground – for 20 runs in 1893, and for 14 a year later. In the game of 1893, his day's figures were seventeen for 40. When he made his first appearance for Hampstead he was in his thirty-eight year, yet he took as many as 951 wickets for the club for 7.5 runs each. In 1894 he claimed 200 wickets for the side for an average of 5.90.

## RECOLLECTIONS OF MR F. R. SPOFFORTH, 1926

### By Lord Harris

I was talking to Mr Noble early in the season at The Oval, and he told me that Spofforth was seriously ill, and then put to me the astonishing question, "Was he a great bowler?" It was about equivalent to asking if W.G. was a great bat. "About the best I ever played", was my reply: "but did you never see him?" It was another shock to find that Noble, with whom I had never played, had never seen him bowl. Later on I went down to see Spofforth, and we had a chat about old times; he was keenly interested in past as well as present times, but as I left the room he said, "The doctors say I shall see the first Test match; but I made my reputation in May; you knocked me out in May; and I shall go out in May." He actually passed away in the first days of June.

Now what he described as my "knocking him out", was a very curious coincident. If anyone cares to look at the cricket records of 1885 and 1887, he will find in Australians v Gentlemen of England, at Lord's, in 1884: F. R. Spofforth absent 0, and absent 0, and in 1886, F. R. Spofforth retired hurt 0, and that he did not bowl at all in the second innings.

I have recorded in "A few Short Runs", and I can but repeat that on each occasion I hit a ball back which injured his right hand; and he always said that he was never the same bowler after the second injury. He followed up his ball very far, and as I probably jumped in, he was very close, too close to put his hand in exactly the right place; else he was ordinarily a very good field to his own bowling, but so full of nerves, that a hard blow made more difference to him than to many.

An amusing illustration of this sensitiveness occurred at Canterbury, in 1886, in Kent v Australians. I was in with G. G. Hearne, who would always run at a nod from me. Old Spof had been rather upset about the wicket-keeping; a ball was thrown in badly from long field, which hurt him; he went dancing about wringing his hand, and at last danced on the opposite side of the wicket to where the ball was lying close to the wicket, and we ran, much to the amusement of the crowd.

It is a common misconception, amongst those who did not see or play him, that he was a very fast bowler. He may have been in Australia before his first visit to England, in 1878, but he was far too knowledgeable on our slower wickets, and 1878 was little better than a mud lark, to depend on pace. He could bowl a very fast ball, and did, as often perhaps as once an over; but what he depended on was what he termed the "judgment" ball; medium pace, but with great variety of pace, and therefore of flight, and a strong break from the off. He could break slightly from leg, I believe, though I cannot remember his doing so; and the rumour went round amongst us who had to face him for the first time, that if he was going to break from the off, he held the ball at the tips of his fingers; if from leg, in the palm of his hand. In my opinion what deceived the batsman, was that he came up at a great pace and then bowled a much slower ball than his pace up to the wicket led one to expect. Consequently the batsman played rather too quickly, cocked the ball up a bit, and he was so close up, and judged the direction the ball would come off the bat so well, that he brought off the catch and bowl very frequently; and if it did not come off in his direction, the break would take it round to silly mid-on, where Boyle was waiting for and seldom missed it. Indeed, with Spof bowling, Blackham at the wicket, and Boyle at short leg, the forward type of play on slow wickets almost certainly led to disaster. That he was a great bowler cannot be disputed, his performances on the tours he took part in were astonishing, as shown elsewhere in this volume.

There were two signs which pretty clearly indicate what the public thought of him; his title "The Demon" bowler; and that he was singled out amongst cricketers for a cartoon in "Vanity Fair". In after years there were quite a number of cricketers similarly honoured by that paper, but in his day it was a rarity.

I have said that he came up to the wicket very fast, and he followed up straight down the wicket, thus, left foot on or about the popping crease, right foot well on to the half-volley pitch, and then both feet plump on the awkward pitch; and when wickets were soft, he undoubtedly made a mess of the pitch. In those days we were not so particular as cricketers are now; we took such happenings as the "rubs" of the game; but in his case we used to remonstrate, and Spof's indignation was deep seated and high voiced. "Look at my heels, no spikes", was his retort; which was true, but the heels were high.

At Sydney in 1878-79, we had made a very good start. I was in, and could not imagine why they did not put Evans, a most accurate bowler, on to bowl at the hole Spof had made. At last they did, and I said to Murdoch, who was keeping wicket, "This innings is over", and we were out for some 40 more. Evans kept on finding the broken spot. He was much more thought of than Spofforth in Australia, and was a much better cricketer all round; but was not successful when he came home, partly due to ill-health. Spofforth was of no great worth as a bat, and was never conspicuous in the field; he seemed to concentrate on his bowling, and I think did really study his opponents' weak points, and work at them; and in after years it was interesting to get him to talk about his performances, which, when we met at Lord's, he was quite ready to do.

I was playing for ten years abroad and at home against those great medium pace Australian bowlers, Allan, Garrett, Palmer, Giffen, Turner, and Ferris, as well as Spofforth, and I have of course also played such great English medium pace bowlers as Alfred Shaw, Watson, Jim Lillywhite, Lohmann, C. T. Studd and W. G. Grace, and I am quite satisfied and always have been, that Spofforth was the most difficult of them all, because he concealed so well the pace of the ball. What he could have done on the easy wickets of the present day, no one can say, but I am sure he could have adapted his bowling to them; and does it matter? What we must judge performances by are the circumstances and conditions of the time when they were done, and taking those as the criteria, I do not see how any bowler can be held to be better than was F. R. Spofforth.

## By The Earl of Darnley

I well remember the first time that I encountered the Demon bowler – in the Cambridge v Australian match, at Lord's, in 1878. We had all been warned by our captain, the Hon. Edward Lyttelton who had, I think, recently made a big score against the Australians, to watch Spofforth's bowling hand as he came to the wicket. If the wrist was bent, one was to expect a slower ball with break back; if the wrist was straight, a very fast ball, and not improbably a "yorker".

In some of the accounts recently published of Spofforth's bowling it was said that he was never a really fast bowler. I believe this statement to be quite incorrect. If my memory does not deceive me, there were two very distinct stages in his bowling. When he first came to England in 1878, his bowling was very fast indeed, almost as fast as the fastest we have seen, with occasional very well-disguised slower ones, which were very deceiving to the batsman and caused many a premature forward stroke and retirement of the batsman – caught and bowled.

After 1878 he greatly moderated his pace, and relied more on the fast-medium ball of wonderfully good length and considerable break back, with the occasional variation of the very fast one, including a particularly deadly "yorker".

I should imagine that the nickname of "Demon" arose from the terrifying aspect of his final bound at the wicket when delivering the ball – long lean arms whirling through the air from a commanding height, and a long stride coming down with great force and damaging effect on a very awkward spot for a breaking-back ball bowled from the other end. The long arms seemed to be whirling round at much the same speed whether the ball was coming fast or slow, and he had practised these disguises of pace to great perfection.

Some of his bowling success may be traced to certain physical attributes of an unusual character – very tall, 6ft 3in, broad shouldered, but unusually lean and sinewy and carrying very little weight. A year or two ago, he told me that at his best he only weighed 11 stone 7 lbs. His early life on horse-back in the Australian bush gave to him the lasting power which made him incomparably the best stayer of any fast or medium pace bowler that I can remember. Though of so comparatively light build, he was exceptionally strong, and one of his feats was to support Bonnor, weighing over 16 stone, on the calf of his leg, held horizontally backwards at right angles to the upright leg – no mean feat. He and Bonnor were the two fastest hundred yard runners in the Australian elevens of those days, one weighing some 5 stone more than the other.

In addition to these physical features, no bowler that I ever saw had a more graceful, spacious sweep of the arm, and his delivery gave a most satisfactory sensation of perfection of pace and power combined. Unlike most of the modern fast bowlers, his run up to the wicket was only of average length, and his pace and power owed nothing to the impetus of an abnormally long run.

One of the very best bowlers that the last 50 years have seen, unquestionably; possibly the best of all. A cheery and amusing companion, withal, amongst his fellow cricketers. Fond of a good story, and, like many of his compatriots, not inclined to understatement. His old cricketing friends will cherish a very kindly recollection of his unique personality.

### By Mr C. I. Thornton

I first met F. R. Spofforth on the Orleans Club ground at Twickenham where the Australians of 1878 met a team which I had got together. My side included I. D. Walker, W. Yardley, W. N. Powys, D. Q. Steel and three professionals – Fred Wild, the Nottinghamshire wicket-keeper, Arnold Rylott of Leicestershire, and Ted Barratt of Surrey. Barratt took twelve wickets and when the game was left drawn we wanted only 75 to win and had eight wickets to fall. In the "seventies" and "eighties" I knew Spofforth well and played a lot of cricket with him. He was a first-rate judge of the game and certainly the best bowler of the "dodgy" class I ever saw, as he varied his run up to the wicket and you could never tell what paced ball was coming along. Still he never stuck me up as much as did Ferris and Giffen. To get Spofforth and E. M. Grace on a side was to ensure a pleasant day's cricket if not necessarily a successful one. Spofforth was at his happiest at country matches where his stories – always told with an air of sincerity – used to amuse people immensely. One special one that never failed to please used to be given in the following circumstances. I would say to him at lunch "How did you learn to be such a fine short-slip, Spoff?" And he would reply "When I was quite young I made a boy, when out for a walk, throw stones into a hedge, and as the sparrows flew out, I caught 'em."

FRANK HOWE SUGG, who died on May 29, 1933, was born at Ilkeston on January 11, 1862. A fine enterprising batsman, especially strong in driving and square-leg hitting, and a brilliant outfield, who not only covered a lot of ground but possessed a very safe pair of hands, he had the experience – very unusual in modern days – of playing for three different counties. He appeared for Yorkshire in 1883, for Derbyshire – his native county – in 1884, 1885 and 1886, and for thirteen seasons subsequently, having qualified by residence, he assisted Lancashire. While doing little as a member of the Yorkshire team, he rendered capital service to Derbyshire, running second in the averages one year to L. C. Docker, and in another to W. Chatterton, while amongst his scores was one of 187 against Hampshire at Southampton. His great work, however, was accomplished for Lancashire. Standing six feet high, he possessed very quick sight and, if his methods tended to make him a poor starter, no one was more likely on a bad wicket to turn the fortunes of a game. Altogether for Lancashire he scored 10,375 runs with an average of

26. He played in 1896 an innings of 220 against Gloucestershire and on five other occasions exceeded 150, his hundreds in first-class cricket numbering sixteen in all. In the game with Somerset at Taunton in 1899, he and G. R. Baker hit up 50 runs off three consecutive overs, Sugg, in one of these, registering five 4s. Sugg appeared several times for the Players against the Gentlemen and in 1888 took part in Test matches against Australia at The Oval and at Manchester. His recollections of these two games must have been very happy, for at The Oval, where he made 31, the Australians were dismissed for 80 and 100, England winning in a single innings, and at Manchester, where he scored 24, Australia's totals were 81 and 70, and again England triumphed with an innings to spare. Some time after the close of his career Sugg officiated as an umpire in first-class matches. Lancashire gave him their match with Kent at Old Trafford in 1897 as a benefit. Frank Sugg was equally good at Association football and he gained fame with Sheffield Wednesday, Derby County, Burnley and Bolton Wanderers, being captain of the first three teams. Such was his versatility in sport that, besides his prowess at cricket and football, he excelled as a long distance swimmer and joined with Burgess and Heaton in swims; he held the record for throwing the cricket ball; reached the final of the Liverpool amateur billiards championship; won prizes all over the country for rifle shooting, bowls, and putting the shot, and was famed as a weight lifter.

REV. FRANCIS W. TERRY, who was born at Wells, Somerset, in 1863, died at Mimico, Ontario, on October 5, 1936. In 1882 at Taunton, he scored 22 and 77 not out for Somerset against MCC. He played in the Oxford freshmen's match in 1881, and for Merton College made many centuries but failed to get his Blue. Going to Canada, he played several times against United States and in 1895 scored 111 in the representative match. During 1892, he scored 1,509 runs in all matches which stood as a Canadian record until 1935. He accomplished an extraordinary performance at London, Ontario, on July 4, 1895, when playing for Ontario Hospital against Forest Club, he scored 130 not out in a total of 149. There were six extras, one score of eight, nine men making 5 runs between them. Mr Terry hit twenty-seven 4s in this wonderful display. He also took two wickets for 18 runs, with his right-hand medium-pace bowling, stumped one man and caught another – altogether enjoying a large share in a victory by an innings and 45 runs. Mr George W. Harvey, the scorer in this match, supplied these details.

CANON THE REV. CHARLES THEOBALD, born on July 4, 1831, died at Chichester on January 27, 1930, in his 99th year. A good bat and smart field at cover point and long leg, he was in the Winchester eleven of 1848, playing at Lord's against both Harrow and Eton. In the following season, when he was possibly the side's best batsman, he was kept out of the game by an injured foot. He did not obtain his Blue for Oxford for, being one of sixteen children, the expense of joining the Magdalen Club, membership of which was then considered almost essential to obtain such distinction, could not be afforded. Canon Theobald lived to become the oldest Wykehamist and the oldest public school cricketer.

MR PERCY FRANCIS THOMAS, who wrote about cricket during the last 40 years as "H.P.T." and "Hippo-Pott-Thomas" died at Cricklewood on October 13, 1931. Born on May 27, 1866, at Woolwich, he was the author of several booklets, the best known being a series on "Early Cricket", which already rank as classics. He was a learned student of cricket lore and a man of much humour.

MR CHARLES INGLIS THORNTON, born at Llanwarne, Herefordshire, on March 20, 1850, died suddenly in London on December 10, 1929, aged 79. With his death there passed a great personality in the history of cricket. He had long given up active participation in the game, but in his day he was one of the biggest – if not actually the mightiest of all time – of hitters. To the present generation he was only a name, but in the memories of those who, like Lord Harris and Mr A. J. Webbe, were his contemporaries, his famous deeds must remain firmly implanted. He went to Eton in 1861, to the Rev. G. R. Dupuis's house, and was in the eleven in 1866, 1867, and 1868, being captain in his last year. He also played in Oppidan and Mixed Wall and Field XI's, won the school fives and was keeper in 1867 and 1868, and won the double rackets and putting the weight in 1868, and throwing the cricket ball in 1867. Going up to Trinity College, Cambridge, he played in the eleven four times from 1869, being captain in 1872, the year that Cambridge, thanks to a fine innings of 130 by W. Yardley and some effective bowling of W. N. Powys, beat Oxford in an innings. Thornton was on the winning side for Cambridge three times out of four. The year that Oxford won was in 1871, when S. E. Butler took all ten wickets in the first innings of Cambridge. Thornton also played from 1867 onwards for Kent, and a little for Middlesex in the middle seventies. To him more than to anybody else was due the success of the annual Scarborough festival. He was largely instrumental in starting it, and although he had long given up cricket he never lost his interest in the famous week, even until last season. To mark the esteem in which he was held and to recognise his services to the Scarborough festival, which had then been in existence a quarter of a century, he was, in 1894, presented with a silver loving-cup subscribed for by the members of the Scarborough Cricket Club. He received another presentation in 1921 and was also given the freedom of the borough.

Like many others of his day, Thornton always regarded cricket more as a game than as a serious business. Adventurous by nature, he felt that in cricket he could indulge this spirit to the full. Whenever he was captain he liked going in first. Individual in style, he jumped quickly to the ball in making his magnificent drives, and in this respect differed from the famous Australian hitters, Bonnor, McDonnell and Lyons, all of whom were fast-footed. In his brilliant career he put together many scores of a hundred in remarkable time, and the length of some of his drives was enormous. It is on record, for instance, that in the North v South match at Canterbury in 1871, he hit a ball from W. M. Rose a strictly measured 152 yards, while at the practice nets at Hove the same year he sent it 168 yards 2 feet and 162 yards. Playing against Harrow at Lord's in 1868, he drove the ball over the old pavilion, and at The Oval he accomplished the same feat, while it is noted that at Canterbury he hit V. E. Walker out of the ground each ball of an over. The over then consisted of four balls.

A good story is told of him when, visiting the neighbourhood of Oakham school and going to the cricket ground, he was asked to play as a substitute. Nobody at the time knew who he was, but they had reason to before the day was out, for in the second innings he scored 188 out of 216 in two hours, sending the ball out of the ground thirteen times. Hitting the ball out of the ground was a feat he always took a delight in accomplishing. On one occasion at Scarborough, off the bowling of A. G. Steel, he drove a ball over a four-storeyed house into the adjoining street, called Trafalgar Square.

To slow bowlers Thornton was a terror, and on James Southerton, in particular, he was generally very severe. He often threatened to hit Southerton out of The Oval, and at length succeeded. As the ball sailed over the fence Thornton dropped his bat, put his hands on his hips, and laughed uproariously, saying, "I told you I would do it, Jim." Southerton shook his head, and replied, "Quite right, Mr Thornton, but I shall get you out." And get him out he did. As a matter of fact he hit Southerton twice over the pavilion, once over the scoring-box, and also for a 2 in a four ball over, and, altogether, he hit out of three sides of The Oval. Once, in a match between Kent and Nottinghamshire, Thornton hit a ball back to Shaw, who, although knocked off his feet, held it and thus brought off a marvellous catch. In the power and consistency of his driving, Thornton was by himself, constantly bringing off hits that have become more or less historic in the game. As showing the difference between cricket in his days and now, he took part, in six seasons for Kent, in only eighteen matches. Still, in 34 innings he got three hundreds. Probably his finest exhibitions in the latter part of his career were a couple of hundreds at Scarborough for the Gentlemen of England against I Zingari. In the game of 1866, he made 107 out of 133 in seventy minutes in 29 hits – eight 6s, twelve 4s, two 2s and seven singles. A. G. Steel was among the bowlers on that occasion. Thornton stood 6ft and had rather sloping shoulders, so that he was admirably proportioned for the batting style he loved.

In business Thornton was in the timber trade for 35 years, and retired in 1912. A keen motorist, he was also extremely fond of travelling, having been all through Japan, Siberia, and Russia. When the war broke out he was in Berlin, and was very nearly caught. In his book, *East and West and Home Again*, he described a trip round the world. He had been a member of the MCC and of the Orleans Club for fifty years. He married Fanny, daughter of Mr Charles Dowell, of Croydon, but left no children.

## C. I. THORNTON, 1929

### By Lord Harris

Charles Inglis Thornton, my very dear old friend and comrade, was nicknamed "Bun and Jam" at Eton – afterwards abbreviated to "Buns" – because of an amusing incident, when, as a lower boy, he was brought up to be tried in Upper Club. He was fielding long-leg, close to the raised road, along which one of the "Cads" was passing with his basket or barrow of comestibles. Some say it was Bryan who wheeled a barrow and certainly purveyed buns and jam; others that it was Levi who carried a basket, but I do not remember his selling this particular edible. Thornton, in an interval when a wicket was down, bought a bun and jam, and commenced consuming it. It lasted long enough for play to be resumed. A high catch was hit to him, which I fancy he caught. What happened to the bun I never heard for certain. Some say he swallowed it, others that he dropped it, others again that he crammed it, jam and all, into his trousers pocket. Anyhow it earned him his nickname. Years afterwards he was playing in a Whit Monday match at Lord's and got "spectacles", and Green Lubbock suggested he should in future be known as "Whit Monday buns".

His home during his Eton days was with his uncle and aunt – the venerable Archdeacon of Canterbury and Mrs Harrison – in the precincts. Consequently he and I, as soon as we became acquainted, about 1866, saw much of each other and became very close friends. We played much local cricket together at Canterbury, and at various country houses, and he was a regular member of my eleven at Belmont. We did a lot of hunting and shooting together. He was a very bold and hard rider on not very good – certainly not expensive – horses. His cousin, P. M. Thornton ("Friday") who won the half mile amateur championship in 1869, and afterwards became MP for Clapham, was also an undaunted rider and sometimes accompanied us: and "Buns" had only to say "Friday, you daren't jump that", for "Friday" to go at and negotiate it. One very hard winter, with snow on the ground, we made an expedition after wild duck in the marshes below Sittingbourne, and "Buns", having read or heard of Jack Mytton's eccentricities, borrowed a night-gown from my father's housekeeper: arrayed in which, to the amusement of the keepers, he essayed to stalk – unsuccessfully if I remember right – the watchful birds.

It was a bitter blow to me when I took up the captaincy of the Kent eleven in 1874 to find that he and C. J. Ottaway had decided to transfer their support to Middlesex. They had gone into business in London, so perhaps it was natural. Thornton had played for Kent from 1867 to 1872 in eighteen matches, with 34 innings averaging 29.06 – a very good one in those days – his highest scores being 124 in 1869 and 111 in 1871. But I see he told Mr Bettesworth that the innings he enjoyed most was 107 at Scarborough in 1886 against I Z for Gentlemen of England. He made this great innings in 29 hits, which illustrates my contention, supported by many reliable authorities, that he hit more balls very hard than any batsmen I have known.

I see in the same interview he told Mr Bettesworth that the bowler he most dreaded was Barratt of Surrey, a very slow left-hand bowler with a great break – a remark I can't understand, for playing with him for Kent v Surrey, he said to me "Come in first to see who can hit old Barratt the furthest" – a rivalry I couldn't allow to be reasonable but I subsequently claimed that I'd hit him the hardest, for I hit a "c and b" back to him, was caught off his wrist at mid-off and Barratt did not bowl another ball in the match. He was full of fun in everyday life as well as at cricket, and the stories of his jests are innumerable. He will be sadly missed by that little coterie who sat of mornings by the entrance gate to the pavilion at Lord's.

That he was a very great cricketer is indisputable. Between 1869 and 1889 he was playing for Kent, Middlesex, Gentlemen of England, Gentlemen of the South, Cambridge University and the South, and in those years played 25 innings of 50 and over, including five centuries in years when centuries were not as common as nowadays. He was a magnificent field in his best days and a very long thrower, and his fast underhand grubs, with a curve all the way from leg, wanted careful watching. He went on first at The Oval for the Gentlemen (or Gentlemen of the South) v Players and took the first two wickets.

The feat which gained him great celebrity was his hit over the pavilion at Lord's in Eton v Harrow in 1868. I was in with him at the time and thought we must make a big score, but the next ball – a dead shooter, of which there were plenty that day – took his wicket. I see it is related of him that he hit V. E. Walker out of the Canterbury ground four times in one over. I saw the over, and I can see him now jumping in and the ball sailing away, but I doubt each ball going out of the ground – one or two perhaps, and all over the ring, but out of the ground I doubt. He was hitting them towards the pavilion, but his biggest hit at Canterbury I should say was on another occasion from the other end out of the ground – a very long carry.

By way of chaff his friends used to ask him if he thought he'd ever hit as far as Bonnor, who was a somewhat self-sufficient batsman, but it is recorded in Lillywhite's annual of 1898 that, next to Mr Fellowes' hit of 175 yards on the Christ Church ground at Oxford, the two next authenticated hits are 168 yards 2 feet and 162 yards – both by Thornton in practice at Brighton – measured at the time by that devoted cricketer, the Rev. James Pycroft, so he could treat our chaff with good humoured contempt.

Thornton made such a success of Scarborough cricket that he was accorded the singular honour of the freedom of the borough. So by encouragement, as well as by his own brilliant play, he has left his mark amongst the great cricketers of, I think I may say, all time.

MR RICHARD THORNTON ("PARSON") THORNTON, born at Folkestone on March 28, 1853, died at Eastbourne on May 30, 1928, aged 75. A brother of Messrs A. J. and W. A. Thornton, he was a free-hitting bat and could bowl both slow-round and lobs. With the latter he was very successful indeed in club games. His earliest experience of county cricket was for Devon, and for Dorset and Wiltshire sides, but in 1881 he played in the first of his 46 matches for Kent. With 79 against Surrey at The Oval in 1885 as his highest score, he made 1,495 runs for the last-mentioned team with an average of 21.66. When he visited America with Mr E. J. Sanders' team in 1885 he played an innings of 107 against Philadelphia, and when a Philadelphian side came to England four years later he scored 111 at their expense for MCC at Lord's. Among his many large innings in club games were 201 not out for Sidmouth, 207 for Blue Mantles, and 200 not out for Mote Park. In 1895 he went to Portugal with Mr T. Westray's team. In a match at Southborough he once made hits for 7 and 8 off consecutive balls from Mr A. F. J. Ford. He and D. D. Pontifex, both of whom wore spectacles, made 222 together for the first wicket of Incogniti v Gentlemen of Sussex at Hove in 1885. Whilst at Oxford Mr Thornton obtained his Blue for Association football, but not for cricket.

MR HUGH TRUMBLE, died at Melbourne on August 14, 1938, aged 71. Improving almost beyond belief each succeeding time he came to England, Hugh Trumble has been very properly placed among the most accomplished of Australian bowlers. Exceptionally tall, he made the most of his height by bringing the ball over at the full extent of his right arm so that "flighting", a new term since his days, came in the natural delivery. Length, with either leg or off-break, and pace slightly varied to medium were the means employed by Trumble and experience enabled him to deceive the best batsmen on perfect pitches while, given any help from the state of the turf, he was deadly. After doing moderately in 1890, when Turner and Ferris were in their prime, he stood out as a front rank bowler in 1893 and his other three tours, at similar intervals, increased his reputation in England. Such consistent form did he show that his figures in the four tours after his quiet start read – 123 wickets at 16.39; 148 at 15.81; 142 at 18.43; and 140 at 14.27. His success in 1899 was not confined to bowling, for he scored 1,183 runs with average 27.51, so proving himself quite as valuable an all-rounder as M. A. Noble, particularly as he was a fine slip fieldsman.

Trumble in matches against England had the unequalled record in these Tests of 141 wickets at 20.88 each and a batting average of nearly 20 for an aggregate of 838 runs. When A. C. MacLaren led England in 1901-02, Trumble took 28 wickets; in the following summer 26 at 14.26 and against the first official MCC team captained by P. F. Warner in the winter of 1903-04 his return for the Tests was 24 wickets at 16.58. Only Trumble had done the hat trick twice against England, each at Melbourne in the last two tours mentioned. His best Test performances were twelve wickets for 89 at The Oval in 1896; ten for 128 at Manchester, when Australia won by 3 runs; and twelve for 173 also in 1902 at The Oval where England won by one wicket, these three matches being among the most remarkable between the two countries. In England's first innings at The Oval in 1902, he dismissed A. C. MacLaren, L. C. H. Palairet, J. T. Tyldesley, T. Hayward, L. C. Braund, G. L. Jessop, G. H. Hirst and A. A. Lilley – eight wickets – at a cost of only 65 runs. He also bowled unchanged while England were getting the 263 runs required for victory.

For Victoria in Sheffield Shield matches, Trumble took 159 wickets at 20.67 and scored 1,150 runs, average 22.54. For some twenty years Trumble was secretary of the Melbourne Cricket Club where his knowledge of the game and happy spirit made him universally popular.

JOHN THOMAS TYLDESLEY, one of England's greatest batsmen, who had been in weak health for some years, died on November 27, 1930. On the morning of his death he was putting on his boots before going to his business at Deansgate, Manchester, when he collapsed and died. He had carried on his duties as coach at Old Trafford until the end of last summer. Born at Roe Green, Worsley, on November 22, 1873, he was just 57 years of age at the time of his death. Tyldesley received his early training in Lancashire club cricket – a very stiff school – and was a well-equipped batsman when he first appeared for Lancashire in 1895. In his second match he scored 152 not out against Warwickshire on the Edgbaston ground – the scene of many triumphs for him in subsequent years. He did nothing else of much note that summer – he was not given a trial until the middle of July – but two years later he made over 1,000 runs, and he achieved that performance for nineteen consecutive seasons. Four times he scored over 2,000 runs, and in 1901 he had an aggregate of 3,041, his innings including nine separate centuries, eight of which were made for Lancashire, and his average being 55. In two seasons – 1897 and 1904 – he played three successive innings of a hundred, and on three occasions he made two separate hundreds in the same match. These scores were 106 and 100 not out for Lancashire against Warwickshire in 1897, 121 and 100 not out in a North and South match in 1900, and 136 and 101 for Lancashire against Hampshire in 1910. His highest innings – all for his county – were:

295* v Kent, at Manchester, 1906
272  v Derbyshire, at Chesterfield, 1919
253  v Kent, at Canterbury, 1914
250  v Nottinghamshire, at Trent Bridge, 1905
249  v Leicestershire, at Leicester, 1899
248  v Worcestershire, at Liverpool, 1903
243  v Leicestershire, at Leicester, 1908
225  v Nottinghamshire, at Trent Bridge, 1904

221  v Nottinghamshire, at Trent Bridge, 1901
210  v Somerset, at Bath, 1904
210  v Surrey, at The Oval, 1913
209  v Warwickshire, at Edgbaston, 1907
200  v Derbyshire, at Manchester, 1898

  * *Signifies not out.*

Altogether in the course of his brilliant career he scored 37,803 runs in first-class matches with an average of nearly 41 and made eighty-six separate centuries. He played frequently in Gentlemen v Players matches and in 1901 made 140 at Lord's. He also took a leading part in Test match cricket between 1899 and 1909, appearing for England in sixteen games in this country and going out to Australia with A. C. MacLaren's team in 1901-02 and with the MCC's side two years later. In England he made three hundreds against Australia, scoring 138 at Birmingham in 1902 (after the side had started in disastrous fashion), 100 at Leeds in 1905, and 112 not out at The Oval in the latter year. In all he scored 1,661 runs in Test matches with an average of 30. Tyldesley was a member of the team Lord Hawke took out to South Africa in the winter of 1898-99. He scored 742 runs during the tour with an average of 32. Among his innings was one of 112 in a Test match at Cape Town. There were few batsmen more attractive to watch than John Tyldesley. He was exceptionally quick on his feet and so always appeared to have plenty of time in which to make his strokes. Essentially a batsman of enterprise, when he went forward to the ball it was nearly always to hit. He also possessed a very strong defence and had at his command practically all the strokes in the game. His ability to adapt himself to circumstances was emphasised in a Test match at The Oval in 1905, when Armstrong, bowling well outside the leg-stump with an off-break, reduced to impotence a number of batsmen, but not Tyldesley, who drew back and cut him. One of the best of outfieldsmen, he was very fast, picked the ball up cleanly, and had a very accurate return, in addition to being a very sure catch.

His benefit match, against Yorkshire at Manchester in 1906, yielded a profit of £3,105. Ernest Tyldesley, the Lancashire batsman, is a younger brother of John Tyldesley.


MR EDWARD FERDINANDO SUTTON TYLECOTE, one of the best batsman wicket-keepers of all time, died at Hunstanton on March 15, 1938, aged 88. He showed such exceptional form as a boy that he was in the Clifton College eleven five years, finishing as captain in 1868. That summer he made the then record score of 404 during three spells of two hours each for Modern v Classical, carrying his bat through an innings of 630. He got his Blue at Oxford as a freshman and his second experience against Cambridge was in the "Cobden match". Next year he led the Dark Blues to victory by eight wickets, but in his secor ' season as captain, Cambridge won by an innings and 166, William Yardley setting up a  :cord with his second hundred in university matches. Mr Tylecote was the oldest living university captain.

When a mathematical tutor at Royal Military Academy, Tylecote played for Kent and perhaps his best performance for the county was a perfect not out hundred against the 1882 Australian team, when T. W. Garrett – still alive, aged 80 – and G. E. Palmer were carrying all before them. W. H. Patterson, the present chairman of the Kent county committee, played a fine second innings in the same match. Tylecote also assisted Bedfordshire, the county of his birth.

Tylecote went to Australia at the end of the 1882 season with the Hon. Ivo Bligh's team which won two out of three matches against W. L. Murdoch's touring side. He scored 66 in the deciding encounter which gave the Englishmen the rubber. Played for his wicket-keeping in the 1886 matches against Australia at Lord's and The Oval he helped in two victories, each by an innings. He appeared several times for the Gentlemen against the Players during a period of sixteen years, ending with that of 1886 when, though 37 years of age, he was probably at his best behind the stumps. He showed exceptionally fine form against the Players at Lord's in 1883, his 107 being a faultless display of two and a half hours' stylish batting, notable for offside strokes made with delightful ease. He was only the sixth batsman to hit a century at Lord's for the Gentlemen, the first having been William Ward in 1825.

When keeping wicket he stood close up unless the bowling was exceptionally fast. By his quiet, unobtrusive taking of the ball under the difficult conditions of rough wickets he was very reliable both in catching and stumping. He was one of the first wicket-keepers who dispensed with a long stop. Two brothers of E. F. S. Tylecote, C. B. L., and H. G. both good cricketers, died within a few days of each other in March 1935, aged 88 and 82 respectively; like E. F. S. both captained the Clifton eleven and H. G. was in the Oxford eleven, 1874-77.

MR RUSSELL DONNITHORNE WALKER, died on the 29th of March, 1932. He had been very ill for some time, but the end came quite suddenly, just when he seemed to be rallying and was not without hope of watching one more season's cricket at Lord's. Born on February 13, 1842, he had received many congratulations on completing his 80th year.

Mr A. J. Webbe writes: The passing of Russie Walker has closed a wonderful chapter of English cricket, for he was the last of the famous brothers who will always be remembered as having played the game in the best and most chivalrous spirit.

The Walkers of Southgate founded the Middlesex County Cricket Club, and until "I.D." retired in 1884 the eleven was always captained by one of the brothers. After that V.E. and R.D. followed each other as presidents of the club, so that we may say that Middlesex cricket was run by the family from 1864, when it was started, until the commencement of 1922. Russie was two years in the Harrow cricket and football elevens, and also won the champion racquet. He then proceeded to BNC, Oxford, and was five years in the University XI, also representing Oxford in the single and double racquet contests. For several years he played for the Gentlemen v Players, and, of course, for Middlesex county, though he retired from first-class cricket far too soon, actually making a century in almost his last county match – against Surrey at The Oval, when the match resulted in a tie.

Present-day cricketers will hardly believe that he faced the fastest bowlers – faster than any we have at the present moment – unarmed with either pads or gloves and, strange to say, he was never seriously hurt.

As a racquet and tennis player he was quite at the top of the tree. In both these games, as in his cricket, he played in a most peculiar style, but with great effect. He simply revelled in unorthodoxy. He certainly attained a higher eminence at racquets than he did at tennis, and often said he regretted not having taken up the latter game earlier. It was a great treat in the old days of Prince's Club, in Hans Place, to see him play a single, as he did frequently, with Punch Fairs, the champion racquet player, from whom he used to receive three aces.

He was also a wonderful whist player, but I fancy he never became equally good at bridge. He was a very fine billiard player and frequently had one of the professionals play on his small pocket table at North Villa, Regent's Park.

Indeed he took a keen interest in almost every game up till the very last hour of his life, and the handicap of his long illness seemed if anything to add to his keenness. He struggled up to Lord's – he was a trustee of the MCC – to attend the committee meetings, both of MCC and of the Middlesex CC, and to witness the matches all through the summer of 1921. The absence of his bath chair, which used to be drawn up in front of the Players' dressing room, was greatly noticed last summer. The Middlesex professionals and his old friends had many a pleasant chat there with him.

It seems strange that neither he nor any of the seven brothers ever married. A partial explanation of this is, I think, their wonderful attachment to each other. Never was there a more united family, and Russie was idolized up to the end of his long life by his numerous nephews and nieces – his five sisters were all married, but alas, there is no one to perpetuate the family name. No one had more friends, though, of course, he had outlived most of them; his friendship once gained was wonderfully strong and true, and those friends who, like the writer, have survived him, will treasure his memory to the end of their lives.

He was one of the most generous of men, but, like his brothers, he had a horror of his name appearing in any subscription list, and insisted on remaining anonymous.

Besides his interest in games he was fond of music of the best kind, in former days never missing the concerts which were termed "Monday Pops". In fact, he was all his life a constant attendant at the best concerts and operas. To recall these performances and the numerous great performers that he had met and heard was a great joy to him, and his memory was never at fault.

To what Mr Webbe has written one may add as a matter of record, that Mr Walker was in the Harrow eleven in 1859 and 1860, and in the Oxford eleven from 1861 to 1865, he being the last man who played five times in the university match. A rule was passed in 1865 that no one should play for more than four years. Mr Walker met with little success as a batsman against Cambridge, his best score being 42 in 1861. In the five matches nine wickets fell to his innocent-looking but rather deceptive slow bowling. He had pleasanter recollections of his two matches against Eton. In 1859, when Harrow won in a single innings, he scored 28 and took six wickets, getting rid of R. A. H. Mitchell for 10 and 0, and in the drawn game in 1860 he took five wickets for 37 runs and two for 60. It was often said of him that his style of batting could be neither described nor imitated. It was entirely his own. He assisted the Gentlemen against the Players in ten matches between 1863 and 1868, and had a batting average – very good in those days – of 24. His best score was 92 at The Oval in 1865. He made 63 in his second innings at Lord's in 1866, when the Gentlemen were beaten, after a fine fight, by 38 runs, and in the same year he scored 52, when the Gentlemen followed on and gained their first victory at The Oval.

S. H. P.

**MR JEHANGIR SORABJI WARDEN**, one of the best all-round cricketers the Parsis ever had, was born at Bombay on January 13, 1885, and died there on January 16, 1928, aged 43. He came to the front as a slow left-handed bowler with a big break, and he developed into quite a good bat. In 1911 he toured England with the All India team making 928 runs with an average of 22.09 and taking 94 wickets for 20.42 runs each. In the game with Northumberland at Newcastle-on-Tyne, which the county won by one wicket, he scored 116 and 11 and had analyses of three for 85 and eight for 88. In the quadrangular tournaments in Bombay he invariably made his presence felt with bat or ball, if not with both, and in such cricket he made 528 runs with an average of 40.61 and took 48 wickets for 12.25 apiece. When he carried out his bat for 115 against the Hindus in 1912, the next highest score in the total of 183 was only 15; and when he made 85 v Mohommedans in 1912, he and H. D. Kanga (150) added 209 together for the third wicket. Among his many good bowling figures for the Parsis in great matches were:

  6-11    v Bombay Presidency, at Bombay, 1907
 11-86    (including 6-21), v Bombay Presidency, at Poona, 1908
 12-96    (including 7-40), v Bombay Presidency, at Bombay, 1911
  7-37    v Mohommedans, at Bombay, 1916
 12-112   (including 7-44), v Mohommedans, at Bombay, 1921

For Jorah Bajan v Customs, at Calcutta, in 1920, he took five wickets with the first five balls of the match. He was the author of *Knotty Cricket Problems Solved*.

**WILLIAM WILFRID WHYSALL**, who had reached the height of his fame last season, died in hospital at Nottingham on November 11, 1930. About a fortnight earlier he had fallen on a dance floor and injured his elbow. Septicaemia set in and, although a blood transfusion was performed, he passed away. Born at Woodborough, Nottinghamshire, on October 31, 1887, he was only 43 years of age at the time of his death.

He matured slowly as a cricketer, and not until 1908 was he invited to join the ground staff at Trent Bridge. Two seasons later he made 140 for Nottinghamshire 2nd XI at Trent Bridge against Staffordshire, who had Sydney Barnes to bowl for them. While a useful wicket-keeper, he played for the county as a batsman and, though first tried for Nottinghamshire in 1910, he did not realise expectations until ten years later when, after the long break due to the war, he resumed his place in the side. From that time he forged ahead rapidly until he became the most reliable batsman in the eleven, a position he held unchallenged last summer when he headed the averages with 47.84 for an aggregate of 1,866. During five consecutive summers he had an aggregate of over 2,000 runs in first class matches and in 1929 he made 2,716 runs.

MR SAMUEL MOSES JAMES WOODS, one of the most famous and popular of athletes, a splendid cricketer and a great Rugby football forward, was born at Glenfield near Sydney on April 14, 1867, and died on April 30, 1931, at Taunton. A player of grand physique, cheery disposition, and unflinching courage, he was generally at his best against the strongest and never knew when he was beaten. Although essentially an all-rounder and a most efficient and inspiring captain, it is on his bowling that his fame will chiefly rest. He was fast and accurate and had at his command not only a deadly yorker but also a slow ball which was as formidable and deceptive as any he sent down. Unquestionably he reached a measure of excellence which entitled him to a place among the great fast bowlers of all time.

Essentially a forcing batsman Woods drove tremendously hard especially to the on. He used his reach, great strength and sure eye to hit at the pitch of the ball without leaving his crease. Often he knocked the most accurate bowlers off their length and he could cut any short ball with a swing of his massive shoulders and arms, sending the ball at tremendous speed past cover point. While Woods preferred the fast scoring game he could, in case of need, adopt a sound, correct method and then he excelled in off-side driving. As with age his effectiveness with the ball declined he used the bat to greater purpose. His highest scoring season was 1895 when he made 1,405 runs with an average of 34. This he surpassed four years later with a record of 40 an innings.

He received his early education at Sydney Grammar School and Royston College, Sydney, and at the latter institution showed such ability as a bowler that in 1883 he took 70 wickets for 5 runs each and on one occasion obtained seven wickets in seven balls.

He came to England in 1884 and went to Brighton College where he and G. L. Wilson stood out as two of the best public school cricketers of the season. In the following summer for Brighton College Woods obtained 78 wickets for 7.5 runs apiece, getting fourteen – all bowled – in the match with Lancing College, and, in addition to achieving so much as a bowler, showed no little ability as a hard-hitting batsman while, later on, he developed into a brilliant field at cover point or extra mid-off and a sure catch. He began to play regularly for Somerset in 1887 but a year earlier had figured at Portsmouth in a match between the fifth Australian team and a side got together by G. N. Wyatt, a prominent amateur who appeared first for Gloucestershire, afterwards for Surrey and finally for Sussex. While reaching double figures in each innings and taking two wickets, Woods accomplished nothing of much note on that occasion, but on going up to Cambridge in 1888 he, in the course of very few weeks, made himself certain of his "Blue". For four years he appeared for the university and, during that period, secured 190 wickets for less than 15 runs apiece, while in the four encounters with Oxford at Lord's, of which three were won and one drawn, he obtained 36 wickets for something under 9 runs each. Cricket has presented no more exhilarating sight than the university match of those days with Woods bowling his hardest and Gregor MacGregor keeping wicket in that famous player's masterly fashion.

Woods did little as a batsman against Oxford, but in his last year when Cambridge – set 90 to make to win – had lost eight wickets for 89, he went in and hit the first ball he received to the boundary. He was Cambridge captain in 1890 when the Light Blues proved victorious by seven wickets.

Although earning great fame as a bowler at Cambridge and repeatedly chosen to assist Gentlemen against Players – he and F. S. Jackson bowled unchanged in the match of 1894 and were mainly instrumental in gaining a single innings victory over the professionals – Sam Woods' career was essentially identified with Somerset, for whom he appeared from 1886 to 1907, acting as captain in 1894 and taking over the duties of secretary until 1923. His biggest score was one of 215 which he hit against Sussex at Hove in 1895, the total meanwhile being increased by 282 in two hours and a half. Three years later, on the same ground, he made 143 out of 173 in two hours and a quarter off the Sussex bowlers.

Among his many bowling feats, in addition to his great performances for Gentlemen v Players, was the taking of all ten wickets for 69 runs in an innings for Cambridge against C. I. Thornton's Eleven – fifteen wickets in the match for 88 runs – at Cambridge in 1890. Two years earlier in a contest against another side got together by C. I. Thornton he performed the "hat trick", and in 1891 at The Oval against Surrey he obtained fourteen wickets for 11 runs each.

He played for the Australians in this country several times in 1888 and participated in several tours abroad, going to America in 1891 and to South Africa in 1896-97 with teams led by Lord Hawke, to the West Indies with a side captained by Sir A. Priestley and to America again in 1899 when Ranjitsinhji was in control.

In the course of his career he made nineteen 100's – eighteen of these for Somerset – scored in all 15,499 runs with an average of 23 and took 1,079 wickets for 20 runs apiece. Over six feet in height, he weighed in his cricket days thirteen stone and a half.

His career as a Rugby football player naturally did not extend over so many years as his cricket life, but he attained the highest honours at the winter game, playing for Cambridge against Oxford in 1888 and in the two following years and being "capped" for England thirteen times in the days when there were only three international encounters each season. Four times he played against Scotland between 1890 and 1895, five times against Ireland and four times against Wales. Tremendously strong and very fast, he possessed all the qualities necessary and, in his quickness in breaking away, was, after Frank Evershed, one of the most famous of wing forwards in the comparatively early days of the Rugby game. He also played Rugby for Somerset and appeared at Association football for Sussex. In the war he served in the Somerset Light Infantry and in the Devon Regiment.

**MAJOR EDWARD GEORGE WYNYARD, DSO,** died at the age of 75, at The Red House, Knotty Green, Beaconsfield, Buckinghamshire, on October 30, 1936. Born in India on April 1, 1861, Major Wynyard was educated chiefly at Charterhouse School. He enjoyed a distinguished career in the Army, mainly in the east, before retiring in 1903. He served in the Great War in different staff appointments.

Over six feet in height and finely built, Wynyard was a brilliant player of most games, and excelled on the cricket field, where his commanding figure could not escape attention. In his Hampshire days he usually wore an I Zingari cap of polo shape balanced at the military angle with a strap under the chin. A splendid forcing batsman he played many fine innings, and in 1899 in company with Major R. M. Poore he scored 225 out of 411 added for Hampshire's sixth wicket against Somerset at Taunton. This is still the record stand for the sixth wicket by English batsmen. The runs were made in four hours twenty minutes, and Major Poore finished with 304. Major Wynyard bowled lobs and in this match he took five wickets for 38 runs.

He went to New Zealand in the autumn of 1906 as captain of the MCC touring team, but in the third match he snapped a tendon in his leg and returned home. He captained an MCC amateur team who went to America at the end of our 1907 season. Twice he was compelled to decline invitations to accompany England teams to Australia. He toured South Africa in 1905 and 1909 with the teams led by P. F. Warner and H. D. G. Leveson Gower.

From the time when Hampshire became a first-class county in 1895, Major Wynyard scored 7,572 runs with an average of 34. He excelled in 1894 with an average of 66. Two years later he was in the England eleven which beat Australia at The Oval by 66 runs, the colonials being dismissed by Peel and J. T. Hearne for 44 in the fourth innings. That was the last match in which W. G. Grace led England to victory.

Major Wynyard played his last first-class match in 1912 for MCC against Oxford University, but was regular in his visits to Lord's where, for a time, he assisted in the management. As he appeared first for Hampshire at Lord's against MCC in 1878, his playing career extended over 35 years. He used to say that he made 150 centuries in all kinds of cricket of which he kept a record.

While on service in India, Major Wynyard played many big innings and in one match scored 123 and 106, both not out. When home on leave in 1887, he made 233 for Incogniti against Phœnix Park at Dublin.

A fine, free hitter, Major Wynyard used a great variety of strokes, especially those in front of the wicket. He had a grand drive, a powerful "hook", a good cut, back strokes of a forcing description and a rare pull in making which he dropped to his right knee and drove the ball on the half volley over mid-on. He developed also a special method of hitting left-handed bowling over cover point in most effective fashion. While he could field admirably anywhere, he excelled at slip and at mid-on.

A splendid Association forward, he played in the Old Carthusian eleven who won the Football Association Cup in 1881 by beating Old Etonians in the final tie at The Oval.

CORRECTION: Mr E. L. Bartlett, West Indies, of whom an obituary notice appeared in last year's issue of the *Almanack*, wrote from Bridgetown in March with the assurance "that I am very much alive and fit". It is a pleasure to publish this message sent to me.

S. J. S.

# MISCELLANY

## GRANGE CLUB CENTENARY, 1932

The Grange Cricket Club has been styled the "Marylebone of the North" and, more familiarly and, perhaps more correctly, "the premier club of Scotland". Not with pomp and circumstance but in the modest manner characteristic of the game in Scotland, the Grange Club last year celebrated its centenary. A centenary match was played at Raeburn Place, Edinburgh, the MCC sending to the Scottish capital a team of twelve men who played a two days' match with the Grange, the game ending drawn. The fact that the match was one of twelve men a side accentuated the friendly sentiment, if making the chance of a definite issue somewhat more remote. However, cricket in Edinburgh, as distinct from other parts of Scotland, is essentially a friendly business and the Grange emphasise this element by playing two Scottish clubs each Saturday during the summer and throwing open their doors to such of the public as care to spend their Saturday afternoons in a restful atmosphere. At the same time the Grange boast a proud tradition and it is still the ambition of all Scottish clubs to beat the leading Edinburgh club.

It is on record that the Grange came into being in a rather strange fashion. Some members of a Speculative Society, which met in Edinburgh in the early part of last century, finding a discussion rather dull, fled from the debating room and resolved to form a cricket club. Sir Thomas Dick Lauder, the author of "The Wolf of Badenoch", who was owner of the estate of Grange on the south side of Edinburgh, gave the club the use of a field in his grounds. Hence the name. The Grange, it is on record, played in 1832 two matches with the Brunswick club, a combination of artisans which still exists. The following year the Grange met an eleven of Glasgow on Glasgow Green and sustained defeat. In the same year the Grange engaged as professional and groundsman John Sparks of MCC and All England, who was with the club till his death in 1854.

The club had several habitations prior to entering in 1872 into occupancy of the ground at Raeburn Place which has, for half a century, enjoyed a distinction boasted by no other cricket field in Scotland. Dr W. G. Grace and many other English cricketing notables have played at the Grange ground, which has been visited by practically all the overseas teams coming to this country, the latest such visitors being the South Americans who were with us in 1932. They say at Raeburn Place that it was out of the Grange ground W.G. made his longest hit, but it is over the doings of certain members of the club that cricket enthusiasts on the north side of Edinburgh like best to linger.

The honorary members of the club number six: J. W. Wharton Tod, an old-time cricketer and golfer, Sir Montague Cotterill and L. M. Balfour Melville, who joined the club in 1872, W. K. Aikman, for many years treasurer of the club, and H. D. G. Leverson Gower and H. J. Stevenson, who were given honorary membership on the occasion of the club centenary when Mr Leveson Gower conveyed the congratulations of the MCC and also a donation of £50 "in recognition of what the club had done for cricket in Scotland and for the game generally". Balfour Melville, brilliant cricketer, rugby "cap", amateur golf champion and many other things in sport, is, perhaps, the finest all-round sportsman Scotland has ever produced. He scored 150 runs in the first match played at Raeburn Place and he was playing for Scotland till shortly before the war. Stevenson, an old Edinburgh Academy boy, maintained in a conspicuous manner what is practically a Scottish sports tradition, born of the circumstance that over half a century ago public schools north of the Tweed laid it down that, for the boys, cricket should be the summer, rugby football the winter sport. Stevenson was described in a contemporary reference in the Scottish press as "the greatest football player in the world". Many who have forgotten his football prowess will remember him as one of the most daring lob bowlers who ever trod a cricket pitch. Of his football team mate, R. H. Johnston, Dr Grace said that he was the finest schoolboy wicket-keeper he had ever seen, and that great Fettesian-Lorettonian and Scotland rugby football combination, A. G. G. Asher and A. R. Don Wauchope, respectively Oxford and Cambridge football "blues", were associated in the summer game at Raeburn Place where the fielding of Don Wauchope remedied his later occasional deficiencies as a batsman. These men flourished during a period which has been described as "the golden age of Grange batting".

Golf and other sports have of recent years taken their toll of men who in a former sports generation would have been Grange cricketers but, in the main, the high traditional standard has been maintained, particularly of recent summers, by B. G. W. Atkinson, a Northamptonshire man, who is carrying on the one-thousand-runs-a-year habit begun thirty years ago by a clever Grange cricketer, D. L. A. Smith. Atkinson was some years ago a prominent club footballer in Edinburgh, where he is filling a scholastic appointment, and it was a general belief that, could a Scottish qualification have been established for him, he would to a certainty have been a Scottish rugby "cap". A brilliant three-quarter, no small part of his value as a cricketer is the enterprising way in which he collects his runs. The list of men distinguished in both sports could be extended but mention should be made of some of the many notable professionals at Raeburn Place since the time of Sparks, conspicuous examples being the late Ben Terry, a Nottinghamshire man, Dennett, who played for Gloucestershire, and Keene and Preston, two other men with English county qualifications – in particular Preston, who took over 100 wickets in eight of the nine seasons during which he was with the Grange club.

The Grange were at one time the subject of a good deal of ungenerous criticism. That, nowadays, there is a happier spirit in the game in Scotland is shown by the fact that at their recent annual meeting the Scottish Cricket Union appointed as their president the Hon. R. B. W. Watson as a tribute to the personal qualities of this old Grange cricketer and also in compliment to the premier club in its centenary year.

William Reid

# THE GOOGLY

## THE SCAPEGOAT OF CRICKET

### By B. J. T. Bosanquet

The visit of the South African team has revived interest in the googly. Poor old googly! It has been subjected to ridicule, abuse, contempt, incredulity, and survived them all. Nowadays one cannot read an article on cricket without finding that any deficiencies existing at the present day are attributed to the influence of the googly. If the standard of bowling falls off, it is because too many cricketers devote their time to trying to master it, instead of carrying on with the recognised and hallowed methods of bowling. If batsmen display a marked inability to hit the ball on the offside, or anywhere in front of the wicket, and stand in apologetic attitudes before their wicket, it is said that the googly has made it impossible for them to adopt the old aggressive attitude and make the old scoring strokes.

But, after all, what is the googly? It is merely a ball with an ordinary break produced by an extra-ordinary method. It is quite possible and, in fact, not difficult, to detect, and, once detected, there is no reason why it should not be treated as an ordinary "break-back". However, it is not for me to defend it. Other and more capable hands have taken it up and exploited it, and, if blame is to be allotted, let it be on their shoulders. For me is the task of the historian, and if I appear too much in the role of the "proud parent", I ask forgiveness. In view of many conflicting statements, it may be of interest if I recapitulate the inception and development of the googly.

## BIRTH OF THE GOOGLY

Somewhere about the year 1897 I was playing a game with a tennis ball, known as "Twisti-Twosti". The object was to bounce the ball on a table so that your opponent sitting opposite could not catch it. It soon occurred to me that if one could pitch a ball which broke in a certain direction and with more or less the same delivery make the next ball go in the opposite direction, one would mystify one's opponent. After a little experimenting I managed to do this, and it was so successful that I practised the same thing with a soft ball at "Stump-cricket". From this I progressed to a cricket ball, and about 1899 I had become a "star turn" for the luncheon interval during our matches at Oxford. That is, the most famous batsman on the opposing side was enticed into a net and I was brought up to bowl him two or three leg-breaks. These were followed by an "off-break with more or less the same action. If this pitched on the right place it probably hit him on the knee, everyone shrieked with laughter, and I was led away and locked up for the day.

## RECOGNITION

During this and the following year I devoted a great deal of time to practising the googly at the nets, and occasionally bowled in unimportant matches. The first public recognition we obtained was in July, 1900, for Middlesex v Leicestershire at Lord's. An unfortunate individual (I believe it was Coe) had made 98 when he was clean bowled by a fine specimen which bounced four times. The incident was rightly treated as a joke, and was the subject of ribald comment, but this small beginning marked the start of what came to be termed a revolution in bowling.

From then on progress was slow but sure. We achieved marked success at Nottingham in August, and attracted a certain amount of notice, and my old friends Gregor McGregor and "Plum" Warner were fully alive to future possibilities. At that time I myself always endeavoured to convey the impression that the result was unintentional and accidental, as I did not wish batsmen to be too much on their guard. I even persuaded "Plum" not to write about it, which he nobly refrained from doing for nearly a year! By that time, however, human nature had to be served, and, following on other successes I obtained, he and others began to write it up, and considerable attention was attracted to it as a new development.

## THE SECRET

At this stage I would like to say that it was in reality nothing new in itself. Many leg-break bowlers (including Attewell and E. R. Wilson to my knowledge) had dismissed batsmen with balls which, intended to break one way, had done the opposite. The sole difference was in achieving this result at will; and although leading cricketers and the more knowledgable critics appreciated that this could be done, it was some time before the ignorance and prejudice of others was overcome. The Googly after all (bowled by a right-handed bowler to a right-handed batsman) is nothing more nor less than an ordinary off-break. The method of delivery is the secret of its difficulty, and this merely consisted in turning the wrist over at the moment of delivery far enough to alter the axis of spin, so that a ball which normally delivered would break from leg breaks from the off. That is all there is to it.

To revert to ancient history, from the moment it became generally recognised that a ball could be bowled which left the batsman in doubt as to which way it would break, the fun began. I must confess that in the beginning I persevered with the Googly chiefly because I found that the lot of an average fast-medium bowler on a county side was not a happy one. It generally meant being put on under a sweltering sun, on a plumb wicket, when the other bowlers had failed and the two batsmen were well set. If one was lucky enough to get a wicket, the original bowlers resumed, and unless the same conditions recurred one was not wanted again. If the wicket was difficult, one was never thought of. As a result, partly from a natural disinclination to work hard on hot days (how much more pleasant to walk slowly up to the wicket and gently propel the ball into the air), and partly, I hope, from a sneaking ambition to achieve greater things, I persevered with the Googly. It took any amount of perseverance, but for a year or two the results were more than worth it, for in addition to adding to the merriment of the cricketing world, I found that batsmen who used to grin at the sight of me and grasp their bat firmly by the long handle, began to show a marked preference for the other end!

## PUZZLED AUSTRALIANS

Contemporary history has recorded the progress of the Googly from this period onwards, and I do not propose to enlarge any further on my personal connection with it. There are a few incidents, however, which stand out vividly.

There was the first time it was bowled against the Australians – at Lord's late one evening in 1902 – when I had two overs and saw two very puzzled Australians return to the Pavilion. It rained all next day, and not one of them tumbled to the fact that it was not an accident. The first Googly ever bowled in Australia, in March, 1903; Trumper batting, having made 40 in about twenty minutes. Two leg-breaks were played beautifully to cover, but the next ball (delivered with a silent prayer), pitching in the same place, saw the same graceful stroke played – and struck the middle-stump instead of the bat! W. Gunn stumped when appreciably nearer my wicket than his own! Arthur Shrewsbury complaining that "it wasn't fair". These are a few impressions.

There are two or three bright patches I can recall, as, for instance, in 1904, when in three consecutive matches I got five wickets in each innings v Yorkshire, six in each v Nottinghamshire, and seven in each v Sussex (including Fry and Ranji). There was one week in 1905 in which I had eleven wickets v Sussex at Lord's (and got a hundred in each innings. The double feat is still a record); and during the next three days in the first Test match at Nottingham I got eight out of nine wickets which fell in the second innings, the last man being out just before a thunderstorm broke – and even then if Trumper could have hobbled to the wicket it meant a draw! This recalls the fourth Test match at Sydney in 1904, in which at one period in the second innings I had six for 12, and then got Noble leg-before, and never appealed. The last man was in, and the match won, and there were reasons!

I have the balls used in these two matches, both presented to me by my old friend Dick Lilley, the best wicket-keeper in a big match we have known. There is a good story of Lilley (whom I last saw pigeon-shooting at Monte Carlo in 1914!) in the Gentlemen v Players match at The Oval, in 1904. I got a few wickets in the second innings. Then one of the "Pros" came in and said: "Dick's in next; he's calling us all a lot of rabbits; says he can see every ball you bowl. Do try and get him, and we'll rag his life out". Dick came in. I bowled him two overs of leg-breaks, then changed my action and bowled another leg-break. Dick played it gracefully to fine leg, and it removed his off-stump! I can still hear the reception he got in the dressing-room.

If the preceding lines seem egotistical, let the following be my excuse. Last year a great pal of mine, with whom I have played a lot of cricket, said at a dinner-table: "I know old Bose invented the Googly and that sort of thing, but did he ever get any wickets?" I can truthfully say that after 1905 he didn't, and one over subsequently bowled at Harrow elicited about a quarter of a column of ribald comment in a newspaper, which finished the Googly so far as I am concerned, and I had better finish this article.

## SPIN BOWLING

By A. P. Freeman, Kent XI, 1914-36

In an Interview

The best piece of advice which I offer to the young bowler is: watch and experiment. To my mind, too many bowlers in modern cricket neglect to use their intelligence; their efforts are little more than mechanical. It is absolutely essential that a bowler should study the batsman, not in a casual sort of way, but with proper concentration. I am convinced that I learned most because I spent so much time all through my career in watching both batsmen and other bowlers.

I do not claim to have any wonderful secrets that may account for my harvest of wickets for Kent in season after season. When you are at the top of the tree it is easier to take wickets than in the days of less experience in the art. I know I bowled better as long ago as 1914 than when I was in my supposed prime. Never having received a day's coaching in my life, I am very sure that bowlers are born and not made.

If the ability is there, it can, of course, be brought out and developed, but without natural gifts no one can hope to attain real eminence as a bowler. A length bowler will get wickets in any class of cricket. Action, length, flight, control of pace and finger spin may all be persevered with, but to rise above the common level that natural ability must be there. The experienced player should be able to tell a boy with cricket in him by the way the boy picks up a bat or bowls one or two balls.

So many cricket text-books are available that I do not think it necessary to go at all deeply into the main principles of bowling. The question has often been raised whether bowlers are given sufficient coaching nowadays. My view has been that you can only tell the pupil the "secrets" – by which I mean the fundamental points of bowling – and he must, by thorough practice, do the rest for himself.

Given a natural ability and having developed an easy run up to the wicket, a boy has a good start. No one can hope to succeed without a loose arm, for if the action is at all bad the bowler has much harder work to do. Fast bowlers like McDonald and Larwood have provided admirable examples in post-war cricket of an easy, loose run up and smooth action and the slow bowler, too, must acquire a perfectly natural run up. It is beyond all contradiction that length is the chief part of bowling, and length must be commanded before any attempt at spinning the ball is begun. When I was coaching, I used to draw a line nine feet in front of the wicket and instruct my pupils to bowl to that; I have also laid a sheet of newspaper on the wicket and told the boys to pitch the ball on it. Of course a good length to a tall batsman like Frank Woolley would be a long-hop to a player of the height of, say, Hendren. The aim must be to drop the ball just out of a batsman's reach and to give him as little time as possible to deal with it.

### FINGER-SPIN

The good-coach will stress the importance of learning to change pace without change of action. In my view that is one of the hardest parts of bowling. I know it is the general opinion that the leg-break is the most difficult ball to bowl but, as it is also the most deadly ball, it is worth mastering. The grip of the ball for this is a matter for the individual. I hold it with the first and second fingers round the seam, with the ball resting on the third finger and the thumb steadying the ball and I think one has more command of the ball with this grip. The seam is pointing towards slip. Some people run away with the idea that the grips for the leg-break and googly are different. That is not so. In fact my grip is the same for the top-spinner as well. The difference between the three balls is this: For the top-spinner I hold the ball with the seam pointing straight down the wicket and release it from a position half-way between that for the leg-break and googly. When bowling the googly the wrist is turned over and the ball comes over the top of the little finger from the back of the hand. In this case the ball is held with the seam pointing to fine leg. Some off-break bowlers who are supposed to spin the ball merely do little except turn the wrist. That is rolling the ball – no more. To spin the ball, you must use your fingers. Hold the ball tight with the first finger over the seam and, at the time the ball is leaving the hand, flick it with the fingers.

Freeman's grip for the leg-break

## STUDY THE BATSMAN

If the art of studying the batsman and watching for his weak spots was cultivated more both in county and club cricket, we should not hear so many lamentations about the scarcity of good spin bowlers. It is important to study the batsman right up to the moment of releasing the ball. A movement by him before the ball has left my hand has prompted me to pitch the ball a little wide and often to get him stumped. It may take you half an hour to find out his weakness but it is worth while. Never mind giving a batsman 20 runs or so. Four wickets for a hundred at The Oval always pleased me more than, say, eight for 20 on a bad wicket against a poor side. Humour the batsman if he has a particular hit but be sure you have safe fieldsmen in the position where a catch may be put up. A good captain will always consult the bowler before altering the placing of the field; otherwise he is likely to ruin the bowler's best laid plans.

I always enjoyed pitting my brains against the top-class batsmen. I preferred to bowl to Jack Hobbs more than anybody. He played every ball on its merits, took no liberties and if you got his wicket you earned it. I always knew he would play every ball as it deserved.

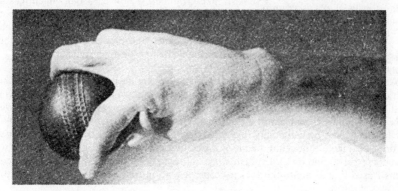

Freeman's grip for the top-spinner. Same as for the leg break but the wrist is turned over more

During the later years of my career in Kent cricket I believe I knew every batsman's weakness. That knowledge, carefully memorised, I was always ready and willing to pass on to younger bowlers in the team. When Warwickshire were playing Kent at Gravesend in the first year Douglas Wright turned out for us, I got a wicket with the last ball of an over and Bates came in to take the next ball from Wright. I suggested to Wright he should bowl a googly first ball: he did and Bates' leg peg went down. Bates said to me afterwards: "You told him, Tich, didn't you, to bowl a googly?" and I admitted the little strategy.

Always be ready to experiment is a good motto for bowlers. If you cannot get a man out try anything. Never be afraid of being hit. If a batsman starts hitting, keep him at it; a little more flight and the batsman may make a mistake. It is when the wicket is "dead" that you need to experiment most. At such times bowl a bit faster but not forgetting to slip in an occasional slow one with the same action. Whenever I am asked to give advice on bowling, I always urge the prime importance of these points of studying the batsman and experimenting.

## THE GOOGLY

I have probably "kidded" more batsmen out than anyone. It may seem a strange thing to say but I got a good many wickets through not bowling the googly. The batsman knew I could bowl it and was always expecting it. Often he became so fidgety trying to watch my hand and to anticipate the googly that he got out in some other way.

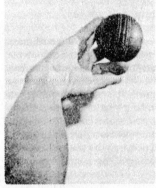

Taken from a position high up behind Freeman's arm, at the moment the googly is being released with the wrist turned completely over The ball is spinning over the little finger

A bowler cannot expect to master the googly without a lot of hard practice. When the late R. O. Schwarz came to England in 1907, round about my eighteenth birthday, I summoned up courage to ask him how to bowl the googly. His advice was, "Just watch me, you will soon see how it is done", and after close observation of his bowling I was optimistic enough to believe I could master it and set to work to practice bowling the googly for two years, winter and summer, before attempting it in the middle. When at last I felt confident that I could keep a length I tried the googly out in a match against Charlton Park and took eight wickets for about 20 runs. W. H. Levett, the Kent wicket-keeper, always said I bowled the googly in two ways. Actually this was not so, but I sometimes released it earlier in my delivery. Also, like Grimmett, I bowled a ball which was not an ordinary googly. Everything else was the same except that, instead of the ball coming from over the back of the hand, it came out between the third and fourth fingers. By using the second method I brought the ball through quicker because I could grip it harder.

A slow bowler, without the support of a good wicket-keeper, would probably find that half of his work was wasted. I have been lucky in playing with such a fine wicket-keeper as Leslie Ames. We made a perfect combination. He knew everything I could do with the ball. Occasionally I beat him but not often. The number of wickets which Ames took off my bowling must be something like a record. I never signalled the googly to Ames but, before he came into the team regularly I used to do so, although I know that most wicket-keepers prefer to find it out for themselves, rather than be given a signal when it is coming. Signs I used to indicate to the wicket-keeper when I meant to bowl a googly were to hitch up the back of my trousers as I walked back after delivering the previous ball or to swing my left hand, holding the ball.

## OPPOSING LEG THEORY

Always try to force the batsman to make shots. That was my plan. Cricket looks so bad when a bowler's policy is aimed at "pegging down" the batsman. I think leg-theory is a sign of weakness on the bowler's part. I only once bowled deliberately outside the leg stump and then with the idea of exposing this negative bowling. We were playing at Tonbridge and Warwickshire's slow left-arm bowler kept on dropping the ball just outside the leg stump. Kent had a bang at him, not with much success, and some of our batsman said, "If he bowls this stuff in the return match, we will ignore it". They did so and although the Warwickshire bowler had a lot of maiden overs he did not get many wickets. When I went on I put all my fieldsmen on the leg side and bowled a few overs outside the leg stump. One man was run out, trying to push the ball to the off, another left a ball alone and it broke and hit the off stump. I don't think a run was scored while I was indulging in this little "retaliation". But it did not please me a bit, because it was so entirely a case of the batsman getting himself out rather than the bowler taking wickets.

A bowler who doesn't like the job will never get on. He should never allow himself to be worried by dropped catches. As soon as you start slacking you are finished. I might have been out of the ordinary but I never got tired all the time I was bowling, no matter how long my spell with the ball. The hotter the weather, the less tired I seemed to become. It was after the day's play that I used to feel the strain. Cold weather, of course, affects the muscles and it takes a long time to get the fingers supple. I believe a good many bowlers are troubled with pains in the wrist and elbow after long hours of spinning the ball, but I can honestly say that I was never affected in this way, nor did I ever have a corn on my hand.

## SOME EXPERIMENTS WORTH TRYING

In my view bowlers do not use the bowling crease as much as they should do. Obviously when this is done the batsman has to contend against the ball coming to him from different angles. I often used to bowl a yard behind the wicket and rely on the art of flighting – making the batsman think the ball is coming up farther than it really is. A slow bowler must be a master of flight. It is not easy to explain how it is done although, of course, it is combined with action and is more or less natural. One of the most dangerous balls is a good length outside the leg stump. A batsman is always liable to over-balance when trying to play this ball and there is a good chance of him being stumped if he misses it. On a sticky wicket you have to bowl almost half-volleys. On a fast wicket you must bowl a bit shorter, for a good length on a fast wicket is a long hop on a slow one. Much the same thing applies when you are bowling to a quick-footed or a slow-footed batsman.

The only time I bowl round the wicket is when I think I can take advantage of broken patches outside the leg stump made by the bowler in his run-up. A left-hander, of course, has to bowl round the wicket to get the right angle. On a wicket where the ball won't turn you must rely on length and flight.

Keep pegging away.

## CRICKET CONUNDRUMS

By A. E. R. Gilligan

Whenever I have given cricket talks in different parts of England, I have always devoted at least a quarter of the time to the many cricket problems and difficulties caused by wrong interpretation of the rules. During my experiences, I have collected quite a useful list of cricket conundrums which I shall discuss in this article.

First of all, I remember being asked rather an important question at a meeting some twelve years ago: "Why doesn't the MCC legislate for many of the doubtful points arising from the Laws of Cricket?" I promised that I would put this problem before the Secretary of the MCC himself and accordingly went to see Mr W. Findlay.

His answer was an excellent one, and I can think of no better way of starting my article than by setting it out here and now. He said: "Why should the MCC legislate for doubtful points arising from the Cricket Laws? Our duty is to see that the Rules of Cricket are made to cover only the rightful interpretation of the very spirit of the game, and anything which borders on unfairness can never be legislated for by the premier cricket club."

I think that everyone will agree that Mr Findlay's outlook on so important a question was absolutely correct and that we should not endeavour to get round the rules by what may be termed unfair methods. Therefore I shall try to keep my cricket conundrums on amusing lines, and prove that all of them are covered by the existing rules of the game.

### ONE BALL: FIVE MEN OUT

Do you know how five men can be dismissed by one ball bowled? Of course, you must allow a certain amount of licence in this respect, but actually several years ago in a county match, when play was due to resume, it was found that one of the overnight not-out batsmen had taken a wrong tube-train, and at half past eleven was miles away from the "scene of conflict".

The umpires, on appeal, ruled that the batsman was "absent" and could not continue his innings. There is the first man out. The next comes in and the bowler delivers a no-ball, which naturally does not count as a legitimate delivery. The striker hits it towards cover-point and calls his partner for a run. His partner, seeing that there is not the slightest chance of a quick single, sends back the striker, who unfortunately slips up and falls to the ground. The ball is returned to the wicket-keeper and No. 2 is run out, still with no legitimate ball being bowled. No. 3 arrives and hits the first ball, a half-volley, with terrific force straight back at his partner, who receives the ball right in the middle of the forehead.

The ball bounces in the air and mid-off catches it easily. No. 3 is out, caught; No. 4 is also out – knocked out – and is carried off the field unconscious, and when No. 5 (who is No. 11 on the batting list) comes to the wicket, he finds he has no one with whom to bat. So there you have five men out with one ball bowled.

## WHO IS OUT?

Now here is another very interesting poser. Jones is bowling to Smith, with Robinson the non-striker. Smith hits a very hard return catch to the bowler, who just touches the ball and deflects it on to the wicket. Robinson is out of his crease and the ball, without touching the ground, riochets off the stumps into the hands of mid-on.

Who is out? Is Smith out, caught, or is Robinson run out?

I have asked over a hundred people this riddle and practically 90 per cent give Robinson run out. I put the point to two first-class umpires, Frank Chester and Jack Newman, last season at Hastings, and they replied simultaneously: "Smith is out, caught"; and that is the correct answer. (MCC have ruled this as "caught" – Editor.)

What about this one? The striker plays the ball a few yards up the wicket and calls his partner for a sharp single. Mid-off dashes in and the striker, seing that a run is impossible, turns back to his crease, but in so doing accidentally kicks the ball into his wicket. With the striker well out of his ground, the bails drop off and the umpire gives him out.

The question before you now is: How is the striker out?

When asked for an immediate decision, many people say: "Oh, he is run out." That is wrong, because the ball has not been touched by any of the fieldsmen after the striker has hit it. Others maintain that he is out, hit wicket. Again that is incorrect, because the ball had broken the wicket. The correct decision is therefore bowled – played on. It is just the same as if the batsman had played the ball on to his foot, from whence it rebounds on to his stumps.

## HALF CAUGHT?

The subject of another conundrum actually happened in a match in New Zealand. The last two batsmen are in, the last ball of the game is about to be delivered, and 2 runs are necessary for victory. The bowler runs up to bowl and sends down a good length ball to the striker, who takes a terrific swipe at it, sending the ball a tremendous way in the air. When it has reached the apex of its flight, the ball breaks in two pieces. Mid-on shouts "Mine" and catches half the ball. "You're out", says the fielder. "No, I am not", retorts the batsman. "The other half of the ball is on the ground".

An appeal is made to the umpire, who rightly decides that this particular delivery should not count and sends for another ball, as much as possible like the one which has been discarded, and play is resumed. The bowler is so excited by the occurrence that he sends down a full toss to leg, the batsman hits it straight to the square-leg boundary, and the match is won by the batting side.

This case was sent to the MCC Committee for a ruling, the result being that the umpire's action was unanimously upheld.

## HOLDING ON!

I remember George Cox, the old Sussex player, telling me of the following remarkable case which was submitted to him. The batting side require 50 runs for victory and the last two men are together, with the last over of the match to be bowled. No. 11 is a complete "rabbit", but manages somehow or other to survive five balls. As the bowler is running up to bowl the final ball, No. 11 waits till the ball is delivered, throws away his bat and turning, holds on the bails with his hands. The ball just snicks the off-stump and travels slowly to the slips.

The batsman removes his hands from the bails, picks up his bat and says: "Well, that is a drawn game".

An appeal is made to the umpire, who scratches his head, and the batsman, noticing this, declares loudly: "There is nothing in the rules which says a batsman cannot hold his bails on".

"Oh, yes, there is", says the umpire. "I give you out for unfair play, Rule 43". So the match is won by the fielding side.

Some years ago, when giving a cricket talk to the Portsmouth Umpires' Association, I was asked to give an instant decision upon this perplexing problem, and I wonder how many of you can do likewise: "How can a batsman hit the ball twice, yet score runs and not be given out by the umpire?"

Knowing that a striker may be out for hitting the ball twice without any attempt at a run being made – that is to say, he hits the ball a second time before it touches the ground, and is out for obstructing the field – I was momentarily at a loss to give the correct answer. Suddenly, like a flash, I remembered, and said: "If the ball has been struck twice lawfully, in defence of his wicket, and an overthrow is made, the striker is entitled to any runs that follow".

A roar of laughter went up, and I thought I had made a mistake until the questioner explained to me that he and his colleagues had gone carefully through the rules before the meeting in the hope of catching me out!

## TEST MATCH CONTRETEMPS

I have already mentioned that, if the umpires agree that a ball in use is unfit for play, they have the right to allow the substitution of another ball as much as possible similar to the one discarded.

I recall that, in the second Test match between England and Australia at Melbourne in 1925, after only 15 runs were on the board – I was bowling at the time – I noticed that a great piece of leather had come off the ball. I immediately showed the ball to Umpire Bob Crockett, who consulted his colleague and a brand new ball was brought out.

Before lunch that day we had no fewer than four new balls with the total no more than 87! When we adjourned, we discovered that, by mistake, a wrong packet of balls had been delivered to the ground and that we had No. 3 grade cricket balls instead of No. 1. It was agreed between "Herby" Collins and myself to play out the first innings with both sides using the No. 3 grade variety, and it is interesting now to record that we used eight new balls before the score reached 200 and Australia had seven.

I do not think that any similar incident can be brought to mind of the ball being changed so frequently in a Test or any other match. It came as quite a relief when we embarked upon the second innings.

## THE MAN WITH THE WOODEN LEG

In conclusion, let me tell you of a problem with Alec Kennedy, Hampshire's noted all-rounder, propounded to members of Frank Mann's MCC team on the outward voyage to South Africa in 1922. This is it. A batsman with his back foot well within his crease hits the ball hard to cover-point and does not move out of his ground. The ball is returned to the wicket-keeper, who whips off the bails; on appeal, the square-leg umpire gives the striker out.

When I replied that it could not be possible for the striker to be given out if his back foot was still inside his crease, Kennedy said: "Oh, yes, he can. You see the batsman has got a wooden leg!"

"But", I expostulated, "even if he has a wooden leg, that is still part and parcel of his body".

Kennedy laughed and replied: "That is quite true; but you see, by virtue of his having a wooden leg, he was entitled to a runner, and the runner was out of his ground. Rule 39 covers that".

There are many more cricket conundrums which puzzle a great number of cricketers, all of them excellently explained in the sixpenny blue edition of the Laws of Cricket with decisions and interpretations authorised by the MCC, so I will not dwell upon any contained therein.

Lastly, let me commend to every cricketer a thorough understanding of the rules of the game, and let us not forget the excellent example of Don Bradman, the Australian captain, who has actually passed an umpire's examination with flying colours.

## CRICKET IN WAR-TIME

### By Maj. H. S. Altham

So long as war was an affair of professional armies, its incidence seems to have had but little effect on cricket.

The first match of which the full score has been preserved – Kent v All England – took place on the Artillery Ground, Finsbury (still the Headquarters of the HAC), on June 18, 1744. England was then engaged in the war of the Austrian Succession, but the game was watched by "a great company", and amongst them the Duke of Cumberland, destined to figure in the following year on the less glorious field of Fontenoy, and Admiral Vernon, seeking, we may conclude, distraction from the memories of his defeat at Cartagena. Nor did the claims of state disturb another great patron of the game, for in 1745 we read of the Earl of Sandwich writing "I'll to your board (of Admiralty) when at leisure from cricket". Again in 1778 when the Empire seemed hastening to dissolution in the War of American Independence, two eminent privy counsellors were violently attacked in a quite unprintable lampoon for continuing to play cricket regardless of the calls of state. Fortunately Mr Churchill was never a cricketer! When the Grande Armée was lining the cliffs at Boulogne in 1804-05, Kent mustered its militia and the Coxheath cricket ground amongst others became a military camp. But so far from war stopping cricket in England, our soldiers took their bats with them; officers of the Light Division got up a match shortly before Busaco, whilst six days before Waterloo the Duke of Richmond was playing near Brussels, only to see the game summarily ended by the appearance of Wellington himself with the Prince of Orange. The terrain of the Crimea hardly favoured cricket, but there is a pleasant story of the Battle of Alma that shows how cricket was never far from some soldiers' minds: The Guards, Rifle Brigade and Black Watch were nearing the top of the rise when a round shot came bounding along and passed through the ranks which had "opened to avoid it in accordance with orders". Sir John Astley tells how "George Duff, a capital chap who was our best wicket-keeper, was just in front of me and I sang out 'Duff, you are keeping wicket, you ought to have stopped that one', and of how he turned and smiling quietly said, 'No, sir, it had a bit too much pace on. You are a long stop, sir, so I left it to you'".

The most striking reflection on cricket and the South African War is supplied by the fact that no reference whatever is to be found to it in the editorial notes of the relevant *Wisden's*. No cricketer of high repute was killed in the war, and of the players who died on service the only memorable names are those of that fine Yorkshire player, Frank Milligan, and the great Australian bowler, J. J. Ferris. I remember, as a boy, seeing pictures of our nurses in South Africa playing cricket, and during the siege of Mafeking one of the Boer commandants suggested to Baden-Powell that there should be a Sunday truce during which his men might come in and meet the garrison in all amity on the cricket field. "B.P." replied that nothing would give him greater pleasure when the present match was over, but at the moment his men were 200 (days) not out and were enjoying their game very much indeed!

The outbreak of the European War of 1914-18 will always be associated in my mind with Lord's. I was up there watching the Lord's Schools v The Rest match and can remember buying an evening paper on the ground and reading in the stop-press column the opening sentences of the speech which Lord Grey was then making in the Commons, and subsequently travelling down from Waterloo to Esher, where I was staying with the Howell brothers, and seeing in the blood-red sunset over the Thames an omen of the years to come. The younger Howell whose batting had dominated the match and for whom no honours in the game seemed unobtainable, fell in the Salient less than a year afterwards.

For most of that August county cricket was played much as usual, though the military authorities commandeered The Oval, and Hobbs' benefit match was staged at Lord's, but then a speech by Lord Roberts and a dignified letter to *The Times* by "W.G." brought the first class game to an end.

Though the 1915 *Wisden* envisaged the possibility of occasional county cricket in the coming summer, no such attempt was made or even seriously contemplated. Every county committee had encouraged the professional staff to join the forces or to engage in some form of war work, in most cases making up to them the difference between their Army pay and allowances and their cricket wage. Yorkshire took the lead in making such war service a condition of re-engagement. But cricketers everywhere needed no urging, and at the annual MCC meeting in May, Lord Hawke as President could claim that 75 per cent of first class cricketers were serving in the Army or Navy (the RFC being then of course a very small body of regular specialists).

At the same meeting he announced the MCC's intention to do all they could to help school cricket and his hope that the headmasters would co-operate to keep the game going. This hope was realised and in one respect at least the war brought real benefit to school cricket; deprived of their usual club opposition the schools naturally turned to each other and many new inter-school fixtures were arranged. Winchester, for instance, who had for 60 years met only one school – Eton – now arranged matches with Charterhouse, Wellington and Bradfield, and the policy, continued after the war, has proved an unqualified success.

The MCC played their part nobly by playing forty-four school matches, and if their sides were often rather long in the tooth this could be off-set by the youth of the school teams; for, in contrast with the far-sighted policy of to-day, no effort was made to prevent boys joining up at a bare eighteen and many were fighting or had been killed in Flanders at a time when they would normally have still been playing cricket for their schools.

Of club cricket, in the ordinary sense of the word, there was virtually none, and the only clubs I have been able to trace as fielding sides, and then only in isolated fixtures against schools, were the Butterflies, Nottinghamshire Amateurs and Hertfordshire County and Ground. But there was plenty of military cricket and the county committees everywhere put their grounds at the disposal of the troops. In many cases too they had turned their buildings to war uses; Lord's accommodated various military units, whilst the staff that remained there spent part of their time in making thousands of hay-nets for horses; the pavilions at Old Trafford, Trent Bridge and Derby became hospitals, whilst the Leicester ground provided a headquarters for a Remount depot and a small-bore rifle range.

At the end of the season a baseball match was played at Lord's between Canadians and London Americans for the benefit of Canadian soldiers' dependants.

But inevitably the chief and melancholy feature of the war issues of *Wisden* was the ever growing Roll of Honour of cricketers; the war was no more than a few months old when it had claimed two young officers who, as boys, had made cricket history – A. E. J. Collins, whose individual score of 628 not out, made when a boy of 13 at Clifton, still stands (in the same match he took eleven wickets), and John Manners, whose fearless hitting had alone made possible the epic Eton victory of "Fowler's year". But from the losses and tragedies of the war cricketers the world over were in 1915 twice distracted – by the deaths of "W.G." and Victor Trumper. I can remember reading of them in France and feeling no real sorrow for W.G. passing Homeric and legendary into the Elysian fields, but an almost personal pain that Trumper's gallant spirit and matchless grace should have been called so early from the world it had enriched.

In 1916 school cricket continued to develop on the lines followed the previous year and Winchester met Harrow for the first time since 1854. The MCC, though only able to play half as many schools as in 1915, wisely decided to revive the Lord's Schools v The Rest match in August. This game saw the appearance of two future county captains in W. G.

Lowndes and M. D. Lyon, and of a very young boy destined to play a great role at Lord's in later years, G. T. S. Stevens. Club cricket received a notable reinforcement in the shape of the Artists Rifles XI, who played a number of matches, chiefly with schools, and thanks to the batting of D. J. Knight and the bowling of E. C. Kirk, carried all before them.

But it was in the north that cricket of first-class standard really survived. The Leagues there kept going and a number of professionals had gravitated to them; interest in their matches was keen, as well it might be with the chance of seeing Barnes bowling at Hobbs. In the four war years the former took 404 wickets in the Bradford League for about 5.5 runs apiece, whiles Hobbs in 1916 had splendid batting figures, and took fifty-nine wickets at very small cost.

The year 1917 saw a great change in sentiment about the game; the nation had by then re-adjusted its life to the state of war and no objection was felt to an attempt to stage some exhibition matches in the cause of charity. Yorkshire had felt their way in that direction the previous year and now played four big games, whilst the MCC bestowed their official blessing by staging two matches at Lord's – The Army v Australian Army, and Navy and Army v Australia and S. Africa; these games, if they produced no outstanding cricket, were very popular. Charity benefited by over £1,000. Two army commanders, Generals Plumer and Horne, wired their good wishes, and Admiral Jellicoe himself came to Lord's.

No fewer than 119 military and school matches were played that year on the Canterbury ground, and Leyton, too, saw much cricket.

The outstanding feature in the school cricket of the year was the bowling of the Wykehamist J. D'E. Firth, who took eight for 48 v Harrow, all ten for 41 v Eton, and with seven for 27 in the last innings at Lord's, pulled the match out of the fire for The Rest. Stevens made further progress, Gibson of Eton and Rotherham of Rugby foreshadowed their future powers, whilst at Uppingham Percy Chapman, though only 16, averaged 111 for ten innings!

The last year of the war saw a further extension of the policy of "Exhibition" matches, both in Yorkshire and in the South.

Three such games were played at Lord's, one at The Oval, and one in September at Folkestone, and if the cricket, as was natural, hardly reached peace-time level the large crowds that attended had their moments of rich reward, in one of Hobbs' very best innings, another, almost as good, by H. W. Taylor, a piece of hurricane hitting by Fender, and the heartening spectacle of "Plum" Warner in the familiar Harlequin cap batting almost as well as ever at the age of forty-four.

School cricket flourished exceedingly and the representative match at Lord's included, besides Stevens and Chapman of the previous year, an exceptionally fine all-rounder from Malvern in N. E. Partridge, and from Tonbridge that brilliant bat and cover point Lionel Hedges. In a further game between a representative schools side and an eleven raised by Captain Warner, Lord Harris delighted everyone by batting for half an hour with relative ease when many, half his age, had been cheaply dismissed.

In this summer a little cricket was even played in France, principally at Étaples, where the old Essex player, Charles McGahey looked after some very respectable matting wickets. I remember one afternoon match in particular which included quite a galaxy of stars, Johnny Douglas, Nigel Haig, Dick Twining, Harry Longman, Donald Knight and poor Reggie Schwartz, who died of influenza just after the armistice. That fine batsman, Colonel H. S. Bush, motored some 100 miles from 2nd Army HQ at St Omer, hit a beautiful four and then off an equally good hit fell to a miraculous catch by Knight at cover, and motored back again.

The game was also played in the Near East where I believe Rockley Wilson bowled the same length as he had bowled everywhere else; but Bernard Darwin at Salonika stuck to golf.

With the biographies of the fallen filling each year more pages in *Wisden*, it would be impossible, and where the sacrifice of all was equal, it would be invidious to pay more than a general tribute to the contribution which cricketers made to final victory, but perhaps I may make one exception. There can never have been a great cricketer less military in temper than Colin Blythe: the artistry of his bowling was but the expression of his sensitive and highly strung temperament, his physique was never strong, but when the call came, he never hesitated, and every year at the Canterbury festival his county have paid tribute at the memorial to his sacrifice.

No one, as the summer of 1918 drew to its close, could have dreamt that next May would see county cricket in full swing again, but so it was. The Advisory Committee, faced in December with the unexpected task of getting the game on its legs again and very doubtful how far public interest would respond to a full-fledged revival, decided on the policy of two day matches, but the season was not many weeks old when everyone realised that the experiment was a mistake, that the fears were unjustified, and that cricket was as popular as ever.

To-day the horizon is again dark, and it is idle to try to look far ahead, but I believe there is a general feeling that the game can and should be kept going wherever possible. With the military service act in operation, and the nation mobilised as never before for its war effort, there is no room for the charge of scrimshanking, and where cricket can be played without interfering with the national effort it can only be good for the national morale. Of course anything like county cricket is out of the question, but the MCC have arranged one or two big charity matches at Lord's with a number of minor matches, and undertaken a long programme against the schools, with the Lord's Schools and the Rest match to end the season at Lord's. The Club Cricket Conference have decided that, with the obvious reservations, the clubs should keep going as much as possible, and with their short hours the northern League matches will justifiably continue to offer excitement and distraction to thousands of workers. In the last war the universities, so far as undergraduates were concerned, virtually ceased to exist: to-day they are full of vigorous life, the undergraduates cannot join up until they are of age, and are very rightly making the best of war conditions. Cambridge, fortunate in having two old Blues in residence, mean to produce a university team and have already arranged a match for charity at Lord's; the situation at Oxford is more difficult, but it is to be hoped that they will try to manage something on the same lines.

A visit to Lord's on a dark December day was a sobering experience; there were sandbags everywhere, and the Long Room was stripped and bare, with its treasures safely stored beneath ground, but the turf was a wondrous green, old Time on the Grand Stand was gazing serenely at the nearest balloon, and one felt that somehow it would take more than totalitarian war to put an end to cricket. *Merses profundo, pulchrior evenit.*

## NOTES ON THE 1939 SEASON

### By R. C. Robertson-Glasgow

So great was the thing which started, for us, on September 3rd last year, so pervasive of our thoughts, homes, even of our pastimes and sports, that to look back on the English cricket season of 1939 is like peeping curiously through the wrong end of a telescope at a very small but very happy world. It is a short six months since Constantine gave the England bowlers such a cracking at The Oval, like a strong man suddenly gone mad in a fielding-practice, but it might be six years, or sixteen; for we have jumped a dimension or two since then in both time and space.

It is true that throughout the season the rumble of war rolled louder and louder, that our guests the West Indies, excepting L. N. Constantine and E. A. Martindale, had to sail for home with seven matches unplayed, that in the county championship several matches had to be abruptly cancelled; but, in a sense, it was a strangely happy season. There may have been more rain than is convenient to fast bowlers, thin shoes, or anxious secretaries; but, as is customary when great issues hang in the balance, men set themselves to a quiet but determined enjoyment. They turned to cricket as to an old friend, who gives you a seat, a glass of beer, and something sane to talk about. Perhaps some of them wondered when, if ever again, they would watch on the Mound at Lord's and borrow from a small boy in a school cap a score card to see what it was all about, and find strange entries and pencilled mysteries; when, once more, they would sit on someone else's sandwiches in the tram that sways to Kennington, or trip over the marquee-ropes at the Saffrons, or smell the sea at Hove, or argue at Old Trafford.

There was much cricket worth the seeing. The advice, both official and unsolicited, given to those who control or direct the county teams, had not, as so often before, rebounded with hardly an echo from the walls of complacency and self-satisfaction. There was a renaissance of the liberal attitude to the game and of the generous technique in batting. The fielding, if we forget a few hours of pandemonium and chaos in the third Test, was of a high standard generally. The bowling, it must be allowed, was at least no worse than in the preceding years. There are two or three English bowlers who are nearly great, and perhaps a dozen who are undeniably good. But few of them are young, as bowlers must be young. There is hardly one man, unless some are lost in the meadows and villages, to cause the batsman to fidget with his cap-peak and shirt-buttons, the wicket-keeper's gloves to go off like an exploded paper-bag, and the spectator to suck in the long-drawn breath. Yes; there is one, K. Farnes, of Essex. But not only is he a bowler of, as it were, high-geared temperament, and difficult to stimulate to utmost powers, but also during most of last summer he was a full-time schoolmaster and had betaken his art at half-pace to the practice-nets.

Of great leg-break bowlers there was none, in the sense that Leonard Braund and, within certain inexplicable limits, Freeman (A. P.) were great; not to mention the masters of leg-break bowling of Australia and South Africa, men who in their prime suffered but little from variation of form, who were often wonderful, and, even when they weren't, yet remained bowlers who mattered. Their very name was worth two or three wickets, and if they had come out of the pavilion with a gouty foot in a carpet-slipper, they would still have been feared, as the sick Napoleon was feared at Waterloo. There was nothing of that sort in England last summer, though there were some half-dozen leg-break bowlers who, if you happened upon them for a half-hour in a match, might almost persuade you into the belief that you had found the right thing at last. There was Sims, of Middlesex; with stuttering run-up but beautifully easy action, almost too easy; he could be difficult, sometimes for overs on end; cheerful, willing, nearly tireless. Something here, surely; but the great moment and the great batsmen have too often found him wanting in the last indefinable gifts of temperament and art. Then Wright, of Kent; more dangerous, at best, than Sims; a vicious spinner of the leg-break at an unusually high speed; less potent and artful in the googly; failing, sometimes, through straining the possibility of spin and so losing length; always clutching at the skirts of greatness, but so far never quite holding on. And Mitchell (T. B.), of Derbyshire; so natural a leg-breaker that the ball almost spins when it sees him; unlike most others of his kind, he resorts often to genuine off-break; a genius, certainly; but quixotic and unreliable, and quite happy suddenly to desert art and purpose to argue privately with invisible fate. There is none quite like him, but his value has too often been frittered away in individualism. F. R. Brown, of Surrey, a very strong player of games, had days of inspirations both as a leg-breaker and a fierce driver. He bowled very finely against West Indies for Surrey at The Oval, sustaining length, direction, and acuteness of spin for long spells. Business prevented him from playing in all matches, but his record was good; eighty-six wickets at 23.34, 946 runs at 33.78. Few genuine amateurs can afford to play regularly, and Brown's form for some years would have been less variable if he had had the opportunity of regular play, for, decidedly unlike some modern cricketers, he has the heart and the will for the grimmest fight, and the optimism to surmount the occasion.

There are others; some of promise and fair performance, some, I fear, unmistakably launched on the irrevocable decline that all bowlers know. Those who may think these judgments of English bowling a little harsh should remind themselves of the steep and rarely crossed hill between county and England form. The great men of the past set no easy standard.

## RICHNESS OF BATTING

The thinness of the bowling was perhaps exaggerated by the richness of the batting. A strict observer, a first-class batsman of a generation ago, considers that the first dozen or so of modern English batsmen are in sum the equals at least of those of his own time, about 1905-14. The old freedom of stroke-play, especially in off-driving and straight hitting, that thing of joy which nature is always urging the real batsman to release, was more often to be found last season, and the poisonous vapours of dullness and dunce-like inaction, which hung over county grounds for heavy years, and, at one time, seemed to have settled for all eternity over Old Trafford in particular, were at last dispersing. It was Paynter who finally drove Calvinistic cricket from his native grounds. Ernest Tyldesley had begun the crusade. His art was above and beyond dry and cautious doctrines, and an eloquent rebuke to the business methods of batting. But he was almost unsupported. In 1939 such batsmen as Iddon, Washbrook, and that accomplished artist, Oldfield, completed the reformation. This new attitude, then, coupled with the loyalty of groundsmen in supporting Marylebone's suggestions for less artificial pitches, gave pleasanter hours to spectators who had deserved some compensation for the hardish seats, for the long, imperfectly explained delays, and the short, imperfectly executed strokes, to which they had, in ever decreasing numbers, become accustomed. Cricketers and committees, even under the shadow of bankruptcy, might continue to remark on the ignorance of spectators, but they could not longer ignore their comparative non-existence. This overdue change, and the discrediting of the Utilitarian method in batting, were the two great victories won by cricket in 1939. But now, of the immediate future no man can speak with more than hope.

The MCC tour to India, which was to have taken place this present winter, was naturally cancelled. A moderately strong, if by no means representative, team had accepted invitations. Some of our best cricketers had decided on rest, in view of the visit to Australia, due in the winter 1940-41, and now most unlikely of achievement. Our guests for this coming summer were to have been the South Africans who, on their last visit, under H. F. Wade in 1935, gave us a rude but helpful shock. This is a severe loss. The virility and gaiety of South African teams have always been refreshing. There was an appalling interlude of funereal proceedings in the Test matches between South Africa and England over there last winter. It will not, I think, happen again. Some notice of the deceased must be given later, but in general the matter, so far as sheer cricket is concerned, is best forgotten. It was, perhaps nobody's fault. The pitches were often ludicrously docile, and there was an unfortunate experiment in a type of Test cricket which has been proved to be supremely suitable to only one set of matches, those between Australia and England in Australia.

At Lord's Mr W. Findlay and Sir Pelham Warner have taken over the respective duties of Secretary and Assistant Secretary to the Marylebone Cricket Club, in the places of Lieut.-Colonel R. S. Rait Kerr and Mr R. Aird, who are absent on military service. The Club is fortunate to be able, at temporary need, to replace two most efficient officers by men whose experience and discretion are so well tried and known. Sir Pelham Warner has given many years and much energy to the playing, the interest, and the furtherance of cricket. Mr Findlay resumes an office which he performed with unfailing tact and conspicuous ability from 1926 to 1936.

It was announced that MCC has contributed three hundred guineas to the British Red Cross Fund, and intend to arrange certain matches to be played during the summer in aid of that organisation. It is also proposed to hold the usual Easter classes at Lord's from 5th April to 24th April. More than forty matches against Schools have been arranged.

In legislation, it is unlikely, war or no war, that any further change or modification of the Rules of Cricket, or advices to captains, secretaries and players, will issue from MCC for some period. The old and bald truth is that any game stands or falls not by its Laws but by the spirit of their interpretation. Neglect of this truth has led, and always will lead, at best to irritation, at worst to grievous quarrels. The Over is likely to remain one of eight balls. It gave rise to discussion and correspondence, some helpful and sensible, much irrelevant but harmless, and a small but diverting section of remarkable mathematical obscurity.

## THE WAR AND CRICKET

As to the possibility or impossibility of playing this summer what is generally known as first-class cricket, I cannot avoid the opinion that there has been in some quarters a deal of cloudy thinking and an over-generous flow of sentiment devoid of reason. Optimism is the thing. So is sense. We must be prepared, as so many are at the moment compelled, to have nothing at all, or nearly nothing. But, in another sense, too, members of county clubs must be prepared – and this is the duty of those who are left behind – to pay, if possible, the full subscription, if not possible, a part of it, to the club to which they belong; in the words that Sir Stanley Jackson addressed to the Yorkshire County Club, "to keep our grounds and facilities for cricket in order ... to keep our organisation in its present efficiency ready for the happier times when the troubled world has returned to normal conditions". On the same question the Surrey County Cricket Club began their circular to members with the same words as were used in their report dated April 14, 1915, the first issued after the start of the last war:

"The Committee are faced with many difficulties and uncertainties in the present National Crisis, and rely on the loyal support of the Members, as heavy current expenses have to be met whether cricket is played or not."

Advice on the spending of private monies is, in general, as improper as it has become unhappily necessary and frequent, but I do not feel that many will turn as lightly as they might in peace-time helping to secure the future of a game that they love. On this point, then, agreement must, I feel, be nearly complete. But on the playing of actual, as opposed to the supporting of future cricket the divergence of view is wide. First, there are those who think that any organised cricket this summer, by those "first-class" cricketers who are too old or too young or unfit for war service, or only temporarily available, is improper ethically. While respecting this view, I cannot agree with it. The idea of having anything remotely resembling the ordinary championship is certainty not only improper but wildly impossible. But I can see no reason or gain in wearing mental sackcloth in advance. Secondly there was – I much doubt if there still is – a view held that county cricket might take place in the form of one three-day match a week, starting on a Saturday, with certain adjustments of the Qualification Rule. But three-day cricket, in peace, was scarcely maintaining the public interest except in matches between the few best, or the locally rivalrous, teams, and how many are going to pay even sixpence to watch cricket for three days between scratch or constantly varying elevens? Again, it was proposed that two-day matches might be played on Saturday and Monday. But why two-day? And why Monday? Few who remember or took part in the two-day matches in the county championship of 1919 will wish to revive them. Gaily undertaken as a bright and promising idea, they proved a dreary disaster; tiresome, unsatisfying, and financially hopeless.

Later, in December 1939, proposals came from Lancashire suggesting groupings for regional cricket in 1940, each group including a proportion of the Minor counties. This carefully thought out, if perhaps over-ambitious scheme, may conceivably prove to be the basis of a simpler programme this summer. I much doubt it. As none can tell who will be available to play any cricket at all, or to what extent the severity of war may strike us, it is useless to make even provisional arrangements for any such programme.

On January 12th this year MCC issued the statement that their Committee was not prepared "at this stage" to take the initiative in the matter of regional cricket, but that if the general feeling was in favour of it, they advised the counties to ask for a meeting of the Advisory County Committee. This wise exhortation to rational procedure was wrongly interpreted by some as an expression of indifference or inertia. In fact, as the conditions then were, and, at the moment of writing, still are, only, so to speak, more so, it was the only decision that could reflect the view of the majority.

No. There is only one solution of the question, unless beyond expectation but not hope, peace returns early, and that is the improvising of one-day matches whenever and wherever possible, in the same spirit that has moved villagers to come out from under the yew-tree and bowl in the place of Tom looking after the calf and bat for Johnson delivering a telegram, and be d——d to the score and the points and the Cup! There will be plenty to play and enough to watch such games. Many would delight to see again a few early-Edwardian drives and a late-Victorian pull or two. And if most of the pence taken at the gate should go to help a greater cause than cricket, so much the better.

## TEDIOUS TESTS

For the notes that follow, on the Test series between South Africa and England in South Africa, winter 1938-39, I am much indebted to an able and vigorous critic, who was an eyewitness of the five principal matches. If the original lucidity of the information should suffer from necessary compression, the fault is not his. It is probably that in the memories of those who took part in this tour little now remains except the entertainment given by a most hospitable people. Which is natural and proper. But annals demand fact; and the warmest enthusiast could not deny, that much of the play in the five Tests was, as earlier remarked, laboured and tedious. The effect of this on spectators accustomed to the brisker pleasures of half-day and one-day cricket can readily be imagined. They saw their sprinters, so to speak, stretched out on a marathon, and most of them were frankly bored – and often said so. In truth, the intensity of the matches was out of all proportion to their meaning. The general standard of skill, too, was unequal to the importance artifically attached to it. The growth was unnatural. And, in the end, the fifth Test match exploded in frustration and farce. For this there were two chief causes; the undue solemnity of proceedings, and the Test pitches which, like certain triumphs of chemistry in England, had so far overstepped perfection as to be of little use to the bowler and to impose some inexplicable narcotic on the batsman. They were plumb, but without pace. Yet the batsmen, with a few exceptions, cannot be wholly aquitted of blame. Some of them nearly slept on the pitch, and it is recorded that the number of half-volleys played by the back stroke was quite dreadful!

On the South African side Melville, the captain, well-known in England as a former captain of Oxford University and Sussex, played a beautiful innings in the fourth Test. He had not been in form. But on this occasion he attacked that wonderfully accurate left-hander, Verity, first on the full pitch, then by hooking; probably the best innings in the series. His fielding was of the highest class and his captaincy, in most trying circumstances, sound. Dalton, a free and wristy batsman, kept to his natural style. Nourse, another attractive player, headed the Test averages for South Africa with 60.28. He scored centuries in the second and fifth Tests. Bruce Mitchell, classical and elegant as ever, averaged 58.25, and seemed happier when not called upon to open the innings. Van der Bijl, a very big man and rather slow of foot, showed an advance in ability, played the faster bowling very stoutly, and was extremely hard to shift. His average was 51.11.

On the English side the averages were generally higher. First Hammond with 87.00. It was remarked that in the Tests he used, in general, his quieter and safer method, scoring mainly from strokes off the back foot. Then Paynter (81.62). He, too, was studious; though the partnership between him (243) and Hammond (120) in the third Test at Durban, which England won by an innings and 13 runs, produced a rare interlude of freedom and gaiety. Valentine (68.75) and Ames (67.80) brought a reviving breath of festival Canterbury to the solemnities, and from them and Hutton (44.16) came most of those strokes which flow instead of being squeezed from the bat. Nor must Gibb (59.12) be forgotten. With a concentration rarely given even to a Yorkshireman, he applied his mind and spectacles to the task. He scored 93 and 106 in the first Test, and 120 in the unfinished second innings of the fifth. He was very slow, but entirely in the fashion.

In bowling, Farnes, the one fast bowler of a high class on either side, was seldom happy with either pitch or climate. But he was accurate always; occasionally hostile. He took sixteen wickets at 32.43 each. Verity, as ever, was extremely steady, taking nineteen wickets at 29.05, so heading the list on both sides. Wright, though fairly steady in length, was unable to spin the ball much. Wilkinson, the other leg-breaker, could neither spin the ball enough nor find any certainty of length. Goddard did a hat trick and Perks had one fine performance, but neither could make much of the pitches. Edrich, at a very fast medium pace, was hard-working and often useful.

The South African bowlers were facing an extremely severe task, and, until they collapsed with weariness or strain in the fifth Test, acquitted themselves well. Langton we know as a resourceful and artistic bowler. Of Gordon, a tall, powerful bowler of inswingers and off-breaks, Hammond spoke with high praise, and remarked especially of his difficulty in the fourth Test, when on a damp pitch he made the ball swing very late away from instead of into the batsman.

England led by one match in the series after four had been played. The fifth was to have been played to a finish. It never ended. Some wished that it had never been begun. Player after player, especially on the South African side, became halt or incapacitated. England had been set the colossal task of scoring 696 runs to win. Quite soon, as "soon" went in this match, with 250 for one wicket on the board, it was obvious that England stood a strong chance of winning. Langton was reduced to bowling half pace and round-arm. The athletic Gordon's powerful springs at last ran down. Newsome was only difficult with a new ball. The captain, Melville, was dead lame. But he could still speak. So on they went. The world of cricket, till now uninterested, suddenly became wildly excited at the prospect of a victory in this weird battle. The days went on, and at last that victory was almost in sight. But the boat for home was growing restive. If it were missed, it meant another week's stay; alternatively, a return by aeroplane. It has been said that MCC would have granted the aeroplane. But, whatever the world was thinking, they were dead sick and tired of it over there. It had lasted for ten weekdays and two Sundays; and all that taking of guard, retaking of guard, walking, running, limping, talking, and throwing, went in the end for nothing. O bathos! But, once more, it is not perhaps the cricket that the teams so much remember; rather, the sun; and friendships renewed or made.

## WEST INDIES IN ENGLAND

I think that the West Indies cricketers enjoyed their tour here last summer, cut short though it was by the war, and often interrupted by rain. They enjoy their cricket, because they mean to do so, because to them the game is a natural, yet important, sort of fun. And this pleasure they communicate, a happy gift, to the spectators. Their matches and scores are set out fair in another part of this volume, but no mathematics can recapture George Headley batting against England in the first Test at Lord's, looking far smaller out there than the hundred and forty odd pounds of weight that he claims, quietly defiant, artistic in cutting, watchful on the line of the ball in defence. In the first innings he made 106 in a total of 277, in the second 107 in a total of 225. None before had ever made a century in each innings of a Test at Lord's. There were some who criticised his style of playing so many strokes off his back foot, and it is true that no batsman, however great, looks so well playing like that; but two forces had combined to push him into the more pragmatic method; weekly play in the League, and the sense that so much depended on his individual success. He was not quite so free as when he came here in 1933, but he showed himself to have no living superior in the square and the late cut. He was wonderful, too, in hooking, and in that very late flick of the ball from thigh or hips to long-leg. I can see a resemblance to Bradman in this stroke; like Bradman, too, he seems to play the ball very late, yet with certainty; but I would not dare to compare him, great batsman as he is, with Bradman in completeness of mastery. He has not, none has, quite the same iron precision or almost heartlessly perfect technique. And I don't think that Headley, as he stood "smiling away like clockwork" at third man, ever reflected seriously on such comparisons.

England won this Test at Lord's by eight wickets, having declared at 404 for five wickets. Hutton (196) and Compton (D.) (120) added 248 for the fourth wicket by fluent and masterful batting. Apart from Cameron, who flighted the ball cleverly from the Pavilion end, and took three wickets for 66 runs, the West Indies bowling was not good. Constantine for once somehow lost himself in eccentric experiments, and it was early apparent that Martindale had declined in speed. J. B. Stollmeyer, only eighteen years of age, opening the innings with his captain, R. S. Grant, made some lovely on-drives in his 59. High promise here. Bowes and Copson both bowled very finely in this match.

The second Test, at Manchester, was ruined by rain. On the first day, in the few overs available, England scored 11 for no wicket, and it needed a Marie Corelli or Ouida to describe how the torrent swirled round the chosen heroes of each country. Hutton and Fagg, the latter having, in my opinion unjustifiably, displaced Gimblett, found it almost as difficult to stand still as the bowlers found it to run. After a strange and not unexciting scramble on the Monday and Tuesday the match was left drawn, as had always seemed probable. Some harshly criticised Hammond's captaincy, suggesting that he might have forced a win. This was rather silly, if expected. Hammond does not rank among the more imaginative England captains. But he is experienced and sound, and he found the correct solutions in a quaint puzzle. At least the West Indies came out of the match with credit increased, Grant, in his 47 in the first innings, attacked the slow bowling with fierce zest. Headley, with 51, batted skilfully enough, but the best achievement was that of Bowes, who, on his thirty-first birthday, took six for 33. In England's first innings Hardstaff batted beautifully for his 76 in a total of 164 for seven wickets declared.

At The Oval, in the third Test, England now leading by one match, West Indies added to the credit carried from Manchester. True, at the end, England led by 220 with seven wickets in hand and Hutton (165) still batting, but it was something to have overtopped England's first innings of 352 by 146 runs. I should doubt if ever in the history of Tests the English bowling has been so lashed and banged and rattled. Headley and Victor Stollmeyer played comfortably enough, but Weekes, the left-hander, then Constantine, "fired indiscriminately". Weekes scored 137 (78 by boundaries) in 135 minutes, and Constantine, soon wearying of mere unorthodoxy, began to aim for sixes over the wicket-keeper. Two, if not three, of England's best bowlers had been unable to accept invitations to play, and the land was naked indeed. At one period, when Compton and Hutton were bowling, it seemed as if all the long-hops and full-pitches in the world were being simultaneously released. Hutton and Hammond put the arithmetic right by adding 264 for the third wicket in England's second innings, and nothing was left but a formal declaration ten minutes from time on the last day.

The West Indies showed themselves to be as a team quite strong, if unreliable – Headley excepted – in batting; only moderately strong in bowling; good, sometimes brilliant, in fielding. Their chief disappointments must have been the weather and the decline in form of Martindale, opening fast bowler, and of Barrow, wicket-keeper and opening batsman of the 1933 tour. Barrow had scored a century in the Manchester Test in that tour, and proved himself a sound wicket-keeper. Unhappily for his team, his batting seemed from the first to be over-anxious last season, and Sealey took his place as wicket-keeper at Manchester and The Oval. Sealey is a natural batsman of many and attractive strokes, also a witty and refreshing conversationalist; but, myself, I do not rank him as a wicket-keeper. Hylton, tall, medium to medium fast, was a clever bowler, with a fluent action and often deceptive flight. His figures do no justice to his skill. R. S. Grant, capable and alert as a captain, took upon himself the task of opening the innings. Within the limits of his skill he performed it well, being free and venturesome in method; but it is as a short-leg that he will be remembered. Here he made some astonishing catches, and his reach was tremendous. On the administration and social side he received tireless and valuable help from Mr J. M. Kidney, the manager, whose wisdom and tact were equally appreciated among English friends and cricketers. J. H. Cameron, who captained the side when Grant was absent, showed a certain maturity of form. He was a most useful all-rounder, and had the advantage of an intimate knowledge of most of his opponents and their methods.

As to Leary Constantine, one of the few unquestioned geniuses of cricket, he shows his greatness by his gift of adaptation. He reached the age of thirty-seven soon after the last Test. And that's not young for a man who bowls, fields, and hits with the best. He no longer bowls fast as a regular habit; just a "fizzer" now and again, to remind the impertinent. But he has kept that curious upward jerk of the head just before delivery, as if to reassure himself that the sky is up to no nonsense. He bowled every variety of medium, medium-slow and medium-fast pace. There are better bowlers in cricket to-day than Constantine, but there's none to equal him for a study in bowling craft. In the Tests there was that one lapse, at Lord's, when he reminded me of a chess-player who had somehow confounded his gambits and made a muddle of the game. At The Oval, in England's first innings, when he took five for 75, he was grand. His fielding, usually in the gulley, is still one of the sights of cricket, as he takes every oddity of bounce with lazy-seeming ease. As a batsman he has somewhat declined. The eye and foot are not quite so quick for those attacks on probability and text-books. But his innings at The Oval, even allowing for the ineptitude of much of the attack, was glorious hitting.

## YORKSHIRE AGAIN

Our own county championship was again won by Yorkshire, Middlesex, who played six matches fewer than the winners, came second; but more than a whole unit behind. Gloucestershire, who had the felicity to beat the champions both home and away, were third. In the previous year they had finished tenth. Their bowling in 1939 was most effective. Goddard, slow-medium, alone of any county cricketer took 200 wickets (200 at 14.86 each). He was finely supported by the two younger bowlers, Scott (121 at 22.89) and Lambert (74 at 26.86). Their captain, Walter Hammond, headed the first-class batting averages for the seventh successive season, an achievement that is unlikely ever to be rivalled. He scored 2,479 runs in all matches at an average of 63.56. As a team they were enterprising in idea and execution.

Essex came fourth, a rise of two places. For the seventh time in eight seasons. Nichols brought off the "double", 1,387 runs and 121 wickets. He was most ably assisted by Kenneth Farnes during the later part of the season. Smith (R.) and Smith (P.), in their different styles, between them took 174 wickets. A varied and strong attack. Avery, a stylish batsman, advanced in ability, averaging 41.71 for 1,335 runs. O'Connor showed little, if any, decline in his powers. The playing of matches in widely separate parts of the county has proved a success. According to latest advice, the secretary, Mr B. K. Castor, absent on war service, has handed over his duties to his wife.

Yorkshire's victory in the championship was assured before the programme was stopped or altered by the war. The captaincy of A. B. Sellers was once more of the highest standard, reflected in the discipline no less than in the tough optimism of his team. Verity (191 wickets at 13.13) headed the first-class bowling averages. There is nothing new that I can say of this greatest among the slower-paced modern left-handers. Bowes, fast-medium to fast, took 122 wickets at 14.48, and, to my mind, has reached in the last two seasons the climax of his powers. The untidiness has gone; the vigour and control remain. Robinson, the off-spinner, showed very good form, taking 120 wickets at 19.07. This was a trio in attack of a total ability a little beyond that to be found in any other county. Hutton and Sutcliffe were a grand opening pair. The older master was occasionally absent recovering from injury, but it was a wonderful performance, in his forty-fifth year, to score 1,416 runs in 29 innings, including, at the end of May and start of June, four consecutive centuries.

Middlesex owed much to the personality and leadership of I. A. R. Peebles. Unlike some captains, he never stretched the bow too tight, but was nevertheless an observant and understanding leader, equally unworried in defeat or success. The batting, even with the brilliant Compton (D.) and the strongly effective Edrich, was never of quite the same solid quality as that of Yorkshire. It was pleasant to note the success as a batsman of J. P. Mann, of Cambridge University, son of the former Middlesex and England captain, F. T. Mann. Jim Smith was as tireless as ever in bowling, and his system of batting was, if anything, more violent and eccentric than ever.

In conclusion, I should wish to end on a note of praise for English batting. There is much to criticise in our cricket. The standard of bowling is low. In some counties the discipline of cricketers is slack. But the batting is very good indeed, and there were stars about last summer, to be seen by those not lost in the mists of pessimism and antiquity. A man could count himself happy to sit down and watch the ripening greatness of Hutton, the airy graces of Hardstaff, and the twinkling feet of Compton. While Hammond, if less flexible and destructive than he was, still looked greater than anything else that we have in the game. Besides these, there were many others last season to show that English batting had tricked its beams anew, and flamed in the forehead of the morning sky.

May I thank those friends and colleagues without whose help these Notes could not have been started: Mr Hubert Preston; Mr Norman Preston, and their colleagues in Pardon's Cricket Reporting Agency, who provided much matter, statistical and general; Mr Frank Thorogood, of the *News Chronicle*; Mr E. W. Swanton, who gave me the benefit of his observation of the MCC tour in South Africa; Sir Pelham Warner and Mr H. S. Altham, whose opinions I asked for, and received on various subjects.

February, 1940

# MISCELLANY, [1936]

A sparrow was killed by a ball bowled by Jahangir Khan in the MCC and Cambridge University match at Lord's. T. N. Pearce, the batsman, managed to play the ball and the bird fell against the stumps without dislodging the bails. The bird is preserved as a relic in the pavilion at Lord's.

In a rain-ruined match at Nottingham, G. O. Allen (Middlesex) batted on each of three days for 6 not out. Actually his innings occupied half an hour.

Hammond of Sussex, when bowling against Kent at Tunbridge Wells, sent the ball direct to James Parks at slip who caught it as Dolphin, the umpire, called wide.

Two instances occurred during the summer of a captain permitting his opponents to alter their side after the start of a match.

At Northampton, A. W. Allen allowed India to bring in M. J. Gopalan for Baqa Jilani, who was indisposed. At Maidstone, A. P. F. Chapman made no objection to Middlesex playing Gray instead of G. O. Allen, who stood down.

Blankets were used to dry the actual pitch at Lord's during the Test Match with India.

In 1836, two professional cricketers, Wenman and Mills, defeated an Isle of Oxney XI at Wittersham, Kent. At the end of that game it was agreed that another of the kind should take place in 100 years time.

The agreement was fulfilled on September 5, 1936, when Ashdown (Kent) and Wensley (Sussex) comprised the professional "team". Oxney batted first, scoring 153; then Wensley (96) and Ashdown (83 not out) made 186, and won by 33 runs.

As many as eight Marlborough College players were lbw (four under the new rule) in the second innings against Cheltenham College at Marlborough. Altogether thirty-four wickets fell in the match and sixteen batsmen were lbw.

# SYDNEY PARDON, 1925

Sydney Herbert Pardon, for thirty-five years editor of *Wisden's Cricketers' Almanack*, died on November 20 after a few hours' illness. Born in 1855, he had recently completed his seventieth year, and yet at that age was as full of enthusiasms as he had been half a century before. Possessed of an extraordinarily good memory, he had a mind stored with interesting information on many subjects, and was always a fascinating companion for young and old. While the game of cricket played the biggest part in his life, he was also a close student of the drama, a devoted supporter of good music, and a keen follower of racing. These were the four things in which he chiefly delighted, and it was always a proud recollection with him that on each of these four subjects he had written special articles for *The Times*. His journalistic experience extended to many forms of sport outside cricket. Upon athletics, rowing, boxing and billiards, he was a mine of information, and used to charm his friends with descriptions, always illuminating and happily phrased, of happenings in bygone days – the running of George and Cummings, the sculling of Hanlan and Trickett, the billiards of John Roberts and William Cook. His joy in racing was peculiarly his own – not the bringing off of a bet successfully, but the triumph of one or other of the big breeding strains, as, for instance, that grandsons of St Simon, or some particular line of Galopin's descendants, had done honour to their pedigree.

A playgoer from his earliest days, Sydney Pardon rarely missed seeing anything in the way of serious drama during a period of fifty years, and was always a fine judge of acting, rather contemptuous of stage accessories, and insistent upon the most polished elocution. Of plays and players during his life-time, and even of those before that period, his knowledge was encyclopædic, and he was equally well-informed about musical matters. Upon this phase of Pardon's acquirements, a leading musical critic wrote: "His detailed and accurate knowledge of the events in cricket had its parallel in regard to music. He could tell you, off-hand, of events in the operatic world, and these not only within his personal experience, but in past history. One often went to him for information as to when and where some eminent vocalist made her appearance in this country, and in what opera, and rarely was he found wanting."

Despite his remarkable attainments in other directions, Sydney Pardon will be chiefly remembered for his writings upon cricket, and his long association with *Wisden's Almanack*. Taken as a small boy to Lord's and The Oval, he developed an absorbing interest in the game, and by the happy accident of circumstances he was able to realise his ambitions while still a young man. Keen and accurate, well-balanced in his conclusions, and gifted with a particularly graceful form of expression, he rapidly built up a name for himself. Steadily his reputation grew until at length all leading cricketers were glad to have his opinions upon the big questions of the day. In years – now happily long distant – when throwing had become very rife, and threatened to invade the best of county elevens, Sydney Pardon fought a great battle for fair bowling, and had no small share in bringing about a healthier state of affairs. Spending his youth in an atmosphere that presumed the superiority of the Englishman in every walk of sport, he mourned over any England failure, yet, however keenly he might feel, nothing but sound and gracious criticism ever emanated from his pen. He treated his calling as a trust, and no power on earth could have made him write anything of which he was not absolutely convinced.

So interesting and pleasantly instructive a companion, Sydney Pardon had naturally a very wide circle of friends in the theatrical, musical, sporting and journalistic worlds. A strong individualist, always level-headed in his judgments, even when his personal sympathies were concerned, and a man of perfect integrity, he had great charm of manner, and by his always interesting speech and never-failing kindness he contributed in no small measure to the happiness of all who knew him. Possessed of mental powers of no common order, he strove untiringly for half a century to give consistently of his best, and certainly his long career brought much honour to his profession.

An old friend asked: "Why didn't he write his reminiscences? They would have made a fine book." Undoubtedly he could have produced a volume, full of interesting information about famous people and outstanding events conveyed in attractive style, and invaluable for its absolute accuracy. It was not to be. Sydney Pardon, in the busy life of a Fleet Street journalist, had neither the time nor the inclination to attempt anything of the kind. All he knew was generously at the disposal of his companions, but, if, with his passing, much has been lost, he has his monument *ære perennius* – and he would have desired no other – in the many *Wisden's Almanacks* which he produced with such ability and loving care.

C. S. C.

Below are some of the many tributes paid at the time of Sydney Pardon's death.

Lord Harris:– "I am concerned to hear of the death of Mr Sydney Pardon, my old friend, and, I might almost say, my old colleague of the cricket field, for we have had very intimate relations for many years. He is a great loss to the cricket world, for he had a most retentive memory and was therefore able, in pursuing his profession, to inform each generation correctly of incidents and players of the past. He had a facile pen, and to me his accounts of matches were always most readable and his criticisms most fair. He was, too, a great judge of the game, and I would as soon have had his opinion on difficult points as anyone I have known. I do not know if he was ever himself a player, but he knew how the game should be played, and was a staunch advocate of the classical style, and a fearless critic of the reverse. There will be many who will miss him much, but none more than I."

Mr A. J. Webbe, the old Harrow, Oxford and Middlesex captain:– "I received only on Friday morning a most charming letter, in which he said that it was sad to think it was fifty years since he and I first met on the old Prince's Ground. For those fifty years, he has said and written nothing but kind things. I shall always remember him with gratitude and affection. What a loss he will be. He was a power in the cricket world and all for good. We cannot think of *Wisden* or, indeed, of cricket generally without him."

Lord Hawke:– "The loss of Sydney Pardon is to cricket journalism nigh irreparable. His knowledge of the game, his retentive memory of the old days, made his articles sought after by all the best papers and they were eagerly devoured by a devoted following. A more kindhearted man I never knew. Is that surprising when his two greatest hobbies were cricket and music? I am not sure but that latterly music did not come first."

Mr P. F. Warner:– "He had such a sane and sound outlook on all cricket matters. He wrote with a charm that was peculiar to himself and had an amazing aptitude for saying a great deal in a few words. I cannot recall in any of the biographies which he wrote – a marked feature of *Wisden* – an unkind word about any cricketer. Criticism was sometimes imperative but the charitable touch was never wanting. On all questions which agitated the cricket world during his long editorship – to ventilate which the pages of *Wisden* were always open – his views were always balanced, one might almost say, judicial. Towards all cricketers with whom he came in contact he showed an amiability of which I, personally, had more than one proof during a long illness. He was a most interesting and many-sided talker. His knowledge of cricket, racing, the drama, the opera, was full and complete and made him at all times a rare companion. His death is a great loss to the cricket world."

Mr F. E. Lacey, Secretary of the MCC:– "All at Lord's are very grieved. We feel we have lost a great supporter, as well as an old and valued friend. His knowledge of cricket was wonderful and he always used his influence in the best interests of the game."

Mr H. D. G. Leveson Gower, of Winchester, Oxford and Surrey:– "His loss to cricket will indeed be severe. No better judge, no fairer critic, no better writer, ever existed."

# INDEX